ous

dictionary

edited by
Miranda Steel

M *ent*
LEGE

OXFORD
UNIVERSITY PRESS

OXFORD
UNIVERSITY PRESS

Great Clarendon Street, Oxford OX2 6DP

Oxford University Press is a department of the University of Oxford.
It furthers the University's objective of excellence in research, scholarship,
and education by publishing worldwide in

Oxford New York

Athens Auckland Bangkok Bogotá Buenos Aires Calcutta
Cape Town Chennai Dar es Salaam Delhi Florence Hong Kong Istanbul
Karachi Kuala Lumpur Madrid Melbourne Mexico City Mumbai
Nairobi Paris São Paulo Singapore Taipei Tokyo Toronto Warsaw

with associated companies in Berlin Ibadan

Oxford is a registered trade mark of Oxford University Press
in the UK and in certain other countries

© Oxford University Press 2000
Database right Oxford Unviersity Press (maker)

First published 2000
Second impression 2000

ISBN 0-19-4315169

3 5 7 9 10 8 6 4 2

Illustrations by Lorna Barnard; Kevin Baverstock; A Biggs; Anna Brookes; David
Burroughs; Andy Cooke; Martin Cox; Mark Dunn; David Eaton; Angelika Elsebach;
Gay Galsworthy; David Haldane; Margaret Heath; Karen Hiscock; Margaret Jones;
Richard Lewington; Jason Lewis; Martin Lonsdale/Hardlines; Vanessa Luff; Kevin
Maddison; Coral Mula; Oxford Illustrators; Fran Sewell; Martin Shovel; Mick Stubbs;
Technical Graphics Department OUP; Harry Venning; Margaret Wellbank; Graham
White; Colin Woolf; Michael Woods

Maps © Oxford University Press

Designed by Danielle Toothill at
Andrew Boag: Typographic problem solving, London

Cover design by Richard Morris

Typeset in Great Britain by Tradespools Ltd, Frome
Printed in China

Contents

Preface

This new edition has been fully revised and updated to make it the perfect study companion for intermediate and upper intermediate learners of English in the 21st century. Our aim has been to produce a dictionary that can be used both in the classroom and for self-study. We have added hundreds of new words and meanings along with new features including a grammar section and new study pages. At the same time we have retained the strengths of the first edition – clear, simple definitions, thousands of examples and grammar patterns, and notes explaining difficult areas of language.

My special thanks go to James Greenan and Alison Waters for their hard work in editing this dictionary with me. Their ideas and contributions have been invaluable throughout the project. I would like to thank Margaret Deuter for her work on the grammar pages and Julie Darbyshire and Jane Taylor for their work on the illustrations. Thanks also go to Sally Wehmeier, the editor of the first edition of *Wordpower* on which this new edition is based. I would also like to acknowledge the contribution made by the many teachers and students who helped us in our research. Finally I am grateful to Frank Keenan and the production team who transformed the edited text into a printed dictionary.

Miranda Steel
Oxford, 2000

Wordpower Workout

How good a dictionary user are you?

All you need to do to find out how an entry works in *Wordpower* is to use your dictionary to answer the questions in this quiz.

1 If an area is suffering from **drought**, what is it lacking?
   A food **B** water **C** air

2 How long is a **fortnight**?
   A one night **B** four nights **C** two weeks

3 *The people were really friendly*. What part of speech is **friendly** in this sentence?
   A adjective **B** adverb **C** preposition

4 What phrasal verb could you use to replace **extinguish** in the following sentence?
   It took firefighters four hours to extinguish the blaze.
   A put away **B** put out **C** put off

5 What is the opposite of **sensible**?
   A senseless **B** insensitive **C** silly

6 If two people meet and get on like **a house on fire** what happens?
   A they fall in love **B** they become good friends **C** they start to argue

7 What does **GP** stand for?
   A guinea pig **B** general practitioner **C** general post

8 Which of the following words does not rhyme with **court**?
   A fought **B** port **C** curt

9 What is the past participle of **lay**?
   A laid **B** lain **C** lay

10 Which syllable is stressed in the word **economize**?
    A the first **B** the second **C** the fourth

11 Which of the following nouns is **countable**?
    A luggage **B** baggage **C** holdall

12 What is the adjective related to **humility**?
    A humble **B** human **C** humid

13 What is the US English word for **fridge**?
    A freezer **B** icebox **C** ice cube

14 What is the plural of **criterion**?
    A criterions **B** criteria **C** criterion

Wordpower Workout

15 When does the verb **eat** take a direct object?
    A always   **B** never   **C** sometimes

16 What part of speech is **square** in this sentence? *You'll have to square it with your manager first.*
    A verb   **B** noun   **C** adjective

17 Which entry in the dictionary tells you the meaning of **square** in the previous question?
    A square¹   **B** square²   **C** square³

18 What is the correct phonetic spelling of **dictionary**?
    A /ˈdɪkʃənri/   **B** /ˈdɪtʃənri/   **C** /ˈdiːkʃɒnri/

19 If something or somebody **gives you the creeps**, how do you feel?
    A excited   **B** frightened   **C** shy

20 Which preposition should go in the space? *How did the children react ____ the news?*
    A with   **B** against   **C** to

Match the definitions on the left with the terms on the right and then number them to show the order in which they would appear in a dictionary entry. The first one has been done for you.

the word in **bold blue** type	example
adj/noun/verb/adv	definition
look forward to sth/doing sth	derivative
*It began to **rain heavily**.*	idiom
(be) above board	part of speech
–heavily	headword 1
/fəˈnetɪks/	phrasal verb
the meaning of the word	pronunciation

Now that you have discovered how to use the entries effectively, the rest of the **Wordpower Workout** will help you make the most of all the other features of your dictionary *and* develop your language skills at the same time.

Wordpower Workout

Finding your way around your dictionary

Getting there quickly
At the top of each page of your dictionary there are two words in blue. These are guide words. They show you the first and the last word on that page and are there to help you find the word you want quickly.

Look at the following guide words and try to think of two words that will appear on each page.

bind – biscuit   **heath – heel**   **smudge – sneer**

Now look at those pages to see if you were right.

Finding the right word
1 When you look up a word in your dictionary, you may not find it in exactly the same form as it appears in the text you are reading. This is because it may be:
   – a comparative or superlative form of an adjective
   – a plural form of a noun
   – a verb ending in -s, -ed, -ing or an irregular form of a verb
   – a derivative

   Under which headword do you think you'll find the meanings of the following words?

example	watched	*watch*	funniest	
	cheaply		children	
	factories		encouragement	
	digging		optimist	
	happiness		older	

2 Look up the word kick. There are two headwords for this word, **kick**[1] and **kick**[2]. They have the same spelling but one is a verb and the other is a noun.

   How many headwords can you find for the following words? Write down the parts of speech (**noun**, **verb**, **adjective**, etc) of the different headwords in the final column.

example	increase	*2 verb, noun*	light	_
	bank	_	blind	_
	film	_	warm	_

Finding the right meaning
In English many words have more than one meaning. Read these sentences, then look at the entries for the word in bold and write down which meaning is being used.

The **film** was based on a true story.
I'm going to make some hot **chocolate**. Would you like some?
Once I've made a promise, I never **break** it.
We had a **light** lunch then went shopping.
I'm still waiting for Barry to **return** that book I lent him.

Wordpower Workout

Picture crossword

Look at the **colour pages** (C1–C8) to find the answers.

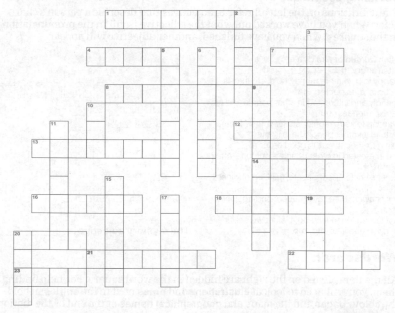

Across

1   the long thick hairs that grow near the mouth of some animals such as a mouse, cat, etc

4   the long sharp teeth of a dog, snake, etc

7   a small building that is used for keeping things in

8   a piece of clothing, similar to trousers, but covering your chest as well as your legs and with straps that go over the shoulders

12 a small red vegetable that is white inside with a strong taste. You eat these in salads.

13 a piece of clothing like a woollen jacket, that fastens at the front

14 small pieces of meat, vegetables, etc that are cooked on a stick

16 a street musician

18 a wild plant with purple flowers and sharp points on its leaves

20 the main long thin part of a plant from which the leaves or flowers grow

21 a young tree

22 a long plastic or paper tube that you can use for drinking through

23 one of the two organs of your body that are inside your chest and are used for breathing

Down

2   one of the small flat pieces of hard material that cover the body of some fish and animals

3   the set of wide bones at the bottom of your back, to which your leg bones are joined

5   one of the parts into which an orange can be divided

6   an umbrella that you use to protect yourself from the sun

9   (used about a drink) containing bubbles of gas

10 the long, green part of some plants, such as peas and beans, that contains the seeds

11 a long jacket with a covering for the head that protects you from the rain or wind

15 an underground room that is used for storing things

17 a small wooden house

19 the room or space under the roof of a house

20 the bottom surface of your foot

Wordpower Workout

Pronunciation

Sounding people out

The definitions on the left all refer to adjectives that describe a person's character. When you have worked out what the adjective is, fill in the pronunciation in the squares. When you have finished, another adjective will appear.

often worried or afraid **n e _ _ _ _ s**
often angry **b a _ – t _ _ _ _ _ _ d**
happy to give more money, help, etc than is
   usual or expected **ge _ _ _ _ _ s**
friendly and interested in other people and new
   experiences **ou _ _ _ _ _ g**
wanting to keep money, etc for yourself rather
   than let other people have it **me _ _**
liking to keep things in good order **ti _ _**
too interested in other people's personal affairs
   no _ y
careful not to upset people; thinking of others
   co _ _ _ _ _ _ _ _ e
not showing thought or understanding; foolish
   si _ _ _
not talking too much about your own abilities,
   good qualities, etc **mo _ _ _ _**

↓

| aʊ | t | g | əʊ | ɪ | ŋ |

The mystery adjective is _____

Wordsearch

All the items listed on the right are hidden in the word square. For help finding them, you will need to look at **illustrations** and **notes** next to the **entries** in bold, the **colour pages** and the **maps** and **geographical names** at the end of the dictionary. **Write down each word when you find it.**

t	s	l	a	u	b	e	r	g	i	n	e
i	w	c	o	c	k	r	o	a	c	h	c
s	a	d	d	l	e	l	a	c	o	r	n
d	r	e	a	d	l	o	c	k	s	m	w
o	m	f	b	j	p	b	o	t	p	h	r
r	o	b	o	e	u	s	d	r	a	k	e
c	l	i	v	e	r	t	o	n	n	e	s
h	s	q	u	o	r	e	e	g	i	s	p
i	s	i	e	v	e	r	g	h	a	n	a
d	r	a	s	t	a	p	l	e	r	n	d
e	b	t	r	n	k	i	f	w	d	c	e
w	e	l	l	i	n	g	t	o	n	y	l

1 a thing you use in the **kitchen** for separating solid food from a liquid
2 a thing that you find in an **office** for fastening papers together
3 a thing you use in the **garden** for digging holes
4 a type of **insect** that lives in damp places
5 the part of a bike that you sit on
6 a purple vegetable
7 the country that has Accra as its capital
8 a wind instrument
9 a type of flower that can be many different colours and shapes
10 a type of dress that many Asian women wear
11 the organ in your body that cleans your blood
12 the capital of New Zealand
13 a group of **bees**
14 a large **shellfish** that we eat
15 a male **duck**
16 the fruit of an **oak** tree
17 a person from Spain
18 this hairstyle ——————→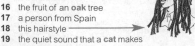
19 the quiet sound that a **cat** makes
20 a female **deer**

Wordpower Workout

Adjectives, nouns and opposites

First, look at the entry for the given word to help you fill in the empty boxes.
Then, complete the sentences below with one of the words from the boxes, and
a preposition if necessary

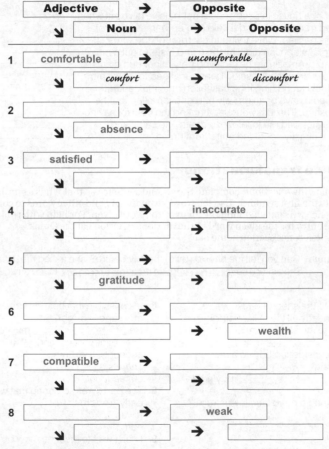

	Adjective →	**Opposite**
	↘ **Noun** →	**Opposite**

	Adjective	Opposite	Noun	Opposite
1	comfortable →	*uncomfortable*		
	↘ *comfort* →	*discomfort*		
2	→			
	↘ absence →			
3	satisfied →			
	↘ →			
4	→	inaccurate		
	↘ →			
5	→			
	↘ gratitude →			
6	→			
	↘ →	wealth		
7	compatible →			
	↘ →			
8	→	weak		
	↘ →			

1 I felt *uncomfortable about* telling her that I didn't like the food.

2 The captain's _____ the team badly affected their confidence.

3 In the survey, 70% of commuters expressed _____ the train service, while 30% said they were happy with it.

4 The article is full of _____. For example, it said that the Olympics were held in 1997.

5 I bought her some flowers to show my _____ all her help.

6 He went bankrupt and spent the rest of his life in _____ .

7 The printer won't work because it's not _____ your computer.

8 My main _____ in French are poor pronunciation and poor grammar.

Wordpower Workout

Spot the error

In each line of the text there is one mistake. <u>Underline</u> the mistake and write the correct word at the end of the line. If you need help in identifying the mistake, look at the page numbered on the right.

For help, look at page

The owner of a house in Leeds could not <u>beleive</u> his eyes when *believe*

he returned from work to find a cold and embarassed burglar   **S11**

laying in his garden. While trying to cut through the wires   **S11**

of the burglar alarm, he did a mistake and instead cut a main   **S23**

electric cable. Amazingly, he recieved only minor burns and   **S25**

cuts. The owner of the flat said, 'I was surprised for how calm   **S11**

he was when I found him. If he has fallen onto the concrete   **S27**

path, he would have been gravely hurt or even killed, but he   **G8**

felt into bushes.' The lucky burglar thanked the man for saving   **S24**

his life: 'He stopped me to freeze to death,' he said, 'and   **773**

because of him, I've decided retire from crime.'   **S28**

        S28

Sentence transformations

For the following questions, complete the second sentence so that it has a similar meaning to the first sentence. Use the word given in **bold** and other words to complete each sentence without changing the form of the word given. For help with this exercise, look at the entry for the given word in the dictionary, or look at the Quick Grammar Reference section at the back.

Example 'Can you tell me how to get to the city centre?' she asked me. (**directions**)
She asked me *for directions /to give her directions* to the city centre.

1 I'm off to the shop because we've drunk nearly all the milk. (**running**)
I'm off to the shop because _____ milk.

2 We're considering buying a new car. (**thinking**)
We're _____ buying a new car.

3 I really had a good time in Australia. (**enjoyed**)
I really _____ in Australia.

4 'Let's all go out and celebrate tonight,' James said. (**suggested**)
James _____ that night.

5 Police are questioning a man in connection with the robbery. (**questioned**)
A man _____ in connection with the robbery.

6 It's possible that he didn't get my message. (**might**)
He _____ my message.

7 There's almost no money left in our account. (**hardly**)
There's _____ left in our account.

8 The party was so boring that we left early. (**such**)
It was _____ that we left early.

9 I can't wait to meet her new boyfriend. (**dying**)
I'm _____ her new boyfriend.

10 I arrived late, so I missed the train. (**earlier**)
If I _____ caught the train.

Wordpower Workout

Fill in the missing words

Complete the following text by writing the correct word or words in each space. The notes below will help you to use your dictionary to find the answers.

Measuring up to 10 feet at the shoulder and (**1**) _____ up to 12 000 lbs, the African elephant is the heaviest land mammal.
It keeps cool by flapping its ears, which circulates cold blood through its body, and by covering itself (**2**) _____ mud or dust, which also helps protect it (**3**) _____ the sun and (**4**) _____ insects.
Numbers have reduced drastically as elephants (**5**) _____ killed for their ivory. This is now illegal but still goes (**6**) _____ . Some are also killed (**7**) _____ farmers, who face the impossible job of keeping elephants (**8**) _____ their crops.
Their tusks are actually two teeth. They are different sizes and shapes depending (**9**) _____ where the elephant lives and what jobs the elephant uses them for. They can be used (**10**) _____ digging, fighting, lifting or removing obstacles.
Most elephants tend to use one tusk more (**11**) _____ the other – like us, they are left- or right-handed.
Female elephants and young males live (**12**) _____ family groups. Typically, a family group consists (**13**) _____ a mother and her daughters and grand-children. Males leave the herd when they (**14**) _____ adults and live (**15**) _____ or in other groups of males.

Where can I find the information to help me?

This dictionary can help you in many different ways. Remember to look in all the possible places that could help you to find the correct word.

Which tense should I use?
Information about grammar including tenses, the passive, nouns and relative clauses is in the Quick Grammar Reference section.

Do I need a gerund or an infinitive?
Look at page S28 Verb patterns. It will tell you about many of the most common ones.

Which preposition?
You can find information about prepositions at the entry for the word.
Example: ask (sb) (about sth); prevent sb (from) (doing sth)

I think I know which word it is but I'm not sure.
Hundreds of usage notes explain the differences between similar words.

It's a phrasal verb but which particle do I need?
Look at the section marked PHRASAL VERBS at the entry for the verb.

Is it an irregular verb?
Check the list on page 773.

Is it an idiom?
Check in the section marked IDIOMS at the entry for one of the main words in it.

Don't forget to look at the example sentences which will show you the most common patterns and collocations of a word.

Aa

A, a¹ /eɪ/ **noun** [C] (*pl* **A's**; **a's** /eɪz/) **1** the first letter of the English alphabet: *'Andy' begins with (an) 'A'.* **2** the highest grade given for an exam or piece of work: *I got an 'A' for my essay.*

★**a²** /ə; *strong form* eɪ/ (also **an** /ən; *strong form* æn/) **indefinite article**

➤ The form **an** is used before a vowel sound.

1 one: *A cup of coffee, please.* • *We've got an apple, a banana and two oranges.* **2** used when you talk about one example of sth for the first time: *I saw a dog chasing a cat this morning. The cat climbed up a tree.* • *Have you got a dictionary* (= any dictionary)? **3** used for saying what kind of person or thing sb/sth is: *He's a doctor.* • *She's a Muslim.* • *You are a clever boy.* • *'Is that an eagle?''No, it's a falcon.'* **4** (used with prices, rates, measurements) each: *I usually drink two litres of water a day.* • *twice a week* • *He was travelling at about 80 miles an hour.* **5** used with some expressions of quantity: *a lot of money* • *a few cars* **6** used when you are talking about a typical example of sth: *An elephant can live for up to eighty years.* •➤ You can also use the plural in this sense: *Elephants can live for up to eighty years.*

➤ For more information about the indefinite article, look at the **Quick Grammar Reference** section at the back of this dictionary.

the AA /ˌeɪ 'eɪ/ **abbr** (in Britain) the Automobile Association; an organization for drivers. If you are a member of the AA and your car breaks down, they will send sb to help you: *My car wouldn't start so I called the AA.*

aback /əˈbæk/ **adv**
  <u>PHRASAL VERB</u> take sb aback → **TAKE**

★**abandon** /əˈbændən/ **verb** [T] **1** to leave sb/sth that you are responsible for, usually permanently: *The bank robbers abandoned the car just outside the city.* **2** to stop doing sth without finishing it or without achieving what you wanted to do: *The search for the missing sailors was abandoned after two days.* –**abandonment noun** [U]

abashed /əˈbæʃt/ **adj** feeling guilty and embarrassed because of sth that you have done: *'I'm sorry', said Ali, looking abashed.*

abattoir /ˈæbətwɑː/ (*Brit*) = **SLAUGHTERHOUSE**

abbey /ˈæbi/ **noun** [C] a large church together with a group of buildings where religious communities of men (**monks**) or women (**nuns**) live or used to live

abbr (also **abbrev**) **abbr** abbreviation

abbreviate /əˈbriːvieɪt/ **verb** [T] to make sth shorter, especially a word or phrase: *'Kilometre' is usually abbreviated to 'km'.* •➤ Look at **abridge**.

abbreviation /əˌbriːviˈeɪʃn/ **noun** [C] a short form of a word or phrase: *In this dictionary 'sth' is the abbreviation for 'something'.*

ABC /ˌeɪ biː ˈsiː/ **noun** [sing] **1** the alphabet; the letters of English from A to Z **2** the simple facts about sth: *an ABC of Gardening*

abdicate /ˈæbdɪkeɪt/ **verb 1** [I] to give up being King or Queen: *The Queen abdicated in favour of her son* (= her son became king). **2** [T] to give sth up, especially power or a position: *to abdicate responsibility* (= to refuse to be responsible for sth) –**abdication** /ˌæbdɪˈkeɪʃn/ **noun** [C,U]

abdomen /ˈæbdəmən/ **noun** [C] a part of your body below the chest, in which the stomach is contained –**abdominal** /æbˈdɒmɪnl/ **adj**

abduct /æbˈdʌkt/ **verb** [T] to take hold of sb and take him/her away illegally: *He has been abducted by a terrorist group.* –**abduction noun** [C,U]

abet /əˈbet/ **verb** [T] (**abetting**; **abetted**)
  <u>IDIOM</u> aid and abet → **AID²**

abhor /əbˈhɔː/ **verb** [T] (**abhorring**; **abhorred**) to hate sth very much: *All civilized people abhor the use of torture.*

abhorrence /əbˈhɒrəns/ **noun** [U] a strong feeling of hate; disgust: *Protesters expressed their abhorrence of war.*

abhorrent /əbˈhɒrənt/ **adj** that makes you feel hate or disgust: *The idea of slavery is abhorrent to us nowadays.*

abide /əˈbaɪd/ **verb**
  <u>IDIOM</u> can't/couldn't abide sb/sth/doing sth to hate sb/sth; to not like sb/sth at all
  <u>PHRASAL VERB</u> abide by sth to obey a law, etc; to do what sb has decided

★**ability** /əˈbɪləti/ **noun** [C,U] (*pl* **abilities**) (an) ability to do sth the mental or physical power or skill that makes it possible to do sth: *an ability to make decisions* • *A person of his ability will have no difficulty getting a job.*

ablaze /əˈbleɪz/ **adj** (not before a noun) burning strongly; completely on fire: *Soldiers used petrol to set the building ablaze.*

★**able** /ˈeɪbl/ **adj 1 be able to do sth** (used as a modal verb) to have the ability, power, opportunity, time, etc to do sth: *Will you be able to come to a meeting next week?* • *I was able to solve the problem quickly.* • *Many men don't feel able to express their emotions.*

➤ In the passive **can/could** are used, not **be able**: *The arrangement can't be changed.* For more information about modal verbs, look at the **Quick Grammar Reference** section at the back of this dictionary.

2 clever; doing your job well: *one of the ablest/most able students in the class* • *an able politician* –**ably** /ˈeɪbli/ **adv**

able-ˈbodied adj physically healthy and strong; having full use of your body

abnormal /æbˈnɔːml/ **adj** different from

a

what is normal or usual, in a way that worries you or that is unpleasant: *abnormal weather conditions* ··➤ opposite **normal** –**abnormally** adv: *abnormally high temperatures*

abnormality /ˌæbnɔːˈmæləti/ noun [C,U] (*pl* **abnormalities**) something that is not normal, especially in a person's body: *He was born with an abnormality of the heart.*

aboard /əˈbɔːd/ adv, prep on or into a train, ship, aircraft or bus: *We climbed aboard the train and found a seat.* ● *Welcome aboard this flight to Caracas.*

abode /əˈbəʊd/ noun [sing] (*written*) the place where you live
IDIOM (of) no fixed abode/address → FIXED

abolish /əˈbɒlɪʃ/ verb [T] to end a law or system officially: *When was capital punishment abolished here?*

abolition /ˌæbəˈlɪʃn/ noun [U] the act of ending a law or system officially: *the abolition of slavery in the US*

abominable /əˈbɒmɪnəbl/ adj very bad; shocking –**abominably** /-əbli/ adv

Aboriginal /ˌæbəˈrɪdʒənl/ (also **Aborigine** /ˌæbəˈrɪdʒəni/) noun [C] a member of the race of people who were the original inhabitants of Australia –**Aboriginal** adj: *Aboriginal traditions*

abort /əˈbɔːt/ [T] verb 1 to end sth before it is complete: *The company aborted the project when they realized it was costing too much.* 2 to make a baby (**foetus**) die before it is born

abortion /əˈbɔːʃn/ noun [C,U] a medical operation that causes a baby to die inside its mother before it is fully developed: *to have an abortion* ● *Abortion is illegal in that country.*

➤ Compare **miscarriage**.

abortive /əˈbɔːtɪv/ adj not completed successfully; failed: *He made two abortive attempts to escape from prison.*

abound /əˈbaʊnd/ verb [I] 1 to exist in large numbers: *Animals abound in the forest.* ● *Rumours abound about the actor's arrest.* 2 **abound with sth** to contain large numbers of sth: *The lake abounds with fish.*

★**about**¹ /əˈbaʊt/ adv 1 (*especially US* **around**) a little more or less than; approximately: *It's about three miles from here to the city centre.* ● *I got home at about half past seven.* 2 (*informal*) almost; nearly: *Dinner's just about ready.* 3 (also **around**) in many directions or places: *I could hear people moving about upstairs.* ● *Don't leave your clothes lying about all over the floor.* 4 (also **around**) (used after certain verbs) without doing anything in particular: *The kids spend most evenings sitting about, bored.* 5 (also **around**) present in a place; existing: *It was very late and there were few people about.* ● *There isn't much good music about these days.*
IDIOM be about to do sth to be going to do sth very soon: *The film's about to start.* ● *I was just about to explain when she interrupted me.*

★**about**² /əˈbaʊt/ prep 1 on the subject of: *Let's talk about something else.* ● *What's your book about?* ● *He told me all about his family.* ● *I don't like it, but there's nothing I can do about it.* 2 (also **around**) in many directions or places; in different parts of sth: *We wandered about the town for an hour or two.* ● *Lots of old newspapers were scattered about the room.* 3 in the character of sb/sth: *There's something about him that I don't quite trust.* ● *I like the food, the climate, and everything else about this country.*
IDIOM how/what about...? 1 (used when asking for information about sb/sth or for sb's opinion or wish): *How about Ruth? Have you heard from her lately?* ● *I'm going to have chicken. What about you?* 2 (used when making a suggestion): *What about going to a film tonight?*

a,bout-ˈturn (*US* **a,bout-ˈface**) noun [C] a complete change of opinion, plan or behaviour: *The government did an about-turn over tax.* ··➤ Look at **U-turn**.

★**above** /əˈbʌv/ prep 1 in a higher place: *The people in the flat above make a lot of noise.* ● *The coffee is in the cupboard above the sink.* 2 in an earlier part (of sth written): *Contact me at the above address/the address above.* ··➤ opposite **below**, but note that **below** is not used before a noun: *Contact me at the address below.* 3 more than a number, amount, price, etc: *children aged 11 and above* ● *A score of 70 and above will get you a grade B.* ● *You must get above 50% to pass.* ● *above-average temperatures* ··➤ opposite **below** ··➤ Look at **over**. 4 with a higher position in an organization, etc: *The person above me is the department manager.* ··➤ opposite **below** 5 too proud to do sth: *He seems to think he's above helping with the cleaning.*
IDIOMS above all (used to emphasize the main point) most importantly: *Above all, stay calm!* (be) above board (used especially about a business deal, etc) honest and open

abrasive /əˈbreɪsɪv/ adj 1 rough and likely to scratch: *Do not use abrasive cleaners on the bath.* 2 (used about a person) rude and rather aggressive

abreast /əˈbrest/ adv **abreast (of sb/sth)** next to or level with sb/sth and going in the same direction: *The soldiers marched two abreast.*
IDIOM be/keep abreast of sth to have all the most recent information about sth

abridge /əˈbrɪdʒ/ verb [T] to make sth (usually a book) shorter by removing parts of it ··➤ Look at **abbreviate**.

★**abroad** /əˈbrɔːd/ adv in or to another country or countries: *They found it difficult to get used to living abroad.* ● *My mother has never been abroad.* ● *She often goes abroad on business.*

abrupt /əˈbrʌpt/ adj 1 sudden and unexpected: *an abrupt change of plan* 2 seeming rude and unfriendly –**abruptly** adv –**abruptness** noun [U]

abscess /ˈæbses/ noun [C] a swelling on or

in the body, containing a poisonous yellow liquid (pus)

abscond /əb'skɒnd/ *verb* [I] (*formal*) **abscond (from sth) (with sth)** to run away from a place where you should stay, sometimes with sth that you should not take: *to abscond from prison* ● *She absconded with all the company's money.*

absence /'æbsəns/ *noun* **1** [C,U] a time when sb is away from somewhere; the fact of being away from somewhere: *Frequent absences due to illness meant he was behind with his work.* ● *I have to make all the decisions in my boss's absence.* **2** [U] the fact of sth/sb not being there; lack: *In the absence of a doctor, try to help the injured person yourself.* ●➤ opposite **presence**

★**absent** /'æbsənt/ *adj* **1** **absent (from sth)** not present somewhere: *He was absent from work because of illness.* ●➤ opposite **present** **2** thinking about sth else; not paying attention: *an absent stare* –**absently** *adv*

absentee /,æbsən'ti:/ *noun* [C] a person who is not in the place where he/she should be

absenteeism /,æbsən'ti:ɪzəm/ *noun* [U] the problem of workers or students often not going to work or school

,absent-'minded *adj* often forgetting or not noticing things, because you are thinking about sth else ●➤ synonym **forgetful** –**absent-mindedly** *adv*

absolute /'æbsəlu:t/ *adj* **1** complete; total: *The whole trip was an absolute disaster.* ● *None of the political parties had an absolute majority* (= more votes, etc than all the other parties together). **2** not measured in comparison with sth else: *Spending on the Health Service has increased in absolute terms.*

★**absolutely** *adv* **1** /'æbsəlu:tli/completely; totally: *It's absolutely freezing outside!* ● *I absolutely refuse to believe that.* ● *He made absolutely no effort* (= no effort at all) *to help me.* **2** /,æbsə'lu:tli/(used when you are agreeing with sb) yes; certainly: *'It is a good idea, isn't it?' 'Oh, absolutely!'*

absolve /əb'zɒlv/ *verb* [T] **absolve sb (from/of sth)** to say formally that sb does not have to take responsibility for sth: *The driver was absolved of any blame for the train crash.*

★**absorb** /əb'zɔ:b; əb'sɔ:b/ *verb* [T] **1** **absorb sth (into sth)** to take in and hold sth (a liquid, heat, etc): *a drug that is quickly absorbed into the bloodstream* ● *Black clothes absorb the sun's heat.* **2** to take sth into the mind and understand it: *I found it impossible to absorb so much information so quickly.* **3** **absorb sth (into sth)** to take sth into sth larger, so that it becomes part of it: *Over the years many villages have been absorbed into the city.* **4** to hold sb's attention completely or interest sb very much: *History is a subject that absorbs her.* **5** to reduce the effect of a sudden violent knock, hit, etc: *The front of the car is designed to absorb most of the impact of a crash.* –**absorption** /əb'zɔ:pʃn; əb'sɔ:pʃn/ *noun* [U]

absorbed /əb'zɔ:bd; əb'sɔ:bd/ *adj* **absorbed (in sth)** giving all your attention to sth: *He was absorbed in his work and didn't hear me come in.*

absorbent /əb'zɔ:bənt; əb'sɔ:bənt/ *adj* able to take in and hold liquid: *an absorbent cloth*

absorbing /əb'zɔ:bɪŋ; əb'sɔ:bɪŋ/ *adj* holding all your interest and attention: *an absorbing book*

abstain /əb'steɪn/ *verb* [I] **1** (*formal*) **abstain (from sth/doing sth)** to stop yourself from doing sth that you enjoy: *The doctor said I should abstain from (drinking) alcohol until I'm better.* ●➤ noun **abstinence 2** (in a vote) to say that you are not voting either for or against sth: *Two people voted in favour, two voted against and one abstained.* ●➤ noun **abstention**

abstention /əb'stenʃn/ *noun* [C,U] the act of not voting either for or against sth

abstinence /'æbstɪnəns/ *noun* [U] (*formal*) stopping yourself from having or doing sth that you enjoy: *The doctor advised total abstinence from alcohol.* ●➤ verb **abstain**

abstract¹ /'æbstrækt/ *adj* **1** existing only as an idea, not as a physical thing: *It is hard to imagine an abstract idea like 'eternity'.* ●➤ opposite **concrete 2** (used about art) not showing people and things as they really look: *an abstract painting*

abstract² /'æbstrækt/ *noun* [C] **1** an example of abstract art **2** a short piece of writing that tells you the main contents of a book, speech, etc

IDIOM **in the abstract** only as an idea, not in real life

absurd /əb'sɜ:d/ *adj* not at all logical or sensible; ridiculous: *It would be absurd to spend all your money on one book.* ● *Don't be absurd! I can't possibly do all this work in one day.* –**absurdity** *noun* [C,U] (*pl* **absurdities**) –**absurdly** *adv*

abundance /ə'bʌndəns/ *noun* [U,sing] a very large quantity of sth: *These flowers grow here in abundance.* ● *There is an abundance of wildlife in the forest.*

abundant /ə'bʌndənt/ *adj* existing in very large quantities; more than enough: *abundant supplies of food* –**abundantly** *adv*

abuse¹ /ə'bju:z/ *verb* [T] **1** to use sth in a bad or dishonest way: *The politician was accused of abusing his position in order to become rich.* **2** to say rude things to sb **3** to treat sb badly, often violently: *The girl had been sexually abused.*

abuse² /ə'bju:s/ *noun* **1** [C,U] using sth in a bad or dishonest way: *an abuse of power* ● *the dangers of drug abuse* **2** [U] rude words, used to insult another person: *The other driver leaned out of the car and hurled abuse at me.* ● *racial abuse* **3** [U] bad, usually violent treatment of sb: *He subjected his children to verbal and physical abuse.* ● *a victim of sexual abuse*

abusive /ə'bju:sɪv/ *adj* using rude language to insult sb: *an abusive remark*

abysmal /ə'bɪzməl/ *adj* very bad; of very poor quality –**abysmally** *adv*

abyss /ə'bɪs/ *noun* [C] a very deep hole that seems to have no bottom

academic[1] /ˌækə'demɪk/ *adj* **1** connected with education, especially in schools and universities: *The academic year begins in September.* **2** connected with subjects of interest to the mind rather than technical or practical subjects: *academic subjects such as History* •➤ opposite **non-academic 3** not connected with reality; not affecting the facts of a situation: *It's academic which one I prefer because I can't have either of them.* –**academically** /-kli/ *adv*

academic[2] /ˌækə'demɪk/ *noun* [C] a person who teaches and/or does research at a university or college

academy /ə'kædəmi/ *noun* [C] (*pl* **academies**) **1** a school for special training: *a military academy* **2** (also **Academy**) an official group of people who are important in art, science or literature: *the Royal Academy of Arts*

accelerate /ək'seləreɪt/ *verb* [I,T] to go faster; to make sth go faster or happen more quickly: *The driver slowed down for the bend then accelerated away.* • *The government plans to accelerate the pace of reform.* –**acceleration** /ək,selə'reɪʃn/ *noun* [U]

accelerator /ək'seləreɪtə/ *noun* [C] the control in a vehicle that you press with your foot in order to make it go faster •➤ picture on page S9

★**accent** /'æksənt; -sent/ *noun* **1** [C,U] a particular way of pronouncing words that is connected with the country, area or social class that you come from: *He speaks with a strong Scottish accent.* **2** [C] the greater force that you give to a particular word or part of a word when you speak: *In the word 'because' the accent is on the second syllable.* **3** [C] (in writing) a mark, usually above a letter, that shows that it has to be pronounced in a certain way **4** [C,usually sing] the particular importance that is given to sth: *In all our products the accent is on quality.*

accentuate /ək'sentʃueɪt/ *verb* [T] to make sth easier to notice: *She uses make-up to accentuate her beautiful eyes.*

★**accept** /ək'sept/ *verb* **1** [I,T] to agree to take sth that sb offers you: *Please accept this small gift.* • *Do I have to pay in cash or will you accept a cheque?* • *Why won't you accept my advice?* **2** [I,T] to say yes to sth or to agree to sth: *Thank you for your invitation. I am happy to accept.* • *He asked her to marry him and she accepted.* • *She has accepted the job.* **3** [I,T] to admit or recognize that sth unpleasant is true: *They refused to accept responsibility for the accident.* **4** [T] to allow sb to join a group, etc: *The university has accepted me on the course.*

acceptable /ək'septəbl/ *adj* **1** that can be allowed: *One or two mistakes are acceptable but no more than that.* **2** good enough; satisfactory: *We hope that you will consider our*

offer acceptable. •➤ opposite **unacceptable** –**acceptability** /ək,septə'bɪləti/ *noun* [U] –**acceptably** /ək'septəbli/ *adv*

acceptance /ək'septəns/ *noun* [C,U] the act of accepting or being accepted: *His ready acceptance of the offer surprised me.* • *He quickly gained acceptance in the group* (= the other people thought of him as equal to them). • *The new methods have received widespread acceptance.*

access[1] /'ækses/ *noun* [U] **1** access (to sth) a way of entering or reaching a place: *Access to the garden is through the kitchen.* **2** access (to sth) the chance or right to use or have sth: *Do you have access to a personal computer?* **3** access (to sb) permission, especially legal or official, to see sb: *They are divorced, but he has regular access to the children.*

access[2] /'ækses/ *verb* [T] to find information on a computer: *Click on the icon to access a file.*

accessible /ək'sesəbl/ *adj* **1** possible to be reached or entered: *The island is only accessible by boat.* **2** easy to get, use or understand: *This television programme aims to make history more accessible to children.* •➤ opposite **inaccessible** –**accessibility** /ək,sesə'bɪləti/ *noun*: *Computers have given people greater accessibility to information.*

accession /æk'seʃn/ *noun* [U] the act of taking a very high position, especially as ruler of a country or head of sth

accessory /ək'sesəri/ *noun* [C] (*pl* **accessories**) **1** an extra item that is added to sth and is useful or attractive but not of great importance: *The car has accessories such as an electronic alarm.* **2** [usually pl] a thing that you wear or carry that matches your clothes, for example a piece of jewellery, a bag, etc **3** an accessory (to sth) (in law) a person who helps sb to do sth illegal

★**accident** /'æksɪdənt/ *noun* [C] an unpleasant event that happens unexpectedly and causes damage, injury or death: *I hope they haven't had an accident.* • *a car accident* • *a fatal accident* (= when sb is killed) • *I didn't mean to kick you, it was an accident.*

IDIOM **by accident** by chance; without intending to: *I knocked the vase over by accident as I was cleaning.*

accidental /ˌæksɪ'dentl/ *adj* happening by chance; not planned: *Police do not know if the explosion was accidental or caused by a bomb.* –**accidentally** /-təli/ *adv*: *She accidentally took the key to the office home with her, so nobody could get in.*

accident-prone *adj* often having accidents

acclaim /ə'kleɪm/ *verb* [T] to express a very high opinion of sth/sb: *a highly acclaimed new film* • *The novel has been acclaimed as a modern classic.* –**acclaim** *noun* [U]: *The film received widespread critical acclaim.*

acclimatize (also **-ise**) /ə'klaɪmətaɪz/ *verb* [I,T] **acclimatize (yourself/sb/sth) (to sth)** to get used to a new climate, a new situation, etc so that it is not a problem any more –**acclimatization** (also **-isation**) /əˌklaɪmətarˈzeɪʃn/ **noun** [U] –**acclimatized** (also **-ised**) **adj**

accolade /ˈækəleɪd/ **noun** [C] a comment, prize, etc that you receive that shows people's high opinion of sth you have done

accommodate /əˈkɒmədeɪt/ **verb** [T] **1** to have enough space for sb/sth, especially for a certain number of people: *Each apartment can accommodate up to six people.* **2** to provide sb with a place to stay, live or work: *During the conference, you will be accommodated in a nearby hotel.* **3** (*formal*) to do or provide what sb wants or needs

accommodating /əˈkɒmədeɪtɪŋ/ **adj** (used about a person) agreeing to do or provide what sb wants: *My boss is very accommodating when I need time off work.*

★**accommodation** /əˌkɒməˈdeɪʃn/ **noun** [U] a place for sb to live or stay: *We lived in rented accommodation before buying this house.* ● *The price of the holiday includes flights and accommodation.*

> **Accommodation** is uncountable. We cannot say, 'I will help you to find an accommodation.' In this case we could say, 'I will help you to find somewhere to live.'

accompaniment /əˈkʌmpənimənt/ **noun** [C] something that goes together with another more important thing: *He only drinks wine as an accompaniment to food.*

★**accompany** /əˈkʌmpəni/ **verb** [T] (*pres part* **accompanying**; *3rd pers sing pres* **accompanies**; *pt, pp* **accompanied**) **1** to go together with sb/sth: *He went to America accompanied by his wife and three children.* ● *Massive publicity accompanied the film's release.* **2** accompany sb (on sth) to play music for a singer or another instrument: *She accompanied him on the guitar.*

accomplice /əˈkʌmplɪs/ **noun** [C] an accomplice (to/in sth) a person who helps sb to do sth bad, especially a crime: *She was charged with being an accomplice to the murder.*

accomplish /əˈkʌmplɪʃ/ **verb** [T] to succeed in doing sth difficult that you planned to do: *I managed to accomplish my goal of writing ten letters in an evening.*

accomplished /əˈkʌmplɪʃt/ **adj** highly skilled at sth: *an accomplished actor*

accomplishment /əˈkʌmplɪʃmənt/ **noun** **1** [U] the act of completing sth successfully: *the accomplishment of a plan* **2** [C] something difficult that sb has succeeded in doing or learning

accord¹ /əˈkɔːd/ **noun** [C] an agreement, especially between countries: *the Helsinki accords on human rights*

IDIOMS **in accord** in agreement about sth

of your own accord without being forced or asked: *He wasn't sacked from his job – he left of his own accord.*

accord² /əˈkɔːd/ **verb** (*formal*) **1** [T] to give

sth to sb **2** [I] accord (with sth) to match; to agree with

accordance /əˈkɔːdns/ **noun**

IDIOM **in accordance with sth** in a way that follows or obeys sth: *to act in accordance with instructions*

accordingly /əˈkɔːdɪŋli/ **adv 1** in a way that is suitable: *I realized that I was in danger and acted accordingly.* **2** (*formal*) therefore; for that reason

★**according to** /əˈkɔːdɪŋ tə; *before vowels* tuː; tu/ **prep 1** as stated by sb; as shown by sth: *According to Mick, it's a brilliant film.* ● *More people now have a high standard of living, according to the statistics.* **2** in a way that matches, follows or depends on sth: *Everything went off according to plan* (= as we had planned it). ● *The salary will be fixed according to age and experience.*

accordion /əˈkɔːdiən/ **noun** [C] a musical instrument that you hold in both hands and play by pulling the two sides apart and then pushing them together, while pressing the keys and/or buttons with your fingers ➹ Look at the note at **piano**. ➹ picture at **music**

accost /əˈkɒst/ **verb** [T] to go up and talk to a stranger in a way that is rude or frightening

★**account**¹ /əˈkaʊnt/ **noun** [C] **1** somebody's report or description of sth that has happened: *She gave the police a full account of the robbery.* **2** (*abbr* **a/c**) the arrangement by which a bank looks after your money for you: *to open/close an account* ● *I have an account with/at Barclays.* ● *I paid the cheque into my bank account.*

> We use a **current** account to pay for things with a **cheque**. We can save money in a **deposit** or **savings** account.

3 [usually pl] a record of all the money that a person or business has received or paid out: *If you are self-employed you have to keep your own accounts.* **4** an arrangement with a shop, etc that allows you to pay for goods or services at a later date: *Most customers settle/pay their account in full at the end of each month.*

IDIOMS **by all accounts** according to what everyone says: *By all accounts, she's a very good doctor.*

by your own account according to what you say yourself: *By his own account, Peter was not very good at his job.*

on account of because of: *Our flight was delayed on account of bad weather.*

on no account; not on any account not for any reason: *On no account should you walk home by yourself.*

take account of sth; take sth into account to consider sth, especially when deciding or judging sth: *We'll take account of your comments.* ● *We'll take your comments into account.*

account² /əˈkaʊnt/ **verb**

PHRASAL VERB **account for sth 1** to explain or give a reason for sth: *How can we account for these changes?* **2** to form the amount that is mentioned: *Sales to Europe accounted for 80% of our total sales last year.*

accountable /ə'kaʊntəbl/ *adj* expected to give an explanation of your actions, etc; responsible: *She is too young to be held accountable for what she did.* –**accountability** /-ə'bɪlɪti/ *noun* [U]

accountancy /ə'kaʊntənsi/ *noun* [U] the work or profession of an accountant

accountant /ə'kaʊntənt/ *noun* [C] a person whose job is to keep or examine the financial accounts of a business, etc

accumulate /ə'kju:mjəleɪt/ *verb* **1** [T] to collect a number or quantity of sth over a period of time: *Over the years, I've accumulated hundreds of books.* **2** [I] to increase over a period of time: *Dust soon accumulates if you don't clean the house for a week or so.* –**accumulation** /ə,kju:mjə'leɪʃn/ *noun* [C,U]

★**accurate** /'ækjərət/ *adj* exact and correct; without mistakes: *He managed to give the police an accurate description of the robbers.* ● *That clock isn't very accurate.* ••➤ opposite **inaccurate** –**accuracy** /'ækjərəsi/ *noun* [U] ••➤ opposite **inaccuracy** –**accurately** *adv*: *It is difficult to estimate the age of these bones accurately.*

accusation /,ækju'zeɪʃn/ *noun* [C,U] a statement saying that sb has done sth wrong

★**accuse** /ə'kju:z/ *verb* [T] **accuse sb (of sth/ doing sth)** to say that sb has done sth wrong or broken the law: *I accused her of cheating.* ● *He was accused of murder and sent for trial.*

the accused /ə'kju:zd/ *noun* [C] (*pl* **the accused**) (used in a court of law) the person who is said to have broken the law

accusing /ə'kju:zɪŋ/ *adj* showing that you think sb has done sth wrong: *He gave me an accusing look.* –**accusingly** *adv*

accustom /ə'kʌstəm/ *verb* [T] **accustom yourself/sb/sth to sth** to make yourself/sb/ sth get used to sth: *It took me a while to accustom myself to working nights.*

accustomed /ə'kʌstəmd/ *adj* **1** **accustomed to sth** if you are accustomed to sth, you are used to it and it is not strange for you: *She's accustomed to travelling a lot in her job.* ● *It took a while for my eyes to get accustomed to the dark room.* **2** (*formal*) usual; regular

ace /eɪs/ *noun* [C] **1** a playing card which has a single shape on it. An ace has either the lowest or the highest value in a game of cards: *the ace of spades* ••➤ Look at the note and picture at **card**. **2** (in tennis) the first hit of the ball (**service**) that the person playing against you cannot hit back: *to serve an ace*

★**ache¹** /eɪk/ *noun* [C,U] a pain that lasts for a long time: *to have toothache/earache/ stomach-ache*

> ➤ **Ache** is often used in compounds. In British English it is usually used without 'a' or 'an': *I've got toothache.* But we always use 'a' with 'headache': *I've got a bad headache.* In US English, ache is usually used with 'a' or 'an', especially when talking about a par-

ticular attack of pain: *I have an awful tooth-ache.*

ache² /eɪk/ *verb* [I] to feel a continuous pain: *His legs ached after playing football.* ● *She was aching all over.*

★**achieve** /ə'tʃi:v/ *verb* [T] **1** to complete sth by hard work and skill: *They have achieved a lot in a short time.* **2** to gain sth, usually by effort or skill: *You have achieved the success you deserve.*

★**achievement** /ə'tʃi:vmənt/ *noun* [C,U] something that you have done successfully, especially through hard work or skill: *She felt that winning the gold medal was her greatest achievement.* ● *He enjoys climbing mountains because it gives him a sense of achievement.*

Achilles' heel /ə,kɪli:z 'hi:l/ *noun* [C] a weak point or fault in sb/sth

★**acid¹** /'æsɪd/ *noun* [C,U] (in chemistry) a liquid substance that can dissolve metal and may burn your skin or clothes. Acids have a pH value of less than 7: *sulphuric acid* ••➤ Look at **alkali** and **base**.

acid² /'æsɪd/ *adj* **1** (used about a fruit, etc) with a sour taste **2** (also **acidic** /ə'sɪdɪk/) containing an acid: *an acid solution* ••➤ Look at **alkaline**.

acidity /ə'sɪdəti/ *noun* [U] the quality of being acid: *to measure the acidity of soil*

acid 'rain *noun* [U] rain that has chemicals in it from factories, etc and that causes damage to trees, buildings and rivers

acknowledge /ək'nɒlɪdʒ/ *verb* [T] **1** to accept or admit that sth is true or exists: *He acknowledged (the fact) that he had made a mistake.* ● *He is acknowledged to be the country's greatest writer.* **2** to show that you have seen or noticed sb/sth or received sth: *The manager sent a card to all the staff to acknowledge their hard work.*

acknowledgement /ək'nɒlɪdʒmənt/ *noun* **1** [U] the act of showing that you have seen or noticed sb/sth: *The president gave a smile of acknowledgement to the photographers.* **2** [C,U] a letter, etc that says that sth has been received or noticed: *I haven't received (an) acknowledgement of my job application yet.* **3** [C] a few words of thanks that an author writes at the beginning or end of a book to the people who have helped him/her

acne /'ækni/ *noun* [U] a skin disease that usually affects young people. When you have acne you get a lot of spots on your face and neck

acorn /'eɪkɔ:n/ *noun* [C] the small nut that grows on a tree (**an oak**), and that grows in a base shaped like a cup

acoustic /ə'ku:stɪk/ *adj* **1** connected with sound or the sense of hearing **2** (of a musical instrument) not electric: *an acoustic guitar* ••➤ picture at **music**

acoustics /ə'ku:stɪks/ *noun* [pl] the qualities of a room, etc that make it good or bad for you to hear music, etc in: *The theatre has excellent acoustics.*

[C] **countable**, a noun with a plural form: *one book, two books*   [U] **uncountable**, a noun with no plural form: *some sugar*

acquaintance /əˈkweɪntəns/ **noun 1** [C] a person that you know but who is not a close friend **2** [U] acquaintance with sb/sth a slight knowledge of sb/sth

acquainted /əˈkweɪntɪd/ **adj** (*formal*) **1** acquainted with sth knowing sth: *I went for a walk to get acquainted with my new neighbourhood.* **2** acquainted (with sb) knowing sb, but usually not very closely

acquiesce /ˌækwiˈes/ **verb** [I] (*written*) acquiesce in/to sth to accept sth without argument, although you may not agree with it –acquiescence /ˌækwiˈesns/ **noun** [U]

acquire /əˈkwaɪə/ **verb** [T] (*formal*) to obtain or buy sth: *She acquired an American accent while living in New York.* • *He's acquired a reputation for being difficult to work with.* • *The company has acquired shares in a rival business.*

acquisition /ˌækwɪˈzɪʃn/ **noun** (*formal*) **1** [U] the act of obtaining or buying sth: *a study of language acquisition in children* **2** [C] something that you have obtained or bought: *This sculpture is the museum's latest acquisition.*

acquit /əˈkwɪt/ **verb** [T] (**acquitting**; **acquitted**) **1** acquit sb (of sth) to state formally that a person is not guilty of a crime: *The jury acquitted her of murder.* •➤ opposite **convict 2** (*formal*) acquit yourself... to behave in the way that is mentioned: *He acquitted himself well in his first match as a professional.* –acquittal /əˈkwɪtl/ **noun** [C,U]

acre /ˈeɪkə/ **noun** [C] a measure of land; 0·405 of a hectare: *a farm of 20 acres/a 20-acre farm*

acrobat /ˈækrəbæt/ **noun** [C] a person who performs difficult movements of the body, especially in a show which travels to different towns (a circus)

acrobatic /ˌækrəˈbætɪk/ **adj** performing or involving difficult movements of the body: *an acrobatic dancer* • *an acrobatic leap* –acrobatically /-kli/ **adv**

acrobatics /ˌækrəˈbætɪks/ **noun** [U] (the art of performing) difficult movements of the body

acronym /ˈækrənɪm/ **noun** [C] an acronym (for sth) a short word that is made from the first letters of a group of words: *TEFL is an acronym for Teaching English as a Foreign Language.*

★**across** /əˈkrɒs/ **adv, prep 1** from one side of sth to the other: *The stream was too wide to jump across.* • *He walked across the field.* • *A smile spread across his face.* • *The river was about 20 metres across.* • *The bank has 800 branches across* (= in all parts of) *the country.* **2** on the other side of sth: *There's a bank just across the road.* • *The house across the road from us is for sale.*

➤ We can use **across** or **over** to mean 'on or to the other side': *I ran across/over the road.* But when we talk about crossing something high, we usually use **over**: *I can't climb over that wall.* With 'room' we usually

use **across**: *I walked across the room to the door.*

IDIOM across the board involving or affecting all groups, members, cases, etc

acrylic /əˈkrɪlɪk/ **noun** [C,U] an artificial material that is used in making clothes and paint

★**act¹** /ækt/ **verb 1** [I] act (on sth) to do sth; to take action: *The doctor knew he had to act quickly to save the child.* • *I'm always giving my brother advice but he never acts on* (= as a result of) *it.* **2** [I] act as sth to perform a particular function: *The man we met on the plane to Tokyo was kind enough to act as our guide.* • *The elephant's trunk acts as a nose, a hand and an arm.* **3** [I] to behave in the way that is mentioned: *Stop acting like a child!* • *Although she was trying to act cool, I could see she was really upset.* • *He hasn't really hurt himself – he's just acting!* • *Ali's acting strangely today – what's wrong with him?* **4** [I,T] to perform in a play or film: *I acted in a play at school.*

★**act²** /ækt/ **noun** [C] **1** a thing that you do: *In a typical act of generosity they refused to accept any money.* • *to commit a violent act*

> Act and action can have the same meaning: *It was a brave act/action.* Act, not action can be followed by of: *It was an act of bravery.* Activity is used for something that is done regularly: *I like outdoor activities such as walking and gardening.*

2 (often Act) one of the main divisions of a play or opera: *How many scenes are there in Act 4?* **3** a short piece of entertainment, especially as part of a show: *Did you enjoy the clowns' act?* **4** (often Act) a law made by a government: *The government passed an act forbidding the keeping of guns.* **5** behaviour that hides your true feelings: *She seems very happy but she's just putting on an act.*

IDIOMS a hard act to follow ➜ **HARD¹**

be/get in on the act become involved in an activity that is becoming popular

get your act together to organize yourself so that you can do sth properly: *If he doesn't get his act together he's going to lose his job.*

in the act (of doing sth) while doing sth, especially sth wrong: *He was looking through the papers on her desk and she caught him in the act.*

acting¹ /ˈæktɪŋ/ **adj** doing the job mentioned for a short time: *James will be the acting director while Henry is away.*

acting² /ˈæktɪŋ/ **noun** [U] the art or profession of performing in plays or films

★**action** /ˈækʃn/ **noun 1** [U] doing things, often for a particular purpose: *Now is the time for action.* • *If we don't take action quickly it'll be too late!* •➤ opposite **inaction 2** [C] something that you do: *The doctor's quick action saved the child's life.* • *They should be judged by their actions, not by what they say.* •➤ Look at the note at act². **3** [sing] the most important events in a story or play: *The action takes place in London during the*

Second World War. **4** [U] exciting things that happen: *There's not much action in this boring town.* ● *I like films with lots of action.* ● *an action-packed film* **5** [U] fighting in a war: *Their son was killed in action.* **6** [sing] the effect that one substance has on another: *They're studying the action of alcohol on the brain.* **7** [C,U] the process of settling an argument in a court of law: *He is going to take legal action against the hospital.*

IDIOMS in action in operation; while working or doing sth: *We shall have a chance to see their new team in action next week.*

into action into operation: *We'll put the plan into action immediately.*

out of action not able to do the usual things; not working: *The coffee machine's out of action again.*

activate /'æktɪveɪt/ **verb** [T] to make sth start working: *A slight movement can activate the car alarm.*

★**active** /'æktɪv/ **adj 1** involved in activity; lively: *My grandfather is very active for his age.* ● *I have a very active social life.* ● *I was at the meeting but I didn't take an active part in the discussion.* ••► opposite **inactive 2** that produces an effect; that is in operation: *an active volcano* (= one that can still erupt) **3** used about the form of a verb or a sentence when the subject of the sentence performs the action of the verb: *In the sentence 'The dog bit him', the verb is active.*

➤ You can also say: 'The verb is in the active'. Look at **passive**.

activist /'æktɪvɪst/ **noun** [C] a person who takes action to cause political or social change, usually as a member of a group: *a protest by environmental activists*

★**activity** /æk'tɪvəti/ **noun** (*pl* **activities**) **1** [U] a situation in which there is a lot of action or movement: *The house was full of activity on the morning of the wedding.* ••► opposite **inactivity 2** [C] something that you do, usually regularly and for enjoyment: *The hotel offers a range of leisure activities.* ••► Look at the note at **act²**.

★**actor** /'æktə/ **noun** [C] a man or woman whose job is to act in a play, film or on television

actress /'æktrəs/ **noun** [C] a woman whose job is to act in a play, film or on television

★**actual** /'æktʃuəl/ **adj** real; that happened: *The actual damage to the car was not as great as we had feared.* ● *They seemed to be good friends but in actual fact they hated each other.*

★**actually** /'æktʃuəli/ **adv 1** really; in fact: *You don't actually believe her, do you?* ● *I can't believe that I'm actually going to America! 2* although it may seem strange: *He actually expected me to cook his meal for him!*

➤ **Actually** is often used in conversation to get somebody's attention or to correct somebody politely: *Actually, I wanted to show you something. Have you got a minute?* ● *We aren't married, actually.* ● *I don't agree*

about the book. I think it's rather good, actually.

In English **actually** does **not** mean 'at the present time'. We use **currently, at present** or **at the moment** instead: *He's currently working on an article about China.* ● *I'm studying for my exams at present.*

acupuncture /'ækjupʌŋktʃə/ **noun** [U] a way of treating an illness or stopping pain by putting thin needles into parts of the body

acute /ə'kjuːt/ **adj 1** very serious; very great: *an acute shortage of food* ● *acute pain* **2** (used about an illness) becoming dangerous very quickly: *acute appendicitis*

➤ Compare **chronic**.

3 (used about feelings or the senses) very strong: *Dogs have an acute sense of smell.* ● *acute hearing* **4** showing that you are able to understand things easily: *The report contains some acute observations on the situation.* –acutely **adv**

a,cute 'angle **noun** [C] an angle of less than 90°

AD /,eɪ 'diː/ **abbr** from the Latin 'anno domini'; used in dates for showing the number of years after the time when Jesus Christ was born: *AD 44* ••► Look at **BC**.

ad /æd/ **noun** (*informal*) = **ADVERTISEMENT**: *I saw your ad in the local paper.*

adage /'ædɪdʒ/ **noun** [C] a well-known phrase expressing sth that is always true about people or the world

adamant /'ædəmənt/ **adj** (*formal*) very sure; refusing to change your mind –adamantly **adv**

★**adapt** /ə'dæpt/ **verb 1** [I,T] adapt (yourself) (to sth) to change your behaviour because the situation you are in has changed: *He was quick to adapt (himself) to the new system.* **2** [T] adapt sth (for sth) to change sth so that you can use it in a different situation: *The bus was adapted for disabled people.* ● *The teacher adapts the coursebook to suit the needs of her students.*

adaptable /ə'dæptəbl/ **adj** able to change to suit new situations

adaptation /,ædæp'teɪʃn/ **noun 1** [C] a play or film that is based on a novel, etc **2** [U] the state or process of changing to suit a new situation

adapted /ə'dæptɪd/ **adj** having all the necessary qualities to do sth: *Chickens are poorly adapted for flight.*

adaptor (also **adapter**) /ə'dæptə/ **noun** [C] **1** a device that allows you to connect more than one piece of electrical equipment to an electricity supply point (**socket**) **2** a device for connecting pieces of electrical equipment that were not designed to be fitted together

★**add** /æd/ **verb 1** [I,T] add (sth) (to sth) to put sth together with sth else, so that you increase the size, number, value, etc: *I added a couple more items to the shopping list.* ● *The noise of the crowd added to the excitement of the race.* **2** [I,T] to put numbers or amounts together so that you get a total: *If you add 3* *and* 3 *together, you get* 6. ● *Add* $8 *to the total, to cover postage and packing.* ● *Ronaldo cost more than all the other players added together.* ● *Don't ask me to work it out – I can't add.* ‣ opposite **subtract**

> We often use the word **plus** when we add two numbers: *2 plus 2 is 4.*

3 [T] to say sth more: *'By the way, please don't tell anyone I phoned you,' she added.*

PHRASAL VERBS **add sth on (to sth)** to include sth: *10% will be added on to your bill as a service charge.*

add up to seem to be a true explanation: *I'm sorry, but your story just doesn't add up.*

add (sth) up to find the total of several numbers: *The waiter hadn't added up the bill correctly.*

add up to sth to have as a total: *How much does all the shopping add up to?*

added /'ædɪd/ **adj** in addition to what is usual; extra: *milk with added vitamins*

'added to prep in addition to sth; as well as

adder /'ædə/ **noun** [C] a small poisonous snake

addict /'ædɪkt/ **noun** [C] a person who cannot stop taking or doing sth harmful: *a drug addict* –**addicted** /ə'dɪktɪd/ **adj addicted (to sth): *He is addicted to heroin.* ‣ synonym **hooked on** –**addiction noun** [C,U]: *the problem of teenage drug addiction*

addictive /ə'dɪktɪv/ **adj** difficult to stop taking or doing: *a highly addictive drug* ● *an addictive game*

★**addition** /ə'dɪʃn/ **noun 1** [U] adding sth, especially two or more numbers ‣ Look at **subtraction. 2** [C] **an addition (to sth)** a person or thing that is added to sth

IDIOM **in addition (to sth)** as well as: *She speaks five foreign languages in addition to English.*

additional /ə'dɪʃənl/ **adj** added; extra: *a small additional charge for the use of the swimming pool* –**additionally** /-ʃənəli/ **adv**

additive /'ædətɪv/ **noun** [C] a substance that is added to sth in small amounts for a special purpose: *food additives* (= to add colour or flavour)

★**address¹** /ə'dres/ **noun** [C] **1** the number of the building and the name of the street and place where sb lives or works: *Let me give you my home/business address.* ● *She no longer lives at this address.* ● *Please inform the office of any change of address.* ● *an address book* (= a small book that you keep the addresses of people you know in) **2** a series of words and/or numbers that tells you where you can find sb/sth using a computer: *What's your e-mail address?* **3** a formal speech that is given to an audience

address² /ə'dres/ **verb** [T] **1 address sth (to sb/sth)** to write the name and address of the person you are sending a letter, etc to: *The parcel was returned because it had been wrongly addressed.* **2** to make an important speech to an audience **3** (*formal*) **address (yourself to) sth** to try to deal with a prob-

lem, etc: *The government is finally addressing the question of corruption.* **4 address sb as sth** to talk or write to sb using a particular name or title: *She prefers to be addressed as 'Ms'.* **5** (*formal*) **address sth to sb** make a comment, etc to sb: *Would you kindly address any complaints you have to the manager.*

adept /ə'dept/ **adj adept (at sth)** very good or skilful at sth ‣ opposite **inept**

adequate /'ædɪkwət/ **adj 1** enough for what you need: *Make sure you take an adequate supply of water with you.* **2** just good enough; acceptable: *Your work is adequate but I'm sure you could do better.* ‣ opposite **inadequate** –**adequacy** /'ædɪkwəsi/ **noun** [U] –**adequately adv**: *The mystery has never been adequately explained.*

adhere /əd'hɪə/ **verb** [I] (*formal*) **1 adhere (to sth)** to stick firmly to sth: *Make sure that the paper adheres firmly to the wall.* **2 adhere to sth** to continue to support an idea, etc; to follow a rule

adherent /əd'hɪərənt/ **noun** [C] somebody who supports a particular idea –**adherence noun** [U]

adhesive¹ /əd'hiːsɪv/ **noun** [C] a substance that makes things stick together: *a fast-drying adhesive*

adhesive² /əd'hiːsɪv/ **adj** that can stick, or can cause two things to stick together; sticky: *He sealed the parcel with adhesive tape.*

ad hoc /ˌæd 'hɒk/ **adj** made or done suddenly for a particular purpose: *They set up an ad hoc committee to discuss the matter.* ● *Staff training takes place occasionally on an ad hoc basis.*

adjacent /ə'dʒeɪsnt/ **adj adjacent (to sth)** situated next to or close to sth: *There was a fire in the adjacent building.* ● *She works in the office adjacent to mine.*

adjectival /ˌædʒek'taɪvl/ **adj** that contains or is used like an adjective: *The adjectival form of 'smell' is 'smelly'.*

★**adjective** /'ædʒɪktɪv/ **noun** [C] (*grammar*) a word that tells you more about a noun: *The adjective 'reserved' is often applied to British people.* ● *What adjective would you use to describe my sister?*

adjoining /ə'dʒɔɪnɪŋ/ **adj** next to or nearest to sth: *A scream came from the adjoining room.*

adjourn /ə'dʒɜːn/ **verb** [I,T] to stop a meeting, a trial, etc for a short time and start it again later: *The meeting adjourned for lunch.* ● *The trial was adjourned until the following week.* –**adjournment noun** [C]

adjudicate /ə'dʒuːdɪkeɪt/ **verb** [I,T] (*written*) to act as an official judge in a competition or to decide who is right when two people or groups disagree about sth

adjudicator /ə'dʒuːdɪkeɪtə/ **noun** [C] a person who acts as a judge, especially in a competition

★**adjust** /ə'dʒʌst/ **verb 1** [T] to change sth slightly, especially because it is not in the right position: *The brakes on my bicycle need* *adjusting.* ● *The seat can be adjusted to different positions.* **2** [I] **adjust (to sth)** to get used to new conditions or a new situation: *She found it hard to adjust to working at night.* –adjustment noun [C,U]: *We'll just* **make** *a few* **minor adjustments** *and the room will look perfect.*

adjustable /ə'dʒʌstəbl/ **adj** that can be adjusted: *an adjustable mirror*

ad lib /ˌæd 'lɪb/ **adj, adv** done or spoken without preparation: *She had to speak ad lib because she couldn't find her notes.* –ad lib **verb** [I] (**ad libbing; ad libbed**): *The singer forgot the words so he had to ad lib.*

admin = ADMINISTRATION

administer /əd'mɪnɪstə/ **verb** [T] (*formal*) **1** to control or manage sth **2** to give sb sth, especially medicine

administration /ədˌmɪnɪ'streɪʃn/ **noun** **1** (also **admin** /'ædmɪn/) [U] the control or the act of managing sth, for example a system, an organization or a business: *The administration of a large project like this is very complicated.* ● *A lot of the teachers' time is taken up by admin.* **2** (also **admin** /'ædmɪn/) [sing] the group of people or part of a company that organizes or controls sth: *the hospital administration* ● *She works in admin, on the second floor.* **3** (often **the Administration**) [C] the government of a country, especially the US: *the Clinton Administration*

administrative /əd'mɪnɪstrətɪv/ **adj** connected with the organization of a country, business, etc, and the way in which it is managed: *London is still the most important administrative centre in Britain.*

administrator /əd'mɪnɪstreɪtə/ **noun** [C] a person whose job is to organize or manage a system, a business, etc

admirable /'ædmərəbl/ **adj** (*formal*) that you admire; excellent –admirably /-əbli/ **adv**: *She dealt with the problem admirably.*

admiral /'ædmərəl/ **noun** [C] the most important officer in the navy

admiration /ˌædmə'reɪʃn/ **noun** [U] admiration **(for/of sb/sth)** a feeling of liking and respecting sb/sth very much: *I have great admiration for what he's done.*

★**admire** /əd'maɪə/ **verb** [T] **admire sb/sth (for sth/doing sth)** to respect or like sb/sth very much; to look at sb/sth with pleasure: *Everyone admired the way he dealt with the problem.* ● *I've always admired her for being such a wonderful mother.* ● *We stopped at the top of the hill to admire the view.*

admirer /əd'maɪərə/ **noun** [C] a person who admires sb/sth: *I've always been a great admirer of her books.*

admiring /əd'maɪərɪŋ/ **adj** feeling or expressing admiration –admiringly **adv**

admission /əd'mɪʃn/ **noun** **1** [C,U] admission **(to sth)** the act of allowing sb to enter a school, club, public place, etc: *Admissions to British universities have increased by 15% this year.* ●➤ Look at **entrance**. **2** [U] the amount of money that you have to pay to enter a

place: *The museum charges half-price admission on Mondays.* **3** [C] a statement that admits that something is true

★**admit** /əd'mɪt/ **verb** (**admitting; admitted**) **1** [I,T] **admit sth; admit to sth/doing sth; admit (that...)** to agree that sth unpleasant is true or that you have done sth wrong: *He refused to admit to the theft.* ● *You should admit your mistake.* ● *After trying four times to pass the exam, I finally* **admitted defeat**. ● *I have to admit (that) I was wrong.* ● *She admitted having broken the computer.* ●➤ opposite **deny 2** [T] **admit sb/sth (into/to sth)** to allow sb/sth to enter; to take sb into a place: *He was admitted to hospital with suspected appendicitis.*

admittance /əd'mɪtns/ **noun** [U] (*formal*) being allowed to enter a place; the right to enter: *The journalist tried to gain admittance to the minister's office.*

admittedly /əd'mɪtɪdli/ **adv** it must be admitted (that...): *The work is very interesting. Admittedly, I do get rather tired.*

adolescence /ˌædə'lesns/ **noun** [U] the period of a person's life between being a child and becoming an adult, between the ages of about 13 and 17 ●➤ Look at **teenager**.

adolescent /ˌædə'lesnt/ **noun** [C] a young person who is no longer a child and not yet an adult, between the ages of about 13 and 17: *the problems of adolescents* ● *an adolescent daughter*

adopt /ə'dɒpt/ **verb 1** [I,T] to take a child into your family and treat him/her as your own child by law: *They couldn't have children so they adopted.* ● *They're hoping to adopt a child.* **2** [T] to take and use sth: *What approach did you adopt when dealing with the problem?* –adopted **adj**: *an adopted child* –adoption **noun** [C,U]: *The number of adoptions has risen in the past year* (= the number of children being adopted).

adoptive /ə'dɒptɪv/ (used about parents) having legally taken a child to live with them as part of their family: *the baby's adoptive parents*

adorable /ə'dɔ:rəbl/ **adj** (used about children or animals) very attractive; lovely

adore /ə'dɔ:/ **verb** [T] **1** to love and admire sb very much: *Kim adores her older sister.* **2** to like sth very much: *She adores children.* –adoration /ˌædə'reɪʃn/ **noun** [U] –adoring **adj**: *his adoring fans*

adorn /ə'dɔ:n/ **verb** [T] **adorn sth (with sth)** to add sth in order to make a thing or person more attractive or beautiful

adrenalin /ə'drenəlɪn/ **noun** [U] a substance that your body produces when you are very angry, frightened or excited and that makes your heart go faster

adrift /ə'drɪft/ **adj** (not before a noun) (used about a boat) not tied to anything or controlled by anyone

★**adult** /'ædʌlt; ə'dʌlt/ **noun** [C] a person or animal that is fully grown: *This film is suitable for both adults and children.* –adult **adj**

adultery /ə'dʌltəri/ **noun** [U] (*formal*) sex

between a married person and sb who is not his/her wife/husband: *to commit adultery*

adulthood /'ædʌlthʊd; ə'dʌlt-/ **noun** [U] the time in your life when you are an adult

advance¹ /əd'vɑːns/ **verb 1** [I] to move forward: *The army advanced towards the city.* ••➤ opposite **retreat 2** [I,T] to make progress or help sth make progress: *Our research has not advanced much recently.*

advance² /əd'vɑːns/ **noun 1** [C,usually sing] forward movement: *the army's advance towards the border* ••➤ opposite **retreat 2** [C,U] progress in sth: *advances in computer technology* **3** [C] an amount of money that is paid to sb before the time when it is usually paid

IDIOM **in advance (of sth)** before a particular time or event: *You should book tickets for the concert well in advance.*

advance³ /əd'vɑːns/ **adj** (only *before* a noun) that happens before sth: *There was no advance warning of the earthquake.*

★**advanced** /əd'vɑːnst/ **adj 1** of a high level: *an advanced English class* **2** highly developed: *a country that is not very advanced industrially*

Ad'vanced level = **A LEVEL**

★**advantage** /əd'vɑːntɪdʒ/ **noun 1** [C] an **advantage (over sb)** something that may help you to do better than other people: *Her experience gave her a big advantage over the other people applying for the job.* ● *Living abroad means he **has the advantage of** being fluent in two languages.* ● *Some runners try to gain an unfair advantage by taking drugs.* **2** [C,U] something that helps you or that will bring you a good result: *the advantages and disadvantages of a plan* ● *The traffic is so bad here that **there is no advantage in** having a car.* ••➤ opposite **disadvantage**

IDIOM **take advantage of sb/sth 1** to make good or full use of sth: *We should take full advantage of these low prices while they last.* **2** to make unfair use of sb or of sb's kindness, etc in order to get what you want: *You shouldn't let him take advantage of you like this.*

advantageous /ˌædvən'teɪdʒəs/ **adj** that will help you or bring you a good result

advent /'ædvent/ **noun** [sing] **1** (*formal*) the fact of sb/sth arriving **2 Advent** (in the Christian year) the four weeks before Christmas

adventure /əd'ventʃə/ **noun** [C,U] an experience or event that is very unusual, exciting or dangerous: *She left home to travel, hoping for excitement and adventure.* ● *Our journey through the jungle was quite an adventure!*

adventurous /əd'ventʃərəs/ **adj 1** (used about a person) liking to try new things or have adventures: *I'm not an adventurous cook – I like to stick to recipes I know.* **2** involving adventure: *For a more adventurous holiday try mountain climbing.*

★**adverb** /'ædvɜːb/ **noun** [C] a word that adds more information about place, time, manner, cause or degree to a verb, an adjective, a

phrase or another adverb: *In 'speak slowly', 'extremely funny', 'arrive late' and 'I know her well', 'slowly', 'extremely', 'late' and 'well' are adverbs.*

adversary /'ædvəsəri/ **noun** [C] (*pl* **adversaries**) (*formal*) an enemy, or an opponent in a competition

adverse /'ædvɜːs/ **adj** (*formal*) making sth difficult for sb: *Our flight was cancelled because of adverse weather conditions.* ••➤ opposite **favourable** ••➤ Look also at **unfavourable**. –**adversely** adv

adversity /əd'vɜːsəti/ **noun** [C,U] (*pl* **adversities**) (*formal*) difficulties or problems

★**advert** /'ædvɜːt/ (*Brit informal*) = **ADVERTISEMENT**

★**advertise** /'ædvətaɪz/ **verb 1** [I,T] to put information in a newspaper, on television, on a picture on the wall, etc in order to persuade people to buy sth, to interest them in a new job, etc: *a poster advertising a new type of biscuit* ● *The job was advertised in the local newspapers.* ● *It's very expensive to advertise on television.* **2** [I] **advertise for sb/sth** to say publicly in a newspaper, on a sign, etc that you need sb to do a particular job, want to buy sth, etc: *The shop is advertising for a part-time sales assistant.* –**advertising noun** [U]: *The magazine gets a lot of money from advertising.* ● *an advertising campaign*

★**advertisement** /əd'vɜːtɪsmənt/ (also *informal* **advert**; **ad**) **noun** [C] a piece of information in a newspaper, on television, a picture on a wall, etc that tries to persuade people to buy sth, to interest them in a new job, etc: *an advertisement for a new brand of washing powder* ● *to put an advertisement in a newspaper*

★**advice** /əd'vaɪs/ **noun** [U] an opinion that you give sb about what he/she should do: *She **took** her doctor's **advice** and gave up smoking.* ● *Let me **give** you some **advice** …*

➤ **Advice** is an uncountable noun, so we cannot say 'an advice' or 'some advices'. We can say: *a piece of advice* and: *a lot of advice.*

advisable /əd'vaɪzəbl/ **adj** (*formal*) that is a good thing to do; sensible: *It is advisable to reserve a seat.* ••➤ opposite **inadvisable**

★**advise** /əd'vaɪz/ **verb 1** [I,T] **advise (sb) (to do sth)**; **advise (sb) (against sth/against doing sth)** to tell sb what you think he/she should do: *I would strongly advise you to take the job.* ● *They advised us not to travel on a Friday.* ● *The newspaper article advised against eating too much meat.* ● *He did what the doctor advised.* ● *She advises the Government on economic affairs.* **2** [T] (*formal*) to officially tell sb sth; to inform sb

adviser (*US* **advisor**) /əd'vaɪzə/ **noun** [C] a person who gives advice to a company, government, etc: *an adviser on economic affairs*

advisory /əd'vaɪzəri/ **adj** giving advice only; not having the power to make decisions

advocate¹ /'ædvəkeɪt/ **verb** [T] (*formal*) to recommend or say that you support a particular plan or action

a

advocate² /'ædvəkət/ **noun** [C] **1** an advocate (of sth) a person who supports a particular plan or action, especially in public **2** a lawyer who defends sb in a court of law

aerial¹ /'eəriəl/ (*US* **antenna**) **noun** [C] a long metal stick on a building, car, etc that receives radio or television signals

aerial² /'eəriəl/ **adj** from or in the air: *an aerial photograph of the town*

aerobics /eə'rəubɪks/ **noun** [U] physical exercises that people do to music: *I do aerobics twice a week to keep fit.* ••➤ picture on page S2

aerodynamics /,eərəudaɪ'næmɪks/ **noun** [U,pl] the scientific study of the way that things move through the air –**aerodynamic adj**: *the aerodynamic design of a racing car*

★**aeroplane** /'eərəpleɪn/ (also **plane**; *US* **airplane**) **noun** [C] a vehicle with wings and one or more engines that can fly through the air: *the noise of an aeroplane flying overhead*

aerosol /'eərəsɒl/ **noun** [C] a container in which a liquid substance is kept under pressure. When you press a button the liquid comes out in a fine spray. ••➤ picture at **spray**

aesthetic /i:s'θetɪk/ (*US also* **esthetic** /es'θetɪk/) **adj** concerned with beauty or art: *The columns are there for purely aesthetic reasons* (= only to look beautiful). –**aesthetically** (*US also* **esthetically**) /-kli/ **adv**: *The design is **aesthetically pleasing** as well as practical.*

afar /ə'fɑː/ **adv** (*written*)
    IDIOM **from afar** from a long distance away

★**affair** /ə'feə/ **noun 1** [C] an event or situation: *The whole affair has been extremely unpleasant.* **2 affairs** [pl] important personal, business, national, etc matters: *the minister for foreign affairs • current affairs* (= the political and social events that are happening at the present time) **3** [sing] something private that you do not want other people to know about: *What happened between us is my affair. I don't want to discuss it.* **4** [C] a sexual relationship between two people, usually when at least one of them is married to sb else: *She's **having an affair with** her boss.*
    IDIOM **state of affairs** → **STATE¹**

★**affect** /ə'fekt/ **verb** [T] **1** make sb/sth change in a particular way; to influence sb/sth: *Her personal problems seem to be affecting her work. • This disease affects the brain.* ••➤ Look at the note at **influence**. **2** to make sb feel very sad, angry, etc: *The whole community was affected by the terrible tragedy.*

    ➤ Notice that **affect** is a verb and **effect** is a noun: *Smoking can affect your health. • Smoking can have a bad effect on your health.*

affected /ə'fektɪd/ **adj** (used about a person or his/her behaviour) not natural or sincere ••➤ opposite **unaffected** –**affectation** /,æfek'teɪʃn/ **noun** [C,U]

★**affection** /ə'fekʃn/ **noun** [C,U] (an) affection (for/towards sb/sth) a feeling of loving or liking sb/sth: *Mark felt great affection for his sister.*

affectionate /ə'fekʃənət/ **adj** showing that you love or like sb very much: *a very affectionate child* –**affectionately adv**

affiliate /ə'fɪlieɪt/ **verb** [T] (usually passive) affiliate sth (to sth) to connect an organization to a larger organization: *Our local club is affiliated to the national association.* –**affiliated adj** –**affiliation** /ə,fɪli'eɪʃn/ **noun** [C,U]

affinity /ə'fɪnəti/ **noun** [C,U] (*pl* **affinities**) **1** (an) affinity (for/with sb/sth) a strong feeling that you like and understand sb/sth, usually because you feel similar to him/her/it in some way: *He had always had an affinity for wild and lonely places.* **2** (an) affinity (with sb/sth); (an) affinity (between A and B) a similar quality in two or more people or things

affirm /ə'fɜːm/ **verb** [T] (*formal*) to say formally or clearly that sth is true or that you support sth strongly –**affirmation** /,æfə'meɪʃn/ **noun** [C,U]

affirmative /ə'fɜːmətɪv/ **adj** (*formal*) meaning 'yes': *an affirmative answer*
    ➤ We can also say: *an answer in the affirmative*
    ••➤ opposite **negative**

afflict /ə'flɪkt/ **verb** [T] (usually passive) (*formal*) afflict sb/sth (with sth) to cause sb/sth to suffer pain, sadness, etc: *He been afflicted with a serious illness since childhood.* –**affliction noun** [C,U]

affluent /'æfluənt/ **adj** having a lot of money: *Hugh comes from a very affluent family.* –**affluence noun** [U]: *Increased exports have brought new affluence.*

★**afford** /ə'fɔːd/ **verb** [T] (usually after *can*, *could* or *be able to*) afford sth/to do sth **1** to have enough money or time to be able to do sth: *We couldn't afford a television in those days. • I've spent more money than I can afford.* **2** to not be able to do sth or let sth happen because it would have a bad result for you: *The other team was very good so we couldn't afford to make any mistakes.* –**affordable adj**: *affordable prices*

affront /ə'frʌnt/ **noun** [C] an affront (to sb/sth) something that you say or do that is insulting to sb/sth

afield /ə'fiːld/ **adv**
    IDIOM **far afield** → **FAR²**

afloat /ə'fləut/ **adj** (not before a noun) **1** on the surface of the water; not sinking: *A life jacket helps you **stay afloat** if you fall in the water.* **2** (used about a business, an economy, etc) having enough money to survive

afoot /ə'fut/ **adj** (not before a noun) being planned or prepared

★**afraid** /ə'freɪd/ **adj** (not before a noun) **1** afraid (of sb/sth); afraid (of doing sth/to do sth) having or showing fear; frightened: *Are you afraid of dogs? • Ben is afraid of going out after dark. • I was too afraid to answer the door.* **2** afraid (that...); afraid (of doing sth) worried about sth: *We were afraid that you would be angry. • to be afraid of*

a

offending sb **3 afraid for sb/sth** worried that sb/sth will be harmed, lost, etc: *When I saw the gun I was afraid for my life.*

➤ Compare **afraid** and **frightened**. You can only use **afraid** after a noun, but you can use **frightened** before or after a noun: *a frightened animal* • *The animal was afraid/frightened.*

[IDIOM] **I'm afraid (that...)** used for saying politely that you are sorry about sth: *I'm afraid I can't come on Sunday.* • *'Is the factory going to close?' 'I'm afraid so.'* • *'Is this seat free?' 'I'm afraid not/it isn't.'*

afresh /ə'freʃ/ *adv* (*formal*) again, in a new way: *to start afresh*

African American *noun* [C] an American citizen whose family was originally from Africa –**African American** *adj*

Afro-Caribbean /ˌæfrəʊ kærɪ'biːən/ *noun* [C] a person whose family came originally from Africa, and who was born or whose parents were born in the Caribbean –**Afro-Caribbean** *adj*

★**after** /'ɑːftə/ *prep, conj, adv* **1** later than sth; at a later time: *Ian phoned just after six o'clock.* • *the week after next* • *I hope to arrive some time after lunch.* • *They arrived at the station after the train had left.* • *After we had finished our dinner, we went into the garden.* • *I went out yesterday morning, and after that I was at home all day.* • *That was in April. Soon after, I heard that he was ill.*

➤ It is more common to use **afterwards** at the end of a sentence: *We played tennis and went to Angela's house afterwards.*

2 ...**after**... repeated many times or continuing for a long time: *day after day* of hot weather • *I've told the children time after time not to do that.* **3** following or behind sb/sth: *Shut the door after you.* • *C comes after B in the alphabet.* **4** looking for or trying to catch or get sb/sth: *The police were after him.* • *Nicky is after a job in advertising.* **5** because of sth: *After the way he behaved I won't invite him here again.* **6** used when sb/sth is given the name of another person or thing: *We called our son William after his grandfather.*

[IDIOM] **after all 1** used when sth is different in reality to what sb expected or thought: *So you decided to come after all!* (= I thought you weren't going to come) **2** used for reminding sb of a certain fact: *She can't understand. After all, she's only two.*

'after-effect *noun* [C] an unpleasant result of sth that comes some time later

aftermath /'ɑːftəmæθ/ *noun* [sing] a situation that is the result of an important or unpleasant event

★**afternoon** /ˌɑːftə'nuːn/ *noun* [C,U] the part of a day between midday and about six o'clock: *I'll see you tomorrow afternoon.* • *What are you doing this afternoon?* • *I studied all afternoon.* • *I usually go for a walk in the afternoon.* • *He goes swimming every afternoon.* • *She arrived at four o'clock in the afternoon.*

• *Tom works two afternoons a week.* • *Are you busy on Friday afternoon?*

➤ Note that when we are talking about a particular afternoon we say **on Monday, Tuesday, Wednesday, etc afternoon**, but when we are talking generally about doing sth at the time of day we say **in the afternoon.**

[IDIOM] **good afternoon** used when you see sb for the first time in the afternoon ·➤ Often we just say *Afternoon: 'Good afternoon, Mrs Davies.' 'Afternoon, Jack.'* Look at the note at **morning.**

aftershave /'ɑːftəʃeɪv/ *noun* [C,U] a liquid with a pleasant smell that men put on their faces after shaving

afterthought /'ɑːftəθɔːt/ *noun* [C, usually sing] something that you think of or add to sth else at a later time

★**afterwards** /'ɑːftəwədz/ (*US also* **afterward**) *adv* at a later time: *He was taken to hospital and died shortly afterwards.* • *Afterwards, I realized I'd made a terrible mistake.*

★**again** /ə'gen; ə'geɪn/ *adv* **1** once more; another time: *Could you say that again, please?* • *She's out at the moment, so I'll phone again later.* • *Don't ever do that again!* **2** in the place or condition that sb/sth was in before: *It's great to be home again.* • *I hope you'll soon be well again.* **3** in addition to sth: *'Is that enough?' 'No, I'd like half as much again, please'* (= one-and-a-half times the original amount).

[IDIOM] **again and again** many times: *He said he was sorry again and again, but she wouldn't listen.*

then/there again used to say that sth you have just said may not happen or be true: *She might pass her test, but then again she might not.*

yet again → **YET**

★**against** /ə'genst; ə'geɪnst/ *prep* **1** being an opponent to sb/sth in a game, competition, etc, or an enemy of sb/sth in a war or fight: *We played football against a school from another district.* **2** not agreeing with or supporting sb/sth: *Are you for or against the plan?* • *She felt that everybody was against her.* ·➤ opposite **with 3** what a law, rule, etc says you must not do: *It's against the law to buy cigarettes before you are sixteen.* **4** to protect yourself from sb/sth: *Take these pills as a precaution against malaria.* **5** in the opposite direction to sth: *We had to cycle against the wind.* **6** touching sb/sth for support: *I put the ladder against the wall.*

★**age¹** /eɪdʒ/ *noun* **1** [C,U] the length of time that sb has lived or that sth has existed: *Ali is seventeen years of age.* • *She left school at the age of sixteen.* • *Children of all ages will enjoy this film.* • *He needs some friends of his own age.*

➤ When you want to ask about somebody's age, you usually say: *How old is she?* and the answer can be: *She's eighteen* or: *She's eighteen years old* but NOT: *She's eighteen years.*

[I] **intransitive**, a verb which has no object: *He laughed.*   [T] **transitive**, a verb which has an object: *He ate an apple.*

a

Here are some examples of other ways of talking about age: *I'm nearly nineteen.* ● *a girl of eighteen* ● *an eighteen-year-old girl* ● *The robber is of medium height and aged about 16 or 17.*

2 [C,U] a particular period in sb's life: *a problem that often develops in* **middle age** ● *Her sons will look after her in her* **old age.** **3** [U] the state of being old: *a face lined with age* ● *The doctor said she* **died of old age.** ◆⋗ Look at **youth. 4** [C] a particular period of history: *the computer age* ● *the history of art through the ages* **5 ages** [pl] (*informal*) a very long time: *We had to wait (for) ages at the hospital.* ● *It's ages since I've done any exercise.*

IDIOMS **the age of consent** the age at which sb can legally agree to have sex

come of age to become an adult in law: *My father gave me a watch when I came of age.*

feel your age → **FEEL¹**

under age not old enough by law to do sth

age² /eɪdʒ/ *verb* [I,T] (*pres part* **ageing** or **aging**; *pt*, *pp* **aged** /eɪdʒd/) to become or look old; to cause sb to look old: *My father seems to have aged a lot recently.* ● *I could see her illness had aged her.* ● *an ageing aunt*

aged 1 /eɪdʒd/**adj** (not before a noun) of the age mentioned: *The woman, aged 26, was last seen at Victoria Station.* **2 the aged** /ˈeɪdʒɪd/ **noun** [pl] very old people

'age group noun [C] people of about the same age: *This club is very popular with the 20-30 age group.*

⋆**agency** /ˈeɪdʒənsi/ **noun** [C] (*pl* **agencies**) **1** a business that provides a particular service: *an advertising agency* **2** (*US*) a government department

agenda /əˈdʒendə/ **noun** [C] a list of matters that need to be discussed or dealt with: *The first item* **on the agenda** *at the meeting will be security.* ● *The government have* **set an agenda** *for reform over the next ten years.*

⋆**agent** /ˈeɪdʒənt/ **noun** [C] **1** a person whose job is to do business for a company or for another person: *Our company's agent in Rio will meet you at the airport.* ● *Most actors and musicians have their own agents.* ● *a travel agent* ● *an estate agent* **2** =**SECRET AGENT**

aggravate /ˈægrəveɪt/ **verb** [T] **1** to make sth worse or more serious **2** (*informal*) to make sb angry or annoyed –**aggravation** /ˌægrəˈveɪʃn/ **noun** [C,U]

aggregate /ˈægrɪgət/ **noun**
IDIOM **on aggregate** in total: *Our team won 3-1 on aggregate.*

aggression /əˈgreʃn/ **noun** [U] **1** angry feelings or behaviour that make you want to attack other people: *People often react to this kind of situation with fear or aggression.* **2** the act of starting a fight or war without reasonable cause

⋆**aggressive** /əˈgresɪv/ **adj 1** ready or likely to fight or argue: *an aggressive dog* ● *Some people get aggressive after drinking alcohol.*

2 using or showing force or pressure in order to succeed: *an aggressive salesman* –**aggressively adv**: *The boys responded aggressively when I asked them to make less noise.*

aggressor /əˈgresə/ **noun** [C] a person or country that attacks sb/sth or starts fighting first

aggrieved /əˈgriːvd/ **adj** (*formal*) upset or angry

agile /ˈædʒaɪl/ **adj** able to move quickly and easily: *Monkeys are extremely agile.* –**agility** /əˈdʒɪləti/ **noun** [U]: *This sport is a test of both physical and mental agility.*

agitate /ˈædʒɪteɪt/ **verb** [I] **agitate (for/ against sth)** to make other people feel very strongly about sth so that they want to help you achieve it: *to agitate for reform*

agitated /ˈædʒɪteɪtɪd/ **adj** worried or excited –**agitation** /ˌædʒɪˈteɪʃn/ **noun** [U]

AGM /ˌeɪ dʒiː ˈem/ **abbr** (*especially Brit*) Annual General Meeting

agnostic /ægˈnɒstɪk/ **noun** [C] a person who is not sure if God exists or not

⋆**ago** /əˈgəʊ/ **adv** in the past; back in time from now: *Patrick left ten minutes ago* (= if it is twelve o'clock now, he left at ten to twelve). ● *That was* **a long time ago.** ● *How long ago did this happen?*

➤ **Ago** is used with the simple past tense and not the present perfect tense: *I arrived in Britain three months ago.* Compare **ago** and **before**. **Ago** means 'before now' and **before** means 'before then' (that is before a particular time in the past): *Anne married Simon two years ago.* ● *She had left her first husband six months before* (= six months before she married Simon).

agonize (also **-ise**) /ˈægənaɪz/ **verb** [I] to worry or think about sth for a long time: *to agonize over a difficult decision*

agonized (also **-ised**) /ˈægənaɪzd/ **adj** showing extreme pain or worry: *an agonized cry*

agonizing (also **-ising**) /ˈægənaɪzɪŋ/ **adj** causing extreme worry or pain: *an agonizing choice* ● *an agonizing headache*

agony /ˈægəni/ **noun** [C,U] (*pl* **agonies**) great pain or suffering: *to be/scream in agony*

agoraphobia /ˌægərəˈfəʊbiə/ **noun** [U] fear of being in public places where there are a lot of people –**agoraphobic adj**

⋆**agree** /əˈgriː/ **verb 1** [I] **agree (with sb/sth); agree (that...)** to have the same opinion as sb/sth: *'I think we should talk to the manager about this.' 'Yes, I agree.'* ● *I agree with Paul.* ● *Do you agree that we should travel by train?* ● *I'm afraid I don't agree.* ◆⋗ opposite **disagree**

➤ Note that we say: *I agree* and: *I don't agree* NOT 'I am agree' or 'I am not agree'. This is incorrect.

2 [I] **agree (to sth/to do sth)** to say yes to sth: *I asked my boss if I could go home early and she agreed.* ● *Alkis has agreed to lend me his car for the weekend.* ◆⋗ opposite **refuse**
3 [I,T] **agree (to do sth); agree (on sth)** to

make an arrangement or decide sth with sb: *They agreed to meet again the following day.* • *Can we agree on a price?* • *We agreed a price of £500.* **4** [I] **agree with sth** to think that sth is right: *I don't agree with experiments on animals.* **5** [I] to be the same as sth: *The two accounts of the accident do not agree.*
[IDIOM] **not agree with sb** (used about food) to make sb feel ill

agreeable /əˈgriːəbl/ *adj* **1** pleasant; nice •→ opposite **disagreeable 2** (*formal*) ready to agree: *If you are agreeable, we would like to visit your offices on 21 May.* –**agreeably** /-əbli/ *adv*: *I was agreeably surprised by the film.*

★**agreement** /əˈgriːmənt/ *noun* **1** [U] the state of agreeing with sb/sth: *She nodded her head in agreement.* • *We are totally in agreement with what you have said.* •→ opposite **disagreement 2** [C] a contract or decision that two or more people have made together: *Please sign the agreement and return it to us.* • *The leaders reached an agreement after five days of talks.* • *We never break an agreement.*

★**agriculture** /ˈægrɪkʌltʃə/ *noun* [U] keeping animals and growing crops for food; farming: *the Minister of Agriculture* –**agricultural** /ˌægrɪˈkʌltʃərəl/ *adj*

ah /ɑː/ *interj* used for expressing surprise, pleasure, understanding, etc: *Ah, there you are.*

aha /ɑːˈhɑː/ *interj* used when you suddenly find or understand sth: *Aha! Now I understand.*

★**ahead** /əˈhed/ *adv, adj* **ahead (of sb/sth) 1** in front of sb/sth: *I could see the other car about half a mile ahead of us.* • *The path ahead looked narrow and steep.* • *Look straight ahead and don't turn round!* **2** before or more advanced than sb/sth: *Inga and Nils arrived a few minutes ahead of us.* • *London is about five hours ahead of New York.* • *The Japanese are way ahead of us in their research.* **3** into the future: *He's got a difficult time ahead of him.* • *We must think ahead and make a plan.* **4** winning in a game, competition, etc: *The goal put Italy 2-1 ahead at half-time.* •→ Look at **behind**.
[IDIOMS] **ahead of your time** so modern that people do not understand you
streets ahead → **STREET**

aid¹ /eɪd/ *noun* **1** [U] help: *to walk with the aid of a stick* • *He had to go to the aid of a child in the river.* •→ Look at **first aid**. **2** [C] a person or thing that helps you: *a hearing aid* • *dictionaries and other study aids* **3** [U] money, food, etc that is sent to a country or to people in order to help them: *We sent aid to the earthquake victims.* • *economic aid*
[IDIOM] **in aid of sb/sth** in order to collect money for sb/sth, especially for a charity: *a concert in aid of Children in Need*

aid² /eɪd/ *verb* [T] (*formal*) to help sb/sth: *Sleep aids recovery from illness.*
[IDIOM] **aid and abet** to help sb to do sth that is not allowed by law

aide /eɪd/ *noun* [C] a person who helps sb

important in the government, etc; an assistant

Aids (also **AIDS**) /eɪdz/ *noun* [U] an illness which destroys the body's ability to fight infection: *He was HIV positive for three years before developing full-blown Aids.* • *to contract Aids* • *the Aids virus*

➤ **Aids** is short for **Acquired Immune Deficiency Syndrome**.

ailing /ˈeɪlɪŋ/ *adj* not in good health; weak: *an ailing economy*

ailment /ˈeɪlmənt/ *noun* [C] (*formal*) any illness that is not very serious

★**aim¹** /eɪm/ *noun* **1** [C] something that you intend to do; a purpose: *Our aim is to open offices in Paris and Rome before the end of the year.* • *His only aim in life is to make money.* **2** [U] the act of pointing sth at sb/sth before trying to hit him/her/it with it: *She picked up the gun, took aim and fired.* • *Jo's aim was good and she hit the target.*

★**aim²** /eɪm/ *verb* **1** [I] **aim to do sth; aim at/for sth** to intend to do or achieve sth: *We aim to leave after breakfast.* • *The company is aiming at a 25% increase in profit.* • *You should always aim for perfection in your work.* **2** [T] **aim sth at sb/sth** to direct sth at a particular person or group: *The advertising campaign is aimed at young people.* **3** [I,T] **aim (sth) (at sb/sth)** to point sth at sb/sth before trying to hit him/her/it with it: *She aimed (the gun) at the target and fired.*
[IDIOM] **be aimed at sth/doing sth** to be intended to achieve sth: *The new laws are aimed at reducing heavy traffic in cities.*

aimless /ˈeɪmləs/ *adj* having no purpose: *an aimless discussion* –**aimlessly** *adv*

ain't /eɪnt/ (*informal*) short for **AM NOT, IS NOT, ARE NOT, HAS NOT, HAVE NOT** •→ **Ain't** is considered to be incorrect English.

★**air¹** /eə/ *noun* **1** [U] the mixture of gases that surrounds the earth and that people, animals and plants breathe: *the pure mountain air* • *Open a window – I need some fresh air.* • *The air was polluted by smoke from the factory.* **2** [U] the space around and above things: *to throw a ball high into the air* • *in the open air* (= outside) **3** [U] travel or transport in an aircraft: *to travel by air* • *an air ticket* **4** [sing] **an air (of sth)** the particular feeling or impression that is given by sb/sth: *She has a confident air.*
[IDIOMS] **a breath of fresh air** → **BREATH**
clear the air → **CLEAR³**
in the air probably going to happen soon: *A feeling of change was in the air.*
in the open air → **OPEN¹**
on (the) air sending out programmes on the radio or television: *This radio station is on the air 24 hours a day.*
vanish, etc into thin air → **THIN¹**

air² /eə/ *verb* **1** [I,T] to put clothes, etc in a warm place or outside in the fresh air to make sure they are completely dry; to become dry in this way: *Put the sheets on the washing line to air.* **2** [I,T] to make a room,

a

etc fresh by letting air into it; to become fresh in this way: *Open the window to air the room.* **3** [T] to tell people what you think about sth: *The discussion gave people a chance to air their views.*

'**air bag** noun [C] a safety device in a car that fills with air if there is an accident. It protects the people sitting in the front.

airbase /'eəbeɪs/ noun [C] an airport for military aircraft

airborne /'eəbɔːn/ adj flying in the air

'**air conditioning** noun [U] the system that keeps the air in a room, building, etc cool and dry —'**air-conditioned** adj: *air-conditioned offices*

★**aircraft** /'eəkrɑːft/ noun [C] (*pl* aircraft) any vehicle that can fly in the air, for example a plane

'**aircraft carrier** noun [C] a ship that carries military aircraft and that has a long flat area where they can take off and land

airfield /'eəfiːld/ noun [C] an area of land where aircraft can land or take off. An airfield is smaller than an airport.

'**air force** noun [C, with sing or pl verb] the part of a country's military organization that fights in the air ••➤ Look at **army** and **navy**.

'**air hostess** (also **hostess**) noun [C] a woman who looks after the passengers on a plane ••➤ synonym **stewardess** ••➤ Look at **air steward**.

'**airing cupboard** noun [C] a warm cupboard that you put clothes, etc in to make sure they are completely dry after being washed

airless /'eələs/ adj not having enough fresh air: *The room was hot and airless.*

airline /'eəlaɪn/ noun [C] a company that provides regular flights for people or goods in aircraft

airliner /'eəlaɪnə/ noun [C] a large plane that carries passengers

airmail /'eəmeɪl/ noun [U] the system for sending letters, packages, etc by plane: *I sent the parcel (by) airmail.*

airplane /'eəpleɪn/ (*US*) = **AEROPLANE**

★**airport** /'eəpɔːt/ noun [C] a place where aircraft can land and take off and that has buildings for passengers to wait in

'**air raid** noun [C] an attack by military aircraft

airsick /'eəsɪk/ adj feeling sick or vomiting as a result of travelling on a plane ••➤ Look at **carsick**, **seasick** and **travel-sick**.

airspace /'eəspeɪs/ noun [U] the part of the sky that is above a country and that belongs to that country by law

'**air steward** noun [C] a man who looks after the passengers on a plane ••➤ Look at **air hostess**.

airstrip /'eəstrɪp/ (also '**landing strip**) noun [C] a narrow piece of land where aircraft can take off and land

airtight /'eətaɪt/ adj that air cannot get into or out of

,**air ,traffic con'troller** noun [C] a person whose job is to organize routes for aircraft, and to tell pilots by radio when they can land and take off

airy /'eəri/ adj having a lot of fresh air inside

aisle /aɪl/ noun [C] a passage between the rows of seats in a church, theatre, etc

ajar /ə'dʒɑː/ adj (not before a noun) (used about a door) slightly open

akin /ə'kɪn/ adj akin to sth similar to sth

à la carte /ˌɑː lɑː 'kɑːt/ adj, adv (used about a meal in a restaurant) where each dish on the list of available dishes (menu) has a separate price and there is not a fixed price for a complete meal

★**alarm**[1] /ə'lɑːm/ noun **1** [U] a sudden feeling of fear or worry: *She jumped up in alarm.* **2** [sing] a warning of danger: *A small boy saw the smoke and raised the alarm.* **3** [C] a machine that warns you of danger, for example by ringing a loud bell: *The burglars set off the alarm when they broke the window.* ● *The fire/burglar alarm went off in the middle of the night.* **4** [C] = **ALARM CLOCK**
  IDIOM a false alarm → **FALSE**

alarm[2] /ə'lɑːm/ verb [T] to make sb/sth feel suddenly frightened or worried

a'larm clock (also **alarm**) noun [C] a clock that you can set to make a noise at a particular time to wake you up: *She set the alarm clock for half past six.* ••➤ picture at **clock**

alarmed /ə'lɑːmd/ adj alarmed (at/by sth) feeling frightened or worried

alarming /ə'lɑːmɪŋ/ adj that makes you frightened or worried —**alarmingly** adv

alas /ə'læs/ interj (*formal*) used for expressing sadness about sth

albeit /ˌɔːl'biːɪt/ conj (*formal*) although: *He finally agreed to come, albeit unwillingly.*

albino /æl'biːnəʊ/ noun [C] (*pl* albinos) a person or animal with very white skin, white hair and pink eyes

album /'ælbəm/ noun [C] **1** a collection of songs on one CD, cassette, etc: *The band are about to release their third album.* ••➤ Look at **single**. **2** a book in which you can keep stamps, photographs, etc that you have collected

★**alcohol** /'ælkəhɒl/ noun [U] **1** the colourless liquid in drinks such as beer and wine that can make you drunk **2** drinks such as beer, whisky, wine, etc that contain alcohol

alcoholic[1] /ˌælkə'hɒlɪk/ adj containing alcohol: *alcoholic drinks* ••➤ opposite **non-alcoholic**

➤ Drinks without alcohol are also called **soft drinks**.

alcoholic[2] /ˌælkə'hɒlɪk/ noun [C] a person who cannot stop drinking large amounts of alcohol

➤ A person who does not drink alcohol at all is a **teetotaller**.

alcoholism /'ælkəhɒlɪzəm/ noun [U] a medical condition that is caused by regularly drinking a large amount of alcohol and not being able to stop

alcove /'ælkəʊv/ **noun** [C] a small area in a room where one part of the wall is further back than the rest of the wall

ale /eɪl/ **noun** [U,C] a type of beer

alert[1] /ə'lɜːt/ **adj** alert (to sth) watching, listening, etc for sth with all your attention: *Security guards must be alert at all times.* • *to be alert to possible changes*

alert[2] /ə'lɜːt/ **noun** [C] a warning of possible danger: *a bomb alert*

IDIOM **on the alert (for sth)** ready or prepared for danger or an attack

alert[3] /ə'lɜːt/ **verb** [T] alert sb (to sth) to warn sb of danger or a problem

'A level (also *formal* **Ad'vanced level**) **noun** [C] an exam that schoolchildren in England, Wales and Northern Ireland take when they are about eighteen. You usually take A levels in two or three subjects and you need good results (grades) if you want to go to university: *How many A levels have you got?* • *I'm doing my A levels this summer.*

➤ Compare **GCSE**.

algae /'ældʒiː; 'ælgiː/ **noun** [pl,with sing or pl verb] very simple plants that grow mainly in water

algebra /'ældʒɪbrə/ **noun** [U] a type of mathematics in which letters and symbols are used to represent numbers

alias[1] /'eɪliəs/ **noun** [C] a false name, for example one that is used by a criminal: *Castorri is known to the police under several aliases.*

alias[2] /'eɪliəs/ **adv** used for giving sb's false name: *Norma Jean Baker, alias Marilyn Monroe*

alibi /'æləbaɪ/ **noun** [C] (*pl* **alibis**) an alibi (for sth) a statement by sb that says you were in a different place at the time of a crime and so cannot be guilty of the crime: *He had a good alibi for the night of the robbery.*

alien[1] /'eɪliən/ **noun** [C] **1** a creature that comes from another planet **2** (*formal*) a person who comes from another country

alien[2] /'eɪliən/ **adj 1** of another country; foreign: *an alien land* **2** alien (to sb) very strange and completely different from your normal experience

alienate /'eɪliəneɪt/ **verb** [T] **1** to make people feel that they cannot share your opinions any more: *The Prime Minister's new policies on defence have alienated many of his supporters.* **2** alienate sb (from sb/sth) to make sb feel that he/she does not belong somewhere or is not part of sth –**alienation** /ˌeɪliə'neɪʃn/ **noun** [U]

alight[1] /ə'laɪt/ **adj** on fire; burning: *A cigarette set the petrol alight.*

➤ **Alight** can only be used after a noun, but you can use **burning** before a noun: *The whole building was alight.* • *a burning building.*

alight[2] /ə'laɪt/ **verb** [I] (*written*) alight (from sth) to get off a bus, train, etc

align /ə'laɪn/ **verb** [T] **1** align sth (with sth) to arrange things in a straight line or so that they are parallel to sth else: *to align the wheels of a car* **2** align yourself with sb to say that you support the opinions of a particular group, country, etc

alignment /ə'laɪnmənt/ **noun 1** [U] arrangement in a straight line or parallel to sth else **2** [C,U] an agreement between political parties, countries, etc to support the same thing

alike /ə'laɪk/ **adj, adv** (not before a noun) **1** very similar: *The two children are very alike.* **2** in the same way: *We try to treat women and men alike in this company.* • *The book is popular with adults and children alike.*

alimony /'æliməni/ **noun** [U] money that you have to pay by law to your former wife or husband after getting divorced

★**alive** /ə'laɪv/ **adj 1** not dead; living: *The young woman was still alive when the ambulance reached the hospital.* • *The quick action of the doctors kept the child alive.*

➤ **Alive** can only be used after a noun, but you can use **living** before a noun: *Are her parents still alive?* • *Does she have any living relatives?*

2 continuing to exist: *Many old traditions are very much alive in this area of the country.* **3** full of life: *In the evening the town really comes alive.*

alkali /'ælkəlaɪ/ **noun** [C,U] a chemical substance that can burn skin when it is dissolved in water. An alkali has a pH value of more than 7. •➤ Look at **acid** and **base**. –**alkaline** **adj**

★**all**[1] /ɔːl/ **determiner, pron 1** the whole of a thing or of a period of time: *All (of) the food has gone.* • *They've eaten all of it.* • *They've eaten it all.* • *This money is all yours.* • *All of it is yours.* • *all week/month/year* • *He worked hard all his life.* **2** every one of a group: *All (of) my children can swim.* • *My children can all swim.* • *She's read all (of) these books.* • *She's read them all.* • *The people at the meeting all voted against the plan.* • *All of them voted against the plan.* **3** everything that; the only thing that: *I wrote down all I could remember.* • *All I've eaten today is one banana.*

IDIOMS **above all → ABOVE**
after all → AFTER
for all 1 in spite of: *For all her wealth and beauty, she was never very happy.* **2** used to show that sth is not important or of no interest or value to you: *For all I know, he's probably remarried by now.*
in all in total: *There were ten of us in all.*
not all that... not very: *The film wasn't all that good.*
(not) at all in any way: *I didn't enjoy it at all.*

➤ We can say **not at all** as a reply when somebody thanks us for something.

a

★**all²** /ɔːl/ **adv 1** completely; very: *He has lived all alone since his wife died.* ● *I didn't watch that programme – I forgot all about it.* ● *They got all excited about it.* **2** (in sport) for each side: *The score was two all.*

IDIOMS **all along** from the beginning: *I knew you were joking all along.*

all the better, harder, etc even better, harder, etc than before: *It will be all the more difficult with two people missing.*

Allah /ˈælə/ the Muslim name for God

allay /əˈleɪ/ **verb** [T] (*formal*) to make sth less strong

the ˌallˈclear noun [sing] a signal telling you that a situation is no longer dangerous

allege /əˈledʒ/ **verb** [T] (*formal*) to say that sb has done sth wrong, but without having any proof that this is true: *The woman alleged that Williams had attacked her with a knife.* –**allegation** /ˌæləˈgeɪʃn/ **noun** [C]: *to make allegations of police corruption* –**alleged** /əˈledʒd/ **adj** (only *before* a noun) –**allegedly** /əˈledʒɪdli/ **adv**: *The man was allegedly shot while trying to escape.*

allegiance /əˈliːdʒəns/ **noun** [U,C] (*formal*) support for a leader, government, belief, etc; loyalty: *Many people switched allegiance and voted against the government.*

allergic /əˈlɜːdʒɪk/ **adj 1** allergic (to sth) having an allergy: *I can't drink cow's milk. I'm allergic to it.* **2** caused by an allergy: *an allergic reaction to house dust*

allergy /ˈælədʒi/ **noun** [C] (*pl* **allergies**) an allergy (to sth) a medical condition that makes you ill when you eat, touch or breathe sth that does not normally make other people ill: *an allergy to cats/shellfish/pollen*

alleviate /əˈliːvieɪt/ **verb** [T] to make sth less strong or bad: *The doctor gave me an injection to alleviate the pain.* –**alleviation** /əˌliːviˈeɪʃn/ **noun** [U]

alley /ˈæli/ (also **alleyway** /ˈæliweɪ/) **noun** [C] a narrow passage between buildings

alliance /əˈlaɪəns/ **noun** [C] an agreement between groups, countries, etc to work together and support each other: *The two parties formed an alliance.* ·➤ Look at **ally**.

allied adj 1 /ˈælaɪd/(used about organizations, countries, etc) having an agreement to work together and support each other **2** /əˈlaɪd/allied (to sth) connected with; existing together with: *The newspaper is closely allied to the government.*

alligator /ˈælɪgeɪtə/ **noun** [C] a large reptile with a long tail and a big mouth with sharp teeth. Alligators live in the lakes and rivers of America and China. ·➤ Look at **crocodile**.

ˌallˈin adj including everything: *an all-in price*

allocate /ˈæləkeɪt/ **verb** [T] allocate sth (to/ for sb/sth) to give sth to sb as his/her share or to decide to use sth for a particular purpose: *The government has allocated half the budget for education.* –**allocation** /ˌæləˈkeɪʃn/ **noun** [C,U]

allot /əˈlɒt/ **verb** [T] (**allotting; allotted**) allot sth (to sb/sth) to give a share of work, time, etc to sb/sth: *Different tasks were allotted to each member of the class.* ● *We all finished the exam in the allotted time.*

allotment /əˈlɒtmənt/ **noun** [C] (*Brit*) a small area of land in a town that you can rent for growing vegetables on

ˈall out adj, adv using all your strength, etc: *an all-out effort*

★**allow** /əˈlaʊ/ **verb** [T] **1** allow sb/sth to do sth; allow sb/sth to give permission for sb/sth to do sth or for sth to happen: *Children under eighteen are not allowed to buy alcohol.* ● *I'm afraid we don't allow people to bring dogs into this restaurant.* ● *Photography is not allowed inside the cathedral.*

➤ Compare **allow**, **permit** and **let**. **Allow** can be used in both formal and informal English. The passive form **be allowed to** is especially common. **Permit** is a formal word and is usually used only in written English. **Let** is an informal word, and very common in spoken English. You **allow sb to do sth** but **let sb do sth** (no 'to'). **Let** cannot be used in the passive: *Visitors are not allowed/permitted to smoke in this area.* ● *Smoking is not allowed/permitted.* ● *I'm not allowed to smoke in my bedroom.* ● *My dad won't let me smoke in my bedroom.*

2 to give permission for sb/sth to be or go somewhere: *No dogs allowed.* ● *I'm only allowed out on Friday and Saturday nights.* **3** allow sb sth to let sb have sth: *My contract allows me four weeks' holiday a year.* **4** allow sb/sth to do sth to make it possible for sb/sth to do sth: *Working part-time would allow me to spend more time with my family.* **5** allow sth (for sb/sth) to provide money, time, etc for sb/sth: *You should allow about 30 minutes for each question.*

PHRASAL VERB **allow for sb/sth** to think about possible problems when you are planning sth and include extra time, money, etc for them: *The journey should take about two hours, allowing for heavy traffic.*

allowance /əˈlaʊəns/ **noun** [C] **1** an amount of sth that you are allowed: *Most flights have a 20kg baggage allowance.* **2** an amount of money that you receive regularly to help you pay for sth that you need

IDIOM **make allowances for sb/sth** to judge a person or his/her actions in a kinder way than usual because he/she has a particular problem or disadvantage

ˌall ˈright (also *informal* **alright**) **interj, adv, adj** (not before a noun) **1** good enough; OK: *Is everything all right?* **2** safe; not hurt; well: *I hope the children are all right.* ● *Do you feel all right?* **3** showing you agree to do what sb has asked; OK: *'Can you get me some stamps?' 'Yes, all right.'*

➤ You say 'That's all right,' when sb thanks you for sth or when sb says sorry for sth he/she has done: *'Thanks for the lift home.' 'That's (quite) all right.'* ● *'I'm so sorry I'm*

[C] **countable**, a noun with a plural form: *one book, two books* [U] **uncountable**, a noun with no plural form: *some sugar*

late.' 'That's all right. We haven't started yet anyway.'

'all-round adj (only before a noun) able to do many different things well; good in many different ways: *a superb all-round athlete* ● *The school aims at the all-round development of the child.*

,all-'rounder noun [C] a person who can do many different things well

allude /əˈluːd/ verb [I] (*formal*) allude to sb/sth to speak about sb/sth in an indirect way –allusion /əˈluːʒn/ noun [C,U]: *He likes to* **make allusions** *to the size of his salary.*

ally /ˈælaɪ/ noun [C] (*pl* **allies**) **1** a country that has an agreement to support another country, especially in a war: *France and its European allies* •➤ Look at **alliance**. **2** a person who helps and supports you, especially when other people are against you: *the Prime Minister's political allies*

almighty /ɔːlˈmaɪti/ adj **1** having the power to do anything: *Almighty God* **2** (only before a noun) (*informal*) very great: *Suddenly we heard the most almighty crash.*

almond /ˈɑːmənd/ noun [C] a kind of bitter tasting nut •➤ picture at **nut**

★**almost** /ˈɔːlməʊst/ adv very nearly; not quite: *By nine o'clock almost everybody had arrived.* ● *Careful! I almost fell into the water then!* ● *The film has almost finished.* ● *She almost always cycles to school.* ● *There's almost nothing left.* ● *Almost all the students passed the exam.*

★**alone** /əˈləʊn/ adj, adv **1** without any other person: *The old man lives alone.* ● *Are you alone? Can I speak to you for a moment?* ● *I don't like walking home alone after dark.*

> ● **Alone** and **lonely** both mean that you are not with other people. **Lonely** (*US* **lonesome**) means that you are unhappy about this, but **alone** does not usually suggest either happiness or unhappiness. **Alone** cannot be used before a noun. You can also use **on your own** and **by yourself** to mean 'alone'. These expressions are more informal and very common in spoken English.

2 (after a noun or pronoun) only: *You alone can help us.* ● *The rent alone takes up most of my salary.*

IDIOMS **go it alone** to start working on your own without the usual help

leave sb/sth alone → **LEAVE¹**

let alone → **LET**

★**along** /əˈlɒŋ/ prep, adv **1** from one end to or towards the other end of sth: *I walked slowly along the road.* ● *David looked along the corridor to see if anyone was coming.* **2** on or beside sth long: *Wild flowers grew along both sides of the river.* ● *Our house is about halfway along the street.* **3** forward: *We moved along slowly with the crowd.* **4** (*informal*) with sb: *We're going for a walk. Why don't you* **come along** *too?*

IDIOMS **all along** → **ALL²**

along with sb/sth together with sb/sth

go along with sb/sth to agree with sb's ideas or plans

alongside /əˌlɒŋˈsaɪd/ adv, prep **1** next to sb/sth or at the side of sth **2** together with sb/sth: *the opportunity to work alongside experienced musicians*

aloof /əˈluːf/ adj **1** not friendly to other people; distant: *Her shyness made her seem aloof.* **2** aloof (from sb/sth) not involved in sth; apart

aloud /əˈlaʊd/ (also ,out 'loud) adv in a normal speaking voice that other people can hear; not silently: *to read aloud from a book*

★**alphabet** /ˈælfəbet/ noun [C] a set of letters in a fixed order that you use when you are writing a language: *There are 26 letters in the English alphabet.*

alphabetical /ˌælfəˈbetɪkl/ adj arranged in the same order as the letters of the alphabet: *The names are listed* **in alphabetical order**. –alphabetically /-kli/ adv

alpine /ˈælpaɪn/ adj of or found in high mountains: *alpine flowers*

★**already** /ɔːlˈredi/ adv **1** used for talking about sth that has happened before now or before a particular time in the past: *'Would you like some lunch?' 'No, I've already eaten, thanks.'* ● *We got there at 6.30 but Marsha had already left.* ● *Sita was already awake when I went into her room.* **2** (used in negative sentences and questions for expressing surprise) so early; as soon as this: *Have you finished already?* ● *Surely you're not going already!*

alright /ɔːlˈraɪt/ (*informal*) = **ALL RIGHT**

★**also** /ˈɔːlsəʊ/ adv (not with negative verbs) in addition; too: *He plays several instruments and also writes music.* ● *Bring summer clothing and also something warm to wear in the evenings.* ● *The food is wonderful, and also very cheap.*

> ● **Too** and **as well** are less formal than **also** and are very common in spoken English. **Also** usually goes before a main verb or after 'is', 'are', 'were', etc: *He also enjoys reading.* ● *He has also been to Australia.* ● *He is also intelligent.* **Too** and **as well** usually go at the end of a phrase or sentence: *I really love this song, and I liked the first one too/as well.*

IDIOM **not only … but also** → **ONLY**

altar /ˈɔːltə/ noun [C] a high table that is the centre of a religious ceremony

alter /ˈɔːltə/ verb [I,T] to make sth different in some way, but without changing it completely; to become different: *We've altered our plan, and will now arrive at 7.00 instead of 8.00.* ● *The village seems to have altered very little in the last twenty years.*

alteration /ˌɔːltəˈreɪʃn/ noun [C,U] (an) alteration (to/in sth) a small change in sb/sth: *We want to* **make a few alterations** *to the house before we move in.*

alternate¹ /ɔːlˈtɜːnət/ adj **1** (used about two types of events, things, etc) happening or following regularly one after the other: *There*

[I] **intransitive**, a verb which has no object: *He laughed.* [T] **transitive**, a verb which has an object: *He ate an apple.*

a

will be alternate periods of sun and showers tomorrow. **2** one of every two: *He works alternate weeks* (= he works the first week, he doesn't work the second week, he works again the third week, etc). –**alternately** adv: *The bricks were painted alternately white and red.*

alternate² /'ɔːltɜːneɪt/ **verb 1** [I] **alternate with sth**; **alternate between A and B** (used about two types of events, things, etc) to happen or follow regularly one after the other: *Busy periods in the hospital alternate with times when there is not much to do.* ● *She seemed to alternate between hating him and loving him.* **2** [T] **alternate A with B** to cause two types of events or things to happen or follow regularly one after the other: *He alternated periods of work with periods of rest.* –**alternation** /ˌɔːltə'neɪʃn/ **noun** [C,U]

alternative¹ /ɔːl'tɜːnətɪv/ **adj** (only *before* a noun) **1** that you can use, do, etc instead of sth else: *The motorway was closed so we had to find an alternative route.* **2** different to what is usual or traditional: *alternative medicine* –**alternatively adv**

alternative² /ɔːl'tɜːnətɪv/ **noun** [C] an alternative (to sth) one of two or more things that you can choose between: *What can I eat as an alternative to meat?* ● *There are several alternatives open to us at the moment.*

★**although** /ɔːl'ðəʊ/ **conj 1** in spite of the fact that: *Although she was tired, she stayed up late watching television.* **2** and yet; but: *I love dogs, although I wouldn't have one as a pet.*

➤ **Though** and **although** are the same but at the end of a sentence it is only possible to use **though**: *She knew all her friends would be at the party. She didn't want to go, though.* **Even though** can be used for emphasis: *She didn't want to go, although/though/even though she knew all her friends would be there.*

altitude /'æltɪtjuːd/ **noun 1** [sing] the height of sth above sea level: *The plane climbed to an altitude of 10000 metres.* **2** [usually pl] a place that is high above sea level: *You need to carry oxygen when you are climbing at high altitudes.*

alto /'æltəʊ/ **noun** [C] (*pl* **altos**) the lowest normal singing voice for a woman, the highest for a man; a woman or man with this voice

★**altogether** /ˌɔːltə'geðə/ **adv 1** completely: *I don't altogether agree with you.* ● *At the age of 55 he stopped working altogether.* ● *This time the situation is altogether different.* **2** including everything; in total: *How much money will I need altogether?* ● *Altogether there were six of us.* **3** when you consider everything; generally: *Altogether, this town is a pleasant place to live.*

➤ **Altogether** is not the same as **all together**. **All together** means 'everything or everybody together': *Put your books all together on the table.* ● *Let's sing. All together now!*

aluminium /ˌæljə'mɪniəm/ (*US* **aluminum** /ə'luːmɪnəm/) (*symbol* **Al**) **noun** [U] a light silver-coloured metal that is used for making cooking equipment, etc: *aluminium foil*

★**always** /'ɔːlweɪz/ **adv 1** at all times; regularly: *I always get up at 6.30.* ● *Why is the train always late when I'm in a hurry?* **2** all through the past until now: *Tony has always been shy.* ● *I've always liked music.* **3** for ever: *I shall always remember this moment.* **4** (only used with continuous tenses) again and again, usually in an annoying way: *She's always complaining about something.* **5** used with 'can' or 'could' for suggesting sth that sb could do, especially if nothing else is possible: *If you haven't got enough money, I could always lend you some.*

➤ **Always** does not usually go at the beginning of a sentence. It usually goes before the main verb or after 'is', 'are', 'were', etc: *He always wears those shoes.* ● *I have always wanted to visit Egypt.* ● *Fiona is always late.* However, **always** can go at the beginning of a sentence when you are telling somebody to do something: *Always stop and look before you cross the road.*

Alzheimer's disease /'æltshaɪməz dɪziːz/ **noun** [sing] a disease that affects the brain and makes you become more and more confused as you get older

a.m. /ˌeɪ 'em/ **abbr 1** (*US* **A.M.**) before midday: *10 am* (= *10 o'clock in the morning*) **2 AM** one of the systems of sending out radio signals

am → BE¹

amalgamate /ə'mælgəmeɪt/ **verb** [I,T] (used especially about organizations, groups, etc) to join together to form a single organization, group, etc –**amalgamation** /əˌmælgə'meɪʃn/ **noun** [C,U]

amass /ə'mæs/ **verb** [T] to collect or put together a large quantity of sth: *We've amassed a lot of information on the subject.*

amateur¹ /'æmətə/ **noun** [C] **1** a person who takes part in a sport or an activity for pleasure, not for money as a job: *Only amateurs can take part in the tournament.* •➤ opposite **professional 2** (usually used when being critical) a person who does not have skill or experience when doing sth

amateur² /'æmətə/ **adj 1** done, or doing sth, for pleasure (not for money as a job): *an amateur production of a play* ● *an amateur photographer* •➤ opposite **professional 2** (also **amateurish** /-rɪʃ/) done without skill or experience: *The painting was an amateurish fake.*

★**amaze** /ə'meɪz/ **verb** [T] to surprise sb very much; to be difficult for sb to believe: *Sometimes your behaviour amazes me!* ● *It amazes me that anyone could be so stupid!*

★**amazed** /ə'meɪzd/ **adj** amazed (at/by sth); amazed (to do sth/that...) very surprised: *I was amazed by the change in his attitude.* ● *She was amazed to discover the truth about her husband.*

amazement /ə'meɪzmənt/ **noun** [U] a feeling

of great surprise: *He looked at me in amazement.* • *To my amazement, I passed the test easily.*

★**amazing** /ə'meɪzɪŋ/ **adj** very surprising and difficult to believe; incredible: *She has shown amazing courage.* • *I've got an amazing story to tell you.* –**amazingly adv**

ambassador /æm'bæsədə/ **noun** [C] an important person who represents his/her country in a foreign country: *the Spanish Ambassador to Britain*

➤ An ambassador lives and works in an **embassy**. Look also at **consul**.

amber /'æmbə/ **noun** [U] **1** a hard clear yellow-brown substance used for making jewellery or objects for decoration **2** a yellow-brown colour: *The three colours in traffic lights are red, amber and green.* –**amber adj**

ambiguity /ˌæmbɪ'gjuːəti/ **noun** [C,U] (*pl* **ambiguities**) the possibility of being understood in more than one way; sth that can be understood in more than one way

ambiguous /æm'bɪgjuəs/ **adj** having more than one possible meaning –**ambiguously adv**

★**ambition** /æm'bɪʃn/ **noun 1** [C] ambition (to do/be sth); ambition (of doing sth) something that you very much want to have or do: *It has always been her ambition to travel the world.* • *He finally achieved his ambition of becoming a doctor.* **2** [U] a strong desire to be successful, to have power, etc: *One problem of young people today is their lack of ambition.*

★**ambitious** /æm'bɪʃəs/ **adj 1** ambitious (to be/do sth) having a strong desire to be successful, to have power, etc: *I'm not particularly ambitious – I'm content with my life the way it is.* • *We are ambitious to succeed.* **2** difficult to achieve or do because it takes a lot of work or effort: *The company have announced ambitious plans for expansion.*

ambivalent /æm'bɪvələnt/ **adj** having or showing a mixture of feelings or opinions about sth or sb –**ambivalence noun** [C,U]

★**ambulance** /'æmbjələns/ **noun** [C] a special vehicle for taking ill or injured people to and from hospital: *the ambulance service*

ambush /'æmbʊʃ/ **noun** [C,U] a surprise attack from a hidden position: *He was killed in an enemy ambush.* • *The robbers were waiting in ambush.* –**ambush verb** [T]

amen /ɑː'men; eɪ'men/ **interj** a word used at the end of prayers by Christians and Jews

amenable /ə'miːnəbl/ **adj** happy to accept sth: *I'm amenable to any suggestions you may have.*

amend /ə'mend/ **verb** [T] to change sth slightly in order to make it better

amendment /ə'mendmənt/ **noun 1** [C] a part that is added or a small change that is made to a piece of writing, especially to a law **2** [U] an act of amending sth

amends /ə'mendz/ **noun** [pl]
IDIOM **make amends** to do sth for sb, that shows that you are sorry for sth bad that you have done before

amenity /ə'miːnəti/ **noun** [C] (*pl* **amenities**) something that makes a place pleasant or easy to live in: *Among the town's amenities are two cinemas and a sports centre.*

★**American** /ə'merɪkən/ **adj** from or connected with the US: *Have you met Bob? He's American.* • *an American accent* –**American noun** [C]: *Millions of Americans visit Britain each year.*

A,merican 'football (*US* **football**) **noun** [U] a game played in the US by two teams of eleven players with a ball that is not round. The players wear hard hats (**helmets**) and other protective clothing and try to carry the ball to the end of the field.

A,merican 'Indian = **NATIVE AMERICAN**

amiable /'eɪmiəbl/ **adj** friendly and pleasant –**amiably /-əbli/ adv**

amicable /'æmɪk **adj** made or done in a friendly way, without argument –**amicably adv**

amid /ə'mɪd/ (also **amidst** /ə'mɪdst/) **prep** (*written*) in the middle of; among

amiss /ə'mɪs/ **adj, adv** wrong; not as it should be: *When I walked into the room I could sense that something was amiss.*
IDIOMS **not come/go amiss** to be useful or pleasant: *Things are fine, although a bit more money wouldn't come amiss.*
take sth amiss to be upset by sth, perhaps because you have understood it in the wrong way: *Please don't take my remarks amiss.*

ammunition /ˌæmju'nɪʃn/ **noun** [U] **1** the supply of bullets, etc that you need to fire from a weapon: *The troops surrendered because they had run out of ammunition.* **2** facts or information that can be used against sb/sth

amnesia /æm'niːziə/ **noun** [U] loss of memory

amnesty /'æmnəsti/ **noun** [C] (*pl* **amnesties**) **1** a time when a government forgives political crimes: *The government has announced an amnesty for all political prisoners.* **2** a time when people can give in illegal weapons without being arrested

★**among** /ə'mʌŋ/ (also **amongst** /ə'mʌŋst/) **prep 1** surrounded by; in the middle of: *I often feel nervous when I'm among strangers.* • *I found the missing letter amongst a heap of old newspapers.* •➤ Look at the note and picture at **between**. **2** in or concerning a particular group of people or things: *Discuss it amongst yourselves and let me know your decision.* • *There is a lot of anger among students about the new law.* • *Among other things, the drug can cause headaches and sweating.* **3** to each one (of a group): *On his death, his money will be divided among his children.*

amoral /ˌeɪ'mɒrəl/ **adj** (used about people or their behaviour) not following any moral rules; not caring about right or wrong •➤ Look at **moral** and **immoral**.

★**amount**[1] /ə'maʊnt/ **noun** [C] **1** the amount of sth is how much of it there is; quantity: *I spent an enormous amount of time preparing for the exam.* • *I have a certain amount of*

a

sympathy with her. ● a large amount of money **2** total or sum of money: You are requested to pay the full amount within seven days.

amount² /əˈmaʊnt/ verb [I] amount to sth **1** to add up to; to total: The cost of the repairs amounted to £5000. **2** to be the same as: Whether I tell her today or tomorrow, it amounts to the same thing.

amp /æmp/ noun [C] **1** (also formal **ampere** /ˈæmpeə/) a unit for measuring electric current **2** = AMPLIFIER

ample /ˈæmpl/ adj **1** enough or more than enough: We've got ample time to make a decision. ● I'm not sure how much the trip will cost, but I should think £500 will be ample. **2** large: There is space for an ample car park. –**amply** /ˈæmpli/ adv

amplifier /ˈæmplɪfaɪə/ (also **amp**) noun [C] a piece of electrical equipment for making sounds louder or signals stronger

amplify /ˈæmplɪfaɪ/ verb [T] (pres part **amplifying**; 3rd pers sing pres **amplifies**; pt, pp **amplified**) **1** to increase the strength of a sound, using electrical equipment **2** to add details to sth in order to explain it more fully –**amplification** /ˌæmplɪfɪˈkeɪʃn/ noun [U]

amputate /ˈæmpjuteɪt/ verb [I,T] to cut off a person's arm, leg, etc for medical reasons: His leg was so badly injured that it had to be amputated from the knee down. –**amputation** /ˌæmpjuˈteɪʃn/ noun [C,U]

★**amuse** /əˈmjuːz/ verb [T] **1** to make sb laugh or smile; to seem funny to sb: Everybody laughed but I couldn't understand what had amused them. **2** to make time pass pleasantly for sb; to stop sb from getting bored: I did some crosswords to amuse myself on the journey. ● I've brought a few toys to amuse the children.

★**amused** /əˈmjuːzd/ adj thinking that sth is funny and wanting to laugh or smile: I was amused to hear his account of what happened. IDIOM **keep sb/yourself amused** to do sth in order to pass time pleasantly and stop sb/yourself getting bored

★**amusement** /əˈmjuːzmənt/ noun **1** [U] the feeling caused by sth that makes you laugh or smile, or by sth that entertains you: Much to the pupils' amusement, the teacher fell off his chair. **2** [C] something that makes time pass pleasantly; an entertainment: The holiday centre offers a wide range of amusements, including golf and tennis.

aˈmusement arcade = ARCADE(2)

★**amusing** /əˈmjuːzɪŋ/ adj causing you to laugh or smile: He's a very amusing person and he makes me laugh a lot. ● The story was quite amusing.

an → A²

anaemia (US anemia) /əˈniːmiə/ noun [U] a medical condition in which there are not enough red cells in the blood –**anaemic** adj

anaesthetic (US **anesthetic**) /ˌænɪsˈθetɪk/ noun [C,U] a substance that stops you feeling pain, for example when a doctor is performing a medical operation on you:

You'll need to be **under anaesthetic** for the operation. ● The dentist gave me a **local anaesthetic** (= one that only affects part of the body and does not make you unconscious). ● Did you have a **general anaesthetic** (= one that makes you unconscious) for your operation?

anaesthetist (US **anesthetist**) /əˈniːsθətɪst/ noun [C] a person with the medical training necessary to give anaesthetic to patients

anaesthetize (also -ise; US **anesthetize**) /əˈniːsθətaɪz/ verb [T] to give an anaesthetic to sb

anagram /ˈænəgræm/ noun [C] a word or phrase that is made by arranging the letters of another word or phrase in a different order: 'Worth' is an anagram of 'throw'.

analogous /əˈnæləgəs/ adj (formal) analogous (to/with sth) similar in some way; that you can compare

analogy /əˈnælədʒi/ noun [C] (pl analogies) an analogy (between A and B) a comparison between two things that shows a way in which they are similar: You could make an analogy between the human body and a car engine.
IDIOM **by analogy** by comparing sth to sth else and showing how they are similar

★**analyse** (US **analyze**) /ˈænəlaɪz/ verb [T] to look at or think about the different parts or details of sth carefully in order to understand or explain it: The water samples are now being analysed in a laboratory. ● to analyse statistics ● She analysed the situation and then decided what to do.

★**analysis** /əˈnæləsɪs/ noun (pl analyses /-siːz/) **1** [C,U] the careful examination of the different parts or details of sth: Some samples of the water were sent to a laboratory for analysis. **2** [C] the result of a careful examination of sth: Your analysis of the situation is different from mine.

analyst /ˈænəlɪst/ noun [C] a person whose job is to examine sth carefully as an expert: a food analyst ● a political analyst

analytical /ˌænəˈlɪtɪkl/ (also **analytic** /ˌænəˈlɪtɪk/) adj using careful examination in order to understand or explain sth

anarchic /əˈnɑːkɪk/ adj without rules or laws

anarchism /ˈænəkɪzəm/ noun [U] the political belief that there should be no government or laws in a country –**anarchist** noun [C]

anarchy /ˈænəki/ noun [U] a situation in which people do not obey rules and laws; a situation in which there is no government in a country: While the civil war went on, the country was in a state of anarchy.

anatomy /əˈnætəmi/ noun (pl anatomies) **1** [U] the scientific study of the structure of human or animal bodies **2** [C] the structure of a living thing: the anatomy of the frog –**anatomical** /ˌænəˈtɒmɪkl/ adj

ancestor /ˈænsestə/ noun [C] a person in your family who lived a long time before you:

My ancestors settled in this country a hundred years ago. ••> Look at **descendant**.

ancestry /'ænsestri/ **noun** [C,U] (*pl ancestries*) all of a person's ancestors: *He is of Irish ancestry.*

anchor¹ /'æŋkə/ **noun** [C] a heavy metal object at the end of a chain that you drop into the water from a boat in order to stop the boat moving

anchor² /'æŋkə/ **verb 1** [I,T] to drop an anchor; to stop a boat moving by using an anchor **2** [T] to fix sth firmly so that it cannot move

ancient /'eɪnʃənt/ **adj 1** belonging to a period of history that is thousands of years in the past: *ancient civilizations* ● *an ancient tradition* **2** very old: *I can't believe he's only 30 – he looks ancient!*

★**and** /ənd; ən; *strong form* ænd/ **conj 1** (used to connect words or parts of sentences) also; in addition to: *a boy and a girl* ● *Do it slowly and carefully.* ● *We were singing and dancing all evening.* ● *Come in and sit down.*

> ➤ When the two things are closely linked, you do not need to repeat the 'a', etc: *a knife and fork* ● *my father and mother*

2 (used when you are saying numbers in sums) in addition to; plus: *Twelve and six is eighteen.*

> ➤ When you are saying large numbers *and* is used after the word 'hundred': *We say 2264 as two thousand, two hundred and sixty-four.*

3 used between repeated words to show that sth is increasing or continuing: *The situation is getting worse and worse.* ● *I shouted and shouted but nobody answered.* **4** used instead of 'to' after certain verbs, for example 'go', 'come', 'try': *Go and answer the door for me, will you?* ● *Why don't you come and stay with us one weekend?* ● *I'll try and find out what's going on.*

anecdote /'ænɪkdəʊt/ **noun** [C] a short interesting story about a real person or event

anemia, anemic (*US*) = **ANAEMIA, ANAEMIC**

anesthetic (*US*) = **ANAESTHETIC**

anew /ə'njuː/ **adv** (*written*) again; in a new or different way: *I wish I could start my life anew!*

angel /'eɪndʒl/ **noun** [C] **1** a spirit who is believed to live in heaven with God. In pictures angels are usually dressed in white, with wings. **2** a person who is very kind

angelic /æn'dʒelɪk/ **adj** looking or acting like an angel –**angelically** /-kli/ **adv**

★**anger¹** /'æŋgə/ **noun** [U] the strong feeling that you have when sth has happened or sb has done sth that you do not like: *He could not hide his anger at the news.* ● *She was shaking with anger.*

anger² /'æŋgə/ **verb** [T] to make sb become angry

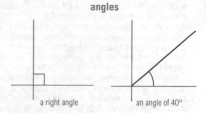
angles

a right angle   an angle of 40°

★**angle¹** /'æŋgl/ **noun** [C] **1** the space between two lines or surfaces that meet, measured in degrees: *a right angle* (= an angle of 90°) ● *at an angle of 40°* ● *The three angles of a triangle add up to 180°.* **2** the direction from which you look at sth: *Viewed from this angle, the building looks bigger than it really is.*

IDIOM **at an angle** not straight

angle² /'æŋgl/ **verb 1** [I,T] to put sth in a position that is not straight; to be in this position: *Angle the lamp towards the desk.* **2** [T] **angle sth (at/to/towards sb)** to show sth from a particular point of view; to aim sth at a particular person or group: *The new magazine is angled at young professional people.*

PHRASAL VERB **angle for sth** to try to make sb give you sth, without asking for it in a direct way: *She was angling for an invitation to our party.*

angler /'æŋglə/ **noun** [C] a person who catches fish as a hobby ••> Look at **fisherman**.

Anglican /'æŋglɪkən/ **noun** [C] a member of the Church of England or of a related church in another English-speaking country –**Anglican adj**

angling /'æŋglɪŋ/ **noun** [U] fishing as a sport or hobby: *He goes angling at weekends.* ••> Look at **fishing**.

Anglo- /'æŋgləʊ/ (in compounds) connected with England or Britain (and another country or countries): *Anglo-American relations*

Anglo-Saxon /ˌæŋgləʊ 'sæksn/ **noun 1** [C] a person whose family originally came from England **2** [C] a person who lived in England before the Norman Conquest (1066) **3** (also **Old English**) [U] the English language before about 1150 –**Anglo-Saxon adj**

★**angry** /'æŋgri/ **adj** (**angrier; angriest**) **angry (with sb) (at/about sth)** feeling or showing anger: *Calm down, there's no need to get angry.* ● *My parents will be angry with me if I get home late.* ● *He's always getting angry about something.* –**angrily adv**

anguish /'æŋgwɪʃ/ **noun** [U] (*written*) great mental pain or suffering –**anguished adj**

angular /'æŋgjələ/ **adj** with sharp points or corners

★**animal** /'ænɪml/ **noun** [C] a living creature that can move and feel. 'Animal' is sometimes used to talk about only creatures with warm blood (**mammals**): *the animal kingdom* ● *Humans are social animals.* ● *farm animals*

a

● *He studied the animals and birds of Southern Africa.* ••➤ picture on page C1

animated /'ænɪmeɪtɪd/ **adj 1** interesting and full of energy: *an animated discussion* **2** (used about films) using a process or method which makes pictures or models appear to move: *an animated cartoon*

animation /ˌænɪ'meɪʃn/ **noun** [U] **1** the state of being full of energy and enthusiasm **2** the method of making films, computer games, etc with pictures or models that appear to move: *computer animation*

★ **ankle** /'æŋkl/ **noun** [C] the part of your body where your foot joins your leg: *The water only came up to my ankles.* ••➤ picture on page C5

annex /ə'neks/ **verb** [T] to take control of another country or region by force –**annexation** /ˌænek'seɪʃn/ **noun** [C,U]

annexe (*especially US* **annex**) /'æneks/ **noun** [C] a building that is joined to a larger one

annihilate /ə'naɪəleɪt/ **verb** [T] to destroy or defeat sb/sth completely –**annihilation** /əˌnaɪə'leɪʃn/ **noun** [U]

anniversary /ˌænɪ'vɜːsəri/ **noun** [C] (*pl* **anniversaries**) a day that is exactly a year or a number of years after a special or important event: *the hundredth anniversary of the country's independence* ● *a wedding anniversary* ••➤ Look at **birthday**.

annotated /'ænəteɪtɪd/ **adj** (used about a book, etc) with notes added to it that explain and give extra information about the contents

★ **announce** /ə'naʊns/ **verb** [T] **1** to make sth known publicly and officially: *They announced that our train had been delayed.* ● *The winners will be announced in next week's paper.* **2** to say sth in a firm or serious way: *She stormed into my office and announced that she was leaving.*

★ **announcement** /ə'naʊnsmənt/ **noun 1** [C] a statement that tells people about sth: *Ladies and gentlemen, I'd like to* **make an announcement**. **2** [sing] an act of telling people about sth

announcer /ə'naʊnsə/ **noun** [C] a person who introduces or gives information about programmes on radio or television

★ **annoy** /ə'nɔɪ/ **verb** [T] to make sb angry or slightly angry: *It really annoys me when you act so selfishly.* ● *Close the door if the noise is annoying you.*

annoyance /ə'nɔɪəns/ **noun 1** [U] the feeling of being annoyed **2** [C] something that annoys sb

★ **annoyed** /ə'nɔɪd/ **adj** feeling angry or slightly angry: *I shall be extremely annoyed if he turns up late again.* ● *She's annoyed with herself for making such a stupid mistake.* ● *He's annoyed that nobody believes him.*

★ **annoying** /ə'nɔɪɪŋ/ **adj** making you feel angry or slightly angry: *It's so annoying that there's no phone near here!* ● *His most annoying habit is always arriving late.*

★ **annual**[1] /'ænjuəl/ **adj 1** happening or done once a year or every year: *the company's annual report* ● *an annual festival* **2** for the period of one year: *What's the average annual salary for a nurse?* ● *the annual sales figures* –**annually adv**

annual[2] /'ænjuəl/ **noun** [C] a book, especially one for children, that is published once each year: *the 1999 Football Annual*

anomalous /ə'nɒmələs/ **adj** different from what is normal: *In a few anomalous cases, these drugs have made people ill.*

anomaly /ə'nɒməli/ **noun** [C] (*pl* **anomalies**) sth that is different from what is normal or usual: *We discovered an anomaly in the sales figures for August.*

anon /ə'nɒn/ **abbr** anonymous; used to show that we don't know who did a piece of writing

anonymity /ˌænə'nɪməti/ **noun** [U] the situation where a person's name is not known

anonymous /ə'nɒnɪməs/ **adj 1** (used about a person) whose name is not known or made public: *An anonymous caller told the police that a robbery was going to take place.* **2** done, written, etc by sb whose name is not known or made public: *He received an anonymous letter.* –**anonymously adv**

anorak /'ænəræk/ **noun** [C] (*Brit*) **1** a short coat with a covering for your head that protects you from rain, wind and cold ••➤ picture on page C6 **2** (*slang*) a person who enjoys learning boring facts: *He's a real anorak – he can name every player in the World Cup.*

anorexia /ˌænə'reksiə/ (also **anorexia nervosa** /ˌænəreksiə nɜː'vəʊsə/) **noun** [U] an illness, especially affecting young women. It makes them afraid of being fat and so they do not eat. –**anorexic adj, noun** [C]

★ **another** /ə'nʌðə/ **determiner, pron 1** one more person or thing of the same kind: *Would you like another drink?* ● *They've got three children already and they're having another.* **2** a different thing or person: *I'm afraid I can't see you tomorrow. Could we arrange another day?* ● *If you've already seen that film, we can go and see another.*

IDIOMS one after another/the other ➔ **ONE**[1]

yet another ➔ **YET**

★ **answer**[1] /'ɑːnsə/ **verb** [I,T] **1** to say or write sth back to sb who has asked you sth or written to you: *I asked her what the matter was but she didn't answer.* ● *I've asked you a question, now please answer me.* ● *Answer all the questions on the form.* ● *He hasn't answered my letter yet* (= written a letter back to me). ● *When I asked him how much he earned, he answered that it was none of my business.* ● *'No!' he answered angrily.*

➤ **Answer** and **reply** are the most common verbs used for speaking or writing in reaction to questions, letters, etc: *I asked him a question but he didn't answer.* ● *I sent my application but they haven't replied yet.* Note that you **answer** a person, a question or a letter (no 'to') but you **reply to** a letter. **Respond** is less common and more formal with this meaning: *Applicants must respond* *within seven days.* It is more commonly used with the meaning of 'reacting in a way that is desired': *Despite all the doctor's efforts the patient did not respond to treatment.*

2 to do sth as a reply: *Can you answer the phone* (= pick up the receiver) *for me, please?* ● *I rang their doorbell but nobody answered.*

PHRASAL VERBS **answer back** to defend yourself against sth bad that has been written or said about you

answer (sb) back to reply rudely to sb

answer for sb/sth 1 to accept responsibility for sth/sb: *Somebody will have to answer for all the damage that has been caused.* **2** to speak in support of sb/sth

★**answer²** /'ɑːnsə/ *noun* [C] **an answer (to sb/sth) 1** something that you say, write or do as a reply: *The answer to your question is that I don't know.* ● *They've made me an offer and I have to give them an answer by Friday.* ● *I wrote to them two weeks ago and I'm still waiting for an answer.* ● *I knocked on the door and waited but there was no answer.* **2** a solution to a problem: *I didn't have any money so the only answer was to borrow some.* **3** a reply to a question in a test or exam: *My answer to question 5 was wrong.* ● *How many answers did you get right?* **4** the correct reply to a question in a test or exam: *What was the answer to question 4?*

IDIOM **in answer (to sth)** as a reply (to sth)

answerable /'ɑːnsərəbl/ **answerable to sb (for sth)** having to explain and give good reasons for your actions to sb; responsible to sb

'answering machine (*Brit* **answerphone** /'ɑːnsəfəʊn/) *noun* [C] a machine that answers the telephone and records messages from the people who call: *I rang him and left a message on his answering machine.*

ant /ænt/ *noun* [C] a very small insect that lives in large groups and works very hard ●► picture at **insect**

antagonism /æn'tægənɪzəm/ *noun* [C,U] antagonism (towards sb/sth); antagonism (between A and B) a feeling of hate and of being against sb/sth —antagonistic /æn,tægə'nɪstɪk/ *adj*

antagonize (also **-ise**) /æn'tægənaɪz/ *verb* [T] to make sb angry or to annoy sb

Antarctic¹ /æn'tɑːktɪk/ *adj* connected with the coldest, most southern parts of the world: *an Antarctic expedition* ●► Look at **Arctic**.

the Antarctic² /æn'tɑːktɪk/ *noun* [sing] the most southern part of the world ●► Look at **the Arctic**. ●► picture at **earth**

antelope /'æntɪləʊp/ *noun* [C] (*pl* **antelope** or **antelopes**) an African animal with horns and long, thin legs that can run very fast

antenatal /,æntɪ'neɪtl/ *adj* connected with the care of

pregnant women: *an antenatal clinic* ● *antenatal care*

antenna /æn'tenə/ *noun* [C] **1** (*pl* **antennae** /-niː/) one of the two long thin parts on the heads of insects and some animals that live in shells. Antennae are used for feeling things with. ●► synonym **feelers** ●► picture at **insect 2** (*pl* **antennas**) (*US*) = **AERIAL¹**

anthem /'ænθəm/ *noun* [C] a song, especially one that is sung on special occasions: *the national anthem* (= the special song of a country)

anthology /æn'θɒlədʒi/ *noun* [C] (*pl* **anthologies**) a book that contains pieces of writing or poems, often on the same subject, by different authors: *an anthology of love poetry*

anthropology /,ænθrə'pɒlədʒi/ *noun* [U] the study of human beings, especially of their origin, development, customs and beliefs —anthropological /,ænθrəpə'lɒdʒɪkl/ *adj*

antibiotic /,æntibaɪ'ɒtɪk/ *noun* [C] a medicine which is used for destroying bacteria and curing infections

antibody /'æntibɒdi/ *noun* [C] (*pl* **antibodies**) a substance that the body produces to fight disease

anticipate /æn'tɪsɪpeɪt/ *verb* [T] to expect sth to happen and prepare for it: *to anticipate a problem* ● *I anticipate that the situation will get worse.*

anticipation /æn,tɪsɪ'peɪʃn/ *noun* [U] **1** the state of expecting sth to happen (and preparing for it): *The government has reduced tax in anticipation of an early general election.* **2** excited feelings about sth that is going to happen: *They queued outside the stadium in excited anticipation.*

anticlimax /,ænti'klaɪmæks/ *noun* [C,U] an event, etc that is less exciting than you had expected or than what has already happened: *When the exams were over we all had a sense of anticlimax.*

anticlockwise /,ænti'klɒkwaɪz/ (*US* **'counter-clockwise**) *adv, adj* in the opposite direction to the movement of the hands of a clock: *Turn the lid anticlockwise/in an anticlockwise direction.* ●► opposite **clockwise**

antics /'æntɪks/ *noun* [pl] funny, strange or silly ways of behaving

antidote /'æntidəʊt/ *noun* [C] **1** a medical substance that is used to prevent a poison or a disease from having an effect: *an antidote to snake bites* **2** anything that helps you to deal with sth unpleasant

antipathy /æn'tɪpəθi/ *noun* [C,U] antipathy (to/towards sb/sth) a strong feeling of not liking sb/sth; dislike

antiperspirant /,ænti'pɜːspərənt/ *noun* [C,U] a liquid that you use to reduce sweating, especially under your arms

antiquated /'æntikweɪtɪd/ *adj* old fashioned and not suitable for the modern world

antique /æn'tiːk/ *adj* very old and therefore unusual and valuable: *an antique vase/table*

a

• *antique furniture/jewellery* –antique **noun** [C]: *an antique shop* (= one that sells antiques) • *That vase is an antique.*

antiquity /æn'tɪkwəti/ **noun** (*pl* **antiquities**) **1** [U] the ancient past, especially the times of the Ancient Greeks and Romans **2** [C, usually pl] a building or object from ancient times: *Greek/Roman antiquities* **3** [U] the state of being very old or ancient

anti-Semitism /ˌænti 'semətɪzəm/ **noun** [U] unfair treatment of Jewish people –anti-Semitic /ˌænti sə'mɪtɪk/

antiseptic /ˌænti'septɪk/ **noun** [C,U] a liquid or cream that prevents a cut, etc from becoming infected: *Put an antiseptic/some antiseptic on that scratch.* –antiseptic **adj**: *antiseptic cream*

antisocial /ˌænti'səʊʃl/ **adj 1** harmful or annoying to other people: *antisocial behaviour* **2** not liking to be with other people

antithesis /æn'tɪθəsɪs/ **noun** [C,U] (*pl* **antitheses** /æn'tɪθəsiːz/) (*formal*) **1** the opposite of sth: *Love is the antithesis of hate.* **2** a difference between two things

antler /'æntlə/ **noun** [C, usually pl] a horn on the head of an adult male animal (a stag): *a pair of antlers* ••➤ picture at **deer** ••➤ picture at **elk**

anus /'eɪnəs/ **noun** [C] the hole through which solid waste substances leave the body ••➤ picture on page C5

anxiety /æŋ'zaɪəti/ **noun** [C,U] (*pl* **anxieties**) a feeling of worry or fear, especially about the future: *a feeling/state of anxiety* • *There are anxieties over the effects of unemployment.*

★**anxious** /'æŋkʃəs/ **adj 1** anxious (about/for sb/sth) worried and afraid: *I'm anxious about my exam.* • *I began to get anxious when they still hadn't arrived at 9 o'clock.* • *an anxious look/expression* **2** causing worry and fear: *For a few anxious moments we thought we'd missed the train.* **3** anxious to do sth; anxious for sth wanting sth very much –anxiously **adv**

★**any** /'eni/ **determiner, pron, adv 1** (used instead of *some* in negative sentences and in questions): *We didn't have any lunch.* • *I speak hardly any* (= almost no) *Spanish.* • *Do you have any questions?* • *I don't like any of his books.* ••➤ Look at the note at **some**. **2** used for saying that it does not matter which thing or person you choose: *Take any book you want.* • *Come round any time – I'm usually in.* • *I'll take any that you don't want.* **3** (used in negative sentences and questions) to any degree: *I can't run any faster.* • *Is your father any better?*

IDIOM **any moment/second/minute/day (now)** very soon: *She should be home any minute now.*

★**anybody** /'enibɒdi/ (also **anyone**) **pron 1** (usually in questions or negative statements) any person: *I didn't know anybody at the party.* • *Is there anybody here who can speak Japanese?* • *Would anybody else* (= any other person) *like to come with me?*

➤ The difference between **somebody** and **anybody** is the same as the difference between **some** and **any**. Look at the notes at **some** and **somebody**.

2 any person, it does not matter who: *Anybody* (= all people) *can learn to swim.* • *Can anybody come, or are there special invitations?*

★**anyhow** /'enihaʊ/ **adv 1** (also **anyway**) (used to add an extra point or reason) in any case: *I don't want to go out tonight, and anyhow I haven't got any money.* **2** (also **anyway**) (used when saying or writing sth which contrasts in one way with what has gone before); nevertheless: *I don't think we'll succeed, but anyhow we can try.* • *I'm afraid I can't come to your party, but thanks anyhow.* **3** (also **anyway**) (used for correcting sth you have just said and making it more accurate) at least: *Everybody wants to be rich – well, most people anyhow.* **4** (also **anyway**) used after a pause in order to change the subject or go back to a subject being discussed before: *Anyhow, that's enough about my problems. How are you?* **5** in a careless way; with no order

★**anyone** /'eniwʌn/ = **ANYBODY**

anyplace /'enipleɪs/ (*US*) = **ANYWHERE**

★**anything** /'eniθɪŋ/ **pron 1** (usually in negative sentences and in questions) one thing (of any kind): *It was so dark that I couldn't see anything at all.* • *There isn't anything interesting in the newspaper today.* • *Did you buy anything?* • *'I'd like a kilo of apples please.' 'Anything else?'* (= any other thing?)

➤ The difference between **something** and **anything** is the same as the difference between **some** and **any**. Look at the note at **some**.

2 any thing or things: it does not matter what: *I'm very hungry – I'll eat anything!* • *I'll do anything you say.*

IDIOMS **anything but** not at all: *Their explanation was anything but clear.*

anything like sb/sth at all similar to sb/sth; nearly: *She isn't anything like her sister, is she?* • *This car isn't anything like as fast as mine.*

as happy, quick, etc as anything (*spoken*) very happy, quick, etc

like anything → **LIKE²**

not come to anything → **COME**

★**anyway** /'eniweɪ/ = **ANYHOW**

★**anywhere** /'eniweə/ (*US also* **anyplace**) **adv 1** (usually in negative sentences or in questions) in, at or to any place: *I can't find my keys anywhere.* • *Is there a post office anywhere near here?* • *You can't buy the book anywhere else* (= in another place).

➤ The difference between **somewhere** and **anywhere** is the same as the difference between **some** and **any**. Look at the note at **some**.

2 any place; it does not matter where: *You can sit anywhere you like.*

apart /ə'pɑːt/ adv **1** away from sb/sth or each other; not together: *The doors slowly slid apart.* • *Stand with your feet apart.* • *The houses are ten metres apart.* • *I'm afraid our ideas are too far apart.* **2** into pieces: *The material was so old that it just fell/came apart in my hands.*

IDIOMS **take sth apart** to separate sth into pieces: *He took the whole bicycle apart.*

tell A and B apart to see the difference between A and B: *It's very difficult to tell the twins apart.*

a'part from (*especially US* **aside from**) prep **1** except for: *I've answered all the questions apart from the last one.* • *There's nobody here apart from me.* **2** as well as; in addition to: *Apart from music, she also loves sport and reading.*

apartheid /ə'pɑːthaɪt/ noun [U] the former official government policy in South Africa of separating people of different races and making them live apart

apartment /ə'pɑːtmənt/ noun [C] **1** (*especially US*) = FLAT²(1) **2** a set of rooms rented for a holiday: *a self-catering apartment*

a'partment block noun [C] (*especially US*) a large building containing several apartments

apathetic /ˌæpə'θetɪk/ adj lacking interest or desire to act: *Many students are apathetic about politics.*

apathy /'æpəθi/ noun [U] the feeling of not being interested in or enthusiastic about anything: *There is widespread apathy towards the elections.*

ape¹ /eɪp/ noun [C] a type of animal like a large monkey with no tail or only a very short tail: *Chimpanzees and gorillas are apes.*

ape² /eɪp/ verb [T] to copy sb/sth, especially in a ridiculous way: *The children were aping the teacher's way of walking.*

aperitif /əˌperə'tiːf/ noun [C] an alcoholic drink that you have before a meal

apiece /ə'piːs/ adv each: *Coates and Winterbotham scored a goal apiece.*

apologetic /əˌpɒlə'dʒetɪk/ adj feeling or showing that you are sorry for sth you have done: *He was most apologetic about his son's bad behaviour.* • *I wrote him an apologetic letter.* –apologetically /-kli/ adv

apologize (also **-ise**) /ə'pɒlədʒaɪz/ verb [I] apologize (to sb) (for sth) to say that you are sorry for sth that you have done: *You'll have to apologize to your teacher for being late.*

➤ When you apologize, the actual words you use are usually '**I'm sorry**'.

apology /ə'pɒlədʒi/ noun [C,U] (*pl* **apologies**) (an) apology (to sb) (for sth) a spoken or written statement that you are sorry for sth you have done, etc: *Please accept our apologies for the delay.* • *a letter of apology*

apostrophe /ə'pɒstrəfi/ noun [C] **1** the sign (') used for showing that you have left a letter or letters out of a word as in 'I'm', 'can't' or 'we'll' **2** the sign (') used for showing who or what sth belongs to as in 'John's chair', 'the boy's room' or 'Russia's President'.

appal (*US* **appall**) /ə'pɔːl/ verb [T] (**appalling**; **appalled**) (usually passive) to shock sb very much –appalling /ə'pɔːlɪŋ/ adj –appallingly adv

apparatus /ˌæpə'reɪtəs/ noun [U] the set of tools, instruments or equipment used for doing a job or an activity

apparent /ə'pærənt/ adj **1** (only *before* a noun) that seems to be real or true but may not be **2** apparent (to sb) clear; easy to see: *It quickly became apparent to us that our teacher could not speak French.*

apparently /ə'pærəntli/ adv according to what people say or to how sth appears, but perhaps not true: *Apparently, he's already been married twice.* • *He was apparently undisturbed by the news.*

appeal¹ /ə'piːl/ verb [I] **1** appeal to sb (for sth); appeal for sth to make a serious request for sth you need or want very much: *Relief workers in the disaster area are appealing for more help and supplies.* • *She appealed to the kidnappers to let her son go.* **2** appeal (to sb) to be attractive or interesting to sb: *The idea of living in the country doesn't appeal to me at all.* **3** appeal to sth to influence sb's feelings or thoughts so that he/she will do sth you want: *We aim to appeal to people's generosity.* **4** appeal (against/for sth) to ask sb in authority to make or change a decision: *He decided to appeal against his conviction.* • *The player fell down and appealed for a penalty.*

appeal² /ə'piːl/ noun **1** [C] a serious request for sth you need or want very much: *The police have made an urgent appeal for witnesses to come forward.* **2** [C] an appeal to sth a suggestion that tries to influence sb's feelings or thoughts so that he/she will do what you want **3** [C] a formal request to sb in authority to change a decision **4** [U] the attraction or interesting quality of sth/sb

appealing /ə'piːlɪŋ/ adj **1** attractive or interesting: *The idea of a lying on a beach sounds very appealing!* **2** showing that you need help, etc: *an appealing look* –appealingly adv

appear /ə'pɪə/ verb [I] **1** appear to be/do sth; appear (that)… to seem: *She appears to be very happy in her job.* • *It appears that you were given the wrong information.* ••➤ adjective **apparent 2** to suddenly be seen; to come into sight: *The bus appeared from round the corner.* ••➤ opposite **disappear 3** to begin to exist: *The disease is thought to have appeared in Africa.* **4** to be published or printed: *The article appeared in this morning's paper.* **5** to perform or speak where you are seen by a lot of people: *to appear on television/in a play*

appearance /ə'pɪərəns/ noun **1** [U] the way that sb/sth looks or seems: *A different hairstyle can completely change your appearance.* • *He gives the appearance of being extremely confident.* **2** [sing] the coming of sb/sth: *the appearance of television in the home in the*

a

1950s **3** [C] an act of appearing in public, especially on stage, television, etc

appendicitis /ə,pendə'saɪtɪs/ **noun** [U] an illness in which your appendix becomes extremely painful and usually has to be removed

appendix /ə'pendɪks/ **noun** [C] **1** (*pl* **appendixes**) a small organ inside your body near your stomach. In humans, the appendix has no real function. **2** (*pl* **appendices** /-dɪsiːz/) a section at the end of a book, etc that gives extra information

appetite /'æpɪtaɪt/ **noun** [C,U] a strong desire for sth, especially food: *Some fresh air and exercise should give you an appetite* (= make you hungry). ● *He has a great **appetite** for work/life.* ● *loss of appetite*
IDIOM whet sb's appetite → WHET

appetizer (also **appetiser**) /'æpɪtaɪzə/ (*especially US*) = STARTER

appetizing (also **appetising**) /'æpɪtaɪzɪŋ/ **adj** (used about food, etc) that looks or smells attractive; making you feel hungry: *an appetizing smell*

applaud /ə'plɔːd/ **verb 1** [I,T] to hit your hands together noisily (**clap**) in order to show that you like sb/sth: *The audience applauded loudly.* ● *The team was applauded as it left the field.* **2** [T] (usually passive) to express approval of sth: *The decision was applauded by everybody.*

applause /ə'plɔːz/ **noun** [U] the noise made by a group of people hitting their hands together (**clapping**) to show their approval and enjoyment: *Let's all give a big **round of applause** to the cook!*

★ **apple** /'æpl/ **noun** [C,U] a hard, round fruit with a smooth green, red or yellow skin: *apple juice* ••> picture on page C3

appliance /ə'plaɪəns/ **noun** [C] a piece of equipment for a particular purpose in the house: *washing machines and other domestic appliances*

applicable /'æplɪkəbl; ə'plɪkəbl/ **adj** (not before a noun) **applicable (to sb/sth)** that concerns sb/sth; relevant to sb/sth: *This part of the form is only applicable to married women.*

applicant /'æplɪkənt/ **noun** [C] a person who makes a formal request for sth (**applies for sth**), especially for a job, a place at a college, university, etc: *There were over 200 applicants for the job.*

application /,æplɪ'keɪʃn/ **noun 1** [C,U] **(an) application (to sb) (for sth)** a formal written request, especially for a job or a place in a school, club, etc: *Applications for the job should be made to the Personnel Manager.* ● *To become a member, fill in the **application form.*** **2** [C,U] the practical use (of sth) **3** [U] hard work; effort

applied /ə'plaɪd/ **adj** (used about a subject) studied in a way that has a practical use ••> opposite **pure**

★ **apply** /ə'plaɪ/ **verb** (*pres part* **applying**; *3rd pers sing pres* **applies**; *pt, pp* **applied**) **1** [I] **apply (to sb) (for sth)** to ask for sth in

writing: *I've applied to that company for a job.* ● *She's applying for a place at university.* **2** [I] **apply (to sb/sth)** to concern or involve sb/sth: *This information applies to all children born after 1997.* **3** [T] **apply sth (to sth)** to make practical use of sth: *new technology which can be applied to solving problems in industry* **4** [T] (usually passive) to use a word, a name, etc to describe sb/sth: *I don't think the term 'music' can be applied to that awful noise.* **5** [T] **apply sth (to sth)** to put or spread sth onto sth: *Apply the cream to the infected area twice a day.* **6** [T] **apply yourself/sth (to sth/doing sth)** to make yourself give all your attention to sth: *to apply your mind to sth*

appoint /ə'pɔɪnt/ **verb** [T] **1 appoint sb (to sth)** to choose sb for a job or position: *The committee have appointed a new chairperson.* ● *He's been appointed (as) assistant to Dr Beale.* **2** (*formal*) **appoint sth (for sth)** to arrange or decide on sth

★ **appointment** /ə'pɔɪntmənt/ **noun 1** [C,U] an **appointment (with sb)** an arrangement to see sb at a particular time: *I have an appointment with Dr Sula at 3 o'clock.* ● *I'd like to **make an appointment** to see the manager.* ● *I realized I wouldn't be able to keep the appointment so I cancelled it.* ● *Visits are by appointment only* (= at a time that has been arranged in advance). **2** [C] a job or a position of responsibility: *a temporary/permanent appointment* **3** [U] **appointment (to sth)** the act of choosing sb for a job

appraisal /ə'preɪzl/ **noun** [C,U] (*formal*) a judgement about the value or quality of sb/sth

appraise /ə'preɪz/ **verb** [T] (*formal*) to judge the value or quality of sb/sth

appreciable /ə'priːʃəbl/ **adj** noticeable or important

★ **appreciate** /ə'priːʃieɪt/ **verb 1** [T] to enjoy sth or to understand the value of sb/sth: *My boss doesn't appreciate me.* ● *I don't appreciate good coffee – it all tastes the same to me.* **2** [T] to understand a problem, situation, etc: *I appreciate your problem but I'm afraid I can't help you.* **3** [T] to be grateful for sth: *Thanks very much. I really appreciate your help.* **4** [I] to increase in value

appreciation /ə,priːʃi'eɪʃn/ **noun** [U] **1** understanding and enjoyment of the value of sth: *I'm afraid I have little appreciation of modern architecture.* **2** the feeling of being grateful for sth: *We bought him a present to show our appreciation for all the work he had done.* **3** understanding of a situation, problem, etc **4** an increase in value

appreciative /ə'priːʃətɪv/ **adj 1** feeling or showing pleasure or admiration: *an appreciative audience* **2 appreciative (of sth)** grateful for sth: *He was very appreciative of our efforts to help.*

apprehensive /,æprɪ'hensɪv/ **adj** worried or afraid that sth unpleasant may happen: *I'm feeling apprehensive about tomorrow's exam.* –**apprehension** /-ʃn/ **noun** [C,U]

apprentice /ə'prentɪs/ **noun** [C] a person who works for low pay, in order to learn the skills needed in a particular job: *an apprentice electrician/chef/plumber*

apprenticeship /ə'prentɪʃɪp/ **noun** [C,U] the state or time of being an apprentice: *He served a two-year apprenticeship as a carpenter.*

★**approach**[1] /ə'prəʊtʃ/ **verb 1** [I,T] to come near or nearer to sb/sth: *The day of the exam approached.* ● *When you approach the village you will see a garage on your left.* **2** [T] to begin to deal with a problem, a situation, etc: *What is the best way to approach this problem?* **3** [T] to speak to sb usually in order to ask for sth: *I'm going to approach my bank manager about a loan.*

approach[2] /ə'prəʊtʃ/ **noun 1** [C] a way of dealing with sb/sth: *Parents don't always know what approach to take with teenage children.* **2** [sing] the act of coming nearer (to sb/sth): *the approach of winter* **3** [C] a request for sth: *The company has made an approach to us for financial assistance.* **4** [C] a road or path leading to sth: *the approach to the village*

approachable /ə'prəʊtʃəbl/ **adj 1** friendly and easy to talk to **2** (not before a noun) that can be reached ••➤ synonym **accessible**

★**appropriate**[1] /ə'prəʊpriət/ **adj** appropriate (for/to sth) suitable or right for a particular situation, person, use, etc: *The matter will be dealt with by the appropriate authorities.* ● *I don't think this film is appropriate for children.* ••➤ opposite **inappropriate** –appropriately **adv**

appropriate[2] /ə'prəʊprieɪt/ **verb** [T] to take sth to use for yourself, usually without permission

★**approval** /ə'pruːvl/ **noun** [U] feeling, showing or saying that you think sth is good; agreement: *Everybody gave their approval to the proposal.*

★**approve** /ə'pruːv/ **verb 1** [I] approve (of sb/sth) to be pleased about sth; to like sb/sth: *His father didn't approve of him becoming a dancer.* ● *Her parents don't approve of her friends.* ••➤ opposite **disapprove 2** [T] to agree formally to sth or to say that sth is correct: *We need to get an accountant to approve these figures.*

approving /ə'pruːvɪŋ/ **adj** showing support or admiration for sth: *'I agree entirely,' he said with an approving smile.* –approvingly **adv**

approx **abbr** (*written*) approximate; approximately

★**approximate** /ə'prɒksɪmət/ **adj** almost correct but not completely accurate: *The approximate time of arrival is 3 o'clock.* ● *I can only give you an approximate idea of the cost.*

★**approximately** /ə'prɒksɪmətli/ **adv** about; roughly: *It's approximately fifty miles from here.*

approximation /ə,prɒksɪ'meɪʃn/ **noun** [C] a number, answer, etc which is nearly, but not exactly, right

Apr **abbr** April: *2 Apr 1993*

apricot /'eɪprɪkɒt/ **noun** [C] a small, round, yellow or orange fruit with a large seed (stone) inside ••➤ picture on page C3

★**April** /'eɪprəl/ **noun** [U,C] (*abbr* **Apr**) the fourth month of the year, coming after March

➤ To see how the months are used in sentences, look at the examples and the note at **January**.

,April 'Fool's Day **noun** [sing] 1 April

➤ On this day it is traditional for people to play tricks on each other, especially by inventing silly stories and trying to persuade other people that they are true. If somebody believes such a story he/she is called an **April Fool**.

apron /'eɪprən/ **noun** [C] a piece of clothing that you wear over the front of your usual clothes in order to keep them clean, especially when cooking ••➤ picture at **overall**

apt /æpt/ **adj 1** suitable in a particular situation: *I thought 'complex' was an apt description of the book.* **2** apt to do sth often likely to do sth

aptitude /'æptɪtjuːd/ **noun** [U,C] aptitude (for sth/for doing sth) natural ability or skill: *She has an aptitude for learning languages.*

aptly /'æptli/ **adv** in an appropriate way; suitably: *The winner of the race was aptly named Alan Speedy.*

aquarium /ə'kweəriəm/ **noun** [C] (*pl* **aquariums** or **aquaria** /-riə/) **1** a glass container filled with water, in which fish and water animals are kept **2** a building where people can go to see fish and other water animals

Aquarius /ə'kweəriəs/ **noun** [C,U] the eleventh sign of the zodiac, the Water Carrier

aquatic /ə'kwætɪk/ **adj** living or taking place in, on or near water: *aquatic plants* ● *windsurfing and other aquatic sports*

★**Arab** /'ærəb/ **noun** [C] a member of a people who lived originally in Arabia and who now live in many parts of the Middle East and North Africa –Arab **adj**: *Arab countries*

★**Arabic** /'ærəbɪk/ **noun** [sing] the language of Arab people

arable /'ærəbl/ **adj** (in farming) connected with growing crops for sale, not keeping animals: *arable land/farmers*

arbitrary /'ɑːbɪtrəri/ **adj** not seeming to be based on any reason or plan: *The choice of players for the team seemed completely arbitrary.* –arbitrarily **adv**

arbitrate /'ɑːbɪtreɪt/ **verb** [I,T] to settle an argument between two people or groups by finding a solution that both can accept –arbitration /,ɑːbɪ'treɪʃn/ **noun** [U]

arc /ɑːk/ **noun** [C] a curved line, part of a circle

arcade /ɑː'keɪd/ **noun** [C] **1** a large covered passage or area with shops along one or both sides: *a shopping arcade* ••➤ picture on page C8 **2** (also **amusement arcade**) a large room with machines and games that you put coins into to play

arch

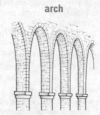

arch¹ /ɑːtʃ/ **noun** [C]
1 a curved structure with straight sides, often supporting a bridge or the roof of a large building, or it may be above a door or window ••➤ Look at **archway**. **2** the curved part at the bottom of your foot

arch² /ɑːtʃ/ **verb** [I,T] to make a curve

archaeological (*US* **archeological**) /ˌɑːkɪəˈlɒdʒɪkl/ **adj** connected with archaeology

archaeologist (*US* **archeologist**) /ˌɑːkɪˈɒlədʒɪst/ **noun** [C] an expert in archaeology

archaeology (*US* **archeology**) /ˌɑːkɪˈɒlədʒi/ **noun** [U] the study of the past, based on objects or parts of buildings that are found in the ground

archaic /ɑːˈkeɪɪk/ **adj** very old-fashioned; no longer used

archbishop /ˌɑːtʃˈbɪʃəp/ **noun** [C] a priest with a very high position, in some branches of the Christian Church, who is responsible for all the churches in a large area of a country: *the Archbishop of Canterbury* (= the head of the Church of England) ••➤ Look at **bishop**.

archer /ˈɑːtʃə/ **noun** [C] a person who shoots pieces of wood or metal with a sharp point (arrows) through the air by pulling back a tight string on a curved piece of wood (a bow) and letting go. In past times this was done in order to kill people, but it is now done as a sport.

archery /ˈɑːtʃəri/ **noun** [U] the sport of shooting arrows

★**architect** /ˈɑːkɪtekt/ **noun** [C] a person whose job is to design buildings

architectural /ˌɑːkɪˈtektʃərəl/ **adj** connected with the design of buildings

architecture /ˈɑːkɪtektʃə/ **noun** [U] **1** the study of designing and making buildings **2** the style or design of a building or buildings: *modern architecture*

archives /ˈɑːkaɪvz/ **noun** [pl] (also **archive** [C]) a collection of historical documents, etc which show the history of a place or an organization; the place where they are kept: *archive material on the First World War*

archway /ˈɑːtʃweɪ/ **noun** [C] a passage or entrance with an arch over it

Arctic¹ /ˈɑːktɪk/ **adj 1** connected with the region around the North Pole (the most northern point of the world) ••➤ Look at **Antarctic**. **2 arctic** extremely cold

the Arctic² /ˈɑːktɪk/ **noun** [sing] the area around the North Pole ••➤ Look at **the Antarctic**.

the ˌArctic ˈCircle noun [sing] a line that we imagine going around the cold area at the top of earth; the line of latitude 66° 30′N ••➤ picture at **earth**

ardent /ˈɑːdnt/ **adj** showing strong feelings, especially a strong liking for sb/sth: *He was an ardent supporter of the Government.* –**ardently adv**

arduous /ˈɑːdjuəs; -dʒu-/ **adj** full of difficulties; needing a lot of effort: *an arduous journey* • *arduous work*

are ➤ BE

★**area** /ˈeəriə/ **noun 1** [C] a part of a town, a country or the world: *Housing is very expensive in the Tokyo area.* • *The wettest areas are in the West of the country.* • *built-up areas* (= where there are a lot of buildings) • *Forests cover a large area of the country.* ••➤ Look at the note at **district**. **2** [C,U] the size of a surface, that you can calculate by multiplying the length by the width: *The area of the office is 35 square metres.* • *The office is 35 square metres in area.* ••➤ Look at **volume**. **3** [C] a space used for a particular activity: *The restaurant has a non-smoking area.* **4** [C] a particular part of a subject or activity: *Training is one area of the business that we could improve.*

arena /əˈriːnə/ **noun** [C] **1** an area with seats around it where public entertainments (sporting events, concerts, etc) are held **2** an area of activity that concerns the public

aren't *short for* ARE NOT

arguable /ˈɑːgjuəbl/ **adj 1** probably true; that you can give reasons for: *It is arguable that all hospital treatment should be free.* **2** probably not true; that you can give reasons against –**arguably** /-əbli/ **adv**: *'King Lear' is arguably Shakespeare's best play.*

★**argue** /ˈɑːgjuː/ **verb 1** [I] argue (with sb) (about/over sth) to say things, often angrily that show that you do not agree with sb about sth: *The couple next door are always arguing.* • *I never argue with my husband about money.* ••➤ Look at **fight¹**(4) and **quarrel²**. **2** [I,T] argue that…; argue (for/against sth) to give reasons that support your opinion about sth: *He argued against buying a new computer.*

★**argument** /ˈɑːgjumənt/ **noun 1** [C,U] an argument (with sb) (about/over sth) an angry discussion between two or more people who disagree with each other: *Sue had an argument with her father about politics.* • *He accepted the decision without argument.*

> A **quarrel** is usually about something less serious.

2 [C] the reason(s) that you give to support your opinion about sth: *What are the arguments for/against lower taxes?*

argumentative /ˌɑːgjuˈmentətɪv/ **adj** often involved in or enjoying arguments

arid /ˈærɪd/ **adj** (used about a climate or land) very dry; with little or no rain

Aries /ˈeəriːz/ **noun** [C,U] the first of the twelve signs of the zodiac, the Ram

arise /əˈraɪz/ **verb** [I] (*pt* **arose** /əˈrəʊz/; *pp*

arisen /əˈrɪzn/) to begin to exist; to appear: *If any problems arise, let me know.*

aristocracy /ˌærɪˈstɒkrəsi/ **noun** [C, with sing or pl verb] (*pl* **aristocracies**) the people of the highest social class who often have special titles ••➤ synonym **nobility**

aristocrat /ˈærɪstəkræt/ **noun** [C] a member of the highest social class, often with a special title –**aristocratic** /ˌærɪstəˈkrætɪk/ **adj**

arithmetic /əˈrɪθmətɪk/ **noun** [U] the kind of mathematics which involves counting with numbers (adding, subtracting, multiplying and dividing): *I'm not very good at **mental arithmetic.***

★**arm**[1] /ɑːm/ **noun** [C] **1** the long part at each side of your body connecting your shoulder to your hand: *He was carrying a newspaper under his arm.* ••➤ picture on page C5 **2** the part of a piece of clothing that covers your arm; a sleeve: *He had a hole in the arm of his jumper.* **3** the part of a chair where you rest your arms

IDIOMS arm in arm with your arm folded around sb else's arm: *The two friends walked arm in arm.* ••➤ picture on page S8

cross/fold your arms to cross your arms in front of your chest: *She folded her arms and waited.* ● *James was sitting with his arms crossed.* ••➤ picture on page S8

twist sb's arm ➤ **TWIST**[1]

with open arms ➤ **OPEN**[1]

arm[2] /ɑːm/ **verb** [I,T] to prepare sb/yourself to fight by supplying or getting weapons ••➤ Look at **armed** and **arms**.

armaments /ˈɑːməmənts/ **noun** [pl] weapons and military equipment

armband /ˈɑːmbænd/ **noun** [C] **1** a piece of material that you wear around your arm: *The captain of the team wears an armband.* **2** a plastic ring filled with air which you can wear on each of your arms when you are learning to swim

armchair /ˈɑːmtʃeə/ **noun** [C] a soft comfortable chair with sides which support your arms ••➤ picture on page C7

armed /ɑːmd/ **adj** carrying a gun or other weapon; involving weapons: *All the terrorists were armed.* ● *armed robbery* ● *the armed forces* (= the army, navy and air force) ••➤ opposite **unarmed**

armful /ˈɑːmfʊl/ **noun** [C] the amount that you can carry in your arms

armhole /ˈɑːmhəʊl/ **noun** [C] the opening in a piece of clothing where your arm goes through

armistice /ˈɑːmɪstɪs/ **noun** [C] an agreement between two countries who are at war that they will stop fighting

armour (*US* **armor**) /ˈɑːmə/ **noun** [U] clothing, often made of metal, that soldiers wore in earlier times to protect themselves: *a suit of armour*

armoured (*US* **armored**) /ˈɑːməd/ **adj** (used about a vehicle) covered with metal to protect it in an attack

armpit /ˈɑːmpɪt/ **noun** [C] the part of the body under the arm at the point where it joins the shoulder ••➤ picture on page C5

arms /ɑːmz/ **noun** [pl] **1** weapons, especially those that are used in war: *a reduction in nuclear arms* **2** =**COAT OF ARMS**

IDIOM up in arms protesting angrily about sth: *The workers were up in arms over the news that the factory was going to close.*

★**army** /ˈɑːmi/ **noun** [C, with sing or pl verb] (*pl* **armies**) **1** the military forces of a country which are trained to fight on land: *the British Army* ● *She joined the army at the age of eighteen.* ● *The army is/are advancing towards the border.* ● *an army officer* ••➤ Look at **air force** and **navy**. **2** a large number of people, especially when involved in an activity together

'A-road noun [C] (*Brit*) a main road, usually not as wide as a motorway

aroma /əˈrəʊmə/ **noun** [C] a smell, especially a pleasant one

arose *past tense* of **ARISE**

★**around** /əˈraʊnd/ **adv, prep 1** (also **about**) in or to various places or directions: *This is our office – David will show you around* (= show you the different parts of it). ● *They wandered around the town, looking at the shops.* **2** moving so as to face in the opposite direction: *Turn around and go back the way you came.* **3** on all sides; forming a circle: *The park has a wall all around.* ● *Gather around so that you can all see.* ● *We sat down around the table.*

➤ In senses **1**, **2** and **3 round** can be used instead of **around**.

4 (also **about**) near a place: *Is there a bank around here?* **5** (also **about**) present or available: *I went to the house but there was nobody around.* **6** (also **about**) approximately: *I'll see you around seven* (= at about 7 o'clock). **7** (also **about**) used for activities with no real purpose: *'What are you doing?' 'Nothing, just lazing around.'*

arouse /əˈraʊz/ **verb** [T] to cause a particular reaction in people: *to arouse sb's curiosity/ interest* –**arousal noun** [U]

arr abbr arrives: *arr York 07.15*

★**arrange** /əˈreɪndʒ/ **verb 1** [T] to put sth in order or in a particular pattern: *The books were arranged in alphabetical order.* ● *Arrange the chairs in a circle.* ● *She arranged the flowers in a vase.* **2** [I,T] arrange (for) sth; arrange to do sth; arrange (sth) with sb to make plans and preparations so that sth can happen in the future: *We're arranging a surprise party for Aisha.* ● *She arranged to meet Stuart after work.* ● *She arranged for her mother to look after the baby.*

★**arrangement** /əˈreɪndʒmənt/ **noun 1** [C, usually pl] plans or preparations for sth that will happen in the future: *Come round this evening and we'll **make arrangements for** the party.* **2** [C,U] an agreement with sb to do sth: *They **have an arrangement** to share the cost of the food.* ● *We both need to use the computer so we'll have to **come to** some*

[I] **intransitive**, a verb which has no object: *He laughed.*   [T] **transitive**, a verb which has an object: *He ate an apple.*

a

arrangement. 3 [C] a group of things that have been placed in a particular pattern: *a flower arrangement*

array /ə'reɪ/ **noun** [C] a large collection of things, especially one that is impressive and is seen by other people

arrears /ə'rɪəz/ **noun** [pl] money that sb owes that he/she should have paid earlier

IDIOMS **be in arrears; fall/get into arrears** to be late in paying money that you owe: *I'm in arrears with the rent.*

be paid in arrears to be paid for work after you have done the work: *You will be paid monthly in arrears.*

★**arrest**[1] /ə'rest/ **verb** [T] when the police arrest sb, they take him/her prisoner in order to question him/her about a crime

★**arrest**[2] /ə'rest/ **noun** [C] the act of arresting sb: *The police **made** ten **arrests** after the riot.* • *The wanted man is now **under arrest** (= has been arrested).*

★**arrival** /ə'raɪvl/ **noun 1** [U] reaching the place to which you were travelling: *On our arrival we were told that our rooms had not been reserved.* **2** [C] people or things that have arrived: *We brought in extra chairs for the late arrivals.*

★**arrive** /ə'raɪv/ **verb** [I] **1** (arrive at/in...) to reach the place to which you were travelling: *We arrived home at about midnight.* • *What time does the train arrive in Newcastle?* • *They arrived at the station ten minutes late.*

➤ Be careful. We use **arrive in** with the name of a town, country, etc and **arrive at** with a place, building, etc

2 to come or happen: *The day of the wedding had finally arrived.*

PHRASAL VERB **arrive at** to reach sth: *We finally arrived at a decision.*

arrogant /'ærəgənt/ **adj** thinking that you are better and more important than other people –**arrogance noun** [U] –**arrogantly adv**

arrow /'ærəʊ/ **noun** [C] **1** a thin piece of wood or metal, with one pointed end and feathers at the other end, that is shot by pulling back the string on a curved piece of wood (a **bow**) and letting go ••➤ Look at **archer**. **2** the sign (→) which is used to show direction

arsenic /'ɑːsnɪk/ **noun** [U] a type of very strong poison

arson /'ɑːsn/ **noun** [U] the crime of setting fire to a building on purpose

arsonist /'ɑːsənɪst/ **noun** [C] a person who deliberately sets fire to a building

★**art** /ɑːt/ **noun 1** [U] the activity or skill of producing things such as paintings, designs, etc; the objects that are produced: *an art class* • *modern art* • *I've never been good at art.* ••➤ Look at **work of art**. **2** [U] a skill or sth that needs skill: *There's an art **to** writing a good letter.* **3 the arts** [pl] activities which involve creating things such as paintings, literature or music **4 arts** [pl] subjects such as history or languages that you study at school or university

➤ We usually contrast **arts** (or **arts subjects**) with **sciences** (or **science subjects**).

artefact /'ɑːtɪfækt/ **noun** [C] an object that is made by a person

artery /'ɑːtəri/ **noun** [C] (*pl* **arteries**) one of the tubes which take blood from the heart to other parts of the body ••➤ Look at **vein**.

arthritis /ɑː'θraɪtɪs/ **noun** [U] a disease which causes swelling and pain in the places where your bones are connected (**joints**), where you bend your arms, fingers, etc

artichoke /'ɑːtɪtʃəʊk/ **noun** [C] a green vegetable with a lot of thick pointed leaves. You can eat the bottom part of the leaves and its centre. ••➤ picture on page C3

★**article** /'ɑːtɪkl/ **noun** [C] **1** an object, especially one of a set: *articles of clothing* **2** a piece of writing in a newspaper or magazine **3** (*grammar*) the words 'a/an' (**the indefinite article**) or 'the' (**the definite article**)

➤ For more information about articles, look at the **Quick Grammar Reference** section at the back of this dictionary.

articulate[1] /ɑː'tɪkjələt/ **adj** good at expressing your ideas clearly ••➤ opposite **inarticulate**

articulate[2] /ɑː'tɪkjuleɪt/ **verb** [I,T] to say sth clearly or to express your ideas or feelings

articulated /ɑː'tɪkjuleɪtɪd/ **adj** (*Brit*) (used about a large vehicle such as a lorry) made of two sections which are joined together

★**artificial** /ˌɑːtɪ'fɪʃl/ **adj** not genuine or natural but made by people: *artificial flowers* –**artificially adv**

ˌ**artificial in'telligence noun** [U] (the study of) the way in which computers can be made to copy the way humans think

artillery /ɑː'tɪləri/ **noun** [U] large, heavy guns that are moved on wheels; the part of the army that uses them

★**artist** /'ɑːtɪst/ **noun** [C] somebody who produces art, especially paintings or drawings

artistic /ɑː'tɪstɪk/ **adj 1** connected with art: *the artistic director of the theatre* **2** showing a skill in art –**artistically** /-kli/ **adv**

artistry /'ɑːtɪstri/ **noun** [U] the skill of an artist

artwork /'ɑːtwɜːk/ **noun 1** [U] photographs, drawings, etc that have been prepared for a book or magazine: *a piece of artwork* **2** [C] a work of art, especially one in a museum or an exhibition

★**as** /əz; *strong form* æz/ **conj, prep, adv 1** while sth else is happening: *The phone rang just as I was leaving the house.* • *As she walked along the road, she thought about her father.* **2 as...as** used for comparing people or things: *Todor's almost as tall as me.* • *Todor's almost as tall as I am.* • *It's not as cold as it was yesterday.* • *I'd like an appointment **as soon as possible**.* • *She earns **twice as much as** her husband.* • *I haven't got as many books as you have.* **3** used for talking about sb/sth's job, role or function: *He works as a train driver.* • *Think of me as your friend, not* as your boss. ● You could use this white sheet as a tablecloth. **4** in a particular way, state, etc; like: *Please do as I tell you.* ● *Leave the room as it is. Don't move anything.* **5** used at the beginning of a comment about what you are saying: *As you know, I've decided to leave at the end of the month.* **6** because: *I didn't buy the dress, as I decided it was too expensive.*

IDIOMS **as for** used when you are starting to talk about a different person or thing: *Gianni's upstairs. As for Andreas, I've no idea where he is.*

as if; as though used for saying how sb/sth appears: *She looks as if/though she's just got out of bed.*

as it were used for saying that sth is only true in a certain way: *She felt, as it were, a stranger in her own house.*

as of; as from starting from a particular time: *As from next week, Tim Shaw will be managing this department.*

as to about a particular thing; concerning: *I was given no instructions as to how to begin.*

ASA /ˌeɪ es 'eɪ/ *abbr* used for indicating the speed of a camera film

asap /ˌeɪ es eɪ 'piː/ *abbr* as soon as possible

asbestos /æsˈbestəs/ *noun* [U] a soft grey material that does not burn and is used to protect against heat

ascend /əˈsend/ *verb* [I,T] (*formal*) to go up ●➤ opposite **descend** –**ascending** *adj*: *The questions are arranged in ascending order of difficulty* (= the most difficult ones are at the end).

ascent /əˈsent/ *noun* [C] **1** the act of climbing or going up: *the ascent of Everest* **2** a path or hill leading upwards: *There was a steep ascent before the path became flat again.* ●➤ opposite **descent**

ascertain /ˌæsəˈteɪn/ *verb* [T] (*formal*) to find sth out

ascribe /əˈskraɪb/ *verb* [T] **ascribe sth to sb/sth** to say that sth was written by or belonged to sb; to say what caused sth: *Many people ascribe this play to Shakespeare.*

★**ash** /æʃ/ *noun* **1** [U] (also **ashes** [pl]) the grey or black powder which is left after sth has burned: *cigarette ash* ● *the ashes of a fire* **2 ashes** [pl] what is left after a dead person has been burned **3** [C] a type of forest tree that grows in cool countries

★**ashamed** /əˈʃeɪmd/ *adj* (not before a noun) **ashamed (of sth/sb/yourself)**; **ashamed that…**; **ashamed to do sth** feeling guilty or embarrassed about sb/sth or because of sth you have done: *She was ashamed of her old clothes.* ● *How could you be so rude? I'm ashamed of you!* ● *She felt ashamed that she hadn't helped him.* ●➤ opposite **unashamed**

ashore /əˈʃɔː/ *adv* onto the land from the sea, a river, etc: *The passengers went ashore for an hour while the ship was in port.*

ashtray /ˈæʃtreɪ/ *noun* [C] a small dish for collecting the powder (**ash**) made when a cigarette burns

Asian /ˈeɪʃn; ˈeɪʒn/ *noun* [C] a person from

Asia or whose family was originally from Asia –**Asian** *adj*

aside /əˈsaɪd/ *adv* **1** on or to one side; out of the way: *We stood aside to let the man go past.* **2** to be kept separately, for a special purpose: *I try to set aside a little money each month.*

a'side from *prep* (*especially US*) = APART FROM

★**ask** /ɑːsk/ *verb* **1** [I,T] **ask (sb) (about sb/ sth)**; **ask sb sth** to put a question to sb in order to find out some information: *We need to ask about tickets.* ● *Can I ask you a question?* ● *Ask him how old he is.* ● *She asked if I wanted tea or coffee.* ● *'What's the time?' he asked.* ● *He asked what the time was.* ● *He asked me the time.* **2** [I,T] **ask (sb) for sth**; **ask sth (of sb)**; **ask sb to do sth** to request that sb gives you sth or does sth for you: *She sat down and asked for a cup of coffee.* ● *Don't ask Joe for money – he hasn't got any.* ● *You are asking too much of him – he can't possibly do all that!* ● *Ring this number and ask for Mrs Khan.* ● *I asked him if he would drive me home.* ● *I asked him to drive me home.* **3** [I,T] to request permission to do sth: *I'm sure she'll let you go if you ask.* ● *He asked to use our phone.* ● *We asked if we could go home early.* **4** [T] **ask sb (to sth)** to invite sb **5** [T] to say the price that you want for sth: *How much are they asking for their car?*

IDIOMS **ask for trouble/it** to behave in a way that will almost certainly cause you problems: *Driving when you're tired is just asking for trouble.*

if you ask me if you want my opinion

PHRASAL VERB **ask after sb** to ask about sb's health or to ask for news of sb: *Tina asked after you today.*

askew /əˈskjuː/ *adv, adj* (not before a noun) not in a straight or level position

★**asleep** /əˈsliːp/ *adj* (not before a noun) not awake; sleeping: *The baby is fast/sound asleep.* ● *It didn't take me long to fall asleep last night.*

➤ Notice that you can only use **asleep** after the noun. **Sleeping** can be used before the noun: *a sleeping child*

●➤ Look at the note at **sleep²**.

asparagus /əˈspærəgəs/ *noun* [U] a plant with long green or white parts (**stems**) that you can cook and eat as a vegetable ●➤ picture on page C3

★**aspect** /ˈæspekt/ *noun* [C] one of the qualities or parts of a situation, idea, problem, etc: *What are the main aspects of your job?*

asphalt /ˈæsfælt/ *noun* [U] a thick black substance that is used for making the surface of roads

asphyxiate /əsˈfɪksieɪt/ *verb* [I,T] to make sb unable to breathe or to be unable to breathe: *He was asphyxiated by the smoke while he was asleep.* –**asphyxiation** /əsˌfɪksiˈeɪʃn/ *noun* [U]

aspire /əˈspaɪə/ *verb* [I] (*formal*) **aspire to sth/to do sth** to have a strong desire to have or do sth: *an aspiring actor* –**aspiration** /ˌæspəˈreɪʃn/ *noun* [C,U]

a

aspirin /ˈæsprɪn; ˈæspərɪn/ **noun** [C,U] a drug used to reduce pain and a high temperature

ass /æs/ = DONKEY

assailant /əˈseɪlənt/ **noun** [C] (*formal*) a person who attacks sb

assassin /əˈsæsɪn/ **noun** [C] a person who kills a famous or important person for money or for political reasons –**assassinate** /əˈsæsɪneɪt/ **verb** [T] •➤ Look at the note at **kill**. –**assassination** /əˌsæsɪˈneɪʃn/ **noun** [C,U]

assault /əˈsɔːlt/ **noun** [C,U] assault (on sb/ sth) a sudden attack on sb/sth –**assault verb** [T]: *He was charged with assaulting a police officer.*

assemble /əˈsembl/ **verb** **1** [I,T] to come together or bring sb/sth together in a group: *I've assembled all the information I need for my essay.* **2** [T] to fit the parts of sth together: *We spent hours trying to assemble our new bookshelves.*

assembly /əˈsembli/ **noun** (*pl* **assemblies**) **1** [C,U] a large group of people who come together for a particular purpose: *school assembly* (= a regular meeting for all the students and teachers of a school) **2** [U] the action of fitting the parts of sth together

as'sembly line noun [C] a line of people and machines in a factory that fit the parts of sth together in a fixed order

assent /əˈsent/ **noun** [U] (*formal*) assent (to sth) official agreement to sth: *The committee gave their assent to the proposed changes.* –**assent verb** [I] assent (to sth)

assert /əˈsɜːt/ **verb** [T] **1** to say sth clearly and firmly **2** to behave in a determined and confident way to make people listen to you or to get what you want: *You ought to assert yourself more.* • *to assert your authority*

assertion /əˈsɜːʃn/ **noun** **1** [C] a statement that says you strongly believe that sth is true **2** [U] the action of showing, using or stating sth strongly

assertive /əˈsɜːtɪv/ **adj** expressing your opinion clearly and firmly so that people listen to you or do what you want –**assertively adv** –**assertiveness noun** [U]

assess /əˈses/ **verb** [T] **1** to judge or form an opinion about sth: *It's too early to assess the effects of the price rises.* **2** assess sth (at sth) to guess or decide the amount or value of sth: *to assess the cost of repairs* –**assessment noun** [C,U]: *I made a careful assessment of the risks involved.*

asset /ˈæset/ **noun** [C] **1** an asset (to sb/sth) a person or thing that is useful to sb/sth: *She's a great asset to the organization.* **2** (usually pl) something of value that a person, company, etc owns

assign /əˈsaɪn/ **verb** [T] **1** assign sth to sb/ sth to give sth to sb for a particular purpose: *We have assigned 20% of our budget to the project.* **2** assign sb to sth to give sb a particular job to do

assignment /əˈsaɪnmənt/ **noun** [C,U] a job or type of work that you are given to do: *The reporter disappeared while on (an) assignment in the war zone.*

assimilate /əˈsɪməleɪt/ **verb** **1** [I,T] assimilate sb/sth (into sth) to become or allow sb/sth to become part of a country, a social group, etc **2** [T] to learn and understand sth: *to assimilate new facts/information/ideas* –**assimilation** /əˌsɪməˈleɪʃn/ **noun** [U]

assist /əˈsɪst/ **verb** [I,T] (*formal*) assist (sb) in/with sth; assist (sb) in doing sth to help: *Volunteers assisted in searching for the boy.*

assistance /əˈsɪstəns/ **noun** [U] (*formal*) help or support: *financial assistance for poorer families* • *She shouted for help but nobody came to her assistance.*

★**assistant** /əˈsɪstənt/ **noun** [C] **1** a person who helps sb in a more important position: *the assistant manager* **2** (*US* **clerk**) a person who sells things to people in a shop: *a shop/ sales assistant*

Assoc (also **assoc**) **abbr** association

★**associate**[1] /əˈsəʊsiət/ **noun** [C] a person that you meet and get to know through your work: *a business associate*

★**associate**[2] /əˈsəʊʃieɪt/ **verb** **1** [T] associate sb/sth (with sb/sth) to make a connection between people or things in your mind: *I always associate the smell of the sea with my childhood.* **2** [I] associate with sb to spend time with sb **3** [T] associate yourself with sth to say that you support sth or agree with sth •➤ opposite **disassociate**

association /əˌsəʊsiˈeɪʃn/ **noun** **1** [U] joining or working with another person or group: *We work in association with our New York office.* **2** [C] a group of people or organizations who work together for a particular purpose: *the National Association of Language Teachers* **3** [C,U] the act of connecting one person or thing with another in your mind

assorted /əˈsɔːtɪd/ **adj** of different types; mixed: *a bowl of assorted fruit*

assortment /əˈsɔːtmənt/ **noun** [C] a group of different things or of different types of the same thing; a mixture: *You'll find a wide assortment of gifts in our shop.*

Asst (also **asst**) **abbr** assistant

★**assume** /əˈsjuːm/ **verb** [T] **1** to accept or believe that sth is true even though you have no proof; to expect sth to be true: *I assume that you have the necessary documents.* • *Everyone assumed Ralph was guilty.* • *Everyone assumed Ralph to be guilty.* **2** to pretend to have or to be sb/sth: *to assume a false name* **3** to begin to use power or to have a powerful position: *to assume control of sth*

assumption /əˈsʌmpʃn/ **noun** **1** [C] something that you accept is true even though you have no proof: *We'll work on the assumption that guests will be hungry when they arrive.* • *It's unfair to make assumptions about a person's character before you know them.* • *a reasonable/false assumption* **2** [U] the assumption of sth the act of taking power or of starting an important job

assurance /əˈʃɔːrəns/ **noun** **1** [C] a promise that sth will certainly happen or be true:

*They gave me an assurance that the work
would be finished by Friday.* **2** (also **self-
assurance**) [U] the belief that you can do or
succeed at sth; confidence

assure /ə'ʃɔː/ **verb** [T] **1** to promise sb that
sth will certainly happen or be true, especially if he/she is worried: *I assure you that it
is perfectly safe.* ● *Let me assure you of my full
support.* **2** to make sth sure or certain: *The
success of the new product assured the survival of the company.*

assured /ə'ʃɔːd/ (also **self-assured**) **adj**
believing that you can do sth or succeed at
sth; confident: *The doctor had a calm and
assured manner.*

asterisk /'æstərɪsk/ **noun** [C] the sign (*) that
you use to make people notice sth in a piece
of writing

asthma /'æsmə/ **noun** [U] a medical condition that makes breathing difficult

asthmatic /æs'mætɪk/ **noun** [C] a person
who has asthma –**asthmatic adj**

astonish /ə'stɒnɪʃ/ **verb** [T] to surprise sb
very much: *She astonished everybody by
announcing her engagement.* –**astonished adj**:
I was astonished by the decision.

astonishing /ə'stɒnɪʃɪŋ/ **adj** very surprising –**astonishingly adv**

astonishment /ə'stɒnɪʃmənt/ **noun** [U]
very great surprise: *He dropped his book in
astonishment.*

astound /ə'staʊnd/ **verb** [T] (usually passive)
to surprise sb very much: *We were astounded
by how well he performed.*

astounded /ə'staʊndɪd/ **adj** feeling or showing great surprise: *We sat in astounded
silence.*

astounding /ə'staʊndɪŋ/ **adj** causing sb to
feel extremely surprised: *an astounding success*

astray /ə'streɪ/ **adv**
IDIOMS **go astray** to become lost or be stolen
lead sb astray → **LEAD¹**

astride /ə'straɪd/ **adv, prep** with one leg on
each side of sth: *to sit astride a horse*

astrologer /ə'strɒlədʒə/ **noun** [C] a person
who is an expert in astrology

astrology /ə'strɒlədʒi/ **noun** [U] the study of
the positions and movements of the stars and
planets and the way that some people believe
they affect people and events ••► Look at
horoscope and **zodiac**.

astronaut /'æstrənɔːt/ **noun** [C] a person
who travels in a spacecraft

astronomer /ə'strɒnəmə/ **noun** [C] a person
who studies astronomy

astronomical /,æstrə'nɒmɪkl/ **adj 1** connected with astronomy **2** extremely large:
astronomical house prices

astronomy /ə'strɒnəmi/ **noun** [U] the scientific study of the sun, moon, stars, etc

astute /ə'stjuːt/ **adj** very clever; good at judging people or situations

asylum /ə'saɪləm/ **noun** [U] protection that a
government gives to people who have left

their own country for political reasons: *to
give sb political asylum*

★**at** /ət; *strong form* æt/ **prep 1** used to show
where sb/sth is or where sth happens: *at the
bottom/top of the page* ● *He was standing at
the door.* ● *Change trains at Chester.* ● *We
were at home all weekend.* ● *Are the children
at school?* ● *'Where's Peter?' 'He's at Sue's.'* (=
at Sue's house) **2** used to show when sth
happens: *I start work at 9 o'clock.* ● *at the
weekend* ● *at night* ● *at Easter* ● *She got married at 18* (= when she was 18). **3** in the
direction of sb/sth: *What are you looking at?*
● *He pointed a gun at the policeman.* ● *Don't
shout at me!* **4** because of sth: *I was surprised
at her behaviour.* ● *We laughed at his jokes.*
5 used to show what sb is doing or what is
happening: *They were hard at work.* ● *The
two countries were at war.* **6** used to show the
price, rate, speed, etc of sth: *We were travelling at about 50 miles per hour.* **7** used with
adjectives that show how well sb/sth does
sth: *She's not very good at French.*

ate *past tense* of **EAT**

atheism /'eɪθiɪzəm/ **noun** [U] the belief that
there is no God –**atheist noun** [C]

athlete /'æθliːt/ **noun** [C] a person who can
run, jump, etc very well, especially one who
takes part in sports competitions, etc

athletic /æθ'letɪk/ **adj 1** connected with athletes or athletics: *athletic ability* **2** (used
about a person) having a fit, strong, and
healthy body

athletics /æθ'letɪks/ **noun** [U] sports such as
running, jumping, throwing, etc

atishoo /ə'tɪʃuː/ **interj** used to represent the
sound that you make when you suddenly
blow air out of your nose (sneeze)

atlas /'ætləs/ **noun** [C] (*pl* **atlases**) a book of
maps: *a road atlas of Europe*

★**atmosphere** /'ætməsfɪə/ **noun 1** [C, usually
sing] **the atmosphere** the mixture of gases
that surrounds the earth or any other star,
planet, etc: *the earth's atmosphere* **2** [sing] the
air in a place: *a smoky atmosphere* **3** [sing]
the mood or feeling of a place or situation:
The atmosphere of the meeting was relaxed.

atmospheric /,ætməs'ferɪk/ **adj 1** connected with the earth's atmosphere **2** creating a particular feeling or emotion:
atmospheric music

atom /'ætəm/ **noun** [C] the smallest part into
which an element can be divided ••► Look at
molecule.

atomic /ə'tɒmɪk/ **adj** of or concerning an
atom or atoms: *atomic physics* ••► Look at
nuclear.

a,tomic 'bomb (also **'atom bomb**) **noun** [C]
a bomb that explodes using the energy that is
produced when an atom or atoms are split

a,tomic 'energy noun [U] the energy that is
produced when an atom or atoms are split.
Atomic energy can be used to produce electricity.

atrocious /ə'trəʊʃəs/ **adj** extremely bad:
atrocious weather –**atrociously adv**

atrocity /əˈtrɒsəti/ **noun** [C,U] (*pl* atroci-ties) (an action of) very cruel treatment of sb/sth: *Both sides were accused of committing atrocities during the war.*

★**attach** /əˈtætʃ/ **verb** [T] **1** attach sth (to sth) to fasten or join sth to sth: *I attached a label to each bag.* ••➤ opposite **detach 2** (usually passive) attach sb/sth to sb/sth to make sb/sth join or belong to sb/sth: *The research centre is attached to the university.* **3** attach sth to sb/sth to think that sth has a particu-lar quality: *Don't attach too much importance to what they say.*

IDIOM (with) no strings attached; without strings → STRING¹

attached /əˈtætʃt/ **adj** attached to sb/sth liking sb/sth very much

attachment /əˈtætʃmənt/ **noun 1** [C] some-thing that you can fit on sth else to make it do a different job: *an electric drill with a range of attachments* **2** [C,U] attachment (to/ for sb/sth) the feeling of liking sb/sth very much: *emotional attachment*

★**attack¹** /əˈtæk/ **noun 1** [C,U] (an) attack (on sb/sth) trying to hurt or defeat sb/sth by using force: *The town was under attack from all sides.* **2** [C,U] (an) attack (on sb/sth) an act of saying strongly that you do not like or agree with sb/sth: *an outspoken attack on government policy* **3** [C] a short period when you suffer badly from a disease, medical con-dition, etc: *an attack of asthma/flu/nerves* **4** [C] trying to score a point in a game of sport

★**attack²** /əˈtæk/ **verb 1** [I,T] to try to hurt or defeat sb/sth by using force: *The child was attacked by a dog.* **2** [T] to say strongly that you do not like or agree with sb/sth: *Steffi attacked Guy's right-wing political views.* **3** [T] to damage or harm sb/sth: *a virus that attacks the nervous system* **4** [I,T] to try to score a point in a game of sport: *This team attacks better than it defends.*

attacker /əˈtækə/ **noun** [C] a person who tries to hurt sb using force: *The victim of the assault didn't recognize his attackers.*

attain /əˈteɪn/ **verb** [T] to succeed in getting or achieving sth, especially after a lot of effort

attainable /əˈteɪnəbl/ **adj** that can be achieved: *realistically attainable targets*

attainment /əˈteɪnmənt/ **noun 1** [U] the act of achieving sth: *the attainment of the govern-ment's objectives* **2** [C] a skill or sth you have achieved

★**attempt¹** /əˈtempt/ **verb** [T] attempt (to do) sth to try to do sth that is difficult: *She was accused of attempted murder* (= she didn't succeed). ● *Don't attempt to make him change his mind.*

★**attempt²** /əˈtempt/ **noun** [C] **1** an attempt (to do sth/at doing sth) an act of trying to do sth: *The thief made no attempt to run away.* ● *I failed the exam once but passed at the second attempt.* ● *They failed in their attempt to reach the North Pole.* **2** an attempt (on sb/sth) trying to attack or beat sb/sth: *an*

attempt on sb's life (= to kill sb)

IDIOM a last-ditch attempt → LAST¹

★**attend** /əˈtend/ **verb 1** [T] to go to or be pre-sent at a place: *Do you attend church regu-larly?* ● *The children attend the local school.* **2** [I] (*formal*) attend to sb/sth to give your care, thought or attention to sb/sth or look after sb/sth: *Please attend to this matter immediately.*

attendance /əˈtendəns/ **noun 1** [U] being present somewhere: *Attendance at lectures is compulsory.* **2** [C,U] the number of people who go to or are present at a place: *There was a poor attendance at the meeting.*

attendant¹ /əˈtendənt/ **noun** [C] a person whose job is to serve or help people in a public place: *a car park attendant*

attendant² /əˈtendənt/ **adj** (only *before* a noun) (*formal*) that goes together with or results from sth: *unemployment and all its attendant social problems*

★**attention¹** /əˈtenʃn/ **noun** [U] **1** watching, listening to or thinking about sb/sth care-fully: *I shouted in order to attract her atten-tion.* ● *Shy people hate to be the centre of attention* (= the person that everybody is watching). ● *to hold sb's attention* (= to keep them interested in sth) **2** special care or action: *The hole in the roof needs urgent atten-tion.* ● *to require medical attention* **3** a pos-ition in which a soldier stands up straight and still: *to stand/come to attention*

IDIOMS catch sb's attention/eye → CATCH¹
draw (sb's) attention to sth → DRAW¹
pay attention → PAY¹

attention² /əˈtenʃn/ **interj** used for asking people to listen to sth carefully

attentive /əˈtentɪv/ **adj** attentive (to sb/sth) watching, listening to or thinking about sb/ sth carefully: *The hotel staff were very atten-tive to our needs.* ••➤ opposite **inattentive** –**attentively adv**: *to listen attentively to sth*

attic /ˈætɪk/ **noun** [C] the space or room under the roof of a house ••➤ Look at **loft**.

★**attitude** /ˈætɪtjuːd/ **noun** [C] an attitude (to/ towards sb/sth) the way that you think, feel or behave: *People's attitude to marriage is changing.* ● *She has a very positive attitude to her work.*

attorney /əˈtɜːni/ (*US*) = LAWYER

★**attract** /əˈtrækt/ **verb** [T] **1** to cause sb/sth to go to sth or give attention to sth: *I waved to attract the waiter's attention.* ● *Moths are attracted to light.* ● *The new film has attracted a lot of publicity.* **2** (usually passive) to cause sb to like sb/sth: *She's attracted to older men.*

attraction /əˈtrækʃn/ **noun 1** [U] a feeling of liking sb/sth: *sexual attraction* **2** [C] sth that is interesting or enjoyable: *The city offers all kinds of tourist attractions.*

★**attractive** /əˈtræktɪv/ **adj 1** that pleases or interests you; that you like: *an attractive part of the country* ● *an attractive idea* **2** (used about a person) beautiful or nice to look at –**attractively adv** –**attractiveness noun** [U]

attribute¹ /əˈtrɪbjuːt/ **verb** [T] attribute sth

to sb/sth to believe that sth was caused or done by sb/sth: *Mustafa attributes his success to hard work.* ● *a poem attributed to Shakespeare*

attribute² /'ætrɪbjuːt/ noun [C] a quality of sb/sth; a feature: *physical attributes*

atypical /ˌeɪ'tɪpɪkl/ adj (*formal*) not typical of a particular type, group, etc: *atypical behaviour* ••➤ opposite **typical**

➤ Compare **untypical**.

aubergine /'əʊbəʒiːn/ (*especially US* **eggplant**) noun [C,U] a long vegetable with dark purple skin ••➤ picture on page C3

auburn /'ɔːbən/ adj (used about hair) reddish-brown

auction¹ /'ɔːkʃn/ noun [C,U] a public sale at which items are sold to the person who offers to pay the most money: *The house was sold at/by auction.*

auction² /'ɔːkʃn/ verb [T] **auction sth (off)** to sell sth at an auction

auctioneer /ˌɔːkʃə'nɪə/ noun [C] a person who organizes the selling at an auction

audible /'ɔːdəbl/ adj that can be heard: *Her speech was barely audible.* ••➤ opposite **inaudible** –**audibly** /-əbli/ adv

★**audience** /'ɔːdiəns/ noun [C] **1** [with sing or pl verb] all the people who are watching or listening to a play, concert, speech, the television, etc: *The audience was/were wild with excitement.* ● *There were only about 200 people in the audience.* **2** a formal meeting with a very important person: *He was granted an audience with the President.*

audio /'ɔːdiəʊ/ adj connected with the recording of sound: *audio equipment* ● *audio tape*

audio-ˈvisual adj using both sound and pictures

audit /'ɔːdɪt/ noun [C] an official examination of the present state of sth, especially of a company's financial records: *to carry out an audit*

audition¹ /ɔː'dɪʃn/ noun [C] a short performance by a singer, actor, etc to find out if he/she is good enough to be in a play, show, etc

audition² /ɔː'dɪʃn/ verb [I,T] **audition (sb) (for sth)** to do or to watch sb do an audition: *I auditioned for a part in the play.*

auditor /'ɔːdɪtə/ noun [C] a person whose job is to examine a company's financial records

auditorium /ˌɔːdɪ'tɔːriəm/ noun [C] (*pl* **auditoriums** or **auditoria**) the part of a theatre, concert hall, etc where the audience sits

Aug abbr August: *10 Aug 1957*

augur /'ɔːgə/ verb
IDIOM **augur well/ill for sb/sth** (*formal*) to be a good/bad sign of what will happen in the future

★**August** /'ɔːgəst/ noun [U,C] (*abbr* **Aug**) the eighth month of the year, coming after July

➤ To see how the months are used in sentences, look at the examples and the note at **January**.

★**aunt** /ɑːnt/ (also *informal* **auntie**; **aunty** /'ɑːnti/) noun [C] the sister of your father or mother; the wife of your uncle: *Aunt Ellen*

au pair /ˌəʊ 'peə/ noun (*Brit*) [C] a person, usually a girl, from another country who comes to live with a family in order to learn the language. An au pair helps to clean the house and looks after the children.

aura /'ɔːrə/ noun [C] (*formal*) the quality that sb/sth seems to have

aural /'ɔːrəl/ adj connected with hearing and listening: *an aural comprehension test* ••➤ Look at **oral**.

auspices /'ɔːspɪsɪz/ noun [pl]
IDIOM **under the auspices of sb/sth** with the help and support of sb/sth

auspicious /ɔː'spɪʃəs/ adj that seems likely to be successful in the future: *She made an auspicious start to her professional career when she won her first race.* ••➤ opposite **inauspicious**

austere /ɒ'stɪə/ adj **1** very simple; without decoration **2** (used about a person) very strict and serious **3** not having anything that makes your life more comfortable: *The nuns lead simple and austere lives.* –**austerity** /ɒ'sterəti/ noun [U]

authentic /ɔː'θentɪk/ adj **1** that you know is real or genuine: *an authentic Van Gogh painting* **2** true or accurate: *an authentic model of the building* –**authenticity** /ˌɔːθen'tɪsəti/ noun [U]

★**author** /'ɔːθə/ noun [C] a person who writes a book, play, etc: *a well-known author of detective novels* –**authorship** noun [U]

authoritarian /ɔːˌθɒrɪ'teəriən/ adj not allowing people the freedom to decide things for themselves: *authoritarian parents*

authoritative /ɔː'θɒrətətɪv/ adj **1** having authority; demanding or expecting that people obey you: *an authoritative tone of voice* **2** that you can trust because it/he/she has a lot of knowledge and information: *They will be able to give you authoritative advice on the problem.*

★**authority** /ɔː'θɒrəti/ noun (*pl* **authorities**) **1** [U] the power and right to give orders and make others obey: *Children often begin to question their parents' authority at a very early age.* ● *You must get this signed by a person in authority* (= who has a position of power). **2** [U] **authority (to do sth)** the right or permission to do sth: *The police have the authority to question anyone they wish.* ● *He was sacked for using a company vehicle without authority.* **3** [C] (often plural) a person, group or government department that has the power to give orders, make official decisions, etc: *I have to report this to the authorities.* **4** [U] a quality that sb has which makes it possible to influence and control other people: *He spoke with authority and everybody listened.* **5** [C] **an authority (on sth)** a person with special knowledge: *He's an authority on criminal law.*

authorize (also **-ise**) /'ɔːθəraɪz/ verb [T] to give official permission for sth or for sb to do sth: *He authorized his secretary to sign letters in his absence.* –authorization (also **-isation**) /ˌɔːθəraɪˈzeɪʃn/ **noun** [U]

autistic /ɔːˈtɪstɪk/ **adj** having a serious mental illness which makes it very difficult to form relationships with other people

autobiography /ˌɔːtəbaɪˈɒɡrəfi/ **noun** [C,U] (*pl* **autobiographies**) the story of a person's life written by that person •➤ Look at **biography**. –autobiographical /ˌɔːtəˌbaɪəˈɡræfɪkl/ **adj**

autograph /ˈɔːtəɡrɑːf/ **noun** [C] the signature of a famous person: *The players stopped outside the stadium to* **sign autographs.** –autograph **verb** [T]: *The whole team have autographed the football.*

automate /ˈɔːtəmeɪt/ **verb** [T] (usually passive) to make sth operate by machine, without needing people

★**automatic**¹ /ˌɔːtəˈmætɪk/ **adj 1** (used about a machine) that can work by itself without direct human control: *an automatic washing machine* **2** done without thinking **3** always happening as a result of a particular action or situation: *All the staff have an automatic right to a space in the car park.* –automatically /-kli/ **adv**: *The lights will come on automatically when it gets dark.*

automatic² /ˌɔːtəˈmætɪk/ **noun** [C] an automatic machine, gun or car: *This car is an automatic* (= has automatic gears).

automation /ˌɔːtəˈmeɪʃn/ **noun** [U] the use of machines instead of people to do work

automobile /ˈɔːtəməbiːl/ (*especially US*) = **CAR**(1)

autonomy /ɔːˈtɒnəmi/ **noun** [U] the right of a person, an organization, a region, etc to govern or control his/her/its own affairs –autonomous /ɔːˈtɒnəməs/ **adj**: *The people in this region want to be completely autonomous.*

autopsy /ˈɔːtɒpsi/ **noun** [C] (*pl* **autopsies**) an examination of a dead body to find out the cause of death

★**autumn** /ˈɔːtəm/ (*US usually* **fall**) **noun** [C,U] the season of the year that comes between summer and winter: *In autumn the leaves on the trees begin to fall.* –autumnal /ɔːˈtʌmnəl/ **adj**

auxiliary /ɔːɡˈzɪliəri/ **adj** (only *before* a noun) giving extra help: *auxiliary nurses/troops/staff*

au͵xiliary ˈverb noun [C] (*grammar*) a verb (for example *be*, *do* or *have*) that is used with a main verb to show tense, etc or to form questions

avail /əˈveɪl/ **noun** [U]

IDIOMS **of little/no avail** not helpful; having little or no effect

to little/no avail without success: *They searched everywhere, but to no avail.*

availability /əˌveɪləˈbɪləti/ **noun** [U] the state of being available: *You will receive the colour you order, subject to availability* (= if it is available).

★**available** /əˈveɪləbl/ **adj 1** available (to sb) (used about things) that you can get, buy,

use, etc: *This information is easily available to everyone at the local library.* ● *Refreshments are available at the snack bar.* **2** (used about people) free to be seen, talked to, etc: *The minister was not available for comment.*

avalanche /ˈævəlɑːnʃ/ **noun** [C] a very large amount of snow that slides quickly down the side of a mountain: *Two skiers are still missing after yesterday's avalanche.*

the avant-garde /ˌævɒŋˈɡɑːd/ **noun** [sing] extremely modern works of art, music or literature, or the artists who create these –avant-garde **adj**

Ave abbr Avenue: *26 Elm Ave*

avenge /əˈvendʒ/ **verb** [T] **avenge sth; avenge yourself on sb** to punish sb for hurting you, your family, etc in some way: *He wanted to avenge his father's murder.* ● *He wanted to avenge himself on his father's murderer.* •➤ Look at **revenge**.

avenue /ˈævənjuː/ **noun** [C] **1** (*abbr* **Ave**) a wide street, especially one with trees or tall buildings on each side: *I live on Tennyson Avenue.* •➤ Look at the note at **road**. **2** a way of doing or getting sth: *We must explore every avenue open to us* (= try every possibility).

★**average**¹ /ˈævərɪdʒ/ **noun 1** [C] the number you get when you add two or more figures together and then divide the total by the number of figures you added: *The average of 14, 3 and 1 is 6* (= 18 divided by 3 is 6). ● *He has scored 93 goals at* **an average of** *1·55 per game.* **2** [sing, U] the normal standard, amount or quality: **On average,** *I buy a newspaper about twice a week.*

★**average**² /ˈævərɪdʒ/ **adj 1** (only *before* a noun) (used about a number) found by calculating the average¹(1): *What's the average age of your students?* **2** normal or typical: *children of* **above/below average** *intelligence*

average³ /ˈævərɪdʒ/ **verb** [T] to do, get, etc a certain amount as an average: *If we average 50 miles an hour we should arrive at about 4 o'clock.*

PHRASAL VERB **average out (at sth)** to result in an average (of sth)

averse /əˈvɜːs/ **adj** (*formal*) **averse to sth** (often with a negative) against or not in favour of sth: *He is not averse to trying out new ideas.*

aversion /əˈvɜːʃn/ **noun** [C] **1** [usually sing] **an aversion (to sb/sth)** a strong feeling of not liking sb/sth: *Some people* **have an aversion to spiders.** **2** a thing that you do not like

avert /əˈvɜːt/ **verb** [T] to prevent sth unpleasant: *The accident could have been averted.*

aviary /ˈeɪviəri/ **noun** [C] (*pl* **aviaries**) a large cage or area in which birds are kept

aviation /ˌeɪviˈeɪʃn/ **noun** [U] the designing, building and flying of aircraft

avid /ˈævɪd/ **adj 1** very enthusiastic about sth (usually a hobby): *an avid collector of antiques* **2** avid for sth wanting to get sth very much: *Journalists crowded round the entrance, avid for news.* –avidly **adv**: *He read avidly as a child.*

avocado /ˌævəˈkɑːdəʊ/ noun [C] (pl avocados) a tropical fruit that is wider at one end than the other, with a hard green skin and a large seed (stone) inside ·➤ picture on page C3

★**avoid** /əˈvɔɪd/ verb [T] **1** avoid (doing sth) to prevent sth happening or to try not to do sth: He always tried to avoid an argument if possible. ● She has to avoid eating fatty food. **2** to keep away from sb/sth: I leave home at 7 o'clock in order to avoid the rush hour. –avoidance noun [U]

avoidable /əˈvɔɪdəbl/ adj that can be prevented; unnecessary ·➤ opposite unavoidable

await /əˈweɪt/ verb [T] (formal) to wait for sb/sth: We sat down to await the arrival of the guests.

awake¹ /əˈweɪk/ verb (pt awoke /əˈwəʊk/; pp awoken /əˈwəʊkən/) [I,T] to wake up; to make sb/sth wake up: I awoke to find that it was already 9 o'clock. ● A sudden loud noise awoke us. ·➤ Wake up is more common than awake.

★**awake²** /əˈweɪk/ adj (not before a noun) not sleeping: I was sleepy this morning but I'm wide awake now. ● They were so tired that they found it difficult to stay awake. ● I hope our singing didn't keep you awake last night. ·➤ opposite asleep

awaken /əˈweɪkən/ verb **1** [I,T] (written) to wake up; to make sb/sth wake up: We were awakened by a loud knock at the door. ·➤ Wake up is much more common than awaken. **2** [T] (formal) to produce a particular feeling, attitude, etc in sb: The film awakened memories of her childhood.
PHRASAL VERB awaken sb to sth to make sb notice or realize sth for the first time: The letter awakened me to the seriousness of the situation.

awakening /əˈweɪkənɪŋ/ noun [sing] **1** the act of starting to feel or understand sth; the start of a feeling, etc: the awakening of an interest in the opposite sex **2** a moment when sb notices or realizes sth for the first time: It was a rude (= unpleasant) awakening when I suddenly found myself unemployed.

★**award¹** /əˈwɔːd/ noun [C] **1** a prize, etc that sb gets for doing sth well: This year the awards for best actor and actress went to two Americans. **2** an amount of money given to sb as the result of a court decision: She received an award of £5000 for damages.

★**award²** /əˈwɔːd/ verb [T] award sth (to sb) to give sth to sb as a prize, payment, etc: She was awarded first prize in the gymnastics competition. ● The court awarded £10000 each to the workers injured in the accident.

★**aware** /əˈweə/ adj **1** aware (of sb/sth); aware (that) knowing about or realizing sth; conscious of sb/sth: I am well aware of the problems you face. ● I suddenly became aware that someone was watching me. ● There is no other entrance, as far as I am aware. ·➤ opposite unaware **2** interested

and informed: Many young people are very politically aware.

awareness /əˈweənəs/ noun [U] knowledge, consciousness or interest: People's awareness of healthy eating has increased in recent years.

awash /əˈwɒʃ/ adj (not before a noun) awash (with sth) covered with water; flooded: (figurative) The city was awash with rumours.

★**away** /əˈweɪ/ adv ·➤ Look also at phrasal verbs, for example give away, take away. **1** away (from sb/sth) to a different place or in a different direction: Go away! I'm busy! ● I asked him a question, but he just looked away. **2** away (from sth) at a particular distance from a place: The village is two miles away from the sea. ● My parents live five minutes away. **3** away (from sth) (used about people) not present; absent: My neighbours are away on holiday at the moment. ● Aki was away from school for two weeks with measles. **4** in the future: Our summer holiday is only three weeks away. **5** into a place where sth is usually kept: Put your books away now. ● They cleared the dishes away (= off the table). ·➤ Contrast throw sth away (= put it in the rubbish bin). **6** continuously, without stopping: They chatted away for hours. **7** (used about a football, etc match) on the other team's ground: Our team's playing away on Saturday. ● an away match/game ·➤ opposite home **8** until sth disappears: The crash of thunder slowly died away. ● He's given most of his money away.
IDIOMS do away with sb/sth to get rid of sb/sth: The government are going to do away with the tax on fuel.
right/straight away immediately; without any delay: I'll phone the doctor right away.

awe /ɔː/ noun [U] in awe; in awe of sb/sth a feeling of respect and either fear or admiration: As a young boy he was very much in awe of his uncle.

'awe-inspiring adj causing a feeling of respect and fear or admiration

awesome /ˈɔːsəm/ adj **1** impressive and sometimes frightening: an awesome task **2** (US slang) very good; excellent

★**awful** /ˈɔːfl/ adj **1** very bad or unpleasant: We had an awful holiday. It rained every day. ● I feel awful – I think I'll go to bed. ● What an awful thing to say! **2** terrible; very serious: I'm afraid there's been some awful news. **3** (only before a noun) (informal) very great: We've got an awful lot of work to do.

awfully /ˈɔːfli/ adv (informal) very; very much: I'm awfully sorry.

awkward /ˈɔːkwəd/ adj **1** difficult to deal with: That's an awkward question. ● You've put me in an awkward position. ● an awkward customer ● The box isn't heavy but it's awkward to carry. **2** not convenient, difficult: My mother always phones at an awkward time. ● This tin-opener is very awkward to clean. **3** embarrassed or embarrassing: I often feel awkward in a group of people. ● There was an awkward silence. **4** not using the body

---

ð then | s so | z zoo | ʃ she | ʒ vision | h how | m man | n no | ŋ sing | l leg | r red | j yes | w wet

b

in the best way; not elegant or comfortable: *I was sitting with my legs in an awkward position.* –**awkwardly** *adv* –**awkwardness noun** [U]

awoke *past tense* of **AWAKE¹**

awoken *past participle* of **AWAKE¹**

awry /ə'raɪ/ *adv*, *adj* (not before a noun) wrong, not in the way that was planned; untidy

axe¹ (*especially US* **ax**) /æks/ *noun* [C] a tool with a wooden handle and a heavy metal head with a sharp edge, used for cutting wood, etc •➤ picture at **garden**

axe² (*especially US* **ax**) /æks/ *verb* [T] **1** to remove sb/sth: *Hundreds of jobs have been axed.* **2** to reduce sth by a great amount: *School budgets are to be axed.* •➤ This verb is used especially in newspapers.

axis /'æksɪs/ *noun* [C] (*pl* **axes** /'æksiːz/) **1** a line we imagine through the middle of an object, around which the object turns: *The earth rotates on its axis.* •➤ picture at **earth** **2** a fixed line used for marking measurements on a diagram (**graph**): *the horizontal/ vertical axis*

axle /'æksl/ *noun* [C] a bar that connects a pair of wheels on a vehicle

Bb

B, b¹ /biː/ *noun* [C] (*pl* **B's**; **b's**) the second letter of the English alphabet: *'Billy' begins with (a) 'B'.*

b² *abbr* born: *J S Bach, b 1685*

BA /ˌbiː 'eɪ/ *abbr* Bachelor of Arts; the degree that you receive when you complete a university or college course in an arts subject •➤ Look at **BSc** and **MA**.

baa /bɑː/ *noun* [sing] the sound that a sheep makes

B & B /ˌbiː ən 'biː/ *abbr* = **BED AND BREAKFAST**

babble¹ /'bæbl/ *noun* [sing] **1** the sound of many voices talking at the same time: *I could hear a babble of voices coming from downstairs.* **2** the sound of water running over stones

babble² /'bæbl/ *verb* [I] **1** to talk quickly or in a way that is difficult to understand **2** to make the sound of water running over stones

babe /beɪb/ *noun* [C] **1** (*especially US slang*) used when talking to sb, especially a girl or young woman: *It's OK, babe.* **2** (*slang*) an attractive young woman **3** (*old-fashioned*) a baby

★**baby** /'beɪbi/ *noun* [C] (*pl* **babies**) **1** a very young child: *I'm going to **have a baby**.* • *She's **expecting a baby** early next year.* • *When's the **baby due**?* (= when will it be born?) • *a baby boy/girl* **2** a very young animal or bird **3** (*US slang*) a person, especially a girl or young woman, that you like or love

'**baby boom** *noun* [usually sing] a time when more babies are born than usual, for example after a war

'**baby boomer** *noun* [C] a person born during a baby boom

'**baby carriage** (*US*) = **PRAM**

babyish /'beɪbiɪʃ/ *adj* suitable for or behaving like a baby: *This book is a bit too babyish for Faruk now.*

babysit /'beɪbisɪt/ *verb* [I] (**babysitting**; *pt*, *pp* **babysat**) to look after a child for a short time while the parents are out: *We have friends who babysit for us if we go out in the evening.* –**babysitter** *noun* [C]

bachelor /'bætʃələ/ *noun* [C] **1** a man who has not yet married

➤ Nowadays **single** is the most usual word that is used to describe a man or a women who is not married: *a single man/woman*

2 a person who has a first university degree: *a Bachelor of Arts/Science*

back to front   inside out

upside down

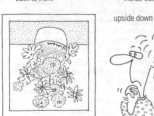

The painting is **upside down**.

★**back¹** /bæk/ *noun* [C] **1** the part of a person's or animal's body between the neck and the bottom: *Do you sleep **on your back** or on your side?* • *She was standing **with** her **back** to me so I couldn't see her face.* • *A camel has a hump on its back.* **2** the part or side of sth that is furthest from the front: *I sat **at the back** of the class.* • *The answers are **in the back** of the book.* • *Write your address **on the back** of the cheque.* **3** the part of a chair that supports your upper body when you sit down: *He put his coat over the back of the chair.*

IDIOMS **at/in the back of your mind** if sth is at the back of your mind, it is in your thoughts but is not the main thing that you are thinking about: *With next week's exam at the back* *of my mind, I couldn't relax and enjoy the film.*

back to front with the back where the front should be: *Wait a minute – you've got your jumper on back to front.* ••➤ Look at **way**¹(3)

behind sb's back without sb's knowledge or agreement: *They criticized her behind her back.* ••➤ opposite **to sb's face**

get off sb's back (*informal*) to stop annoying sb, for example when you keep asking him/her to do sth: *I've told her I'll do the job by Monday, so I wish she'd get off my back!*

know sth like the back of your hand → **KNOW**¹

a pat on the back → **PAT**²

turn your back on sb/sth to refuse to be involved with sb/sth: *He turned his back on his career and went to live in the country.*

★**back²** /bæk/ **adj 1** (only *before* a noun) furthest from the front: *Have you locked the back door?* ● *the back row of the theatre* ● *back teeth* **2** owed from a time in the past: *back pay/rent/taxes*

IDIOM **take a back seat** to allow sb to play a more important or active role than yourself in a particular situation

★**back³** /bæk/ **adv 1** in or to a place or state that sb/sth was in before: *I'm going out now – I'll **be back** about six o'clock.* ● *It started to rain so I **came back** home.* ● *Go back to sleep.* ● *Could I **have** my pen **back**, please?* ● *I've got to **take** these books **back** to the library.* **2** away from the direction you are facing or moving in: *She walked away without **looking back**.* ● *Could everyone **move back** a bit, please?* ••➤ opposite **forward** **3** away from sth; under control: *The police were unable to **keep** the crowds **back**.* ● *She tried to **hold back** her tears.* **4** in return or in reply: *He said he'd **phone** me **back** in half an hour.* **5** in or into the past; ago: *I met him a few years **back**, in Madrid.* ● ***Think back** to your first day at school.*

IDIOM **back and forth** from one place to another and back again, all the time: *Travelling back and forth to work takes up quite a bit of time.*

★**back⁴** /bæk/ **verb 1** [I,T] to move backwards or to make sth move backwards: *I'll have to back into that parking space.* ● *He backed the car into the parking space.* **2** [I] to face sth at the back: *Many of the colleges back onto the river.* **3** [T] to give help or support to sb/sth: *We can go ahead with the scheme if the bank will agree to back us.* **4** [T] to bet money that a particular horse, team, etc will win in a race or game: *Which horse are you backing in the 2 o'clock race?*

PHRASAL VERBS **back away (from sb/sth)** to move backwards because you are afraid, shocked, etc: *He began to back slowly away from the snake.*

back down to stop saying that you are right: *I think you are right to demand an apology. Don't back down now.*

back out (of sth) to decide not to do sth that you had promised to do: *You promised you would come with me. You can't back out of it now!*

back sb/sth up to support sb; to say or show that sth is true: *I'm going to say exactly what I think at the meeting. Will you back me up?* ● *All the evidence backed up what the woman had said.*

back (sth) up to move backwards, especially in a vehicle: *Back up a little so that the other cars can get past.*

back sth up (*computing*) to make a copy of a computer program, etc in case the original one is lost or damaged

,**back 'bench** **noun** [C,usually pl] (*Brit*) a seat in the House of Commons for an ordinary member of Parliament: *to sit on the back benches* – ,**back-'bencher** **noun** [C]

backbone /'bækbəʊn/ **noun 1** [C] the row of small bones that are connected together down the middle of your back ••➤ synonym **spine** ••➤ picture on page C5 **2** [sing] the most important part of sth: *Agriculture is the backbone of the country's economy.*

backcloth /'bækklɒθ/ = **BACKDROP**

backdate /,bæk'deɪt/ **verb** [T] to make a document, cheque or a payment take effect from an earlier date: *The pay rise will be backdated to 1 April.*

backdrop /'bækdrɒp/ (also **backcloth**) **noun** [C] a painted piece of material that is hung behind the stage in a theatre as part of the scenery

backer /'bækə/ **noun** [C] a person, organization or company that gives support to sb, especially financial support

backfire /,bæk'faɪə/ **verb** [I] to have an unexpected and unpleasant result, often the opposite of what was intended

★**background** /'bækgraʊnd/ **noun 1** [sing] the part of a view, scene, picture, etc which is furthest away from the person looking at it: *You can see the mountains **in the background** of the photo.* ••➤ opposite **foreground** **2** [sing] a position where sb/sth can be seen/heard, etc but is not the centre of attention: *The film star's husband prefers to stay in the background.* ● *All the time I was speaking to her, I could hear a child crying **in the background**.* ● *I like to have **background music** when I'm studying.* **3** [sing,U] the facts or events that are connected with a situation: *The talks are taking place against a background of increasing tension.* ● *I need some background information.* **4** [C] the type of family and social class you come from and the education and experience you have: *We get on very well together in spite of our different backgrounds.*

backhand /'bækhænd/ **noun** [sing] a way of hitting the ball in tennis, etc that is made with the back of your hand facing forward ••➤ opposite **forehand**

backing /'bækɪŋ/ **noun** [U] help or support to do sth, especially financial support: *financial backing*

backlash /'bæklæʃ/ **noun** [sing] a strong reaction against a political or social event or development

b

backlog /ˈbæklɒg/ **noun** [C, usually sing] an amount of work, etc that has not yet been done and should have been done already: *Because I've been off sick, I've got a backlog of work to catch up on.*

backpack[1] /ˈbækpæk/ **noun** [C] a large bag, often on a metal frame, that you carry on your back when travelling •➤ synonym **rucksack** •➤ picture at **bag**

backpack[2] /ˈbækpæk/ **verb** [I] to go walking or travelling with your clothes, etc in a backpack

> **Go backpacking** is used when you are talking about spending time backpacking: *We went backpacking round Europe last summer.*

–**backpacker noun** [C]

backside /ˈbæksaɪd/ **noun** [C] (*informal*) the part of your body that you sit on; your bottom

backstage /ˌbækˈsteɪdʒ/ **adv** in the part of a theatre where the actors get dressed, wait to perform, etc

backstroke /ˈbækstrəʊk/ **noun** [U] a style of swimming that you do on your back: *Can you do backstroke?* •➤ picture on page S2

backtrack /ˈbæktræk/ **verb** [I] **1** to go back the same way you came: *We got lost in the wood and had to backtrack.* **2** backtrack (on sth) to change your mind about a plan, promise, etc that you have made: *Unions forced the company to backtrack on its plans to close the factory.*

ˈback-up noun 1 [U] extra help or support that you can get if necessary: *The police officer requested urgent back-up from the rest of the team.* **2** [C] (*computing*) a copy of a computer disk that you can use if the original one is lost or damaged: *Always make a back-up of your files.*

★**backward** /ˈbækwəd/ **adj 1** (only *before* a noun) directed towards the back: *a backward step/glance* •➤ opposite **forward 2** slow to develop or learn: *Our teaching methods are backward compared to some countries.*

backwards /ˈbækwədz/ (also **backward**) **adv 1** towards a place or a position that is behind: *Could everybody take a step backwards?* **2** in the opposite direction to usual: *Can you say the alphabet backwards?* •➤ opposite **forwards**

[IDIOM] **backward(s) and forward(s)** first in one direction and then in the other, all the time: *The dog ran backwards and forwards, barking loudly.*

backwater /ˈbækwɔːtə/ **noun** [C] a place that is away from where most things happen and so it is not affected by new ideas or outside events

backyard /ˌbækˈjɑːd/ **noun** [C] **1** (*Brit*) an area behind a house, usually of concrete or stone, with a wall or fence around it **2** (*US*) the whole area behind the house including the grass area and the garden

bacon /ˈbeɪkən/ **noun** [U] thin pieces of salted or smoked meat from the back or sides of a pig •➤ Look at the note at **meat**.

bacteria /bækˈtɪəriə/ **noun** [pl] very small living things that can only be seen with special equipment (a microscope). Bacteria exist in large numbers in air, water, soil, plants and the bodies of people and animals. Some bacteria cause disease. •➤ Look at **virus**.

★**bad** /bæd/ **adj** (**worse** /wɜːs/, **worst** /wɜːst/) **1** not good; unpleasant: *Our family's had a bad time recently.* • *bad weather* • *I'm afraid I've got some bad news for you.* **2** of poor quality; of a low standard: *Many accidents are caused by bad driving.* • *Some of the company's problems are the result of bad management.* **3** bad (at sth/at doing sth) not able to do sth well or easily; not skilful or reliable: *a bad teacher/driver/cook* • *I've always been bad at sport.* **4** serious; severe: *The traffic was very bad on the way to work.* • *She went home with a bad headache.* • *That was a bad mistake!* **5** (used about food) not fresh or fit to eat; rotten: *These eggs will* **go bad** *if we don't eat them soon.* **6** (used about parts of the body) not healthy; painful: *He's always had a bad heart.* • *Keith's off work with a bad back.* **7** (used about a person or behaviour) not good; morally wrong: *He was not a bad man, just rather weak.* **8** (not before a noun) bad for sb/sth likely to damage or hurt sb/sth: *Sugar is bad for your teeth.* **9** bad (for/to do sth) difficult or not suitable: *This is a bad time to phone – everyone's out to lunch.*

[IDIOMS] **not bad** (*informal*) quite good: *'What was the film like?' 'Not bad.'*

too bad (*informal*) used to show that nothing can be done to change a situation: *'I'd much rather stay at home.' 'Well that's just too bad. We've said we'll go.'*

baddy (also **baddie**) /ˈbædi/ **noun** [C] (*pl* **baddies**) (*informal*) a bad person in a film, book, etc •➤ opposite **goody**

★**badge** /bædʒ/ **noun** [C] a small piece of metal, cloth or plastic with a design or words on it that you wear on your clothing: *The players all have jackets with the club badge on.*

badger /ˈbædʒə/ **noun** [C] an animal with black and white lines on its head that lives in holes in the ground and comes out at night

badge

badge

badge

badger

snout

,bad 'language noun [U] words that are used for swearing: *You'll get into trouble if you use bad language.*

badly /'bædli/ adv (worse /wɜːs/, worst /wɜːst/) 1 in a way that is not good enough; not well: *'Can you speak French?' 'Only very badly.'* ● *She did badly in the exams.* 2 seriously; severely: *He was badly hurt in the accident.* 3 very much: *He badly needed a holiday.*

IDIOM badly off poor; not having enough of sth: *They don't seem too badly off – they have smart clothes and a nice house.* ••➤ opposite well off

badminton /'bædmɪntən/ noun [U] a game for two or four people in which players hit a type of light ball with feathers (shuttlecock) over a high net, using a piece of equipment (a racket), which is held in the hand

,bad-'tempered adj often angry or impatient: *a bad-tempered old man*

baffle /'bæfl/ verb [T] to be impossible to understand; to confuse sb very much: *His illness baffled the doctors.* –baffled adj: *The instructions were so complicated that I was absolutely baffled.* –baffling adj: *I find it baffling how people can enjoy computer magazines.*

★bag¹ /bæg/ noun 1 [C] a container made of paper or thin plastic that opens at the top: *She brought some sandwiches in a plastic bag.* 2 [C] a strong container made from cloth, plastic, leather, etc, usually with one or two handles, used to carry things in when travelling, shopping, etc: *a shopping bag* ● *Have you packed your bags yet?* ● *She took her purse out of her bag* (= handbag). 3 [C] the amount contained in a bag: *She's eaten a whole bag of sweets!* ● *a bag of crisps/sugar/flour* ••➤ picture at container 4 bags [pl]

folds of skin under the eyes, often caused by lack of sleep: *I've got terrible bags under my eyes.* 5 bags [pl] (*Brit*) bags (of sth) a lot (of sth); plenty (of sth): *There's no hurry, we've got bags of time.*

bag² /bæg/ verb [T] (bagging; bagged) (*informal*) to try to get sth for yourself so that other people cannot have it: *Somebody's bagged the seats by the pool!*

bagel /'beɪgl/ noun [C] a type of bread roll in the shape of a ring ••➤ picture at bread

★baggage /'bægɪdʒ/ noun [U] bags, suitcases, etc used for carrying a person's clothes and things on a journey: *excess baggage* (= baggage weighing more than the airline's permitted limit) ● *I went to wait for my suitcase at baggage reclaim* (= the area in an airport where luggage goes after being taken off a plane). ••➤ synonym luggage

baggy /'bægi/ adj (used about a piece of clothing) big; hanging loosely on the body: *a baggy pullover*

bagpipes /'bægpaɪps/ noun [pl] a musical instrument, popular in Scotland, that is played by blowing air through a pipe into a bag and then pressing the bag so that the air comes out of other pipes ••➤ Look at the note at piano.

bail¹ /beɪl/ noun [U] money that sb agrees to pay if a person accused of a crime does not appear in front of the court on the day he/she is called. When bail has been arranged, the accused person can go free until that day: *She was released on bail of £2 000.* ● *The judge set bail at £10 000.* ● *The judge felt that he was a dangerous man and refused him bail.* ● *She was granted bail.*

bail² /beɪl/ verb [T] (usually passive) to be given bail by a court of law

PHRASAL VERB bail sb out 1 to obtain sb's

bags

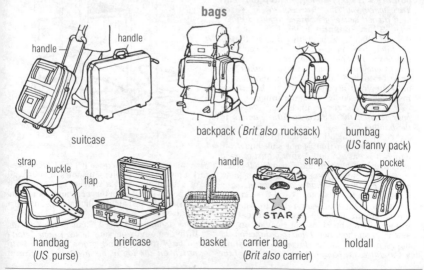

handle — handle

handle

suitcase

backpack (*Brit also* rucksack)

bumbag (*US* fanny pack)

strap — buckle — flap

handle — strap — pocket

handbag (*US* purse)

briefcase

basket

carrier bag (*Brit also* carrier)

holdall

STAR

freedom by paying money to the court: *Her parents went to the police station and bailed her out.* **2** to rescue sb or sth from a difficult situation (especially by providing money): *If you get into trouble don't expect me to bail you out again!*

bailiff /'beɪlɪf/ **noun** [C] an officer whose job is to take the possessions and property of people who cannot pay their debts

bait /beɪt/ **noun** [U] **1** food or sth that looks like food that is put onto a hook to catch fish, or to catch animals or birds **2** something that is used for persuading or attracting sb: *Free offers are often used as bait to attract customers.*

★**bake** /beɪk/ **verb** [I,T] **1** to cook in an oven in dry heat: *I could smell bread baking in the oven.* • *On his birthday she baked him a cake.* •➤ Look at the note at **cook**. **2** to become or to make sth hard by heating it: *The hot sun baked the earth.*

baker /'beɪkə/ **noun 1** [C] a person who bakes bread, cakes, etc to sell in a shop **2 the baker's** [sing] a shop that sells bread, cakes, etc: *Get a loaf at the baker's.*

bakery /'beɪkəri/ **noun** [C] (*pl* **bakeries**) a place where bread, cakes, etc are baked to be sold

baking /'beɪkɪŋ/ **adj** very hot: *The workers complained of the baking heat in the office in the summer.*

★**balance**¹ /'bæləns/ **noun 1** [sing] **(a)** balance **(between A and B)** a situation in which different or opposite things are of equal importance, size, etc: *The course provides a good balance between academic and practical work.* • *Tourism has upset the delicate balance of nature on the island.* **2** [U] the ability to keep steady with an equal amount of weight on each side of the body: *to lose your balance* • *It's very difficult to keep your balance when you start learning to ski.* • *You need a good sense of balance to ride a motor bike.* **3 the balance** [C,sing] the amount that still has to be paid; the amount that is left after some has been used, taken, etc: *You can pay a 10% deposit now, with the balance due in one month.* • *to check your bank balance* (= to find out how much money you have in your account) **4** [C] (*technical*) an instrument used for weighing things

IDIOMS **in the balance** uncertain: *Following poor results, the company's future hangs in the balance.*

(catch/throw sb) off balance (to find or put sb) in a position that is not safe and from which it is easy to fall: *A strong gust of wind caught me off balance and I nearly fell over.*

on balance having considered all sides, facts, etc: *On balance, I've had a pretty good year.*

strike a balance (between A and B) → STRIKE²

★**balance**² /'bæləns/ **verb 1** [I,T] to be or to put sb/sth in a steady position so that the weight of him/her/it is not heavier on one side than on the other: *I had to balance on the top step of the ladder to paint the ceiling.* • *Carefully, she balanced a glass on top of the pile of plates.* **2** [I,T] to have equal totals of money spent and money received: *I must have made a mistake – the accounts don't balance.* • *She is always very careful to balance her weekly budget.* **3** [I,T] balance (sth) (out) (with sth) to have or give sth equal value, importance, etc in relation to other parts: *The loss in the first half of the year was balanced out by the profit in the second half.* **4** [T] balance sth against sth to consider and compare one matter in relation to another: *In planning the new road, we have to balance the benefit to motorists against the damage to the environment.*

balanced /'bælənst/ **adj** keeping or showing a balance so that different things, or different parts of things exist in equal or correct amounts: *I like this newspaper because it gives a balanced view.* • *A balanced diet plays an important part in good health.* •➤ opposite **unbalanced**

balance of 'payments noun [sing] the difference between the amount of money one country receives from other countries from exports, etc and the amount it pays to them for imports and services in a particular period of time

balance of 'power noun [sing] **1** a situation in which political power or military strength is divided between two countries or groups of countries **2** the power that a smaller political party has when the larger parties need its support because they do not have enough votes on their own

balance sheet noun [C] a written statement showing the amount of money and property that a company has, and how much has been received and paid out

balcony

★**balcony** /'bælkəni/ **noun** [C] (*pl* **balconies**) **1** a platform built on an upstairs outside wall of a building, with a wall or rail around it •➤ Look at **patio**, **terrace** and **veranda**. **2** (*especially US*) an area of seats upstairs in a theatre

★**bald** /bɔːld/ **adj 1** (used about people) having little or no hair on your head: *I hope I don't go bald like my father did.* • *He has a bald patch on the top of his head.* •➤ picture at hair **2** (used about sth that is said) simple; without extra words: *the bald truth*

balding /'bɔːldɪŋ/ *adj* starting to lose the hair on your head: *a balding man in his fifties*

bale /beɪl/ *noun* [C] a large quantity of sth pressed tightly together and tied up: *a bale of hay/cloth/paper*

balk /bɔːk/ (*especially US*) = **BAULK**

★**ball** /bɔːl/ *noun* [C] **1** a round object that you hit, kick, throw, etc in games and sports: *a tennis/golf/rugby ball* ● *a football* ·➤ picture at **pool** and on page S2 **2** a round object or a thing that has been formed into a round shape: *a ball of wool* ● *The children threw snowballs at each other.* ● *We had meatballs and pasta for dinner.* **3** one throw, kick, etc of the ball in some sports: *That was a great ball from the defender.* **4** a large formal party at which people dance **5** (*slang*) = **TESTICLE**

IDIOMS **be on the ball** (*informal*) to always know what is happening and be able to react to or deal with it quickly: *With so many new developments, you really have to be on the ball.*

set/start the ball rolling to start sth (an activity, conversation, etc) that involves or is done by a group: *I told a joke first, to set the ball rolling.*

ballad /'bæləd/ *noun* [C] a long song or poem that tells a story, often about love

ball 'bearing *noun* [C] one of a number of metal balls put between parts of a machine to make them move smoothly

ballerina /,bælə'riːnə/ *noun* [C] a woman who dances in ballets

ballet /'bæleɪ/ *noun* **1** [U] a style of dancing that tells a story with music but without words: *He wants to be a ballet dancer.* **2** [C] a performance or work that consists of this type of dancing

'ball game *noun* [C] **1** any game played with a ball **2** (*US*) a baseball match

IDIOM **a (whole) new/different ball game** something completely new or different: *I'm used to working outside, so sitting in an office all day is a whole new ball game for me.*

balloon /bə'luːn/ *noun* [C] **1** a small coloured object that you blow air into and use as a toy or for decoration: *to blow up/burst/pop a balloon* **2** (also **hot-'air balloon**) a large balloon made of material that is filled with gas or hot air so that it can fly through the sky, carrying people in a basket underneath it

ballot /'bælət/ *noun* [C,U] a secret written vote: *The union will hold a ballot on the new pay offer.* ● *The committee are elected by ballot every year.* –**ballot** *verb* [T] **ballot sb (about/on sth)**: *The union is balloting its members on strike action.*

'ballot box *noun* **1** [C] the box into which people put the piece of paper with their vote on **2 the ballot box** [sing] the system of voting in an election: *People will express their opinion through the ballot box.*

ballpark /'bɔːlpɑːk/ *noun* [C] a place where baseball is played

IDIOMS **in the ballpark** (*informal*) (used about figures or amounts) that are within the same limits: *All the bids for the contract were in the same ballpark.*

a ballpark figure/estimate a number, amount, etc that is approximately correct: *We asked the builders for a ballpark figure, to give us an idea of how much it would cost.*

ballpoint /'bɔːlpɔɪnt/ (also **,ballpoint 'pen**) *noun* [C] a pen with a very small metal ball at the end that rolls ink onto paper ·➤ Look at **biro**.

ballroom /'bɔːlruːm; -rʊm/ *noun* [C] a large room used for dancing on formal occasions

,ballroom 'dancing *noun* [U] a formal type of dance in which couples dance together using particular steps and movements

baloney /bə'ləʊni/ *noun* [U] (*US spoken*) nonsense; lies: *Don't give me that baloney!*

bamboo /,bæm'buː/ *noun* [C,U] a tall tropical plant of the grass family. Young bamboo plants (**bamboo shoots**), can be eaten and the hard parts of the plant are used for making furniture, etc: *a bamboo chair* ·➤ picture on page C2

★**ban** /bæn/ *verb* [T] (**banning; banned**) **ban sth; ban sb (from sth/from doing sth)** to officially say that sth is not allowed, often by law: *The government has banned the import of products from that country.* ● *He was fined £500 and banned from driving for a year.* –**ban** *noun* [C] **a ban (on sth)**: *There is a ban on smoking in this office.* ● *to impose/lift a ban*

banal /bə'nɑːl/ *adj* not original or interesting: *a banal comment*

★**banana** /bə'nɑːnə/ *noun* [C] a curved fruit with yellow skin that grows in hot countries: *a bunch of bananas* ·➤ picture on page C3

★**band** /bænd/ *noun* [C] **1** [with sing or pl verb] a small group of musicians who play popular music together, often with a singer or singers: *a rock/jazz band* ● *He plays the drums in a band.* ● *The band has/have announced that it/they is/are going to split up.* **2** [with sing or pl verb] a group of people who do sth together or have the same ideas: *A small band of rebels is/are hiding in the hills.* **3** a thin, flat, narrow piece of material used for fastening sth, or to put round sth: *She rolled up the papers and put an elastic band round them.* **4** a line of colour or material on sth that is different from what is around it: *She wore a red pullover with a green band across the middle.* **5** = **WAVEBAND**

bandage /'bændɪdʒ/ *noun* [C] a long piece of soft white material that you tie round a wound or injury –**bandage** *verb* [T] **bandage sth/sb (up)**: *The nurse bandaged my hand up.* ·➤ picture on next page

bandit /'bændɪt/ *noun* [C] a member of an armed group of thieves, who attack travellers

bandwagon /'bændwægən/ *noun*

IDIOM **climb/jump on the bandwagon** to copy what other people are doing because it is fashionable or successful

★**bang¹** /bæŋ/ *verb* [I,T] **1** to make a loud noise by hitting sth hard, to close sth or to be closed with a loud noise: *Somewhere in the*

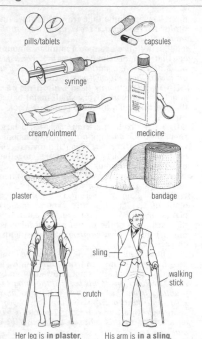

pills/tablets

capsules

syringe

cream/ointment

medicine

plaster

bandage

sling

walking stick

crutch

Her leg is **in plaster**. His arm is **in a sling**.

house, I heard a door bang. ● *He banged his fist on the table and started shouting.* **2** to knock against sth by accident; to hit a part of the body against sth by accident: *Be careful not to bang your head on the ceiling. It's quite low.* ● *As I was crossing the room in the dark I banged into a table.*

★**bang²** /bæŋ/ **noun** [C] **1** a sudden, short, very loud noise: *There was an enormous bang when the bomb exploded.* **2** a short, strong knock or hit, especially one that causes pain and injury: *a nasty bang on the head*

IDIOM **with a bang** in a successful or exciting way: *Our team's season started with a bang when we won our first five matches.*

bang³ /bæŋ/ **adv** (*especially Brit informal*) exactly; directly; right: *Our computers are bang up to date.* ● *The shot was bang on target.*

IDIOM **bang goes sth** (*informal*) used for expressing the idea that sth is now impossible: *'It's raining!' 'Ah well, bang goes our picnic!'*

bang⁴ /bæŋ/ **interj** used to sound like the noise of a gun, etc

banger /'bæŋə/ **noun** [C] (*Brit informal*) **1** a sausage **2** an old car that is in very bad condition: *I'm tired of driving around in that old banger.* **3** a small device (**firework**) that explodes with a short loud noise and is used for fun

bangle /'bæŋgl/ **noun** [C] a circular metal band that is worn round the arm or wrist for

decoration ●● picture at **jewellery**

bangs /bæŋz/ (*US*) = **FRINGE¹**(1)

banish /'bænɪʃ/ **verb** [T] (*formal*) **1** to send sb away (especially out of the country), usually as a punishment: *They were banished from the country for demonstrating against the government.* **2** to make sb/sth go away; to get rid of sb/sth: *She banished all hope of winning from her mind.*

banister (also **bannister**) /'bænɪstə/ **noun** [C] (often plural) the posts and rail at the side of a staircase: *The children loved sliding down the banister at the old house.*

banjo /'bændʒəʊ/ **noun** [C] (*pl* **banjos**) a musical instrument like a guitar, with a long thin neck, a round body and four or more strings ●● Look at the note at **piano**. ●● picture at **music**

★**bank¹** /bæŋk/ **noun** [C] **1** an organization which keeps money safely for its customers; the office or building of such an organization. You can take money out, save, borrow or exchange money at a bank: *My salary is paid directly into my bank.* ● *I need to go to the bank to get some money out.* ● *a bank account/loan* **2** a store of things, which you keep to use later: *a databank* ● *a blood bank in a hospital* **3** the ground along the side of a river or canal: *People were fishing along the banks of the river.* **4** a higher area of ground that goes down or up at an angle, often at the edge of sth or dividing sth: *There were grassy banks on either side of the road.* **5** a mass of cloud, snow, etc: *The sun disappeared behind a bank of clouds.*

bank² /bæŋk/ **verb** [I] **bank (with/at...)** to have an account with a particular bank: *I've banked with Lloyds for years.*

PHRASAL VERB **bank on sb/sth** to expect and trust sb to do sth, or sth to happen: *Our boss might let you have the morning off but I wouldn't bank on it.*

banker /'bæŋkə/ **noun** [C] a person who owns or has an important job in a bank

bank 'holiday noun [C] (*Brit*) a public holiday (not a Saturday or Sunday)

banking /'bæŋkɪŋ/ **noun** [U] the type of business done by banks: *She decided on a career in banking.*

banknote /'bæŋknəʊt/ = **NOTE¹**(4)

★**bankrupt** /'bæŋkrʌpt/ **adj** not having enough money to pay your debts: *The company must cut its costs or it will* **go bankrupt**. –**bankrupt verb** [T]: *The failure of the new product almost bankrupted the firm.*

bankruptcy /'bæŋkrʌptsi/ **noun** [C,U] (*pl* **bankruptcies**) the state of being bankrupt: *The company filed for bankruptcy* (= asked to be officially declared bankrupt) *in 1999.*

'bank statement (also **statement**) **noun** [C] a printed list of all the money going into or out of your bank account during a certain period

banner /'bænə/ **noun** [C] a long piece of cloth with words or signs on it, which can be hung up or carried on two poles: *The demonstrators carried banners saying 'Stop the War'.* ●● picture at **placard**

banquet /'bæŋkwɪt/ noun [C] a formal dinner for a large number of people, usually as a special event at which speeches are made

banter /'bæntə/ noun [U] friendly comments and jokes –banter verb [I]

baptism /'bæptɪzəm/ noun [C,U] a ceremony in which a person becomes a member of the Christian Church by being held under water for a short time or having drops of water put onto his/her head. Often he/she is also formally given a name. ••➤ Look at **christening**. –baptize (also -ise) /bæp'taɪz/ verb [T] ••➤ Look at **christen**.

Baptist /'bæptɪst/ noun, adj (a member) of a Protestant Church that believes that baptism should only be for people who are old enough to understand the meaning of the ceremony and should be done by placing the person fully under water

★**bar¹** /bɑ:/ noun [C] **1** a place where you can buy and drink (especially alcoholic) drinks and sometimes have sth to eat: *a wine/coffee/snack bar*

> In Britain, a bar where you can get alcoholic drinks is not a separate building (except a wine bar), but usually found as part of a pub, hotel, restaurant, etc. In a pub there may be two types of bar. The lounge bar is more comfortable (and often more expensive) than the public bar.

2 a long, narrow, high surface where drinks are served: *She went to the bar and ordered a drink.* • *We sat on stools at the bar.* **3** a bar (of sth) a small block of solid material, longer than it is wide: *a bar of soap/chocolate* **4** a long, thin, straight piece of metal, often placed across a window or door, etc to stop sth from getting through it **5** a bar (to sth) a thing that prevents you from doing sth: *Lack of education is not always a bar to success in business.* **6** one of the short, equal units of time into which music is divided: *If you sing a few bars of the song I might recognize it.* IDIOM **behind bars** (*informal*) in prison: *The criminals are now safely behind bars.*

bar² /bɑ:/ verb [T] (**barring**; **barred**) **1** (usually passive) to close sth with a bar or bars¹(4): *All the windows were barred.* **2** to block a road, path, etc so that nobody can pass: *A line of police officers barred the entrance to the embassy.* **3** bar sb from sth/from doing sth to say officially that sb is not allowed to do, use or enter sth: *He was barred from the club for fighting.*

bar³ /bɑ:/ prep except: *All the seats were taken, bar one.*

barbarian /bɑ:'beəriən/ noun [C] a wild person with no culture, who behaves very badly

barbaric /bɑ:'bærɪk/ adj very cruel and violent: *barbaric treatment of prisoners* –barbarism /'bɑ:bərɪzəm/ noun [U]: *acts of barbarism committed in war*

barbecue /'bɑ:bɪkju:/ (*abbr* BBQ) noun [C] **1** a metal frame on which food is cooked outdoors over an open fire **2** an outdoor party at which food is cooked in this way: *Let's have a barbecue on the beach.* ••➤ Look at **roast²(2)**. –barbecue verb [T]: *barbecued steak*

barbed wire /ˌbɑ:bd 'waɪə/ noun [U] strong wire with sharp points on it: *a barbed wire fence*

barber /'bɑ:bə/ noun **1** [C] a man whose job is to cut men's hair and sometimes to shave them

> Compare **hairdresser**.

2 the barber's [sing] (*Brit*) a shop where men go to have their hair cut

bar code

'**bar code** noun [C] a pattern of thick and thin lines that is printed on things you buy. It contains information that a computer can read.

★**bare** /beə/ adj **1** (used about part of the body) not covered by clothing: *bare arms/feet/shoulders* ••➤ Look at **naked** and **nude**. **2** without anything covering it or in it: *They had taken the painting down, so the walls were all bare.* **3** just enough; the most basic or simple: *You won't pass your exams if you just do the bare minimum.* • *I don't take much luggage when I travel, just the bare essentials.* IDIOM **with your bare hands** without weapons or tools: *She killed him with her bare hands.*

barefoot /'beəfʊt/ adj, adv with nothing (for example shoes, socks, etc) on your feet: *We walked barefoot along the beach.*

barely /'beəli/ adv (used especially after 'can' and 'could' to emphasize that sth is difficult to do) only just; almost not: *I was so tired I could barely stand up.* • *I earn barely enough money to pay my rent.* ••➤ Look at **hardly**.

bargain¹ /'bɑ:gən/ noun [C] **1** something that is cheaper or at a lower price than usual: *At that price, it's an absolute bargain!* • *I found a lot of bargains in the sale.* **2** an agreement between people or groups about what each of them will do for the other or others: *Let's make a bargain – I'll lend you the money if you'll help me with my work.* • *I lent him the money but he didn't keep his side of the bargain.* IDIOMS **into the bargain** (used for emphasizing sth) as well; in addition; also: *They gave me free tickets and a free meal into the bargain.*
strike a bargain (with sb) → STRIKE²

bargain² /'bɑ:gən/ verb [I] bargain (with sb) (about/over/for sth) to discuss prices, conditions, etc with sb in order to reach an agreement that suits each person: *I'm sure that if you bargain with him, he'll drop the price.* • *They bargained over the price.* PHRASAL VERB **bargain for/on sth** (usually in negative sentences) to expect sth to happen and be ready for it: *When I agreed to help him I didn't bargain for how much it would cost me.*

barge¹ /bɑːdʒ/ *noun* [C] a long narrow boat with a flat bottom that is used for carrying goods or people on a canal or river

barge² /bɑːdʒ/ *verb* [I,T] to push people out of the way in order to get past them: *He barged (his way) angrily through the crowd.*

baritone /'bærɪtəʊn/ *noun* [C] a male singing voice that is fairly low; a man with this voice

➤ Baritone is between **tenor** and **bass**.

bark¹ /bɑːk/ *noun* **1** [U] the hard outer covering of a tree ••➤ picture on page C2 **2** [C] the short, loud noise that a dog makes: *The dog next door has a very loud bark.*

★**bark²** /bɑːk/ *verb* **1** [I] bark (at sb/sth) (used about dogs) to make a loud, short noise or noises **2** [I,T] bark (sth) (out) (at sb) to speak to sb in a loud voice in an angry or aggressive way: *The boss came in, barked out some orders and left again.*

barley /'bɑːli/ *noun* [U] **1** a plant that produces grain that is used for food or for making beer and other drinks **2** the grain produced by this plant ••➤ picture at **cereal**

barmaid /'bɑːmeɪd/ *noun* [C] a woman who serves drinks from behind a bar in a pub, etc

barman /'bɑːmən/ *noun* [C] (*pl* -men /-mən/) (*US* **bartender**) a man who serves drinks from behind a bar in a pub, etc

bar mitzvah /ˌbɑː 'mɪtsvə/ *noun* [C] a ceremony in the Jewish religion for a boy who is about 13 years old. After the ceremony, he is considered an adult.

➤ The same ceremony for a 13-year-old Jewish girl is called a **bat mitzvah**.

barn

barn /bɑːn/ *noun* [C] a large building on a farm in which crops or animals are kept

barometer /bə'rɒmɪtə/ *noun* [C] **1** an instrument that measures air pressure and indicates changes in weather **2** something that indicates the state of sth (a situation, a feeling, etc): *Results of local elections are often a barometer of the government's popularity.*

baron /'bærən/ *noun* [C] **1** a man of a high social position in Britain; a nobleman **2** a person who controls a large part of a particular industry or type of business: *drug/oil barons*

baroness /'bærənəs/ *noun* [C] a woman of a high social position; the wife of a baron

barracks /'bærəks/ *noun* [C, with sing or pl verb] (*pl* **barracks**) a building or group of buildings in which soldiers live: *Guards were on duty at the gate of the barracks.*

barrage /'bærɑːʒ/ *noun* [C] **1** a continuous attack on a place with a large number of guns **2** a large number of questions, comments, etc, directed at a person very quickly: *The*

minister faced a barrage of questions from reporters.

barrel /'bærəl/ *noun* [C] **1** a large, round, wooden, plastic or metal container for liquids, that has a flat top and bottom and is wider in the middle: *a beer/wine barrel* • *The price of oil is usually given per barrel.* **2** the long metal part of a gun like a tube through which the bullets are fired

barren /'bærən/ *adj* **1** (used about land or soil) not good enough for plants to grow on **2** (used about trees or plants) not producing fruit or seeds

barricade /ˌbærɪ'keɪd/ *noun* [C] an object or line of objects that is placed across a road, entrance, etc to stop people getting through: *The demonstrators put up barricades to keep the police away.* –**barricade** *verb* [T]

barricade yourself in to defend yourself by putting up a barricade: *Demonstrators took over the building and barricaded themselves in.*

★**barrier** /'bæriə/ *noun* [C] **1** an object that keeps people or things separate or prevents them moving from one place to another: *The crowd were all kept behind barriers.* • *The mountains form a natural barrier between the two countries.* ••➤ Look at **crash barrier**. **2** a barrier (to sth) something that causes problems or makes it impossible for sth to happen: *When you live in a foreign country, the language barrier is often the most difficult problem to overcome.*

barring /'bɑːrɪŋ/ *prep* except for; unless there is/are: *Barring any unforeseen problems, we'll be moving house in a month.*

barrister /'bærɪstə/ *noun* [C] (in English law) a lawyer who is trained to speak for you in the higher courts ••➤ Look at the note at **lawyer**.

barrow /'bærəʊ/ *noun* [C] (*Brit*) **1** a small thing on two wheels on which fruit, vegetables, etc are moved or sold in the street, especially in markets **2** =**WHEELBARROW**

barstaff /'bɑːstɑːf/ *noun* [U, with pl verb] the people who serve drinks from behind a bar in a pub, etc: *The barstaff are very friendly here.* ••➤ Look at **barmaid** and **barman**.

barter /'bɑːtə/ *verb* [I,T] barter sth (for sth); barter (with sb) (for sth) to exchange goods, services, property, etc for other goods, etc, without using money: *The farmer bartered his surplus grain for machinery.* • *The prisoners bartered with the guards for writing paper and books.* –**barter** *noun* [U]

★**base¹** /beɪs/ *noun* [C] **1** the lowest part of sth, especially the part on which it stands or at which it is fixed or connected to sth: *the base of a column/glass/box* • *I felt a terrible pain at the base of my spine.* **2** an idea, fact, etc from which sth develops or is made: *With these ingredients as a base, you can create all sorts of interesting dishes.* • *The country needs a strong economic base.* **3** a place used as a centre from which activities are done or controlled: *This hotel is an ideal base for touring the region.* **4** a military centre from which the armed forces operate: *an army base* **5** (in baseball) one of the four points that a runner must touch

★**base²** /beɪs/ **verb** [T] (usually passive) **base sb/sth in...** to make one place the centre from which sb/sth can work or move around: *I'm based in New York, although my job involves a great deal of travel.* ● *a Cardiff-based company*

PHRASAL VERB **base sth on/sth** to form or develop sth from a particular starting point or source: *This film is based on a true story.*

baseball /ˈbeɪsbɔːl/ **noun** [U] a team game that is popular in the US in which players hit the ball with a bat and run round four points (**bases**). They have to touch all four bases in order to score a point (**run**).

basement /ˈbeɪsmənt/ **noun** [C] a room or rooms in a building, partly or completely below ground level: *a basement flat* ••➤ Look at **cellar**.

bases 1 *plural* of **BASIS 2** *plural* of **BASE¹**

bash¹ /bæʃ/ **verb** (*informal*) **1** [I,T] to hit sb/sth very hard: *I didn't stop in time and bashed into the car in front.* **2** [T] to criticize sb/sth strongly: *The candidate continued to bash her opponent's policies.*

bash² /bæʃ/ **noun** [C] **1** a hard hit: *He gave Alex a bash on the nose.* **2** (*informal*) a large party or celebration: *Are you going to Gary's birthday bash?*

IDIOM **have a bash (at sth/at doing sth)** (*Brit spoken*) to try: *I'll get a screwdriver and have a bash at mending the light.*

bashful /ˈbæʃfl/ **adj** shy and embarrassed

★**basic** /ˈbeɪsɪk/ **adj 1** forming the part of sth that is most necessary and from which other things develop: *The basic question is, can we afford it?* ● *basic information/facts/ideas* **2** of the simplest kind or level; including only what is necessary without anything extra: *This course teaches basic computer skills.* ● *The basic pay is £200 a week – with extra for overtime.*

★**basically** /ˈbeɪsɪkli/ **adv** used to say what the most important or most basic aspect of sb/sth is: *The new design is basically the same as the old one.*

basics /ˈbeɪsɪks/ **noun** [pl] the simplest or most important facts or aspects of sth; things that you need the most: *So far, I've only learnt the basics of computing.*

★**basin** /ˈbeɪsn/ **noun** [C] **1** =WASHBASIN **2** a round open bowl often used for mixing or cooking food **3** an area of land from which water flows into a river: *the Amazon Basin*

★**basis** /ˈbeɪsɪs/ **noun** (*pl* **bases** /ˈbeɪsiːz/) **1** [sing] the principle or reason which lies behind sth: *We made our decision on the basis of the reports which you sent us.* **2** [sing] the way sth is done or organized: *They meet on a regular basis.* **3** [C] a starting point, from which sth can develop: *She used her diaries as a basis for her book.*

bask /bɑːsk/ **verb** [I] **bask (in sth) 1** to sit or lie in a place where you can enjoy the

warmth: *The snake basked in the sunshine on the rock.* **2** to enjoy the good feelings you have when other people admire you, give you a lot of attention, etc: *The team was still basking in the glory of winning the cup.*

★**basket** /ˈbɑːskɪt/ **noun** [C] **1** a container for carrying or holding things, made of thin pieces of material such as wood, plastic or wire that bends easily: *a waste-paper basket* ● *a shopping basket* ● *a clothes/laundry basket* (in which you put dirty clothes before they are washed) ••➤ picture at **bag 2** a net that hangs from a metal ring high up at each end of a basketball court ••➤ picture on page S2 **3** a score of one, two or three points in basketball, made by throwing the ball through one of the nets

IDIOM **put all your eggs in one basket** → **EGG¹**

basketball /ˈbɑːskɪtbɔːl/ **noun** [U] a game for two teams of five players. There is a net (**basket**) fixed to a metal ring high up at each end of the court and the players try to throw a ball through the other team's net in order to score points (**baskets**).

bass /beɪs/ **noun 1** [U] the lowest part in music **2** [C] the lowest male singing voice; a singer with this kind of voice ••➤ Look at **tenor** and **baritone**. **3** = **DOUBLE BASS 4** [C] (also **bass guitar**) an electric guitar which plays very low notes ••➤ Look at the note at **piano**. –**bass adj** (only *before* a noun): *a bass drum* ● *Can you sing the bass part in this song?*

bassoon /bəˈsuːn/ **noun** [C] a musical instrument that you blow which makes a very deep sound ••➤ Look at the note at **piano**. ••➤ picture at **music**

bat¹ /bæt/ **noun** [C] **1** a piece of wood for hitting the ball in sports such as table tennis, cricket or baseball: *a cricket bat* ••➤ Look at **club**, **racket** and **stick**. ••➤ picture on page S2 **2** a small animal, like a mouse with wings, which flies and hunts at night

bat

IDIOM **off your own bat** without anyone asking you or helping you

bat² /bæt/ **verb** [I] (**batting**; **batted**) (used about one player or a whole team) to have a turn hitting the ball in sports such as cricket or baseball

IDIOM **not bat an eyelid**; (*US*) **not bat an eye** to show no surprise or embarrassment when sth unusual happens

batch /bætʃ/ **noun** [C] a number of things or people which belong together as a group: *The bus returned to the airport for the next batch of tourists.*

bated /ˈbeɪtɪd/ **adj**

IDIOM **with bated breath** excited or afraid, because you are waiting for sth to happen

★**bath¹** /bɑːθ/ **noun 1** [C] (also **bathtub** /ˈbɑːθtʌb/) a large container for water in which you sit to wash your body: *Can you* *answer the phone? I'm in the bath!* • ➤ picture on page C7 **2** [sing] an act of washing the whole of your body when you sit or lie in a bath filled with water: *to* **have a bath** • (*especially US*) *Would you prefer to* **take a bath** *or a shower?* **3 baths** [pl] (*Brit old-fashioned*) a public building where you can go to swim; a public place where people went in past times to have a wash or a bath: *Roman baths*

bath² /bɑːθ/ **verb 1** [T] to give sb a bath: *bath the baby* **2** [I] (*old-fashioned*) to have a bath: *I prefer to bath in the mornings.*

bathe /beɪð/ **verb 1** [T] to wash or put part of the body in water, often for medical reasons: *She bathed the wound with antiseptic.* **2** [I] (*old-fashioned*) to swim in the sea or in a lake or river • ➤ Look at **sunbathe**.

bathed /beɪðd/ **adj** (*written*) **bathed in sth** (not before a noun) covered with sth: *The room was bathed in moonlight.*

bathrobe /'bɑːθrəʊb/ = **DRESSING GOWN**

★**bathroom** /'bɑːθruːm; -rʊm/ **noun** [C] **1** a room where there is a bath, a place to wash your hands (a **washbasin**), and sometimes a toilet • ➤ picture on page C7 **2** (*US*) a room with a toilet • ➤ Look at the note at **toilet**.

bathtub /'bɑːθtʌb/ = **BATH¹**(1)

baton /'bætɒn/ **noun** [C] **1** = **TRUNCHEON 2** a short thin stick used by the leader of an orchestra **3** a stick which a runner in a race (a **relay race**) passes to the next person in the team

batsman /'bætsmən/ **noun** [C] (*pl* **-men** /-mən/) (in cricket) one of the two players who hit the ball to score points (**runs**).

battalion /bə'tæliən/ **noun** [C] a large unit of soldiers that forms part of a larger unit in the army

batter¹ /'bætə/ **verb** [I,T] to hit sb/sth hard, many times: *The wind battered against the window.* • *He battered the door down.*

batter² /'bætə/ **noun** [U] a mixture of flour, eggs and milk used to cover food such as fish, vegetables, etc before frying them

battered /'bætəd/ **adj** no longer looking new; damaged or out of shape: *a battered old hat*

★**battery** **noun** (*pl* **batteries**) **1** /'bætri/[C] a device which provides electricity for a toy, radio, car, etc: *to recharge* **a flat battery** (= no longer producing electricity) • ➤ picture at **light 2** /'bætri/[C] (*Brit*) a large number of very small cages in which chickens, etc are kept on a farm: *a battery hen/farm* • ➤ Look at **free-range**. **3** /'bætəri/[U] the crime of attacking sb physically: *He was charged with* **assault and battery**.

★**battle¹** /'bætl/ **noun 1** [C,U] a fight, especially between armies in a war: *the battle of Trafalgar* • *to die/be killed* **in battle 2** [C] a battle (**with sb**) (**for sth**) a competition, argument or fight between people or groups of people trying to win power or control: *a legal battle for custody of the children* **3** [C,usually sing] a battle (**against/for sth**) a determined effort to solve a difficult problem or to succeed in a difficult situation: *After three years she lost*

her battle against cancer.

IDIOM a losing battle → **LOSE**

battle² /'bætl/ **verb** [I] **battle (with/against sb/sth) (for sth)**; **battle (on)** to try very hard to achieve sth difficult or to deal with sth unpleasant or dangerous: *Mark is battling with his maths homework.* • *The little boat battled against the wind.* • *The two brothers were battling for control of the family business.* • *Life is hard at the moment but we're battling on.*

battlefield /'bætlfiːld/ (also **battleground** /'bætlɡraʊnd/) **noun** [C] the place where a battle is fought

battleship /'bætlʃɪp/ **noun** [C] the largest type of ship used in war

bauble /'bɔːbl/ **noun** [C] **1** a piece of cheap jewellery **2** a decoration in the shape of a ball that is hung on a Christmas tree

baulk (*especially US* **balk**) /bɔːk/ **verb** [I] **baulk (at sth)** to not want to do or agree to sth because it seems too difficult, dangerous or unpleasant: *She liked horses, but she baulked at trying to ride one.*

bawl /bɔːl/ **verb** [I,T] to shout or cry loudly

★**bay** /beɪ/ **noun** [C] **1** a part of the coast where the land goes in to form a curve: *the Bay of Bengal* • *The harbour was in a sheltered bay.* **2** a part of a building, aircraft or area which has a particular purpose: *a parking/loading bay*

IDIOM **hold/keep sb at bay** to stop sb dangerous from getting near you; to prevent a situation or problem from getting worse

bayonet /'beɪənət/ **noun** [C] a knife that can be fixed to the end of a gun

bay 'window **noun** [C] a window in a part of a room that sticks out from the wall of a house

bazaar /bə'zɑː/ **noun** [C] **1** (in some eastern countries) a market **2** (*Brit*) a sale where the money that is made goes to charity: *The school held a bazaar to raise money for the homeless.*

BBC /ˌbiː biː 'siː/ **abbr** the British Broadcasting Corporation; one of the national radio and television companies in Britain: *a BBC documentary* • *watch a programme on BBC1*

BBQ **abbr** = **BARBECUE**

BC /ˌbiː 'siː/ **abbr** before Christ; used in dates to show the number of years before the time when Christians believe Jesus Christ was born: *300 BC* • ➤ Look at **AD**.

★**be¹** /bi; *strong form* biː/ **verb 1** [T] **there is/are** to exist; to be present: *I tried phoning them but there was no answer.* • *There are some people outside.* • *There are a lot of trees in our garden.* **2** [I] used to give the position of sb/sth or the place where sb/sth is situated: *Katrina's in her office.* • *Where are the scissors?* • *The bus stop is five minutes' walk from here.* • *St Tropez is on the south coast.* **3** [I] used to give the date or age of sb/sth or to talk about time: *My birthday is on April 24th.* • *It's 6 o'clock.* • *It was Tuesday yesterday.* • *Sue'll be 21 in June.* • *He's older than Miranda.* • *It's ages since I last saw him.* **4** [I] used when you are giving the name of people or things, describing them or giving more information about them: *This is my father, John.* • *I'm Alison.* • *He's Italian. He's from Milan.* • *He's a doctor.* • *What's that?* • *A lion is a mammal.* • *'What colour is your car?' 'It's green.'* • *How much was your ticket?* • *The film was excellent.* • *She's very friendly.* • *'How is your wife?' 'She's fine, thanks.'* **5** [I] (only used in the perfect tenses) to go to a place (and return): *Have you ever **been** to Japan?*

➤ Compare **has/have gone**: *Julia's gone to the doctor's* (= she hasn't returned yet). • *Julia's **been** to the doctor's today* (= she has returned).

IDIOMS **be yourself** to act naturally: *Don't be nervous; just be yourself and the interview will be fine.*

-to-be (used to form compound nouns) future: *his bride-to-be* • *mothers-to-be* (= pregnant women)

present tense	past tense
I am (I'm)	I was
you are (you're)	you were
he/she/it is (he's/she's/it's)	he/she/it was
we are (we're)	we were
you are (you're)	you were
they are (they're)	they were
past participle	been
present participle	being
negative short forms	aren't, isn't, wasn't, weren't

★**be²** /bi; *strong form* bi:/ **auxiliary verb 1** used with a past participle to form the passive; used with a present participle to form the continuous tenses ·➤ Look at the **Quick Grammar Reference** section at the back of this dictionary. **2 be to do sth** used to show that sth must happen or that sth has been arranged: *You are to leave here at 10 o'clock at the latest.* **4 if sb/sth were to do sth** used to show that sth is possible but not very likely: *If they were to offer me the job, I'd probably take it.*

★**beach** /bi:tʃ/ **noun** [C] an area of sand or small stones beside the sea: *to sit **on the beach*** ·➤ picture on page C8

beacon /'bi:kən/ **noun** [C] a fire or light on a hill or tower, often near the coast, which is used as a signal

bead /bi:d/ **noun** [C] **1** a small round piece of wood, glass or plastic with a hole in the middle for putting a string through to make jewellery, etc **2 beads** [pl] a circular piece of jewellery (**a necklace**) made of beads ·➤ picture at **jewellery 3** a drop of liquid: *There were **beads** of **sweat** on his forehead.*

★**beak** /bi:k/ **noun** [C] the hard pointed part of a bird's mouth ·➤ picture on page C1

beaker /'bi:kə/ **noun** [C] **1** a plastic or paper drinking cup, usually without a handle ·➤ picture at **cup 2** a glass container used in scientific experiments, etc for pouring liquids

beam¹ /bi:m/ **noun** [C] **1** a line of light: *the beam of a torch* • *The car's headlights were **on full beam*** (= giving the most light possible and not directed downwards). • *a laser beam* **2** a long piece of wood, metal, etc that is used to support weight, for example in the floor or ceiling of a building **3** a happy smile

beam² /bi:m/ **verb 1** [I] **beam (at sb/sth)** to smile happily: *I looked at Sam and he beamed back at me.* **2** [T] to send out radio or television signals: *The programme was beamed live by satellite to many different countries.* **3** [I] to send out light and warmth: *The sun beamed down on them.*

★**bean** /bi:n/ **noun** [C] **1** the seeds or seed containers (**pods**) from a climbing plant which are eaten as vegetables: *soya beans* • *a tin of baked beans* (= beans in a tomato sauce) • *green beans* ·➤ picture on page C3 **2** similar seeds from other plants: *coffee beans*
IDIOMS **full of beans/life** → **FULL¹**
spill the beans → **SPILL**

★**bear¹** /beə/ **noun** [C] a large, heavy wild animal with thick fur and sharp teeth: *a polar/grizzly/brown bear* ·➤ Look at **teddy bear**.

★**bear²** /beə/ **verb** (*pt* **bore** /bɔ:/; *pp* **borne** /bɔ:n/) **1** [T] (used with *can/could* in negative sentences or in questions) to be able to accept and deal with sth unpleasant: *I can't bear spiders.* • *She couldn't bear the thought of anything happening to him.* • *How can you bear to listen to that music?* • *The pain was almost more than he could bear.* ·➤ synonym **stand** or **endure 2** [T] **not bear sth/doing sth** to not be suitable for sth; to not allow sth: *These figures won't bear close examination* (= when you look closely you will find mistakes). • *What I would do if I lost my job **doesn't bear thinking about*** (= is too unpleasant to think about). **3** [T] (*formal*) to take responsibility for sth: *Customers will bear the full cost of the improvements.* **4** [T] to have a feeling, especially a negative feeling: *Despite what they did, she **bears** no **resentment** towards them.* • *He's not the type to **bear a grudge** against anyone.* **5** [T] to support the weight of sth: *Twelve pillars bear the weight of the roof.* **6** [T] (*formal*) to show sth; to carry sth so that it can be seen: *The waiters came in bearing trays of food.* • *He still **bears the scars** of his accident.* • *She **bore a** strong **resemblance** to her mother* (= she looked like her). **7** [T] (*written*) to give birth to children: *She bore him four children, all sons.*

➤ A more common expression is 'She had four children.' When you talk about a person's own birth you use **be born**: *Robert was born in 1996.*

8 [I] to turn or go in the direction that is mentioned: *Where the road forks, bear left.*
IDIOMS **bear the brunt of sth** to suffer the main force of sth: *Her sons usually bore the brunt of her anger.*

b

bear fruit to be successful; to produce results: *At last our hard work is beginning to bear fruit.*

bear in mind (that); bear/keep sb/sth in mind → **MIND**¹

bear witness (to sth) to show evidence of sth: *The burning buildings and empty streets bore witness to a recent attack.*

PHRASAL VERBS **bear down (on sb/sth) 1** to move closer to sb/sth in a frightening way: *We could see the hurricane bearing down on the town.* **2** to push down hard on sb/sth

bear sb/sth out to show that sb is correct or that sth is true: *The evidence bears out my theory.*

bear up to be strong enough to continue at a difficult time: *How is he bearing up after his accident?*

bear with sb/sth to be patient with: *Bear with me – I won't be much longer.*

bearable /'beərəbl/ **adj** that you can accept or deal with, although unpleasant: *It was extremely hot but the breeze made it more bearable.* ·➤ opposite **unbearable**

★**beard** /bɪəd/ **noun** [C,U] the hair which grows on a man's cheeks and chin: *I'm going to grow a beard.* ·➤ Look at **goatee** and **moustache.** ·➤ picture at **hair**

bearded /'bɪədɪd/ **adj** with a beard

bearer /'beərə/ **noun** [C] a person who carries or brings sth: *I'm sorry to be the bearer of bad news.*

bearing /'beərɪŋ/ **noun 1** [U,sing] **(a) bearing on sth** a relation or connection to the subject being discussed: *Her comments **had no bearing** on our decision.* **2** [U,sing] the way in which sb stands or moves: *a man of dignified bearing* **3** [C] a direction measured from a fixed point using a special instrument (a compass)

IDIOMS **get/find your bearings** to become familiar with where you are

lose your bearings → **LOSE**

beast /biːst/ **noun** [C] (*formal*) an animal, especially a large one: *a wild beast*

★**beat**¹ /biːt/ **verb** (*pt* **beat**; *pp* **beaten** /'biːtn/) **1** [T] **beat sb (at sth); beat sth** to defeat sb; to be better than sth: *He always beats me at tennis.* ● *We're hoping to beat the world record.* ● *If you want to keep fit, you can't beat swimming.* **2** [I,T] to hit many times, usually very hard: *The man was beating the donkey with a stick.* ● *The rain was beating on the roof of the car.* **3** [I,T] to make a regular sound or movement: *Her **heart beat** faster as she ran to pick up her child.* ● *We could hear the drums beating in the distance.* ● *The bird **beat its wings** (= moved them up and down quickly).* **4** [T] to mix quickly with a fork, etc: *Beat the eggs and sugar together.*

IDIOMS **beat about the bush** to talk about sth for a long time without mentioning the main point: *Stop beating about the bush and tell me how much money you need.*

(it) beats me (*spoken*) I do not know: *It beats me where he's gone.* ● *'Why is she angry?' 'Beats me!'*

off the beaten track in a place where people do not often go

PHRASAL VERBS **beat sb/sth off** to fight until sb/sth goes away: *The thieves tried to take his wallet but he beat them off.*

beat sb to sth to get somewhere or do sth before sb else: *She beat me back to the house.* ● *I wanted to ring him first but Aisha beat me to it.*

beat sb up to attack sb by hitting or kicking him/her many times: *He was badly beaten up outside the pub last night.*

beat² /biːt/ **noun 1** [C] a single hit on sth such as a drum or the movement of sth, such as your heart; the sound that this makes: *Her heart skipped a beat when she saw him.* **2** [sing] a series of regular hits on sth such as a drum, or of movements of sth; the sound that this makes: *the beat of the drums* ·➤ Look at **heartbeat. 3** [C] the strong rhythm that a piece of music has **4** [sing] the route along which a police officer regularly walks: *Having more policemen **on the beat** helps reduce crime.*

beating /'biːtɪŋ/ **noun** [C] **1** a punishment that you give to sb by hitting him/her: *The boys got a beating when they were caught stealing.* **2** a defeat

IDIOM **take a lot of/some beating** to be so good that it would be difficult to find sth better: *Mary's cooking takes some beating.*

beautician /bju:'tɪʃn/ **noun** [C] a person whose job is to improve the way people look with beauty treatments, etc

★**beautiful** /'bju:tɪfl/ **adj** very pretty or attractive; giving pleasure to the senses: *The view from the top of the hill was really beautiful.* ● *What a beautiful day – the weather's perfect!* ● *He has a beautiful voice.* ● *A beautiful perfume filled the air.* ● *a beautiful woman*

➤ **Beautiful** is usually used for women and girls. It is stronger than **pretty**, which is also used of women and girls only. Men are described as **handsome** or **good-looking.**

–**beautifully** /-fli/ **adv**: *He plays the piano beautifully.* ● *She was beautifully dressed.*

★**beauty** /'bju:ti/ **noun** (*pl* **beauties**) **1** [U] the quality which gives pleasure to the senses; the state of being beautiful: *I was amazed by the beauty of the mountains.* ● *music of great beauty* **2** [C] a beautiful woman: *She grew up to be a beauty.* **3** [C] a particularly good example of sth: *Look at this tomato – it's a beauty!*

'**beauty spot** **noun** [C] (*Brit*) a place in the countryside which is famous for its attractive scenery

beaver

beaver /'biːvə/ **noun** [C] an animal with brown fur, a wide, flat tail and sharp teeth. It lives in water and on land and uses branches to build walls across rivers to hold back the water (**dams**).

became *past tense* of **BECOME**

★**because** /bɪˈkɒz/ **conj** for the reason that: *They didn't go for a walk because it was raining.*

★**be'cause of prep** as a result of; on account of: *They didn't go for a walk because of the rain.*

beck /bek/ **noun**
  IDIOM **at sb's beck and call** always ready to obey sb's orders

beckon /ˈbekən/ **verb** [I,T] to show sb with a movement of your finger or hand that you want him/her to come closer: *She beckoned me over to speak to her.*

★**become** /bɪˈkʌm/ **verb** [I] (*pt* **became** /bɪˈkeɪm/; *pp* **become**) to begin to be sth: *Mr Saito became Chairman in 1998.* • *She wants to become a pilot.* • *They became friends.* • *She became nervous as the exam date came closer.* • *He is becoming more like you every day.* ·•➤ **Get** is also used with adjectives in this sense: *She got nervous as the exam date came closer.* • *He's getting more like you every day.* It is very common in conversation and is less formal than **become**.
  PHRASAL VERB **become of sb/sth** to happen to sb/sth: *What became of Alima? I haven't seen her for years!*

BEd /ˌbiː ˈed/ **abbr** Bachelor of Education; a degree in education for people who want to be teachers and do not already have a degree in a particular subject

★**bed¹** /bed/ **noun** **1** [C,U] a piece of furniture that you lie on when you sleep: *to make the bed* (= to arrange the sheets, etc so that the bed is tidy and ready for sb to sleep in) • *What time do you usually go to bed?* • *She was lying on the bed* (= on top of the covers). • *When he rang I was already in bed* (= under the covers). • *It's late. It's time for bed.* • *to get into/out of bed* ·•➤ picture on page C7

  ➤ A bed for one person is called a **single bed** and a bed for a couple to share is a **double bed**. Two single beds next to each other in the same room are called **twin beds**. A room in a hotel with twin beds is called a **twin-bedded** room. Two single beds built as a unit with one above the other, used especially by children, are called **bunk beds**.

2 -bedded having the type or number of beds mentioned: *a twin-bedded room* **3** [C] the ground at the bottom of a river or the sea: *the seabed* **4** =**FLOWER BED**
  IDIOM **bed and breakfast; B & B** a place to stay in a private house or small hotel that consists of a room for the night and breakfast; a place that provides this
  go to bed with sb (*informal*) to have sex with sb

bed² /bed/ **verb** [T] (**bedding; bedded**) to fix sth firmly in sth
  PHRASAL VERB **bed down** to sleep in a place where you do not usually sleep: *We couldn't find a hotel so we bedded down for the night in the van.*

bedclothes /ˈbedkləʊðz/ (*Brit also* '**bedcovers**) **noun** [pl] the sheets, covers, etc that you put on a bed

bedding /ˈbedɪŋ/ **noun** [U] everything that you put on a bed and need for sleeping

bedraggled /bɪˈdrægld/ **adj** very wet and untidy or dirty: *bedraggled hair*

bedridden /ˈbedrɪdn/ **adj** being too old or ill to get out of bed

★**bedroom** /ˈbedruːm; -rʊm/ **noun** [C] a room which is used for sleeping in: *You can sleep in the spare bedroom.* • *a three-bedroom house* ·•➤ picture on page C7

bedside /ˈbedsaɪd/ **noun** [sing] the area that is next to a bed: *She sat at his bedside all night long.* • *A book lay open on the bedside table.* ·•➤ picture on page C7

bedsit /ˈbedsɪt/ (*also* '**bedsitter**) **noun** [C] (*Brit*) a rented room which is used for both living and sleeping in

bedspread /ˈbedspred/ **noun** [C] an attractive

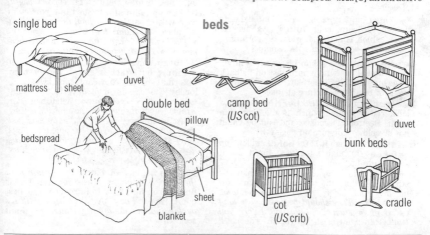

beds

single bed

mattress · sheet · duvet

double bed
pillow

camp bed
(*US* cot)

bedspread

sheet

blanket

bunk beds

duvet

cot
(*US* crib)

cradle

cover for a bed that you put on top of the sheets and other covers ··➤ picture at **bed**

bedtime /'bedtaɪm/ **noun** [U] the time that you normally go to bed

★ **bee** /biː/ **noun** [C] a black and yellow insect that lives in large groups and that makes a sweet substance that we eat (honey)

> A large number of bees together is a **swarm**. Bees **buzz** or **hum** when they make a noise. They may **sting** if they are angry. Look also at **beehive**.

··➤ picture at **honeycomb** ··➤ picture at **insect**

beech /biːtʃ/ **noun 1** (also '**beech tree**) [C] a large tree that produces small three-sided nuts **2** [U] the wood from this tree

★ **beef** /biːf/ **noun** [U] the meat from a cow: *a slice of roast beef* ··➤ Look at the note at **meat**.

beefburger /'biːfbɜːgə/ **noun** [C] beef that has been cut up small and pressed into a flat round shape ··➤ Look at **hamburger**.

beefy /'biːfi/ **adj** having a strong body with big muscles

beehive /'biːhaɪv/ (also **hive**) **noun** [C] a type of box that people use for keeping bees in

★ **been** /biːn/ *past participle* of **BE, GO¹**

> **Been** is used as the past participle of both **be** and **go**: *I've never been seriously ill.* • *I've never been to Lisbon.* **Gone** is also a past participle of **go**. Note the difference in meaning: *I'm cold because I've just been outside* (= I'm here now). • *Jim's not here, I'm afraid – he's just gone out* (= he's not here now).

beep /biːp/ **noun** [C] **beep** '**beep** a short high noise, for example made by the horn of a car –**beep verb** [I,T]: *I beeped my horn at the dog, but it wouldn't get off the road.*

beeper /'biːpə/ *(US)* → **BLEEPER**

★ **beer** /bɪə/ **noun 1** [U] a type of alcoholic drink that is made from grain **2** [C] a type or glass of beer

> **Lager** is a type of light-coloured beer, which is drunk cold. **Bitter** is a darker beer, which is drunk at room temperature. **Shandy** is beer mixed with lemonade.

beetle /'biːtl/ **noun** [C] an insect, often large, shiny and black, with a hard case on its back covering its wings. There are many different types of beetle. ··➤ picture at **insect**

beetroot /'biːtruːt/ *(US* **beet)** **noun** [C,U] a dark red vegetable which is the root of a plant. Beetroot is cooked and can be eaten hot or cold. ··➤ picture on page C3

befall /bɪˈfɔːl/ **verb** [I,T] *(pt* **befell** /bɪˈfel/; *pp* **befallen** /bɪˈfɔːlən/) *(written)* (used about sth bad) to happen to sb

★ **before¹** /bɪˈfɔː/ **prep, conj 1** earlier than sb/sth; earlier than the time that: *You can call me any time before 10 o'clock.* • *the week before last* • *They should be here before long* (= soon). • *Turn the lights off before you leave.* **2** in front of sb/sth (in an order): *'H'*

comes before 'N' in the alphabet. • *A very difficult task lies before us.* • *a company that puts profit before safety* (= thinks profit is more important than sth/sb) **3** *(formal)* in a position in front of sb/sth: *They knelt before the altar.* • *You will appear before the judge tomorrow.* **4** rather than: *I'd die before I apologized to him!*

★ **before²** /bɪˈfɔː/ **adv** at an earlier time; already: *I think we've met somewhere before.* • *It was fine yesterday but it rained the day before.*

beforehand /bɪˈfɔːhænd/ **adv** at an earlier time than sth: *If you visit us, phone beforehand to make sure we're in.*

befriend /bɪˈfrend/ **verb** [T] *(written)* to become sb's friend; to be kind to sb

beg /beg/ **verb** [I,T] (**begging**; **begged**) **1** beg (sb) for sth; beg (sb) to do sth to ask sb for sth strongly, or with great emotion: *He begged for forgiveness.* • *We begged him to lend us the money.* ··➤ synonym **entreat** or **implore 2** beg (for) sth (from sb) to ask people for food, money, etc because you are very poor: *There are people begging for food in the streets.*

[IDIOM] **I beg your pardon** *(formal)* **1** I am sorry: *I beg your pardon. I picked up your bag by mistake.* **2** used for asking sb to repeat sth because you did not hear it properly

began *past tense of* **BEGIN**

beggar /'begə/ **noun** [C] a person who lives by asking people for money, food, etc on the streets

★ **begin** /bɪˈgɪn/ **verb** *(pres part* **beginning**; *pt* **began** /bɪˈgæn/; *pp* **begun** /bɪˈgʌn/) **1** [I,T] to start doing sth; to do the first part of sth: *Shall I begin or will you?* • *I began* (= started reading) *this novel last month and I still haven't finished it.* • *When did he begin his lesson?* • *When do you begin work?* • *We began writing to each other in 1980.* • *The carpet is beginning to look dirty.* **2** [I] to start to happen or exist, especially from a particular time: *What time does the concert begin?* **3** [I] begin (with sth) to start in a particular way, with a particular event, or in a particular place: *My name begins with 'W' not 'V'.* • *The fighting began with an argument about money.* • *This is where the footpath begins.*

> **Begin** and **start** are very similar in meaning but **start** is more often used in informal speech. They can be followed by *to* or by the *-ing* form of a verb: *The baby began/started crying/to cry.* When **begin** or **start** are themselves in the *-ing* form they must be followed by *to*: *The baby was just beginning/starting to cry.* In some meanings only **start** can be used: *I couldn't start the car.* • *We'll have to start* (= leave) *early if we want to be in Dover by 8 o'clock.*

[IDIOM] **to begin with 1** at first: *To begin with they were very happy.* **2** used for giving your first reason for sth or to introduce your first point: *We can't possibly go. To begin with it's too far and we can't afford it either.* –**beginner noun** [C]

b

★**beginning** /bɪ'gɪnɪŋ/ **noun** [C] the first part of sth; the time when or the place where sth starts: *I've read the article from beginning to end.* • *We're going away at the beginning of the school holidays.*

begrudge /bɪ'grʌdʒ/ **verb** [T] **begrudge (sb) sth 1** to feel angry or upset because sb has sth that you think that he/she should not have: *He's worked hard. I don't begrudge him his success.* **2** to be unhappy that you have to do sth: *I begrudge paying so much money in tax each month.*

behalf /bɪ'hɑːf/ **noun**
IDIOM **on behalf of sb; on sb's behalf** for sb; as the representative of sb: *Emma couldn't be present so her husband accepted the prize on her behalf.* • *I would like to thank you all on behalf of my colleagues and myself.*

★**behave** /bɪ'heɪv/ **verb 1** [I] **behave well, badly, etc (towards sb)** to act in a particular way: *Don't you think that Ellen has been behaving very strangely recently?* • *I think you behaved very badly towards your father.* • *He behaves as if/though he was the boss.* **2** [I,T] **behave (yourself)** to act in the correct or appropriate way: *I want you to behave yourselves while we're away.* •➤ opposite **misbehave 3** ~~-behaved~~ (used to form compound adjectives) behaving in the way mentioned: *a well-behaved child* • *a badly-behaved class*

★**behaviour** (*US* **behavior**) /bɪ'heɪvjə/ **noun** [U] the way that you act or behave: *He was sent out of the class for bad behaviour.*

★**behind** /bɪ'haɪnd/ **prep, adv 1** in, at or to the back of sb/sth: *There's a small garden behind the house.* • *The sun went behind a cloud.* • *You go on ahead. I'll follow on behind.* • *Look behind you before you drive off.* • *He ran off but the police were close behind.* **2 behind (in/with) (sth)** later or less good than sb/sth; making less progress than sb/sth: *The train is twenty minutes behind schedule.* • *Jane is behind the rest of the class in maths.* • *We are a month behind with the rent.* •➤ Look at **ahead. 3** supporting or agreeing with sb/sth: *Whatever she decides, her family will be behind her.* **4** responsible for causing or starting sth: *What is the reason behind his sudden change of opinion?* **5** used to say that sth is in sb's past: *It's time you put your problems behind you* (= forgot about them). **6** in the place where sb/sth is or was: *Oh no! I've left the tickets behind* (= at home).

beige /beɪʒ/ **adj, noun** [U] (of) a light brown colour

being[1] ➤ BE

being[2] /'biːɪŋ/ **noun 1** [U] the state of existing; existence: *When did the organization come into being?* **2** [C] a living person or thing: *a human being*

belated /bɪ'leɪtɪd/ **adj** coming late: *a belated apology* –**belatedly** **adv**: *They have realized, rather belatedly, that they have made a mistake.*

belch /beltʃ/ **verb 1** [I] to let gas out from your stomach through your mouth with a

sudden noise **2** [T] to send out a lot of smoke, etc: *The volcano belched smoke and ashes.* –**belch noun** [C]

belie /bɪ'laɪ/ **verb** [T] (*pres part* **belying**; *3rd pers sing pres* **belies**; *pt, pp* **belied**) to give an idea of sth that is false or not true: *His smiling face belied his true feelings.*

★**belief** /bɪ'liːf/ **noun 1** [sing,U] **belief in sb/sth** a feeling that sb/sth is true, morally good or right, or that sb/sth really exists: *She has lost her belief in God.* •➤ Look at **disbelief. 2** [sing,U] (*formal*) **belief (that…)** something you accept as true; what you believe: *It's my belief that people are basically good.* • *There is a general belief that things will soon get better.* • *Contrary to popular belief* (= in spite of what many people think) *the north of the country is not poorer than the south.* **3** [C] an idea about religion, politics, etc: *Divorce is contrary to their religious beliefs.*
IDIOM **beyond belief** (in a way that is) too great, difficult, etc to be believed: *The amount of money we owe has increased beyond belief.*

believable /bɪ'liːvəbl/ **adj** that can be believed •➤ opposite **unbelievable**

★**believe** /bɪ'liːv/ **verb** (not used in the continuous tenses) **1** [T] to feel sure that sth is true or that sb is telling the truth: *He said he hadn't taken any money but I didn't believe him.* • *Nobody believes a word she says.* •➤ opposite **disbelieve 2** [T] **believe (that)…** to think that sth is true or possible, although you are not certain: *I believe they have moved to Italy.* • *'Does Pat still work there?' 'I believe so.'* • *The escaped prisoner is believed to be in this area.* • *Four people are still missing, believed drowned.* **3** don't/can't **believe sth** used to show anger or surprise at sth: *I can't believe (that) you're telling me to do it again!* **4** [I] to have religious beliefs

➤ Although this verb is not used in the continuous tenses, it is common to see the present participle (= *-ing* form): *Believing the house to be empty, she quietly let herself in.*

IDIOMS **believe it or not** it may be surprising but it is true: *Believe it or not, English food can sometimes be quite good.*
give sb to believe/understand (that) (often passive) to give sb the impression or idea that sth is true: *I was given to believe that I had got the job.*
PHRASAL VERBS **believe in sb/sth** to be sure that sb/sth exists: *Do you believe in God?* • *Most young children believe in Father Christmas.*
believe in sb/sth; believe in doing sth to think that sb/sth is good or right: *They need a leader they can believe in.* • *He doesn't believe in killing animals for their fur.*

believer /bɪ'liːvə/ **noun** [C] a person who has religious beliefs
IDIOM **be a (great/firm) believer in sth** to think that sth is good or right: *He is a great believer in getting things done on time.*

belittle /bɪ'lɪtl/ **verb** [T] to make sb or the

things he/she does, seem unimportant or not very good

★**bell** /bel/ noun [C] **1** a metal object, often shaped like a cup, that makes a ringing sound when it is hit by a small piece of metal inside it: *the sound of church bells* ● *Her voice came back* **clear as a bell**. ·➤ picture on page S9 **2** an electrical device that makes a ringing sound when the button on it is pushed; the sound that it makes: *Ring the doorbell and see if they're in.*
IDIOM ring a bell → RING²

bellow /'beləʊ/ verb **1** [I,T] bellow (sth) (at sb) to shout in a loud deep voice, especially because you are angry **2** [I] to make a deep low sound, like an animal (a bull) –bellow noun [C]

belly /'beli/ noun [C] (*pl* bellies) the stomach or the front part of your body between your chest and your legs

'**belly button** (*informal*) = NAVEL

★**belong** /bɪ'lɒŋ/ verb [I] **1** belong to sb to be owned by sb: *Who does this pen belong to?* ● *Don't take anything that doesn't belong to you.* **2** belong to sth to be a member of a group or organization: *Do you belong to any political party?* **3** to have a right or usual place: *The plates belong in the cupboard over there.* ● *It took quite a long time before we felt we belonged in the village* (= until we felt comfortable).

belongings /bɪ'lɒŋɪŋz/ noun [pl] the things that you own that can be moved, that is, not land and buildings: *They lost all their belongings in the fire.*

beloved /bɪ'lʌvd; bɪ'lʌvɪd/ adj (*formal*) much loved: *They had always intended to return to their beloved Ireland.*
➤ When 'beloved' comes before a noun, the pronunciation is /bɪ'lʌvɪd/.

★**below** /bɪ'ləʊ/ prep, adv at or to a lower position or level than sb/sth: *Do not write below this line.* ● *The temperature fell below freezing during the night.* ● *Her marks in the exam were below average.* ● *I don't live on the top floor. I live on the floor below.* ● *temperatures of 30° and below* ·➤ Look at the note at **under**. ·➤ opposite **above**

★**belt¹** /belt/ noun [C] **1** a thin piece of cloth, leather, etc that you wear around your waist: *I need a belt to keep these trousers up.* ·➤ picture on page C6 ·➤ Look at **seat belt**. **2** a long narrow piece of rubber, cloth, etc in a circle, that is used for carrying things along or for making parts of a machine move: *The suitcases were carried round on a* **conveyor belt**. ● *the* **fan belt** *of a car* (= that operates the machinery that cools a car engine) **3** an area of land that has a particular quality or where a particular group of people live: *the* **green belt** *around London* (= an area of countryside where you are not allowed to build houses, factories, etc) ● *the commuter belt*
IDIOMS below the belt (*informal*) unfair or cruel: *That remark was rather below the belt.*
tighten your belt → TIGHTEN

under your belt (*informal*) that you have already done or achieved: *She's already got four tournament wins under her belt.*

belt² /belt/ verb [T] (*informal*) **1** to hit sb hard **2** to run or go somewhere very fast: *I was belting along on my bicycle.*
PHRASAL VERBS belt sth out to sing, shout or play sth loudly: *In the restaurant, loudspeakers were belting out Spanish pop music.*
belt up (*slang*) used to tell sb rudely to be quiet: *Belt up! I can't think with all this noise.*

bemused /bɪ'mju:zd/ adj confused and unable to think clearly

★**bench** /bentʃ/ noun [C] **1** a long wooden or metal seat for two or more people, often outdoors: *a park bench* **2** (in the British parliament) the seats where a particular group of politicians sit: *the Government* **front bench** ● *the Labour* **back benches** **3** a long narrow table that people work at; for example, in a factory

benchmark /'bentʃmɑːk/ noun [C] a standard that other things can be compared to: *These new safety features set a benchmark for other manufacturers to follow.*

★**bend¹** /bend/ verb (*pt, pp* bent /bent/) **1** [T] to make sth that was straight into a curved shape: *to bend a piece of wire into an S shape* ● *It hurts when I bend my knee.* **2** [I] to be or become curved: *The road bends to the left here.* **3** [I] to move your body forwards and downwards: *He* **bent down** *to tie up his shoelaces.* ·➤ picture on page S2
IDIOM bend the rules to do sth that is not normally allowed by the rules

★**bend²** /bend/ noun [C] a curve or turn, for example in a road: *a sharp bend in the road*
IDIOM round the bend (*informal*) crazy; mad: *His behaviour is* **driving me round the bend** (= annoying me very much).

★**beneath** /bɪ'niːθ/ prep, adv **1** in, at or to a lower position than sb/sth; under: *The ship disappeared beneath the waves.* ● *He seemed a nice person but there was a lot of anger beneath the surface.* ·➤ Look at the note at **under**. **2** not good enough for sb: *She felt that cleaning for other people was beneath her.*

benefactor /'benɪfæktə/ noun [C] a person who helps or gives money to a person or an organization

beneficial /ˌbenɪ'fɪʃl/ adj beneficial (to sb/ sth) having a good or useful effect: *A good diet is beneficial to health.*

★**benefit¹** /'benɪfɪt/ noun **1** [U,C] an advantage or useful effect that sth has: *A change in the law would be to everyone's benefit.* ● *I can't see the* **benefit of** *doing things this way.* ● *the benefits of modern technology* **2** [U] (*Brit*) money that the government gives to people who are ill, poor, unemployed, etc: *child/ sickness/housing benefit* ● *I'm not entitled to unemployment benefit.* **3** [C,usually pl] advantages that you get from your company in addition to the money you earn: *a company car and other benefits*
IDIOMS for sb's benefit especially to help, please, etc sb: *For the benefit of the new-*

comers, I will start again.

give sb the benefit of the doubt to believe what sb says although there is no proof that it is true

benefit² /'benɪfɪt/ *verb* (**benefiting**; **benefited** or **benefitting**; **benefitted**) **1** [T] to produce a good or useful effect: *The new tax laws will benefit people on low wages.* **2** [I] **benefit (from sth)** to receive an advantage from sth: *Small businesses have benefited from the changes in the law.*

benevolent /bə'nevələnt/ *adj* (*formal*) kind, friendly and helpful to others –**benevolence** *noun* [U]

benign /bɪ'naɪn/ *adj* **1** (used about people) kind or gentle **2** (used about a disease, etc) not dangerous: *a benign tumour* ••➤ opposite **malignant**

bent¹ *past tense, past participle* of **BEND¹**

bent² /bent/ *adj* **1** not straight: *Do this exercise with your knees bent.* • *This knife is bent.* • *It was so funny we were bent double with laughter.* **2** (*Brit informal*) (used about a person in authority) dishonest; corrupt: *a bent policeman*

IDIOM **bent on sth/on doing sth** wanting to do sth very much; determined: *They seem bent on moving house, whatever the difficulties.*

bent³ /bent/ *noun* [sing] **a bent for sth/doing sth** a natural skill at sth or interest in sth: *She has a bent for music.*

bequeath /bɪ'kwi:ð/ *verb* [T] (*formal*) **bequeath sth (to sb)** to arrange for sth to be given to sb after you have died: *He bequeathed £1000 to his favourite charity.* ••➤ **Leave** is a more common word.

bequest /bɪ'kwest/ *noun* [C] (*formal*) something that you arrange to be given to sb after you have died: *He left a bequest to each of his grandchildren.*

bereaved /bɪ'ri:vd/ *adj* **1** having lost a relative or close friend who has recently died **2 the bereaved** *noun* [pl] the people whose relative or close friend has died recently

bereavement /bɪ'ri:vmənt/ *noun* (*formal*) **1** [U] the state of having lost a relative or close friend who has recently died **2** [C] the death of a relative or close friend: *There has been a bereavement in the family.*

beret /'bereɪ/ *noun* [C] a soft flat round hat ••➤ picture at **hat**

★**berry** /'beri/ *noun* [C] (*pl* **berries**) a small soft fruit with seeds: *Those berries are poisonous.* • *a raspberry/strawberry/blueberry*

berserk /bə'zɜ:k/ *adj* (not before a noun) very angry; crazy: *If the teacher finds out what you've done he'll* **go berserk**.

berth /bɜ:θ/ *noun* [C] **1** a place for sleeping on a ship or train: *a cabin with four berths* **2** a place where a ship can stop and stay

beset /bɪ'set/ (*pres part* **besetting**; *pt, pp* **beset**) *verb* [T] (*written*) to affect sb/sth in a bad way: *The team has been beset by injuries all season.*

★**beside** /bɪ'saɪd/ *prep* at the side of, or next to sb/sth: *Come and sit beside me.* • *He kept his bag close beside him at all times.*

IDIOMS **beside the point** not connected with the subject you are discussing

beside yourself (with sth) not able to control yourself because of a very strong emotion: *Emily was almost beside herself with grief.*

besides /bɪ'saɪdz/ *prep, adv* in addition to or as well as sb/sth; also: *There will be six people coming, besides you and David.* • *I don't want to go out tonight. Besides, I haven't got any money.*

besiege /bɪ'si:dʒ/ *verb* [T] **1** to surround a place with an army **2** (usually passive) (used about sth unpleasant or annoying) to surround sb/sth in large numbers: *The actor was besieged by fans and reporters.*

besotted /bɪ'sɒtɪd/ *adj* (not before a noun) **besotted (with/by sb/sth)** so much in love with sb/sth that you cannot think or behave normally

★**best¹** /best/ *adj* (the superlative of *good*) of the highest quality or level; most suitable: *His latest book is by far his best.* • *I'm going to wear my best shirt to the interview.* • *Who in the class is best at maths?* • *It's best to arrive early if you want a good seat.* • *What's the best way to get to York from here?* • *Who's your best friend?*

IDIOMS **your best bet** (*informal*) the most sensible or appropriate thing for you to do in a particular situation: *There's nowhere to park in the city centre. Your best bet is to go in by bus.*

the best/better part of sth → **PART¹**

★**best²** /best/ *adv* (the superlative of *well*) to the greatest degree; most: *He works best in the morning.* • *Which of these dresses do you like best?* • *one of Britain's best-loved TV stars*

IDIOM **as best you can** as well as you can even if it is not perfectly

★**best³** /best/ *noun* [sing] **the best** the person or thing that is of the highest quality or level or better than all others: *When you pay that much for a meal you expect the best.* • *Even the best of us make mistakes sometimes.* • *I think James is the best!* • *They are the best of friends.* • *The best we can hope for is that the situation doesn't get any worse.* ••➤ Look at **second-best**.

IDIOMS **all the best** (*informal*) used when you are saying goodbye to sb and wishing him/her success: *All the best! Keep in touch, won't you?*

at best if everything goes as well as possible; taking the most hopeful view: *We won't be able to deliver the goods before March, or, at best, the last week in February.*

at its/your best in its/your best state or condition: *This is an example of Beckett's work at its best.* • *No one is at their best first thing in the morning.*

be (all) for the best to be good in the end even if it does not seem good at first: *I didn't get the job, but I'm sure it's all for the best.*

bring out the best/worst in sb to show sb's

best/worst qualities: *The crisis really brought out the best in Tony.*

do/try your best to do all or the most that you can

look your best to look as beautiful or attractive as possible

make the best of sth/a bad job to accept a difficult situation and try to be as happy as possible

best 'man noun [sing] a man who helps and supports the man who is getting married (bridegroom) at a wedding •➤ Look at the note at **wedding**.

best-'seller noun [C] a book or other product that is bought by large numbers of people –'**best-selling** adj: *a best-selling novel*

★**bet¹** /bet/ verb [I,T] (*pres part* **betting**; *pt, pp* **bet** or **betted**) **1** bet (sth) (on sth) to risk money on a race or an event by trying to predict the result. If you are right, you win money: *I wouldn't bet on them winning the next election.* • *I bet him £10 he couldn't stop smoking for a week.* •➤ synonym **gamble** or **put money on sth 2** (*spoken*) used to say that you are almost certain that sth is true or that sth will happen: *I bet he arrives late – he always does.* • *I bet you're worried about your exam, aren't you?*

IDIOM **you bet** (*spoken*) a way of saying 'Yes, of course!': *'Are you coming too?' 'You bet (I am)!'*

bet² /bet/ noun [C] **1** an act of betting: *Did you have a bet on that race?* • *to win/lose a bet* **2** an opinion: *My bet is that he's missed the train.*

IDIOMS **your best bet** → **BEST¹**

hedge your bets → **HEDGE²**

betide /bɪ'taɪd/ verb

IDIOM **woe betide sb** → **WOE**

betray /bɪ'treɪ/ verb [T] **1** to give information about sb/sth to an enemy; to make a secret known: *She betrayed all the members of the group to the secret police.* • *He refused to betray their plans.* • *to betray your country* •➤ Look at the note at **traitor**. **2** to hurt sb who trusts you, especially by not being loyal or faithful to him/her: *If you take the money you'll betray her trust.* • *When parents get divorced the children often feel betrayed.* **3** to show a feeling or quality that you would like to keep hidden: *Her steady voice did not betray the emotion she was feeling.* –**betrayal** /bɪ'treɪəl/ noun [C,U]

★**better¹** /'betə/ adj **1** (the comparative of *good*) better than sb/sth of a higher quality or level or more suitable for sb/sth: *I think her second novel was much better than her first.* • *He's far better at English than me.* • *It's a long way to drive. It would be better to take the train.* • *You'd be better getting the train than driving.* **2** (the comparative of *well*) less ill; fully recovered from an illness: *You can't go swimming until you're better.*

★**better²** /'betə/ adv (the comparative of *well*) in a better way; to a greater or higher degree: *I think you could have done this better.* • *Syl-*

vie speaks English better than I do.

IDIOMS **(be) better off 1** to be in a more pleasant or suitable situation: *You look terrible. You'd be better off at home in bed.* **2** (comparative of *well off*) with more money: *We're much better off now I go out to work too.*

the best/better part of sth → **PART¹**

you, etc had better you should; you ought to: *I think we'd better go before it gets dark.* • *You'd better take a pen and paper – you might want to take notes.*

know better (than that/than to do sth) → **KNOW¹**

think better of (doing) sth → **THINK**

★**better³** /'betə/ noun [sing] something that is of higher quality: *The hotel wasn't very good. I must say we'd expected better.*

IDIOM **get the better of sb/sth** to defeat or be stronger than sb/sth: *When we have an argument she always gets the better of me.*

betting shop noun [C] a shop where you can go to put money on a race or an event •➤ Look at **bookmaker's**.

between/among

a plant growing
between the slabs

a plant growing
among the rocks

★**between** /bɪ'twiːn/ prep, adv **1** between A and B; in between in the space in the middle of two things, people, places etc: *I was sitting between Sam and Charlie.* • *a village between Cambridge and Ely* • *She was standing in between the desk and the wall.* **2** between A and B; in between (used about two amounts, distances, ages, times, etc) at a point that is greater or later than the first and smaller or earlier than the second; somewhere in the middle: *They said they would arrive between 4 and 5 o'clock.* • *They've got this shirt in size 10 and size 16, but nothing in between.* **3** from one place to another and back again: *There aren't any direct trains between here and Manchester.* **4** involving or connecting two people, groups or things: *There's some sort of disagreement between them.* • *There may be a connection between the two crimes.* **5** choosing one and not the other (of two things): *to choose between two jobs* • *What's the difference between 'some' and 'any'?* **6** by putting together the actions, efforts, etc of two or more people: *Between us we saved up enough money to buy a car.* **7** giving each person a share: *The money was divided equally between the two children.* • *We ate all the chocolates between us.*

➤ **Between** is usually used of two people or things: *sitting between her mother and father*

• *between the ages of 12 and 14.* However, **between** can sometimes be used of more than two when the people or things are being considered as individuals, especially when the meaning is that of number 7 (above): *We drank a bottle of wine between the three of us.* **Among** is always used of more than two people or things considered as a group rather than as individuals: *You're among friends here.*

beverage /'bevərɪdʒ/ **noun** [C] (*written*) a drink

beware /bɪ'weə/ **verb** [I] (only in the imperative or infinitive) **beware (of sb/sth)** (used for giving a warning) to be careful: *Beware of the dog!* (= written on a sign) • *We were told to beware of strong currents in the sea.*

bewilder /bɪ'wɪldə/ **verb** [T] to confuse and surprise: *I was completely bewildered by his sudden change of mood.* –**bewildered** adj: *a bewildered expression* –**bewildering** adj: *a bewildering experience* –**bewilderment** noun [U]: *to stare at sb in bewilderment*

bewitch /bɪ'wɪtʃ/ **verb** [T] to attract and interest sb very much

★**beyond** /bɪ'jɒnd/ **prep, adv 1** on or to the other side of: *beyond the distant mountains* • *We could see the mountains and the sea beyond.* **2** further than; later than: *Does the motorway continue beyond Birmingham?* • *Most people don't go on working beyond the age of 65.* **3** more than sth: *The house was far beyond what I could afford.* • *I haven't heard anything beyond a few rumours.* **4** used to say that sth is not possible: *The car was completely beyond repair* (= too badly damaged to repair). • *The situation is beyond my control.* **5** too far or too advanced for sb/sth: *The activity was beyond the students' abilities.*
[IDIOM] **be beyond sb** (*informal*) to be impossible for sb to understand or imagine: *Why she wants to go and live there is quite beyond me.*

bias¹ /'baɪəs/ **noun** (*pl* **biases**) **1** [C,U] a strong feeling of favour towards or against one group of people, or on one side in an argument, often not based on fair judgement or facts: *a bias against women drivers* • *The BBC has been accused of **political bias**.* **2** [C, usually sing] an interest in one thing more than others; a special ability: *a course with a strong scientific bias*

bias² /'baɪəs/ **verb** [T] (**biasing**; **biased** or **biassing**; **biassed**) to influence sb/sth, especially unfairly; to give an advantage to one group, etc: *Good newspapers should not be biased towards a particular political party.* –**biased** adj: *a biased report*

bib /bɪb/ **noun** [C] a piece of cloth or plastic that a baby or small child wears under the chin to protect its clothes while it is eating

the Bible /'baɪbl/ **noun** [C] the book of great religious importance to Christian and Jewish people –**biblical** /'bɪblɪkl/ adj

bibliography /ˌbɪbli'ɒɡrəfi/ **noun** [C] (*pl* **bibliographies**) **1** a list of the books and articles that a writer used when he/she was writing a particular book or article **2** a list of books on a particular subject

bicentenary /ˌbaɪsen'ti:nəri/ (*US* **bicentennial** /ˌbaɪsen'teniəl/) **noun** [C] (*pl* **bicentenaries**) the day or the year two hundred years after sth happened or began: *the bicentenary of the French Revolution*

biceps /'baɪseps/ **noun** [C] (*pl* **biceps**) the large muscle at the front of the upper part of your arms

bicker /'bɪkə/ **verb** [I] to argue about unimportant things: *My parents are always bickering about money.*

★**bicycle** /'baɪsɪkl/ (also **bike**) **noun** [C] a vehicle with two wheels, which you sit on and ride by moving your legs •➤ Look at the note at **bike**. A **cyclist** is a person who rides a bicycle. •➤ picture on page S9

bid¹ /bɪd/ **verb** (**bidding**; *pt, pp* **bid**) [I,T] **bid (sth) (for sth)** to offer to pay a particular price for sth, especially at a public sale where things are sold to the person who offers most money (an **auction**): *I wanted to buy the vase but another man was **bidding against** me.* • *Somebody bid £5000 for the painting.*

bid² /bɪd/ **noun** [C] **1** a bid (for sth); a bid (to do sth) an effort to do, obtain, etc sth; an attempt: *His bid for freedom had failed.* • *Tonight the Ethiopian athlete will **make a bid** to break the world record.* **2** an offer by a person or a business company to pay a certain amount of money for sth: *Granada mounted a hostile **takeover bid*** (= when one company tries to buy another company) *for Forte.* • *At the auction we **made a bid** of £100 for the chair.* **3** (*especially US*) = **TENDER²** –**bidder** noun [C]: *The house was sold to the highest bidder* (= the person who offered the most money).

bide /baɪd/ **verb**
[IDIOM] **bide your time** to wait for a good opportunity: *I'll bide my time until the situation improves.*

bidet /'bi:deɪ/ **noun** [C] a large bowl in the bathroom that you can sit on in order to wash your bottom

biennial /baɪ'eniəl/ **adj** happening once every two years

★**big** /bɪɡ/ **adj** (**bigger**; **biggest**) **1** large; not small: *a big house/town/salary* • *This dress is too big for me.* **2** great or important: *They had a big argument yesterday.* • *That was the biggest decision I've ever had to make.* • *some of the big names in Hollywood* **3** (only *before* a noun) (*informal*) older: *a big brother/sister*

> **Big** and **large** can both be used when talking about size or number. **Large** is more formal and is not usually used for describing people: *a big/large house* • *a big baby*. **Great** is mostly used when talking about the importance, quality, etc of a person or thing: *a great occasion/musician*. It can also be used with uncountable nouns to mean 'a lot of': *great happiness/care/sorrow*. It can also be used to emphasize an adjective of size, quantity, etc. Look at **great¹**(4).

b

••➤ opposite **small**

IDIOMS **Big Deal!** (*informal*) used to say that you think sth is not important or interesting: *'Look at my new bike!' 'Big deal! It's not as nice as mine.'*
a big deal/no big deal (*informal*) something that is (not) very important or exciting: *Birthday celebrations are a big deal in our family.* ● *A 2% pay increase is no big deal.*
give sb a big hand → HAND¹

bigamy /'bɪgəmi/ **noun** [U] the crime of being married to two people at the same time –**bigamist noun** [C]

'big-head (*informal*) **noun** [C] a person who thinks he/she is very important or clever because of sth he/she has done –**big-'headed adj**

'big mouth (*informal*) **noun** [C] a person who talks too much and cannot keep a secret

bigot /'bɪgət/ **noun** [C] a person who has very strong and unreasonable opinions and refuses to change them or listen to other people: *a religious/racial bigot* –**bigoted adj** –**bigotry** /'bɪgətri/ **noun** [U]

the 'big time noun [sing] success; fame: *This is the role that could help her make it to the big time in Hollywood.*

'big time¹ adv (*especially US slang*) very much: *You screwed up big time, Wayne!*

'big-time² adj (only *before* a noun) important or famous: *a big-time drug dealer/politician*

★**bike** /baɪk/ **noun** [C] a bicycle or a motorbike: *Hasan's just learnt to ride a bike.*

➤ Note that we **go on** a/your **bike** or **by bike**. You can also use the verbs **ride** and **cycle**.

••➤ picture on page S9

bikini /bɪ'ki:ni/ **noun** [C] a piece of clothing, in two pieces, that women wear for swimming ••➤ picture on page C6

bilingual /ˌbaɪ'lɪŋgwəl/ **adj 1** having or using two languages: *a bilingual dictionary* ••➤ Look at **monolingual**. **2** able to speak two languages equally well: *Our children are bilingual in English and Spanish.*

★**bill¹** /bɪl/ **noun 1** [C] (*US* **check**) a piece of paper that shows how much money you owe for goods or services: *an electricity bill* ● *Can I have the bill, please?* (= in a restaurant) ● *to pay a bill* **2** [C] (*US*) = NOTE¹(4): *a ten-dollar bill* **3** [C] a plan for a possible new law: *The bill was passed/defeated.* **4** [sing] the programme of entertainment offered in a show, concert, etc: *Which bands are on the bill at the festival?* **5** [C] a bird's beak ••➤ picture on page C1

IDIOM **foot the bill** → FOOT²

bill² /bɪl/ **verb** [T] (usually passive) **bill sb/sth as sth** to describe sb/sth to the public in an advertisement, etc: *This young player is being billed as 'the new Pele'.*

billboard /'bɪlbɔ:d/ (*Brit* also **hoarding**) **noun** [C] a large board near a road where advertisements are put

billfold /'bɪlfəʊld/ (*US*) = WALLET

billiards /'bɪliədz/ **noun** [U] a game played on

a big table covered with cloth. You use a long stick (**a cue**) to hit three balls against each other and into pockets at the corners and sides of the table: *to have a game of/play billiards* ••➤ Note that when **billiard** comes before another noun it has no 's': *a billiard table* ••➤ Look at **snooker** and **pool¹**(5).

★**billion** /'bɪljən/ **number** 1 000 000 000: *billions of dollars*

➤ Notice that when you are counting you use billion without 's': *three billion yen* Formerly, 'billion' was used with the meaning 'one million million'. We now say **trillion** for this.
For more information about numbers look at the special section on numbers at the back of this dictionary.

billow /'bɪləʊ/ **verb** [I] **1** to fill with air and move in the wind: *curtains billowing in the breeze* **2** to move in large clouds through the air: *Smoke billowed from the chimneys.*

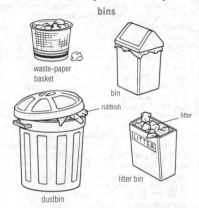
bins

waste-paper basket
bin
rubbish
litter
litter bin
dustbin

bin /bɪn/ **noun** [C] **1** a container that you put rubbish in: *to throw sth in the bin* ● *a litter bin* ● *The dustmen come to empty the bins on Wednesdays.* **2** a container, usually with a lid, for storing bread, flour, etc: *a bread bin*

binary system /'baɪnəri sɪstəm/ **noun** [sing] (*technical*) a system of numbers using only the numbers 0 and 1. It is used especially with computers.

bind¹ /baɪnd/ **verb** [T] (*pt, pp* **bound** /baʊnd/) **1 bind sb/sth (to sb/sth); bind A and B (together)** to tie or fasten with string or rope: *They bound the prisoner's hands behind his back.* **2 bind A to B; bind A and B (together)** to unite people, organizations, etc so that they live or work together more happily or with better effect: *The two countries are bound together by a common language.* **3 bind sb (to sth)** to force sb to do sth by making him/her promise to do it or by making it his/her duty to do it: *to be bound by a law/an agreement* ● *The contract binds you to completion of the work within two years.* **4** (usually passive) to fasten sheets of paper into a cover to form a book: *The book was bound in leather*.

bind² /baɪnd/ **noun** [sing] (*Brit informal*) something that you find boring or annoying; a nuisance: *I find housework a real bind.*

binding¹ /'baɪndɪŋ/ **adj** making it necessary for sb to do sth he/she has promised or to obey a law, etc: *This contract is legally binding*.

binding² /'baɪndɪŋ/ **noun 1** [C] a cover that holds the pages of a book together **2** [C,U] material that you fasten to the edge of sth to protect or decorate it **3 bindings** [pl] (used in skiing) a device that fastens a ski boot to a ski •➤ Look at **picture** at **ski**

binge¹ /bɪndʒ/ **noun** [C] (*informal*) a period of eating or drinking too much: *to˙go on a binge*

binge² /bɪndʒ/ **verb** [I] (*pres part* **bingeing** or **binging**) (*informal*) binge (on sth) to eat or drink too much, especially without being able to control yourself: *When she's depressed she binges on chocolate*

bingo /'bɪŋgəʊ/ **noun** [U] a game in which each player has a different card with numbers on it. The person in charge of the game calls numbers out and the winner is the first player to have all the numbers on their card called out.

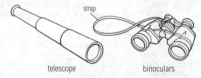

telescope   binoculars

binoculars /bɪ'nɒkjələz/ **noun** [pl] an instrument with two glass parts (**lenses**) which you look through in order to make objects in the distance seem nearer: *a pair of binoculars* •➤ Look at **telescope**.

biochemistry /ˌbaɪəʊ'kemɪstri/ **noun** [U] the study of the chemistry of living things

biodegradable /ˌbaɪəʊdɪ'greɪdəbl/ **adj** that can be absorbed back into the earth naturally and so not harm the environment •➤ opposite **non-biodegradable**

biogas /'baɪəgæs/ **noun** [U] gas produced by natural waste, that can be used as fuel

biographer /baɪ'ɒɡrəfə/ **noun** [C] a person who writes the story of sb else's life

biography /baɪ'ɒɡrəfi/ **noun** [C,U] (*pl* **biographies**) the story of a person's life written by sb else: *a biography of Napoleon* • *I enjoy reading science fiction and biography*. •➤ Look at **autobiography**. –**biographical** /ˌbaɪə'ɡræfɪkl/ **adj**

biological /ˌbaɪə'lɒdʒɪkl/ **adj 1** connected with the scientific study of animals, plants and other living things: *biological research* **2** involving the use of living things to destroy or damage other living things: *biological weapons*

biology /baɪ'ɒlədʒi/ **noun** [U] the scientific study of living things •➤ Look at **botany** and **zoology**. –**biologist noun** [C]

birch /bɜːtʃ/ **noun 1** (also **birch tree**) [C] a type of tree with smooth thin branches **2** [U] the wood from this tree

★**bird** /bɜːd/ **noun** [C] a creature with feathers and wings which can (usually) fly •➤ picture on page C1

➤ Birds **fly** and **sing**. They build **nests** and lay **eggs**.

IDIOM **kill two birds with one stone** → **KILL¹**

,**bird of 'prey noun** [C] a bird that kills and eats other animals and birds

birdwatcher /'bɜːdwɒtʃə/ **noun** [C] a person who studies birds in their natural surroundings •➤ The formal word is **ornithologist**. –**birdwatching noun** [U]

biro™ /'baɪrəʊ/ **noun** [C] (*pl* **biros**) a type of pen in which ink comes out of a small metal ball at the end •➤ Look at **ballpoint**.

★**birth** /bɜːθ/ **noun 1** [C,U] being born; coming out of a mother's body: *It was a difficult birth.* • *The baby weighed 3 kilos at birth* (= when it was born). • *What's your date of birth?* (= the date on which you were born) **2** [U] the country you belong to: *She's always lived in England but she's German by birth.* **3** [sing] the beginning of sth: *the birth of an idea*

IDIOM **give birth (to sb)** to produce a baby: *She gave birth to her second child at home.*

'**birth certificate noun** [C] an official document that states the date and place of a person's birth and the names of his/her parents

'**birth control noun** [U] ways of limiting the number of children you have •➤ Look at **contraception** and **family planning**.

★**birthday** /'bɜːθdeɪ/ **noun** [C] the day in each year which is the same date as the one when you were born: *My birthday's on November 15th.* • *my eighteenth birthday* • *a birthday present/card/cake*

➤ An **anniversary** is not the same as a **birthday**. It is the day in each year which is the same date as an important past event: *our wedding anniversary* • *the anniversary of the end of the war.*
When it is a person's birthday we say **Happy Birthday!** If we know the person well we send a special card to him/her or a present. Your eighteenth birthday is an important occasion when you legally become an adult.

birthmark /'bɜːθmɑːk/ **noun** [C] a red or brown mark on a person's body that has been there since he/she was born

birthplace /'bɜːθpleɪs/ **noun 1** [C] the house or town where a person was born **2** [sing] the place where sth began: *Greece is the birthplace of the Olympic Games.*

'**birth rate noun** [C] the number of babies born in a particular group of people during a particular period of time

★**biscuit** /'bɪskɪt/ **noun** [C] **1** a (*US* **cookie**) a type of small cake that is thin, hard and usually sweet: *a chocolate biscuit* • *a packet of biscuits* •➤ picture at **cake 2** (*US*) a type of small simple cake that is not sweet

b

bisexual /ˌbaɪˈsekʃuəl/ **adj** sexually attracted to both men and women •➤ Look at **heterosexual** and **homosexual**.

bishop /ˈbɪʃəp/ **noun** [C] a priest with a high position in some branches of the Christian Church, who is responsible for all the churches in a city or a district •➤ Look at **archbishop**.

★ **bit¹** /bɪt/ **noun 1 a bit** [sing] slightly, a little: *I was a bit annoyed with him.* ● *I'm afraid I'll be a little bit late tonight.* ● *Could you be a bit quieter, please?* **2 a bit** [sing] a short time or distance: *Could you move forward a bit?* ● *I'm just going out for a bit.* **3 a bit** [sing] (*informal*) a lot: *It must have rained quite a bit during the night.* **4** [C] a bit of sth a small piece, amount or part of sth: *There were bits of broken glass all over the floor.* ● *Could you give me a bit of advice?* ● *Which bit of the film did you like best?* **5** [C] (*computing*) the smallest unit of information that is stored in a computer's memory **6** [C] a metal bar that you put in a horse's mouth when you ride it •➤ picture at **horse**

IDIOMS **bit by bit** slowly or a little at a time: *Bit by bit we managed to get the information we needed.*

a bit much (*informal*) annoying or unpleasant: *It's a bit much expecting me to work on Sundays.*

a bit of a (*informal*) rather a: *I've got a bit of a problem...*

bits and pieces (*informal*) small things of different kinds: *I've finished packing except for a few bits and pieces.*

do your bit (*informal*) to do your share of sth; to help with sth: *It won't take long to finish if we all do our bit.*

not a bit not at all: *The holiday was not a bit what we had expected.*

to bits 1 into small pieces: *She angrily tore the letter to bits.* **2** very; very much: *I was thrilled to bits when I won the competition.*

bit² past tense of **BITE¹**

bitch¹ /bɪtʃ/ **verb** [I] (*informal*) **bitch (about sb/sth)** to say unkind and critical things about sb, especially when he/she is not there: *She's not the kind of person who would bitch about you behind your back.*

bitch² /bɪtʃ/ **noun** [C] a female dog

bitchy /ˈbɪtʃi/ **adj** talking about other people in an unkind way: *a bitchy remark*

★ **bite¹** /baɪt/ **verb** (*pt* **bit** /bɪt/; *pp* **bitten** /ˈbɪtn/) **1** [I,T] **bite (into sth)**; **bite (sb/sth)** to cut or attack sb/sth with your teeth: *Don't worry about the dog – she never bites.* ● *The cat bit me.* ● *He picked up the bread and bit into it hungrily.* •➤ picture at **lick 2** [T] (used about some insects and animals) to push a sharp point into your skin and cause pain: *He was bitten by a snake/mosquito/spider.*

➤ Wasps, bees and jellyfish do not **bite** you. They **sting** you.

3 [I] to begin to have an unpleasant effect: *In the South the job losses are starting to bite.*

IDIOM **bite sb's head off** to answer sb in a very angry way

★ **bite²** /baɪt/ **noun 1** [C] a piece of food that you can put into your mouth: *She took a big bite of the apple.* **2** [C] a painful place on the skin made by an insect, snake, dog, etc: *I'm covered in mosquito bites.* **3** [sing] (*informal*) a small meal; a snack: *Would you like a bite to eat before you go?*

bitten past tense of **BITE¹**

★ **bitter¹** /ˈbɪtə/ **adj 1** caused by anger or hatred: *a bitter quarrel* **2 bitter (about sth)** (used about a person) very unhappy or angry about sth that has happened because you feel you have been treated unfairly: *She was very bitter about not getting the job.* **3** causing unhappiness or anger for a long time; difficult to accept: *Failing the exam was a bitter disappointment to him.* ● *I've learnt from bitter experience not to trust him.* **4** having a sharp, unpleasant taste; not sweet: *bitter coffee* **5** (used about the weather) very cold: *a bitter wind* –**bitterness** **noun** [U] anger and unhappiness as a result of sth bad happening

bitter² /ˈbɪtə/ **noun** [U] (*Brit*) a type of dark beer that is popular in Britain: *A pint of bitter, please.*

bitterly /ˈbɪtəli/ **adv 1** (used for describing strong negative feelings or cold weather) extremely: *bitterly disappointed/resentful/disappointed* ● *a bitterly cold winter/wind* **2** in an angry and disappointed way: *'I've lost everything,' he said bitterly.*

bitty /ˈbɪti/ **adj** made up of lots of parts which do not seem to be connected: *Your essay is rather bitty.*

bizarre /bɪˈzɑː/ **adj** very strange: *The story had a most bizarre ending.*

bk (*pl* **bks**) **abbr** book

★ **black¹** /blæk/ **adj 1** of the darkest colour, like night or coal **2** belonging to a race of people with dark skins: *the black population of Britain* ● *black culture* **3** (used about coffee or tea) without milk or cream: *black coffee with sugar* **4** very angry: *to give sb a black look* **5** (used about a situation) without hope; depressing: *The economic outlook for the coming year is rather black.* **6** funny in a cruel or unpleasant way: *The film was a black comedy.*

IDIOMS **black and blue** covered with blue, brown or purple marks on the body (**bruises**) because you have been hit by sb/sth

black and white (used about television, photographs, etc) showing no colours except black, white and grey

★ **black²** /blæk/ **noun 1** [U] the darkest colour, like night or coal: *People often wear black* (= black clothes) *at funerals.* **2** (usually **Black**) [C] a person who belongs to a race of people with dark skins –**blackness** **noun** [U]

IDIOMS **be in the black** to have some money in the bank •➤ opposite **be in the red**

in black and white in writing or in print: *I won't believe we've got the contract till I see it in black and white.*

black³ /blæk/ **verb**

PHRASAL VERB **black out** to lose consciousness for a short time

blackberry /'blækbəri/ *noun* [C] (*pl black-berries*) a small black fruit that grows wild on bushes •⇥ picture on page C3

blackbird /'blækbɜːd/ *noun* [C] a common European bird. The male is black with a yellow beak and the female is brown.

blackboard /'blækbɔːd/ (*US* **chalkboard**) *noun* [C] a piece of dark board used for writing on with chalk, which is used in a class

blackcurrant /ˌblækˈkʌrənt/ *noun* [C] a small round black fruit that grows on bushes

blacken /'blækən/ *verb* [T] **1** to make sth black **2** to make sth seem bad, by saying unpleasant things about it: *to blacken sb's name*

black 'eye *noun* [C] an area of dark-coloured skin around sb's eye where he/she has been hit: *He got a black eye in the fight.*

blackhead /'blækhed/ *noun* [C] a small spot on the skin with a black centre

blacklist /'blæklɪst/ *noun* [C] a list of people, companies, etc who are considered bad or dangerous: *to be on sb's blacklist* –**blacklist** *verb* [T]: *She was blacklisted by all the major Hollywood studios.*

black 'magic *noun* [U] a type of magic that is used for evil purposes

blackmail /'blækmeɪl/ *noun* [U] the crime of forcing a person to give you money or do sth for you, usually by threatening to make known sth which they want to keep secret –**blackmail** *verb* [T] **blackmail sb (into doing sth)** –**blackmailer** *noun* [C]

black 'market *noun* [usually sing] the buying and selling of goods or foreign money in a way that is not legal: *to buy/sell sth on the black market*

blackout /'blækaʊt/ *noun* [C] **1** a period of time during a war, when all lights must be turned off or covered so that the enemy cannot see them **2** a period when you lose consciousness for a short time: *to have a blackout*

blacksmith /'blæksmɪθ/ *noun* [C] a person whose job is to make and repair things made of iron

bladder /'blædə/ *noun* [C] the part of your body where waste liquid (**urine**) collects before leaving your body •⇥ picture on page C5

★**blade** /bleɪd/ *noun* [C] **1** the flat, sharp part of a knife, etc •⇥ picture at **garden**, **penknife** and **scissors 2** one of the flat, wide parts that turn round very quickly on an aircraft, etc **3** a long, thin leaf of grass: *a blade of grass*

★**blame** /bleɪm/ *verb* [T] **1** **blame sb (for sth)**; **blame sth on sb/sth** to think or say that a certain person or thing is responsible for sth bad that has happened: *The teacher blamed me for the accident.* • *Some people blame the changes in the climate on pollution.* **2** not **blame sb (for sth)** to think that sb is not wrong to do sth; to understand sb's reason for doing sth: *I don't blame you for feeling fed up.*

IDIOMS **be to blame (for sth)** to be responsible

for sth bad: *The police say that careless driving was to blame for the accident.*

shift the blame/responsibility (for sth) (onto sb) → **SHIFT¹**

blame² /bleɪm/ *noun* [U] blame (for sth) responsibility for sth bad: *The government must take the blame for the economic crisis.* • *The report put the blame on rising prices.* • *Why do I always get the blame?*

blameless /'bleɪmləs/ *adj* (*written*) not guilty; that should not be blamed: *He insisted that his wife was blameless and hadn't known about his crimes.*

bland /blænd/ *adj* **1** ordinary or not very interesting: *a rather bland style of writing* **2** (used about food) mild or lacking in taste **3** not showing any emotion –**blandly** *adv*

★**blank¹** /blæŋk/ *adj* **1** empty, with nothing written, printed or recorded on it: *a blank video/cassette/piece of paper/page* **2** without feelings, understanding or interest: *a blank expression on his face* • *My mind went blank when I saw the exam questions* (= I couldn't think properly or remember anything). –**blankly** *adv*: *She stared at me blankly, obviously not recognizing me.*

blank² /blæŋk/ *noun* [C] an empty space: *Fill in the blanks in the following exercise.* • (*figurative*) *I couldn't remember his name – my mind was a complete blank.*

IDIOM **draw a blank** → **DRAW¹**

blank 'cheque *noun* [C] a cheque that has been signed but that has an empty space so that the amount to be paid can be written in later

★**blanket¹** /'blæŋkɪt/ *noun* [C] **1** a cover made of wool, etc that is put on beds to keep people warm •⇥ picture at **bed 2** a thick layer or covering of sth: *a blanket of snow* – *verb* [T] **blanket sth (in/with sth)**: *The countryside was blanketed in snow.*

IDIOM **a wet blanket** → **WET¹**

blanket² /'blæŋkɪt/ *adj* (only *before* a noun) affecting everybody or everything: *There is a blanket ban on journalists reporting the case.*

blare /bleə/ *verb* [I,T] **blare (sth) (out)** to make a loud, unpleasant noise: *Car horns were blaring in the street outside.* • *The loudspeaker blared out pop music.* –**blare** *noun* [U, sing]: *the blare of a siren*

blasphemy /'blæsfəmi/ *noun* [U] writing or speaking about God in a way that shows a lack of respect –**blasphemous** /'blæsfəməs/ *adj*

blast¹ /blɑːst/ *noun* [C] **1** an explosion, especially one caused by a bomb **2** a sudden strong current of air: *a blast of cold air* **3** a loud sound made by a musical instrument, etc: *The driver gave a few blasts on his horn.*

blast² /blɑːst/ *verb* [T] **1** to make a hole, a tunnel, etc in sth with an explosion: *They blasted a tunnel through the mountainside.* **2** to criticize sth very strongly: *Union leaders last night blasted the government's proposals.*

PHRASAL VERB **blast off** (used about a spacecraft) to leave the ground; to take off

b

blast-off noun [U] the time when a spacecraft leaves the ground

blatant /'bleɪtnt/ adj very clear or obvious: *a blatant lie* ••► This word is used in a critical way. –**blatantly** adv

blaze¹ /bleɪz/ noun **1** [C] a large and often dangerous fire: *It took firefighters four hours to put out the blaze.* **2** [sing] a blaze of sth a very bright show of light or colour: *In the summer the garden was a blaze of colour.* • *The new theatre was opened in **a blaze of publicity*** (= the media gave it a lot of attention).

blaze² /bleɪz/ verb [I] **1** to burn with bright strong flames **2** blaze (with sth) to be extremely bright; to shine brightly: *I woke up to find that the room was blazing with sunshine.* • (*figurative*) *'Get out!' she shouted, her eyes blazing with anger.*

blazer /'bleɪzə/ noun [C] a jacket, especially one that has the colours or sign (badge) of a school, club or team on it: *a school blazer* ••► picture on page C6

bleach¹ /bliːtʃ/ verb [T] to make sth white or lighter in colour by using a chemical or by leaving it in the sun

bleach² /bliːtʃ/ noun [C,U] a strong chemical substance used for making clothes, etc whiter or for cleaning things

bleak /bliːk/ adj **1** (used about a situation) bad; not encouraging or hopeful: *a bleak future for the next generation* **2** (used about a place) cold, empty and grey: *the bleak Arctic landscape* **3** (used about the weather) cold and grey: *a bleak winter's day* –**bleakly** adv –**bleakness** noun [U]

bleary /'blɪəri/ adj (used about the eyes) red, tired and unable to see clearly: *We were all rather bleary-eyed after the journey.* –**blearily** adv

bleat /bliːt/ verb **1** [I] to make the sound of a sheep **2** [I,T] to speak in a weak or complaining voice –**bleat** noun [C]

★**bleed** /bliːd/ verb [I] (*pt, pp* **bled** /bled/) to lose blood –**bleeding** noun [U]: *He wrapped a scarf around his arm to stop the bleeding.*

bleep¹ /bliːp/ noun [C] a short, high sound made by a piece of electronic equipment

bleep² /bliːp/ verb **1** [I] (used about machines) to make a short high sound: *Why is the computer bleeping?* **2** (*US also* **beep**) [T] to attract a person's attention using an electronic machine: *Please bleep the doctor on duty immediately.*

bleeper /'bliːpə/ (*US* **beeper**) noun [C] a small piece of electronic equipment that bleeps to let a person (for example a doctor) know when sb is trying to contact him/her ••► synonym **pager**

blemish /'blemɪʃ/ noun [C] a mark that spoils the way sth looks –**blemish** verb (*figurative*): *The defeat has blemished the team's perfect record.*

blend¹ /blend/ verb **1** [T] blend A with B; blend A and B (together) to mix: *First blend the flour and the melted butter together.* **2** [I]

blend (in) with sth to combine with sth in an attractive or suitable way: *The new room is decorated to blend in with the rest of the house.* **3** [I] blend (into sth) to match or be similar to the surroundings sb/sth is in: *These animals' ability to blend into their surroundings provides a natural form of defence.*

blend² /blend/ noun [C] a mixture: *He had the right blend of enthusiasm and experience.*

blender /'blendə/ (*Brit* **liquidizer**) noun [C] an electric machine that is used for making food into liquid ••► picture at **mixer**

bless /bles/ verb [T] (*pt, pp* **blessed** /blest/) to ask for God's help and protection for sb/sth

IDIOMS **be blessed with sth/sb** to be lucky enough to have sth/sb: *The West of Ireland is an area blessed with many fine sandy beaches.*

Bless you! what you say to a person who has a cold and has just made a noise through his/her nose (**sneezed**)

blessed /'blesɪd/ adj **1** having God's help and protection: *the Blessed Virgin Mary* **2** (in religious language) lucky; fortunate: *Blessed are the pure in heart.* **3** (*formal*) giving great pleasure: *The cool breeze brought **blessed** relief from the heat.*

blessing /'blesɪŋ/ noun [C] **1** a thing that you are grateful for or that brings happiness: *It's a great blessing that we have two healthy children.* • *Not getting that job was **a blessing in disguise*** (= something which seems unlucky but turns out to be a good thing). **2** [usually sing] approval or support: *They got married without their parents' blessing.* **3** [usually sing] (a prayer asking for) God's help and protection: *The priest said a blessing.*

blew *past tense* of **BLOW¹**

★**blind¹** /blaɪnd/ adj **1** unable to see: *a blind person* • *to be completely/partially blind* ••► People are sometimes described as **partially sighted** or **visually impaired** rather than **blind**. **2** blind (to sth) not wanting to notice or understand sth: *He was completely blind to her faults.* **3** without reason or thought: *He drove down the motorway in **a blind panic**.* **4** impossible to see round: *You should never overtake on **a blind corner**.* –**blindly** adv –**blindness** noun [U]

IDIOM **turn a blind eye (to sth)** to pretend not to notice sth bad is happening so that you do not have to do anything about it

blind² /blaɪnd/ verb [T] **1** to make sb unable to see: *Her grandfather had been blinded in an accident* (= permanently). • *Just for a second I was blinded by the sun* (= for a short time). **2** blind sb (to sth) to make sb unable to think clearly or behave in a sensible way

blind³ /blaɪnd/ noun **1** [C] a piece of cloth or other material that you pull down to cover a window ••► picture at **curtain 2 the blind** noun [pl] people who are unable to see

blind 'date noun [C] an arranged meeting between a man and a woman who have never met before to see if they like each other enough to begin a romantic relationship

blindfold /'blaɪndfəʊld/ noun [C] a piece of cloth, etc that is used for covering sb's eyes –**blindfold** verb [T]

'**blind spot** noun [C] **1** the part of the road just behind you that you cannot see when driving a car **2** if you have a blind spot about sth, you cannot understand or accept it

blink /blɪŋk/ verb **1** [I,T] to shut your eyes and open them again very quickly: *Oh dear! You blinked just as I took the photograph!* •➤ Look at **wink**. **2** [I] (used about a light) to come on and go off again quickly –**blink** noun [C]

blip /blɪp/ noun [C] **1** a light flashing on the screen of a piece of equipment, sometimes with a short high sound **2** a small problem that does not last for long

bliss /blɪs/ noun [U] perfect happiness –**blissful** /-fl/ adj –**blissfully** /-fəli/ adv

blister¹ /'blɪstə/ noun [C] a small painful area of skin that looks like a bubble and contains clear liquid. Blisters are usually caused by rubbing or burning.

blister² /'blɪstə/ verb [I,T] **1** to get or cause blisters **2** to swell and crack or to cause sth to do this: *The paint is starting to blister.*

blistering /'blɪstərɪŋ/ adj very strong or extreme: *the blistering midday heat* • *The runners set off at a blistering pace.*

blitz /blɪts/ noun [C] a blitz (on sth) a sudden effort or attack on sb/sth: *The police are planning a blitz on vandalism.*

blizzard /'blɪzəd/ noun [C] a very bad storm with strong winds and a lot of snow •➤ Look at the note at **storm**.

bloated /'bləʊtɪd/ adj unusually large and uncomfortable because of liquid, food or gas inside: *I felt a bit bloated after all that food.*

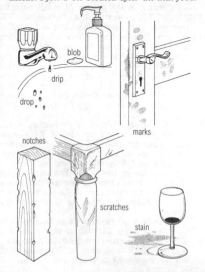

blob

drip

drop

notches

marks

scratches

stain

blob /blɒb/ noun [C] a small drop of a thick liquid: *a blob of paint/cream/ink*

bloc /blɒk/ noun [C,with sing or pl verb] a group of countries that work closely together because they have the same political interests

★**block¹** /blɒk/ noun [C] **1** a large, heavy piece of sth, usually with flat sides: *a block of wood* • *huge concrete blocks* **2** a large building that is divided into separate flats or offices: *a block of flats* •➤ Look at **apartment block** and **office block**. **3** a group of buildings in a town which has streets on all four sides: *The restaurant is three blocks away.* **4** a quantity of sth or an amount of time that is considered as a single unit: *The class is divided into two blocks of fifty minutes.* **5** [usually sing] a thing that makes movement or progress difficult or impossible: *a block to further progress in the talks* •➤ Look at **roadblock**.
  IDIOM **have a block (about sth)** to be unable to think or understand sth properly: *I had a complete mental block. I just couldn't remember his name.*

★**block²** /blɒk/ verb [T] **1** block sth (up) to make it difficult or impossible for sb/sth to pass: *Many roads are completely blocked by snow.* **2** to prevent sth from being done: *The management tried to block the deal.* **3** to prevent sth from being seen by sb: *Get out of the way, you're blocking the view!*
  PHRASAL VERBS **block sth off** to separate one area from another with sth solid: *This section of the motorway has been blocked off by the police.*
  block sth out to try not to think about sth unpleasant: *She tried to block out the memory of the crash.*

blockade /blɒ'keɪd/ noun [C] a situation in which a place is surrounded by soldiers or ships in order to prevent goods or people from reaching it –**blockade** verb [T]

blockage /'blɒkɪdʒ/ noun [C] a thing that is preventing sth from passing; the state of being blocked: *a blockage in the drainpipe* • *There are blockages on some major roads.*

blockbuster /'blɒkbʌstə/ noun [C] a book or film with an exciting story which is very successful and popular

block 'capital noun [C,usually pl] a big letter such as 'A' (not 'a'): *Please write your name in block capitals.*

bloke /bləʊk/ noun [C] (*Brit slang*) a man: *He's a really nice bloke.*

blond (also **blonde**) /blɒnd/ noun [C], adj (a person) with fair or yellow hair: *Most of our family have blond hair.*

  ➤ When describing women the spelling **blonde** is used: *She's tall, slim and blonde.* The noun is usually only used of women and is spelled **blonde**: *She's a blonde.* Look also at **brunette**.

★**blood** /blʌd/ noun [U] the red liquid that flows through your body: *The heart pumps blood around the body.* •➤ Look at **bleed**.
  IDIOMS **in your blood** a strong part of your

b

character: *A love of the countryside was in his blood.*

in cold blood → COLD¹

shed blood → SHED²

your (own) flesh and blood → FLESH

bloodbath /'blʌdbɑːθ/ noun [sing] an act of violently killing many people

blood-curdling adj very frightening: *a blood-curdling scream*

blood donor noun [C] a person who gives some of his/her blood for use in medical operations

blood group (also **blood type**) noun [C] any of several different types of human blood: *'What blood group are you?' 'O.'*

bloodless /'blʌdləs/ adj **1** without killing or violence: *a bloodless coup* **2** (used about a part of the body) very pale

blood pressure noun [U] the force with which the blood travels round the body: *to have high/low blood pressure*

bloodshed /'blʌdʃed/ noun [U] the killing or harming of people: *Both sides in the war want to avoid further bloodshed.*

bloodshot /'blʌdʃɒt/ adj (used about the white part of the eyes) full of red lines, for example when sb is tired

blood sport noun [C] a sport in which animals or birds are killed

bloodstain /'blʌdsteɪn/ noun [C] a mark or spot of blood on sth –bloodstained adj

bloodstream /'blʌdstriːm/ noun [sing] the blood as it flows through the body: *drugs injected straight into the bloodstream*

bloodthirsty /'blʌdθɜːsti/ adj wanting to use violence or to watch scenes of violence

blood transfusion noun [C] the process of putting new blood into a person's body

blood vessel noun [C] any of the tubes in your body which blood flows through
•➤ Look at **vein**, **artery** and **capillary**.

bloody /'blʌdi/ adj (bloodier; bloodiest) **1** involving a lot of violence and killing: *a bloody war* **2** covered with blood: *a bloody knife* **3** also adv (*Brit slang*) a swear word used for emphasizing a comment or an angry statement: *The bloody train was late again this morning.* • *What a bloody stupid thing to say!* • *We had a bloody good time.* •➤ Many people find this word offensive.

bloody-minded adj (*Brit informal*) (used about a person) deliberately difficult; not helpful –bloody-mindedness noun [U]

bloom¹ /bluːm/ noun [C] a flower
IDIOM in bloom with its flowers open: *All the wild plants are in bloom.*

bloom² /bluːm/ verb [I] to produce flowers: *This shrub blooms in May.*

blossom¹ /'blɒsəm/ noun [C,U] a flower or a mass of flowers, especially on a fruit tree in the spring: *The apple tree is in blossom.*
•➤ picture on page C2

blossom² /'blɒsəm/ verb [I] **1** (used especially about trees) to produce flowers **2** blossom (into sth) to become more healthy,

confident or successful: *This young runner has blossomed into a top-class athlete.*

blot¹ /blɒt/ noun [C] **1** a spot of sth, especially one made by ink on paper; a stain **2** a blot on sth a thing that spoils your happiness or other people's opinion of you

blot² /blɒt/ verb [T] (blotting; blotted) **1** to make a spot or a mark on sth, especially ink on paper **2** to remove liquid from a surface by pressing soft paper or cloth on it
PHRASAL VERB blot sth out to cover or hide sth: *Fog blotted out the view completely.* • *She tried to blot out the memory of what happened.*

blotch /blɒtʃ/ noun [C] a temporary mark or an area of different colour on skin, plants, material, etc: *The blotches on her face showed that she had been crying.* –blotchy (also blotched) adj

blotting paper noun [U] soft paper that you use for drying wet ink after you have written sth on paper

★**blouse** /blaʊz/ noun [C] a piece of clothing like a shirt, that women wear •➤ picture on page C6

blow/suck

blowing   sucking

★**blow¹** /bləʊ/ verb (*pt* blew /bluː/; *pp* blown /bləʊn/) **1** [I,T] (used about wind, air, etc) to be moving or to cause sth to move: *A gentle breeze was blowing.* **2** [I] to move because of the wind or a current of air: *The balloons blew away.* • *My papers blew all over the garden.* **3** [I] to send air out of the mouth: *The policeman asked me to blow into the Breathalyser.* **4** [T] to make or shape sth by blowing air out of your mouth: *to blow bubbles/smoke rings* • *to blow (sb) a kiss* (= to kiss your hand and pretend to blow the kiss towards sb) **5** [I,T] to produce sound from a musical instrument, etc by blowing air into it: *The referee's whistle blew for the end of the match.* • *He blew a few notes on the trumpet.* **6** [T] (*informal*) to waste an opportunity: *I think I've blown my chances of promotion.* • *You had your chance and you blew it.* **7** [T] (*informal*) blow sth (on sth) to spend or waste a lot of money on sth: *She blew all her savings on a trip to China.* **8** [I,T] used about a thin piece of wire in an electrical system (a fuse) to stop working suddenly because the electric current is too strong; to make sth do this: *A fuse has blown.* • *I think the kettle's blown a fuse.*
IDIOM blow your nose to clear your nose by blowing strongly through it into a piece of cloth (handkerchief) •➤ picture at sneeze
PHRASAL VERBS blow over to disappear without having a serious effect: *The scandal will*

soon *blow over*.
  blow up 1 to explode or to be destroyed in an explosion: *The car blew up when the door was opened.* **2** to start suddenly and strongly: *A storm blew up in the night.* • *A huge row blew up about money.* **3** (*informal*) to become very angry: *The teacher blew up when I said I'd forgotten my homework.*
  blow sth up 1 to make sth explode or to destroy sth in an explosion: *The terrorists tried to blow up the plane.* **2** to fill sth with air or gas: *to blow up a balloon* **3** to make a photograph bigger

★ **blow²** /bləʊ/ **noun** [C] **1** a hard hit from sb's hand, a weapon, etc: *She aimed a blow at me.* **2** a blow (to sb/sth) a sudden shock or disappointment: *It was a blow when I didn't get the job.* **3** an act of blowing: *Give your nose a blow!*
  IDIOMS a **blow-by-blow account, description, etc (of sth)** an account, etc of an event that gives the exact details of it
  come to blows (with sb) (over sth) to start fighting or arguing (about sth)
  deal sb/sth a blow; deal a blow to sb/sth → **DEAL¹**

'blow-dry verb [T] (*pt, pp* **blow-dried**) to dry and shape sb's hair by holding a machine that produces hot air (a **hairdryer**) in your hand, and a brush

blown *past participle* of **BLOW¹**

blowout /'bləʊaʊt/ **noun** [C] (*informal*) **1** a burst tyre; a puncture: *We had a blowout on the motorway.* **2** a very large meal at which people eat too much; a large party or social event

★ **blue¹** /bluː/ **adj 1** having the colour of a clear sky when the sun shines: *His eyes were bright blue.* • *light/dark blue* **2** (*informal*) (often used in songs) sad
  IDIOMS black and blue → **BLACK¹**
  once in a blue moon → **ONCE**

★ **blue²** /bluː/ **noun 1** [C,U] the colour of a clear sky when the sun shines: *a deep blue* • *dressed in blue* (= blue clothes) **2** the blues [pl,with sing or pl verb] a type of slow sad music: *a blues singer* **3** the blues [pl] (*informal*) a feeling of great sadness; depression: *to have the blues*
  IDIOM out of the blue suddenly; unexpectedly: *I didn't hear from him for years and then this letter came out of the blue.*

'blue-collar adj doing or involving physical work with the hands rather than office work •➤ Look at **white-collar**.

blueprint /'bluːprɪnt/ **noun** [C] a photographic plan or a description of how to make, build or achieve sth

bluff¹ /blʌf/ **verb** [I,T] to try to make people believe that sth is true when it is not, usually by appearing very confident: *They tried to bluff their parents into believing there was no school that day.*
  IDIOM bluff your way in, out, through, etc sth to trick sb in order to get into, out of a place, etc: *We managed to bluff our way into the stadium by saying we were journalists.*

bluff² /blʌf/ **noun** [U,C] making sb believe that you will do sth when you really have no intention of doing it, or that you know sth when, in fact, you do not know it
  IDIOM call sb's bluff → **CALL¹**

bluish (also **blueish**) /'bluːɪʃ/ **adj** (*informal*) slightly blue: *bluish green*

blunder¹ /'blʌndə/ **noun** [C] a stupid mistake: *I'm afraid I've made a terrible blunder.*

blunder² /'blʌndə/ **verb** [I] to make a stupid mistake
  PHRASAL VERB blunder about, around, etc to move in an uncertain or careless way, as if you cannot see where you are going: *We blundered about in the dark, trying to find the light switch.*

blunt /blʌnt/ **adj 1** (used about a knife, pencil, tool, etc) without a sharp edge or point: *blunt scissors* •➤ opposite **sharp 2** (used about a person, comment, etc) very direct; saying what you think without trying to be polite: *I'm sorry to be so blunt, but I'm afraid you're just not good enough.* –**blunt verb** [T] –**bluntly adv** –**bluntness noun** [U]

blur¹ /blɜː/ **noun** [C,usually sing] something that you cannot see clearly or remember well: *Without my glasses, their faces were just a blur.*

blur² /blɜː/ **verb** [I,T] (**blurring**; **blurred**) to become or to make sth less clear: *The words on the page blurred as tears filled her eyes.* –**blurred adj**

blurt /blɜːt/ **verb**
  PHRASAL VERB blurt sth out to say sth suddenly or without thinking: *We didn't want to tell Mum but Ann blurted the whole thing out.*

blush /blʌʃ/ **verb** [I] to become red in the face, especially because you are embarrassed or feel guilty: *She blushed with shame.* –**blush noun** [C,usually sing]

blusher /'blʌʃə/ **noun** [U,C] a coloured cream or powder that some people put on their cheeks to give them more colour

blustery /'blʌstəri/ **adj** (used to describe the weather) with strong winds: *The day was cold and blustery.*

BO /ˌbiː 'əʊ/ **abbr** body odour

boar /bɔː/ **noun** [C] (*pl* **boar** or **boars**) **1** a male pig **2** a wild pig •➤ Look at the note at **pig**.

★ **board¹** /bɔːd/ **noun 1** [C] a long, thin, flat piece of wood used for making floors, walls, etc: *The old house needed new floorboards.* **2** [C] a thin flat piece of wood, etc used for a particular purpose: *an ironing board* • *a surfboard* • *a noticeboard* • *board games* (= games you play on a board) **3** [C,with sing or pl verb] a group of people who control an organization, company, etc: *The board of directors is/are meeting to discuss the firm's future.* • *a board meeting* **4** [U] the meals that are provided when you stay in a hotel, etc: *The prices are for a double room and full board* (= all the meals).
  IDIOMS above board → **ABOVE**
  across the board → **ACROSS**

[I] **intransitive**, a verb which has no object: *He laughed.*   [T] **transitive**, a verb which has an object: *He ate an apple.*

b

on board on a ship or an aircraft: *All the passengers were safely on board.*

board² /bɔːd/ *verb* [I,T] to get on a plane, ship, bus, etc: *We said goodbye and boarded the train.* ● *Lufthansa flight LH120 to Hamburg is now boarding* (= ready to take passengers) *at Gate 27.*

PHRASAL VERB **board sth up** to cover with boards¹(1): *Nobody lives there now – it's all boarded up.*

boarder /'bɔːdə/ *noun* [C] (*Brit*) **1** a child who lives at school and goes home for the holidays. **2** a person who pays to live at sb's house ••► Look at **lodger**.

'boarding card *noun* [C] a card that you must show in order to get on a plane or ship

'boarding house *noun* [C] a private house where you can pay to stay and have meals for a period of time

'boarding school *noun* [C] a school that schoolchildren live at while they are studying, going home only in the holidays

boardroom /'bɔːdruːm; -rʊm/ *noun* [C] the room where the group of people in charge of a company or organization (the board of directors) meets

boast /bəʊst/ *verb* **1** [I] to talk with too much pride about sth that you have or can do: *I wish she wouldn't boast about her family so much.* **2** [T] (used about a place) to have sth that it can be proud of: *The town boasts over a dozen restaurants.* –**boast** *noun* [C]

boastful /'bəʊstfl/ *adj* (used about a person or the things that he/she says) showing too much pride

boats

rowing boat
(US rowboat)

oar

paddle

canoe
(also kayak)

life jacket

dinghy

★**boat** /bəʊt/ *noun* [C] **1** a small vehicle that is used for travelling across water: *The cave can only be reached by boat/ in a boat.* ● *a rowing/fishing/motor boat* **2** any ship: *When does the next boat to France sail?*

IDIOM **rock the boat** → ROCK²

bob /bɒb/ *verb* (**bobbing**; **bobbed**) [I,T] to move quickly up and down; to make sth do

this: *The boats in the harbour were bobbing up and down in the water.* ● *She bobbed her head down below the top of the wall.*

PHRASAL VERB **bob up** to appear suddenly from behind or under sth: *He disappeared and then bobbed up again on the other side of the pool.*

bobsleigh /'bɒbsleɪ/ (*US* **bobsled** /'bɒbsled/) *noun* [C] a racing vehicle for two or more people that slides over snow along a track ••► Look at **sleigh**, **sledge** and **toboggan**.

bode /bəʊd/ *verb*

IDIOM **bode well/ill (for sb/sth)** to be a sign that sb/sth will have a good/bad future

bodily¹ /'bɒdəli/ *adj* of the human body; physical: *First we must attend to their bodily needs* (= make sure that they have a home, enough to eat, etc).

bodily² /'bɒdɪli/ *adv* by taking hold of the body: *She picked up the child and carried him bodily from the room.*

★**body** /'bɒdi/ *noun* (*pl* **bodies**) **1** [C] the whole physical form of a person or animal: *the human body* **2** [C] the part of a person that is not his/her legs, arms or head: *She had injuries to her head and body.* **3** [C] a dead person: *The police have found a body in the canal.* **4** [C, with sing or pl verb] a group of people who work or act together, especially in an official way: *The governing body of the college meets/meet once a month.* **5** [sing] the main part of sth: *We agree with the body of the report, although not with certain details.* **6** [C] (*formal*) an object: *The doctor removed a foreign body from the child's ear.*

IDIOM **in a body** all together

bodybuilding /'bɒdɪbɪldɪŋ/ *noun* [U] making the muscles of the body stronger and larger by exercise –**bodybuilder** *noun* [C]

bodyguard /'bɒdɪgɑːd/ *noun* [C] a person or group of people whose job is to protect sb

'body language *noun* [U] showing how you feel by the way you move, stand, sit, etc, rather than by what you say: *I could tell by his body language that he was scared.*

'body odour *noun* [U] (*abbr* **BO**) the unpleasant smell from a person's body, especially of sweat

bodywork /'bɒdiwɜːk/ *noun* [U] the main outside structure of a vehicle, usually made of painted metal

bog /bɒg/ *noun* [C,U] an area of ground that is very soft and wet: *a peat bog*

bogey /'bəʊgi/ *noun* [C] **1** something that causes fear, often without reason **2** a piece of the sticky substance (mucus) that forms inside your nose

bogged 'down *adj* **1** (used about a vehicle) not able to move because it has sunk into soft ground **2** (used about a person) not able to make any progress: *We got bogged down in a long discussion and didn't have time to make any decisions.*

boggle /'bɒgl/ *verb* [I] to be unable to imagine sth; impossible to imagine or believe: *'What will happen if his plan doesn't* *work?' 'The mind boggles!'* ••➤ Look also at **mind-boggling**.

boggy /'bɒgi/ **adj** (used about land) soft and wet, so that your feet sink into it

bogus /'bəʊgəs/ **adj** pretending to be real or genuine: *a bogus policeman*

★**boil**[1] /bɔɪl/ **verb 1** [I] (used about a liquid) to reach a high temperature where bubbles rise to the surface and the liquid changes to a gas: *Water boils at 100°C.* • *The kettle's boiling.* **2** [T] to heat a liquid until it boils and let it keep boiling: *Boil all drinking water for five minutes.* **3** [I,T] to cook (sth) in boiling water: *Put the potatoes on to boil, please.* • *to boil an egg* **4** [I] (used about a person) to feel very angry: *She was boiling with rage.*

PHRASAL VERBS **boil down to sth** to have sth as the most important point: *What it all boils down to is that you don't want to spend too much money.*

boil over 1 (used about a liquid) to boil and flow over the sides of a pan: *You let the soup boil over.* **2** (used about an argument or sb's feelings) to become more serious or angry

boil[2] /bɔɪl/ **noun 1** [sing] a period of boiling; the point at which a liquid boils: *You'll have to give those shirts a boil to get them clean.* **2** [C] a small, painful swelling under your skin, with a red or yellow top

boiler /'bɔɪlə/ **noun** [C] a container in which water is heated to provide hot water or heating in a building or to produce steam in an engine

'boiler suit noun [C] (*US* **coveralls**) a piece of clothing that you wear over your normal clothes to protect them when you are doing dirty work

boiling /'bɔɪlɪŋ/ (also **boiling 'hot**) **adj** (*informal*) very hot: *Open a window – it's boiling hot in here.* • *Can I open a window? I'm boiling.*

'boiling point noun [C] the temperature at which a liquid starts to boil

boisterous /'bɔɪstərəs/ **adj** (used about a person or behaviour) noisy and full of energy: *Their children are very nice but they can get a bit too boisterous.*

★**bold** /bəʊld/ **adj 1** (used about a person or his/her behaviour) confident and not afraid: *Not many people are bold enough to say exactly what they think.* **2** that you can see clearly: *bold, bright colours* **3** (used about printed letters) in thick, dark type: *Make the important text bold.* –**bold noun** [U]: *The important words are highlighted in bold.* –**boldly adv** –**boldness noun** [U]

bollard /'bɒlɑːd/ **noun** [C] a short thick post that is used to stop motor vehicles from going into an area that they are not allowed to enter

bolshie (also **bolshy**) /'bɒlʃi/ **adj** (*Brit informal*) (used about a person) bad-tempered and often refusing to do what people ask him/her to do

bolster /'bəʊlstə/ **verb** [T] **bolster sb/sth (up)** to support or encourage sb/sth; to make sth stronger: *His remarks did nothing to bolster my confidence.*

bolt[1] /bəʊlt/ **noun** [C] **1** a small piece of metal that is used with another piece of metal (a nut) for fastening things together **2** a bar of metal that you can slide across the inside of the door to fasten it

bolt[2] /bəʊlt/ **verb 1** [I] (used especially about a horse) to run away very suddenly, usually in fear **2** [T] **bolt sth (down)** to eat sth very quickly: *She bolted down a sandwich and dashed out of the house.* **3** [T] to fasten one thing to another using a bolt[1](1): *All the tables have been bolted to the floor so that nobody can steal them.* **4** [T] to fasten a door, etc with a bolt[1](2): *Make sure that the door is locked and bolted.*

bolt[3] /bəʊlt/ **adv**

IDIOM **bolt upright** sitting or standing very straight

★**bomb**[1] /bɒm/ **noun 1** [C] a container that is filled with material that will explode when it is thrown or dropped, or when a device inside it makes it explode: *Fortunately, the car bomb failed to go off.* **2 the bomb** [sing] nuclear weapons: *How many countries have the bomb now?* **3 a bomb** [sing] (*informal*) a lot of money: *That car must have cost you a bomb!*

bomb[2] /bɒm/ **verb 1** [T] to attack a city, etc with bombs: *Enemy forces have bombed the bridge.* **2** (*Brit informal*) **bomb along, down, up, etc** to move along very fast in the direction mentioned, especially in a vehicle: *He was bombing along at 100 miles an hour when the police stopped him.*

bombard /bɒm'bɑːd/ **verb** [T] to attack a place with bombs or guns: *They bombarded the city until the enemy surrendered.* • (*figurative*) *The reporters bombarded the minister with questions.* –**bombardment noun** [C,U]: *The main radio station has come under enemy bombardment.*

'bomb disposal noun [U] the removing or exploding of bombs in order to make an area safe: *a bomb disposal expert*

bomber /'bɒmə/ **noun** [C] **1** a type of plane that drops bombs **2** a person who makes a bomb explode in a public place

bombshell /'bɒmʃel/ **noun** [C,usually sing] an unexpected piece of news, usually about sth unpleasant: *The chairman dropped a bombshell when he said he was resigning.*

bona fide /ˌbəʊnə 'faɪdi/ **adj** real or genuine: *This car park is for the use of bona fide customers only.*

bond /bɒnd/ **noun 1** [C] something that joins two or more people or groups of people together, such as a feeling of friendship: *Our two countries are united by bonds of friendship.* **2** [C] a certificate that you can buy from a government or company that promises to

b

pay you interest on the money you have given: *government bonds*

★**bone**[1] /bəʊn/ **noun 1** [C] one of the hard parts inside the body of a person or animal that are covered with muscle, skin, etc: *He's broken a bone in his hand.* ● *This fish has got a lot of bones in it.* **2** [U] the substance that bones are made of

IDIOMS **have a bone to pick with sb** to have sth that you want to complain to sb about

make no bones about (doing) sth to do sth in an open honest way without feeling nervous or worried about it: *She made no bones about telling him exactly what she thought about him.*

bone[2] /bəʊn/ **verb** [T] to take the bones out of sth: *to bone a fish*

bone-'dry adj completely dry: *Give that plant some water – it's bone-dry.*

'bone marrow (also **marrow**) **noun** [U] the soft substance that is inside the bones of a person or animal

bonfire /'bɒnfaɪə/ **noun** [C] a large fire that you build outside to burn rubbish, as part of a festival, etc

'Bonfire Night noun [C] in Britain, the night of 5 November

➤ On this day people in Britain light fireworks and burn a model of a man called a **guy** on top of a bonfire, to celebrate the failure of Guy Fawkes to blow up the Houses of Parliament in the seventeenth century.

bonkers /'bɒŋkəz/ **adj** (*slang*) crazy; mad: *I'd go bonkers if I worked here full-time.*

bonnet /'bɒnɪt/ (*US* **hood**) **noun** [C] **1** the front part of a car that covers the engine ●➤ picture on page S9 **2** a type of hat which covers the sides of the face and is fastened with strings under the chin

bonus /'bəʊnəs/ **noun** (*pl* **bonuses**) **1** a payment that is added to what is usual: *All our employees receive an annual bonus.* **2** something good that you get in addition to what you expect: *I enjoy my job, and having my own office is **an added bonus**.*

bony /'bəʊni/ **adj** so thin that you can see the shape of the bones: *long bony fingers*

boo /buː/ **interj, noun** [C] (*pl* **boos**) **1** a sound you make to show that you do not like sb/sth: *The minister's speech was met with boos from the audience.* **2** a sound you make to frighten or surprise sb: *He jumped out from behind the door and said 'boo'.* **–boo verb** [I,T]

boob /buːb/ **noun** [C] (*slang*) **1** a woman's breast **2** a silly mistake **–boob verb** [I]: *I'm afraid I've boobed again.*

booby prize /'buːbi praɪz/ (also **wooden spoon**) **noun** [C] a prize that is given as a joke to the person or team that comes last in a competition

booby trap /'buːbi træp/ **noun** [C] a device that will kill, injure or surprise sb when he/she touches the object that it is connected to **–booby-trap verb** [T]

★**book**[1] /bʊk/ **noun 1** [C] a written work that is published as printed pages fastened together inside a cover, or in electronic form: *I'm reading a book on astrology.* ● *She's writing a book about her life abroad.* ● *Do you have any books by William Golding?* ● *hardback/paperback books* **2** [C] a number of pieces of paper, fastened together inside a cover, for people to write or draw on: *Please write down all the new vocabulary in your exercise books.* ● *a notebook* ● *a sketch book* **3** [C] a number of things fastened together in the form of a book: *a book of stamps* ● *a chequebook* **4 books** [pl] the records that a company, etc, keeps of the amount of money it spends and receives: *We employ an accountant to **keep the books**.*

IDIOMS **be in sb's good/bad books** (*informal*) to have sb pleased/angry with you: *He's been in his girlfriend's bad books since he forgot her birthday.*

by the book exactly according to the rules: *A policeman must always do things by the book.*

(be) on sb's books (to be) on the list of an organization: *The employment agency has hundreds of qualified secretaries on its books.*

★**book**[2] /bʊk/ **verb 1** [I,T] to arrange to have or do sth at a particular time: *Have you booked a table, sir?* ● *to book a seat on a plane/train/bus* ● *I've booked a hotel room for you/I've booked you a hotel room.* ● *I'm sorry, but this evening's performance is fully booked* (= there are no seats left). **2** [T] to officially write down the name of a person who has done sth wrong: *The police booked her for* (= charged her with) *dangerous driving.* ● *The player was booked for a foul and then sent off for arguing.*

PHRASAL VERBS **book in** to say that you have arrived at a hotel, etc, and sign your name on a list

book sb in to arrange a room for sb at a hotel, etc in advance: *I've booked you in at the George Hotel.*

bookcase /'bʊkkeɪs/ **noun** [C] a piece of furniture with shelves to keep books on ●➤ picture on page C7

bookie /'bʊki/ (*informal*) = **BOOKMAKER**

booking /'bʊkɪŋ/ **noun** [C,U] the arrangement that you make in advance to have a hotel room, a seat on a plane, etc: *Did you manage to **make a booking**?* ● *No advance booking is necessary.*

'booking office noun [C] an office where you buy tickets

bookkeeping /'bʊkkiːpɪŋ/ **noun** [U] keeping the accounts of the money that a company, etc, spends or receives

booklet /'bʊklət/ **noun** [C] a small thin book, usually with a soft cover, that gives information about sth

bookmaker /'bʊkmeɪkə/ (also *informal* **bookie**) **noun** [C] **1** a person whose job is to take bets on horse races, etc **2 bookmaker's** [sing] a shop, etc where you can bet money on a race or an event ●➤ Look at **betting shop.**

b

bookmark /'bʊkmɑːk/ noun [C] **1** a narrow piece of card, etc that you put between the pages of a book so that you can find the same place again easily **2** a file from the Internet that you have stored on your computer

bookseller /'bʊkselə/ noun [C] a person whose job is selling books

bookshop /'bʊkʃɒp/ (US **bookstore**) noun [C] a shop that sells books ••➤ Look at **library**.

bookstall /'bʊkstɔːl/ (US **'news-stand**) noun [C] a type of small shop, which is open at the front, selling newspapers, magazines and books, for example on a station

bookworm /'bʊkwɜːm/ noun [C] a person who likes reading books very much

boom¹ /buːm/ noun [C] **1** a period in which sth increases or develops very quickly: *There was a boom in car sales in the 1980s.* **2** [usually sing] a loud deep sound: *the boom of distant guns*

boom² /buːm/ verb **1** [I,T] boom (sth) (out) to make a loud deep sound: *The loudspeaker boomed out instructions to the crowd.* **2** [I] to grow very quickly in size or value: *Business is booming in the computer industry.*

boomerang /'buːməræŋ/ noun [C] a curved piece of wood that returns to you when you throw it in a particular way

boon /buːn/ noun [C] a thing that is very helpful and that you are grateful for

boost¹ /buːst/ verb [T] to increase sth in number, value or strength: *If we lower the price, that should boost sales.* • *The good exam result boosted her confidence.*

boost² /buːst/ noun [C] something that encourages people; an increase: *The fall in the value of the pound has led to a boost in exports.* • *The president's visit gave a boost to the soldiers' morale.*

★**boot¹** /buːt/ noun [C] **1** a type of shoe that covers your foot completely and sometimes part of your leg: *ski boots* • *walking/climbing boots* • *football boots* ••➤ picture at **shoe** and **ski 2** (US **trunk**) the part of a car where you put luggage, usually at the back ••➤ picture on page S9

boot² /buːt/ verb (informal) **1** [T] to kick sth/sb hard: *He booted the ball over the fence.* **2** [I,T] to make a computer ready for use when it is first switched on
PHRASAL VERB **boot sb/sth out** to force sb/sth to leave a place: *The boys were booted out of the club for fighting.*

booth /buːð/ noun [C] a small enclosed place with thin walls that divide it from the rest of the room or area: *a phone booth*

booty /'buːti/ noun [U] things that are taken by thieves or captured by soldiers in a war

booze¹ /buːz/ noun [U] (informal) alcohol

booze² /buːz/ verb [I] (informal) to drink a lot of alcohol: *He went out boozing with some friends on Saturday.*

'booze-up noun [C] (Brit informal) an occasion when people drink a lot of alcohol

★**border¹** /'bɔːdə/ noun [C] **1** a line that divides two countries, etc; the land close to this line: *The refugees escaped **across/over the border**.* • *the Moroccan border* • *the border between France and Italy* • *Italy's border with France*

➤ We use **border** and **frontier** to talk about the line that divides two countries or states. We usually use **border** to talk about natural divisions: *The river forms the border between the two countries.* **Boundary** is usually used for the line that divides smaller areas: *the county boundary*

2 a band or narrow line around the edge of sth, often for decoration: *a white tablecloth with a blue border*

border² /'bɔːdə/ verb [T] to form a border to an area; to be on the border of an area: *The road was bordered with trees.*
PHRASAL VERB **border on sth 1** to be almost the same as sth: *The dictator's ideas bordered on madness.* **2** to be next to sth: *Our garden borders on the railway line.*

borderline /'bɔːdəlaɪn/ noun [sing] the line that marks a division between two different cases, conditions, etc: *He's **a borderline case** – he may pass the exam or he may fail.*

★**bore¹** /bɔː/ verb **1** [T] to make sb feel bored, especially by talking too much: *I hope I'm not boring you.* **2** [I,T] to make a long deep hole with a tool: *This drill can bore (a hole) through solid rock.* **3** past tense of **BEAR²**

bore² /bɔː/ noun **1** [C] a person who talks a lot in a way that is not interesting **2** [sing] (informal) something that you have to do so that you do not find interesting: *It's such a bore having to learn these lists of irregular verbs.*

bored /bɔːd/ adj **bored (with sth)** feeling tired and perhaps slightly annoyed because sth is not interesting or because you do not have anything to do: *I'm bored with eating the same thing every day.* • *The children **get bored** on long journeys.* • *He gave a **bored** yawn.* • *The play was awful – we were **bored stiff** (= extremely bored).*

➤ If you have nothing to do, or if what you are doing does not interest you, then you are **bored**. The person or thing that makes you feel like this is **boring**.

boredom /'bɔːdəm/ noun [U] the state of being bored: *I sometimes eat out of boredom.*

boring /'bɔːrɪŋ/ adj not at all interesting; dull: *a boring film/job/speech/man* ••➤ Look at the note at **bored**.

★**born¹** /bɔːn/ verb **be born** to come into the world by birth; to start existing: *Where were you born?* • *I was born in London, but I grew up in Leeds.* • *I'm going to give up work after the baby is born.* • *The idea of free education for all was born in the nineteenth century.* • *His unhappiness was **born out of** a feeling of frustration.*

born² /bɔːn/ adj **1** having a natural ability to do sth: *She's a born leader.* **2 -born** (used to form compound adjectives) born in the place or state mentioned: *This Kenyan-born athlete now represents Denmark.*

b

,born-a'gain adj (only *before* a noun) having found new, strong religious belief: *a born-again Christian*

borne /bɔːn/ *past participle* of **BEAR**²

borough /'bʌrə/ *noun* [C] a town, or an area inside a large town, that has some form of local government

borrow/lend

She's **lending** her son some money.

He's **borrowing** some money from his mother.

★**borrow** /'bɒrəʊ/ *verb* [I,T] **borrow (sth) (from/off sb/sth) 1** to take or receive sth from sb/sth that you intend to give back, usually after a short time: *I had to borrow from the bank to pay for my car.* ● *We'll have to borrow a lot of money to buy a car.* ● *Could I borrow your pen for a minute?* ● *He's always borrowing off his mother.* ● *I borrowed a book from the library.*

➤ Be careful not to confuse **borrow** with its opposite **lend**.

2 to take sth and use it as your own; to copy sth: *That idea is borrowed from another book.*

borrower /'bɒrəʊə/ *noun* [C] a person who borrows sth

bosom /'bʊzəm/ *noun* **1** [sing] (*formal*) a person's chest, especially a woman's breasts: *She clutched the child to her bosom.* **2** [C] a woman's breast

IDIOM **in the bosom of sth** close to; with the protection of: *He was glad to be back in the bosom of his family.*

,bosom 'friend *noun* [C] a very close friend

★**boss**¹ /bɒs/ *noun* [C] (*informal*) a person whose job is to give orders to others at work; an employer; a manager: *I'm going to ask the boss for a day off work.* ● *OK. You're the boss* (= you make the decisions).

boss² /bɒs/ *verb* [T] **boss sb (about/around)** to give orders to sb, especially in an annoying way: *I wish you'd stop bossing me around.*

bossy /'bɒsi/ *adj* liking to give orders to other people, often in an annoying way: *Don't be so bossy!* –**bossily** *adv* –**bossiness** *noun* [U]

botanist /'bɒtənɪst/ *noun* [C] a person who studies plants

botany /'bɒtəni/ *noun* [U] the scientific study of plants ••➤ Look at **biology** and **zoology**. –**botanical** /bə'tænɪkl/ *adj*: *botanical gardens* (= a type of park where plants are grown for scientific study)

botch /bɒtʃ/ *verb* [T] **botch sth (up)** to do sth badly; to make a mess of sth: *I've completely botched up this typing, I'm afraid.*

★**both** /bəʊθ/ **determiner, pron, adv 1** the two; the one as well as the other: *Both women were French.* ● *Both the women were French.* ● *Both of the women were French.* ● *I liked them both.* ● *We were both very tired.* ● *Both of us were tired.* ● *I've got two sisters. They both live in London/Both of them live in London.*

➤ Note that we CANNOT say: *the both women* or: *my both sisters.*

2 both...and... not only...but also...: *Both he and his wife are vegetarian.*

★**bother**¹ /'bɒðə/ *verb* **1** [T] to disturb, annoy or worry sb: *I'm sorry to bother you, but could I speak to you for a moment?* ● *Don't bother Geeta with that now – she's busy.* ••➤ synonym **trouble 2** [I] **bother (to do sth/doing sth); bother (about/with sth)** (usually negative) to make the effort to do sth: *'Shall I make you something to eat?' 'No, don't bother – I'm not hungry.'* ● *He didn't even bother to say thank you.* ● *Don't bother waiting for me – I'll catch you up later.* ● *Don't bother about the washing-up. I'll do it later.*

IDIOMS **can't be bothered (to do sth)** used to say that you do not want to spend time or energy doing sth: *I can't be bothered to do my homework now. I'll do it tomorrow.*

not be bothered (about sth) (*especially Brit informal*) to think that sth is not important: *'What would you like to do this evening?' 'I'm not bothered really.'*

bother² /'bɒðə/ *noun* [U] trouble or difficulty: *Thanks for all your help. It's saved me a lot of bother.*

bothered /'bɒðəd/ *adj* worried about sth: *Sam doesn't seem too bothered about losing his job.*

★**bottle**¹ /'bɒtl/ *noun* [C] **1** a glass or plastic container with a narrow neck for keeping liquids in: *a beer bottle* ● *an empty bottle* **2** the amount of liquid that a bottle can hold: *a bottle of beer* ••➤ picture at **container**

bottle² /'bɒtl/ *verb* [T] to put sth into bottles: *After three or four months the wine is bottled.* ● *bottled water* (= that you can buy in bottles)

PHRASAL VERB **bottle sth up** to not allow yourself to express strong emotions: *You'll make yourself ill if you keep your feelings bottled up.*

'bottle bank *noun* [C] a large container in a public place where people can leave their empty bottles so that the glass can be used again (**recycled**)

bottleneck /'bɒtlnek/ *noun* [C] **1** a narrow piece of road that causes traffic to slow down or stop **2** something that slows down progress, especially in business or industry

★**bottom**¹ /'bɒtəm/ *noun* **1** [C,usually sing] the lowest part of sth: *The house is **at the bottom** of a hill.* ● *I think I've got a pen **in the bottom** of my bag.* ● *The sea is so clear that you can see the bottom.* **2** [C] the flat surface on the outside of an object, on which it stands: *There's a label **on the bottom** of the box.*

---

3 [sing] the far end of sth: *The bus stop is at the bottom of the road.* **4** [sing] the lowest position in relation to other people, teams, etc: *She started at the bottom and now she's the Managing Director.* **5** [C] the part of your body that you sit on: *He fell over and landed on his bottom.* ••► picture on page C5 **6** bottoms [pl] the lower part of a piece of clothing that is in two parts: *pyjama bottoms* • *track suit bottoms*

IDIOMS **be at the bottom of sth** to be the cause of sth: *I'm sure Molly Potter is at the bottom of all this.*

from the (bottom of your) heart → HEART

get to the bottom of sth to find out the real cause of sth

bottom² /'bɒtəm/ **adj** in the lowest position: *the bottom shelf* • *I live on the bottom floor.*

bottomless /'bɒtəmləs/ **adj** very deep; without limit

,bottom 'line **noun** [sing] **1** the bottom line the most important thing to consider when you are discussing or deciding sth, etc: *A musical instrument should look and feel good, but the bottom line is how it sounds.* **2** the final profit or loss that a company has made in a particular period of time **3** the lowest price that sb will accept for sth

bough /baʊ/ **noun** [C] one of the main branches of a tree

bought /bɔːt/ *past tense, past participle of* BUY¹

boulder /'bəʊldə/ **noun** [C] a very large rock

boulevard /'buːləvɑːd/ **noun** [C] a wide street in a city often with trees on each side

bounce /baʊns/ **verb** **1** [I,T] (used about a ball, etc) to move away quickly after it has hit a hard surface; to make a ball do this: *The stone bounced off the wall and hit her on the head.* • *A small boy came down the street, bouncing a ball.* **2** [I] to jump up and down continuously: *The children were bouncing on their beds.* ••► picture at **hop 3** [I,T] (used about a cheque) to be returned by a bank without payment because there is not enough money in the account –**bounce** **noun** [C]

PHRASAL VERB **bounce back** to become healthy, successful or happy again after an illness, a failure, or a disappointment

bouncy /'baʊnsi/ **adj** **1** that bounces well or that can make things bounce: *a bouncy ball/ surface* **2** (used about a person) full of energy; lively: *She's a very bouncy person.*

bound¹ /baʊnd/ **adj** **1** bound to do sth certain to do sth: *You've done so much work that you're bound to pass the exam.* **2** (not before a noun) having a legal or moral duty to do sth: *The company is bound by UK employment law.* • *She felt bound to refuse the offer.* **3** bound (for...) travelling to a particular place: *a ship bound for Australia*

IDIOM **bound up with sth** very closely connected with sth

bound² /baʊnd/ **verb** [I] to run quickly with long steps: *She bounded out of the house to meet us.* –**bound** **noun** [C]: *With a couple of bounds he had crossed the room.*

bound³ *past tense, past participle of* BIND¹

★**boundary** /'baʊndri/ **noun** [C] (*pl* boundaries) a real or imagined line that marks the limits of sth and divides it from other places or things: *The main road is the boundary between the two districts.* • *Scientists continue to push back the boundaries of human knowledge.* ••► Look at the note at **border**.

boundless /'baʊndləs/ **adj** having no limit: *boundless energy*

bounds /baʊndz/ **noun** [pl] limits that cannot or should not be passed: *Price rises must be kept within reasonable bounds.*

IDIOM **out of bounds** not to be entered by sb: *This area is out of bounds to all staff.*

bouquet /bu'keɪ/ **noun** [C] a bunch of flowers that is arranged in an attractive way

bourbon /'bɜːbən/ **noun** [C,U] a type of strong alcoholic drink (whisky) that is made mainly in the US

the bourgeoisie /ˌbɔːʒwɑːˈziː/ **noun** [sing, with sing or pl verb] a class of people in society who are interested mainly in having more money and a higher social position –**bourgeois** /'bʊəʒwɑː/ **adj**: *bourgeois attitudes/ideas/values*

bout /baʊt/ **noun** [C] **1** a short period of great activity: *a bout of hard work* **2** a period of illness: *I'm just recovering from a bout of flu.*

boutique /buːˈtiːk/ **noun** [C] a small shop that sells fashionable clothes or expensive presents

bovine /'bəʊvaɪn/ **adj** (*technical*) connected with cows: *bovine diseases*

★**bow¹** /baʊ/ **verb 1** [I,T] bow (sth) (to sb) to bend your head or the upper part of your body forward and down, as a sign of respect: *The speaker bowed to the guests and left the stage.* • *He bowed his head respectfully.* **2** [I] bow to sb/sth to accept sth: *I do not think the unions should bow to pressure from the Government.*

PHRASAL VERB **bow out (of sth/as sth)** to leave an important position or stop taking part in sth: *After a long and successful career, she has decided to bow out of politics.* • *He finally bowed out as chairman after ten years.*

bow² /baʊ/ **noun** [C] **1** an act of bowing¹(1): *The director of the play came on stage to take a bow.* **2** the front part of a ship ••► Look at **stern**.

bow³ /bəʊ/ **noun** [C] **1** a knot with two loose roundish parts and two loose ends that you use when you are tying shoes, etc: *He tied his laces in a bow.* ••► picture at **loop 2** a weapon for shooting arrows. A bow is a curved piece of wood that is held in shape by a tight string. **3** a long thin piece of wood with string stretched across it that you use for playing some musical instruments: *a violin bow* ••► picture at **music**

★**bowel** /'baʊəl/ **noun** [C,usually pl] one of the tubes that carries waste food away from your stomach to the place where it leaves your body

---

[I] **intransitive**, a verb which has no object: *He laughed.*   [T] **transitive**, a verb which has an object: *He ate an apple.*

bowl

★**bowl¹** /bəʊl/ **noun** [C] **1** a deep round dish without a lid that is used for holding food or liquid: *a soup bowl* **2** the amount of sth that is in a bowl: *I usually have a bowl of cereal for breakfast.* **3** a large plastic container that is used for washing dishes, washing clothes, etc

bowl² /bəʊl/ **verb** [I,T] (in cricket) to throw the ball in the direction of the person with the bat

<u>PHRASAL VERB</u> **bowl sb over 1** to knock sb down when you are moving quickly **2** to surprise sb very much in a pleasant way: *I was absolutely bowled over by the beautiful scenery.*

bow legs /bəʊ 'legz/ **noun** [pl] legs that curve out at the knees –**bow-legged** /ˌbəʊ 'legɪd/ **adj**

bowler /'bəʊlə/ **noun** [C] **1** (also **bowler 'hat**, *US* **derby**) a round hard black hat, usually worn by men ••➤ picture at **hat 2** (in cricket) the player who throws (**bowls**) the ball in the direction of the person with the bat

bowling /'bəʊlɪŋ/ **noun** [U] a game in which you roll a heavy ball down a special track (a **lane**) towards a group of wooden objects (**pins**) and try to knock them all down: *to go bowling*

bowls /bəʊlz/ **noun** [U] a game in which you try to roll large wooden balls as near as possible to a smaller ball: *to play bowls*

bow tie /ˌbəʊ 'taɪ/ **noun** [C] a tie in the shape of a bow³(1), that is worn by men, especially on formal occasions ••➤ picture on page C6

★**box¹** /bɒks/ **noun 1** [C] a square or rectangular container for solid objects. A box often has a lid: *a cardboard box* ● *a shoebox* ••➤ picture at **container 2** [C] a box and the things inside it: *a box of chocolates/matches/tissues* **3** [C] an empty square or rectangular space on a form in which you have to write sth: *Write your full name in the box below.* **4** [C] a small enclosed area that is used for a particular purpose: *a telephone box* ● *the witness box* (= in a court of law) **5 the box** [sing] (*Brit informal*) television: *What's on the box tonight?*

★**box²** /bɒks/ **verb 1** [I,T] to fight in the sport of boxing **2** [T] to put sth into a box: *a boxed set of CDs*

<u>PHRASAL VERB</u> **box sb/sth in** to prevent sb from getting out of a small space: *Someone parked behind us and boxed us in.*

boxer /'bɒksə/ **noun** [C] a person who does boxing as a sport

'boxer shorts (also **boxers**) **noun** [pl] shorts that men use as underwear

boxing /'bɒksɪŋ/ **noun** [U] a sport in which two people fight by hitting each other with their hands inside large gloves: *the world middleweight boxing champion* ● *boxing gloves* ••➤ picture on page S2

★**'Boxing Day noun** [C] (*Brit*) the day after Christmas Day; 26 December

➤ In England and Wales Boxing Day is a public holiday.

'box number noun [C] a number used as an address, especially in newspaper advertisements

'box office noun [C] the place in a cinema, theatre, etc where the tickets are sold

★**boy** /bɔɪ/ **noun** [C] a male child or a young man: *They've got three children – two boys and a girl.* ● *I used to play here when I was a boy.*

boycott /'bɔɪkɒt/ **verb** [T] to refuse to buy things from a particular company, take part in an event, etc because you strongly disapprove of it: *Several countries boycotted the Olympic Games in protest.* –**boycott noun** [C]: *a boycott of the local elections*

boyfriend /'bɔɪfrend/ **noun** [C] a man or boy with whom a person has a romantic and/or sexual relationship

boyhood /'bɔɪhʊd/ **noun** [U] the time of being a boy: *My father told me some of his boyhood memories.*

boyish /'bɔɪɪʃ/ **adj** like a boy: *a boyish smile*

Boy 'Scout = scout(1)

★**bra** /brɑː/ **noun** [C] a piece of clothing that women wear under their other clothes to support their breasts

brace¹ /breɪs/ **noun 1** [C] a metal frame that is fixed to a child's teeth in order to make them straight **2 braces** (*US* **suspenders**) [pl] a pair of straps that go over your shoulders to hold your trousers up

brace² /breɪs/ **verb** [T] **brace sth/yourself (for sth)** to prepare yourself for sth unpleasant: *You'd better brace yourself for some bad news.*

★**bracelet** /'breɪslət/ **noun** [C] a piece of jewellery, for example a metal chain or band, that you wear around your wrist or arm ••➤ picture at **jewellery**

bracing /'breɪsɪŋ/ **adj** making you feel healthy and full of energy: *bracing sea air*

bracket¹ /'brækɪt/ **noun** [C] **1** [usually pl] (*especially US* **parenthesis**) one of two marks, () or [ ], that you put round extra information in a piece of writing: *A translation of each word is given in brackets.* **2** age, income, price, etc bracket prices, ages, etc which are between two limits: *to be in a high income bracket* **3** a piece of metal or wood that is fixed to a wall and used as a support for a shelf, lamp, etc

bracket² /'brækɪt/ **verb** [T] **1** to put brackets¹(1) round a word, number, etc **2 bracket A and B (together); bracket A with B** to think of two or more people or things as similar in some way

brag /bræg/ **verb** [I] (**bragging; bragged**) **brag (to sb) (about/of sth)** to talk too proudly about sth: *She's always bragging to her friends about how clever she is.*

braid /breɪd/ **noun 1** [U] thin coloured rope

that is used to decorate military uniforms, etc 2 (US) = **PLAIT** ••➤ picture at **hair**

Braille /breɪl/ *noun* [U] a system of printing, using little round marks that are higher than the level of the paper they are on and which blind people can read by touching them: *The signs were written in Braille.*

★**brain** /breɪn/ *noun* **1** [C] the part of your body inside your head that controls your thoughts, feelings and movements: *He suffered serious brain damage in a road accident.* ● *a brain surgeon* ••➤ picture on page C5 **2** [C,U] the ability to think clearly; intelligence: *She has a very quick brain and learns fast.* ● *He hasn't got the brains to be a doctor.* **3** [C] (*informal*) a very clever person: *He's one of the best brains in the country.* **4 the brains** [sing] the person who plans or organizes sth: *She's the real brains in the organization.*

IDIOMS **have sth on the brain** (*informal*) to think about sth all the time: *I've had that song on the brain all day.*

rack your brains → **RACK²**

brainchild /'breɪntʃaɪld/ *noun* [sing] the idea or invention of a particular person: *The music festival was the brainchild of a young teacher.*

'**brain-dead** *adj* **1** having serious brain damage and needing a machine to stay alive **2** (*informal*) unable to think clearly; stupid: *He's brain-dead from watching too much TV.*

brainless /'breɪnləs/ *adj* (*informal*) very silly; stupid

brainstorm¹ /'breɪnstɔːm/ *noun* [C] **1** a moment of sudden confusion: *I had a brainstorm in the exam and couldn't answer any questions.* **2** (US) = **BRAINWAVE**

brainstorm² /'breɪnstɔːm/ *verb* [I,T] to solve a problem or make a decision by thinking of as many ideas as possible in a short time: *We'll spend five minutes brainstorming ideas on how we can raise money.*

brainwash /'breɪnwɒʃ/ *verb* [T] **brainwash sb (into doing sth)** to force sb to believe sth by using strong mental pressure: *Television advertisements try to brainwash people into buying things that they don't need.* –**brainwashing** *noun* [U]

brainwave /'breɪnweɪv/ (US **brainstorm**) *noun* [C] (*informal*) a sudden clever idea: *If I have a brainwave, I'll let you know.*

brainy /'breɪni/ *adj* (*informal*) intelligent

braise /breɪz/ *verb* [T] to cook meat or vegetables slowly in a little liquid in a covered dish

★**brake¹** /breɪk/ *noun* [C] **1** the part of a vehicle that makes it go slower or stop: *She put her foot on the brake and just managed to stop in time.* ••➤ picture on page S9 **2** something that makes sth else slow down or stop: *The Government must try to put a brake on inflation.*

brake² /breɪk/ *verb* [I] to make a vehicle go slower or stop by using the brakes: *If the driver hadn't braked in time, the car would have hit me.*

bran /bræn/ *noun* [U] the brown outer covering of grains that is left when the grain is made into flour

★**branch¹** /brɑːntʃ/ *noun* [C] **1** one of the main parts of a tree that grows out of the thick central part (**trunk**) ••➤ picture on page C2 **2** an office, shop, etc that is part of a larger organization: *The company I work for has branches in Paris, Milan and New York.* **3** a part of an academic subject: *Psychiatry is a branch of medicine.*

branch² /brɑːntʃ/ *verb*

PHRASAL VERBS **branch off** (used about a road) to leave a larger road and go off in another direction: *A bit further on, the road branches off to the left.*

branch out (into sth) to start doing sth new and different from the things you usually do: *The band has recently branched out into acting.*

★**brand¹** /brænd/ *noun* [C] **1** the name of a product that is made by a particular company: *a well-known brand of coffee* **2** a particular type of sth: *a strange brand of humour*

brand² /brænd/ *verb* [T] **1** to mark an animal with a hot iron to show who owns it **2 brand sb (as sth)** to say that sb has a bad character so that people have a bad opinion of him/her: *She was branded as a troublemaker after she complained about her long working hours.*

brandish /'brændɪʃ/ *verb* [T] to wave sth in the air in an aggressive or excited way: *The robber was brandishing a knife.*

,**brand 'new** *adj* completely new

brandy /'brændi/ *noun* [C,U] (*pl* **brandies**) a strong alcoholic drink that is made from wine

brash /bræʃ/ *adj* too confident and direct: *Her brash manner makes her unpopular with strangers.* –**brashness** *noun* [U]

brass /brɑːs/ *noun* **1** [U] a hard yellow metal that is a mixture of two other metals (**copper** and **zinc**): *brass buttons on a uniform* **2** [sing, with sing or pl verb] the group of musical instruments that are made of brass: *the brass section in an orchestra*

brat /bræt/ *noun* [C] a child who behaves badly and annoys you

bravado /brə'vɑːdəʊ/ *noun* [U] a confident way of behaving that is intended to impress people, sometimes as a way of hiding a lack of confidence

★**brave¹** /breɪv/ *adj* **1** ready to do things that are dangerous or difficult without showing fear: *the brave soldiers who fought in the war* ● *'This may hurt a little, so try and be brave,' said the dentist.* **2** needing or showing courage: *a brave decision* ••➤ synonym **gallant** –**bravely** *adv: The men bravely defended the town for three days.*

brave² /breɪv/ *verb* [T] to face sth unpleasant, dangerous or difficult without showing fear: *She braved the rain and went out into the street.*

bravery /'breɪvəri/ *noun* [U] actions that are brave: *After the war he received a medal for bravery.*

b

bravo /ˌbrɑːˈvəʊ/ **interj** a word that people shout to show that they have enjoyed sth that sb has done, for example a play

brawl /brɔːl/ **noun** [C] a noisy fight among a group of people, usually in a public place –**brawl verb** [I]: *We saw some football fans brawling in the street.*

brawn /brɔːn/ **noun** [U] physical strength: *To do this kind of job you need more brawn than brain* (= you need to be strong rather than clever). –**brawny adj**: *He folded his brawny arms across his chest.*

brazen /ˈbreɪzn/ **adj** without embarrassment, especially in a way which shocks people: *Don't believe a word she says - she's a brazen liar!* –**brazenly adv**: *He brazenly admitted he'd been having an affair.*

Bra'zil nut noun [C] a nut that we eat with a very hard shell •➤ picture at **nut**

breach¹ /briːtʃ/ **noun 1** [C,U] **breach (of sth)** an act that breaks an agreement, a law, etc: *Giving private information about clients is a breach of confidence.* • *The company was found to be in breach of contract.* **2** [C] a break in friendly relations between people, groups, etc: *The incident caused a breach between the two countries.* **3** [C] an opening in a wall, etc that defends or protects sb/sth: *The waves made a breach in the sea wall.*

breach² /briːtʃ/ **verb** [T] **1** to break an agreement, a law, etc: *He accused the Government of breaching international law.* **2** to make an opening in a wall, etc that defends or protects sb/sth

bread

French bread

bagel

roll

slice

croissant

crust

loaf of bread

★**bread** /bred/ **noun** [U] a type of food made from flour and water mixed together and baked in an oven. Another substance (yeast) is usually added to make the bread rise: *a piece/slice of bread*

> A **loaf** of bread is bread that has been shaped and cooked in one piece. **Wholemeal** bread is made from flour that contains all the grain.

•➤ picture on page C4

breadcrumbs /ˈbredkrʌmz/ **noun** [pl] very small bits of bread that are used in cooking

★**breadth** /bredθ/ **noun 1** [C,U] the distance between the two sides of sth: *We measured the length and breadth of the garden.* **2** [U] the wide variety of things, subjects, etc that sth includes: *I was amazed by the breadth of her*

knowledge. •➤ adjective **broad**

the length and breadth of sth → **LENGTH**

breadwinner /ˈbredwɪnə/ **noun** [C, usually sing] the person who earns most of the money that his/her family needs: *When his dad died, Steve became the breadwinner.*

★**break¹** /breɪk/ **verb** (*pt* **broke** /brəʊk/; *pp* **broken** /ˈbrəʊkən/) **1** [I,T] to separate, or make sth separate, into two or more pieces: *She dropped the vase onto the floor and it broke.* • *He broke his leg in a car accident.* •➤ picture at **chip 2** [I,T] (used about a machine, etc) to stop working; to stop a machine, etc working: *The photocopier has broken.* • *Be careful with my camera – I don't want you to break it.* **3** [T] to do sth that is against the law, or against what has been agreed or promised: *to break the law/rules/ speed limit* • *Don't worry – I never break my promises.* **4** [I,T] to stop doing sth for a short time: *Let's break for coffee now.* • *We decided to break the journey and stop for lunch.* **5** [T] to make sth end: *Once you start smoking it's very difficult to break the habit.* • *Suddenly, the silence was broken by the sound of a bird singing.* **6** [I] to begin: *The day was breaking as I left the house.* • *We ran indoors when the storm broke.* • *When the story broke in the newspapers, nobody could believe it.* **7** [I] (used about a wave) to reach its highest point and begin to fall: *I watched the waves breaking on the rocks.* **8** [I] (used about the voice) to change suddenly: *Most boys' voices break when they are 13 or 14 years old.* • *His voice was breaking with emotion as he spoke.*

> For idioms containing **break**, look at the entries for nouns, adjectives, etc. For example, **break even** is at **even**.

PHRASAL VERBS **break away (from sb/sth) 1** to escape suddenly from sb who is holding you **2** to leave a political party, state, etc in order to form a new one

break down 1 (used about a vehicle or machine) to stop working: *Akram's car broke down on the way to work this morning.* **2** (used about a system, discussion, etc) to fail: *Talks between the two countries have completely broken down.* **3** to lose control of your feelings and start crying: *He broke down in tears when he heard the news.*

break sth down 1 to destroy sth by using force: *The police had to break down the door to get into the house.* **2** to make a substance separate into parts or change into a different form in a chemical process: *Food is broken down in our bodies by the digestive system.*

break in to enter a building by force, usually in order to steal sth

break in (on sth) to interrupt when sb else is speaking: *The waiter broke in on our conversation to tell me I had a phone call.*

break into sth 1 to enter a place that is closed: *Thieves broke into his car and stole the radio.* • (*figurative*) *The company is trying to break into the Japanese market.* **2** to start doing sth suddenly: *to break into song/a run*

break off to suddenly stop doing or saying sth: *He started speaking and then broke off in the middle of a sentence.*
break (sth) off to remove a part of sth by force; to be removed in this way: *Could you break off another bit of chocolate for me?*
break sth off to end a relationship suddenly: *After a bad argument, they decided to **break off** their **engagement**.*
break out (used about fighting, wars, fires, etc) to start suddenly
break out in sth to suddenly have a skin problem: *to break out in spots/a rash*
break out (of sth) to escape from a prison, etc
break through (sth) to manage to get past sth that is stopping you: *The protesters were trying to break through the line of police.*
break up 1 (used about events that involve a group of people) to end or finish: *The meeting broke up just before lunch.* **2** (*Brit*) to start school holidays: *When do you break up for the summer holidays?*
break up (with sb) to end a relationship with a wife, husband, girlfriend or boyfriend: *She's broken up with her boyfriend.*
break (sth) up to separate into parts: *The ship broke up on the rocks.*
break sth up to end an event by separating the people who are involved in it: *The police arrived and broke up the fight.*
break with sth to end a relationship or connection with sb/sth: *to break with tradition/ the past*

★**break²** /breɪk/ *noun* [C] **1** a place where sth has been broken: *a break in a pipe* **2** an opening or space in sth: *Wait for a break in the traffic before you cross the road.* **3** a short period of rest: *We worked all day without a break.* • *to take a break* ••➤ Look at the note at **interval**. **4 break (in sth); break (with sb/sth)** a change from what usually happens or an end to sth: *The incident led to a break in diplomatic relations.* • *She wanted to make a complete break with the past.* **5** (*informal*) a piece of good luck: *to give sb a break* (= to help sb by giving him/her a chance to be successful)
IDIOMS **break of day** the time when light first appears in the morning; dawn
give sb a break 1 used to tell sb to stop saying things that are annoying or not true: *Give me a break and stop nagging, OK!* **2** (*especially US*) to be fair to sb

breakage /'breɪkɪdʒ/ *noun* [C, usually pl] something that has been broken: *Customers must pay for any breakages*

breakaway /'breɪkəweɪ/ *adj* (only *before* a noun) (used about a political group, an organization, or a part of a country) that has separated from a larger group or country
–**breakaway** *noun* [C]

breakdown /'breɪkdaʊn/ *noun* [C] **1** a time when a vehicle, machine, etc stops working: *I hope we don't **have a breakdown** on the motorway.* **2** the failure or end of sth: *The breakdown of the talks means that a strike is likely.* **3** = **NERVOUS BREAKDOWN 4** a list of all

the details of sth: *I would like a full break-down of how the money was spent.*

★**breakfast** /'brekfəst/ *noun* [C,U] the meal which you have when you get up in the morning: *to **have breakfast*** • *What do you usually have **for** breakfast?* • *to eat a big breakfast*

➤ In a hotel an **English** breakfast means cereal, fried eggs, bacon, sausages, tomatoes, toast, etc. A **Continental** breakfast means bread and jam with coffee.

IDIOM **bed and breakfast** ➔ **BED¹**

'**break-in** *noun* [C] the act of entering a building by force, especially in order to steal sth: *The police say there have been several break-ins in this area.*

breakneck /'breɪknek/ *adj* (only *before* a noun) very fast and dangerous: *He drove her to the hospital **at breakneck speed**.*

breakthrough /'breɪkθruː/ *noun* [C] a breakthrough (in sth) an important discovery or development: *Scientists are hoping to **make a breakthrough** in cancer research.*

'**break-up** *noun* [C] **1** the end of a relationship between two people: *the break-up of a marriage* **2** the separation of a group or organization into smaller parts: *the break-up of the Soviet Union*

★**breast** /brest/ *noun* [C] **1** one of the two soft round parts of a woman's body that can produce milk **2** a word used especially in literature for the top part of the front of your body, below the neck **3** the front part of the body of a bird ••➤ picture on page C1

breastfeed /'brestfiːd/ *verb* [I,T] (*pt, pp* **breastfed**) to feed a baby with milk from the breast

breaststroke /'breststrəʊk/ *noun* [U] a style of swimming on your front in which you start with your hands together, push both arms forward and then move them out and back through the water: *to **do (the) breaststroke*** ••➤ Look at **backstroke**, **butterfly** and **crawl**. ••➤ picture on page S2

★**breath** /breθ/ *noun* **1** [U] the air that you take into and blow out of your lungs: *to **have bad breath*** (= breath which smells unpleasant) **2** [C] an act of taking air into or blowing air out of your lungs: *Take a few deep breaths before you start running.*
IDIOMS **a breath of fresh air** the clean air which you breathe outside, especially when compared to the air inside a room or building: *Let's go for a walk. I need a breath of fresh air.* • (*figurative*) *James's happy face is like a breath of fresh air in that miserable place.*
catch your breath ➔ **CATCH¹**
get your breath (again/back) to rest after physical exercise so that your breathing returns to normal
hold your breath to stop breathing for a short time, for example when you are swimming or because of fear or excitement: *We all held our breath as we waited for her reply.*
(be/get) out of/short of breath (to be/start)

b

breathing very quickly, for example after physical exercise

say sth, speak, etc under your breath to say sth very quietly, usually because you do not want people to hear you

take your breath away to surprise sb very much: *The spectacular view took our breath away.* ••➤ adjective **breathtaking**

take a deep breath → DEEP¹

with bated breath → BATED

breathalyse (*US* **breathalyze**) /'breθəlaɪz/ verb [T] to test the breath of a driver with a special machine (a **breathalyser**) to measure how much alcohol he/she has drunk

★**breathe** /briːð/ verb [I,T] to take air, etc into your lungs and blow it out again: *Breathe out as you lift the weight and breathe in as you lower it.* • *I hate having to breathe (in) other people's cigarette smoke.* –**breathing** noun [U]: *heavy/irregular breathing* • *These deep breathing exercises will help you relax.*

IDIOM **not breathe a word (of/about sth) (to sb)** to not tell sb about sth that is secret: *If you breathe a word of this to my mother, I'll never speak to you again!*

breather /'briːðə/ noun [C] (*informal*) a short rest: *to have/take a breather*

breathless /'breθləs/ adj **1** having difficulty breathing: *I was hot and breathless when I got to the top of the hill.* **2** not able to breathe because you are so excited, frightened, etc: *to be breathless with excitement* –**breathlessly** adv

breathtaking /'breθteɪkɪŋ/ adj extremely surprising, beautiful, etc: *breathtaking scenery*

'breath test noun [C] a test by the police on the breath of a driver to measure how much alcohol he/she has drunk

breed¹ /briːd/ verb (*pt, pp* **bred** /bred/) **1** [I] (used about animals) to have sex and produce young animals: *Many animals won't breed in zoos.* ••➤ synonym **mate 2** [T] to keep animals or plants in order to produce young from them: *These cattle are bred to produce high yields of milk.* **3** [T] to cause sth: *This kind of thinking breeds intolerance.* –**breeding** noun [U]

breed² /briːd/ noun [C] a particular variety of an animal: *a breed of cattle/dog*

breeder /'briːdə/ noun [C] a person who breeds animals or plants: *a dog breeder*

'breeding ground noun [C] **1** a place where wild animals go to breed **2** a place where sth can develop: *a breeding ground for crime*

breeze¹ /briːz/ noun [C] a light wind: *A warm breeze was blowing.*

breeze² /briːz/ verb [I] **breeze along, in, out,** etc to move in a confident and relaxed way: *He just breezed in twenty minutes late without a word of apology.*

breezy /'briːzi/ adj **1** with a little wind

2 happy and relaxed: *You're bright and breezy this morning!*

brevity /'brevəti/ noun [U] the state of being short or quick ••➤ adjective **brief**

brew /bruː/ verb **1** [T] to make beer **2** [T] to make a drink of tea or coffee by adding hot water: *to brew a pot of tea* **3** [I] (used about tea) to stand in hot water before it is ready to drink: *Leave it to brew for a few minutes.*

IDIOM **be brewing** (used about sth bad) to develop or grow: *There's **trouble brewing**.*

brewery /'bruːəri/ noun [C] (*pl* **breweries**) a place where beer is made

bribe /braɪb/ noun [C] money, etc that is given to sb such as an official to persuade him/her to do sth to help you that is wrong or dishonest: *to accept/take bribes* –**bribe** verb [T] **bribe sb (with sth)**: *They got a visa by bribing an official.* –**bribery** /'braɪbəri/ noun [U]

bric-a-brac /'brɪk ə bræk/ noun [U] small items of little value, for decoration in a house ••➤ picture on page C8

★**brick** /brɪk/ noun [C,U] a hard block of baked clay that is used for building houses, etc: *a lorry carrying bricks* • *a house built of red brick* ••➤ picture on page C7

bricklayer /'brɪkleɪə/ noun [C] a person whose job is to build walls with bricks

brickwork /'brɪkwɜːk/ noun [U] the part of a building that is made of bricks

bridal /'braɪdl/ adj (only *before* a noun) connected with a bride

★**bride** /braɪd/ noun [C] a woman on or just before her wedding day: *a **bride-to-be** (= a woman whose wedding is soon)* ••➤ Look at the note at **wedding**.

★**bridegroom** /'braɪdɡruːm/ (also **groom**) noun [C] a man on or just before his wedding day ••➤ Look at the note at **wedding**.

bridesmaid /'braɪdzmeɪd/ noun [C] a woman or girl who helps a woman on her wedding day (**the bride**) ••➤ Look at the note at **wedding**.

★**bridge¹** /brɪdʒ/ noun **1** [C] a structure that carries a road or railway across a river, valley, road or railway: *a bridge over the River Danube* **2** [sing] the high part of a ship where the captain and the people who control the ship stand **3** [U] a card game for four people

bridge² /brɪdʒ/ verb [T] to build a bridge over sth

IDIOM **bridge a/the gap** to fill a space between two people, groups or things or to bring them closer together: *Baby food bridges the gap between milk and solid food.*

bridle /'braɪdl/ noun [C] the leather straps that you put on a horse's head so that you can control it when you are riding it ••➤ picture at **horse**

★**brief¹** /briːf/ adj short or quick: *a brief description* • *Please be brief. We don't have*

much time. ••➤ **noun brevity**

IDIOM **in brief** using only a few words: *In brief, the meeting was a disaster.*

brief² /briːf/ **noun** [C] instructions or information about a job or task: *He was given the brief of improving the image of the organization.*

brief³ /briːf/ **verb** [T] to give sb information or instructions about sth: *The minister has been fully briefed on what questions to expect.*

briefcase /'briːfkeɪs/ **noun** [C] a flat case that you use for carrying papers, etc, especially when you go to work ••➤ picture at **bag**

briefing /'briːfɪŋ/ **noun** [C,U] instructions or information that you are given before sth happens: *a press/news briefing* (= where information is given to journalists)

briefly /'briːfli/ **adv 1** for a short time; quickly: *She glanced briefly at the letter.* **2** using only a few words: *I'd like to comment very briefly on that last statement.*

briefs /briːfs/ **noun** [pl] pants for men or women ••➤ Note that we say *a pair of briefs*.

brigade /brɪˈgeɪd/ **noun** [C] **1** a unit of soldiers in the army **2** a group of people who work together for a particular purpose: *the fire brigade*

brigadier /ˌbrɪgəˈdɪə/ **noun** [C] an important officer in the army

★ **bright** /braɪt/ **adj 1** having a lot of light: *a bright, sunny day* • *eyes bright with happiness* **2** (used about a colour) strong and easy to see: *a bright yellow jumper* ••➤ opposite **soft 3** clever, or able to learn things quickly: *a bright child* • *a **bright idea*** **4** likely to be pleasant or successful: *The future looks bright.* **5** happy; cheerful –**brightly** adv: *brightly-coloured clothes* –**brightness noun** [U] IDIOM **look on the bright side → LOOK¹**

brighten /'braɪtn/ **verb** [I,T] **brighten (sth) (up)** to become brighter or happier; to make sth brighter: *His face brightened when he saw her.* • *to brighten up sb's day* (= make it happier)

★ **brilliant** /'brɪliənt/ **adj 1** having a lot of light; very bright: *brilliant sunshine* **2** very clever, skilful or successful: *a brilliant young scientist* • *That's a brilliant idea!* **3** (*informal*) very good: *That was a brilliant film!* –**brilliance noun** [U] –**brilliantly adv**

brim¹ /brɪm/ **noun** [C] **1** the top edge of a cup, glass, etc: *The cup was full to the brim.* **2** the bottom part of a hat that is wider than the rest ••➤ picture at **hat**

brim² /brɪm/ **verb** [I] (**brimming; brimmed**) **brim (with sth)** to be full of sth: *His eyes were brimming with tears.*
PHRASAL VERB **brim over (with sth)** (used about a cup, glass, etc) to have more liquid than it can hold: *The bowl was brimming over with water.* • (*figurative*) *to be brimming over with health/happiness*

Bring the newspaper.

Fetch the newspaper.

Take the newspaper.

★ **bring** /brɪŋ/ **verb** [T] (*pt, pp* **brought** /brɔːt/) **1** to carry or take sb/sth to a place with you: *Is it all right if I bring a friend to the party?* • *Could you bring us some water, please?* • (*figurative*) *He will bring valuable skills and experience to the team.* • *My sister went to Spain on holiday and brought me back a T-shirt.* **2** to move sth somewhere: *She brought the book down off the shelf.* • *Louis brought a photo out of his wallet and showed it to us.* **3** to cause or result in sth: *The sight of her brought a smile to his face.* • *Money doesn't always bring happiness.* **4** to cause sb/sth to be in a certain place or condition: *Their screams brought people running from all directions.* • *Add water to the mixture and bring it to the boil.* • *An injury can easily **bring** an athlete's career **to an end.*** **5 bring yourself to do sth** to force yourself to do sth: *The film was so horrible that I couldn't bring myself to watch it.*

➤ For idioms containing **bring**, look at the entries for the nouns, adjectives, etc, for example **bring up the rear** is at **rear**.

PHRASAL VERBS **bring about** to cause sth to happen: *to bring about changes in people's lives*

bring sth back 1 to cause sth that existed before to be introduced again: *Nobody wants to bring back the days of child labour.* **2** to cause sb to remember sth: *The photographs brought back memories of his childhood.*

bring sb/sth down to defeat sb/sth; to make sb/sth lose a position of power: *to bring down the government*

bring sth down to make sth lower in level: *to bring down the price of sth*

[I] **intransitive**, a verb which has no object: *He laughed.*   [T] **transitive**, a verb which has an object: *He ate an apple.*

b

bring sth forward 1 to move sth to an earlier time: *The date of the meeting has been brought forward by two weeks.* •➤ opposite **put sth back 2** to suggest sth for discussion **bring sb in** to ask or employ sb to do a particular job: *A specialist was brought in to set up the new computer system.*
bring sth in to introduce sth: *The government have brought in a new law on dangerous dogs.*
bring sth off to manage to do sth difficult: *The team brought off an amazing victory.*
bring sth on to cause sth: *Her headaches are brought on by stress.*
bring sth out to produce sth or cause sth to appear: *When is the company bringing out its next new model?*
bring sb round to make sb become conscious again: *I splashed cold water on his face to try to bring him round.*
bring sb round (to sth) to persuade sb to agree with your opinion: *After a lot of discussion we finally brought them round to our point of view.*
bring sth round to sth to direct a conversation to a particular subject: *I finally brought the conversation round to the subject of money.*
bring sb up to look after a child until he/she is adult and to teach him/her how to behave: *After her parents were killed the child was brought up by her uncle.* • *a well-brought-up child*
bring sth up 1 to be sick so that food that you have swallowed comes back out of your mouth; to vomit **2** to introduce sth into a discussion or conversation: *I intend to bring the matter up at the next meeting.*

brink /brɪŋk/ **noun** [sing] **the brink (of sth)** if you are on the brink of sth, you are almost in a very new, exciting or dangerous situation: *Just when the band were on the brink of becoming famous, they split up.*

brisk /brɪsk/ **adj 1** quick or using a lot of energy; busy: *They set off at a brisk pace.* • *Trading has been brisk this morning.* **2** confident and practical; wanting to get things done quickly –**briskly adv** –**briskness noun** [U]

bristle¹ /ˈbrɪsl/ **noun** [C] **1** a short thick hair: *The bristles on my chin hurt the baby's face.* **2** one of the short thick hairs of a brush

bristle² /ˈbrɪsl/ **verb** [I] **1** (used about hair or an animal's fur) to stand up straight because of fear, anger, cold, etc **2 bristle (with sth) (at sb/sth)** to show that you are angry
PHRASAL VERB **bristle with sth** to be full of sth

Brit /brɪt/ **noun** [C] (*informal*) a British person

★**Britain** /ˈbrɪtn/ = **GREAT BRITAIN** •➤ Look at the note at **United Kingdom**.

★**British** /ˈbrɪtɪʃ/ **adj 1** of the United Kingdom (= Great Britain and Northern Ireland): *British industry* • *to hold a British passport* **2 the British noun** [pl] the people of the United Kingdom

the British Isles noun [pl] Great Britain and Ireland with all the islands that are near their coasts •➤ note that the British Isles are only a geographical unit, not a political unit

Briton /ˈbrɪtn/ **noun** [C] a person who comes from Great Britain

➤ This is normally only used in newspapers, or when talking about the inhabitants of Britain in earlier times: *Three Britons killed in air crash.* • *the Ancient Britons.* Otherwise we say 'a British man', 'a British woman'.

brittle /ˈbrɪtl/ **adj** hard but easily broken: *The bones become brittle in old age.*

broach /brəʊtʃ/ **verb** [T] to start talking about a particular subject, especially one which is difficult or embarrassing: *How will you broach the subject of the money he owes us?*

'**B-road noun** [C] (in Britain) a road that is not as wide or important as a motorway or a main road (A-road): *We drove the whole way on B-roads.*

★**broad** /brɔːd/ **adj 1** wide: *a broad street/river* • *broad shoulders* • *a broad smile*

➤ Wide is more often used than broad when you are talking about the distance between one side of something and the other: *The gate is four metres wide.*

•➤ opposite **narrow** •➤ **noun breadth**
2 including many different people or things: *We sell a broad range of products.* **3** without a lot of detail; general: *I'll explain the new system in broad terms.* **4** (used about the way sb speaks) very strong: *She has a broad Somerset accent.*
IDIOM **(in) broad daylight** during the day, when it is easy to see: *He was attacked in broad daylight.*

,**broad 'bean noun** [C] a type of large flat green bean that can be cooked and eaten

★**broadcast** /ˈbrɔːdkɑːst/ **verb** [I,T] (*pt, pp* **broadcast**) to send out radio or television programmes: *The Olympics are broadcast live around the world.* –**broadcast noun** [C]: *The next news broadcast is at 9 o'clock.*

broadcaster /ˈbrɔːdkɑːstə/ **noun** [C] a person who speaks on the radio or on television

broaden /ˈbrɔːdn/ **verb** [I,T] **broaden (sth) (out)** to become wider; to make sth wider: *The river broadens out beyond the bridge.* • (*figurative*) *Travel broadens the mind* (= it makes you understand other people better).

broadly /ˈbrɔːdli/ **adv 1** (used to describe a way of smiling) with a big, wide smile: *He smiled broadly as he shook everyone's hand.* **2** generally: *Broadly speaking, the scheme will work as follows...*

,**broad-'minded adj** happy to accept beliefs and ways of life that are different from your own •➤ opposite **narrow-minded**

broccoli /ˈbrɒkəli/ **noun** [U] a thick green plant with green or purple flower heads that can be cooked and eaten •➤ picture on page C3

brochure /ˈbrəʊʃə/ **noun** [C] a small book with pictures and information about sth

broil /brɔɪl/ **verb** [T] (*especially US*) = **GRILL²**

broke¹ *past tense of* **BREAK¹**

broke² /brəʊk/ **adj** (not before a noun) (*informal*) having no money: *I can't come out tonight – I'm absolutely broke.*

broken¹ *past participle* of **BREAK¹**

★**broken²** /'brəʊkən/ **adj 1** damaged or in pieces; not working: *The washing machine's broken.* ● *Watch out! There's broken glass on the floor.* ● *a broken leg* ● *How did the window* **get broken**? •➤ picture at **chip 2** (used about a promise or an agreement) not kept **3** not continuous; interrupted: *a broken line* ● *a broken night's sleep* **4** (used about a foreign language) spoken slowly with a lot of mistakes: *to speak in broken English*

broken-'down adj 1 in a very bad condition: *a broken-down old building* **2** (used about a vehicle) not working: *A broken-down bus was blocking the road.*

broken-'hearted = **HEARTBROKEN**

broken 'home noun [C] a family in which the parents do not live together, for example because they are divorced: *Many of the children came from broken homes.*

broker /'brəʊkə/ **noun** [C] a person who buys and sells things, for example shares in a business, for other people: *an insurance broker*

brolly /'brɒli/ **noun** [C] (*pl* **brollies**) (*Brit informal*) = **UMBRELLA**

bronchitis /brɒŋ'kaɪtɪs/ **noun** [U] an illness of the tubes leading to the lungs (bronchial tubes) that causes a very bad cough

bronze /brɒnz/ **noun 1** [U] a reddish-brown metal that is made by mixing tin with another metal (copper) **2** [U] the colour of bronze **3** = **BRONZE MEDAL** –**bronze adj**

bronzed /brɒnzd/ **adj** having skin that has been turned brown, in an attractive way, by the sun

bronze 'medal noun [C] a round piece of bronze that you get as a prize for coming third in a race or a competition •➤ Look at **gold** and **silver medal**.

brooch /brəʊtʃ/ **noun** [C] a piece of jewellery with a pin at the back that women wear on their clothes •➤ picture at **jewellery**

brood¹ /bruːd/ **verb** [I] **1** brood (on/over/about sth) to worry, or to think a lot about sth that makes you worried or sad: *to brood on a failure* **2** (used about a female bird) to sit on her eggs

brood² /bruːd/ **noun** [C] all the young birds that belong to one mother

broody /'bruːdi/ **adj 1** (used about a woman) wanting to have a baby **2** (used about a female bird) ready to have or sit on eggs: *a broody hen*

brook /brʊk/ **noun** [C] a small flow of water (stream)

broom /bruːm/ **noun** [C] a brush with a long handle that you use for removing (sweeping) dirt from the floor •➤ picture at **brush**

broomstick /'bruːmstɪk/ **noun** [C] the handle of a broom

Bros abbr (used in the name of companies) Brothers: *Wentworth Bros Ltd*

broth /brɒθ/ **noun** [U] thin soup: *chicken broth*

brothel /'brɒθl/ **noun** [C] a place where men can go and pay to have sex with a woman (a prostitute)

★**brother** /'brʌðə/ **noun** [C] **1** a man or boy who has the same parents as another person: *Michael and Jim are brothers.* ● *Michael is Jim's brother.* ● *a younger/older brother* •➤ Look at **half-brother** and **stepbrother**. Notice that there is no common English word that means 'both brothers and sisters': *Have you got any brothers and sisters?* The word **sibling** is very formal. **2** a man who is a member of a Christian religious community **3** (*informal*) a man who you feel close to because he is a member of the same society, group, etc as you

brotherhood /'brʌðəhʊd/ **noun 1** [U] a feeling of great friendship and understanding between people: *the brotherhood of man* (= a feeling of friendship between all the people in the world) **2** [C, with sing or pl verb] a organization which is formed for a particular, often religious, purpose

'brother-in-law noun [C] (*pl* **brothers-in-law**) **1** the brother of your husband or wife **2** the husband of your sister

brotherly /'brʌðəli/ **adj** showing feelings of love and kindness that you would expect a brother to show: *brotherly love/advice*

brought *past tense, past participle* of **BRING**

brow /braʊ/ **noun** [C] **1** [usually pl] = **EYEBROW** **2** = **FOREHEAD 3** [sing] the top part of a hill: *Suddenly a car came over the brow of the hill.*

brown¹ /braʊn/ **noun, adj** [C,U] (of) the colour of earth or wood: *brown eyes/hair* ● *the yellows and browns of the trees in autumn* ● *You don't look nice in brown* (= in brown clothes). **2** having skin that the sun has made darker: *Although I often sunbathe, I never seem to* **go brown**.

brown² /braʊn/ **verb** [I,T] to become or make sth become brown: *Brown the meat in a frying pan.*

brownie /'braʊni/ **noun** [C] **1 Brownie** a young girl who is a member of the junior part of the Girl Guides organization **2** a type of heavy chocolate cake that often contains nuts

brown 'paper noun [U] strong, thick paper used for putting round packages, etc: *I wrapped the books in brown paper and tied the package with string.*

browse /braʊz/ **verb 1** [I] to spend time pleasantly, looking round a shop, without a clear idea of what you are looking for: *I spent hours browsing in the local bookshop.* **2** [I] browse through sth to look through a book or magazine without reading every part or studying it carefully: *I enjoyed browsing through the catalogue but I didn't order anything.* **3** [T] (*computing*) to look for and read information on a computer: *I've just been browsing the Internet for information on Iceland.* –**browse noun** [sing]

browser /'braʊzə/ **noun** [C] (*computing*) a computer program that lets you look at

b

words and pictures from other computer systems by receiving information through telephone wires: *an Internet browser*

★**bruise** /bruːz/ *noun* [C] a blue, brown or purple mark that appears on the skin after sb has fallen, been hit, etc ••➤ A bruise on your eye is a **black eye**. –**bruise** *verb* [I,T]: *I fell over and bruised my arm.* ● *Handle the fruit carefully or you'll bruise it.* ● *I've got the sort of skin that bruises easily.*

brunette /bruːˈnet/ *noun* [C] a white woman with dark brown hair ••➤ Look at **blond**.

brunt /brʌnt/ *noun*
IDIOM **bear the brunt of sth** → **BEAR²**

brushes

hairbrush
nail brush
brush
dustpan
brush/broom
paintbrushes
toothbrush

★**brush¹** /brʌʃ/ *noun* **1** [C]. an object that is used for cleaning things, painting, tidying your hair, etc: *I took a brush and swept the snow from the path.* ● *a toothbrush* ● *a paintbrush* ● *a hairbrush* **2** [sing] an act of cleaning, tidying the hair, etc with a brush: *The floor needs a brush.*
IDIOM **(have) a brush with sb/sth** (to have or almost have) an unpleasant meeting with sb/sth: *My only brush with the law was when I was stopped for speeding.*

★**brush²** /brʌʃ/ *verb* **1** [T] to clean, tidy, etc sth with a brush: *Make sure you **brush** your teeth twice a day.* ● *Brush your hair before you go out.* ••➤ Look at the note at **clean²**. **2** [I,T] to touch sb/sth lightly when passing: *Her hand brushed his cheek.* ● *Leaves brushed against the car as we drove along the narrow road.*
PHRASAL VERBS **brush sb/sth aside 1** to refuse to pay attention to sb/sth: *She brushed aside the protests and continued with the meeting.* **2** to push past sb/sth: *He hurried through the crowd, brushing aside the reporters who tried to stop him.*
brush sth off (sth)/away to remove sth with a brush or with the hand, as if using a brush: *I brushed the dust off my jacket.*
brush sth up/brush up on sth to study or practise sth in order to get back knowledge or skill that you had before and have lost: *She took a course to brush up her Spanish.*

'**brush-off** *noun*
IDIOM **give sb the brush-off** to refuse to be friendly to sb: *I'd ask her to go out with me but I'm scared she'd give me the brush-off.*

brusque /bruːsk/ *adj* using very few words and sounding rude: *He gave a brusque 'No comment!' and walked off.* –**brusquely** *adv*

Brussels sprout /ˌbrʌslz ˈspraʊt/ (also **sprout**) *noun* [C, usually pl] a small round green vegetable that looks like another vegetable (a **cabbage**), but is much smaller ••➤ picture on page C3

brutal /ˈbruːtl/ *adj* very cruel and/or violent: *a brutal murder* ● *a brutal dictatorship* –**brutally** *adv*: *He was brutally honest and told her that he didn't love her any more.*

brutality /bruːˈtæləti/ *noun* [C,U] (*pl* **brutalities**) very cruel and violent behaviour

brute¹ /bruːt/ *noun* [C] **1** a cruel, violent man **2** a large strong animal: *That dog of theirs is an absolute brute.*

brute² /bruːt/ *adj* using strength to do sth rather than thinking about it: *I think you'll have to use **brute force** to get this window open.*

BSc /ˌbiː es ˈsiː/ *abbr* Bachelor of Science; the degree that you receive when you complete a university or college course in a science subject ••➤ Look at **BA** and **MSc**.

BSE /ˌbiː es ˈiː/ (also *informal* **mad 'cow disease**) *noun* [U] bovine spongiform encephalopathy; a disease of cows which affects their brains and usually kills them ••➤ Look at **CJD**.

BST /ˌbiː es ˈtiː/ *abbr* British Summer Time; the system used in Britain between March and October, when clocks are put one hour earlier than Greenwich Mean Time

BTEC /ˈbiː tek/ *noun* [C] an exam for young people who have left secondary school and are training in commercial or technical subjects: *She's doing a BTEC in design.*

bubble

bubble
sparkling
bubble
fizzy
still

★**bubble¹** /ˈbʌbl/ *noun* [C] a ball of air or gas, in liquid or floating in the air: *We knew where there were fish because of the bubbles on the surface.*

bubble² /ˈbʌbl/ *verb* [I] **1** to produce bubbles or to rise with bubbles: *Cook the pizza until*

b

the cheese starts to bubble. • *The clear water bubbled up out of the ground.* **2 bubble (over) (with sth)** to be full of happy feelings

bubble bath *noun* [U] a liquid that you can add to the water in a bath to produce a mass of white bubbles

bubblegum /ˈbʌblgʌm/ *noun* [U] a sticky sweet that you eat but do not swallow and that can be blown into bubbles out of the mouth ••➤ Look at **chewing gum**.

bubbly /ˈbʌbli/ *adj* **1** full of bubbles **2** (used about a person) happy and full of energy

buck¹ /bʌk/ *noun* [C] **1** (*US informal*) a US dollar: *Could you lend me a few bucks?* **2** (*pl* **buck** or **bucks**) the male of certain types of animal (**rabbits** and **deer**) ••➤ Look at the note at **deer**.

> **IDIOM pass the buck →** **PASS¹**

buck² /bʌk/ *verb* [I] (used about a horse) to jump into the air or to kick the back legs in the air

> **PHRASAL VERB buck (sb/sth) up** (*informal*) to feel or to make sb feel better or happier: *Drink this – it'll buck you up.* • *Unless you buck your ideas up* (= become more sensible and serious)*, you'll never pass the exam.*

bucket   polish   duster

mop

cloth   rubber gloves   sponge

★**bucket** /ˈbʌkɪt/ *noun* [C] **1** a round, open container, usually made of metal or plastic, with a handle, that is used for carrying sth **2** (also **bucketful**) the amount that a bucket contains: *How many buckets of water do you think we'll need?*

> **IDIOM a drop in the bucket →** **DROP²**

buckle¹ /ˈbʌkl/ *noun* [C] a piece of metal or plastic at the end of a belt or strap that is used for fastening it ••➤ picture at **bag** and **shoe**

buckle² /ˈbʌkl/ *verb* [I,T] **1** to fasten or be fastened with a buckle **2** to bend because of heat, force, weakness, etc: *Some railway lines buckled in the heat.*

bud /bʌd/ *noun* [C] a small lump on a tree or plant that opens and develops into a flower or leaf: *rosebuds* ••➤ picture on page C2

> **IDIOM nip sth in the bud →** **NIP**

Buddhism /ˈbʊdɪzəm/ *noun* [U] an Asian religion that was started in India by Buddha

Buddhist /ˈbʊdɪst/ *noun* [C] a person whose religion is Buddhism –**Buddhist** *adj*: *a Buddhist temple*

budding /ˈbʌdɪŋ/ *adj* wanting or starting to develop and be successful: *Have you got any tips for budding young photographers?*

buddy /ˈbʌdi/ *noun* [C] (*pl* **buddies**) (*informal*) a friend, especially a male friend of a man

budge /bʌdʒ/ *verb* [I,T] **1** to move or make sth move a little: *I tried as hard as I could to loosen the screw but it simply wouldn't budge.* • *We just couldn't budge the car when it got stuck in the mud.* **2** to change or make sb change a firm opinion: *Neither side in the dispute is prepared to budge.*

budgerigar /ˈbʌdʒərɪgɑː/ (also *informal* **budgie**) *noun* [C] a small, brightly-coloured bird that people often keep as a pet in a cage

★**budget¹** /ˈbʌdʒɪt/ *noun* [C,U] **1** a plan of how to spend an amount of money over a particular period of time; the amount of money that is mentioned: *What's your monthly budget for food?* • *a country's defence budget* • *The work was finished on time and within budget.* • *The builders are already 20% over budget.* **2** (also **Budget**) a statement by a government saying how much money it plans to spend on particular things in the next year and how it plans to collect money: *Do you think taxes will go up in this year's budget?*

budget² /ˈbʌdʒɪt/ *verb* [I,T] **budget (sth) (for sth)** to plan carefully how much money to spend on sth: *The government has budgeted £10 billion for education.*

budget³ /ˈbʌdʒɪt/ *adj* (*informal*) (used in advertisements) very cheap: *budget holidays*

budgie /ˈbʌdʒi/ (*informal*) = **BUDGERIGAR**

buff /bʌf/ *noun* [C] (*informal*) a person who knows a lot about a particular subject and is very interested in it: *a film/computer buff*

buffalo /ˈbʌfələʊ/ *noun* [C] (*pl* **buffalo** or **buffaloes**) a large wild animal that looks like a cow with long curved horns: *a herd of buffalo*

buffer /ˈbʌfə/ *noun* [C] **1** a thing or person that reduces the unpleasant effects of sth or prevents violent contact between two things, people, etc: *UN forces are acting as a buffer between the two sides in the war.* **2** a flat round piece of metal with a spring behind it that is on the front or back of a train or at the end of a railway track. Buffers reduce the shock when sth hits them.

buffet¹ /ˈbʊfeɪ/ *noun* [C] **1** a meal (usually at a party or a special occasion) at which food is placed on a long table and people serve themselves: *Lunch was a cold buffet.* • *a buffet lunch* **2** part of a train where passengers can buy food and drinks; a cafe at a station

buffet² /ˈbʌfɪt/ *verb* [T] to knock or push sth in a rough way from side to side: *The boat was buffeted by the rough sea.*

bug¹ /bʌg/ *noun* **1** [C] (*especially US*) any

b

small insect **2** [C] an illness that is not very serious and that people get from each other: *I don't feel very well – I think I've got the bug that's going round.* **3** [C] something wrong in a system or machine, especially a computer: *There's a bug in the software.* **4** usually **the-...bug** [sing] (*informal*) a sudden interest in sth: *They've been bitten by the golf bug.* **5** [C] a very small device (microphone) that is hidden and secretly records people's conversations

bug² /bʌg/ **verb** [T] (**bugging; bugged**) **1** to hide a very small device (microphone) somewhere so that people's conversations can be recorded secretly: *Be careful what you say. This room is bugged.* **2** (*informal*) to annoy or worry sb: *It bugs him that he's not as successful as his brother.*

buggy /ˈbʌgi/ (*pl* **buggies**) (*Brit*) = PUSH-CHAIR

★**build¹** /bɪld/ **verb** (*pt, pp* **built** /bɪlt/) **1** [T] to make sth by putting pieces, materials, etc together: *They've built a new bridge across the river.* ● *The house is built of stone.* **2** [I] to use land for building on: *There's plenty of land to build on around here.* **3** [T] to develop or increase sth: *The government is trying to build a more modern society.* ● *This book claims to help people to build their self-confidence.*

PHRASAL VERBS **build sth in/on; build sth into/ onto sth** to make sth a part of sth else: *They've made sure that a large number of checks are built into the system.* ● *We're planning to build two more rooms onto the back of the house.*

build on sth to use sth as a base from which you can make further progress: *Now that we're beginning to make a profit, we must build on this success.*

build sth on sth to base sth on sth: *a society built on the principle of freedom and democracy*

build up (to sth) to become greater in amount or number; to increase: *The traffic starts to build up at this time of day.*

build sth up 1 to make sth seem more important or greater than it really is: *I don't think it's a very serious matter, it's just been built up in the newspapers.* **2** to increase or develop sth over a period: *You'll need to build up your strength again slowly after the operation.*

build² /bɪld/ **noun** [C,U] the shape and size of sb's body: *She has a very athletic build.* [U]

    ► Compare **build** and **figure**. **Build** usually describes size in connection with strength and muscle and is used for both men and women. **Figure** usually describes shape, especially whether it is attractive or not, and is usually used only for women.

builder /ˈbɪldə/ **noun** [C] a person whose job is to build houses and other buildings

★**building** /ˈbɪldɪŋ/ **noun 1** [C] a structure, such as a house, shop or school, that has a roof and walls: *There are a lot of very old buildings in this town.* **2** [U] the process or

business of making buildings: *building materials* ● *the building industry*

'building site noun [C] an area of land on which a building is being built

'building society noun [C] (*Brit*) an organization like a bank with which people can save money and which lends money to people who want to buy a house

'build-up noun [C, usually sing] **1 a build-up (of sth)** an increase of sth over a period: *The build-up of tension in the area has made war seem more likely.* **2 a build-up (to sth)** a period of preparation or excitement before an event: *The players started to get nervous in the build-up to the big game.*

-built /bɪlt/ (used to form compound adjectives) having a body with the shape and size mentioned: *a tall well-built man*

built-'in adj that is a part of sth and cannot be removed: *built-in cupboards*

built-'up adj covered with buildings: *a built-up area*

bulb /bʌlb/ **noun** [C] **1** (also **'light bulb**) the glass part of an electric lamp that gives out light: *The bulb's gone* (= it no longer works) *in this lamp.* ◈ picture at **light 2** the round root of certain plants: *a tulip bulb* ◈ picture on page C2

bulbous /ˈbʌlbəs/ **adj** fat, round and ugly: *a bulbous red nose*

bulge¹ /bʌldʒ/ **noun** [C] a round lump that sticks out on sth ◈ picture at **bump**

bulge² /bʌldʒ/ **verb** [I] **1** to stick out in a lump from sth that is usually flat: *My stomach is starting to bulge. I must get more exercise.* **2 bulge (with sth)** to be full of sth: *His bags were bulging with presents for the children.*

bulging /ˈbʌldʒɪŋ/ **adj 1** sticking out: *He had a thin face and rather bulging eyes.* **2** very full: *She came home with bulging carrier bags.*

bulk /bʌlk/ **noun 1 the bulk (of sth)** [sing] the main part of sth; most of sth: *The bulk of the work has been done, so we should finish this week.* **2** [U] the size, quantity or weight of sth large: *The cupboard isn't especially heavy – it's its bulk that makes it hard to move.* ● *He slowly lifted his vast bulk out of the chair.*

IDIOM **in bulk** in large quantities: *If you buy in bulk, it's 10% cheaper.*

bulky /ˈbʌlki/ **adj** large and heavy and therefore difficult to move or carry: *a bulky parcel*

bull /bʊl/ **noun** [C] **1** an adult male of the cow family ◈ Look at the note and picture at **cow. 2** the male of certain other animals (the whale and the elephant)

bulldog /ˈbʊldɒg/ **noun** [C] a strong dog with short legs, a large head and a short, thick neck

bulldoze /ˈbʊldəʊz/ **verb** [T] to make ground flat or knock down a building with a bulldozer: *The old buildings were bulldozed and new ones were built.*

bulldozer /'bʊldəʊzə/ **noun** [C] a large, powerful vehicle with a broad piece of metal at the front, used for clearing ground or knocking down buildings

★**bullet** /'bʊlɪt/ **noun** [C] a small metal object that is fired from a gun: *The bullet hit her in the arm.* • *a bullet wound*

bulletin /'bʊlətɪn/ **noun** [C] **1** a short news report on TV or radio; an official statement about a situation: *The next news bulletin on this channel is at nine o'clock.* **2** a short newspaper that a club or an organization produces: *As a member of the fan club, she receives a monthly bulletin.*

'**bulletin board** (*US*) = NOTICEBOARD

bulletproof /'bʊlɪtpruːf/ **adj** made of a strong material that stops bullets from passing through it

bullfight /'bʊlfaɪt/ **noun** [C] a traditional public entertainment, especially in Spain, Portugal and Latin America, in which an animal (a bull) is fought and often killed –**bullfighter noun** [C] –**bullfighting noun** [U]

bullion /'bʊliən/ **noun** [U] bars of gold or silver: *The dollar price of gold bullion has risen by more than 10%.*

'**bull's-eye noun** [C] the centre of a round object (target) that you shoot or throw things at in certain sports, or a shot that hits this

bully¹ /'bʊli/ **noun** [C] (*pl* **bullies**) a person who uses his/her strength or power to hurt or frighten people who are weaker

bully² /'bʊli/ **verb** [T] (*pres part* **bullying**; *3rd pers sing pres* **bullies**; *pt, pp* **bullied**) bully sb (into doing sth) to use your strength or power to hurt or frighten sb who is weaker or to make them do sth: *Don't try to bully me into making a decision.* –**bullying noun** [U]: *Bullying is a serious problem in many schools.*

bum /bʌm/ **noun** [C] (*informal*) **1** (*Brit*) the part of your body on which you sit; bottom **2** (*especially US*) an insulting word for a person who lives on the street **3** (*especially US*) a lazy or useless person

bumbag /'bʌmbæg/ (*US* '**fanny pack**) **noun** [C] (*informal*) a small bag worn around the waist to keep money, etc in •➤ picture at **bag**

bump¹ /bʌmp/ **verb 1** [I] bump against/into sb/sth to hit sb/sth by accident when you are moving: *She bumped into a lamp post because she wasn't looking where she was going.* **2** [T] bump sth (against/on sth) to hit sth against or on sth by accident: *I bumped my knee on the edge of the table.* **3** [I] to move along over a rough surface: *The car bumped along over the track to the farm.*

PHRASAL VERBS bump into sb to meet sb by chance: *I bumped into a old friend on the bus today.*

bump sb off (*slang*) to murder sb

bump sth up (*informal*) to increase or make sth go up: *All this publicity will bump up sales of our new product.*

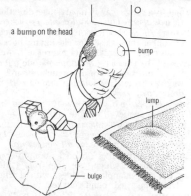

a bump on the head

bump

lump

a bag bulging with presents   a lump under the rug

bump² /bʌmp/ **noun** [C] **1** the action or sound of sth hitting a hard surface: *She fell and hit the ground with a bump.* **2** a lump on the body, often caused by a hit **3** a part of a surface that is higher than the rest of it: *There are a lot of bumps in the road, so drive carefully.*

bumper¹ /'bʌmpə/ **noun** [C] the bar fixed to the front and back of a motor vehicle to protect it if it hits sth

bumper² /'bʌmpə/ **adj** larger than usual: *The unusually fine weather has produced a bumper harvest this year.*

bumpy /'bʌmpi/ **adj** not flat or smooth: *a bumpy road* • *Because of the stormy weather, it was a very bumpy flight.* •➤ opposite **smooth**

bun /bʌn/ **noun** [C] **1** a small round sweet cake: *a currant bun* •➤ picture at **cake 2** a small soft bread roll: *a hamburger bun* **3** hair fastened tightly into a round shape at the back of the head: *She wears her hair in a bun.* •➤ picture at **hair**

bunch¹ /bʌntʃ/ **noun 1** [C] a number of things, usually of the same type, fastened or growing together: *He bought her a bunch of flowers for her birthday.* • *a bunch of bananas/grapes* • *a bunch of keys* **2 bunches** [pl] long hair that is tied on each side of the head •➤ picture at **hair 3** [C, with sing or pl verb] (*informal*) a group of people: *My colleagues are the best bunch of people I've ever worked with.*

bunch² /bʌntʃ/ **verb** [I,T] bunch (sth/sb) (up/together) to stay together in a group; to form sth into a group or bunch: *The runners bunched up as they came round the final bend.* • *He kept his papers bunched together in his hand.*

bundle¹ /'bʌndl/ **noun** [C] a number of things tied or folded together: *a bundle of letters with an elastic band round them*

bundle² /'bʌndl/ **verb** [T] **1** bundle sth (up) to make or tie a number of things together: *I bundled up the old newspapers and threw them away.* **2** to put or push sb or sth quickly and in a rough way in a particular direction: *He was arrested and bundled into a police car.*

bung[1] /bʌŋ/ noun [C] a round piece of wood or rubber that is used for closing the hole in some types of container (a barrel or a jar)

bung[2] /bʌŋ/ verb [T] (*Brit informal*) to put or throw sth somewhere in a rough or careless way: *We bunged the suitcases into the car and drove away.*

bungalow /'bʌŋɡələʊ/ noun [C] a house that is all on one level, without stairs

bunged 'up adj (*informal*) blocked, so that nothing can get through: *I feel terrible – I've got a cold and my nose is all bunged up.*

bungee jumping /'bʌndʒi dʒʌmpɪŋ/ noun [U] a sport in which you jump from a high place, for example a bridge, with a thick elastic rope tied round your feet

bungle /'bʌŋɡl/ verb [I,T] to do sth badly or fail to do sth: *a bungled robbery*

bunk /bʌŋk/ noun [C] **1** a bed that is fixed to a wall, for example on a ship or train **2** (also **'bunk bed**) one of a pair of single beds built as a unit with one above the other •➤ Look at the note and picture at **bed**.

<u>IDIOM</u> **do a bunk** (*Brit informal*) to run away or escape; to leave without telling anyone

bunker /'bʌŋkə/ noun [C] **1** a strong underground building that gives protection in a war **2** a hole filled with sand on a golf course

bunny /'bʌni/ noun [C] (*pl* **bunnies**) (used by and to small children) a rabbit

buoy[1] /bɔɪ/ noun [C] a floating object, fastened to the bottom of the sea or a river, that shows the places where it is dangerous for boats to go

buoy[2] /bɔɪ/ verb [T] buoy sb/sth (up) **1** to keep sb happy and confident: *His encouragement buoyed her up during that difficult period.* **2** to keep sth at a high level: *Share prices were buoyed by news of a takeover.*

buoyant /'bɔɪənt/ adj **1** (used about a material) floating or able to float **2** happy and confident: *The team were in buoyant mood after their win.* **3** (used about prices, business activity, etc) staying at a high level or increasing, so that people make more money: *Despite the recession, the property market remained buoyant.* –buoyancy /-ənsi/ noun [U]: *the buoyancy of the German economy*

★**burden**[1] /'bɜːdn/ noun [C] **1** something that is heavy and difficult to carry **2** a responsibility or difficult task that causes a lot of work or worry: *Having to make all the decisions is a terrible burden for me.* ● *I don't want to be a burden to my children when I'm old.*

burden[2] /'bɜːdn/ verb [T] burden sb/yourself (with sth) to give sb/yourself a responsibility or task that causes a lot of work or worry

bureau /'bjʊərəʊ/ noun [C] (*pl* **bureaux** or **bureaus** /-rəʊz/) **1** (*especially US*) one of certain government departments: *the Federal Bureau of Investigation* **2** an organization that provides information: *a tourist information bureau* **3** (*Brit*) a writing desk with drawers and a lid

bureaucracy /bjʊə'rɒkrəsi/ noun (*pl* **bureaucracies**) **1** [U] (often used in a critical way) the system of official rules that an organization has for doing sth, that people often think is too complicated: *Getting a visa involves a lot of unnecessary bureaucracy.* **2** [C,U] a system of government by a large number of officials who are not elected; a country with this system –bureaucratic /ˌbjʊərə'krætɪk/ adj connected with a bureaucracy, especially when it follows official rules too closely: *You have to go through a complex bureaucratic procedure if you want to get your money back.*

bureaucrat /'bjʊərəkræt/ noun [C] (often used in a critical way) an official in an organization or government department

bureau de change /ˌbjʊərəʊ də 'ʃɑːnʒ/ noun [C] (*pl* **bureaux de change**) (*Brit*) an office at an airport, in a hotel, etc where you can change the money of one country to the money of another country

burger /'bɜːɡə/ = HAMBURGER(1)

-burger /'bɜːɡə/ (in compounds) **1** a hamburger with sth else on top: *a cheeseburger* **2** something that is cooked like and looks like a hamburger, but is made of sth else: *a veggie burger*

burglar /'bɜːɡlə/ noun [C] a person who enters a building illegally in order to steal: *The burglars broke in by smashing a window.* •➤ Look at the note at **thief**. –burgle /'bɜːɡl/ verb [T]: *Our flat was burgled while we were out.*

'burglar alarm noun [C] a piece of equipment, usually fixed on a wall, that makes a loud noise if a thief enters a building

burglary /'bɜːɡləri/ noun [C,U] (*pl* **burglaries**) the crime of entering a building illegally in order to steal: *There was a burglary next door last week.* ● *He is in prison for burglary.*

burial /'beriəl/ noun [C,U] the ceremony when a dead body is put in the ground (buried): *The burial took place on Friday.* •➤ Look at the note at **funeral**.

burly /'bɜːli/ adj (used about a person or his/her body) strong and heavy

★**burn**[1] /bɜːn/ verb (*pt, pp* **burnt** /bɜːnt/ or **burned** /bɜːnd/) **1** [T] to destroy, damage or injure sb/sth with fire or heat: *We took all the rubbish outside and burned it.* ● *It was a terrible fire and the whole building was burnt to the ground* (= completely destroyed). ● *If you get too close to the fire you'll burn yourself.* ● *The people inside the building couldn't get out and they were all burnt to death.* **2** [I] to be destroyed, damaged or injured by fire or heat: *If you leave the cake in the oven for much longer, it will burn.* ● *I can't spend too much time in the sun because I burn easily.* ● *They were trapped by the flames and they burned to death.* **3** [T] to produce a hole or mark in or on sth by burning: *He dropped his cigarette and it burned a hole in the carpet.* **4** [I] to be on fire: *Firemen raced to the burning building.* **5** [T] to use sth as fuel: *an oil-burning lamp* **6** [I] to produce light: *I don't think he* went to bed at all – I could see his light burning all night. **7** [I] to feel very hot and painful: *You have a temperature, your fore-head's burning.* **8** [I] **burn (with sth)** to be filled with a very strong feeling: *She was burning with indignation.*

IDIOM **sb's ears are burning** → **EAR**

PHRASAL VERBS **burn down** (used about a build-ing) to be completely destroyed by fire: *The fire could not be brought under control and the school burned down.*
burn sth down to completely destroy a build-ing by fire: *The house was burnt down in a fire some years ago.*
burn (sth) off to remove sth or to be removed by burning
burn sth out (usually passive) to completely destroy sth by burning: *the burnt-out wreck of a car*
burn yourself out (usually passive) to work, etc, until you have no more energy or strength: *I've been studying so hard recently I feel completely burned out.*
burn (sth) up to destroy or to be destroyed by fire or strong heat: *The space capsule burnt up on its re-entry into the earth's atmosphere.*

burn² /bɜːn/ *noun* [C] damage or an injury caused by fire or heat: *He was taken to hos-pital with **minor burns.*** *• There's a cigarette burn on the carpet.*

burning /'bɜːnɪŋ/ *adj* (only *before* a noun) **1** (used about a feeling) extremely strong: *a burning ambition/desire* **2** very important or urgent: *a burning issue/question* **3** feeling very hot: *the burning sun*

burp /bɜːp/ *verb* [I] to make a noise with the mouth when air rises from the stomach and is forced out: *He sat back when he had fin-ished his meal and burped loudly.* –**burp** *noun* [C]

burrow¹ /'bʌrəʊ/ *noun* [C] a hole in the ground made by certain animals, for example rabbits, in which they live

burrow² /'bʌrəʊ/ *verb* [I] to dig a hole in the ground, to make a tunnel or to look for sth: *These animals burrow for food.* *• (figurative) She burrowed in her handbag for her keys.*

bursar /'bɜːsə/ *noun* [C] the person who man-ages the financial matters of a school, college or university

bursary /'bɜːsəri/ *noun* [C] (*pl* **bursaries**) a sum of money given to a specially chosen student to pay for his/her studies at a college or university

★**burst¹** /bɜːst/ *verb* (*pt, pp* **burst**) **1** [I,T] to break open suddenly and violently, usually because there is too much pressure inside; to cause this to happen: *The ball burst when I kicked it.* *• You'll burst that tyre if you blow it up any more.* *• (figurative) If I eat any more I'll burst!* *• If it rains much more, the river will burst its banks.* **2** [I] **burst into, out of, through, etc** to move suddenly in a particu-lar direction, often using force: *She burst into the manager's office and demanded to speak to him.*

IDIOMS **be bursting (with sth)** to be very full

of sth: *I packed so many clothes that my suit-case was bursting.* *• She was bursting with pride when she won the race.*
be bursting to do sth to want to do sth very much: *I'm bursting to tell someone the news but it's a secret.*
burst (sth) open to open or make sth open suddenly or violently: *Suddenly the doors burst open and five police officers rushed in.*

PHRASAL VERBS **burst in on sb/sth** to interrupt sb/sth by arriving suddenly: *The police burst in on the gang as they were counting the money.*
burst into sth to start doing sth suddenly: *On hearing the news she **burst into tears** (= started crying). • The lorry hit a wall and **burst into flames** (= started burning).*
burst out 1 to start doing sth suddenly: *He looked so ridiculous that I **burst out laugh-ing.*** **2** to say sth suddenly and with strong feeling: *Finally she burst out, 'I can't stand it any more!'*

burst² /bɜːst/ *noun* [C] **1** a short period of a particular activity, that often starts sud-denly: *a burst of energy/enthusiasm/speed* *• a burst of applause/gunfire* *• He prefers to work in short bursts.* **2** an occasion when sth bursts or explodes; a crack or hole caused by this: *a burst in a water pipe*

★**bury** /'beri/ *verb* [T] (*pres part* **burying**; *3rd pers sing pres* **buries**; *pt, pp* **buried**) **1** to put a dead body in the ground: *She wants to be buried in the village graveyard.* **2** to put sth in a hole in the ground and cover it: *Our dog always buries its bones in the garden.* **3** (usu-ally passive) to cover or hide sth/sb: *At last I found the photograph, buried at the bottom of a drawer.* *• (figurative) Aisha was buried in a book and didn't hear us come in.*

★**bus** /bʌs/ *noun* [C] (*pl* **buses**) a big public vehicle which takes passengers along a fixed route and stops regularly to let people get on and off: *Where do you usually get on/off the bus?* *• We'll have to hurry up if we want to **catch the 9 o'clock bus.*** *• We'd better run or we'll **miss the bus.***

➤ The **bus driver** may also take the money (your **fare**) and give you your **ticket**, or there may be a **conductor** who collects the fares. You can get on or off at a **bus stop** and the place where most bus routes start is the **bus station**. Note that we travel **on the bus** or **by bus**: *'How do you get to work?' 'On the bus.'*

★**bush** /bʊʃ/ *noun* **1** [C] a plant like a small, thick tree with many low branches: *a rose bush* *• The house was surrounded by thick bushes.* **2** (often **the bush**) [U] wild land that has not been cleared, especially in Africa and Australia

IDIOM **beat about the bush** → **BEAT¹**

bushy /'bʊʃi/ *adj* growing thickly: *bushy hair/eyebrows*

busier, busiest, busily → **BUSY¹**

★**business** /'bɪznəs/ *noun* **1** [U] buying and selling as a way of earning money; com-merce: *She's planning to **set up in business*** as a hairdresser. • *I'm going to* **go into business** *with my brother.* • *They are very easy to* **do business with. 2** [U] the work that you do as your job: *The manager will be away on* **business** *next week.* • *a business trip* **3** [U] the number of customers that a person or company has had: *Business has been good for the time of the year.* **4** [C] a firm, a shop, a factory, etc which produces or sells goods or provides a service: *She aims to* **start a business** *of her own.* • *Small businesses are finding it hard to survive at the moment.* **5** [U] something that concerns a particular person: *The friends I choose are my business, not yours.* • *Our business is to collect the information, not to comment on it.* • *'How much did it cost?' 'It's* **none of your business***!'* (= I don't want to tell you. It's private.) **6** [U] important matters that need to be dealt with or discussed: *First we have some unfinished business from the last meeting to deal with.* **7** [sing] a situation or an event, especially one that is strange or unpleasant: *The divorce was an awful business.* • *I found the whole business very depressing.*

IDIOMS **get down to business** to start the work that has to be done: *Let's just have a cup of coffee before we get down to business.*

go out of business to have to close because there is no more money available: *The shop went out of business because it couldn't compete with the new supermarket.*

have no business to do sth/doing sth to have no right to do sth: *You have no business to read/reading my letters without asking me.*

mind your own business → MIND²

monkey business → MONKEY

businesslike /'bɪznəslaɪk/ *adj* dealing with matters in a direct and practical way, without trying to be friendly: *She has a very businesslike manner.*

businessman /'bɪznəsmæn; 'bɪznəsmən/ *noun* [C] (*pl* **-men** /-mən; -men/) **1** a man who works in business, especially in a top position **2** a man who is skilful at dealing with money

business studies *noun* [U] the study of how to control and manage a company: *a course in business studies*

businesswoman /'bɪznəswʊmən/ *noun* [C] (*pl* **-women** /-wɪmɪn/) **1** a woman who works in business, especially in a top position **2** a woman who is skilful at dealing with money

busk /bʌsk/ *verb* [I] to sing or play music in the street so that people will give you money

busker /'bʌskə/ *noun* [C] a street musician •➤ picture on page C8

bust¹ /bʌst/ *verb* (*pt, pp* **bust** or **busted**) (*informal*) **1** [T] to break or damage sth so that it cannot be used **2** [T] to arrest sb: *He was busted for possession of heroin.*

bust² /bʌst/ *adj* (not before a noun) (*informal*) broken or not working: *The zip on these trousers is bust.*

IDIOM **go bust** (*informal*) (used about a business) to close because it has lost so much

money: *During the recession thousands of businesses went bust.*

bust³ /bʌst/ *noun* [C] **1** a model in stone, etc of a person's head, shoulders and chest **2** a woman's breasts; the measurement round a woman's chest: *This blouse is a bit too tight around the bust.* **3** (*informal*) an unexpected visit by the police in order to arrest people for doing sth illegal: *a drugs bust*

bustle¹ /'bʌsl/ *verb* **1** [I,T] to move in a busy, noisy or excited way; to make sb move somewhere quickly: *He bustled about the kitchen making tea.* • *They bustled her out of the room before she could see the body.* **2** [I] **bustle (with sth)** to be full of people, noise or activity: *The streets were bustling with shoppers.*

bustle² /'bʌsl/ *noun* [U] excited and noisy activity: *She loved the bustle of city life.*

bust-up *noun* [C] (*informal*) an argument: *He had a bust-up with his boss over working hours.*

★**busy¹** /'bɪzi/ *adj* (**busier; busiest**) **1** **busy (at/with sth); busy (doing sth)** having a lot of work or tasks to do; not free; working on sth: *Mr Khan is busy until 4 o'clock but he could see you after that.* • *Don't disturb him. He's busy.* • *She's busy with her preparations for the party.* • *We're busy decorating the spare room before our visitors arrive.* **2** (used about a period of time) full of activity and things to do: *I've had rather a busy week.* **3** (used about a place) full of people, movement and activity: *The town centre was so busy that you could hardly move.* **4** (*especially US*) (used about a telephone) being used: *The line's busy at the moment. I'll try again later.* –**busily** *adv*: *When I came in she was busily writing something at her desk.*

IDIOM **get busy** to start working: *We'll have to get busy if we're going to be ready in time.*

busy² /'bɪzi/ *verb* [T] (*pres part* **busying**; *3rd pers sing pres* **busies**; *pt, pp* **busied**) **busy yourself with sth; busy yourself doing sth** to keep yourself busy; to find sth to do

busybody /'bɪzibɒdi/ *noun* [C] (*pl* **busybodies**) a person who is too interested in other people's private lives

★**but¹** /bət; *strong form* bʌt/ *conj* **1** used for introducing an idea which contrasts with or is different from what has just been said: *The weather will be sunny but cold.* • *Theirs is not the first but the second house on the left.* • *James hasn't got a car but his sister has.* **2** however; and yet: *She's been learning Italian for five years but she doesn't speak it very well.* • *I'd love to come but I can't make it till 8 o'clock.* **3** used when you are saying sorry for sth: *Excuse me, but is your name David Harries?* • *I'm sorry, but I can't stay any longer.* **4** used for introducing a statement that shows that you are surprised or annoyed or that you disagree: *'Here's the book you lent me.' 'But it's all dirty and torn!'* • *But that's not possible!*

IDIOM **but then** however; on the other hand: *We could go swimming. But then perhaps it's* too cold. • *He's brilliant at the piano. But then so was his father* (= however, this is not surprising because...).

★**but²** /bət; *strong form* bʌt/ **prep** except: *I've told no one but you about this.* • *We've had nothing but trouble with this washing machine!*

IDIOM **but for sb/sth** except for or without sb/sth: *We wouldn't have managed but for your help.*

★**butcher¹** /'bʊtʃə/ **noun** [C] **1** a person who sells meat: *The butcher cut me four lamb chops.* • *She went to the butcher's for some sausages.*

> Note that **the butcher** is the person who runs the shop and **the butcher's** is the shop.

2 a person who kills a lot of people in a cruel way

butcher² /'bʊtʃə/ **verb** [T] to kill a lot of people in a cruel way

butchery /'bʊtʃəri/ **noun** [U] cruel killing

butler /'bʌtlə/ **noun** [C] a person who works in a very large house, whose main duty is to organize and serve food and wine

butt¹ /bʌt/ **verb** [T] to hit sb/sth with the head
PHRASAL VERB **butt in (on sb/sth)** to interrupt sb/sth or to join in sth without being asked: *I'm sorry to butt in but could I speak to you urgently for a minute?*

butt² /bʌt/ **noun** [C] **1** the thicker, heavier end of a weapon or tool: *the butt of a rifle* **2** a short piece of a cigarette which is left when it has been smoked **3** (*especially US informal*) the part of your body that you sit on; your bottom: *Get up off your butt and do some work!* **4** a person who is often laughed at or talked about in an unkind way: *Fat children are often the butt of other children's jokes.* **5** the act of hitting sb with your head

★**butter¹** /'bʌtə/ **noun** [U] a soft yellow fat that is made from cream and used for spreading on bread, etc or in cooking: *Do you prefer butter or low-fat spread?* • *First, melt a little butter in the pan.* ••➤ picture on page C4

butter² /'bʌtə/ **verb** [T] to spread butter on bread, etc: *I'll cut the bread and you butter it.* • *hot buttered toast*

butterfly /'bʌtəflaɪ/ **noun 1** [C] (*pl* **butterflies**) an insect with a long, thin body and four brightly coloured wings: *Caterpillars develop into butterflies.* ••➤ picture at **insect** **2** [sing] a style of swimming in which both arms are brought over the head at the same time, and the legs move up and down together
IDIOM **have butterflies (in your stomach)** (*informal*) to feel very nervous before doing sth

buttermilk /'bʌtəmɪlk/ **noun** [U] the liquid that is left when butter is separated from milk

buttock /'bʌtək/ **noun** [C, usually pl] one of the two parts of your body which you sit on

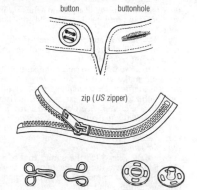

button   buttonhole

zip (*US* zipper)

hook and eye   popper (*US* snap)

★**button** /'bʌtn/ **noun** [C] **1** a small, often round, piece of plastic, wood or metal that you use for fastening your clothes: *One of the buttons on my jacket has come off.* • *This blouse is too tight – I can't fasten the buttons.* **2** a small part of a machine, etc that you press in order to operate sth: ***Press the button** to ring the bell.* • *To dial the same number again, **push the 'redial' button**.* • *Which button turns the volume down?* • *To print a file, simply click on the 'print' button.* • *Double click the right mouse button.* ••➤ picture at **handle** and **telephone**

buttonhole /'bʌtnhəʊl/ **noun** [C] **1** a hole in a piece of clothing that you push a button through in order to fasten it ••➤ picture at **button 2** (*Brit*) a flower worn in the buttonhole of a coat or jacket

★**buy¹** /baɪ/ **verb** [T] (*pt, pp* **bought** /bɔːt/) **buy sth (for sb); buy sb sth** to get sth by paying money for it: *I'm going to buy a new dress for the party.* • *We bought this book for you in London.* • *Can I buy you a coffee?* • *He bought the car from a friend.* • *Did you buy your car new or second-hand?* • *He bought the necklace as a present for his wife.*
IDIOM **buy time** to do sth in order to delay an event, a decision, etc: *He took a few days' holiday in order to buy some time before giving them his final decision.*
PHRASAL VERBS **buy sb off** (*informal*) to pay sb money, especially dishonestly, to stop him/her from doing sth you do not want him/her to do: *The construction company tried to buy off the opposition by offering them discounts on the properties they were planning to build.* **buy sb out** to pay sb for his/her share in a house, business, etc in order to get full control of it yourself: *After the divorce, she bought him out and kept the house for herself.*

buy² /baɪ/ **noun** [C] an act of buying sth or a thing that you can buy: *I think your house was a very good buy* (= worth the money you paid).

buyer /'baɪə/ **noun** [C] **1** a person who is buying sth or may buy sth: *I think we've found a*

b

buyer for our house! **2** a person whose job is to choose and buy goods to be sold in a large shop

buyout /'baɪaʊt/ **noun** [C] the act of buying enough or all of the shares in a company in order to get control of it

buzz¹ /bʌz/ **verb 1** [I] to make the sound that bees, etc make when flying: *A large fly was buzzing against the windowpane.* **2** [I] **buzz (with sth)** to be full of excitement, activity, thoughts, etc: *Her head was buzzing with questions that she wanted to ask.* ● *The room was buzzing with activity.* **3** [I,T] to call sb by using an electric bell, etc: *The doctor will buzz for you when he's ready.*

buzz² /bʌz/ **noun 1** [C] the sound that a bee, etc makes when flying: *the buzz of insects* **2** [sing] the low sound made by many people talking at the same time: *I could hear the buzz of conversation in the next room.* **3** [sing] (*informal*) a strong feeling of excitement or pleasure: *a buzz of expectation* ● *Flying on Concorde gave him a real buzz.* ● *She gets a buzz out of shopping for expensive clothes.*

buzzer /'bʌzə/ **noun** [C] a piece of equipment that makes a buzzing sound: *Press your buzzer if you know the answer to a question.*

buzzword /'bʌzwɜːd/ **noun** [C] a word or phrase, especially one connected with a particular subject, that has become fashionable and popular: *Self-organization is the current buzzword.*

*★ **by** /baɪ/ **prep, adv 1** beside; very near: *Come and sit by me.* ● *We stayed in a cottage by the sea.* ● *The shops are close by.* **2** past: *He walked straight by me without speaking.* ● *We stopped to let the ambulance get by.* **3** not later than; before: *I'll be home by 7 o'clock.* ● *He should have telephoned by now/by this time.* **4** (usually without *the*) during a period of time; in particular circumstances: *By day we covered about thirty miles and by night we rested.* ● *The electricity went off so we had to work by candlelight.* **5** used after a passive verb for showing who or what did or caused sth: *She was knocked down by a car.* ● *The event was organized by local people.* ● *I was deeply shocked by the news.* ● *Who was the book written by?/Who is the book by?* **6** through doing or using sth; by means of sth: *You can get hold of me by phoning this number.* ● *Will you be paying by cheque?* ● *The house is heated by electricity.* ● 'How do you go to work?' 'By train, usually.' ● *by bus/car/plane/bicycle* ● *We went in by the back door.* **7** as a result of sth; due to sth: *I got on the wrong bus by mistake/accident.* ● *I met an old friend by chance.* **8** according to sth; with regard to sth: *It's 8 o'clock by my watch.* ● *By law you have to attend school from the age of five.* ● *She's French by birth.* ● *He's a doctor*

by profession. **9** used for multiplying or dividing: *4 multiplied by 5 is 20.* ● *6 divided by 2 is 3.* **10** used for showing the measurements of an area: *The table is six feet by three feet* (= six feet long and three feet wide). **11** (often used with *the*) in the quantity or period mentioned: *You can rent a car by the day, the week or the month.* ● *Copies of the book have sold by the million.* ● *They came in one by one.* ● *Day by day she was getting better.* **12** to the amount mentioned: *Prices have gone up by 10 per cent.* ● *I missed the bus by a few minutes.* **13** (used with a part of the body or an article of clothing) holding: *He grabbed me by the arm.*

IDIOMS **by and large** → **LARGE**
by the way → **WAY**¹

bye /baɪ/ (also **bye-bye** /'baɪbaɪ/) **interj** (*informal*) goodbye: *Bye! See you tomorrow.*

'by-election noun [C] an election to choose a new Member of Parliament for a particular town or area (a constituency). It is held when the former member has died or left suddenly. ••► Look at **general election**.

bygone /'baɪgɒn/ **adj** (only *before* a noun) that happened a long time ago: *a bygone era*

bygones /'baɪgɒnz/ **noun** [pl]
IDIOM **let bygones be bygones** to decide to forget disagreements or arguments that happened in the past

bypass¹ /'baɪpɑːs/ **noun** [C] **1** a road which traffic can use to go round a town, instead of through it ••► Look at **ring road**. **2** (*medical*) an operation on the heart to send blood along a different route so that it does not go through a part which is damaged or blocked: *a triple bypass operation* ● *heart bypass surgery*

bypass² /'baɪpɑːs/ **verb** [T] to go around or to avoid sth using a bypass: *Let's try to bypass the city centre.* ● (*figurative*) *It's no good trying to bypass the problem.*

'by-product noun [C] **1** something that is formed during the making of sth else **2** something that happens as the result of sth else

bystander /'baɪstændə/ **noun** [C] a person who is standing near and sees sth that happens, without being involved in it: *Several innocent bystanders were hurt when the two gangs attacked each other.*

byte /baɪt/ **noun** [C] (*computing*) a unit of information that can represent one item, such as a letter or a number. A byte is usually made up of a series of eight smaller units (bits).

byword /'baɪwɜːd/ **noun** [usually sing] **1** a **byword for sth** a person or a thing that is a typical or well-known example of a particular quality: *A limousine is a byword for luxury.* **2** (*especially US*) a word or phrase that is often used

---

Cc

C, c¹ /siː/ noun [C] (*pl* **C's; c's**) the third letter of the English alphabet: *'Car' begins with (a) 'C'.*

c² /siː/ **abbr 1** C Celsius; centigrade: *Water freezes at 0°C.* **2** (before dates) about; approximately: *c 1770*

cab /kæb/ noun [C] **1** (*especially US*) = TAXI¹: *Let's take a cab/go by cab.* **2** the part of a lorry, train, bus, etc where the driver sits

cabaret /'kæbəreɪ/ noun [C,U] entertainment with singing, dancing, etc in a restaurant or club

★**cabbage** /'kæbɪdʒ/ noun [C,U] a large round vegetable with thick green, dark red or white leaves: *Cabbages are easy to grow.* ● *Do you like cabbage?* ••➤ picture on page C3

cabin /'kæbɪn/ noun [C] **1** a small room in a ship or boat, where a passenger sleeps **2** the part of a plane where the passengers sit **3** a small wooden house; a hut: *a log cabin* ••➤ picture on page C8

cabinet /'kæbɪnət/ noun [C] **1** a cupboard with shelves or drawers, used for storing things: *a medicine cabinet* ● *a filing cabinet* ••➤ picture on page S6 **2** (also **the Cabinet**) [with sing or pl verb] the most important ministers in a government, who have regular meetings with the Prime Minister: *The Cabinet is/are meeting today to discuss the crisis.*

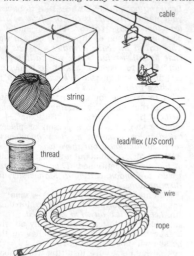

cable

string

thread

lead/flex (*US* cord)

wire

rope

cable /'keɪbl/ noun **1** [C] a thick strong metal rope **2** [C,U] a set of wires covered with plastic, etc, for carrying electricity or signals:

underground/overhead cables ● *a telephone cable* ● *two metres of cable* ••➤ picture on page C8 **3** = CABLE TELEVISION

'cable car noun [C] a vehicle like a box that hangs on a moving metal rope (cable) and carries passengers up and down a mountain ••➤ picture on page C8

,cable 'television noun [U] a system of sending out television programmes along wires instead of by radio signals

cackle /'kækl/ verb [I] to laugh in a loud, unpleasant way –**cackle** noun [C]

cactus /'kæktəs/ noun [C] (*pl* **cactuses** or **cacti** /'kæktaɪ/) a type of plant that grows in hot, dry areas, especially deserts. A cactus has a thick central part (stem) and sharp points (prickles) but no leaves. ••➤ picture on page C2

cadet /kə'det/ noun [C] a young person who is training to be in the army, navy, air force or police

cadge /kædʒ/ verb [I,T] (*informal*) **cadge (sth) (from/off sb)** to try to persuade sb to give or lend you sth: *He's always trying to cadge money off me.*

Caesarean (also **-rian;** *US* also **cesarean**) /siˈzeərian/ noun [C] a medical operation in which an opening is cut in a mother's body in order to take out the baby when a normal birth would be impossible or dangerous: *to have a Caesarean*

> This operation is also called a **Caesarean section** or in US English a **C-section**.

★**cafe** /'kæfeɪ/ noun [C] a small restaurant that serves drinks and light meals

> In Britain, a cafe does not normally serve alcoholic drinks, which are served in a **pub** or **bar**.

••➤ picture on page C8

cafeteria /ˌkæfə'tɪəriə/ noun [C] a restaurant, especially one for staff or workers, where people collect their meals themselves and carry them to their tables ••➤ Look at **canteen**.

caffeine /'kæfiːn/ noun [U] the substance found in coffee and tea that makes you feel more awake and full of energy ••➤ Look at **decaffeinated**.

★**cage** /keɪdʒ/ noun [C] a box made of bars or wire, or a space surrounded by wire or metal bars, in which a bird or animal is kept so that it cannot escape: *a birdcage* –**cage** verb [T] –**caged** /keɪdʒd/ adj: *He felt like a caged animal in the tiny office.*

cagey /'keɪdʒi/ adj (*informal*) **cagey (about sth)** not wanting to give information or to talk about sth

cagoule /kə'guːl/ noun [C] a long jacket with a covering for the head (hood) that protects you from the rain or wind ••➤ picture on page C6

cakes

cake muffin icing

slice

bun

eclair

crumbs

crackers doughnut biscuits

★**cake**[1] /keɪk/ *noun* **1** [C,U] a sweet food made by mixing flour, eggs, butter, sugar, etc together and baking the mixture in the oven: *to make/bake a cake* ● *a wedding cake* ● *a piece/slice of birthday cake* ● *Would you like some more cake?* **2** [C] a mixture of other food, cooked in a round, flat shape: *fish/potato cakes*

IDIOMS **have your cake and eat it** to enjoy the advantages of sth without its disadvantages; to have both things that are available: *You can't go out every night and pass your exams. You can't have your cake and eat it.*

a piece of cake → PIECE[1]

cake[2] /keɪk/ *verb* [T] (usually passive) **cake sth (in/with sth)** to cover sth thickly with a substance that becomes hard when it dries: *boots caked in mud*

calamity /kə'læməti/ *noun* [C,U] (*pl* **calamities**) a terrible event that causes a lot of damage or harm

★**calculate** /'kælkjuleɪt/ *verb* [T] **1** to find sth out by using mathematics; to work sth out: *It's difficult to calculate how long the project will take.* **2** to consider or expect sth: *We calculated that the advantages would be greater than the disadvantages.*

IDIOM **be calculated to do sth** to be intended or designed to do sth: *His remark was clearly calculated to annoy me.*

calculating /'kælkjuleɪtɪŋ/ *adj* planning things in a very careful way in order to achieve what you want, without considering other people: *Her cold, calculating approach made her many enemies.*

calculation /ˌkælkju'leɪʃn/ *noun* **1** [C,U] finding an answer by using mathematics: *I'll have to do a few calculations before telling you how much I can afford.* ● *Calculation of the exact cost is impossible.* **2** [U] (*formal*) careful planning in order to achieve what you want, without considering other people: *His actions were clearly the result of deliberate calculation.*

calculator /'kælkjuleɪtə/ *noun* [C] a small electronic machine used for calculating figures: *a pocket calculator*

caldron (*especially US*) = CAULDRON

★**calendar** /'kælɪndə/ *noun* [C] **1** a list that shows the days, weeks and months of a particular year

> A **calendar** is often hung on a wall and may have a separate page for each month, sometimes with a picture or photograph. A

diary is a little book which you can carry around with you and which has spaces next to the dates so that you can write in appointments, etc.

•➤ picture on page S6 **2** a system for dividing time into fixed periods and for marking the beginning and end of a year: *the Muslim calendar* **3** a list of dates and events in a year that are important in a particular area of activity: *Wimbledon is a major event in the sporting calendar.*

ˌ**calendar 'month** = MONTH(1)

ˌ**calendar 'year** = YEAR(1)

calf /kɑːf/ *noun* [C] (*pl* **calves** /kɑːvz/) **1** a young cow •➤ Look at the note and picture at COW.

> The meat from a calf is called **veal**. Look at the note at **meat**.

2 the young of some other animals, for example elephants **3** the back of your leg, below your knee: *I've strained a calf muscle.* •➤ picture on page C5

calibre (*US* **caliber**) /'kælɪbə/ *noun* [sing,U] the quality or ability of a person or thing: *The company's employees are of (a) high calibre.*

★**call**[1] /kɔːl/ *verb* **1** [I,T] **call (out) to sb; call (sth) (out)** to say sth loudly or to shout in order to attract attention: *'Hello, is anybody there?' she called.* ● *He called out the names and the winners stepped forward.* ● *I could hear a man calling his dog.* **2** [I,T] = RING[2](1): *Who's calling, please?* ● *I'll call you tomorrow.* ● *We're just in the middle of dinner. Can I call you back later?* **3** **be called** to have as your name: *His wife is called Silvia.* ● *What was that village called?* **4** [T] to name or describe a person or thing in a certain way: *They called the baby Freddie.* ● *It was very rude to call her fat.* ● *Are you calling me a liar?* **5** [T] to order or ask sb to come to a certain place: *Can you call everybody in for lunch?* ● *I think we had better call the doctor.* **6** [T] to arrange for sth to take place at a certain time: *to call a meeting/an election/a strike* **7** [I] **call (in/round) (on sb/at...)** to make a short visit to a person or place: *I called in on Mike on my way home.* ● *We called at his house but there was nobody in.* **8** [I] **call at...** (used about a train, etc) to stop at the places mentioned: *This is the express service to London, calling at Manchester and Birmingham.*

IDIOMS **bring/call sb/sth to mind** → MIND[1]

call it a day (*informal*) to decide to stop doing sth: *Let's call it a day. I'm exhausted.*

call sb's bluff to tell sb to actually do what he/she is threatening to do (believing that he/she will not risk doing it)

call sb names to use insulting words about sb

call the shots/tune (*informal*) to be in a position to control a situation and make decisions about what should be done

PHRASAL VERBS **call by** (*informal*) to make a short visit to a place or person as you pass: *I'll call by to pick up the book on my way to work.*

call for sb (*Brit*) to collect sb in order to go somewhere together: *I'll call for you when it's time to go.*

call for sth to demand or need sth: *The crisis calls for immediate action.* ● *This calls for a celebration!*

call sth off to cancel sth: *The football match was called off because of the bad weather.*

call sb out to ask sb to come, especially to an emergency: *We had to call out the doctor in the middle of the night.*

call sb up 1 (*especially US*) to telephone sb: *He called me up to tell me the good news.* **2** to order sb to join the army, navy or air force: *All men under 30 were called up to fight in the war.*

call sth up to look at sth that is stored in a computer: *The bank clerk called up my account details on screen.*

⋆**call²** /kɔːl/ **noun 1** (also **'phone call**) [C] an act of telephoning or a conversation on the telephone: *Were there any calls for me while I was out?* ● *I'll give you a call at the weekend.* ● *to make a local call* ● *a long-distance call* **2** [C] a loud sound that is made to attract attention; a shout: *a call for help* ● *That bird's call is easy to recognize.* **3** [C] a short visit, especially to sb's house: *We could pay a call on Dave on our way home.* ● *The doctor has several calls to make this morning.* **4** [C] a request, demand for sth: *There have been calls for the President to resign.* **5** [C,U] **call for sth** a need for sth: *The doctor said there was no call for concern.*

IDIOMS **at sb's beck and call** → BECK

(be) on call to be ready to work if necessary: *Dr Young will be on call this weekend.*

CALL³ /kɔːl/ **abbr** computer-assisted language learning

'call box = TELEPHONE BOX

caller /'kɔːlə/ **noun** [C] a person who telephones or visits sb

callous /'kæləs/ **adj** not caring about the suffering of other people

⋆**calm¹** /kɑːm/ **adj 1** not excited, worried or angry; quiet: *Try to keep calm – there's no need to panic.* ● *She spoke in a calm voice.* ● *The city is calm again after last night's riots.* **2** without big waves: *a calm sea* ⋅➤ opposite **rough 3** without much wind: *calm weather* –**calmly** **adv** –**calmness noun** [U]

calm² /kɑːm/ **verb** [I,T] **calm (sb/sth) (down)** to become or to make sb quiet or calm: *Calm down! Shouting at everybody won't help.* ● *I did some breathing exercises to calm my nerves.*

calm³ /kɑːm/ **noun** [C,U] a period of time or a state when everything is peaceful: *After living in the city, I enjoyed the calm of country life.*

Calor gas™ /'kælə gæs/ **noun** [U] gas that is kept in special bottles and used for cooking, heating, etc

calorie /'kæləri/ **noun** [C] a unit for measur-ing the energy value of food: *A fried egg contains about 100 calories.* ● *a low-calorie drink/yoghurt/diet*

calves plural of CALF

camcorder /'kæmkɔːdə/ **noun** [C] a camera that you can carry around and use for record-ing pictures and sound on a video cassette

came past tense of COME

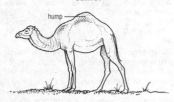

camel

hump

⋆**camel** /'kæml/ **noun** [C] an animal that lives in the desert and has a long neck and either one or two large masses of fat (**humps**) on its back. It is used for carrying people and goods.

cameo /'kæmiəʊ/ **noun** [C] (*pl* **cameos**) **1** a small part in a film or play that is usually played by a famous actor: *Sean Connery plays a cameo role as the dying king.* **2** a piece of jewellery that has a design in one colour and a background in a different colour

camera

flash

tripod

zoom

lens

roll of film

⋆**camera** /'kæmərə/ **noun** [C] a piece of equip-ment that you use for taking photographs or moving pictures: *I need a new film for my camera.* ● *a video/television camera*

cameraman /'kæmrəmən/ **noun** [C] (*pl* **-men** /-mən/) a person whose job is to oper-ate a camera for a film or a television com-pany ⋅➤ Look at **photographer**.

camouflage /'kæməflɑːʒ/ **noun** [U] **1** mater-ials or colours that soldiers use to make themselves and their equipment difficult to see **2** the way in which an animal's colour or shape matches its surroundings and makes it difficult to see: *The polar bear's white fur provides effective camouflage against the snow.* –**camouflage verb** [T]

camp¹ /kæmp/ **noun** [C,U] a place where people live in tents or simple buildings away from their usual home: *a refugee camp* • *The climbers set up camp at the foot of the mountain.*

★**camp**² /kæmp/ **verb** [I] **camp (out)** to sleep without a bed, especially outside in a tent: *We camped next to a river.* ••➤ **Go camping** is a common way of talking about camping for pleasure: *They went camping in France last year.*

★**campaign**¹ /kæm'peɪn/ **noun** [C] **1** a plan to do a number of things in order to achieve a special aim: *to launch an advertising/election campaign* **2** a planned series of attacks in a war

★**campaign**² /kæm'peɪn/ **verb** [I] **campaign (for/against sb/sth)** to take part in a planned series of activities in order to make sth happen or to prevent sth: *Local people are campaigning for lower speed limits in the town.* –**campaigner** **noun** [C]: *an animal rights campaigner*

'**camp bed** (*US* **cot**) **noun** [C] a light, narrow bed that you can fold up and carry easily ••➤ picture at **bed**

camper /'kæmpə/ **noun** [C] **1** a person who stays in a tent on holiday **2** (*Brit also* **camper van**) a motor vehicle in which you can sleep, cook, etc while on holiday

camping /'kæmpɪŋ/ **noun** [U] sleeping or spending a holiday in a tent: *Camping is cheaper than staying in hotels.* • *to go on a camping holiday*

campsite /'kæmpsaɪt/ **noun** [C] a place where you can stay in a tent

campus /'kæmpəs/ **noun** [C,U] (*pl* **campuses**) the area of land where the main buildings of a college or university are: *the college campus*

★**can**¹ /kən; *strong form* kæn/ **modal verb** (*negative* **cannot** /'kænɒt/; *short form* **can't** /kɑːnt/; *pt* **could** /kəd/ *strong form* /kʊd/; *negative* **could not** *short form* **couldn't** /'kʊdnt/) **1** used for showing that it is possible for sb/sth to do sth or that sb/sth has the ability to do sth: *Can you ride a bike?* • *He can't speak French.*

➤ **Can** has no infinitive or participle forms. To make the future and perfect tenses, we use **be able to**: *He's been able to swim for almost a year.* **Could have** is used when we say that somebody had the ability to do something but did not do it: *She could have passed the exam but she didn't really try.*

2 used to ask for or give permission: *Can I have a drink, please?* • *He asked if he could have a drink.*

➤ When we are talking about general permission in the past **could** is used: *I could do anything I wanted when I stayed with my grandma.* When we are talking about one particular occasion we do not use **could**: *I was allowed to visit him in hospital yesterday.*

3 used to ask sb to do sth: *Can you help me carry these books?* **4** used for offering to do sth: *Can I help at all?*

➤ For more information about modal verbs, look at the **Quick Grammar Reference** section at the back of this dictionary.

5 used to talk about sb's typical behaviour or of a typical effect: *You can be very annoying.* • *Wasp stings can be very painful.* **6** used in the negative for saying that you are sure sth is not true: *That can't be Maria – she's in London.* • *Surely you can't be hungry. You've only just had lunch.* **7** used with the verbs 'feel', 'hear', 'see', 'smell', 'taste'

➤ These verbs are not used in the continuous tenses. If we want to talk about seeing, hearing, etc at a particular moment, we use **can**: *I can smell something burning.* NOT *I'm smelling...*

★**can**² /kæn/ **noun** [C] **1** a metal or plastic container that is used for holding or carrying liquid: *an oil can* • *a watering can* **2** a metal container in which food or drink is kept without air so that it stays fresh: *a can of sardines* • *a can of beer* ••➤ picture at **container**

➤ In British English we usually use the word **tin** when it contains food. **Can** is used for drinks.

can³ /kæn/ **verb** [T] (**canning**; **canned**) to put food, drink, etc into a can in order to keep it fresh for a long time: *canned fruit*

★**canal** /kə'næl/ **noun** [C] **1** a deep cut that is made through land so that boats or ships can travel along it or so that water can flow to an area where it is needed: *the Panama Canal* **2** one of the tubes in the body through which food, air, etc passes

canary /kə'neəri/ **noun** [C] (*pl* **canaries**) a small yellow bird that sings and is often kept in a cage as a pet

★**cancel** /'kænsl/ **verb** [T] (**cancelling; cancelled**: *US* **canceling; canceled**) **1** to decide that sth that has been planned or arranged will not happen: *All flights have been cancelled because of the bad weather.* ••➤ Look at **postpone**. **2** to stop sth that you asked for or agreed to: *to cancel a reservation* • *I wish to cancel my order for these books.*

PHRASAL VERB **cancel (sth) out** to be equal to or have an equal effect: *What I owe you is the same as what you owe me, so our debts cancel each other out.*

cancellation /ˌkænsə'leɪʃn/ **noun** [C,U] the act of cancelling sth: *We had to make a last-minute cancellation.*

cancer /'kænsə/ **noun** [C,U] **1** a very serious disease in which lumps grow in the body: *She has lung cancer.* • *He died of cancer.* **2 Cancer** the fourth sign of the zodiac, the Crab

cancerous /'kænsərəs/ **adj** (used especially about a part of the body or sth growing in the body) having cancer: *a cancerous growth* • *cancerous cells*

candid /'kændɪd/ **adj** saying exactly what you think; frank ••➤ **noun** **candour** –**candidly** **adv**

candidacy /ˈkændɪdəsi/ **noun** [U] being a candidate

★**candidate** /ˈkændɪdət/ **noun** [C] **1** a person who makes a formal request to be considered for a job or wants to be elected to a particular position: *We have some very good candidates for the post.* **2** a person who is taking an exam

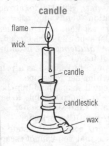

candle

flame
wick
candle
candlestick
wax

candle /ˈkændl/ **noun** [C] a round stick of solid oil or fat (wax) with a piece of string (a wick) through the middle that you can burn to give light: *to light/blow out a candle*

candlelight /ˈkændllaɪt/ **noun** [U] light that comes from a candle: *They had dinner by candlelight.*

candlestick /ˈkændlstɪk/ **noun** [C] an object for holding a candle or candles ••➤ picture at **candle**

candour (*US* **candor**) /ˈkændə/ **noun** [U] the quality of being honest; saying exactly what you think ••➤ adjective **candid**

candy /ˈkændi/ **noun** [C,U] (*pl* **candies**) (*US*) = **SWEET²**(1): *You eat too much candy.*

cane /keɪn/ **noun 1** [C,U] the long central part of certain plants (bamboo or sugar) that is like a tube and is used as a material for making furniture, etc: *sugar cane* ● *a cane chair* **2** [C] a stick that is used to help sb walk

canine /ˈkeɪnaɪn/ **adj** connected with dogs

canister /ˈkænɪstə/ **noun** [C] a small round metal container: *a gas canister*

cannabis /ˈkænəbɪs/ **noun** [U] a drug made from a plant (hemp) that some people smoke for pleasure, but which is illegal in many countries

cannibal /ˈkænɪbl/ **noun** [C] a person who eats other people –**cannibalism** /ˈkænɪbəlɪzəm/ **noun** [U]

cannon /ˈkænən/ **noun** [C] (*pl* **cannon** or **cannons**) **1** a large gun on a ship, army vehicle, aircraft, etc **2** a large, simple gun that was used in past times for firing large stone or metal balls (cannon balls)

cannot /ˈkænɒt/ *negative of* **CAN¹**

canoe /kəˈnuː/ **noun** [C] a light, narrow boat for one or two people that you can move through the water using a flat piece of wood (a paddle) ••➤ Look at **kayak**. ••➤ picture at **boat** –**canoe verb** [I] (*pres part* **canoeing**; *3rd pers sing pres* **canoes**; *pt, pp* **canoed**): *They canoed down the river.* ••➤ When we are talking about spending time in a canoe it is more usual to say **go canoeing**: *We're going canoeing on the river tomorrow.*

canon /ˈkænən/ **noun** [C] a Christian priest who works in a large church (cathedral)

canopy /ˈkænəpi/ **noun** [C] (*pl* **canopies**) a cover that hangs or spreads above sth: *The*

highest branches in the rainforest form a dense canopy. ● *a parachute canopy*

can't *short for* **CANNOT**

canteen /kænˈtiːn/ **noun** [C] the place in a school, factory, office, etc where the people who work there can get meals: *the staff canteen* ••➤ Look at **cafeteria**.

canter /ˈkæntə/ **verb** [I] (used about a horse and its rider) to run fairly fast but not very: *We cantered along the beach.* –**canter noun** [sing] ••➤ Look at **gallop** and **trot**.

canvas /ˈkænvəs/ **noun 1** [U] a type of strong cloth that is used for making sails, bags, tents, etc **2** [C] a piece of strong cloth for painting a picture on

canvass /ˈkænvəs/ **verb 1** [I,T] **canvass (sb) (for sth)** to try to persuade people to vote for a particular person or party in an election or to support sb/sth: *to canvass for votes* ● *He's canvassing for the Conservative Party.* ● *The Prime Minister is trying to canvass support for the plan.* **2** [T] to find out what people's opinions are about sth

canyon /ˈkænjən/ **noun** [C] a deep valley with very steep sides

★**cap¹** /kæp/ **noun** [C] **1** a soft hat that has a part sticking out at the front (peak): *a baseball cap* ••➤ picture at **hat 2** a soft hat that is worn for a particular purpose: *a shower cap* **3** a hat that is given to a player who is chosen to play for his/her country: *He won his first cap against France.* **4** a covering for the end or top of sth: *Please put the cap back on the bottle.* ••➤ Look at the note at **top¹**. ••➤ picture at **container**

cap² /kæp/ **verb** [T] (**capping**; **capped**) **1** to cover the top of sth: *mountains capped with snow* **2** to limit the amount of money that can be spent on sth **3** to follow sth with sth bigger or better **4** (*sport*) to choose a player to represent his/her country

IDIOM **to cap it all** as a final piece of bad luck: *I had a row with my boss, my bike was stolen, and now to cap it all I've lost my keys!*

capability /ˌkeɪpəˈbɪləti/ **noun** [C,U] (*pl* **capabilities**) **capability (to do sth/of doing sth)** the quality of being able to do sth: *Animals in the zoo have lost the capability to catch/of catching food for themselves.* ● *I tried to fix the computer, but it was **beyond** my capabilities.*

★**capable** /ˈkeɪpəbl/ **adj 1** **capable of (doing) sth** having the ability or qualities necessary to do sth: *He's capable of passing the exam if he tries harder.* ● *That car is capable of 180 miles per hour.* ● *I do not believe that she's capable of stealing.* **2** having a lot of skill; good at doing sth: *She's a very capable teacher.* ••➤ opposite **incapable** –**capably adv**

capacity /kəˈpæsəti/ **noun** (*pl* **capacities**) **1** [sing,U] the amount that a container or space can hold: *The tank has a capacity of 1000 litres.* ● *The stadium was **filled** to capacity.* **2** [sing] a capacity (for sth/for doing sth); a capacity (to do sth) the ability to understand or do sth: *That book is beyond the capacity of young children.* ● *a capacity for* hard work/for learning languages **3** [C] the official position that sb has: *In his capacity as chairman of the council...* **4** [sing, U] the amount that a factory or machine can produce: *The power station is working at full capacity.*

cape /keɪp/ **noun** [C] **1** a piece of clothing with no sleeves that hangs from your shoulders •➤ Look at **cloak**. **2** a piece of high land that sticks out into the sea: *the Cape of Good Hope*

★**capital**¹ /'kæpɪtl/ **noun 1** (also **capital city**) [C] the town or city where the government of a country is: *Madrid is the capital of Spain.* **2** [U] an amount of money that you use to start a business or to put in a bank, etc so that you earn more money (**interest**) on it: *When she had enough capital, she bought a shop.* **3** (also **capital letter**) [C] the large form of a letter of the alphabet: *Write your name in capitals.* **4** [C] a place that is well-known for a particular thing: *Niagara Falls is the honeymoon capital of the world.*

capital² /'kæpɪtl/ **adj 1** connected with punishment by death: *a capital offence* (= a crime for which sb can be sentenced to death) **2** (used about letters of the alphabet) written in the large form: *'David' begins with a capital 'D'.*

capital in'vestment noun [U] money that a business spends on buildings, equipment, etc

capitalism /'kæpɪtəlɪzəm/ **noun** [U] the economic system in which businesses are owned and run for profit by individuals and not by the state •➤ Look at **communism**, **Marxism** and **socialism**. –**capitalist noun** [C], **adj**

capitalize (also **-ise**) /'kæpɪtəlaɪz/ **verb**
PHRASAL VERB **capitalize on sth** to use sth to your advantage: *We can capitalize on the mistakes that our rivals have made.*

capital 'punishment noun [U] punishment by death for serious crimes •➤ Look at **death penalty** and compare **corporal punishment**.

capitulate /kə'pɪtʃuleɪt/ **verb** [I] (*formal*) to stop fighting and accept that you have lost; to give in to sb –**capitulation** /kə,pɪtʃu'leɪʃn/ **noun** [C, U]

capricious /kə'prɪʃəs/ **adj** changing behaviour suddenly in a way that is difficult to predict: *a capricious actor*

Capricorn /'kæprɪkɔːn/ **noun** [C, U] the tenth sign of the zodiac, the Goat

capsize /kæp'saɪz/ **verb** [I, T] (used about boats) to turn over in the water: *The canoe capsized.* • *A big wave capsized the yacht.*

capsule /'kæpsjuːl/ **noun** [C] **1** a very small closed tube of medicine that you swallow •➤ picture at **bandage 2** a container that is closed so that air, water, etc cannot enter

Capt abbr Captain; a rank in the British and American armies

★**captain**¹ /'kæptɪn/ **noun** [C] **1** the person who is in command of a ship or an aircraft **2** a person who is the leader of a group or team: *Who's (the) captain of the French team?*

3 an officer at a middle level in the army or navy

captain² /'kæptɪn/ **verb** [T] to be the captain of a group or team

caption /'kæpʃn/ **noun** [C] the words that are written above or below a picture, photograph, etc to explain what it is about

captivate /'kæptɪveɪt/ **verb** [T] to attract and hold sb's attention –**captivating adj**

captive¹ /'kæptɪv/ **adj** kept as a prisoner; (used about animals) kept in a cage, etc: (*figurative*) *a captive audience* (= listening because they cannot leave)
IDIOMS **hold sb captive** to keep sb as a prisoner and not allow him/her to escape
take sb captive to catch sb and hold him/her as your prisoner •➤ It is also possible to say **hold sb prisoner** and **take sb prisoner**.

captive² /'kæptɪv/ **noun** [C] a prisoner

captivity /kæp'tɪvəti/ **noun** [U] the state of being kept in a place that you cannot escape from: *Wild animals are often unhappy in captivity.*

captor /'kæptə/ **noun** [C] a person who takes or keeps a person as a prisoner

capture¹ /'kæptʃə/ **verb** [T] **1** to take a person or animal prisoner: *The lion was captured and taken back to the zoo.* **2** to take control of sth: *The town has been captured by the rebels.* • *The company has captured 90% of the market.* **3** to make sb interested in sth: *The story captured the children's imagination/interest/attention.* **4** to succeed in representing or recording sth in words, pictures, etc: *This poem captures the atmosphere of the carnival.* • *The robbery was captured on video.*

capture² /'kæptʃə/ **noun** [U] the act of capturing sth or being captured

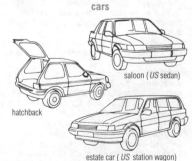

cars

saloon (*US* sedan)

hatchback

estate car (*US* station wagon)

★**car** /kɑː/ **noun** [C] **1** (*especially US* **automobile**) a road vehicle with four wheels that can carry a small number of people: *a new/second-hand car* • *Where can I park the car?* • *They had a car crash.* • *to get into/out of a car*

➤ Note that we go **in the car** or **by car**. You can also use the verb **drive**: *I come to work in the car/by car.* • *I drive to work.*

•➤ picture on page S9 **2** (*Brit*) a section of a train that is used for a particular purpose: *a dining/sleeping car* **3** (*US*) = **CARRIAGE**(1)

carafe /kə'ræf/ noun [C] a glass container like a bottle with a wide neck, in which wine or water is served •➤ picture at **jug**

caramel /'kærəmel/ noun **1** [U] burnt sugar that is used to add flavour and colour to food **2** [C,U] a type of sticky sweet that is made from boiled sugar, butter and milk

carat (*US* **karat**) /'kærət/ noun [C] a unit for measuring how pure gold is or how heavy jewels are: *a 20-carat gold ring*

caravan

★**caravan** /'kærəvæn/ noun [C] **1** (*US* **trailer**) a large vehicle that is pulled by a car. You can sleep, cook, etc in a caravan when you are travelling or on holiday. •➤ When we are talking about using a caravan for holidays we say **go caravanning**. **2** a group of people and animals that travel together, for example across a desert

carbohydrate /,kɑ:bəʊ'haɪdreɪt/ noun [C,U] one of the substances in food, for example sugar, that gives your body energy: *Athletes need a diet that is high in carbohydrate.* ● *Bread, potatoes and rice all contain carbohydrates.*

carbon /'kɑ:bən/ noun [U] (*symbol* **C**) a chemical substance that is found in all living things, and also in diamonds, coal, petrol, etc

,**carbon 'copy** noun [C] **1** a copy of a letter, etc that was made using special paper (**carbon paper**) **2** an exact copy of sth

,**carbon di'oxide** noun [U] (*symbol* CO_2) a gas that has no colour or smell that people and animals breathe out of their lungs

,**carbon mon'oxide** noun [U] (*symbol* **CO**) a poisonous gas. Motor vehicles produce a lot of carbon monoxide.

'**carbon paper** noun [U] thin paper with a dark substance on one side that you put between two sheets of paper to make a copy of what you are writing

,**car 'boot sale** noun [C] an outdoor sale where people sell things they do not want from the back of their cars

carburettor (*US* **carburetor**) /,kɑ:bə'retə/ noun [C] the piece of equipment in a car's engine that mixes petrol and air

carcass /'kɑ:kəs/ noun [C] the dead body of an animal •➤ Look at **corpse**.

★**card** /kɑ:d/ noun **1** [U] thick rigid paper **2** [C] a piece of card or plastic that has information on it: *Here is my business card in case you need to contact me.* ● *a membership/identity/credit card* **3** [C] a piece of card with a picture on it that you use for sending a special message to sb: *a Christmas/birthday card* ● *a*

cards

pack of cards   cards   suits

◆ diamonds
♥ hearts
♣ clubs
♠ spades

jack   queen   king   ace   joker

get-well card (= one that you send to sb who is ill) **4** (also **playing card**) [C] one of a set of 52 small pieces of card with shapes or pictures on them that are used for playing games: *a pack of cards* **5 cards** [pl] games that are played with cards: *Let's play cards.* ● *Let's have a game of cards.* ● *I never win at cards!*

➤ A **pack** of cards is divided into four **suits**, two red (**hearts** and **diamonds**) and two black (**clubs** and **spades**). Each suit has an **ace**, a **king**, a **queen**, a **jack** and nine other cards, numbered from 2 to 10. Before we play cards we **shuffle**, **cut** and **deal** the cards.

IDIOM on the cards; (*US*) **in the cards** (*informal*) likely to happen: *Their marriage break-up has been on the cards for some time now.*

★**cardboard** /'kɑ:dbɔ:d/ noun [U] very thick paper that is used for making boxes, etc: *The goods were packed in cardboard boxes.*

cardiac /'kɑ:diæk/ adj (*formal*) connected with the heart: *cardiac surgery* ● *a cardiac arrest* (= when the heart stops temporarily or permanently)

cardigan /'kɑ:dɪgən/ noun [C] a piece of clothing like a woollen jacket, that fastens at the front •➤ picture on page C6 •➤ Look at the note at **sweater**.

cardinal /'kɑ:dɪnl/ noun [C] **1** a priest at a high level in the Roman Catholic church **2** (also ,**cardinal 'number**) a whole number, for example 1, 2, 3 that shows quantity •➤ Look at **ordinal**.

★**care¹** /keə/ noun **1** [U] **care (for sb)** looking after sb/sth so that he/she/it has what he/she/it needs for his/her/its health and protection: *All the children in their care were healthy and happy.* ● *This hospital provides free medical care.* ● *She's in intensive care* (= the part of the hospital for people who are very seriously ill). ● *skin/hair care products* **2** [U] **care (over sth/in doing sth)** thinking about what you are doing so that you do it well or do not make a mistake: *You should take more care over your homework.* ● *This* *box contains glasses – please handle it with care.* **3** [C,U] something that makes you feel worried or unhappy: *Since Charlie retired he doesn't have a care in the world.* • *It was a happy life, free from care.*

IDIOMS in care (used about children) living in a home which is organized by the government or the local council, and not with their parents: *They were taken into care after their parents died.*

take care (that.../to do sth) to be careful: *Goodbye and take care!* • *Take care that you don't spill your tea.* • *He took care not to arrive too early.*

take care of sb/sth to deal with sb/sth; to organize or arrange sth: *I'll take care of the food for the party.*

take care of yourself/sb/sth to keep yourself/ sb/sth safe from injury, illness, damage, etc; to look after sb/sth: *My mother took care of me when I was ill.* • *She always takes great care of her books.*

★ **care²** /keə/ **verb** [I,T] care (about sb/sth) to be worried about or interested in sb/sth: *Money is the thing that she cares about most.* • *He really cares about his staff.* • *I don't care what you do.*

IDIOMS I, etc couldn't care less (*informal*) it does not matter to me, etc at all: *I couldn't care less what Barry thinks.*

who cares? (*informal*) nobody is interested; it is not important to anyone: *'I wonder who'll win the match.' 'Who cares?'*

would you care for.../to do sth (*formal*) a polite way to ask if sb would like sth or would like to do sth

PHRASAL VERBS care for sb to look after sb: *Who cared for her while she was ill?*

care for sb/sth to like or love sb/sth: *She still cares for Liam although he married someone else.* • *I don't care for that colour very much.*

★ **career¹** /kə'rɪə/ **noun** [C] **1** the series of jobs that sb has in a particular area of work: *Sarah is considering a career in engineering.* • *a successful career in politics* **2** the period of your life that you spend working: *She spent most of her career working in India.*

career² /kə'rɪə/ **verb** [I] to move quickly and in a dangerous way: *The car careered off the road and crashed into a wall.*

carefree /'keəfri:/ **adj** with no problems or worries

★ **careful** /'keəfl/ **adj 1** careful (of/with sth); careful (to do sth) thinking about what you are doing so that you do not have an accident or make mistakes, etc: **Be careful!** *There's a car coming.* • *Please be very careful of the traffic.* • *Be careful with that knife – it's very sharp.* • *That ladder doesn't look very safe. Be careful you don't fall.* • *I was careful not to say anything about the money.* • *a careful driver* **2** giving a lot of attention to details to be sure sth is right: *I'll need to give this matter some careful thought.* • *a careful worker* –carefully /'keəfəli/ **adv**: *Please listen carefully. It's important that you remember all this.*

★ **careless** /'keələs/ **adj 1** careless (about/ with sth) not thinking enough about what you are doing so that you make mistakes: *Jo's very careless.* • *The accident was caused by careless driving.* **2** resulting from a lack of thought or attention to detail: *a careless mistake* –carelessly **adv**: *She threw her coat carelessly on the chair.* –carelessness **noun** [U]

carer /'keərə/ (*US* **caregiver** /'keəgɪvə/) **noun** [C] a person who regularly looks after sb who is unable to look after himself/herself because of age, illness, etc

caress /kə'res/ **verb** [T] to touch sb/sth in a gentle and loving way –caress **noun** [C]

caretaker /'keəteɪkə/ (*US* **janitor**) **noun** [C] a person whose job is to look after a large building, for example a school or a block of flats

★ **cargo** /'kɑːgəʊ/ **noun** [C,U] (*pl* **cargoes**: *US also* **cargos**) the goods that are carried in a ship or aircraft: *Luggage is carried in the cargo hold of the plane.* • *a cargo ship*

the Caribbean /ˌkærɪ'bɪən/ **noun** [sing] the area in the Caribbean Sea where the group of islands called the West Indies are situated –Caribbean **adj**

caricature /'kærɪkətʃʊə/ **noun** [C] a picture or description of sb that makes his/her appearance or behaviour funnier and more extreme than it really is: *Many of the people in the book are caricatures of the author's friends.*

caring /'keərɪŋ/ **adj** showing that you care about other people: *We must work towards a more caring society.*

carnation /kɑː'neɪʃn/ **noun** [C] a white, pink or red flower with a pleasant smell •⁕ picture on page C2

carnival /'kɑːnɪvl/ **noun** [C] a public festival that takes place in the streets with music and dancing: *the carnival in Rio*

carol /'kærəl/ **noun** [C] a Christian religious song that people sing at Christmas

carousel /ˌkærə'sel/ **noun** [C] **1** (*US*) = MERRY-GO-ROUND **2** a moving belt at an airport that carries luggage for passengers to collect

'**car park** (*US* '**parking lot**) **noun** [C] an area or building where you can leave your car: *a multi-storey car park*

★ **carpenter** /'kɑːpəntə/ **noun** [C] a person whose job is to make things from wood •⁕ Look at **joiner**.

carpentry /'kɑːpəntri/ **noun** [U] the skill or work of a carpenter

★ **carpet** /'kɑːpɪt/ **noun 1** [C,U] (a piece of) thick material that is used for covering floors and stairs: *a fitted carpet* (= one that is cut to the exact shape of a room) • *a square metre of carpet* •⁕ Look at **rug**. **2** [C] a thick layer of sth that covers the ground: *The fields were under a carpet of snow.* –carpeted **adj**: *All the rooms are carpeted.*

★ **carriage** /'kærɪdʒ/ **noun** [C] **1** (also **coach**, *US* **car**) one of the separate parts of a train where people sit: *a first-class carriage* **2** (also coach) a vehicle with wheels that is pulled by horses

carriageway /'kærɪdʒweɪ/ noun [C] (*Brit*) one of the two sides of a motorway or main road on which vehicles travel in one direction only: *the southbound carriageway of the motorway* •➤ Look at **dual carriageway**.

carrier /'kæriə/ noun [C] **1** (in business) a company that transports people or goods: *the Dutch carrier, KLM* **2** a military vehicle or ship that is used for transporting soldiers, planes, weapons, etc: *an aircraft carrier* **3** a person or animal that can give an infectious disease to others but does not show the signs of the disease: *Some insects are carriers of tropical diseases.* **4** (*Brit*) = CARRIER BAG

'**carrier bag** (*Brit also* **carrier**) noun [C] a plastic or paper bag for carrying shopping •➤ picture at **bag**

★**carrot** /'kærət/ noun **1** [C,U] a long thin orange vegetable that grows under the ground: *A pound of carrots, please.* • *grated carrot* •➤ picture on page C3 **2** [C] something attractive that is offered to sb in order to persuade him/her to do sth: *The management have offered them the carrot of a £500 bonus if they agree to work extra hours.*

★**carry** /'kæri/ verb (*pres part* **carrying**; *3rd pers sing pres* **carries**; *pt, pp* **carried**) **1** [T] to hold sb/sth in your hand, arms or on your back while you are moving from one place to another: *Could you carry this bag for me? It's terribly heavy.* • *She was carrying a rucksack on her back.*

> You use **wear**, not **carry**, to talk about having clothes, jewellery, etc on your body: *He was wearing a black jacket.*

2 [T] to have sth with you as you go somewhere: *I never carry much money with me when I go to London.* • *Do the police carry guns in your country?* **3** [T] to transport sb/sth from one place to another: *A train carrying hundreds of passengers crashed yesterday.* • *Strong winds carried the boat off course.* **4** [T] to have an infectious disease that can be given to others, usually without showing any signs of the disease yourself: *Rats carry all sorts of diseases.* **5** [T] (usually passive) to officially approve of sth in a meeting, etc, because the largest number of people vote for it: *The motion was carried by 12 votes to 9.* **6** [I] (used about a sound) to reach a long distance: *You'll have to speak louder if you want your voice to carry to the back of the room.*

IDIOMS **be/get carried away** to be so excited that you forget what you are doing: *I got so carried away watching the race that I forgot how late it was.*

carry weight to have influence on the opinion of sb else: *Nick's views carry a lot of weight with our manager.*

PHRASAL VERBS **carry it/sth off** to succeed in doing sth difficult: *He felt nervous before he started his speech but he carried it off very well.*

carry on (with sth/doing sth) to continue: *They ignored me and carried on with their conversation.* • *She intends to carry on studying after the course has finished.*

carry on sth to do an activity: *to carry on a conversation/a business*

carry out sth 1 to do sth that you have been ordered to do: *The soldiers carried out their orders without question.* **2** to do a task, repair, etc: *to carry out tests/an investigation*

carrycot /'kærɪkɒt/ noun [C] a small bed, like a box with handles, that you can carry a baby in •➤ picture at **pram**

'**carry-on** noun [C] (*especially US*) a small piece of luggage that you can take onto a plane with you

carsick /'kɑːsɪk/ adj feeling sick or vomiting as a result of travelling in a car: *to get/feel/be carsick* •➤ Look at **airsick**, **seasick** and **travel-sick**.

cart[1] /kɑːt/ noun [C] a vehicle with wheels that is used for transporting things

cart[2] /kɑːt/ verb [T] (*informal*) to take or carry sth/sb somewhere, often with difficulty: *We left our luggage at the station because we didn't want to cart it around all day.*

cartilage /'kɑːtɪlɪdʒ/ noun [C,U] a strong substance in the places where your bones join

carton /'kɑːtn/ noun [C] a small container made of cardboard or plastic: *a carton of milk/orange juice* •➤ picture at **container**

cartoon /kɑː'tuːn/ noun [C] **1** a funny drawing, especially in a newspaper or magazine **2** a film that tells a story by using moving drawings instead of real people and places

cartoonist /kɑː'tuːnɪst/ noun [C] a person who draws cartoons

cartridge /'kɑːtrɪdʒ/ noun [C] **1** a small tube that contains explosive powder and a bullet. You put a cartridge into a gun when you want to fire it. **2** a closed container that holds sth that is used in a machine, for example film for a camera, ink for printing, etc. Cartridges can be removed and replaced when they are finished or empty.

carve /kɑːv/ verb **1** [I,T] carve (sth) (out of sth) to cut wood or stone in order to make an object or to put a pattern or writing on it: *The statue is carved out of marble.* • *He carved his name on the desk.* **2** [T] to cut a piece of cooked meat into slices: *to carve a chicken*

carving /'kɑːvɪŋ/ noun [C,U] an object or design that has been carved: *There are ancient carvings on the walls of the cave.*

cascade[1] /kæ'skeɪd/ noun [C] **1** water that flows down the side of a mountain, etc (a waterfall) **2** a large quantity of sth that falls or hangs down: *a cascade of blond hair*

cascade[2] /kæ'skeɪd/ verb [I] to fall or hang down, especially in large amounts or in stages: *Water cascaded from the roof.*

★**case** /keɪs/ noun **1** [C] a particular situation or example of sth: *In some cases, people have had to wait two weeks for a doctor's appointment.* • *Most of us travel to work by tube – or,* *in Jim's **case**, by train and tube.* ● *Cases of the disease are very unusual in this country.* **2 the case** [sing] the true situation: *The man said he worked in Cardiff, but we discovered later that this was not the case.* **3** [C] a crime or legal matter: *The police deal with hundreds of murder cases a year.* ● *The case will come to court in a few months.* **4** [C, usually sing] the facts and reasons that support one side in a discussion or legal matter: *She tried to **make a case for** shorter working hours, but the others disagreed.* **5** [C] (especially in compounds) a container or cover for sth: *a pencil case* ● *a pillowcase* ● *a bookcase* ● *But put her glasses back in the case.* **6** = **SUITCASE**: *Would you like me to carry your case?*

IDIOMS **(be) a case of sth/doing sth** a situation in which sth is needed: *There's no secret to success in this business. It's just a case of hard work.*

in any case whatever happens or has happened; anyway: *I don't know how much tickets for the match cost, but I'm going in any case.*

in case because sth might happen: *I think I'll take an umbrella in case it rains.* ● *I wasn't intending to buy anything but I took my cheque book just in case.*

in case of sth (*formal*) if sth happens: *In case of fire, break this glass.*

in that case if that is the situation: *'I'm busy on Tuesday.' 'Oh well, in that case we'll have to meet another day.'*

prove your/the case/point → **PROVE**

'**case study** noun [C] a detailed study of a person, group, situation, etc over a period of time

★**cash¹** /kæʃ/ noun [U] **1** money in the form of coins or notes and not cheques, plastic cards, etc: *Would you prefer me to pay **in cash** or by cheque?* ● *How much cash have you got with/on you?*

➤ We use **cash** when we are talking about coins and notes, but **change** when we are talking about coins only.

2 (*informal*) money in any form: *I'm a bit short of cash this month so I can't afford to go out much.* ••➤ picture at **money**

cash² /kæʃ/ verb [T] to exchange a cheque, traveller's cheque, etc for coins and notes: *I'm just going to the bank to cash a cheque.*

PHRASAL VERB **cash in (on sth)** to take advantage of a situation

cashback /'kæʃbæk/ noun [U] **1** an offer of money as a present that is made by some banks, companies selling cars, etc in order to persuade customers to do business with them **2** a system in some shops (supermarkets), which allows the customer to take money out of his/her bank account at the same time as paying for the goods with a special card (cash card).

'**cash card** (*US* ATM card) noun [C] a plastic card given by a bank to its customers so that they can get money from a special machine (cash machine) in or outside a bank ••➤ Look at **cheque card** and **credit card**.

'**cash desk** noun [C] the place in a large shop where you pay for things

cashew /'kæʃuː/ (also **cashew nut**) noun [C] a small curved nut that we eat ••➤ picture at **nut**

'**cash flow** noun [sing] the movement of money into and out of a business as goods are bought and sold: *The company had cash-flow problems and could not pay its bills.*

cashier /kæ'ʃɪə/ noun [C] the person in a bank, shop, etc that customers pay money to or get money from

'**cash machine** (also '**cash dispenser**; **cashpoint**; *US also* **ATM** /,eɪ tiː 'em/) noun [C] a machine inside or outside a bank that you can get money from at any time of day by putting in a special card (cash card)

cashmere /'kæʃmɪə/ noun [U] a type of wool that is very fine and soft

casino /kə'siːnəʊ/ noun [C] (*pl* **casinos**) a place where people play roulette and other games in which you can win or lose money

cask /kɑːsk/ noun [C] a large wooden container in which alcoholic drinks, etc are stored

casserole /'kæsərəʊl/ noun **1** [C,U] a type of food that you make by cooking meat and vegetables in a liquid for a long time in the oven: *chicken casserole* **2** [C] a large dish with a lid for cooking casseroles in ••➤ picture at **pan**

★**cassette** /kə'set/ noun [C] a small flat case with tape inside that you use for recording and playing music and other sounds: *to put on/play/listen to a cassette*

➤ Another word for **cassette** is **tape**. When you want to go back to the beginning of a cassette you **rewind** it. When you want to go forward you **fast forward** it. ••➤ Look at **video**.

cas'sette recorder noun [C] a machine that you use for recording and playing cassettes

cast¹ /kɑːst/ verb (*pt, pp* **cast**) **1** [T] (often passive) to choose an actor for a particular role in a play, film, etc: *She always seems to be cast in the same sort of role.* **2** [I,T] to throw a fishing line or net into the water

IDIOMS **cast doubt on sth** to make people less sure about sth: *The newspaper report casts doubt on the truth of the Prime Minister's statement.*

cast an eye/your eye(s) over sb/sth to look at sb/sth quickly

cast light on sth to help to explain sth: *Can you cast any light on the problem?*

cast your mind back to make yourself remember sth: *She cast her mind back to the day she met her husband.*

cast a shadow (across/over sth) to cause an area of shade to appear somewhere: (*figurative*) *The accident cast a shadow over the rest of the holiday* (= stopped people enjoying it fully).

cast a/your vote to vote: *The MPs will cast*

their votes in the leadership election tomorrow.
PHRASAL VERB cast **around/about for sth** to try
to find sth: *Jack cast around desperately for a
solution to the problem.*

cast² /kɑːst/ **noun** [C,with sing or pl verb] all
the actors in a play, film, etc: *The entire cast
was/were excellent.*

castaway /ˈkɑːstəweɪ/ **noun** [C] a person
who is left alone somewhere after his/her
ship has sunk

caste /kɑːst/ **noun** [C,U] a social class or
group based on your position in society, how
much money you have, family origin, etc; the
system of dividing people in this way: *Hindu
society is based on a caste system.*

,**cast 'iron** **noun** [U] a hard type of iron

,**cast-'iron** **adj** made of cast iron: (*figurative*)
a cast-iron alibi (= one that people cannot
doubt)

★**castle** /ˈkɑːsl/ **noun** [C] a large building with
high walls and towers that was built in the
past to defend people against attack: *a medieval castle* ● *Edinburgh Castle*

'**cast-off** **noun** [C,usually pl] a piece of clothing that you no longer want and that you give
to sb else or throw away: *When I was little I
had to wear my sister's cast-offs.*

castrate /kæˈstreɪt/ **verb** [T] to remove part
of the sexual organs of a male animal so that
it cannot produce young ••➤ Look at **neuter²**.
–**castration** /kæˈstreɪʃn/ **noun** [U]

casual /ˈkæʒuəl/ **adj 1** relaxed and not worried; not showing great effort or interest: *I'm
not happy about your casual attitude to your
work.* ● *It was only a casual remark so I don't
know why he got so angry.* **2** (used about
clothes) not formal: *I always change into casual clothes as soon as I get home from work.*
3 (used about work) done only for a short
period; not regular or permanent: *Most of the
building work was done by casual labour.* ● *a
casual job* –**casually** /ˈkæʒuəli/ **adv**: *She
walked in casually and said, 'I'm not late, am
I?'* ● *Dress casually, it won't be a formal
party.*

casualty /ˈkæʒuəlti/ **noun** (*pl* **casualties**)
1 [C] a person who is killed or injured in a
war or an accident: *After the accident the
casualties were taken to hospital.* **2** [C] a person or thing that suffers as a result of sth
else: *Many small companies became casualties
of the economic crisis.* **3** (also '**casualty
department**, *US* e'**mergency room**; **ER**)
[U] the part of a hospital where people who
have been injured in accidents are taken for
immediate treatment

★**cat** /kæt/ **noun** [C] **1** a small animal with soft
fur that people often keep as a pet **2** a wild
animal of the cat family: *the big cats* (= lions,
tigers, etc)

> ➤ A young cat is called a **kitten**. A male cat
is called a **tom**. When a cat makes a soft
sound of pleasure, it **purrs**. When it makes
a louder sound, it **miaows**.

catalogue (*US* **catalog**) /ˈkætəlɒg/ **noun** [C]
1 a list of all the things that you can buy, see,

etc somewhere **2** a series, especially of bad
things: *a catalogue of disasters/errors/injur-
ies* –**catalogue verb** [T]: *She started to catalogue all the new library books.*

catalytic converter /ˌkætəˌlɪtɪk kən-
ˈvɜːtə/ **noun** [C] a device used in motor
vehicles to reduce the damage caused to the
environment by poisonous gases

catapult¹ /ˈkætə-
pʌlt/ (*US* **sling-
shot**) **noun** [C] a
Y-shaped stick with
a piece of elastic
tied to each side
that is used by chil-
dren for shooting
stones

catapult² /ˈkætə-
pʌlt/ **verb** [T] to throw sb/sth suddenly and
with great force: *When the car crashed the
driver was catapulted through the windscreen.*
● (*figurative*) *The success of his first film catapulted him to fame.*

cataract /ˈkætərækt/ **noun** [C] a white area
that grows over the eye as a result of disease

catarrh /kəˈtɑː/ **noun** [U] a thick liquid that
forms in the nose and throat when you have
a cold

catastrophe /kəˈtæstrəfi/ **noun** [C] **1** a sudden disaster that causes great suffering or
damage: *major catastrophes such as floods
and earthquakes* **2** an event that causes great
difficulty, disappointment, etc: *It'll be a catastrophe if I fail the exam again.* –**catastrophic**
/ˌkætəˈstrɒfɪk/ **adj**: *The war had a catastrophic effect on the whole country.*

★**catch¹** /kætʃ/ **verb** (*pt, pp* **caught** /kɔːt/)
1 [T] to take hold of sth that is moving, usually with your hand or hands: *The dog caught
the ball in its mouth.* **2** [T] to capture sb/sth
that you have been following or looking for:
*Two policemen ran after the thief and caught
him at the end of the street.* ● *to catch a fish*
3 [T] to notice or see sb doing sth bad: *I
caught her taking money from my purse.* **4** [T]
to get on a bus, train, plane, etc: *I caught the
bus into town.* ••➤ opposite **miss 5** [T] to be in
time for sth; not to miss sb/sth: *We arrived
just in time to catch the beginning of the film.*
● *I'll phone her now. I might just catch her
before she leaves the office.* **6** [I,T] to become
or cause sth to become accidentally connected to or stuck in sth: *His jacket caught on
a nail and ripped.* ● *If we leave early we won't
get caught in the traffic.* **7** [T] to hit sb/sth:
The branch caught him on the head. **8** [T] to
get an illness: *to catch a cold/flu/measles*
9 [T] to hear or understand sth that sb says:
*I'm sorry, I didn't quite catch what you said.
Could you repeat it?*
IDIOMS catch **sb's attention/eye** to make sb
notice sth: *I tried to catch the waiter's eye so
that I could get the bill.*
catch **your breath 1** to rest after physical
exercise so that your breathing returns to
normal: *I had to sit down at the top of the hill
to catch my breath.* **2** to breathe in suddenly

because you are surprised

catch your death (of cold) to get very cold: *Don't go out without a coat – you'll catch your death!*

catch fire to start burning, often accidentally: *Nobody knows how the building caught fire.*

catch sb red-handed to find sb just as he/she is doing sth wrong: *The police caught the burglars red-handed with the stolen jewellery.*

catch sight/a glimpse of sb/sth to see sb/sth for a moment: *We waited outside the theatre, hoping to catch a glimpse of the actress.*

catch the sun 1 to shine brightly in the sunlight: *The panes of glass flashed as they caught the sun.* **2** to become burned or brown in the sun: *Your face looks red. You've really caught the sun, haven't you?*

PHRASAL VERBS **catch on** (*informal*) **1** to become popular or fashionable: *The idea has never really caught on in this country.* **2** to understand or realize sth: *She's sometimes a bit slow to catch on.*

catch sb out to cause sb to make a mistake by asking a clever question: *Ask me anything you like – you won't catch me out.*

catch up (with sb); catch sb up to reach sb who is in front of you: *Sharon's missed so much school she'll have to work hard to catch up with the rest of the class.* • *Go on ahead, I'll catch you up in a minute.*

catch up on sth to spend time doing sth that you have not been able to do for some time: *I'll have to go into the office at the weekend to catch up on my work.*

be/get caught up in sth to be or get involved in sth, usually without intending to: *I seem to have got caught up in a rather complicated situation.*

catch² /kætʃ/ **noun** [C] **1** an act of catching sth, for example a ball **2** the amount of fish that sb has caught: *The fishermen brought their catch to the harbour.* **3** a device for fastening sth and keeping it closed: *I can't close my suitcase – the catch is broken.* • *a window catch* **4** a hidden disadvantage or difficulty in sth that seems attractive: *It looks like a good offer but I'm sure there must be a catch in it.*

catchment area /'kætʃmənt eəriə/ **noun** [C] the area from which a school gets its students, a hospital gets its patients, etc

catchphrase /'kætʃfreɪz/ **noun** [C] a phrase that becomes famous for a while because it is used by a famous person

catchy /'kætʃi/ **adj** (used about a tune or song) easy to remember

categorical /ˌkætə'gɒrɪkl/ **adj** very definite: *The answer was a categorical 'no'.* –**categorically** /-kli/ **adv**: *The Minister categorically denied the rumour.*

categorize (also **-ise**) /'kætəgəraɪz/ **verb** [T] to divide people or things into groups; to say that sb/sth belongs to a particular group

★**category** /'kætəgəri/ **noun** [C] (*pl* **categories**) a group of people or things that are similar to each other: *This painting won first prize in the junior category.* • *These books are divided into categories according to subject.*

cater /'keɪtə/ **verb** [I] **1 cater for sb/sth; cater to sth** to provide what sb/sth needs or wants: *We need a hotel that caters for small children.* • *The menu caters to all tastes.* **2** to provide and serve food and drink at an event or in a place that a lot of people go to: *Our firm caters for the 5000 staff and visitors at the festival.*

caterer /'keɪtərə/ **noun** [C] a person or business that provides food and drink at events or in places that a lot of people go to

catering /'keɪtərɪŋ/ **noun** [U] the activity or business of providing food and drink at events or in places that a lot of people go to: *the hotel and catering industry* • *Who's going to do the catering at the wedding?*

caterpillar /'kætəpɪlə/ **noun** [C] a small hairy animal with a long body and a lot of legs, which eats the leaves of plants. A caterpillar later becomes an insect with large, often colourful wings (a **butterfly** or a **moth**). •➤ picture at **insect**

cathedral /kə'θiːdrəl/ **noun** [C] a large church that is the most important one in a district

Catholic /'kæθlɪk/ = **ROMAN CATHOLIC** –**Catholicism** /kə'θɒləsɪzəm/ = **ROMAN CATHOLICISM**

cattle /'kætl/ **noun** [pl] male and female cows, for example on a farm: *a herd of cattle* (= a group of them) •➤ Look at the note at **cow**.

caught *past tense, past participle* of **CATCH¹**

cauldron (also **caldron**) /'kɔːldrən/ **noun** [C] a large, deep, metal pot that is used for cooking things over a fire

cauliflower /'kɒliflaʊə/ **noun** [C,U] a large vegetable with green leaves and a round white centre that you eat when it is cooked •➤ picture on page C3

★**cause¹** /kɔːz/ **noun 1** [C] a thing or person that makes sth happen: *The police do not know the cause of the accident.* • *Smoking is one of the causes of heart disease.* **2** [U] **cause (for sth)** reason for feeling sth or behaving in a particular way: *The doctor assured us that there was no cause for concern.* • *I don't think you have any real cause for complaint.* **3** [C] an idea or organization that a group of people believe in and support: *We are all committed to the cause of racial equality.*

IDIOMS **a lost cause** → **LOST²**

be for/in a good cause to be worth doing because it will help other people

★**cause²** /kɔːz/ **verb** [T] to make sth happen: *The fire was caused by an electrical fault.* • *High winds caused many trees to fall during the night.* • *Is your leg causing you any pain?*

caustic /'kɔːstɪk/ **adj 1** (used about a substance) able to burn or destroy things by chemical action **2** critical in a cruel way: *a caustic remark*

caution¹ /'kɔːʃn/ **noun 1** [U] great care, because of possible danger: *Any advertisement that asks you to send money should be treated with caution.* **2** [C] a spoken warning that a judge or police officer gives to sb who has committed a small crime

caution² /ˈkɔːʃn/ verb [I,T] **1** caution (sb) against sth to warn sb not to do sth: *The President's advisers have cautioned against calling an election too early.* **2** to give sb an official warning: *Dixon was cautioned by the referee for wasting time.*

cautionary /ˈkɔːʃənəri/ adj giving a warning: *The teacher told us a cautionary tale about a girl who cheated in her exams.*

★**cautious** /ˈkɔːʃəs/ adj taking great care to avoid possible danger or problems: *I'm very cautious about expressing my opinions in public.* –cautiously adv

cavalry /ˈkævlri/ noun [sing,with sing or pl verb] the part of the army that fought on horses in the past; the part of the modern army that uses heavily protected vehicles

cave¹ /keɪv/ noun [C] a large hole in the side of a cliff or hill, or under the ground: *When it started to rain, we ran to shelter in a cave.*

cave² /keɪv/ verb

PHRASAL VERB cave in **1** to fall in: *The roof of the tunnel had caved in and we could go no further.* **2** to suddenly stop arguing or being against sth: *He finally caved in and agreed to the plan.*

cavern /ˈkævən/ noun [C] a large, deep hole in the side of a hill or under the ground; a big cave

caviar (also **caviare**) /ˈkævɪɑː/ noun [U] the eggs of a large fish (a sturgeon) that we eat. Caviar is usually very expensive.

cavity /ˈkævəti/ noun [C] (*pl* cavities) an empty space inside sth solid: *a cavity in a tooth* • *a wall cavity*

CBI /ˌsiː biː ˈaɪ/ abbr the Confederation of British Industry; an employer's association

cc /ˌsiː ˈsiː/ abbr cubic centimetre(s): *a 1200cc engine*

CCTV /ˌsiː siː tiː ˈviː/ abbr closed-circuit television

CD /ˌsiː ˈdiː/ (also **compact disc**) noun [C] a small, round piece of hard plastic on which sound is recorded or information stored. You play a CD on a special machine (CD player).

CD-ROM /ˌsiː diː ˈrɒm/ abbr a compact disc which has a lot of information recorded on it. The information cannot be changed or removed.

cease /siːs/ verb [I,T] (*formal*) to stop or end: *Fighting in the area has now ceased.* • *That organization has ceased to exist.*

ceasefire /ˈsiːsfaɪə/ noun [C] an agreement between two groups to stop fighting each other •➤ Look at truce.

ceaseless /ˈsiːsləs/ adj continuing for a long time without stopping –ceaselessly adv

cede /siːd/ verb [T] (*written*) to give land or control of sth to another country or person

★**ceiling** /ˈsiːlɪŋ/ noun [C] **1** the top surface of the inside of a room: *a room with a high/low ceiling* **2** a top limit: *The Government has put a 10% ceiling on wage increases.*

★**celebrate** /ˈselɪbreɪt/ verb [I,T] to do sth to show that you are happy about sth that has happened or because it is a special day: *When I got the job we celebrated by going out for a meal.* • *Nora celebrated her 90th birthday yesterday.* –celebratory /ˌseləˈbreɪtəri/ adj: *We went out for a celebratory meal after the match.*

celebrated /ˈselɪbreɪtɪd/ adj (*formal*) famous: *a celebrated poet*

celebration /ˌselɪˈbreɪʃn/ noun [C,U] the act or occasion of doing sth enjoyable because sth good has happened or because it is a special day: *Christmas celebrations* • *I think this is an occasion for celebration!*

celebrity /səˈlebrəti/ noun [C] (*pl* celebrities) a famous person: *a TV celebrity*

celery /ˈseləri/ noun [U] a vegetable with long green and white sticks that can be eaten without being cooked: *a stick of celery* •➤ picture on page C3

celibate /ˈselɪbət/ adj (*formal*) never having sexual relations, often because of religious beliefs –celibacy /ˈselɪbəsi/ noun [U]

cell /sel/ noun [C] **1** the smallest living part of an animal or a plant: *The human body consists of millions of cells.* • *red blood cells* **2** a small room in a prison or police station in which a prisoner is locked

cellar /ˈselə/ noun [C] an underground room that is used for storing things •➤ Look at basement. •➤ picture on page C7

cellist /ˈtʃelɪst/ noun [C] a person who plays the cello

cello /ˈtʃeləʊ/ noun [C] (*pl* cellos) a large musical instrument with strings. You sit down to play it and hold it between your knees. •➤ Look at the note at piano. •➤ picture at music

cellophane™ /ˈseləfeɪn/ = CLING FILM

cellphone /ˈselfəʊn/ (also cellular phone) = MOBILE PHONE

cellular /ˈseljələ/ adj consisting of cells (1): *cellular tissue*

★**Celsius** /ˈselsiəs/ (also **Centigrade**) adj (*abbr* C) the name of a scale for measuring temperatures, in which water freezes at 0° and boils at 100°: *The temperature tonight will fall to 7°C.* •➤ We say 'seven degrees Celsius'. Look also at Fahrenheit.

Celtic /ˈkeltɪk/ adj connected with the people (the Celts) who lived in Wales, Scotland, Ireland and Brittany in ancient times, or with their culture

cement¹ /sɪˈment/ noun [U] a grey powder, that becomes hard after it is mixed with water and left to dry. It is used in building for sticking bricks or stones together or for making very hard surfaces.

cement² /sɪˈment/ verb [T] **1** to join two things together using cement, or a strong sticky substance **2** to make a relationship, agreement, etc very strong: *This agreement has cemented the relationship between our two countries.*

[I] **intransitive**, a verb which has no object: *He laughed.*   [T] **transitive**, a verb which has an object: *He ate an apple.*

cemetery /'semətri/ **noun** [C] (*pl cemeteries*) a place where dead people are buried, especially a place that does not belong to a church ••➤ Look at **graveyard** and **churchyard**.

censor¹ /'sensə/ **verb** [T] to remove the parts of a book, film, etc that might offend people or that are considered politically dangerous: *The soldier's letters home had to be censored.* –**censorship noun** [U]: *state censorship of radio and television programmes*

censor² /'sensə/ **noun** [C] an official who censors books, films, etc: *All films have to be examined by the board of film censors.*

censure /'senʃə/ **verb** [T] (*written*) to tell sb, in a strong and formal way, that he/she has done sth wrong: *The attorney was censured for not revealing the information earlier.* –**censure noun** [U]

census /'sensəs/ **noun** [C] (*pl censuses*) an official count of the people who live in a country, including information about their ages, jobs, etc

★**cent** /sent/ **noun** [C] (*abbr* **c, ct**) a unit of money that is worth 100th part of a US dollar or of the main unit of money in some other countries ••➤ Look at **per cent**.

centenary /sen'ti:nəri/ **noun** [C] (*pl centenaries*) (*US* **centennial** /sen'teniəl/) the year that comes exactly one hundred years after an important event or the beginning of sth: *2001 is the centenary of Disney's birth.*

center (*US*) = **CENTRE**

centigrade /'sentigreid/ = **CELSIUS**

★**centimetre** (*US* **centimeter**) /'sentimi:tə/ **noun** [C] (*abbr* **cm**) a measure of length. There are 100 centimetres in a metre.

★**central** /'sentrəl/ **adj 1** in the centre of sth: *a map of central Europe* • *Our flat is very central* (= near the centre of the city and therefore very convenient). **2** most important; main: *The film's central character is a fifteen-year-old girl.* **3** (only *before* a noun) having control over all other parts: *central government* (= the government of a whole country, not local government) • *the central nervous system*

,**central 'heating noun** [U] a system for heating a building from one main point. Air or water is heated and carried by pipes to all parts of the building.

centralize (also **-ise**) /'sentrəlaiz/ **verb** [T] (usually passive) to give control of all the parts of a country or organization to a group of people in one place: *Our educational system is becoming increasingly centralized.* –**centralization** (also **-isation**) /ˌsentrəlai-'zeiʃn/ **noun** [U]

centrally /'sentrəli/ **adv** in or from the centre: *a centrally located hotel* (= near the centre of the town)

★**centre¹** (*US* **center**) /'sentə/ **noun 1** [C, usually sing] the middle point or part of sth: *I work in the centre of London.* • *Which way is the town centre, please?* • *She hit the target dead centre* (= exactly in the centre). ••➤ Look at the note at **middle**. **2** [C] a building or place where a particular activity or service is based: *a sports/health/shopping centre* • *This university is a centre of excellence for medical research.* **3** [C] a place where sb/sth is collected together; the point towards which sth is directed: *major urban/industrial centres* • *She always likes to be the centre of attention.* • *You should bend your legs to keep a low centre of gravity.* **4** [sing, with sing or pl verb] a political position that is not extreme: *Her views are left of centre.*

centre² (*US* **center**) /'sentə/

PHRASAL VERB **centre on/around sb/sth** to have sb/sth as its centre: *The life of the village centres on the church, the school and the pub.*

-centric /'sentrik/ (used in compounds) concentrating on or interested in the thing mentioned: *eurocentric policies* (= concerned with Europe)

★**century** /'sentʃəri/ **noun** [C] (*pl centuries*) **1** a particular period of 100 years that is used for giving dates: *We live in the 21st century* (= the period between the years 2000 and 2099). **2** any period of 100 years: *People have been making wine in this area for centuries.*

ceramic /sə'ræmik/ **adj** made of clay that has been baked: *ceramic tiles* –**ceramic noun** [C]: *an exhibition of ceramics by Picasso*

cereals

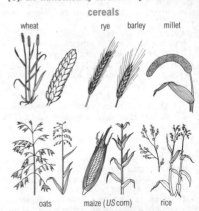

wheat   rye   barley   millet

oats   maize (*US* corn)   rice

★**cereal** /'siəriəl/ **noun** [C,U] **1** any type of grain that can be eaten or made into flour, or the grass that the grain comes from: *Wheat, barley and rye are cereals.* **2** a food that is made from grain, often eaten for breakfast with milk: *a bowl of cereal* ••➤ picture on page C4

cerebral /'serəbrəl/ **adj** of the brain

ceremonial /ˌseri'məuniəl/ **adj** connected with a ceremony: *a ceremonial occasion* –**ceremonially** /-niəli/ **adv**

★**ceremony** /'serəməni/ **noun** (*pl ceremonies*) **1** [C] a formal public or religious event: *the opening ceremony of the Olympic Games* • *a wedding ceremony* **2** [U] formal behaviour, speech, actions, etc that are expected on special occasions: *The new hospital was opened* **with great ceremony**.

★**certain** /'sɜːtn/ *adj* **1** (not before a noun) certain (that...); certain (of sth) completely sure; without any doubts: *She's absolutely certain that there was somebody outside her window.* ● *We're not quite certain what time the train leaves.* ● *I'm certain of one thing – he didn't take the money.* **2** certain (that...); certain (to do sth) sure to happen or to do sth; definite: *It is almost certain that unemployment will increase this year.* ● *The Director is certain to agree.* ● *We must rescue them today, or they will face certain death.* ••➤ Look at the note at **sure**. **3** (only *before* a noun) used for talking about a particular thing or person without naming them: *You can only contact me at certain times of the day.* ● *There are certain reasons why I'd prefer not to meet him again.* **4** (only *before* a noun) some, but not very much: *I suppose I have* **a certain amount** *of respect for Mr Law.* **5** noticeable but difficult to describe: *There was a certain feeling of autumn in the air.* **6** (*formal*) used before a person's name to show that you do not know him/her: *I received a letter from a certain Mrs Berry.*

IDIOMS **for certain** without doubt: *I don't know for certain what time we'll arrive.*

make certain (that...) **1** to do sth in order to be sure that sth else happens: *They're doing everything they can to make certain that they win.* **2** to do sth in order to be sure that sth is true: *We'd better phone Akram before we go to make certain he's expecting us.*

certainly /'sɜːtnli/ *adv* **1** without doubt; definitely: *The number of students will certainly increase after 2001.* **2** (used in answer to questions) of course: *'Do you think I could borrow your notes?' 'Certainly.'*

certainty /'sɜːtnti/ *noun* (*pl* **certainties**) **1** [U] the state of being completely sure about sth: *We can't say with certainty that there is life on other planets.* ••➤ opposite **uncertainty** **2** [C] something that is sure to happen: *It's now almost a certainty our team will win the league.*

★**certificate** /sə'tɪfɪkət/ *noun* [C] an official piece of paper that says that sth is true or correct: *a birth/marriage/medical certificate*

certify /'sɜːtɪfaɪ/ *verb* [T] (*pres part* **certifying**; *3rd pers sing pres* **certifies**; *pt, pp* **certified**) **1** to say formally that sth is true or correct: *We need someone to certify that this is her signature.* **2** to give sb a certificate to show that he/she has successfully completed a course of training for a particular profession: *a certified accountant*

cesarean (*US*) = **CAESAREAN**

cf *abbr* compare

CFC /ˌsiː ef 'siː/ *noun* [C,U] chlorofluorocarbon; a type of gas found, for example, in cans of spray which is harmful to the earth's atmosphere ••➤ Look at **ozone layer**.

ch *abbr* chapter

★**chain**[1] /tʃeɪn/ *noun* **1** [C,U] a line of metal rings that are joined together: *a bicycle chain*

● *She was wearing a silver chain round her neck.* ● *a length of chain* ••➤ picture at **jewellery**, **key**, **padlock** and on page S9 **2** [C] a series of connected things or people: *a chain of mountains/a mountain chain* ● *The book examines the complex* **chain of events** *that led to the Russian Revolution.* ● *The Managing Director is at the top of the* **chain of command**. **3** [C] a group of shops, hotels, etc that are owned by the same company: *a chain of supermarkets* ● *a fast-food chain*

chain[2] /tʃeɪn/ *verb* [T] chain sb/sth (to sth); chain sb/sth (up) to fasten sb/sth to sth else with a chain: *The dog is kept chained up outside.*

'chain-smoke *verb* [I] to smoke continuously, lighting one cigarette after another –**chain-smoker** *noun* [C]

'chain store *noun* [C] one of a number of similar shops that are owned by the same company

★**chair**[1] /tʃeə/ *noun* **1** [C] a piece of furniture for one person to sit on, with a seat, a back and four legs: *a kitchen chair* ● *an armchair* ••➤ picture on page C7 **2** [sing] the person who is controlling a meeting: *Please address your questions to the chair.* **3** [C] the position of being in charge of a department in a university: *She holds the chair of economics at London University.*

chair[2] /tʃeə/ *verb* [T] to be the chairman or chairwoman of a meeting: *Who's chairing the meeting this evening?*

★**chairman** /'tʃeəmən/ *noun* [C] (*pl* **-men** /-men/) **1** the head of a company or other organization **2** a person who controls a meeting –**chairmanship** *noun* [sing]

chairperson /'tʃeəpɜːsn/ *noun* [C] (*pl* **-persons**) a person who controls a meeting

chairwoman /'tʃeəwʊmən/ *noun* [C] (*pl* **-women** /-wɪmɪn/) a woman who controls a meeting

chalet /'ʃæleɪ/ *noun* [C] a wooden house, especially one built in a mountain area or used by people on holiday

chalk[1] /tʃɔːk/ *noun* **1** [U] a type of soft white rock: *chalk cliffs* **2** [C,U] a small stick of soft white or coloured rock that is used for writing or drawing

chalk[2] /tʃɔːk/ *verb* [I,T] to write or draw sth with chalk: *Somebody had chalked a message on the wall.*

PHRASAL VERB **chalk sth up** to succeed in getting sth: *The team has chalked up five wins this summer.*

chalkboard /'tʃɔːkbɔːd/ (*US*) = **BLACKBOARD**

★**challenge**[1] /'tʃælɪndʒ/ *noun* [C] **1** something new and difficult that forces you to make a lot of effort: *I'm finding my new job an exciting challenge.* ● *The company will have to* **face** *many* **challenges** *in the coming months.* ● *How will this government* **meet the challenge** *of rising unemployment?* **2** a challenge (to sb) (to do sth) an invitation from sb to fight, play, argue, etc against him/her: *The Prime Minister should accept our challenge and call a new election now.*

★challenge² /'tʃælɪndʒ/ *verb* [T] **1** challenge sb (to sth/to do sth) to invite sb to fight, play, argue, etc against you: *They've challenged us to a football match this Saturday.* **2** to question if sth is true, right, etc, or not: *She hates anyone challenging her authority.*

challenger /'tʃælɪndʒə/ *noun* [C] a person who invites you to take part in a competition, because he/she wants to win a title or position that you hold

challenging /'tʃælɪndʒɪŋ/ *adj* forcing you to make a lot of effort: *a challenging job*

chamber /'tʃeɪmbə/ *noun* [C] **1** an organization that makes important decisions, or the room or building where it meets: *a council chamber* **2** a closed space in the body, a machine, etc: *the four chambers of the heart* **3** a room that is used for a particular purpose: *a burial chamber*

chambermaid /'tʃeɪmbəmeɪd/ *noun* [C] a woman whose job is to clean and tidy hotel bedrooms

'chamber music *noun* [U] a type of music (classical music) that is written for a small group of instruments

champagne /ʃæm'peɪn/ *noun* [U,C] a French white wine which has a lot of bubbles in it and is often very expensive

★champion¹ /'tʃæmpiən/ *noun* [C] **1** a person, team, etc that has won a competition: *a world champion* • *a champion swimmer* **2** a person who speaks and fights for a particular group, idea, etc: *a champion of free speech*

champion² /'tʃæmpiən/ *verb* [T] to support or fight for a particular group or idea: *to champion the cause of human rights*

championship /'tʃæmpiənʃɪp/ *noun* [C] (often plural) a competition or series of competitions to find the best player or team in a sport or game: *the World Hockey Championships*

★chance¹ /tʃɑːns/ *noun* **1** [C] a chance of (doing) sth; a chance (that...) a possibility: *I think there's a good chance that she'll be the next Prime Minister.* • *to have a slim/an outside chance of success* • *I think we **stand a good chance** of winning the competition.* • *Is there any chance of getting tickets for tonight's concert?* **2** [C] chance (of doing sth/to do sth) an opportunity: *If somebody invited me to America, I'd jump at the chance* (= accept enthusiastically). • *Be quiet and **give her a chance** to explain.* • *I think you should tell him now. You may not **get another chance**.* •➤ Look at the note at **occasion**. **3** [C] a risk: *We may lose some money but we'll just have to take that chance.* • *Fasten your seat-belt – you shouldn't take (any) chances.* • *I didn't want to **take a chance on** anyone seeing me, so I closed the curtains.* **4** [U] luck; the way that some things happen without any cause that you can see or understand: *We have to plan every detail – I don't want to **leave anything to chance**.* • *We met **by chance** (= we had not planned to meet) as I was walking down the street.*

IDIOMS **by any chance** (used for asking sth politely) perhaps or possibly: *Are you, by any chance, going into town this afternoon?*

the chances are (that)... (*informal*) it is probable that...: *The chances are that it will rain tomorrow.*

no chance (*informal*) there is no possibility of that happening: *'Perhaps your mother will give you the money.' 'No chance!'*

on the off chance in the hope that sth might happen, although it is not very likely: *I didn't think you'd be at home, but I just called in on the off chance.*

chance² /tʃɑːns/ *verb* **1** [T] (*informal*) chance sth/doing sth to risk sth: *It might be safe to leave the car here, but I'm not going to chance it.* **2** [I] (*formal*) chance to do sth to do sth without planning or trying to do it: *I chanced to see the drawer on his desk.*

chance³ /tʃɑːns/ *adj* (only *before* a noun) not planned: *a chance meeting*

chancellor /'tʃɑːnsələ/ *noun* [C] **1** the head of the government in some countries: *the German chancellor* **2** (also ,**Chancellor of the Ex'chequer**) (*Brit*) the government minister who makes decisions about taxes and government spending

chandelier /,ʃændə'lɪə/ *noun* [C] a large round frame with many branches for lights or candles, that hangs from the ceiling and is decorated with small pieces of glass

★change¹ /tʃeɪndʒ/ *verb* **1** [I,T] to become different or to make sb/sth different; to alter: *This town has changed a lot since I was young.* • *Our plans have changed – we leave in the morning.* • *His lottery win has not changed him at all.* **2** [I,T] change (sb/sth) to/into sth; change (from A) (to/into B) to become a different thing; to make sb/sth take a different form: *The traffic lights changed from green to red.* • *They changed the spare bedroom into a study.* • *The new job changed him into a more confident person.* **3** [T] change sth (for sth) to take, have or use sth instead of sth else: *Could I change this blouse for a larger size?* • *to change jobs* • *to change a wheel on a car* • *to change direction* • *Can I change my appointment from Wednesday to Thursday?* **4** [T] to change sth (with sb) (used with a plural noun) to exchange sth with sb, so that you have what he/she had, and he/she has what you had; to swap: *The teams change ends at half-time.* • *If you want to sit by the window I'll change seats with you.* **5** [I,T] change (out of sth) (into sth) to take off your clothes and put different ones on: *He's changed his shirt.* • *I had a shower and changed before going out.* • *She changed out of her work clothes and into a clean dress.*

➤ **Get changed** is a common expression meaning 'to change your clothes': *You can get changed in the bedroom.*

6 [T] to put clean things onto sb/sth: *The baby's nappy needs changing.* • *to change the bed* (= to put clean sheets on) **7** [T] change sth (for/into sth) to give sb money and receive the same amount back in money of a different type: *Can you change a ten-pound*

note for two fives? • I'd like to change fifty pounds into US dollars. **8** [I,T] to get out of one bus, train, etc and get into another: *Can we get to London direct or do we have to change (trains)?*

IDIOMS **change hands** to pass from one owner to another

change your mind to change your decision or opinion: *I'll have the green one. No, I've changed my mind – I want the red one.*

change/swap places (with sb) → PLACE¹

change the subject to start talking about sth different

change your tune (*informal*) to change your opinion or feelings about sth

change your ways to start to live or behave in a different and better way from before

chop and change → CHOP¹

PHRASAL VERB **change over (from sth) (to sth)** to stop doing or using one thing and start doing or using sth else: *The theatre has changed over to a computerized booking system.*

★**change²** /tʃeɪndʒ/ *noun* **1** [C,U] **change (in/to sth)** the process of becoming or making sth different: *There was little change in the patient's condition overnight.* • *After two hot summers, people were talking about a change in the climate.* **2** [C] **a change (of sth)** something that you take, have or use instead of sth else: *We must notify the bank of our change of address.* • *I packed my toothbrush and a change of clothes.* **3** [U] the money that you get back if you pay more than the amount sth costs: *If a paper costs 60p and you pay with a pound coin, you will get 40p change.* **4** [U] coins of low value: *He needs some change for the phone.* • *Have you got change for a twenty-pound note?* (= coins or notes of lower value that together make twenty pounds)

IDIOMS **a change for the better/worse** a person, thing or situation that is better/worse than the one before

a change of heart a change in your opinion or the way that you feel

for a change in order to do sth different from usual: *I usually cycle to work, but today I decided to walk for a change.*

make a change to be enjoyable or pleasant because it is different from what you usually do

changeable /'tʃeɪndʒəbl/ *adj* likely to change; often changing: *English weather is very changeable.*

changeover /'tʃeɪndʒəʊvə/ *noun* [C] a change from one system to another

'**changing room** *noun* [C] a room for changing clothes in, for example before or after playing sport

★**channel¹** /'tʃænl/ *noun* [C] **1** a television station: *Which channel is the film on?* •➤ Look at **station¹**(4) **2** a band of radio waves for sending out radio or television programmes: *terrestrial/satellite channels* **3** a way or route along which news, information, etc is sent: *a channel of communication* • *You have to*

order new equipment through the official channels. **4** an open passage along which liquids can flow: *a drainage channel* **5** the part of a river, sea, etc which is deep enough for boats to pass through **6 the Channel** (also **the English Channel**) the sea between England and France

channel² /'tʃænl/ *verb* [T] (**channelling**; **channelled**; *US also* **channeling**; **channeled**) to make sth move along a particular path or route: *Water is channelled from the river to the fields.* • (*figurative*) *You should channel your energies into something constructive.*

the Channel Tunnel *noun* [sing] the tunnel under the sea that connects England and France

chant¹ /tʃɑːnt/ *noun* **1** [C] a word or phrase that is sung or shouted many times: *A chant of 'we are the champions' went round the stadium.* **2** [C,U] a usually religious song with only a few notes that are repeated many times

chant² /tʃɑːnt/ *verb* [I,T] to sing or shout a word or phrase many times: *The protesters marched by, chanting slogans.*

chaos /'keɪɒs/ *noun* [U] a state of great disorder; confusion: *The country was in chaos after the war.* • *The heavy snow has caused chaos on the roads.*

chaotic /keɪ'ɒtɪk/ *adj* in a state of chaos: *With no one in charge the situation became chaotic.*

chap /tʃæp/ *noun* [C] (*especially Brit informal*) a man or boy

chapel /'tʃæpl/ *noun* [C,U] a small building or room that is used by some Christians as a church or for prayer: *a Methodist chapel*

chaperone /'ʃæpərəʊn/ *noun* [C] in the past, an older person, usually a woman, who went to public places with a young woman who was not married, to look after her and to make sure that she behaved correctly –chaperone *verb* [T]

★**chapter** /'tʃæptə/ *noun* [C] one of the parts into which a book is divided: *Please read Chapter 2 for homework.* • (*figurative*) *The last few years have been a difficult chapter in the country's history.*

★**character** /'kærəktə/ *noun* **1** [C,usually sing, U] the qualities that make sb/sth different from other people or things; the nature of sb/sth: *Although they are twins, their characters are quite different.* • *These two songs are very different in character.* **2** [U] strong personal qualities: *The match developed into a test of character rather than just physical strength.* **3** [U] qualities that make sb/sth interesting: *Modern houses often seem to lack character.* **4** [U] the good opinion that people have of you: *The article was a vicious attack on the President's character.* **5** [C] (*informal*) an interesting, amusing, strange or unpleasant person: *Neil's quite a character – he's always making us laugh.* • *I saw a suspicious-looking character outside the bank, so I called the police.* **6** [C] a person in a book, story, etc: *The main character in the film is a boy who meets an alien.* **7** [C] a letter or sign that you use when you are writing or printing: *Chinese characters*

IDIOM **in/out of character** typical/not typical of sb/sth: *Emma's rude reply was completely out of character.*

characteristic¹ /ˌkærəktə'rɪstɪk/ **noun** [C] **a characteristic of (sb/sth)** a quality that is typical of sb/sth and that makes him/her/it different from other people or things: *The chief characteristic of fish is they live in water.*

characteristic² /ˌkærəktə'rɪstɪk/ **adj** characteristic of (sb/sth) very typical of sb/sth: *The flat landscape is characteristic of this part of the country.* ••➤ opposite **uncharacteristic** –characteristically /-kli/ **adv**: *'No' he said, in his characteristically direct manner.*

characterize (also **-ise**) /'kærəktəraɪz/ **verb** [T] (*formal*) **1** (often passive) to be typical of sb/sth: *the tastes that characterize Thai cooking* **2** characterize sb/sth (as sth) to describe what sb/sth is like: *The President characterized the meeting as friendly and positive.*

charade /ʃə'rɑːd/ **noun 1** [C] a situation or event that is clearly false but in which people pretend to do or be sth: *They pretend to be friends but it's all a charade. Everyone knows they hate each other.* **2 charades** [U] a party game in which people try to guess the title of a book, film, etc that one person must represent using actions but not words

charcoal /'tʃɑːkəʊl/ **noun** [U] a black substance that is produced from burned wood. It can be used for drawing or as a fuel.

★**charge¹** /tʃɑːdʒ/ **noun 1** [C,U] the price that you must pay for sth: *The hotel makes a small charge for changing currency.* • *We deliver free of charge.* ••➤ Look at the note at **price**. **2** [C,U] a statement that says that sb has done sth illegal or bad: *He was arrested on a charge of murder.* • *The writer dismissed the charge that his books were childish.* **3** [U] a position of control over sb/sth; responsibility for sb/sth: *Who is in charge of the office while Alan's away?* • *The assistant manager had to take charge of the team when the manager resigned.* **4** [C] a sudden attack where sb/sth runs straight at sb/sth else **5** [C] the amount of electricity that is put into a battery or carried by a substance: *a positive/negative charge*

IDIOMS **bring/press charges (against sb)** to formally accuse sb of a crime so that there can be a trial in a court of law

reverse the charges ➤ **REVERSE¹**

charge² /tʃɑːdʒ/ **verb 1** [I,T] **charge (sb/sth) for sth** to ask sb to pay a particular amount of money: *We charge £35 per night for a single room.* • *They forgot to charge us for the drinks.* ••➤ Look at **overcharge**. **2** [T] **charge sb (with sth)** to accuse sb officially of doing sth which is against the law: *Six men have been charged with attempted robbery.* **3** [I,T] to run straight at sb/sth, or in a particular direction, in an aggressive or noisy way: *The*

bull put its head down ready to charge (us). • *The children charged into the room.* **4** [T] to put electricity into sth: *to charge a battery* ••➤ Look at **recharge**.

chariot /'tʃæriət/ **noun** [C] an open vehicle with two wheels that was pulled by a horse or horses in ancient times

charisma /kə'rɪzmə/ **noun** [U] a powerful personal quality that some people have to attract and influence other people: *The president is not very clever, but he has great charisma.* –charismatic /ˌkærɪz'mætɪk/ **adj**

charitable /'tʃærətəbl/ **adj 1** kind; generous: *Some people accused him of lying, but a more charitable explanation was that he had made a mistake.* **2** connected with a charity

★**charity** /'tʃærəti/ **noun** (*pl* **charities**) **1** [C,U] an organization that collects money to help people who are poor, sick, etc or to do work that is useful to society: *We went on a sponsored walk to raise money for charity.* [C] **2** [U] kindness towards other people: *to act out of charity*

'**charity shop noun** [C] a shop that sells clothes, books, etc given by people to make money for charity

★**charm¹** /tʃɑːm/ **noun 1** [C,U] a quality that pleases and attracts people: *The charm of the island lies in its unspoilt beauty.* • *Barry found it hard to resist Linda's charms.* **2** [C] something that you wear because you believe it will bring you good luck: *a necklace with a lucky charm on it*

★**charm²** /tʃɑːm/ **verb** [T] **1** to please and attract sb: *Her drawings have charmed children all over the world.* **2** to protect sb/sth as if by magic: *He has led a charmed life, surviving serious illness and a plane crash.*

charming /'tʃɑːmɪŋ/ **adj** very pleasing or attractive: *a charming old church* –charmingly **adv**

charred /tʃɑːd/ **adj** burnt black by fire

chart¹ /tʃɑːt/ **noun 1** [C] a drawing which shows information in the form of a diagram, etc: *a temperature chart* • *This chart shows the company's sales for this year.* ••➤ Look at **pie chart** and **flow chart**. **2** [C] a map of the sea or the sky: *navigation charts* **3 the charts** [pl] an official list of the songs or CDs, etc, that have sold the most in a particular week

chart² /tʃɑːt/ **verb** [T] **1** to follow or record sth carefully and in detail: *This television series charts the history of the country since independence.* **2** to make a map of one area of the sea or sky: *an uncharted coastline*

charter¹ /'tʃɑːtə/ **noun** [C,U] **1** a written statement of the rights, beliefs and purposes of an organization or a particular group of people: *The club's charter does not permit women to become members.* **2** the renting of a ship, plane, etc for a particular purpose or for a particular group of people: *a charter airline*

charter² /'tʃɑːtə/ **verb** [T] to rent a ship, plane, etc for a particular purpose or for a particular group of people: *As there was no* *regular service to the island we had to charter a boat.*

chartered /'tʃɑːtəd/ **adj** (only *before* a noun) (used about people in certain professions) fully trained; having passed all the necessary exams: *a chartered accountant*

'**charter flight** **noun** [C] a flight in which all seats are paid for by a travel company and then sold to their customers, usually at a lower price than an ordinary (scheduled) flight

★**chase**¹ /tʃeɪs/ **verb 1** [I,T] chase (after) sb/ sth to run after sb/sth in order to catch him/her/it: *The dog chased the cat up a tree.* • *The police car chased after the stolen van.* **2** [I] to run somewhere fast: *The kids were chasing around the park.*

★**chase**² /tʃeɪs/ **noun** [C] the act of following sb/sth in order to catch him/her/it: *an exciting car chase*

  IDIOM **give chase** to begin to run after sb/sth in order or to try to catch him/her/it: *The robber ran off and the policeman gave chase.*

chasm /'kæzəm/ **noun** [C] **1** a deep hole in the ground **2** a wide difference of feelings, interests, etc between two people or groups

chassis /'ʃæsi/ **noun** [C] (*pl* **chassis** /'ʃæsi/) the metal frame of a vehicle onto which the other parts fit

chaste /tʃeɪst/ **adj** (*old-fashioned*) **1** not involving thoughts and feelings about sex: *She gave him a chaste kiss on the cheek.* **2** never having had a sexual relationship, or only with your husband/wife –**chastity** /'tʃæstəti/ **noun** [U]

chat¹ /tʃæt/ **verb** [I] (**chatting**; **chatted**) chat (with/to sb) (about sth) to talk to sb in a friendly, informal way: *The two grandmothers sat chatting about the old days.*

  PHRASAL VERB **chat sb up** (*Brit informal*) to talk to sb in a friendly way because you are sexually attracted to him/her

chat² /tʃæt/ **noun** [C,U] a friendly informal conversation: *I'll have a chat with Jim about the arrangements.*

'**chat show** **noun** [C] a television or radio programme on which well-known people are invited to talk about themselves

chatter /'tʃætə/ **verb** [I] **1** to talk quickly or for a long time about sth unimportant: *The children were laughing and chattering excitedly.* **2** (used about your teeth) to knock together because you are cold or frightened –**chatter noun** [U]

chatty /'tʃæti/ **adj 1** talking a lot in a friendly way **2** in an informal style: *a chatty letter*

chauffeur /'ʃəʊfə/ **noun** [C] a person whose job is to drive a car for sb else: *a chauffeur-driven limousine* –**chauffeur verb** [T]

★**cheap**¹ /tʃiːp/ **adj 1** low in price, costing little money: *Oranges are cheap at the moment.* • *Computers are getting cheaper all the time.* •➔ synonym **inexpensive** •➔ opposite **expensive 2** charging low prices: *a cheap hotel/restaurant* **3** low in price and quality and therefore not attractive: *The clothes in*

that shop look cheap.

  IDIOM **dirt cheap** → **DIRT**

cheap² /tʃiːp/ **adv** (*informal*) for a low price: *I got this coat cheap in the sale.*

  IDIOM **be going cheap** (*informal*) be on sale at a lower price than usual

cheaply /'tʃiːpli/ **adv** for a low price

★**cheat**¹ /tʃiːt/ **verb 1** [T] to trick sb, especially when that person trusts you; to deceive sb: *The shopkeeper cheated customers by giving them too little change.* **2** [I] cheat (at sth) to act in a dishonest or unfair way in order to get an advantage for yourself: *Paul was caught cheating in the exam.* • *to cheat at cards* **3** [I] cheat (on sb) to not be faithful to your husband, wife or regular partner by having a secret sexual relationship with sb else

  PHRASAL VERB **cheat sb (out) of sth** to take sth from sb in a dishonest or unfair way: *They tried to cheat the old lady out of her savings.*

cheat² /tʃiːt/ **noun** [C] a person who cheats

★**check**¹ /tʃek/ **verb 1** [I,T] check (sth) (for sth) to examine or test sth in order to make sure that it is safe or correct, in good condition, etc: *Check your work for mistakes before you hand it in.* • *The doctor X-rayed me to check for broken bones.* **2** [I,T] check (sth) (with sb) to make sure that sth is how you think it is: *You'd better check with Tim that it's OK to borrow his bike.* • *I'll phone and check what time the bus leaves.* **3** [T] to stop or make sb/sth stop or go more slowly: *She almost told her boss what she thought of him, but checked herself in time.* • *Phil checked his pace as he didn't want to tire too early.* **4** [T] (*US*) = **TICK**¹(2)

  PHRASAL VERBS **check in (at...); check into...** to go to a desk in a hotel or an airport and tell an official that you have arrived

check sth off to mark names or items on a list: *The boxes were all checked off as they were unloaded.*

check (up) on sb/sth to find out how sb/sth is: *We call my grandmother every evening to check up on her.*

check up on sb/sth to make sure that sb/sth is working correctly, behaving well, etc, especially if you think he/she/it is not

check out (of...) to pay your bill and leave a hotel

check sb/sth out 1 to find out more information about sb/sth, especially to find out if sth is true or not: *We need to check out these rumours of possible pay cuts.* **2** (*especially US slang*) to look at sth, especially to find out if you like him/her/it: *I'm going to check out that new club tonight.*

★**check**² /tʃek/ **noun 1** [C] a check (on sth) a close look at sth to make sure that it is safe, correct, in good condition, etc: *We **carry out/do** regular **checks** on our products to make sure that they are of high quality.* • *I don't go to games, but I like to **keep a check** on my team's results.* **2** [C,U] a pattern of squares, often of different colours: *a check jacket* • *a pattern of blue and red checks* **3** [U] the situation in a particular game (chess), in which a player must move to protect his/her king •➤ Look at **checkmate**. **4** (*US*) = CHEQUE **5** (*US*) = BILL¹(1) **6** (*US*) = TICK²(1)

IDIOM hold/keep sth in check to stop sth from advancing or increasing too quickly: *government measures to keep inflation in check*

checkbook (*US*) = CHEQUEBOOK

checked /tʃekt/ **adj** with a pattern of squares: *a red-and-white checked tablecloth*

checkers /'tʃekəz/ (*US*) = DRAUGHT¹(2)

'**check-in** **noun** [C] **1** the act of checking in at an airport: *Our check-in time is 10.30 am.* **2** the place where you check in at an airport

'**checking account** (*US*) = CURRENT ACCOUNT

checklist /'tʃeklɪst/ **noun** [C] a list of things that you must do or have

checkmate /ˌtʃek'meɪt/ **noun** [U] the situation in a particular game (chess), in which you cannot protect your king and so have lost the game •➤ Look at **check²**(3).

checkout /'tʃekaʊt/ **noun** [C] the place in a large food shop (supermarket) where you pay

checkpoint /'tʃekpɔɪnt/ **noun** [C] a place where all people and vehicles must stop and be checked: *an army checkpoint*

'**check-up** **noun** [C] a general medical examination to make sure that you are healthy

cheddar /'tʃedə/ **noun** [U] a type of hard yellow cheese

★**cheek** /tʃiːk/ **noun** **1** [C] either side of the face below your eyes •➤ picture on page C5 **2** [U] (*Brit*) rude behaviour; lack of respect: *He's got a cheek, asking to borrow money again!*

IDIOM (with) tongue in cheek → TONGUE

cheekbone /'tʃiːkbəʊn/ **noun** [C] the bone below your eye •➤ picture on page C5

cheeky /'tʃiːki/ **adj** (*Brit*) (**cheekier**; **cheekiest**) not showing respect; rude: *Don't be so cheeky! Of course I'm not fat!* –**cheekily** adv

★**cheer¹** /tʃɪə/ **verb** **1** [I,T] to shout to show that you like sth or to encourage sb who is taking part in competition, sport, etc: *Everyone cheered the winner as he crossed the finishing line.* **2** [T] to make sb happy or more hopeful: *They were all cheered by the good news.*

PHRASAL VERBS **cheer sb on** to shout in order to encourage sb in a race, competition, etc: *As the runners started the last lap the crowd cheered them on.*

cheer (sb/sth) up to become or to make sb happier; to make sth look more attractive: *Cheer up! Things aren't that bad.* • *A few pictures would cheer this room up a bit.*

★**cheer²** /tʃɪə/ **noun** [C] a loud shout to show that you like sth or to encourage sb who is taking part in a competition, sport, etc: *The crowd gave a cheer when the president appeared.*

★**cheerful** /'tʃɪəfl/ feeling happy; showing that you are happy: *Caroline is always very cheerful.* • *a cheerful smile* –**cheerfully** /-fəli/ **adv** –**cheerfulness** **noun** [U]

cheerio /ˌtʃɪəri'əʊ/ **interj** (*Brit informal*) goodbye

cheerleader /'tʃɪəliːdə/ **noun** [C] (especially in the US) one of a group of girls or women at a sports match who wear special uniforms and shout, dance, etc in order to encourage people to support the players

cheers /tʃɪəz/ **interj** (*informal*) **1** used to express good wishes before you have an alcoholic drink: *'Cheers,' she said, raising her wine glass.* **2** (*Brit*) goodbye **3** (*Brit*) thank you

cheery /'tʃɪəri/ **adj** happy and smiling: *a cheery remark/wave/smile* –**cheerily** adv

★**cheese** /tʃiːz/ **noun 1** [U] a type of food made from milk. Cheese is usually white or yellow in colour and can be soft or hard: *a piece of cheese* • *a cheese sandwich* •➤ picture on page C4 **2** [C] a type of cheese: *a wide selection of cheeses*

cheesecake /'tʃiːzkeɪk/ **noun** [C,U] a type of cake that is made from soft cheese and sugar on a pastry or biscuit base, often with fruit on top

cheetah /'tʃiːtə/ **noun** [C] a large wild cat with black spots that can run very fast •➤ picture at **lion**

chef /ʃef/ **noun** [C] a professional cook, especially the head cook in a hotel, restaurant, etc

★**chemical¹** /'kemɪkl/ **adj** connected with chemistry; involving changes to the structure of a substance: *a chemical reaction* –**chemically** /-kli/ **adv**

★**chemical²** /'kemɪkl/ **noun** [C] a substance that is used or produced in a chemical process: *Sulphuric acid is a dangerous chemical.* • *chemical weapons/warfare*

★**chemist** /'kemɪst/ **noun** [C] **1** (also **pharmacist**, *US* **druggist**) a person who prepares and sells medicines **2** **the chemist's** (*US* **drugstore**) a shop that sells medicines, soap, camera film, etc: *I got my tablets from the chemist's.* **3** a person who is a specialist in chemistry

★**chemistry** /'kemɪstri/ **noun** [U] **1** the scientific study of the structure of substances and what happens to them in different conditions or when mixed with each other: *We did an experiment in the chemistry lesson today.* **2** the structure of a particular substance

★**cheque** (*US* **check**) /tʃek/ **noun** [C,U] a piece of paper printed by a bank that you sign and use to pay for things: *She wrote out a cheque for £20.* • *I went to the bank to **cash a cheque**.* • *Can I **pay by cheque**?* •➤ picture at **money**

chequebook (*US* **checkbook**) /'tʃekbʊk/ **noun** [C] a book of cheques

'**cheque card** **noun** [C] (*Brit*) a small plastic card that you show when you pay with a cheque as proof that your bank will pay the amount on the cheque ••➤ Look at **cash card** and **credit card**.

cherish /'tʃerɪʃ/ **verb** [T] **1** to love sb/sth and look after him/her/it carefully: *The ring was her most cherished possession.* **2** to keep a thought, feeling, etc in your mind and think about it often: *a cherished memory*

cherry /'tʃeri/ **noun** [C] (*pl* **cherries**) **1** a small round black or red fruit that has a stone inside it ••➤ picture on page C3 **2** (also **'cherry tree**) the tree that produces cherries

chess /tʃes/ **noun** [U] a game for two people that is played on a board with 64 black and white squares (a **chessboard**). Each player has sixteen pieces which can be moved according to fixed rules: *Can you play chess?*

★**chest** /tʃest/ **noun** [C] **1** the top part of the front of your body ••➤ picture on page C5 **2** a large strong box that is used for storing or carrying things ••➤ picture on page C7

> IDIOM **get sth off your chest** (*informal*) to talk about sth that you have been thinking or worrying about

chestnut /'tʃesnʌt/ **noun** [C] **1** (also **'chestnut tree**) a tree with large leaves that produces smooth brown nuts in shells with sharp points on the outside **2** a smooth brown nut from the chestnut tree. You can eat some chestnuts: *roast chestnuts* ••➤ Look at **conker**. ••➤ picture at **nut**

chest of 'drawers noun [C] a piece of furniture with drawers in it that is used for storing clothes, etc ••➤ picture on page C7

★**chew** /tʃuː/ **verb** [I,T] **1** to break up food in your mouth with your teeth before you swallow it **2 chew (on) sth** to bite sth continuously with the back teeth: *The dog was chewing on a bone.*

'chewing gum (also **gum**) **noun** [U] a sweet sticky substance that you chew in your mouth but do not swallow ••➤ Look at **bubblegum**.

chewy /'tʃuːi/ **adj** (used about food) difficult to break up with your teeth before it can be swallowed: *chewy meat/toffee*

chic /ʃiːk/ **adj** fashionable and elegant –**chic noun** [U]

chick /tʃɪk/ **noun** [C] a baby bird, especially a young chicken ••➤ picture at **chicken**

chickens

cock   chick   hen

★**chicken¹** /'tʃɪkɪn/ **noun 1** [C] a bird that people often keep for its eggs and its meat **2** [U] the meat of this bird: *chicken soup*

> Notice that chicken is the general word for the bird and its meat. A male chicken is called a **cock** (*US* **rooster**), a female is called a **hen** and a young bird is called a **chick**.

> IDIOM **Don't count your chickens (before they're hatched)** → **COUNT¹**

chicken² /'tʃɪkɪn/ **verb**

> PHRASAL VERB **chicken out (of sth)** (*informal*) to decide not to do sth because you are afraid: *Mark chickened out of swimming across the river when he saw how far it was.*

chickenpox /'tʃɪkɪnpɒks/ **noun** [U] a disease, especially of children. When you have chickenpox you feel very hot and get red spots on your skin that make you want to scratch.

chicory /'tʃɪkəri/ (*US* **endive**) **noun** [U] a small pale green plant with bitter leaves that can be eaten cooked or not cooked

chief¹ /tʃiːf/ **adj** (only *before* a noun) **1** most important; main: *One of the chief reasons for his decision was money.* **2** of the highest level or position: *the chief executive of a company*

★**chief²** /tʃiːf/ **noun** [C] **1** the person who has command or control over an organization: *the chief of police* **2** the leader of a tribe

chiefly /'tʃiːfli/ **adv** mainly; mostly: *His success was due chiefly to hard work.*

chieftain /'tʃiːftən/ **noun** [C] the leader of a tribe: *a twelfth-century Scottish chieftain*

chiffon /'ʃɪfɒn/ **noun** [U] a very thin, transparent type of cloth used for making clothes, etc

chilblain /'tʃɪlbleɪn/ **noun** [C] a painful red area on your foot, hand, etc that is caused by cold weather

★**child** /tʃaɪld/ **noun** [C] (*pl* **children** /'tʃɪldrən/) **1** a young boy or girl who is not yet an adult: *A group of children were playing in the park.* • *a six-year-old child* **2** a son or daughter of any age: *She has two children but both are married and have moved away.*

> An **only child** is a child who has no brothers or sisters. A couple may **adopt** a child who is not their own son or daughter (for example if the child's parents are dead). A **foster child** is looked after for a certain period of time by a family that is not his/her own.

childbirth /'tʃaɪldbɜːθ/ **noun** [U] the act of giving birth to a baby: *His wife died **in childbirth**.*

childcare /'tʃaɪldkeə/ **noun** [U] the job of looking after children, especially while the parents are at work: *Some employers provide childcare facilities.*

childhood /'tʃaɪldhʊd/ **noun** [C,U] the time when you are a child: *Harriet had a very unhappy childhood.* • *childhood memories*

childish /'tʃaɪldɪʃ/ **adj** like a child –**childishly adv**

> If you say that people or their behaviour are **childish**, you mean that they are like children in some way: *His childlike enthusiasm delighted us all.* If you say that an

adult's behaviour is **childish**, you are criticizing it because you think it is silly: *Don't be so childish! You can't always have everything you want.*

childless /'tʃaɪldləs/ **adj** having no children

childlike /'tʃaɪldlaɪk/ **adj** like a child ••➤ Look at **childish**.

childminder /'tʃaɪldmaɪndə/ **noun** [C] (*Brit*) a person whose job is to look after a child while his/her parents are at work

'**children's home noun** [C] an institution where children live whose parents cannot look after them

chili (*US*) = **CHILLI**

chill¹ /tʃɪl/ **noun 1** [sing] an unpleasant cold feeling: *There's a chill in the air.* ● (*figurative*) *A chill of fear went down my spine.* **2** [C] (*informal*) an common illness that affects your nose and throat; a cold: *to catch a chill*

chill² /tʃɪl/ **verb** [I,T] to become or to make sb/sth colder: *It's better to chill white wine before you serve it.*

chilli (*US* **chili**) /'tʃɪli/ **noun** [C,U] (*pl* **chillies**; *US* **chilies**) a small green or red vegetable that has a very strong hot taste: *chilli powder* ••➤ picture on page C3

chilling /'tʃɪlɪŋ/ **adj** frightening: *a chilling ghost story*

chilly /'tʃɪli/ **adj** (**chillier**; **chilliest**) (used about the weather but also about people) too cold to be comfortable: *It's a chilly morning. You need a coat on.* ● *We got a very chilly reception* (= unfriendly)

chime /tʃaɪm/ **verb** [I,T] (used about a bell or clock) to ring –**chime noun** [C]

PHRASAL VERB **chime in (with sth)** (*informal*) to interrupt a conversation and add your own comments

★**chimney** /'tʃɪmni/ **noun** [C] a pipe through which smoke or steam is carried up and out through the roof of a building ••➤ picture on page C7

'**chimney sweep noun** [C] a person whose job is to clean the inside of chimneys with long brushes

chimpanzee /ˌtʃɪmpæn'ziː/ (also *informal* **chimp** /tʃɪmp/) **noun** [C] a small intelligent animal like a monkey but without a tail (an **ape**), which is found in Africa

★**chin** /tʃɪn/ **noun** [C] the part of your face below your mouth ••➤ picture on page C5

china /'tʃaɪnə/ **noun** [U] **1** white clay of good quality that is used for making cups, plates, etc: *a china vase* **2** cups, plates, etc that are made from china

chink /tʃɪŋk/ **noun** [C] a small narrow opening: *Daylight came in through a chink between the curtains.*

chintz /tʃɪnts/ **noun** [U] a shiny cotton cloth with a printed design, usually of flowers, which is used for making curtains, covering furniture, etc

chips

chips (*US* French fries)   crisps (*US* chips)

★**chip¹** /tʃɪp/ **noun** [C] **1** the place where a small piece of stone, glass, wood, etc has broken off sth: *This dish has a chip in it.* **2** a small piece of stone, glass, wood, etc that has broken off sth **3** (*US* **French fry**) [usually pl] a thin piece of potato that is fried in hot fat or oil ••➤ picture on page C4 **4** (also **potato chip**) (*US*) = **CRISP²** **5** =**MICROCHIP** **6** a flat round piece of plastic that you use instead of money when you are playing some games

IDIOM **have a chip on your shoulder (about sth)** (*informal*) to feel angry about sth that happened a long time ago because you think it is unfair: *My dad still has a chip on his shoulder about being thrown out of school.*

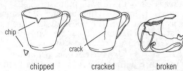

chip   crack

chipped   cracked   broken

chip² /tʃɪp/ **verb** [I,T] (**chipping**; **chipped**) **1** to break a small piece off the edge or surface of sth: *They chipped the paint trying to get the table through the door.* **2** (in sport) to kick or hit a ball a short distance through the air

PHRASAL VERB **chip in (with sth)** (*informal*) **1** to interrupt when sb else is talking **2** to give some money as part of the cost of sth: *We all chipped in and bought him a present when he left.*

'**chip shop** (also **chippy** /'tʃɪpi/) **noun** [C] (in Britain) a shop that cooks and sells fish and chips and other fried food to take away and eat

chiropodist /kɪ'rɒpədɪst/ (*US* **podiatrist**) **noun** [C] a person whose job is to look after people's feet

chirp /tʃɜːp/ **verb** [I] (used about small birds and some insects) to make short high sounds

chisel /'tʃɪzl/ **noun** [C] a tool with a sharp end that is used for cutting or shaping wood or stone ••➤ picture at **tool**

chivalry /'ʃɪvəlri/ **noun** [U] polite and kind behaviour by men which shows respect towards women –**chivalrous** /'ʃɪvlrəs/ **adj**

chive /tʃaɪv/ **noun** [C,usually pl] a long thin green plant that tastes like onion and is used in cooking

chlorine /'klɔːriːn/ **noun** [U] (*symbol* **Cl**) a greenish-yellow gas with a strong smell, that is used for making water safe to drink or to swim in

chock-a-block /ˌtʃɒk ə 'blɒk/ **adj** (not before a noun) completely full: *The High Street was chock-a-block with shoppers.*

chocoholic /ˌtʃɒkə'hɒlɪk/ **noun** [C] a person who loves chocolate and eats a lot of it

★**chocolate** /'tʃɒklət/ **noun 1** [U] a sweet brown substance made from seeds (cocoa beans) that you can eat as a sweet or use to give flavour to food and drinks: *a bar of milk/plain chocolate* • *a chocolate milkshake* **2** [C] a small sweet that is made from or covered with chocolate: *a box of chocolates* **3** [C,U] a drink made from powdered chocolate with hot milk or water: *a mug of hot chocolate* **4** [U] a dark brown colour

★**choice¹** /tʃɔɪs/ **noun 1** [C] a choice (between A and B) an act of choosing between two or more people or things: *David was forced to make a choice between moving house and losing his job.* **2** [U] the right or chance to choose: *There is a rail strike so we have no choice but to cancel our trip.* • *to have freedom of choice* ••➤ synonym **option 3** [C,U] two or more things from which you can or must choose: *This cinema offers a choice of six different films every night.* **4** [C] a person or thing that is chosen: *Barry would be my choice as team captain.* ••➤ verb **choose**
IDIOM **out of/from choice** because you want to; of your own free will: *I wouldn't have gone to America out of choice. I was sent there on business.*

choice² /tʃɔɪs/ **adj** of very good quality: *choice beef*

choir /'kwaɪə/ **noun** [C, with sing or pl verb] a group of people who sing together in churches, schools, etc

★**choke¹** /tʃəʊk/ **verb 1** [I,T] choke (on sth) to be or to make sb unable to breathe because sth is stopping air getting into the lungs: *She was choking on a fish bone.* • *The smoke choked us.* ••➤ Look at **strangle. 2** [T] (usually passive) choke sth (up) (with sth) to fill a passage, space, etc, so that nothing can pass through: *The roads to the coast were choked with traffic.*
PHRASAL VERB **choke sth back** to hide or control a strong emotion: *to choke back tears/anger*

choke² /tʃəʊk/ **noun** [C] **1** the device in a car, etc that controls the amount of air going into the engine. If you pull out the choke it makes it easier to start the car. ••➤ picture on page S9 **2** an act or the sound of sb choking: *A tiny choke of laughter escaped her.*

cholera /'kɒlərə/ **noun** [U] a serious disease that causes stomach pains and vomiting and can cause death. Cholera is most common in hot countries and is carried by water.

cholesterol /kə'lestərɒl/ **noun** [U] a substance that is found in the blood, etc of people and animals. Too much cholesterol is thought to be a cause of heart disease

★**choose** /tʃuːz/ **verb** [I,T] (*pt* chose /tʃəʊz/; *pp* chosen /'tʃəʊzn/) **1** choose (between A and/or B); choose (A) (from B); choose sb/sth as sth to decide which thing or person

you want out of the ones that are available: *Choose carefully before you make a final decision.* • *Amy had to choose between getting a job or going to college.* • *The viewers chose this programme as their favourite.* **2** choose (to do sth) to decide or prefer to do sth: *You are free to leave whenever you choose.* • *They chose to resign rather than work for the new manager.* ••➤ noun **choice**
IDIOM **pick and choose →** **PICK¹**

choosy /'tʃuːzi/ **adj** (*informal*) (used about a person) difficult to please

★**chop¹** /tʃɒp/ **verb** [T] (chopping; chopped) chop sth (up) (into sth) to cut sth into pieces with a knife, etc: *finely chopped herbs* • *Chop the onions up into small pieces.*
IDIOM **chop and change** to change your plans or opinions several times
PHRASAL VERBS **chop sth down** to cut a tree, etc at the bottom so that it falls down
chop sth off (sth) to remove sth from sth by cutting it with a knife or a sharp tool

chop² /tʃɒp/ **noun** [C] **1** a thick slice of meat with a piece of bone in it ••➤ Look at **steak**. ••➤ picture on page C4 **2** an act of chopping sth: *a karate chop*

chopper /'tʃɒpə/ **noun** [C] (*informal*) = **HELICOPTER**

'**chopping board noun** [C] a piece of wood or plastic used for cutting meat or vegetables on ••➤ picture at **kitchen**

choppy /'tʃɒpi/ **adj** (used about the sea) having a lot of small waves, slightly rough

chopsticks /'tʃɒpstɪks/ **noun** [pl] two thin sticks made of wood or plastic, that people in China, Japan, etc use for picking up food to eat

choral /'kɔːrəl/ **adj** music written for or involving a group of singers (a choir)

chord /kɔːd/ **noun** [C] two or more musical notes that are played at the same time

chore /tʃɔː/ **noun** [C] a job that is not interesting but that you must do: *household chores*

choreograph /'kɒriəɡrɑːf/ **verb** [T] to design and arrange the movements of a dance –**choreographer noun** [C]

choreography /ˌkɒri'ɒɡrəfi/ **noun** [U] the arrangement of movements for a dance performance

chorus¹ /'kɔːrəs/ **noun** [C] **1** the part of a song that is repeated at the end of each verse ••➤ synonym **refrain 2** a piece of music, usually part of a larger work, that is written for a large group of people (a choir) to sing **3** [with sing or pl verb] a large group of people who sing together **4** [with sing or pl verb] the singers and dancers in a musical show who do not play the main parts **5** a chorus of sth [sing] something that a lot of people say together: *a chorus of cheers/criticism/disapproval*

chorus² /'kɔːrəs/ **verb** [T] (used about a group of people) to sing or say sth together: *'That's not fair!' the children chorused.*

chose *past tense* of **CHOOSE**
chosen *past participle* of **CHOOSE**

Christ /kraɪst/ (also **Jesus; Jesus Christ** /ˌdʒiːzəs ˈkraɪst/) *noun* the man who Christians believe is the son of God and who established the Christian religion

christen /ˈkrɪsn/ *verb* [T] **1** to give a person, usually a baby, a name during a Christian ceremony in which he/she is made a member of the Church: *The baby was christened Simon Mark.* •➤ Look at **baptize**. **2** to give sb/sth a name: *People drive so dangerously on this stretch of road that they've christened it 'The Mad Mile'.*

christening /ˈkrɪsnɪŋ/ *noun* [C] the church ceremony in the Christian religion in which a baby is given a name •➤ Look at **baptism**.

★**Christian** /ˈkrɪstʃən/ *noun* [C] a person whose religion is Christianity –**Christian** *adj*

Christianity /ˌkrɪstiˈænəti/ *noun* [U] the religion that is based on the teachings of Jesus Christ

★**Christmas** /ˈkrɪsməs/ *noun* **1** [C,U] the period of time before and after 25 December: *Where are you spending Christmas this year?* **2 Christmas Day** [C] a public holiday on 25 December. It is the day on which Christians celebrate the birth of Christ each year. •➤ Christmas is sometimes written as **Xmas** in informal English.

'**Christmas card** *noun* [C] a card with a picture on the front and a message inside that people send to their friends and relatives at Christmas

,**Christmas 'carol** = **CAROL**

,**Christmas 'cracker** = **CRACKER**(2)

,**Christmas 'dinner** *noun* [C] the traditional meal eaten on Christmas Day: *We had a traditional Christmas dinner that year, with roast turkey, Christmas pudding and all the trimmings.*

,**Christmas 'Eve** *noun* [C] 24 December, the day before Christmas Day

,**Christmas 'pudding** *noun* [C,U] a sweet dish made from dried fruit and eaten hot with sauce at Christmas dinner

'**Christmas tree** *noun* [C] a real or artificial tree, which people bring into their homes and cover with coloured lights and decorations at Christmas

chrome /krəʊm/ (also **chromium** /ˈkrəʊmiəm/) *noun* [U] a hard shiny metal that is used for covering other metals

chromosome /ˈkrəʊməsəʊm/ *noun* [C] a part of a cell in living things that decides the sex, character, shape, etc that a person, an animal or a plant will have

chronic /ˈkrɒnɪk/ *adj* (used about a disease or a problem) that continues for a long time: *There is a chronic shortage of housing in the city.*

▶ Compare **acute**.

–**chronically** /-kli/ *adv*

chronicle /ˈkrɒnɪkl/ *noun* [C] (often plural) a written record of historical events describing them in the order in which they happened

chronological /ˌkrɒnəˈlɒdʒɪkl/ *adj*

arranged in the order in which the events happened: *This book describes the main events in his life in chronological order.* –**chronologically** /-kli/ *adv*

chrysalis /ˈkrɪsəlɪs/ (*pl* **chrysalises**) *noun* [C] the form of an insect, (a butterfly or a moth), while it is changing into an adult inside a hard case, also called a chrysalis •➤ picture at **insect**

chrysanthemum /krɪˈsænθəməm/ *noun* [C] a large garden flower which is brightly coloured and shaped like a ball •➤ picture on page C2

chubby /ˈtʃʌbi/ *adj* slightly fat in a pleasant way: *a baby with chubby cheeks*

chuck /tʃʌk/ *verb* [T] (*informal*) to throw sth in a careless way: *You can chuck those old shoes in the bin.*

PHRASAL VERBS **chuck sth in** to give sth up: *He's chucked his job in because he was fed up.*
chuck sb out (of sth) to force sb to leave a place: *They were chucked out of the cinema for making too much noise.*

chuckle /ˈtʃʌkl/ *verb* [I] to laugh quietly: *Bruce chuckled to himself as he read the letter.* –**chuckle** *noun* [C]

chug /tʃʌg/ *verb* [I] (**chugging; chugged**) **1** (used about a machine or engine) to make short repeated sounds while it is working or moving slowly **2 chug along, down, up, etc** to move in a particular direction making this sound: *The train chugged out of the station.*

chunk /tʃʌŋk/ *noun* [C] a large or thick piece of sth: *chunks of bread and cheese*

chunky /ˈtʃʌŋki/ *adj* **1** thick and heavy: *chunky jewellery* **2** (used about a person) short and strong: *He was a short man with chunky legs.* **3** (used about food) containing thick pieces: *chunky banana milkshake*

★**church** /tʃɜːtʃ/ *noun* **1** [C,U] a building where Christians go to pray, etc: *Do you go to church regularly?*

▶ Notice that when you are talking about going to a ceremony (a service) in a church you say 'in church', 'to church' or 'at church' without 'a' or 'the': *Was Mrs Stevens at church today?*

2 Church [C] a particular group of Christians: *the Anglican/Catholic/Methodist/Church* **3 (the) Church** [sing] the ministers or the institution of the Christian religion: *the conflict between Church and State*

churchgoer /ˈtʃɜːtʃɡəʊə/ *noun* [C] a person who goes to church regularly

the ,Church of 'England (*abbr* **C of E**) *noun* [sing] the Protestant Church, which is the official church in England, whose leader is the Queen or King •➤ Look at **Anglican**.

churchyard /ˈtʃɜːtʃjɑːd/ *noun* [C] the area of land that is around a church •➤ Look at **cemetery** and **graveyard**.

churn /tʃɜːn/ *verb* **1** [I,T] **churn (sth) (up)** to move, or to make water, mud, etc move around violently: *The dark water churned beneath the huge ship.* • *Vast crowds had churned the field into a sea of mud.* **2** [I] if your stomach churns or sth makes it churn, you feel sick because you are disgusted or nervous: *Reading about the murder in the paper made my stomach churn.* **3** [T] to make butter from milk or cream

PHRASAL VERB **churn sth out** (*informal*) to produce large numbers of sth very quickly: *Modern factories can churn out cars at an amazing speed.*

chute /ʃuːt/ *noun* [C] a passage down which you can drop or slide things, so that you do not have to carry them: *a laundry/rubbish chute* (from the upper floors of a high building) ● *a water chute* (at a swimming pool)

chutney /ˈtʃʌtni/ *noun* [U] a thick sweet sauce that is made from fruit or vegetables. You eat chutney cold with cheese or meat.

CIA /ˌsiː aɪ ˈeɪ/ *abbr* the Central Intelligence Agency; the US government organization that tries to discover secret information about other countries

ciabatta /tʃəˈbætə/ *noun* [U,C] a type of heavy Italian bread; a whole piece (loaf) of this

cider /ˈsaɪdə/ *noun* [U] **1** (*Brit*) an alcoholic drink made from apples: *dry/sweet cider* **2** (*US*) a drink made from apples that does not contain alcohol

cigar /sɪˈɡɑː/ *noun* [C] a roll of dried tobacco leaves that people smoke. Cigars are larger than cigarettes

cigarette /ˌsɪɡəˈret/ *noun* [C] tobacco in a tube of thin white paper that people smoke: *a packet of cigarettes*

ciga'rette lighter (also **lighter**) *noun* [C] an object which produces a small flame for lighting cigarettes, etc

cinder /ˈsɪndə/ *noun* [C] a very small piece of burning coal, wood, etc

★ **cinema** /ˈsɪnəmə/ *noun* **1** [C] (*Brit*) a place where you go to see a film: *What's on at the cinema this week?*

➤ In US English, you use **movie theater** to talk about the building where films are shown but **the movies** when you are talking about going to see a film there: *There are five movie theaters in this town.* ● *Let's go to the movies this evening.*

2 [U] films in general; the film industry: *one of the great successes of British cinema*

cinnamon /ˈsɪnəmən/ *noun* [U] a sweet brown powder that is used for giving flavour to food

circa /ˈsɜːkə/ *prep* (*abbr* c) (*written*) (used with dates) about; approximately: *The vase was made circa 600 AD.*

circle

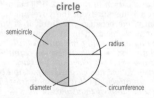

semicircle

radius

diameter

circumference

★ **circle**[1] /ˈsɜːkl/ *noun* **1** [C] a round shape like a ring: *The children were drawing circles and squares on a piece of paper.* ● *We all stood in a circle and held hands.* **2** [C] a flat, round area: *She cut out a circle of paper.* ·➤ picture at **shape** **3** [C] a group of people who are friends, or who have the same interest or profession: *He has a large circle of friends.* ● *Her name was well known in artistic circles.* **4 the (dress) circle** (*US* **balcony**) [sing] an area of seats that is upstairs in a cinema, theatre, etc

IDIOM **a vicious circle** → **VICIOUS**

★ **circle**[2] /ˈsɜːkl/ *verb* **1** [I,T] to move, or to move round sth, in a circle: *The plane circled the town several times before it landed.* **2** [T] to draw a circle round sth: *There are three possible answers to each question. Please circle the correct one.*

circuit /ˈsɜːkɪt/ *noun* **1** [C] a circular journey or track round sth: *The cars have to complete ten circuits of the track.* **2** [C] a complete circular path that an electric current can flow around **3** [sing] a series of sports competitions, meetings or other organized events that are regularly visited by the same people: *She's one of the best players on the tennis circuit.*

★ **circular**[1] /ˈsɜːkjələ/ *adj* **1** round and flat; shaped like a circle: *a circular table* **2** (used about a journey, etc) moving round in a circle: *a circular tour of Oxford*

circular[2] /ˈsɜːkjələ/ *noun* [C] a printed letter, notice or advertisement that is sent to a large number of people

circulate /ˈsɜːkjəleɪt/ *verb* [I,T] **1** to go or be passed from one person to another: *Rumours were circulating about the Minister's private life.* ● *We've circulated a copy of the report to each department.* **2** (used about a substance) to move or make sth move round continuously: *Blood circulates round the body.*

circulation /ˌsɜːkjəˈleɪʃn/ *noun* **1** [U] the movement of blood around the body: *If you have bad circulation, your hands and feet get cold easily.* **2** [U] the passing of sth from one person or place to another: *the circulation of news/information/rumours* ● *Old five pence coins are no longer in circulation* (= being used by people). **3** [C] the number of copies of a newspaper, magazine, etc that are sold each time it is produced: *This newspaper has a circulation of over a million.*

circumcise /ˈsɜːkəmsaɪz/ *verb* [T] to cut off the skin at the end of a man's sexual organ (penis) or to remove part of a woman's sexual organs (clitoris), for religious or sometimes (in the case of a man) medical reasons —**circumcision** /ˌsɜːkəmˈsɪʒn/ *noun* [C,U]

circumference /səˈkʌmfərəns/ *noun* [C,U] the distance round a circle or sth circular: *The Earth is about 40000 kilometres in circumference.* ·➤ Look at **diameter** and **radius**. ·➤ picture at **circle**

★ **circumstance** /ˈsɜːkəmstəns/ *noun* **1** [C, usually pl] the facts and events that affect what happens in a particular situation: *Police* *said there were no **suspicious circumstances** surrounding the boy's death.* ● *In normal circumstances I would not have accepted the job, but at that time I had very little money.* **2 circumstances** [pl] (*formal*) the amount of money that you have: *The company has promised to repay the money when its financial circumstances improve.*

IDIOMS **in/under no circumstances** never; not for any reason: *Under no circumstances should you enter my office.*

in/under the circumstances as the result of a particular situation: *My father was ill at that time, so under the circumstances I decided not to go on holiday.* ● *It's not an ideal solution, but it's the best we can do in the circumstances.*

circumstantial /ˌsɜːkəmˈstænʃl/ **adj** (used in connection with the law) containing details and information that strongly suggest sth is true but are not actual proof of it: *circumstantial evidence*

★**circus** /ˈsɜːkəs/ **noun** [C] a show performed in a large tent by a company of people and animals

CIS /ˌsiː aɪ ˈes/ **abbr** the Commonwealth of Independent States ●▶ Look at **USSR**.

cistern /ˈsɪstən/ **noun** [C] a container for storing water, especially one that is connected to a toilet

cite /saɪt/ **verb** [T] (*formal*) to mention sth or use sb's exact words as an example to support, or as proof of, what you are saying: *She cited a passage from the President's speech.*

★**citizen** /ˈsɪtɪzn/ **noun** [C] **1** a person who is legally accepted as a member of a particular country: *She was born in Japan, but became an American citizen in 1981.* **2** a person who lives in a town or city: *the citizens of Paris* ●▶ Look at **senior citizen**.

citizenship /ˈsɪtɪzənʃɪp/ **noun** [U] the state of being a citizen of a particular country: *After living in Spain for twenty years, he decided to apply for Spanish citizenship.*

citrus /ˈsɪtrəs/ **adj** used to describe fruit such as oranges and lemons

★**city** /ˈsɪti/ **noun** (*pl* **cities**) **1** [C] a large and important town: *Venice is one of the most beautiful cities in the world.* ● *Many people are worried about housing conditions in Britain's inner cities* (= the central parts where there are often social problems). ● *the city centre* **2 the City** [sing] the oldest part of London, which is now Britain's financial centre

civic /ˈsɪvɪk/ **adj** officially connected with a city or town: *civic pride* (= feeling proud because you belong to a particular town or city) ● *civic duties* ● *the civic centre* (= the area where the public buildings are in a town)

civil /ˈsɪvl/ **adj 1** (only *before* a noun) connected with the people who live in a country: *civil disorder* (= involving groups of people within the same country) **2** (only *before* a noun) connected with the state, not with the army or the Church: *civil engineering* (= the

designing and building of roads, railways, bridges, etc) ● *a civil wedding* (= not a religious one) **3** (only *before* a noun) (in law) connected with the personal legal matters of ordinary people, and not criminal law: *civil courts* **4** polite, but not very friendly: *I know you don't like the director, but do try and be civil to him.* –civilly /ˈsɪvəli/ **adv**

★**civilian** /səˈvɪliən/ **noun** [C] a person who is not in the army, navy, air force or police force: *Two soldiers and one civilian were killed when the bomb exploded.*

★**civilization** (also **civilisation**) /ˌsɪvəlaɪˈzeɪʃn/ **noun 1** [C,U] a society which has its own highly developed culture and way of life: *the civilizations of ancient Greece and Rome* ● *Western civilization* **2** [U] an advanced state of social and cultural development, or the process of reaching this state: *the civilization of the human race* **3** [U] all the people in the world and the societies they live in considered as a whole: *Global warming poses a threat to the whole of civilization.*

civilize (also **-ise**) /ˈsɪvəlaɪz/ **verb** [T] to make people or a society develop from a low social and cultural level to a more advanced one

★**civilized** (also **-ised**) /ˈsɪvəlaɪzd/ **adj 1** (used about a society) well-organized; having a high level of social and cultural development **2** polite and reasonable: *a civilized conversation*

civil 'rights (also **civil 'liberties**) **noun** [pl] a person's legal right to freedom and equal treatment in society, whatever his/her sex, race or religion: *the civil rights leader Martin Luther King*

civil 'servant noun [C] (*especially Brit*) a person who works for the government's or State's own organization (**the civil service**)

the civil 'service noun [sing] all the government departments (except for the armed forces) and all the people who work in them

civil 'war noun [C,U] a war between groups of people who live in the same country

CJD /ˌsiː dʒeɪ ˈdiː/ **abbr** Creutzfeldt-Jakob disease; a disease of the brain caused by eating infected meat ●▶ Look at **BSE**.

cl abbr centilitre(s)

clad /klæd/ **adj** (not *before* a noun) (*old-fashioned*) dressed (in); wearing a particular type of clothing: *The children were warmly clad in coats, hats and scarves.*

★**claim¹** /kleɪm/ **verb 1** [T] **claim (that); claim (to be sth)** to say that sth is true, without having any proof: *Colin claims the book belongs to him.* ● *The woman claims to be the oldest person in Britain.* **2** [I,T] **claim (for sth)** to ask for sth from the government, a company, etc because you think it is your legal right to have it, or it belongs to you: *The police are keeping the animal until somebody claims it.* ● *Don't forget to claim for your travel expenses when you get back.* ● (*figurative*) *No one has claimed responsibility for the bomb attack.* **3** [T] to cause death: *The earthquake claimed thousands of lives.*

★ **claim**[2] /kleɪm/ **noun** [C] **1** a claim (that) a statement that sth is true, which does not have any proof: *I do not believe the Government's claim that they can reduce unemployment by the end of the year.* **2** a claim (to sth) the right to have sth: *You will have to prove your claim to the property in a court of law.* **3** a claim (for sth) a demand for money that you think you have a right to, especially from the government, a company, etc: *to make an insurance claim ● After the accident he decided to put in a claim for compensation.*
IDIOM **stake a/your claim** → **STAKE**[2]

claimant /'kleɪmənt/ **noun** [C] a person who believes he/she has the right to have sth: *The insurance company refused to pay the claimant any money.*

clairvoyant /kleə'vɔɪənt/ **noun** [C] a person who some people believe has special mental powers and can see what will happen in the future

clam[1] /klæm/ **noun** [C] a type of shellfish that can be eaten ••▶ picture at **shellfish**

clam[2] /klæm/ **verb** (**clamming**; **clammed**)
PHRASAL VERB **clam up (on sb)** (*informal*) to stop talking and refuse to speak especially when sb asks you about sth

clamber /'klæmbə/ **verb** [I] clamber up, down, out etc to move or climb with difficulty, usually using both your hands and feet: *She managed to clamber up the over the wall.*

clammy /'klæmi/ **adj** cold, slightly wet and sticky in an unpleasant way: *clammy hands*

clamour (*US* **clamor**) /'klæmə/ **verb** [I] clamour for sth to demand sth in a loud or angry way: *The public are clamouring for an answer to all these questions.* –**clamour** (*US* **clamor**) **noun** [sing]: *the clamour of angry voices*

clamp

clamp[1] /klæmp/ **noun** [C] **1** a tool that you use for holding two things together very tightly **2** (also **wheel clamp**) (*Brit*) a metal object that is fixed to the wheel of a car that has been parked illegally, so that it cannot drive away

clamp[2] /klæmp/ **verb** [T] **1** clamp A and B (together); clamp A to B to fasten two things together with a clamp: *The metal rods were clamped together. ● Clamp the wood to the table so that it doesn't move.* **2** to hold sth very firmly in a particular position: *Her lips were clamped tightly together.* **3** to fix a metal object to the wheel of a vehicle that has been parked illegally, so that it cannot move: *Oh no! My car's been clamped.*
PHRASAL VERB **clamp down on sb/sth** (*informal*) to take strong action in order to stop or control sth: *The police are clamping down on people who drink and drive.*

clampdown /'klæmpdaʊn/ **noun** [C] strong action to stop or control sth: *a clampdown on tax evasion*

clan /klæn/ **noun** [C, with sing or pl verb] a group of families who are related to each other, especially in Scotland

clandestine /klæn'destɪn/ **adj** (*formal*) secret and often not legal: *a clandestine meeting*

clang /klæŋ/ **verb** [I,T] to make or cause sth metal to make a loud ringing sound: *The iron gates clanged shut.* –**clang noun** [C]

clank /klæŋk/ **verb** [I,T] to make or cause sth metal to make a loud unpleasant sound: *The lift clanked its way up to the seventh floor.* –**clank noun** [C]

★ **clap**[1] /klæp/ **verb** (**clapping**; **clapped**) **1** [I,T] to hit your hands together many times, usually to show that you like sth: *The audience clapped as soon as the singer walked onto the stage.* **2** [T] to put sth onto sth quickly and firmly: *'Oh no, I shouldn't have said that,' she said, clapping a hand over her mouth.*

clap[2] /klæp/ **noun** [C] **1** a sudden loud noise: *a clap of thunder* **2** an act of clapping

clarification /ˌklærəfɪ'keɪʃn/ **noun** [U] an act of making sth clear and easier to understand: *We'd like some clarification of exactly what your company intends to do.* ••▶ Look at **clarity**.

clarify /'klærəfaɪ/ **verb** [T] (*pres part* **clarifying**; *3rd pers sing pres* **clarifies**; *pt, pp* **clarified**) to make sth become clear and easier to understand: *I hope that what I say will clarify the situation.* ••▶ adjective **clear**

clarinet /ˌklærə'net/ **noun** [C] a musical instrument that is made of wood. You play a clarinet by blowing through it. ••▶ Look at the note at **piano**. ••▶ picture at **music**

clarity /'klærəti/ **noun** [U] the quality of being clear and easy to understand: *clarity of expression* ••▶ Look at **clarification**.

clash[1] /klæʃ/ **verb 1** [I] clash (with sb) (over sth) to fight or disagree seriously about sth: *A group of demonstrators clashed with police outside the Town Hall.* **2** [I] clash (with sth) (used about two events) to happen at the same time: *It's a pity the two concerts clash. I wanted to go to both of them.* **3** [I] clash (with sth) (used about colours, etc) to not match or look nice together: *I don't think you should wear that tie – it clashes with your shirt.* **4** [I,T] (used about two metal objects) to hit together with a loud noise; to cause two metal objects to do this: *Their swords clashed.*

clash[2] /klæʃ/ **noun** [C] **1** a fight or serious disagreement: *a clash between police and demonstrators* **2** a big difference: *a clash of opinions ● There was a personality clash between the two men* (= they did not get well on together or like each other). **3** a loud noise, made by two metal objects hitting each other

clasp[1] /klɑːsp/ **noun** [C] an object, usually of

metal, which fastens or holds sth together: *the clasp on a necklace/brooch/handbag*

clasp² /klɑːsp/ *verb* [T] to hold sb/sth tightly: *Kevin clasped the child in his arms.*

★**class**¹ /klɑːs/ *noun* **1** [C, with sing or pl verb] a group of students who are taught together: *Jane and I are in the same class at school.* ● *The whole class is/are going to the theatre tonight.* **2** [C,U] a lesson: *Classes begin at 9 o'clock in the morning.* ● *We watched an interesting video in class* (= during the lesson) *yesterday.* **3** [U,C] the way people are divided into social groups; one of these groups: *The idea of class still divides British society.* ● *class differences* [with sing or pl verb] **4** [C] (*technical*) a group of animals, plants, words, etc of a similar type: *There are several different classes of insects.* **5** [U] (*informal*) high quality or style: *Pele was a football player of great class.* **6** [C] (used to form compound adjectives) of a certain level of quality: *a first-class carriage on a train* **7** [C] (*Brit*) (used to form compound adjectives) a mark that you are given when you pass your final university exam: *a first-/second-/third-class degree*

class² /klɑːs/ *verb* [T] class sb/sth (as sth) to put sb/sth in a particular group or type: *Certain animals and plants are now classed as 'endangered species'.*

classic¹ /ˈklæsɪk/ *adj* (usually *before* a noun) **1** typical: *It was a classic case of bad management.* **2** (used about a book, play, etc) important and having a value that will last: *the classic film 'Gone With The Wind'*

classic² /ˈklæsɪk/ *noun* **1** [C] a famous book, play, etc which has a value that will last: *All of Charles Dickens' novels are classics.* **2 Classics** [U] the study of ancient Greek and Roman language and literature

classical /ˈklæsɪkl/ *adj* (usually *before* a noun) **1** (used about music) serious and having a value that lasts: *I prefer classical music to pop.* •➤ Look at **jazz**, **pop** and **rock**. **2** traditional, not modern: *classical ballet* **3** connected with ancient Greece or Rome: *classical architecture* –**classically** /-kli/ *adv*

classified /ˈklæsɪfaɪd/ *adj* officially secret: *classified information*

,**classified ad'vertisement** (*Brit informal* ,**classified 'ad**; ,**small ad**) *noun* [usually pl] a small advertisement that you put in a newspaper if you want to buy or sell sth, employ sb, find a flat, etc

classify /ˈklæsɪfaɪ/ *verb* [T] (*pres part* **classifying**; *3rd pers sing pres* **classifies**; *pt, pp* **classified**) classify sb/sth (as sth) to put sb/sth into a group with other people or things of a similar type: *Would you classify it as an action film or a thriller?* –**classification** /ˌklæsɪfɪˈkeɪʃn/ *noun* [C,U]: *the classification of the different species of butterfly*

classmate /ˈklɑːsmeɪt/ *noun* [C] a person who is in the same class as you at school or college

classroom /ˈklɑːsruːm; -rʊm/ *noun* [C] a

room in a school, college, etc where lessons are taught

classy /ˈklɑːsi/ *adj* (**classier**; **classiest**) (*informal*) of high quality or style; expensive and fashionable: *a classy restaurant*

clatter /ˈklætə/ *verb* [I,T] to make or cause sth hard to make a series of short loud repeated sounds: *The horses clattered down the street.* –**clatter** *noun* [usually sing]

clause /klɔːz/ *noun* [C] **1** one of the sections of a legal document that says that sth must or must not be done **2** (*grammar*) a group of words that includes a subject and a verb. A clause is usually only part of a sentence: *The sentence, 'After we had finished eating, we watched a film on the video,' contains two clauses.*

claustrophobia /ˌklɔːstrəˈfəʊbiə/ *noun* [U] fear of being in a small or enclosed space

claustrophobic /ˌklɔːstrəˈfəʊbɪk/ *adj* **1** extremely afraid of small, enclosed spaces: *I always feel claustrophobic in lifts.* **2** used about sth that makes you feel afraid in this way: *a claustrophobic little room*

claw¹ /klɔː/ *noun* [C] **1** one of the long curved nails on the end of an animal's or a bird's foot •➤ picture on page C1 **2** one of a pair of long, sharp fingers that certain types of shellfish and some insects have. They use them for holding or picking things up: *the claws of a crab*

claw² /klɔː/ *verb* [I,T] claw (at) sb/sth to scratch or tear sb/sth with claws or with your fingernails: *The cat was clawing at the furniture.*

clay /kleɪ/ *noun* [U] heavy earth that is soft and sticky when it is wet and becomes hard when it is baked or dried: *clay pots*

★**clean**¹ /kliːn/ *adj* **1** not dirty: *The whole house was beautifully clean.* ● *Cats are very clean animals.* **2** (used about humour) not about sex, etc; not dirty: *a clean joke* •➤ opposite for senses 1 and 2 **dirty** **3** having no record of offences or crimes: *a clean driving licence*

IDIOM **a clean sweep** a complete victory in a sports competition, election, etc that you get by winning all the different parts of it: *The Russians made a clean sweep of all the gymnastics events.* •➤ noun **cleanliness**

★**clean**² /kliːn/ *verb* **1** [T] to remove dirt, dust and marks from sth: *to clean the windows* ● *Don't forget to clean your teeth!*

➤ **Clean** is a general word for removing dirt from something. If you **wash** something you clean it with water and often soap. You can **wipe** a surface by rubbing it with a wet cloth; you **dust** a surface by rubbing it with a dry cloth. If you **brush** something you clean it with a brush that has a short handle; if you **sweep** the floor you use a brush with a long handle.

2 [I,T] to make the inside of a house, office, etc free from dust and dirt: *Mr Burrows comes in to clean after office hours.* •➤ **Do the cleaning** is often used instead of clean: *I do* *the cleaning once a week.*

PHRASAL VERBS **clean sth out** to clean the inside of sth: *I'm going to clean out all the cupboards next week.*

clean (sth) up to remove all the dirt from a place that is particularly dirty: *I'm going to clean up the kitchen before Mum and Dad get back.* • *Oh no, you've spilt coffee on the new carpet! Can you clean it up?* •➤ Look at **dry-clean** and **spring-clean**.

clean³ /kliːn/ *adv* (*informal*) completely: *I clean forgot it was your birthday.*

IDIOMS **come clean (with sb) (about sth)** (*informal*) to tell the truth about sth that you have been keeping secret: *She decided to come clean with Martin about her relationship with Tom.*

go clean out of your mind to be completely forgotten

cleaner /ˈkliːnə/ *noun* **1** [C] a person whose job is to clean the rooms and furniture inside a house or other building: *an office cleaner* **2** [C] a substance or a special machine that you use for cleaning sth: *liquid floor cleaners* • *a carpet cleaner* •➤ Look at **vacuum cleaner**. **3 the cleaner's** = DRY-CLEANER'S

cleanliness /ˈklenlinəs/ *noun* [U] being clean or keeping things clean: *High standards of cleanliness are important in a hotel kitchen.*

cleanly /ˈkliːnli/ *adv* easily or smoothly in one movement: *The knife cut cleanly through the rope.*

cleanse /klenz/ *verb* [T] to clean your skin or a wound •➤ Look at **ethnic cleansing**.

cleanser /ˈklenzə/ *noun* [C] a substance that you use for cleaning your skin, especially your face

clean-ˈshaven *adj* (used about men) having recently shaved

★**clear¹** /klɪə/ *adj* **1** easy to see, hear or understand: *His voice wasn't very clear on the telephone.* • *She gave me clear directions on how to get there.* **2 clear (about/on sth)** sure or definite; without any doubts or confusion: *I'm not quite clear about the arrangements for tomorrow.* •➤ verb **clarify 3 clear (to sb)** obvious: *There are clear advantages to the second plan.* • *It was clear to me that he was not telling the truth.* **4** easy to see through: *The water was so clear that we could see the bottom of the lake.* **5 clear (of sth)** free from things that are blocking the way: *The police say that most roads are now clear of snow.* **6** free from marks: *a clear sky* (= without clouds) • *a clear skin* (= without spots) **7** free from guilt: *It wasn't your fault. You can have a completely clear conscience.*

IDIOM **make yourself clear; make sth clear/plain (to sb)** to speak so that there can be no doubt about what you mean: *'I do not want you to go to that concert,' said my mother. 'Do I make myself clear?'* • *He made it quite clear that he was not happy with the decision.*

★**clear²** /klɪə/ *adv* **1** =CLEARLY(1): *We can hear the telephone loud and clear from here.* **2 clear (of sth)** away from sth; not touching

sth: *stand clear of the doors* (= on a train)

IDIOM **keep/stay/steer clear (of sb/sth)** to avoid sb/sth because he/she/it may cause problems: *It's best to keep clear of the town centre during the rush hour.*

★**clear³** /klɪə/ *verb* **1** [T] to remove sth that is not wanted or needed: *to clear the roads of snow/to clear snow from the roads* • *It's your turn to clear the table* (= to take away the dirty plates, etc after a meal). **2** [I] (used about smoke, etc) to disappear: *The fog slowly cleared and the sun came out.* **3** [I] (used about the sky, the weather or water) to become free of clouds, rain, or mud: *After a cloudy start, the weather will clear during the afternoon.* **4** [T] **clear sb (of sth)** to provide proof that sb is innocent of sth: *The man has finally been cleared of murder.* **5** [T] to jump over or get past sth without touching it **6** [T] to give official permission for a plane, ship, etc to enter or leave a place: *At last the plane was cleared for take-off.* **7** [T] **clear sth (with sb)** to get official approval for sth to be done: *I'll have to clear it with the manager before I can refund your money.* **8** [I] (used about a cheque) to go through the system that moves money from one account to another: *The cheque will take three days to clear.*

IDIOMS **clear the air** to improve a difficult or tense situation by talking honestly about worries, doubts, etc: *I'm sure if you discuss your feelings with her it will help to clear the air between you.*

clear your throat to cough slightly in order to make it easier to speak

PHRASAL VERBS **clear off** (*informal*) used to tell sb to go away

clear sth out to tidy sth and throw away things that you do not want

clear up (used about the weather or an illness) to get better: *We can go out for a walk if it clears up later on.* • *The doctor told him to stay at home until his cold cleared up.*

clear (sth) up to make sth tidy: *Make sure you clear up properly before you leave.*

clear sth up to find the solution to a problem, cause of confusion, etc: *There's been a slight misunderstanding but we've cleared it up now.*

clearance /ˈklɪərəns/ *noun* [U] **1** the removing of sth that is old or not wanted: *The shop is having a clearance sale* (= selling things cheaply in order to get rid of them). **2** the distance between an object and something that is passing under or beside it, for example a ship or vehicle: *There was not enough clearance for the bus to pass under the bridge safely.* **3** official permission for sb/sth to do sth: *She was given clearance to work at the nuclear research establishment.*

clear-ˈcut *adj* definite and easy to see or understand

clear-ˈheaded *adj* able to think clearly, especially if there is a problem

clearing /ˈklɪərɪŋ/ *noun* [C] a small area without trees in the middle of a wood or forest

clearly /ˈklɪəli/ *adv* **1** in a way that is easy to

see, hear or understand: *It was so foggy that we couldn't see the road clearly.* **2** in a way that is not confused: *I'm so tired that I can't think clearly.* **3** without doubt; obviously: *She clearly doesn't want to speak to you any more.*

,clear-'sighted **adj** able to understand situations well and to see what might happen in the future

cleavage /'kli:vɪdʒ/ **noun** [C,U] the space between a woman's breasts

clef /klef/ **noun** [C] (in music) a sign (𝄞,𝄢) at the beginning of a line of written music that shows the area of sound that the notes are in: *the bass/treble clef*

clementine /'klemənti:n/ **noun** [C] a type of small orange

clench /klentʃ/ **verb** [T] to close or hold tightly: *She clenched her fists and looked as if she was going to hit him.*

clergy /'klɜːdʒi/ **noun** [pl] the people who perform religious ceremonies in the Christian church: *a member of the clergy*

clergyman /'klɜːdʒimən/ **noun** [C] (*pl* **-men** /-mən; -men/) a male member of the clergy

clergywoman /'klɜːdʒiwʊmən/ **noun** [C] (*pl* **-women** /-wɪmɪn/) a female member of the clergy

clerical /'klerɪkl/ **adj 1** connected with the work of a clerk in an office: *clerical work* **2** connected with the clergy

★**clerk** /klɑːk/ **noun** [C] **1** a person whose job is to do written work or look after records or accounts in an office, bank, court of law, etc **2** (also **sales clerk**) (*US*) = **SHOP ASSISTANT**

★**clever** /'klevə/ **adj 1** able to learn, understand or do sth quickly and easily; intelligent: *a clever student* ● *How clever of you to mend my watch!* **2** (used about things, ideas, etc) showing skill or intelligence: *a clever device* ● *a clever plan* –**cleverly adv** –**cleverness noun** [U]

cliché /'kli:ʃeɪ/ **noun** [C] a phrase or idea that has been used so many times that it no longer has any real meaning or interest

click¹ /klɪk/ **verb 1** [I,T] to make a short sharp sound; to cause sth to do this: *The door clicked shut.* ● *He clicked his fingers at the waiter.* **2** [I,T] click (on sth) (*computing*) to press one of the buttons on a mouse: *To open a file, click on the menu.* ● *Position the pointer and double click the left-hand mouse button* (= press it twice very quickly). **3** [I] (*Brit informal*) (used about two people) to become friendly immediately: *We met at a party and just clicked.* **4** [I] (*informal*) (used about a problem, etc) to become suddenly clear or understood: *Once I'd found the missing letter, everything clicked into place.*

click² /klɪk/ **noun** [C] **1** a short sharp sound: *the click of a switch* **2** (*computing*) the act of pressing the button on a computer mouse

★**client** /'klaɪənt/ **noun** [C] **1** somebody who receives a service from a professional person, for example a lawyer **2** (*computing*) one of a number of computers that is connected to a special computer (**server**) that stores shared information

➤ Be careful. **Client** cannot be used for people in shops or restaurants. Those people are **customers**. **Clientele** is a general, formal word that includes both clients and customers.

clientele /ˌkli:ən'tel/ **noun** [U] all the customers, guests or clients who regularly go to a particular shop, hotel, organization, etc •➤ This word is more formal than similar words such as **customers** or **guests**.

★**cliff** /klɪf/ **noun** [C] a high, very steep area of rock, especially one next to the sea •➤ picture on page C8

★**climate** /'klaɪmət/ **noun** [C] **1** the normal weather conditions of a particular region: *a dry/humid/tropical climate* **2** the general opinions, etc that people have at a particular time: *What is the current climate of opinion regarding the death penalty?* ● *the political climate*

climatic /klaɪ'mætɪk/ **adj** connected with the climate (1)

climax /'klaɪmæks/ **noun** [C] the most important and exciting part of a book, play, piece of music, event, etc: *The novel reaches a dramatic climax in the final chapter.* –**climax verb** [I]

★**climb¹** /klaɪm/ **verb 1** [I,T] climb (up) (sth) to move up towards the top of sth: *to climb a tree/mountain/rope* ● *She climbed the stairs to bed.* ● *to climb up a ladder* **2** [I] to move, with difficulty or effort, in the direction mentioned: *I managed to climb out of the window.* **3** [I] to go up mountains, etc as a sport •➤ **Go climbing** is a common way of talking about climbing for pleasure: *I go climbing in the Alps most summers.* **4** [I] to rise to a higher position: *The plane climbed steadily.* ● *The road climbed steeply up the side of the mountain.* ● (*figurative*) *The value of the dollar climbed against the pound.*

IDIOM **climb/jump on the bandwagon** → **BANDWAGON**

PHRASAL VERB **climb down (over sth)** (*informal*) to admit that you have made a mistake; to change your opinion about sth in an argument

climb² /klaɪm/ **noun** [C] an act of climbing or a journey made by climbing: *The monastery could only be reached by a three-hour climb.*

climbdown /'klaɪmdaʊn/ **noun** [C] an act of admitting you have been wrong; a change of opinion in an argument: *a government climbdown*

climber /'klaɪmə/ **noun** [C] a person who climbs mountains as a sport

clinch /klɪntʃ/ **verb** [T] (*informal*) to finally manage to get what you want in an argument or business agreement: *to clinch a deal*

cling /klɪŋ/ **verb** [I] (*pt, pp* **clung** /klʌŋ/) **1** cling (on) to sb/sth; cling together to hold on tightly to sb/sth: *She clung to the rope with all her strength.* ● *They clung together for warmth.* **2** cling (on) to sth to continue to believe sth, often when it is not reasonable to do so: *They were still clinging to the hope that the girl would be found alive.* **3 cling to sb/ sth** to stick firmly to sth: *Her wet clothes clung to her.* **–clingy adj:** *a clingy child* (= that does not want to leave its parents) ● *a clingy sweater*

'cling film noun [U] thin transparent plastic used for covering food to keep it fresh

clinic /'klɪnɪk/ **noun** [C] **1** a small hospital or a part of a hospital where you go to receive special medical treatment: *He's being treated at a private clinic.* ● *an ante-natal clinic* **2** a time when a doctor sees patients and gives special treatment or advice: *Dr Greenall's clinic is from 2 to 4 on Mondays.*

clinical /'klɪnɪkl/ **adj 1** connected with the examination and treatment of patients at a clinic or hospital: *Clinical trials of the new drug have proved successful.* **2** (used about a person) cold and not emotional

clinically /'klɪnɪkli/ **adv 1** according to medical examination: *to be clinically dead* **2** in a cold way; without showing any emotion

clink /klɪŋk/ **noun** [sing] the short sharp ringing sound that objects made of glass, metal, etc make when they touch each other: *the clink of glasses* **–clink verb** [I,T]

clip¹ /klɪp/ **noun** [C] **1** a small object, usually made of metal or plastic, used for holding things together: *a paper clip* ● *a hairclip* **2** a small section of a film that is shown so that people can see what the rest of the film is like **••➤** Look at **trailer**. **3** (*informal*) a quick hit with the hand: *She gave the boy a clip round the ear.* **4** an act of cutting sth

clip² /klɪp/ **verb** (**clipping; clipped**) **1** [I,T] to be fastened with a clip; to fasten sth to sth else with a clip: *Clip the photo to the letter, please.* **2** [T] to cut sth, especially by cutting small parts off: *The hedge needs clipping.* **3** [T] to hit sb/sth quickly: *My wheel clipped the pavement and I fell off my bike.*

clippers /'klɪpəz/ **noun** [pl] a small metal tool used for cutting things, for example hair or fingernails: *a pair of nail clippers* **••➤** picture at **scissors**

clipping /'klɪpɪŋ/ (*US* = **CUTTING¹**(1))

clique /kli:k/ **noun** [C] a small group of people with the same interests who do not want others to join their group

clitoris /'klɪtərɪs/ **noun** [C] the small part of the female sex organs which becomes larger when a woman is sexually excited

cloak /kləʊk/ **noun 1** [C] a type of loose coat without sleeves that was more common in former times **••➤** Look at **cape**. **2** [sing] a thing that hides sth else: (*figurative*) *a cloak of mist*

cloakroom /'kləʊkru:m/ **noun** [C] a room near the entrance to a building where you can leave your coat, bags, etc

clobber /'klɒbə/ **verb** [T] (*Brit informal*) to hit sb hard

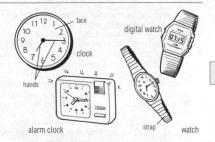

face   digital watch

clock

hands

alarm clock   strap   watch

★clock¹ /klɒk/ **noun** [C] **1** an instrument that shows you what time it is: *an alarm clock* ● *a church clock* **••➤** Look at **watch**. **2** an instrument in a car that measures how far it has travelled: *My car has only 10 000 miles on the clock.*

IDIOMS against the clock to do sth fast in order to finish it before a certain time: *It was a race against the clock to get the building work finished on time.*

around/round the clock all day and all night: *They are working round the clock to repair the bridge.*

put the clock/clocks forward/back to change the time, usually by one hour, at the beginning/end of summer

clock² /klɒk/ **verb**

PHRASAL VERBS clock in/on; clock off to record the time that you arrive at or leave work, especially by putting a card into a type of clock

clock sth up to achieve a certain number or total: *Our car clocked up over 2000 miles while we were on holiday.*

clockwise /'klɒkwaɪz/ **adv, adj** in the same direction as the hands of a clock: *Turn the handle clockwise.* ● *to move in a clockwise direction* **••➤** opposite *Brit* **anticlockwise**, *US* **counter-clockwise**.

clockwork /'klɒkwɜ:k/ **noun** [U] a type of machinery found in certain toys, etc that you operate by turning a key: *a clockwork toy* ● *The plan went like clockwork* (= smoothly and without any problems).

clog /klɒg/ **noun** [C] a type of shoe made completely out of wood or with a thick wooden base

clog² /klɒg/ **verb** (**clogging; clogged**) [I,T] **clog (sth) (up) (with sth)** to block or become blocked: *The drain is always clogging up.* ● *The roads were clogged with traffic.*

clone /kləʊn/ **noun** [C] an exact copy of a plant or animal that is produced from one of its cells by scientific methods **–clone verb:** *A team from the UK were the first to successfully clone an animal.*

★close¹ /kləʊz/ **verb** [I,T] **1** to shut: *The door closed quietly.* ● *to close a door/window* ● *Close your eyes – I've got a surprise.* **2** to be, or to make sth, not open to the public: *What time do the shops close?* ● *The police have closed the road to traffic.* **3** to end or to bring sth to an end: *The meeting closed at 10pm.*

• *Detectives have closed the case on the missing girl.* •➤ opposite **open**

PHRASAL VERBS **close (sth) down** to stop all business or work permanently at a shop or factory: *The factory has had to close down.* • *Health inspectors have closed the restaurant down.*

close in (on sb/sth) to come nearer and gradually surround sb/sth, especially in order to attack: *The army is closing in on the enemy troops.*

close sth off to prevent people from entering a place or an area: *The police closed off the city centre because of a bomb alert.*

⋆**close²** /kləʊz/ **noun** [sing] the end, especially of a period of time or an activity: *the close of trading on the stock market* •➤ opposite **open**

IDIOM **bring sth/come/draw to a close** to end: *The chairman brought the meeting to a close.* • *The guests began to leave as the evening drew to a close.*

⋆**close³** /kləʊs/ **adj, adv 1** (not before a noun) **close (to sb/sth); close (together)** near: *Is our hotel close to the beach?* • *The tables are quite close together.* • *to follow close behind someone* • *I held her close* (= tightly). **2** (used about a friend, etc) known very well and liked: *They invited only close friends to the wedding.* **3** near in a family relationship: *a close relative* **4** (used about a competition, etc) only won by a small amount: *a close match* •➤ Look at the note at **near¹**. **5** careful; thorough: *On close examination, you could see that the banknote was a forgery.* **6** (used about the weather, etc) heavy and with little movement of air: *It's so close today that there might be a storm.* –**closely** adv: *to watch sb closely* • *The insect closely resembles a stick.* –**closeness** noun [U]

IDIOMS **a close shave/thing** a bad thing that almost happened: *I wasn't injured, but it was a close shave.*

at close quarters at or from a position that is very near

close by (sb/sth) at a short distance from sb/sth: *She lives close by.*

close/near/dear to sb's heart → **HEART**

close on nearly; almost: *He was born close on a hundred years ago.*

close up (to sb/sth) at or from a very short distance to sb/sth: *You can't tell it's a forgery until you look at it close up.*

come close (to sth/to doing sth) to almost do sth: *We didn't win but we came close.*

close⁴ /kləʊs/ **noun** [C] part of the name of a street: *5 Devon Close*

⋆**closed** /kləʊzd/ **adj** not open; shut: *Keep your mouth closed.* • *The supermarket is closed.* •➤ opposite **open**

closed-circuit television (*abbr* **CCTV**) **noun** [C,U] a type of television system used inside a building, for example a shop, to protect it from crime

closet /ˈklɒzɪt/ **noun** [C] (*especially US*) a large cupboard that is built into a room

close-up /ˈkləʊsʌp/ **noun** [C] a photograph or film of sb/sth that you take from a very short distance away: *Here's a close-up of Mike.*

'closing time **noun** [C] the time when a shop, pub, etc closes

closure /ˈkləʊʒə/ **noun** [C,U] the permanent closing, for example of a business: *The firm is threatened with closure.*

clot¹ /klɒt/ **noun** [C] a lump formed by blood as it dries: *They removed a blood clot from his brain.*

clot² /klɒt/ **verb** [I,T] (**clotting; clotted**) to form or cause blood to form thick lumps: *a drug that stops blood from clotting during operations*

⋆**cloth** /klɒθ/ **noun** (*pl* **cloths** /klɒθs/) **1** [U] a material made of cotton, wool, etc that you use for making clothes, curtains, etc: *a metre of cloth* **2** [C] a piece of material that you use for a particular purpose: *a tablecloth* • *Where can I find a cloth to wipe this water up?* •➤ picture at **bucket**

clothe /kləʊð/ **verb** [T] to provide clothes for sb: *to feed and clothe a child*

clothed /kləʊðd/ **adj** **clothed (in sth)** dressed; wearing sth: *He was clothed in leather from head to foot.*

⋆**clothes** /kləʊðz/ **noun** [pl] the things that you wear, for example trousers, shirts, dresses, coats, etc: *Take off those wet clothes.* • *She was wearing new clothes.* •➤ Look at **garment**.

➤ Remember that **clothes** is always plural. We can use an **item/piece/article of clothing** to describe a single thing that you wear: *A kilt is an item of clothing worn in Scotland.*

'clothes line **noun** [C] a thin rope that you hang clothes on so that they can dry

'clothes peg (*US* **'clothes pin**) = **PEG¹**(3)

⋆**clothing** /ˈkləʊðɪŋ/ **noun** [U] the clothes that you wear, especially for a particular activity: *You will need waterproof/outdoor/winter clothing.* •➤ **Clothing** is a more formal word than **clothes**.

clotted 'cream **noun** [U] (*Brit*) a type of thick rich cream

⋆**cloud¹** /klaʊd/ **noun 1** [C,U] a mass of very small drops of water that floats in the sky and is usually white or grey: *The sun disappeared behind a cloud.* • *A band of thick cloud is spreading from the west.* **2** [C] a mass of smoke, dust, sand, etc: *Clouds of smoke were pouring from the burning building.*

IDIOMS **every cloud has a silver lining** even a very bad situation has a positive or hopeful side

under a cloud with the disapproval of the people around you: *She left her job under a cloud because she'd been accused of stealing.*

cloud² /klaʊd/ **verb 1** [I,T] to become or make sth difficult to see through: *His eyes clouded with tears.* **2** [T] to make sth less clear or easy to understand: *Her personal involvement in the case was beginning to cloud her judgement.* **3** [T] to make sth less enjoyable; to spoil: *Illness has clouded the last few years of* *his life.*

PHRASAL VERB **cloud over** (used about the sky) to become full of clouds

cloudburst /'klaʊdbɜ:st/ noun [C] a sudden heavy fall of rain

cloudless /'klaʊdləs/ adj (used about the sky, etc) clear; without any clouds

cloudy /'klaʊdi/ adj **1** (used about the sky, etc) full of clouds **2** (used about liquids, etc) not clear: *cloudy water*

clout /klaʊt/ noun (*informal*) **1** [C] a hard hit, usually with the hand: *to give someone a clout* **2** [U] influence and power: *He's an important man – he has a lot of clout in the company.*

clove /kləʊv/ noun [C] **1** the small dried flower of a tropical tree, used to give a special flavour in cooking **2** one of the small separate sections of a vegetable root (**garlic**)

clover /'kləʊvə/ noun [C] a small plant with pink or white flowers and leaves with three parts to them ••➤ picture on page C2

> Sometimes clover leaves have four parts and it is thought to be very lucky if you find one of these.

clown¹ /klaʊn/ noun [C] **1** a person who wears funny clothes and a big red nose and does silly things to make people (especially children) laugh **2** a person who makes jokes and does silly things to make the people around him/her laugh: *At school, Jan was always the class clown.*

clown² /klaʊn/ verb [I] **clown** (**about/ around**) to act in a funny or foolish way: *Stop clowning around and get some work done!*

★**club¹** /klʌb/ noun **1** [C] a group of people who meet regularly to share an interest, do sport, etc; the place where they meet: *to join a club* • *to be a member of a club* • *a tennis/football/golf club* **2** (also **nightclub**) [C] a place where you can go to dance and drink late at night **3** [C] a heavy stick, usually with one end that is thicker than the other, used as a weapon **4** [C] a long stick that is specially shaped at one end and used for hitting a ball when playing golf ••➤ picture on page S2 ••➤ Look at **bat**, **racket** and **stick**. **5 clubs** [pl] the group (**suit**) of playing cards with black three-leafed shapes on them: *the two/ace/queen of clubs* ••➤ Look at the note and picture at **card**. **6** [C] one of the cards from this suit: *I played a club.*

club² /klʌb/ verb (**clubbing**; **clubbed**) **1** [T] to hit sb/sth hard with a heavy object **2** [I] **go clubbing** to go dancing and drinking in a club: *She goes clubbing every Saturday.*

PHRASAL VERB **club together** (**to do sth**) to share the cost of sth, for example a present: *We clubbed together to buy him a leaving present.*

cluck /klʌk/ noun [C] the noise made by a chicken –**cluck** verb [I]

clue /klu:/ noun [C] a **clue** (**to sth**) a piece of information that helps you solve a problem or a crime, answer a question, etc: *The police were looking for clues to his disappearance.*

• *the clues for solving a crossword puzzle*

IDIOM **not have a clue** (*informal*) to know nothing about sth

clued-up /,klʌd 'ʌp/ (*US also* ,**clued-'in**) adj **clued-up** (**on sth**) knowing a lot about sth: *I'm not really clued-up on the technical details.*

clueless /'klu:ləs/ adj (*informal*) not able to understand; stupid: *I'm absolutely clueless about computers.*

clump /klʌmp/ noun [C] a small group of plants or trees, growing together

clumsy /'klʌmzi/ adj (**clumsier**; **clumsiest**) **1** (used about a person) careless and likely to knock into, drop or break things: *She undid the parcel with clumsy fingers.* **2** (used about a comment, etc) likely to upset or offend people: *He made a clumsy apology.* **3** large, difficult to use, and not attractive in design: *a clumsy piece of furniture* –**clumsily** adv –**clumsiness** noun [U]

clung *past tense, past participle* of **CLING**

cluster¹ /'klʌstə/ noun [C] a group of people, plants or things that stand or grow close together: *a cluster of schoolchildren*

cluster² /'klʌstə/ verb

PHRASAL VERB **cluster around sb/sth** to form a group around sb/sth: *The tourists clustered around their guide.*

clutch¹ /klʌtʃ/ verb [T] to hold sth tightly, especially because you are in pain, afraid or excited: *He clutched his mother's hand in fear.* **PHRASAL VERB** **clutch at sth** to try to take hold of sth: *She clutched at the money but the wind blew it away.*

clutch² /klʌtʃ/ noun **1** [C] the part of a vehicle, etc that you press with your foot when you are driving in order to change the speed (**gear**); the part of the engine that it is connected to: *to press/release the clutch* ••➤ picture on page S9 **2 clutches** [pl] power or control over sb: *He fell into the enemy's clutches.*

clutter¹ /'klʌtə/ noun [U] things that are where they are not wanted or needed and make a place untidy: *Who left all this clutter on the floor?* –**cluttered** adj: *a cluttered desk*

clutter² /'klʌtə/ verb [T] **clutter sth** (**up**) to cover or fill sth with lots of objects in an untidy way: *Don't leave those books there – they're cluttering up the table.*

cm abbr centimetre(s)

Co abbr **1** company: *W Smith & Co* **2** county: *Co Down*

c/o abbr (used for addressing a letter to somebody who is staying at another person's house) care of: *Andy Kirkham, c/o Mrs Potter*

★**coach¹** /kəʊtʃ/ noun [C] **1** a person who trains people to compete in certain sports: *a tennis coach* **2** (*Brit*) a comfortable bus used for long journeys: *It's cheaper to travel by coach than by train.* **3** =**CARRIAGE**(1) **4** a large vehicle with four wheels pulled by horses, used in the past for carrying passengers ••➤ Look at **carriage** and **car**.

coach² /kəʊtʃ/ verb [I,T] **coach sb** (**in/for**

C

sth) to train or teach sb, especially to compete in a sport or pass an exam: *She is being coached for the Olympics by a former champion.*

★**coal** /kəʊl/ noun **1** [U] a type of black mineral that is dug (mined) from the ground and burned to give heat: *a lump of coal* ● *a coal fire* **2 coals** [pl] burning pieces of coal ••➤ picture at **fireplace**

coalition /ˌkəʊəˈlɪʃn/ noun [C, with sing or pl verb] a government formed by two or more political parties working together: *a coalition between the socialists and the Green Party*

'**coal mine** (also **pit**) noun [C] a place, usually underground, where coal is dug from the ground ••➤ Look at **colliery**.

'**coal miner** (also **miner**) noun [C] a person whose job is to dig coal from the ground

coarse /kɔːs/ adj **1** consisting of large pieces; rough, not smooth: *coarse salt* ● *coarse cloth* ••➤ opposite **fine 2** (used about a person or his/her behaviour) rude, likely to offend people; having bad manners: *His coarse remarks about women offended her.* –**coarsely** adv: *Chop the onion coarsely* (= into pieces which are not too small). ● *He laughed coarsely.*

coarsen /ˈkɔːsn/ verb [I,T] to become or to make sth coarse

★**coast**[1] /kəʊst/ noun [C] the area of land that is next to or close to the sea: *After sailing for an hour we could finally see the coast.* ● *Scarborough is on the east coast.*

coast[2] /kəʊst/ verb [I] **1** to travel in a car, on a bicycle, etc (especially down a hill) without using power **2** to achieve sth without much effort: *They coasted to victory.*

coastal /ˈkəʊstl/ adj on or near a coast: *coastal areas*

coastguard /ˈkəʊstɡɑːd/ noun [C] a person or group of people whose job is to watch the sea near the coast in order to help people or ships that are in danger or to stop illegal activities

coastline /ˈkəʊstlaɪn/ noun [C] the edge or shape of a coast: *a rocky coastline*

★**coat**[1] /kəʊt/ noun [C] **1** a piece of clothing that you wear over your other clothes to keep warm when you are outside: *Put your coat on – it's cold outside.* ••➤ Look at **overcoat** and **raincoat**. ••➤ picture on page C6 **2** the fur or hair covering an animal's body: *a dog with a smooth coat* **3** a layer of sth covering a surface: *The walls will probably need two coats of paint.*

coat[2] /kəʊt/ verb [T] **coat** sth (**with/in** sth) to cover sth with a layer of sth: *biscuits coated with milk chocolate*

'**coat hanger** = HANGER

coating /ˈkəʊtɪŋ/ noun [C] a thin layer of sth that covers sth else: *wire with a plastic coating*

ˌ**coat of** '**arms** (also **arms**) noun [C] a design that is used as the symbol of a family, a town, a university, etc

coax /kəʊks/ verb [T] **coax** sb (**into/out of** sth/doing sth); **coax** sth **out of/from** sb to persuade sb gently: *The child wasn't hungry, but his mother coaxed him into eating a little.* ● *At last he coaxed a smile out of her.*

cobble /ˈkɒbl/ verb
PHRASAL VERB **cobble** sth **together** to make sth or put sth together quickly and without much care

cobbler /ˈkɒblə/ noun [C] (*old-fashioned*) a person who repairs shoes

cobbles /ˈkɒblz/ (also **cobblestones** /ˈkɒblstəʊnz/) noun [pl] small rounded stones used (in the past) for covering the surface of streets –**cobbled** adj

cobra /ˈkəʊbrə/ noun [C] a poisonous snake that can spread out the skin at the back of its neck. Cobras live in India and Africa.

cobweb /ˈkɒbweb/ noun [C] a net of threads made by a spider in order to catch insects

cocaine /kəʊˈkeɪn/ (also *informal* **coke**) noun [U] a dangerous drug that some people take for pleasure but which is difficult to stop using (addictive)

cock[1] /kɒk/ noun [C] **1** (*US* **rooster**) an adult male chicken ••➤ Look at the note and picture at **chicken**. **2** an adult male bird of any type

cock[2] /kɒk/ verb [T] to hold up a part of the body: *The horse cocked its ears on hearing the noise.*
PHRASAL VERB **cock** sth **up** (*Brit slang*) to do something very badly and spoil sth ••➤ Look at **cock-up**.

cock-a-doodle-doo /ˌkɒk ə ˌduːdl ˈduː/ noun [sing] the noise made by an adult male chicken (cock)

cockerel /ˈkɒkərəl/ noun [C] a young male chicken

cockney /ˈkɒkni/ noun **1** [C] a person who was born and grew up in the East End of London **2** [U] the way of speaking English that is typical of people living in this area: *a cockney accent*

cockpit /ˈkɒkpɪt/ noun [C] **1** the part of a plane where the pilot sits **2** the part of a racing car where the driver sits

cockroach /ˈkɒkrəʊtʃ/ (*US* **roach**) noun [C] a large dark brown insect, usually found in dirty or slightly wet places ••➤ picture at **insect**

cocktail /ˈkɒkteɪl/ noun [C] **1** a drink made from a mixture of alcoholic drinks and fruit juices **2** a mixture of small pieces of food that is served cold: *a prawn cocktail*

'**cock-up** noun [C] (*slang*) something that was badly done; a mistake that spoils sth ••➤ Look at **cock**[2].

cocoa /ˈkəʊkəʊ/ noun **1** [U] a dark brown powder made from the seeds of a tropical tree and used in making chocolate **2** [C,U] a hot drink made from this powder mixed with milk or water; a cup of this drink: *a cup of cocoa*

coconut /ˈkəʊkənʌt/ **noun** [C,U] a large tropical fruit with a hard, hairy shell •➤ picture on page C3

cod /kɒd/ **noun** [C,U] (*pl* **cod**) a large sea fish that lives in the North Atlantic that you can eat

code[1] /kəʊd/ **noun 1** [C,U] a system of words, letters, numbers, etc that are used instead of the real letters or words to make a message or information secret: *They managed to break/crack the enemy code* (= find out what it means). • *They wrote letters to each other in code.* •➤ Look at **bar code**. **2** [C] a group of numbers, letters, etc that is used for identifying sth: *What's the code* (= the telephone number) *for Stockholm?* •➤ Look at **bar code**. **3** [C] a set of rules for behaviour: *a code of practice* (= a set of standards agreed and accepted by a particular profession) • *the Highway Code* (= the rules for driving on the roads)

code[2] /kəʊd/ **verb** [T] **1** (also **encode**) to put or write sth in code[1](1): *coded messages* •➤ opposite **decode 2** to use a particular system for identifying things: *The files are colour-coded: blue for Europe, green for Africa.*

coerce /kəʊˈɜːs/ **verb** [T] (*formal*) **coerce sb (into sth/doing sth)** to force sb to do sth, for example by threatening him/her –**coercion** /kəʊˈɜːʃn/ **noun** [U]

coexist /ˌkəʊɪɡˈzɪst/ **verb** [I] to live or be together at the same time or in the same place as sb/sth –**coexistence noun** [U]

C of E /ˌsiː əv ˈiː/ **abbr** Church of England

★**coffee** /ˈkɒfi/ **noun 1** [U] the cooked beans (**coffee beans**) of a tropical tree, made into powder and used for making a drink: *Coffee is the country's biggest export.* • *coffee beans* **2** [U] a drink made by adding hot water to this powder: *Would you prefer tea or coffee?* • *a cup of coffee* **3** [C] a cup of this drink: *Two coffees please.* •➤ picture on page C4

> **Black coffee** is made without milk; **white coffee** is with milk. **Decaffeinated coffee** has had the caffeine taken out. Coffee can be **weak** or **strong**. **Instant coffee** is sold in a jar and made by pouring hot water or milk onto coffee powder in a cup. **Fresh coffee** is made in a coffee pot from coffee beans that have just been ground.

ˈ**coffee bar** (also ˈ**coffee shop**) **noun** [C] (*Brit*) a place in a hotel, a large shop, etc, where simple food, coffee, tea and other drinks without alcohol are served

ˈ**coffee pot noun** [C] a container in which coffee is made and served •➤ picture on page C4

ˈ**coffee table noun** [C] a small low table for putting magazines, cups, etc, on •➤ picture on page C7

coffin /ˈkɒfɪn/ **noun** [C] (*US* **casket**) a box in which a dead body is buried or burned (**cremated**) •➤ Look at the note at **funeral**.

cogs

cog /kɒɡ/ **noun** [C] one of a series of teeth on the edge of a wheel that fit into the teeth on the next wheel and cause it to move

cognac /ˈkɒnjæk/ **noun 1** [U] a type of strong alcoholic drink (**brandy**) that is made in France **2** [C] a glass of this drink

cohabit /kəʊˈhæbɪt/ **verb** [I] (*formal*) (used about a couple) to live together as if they are married

coherent /kəʊˈhɪərənt/ **adj** clear and easy to understand •➤ opposite **incoherent** –**coherence noun** [U] –**coherently adv**

cohesion /kəʊˈhiːʒn/ **noun** [U] the ability to stay or fit together well: *What the team lacks is cohesion – all the players play as individuals.*

coil[1] /kɔɪl/ **verb** [I,T] to make sth into a round shape: *a snake coiled under a rock*

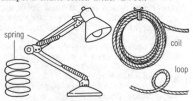
spring
coil
loop

coil[2] /kɔɪl/ **noun** [C] a length of rope, wire, etc that has been made into a round shape: *a coil of rope*

★**coin**[1] /kɔɪn/ **noun** [C] a piece of money made of metal: *a pound coin* •➤ picture at **money**

coin[2] /kɔɪn/ **verb** [T] to invent a new word or phrase: *Who was it who coined the phrase 'a week is a long time in politics'?*

coincide /ˌkəʊɪnˈsaɪd/ **verb** [I] **coincide (with sth) 1** (used about events) to happen at the same time as sth else: *The Queen's visit is timed to coincide with the country's centenary celebrations.* **2** to be exactly the same or very similar: *Our views coincide completely.*

coincidence /kəʊˈɪnsɪdəns/ **noun** [C,U] two or more similar things happening at the same time by chance, in a surprising way: *We hadn't planned to meet, it was just coincidence.*

coincidental /kəʊˌɪnsɪˈdentl/ **adj** resulting from two similar or related events happening at the same time by chance –**coincidentally** /-təli/ **adv**

coke /kəʊk/ **noun** [U] **1** a solid black substance produced from coal and used as a fuel **2** =**COCAINE**

Col **abbr** Colonel

cola /ˈkəʊlə/ **noun** [C,U] a brown, sweet cold drink that does not contain alcohol; a glass or can of this

colander /ˈkʌləndə/ **noun** [C] a metal or plastic bowl with a lot of small holes in it that is used for removing water from food that has been boiled or washed •➤ picture at **kitchen**

★**cold**[1] /kəʊld/ **adj 1** having a low temperature; not hot or warm: *I'm not going into the sea, the water's too cold.* ● *Shall I put the heating on? I'm cold.*

➤ Compare **cold**, **hot**, **cool**, and **warm**. **Cold** indicates a lower temperature than **cool** and may describe a temperature that is unpleasantly low: *a terribly cold winter.* **Cool** means 'fairly cold' and may describe a pleasantly low temperature: *It's terribly hot outside but it's nice and cool in here.* **Hot** indicates a higher temperature than **warm** and may describe a temperature that is unpleasantly high: *I can't drink this yet, it's too hot.* **Warm** means 'fairly hot' and may describe a pleasantly high temperature: *Come and sit by the fire, you'll soon get warm again.*

2 (used about food or drink) not heated or cooked; having become cold after being heated or cooked: *a cold drink* ● *Have your soup before it gets cold.* **3** (used about a person or sb's behaviour) very unfriendly; not showing kindness, understanding, etc: *She gave him a cold, hard look.*

IDIOMS **cold turkey** suddenly and completely, without getting used to sth gradually: *I gave up smoking cold turkey.*

get/have cold feet (*informal*) to become/be afraid to do sth: *She started to get cold feet as her wedding day approached.*

in cold blood in a cruel way and without pity: *to kill sb in cold blood*

★**cold**[2] /kəʊld/ **noun 1** [sing,U] lack of heat; low temperature; cold weather: *We walked home in the snow, shivering with cold.* ● *Come on, let's get out of the cold and go indoors.* **2** [C,U] a common illness of the nose and throat. When you have a cold you have a sore throat and often cannot breathe through your nose: *I think I'm getting a cold.* ● *Wear some warm clothes when you go out or you'll* **catch cold**.

,**cold-'blooded adj 1** having a blood temperature that changes with the temperature of the surroundings: *Reptiles are cold-blooded.* •➤ Look at **warm-blooded**. **2** cruel; having or showing no pity: *cold-blooded killers*

,**cold-'hearted adj** unkind; showing no kindness, understanding, etc

coldly /'kəʊldli/ **adv** in an unfriendly way; in a way that shows no kindness or understanding

coldness /'kəʊldnəs/ **noun** [U] the lack of warm feelings; unfriendly behaviour

colic /'kɒlɪk/ **noun** [U] pain in the stomach area, which especially babies get

collaborate /kə'læbəreɪt/ **verb** [I] **1** collaborate (with sb) (on sth) to work together (with sb), especially to create or produce sth: *She collaborated with another author on the book.* **2** collaborate (with sb) to help the enemy forces who have taken control of your country •➤ This word shows disapproval. –**collaboration** /kə,læbə'reɪʃn/ **noun** [U]

–**collaborator noun** [C]

collage /'kɒlɑːʒ/ **noun** [C,U] a picture made by fixing pieces of paper, cloth, photographs, etc onto a surface; the art of making a picture like this

★**collapse**[1] /kə'læps/ **verb** [I] **1** to fall down or break into pieces suddenly: *A lot of buildings collapsed in the earthquake.* **2** (used about a person) to fall down, usually because you are very ill, and perhaps become unconscious: *The winner collapsed at the end of the race.* **3** (used about a business, plan, etc) to fail suddenly or completely: *The company collapsed, leaving hundreds of people out of work.* **4** to fold sth or be folded into a shape that uses less space

collapse[2] /kə'læps/ **noun 1** [C,U] the sudden or complete failure of sth, such as a business, plan, etc: *The peace talks were on the brink/ verge of collapse.* **2** [sing,U] (used about a building) a sudden fall: *the collapse of the motorway bridge* **3** [sing,U] (used about a person) a medical condition when a person becomes very ill and suddenly falls down

collapsible /kə'læpsəbl/ **adj** that can be folded into a shape that makes sth easy to store: *a collapsible bed*

★**collar**[1] /'kɒlə/ **noun** [C] **1** the part of a shirt, coat, dress, etc that fits round the neck and is often folded over: *a coat with a fur collar* •➤ picture at **lace** •➤ Look at **dog collar**, **blue-collar** and **white-collar**. **2** a band of leather that is put round an animal's neck (especially a dog or cat)

collar[2] /'kɒlə/ **verb** [T] (*informal*) to catch hold of sb who does not want to be caught: *The police officer collared the thief.*

collarbone /'kɒləbəʊn/ **noun** [C] one of the two bones that connect your chest bones to your shoulder •➤ picture on page C5

collateral /kə'lætərəl/ **noun** [C] property or sth valuable that you agree to give if you cannot pay back money that you have borrowed

★**colleague** /'kɒliːɡ/ **noun** [C] a person who works at the same place as you

★**collect**[1] /kə'lekt/ **verb 1** [T] to bring a number of things together: *All the exam papers will be collected at the end.* **2** [T] to get and keep together a number of objects of a particular type over a period of time as a hobby: *He used to collect stamps.* **3** [I,T] to ask for money from a number of people: *to collect for charity* ● *The landlord collects the rent at the end of each month.* **4** [I] to come together; gather: *A crowd collected to see what was going on.* **5** [T] (*especially Brit*) to go and get sb/sth from a particular place; to pick sb/sth up: *to collect the children from school* **6** [T] collect yourself/sth to get control of yourself, your feelings, thoughts, etc: *She collected herself and went back into the room as if nothing had happened.* ● *I tried to* **collect my thoughts** *before the exam.*

collect[2] /kə'lekt/ **adj, adv** (*US*) (used about a telephone call) to be paid for by the person who receives the call: *a collect call* ● *She called me collect.* •➤ In British English, we make a reverse-charge call or reverse the charges.

collected /kə'lektɪd/ *adj* calm and in control of yourself, your feelings, thoughts, etc: *She felt cool, calm and collected before the interview.*

★**collection** /kə'lekʃn/ *noun* **1** [C] a group of objects of a particular type that sb has collected as a hobby: *a stamp collection* **2** [C,U] the act of getting sth from a place or from people: *rubbish collections* **3** [C] a group of people or things: *a large collection of papers on the desk* **4** [C] a number of poems, stories, letters, etc published together in one book: *a collection of modern poetry* **5** [C] the act of asking for money from a number of people (for charity, in church, etc): *a collection for the poor* **6** [C] a variety of new clothes or items for the home that are specially designed and sold at a particular time: *Armani's stunning new autumn collection*

collective[1] /kə'lektɪv/ *adj* shared by a group of people together; not individual: *collective responsibility* –collectively *adv*: *We took the decision collectively at a meeting.*

collective[2] /kə'lektɪv/ *noun* [C, with sing or pl verb] an organization or business that is owned and controlled by the people who work in it

collector /kə'lektə/ *noun* [C] (often in compounds) a person who collects things as a hobby or as part of his/her job: *a stamp collector* ● *a ticket/rent/tax collector*

★**college** /'kɒlɪdʒ/ *noun* **1** [C,U] an institution where you can study after you leave school (at the age of 16): *an art college* ● *a sixth-form college* (= an institution where pupils aged 16 to 18 can prepare for A Levels) ● *She's studying Spanish at the college of further education* (= a college that is not a university where people who have left school can study).

> We talk about **college**, without **the**, when we mean that somebody is attending a college or university as a student: *He's at college in York.* ● *She's going to college in October.* but not if somebody goes there for any other reason: *I went to an art exhibition at the college last night.*

2 [C] (in Britain) one of the separate institutions into which certain universities are divided: *Kings College, London* **3** [C] (in the US) a university, or part of one, where students can study for a degree

collide /kə'laɪd/ *verb* [I] collide (with sb/sth) to crash; to hit sb/sth very hard while moving: *He ran along the corridor and collided with his teacher.*

colliery /'kɒliəri/ *noun* [C] (*pl* collieries) (*especially Brit*) a coal mine and its buildings

collision /kə'lɪʒn/ *noun* [C,U] a crash; an occasion when things or people collide: *It was a head-on collision and the driver was killed instantly.*
[IDIOM] be on a collision course (with sb/sth) **1** to be in a situation which is certain to end in a disagreement or argument: *I'm not sur-*prised they're arguing – they've been on a collision course over money all week. **2** to be moving in a direction which is certain to cause a crash: *The ship was on a collision course with an iceberg.*

colloquial /kə'ləʊkwiəl/ *adj* (used about words, phrases, etc) used in spoken conversation, not in formal situations –colloquially /-kwiəli/ *adv*

collusion /kə'luːʒn/ *noun* [U] (*formal*) secret agreement, especially in order to do sth dishonest: *The drugs were brought into the country with the collusion of customs officials.*

cologne /kə'ləʊn/ = EAU DE COLOGNE

colon /'kəʊlən/ *noun* [C] the mark (:) used before a list, an explanation, an example, etc

colonel /'kɜːnl/ *noun* [C] an officer of a high level in the army

colonial /kə'ləʊniəl/ *adj* connected with or belonging to a country that controls another country (colony): *Spain used to be a major colonial power.*

colonialism /kə'ləʊniəlɪzəm/ *noun* [U] the practice by which a powerful country controls another country or countries, in order to become richer

colonist /'kɒlənɪst/ *noun* [C] a person who goes to live in a country that has become a colony

colonize (also -ise) /'kɒlənaɪz/ *verb* [T] to take control of another country or place and make it a colony –colonization (also -isation) /ˌkɒlənaɪ'zeɪʃn/ *noun* [U]

colony /'kɒləni/ *noun* [C] (*pl* colonies) **1** a country or area that is ruled by another, more powerful country **2** [with sing or pl verb] a group of people who go to live permanently in another country but keep their own habits and traditions **3** a group of the same type of animals, insects or plants living or growing in the same place: *a colony of ants*

color (*US*) = COLOUR

colossal /kə'lɒsl/ *adj* extremely large: *a colossal building* ● *a colossal amount of money*

★**colour**[1] (*US* color) /'kʌlə/ *noun* **1** [C,U] the fact that sth is red, green, yellow, blue, etc: *'What colour is your car?' 'Red.'* ● *What colours do the Swedish team play in?* ● *a dark/deep colour* ● *a bright colour* ● *a light/pale colour* ● *Those flowers certainly give the room a bit of colour.*

> We say that a thing is a certain colour, not that it has a colour.

2 [U] the use of all the colours, not just black and white: *All the pictures in the book are in colour.* ● *a colour television* **3** [U] a red or pink colour in your face, particularly when it shows how healthy you are or that you are embarrassed: *You look much better now, you've got a bit more colour.* ● *Colour flooded her face when she thought of what had happened.* **4** [U] interesting or exciting details: *It's a busy area, full of activity and colour.*
[IDIOMS] off colour ill
with flying colours → FLYING

[I] **intransitive**, a verb which has no object: *He laughed.*   [T] **transitive**, a verb which has an object: *He ate an apple.*

C

★colour² (*US* **color**) /'kʌlə/ **verb** [T] **1** to put colour on sth, for example by painting it: *Colour the picture with your crayons.* ● *The area coloured yellow on the map is desert.* **2** to influence thoughts, opinions, etc: *You shouldn't let one bad experience colour your attitude to everything.*

PHRASAL VERB **colour sth in** to fill a shape, a picture, etc with colour using pencils, paint, etc: *The children were colouring in pictures of animals.*

'colour-blind **adj** unable to see certain colours, especially red and green

coloured /'kʌləd/ (*US* **colored**) **adj 1** having colour or a particular colour: *a coffee-coloured dress* ● *brightly-coloured lights* **2** (used about a person) belonging to a race that does not have white skin •➤ This word is considered offensive nowadays. To refer to a person belonging to a particular racial group, you should use *black*, *Asian*, etc as appropriate.

colourful (*US* **colorful**) /'kʌlə(r)fl/ **adj 1** with bright colours; full of colour: *a colourful shirt* **2** full of interest or excitement: *a colourful story* ● *He has a rather colourful past.*

colouring (*US* **coloring**) /'kʌlərɪŋ/ **noun 1** [U] the colour of a person's hair, skin, etc: *to have a fair/dark colouring* **2** [C,U] a substance that is used to give a particular colour to sth, especially food

colourless (*US* **colorless**) /'kʌlələs/ **adj 1** without any colour: *a colourless liquid, like water* **2** not interesting or exciting; dull

'colour scheme **noun** [C] the way in which colours are arranged, especially in a room

colt /kəʊlt/ **noun** [C] a young male horse

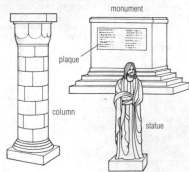

monument

plaque

column

statue

★column /'kɒləm/ **noun** [C] **1** a tall solid vertical post made of stone, supporting or decorating a building or standing alone: *Nelson's Column is a monument in London.* **2** something that has the shape of a column: *a column of smoke* (=smoke rising straight up) **3** one of the vertical sections into which a printed page, especially in a newspaper, is divided **4** a piece of writing in a newspaper or magazine that is part of a regular series or always written by the same writer: *the*

travel/gossip column **5** a series of numbers written one under the other: *to add up a column of figures* **6** a long line of people, vehicles, etc, one following another: *a column of troops*

columnist /'kɒləmnɪst/ **noun** [C] a journalist who writes regular articles in a newspaper or magazine: *a gossip columnist*

coma /'kəʊmə/ **noun** [C] a deep unconscious state, often lasting for a long time and caused by serious illness or injury

comatose /'kəʊmətəʊs/ **adj 1** (*informal*) deeply asleep: *He had drunk a bottle of vodka and was comatose.* **2** (*medical*) deeply unconscious; in a coma

★comb¹ /kəʊm/ **noun 1** [C] a flat piece of metal or plastic with teeth that you use for making your hair tidy **2** [C, usually sing] an act of combing the hair: *Give your hair a comb before you go out.*

comb² /kəʊm/ **verb** [T] **1** to make your hair tidy using a comb **2 comb sth (for sb/sth)** to search an area carefully: *Police are combing the woodland for the murder weapon.*

combat¹ /'kɒmbæt/ **noun** [C,U] a fight, especially in war: *unarmed combat* (= without weapons)

combat² /'kɒmbæt/ **verb** [T] to fight against sth; to try to stop or defeat sth: *to combat terrorism* ● *new medicines to combat heart disease*

combatant /'kɒmbətənt/ **noun** [C] a person who takes part in fighting, especially in war

★combination /ˌkɒmbɪ'neɪʃn/ **noun** [C,U] a number of people or things mixed or joined together; a mixture: *The team manager still hasn't found the right combination of players.* ● *On this course, you may study French in combination with Spanish or Italian.*

★combine¹ /kəm'baɪn/ **verb 1** [I,T] **combine (with sb/sth)** to join or mix two or more things together: *The two organizations combined to form one company.* ● *Bad planning, combined with bad luck, led to the company's collapse.* **2** [T] **combine A and/with B** to do or have two or more things at the same time: *This car combines speed and reliability.*

combine² /'kɒmbaɪn/ (*Brit also* **ˌcombine 'harvester**) **noun** [C] a large farm machine that both cuts corn and separates the grain from the rest of the plant •➤ Look at **harvest.**

combined /kəm'baɪnd; kəm'baɪnz/ **adj** done by a number of people joining together, resulting from the joining of two or more things: *The combined efforts of the emergency services prevented a major disaster.*

combustion /kəm'bʌstʃən/ **noun** [U] the process of burning

★come /kʌm/ **verb** [I] (*pt* **came** /keɪm/; *pp* **come**) **1** to move to or towards the person who is speaking or the place that sb is talking about: *Come here, please.* ● *Come and see what I've found.* ● *I hope you can come to my party.* ● *They're coming to stay for a week.* ● *The children came running into the room.* **2 come (to...)** to arrive somewhere or reach a particular place or time: *What time are you coming home?* • *Has the newspaper come yet?* • *After a few hours in the jungle, we came to a river* • *Her hair comes down to her waist.* • *The water in the pool came up to our knees.* • *The time has come to say goodbye.* **3** to be in a particular position in a series: *March comes after February.* • *Charlie came second in the exam.* • *I can't wait to find out what comes next in the story.* **4 come in sth** to be available: *This blouse comes in a choice of four colours.* • *Do these trousers come in a larger size?* **5** to be produced by or from sth: *Wool comes from sheep.* **6** to become open or loose: *Your blouse has come undone.* • *Her hair has come untied.* **7 come to do sth** used for talking about how, why or when sth happened: *How did you come to lose your passport?* **8 come to/into sth** to reach a particular state: *We were all sorry when the holiday came to an end.* • *The military government came to power in a coup d'état.*

➤ For other idioms containing **come**, look at the entries for the nouns, adjectives, etc, for example **come to a head** is at **head**.

IDIOMS **come and go** to be present for a short time and then go away: *The pain in my ear comes and goes.*

come easily/naturally to sb to be easy for sb to do: *Apologizing does not come easily to her.*

come to nothing; not come to anything to fail; to not be successful: *Unfortunately, all his efforts came to nothing.*

how come...? (*informal*) why or how: *How come you're back so early?*

to come (used after a noun) in the future: *You'll regret it in years to come.*

when it comes to sth/to doing sth when it is a question of sth: *When it comes to value for money, these prices are hard to beat.*

PHRASAL VERBS **come about** to happen: *How did this situation come about?*

come across/over (as sth) to make an impression of a particular type: *Elizabeth comes across as being rather shy.*

come across sb/sth to meet or find sb/sth by chance: *I came across this book in a second-hand shop.* •➤ synonym **encounter**

come along 1 to arrive or appear: *An old man was coming along the road.* **2** =COME ON (2) **3** =COME ON(3)

come apart to break into pieces: *This old coat is coming apart at the seams.*

come away (from sth) to become loose or unfastened: *The wallpaper is coming away from the wall in the corner.*

come away with sth to leave a place with a particular opinion or feeling: *We came away with a very favourable impression of Cambridge.*

come back 1 to return: *I don't know what time I'll be coming back.* **2** to become popular or fashionable again: *Flared trousers are coming back again.*

come back (to sb) to be remembered: *When I went to Italy again, my Italian started to come back to me.*

come before sb/sth to be more important than sb/sth else: *Mark feels his family comes before his career.*

come between sb and sb to damage the relationship between two people: *Arguments over money came between the two brothers.*

come by sth to manage to get sth: *Fresh vegetables are hard to come by in the winter.*

come down 1 to fall down: *The power lines came down in the storm.* **2** (used about an aircraft or spacecraft) to land: *The helicopter came down in a field.* **3** (used about prices) to become lower: *The price of land has come down in the past year.*

come down to sth/to doing sth (*informal*) to be able to be explained by a single important point: *It all comes down to having the right qualifications.*

come down with sth to become ill with sth: *I think I'm coming down with flu.*

come forward to offer help: *The police are asking witnesses to come forward.*

come from... to live in or have been born in a place: *Where do you come from originally?*

come from (doing) sth to be the result of sth: *'I'm tired.' 'That comes from all the late nights you've had.'*

come in 1 to enter a place: *Come in and sit down.* **2** (used about the tides of the sea) to move towards the land and cover the beach •➤ Look at **tide**[1]. **3** to become popular or fashionable: *Punk fashions came in in the seventies.* **4** (used about news or information) to be received: *Reports are coming in of fighting in Beirut.*

come in for sth to receive sth, especially sth unpleasant: *The government came in for a lot of criticism.*

come of sth/of doing sth to be the result of sth: *We've written to several companies asking for help but nothing has come of it yet.*

come off 1 to be able to be removed: *Does the hood come off?* **2** (*informal*) to be successful: *The deal seems unlikely to come off.* **3** (*informal*) (followed by an adverb) to be in a good, bad, etc situation as a result of sth: *Unfortunately, Dennis came off worst in the fight.*

come off (sth) 1 to fall off sth: *Kim came off her bicycle and broke her leg.* **2** to become removed from sth: *One of the legs has come off this table.*

come off it (*spoken*) used to say that you do not believe sb/sth or that you strongly disagree with sb: *'I thought it was quite a good performance.' 'Oh, come off it – it was awful!'*

come on 1 to start to act, play in a game of sport, etc: *The audience jeered every time the villain came on.* • *The substitute came on in the second half.* **2** (also **come along**) to make progress or to improve: *Your English is coming on nicely.* **3 Come on!** (also **Come along!**) used to tell sb to hurry up, try harder, etc: *Come on or we'll be late!* **4** to begin: *I think I've got a cold coming on.*

come out 1 to appear; to be published: *The rain stopped and the sun came out.* • *The report came out in 1998.* **2** to become known: *It was only after his death that the truth came* *out.* **3** (used about a photograph, etc) to be produced successfully: *Only one of our photos came out.*

come out (of sth) to be removed from sth: *Red wine stains don't come out easily.*

come out against sth to say in public that you do not like or agree with sth: *The Prime Minister came out against capital punishment.*

come out in sth to become covered in spots, etc: *Heat makes him come out in a rash.*

come out with sth to say sth unexpectedly: *The children came out with all kinds of stories.*

come over = COME ACROSS/OVER

come over (to...) (from...) to visit people or a place a long way away: *They've invited us to come over to Australia for a holiday.*

come over sb (used about a feeling) to affect sb: *A feeling of despair came over me.*

come round 1 (used about an event that happens regularly) to happen: *The end of the holidays always comes round very quickly.* **2** (also **come to**) to become conscious again ••► opposite **pass out**

come round (to...) to visit a person or place not far away: *Do you want to come round for lunch on Saturday?*

come round (to sth) to change your opinion so that you agree with sb/sth: *They finally came round to our way of thinking.*

come through (used about news, information, etc) to arrive: *The football results are just coming through.*

come through (sth) to escape injury or death in a dangerous situation, illness, etc: *to come through an enemy attack*

come to = COME ROUND(2)

come to sth 1 to equal or total a particular amount: *The bill for the meal came to £35.* **2** to result in a bad situation: *We will sell the house to pay our debts if we have to but we hope it won't come to that.*

come under to be included in a particular section, department, etc: *Garages that sell cars come under 'car dealers' in the telephone book.*

come up 1 to happen or be going to happen in the future: *Something's come up at work so I won't be home until late tonight.* **2** to be discussed or mentioned: *The subject of religion came up.* **3** (used about the sun and moon) to rise **4** (used about a plant) to appear above the soil

come up against sb/sth to find a problem or difficulty that you have to deal with: *I had to stop when I came up against a high fence.*

come up to sth to be as good as usual or as necessary: *This piece of work does not come up to your usual standard.*

come up with sth to find an answer or solution to sth: *Engineers have come up with new ways of saving energy.*

comeback /'kʌmbæk/ **noun** [C] a return to a position of strength or importance that you had before: *The former world champion is hoping to make a comeback.*

comedian /kə'miːdiən/ (also **comic**) **noun**

[C] a person whose job is to entertain people and make them laugh, for example by telling jokes ••► A female comedian is sometimes called a **comedienne**.

comedown /'kʌmdaʊn/ **noun** [C, usually sing] (*informal*) a loss of importance or social position: *It's a bit of a comedown for her having to move to a smaller house.*

comedy /'kɒmədi/ **noun** (*pl* **comedies**) **1** [C] an amusing play, film, etc that has a happy ending ••► Look at **tragedy**. **2** [U] the quality of being amusing or making people laugh

comet /'kɒmɪt/ **noun** [C] an object in space that looks like a bright star with a tail and that moves around the sun

★**comfort**[1] /'kʌmfət/ **noun 1** [U] the state of having everything your body needs, or of having a pleasant life: *Most people expect to live in comfort in their old age.* • *to travel in comfort* **2** [U] the feeling of being physically relaxed and in no pain: *This car has been specially designed for extra comfort.* ••► opposite **discomfort**. **3** [U] help or kindness to sb who is suffering: *I tried to offer a few words of comfort.* **4 be a comfort (to sb)** [sing] a person or thing that helps you when you are very sad or worried: *You've been a real comfort to me.* **5** [C] something that makes your life easier or more pleasant: *the comforts of home*

comfort[2] /'kʌmfət/ **verb** [T] to try to make sb feel less worried or unhappy: *to comfort a crying child*

★**comfortable** /'kʌmftəbl/ **adj 1** (also *informal* **comfy**) that makes you feel physically relaxed and in no pain; that provides you with everything your body needs: *a comfortable temperature* (= not too hot or too cold) • *Sit down and make yourselves comfortable.* • *a comfortable pair of shoes* ••► opposite **uncomfortable**. **2** not having or causing worry, difficulty, etc: *He did not feel comfortable in the presence of so many women.* **3** having or providing enough money for all your needs: *They are not wealthy but they're quite comfortable.* –**comfortably** adv: *Jon was sitting comfortably in the armchair.* • *You can't live comfortably on such low wages.*

comic[1] /'kɒmɪk/ **adj** that makes you laugh; connected with comedy: *a comic scene in a play*

comic[2] /'kɒmɪk/ **noun** [C] **1** =COMEDIAN **2** (*especially US* **comic book**) a magazine for children that tells stories through pictures

comical /'kɒmɪkl/ **adj** that makes you laugh; funny –**comically** /-kli/ **adv**

'comic strip (also **'strip cartoon**) **noun** [C] a short series of pictures that tell a funny story, for example in a newspaper

coming /'kʌmɪŋ/ **noun** [C] the moment when sth new arrives or begins: *The coming of the computer meant the loss of many jobs.* –**coming** adj: *We've got a lot of plans for the coming year.*

comma /'kɒmə/ **noun** [C] the mark (,) used

for dividing parts of a sentence or items in a list

★**command**¹ /kəˈmɑːnd/ *verb* **1** [I,T] (*formal*) command (sb to do sth) to tell or order sb to do sth: *I command you to leave now!* **2** command sb/sth [T] to control or be in charge of sb/sth: *to command a ship/regiment/army* **3** [T] to deserve and get sth: *The old man commanded great respect.*

★**command**² /kəˈmɑːnd/ *noun* **1** [C] an order: *The captain's commands must be obeyed without question.* **2** [U] control over sb/sth: *Who is in command of the expedition?* • *to take command of a situation* **3** [sing] the state of being able to do or use sth well: *She has a good command of French.*

IDIOMS **at/by sb's command** (*formal*) because you were ordered by sb: *At the command of their officer the troops opened fire.*

be at sb's command to be ready to obey sb: *I'm completely at your command.*

commandeer /ˌkɒmənˈdɪə/ *verb* [T] to take control or possession of sth for military or police use

commander /kəˈmɑːndə/ *noun* [C] **1** a person who controls or is in charge of a military organization or group **2** (*Brit*) an officer at a fairly high level in the navy

commanding /kəˈmɑːndɪŋ/ *adj* **1** in charge or having control of sb/sth: *Who is your commanding officer?* **2** strong or powerful: *to speak in a commanding tone of voice*

commandment (also **Commandment**) /kəˈmɑːndmənt/ *noun* [C] (*formal*) one of the ten important laws that Christian people should obey

commando /kəˈmɑːndəʊ/ *noun* [C] (*pl* **commandos**) one of a group of soldiers who is trained to make sudden attacks in enemy areas

commemorate /kəˈmeməreɪt/ *verb* [T] to exist or take place in order to make people remember a special event: *a statue commemorating all the soldiers who died in the last war* –**commemoration** /kəˌmeməˈreɪʃn/ *noun* [C,U]: *The concerts were held in commemoration of the 200th anniversary of Mozart's death.*

commence /kəˈmens/ *verb* [I,T] (*formal*) commence sth/doing sth to start or begin –**commencement** *noun* [C,U]

commend /kəˈmend/ *verb* [T] (*formal*) to say officially that sb/sth is very good: *Dean was commended for his excellent work.*

commendable /kəˈmendəbl/ *adj* (*formal*) that people think is good: *She acted with commendable honesty and fairness.*

★**comment**¹ /ˈkɒment/ *noun* [C,U] comment (on sth) something that you say or write that gives your opinion or feeling about sth: *The chancellor was not available for comment.* • *I heard someone make a rude comment about my clothes.* •➤ Look at **observation** and **remark**.

IDIOM **no comment** used in reply to a question when you do not want to say anything at all: *'Mr President, how do you feel about these latest developments?' 'No comment.'*

comment² /ˈkɒment/ *verb* [I,T] comment (on sth) to sat what you think or feel about sth: *Several people commented on how ill David looked.*

commentary /ˈkɒməntri/ *noun* (*pl* **commentaries**) **1** [C,U] a spoken description on the radio or television of sth as it is happening: *a sports commentary* **2** [C] a written explanation or discussion of sth such as a book or play **3** [C] something that shows what sth is like: *This drug scandal is a sad commentary on the state of the sport.*

commentate /ˈkɒmənteɪt/ *verb* [I] commentate (on sth) to give a spoken description on the radio or television of sth as it is happening

commentator /ˈkɒmənteɪtə/ *noun* [C] **1** a person who commentates on sth: *a sports commentator* **2** a person who gives his/her opinion about sth on the radio, on television or in a newspaper: *a political commentator*

commerce /ˈkɒmɜːs/ *noun* [U] the business of buying and selling things

★**commercial**¹ /kəˈmɜːʃl/ *adj* **1** connected with buying and selling goods and services: *commercial law* **2** making or trying to make money: *Although it won a lot of awards, the film was not a commercial success.* **3** selling sth or sold in large quantities to the public: *commercial airlines* • *commercial products* –**commercially** /-ʃəli/: *The factory was closed down because it was no longer commercially viable.*

commercial² /kəˈmɜːʃl/ *noun* [C] an advertisement on television or the radio: *a commercial break* (= a space between television programmes when commercials are shown)

commercialism /kəˈmɜːʃəlɪzəm/ *noun* [U] the attitude that making money is more important than anything else

commercialize (also **-ise**) /kəˈmɜːʃəlaɪz/ *verb* [T] to try to make money out of sth, even if it means spoiling it: *Christmas has become very commercialized over recent years.* –**commercialization** (also **-isation**) /kəˌmɜːʃəlaɪˈzeɪʃn/ *noun* [U]

commiserate /kəˈmɪzəreɪt/ *verb* [I] (*formal*) commiserate (with sb) (on/over/for sth) to feel sorry for and show understanding towards sb who is unhappy or in difficulty: *I commiserated with Debbie over losing her job.*

commission¹ /kəˈmɪʃn/ *noun* **1** (often **Commission**) [C, with sing or pl verb] an official group of people who are asked to find out about sth: *A Commission was appointed to investigate the causes of the accident.* **2** [C,U] money that you get for selling sth: *Agents get 10% commission on everything they sell.* **3** [C,U] money that a bank, etc charges for providing a particular service: [U] **3** [C] a formal request to an artist, writer, etc to produce a piece of work: *He received a commission to write a play for the festival.*

commission² /kəˈmɪʃn/ *verb* [T] commission sb (to do sth); commission sth (from sb) to ask an artist, writer, etc to do a piece of work: *to commission an architect to design a building*

commissioner /kə'mɪʃənə/ **noun** [C] the head of the police or of a government department in some countries

★**commit** /kə'mɪt/ **verb** [T] (**committing**; **committed**) **1** to do sth bad or illegal: *to commit a crime* • *to commit suicide* **2** commit sb/yourself (to sth/to doing sth) to make a definite agreement or promise to do sth: *I can't commit myself to helping you tomorrow.* **3** commit yourself (on sth) to make a decision or give an opinion publicly so that it is then difficult to change it: *I'm not going to commit myself on who will win the election.* •➤ Look at **noncommittal**. **4** (*formal*) to decide to use money or time in a certain way: *The government has committed £2 billion to education.* **5** (*formal*) commit sb to sth to send sb to a prison, mental hospital, etc

commitment /kə'mɪtmənt/ **noun 1** [U] commitment (to sth) being prepared to give a lot of your time and attention to sth because you believe it is right or important: *I admire Gary's commitment to protecting the environment.* **2** [C,U] a promise or agreement to do sth; a responsibility: *When I make a commitment I always stick to it.* • *Helen now works fewer hours because of family commitments.*

committed /kə'mɪtɪd/ **adj** committed (to sth) prepared to give a lot of your time and attention to sth because you believe it is right or important: *The company is committed to providing quality products.*

★**committee** /kə'mɪti/ **noun** [C,with sing or pl verb] a group of people who have been chosen to discuss sth or decide sth: *to be/sit on a committee* • *The planning committee meets/meet twice a week.*

commodity /kə'mɒdəti/ **noun** [C] (*pl* **commodities**) a product or material that can be bought and sold: *Salt was once a very valuable commodity.*

★**common**[1] /'kɒmən/ **adj 1** happening or found often or in many places; usual: *Pilot error is the commonest/most common cause of plane crashes.* • *The daisy is a common wild flower.* **2** common (to sb/sth) shared by or belonging to two or more people or groups; shared by most or all people: *This type of behaviour is common to most children of that age.* • *We have a common interest in gardening.* **3** (only *before* a noun) not special; ordinary: *The officers had much better living conditions than the common soldiers.* **4** (*Brit informal*) having or showing a lack of education: *Don't speak like that. It's common!* •➤ opposite for senses 1 and 3 **uncommon**
IDIOM be common/public knowledge → KNOWLEDGE

common[2] /'kɒmən/ **noun** [C] an area of open land that anyone can use
IDIOMS have sth in common (with sb/sth) to share sth with sb/sth else: *to have a lot in common with sb*

in common with sb/sth (*formal*) in the same way as sb/sth else; like sb/sth: *This company, in common with many others, is losing a lot of money.*

,common 'ground **noun** [U] beliefs, interests, etc that two or more people or groups share

,common 'law **noun** [U] laws in England that are based on decisions that judges have made, not laws that were made by Parliament

commonly /'kɒmənli/ **adv** normally; usually

commonplace /'kɒmənpleɪs/ **adj** not exciting or unusual; ordinary: *Foreign travel has become commonplace in recent years.*

'common room **noun** [C] a room in a school, university, etc where students or teachers can go to relax when they are not in class

the Commons /'kɒmənz/ = **THE HOUSE OF COMMONS** •➤ Look at the note at **Parliament**.

,common 'sense **noun** [U] the ability to make good sensible decisions or to behave in a sensible way

the Commonwealth /'kɒmənwelθ/ **noun** [sing] the group of countries that once formed the British Empire and that work together in a friendly way

commotion /kə'məʊʃn/ **noun** [sing,U] great noise or excitement

communal /kə'mju:nl; 'kɒmjənl/ **adj** shared by a group of people: *a communal kitchen*

commune /'kɒmju:n/ **noun** [C,with sing or pl verb] a group of people, not from the same family, who live together and share their property and responsibilities

★**communicate** /kə'mju:nɪkeɪt/ **verb 1** [I,T] to share and exchange information, ideas or feelings with sb: *Parents often have difficulty communicating with their teenage children.* • *Our boss is good at communicating her ideas to the team.* **2** [T] (*formal*) (usually passive) to pass a disease from one person or animal to another **3** [I] to lead from one place to another: *two rooms with a communicating door*

★**communication** /kə,mju:nɪ'keɪʃn/ **noun 1** [U] the act of sharing or exchanging information, ideas or feelings: *Radio is the only means of communication in remote areas.* • *We are in regular communication with our head office in New York.* **2** communications [pl] the methods that are used for travelling to and from a place or for sending messages between places: *The telephone lines are down so communications are very difficult.* **3** [C] (*formal*) a message: *a communication from head office*

communicative /kə'mju:nɪkətɪv/ **adj** willing and able to talk and share ideas, etc: *Paolo has excellent communicative skills.*

communion /kə'mju:niən/ **noun** [U] **1** (*formal*) the sharing of thoughts or feelings **2** Communion a Christian church ceremony in which people share bread and wine

communiqué /kə'mju:nɪkeɪ/ **noun** [C] (*written*) an official statement, especially from a government, a political group, etc

communism /'kɒmjunɪzəm/ **noun** [U] the political system in which the state owns and controls all factories, farms, services etc and aims to treat everyone equally ••➤ Look at **Marxism**, **socialism** and **capitalism**.

communist (also **Communist**) /'kɒmjənɪst/ **noun** [C] a person who believes in or supports communism; a member of the Communist Party —**communist** (also **Communist**) **adj**: *communist sympathies*

★**community** /kə'mju:nəti/ **noun** (*pl* **communities**) **1 the community** [sing] all the people who live in a particular place, area, etc when considered as a group: *Recent increases in crime have disturbed the whole community.* **2** [C,with sing or pl verb] a group of people who have sth in common: *the Asian community in Britain* • *the business community* **3** [U] the feeling of belonging to a group in the place where you live: *There is a strong sense of community in the neighbourhood.*

com'munity centre **noun** [C] a building that local people can use for meetings, classes, sports, etc

commute /kə'mju:t/ **verb** [I] to travel a long distance from home to work every day: *A lot of people commute to London from nearby towns.* –**commuter** **noun** [C]

compact /kəm'pækt/ **adj** small and easy to carry: *a compact camera*

compact 'disc = **CD**

companion /kəm'pæniən/ **noun** [C] a person or animal with whom you spend a lot of time or go somewhere: *a travelling companion*

companionship /kəm'pæniənʃɪp/ **noun** [U] the pleasant feeling of having a friendly relationship with sb and not being alone

★**company** /'kʌmpəni/ **noun** (*pl* **companies**) **1** [C,with sing or pl verb] a business organization selling goods or services: *The company is/are planning to build a new factory.*

➤ In names company is written with a capital letter. The abbreviation is **Co**: *the Walt Disney Company* • *Milton & Co*

2 [C,with sing or pl verb] a group of actors, singers, dancers, etc: *a ballet company* • *the Royal Shakespeare Company* **3** [U] being with a person: *I always enjoy Rachel's company.* • *Jeff is very good company* (= pleasant to be with). **4** [U] a visitor or visitors: *Sorry, I wouldn't have called if I'd known you had company.*

IDIOMS **keep sb company** to go or be with sb so that he/she is not alone: *She was nervous so I went with her to keep her company.*

part company ➔ **PART²**

comparable /'kɒmpərəbl/ **adj** **comparable (to/with sb/sth)** of a similar standard or size; that can be compared with sth: *The population of Britain is comparable to that of France.* • *A comparable flat in my country would be a lot cheaper.*

comparative¹ /kəm'pærətɪv/ **adj** **1** that compares things of the same kind: *a comparative study of systems of government* **2** compared with sth else or with what is usual or normal: *He had problems with the written exam but passed the practical exam with comparative ease.* **3** (*grammar*) (used about the form of an adjective or adverb) expressing a greater amount, quality, size, etc: *'Hotter' and 'more quickly' are the comparative forms of 'hot' and 'quickly'.*

comparative² /kəm'pærətɪv/ **noun** [C] (*grammar*) the form of an adjective or adverb that expresses a greater amount, quality, size, etc: *'Bigger' is the comparative of 'big'.*

comparatively /kəm'pærətɪvli/ **adv** when compared with sth else or with what is usual; fairly: *The disease is comparatively rare nowadays.*

★**compare** /kəm'peə/ **verb** **1** [T] **compare A and B; compare A with/to B** to consider people or things in order to see how similar or how different they are: *I'm quite a patient person, compared with him.* • *Compared to the place where I grew up, this town is exciting.* • *When the police compared the two letters, they realized that they had been written by the same person.* **2** [T] **compare A to B** to say that sb/sth is similar to sb/sth else: *When it was built, people compared the stadium to a spaceship.* **3** [I] **compare (with/to sb/sth)** to be as good as sb/sth: *Her last film was brilliant but this one simply doesn't compare.* • *There is nothing to compare with the taste of bread fresh from the oven.*

IDIOM **compare notes (with sb)** to discuss your opinions, ideas, experiences, etc with sb else: *At the beginning of term we met and compared notes about the holidays.*

★**comparison** /kəm'pærɪsn/ **noun** [C,U] a act of comparing; a statement in which people or things are compared: *Put the new one and the old one side by side, for comparison.* • *It's hard to make comparisons between two athletes from different sports.*

IDIOM **by/in comparison (with sb/sth)** when compared: *In comparison with many other people, they're quite well-off.*

compartment /kəm'pɑ:tmənt/ **noun** [C] **1** one of the separate sections into which some larger parts of a train (carriages) are divided: *a first-class compartment* **2** one of the separate sections into which certain containers are divided: *The drugs were discovered in a secret compartment in his suitcase.*

★**compass** /'kʌmpəs/ **noun** [C] **1** an instrument for finding direction, with a needle that always points north: *They had to find their way back to the camp using a map and a compass.* **2** **compasses** [pl] a V-shaped instrument that is used for drawing circles: *a pair of compasses*

compassion /kəm'pæʃn/ **noun** [U] compassion (for sb) understanding or pity for sb who is suffering: *to have/feel/show compassion* –**compassionate** /-ʃənət/ **adj**

compatible /kəm'pætəbl/ **adj** **compatible (with sb/sth)** suitable to be used together, or

---

[I] **intransitive**, a verb which has no object: *He laughed.*   [T] **transitive**, a verb which has an object: *He ate an apple.*

to live or exist together: *These two computer systems are not compatible.* • *Lee's diet is not compatible with his active lifestyle.* •➤ opposite **incompatible** –compatibility /kəm͵pætə-'bɪləti/ **noun** [U]

compatriot /kəm'pætriət/ **noun** [C] a person who comes from the same country as you

compel /kəm'pel/ **verb** [T] (**compelling**; **compelled**) (*formal*) compel sb to do sth to force sb to do sth: *I felt compelled to tell her what I really thought of her.*

compelling /kəm'pelɪŋ/ **adj** that forces or persuades you to do or to believe sth: *compelling evidence* •➤ noun **compulsion**

compensate /'kɒmpenseɪt/ **verb 1** [I] compensate (for sth) to remove or reduce the bad effect of sth: *His willingness to work hard compensates for his lack of skill.* **2** [I,T] compensate (sb) (for sth) to pay sb money because you have injured him/her or lost or damaged his/her property: *The airline sent me a cheque to compensate for losing my luggage.*

compensation /͵kɒmpen'seɪʃn/ **noun 1** [U] compensation (for sth) money that you pay to sb because you have injured him/her or lost or damaged his/her property: *I got £5000 (in) compensation for my injuries.* **2** [C,U] a fact or action that removes or reduces the bad effect of sth: *City life can be very tiring but there are compensations* (= good things about it).

compère /'kɒmpeə/ **noun** [C] (*Brit*) a person who entertains the audience and introduces the different performers in a show –compère **verb** [T]: *Who compèred the show?*

★**compete** /kəm'piːt/ **verb** [I] compete (in sth) (against/with sb) (for sth) to try to win or achieve sth, or to try to be better than sb else: *The world's best athletes compete in the Olympic Games.* • *We'll be competing against seven other teams for the trophy.* • *As children, they always used to compete with each other.* • *Supermarkets have such low prices that small shops just can't compete.*

competence /'kɒmpɪtəns/ **noun** [U] the fact of having the ability or skill that is needed for sth: *She quickly proved her competence in her new position.* •➤ opposite **incompetence**

competent /'kɒmpɪtənt/ **adj 1** having the ability or skill needed for sth: *a highly competent player* • *She is competent at her job.* •➤ opposite **incompetent 2** good enough, but not excellent: *The singer gave a competent, but not particularly exciting, performance.* –competently **adv**

★**competition** /͵kɒmpə'tɪʃn/ **noun 1** [C] an organized event in which people try to win sth: *to go in for/enter a competition* • *They hold a competition every year to find the best young artist.* • *He came second in an international piano competition.* **2** [U] a situation where two or more people or organizations are trying to achieve, obtain, etc the same thing or to be better than sb else: *He is in competition with three other people for promotion.* • *There was fierce competition*

among the players for places in the team. **3 the competition** [sing, with sing or pl verb] the other people, companies, etc who are trying to achieve the same as you: *If we are going to succeed, we must offer a better product than the competition.*

competitive /kəm'petɪtɪv/ **adj 1** involving people or organizations competing against each other: *The travel industry is a highly competitive business.* • *competitive sports* **2** able to be as successful as or more successful than others: *They are trying to make the company competitive in the international market.* • *Our prices are highly competitive* (= as low as or lower than those of the others). **3** (used about people) wanting very much to win or to be more successful than others: *She's a very competitive player.* –competitively **adv**: *Their products are competitively priced.* –competitiveness **noun** [U]

competitor /kəm'petɪtə/ **noun** [C] a person or organization that is competing against others: *There are ten competitors in the first race.* • *Two local companies are our main competitors.*

compilation /͵kɒmpɪ'leɪʃn/ **noun 1** [C] a collection of pieces of music, writing, film, etc that are taken from different places and put together: *A compilation CD of the band's greatest hits.* **2** [U] the act of compiling sth

compile /kəm'paɪl/ **verb** [T] to collect information and arrange it in a list, book, etc: *to compile a dictionary/a report/a list*

complacent /kəm'pleɪsnt/ **adj** feeling too satisfied with yourself or with a situation, so that you think that there is no need to worry: *He had won his matches so easily that he was in danger of becoming complacent.* –complacency /kəm'pleɪsnsi/ **noun** [U] –complacently **adv**

★**complain** /kəm'pleɪn/ **verb** [I] **1** complain (to sb) (about sth/that...) to say that you are not satisfied with or happy about sth: *People are always complaining about the weather.* • *We complained to the hotel manager that the room was too noisy.* •➤ Look at the notes at **grumble** and **protest. 2** (*formal*) complain of sth to say that you have a pain or illness: *He went to the doctor, complaining of chest pains.*

★**complaint** /kəm'pleɪnt/ **noun** complaint (about sth); complaint (that...) **1** [C] a statement that you are not satisfied with sth: *You should make a complaint to the company that made the machine.* **2** [U] the act of complaining: *I wrote a letter of complaint to the manager about the terrible service I had received.* • *Jim's behaviour never gave the teachers cause for complaint.* **3** [C] an illness or disease: *a heart complaint*

complement[1] /'kɒmplɪmənt/ **noun** [C] (*formal*) **1** a thing that goes together well with sth else: *A cream sauce is the perfect complement to this dessert.* **2** the total number that makes a group complete: *Without a full complement of players, the team will not be able to take part in the match.* **3** (*grammar*) a word or words, especially a noun or adjective, used after a verb such as 'be' or 'become' and describing the subject of that verb: *In 'He's friendly' and 'He's a fool', 'friendly' and 'fool' are complements.*

complement² /'kɒmplɪmənt/ **verb** [T] to go together well with: *The colours of the furniture and the carpet complement each other.*

complementary /ˌkɒmplɪ'mentri/ **adj** going together well with sb/sth; adding sth which the other person or thing does not have: *They work well together because their skills are complementary: he's practical and she's creative.*

★**complete¹** /kəm'pliːt/ **adj** **1** having or including all parts; with nothing missing: *I gave a complete list of the stolen items to the police.* ● *The book explains the complete history of the place.* **2** (not before a noun) finished or ended: *The repair work should be complete by Friday.* •➤ opposite for senses 1 and 2 **incomplete** **3** complete (with sth) including sth extra, in addition to what is expected: *The computer comes complete with instruction manual and printer.* **4** (only before a noun) as great as possible; total; in every way: *It was a complete waste of time.* ● *The room is a complete mess.* –completeness **noun** [U]

★**complete²** /kəm'pliːt/ **verb** [T] **1** to make sth whole: *We need two more players to complete the team.* **2** to finish sth; to bring sth to an end: *When the building has been completed, it will look impressive.* ● *He completed his teacher training course in June 1997.* **3** to write all the necessary information on sth (for example a form): *Please complete the following in capital letters.*

completely /kəm'pliːtli/ **adv** in every way; fully; totally: *The building was completely destroyed by fire.*

completion /kəm'pliːʃn/ **noun** [U] (*formal*) the act of finishing sth or the state of being finished: *You will be paid on completion of the work.* ● *The new motorway is due for completion within two years.*

★**complex¹** /'kɒmpleks/ **adj** made up of several connected parts and often difficult to understand; complicated: *a complex problem/subject*

complex² /'kɒmpleks/ **noun** [C] **1** a group of connected things, especially buildings: *a shopping/sports complex* **2** a complex (about sth) a mental problem that makes sb worry a lot about sth: *He's got a complex about his height.* ● *an inferiority complex*

complexion /kəm'plekʃn/ **noun** [C] **1** the natural colour and quality of the skin on your face: *a dark/fair complexion* ● *a healthy complexion* **2** [usually sing] the general nature or character of sth: *These announcements put a different complexion on our situation.*

complexity /kəm'pleksəti/ **noun** (*pl* **complexities**) **1** [U] the state of being complex and difficult to understand: *an issue of great complexity* **2** [C] one of the many details that

make sth complicated: *I haven't time to explain the complexities of the situation now.*

compliant /kəm'plaɪənt/ **adj** (*formal*) compliant (with sth) working or done in agreement with particular rules, orders, etc: *All new products must be compliant with EU specifications.* –compliance **noun** [U]: *A hard hat must be worn at all times **in compliance with** safety regulations.*

★**complicate** /'kɒmplɪkeɪt/ **verb** [T] to make sth difficult to understand or deal with: *Let's not complicate things by adding too many details.* –complicated **adj**: *a novel with a very complicated plot*

complication /ˌkɒmplɪ'keɪʃn/ **noun** [C] **1** something that makes a situation hard to understand or to deal with: *Unless there are any unexpected complications, I'll be arriving next month.* **2** a new illness that you get when you are already ill: *Unless he develops complications, he'll be out of hospital in a week.*

complicity /kəm'plɪsəti/ **noun** [U] (*formal*) the fact of being involved with sb else in a crime

compliment¹ /'kɒmplɪmənt/ **noun** **1** [C] a compliment (on sth) a statement or action that shows admiration for sb: *People often **pay** her **compliments** on her piano playing.* **2** **compliments** [pl] (*formal*) used to say that you like sth or to thank sb for sth: *Tea and coffee are provided with the compliments of the hotel management* (= without charge).

compliment² /'kɒmplɪment/ **verb** [T] compliment sb (on sth) to say that you think sb/sth is very good: *She complimented them on their smart appearance.*

complimentary /ˌkɒmplɪ'mentri/ **adj** **1** showing that you think sb/sth is very good: *He made several complimentary remarks about her work.* **2** given free of charge: *a complimentary theatre ticket*

comply /kəm'plaɪ/ **verb** [I] (*pres part* **complying**; *3rd pers sing pres* **complies**; *pt, pp* **complied**) (*formal*) comply (with sth) to obey an order or request: *All office buildings must comply with the fire and safety regulations.*

component /kəm'pəʊnənt/ **noun** [C] one of several parts of which sth is made: *The human eye has two main components.* ● *the components of a machine/system* –component **adj**: *the component parts of an engine*

compose /kəm'pəʊz/ **verb** **1** [T] to be the parts that together form sth: *the parties that compose the coalition government* **2** [I,T] to write music: *Mozart composed forty-one symphonies.* **3** [T] to produce a piece of writing, using careful thought: *I sat down and composed a letter of reply.* **4** [T] to make yourself, your feelings, etc become calm and under control: *The news came as such a shock that it took me a while to **compose myself**.*

composed /kəm'pəʊzd/ **adj** **1** composed of sth made or formed from several different parts, people, etc: *The committee is composed* *of politicians from all parties.* **2** calm, in control of your feelings: *Although he felt very nervous, he managed to appear composed.*

composer /kəm'pəʊzə/ **noun** [C] a person who writes music

composite /'kɒmpəzɪt/ **adj** consisting of different parts or materials –**composite noun** [C]

composition /ˌkɒmpə'zɪʃn/ **noun 1** [U] the parts that form sth; the way in which the parts of sth are arranged: *the chemical composition of a substance* • *the composition of the population* **2** [C] a piece of music that has been written by sb: *Chopin's best-known compositions* **3** [U] the act or skill of writing a piece of music or text: *She studied both musical theory and composition.* **4** [C] a short piece of writing done at school, in an exam, etc: *Write a composition of about 300 words on one of the following subjects.*

compost /'kɒmpɒst/ **noun** [U] a mixture of dead plants, old food, etc that is added to soil to help plants grow

composure /kəm'pəʊʒə/ **noun** [U] the state of being calm and having your feelings under control: *The goalkeeper couldn't regain his composure after his mistake.*

compound¹ /'kɒmpaʊnd/ **noun** [C] **1** something that consists of two or more things or substances combined together: *a chemical compound* **2** (*grammar*) a word or phrase consisting of two or more parts that combine to make a single meaning: *'Car park' and 'bad-tempered' are compounds.* **3** an area of land with a group of buildings on it, surrounded by a wall or fence

compound² /kəm'paʊnd/ **verb** [T] to make sth such as a problem worse

comprehend /ˌkɒmprɪ'hend/ **verb** [T] (*formal*) to understand sth completely: *She's too young to comprehend what has happened.*

comprehensible /ˌkɒmprɪ'hensəbl/ **adj** easy to understand: *The book is written in clear, comprehensible language.* ••➤ opposite **incomprehensible**

comprehension /ˌkɒmprɪ'henʃn/ **noun 1** [U] (*formal*) the ability to understand: *The horror of war is beyond comprehension.* ••➤ opposite **incomprehension 2** [C,U] an exercise that tests how well you understand spoken or written language: *a listening comprehension*

comprehensive¹ /ˌkɒmprɪ'hensɪv/ **adj 1** including everything or nearly everything that is connected with a particular subject: *a guide book giving comprehensive information on the area* **2** (*Brit*) (used about education) educating children of all levels of ability in the same school: *a comprehensive education system*

comprehensive² /ˌkɒmprɪ'hensɪv/ (also **compre'hensive school**) **noun** [C] (*Brit*) a secondary school in which children of all levels of ability are educated: *I went to the local comprehensive.*

comprehensively /ˌkɒmprɪ'hensɪvli/ **adv** completely; thoroughly

compress /kəm'pres/ **verb** [T] **compress** sth (into sth) to make sth fill less space than usual: *Divers breathe compressed air from tanks.* • *He found it hard to compress his ideas into a single page.* –**compression** /kəm'preʃn/ **noun** [U]

comprise /kəm'praɪz/ **verb** [T] **1** to consist of; to have as parts or members: *a house comprising three bedrooms, kitchen, bathroom and a living room* **2** to form or be part of sth: *Women comprise 62% of the staff.*

compromise¹ /'kɒmprəmaɪz/ **noun** [C,U] a compromise (between/on sth) an agreement that is reached when each person gets part, but not all, of what he/she wanted: *to reach a compromise* • *Both sides will have to be prepared to make compromises.*

compromise² /'kɒmprəmaɪz/ **verb 1** [I] **compromise (with sb) (on sth)** to accept less than you want or are aiming for, especially in order to reach an agreement: *Unless both sides are prepared to compromise, there will be no peace agreement.* • *The company never compromises on the quality of its products.* **2** [T] **compromise sb/sth/yourself** to put sb/sth/yourself in a bad or dangerous position, especially by doing sth that is not very sensible: *He compromised himself by accepting money from them.*

compulsion /kəm'pʌlʃn/ **noun 1** [U] the act of forcing sb to do sth or being forced to do sth: *There is no compulsion to take part. You can decide yourself.* ••➤ verb **compel 2** [C] a strong desire that you cannot control, often to do sth that you should not do; an urge: *Tony sometimes felt a strong compulsion to tell lies.*

compulsive /kəm'pʌlsɪv/ **adj 1** (used about a bad or harmful habit) caused by a strong desire that you cannot control: *compulsive eating* **2** (used about a person) having a bad habit that he/she cannot control: *a compulsive gambler/shoplifter* **3** so interesting or exciting that you cannot take your attention away from it: *This book makes compulsive reading.* –**compulsively adv**

★**compulsory** /kəm'pʌlsəri/ **adj** that must be done, by law, rules, etc; obligatory: *Maths and English are compulsory subjects on this course.* • *It is compulsory to wear a hard hat on the building site.* ••➤ Something that you do not have to do is **non-compulsory**, **voluntary** or **optional**.

compute /kəm'pjuːt/ **verb** [T] (*formal*) to calculate sth

★**computer** /kəm'pjuːtə/ **noun** [C] an electronic machine that can store, find and arrange information, calculate amounts and control other machines: *The bills are all done by computer.* • *a computer program* • *a home/personal computer* • *computer software/games* • *First of all, the details are fed into a computer.* ••➤ picture on page S7

computerize (also **-ise**) /kəm'pjuːtəraɪz/ **verb** [T] to use computers to do a job or to store information: *The whole factory has been computerized.* • *We have now computerized* *the library catalogue.* –computerization (also -isation) /kəm,pju:tərɑɪ'zeɪʃn/ noun [U]

com,puter-'literate adj able to use a computer

computing /kəm'pju:tɪŋ/ noun [U] the use of computers: *She did a course in computing.*

Con (also **Cons**) abbr (in British politics) Conservative

con¹ /kɒn/ verb [T] (**conning; conned**) (*informal*) **con sb (into doing sth/out of sth)** to cheat sb, especially in order to get money: *He conned her into investing in a company that didn't really exist.* ● *The old lady was conned out of her life savings.*

con² /kɒn/ noun [C] (*informal*) a trick, especially in order to cheat sb out of some money

IDIOM **the pros and cons** → PRO

concave /kɒn'keɪv/ adj having a surface that curves towards the inside of sth, like the inside of a bowl ●● Look at **convex**.

conceal /kən'si:l/ verb [T] (*formal*) **conceal sth/sb (from sb/sth)** to hide sb/sth; to prevent sb/sth from being seen or discovered: *She tried to conceal her anger from her friend.* –concealment noun [U]: *the concealment of the facts of the case*

concede /kən'si:d/ verb [T] (*formal*) **1** to admit that sth is true although you do not want to: *When it was clear that he would lose the election, he conceded defeat.* ● *She conceded that the problem was mostly her fault.* **2 concede sth (to sb)** to allow sb to take sth although you do not want to: *They lost the war and had to concede territory to their enemy.* ●● noun **concession**

conceit /kən'si:t/ noun [U] too much pride in yourself and your abilities and importance –conceited adj: *He's so conceited – he thinks he's the best at everything!*

conceivable /kən'si:vəbl/ adj possible to imagine or believe: *I made every conceivable effort to succeed.* ●● opposite **inconceivable** –conceivably /-əbli/ adv: *She might just conceivably be telling the truth.*

conceive /kən'si:v/ verb **1** [T] (*formal*) to think of a new an idea or plan: *He conceived the idea for the novel during his journey through India.* **2** [I,T] (*formal*) **conceive (of) sb/sth (as sth)** to think about sb/sth in a particular way; to imagine: *He started to conceive of the world as a dangerous place.* **3** [I,T] to become pregnant ●● noun **conception**

★**concentrate** /'kɒnsntreɪt/ verb [I,T] **1 concentrate (sth) (on sth/doing sth)** to give all your attention or effort to sth: *I need to concentrate on passing this exam.* ● *I tried to concentrate my thoughts on the problem.* **2** to come together or to bring people or things together in one place: *Most factories are concentrated in one small area of the town.*

concentrated /'kɒnsntreɪtɪd/ adj **1** showing determination: *With one concentrated effort we can finish the work by tonight.* **2** made stronger by the removal of some liquid: *This is concentrated orange juice. You have to add water before you drink it.* ●● opposite **dilute**

★**concentration** /,kɒnsn'treɪʃn/ noun **1** [U] **concentration (on sth)** the ability to give all your attention or effort to sth: *This type of work requires total concentration.* ● *Don't lose your concentration or you might make a mistake.* **2** [C] **concentration (of sth)** a large amount of people or things in one place: *There is a high concentration of chemicals in the drinking water here.*

,**concen'tration camp** noun [C] a prison (usually a number of buildings inside a high fence) where political prisoners are kept in very bad conditions

concentric /kən'sentrɪk/ adj (used about circles of different sizes) having the same centre point

★**concept** /'kɒnsept/ noun [C] **the concept (of sth/that...)** an idea; a basic principle: *It is difficult to grasp the concept of eternity.* –conceptual /kən'septʃʊəl/ adj

conception /kən'sepʃn/ noun [C,U] **1 (a) conception (of sth)** an understanding of how or what sth is: *We have no real conception of what people suffered during the war.* **2** the process of forming an idea or a plan **3** the moment when a woman or female animal becomes pregnant ●● verb **conceive**

★**concern¹** /kən'sɜ:n/ verb [T] **1** to affect or involve sb/sth: *This does not concern you. Please go away.* ● *It is important that no risks are taken where safety is concerned.* **2** to be about sth: *The main problem concerns the huge cost of the project.* **3** to worry sb: *What concerns me is that we have no long-term plan.* **4 concern yourself with sth** to give your attention to sth: *You needn't concern yourself with the hotel booking. The travel agent will take care of it.*

IDIOMS **be concerned in sth** to have a connection with or be involved in sth: *She was concerned in a drugs case some years ago.*

be concerned with sth to be about sth: *Tonight's programme is concerned with the effects of the law on ordinary people..*

★**concern²** /kən'sɜ:n/ noun **1** [C,U] **concern (for/about/over sb/sth); concern (that...)** a feeling of worry; sth that causes worry: *The safety officer assured us that there was no cause for concern.* ● *My main concern is that we'll run out of money.* **2** [C] something that is important to you or that involves you: *Financial matters are not my concern.* **3** [C] a company or business: *a large industrial concern*

IDIOM **a going concern** → GOING²

concerned /kən'sɜ:nd/ adj **concerned (about/for sth); concerned (that...)** worried and feeling concern about sth: *If you are concerned about your baby's health you should consult a doctor immediately.* ●● opposite **unconcerned**

concerning /kən'sɜ:nɪŋ/ prep about; on the subject of: *She refused to answer questions concerning her private life.*

★**concert** /'kɒnsət/ noun [C] a performance of music: *The band is on tour doing concerts all*

c

over the country. ••➤ Look also at **recital.**

IDIOM in concert (with sb/sth) (*formal*) working together with sb/sth

concerted /kən'sɜːtɪd/ *adj* done by a group of people working together: *We must all make a concerted effort to finish the work on time.*

concertina /ˌkɒnsə'tiːnə/ *noun* [C] a musical instrument that you hold in your hands and play by pressing the ends together and pulling them apart ••➤ A concertina is like a small **accordion.** ••➤ Look at the note at **piano.** ••➤ picture at **music**

concerto /kən'tʃɜːtəʊ/ *noun* [C] (*pl* **concertos**) a piece of music for an orchestra with one instrument playing an important part (**solo**): *Mozart's second piano concerto*

concession /kən'seʃn/ *noun* **1** [C,U] (a) concession (to sb/sth) something that you agree to do in order to end an argument: *Employers have been forced to **make concessions** to the union.* ••➤ verb **concede 2** [C] a lower price for certain groups of people: *Concessions are available for students and pensioners.*

concessionary /kən'seʃənəri/ *adj* having a lower price for certain groups of people: *a concessionary fare*

conciliation /kənˌsɪli'eɪʃn/ *noun* [U] the process of ending an argument or disagreement: *All attempts at conciliation have failed and civil war seems inevitable.*

conciliatory /kən'sɪliətəri/ *adj* that tries to end an argument or disagreement: *a conciliatory speech/gesture*

concise /kən'saɪs/ *adj* giving a lot of information in a few words; brief: *He gave a clear and concise summary of what had happened.* –**concisely** *adv* –**conciseness** *noun* [U]

conclude /kən'kluːd/ *verb* **1** [T] conclude sth from sth to form an opinion as the result of thought or study: *From the man's strange behaviour I concluded that he was drunk.* **2** [I,T] (*formal*) to end or to bring sth to an end: *The Prince concluded his tour with a visit to a charity concert.* **3** [T] conclude sth (with sb) to formally arrange or agree to sth: *conclude a business deal/treaty*

★**conclusion** /kən'kluːʒn/ *noun* **1** [C] the conclusion (that...) an opinion that you reach after thinking about sth carefully: *After trying to phone Bob for days, I came to the conclusion that he was on holiday.* • *Have you reached any conclusions from your studies?* **2** [C,usually sing] (*formal*) an end to sth: *Let us hope the peace talks reach a successful conclusion.* **3** [U] an act of arranging or agreeing to sth formally: *The summit ended with the conclusion of an arms-reduction treaty.*

IDIOMS a foregone conclusion → **FOREGONE** in conclusion finally; lastly jump to conclusions → **JUMP¹**

conclusive /kən'kluːsɪv/ *adj* that shows sth is definitely true or real: *The blood tests gave conclusive proof of Robson's guilt.* ••➤ opposite **inconclusive** –**conclusively** *adv*

concoct /kən'kɒkt/ *verb* [T] **1** to make sth unusual by mixing different things together **2** to make up or invent sth (an excuse, a story, etc) –**concoction** /kən'kɒkʃn/ *noun* [C]

concourse /'kɒŋkɔːs/ *noun* [C] a large hall or space inside a building such as a station or an airport

concrete¹ /'kɒŋkriːt/ *adj* real or definite; not only existing in the imagination: *Can you give me a concrete example of what you mean?* ••➤ opposite **abstract** –**concretely** *adv*

concrete² /'kɒŋkriːt/ *noun* [U] a hard substance made from cement mixed with sand, water, small stones (**gravel**), etc, that is used in building: *a modern office building of glass and concrete* • *a concrete floor/bridge*

concrete³ /'kɒŋkriːt/ *verb* [T] concrete sth (over) to cover sth with concrete

concur /kən'kɜː/ *verb* [I] (**concurring; concurred**) (*formal*) to agree

concurrent /kən'kʌrənt/ *adj* existing or happening at the same time as sth else –**concurrently** *adv*: *The semi-finals are played concurrently, so it is impossible to watch both.*

concuss /kən'kʌs/ *verb* [T] (usually passive) to injure sb's brain by hitting his/her head: *I was slightly concussed when I fell off my bicycle.* –**concussion** /kən'kʌʃn/ *noun* [U]

★**condemn** /kən'dem/ *verb* [T] **1** condemn sb/sth (for/as sth) to say strongly that you think sb/sth is very bad or wrong: *A government spokesman condemned the bombing as a cowardly act of terrorism.* **2** condemn sb (to sth/to do sth) to say what sb's punishment will be; to sentence sb: *The murderer was condemned to death.* • (*figurative*) *Their poor education condemns them to a series of low-paid jobs.* **3** condemn sth (as sth) to say officially that sth is not safe enough to use: *The building was condemned as unsafe and was demolished.*

condemnation /ˌkɒndem'neɪʃn/ *noun* [C,U] the act of condemning sth; a statement that condemns: *The bombing brought condemnation from all around the world.*

condensation /ˌkɒnden'seɪʃn/ *noun* [U] small drops of liquid that are formed when warm air touches a cold surface

condense /kən'dens/ *verb* **1** [I,T] to change or make sth change from gas to liquid: *Steam condenses into water when it touches a cold surface.* ••➤ Look at **evaporate. 2** [T] condense sth (into sth) to make smaller or shorter so that it fills less space: *We'll have to condense these three chapters into one.*

condescend /ˌkɒndɪ'send/ *verb* [I] **1** condescend (to sb) to behave towards sb in a way that shows that you think you are better or more important than him/her; to patronize sb **2** condescend (to do sth) to do sth that you believe is below your level of importance: *Celia only condescends to speak to me when she wants me to do something for her.* –**condescending** *adj*: *a condescending smile* –**condescension** /ˌkɒndɪ'senʃn/ *noun* [U]

★**condition**¹ /kən'dɪʃn/ noun **1** [U,sing] the state that sb/sth is in: *to be in poor/good/ excellent condition* ● *He looks really ill. He is certainly not in a condition to drive home.* **2** [C] something that must happen so that sth else can happen or be possible: *One of the conditions of the job is that you agree to work on Sundays.* ● *He said I could borrow his bike on one condition – that I didn't let anyone else ride it.* **3 conditions** [pl] the situation or surroundings in which people live, work or do things: *The prisoners were kept* **in** *terrible conditions.* ● *poor living/housing/working conditions* **4** [C] a medical problem that you have for a long time: *to have a heart/lung condition*

IDIOMS **on condition (that...)** only if: *I agreed to help on condition that I got half the profit.*

on no condition (*formal*) not for any reason: *On no condition must the press find out about this.*

out of condition not physically fit

condition² /kən'dɪʃn/ verb [T] to affect or control the way that sb/sth behaves: *Boys are conditioned to feel that they are stronger than girls.*

★**conditional** /kən'dɪʃənl/ adj **1 conditional (on/upon sth)** that only happens if sth else is done or happens first: *My university place is conditional on my getting good marks in the exams.* ••➤ opposite **unconditional 2** (*grammar*) describing a situation that must exist before sth else can happen. A conditional sentence often contains the word 'if': *'Unless you study, you won't pass the exam' is a conditional sentence.*

➤ For more information about conditional sentences, look at the **Quick Grammar Reference** section at the back of this dictionary.

–conditionally /-ʃənəli/ adv

conditioner /kən'dɪʃənə/ noun [C,U] a substance that keeps sth in a good condition: *Do you use conditioner on your hair?*

condolence /kən'dəʊləns/ noun [pl,U] an expression of how sorry you feel for sb whose relative or close friend has just died: *offer your condolences* ● *a message of condolence*

condom /'kɒndɒm/ (also *informal* **rubber**) noun [C] a thin rubber covering that a man wears over his sexual organ during sex to prevent the woman from becoming pregnant or as protection against disease

condominium /ˌkɒndə'mɪniəm/ (also *informal* **condo** /'kɒndəʊ/) noun [C] (*US*) a flat or block of flats owned by the people who live in them

condone /kən'dəʊn/ verb [T] to accept or agree with sth that most people think is wrong: *I can never condone violence – no matter what the circumstances are.*

conducive /kən'djuːsɪv/ adj (*formal*) conducive (to sth) helping or making sth happen: *This hot weather is not conducive to hard work.*

conduct¹ /kən'dʌkt/ verb [T] **1** (*formal*) to organize and do sth, especially research: *to conduct tests/a survey/an inquiry* **2** to stand in front of an orchestra and direct the musicians **3** (*formal*) **conduct yourself well, badly, etc** to behave in a particular way **4** to allow heat or electricity to pass along or through sth: *Rubber does not conduct electricity.*

conduct² /'kɒndʌkt/ noun [U] **1** a person's behaviour: *His conduct has always been of the highest standard.* ● *a code of conduct* (= a set of rules for behaviour) **2** (*formal*) **conduct of sth** the act of controlling or organizing sth: *She was criticized for her conduct of the bank's affairs.*

conductor /kən'dʌktə/ noun [C] **1** a person who stands in front of an orchestra and directs the musicians **2** (*Brit*) a person whose job is to collect money from passengers on a bus or to check their tickets **3** (*US*) = **GUARD**¹ (5) **4** a substance that allows heat or electricity to pass through or along it

cone /kəʊn/ noun [C] **1** a shape or object that has a round base and a point at the top: *traffic cones* ● *an ice cream cone* ••➤ adjective **conical** ••➤ picture at **cube 2** the hard fruit of some trees (**pine** and **fir**) ••➤ picture on page C2 ••➤ Look at **conifer**.

confectionery /kən'fekʃənəri/ noun [U] sweets, cakes, chocolates, etc

confederation /kənˌfedə'reɪʃn/ noun [C,U] an organization of smaller groups which have joined together: *a confederation of independent republics*

confer /kən'fɜː/ verb (**conferring**; **conferred**) **1** [I] confer (with sb) (on/about sth) to discuss sth with sb before making a decision: *The President is conferring with his advisers.* **2** [T] (*written*) confer sth (on sb) to give sb a special right or advantage

★**conference** /'kɒnfərəns/ noun [C] a large official meeting, often lasting several days, at which members of an organization, profession, etc meet to discuss important matters: *an international conference on global warming*

★**confess** /kən'fes/ verb [I,T] confess (to sth/to doing sth); confess (sth) (to sb) to admit that you have done sth bad or wrong: *The young woman confessed to the murder of her boyfriend/to murdering her boyfriend.* ● *They confessed to their mother that they had spent all the money.* ••➤ Look at **own up (to sth).** It is less formal.

confession /kən'feʃn/ noun [C,U] an act of admitting that you have done sth bad or wrong: *The police persuaded the man to make a full confession.*

confetti /kən'feti/ noun [U] small pieces of coloured paper that people throw over a man and woman who have just got married

confide /kən'faɪd/ verb [T] **confide sth to sb** to tell sb sth that is secret: *She did not confide her love to anyone – not even to her best friend.*

PHRASAL VERB **confide in sb** to talk to sb that you trust about sth secret or private

C

[I] **intransitive**, a verb which has no object: *He laughed.*   [T] **transitive**, a verb which has an object: *He ate an apple.*

★**confidence** /'kɒnfɪdəns/ noun [U] **1** confidence (in sb/sth) trust or strong belief in sb/sth: *The public is losing confidence in the present government.* ● *I have every confidence in Emily's ability to do the job.* **2** the feeling that you are sure about your own abilities, opinion, etc: *I didn't have the confidence to tell her I thought she was wrong.* ● *to be full of confidence* ● *'Of course we will win,' the team captain said with confidence.* ••➤ Look at **self-confidence**. **3** a feeling of trust in sb to keep sth a secret: *The information was given to me in strict confidence.* ● *It took a while to win/gain her confidence.*

'**confidence trick** noun [C] a way of getting money by cheating sb

★**confident** /'kɒnfɪdənt/ adj confident (of sth/that...); confident (about sth) feeling or showing that you are sure about your own abilities, opinions, etc: *Kate feels confident of passing/that she can pass the exam.* ● *to be confident of success* ● *You should feel confident about your own abilities.* ● *Dillon has a very confident manner.* ••➤ Look at **self-confident**. –**confidently** adv: *She stepped confidently onto the stage and began to sing.*

confidential /ˌkɒnfɪ'denʃl/ adj secret; not to be shown or told to other people: *The letter was marked 'private and confidential'.* –**confidentiality** /ˌkɒnfɪˌdenʃi'æləti/ noun [U] –**confidentially** /-ʃəli/ adv

confine /kən'faɪn/ verb [T] **1** confine sb/sth (in/to sth) to keep a person or animal in a particular, usually small, place: *The prisoners are confined to their cells for long periods at a time.* **2** confine sb/sth/yourself to sth to stay within the limits of sth: *Please confine your questions to the topic we are discussing.*

confined /kən'faɪnd/ adj (used about a space) very small

confinement /kən'faɪnmənt/ noun [U] being kept in a small space: *to be kept in solitary confinement* (= in a prison)

confines /'kɒnfaɪnz/ noun [pl] (*formal*) the limits of sth: *Patients are not allowed beyond the confines of the hospital grounds.*

★**confirm** /kən'fɜ:m/ verb [T] **1** to say or show that sth is true; to make sth definite: *Seeing the two of them together confirmed our suspicions.* ● *Can you confirm that you will be able to attend?* **2** to accept sb as a full member of a Christian Church in a special ceremony: *He was confirmed at the age of thirteen.* –**confirmation** /ˌkɒnfə'meɪʃn/ noun: *We are waiting for confirmation of the report.*

confirmed /kən'fɜ:md/ adj (only *before* a noun) fixed in a particular habit or way of life: *a confirmed bachelor*

confiscate /'kɒnfɪskeɪt/ verb [T] to take sth away from sb as a punishment: *Any cigarettes found in school will be confiscated.* –**confiscation** /ˌkɒnfɪ'skeɪʃn/ noun [C,U]

★**conflict**[1] /'kɒnflɪkt/ noun [C,U] **1** (a) conflict with sb/sth (over sth) a fight or an argument: *an armed conflict* ● *The new laws have brought the Government into conflict with the unions over pay increases.* **2** a difference between two or more ideas, wishes, etc: *Many women have to cope with the conflict between their career and their family.* ● *a conflict of interests*

conflict[2] /kən'flɪkt/ verb [I] A and B conflict; A conflicts with B to disagree with or be different from sb/sth: *The statements of the two witnesses conflict.* ● *John's statement conflicts with yours.* ● *conflicting results*

conform /kən'fɔ:m/ verb [I] conform (to sth) **1** to obey a rule or law: *This building does not conform to fire regulations.* **2** to behave in the way that other people and society expect you to behave: *Children are under a lot of pressure to conform when they first start school.* –**conformity** /kən'fɔ:məti/ noun [U]

conformist /kən'fɔ:mɪst/ noun [C] a person who behaves in the way that people are expected to behave by society ••➤ opposite **non-conformist**

confront /kən'frʌnt/ verb [T] **1** confront sth; confront sb with sb/sth to think about, or to make sb think about, sth that is difficult or unpleasant: *to confront a problem/difficulty/issue* ● *When the police confronted him with the evidence, he confessed.* **2** to stand in front of sb, for example because you want to fight him/her: *The unarmed demonstrators were confronted by a row of soldiers.*

confrontation /ˌkɒnfrʌn'teɪʃn/ noun [C,U] a fight or an argument

★**confuse** /kən'fju:z/ verb [T] **1** (usually passive) to make sb unable to think clearly or to know what to do: *He confused everybody with his pages of facts and figures.* **2** confuse A and/with B to mistake sb/sth for sb/sth else: *I often confuse Lee with his brother. They look very much alike.* **3** to make sth complicated: *The situation is confused by the fact that so many organizations are involved.*

★**confused** /kən'fju:zd/ adj **1** not able to think clearly: *When he regained consciousness he was dazed and confused.* **2** difficult to understand: *The article is very confused – I don't know what the main point is.* –**confusedly** /-ədli/ adv

★**confusing** /kən'fju:zɪŋ/ adj difficult to understand: *Her instructions were contradictory and confusing.* –**confusingly** adv

★**confusion** /kən'fju:ʒn/ noun [U] **1** the state of not being able to think clearly or not understanding sth: *He stared in confusion at the exam paper.* ● *There is still a great deal of confusion as to the true facts.* **2** a state of disorder: *Their unexpected visit threw all our plans into confusion.* **3** the act of mistaking sb/sth for sb/sth else: *To avoid confusion, all luggage should be labelled with your name and destination.*

congeal /kən'dʒi:l/ verb [I,T] (used about a liquid) to become solid; to make a liquid solid: *congealed blood*

congenial /kən'dʒi:niəl/ adj (*formal*) pleasant: *We spent an evening in congenial company.*

congenital /kən'dʒenɪtl/ adj (used about a

disease) beginning at and continuing since birth

congested /kən'dʒestɪd/ **adj** so full of sth that nothing can move: *The streets of London are congested with traffic.* —congestion /kən'dʒestʃən/ **noun** [U]: *severe traffic congestion*

conglomerate /kən'ɡlɒmərət/ **noun** [C] a large firm made up of several different companies

conglomeration /kən,ɡlɒmə'reɪʃn/ **noun** [C] a group of many different things that have been brought together

★**congratulate** /kən'ɡrætʃuleɪt/ **verb** [T] congratulate sb (on sth) to tell sb that you are pleased about sth he/she has done; to praise sb: *I congratulated Sue on passing her driving test.*

★**congratulations** /kən,ɡrætʃu'leɪʃnz/ **noun** [pl] used for telling sb that you are pleased about sth he/she has done: *Congratulations on the birth of your baby boy!*

congregate /'kɒŋɡrɪɡeɪt/ **verb** [I] to come together in a crowd or group

congregation /,kɒŋɡrɪ'ɡeɪʃn/ **noun** [C,with sing or pl verb] the group of people who attend a particular church

★**congress** /'kɒŋɡres/ **noun** [C] **1** a large formal meeting or series of meetings: *a medical congress* **2 Congress** the name in some countries (for example the US) for the group of people who are elected to make the laws
> The US Congress is made up of the **Senate** and the **House of Representatives.**

congressional /kən'ɡreʃənl/ **adj** connected with a congress or Congress

conical /'kɒnɪkl/ **adj** having a round base and getting narrower towards a point at the top ••> noun **cone**

conifer /'kɒnɪfə; 'kəʊn-/ **noun** [C] a tree with short, very thin leaves (needles) that stay green all through the year and that has hard brown fruit (cones) –coniferous /kə'nɪfərəs/ **adj**

conjecture /kən'dʒektʃə/ **verb** [I,T] (*formal*) to guess about sth without real proof or evidence –conjecture **noun** [C,U]

conjugate /'kɒndʒəɡeɪt/ **verb** [T] to give the different forms of a verb –conjugation /,kɒndʒu'ɡeɪʃn/ **noun** [C,U]

conjunction /kən'dʒʌŋkʃn/ **noun** [C] a word that is used for joining other words, phrases or sentences: *'And', 'but' and 'or' are conjunctions.*
IDIOM in conjunction with sb/sth together with sb/sth

conjure /'kʌndʒə/ **verb** [I] to do tricks by clever, quick hand movements, that appear to be magic –conjuring **noun** [U]
PHRASAL VERB conjure sth up **1** to cause an image to appear in your mind: *Hawaiian music conjures up images of sunshine, flowers and sandy beaches.* **2** to make sth appear quickly or suddenly: *Mum can conjure up a meal out of almost anything.*

conjuror (also **conjurer**) /'kʌndʒərə/ **noun**

[C] a person who does clever tricks that appear to be magic ••> Look at **magician.**

conker /'kɒŋkə/ (*Brit informal*) (also **horse chestnut**) **noun** [C] the seed of the horse chestnut tree, used in a children's game (conkers)

★**connect** /kə'nekt/ **verb 1** [I,T] connect (sth) (up) (to/with sth) to be joined to sth; to join sth to sth else: *The tunnels connect (up) ten metres further on.* ● *The printer is connected to the computer.* ● *This motorway connects Oxford with Birmingham.* ••> Look at **disconnect.** **2** [T] connect sb/sth (with sb/sth) to have an association with sb/sth else; to realize or show that sb/sth is involved with sb/sth else: *There was no evidence that she was connected with the crime.* **3** [I] connect (with sth) (used about a bus, train, plane, etc) to arrive at a particular time so that passengers can change to another bus, train, plane, etc: *a connecting flight*

★**connection** /kə'nekʃn/ **noun 1** [C] a connection between A and B; a connection with/to sth an association or relationship between two or more people or things: *Is there any connection between the two organizations?* ● *What's your connection with Brazil? Have you worked there?* **2** [C] a place where two wires, pipes, etc join together: *The radio doesn't work. There must be a loose connection somewhere.* **3** [C] a bus, train, plane, etc that leaves soon after another arrives: *Our bus was late so we missed our connection.*
IDIOMS in connection with sb/sth (*formal*) about or concerning: *I am writing to you in connection with your application.*
in this/that connection (*formal*) about or concerning this/that

connive /kə'naɪv/ **verb** [I] connive at sth; connive (with sb) (to do sth) to work secretly with sb to do sth that is wrong; to do nothing to stop sb doing sth wrong: *The two parties connived to get rid of the president.*

connoisseur /,kɒnə'sɜː/ **noun** [C] a person who knows a lot about art, good food, music, etc

connotation /,kɒnə'teɪʃn/ **noun** [C] an idea expressed by a word in addition to its main meaning: *'Spinster' means a single woman but it has negative connotations.*

★**conquer** /'kɒŋkə/ **verb** [T] **1** to take control of a country or city and its people by force, especially in a war: *Napoleon's ambition was to conquer Europe.* ● (*figurative*) *The young singer conquered the hearts of audiences all over the world.* **2** to succeed in controlling or dealing with a strong feeling, problem, etc: *She's trying to conquer her fear of flying.*

conqueror /'kɒŋkərə/ **noun** [C] a person who has conquered (1) sth

conquest /'kɒŋkwest/ **noun 1** [C,U] an act of conquering sth: *the Norman conquest* (= of England in 1066) ● *the conquest of Mount Everest* **2** [C] an area of land that has been taken in a war

conscience /'kɒnʃəns/ **noun** [C,U] the part

of your mind that tells you if what you are doing is right or wrong: *a clear/a guilty conscience*

IDIOM **have sth on your conscience** to feel guilty because you have done sth wrong

conscientious /ˌkɒnʃiˈenʃəs/ *adj* **1** (used about people) careful to do sth correctly and well: *He's a conscientious worker.* **2** (used about actions) done with great care and attention: *conscientious work* –**conscientiously** *adv*

conscientious ob'jector *noun* [C] a person who refuses to join the army, etc because he/she believes it is morally wrong to kill other people

★**conscious** /ˈkɒnʃəs/ *adj* **1** able to see, hear, feel, etc things; awake: *The injured driver was still conscious when the ambulance arrived.* ∙∙➤ opposite **unconscious 2** conscious (of sth/that...) noticing or realizing that sth exists; aware of sth: *She didn't seem conscious of the danger.* ● *Bill suddenly became conscious that someone was following him.* **3** that you do on purpose or for a particular reason: *We made a conscious effort to treat both children equally.* ∙∙➤ Look at **deliberate**. It has a similar meaning. –**consciously** *adv*

★**consciousness** /ˈkɒnʃəsnəs/ *noun* **1** [U] the state of being able to see, hear, feel, etc: *As he fell, he hit his head and lost consciousness.* ● *She regained consciousness after two weeks in a coma.* **2** [U,sing] consciousness (of sth) the state of realizing or noticing that sth exists: *There is (a) growing consciousness of the need to save energy.*

conscript¹ /kənˈskrɪpt/ *verb* [T] to make sb join the army, navy or air force –**conscription** *noun* [U]

conscript² /ˈkɒnskrɪpt/ *noun* [C] a person who has been conscripted ∙∙➤ Look at **volunteer¹**(2).

consecrate /ˈkɒnsɪkreɪt/ *verb* [T] to state formally in a special ceremony that a place or an object can be used for religious purposes –**consecration** /ˌkɒnsɪˈkreɪʃn/ *noun* [C,U]

consecutive /kənˈsekjətɪv/ *adj* coming or happening one after the other: *This is the team's fourth consecutive win.* –**consecutively** *adv*

consensus /kənˈsensəs/ *noun* [sing,U] (a) consensus (among/between sb) (on/about sth) agreement among a group of people: *to reach a consensus* ● *There is no consensus among experts about the causes of global warming.*

consent¹ /kənˈsent/ *verb* [I] consent (to sth) to agree to sth; to allow sth to happen

consent² /kənˈsent/ *noun* [U] agreement; permission: *The child's parents had to give their consent to the operation.*

IDIOM **the age of consent** → **AGE¹**

★**consequence** /ˈkɒnsɪkwəns/ *noun* **1** [C] something that happens or follows as a result of sth else: *Many people may lose their jobs as*

a consequence of recent poor sales. **2** [U] (*formal*) importance: *It is of no consequence.*

consequent /ˈkɒnsɪkwənt/ *adj* (*formal*) (only *before* a noun) following as the result of sth else: *The lack of rain and consequent poor harvests have led to food shortages.* –**consequently** *adv*: *She didn't work hard enough, and consequently failed the exam.*

conservation /ˌkɒnsəˈveɪʃn/ *noun* [U] **1** the protection of the natural world: *Conservation groups are protesting against the plan to build a road through the forest.* **2** not allowing sth to be wasted, damaged or destroyed: *the conservation of energy* ∙∙➤ verb **conserve**

conservationist /ˌkɒnsəˈveɪʃənɪst/ *noun* [C] a person who believes in protecting the natural world

conservatism /kənˈsɜːvətɪzəm/ *noun* [U] **1** the disapproval of new ideas and change **2** usually **Conservatism** the beliefs of the Conservative Party

★**conservative¹** /kənˈsɜːvətɪv/ *adj* **1** not liking change; traditional **2** (**Conservative**) connected with the British Conservative Party: *Conservative voters* **3** (used when you are guessing how much sth costs) lower than the real figure or amount: *Even a conservative estimate would put the damage at about £4000 to repair.* –**conservatively** *adv*

conservative² /kənˈsɜːvətɪv/ *noun* [C] **1** a person who does not like change **2** (usually **Conservative**) a member of the British Conservative Party

Con'servative Party *noun* [C] one of the main political parties in Britain. The Conservative Party supports a free market and is opposed to the state controlling industry ∙∙➤ Look at **Labour Party** and **Liberal Democrats**.

conservatory /kənˈsɜːvətri/ *noun* [C] (*pl* **conservatories**) a room with a glass roof and walls often built onto the outside of a house

conserve /kənˈsɜːv/ *verb* [T] to avoid wasting sth: *to conserve water* ∙∙➤ noun **conservation**

★**consider** /kənˈsɪdə/ *verb* [T] **1** consider sb/sth (for/as sth); consider doing sth to think about sth carefully, often before making a decision: *She had never considered nursing as a career.* ● *We're considering going to Spain for our holidays.* **2** consider sb/sth (as/to be) sth; consider that... to think about sb/sth in a particular way: *He considered the risk (to be) too great.* ● *He considered that the risk was too great.* ● *Jane considers herself an expert on the subject.* **3** to remember or pay attention to sth, especially sb's feelings: *I can't just move abroad. I have to consider my family.*

★**considerable** /kənˈsɪdərəbl/ *adj* great in amount or size: *A considerable number of people preferred the old building to the new one.* –**considerably** /-əbli/ *adv*: *This flat is considerably larger than our last one.*

considerate /kənˈsɪdərət/ *adj* careful not to upset people; thinking of others: *It was very* *considerate of you to offer to drive me home.* ∙► opposite **inconsiderate**

★**consideration** /kən₁sɪdə'reɪʃn/ **noun 1** [U] (*formal*) an act of thinking about sth carefully or for a long time: *I have given some consideration to the idea but I don't think it would work.* **2** [C] something that you think about when you are making a decision: *If he changes his job, the salary will be an important consideration.* **3** [U] consideration (**for sb/sth**) the quality of thinking about what other people need or feel: *Most drivers show little consideration for cyclists.*

IDIOM **take sth into consideration** to think about sth when you are forming an opinion or making a decision

considering /kən'sɪdərɪŋ/ **prep, conj** (used for introducing a surprising fact) when you think about or remember sth: *Considering you've only been studying for a year, you speak English very well.*

consign /kən'saɪn/ **verb** [T] (*formal*) consign sb/sth **to** sth to put or send sb/sth somewhere, especially in order to get rid of him/her/it: *I think I can consign this junk mail straight to the bin.*

consignment /kən'saɪnmənt/ **noun** [C] goods that are being sent to sb/sth: *a new consignment of books*

★**consist** /kən'sɪst/ **verb** (not used in the continuous tenses)

PHRASAL VERBS **consist in** sth to have sth as its main point: *Her job consisted in welcoming the guests as they arrived.*
consist of sth to be formed or made up of sth: *The band consists of a singer, two guitarists and a drummer.*

➤ Although this verb is not used in the continuous tenses, it is common to see the present participle (= *-ing* form): *It's a full-time course consisting of six different modules.*

consistency /kən'sɪstənsi/ **noun** (*pl* consistencies) **1** [U] the quality of always having the same standard, opinions, behaviour, etc: *Your work lacks consistency. Sometimes it's excellent but at other times it's full of mistakes.* ∙► opposite **inconsistency 2** [C,U] how thick or smooth a liquid substance is: *The mixture should have a thick, sticky consistency.*

consistent /kən'sɪstənt/ **adj 1** always having the same opinions, standard, behaviour, etc; not changing **2** consistent (**with** sth) agreeing with or similar to sth: *I'm afraid your statement is not consistent with what the other witnesses said.* ∙► opposite **inconsistent** –**consistently** **adv**: *We must try to maintain a consistently high standard.*

consolation /₁kɒnsə'leɪʃn/ **noun** [C,U] a thing or person that makes you feel better when you are sad; a comfort: *It was some consolation to me to know that I wasn't the only one who had failed the exam.*

console /kən'səʊl/ **verb** [T] to make sb happier when he/she is very sad or disappointed; to comfort sb

consolidate /kən'sɒlɪdeɪt/ **verb** [I,T] to become or to make sth firmer or stronger: *We're going to consolidate what we've learnt so far by doing some revision exercises today.* –**consolidation** /kən₁sɒlɪ'deɪʃn/ **noun** [U]

consonant /'kɒnsənənt/ **noun** [C] any of the letters of the English alphabet except a, e, i, o, and u: *The letters 't', 'm', 's' and 'b' are all consonants.* ∙► Look at **vowel**.

consortium /kən'sɔːtiəm/ **noun** [C] (*pl* consortiums or consortia /-tiə/) a group of companies that work closely together for a particular purpose

conspicuous /kən'spɪkjuəs/ **adj** easily seen or noticed ∙► opposite **inconspicuous** –**conspicuously** **adv**

conspiracy /kən'spɪrəsi/ **noun** [C,U] (*pl* conspiracies) a secret plan by a group of people to do sth bad or illegal: *a conspiracy against the president*

conspirator /kən'spɪrətə/ **noun** [C] a member of a group of people who are planning to do sth bad or illegal

conspire /kən'spaɪə/ **verb** [I] **1** conspire (**with** sb) (**to do** sth) to plan to do sth bad or illegal with a group of people: *A group of terrorists were conspiring to blow up the plane.* **2** conspire (**against** sb/sth) (used about events) to seem to work together to make sth bad happen: *When we both lost our jobs in the same week, we felt that everything was conspiring against us.*

constable /'kʌnstəbl/ = **POLICE CONSTABLE**

constabulary /kən'stæbjələri/ **noun** [C] (*pl* constabularies) the police force of a particular area: *the West Yorkshire Constabulary*

★**constant** /'kɒnstənt/ **adj 1** happening or existing all the time or again and again: *The constant noise gave me a headache.* **2** that does not change: *You use less petrol if you drive at a constant speed.*

constantly /'kɒnstəntli/ **adv** always; again and again: *The situation is constantly changing.*

constellation /₁kɒnstə'leɪʃn/ **noun** [C] a group of stars that forms a pattern and has a name

consternation /₁kɒnstə'neɪʃn/ **noun** [U] a feeling of shock or worry: *We stared at each other* **in consternation**.

constipated /'kɒnstɪpeɪtɪd/ **adj** not able to empty waste from your body –**constipation** /₁kɒnstɪ'peɪʃn/ **noun** [U]: *to suffer from/have constipation*

constituency /kən'stɪtjuənsi/ **noun** [C] (*pl* constituencies) a district and the people who live in it that a politician represents

constituent /kən'stɪtjuənt/ **noun** [C] **1** one of the parts that form sth: *Hydrogen and oxygen are the constituents of water.* **2** a person who lives in the district that a politician represents

constitute /'kɒnstɪtjuːt/ **verb** [T] (*formal*) (not used in the continuous tenses) **1** to be one of the parts that form sth: *Women consti-tute a high proportion of part-time workers.* **2** to be considered as sth; to be equal to sth: *The presence of the troops constitutes a threat to peace.*

➤ Although this verb is not used in the continuous tenses, it is common to see the present participle (= *-ing* form): *Management has to fix a maximum number of hours as constituting a day's work.*

constitution /ˌkɒnstɪˈtjuːʃn/ *noun* **1** [C] the basic laws or rules of a country or organization: *the United States constitution* **2** [U] the way the parts of sth are put together; the structure of sth: *the constitution of DNA*

constitutional /ˌkɒnstɪˈtjuːʃənl/ *adj* connected with or allowed by the constitution of a country, etc: *It is not constitutional to imprison a person without trial.*

constrain /kənˈstreɪn/ *verb* [T] (*formal*) **constrain sb/sth (to do sth)** to limit sb/sth; to force sb/sth to do sth: *The company's growth has been constrained by high taxes.*

constraint /kənˈstreɪnt/ *noun* [C,U] something that limits you; a restriction: *There are always some financial constraints on a project like this.*

constrict /kənˈstrɪkt/ *verb* [I,T] **1** to become or make sth tighter, narrower or less: *She felt her throat constrict with fear.* • *The valve constricts the flow of air.* **2** to limit a person's freedom to do sth –**constriction** *noun* [C,U]

construct /kənˈstrʌkt/ *verb* [T] to build or make sth: *Early houses were constructed out of mud and sticks.* •➤ **Construct** is more formal than **build**.

★**construction** /kənˈstrʌkʃn/ *noun* **1** [U] the act or method of building or making sth: *A new bridge is now **under construction**.* • *He works in the construction industry.* **2** [C] (*formal*) something that has been built or made; a building: *The new pyramid was a construction of glass and steel.* **3** [C] the way that words are used together in a phrase or sentence: *a grammatical construction*

constructive /kənˈstrʌktɪv/ *adj* useful or helpful: *constructive suggestions/criticisms/advice* –**constructively** *adv*

construe /kənˈstruː/ *verb* [T] (*formal*) **construe sth (as sth)** to understand the meaning of sth in a particular way: *Her confident manner is often construed as arrogance.* •➤ Look at **misconstrue**.

consul /ˈkɒnsl/ *noun* [C] an official who works in a foreign city helping people from his/her own country who are living or visiting there •➤ Look at **ambassador**. –**consular** /ˈkɒnsjələ/ *adj*

consulate /ˈkɒnsjələt/ *noun* [C] the building where a consul works •➤ Look at **embassy**.

consult /kənˈsʌlt/ *verb* **1** [T] **consult sb/sth (about sth)** to ask sb for some information or advice, or to look for it in a book, etc: *If the symptoms continue, consult your doctor.* **2** [I] **consult with sb** to discuss sth with sb: *Harry*

consulted with his brothers before selling the family business.

consultancy /kənˈsʌltənsi/ *noun* **1** [C] a company that gives expert advice on a particular subject **2** [U] expert advice that sb is paid to provide on a particular subject

consultant /kənˈsʌltənt/ *noun* [C] **1** a person who gives advice to people on business, law, etc: *a firm of management consultants* **2** (*Brit*) a hospital doctor who is a specialist in a particular area of medicine: *a consultant psychiatrist*

consultation /ˌkɒnslˈteɪʃn/ *noun* [C,U] **1** a discussion between people before a decision is taken: *Diplomats met for consultations on the hostage crisis.* • *The measures were introduced without consultation.* **2** (*formal*) meeting sb to get information or advice, or looking for it in a book: *a consultation with a doctor*

consume /kənˈsjuːm/ *verb* [T] (*formal*) **1** to use sth such as fuel, energy or time: *This car consumes a lot of petrol.* **2** to eat or drink sth: *Wrestlers can consume up to 10000 calories in a day.* •➤ *noun* **consumption** **3** (used about fire) to destroy sth **4** (used about an emotion) to affect sb very strongly: *She was consumed by grief when her son was killed.*

★**consumer** /kənˈsjuːmə/ *noun* [C] a person who buys things or uses services

consuming /kənˈsjuːmɪŋ/ *adj* (only before a noun) that takes up a lot of your time and attention: *Sport is her consuming passion.*

consummate[1] /ˈkɒnsəmət/ *adj* (only before a noun) (*formal*) extremely skilled; a perfect example of its kind: *a consummate performer/professional*

consummate[2] /ˈkɒnsəmeɪt/ *verb* [T] (*formal*) to make a marriage or relationship complete by having sex –**consummation** /ˌkɒnsəˈmeɪʃn/ *noun* [C,U]

consumption /kənˈsʌmpʃn/ *noun* [U] **1** the amount of fuel, etc that sth uses: *a car with low fuel consumption* **2** the act of using, eating, etc sth: *The meat was declared unfit for human consumption* (= for people to eat). •➤ *verb* **consume**

cont (also **contd**) *abbr* continued: *cont on p 91*

★**contact**[1] /ˈkɒntækt/ *noun* **1** [U] contact (with sb/sth) meeting, talking to or writing to sb else: *They are trying to **make contact** with the kidnappers.* • *We **keep in contact** with our office in New York.* • *It's a pity to **lose contact** with old schoolfriends.* **2** [U] contact (with sb/sth) the state of touching sb/sth: *This product should not **come into contact** with food.* **3** [C] a person that you know who may be able to help you: *business contacts*

contact[2] /ˈkɒntækt/ *verb* [T] to telephone or write to sb: *Is there a phone number where I can contact you?*

'contact lens *noun* [C] a small piece of plastic that fits onto your eye to help you to see better •➤ picture at **glasses**

contagious /kənˈteɪdʒəs/ *adj* (used about a disease) that you can get by touching sb/sth:

containers

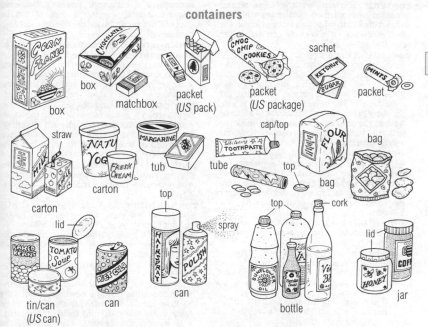

box
box
matchbox
packet (US pack)
packet (US package)
sachet
packet

straw
carton
carton
lid
tub
tube
cap/top
top
bag
bag
top
cork
top
spray
flour
tin/can (US can)
can
can
bottle
lid
jar

Smallpox is a highly contagious disease. ● (*figurative*) *Her laugh is contagious.* •➤ Look at the note at **infectious**. –**contagion** /kən'teɪdʒən/ **noun** [U]

✳contain /kən'teɪn/ **verb** [T] (not used in the continuous tenses) **1** to have sth inside or as part of itself: *Each box contains 24 tins.* **2** to keep sth within limits; to control sth: *efforts to contain inflation* ● *She found it hard to contain her anger.*

➤ Although this verb is not used in the continuous tenses, it is common to see the present participle (= -ing form): *petrol containing lead*

➤ **Contain** or **include**? We use **contain** to talk about objects which have other things inside them: *a jar containing olives* ● *This film contains violent scenes.* We use **include** to show that sb/sth forms part of a whole or belongs to something: *a team of seven people including a cameraman and a doctor* ● *The price of the holiday includes accommodation.*

✳container /kən'teɪnə/ **noun** [C] **1** a box, bottle, packet, etc in which sth is kept: *a plastic container* **2** a large metal box that is used for transporting goods by sea, road or rail: *a container lorry/ship*

contaminate /kən'tæmɪneɪt/ **verb** [T] to add a substance which will make sth dirty or harmful: *The town's drinking water was contaminated with poisonous chemicals.* –**contamination** /kən,tæmɪ'neɪʃn/ **noun** [U]

contemplate /'kɒntəmpleɪt/ **verb** [T] **1** to think carefully about sth or the possibility of doing sth: *Before her illness she had never contemplated retiring.* **2** to look at sb/sth, often quietly or for a long time –**contemplation** /,kɒntəm'pleɪʃn/ **noun** [U]

✳contemporary¹ /kən'temprəri/ **adj 1** belonging to the same time as sb/sth else: *The programme includes contemporary film footage of the First World War.* **2** of the present time; modern: *contemporary music/art/society*

contemporary² /kən'temprəri/ **noun** [C] (*pl* **contemporaries**) a person who lives or does sth at the same time as sb else

contempt /kən'tempt/ **noun** [U] **contempt (for sb/sth)** the feeling that sb/sth does not deserve any respect or is without value: *The teacher treated my question with contempt.* –**contemptuous** /kən'temptʃuəs/ **adj**: *The boy just gave a contemptuous laugh when I asked him to be quiet.*

contend /kən'tend/ **verb 1** [I] **contend with/against sb/sth** to have to deal with a problem or a difficult situation: *She's had a lot of problems to contend with.* **2** [T] (*formal*) to say or argue that sth is true: *The young man contended that he was innocent.* **3** [I] **contend (for sth)** to compete against sb to win or gain sth: *Two athletes are contending for first place.*

contender /kən'tendə/ **noun** [C] a person who may win a competition: *There are only two serious contenders for the leadership.*

I] **intransitive**, a verb which has no object: *He laughed.*   [T] **transitive**, a verb which has an object: *He ate an apple.*

C

★**content**¹ /kən'tent/ **adj** (not before a noun) content (with sth); content to do sth happy or satisfied with what you have or do: *I don't need a new car – I'm perfectly content with the one I've got.*

★**content**² /'kɒntent/ **noun 1 contents** [pl] the thing or things that are inside sth: *Add the contents of this packet to a pint of cold milk and mix well.* **2** [sing] the main subject, ideas, etc of a book, article, television programme, etc: *The content of the essay is good, but there are too many grammatical mistakes.* **3** [sing] the amount of a particular substance that sth contains: *Many processed foods have a high sugar content.*

content³ /kən'tent/ **noun** [sing]
IDIOM **to your heart's content** → **HEART**

content⁴ /kən'tent/ **verb** [T] content yourself with sth to accept sth even though it was not exactly what you wanted: *The restaurant was closed, so we had to content ourselves with a sandwich.*

contented /kən'tentɪd/ **adj** happy or satisfied: *The baby gave a contented chuckle.* –**contentedly adv**

contention /kən'tenʃn/ **noun 1** [U] (*formal*) arguing; disagreement **2** [C] (*formal*) your opinion; sth that you say is true: *The government's contention is that unemployment will start to fall next year.*
IDIOM **in contention (for sth)** having a chance of winning a competition: *Four teams are still in contention for the cup.*

contentious /kən'tenʃəs/ **adj** likely to cause argument: *a contentious issue*

contentment /kən'tentmənt/ **noun** [U] a feeling of happy satisfaction

★**contest**¹ /'kɒntest/ **noun** [C] a competition to find out who is the best, strongest, most beautiful, etc: *I've decided to enter that writing contest.* ● *The by-election will be a contest between the two main parties.*

contest² /kən'test/ **verb** [T] **1** to take part in a competition or try to win sth: *Twenty-four teams will contest next year's World Cup.* **2** to say that sth is wrong or that it was not done properly: *They contested the decision, saying that the judges had not been fair.*

contestant /kən'testənt/ **noun** [C] a person who takes part in a contest: *Four contestants appear on the quiz show each week.*

★**context** /'kɒntekst/ **noun** [C,U] **1** the situation in which sth happens or that caused sth to happen: *To put our company in context, we are now the third largest in the country.* **2** the words that come before or after a word, phrase or sentence that help you to understand its meaning: *You can often guess the meaning of a word from its context.* ● *Taken out of context, his comment made no sense.*

★**continent** /'kɒntɪnənt/ **noun 1** [C] one of the seven main areas of land on the Earth: *Asia, Africa and Antarctica are continents.* **2 the Continent** [sing] (*Brit*) the main part of Europe not including the British Isles

continental /ˌkɒntɪ'nentl/ **adj 1** connected with or typical of a continent: *Moscow has a continental climate: hot summers and cold winters.* **2** (*Brit*) connected with the main part of Europe not including the British Isles: *continental holidays*

contingency /kən'tɪndʒənsi/ **noun** [C] (*pl* **contingencies**) a possible future situation or event: *We'd better make contingency plans just in case something goes wrong.* ● *We've tried to prepare for every possible contingency.*

contingent /kən'tɪndʒənt/ **noun** [C,with sing or pl verb] **1** a group of people from the same country, organization, etc who are attending an event: *the Irish contingent at the conference* **2** a group of armed forces forming part of a larger force

continual /kən'tɪnjuəl/ **adj** happening again and again: *His continual phone calls started to annoy her.* •→ Look at **incessant**. –**continually adv**

continuation /kənˌtɪnju'eɪʃn/ **noun** [sing,U] something that continues or follows sth else; the act of making sth continue: *The team are hoping for a continuation of their recent good form.* ● *Continuation of the current system will be impossible.*

★**continue** /kən'tɪnju:/ **verb 1** [I] to keep happening or existing without stopping: *If the pain continues, see your doctor.* **2** [I,T] continue (doing/to do sth); continue (with sth) to keep doing sth without stopping: *They ignored me and continued their conversation.* ● *He continued working/to work late into the night.* ● *Will you continue with the lessons after the exam?* **3** [I,T] to begin to do or say sth again after you had stopped: *The meeting will continue after lunch.* **4** [I,T] to go further in the same direction: *The next day we continued our journey.*

continued /kən'tɪnju:d/ **adj** going on without stopping: *There are reports of continued fighting near the border.*

continuity /ˌkɒntɪ'nju:əti/ **noun** [U] the fact of continuing without stopping or of staying the same: *The pupils will have the same teacher for two years to ensure continuity.*

★**continuous** /kən'tɪnjuəs/ **adj** happening or existing without stopping: *There was a continuous line of cars stretching for miles.* –**continuously adv**: *It has rained continuously here for three days.*

the con'tinuous tense (also **the progressive tense**) **noun** [C] (*grammar*) the form of a verb such as 'I am waiting', 'I was waiting' or 'I have been waiting' which is made from a part of 'be' and a verb ending in '-ing' and is used to describe an action that continues for a period of time

➤ For more information about the continuous tense, look at the **Quick Grammar Reference** section at the back of this dictionary.

contort /kən'tɔ:t/ **verb** [I,T] to move or to make sth move into a strange or unusual shape: *His face contorted/was contorted with pain.* –**contortion noun** [C]

contour /'kɒntʊə/ **noun** [C] **1** the shape of the outer surface of sth: *I could just make out the contours of the house in the dark.* **2** (also 'contour line) a line on a map joining places of equal height

contraception /ˌkɒntrə'sepʃn/ **noun** [U] the ways of preventing a woman from becoming pregnant: *a reliable form of contraception* •➤ Look at **birth control** and **family planning**.

contraceptive /ˌkɒntrə'septɪv/ **noun** [C] a drug or a device that prevents a woman from becoming pregnant –contraceptive **adj**

★**contract¹** /'kɒntrækt/ **noun** [C] a written legal agreement: *They signed a three-year contract with a major record company.* • *a temporary contract*

contract² /kən'trækt/ **verb 1** [I,T] to become or to make sth smaller or shorter: *Metals contract as they cool.* •➤ opposite **expand** **2** [T] to get an illness or disease, especially a serious one: *to contract pneumonia* **3** [I,T] to make a written legal agreement with sb to do sth: *His firm has been contracted to supply all the furniture for the new building.*
PHRASAL VERB **contract sth out (to sb)** to arrange for work to be done by sb outside your own company

contraction /kən'trækʃn/ **noun 1** [U] the process of becoming or of making sth become smaller or shorter: *the expansion and contraction of a muscle* **2** [C] a strong movement of the muscles that happens to a woman as her baby is born **3** [C] a shorter form of a word or words: *'Mustn't' is a contraction of 'must not'.*

contractor /kən'træktə/ **noun** [C] a person or company that has a contract to do work or provide goods or services for another company

contractual /kən'træktʃuəl/ **adj** connected with or included in a contract

contradict /ˌkɒntrə'dɪkt/ **verb** [T] to say that sth is wrong or not true; to say the opposite of sth: *These instructions seem to contradict previous ones.*

contradiction /ˌkɒntrə'dɪkʃn/ **noun** [C,U] a statement, fact or action that is opposite to or different from another one: *There were a number of contradictions in what he told the police.* • *This letter is in complete contradiction to their previous one.*

contradictory /ˌkɒntrə'dɪktəri/ **adj** being opposite to or not matching sth else: *Contradictory reports appeared in the newspapers.*

contraflow /'kɒntrəfləʊ/ **noun** [C] the system that is used when one half of a wide road is closed for repairs, and traffic going in both directions has to use the other side

contralto /kən'træltəʊ/ **noun** [C,U] the lowest female singing voice; a woman with this voice

contraption /kən'træpʃn/ **noun** [C] a strange or complicated piece of equipment: *The first aeroplanes were dangerous contraptions.*

contrary¹ /'kɒntrəri/ **adj 1** (only *before* a noun) completely different; opposite: *I thought it was possible, but she took the contrary view.* **2** contrary to completely different from; opposite to; against: *Contrary to popular belief* (= to what many people think), *not all boxers are stupid.*

contrary² /'kɒntrəri/ **noun**
IDIOMS **on the contrary** the opposite is true; certainly not: *'You look as if you're not enjoying yourself.' 'On the contrary, I'm having a great time.'*
to the contrary (*formal*) saying the opposite: *Unless I hear anything to the contrary, I shall assume that the arrangements haven't changed.*

★**contrast¹** /'kɒntrɑːst/ **noun 1** [U] comparison between two people or things that shows the differences between them: *In contrast to previous years, we've had a very successful summer.* **2** [C,U] (a) contrast (to/with sb/sth); (a) contrast (between A and B) a clear difference between two things or people that is seen when they are compared: *There is a tremendous contrast between the climate in the valley and the climate in the hills.* **3** [C] something that is clearly different from sth else when the two things are compared: *This house is quite a contrast to your old one!*

★**contrast²** /kən'trɑːst/ **verb 1** [T] contrast (A and/with B) to compare people or things in order to show the differences between them: *The film contrasts his poor childhood with his later life as a millionaire.* **2** [I] contrast with sb/sth to be clearly different when compared: *This comment contrasts sharply with his previous remarks.*

contravene /ˌkɒntrə'viːn/ **verb** [T] (*formal*) to break a law or a rule –contravention /ˌkɒntrə'venʃn/ **noun** [C,U]

★**contribute** /'kɒntrɪbjuːt; kən'trɪbjuːt/ **verb** contribute (sth) (to/towards sth) **1** [I,T] to give a part of the total, together with others: *Would you like to contribute towards our collection for famine relief?* • *The research has contributed a great deal to our knowledge of cancer.* **2** [I] to be one of the causes of sth: *It is not known whether the bad weather contributed to the accident.* **3** [I,T] to write articles for a magazine or newspaper

contribution /ˌkɒntrɪ'bjuːʃn/ **noun** [C] a contribution (to/toward sth) something that you give, especially money or help, or do together with other people: *If we all make a small contribution, we'll be able to buy Ray a good present.*

contributor /kən'trɪbjətə/ **noun** [C] a person who contributes to sth

contributory /kən'trɪbjətəri/ **adj** helping to cause or produce sth: *Alcohol was a contributory factor in her death.*

contrive /kən'traɪv/ **verb** [T] **1** to manage to do sth, although there are difficulties: *If I can contrive to get off work early, I'll see you later.* **2** to plan or invent sth in a clever and/or dishonest way: *He contrived a scheme to cheat insurance companies.*

contrived /kən'traɪvd/ **adj** hard to believe;

not natural or realistic: *The ending of the film seemed rather contrived.*

★ **control¹** /kən'trəʊl/ **noun 1** [U] control (of/ over sb/sth) power and ability to make sb/ sth do what you want: *Rebels managed to **take control** of the radio station.* • *Some teachers find it difficult to **keep control** of their class.* • *He **lost control** of the car and crashed.* • *I was late because of circumstances **beyond** my **control.*** **2** [C,U] (a) control (on/ over sth) a limit on sth; a way of keeping sb/sth within certain limits: *price controls* • *The faults forced the company to review its **quality control** procedures.* **3** [C] one of the parts of a machine that is used for operating it: *the controls of an aeroplane/a TV* • *a control panel* **4** [sing] the place from which sth is operated or where sth is checked: *We went through passport control and then got onto the plane.*

IDIOMS **be in control (of sth)** to have the power or ability to deal with sth: *The police are again in control of the area following last night's violence.*

be/get out of control to be/become impossible to deal with: *The demonstration got out of control and fighting broke out.*

under control being dealt with successfully: *It took several hours to bring the fire under control.*

★ **control²** /kən'trəʊl/ **verb** [T] (**controlling**; **controlled**) **1** to have power and ability to make sb/sth do what you want: *One family controls the company.* • *Police struggled to control the crowd.* • *I couldn't control myself any longer and burst out laughing.* **2** to keep sth within certain limits: *measures to control price rises* –**controller** noun [C]: *air traffic controllers*

controversial /ˌkɒntrə'vɜːʃl/ **adj** causing public discussion and disagreement: *a controversial issue/decision/plan*

controversy /'kɒntrəvɜːsi; kən'trɒvəsi/ **noun** [C,U] (*pl* **controversies**) public discussion and disagreement about sth: *The plans for changing the city centre caused a great deal of controversy.*

conurbation /ˌkɒnɜː'beɪʃn/ **noun** [C] a very large area of houses and other buildings where towns have grown and joined together

convalesce /ˌkɒnvə'les/ **verb** [I] to rest and get better over a period of time after an illness –**convalescence** /ˌkɒnvə'lesns/ **noun** [sing,U] –**convalescent** /ˌkɒnvə'lesnt/ **adj**

convene /kən'viːn/ **verb** [I,T] (*formal*) to come together or to bring people together for a meeting, etc

convenience /kən'viːniəns/ **noun 1** [U] the quality of being easy, useful or suitable for sb: *a building designed **for the convenience of** disabled people* • *For convenience, you can pay for everything at once.* **2** [C] something that makes things easier, quicker or more comfortable: *houses with all the modern conveniences* (= central heating, hot water, etc) **3** [C] (*Brit*) a public toilet

con'venience food noun [C,U] food that

you buy frozen or in a box or can, that you can prepare very quickly and easily

★ **convenient** /kən'viːniənt/ **adj 1** suitable or practical for a particular purpose; not causing difficulty: *I'm willing to meet you on any day that's convenient for you.* • *It isn't convenient to talk at the moment, I'm in the middle of a meeting.* ••➤ opposite **inconvenient** **2** close to sth; in a useful position: *Our house is convenient for the shops.* –**conveniently adv**

convent /'kɒnvənt/ **noun** [C] a place where women (**nuns**) live in a religious community ••➤ Look at **monastery**.

convention /kən'venʃn/ **noun 1** [C,U] a traditional way of behaving or of doing sth: *A speech by the bride's father is one of the conventions of a wedding.* • *The film shows no respect for convention.* **2** [C] a large meeting of the members of a profession, political party, etc; a conference: *the Democratic Party Convention* **3** [C] a formal agreement, especially between different countries: *the Geneva Convention*

conventional /kən'venʃənl/ **adj** always behaving in a traditional or normal way: *conventional attitudes* • *I quite like him but he's so conventional* (= boring, because of this). ••➤ opposite **unconventional** –**conventionally** /-ʃənəli/ **adv**

converge /kən'vɜːdʒ/ **verb** [I] converge (on sb/sth) (used about two or more people or things) to move towards each other or meet at the same point from different directions: *Fans from all over the country converge on the village during the annual music festival.*

conversant /kən'vɜːsnt/ **adj** (*formal*) conversant with sth knowing about sth; familiar with sth: *All employees should be conversant with basic accounting.*

★ **conversation** /ˌkɒnvə'seɪʃn/ **noun** [C,U] a talk between two or more people: *I **had a long conversation** with her about her plans for the future.* • *His job is his only **topic of conversation.***

IDIOM **deep in thought/conversation** ➔ **DEEP¹**

converse /kən'vɜːs/ **verb** [I] (*formal*) to talk to sb; to have a conversation

conversely /'kɒnvɜːsli/ **adv** (*formal*) in a way that is opposite to sth: *People who earn a lot of money have little time to spend it. Conversely, many people with limitless time do not have enough money to do what they want.*

conversion /kən'vɜːʃn/ **noun** (a) conversion (from sth) (into/to sth) **1** [C,U] the act or process of changing from one form, system or use to another: *a conversion table for miles and kilometres* **2** [C,U] becoming a member of a different religion

convert¹ /kən'vɜːt/ **verb** [I,T] **1** convert (sth) (from sth) (into/to sth) to change from one form, system or use to another: *a sofa that converts into a double bed* • *How do you convert pounds into kilos?* **2** convert (sb) (from sth) (to sth) to change or to persuade sb to change to a different religion: *As a young man he converted to Islam.* • *to convert people to Christianity*

convert² /'kɒnvɜːt/ *noun* [C] **a convert (to sth)** a person who has changed his/her religion

convertible¹ /kən'vɜːtəbl/ *adj* able to be changed into another form: *convertible currencies* (= those that can be exchanged for other currencies)

convertible² /kən'vɜːtəbl/ *noun* [C] a car with a roof that can be folded down or taken off

convex /'kɒnveks/ *adj* having a surface that curves towards the outside of sth, like an eye: *a convex lens* ••➤ Look at **concave**.

convey /kən'veɪ/ *verb* [T] **1 convey sth (to sb)** to make ideas, thoughts, feelings, etc known to sb: *The film conveys a lot of information but in an entertaining way.* ● *Please convey my sympathy to her at this sad time.* **2** (*formal*) to take sb/sth from one place to another, especially in a vehicle

con'veyor belt *noun* [C] a moving belt that carries objects from one place to another, for example in a factory

convict¹ /kən'vɪkt/ *verb* [T] **convict sb (of sth)** to say officially in a court of law that sb is guilty of a crime: *He was convicted of armed robbery and sent to prison.* ••➤ opposite **acquit**

convict² /'kɒnvɪkt/ *noun* [C] a person who has been found guilty of a crime and put in prison

conviction /kən'vɪkʃn/ *noun* **1** [C,U] the action of finding sb guilty of a crime in a court of law: *He has several previous convictions for burglary.* **2** [C] a very strong opinion or belief: *religious convictions* **3** [U] the feeling of being certain about what you are doing: *He played without conviction and lost easily.*

★**convince** /kən'vɪns/ *verb* [T] **1 convince sb (of sth/that...)** to succeed in making sb believe sth: *She convinced him of the need to go back.* ● *I couldn't convince her that I was right.* **2 convince sb (to do sth)** to persuade sb to do sth: *The salesman convinced them to buy a new cooker.*

★**convinced** /kən'vɪnst/ *adj* (not before a noun) completely sure about sth: *He's convinced of his ability to win.*

★**convincing** /kən'vɪnsɪŋ/ *adj* **1** able to make sb believe sth: *Her explanation for her absence wasn't very convincing.* **2** (used about a victory) complete; clear: *a convincing win* –**convincingly** *adv*

convoy /'kɒnvɔɪ/ *noun* [C,U] a group of vehicles or ships travelling together: *a convoy of lorries* ● *warships travelling in convoy*

convulse /kən'vʌls/ *verb* [I,T] to make sudden violent movements that you cannot control; to cause sb to move in this way: *He was convulsed with pain.*

convulsion /kən'vʌlʃn/ *noun* [C,usually pl] a sudden violent movement that you cannot control: *Children sometimes have convulsions when they are ill.*

coo /kuː/ *verb* [I] **1** to make a soft low sound

like a bird (a **dove**) **2** to speak in a soft, gentle voice: *He went to the cot and cooed over the baby.*

★**cook¹** /kʊk/ *verb* **1** [I,T] to prepare food for eating by heating it: *My mother taught me how to cook.* ● *The sauce should be cooked on low heat for twenty minutes.* ● *He cooked us a meal.* **2** [I] (used about food) to be prepared for eating by being heated: *I could smell something cooking in the kitchen.*

➤ Food can be cooked in various ways: by **boiling** in a saucepan of hot water; by **frying** in a frying pan with hot oil or fat; or by **grilling** under a grill, which heats the food from above. We can **toast** bread under a grill or in a toaster to make it crisp and brown. Cakes and bread are **baked** in the oven, but we use the word **roast** for cooking meat or potatoes in the oven.

PHRASAL VERB **cook sth up** (*informal*) to invent sth that is not true: *She cooked up an excuse for not arriving on time.*

cook² /kʊk/ *noun* [C] a person who cooks: *My sister is an excellent cook.*

cookbook /'kʊkbʊk/ = **COOKERY BOOK**

★**cooker** /'kʊkə/ *noun* [C] a large piece of kitchen equipment for cooking using gas or electricity. It consists of an oven, a flat top on which pans can be placed and often a device which heats the food from above (a **grill**). ••➤ picture on page C7

cookery /'kʊkəri/ *noun* [U] the skill or activity of preparing and cooking food: *Chinese/French/Italian cookery*

'cookery book (also **cookbook**) *noun* [C] a book that gives instructions on cooking and how to cook individual dishes (**recipes**)

cookie /'kʊki/ (*US*) = **BISCUIT**

★**cooking** /'kʊkɪŋ/ *noun* [U] **1** the preparation of food for eating: *Cooking is one of her hobbies.*

➤ A common way of talking about the activity of preparing food is **do the cooking**: *In our house, I do the cleaning and my husband does the cooking.*

2 food produced by cooking: *He missed his mother's cooking when he left home.*

★**cool¹** /kuːl/ *adj* **1** fairly cold; not hot or warm: *It was a cool evening so I put on a pullover.* ● *What I'd like is a long cool drink.* ••➤ Look at the note at **cold¹**. **2** calm; not excited or angry: *She always manages to remain cool under pressure.* **3** unfriendly; not showing interest: *When we first met, she was rather cool towards me, but later she became friendlier.* **4** (*slang*) very good or fashionable: *Those are cool shoes you're wearing!*

★**cool²** /kuːl/ *verb* **1** [I,T] **cool (sth/sb) (down/off)** to lower the temperature of sth; to become cool¹(1): *Let the soup cool (down).* ● *After the game we needed to cool off.* ● *A nice cold drink will soon cool you down.* **2** [I] (used about feelings) to become less strong

PHRASAL VERB **cool (sb) down/off** to become or make sb calmer

cool³ /kuːl/ noun [sing] **the cool** a cool temperature or place; the quality of being cool: *We sat in the cool of a cafe, out of the sun.*
IDIOM **keep/lose your cool** to stay calm/to stop being calm and become angry, nervous, etc

cooling-'off period noun [C] a period of time when sb can think again about a decision that he/she has made

coolly /'kuːlli/ adv in a calm way; without showing much interest or excitement: *At first she was very angry; then she explained the problem coolly.*

coolness /'kuːlnəs/ noun [U] the quality or state of being cool: *the coolness of the water* • *his coolness under stress* • *their coolness towards strangers*

coop /kuːp/ verb
PHRASAL VERB **coop sb/sth up (in sth)** to keep sb/sth inside a small space: *The children were cooped up indoors all day because the weather was so bad.*

cooperate (*Brit also* **co-operate**) /kəʊ-ˈɒpəreɪt/ verb [I] **cooperate (with sb/sth) 1** to work with sb else to achieve sth: *Our company is cooperating with a Danish firm on this project.* **2** to be helpful by doing what sb asks you to do: *If everyone cooperates by following the instructions, there will be no problem.*

cooperation (*Brit also* **co-operation**) /kəʊ-ˌɒpəˈreɪʃn/ noun [U] **1 cooperation (with sb)** working together with sb else to achieve sth: *Schools are working in close cooperation with parents to improve standards.* **2** help that you give by doing what sb asks you to do: *The police asked the public for their cooperation in the investigation.*

cooperative¹ (*Brit also* **co-operative**) /kəʊˈɒpərətɪv/ adj **1** done by people working together: *a cooperative business venture* **2** helpful; doing what sb asks you to do: *My firm were very cooperative and allowed me to have time off.* •➤ opposite **uncooperative**

cooperative² (*Brit also* **co-operative**) /kəʊˈɒpərətɪv/ noun [C] a business or organization that is owned and run by all of the people who work for it: *a workers' cooperative*

coordinate¹ (*Brit also* **co-ordinate**) /kəʊ-ˈɔːdɪneɪt/ verb [T] to organize different things or people so that they work together: *It is her job to coordinate the various departments.*

coordinate² (*Brit* **co-ordinate**) /kəʊ-ˈɔːdɪnət/ noun [C] one of the two sets of numbers and/or letters that are used for finding the position of a point on a map

coordination (*Brit also* **co-ordination**) /kəʊˌɔːdɪˈneɪʃn/ noun [U] **1** the organization of different things or people so that they work together **2** the ability to control the movements of your body properly: *Children's coordination improves as they get older.*

coordinator (*Brit also* **co-ordinator**) /kəʊ-ˈɔːdɪneɪtə/ noun [C] a person who is responsible for organizing different things or people so that they work together

cop¹ /kɒp/ (also **copper**) noun [C] (*informal*) a police officer

cop² /kɒp/ verb (**copping**; **copped**) (*informal*)
PHRASAL VERB **cop out (of sth)** to avoid sth that you should do, because you are afraid or lazy: *She was going to help me with the cooking but she copped out at the last minute.*

cope /kəʊp/ verb [I] **cope (with sb/sth)** to deal successfully with a difficult matter or situation: *She sometimes finds it difficult to cope with all the pressure at work.*

copious /'kəʊpiəs/ adj in large amounts; plentiful: *She made copious notes at the lecture.* –**copiously** adv

'cop-out noun [C] (*informal*) a way of avoiding sth that you should do

copper /'kɒpə/ noun **1** [U] a common reddish-brown metal: *water pipes made of copper* **2** [C] (*Brit*) a coin of low value made of brown metal: *I only had a few coppers left.* **3** =**cop¹**

copse /kɒps/ noun [C] a small area of trees or bushes

copulate /'kɒpjuleɪt/ verb [I] (*formal*) (used especially about animals) to have sex –**copulation** /ˌkɒpjuˈleɪʃn/ noun [U]

★**copy¹** /'kɒpi/ noun [C] (*pl* **copies**) **1** something that is made to look exactly like sth else: *I kept a copy of the letter I wrote.* • *the master copy* (= the original piece of paper from which copies are made) • *to make a copy of a computer file* •➤ Look at **photocopy**. **2** one book, newspaper, record, etc of which many have been printed or produced: *I managed to buy the last copy of the book left in the shop.*

★**copy²** /'kɒpi/ verb (*pres part* **copying**; *3rd pers sing pres* **copies**; *pt, pp* **copied**) **1** [T] to make sth exactly the same as sth else: *The children copied pictures from a book.* • *It is illegal to copy videos.* **2** [T] **copy sth (down/out)** to write down sth exactly as it is written somewhere else: *I copied down the address on the brochure.* • *I copied out the letter more neatly.* **3** [T] = **photocopy 4** [T] to do or try to do the same as sb else; to imitate: *She copies everything her friends do.* **5** [I] **copy (from sb)** to cheat in an exam or test by writing what sb else has written: *He was caught copying from another student in the exam.*

copyright /'kɒpiraɪt/ noun [C,U] the legal right to be the only person who may print, copy, perform, etc a piece of original work, such as a book, a song or a computer program

coral /'kɒrəl/ noun [U] a hard red, pink or white substance that forms in the sea from the bones of very small sea animals: *a coral reef* (= a line of rock in the sea formed by coral)

cord /kɔːd/ noun **1** [C,U] (a piece of) strong, thick string **2** [C,U] (*especially US*) (a piece of) wire covered with plastic; flex •➤ picture at **cable 3 cords** [pl] trousers made of a thick soft cotton cloth (**corduroy**)

cordial /'kɔːdiəl/ adj pleasant and friendly: *a cordial greeting/smile* –**cordially** /-diəli/ adv

cordless /'kɔːdləs/ adj without a cord (2): *a cordless phone/kettle/iron*

cordon¹ /'kɔːdn/ noun [C] a line or ring of police or soldiers that prevents people from entering an area

cordon² /'kɔːdn/ verb

PHRASAL VERB **cordon sth off** to stop people entering an area by surrounding it with a ring of police or soldiers: *The street where the bomb was discovered was quickly cordoned off.*

corduroy /'kɔːdərɔɪ/ noun [U] a thick soft cotton cloth with lines on it, used for making clothes: *a corduroy jacket*

core /kɔː/ noun **1** [C] the hard centre of certain fruits, containing seeds: *an apple core* **2** [sing] the central or most important part of sth: *the core curriculum* (= the subjects that all pupils have to study) ● *What's the core issue here?* **3** [C] the central part of a planet: *the earth's core*

IDIOM **to the core** completely; in every way: *The news shook him to the core* (= shocked him very much).

cork /kɔːk/ noun **1** [U] a light soft material which comes from the outside of a type of tree: *cork floor tiles* **2** [C] a round piece of cork that you push into the end of a bottle to close it, especially a bottle of wine ••➤ picture at **container**

corkscrew /'kɔːkskruː/ noun [C] a tool that you use for pulling corks (2) out of bottles

★**corn** /kɔːn/ noun **1** [U] (*especially Brit*) any plant that is grown for its grain, such as wheat; the seeds from these plants: *a field of corn* ● *a corn field* **2** [U] (*US*) = MAIZE ••➤ picture at **cereal 3** [C] a small, painful area of hard skin on the toe

corner

The car is **in the corner**.

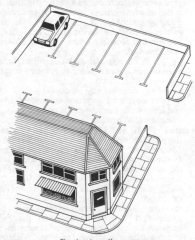

The shop is **on the corner**.

★**corner**¹ /'kɔːnə/ noun [C] **1** a place where two lines, edges, surfaces or roads meet: *Put the lamp in the corner of the room* ● *Write your address in the top right-hand corner.* ● *The shop is on the corner of Wall Street and Long Road.* ● *He went round the corner at top speed.* **2** a quiet or secret place or area: *a remote corner of Scotland* **3** a difficult situation from which you cannot escape: *to get yourself into a corner* **4** (used in football) a free kick from the corner of the field

IDIOMS **cut corners** to do sth quickly and not as well as you should

(just) round the corner very near: *There's a phone box just round the corner.*

★**corner**² /'kɔːnə/ verb [T] **1** to get a person or an animal into a position from which he/she/it cannot escape: *He cornered me at the party and started telling me all his problems.* **2** to get control in a particular area of business so that nobody else can have any success in it: *That company's really cornered the market in health foods.*

cornflakes /'kɔːnfleɪks/ noun [pl] food made of small pieces of dried corn and eaten with milk for breakfast

cornflour /'kɔːnflaʊə/ noun [U] very fine flour often used to make sauces, etc thicker

corn on the 'cob noun [U] corn that is cooked with all the yellow grains still on the inner part and eaten as a vegetable

corny /'kɔːni/ adj (*informal*) too ordinary or familiar to be interesting or amusing: *a corny joke*

coronary¹ /'kɒrənri/ adj connected with the heart

coronary² /'kɒrənri/ noun [C] (*pl* **coronaries**) a type of heart attack

coronation /ˌkɒrə'neɪʃn/ noun [C] an official ceremony at which sb is made a king or queen

coroner /'kɒrənə/ noun [C] a person whose job is to find out the causes of death of people who have died in violent or unusual ways

Corp abbr (*US*) Corporation: *West Coast Motor Corp*

corporal /'kɔːpərəl/ noun [C] a person at a low level in the army or air force

corporal 'punishment noun [U] the punishment of people by hitting them, especially the punishment of children by parents or teachers ••➤ Look at **capital punishment**.

corporate /'kɔːpərət/ adj of or shared by all the members of a group or organization: *corporate responsibility*

corporation /ˌkɔːpə'reɪʃn/ noun [C, with sing or pl verb] **1** a large business company: *multinational corporations* ● *the British Broadcasting Corporation* **2** (*Brit*) a group of people elected to govern a particular town or city

corps /kɔː/ noun [C, with sing or pl verb] (*pl* **corps** /kɔːz/) **1** a part of an army with special duties: *the medical corps* **2** a group of people involved in a special activity: *the diplomatic corps*

corpse /kɔːps/ noun [C] a dead body, especially of a person ••➤ Look at **carcass**.

★**correct¹** /kəˈrekt/ adj **1** with no mistakes; right or true: *Well done! All your answers were correct.* • *Have you got the correct time, please?* **2** (used about behaviour, manners, dress, etc) suitable, proper or right: *What's the correct form of address for a vicar?* ••➤ opposite for senses 1 and 2 **incorrect** –**correctly** adv –**correctness** noun [U]

★**correct²** /kəˈrekt/ verb [T] **1** to make a mistake, fault, etc right or better: *to correct a spelling mistake* • *to correct a test* (= mark the mistakes in it) **2** to tell sb what mistakes he/she is making or what faults he/she has: *He's always correcting me when I'm talking to people.* –**correction** noun [C,U]: *Some parts of the report needed correction.*

corrective /kəˈrektɪv/ adj intended to make sth right that is wrong: *to take corrective action*

correlate /ˈkɒrəleɪt/ verb [I,T] to have or to show a relationship or connection between two or more things –**correlation** /ˌkɒrəˈleɪʃn/ noun [C,U]: *There is a correlation between a person's diet and height.*

correspond /ˌkɒrəˈspɒnd/ verb [I] **1** correspond (to/with sth) to be the same as or equal to sth; to match: *Does the name on the envelope correspond with the name inside the letter?* **2** (formal) correspond (with sb) to write letters to and receive them from sb: *They corresponded for a year before they got married.*

correspondence /ˌkɒrəˈspɒndəns/ noun **1** [U] (formal) the act of writing letters; the letters themselves: *There hasn't been any correspondence between them for years.* **2** [C,U] a close connection or relationship between two or more things: *There is no correspondence between the two sets of figures.*

correspondent /ˌkɒrəˈspɒndənt/ noun [C] **1** a person who provides news or writes articles for a newspaper, etc, especially from a foreign country: *our Middle East correspondent, Andy Jenkins* **2** a person who writes letters to sb

corresponding /ˌkɒrəˈspɒndɪŋ/ adj (only before a noun) related or similar to sth: *Sales are up 10% compared with the corresponding period last year.* –**correspondingly** adv

★**corridor** /ˈkɒrɪdɔː/ noun [C] a long narrow passage in a building or train, with doors that open into rooms, etc

corroborate /kəˈrɒbəreɪt/ verb [T] (formal) to support a statement, idea, etc by providing new evidence: *The witness corroborated Mr Patton's statement about the night of the murder.* –**corroboration** /kəˌrɒbəˈreɪʃn/ noun [U]

corrode /kəˈrəʊd/ verb [I,T] (used about metals) to become weak or to be destroyed by chemical action; to cause a metal to do this: *Parts of the car were corroded by rust.* –**corrosion** /kəˈrəʊʒn/ noun [U] –**corrosive** /kəˈrəʊsɪv/ adj

corrugated /ˈkɒrəɡeɪtɪd/ adj (used about metal or cardboard) shaped into folds

corrupt¹ /kəˈrʌpt/ adj doing or involving illegal or dishonest things in exchange for money, etc: *corrupt officials who accept bribes* • *corrupt business practices*

corrupt² /kəˈrʌpt/ verb [T] to cause sb/sth to start behaving in a dishonest or immoral way: *Too many people are corrupted by power.*

corruption /kəˈrʌpʃn/ noun [U] **1** dishonest or immoral behaviour or activities: *There were accusations of corruption among senior police officers.* **2** the process of making sb/sth corrupt

corset /ˈkɔːsɪt/ noun [C] a piece of clothing that some women wear pulled tight around their middle to make them look thinner

cosmetic¹ /kɒzˈmetɪk/ noun [usually pl] a substance that you put on your face or hair to make yourself look more attractive ••➤ Look at **make-up**.

cosmetic² /kɒzˈmetɪk/ adj **1** used or done in order to make your face or body more attractive: *cosmetic products* • *cosmetic surgery* **2** done in order to improve only the appearance of sth, without changing it in any other way: *changes in government policy which are purely cosmetic*

cosmic /ˈkɒzmɪk/ adj connected with space or the universe

cosmopolitan /ˌkɒzməˈpɒlɪtən/ adj **1** containing people from all over the world: *a cosmopolitan city* **2** influenced by the culture of other countries: *a cosmopolitan and sophisticated young woman*

the cosmos /ˈkɒzmɒs/ noun [sing] the universe

★**cost¹** /kɒst/ noun **1** [C,U] the money that you have to pay for sth: *The cost of petrol has gone up again.* • *The hospital was built at a cost of £10 million.* • *The damage will have to be repaired regardless of cost.* ••➤ Look at the note at **price**. **2** [sing,U] what you have to give or lose in order to obtain sth else: *He achieved great success but only at the cost of a happy family life.* **3 costs** [pl] the amount of money that the losing side has to pay to the winning side in a court of law: *a £250 fine and £100 costs*

IDIOMS **at all costs/at any cost** using whatever means are necessary to achieve sth: *We must win at all costs.*

cover the cost (of sth) → **COVER¹**

to your cost in a way that is unpleasant or bad for you: *Life can be lonely at university, as I found out to my cost.*

★**cost²** /kɒst/ verb [T] (pt, pp cost) **1** to have the price of: *How much does a return ticket to London cost?* • *We'll take the bus – it won't cost much.* • (informal) *How much did your car cost you?* **2** to make you lose sth: *That one mistake cost him his job.*

IDIOM **cost the earth/a fortune** to be very expensive

co-star /ˈkəʊstɑː/ verb (**co-starring**; **co-starred**) **1** [T] (used about a film, play, etc) to have two or more famous actors as its stars: *a film co-starring Leonardo di Caprio and Kate Winslett* **2** [I] (used about actors) to be one of two or more stars in a film, play, etc: *Kate Winslett co-stars with Leonardo di Caprio in the film.* –co-star noun: *His co-star was Marilyn Monroe.*

costly /'kɒstli/ adj (**costlier**, **costliest**) **1** costing a lot of money; expensive: *a costly repair bill* **2** involving great loss of time, effort, etc: *a costly mistake*

costume /'kɒstjuːm/ noun [C,U] **1** a set or style of clothes worn by people in a particular country or in a particular historical period: *17th century costume* ● *Welsh national costume* **2** clothes that an actor, etc wears in order to look like sth else: *One of the children was dressed in a pirate's costume.* ● *The last rehearsal of the play will be done in costume.* **3** (*Brit*) = SWIMSUIT

cosy /'kəʊzi/ adj (**cosier**, **cosiest**) (*US* **cozy**) warm and comfortable: *The room looked cosy and inviting in the firelight.*

cot /kɒt/ (*US* **crib**) noun [C] **1** a bed with high sides for a baby **2** (*US*) = CAMP BED ••➤ picture at **bed**

cottage /'kɒtɪdʒ/ noun [C] a small and usually old house, especially in the country

cottage 'cheese noun [U] a type of soft white cheese in small wet lumps

★**cotton** /'kɒtn/ noun [U] **1** a natural cloth or thread made from the thin white hairs of the cotton plant: *a cotton shirt* ••➤ picture at **knit 2** (*US*) = COTTON WOOL

cotton 'wool noun [U] a soft mass of cotton, used for cleaning the skin, cuts, etc

couch¹ /kaʊtʃ/ noun [C] a long seat, often with a back and arms, for sitting or lying on: *They were sitting on the couch in the living room.*

couch² /kaʊtʃ/ verb [T] (usually passive) (*formal*) to express a thought, idea, etc in the way mentioned: *His reply was couched in very polite terms.*

★**cough¹** /kɒf/ verb **1** [I] to send air out of your throat and mouth with a sudden loud noise, especially when you have a cold, have sth in your throat, etc: *Cigarette smoke makes me cough.* ••➤ picture at **sneeze 2** [T] cough (up) sth to send sth out of your throat and mouth with a sudden loud noise: *When I started coughing (up) blood I called the doctor.*

PHRASAL VERB cough (sth) up (*informal*) to give money when you do not want to: *Come on, cough up what you owe me!*

cough² /kɒf/ noun [C] **1** an act or the sound of coughing: *He gave a nervous cough before he started to speak.* **2** an illness or infection that makes you cough a lot: *Kevin's got a bad cough.*

★**could** /kəd; *strong form* kʊd/ modal verb (*negative* **could not**; *short form* **couldn't** /'kʊdnt/) **1** used for saying that sb had the ability or was allowed to do sth: *I could run three miles without stopping when I was younger.* ● *Elena said we could stay at her house.*

➤ If something was possible on one occasion in the past, use **was/were able to** or

managed to: *The firemen were able to/managed to rescue the children.* But in negative sentences **could not** can be used, too: *The firemen couldn't rescue the children.*

2 used for saying that sth may be or may have been possible: *I could do it now if you like.* ● *She could be famous one day.* ● *He could have gone to university but he didn't want to.* ● *You could have said you were going to be late!* (= I'm annoyed that you didn't) **3** used for asking permission politely: *Could I possibly borrow your car?* **4** used for asking sb politely to do sth for you: *Could you open the door? My hands are full.*

➤ For more information about modal verbs, look at the **Quick Grammar Reference** section at the back of this dictionary.

5 used for making a suggestion: *'What do you want to do tonight?' 'We could go to the cinema or we could just stay in.'* **6** used with the verbs 'feel', 'hear', 'see', 'smell', 'taste'

➤ These verbs are not used in the continuous tenses. If we want to talk about seeing, hearing, etc at a particular moment in the past, we use **could**: *We could hear/see children playing outside.*(NOT *We were hearing...*)

★**council** (also **Council**) /'kaʊnsl/ noun [C, with sing or pl verb] **1** a group of people who are elected to govern an area such as a town or county: *The city council has/have decided to build a new road.* ● *a council house* (= one that a council owns and lets to people who do not have much money) ● *My dad's on the local council.* **2** a group of people chosen to give advice, manage affairs, etc for a particular organization or activity: *the Arts Council*

councillor /'kaʊnsələ/ noun [C] a member of a council: *to elect new councillors*

counsel¹ /'kaʊnsl/ verb [T] (**counselling**; **counselled**: *US* **counseling**; **counseled**) **1** to give professional advice and help to sb with a problem **2** (*written*) to tell sb what you think he/she should do; to advise: *Mr Dean's lawyers counselled him against making public statements.*

counsel² /'kaʊnsl/ noun [U] **1** (*written*) advice **2** a lawyer who speaks in a court of law: *the counsel for the defence/prosecution*

counselling (*US* **counseling**) /'kaʊnsəlɪŋ/ noun [U] professional advice and help given to people with problems: *Many students come to us for counselling.*

counsellor (*US* **counselor**) /'kaʊnsələ/ noun [C] a person whose job is to give advice: *a marriage counsellor*

★**count¹** /kaʊnt/ verb **1** [I] to say numbers one after another in order: *Close your eyes and count (up) to 20.* **2** [T] count sth to calculate the total number or amount of sth: *The teacher counted the children as they got on the bus.* **3** [T] to include sb/sth when you are calculating an amount or number: *There were thirty people on the bus, not counting the driver.* **4** [I] count (for sth) to be important or valuable: *I sometimes think my opinion*

C

counts for nothing at work. **5** [I] **count (as sth)** to be valid or accepted: *The referee had already blown his whistle so the goal didn't count.* • *Will my driving licence count as identification?* **6** [I,T] to consider sb/sth in a particular way: *You should count yourself lucky to have a good job.* • *On this airline, children over 12 count/are counted as adults.*

IDIOM **Don't count your chickens (before they're hatched)** used to say that you should not be too confident that sth will be successful because sth might still go wrong

PHRASAL VERBS **count against sb** to be considered as a disadvantage: *Do you think my age will count against me?*

count on sb/sth to expect sth with confidence; to depend on sb/sth: *Can I count on you to help me?*

count sb/sth out 1 to count things slowly, one by one: *She carefully counted out the money into my hand.* **2** (*informal*) to not include sb/sth: *If you're going swimming, you can count me out!*

count² /kaʊnt/ *noun* [C] **1** [usually sing] an act of counting or a number that you get after counting: *At the last count, there were nearly 2 million unemployed.* • *On the count of three, all lift together.* **2** [usually pl] a point that is made in a discussion, argument, etc: *I proved her wrong on all counts.*

IDIOM **keep/lose count (of sth)** to know/not know how many there are of sth: *I've lost count of the number of times he's told that joke!*

countable /'kaʊntəbl/ *adj* (*grammar*) that can be counted: *'Chair' is a countable noun, but 'sugar' isn't.* • *Countable nouns are marked* [C] *in this dictionary.* ••➤ opposite **uncountable**

➤ For more information about countable nouns, look at the **Quick Grammar Reference** section at the back of this dictionary.

countdown /'kaʊntdaʊn/ *noun* [C] the act of saying numbers backwards to zero just before sth important happens: *the countdown to the lift-off of a rocket* • (*figurative*) *The countdown to this summer's Olympic Games has started.*

counter¹ /'kaʊntə/ *noun* [C] **1** a long, flat surface in a shop, bank, etc, where customers are served: *The man behind the counter in the bank was very helpful.* **2** a small object (usually round and made of plastic) that is used in some games to show where a player is on the board **3** an electronic device for counting sth

counter² /'kaʊntə/ *verb* [I,T] **1** to reply or react to criticism: *He countered our objections with a powerful defence of his plan.* **2** to try to reduce or prevent the bad effects of sth: *The shop has installed security cameras to counter theft.*

counter³ /'kaʊntə/ *adv* **counter to sth** in the opposite direction to sth: *The results of these experiments run counter to previous findings.*

counteract /ˌkaʊntər'ækt/ *verb* [T] to reduce the effect of sth by acting against it: *measures to counteract traffic congestion*

'counter-attack *noun* [C] an attack made in reaction to an enemy or opponent's attack –**counter-attack** *verb* [I,T]

counter-'clockwise (*US*) = **ANTICLOCK-WISE**

counterfeit /'kaʊntəfɪt/ *adj* not genuine, but copied so that it looks like the real thing: *counterfeit money*

counterfoil /'kaʊntəfɔɪl/ *noun* [C] the part of a cheque, ticket, etc that you keep when you give the other part to sb else

counterpart /'kaʊntəpɑːt/ *noun* [C] a person or thing that has a similar position or function in a different country or organization: *the French President and his Italian counterpart* (= the Italian President)

counter-pro'ductive *adj* having the opposite effect to the one you want: *It can be counter-productive to punish children.*

countless /'kaʊntləs/ *adj* (only *before* a noun) very many: *I've tried to phone him countless times but he's not there.*

★**country** /'kʌntri/ *noun* (*pl* **countries**) **1** [C] an area of land with its own people, government, etc: *France, Spain and other European countries* • *There was snow over much of the country during the night.*

➤ **State** is used for talking about a country as an organized political community controlled by one government. It can also mean the government itself: *a politically independent state* • *the member states of the EU* • *You get a pension from the state when you retire.* • *state education.* **Land** is more formal or literary: *Explorers who set out to discover new lands.*

2 the country [sing] the people who live in a country: *a survey to find out what the country really thinks* **3 the country** [sing] land which is away from towns and cities: *Do you live in a town or the in the country?*

➤ The word **countryside** also refers to areas of land that are away from towns but it emphasizes the natural features such as hills, rivers, trees, etc that you find there: *beautiful countryside* • *the destruction of the countryside by new roads.* Look also at the note at **scenery**.

4 [U] an area of land: *We looked down over miles of open country.* • *hilly country* ••➤ synonym **terrain 5** =**COUNTRY AND WESTERN**

country and 'western *noun* [U] a type of popular music based on traditional music from southern and western US

countryman /'kʌntrimən/ *noun* [C] (*pl* -**men** /-mən/) a person from your own country (1): *The Italian Castorri beat his fellow countryman Rossi in the final.*

the countryside /'kʌntrɪsaɪd/ *noun* [U, sing] land which is away from towns and cities, where there are fields, woods, etc: *From the hill there is a magnificent view of the surrounding countryside.* ••➤ Look at the note at **country**.

county /'kaʊnti/ *noun* [C] (*pl* **counties**) an area in Britain, Ireland or the US which has its own local government: *the county of Nottinghamshire* ● *Orange County, California*

➤ Compare **province** and **state**¹(4).

coup /ku:/ *noun* [C] **1** (also **coup d'état** /ku: deɪ'tɑ:/) a sudden, illegal and often violent change of government: *a coup to overthrow the President* ● *an attempted coup* (= one which fails to succeed) **2** a clever and successful thing to do: *Getting that promotion was a real coup.*

★**couple**¹ /'kʌpl/ *noun* [C, with sing or pl verb] two people who are together because they are married or in a relationship: *a married couple* ● *Is/Are that couple over there part of our group?* ●➤ Look also at **pair**.

IDIOM **a couple of people/things 1** two people/things: *I need a couple of glasses.* **2** a few: *I last saw her a couple of months ago.*

couple² /'kʌpl/ *verb* [T] (usually passive) to join or connect sb/sth to sb/sth else: *The fog, coupled with the amount of traffic on the roads, made driving very difficult.*

coupon /'ku:pɒn/ *noun* [C] **1** a small piece of paper which you can use to buy goods at a lower price, or which you can collect and then exchange for goods: *a coupon worth 10% off your next purchase* **2** a printed form in a newspaper or magazine which you use to order goods, enter a competition, etc

★**courage** /'kʌrɪdʒ/ *noun* [U] the ability to control fear in a situation that may be dangerous or unpleasant; bravery: *It took real courage to go back into the burning building.* ● *She showed great courage all through her long illness.* –**courageous** /kə'reɪdʒəs/ *adj*

IDIOM **pluck up courage** ➜ **PLUCK**¹

courgette /kɔː'ʒet/ *noun* [C] (*especially US* **zucchini**) a long vegetable with dark green skin that is white inside ●➤ picture on page C3

courier /'kʊriə/ *noun* [C] **1** a person whose job is to carry letters, important papers, etc, especially when they are urgent: *The package was delivered by motorcycle courier.* **2** a person whose job is to look after a group of tourists

★**course** /kɔːs/ *noun* **1** [C] a course (in/on sth) a complete series of lessons or studies: *I've decided to enrol on a computer course.* ● *I'm going to take/do a course in self-defence.* **2** [C,U] the route or direction that sth, especially an aircraft, ship or river, takes: *The hijackers forced the captain to change course and head for Cuba.* ● *to be on/off course* (= going in the right/wrong direction) ● (*figurative*) *I'm on course* (= making the right amount of progress) *to finish this work by the end of the week.* ● *The road follows the course of the river.* **3** (also **course of action**) [C] a way of dealing with a particular situation: *In that situation resignation was the only course open to him.* **4** [sing] the development of sth over a period of time: *events that changed the course of history* ● *In the normal course of*

events (= the way things normally happen) *such problems do not arise.* **5** [C] the first, second, third, etc separate part of a meal: *a three-course lunch* ● *I had chicken for the main course.* **6** [C] an area where golf is played or where certain types of race take place: *a golf course* ● *a racecourse* **7** [C] a **course (of sth)** a series of medical treatments: *The doctor put her on a course of tablets.*

IDIOM **be on a collision course (with sb/sth)** ➜ **COLLISION**

in the course of sth during sth: *He mentioned it in the course of conversation.*

in the course of time when enough time has passed; eventually

in due course ➜ **DUE**¹

a matter of course ➜ **MATTER**¹

of course naturally; certainly: *Of course, having children has changed their lives a lot.* ● '*Can I use your phone?*' '*Of course (you can).*' ● '*You're not annoyed with me, are you?*' '*Of course (I'm) not.*'

coursebook /'kɔːsbʊk/ *noun* [C] a book for studying from that is used regularly in class

★**court**¹ /kɔːt/ *noun* **1** [C,U] a place where legal trials take place and crimes, etc are judged: *A man has been charged and will appear in court tomorrow.* ● *Bill's company are refusing to pay him so he's decided to take them to court.* **2 the court** [sing] the people in a court, especially those taking part in the trial: *Please tell the court exactly what you saw.* **3** [C,U] an area where certain ball games are played: *a tennis/squash/badminton court*

➤ Compare **pitch**¹.

court² /kɔːt/ *verb* [T] **1** to try to gain sb's support by paying special attention to him/her: *Politicians from all parties will be courting voters this week.* **2** to do sth that might have a very bad effect: *Britain is courting ecological disaster if it continues to dump waste in the North Sea.*

courteous /'kɜːtiəs/ *adj* polite and pleasant, showing respect for other people ●➤ opposite **discourteous** –**courteously** *adv*

courtesy /'kɜːtəsi/ *noun* (*pl* **courtesies**) **1** [U] polite and pleasant behaviour that shows respect for other people: *She didn't even have the courtesy to say that she was sorry.* **2** [C] (*formal*) a polite thing that you say or do when you meet people in formal situations: *The two presidents exchanged courtesies before their meeting.*

IDIOM **(by) courtesy of sb** (*formal*) with the permission or because of the kindness of sb: *These pictures are being shown by courtesy of BBC TV.*

court martial *noun* [C] a military court that deals with matters of military law; a trial that takes place in such a court: *His case will be heard by a court martial.* –**court-martial** *verb* [T]

court of law = **COURT**¹(1)

courtship /'kɔːtʃɪp/ noun [C,U] (old-fashioned) the relationship between a man and a woman before they get married

courtyard /'kɔːtjɑːd/ noun [C] an area of ground, without a roof, that has walls or buildings around it, for example in a castle or between houses or flats

★**cousin** /'kʌzn/ (also ˌfirst 'cousin) noun [C] the child of your aunt or uncle: *Paul and I are cousins.*

➤ The same word is used for both male and female cousins. A **second cousin** is the child of your cousin.

cove /kəʊv/ noun [C] a small area of the coast where the land curves round so that it is protected from the wind, etc: *a sandy cove*

★**cover**[1] /'kʌvə/ verb [T] **1 cover sb/sth (up/over) (with sth)** to put sth on or in front of sth to hide or protect it: *Could you cover the food and put it in the fridge?* ● *She couldn't look any more and covered her eyes.* ● *I covered the floor with newspaper before I started painting.* ● (figurative) *Paula laughed to cover* (= hide) *her embarrassment.* ⸱⸱➤ opposite **uncover 2 cover sb/sth in/with sth** to be on the surface of sth; to make sth do this: *A car went through the puddle and covered me with mud.* ● *Graffiti covered the walls.* ● *The eruption of the volcano covered the town in a layer of ash.* **3** to fill or spread over a certain area: *The floods cover an area of about 15000 square kilometres.* **4** to include or to deal with sth: *All the papers covered the election in depth.* ● *The course covered both British and European history.* **5** to travel a certain distance: *We covered about 500 kilometres that day.* **6** to be enough money for sth: *We'll give you some money to cover your expenses.* **7 cover sb/sth against/for sth** to protect sb/sth by insurance: *The insurance policy covers us for any damage to our property.* **8 cover (for sb)** to do sb's job while he/she is away from work: *Matt's phoned in sick so we'll have to find someone to cover (for him).*

IDIOM **cover the cost (of sth)** to have or make enough money to pay for sth: *We made so little money at our school dance that we didn't even cover the cost of the band.*

PHRASAL VERBS **cover (sth) up** to prevent people hearing about a mistake or sth bad: *The police have been accused of trying to cover up the facts of the case.*

cover up for sb to hide a person's mistakes or crimes in order to protect him/her: *His wife covered up for him to protect the police.*

★**cover**[2] /'kʌvə/ noun **1** [C] something that is put on or over sth, especially in order to protect it: *a plastic cover for a computer* ● *a duvet cover* **2** [C] the outside part of a book or magazine: *I read the magazine from cover to cover* (= from beginning to end). **3** [U] **cover (against sth)** insurance against sth, so that if sth bad happens you get money or help in return: *The policy provides cover against theft.* **4** [U] protection from the weather, damage, etc; shelter: *When the storm started we*

had to **take cover** in a shop doorway. ● *When the gunfire started everyone **ran for cover**.* **5 the covers** [pl] the sheets, etc on a bed **6** [C,U] a **cover (for sth)** something that hides what sb is really doing: *The whole company was just a cover for all kinds of criminal activities.* ● *police officers working **under cover** 7* [U] doing sb's job for him/her while he/she is away from work: *Joanne's off next week so we'll have to arrange cover.*

IDIOM **under (the) cover of sth** hidden by sth: *They attacked under cover of darkness.*

coverage /'kʌvərɪdʒ/ noun [U] **1** the act or amount of reporting on an event in newspapers, on television, etc: *TV coverage of the Olympic Games was excellent.* **2** the amount or quality of information included in a book, magazine, etc: *The grammar section provides coverage of all the most problematic areas.*

coveralls /'kʌvərɔːlz/ (US) = **OVERALL**[2](2)

covered /'kʌvəd/ adj **1 covered in/with sth** having a large or a large amount of sth on sb/sth: *She was covered in mud/sweat/dust.* ● *nuts covered with chocolate* **2** having a cover, especially a roof: *a covered shopping centre*

covering /'kʌvərɪŋ/ noun [C] something that covers the surface of sth: *There was a thick covering of dust over everything.*

ˌ**covering 'letter** noun [C] a letter that you send with a package, etc that gives more information about it: *To apply for the job, send your CV with a covering letter.*

covert /'kʌvət/ adj done secretly: *a covert police operation* –**covertly** adv

'**cover-up** noun [C] an act of preventing sth bad or dishonest from becoming known: *Several newspapers have claimed that there has been a government cover-up.*

covet /'kʌvət/ verb [T] (formal) to want to have sth very much (especially sth that belongs to sb else)

COWS

★**cow** /kaʊ/ noun [C] **1** a large female animal that is kept on farms to produce milk: *to milk a cow* ● *a herd of cows*

➤ **Cow** is often used for both male and female animals. The special word for a male is **bull**. A male that cannot produce any young and which was used in past times for pulling heavy loads is an **ox**. A young cow is a **calf**. A number of cows together can be called **cattle**. Look at the note at **meat**.

2 the adult female of certain large animals, for example elephants

coward /'kaʊəd/ noun [C] a person who has no courage and is afraid in dangerous or unpleasant situations: *I hate going to the dentist's because I'm a terrible coward.* –**cowardly** adj

cowardice /'kaʊədɪs/ **noun** [U] a lack of courage; behaviour that shows that you are afraid

cowboy /'kaʊbɔɪ/ **noun** [C] **1** a man whose job is to look after cows (usually on a horse) in certain parts of the US **2** (*Brit informal*) a person in business who is not honest or who does work badly: *a cowboy builder*

cower /'kaʊə/ **verb** [I] to move back or into a low position because of fear: *The dog cowered under the table when the storm started.*

coy /kɔɪ/ **adj 1** pretending to be shy or innocent: *She lifted her head a little and gave him a coy smile.* **2** not wanting to give information about sth or to answer questions that tell people too much about you: *Don't be coy, tell me how much you earn.* –**coyly** adv

cozy (*US*) = **cosy**

crab /kræb/ **noun** [C,U] a sea animal with a flat shell and ten legs. The front two legs have long curved points (pincers) on them. Crabs move sideways; the meat from a crab ·•➤ picture at **shellfish**

★**crack¹** /kræk/ **verb 1** [I,T] to break or to make sth break so that a line appears on the surface, but without breaking into pieces: *Don't put boiling water into that glass – it'll crack.* • *The stone cracked the windscreen but didn't break it.* ·•➤ picture at **chip 2** [T] to break sth open: *Crack two eggs into a bowl.* **3** [I,T] to make a sudden loud, sharp sound; to cause sth to make this sound: *to crack a whip/your knuckles* **4** [T] to hit a part of your body against sth; to hit somebody with sth: *She stood up and cracked her head on the cupboard door.* • *She cracked the thief over the head with her umbrella.* **5** [I] to no longer be able to deal with pressure and so lose control: *He cracked under the strain of all his problems.* **6** [I] (used about sb's voice) to suddenly change in a way that is not controlled: *Her voice cracked as she spoke about her parent's death.* **7** [T] (*informal*) to solve a problem: *to crack a code* • *The police have cracked an international drug-smuggling ring.* **8** [T] to tell or make a joke: *Stop cracking jokes and do some work!*

IDIOM **get cracking** (*Brit informal*) to start doing sth immediately: *I have to finish this job today so I'd better get cracking.*

PHRASAL VERBS **crack down (on sb/sth)** (used about people in authority) to start dealing strictly with bad or illegal behaviour: *The police have started to crack down on drug dealers.*

crack up 1 (*informal*) to be unable to deal with pressure and so lose control and become mentally ill: *He cracked up when his wife left him.* **2** (*slang*) to suddenly start laughing, especially when you should be serious

★**crack²** /kræk/ **noun 1** [C] a line on the surface of sth where it has broken, but not into separate pieces: *a pane of glass with a crack in it* • (*figurative*) *They had always seemed*

happy together, but then cracks began to appear in their relationship. ·•➤ picture at **chip 2** [C] a narrow opening: *a crack in the curtains* **3** [C] a sudden loud, sharp sound: *There was a loud crack as the gun went off.* **4** [C] a hard hit on a part of the body: *Suddenly a golf ball gave him a nasty crack on the head.* **5** [C] (*informal*) an amusing, often critical, comment; a joke: *She made a crack about his bald head and he got angry.* **6** [U] a dangerous and illegal drug that some people take for pleasure and cannot then stop taking

IDIOMS **the crack of dawn** very early in the morning

have a crack (at sth/at doing sth) (*informal*) to try to do sth: *I'm not sure how to play but I'll have a crack at it.*

crack³ /kræk/ **adj** (used about soldiers or sports players) very well-trained and skilful: *crack troops* • *He's a crack shot* (= very accurate at shooting) *with a rifle.*

crackdown /'krækdaʊn/ **noun** [C] action to stop bad or illegal behaviour: *Fifty people have been arrested in a police crackdown on street crime.*

cracker /'krækə/ **noun** [C] **1** a thin dry biscuit that is often eaten with cheese ·•➤ picture at **cake 2** (also **Christmas cracker**) a cardboard tube covered in coloured paper and containing a small present. Crackers are pulled apart by two people, each holding one end, at Christmas parties. They make a loud noise as they break. **3** (*Brit informal*) a very good example of sth: *That story he told was a real cracker.*

crackle /'krækl/ **verb** [I] to make a series of short, sharp sounds: *The radio started to crackle and then it stopped working.* –**crackle** noun [sing]: *the crackle of dry wood burning*

cradle¹ /'kreɪdl/ **noun** [C] a small bed for a baby. Cradles can often be moved from side to side. ·•➤ picture at **bed**

cradle² /'kreɪdl/ **verb** [T] to hold sb/sth carefully and gently in your arms

craft /krɑːft/ **noun 1** [C,U] a job or activity for which you need skill with your hands: *an arts and crafts exhibition* • *I studied craft and design at school.* ·•➤ Look at **handicraft. 2** [C] any job or activity for which you need skill: *He regards acting as a craft.* **3** [C] (*pl* **craft**) a boat, aircraft or spacecraft

craftsman /'krɑːftsmən/ **noun** [C] (*pl* **-men** /-mən/) a person who makes things skilfully, especially with his/her hands

craftsmanship /'krɑːftsmənʃɪp/ **noun** [U] the skill used by sb to make sth of high quality with his/her hands

crafty /'krɑːfti/ **adj** clever at getting or achieving things by using unfair or dishonest methods –**craftily** adv

crag /kræg/ **noun** [C] a steep, rough rock on a hill or mountain

craggy /'krægi/ **adj 1** having a lot of steep rough rock **2** (used about a man's face) strong and with deep lines, especially in an attractive way

cram /kræm/ **verb** (**cramming**; **crammed**)

1 [T] to push people or things into a small space: *I managed to cram all my clothes into the bag but I couldn't close it.* • *We only spent two days in Rome but we managed to cram a lot of sightseeing in.* **2** [I] to move, with a lot of other people, into a small space: *He only had a small car but they all managed to cram in.* **3** [I] to study very hard and learn a lot in a short time before an exam: *She's cramming for her exams.*

crammed /kræmd/ *adj* very or too full: *That book is crammed with useful information.*

cramp /kræmp/ *noun* [U] a sudden pain that you get in a muscle, that makes it difficult to move

cramped /kræmpt/ *adj* not having enough space: *The flat was terribly cramped with so many of us living there.*

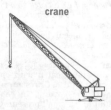

crane

crane¹ /kreɪn/ *noun* [C] a large machine with a long metal arm that is used for moving or lifting heavy objects

crane² /kreɪn/ *verb* [I,T] to stretch your neck forward in order to see or hear sth: *We all craned forward to get a better view.*

crank /kræŋk/ *noun* [C] a person with strange ideas or who behaves in a strange way: *Lots of cranks phoned the police confessing to the murder.*

cranny /ˈkræni/ *noun* [C] (*pl* **crannies**) a small opening in a wall, rock, etc
 IDIOM **every nook and cranny → NOOK**

crap /kræp/ *noun* [U] (*slang*) a very rude word meaning nonsense or rubbish ••➤ Many people find this word offensive.

★**crash¹** /kræʃ/ *verb* **1** [I,T] to have an accident in a vehicle; to drive a vehicle into sth: *He braked too late and crashed into the car in front.* **2** [I] to hit sth hard, making a loud noise: *The tree crashed to the ground.* **3** [I] to make a loud noise: *I could hear thunder crashing outside.* **4** [I] (used about money or business) to suddenly lose value or fail **5** [I] (used about a computer) to suddenly stop working: *We lost the data when the computer crashed.*

★**crash²** /kræʃ/ *noun* [C] **1** a sudden loud noise made by sth breaking, hitting sth, etc: *I heard a crash and ran outside.* **2** an accident when a car or other vehicle hits sth and is damaged: *a car/plane crash* **3** (used about money or business) a sudden fall in the value or price of sth: *the Stock Market crash of 1987* **4** a sudden failure of a machine, especially a computer

crash³ /kræʃ/ *adj* done in a very short

period of time: *She did a **crash course** in Spanish before going to work in Madrid.*

'crash barrier *noun* [C] a fence that keeps people or vehicles apart, for example when there are large crowds or between the two sides of the road

'crash helmet *noun* [C] a hard hat worn by motorbike riders, racing drivers, etc ••➤ picture at **hat**

ˌcrash-'land *verb* [I] to land a plane in a dangerous way in an emergency –**crash-landing** *noun* [C]: *to make a crash-landing*

crass /kræs/ *adj* stupid, showing that you do not understand sth: *It was a crass comment to make when he knew how upset she was.*

crate /kreɪt/ *noun* [C] a large box in which goods are carried or stored

crater /ˈkreɪtə/ *noun* [C] **1** a large hole in the ground: *The bomb left a large crater.* • *craters on the moon* **2** the hole in the top of a mountain through which hot gases and liquid rock are forced (a volcano) ••➤ picture at **volcano**

cravat /krəˈvæt/ *noun* [C] a wide piece of cloth that some men tie around their neck and wear inside the collar of their shirt

crave /kreɪv/ *verb* [I,T] **crave (for) sth** to want and need to have sth very much: *Sometimes I really crave for some chocolate.*

craving /ˈkreɪvɪŋ/ *noun* [C] a strong desire for sth: *When she was pregnant she used to have cravings for all sorts of peculiar food.*

★**crawl¹** /krɔːl/ *verb* [I] **1** to move slowly with your body on or close to the ground, or on your hands and knees: *Their baby has just started to crawl.* • *An insect crawled across the floor.*

crawl

2 (used about vehicles) to move very slowly: *The traffic crawls through the centre of town in the rush-hour.* **3** (*informal*) **crawl (to sb)** to be very polite or pleasant to sb in order to be liked or to gain sth: *He only got promoted because he crawled to the manager.*
 IDIOM **be crawling with sth** to be completely full of or covered with unpleasant animals: *The kitchen was crawling with insects.* • (*figurative*) *The village is always crawling with tourists at this time of year.*

crawl² /krɔːl/ *noun* **1** [sing] a very slow speed: *The traffic slowed to a crawl.* **2** (often **the crawl**) [sing,U] a style of swimming which you do on your front. When you do the crawl, you move first one arm and then the other over your head, turn your face to one side so that you can breathe and kick up and down with your legs. ••➤ picture on page S2

crayon /ˈkreɪən/ *noun* [C,U] a soft, thick, coloured pencil that is used for drawing or writing, especially by children –**crayon** *verb* [I,T]

craze /kreɪz/ *noun* [C] a **craze (for sth) 1** a strong interest in sth, that usually only lasts for a short time: *There was a craze for that* *kind of music last year.* **2** something that a lot of people are very interested in: *Pocket TVs are the latest craze among teenagers.*

★**crazy** /'kreɪzi/ *adj* (**crazier**; **craziest**) (*informal*) **1** very silly or foolish: *You must be crazy to turn down such a wonderful offer.* **2** very angry: *She goes crazy when people criticize her.* **3** crazy about sb/sth liking sb/sth very much: *He's always been crazy about horses.* **4** showing great excitement: *The fans went crazy when their team scored the first goal.* –**crazily** *adv* –**craziness** *noun* [U]

creak /kriːk/ *verb* [I] to make the noise of wood bending or of sth not moving smoothly: *The floorboards creaked when I walked across the room.* –**creak** *noun* [C] –**creaky** *adj*: *creaky stairs*

★**cream¹** /kriːm/ *noun* **1** [U] the thick yellowish-white liquid that rises to the top of milk: *coffee with cream* • *whipped cream* (= cream that has been beaten) ·➤ picture on page C4 **2** [C,U] a substance that you rub into your skin to keep it soft or as a medical treatment: (*an*) *antiseptic cream* ·➤ picture at **bandage** **3 the cream** [sing] the best part of sth or the best people in a group

cream² /kriːm/ *adj*, *noun* [U] (of) a yellowish-white colour

cream³ /kriːm/ *verb* [PHRASAL VERB] **cream sb/sth off** to take away the best people or part from sth for a particular purpose: *The big clubs cream off the country's best young players.*

creamy /'kriːmi/ *adj* (**creamier**; **creamiest**) **1** containing cream; thick and smooth like cream: *a creamy sauce* **2** having a light colour like cream: *creamy skin*

crease¹ /kriːs/ *noun* [C] **1** an untidy line on paper, material, a piece of clothing, etc that should not be there: *Your shirt needs ironing, it's full of creases.* • *When I unrolled the poster, there was a crease in it.* **2** a tidy straight line that you make in sth, for example when you fold it in: *He had a sharp crease in his trousers.*

crease² /kriːs/ *verb* [I,T] to get creases; to make sth get creases: *Hang up your jacket or it will crease.* • *Crease the paper carefully down the middle.*

★**create** /kri'eɪt/ *verb* [T] to cause sth new to happen or exist: *a plan to create new jobs in the area* • *He created a bad impression at the interview.*

creation /kri'eɪʃn/ *noun* **1** [U] the act of causing sth new to happen or exist: *the creation of new independent states* **2** (usually **the Creation**) [sing] the act of making the whole universe, as described in the Bible **3** [C] something new that sb has made or produced: *This dish is a new creation – I didn't use a recipe.*

creative /kri'eɪtɪv/ *adj* **1** using skill or imagination to make or do new things: *She's a fantastic designer – she's so creative.* **2** connected with producing new things: *His creative life went on until he was well over 80.* –**creatively** *adv*

creativity /ˌkriːeɪ'tɪvəti/ *noun* [U] the ability to make or produce new things using skill or imagination: *We want teaching that encourages children's creativity.*

creator /kri'eɪtə/ *noun* [C] a person who makes or produces sth new: *He was the creator of some of the best-known characters in literature.*

★**creature** /'kriːtʃə/ *noun* [C] a living thing such as an animal, a bird, a fish or an insect, but not a plant: *sea creatures*

crèche /kreʃ/ *noun* [C] a place where small children are looked after while their parents are working, shopping, etc

credentials /krə'denʃlz/ *noun* [pl] **1** the qualities, experience, etc that make sb suitable for sth: *He has the perfect credentials for the job.* **2** a document that is proof that you have the training, education, etc necessary to do sth, or proof that you are who you say you are

credibility /ˌkredə'bɪləti/ *noun* [U] the quality that sb has that makes people believe or trust him/her: *The Prime Minister had lost all credibility and had to resign.*

credible /'kredəbl/ *adj* **1** that you can believe: *It's hardly credible that such a thing could happen without him knowing it.* ·➤ opposite **incredible** **2** that seems possible: *We need to think of a credible alternative to nuclear energy.*

★**credit¹** /'kredɪt/ *noun* **1** [U] a way of buying goods or services and not paying for them until later: *I bought the television on credit.* **2** [C,U] a sum of money that a bank, etc lends to sb: *The company was not able to get any further credit and went bankrupt.* **3** [U] having money in an account at a bank: *No bank charges are made if your account remains in credit.* **4** [C] a payment made into an account at a bank: *There have been several credits to her account over the last month.* ·➤ opposite **debit** **5** [U] an act of saying that sb has done sth well: *He got all the credit for the success of the project.* • *I can't take any credit; the others did all the work.* • *She didn't do very well but at least give her credit for trying.* **6** [sing] a credit to sb/sth a person or thing that you should be proud of: *She is a credit to her school.* **7 the credits** [pl] the list of the names of the people who made a film or TV programme, shown at the beginning or end of the film **8** [C] (*US*) a part of a course at a college or university, that a student has completed successfully

[IDIOMS] **do sb credit** (used about sb's qualities or achievements) to be so good that people should be proud of him/her: *His courage and optimism do him credit.*

(be) to sb's credit used for showing that you approve of sth that sb has done, although you have criticized him/her for sth else: *The company, to its credit, apologized and refunded my money.*

have sth to your credit to have finished sth that is successful: *He has three best-selling novels to his credit.*

credit[2] /'kredɪt/ *verb* [T] **1** to add money to a bank account: *Has the cheque been credited to my account yet?* **2 credit sb/sth with sth; credit sth to sb/sth** to believe or say that sb/sth has a particular quality or has done something well: *Of course I wouldn't do such a stupid thing – credit me with a bit more sense than that!* **3** (especially in negative sentences and questions) to believe sth: *I simply cannot credit that he has made the same mistake again!*

creditable /'kredɪtəbl/ *adj* of a quite good standard that cannot be criticized, though not excellent: *It was a creditable result considering that three players were injured.*

'**credit card** *noun* [C] a small plastic card that allows sb to get goods or services without using money. You usually receive a bill once a month for what you have bought: *Can I pay by credit card?* •➤ Look at **cash card** and **cheque card**. •➤ picture at **money**

creditor /'kredɪtə/ *noun* [C] a person or company from whom you have borrowed money

creed /kriːd/ *noun* [C] a set of beliefs or principles (especially religious ones) that strongly influence sb's life

creek /kriːk/ *noun* [C] **1** (*Brit*) a narrow piece of water where the sea flows into the land **2** (*US*) a small river; a stream

creep[1] /kriːp/ *verb* [I] (*pt, pp* **crept** /krept/) **1** to move very quietly and carefully so that nobody will notice you: *She crept into the room so as not to wake him up.* **2** to move forward slowly: *The traffic was only creeping along.*

> IDIOM **make your flesh creep** → **FLESH**

> PHRASAL VERB **creep in** to begin to appear: *All sorts of changes are beginning to creep into the education system.*

creep[2] /kriːp/ *noun* [C] (*informal*) a person that you do not like because they try too hard to be liked by people in authority

> IDIOM **give sb the creeps** (*informal*) to make sb feel frightened or nervous: *There's something about him that gives me the creeps.*

creeper /'kriːpə/ *noun* [C] a plant that grows up trees or walls or along the ground

creepy /'kriːpi/ *adj* (*informal*) that makes you feel nervous or frightened

cremate /krə'meɪt/ *verb* [T] to burn the body of a dead person as part of a funeral service –**cremation** /krə'meɪʃn/ *noun* [C,U] •➤ Look at the note at **funeral**.

crematorium /ˌkremə'tɔːriəm/ *noun* [C] a building in which the bodies of dead people are burned

Creole (also **creole**) /'kriːəʊl/ *noun* **1** [C] a person who was born in the Caribbean whose family originally came from Europe and Africa **2** [C] a person whose relatives (ancestors) were among the first Europeans to live in the Caribbean and South America, or among the first French or Spanish people to live in the southern states of the US: *the Creole cooking of New Orleans* **3** [U,C] a language that was originally a mixture of a

European language and a local, especially African, language

crept *past tense, past participle* of **CREEP**[1]

crescendo /krə'ʃendəʊ/ *noun* [C] (*pl* **crescendos**) a noise or piece of music that gets louder and louder

crescent /'kresnt/ *noun* [C] **1** a curved shape that is pointed at both ends, like the moon in its first and last stages •➤ picture at **shape 2** a street that is curved

cress /kres/ *noun* [U] a small plant with very small green leaves that does not need to be cooked and is eaten in salads and sandwiches

crest /krest/ *noun* [C] **1** a group of feathers on the top of a bird's head •➤ picture on page C1 **2** the top of a hill **3** the white part at the top of a wave

crestfallen /'krestfɔːlən/ *adj* sad or disappointed

crevasse /krə'væs/ *noun* [C] a deep crack in a very thick layer of ice

crevice /'krevɪs/ *noun* [C] a narrow crack in a rock, wall, etc

★**crew** /kruː/ *noun* [C,with sing or pl verb] **1** all the people who work on a ship, aircraft, etc **2** a group of people who work together: *a camera crew* (= people who film things for television, etc)

crib[1] /krɪb/ (*especially US*) = **COT**

crib[2] /krɪb/ *verb* [I,T] (**cribbing; cribbed**) **crib (sth) (from/off sb)** to copy sb else's work and pretend it is your own

crick /krɪk/ *noun* [sing] a pain in your neck, back, etc that makes it difficult for you to move easily –**crick** *verb* [T]: *I've cricked my neck.*

cricket /'krɪkɪt/ *noun* **1** [U] a game that is played with a bat and ball on a large area of grass by two teams of eleven players

> In cricket the **bowler** bowls the ball to the **batsman** who tries to hit it with a **bat** and then score a **run** by running from one end of the pitch to the other.

2 [C] an insect that makes a loud noise by rubbing its wings together

cricketer /'krɪkɪtə/ *noun* [C] a person who plays cricket

★**crime** /kraɪm/ *noun* **1** [C] something which is illegal and which people are punished for, for example by being sent to prison: *to commit a crime* **2** [U] illegal behaviour or activities: *There has been an increase in car crime recently.* ● *to fight crime* **3** (usually **a crime**) [sing] something that is morally wrong: *It is a crime to waste food when people are starving.*

★**criminal**[1] /'krɪmɪnl/ *noun* [C] a person who has done something illegal

★**criminal**[2] /'krɪmɪnl/ *adj* **1** (only *before* a noun) connected with crime: *Deliberate damage to public property is a criminal offence.* ● *criminal law* **2** morally wrong: *a criminal waste of taxpayers' money*

crimson /'krɪmzn/ *adj, noun* [U] (of) a dark red colour

cringe /krɪndʒ/ *verb* [I] **1** to feel embarrassed: *awful family photographs which* **make** *you cringe* **2** to move away from sb/sth because you are frightened: *The dog cringed in terror when the man raised his arm.*

crinkle /'krɪŋkl/ *verb* [I,T] crinkle (sth) (up) to have, or to make sth have, thin folds or lines in it: *He crinkled the silver paper up into a ball.* –crinkly /'krɪŋkli/ *adj*: *crinkly material*

cripple /'krɪpl/ *verb* [T] to damage sth badly: *The recession has crippled the motor industry.*

crippling /'krɪplɪŋ/ *adj* that causes very great damage or has a very bad effect: *They had crippling debts and had to sell their house.*

crisis /'kraɪsɪs/ *noun* [C,U] (*pl* **crises** /-si:z/) a time of great danger or difficulty; the moment when things change and either improve or get worse: *the international crisis caused by the invasion* ● *a friend you can rely on in times of crisis*

crisp¹ /krɪsp/ *adj* **1** pleasantly hard and dry: *Store the biscuits in a tin to keep them crisp.* **2** firm and fresh or new: *a crisp salad/apple* ● *a crisp cotton dress* **3** (used about the air or weather) cold and dry: *a crisp winter morning* **4** (used about the way sb speaks) quick, clear but not very friendly: *a crisp reply* –crisply *adv*: *'I disagree,' she said crisply.* –crispy *adj* (*informal*) = CRISP¹(1,2)

crisp² /krɪsp/ (*US* chip; po'tato chip) *noun* [C] a very thin piece of potato that is fried in oil, dried and then sold in packets. Crisps usually have salt or another flavouring on them: *a packet of crisps* ••➤ picture at **chip**

criss-cross /'krɪs krɒs/ *adj* (only *before* a noun) with many straight lines that cross over each other: *a criss-cross pattern* –criss-cross *verb* [I,T]: *Many footpaths criss-cross the countryside.*

criterion /kraɪˈtɪəriən/ *noun* [C] (*pl* **criteria** /-riə/) the standard that you use when you make a decision or form an opinion about sb/sth: *What are the criteria for deciding who gets a place on the course?*

critic /'krɪtɪk/ *noun* [C] **1** a person who says what is bad or wrong with sb/sth: *He is a long-standing critic of the council's transport policy.* **2** a person whose job is to give his/her opinion about a play, film, book, work of art, etc: *a film/restaurant/art critic*

★**critical** /'krɪtɪkl/ *adj* **1** critical (of sb/sth) saying what is wrong with sb/sth: *The report was very critical of safety standards on the railways.* **2** (only *before* a noun) describing the good and bad points of a play, film, book, work of art, etc: *a critical guide to this month's new films* **3** dangerous or serious: *The patient is **in a critical condition**.* **4** very important; at a time when things can suddenly become better or worse: *The talks between the two leaders have **reached a critical stage**.* –critically /-kli/ *adv*: *a critically ill patient* ● *a critically important decision*

★**criticism** /'krɪtɪsɪzəm/ *noun* **1** [C,U] (an expression of) what you think is bad about sb/sth: *The council has **come in for** severe criticism over the plans.* **2** [U] the act of

describing the good and bad points of a play, film, book, work of art, etc: *literary criticism*

★**criticize** (also **-ise**) /'krɪtɪsaɪz/ *verb* [I,T] criticize (sb/sth) (for sth) to say what is bad or wrong with sb/sth: *The doctor was criticized for not sending the patient to hospital.*

critique /krɪˈtiːk/ *noun* [C] a piece of writing that describes the good and bad points of sb/sth

croak /krəʊk/ *verb* [I] to make a harsh low noise like a particular animal (a frog) –croak *noun* [C]

crochet /'krəʊʃeɪ/ *noun* [U] a way of making clothes, cloth, etc by using wool or cotton and a needle with a hook at one end –crochet *verb* [I,T] (*pt, pp* crocheted /-ʃeɪd/) ••➤ Look at **knit**.

crockery /'krɒkəri/ *noun* [U] cups, plates and dishes ••➤ Look at **cutlery**.

crocodile /'krɒkədaɪl/ *noun* [C] a large reptile with a long tail and a big mouth with sharp teeth. Crocodiles live in rivers and lakes in hot countries. ••➤ Look at **alligator**.

croissant /'krwæsɒ̃/ *noun* [C] a type of bread roll, shaped in a curve, that is often eaten with butter for breakfast ••➤ picture at **bread**

crony /'krəʊni/ *noun* [C] (*pl* **cronies**) (*informal*) (often used in a critical way) a friend

crook /krʊk/ *noun* [C] **1** (*informal*) a dishonest person; a criminal **2** a bend or curve in sth: *the crook of your arm* (= the inside of your elbow)

crooked /'krʊkɪd/ *adj* **1** not straight or even: *That picture is crooked.* ● *crooked teeth* **2** (*informal*) not honest: *a crooked accountant*

★**crop¹** /krɒp/ *noun* **1** [C] all the grain, fruit, vegetables, etc of one type that a farmer grows at one time: *a crop of apples* **2** [C, usually pl] plants that are grown on farms for food: *Rice and soya beans are the main crops here.* **3** [sing] a number of people or things which have appeared at the same time: *the recent crop of movies about aliens*

crop² /krɒp/ *verb* (cropping; cropped) **1** [T] to cut sth very short: *cropped hair* **2** [I] to produce a crop¹(1)

PHRASAL VERB crop up to appear suddenly, when you are not expecting it: *We should have finished this work yesterday but some problems cropped up.*

cropper /'krɒpə/ *noun*

IDIOM come a cropper (*informal*) **1** to fall over or have an accident **2** to fail

★**cross¹** /krɒs/ *noun* [C] **1** a mark that you make by drawing one line across another (× or x). The sign is used for showing the position of sth, for showing that sth is not correct, etc: *I drew a cross on the map to show where our house is.* ● *Incorrect answers were marked with a cross.* ••➤ picture at **tick** **2** (also **the Cross**) the two pieces of wood in the shape of a cross on which people were killed as a punishment in former times, or something in this shape that is used as a symbol of the Christian religion: *She wore a* gold cross round her neck. •➤ Look at **crucifix**. **3** [usually sing] a cross (between A and B) something (especially a plant or an animal) that is a mixture of two different types of thing: *a fruit which is a cross between a peach and an apple* **4** (in sports such as football) a kick or hit of the ball that goes across the front of the goal

IDIOM **noughts and crosses** → NOUGHT

★**cross²** /krɒs/ *verb* **1** [I,T] **cross (over) (from sth/to sth)** to go from one side of sth to the other: *to cross the road* • *Where did you cross the border?* • *Which of the runners crossed the finishing line first?* **2** [I] (used about lines, roads, etc) to pass across each other: *The two roads cross just north of the village.* **3** [T] to put sth across or over sth else: *to cross your arms* •➤ picture on page S8 **4** [T] to make sb angry by refusing to do what he/she wants you to do: *He's an important man. It could be dangerous to cross him.* **5** [T] **cross sth with sth** to produce a new type of plant or animal by mixing two different types: *If you cross a horse with a donkey, you get a mule.* **6** [I,T] (in sports such as football and hockey) to pass the ball across the front of the goal

IDIOMS **cross my heart (and hope to die)** (*spoken*) used for emphasizing that what you are saying is true

cross your fingers; keep your fingers crossed → FINGER¹

cross your mind (used about a thought, idea, etc) to come into your mind: *It never once crossed my mind that she was lying.*

PHRASAL VERBS **cross sth off (sth)** to remove sth from a list, etc by drawing a line through it: *Cross Dave's name off the guest list – he can't come.*

cross sth out to draw a line through sth that you have written because you have made a mistake, etc: *to cross out a spelling mistake*

cross³ /krɒs/ *adj* (*informal*) **cross (with sb) (about sth)** angry or annoyed: *I was really cross with her for leaving me with all the work.* •➤ **Cross** is less formal than **angry**. –**crossly** *adv*: *'Be quiet,' Dad said crossly.*

crossbar /'krɒsbɑː/ *noun* [C] **1** the piece of wood over the top of a goal in football, etc **2** the metal bar that joins the front and back of a bicycle •➤ picture on page S9

,**cross-'country** *adj, adv* across fields and natural land; not using roads or tracks: *We walked about 10 miles cross-country before we saw a village.*

,**cross-e'xamine** *verb* [T] to ask sb questions in a court of law, etc in order to find out the truth about sth: *The witness was cross-examined for two hours.* –,**cross-e,xami'nation** *noun* [C,U]

'**cross-eyed** *adj* having one or both your eyes looking towards your nose

crossfire /'krɒsfaɪə/ *noun* [U] a situation in which guns are being fired from two or more different directions: *The journalist was killed in crossfire.* • (*figurative*) *When my parents argued, I sometimes got caught in the crossfire.*

crossing /'krɒsɪŋ/ *noun* [C] **1** a place where you can cross over sth: *You should cross the road at the pedestrian crossing.* • *a border crossing* **2** (*Brit* **level crossing**) a place where a road and a railway line cross each other **3** a journey from one side of a sea or river to the other: *We had a rough crossing.*

cross-legged /,krɒs 'legd/ *adj, adv* sitting on the floor with your legs pulled up in front of you and with one leg or foot over the other: *to sit cross-legged* •➤ picture on page S8

,**cross-'purposes** *noun*

IDIOM **at cross-purposes** a state of confusion between people who are talking about different things but think they are talking about the same thing

'**cross-reference** *noun* [C] a note in a book that tells you to look in another place in the book for more information

crossroads /'krɒsrəʊdz/ *noun* [C] (*pl* **crossroads**) a place where two or more roads cross each other: *When you come to the next crossroads turn right.* •➤ picture at **roundabout**

'**cross section** *noun* [C] **1** a picture of what the inside of sth would look like if you cut through it: *a cross-section of the human brain* **2** a number of people, etc that come from the different parts of a group, and so can be considered to represent the whole group: *The families we studied were chosen to represent a cross-section of society.*

crosswalk /'krɒswɔːk/ (*US*) = PEDESTRIAN CROSSING

★**crossword** /'krɒswɜːd/ (also '**crossword puzzle**) *noun* [U] a word game in which you have to write the answers to questions (**clues**) in square spaces, which are arranged in a pattern: *Every morning I try to **do the crossword** in the newspaper.*

crotch /krɒtʃ/ (also **crutch**) *noun* [C] the place where your legs, or a pair of trousers, join at the top

crouch /kraʊtʃ/ *verb* [I] **crouch (down)** to bend your legs and body so that you are close to the ground: *He crouched down behind the sofa.* •➤ picture at **kneel**

crow¹ /krəʊ/ *noun* [C] a large black bird that makes a loud noise

IDIOM **as the crow flies** (used for describing distances) in a straight line: *It's a kilometre as the crow flies but three kilometres by road.*

crow² /krəʊ/ *verb* [I] **1** to make a loud noise like a male chicken (**cock**) makes **2** (*informal*) to speak very proudly about sth; to boast

crowbar /'krəʊbɑː/ *noun* [C] a long iron bar that is used for forcing sth open

★**crowd¹** /kraʊd/ *noun* **1** [C, with sing or pl verb] a large number of people in one place: *The crowd was/were extremely noisy.* • *He pushed his way through the crowd.* • *I go shopping early in the morning to avoid the crowds.* **2** **the crowd** [sing] ordinary people: *He wears weird clothes because he wants to **stand out from the crowd**.* **3** [C, with sing or pl verb] (*informal*) a group of people who know each other: *John, Linda and Barry will be there – all the usual crowd.*

*crowd² /kraʊd/ **verb 1** [I] **crowd around/ round (sb)** (used about a lot of people) to stand in a large group around sb/sth: *Fans crowded round the singer hoping to get his autograph.* **2** [T] (used about a lot of people) to fill an area: *Groups of tourists crowded the main streets.* ● (*figurative*) *Memories crowded her mind.*

PHRASAL VERBS **crowd into sth; crowd in** to go into a small place and make it very full: *Somehow we all crowded into their small living room.*

crowd sb/sth into sth; crowd sb/sth in to put a lot of people into a small place: *Ten prisoners were crowded into one small cell.*

crowd sth out; crowd sb/sth out (of sth) to completely fill a place so that nobody else can enter: *Students crowd out the cafe at lunchtimes.* ● *Smaller companies are being crowded out of the market.*

crowded /'kraʊdɪd/ **adj** full of people: *a crowded bus* ● *people living in poor and crowded conditions*

crown¹ /kraʊn/ **noun 1** [C] a circle made of gold and jewels, that a king or queen wears on his/her head on official occasions **2 the Crown** [sing] the state as represented by a king or queen: *an area of land belonging to the Crown* **3** [sing] the top of your head or of a hat ●➤ picture at **hat 4** [sing] the top of a hill

crown² /kraʊn/ **verb** [T] **1** to put a crown on the head of a new king or queen in an official ceremony: *Elizabeth was crowned in 1952.* ● (*figurative*) *the newly crowned British champion* **2** (often passive) **crown sth (with sth)** to have or put sth on the top of sth: *The mountain was crowned with snow.* ● (*figurative*) *Her years of hard work were finally crowned with success.*

crowning /'kraʊnɪŋ/ **adj** (only *before* a noun) the best or most important: *Winning the World Championship was the crowning moment of her career.*

*crucial /'kru:ʃl/ **adj crucial (to/for sth)** extremely important; vital: *Early diagnosis of the illness is crucial for successful treatment.* –**crucially** /-ʃəli/ **adv**

crucifix /'kru:səfɪks/ **noun** [C] a small model of a cross with a figure of Jesus on it

crucifixion /ˌkru:sə'fɪkʃn/ **noun** [C,U] the act of crucifying sb: *the Crucifixion of Christ*

crucify /'kru:sɪfaɪ/ **verb** [T] (*pres part* **crucifying**; *3rd pers sing pres* **crucifies**; *pt, pp* **crucified**) to kill sb by nailing or tying him/her to a cross

crude /kru:d/ **adj 1** simple and basic, without much detail, skill, etc: *The method was crude but very effective.* ● *She explained how the system worked in crude terms.* **2** referring to sex or the body in a way that would offend many people: *He's always telling crude jokes.* **3** in its natural state, before it has been treated with chemicals: *crude oil* –**crudely** **adv**: *a crudely drawn face*

*cruel /'kru:əl/ **adj** (**crueller**; **cruellest**) causing physical or mental pain or suffering to sb/sth: *I think it's cruel to keep animals in cages.* ● *a cruel punishment* –**cruelly** /'kru:əli/ **adv**

*cruelty /'kru:əlti/ **noun** (*pl* **cruelties**) **1** [U] **cruelty (to sb/sth)** cruel behaviour: *cruelty to children* **2** [C,usually pl] a cruel act: *the cruelties of war*

cruise¹ /kru:z/ **verb** [I] **1** to travel by boat, visiting a number of places, as a holiday: *to cruise around the Caribbean* **2** to stay at the same speed in a car, plane, etc: *cruising at 80 kilometres an hour*

cruise² /kru:z/ **noun** [C] a holiday in which you travel on a ship and visit a number of different places: *They're planning to go on a cruise.*

cruiser /'kru:zə/ **noun** [C] **1** a large fast ship used in a war **2** a motor boat which has room for people to sleep in it

crumb /krʌm/ **noun** [C] a very small piece of bread, cake or biscuit ●➤ picture at **cake**

crumble /'krʌmbl/ **verb** [I,T] **crumble (sth) (up)** to break or make sth break into very small pieces: *The walls of the church are beginning to crumble.* ● *We crumbled up the bread and threw it to the birds.* ● (*figurative*) *Support for the government is beginning to crumble.* –**crumbly** **adj**: *This cheese has a crumbly texture.*

crumple /'krʌmpl/ **verb** [I,T] **crumple (sth) (into sth); crumple (sth) (up)** to be pressed or to press sth into an untidy shape: *The front of the car crumpled when it hit the wall.* ● *She crumpled the letter into a ball and threw it away.*

crunch¹ /krʌntʃ/ **verb 1** [T] **crunch sth (up)** to make a loud noise when you are eating sth hard: *to crunch an apple* **2** [I] to make a loud noise like the sound of sth being crushed: *We crunched through the snow.* –**crunchy** **adj**: *a crunchy apple*

crunch² /krʌntʃ/ **noun** [sing] an act or noise of crunching: *There was a loud crunch as he sat on the box of eggs.*

IDIOM **if/when it comes to the crunch** if/ when you are in a difficult situation and must make a difficult decision: *If it comes to the crunch, I'll stay and fight.*

crusade /kru:'seɪd/ **noun** [C] **1** a fight for sth that you believe to be good or against sth that you believe to be bad: *Mr Khan is leading a crusade against drugs in his neighbourhood.* **2 Crusade** one of the wars fought in Palestine by European Christians against Muslims in the Middle Ages –**crusader** **noun** [C]

crush¹ /krʌʃ/ **verb** [T] **1** to press sb/sth hard so that he/she/it is broken, damaged or injured: *Most of the eggs got crushed when she sat on them.* ● *He was crushed to death by a lorry.* **2 crush sth (up)** to break sth into very small pieces or a powder: *Crush the garlic and fry in oil.* ●➤ picture at **squeeze 3** to defeat sb/sth completely: *The army was sent in to crush the rebellion.*

crush² /krʌʃ/ **noun 1** [sing] a large group of

people in a small space: *There was such a crush that I couldn't get near the bar.* **2** [C] (*informal*) **a crush (on sb)** a strong feeling of love for sb that only usually lasts for a short time: *Maria had a huge crush on her teacher.*

crushing /'krʌʃɪŋ/ **adj** (only *before* a noun) that defeats sb/sth completely; very bad: *a crushing defeat*

crust /krʌst/ **noun** [C,U] **1** the hard part on the outside of a piece of bread, a pie, etc ••➤ picture at **bread 2** a hard layer on the outside of sth: *the earth's crust*

crusty /'krʌsti/ **adj 1** having a hard crust (1): *crusty bread* **2** (*informal*) bad-tempered and impatient: *a crusty old man*

crutch /krʌtʃ/ **noun** [C] **1** a type of stick that you put under your arm to help you walk when you have hurt your leg or foot: *She was on crutches for two months after she broke her ankle.*

➤ Compare **walking stick**.

••➤ picture at **bandage 2** =**CROTCH**

crux /krʌks/ **noun** [sing] the most important or difficult part of a problem: *The crux of the matter is how to stop this from happening again.*

★**cry¹** /kraɪ/ **verb** (*pres part* **crying**; *3rd pers sing pres* **cries**; *pt, pp* **cried**) **1** [I] to make a noise and produce tears in your eyes, for example because you are unhappy or have hurt yourself: *The baby never stops crying.* ● *The child was crying for* (= because she wanted) *her mother.* **2** [I,T] **cry (out)** to shout or make a loud noise: *We could hear someone crying for help.* ● *'Look,' he cried, 'There they are.'*

IDIOMS **a shoulder to cry on** ➔ **SHOULDER¹**

cry your eyes out to cry a lot for a long time

PHRASAL VERB **cry out for sth** to need sth very much: *Birmingham is crying out for a new transport system.*

★**cry²** /kraɪ/ **noun** (*pl* **cries**) **1** [C] a shout or loud high noise: *the cries of the children in the playground* ● *We heard Adam give a cry of pain as the dog bit him.* ● (*figurative*) *Her suicide attempt was really a cry for help.* **2** [sing] an act of crying¹(1): *After a good cry I felt much better.*

IDIOM **a far cry from sth/from doing sth** ➔ **FAR¹**

crying /'kraɪɪŋ/ **adj** (only *before* a noun) (used to talk about a bad situation) very great: *There's a crying need for more doctors.* ● *It's a crying shame that so many young people can't find jobs.*

crypt /krɪpt/ **noun** [C] a room that is under a church, where people were sometimes buried in the past

cryptic /'krɪptɪk/ **adj** having a hidden meaning that is not easy to understand; mysterious: *a cryptic message/remark* –**cryptically** /-kli/ **adv**

crystal /'krɪstl/ **noun 1** [C] a regular shape that some mineral substances form when they become solid: *salt crystals* **2** [U] a clear mineral that can be used in making jewellery **3** [U] very high-quality glass: *a crystal vase*

crystal 'ball noun [C] a glass ball in which some people say you can see what will happen in the future

crystal 'clear adj 1 (used about water, glass, etc) that you can see through perfectly **2** very easy to understand: *The meaning is crystal clear.*

cu abbr cubic: *a volume of 3 cu ft*

cub /kʌb/ **noun** [C] **1** a young bear, lion, etc ••➤ picture at **lion 2 the Cubs** [pl] the part of the Boy Scout organization that is for younger boys **3 Cub** (also **Cub Scout**) [C] a member of the Cubs

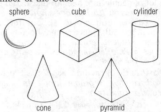

sphere   cube   cylinder

cone   pyramid

cube¹ /kjuːb/ **noun** [C] **1** a solid shape that has six equal square sides **2** the number that you get if you multiply a number by itself twice: *the cube of 5* (5^3) *is 125* (= 5 x 5 x 5).

cube² /kjuːb/ **verb** [T] (usually *passive*) to multiply a number by itself twice: *Four cubed* (4^3) *is 64* (= 4 x 4 x 4).

cubic /'kjuːbɪk/ **adj** a measure of volume expressed as a cube¹(2): *If a box is 4cm long, 4cm wide and 4cm high, its volume is 64 cubic centimetres.* ● *The lake holds more than a million cubic metres of water.*

cubicle /'kjuːbɪkl/ **noun** [C] a small room that is made by separating off part of a larger room: *There are cubicles at the swimming pool for changing your clothes.*

cuckoo /'kʊkuː/ **noun** [C] a bird which makes a sound like its name and which leaves its eggs with another bird's eggs in its nest

cucumber /'kjuːkʌmbə/ **noun** [C,U] a long, thin vegetable with a dark green skin that does not need to be cooked ••➤ picture on page C3

cuddle /'kʌdl/ **verb** [I,T] to hold sb/sth closely in your arms: *The little girl was cuddling her favourite doll.* –**cuddle noun**: *He gave the child a cuddle and kissed her goodnight.*

PHRASAL VERB **cuddle up (to/against sb/sth); cuddle up (together)** to move close to sb and sit or lie in a comfortable position: *They cuddled up together for warmth.*

cuddly /'kʌdli/ **adj** soft and pleasant to hold close to you: *a cuddly toy*

cue /kjuː/ **noun** [C] **1** a word or movement that is the signal for sb else to say or do sth, especially in a play: *When Julia puts the tray on the table, that's your cue to come on stage.*

2 an example of how to behave: *I'm not sure how to behave at a Japanese wedding, so I'll take my cue from the hosts.* **3** a long, thin wooden stick used to hit the ball in some games that are played on a special table (**snooker** and **billiards**) ▪▸ picture at **pool** and on page S2

IDIOM (**right**) **on cue** at exactly the moment expected: *Just as I was starting to worry about Stan, he phoned right on cue.*

cuff /kʌf/ *noun* [C] **1** the end part of a sleeve, which often fastens at the wrist ▪▸ picture on page C6 **2 cuffs** [pl] = **HANDCUFFS 3** a light hit with the open hand

IDIOM **off the cuff** (used about sth you say) without thought or preparation before that moment: *I haven't got the figures here, but, off the cuff, I'd say the rise is about 10%.*

cufflink /'kʌflɪŋk/ *noun* [usually pl] one of a pair of small objects used instead of a button to fasten a shirt sleeve together at the wrist

cuisine /kwɪ'ziːn/ *noun* [U] (*formal*) the style of cooking of a particular country, restaurant, etc: *Italian cuisine* ▪▸ A less formal word is **cooking**.

cul-de-sac /'kʌl də sæk/ *noun* [C] (*pl* **cul-de-sacs**) a street that is closed at one end

culinary /'kʌlɪnəri/ *adj* (*formal*) connected with cooking

cull /kʌl/ *verb* [T] **1** to kill a number of animals in a group to prevent the group from becoming too large **2** to collect information, ideas, etc, from different places: *I managed to cull some useful addresses from the Internet.* –**cull** *noun* [C]: *a deer cull*

culminate /'kʌlmɪneɪt/ *verb* [I] (*formal*) **culminate in sth** to reach a final result: *The team's efforts culminated in victory in the championships.* –**culmination** /ˌkʌlmɪ'neɪʃn/ *noun* [sing]: *The joint space mission was the culmination of years of research.*

culpable /'kʌlpəbl/ *adj* (*formal*) responsible for sth bad that has happened

culprit /'kʌlprɪt/ *noun* [C] a person who has done sth wrong

cult /kʌlt/ *noun* [C] **1** a type of religion or religious group, especially one that is considered unusual **2** a person or thing that has become popular with a particular group of people: *cult movies*

cultivate /'kʌltɪveɪt/ *verb* [T] **1** to prepare and use land for growing plants for food or to sell: *to cultivate the soil* **2** to grow plants for food or to sell: *Olives have been cultivated for centuries in Mediterranean countries.* **3** to try hard to develop a friendship with sb: *He cultivated links with colleagues abroad.* –**cultivation** /ˌkʌltɪ'veɪʃn/ *noun* [U]

cultivated /'kʌltɪveɪtɪd/ *adj* **1** well educated, with good manners **2** (used about land) used for growing plants for food or to sell **3** (used about plants) grown on a farm, not wild

★**cultural** /'kʌltʃərəl/ *adj* **1** connected with the customs, ideas, beliefs, etc of a society or country: *The country's cultural diversity is a result of taking in immigrants from all over the world.* ▪▸ Look at **multicultural**. **2** connected with art, music, literature, etc: *The city has a rich cultural life, with many theatres, concert halls and art galleries.* –**culturally** /-rəli/ *adv*

★**culture** /'kʌltʃə/ *noun* **1** [C,U] the customs, ideas, beliefs, etc of a particular society, country, etc: *the language and culture of the Aztecs* ● *people from many different cultures* **2** [U] art, literature, music, etc: *London has always been a centre of culture.*

cultured /'kʌltʃəd/ *adj* well-educated, showing a good knowledge of art, music, literature, etc

'**culture shock** *noun* [U] a feeling of confusion, etc that you may have when you go to live in or visit a country that is very different from your own

cumbersome /'kʌmbəsəm/ *adj* **1** heavy and difficult to carry, use, wear, etc **2** (used about a system, etc) slow and complicated: *cumbersome legal procedures*

cumulative /'kjuːmjələtɪv/ *adj* increasing steadily in amount, degree, etc: *a cumulative effect*

cunning /'kʌnɪŋ/ *adj* clever in a dishonest or bad way: *He was as cunning as a fox.* ● *a cunning trick* ▪▸ synonym **sly** or **wily** –**cunning** *noun* [U] –**cunningly** *adv*

cup and saucer   mug

beaker   plastic cup/ beaker

wine glass   beer glass

★**cup¹** /kʌp/ *noun* [C] **1** a small container usually with a handle, used for drinking liquids: *a teacup* ● *a cup of coffee* **2** (in sport) a large metal cup given as a prize; the competition for such a cup: *Our team won the cup in the basketball tournament.* ● *the World Cup* ••➤ picture at **medal 3** an object shaped like a cup: *an eggcup*

IDIOM **not sb's cup of tea** not what sb likes or is interested in: *Horror films aren't my cup of tea.*

cup[2] /kʌp/ **verb** [T] (**cupping**; **cupped**) to form sth, especially your hands, into the shape of a cup; to hold sth with your hands shaped like a cup: *I cupped my hands to take a drink from the stream.*

★**cupboard** /'kʌbəd/ **noun** [C] a piece of furniture, usually with shelves inside and a door or doors at the front, used for storing food, clothes, etc ••➤ picture on page C7

cupful /'kʌpfʊl/ **noun** [C] the amount that a cup will hold: *two cupfuls of water*

curable /'kjʊərəbl/ **adj** (used about a disease) that can be made better ••➤ opposite **incurable**

curator /kjʊə'reɪtə/ **noun** [C] a person whose job is to look after the things that are kept in a museum

curb[1] /kɜːb/ **verb** [T] to limit or control sth, especially sth bad: *He needs to learn to curb his anger.*

curb[2] /kɜːb/ **noun** [C] **1** a curb (on sth) a control or limit on sth: *a curb on local government spending* **2** (*especially US*) = **KERB**

curdle /'kɜːdl/ **verb** [I,T] (used about liquids) to turn sour or to separate into different parts; to make something do this: *I've curdled the sauce.* ••➤ Look at **blood-curdling.**

★**cure**[1] /kjʊə/ **verb** [T] **1** cure sb (of sth) to make sb healthy again after an illness: *The treatment cured him of cancer.* **2** to make an illness, injury, etc end or disappear: *It is still not possible to cure the common cold.* ● (*figurative*) *The plumber cured the problem with the central heating.* **3** to make certain types of food last longer by drying, smoking or salting them: *cured ham*

cure[2] /kjʊə/ **noun** [C] a cure (for sth) **1** a medicine or treatment that can cure an illness, etc: *There is no cure for this illness.* **2** a return to good health; the process of being cured: *The new drug brought about a miraculous cure.*

curfew /'kɜːfjuː/ **noun** [C] **1** a time after which people are not allowed to go outside their homes, for example during a war: *The government imposed a dusk-to-dawn curfew.* **2** (*US*) a time when children must arrive home in the evening: *She has a ten o'clock curfew.*

curiosity /ˌkjʊəri'ɒsəti/ **noun** (*pl* **curiosities**) **1** [U] a desire to know or learn: *I was full of curiosity about their plans.* ● *Out of curiosity, he opened her letter.* **2** [C] an unusual and interesting person or thing: *The museum was full of historical curiosities.*

★**curious** /'kjʊəriəs/ **adj 1** curious (about sth); curious (to do sth) wanting to know or learn sth: *They were very curious about the people who lived upstairs.* ● *He was curious to know how the machine worked.* **2** unusual or

strange: *It was curious that she didn't tell anyone about the incident.* –curiously **adv**

curl[1] /kɜːl/ **verb 1** [I,T] to form or to make sth form into a curved or round shape: *Does your hair curl naturally?* **2** [I] to move round in a curve: *The snake curled around his arm.* ● *Smoke curled up into the sky.*

PHRASAL VERB **curl up** to pull your arms, legs and head close to your body: *The cat curled up in front of the fire.*

curl[2] /kɜːl/ **noun** [C] **1** a piece of hair that curves round: *Her hair fell in curls round her face.* **2** a thing that has a curved round shape: *a curl of blue smoke*

curler /'kɜːlə/ **noun** [C] a small plastic or metal tube that you roll your hair around in order to make it curly

curly /'kɜːli/ **adj** full of curls; shaped like a curl: *curly hair* ••➤ opposite **straight.** ••➤ picture at **hair**

currant /'kʌrənt/ **noun** [C] **1** a very small dried grape used to make cakes, etc **2** (often in compounds) one of several types of small soft fruit: *blackcurrants*

★**currency** /'kʌrənsi/ **noun** (*pl* **currencies**) **1** [C,U] the system or type of money that a particular country uses: *The currency of Argentina is the austral.* ● *foreign currency* ● *a weak/strong/stable currency* **2** [U] the state of being believed, accepted or used by many people: *The new ideas soon gained currency.*

★**current**[1] /'kʌrənt/ **adj 1** of the present time; happening now: *current fashions/events* **2** generally accepted; in common use: *Is this word still current?*

current[2] /'kʌrənt/ **noun 1** [C] a continuous flowing movement of water, air, etc: *to swim against/with the current* ● (*figurative*) *a current of anti-government feeling* **2** [U] the flow of electricity through a wire, etc

ˌ**current acˈcount** (*US* ˌ**checking account**) **noun** [C] a bank account from which you can take out your money when you want, with a cheque book or cash card

ˌ**current afˈfairs noun** [pl] important political or social events that are happening at the present time

currently /'kʌrəntli/ **adv** at present; at the moment: *He is currently working in Spain.* ••➤ Look at the note at **actually.**

curriculum /kə'rɪkjələm/ **noun** [C] (*pl* **curriculums** or **curricula** /-lə/) all the subjects that are taught in a school, college or university; the contents of a particular course of study: *Latin is not on the curriculum at our school.* ••➤ Look at **syllabus.**

curriculum vitae /kəˌrɪkjələm 'viːtaɪ/ = **CV**

curry /'kʌri/ **noun** [C,U] (*pl* **curries**) an Indian dish of meat, vegetables, etc containing a lot of spices usually served with rice: *a hot/mild curry* –curried **adj**: *curried chicken*

ˈ**curry powder noun** [U] a fine mixture of strongly flavoured spices that is used to make curry

curse¹ /kɜːs/ noun [C] **1** a word used for expressing anger; a swear word **2** a word or words expressing a wish that sth terrible will happen to sb: *The family seemed to be under a curse* (= lots of bad things happened to them). **3** something that causes great harm: *the curse of drug addiction*

curse² /kɜːs/ verb **1** [I,T] curse (sb/sth) (for sth) to swear at sb/sth; to use rude language to express your anger: *He dropped the box, cursing himself for his clumsiness.* **2** [T] to use a magic word or phrase against sb because you wish him/her harm: *She cursed his family.*

cursor /'kɜːsə/ noun [C] (*computing*) a small sign on a computer screen that shows the position you are at ·➤ picture on page S7

cursory /'kɜːsəri/ adj quick and short; done in a hurry: *a cursory glance*

curt /kɜːt/ adj short and not polite: *She gave him a curt reply and slammed the phone down.* –curtly adv –curtness noun [U]

curtail /kɜːˈteɪl/ verb [T] (*formal*) to make sth shorter or smaller; to reduce: *I had to curtail my answer as I was running out of time.* –curtailment noun [C,U]

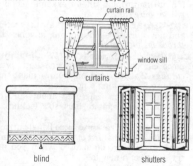

curtain rail

window sill

curtains

blind   shutters

★**curtain** /'kɜːtn/ noun [C] **1** (*US also* drape) a piece of material that you can move to cover a window, etc: *Could you draw the curtains, please?* (= Could you open/close the curtains) • *The curtain goes up at 7pm* (= in a theatre, the play begins). **2** a thing that covers or hides sth: *a curtain of mist*

curtsy (*also* curtsey) /'kɜːtsi/ noun [C] (*pl* curtsies *or* curtseys) a movement made by a person as a sign of respect, done by bending the knees, with one foot behind the other –curtsy (*also* curtsey) verb [I]

★**curve¹** /kɜːv/ noun [C] a line that bends round: *a curve on a graph* ·➤ picture at **line**

curve² /kɜːv/ verb [I,T] to bend or to make sth bend in a curve: *The bay curved round to the south.* • *a curved line* ·➤ picture at **line**

cushion¹ /'kʊʃn/ noun [C] **1** a bag filled with soft material, for example feathers, which you put on a chair, etc to make it more comfortable ·➤ A cushion on a bed is a pillow. **2** something that acts or is shaped like a cushion: *A hovercraft rides on a cushion of air.*

cushion² /'kʊʃn/ verb [T] **1** to make a fall, hit, etc less painful: *The snow cushioned his fall.* **2** to reduce the unpleasant effect of sth: *She spent her childhood on a farm, cushioned from the effects of the war.*

cushy /'kʊʃi/ adj (*informal*) too easy, needing little effort (in a way that seems unfair to others): *a cushy job*

custard /'kʌstəd/ noun [U] a sweet yellow sauce made from milk, eggs and sugar. In Britain it is eaten hot or cold with sweet dishes ·➤ picture on page C4

custodian /kʌˈstəʊdiən/ noun [C] **1** (*formal*) a person who looks after sth, especially a museum, library, etc **2** (*US*) = CARETAKER

custody /'kʌstədi/ noun [U] **1** the legal right or duty to take care of sb/sth: *After the divorce, the mother had custody of the children.* **2** the state of being guarded, or kept in prison temporarily, especially by the police: *The man was kept in custody until his trial.*

★**custom** /'kʌstəm/ noun **1** [C,U] a way of behaving which a particular group or society has had for a long time: *It's the custom in Britain for a bride to throw her bouquet to the wedding guests.* • *according to local custom* ·➤ Look at the note at **habit**. **2** [sing] (*formal*) something that a person does regularly: *It's my custom to drink tea in the afternoon.* **3** [U] (*Brit*) commercial activity; the practice of people buying things regularly from a particular shop, etc: *The local shop lost a lot of custom when the new supermarket opened.* ·➤ Look at **customs**.

customary /'kʌstəməri/ adj according to custom; usual: *Is it customary to send cards at Christmas in your country?*

★**customer** /'kʌstəmə/ noun [C] **1** a person who buys goods or services in a shop, restaurant, etc: *The shop assistant was serving a customer.* ·➤ Look at **client**. **2** (*informal*) (after certain adjectives) a person: *a tough/an awkward/an odd/ customer*

★**customs** (*also* Customs) /'kʌstəmz/ noun [pl] the place at an airport, etc where government officials check your luggage to make sure you are not bringing goods into the country illegally: *a customs officer* ·➤ Look at **excise**.

★**cut¹** /kʌt/ verb (*pres part* cutting; *pt, pp* cut) **1** [I,T] to make an opening, wound or mark in sth using a sharp tool, for example a pair of scissors or a knife: *Be careful not to cut yourself on that broken glass!* • *This knife doesn't cut very well.* **2** [T] cut sth (from sth) to remove sth or a part of sth, using a knife, etc: *She cut two slices of bread (from the loaf).* **3** [T] cut sth (in/into sth) to divide sth into pieces with a knife, etc: *She cut the cake into eight (pieces).* • *He cut the rope in two.* **4** [T] to make sth shorter by using scissors, etc: *I cut my own hair.* • *to have your hair cut* (= at the hairdresser's). • *to cut the grass* **5** [T] to make or form sth by removing material with a sharp tool: *She cut a hole in the card and pushed the string through.* • *They cut a path through the jungle.* **6** [T] to reduce sth or make it shorter; to remove sth: *to cut taxes/ costs/spending* ● *Several violent scenes in the film were cut.* **7** [T] (*computing*) to remove a piece of text from the screen: *Use the **cut and paste** buttons to change the order of the paragraphs.* **8** [I] **cut across, along, through,** etc (sth) to go across, etc sth, in order to make your route shorter: *It's much quicker if we cut across the field.* **9** [T] (*spoken*) to stop sth: *Cut the chat and get on with your work!* **10** [T] to deeply offend sb or hurt his/her feelings: *His cruel remarks cut her deeply.*

➤ For other idioms containing **cut** look at the entries for the nouns, adjectives, etc, for example **cut corners** is at **corner**.

PHRASAL VERBS **cut across sth** to affect or be true for different groups that usually remain separate: *The question of aid for the earthquake victims cuts across national boundaries.*
cut sth back; cut back (on sth) to reduce sth: *to cut back on public spending*
cut sth down 1 to make sth fall down by cutting it: *to cut down a tree* **2** to make sth shorter: *I have to cut my essay down to 2000 words.*
cut sth down; cut down (on sth) to reduce the quantity or amount of sth; to do sth less often: *You should cut down on fatty foods.*
cut in (on sb/sth) to interrupt sb/sth: *She kept cutting in on our conversation.*
cut sb off (often passive) to stop or interrupt sb's telephone conversation: *We were cut off before I could give her my message.*
cut sb/sth off (often passive) to stop the supply of sth to sb: *The electricity/gas/water has been cut off.*
cut sth off to block a road, etc so that nothing can pass: *We must cut off all possible escape routes.*
cut sth off (sth) to remove sth from sth larger by cutting: *Be careful you don't cut your fingers off using that electric saw.*
cut sb/sth off (from sb/sth) (often passive) to prevent sb/sth from moving from a place or contacting people outside: *The farm was cut off from the village by heavy snow.*
cut sth open to open sth by cutting: *She fell and cut her head open.*
cut sth out 1 to remove sth or to form sth into a particular shape by cutting: *He cut the job advertisement out of the newspaper.* **2** to not include sth: *Cut out the boring details!* **3** (*especially US informal*) to stop saying or doing sth that annoys sb: *Cut that out and leave me alone!* **4** (*informal*) to stop doing or using sth: *You'll only lose weight if you cut out sweet things from your diet.*
be cut out for sth; be cut out to be sth to have the qualities needed to do sth; to be suitable for sth/sb: *You're not cut out to be a soldier.*
cut sth up to cut sth into small pieces with a knife, etc

★**cut²** /kʌt/ *noun* [C] **1** an injury or opening in the skin made with a knife, etc: *He had a deep cut on his forehead.* **2** an act of cutting: *to have a cut and blow-dry* (= at a hairdresser's)

3 a cut (in sth) a reduction in size, amount, etc: *a cut in government spending* ● *a power cut* (= when the electric current is stopped temporarily) **4** a piece of meat from a particular part of an animal: *cheap cuts of lamb* **5** (*informal*) a share of the profits from sth, especially sth dishonest ••➤ Look at **short cut**.

cutback /ˈkʌtbæk/ *noun* [C] a reduction in amount or number: *The management were forced to make cutbacks in staff.*

cute /kjuːt/ *adj* attractive; pretty: *Your little girl is so cute!* ● *a cute smile*

cutlery /ˈkʌtləri/ *noun* [U] the knives, forks and spoons that you use for eating food ••➤ Look at **crockery**.

cutlet /ˈkʌtlət/ *noun* [C] a small, thick piece of meat, often with bone in it, that is cooked

'**cut-off** *noun* [C] the level or time at which sth stops: *The cut-off date is 12 May. After that we'll end the offer.*

'**cut-price** (*US* '**cut-rate**) *adj* sold at a reduced price; selling goods at low prices: *cut-price offers* ● *a cut-price store*

cutters /ˈkʌtəz/ *noun* [pl] a tool that you use for cutting through sth, for example metal: *a pair of wire cutters*

'**cut-throat** *adj* caring only about success and not worried about hurting anyone: *cut-throat business practices*

cutting¹ /ˈkʌtɪŋ/ *noun* [C] **1** (*US* **clipping**) a piece cut out from a newspaper, etc: *press cuttings* **2** a piece cut off from a plant that you use for growing a new plant

cutting² /ˈkʌtɪŋ/ *adj* (used about sth you say) unkind; meant to hurt sb's feelings: *a cutting remark*

CV /ˌsiː ˈviː/ (*US* **résumé**) *noun* [sing] curriculum vitae; a formal list of your education and work experience, often used when you are trying to get a new job

cwt *abbr* a hundred weight; a measure of weight, about 50.8 kg

cyanide /ˈsaɪənaɪd/ *noun* [U] a poisonous chemical

cybercafe /ˈsaɪbəkæfeɪ/ *noun* [C] a cafe with computers where customers can pay to use the Internet

cyberspace /ˈsaɪbəspeɪs/ *noun* [U] a place that is not real, where electronic messages exist while they are being sent from one computer to another

★**cycle¹** /ˈsaɪkl/ *noun* [C] **1** a series of events, etc that happen again and again in the same order: *the life cycle of a frog* **2** a bicycle or motor cycle: *a cycle shop* ••➤ synonym **bike**

cycle² /ˈsaɪkl/ *verb* [I] to ride a bicycle: *He usually cycles to school.* ••➤ **Go cycling** is a common way of talking about cycling for pleasure: *We go cycling most weekends.*

cyclic /ˈsaɪklɪk/ (also **cyclical** /ˈsɪklɪkl/) *adj* following a repeated pattern

cyclist /ˈsaɪklɪst/ *noun* [C] a person who rides a bicycle

cyclone /ˈsaɪkləʊn/ *noun* [C] a violent wind

that moves in a circle causing a storm ••➤ Look at the note at **storm**.

cylinder /ˈsɪlɪndə/ **noun** [C] **1** an object shaped like a tube ••➤ picture at **cube 2** a tube-shaped part of an engine, for example in a car –**cylindrical** /səˈlɪndrɪkl/ **adj**

cymbal /ˈsɪmbl/ **noun** [C, usually pl] one of a pair of round metal plates used as a musical instrument. Cymbals make a loud ringing sound when you hit them together or with a stick. ••➤ picture at **music**

cynic /ˈsɪnɪk/ **noun** [C] a person who believes that people only do things for themselves, rather than to help others: *Don't be such a cynic. He did it to help us, not for the money.* –**cynical** /ˈsɪnɪkl/ **adj**: *a cynical remark* –**cynically** /-kli/ **adv** –**cynicism** /ˈsɪnɪsɪzem/ **noun** [U]

Cyrillic /sɪˈrɪlɪk/ **noun** [U] the alphabet that is used in languages such as Russian

cyst /sɪst/ **noun** [C] a swelling or a lump filled with liquid in the body or under the skin

D d

D, d¹ /diː/ **noun** [C] (*pl* **D's; d's**) the fourth letter of the English alphabet: *'David' begins with (a) 'D'.*

d² **abbr** died: *W A Mozart, d 1791*

dab¹ /dæb/ **verb** [I,T] (**dabbing; dabbed**) to touch sth lightly, usually several times: *He dabbed the cut with some cotton wool.*

PHRASAL VERB **dab sth on/off (sth)** to put sth on or to remove sth lightly: *to dab some antiseptic on a wound*

dab² /dæb/ **noun** [C] **1** a light touch: *She gave her eyes a dab with a handkerchief.* **2** a small quantity of sth that is put on a surface: *a dab of paint/perfume*

dabble /ˈdæbl/ **verb 1** [I] to become involved in sth in a way that is not very serious: *to dabble in politics* **2** [T] to put your hands, feet, etc in water and move them around: *We sat on the bank and dabbled our toes in the river.*

★**dad** /dæd/ **noun** [C] (*informal*) father: *Is that your dad? • Come on, Dad!*

★**daddy** /ˈdædi/ **noun** (*pl* **daddies**) (*informal*) (used by children) father: *I want my daddy!*

daffodil /ˈdæfədɪl/ **noun** [C] a tall yellow flower that grows in the spring ••➤ picture on page C2

daft /dɑːft/ **adj** (*informal*) silly; foolish: *Don't be daft. • a daft idea*

dagger /ˈdægə/ **noun** [C] a type of knife used as a weapon, especially in past times ••➤ picture at **spear**

★**daily¹** /ˈdeɪli/ **adj, adv** done, made or happening every day: *a daily routine/delivery/newspaper • Our airline flies to Japan daily.*

daily² /ˈdeɪli/ **noun** [C] (*pl* **dailies**) (*informal*) a newspaper that is published every day except Sunday

dainty /ˈdeɪnti/ **adj 1** small and pretty: *a dainty lace handkerchief* **2** (used about a person's movements) very careful in a way that tries to show good manners: *Veronica took a dainty bite of the giant hot dog.* –**daintily adv**

dairy¹ /ˈdeəri/ **noun** [C] (*pl* **dairies**) **1** a place on a farm where milk is kept and butter, cheese, etc are made **2** a company which sells milk, butter, eggs, etc

dairy² /ˈdeəri/ **adj** (only *before* a noun) **1** made from milk: *dairy products/produce* (= milk, butter, cheese, etc) **2** connected with the production of milk: *dairy cattle • a dairy farm*

daisy /ˈdeɪzi/ **noun** [C] (*pl* **daisies**) a small white flower with a yellow centre, which usually grows wild in grass ••➤ picture on page C2

dam /dæm/ **noun** [C] a wall built across a river to hold back the water and form a lake (reservoir) behind it –**dam verb** [T]

★**damage¹** /ˈdæmɪdʒ/ **noun 1** [U] damage (to sth) harm or injury caused when sth is broken or spoiled: *Earthquakes can **cause** terrible **damage** in urban areas. • It will take weeks to **repair the damage** done by the vandals.* **2 damages** [pl] money that you can ask for if sb damages sth of yours or hurts you: *Mrs Rees, who lost a leg in the crash, was awarded damages of £100000.*

★**damage²** /ˈdæmɪdʒ/ **verb** [T] to spoil or harm sth, for example by breaking it: *The roof was damaged by the storm.* –**damaging adj**: *These rumours could be damaging to her reputation.*

dame /deɪm/ **noun** [C] **Dame** (*Brit*) a title given to a woman as an honour because of sth special that she has done: *Dame Agatha Christie*

damn¹ /dæm/ **verb** [I,T] (*slang*) a swear word that people use to show that they are angry: *Damn (it!) I've left my money behind.*

damn² /dæm/ (also **damned**) **adj, adv** (*slang*) **1** (a swear word that people use for emphasizing what they are saying) very: *Read it! It's a damn good book.* **2** a swear word that people use to show that they are angry: *Some damn fool has parked too close to me.*

damn³ /dæm/ **noun**

IDIOM **not give a damn (about sb/sth)** (*slang*) not care at all: *I don't give a damn what he thinks about me.*

damning /ˈdæmɪŋ/ **adj** that criticizes sth very much: *There was a damning article about the book in the newspaper.*

★**damp¹** /dæmp/ **adj** a little wet: *The house had been empty and felt rather damp.* –**damp noun** [U]: *She hated the damp and the cold of the English climate.* ••➤ Look at the note at **wet**.

damp² /dæmp/ **verb** [T] **damp sth (down) 1** to make a fire burn less strongly or stop burning: *He tried to damp (down) the flames.* **2** to make sth less strong or urgent: *He tried to damp down their expectations in case they failed.*

[I] **intransitive**, a verb which has no object: *He laughed.*   [T] **transitive**, a verb which has an object: *He ate an apple.*

dampen /'dæmpən/ **verb** [T] **1** to make sth less strong or urgent: *Even the awful weather did not dampen their enthusiasm for the trip.* **2** to make sth a little wet: *He dampened his hair to try to stop it sticking up.*

★**dance**[1] /dɑːns/ **noun 1** [C] a series of steps and movements which you do to music **2** [U] dancing as a form of art or entertainment: *She's very interested in modern dance.* **3** [C] (*old-fashioned*) a social meeting at which people dance with each other: *My parents met at a dance.*

★**dance**[2] /dɑːns/ **verb 1** [I,T] to move around to the rhythm of music by making a series of steps: *I can't dance very well.* ● *to dance the samba* **2** [I] to jump and move around with energy: *She was dancing up and down with excitement.*

dancer /'dɑːnsə/ **noun** [C] a person who dances, often as a job: *a ballet dancer* ● *She's a good dancer.*

dandelion /'dændɪlaɪən/ **noun** [C] a small wild plant with a bright yellow flower ••> picture on page C2

dandruff /'dændrʌf/ **noun** [U] small pieces of dead skin in the hair, that look like white powder

★**danger** /'deɪndʒə/ **noun 1** [U,C] the chance that sb/sth may be hurt, killed or damaged or that sth bad may happen: *When he saw the men had knives, he realized his life was in danger.* ● *The men kept on running until they thought they were out of danger.* ● *If things carry on as they are, there's a danger that the factory may have to close.* **2** [C] a danger (to sb/sth) a person or thing that can cause injury, pain or damage to sb: *Drunk drivers are a danger to everyone on the road.*

★**dangerous** /'deɪndʒərəs/ **adj** likely to cause injury or damage: *a dangerous animal/road/illness* ● *Police warn that the man is highly dangerous.* –**dangerously** **adv**: *He was standing dangerously close to the cliff edge.*

dangle /'dæŋgl/ **verb** [I,T] to hang freely; to hold sth so that it hangs down in this way: *She sat on the fence with her legs dangling.* ● *The police dangled a rope from the bridge and the man grabbed it.*

dank /dæŋk/ **adj** wet, cold and unpleasant

★**dare**[1] /deə/ **verb 1** [I] (usually in negative sentences) dare (to) do sth to have enough courage to do sth: *Nobody dared (to) speak.* ● *I daren't ask her to lend me any more money.* ● *We were so frightened that we didn't dare (to) go into the room.*

➤ The negative is **dare not** (usually **daren't** /deənt/) or **do not/does not** (= **don't/doesn't**) **dare**. In the past tense it is **did not** (**didn't**) **dare**.

2 [T] dare sb (to do sth) to ask or tell sb to do sth in order to see if he/she has the courage to do it: *Can you jump off that wall? Go on, I dare you!* ● *He dared his friend to put a mouse in the teacher's bag.*

IDIOMS **don't you dare** used for telling sb very strongly not to do sth: *Don't you dare tell my parents about this!*

how dare you used when you are angry about sth that sb has done: *How dare you speak to me like that!*

I dare say used when you are saying sth is probable: *'I think you should accept the offer.' 'I dare say you're right.'*

★**dare**[2] /deə/ **noun** [C,usually sing] something dangerous that sb asks you to do, to see if you have the courage to do it: *'Why did you try to swim across the river?' 'For a dare.'*

daredevil /'deədevl/ **noun** [C] a person who likes to do dangerous things

daring /'deərɪŋ/ **adj** involving or taking risks; brave: *a daring attack* –**daring noun** [U]: *The climb required skill and daring.*

★**dark**[1] /dɑːk/ **adj 1** with no light or very little light: *It was a dark night, with no moon.* ● *What time does it get dark in winter?* **2** (used about a colour) not light; nearer black than white: *dark blue* ••> opposite **light** or **pale** **3** (*especially Brit*) (used about a person's hair, skin or eyes) brown or black; not fair: *She was small and dark with brown eyes.* **4** (only *before* a noun) hidden and frightening; mysterious: *He seemed friendly, but there was a dark side to his character.* **5** (only *before* a noun) sad; without hope: *the dark days of the recession*

★**dark**[2] /dɑːk/ **noun** [sing] **the dark** the state of having no light: *He's afraid of the dark.* ● *Why are you sitting alone in the dark?*

IDIOMS **before/after dark** before /after the sun goes down in the evening

(be/keep sb) in the dark (about sth) (be/keep sb) in a position of not knowing about sth: *Don't keep me in the dark. Tell me!*

darken /'dɑːkən/ **verb** [I,T] to become or to make sth darker: *The sky suddenly darkened and it started to rain.*

dark 'glasses = SUNGLASSES

darkness /'dɑːknəs/ **noun** [U] the state of being dark: *We sat in total darkness, waiting for the lights to come back on.*

darkroom /'dɑːkruːm; -rʊm/ **noun** [C] a room that can be made completely dark so that film can be taken out of a camera and photographs can be produced there

darling /'dɑːlɪŋ/ **noun** [C] a word that you say to sb you love

darn /dɑːn/ **verb** [I,T] to repair a hole in clothes by sewing across it in one direction and then in the other: *I hate darning socks.*

dart[1] /dɑːt/ **noun 1** [C] an object like a small arrow. It is thrown in a game or shot as a weapon: *The keeper fired a tranquillizer dart into the tiger to send it to sleep.* **2** darts [U] a game in which you throw darts at a round board with numbers on it (a **dartboard**)

dart[2] /dɑːt/ **verb** [I,T] to move or make sth move suddenly and quickly in a certain direction: *A rabbit darted across the field.* ● *She darted an angry glance at me.*

dash[1] /dæʃ/ **noun 1** [sing] an act of going somewhere suddenly and quickly: *Suddenly the prisoner made a dash for the door.* **2** [C, usually sing] a small amount of sth that you add to sth else: *a dash of lemon juice* **3** [C] a small horizontal line (–) used in writing, especially for adding extra information •➤ Look at **hyphen**.

dash² /dæʃ/ *verb* **1** [I] to go somewhere suddenly and quickly: *We all dashed for shelter when it started to rain.* • *I must dash – I'm late.* **2** [I,T] to hit sth with great force; to throw sth so that it hits sth else very hard: *She dashed her racket to the ground.*

IDIOM **dash sb's hopes (of sth/of doing sth)** to completely destroy sb's hopes of doing sth: *The accident dashed his hopes of becoming a pianist.*

PHRASAL VERB **dash sth off** to write or draw sth very quickly: *I dashed off a note to my boss and left.*

dashboard /'dæʃbɔːd/ *noun* [C] the part in a car in front of the driver where most of the switches, etc are •➤ picture on page S9

★**data** /'deɪtə; 'dɑːtə/ *noun* [U,pl] facts or information: *to gather/collect data* • *data capture/ retrieval* (= ways of storing and looking at information on a computer)

database /'deɪtə-; 'deɪtəbeɪs/ *noun* [C] a large amount of data that is stored in a computer and can easily be used, added to, etc

★**date¹** /deɪt/ *noun* **1** [C] a particular day of the month or year: *What's the date today?/What date is it today?/What's today's date?* • *What's your **date** of birth?* • *We'd better **fix a date** for the next meeting.* **2** [sing] a particular time: *We can discuss this **at a later date.*** •➤ Look at **sell-by date**. **3** [C] an arrangement to meet sb, especially a boyfriend or girlfriend: *Shall we **make a date** to have lunch together?* • *I've got a date with Roxanne on Friday night.* •➤ Look at **blind date**. **4** [C] a small, sweet, dark brown fruit that comes from a tree which grows in hot countries •➤ picture on page C3

IDIOMS **out of date 1** not fashionable; no longer useful: *out-of-date methods/machinery* **2** no longer able to be used: *I must renew my passport. It's out of date.*

to date (*formal*) until now: *We've had very few complaints to date.*

up to date 1 completely modern: *The new kitchen will be right up to date, with all the latest gadgets.* **2** with all the latest information; having done everything that you should: *In this report we'll bring you up to date with the latest news from the area.*

★**date²** /deɪt/ *verb* **1** [T] to discover or guess how old sth is: *The skeleton has been dated at about 3000 BC.* **2** [T] to write the day's date on sth: *The letter is dated 24 March, 2000.* **3** [I,T] to seem, or to make sb/sth seem, unfashionable: *We chose a simple style so that it wouldn't date as quickly.*

PHRASAL VERB **date back to...; date from...** to have existed since...: *The house dates back to the seventeenth century.* • *photographs dating from before the war*

dated /'deɪtɪd/ *adj* unfashionable: *This sort of jacket looks rather dated now.*

★**daughter** /'dɔːtə/ *noun* [C] a female child: *I have two sons and one daughter.* • *Janet's daughter is a doctor.*

'**daughter-in-law** *noun* [C] (*pl* **daughters-in-law**) the wife of your son

daunt /dɔːnt/ *verb* [T] (usually passive) to frighten or to worry sb by being too big or difficult: *Don't be daunted by all the controls – in fact it's a simple machine to use.* —**daunting** *adj*: *a daunting task*

dawdle /'dɔːdl/ *verb* [I] to go somewhere very slowly: *Stop dawdling! We've got to be there by two.*

dawn¹ /dɔːn/ *noun* **1** [U,C] the early morning, when light first appears in the sky: *before/at dawn* • *Dawn was breaking* (= it was starting to get light) *as I set off to work.* **2** [sing] the beginning: *the dawn of civilization*

IDIOM **the crack of dawn →** CRACK²

dawn² /dɔːn/ *verb* [I] **1** (*formal*) to begin to grow light, after the night: *The day dawned bright and cold.* • (*figurative*) *A new era of peace is dawning.* **2 dawn (on sb)** to become clear (to sb): *Suddenly it dawned on her. 'Of course!' she said. 'You're Mike's brother!'*

★**day** /deɪ/ *noun* **1** [C] a period of 24 hours. Seven days make up a week: *'What day is it today?' 'Tuesday.'* • *We went to Italy for ten days.* • *We're meeting again the day after tomorrow/in two days' time.* • *The next/following day I saw Mark again.* • *I'd already spoken to him the day before/the previous day.* • *I have to take these pills twice a day.* • *I work six days a week. Sunday's my day off* (= when I do not work). **2** [C,U] the time when the sky is light; not night: *The days were warm but the nights were freezing.* • *It's been raining all day (long).* • *Owls sleep by day* (= during the day) *and hunt at night.* **3** [C] the hours of the day when you work: *She's expected to work a seven-hour day.* **4** [C] (also **days**) a particular period of time in the past: *in Shakespeare's day* • *There weren't so many cars in those days*

IDIOMS **at the end of the day →** END¹

break of day → BREAK²

call it a day → CALL¹

day by day every day; as time passes: *Day by day, she was getting a little bit stronger.*

day in, day out every day, without any change: *He sits at his desk working, day in, day out.*

day-to-day happening as a normal part of each day; usual

from day to day; from one day to the next within a short period of time: *Things change so quickly that we never know what will happen from one day to the next.*

have a field day → FIELD DAY

it's early days (yet) → EARLY

make sb's day (*informal*) to make sb very happy

one day; some day at some time in the future: *Some day we'll go back and see all our old friends.*

the other day a few days ago; recently: *I bumped into him in town the other day.*

ð **then** | s **so** | z **zoo** | ʃ **she** | ʒ **vision** | h **how** | m **man** | n **no** | ŋ **sing** | l **leg** | r **red** | j **yes** | w **wet**

the present day → **PRESENT¹**
these days in the present age; nowadays

daybreak /'deɪbreɪk/ **noun** [U] the time in the early morning when light first appears; dawn

daydream /'deɪdriːm/ **noun** [C] thoughts that are not connected with what you are doing; often pleasant scenes in your imagination: *The child stared out of the window, lost in a daydream.* –**daydream** **verb** [I]: *Don't just sit there daydreaming – do some work!*

daylight /'deɪlaɪt/ **noun** [U] the light that there is during the day: *The colours look quite different in daylight.* • *daylight hours*
IDIOM **broad daylight** → **BROAD**

,day re'turn **noun** [C] (*Brit*) a train or bus ticket for going somewhere and coming back on the same day. It is cheaper than a normal return ticket.

daytime /'deɪtaɪm/ **noun** [U] the time when it is light; not night: *These flowers open in the daytime and close again at night.* • *daytime TV*

daze /deɪz/ **noun**
IDIOM **in a daze** unable to think or react normally; confused

dazed /deɪzd/ **adj** unable to think or react normally; confused: *He had a dazed expression on his face.*

dazzle /'dæzl/ **verb** [T] (usually passive) **1** (used about a bright light) to make sb unable to see for a short time: *She was dazzled by the other car's headlights.* **2** to impress sb very much: *He had been dazzled by her beauty.* –**dazzling** **adj**: *a dazzling light*

★dead¹ /ded/ **adj 1** no longer alive: *My father's dead. He died two years ago.* • *Police found a dead body under the bridge.* • *The man was shot dead by a masked gunman.* • *dead leaves* •➤ **noun death**, **verb die 2** no longer used; finished: *Latin is a dead language.* •➤ opposite **living 3** (not before a noun) (used about a part of the body) no longer able to feel anything: *Oh no, my foot's gone dead. I was sitting on it for too long.* **4** (not before a noun) (used about a piece of equipment) no longer working: *I picked up the telephone but the line was dead.* • *This battery's dead.* **5** without movement, activity or interest: *This town is completely dead after 11 o'clock at night.* **6** (only *before* a noun) complete or exact: *a dead silence/calm* • *The arrow hit the dead centre of the target.*
IDIOMS **a dead end 1** a street that is only open at one end **2** a point, situation, etc from which you can make no further progress: *a dead-end job* (= one that offers no chance of promotion)
drop dead → **DROP¹**

dead² /ded/ **the dead noun** [pl] people who have died: *A church service was held in memory of the dead.*
IDIOM **in the dead of night** in the middle of the night, when it is very dark and quiet

dead³ /ded/ **adv** completely, exactly or very: *The car made a strange noise and then stopped dead.* • *He's dead keen to start work.*

deaden /'dedn/ **verb** [T] to make sth less strong, painful, etc: *They gave her drugs to try and deaden the pain.*

,dead 'heat **noun** [C] the result of a race when two people, etc finish at exactly the same time

deadline /'dedlaɪn/ **noun** [C] a time or date before which sth must be done or finished: *I usually set myself a deadline when I have a project to do.* • *A journalist is used to having to meet deadlines.*

deadlock /'dedlɒk/ **noun** [sing,U] a situation in which two sides cannot reach an agreement: *Talks have reached (a) deadlock.* • *to try to break the deadlock*

deadly /'dedli/ **adj, adv (deadlier; deadliest) 1** causing or likely to cause death: *a deadly poison/weapon/disease* **2** very great; complete: *They're deadly enemies.* **3** completely; extremely: *I'm not joking. In fact I'm deadly serious.* **4** extremely accurate, so that no defence is possible: *That player is deadly when he gets in front of the goal.*

deadpan /'dedpæn/ **adj** without any expression on your face or in your voice: *He told the joke with a completely deadpan face.*

★deaf /def/ **adj 1** unable to hear anything or unable to hear very well: *You'll have to speak louder. My father's a bit deaf.* • *to go deaf* **2 the deaf noun** [pl] people who cannot hear **3** deaf to sth not wanting to listen to sth: *I've told her what I think but she's deaf to my advice.* –**deafness noun** [U]

deafen /'defn/ **verb** [T] (usually passive) to make sb unable to hear by making a very loud noise: *We were deafened by the loud music.* –**deafening** **adj**: *deafening music*

★deal¹ /diːl/ **verb** (*pt, pp* **dealt** /delt/) **1** [I,T] deal (sth) (out); deal (sth) (to sb) to give cards to players in a game of cards: *Start by dealing seven cards to each player.* **2** [I] deal (in sth); deal (with sb) to do business, especially buying and selling goods: *He deals in second-hand cars.* • *Our firm deals with customers all over the world.* **3** [I,T] (*informal*) to buy and sell illegal drugs
IDIOM **deal sb/sth a blow; deal a blow to sb/sth 1** to hit sb/sth: *He was dealt a nasty blow to the head in the accident.* **2** to give sb a shock, etc: *This news dealt a terrible blow to my father.*
PHRASAL VERBS **deal sth out** to give sth to a number of people: *The profits will be dealt out among us.*
deal with sb to treat sb in a particular way; to handle sb: *He's a difficult man. Nobody quite knows how to deal with him.*
deal with sth 1 to take suitable action in a particular situation in order to solve a problem, complete a task, etc; to handle sth: *My secretary will deal with my correspondence while I'm away.* **2** to have sth as its subject: *This chapter deals with letter-writing.*

★deal² /diːl/ **noun** [C] **1** an agreement or arrangement, especially in business: *We're hoping to do a deal with an Italian company.* • *Let's make a deal not to criticize each* *other's work.* ● *'I'll help you with your essay if you'll fix my bike.' 'OK, it's a deal!'* **2** the way that sb is treated: *With high fares and unreliable services, rail users are getting a raw deal.* ● *The new law aims to give pensioners a fair deal.* **3** the action of giving cards to players in a card game

IDIOMS **a big deal/no big deal →** BIG
a good/great deal (of sth) a lot (of sth): *I've spent a great deal of time on this report.*

dealer /'di:lə/ noun [C] **1** a person whose business is buying and selling things: *a dealer in gold and silver* ● *a drug dealer* **2** the person who gives the cards to the players in a game of cards

dealing /'di:lɪŋ/ noun **1 dealings** [pl] relations, especially in business: *We had some dealings with that firm several years ago.*
2 [U] buying and selling: *share dealing*

dealt *past tense, past participle of* DEAL¹

★**dear¹** /dɪə/ adj **1** used at the beginning of a letter before the name or title of the person you are writing to: *Dear Sarah, ...* ● *Dear Sir or Madam, ...* **2 dear (to sb)** loved by or important to sb: *It was a subject that was very dear to him.* ● *She's one of my dearest friends.* **3** (*Brit*) expensive: *How can people afford to smoke when cigarettes are so dear?*

IDIOM **close/dear/near to sb's heart →** HEART

dear² /dɪə/ interj **1** used for expressing disappointment, sadness, surprise, etc: *Dear me! Aren't you ready?* **2** (*old-fashioned*) used when speaking to sb you know well: *Would you like a cup of tea, dear?*

dearly /'dɪəli/ adv **1** very much: *I'd dearly like to go there again.* **2** (*formal*) in a way that causes damage or suffering, or costs a lot of money: *I've already paid dearly for that mistake.*

dearth /dɜːθ/ noun [sing] **a dearth (of sb/sth)** a lack of sth; not enough of sth: *There's a dearth of young people in the village.*

★**death** /deθ/ noun **1** [C,U] the end of sb/sth's life; dying: *There were two deaths and many other people were injured in the accident.* ● *The police do not know the cause of death.* ● *There was no food and people were starving to death.* ••► adjective **dead**, verb **die 2** [U] the end (of sth): *the death of communism*

IDIOMS **catch your death →** CATCH¹
a matter of life and/or death → MATTER¹
put sb to death (usually passive) (*formal*) to kill sb as a punishment, in past times
sick to death of sb/sth → SICK¹
sudden death → SUDDEN

deathly /'deθli/ adj, adv like death: *There was a deathly silence.*

'death penalty noun [sing] the legal punishment of being killed for a crime ••► Look at **capital punishment**.

'death toll noun [C] the number of people killed in a disaster, war, accident, etc

debase /dɪ'beɪs/ verb [T] (usually passive) (*formal*) to reduce the quality or value of sth

debatable /dɪ'beɪtəbl/ adj not certain; that you could argue about: *It's debatable whether people have a better lifestyle these days.*

debate¹ /dɪ'beɪt/ noun **1** [C] a formal argument or discussion of a question at a public meeting or in Parliament **2** [U] general discussion about sth expressing different opinions: *There's been a lot of debate about the cause of acid rain.*

debate² /dɪ'beɪt/ verb **1** [I,T] to discuss sth in a formal way or at a public meeting **2** [T] to think about or discuss sth before deciding what to do: *They debated whether to go or not.*

debit¹ /'debɪt/ noun [C] an amount of money paid out of a bank account ••► opposite **credit¹** ••► Look at **direct debit**.

debit² /'debɪt/ verb [T] to take an amount of money out of a bank account, etc usually as a payment; to record this

debris /'debri:/ noun [U] pieces from sth that has been destroyed, especially in an accident

★**debt** /det/ noun **1** [C] an amount of money that you owe to sb: *She borrowed a lot of money and she's still paying off the debt.* **2** [U] the state of owing money: *After he lost his job, he got into debt.* **3** [C, usually sing] (*formal*) something that you owe sb, for example because he/she has helped or been kind to you: *In his speech he acknowledged his debt to his family and friends for their support.*

IDIOMS **be in/out of debt** to owe/not owe money
be in sb's debt (*formal*) to feel grateful to sb for sth that he/she has done for you

debtor /'detə/ noun [C] a person who owes money

début (also **debut**) /'deɪbju:/ noun [C] a first appearance in public of an actor, etc: *She made her début in London in 1959.*

Dec abbr December: *5 Dec 1999*

decade /'dekeɪd; dɪ'keɪd/ noun [C] a period of ten years

decadence /'dekədəns/ noun [U] behaviour, attitudes, etc that show low moral standards
–**decadent** /'dekədənt/ adj: *a decadent society*

decaffeinated /ˌdi:'kæfɪneɪtɪd/ adj (used about coffee or tea) with most or all of the substance that makes you feel awake and gives you energy (**caffeine**) removed

decapitate /dɪ'kæpɪteɪt/ verb [T] (*formal*) to cut off a person's head

★**decay¹** /dɪ'keɪ/ verb [I] **1** to become bad or be slowly destroyed: *the decaying carcass of a dead sheep* ••► synonym **rot 2** to become weaker or less powerful: *His business empire began to decay.* –**decayed** adj: *a decayed tooth*

decay² /dɪ'keɪ/ noun [U] the process or state of being slowly destroyed: *tooth decay* ● *The old farm was in a terrible state of decay.*

the deceased /dɪ'si:st/ noun [sing] (*formal*) a person who has died, especially one who has died recently: *Many friends of the deceased were present at the funeral.*
–**deceased** adj

deceit /dɪ'si:t/ noun [U] dishonest behaviour; trying to make sb believe sth that is not true: *Their marriage eventually broke up because she was tired of his lies and deceit.*

deceitful /dɪ'si:tfl/ adj dishonest; trying to

make sb believe sth that is not true –**deceit-fully** /-fəli/ **adv** –**deceitfulness noun** [U]

★**deceive** /dɪˈsiːv/ **verb** [T] **deceive sb/yourself (into doing sth)** to try to make sb believe sth that is not true: *He deceived his mother into believing that he had earned the money, not stolen it.* ● *You're deceiving yourself if you think there's an easy solution to the problem.* •➤ **noun deception** or **deceit**

★**December** /dɪˈsembə/ **noun** [U,C] (*abbr* **Dec**) the twelfth month of the year, coming after November •➤ To see how the months are used in sentences, look at the examples and the note at **January**.

decency /ˈdiːsnsi/ **noun** [U] moral or correct behaviour: *She had the decency to admit that it was her fault.*

decent /ˈdiːsnt/ **adj** 1 being of an acceptable standard; satisfactory: *All she wants is a decent job with decent wages.* 2 (used about people or behaviour) honest and fair; treating people with respect 3 not likely to offend or shock sb: *I can't come to the door, I'm not decent* (= I'm not dressed). •➤ opposite **indecent** –**decently adv**

deception /dɪˈsepʃn/ **noun** [C,U] making sb believe or being made to believe sth that is not true: *He had obtained the secret papers by deception.* •➤ **verb deceive**

deceptive /dɪˈseptɪv/ **adj** likely to give a false impression or to make sb believe sth that is not true: *The water is deceptive. It's much deeper than it looks.* –**deceptively adv**: *She made the task sound deceptively easy.*

decibel /ˈdesɪbel/ **noun** [C] a measurement of how loud a sound is

★**decide** /dɪˈsaɪd/ **verb** 1 [I,T] **decide (to do sth); decide against (doing) sth; decide about/on sth; decide that...** to think about two or more possibilities and choose one of them: *There are so many to choose from – I can't decide!* ● *We've decided not to invite Isabel.* ● *She decided against borrowing the money.* ● *They decided on a name for the baby.* ● *He decided that it was too late to go.* ● *The date hasn't been decided yet.* 2 [T] to influence sth so that it produces a particular result: *Your votes will decide the winner.* 3 [T] to cause sb to make a decision: *What finally decided you to leave?* •➤ **noun decision**, adjective **decisive**

decided /dɪˈsaɪdɪd/ **adj** clear; definite: *There has been a decided improvement in his work.* •➤ opposite **undecided** –**decidedly adv**

deciduous /dɪˈsɪdʒuəs/ **adj** (used about a tree) of a type that loses its leaves every autumn •➤ Look at **evergreen**.

decimal[1] /ˈdesɪml/ **adj** based on or counted in units of ten: *decimal currency*

decimal[2] /ˈdesɪml/ **noun** [C] part of a number, written after a kind of full stop (**decimal point**): *Three quarters expressed as a decimal is 0·75.*

decipher /dɪˈsaɪfə/ **verb** [T] to succeed in reading or understanding sth that is not clear: *It's impossible to decipher his handwriting.*

★**decision** /dɪˈsɪʒn/ **noun** 1 [C,U] **a decision (to do sth); a decision on/about sth; a decision that...** a choice or judgement that you make after thinking about various possibilities: *Have you made a decision yet?* ● *I realize now that I made the wrong decision.* ● *There were good reasons for his decision to leave.* ● *I took the decision that I believed to be right.* 2 [U] being able to decide clearly and quickly: *We are looking for someone with decision for this job.* •➤ **verb decide**

decisive /dɪˈsaɪsɪv/ **adj** 1 making sth certain or final: *the decisive battle of the war* 2 having the ability to make clear decisions quickly: *It's no good hesitating. Be decisive.* •➤ opposite **indecisive** •➤ **verb decide** –**decisively adv** –**decisiveness noun** [U]

deck /dek/ **noun** [C] 1 one of the floors of a ship or bus 2 (*US*) = **pack**[1](6): *a deck of cards* **IDIOM on deck** on the part of a ship which you can walk on outside: *I'm going out on deck for some fresh air.*

deckchair /ˈdektʃeə/ **noun** [C] a chair that you use outside, especially on the beach. You can fold it up and carry it.

★**declaration** /ˌdekləˈreɪʃn/ **noun** 1 [C,U] an official statement about sth: *In his speech he made a strong declaration of support for the rebels.* ● *a declaration of war* 2 [C] a written statement giving information on goods or money you have earned, on which you have to pay tax: *a customs declaration*

★**declare** /dɪˈkleə/ **verb** [T] 1 to state sth publicly and officially or to make sth known in a firm, clear way: *to declare war on another country* ● *I declare that the winner of the award is Joan Taylor.* 2 to give information about goods or money you have earned, on which you have to pay tax: *You must declare all your income on this form.*

decline[1] /dɪˈklaɪn/ **verb** 1 [I] to become weaker, smaller or less good: *declining profits* ● *The standard of education has declined in this country.* 2 [I,T] (*formal*) to refuse, usually politely: *Thank you for the invitation but I'm afraid I have to decline.*

decline[2] /dɪˈklaɪn/ **noun** [C,U] **(a) decline (in sth)** a process or period of becoming weaker, smaller or less good: *a decline in sales* ● *As an industrial power, the country is in decline.*

decode /ˌdiːˈkəʊd/ **verb** [T] to find the meaning of a secret message (**code**) •➤ opposite **encode**

decoder /ˌdiːˈkəʊdə/ **noun** [C] a device that changes electronic signals into a form that can be understood: *a satellite/video decoder*

decompose /ˌdiːkəmˈpəʊz/ **verb** [I,T] to slowly be destroyed by natural chemical processes: *The body was so badly decomposed that it couldn't be identified.*

décor /ˈdeɪkɔː/ **noun** [U,sing] the style in which the inside of a building is decorated

★**decorate** /ˈdekəreɪt/ **verb** 1 [T] **decorate sth (with sth)** to add sth in order to make a thing more attractive to look at: *Decorate the cake with cherries and nuts.* 2 [I,T] (*especially Brit*) to put paint and/or coloured paper onto walls, ceilings and doors in a room or building –**decorator** noun [C] a person whose job is to paint and decorate houses and buildings

decoration /ˌdekəˈreɪʃn/ noun 1 [C,U] something that is added to sth in order to make it look more attractive 2 [U] the process of decorating a room or building; the style in which sth is decorated: *The house is in need of decoration.*

decorative /ˈdekərətɪv/ adj attractive or pretty to look at: *The cloth had a decorative lace edge.*

decoy /ˈdiːkɔɪ/ noun [C] a person or object that is used in order to trick sb/sth into doing what you want, going where you want, etc –**decoy** verb [T]

★**decrease**[1] /dɪˈkriːs/ verb [I,T] to become or to make sth smaller or less: *Profits have decreased by 15%.* ● *Decrease speed when you are approaching a road junction.* ••➤ opposite **increase**

★**decrease**[2] /ˈdiːkriːs/ noun [C,U] (a) **decrease (in sth)** the process of becoming or making sth smaller or less; the amount that sth is reduced by: *a 10% decrease in sales*

decree /dɪˈkriː/ noun [C] an official order given by a government, a ruler, etc –**decree** verb [T] (*pt, pp* **decreed**)

decrepit /dɪˈkrepɪt/ adj (used about a thing or person) old and in very bad condition or poor health

dedicate /ˈdedɪkeɪt/ verb [T] 1 **dedicate sth to sth** to give all your energy, time, efforts, etc to sth: *He dedicated his life to helping the poor.* 2 **dedicate sth to sb** to say that sth is specially for sb: *He dedicated the book he had written to his brother.*

dedicated /ˈdedɪkeɪtɪd/ adj giving a lot of your energy, time, efforts, etc to sth that you believe to be important: *dedicated nurses and doctors*

dedication /ˌdedɪˈkeɪʃn/ noun 1 [U] wanting to give your time and energy to sth because you feel it is important: *I admire her dedication to her career.* 2 [C] a message at the beginning of a book or piece of music saying that it is for a particular person

deduce /dɪˈdjuːs/ verb [T] to form an opinion using the facts that you already know: *From his name I deduced that he was Polish.* ••➤ noun **deduction**

deduct /dɪˈdʌkt/ verb [T] **deduct sth (from sth)** to take sth such as money or points away from a total amount: *Marks will be deducted for untidy work.*

deduction /dɪˈdʌkʃn/ noun [C,U] 1 something that you work out from facts that you already know; the ability to think in this way: *It was a brilliant piece of deduction by the detective.* ••➤ verb **deduce** 2 **deduction (from sth)** taking away an amount or number from a total; the amount or number taken away from the total: *What is your total income after deductions?* (= when tax, insurance, etc are taken away) ••➤ verb **deduct**

deed /diːd/ noun [C] 1 (*formal*) something that you do; an action: *a brave/good/evil deed*

2 a legal document that shows that you own a house or building

deem /diːm/ verb [T] (*formal*) to have a particular opinion about sth: *He did not even deem it necessary to apologize.*

★**deep**[1] /diːp/ adj 1 going a long way down from the surface: *to dig a deep hole* ● *That's a deep cut.* ● *a coat with deep pockets* ••➤ noun **depth** ••➤ picture at **shallow** 2 going a long way from front to back: *deep shelves* 3 measuring a particular amount from top to bottom or from front to back: *The water is only a metre deep at this end of the pool.* ● *shelves 40 centimetres deep* 4 (used about sounds) low: *a deep voice* 5 (used about colours) dark; strong: *a deep red* 6 (used about an emotion) strongly felt: *He felt a very deep love for the child.* 7 (used about sleep) not easy to wake from: *I was in a deep sleep and didn't hear the phone ringing for ages.* 8 dealing with difficult subjects or details; thorough: *His books show a deep understanding of human nature.* –**the deep** noun: *in the deep of the night* (= in the middle of the night) ● *the deep* (= a literary way of referring to the sea) –**deeply** adv: *a deeply unhappy person* ● *to breathe deeply*

IDIOMS **deep in thought/conversation** thinking very hard or giving sb/sth your full attention

take a deep breath to breathe in a lot of air, especially in preparation for doing something difficult: *He took a deep breath then walked on stage.*

★**deep**[2] /diːp/ adv a long way down or inside sth: *He gazed deep into her eyes.* ● *He dug his hands deep into his pockets.*

IDIOMS **deep down** in what you really think or feel: *I tried to appear optimistic but deep down I knew there was no hope.*

dig deep → **DIG**[1]

deepen /ˈdiːpən/ verb [I,T] to become or to make sth deep or deeper: *The river deepens here.*

deep-ˈfreeze = **FREEZER**

deep-ˈrooted (also **deep-ˈseated**) adj strongly felt or believed and therefore difficult to change: *deep-rooted fears*

deer

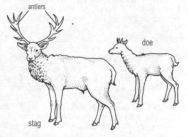

antlers · doe · stag

deer /dɪə/ noun [C] (*pl* **deer**) a large wild grass-eating animal. The male has large horns shaped like branches (**antlers**). ••➤ Note on next page

---

➤ A male deer is called a **buck** or, especially if it has fully-grown antlers, a **stag**. The female is a **doe** and a young deer a **fawn**. **Venison** is the meat from deer.

deface /dɪˈfeɪs/ verb [T] to spoil the way sth looks by writing on or marking its surface

default¹ /dɪˈfɔːlt/ noun [sing] (*computing*) a course of action taken by a computer when it is not given any other instruction

IDIOM **by default** because nothing happened, not because of successful effort: *They won by default, because the other team didn't turn up.*

default² /dɪˈfɔːlt/ verb [I] **1** default (on sth) to not do sth that you should do by law: *If you default on the credit payments (= you don't pay them), the car will be taken back.* **2** (*computing*) default (to sth) to take a particular course of action when no other command is given

★**defeat¹** /dɪˈfiːt/ verb [T] **1** to win a game, a fight, a vote, etc against sb; to beat sb: *The army defeated the rebels after three days of fighting.* ● *In the last match France defeated Wales.* **2** to be too difficult for sb to do or understand: *I've tried to work out what's wrong with the car but it defeats me.* **3** to prevent sth from succeeding: *The local residents are determined to defeat the council's building plans.*

defeat² /dɪˈfiːt/ noun **1** [C] an occasion when sb fails to win or be successful against sb else: *This season they have had two victories and three defeats.* **2** [U] the act of losing or not being successful: *She refused to admit defeat and kept on trying.*

defeatism /dɪˈfiːtɪzəm/ noun [U] the attitude of expecting sth to end in failure

defeatist /dɪˈfiːtɪst/ adj expecting not to succeed: *a defeatist attitude/view* –**defeatist** noun [C]: *Don't be such a defeatist, we haven't lost yet!*

defecate /ˈdefəkeɪt/ verb [I] (*formal*) to get rid of waste from the body; to go to the toilet

defect¹ /ˈdiːfekt/ noun [C] sth that is wrong with or missing from sb/sth: *a speech defect* ● *defects in the education system* –**defective** /dɪˈfektɪv/ adj

defect² /dɪˈfekt/ verb [I] to leave your country, a political party, etc and join one that is considered to be the enemy –**defection** noun [C,U]

★**defence** (*US* **defense**) /dɪˈfens/ noun **1** [U] something that you do or say to protect sb/sth from attack, bad treatment, criticism, etc: *Would you fight in defence of your country?* ● *When her brother was criticized she leapt to his defence.* ● *I must say in her defence that I have always found her very reliable.* •➤ Look at **self-defence**. **2** [C] a defence (against sth) something that protects sb/sth from sth, or that is used to fight against attack: *the body's defences against disease* **3** [U] the military equipment, forces, etc for protecting a country: *Spending on defence needs to be reduced.* **4** [C] (in law) an argument in support of the accused person in a

court of law: *His defence was that he was only carrying out orders.* **5** (**the defence**) [sing, with sing or pl verb] (in law) the lawyer or lawyers who are acting for the accused person in a court of law: *The defence claims/ claim that many of the witnesses were lying.* •➤ Look at **the prosecution**. **6** usually **the defence** [sing,U] (in sport) action to prevent the other team scoring; the players who try to do this: *She plays in defence.*

defenceless /dɪˈfensləs/ adj unable to defend yourself against attack

★**defend** /dɪˈfend/ verb **1** [T] defend sb/sth/ yourself (against/from sb/sth) to protect sb/ sth from harm or danger: *Would you be able to defend yourself if someone attacked you in the street?* **2** [T] defend sb/sth/yourself (against/from sb/sth) to say or write sth to support sb/sth that has been criticized: *The minister went on television to defend the government's policy.* **3** [T] (in law) to speak for sb who is accused of a crime in a court of law **4** [I,T] (in sport) to try to stop the other team or player scoring: *They defended well and managed to hold onto their lead.* **5** [T] to take part in a competition that you won before and try to win it again: *She successfully defended her title.* ● *He is the defending champion.*

defendant /dɪˈfendənt/ noun [C] a person who is accused of a crime in a court of law

defender /dɪˈfendə/ noun [C] a person who defends sb/sth, especially in sport

defense (*US*) = DEFENCE

defensive¹ /dɪˈfensɪv/ adj **1** that protects sb/sth from attack: *The troops took up a defensive position.* •➤ opposite **offensive** **2** showing that you feel that sb is criticizing you: *When I asked him about his new job, he became very defensive and tried to change the subject.*

defensive² /dɪˈfensɪv/ noun

IDIOM **on the defensive** acting in a way that shows that you expect sb to attack or criticize you: *My questions about her past immediately put her on the defensive.*

defer /dɪˈfɜː/ verb [T] (**deferring**; **deferred**) (*formal*) to leave sth until a later time: *She deferred her place at university for a year.*

deference /ˈdefərəns/ noun [U] polite behaviour that you show towards sb/sth, usually because you respect him/her

IDIOM **in deference to sb/sth** because you respect and do not wish to upset sb: *In deference to her father's wishes, she didn't mention the subject again.*

defiance /dɪˈfaɪəns/ noun [U] open refusal to obey sb/sth: *an act of defiance* ● *He continued smoking in defiance of the doctor's orders.* •➤ verb **defy**

defiant /dɪˈfaɪənt/ adj showing open refusal to obey sb/sth •➤ verb **defy** –**defiantly** adv

deficiency /dɪˈfɪʃnsi/ noun (pl **deficiencies**) deficiency (in/of sth) **1** [C,U] the state of not having enough of sth; a lack: *a deficiency of vitamin C* **2** [C] a fault or a weakness in sb/sth: *The problems were caused by defi-ciencies in the design.*

deficient /dɪˈfɪʃnt/ **adj** **1** deficient (in sth) not having enough of sth: *food that is deficient in minerals* **2** not good enough or not complete

deficit /ˈdefɪsɪt/ **noun** [C] the amount by which the money you receive is less than the money you have spent: *a trade deficit*

define /dɪˈfaɪn/ **verb** [T] **1** to say exactly what a word or idea means: *How would you define 'happiness'?* **2** to explain the exact nature of sth clearly: *We need to define the problem before we can attempt to solve it.*

★**definite** /ˈdefɪnət/ **adj** **1** fixed and unlikely to change; certain: *I'll give you a definite decision in a couple of days.* •➤ opposite **indefinite** **2** clear; easy to see or notice: *There has been a definite change in her attitude recently.*

the ˌdefinite ˈarticle **noun** [C] (*grammar*) the name used for the word 'the' •➤ Look at **the indefinite article**.

> For more information about the definite article, look at the **Quick Grammar Reference** section at the back of this dictionary.

definitely /ˈdefɪnətli/ **adv** certainly; without doubt: *I'll definitely consider your advice.*

definition /ˌdefɪˈnɪʃn/ **noun** [C,U] a description of the exact meaning of a word or idea

definitive /dɪˈfɪnɪtɪv/ **adj** in a form that cannot be changed or that cannot be improved: *This is the definitive version.* • *the definitive performance of Hamlet* –**definitively** **adv**

deflate /ˌdiːˈfleɪt/ **verb** **1** [I,T] to become or to make sth smaller by letting the air or gas out of it: *The balloon slowly deflated.* •➤ opposite **inflate** **2** [T] to make sb feel less confident, proud or excited: *I felt really deflated when I got my exam results.*

deflect /dɪˈflekt/ **verb** **1** [I,T] to change direction after hitting sb/sth; to make sth change direction in this way: *The ball deflected off a defender and into the goal.* **2** [T] to turn sb's attention away from sth: *Nothing could deflect her from her aim.*

deflection /dɪˈflekʃn/ **noun** [C,U] a change of direction after hitting sb/sth

deforestation /ˌdiːˌfɒrɪˈsteɪʃn/ **noun** [U] cutting down trees over a large area

deform /dɪˈfɔːm/ **verb** [T] to change or spoil the natural shape of sth

deformed /dɪˈfɔːmd/ **adj** having a shape that is not normal because it has grown wrongly

deformity /dɪˈfɔːməti/ **noun** (*pl* **deformities**) [C,U] the condition of having a part of the body that is an unusual shape because of disease, injury, etc: *The drug caused women to give birth to babies with severe deformities.*

defraud /dɪˈfrɔːd/ **verb** [T] defraud sb (of sth) to get sth from sb in a dishonest way: *He defrauded the company of millions.*

defrost /ˌdiːˈfrɒst/ **verb** **1** [T] to remove the ice from sth: *to defrost a fridge* **2** [I,T] (used about frozen food) to return to a normal temperature; to make food do this: *Defrost the*

chicken thoroughly before cooking. •➤ Look at **de-ice**.

deft /deft/ **adj** (used especially about movements) skilful and quick –**deftly** **adv**

defunct /dɪˈfʌŋkt/ **adj** no longer existing or in use

defuse /ˌdiːˈfjuːz/ **verb** [T] **1** to remove part of a bomb so that it cannot explode: *Army experts defused the bomb safely.* **2** to make a situation calmer or less dangerous: *She defused the tension by changing the subject.*

defy /dɪˈfaɪ/ **verb** [T] (*pp* **defying**; *3rd pers sing pres* **defies**; *pt, pp* **defied**) **1** to refuse to obey sb/sth: *She defied her parents and continued seeing him.* •➤ adjective **defiant**, noun **defiance** **2** defy sb to do sth to ask sb to do sth that you believe to be impossible: *I defy you to prove me wrong.* **3** to make sth impossible or very difficult: *It's such a beautiful place that it defies description.*

degenerate[1] /dɪˈdʒenəreɪt/ **verb** [I] to become worse, lower in quality, etc: *The calm discussion degenerated into a nasty argument.* –**degeneration** /dɪˌdʒenəˈreɪʃn/ **noun** [U]

degenerate[2] /dɪˈdʒenərət/ **adj** having moral standards that have fallen to a very low level

degradation /ˌdegrəˈdeɪʃn/ **noun** [U] **1** the action of making sb be less respected; the state of being less respected: *the degradation of being in prison* **2** causing the condition of sth to become worse: *environmental degradation*

degrade /dɪˈgreɪd/ **verb** [T] to make people respect sb less: *It's the sort of film that really degrades women.* –**degrading** **adj**

★**degree** /dɪˈgriː/ **noun** **1** [C] a measurement of temperature: *Water boils at 100 degrees Celsius (100°C).* • *three degrees below zero/minus three degrees (-3°)* **2** [C] a measurement of angles: *a forty-five degree (45°) angle* • *An angle of 90 degrees is called a right angle.* **3** [C,U] (used about feelings or qualities) a certain amount or level: *There is always a degree of risk involved in mountaineering.* • *I sympathize with her to some degree.* **4** [C] an official document gained by successfully completing a course at university or college: *She's got a degree in Philosophy.* • *to do a Chemistry degree*

> In Britain **degree** is the usual word for the qualification you get when you complete and pass a university course. You can study for a **diploma** at other types of college. The courses may be shorter and more practical than degree courses. The best result you can get in a British university degree is a **first**, followed by a **two-one**, a **two-two**, a **third**, a **pass**, and a **fail**.

dehydrate /ˌdiːhaɪˈdreɪt/ **verb** **1** [T] (usually passive) to remove all the water from sth: *Dehydrated vegetables can be stored for months.* **2** [I,T] to lose too much water from your body: *If you run for a long time in the heat, you start to dehydrate.* –**dehydration**

/ˌdiːhaɪˈdreɪʃn/ **noun** [U]: *Several of the runners were suffering from severe dehydration.*

de-ice /ˌdiː 'aɪs/ **verb** [T] to remove the ice from sth: *The car windows need de-icing.* ⋅► Look at **defrost**.

deign /deɪn/ **verb** [T] **deign to do sth** to do sth although you think you are too important to do it: *He didn't even deign to look up when I entered the room.*

deity /'deɪəti/ **noun** [C] (*pl* **deities**) (*formal*) a god

dejected /dɪ'dʒektɪd/ **adj** very unhappy, especially because you are disappointed: *The fans went home dejected after watching their team lose.* –**dejectedly adv** –**dejection noun** [U]

★**delay¹** /dɪ'leɪ/ **verb 1** [T] to make sth/sb slow or late: *The plane was delayed for several hours because of bad weather.* **2** [I,T] **delay (sth/doing sth)** to decide not to do sth until a later time: *I was forced to delay the trip until the following week.*

delay² /dɪ'leɪ/ **noun** [C,U] a situation or period of time where you have to wait: *Delays are likely on the roads because of heavy traffic.* ● *If you smell gas, report it without delay* (= immediately).

delegate¹ /'delɪɡət/ **noun** [C] a person who has been chosen to speak or take decisions for a group of people, especially at a meeting

delegate² /'delɪɡeɪt/ **verb** [I,T] to give sb with a lower job or position a particular task to do: *You can't do everything yourself. You must learn how to delegate.*

delegation /ˌdelɪˈɡeɪʃn/ **noun 1** [C, with sing or pl verb] a group of people who have been chosen to speak or take decisions for a larger group of people, especially at a meeting: *The British delegation walked out of the meeting in protest.* **2** [U] giving sb with a lower job or position a particular task to do

delete /dɪ'liːt/ **verb** [T] to remove sth that is written –**deletion** /dɪ'liːʃn/ **noun** [C,U]

★**deliberate¹** /dɪ'lɪbərət/ **adj 1** done on purpose; planned: *Was it an accident or was it deliberate?* ⋅► synonym **intentional 2** done slowly and carefully, without hurrying: *She spoke in a calm, deliberate voice.*

deliberate² /də'lɪbəreɪt/ **verb** [I,T] (*formal*) to think about or discuss sth fully before making a decision: *The judges deliberated for an hour before announcing the winner.*

★**deliberately** /dɪ'lɪbərətli/ **adv 1** on purpose; intentionally: *I didn't break it deliberately, it was an accident.* ⋅► synonym **purposely 2** slowly and carefully, without hurrying

deliberation /dɪˌlɪbəˈreɪʃn/ **noun** (*formal*) **1** [C,U] discussion or thinking about sth in detail: *After much deliberation I decided to reject the offer.* **2** [U] the quality of being very slow and careful in what you say and do: *He spoke with great deliberation.*

delicacy /'delɪkəsi/ **noun** (*pl* **delicacies**) **1** [U] the quality of being easy to damage or break **2** [U] great care; a gentle touch: (*figurative*) *Be tactful! It's a matter of some delicacy.* **3** [C] a type of food that is considered particularly good: *Try this dish, it's a local delicacy.*

★**delicate** /'delɪkət/ **adj 1** easy to damage or break: *delicate skin* ● *the delicate mechanisms of a watch* **2** frequently ill or hurt: *He was a delicate child and often in hospital.* **3** (used about colours, flavours, etc) light and pleasant; not strong: *a delicate shade of pale blue* **4** needing skilful treatment and care: *Repairing this is going to be a very delicate operation.* –**delicately adv**: *She stepped delicately over the broken glass.*

delicatessen /ˌdelɪkə'tesn/ **noun** [C] a shop that sells special, unusual or foreign foods, especially cold cooked meat, cheeses, etc

★**delicious** /dɪ'lɪʃəs/ **adj** having a very pleasant taste or smell: *This soup is absolutely delicious.*

delight¹ /dɪ'laɪt/ **noun 1** [U] great pleasure; joy: *She laughed with delight as she opened the present.* **2** [C] something that gives sb great pleasure: *The story is a delight to read.* –**delightful** /-fl/ **adj**: *a delightful view* –**delightfully** /-fəli/ **adv**

★**delight²** /dɪ'laɪt/ **verb** [T] to give sb great pleasure: *She delighted the audience by singing all her old songs.*

PHRASAL VERB **delight in sth/in doing sth** to get great pleasure from sth: *He delights in playing tricks on people.*

delighted /dɪ'laɪtɪd/ **adj delighted (at/with/about sth); delighted to do sth/that...** extremely pleased: *She was delighted at getting the job/that she got the job.* ● *They're absolutely delighted with their baby.*

delinquency /dɪ'lɪŋkwənsi/ **noun** [U] (*formal*) bad or criminal behaviour, especially among young people

delinquent /dɪ'lɪŋkwənt/ **adj** (*formal*) (usually used about a young person) behaving badly and often breaking the law –**delinquent noun** [C]: *a juvenile delinquent*

delirious /dɪ'lɪriəs/ **adj 1** speaking or thinking in a crazy way, often because of illness **2** extremely happy: *I was absolutely delirious when I passed the exam.* –**deliriously adv**

★**deliver** /dɪ'lɪvə/ **verb 1** [I,T] to take sth (goods, letters, etc) to the place requested or to the address on it: *Your order will be delivered within five days.* ● *We deliver free within the local area.* **2** [T] to help a mother to give birth to her baby: *to deliver a baby* **3** [T] (*formal*) to say sth formally: *to deliver a speech/lecture/warning* **4** [I] **deliver (on sth)** (*informal*) to do or give sth that you have promised: *The new leader has made a lot of promises, but can he deliver on them?*

IDIOM **come up with/deliver the goods** → **GOODS**

delivery /dɪ'lɪvəri/ **noun** (*pl* **deliveries**) **1** [U] the act of taking sth (goods, letters, etc) to the place or person who has ordered it or whose address is on it: *Please allow 28 days for delivery.* ● *a delivery van* **2** [C] an occasion when sth is delivered: *Is there a delivery here on Sundays?* **3** [C] something (goods, letters, etc) that is delivered: *The shop is waiting for a new delivery of apples.* **4** [C] the process of giving birth to a baby: *an easy delivery*

delta /'deltə/ **noun** [C] an area of flat land shaped like a triangle where a river divides into smaller rivers as it goes into the sea

delude /dɪ'luːd/ **verb** [T] to make sb believe sth that is not true: *If he thinks he's going to get rich quickly, he's deluding himself.* **··>** noun delusion

deluge[1] /'deljuːdʒ/ **noun** [C] **1** a sudden very heavy fall of rain; a flood **2** a deluge (of sth) a very large number of things that happen or arrive at the same time: *The programme was followed by a deluge of complaints from the public.*

deluge[2] /'deljuːdʒ/ **verb** [T] (usually passive) to send or give sb/sth a very large quantity of sth, all at the same time: *They were deluged with applications for the job.*

delusion /dɪ'luːʒn/ **noun** [C,U] a false belief: *He seems to be **under the delusion** that he's popular.* **··>** verb delude

de luxe /ˌdə 'lʌks/ **adj** of extremely high quality and more expensive than usual: *a de luxe hotel*

delve /delv/ **verb** [I] delve into sth to search inside sth: *She delved into the bag and brought out a tiny box.* ● *(figurative) We must delve into the past to find the origins of the custom.*

★**demand**[1] /dɪ'mɑːnd/ **noun 1** [C] a demand (for sth/that...) a strong request or order that must be obeyed: *a demand for changes in the law* ● *I was amazed by their demand that I should leave immediately.* **2** demands [pl] something that sb makes you do, especially sth that is difficult or tiring: *Running a marathon **makes huge demands** on the body.* **3** [U,sing] demand (for sth/sb) the desire or need for sth among a group of people: *We no longer sell that product because there is no demand for it.*

IDIOMS in demand wanted by a lot of people: *I'm in demand this weekend – I've had three invitations!*

on demand whenever you ask for it: *This treatment is available from your doctor on demand.*

★**demand**[2] /dɪ'mɑːnd/ **verb** [T] **1** demand to do sth/that...; demand sth to ask for sth in an extremely firm or aggressive way: *I walked into the office and demanded to see the manager.* ● *She demanded that I pay her immediately.* ● *Your behaviour was disgraceful and I demand an apology.* **2** to need sth: *a sport that demands skill as well as strength*

demanding /dɪ'mɑːndɪŋ/ **adj 1** (used about a job, task, etc) needing a lot of effort, care, skill, etc: *It will be a demanding schedule – I have to go to six cities in six days.* **2** (used about a person) always wanting attention or expecting very high standards of people: *Young children are very demanding.* ● *a demanding boss*

demise /dɪ'maɪz/ **noun** [sing] **1** the end or

failure of sth: *Poor business decisions led to the company's demise.* **2** *(written)* the death of a person

★**democracy** /dɪ'mɒkrəsi/ **noun** (*pl* democracies) **1** [U] a system in which the government of a country is elected by the people **2** [C] a country that has this system **3** [U] the right of everyone in an organization, etc to be treated equally and to vote on matters that affect them: *There is a need for more democracy in the company.*

democrat /'deməkræt/ **noun** [C] **1** a person who believes in and supports democracy **2** Democrat a member or supporter of the Democratic Party of the US **··>** Look at **Republican**.

★**democratic** /ˌdeməˈkrætɪk/ **adj 1** based on the system of democracy: *democratic elections* ● *a democratic government* **2** having or supporting equal rights for all people: *a democratic decision* (= made by all the people involved) –democratically /-kli/ **adv**: *a democratically elected government*

the ˌDemoˈcratic Party noun [sing] one of the two main political parties of the US

  ➤ The other main party is the Republican Party.

demolish /dɪ'mɒlɪʃ/ **verb** [T] to destroy sth, for example a building: *The old shops were demolished and a supermarket was built in their place.* ● *(figurative) She demolished his argument in one sentence.* –demolition /ˌdeməˈlɪʃn/ **noun** [C,U]

demon /'diːmən/ **noun** [C] an evil spirit

★**demonstrate** /'demənstreɪt/ **verb 1** [T] demonstrate sth (to sb) to show sth clearly by giving proof: *Using this chart, I'd like to demonstrate to you what has happened to our sales.* **2** [I,T] demonstrate sth (to sb) to show and explain to sb how to do sth or how sth works: *The crew demonstrated the use of life-jackets just after take-off.* ● *I'm not sure what you mean – could you demonstrate?* **3** [I] demonstrate (against/for sb/sth) to take part in a public protest for or against sb/sth: *Enormous crowds have been demonstrating against the government.*

★**demonstration** /ˌdemənˈstreɪʃn/ **noun 1** [C,U] something that shows clearly that sth exists or is true: *This accident is a clear demonstration of the system's faults.* **2** [C,U] an act of showing or explaining to sb how to do sth or how sth works: *The salesman gave me a demonstration of what the computer could do.* **3** [C] a demonstration (against/for sb/sth) a public protest for or against sb/sth: *demonstrations against a new law*

demonstrative /dɪ'mɒnstrətɪv/ **adj** (used about a person) showing feelings, especially loving feelings, in front of other people

demonstrator /'demənstreɪtə/ **noun** [C] a person who takes part in a public protest

demoralize (also **-ise**) /dɪ'mɒrəlaɪz/ **verb** [T] to make sb lose confidence or the courage to continue doing sth: *Repeated defeats demoralized the team.* –demoralization (also -isation) /dɪˌmɒrəlaɪˈzeɪʃn/ **noun** [U] –demoralizing (also **demoralising**) **adj**: *Constant criticism can be extremely demoralizing.*

demure /dɪˈmjʊə/ **adj** (used especially about a girl or young woman) shy, quiet and polite

den /den/ **noun** [C] **1** the place where certain wild animals live, for example lions **2** a secret place, especially for illegal activities: *a gambling den*

denial /dɪˈnaɪəl/ **noun 1** [C] a statement that sth is not true: *The minister issued a denial that he was involved in the scandal.* **2** [C,U] (a) denial (of sth) refusing to allow sb to have or do sth: *a denial of personal freedom* **3** [U] a refusal to accept that sth unpleasant or painful has happened: *He's been in denial ever since the accident.* ·➤ verb **deny**

denim /ˈdenɪm/ **noun** [U] a thick cotton material (often blue) that is used for making clothes, especially trousers (**jeans**): *a denim jacket*

denomination /dɪˌnɒmɪˈneɪʃn/ **noun** [C] one of the different religious groups that you can belong to

denote /dɪˈnəʊt/ **verb** [T] to mean or be a sign of sth: *In algebra the sign x always denotes an unknown quantity.*

denounce /dɪˈnaʊns/ **verb** [T] to say publicly that sth is wrong; to be very critical of a person in public: *The actor has been denounced as a bad influence on young people.* ·➤ noun **denunciation**

dense /dens/ **adj 1** containing a lot of things or people close together: *dense forests* ● *areas of dense population* **2** difficult to see through: *dense fog* **3** (*informal*) not intelligent; stupid –densely **adv**: *densely populated areas*

density /ˈdensəti/ **noun** (*pl* **densities**) **1** [U] the number of things or people in a place in relation to its area: *There is a high density of wildlife in this area.* **2** [C,U] (*technical*) the relation of the weight of a substance to its size: *Lead has a high density.*

dent[1] /dent/ **noun** [C] a place where a flat surface, especially metal, has been hit and damaged but not broken: *This tin's got a dent in it.*

dent[2] /dent/ **verb** [T] to damage a flat surface by hitting it but not breaking it: *I hit a wall and dented the front of the car.*

dental /ˈdentl/ **adj** connected with teeth: *dental care/treatment*

★**dentist** /ˈdentɪst/ **noun 1** [C] a person whose job is to look after people's teeth **2 the dentist's** [sing] the place where a dentist works: *I have to go to the dentist's today.*

dentures /ˈdentʃəz/ = **FALSE TEETH**

denunciation /dɪˌnʌnsiˈeɪʃn/ **noun** [C,U] an expression of strong disapproval of sb/sth in public ·➤ verb **denounce**

★**deny** /dɪˈnaɪ/ **verb** [T] (*pres part* **denying**; *3rd pers sing pres* **denies**; *pt, pp* **denied**) **1** deny sth/doing sth; deny that… to state that sth is not true; to refuse to admit or accept sth: *In*

court he denied all the charges. ● *She denied telling lies/that she had told lies.* ·➤ opposite **admit 2** (*formal*) deny sb sth; deny sth (to sb) to refuse to allow sb to have sth: *She was denied permission to remain in the country.* ·➤ noun **denial**

deodorant /diˈəʊdərənt/ **noun** [C,U] a chemical substance that you put onto your body to prevent bad smells

dep **abbr** departs: *dep London 15.32*

depart /dɪˈpɑːt/ **verb** [I] (*formal*) to leave a place, usually at the beginning of a journey: *Ferries depart for Spain twice a day.* ● *The next train to the airport departs from platform 2.* ·➤ noun **departure** ·➤ Look at the note at **leave**[1].

★**department** /dɪˈpɑːtmənt/ **noun** [C] (*abbr* **Dept**) **1** one of the sections into which an organization (for example) a school or a business) is divided: *the Modern Languages department* ● *She works in the accounts department.* **2** a division of the government responsible for a particular subject; a ministry: *the Department of Health*

departmental /ˌdiːpɑːtˈmentl/ **adj** concerning a department: *There is a departmental meeting once a month.*

deˈpartment store **noun** [C] a large shop that is divided into sections selling different types of goods

★**departure** /dɪˈpɑːtʃə/ **noun** [C,U] **1** leaving or going away from a place: *Helen's sudden departure meant I had to do her job as well as mine.* ● *Passengers should check in at least one hour before departure.* ·➤ verb **depart 2** a departure (from sth) an action which is different from what is usual or expected: *a departure from normal practice*

★**depend** /dɪˈpend/ **verb**
IDIOM that depends; it (all) depends (used alone or at the beginning of a sentence) used to say that you are not certain of sth until other things have been considered: *'Can you lend me some money?' 'That depends. How much do you want?'* ● *I don't know whether I'll see him. It depends what time he gets here.*
PHRASAL VERBS depend on sb/sth to be able to trust sb/sth to do sth; to rely on sb/sth: *If you ever need any help, you know you can depend on me.* ● *You can't depend on the trains. They're always late.* ● *I was depending on getting the money today.*
depend on sb/sth (for sth) to need sb/sth to provide sth: *Our organization depends on donations from the public.*
depend on sth to be decided or influenced by sb/sth: *His whole future depends on these exams.*

dependable /dɪˈpendəbl/ **adj** that can be trusted; reliable: *The bus service is very dependable.*

dependant (*especially US* **dependent**) /dɪˈpendənt/ **noun** [C] a person who depends on sb else for money, a home, food, etc: *insurance cover for you and all your dependants*

dependence /dɪˈpendəns/ **noun** [U] dependence on sb/sth the state of needing sb/sth: *The country wants to reduce its dependence on imported oil.*

dependency /dɪˈpendənsi/ **noun** [U] the state of being dependent on sb/sth; the state of being unable to live without sth, especially a drug

★**dependent** /dɪˈpendənt/ **adj 1** dependent (on sb/sth) needing sb/sth to support you: *The industry is heavily dependent on government funding.* ● *Do you have any dependent children?* **2** dependent on sb/sth influenced or decided by sth: *The price you pay is dependent on the number in your group.* •➤ opposite **independent**

depict /dɪˈpɪkt/ **verb** [T] **1** to show sb/sth in a painting or drawing: *a painting depicting a country scene* **2** to describe sb/sth in words: *The novel depicts rural life a century ago.*

deplete /dɪˈpliːt/ **verb** [T] to reduce the amount of sth so that there is not much left: *We are depleting the world's natural resources.* –depletion /dɪˈpliːʃn/ **noun** [U]

deplorable /dɪˈplɔːrəbl/ **adj** (*formal*) morally bad and deserving disapproval: *They are living in deplorable conditions.* –deplorably /-əbli/ **adv**

deplore /dɪˈplɔː/ **verb** [T] (*formal*) to feel or say that sth is morally bad: *I deplore such dishonest behaviour.*

deploy /dɪˈplɔɪ/ **verb** [T] **1** to put soldiers or weapons in a position where they are ready to fight **2** to use sth in a useful and successful way –deployment **noun** [U]: *the deployment of troops*

deport /dɪˈpɔːt/ **verb** [T] to force sb to leave a country because he/she has no legal right to be there: *A number of illegal immigrants have been deported.* –deportation /ˌdiːpɔːˈteɪʃn/ **noun** [C,U]

depose /dɪˈpəʊz/ **verb** [T] to remove a ruler or leader from power: *There was a revolution and the dictator was deposed.*

deposit[1] /dɪˈpɒzɪt/ **verb** [T] **1** to put sth down somewhere: *He deposited his bags on the floor and sat down.* **2** (used about liquid or a river) to leave sth lying on a surface, as the result of a natural or chemical process: *mud deposited by a flood* **3** to put money into an account at a bank: *He deposited £20 a week into his savings account.* **4** deposit sth (in sth); deposit sth (with sb/sth) to put sth valuable in an official place where it is safe until needed again: *Valuables can be deposited in the hotel safe.*

deposit[2] /dɪˈpɒzɪt/ **noun** [C] **1** a deposit (on sth) a sum of money which is the first payment for sth, with the rest of the money to be paid later: *Once you have paid a deposit, the booking will be confirmed.* **2** a deposit (on sth) [usually sing] a sum of money that you pay when you rent sth and get back when you return it without damage: *Boats can be hired for £5 an hour, plus £20 deposit.* **3** a sum of money paid into a bank account **4** a substance that has been left on a surface or in the ground as the result of a natural or chemical process: *mineral deposits*

de'posit account **noun** [C] (*Brit*) a type of bank account where your money earns interest. You cannot take money out of a deposit account without arranging it first with the bank.

depot /ˈdepəʊ/ **noun** [C] **1** a place where large numbers of vehicles (buses, lorries, etc) are kept when not in use **2** a place where large amounts of food, goods or equipment are stored **3** (*US*) a small bus or railway station

depreciate /dɪˈpriːʃieɪt/ **verb** [I] to become less valuable over a period of time: *New cars start to depreciate the moment they are on the road.* –depreciation /dɪˌpriːʃiˈeɪʃn/ **noun** [C,U]

depress /dɪˈpres/ **verb** [T] **1** to make sb unhappy and without hope or enthusiasm: *The thought of going to work tomorrow really depresses me.* **2** (used about business) to cause sth to become less successful: *The reduction in the number of tourists has depressed local trade.* **3** (*formal*) to press sth down on a machine, etc: *To switch off the machine, depress the lever.* –depressing **adj**: *The thought of growing old alone is very depressing.* –depressingly **adv**

depressed /dɪˈprest/ **adj 1** very unhappy, often for a long period of time: *He's been very depressed since he lost his job.* **2** (used about a place or an industry) without enough business or jobs

★**depression** /dɪˈpreʃn/ **noun 1** [U] a feeling of unhappiness that lasts for a long time. Depression can be a medical condition and may have physical signs, for example being unable to sleep, etc: *clinical/post-natal depression* **2** [C,U] a period when the economic situation is bad, with little business activity and many people without a job: *The country was in the grip of (an) economic depression.* **3** [C] a part of a surface that is lower than the parts around it: *Rainwater collects in shallow depressions in the ground.*

deprive /dɪˈpraɪv/ **verb** [T] deprive sb/sth of sth to prevent sb/sth from having sth; to take away sth from sb: *The prisoners were deprived of food.* –deprivation /ˌdeprɪˈveɪʃn/ **noun** [C,U]

deprived /dɪˈpraɪvd/ **adj** not having enough of the basic things in life, such as food, money, etc: *He came from a deprived background.*

Dept **abbr** department: *the Sales Dept*

★**depth** /depθ/ **noun 1** [C,U] the distance down from the top to the bottom of sth: *The hole should be 3cm in depth.* **2** [C,U] the distance from the front to the back of sth: *the depth of a shelf* •➤ picture at **length 3** [U] the amount of emotion, knowledge, etc that a person has: *He tried to convince her of the depth of his feelings for her.* **4** [usually pl] the deepest, most extreme or serious part of sth: *in the depths of winter* (= when it is coldest) •➤ adjective **deep**

IDIOMS **in depth** looking at all the details; in a thorough way: *to discuss a problem in depth*

out of your depth 1 (*Brit*) in water that is too deep for you to stand up in **2** in a situation

d

---

that is too difficult for you: *When they start discussing politics I soon get out of my depth.*

deputation /ˌdepjə'teɪʃn/ **noun** [C,with sing or pl verb] a group of people sent to sb to act or speak for others

deputize (also **-ise**) /'depjətaɪz/ **verb** [I] **deputize (for sb)** to act for sb in a higher position, who is away or unable to do sth

★**deputy** /'depjəti/ **noun** [C] (*pl* **deputies**) the second most important person in a particular organization, who does the work of his/her manager if the manager is away: *the deputy head of a school*

derail /dɪ'reɪl/ **verb** [T] to cause a train to come off a railway track

derailment /dɪ'reɪlmənt/ **noun** [C,U] an occasion when sth causes a train to come off a railway track

deranged /dɪ'reɪndʒd/ **adj** thinking and behaving in a way that is not normal, especially because of mental illness

derby /'dɑːbi/ **noun** [C] (*pl* **derbies**) **1** (*Brit*) a race or sports competition: *a motorcycle derby* **2** (*Brit*) **the Derby** a horse race which takes place every year at Epsom **3** (*US*) = **BOWLER**(1)

derelict /'derəlɪkt/ **adj** no longer used and in bad condition: *a derelict house*

deride /dɪ'raɪd/ **verb** [T] to say that sb/sth is ridiculous; to laugh at sth in a cruel way –**derision** /dɪ'rɪʒn/ **noun** [U]: *Her comments were met with derision.* –**derisive** /dɪ'raɪsɪv/ **adj**: *'What rubbish!' he said with a derisive laugh.*

derisory /dɪ'raɪsəri/ **adj** too small or of too little value to be considered seriously: *Union leaders rejected the derisory pay offer.*

derivation /ˌderɪ'veɪʃn/ **noun** [C,U] the origin from which a word or phrase has developed

derivative /dɪ'rɪvətɪv/ **noun** [C] a form of sth (especially a word) that has developed from the original form: *'Sadness' is a derivative of 'sad.'*

derive /dɪ'raɪv/ **verb 1** [T] (*formal*) **derive sth from sth** to get sth (especially a feeling or an advantage) from sth: *I derive great satisfaction from my work.* **2** [I,T] (used about a name or word) to come from sth; to have sth as its origin: *The town derives its name from the river on which it was built.*

derogatory /dɪ'rɒgətri/ **adj** expressing a lack of respect for, or a low opinion of sth: *derogatory comments about the standard of my work*

descend /dɪ'send/ **verb** [I,T] (*formal*) to go down to a lower place; to go down sth: *The plane started to descend and a few minutes later we landed.* • *She descended the stairs slowly.* •➤ opposite **ascend**

IDIOM **be descended from sb** to have sb as a relative in past times: *He says he's descended from a Russian prince.*

descendant /dɪ'sendənt/ **noun** [C] a person who belongs to the same family as sb who lived a long time ago: *Her family are descend-*

ants of one of the first Englishmen to arrive in America. •➤ Look at **ancestor**.

descent /dɪ'sent/ **noun 1** [C] a movement down to a lower place: *The pilot warned us that we were about to begin our descent.* **2** [U] a person's family origins: *He is of Italian descent.*

★**describe** /dɪ'skraɪb/ **verb** [T] **describe sb/ sth (to/for sb); describe sb/sth (as sth)** to say what sb/sth is like, or what happened: *Can you describe the bag you lost?* • *It's impossible to describe how I felt.* • *The thief was described as tall, thin, and aged about twenty.*

★**description** /dɪ'skrɪpʃn/ **noun 1** [C,U] a picture in words of sb/sth or of sth that happened: *The man gave the police a detailed description of the burglar.* **2** [C] a type or kind of sth: *It must be a tool of some description, but I don't know what it's for.*

descriptive /dɪ'skrɪptɪv/ **adj** that describes sb/sth, especially in a skilful or interesting way: *a piece of descriptive writing* • *She gave a highly descriptive account of the journey.*

desert[1] /dɪ'zɜːt/ **verb 1** [T] to leave sb/sth, usually for ever: *Many people have deserted the countryside and moved to the towns.* **2** [I,T] (used especially about sb in the armed forces) to leave without permission: *He deserted because he didn't want to fight.* –**desertion noun** [C,U]

★**desert**[2] /'dezət/ **noun** [C,U] a large area of land, usually covered with sand, that is hot and has very little water and very few plants

deserted /dɪ'zɜːtɪd/ **adj** empty, because all the people have left: *a deserted house*

deserter /dɪ'zɜːtə/ **noun** [C] a person who leaves the armed forces without permission

desert 'island noun [C] an island, especially a tropical one, where nobody lives

★**deserve** /dɪ'zɜːv/ **verb** [T] (not used in the continuous tenses) to earn sth, either good or bad, because of sth that you have done: *We've done a lot of work and we deserve a break.* • *He deserves to be punished severely for such a crime.*

➤ Although this verb is not used in the continuous tenses, it is common to see the present participle (= -*ing* form): *There are other aspects of the case deserving attention.*

deservedly /dɪ'zɜːvɪdli/ **adv** in a way that is right because of what sb has done: *He deservedly won the Best Actor award.*

deserving /dɪ'zɜːvɪŋ/ **adj** **deserving (of sth)** that you should give help, money, etc to: *This charity is a most deserving cause.*

★**design**[1] /dɪ'zaɪn/ **noun 1** [U] the way in which sth is planned and made or arranged: *Design faults have been discovered in the car.* **2** [U] the process and skill of making drawings that show how sth should be made, how it will work, etc: *to study industrial design* • *graphic design* **3** [C] a design (for sth) a drawing or plan that shows how sth should be made, built, etc: *The architect showed us her design for the new theatre.* **4** [C] a pattern of lines, shapes, etc that decorate sth: *a T-shirt with a geometric design on it* ••➤ synonym **pattern**

★**design²** /dɪˈzaɪn/ **verb 1** [I,T] to plan and make a drawing of how sth will be made: *to design cars/dresses/houses* **2** [T] to invent, plan and develop sth for a particular purpose: *The bridge wasn't designed for such heavy traffic.*

designate /ˈdezɪɡneɪt/ **verb** [T] (often passive) (*formal*) **1 designate sth (as)** sth to give sth a name to show that it has a particular purpose: *This has been designated (as) a conservation area.* **2 designate sb (as)** sth to choose sb to do a particular job or task: *Who has she designated (as) her deputy?* **3** to show or mark sth: *These arrows designate the emergency exits.*

designer /dɪˈzaɪnə/ **noun** [C] a person whose job is to make drawings or plans showing how sth will be made: *a fashion/jewellery designer* • *designer jeans* (= made by a famous designer)

desirable /dɪˈzaɪərəbl/ **adj 1** wanted, often by many people; worth having: *Experience is desirable but not essential for this job.* **2** sexually attractive ••➤ opposite **undesirable**

desire¹ /dɪˈzaɪə/ **noun** [C,U] (a) **desire (for sth/to do sth) 1** the feeling of wanting sth very much; a strong wish: *the desire for a peaceful solution to the crisis* • *I have no desire to visit that place again.* **2** the wish for a sexual relationship with sb

desire² /dɪˈzaɪə/ **verb** [T] **1** (*formal*) (not used in the continuous tenses) to want; to wish for: *They have everything they could possibly desire.* • *The service in the restaurant left a lot to be desired* (= was very bad). **2** to find sb/sth sexually attractive

> ➤ Although this verb is not used in the continuous tenses, it is common to see the present participle (= -*ing* form): *Not desiring another argument, she turned away.*

★**desk** /desk/ **noun** [C] **1** a type of table, often with drawers, that you sit at to write or work: *The pupils took their books out of their desks.* • *He used to be a pilot but now he has **a desk job*** (= he works in an office). **2** a table or place in a building where a particular service is provided: *an information desk* • *Take your suitcases and tickets to the check-in desk.*

desktop /ˈdesktɒp/ **noun** [C] **1** the top of a desk **2** a computer screen on which you can see symbols (icons) showing the programs, information, etc that are available to be used **3** (also **desktop comˈputer**) a computer that can fit on a desk ••➤ Look at **laptop**.

desktop ˈpublishing (*abbr* DTP) **noun** [U] the use of a small computer and a machine for printing, to produce books, magazines and other printed material

desolate /ˈdesələt/ **adj 1** (used about a place) empty in a way that seems very sad: *desolate wasteland* **2** (used about a person) lonely, very unhappy and without hope

–**desolation** /ˌdesəˈleɪʃn/ **noun** [U]: *a scene of desolation.* • *He felt utter desolation when his wife died.*

despair¹ /dɪˈspeə/ **noun** [U] the state of having lost all hope: *I felt like giving up **in despair**.* –**despairing** adj: *a despairing cry* ••➤ Look at **desperate**.

despair² /dɪˈspeə/ **verb** [I] **despair (of sb/sth)** to lose all hope that sth will happen: *We began to despair of ever finding somewhere to live.*

despatch /dɪˈspætʃ/ = **DISPATCH**

★**desperate** /ˈdespərət/ **adj 1** out of control and ready to do anything to change the situation you are in because it is so terrible: *She became desperate when her money ran out.* **2** done with little hope of success, as a last thing to try when everything else has failed: *I made a desperate attempt to persuade her to change her mind.* **3 desperate (for sth/to do sth)** wanting or needing sth very much: *Let's go into a cafe. I'm desperate for a drink.* **4** terrible, very serious: *There is a desperate shortage of skilled workers.* –**desperately** adv: *She was desperately* (= extremely) *unlucky not to win.* –**desperation** /ˌdespəˈreɪʃn/ **noun** [U]

despicable /dɪˈspɪkəbl/ **adj** very unpleasant or evil: *a despicable act of terrorism*

despise /dɪˈspaɪz/ **verb** [T] to hate sb/sth very much: *I despise him for lying to me.*

despite /dɪˈspaɪt/ **prep** without being affected by the thing mentioned: *Despite having very little money, they enjoy life.* • *The scheme went ahead despite public opposition.* ••➤ synonym **in spite of**

despondent /dɪˈspɒndənt/ **adj despondent (about/over sth)** without hope; expecting no improvement: *She was becoming increasingly despondent about finding a job.* –**despondency** /dɪˈspɒndənsi/ **noun** [U]

dessert /dɪˈzɜːt/ **noun** [C,U] something sweet that is eaten after the main part of a meal: *What would you like **for dessert** – ice cream or fresh fruit?* ••➤ Look at **pudding** and **sweet**.

dessertspoon /dɪˈzɜːtspuːn/ **noun** [C] a spoon used for eating sweet food after the main part of a meal

destabilize /ˌdiːˈsteɪbəlaɪz/ **verb** [T] to make a system, government, country, etc become less safe and successful: *Terrorist attacks were threatening to destabilize the government.* ••➤ Look at **stabilize**.

destination /ˌdestɪˈneɪʃn/ **noun** [C] the place where sb/sth is going: *I finally reached my destination two hours late.* • *popular holiday destinations like the Bahamas*

destined /ˈdestɪnd/ **adj 1 destined for sth/to do sth** having a future that has been decided or planned at an earlier time: *I think she is destined for success.* • *He was destined to become one of the country's leading politicians.* **2 destined for...** travelling towards a particular place: *I boarded a bus destined for New York.*

destiny /ˈdestəni/ **noun** (*pl* **destinies**) **1** [C] the things that happen to you in your life,

d

especially things that you cannot control: *She felt that it was her destiny to be a great singer.* **2** [U] a power that people believe controls their lives; fate

destitute /'destɪtjuːt/ **adj** without any money, food or a home –**destitution** /ˌdestɪ-'tjuːʃn/ **noun** [U]

★**destroy** /dɪ'strɔɪ/ **verb** [T] **1** to damage sth so badly that it can no longer be used or no longer exists: *The building was destroyed by fire.* • *The defeat destroyed his confidence.* **2** to kill an animal, especially because it is injured or dangerous: *The horse broke its leg and had to be destroyed.*

destroyer /dɪ'strɔɪə/ **noun** [C] **1** a small ship that is used when there is a war **2** a person or thing that destroys sth

★**destruction** /dɪ'strʌkʃn/ **noun** [U] the action of destroying sth: *The war brought death and destruction to the city.* • *the destruction of the rainforests*

destructive /dɪ'strʌktɪv/ **adj** causing a lot of harm or damage: *destructive weapons* • *the destructive effects of drink and drugs*

detach /dɪ'tætʃ/ **verb** [T] detach sth (from sth) to separate sth from sth it is connected to: *Detach the form at the bottom of the page and send it to this address...* ••➤ opposite **attach**

detachable /dɪ'tætʃəbl/ **adj** that can be separated from sth it is connected to: *a coat with a detachable hood*

detached /dɪ'tætʃt/ **adj** **1** (used about a house) not joined to any other house **2** not being or not feeling personally involved in sth; without emotion

detachment /dɪ'tætʃmənt/ **noun** **1** [U] the fact or feeling of not being personally involved in sth **2** [C] a group of soldiers who have been given a particular task away from the main group

★**detail**¹ /'diːteɪl/ **noun** [C,U] one fact or piece of information: *Just give me the basic facts. Don't worry about the details.* • *On the application form you should give details of your education and experience.* • *The work involves close attention to detail.* –**detailed** **adj**: *a detailed description*

<u>IDIOMS</u> **go into detail(s)** to talk or write about the details of sth; to explain sth fully: *I can't go into detail now because it would take too long.*

in detail including the details; thoroughly: *We haven't discussed the matter in detail yet.*

detail² /'diːteɪl/ **verb** [T] to give a full list of sth; to describe sth completely: *He detailed all the equipment he needed for the job.*

detain /dɪ'teɪn/ **verb** [T] to stop sb from leaving a place; to delay sb: *A man has been detained by the police for questioning* (= kept at the police station). • *Don't let me detain you if you're busy.* ••➤ Look at **detention**.

detect /dɪ'tekt/ **verb** [T] to notice or discover sth that is difficult to see, feel, etc: *I detected a slight change in his attitude.* • *Traces of blood were detected on his clothes.* –**detection** **noun**

[U]: *The crime escaped detection* (= was not discovered) *for many years.*

★**detective** /dɪ'tektɪv/ **noun** [C] a person, especially a police officer, who tries to solve crimes

de'tective story **noun** [C] a story about a crime in which sb tries to find out who the guilty person is

detector /dɪ'tektə/ **noun** [C] a machine that is used for finding or noticing sth: *a smoke/ metal/lie detector*

detention /dɪ'tenʃn/ **noun** [U,C] **1** the act of stopping a person leaving a place, especially by keeping him/her in prison: *They were kept in detention for ten days.* **2** the punishment of being kept at school after the other schoolchildren have gone home ••➤ verb **detain**

deter /dɪ'tɜː/ **verb** [T] (**deterring**; **deterred**) deter sb (from doing sth) to make sb decide not to do sth, especially by telling him/her that it would have bad results: *The council is trying to deter visitors from bringing their cars into the city centre.* ••➤ noun **deterrent**

detergent /dɪ'tɜːdʒənt/ **noun** [C,U] a chemical liquid or powder that is used for cleaning things

deteriorate /dɪ'tɪəriəreɪt/ **verb** [I] to become worse: *The political tension is deteriorating into civil war.* –**deterioration** /dɪˌtɪəriə'reɪʃn/ **noun** [C,U]

★**determination** /dɪˌtɜːmɪ'neɪʃn/ **noun** [U] **1** determination (to do sth) the quality of having firmly decided to do sth, even if it is very difficult: *her determination to win* • *You need great determination to succeed in business.* **2** (*formal*) the process of deciding sth officially: *the determination of future government policy*

determine /dɪ'tɜːmɪn/ **verb** [T] **1** (*formal*) to discover the facts about sth: *We need to determine what happened immediately before the accident.* **2** to make sth happen in a particular way or be of a particular type: *The results of the tests will determine what treatment you need.* • *Age and experience will be determining factors in our choice of candidate.* **3** (*formal*) to decide sth officially: *A date for the meeting has yet to be determined.*

★**determined** /dɪ'tɜːmɪnd/ **adj** **determined (to do sth)** having firmly decided to do sth or to succeed, even if it is difficult: *He is determined to leave school, even though his parents want him to stay.* • *She's a very determined athlete.*

determiner /dɪ'tɜːmɪnə/ **noun** [C] (*grammar*) a word that comes before a noun to show how the noun is being used: *'Her', 'most' and 'those' are all determiners.*

deterrent /dɪ'terənt/ **noun** [C] something that should stop you doing sth: *Their punishment will be a deterrent to others.* ••➤ verb **deter** –**deterrent** **adj**

detest /dɪ'test/ **verb** [T] to hate or not like sb/sth at all: *They absolutely detest each other.*

detonate /'detəneɪt/ **verb** [I,T] to explode or to make a bomb, etc explode

detour /'di:tʊə/ **noun** [C] **1** a longer route from one place to another that you take in order to avoid sth/sb or in order to see or do sth: *Because of the accident we had to make a five-kilometre detour.* **2** (US) = **DIVERSION**(2)

detract /dɪ'trækt/ **verb** [I] detract from sth to make sth seem less good or important: *These criticisms in no way detract from the team's achievements.*

detriment /'detrɪmənt/ **noun**
IDIOM to the detriment of sb/sth harming or damaging sb/sth: *Doctors claim that the changes will be to the detriment of patients.* –detrimental /ˌdetrɪ'mentl/ **adj**: *Too much alcohol is detrimental to your health.*

deuce /dju:s/ **noun** [U] a score of 40 points to each player in a game of tennis

devalue /ˌdi:'vælju:/ **verb** [T] **1** to reduce the value of the money of one country in relation to the value of the money of other countries: *The pound has been devalued against the dollar.* **2** to reduce the value or importance of sth: *The refusal of the top players to take part devalues this competition.* –devaluation /di:ˌvælju'eɪʃn/ **noun** [U]

devastate /'devəsteɪt/ **verb** [T] **1** to destroy sth or damage it badly: *a land devastated by war* **2** to make sb extremely upset and shocked: *This tragedy has devastated the community.* –devastation /ˌdevə'steɪʃn/ **noun** [U]: *a scene of total devastation*

devastated /'devəsteɪtɪd/ **adj** extremely shocked and upset: *They were devastated when their baby died.*

devastating /'devəsteɪtɪŋ/ **adj 1** that destroys sth completely: *a devastating explosion* **2** that shocks or upsets sb very much: *The closure of the factory was a devastating blow to the workers.*

★**develop** /dɪ'veləp/ **verb 1** [I,T] to grow slowly, increase, or change into sth else; to make sb/sth do this: *to develop from a child into an adult* ● *a scheme to help pupils develop their natural talents* ● *Scientists have developed a drug against this disease.* ● *Over the years, she's developed her own unique singing style.* **2** [I] to begin to have a problem or disease; to start to affect sth: *to develop cancer/Aids* ● *Trouble is developing along the border.* **3** [T] to make an idea, a story, etc clearer or more detailed by writing or talking about it more: *She went on to develop this theme later in the lecture.* **4** [T] to make pictures or negatives from a piece of film by using special chemicals: *to develop a film* **5** [T] to build houses, shops, factories, etc on a piece of land: *This site is being developed for offices.*

developed /dɪ'veləpt/ **adj** of a good level or standard: *a highly developed economy*

developer /dɪ'veləpə/ (also 'property developer) **noun** [C] a person or company that builds houses, shops, etc on a piece of land

developing /dɪ'veləpɪŋ/ **adj** (used about a poor country) that is trying to develop or improve its economy: *a developing country* ● *the developing world*

★**development** /dɪ'veləpmənt/ **noun 1** [U] the process of becoming bigger, stronger, better etc, or of making sb/sth do this: *the development of tourism in Cuba* ● *a child's intellectual development* **2** [U,C] the process of creating sth more advanced; a more advanced product: *She works in research and development for a drug company.* ● *the latest developments in space technology* **3** [C] a new event that changes a situation: *This week has seen a number of new developments in the Middle East.* **4** [C,U] a piece of land with new buildings on it; the process of building on a piece of land: *a new housing development* ● *The land has been bought for development.*

deviate /'di:vieɪt/ **verb** [I] deviate (from sth) to change or become different from what is normal or expected: *He never once deviated from his original plan.*

deviation /ˌdi:vi'eɪʃn/ **noun** [C,U] a difference from what is normal or expected, or from what is approved of by society: *sexual deviation* ● *a deviation from our usual way of doing things*

★**device** /dɪ'vaɪs/ **noun** [C] **1** a tool or piece of equipment made for a particular purpose: *a security device which detects any movement* ● *labour-saving devices such as washing machines and vacuum cleaners* •➤ Look at the note at **tool**. **2** a clever method for getting the result you want: *Critics dismissed the speech as a political device for winning support.*

devil /'devl/ **noun** [C] **1 the Devil** the most powerful evil being, according to the Christian, Jewish and Muslim religions •➤ Look at **Satan**. **2** an evil being; a spirit **3** (*spoken*) a word used to show pity, anger, etc when you are talking about a person: *The poor devil died in hospital two days later.* ● *Those kids can be little devils sometimes.*
IDIOMS be a devil used to encourage sb to do sth that he/she is not sure about doing: *Go on, be a devil – buy both of them.*
speak/talk of the devil used when the person who is being talked about appears unexpectedly

devious /'di:viəs/ **adj** clever but not honest or direct: *I wouldn't trust him – he can be very devious.* ● *a devious trick/plan* –deviously **adv**

devise /dɪ'vaɪz/ **verb** [T] to invent a new way of doing sth: *They've devised a plan for keeping traffic out of the city centre.*

devoid /dɪ'vɔɪd/ **adj** (*formal*) devoid of sth not having a particular quality; without sth: *devoid of hope/ambition/imagination*

devolution /ˌdi:və'lu:ʃn/ **noun** [U] the movement of political power from central to local government

devote /dɪ'vəʊt/ **verb** [T] devote yourself/sth to sb/sth to give a lot of time, energy, etc to sb/sth: *She gave up work to devote herself full-time to her music.* ● *Schools should devote more time to science subjects.*

devoted /dɪ'vəʊtɪd/ **adj** devoted (to sb/sth)

d

loving sb/sth very much; completely loyal to sb/sth: *Neil's absolutely devoted to his wife.*

devotee /ˌdevəˈtiː/ noun [C] a devotee (of sb/sth) a person who likes sb/sth very much: *Devotees of science fiction will enjoy this new film.*

devotion /dɪˈvəʊʃn/ noun [U] devotion (to sb/sth) **1** great love for sb/sth: *a mother's devotion to her children* **2** the act of giving a lot of your time, energy, etc to sb/sth: *devotion to duty* **3** very strong religious feeling

devour /dɪˈvaʊə/ verb [T] **1** to eat sth quickly because you are very hungry **2** to do or use sth quickly and completely: *Lisa devours two or three novels a week.*

devout /dɪˈvaʊt/ adj very religious: *a devout Muslim family* –**devoutly** adv

dew /djuː/ noun [U] small drops of water that form on plants, leaves, etc during the night

dexterity /dekˈsterəti/ noun [U] skill at doing things, especially with your hands

diabetes /ˌdaɪəˈbiːtiːz/ noun [U] a serious disease in which a person's body cannot control the level of sugar in the blood

diabetic¹ /ˌdaɪəˈbetɪk/ noun [C] a person who suffers from diabetes

diabetic² /ˌdaɪəˈbetɪk/ adj connected with diabetes or diabetics: *diabetic chocolate* (= safe for diabetics)

diagnose /ˈdaɪəgnəʊz/ verb [T] diagnose sth (as sth); diagnose sb as/with sth to find out and say exactly what illness a person has or what the cause of a problem is: *His illness was diagnosed as bronchitis.* ● *I've been diagnosed as (a) diabetic/with diabetes.* ● *After a couple of minutes I diagnosed the trouble – a flat battery.*

diagnosis /ˌdaɪəgˈnəʊsɪs/ noun [C,U] (*pl* diagnoses /-siːz/) the act of saying exactly what illness a person has or what the cause of a problem is: *to **make a diagnosis***

diagonal /daɪˈæɡənl/ adj (used about a straight line) joining two sides of sth at an angle that is not 90° or vertical or horizontal: *Draw a diagonal line from one corner of the square to the opposite corner.* ●▶ picture at **line** –**diagonally** /-nəli/ adv

diagram /ˈdaɪəɡræm/ noun [C] a simple picture that is used to explain how sth works or what sth looks like: *a diagram of the body's digestive system*

dial¹ /ˈdaɪəl/ noun [C] **1** the round part of a clock, watch, control on a machine, etc that shows a measurement of time, amount, temperature, etc: *a dial for showing air pressure* **2** the round control on a radio, cooker, etc that you turn to change sth **3** the round part with holes in it on some older telephones that you turn to call a number.

dial² /ˈdaɪəl/ verb [I,T] (dialling; dialled: US dialing; dialed) to push the buttons or move the dial on a telephone in order to make a telephone number: *You can now dial direct to Singapore.* ● *to dial the wrong number*

dialect /ˈdaɪəlekt/ noun [C,U] a form of a language that is spoken in one part of a country: *a local dialect*

★**dialogue** (*US* dialog) /ˈdaɪəlɒɡ/ noun [C,U] **1** (a) conversation between people in a book, play, etc: *This movie is all action, with very little dialogue.* ● *On the tape you will hear a short dialogue between a shop assistant and a customer.* **2** (a) discussion between people who have different opinions: (a) *dialogue between the major political parties*

diameter /daɪˈæmɪtə/ noun [C] a straight line that goes from one side to the other of a circle, passing through the centre ●▶ Look at **radius** and **circumference**. ●▶ picture at **circle**

★**diamond** /ˈdaɪəmənd/ noun **1** [C,U] a hard, bright precious stone which is very expensive and is used for making jewellery. A diamond usually has no colour. **2** [C] a flat shape that has four sides of equal length and points at two ends ●▶ picture at **shape 3 diamonds** [pl] the group (suit) of playing cards with red shapes like diamonds(2) on them: *the seven of diamonds* ●▶ Look at the note and picture at **card**. **4** [C] one of the cards from this suit: *I haven't got any diamonds.* **5** [U] celebrating the 60th anniversary of sth: *This year's their diamond wedding.* ●▶ Look at **silver** and **golden**.

diaper /ˈdaɪəpə/ (*US*) = NAPPY

diaphragm /ˈdaɪəfræm/ noun [C] **1** the muscle between your lungs and your stomach that helps you to breathe **2** a thin piece of rubber that a woman puts inside her body before having sex to stop her having a baby

diarrhoea (*US* diarrhea) /ˌdaɪəˈrɪə/ noun [U] an illness that causes you to get rid of waste material (faeces) from your body very often and in a more liquid form than usual

★**diary** /ˈdaɪəri/ noun [C] (*pl* diaries) **1** a book in which you write down things that you have to do, remember, etc: *I'll just check in my diary to see if I'm free that weekend.* ●▶ Look at the note at **calendar**. **2** a book in which you write down what happens to you each day: *Do you keep a diary?*

dice /daɪs/ noun [C] (*pl* dice) a small square object with a different number of spots (from one to six) on each side, used in certain games: ***Throw the dice*** to see who goes first.

dictate /dɪkˈteɪt/ verb **1** [I,T] dictate (sth) (to sb) to say sth aloud so that sb else can write or type it: *to dictate a letter to a secretary* **2** [I,T] dictate (sth) (to sb) to tell sb what to do in a way that seems unfair: *Parents can't dictate to their children how they should run their lives.* **3** [T] to control or influence sth: *The kind of house people live in is usually dictated by how much they earn.*

dictation /dɪkˈteɪʃn/ noun [C,U] spoken words that sb else must write or type: *We had a dictation in English today* (= a test in which we had to write down what the teacher said).

dictator /dɪkˈteɪtə/ noun [C] a ruler who has total power in a country, especially one who rules the country by force –**dictatorship** noun [C,U]: *a military dictatorship*

★**dictionary** /'dɪkʃənri/ **noun** [C] (*pl* **diction-aries**) **1** a book that contains a list of the words in a language in the order of the alphabet and that tells you what they mean, in the same or another language: *to look up a word in a dictionary* • *a bilingual/monolingual dictionary* **2** a book that lists the words connected with a particular subject and tells you what they mean: *a dictionary of idioms* • *a medical dictionary*

did *past tense of* **DO**

didn't *short for* **DID NOT**

★**die** /daɪ/ **verb** (*pres part* **dying**; *3rd pers sing pres* **dies**; *pt, pp* **died**) **1** [I,T] die (from/of sth) to stop living: *My father died when I was three.* • *Thousands of people have died from this disease.* • *to die of hunger* • *to die for what you believe in* • *to die a natural/violent death* ···➤ adjective **dead**, noun **death**. **2** [I] to stop existing; to disappear: *The old customs are dying.* • *Our love will never die.*

[IDIOMS] be dying for sth/to do sth (*spoken*) to want sth/to do sth very much: *I'm dying for a cup of coffee.*

die hard to change or disappear only slowly or with difficulty: *Old attitudes towards women die hard.*

to die for (*informal*) if you think that sth is to die for, you really want it and would do anything to get it: *They have a house in town that's to die for.*

die laughing to find sth very funny: *I thought I'd die laughing when he told that joke.*

[PHRASAL VERBS] die away to slowly become weaker before stopping or disappearing: *The sound of the engine died away as the car drove into the distance.*

die down to slowly become less strong: *Let's wait until the storm dies down before we go out.*

die off to die one by one until there are none left

die out to stop happening or disappear: *The use of horses on farms has almost died out in this country.*

diesel /'di:zl/ **noun 1** [U] a type of heavy oil used in some engines instead of petrol: *a diesel engine* • *a taxi that runs on diesel* **2** [C] a vehicle that uses diesel: *My new car's a diesel.* ···➤ Look at **petrol**.

★**diet¹** /'daɪət/ **noun 1** [C,U] the food that a person or animal usually eats: *They live on a diet of rice and vegetables.* • *I always try to have a healthy, balanced diet* (= including all the different types of food that our body needs). • *Poor diet is a cause of ill health.* **2** [C] certain foods that a person who is ill, or who wants to lose weight is allowed to eat: *a low-fat diet* • *a sugar-free diet* –dietary /'daɪətəri/ **adj**: *dietary habits/requirements*

[IDIOM] be/go on a diet to eat only certain foods or a small amount of food because you want to lose weight

diet² /'daɪət/ **verb** [I] to try to lose weight by eating less food or only certain kinds of food: *You've lost some weight. Have you been dieting?*

differ /'dɪfə/ **verb** [I] **1** differ (from sb/sth) to be different: *How does this car differ from the more expensive model?* **2** differ (with sb) (about/on sth) to have a different opinion: *I'm afraid I differ with you on that question.*

★**difference** /'dɪfrəns/ **noun 1** [C] a difference (between A and B) the way that people or things are not the same or the way that sb/sth has changed: *What's the difference between this computer and that cheaper one?* • *From a distance it's hard to tell the difference between the twins.* **2** [C,U] difference (in sth) (between A and B) the amount by which people or things are not the same or by which sb/sth has changed: *There's an age difference of three years between the two children.* • *There's very little difference in price since last year.* • *We gave a 30% deposit and must pay the difference when the work is finished* (= the rest of the money). **3** [C] a disagreement that is not very serious: *All couples have their differences from time to time.* • *There was a difference of opinion over how much we owed.*

[IDIOMS] make a, some, etc difference (to sb/sth) to have an effect (on sb/sth): *Marriage made a big difference to her life.*

make no difference (to sb/sth); not make any difference to not be important (to sb/sth); to have no effect: *It makes no difference to us if the baby is a girl or a boy.*

split the difference → **SPLIT¹**

★**different** /'dɪfrənt/ **adj 1** different (from/to sb/sth) not the same: *The play was different from anything I had seen before.* • *The two houses are very different in style.* • *You'd look completely different with short hair.* • *When Ulf started school in this country, the other kids were cruel to him because he was different.* ···➤ opposite **similar**

➤ In US English **different than** is also used.

2 separate; individual: *This coat is available in three different colours.* –differently **adv**: *I think you'll feel differently about it tomorrow.*

differentiate /ˌdɪfə'renʃieɪt/ **verb 1** [I,T] differentiate between A and B; differentiate A (from B) to see or show how things are different: *It is hard to differentiate between these two types of seed.* **2** [T] differentiate sth (from sth) to make one thing different from another: *The coloured feathers differentiate the male bird from the plain brown female.* **3** [T] to treat one person or group differently from another: *We don't differentiate between the two groups – we treat everybody alike.* ···➤ synonym **distinguish**

★**difficult** /'dɪfɪkəlt/ **adj 1** difficult (for sb) (to do sth) not easy to do or understand: *a difficult test/problem* • *I find it difficult to get up early in the morning.* • *It was difficult for us to hear the speaker.* • *I'm in a difficult situation. Whatever I do, somebody will be upset.* **2** (used about a person) not friendly, reasonable or helpful: *a difficult customer*

d

d

★**difficulty** /'dɪfɪkəlti/ **noun** (*pl* **difficulties**)
1 [U,C] difficulty (in sth/in doing sth) a problem; a situation that is hard to deal with: *I'm sure you won't **have** any **difficulty** getting a visa for America.* • *We **had no difficulty** selling our car.* • *We found a hotel **without difficulty**.* • ***With difficulty**, I managed to persuade Alice to lend us the money.* • *I could see someone **in difficulty** in the water so I went to help them.* • *If you borrow too much money you may **get into** financial **difficulties**.* **2** [U] how hard sth is to do or to deal with: *The questions start easy and then increase in difficulty.*

diffident /'dɪfɪdənt/ **adj** not having confidence in your own strengths or abilities: *He has a very diffident manner.* –**diffidence noun** [U]

dig
spade

★**dig¹** /dɪg/ **verb** [I,T] (*pres part* **digging**; *pt, pp* **dug** /dʌg/) to move earth and make a hole in the ground: *The children are busy digging in the sand.* • *to dig a hole*

IDIOMS **dig deep** to try harder, give more, go further, etc than is usually necessary: *Charities for the homeless are asking people to dig deep into their pockets in this cold weather.*

dig your heels in to refuse to do sth or to change your mind about sth: *The union dug its heels in and waited for a better pay offer.*

PHRASAL VERBS **dig (sth) in**; **dig sth into sth** to push or press (sth) into sb/sth: *My neck is all red where my collar is digging in.* • *He dug his hands deep into his pockets.*

dig sb/sth out (of sth) **1** to get sb/sth out of sth by moving the earth, etc that covers him/her/it: *Rescue workers dug the survivors out of the rubble.* **2** to get or find sb/sth by searching: *Bill went into the attic and dug out some old photos.*

dig sth up **1** to remove sth from the earth by digging: *to dig up potatoes* **2** to make a hole or take away soil by digging: *Workmen are digging up the road in front of our house.* **3** to find information by searching or studying: *Newspapers have dug up some embarrassing facts about his private life.*

dig² /dɪg/ **noun 1** [C] a hard push: *to give sb a dig in the ribs* (= with your elbow) **2** [C] something that you say to upset sb: *The others kept **making digs** at him because of the way he spoke.* **3** [C] an occasion or place where a group of people try to find things of historical or scientific interest in the ground in order to study them: *an archaeological dig*

★**digest** /daɪ'dʒest/ **verb** [T] **1** to change food in your stomach so that it can be used by the body: *I'm not going to go swimming until I've digested my lunch.* **2** to think about new information so that you understand it fully:

The lecture was interesting, but too much to digest all at once.

digestion /daɪ'dʒestʃən/ **noun** [C,U] the process of changing food in your stomach so that it can be used by the body –**digestive** /daɪ'dʒestɪv/ **adj**: *the digestive system*

digit /'dɪdʒɪt/ **noun** [C] any of the numbers from 0 to 9: *a six-digit telephone number*

digital /'dɪdʒɪtl/ **adj 1** using an electronic system that uses the numbers 1 and 0 to record sound or store information, and that gives high-quality results: *a digital recording* **2** showing information by using numbers: *a digital watch* ••➤ picture at **clock**

dignified /'dɪgnɪfaɪd/ **adj** behaving in a calm, serious way that makes other people respect you: *dignified behaviour* ••➤ opposite **undignified**

dignity /'dɪgnəti/ **noun** [U] **1** calm, serious behaviour that makes other people respect you: *to behave **with dignity*** **2** the quality of being serious and formal: *the quiet dignity of the funeral service*

digress /daɪ'gres/ **verb** [I] (*formal*) to stop talking or writing about the main subject under discussion and start talking or writing about another less important one –**digression** /daɪ'greʃn/ **noun** [C,U]

dike → DYKE

dilapidated /dɪ'læpɪdeɪtɪd/ **adj** (used about buildings, furniture, etc) old and broken –**dilapidation** /dɪ,læpɪ'deɪʃn/ **noun** [U]

dilemma /dɪ'lemə/ **noun** [C] a situation in which you have to make a difficult choice between two or more things: *Doctors **face a** moral **dilemma** of when to keep patients alive artificially and when to let them die.* • *to be **in a dilemma***

dilute /daɪ'luːt/ **verb** [T] **dilute sth (with sth)** to make a liquid weaker by adding water or another liquid –**dilute adj**

dim¹ /dɪm/ **adj** (**dimmer**; **dimmest**) **1** not bright or easy to see; not clear: *The light was too dim to read by.* • *a dim shape in the distance* • *My memories of my grandmother are quite dim.* **2** (*informal*) not very clever; stupid: *He's a bit dim.* **3** (*informal*) (used about a situation) not hopeful: *The prospects of the two sides reaching an agreement look dim.* –**dimly adv**

dim² /dɪm/ **verb** [I,T] (**dimming**; **dimmed**) to become or make sth less bright or clear: *The lights dimmed.* • *to dim the lights*

dime /daɪm/ **noun** [C] a coin used in the US and Canada that is worth ten cents

dimension /daɪ'menʃn/ **noun** [C,U] a measurement of the length, width or height of sth **2 dimensions** [pl] the size of sth including its length, width and height: *to measure the dimensions of a room* • (*figurative*) *The full dimensions of this problem are only now being recognized.* **3** [C] something that affects the way you think about a problem or situation: *to add a new dimension to a problem/situation* **4 -dimensional** /-ʃənəl/ (used to form compound adjectives) having the number of dimensions mentioned: *a three-dimensional object*

diminish /dɪ'mɪnɪʃ/ **verb** [I,T] (*formal*) to become or to make sth smaller or less important; decrease: *The world's rainforests are diminishing fast.* • *The bad news did nothing to diminish her enthusiasm for the plan.*

diminutive /dɪ'mɪnjətɪv/ **adj** (*formal*) much smaller than usual

dimple /'dɪmpl/ **noun** [C] a round area in the skin on your cheek, etc, which often only appears when you smile

din /dɪn/ **noun** [sing] a lot of unpleasant noise that continues for some time

dine /daɪn/ **verb** [I] (*formal*) to eat a meal, especially in the evening: *We dined at an exclusive French restaurant.*
PHRASAL VERB **dine out** to eat in a restaurant

diner /'daɪnə/ **noun** [C] **1** a person who is eating at a restaurant **2** (*US*) a restaurant that serves simple, cheap food

dinghy /'dɪŋgi/ **noun** [C] (*pl* **dinghies**) **1** a small boat that you sail •➤ Look at **yacht**. **2** a small open boat, often used to take people to land from a larger boat •➤ picture at **boat**

dingy /'dɪndʒi/ **adj** dirty and dark: *a dingy room/hotel*

'**dining room noun** [C] a room where you eat meals •➤ picture on page C7

★**dinner** /'dɪnə/ **noun 1** [C,U] the main meal of the day, eaten either at midday or in the evening: *Would you like to go out for/to dinner one evening?* • *I never eat a big dinner.* • *What's for dinner, Mum?* **2** [C] a formal occasion in the evening during which a meal is served: *The club is holding its annual dinner next week.*

'**dinner jacket** (*US* **tuxedo**) **noun** [C] a black or white jacket that a man wears on formal occasions. A dinner jacket is usually worn with a special tie (a bow tie).

dinosaur /'daɪnəsɔː/ **noun** [C] one of a number of very large animals that disappeared from the earth (became extinct) millions of years ago: *dinosaur fossils* •➤ picture on page C8

Dip[1] **abbr** diploma

dip[2] /dɪp/ **verb** (**dipping**; **dipped**) **1** [T] dip sth (into sth); dip sth (in) to put sth into liquid and immediately take it out again: *Julie dipped her toe into the pool to see how cold it was.* **2** [I,T] to go down or make sth go down to a lower level: *The road suddenly dipped down to the river.* • *The company's sales have dipped disastrously this year.*
PHRASAL VERB **dip into sth 1** to use part of an amount of sth that you have: *Tim had to dip into his savings to pay for his new suit.* **2** to read parts, but not all, of sth: *I've only dipped into the book. I haven't read it all the way through.*

dip[3] /dɪp/ **noun 1** [C] a fall to a lower level, especially for a short time: *a dip in sales/temperature* **2** [C] an area of lower ground: *The cottage was in a dip in the hills.* **3** [C] (*informal*) a short swim: *We went for a dip*

before breakfast. **4** [C,U] a thick sauce into which you dip biscuits, vegetables, etc before eating them: *a cheese/chilli dip*

diphtheria /dɪf'θɪəriə/ **noun** [U] a serious disease of the throat that makes it difficult to breathe

diphthong /'dɪfθɒŋ/ **noun** [C] two vowel sounds that are pronounced together to make one sound, for example the /aɪ/ sound in 'fine'

diploma /dɪ'pləʊmə/ **noun** [C] a diploma (in sth) a certificate that you receive when you complete a course of study, often at a college: *I'm studying for a diploma in hotel management.* •➤ Look at the note at **degree**.

diplomacy /dɪ'pləʊməsi/ **noun** [U] **1** the activity of managing relations between different countries: *If diplomacy fails, there is a danger of war.* **2** skill in dealing with people without upsetting or offending them: *He handled the tricky situation with tact and diplomacy.*

diplomat /'dɪpləmæt/ **noun** [C] an official who represents his/her country in a foreign country: *a diplomat at the embassy in Rome*

diplomatic /ˌdɪplə'mætɪk/ **adj 1** connected with diplomacy(1): *to break off diplomatic relations* **2** skilful at dealing with people: *He searched for a diplomatic reply so as not to offend her.* –**diplomatically** /-kli/ **adv**

dire /'daɪə/ **adj** (*formal*) very bad or serious; terrible: *dire consequences/poverty*
IDIOM **be in dire straits** to be in a very difficult situation: *The business is in dire straits financially.*

★**direct**[1] /daɪ'rekt; dɪ-/ **adj, adv 1** with nobody/ nothing in between; not involving anyone/ anything else: *The British Prime Minister is in direct contact with the US President.* • *a direct attack on the capital* • *As a direct result of the new road, traffic jams in the centre have been reduced.* • *You should protect your skin from direct sunlight.* **2** going from one place to another without turning or stopping; straight: *a direct flight to Hong Kong* • *This bus goes direct to London.* **3** saying what you mean; clear: *Politicians never give a direct answer to a direct question.* • *She sometimes offends people with her direct way of speaking.* •➤ opposite for senses 1, 2 and 3 **indirect 4** (only *before* a noun) complete; exact: *What she did was in direct opposition to my orders.*

★**direct**[2] /daɪ'rekt; dɪ-/ **verb** [T] **1** direct sth to/towards sb/sth; direct sth at sb/sth to point or send sth towards sb/sth or in a particular direction: *In recent weeks the media's attention has been directed towards events abroad.* • *The advert is directed at young people.* • *The actor directed some angry words at a photographer.* **2** to manage or control sb/sth: *A policeman was in the middle of the road, directing the traffic.* • *to direct a play/film* **3** direct sb (to...) to tell or show sb how to get somewhere: *I was directed to an office at the end of the corridor.* •➤ Look at the note at **lead**[1](1). **4** (*formal*) to tell or order sb to do sth: *Take the tablets as directed by your doctor.*

di,rect 'debit noun [C,U] an order to your bank that allows sb else to take a particular amount of money out of your account on certain dates

★**direction** /daɪˈrekʃn; dɪ-/ noun **1** [C,U] the path, line or way along which a person or thing is moving, looking, pointing, developing, etc: *A woman was seen running in the direction of the station.* ● *We met him coming in the opposite direction.* ● *I think the new speed limit is still too high, but at least it's a step in the right direction.* ● *I think the wind has changed direction.* ● *I've got such a hopeless sense of direction – I'm always getting lost.* **2** [C,U] a purpose; an aim: *I want a career that gives me a (sense of) direction in life.* **3** [usually pl] information or instructions about how to do sth or how to get to a place: *I'll give you directions to my house.* **4** [U] the act of managing or controlling sth: *This department is under the direction of Mrs Walters.*

directive /daɪˈrektɪv; dɪ-/ noun [C] an official order to do sth: *an EU directive on safety at work*

directly¹ /daɪˈrektli; dɪ-/ adv **1** in a direct line or way: *The bank is directly opposite the supermarket.* ● *He refused to answer my question directly.* ● *Lung cancer is directly related to smoking.* •➤ opposite **indirectly 2** immediately; very soon: *Wait where you are. I'll be back directly.*

directly² /daɪˈrektli; dɪ-/ conj as soon as: *I phoned him directly I heard the news.*

di,rect 'object noun [C] (*grammar*) a noun or phrase that is affected by the action of a verb: *In the sentence 'Anna bought a record', 'a record' is the direct object.* •➤ Look at **indirect object.**

➤ For more information about direct objects, look at the **Quick Grammar Reference** section at the back of this dictionary.

★**director** /daɪˈrektə; dɪ-/ noun [C] **1** a person who manages or controls a company or organization: *the managing director of Rolls Royce* ● *She's on the board of directors* (= group of directors) *of a large computer company.* **2** a person who is responsible for a particular activity or department in a company, a college, etc: *the director of studies of a language school* **3** a person who tells the actors, etc what to do in a film, play, etc: *a film/theatre director*

directory /daɪˈrektəri; dɪ-/ noun [C] (*pl* **directories**) a list of names, addresses and telephone numbers in the order of the alphabet: *the telephone directory* ● *I tried to look up Joe's number but he's ex-directory* (= he has chosen not to be listed in the telephone directory).

di,rect 'speech noun [U] (*grammar*) the actual words that a person said •➤ Look at **indirect speech.**

➤ For more information about direct speech, look at the **Quick Grammar Reference** section at the back of this dictionary.

★**dirt** /dɜːt/ noun [U] **1** a substance that is not clean, such as dust or mud: *His face and hands were covered in dirt.* **2** earth or soil: *a dirt track* **3** damaging information about sb: *The press are always trying to dig up dirt on the President's love life.*

IDIOM **dirt cheap** extremely cheap

★**dirty¹** /ˈdɜːti/ adj (**dirtier**; **dirtiest**) **1** not clean: *Your hands are dirty. Go and wash them!* ● *Gardening is dirty work* (= it makes you dirty). •➤ opposite **clean 2** referring to sex in a way that may upset or offend people: *to tell a dirty joke* **3** unpleasant or dishonest: *He's a dirty player.* ● *He doesn't sell the drugs himself – he gets kids to do his dirty work for him.* –**dirty** adv

IDIOMS **a dirty word** an idea or thing that you do not like or agree with: *Work is a dirty word to Frank.*

play dirty (*informal*) to behave or to play a game in an unfair or dishonest way

dirty² /ˈdɜːti/ verb [I,T] (*pres part* **dirtying**; *3rd pers sing pres* **dirties**; *pt, pp* **dirtied**) to become or to make sth dirty •➤ opposite **clean**

disability /ˌdɪsəˈbɪləti/ noun (*pl* **disabilities**) **1** [U] the state of being unable to use a part of your body properly, usually because of injury or disease: *physical/mental disability* **2** [C] something that makes you unable to use a part of your body properly: *Because of his disability, he needs constant care.*

disable /dɪsˈeɪbl/ verb [T] (often passive) to make sb unable to use part of his/her body properly, usually because of injury or disease: *Many soldiers were disabled in the war.*

disabled /dɪsˈeɪbld/ adj **1** unable to use a part of your body properly: *A car accident left her permanently disabled.* **2 the disabled** noun [pl] people who are disabled: *The hotel has improved facilities for the disabled.*

★**disadvantage** /ˌdɪsədˈvɑːntɪdʒ/ noun [C] **1** something that may make you less successful than other people: *Your qualifications are good. Your main disadvantage is your lack of experience.* **2** something that is not good or that causes problems: *The main disadvantage of the job is the long hours.* ● *What are the advantages and disadvantages of nuclear power?* •➤ opposite **advantage**

IDIOMS **put sb/be at a disadvantage** to put sb/be in a situation where he/she/you may be less successful than other people: *The fact that you don't speak the language will put you at a disadvantage in France.*

to sb's disadvantage (*formal*) not good or helpful for sb: *The agreement will be to your disadvantage – don't accept it.*

disadvantaged /ˌdɪsədˈvɑːntɪdʒd/ adj in a bad social or economic situation; poor: *extra help for the most disadvantaged members of society*

disadvantageous /ˌdɪsædvænˈteɪdʒəs/ adj

causing sb to be in a worse situation compared to other people

★**disagree** /ˌdɪsəˈɡriː/ verb [I] **1** disagree (with sb/sth) (about/on sth) to have a different opinion from sb/sth; to not agree: *Noel often disagrees with his father about politics.* • *They strongly disagreed with my idea.* • *'We have to tell him.' 'No, I disagree. I don't think we should tell him at all.'* **2** to be different: *These two sets of statistics disagree.* ••➤ opposite **agree**

PHRASAL VERB disagree with sb (used about sth you have eaten or drunk) to make you feel ill; to have a bad effect on you

disagreeable /ˌdɪsəˈɡriːəbl/ adj (*formal*) unpleasant ••➤ opposite **agreeable** –**disagreeably** /-əbli/ adv

disagreement /ˌdɪsəˈɡriːmənt/ noun [C,U] disagreement (with sb) (about/on/over sth) a situation in which people have a different opinion about sth and often also argue: *It's normal for couples to **have disagreements.*** • *Mandy resigned after a disagreement with her boss.* • *The conference ended in disagreement.* ••➤ opposite **agreement**

disallow /ˌdɪsəˈlaʊ/ verb [T] to not allow or accept sth: *The goal was disallowed because the player was offside.*

★**disappear** /ˌdɪsəˈpɪə/ verb [I] **1** to become impossible to see or to find; vanish: *He walked away and disappeared into a crowd of people.* • *My purse was here a moment ago and now it's disappeared.* **2** to stop existing; vanish: *Plant and animal species are disappearing at an alarming rate.* ••➤ opposite **appear** –**disappearance** noun [C,U]: *The mystery of her disappearance was never solved.*

disappoint /ˌdɪsəˈpɔɪnt/ verb [T] to make sb sad because what he/she had hoped for has not happened or is less good, interesting, etc then he/she had hoped: *I'm sorry to disappoint you but I'm afraid you haven't won the prize.*

★**disappointed** /ˌdɪsəˈpɔɪntɪd/ adj disappointed (about/at sth); disappointed (in/with sb/sth); disappointed that... sad because you/sb/sth did not succeed or because sth was not as good, interesting, etc as you had hoped: *Lucy was deeply disappointed at not being chosen for the team.* • *We were disappointed with our hotel.* • *I'm disappointed in you. I thought you could do better.* • *They are very disappointed that they can't stay longer.* • *I was disappointed to hear that you can't come to the party.*

★**disappointing** /ˌdɪsəˈpɔɪntɪŋ/ adj making you feel sad because sth was not as good, interesting, etc as you had hoped: *It has been a disappointing year for the company.* –**disappointingly** adv

★**disappointment** /ˌdɪsəˈpɔɪntmənt/ noun **1** [U] the state of being disappointed: *To his great disappointment he failed to get the job.* **2** [C] a disappointment (to sb) a person or thing that disappoints you: *She has suffered many disappointments in her career.*

disapproval /ˌdɪsəˈpruːvl/ noun [U] a feeling that sth is bad or that sb is behaving badly: *She shook her head **in disapproval.***

★**disapprove** /ˌdɪsəˈpruːv/ verb [I] disapprove (of sb/sth) to think that sb/sth is bad, foolish, etc: *His parents strongly disapproved of him leaving college before he had finished his course.* –**disapproving** adj: *After he had told the joke there was a disapproving silence.* –**disapprovingly** adv: *David frowned disapprovingly when I lit a cigarette.*

disarm /dɪsˈɑːm/ verb **1** [T] to take weapons away from sb: *The police caught and disarmed the terrorists.* **2** [I] (used about a country) to reduce the number of weapons it has **3** [T] to make sb feel less angry: *Jenny could always disarm the teachers with a smile.*

disarmament /dɪsˈɑːməmənt/ noun [U] reducing the number of weapons that a country has: *nuclear disarmament*

disassociate = **DISSOCIATE**

★**disaster** /dɪˈzɑːstə/ noun **1** [C] an event that causes a lot of harm or damage: *earthquakes, floods and other natural disasters* **2** [C,U] a terrible situation or event: *Losing your job is unpleasant, but it's not a disaster.* • *This year's lack of rain could **spell disaster** for the region.* **3** [C,U] (*informal*) a complete failure: *The school play was an absolute disaster. Everything went wrong.* –**disastrously** adv: *The plan went disastrously wrong.*

disastrous /dɪˈzɑːstrəs/ adj terrible, harmful or failing completely: *Our mistake had disastrous results.*

disband /dɪsˈbænd/ verb [I,T] to stop existing as a group; to separate

disbelief /ˌdɪsbɪˈliːf/ noun [U] the feeling of not believing sb/sth: *'It can't be true!' he shouted **in disbelief.***

disbelieve /ˌdɪsbɪˈliːv/ verb [T] to think that sth is not true or that sb is not telling the truth: *I have no reason to disbelieve her.* ••➤ opposite **believe**

disc (*especially US* **disk**) /dɪsk/ noun [C] **1** a round flat object **2** = **DISK 3** one of the pieces of thin strong material (cartilage) between the bones in your back

discard /dɪsˈkɑːd/ verb [T] (*formal*) to throw sth away because it is not useful

discern /dɪˈsɜːn/ verb [T] to see or notice sth with difficulty: *I discerned a note of anger in his voice.* –**discernible** adj: *The shape of a house was just discernible through the mist.*

discerning /dɪˈsɜːnɪŋ/ adj able to recognize the quality of sb/sth: *The discerning music lover will appreciate the excellence of this recording.*

discharge[1] /dɪsˈtʃɑːdʒ/ verb [T] **1** to send sth out (a liquid, gas, etc): *Smoke and fumes are discharged from the factory.* **2** to allow sb officially to leave; to send sb away: *to discharge sb from hospital* **3** to do sth that you have to do: *to discharge a duty/task*

discharge[2] /ˈdɪstʃɑːdʒ/ noun [C,U] **1** the action of sending sb/sth out or away: *The discharge of oil from the leaking tanker could not be prevented.* • *The wounded soldier was* given a medical discharge. **2** a substance that has come out of somewhere: *yellowish discharge from a wound*

disciple /dɪ'saɪpl/ noun [C] a person who follows a teacher, especially a religious one

disciplinary /ˌdɪsə'plɪnəri/ adj connected with punishment for breaking rules

★**discipline**[1] /'dɪsəplɪn/ noun **1** [U] the practice of training people to obey rules and behave well: *A good teacher must be able to* **maintain discipline** *in the classroom.* **2** [U] the practice of training your mind and body so that you control your actions and obey rules; a way of doing this: *It takes a lot of* **self-discipline** *to study for three hours a day.* • *Having to get up early every day is good discipline for a child.* **3** [C] a subject of study; a type of sporting event: *Barry's a good all-round athlete, but the long jump is his strongest discipline.*

discipline[2] /'dɪsəplɪn/ verb [T] **1** to train sb to obey and to behave in a controlled way: *You should discipline yourself to practise the piano every morning.* **2** to punish sb

'**disc jockey** = **DJ**

disclaim /dɪs'kleɪm/ verb [T] to say that you do not have sth; deny: *to disclaim responsibility/knowledge*

disclose /dɪs'kləʊz/ verb [T] (*formal*) to tell sth to sb or to make sth known publicly: *The newspapers did not disclose the victim's name.*

disclosure /dɪs'kləʊʒə/ noun [C,U] making sth known; the facts that are made known: *the disclosure of secret information* • *He resigned following disclosures about his private life.*

disco /'dɪskəʊ/ noun [C] (*pl* **discos**) (*old-fashioned*) a place, party, etc where people dance to pop music: *Are you going to the school disco?* •➤ Look at **club**[1](2).

discolour (*US* **discolor**) /dɪs'kʌlə/ verb [I,T] to change or to make sth change colour (often by the effect of light, age or dirt)

discomfort /dɪs'kʌmfət/ noun **1** [U] a slight feeling of pain: *There may be some discomfort after the operation.* •➤ opposite **comfort 2** [U] a feeling of embarrassment: *I could sense John's discomfort when I asked him about his job.*

disconcert /ˌdɪskən'sɜːt/ verb [T] (usually passive) to make sb feel confused or worried: *She was disconcerted when everyone stopped talking and looked at her.* –**disconcerting** adj –**disconcertingly** adv

disconnect /ˌdɪskə'nekt/ verb [T] **1** to stop a supply of water, gas or electricity going to a piece of equipment or a building: *If you don't pay your gas bill your supply will be disconnected.* **2** to separate sth from sth: *The brake doesn't work because the cable has become disconnected from the lever.*

discontent /ˌdɪskən'tent/ (also **discontentment** /ˌdɪskən'tentmənt/) noun [U] the state of being unhappy with sth: *The management could sense growing discontent among the staff.* –**discontented** adj: *to be/feel discontented*

discontinue /ˌdɪskən'tɪnjuː/ verb [T] (*formal*) to stop sth or stop producing sth

discord /'dɪskɔːd/ noun (*formal*) [U] disagreement or argument

discordant /dɪs'kɔːdənt/ adj that spoils a general feeling of agreement: *Her criticism was the only discordant note in the discussion.*

discount[1] /'dɪskaʊnt/ noun [C,U] a lower price than usual; reduction: *Staff get 20% discount on all goods.* • *Do you give a discount for cash?*

discount[2] /dɪs'kaʊnt/ verb [T] to consider sth not true or not important: *I think we can discount that idea. It's just not practical.*

discourage /dɪs'kʌrɪdʒ/ verb [T] **discourage sb (from doing sth)** to stop sb doing sth, especially by making him/her realize that it would not be successful or a good idea: *I tried to discourage Jake from giving up his job.* • *Don't let these little problems discourage you.* •➤ opposite **encourage** –**discouraged** adj: *After failing the exam again Paul felt very discouraged.* –**discouraging** adj: *Constant criticism can be very discouraging.*

discouragement /dɪs'kʌrɪdʒmənt/ noun [C,U] a thing that makes you not want to do sth; the action of trying to stop sb from doing sth: *the government's discouragement of smoking*

★**discover** /dɪ'skʌvə/ verb [T] **1** to find or learn sth that nobody had found or knew before: *Who discovered the lost city of Machu Picchu?* • *Scientists are hoping to discover the cause of the epidemic.* **2** to find or learn sth without expecting to or that sb does not want you to find: *I think I've discovered why the computer won't print out.* • *The police discovered drugs hidden under the floor.* –**discoverer** noun [C]: *Parkinson's disease was named after its discoverer.*

discovery /dɪ'skʌvəri/ noun (*pl* **discoveries**) **1** [U] the act of finding sth: *The discovery of X-rays changed the history of medicine.* **2** [C] something that has been found: *scientific discoveries*

discredit /dɪs'kredɪt/ verb [T] to make people stop respecting or believing sb/sth: *Journalists are trying to discredit the President by inventing stories about his love life.* –**discredit** noun [U]

discreet /dɪ'skriːt/ adj careful in what you say and do so as not to cause embarrassment or difficulty for sb: *I don't want anyone to find out about our agreement, so please be discreet.* –**discreetly** adv •➤ noun **discretion** •➤ opposite **indiscreet**

discrepancy /dɪs'krepənsi/ noun [C,U] (*pl* **discrepancies**) a difference between two things that should be the same: *Something is wrong here. There is a discrepancy between these two sets of figures.*

discretion /dɪ'skreʃn/ noun [U] **1** the freedom and power to make decisions by yourself: *You must decide what is best. Use your discretion.* **2** care in what you say and do so as not to cause embarrassment or difficulty for sb: *This is confidential but I know I can*

rely on your discretion. •> adjective discreet
IDIOM **at sb's discretion** depending on what
sb thinks or decides: *Pay increases are
awarded at the discretion of the director.*

discriminate /dɪˈskrɪmɪneɪt/ **verb 1** [I] discriminate (against sb) to treat one person or
group worse than others: *It is illegal to discriminate against any ethnic or religious
group.* **2** [I,T] discriminate (between A and
B) to see or make a difference between two
people or things: *The immigration law dis-
criminates between political and economic
refugees.*

discrimination /dɪˌskrɪmɪˈneɪʃn/ **noun** [U]
1 discrimination (against sb) treating one
person or group worse than others: *sexual/
racial/religious discrimination* • *Discrimination against disabled people is illegal.*
2 (*formal*) the state of being able see a difference between two people or things: *discrimination between right and wrong*

discus /ˈdɪskəs/ **noun 1** [C] a heavy round
flat object that is thrown as a sport **2 the
discus** [sing] the sport or event of throwing
a discus as far as possible

★**discuss** /dɪˈskʌs/ **verb** [T] discuss sth (with
sb) to talk or write about sth seriously or
formally: *I must discuss the matter with my
parents before I make a decision.*

★**discussion** /dɪˈskʌʃn/ **noun** [C,U] the process of talking about sth seriously or deeply:
*After much discussion we all agreed to share
the cost.* • *We had a long discussion about art.*
IDIOM **under discussion** being talked about:
*Plans to reform the Health Service are under
discussion in Parliament.*

disdain /dɪsˈdeɪn/ **noun** [U] the feeling that
sb/sth is not good enough to be respected:
*Monica felt that her boss always **treated** her
ideas **with disdain**.* –disdainful /-fl/ **adj**
–disdainfully /-fəli/ **adv**

★**disease** /dɪˈziːz/ **noun** [C,U] an illness of the
body in humans, animals or plants: *an infec-
tious/contagious disease* • *These children suffer from a rare disease.* • *Rats and flies
spread disease.* • *Smoking causes heart disease.* –diseased **adj**: *His diseased kidney had to
be removed.*

➤ **Illness** and **disease** can be used in a
similar way. However, we use **disease** to
describe a type of illness which has a name
and is recognized by certain symptoms. Diseases may be caused by bacteria, viruses,
etc, and you can often catch and pass them
on to others. **Illness** is used to describe the
general state of being ill and the time during which you are not well.

disembark /ˌdɪsɪmˈbɑːk/ **verb** [I] (*formal*) to
get off a ship or an aircraft •> opposite
embark –disembarkation /ˌdɪsˌembɑːˈkeɪʃn/
noun [U]

disenchanted /ˌdɪsɪnˈtʃɑːntɪd/ **adj** having
lost your good opinion of sb/sth: *Fans are
already becoming disenchanted with the new
team manager.* –disenchantment **noun** [U]

disentangle /ˌdɪsɪnˈtæŋgl/ **verb** [T] to free

sb/sth that had become connected to sb/sth
else in a confused and complicated way: *My
coat got caught up in some bushes and I
couldn't disentangle it.* • (*figurative*) *Listening to the woman's story, I found it hard to
disentangle the truth from the lies.*

disfigure /dɪsˈfɪgə/ **verb** [T] to spoil the
appearance of sb/sth: *His face was permanently disfigured by the fire.*

disgrace¹ /dɪsˈgreɪs/ **noun 1** [U] the state of
not being respected by other people, usually
because you have behaved badly: *She left the
company **in disgrace** after admitting stealing
from colleagues.* **2** [sing] a disgrace (to sb/
sth) a person or thing that gives a very bad
impression and makes you feel sorry and
embarrassed: *The streets are covered in litter.
It's a disgrace!* • *Teachers who hit children
are a disgrace to their profession.*

disgrace² /dɪsˈgreɪs/ **verb** [T] to behave
badly in a way that makes you or other
people feel sorry and embarrassed: *My
brother disgraced himself by starting a fight
at the wedding.*

disgraceful /dɪsˈgreɪsfl/ **adj** very bad, making other people feel sorry and embarrassed:
*The behaviour of the team's fans was abso-
lutely disgraceful.* –disgracefully /-fəli/ **adv**

disgruntled /dɪsˈgrʌntld/ **adj** disappointed
and annoyed

disguise¹ /dɪsˈgaɪz/ **verb** [T] disguise sb/sth
(as sb/sth) to change the appearance, sound,
etc of sb/sth so that people cannot recognize
him/her/it: *They disguised themselves as fishermen and escaped in a boat.* • (*figurative*)
His smile disguised his anger.

disguise² /dɪsˈgaɪz/ **noun** [C,U] a thing that
you wear or use to change your appearance
so that nobody recognizes you: *She is so famous that she has to go shopping **in disguise**.*
• *The robbers were wearing heavy disguises
so that they could not be identified.*

disgust¹ /dɪsˈgʌst/ **noun** [U] disgust (at sth)
a strong feeling of not liking or approving of
sth/sb that you feel is unacceptable, or sth/sb
that looks, smells, etc unpleasant: *The film
was so bad that we walked out **in disgust**.*
• *Much to my disgust, I found a hair in my
soup.*

disgust² /dɪsˈgʌst/ **verb** [T] **1** to cause a
strong feeling of not liking or approving of
sb/sth: *Cruelty towards animals absolutely
disgusts me.* **2** to make sb feel sick: *The way
he eats with his mouth open completely disgusts me.*

disgusted /dɪsˈgʌstɪd/ **adj** disgusted (at/
with sb/sth) not liking or approving of sb/sth
at all: *We were disgusted at the standard of
service we received.*

disgusting /dɪsˈgʌstɪŋ/ **adj** very unpleasant:
What a disgusting smell!

disgustingly /dɪsˈgʌstɪŋli/ **adv 1** (often
used to show you are jealous of sb/sth)
extremely: *Our neighbours are disgustingly
rich.* **2** in a way that you do not like or
approve of or that makes you feel sick: *The
kitchen was disgustingly dirty.*

d

d

★**dish**¹ /dɪʃ/ **noun 1** [C] a round container for food that is deeper than a plate **2** [C] a type of food prepared in a particular way: *The **main** dish was curry. It was served with a selection of **side dishes**.* ● *Paella is a typical Spanish dish, made with rice and shellfish.* **3 the dishes** [pl] all the plates, cups, etc that you use during a meal: *I'll cook and you can wash the dishes.* **4** = SATELLITE DISH

dish² /dɪʃ/ **verb**

PHRASAL VERBS **dish sth out** (*informal*) to give away a lot of sth: *to dish out advice*
dish sth up (*informal*) to serve food

disheartened /dɪs'hɑːtnd/ **adj** sad or disappointed

disheartening /dɪs'hɑːtnɪŋ/ **adj** making you lose hope and confidence; causing disappointment ●◆ opposite **heartening**

dishevelled (*US* **disheveled**) /dɪ'ʃevld/ **adj** (used about a person's appearance) very untidy

dishonest /dɪs'ɒnɪst/ **adj** that you cannot trust; likely to lie, steal or cheat ●◆ opposite **honest** – **dishonestly adv** – **dishonesty noun** [U] ●◆ opposite **honesty**

dishonour¹ (*US* **dishonor**) /dɪs'ɒnə/ **noun** [U,sing] (*formal*) the state of no longer being respected, especially because you have done sth bad: *Her illegal trading has **brought dishonour on** the company.* ●◆ opposite **honour** – **dishonourable** /-'nərəbl/ **adj** ●◆ opposite **honourable**

dishonour² (*US* **dishonor**) /dɪs'ɒnə/ **verb** [T] (*formal*) to do sth bad that makes people stop respecting you or sb/sth close to you

dishwasher /'dɪʃwɒʃə/ **noun** [C] a machine that washes plates, cups, knives, forks, etc

disillusion /ˌdɪsɪ'luːʒn/ **verb** [T] to destroy sb's belief in or good opinion of sth/sb – **disillusion** (also **disillusionment**) **noun** [U]: *I feel increasing disillusion with the government.*

disillusioned /ˌdɪsɪ'luːʒnd/ **adj** disappointed because sb/sth is not as good as you first thought: *She's disillusioned with nursing.*

disinfect /ˌdɪsɪn'fekt/ **verb** [T] to clean sth with a liquid that destroys bacteria: *to disinfect a wound* – **disinfection noun** [U]

disinfectant /ˌdɪsɪn'fektənt/ **noun** [C,U] a substance that destroys bacteria and is used for cleaning

disintegrate /dɪs'ɪntɪgreɪt/ **verb** [I] to break into many small pieces: *The spacecraft exploded and disintegrated.* – **disintegration** /ˌdɪsˌɪntɪ'greɪʃn/ **noun** [U]: *the disintegration of the empire*

disinterested /dɪs'ɪntrəstɪd/ **adj** fair, not influenced by personal feelings: *disinterested advice* ●◆ Look at **uninterested**. It has a different meaning.

disjointed /dɪs'dʒɔɪntɪd/ **adj** (used especially about ideas, writing or speech) not clearly connected and therefore difficult to follow – **disjointedly adv**

disk /dɪsk/ **noun** [C] **1** (*US*) = DISC **2** (*comput-*

ing) a flat piece of plastic that stores information for use by a computer ●◆ Look at **floppy disk** and **hard disk**.

'**disk drive noun** [C] (*computing*) a piece of electrical equipment that passes information to or from a computer disk ●◆ picture on page S7

diskette /dɪs'ket/ = FLOPPY DISK

dislike¹ /dɪs'laɪk/ **verb** [T] dislike (doing) sth to think that sb/sth is unpleasant: *I really dislike flying.* ● *What is it that you dislike about living here?* ●◆ opposite **like**

dislike² /dɪs'laɪk/ **noun** [U,sing] (a) dislike (of/for sb/sth) the feeling of not liking sb/sth: *She couldn't hide her dislike for him.* ● *He seems to have a strong dislike of hard work.*
IDIOM **take a dislike to sb/sth** to start disliking sb/sth: *He took an instant dislike to his boss.*

dislocate /'dɪsləkeɪt/ **verb** [T] to put sth (usually a bone) out of its correct position: *He dislocated his shoulder during the game.* – **dislocation** /ˌdɪslə'keɪʃn/ **noun** [C,U]

dislodge /dɪs'lɒdʒ/ **verb** [T] dislodge sth (from sth) to make sb/sth move from its correct fixed position: *The strong wind dislodged several tiles from the roof.*

disloyal /dɪs'lɔɪəl/ **adj** disloyal (to sb/sth) not supporting your friends, family, country etc; doing sth that will harm them: *It was disloyal to your friends to repeat their conversation to Peter.* ●◆ opposite **loyal** – **disloyalty** /-'lɔɪəlti/ **noun** [C,U] (*pl* **disloyalties**)

dismal /'dɪzməl/ **adj 1** causing or showing sadness; depressing: *dismal surroundings* ●◆ synonym **miserable 2** (*informal*) of low quality; poor: *a dismal standard of work*

dismantle /dɪs'mæntl/ **verb** [T] to take sth to pieces; to separate sth into the parts it is made from: *The photographer dismantled his equipment and packed it away.*

dismay /dɪs'meɪ/ **noun** [U] a strong feeling of disappointment and sadness: *I realized to my dismay that I was going to miss the plane.* – **dismay verb** [T] (usually passive): *I was dismayed to hear that my old school had been knocked down.*

dismember /dɪs'membə/ **verb** [T] to cut a dead body into pieces

dismiss /dɪs'mɪs/ **verb** [T] **1** dismiss sb/sth (as sth) to decide not to think about sth/sb: *He dismissed the idea as nonsense.* **2** dismiss sb (from sth) to order an employee to leave his/her job: *He was dismissed for refusing to obey orders.*

➤ **Fire** and **sack** are less formal words for **dismiss.**

3 to send sb away: *The lesson ended and the teacher dismissed the class.* **4** (used in law) to say that a trial or court case should not continue, usually because there is not enough evidence: *The case was dismissed.* – **dismissal** /dɪs'mɪsl/ **noun** [C,U]: *She was hurt at their dismissal of her offer of help.* ● *a case of unfair dismissal*

dismissive /dɪs'mɪsɪv/ **adj** dismissive (of

sb/sth) saying or showing that you think that sb/sth is not worth considering seriously: *The boss was dismissive of all the efforts I had made.* –dismissively **adv**

dismount /dɪsˈmaʊnt/ **verb** [I] to get off sth that you ride (a horse, a bicycle, etc) ∙∙➤ opposite **mount**

disobedient /ˌdɪsəˈbiːdiənt/ **adj** refusing or failing to obey ∙∙➤ opposite **obedient** –disobedience **noun** [U]

disobey /ˌdɪsəˈbeɪ/ **verb** [I,T] to refuse to do what you are told to do: *He was punished for disobeying orders.* ∙∙➤ opposite **obey**

disorder /dɪsˈɔːdə/ **noun 1** [U] an untidy, confused or badly organized state: *His financial affairs are in complete disorder.* ∙∙➤ opposite **order 2** [U] violent behaviour by a large number of people: *Disorder broke out on the streets of the capital.* **3** [C,U] an illness in which the mind or part of the body is not working properly: *treatment for eating disorders such as anorexia* ● *a kind of mental disorder*

disordered /dɪsˈɔːdəd/ **adj** untidy, confused or badly organized

disorderly /dɪsˈɔːdəli/ **adj 1** (used about people or behaviour) out of control and violent; causing trouble in public: *They were arrested for being drunk and disorderly.* **2** untidy ∙∙➤ opposite **orderly**

disorganization (also **disorganisation**) /dɪsˌɔːgənaɪˈzeɪʃn/ **noun** ∙∙➤ opposite **organization**

disorganized /dɪsˈɔːgənaɪzd/ (also **-ised**) **adj** badly planned; not able to plan well ∙∙➤ opposite **organized**

disorientate /dɪsˈɔːriənteɪt/ (*especially US* **disorient** /dɪsˈɔːrient/) **verb** [T] to make sb become confused about where he/she is: *The road signs were very confusing and I soon became disorientated.* –disorientation /dɪsˌɔːriənˈteɪʃn/ ˌnoun [U]

disown /dɪsˈəʊn/ **verb** [T] to say that you no longer want to be connected with or responsible for sb/sth: *When he was arrested, his family disowned him.*

disparage /dɪˈspærɪdʒ/ **verb** [T] (*formal*) to talk about sb/sth in a critical way; to say that sb/sth is of little value or importance –disparaging **adj**: *disparaging remarks*

dispatch (*Brit also* **despatch**) /dɪˈspætʃ/ **verb** [T] (*formal*) to send sb/sth to a place: *Your order will be dispatched within 7 days.*

dispel /dɪˈspel/ **verb** [T] (**dispelling**; **dispelled**) to make sth, especially a feeling or a belief, disappear: *His reassuring words dispelled all her fears.*

dispensable /dɪˈspensəbl/ **adj** not necessary: *I suppose I'm dispensable. Anybody could do my job.* ∙∙➤ opposite **indispensable**

dispense /dɪˈspens/ **verb** [T] (*formal*) to give or provide people with sth: *a machine that dispenses hot and cold drinks*
PHRASAL VERB **dispense with sb/sth** to get rid

of sb/sth that is not necessary: *They decided to dispense with luxuries and live a simple life.*

dispenser /dɪˈspensə/ **noun** [C] a machine or container from which you can get sth: *a cash dispenser at a bank* ● *a soap dispenser*

disperse /dɪˈspɜːs/ **verb** [I,T] to separate and go in different directions; to make sb/sth do this: *When the meeting was over, the group dispersed.* ● *The police arrived and quickly dispersed the crowd.*

dispirited /dɪˈspɪrɪtɪd/ **adj** having lost confidence or hope; depressed

displace /dɪsˈpleɪs/ **verb** [T] **1** to remove and take the place of sb/sth: *She hoped to displace Seles as the top tennis player in the world.* **2** to force sb/sth to move from the usual or correct place: *refugees displaced by the war*

★**display¹** /dɪˈspleɪ/ **verb** [T] **1** to put sth in a place where people will see it or where it will attract attention: *Posters for the concert were displayed throughout the city.* **2** to show signs of sth (for example a feeling or a quality): *She displayed no interest in the discussion.*

★**display²** /dɪˈspleɪ/ **noun** [C] **1** an arrangement of things in a public place for people to see: *a window display in a shop* **2** a public event in which sth is shown in action: *a firework display* **3** behaviour that shows a particular feeling or quality: *a sudden display of aggression* **4** (*computing*) words, pictures, etc that can be seen on a computer screen
IDIOM **on display** in a place where people will see it and where it will attract attention: *Treasures from the sunken ship were put on display at the museum.*

displease /dɪsˈpliːz/ **verb** [T] (*formal*) to annoy sb or to make sb angry or upset –displeased **adj** ∙∙➤ opposite **pleased**

displeasure /dɪsˈpleʒə/ **noun** [U] (*formal*) the feeling of being annoyed or not satisfied: *I wrote to express my displeasure at not having been informed sooner.*

disposable /dɪˈspəʊzəbl/ **adj** made to be thrown away after being used once or for a short time: *a disposable razor*

disposal /dɪˈspəʊzl/ **noun** [U] the act of getting rid of sth or throwing sth away: *the disposal of dangerous chemical waste* ● *bomb disposal*
IDIOM **at sb's disposal** available for sb to use at any time

dispose /dɪˈspəʊz/ **verb**
PHRASAL VERB **dispose of sb/sth** to throw away or sell sth; to get rid of sb/sth that you do not want

disproportionate /ˌdɪsprəˈpɔːʃənət/ **adj** disproportionate (to sth) too large or too small when compared to sth else: *Her salary is disproportionate to the amount of work she has to do.* –disproportionately **adv**

disprove /ˌdɪsˈpruːv/ **verb** [T] to show that sth is not true

★**dispute¹** /ˈdɪspjuːt; dɪˈspjuːt/ **noun** [C,U] (a) dispute (between A and B) (over/about sth) a disagreement or argument between two people, groups or countries: *There was some dispute between John and his boss about*

ð **then** | s **so** | z **zoo** | ʃ **she** | ʒ **vision** | h **how** | m **man** | n **no** | ŋ **sing** | l **leg** | r **red** | j **yes** | w **wet**

whose fault it was. ● *a pay dispute*

IDIOM **in dispute** in a situation of arguing or being argued about: *He is in dispute with the tax office about how much he should pay.*

dispute² /dɪ'spjuːt/ **verb** [T] to argue about sth and to question if it is true or right: *The player disputed the referee's decision.*

disqualify /dɪs'kwɒlɪfaɪ/ **verb** [T] (*pres part* **disqualifying**; *3rd pers sing pres* **disqualifies**; *pt, pp* **disqualified**) disqualify sb (from sth/doing sth); disqualify sb (for sth) to officially prevent sb from doing sth or taking part in sth, usually because he/she has broken a rule or law: *He was disqualified from driving for two years.* ● *The team were disqualified for cheating.* –**disqualification** /dɪs,kwɒlɪfɪ'keɪʃn/ **noun** [C,U]

disregard /,dɪsrɪ'gɑːd/ **verb** [T] to take no notice of sb/sth; to treat sth as unimportant: *These are the latest instructions. Please disregard any you received before.* –**disregard noun** [U,sing] disregard (for sb/sth): *He rushed into the burning building with complete disregard for his own safety.*

disrepair /,dɪsrɪ'peə/ **noun** [U] the state of being in bad condition because repairs have not been made: *Over the years the building fell into disrepair.*

disreputable /dɪs'repjətəbl/ **adj** not to be trusted; well-known for being bad or dishonest: *disreputable business methods* ••► opposite **reputable**

disrepute /,dɪsrɪ'pjuːt/ **noun** [U] the situation when people no longer respect sb/sth: *Such unfair decisions bring the legal system into disrepute.*

disrespect /,dɪsrɪ'spekt/ **noun** [U] disrespect (for/to sb/sth) a lack of respect for sb/sth that is shown in what you do or say ••► opposite **respect** –**disrespectful** /-fl/ **adj** ••► opposite **respectful** –**disrespectfully** /-fəli/ **adv**

disrupt /dɪs'rʌpt/ **verb** [T] to stop sth happening as or when it should: *The strike severely disrupted flights to Spain.* –**disruption noun** [C,U] –**disruptive** /dɪs'rʌptɪv/ **adj**

dissatisfaction /,dɪs,sætɪs'fækʃn/ **noun** [U] dissatisfaction (with/at sb/sth) the feeling of not being satisfied or pleased: *There is some dissatisfaction among teachers with the plans for the new exam.* ••► opposite **satisfaction**

dissatisfied /dɪs'sætɪsfaɪd/ **adj** dissatisfied (with sb/sth) not satisfied or pleased: *complaints from dissatisfied customers* ••► opposite **satisfied**

dissect /dɪ'sekt/ **verb** [T] to cut up a dead body, a plant, etc in order to study it –**dissection noun** [C,U]

dissent¹ /dɪ'sent/ **noun** [U] (*formal*) disagreement with official or generally agreed ideas or opinions: *There is some dissent within the Labour Party on these policies.*

dissent² /dɪ'sent/ **verb** [I] (*formal*) dissent (from sth) to have opinions that are different to those that are officially held –**dissenting adj**

dissertation /,dɪsə'teɪʃn/ **noun** [C] a long piece of writing on sth that you have studied, especially as part of a university degree ••► Look at **thesis**.

disservice /dɪs'sɜːvɪs/ **noun** [U,sing]

IDIOM **do (a) disservice to sb/sth** to do sth that harms sb and the opinion other people have of him/her: *The minister's comments do the teaching profession a great disservice.*

dissident /'dɪsɪdənt/ **noun** [C] a person who strongly disagrees with and criticizes his/her government, especially in a country where it is dangerous to do this: *left-wing dissidents* –**dissidence noun** [U]

dissimilar /dɪ'sɪmɪlə/ **adj** dissimilar (from/to sb/sth) not the same; different: *The situation you're in is not dissimilar to mine.* ••► opposite **similar**

dissociate /dɪ'səʊʃieɪt; -'səʊs-/ (also **disassociate** /,dɪsə'səʊʃieɪt; -'səʊs-/) **verb** [T] dissociate sb/sth/yourself (from sth) to show that you are not connected with or do not support sb/sth; to show that two things are not connected with each other: *She dissociated herself from the views of the extremists in her party.* ••► opposite **associate**

dissolve /dɪ'zɒlv/ **verb** [I,T] (used about a solid) to become or to make sth become liquid: *Sugar dissolves in water.* ● *Dissolve two tablets in cold water.*

dissuade /dɪ'sweɪd/ **verb** [T] dissuade sb (from doing sth) to persuade sb not to do sth: *I tried to dissuade her from spending the money, but she insisted.* ••► opposite **persuade**

★**distance¹** /'dɪstəns/ **noun** 1 [C,U] the amount of space between two places or things: *The map tells you the distances between the major cities.* ● *We can walk home from here, it's no distance* (= it isn't far). ● *The house is within walking distance of the shops.* 2 [sing] a point that is a long way from sb/sth: *At this distance I can't read the number on the bus.* ● *From a distance the village looks quite attractive.*

IDIOMS **in the distance** far away: *I could just see Paul in the distance.*

keep your distance to stay away from sb/sth: *Rachel's got a bad cold so I'm keeping my distance until she gets better.*

within striking distance → **STRIKE²**

distance² /'dɪstəns/ **verb** [T] distance yourself from sb/sth to become less involved or connected with sb/sth: *She was keen to distance herself from the views of her colleagues.*

★**distant** /'dɪstənt/ **adj** 1 a long way away in space or time: *travel to distant parts of the world* ● *in the not-too-distant future* (= quite soon) 2 (used about a relative) not closely related: *a distant cousin* 3 not very friendly: *He has a rather distant manner and it's hard to get to know him well.* 4 seeming to be thinking about sth else: *She had a distant look in her eyes and clearly wasn't listening to me.*

distaste /dɪs'teɪst/ **noun** [U,sing] not liking sth; the feeling that sb/sth is unpleasant or offends you: *She looked around the dirty kitchen with distaste.*

distasteful /dɪsˈteɪstfl/ adj unpleasant or causing offence: *a distasteful remark*

distil (*US* **distill**) /dɪˈstɪl/ verb [T] (**distilling**; **distilled**) to make a liquid pure by heating it until it becomes a gas and then collecting the liquid that forms when the gas cools

distillery /dɪˈstɪləri/ noun [C] (*pl* **distilleries**) a factory where strong alcoholic drink is made by the process of distilling

★**distinct** /dɪˈstɪŋkt/ adj **1** clear; easily seen, heard or understood: *There has been a distinct improvement in your work recently.* ● *I had **the distinct impression** that she was lying.* **2** distinct (from sth) clearly different: *Her books fall into two distinct groups: the novels and the travel stories.* ● *This region, as distinct from other parts of the country, relies heavily on tourism.* •➤ opposite for both senses **indistinct**

★**distinction** /dɪˈstɪŋkʃn/ noun **1** [C,U] (a) distinction (between A and B) a clear or important difference between things or people: *We must **make a distinction** between classical and popular music here.* **2** [C,U] the quality of being excellent; fame for what you have achieved: *a violinist **of distinction*** **3** [C] the highest mark that is given to students in some exam for excellent work: *James got a distinction in maths.*
▨**IDIOM** **draw a distinction between sth and sth → DRAW¹**

distinctive /dɪˈstɪŋktɪv/ adj clearly different from others and therefore easy to recognize: *The soldiers were wearing their distinctive red berets.* –**distinctively** adv

distinctly /dɪˈstɪŋktli/ adv **1** clearly: *I distinctly heard her say that she would be here on time.* **2** very; particularly: *His behaviour has been distinctly odd recently.*

★**distinguish** /dɪˈstɪŋgwɪʃ/ verb **1** [I,T] distinguish between A and B; distinguish A from B to recognize the difference between two things or people: *He doesn't seem able to distinguish between what's important and what isn't.* ● *People who are colour-blind often can't distinguish red from green.* •➤ synonym **differentiate 2** [T] distinguish A (from B) to make sb/sth different from others: *distinguishing features* (= things by which sb/sth can be recognized) ● *The power of speech distinguishes humans from animals.* **3** [T] to see, hear or recognize with effort: *I listened carefully but they were too far away for me to distinguish what they were saying.* **4** [T] distinguish yourself to do sth which causes you to be noticed and admired: *She distinguished herself in the exams.*

distinguishable /dɪˈstɪŋgwɪʃəbl/ adj **1** possible to recognize as different from sb/sth else: *The male bird is distinguishable from the female by the colour of its beak.* **2** possible to see, hear or recognize with effort: *The letter is so old that the signature is barely distinguishable.* •➤ opposite **indistinguishable**

distinguished /dɪˈstɪŋgwɪʃt/ adj important,

successful and respected by other people: *a distinguished guest*

distort /dɪˈstɔːt/ verb [T] **1** to change the shape or sound of sth so that it seems strange or is not clear: *Her face was distorted with grief.* **2** to change sth and show it falsely: *Foreigners are often given a distorted view of this country.* –**distortion** noun [C,U]

distract /dɪˈstrækt/ verb [T] distract sb (from sth) to take sb's attention away from sth: *Could you stop talking please? You're distracting me from my work.*

distracted /dɪˈstræktɪd/ adj unable to give your full attention to sth because you are worried or thinking about sth else

distraction /dɪˈstrækʃn/ noun [C,U] something that takes your attention away from what you were doing or thinking about: *I find it hard to work at home because there are so many distractions.*
▨**IDIOM** **to distraction** with the result that you become upset, excited, or angry and unable to think clearly: *The noise of the traffic outside at night is driving me to distraction.*

distraught /dɪˈstrɔːt/ adj extremely sad and upset

distress¹ /dɪˈstres/ noun [U] **1** the state of being very upset or of suffering great pain or difficulty: *She was **in such distress** that I didn't want to leave her on her own.* **2** the state of being in great danger and needing immediate help: *The ship's captain radioed that it was **in distress**.*

distress² /dɪˈstres/ verb [T] to make sb very upset or unhappy: *Try not to say anything to distress the patient further.* –**distressed** adj: *She was too distressed to talk.* –**distressing** adj: *a distressing experience/illness*

★**distribute** /dɪˈstrɪbjuːt; ˈdɪstrɪbjuːt/ verb [T] **1** distribute sth (to/among sb/sth) to give things to a number of people: *Tickets will be distributed to all club members.* ● *They distributed emergency food supplies to the areas that were most in need.* **2** to transport and supply goods to shops, companies, etc: *Which company distributes this product in your country?* **3** to spread sth equally over an area: *Make sure that the weight is **evenly distributed**.*

★**distribution** /ˌdɪstrɪˈbjuːʃn/ noun **1** [sing,U] the act of giving or transporting sth to a number of people or places: *the distribution of food parcels to the refugees* **2** [sing,U] the way sth is shared out; the pattern in which sth is found: *a map to show the distribution of rainfall in Africa*

distributor /dɪˈstrɪbjətə/ noun [C] a person or company that transports and supplies goods to a number of shops and companies

★**district** /ˈdɪstrɪkt/ noun [C] **1** a part of a town or country that is special for a particular reason or is of a particular type: *rural districts* ● *the financial district of the city* **2** an official division of a town or country: *the district council* ● *postal districts*

d

> A **district** may be part of a town or country, and it may have fixed boundaries: *the district controlled by a council.* A **region** is larger, usually part of a country only and may not have fixed boundaries: *the industrial regions of the country.* An **area** is the most general term and is used with the same meaning as both **district** and **region**: *the poorer areas of a town* ● *an agricultural area of the country.* We use **part** more often when we are talking about a section of a town: *Which part of Paris do you live in?*

distrust /dɪs'trʌst/ **noun** [U,sing] (a) **distrust (of sb/sth)** the feeling that you cannot believe sb/sth; a lack of trust –**distrust verb** [T]: *She distrusts him because he lied to her once before.*

> Compare **mistrust**.

–**distrustful adj**

★**disturb** /dɪ'stɜːb/ **verb** [T] **1** to interrupt sb while he/she is doing sth or sleeping; to spoil a peaceful situation: *I'm sorry to disturb you but there's a phone call for you.* ● *Their sleep was disturbed by a loud crash.* **2** to cause sb to worry: *It disturbed her to think that he might be unhappy.* **3** to move sth or change its position: *I noticed a number of things had been disturbed and realized that there had been a burglary.*

disturbance /dɪ'stɜːbəns/ **noun** [C,U] something that makes you stop what you are doing, or that upsets the normal condition of sth: *They were arrested for causing a disturbance (= fighting) in the town centre.* ● *emotional disturbance*

disturbed /dɪ'stɜːbd/ **adj** having mental or emotional problems: *a school for disturbed young people*

disturbing /dɪ'stɜːbɪŋ/ **adj** making you worried or upset: *I found the film about Aids very disturbing.*

disuse /dɪs'juːs/ **noun** [U] the state of not being used any more: *The farm buildings had been allowed to fall into disuse.*

disused /ˌdɪs'juːzd/ **adj** not used any more: *a disused railway line*

ditch¹ /dɪtʃ/ **noun** [C] a long narrow hole that has been dug into the ground, especially along the side of a road or field for water to flow along

IDIOM **a last-ditch attempt** → **LAST¹**

ditch² /dɪtʃ/ **verb** [T] (*informal*) to get rid of or leave sb/sth: *She ditched her old friends when she became famous.*

dither /'dɪðə/ **verb** [I] to be unable to decide sth; to hesitate: *Stop dithering and make up your mind!*

ditto /'dɪtəʊ/ **noun** [C] (represented by the mark (") and used instead of repeating the thing written above it) the same –**ditto adv**: *'I'm starving.' 'Ditto (= me too).'*

divan /dɪ'væn/ **noun** [C] (*Brit*) a type of bed with only a thick base to lie on but no frame at either end

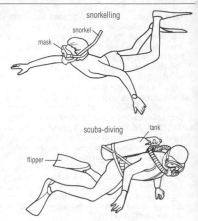

snorkelling
snorkel
mask
scuba-diving
tank
flipper

★**dive¹** /daɪv/ **verb** [I] (*pt* **dived**; *US also* **dove** /dəʊv/; *pp* **dived**) **1 dive (off/from sth) (into sth)**; **dive in** to jump into water with your arms and head first: *In Acapulco, men dive off the cliffs into the sea.* ● *A passer-by dived in and saved the drowning man.* ·❯ picture on page S2 **2** to swim under the surface of the sea, a lake, etc: *people diving for pearls* ● *I'm hoping to go diving on holiday.* **3** to move quickly and suddenly downwards: *He dived under the table and hid there.* ● *The goalkeeper dived to save the penalty.*

PHRASAL VERB **dive into sth** to put your hand quickly into a pocket or bag in order to find or get sth: *She dived into her bag and brought out an old photograph.*

dive² /daɪv/ **noun** [C] **1** the act of diving into water **2** a quick and sudden downwards movement: *Despite a desperate dive, the goalkeeper couldn't stop the ball.*

diver /'daɪvə/ **noun** [C] **1** a person who swims under the surface of water using special equipment **2** a person who jumps into water with his/her arms and head first

diverge /daɪ'vɜːdʒ/ **verb** [I] **diverge (from sth)** **1** (used about roads, lines, etc) to separate and go in different directions: *The paths suddenly diverged and I didn't know which one to take.* **2** to be or become different: *Attitudes among teachers diverge on this question.*

diverse /daɪ'vɜːs/ **adj** very different from each other: *people from diverse social backgrounds* ● *My interests are very diverse.* ·❯ noun **diversity**

diversify /daɪ'vɜːsɪfaɪ/ **verb** [I] (*pres part* **diversifying**; *3rd pers sing pres* **diversifies**; *pt, pp* **diversified**) **diversify (sth) (into sth)** to increase or develop the number or types of sth: *To remain successful in the future, the company will have to diversify.* ● *Latin diversified into several different languages.* –**diversification** /daɪˌvɜːsɪfɪ'keɪʃn/ **noun** [C,U]

diversion /daɪ'vɜːʃn/ **noun** **1** [C,U] the act of changing the direction or purpose of sth, especially in order to solve or avoid a problem: *the diversion of a river to prevent* *flooding* • *the diversion of government funds to areas of greatest need* **2** [C] (*US* **detour**) a different route which traffic can take when a road is closed: *For London, follow the diversion.* **3** [C] something that takes your attention away from sth: *Some prisoners created a diversion while others escaped.*

diversity /daɪ'vɜːsəti/ **noun** [U] the wide variety of sth: *cultural and ethnic diversity*

divert /daɪ'vɜːt/ **verb** [T] **divert sb/sth (from sth) (to sth); divert sth (away from sth)** to change the direction or purpose of sb/sth, especially to avoid a problem: *During the road repairs, all traffic is being diverted.* • *Government money was diverted from defence to education.* • *Politicians often criticise each other to divert attention away from their own mistakes.*

★**divide**[1] /dɪ'vaɪd/ **verb 1** [I,T] **divide (sth) (up) (into sth)** to separate into different parts: *The egg divides into two cells.* • *The house was divided up into flats.* **2** [T] **divide sth (out/up) (between/among sb)** to separate sth into parts and give a part to each of a number of people: *The robbers divided the money out between themselves.* • *When he died, his property was divided up among his children.* **3** [T] **divide sth (between A and B)** to use different parts or amounts of sth for different purposes: *They divide their time between their two homes.* **4** [T] to separate two places or things: *The river divides the old part of the city from the new.* **5** [T] to cause people to disagree: *The question of immigration has divided the country.* **6** [T] **divide sth by sth** to calculate how many times a number will go into another number: *10 divided by 5 is 2.* •➤ opposite **multiply**

divide[2] /dɪ'vaɪd/ **noun** [C] **a divide (between A and B)** a difference between two groups of people that separates them from each other: *a divide between the rich and the poor*

di̩vided 'highway (*US*) = **DUAL CARRIAGEWAY**

dividend /'dɪvɪdend/ **noun** [C] a part of a company's profits that is paid to the people who own shares in it (**shareholders**)

divine /dɪ'vaɪn/ **adj** connected with God or a god

diving /'daɪvɪŋ/ **noun** [U] the activity or sport of jumping into water or swimming under the surface of the sea, a lake, etc

'diving board noun [C] a board at the side of a swimming pool from which people can jump into the water

divisible /dɪ'vɪzəbl/ **adj** that can be divided: *12 is divisible by 3.*

★**division** /dɪ'vɪʒn/ **noun 1** [U,sing] **division (of sth) (into sth); division (of sth) (between A and B)** the separation of sth into different parts; the sharing of sth between different people, groups, places, etc: *There is a growing economic division between the north and south of the country.* • *an unfair division of the profits* **2** [U] dividing one number by another: *the teaching of multiplication and division* **3** [C] a **division (in/within sth); a division**

(**between A and B**) a disagreement or difference of opinion between sb/sth: *deep divisions within the Labour Party* **4** [C] a part or section of an organization: *the company's sales division* • *the First Division* (= of the football league) **5** [C] a line that separates sth; a border: *The river marks the division between the two counties.*

divisive /dɪ'vaɪsɪv/ **adj** (*formal*) likely to cause disagreements or arguments between people: *a divisive policy*

★**divorce**[1] /dɪ'vɔːs/ **noun** [C,U] the legal end of a marriage: *to get a divorce*

★**divorce**[2] /dɪ'vɔːs/ **verb** [T] **1** to legally end your marriage to sb: *My parents got divorced when I was three.* • *She divorced him a year after their marriage.* **2** **divorce sb/sth from sth** to separate sb/sth from sth: *Sometimes these modern novels seem completely divorced from everyday life.* –divorced **adj**

divorcee /dɪˌvɔː'siː/ **noun** [C] a person who is divorced

divulge /daɪ'vʌldʒ/ **verb** [T] (*formal*) to tell sth that is secret: *The phone companies refused to divulge details of their costs.*

Diwali /diː'wɑːli/ **noun** [sing] a festival in several Indian religions that takes place in October or November, in which people decorate their homes with lights

DIY /ˌdiː aɪ 'waɪ/ **abbr** do it yourself; the activity of making and repairing things yourself around your home: *a DIY expert*

dizzy /'dɪzi/ **adj 1** feeling as if everything is turning round and that you might fall: *I feel/get dizzy in high places.* **2** very great; extreme: *the dizzy pace of life in London* • *The following year, the band's popularity reached dizzy heights.* –dizziness **noun** [U]

DJ /ˌdiː 'dʒeɪ/ (also **disc jockey**) **noun** [C] a person who plays records and talks about music on the radio or in a club

★**do**[1] /də; *strong form* duː/ **auxiliary verb 1** used with other verbs to form questions and negative sentences, also in short answers and short questions at the end of a sentence (**question tags**) •➤ Look at the **Quick Grammar Reference** section at the back of this dictionary. **2** used for emphasizing the main verb: *I can't find the receipt now but I'm sure I did pay the phone bill.* **3** used to avoid repeating the main verb: *He earns a lot more than I do.* • *She's feeling much better than she did last week.*

★**do**[2] /duː/ **verb 1** [T] to perform an action, activity or job: *What are you doing?* • *What is the government doing about pollution* (= what action are they taking)? • *What do you do* (= what is your job)? • *Have you done your homework?* • *I do twenty minutes' exercise every morning.* • *to do the cooking/cleaning/ironing* • *to do judo/aerobics/windsurfing* • *What did you do with the keys* (= where did you put them)? **2** [I] to make progress or develop; to improve sth: *'How's your daughter doing at school?' 'She's doing well.'* • *Last week's win has done wonders for the team's*

---

present tense	past tense
I do	I did
you do	you did
he/she/it does	he/she/it did
we do	we did
you do	you did
they do	they did
past participle	done
present participle	doing
negative short forms	don't, doesn't, didn't

confidence. ● *This latest scandal will do **nothing for** (= will harm) this government's reputation.* **3** [T] to make or produce sth: *The photocopier does 60 copies a minute.* ● *to do a painting/drawing* **4** [T] to provide a service: *Do you do eye tests here?* **5** [T] to study sth or find the answer to sth: *to do French/a course/a degree* ● *I can't do question three.* **6** [T] to travel a certain distance or at a certain speed: *This car does 120 miles per hour.* ● *I normally do about five miles when I go running.* **7** [T] to have a particular effect: *A holiday will do you good.* ● *The storm did a lot of damage.* **8** [I,T] to be enough or suitable: *If you haven't got a pen, a pencil will do.*

IDIOMS **be/have to do with sb/sth** to be connected with sb/sth: *I'm not sure what Paola's job is, but I think it's something to do with animals.* ● *'How much do you earn?' 'It's nothing to do with you!'*

could do with sth to want or need sth: *I could do with a holiday.*

how do you do? → HOW

make do with sth → MAKE¹

PHRASAL VERBS **do away with sth** to get rid of sth: *Most European countries have done away with their royal families.*

do sb out of sth to prevent sb having sth in an unfair way; to cheat sb: *They've done me out of my share of the money!*

do sth up 1 to fasten a piece of clothing: *Hurry up. Do up your jacket and we can go!* **2** to repair a building and make it more modern: *They're doing up the old cottage.*

do without (sth) to manage without having sth: *If there isn't any coffee left, we'll just have to do without.*

do³ /duː/ *noun* [C] (*pl* **dos** /dʌːz/) (*Brit informal*) a party or other social event: *We're having a bit of a do to celebrate Tim's birthday.*

IDIOM **dos and don'ts** things that you should and should not do: *the dos and don'ts of mountain climbing*

docile /'dəʊsaɪl/ *adj* (used about a person or animal) quiet and easy to control

dock¹ /dɒk/ *noun* **1** [C,U] an area of a port where ships stop to be loaded, repaired, etc **2 docks** [pl] a group of docks with all the buildings, offices, etc that are around them: *He works down at the docks.* **3** [C, usually sing] the place in a court of law where the person who is accused sits or stands **4** (*US*) = **LANDING STAGE**

dock² /dɒk/ *verb* **1** [I,T] (used about a ship) to sail into a port and stop at the dock: *The ship had docked/was docked at Lisbon.* **2** [T] to take away part of the money sb earns, especially as a punishment: *They've docked £20 off my wages because I was late.*

★**doctor¹** /'dɒktə/ *noun* (*abbr* **Dr**) **1** [C] a person who has been trained in medicine and who treats people who are ill: *Our family doctor is Dr Young.* ● *I've got a doctor's appointment at 10 o'clock.*

➤ A doctor **sees** or **treats** his/her **patients**. He/she may **prescribe** treatment or **medicine**. This is written on a **prescription**.

2 the doctor's [sing] the place where a doctor sees his/her patients; a doctor's surgery: *I'm going to the doctor's today.* **3** [C] a person who has got the highest degree from a university (doctorate): *a Doctor of Philosophy*

doctor² /'dɒktə/ *verb* [T] **1** to change sth that should not be changed in order to gain an advantage: *The results of the survey had been doctored.* **2** to add sth harmful to food or drink

doctorate /'dɒktərət/ *noun* [C] the highest university degree

doctrine /'dɒktrɪn/ *noun* [C,U] a set of beliefs that is taught by a church, political party, etc

★**document** /'dɒkjumənt/ *noun* [C] an official piece of writing which gives information, proof or evidence: *Her solicitor asked her to read and sign a number of documents.*

documentary /ˌdɒkju'mentri/ *noun* [C] (*pl* **documentaries**) a film or television or radio programme that gives facts or information about a particular subject: *Did you see that documentary on Sri Lanka?*

doddle /'dɒdl/ *noun* [sing] (*Brit informal*) something that is very easy to do: *The exam was an absolute doddle!*

dodge¹ /dɒdʒ/ *verb* **1** [I,T] to move quickly in order to avoid sb/sth: *I had to dodge between the cars to cross the road.* **2** [T] to avoid doing sth that you should do: *Don't try to dodge your responsibilities.*

dodge² /dɒdʒ/ *noun* [C] (*informal*) a clever way of avoiding sth: *The man had been involved in a massive tax dodge.*

dodgy /'dɒdʒi/ *adj* (**dodgier**, **dodgiest**) (*Brit informal*) involving risk; not honest or not to be trusted: *a dodgy business deal* ● *This meat looks a bit dodgy – when did we buy it?*

doe /dəʊ/ *noun* [C] the female of certain types of animal (deer and rabbits) ••➤ Look at the note and picture at **deer**.

does → DO

doesn't *short for* **DOES NOT**

★**dog¹** /dɒg/ *noun* [C] **1** an animal that many people keep as a pet, or for working on farms, hunting, etc

➤ A dog can **bark**, **growl** or **whine**. Dogs **wag** their tails when they are happy.

2 a male dog or other animal (fox)

dog² /dɒg/ *verb* [T] (**dogging**; **dogged**) to

follow sb closely: *A shadowy figure was dogging their every move.* ● (*figurative*) *Bad luck and illness have dogged her career from the start.*

'dog collar noun [C] (*informal*) a white collar that is worn by priests in the Christian church

'dog-eared adj (used about a book or piece of paper) in bad condition with untidy corners and edges because it has been used a lot

dogged /'dɒɡɪd/ adj refusing to give up even when sth is difficult: *I was impressed by his dogged determination to succeed.* –doggedly adv: *She doggedly refused all offers of help.*

dogma /'dɒɡmə/ noun [C,U] a belief or set of beliefs that people are expected to accept as true without questioning

dogmatic /dɒɡ'mætɪk/ adj being certain that your beliefs are right and that others should accept them, without considering other opinions or evidence –dogmatically /-kli/ adv

dogsbody /'dɒɡzbɒdi/ noun [C] (*pl dogsbodies*) (*Brit informal*) a person who has to do the boring or unpleasant jobs that no one else wants to do and who is considered less important than other people

doldrums /'dɒldrəmz/ noun [pl]
IDIOM **in the doldrums 1** not active or busy: *Business has been in the doldrums recently.* **2** sad or unhappy

dole¹ /dəʊl/ verb (*informal*)
PHRASAL VERB **dole sth out** to give sth, especially food, money, etc in small amounts to a number of people

the dole² /dəʊl/ noun [sing] (*Brit informal*) money that the State gives every week to people who are unemployed: *I lost my job and had to go on the dole.*

doleful /'dəʊlfl/ adj sad or unhappy: *She looked at him with doleful eyes.* –dolefully /-fəli/ adv

doll /dɒl/ noun [C] a child's toy that looks like a small person or a baby

＊**dollar** /'dɒlə/ noun **1** [C] (*symbol* $) a unit of money in some countries, for example the US, Canada and Australia ⋯➤ There are 100 **cents** in a dollar. **2** [C] a note or coin that is worth one dollar **3 the dollar** [sing] the value of the US dollar on international money markets

dollop /'dɒləp/ noun [C] (*informal*) a lump of sth soft, especially food: *a dollop of ice cream*

dolphin /'dɒlfɪn/ noun [C] an intelligent animal that lives in the sea and looks like a large fish. Dolphins usually swim in large groups (schools).

domain /də'meɪn; dəʊ-/ noun [C] an area of knowledge or activity: *I don't know – that's outside my domain.* ● *This issue is now in the public domain* (= the public knows about it).

dome /dəʊm/ noun [C] a round roof on a building: *the dome of St Paul's in London*

＊**domestic** /də'mestɪk/ adj **1** not international; only within one country: *domestic flights* ● *domestic affairs/politics* **2** (only

before a noun) connected with the home or family: *domestic chores/tasks* ● *the growing problem of domestic violence* (= violence between members of the same family) ● *domestic water/gas/electricity supplies* **3** (used about animals) kept as pets or on farms; not wild: *domestic animals such as cats, dogs and horses* **4** (used about a person) enjoying doing things in the home, such as cooking and cleaning

domesticated /də'mestɪkeɪtɪd/ adj **1** (used about animals) happy being near people and being controlled by them **2** (used about people) able to do or good at cleaning the house, cooking, etc: *Men are expected to be much more domesticated nowadays.*

dominance /'dɒmɪnəns/ noun [U] control or power: *Japan's dominance of the car industry*

dominant /'dɒmɪnənt/ adj more powerful, important or noticeable than others: *His mother was the dominant influence in his life.*

dominate /'dɒmɪneɪt/ verb **1** [I,T] to be more powerful, important or noticeable than others: *The Italian team dominated throughout the second half of the game.* ● *She always tends to dominate the conversation.* **2** [T] (used about a building or place) to be much higher than everything else: *The cathedral dominates the area for miles around.* –domination /ˌdɒmɪ'neɪʃn/ noun [U]

domineering /ˌdɒmɪ'nɪərɪŋ/ adj having a very strong character and wanting to control other people

dominion /də'mɪnɪən/ noun (*formal*) **1** [U] the power to rule and control: *to have dominion over an area* **2** [C] an area controlled by one government or ruler: *the dominions of the Roman empire*

dominoes

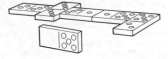

domino /'dɒmɪnəʊ/ noun [C] (*pl dominoes*) one of a set of small flat pieces of wood or plastic, marked on one side with two groups of spots representing numbers, that are used for playing a game (dominoes)

donate /dəʊ'neɪt/ verb [T] donate sth (to sb/sth) to give money or goods to an organization, especially one for people or animals who need help: *She donated a large sum of money to Cancer Research.*

donation /dəʊ'neɪʃn/ noun [C] money, etc that is given to a person or an organization such as a charity, in order to help people or animals in need

done¹ past participle of **DO²**

＊**done²** /dʌn/ adj (not before a noun) **1** finished: *I've got to go out as soon as this job is done.* **2** (used about food) cooked enough: *The meat's ready but the vegetables still aren't done.*

d

IDIOM **over and done with** completely finished; in the past

done³ /dʌn/ **interj** used for saying that you accept an offer: *'I'll give you twenty pounds for it.' 'Done!'*

donkey

donkey /'dɒŋki/ **noun** [C] (also **ass**) an animal like a small horse, with long ears

IDIOM **donkey's years** (*Brit informal*) a very long time: *They've been going out together for donkey's years.*

donor /'dəʊnə/ **noun** [C] **1** a person who gives blood or a part of his/her own body for medical use: *a blood/kidney donor* **2** somebody who gives money or goods to an organization that helps people or animals

don't → **DO**

doodle /'du:dl/ **verb** [I] to draw lines, patterns, etc without thinking, especially when you are bored – **doodle noun** [C]

doom /du:m/ **noun** [U] death or a terrible event in the future which you cannot avoid: *a sense of impending doom* (= that something bad is going to happen) • *Don't listen to her. She's always full of doom and gloom* (= expecting bad things to happen). – **doomed adj**: *The plan was doomed from the start.*

★**door** /dɔ:/ **noun** [C] **1** a piece of wood, glass, etc that you open and close to get in or out of a room, building, car, etc: *to open/shut/close the door* • *to answer the door* (= to open the door when sb knocks or rings the bell) • *Have you bolted/locked the door?* • *I could hear someone knocking on the door.* • *the front/back door* • *the fridge door* ·›➤ picture on page S9 **2** the entrance to a building, room, car, etc: *I looked through the door and saw her sitting there.*

IDIOMS **(from) door to door** (from) house to house: *The journey takes about five hours, door to door.* • *a door-to-door salesman* (= a person who visits people in their homes to try and sell them things)

next door (to sb/sth) in the next house, room, etc: *Do you know the people who live next door?*

out of doors outside: *Shall we eat out of doors today?* ·›➤ synonym **outdoors** ·›➤ opposite **indoors**

doorbell /'dɔ:bel/ **noun** [C] a bell on the outside of a house which you ring when you want to go in

doormat /'dɔ:mæt/ **noun** [C] **1** a piece of material on the floor in front of a door which you can clean your shoes on before going inside **2** (*informal*) a person who allows other people to treat him/her badly without complaining

doorstep /'dɔ:step/ **noun** [C] a step in front of a door outside a building

IDIOM **on your/the doorstep** very near to you: *The sea was right on our doorstep.*

doorway /'dɔ:weɪ/ **noun** [C] an opening filled by a door leading into a building, room, etc: *She was standing in the doorway.*

dope¹ /dəʊp/ **noun** (*informal*) **1** [U] an illegal drug, especially cannabis or marijuana **2** [C] a stupid person: *What a dope!*

dope² /dəʊp/ **verb** [T] to give a drug secretly to a person or animal, especially to make them sleep

dopey /'dəʊpi/ **adj 1** tired and not able to think clearly, especially because of drugs, alcohol or lack of sleep **2** (*informal*) stupid; not intelligent

dormant /'dɔ:mənt/ **adj** not active for some time: *a dormant volcano*

dormitory /'dɔ:mətri/ **noun** [C] (*pl* **dormitories**) (also **dorm**) **1** a large bedroom with a number of beds in it, especially in a school, etc **2** (*US*) a building at a college or university where students live

dosage /'dəʊsɪdʒ/ **noun** [C, usually sing] the amount of a medicine you should take over a period of time: *The recommended dosage is one tablet every four hours.*

dose¹ /dəʊs/ **noun** [C] **1** an amount of medicine that you take at one time: *You should take a large dose of this cough medicine before going to bed.* ·›➤ Look at **overdose**. **2** an amount of sth, especially sth unpleasant: *a dose of the flu* • *I can only stand him in small doses.*

dose² /dəʊs/ **verb** [T] to give sb/yourself a medicine or drug: *She dosed herself with aspirin and went to work.*

doss /dɒs/ **verb** (*Brit slang*)

PHRASAL VERBS **doss down** to lie down to sleep, without a proper bed: *Do you mind if I doss down on your floor tonight?*

doss about/around to waste time not doing very much: *We just dossed about in class yesterday.*

★**dot**¹ /dɒt/ **noun** [C] **1** a small, round mark, like a full stop: *a white dress with black dots* • *The letters i and j have dots above them.*

➤ We use **dot** when we say a person's e-mail address. For the address written as **ann@smithuni.co.uk** we would say 'Ann at smithuni **dot** co **dot** uk'.

2 something that looks like a dot: *He watched until the aeroplane was just a dot in the sky.*

IDIOM **on the dot** (*informal*) at exactly the right time or at exactly the time mentioned: *Lessons start at 9 o'clock on the dot.*

dot² /dɒt/ **verb** [T] (**dotting; dotted**) (usually passive) to mark with a dot

IDIOMS **be dotted about/around** to be spread over an area: *There are restaurants dotted about all over the centre of town.*

be dotted with to have several things or people in or on it: *a hillside dotted with sheep*

dote /dəʊt/ **verb** [I] **dote on sb/sth** to have or show a lot of love for sb/sth and think he/

she/it is perfect: *He's always doted on his eldest son.* –**doting** adj: *doting parents*

dotted 'line noun [C] a line of small round marks (**dots**) which show where sth is to be written on a form, etc: *Sign on the dotted line.* •➤ picture at **line**

★**double**[1] /'dʌbl/ adj, determiner **1** twice as much or as many (as usual): *His income is double hers.* ● *We'll need double the amount of wine.* **2** having two equal or similar parts: *double doors* ● *Does 'necessary' have (a) double 's'?* ● *My phone number is two four double three four* (= 24334). **3** made for or used by two people or things: *a double garage* •➤ Look at the note at **bed**[1].

★**double**[2] /'dʌbl/ adv in twos or two parts: *When I saw her with her twin sister I thought I was **seeing double**.*

★**double**[3] /'dʌbl/ noun **1** [U] twice the (usual) number or amount: *When you work overtime, you get paid double.* **2** [C] a glass of strong alcoholic drink containing twice the usual amount **3** [C] a person who looks very much like another: *I thought it was you I saw in the supermarket. You must have a double.* **4** [C] an actor who replaces another actor in a film to do dangerous or other special things **5** [C] a bedroom for two people in a hotel, etc •➤ Look at **single**[2](3). **6 doubles** [pl] in some sports, for example tennis) with two pairs playing: *the Men's Doubles final* •➤ Look at **single**[2](4).

★**double**[4] /'dʌbl/ verb **1** [I,T] to become or to make sth twice as much or as many; to multiply by two: *The price of houses has almost doubled.* ● *Think of a number and double it.* **2** [I] double (up) as sth to have a second use or function: *The small room doubles (up) as a study.*

PHRASAL VERB **double (sb) up/over** (to cause sb) to bend the body: *to be doubled up with pain/laughter*

,**double 'bass** (also **bass**) noun [C] the largest musical instrument with strings, that you can play either standing up or sitting down •➤ Look at the note at **piano**. •➤ picture at **music**

,**double-'breasted** adj (used about a coat or jacket) having two rows of buttons down the front

,**double-'check** verb [I,T] to check sth again, or with great care

,**double-'cross** verb [T] to cheat sb who believes that he/she can trust you after you have agreed to do sth dishonest together

,**double-'decker** noun [C] a bus with two floors

,**double 'Dutch** noun [U] conversation or writing that you cannot understand at all: *The listening comprehension in the exam was really hard. It all sounded like double Dutch to me!*

,**double 'figures** noun [U] a number that is more than nine: *Inflation is now **in double figures**.*

,**double 'glazing** noun [U] two layers of glass in a window to keep a building warm or quiet –,**double-'glazed** adj

doubly /'dʌbli/ adv **1** in two ways: *He was doubly blessed with both good looks and talent.* **2** more than usually: *I made doubly sure that the door was locked.*

★**doubt**[1] /daʊt/ noun [C,U] doubt (about sth); doubt that …; doubt as to sth (a feeling of) uncertainty: *If you have any doubts about the job, feel free to ring me and discuss them.* ● *There's some doubt that Jan will pass the exam.*

IDIOMS **cast doubt on sth** → CAST[1]
give sb the benefit of the doubt → BENEFIT[1]
in doubt not sure or definite
no doubt (used when you expect sth to happen but you are not sure that it will) probably: *No doubt she'll write when she has time.*
without (a) doubt definitely: *It was, without doubt, the coldest winter for many years.*

★**doubt**[2] /daʊt/ verb [T] to think sth is unlikely or to feel uncertain (about sth): *She never doubted that he was telling the truth.* ● *He had never doubted her support.*

doubtful /'daʊtfl/ adj **1** unlikely or uncertain: *It's doubtful whether/if we'll finish in time.* ● *It was doubtful that he was still alive.* **2** doubtful (about sth/about doing sth) (used about a person) not sure: *He still felt doubtful about his decision.* –**doubtfully** /-fəli/ adv: *'I suppose it'll be all right,' she said doubtfully.*

doubtless /'daʊtləs/ adv almost certainly: *Doubtless she'll have a good excuse for being late!*

dough /dəʊ/ noun [U] **1** a mixture of flour, water, etc used for baking into bread, etc **2** (*informal*) money

doughnut (*US* **donut**) /'dəʊnʌt/ noun [C] a small cake in the shape of a ball or a ring, made from a sweet dough cooked in very hot oil •➤ picture at **cake**

dour /dʊə/ adj (used about a person's manner or expression) cold and unfriendly

douse (also **dowse**) /daʊs/ verb [T] **1** douse sth (with sth) to stop a fire from burning by pouring liquid over it: *The firefighters managed to douse the flames.* **2** douse sb/sth (in/with sth) to cover sb/sth with liquid: *to douse yourself in perfume* (= wear too much of it)

dove[1] /dʌv/ noun [C] a type of white bird, often used as a sign of peace

dove[2] /dəʊv/ (*US*) past tense of **DIVE**[1]

dowdy /'daʊdi/ adj (used about a person or the clothes he/she wears) not attractive or fashionable

★**down**[1] /daʊn/ adv, prep **1** to or at a lower level or place; from the top towards the bottom of sth: *Can you get that book down from the top shelf?* ● *'Where's Mary?' 'She's down in the basement.'* ● *Her hair hung down her back.* ● *The rain was running down the window.* **2** along: *We sailed down the river towards the sea.* ● *'Where's the nearest garage?' 'Go down this road and take the first turning on the right.'* **3** from a standing or vertical position to a sitting or horizontal

d

one: *I think I'll sit/lie down.* **4** to or in the south: *We went down to Devon for our holiday.* **5** used for showing that the level, amount, strength, etc of sth is less or lower: *Do you mind if I turn the heating down a bit?* **6** (written) on paper: *Put these dates down in your diary.* **7** down to sb/sth even including: *We had everything planned down to the last detail.*

IDIOMS be down to sb to be sb's responsibility: *When my father died it was down to me to look after the family's affairs.*

be down to sth to have only the amount mentioned left: *I need to do some washing – I'm down to my last shirt.*

down and out having no money, job or home

down under (*informal*) (in) Australia

down² /daʊn/ *verb* [T] (*informal*) to finish a drink quickly: *She **downed** her drink **in one** (= she drank the whole glass without stopping).

down³ /daʊn/ *adj* **1** sad: *You're looking a bit down today.* **2** lower than before: *Unemployment figures are down again this month.* **3** (used about computers) not working: *I can't access the file as our computers have been down all morning.*

down⁴ /daʊn/ *noun* [U] very soft feathers: *a duvet filled with duck down*

IDIOM ups and downs → UP

'down-and-out *noun* [C] a person who has got no money, job or home

downcast /'daʊnkɑːst/ *adj* **1** (used about a person) sad and without hope **2** (used about eyes) looking down

downfall /'daʊnfɔːl/ *noun* [sing] a loss of a person's money, power, social position, etc; the thing that causes this: *The government's downfall seemed inevitable.* ● *Greed was her downfall.*

downgrade /ˌdaʊn'ɡreɪd/ *verb* [T] down-grade sb/sth (from sth) (to sth) to reduce sb/sth to a lower level or position of importance: *Tom's been downgraded from manager to assistant manager.*

downhearted /ˌdaʊn'hɑːtɪd/ *adj* sad

downhill /ˌdaʊn'hɪl/ *adj, adv* (going) in a downward direction; towards the bottom of a hill: *It's an easy walk. The road runs downhill most of the way.* ••➤ opposite **uphill**

IDIOM go downhill to get worse: *Their relationship has been going downhill for some time now.*

download /ˌdaʊn'ləʊd/ *verb* [T] to copy a computer file, etc from a large computer system to a smaller one

downmarket /ˌdaʊn'mɑːkɪt/ *adj, adv* cheap and of low quality: *a downmarket newspaper*

downpour /'daʊnpɔː/ *noun* [C] a heavy, sudden fall of rain

downright /'daʊnraɪt/ *adj* (only *before* a noun) (used about sth bad or unpleasant) complete: *The holiday was a downright disaster.* –downright *adv*: *The way he spoke to me was downright rude!*

downside /'daʊnsaɪd/ *noun* [C, usually sing]

the disadvantages or negative aspects of sth: *All good ideas have a downside.*

Down's syndrome /'daʊnz sɪndrəʊm/ *noun* [U] a condition that a person is born with. People with this condition have a flat, wide face and lower than average intelligence.

★**downstairs** /ˌdaʊn'steəz/ *adv, adj* towards or on a lower floor of a house or building: *He fell downstairs and broke his arm.* ● *Dad's downstairs, in the kitchen.* ● *a downstairs toilet* ••➤ opposite **upstairs**

downstream /ˌdaʊn'striːm/ *adv* in the direction in which a river flows: *We were rowing downstream.* ••➤ opposite **upstream**

down-to-'earth *adj* (used about a person) sensible, realistic and practical

downtrodden /'daʊntrɒdn/ *adj* (used about a person) made to suffer bad treatment or living conditions by people in power, but being too tired, poor, ill, etc to change this

downturn /'daʊntɜːn/ *noun* [usually sing] a downturn (in sth) a drop in the amount of business that is done; a time when the economy becomes weaker: *a downturn in sales/trade/business* ••➤ opposite **upturn**

★**downward** /'daʊnwəd/ *adj, adv* (only *before* a noun) towards the ground or a lower level: *a downward movement* –downwards /'daʊnwədz/ *adv*: *She laid the picture face downwards on the table.* ••➤ opposite **upward(s)**

dowry /'daʊri/ *noun* [C] (*pl* dowries) an amount of money or property which, in some countries, a woman's family gives to the man she is marrying

dowse = **DOUSE**

doz *abbr* dozen

doze¹ /dəʊz/ *verb* [I] to sleep lightly and/or for a short time: *He was dozing in front of the television.* –doze *noun* [sing]

PHRASAL VERB doze off to go to sleep, especially during the day: *I'm sorry – I must have dozed off for a minute.*

★**dozen** /'dʌzn/ (*abbr* doz) *noun* [C] (*pl* dozen) twelve or a group of twelve: *A dozen eggs, please.* ● *half a dozen* (= six) ● *two dozen sheep*

IDIOM dozens (of sth) (*informal*) very many: *I've tried phoning her dozens of times.*

dozy /'dəʊzi/ *adj* **1** wanting to sleep; not feeling awake: *The wine had made her rather dozy.* **2** (*Brit informal*) stupid; not intelligent: *You dozy thing – look what you've done!*

Dr *abbr* doctor: *Dr Timothy Woodhouse*

drab /dræb/ *adj* not interesting or attractive: *a drab grey office building*

draft¹ /drɑːft/ *noun* [C] **1** a piece of writing, etc which will probably be changed and improved; not the final version: *the first draft of a speech/essay* **2** a written order to a bank to pay money to sb: *Payment must be made by bank draft.* **3** (*US*) = **DRAUGHT**¹(1)

draft² /drɑːft/ *verb* [T] **1** to make a first or early copy of a piece of writing: *I'll draft a letter and show it to you before I type it. **2** (*US*) (usually passive) to force sb to join the armed forces: *He was drafted into the army.*

drafty (*US*) = **DRAUGHTY**

⋆**drag**[1] /dræg/ **verb** (**dragging**; **dragged**) **1** [T] to pull sb/sth along with difficulty: *The box was so heavy we had to drag it along the floor.* ⋅► picture at **pull 2** [T] to make sb come or go somewhere: *She's always trying to drag me along to museums and galleries, but I'm not interested.* **3** [I] **drag (on)** to be boring or to seem to last a long time: *The speeches dragged on for hours.* **4** [T] (*computing*) to move sth across the screen of the computer using the mouse: *Click on the file and drag it into the new folder.*

PHRASAL VERBS **drag sth out** to make sth last longer than necessary: *Let's not drag this decision out – shall we go or not?*

drag sth out (of sb) to force or persuade sb to give you information

drag[2] /dræg/ **noun 1** [sing] (*informal*) a person or thing that is boring or annoying: *'The car's broken down.' 'Oh no! What a drag!'* **2** [U] women's clothes worn by a man, especially as part of a show, etc: *men in drag* **3** [C] an act of breathing in cigarette smoke: *He took a long drag on his cigarette.*

dragon /'drægən/ **noun** [C] (in stories) an large animal with wings, which can breathe fire

⋆**drain**[1] /dreɪn/ **noun** [C] a pipe or hole in the ground for dirty water, etc goes down to be carried away ⋅► picture on page C7

IDIOMS **a drain on sb/sth** something that uses up time, money, strength, etc: *The cost of travelling is a great drain on our budget.*

(go) down the drain (*informal*) (to be) wasted: *All that hard work has gone down the drain.*

⋆**drain**[2] /dreɪn/ **verb 1** [I,T] to become empty or dry as liquid flows away and disappears; to make sth dry or empty in this way: *The whole area will have to be drained before it can be used for farming.* ● *Drain the pasta and add the sauce.* **2** [I,T] **drain (from/out of sth)**; **drain sth (away/off)** to flow away; to make a liquid flow away: *The sink's blocked – the water won't drain away at all.* ● *The plumber had to drain the water from the heating system.* ● (*figurative*) *He felt all his anger begin to drain away.* **3** [T] to drink all the liquid in a glass, cup, etc: *He drained his glass in one gulp.* **4** [T] **drain sb/sth (of sth)** to make sb/sth weaker, poorer, etc by slowly using all the strength, money, etc available: *My mother's hospital expenses were slowly draining my funds.* ● *The experience left her emotionally drained.*

drainage /'dreɪnɪdʒ/ **noun** [U] a system used for making water, etc flow away from a place

'**draining board noun** [C] the place in the kitchen where you put plates, cups, knives, etc to dry after washing them ⋅► picture on page C7

drainpipe /'dreɪnpaɪp/ **noun** [C] a pipe which goes down the side of a building and carries

water from the roof into a hole in the ground (**drain**) ⋅► picture on page C7

drama /'drɑːmə/ **noun 1** [C] a play for the theatre, radio or television: *a contemporary drama* **2** [U] plays as a form of writing; the performance of plays: *He wrote some drama, as well as poetry.* **3** [C,U] an exciting event; exciting things that happen: *a real-life courtroom drama*

⋆**dramatic** /drə'mætɪk/ **adj 1** noticeable or sudden and often surprising: *a dramatic change/increase/fall/improvement* **2** exciting or impressive: *the film's dramatic opening scene* **3** connected with plays or the theatre: *Shakespeare's dramatic works* **4** (used about a person, a person's behaviour, etc) showing feelings, etc in a very obvious way because you want other people to notice you: *Calm down. There's no need to be so dramatic about everything!* –**dramatically** /-kli/ **adv**

dramatist /'dræmətɪst/ **noun** [C] a person who writes plays for the theatre, radio or television

dramatize (also **-ise**) /'dræmətaɪz/ **verb 1** [T] to make a book, an event, etc into a play: *The novel has been dramatized for television.* **2** [I,T] to make sth seem more exciting or important than it really is: *The newspaper was accused of dramatizing the situation.* –**dramatization** (also **-isation**) /ˌdræmətaɪ'zeɪʃn/ **noun** [C,U]

drank *past tense of* **DRINK**[1]

drape /dreɪp/ **verb** [T] **1 drape sth round/over sth** to put a piece of material, clothing, etc loosely on sth: *He draped his coat over the back of his chair.* **2 drape sb/sth (in/with sth)** (usually passive) to cover sb/sth (with cloth, etc): *The furniture was draped in dustsheets.* –**drape noun** [C] (*US*) = **CURTAIN**

drastic /'dræstɪk/ **adj** extreme, and having a sudden very strong effect: *There has been a drastic rise in crime in the area.* –**drastically** /-kli/ **adv**

draught[1] /drɑːft/ **noun 1** (*US* **draft**) [C] a flow of cold air that comes into a room: *Can you shut the door? There's a draught in here.* **2 draughts** (*US* **checkers**) [U] a game for two players that you play on a black and white board using round black and white pieces –**draughty adj**

draught[2] /drɑːft/ **adj** (used about beer, etc) served from a large container (**a barrel**) rather than in a bottle: *draught beer*

draughtsman (*US* **draftsman** /'drɑːftsmən/) **noun** [C] (*pl* **-men** /-mən/) a person whose job is to do technical drawings

⋆**draw**[1] /drɔː/ **verb** (*pt* **drew** /druː/; *pp* **drawn** /drɔːn/) **1** [I,T] to do a picture or diagram of sth with a pencil, pen, etc but not paint: *Shall I draw you a map of how to get there?* ● *I'm good at painting but I can't draw.* **2** [I] to move in the direction mentioned: *The train drew into the station* ● *I became more anxious as my exams drew nearer.* **3** [T] **draw sth out of/from sth** to pull sth/sb into a new position or in the direction mentioned: *She drew the letter out of her pocket and handed it to me.*

[I] **intransitive**, a verb which has no object: *He laughed.*   [T] **transitive**, a verb which has an object: *He ate an apple.*

• to draw (= open or close) the curtains • He drew me by the hand into the room. **4** [T] draw sth (from sth) to learn or decide sth as a result of study, research or experience: Can we **draw** any **conclusions** from this survey? • There are important **lessons to be drawn** from this tragedy. **5** [T] draw sth (from sb/sth) to get or take sth from sb/sth: He draws the inspiration for his stories from his family. **6** [T] draw sth (from sb); draw sb (to sb/sth) to make sb react to or be interested in sb/sth: The advertisement has drawn criticism from people all over the country. • The musicians drew quite a large crowd. **7** [I,T] to finish a game, competition, etc with equal scores so that neither person or team wins: The two teams drew. • The match was drawn.

IDIOMS **bring sth/come/draw to an end** → END¹

draw (sb's) attention to sth to make sb notice sth: The article draws attention to the problem of homelessness.

draw a blank to get no result or response: Detectives investigating the case have drawn a blank so far.

draw a distinction between sth and sth to show how two things are different

draw the line at sth to say 'no' to sth even though you are happy to help in other ways: I do most of the cooking but I draw the line at washing up as well!

draw lots to decide sth by chance: They drew lots to see who should stay behind.

PHRASAL VERBS **draw in** to get dark earlier as winter arrives: The days/nights are drawing in.

draw out (used about days) to get longer in the spring

draw sth out to take money out of a bank account: How much money do I need to draw out?

draw up (used about a car, etc) to drive up and stop in front of or near sth: A police car drew up outside the building.

draw sth up to prepare and write a document, list, etc: Our solicitor is going to draw up the contract.

draw² /drɔː/ noun [C] **1** a result of a game or competition in which both players or teams get the same score so that neither of them wins: The match **ended in a draw**. **2** an act of deciding sth by chance by pulling out names or numbers from a bag, etc: She won her bike in a prize draw.

drawback /'drɔːbæk/ noun [C] a disadvantage or problem: His lack of experience is a major drawback.

★**drawer** /drɔː/ noun [C] a container which forms part of a piece of furniture such as a desk, that you can pull out to put things in: There's some paper in the top drawer of my desk.

★**drawing** /'drɔːɪŋ/ noun **1** [C] a picture made with a pencil, pen, etc but not paint ••➤ Look at the note at **painting**. **2** [U] the art of drawing pictures: She's good at drawing and painting.

'**drawing pin** (US **thumbtack**) noun [C] a short pin with a flat top, used for fastening paper, etc to a board or wall ••➤ picture at **pin** and on page S6

'**drawing room** noun [C] (old-fashioned) a living room, especially in a large house

drawl /drɔːl/ verb [I,T] to speak slowly, making the vowel sounds very long –**drawl** noun [sing]: to speak with a drawl

drawn¹ past participle of DRAW¹

drawn² /drɔːn/ adj (used about a person or his/her face) looking tired, worried or ill: She looked pale and drawn after the long journey.

,**drawn-'out** adj lasting longer than necessary: long drawn-out negotiations

dread¹ /dred/ verb [T] to be very afraid of or worried about sth: I'm dreading the exams. • She dreaded having to tell him what had happened. • I **dread to think** what my father will say. –**dreaded** adj

dread² /dred/ noun [U,sing] great fear: He lived **in dread of** the same thing happening to him one day.

dreadful /'dredfl/ adj very bad or unpleasant: We had a dreadful journey – traffic jams all the way! • I'm afraid there's been a dreadful (= very serious) mistake.

dreadfully /'dredfəli/ adv **1** very; extremely: I'm dreadfully sorry, I didn't mean to upset you. **2** very badly: The party went dreadfully and everyone left early.

dreadlocks /'dredlɒks/ noun [pl] hair worn in long thick pieces, especially by some black people ••➤ picture at **hair**

★**dream¹** /driːm/ noun **1** [C] a series of events or pictures which happen in your mind while you are asleep: I **had** a strange **dream** last night. • That horror film has given me **bad dreams**. ••➤ Look at **nightmare**. **2** [C] something that you want very much to happen, although it is not likely: His dream was to give up his job and live in the country. • My dream house would have a huge garden and a swimming pool. • Becoming a professional dancer was **a dream come true** for Nicola. **3** [sing] a state of mind in which you are not thinking about what you are doing: You've been in a dream all morning!

★**dream²** /driːm/ verb (pt, pp **dreamed** /driːmd/ or **dreamt** /dremt/) **1** [I,T] dream (about sb/sth) to see or experience pictures and events in your mind while you are asleep: I dreamt about the house that I lived in as a child. • I dreamed that I was running but I couldn't get away. ••➤ Look at **daydream**. **2** [I] dream (about/of sth/doing sth) to imagine sth that you would like to happen: I've always dreamt about winning lots of money. **3** [I] dream (of doing sth/that...) to imagine that sth might happen: I **wouldn't dream of** telling Stuart that I don't like his music. • When I watched the Olympics on TV, I never dreamt that one day I'd be here competing!

PHRASAL VERB **dream sth up** (informal) to think of a plan, an idea, etc, especially sth strange: Which of you dreamt up that idea?

dreamer /'dri:mə/ noun [C] a person who thinks a lot about ideas, plans, etc which may never happen instead of thinking about real life

dreamy /'dri:mi/ adj looking as though you are not paying attention to what you are doing because you are thinking about sth else: *a dreamy look/expression* –**dreamily** adv

dreary /'drɪəri/ adj (**drearier**; **dreariest**) not at all interesting or attractive; boring: *His dreary voice sends me to sleep.*

dredge /dredʒ/ verb [T] to clear the mud, etc from the bottom of a river, canal, etc using a special machine

PHRASAL VERB **dredge sth up** to mention sth unpleasant from the past that sb would like to forget: *The newspaper had dredged up all sorts of embarrassing details about her private life.*

dregs /dregz/ noun [pl] **1** the last drops in a container of liquid, containing small pieces of solid waste **2** the worst and most useless part of sth: *These people were regarded as the dregs of society.*

drench /drentʃ/ verb [T] (usually passive) to make sb/sth completely wet: *Don't go out while it's raining so hard or you'll get drenched.*

★**dress¹** /dres/ noun **1** [C] a piece of clothing worn by a girl or a woman. It covers the body from the shoulders to the knees or below. •➤ picture on page C6 **2** [U] clothes for either men or women: *formal/casual dress* ● *He was wearing Bulgarian national dress.*

★**dress²** /dres/ verb **1** [I,T] to put clothes on sb or yourself: *He dressed quickly and left the house.* ● *My husband dressed the children while I got breakfast ready.* ● *Hurry up, Simon! Aren't you dressed yet?* •➤ opposite **undress.** •➤ It is more common to say **get dressed** than **dress. 2** [I] to put or have clothes on, in the way or style mentioned: *to dress well/badly/casually* ● *to be well dressed/badly/casually dressed* **3** [T] to put a clean covering on the place on sb's body where he/she has been hurt: *to dress a wound*

IDIOM **(be) dressed in sth** wearing sth: *The people at the funeral were all dressed in black.*

PHRASAL VERB **dress up 1** to put on special clothes, especially in order to look like sb/sth else: *The children decided to dress up as pirates.* **2** to put on formal clothes, usually for a special occasion: *You don't need to dress up for the party.*

dresser /'dresə/ noun [C] (*especially Brit*) a piece of furniture with cupboards at the bottom and shelves above. It is used for holding dishes, cups, etc •➤ picture on page C7

dressing /'dresɪŋ/ noun **1** [C] a covering that you put on a part of sb's body that has been hurt to protect it and keep it clean **2** [C,U] a sauce for food, especially for salads

'dressing gown (also **bathrobe** *US* **robe**) noun [C] a piece of clothing like a loose coat with a belt, which you wear before or after a bath, before you get dressed in the morning, etc

'dressing table noun [C] a piece of furniture in a bedroom, which has drawers and a mirror •➤ picture on page C7

drew *past tense* of **DRAW¹**

dribble /'drɪbl/ verb **1** [I,T] (used about a liquid) to move downwards in a thin flow; to make a liquid move in this way: *The paint dribbled down the side of the pot.* **2** [I] to allow liquid (saliva) to run out of the mouth: *Small children often dribble.* **3** [I] (used in ball games) to make a ball move forward by using many short kicks or hits: *Ronaldo dribbled round the goalkeeper and scored.*

dried¹ *past tense, past participle* of **DRY²**

dried² /draɪd/ adj (used about food) with all the liquid removed from it: *dried milk* ● *dried fruit*

drier¹ adj → **DRY¹**

drier² (also **dryer**) /'draɪə/ noun [C] a machine that you use for drying sth: *a hairdrier*

drift¹ /drɪft/ verb [I] **1** to be carried or moved along by wind or water: *The boat drifted out to sea.* **2** to move slowly or without any particular purpose: *He drifted from room to room.* ● *She drifted into acting almost by accident.* **3** (used about snow or sand) to be moved into piles by wind or water: *The snow drifted up to two metres deep in some places.*

PHRASAL VERB **drift apart** to slowly become less close or friendly with sb

drift² /drɪft/ noun **1** [C] a slow movement towards sth: *the country's drift into economic decline* **2** [sing] the general meaning of sth: *I don't understand all the details of the plan but I get the drift.* **3** [C] a pile of snow or sand that was made by wind or water

drill¹ /drɪl/ noun **1** [C] a tool or machine that is used for making holes in things: *a dentist's drill* •➤ picture at **tool 2** [U] exercise in marching, etc that soldiers do **3** [C] something that you repeat many times in order to learn sth **4** [C,U] practice for what you should do in an emergency: *a fire drill*

drill² /drɪl/ verb [I,T] **1** to make a hole in sth with a drill: *to drill a hole in sth* ● *to drill for oil* **2** to teach sb by making him/her repeat sth many times

drily (also **dryly**) /'draɪli/ adv (used about the way sb says sth) in an amusing way that sounds serious: *'I can hardly contain my excitement,' Peter said drily* (= he was not excited at all).

★**drink¹** /drɪŋk/ verb (*pt* **drank** /dræŋk/; *pp* **drunk** /drʌŋk/) **1** [I,T] to take liquid into your body through your mouth: *Would you like anything to drink?* ● *We sat drinking coffee and chatting for hours.* **2** [I,T] to drink alcohol: *I never drink and drive so I'll have an orange juice.* ● *What do you drink – beer or wine?* ● *Her father used to drink heavily but he's teetotal now.*

PHRASAL VERBS **drink to sb/sth** to wish sb/sth good luck by holding your glass up in the air before you drink: *We all drank to the future of* *the bride and groom.* ••► Look at **toast**².

drink (sth) up to finish drinking sth: *Drink up your tea – it's getting cold.*

★**drink**² /drɪŋk/ **noun** [C,U] **1** liquid for drinking: *Can I **have a drink** please?* • *a drink of milk* • *soft drinks* (= cold drinks without alcohol) **2** alcoholic drink: *He's got a drink problem.* • *Shall we **go for a drink**?*

,**drink-'driver** (also ,**drunk-'driver**) **noun** [C] a person who drives after drinking too much alcohol –**drink-driving noun** [U]: *He was convicted of drink-driving and was banned for two years.*

drinker /'drɪŋkə/ **noun** [C] a person who drinks a lot of sth, especially alcohol: *a heavy drinker* • *I'm not a big coffee drinker.*

drinking /'drɪŋkɪŋ/ **noun** [U] drinking alcohol: *Her drinking became a problem.*

'**drinking water noun** [U] water that is safe to drink

drip¹ /drɪp/ **verb** (**dripping**; **dripped**) **1** [I] (used about a liquid) to fall in small drops: *Water was dripping down through the roof.* **2** [I,T] to produce drops of liquid: *The tap is dripping.* • *Her finger was dripping blood.*

drip² /drɪp/ **noun 1** [sing] the act or sound of water dripping **2** [C] a drop of water that falls down from sb/sth: *We put a bucket under the hole in the roof to catch the drips.* ••► picture at **blob 3** [C] a piece of medical equipment, like a tube, that is used for putting liquid food or medicine straight into a person's blood: *She's on a drip.*

★**drive**¹ /draɪv/ **verb** (*pt* **drove** /drəʊv/; *pp* **driven** /'drɪvn/) **1** [I,T] to control or operate a car, train, bus, etc: *Can you drive?* • *to drive a car/train/bus/lorry* **2** [I,T] to go or take sb somewhere in a car, etc: *I usually drive to work.* • *We drove Aisha to the airport.* **3** [T] to force people or animals to move in a particular direction: *The dogs drove the sheep into the field.* **4** [T] to force sth into a particular position by hitting it: *to drive a post into the ground* **5** [T] to cause sb to be in a particular state or to do sth: *His constant stupid questions drive me mad.* • *to drive sb to despair* **6** [T] to make sb/sth work very hard: *You shouldn't drive yourself so hard.* **7** [T] to make a machine work, by giving it power: *What drives the wheels in this engine?*

IDIOMS **be driving at** (*informal*) to want to say sth; to mean: *I'm afraid I don't understand what you are driving at.*

drive sth home (to sb) to make sth clear so that people understand it

PHRASAL VERBS **drive off** (used about a car, driver, etc) to leave

drive sb/sth off to make sb/sth go away: *They kept a large dog outside to drive off burglars.*

★**drive**² /draɪv/ **noun 1** [C] a journey in a car: *The supermarket is only a five-minute drive away.* • *Let's go for a drive.* **2** [C] a wide path or short road that leads to the door of a house: *We keep our car on the drive.* ••► picture on page C7 **3** [C] a street, usually where people live: *They live at 23 Woodlands Drive.* **4** [C] a big effort by a group of people in order to achieve sth: *The company is launching (big sales drive.* **5** [U] the energy and determination you need to succeed in doing sth You need lots of drive to run your own com pany.* **6** [C,U] a strong natural need or desire *a strong sex drive* **7** [C] (in sport) a long har• hit: *This player has the longest drive in golf* **8** [C] (*computing*) the part of a computer tha reads and stores information: *a 224 MB har• drive* • *a CD drive* ••► Look at **disk drive 9** [U] the equipment in a vehicle that take• power from the engine to the wheels: *a ca• with four-wheel drive*

'**drive-by adj** (*US*) (only *before* a noun) (used about a shooting) done from a moving car *drive-by killings*

'**drive-in noun** [C] (*US*) a place where you car eat, watch a film, etc in your car

driven *past participle* of **DRIVE**¹

★**driver** /'draɪvə/ **noun** [C] a person who drives a vehicle: *a bus/train driver*

'**drive-through noun** [C] (*especially US*) a• restaurant, bank, etc where you can be served without getting out of your car

★**driving**¹ /'draɪvɪŋ/ **noun** [U] the action or skill of controlling a car, etc: *She was arrested for dangerous driving.* • *Joe's having driving lessons.* • *She works as a driving instructor.* • *a driving school* • *Did you pass your driving test first time?* • *How long have you had a driving licence* (= an official piece of paper that says you are allowed to drive a car, etc)?

driving² /'draɪvɪŋ/ **adj** very strong: *driving rain* • *driving ambition* • *Who's the driving force behind this plan?*

drizzle /'drɪzl/ **noun** [U] light rain with very small drops –**drizzle verb** [I] ••► Look at the note at **weather**.

drone /drəʊn/ **verb** [I] to make a continuous low sound: *the sound of the tractors droning away in the fields*

PHRASAL VERB **drone on** to talk in a flat or boring voice: *We had to listen to the chairman drone on about sales for hours.* –**drone noun** [sing]

drool /druːl/ **verb** [I] **1** to let liquid (saliva) come out from the mouth, usually at the sight or smell of sth good to eat **2 drool (over sb/sth)** to show in a silly or exaggerated way that you want or admire sb/sth very much: *teenagers drooling over photographs of their favourite pop stars*

droop /druːp/ **verb** [I] to bend or hang downwards, especially because of weakness or because you are tired: *The flowers were drooping without water.* –**drooping adj**: *a drooping moustache*

★**drop**¹ /drɒp/ **verb** (**dropping**; **dropped**) **1** [T] to let sth fall: *That vase was very expensive. Whatever you do, don't drop it!* **2** [I] to fall: *The parachutist dropped safely to the ground.* • *At the end of the race she dropped to her knees exhausted.* **3** [I,T] to become lower; to make sth lower: *The temperature will drop to minus 3 overnight.* • *They ought to drop*

drop

their prices. ● to drop your voice (= speak more quietly) **4** [T] drop sb/sth (off) to stop your car, etc so that sb can get out, or in order to take sth out: *Drop me off at the traffic lights, please.* ● *I'll drop the parcel at your house.* **5** [T] drop sb/sth (from sth) to no longer include sb/sth in sth: *Joe has been dropped from the team.* **6** [T] to stop doing sth: *I'm going to drop geography next term* (= stop studying it).

IDIOMS drop dead (*informal*) to die suddenly drop sb a line (*informal*) to write a letter to sb: *Do drop me a line when you've time.*

PHRASAL VERBS drop back; drop behind (sb) to move into a position behind sb else, because you are moving more slowly: *Towards the end of the race she dropped behind the other runners.*

drop by; drop in (on sb) to go to sb's house on an informal visit or without having told him/her you were coming: *We were in the area so we thought we'd drop in and see you.*

drop off (*informal*) to fall into a light sleep: *I dropped off in front of the television.*

drop out (of sth) to leave or stop doing sth before you have finished: *His injury forced him to drop out of the competition.*

★**drop²** /drɒp/ **noun 1** [C] a very small amount of liquid that forms a round shape: *a drop of blood/rain* •➤ picture at **blob 2** [C, usually sing] a small amount of liquid: *I just have a drop of milk in my coffee.* **3** [sing] a fall to a smaller amount or level: *The job is much more interesting but it will mean a drop in salary.* ● *a drop in prices/temperature* **4** [sing] a distance down from a high point to a lower point: *a sheer drop of 40 metres to the sea* **5 drops** [pl] liquid medicine that you put into your eyes, ears or nose: *The doctor prescribed me drops to take twice a day.*

IDIOMS a drop in the ocean; (*US*) a drop in the bucket an amount of sth that is too small or unimportant to make any real difference to a situation: *The money we made was a drop in the ocean compared to the amount we need.*

at the drop of a hat immediately; without having to stop and think about it

'**drop-dead** adv (*informal*) used before an adjective to emphasize how attractive sb/sth is: *She's drop-dead gorgeous.*

'**drop-out** noun [C] **1** a person who leaves school, university, etc before finishing his/ her studies **2** a person who does not accept the ideas and ways of behaving of the rest of society

droppings /'drɒpɪŋz/ noun [pl] waste material from the bodies of small animals or birds

drought /draʊt/ noun [C,U] a long period without rain: *Drought has affected many countries in Africa.*

drove *past tense* of **DRIVE¹**

★**drown** /draʊn/ **verb 1** [I,T] to die in water because it is not possible to breathe; to make sb die in this way: *The girl fell into the river and drowned.* ● *Twenty people were drowned in the floods.* **2** [T] drown sb/sth (out) (used about a sound) to be so loud that you cannot hear sb/sth else: *His answer was drowned out by the music.*

drowsy /'draʊzi/ adj not completely awake; sleepy: *The heat made me feel drowsy.* –**drowsily** adv –**drowsiness** noun [U]

drudgery /'drʌdʒəri/ noun [U] hard and boring work

★**drug¹** /drʌg/ noun [C] **1** a chemical which people use to give them pleasant or exciting feelings. It is illegal in many countries to use drugs: *He doesn't drink or take drugs.* ● *She suspected her son was on drugs.* ● *hard drugs such as heroin and cocaine* ● *soft drugs* **2** a chemical which is used as a medicine: *drug companies* ● *Some drugs can only be obtained with a prescription from a doctor.*

drug² /drʌg/ verb [T] (**drugging**; **drugged**) **1** to give a person or animal a chemical to make him/her/it fall asleep or unconscious: *The lion was drugged before the start of the journey.* **2** to put a drug into food or drink: *I think his drink was drugged.*

'**drug addict** noun [C] a person who cannot stop taking drugs –**drug addiction** noun [U]

druggist /'drʌgɪst/ (*US*) = **CHEMIST**(2)

drugstore /'drʌgstɔː/ (*US*) = **CHEMIST**(2)

★**drum¹** /drʌm/ noun [C] **1** a musical instrument like an empty container with plastic or skin stretched across the ends. You play a drum by hitting it with your hands or with sticks: *She plays the drums in a band.* •➤ Look at the note at **piano**. •➤ picture at **music 2** a round container: *an oil drum*

drum² /drʌm/ verb (**drumming**; **drummed**) **1** [I] to play a drum **2** [I,T] to make a noise like a drum by hitting sth many times: *to drum your fingers on the table* (= because you are annoyed, impatient, etc)

PHRASAL VERBS drum sth into sb to make sb remember sth by repeating it many times: *Road safety should be drummed into children from an early age.*

drum sth up to try to get support or business: *to drum up more custom*

drummer /'drʌmə/ noun [C] a person who plays a drum or drums

drumstick /'drʌmstɪk/ noun [C] **1** a stick used for playing the drums **2** the lower leg of a chicken or similar bird that we cook and eat

★**drunk¹** /drʌŋk/ adj (not before a noun) having drunk too much alcohol: *to get drunk* –**drunk** (also *old-fashioned* **drunkard**) **noun** [C]: *There were two drunks asleep under the bridge.*

drunk² *past participle* of **DRINK¹**

drunken /'drʌŋkən/ adj (only *before* a noun) **1** having drunk too much alcohol: *drunken drivers* **2** showing the effects of too much

alcohol: *drunken singing* –**drunkenly** adv
–**drunkenness** noun [U]

★**dry¹** /draɪ/ adj (**drier**; **driest**) **1** without
liquid in it or on it; not wet: *The washing
isn't dry yet.* ● *The paint is dry now.* ● *Rub
your hair dry with a towel.* **2** having little or
no rain: *a hot, dry summer* ● *a dry climate*
••➔ opposite for senses 1 and 2 **wet 3** (used
about hair or skin) not having enough natural oil **4** (used about wine) not sweet **5** (used
about what sb says, or sb's way of speaking)
amusing, although it sounds serious: *a dry
sense of humour* **6** boring: *dry legal documents* **7** without alcohol; where no alcohol is
allowed: *Saudi Arabia is a dry country.*
–**dryness** noun [U]
> IDIOM be left high and dry → **HIGH¹**

★**dry²** /draɪ/ verb [I,T] (*pres part* **drying**; *3rd
pers sing pres* **dries**; *pt, pp* **dried**) to become
dry; to make sth dry: *I hung my shirt in the
sun to dry.* ● *to dry your hands on a towel*
> PHRASAL VERBS **dry (sth) out** to become or
make sth become completely dry: *Don't allow
the soil to dry out.*
dry up 1 (used about a river, etc) to have no
more water in it **2** to stop being available:
*Because of the recession a lot of building work
has dried up.* **3** to forget what you were going
to say, for example because you are very
nervous: *When he came on stage and saw the
audience, he dried up completely.*
dry (sth) up to dry plates, knives, forks, etc
with a towel after they have been washed

dry-ˈclean verb [T] to clean clothes using
special chemicals, without using water

dry-ˈcleaner's (also **cleaner's**) noun [C]
the shop where you take your clothes to be
cleaned

dry ˈland noun [U] land, not the sea: *I was
glad to be back on dry land again.*

DTP /ˌdiːtiːˈpiː/ abbr desktop publishing

dual /ˈdjuːəl/ adj (only *before* a noun) having
two parts; double: *to have dual nationality*

dual ˈcarriageway (*US* **divided highway**) noun [C] a wide road that has an area of
grass or a fence in the middle to separate the
traffic going in one direction from the traffic
going in the other direction

dub /dʌb/ verb [T] (**dubbing**; **dubbed**) **1** to
give sb/sth a new or amusing name (a **nickname**): *Bill Clinton was dubbed 'Slick Willy'.*
2 dub sth (into sth) to change the sound in a
film so that what the actors said originally is
spoken by actors using a different language: *I
don't like foreign films when they're dubbed
into English. I prefer subtitles.* **3** to make a
piece of music by mixing different pieces of
recorded music together

dubious /ˈdjuːbiəs/ adj **1 dubious (about
sth/about doing sth)** not sure or certain: *I'm
very dubious about whether we're doing the
right thing.* **2** that may not be honest or safe:
dubious financial dealings –**dubiously** adv

duchess /ˈdʌtʃəs/ noun [C] a woman who
has the same position as a duke, or who is
the wife of a duke

duck
goose
swan

★**duck¹** /dʌk/ noun (*pl* **duck** or **ducks**) **1** [C] a
common bird that lives on or near water.
Ducks have short legs, special (**webbed**) feet
for swimming and a wide beak. **2** [C] a female
duck
> ➤ A male duck is called a **drake** and a
young duck is a **duckling**. The sound a
duck makes is a **quack**.
3 [U] the meat of a duck: *roast duck with
orange sauce*

duck² /dʌk/ verb **1** [I,T] to move your head
down quickly so that you are not seen or hit
by sb/sth: *The boys ducked out of sight behind
a hedge.* ● *I had to duck my head down to
avoid the low doorway.* **2** [I,T] (*informal*)
duck (out of) sth to try to avoid sth difficult
or unpleasant: *She tried to duck out of apologizing.* ● *The President is trying to duck
responsibility for the crisis.* **3** [T] to push sb's
head under water for a short time, especially
when playing: *The kids were ducking each
other in the pool.*

duct /dʌkt/ noun [C] a tube that carries
liquid, gas, etc: *They got into the building
through the air duct.* ● *tear ducts* (= in the
eye)

dud /dʌd/ noun [C] (*informal*) a thing that
cannot be used because it is not real or does
not work properly: *a dud cheque/coin/fire-
work*

dude /duːd/ noun [C] (*especially US slang*) a
man

★**due¹** /djuː/ adj **1** (not *before* a noun) expected
or planned to happen or arrive: *The conference is due to start in four weeks' time.* ● *What
time is the next train due (in)?* ● *The baby is
due in May.* **2** (not *before* a noun) having to
be paid: *The rent is due on the fifteenth of each
month.* **3 due (to sb)** that is owed to you
because it is your right to have it: *Make sure
you claim all the benefits that are due to you.*
4 due to sb/sth caused by or because of sb/
sth: *His illness is probably due to stress.* **5 due
for sth** expecting sth or having the right to
sth: *I think that I'm due for a pay rise.*
> IDIOM **in due course** at some time in the
future, quite soon: *All applicants will be
informed of our decision in due course.*

due² /djuː/ adv (used before 'north', 'south',
'east' and 'west') exactly: *The aeroplane was
flying due east.*

[C] **countable**, a noun with a plural form: *one book, two books*   [U] **uncountable**, a noun with no plural form: *some sugar*

Animals

Animals

muzzle
ear
fur
tail
whiskers
fangs
paw
claw
pad
hind or back legs
front legs
antlers
horn
hoof
toes
tusk
trunk

Birds

crest
beak
wing
chick
shell
breast
bill
tail
feather
leg
claw
nest
egg
webbed foot

Fish

tail
fin
scales
gills

Insects

antennae
wing
leg
egg
grub

Plants

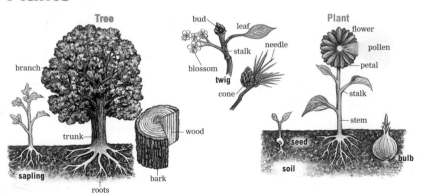

- tree
  - branch
  - trunk
  - wood
  - sapling
  - roots
  - bark
- bud
- leaf
- blossom
- stalk
- twig
- needle
- cone
- flower
- pollen
- petal
- stalk
- stem
- seed
- soil
- bulb

Types of plants and flower

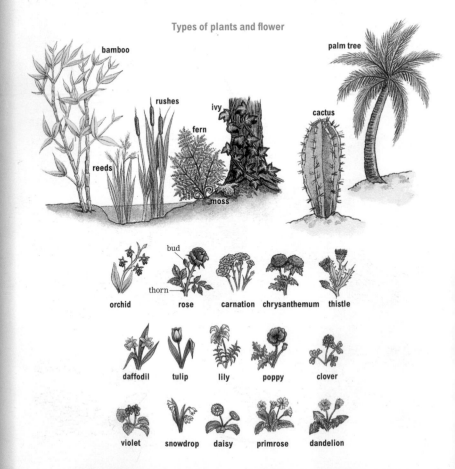

- bamboo
- reeds
- rushes
- fern
- ivy
- moss
- cactus
- palm tree

- orchid
- bud
- thorn
- rose
- carnation
- chrysanthemum
- thistle

- daffodil
- tulip
- lily
- poppy
- clover

- violet
- snowdrop
- daisy
- primrose
- dandelion

Fruit and Vegetables

stalk
apple
pear
skin
banana

orange
lemon
grapefruit
pip
peel
lime
segment

apricot
peach
plum
cherry

papaya/pawpaw
mango
avocado
stone
white grapes
pip
gooseberry
raspberry
blackberry
shell
fig
kiwi fruit
black grapes
date
olive
coconut
pineapple
watermelon
melon
seed

garlic
leek
spring onion
onion
carrot
parsnip
beetroot (US beet)
turnip
radish
swede
peel
potato

pumpkin
aubergine
(esp US eggplant)
marrow
courgette
(esp US zucchini)
tomato
cucumber
chilli pepper
green pepper
red pepper
broccoli
stalk
artichoke
mushroom
cauliflower

asparagus
spinach
leaf
celery
lettuce
Brussels sprout
cabbage
green beans
beans
pod
pea
sweet corn (US corn)

Food and Drink

crust
loaf of bread
flour
slice
honey   jam   marmalade   yoghurt
butter
cereal   margarine

soup   omelette   eggs   quiche   rice   salad   sauce   spaghetti/pasta

ketchup   mustard
hamburger/burger   hot dog   sandwiches   chips (US French fries)   crisps (US potato chips)   pizza   slice

kebabs   chicken   steak   chops   fish   sausages

Desserts

tart
gateau
pie   custard   cream   sauce   pancakes   wafer   ice cream   cheese   biscuits   cheese and biscuits

Drinks

teapot
teabag
sugar lump
fresh coffee
sugar   coffee pot   instant coffee   sparkling   still   mineral water   soft drinks   straw   fruit juice   fizzy drink (US soda)   milkshake

due³ /djuː/ **noun**

> IDIOM **give sb his/her due** to be fair to a person: *She doesn't work very quickly, but to give Sarah her due, she is very accurate.*

duel /'djuːəl/ **noun** [C] a formal type of fight with guns or other weapons which was used in the past to decide an argument between two men

duet /dju'et/ (also **duo**) **noun** [C] a piece of music for two people to sing or play •➤ Look at **solo**.

duffel coat (also **duffle coat**) /'dʌflkəʊt/ **noun** [C] a coat made of heavy woollen cloth with a covering for the head (a **hood**). A duffle coat has special long buttons (**toggles**).

dug *past tense, past participle of* **DIG¹**

duke /djuːk/ (also **Duke**) **noun** [C] a man of the highest social position •➤ Look at **duchess**.

★**dull** /dʌl/ **adj 1** not interesting or exciting; boring: *Miss Potter's lessons are always so dull.* **2** not bright: *a dull and cloudy day* **3** not loud, sharp or strong: *Her head hit the floor with a dull thud.* • *a dull pain* •➤ opposite **sharp** –**dullness noun** [U] –**dully adv**

duly /'djuːli/ **adv** (*formal*) in the correct or expected way: *We all duly assembled at 7.30 as agreed.*

dumb /dʌm/ **adj 1** not able to speak: *to be deaf and dumb* • (*figurative*) *They were struck dumb with amazement.* **2** (*informal*) stupid: *What a dumb thing to do!* –**dumbly adv**: *Ken did all the talking, and I just nodded dumbly.*

dumbfounded /dʌm'faʊndɪd/ **adj** very surprised

dummy

dummy /'dʌmi/ **noun** [C] (*pl* **dummies**) **1** a model of the human body used for putting clothes on in a shop window or while you are making clothes: *a tailor's dummy* **2** (*informal*) a stupid person: *Don't just stand there like a dummy – help me!* **3** (*US* **pacifier**) a rubber object that you put in a baby's mouth to keep him/her quiet and happy **4** something that is made to look like sth else but that is not the real thing: *The robbers used dummy handguns in the raid.*

dump¹ /dʌmp/ **verb** [T] **1** to get rid of sth that you do not want, especially in a place which is not suitable: *Nuclear waste should not be dumped in the sea.* • (*figurative*) *I wish you wouldn't keep dumping the extra work on me.* **2** to put something down quickly or in a careless way: *The children dumped their coats and bags in the hall and ran off to play.* **3** (*informal*) to get rid of sb, especially a boyfriend or girlfriend: *Did you hear that Laura dumped Chris last night?*

dump² /dʌmp/ **noun** [C] **1** a place where rubbish or waste material from factories, etc is left: *a rubbish dump* **2** (*informal*) a place that

is very dirty, untidy or unpleasant: *The flat is cheap but it's a real dump.* •➤ synonym **tip**

> IDIOM **down in the dumps** unhappy or sad

dumpling /'dʌmplɪŋ/ **noun** [C] a small ball of flour and fat (**dough**) that is cooked and usually eaten with meat

dune /djuːn/ (also **sand dune**) **noun** [C] a low hill of sand by the sea or in the desert

dung /dʌŋ/ **noun** [U] waste material from the bodies of large animals: *cow dung*

dungarees /ˌdʌŋɡə'riːz/ (*US* **overalls**) **noun** [pl] a piece of clothing, similar to trousers, but covering your chest as well as your legs and with straps that go over the shoulders: *a pair of dungarees* •➤ picture on page C6

dungeon /'dʌndʒən/ **noun** [C] an old underground prison, especially in a castle

duo /'djuːəʊ/ **noun** [C] **1** two people playing music or singing together **2** =**DUET**

dupe /djuːp/ **verb** [T] to lie to sb in order to make him/her believe sth or do sth: *The woman was duped into carrying the drugs.*

duplicate¹ /'djuːplɪkeɪt/ **verb** [T] **1** to make an exact copy of sth **2** to do sth that has already been done: *We don't want to duplicate the work of other departments.* –**duplication** /ˌdjuːplɪ'keɪʃn/ **noun** [U]

duplicate² /'djuːplɪkət/ **noun** [C] something that is exactly the same as sth else –**duplicate adj** (only *before* a noun): *a duplicate key*

> IDIOM **in duplicate** with two copies (for example of an official piece of paper) that are exactly the same: *The contract must be in duplicate.*

durable /'djʊərəbl/ **adj** that can last a long time: *a durable fabric* –**durability** /ˌdjʊərə'bɪləti/ **noun** [U]

duration /dju'reɪʃn/ **noun** [U] the time that sth lasts: *Please remain seated for the duration of the flight.*

duress /dju'res/ **noun** [U] threats or force that are used to make sb do sth: *He signed the confession under duress.*

★**during** /'djʊərɪŋ/ **prep** within the period of time mentioned: *During the summer holidays we went swimming every day.* • *Grandpa was taken very ill during the night.*

> ➤ Notice that you use **during** to say when something happens and **for** to say how long something lasts: *I went shopping during my lunch break. I was out for about 25 minutes.*

dusk /dʌsk/ **noun** [U] the time in the evening when the sun has already gone down and it is nearly dark •➤ Look at **dawn** and **twilight**.

★**dust¹** /dʌst/ **noun** [U] very small pieces of dry dirt, sand, etc in the form of a powder: *a thick layer of dust* • *chalk/coal dust* • *The tractor came up the track in a cloud of dust.* • *a speck* (= small piece) *of dust* –**dusty adj**: *This shelf has got very dusty.*

★**dust²** /dʌst/ **verb** [I,T] to clean a room, furniture, etc by removing dust with a cloth: *Let me dust those shelves before you put the books on them.* •➤ Look at the note at **clean²**.

dustbin /'dʌstbɪn/ (*US* **garbage can;**

trash can) noun [C] a large container for rubbish that you keep outside your house ••➤ picture at **bin**

duster /'dʌstə/ noun [C] a soft dry cloth that you use for cleaning furniture, etc ••➤ picture at **bucket**

dustman /'dʌstmən/ noun [C] (pl -men /-mən/) a person whose job is to take away the rubbish that people put in large containers outside the house (**dustbins**)

dustpan /'dʌstpæn/ noun [C] a flat container with a handle into which you brush dirt from the floor: *Where do you keep your dustpan and brush?* ••➤ picture at **brush**

Dutch /dʌtʃ/ adj from the Netherlands ••➤ Look at the section on geographical names at the back of this dictionary.

dutiful /'djuːtɪfl/ adj happy to respect and obey sb: *a dutiful son*

★**duty** /'djuːti/ noun (pl **duties**) **1** [C,U] something that you have to do because people expect you to do it or because you think it is right: *A soldier must do his duty.* ● *a sense of moral duty* **2** [C,U] the tasks that you do when you are at work: *the duties of a policeman* ● *Which nurses are on night duty this week?* **3** [C] a tax that you pay, especially on goods that you bring into a country

IDIOM **on/off duty** (used about doctors, nurses, police officers, etc) to be working/not working: *The porter's on duty from 8 till 4.* ● *What time does she go off duty?*

,duty-'free adj, adv (used about goods) that you can bring into a country without paying tax: *an airport duty-free shop* ● *How much wine can you bring into Britain duty-free?* ••➤ Look at **tax-free**.

duvet /'duːveɪ/ noun [C] a thick cover filled with feathers or another soft material that you sleep under to keep warm in bed ••➤ Look at **eiderdown** and **quilt**. ••➤ picture at **bed**

dwarf¹ /dwɔːf/ noun [C] (pl **dwarfs** or **dwarves** /dwɔːvz/) **1** a person, animal or plant that is much smaller than the usual size **2** (in children's stories) a very small person

dwarf² /dwɔːf/ verb [T] (used about a large object) to make sth seem very small in comparison: *The skyscraper dwarfs all the other buildings around.*

dwell /dwel/ verb [I] (pt, pp **dwelt** /dwelt/ or **dwelled**) (old-fashioned, formal) to live or stay in a place

PHRASAL VERB **dwell on/upon sth** to think or talk a lot about sth that it would be better to forget: *I don't want to dwell on the past. Let's think about the future.*

dweller /'dwelə/ noun [C] (often in compounds) a person or animal that lives in the place mentioned: *city-dwellers*

dwelling /'dwelɪŋ/ noun [C] (formal) the place where a person lives; a house

dwindle /'dwɪndl/ verb [I] **dwindle (away)** to become smaller or weaker: *Their savings dwindled away to nothing.*

dye¹ /daɪ/ verb [T] (pres part **dyeing**; 3rd pers sing pres **dyes**; pt, pp **dyed**) to make sth a different colour: *Does she dye her hair?* ● *I'm going to dye this blouse black.*

dye² /daɪ/ noun [C,U] a substance that is used to change the colour of sth

dying present participle of **DIE**

dyke (also **dike**) /daɪk/ noun [C] **1** a long thick wall that is built to prevent the sea or a river from flooding low land **2** (especially Brit) a long narrow space dug in the ground and used for taking water away from land

dynamic /daɪ'næmɪk/ adj **1** (used about a person) full of energy and ideas; active **2** (used about a force or power) that causes movement –**dynamism** /'daɪnəmɪzəm/ noun [U]

dynamite /'daɪnəmaɪt/ noun [U] **1** a powerful explosive substance **2** a thing or person that causes great excitement, shock, etc: *His news was dynamite.*

dynamo /'daɪnəməʊ/ noun [C] (pl **dynamos**) a device that changes energy from the movement of sth such as wind or water into electricity

dynasty /'dɪnəsti/ noun [C] (pl **dynasties**) a series of rulers who are from the same family: *the Ming dynasty in China*

dysentery /'dɪsəntri/ noun [U] a serious disease which causes you to get rid of waste material from your body very often in liquid form (**to have diarrhoea**), and to lose blood

dyslexia /dɪs'leksiə/ noun [U] a difficulty that some people have with reading and spelling –**dyslexic** noun [C], adj

Ee

E, e¹ /iː/ noun [C] (pl **E's**; **e's**) the fifth letter of the English alphabet: *'Egg' begins with (an) 'E'.*

E² abbr east(ern): *E Asia*

ea abbr each

★**each** /iːtʃ/ determiner, pron every individual person or thing: *Each lesson lasts an hour.* ● *Each of the lessons lasts an hour.* ● *The lessons each last an hour.* ● *These T-shirts are £5 each.*

each other

He's looking at himself.

They're looking at **each other**.

★ **,each 'other** pron used for saying that A does the same thing to B as B does to A: *Emma and Dave love each other very much* (= Emma loves Dave and Dave loves Emma). • *We looked at each other.*

★ **eager** /'i:gə/ adj eager (to do sth); eager (for sth) full of desire or interest; keen: *We're all eager to start work on the new project.* • *eager for success* –**eagerly** adv –**eagerness** noun [U]

eagle /'i:gl/ noun [C] a very large bird that can see very well. It eats small birds and animals.

EAP /,i: eɪ 'pi:/ abbr English for Academic Purposes

★ **ear** /ɪə/ noun 1 [C] one of the two parts of the body of a person or animal that are used for hearing •➤ picture on pages C1 and C5 2 [sing] an ear (for sth) an ability to recognize and repeat sounds, especially in music or language: *Yuka has a good ear for languages.* 3 [C] the top part of a plant that produces grain: *an ear of corn*

IDIOMS **sb's ears are burning** used when a person thinks that other people are talking about him/her, especially in an unkind way

play (sth) by ear to play a piece of music that you have heard without using written notes: *She can read music, but she can also play by ear.*

go in one ear and out the other (used about information, etc) to be forgotten quickly: *Everything I tell him seems to go in one ear and out the other.*

play it by ear to decide what to do as things happen, instead of planning in advance: *We don't know what Alan's reaction will be, so we'll just have to play it by ear.*

prick up your ears → PRICK¹

earache /'ɪəreɪk/ noun [U] a pain in your ear: *I've got earache.* •➤ Look at the note at **ache**.

eardrum /'ɪədrʌm/ noun [C] a thin piece of skin inside the ear that is tightly stretched and that allows you to hear sound

earl /ɜːl/ noun [C] a British man of a high social position

'ear lobe noun [C] the round soft part at the bottom of your ear

★ **early** /'ɜːli/ adj, adv (earlier; earliest) 1 near the beginning of a period of time, a piece of work, a series, etc: *I have to get up early on weekday mornings.* • *I think John's in his early twenties.* • *The project is still in its early stages.* 2 before the usual or expected time: *She arrived five minutes early for her interview.*

IDIOMS **at the earliest** not before the date or time mentioned: *I can repair it by Friday at the earliest.*

it's early days (yet) used to say that it is too soon to know how a situation will develop

the early hours very early in the morning in the hours after midnight

an early/a late night → NIGHT

early on soon after the beginning: *He achieved fame early on in his career.*

an early riser a person who usually gets up early in the morning

earmark /'ɪəmɑːk/ verb [T] earmark sb/sth (for sth/sb) to choose sb/sth to do sth in the future: *Everybody says Elena has been earmarked as the next manager.*

★ **earn** /ɜːn/ verb [T] 1 to get money by working: *How much does a dentist earn?* • *I earn £20000 a year.* • *It's hard to earn a living as an artist.* 2 to win the right to sth, for example by working hard: *The team's victory today has earned them a place in the final.* 3 to get money as profit or interest on money you have in a bank, lent to sb, etc: *How much interest will my savings earn in this account?*

earnest /'ɜːnɪst/ adj serious or determined: *He's such an earnest young man – he never makes a joke.* • *They were having a very earnest discussion.* –**earnestly** adv

IDIOM **in earnest 1** serious and sincere about what you are going to do: *He was in earnest about wanting to leave university.* **2** happening more seriously or with more force than before: *After two weeks work began in earnest on the project.*

earnings /'ɜːnɪŋz/ noun [pl] the money that a person earns by working: *Average earnings have increased by 5%.*

earphones /'ɪəfəʊnz/ noun [pl] a piece of equipment that fits over or in the ears and is used for listening to music, the radio, etc

earring /'ɪərɪŋ/ noun [C] a piece of jewellery that is worn in or on the lower part of the ear: *Do these earrings clip on or are they for pierced ears?* •➤ picture at **jewellery**

earshot /'ɪəʃɒt/ noun [U]

IDIOM **(be) out of/within earshot** where a person cannot/can hear: *Wait until he's out of earshot before you say anything about him.*

the earth

northern hemisphere
Tropic of Cancer
axis
North Pole
Arctic Circle
line of longitude
Tropic of Capricorn
equator
South Pole
line of latitude
Antarctic Circle
southern hemisphere

★ **earth¹** /ɜːθ/ noun 1 (also **the earth**; **the Earth**) [sing] the world; the planet on which we live: *life on earth* • *The earth goes round the sun.* 2 [sing] the surface of the world; land: *The spaceship fell towards earth.* • *I could feel the earth shake when the earthquake started.* 3 [U] the substance that plants grow in; soil: *The earth around here is very fertile.* •➤ Look at the note at **ground**. **4** [C, usually sing] (*US* **ground**) a wire that makes a piece of electrical equipment safer by connecting it to the ground

IDIOMS **charge/pay the earth** (*informal*) to charge/pay a very large amount of money: *Dan must have paid the earth for that new car.*

cost the earth/a fortune → **COST²**

how/why/where/who etc on earth (*informal*) used for emphasizing sth or expressing surprise: *Where on earth have you been?*

earth² /ɜːθ/ (*US* **ground**) **verb** [T] to make a piece of electrical equipment safer by connecting it to the ground with a wire: *Make sure the plug is earthed.*

earthquake /ˈɜːθkweɪk/ (also *informal* **quake**) **noun** [C] violent movement of the earth's surface

earthworm /ˈɜːθwɜːm/ **noun** [C] a small, long, thin animal with no legs or eyes that lives in the soil

ease¹ /iːz/ **noun** [U] a lack of difficulty: *She answered the questions with ease.* •➤ adjective **easy** •➤ opposite **unease**

IDIOM **(be/feel) at (your) ease** to be/feel comfortable, relaxed, etc: *They were all so kind and friendly that I felt completely at ease.*

ease² /iːz/ **verb 1** [I,T] to become or make sth less painful or serious: *The pain should ease by this evening.* • *This money will ease their financial problems a little.* •➤ adjective **easy 2** [T] to move sth slowly and gently: *He eased the key into the lock.*

IDIOM **ease sb's mind** to make sb feel less worried: *The doctor tried to ease her mind about her son's illness.*

PHRASAL VERBS **ease off** to become less strong or unpleasant: *Let's wait until the rain eases off.*

ease up to work less hard: *Ease up a bit or you'll make yourself ill!*

easel /ˈiːzl/ **noun** [C] a wooden frame that holds a picture while it is being painted

easily /ˈiːzəli/ **adv 1** without difficulty: *I can easily ring up and check the time.* **2** easily the best, worst, nicest, etc without doubt: *It's easily his best novel.*

★ **east¹** /iːst/ **noun** [sing] (*abbr* **E**) **1** (also **the east**) the direction you look towards in order to see the sun rise; one of the four main directions that we give names to (**the points of the compass**): *Which way is east?* • *a cold wind from the east* • *Which county is to the east of Oxfordshire?* •➤ picture at **north 2 the east** the part of any country, city, etc that is further to the east than the other parts: *Norwich is in the east of England.* **3 the East** the countries of Asia, for example China and Japan •➤ Look at **the Far East** and **the Middle East**.

east² /iːst/ (also **East**) **adj, adv** in or towards the east or from the east: *They headed east.* • *the East Coast of America* • *We live east of the city.* • *an east wind*

eastbound /ˈiːstbaʊnd/ **adj** travelling or leading towards the east: *The eastbound carriageway of the motorway is blocked.*

★ **Easter** /ˈiːstə/ **noun** [U] a festival on a Sunday in March or April when Christians celebrate Christ's return to life; the time before and after Easter Sunday: *the Easter holidays* • *Are you going away at Easter?*

Easter egg noun [C] an egg, usually made of chocolate, that you give as a present at Easter

easterly /ˈiːstəli/ **adj 1** towards or in the east: *They travelled in an easterly direction.* **2** (used about winds) coming from the east: *cold easterly winds*

★ **eastern** (also **Eastern**) /ˈiːstən/ **adj 1** of, in or from the east of a place: *Eastern Scotland* • *the eastern shore of the lake* **2** from or connected with the countries of the East: *Eastern cookery* (= that comes from Asia)

eastward /ˈiːstwəd/ **adj** (also **eastwards**) **adj, adv** towards the east: *to travel in an eastward direction* • *The Amazon flows eastwards.*

★ **easy¹** /ˈiːzi/ **adj** (**easier**; **easiest**) **1** not difficult: *an easy question* • *It isn't easy to explain the system.* • *The system isn't easy to explain.* •➤ opposite **hard 2** comfortable, relaxed and not worried: *an easy life* • *My mind's easier now.* •➤ opposite **uneasy** •➤ noun, verb **ease**

IDIOMS **free and easy** → **FREE¹**

I'm easy (*informal*) used to say that you do not have a strong opinion when sb offers you a choice: *'Would you like to go first or second?' 'I'm easy.'*

★ **easy²** /ˈiːzi/ **adv** (**easier**; **easiest**)

IDIOMS **easier said than done** (*spoken*) more difficult to do than to talk about: *'You should get her to help you.' 'That's easier said than done.'*

go easy on sb/on/with sth (*informal*) **1** to be gentle or less strict with sb: *Go easy on him; he's just a child.* **2** to avoid using too much of sth: *Go easy on the salt; it's bad for your heart.*

take it/things easy to relax and not work too hard or worry too much

easy 'chair noun [C] a large comfortable chair with arms

easy-'going adj (used about a person) calm, relaxed and not easily worried or upset by what other people do: *Her parents are very easy-going. They let her do what she wants.*

★ **eat** /iːt/ **verb** (*pt* **ate** /et/; *pp* **eaten** /ˈiːtn/) **1** [I,T] to put food into your mouth, then bite and swallow it: *Who ate all the biscuits?* • *Eat your dinner up, Joe* (= finish it all). • *She doesn't eat properly. No wonder she's so thin.* **2** [I] to have a meal: *What time shall we eat?*

IDIOMS **have sb eating out of your hand** to have control and power over sb

have your cake and eat it → **CAKE¹**

PHRASAL VERBS **eat sth away/eat away at sth** to damage or destroy sth slowly over a period of time: *The sea had eaten away at the cliff.*

eat out to have a meal in a restaurant: *Would you like to eat out tonight?*

eater /ˈiːtə/ **noun** [C] a person who eats in a

particular way: *My uncle's a big eater* (= he eats a lot). ● *We're not great meat eaters.*

eau de cologne /ˌəʊdəkə'ləʊn/ (also **cologne**) *noun* [U] a type of pleasant smelling liquid (**perfume**) that is not very strong

eaves /i:vz/ *noun* [pl] the edges of a roof that stick out over the walls: *There's a bird's nest under the eaves.* ••➤ picture on page C7

eavesdrop /'i:vzdrɒp/ *verb* [I] (**eavesdropping**; **eavesdropped**) eavesdrop (on sb/sth) to listen secretly to other people talking: *They caught her eavesdropping on their conversation.*

ebb¹ /eb/ *verb* [I] **1** (used about sea water) to flow away from the land, which happens twice a day ••➤ synonym **go out 2** ebb (away) (used about a feeling, etc) to become weaker: *The crowd's enthusiasm began to ebb.*

the ebb² /eb/ *noun* [sing] the time when sea water flows away from the land

> The movement of sea water twice a day is called the **tide**. The opposite of **ebb tide** is **high tide**.

IDIOM **the ebb and flow (of sth)** (used about a situation, noise, feeling, etc) a regular increase and decrease in the progress or strength of sth

ebony /'ebəni/ *noun* [U] a hard black wood

eccentric /ɪk'sentrɪk/ *adj* (used about people or their behaviour) strange or unusual: *People said he was mad but I think he was just eccentric.* –**eccentric** *noun* [C]: *She's just an old eccentric.* –**eccentricity** /ˌeksen'trɪsəti/ *noun* [C,U] (*pl* **eccentricities**)

echo¹ /'ekəʊ/ *noun* [C] (*pl* **echoes**) a sound that is repeated as it is sent back off a surface such as the wall of a tunnel: *I could hear the echo of footsteps somewhere in the distance.*

echo² /'ekəʊ/ *verb* **1** [I] (used about a sound) to be repeated; to come back as an echo: *Their footsteps echoed in the empty church.* **2** [I,T] echo sth (back); echo (with/to sth) to repeat or send back a sound; to be full of a particular sound: *The tunnel echoed back their calls.* ● *The hall echoed with their laughter.* **3** [T] to repeat what sb has said, done or thought: *The child echoed everything his mother said.* ● *The newspaper article echoed my views completely.*

eclair /ɪ'kleə/ *noun* [C] a type of long thin cake, usually filled with cream and covered with chocolate ••➤ picture at **cake**

eclipse

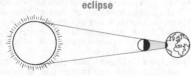

eclipse¹ /ɪ'klɪps/ *noun* [C] an occasion when the moon or the sun seems to completely or partly disappear, because one of them is passing between the other and the earth: *a total/ partial eclipse of the sun*

eclipse² /ɪ'klɪps/ *verb* [T] (used about the moon, etc) to cause an eclipse of the sun, etc

eco-friendly /'ikəʊ frendli/ *adj* not harmful to the environment: *eco-friendly products/fuel*

ecologist /i'kɒlədʒɪst/ *noun* [C] a person who studies or is an expert in ecology

ecology /i'kɒlədʒi/ *noun* [U] the relationship between living things and their surroundings; the study of this subject –**ecological** /ˌi:kə'lɒdʒɪkl/ *adj*: *an ecological disaster* –**ecologically** *adv*

★**economic** /ˌi:kə'nɒmɪk; ˌekə-/ *adj* **1** (only *before* a noun) connected with the supply of money, business, industry, etc: *The country faces growing economic problems.* **2** producing a profit: *The mine was closed because it was not economic.* ••➤ Look at **economical**. It has a different meaning. ••➤ opposite **uneconomic** –**economically** /ˌi:kə'nɒmɪkli; ˌekə-/ *adv*: *The country was economically very underdeveloped.*

economical /ˌi:kə'nɒmɪkl; ˌekə-/ *adj* that costs or uses less time, money, fuel, etc than usual: *an economical car to run* ••➤ Look at **economic**. It has a different meaning. ••➤ opposite **uneconomical** –**economically** /ˌi:kə'nɒmɪkli; ˌekə-/ *adv*: *The train service could be run more economically.*

economics /ˌi:kə'nɒmɪks; ˌekə-/ *noun* [U] the study or principles of the way money, business and industry are organized: *a degree in economics* ● *the economics of a company*

economist /ɪ'kɒnəmɪst/ *noun* [C] a person who studies or is an expert in economics

economize (also **-ise**) /ɪ'kɒnəmaɪz/ *verb* [I] economize (on sth) to save money, time, fuel, etc; to use less of sth

★**economy** /ɪ'kɒnəmi/ *noun* (*pl* **economies**) **1** (also **the economy**) [C] the operation of a country's money supply, commercial activities and industry: *There are signs of improvement in the economy.* ● *the economies of America and Japan* **2** [C,U] careful spending of money, time, fuel, etc; trying to save, not waste sth: *Our department is making economies in the amount of paper it uses.* ● *economy class* (= the cheapest class of air travel)

ecstasy /'ekstəsi/ *noun* [C,U] (*pl* **ecstasies**) a feeling or state of great happiness: *to be in ecstasy* ● *She went into ecstasies about the ring he had bought her.*

ecstatic /ɪk'stætɪk/ *adj* extremely happy

ecu (also **ECU**) /'ekju:; 'eɪkju:/ (*pl* **ecus**; **ecu**) *noun* [C] (until 1999) money used for business and commercial activities between member countries of the European Union. Ecu is short for (European Currency Unit)

eczema /'eksɪmə/ *noun* [U] a disease which makes your skin red and dry so that you want to scratch it

ed *abbr* edited by; edition; editor

eddy /'edi/ *noun* [C] (*pl* **eddies**) a circular movement of water, wind, dust, etc

★**edge**¹ /edʒ/ *noun* [C] **1** the place where sth, especially a surface, ends: *the edge of a table* ● *The leaves were brown and curling at the edges.* ● *I stood at the water's edge.* **2** the sharp cutting part of a knife, etc

IDIOMS **an/the edge on/over sb/sth** a small advantage over sb/sth: *She knew she had the edge over the other candidates.*

(be) on edge to be nervous, worried or quick to become upset or angry: *I'm a bit on edge because I get my exam results today.*

edge² /edʒ/ **verb 1** [T] (usually passive) **edge sth (with sth)** to put sth along the edge of sth else: *The cloth was edged with lace.* **2** [I,T] **edge (your way/sth) across, along, away, back,** etc to move yourself/sth somewhere slowly and carefully: *We edged closer to get a better view.* ● *She edged her chair up to the window.*

edgeways /'edʒweɪz/ (also **edgewise** /-waɪz/) **adv**

IDIOM **not get a word in edgeways → WORD¹**

edgy /'edʒi/ **adj** (*informal*) nervous, worried or quick to become upset or angry: *You seem very edgy. What's bothering you?*

edible /'edəbl/ **adj** good or safe to eat: *Are these mushrooms edible?* •➤ opposite **inedible**

edifice /'edɪfɪs/ **noun** [C] (*formal*) a large impressive building

edit /'edɪt/ **verb** [T] **1** to prepare a piece of writing to be published, making sure that it is correct, the right length, etc **2** to prepare a film, television or radio programme by cutting and arranging filmed material in a particular order **3** to be in charge of a newspaper, magazine, etc

edition /ɪ'dɪʃn/ **noun** [C] **1** the form in which a book is published; all the books, newspapers, etc published in the same form at the same time: *a paperback/hardback edition* ● *the morning edition of a newspaper* **2** one of a series of newspapers, magazines, television or radio programmes: *And now for this week's edition of 'Panorama'*...

★**editor** /'edɪtə/ **noun** [C] **1** the person who is in charge of all or part of a newspaper, magazine, etc and who decides what should be included: *the financial editor* ● *Who is the editor of 'The Times'?* **2** a person whose job is to prepare a book to be published by checking for mistakes and correcting the text **3** a person whose job is to prepare a film, television programme, etc for showing to the public by cutting and putting the filmed material in the correct order

editorial /,edɪ'tɔːriəl/ **noun** [C] an article in a newspaper, usually written by the head of the newspaper (**editor**), giving an opinion on an important subject

educate /'edʒukeɪt/ **verb** [T] to teach or train sb, especially in school: *Young people should be educated to care for their environment.* ● *All their children were educated at private schools.*

educated /'edʒukeɪtɪd/ **adj** having studied and learnt a lot of things to a high standard: *a highly educated woman*

★**education** /,edʒu'keɪʃn/ **noun** [C, usually sing, U] the teaching or training of people, especially in schools: *primary, secondary, higher, adult education* ● *She received an*

excellent education. –**educational** /-ʃənl/ **adj**: *an educational toy/visit/experience*

eel /iːl/ **noun** [C] a long fish that looks like a snake

eerie (also **eery**) /'ɪəri/ **adj** strange and frightening: *an eerie noise* –**eerily adv** –**eeriness noun** [U]

★**effect** /ɪ'fekt/ **noun 1** [C,U] **(an) effect (on sb/sth)** a change that is caused by sth; a result: *the effects of acid rain on the lakes and forests* ● *Her shouting had little or no effect on him.* ● *Despite her terrible experience, she seems to have suffered no ill effects.* •➤ Look at **after-effect** and **side-effect** and at the note at **affect**. **2** [C,U] a particular look, sound or impression that an artist, writer, etc wants to create: *How does the artist create the effect of moonlight?* ● *He likes to say things just for effect* (= to impress people). **3 effects** [pl] (*formal*) your personal possessions

IDIOMS **come into effect** (used especially about laws or rules) to begin to be used

in effect 1 in fact; for all practical purposes: *Though they haven't made an official announcement, she is, in effect, the new director.* **2** (used about a rule, a law, etc) in operation; in use: *The new rules will be in effect from next month.*

take effect 1 (used about a drug, etc) to begin to work; to produce the result you want: *The anaesthetic took effect immediately.* **2** (used about a law, etc) to come into operation: *The ceasefire takes effect from midnight.*

to this/that effect with this/that meaning: *I told him to leave her alone, or words to that effect.*

★**effective** /ɪ'fektɪv/ **adj 1** successfully producing the result that you want: *a medicine that is effective against the common cold* ● *That picture would look more effective on a dark background.* •➤ opposite **ineffective 2** real or actual, although perhaps not official: *The soldiers gained effective control of the town.* –**effectiveness noun** [U]

effectively /ɪ'fektɪvli/ **adv 1** in a way that successfully produces the result you wanted: *She dealt with the situation effectively.* **2** in fact; in reality: *It meant that, effectively, they had lost.*

effeminate /ɪ'femɪnət/ **adj** (used about a man or his behaviour) like a woman

★**efficient** /ɪ'fɪʃnt/ **adj** able to work well without making mistakes or wasting time and energy: *Our secretary is very efficient.* ● *You must find a more efficient way of organizing your time.* •➤ opposite **inefficient** –**efficiency** /ɪ'fɪʃnsi/ **noun** [U] –**efficiently adv**

effluent /'efluənt/ **noun** [U] liquid waste, especially chemicals produced by factories

★**effort** /'efət/ **noun 1** [U] the physical or mental strength or energy that you need to do sth; sth that takes a lot of energy: *They have put a lot of effort into their studies this year.* ● *He made no effort to contact his parents.* **2** [C] **an effort (to do sth)** something that is done with difficulty or that takes a lot of energy: *It was a real effort to stay awake in the lecture.*

effortless /'efətləs/ **adj** needing little or no effort so that sth seems easy –**effortlessly adv**

EFL /ˌiː ef 'el/ **abbr** English as a Foreign Language

eg /ˌiː 'dʒiː/ **abbr** for example: *popular sports, eg football, tennis, swimming*

egalitarian /iˌɡælɪ'teəriən/ **adj** (used about a person, system, society, etc) following the principle that everyone should have equal rights

egg
white
yolk
eggshell

★**egg**¹ /eɡ/ **noun 1** [C] an almost round object with a hard shell that contains a young bird, reptile or insect •➤ picture at **insect**

➤ A female bird **lays** her eggs and then **sits on** them until they **hatch**.

2 [C,U] a bird's egg, especially one from a chicken, etc that we eat

➤ Eggs may be **boiled**, **fried**, **poached** or **scrambled**.

3 [C] (in women and female animals) the small cell that can join with a male seed (**sperm**) to make a baby

IDIOM **put all your eggs in one basket** to risk everything by depending completely on one thing, plan, etc instead of giving yourself several possibilities

egg² /eɡ/ **verb**

PHRASAL VERB **egg sb on (to do sth)** to encourage sb to do sth that he/she should not do

eggcup /'eɡkʌp/ **noun** [C] a small cup for holding a boiled egg

eggplant /'eɡplɑːnt/ (*especially US*) = **AUBERGINE**

eggshell /'eɡʃel/ **noun** [C,U] the hard outside part of an egg •➤ picture at **egg**

ego /'eɡəʊ/ **noun** [C] (*pl* **egos**) the (good) opinion that you have of yourself: *It was a blow to her ego when she lost her job.*

egocentric /ˌeɡəʊ'sentrɪk/ **adj** thinking only about yourself and not what other people need or want; selfish

egoism /'eɡəʊɪzəm; 'iːɡ-/ (also **egotism** /'eɡətɪzəm; 'iːɡ-/) **noun** [U] thinking about yourself too much; selfishness –**egoist** /'eɡəʊɪst; 'iːɡ-/ (also **egotist** /'eɡətɪst; 'iːɡə-/) **noun** [C]: *I hate people who are egoists.* –**egoistic** /ˌeɡəʊ'ɪstɪk/ (also **egotistical** /ˌeɡə'tɪstɪkl; ˌiːɡə-/) **adj**

eh /eɪ/ **interj** (*Brit informal*) **1** used for asking sb to agree with you: *'Good party, eh?'* **2** used for asking sb to repeat sth: *'Did you like the film?' 'Eh?' 'I asked if you liked the film.'*

Eid (also **Id**) /iːd/ **noun** [sing] any of several Muslim festivals, especially one that celebrates the end of a month when people do not eat during the day (**Ramadan**)

eiderdown /'aɪdədaʊn/ **noun** [C] a covering for a bed filled with soft feathers (**down**),

usually used on top of other coverings for the bed •➤ Look at **duvet**.

★**eight** /eɪt/ **number 1** 8

➤ For examples of how to use numbers in sentences, look at **six**.

2 eight- (used to form compounds) having eight of sth: *an eight-sided shape*

★**eighteen** /ˌeɪ'tiːn/ **number** 18

➤ For examples of how to use numbers in sentences, look at **six**.

eighteenth /ˌeɪ'tiːnθ/ **pron, determiner, adv** 18th •➤ Look at the examples at **sixth**.

eighth¹ /eɪtθ/ **noun** [C] the fraction ⅛; one of eight equal parts of sth

eighth² /eɪtθ/ **pron, determiner, adv** 8th •➤ Look at the examples at **sixth**.

eightieth /'eɪtiəθ/ **pron, determiner, adv** 80th •➤ Look at the examples at **sixth**.

★**eighty** /'eɪti/ **number** 80

➤ For examples of how to use numbers in sentences, look at **sixty**.

★**either**¹ /'aɪðə; 'iːðə/ **determiner, pron 1** one or the other of two; it does not matter which: *You can choose either soup or salad, but not both.* ● *You can ask either of us for advice.* ● *Either of us is willing to help.* **2** both: *It is a pleasant road, with trees on either side.*

★**either**² /'aɪðə; 'iːðə/ **adv 1** (used after two negative statements) also: *I don't like Pat and I don't like Nick much either.* ● *'I can't remember his name.' 'I can't either.'*

➤ We can also say **neither can I**. Look at **too** for agreement with positive statements.

2 used for emphasizing a negative statement: *The restaurant is quite good. And it's not expensive either.*

either³ /'aɪðə; 'iːðə/ **conj either...or...** used when you are giving a choice, usually of two things: *I can meet you either Thursday or Friday.* ● *Either you leave or I do.* ● *You can either write or phone.*

ejaculate /i'dʒækjuleɪt/ **verb 1** [I] to send out liquid (**semen**) from the male sexual organ (**penis**) **2** [I,T] (*old-fashioned*) to say sth suddenly –**ejaculation** /iˌdʒækju'leɪʃn/ **noun** [C,U]

eject /i'dʒekt/ **verb 1** [T] (*formal*) (often passive) **eject sb (from sth)** to push or send sb/sth out of a place (usually with force): *The protesters were ejected from the building.* **2** [I,T] to remove a tape, disk etc from a machine, usually by pressing a button: *To eject the CD, press this button.* ● *After recording for three hours the video will eject automatically.* **3** [I] to escape from an aircraft that is going to crash

eke /iːk/ **verb**

PHRASAL VERB **eke sth out** to make a small amount of sth last a long time

elaborate¹ /ɪ'læbərət/ **adj** very complicated; done or made very carefully: *an elaborate pattern* ● *elaborate plans*

elaborate² /ɪ'læbəreɪt/ **verb** [I] (*formal*)

[I] **intransitive**, a verb which has no object: *He laughed.*   [T] **transitive**, a verb which has an object: *He ate an apple.*

elaborate (on sth) to give more details about sth: *Could you elaborate on that idea?*

elapse /ɪ'læps/ **verb** [I] (*formal*) (used about time) to pass

elastic¹ /ɪ'læstɪk/ **noun** [U] material with rubber in it which can stretch

elastic² /ɪ'læstɪk/ **adj 1** (used about material, etc) that returns to its original size and shape after being stretched **2** that can be changed; not fixed: *Our rules are quite elastic.*

e,lastic 'band = RUBBER BAND

elated /i'leɪtɪd/ **adj** very happy and excited –**elation** /i'leɪʃn/ **noun** [U]

★**elbow¹** /'elbəʊ/ **noun** [C] **1** the place where the bones of your arm join and your arm bends ••➤ picture on page C5 **2** the part of the sleeve of a coat, jacket, etc that covers the elbow

elbow² /'elbəʊ/ **verb** [T] to push sb with your elbow: *She elbowed me out of the way.* ••➤ picture on page S8

'elbow room noun [U] enough space to move freely

★**elder¹** /'eldə/ **adj** (only *before* a noun) older (of two members of a family): *My elder daughter is at university now but the other one is still at school.* ● *an elder brother/sister*

elder² /'eldə/ **noun 1** [sing] **the elder** the older of two people: *Who is the elder of the two?* **2 my, etc elder** [sing] a person who is older than me, etc: *He is her elder by several years.* **3 elders** [pl] older people: *Do children still respect the opinions of their elders?*

elderly /'eldəli/ **adj 1** (used about a person) old ••➤ This is a polite way of saying 'old'. **2 the elderly noun** [pl] old people in general: *The elderly need special care in winter.* ••➤ Look at **old**.

★**eldest** /'eldɪst/ **adj, noun** [C] (the) oldest (of three or more members of a family): *Their eldest child is a boy.* ● *John's got 4 boys. The eldest has just gone to university.*

•★**elect** /ɪ'lekt/ **verb** [T] **1 elect sb (to sth); elect sb (as sth)** to choose sb to have a particular job or position by voting for him/her: *He was elected to Parliament in 1970.* ● *The committee elected her as their representative.* **2** (*formal*) **elect to do sth** to decide to do sth

★**election** /ɪ'lekʃn/ **noun** [C,U] (the time of) choosing a Member of Parliament, President, etc by voting: *In America, presidential elections are held every four years.* ● *If you're interested in politics why not stand for election yourself?*

➤ In Britain, **general elections** are held about every five years. Sometimes **by-elections** are held at other times. In each region (**constituency**) voters must choose one person from a list of **candidates**.

elector /ɪ'lektə/ **noun** [C] a person who has the right to vote in an election ••➤ **Voter** is a more common word. –**electoral** /ɪ'lektərəl/ **adj**: *the electoral register/roll* (= the list of electors in an area)

electorate /ɪ'lektərət/ **noun** [C, with sing or pl verb] all the people who can vote in a region, country, etc

★**electric** /ɪ'lektrɪk/ **adj 1** producing or using electricity: *an electric current* ● *an electric kettle* **2** very exciting: *The atmosphere in the room was electric.*

★**electrical** /ɪ'lektrɪkl/ **adj** of or about electricity: *an electrical appliance* (= a machine that uses electricity) ● *an electrical engineer* (= a person who produces electrical systems and equipment)

the e,lectric 'chair noun [sing] a chair used in some countries for killing criminals with a very strong electric current

★**electrician** /ɪ,lek'trɪʃn/ **noun** [C] a person whose job is to make and repair electrical systems and equipment

★**electricity** /ɪ,lek'trɪsəti/ **noun** [U] a type of energy that we use to make heat, light and power to work machines, etc: *Turn that light off. We don't want to waste electricity.*

➤ Electricity is usually **generated** in **power stations**. It may also be produced by **generators** or by **batteries**.

e,lectric 'razor = SHAVER

e,lectric 'shock (also **shock**) **noun** [C] a sudden painful feeling that you get if electricity goes through your body

electrify /ɪ'lektrɪfaɪ/ **verb** [T] (*pres part* **electrifying**; *3rd pers sing pres* **electrifies**; *pt, pp* **electrified**) **1** to supply sth with electricity: *The railways are being electrified.* **2** to make sb very excited: *Ronaldo electrified the crowd with his pace and skill.*

electrocute /ɪ'lektrəkjuːt/ **verb** [T] to kill sb with electricity that goes through the body –**electrocution** /ɪ,lektrə'kjuːʃn/ **noun** [U]

electrode /ɪ'lektrəʊd/ **noun** [C] one of two points (**terminals**) where an electric current enters or leaves a battery, etc

★**electronic** /ɪ,lek'trɒnɪk/ **adj 1** using electronics: *electronic equipment* ● *This dictionary is available in electronic form* (= on a computer disk). **2** done using a computer: *electronic banking/shopping* –**electronically** /-kli/ **adv**

electronics /ɪ,lek'trɒnɪks/ **noun** [U] the technology used to produce computers, radios, etc: *the electronics industry*

elegant /'elɪgənt/ **adj** having a good or attractive style: *She looked very elegant in her new dress.* ● *an elegant coat* –**elegance** /'elɪgəns/ **noun** [U] –**elegantly adv**

★**element** /'elɪmənt/ **noun 1** [C] one important part of sth: *Cost is an important element when we're thinking about holidays.* **2** [C, usually sing] **an element of sth** a small amount of sth: *There was an element of truth in what he said.* **3** [C] people of a certain type: *The criminal element at football matches causes a lot of trouble.* **4** [C] one of the simple chemical substances, for example iron, gold, etc **5** [C] the metal part of a piece of electrical equipment that produces heat **6 the elements** [pl] (bad) weather: *to be exposed to the elements* IDIOM **in/out of your element** in a situation where you feel comfortable/uncomfortable: *Bill's in his element speaking to a large group of people, but I hate it.*

★**elementary** /ˌelɪˈmentri/ *adj* **1** connected with the first stages of learning sth: *an elementary course in English* ● *a book for elementary students* **2** basic; not difficult: *elementary physics*

ˌele'mentary school *noun* [C] (*US*) a school for children aged six to eleven

elephant

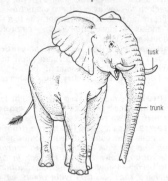

tusk

trunk

★**elephant** /ˈelɪfənt/ *noun* [C] a very large grey animal with big ears, two long curved teeth (**tusks**) and a long nose (**trunk**)

elevate /ˈelɪveɪt/ *verb* [T] (*formal*) to move sb/sth to a higher place or more important position: *an elevated platform* ● *He was elevated to the Board of Directors.*

elevation /ˌelɪˈveɪʃn/ *noun* **1** [C,U] (*formal*) the process of moving to a higher place or more important position: *his elevation to the presidency* **2** [C] the height of a place (above sea-level): *The city is at an elevation of 2000 metres.*

elevator /ˈelɪveɪtə/ (*US*) = **LIFT²**(1)

★**eleven** /ɪˈlevn/ *number* 11

➤ For examples of how to use numbers in sentences, look at **six**.

eleventh /ɪˈlevnθ/ *pron, determiner, adv* 11th
··➤ Look at the examples at **sixth**.

elf /elf/ *noun* [C] (*pl* **elves** /elvz/) (in stories) a small creature with pointed ears who has magic powers

elicit /iˈlɪsɪt/ *verb* [T] (*formal*) **elicit sth (from sb)** to manage to get information, facts, a reaction, etc from sb

eligible /ˈelɪdʒəbl/ *adj* **eligible (for sth/to do sth)** having the right to do or have sth: *In Britain, you are eligible to vote when you are eighteen.* ··➤ opposite **ineligible**

eliminate /ɪˈlɪmɪneɪt/ *verb* [T] **1** to remove sb/sth that is not wanted or needed: *We must try and eliminate the problem.* **2** (often passive) to stop sb going further in a competition, etc: *The school team was eliminated in the first round of the competition.* –**elimination** /ɪˌlɪmɪˈneɪʃn/ *noun* [U]

élite /eɪˈliːt/ *noun* [C, with sing or pl verb] a social group that is thought to be the best or most important because of its power, money, intelligence, etc: *an intellectual élite* ● *an élite group of artists*

élitism /eɪˈliːtɪzəm/ *noun* [U] the belief that some people should be treated in a special way –**élitist** /-tɪst/ *noun* [C], *adj*

elk

antlers

elk /elk/ (*US* **moose**) *noun* [C] a very large wild animal (**deer**) with large flat horns (**antlers**)

elm /elm/ (also 'elm tree) *noun* [C] a tall tree with broad leaves

elongated /ˈiːlɒŋgeɪtɪd/ *adj* long and thin

elope /ɪˈləʊp/ *verb* [I] **elope (with sb)** to run away secretly to get married

eloquent /ˈeləkwənt/ *adj* (*formal*) able to use language and express your opinions well, especially when you speak in public –**eloquence** *noun* [U] –**eloquently** *adv*

★**else** /els/ *adv* (used after words formed with *any-, no-, some-* and after question words) another, different person, thing or place: *This isn't mine. It must be someone else's.* ● *Was it you who phoned me, or somebody else?* ● *Everybody else is allowed to stay up late.* ● *You'll have to pay. Nobody else will.* ● *What else would you like?* ● *I'm tired of that cafe – shall we go somewhere else for a change?*

IDIOM **or else** otherwise; if not: *You'd better go to bed now or else you'll be tired in the morning.* ● *He's either forgotten or else he's decided not to come.*

★**elsewhere** /ˌelsˈweə/ *adv* in or to another place: *He's travelled a lot – in Europe and elsewhere.*

ELT /ˌiː el ˈtiː/ *abbr* English Language Teaching

elude /iˈluːd/ *verb* [T] (*formal*) **1** to manage to avoid being caught: *The escaped prisoner eluded the police for three days.* **2** to be difficult or impossible to remember: *I remember his face but his name eludes me.*

elusive /iˈluːsɪv/ *adj* not easy to catch, find or remember

elves *plural of* **ELF**

'em /əm/ *pron* (*informal*) = **THEM**

emaciated /ɪˈmeɪsieɪtɪd/ *adj* extremely thin and weak because of illness, lack of food, etc –**emaciation** /ɪˌmeɪsiˈeɪʃn/ *noun* [U]

e

e-mail /ˈiːmeɪl/ **noun** [C,U] electronic messages that are sent from one computer to another; the system for sending these: *I'll send you an e-mail as soon as I hear any news.* ● *Did you get my e-mail?* ● *Have you got e-mail on your computer?* –e-mail **verb** [T]: *I'll e-mail the information to you*

emancipate /ɪˈmænsɪpeɪt/ **verb** [T] (*formal*) to give sb the same legal, social and political rights as other people –emancipation /ɪˌmænsɪˈpeɪʃn/ **noun** [U]

embankment /ɪmˈbæŋkmənt/ **noun** [C] a wall of stone or earth that is built to stop a river from flooding or to carry a road or railway

embargo /ɪmˈbɑːɡəʊ/ **noun** [C] (*pl* **embargoes**) an official order to stop doing business with another country: *to impose an embargo on sth* ● *to lift/remove an embargo*

embark /ɪmˈbɑːk/ **verb** [I] to get on a ship: *Passengers with cars must embark first.* ●► opposite **disembark** –embarkation /ˌembɑːˈkeɪʃn/ **noun** [C,U]

PHRASAL VERB **embark on sth** (*formal*) to start sth (new): *I'm embarking on a completely new career.*

embarrass /ɪmˈbærəs/ **verb** [T] to make sb feel uncomfortable or shy: *Don't ever embarrass me in front of my friends again!* ● *The Minister's mistake embarrassed the government.*

★**embarrassed** /ɪmˈbærəst/ **adj** feeling uncomfortable or shy because of sth silly you have done, because people are looking at you, etc: *I felt so embarrassed when I dropped my glass.*

★**embarrassing** /ɪmˈbærəsɪŋ/ **adj** making you feel uncomfortable or shy: *an embarrassing question/mistake/situation* –embarrassingly **adv**

embarrassment /ɪmˈbærəsmənt/ **noun** **1** [U] the feeling you have when you are embarrassed **2** [C] a person or thing that makes you embarrassed

embassy /ˈembəsi/ **noun** [C] (*pl* **embassies**) (the official building of) a group of officials (**diplomats**) and their head (**ambassador**), who represent their government in a foreign country ●► Look at **consulate**.

embed /ɪmˈbed/ **verb** [T] (**embedding**; **embedded**) (usually passive) to fix sth firmly and deeply (in sth else): *The axe was embedded in the piece of wood.*

ember /ˈembə/ **noun** [C,usually pl] a piece of wood or coal that is not burning, but is still red and hot after a fire has died

embezzle /ɪmˈbezl/ **verb** [T] to steal money that you are responsible for or that belongs to your employer –embezzlement **noun** [U]

emblem /ˈembləm/ **noun** [C] an object or symbol that represents sth: *The dove is the emblem of peace.*

embody /ɪmˈbɒdi/ **verb** [T] (*pres part* **embodying**; *3rd pers sing pres* **embodies**; *pp, pt* **embodied**) (*formal*) **1** to be a very good example of sth: *To me she embodies all*

the best qualities of a teacher. **2** to include or contain sth: *This latest model embodies many new features.* –embodiment **noun** [C]: *She is the embodiment of a caring mother.*

embrace /ɪmˈbreɪs/ **verb** **1** [I,T] to put your arms around sb as a sign of love, happiness, etc **2** [T] (*formal*) to include: *His report embraced all the main points.* **3** [T] (*formal*) to accept sth with enthusiasm: *She embraced Christianity in her later years.* –embrace **noun** [C]: *He held her in a warm embrace.*

embroider /ɪmˈbrɔɪdə/ **verb** **1** [I,T] to decorate cloth by sewing a pattern or picture on it **2** [T] to add details that are not true to a story to make it more interesting –embroidery /-dəri/ **noun** [U]

embryo /ˈembriəʊ/ **noun** [C] (*pl* **embryos** /-əʊz/) a baby, an animal or a plant in the early stages of development before birth ●► Look at **foetus**. –embryonic /ˌembriˈɒnɪk/ **adj**

emerald /ˈemərəld/ **noun** [C] a bright green precious stone –emerald (also **emerald green**) **adj**: *an emerald green dress*

emerge /iˈmɜːdʒ/ **verb** [I] **emerge (from sth)** **1** to appear or come out from somewhere: *A man emerged from the shadows.* ● (*figurative*) *The country emerged from the war in ruins.* **2** to become known: *During investigations it emerged that she was lying about her age.* –emergence /-dʒəns/ **noun** [U]: *the emergence of Aids in the 1980s*

★**emergency** /iˈmɜːdʒənsi/ **noun** [C,U] (*pl* **emergencies**) a serious event that needs immediate action: *In an emergency phone 999 for help.* ● *The government has declared a state of emergency.* ● *an emergency exit*

e'mergency room (*US*) = **CASUALTY**(3)

emigrant /ˈemɪɡrənt/ **noun** [C] a person who has gone to live in another country ●► Look at **immigrant**.

emigrate /ˈemɪɡreɪt/ **verb** [I] to leave your own country to go and live in another: *They emigrated from Ireland to Australia twenty years ago.* –emigration /ˌemɪˈɡreɪʃn/ **noun** [C,U] ●► Look at **immigrant**, **immigration** and **migrate**.

eminent /ˈemɪnənt/ **adj** (*formal*) (used about a person) famous and important: *an eminent scientist*

eminently /ˈemɪnəntli/ **adv** (*formal*) very; extremely: *She is eminently suitable for the job.*

emit /iˈmɪt/ **verb** [T] (**emitting**; **emitted**) (*formal*) to send out sth, for example a smell, a sound, smoke, heat or light: *The animal emits a powerful smell when scared.* –emission /iˈmɪʃn/ **noun** [C,U]: *sulphur dioxide emissions from power stations*

★**emotion** /iˈməʊʃn/ **noun** [C,U] a strong feeling such as love, anger, fear, etc: *to control/express your emotions* ● *His voice was filled with emotion.* ● *He showed no emotion as the police took him away.*

★**emotional** /iˈməʊʃənl/ **adj** **1** connected with people's feelings: *emotional problems* **2** causing strong feelings: *He gave an emotional* *speech.* **3** having strong emotions and showing them in front of people: *She always gets very emotional when I leave.* –emotionally /-ʃənəli/ **adv**: *She felt physically and emotionally drained after giving birth.*

emotive /i'məʊtɪv/ **adj** causing strong feelings: *emotive language* • *an emotive issue*

empathy /'empəθi/ **noun** [C,U] empathy (with/for sb/sth); empathy (between A and B) the ability to imagine how another person is feeling and so understand his/her mood: *Some adults have (a) great **empathy** with children.* –empathize (also **-ise**) /'empəθaɪz/ **verb** [I] empathize (with sb/sth): *He's a popular teacher because he empathizes with his students.*

emperor /'empərə/ **noun** [C] the ruler of an empire

★**emphasis** /'emfəsɪs/ **noun** [C,U] (*pl* **emphases** /-siːz/) **1** emphasis (on sth) (giving) special importance or attention to sth: *There's a lot of emphasis on science at our school.* • *You should **put** a greater **emphasis** on quality rather than quantity when you write.* **2** the force that you give to a word or phrase when you are speaking; a way of writing a word to show that it is important: *In the word 'photographer' the emphasis is on the second syllable.* • *I underlined the key phrases of my letter for emphasis.* ••➤ synonym **stress**¹

★**emphasize** (also **-ise**) /'emfəsaɪz/ **verb** [T] emphasize (that...) to put emphasis on sth: *They emphasized that healthy eating is important.* • *They emphasized the importance of healthy eating.* ••➤ synonym **stress**²

emphatic /ɪm'fætɪk/ **adj** said or expressed in a strong way: *an emphatic refusal* –emphatically /-kli/ **adv**

empire /'empaɪə/ **noun** [C] **1** a group of countries that is governed by one country: *the Roman Empire* ••➤ Look at **emperor** and **empress**. **2** a very large company or group of companies

empirical /ɪm'pɪrɪkl/ **adj** (*formal*) based on experiments and practical experience, not on ideas: *empirical evidence*

★**employ** /ɪm'plɔɪ/ **verb** [T] **1** employ sb (in/on sth); employ sb (as sth) to pay sb to work for you: *He is employed as a lorry driver.* • *They employ 600 workers.* • *Three people are employed on the task of designing a new computer system.* ••➤ Look at **unemployed**. **2** (*formal*) employ sth (as sth) to use: *In an emergency, an umbrella can be employed as a weapon.*

employee /ɪm'plɔɪiː/ **noun** [C] a person who works for sb: *The factory has 500 employees.*

employer /ɪm'plɔɪə/ **noun** [C] a person or company that employs other people

employment /ɪm'plɔɪmənt/ **noun** [U] **1** the state of having a paid job: *to be in/out of employment* • *This bank can **give employment to** ten extra staff.* • *It is difficult to **find employment** in the north of the country.* ••➤ Look at **unemployment** and at the note

at **work**¹. **2** (*formal*) the use of sth: *the employment of force*

em'ployment agency noun [C] a company that helps people to find work and other companies to find workers

empower /ɪm'paʊə/ **verb** [T] (*formal*) (usually passive) to give sb power or authority (to do sth) –empowerment **noun** [U]

empress /'emprəs/ **noun** [C] **1** a woman who rules an empire **2** the wife of a man who rules an empire (**emperor**)

★**empty**¹ /'empti/ **adj** **1** having nothing or nobody inside it: *an empty box* • *The bus was half empty.* **2** without meaning or value: *It was an empty threat* (= it was not meant seriously). • *My life feels empty now the children have left home.* –emptiness /'emptinəs/ **noun** [U]

★**empty**² /'empti/ **verb** (*pres part* **emptying**; *3rd pers sing pres* **empties**; *pt, pp* **emptied**) **1** [T] empty sth (out/out of sth) to remove everything that is inside a container, etc: *I've emptied a wardrobe for you to use.* • *Luke emptied everything out of his desk and left.* **2** [I] to become empty: *The cinema emptied very quickly once the film was finished.*

empty-'handed adj without getting what you wanted; without taking sth to sb: *The robbers fled empty-handed.*

EMU /ˌiː em 'juː/ **abbr** Economic and Monetary Union (of the countries of the European Union) ••➤ Look at **euro**.

emulate /'emjuleɪt/ **verb** [T] (*formal*) to try to do sth as well as, or better than, sb ••➤ A less formal word is **copy**.

★**enable** /ɪ'neɪbl/ **verb** [T] enable sb/sth to do sth to make it possible for sb/sth to do sth: *The new law has enabled more women to return to work.*

enamel /ɪ'næml/ **noun** [U] **1** a hard, shiny substance used for protecting or decorating metal, etc: *enamel paint* **2** the hard white outer covering of a tooth

enc (also **encl**) **abbr** (used at the end of a business letter to show that there is sth else in the envelope with the letter) enclosed

enchanted /ɪn'tʃɑːntɪd/ **adj** **1** (in stories) affected by magic powers **2** (*formal*) pleased or very interested: *The audience was enchanted by her singing.*

enchanting /ɪn'tʃɑːntɪŋ/ **adj** very nice or pleasant; attractive

encircle /ɪn'sɜːkl/ **verb** [T] (*formal*) to make a circle round sth; to surround: *London is encircled by the M25 motorway.*

★**enclose** /ɪn'kləʊz/ **verb** [T] **1** enclose sth (in sth) (usually passive) to surround sth with a wall, fence, etc; to put one thing inside another: *The jewels were enclosed in a strong box.* • *He gets very nervous in enclosed spaces.* **2** to put sth in an envelope, package, etc with sth else: *Can I enclose a letter with this parcel?* • *Please find enclosed a cheque for £100.*

enclosure /ɪn'kləʊʒə/ **noun** [C] **1** a piece of land inside a wall, fence, etc that is used for a particular purpose: *a wildlife enclosure*

2 something that is placed inside an envelope together with the letter

encode /ɪnˈkəʊd/ = CODE²(1)

encore¹ /ˈɒŋkɔː/ **interj** called out by an audience that wants the performers in a concert, etc to sing or play sth extra

encore² /ˈɒŋkɔː/ **noun** [C] a short, extra performance at the end of a concert, etc

encounter¹ /ɪnˈkaʊntə/ **verb** [T] **1** to experience sth (a danger, difficulty, etc): *I've never encountered any discrimination at work.* •➤ synonym **meet with 2** (*formal*) to meet sb unexpectedly; to experience or find sth unusual or new •➤ synonym **come across**

encounter² /ɪnˈkaʊntə/ **noun** [C] an encounter (with sb/sth); an encounter (between A and B) an unexpected (often unpleasant) meeting or event: *I've had a number of close encounters* (= situations which could have been dangerous) *with bad drivers.*

★**encourage** /ɪnˈkʌrɪdʒ/ **verb** [T] **1** encourage sb/sth (in sth/to do sth) to give hope, support or confidence to sb: *The teacher encouraged her students to ask questions.* **2** to make sth happen more easily: *The government wants to encourage new businesses.* •➤ opposite **discourage** —**encouragement** **noun** [C,U] —**encouraging** **adj**

encroach /ɪnˈkrəʊtʃ/ **verb** [I] (*formal*) encroach (on/upon sth) to use more of sth than you should: *I do hope that I am not encroaching too much upon your free time.*

encyclopedia (also **encyclopaedia**) /ɪnˌsaɪkləˈpiːdiə/ **noun** [C] (*pl* **encyclopedias**) a book or set of books that gives information about very many subjects, arranged in the order of the alphabet (= from A to Z)

★**end¹** /end/ **noun** [C] **1** the furthest or last part of sth; the place or time where sth stops: *My house is at the end of the street.* • *There are some seats at the far end of the room.* • *I'm going on holiday at the end of October.* • *He promised to give me an answer by the end of the week.* • *She couldn't wait to hear the end of the story.*

> ➤ **End** is sometimes used before another noun: *the end house* • *the end seat*
> ➤ The idiom **in the end** refers to time and means 'finally': *We were too tired to cook, so in the end we decided to eat out.* **At the end of sth** refers to the last part of a book, film, class, etc, at the point where it is about to finish: *At the end of the meal we had a row about who should pay for it.*

•➤ Look at the noun **finish**. It is used to mean **end** only in connection with races and competitions. **2** (*formal*) an aim or purpose: *They were prepared to do anything to achieve their ends.* **3** a little piece of sth that is left after the rest has been used: *a cigarette end.* IDIOMS **at an end** (*formal*) finished or used up: *Her career is at an end.*

at the end of your tether having no more patience or strength

at the end of the day (*spoken*) used to say the most important fact in a situation: *At the end of the day, you have to make the decision yourself.*

at a loose end ➔ LOOSE¹

at your wits' end ➔ WIT

bring sth/come/draw to an end (to cause sth) to finish: *His stay in England was coming to an end.*

a dead end ➔ DEAD¹

end to end in a line with the ends touching: *They put the tables end to end.*

in the end at last; finally: *He wanted to get home early but in the end it was midnight before he left.*

make ends meet to have enough money for your needs: *It's hard for us to make ends meet.*

make sb's hair stand on end ➔ HAIR

a means to an end ➔ MEANS

no end of sth (*spoken*) too many or much; a lot of sth: *She has given us no end of trouble.*

odds and ends ➔ ODDS

on end (used about time) continuously: *He sits and reads for hours on end.*

put an end to sth to stop sth from happening any more

★**end²** /end/ **verb** [I,T] end (in/with sth) (to cause sth) to finish: *The road ends here.* • *How does this story end?* • *The match ended in a draw.* • *I think we'd better end this conversation now.*

PHRASAL VERB **end up (as sth); end up (doing sth)** to find yourself in a place/situation that you did not plan or expect: *We got lost and ended up in the centre of town.* • *She had always wanted to be a writer but ended up as a teacher.* • *There was nothing to eat at home so we ended up getting a takeaway.*

endanger /ɪnˈdeɪndʒə/ **verb** [T] to cause danger to sb/sth: *Smoking endangers your health.*

endangered /ɪnˈdeɪndʒəd/ **adj** (used about animals, plants, etc) in danger of disappearing from the world (becoming extinct): *The giant panda is an endangered species.*

endear /ɪnˈdɪə/ **verb** [T] (*formal*) endear sb/ yourself to sb to make sb/yourself liked by sb: *She managed to endear herself to everybody by her kindness.* —**endearing** **adj** —**endearingly** **adv**

endeavour (US **endeavor**) /ɪnˈdevə/ **verb** [I] (*formal*) endeavour (to do sth) to try hard: *She endeavoured to finish her work on time.* —**endeavour** **noun** [C,U]

★**ending** /ˈendɪŋ/ **noun** [C] **1** the end (of a story, play, film, etc): *That film made me cry but I was pleased that it had a happy ending.* **2** (*grammar*) the last part of a word, which can change: *When nouns end in -ch or -sh or -x, the plural ending is -es not -s.*

endive /ˈendaɪv/ (US) = CHICORY

★**endless** /ˈendləs/ **adj 1** very large in size or amount and seeming to have no end: *The possibilities are endless.* **2** lasting for a long time and seeming to have no end: *Our plane was delayed for hours and the wait seemed endless.* •➤ synonym **interminable** —**endlessly** **adv**

endorse /ɪnˈdɔːs/ **verb** [T] **1** to say publicly

that you give official support or agreement to a plan, statement, decision, etc: *Members of all parties endorsed a ban on firearms.* **2** (*Brit*) (usually passive) to add a note to the document which allows you to drive a vehicle (driving licence) to say that the driver has broken the law –**endorsement** **noun** [C,U]

'end product **noun** [C] something that is produced by a particular process or activity

endurance /ɪn'djʊərəns/ **noun** [U] the ability to continue doing sth painful or difficult for a long period of time without complaining

endure /ɪn'djʊə/ **verb** (*formal*) **1** [T] to suffer sth painful or uncomfortable, usually without complaining: *She endured ten years of loneliness.* ••➤ synonym **bear 2** [I] to continue ••➤ synonym **last** –**enduring adj**

★**enemy** /'enəmi/ **noun** (*pl* **enemies**) **1** [C] a person who hates and tries to harm you: *They used to be friends but became bitter enemies.* ● *He has made several enemies during his career.* ••➤ noun **enmity**. **2 the enemy** [with sing or pl verb] the army or country that your country is fighting against: *The enemy is/are approaching.* ● *enemy forces*

★**energetic** /ˌenə'dʒetɪk/ **adj** full of or needing energy and enthusiasm: *Jogging is a very energetic form of exercise.* –**energetically** /-kli/ **adv**

★**energy** /'enədʒi/ **noun** (*pl* **energies**) **1** [U] the ability to be very active or do a lot of work without getting tired: *Children are usually full of energy.* **2** [U] the power that comes from coal, electricity, gas, etc that is used for producing heat, driving machines, etc: *nuclear energy* **3 energies** [pl] the effort and attention that you give to doing sth: *She devoted all her energies to helping the blind.*

enforce /ɪn'fɔːs/ **verb** [T] to make people obey a law or rule or do sth that they do not want to: *How will they enforce the new law?* –**enforced adj**: *enforced redundancies* –**enforcement noun** [U]

engage /ɪn'ɡeɪdʒ/ **verb** [T] (*formal*) **1** to interest or attract sb: *You need to engage the students' attention right from the start.* **2 engage sb (as sth)** to give work to sb: *They engaged him as a cook.* **3 engage (with sth)** to make parts of a machine fit together: *Engage the clutch before selecting a gear.* PHRASAL VERB **engage in sth** to take part in sth: *I don't engage in that kind of gossip!*

★**engaged** /ɪn'ɡeɪdʒd/ **adj 1** (*formal*) **engaged (in/on sth)** (used about a person) busy doing sth: *They are engaged in talks with the Irish government.* **2 engaged (to sb)** having agreed to get married: *We've just got engaged.* ● *Susan is engaged to Jim.* **3** (*US* **busy**) (used about a telephone) in use: *I can't get through – the line is engaged.* **4** (used about a toilet) in use ••➤ opposite **vacant**

engagement /ɪn'ɡeɪdʒmənt/ **noun** [C] **1** an agreement to get married; the time when you are engaged: *He broke off their engagement.* **2** (*formal*) an arrangement to go somewhere

or do sth at a fixed time; an appointment: *I can't come on Tuesday as I have a prior engagement.*

en'ɡagement ring **noun** [C] a ring, usually with precious stones in it, that a man gives to a woman when they agree to get married

★**engine** /'endʒɪn/ **noun** [C] **1** the part of a vehicle that produces power to make the vehicle move: *This engine runs on diesel.* ● *a car/jet engine* ••➤ Look at the note at **motor**. ••➤ picture at **motorbike 2** (also **locomotive**) a vehicle that pulls a railway train

'engine driver (also **'train driver**, *US* **engineer**) **noun** [C] a person whose job is to drive a railway engine

★**engineer**[1] /ˌendʒɪ'nɪə/ **noun** [C] **1** a person whose job is to design, build or repair engines, machines, etc: *a civil/chemical/electrical/mechanical engineer* **2** (*US*) = **ENGINE DRIVER**

engineer[2] /ˌendʒɪ'nɪə/ **verb** [T] (*formal*) to arrange for sth to happen by careful secret planning: *Her promotion was engineered by her father.*

engineering /ˌendʒɪ'nɪərɪŋ/ **noun** [U] (the study of) the work that is done by an engineer: *mechanical/civil/chemical engineering*

★**English**[1] /'ɪŋɡlɪʃ/ **noun 1** [U] the language that is spoken in Britain, the US, Australia, etc: *Do you speak English?* ● *I've been learning English for 5 years.* **2 the English** [pl] the people of England

English[2] /'ɪŋɡlɪʃ/ **adj** belonging to England, the English people, the English language, etc: *English history* ● *the English countryside*

➤ Be careful. The people of Scotland (the Scots) and of Wales (the Welsh) are **British** not English. Look at the note at **United Kingdom**.

Englishman /'ɪŋɡlɪʃmən/ **noun** [C] (*pl* -**men** /-mən; -men/) a person who comes from England or whose parents are English

➤ We normally say: *'I'm English'* not *'I'm an Englishman.'* You can also refer to a woman from England as an **Englishwoman** but this is not commonly used.

engrave /ɪn'ɡreɪv/ **verb** [T] **engrave B on A**; **engrave A with B** to cut words or designs on metal, stone, etc: *His name is engraved on the cup.* ● *The cup is engraved with his name.*

engraving /ɪn'ɡreɪvɪŋ/ **noun** [C,U] a design that is cut into a piece of metal or stone; a picture made from this

engrossed /ɪn'ɡrəʊst/ **adj** **engrossed (in/ with sth)** so interested in sth that you give it all your attention: *She was completely engrossed in her book.*

enhance /ɪn'hɑːns/ **verb** [T] (*formal*) to improve sth or to make sth look better

enigma /ɪ'nɪɡmə/ **noun** [C] (*pl* **enigmas**) a person, thing or situation that is difficult to understand –**enigmatic** /ˌenɪɡ'mætɪk/ **adj**

★**enjoy** /ɪn'dʒɔɪ/ **verb** [T] **1 enjoy sth/enjoy doing sth** to get pleasure from sth: *I really enjoyed that meal.* ● *He enjoys listening to*

e

music while he's driving. **2 enjoy yourself** to be happy; to have a good time: *I enjoyed myself at the party last night.*

enjoyable /ɪnˈdʒɔɪəbl/ *adj* giving pleasure

enjoyment /ɪnˈdʒɔɪmənt/ *noun* [U,C] pleasure or a thing which gives pleasure: *She gets a lot of enjoyment from teaching.* ● *One of her main enjoyments is foreign travel.*

enlarge /ɪnˈlɑːdʒ/ *verb* [I,T] to make sth or to become bigger: *I'm going to have this photo enlarged.*

PHRASAL VERB **enlarge on sth** to say or write more about sth

enlargement /ɪnˈlɑːdʒmənt/ *noun* [C,U] making sth bigger or sth that has been made bigger: *an enlargement of a photo*

enlighten /ɪnˈlaɪtn/ *verb* [T] (*formal*) to give sb information so that he/she understands sth better

enlightened /ɪnˈlaɪtnd/ *adj* having an understanding of people's needs, a situation, etc that shows a modern attitude to life

enlist /ɪnˈlɪst/ *verb* **1** [T] to get help, support, etc: *We need to enlist your support.* **2** [I,T] to join the army, navy or air force; to make sb a member of the army, etc: *They enlisted as soon as war was declared.*

enmity /ˈenməti/ *noun* [U] the feeling of hatred towards an enemy

enormity /ɪˈnɔːməti/ *noun* [sing] (*formal*) the very great size, effect, etc of sth; the fact that sth is very serious: *the enormity of a task/decision/problem*

★**enormous** /ɪˈnɔːməs/ *adj* very big or very great: *an enormous building* ● *enormous pleasure* –**enormously** *adv*

★**enough¹** /ɪˈnʌf/ *determiner, pron* **1** as much or as many of sth as necessary: *We've saved enough money to buy a computer.* ● *Not everybody can have a book – there aren't enough.* ● *If enough of you are interested, we'll arrange a trip to the theatre.* **2** as much or as many as you want: *I've had enough of living in a city* (= I don't want to live in a city any more). ● *Don't give me any more work. I've got quite enough already.*

★**enough²** /ɪˈnʌf/ *adv* (used *after* verbs, adjectives and adverbs) **1** to the necessary amount or degree; sufficiently: *You don't practise enough.* ● *He's not old enough to travel alone.* ● *Does she speak Italian well enough to get the job?* •➤ picture at **too 2** quite, but not very: *She plays well enough, for a beginner.*

IDIOMS **fair enough** → **FAIR¹**

funnily, strangely, etc used it is funny, etc that...: *Funnily enough, I thought exactly the same myself.*

sure enough → **SURE**

★**enquire** (also **inquire**) /ɪnˈkwaɪə/ *verb* (*formal*) [I,T] **enquire (about sb/sth)** to ask for information about sth: *Could you enquire when the trains to Cork leave?* ● *We need to enquire about hotels in Vienna.*

PHRASAL VERBS **enquire after sb** to ask about sb's health

enquire into sth to study sth in order to find

out all the facts: *The journalist enquired into the politician's financial affairs.*

enquirer /ɪnˈkwaɪərə/ *noun* [C] (*formal*) a person who asks for information

enquiring /ɪnˈkwaɪərɪŋ/ *adj* **1** interested in learning new things: *We should encourage children to have an enquiring mind.* **2** asking for information: *He gave me an enquiring look.* –**enquiringly** *adv*

★**enquiry** (also **inquiry**) /ɪnˈkwaɪəri/ *noun* (*pl* **enquiries**) **1** [C] (*formal*) an enquiry (about/concerning/into sb/sth) a question that you ask about sth: *I'll make some enquiries into English language courses in Oxford.* **2** [U] the act of asking about sth: *After weeks of enquiry he finally found what he was looking for.* **3** [C] enquiry (into sth) an official process to find out the cause of sth: *After the accident there was an enquiry into safety procedures.*

enrage /ɪnˈreɪdʒ/ *verb* [T] (*formal*) to make sb very angry

enrich /ɪnˈrɪtʃ/ *verb* [T] **1** to improve the quality, flavour, etc of sth: *These cornflakes are enriched with vitamins/are vitamin-enriched.* **2** to make sb/sth rich or richer •➤ opposite **impoverish**

enrol (*US* **enroll**) /ɪnˈrəʊl/ *verb* [I,T] (**enrolling; enrolled**) to become or to make sb a member of a club, school, etc: *They enrolled 100 new students last year.* ● (*Brit*) *I've enrolled on an Italian course.* –**enrolment** (*US* **enrollment**) *noun* [U]: *Enrolment for the course will take place next week.*

en route /ˌɒn ˈruːt/ *adv* **en route (from...) (to...); en route (for...)** on the way; while travelling from/to a place: *The car broke down when we were en route for Dover.*

ensue /ɪnˈsjuː/ *verb* [I] (*formal*) to happen after (and often as a result of) sth else

en suite /ˌɒn ˈswiːt/ *adj, adv* (used about a bedroom and bathroom) forming one unit: *The bedroom has a bathroom en suite.*

ensure (*US* **insure**) /ɪnˈʃɔː/ *verb* [T] to make sure that sth happens or is definite: *Please ensure that the door is locked before you leave.*

entail /ɪnˈteɪl/ *verb* [T] (*formal*) to make sth necessary; to involve sth: *The job sounds interesting but I'm not sure what it entails.*

entangled /ɪnˈtæŋgld/ *adj* caught in sth else: *The bird was entangled in the net.* ● (*figurative*) *I've got myself entangled in some financial problems.*

★**enter** /ˈentə/ *verb* **1** [I,T] (*formal*) to come or go into a place: *Don't enter without knocking.* ● *They all stood up when he entered the room.* •➤ nouns **entrance** and **entry**

➤ Note that **enter** is used without a preposition. **Come into** and **go into** are much more common.

2 [T] to become a member of sth, especially a profession or an institution: *She entered the legal profession in 1998.* ● *to enter school/college/university* •➤ noun **entrant 3** [T] to begin or become involved in an activity, a situation, etc: *When she entered the relation-*

ship, she had no idea he was already married. • *We have just entered a new phase in international relations.* **4** [I,T] **enter (for) sth; enter sb (in/for sth)** to put your name or sb's name on the list for an exam, race, competition, etc: *I entered a competition in the Sunday paper and I won £20!* **5** [T] **enter sth (in/into/ on/onto sth)** to put names, numbers, details, etc in a list, book, computer, etc: *I've entered all the data onto the computer.* • *Enter your password and press return.*

PHRASAL VERBS **enter into sth 1** to start to think or talk about sth: *I don't want to enter into details now.* **2** to be part of sth; to be involved in sth: *This is a business matter. Friendship doesn't enter into it.*

enter into sth (with sb) to begin sth: *The government has entered into negotiations with the unions.*

enterprise /'entəpraɪz/ noun **1** [C] a new plan, project, business, etc: *It's a very exciting new enterprise.* • *a new industrial enterprise* **2** [U] the ability to think of new projects or create new businesses and make them successful: *We need men and women of enterprise and energy.*

enterprising /'entəpraɪzɪŋ/ adj having or showing the ability to think of new projects or new ways of doing things and make them successful: *One enterprising farmer opened up his field as a car park and charged people to park there.*

★**entertain** /ˌentə'teɪn/ verb **1** [T] **entertain (sb) (with sth)** to interest and amuse sb in order to please him/her: *I find it very hard to keep my class entertained on a Friday afternoon.* **2** [I,T] to welcome sb as a guest, especially to your home; to give sb food and drink: *They entertain a lot./They do a lot of entertaining.*

entertainer /ˌentə'teɪnə/ noun [C] a person whose job is to amuse people, for example by singing, dancing or telling jokes: *a street entertainer*

entertaining /ˌentə'teɪnɪŋ/ adj interesting and amusing

★**entertainment** /ˌentə'teɪnmənt/ noun [U,C] film, music, etc used to interest and amuse people: *There isn't much entertainment for young people in this town.* • *There's a full programme of entertainments every evening.*

enthral (*US* **enthrall**) /ɪn'θrɔːl/ verb [T] (**enthralling**; **enthralled**) to hold sb's interest and attention completely: *He was enthralled by her story.* –**enthralling** adj

★**enthusiasm** /ɪn'θjuːziæzəm/ noun [U] **enthusiasm (for/about sth/doing sth)** a strong feeling of excitement or interest in sth and a desire to become involved in it: *Jan showed great enthusiasm for the new project.*

enthusiast /ɪn'θjuːziæst/ noun [C] a person who is very interested in an activity or subject

★**enthusiastic** /ɪnˌθjuːzi'æstɪk/ adj enthusiastic (about sth/doing sth) full of excitement and interest in sth –**enthusiastically** /-kli/ adv

entice /ɪn'taɪs/ verb [T] **entice sb (into sth/ doing sth)** to persuade sb to do sth or to go somewhere by offering him/her something nice: *Advertisements try to entice people into buying more things than they need.* –**enticement** noun [C,U]

enticing /ɪn'taɪsɪŋ/ adj attractive and interesting

★**entire** /ɪn'taɪə/ adj (only *before* a noun) whole or complete: *He managed to read the entire book in two days.*

➤ **Entire** is stronger than **whole**.

–**entirely** adv: *I entirely agree with you.* –**entirety** /ɪn'taɪərəti/ noun [U]: *We must consider the problem in its entirety* (= as a whole).

entitle /ɪn'taɪtl/ verb [T] **entitle sb (to sth)** (usually passive) to give sb the right to have or do sth: *I think I'm entitled to a day's holiday – I've worked hard enough.*

entitled /ɪn'taɪtld/ adj (used about books, plays, etc) with the title: *Duncan's first book was entitled 'Aquarium'.*

entity /'entəti/ noun [C] (*pl* **entities**) something that exists separately from sth else and has its own identity: *The kindergarten and the school are in the same building but they're really separate entities.*

★**entrance** /'entrəns/ noun **1** [C] **the entrance (to/of sth)** the door, gate or opening where you go into a place: *I'll meet you at the entrance to the theatre.* **2** [C] **entrance (into/ onto sth)** the act of coming or going into a place, especially in a way that attracts attention: *He made a dramatic entrance onto the stage.* •➤ **Entry** can be used with the same meaning. •➤ opposite for senses **1** and **2** **exit 3** [U] **entrance (to sth)** the right to enter a place: *They were refused entrance to the disco because they were wearing shorts.* • *an entrance fee* •➤ **Entry** can be used with the same meaning. Look at **admission**, **admittance**. **4** [U] **entrance (into/to sth)** permission to join a club, society, university, etc: *You don't need to take an entrance exam to get into university.* •➤ Look at **admission**.

entrant /'entrənt/ noun [C] a person who enters a profession, competition, exam, university, etc

entreat /ɪn'triːt/ verb [T] (*formal*) to ask sb to do sth, often in an emotional way •➤ synonym **beg**

entrust /ɪn'trʌst/ verb [T] (*formal*) **entrust A with B/entrust B to A** to make sb responsible for sth: *I entrusted Rachel with the arrangements for the party./I entrusted the arrangements for the party to Rachel.*

★**entry** /'entri/ noun (*pl* **entries**) **1** [C] the act of coming or going into a place: *The thieves forced an entry into the building.* •➤ synonym **entrance 2** [U] **entry (to/into sth)** the right to enter a place: *The immigrants were refused entry at the airport.* • *The sign says 'No Entry'.* • *an entry visa* •➤ synonym **entrance**. Look at **admission** and **admittance**. **3** [U] the right to take part in sth or become a member of a group: *countries seeking into the European Union* **4** [C] a person or thing that is entered for a competition, etc: *There were fifty entries for the Eurovision song contest.* ● *The winning entry is number 45!* **5** [C] one item that is written down in a list, diary, account book, dictionary, etc: *an entry in a diary* ● *You'll find 'ice-skate' after the entry for 'ice'.* **6** [C] (*US*) a door, gate, passage, etc where you enter a building, etc ••➤ synonym **entrance**

envelop /ɪnˈveləp/ **verb** [T] (*formal*) to cover or surround sb/sth completely (in sth): *The hills were enveloped in mist.*

★**envelope** /ˈenvələʊp; ˈɒn-/ **noun** [C] the paper cover for a letter

> ➤ After writing a letter you **address** the envelope, **seal** it and stick a stamp in the top right-hand corner.

••➤ Look at **stamped/self-addressed envelope**. ••➤ picture on page S6

enviable /ˈenviəbl/ **adj** (used about sth that sb else has and that you would like) attractive ••➤ opposite **unenviable** ••➤ verb and noun **envy**

envious /ˈenviəs/ **adj** envious (of sb/sth) wanting sth that sb else has: *She was envious of her sister's success.* ••➤ synonym **jealous** ••➤ verb and noun **envy** –**enviously** **adv**

★**environment** /ɪnˈvaɪrənmənt/ **noun 1** [C,U] the conditions in which you live, work, etc: *a pleasant working environment* **2 the environment** [sing] the natural world, for example the land, air and water, in which people, animals and plants live: *We need stronger laws to protect the environment.* ••➤ Look at page S4. ••➤ Look at **surroundings**. –**environmental** /ɪnˌvaɪrənˈmentl/ **adj**: *environmental science* –**environmentally** /-təli/ **adv**: *These products are environmentally friendly.*

environmentalist /ɪnˌvaɪrənˈmentəlɪst/ **noun** [C] a person who wants to protect the environment

envisage /ɪnˈvɪzɪdʒ/ **verb** [T] (*formal*) to think of sth as being possible in the future; to imagine: *I don't envisage any problems with this.*

envoy /ˈenvɔɪ/ **noun** [C] a person who is sent by a government with a message to another country

★**envy**[1] /ˈenvi/ **noun** [U] envy (of sb); envy (at/of sth) the feeling that you have when sb else has sth that you want: *It was difficult for her to hide her envy of her friend's success.* IDIOM **be the envy of sb** to be the thing that causes sb to feel envy: *The city's transport system is the envy of many of its European neighbours.* ••➤ Look at **enviable** and **envious**.

envy[2] /ˈenvi/ **verb** [T] (*pres part* **envying**; *3rd pers sing pres* **envies**; *pt, pp* **envied**) envy (sb) (sth) to want sth that sb else has; to feel envy: *I've always envied your good luck.* ● *I don't envy you that job* (= I'm glad that I don't have it).

epic /ˈepɪk/ **adj** very long and exciting: *an epic struggle/journey* –**epic** **noun** [C]: *The film 'Glory' is an American Civil War epic.*

epidemic /ˌepɪˈdemɪk/ **noun** [C] a large number of people or animals suffering from the same disease at the same time

epilepsy /ˈepɪlepsi/ **noun** [U] a disease of the brain that can cause a person to become unconscious (sometimes with violent movements that he/she cannot control)

epileptic /ˌepɪˈleptɪk/ **noun** [C] a person who suffers from epilepsy –**epileptic** **adj**: *an epileptic fit*

epilogue /ˈepɪlɒg/ (*US* **epilog**) **noun** [C] a short piece that is added at the end of a book, play, etc and that comments on what has gone before ••➤ Look at **prologue**.

episode /ˈepɪsəʊd/ **noun** [C] **1** one separate event in sb's life, a novel, etc: *That's an episode in my life I'd rather forget.* **2** one part of a television or radio story that is shown in several parts (a **serial**)

epitaph /ˈepɪtɑːf/ **noun** [C] words that are written or said about a dead person, especially words written on a stone where he/she is buried

epitome /ɪˈpɪtəmi/ **noun** [sing] the epitome (of sth) a perfect example of sth: *Her clothes are the epitome of good taste.*

epitomize (also **-ise**) /ɪˈpɪtəmaɪz/ **verb** [T] to be typical of sth: *This building epitomizes modern trends in architecture.*

epoch /ˈiːpɒk/ **noun** [C] a period of time in history (that is important because of special events, characteristics, etc)

★**equal**[1] /ˈiːkwəl/ **adj 1** equal (to sb/sth) the same in size, amount, value, number, level, etc: *This animal is equal in weight to a small car.* ● *They are equal in weight.* ● *They are of equal weight.* ● *Divide it into two equal parts.* ••➤ opposite **unequal 2** having the same rights or being treated the same as other people: *This company has an equal opportunities policy* (= gives the same chance of employment to everyone). **3** (*formal*) equal to sth having the strength, ability etc to do sth: *I'm afraid Bob just isn't equal to the job.* IDIOM **be on equal terms (with sb)** to have the same advantages and disadvantages as sb else

equal[2] /ˈiːkwəl/ **verb** [T] (**equalling**; **equalled**: *US* **equaling**; **equaled**) **1** (used about numbers, etc) to be the same as sth: *44 plus 17 equals 61 is written: 44 + 17 = 61.* **2** to be as good as sb/sth: *He ran an excellent race, equalling the world record.*

equal[3] /ˈiːkwəl/ **noun** [C] a person who has the same ability, rights, etc as you do: *to treat sb as an equal*

★**equality** /iˈkwɒləti/ **noun** [U] the situation in which everyone has the same rights and advantages: *racial equality* (= between people of different races) ••➤ opposite **inequality**

equalize (also **-ise**) /ˈiːkwəlaɪz/ **verb** [I] (*sport*) to reach the same number of points as your opponent

★**equally** /'i:kwəli/ **adv 1** to the same degree or amount: *They both worked equally hard.* **2** in equal parts: *His money was divided equally between his children.* **3** (*formal*) (used when you are comparing two ideas or commenting on what you have just said) at the same time; but/and also: *I do not think what he did was right. Equally, I can understand why he did it.*

equate /i'kweɪt/ **verb** [T] **equate sth (with sth)** to consider one thing as being the same as sth else: *You can't always equate money with happiness.*

equation /ɪ'kweɪʒn/ **noun** [C] (in mathematics) a statement that two quantities are equal: $2x + 5 = 11$ *is an equation.*

the equator (also **the Equator**) /ɪ'kweɪtə/ **noun** [sing] the imagined line around the earth at an equal distance from the North and South Poles: *north/south of the Equator* • *The island is on the equator.* •➤ picture at **earth**

equestrian /ɪ'kwestriən/ **adj** (*formal*) connected with horse riding

equip /ɪ'kwɪp/ **verb** [T] (**equipping**; **equipped**) equip sb/sth (with sth) **1** (usually passive) to supply sb/sth with what is needed for a particular purpose: *We shall equip all schools with new computers over the next year.* • *The flat has a **fully-equipped** kitchen.* **2** to prepare sb for a particular task: *The course equips students with all the skills necessary to become a chef.*

★**equipment** /ɪ'kwɪpmənt/ **noun** [U] the things that are needed to do a particular activity: *office/sports/computer equipment*

➤ Note that **equipment** is uncountable. We have to say 'a piece of equipment' if we are talking about one item: *a very useful piece of kitchen equipment.*

equivalent /ɪ'kwɪvələnt/ **adj** equivalent (to sth) equal in value, amount, meaning, importance, etc: *The British House of Commons is roughly equivalent to the American House of Representatives.* –**equivalent noun** [C]: *There is no English equivalent to the French 'bon appétit'.*

er /ɜː/ **interj** used in writing to show the sound that sb makes when he/she cannot decide what to say next

era /'ɪərə/ **noun** [C] a period of time in history (that is special for some reason): *We are living in the era of the computer.*

eradicate /ɪ'rædɪkeɪt/ **verb** [T] (*formal*) to destroy or get rid of sth completely: *Scientists have completely eradicated some diseases, such as smallpox.* –**eradication** /ɪ,rædɪ'keɪʃn/ **noun** [U]

erase /ɪ'reɪz/ **verb** [T] (*formal*) to remove sth completely (a pencil mark, a recording on tape, a computer file, etc): (*figurative*) *He tried to erase the memory of those terrible years from his mind.* •➤ We usually say **rub out** a pencil mark. –**eraser** (*especially US*) = **RUBBER**(2)

erect[1] /ɪ'rekt/ **adj 1** standing straight up: *He stood with his head erect.* •➤ synonym **upright 2** (used about the male sexual organ) hard and standing up because of sexual excitement

erect[2] /ɪ'rekt/ **verb** [T] (*formal*) to build sth or to stand sth straight up: *to erect a statue* • *Huge TV screens were erected above the stage.*

erection /ɪ'rekʃn/ **noun 1** [C] if a man has an erection, his sexual organ (**penis**) becomes hard and stands up because he is sexually excited: *to get/have an erection* **2** [U] (*formal*) the act of building sth or standing sth straight up

erode /ɪ'rəʊd/ **verb** [T] (usually passive) (used about the sea, the weather, etc) to destroy sth slowly: *The cliff has been eroded by the sea.* –**erosion** /ɪ'rəʊʒn/ **noun** [U]: *the erosion of rocks by the sea*

erotic /ɪ'rɒtɪk/ **adj** causing sexual excitement: *an erotic film/poem/dream*

err /ɜː/ **verb** [I] (*formal*) to be or do wrong; to make mistakes

IDIOM **err on the side of sth** to do more of sth than is necessary in order to avoid the opposite happening: *It is better to err on the side of caution* (= it is better to be too careful rather than not careful enough).

errand /'erənd/ **noun** [C] (*old-fashioned*) a short journey to take or get sth for sb, for example to buy sth from a shop

erratic /ɪ'rætɪk/ **adj** (used about a person's behaviour, or about the quality of sth) changing without reason; that you can never be sure of: *Jones is a talented player but he's very erratic* (= sometimes he plays well, sometimes badly). –**erratically** /-kli/ **adv**

★**error** /'erə/ **noun 1** [C] (*formal*) a mistake: *The telephone bill was far too high due to a computer error.* • *an error of judgement* • *to make an error*

➤ **Error** is more formal than **mistake**. There are some expressions such as *error of judgement, human error* where only **error** can be used.

2 [U] the state of being wrong: *The letter was sent to you in error.* • *The accident was the result of **human error**.*

IDIOM **trial and error** → **TRIAL**

erupt /ɪ'rʌpt/ **verb** [I] **1** (used about a volcano) to explode and throw out fire, rock that has melted (**lava**), smoke, etc **2** (used about violence, shouting, etc) to start suddenly: *The demonstration erupted into violence.* **3** (used about a person) to suddenly become very angry: *George erupted when he heard the news.* –**eruption noun** [C,U]: *a volcanic eruption*

escalate /'eskəleɪt/ **verb** [I,T] **1** escalate (sth) (into sth) (to cause sth) to become stronger or more serious: *The demonstrations are escalating into violent protest in all the major cities.* • *The terrorist attacks escalated tension in the capital.* **2** (to cause sth) to become greater or higher; to increase: *The* *cost of housing has escalated in recent years.* –escalation /ˌeskəˈleɪʃn/ **noun** [C,U]

escalator /ˈeskəleɪtə/ **noun** [C] a moving staircase in a shop, etc

escapade /ˌeskəˈpeɪd/ **noun** [C] an exciting adventure that may be dangerous

★**escape¹** /ɪˈskeɪp/ **verb 1** [I] escape (from sb/sth) to manage to get away from a place where you do not want to be; to get free: *Two prisoners have escaped.* ● *They managed to escape from the burning building.* **2** [I,T] to manage to avoid sth dangerous or unpleasant: *The two men in the other car escaped unhurt in the accident.* ● *David Smith escaped injury when his car skidded off the road.* ● *to escape criticism/punishment* **3** [T] to be forgotten or not noticed by sb: *His name escapes me.* ● *to escape sb's notice* **4** [I] (used about gases or liquids) to come or get out of a container, etc: *There's gas escaping somewhere.* –escaped **adj**: *an escaped prisoner*

★**escape²** /ɪˈskeɪp/ **noun 1** [C,U] escape (from sth) the act of escaping (1,2): *There have been twelve escapes from the prison this year.* ● *She had a narrow/lucky escape when a lorry crashed into her car.* ● *When the guard fell asleep they were able to make their escape.* ••➤ Look also at **fire escape**. **2** [U,sing] something that helps you forget your normal life: *For him, listening to music is a means of escape.* ● *an escape from reality*

escort¹ /ˈeskɔːt/ **noun** [C] **1** [with sing or pl verb] one or more people or vehicles that go with and protect sb/sth, or that go with sb/ sth as an honour: *an armed escort* ● *He arrived under police escort.* **2** (*formal*) a person who takes sb to a social event **3** a person, especially a woman, who is paid to go out socially with sb: *an escort agency*

escort² /esˈkɔːt/ **verb** [T] **1** to go with sb as an escort(1): *The President's car was escorted by several police cars.* **2** to take sb somewhere: *Philip escorted her to the door.*

Eskimo /ˈeskɪməʊ/ (*old-fashioned*) = **INUIT** ••➤ Inuits prefer not to be called Eskimos.

ESL /ˌiː es ˈel/ **abbr** English as a Second Language

esp **abbr 1** especially **2 ESP** /ˌiː es ˈpiː/ English for Specific/Special Purposes; the teaching of English to people who need it for a special reason, such as scientific study, engineering, etc

especial /ɪˈspeʃl/ **adj** (only *before* a noun) (*formal*) not usual; special: *This will be of especial interest to you.*

★**especially** /ɪˈspeʃəli/ **adv 1** more than other things, people, situations, etc; particularly: *She loves animals, especially dogs.* ● *Teenage boys especially can be very competitive.* ● *He was very disappointed with his mark in the exam, especially as he had worked so hard for it.* **2** for a particular purpose or person: *I made this especially for you.* ••➤ A less formal word is **specially**. **3** very (much): *It's not an especially difficult exam.* ● *'Do you like jazz?' 'Not especially.'*

espionage /ˈespiənɑːʒ/ **noun** [U] the act of finding out secret information about another country or organization ••➤ verb spy

Esq **abbr** (*especially Brit formal*) Esquire; used when you are writing a man's name on an envelope: *Edward Hales, Esq*

➤ This is old-fashioned and many people now prefer to write: *Mr Edward Hales.*

★**essay** /ˈeseɪ/ **noun** [C] an essay (on/about sth) a short piece of writing on one subject: *We have to write a 1000-word essay on tourism for homework.*

essence /ˈesns/ **noun 1** [U] the basic or most important quality of sth: *The essence of the problem is that there is not enough money available.* ● *Although both parties agree in essence, some minor differences remain.* **2** [C,U] a substance (usually a liquid) that is taken from a plant or food and that has a strong smell or taste of that plant or food: *coffee/vanilla essence*

★**essential** /ɪˈsenʃl/ **adj** completely necessary; that you must have or do: *essential medical supplies* ● *Maths is essential for a career in computers.* ● *It is essential that all school-leavers should have a qualification.* –essential **noun** [C,usually pl]: *food, and other essentials such as clothing and heating*

★**essentially** /ɪˈsenʃəli/ **adv** when you consider the basic or most important part of sth; basically: *The problem is essentially one of money.*

★**establish** /ɪˈstæblɪʃ/ **verb** [T] **1** to start or create an organization, a system, etc: *The school was established in 1875.* ● *Before we start on the project we should establish some rules.* **2** to start a formal relationship with sb/sth: *The government is trying to establish closer links between the two countries.* **3** establish sb/sth (as sth) to become accepted and recognized as sth: *She has been trying to establish herself as a novelist for years.* **4** to discover or find proof of the facts of a situation: *The police have not been able to establish the cause of the crash.*

★**establishment** /ɪˈstæblɪʃmənt/ **noun 1** [C] (*formal*) an organization, a large institution or a hotel: *an educational establishment* **2 the Establishment** [sing] the people in positions of power in a country, who usually do not support change **3** [U] the act of creating or starting a new organization, system, etc: *the establishment of new laws on taxes*

★**estate** /ɪˈsteɪt/ **noun** [C] **1** a large area of land in the countryside that is owned by one person or family: *He owns a large estate in Scotland.* **2** (*Brit*) an area of land that has a lot of houses or factories of the same type on it: *an industrial estate* (= where there are a lot of factories) ● *a housing estate* **3** all the money and property that sb leaves when he/she dies

es'tate agent (*US realtor; real estate agent*) **noun** [C] a person whose job is to buy and sell houses and land for other people

es'tate car (*US station wagon*) **noun** [C] a car with a door at the back and a long area for luggage behind the back seat ••➤ picture at **car**

esteem /ɪˈstiːm/ **noun** [U] (*formal*) great respect; a good opinion of sb

esthetic (*US*) = **AESTHETIC**

★**estimate**¹ /ˈestɪmət/ **noun** [C] **1** an estimate (of sth) a guess or judgement about the size, cost, etc of sth, before you have all the facts and figures: *Can you give me **a rough estimate** of how many people will be at the meeting?* • *At a conservative estimate* (= the real figure will probably be higher)*, the job will take six months to complete.* **2** an estimate (for sth/doing sth) a written statement from a person who is going to do a job for you, for example a builder or a painter, telling you how much it will cost: *They gave me an estimate for repairing the roof.* ••➤ Look at **quotation**.

IDIOM a ballpark figure/estimate → **BALLPARK**

★**estimate**² /ˈestɪmeɪt/ **verb** [T] **estimate sth (at sth); estimate that…** to calculate the size, cost, etc of·sth approximately, before you have all the facts and figures: *The police estimated the crowd at 10000.* • *She estimated that the work would take three months.*

estimation /ˌestɪˈmeɪʃn/ **noun** [U] (*formal*) opinion or judgement: *Who is to blame, in your estimation?*

estranged /ɪˈstreɪndʒd/ **adj 1** no longer living with your husband/wife: *her estranged husband* **2** **estranged (from sb)** no longer friendly or in contact with sb who was close to you: *He became estranged from his family following an argument.*

estuary /ˈestʃuəri/ **noun** [C] (*pl estuaries*) the wide part (**mouth**) of a river where it joins the sea

etc **abbr** etcetera; and so on, and other things of a similar kind: *sandwiches, biscuits, cakes, etc*

eternal /ɪˈtɜːnl/ **adj 1** without beginning or end; existing or continuing for ever: *Some people believe in eternal life* (= after death). **2** happening too often; seeming to last for ever: *I'm tired of these eternal arguments!* –**eternally** /-əli/ **adv**: *I'll be **eternally grateful** if you could help me.*

eternity /ɪˈtɜːnəti/ **noun 1** [U] time that has no end; the state or time after death **2** an eternity [sing] a period of time that never seems to end: *It seemed like an eternity before the ambulance arrived.*

ethical /ˈeθɪkl/ **adj 1** connected with beliefs of what is right or wrong: *That is an ethical problem.* **2** morally correct: *Although she didn't break the law, her behaviour was certainly not ethical.*

ethics /ˈeθɪks/ **noun 1** [U] the study of what is right and wrong in human behaviour **2** [pl] beliefs about what is morally correct or acceptable: *The medical profession has its own **code of ethics**.*

ethnic /ˈeθnɪk/ **adj** connected with or typical of a particular race or religion: *ethnic minorities* • *ethnic food/music/clothes*

ˌ**ethnic ˈcleansing** **noun** [U] the policy of

forcing people of a certain race or religion to leave an area or country

etiquette /ˈetɪket/ **noun** [U] the rules of polite and correct behaviour: *social/professional etiquette*

etymology /ˌetɪˈmɒlədʒi/ **noun** (*pl etymologies*) **1** [U] the study of the origins and history of words and their meanings **2** [C] an explanation of the origin and history of a particular word

euphemism /ˈjuːfəmɪzəm/ **noun** [C,U] (using) a polite word or expression instead of a more direct one when you are talking about sth that is unpleasant or embarrassing: *'Pass away' is a euphemism for 'die'.*

euphoria /juːˈfɔːriə/ **noun** [U] (*formal*) an extremely strong feeling of happiness

euro /ˈjʊərəʊ/ **noun** [C] (*symbol €*) (since 1999) a unit of money used in several countries of the European Union: *The price is given in dollars or euros.* ••➤ Look at **EMU**.

Eurocheque /ˈjʊərəʊtʃek/ **noun** [C] a cheque that can be used in many European countries

★**European**¹ /ˌjʊərəˈpiːən/ **adj** of or from Europe: *European languages*

★**European**² /ˌjʊərəˈpiːən/ **noun** [C] a person from a European country

the Euroˌpean ˈUnion noun [sing] (*abbr* **EU**) an economic and political association of certain European countries

euthanasia /ˌjuːθəˈneɪziə/ **noun** [U] the practice (illegal in most countries) of killing without pain sb who wants to die because he/she is suffering from a disease that cannot be cured

evacuate /ɪˈvækjueɪt/ **verb** [T] to move people from a dangerous place to somewhere safer; to leave a place because it is dangerous: *Thousands of people were evacuated from the war zone.* • *The village had to be evacuated when the river burst its banks.* –**evacuation** /ɪˌvækjuˈeɪʃn/ **noun** [C,U]

evade /ɪˈveɪd/ **verb** [T] **1** to manage to escape from or to avoid meeting sb/sth: *They managed to evade capture and escaped to France.* **2** to avoid dealing with or doing sth: *to evade responsibility* • *I asked her directly, but she evaded the question.* ••➤ noun **evasion**

evaluate /ɪˈvæljueɪt/ **verb** [T] (*formal*) to study the facts and then form an opinion about sth: *We evaluated the situation very carefully before we made our decision.* –**evaluation** /ɪˌvæljuˈeɪʃn/ **noun** [C,U]

evaporate /ɪˈvæpəreɪt/ **verb** [I] **1** (used about a liquid) to change into steam or gas and disappear: *The water evaporated in the sunshine.* ••➤ Look at **condense**. **2** to disappear completely: *All her confidence evaporated when she saw the exam paper.* –**evaporation** /ɪˌvæpəˈreɪʃn/ **noun** [U]

evasion /ɪˈveɪʒn/ **noun** [C,U] **1** the act of avoiding sth that you should do: *He has been sentenced to two years' imprisonment for **tax evasion**.* • *an evasion of responsibility* **2** a statement that avoids dealing with a question

e

or subject in a direct way: *The President's reply was full of evasions.* •➤ verb **evade**

evasive /ɪ'veɪsɪv/ **adj** trying to avoid sth; not direct: *Ann gave an evasive answer.*

eve /iːv/ **noun** [C] the day or evening before a religious festival, important event, etc: *Christmas Eve* ● *He injured himself on the eve of the final.*

★**even¹** /'iːvn/ **adj 1** flat, level or smooth: *The game must be played on an even surface.* **2** not changing; regular: *He's very even-tempered – in fact I've never seen him angry.* **3** (used about a competition, etc) equal, with one side being as good as the other: *The contest was very even until the last few minutes of the game.* •➤ opposite for senses **1**, **2** and **3** **uneven 4** (used about numbers) that can be divided by two: *2, 4, 6, 8, 10, etc are even numbers.* •➤ opposite **odd**

IDIOMS **be/get even (with sb)** (*informal*) to hurt or harm sb who has hurt or harmed you **break even** to make neither a loss nor a profit

★**even²** /'iːvn/ **adv 1** used for emphasizing sth that is surprising: *It isn't very warm here even in summer.* ● *He didn't even open the letter.* **2 even more, less, bigger, nicer, etc** used when you are comparing things, to make the comparison stronger: *You know even less about it than I do.* ● *It is even more difficult that I expected.* ● *We are even busier than yesterday.*

IDIOMS **even if** used for saying that what follows 'if' makes no difference: *I wouldn't ride a horse, even if you paid me.*

even so (used for introducing a new idea, fact, etc that is surprising) in spite of that; nevertheless: *There are a lot of spelling mistakes; even so it's quite a good essay.*

even though although: *I like her very much even though she can be very annoying.* •➤ Look at the note at **although**.

★**evening** /'iːvnɪŋ/ **noun** [C,U] the part of the day between the afternoon and the time that you go to bed: *What are you doing this evening?* ● *We were out yesterday evening.* ● *I went to the cinema on Saturday evening.* ● *Tom usually goes swimming on Wednesday evenings.* ● *Most people watch television in the evening.* ● *an evening class* (= a course of lessons for adults that takes place in the evening)

IDIOM **good evening** used when you see sb for the first time in the evening •➤ Often we just say *Evening*: *'Good evening, Mrs Wilson.' 'Evening, Mr Mills.'*

★**evenly** /'iːvnli/ **adv** in a smooth, regular or equal way: *The match was very evenly balanced.* ● *Spread the cake mixture evenly in the tin.*

★**event** /ɪ'vent/ **noun** [C] **1** something that happens, especially sth important or unusual: *a historic event* ● *The events of the past few days have made things very difficult for the Government.* **2** a planned public or social occasion: *a fund-raising event* **3** one of the races, competitions, etc in a sports programme: *The next*

event is the 800 metres.

IDIOMS **at all events/in any event** whatever happens: *I hope to see you soon, but in any event I'll phone you on Sunday.*

in the event of sth (*formal*) if sth happens: *In the event of fire, leave the building as quickly as possible.*

★**eventful** /ɪ'ventfl/ **adj** full of important, dangerous, or exciting things happening

eventual /ɪ'ventʃuəl/ **adj** (only *before* a noun) happening as a result at the end of a period of time or of a process: *It is impossible to say what the eventual cost will be.*

★**eventually** /ɪ'ventʃuəli/ **adv** in the end; finally: *He eventually managed to persuade his parents to let him buy a motor bike.* •➤ synonym **finally**

★**ever¹** /'evə/ **adv 1** (used in questions and negative sentences, when you are comparing things, and in sentences with 'if') at any time: *Do you ever wish you were famous?* ● *Nobody ever comes to see me.* ● *She hardly ever* (= almost never) *goes out.* ● *Today is hotter than ever.* ● *This is the best meal I have ever had.* ● *If you ever visit England, you must come and stay with us.* **2** (used in questions with verbs in the perfect tenses) at any time up to now: *Have you ever been to Spain?* **3** used with a question that begins with 'when', 'where', 'who', 'how', etc, to show that you are surprised or shocked: *How ever did he get back so quickly?* ● *What ever were you thinking about when you wrote this?* •➤ Look at **whatever, whenever, however,** etc.

IDIOMS **(as) bad, good, etc as ever** (as) bad, good, etc as usual or as always: *In spite of his problems, Andrew is as cheerful as ever.*

ever after (used especially at the end of stories) from that moment on for always: *The prince married the princess and they lived happily ever after.*

ever since... all the time from...until now: *She has had a car ever since she was at university.*

ever so/ever such (a) (*Brit informal*) very: *He's ever so kind.* ● *He's ever such a kind man.*

for ever → FOREVER(1)

ever-² /'evə/ (in compounds) always; continuously: *the ever-growing problem of pollution*

evergreen /'evəgriːn/ **noun** [C], **adj** (a tree or bush) with green leaves all through the year •➤ Look at **deciduous**.

everlasting /,evə'lɑːstɪŋ/ **adj** (*formal*) continuing for ever; never changing: *everlasting life/love*

★**every** /'evri/ **determiner 1** (used with singular nouns) all of the people or things in a group of three or more: *She knows every student in the school.* ● *There are 200 students in the school, and she knows every one of them.* ● *I've read every book in this house.* ● *You were out every time I phoned.* •➤ Look at note at **everybody. 2** all that is possible: *You have every chance of success.* ● *She had every reason to be angry.* **3** used for saying how often sth happens: *We see each other every day.*

● *Take the medicine every four hours* (= at 8, 12, 4 o'clock, etc). ● *I work every other day* (= on Monday, Wednesday, Friday, etc). ● *One in every three marriages ends in divorce.*

★**everybody** /'evribɒdi/ (also **everyone** /'evriwʌn/) **pron** [with sing verb] every person; all people: *Is everybody here?* ● *The police questioned everyone who was at the party.* ● *I'm sure everybody else* (= all the other people) *will agree with me.*

➤ **Everyone** is only used about people and is not followed by 'of'. **Every one** means 'each person or thing' and is often followed by 'of': *Every one of his records has been successful.* Look also at the note at **somebody**.

everyday /'evrideɪ/ **adj** (only *before* a noun) normal or usual: *The computer is now part of everyday life.*

everyplace /'evripleɪs/ (*US*) = **EVERYWHERE**

★**everything** /'evriθɪŋ/ **pron** [with sing verb] **1** each thing; all things: *Sam lost everything in the fire.* ● *Everything is very expensive in this shop.* ● *We can leave everything else* (= all the other things) *until tomorrow.* **2** the most important thing: *Money isn't everything.*

everywhere /'evriweə/ **adv** in or to every place: *I've looked everywhere, but I still can't find it.*

evict /ɪ'vɪkt/ **verb** [T] to force sb (officially) to leave the house or land which he/she is renting: *They were evicted for not paying the rent.* –**eviction noun** [C,U]

★**evidence** /'evɪdəns/ **noun** [U] evidence (of/ for sth); evidence that… the facts, signs, etc that make you believe that sth is true: *There was no evidence of a struggle in the room.* ● *There was not enough evidence to prove him guilty.* ● *Her statement to the police was used in evidence against him.* ● *The witnesses to the accident will be asked to give evidence in court.* ● *You have absolutely no evidence for what you're saying!*

➤ Note that **evidence** is uncountable. We use **piece** if we are talking about a single item of evidence: *One piece of evidence is not enough to prove somebody guilty.*

IDIOM (to be) in evidence that you can see; present in a place: *When we arrived there was no ambulance in evidence.*

evident /'evɪdənt/ **adj** clear (to the eye or mind); obvious: *It was evident that the damage was very serious.*

evidently /'evɪdəntli/ **adv 1** clearly; that can be easily seen or understood: *She was evidently extremely shocked at the news.* **2** according to what people say: *Evidently he has decided to leave.*

evil¹ /'iːvl/ **adj** morally bad; causing trouble or harming people: *In the play Richard is portrayed as an evil king.*

evil² /'iːvl/ **noun** [C,U] a force that causes bad or harmful things to happen: *The play is about the good and evil in all of us.* ● *Drugs and alcohol are two of the evils of modern*

society.

IDIOM the lesser of two evils → **LESSER**

evoke /ɪ'vəʊk/ **verb** [T] (*formal*) to produce a memory, feeling, etc in sb: *For me, that music always evokes hot summer evenings.* ● *Her novel evoked a lot of interest.*

evolution /ˌiːvə'luːʃn; ˌev-/ **noun** [U] **1** the development of plants, animals, etc over many thousands of years from simple early forms to more advanced ones: *Darwin's theory of evolution* **2** the gradual process of change and development of sth: *Political evolution is a slow process.*

evolve /i'vɒlv/ **verb 1** [I,T] (*formal*) to develop or to make sth develop gradually, from a simple to a more advanced form: *His style of painting has evolved gradually over the past 20 years.* **2** [I] develop (from sth) (used about plants, animals, etc) to develop over many thousands of years from simple forms to more advanced ones

ewe /juː/ **noun** [C] a female sheep ••➤ Look at the note at **sheep**. ••➤ picture at **goat**

★**exact**¹ /ɪg'zækt/ **adj 1** (completely) correct; accurate: *He's in his mid-fifties. Well, 56 to be exact.* ● *I can't tell you the exact number of people who are coming.* ● *She's the exact opposite of her sister.* **2** able to work in a way that is completely accurate: *You need to be very exact when you calculate the costs.* –**exactness noun** [U]

exact² /ɪg'zækt/ **verb** [T] (*formal*) exact sth (from sb) to demand and get sth from sb

exacting /ɪg'zæktɪŋ/ **adj** needing a lot of care and attention; difficult: *exacting work*

★**exactly** /ɪg'zæktli/ **adv 1** (used to emphasize that sth is correct in every way) just: *You've arrived at exactly the right moment.* ● *I found exactly what I wanted.* **2** used to ask for, or give, completely correct information: *He took exactly one hour to finish.* ••➤ synonym **precisely 3** (*spoken*) (used for agreeing with a statement) yes; you are right: *'I don't think she's old enough to travel on her own.' 'Exactly.'*

IDIOM not exactly (*spoken*) **1** (used when you are saying the opposite of what you really mean) not really; not at all: *He's not exactly the most careful driver I know.* **2** (used as an answer to say that sth is almost true): *'So you think I'm wrong?' 'No, not exactly, but …'*

★**exaggerate** /ɪg'zædʒəreɪt/ **verb** [I,T] to make sth seem larger, better, worse, etc than it really is: *Don't exaggerate. I was only two minutes late, not twenty.* ● *The problems have been greatly exaggerated.* –**exaggeration** /ɪgˌzædʒə'reɪʃn/ **noun** [C,U]: *It's rather an exaggeration to say that all the students are lazy.*

★**exam** /ɪg'zæm/ (also *formal* **examination**) **noun** [C] a written, spoken or practical test of what you know or can do: *an English exam* ● *the exam results* ● *to do/take/sit an exam* ● *to pass/fail an exam*

➤ A **test** is less formal and usually shorter than an exam.

e

★**examination** /ɪgˌzæmɪˈneɪʃn/ **noun 1** [C,U] the act of looking at sth carefully, especially to see if there is anything wrong or to find the cause of a problem: *On close examination, it was found that the passport was false.* ● *a medical examination* **2** [C] (*formal*) = **EXAM**

★**examine** /ɪgˈzæmɪn/ **verb** [T] **1** to consider or study an idea, a subject, etc very carefully: *These theories will be examined in more detail later on in the lecture.* **2 examine sb/sth (for sth)** to look at sb/sth carefully in order to find out sth: *The detective examined the room for clues.* **3** (*formal*) **examine sb (in/on sth)** to test what sb knows or can do: *You will be examined on everything that has been studied in the course.*

examiner /ɪgˈzæmɪnə/ **noun** [C] a person who tests sb in an exam

★**example** /ɪgˈzɑːmpl/ **noun** [C] **1** an example (of sth) something such as an object, a fact or a situation which shows, explains or supports what you say: *I don't quite understand you. Can you give me an example of what you mean?* ● *This is a typical example of a Victorian house.* **2** an example (to sb) a person or thing or a type of behaviour that is good and should be copied: *Joe's bravery should be an example to us all.*

IDIOMS **follow sb's example/lead** → **FOLLOW**

for example (*abbr* eg) used for giving a fact, situation, etc, which explains or supports what you are talking about: *In many countries, Italy, for example, family life is much more important than here.*

set a(n) (good/bad) example (to sb) to behave in a way that should/should not be copied: *Parents should always take care when crossing roads in order to set a good example to their children.*

exasperate /ɪgˈzæspəreɪt/ **verb** [T] to make sb angry; to annoy sb very much: *She was exasperated by the lack of progress.* –**exasperating adj**: *an exasperating problem* –**exasperation** /ɪgˌzæspəˈreɪʃn/ **noun** [U]: *She finally threw the book across the room in exasperation.*

excavate /ˈekskəveɪt/ **verb** [I,T] to dig in the ground to look for old objects or buildings that have been buried for a long time; to find sth by digging in this way: *A Roman villa has been excavated in a valley near the village.* –**excavation** /ˌekskəˈveɪʃn/ **noun** [C,U]: *Excavations on the site have revealed Saxon objects.*

exceed /ɪkˈsiːd/ **verb** [T] **1** to be more than a particular number or amount: *The weight should not exceed 20 kilos.* **2** to do more than the law, a rule, an order, etc allows you to do: *He was stopped by the police for exceeding the speed limit* (= driving faster than is allowed). •➤ Look at **excess** and **excessive**.

exceedingly /ɪkˈsiːdɪŋli/ **adv** (*formal*) very: *an exceedingly difficult problem*

excel /ɪkˈsel/ **verb** [I] (**excelling; excelled**) (*formal*) **1 excel (in/at sth/doing sth)** to be very good at doing sth: *Anne excels at sports.* **2 excel yourself** (*Brit*) to do sth even better

than you usually do: *Rick's cooking is always good but this time he really excelled himself.*

excellence /ˈeksələns/ **noun** [U] the quality of being very good: *The head teacher said that she wanted the school to be a centre of academic excellence.*

★**excellent** /ˈeksələnt/ **adj** very good; of high quality: *He speaks excellent French.* –**excellently adv**

★**except**[1] /ɪkˈsept/ **prep except (for) sb/sth; except that...** not including sb/sth; apart from the fact that: *The museum is open every day except Mondays.* ● *I can answer all of the questions except for the last one.* ● *It was a good hotel except that it was rather noisy.*

except[2] /ɪkˈsept/ **verb** [T] (*formal*) **except sb/sth (from sth)** (often passive) to leave sb/sth out; to not include sb/sth: *Nobody is excepted from helping with the housework.* –**excepting prep**: *I swim every day excepting Sundays.*

★**exception** /ɪkˈsepʃn/ **noun** [C] a person or thing that is not included in a general statement: *Most of his songs are awful but this one is an exception.* ● *Everybody was poor as a student and I was no exception.*

IDIOMS **make an exception (of sb/sth)** to treat sb/sth differently: *We don't usually allow children under 14 but we'll make an exception in your case.*

with the exception of except for; apart from: *He has won every major tennis championship with the exception of Wimbledon.*

without exception in every case; including everyone/everything: *Everybody without exception must take the test.*

exceptional /ɪkˈsepʃənl/ **adj** very unusual; unusually good: *You will only be allowed to leave early in exceptional circumstances.* –**exceptionally** /-ʃənəli/ **adv**: *The past year has been exceptionally difficult for us.*

excerpt /ˈeksɜːpt/ **noun** [C] a short piece taken from a book, film, piece of music, etc

excess[1] /ɪkˈses/ **noun** [sing] **an excess (of sth)** more of sth than is necessary or usual; too much of sth: *An excess of fat in your diet can lead to heart disease.*

IDIOM **in excess of** more than: *Her debts are in excess of £1000.* •➤ **verb exceed**

excess[2] /ˈekses/ **adj** (only *before* a noun) more than is usual or allowed; extra: *Cut any excess fat off the meat.* •➤ **verb exceed**

excessive /ɪkˈsesɪv/ **adj** too much; too great or extreme: *He was driving at excessive speed when he crashed.* –**excessively adv**

★**exchange**[1] /ɪksˈtʃeɪndʒ/ **noun 1** [C,U] giving or receiving sth in return for sth else: *a useful exchange of information* ● *We can offer free accommodation in exchange for some help in the house.* **2** [U] the relation in value between kinds of money used in different countries: *What's the exchange rate/rate of exchange for dollars?* ● *Most of the country's foreign exchange comes from oil.* •➤ Look at **Stock Exchange**. **3** [C] a visit by a group of students or teachers to another country and a return visit by a similar group from that country: *She went on an exchange to Germany when she was sixteen.* **4** [C] an angry conversation or argument: *She ended up having a* **heated exchange** *with her neighbours about the noise the night before.*

★**exchange²** /ɪks'tʃeɪndʒ/ **verb** [T] **exchange A for B**; **exchange sth (with sb)** to give or receive sth in return for sth else: *I would like to exchange this skirt for a bigger size.* ● *Claire and Molly exchanged addresses with the boys.* ● *They exchanged glances* (= they looked at each other).

excise /'eksaɪz/ **noun** [U] a government tax on certain goods that are produced or sold inside a country, for example tobacco, alcohol, etc ••➤ Look at **customs**.

excitable /ɪk'saɪtəbl/ **adj** easily excited

excite /ɪk'saɪt/ **verb** [T] **1** to make sb feel happy and enthusiastic or nervous: *Don't excite the baby too much or we'll never get him off to sleep.* **2** to make sb react in a particular way: *The programme excited great interest.*

★**excited** /ɪk'saɪtɪd/ **adj** **excited (about/at/by sth)** feeling or showing happiness and enthusiasm; not calm: *Are you getting excited about your holiday?* ● *We're all very excited at the thought of moving house.* –**excitedly adv**

★**excitement** /ɪk'saɪtmənt/ **noun** [U] the state of being excited, especially because sth interesting is happening or will happen: *There was* **great excitement** *as the winner's name was announced.* ● *The match was* **full of excitement** *until the very last minute.*

★**exciting** /ɪk'saɪtɪŋ/ **adj** causing strong feelings of pleasure and interest: *That's very exciting news.* ● *Berlin is one of the most exciting cities in Europe.*

exclaim /ɪk'skleɪm/ **verb** [I,T] to say sth suddenly and loudly because you are surprised, angry, etc: *'I just don't believe it!' he exclaimed.*

exclamation /ˌeksklə'meɪʃn/ **noun** [C] a short sound, word or phrase that you say suddenly because of a strong emotion, pain, etc: *'Ouch!' is an exclamation.* ••➤ synonym **interjection**

ˌexcla'mation mark (*US* ˌexcla'mation point) **noun** [C] a mark (!) that is written after an exclamation

★**exclude** /ɪk'skluːd/ **verb** [T] (not used in the continuous tenses) **1** to leave out; not include: *The price excludes all extras such as drinks or excursions.* **2** **exclude sb/sth (from sth)** to prevent sb/sth from entering a place or taking part in sth: *Women are excluded from the temple.* ● *Jake was excluded from the game for cheating.* ••➤ opposite **include 3** to decide that sth is not possible: *The police had* **excluded the possibility** *that the child had run away.*

★**excluding** /ɪk'skluːdɪŋ/ **prep** leaving out; without: *Lunch costs £10 per person excluding drinks.* ••➤ opposite **including**

exclusion /ɪk'skluːʒn/ **noun** [U] keeping or leaving sb/sth out

exclusive¹ /ɪk'skluːsɪv/ **adj** **1** (only *before* a noun) only to be used by or given to one

person, group, etc; not to be shared: *This car is for the Director's exclusive use.* ● *Tonight we are showing an exclusive interview with the new leader of the Labour Party* (= on only one television or radio station). **2** expensive and not welcoming people who are thought to be of a lower social class: *an exclusive restaurant* ● *a flat in an exclusive part of the city* **3** **exclusive of sb/sth** not including sb/sth; without: *Lunch costs £7 per person exclusive of drinks.*

exclusive² /ɪk'skluːsɪv/ **noun** [C] a newspaper story that is given to and published by only one newspaper

exclusively /ɪk'skluːsɪvli/ **adv** only; not involving anyone/anything else: *The swimming pool is reserved exclusively for members of the club.*

excrement /'ekskrɪmənt/ **noun** [U] (*formal*) the solid waste material that you get rid of when you go to the toilet ••➤ synonym **faeces**

excrete /ɪk'skriːt/ **verb** [T] (*formal*) to get rid of solid waste material from the body

excruciating /ɪk'skruːʃieɪtɪŋ/ **adj** extremely painful

excursion /ɪk'skɜːʃn/ **noun** [C] a short journey or trip that a group of people make for pleasure: *to* **go on an excursion** *to the seaside* ••➤ Look at the note at **travel**.

excusable /ɪk'skjuːzəbl/ **adj** that you can forgive: *an excusable mistake* ••➤ opposite **inexcusable**

★**excuse¹** /ɪk'skjuːs/ **noun** [C] an excuse (for sth/doing sth) a reason (that may or may not be true) that you give in order to explain your behaviour: *There's* **no excuse for** *rudeness.* ● *He always* **finds an excuse** *for not helping with the housework.* ● *to* **make an excuse**

★**excuse²** /ɪk'skjuːz/ **verb** [T] **1** **excuse sb/sth (for sth/for doing sth)** to forgive sb for sth he/she has done wrong that is not very serious: *Please excuse the interruption but I need to talk to you.* **2** to explain sb's bad behaviour and make it seem less bad: *Nothing can excuse such behaviour.* **3** **excuse sb (from sth)** to free sb from a duty, responsibility, etc: *She excused herself* (= asked if she could leave) *and left the meeting early.*

> ➤ The expression **excuse me** is used when you interrupt somebody or when you want to start talking to somebody that you don't know: *Excuse me, can you tell me the way to the station?* In US English and occasionally in British English **excuse me** is used when you apologize for something: *Did I tread on your toe? Excuse me.*

execute /'eksɪkjuːt/ **verb** [T] **1** **execute sb (for sth)** (usually passive) to kill sb as an official punishment: *He was executed for murder.* **2** (*formal*) to perform a task, etc or to put a plan into action –**execution** /ˌeksɪ'kjuːʃn/ **noun** [C,U]

executioner /ˌeksɪ'kjuːʃənə/ **noun** [C] a person whose job is to execute criminals

executive[1] /ɪgˈzekjətɪv/ **adj 1** (used in connection with people in business, government, etc) concerned with managing, making plans, decisions, etc: *an executive director of the company* • *executive decisions/jobs/duties* **2** (used about goods, buildings, etc) designed to be used by important business people: *an executive briefcase*

executive[2] /ɪgˈzekjətɪv/ **noun 1** [C] a person who has an important position as a manager of a business or organization: *She's a senior executive in a computer company.* **2** [sing] the group of people who are in charge of an organization or a company

exemplary /ɪgˈzempləri/ **adj** very good; that can be an example to other people: *exemplary behaviour*

exemplify /ɪgˈzemplɪfaɪ/ **verb** [T] (*pres part* **exemplifying**; *3rd pers sing pres* **exemplifies**; *pt, pp* **exemplified**) to be a typical example of sth

exempt[1] /ɪgˈzempt/ **adj** (not before a noun) exempt (from sth) free from having to do sth or pay for sth: *Children under 16 are exempt from dental charges.* –**exemption** /ɪgˈzempʃn/ **noun** [C,U]

exempt[2] /ɪgˈzempt/ **verb** [T] (*formal*) **exempt sb/sth (from sth)** to say officially that sb does not have to do sth or pay for sth

★**exercise**[1] /ˈeksəsaɪz/ **noun 1** [U] physical or mental activity that keeps you healthy and strong: *The doctor advised him to take regular exercise.* • *Swimming is a good form of exercise.* **2** [C] (often plural) a movement or activity that you do in order to stay healthy or to become skilled at sth: *I do keep-fit exercises every morning.* • *breathing/stretching/relaxation exercises* **3** [C] a piece of work that is intended to help you learn or practise sth: *an exercise on phrasal verbs* **4** [C] an exercise in sth an activity or a series of actions that have a particular aim: *The project is an exercise in getting the best results at a low cost.* **5** [U] (*formal*) exercise of sth the use of sth, for example a power, right, etc: *the exercise of patience/judgement/discretion* **6** [C, usually pl] a series of activities by soldiers to practise fighting: *military exercises*

★**exercise**[2] /ˈeksəsaɪz/ **verb 1** [I] to do some form of physical activity in order to stay fit and healthy: *It is important to exercise regularly.* **2** [T] to make use of sth, for example a power, right, etc: *You should exercise your right to vote.*

exert /ɪgˈzɜːt/ **verb** [T] **1** to make use of sth, for example influence, strength, etc, to affect sb/sth: *Parents exert a powerful influence on their children's opinions.* **2** **exert yourself** to make a big effort: *You won't make any progress if you don't exert yourself a bit more.*

exertion /ɪgˈzɜːʃn/ **noun** [U,C] using your body in a way that takes a lot of effort; sth that you do that makes you tired: *At his age physical exertion was dangerous.* • *I'm tired after the exertions of the past few days.*

exhale /eksˈheɪl/ **verb** [I] (*formal*) to breathe out so that the air leaves your lungs ••➤ opposite **inhale**

exhaust[1] /ɪgˈzɔːst/ **noun 1** [U] the waste gas that comes out of a vehicle, an engine or a machine: *car exhaust fumes/emissions* **2** [C] (also **exhaust pipe**; *US* **tailpipe**) a pipe (particularly at the back of a car) through which waste gas escapes from an engine or machine ••➤ picture on page S9

★**exhaust**[2] /ɪgˈzɔːst/ **verb** [T] **1** to make sb very tired: *The long journey to work every morning exhausted him.* **2** to use sth up completely; to finish sth: *All the supplies of food have been exhausted.* **3** to say everything you can about a subject, etc: *Well, I think we've exhausted that topic.*

★**exhausted** /ɪgˈzɔːstɪd/ **adj** very tired

★**exhausting** /ɪgˈzɔːstɪŋ/ **adj** making sb very tired: *Teaching young children is exhausting work.*

exhaustion /ɪgˈzɔːstʃən/ **noun** [U] the state of being extremely tired

exhaustive /ɪgˈzɔːstɪv/ **adj** including everything possible: *This list is certainly not exhaustive.*

exhibit[1] /ɪgˈzɪbɪt/ **noun** [C] an object that is shown in a museum, etc or as a piece of evidence in a court of law

exhibit[2] /ɪgˈzɪbɪt/ **verb** [T] **1** to show sth in a public place for people to enjoy or to give them information: *His paintings have been exhibited in the local art gallery.* **2** (*formal*) to show clearly that you have a particular quality, feeling. etc: *The refugees are exhibiting signs of exhaustion and stress.*

★**exhibition** /ˌeksɪˈbɪʃn/ **noun 1** [C] a collection of objects, for example works of art, that are shown to the public: *an exhibition of photographs* • *Her paintings will be on exhibition in London for the whole of April.* **2** [C] an occasion when a particular skill is shown to the public: *We saw an exhibition of Scottish dancing last night.* **3** [sing] (*formal*) the act of showing a quality, feeling, etc: *The game was a superb exhibition of football at its best.*

exhibitor /ɪgˈzɪbɪtə/ **noun** [C] a person, for example an artist, a photographer, etc, who shows his/her work to the public

exhilarate /ɪgˈzɪləreɪt/ **verb** [T] (usually passive) to make sb feel very excited and happy: *We felt exhilarated by our walk along the beach.* –**exhilarating adj** –**exhilaration** /ɪgˌzɪləˈreɪʃn/ **noun** [U]

exile /ˈeksaɪl/ **noun 1** [U] the state of being forced to live outside your own country (especially for political reasons): *He went into exile after the revolution of 1968.* • *They lived in exile in London for many years.* **2** [C] a person who is forced to live outside his/her own country (especially for political reasons) ••➤ Look at **refugee.** –**exile verb** [T] (usually passive): *After the revolution the king was exiled.*

★**exist** /ɪgˈzɪst/ **verb** [I] **1** (not used in the continuous tenses) to be real; to be found in the real world; to live: *Dreams only exist in our*

imagination. • *Fish cannot exist out of water.*
2 exist (on sth) to manage to live: *I don't know how she exists on the wage she earns.*

existence /ɪg'zɪstəns/ **noun 1** [U] the state of existing: *This is the oldest human skeleton in existence.* • *How did the universe come into existence?* **2** [sing] a way of living, especially when it is difficult: *They lead a miserable existence in a tiny flat in London.*

existing /ɪg'zɪstɪŋ/ **adj** (only *before* a noun) that is already there or being used; present: *Under the existing law you are not allowed to work in this country.*

★**exit**[1] /'eksɪt; 'egzɪt/ **noun** [C] **1** a door or way out of a public building or vehicle: *The emergency exit is at the back of the bus.* **2** the act of leaving sth: *If I see her coming I'll make a quick exit.* • *an exit visa* (= one that allows you to leave a country) ••➤ opposite for senses 1 and 2 **entrance 3** a place where traffic can leave a road or a motorway to join another road: *At the roundabout take the third exit.*

exit[2] /'eksɪt; 'egzɪt/ **verb** [I,T] (*formal*) to leave a place: *He exited through the back door.* • *I exited the database and switched off the computer.*

exonerate /ɪg'zɒnəreɪt/ **verb** [T] (*formal*) (often passive) to say officially that sb was not responsible for sth bad that happened

exorbitant /ɪg'zɔːbɪtənt/ **adj** (*formal*) (used about the cost of sth) much more expensive than it should be

exotic /ɪg'zɒtɪk/ **adj** unusual or interesting because it comes from a different country or culture: *exotic plants/animals/fruits*

★**expand** /ɪk'spænd/ **verb** [I,T] to become or to make sth bigger: *Metals expand when they are heated.* • *We hope to expand our business this year.* ••➤ opposite **contract**
PHRASAL VERB **expand on sth** to give more details of a story, plan, idea, etc

expanse /ɪk'spæns/ **noun** [C] a large open area (of land, sea, sky, etc): *I lay on my back and stared up at the vast expanse of blue sky.*

★**expansion** /ɪk'spænʃn/ **noun** [U] the action of becoming bigger or the state of being bigger than before: *The rapid expansion of the university has caused a lot of problems.*

expansive /ɪk'spænsɪv/ **adj** (*formal*) (used about a person) who talks a lot in an interesting way; friendly

expatriate /,eks'pætriət/ (also *informal* **expat**) **noun** [C] a person who lives outside his/her own country: *American expatriates in London*

★**expect** /ɪk'spekt/ **verb** [T] **1** to think or believe that sb/sth will come or that sth will happen: *She was expecting a letter from the bank this morning but it didn't come.* • *I expect that it will rain this afternoon.* • *I know the food's not so good, but what did you expect from such a cheap restaurant?* (= it's not surprising) • *She's expecting a baby in the spring* (= she's pregnant). ••➤ Look at the note at **wait**[1]. **2 expect sth (from sb); expect sb to do sth** to feel confident that you will get sth from sb or that he/she will do what

you want: *He expects a high standard of work from everyone.* • *Factory workers are often expected to work at nights.* **3** (*Brit*) (not used in the continuous tenses) to think that sth is true or correct; to suppose: *'Whose is this suitcase?' 'Oh it's Maureen's, I expect.'* • *'Will you be able to help me later on?' 'I expect so.'*

➤ Although this verb is not used in the continuous tenses, it is common to see the present participle (= *-ing* form): *She flung the door open, expecting to see Richard standing there.*

expectancy /ɪk'spektənsi/ **noun** [U] the state of expecting sth to happen; hope: *a look/feeling of expectancy* ••➤ Look at **life expectancy**.

expectant /ɪk'spektənt/ **adj 1** thinking that sth good will happen; hopeful: *an expectant audience* • *expectant faces* **2** pregnant: *Expectant mothers need a lot of rest.* –**expectantly** **adv**

expectation /,ekspek'teɪʃn/ **noun** (*formal*) **1** [U] expectation (of sth) the belief that sth will happen or come: *The dog was sitting under the table in expectation of food.* **2** [C, usually pl] hope for the future: *They had great expectations for their daughter, but she didn't really live up to them.*
IDIOMS **against/contrary to (all) expectation(s)** very different to what was expected: *Contrary to all expectations, Val won first prize.*
not come up to (sb's) expectations to not be as good as expected

expedient /ɪk'spiːdiənt/ **adj** (*formal*) (used about an action) convenient or helpful for a purpose, but possibly not completely honest or moral: *The government decided that it was expedient not to increase taxes until after the election.* –**expediency** /-ənsi/ **noun** [U]

expedition /,ekspə'dɪʃn/ **noun** [C] **1** a long journey for a special purpose: *a scientific expedition to Antarctica* **2** a short journey that you make for pleasure: *a fishing expedition*

expel /ɪk'spel/ **verb** [T] (**expelling**; **expelled**) **1** to force sb to leave a country, school, club, etc: *The government has expelled all foreign journalists.* • *The boy was expelled from school for smoking.* **2** to send sth out by force: *to expel air from the lungs* ••➤ noun **expulsion**

expend /ɪk'spend/ **verb** [T] (*formal*) **expend sth (on sth)** to spend or use money, time, care, etc in doing sth: *I have expended a lot of time and energy on that project.*

expendable /ɪk'spendəbl/ **adj** (*formal*) not considered important enough to be saved: *In a war human life is expendable.*

expenditure /ɪk'spendɪtʃə/ **noun** [U, sing] (*formal*) the act of spending money; the amount of money that is spent: *Government expenditure on education is very low.*

★**expense** /ɪk'spens/ **noun 1** [C,U] the cost of sth in time or money: *Running a car is a great expense.* • *The movie was filmed in Tahiti at great expense.* **2 expenses** [pl] money

that is spent for a particular purpose: *You can claim back your travelling expenses.*
IDIOMS **at sb's expense 1** with sb paying; at sb's cost: *My trip is at the company's expense.* **2** against sb, so that he/she looks silly: *They were always making jokes at Paul's expense.*
at the expense of sth harming or damaging sth: *He was a successful businessman, but it was at the expense of his family life.*

★**expensive** /ɪk'spensɪv/ *adj* costing a lot of money: *Houses are very expensive in this area.* •➤ opposite **inexpensive** or **cheap** –**expensively** *adv*

★**experience**[1] /ɪk'spɪəriəns/ *noun* **1** [U] the things that you have done in your life; the knowledge or skill that you get from seeing or doing sth: *We all learn by experience.* • *She has five years' teaching experience.* • *I know from experience what will happen.* **2** [C] something that has happened to you (often something unusual or exciting): *She wrote a book about her experiences in Africa.*

experience[2] /ɪk'spɪəriəns/ *verb* [T] to have sth happen to you; to feel: *It was the first time I'd ever experienced failure.* • *to experience pleasure/pain/difficulty*

★**experienced** /ɪk'spɪəriənst/ *adj* having the knowledge or skill that is necessary for sth: *He's an experienced diver.* •➤ opposite **inexperienced**

★**experiment**[1] /ɪk'sperɪmənt/ *noun* [C,U] a scientific test that is done in order to get proof of sth or new knowledge: *to carry out/ perform/conduct/do an experiment* • *We need to prove this theory by experiment.* –**experimentally** /-təli/ *adv*

experiment[2] /ɪk'sperɪmənt/ *verb* [I] experiment (on/with sth) to do tests to see if sth works or to try to improve it: *Is it really necessary to experiment on animals?* • *We're experimenting with a new timetable this month.*

experimental /ɪk,sperɪ'mentl/ *adj* connected with experiments or trying new ideas: *We're still at the experimental stage with the new product.* • *experimental schools*

★**expert** /'eksp3:t/ *noun* [C] an expert (at/in/on sth) a person who has a lot of special knowledge or skill: *She's a leading expert in the field of genetics.* • *a computer expert* • *Let me try – I'm an expert at parking cars in small spaces.* –**expert** *adj*: *He's an expert cook.* • *I think we should get expert advice on the problem.* –**expertly** *adv*

expertise /,eksp3:'ti:z/ *noun* [U] a high level of special knowledge or skill: *I was amazed at his expertise on the word processor.*

expire /ɪk'spaɪə/ *verb* [I] (*formal*) (used about an official document, agreement, etc) to come to the end of the time when you can use it or in which it has effect: *My passport's expired. I'll have to renew it.* •➤ A less formal expression is **run out.**

expiry /ɪk'spaɪəri/ *noun* [U] the end of a period when you can use sth: *The expiry date on this yoghurt was 20 November.*

★**explain** /ɪk'spleɪn/ *verb* [I,T] explain (sth) (to sb) **1** to make sth clear or easy to understand: *She explained how I should fill in the form.* • *I don't understand this. Can you explain it to me?*

➤ Note that you have to say 'Explain **it to me**' NOT 'Explain me it'. This is wrong.

2 to give a reason for sth: *'This work isn't very good.' 'I wasn't feeling very well.' 'Oh, that explains it then.'* • *The manager explained to the customers why the goods were late.*
IDIOM **explain yourself 1** to give reasons for your behaviour, especially when it has upset sb **2** to say what you mean in a clear way
PHRASAL VERB **explain sth away** to give reasons why sth is not your fault or is not important

★**explanation** /,eksplə'neɪʃn/ *noun* **1** [C,U] an explanation (for sth) a statement, fact or situation that gives a reason for sth: *He could not give an explanation for his behaviour.* **2** [C] a statement or a piece of writing that makes sth easier to understand: *That idea needs some explanation.*

explanatory /ɪk'splænətri/ *adj* giving an explanation: *There are some explanatory notes at the back of the book.* • *Those instructions are self-explanatory* (= they don't need explaining).

explicable /ɪk'splɪkəbl; 'eksplɪkəbl/ *adj* that can be explained: *Barry's strange behaviour is only explicable in terms of the stress he is under.* •➤ opposite **inexplicable**

explicit /ɪk'splɪsɪt/ *adj* **1** clear, making sth easy to understand: *I gave you explicit instructions not to touch anything.* • *She was quite explicit about her feelings on the subject.* •➤ Look at **implicit.** **2** not hiding anything: *Some of the sex scenes in that TV play were very explicit.* –**explicitly** *adv*: *He was explicitly forbidden to stay out later than midnight.*

★**explode** /ɪk'spləud/ *verb* [I,T] to burst with a loud noise: *The bomb exploded without warning.* • *The army exploded the bomb at a safe distance from the houses.* • (*figurative*) *My father exploded* (= became very angry) *when I told him how much the car would cost to repair.* •➤ *noun* **explosion**

★**exploit**[1] /ɪk'splɔɪt/ *verb* [T] **1** to use sth or to treat sb unfairly for your own advantage: *Some employers exploit foreign workers, making them work long hours for low pay.* **2** to develop sth or make the best use of sth: *This region has been exploited for oil for fifty years.* • *Solar energy is a source of power that needs to be exploited more fully.* –**exploitation** /,eksplɔɪ'teɪʃn/ *noun* [U]: *They're making you work 80 hours a week? That's exploitation!*

exploit[2] /'eksplɔɪt/ *noun* [C] something exciting or interesting that sb has done

exploration /,eksplə'reɪʃn/ *noun* [C,U] the act of travelling around a place in order to learn about it: *space exploration*

exploratory /ɪk'splɒrətri/ *adj* done in order to find sth out: *The doctors are doing some* *exploratory tests to try and find out what's wrong.*

★explore /ɪkˈsplɔː/ **verb** [I,T] to travel around a place, etc in order to learn about it: *They went on an expedition to explore the River Amazon.* • *I've never been to Paris before – I'm going out to explore.* • (*figurative*) *We need to explore* (= look carefully at) *all the possibilities before we decide.*

explorer /ɪkˈsplɔːrə/ **noun** [C] a person who travels round a place in order to learn about it

★explosion /ɪkˈspləʊʒn/ **noun** [C] **1** a sudden and extremely violent bursting: *Two people were killed in the explosion.* **2** a sudden dramatic increase in sth: *the population explosion* ••➤ verb **explode**

explosive¹ /ɪkˈspləʊsɪv/ **adj 1** capable of exploding and therefore dangerous: *Hydrogen is highly explosive.* **2** causing strong feelings or having dangerous effects: *The situation is explosive. We must do all we can to calm people down.*

explosive² /ɪkˈspləʊsɪv/ **noun** [C] a substance that is used for causing explosions

★export¹ /ɪkˈspɔːt/ **verb** [I,T] **1** to send goods, etc to another country, usually for sale: *India exports tea and cotton.* ••➤ opposite **import** **2** (*computing*) to move information from one program to another

★export² /ˈekspɔːt/ **noun 1** [U] sending goods to another country for sale: *Most of our goods are produced for export.* • *the export trade* **2** [C, usually pl] something that is sent to another country for sale: *What are Brazil's main exports?* ••➤ opposite **import** –**exporter** **noun** [C]: *Japan is the largest exporter of electronic goods.* ••➤ opposite **importer**

expose /ɪkˈspəʊz/ **verb** [T] **1** **expose sth (to sb); expose sb/sth (as sth)** to show sth that is usually hidden; to tell sth to sb that has been kept secret: *She didn't want to expose her true feelings to her family.* • *The politician was exposed as a liar on TV.* **2** **expose sb/sth to sth** to put sb/sth or yourself in a situation that could be difficult or dangerous: *to be exposed to radiation/danger* **3** **expose sb to sth** to give sb the chance to experience sth: *I like jazz because I was exposed to it as a child.* **4** (in photography) to allow light onto the film inside a camera when taking a photograph

exposed /ɪkˈspəʊzd/ **adj** (used about a place) not protected from the wind and bad weather

exposure /ɪkˈspəʊʒə/ **noun 1** [U,C] the act of making sth public; the thing that is made public: *The new movie has been given a lot of exposure in the media.* • *The politician resigned because of the exposures about his private life.* **2** [U] being allowed or forced to experience sth: *Exposure to radiation is almost always harmful.* • *Television can give children exposure to other cultures from an early age.* **3** [U] a harmful condition when a person becomes very cold because he/she has been outside in very bad weather: *The climbers all died of exposure.* **4** [C] the amount of

film that is used when you take one photograph: *How many exposures are there on this film?*

★express¹ /ɪkˈspres/ **verb** [T] **1** to show sth such as a feeling or an opinion by words or actions: *I found it very hard to express what I felt about her.* • *to express fears/concern about sth* **2** **express yourself** to say or write your feelings, opinions, etc: *I don't think she expresses herself very well in that article.*

express² /ɪkˈspres/ **adj, adv 1** going or sent quickly: *an express coach* • *We'd better send the parcel express if we want it to get there on time.* **2** (used about a wish, command, etc) clearly and definitely stated: *It was her express wish that he should have the picture after her death.*

express³ /ɪkˈspres/ (also **ex‚press 'train**) **noun** [C] a fast train that does not stop at all stations

★expression /ɪkˈspreʃn/ **noun 1** [C,U] something that you say that shows your opinions or feelings: *Freedom of expression is a basic human right.* • *an expression of gratitude/ sympathy/anger* **2** [C] the look on a person's face that shows what he/she is thinking or feeling: *He had a puzzled expression on his face.* **3** [C] a word or phrase with a particular meaning: *'I'm starving' is an expression meaning 'I'm very hungry'.* • *a slang/an idiomatic expression*

expressive /ɪkˈspresɪv/ **adj** showing feelings or thoughts: *That is a very expressive piece of music.* • *Dave has a very expressive face.* –**expressively adv**

expressly /ɪkˈspresli/ **adv 1** clearly; definitely: *I expressly told you not to do that.* **2** for a special purpose; specially: *These scissors are expressly designed for left-handed people.*

expressway /ɪkˈspresweɪ/ (*US*) = MOTOR-WAY

expulsion /ɪkˈspʌlʃn/ **noun** [C,U] the act of making sb leave a place or an institution: *There have been three expulsions from school this year.* ••➤ verb **expel**

exquisite /ˈekskwɪzɪt; ɪkˈskwɪzɪt/ **adj** extremely beautiful and pleasing: *She has an exquisite face.* • *I think that ring is exquisite.*

ext **abbr** extension number of a telephone: *ext 3492*

★extend /ɪkˈstend/ **verb 1** [T] to make sth longer or larger (in space or time): *Could you extend your visit for a few days?* • *We're planning to extend the back of the house to give us more space.* • *Since my injury I can't extend this leg fully* (= make it completely straight). **2** [I] to cover the area or period of time mentioned: *The desert extends over a huge area of the country.* • *The company is planning to extend its operations into Asia.* **3** [T] (*formal*) to offer sth to sb: *to extend hospitality/a warm welcome/an invitation to sb*

extension /ɪkˈstenʃn/ **noun** [C] **1** an extra period of time that you are allowed for sth: *I've applied for an extension to my work permit.* **2** a part that is added to a building: *They're building an extension on the hospital.*

3 a telephone that is connected to a central phone in a house or to a central point (**switchboard**) in a large office building: *What's your extension number?* • *Can I have extension 4342, please?*

extensive /ɪk'stensɪv/ adj large in area or amount: *The house has extensive grounds.* • *Most of the buildings suffered extensive damage.* –**extensively** adv

★**extent** /ɪk'stent/ noun [U] the extent of sth the length, area, size or importance of sth: *I was amazed at the extent of his knowledge.* • *The full extent of the damage is not yet known.*

IDIOMS **to a certain/to some extent** used to show that sth is only partly true: *I agree with you to a certain extent but there are still a lot of points I disagree with.*

to what extent how far; how much: *I'm not sure to what extent I believe her.*

exterior¹ /ɪk'stɪəriə/ adj on the outside: *the exterior walls of a house* ••➤ opposite **interior**

exterior² /ɪk'stɪəriə/ noun [C] the outside of sth; the appearance of sb/sth: *The exterior of the house is fine but inside it isn't in very good condition.* • *Despite his calm exterior, Steve suffers badly from stress.*

exterminate /ɪk'stɜːmɪneɪt/ verb [T] to kill a large group of people or animals: *Once cockroaches infest a building, they are very hard to exterminate.* –**extermination** /ɪkˌstɜːmɪ'neɪʃn/ noun [U]

★**external** /ɪk'stɜːnl/ adj **1** connected with the outside of sth: *The cream is for external use only* (= to be used on the skin). **2** coming from another place: *You will be tested by an external examiner.* ••➤ opposite **internal**

extinct /ɪk'stɪŋkt/ adj **1** (used about a type of animal, plant, etc) no longer existing: *Tigers are nearly extinct in the wild.* **2** (used about a volcano) no longer active –**extinction** /ɪk'stɪŋkʃn/ noun [U]: *The giant panda is in danger of extinction.*

extinguish /ɪk'stɪŋgwɪʃ/ verb [T] (*formal*) to cause sth to stop burning: *The fire was extinguished very quickly.* ••➤ A less formal expression is **put out**. –**extinguisher** = FIRE EXTINGUISHER

extort /ɪk'stɔːt/ verb [T] (*formal*) extort sth (from sb) to get sth by using threats or violence: *The gang were found guilty of extorting money from small businesses.* –**extortion** noun [U]

extortionate /ɪk'stɔːʃənət/ adj (used especially about prices) much too high

★**extra¹** /'ekstrə/ adj, adv more than is usual, expected, or than exists already: *I'll need some extra money for the holidays.* • *'What size is this sweater?' 'Extra large.'* • *Is wine included in the price of the meal or is it extra?* • *I tried to be extra nice to him yesterday because it was his birthday.*

extra² /'ekstrə/ noun [C] **1** something that costs more, or that is not normally included: *Optional extras such as colour printer, scanner and modem are available on top of the basic package.* **2** a person in a film, etc who

has a small unimportant part, for example in a crowd

extract¹ /ɪk'strækt/ verb [T] (*formal*) to take sth out, especially with difficulty: *I think this tooth will have to be extracted.* • *I wasn't able to extract an apology from her.*

extract² /'ekstrækt/ noun [C] a part of a book, piece of music, etc, that has often been specially chosen to show sth: *The newspaper published extracts from the controversial novel.*

extraction /ɪk'strækʃn/ noun (*formal*) **1** [C,U] the act of taking sth out: *extraction of salt from the sea* • *Dentists report that children are requiring fewer extractions.* **2** [U] family origin: *He's an American but he's of Italian extraction.*

extra-curricular /ˌekstrə kə'rɪkjələ/ adj not part of the normal course of studies (**curriculum**) in a school or college: *The school offers many extra-curricular activities such as sport, music, drama, etc.*

extradite /'ekstrədaɪt/ verb [T] to send a person who may be guilty of a crime from the country in which he/she is living to the country which wants to put him/her on trial for the crime: *The suspected terrorists were captured in Spain and extradited to France.* –**extradition** /ˌekstrə'dɪʃn/ noun [C,U]

★**extraordinary** /ɪk'strɔːdnri/ adj **1** very unusual: *She has an extraordinary ability to whistle and sing at the same time.* **2** not what you would expect in a particular situation; very strange: *That was extraordinary behaviour for a teacher!* ••➤ opposite **ordinary** –**extraordinarily** /ɪk'strɔːdnrəli/ adv: *He was an extraordinarily talented musician.*

extravagant /ɪk'strævəgənt/ adj **1** spending or costing too much money: *He's terribly extravagant – he travels everywhere by taxi.* • *an extravagant present* **2** exaggerated; more than is usual, true or necessary: *The advertisements made extravagant claims for the new medicine.* –**extravagance** noun [C,U] –**extravagantly** adv

★**extreme** /ɪk'striːm/ adj **1** (only *before* a noun) the greatest or strongest possible: *You must take extreme care when driving at night.* • *extreme heat/difficulty/poverty* **2** much stronger than is considered usual, acceptable, etc: *Her extreme views on immigration are shocking to most people.* **3** (only *before* a noun) as far away as possible from the centre in the direction mentioned: *There could be snow in the extreme north of the country.* • *politicians on the extreme left of the party* ••➤ Look at **moderate** and **radical**. –**extreme** noun [C]: *Alex used to be very shy but now she's gone to the opposite extreme.*

extremely /ɪk'striːmli/ adv very: *Listen carefully because this is extremely important.*

ex'treme sport noun [C] a very dangerous sport or activity which some people do for fun: *The first day of the extreme sports championships featured white-water rafting.*

extremist /ɪk'striːmɪst/ noun [C] a person who has extreme political opinions ••➤ Look at **moderate** and **radical**. –extremism noun [U]

extremity /ɪk'streməti/ noun [C] (*pl* **extremities**) the part of sth that is furthest from the centre

extricate /'ekstrɪkeɪt/ verb [T] to manage to free sb/sth from a difficult situation or position: *I finally managed to extricate myself from the meeting by saying that I had a train to catch.*

extrovert /'ekstrəvɜːt/ noun [C] a person who is confident and full of life and who prefers being with other people to being alone •➤ opposite **introvert**

exuberant /ɪg'zjuːbərənt/ adj (used about a person or his/her behaviour) full of energy and excitement –exuberance noun [U]

★**eye**[1] /aɪ/ noun [C] **1** one of the two organs of your body that you use to see with: *She opened/closed her eyes.* ● *He's got blue eyes.* •➤ picture on page C5

➤ If somebody hits you on the eye you might get a **black eye**. When you close both eyes very quickly and open them again you **blink**. To close one eye quickly and open it again is to **wink**.

2 the ability to see sth: *He has **sharp eyes** (= he can see very well).* ● *She has **an eye for detail** (= she notices small details).* **3** the hole at one end of a needle that the thread goes through

IDIOMS an eye for an eye used to say that you should punish sb by doing to him/her what he/she has done to sb else

as far as the eye can see ➤ FAR[2]

be up to your eyes in sth (*informal*) to have more of sth than you can easily do or manage: *I can't come out with you tonight – I'm up to my eyes in work.*

before sb's very eyes in front of sb so that he/she can clearly see what is happening

cast an eye/your eye(s) over sb/sth ➤ CAST[1]

catch sb's attention/eye ➤ CATCH[1]

cry your eyes out ➤ CRY[1]

have (got) your eye on sb to watch sb carefully to make sure that he/she does nothing wrong

have (got) your eye on sth to be thinking about buying sth: *I've got my eye on a suit that I saw in the sales.*

in the eyes of sb/in sb's eyes in the opinion of sb: *She was still a child in her mother's eyes.*

in the public eye ➤ PUBLIC[1]

keep an eye on sb/sth to make sure that sb/sth is safe; to look after sb/sth: *Please could you keep an eye on the house while we're away?*

keep an eye open/out (for sb/sth) to watch or look out for sb/sth: *I've lost my ring – could you keep an eye out for it?*

keep your eyes peeled/skinned (for sb/sth) to watch carefully for sb/sth: *Keep your eyes peeled for the turning to the village.*

look sb in the eye ➤ LOOK[1]

the naked eye ➤ NAKED

not bat an eye ➤ BAT[2]

see eye to eye (with sb) ➤ SEE

set eyes on sb/sth ➤ SET[1]

turn a blind eye ➤ BLIND[1]

with your eyes open knowing what you are doing: *You went into the new job with your eyes open, so you can't complain now.*

eye[2] /aɪ/ verb [T] (*pres part* eyeing or eying; *pt, pp* eyed) to look at sb/sth closely: *She eyed him with suspicion.*

eyeball /'aɪbɔːl/ noun [C] the whole of your eye (including the part which is hidden inside the head)

eyebrow /'aɪbraʊ/ noun [C] the line of hair that is above your eye •➤ picture on page C5

IDIOM raise your eyebrows ➤ RAISE

'**eye-catching** adj (used about a thing) attracting your attention immediately because it is interesting, bright or pretty

eyeglasses /'aɪglɑːsɪz/ (*US*) = GLASSES

eyelash /'aɪlæʃ/ (also **lash**) noun [C] one of the hairs that grow on the edges of your eyelids •➤ picture on page C5

'**eye level** adj at the same height as sb's eyes when he/she is standing up: *an eye-level grill*

eyelid /'aɪlɪd/ (also **lid**) noun [C] the piece of skin that can move to cover your eye •➤ picture on page C5

IDIOM not bat an eyelid ➤ BAT[2]

'**eye-opener** noun [C] something that makes you realize the truth about sth: *That television programme about the inner cities was a real eye-opener.*

eyeshadow /'aɪʃædəʊ/ noun [U] colour that is put on the skin above the eyes to make them look more attractive

eyesight /'aɪsaɪt/ noun [U] the ability to see: *good/poor eyesight*

eyesore /'aɪsɔː/ noun [C] something that is ugly and unpleasant to look at: *All this litter in the streets is a real eyesore.*

eyewitness /'aɪwɪtnəs/ = WITNESS[1](1)

Ff

F, f[1] /ef/ noun [C] (*pl* **F's; f's**) the sixth letter of the English alphabet: *'Father' begins with (an) 'F'.*

F[2] abbr **1** Fahrenheit: *Water freezes at 32°F* **2** (also **fem**) female; feminine

FA /ˌef 'eɪ/ abbr (*Brit*) the Football Association: *the FA Cup*

fable /'feɪbl/ noun [C] a short story that teaches a lesson (a **moral**) and that often has animals as the main characters: *Aesop's fables*

fabric /'fæbrɪk/ noun **1** [C,U] (a type of) cloth or soft material that is used for making clothes, curtains, etc: *cotton fabrics* **2** [sing] the basic structure of a building or system:

The Industrial Revolution changed the fabric of society.

fabulous /'fæbjələs/ **adj 1** very good; excellent: *It was a fabulous concert.* **2** very great: *fabulous wealth/riches/beauty*

façade (also **facade**) /fə'sɑːd/ *noun* [C] **1** the front wall of a large building that you see from the outside **2** the way sb/sth appears to be, which is not the way he/she/it really is: *His good humour was just a façade.*

★**face¹** /feɪs/ *noun* [C] **1** the front part of your head; the expression that is shown on it: *Go and wash your face.* ● *She has a very pretty face.* ● *He came in with a smile on his face.* ● *Her face lit up* (= showed happiness) *when John came into the room.* **2** the front or one side of sth: *the north face of the mountain* ● *He put the cards face up/down on the table.* ● *a clock face* ••➤ picture at **clock 3 -faced** (used to form compound adjectives) having the type of face or expression mentioned: *red/round/sour-faced*
IDIOMS face to face (with sb/sth) close to and looking at sb/sth
keep a straight face ➔ **STRAIGHT¹**
lose face ➔ **LOSE**
make/pull faces/a face (at sb) to make an expression that shows that you do not like sb/sth: *When she saw what was for dinner she pulled a face.*
make/pull faces to make rude expressions with your face: *The children made faces behind the teacher's back.*
save face ➔ **SAVE¹**
to sb's face if you say sth to sb's face, you do it when that person is with you: *I wanted to say that I was sorry to her face, not on the phone.* ••➤ opposite **behind sb's back**

★**face²** /feɪs/ *verb* [T] **1** to have your face or front pointing towards sb/sth or in a particular direction: *The garden faces south.* ● *Can you all face the front, please?* **2** to have to deal with sth unpleasant; to deal with sb in a difficult situation: *I can't face another argument.* ● *He couldn't face going to work yesterday – he felt too ill.* **3** to need attention or action from sb: *There are several problems facing the government.* ● *We are faced with a difficult decision.*
IDIOM let's face it (*informal*) we must accept it as true: *Let's face it, we can't afford a holiday this year.*
PHRASAL VERB face up to sth to accept a difficult or unpleasant situation and do sth about it: *She had to face up to the fact that she was wrong.*

facecloth /'feɪsklɒθ/ (also **flannel**) *noun* [C] a small square towel that is used for washing the face, hands, etc

faceless /'feɪsləs/ *adj* without individual character or identity: *faceless civil servants*

facelift /'feɪslɪft/ *noun* [C] a medical operation that makes your face look younger ••➤ Look at **plastic surgery**.

facet /'fæsɪt/ *noun* [C] **1** one part or particular aspect of sth: *There are many facets to this* *argument* (= points that must be considered) **2** one side of a precious stone

facetious /fə'siːʃəs/ *adj* trying to be amusing about a subject or at a time that is not appropriate so that other people become annoyed: *He kept making facetious remarks during the lecture.* –**facetiously adv**

face 'value *noun* [U,sing] the cost or value that is shown on the front of stamps, coins etc
IDIOM take sb/sth at (its, his, etc) face value to accept sb/sth as it, she, he, etc appears to be: *Don't take his story at face value. There's something he hasn't told us yet.*

facial /'feɪʃl/ *adj* connected with a person's face: *a facial expression* ● *facial hair*

facile /'fæsaɪl/ *adj* (used about a comment, argument, etc) not carefully thought out

facilitate /fə'sɪlɪteɪt/ *verb* [T] (*formal*) to make sth possible or easier

★**facility** /fə'sɪləti/ *noun* (*pl* **facilities**) **1 facilities** [pl] a service, building, piece of equipment, etc that makes it possible to do sth: *Our town has excellent sports facilities* (= a stadium, swimming pool, etc). **2** [C] an extra function or ability that a machine, etc may have: *This word processor has a facility for checking spelling.*

facsimile /fæk'sɪməli/ *noun* [C,U] an exact copy of a picture, piece of writing, etc ••➤ Look at **fax**.

★**fact** /fækt/ *noun* **1** [C] something that you know has happened or is true: *It is a scientific fact that light travels faster than sound.* ● *We need to know all the facts before we can decide.* ● *I know for a fact that Peter wasn't ill yesterday.* ● *The fact that I am older than you makes no difference at all.* ● *You must face facts and accept that he has gone.* **2** [U] true things; reality: *The film is based on fact.* ••➤ opposite **fiction**
IDIOMS as a matter of fact ➔ **MATTER¹**
the fact (of the matter) is (that)... the truth is that...: *I would love a car, but the fact is that I just can't afford one.*
facts and figures detailed information: *Before we make a decision, we need some more facts and figures.*
a fact of life something unpleasant that you must accept because you cannot change it: *Most people now see unemployment as just another fact of life.*
the facts of life the details of sexual behaviour and how babies are born
hard facts ➔ **HARD¹**
in (actual) fact 1 (used for emphasizing that sth is true) really; actually: *I thought the lecture would be boring but in actual fact it was rather interesting.* **2** used for introducing more detailed information: *It was cold. In fact it was freezing.*

factor /'fæktə/ *noun* [C] **1** one of the things that influences a decision, situation, etc: *His unhappiness at home was a major factor in his decision to go abroad.* **2** (*technical*) (in mathematics) a whole number (except 1) by which a larger number can be divided: *2, 3, 4 and 6 are factors of 12.*

★**factory** /'fæktri; -təri/ **noun** [C] (*pl* **factories**) a building or group of buildings where goods are made in large quantities by machine

factual /'fæktʃuəl/ **adj** based on or containing things that are true or real: *a factual account of the events* ••➤ Look at **fictional**.

faculty /'fæklti/ **noun** [C] (*pl* **faculties**) **1** one of the natural abilities of a person's body or mind: *the faculty of hearing/sight/speech* **2** (also **Faculty**) one department in a university, college, etc: *the Faculty of Law/Arts* ••➤ **The Faculty** can also mean the teaching staff of a university or college department and is then used with either a singular or a plural verb: *The Faculty has/have been invited to the meeting.*

fad /fæd/ **noun** [C] (*informal*) a fashion, interest, etc that will probably not last long

★**fade** /feɪd/ **verb 1** [I,T] to become or make sth become lighter in colour or less strong or fresh: *Jeans fade when you wash them.* ● *Look how the sunlight has faded these curtains.* **2** [I] **fade (away)** to disappear slowly (from sight, hearing, memory, etc): *The cheering of the crowd faded away.* ● *The smile faded from his face.*

faeces (*US* **feces**) /'fiːsiːz/ **noun** [pl] (*technical*) the solid waste material that you get rid of when you go to the toilet

fag /fæg/ **noun** [C] **1** (*Brit*) (*slang*) a cigarette **2** [sing] (*informal*) a piece of work that you do not want to do: *I've got to wash the car. What a fag!*

Fahrenheit /'færənhaɪt/ **noun** [U] (*abbr* **F**) the name of a scale which measures temperatures: *Water freezes at 32° Fahrenheit (32°F).* ••➤ Look at **Celsius**.

★**fail¹** /feɪl/ **verb 1** [I,T] to not be successful in sth: *She failed her driving test.* ● *I feel that I've failed – I'm 25 and I still haven't got a steady job.* ••➤ Look at **pass** and **succeed**. **2** [T] to decide that sb is not successful in a test, exam, etc: *The examiners failed half of the candidates.* ••➤ opposite **pass 3** [I] **fail to do sth** to not do sth: *She never fails to do her homework.* **4** [I,T] to not be enough or not do what people are expecting or wanting: *If the crops fail, people will starve.* ● *I think the government has failed us.* **5** [I] (used about health, eyesight, etc) to become weak: *His health is failing.* **6** [I] to stop working: *My brakes failed on the hill but I managed to stop the car.*

fail² /feɪl/ **noun** [C] the act not being successful in an exam ••➤ opposite **pass**

IDIOM **without fail** always, even if there are difficulties: *The postman always comes at 8 o'clock without fail.*

failing¹ /'feɪlɪŋ/ **noun** [C] a weakness or fault: *She's not very patient – that's her only failing.*

failing² /'feɪlɪŋ/ **prep** if sth is not possible: *Ask Jackie to go with you, or failing that, try Anne.*

★**failure** /'feɪljə/ **noun 1** [U] lack of success: *All my efforts ended in failure.* **2** [C] a person or thing that is not successful: *His first attempt at skating was a miserable failure.* ••➤ opposite for senses 1 and 2 **success 3** [C,U] **failure to do sth** not doing sth that people expect you to do: *I was very disappointed at his failure to come to the meeting.* **4** [C,U] an example of sth not working properly: *She died of heart failure.* ● *There's been a failure in the power supply.*

★**faint¹** /feɪnt/ **adj 1** (used about things that you can see, hear, feel, etc) not strong or clear: *a faint light/sound* ● *There is still a faint hope that they will find more people alive.* **2** (used about people) almost losing consciousness; very weak: *I feel faint – I'd better sit down.* **3** (used about actions, etc) done without much effort: *He made a faint protest.*

IDIOM **not have the faintest/foggiest (idea)** to not know at all: *I haven't the faintest idea where they've gone.*

faint² /feɪnt/ **verb** [I] to lose consciousness

★**fair¹** /feə/ **adj, adv 1** appropriate and acceptable in a particular situation: *That's a fair price for that house.* ● *I think it's fair to say that the number of homeless people is increasing.* **2** **fair (to/on sb)** treating each person or side equally, according to the law, the rules, etc: *That's not fair – he got the same number of mistakes as I did and he's got a better mark.* ● *It wasn't fair on her to ask her to stay so late.* ● *a fair trial* ••➤ opposite for senses 1 and 2 **unfair 3** quite good, large, etc: *They have a fair chance of success.* **4** (used about the skin or hair) light in colour: *Chloe has fair hair and blue eyes.* **5** (used about the weather) good, without rain

IDIOMS **fair enough** (*spoken*) used to show that you agree with what sb has suggested

fair play equal treatment of both/all sides according to the rules: *The referee is there to ensure fair play during the match.*

(more than) your fair share of sth (more than) the usual or expected amount of sth: *We've had more than our fair share of trouble this year.*

fair² /feə/ **noun** [C] **1** (also **funfair**) a type of entertainment in a field or park. At a fair you can ride on machines or try and win prizes at games. Fairs usually travel from town to town. **2** a large event where people, businesses, etc show and sell their goods: *a trade fair* ● *the Frankfurt book fair*

fairground /'feəgraʊnd/ **noun** [C] a large outdoor area where fairs are held

fair-'haired adj with light-coloured hair; blonde

★**fairly** /'feəli/ **adv 1** in an acceptable way; in a way that treats people equally or according to the law, rules, etc: *I felt that the teacher didn't treat us fairly.* ••➤ opposite **unfairly 2** quite, not very: *He is fairly tall.* ••➤ Look at the note at **rather**.

fairness /'feənəs/ **noun** [U] treating people equally or according to the law, rules, etc

---

[I] **intransitive**, a verb which has no object: *He laughed.*   [T] **transitive**, a verb which has an object: *He ate an apple.*

fairy /ˈfeəri/ **noun** [C] (*pl* **fairies**) (in stories) a small creature with wings and magic powers

'fairy tale (also **'fairy story**) **noun** [C] a story that is about fairies, magic, etc

★**faith** /feɪθ/ **noun 1** [U] faith (in sb/sth) strong belief (in sb/sth); trust: *I've got great/little faith in his ability to do the job.* ● *I have lost faith in him.* **2** [U] strong religious belief: *I've lost my faith.* **3** [C] a particular religion: *the Jewish faith*

IDIOM **in good faith** with honest reasons for doing sth: *I bought the car in good faith. I didn't know it was stolen.*

★**faithful** /ˈfeɪθfl/ **adj** faithful (to sb/sth) **1** always staying with and supporting a person, organization or belief; loyal: *Peter has been a faithful friend.* ● *He was always faithful to his wife* (= he didn't have sexual relations with anyone else). •➤ synonym **loyal** •➤ opposite **unfaithful 2** true to the facts; accurate: *a faithful description* –**faithfully** /-fəli/ **adv**

➤ **Yours faithfully** is used to end formal letters.

–**faithfulness noun** [U] •➤ Look also at **fidelity**.

fake¹ /feɪk/ **noun** [C] **1** a work of art, etc that seems to be real or genuine but is not **2** a person who is not really what he/she appears to be –**fake adj**: *a fake passport*

fake² /feɪk/ **verb** [T] **1** to copy sth and try to make people believe it is the real thing: *He faked his father's signature.* **2** to make people believe that you are feeling sth that you are not: *I faked surprise when he told me the news.*

falcon /ˈfɔːlkən/ **noun** [C] a bird with long pointed wings that kills and eats other animals (**a bird of prey**). Falcons can be trained to hunt.

★**fall¹** /fɔːl/ **verb** [I] (*pt* **fell** /fel/; *pp* **fallen** /ˈfɔːlən/) **1** to drop down towards the ground: *He fell off the ladder onto the grass.* ● *The rain was falling steadily.* **2** fall (down/over) to suddenly stop standing and drop to the ground: *She slipped on the ice and fell.* ● *The little boy fell over and hurt his knee.* **3** to hang down: *Her hair fell down over her shoulders.* **4** to become lower or less: *The temperature is falling.* ● *The price of coffee has fallen again.* •➤ opposite **rise 5** to be defeated: *The Government fell because of the scandal.* **6** (*written*) to be killed (in battle): *Millions of soldiers fell in the war.* **7** to change into a different state; to become: *He fell asleep on the sofa.* ● *They fell in love with each other in Spain.* ● *I must get some new shoes – these ones are falling to pieces.* **8** (*formal*) to come or happen: *My birthday falls on a Sunday this year.* **9** to belong to a particular group, type, etc: *Animals fall into two groups, those with backbones and those without.*

IDIOMS **fall flat** → **FLAT¹**

fall/slot into place → **PLACE¹**

fall short (of sth) → **SHORT¹**

PHRASAL VERBS **fall apart** to break (into pieces): *My car is falling apart.*

fall back on sb/sth to use sb/sth when you are in difficulty: *When the electricity was cut off we fell back on candles.*

fall for sb (*informal*) to be strongly attracted to sb; to fall in love with sb

fall for sth (*informal*) to be tricked into believing sth that is not true: *He makes excuses and she falls for them every time.*

fall out (with sb) to argue and stop being friendly (with sb)

fall through to fail or not happen: *Our trip to Japan has fallen through.*

★**fall²** /fɔːl/ **noun 1** [C] an act of falling down or off sth: *She had a nasty fall from her horse.* **2** [C] a fall (of sth) the amount of sth that has fallen or the distance that sth has fallen: *We have had a heavy fall of snow.* ● *a fall of four metres* **3** [C] a fall (in sth) a decrease (in value, quantity, etc): *There has been a sharp fall in the price of oil.* •➤ synonym **drop** •➤ opposite **rise 4** [sing] the fall of sth a (political) defeat; a failure: *the fall of the Roman Empire* **5 falls** [pl] a large amount of water that falls from a height down the side of a mountain, etc; a waterfall: *Niagara Falls*

fall³ /fɔːl/ (*US*) = **AUTUMN**

fallacy /ˈfæləsi/ **noun** (*pl* **fallacies**) [C,U] (*formal*) a false belief or a wrong idea: *It's a fallacy to believe that money brings happiness* (= it's not true).

fallen *past participle* of **FALL¹**

fallible /ˈfæləbl/ **adj** able or likely to make mistakes: *Even our new computerized system is fallible.* •➤ opposite **infallible**

fallout /ˈfɔːlaʊt/ **noun** [U] dangerous waste that is carried in the air after a nuclear explosion

★**false** /fɔːls/ **adj 1** not true; incorrect: *I think the information you have been given is false.* ● *I got a completely false impression of him from our first meeting.* •➤ opposite **true 2** not real; artificial: *false hair/eyelashes/teeth* •➤ opposite **real** or **natural 3** not genuine, but made to look real in order to trick people: *This suitcase has a false bottom.* ● *a false name/passport* **4** (used about sb's behaviour or expression) not sincere or honest: *a false smile* ● *false modesty*

IDIOMS **a false alarm** a warning about a danger that does not happen

a false friend a word in another language that looks similar to a word in your own but has a different meaning

under false pretences pretending to be or to have sth in order to trick people: *She got into the club under false pretences – she isn't a member at all!*

false 'teeth (also **dentures**) **noun** [pl] artificial teeth that are worn by sb who has lost his/her natural teeth

falsify /ˈfɔːlsɪfaɪ/ **verb** [T] (*pres part* **falsifying**; *3rd pers sing pres* **falsifies**; *pt, pp* **falsified**) (*formal*) to change a document, information, etc so that it is no longer true in order to trick sb: *to falsify data/records/accounts*

falter /ˈfɔːltə/ **verb** [I] **1** to become weak or

move in a way that is not steady: *The engine faltered and stopped.* **2** to lose confidence and determination: *Sampras faltered and missed the ball.*

★**fame** /feɪm/ noun [U] being known or talked about by many people because of what you have achieved: *Pop stars achieve fame at a young age.* ● *The town's only **claim to fame** is that there was a riot there.*

famed /feɪmd/ adj famed (for sth) well-known (for sth): *Welsh people are famed for their singing.* •➤ Look at **famous**, which is the more usual word.

★**familiar** /fəˈmɪliə/ adj **1** familiar (to sb) well-known to you; often seen or heard and therefore easy to recognize: *to look/sound familiar* ● *Chinese music isn't very familiar to people in Europe.* ● *It was a relief to see a familiar face in the crowd.* **2** familiar with sth having a good knowledge of sth: *People in Europe aren't very familiar with Chinese music.* •➤ opposite for senses 1 and 2 **unfamiliar** **3** familiar (with sb) (used about a person's behaviour) too friendly and informal: *I was annoyed by the waiter's familiar behaviour.*

familiarity /fəˌmɪliˈærəti/ noun [U] **1** familiarity (with sth) having a good knowledge of sth: *His familiarity with the area was an advantage.* **2** being too friendly and informal

familiarize (also **-ise**) /fəˈmɪliəraɪz/ verb [T] familiarize sb/yourself (with sth) to teach sb about sth or learn about sth until you know it well: *I want to familiarize myself with the plans before the meeting.*

★**family** /ˈfæməli/ noun (*pl* **families**) **1** [C,with sing or pl verb] a group of people who are related to each other: *I have quite a large family.*

➤ Sometimes we use 'family' to mean 'parents and their children' (a **nuclear family**), sometimes we use it to include other relatives, for example grandparents, aunts, uncles, etc (an **extended family**). **Family** is used with a singular verb when we are talking about it as a unit: *Almost every family in the village owns a television.* A plural verb is used when we are thinking about the members of a family as individuals: *My family are all very tall.* **Family** can be used before another noun to describe things that are suitable for or that can be used by all the family: *family entertainment* ● *the family car*

2 [C,U] children: *Do you have any family?* ● *We are planning to **start a family** next year* (= to have our first baby). ● *to bring up/raise a family* **3** [C] a group of animals, plants, etc that are of a similar type: *Lions belong to the cat family.*

IDIOM **run in the family** to be found very often in a family: *Red hair runs in the family.*

'**family name** noun [C] the name that is shared by members of a family; surname •➤ Look at the note at **name**.

family '**planning** noun [U] controlling the

number of children you have by using birth control •➤ Look at **contraception**.

family '**tree** noun [C] a diagram that shows the relationships between different members of a family over a long period of time: *How far back can you trace your family tree?*

famine /ˈfæmɪn/ noun [C,U] a lack of food over a long period of time in a large area that can cause the death of many people: *There is a severe famine in many parts of Africa.* ● *The long drought* (= a lack or rain or water) *was followed by famine.*

famished /ˈfæmɪʃt/ adj (*informal*) (not before a noun) very hungry: *When's lunch? I'm famished!*

★**famous** /ˈfeɪməs/ adj famous (for sth) well-known to many people: *a famous singer* ● *Glasgow is famous for its museums and art galleries.* •➤ Look at **infamous** and **notorious** which mean 'famous for being bad'.

famously /ˈfeɪməsli/ adv in a way that is famous: *the words he famously uttered just before he died*

IDIOM **get on/along famously** to have a very good relationship with sb, especially from the first meeting

fans

★**fan**¹ /fæn/ noun [C] **1** somebody who admires and is very enthusiastic about a sport, a film star, a singer, etc: *football fans* ● *He's a Van Morrison fan.* ● *fan mail* (= letters from fans to the person they admire) **2** a machine with parts that turn around very quickly to create a current of cool or warm air: *an electric fan* ● *a fan heater* **3** an object in the shape of a half-circle made of paper, feathers, etc that you wave in your hand to create a current of cool air

fan² /fæn/ verb [T] (**fanning**; **fanned**) **1** to make air blow on sb/sth by waving a fan¹(3), your hand, etc in the air: *She used a newspaper to fan her face.* **2** to make a fire burn more strongly by blowing on it: *The strong wind really fanned the flames.*

PHRASAL VERB **fan out** to spread out: *The police fanned out across the field.*

fanatic /fəˈnætɪk/ noun [C] a person who is very enthusiastic about sth and may have extreme or dangerous opinions (especially about religion or politics): *a religious fanatic* ● *She's a health-food fanatic.* •➤ synonym **fiend** or **freak** –**fanatical** /-kl/ (also **fanatic**) adj: *He's fanatical about keeping things tidy.* –**fanatically** /-kli/ adv –**fanaticism** /-tɪsɪzəm/ noun [C,U]

'**fan belt** noun [C] the belt that operates the machinery that cools a car engine

fancy¹ /ˈfænsi/ verb (*pres part* **fancying**; *3rd*

pers sing pres **fancies**; *pt, pp* **fancied**) **1** [T] (*Brit informal*) to like the idea of having or doing sth; to want sth or to want to do sth: *What do you fancy to eat?* ● *I don't fancy going out in this rain.* **2** [T] (*Brit informal*) to be sexually attracted to sb: *Jack keeps looking at you. I think he fancies you.* **3** [T] **fancy yourself (as) sth** to think that you would be good at sth; to think that you are sth (although this may not be true): *He fancied himself (as) a poet.*

fancy[2] /'fænsi/ **adj** not simple or ordinary: *My father doesn't like fancy food.* ● *I just want a pair of black shoes – nothing fancy.*

fancy[3] /'fænsi/ **noun**
IDIOMS **take sb's fancy** to attract or please sb: *If you see something that takes your fancy I'll buy it for you.*
take a fancy to sb/sth to start liking sb/sth: *I think that Laura's really taken a fancy to you.*

fancy 'dress noun [U] special clothes that you wear to a party at which people dress up to look like a different person (for example from history or a story): *It was a Hallowe'en party and everyone went in fancy dress.*

fanfare /'fænfeə/ **noun** [C] a short loud piece of music that is used for introducing sb important, for example a king or queen

fang /fæŋ/ **noun** [C] a long sharp tooth of a dog, snake, etc •➤ picture on page C1

fanny pack /'fænipæk/ (*US*) = BUMBAG

fantasize (also **-ise**) /'fæntəsaɪz/ **verb** [I,T] to imagine sth that you would like to happen: *He liked to fantasize that he had won a gold medal at the Olympics.*

fantastic /fæn'tæstɪk/ **adj 1** (*informal*) very good; excellent: *She's a fantastic swimmer.* **2** strange and difficult to believe: *a story full of fantastic creatures from other worlds* **3** (*informal*) very large or great: *A Rolls Royce costs a fantastic amount of money.* –**fantastically** /-kli/ **adv**

fantasy /'fæntəsi/ **noun** [C,U] (*pl* **fantasies**) situations that are not true, that you just imagine: *I have a fantasy about going to live in the Bahamas.* ● *They live in a world of fantasy.* •➤ Look at the note at **imagination**.

fanzine /'fænziːn/ **noun** [C] a magazine that is written by and for people (**fans**) who like a particular sports team, singer, etc

FAQ /ˌef eɪ 'kjuː/ **noun** [C] a document on the Internet that contains the most *frequently asked questions* about a subject and the answers to these questions

★**far**[1] /fɑː/ **adj** (**farther** /'fɑːðə/ or **further** /'fɜːðə/, **farthest** /'fɑːðɪst/ or **furthest** /'fɜːðɪst/) **1** distant; a long way away: *Let's walk – it's not far.* **2** (only *before* a noun) the most distant of two or more things: *the far side of the river* **3** (only *before* a noun) a long way from the centre in the direction mentioned: *politicians from the far left of the party* IDIOM **a far cry from sth/from doing sth** an experience that is very different from sth/doing sth

★**far**[2] /fɑː/ **adv** (**farther** /'fɑːðə/ or **further** /'fɜːðə/, **farthest** /'fɑːðɪst/ or **furthest**

/'fɜːðɪst/) **1** (at) a distance: *London's not far from here.* ● *How far did we walk yesterday?* ● *If we sit too far away from the screen I won't be able to see the film.* ● *I can't swim as far as you.*

➤ **Far** in this sense is usually used in negative sentences and questions. In positive sentences we say **a long way**: *It's a long way from here to the sea.* Some sentences have a negative meaning although they are positive in form. **Far** can be used in them: *Let's get a bus. It's much too far to walk.*

2 (before comparative adjectives) very much: *She's far more intelligent than I thought.* ● *There's far too much salt in this soup.* **3** (to) a certain degree: *How far have you got with your homework?* ● *The company employs local people as far as possible.* **4** a long time: *We danced far into the night.*
IDIOMS **as far as** to the place mentioned but not further: *We walked as far as the river and then turned back.*
as/so far as used for giving your opinion or judgement of a situation: *As far as I know, she's not coming, but I may be wrong.* ● *As far as school work is concerned, he's hopeless.* ● *As far as I'm concerned, this is the most important point.* ● *As far as I can see, the accident was John's fault, not Ann's.*
as far as the eye can see to the furthest place you can see
by far (used for emphasizing comparative or superlative words) by a large amount: *Carmen is by far the best student in the class.*
far afield far away, especially from where you live or from where you are staying: *We decided to hire a car in order to explore further afield.*
far from doing sth instead of doing sth: *Far from enjoying the film, he fell asleep in the middle.*
far from sth almost the opposite of sth; not at all: *He's far from happy* (= he's very sad or angry).
far from it (*informal*) certainly not; just the opposite: '*Did you enjoy your holiday?*' '*No, far from it. It was awful.*'
few and far between → FEW
go far 1 to be enough: *This food won't go very far between three of us.* **2** to be successful in life: *Dan is very talented and should go far.*
go too far to behave in a way that causes trouble or upsets other people: *He's always been naughty but this time he's gone too far.*
so far until now: *So far the weather has been good but it might change.*
so far so good (*spoken*) everything has gone well until now

faraway /'fɑːrəweɪ/ **adj 1** (*written*) a great distance away: *He told us stories of faraway countries.* **2** (used about a look in a person's eyes) as if you are thinking of sth else: *She stared out of the window with a faraway look in her eyes.*

farce /fɑːs/ **noun** [C] **1** something important or serious that is not organized well or treated with respect: *The meeting was a farce – everyone was shouting at the same time.* **2** a funny play for the theatre full of ridiculous situations –**farcical** /'fɑːsɪkl/ **adj**

★**fare**¹ /feə/ **noun** [C] the amount of money you pay to travel by bus, train, taxi, etc: *What's the fare to Birmingham?* • *Adults pay **full fare**, children pay **half fare**.*

fare² /feə/ **verb** [I] (*formal*) to be successful or not successful in a particular situation: *How did you fare in your examination?* (= did you do well or badly?)

the ˌFar ˈEast noun [sing] China, Japan and other countries in E and SE Asia •➤ Look at **the Middle East**.

farewell /ˌfeə'wel/ **interj** (*old-fashioned*) goodbye –**farewell noun** [C]: *He said his farewells and left.*

ˌfar-ˈfetched **adj** not easy to believe: *It's a good book but the story's too far-fetched.*

★**farm**¹ /fɑːm/ **noun** [C] an area of land with fields and buildings that is used for growing crops and keeping animals: *to work **on a farm*** • *farm buildings/workers/animals*

★**farm**² /fɑːm/ **verb** [I,T] to use land for growing crops or keeping animals: *She farms 200 acres.*

farmer /'fɑːmə/ **noun** [C] a person who owns or manages a farm

farmhouse /'fɑːmhaʊs/ **noun** [C] the house on a farm where the farmer lives

farming /'fɑːmɪŋ/ **noun** [U] managing a farm or working on it: *farming methods/areas*

farmyard /'fɑːmjɑːd/ **noun** [C] an outside area near a farmhouse surrounded by buildings or walls

ˌfar-ˈreaching **adj** having a great influence on a lot of other things: *far-reaching changes*

ˌfar-ˈsighted **adj 1** being able to see what will be necessary in the future and making plans for it **2** (*US*) = **LONG-SIGHTED**

fart /fɑːt/ **verb** [I] (*informal*) to suddenly let gas from the stomach escape from your bottom –**fart noun** [C]

★**farther** /'fɑːðə/ *comparative* of **FAR** •➤ Look at the note at **further**.

★**farthest** /'fɑːðɪst/ (also **furthest**) *superlative* of **FAR**

★**fascinate** /'fæsɪneɪt/ **verb** [T] to attract or interest sb very much: *Chinese culture has always fascinated me.* –**fascinating adj** –**fascination** /ˌfæsɪ'neɪʃn/ **noun** [C,U]

fascism (also **Fascism**) /'fæʃɪzəm/ **noun** [U] an extreme (right-wing) political system –**fascist** (also **Fascist**) /'fæʃɪst/ **noun** [C], **adj**

★**fashion** /'fæʃn/ **noun 1** [C,U] the style of dressing or behaving that is the most popular at a particular time: *What is **the latest fashion** in hairstyles?* • *a fashion show/model/ magazine* • *Jeans are always **in fashion**.* • *I think hats will **come back into fashion**.* • *That colour is **out of fashion** this year.* **2** [sing] the way you do sth: *Watch him. He's been behaving **in a very strange fashion**.*

★**fashionable** /'fæʃnəbl/ **adj 1** popular or in a popular style at the time: *a fashionable area/dress/opinion* **2** considering fashion to be important: *fashionable society* •➤ opposite

unfashionable or **old-fashioned** –**fashionably** /-əbli/ **adv**

★**fast**¹ /fɑːst/ **adj 1** able to move or act at great speed: *a fast car/worker/runner/reader* •➤ Look at the note at **quick**. **2** (used about a clock or watch) showing a time that is later than the real time: *The clock is five minutes fast.* •➤ opposite **slow 3** (used about camera film) very sensitive to light, and therefore good for taking photographs in poor light or of things that are moving quickly **4** (only *after* a noun) firmly fixed: *He made the boat fast* (= he tied it to something) *before he got out.* • *Do you think the colour in this T-shirt is fast* (= will not come out when washed)?
IDIOMS **fast and furious** very fast and exciting

hard and fast → HARD¹

fast² /fɑːst/ **adv** firmly or deeply: *Sam was **fast asleep** by ten o'clock.* • *Our car was **stuck fast** in the mud.*

fast³ /fɑːst/ **verb** [I] to eat no food for a certain time, usually for religious reasons: *Muslims fast during Ramadan.* –**fast noun** [C]

★**fasten** /'fɑːsn/ **verb 1** [I,T] **fasten sth (up)** to close or join the two parts of sth; to become closed or joined: *Please fasten your seat belts.* • *Fasten your coat up – it's cold outside.* • *My dress fastens at the back.* **2** [T] **fasten sth (on/to sth)**; **fasten A and B (together)** to fix or tie sth to sth, or two things together: *Fasten this badge on your jacket.* • *How can I fasten these pieces of wood together?* **3** [T] to close or lock sth firmly so that it will not open: *Close the window and fasten it securely.*

fastener /'fɑːsnə/ (also **fastening** /'fɑːsnɪŋ/) **noun** [C] something that fastens things together

ˌfast ˈfood **noun** [U] food that can be served very quickly in special restaurants and is often taken away to be eaten in the street: *a fast food restaurant*

ˌfast ˈforward **verb** [T] to make a video tape or a cassette go forward quickly without playing it –**fast forward noun** [U]: *Press fast forward to advance the tape.* • *the fast-forward button* •➤ Look at **rewind**.

fastidious /fæ'stɪdiəs/ **adj** difficult to please; wanting everything to be perfect

★**fat**¹ /fæt/ **adj** (**fatter**; **fattest**) **1** (used about people's or animal's bodies) weighing too much; covered with too much flesh: *You'll get fat if you eat too much.* •➤ opposite **thin**

> It is not very polite to describe a person as **fat**. More polite words are **plump, stout** or **overweight**.

2 (used about a thing) thick or full: *a fat wallet/book*

★**fat**² /fæt/ **noun 1** [U] the soft white substance under the skins of animals and people: *I don't like meat with too much fat on it.* •➤ adjective **fatty 2** [C,U] the substance containing oil that we obtain from animals, plants or seeds and use for cooking: *Cook the onions in a little fat.*

★**fatal** /ˈfeɪtl/ adj **1** causing or ending in death: *a fatal accident/disease* ••➤ Look at **mortal**. **2** causing trouble or a bad result: *She made the fatal mistake of trusting him.* –**fatally** adv: *fatally injured*

fatality /fəˈtæləti/ noun [C] (*pl* **fatalities**) a person's death caused by an accident, in war, etc: *There were no fatalities in the fire.*

★**fate** /feɪt/ noun **1** [U] the power that some people believe controls everything that happens: *It was fate that brought them together again after twenty years.* **2** [C] your future; something that happens to you: *Both men suffered the same fate – they both lost their jobs.* ••➤ synonym **fortune**

fateful /ˈfeɪtfl/ adj having an important effect on the future: *a fateful decision*

★**father**[1] /ˈfɑːðə/ noun [C] **1** a person's male parent: *John looks exactly like his father.* **2** **Father** the title of certain priests: *Father O'Reilly*

father[2] /ˈfɑːðə/ verb [T] to become a father: *to father a child*

Father Christmas (also **Santa Claus**) an old man with a red coat and a long white beard who, children believe, brings presents at Christmas

fatherhood /ˈfɑːðəhʊd/ noun [U] the state of being a father

father-in-law noun [C] (*pl* **fathers-in-law**) the father of your husband or wife

fatherly /ˈfɑːðəli/ adj like or typical of a father: *Would you like a piece of fatherly advice?*

fathom /ˈfæðəm/ verb [T] (usually in the negative) to understand sth: *I can't fathom what he means.*

fatigue /fəˈtiːɡ/ noun [U] **1** the feeling of being extremely tired: *He was suffering from mental and physical fatigue.* **2** weakness in metals caused by a lot of use: *The plane crash was caused by metal fatigue in a wing.*

fatten /ˈfætn/ verb [T] **fatten sb/sth (up)** to make sb/sth fatter: *He's fattening the pigs up for market.*

fattening /ˈfætnɪŋ/ adj (used about food) that makes people fat: *Chocolate is very fattening.*

fatty /ˈfæti/ adj (**fattier, fattiest**) (used about food) having a lot of fat in or on it

faucet /ˈfɔːsɪt/ (*US*) = **TAP**[2](1)

★**fault**[1] /fɔːlt/ noun **1** [C] something wrong or not perfect in a person's character or in a thing: *One of my faults is that I'm always late.* ••➤ Look at the note at **mistake**. **2** [U] responsibility for a mistake: *It will be your own fault if you don't pass your exams.*
IDIOMS **be at fault** to be wrong or responsible for a mistake: *The other driver was at fault – he didn't stop at the traffic lights.*
find fault (with sb/sth) → **FIND**[1]

fault[2] /fɔːlt/ verb [T] to find sth wrong with sb/sth: *It was impossible to fault her English.*

faultless /ˈfɔːltləs/ adj without any mistakes; perfect: *The pianist gave a faultless performance.*

faulty /ˈfɔːlti/ adj (used especially about electricity or machinery) not working properly: *a faulty switch*

fauna /ˈfɔːnə/ noun [U] all the animals of an area or a period of time: *the flora and fauna of South America* ••➤ Look at **flora**.

faux pas /ˌfəʊ ˈpɑː/ noun [C] (*pl* **faux pas** /ˌfəʊ ˈpɑːz/) something you say or do that is embarrassing or offends people: *to make a faux pas*

★**favour**[1] (*US* **favor**) /ˈfeɪvə/ noun **1** [C] something that helps sb: *Would you do me a favour and post this letter for me?* ● *Could I ask you a favour?* ● *Are they paying you for the work, or are you doing it as a favour?* **2** [U] favour (with sb) liking or approval: *I'm afraid I'm out of favour with my neighbour since our last argument.* ● *The new boss's methods didn't find favour with the staff.*
IDIOMS **in favour of sb/sth** in agreement with: *Are you in favour of private education?*
in sb's favour to the advantage of sb: *The committee decided in their favour.*

★**favour**[2] (*US* **favor**) /ˈfeɪvə/ verb [T] **1** to support sb/sth; to prefer: *Which suggestion do you favour?* **2** to treat one person very well and so be unfair to others: *Parents must try not to favour one of their children.*

favourable (*US* **favorable**) /ˈfeɪvərəbl/ adj **1** showing liking or approval: *He made a favourable impression on the interviewers.* **2** (often used about the weather) suitable or helpful: *Conditions are favourable for skiing today.* ••➤ opposite **unfavourable** or **adverse** –**favourably** (*US* **favorably**) /-əbli/ adv

★**favourite**[1] (*US* **favorite**) /ˈfeɪvərɪt/ adj liked more than any other: *What is your favourite colour?* ● *Who is your favourite singer?*

favourite[2] (*US* **favorite**) /ˈfeɪvərɪt/ noun [C] **1** a person or thing that you like more than any others: *The other kids were jealous of Rose because she was the teacher's favourite.* **2** **favourite (for sth/to do sth)** the horse, team, competitor, etc who is expected to win: *Mimms is the hot favourite for the leadership of the party.* ••➤ opposite **outsider**

favouritism /ˈfeɪvərɪtɪzəm/ (*US* **favoritism**) /ˈfeɪvərɪtɪzəm/ noun [U] giving unfair advantages to the person or people that you like best: *The referee was accused of showing favouritism to the home side.*

fawn[1] /fɔːn/ adj, noun [U] (of) a light yellowish-brown colour

fawn[2] /fɔːn/ noun [C] a young animal (deer) ••➤ Look at the note at **deer**.

fax[1] /fæks/ noun [C,U] **1** a copy of a letter, etc that you can send by telephone lines using a special machine: *They need an answer today so I'll send a fax.* ● *They contacted us by fax.* **2** [C] (also **fax machine**) the machine that you use for sending faxes: *Have you got a fax?* ● *What's your fax number?*

fax[2] /fæks/ verb [T] **fax sth (to sb)**; **fax sb (sth)** to send sb a fax: *We will fax our order to you tomorrow.* ● *I've faxed her a copy of the letter.*

faze /feɪz/ verb [T] (*informal*) to make sb

worried or nervous: *He doesn't get fazed by things going wrong.*

FBI /,ef bi: 'aɪ/ **abbr** (*US*) Federal Bureau of Investigation; the section of the US Justice Department which investigates crimes that are against the laws of the US as a whole, such as bank robbery and terrorism

FC /,ef 'si:/ **abbr** (*Brit*) Football Club: *Everton FC*

FCO /,efsi:'əʊ/ **abbr** Foreign and Commonwealth Office

★**fear**¹ /fɪə/ **noun** [C,U] the feeling that you have when sth dangerous, painful or frightening might happen: *He was shaking **with fear** after the accident.* • *People in this area live in constant fear of crime.* • *This book helped me overcome my fear of dogs.* • *She showed no fear.* • *My fears for his safety were unnecessary.* IDIOM **no fear** (*spoken*) (used when answering a suggestion) certainly not

★**fear**² /fɪə/ **verb 1** [T] to be afraid of sb/sth or of doing sth: *We all fear illness and death.* **2** [T] to feel that something bad might happen or might have happened: *The government fears that it will lose the next election.* • *Thousands of people are feared dead in the earthquake.* PHRASAL VERB **fear for sb/sth** to be worried about sb/sth: *Parents often fear for the safety of their children.*

fearful /'fɪəfl/ **adj** (*formal*) **1 fearful (of sth/ doing sth); fearful that...** afraid or worried about sth: *You should never be fearful of starting something new.* • *They were fearful that they would miss the plane.* •➤ Look at **frightened** and **scared** and the note at **afraid**. These words are much more common. **2** terrible: *the fearful consequences of war* –**fearfully** /-fəli/ **adv** –**fearfulness noun** [U]

fearless /'fɪələs/ **adj** never afraid –**fearlessly adv** –**fearlessness noun** [U]

feasible /'fi:zəbl/ **adj** possible to do: *a feasible plan* –**feasibility** /,fi:zə'bɪləti/ **noun** [U]

feast /fi:st/ **noun** [C] a large, special meal, especially to celebrate sth –**feast verb** [I] **feast (on sth)**: *They feasted on exotic dishes.*

feat /fi:t/ **noun** [C] something you do that shows great strength, skill or courage: *That new bridge is a remarkable feat of engineering.* • *Persuading Helen to give you a pay rise was no mean feat* (= difficult to do).

★**feather** /'feðə/ **noun** [C] one of the light, soft things that grow in a bird's skin and cover its body •➤ picture on page C1

★**feature**¹ /'fi:tʃə/ **noun** [C] **1** an important or noticeable part of sth: *Mountains and lakes are the main features of the landscape of Wales.* • *Noise is a feature of city life.* **2** a part of the face: *Her eyes are her best feature.* **3** a **feature (on sth)** a newspaper or magazine article or television programme about sth: *There's a feature on kangaroos in this magazine.* **4** (also **feature film**) a long film that tells a story –**featureless adj**: *dull, featureless landscape*

feature² /'fi:tʃə/ **verb 1** [T] to include sb/sth as an important part: *The film features many well-known actors.* **2** [I] **feature in sth** to have

a part in sth: *Does marriage feature in your future plans?* •➤ synonym **figure**

Feb abbr February: *18 Feb 1993*

★**February** /'februəri/ **noun** [U,C] (*abbr* **Feb**) the second month of the year, coming after January

➤ To see how the months are used in sentences, look at the examples and the note at **January**.

feces (*US*) = **FAECES**

fed *past tense, past participle* of **FEED**¹

federal /'fedərəl/ **adj 1** organized as a federation: *a federal system of rule* **2** connected with the central government of a federation: *That is a federal not a state law.*

federation /,fedə'reɪʃn/ **noun** [C] a group of states, etc that have joined together to form a single group

fed 'up adj (*informal*) (not before a noun) **fed up (with/of sb/sth/doing sth)** bored or unhappy; tired of sth: *What's the matter? You look really fed up.* • *I'm fed up with waiting for the phone to ring.*

★**fee** /fi:/ **noun** [C] **1** (usually plural) the money you pay for professional advice or service from private doctors, lawyers, schools, universities, etc: *We can't afford private school fees.* • *Most ticket agencies will **charge a** small **fee**.* **2** the cost of an exam, the cost of becoming a member of a club, the amount you pay to go into certain buildings, etc: *How much is the entrance fee?* •➤ Look at the note at **pay**².

feeble /'fi:bl/ **adj 1** with no energy or power; weak: *a feeble old man* • *a feeble cry* **2** not able to make sb believe sth: *a feeble argument/excuse*

★**feed**¹ /fi:d/ **verb** (*pt, pp* fed /fed/) **1** [T] **feed sb/sth (on) (sth)** to give food to a person or an animal: *Don't forget to feed the dog.* • *I can't come yet. I haven't fed the baby.* • *Some of the snakes in the zoo are fed (on) rats.* **2** [I] **feed (on sth)** (used about animals or babies) to eat: *What do horses feed on in the winter?* • *Bats feed at night.* **3** [T] **feed A (with B); feed B into/to/through A** to supply sb/sth with sth; to put sth into sth else: *This channel feeds us with news and information 24 hours a day.* • *Metal sheets are fed through the machine one at a time.*

feed² /fi:d/ **noun 1** [C] a meal for an animal or a baby: *When's the baby's next feed due?* **2** [U] food for animals: *cattle feed*

feedback /'fi:dbæk/ **noun** [U] information or comments about sth that you have done which tells you how good or bad it is: *The teacher spent five minutes with each of us to give us feedback on our homework.*

★**feel**¹ /fi:l/ **verb** (*pt, pp* felt /felt/) **1** [I] (usually with an adjective) to be in the state that is mentioned: *to feel cold/sick/tired/happy* • *How are you feeling today?* • *You'll feel better in the morning.* **2** [I] used to say how something seems to you when you touch, see, smell, experience, etc it: *My new coat feels like leather but it's not.* • *He felt as if he had* been there before. ● *My head feels as though it will burst.* ● *I felt (that) it was a mistake not to ask her advice.*

> ' **It**' is often used as the subject of **feel** in this sense: *It feels as if it is going to snow soon.*

3 [T] to notice or experience sth physical or emotional: *I damaged nerves and now I can't feel anything in this hand.* ● *I felt something crawling up my back.* ● *I don't feel any sympathy for Matt at all.* ● *You could feel the tension in the courtroom.* **4** [T] to touch sth in order to find out what it is like: *Feel this material. Is it cotton or silk?* ● *I felt her forehead to see if she had a temperature.* **5** [I] **feel (about) (for sb/sth)** to try to find something with your hands instead of your eyes: *She felt about in the dark for the light switch.* **6** [T] to be affected by sth: *Do you feel the cold in winter?* ● *She felt it badly when her mother died.*

IDIOMS **feel free (to do sth)** (*informal*) used to tell sb he/she is allowed to do sth: *Feel free to use the phone.*

feel like sth/doing sth to want sth or to want to do sth: *Do you feel like going out?*

feel your age to realize that you are getting old, especially compared to other younger people around you

not feel yourself to not feel healthy or well

PHRASAL VERBS **feel for sb** to understand sb's feelings and situation and feel sorry for him/her: *I really felt for him when his wife died.*

feel up to sth/to doing sth to have the strength and the energy to do or deal with sth: *I really don't feel up to eating a huge meal.*

★**feel²** /fiːl/ *noun* [sing] **1** the impression something gives you when you touch it; the impression that a place or situation gives you: *You can tell it's wool by the feel.* ● *The town has a friendly feel.* **2** an act of touching sth in order to learn about it: *Let me have a feel of that material.*

feelers /'fiːləz/ *noun* [pl] the long thin parts at the front of an insect's head that it uses to feel things •➤ synonym **antennae**

★**feeling** /'fiːlɪŋ/ *noun* **1** [C] **a feeling (of sth)** something that you feel in your mind or body: *a feeling of hunger/happiness/fear/helplessness* ● *I've got a funny feeling in my leg.* **2** [sing] a belief or idea that sth is true or is likely to happen: *I get the feeling that Ian doesn't like me much.* ● *I have a nasty feeling that Jan didn't get our message.* **3** [C,U] **feeling(s) (about/on sth)** an attitude or opinion about sth: *What are your feelings on this matter?* ● *My own feeling is that we should postpone the meeting.* ● *Public feeling seems to be against the new road.* **4** [U,C, usually pl] a person's emotions; strong emotion: *I have to tell Jeff his work's not good enough but I don't want to hurt his feelings.* ● *Let's practise that song again, this time with feeling.* **5** [C,U] **(a) feeling/feelings (for sb/sth)** love or understanding for sb/sth: *She doesn't have much (of a) feeling for music.* ● *He still has feelings for*

his ex-wife. **6** [U] the ability to feel in your body: *After the accident he lost all feeling in his legs.*

IDIOMS **bad/ill feeling** unhappy relations between people: *The decision caused a lot of bad feeling at the factory.*

no hard feelings → **HARD¹**

feet *plural of* **FOOT¹**

feline /'fiːlaɪn/ *adj* connected with an animal of the cat family; like a cat

fell¹ *past tense of* **FALL¹**

fell² /fel/ *verb* [T] to cut down a tree

fellow¹ /'feləʊ/ *noun* [C] **1** a member of an academic or professional organization, or of certain universities: *a fellow of the Royal College of Surgeons* **2** a person who is paid to study a particular thing at a university: *Jill is a research fellow in the biology department* **3** (*old-fashioned*) a man

fellow² /'feləʊ/ *adj* (only *before* a noun) another or others like yourself in the same situation: *Her fellow students were all older than her.* ● *fellow workers/passengers/citizens*

fellowship /'feləʊʃɪp/ *noun* **1** [U] a feeling of friendship between people who share an interest **2** [C] a group or society of people who share the same interest or belief **3** [C] the position of a college or university fellow

felt¹ *past tense, past participle of* **FEEL¹**

felt² /felt/ *noun* [U] a type of soft cloth made from wool, etc which has been pressed tightly together: *a felt hat*

felt-tip 'pen (also **felt 'tip**) *noun* [C] a type of pen with a point made of felt

★**female¹** /'fiːmeɪl/ *adj* **1** being a woman or a girl: *a female artist/employer/student* **2** being of the sex that produce eggs or give birth to babies: *a female cat* **3** (used about plants and flowers) that can produce fruit

female² /'fiːmeɪl/ *noun* [C] **1** an animal that can produce eggs or give birth to babies; a plant that can produce fruit **2** a woman or a girl

> **Female** and **male** are used only to describe the sex of a creature. To describe the qualities we think of as typical of females and males, we use **feminine** and **masculine**.

★**feminine** /'femənɪn/ *adj* **1** typical of or looking like a woman; connected with women: *My daughter always dresses like a boy. She hates looking feminine.* •➤ Look at **masculine** and the note at **female**. **2** (*abbr* **fem**) (*grammar*) (in English) of the forms of words used to describe females: *'Lioness' is the feminine form of 'lion'.* **3** (*abbr* **fem**) (*grammar*) (in the grammar of some languages) belonging to a certain class of nouns, adjectives or pronouns: *The German word for a flower is feminine.* •➤ Look at **masculine** and **neuter**. –femininity /ˌfemə'nɪnəti/ *noun* [U]

feminism /'femənɪzəm/ *noun* [U] the belief that women should have the same rights and opportunities as men –feminist /'femənɪst/ noun [C], adj

fence¹ /fens/ noun [C] a line of wooden or metal posts joined by wood, wire, metal, etc to divide land or to keep in animals •➤ picture on page C7

IDIOM **sit on the fence** → **SIT**

fence² /fens/ verb **1** [T] to surround land with a fence **2** [I] to fight with a long thin pointed weapon (a foil) as a sport

PHRASAL VERBS **fence sb/sth in 1** to surround sb/sth with a fence: *They fenced in their garden to make it more private.* **2** to restrict sb's freedom: *She felt fenced in by so many responsibilities.*

fence sth off to separate one area from another with a fence

fencing /'fensɪŋ/ noun [U] the sport of fighting with long thin pointed weapons (foils)

fend /fend/ verb

PHRASAL VERBS **fend for yourself** to look after yourself without help from anyone else: *It's time Ben left home and learned to fend for himself.*

fend sb/sth off to defend yourself from sb/sth that is attacking you: *Politicians usually manage to fend off awkward questions.*

fender /'fendə/ noun [C] **1** (*US*) = **WING**(4) **2** a low metal frame in front of an open fire that stops coal or wood falling out

ferment¹ /fə'ment/ verb [I,T] to change or make the chemistry of sth change, especially sugar changing to alcohol: *The wine is starting to ferment.*

ferment² /'fɜːment/ noun [U] a state of political or social excitement and change: *The country is in ferment and nobody's sure what will happen next.*

fern /fɜːn/ noun [C] a green plant with no flowers and a lot of long thin leaves •➤ picture on page C2

ferocious /fə'rəʊʃəs/ adj very aggressive and violent: *a ferocious beast/attack/storm/war* –**ferociously** adv

ferocity /fə'rɒsəti/ noun [U] violence; cruel and aggressive behaviour •➤ adjective **fierce**

ferry¹ /'feri/ noun [C] (*pl* ferries) a boat that carries people, vehicles or goods across a river or across a narrow part of the sea: *a car ferry*

ferry² /'feri/ verb [T] (*pres part* ferrying; *3rd pers sing pres* ferries; *pt, pp* ferried) to carry people or goods in a boat or other vehicle from one place to another, usually for a short distance: *Could you ferry us across to the island? • We share the job of ferrying the children to school.*

fertile /'fɜːtaɪl/ adj **1** (used about land or soil) that plants grow well in **2** (used about people, animals or plants) that can produce babies, fruit or new plants **3** (used about a person's mind) full of ideas: *a fertile imagination* •➤ opposite **infertile**. Look at **sterile**. –**fertility** /fə'tɪləti/ noun [U]: *Nowadays women can take drugs to increase their fertility (= their chances of having a child).* •➤ opposite **infertility**

fertilize (also **-ise**) /'fɜːtəlaɪz/ verb [T] **1** (*technical*) to put a male seed into an egg, a plant or a female animal so that a baby, fruit or a young animal starts to develop **2** to put natural or artificial substances on soil in order to make plants grow better –**fertilization** (also **-isation**) /ˌfɜːtəlaɪ'zeɪʃn/ noun [U]

fertilizer (also **-iser**) /'fɜːtɪlaɪzə/ noun [C,U] a natural or chemical substance that is put on land or soil to make plants grow better •➤ Look at **manure**.

fervent /'fɜːvənt/ adj having or showing very strong feelings about sth: *She's a fervent believer in women's rights. • a fervent belief/hope/desire* –**fervently** adv

fervour (*US* fervor) /'fɜːvə/ noun [U] very strong feelings about sth; enthusiasm

fester /'festə/ verb [I] **1** (used about a cut or an injury) to become infected: *a festering sore/wound* **2** (used about an unpleasant situation, feeling or thought) to become more unpleasant because you do not deal with it successfully

festival /'festɪvl/ noun [C] **1** a series of plays, films, musical performances, etc often held regularly in one place: *the Cannes Film Festival • a jazz festival* **2** a day or time when people celebrate sth (especially a religious event): *Christmas is an important Christian festival.*

festive /'festɪv/ adj happy, because people are enjoying themselves celebrating sth: *the festive season* (= Christmas)

festivity /fe'stɪvəti/ noun (*pl* festivities) **1** [pl] happy events when people celebrate sth: *The festivities went on until dawn.* **2** [U] being happy and celebrating sth: *The wedding was followed by three days of festivity.*

fetch /fetʃ/ verb [T] **1** (*especially Brit*) to go to a place and bring back sb/sth: *Shall I fetch you your coat?/Shall I fetch your coat for you?* •➤ picture at **bring 2** (used about goods) to be sold for the price mentioned: *'How much will your car fetch?' 'It should fetch about £900.'*

fête /feɪt/ noun [C] an outdoor event with competitions, entertainment and things to buy, often organized to make money for a particular purpose: *the school/village/church fête*

fetus (*US*) = **FOETUS**

feud /fjuːd/ noun [C] a feud (between A and B); a feud (with sb) (over sb/sth) an angry and serious argument between two people or groups that continues over a long period of time: *a family feud* (= within a family or between two families) –**feud** verb [I]

feudal /'fjuːdl/ adj connected with the system of feudalism: *the feudal system*

feudalism /'fjuːdəlɪzəm/ noun [U] the social system which existed in the Middle Ages in Europe, in which people worked and fought for a person who owned land and received land and protection from him in return

fever /'fiːvə/ noun **1** [C,U] a condition of the body when it is too hot because of illness: *A high fever can be dangerous, especially in* *small children.*

➤ When somebody's body is very hot we normally say that he/she **has a temperature**.

2 [sing] **a fever (of sth)** a state of nervous excitement

feverish /'fiːvərɪʃ/ *adj* **1** suffering from or caused by a fever: *a feverish cold/dream* **2** (usually *before* a noun) showing great excitement –**feverishly** *adv*

★**few** /fjuː/ *determiner, adj, pron* (used with a plural countable noun and a plural verb) **1** not many: *Few people live to be 100.* ● *There are fewer cars here today than yesterday.* ● *Few of the players played really well.* **2 a few** a small number of; some: *a few people* ● *a few hours/days/years* ● *I'll meet you later. I've got a few things to do first.* ● *I knew a few of the people there.* •➤ Look at the note at **less**.

IDIOMS **few and far between** not happening very often; not common: *Pubs are a bit few and far between in this area.*

a good few; quite a few quite a lot: *It's been a good few years since I saw him last.*

ff *abbr* used to show that sth starts on a particular page or line and continues for several pages or lines more: *British Politics, p10ff*

★**fiancé** (*fem* **fiancée**) /fɪ'ɒnseɪ/ *noun* [C] a person who has promised to marry sb: *This is my fiancée Liz. We got engaged a few weeks ago.*

fiasco /fi'æskəʊ/ *noun* [C] (*pl* **fiascos**: *US also* **fiascoes**) an event that does not succeed, often in a way that causes embarrassment: *Our last party was a complete fiasco.*

fib /fɪb/ *noun* [C] (*informal*) something you say that is not true: *Please don't tell fibs.* •➤ synonym **lie** –**fib** *verb* [I] (**fibbing**; **fibbed**)

➤ **Fib** is used when the lie does not seem very important.

fibre (*US* **fiber**) /'faɪbə/ *noun* **1** [U] parts of plants that you eat which are good for you because they help to move food quickly through your body: *Wholemeal bread is **high in fibre**.* **2** [C,U] a material or a substance that is made from natural or artificial threads

➤ **Natural** fibres are, for example, cotton and wool. **Man-made** or **synthetic** fibres are nylon, polyester, etc.

3 [C] one of the thin threads which form a natural or artificial substance: *cotton/wood/nerve/muscle fibres*

fibreglass (*US* **fiberglass**) /'faɪbəglɑːs/ (also **glass** 'fibre) *noun* [U] a material made from small threads of plastic or glass, used for making small boats, parts of cars, etc

fickle /'fɪkl/ *adj* always changing your mind or your feelings so you cannot be trusted: *a fickle friend*

★**fiction** /'fɪkʃn/ *noun* [U] stories, novels, etc which describe events and people that are not real: *I don't read much fiction.* •➤ opposite **non-fiction**. Look at **fact**.

➤ Fiction is one type of **literature**. Look at **drama** and **poetry**.

fictional /'fɪkʃənl/ *adj* not real or true; only existing in stories, novels, etc: *The book gav a fictional account of a doctor's life.* •➤ Look at **factual**.

fictitious /fɪk'tɪʃəs/ *adj* invented; not real The novel is set in a fictitious village calle Paradise.

fiddle¹ /'fɪdl/ *noun* [C] (*informal*) **1** = VIOLIN **2** (*Brit*) a dishonest action, especially one connected with money: *a tax fiddle*

fiddle² /'fɪdl/ *verb* **1** [I] **fiddle (about/around) (with sth)** to play with sth carelessly, because you are nervous or not thinking: *He sat ner vously, fiddling with a pencil.* **2** [T] (*informal* to change the details or facts of sth (busines accounts, etc) in order to get money dishon estly: *She fiddled her expenses form.*

fiddly /'fɪdli/ *adj* difficult to do or manage with your hands (because small o complicated parts are involved)

fidelity /fɪ'deləti/ *noun* [U] **1** (*formal*) fidelity **(to sb/sth)** the quality of being faithful, espe cially to a wife or husband by not having a sexual relationship with anyone else •➤ A less formal word is **faithfulness**. •➤ opposite **infidelity 2** (used about translations, the reproduction of music, etc) the quality o being accurate or close to the origina •➤ Look at **hi-fi**.

fidget /'fɪdʒɪt/ *verb* [I] **fidget (with sth)** to keep moving your body, hands or feet because you are nervous, bored, excited, etc *She fidgeted nervously with her keys* –**fidgety** *adj*

★**field¹** /fiːld/ *noun* [C] **1** an area of land or a farm, usually surrounded by fences or walls used for growing crops or keeping animals in **2** an area of study or knowledge: *He's an expert in the field of economics.* ● *That question is outside my field* (= not one of the subjects that I know about). **3** an area of land used for sports, games or some other activity *a football field* ● *an airfield* (= where aero planes land and take off) ● *a battlefield* •➤ Look at **pitch**. **4** an area affected by or included in sth: *a magnetic field* ● *It's outside my field of vision* (= I can't see it). **5** an area of land where oil, coal or other minerals are found: *a coalfield* ● *a North Sea oilfield*

field² /fiːld/ *verb* **1** [I,T] (in cricket, baseball, etc) to (be ready to) catch and throw back the ball after sb has hit it

➤ When one team is **fielding**, the other is **batting**.

2 [T] to choose a team for a game of football, cricket, etc: *New Zealand is fielding an excellent team for the next match.*

'**field day** *noun*

IDIOM **have a field day** to get the opportunity to do sth you enjoy, especially sth other people disapprove of: *The newspapers always have a field day when there's a political scandal.*

'**field event** *noun* [C] a sport, such as jumping and throwing, that is not a race and does not involve running ••► Look at **track event**.

fieldwork /'fi:ldwɜ:k/ noun [U] practical research work done outside school, college, etc

fiend /fi:nd/ noun [C] **1** a very cruel person **2** (*informal*) a person who is very interested in one particular thing: *a health fiend* ••► synonym **fanatic**

fiendish /'fi:ndɪʃ/ adj **1** very unpleasant or cruel **2** (*informal*) clever and complicated: *a fiendish plan* –**fiendishly** adv

★**fierce** /fɪəs/ adj **1** angry, aggressive and frightening: *The house was guarded by fierce dogs.* **2** very strong; violent: *fierce competition for jobs* • *a fierce attack* ••► noun **ferocity** –**fiercely** adv

fiery /'faɪəri/ adj **1** looking like fire: *She has fiery red hair.* **2** quick to become angry: *a fiery temper*

★**fifteen** /ˌfɪf'ti:n/ number 15

➤ For examples of how to use numbers in sentences, look at **six**.

fifteenth /ˌfɪf'ti:nθ/ pron, determiner, adv 15th ••► Look at the examples at **sixth**.

★**fifth**[1] /fɪfθ/ pron, determiner, adv 5th ••► Look at the examples at **sixth**.

fifth[2] /fɪfθ/ noun [C] the fraction ⅕; one of five equal parts of sth

fiftieth /'fɪftiəθ/ pron, determiner, adv 50th ••► Look at the examples at **sixth**.

★**fifty** /'fɪfti/ number 50

➤ For examples of how to use numbers in sentences, look at **six**.

ˌ**fifty-'fifty** adj, adv equal or equally (between two people, groups, etc): *You've got a fifty-fifty chance of winning.* • *We'll divide the money fifty-fifty.*

fig[1] /fɪg/ noun [C] (a type of tree with) a soft sweet fruit full of small seeds that grows in warm countries and is often eaten dried ••► picture on page C3

fig[2] abbr **1** figure, illustration: *See diagram at fig 2.* **2** figurative(ly)

★**fight**[1] /faɪt/ verb (*pt, pp* **fought** /fɔ:t/) **1** [I,T] fight (against sb) to use physical strength, guns, weapons, etc against sb/sth: *They gathered soldiers to fight the invading army.* • *My younger brothers were always fighting.* **2** [I,T] fight (against sth) to try very hard to stop or prevent sth: *to fight a fire/a decision/prejudice* • *to fight against crime/disease* **3** [I] fight (for sth/to do sth) to try very hard to get or keep sth: *to fight for your rights* **4** [I] fight (with sb) (about/over sth) to argue: *It's not worth fighting about money.* ••► Look at **argue** and **quarrel**[2]

PHRASAL VERB **fight back** to protect yourself with actions or words by attacking sb who has attacked you: *If he hits you again, fight back!*

★**fight**[2] /faɪt/ noun **1** [C] a fight (with sb/sth); a fight (between A and B) the act of using physical force against sb/sth: *Don't get into a fight at school, will you?* • *Fights broke out*

between rival groups of fans. **2** a fight (against/for sth) (to do sth) [sing] the work done trying to destroy, prevent or achieve sth: *Workers won their fight against the management to stop the factory from closing down.* **3** (*especially US*) a fight (with sb/sth) (about/over sth) an argument about sth: *I **had a fight** with my mum over what time I had to be home.* **4** [U] the desire to continue trying or fighting: *I've had some bad luck but I've still got plenty of fight in me.*

IDIOM **pick a fight** → **PICK**[1]

fighter /'faɪtə/ noun [C] **1** (also **fighter plane**) a small fast military aircraft used for attacking enemy aircraft: *a fighter pilot* • *a jet fighter* **2** a person who fights in a war or in sport (a **boxer**)

figurative /'fɪɡərətɪv/ adj (*abbr* **fig**) (used about a word or an expression) not used with its exact meaning but used for giving an imaginative description or a special effect: *'He exploded with rage' is a figurative use of the verb 'to explode'.* ••► Look at **literal** and **metaphor**. –**figuratively** adv

★**figure**[1] /'fɪɡə/ noun [C] **1** an amount (in numbers) or a price: *The unemployment figures are lower this month.* • *What sort of figure are you thinking of for your house?* **2** a written sign for a number (0 to 9): *Write the numbers in figures, not words.* • *He has a six-figure income/an income in six figures* (= £100000 or more). • *Interest rates are now down to single figures* (= less than 10%). • *double figures* (= 10 to 99) **3 figures** [pl] (*informal*) mathematics: *I don't **have a head for figures** (= I'm not very good with numbers).* **4** a well-known or important person: *an important political figure* **5** the shape of the human body, especially a woman's body that is attractive: *She's got a beautiful slim figure.* ••► Look at the note at **build**[2]. **6** a person that you cannot see very clearly or do not know: *Two figures were coming towards us in the dark.* • *There were two figures on the photo that I didn't recognize.* **7** (*abbr* **fig**) a diagram or picture used in a book to explain sth: *Figure 3 shows the major cities of Italy.*

IDIOMS **a ballpark figure/estimate** → **BALLPARK** **facts and figures** → **FACT** **in round figures/numbers** → **ROUND**[1]

figure[2] /'fɪɡə/ verb **1** [I] figure (as sth) (in/among sth) to be included in sth; to be an important part of sth: *Women don't figure much in his novels.* ••► synonym **feature 2** [T] figure (that) (*especially US*) to think or guess sth: *I figured he was here because I saw his car outside.*

IDIOM **it/that figures** (*informal*) that is what I expected

PHRASAL VERBS **figure on sth/on doing sth** (*especially US*) to include sth in your plans: *I figure on arriving in New York on Wednesday.* **figure sb/sth out** to find an answer to sth or to understand sb: *I can't figure out why she married him in the first place.*

ˌ**figure of 'eight** (*US* ˌfigure 'eight) noun

[C] (*pl* **figures of eight**) something in the shape of an 8

ˌfigure of ˈspeech *noun* [C] (*pl* **figures of speech**) a word or expression used not with its original meaning but in an imaginative way to make a special effect

★**file**[1] /faɪl/ *noun* [C] **1** a box or a cover that is used for keeping papers together •➤ picture on page S6 **2** a collection of information or material on one subject that is stored together in a computer or on a disk, with a particular name: *to open/close a file* • *to create/delete/save/copy a file* **3** a file (on sb/sth) a collection of papers or information about sb/sth kept inside a file: *The police are now keeping a file on all known football hooligans.* **4** a metal tool with a rough surface used for shaping hard substances or for making surfaces smooth: *a nail file*

IDIOMS **on file** kept in a file: *We have all the information you need on file.*

in single file in a line, one behind the other **the rank and file** → **RANK**[1]

file[2] /faɪl/ *verb* **1** [T] **file sth (away)** to put and keep documents, etc in a particular place so that you can find them easily; to put sth into a file: *I filed the letters away in a drawer.* **2** [I] file in, out, past, etc to walk or march in a line: *The children filed out of the classroom.* **3** [T] **file sth (away, down, etc)** to shape sth hard or make sth smooth with a file: *to file your nails*

★**fill** /fɪl/ *verb* **1** [I,T] **fill (sth/sb) (with sth)** to make sth full or to become full: *Can you fill the kettle for me?* • *The news filled him with excitement.* • *The room filled with smoke within minutes.* **2** [T] to take a position or to use up your time doing sth: *I'm afraid that teaching post has just been filled* (= somebody has got the job).

PHRASAL VERBS **fill sth in** (*US also* **fill sth out**) **1** to complete a form, etc by writing information on it: *Could you fill in the application form, please?* **2** to fill a hole or space completely to make a surface flat: *You had better fill in the cracks in the wall before you paint it.*

fill (sth) up to become or to make sth completely full: *There weren't many people at first but then the room filled up.*

fillet (*US* **filet**) /ˈfɪlɪt/ *noun* [C,U] a piece of meat or fish with the bones taken out

filling[1] /ˈfɪlɪŋ/ *noun* **1** [C] the material that a dentist uses to fill a hole in a tooth: *a gold filling* **2** [C,U] the food inside a sandwich, pie, cake, etc

filling[2] /ˈfɪlɪŋ/ *adj* (used about food) that makes you feel full: *Pasta is very filling.*

★**film**[1] /fɪlm/ *noun* **1** (*US also* **movie**) [C] a story, play, etc shown in moving pictures at the cinema or on television: *Let's go to the cinema – there's a good film on this week.* • *watch a film* on TV • *to see a film* at the cinema • *a horror/documentary/feature film* • *a film director/producer/critic* **2** [C,U] the art or business of making films: *She's studying film and theatre.* • *the film industry* **3** [U] moving pictures of real events: *The pro-*

gramme included film of the town one hundred years ago. **4** [C,U] a roll of thin plastic that you use in a camera to take photographs: *to have a film developed* • *Fast film is better if there's not much light.* •➤ picture at **camera 5** [usually sing] a thin layer of a substance or material: *The oil forms a film on the surface of the water.*

★**film**[2] /fɪlm/ *verb* [I,T] to record moving pictures of an event, story, etc with a camera: *A lot of westerns are filmed in Spain.* • *The man was filmed stealing from the shop.*

ˈfilm star *noun* [C] a person who is a well-known actor in films

filter[1] /ˈfɪltə/ *noun* [C] **1** a device for holding back solid substances from a liquid or gas that passes through it: *a coffee filter* • *an oil filter* **2** a piece of coloured glass used with a camera to hold back some types of light

filter[2] /ˈfɪltə/ *verb* **1** [T] to pass a liquid through a filter: *Do you filter your water?* **2** [I] filter in, out, through, etc to move slowly and/or in small amounts: *Sunlight filtered into the room through the curtains.* • (*figurative*) *News of her illness filtered through to her friends.*

PHRASAL VERB **filter sb/sth out (of sth)** to remove sth that you do not want from a liquid, light, etc using a special device or substance: *This chemical filters impurities out of the water.* • (*figurative*) *This test is designed to filter out weaker candidates before the interview stage.*

filth /fɪlθ/ *noun* [U] **1** unpleasant dirt: *The room was covered in filth.* **2** sexual words or pictures that cause offence

filthy /ˈfɪlθi/ *adj* (**filthier; filthiest**) **1** very dirty **2** (used about language, books, films, etc) connected with sex, and causing offence

fin /fɪn/ *noun* [C] **1** one of the parts of a fish that it uses for swimming •➤ picture on page C1 **2** a flat, thin part that sticks out of an aircraft, a vehicle, etc to improve its balance and movement through the air or water

★**final**[1] /ˈfaɪnl/ *adj* **1** (only *before* a noun) last (in a series): *This will be the final lesson of our course.* • *I don't want to miss the final episode of that serial.* **2** not to be changed: *The judge's decision is always final.* • *I'm not lending you the money, and that's final!*

IDIOM **the last/final straw** → **STRAW**

★**final**[2] /ˈfaɪnl/ *noun* **1** [C] the last game or match in a series of competitions or sporting events: *The first two runners in this race go through to the final.* •➤ Look at **semi-final**. **2** finals [pl] the exams you take in your last year at university: *I'm taking my finals in June.*

finale /fɪˈnɑːli/ *noun* [C] the last part of a piece of music, an opera, a show, etc

finalist /ˈfaɪnəlɪst/ *noun* [C] a person who is in the final[2](1) of a competition •➤ Look at **semi-finalist**.

finalize (also **-ise**) /ˈfaɪnəlaɪz/ *verb* [T] to make firm decisions about plans, dates, etc: *Have you finalized your holiday arrangements yet?*

★**finally** /'faɪnəli/ *adv* **1** after a long time or delay: *It was getting dark when the plane finally took off.* ••➤ synonym **eventually** **2** used to introduce the last in a list of things: *Finally, I would like to say how much we have all enjoyed this evening.* ••➤ synonym **lastly** **3** in a definite way so that sth will not be changed: *We haven't decided finally who will get the job yet.*

★**finance**¹ /'faɪnæns/ *noun* **1** [U] the money you need to start or support a business, etc: *How will you raise the finance to start the project?* **2** [U] the activity of managing money: *Who is the new Minister of Finance?* ● *an expert in finance* **3 finances** [pl] the money a person, company, country, etc has to spend: *What are our finances like at the moment?* (= how much money have we got?)

finance² /'faɪnæns; fə'næns/ *verb* [T] to provide the money to pay for sth: *Your trip will be financed by the company.*

financial /faɪ'nænʃl; fə'næ-/ *adj* connected with money: *The business got into financial difficulties.* –**financially** *adv* /-ʃəli/

finch /fɪntʃ/ *noun* [C] a small bird with a short strong beak

★**find**¹ /faɪnd/ *verb* [T] (*pt, pp* **found** /faʊnd/) **1** to discover sth that you want or that you have lost after searching for it: *Did you find the pen you lost?* ● *After six months she finally found a job.* ● *Scientists haven't yet found a cure for colds.* ● *I hope you find an answer to your problem.*

➤ Notice the expressions **find the time**, **find the money**: *I never seem to find the time to write letters these days.* ● *We'd like to go on holiday but we can't find the money.*

2 to discover sth by chance: *I've found a piece of glass in this milk.* ● *We went into the house and found her lying on the floor.* ● *This animal can be found* (= exists) *all over the world.* **3** to have an opinion about sth because of your own experience: *I find that book very difficult to understand.* ● *We didn't find the film at all funny.* ● *How are you finding life as a student?* **4** to suddenly realize or see sth: *I got home to find that I'd left the tap on all day.* ● *Ben turned a corner and suddenly found himself in the port.* **5** to arrive somewhere naturally: *These birds find their way to Africa every winter.*

IDIOMS **find fault (with sb/sth)** to look for things that are wrong with sb/sth and complain about them: *Monica wouldn't make a good teacher because she's always finding fault with people.*

find your feet to become confident and independent in a new situation: *Don't worry if the job seems difficult at first – you'll soon find your feet.*

PHRASAL VERBS **find (sth) out** to get some information; to discover a fact: *Have you found out how much the tickets cost?* ● *I later found out that Will had been lying to me.*

find sb out to discover that sb has done sth wrong: *He had used a false name for years before they found him out.*

find² /faɪnd/ *noun* [C] a thing or a person that has been found, especially one that is valuable or useful: *Archaeologists made some interesting finds when they dug up the field.* ● *This new young player is quite a find!*

finder /'faɪndə/ *noun* [C] a person or thing that finds sth

finding /'faɪndɪŋ/ *noun* [C, usually pl] information that is discovered as a result of research into sth: *the findings of a survey/report/committee*

★**fine**¹ /faɪn/ *adj* **1** in good health, or happy and comfortable: *'How are you?' 'Fine thanks.'* ● *'Do you want to change places?' 'No I'm fine here, thanks.'* **2** all right; acceptable: *'Do you want some more milk in your coffee?' 'No that's fine, thanks.'* ● *Don't cook anything special – a sandwich will be fine.* ● *The hotel rooms were fine but the food was awful.*

➤ We do not use meanings **1** and **2** in questions or in the negative form, so you CANNOT say 'Are you fine?' or 'This isn't fine'.

3 (used about weather) bright with sunlight; not raining: *Let's hope it stays fine for the match tomorrow.* **4** (only *before* a noun) of very good quality, beautiful, well-made: *a fine piece of work* ● *fine detail/carving/china* **5** very thin or narrow: *That hairstyle's no good for me – my hair's too fine.* ● *You must use a fine pencil for the diagrams.* ••➤ opposite **thick 6** made of very small pieces, grains, etc: *Salt is finer than sugar.* ••➤ opposite **coarse 7** difficult to notice or understand: *I couldn't understand the finer points of his argument.* ● *There's a fine line between being reserved and being unfriendly.*

★**fine**² /faɪn/ *noun* [C] a sum of money that you have to pay for breaking a law or rule: *a parking fine* ● *You'll get a fine if you park your car there.* –**fine** *verb* [T] **fine sb (for sth/doing sth)**: *He was fined £50 for driving without lights.*

finely /'faɪnli/ *adv* **1** into small pieces: *The onions must be finely chopped for this recipe.* **2** very accurately: *a finely tuned instrument*

★**finger**¹ /'fɪŋgə/ *noun* [C] one of the five parts at the end of each hand: *little finger, ring finger, middle finger, forefinger (or index finger), thumb* ••➤ picture on page C5

➤ Sometimes we think of the thumb as one of the fingers, sometimes we contrast it: *Hold the pen between your finger and thumb.* The five parts at the end of each foot are called **toes**.

IDIOMS **cross your fingers; keep your fingers crossed** to hope that sb/sth will be successful or lucky: *I'll keep my fingers crossed for you in your exams.* ● *There's nothing more we can do now – just cross our fingers and hope for the best.*

have green fingers → GREEN¹
snap your fingers → SNAP¹

finger² /'fɪŋgə/ *verb* [T] to touch or feel sth with your fingers

---

[I] **intransitive**, a verb which has no object: *He laughed.*   [T] **transitive**, a verb which has an object: *He ate an apple.*

fingermark /ˈfɪŋgəmɑːk/ noun [C] a mark on sth made by a dirty finger

fingernail /ˈfɪŋgəneɪl/ (also **nail**) noun [C] the hard parts on the ends of the fingers ••➤ picture on page C5

fingerprint /ˈfɪŋgəprɪnt/ noun [C] the mark made by the skin of a finger, used for identifying people: *The burglar left his fingerprints all over the house.* ••➤ picture at **footprint**

fingertip /ˈfɪŋgətɪp/ noun [C] the end of a finger

IDIOM **have sth at your fingertips** to have sth ready for quick and easy use: *They asked some difficult questions but luckily I had all the facts at my fingertips.*

★**finish¹** /ˈfɪnɪʃ/ verb **1** [I,T] finish (sth/doing sth) to complete sth or reach the end of sth: *What time does the film finish?* • *Haven't you finished yet? You've taken ages!* • *The Ethiopian runner won and the Kenyans finished second and third.* • *Finish your work quickly!* • *Have you finished typing that letter?* **2** [T] finish sth (off/up) to eat, drink or use the last part of sth: *Finish up your milk, Tony!* • *Who finished off all the bread?* **3** [T] finish sth (off) to complete the last details of sth or make sth perfect: *He stayed up all night to finish off the article he was writing.* • *He's just **putting the finishing touches** to his painting.*

PHRASAL VERBS finish sb/sth off (*informal*) to kill sb/sth; to be the thing that makes sb unable to continue: *The cat played with the mouse before finishing it off.* • *I was very tired towards the end of the race, and that last hill finished me off.*
finish with sb/sth **1** to stop needing or using sb/sth: *I'll borrow that book when you've finished with it.* **2** (*informal*) to end a relationship with sb: *Sally's not going out with David any more – she finished with him last week.*

finish² /ˈfɪnɪʃ/ noun [C] **1** the last part or end of sth: *There was a dramatic finish to the race when two runners fell.* • *I enjoyed the film from start to finish.* **2** the last covering of paint, polish, etc that is put on a surface to make it look good

★**finished** /ˈfɪnɪʃt/ adj **1** (not before a noun) finished (with sb/sth) having stopped doing sth, using sth or dealing with sb/sth: *'Are you using the computer?' 'Yes, I won't be finished with it for another hour or so.'* **2** (not before a noun) not able to continue: *The business is finished – there's no more money.* **3** made; completed: *the finished product/article*

finite /ˈfaɪnaɪt/ adj having a definite limit or a fixed size: *The world's resources are finite.* ••➤ opposite **infinite**

fir /fɜː/ (also **ˈfir tree**) noun [C] a tree with thin leaves (**needles**) that do not fall off in winter

ˈfir cone noun [C] the fruit of the fir tree

★**fire¹** /ˈfaɪə/ noun **1** [C,U] burning and flames, especially when it destroys and is out of control: *Firemen struggled for three hours to **put out the fire**.* • *It had been a dry summer so* there were many forest fires. • *In very ho̶ weather, dry grass can **catch fire** (= star̶ burning).* • *Did someone **set fire to** that pil̶ of wood?* • *Help! The frying pan's **on fire**.* **2** [C] burning wood or coal used for warming people or cooking food: *They tried to **light a̶ fire** to keep warm.* • *It's cold – don't let the fir̶ go out!* **3** [C] a machine for heating a room etc: *a gas/an electric fire* **4** [U] shooting from guns: *The soldiers came **under fire** from al̶ sides.* • *I could hear gunfire in the distance.*

IDIOMS **get on/along like a house on fire** → **HOUSE¹**

open fire → **OPEN²**

come/be under fire be strongly criticized: *The government has come under fire from al̶ sides for its foreign policy.*

fire² /ˈfaɪə/ verb **1** [I,T] fire (sth) (at sb/sth); fire (sth) (on/into sb/sth) to shoot bullets, etc from a gun or other weapon: *Can you hear the guns firing?* • *The soldiers fired on the crowd, killing twenty people.* • *She fired an arrow at the target.* • (*figurative*) *If you stop firing questions at me I might be able to answer!* **2** [T] (*informal*) to remove an employee from a job: *He was fired for always being late.* **3** [T] fire sb with sth to produce a strong feeling in sb: *Her speech fired me with determination.*

ˈfire alarm noun [C] a bell or other signal to warn people that there is a fire

firearm /ˈfaɪərɑːm/ noun [C] a gun that you can carry

ˈfire brigade (*US* **ˈfire department**) noun [C, with sing or pl verb] an organization of people trained to deal with fires

-fired /ˈfaɪəd/ (in compounds) using the fuel mentioned: *gas-fired central heating*

ˈfire engine noun [C] a special vehicle that carries equipment for dealing with large fires

ˈfire escape noun [C] a special staircase on the outside of a building that people can go down if there is a fire

ˈfire extinguisher (also **extinguisher**) noun [C] a metal container with water or chemicals inside that you use for stopping small fires

firefighter /ˈfaɪəfaɪtə/ noun [C] a person whose job is to stop fires

firelight /ˈfaɪəlaɪt/ noun [U] the light that comes from a fire

fireman /ˈfaɪəmən/ (*pl* **-men** /-mən/) = **FIRE-FIGHTER**

fireplace /ˈfaɪəpleɪs/ noun [C] the open place in a room where you light a fire

fireside /ˈfaɪəsaɪd/ noun [sing] the part of a room beside the fire: *Come and sit by the fireside.*

ˈfire station noun [C] a building where fire-fighters wait to be called, and where the vehicles that they use are kept

firewood /ˈfaɪəwʊd/ noun [U] wood used for burning on fires

---

fireplace

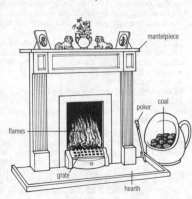

mantelpiece

poker | coal

flames

grate

hearth

firework /'faɪəwɜːk/ **noun** [C] a small object that burns or explodes with coloured lights and loud sounds, used for entertainment

fireworks

rocket

'firing squad noun [C] a group of soldiers who have been ordered to shoot and kill a prisoner

★**firm¹** /fɜːm/ **adj**
1 able to stay the same shape when pressed; quite hard: *a firm mattress* ● *firm muscles*
2 strong and steady or not likely to change: *She kept a firm grip on her mother's hand.* ● *a firm commitment/ decision/offer* **3** firm (with sb) strong and in control: *He's very firm with his children.* ● *You have to show the examiner that you have a firm grasp* (= good knowledge) *of grammar.* –firmly **adv** –firmness **noun** [U]
IDIOM a firm hand strong control or discipline: *Those children need a teacher with a firm hand.*

★**firm²** /fɜːm/ **noun** [C, with sing or pl verb] a business company: *Which firm do you work for?*

★**first¹** /fɜːst/ **determiner** coming before all others; that has not happened before: *She's expecting her first baby.* ● *the first half of the game* ● *You've won first prize!* ● *What were your first impressions of this country when you arrived?* ● *King Charles I* (= King Charles the First) •➤ Look at **one**.
IDIOMS **at first glance/sight** when first seen or examined: *The task seemed impossible at first glance, but it turned out to be quite easy.*
first/last thing → THING

★**first²** /fɜːst/ **adv 1** before any others: *Sue arrived first at the party.* ● *Mike's very competitive – he always wants to come first when he plays a game.* ● *Do you want to go first or*

second? **2** before doing anything else: *I'll come out later. I've got to finish my homework first.* **3** the time before all the other times; for the first time: *Where did you first meet your husband?* **4** at the beginning: *When I first started my job I hated it.* **5** used for introducing the first thing in a list: *There are several people I would like to thank: First, my mother.*
•➤ synonym **firstly**
IDIOMS **at first** at the beginning: *At first I thought he was joking, but then I realized he was serious.*
come first to be more important to sb than anything else: *Although she enjoys her job, her family has always come first.*
first and foremost more than anything else; most importantly: *He worked in television but he was a stage actor first and foremost.*
first come, first served (*informal*) people will be dealt with, served, seen, etc strictly in the order in which they arrive: *Tickets can be bought here on a first come, first served basis.*
first of all as the first thing (to be done or said): *In a moment I'll introduce our guest speaker, but first of all, let me thank you all for coming.*
first off (*informal*) before anything else: *First off, let's decide who does what.*
head first → HEAD¹

★**first³** /fɜːst/ **noun, pron 1** [sing] the first person or thing: *Are we the first to arrive?* ● *They enjoyed the holiday – their first for ten years.* **2 a first** [sing] an important event that is happening for the first time: *This operation is a first in medical history.* **3** [C] (*Brit*) the highest mark given for a university degree: *He got a first in History.*
IDIOM **from the (very) first** from the beginning: *They hated each other from the first.*

first 'aid noun [U] medical help that you give to sb who is hurt or ill before the doctor arrives: *a first aid kit/course* ● *to give sb first aid*

first 'class adj, adv 1 excellent; of the best quality: *a first-class player* ● *This book is really first class.* **2** giving or using the best and most expensive type of service: *He always travels first class.* ● *Ten first-class stamps, please.*

the first 'floor noun [C] **1** (*Brit*) the floor of a building above the one on street level (**the ground floor**): *I live in a flat on the first floor.* ● *a first-floor flat* **2** (*US*) the floor of a building on street level

first 'gear noun [C] the lowest gear on a car, bicycle, etc: *To move off, put the car into first gear and slowly release the clutch.*

first-hand /ˌfɜːst 'hænd/ **adj, adv** (used about information, experience, a story, etc) heard, seen or learnt by yourself, not from other people: *He gave me a first-hand account of the accident* (= he had seen it). ● *I've experienced the problem first-hand, so I know how you feel.*

firstly /'fɜːstli/ **adv** used to introduce the first point in a list: *They were angry firstly because they had to pay extra, and secondly because no one had told them about it.* •➤ synonym **first**

'first name noun [C] the first of your names that come before you family name: *'What's Mr Munn's first name?' 'Robert, I think.'* •➤ Look at the note at **name**¹.

the ,first 'person noun [sing] **1** (*grammar*) the words such as 'I', 'me', 'we', and the verb forms that go with them: *'I am' is the first person singular of the verb 'to be'.* **2** the style of telling a story as if it happened to you: *The author writes in the first person.*

,first-'rate adj excellent; of the best quality

★**fish**¹ /fɪʃ/ noun (*pl* **fish** or **fishes**) **1** [C] an animal that lives and breathes in water and swims: *How many fish have you caught?* • *I went diving on holiday – it was fantastic to see so many different fishes* (= types or species of fish). •➤ picture on page C1

➤ The plural form **fish** is more common. **Fishes** is used when we are talking about different types of fish.

2 [U] fish as food: *We're having fish for dinner.* •➤ picture on page C4

➤ In Britain a common type of fast food is **fish and chips** which we buy at a **fish and chip shop**.

★**fish**² /fɪʃ/ verb [I] **1** fish (for sth) to try to catch fish: *He's fishing for trout.* • *They often go fishing at weekends.* **2** fish (around) (in sth) (for sth) to search for sth in water or in a deep or hidden place: *She fished (around) for her keys in the bottom of her bag.*

PHRASAL VERBS **fish for sth** to try to get sth you want in an indirect way: *to fish for an invitation*

fish sth out (of sth) to take or pull sth out (of sth) especially after searching for it: *After the accident they fished the car out of the canal.*

fisherman /'fɪʃəmən/ noun [C] (*pl* **-men** /-men/) a person who catches fish either as a job or as a sport •➤ Look at **angler**.

fishing /'fɪʃɪŋ/ noun [U] catching fish as a job, sport or hobby: *Fishing is a major industry in Iceland.* •➤ Look at **angling**.

'fishing rod noun [C] a long thin stick with a long thread (**line**) and a hook on it for catching fish

fishmonger /'fɪʃmʌŋgə/ noun (*Brit*) **1** [C] a person whose job is to sell fish **2 the fishmonger's** [sing] a shop that sells fish

fishy /'fɪʃi/ adj **1** tasting or smelling like a fish: *a fishy smell* **2** (*informal*) seeming suspicious or dishonest: *The police thought the man's story sounded extremely fishy.*

fist /fɪst/ noun [C] a hand with the fingers closed together tightly: *She clenched her fists in anger.*

★**fit**¹ /fɪt/ verb (**fitting**; **fitted**) **1** [I,T] to be the right size or shape for sb/sth: *These jeans fit very well.* • *This dress doesn't fit me any more.* • *This key doesn't fit in the lock.* **2** [T] fit (sb/sth) in/into/on/onto sth to find or have enough space for sb/sth: *I can't fit into these trousers any more.* • *Can you fit one more person in the car?* • *I can't fit all these books onto the shelf.* **3** [T] to put or fix sth in the right place: *The builders are fitting new win-*

dows today. • *I can't fit these pieces of the model together.* **4** [T] to be or make sb/sth right or suitable: *I don't think Ruth's fitted for such a demanding job.* • *That description fits Jim perfectly.*

PHRASAL VERBS **fit sb/sth in; fit sb/sth in/into sth** to find time to see sb or to do sth: *The doctor managed to fit me in this morning.* • *You're tired because you're trying to fit too much into one day.*

fit in (with sb/sth) to be able to live, work, etc in an easy and natural way (with sb/sth): *The new girl found it difficult to fit in (with the other children) at school.*

★**fit**² /fɪt/ adj (**fitter**; **fittest**) **1** fit (for sth/to do sth) strong and in good physical health (especially because of exercise): *Swimming is a good way to keep fit.* • *My dad's almost recovered from his illness, but he's still not fit enough for work.* • *She goes to keep-fit classes.* •➤ opposite **unfit 2** fit (for sb/sth); fit to do sth good enough; suitable: *Do you think she is fit for the job?* • *These houses are not fit (for people) to live in.*

fit³ /fɪt/ noun **1** [C] a sudden attack of an illness, in which sb loses consciousness and his/her body may make violent movements: *to have fits* **2** [C] a sudden short period of coughing, laughter, etc that you cannot control: *a fit of laughter/anger* **3** [sing] (usually after an adjective) the way in which sth (for example a piece of clothing) fits: *a good/bad/tight/loose fit*

fitness /'fɪtnəs/ noun [U] **1** the condition of being strong and healthy: *Fitness is important in most sports.* **2** fitness for sth/to do sth the quality of being suitable: *The directors were not sure about his fitness for the job.*

fitted /'fɪtɪd/ adj made or cut to fit a particular space and fixed there: *a fitted carpet* • *a fitted kitchen* (= one with fitted cupboards)

fitting¹ /'fɪtɪŋ/ adj **1** (*formal*) right; suitable: *It would be fitting for the Olympics to be held in Greece, as that is where they originated.* **2 -fitting** used in compounds to describe how clothes, etc fit: *a tight-fitting dress* • *loose-fitting trousers*

fitting² /'fɪtɪŋ/ noun [C,usually pl] the things that are fixed in a building or on a piece of furniture but that can be changed or moved if necessary •➤ Look at **fixture**.

★**five** /faɪv/ number **1** 5 •➤ Look at **fifth** (= 5th).

➤ For examples of how to use numbers in sentences, look at **six**.

2 five- (used in compounds) having five of the thing mentioned: *a five-day week* • *a five-hour flight*

fiver /'faɪvə/ noun [C] (*Brit informal*) a five-pound note; £5

★**fix**¹ /fɪks/ verb [T] **1** to put sth firmly in place so that it will not move: *Can you fix this new handle to the door?* • (*figurative*) *I found it difficult to keep my mind fixed on my work.* **2** to repair sth: *The electrician's coming to fix the cooker.* •➤ synonym **repair 3** fix sth (up) to decide or arrange sth: *We need to fix the*

price. • *Have you fixed (up) a date for the party?* **4** fix sth (up) to get sth ready: *They're fixing up their spare room for the new baby.* **5** (usually passive) (*informal*) to arrange the result of sth in a way that is not honest or fair: *Fans of the losing team suspected that the match had been fixed.* **6** fix sth (for sb) (*especially US*) to prepare sth (especially food or drink): *Can I fix you a drink/a drink for you?*
PHRASAL VERB fix sb up (with sth) (*informal*) to arrange for sb to have sth: *I can fix you up with a place to stay.*

fix² /fɪks/ *noun* **1** [C] a solution to a problem, especially one that is easy or temporary: *There's no quick fix to this problem.* **2** [usually sing] (*informal*) a difficult situation: *I was in a real fix – I'd locked the car keys inside the car.* **3** [usually sing] (*informal*) a result that is dishonestly arranged

fixation /fɪk'seɪʃn/ *noun* [C] a fixation (with sth) an interest in sth that is too strong and not normal: *I'm tired of James's fixation with football.*

fixed /fɪkst/ *adj* **1** already decided: *a fixed date/price/rent* •▸ opposite **movable** **2** not changing: *He has such fixed ideas that you can't discuss anything with him.*
IDIOM (of) no fixed abode/address (*formal*) (with) no permanent place to live: *Daniel Stephens, of no fixed abode, was found guilty of robbery.*

fixture /'fɪkstʃə/ *noun* [C] **1** a sporting event arranged for a particular day: *to arrange/cancel/play a fixture* **2** [usually pl] a piece of furniture or equipment that is fixed in a house or building and sold with it: *Does the price of the house include fixtures and fittings?* •▸ Look at **fitting**.

fizz /fɪz/ *noun* [U] the bubbles in a liquid and the sound they make: *This lemonade's lost its fizz.* –fizz *verb* [I]

fizzle /'fɪzl/ *verb*
PHRASAL VERB fizzle out to end in a weak or disappointing way: *The game started well but it fizzled out in the second half.*

fizzy /'fɪzi/ *adj* (used about a drink) containing many small bubbles of gas

> Wine or mineral water that contains bubbles is usually described as **sparkling**, not fizzy.

•▸ picture at **bubble** •▸ Look at **still**.

fizzy 'drink (*US* **soda**) *noun* [C] a sweet non-alcoholic drink that contains many small bubbles •▸ picture on page C4

fjord /'fiː.ɔːd/ *noun* [C] a long narrow piece of sea between cliffs, especially in Norway

flabbergasted /'flæbəgɑːstɪd/ *adj* (*informal*) extremely surprised and/or shocked

flabby /'flæbi/ *adj* having too much soft fat instead of muscle: *a flabby stomach*

★**flag¹** /flæg/ *noun* [C] a piece of cloth with a pattern or picture on it, often tied to a pole (flagpole) or rope and used as a symbol of a country, club, etc or as a signal

flag² /flæg/ *verb* [I] (flagging; flagged) to become tired or less strong
PHRASAL VERB flag sb/sth down to wave to sb in a car to make him/her stop: *to flag down a taxi*

flagrant /'fleɪɡrənt/ *adj* (only *before* a noun) (used about an action) shocking because it is done in a very obvious way and shows no respect for people, laws, etc

flail /fleɪl/ *verb* [I,T] to wave or move about without control: *The insect's legs were flailing in the air.* • *Don't flail your arms about like that – you might hurt someone.*

flair /fleə/ *noun* **1** (a) flair for sth [sing] a natural ability to do sth well: *She has a flair for languages.* **2** [U] the quality of being interesting or having style: *That poster is designed with her usual flair.*

flak /flæk/ *noun* [U] (*informal*) criticism: *He'll get some flak for missing that goal.*

flake¹ /fleɪk/ *noun* [C] a small thin piece of sth: *snowflakes* • *flakes of paint*

flake² /fleɪk/ *verb* [I] flake (off) to come off in flakes: *This paint is very old – it's beginning to flake (off).*

flamboyant /flæm'bɔɪənt/ *adj* **1** (used about a person) acting in a loud, confident way that attracts attention: *a flamboyant gesture/style/personality* **2** bright and easily noticed: *flamboyant colours* –flamboyance *noun* [U] –flamboyantly *adv*

★**flame** /fleɪm/ *noun* [C,U] an area of bright burning gas that comes from sth that is on fire: *The flame of the candle flickered by the open window.* • *The house was in flames when the fire engine arrived.* • *The piece of paper burst into flames in the fire* (= suddenly began to burn strongly). •▸ picture at **candle** and **fireplace**

flaming /'fleɪmɪŋ/ *adj* (only *before* a noun) **1** (used about anger, an argument, etc) violent: *We had a flaming argument over the bills.* **2** burning brightly **3** (*slang*) used as a mild swear word: *I can't get in – I've lost the flaming key.* **4** (used about colours, especially red) very bright: *flaming red hair* • *a flaming sunset*

flamingo /flə'mɪŋɡəʊ/ *noun* [C] a large pink and red bird that has long legs and stands in water

flammable /'flæməbl/ *adj* able to burn easily •▸ **Inflammable** has the same meaning as flammable and is more common. •▸ opposite **non-flammable**

flan /flæn/ *noun* [C,U] a round open pie that is filled with fruit, cheese, vegetables, etc

flank¹ /flæŋk/ *noun* [C] **1** the side of an animal's body **2** the parts of an army at the sides in a battle

flank² /flæŋk/ *verb* [T] (usually passive) to be placed at the side or sides of: *The road was flanked by trees.*

flannel /'flænl/ *noun* **1** [U] a type of soft woollen cloth **2** =FACECLOTH

flap¹ /flæp/ *noun* [C] a piece of material, paper, etc that is fixed to sth at one side only, often covering an opening: *the flap of an* *envelope* ··➤ picture at **bag** and **tent**

IDIOM **be in/get into a flap** (*informal*) to be in/get into a state of worry or excitement

flap² /flæp/ **verb** (**flapping**; **flapped**) **1** [I,T] to move (sth) up and down or from side to side, especially in the wind: *The sails were flapping in the wind.* ● *The bird flapped its wings and flew away.* **2** [I] (*informal*) to become worried or excited: *Stop flapping – it's all organized!*

flare¹ /fleə/ **verb** [I] to burn for a short time with a sudden bright flame

PHRASAL VERB **flare up 1** (used about a fire) to suddenly burn more strongly **2** (used about violence, anger, etc) to start suddenly or to become suddenly worse

flare² /fleə/ **noun 1** [sing] a sudden bright light or flame **2** [C] a thing that produces a bright light or flame, used especially as a signal

flared /fleəd/ **adj** (used about trousers and skirts) becoming wider towards the bottom

★**flash¹** /flæʃ/ **verb 1** [I,T] to produce or make sth produce a sudden bright light for a short time: *The neon sign above the door flashed on and off all night.* ● *That lorry driver's flashing his lights at us* (= in order to tell us sth). **2** [I] to move very fast: *I saw something flash past the window.* ● *Thoughts kept flashing through my mind and I couldn't sleep.* **3** [T] to show sth quickly: *The detective flashed his card and went straight in.* **4** [T] to send sth by radio, television, etc: *The news of the disaster was flashed across the world.*

PHRASAL VERB **flash back** (used about a person's thoughts) to return suddenly to a time in the past: *Something he said made my mind flash back to my childhood.*

★**flash²** /flæʃ/ **noun 1** [C] a sudden bright light that comes and goes quickly: *a flash of lightning* **2** [C] **a flash (of sth)** a sudden strong feeling or idea: *a flash of inspiration* ● *The idea came to me in a flash.* **3** [C,U] a bright light that you use with a camera for taking photographs when it is dark; the device for producing this light ··➤ picture at **camera**

IDIOMS **in/like a flash** very quickly

(as) quick as a flash → **QUICK¹**

flashback /'flæʃbæk/ **noun** [C,U] a part of a film, play, etc that shows sth that happened before the main story

flashlight /'flæʃlaɪt/ (*US*) = **TORCH**(1)

flashy /'flæʃi/ **adj** (**flashier**; **flashiest**) attracting attention by being very big, bright and expensive: *a flashy sports car*

flask /flɑːsk/ **noun** [C] **1** (also **Thermos**™) (*Brit*) a type of container for keeping a liquid hot or cold **2** a bottle with a narrow neck that is used for storing and mixing chemicals in scientific work

★**flat¹** /flæt/ **adj**, **adv** (**flatter**; **flattest**) **1** smooth and level, with no parts that are higher than the rest: *The countryside in Essex is quite flat* (= there are not many hills). ● *I need a flat surface to write this letter on.* ● *a flat roof* ● *She lay flat on her back in the sunshine.* ● *He fell flat on his face* in the

mud. **2** not high or deep: *You need flat shoes for walking.* ● *a flat dish* **3** without much interest or energy: *Things have been a bit flat since Alex left.* **4** (only *before* a noun) (used about sth that you say or decide) that will not change; firm: *He answered our request with a flat 'No!'* **5** (in music) half a note lower than the stated note ··➤ Look at **sharp**. **6** (in music) lower than the correct note: *That last note was flat. Can you sing it again?* ● *You're singing flat.* ··➤ Look at **sharp**. **7** (used about a drink) not fresh because it has lost its bubbles: *Open a new bottle. That lemonade has gone flat.* **8** (*Brit*) (used about a battery) no longer producing electricity; not working: *We couldn't start the car because the battery was completely flat.* **9** (used about a tyre) without enough air in it: *This tyre looks flat – has it got a puncture?* **10** (used about the cost of sth) that is the same for everyone; that is fixed: *We charge a flat fee of £20, however long you stay.* **11** (used for emphasizing how quickly sth is done) in exactly the time mentioned and no longer: *She can get up and out of the house in ten minutes flat.*

IDIOMS **fall flat** (used about a joke, a story, an event, etc) to fail to produce the effect that you wanted

flat out as fast as possible; without stopping: *He's been working flat out for two weeks and he needs a break.*

flat² /flæt/ **noun 1** [C] (*especially US* **apartment**) a set of rooms that is used as a home (usually in a large building): *Do you rent your flat or have you bought it?*

➤ **Apartment** is the normal word in US English. In British English we say **apartment** when talking about a flat we are renting for a holiday, etc rather than to live in: *We're renting an apartment in the South of France.*
You **rent** a flat from a **landlord/landlady**. The landlord/lady **lets** the flat to you, the **tenant**. The money you have to pay is called **rent**. Your flat may be **furnished** or **unfurnished**. A tall modern building that contains many flats is a **block of flats**. A person who shares the flat with you is your **flatmate**.

2 [C] (*symbol* ♭) (in music) a note which is half a note lower than the note with the same letter ··➤ Look at **sharp**. **3** [sing] **the flat (of sth)** the flat part or side of sth: *the flat of your hand* **4** [C] (*especially US*) a tyre on a vehicle that has no air in it

flatly /'flætli/ **adv 1** in a direct way; absolutely: *He flatly denied the allegations.* **2** in a way that shows no interest or emotion

flatten /'flætn/ **verb** [I,T] **flatten (sth) (out)** to become or make sth flat: *The countryside flattens out as you get nearer the sea.* ● *The storms have flattened crops all over the country.*

flatter /'flætə/ **verb** [T] **1** to say nice things to sb, often in a way that is not sincere, because you want to please him/her or because you want to get an advantage for yourself **2** flatter yourself (that) to choose to believe sth good about yourself although other people may not think the same: *He flatters himself that he speaks fluent French.* **3** (usually passive) to give pleasure or honour to sb: *I felt very flattered when they gave me the job.*

flattering /ˈflætərɪŋ/ **adj** making sb look or sound more attractive or important than he/ she really is

flattery /ˈflætəri/ **noun** [U] saying good things about sb/sth that you do not really mean

flaunt /flɔːnt/ **verb** [T] to show sth that you are proud of so that other people will admire it

flautist /ˈflɔːtɪst/ (*US* **flutist**) **noun** [C] a person who plays a musical instrument that you blow into (a flute)

★**flavour¹** (*US* **flavor**) /ˈfleɪvə/ **noun** [C,U] **1** the taste (of food): *Do you think a little salt would improve the flavour?* • *ten different flavours of yoghurt* • *yoghurt in ten different flavours* **2** [sing] an idea of the particular quality or character of sth: *This video will give you a flavour of what the city is like.*

flavour² (*US* **flavor**) /ˈfleɪvə/ **verb** [T] to give flavour to sth: *Add a little nutmeg to flavour the sauce.* • *strawberry-flavoured milkshake*

flavouring (*US* **flavoring**) /ˈfleɪvərɪŋ/ **noun** [C,U] something that you add to food or drink to give it a particular taste: *This orange juice contains no artificial flavourings.*

flaw /flɔː/ **noun** [C] **1** a flaw (in sth) a mistake in sth that makes it not good enough or not function as it should: *There are some flaws in her argument.* **2** a mark or crack in an object that means that it is not perfect **3** a flaw (in sb/sth) a bad quality in sb's character: *His only real flaw is impatience.* –flawed **adj**: *I think your plan is flawed.*

flawless /ˈflɔːləs/ **adj** perfect; with no faults or mistakes: *a flawless diamond*

flea /fliː/ **noun** [C] a very small jumping insect without wings that lives on animals, for example cats and dogs. Fleas bite people and animals and make them scratch.

ˈflea market noun [C] a market, often in a street, that sells old and used goods

fleck /flek/ **noun** [C,usually pl] a very small mark on sth; a very small piece of sth: *After painting the ceiling, her hair was covered with flecks of blue paint.*

flee /fliː/ **verb** [I,T] (*pt, pp* **fled** /fled/) flee (to…/into…); flee (from) sb/sth to run away or escape from sth: *The robbers fled the country with £100000.*

fleet /fliːt/ **noun** [C,with sing or pl verb] **1** a group of ships or boats that sail together: *a fishing fleet* **2** a fleet (of sth) a group of vehicles (especially taxis, buses or aircraft) that are travelling together or owned by one person

★**flesh** /fleʃ/ **noun** [U] **1** the soft part of a human or animal body (between the bones and under the skin) • ➤ The flesh of animals that we eat is called **meat**. **2** the part of a

fruit or vegetable that is soft and can be eaten

ℹ️ IDIOMS your (own) flesh and blood a member of your family

in the flesh in person, not on television, in a photograph, etc

make your flesh creep to make you feel disgusted and/or nervous: *The way he smiled made her flesh creep.*

flew *past tense* of FLY¹

flex¹ /fleks/ (*especially US* **cord**) **noun** [C,U] (a piece of) wire inside a plastic tube, used for carrying electricity to electrical equipment • ➤ picture at **cable**

➤ At the end of a flex there is a **plug** which you fit into a **socket** or a **power point**.

flex² /fleks/ **verb** [T] to bend or move a leg, arm, muscle, etc in order to exercise it

flexible /ˈfleksəbl/ **adj 1** able to bend or move easily without breaking **2** that can be changed easily: *flexible working hours* • ➤ opposite **inflexible** –flexibility /ˌfleksəˈbɪləti/ **noun** [U]

flick

flick /flɪk/ **verb 1** [T] flick sth (away, off, onto, etc) to hit sb/ sth lightly and quickly with your finger or hand in order to move it: *She flicked the dust off her jacket.* • *Please don't flick ash on the carpet.* **2** [I,T] flick (sth) (away, off, out, etc) to move, or to make sth move, with a quick sudden movement: *She flicked the switch and the light came on.* –flick **noun** [C]

ℹ️ PHRASAL VERB flick/flip through sth to turn over the pages of a book, magazine, etc quickly without reading everything

flicker¹ /ˈflɪkə/ **verb** [I] **1** (used about a light or a flame) to keep going on and off as it burns or shines: *The candle flickered and went out.* **2** (used about a feeling, thought, etc) to appear for a short time: *A smile flickered across her face.* **3** to move lightly and quickly up and down: *His eyelids flickered for a second and then he lay still.*

flicker² /ˈflɪkə/ **noun** [C,usually sing] **1** a light that shines on and off quickly: *the flicker of the television/flames* **2** a small, sudden movement of part of the body **3** a feeling of sth that only lasts for a short time: *a flicker of hope/ interest/doubt*

flies → FLY

★**flight** /flaɪt/ **noun 1** [C] a journey by air: *to book a flight* • *a direct/scheduled/charter flight* • *They met on a flight to Australia.* • *a manned space flight to Mars* **2** [C] an aircraft that takes you on a particular journey: *Flight number 340 from London to New York is boarding now* (= is ready for passengers to get on it). **3** [U] the action of flying: *It's unusual to see swans in flight* (= when they are flying). **4** [C] a number of stairs or steps going up or down: *a flight of stairs* **5** [C,U] the action of running away or escaping from a dangerous or difficult situation: *the refugees' flight from the war zone*

flimsy /'flɪmzi/ *adj* **1** not strong; easily broken or torn: *a flimsy bookcase* • *a flimsy blouse* **2** weak; not making you believe that sth is true: *He gave a flimsy excuse for his absence.*

flinch /flɪntʃ/ *verb* [I] **1** flinch (at sth); flinch (away) to make a sudden movement backwards because of sth painful or frightening: *She couldn't help flinching away as the dentist came towards her with the drill.* **2** flinch from sth/doing sth to avoid doing sth because it is unpleasant: *She didn't flinch from telling him the whole truth.*

fling¹ /flɪŋ/ *verb* [T] (*pt, pp* flung /flʌŋ/) to throw sb/sth suddenly and carelessly or with great force: *He flung his coat on the floor.*

fling² /flɪŋ/ *noun* [C] a short period of fun and pleasure

flint /flɪnt/ *noun* **1** [U] very hard grey stone that produces small flames (sparks) when you hit it against steel **2** [C] a small piece of flint or metal that is used to produce sparks (for example in a cigarette lighter)

flip /flɪp/ *verb* (flipping; flipped) **1** [I,T] to turn (sth) over with a quick movement: *She flipped the book open and started to read.* **2** [T] to throw sth into the air and make it turn over: *Let's flip a coin to see who starts.* **3** [I] flip (out) (*spoken*) to become very angry or excited: *When his father saw the damage to the car he flipped.*
PHRASAL VERB flick/flip through sth → **FLICK**

flip-flop (*US* thong) *noun* [usually pl] a simple open shoe with a thin strap that goes between your big toe and the toe next to it

flippant /'flɪpənt/ (also *informal* flip) *adj* not serious enough about things that are important

flipper /'flɪpə/ *noun* [C] **1** a flat arm that is part of the body of some sea animals which they use for swimming: *Seals have flippers.* •➤ picture at **seal** **2** a rubber shoe shaped like an animal's flipper that people wear so that they can swim better, especially under water: *a pair of flippers* •➤ picture at **dive**

flipping /'flɪpɪŋ/ *adj, adv* (*slang*) used as a mild way of swearing: *When's the flipping bus coming?*

flirt¹ /flɜːt/ *verb* [I] flirt (with sb) to behave in a way that suggests you find sb attractive and are trying to attract him/her: *Who was that boy Irene was flirting with at the party?* • (*figurative*) *to flirt with death/danger/disaster*
PHRASAL VERB flirt with sth to think about doing sth (but not very seriously): *She had flirted with the idea of becoming a teacher for a while.*

flirt² /flɜːt/ *noun* [C] a person who often flirts with people

flit /flɪt/ *verb* [I] (flitting; flitted) flit (from A to B); flit (between A and B) to fly or move quickly from one place to another without staying anywhere for long: *She flits from one job to another.*

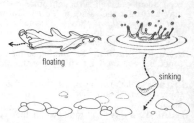

float/sink

floating

sinking

★**float**¹ /fləʊt/ *verb* **1** [I] to move slowly through air or water: *The boats were floating gently down the river.* • *The smell of freshly-baked bread floated in through the window.* **2** [I] float (in/on sth) to stay on the surface of a liquid and not sink: *Wood floats in water.* **3** [T] to sell shares in a company or business for the first time: *The company was floated on the stock market in 1999.* **4** [I,T] (used in economics) to allow the value of a country's money to change freely according to the value of the money of other countries

float² /fləʊt/ *noun* [C] **1** a lorry or other vehicle that is decorated and used in a celebration that travels through the streets: *a carnival float* **2** a light object used in fishing that moves on the water when a fish has been caught **3** a light object used for helping people to learn to swim

floating /'fləʊtɪŋ/ *adj* not fixed; not living permanently in one place: *London's floating population*

flock¹ /flɒk/ *noun* [C] **1** a group of sheep or birds •➤ Look at **herd**. **2** a large number of people: *Flocks of tourists visit London every summer.*

flock² /flɒk/ *verb* [I] (used about people) to go or meet somewhere in large numbers: *People are flocking to her latest exhibition.*

flog /flɒg/ *verb* [T] (flogging; flogged) **1** (usually passive) to hit sb hard several times with a stick or a long thin piece of leather (whip) as a punishment **2** (*Brit informal*) to sell sth

flogging /'flɒgɪŋ/ *noun* [C,U] the act of hitting sb several times with a long thin piece of leather (whip) or a stick as a punishment

★**flood**¹ /flʌd/ *verb* [I,T] **1** to fill a place with water; to be filled or covered with water: *I left the taps on and flooded the bathroom.* • *The River Trent floods almost every year.* **2** flood in/into/out of sth to go somewhere in large numbers: *Since the television programme was shown, phone calls have been flooding into the studio.* **3** (used about a thought, feeling, etc) to fill sb's mind suddenly: *At the end of the day all his worries came flooding back.*

★**flood**² /flʌd/ *noun* [C] **1** a large amount of water that has spread from a river, the sea, etc that covers an area which should be dry: *Many people have been forced to leave their homes because of the floods.* **2** a flood (of sth)

a large number or amount: *She received a flood of letters after the accident.*

floodlight /'flʌdlaɪt/ **noun** [C] a powerful light that is used for lighting places where sports are played, the outside of public buildings, etc

floodlit /'flʌdlɪt/ **adj** lit by powerful lights (floodlights): *a floodlit hockey match*

★**floor**¹ /flɔː/ **noun 1** [C, usually sing] the flat surface that you walk on indoors: *Don't come in – there's broken glass on the floor!* ● *a wooden/concrete/marble floor* •➤ Look at the note at **ground**. **2** [C] all the rooms that are on the same level of a building: *My office is on the second floor.*

> In Britain, the **ground floor** is the floor at street level, and the floor above is the **first floor**. In US English the **first floor** is the floor at street level.

3 [C, usually sing] the ground or surface at the bottom of the sea, a forest, etc: *the ocean/valley/cave/forest floor*

floor² /flɔː/ **verb** [T] (*informal*) to surprise or confuse sb completely with a question or a problem: *Some of the questions I was asked in the interview completely floored me.*

floorboard /'flɔːbɔːd/ **noun** [C] one of the long wooden boards used to make a floor

flop¹ /flɒp/ **verb** [I] (**flopping; flopped**) **1** flop into, onto sth; flop (down/back) to sit or lie down in a sudden and careless way because you are very tired: *I was so tired that all I could do was flop onto the sofa and watch TV.* **2** flop around, back, down, etc to move, hang or fall in a careless way without control: *I can't bear my hair flopping in my eyes.* **3** (used about a book, film, record, etc) to be a complete failure with the public

flop² /flɒp/ **noun** [C] (used about a film, play, party, etc) something that is not a success; a failure: *Her first novel was very successful but her second was a flop.* ● *a box-office flop*

floppy /'flɒpi/ **adj** soft and hanging downwards; not rigid: *a floppy hat*

floppy '**disk** (also **floppy** or **diskette**) **noun** [C] a square piece of plastic that can store information from a computer: *Don't forget to back up your files onto a floppy disk.* •➤ Look at **hard disk**. •➤ picture on page S7

flora /'flɔːrə/ **noun** [pl] all the plants growing in a particular area: *He's studying the flora and fauna* (= the plants and animals) *of South America.* •➤ Look at **fauna**.

floral /'flɔːrəl/ **adj** decorated with a pattern of flowers, or made with flowers

florist /'flɒrɪst/ **noun 1** [C] a person who has a shop that sells flowers **2 the florist's** [sing] a shop that sells flowers

flounder /'flaʊndə/ **verb** [I] **1** to find it difficult to speak or act (usually in a difficult or embarrassing situation): *The questions they asked her at the interview had her floundering helplessly.* **2** to have a lot of problems and be in danger of failing completely: *By the late nineties, the business was floundering.* **3** to

move with difficulty, for example when trying to get out of some water, wet earth, etc

★**flour** /'flaʊə/ **noun** [U] a very thin powder made from wheat or other grain and used for making breads, cakes, biscuits, etc •➤ picture on page C4

flourish¹ /'flʌrɪʃ/ **verb 1** [I] to be strong and healthy; to develop in a successful way: *a flourishing business* **2** [T] to wave sth in the air so that people will notice it: *He proudly flourished two tickets for the concert.*

flourish² /'flʌrɪʃ/ **noun** [C] an exaggerated movement: *He opened the door for her with a flourish.*

flout /flaʊt/ **verb** [T] to refuse to obey or accept sth: *to flout the rules of the organization* ● *to flout sb's advice*

★**flow**¹ /fləʊ/ **noun** [sing] a flow (of sth/sb) **1** a steady, continuous movement of sth/sb: *Press hard on the wound to stop the flow of blood.* **2** a supply of sth: *the flow of information between the school and the parents* **3** the way in which words, ideas, etc are joined together smoothly: *Once Charlie's in full flow, it's hard to stop him talking.*

IDIOM the ebb and flow (of sth) ➜ **EBB**²

★**flow**² /fləʊ/ **verb** [I] **1** to move in a smooth and continuous way (like water): *This river flows south into the English Channel.* ● *a fast-flowing stream* ● *Traffic began to flow normally again after the accident.* **2** (used about words, ideas, actions, etc) to be joined together smoothly: *As soon as we sat down at the table, the conversation began to flow.* **3** (used about hair and clothes) to hang down in a loose way: *a long flowing dress.*

'**flow chart** (also '**flow diagram**) **noun** [C] a diagram that shows the connections between different stages of a process or parts of a system

★**flower**¹ /'flaʊə/ **noun** [C] **1** the coloured part of a plant or tree from which seeds or fruit grow •➤ picture on page C2

> A flower consists of several **petals**. It grows from a **bud** on the end of a **stem**.

2 a plant that is grown for its flowers: *to grow flowers*

> We **pick** flowers and **arrange** them in a vase. Flowers that are given or carried on a special occasion are called a **bouquet**.

★**flower**² /'flaʊə/ **verb** [I] to produce flowers: *This plant flowers in late summer.*

'**flower bed noun** [C] a piece of ground in a garden or park where flowers are grown •➤ picture on page C7

flowerpot /'flaʊəpɒt/ **noun** [C] a pot in which a plant can be grown

★**flowery** /'flaʊəri/ **adj 1** covered or decorated with flowers: *a flowery dress/hat/pattern* **2** (used about a style of speaking or writing) using long, difficult words when they are not necessary

flown *past participle* of **FLY**¹

fl oz abbr fluid ounce(s)

★**flu** /fluː/ (also *formal* **influenza**) **noun** [U] an illness that is like a bad cold but more serious. You usually feel very hot and your arms and legs hurt.

fluctuate /ˈflʌktʃueɪt/ **verb** [I] fluctuate (between A and B) (used about prices and numbers, or people's feelings) to change frequently from one thing to another: *The number of students fluctuates between 100 and 150.* –fluctuation /ˌflʌktʃuˈeɪʃn/ **noun** [C,U]

fluent /ˈfluːənt/ **adj 1** fluent (in sth) able to speak or write a foreign language easily and accurately: *After a year in France she was fluent in French.* **2** (used about speaking, reading or writing) expressed in a smooth and accurate way: *He speaks fluent German.* –fluency /ˈfluːənsi/ **noun** [U]: *My knowledge of Japanese grammar is good but I need to work on my fluency.* –fluently **adv**

fluff /flʌf/ **noun** [U] **1** very small pieces of wool, cotton, etc that form into balls and collect on clothes and other surfaces **2** the soft new fur on young animals or birds

fluffy /ˈflʌfi/ **adj 1** covered in soft fur: *a fluffy kitten* **2** that looks or feels very soft and light: *fluffy clouds/towels*

fluid¹ /ˈfluːɪd/ **noun** [C,U] a substance that can flow; a liquid: *The doctor told her to drink plenty of fluids.* • *cleaning fluid*

fluid² /ˈfluːɪd/ **adj 1** able to flow smoothly like a liquid: (*figurative*) *I like her fluid style of dancing.* **2** (used about plans, etc) able to change or likely to be changed

fluid 'ounce **noun** [C] (*abbr* fl oz) a measure of liquid; in Britain, 0·0284 of a litre; in the US, 0·0295 of a litre.

> For more information about measurements look at the special section on numbers at the back of this dictionary.

fluke /fluːk/ **noun** [C,usually sing] (*informal*) a surprising and lucky result that happens by accident, not because you have been clever or skilful: *The result was no fluke. The better team won.*

flung *past tense, past participle* of **FLING¹**

fluorescent /ˌfluəˈresnt/ **adj 1** producing a bright white light: *fluorescent lighting* **2** very bright; seeming to shine: *fluorescent pink paint*

fluoride /ˈflɔːraɪd/ **noun** [U] a chemical substance that can be added to water or toothpaste to help prevent bad teeth

flurry /ˈflʌri/ **noun** [C] (*pl* flurries) **1** a short time in which there is suddenly a lot of activity: *a flurry of excitement/activity* **2** a sudden short fall of snow or rain

flush¹ /flʌʃ/ **verb 1** [I] (used about a person or his/her face) to go red: *Susan flushed and could not hide her embarrassment.* •➤ A more common word is **blush**. **2** [T] to clean a toilet by pressing or pulling a handle that sends water into the toilet: *Please remember to flush the toilet.* **3** [I] (used about a toilet) to be cleaned with a short flow of water: *The toilet won't flush.* **4** [T] flush sth away, down, etc to get rid of sth in a flow of water: *You can't flush tea leaves down the sink – they'll block it.*

flush² /flʌʃ/ **noun** [C,usually sing] **1** a hot feeling or red colour that you have in your face when you are embarrassed, excited, angry, etc: *The cold wind brought a flush to our cheeks.* • *a flush of anger* **2** the act of cleaning a toilet with a quick flow of water; the system for doing this

flushed /flʌʃt/ **adj** with a hot red face: *You look very flushed. Are you sure you're all right?*

fluster /ˈflʌstə/ **verb** [T] (usually passive) to make sb feel nervous and confused (because there is too much to do or not enough time): *Don't get flustered – there's plenty of time.* –fluster **noun** [C]: *I always get in a fluster before exams.*

flute /fluːt/ **noun** [C] a musical instrument like a pipe that you hold sideways and play by blowing over a hole at one side •➤ Look at the note at **piano**. •➤ picture at **music** –flutist /ˈfluːtɪst/ (*US*) = **FLAUTIST**

flutter¹ /ˈflʌtə/ **verb 1** [I,T] to move or make sth move quickly and lightly, especially through the air: *The flags were fluttering in the wind.* • *The bird fluttered its wings and tried to fly.* **2** [I] your heart or stomach flutters when you feel nervous and excited

flutter² /ˈflʌtə/ **noun** [C,usually sing] **1** a quick, light movement: *the flutter of wings/ eyelids* **2** (*Brit slang*) a bet on a race, etc: *I sometimes have a flutter on the horses.*

★fly¹ /flaɪ/ **verb** (*pres part* flying; *3rd pers sing pres* flies; *pt* flew /fluː/; *pp* flown /fləʊn/) **1** [I,T] (used about a bird, insect, aircraft, etc) to move through the air: *This bird has a broken wing and can't fly.* • *Concorde can fly (across) the Atlantic in three hours.* **2** [I,T] to travel or carry sth in an aircraft, etc: *My daughter is flying (out) to Singapore next week.* • *Supplies of food were flown (in) to the starving people.* **3** [I,T] (used about a pilot) to control an aircraft: *You have to have special training to fly a jumbo jet.* **4** [I] to move quickly or suddenly, especially through the air: *A large stone came flying through the window.* • *I slipped and my shopping went flying everywhere.* • *Suddenly the door flew open and Mark came running in.* • (*figurative*) *The weekend has just flown by and now it's Monday again.* **5** [I,T] to move about in the air; to make sth move about in the air: *The flags are flying.* • *to fly a flag/kite* •➤ **noun** flight

IDIOMS **as the crow flies** → **CROW¹**

fly off the handle (*informal*) to become very angry in an unreasonable way

let fly (at sb/sth) 1 to shout angrily at sb **2** to hit sb in anger: *She let fly at him with her fists.*

★fly² /flaɪ/ **noun** [C] **1** (*pl* flies) a small insect with two wings: *Flies buzzed round the dead cow.* •➤ picture at **insect 2** (also **flies** [pl]) an opening down the front of a pair of trousers that fastens with buttons or another device (a zip) and is covered with a narrow piece of material •➤ picture on page C6

flying /ˈflaɪɪŋ/ **adj** able to fly: *flying insects*
  IDIOMS **with flying colours** with great success; very well: *Martin passed the exam with flying colours.*
  get off to a flying start to begin sth well; to make a good start

,**flying 'saucer** *noun* [C] a round spacecraft that some people claim to have seen and that they believe comes from another planet

,**flying 'visit** *noun* [C] a very quick visit: *I can't stop. This is just a flying visit.*

flyover /ˈflaɪəʊvə/ (*US* **overpass**) *noun* [C] a type of bridge that carries a road over another road

FM /ˌef ˈem/ *abbr* frequency modulation; one of the systems of sending out radio signals

foal /fəʊl/ *noun* [C] a young horse ••➤ Look at the note at **horse**.

foam[1] /fəʊm/ *noun* [U] **1** (also ,**foam 'rubber**) a soft light rubber material that is used inside seats, cushions, etc: *a foam mattress* **2** a mass of small air bubbles that form on the surface of a liquid: *white foam on the tops of the waves* **3** an artificial substance that is between a solid and a liquid and is made from very small bubbles: *shaving foam*

foam[2] /fəʊm/ *verb* [I] to produce foam: *We watched the foaming river below.*

fob /fɒb/ *verb* (**fobbing; fobbed**)
  PHRASAL VERB **fob sb off (with sth)** **1** to try to stop sb asking questions or complaining by telling him/her sth that is not true: *Don't let them fob you off with any more excuses.* **2** to try to give sb something that he/she does not want: *Don't try to fob me off with that old car – I want a new one.*

focal point /ˌfəʊkl ˈpɔɪnt/ *noun* [sing] the centre of interest or activity

focus[1] /ˈfəʊkəs/ *verb* [I,T] (**focusing; focused** or **focussing; focussed**) **focus (sth) (on sth)** **1** to give all your attention to sth: *to focus on a problem* **2** (used about your eyes or a camera) to change or be changed so that things can be seen clearly: *Gradually his eyes focused.* • *I focussed (the camera) on the person in the middle of the group.*

focus[2] /ˈfəʊkəs/ *noun* [C, usually sing] the centre of interest or attention; special attention that is given to sb/sth: *The school used to be the focus of village life.*
  IDIOM **in focus/out of focus** (used about a photograph or sth in a photograph) clear/not clear: *This picture is so badly out of focus that I can't recognize anyone.*

fodder /ˈfɒdə/ *noun* [U] food that is given to farm animals

foe /fəʊ/ *noun* [C] (*written*) an enemy

foetus (*US* **fetus**) /ˈfiːtəs/ *noun* [C] (*pl* **foetuses; fetuses**) a young human or animal that is still developing in its mother's body

  ➤ An **embryo** is at an earlier stage of development.

fog /fɒg/ *noun* [U,C] thick white cloud that forms close to the land or sea. Fog makes it difficult for us to see: *Patches of dense fog are making driving dangerous.* • *Bad fogs are common in November.*

  ➤ **Fog** is thicker than **mist**. **Haze** is caused by heat. **Smog** is caused by pollution. Look at the note at **weather**.

foggy /ˈfɒgi/ *adj* (**foggier; foggiest**) used to describe the weather when there is fog
  IDIOM **not have the faintest/foggiest (idea)**
  ➔ **FAINT**[1]

foil[1] /fɔɪl/ (also **tinfoil**) *noun* **1** [U] metal that has been made into very thin sheets, used for putting around food: *aluminium foil* **2** [C] a long, thin, pointed weapon used in a type of fighting sport (**fencing**)

foil[2] /fɔɪl/ *verb* [T] to prevent sb from succeeding, especially with a plan; to prevent a plan from succeeding: *The prisoners were foiled in their attempt to escape.*

foist /fɔɪst/ *verb*
  PHRASAL VERB **foist sth on/upon sb** to force sb to accept sth that he/she does not want: *Jeff had a lot of extra work foisted on him when his boss was away.*

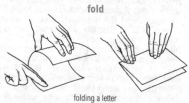

fold

folding a letter

★**fold**[1] /fəʊld/ *verb* **1** [T] **fold sth (up)** to bend one part of sth over another part in order to make it smaller, tidier, etc: *He folded the letter into three before putting it into the envelope.* • *Fold up your clothes neatly, please.* ••➤ opposite **unfold** **2** [I] **fold (up)** to be able to be made smaller in order to be carried or stored more easily: *This table folds up flat.* • *a folding bed* **3** [I] **fold A in B; fold B round/over A** to put sth around sth else: *I folded the photos in a sheet of paper and put them away.* **4** [I] (used about a business, a play in the theatre, etc) to close because it is a failure
  IDIOM **cross/fold your arms** ➔ **ARM**[1]

★**fold**[2] /fəʊld/ *noun* [C] **1** the mark or line where sth has been folded **2** a curved shape that is made when there is more material, etc than is necessary to cover sth: *the folds of a dress/curtain* **3** a small area inside a fence where sheep are kept together in a field

folder /ˈfəʊldə/ *noun* [C] **1** a cardboard or plastic cover that is used for holding papers, etc **2** a collection of information or files on one subject that is stored in a computer or on a disk

foliage /ˈfəʊliɪdʒ/ *noun* [U] (*formal*) all the leaves of a tree or plant

folk[1] /fəʊk/ *noun* **1** (*US* **folks**) [pl] (*informal*) people in general: *Some folk are never satisfied.* **2** [pl] a particular type of people: *Old folk often don't like change.* • *country folk* **3 folks** [pl] (*informal*) used as a friendly way of addressing more than one person: *What shall we do today, folks?* **4 folks** [pl] (*informal*) your parents or close relatives: *How are your folks?* **5** [U] music in the traditional style of a country or community: *Do you like Irish folk?*

folk² /fəʊk/ **adj** traditional in a community; of a traditional style: *Robin Hood is an English folk hero.* • *folk music* • *a folk song*

folklore /'fəʊklɔː/ **noun** [U] traditional stories and beliefs

★**follow** /'fɒləʊ/ **verb 1** [I,T] to come, go or happen after sb/sth: *You go first and I'll follow (on) later.* • *The dog followed her (around) wherever she went.* • *I'll have soup followed by spaghetti.* **2** [T] to go along a road, etc; to go in the same direction as sth: *Follow this road for a mile and then turn right at the pub.* • *The road follows the river for a few miles.* **3** [T] to do sth or to happen according to instructions, an example, what is usual, etc: *When lighting fireworks, it is important to* **follow the instructions** *carefully.* • *The day's events followed the usual pattern.* **4** [I,T] to understand the meaning of sth: *The children couldn't follow the plot of that film.* **5** [T] to keep watching or listening to sth as it happens or develops: *The film follows the career of a young dancer.* • *Have you been following the tennis championships?* **6** [I] **follow (on) (from sth)** to be the logical result of sth; to be the next logical step after sth: *It doesn't follow that old people can't lead active lives.* • *Intermediate Book One follows on from Elementary Book Two.*
> IDIOMS **a hard act to follow** → **HARD¹**
> **as follows** used for introducing a list: *The names of the successful candidates are as follows...*
> **follow in sb's footsteps** to do the same job as sb else who did it before you: *He followed in his father's footsteps and joined the army.*
> **follow sb's example/lead** to do what sb else has done or decided to do
> **follow suit** to do the same thing that sb else has just done
> **follow your nose** to go straight forward: *Turn right at the lights and after that just follow your nose until you get to the village.*
> PHRASAL VERBS **follow sth through** to continue doing sth until it is finished
> **follow sth up 1** to take further action about sth: *You should follow up your letter with a phone call.* **2** to find out more about sth: *We need to follow up the story about the school.*

follower /'fɒləʊə/ **noun** [C] a person who follows or supports a person, belief, etc

following¹ /'fɒləʊɪŋ/ **adj 1** next (in time): *He became ill on Sunday and died the following day.* **2** that are going to be mentioned next: *Please could you bring the following items to the meeting...*

following² /'fɒləʊɪŋ/ **noun 1** [sing] a group of people who support or admire sth: *The Brazilian team has a large following all over the world.* **2 the following** [pl] the people or things that are going to be mentioned next:

The following are the winners of the competition...

following³ /'fɒləʊɪŋ/ **prep** after; as a result of: *Following the riots many students have been arrested.*

'follow-up noun [C] something that is done as a second stage to continue or develop sth: *As a follow-up to the television series, the BBC is publishing a book.*

folly /'fɒli/ **noun** [C,U] (*pl* **follies**) (*formal*) an act that is not sensible and may have a bad result: *It would be folly to ignore their warnings.*

★**fond** /fɒnd/ **adj 1** (not before a noun) **fond of sb/sth; fond of doing sth** liking a person or thing, or liking doing sth: *Elephants are very fond of bananas.* • *I'm not very fond of getting up early.* • *Teachers often* **grow fond** *of their students.* **2** (only *before* a noun) kind and loving: *I have* **fond memories** *of my grandmother.*

fondle /'fɒndl/ **verb** [T] to touch sb/sth gently in a loving or sexual way

fondly /'fɒndli/ **adv** in a loving way: *Miss Murphy will be fondly remembered by all her former students.*

fondness /'fɒndnəs/ **noun** [U,sing] **(a) fondness (for sb/sth)** a liking for sb/sth: *I've always had a fondness for cats.* • *My grandmother talks about her schooldays* **with fondness***.*

★**food** /fuːd/ **noun 1** [U] something that people or animals eat: *Food and drink will be provided after the meeting.* • *There is a shortage of food in some areas.* **2** [C,U] a particular type of food that you eat: *My favourite food is pasta.* • *Have you ever had Japanese food?* • *baby food* • *dog food* • *health foods*

'food poisoning noun [U] an illness that is caused by eating food that is bad

'food processor noun [C] an electric machine that can mix food and also cut food into small pieces ••➤ picture at **mixer**

foodstuff /'fuːdstʌf/ **noun** [C,usually pl] a substance that is used as food: *There has been a sharp rise in the cost of basic foodstuffs.*

★**fool¹** /fuːl/ **noun** [C] a person who is silly or who acts in a silly way: *I felt such a fool when I realized my mistake.* •➤ Look at **April Fool**.
> IDIOM **make a fool of sb/yourself** to make sb/yourself look foolish or silly: *Barry got drunk and made a complete fool of himself.*

★**fool²** /fuːl/ **verb 1** [T] **fool sb (into doing sth)** to trick sb: *Don't be fooled into believing everything that the salesman says.* **2** [I] to speak without being serious: *You didn't really believe me when I said I was going to America, did you? I was only fooling.*
> PHRASAL VERB **fool about/around** to behave in a silly way: *Stop fooling around with that knife or someone will get hurt!*

foolhardy /'fuːlhɑːdi/ **adj** taking unnecessary risks

★**foolish** /'fuːlɪʃ/ **adj 1** silly; not sensible: *I was foolish enough to trust him.* **2** looking silly or feeling embarrassed: *I felt a bit foolish when I*

couldn't remember the man's name. –**foolishly**
adv: *I foolishly agreed to lend him money.*
–**foolishness** noun [U]

foolproof /'fu:lpru:f/ adj not capable of
going wrong or being wrongly used: *Our
security system is absolutely foolproof.*

★**foot¹** /fʊt/ noun [C] (*pl* **feet** /fiːt/) **1** the lowest part of the body, at the end of the leg, on
which a person or animal stands: *People usually get to their feet* (= stand up) *for the
national anthem.* • *I usually go to school on
foot* (= walking). • *I need to sit down – I've
been on my feet all day.* • *There's broken
glass on the floor, so don't walk around in
bare feet* (= without shoes and socks). • *She
sat by the fire and the dog sat at her feet.* • *a
foot brake/pedal/pump* (= one that is operated by your foot) •➤ picture on page C5
2 -footed (used to form compound adjectives
and adverbs) having or using the type of foot
or number of feet mentioned: *There are no
left-footed players in the team.* • *a four-footed
creature* **3** the part of a sock, etc that covers
the foot **4** [sing] **the foot of sth** the bottom of
sth: *There's a note at the foot of the page.* • *the
foot of the stairs* • *the foot of the bed*
•➤ opposite **top 5** (*abbr* **ft**) a measurement of
length; 30·48 centimetres: '*How tall are you?*'
'*Five foot six (inches).*' • *a six-foot high wall*

➤ For more information about measurements look at the special section on numbers at the back of this dictionary.

IDIOMS **back on your feet** completely healthy
again after an illness or a time of difficulty
be rushed/run off your feet to be extremely
busy; to have too many things to do: *Over
Christmas we were rushed off our feet at work.*
fall/land on your feet to be lucky in finding
yourself in a good situation, or in getting out
of a difficult situation: *I really landed on my
feet getting such a good job with so little
experience.*
find your feet → FIND¹
get/have cold feet → COLD¹
get/start off on the right/wrong foot (with sb)
(*informal*) to start a relationship well/badly:
*I seem to have got off on the wrong foot with
the new boss.*
have one foot in the grave (*informal*) to be
so old or ill that you are not likely to live
much longer
put your foot down (*informal*) to say firmly
that sth must (not) happen: *I put my foot
down and told Andy he couldn't use our car
any more.*
put your foot in it (*informal*) to say or do sth
that makes sb embarrassed or upset
put your feet up to sit down and relax, especially with your feet off the floor and supported: *I'm so tired that I just want to go home
and put my feet up.*
set foot in/on sth → SET¹
stand on your own (two) feet to take care of
yourself without help; to be independent
under your feet in the way; stopping you
from working, etc: *Would somebody get these*

children out from under my feet and take them
to the park?

foot² /fʊt/ verb
IDIOM **foot the bill (for sth)** to pay (for sth)

footage /'fʊtɪdʒ/ noun [U] part of a film
showing a particular event: *The documentary
included footage of the assassination of
Kennedy.*

★**football** /'fʊtbɔːl/ noun **1** (also **soccer**) [U] a
game that is played by two teams of eleven
players who try to kick a round ball into a
goal: *a football pitch/match*

➤ In the US **soccer** is the usual word for
this game since Americans use the word
football to refer to **American Football**.

2 [C] the large round ball that is used in this
game

★**footballer** /'fʊtbɔːlə/ noun [C] a person who
plays football: *a talented footballer*

'**football pools** (also **the pools**) noun [pl] a
game in which people bet money on the
results of football matches and can win large
amounts of money

foothold /'fʊthəʊld/ noun [C] a place where
you can safely put your foot when you are
climbing: (*figurative*) *We need to get a foothold in the European market.*

footing /'fʊtɪŋ/ noun [sing] **1** being able to
stand firmly on a surface: *Climbers usually
attach themselves to a rope in case they lose
their footing.* • (*figurative*) *The company is
now on a firm footing and should soon show
a profit.* **2** the level or position of sb/sth (in
relation to sb/sth else): *to be on an equal
footing with sb*

footnote /'fʊtnəʊt/ noun [C] an extra piece of
information that is added at the bottom of a
page in a book

footpath /'fʊtpɑːθ/ noun [C] a path for people
to walk on: *a public footpath*

footprints   fingerprint

footprint /'fʊtprɪnt/ noun [C] a mark that is
left on the ground by a foot or a shoe •➤ Look
at **track**.

footstep /'fʊtstep/ noun [C] the sound of sb
walking: *I heard his footsteps in the hall.*
IDIOM **follow in sb's footsteps → FOLLOW**

footwear /'fʊtweə/ noun [U] boots or shoes

★**for¹** /fə; *strong form* fɔː/ prep **1** showing the
person that will use or have sth: *Here is a
letter for you.* • *He made lunch for them.* • *It's
a book for children.* **2** in order to do, have or
get sth: *What's this gadget for?* • *What did
you do that for?* (= Why did you do that?)
• *Do you learn English for your job or for
fun?* • *She asked me for help.* • *Phone now for*

information. ● *to go for a walk/swim/drink* **3** in order to help sb/sth: *What can I do for you?* ● *You should take some medicine for your cold.* ● *Doctors are fighting for his life.* ● *shampoo for dry hair* **4** in support of (sb/sth): *Are you for or against shops opening on Sundays?* **5** meaning sth or representing sb/sth: *What's the 'C' for in 'BBC'?* ● *What's the Russian for 'window'?* ● *She plays hockey for England.* **6** showing the place that sb/sth will go to: *Is this the train for Glasgow?* ● *They set off for the shops.* **7** (showing a reason) as a result of: *Ben didn't want to come for some reason.* ● *He was sent to prison for robbery.* ● *I couldn't speak for laughing.* **8** (showing the price or value of sth); in exchange for: *I bought this car for £2000.* ● *You get one point for each correct answer.* ● *I want to exchange this sweater for a larger one.* ● *The officer was accused of giving secret information for cash.* **9** showing a length of time: *I'm going away for a few days.* ● *for a while/a long time/ages* ● *They have left the town for good* (= they will not return). ● *He was in prison for 20 years* (= he is not in prison now). ● *He has been in prison for 20 years* (= he is still in prison).

> ➤ **Since** is used with a point in time for showing when something began: *He has been in prison since 1982.* **Ago** is also used for showing when something began: *He went to prison 20 years ago.*

10 showing how many times sth has happened: *I'm warning you for the last time.* ● *I met him for the second time yesterday.* **11** at a particular, fixed time: *What did they give you for your birthday?* ● *Shall we have eggs for breakfast?* ● *I'm going to my parents' for Christmas.* ● *The appointment is for 10.30.* **12** showing a distance: *He walked for ten miles.* **13** (after an adjective) showing how usual, suitable, difficult, etc sb/sth is in relation to sb/sth else: *She's tall for her age.* ● *It's quite warm for January.* ● *It's unusual for Alex to be late.* ● *I think Sandra is perfect for this job.*

IDIOMS **be (in) for it** (*Brit informal*) to be going to get into trouble or be punished: *If you arrive late again you'll be in for it.*

for all in spite of: *For all his money, he's a very lonely man.*

for ever → FOREVER(1)

for² /fə; *strong form* fɔː/ *conj* (*formal*) because: *The children soon lost their way, for they had never been in the forest alone before.*

★**forbid** /fəˈbɪd/ *verb* [T] (*pres part* **forbidding** *pt* **forbade** or **forbad** /fəˈbæd/; *pp* **forbidden** /fəˈbɪdn/) **1** (usually passive) to not allow sth: *Smoking is forbidden inside the building.* **2** forbid sb to do sth to order sb not to do sth: *My parents forbade me to see Tim again.*

forbidding /fəˈbɪdɪŋ/ *adj* looking unfriendly or frightening: *The coast near the village is rather grey and forbidding.*

★**force¹** /fɔːs/ *noun* **1** [U] physical strength or power: *The force of the explosion knocked*

them to the ground. ● *The police used force to break up the demonstration.* **2** [U] power and influence: *the force of public opinion* **3** [C] a person or thing that has power or influence: *Britain is no longer a major force in international affairs.* ● *Julia has been the driving force behind the company's success.* **4** [C] a group of people who are trained for a particular purpose: *a highly trained workforce* ● *the police force* **5** (usually plural) the soldiers and weapons that an army, etc has: *the armed forces* **6** [C,U] (*technical*) a power that can cause change or movement: *the force of gravity*

IDIOMS **bring sth/come into force** to start using a new law, etc; to start being used: *The government want to bring new anti-pollution legislation into force next year.*

force of habit if you do sth from or out of force of habit you do it in a particular way because you have always done it that way in the past

in force 1 (used about people) in large numbers: *The police were present in force at the football match.* **2** (used about a law, rule, etc) being used: *The new speed limit is now in force.*

join forces (with sb) to work together in order to achieve a shared goal: *The two companies joined forces to win the contract.*

★**force²** /fɔːs/ *verb* [T] **1** force sb (to do sth); force sb (into sth/doing sth) to make sb do sth that he/she does not want to do: *She forced herself to speak to him.* ● *The President was forced into resigning.* **2** to use physical strength to sth or to move sth: *The window had been forced (open).* ● *We had to force our way through the crowd.* **3** to make sth happen when it will not happen naturally: *to force a smile/laugh* ● *To force the issue, I gave him until midday to decide.*

forceful /ˈfɔːsfl/ *adj* having the power to persuade people: *He has a very forceful personality.* ● *a forceful speech*

forceps /ˈfɔːseps/ *noun* [pl] a special instrument that looks like a pair of scissors but is not sharp. Forceps are used by doctors for holding things firmly: *a pair of forceps*

forcible /ˈfɔːsəbl/ *adj* (only *before* a noun) done using (physical) force: *The police made a forcible entry into the building.* –**forcibly** /ˈfɔːsəbli/ *adv*: *The squatters were forcibly removed by the police.*

ford /fɔːd/ *noun* [C] a place in a river where you can walk or drive across because the water is not deep

fore /fɔː/ *noun*

IDIOM **be/come to the fore** to be in or get into an important position so that you are noticed by people

forearm /ˈfɔːrɑːm/ *noun* [C] the lower part of your arm •➤ picture on page C5

foreboding /fɔːˈbəʊdɪŋ/ *noun* [U, sing] a strong feeling that danger or trouble is coming: *She was suddenly filled with a sense of foreboding.*

★**forecast** /ˈfɔːkɑːst/ **verb** [T] (*pt, pp* **forecast**) to say (with the help of information) what will probably happen in the future: *The Chancellor did not forecast the sudden rise in inflation.* ● *Rain has been forecast for tomorrow.* –forecast **noun** [C]: *a sales forecast for the coming year* ••> Look at **weather forecast**.

forecourt /ˈfɔːkɔːt/ **noun** [C] a large open area in front of a building such as a hotel or petrol station

forefinger /ˈfɔːfɪŋɡə/ (also **index finger**) **noun** [C] the finger next to the thumb

forefront /ˈfɔːfrʌnt/ **noun** [sing] the leading position; the position at the front: *Our department is right at the forefront of scientific research.*

forego = FORGO

foregone /ˈfɔːɡɒn/ **adj**
IDIOM a foregone conclusion a result that is or was certain to happen

foreground /ˈfɔːɡraʊnd/ **noun** [sing] **1** the part of a view, picture, photograph, etc that appears closest to the person looking at it: *Notice the artist's use of colour in the foreground of the picture.* **2** a position where you will be noticed most: *He likes to be in the foreground at every meeting.* ••> opposite **background**

forehand /ˈfɔːhænd/ **noun** [C] a way of hitting the ball in tennis, etc that is made with the inside of your hand facing forward ••> opposite **backhand**

★**forehead** /ˈfɔːhed; ˈfɒrɪd/ (also **brow**) **noun** [C] the part of a person's face above the eyes and below the hair ••> picture on page C5

★**foreign** /ˈfɒrən/ **adj 1** belonging to or connected with a country that is not your own: *a foreign country/coin/accent* ● *to learn a foreign language* **2** (only *before* a noun) dealing with or involving other countries: *foreign policy* (= government decisions concerning other countries) ● *foreign affairs/news/trade* ● *the French Foreign Minister* **3** (used about an object or a substance) not being where it should be: *The X-ray showed up a foreign body* (= object) *in her stomach.*

the ˌForeign and ˌCommonwealth Office (*abbr* FCO) **noun** [sing,with sing or pl verb] the British government department that deals with relations with other countries ••> Many people still refer to this department by its old name **the Foreign Office**.

★**foreigner** /ˈfɒrənə/ **noun** [C] a person who belongs to a country that is not your own

ˌforeign exˈchange **noun** [C,U] the system of buying and selling money from a different country; the place where it is bought and sold

the ˌForeign ˈSecretary **noun** [C] the person in the government who is responsible for dealing with foreign countries ••> Look at **Home Secretary**.

foremost /ˈfɔːməʊst/ **adj** most famous or important; best: *Laurence Olivier was among the foremost actors of the last century.*
IDIOM first and foremost → FIRST²

forename /ˈfɔːneɪm/ **noun** [C] (*formal*) your first name, that is given to you when you are born ••> Look at the note at **name**.

forensic /fəˈrenzɪk/ **adj** (only *before* a noun) using scientific tests to find out about a crime: *The police are carrying out forensic tests to try and find out the cause of death.*

forerunner /ˈfɔːrʌnə/ **noun** [C] a forerunner (of sb/sth) a person or thing that is an early example or a sign of sth that appears or develops later: *Country music was undoubtedly one of the forerunners of rock and roll.*

foresee /fɔːˈsiː/ **verb** [T] (*pt* **foresaw** /fɔːˈsɔː/; *pp* **foreseen** /fɔːˈsiːn/) to know or guess that sth is going to happen in the future: *Nobody could have foreseen the result of the election.* ••> Look at **unforeseen**.

foreseeable /fɔːˈsiːəbl/ **adj** that can be expected; that you can guess will happen: *These problems were foreseeable.* ● *The weather won't change in the foreseeable future* (= as far ahead as we can see).

foresight /ˈfɔːsaɪt/ **noun** [U] the ability to see what will probably happen in the future and to use this knowledge to make careful plans: *My neighbour had the foresight to move house before the new motorway was built.* ••> Look at **hindsight**.

foreskin /ˈfɔːskɪn/ **noun** [C] the piece of skin that covers the end of the male sexual organ

★**forest** /ˈfɒrɪst/ **noun** [C,U] a large area of land covered with trees: *the tropical rainforests of South America* ● *a forest fire*

> A **forest** is larger than a **wood**. A **jungle** is a forest in a tropical part of the world.

forestall /fɔːˈstɔːl/ **verb** [T] to take action to prevent sb from doing sth or sth from happening

forestry /ˈfɒrɪstri/ **noun** [U] the science of planting and taking care of trees in forests

forethought /ˈfɔːθɔːt/ **noun** [U] careful thought about, or preparation for, the future

★**forever** /fərˈevə/ **adv 1** (also **for ever**) for all time; permanently: *I wish the holidays would last forever!* ● *I realized that our relationship had finished forever.* **2** (only used with continuous tenses) very often; in a way which is annoying: *Our neighbours are forever having noisy parties.*

foreword /ˈfɔːwɜːd/ **noun** [C] a piece of writing at the beginning of a book that introduces the book and/or its author

forfeit /ˈfɔːfɪt/ **verb** [T] to lose sth or have sth taken away from you, usually because you have done sth wrong: *Because of his violent behaviour he forfeited the right to visit his children.* –forfeit **noun** [C]

forgave *past tense* of FORGIVE

forge¹ /fɔːdʒ/ **verb** [T] **1** to make an illegal copy of sth: *to forge a signature/banknote/passport/cheque* ••> Look at **counterfeit**. **2** to put a lot of effort into making sth strong and successful: *Our school has forged links with a school in Romania.*
PHRASAL VERB **forge ahead** to go forward or make progress quickly: *I think it's now time*

to forge ahead with our plans to open a new shop.

forge² /fɔːdʒ/ **noun** [C] a place where objects are made by heating and shaping metal

forgery /ˈfɔːdʒəri/ **noun** (pl **forgeries**) **1** [U] the crime of illegally copying a document, signature, painting, etc **2** [C] a document, signature, picture, etc that is a copy of the real one

★**forget** /fəˈget/ **verb** (pt **forgot** /fəˈgɒt/; pp **forgotten** /fəˈgɒtn/) **1** [T] forget (doing) sth to not be able to remember sth: *I've forgotten what I was going to say.* • *I've forgotten her telephone number.* • *He forgot that he had invited her to the party.* • *I'll never forget meeting my husband for the first time.* **2** [I,T] forget (about) sth; forget to do sth to fail to remember to do sth that you ought to have done: *'Why didn't you come to the party?' 'Oh dear! I completely forgot about it!'* • *'Did you feed the cat?' 'Sorry, I forgot.'* • *Don't forget to do your homework!* **3** [T] to fail to bring sth with you: *When my father got to the airport he realized he'd forgotten his passport.*

➤ When we are talking about something we have forgotten, and we want to say **where** it is, we have to use the word **leave**. We CANNOT say: *'He forgot his passport at home'.* We have to say: *'He left his passport at home'.*

4 [T] forget (about) sb/sth; forget about doing sth to make an effort to stop thinking about sb/sth; to stop thinking that sth is possible: *Forget about your work and enjoy yourself!* • *'I'm sorry I shouted at you.' 'Forget it.'* (= don't worry about it)

forgetful /fəˈgetfl/ **adj** often forgetting things: *My mother's nearly 80 and she's starting to get a bit forgetful.* ∙➤ synonym **absent-minded**

forgivable /fəˈgɪvəbl/ **adj** that can be forgiven

★**forgive** /fəˈgɪv/ **verb** [T] (pt **forgave** /fəˈgeɪv/; pp **forgiven** /fəˈgɪvn/) **1** forgive sb/yourself (for sth/for doing sth) to stop being angry towards sb for sth that he/she has done wrong: *I can't forgive his behaviour last night.* • *I can't forgive him for his behaviour last night.* • *I can't forgive him for behaving like that last night.* **2** forgive me (for doing sth) used for politely saying sorry: *Forgive me for asking, but where did you get that dress?* –**forgiveness** **noun** [U]: *He begged for forgiveness for what he had done.*

forgiving /fəˈgɪvɪŋ/ **adj** ready and able to forgive

forgo (also **forego**) /fɔːˈgəʊ/ **verb** [T] (pt **forwent** /fɔːˈwent/; pp **forgone** /fɔːˈgɒn/) (*formal*) to decide not to have or do sth that you want

forgot past tense of **FORGET**

forgotten past participle of **FORGET**

★**fork¹** /fɔːk/ **noun** [C] **1** a small metal object with a handle and two or more points (**prongs**) that you use for lifting food to your mouth when eating: *a knife and fork* **2** a large

tool with a handle and three or more points (**prongs**) that you use for digging the ground: *a garden fork* ∙➤ picture at **garden 3** a place where a road, river, etc divides into two parts; one of these parts: *After about two miles you'll come to a fork in the road.*

★**fork²** /fɔːk/ **verb** [I] **1** (used about a road, river, etc) to divide into two parts: *Bear right where the road forks at the top of the hill.* **2** to go along the left or right fork of a road: *Fork right up the hill.*

PHRASAL VERB **fork out (for sth)** (*informal*) to pay for sth when you do not want to: *I forked out over £20 for that book.*

forlorn /fəˈlɔːn/ **adj** lonely and unhappy; not cared for

★**form¹** /fɔːm/ **noun 1** [C] a particular type or variety of sth or a way of doing sth: *Swimming is an excellent form of exercise.* • *We never eat meat in any form.* **2** [C,U] the shape of sb/sth: *The articles will be published in book form.* **3** [C] an official document with questions on it and spaces where you give answers and personal information: *an entry form for a competition* • *to fill in an application form* **4** [C] a class in a school

➤ In Britain, the years at secondary school used to be called **first/second/third, etc form** but now they are called **Year 7** to **Year 11**. However the last two years of school (for pupils aged between 16 and 18) are still referred to as the **sixth form**.

5 [C] (*grammar*) a way of spelling or changing a word in a sentence: *the irregular forms of the verbs* • *The plural form of mouse is mice.* **6** [U] the state of being fit and strong for a sports player, team, etc: *to be in/out of form* **7** [U] how well sb/sth is performing at a particular time, for example in sport or business: *to be on/off form* • *On present form the Italian team should win easily.*

IDIOM **true to form** → **TRUE**

★**form²** /fɔːm/ **verb 1** [I,T] to begin to exist or to make sth exist: *A pattern was beginning to form in the monthly sales figures.* • *These tracks were formed by rabbits.* **2** [T] to make or organize sth: *to form a government* • *In English we usually form the past tense by adding '-ed'.* **3** [T] to become or make a particular shape: *The police formed a circle around the house.* • *to form a line/queue* **4** [T] to be the thing mentioned: *Seminars form the main part of the course.* • *The survey formed part of a larger programme of market research.* **5** [T] to begin to have or think sth: *I haven't formed an opinion about the new boss yet.* • *to form a friendship*

★**formal** /ˈfɔːml/ **adj 1** (used about language or behaviour) used when you want to appear serious or official and in situations in which you do not know the other people very well: *'Yours faithfully' is a formal way of ending a letter.* • *She has a very formal manner – she doesn't seem to be able to relax.* • *a formal occasion* (= one where you must behave politely and wear the clothes that people think are suitable)

> ➤ In this dictionary some words and phrases are marked *(formal)* or *(informal)*. This will help you to choose the right word for a particular situation. Often there is an informal or neutral word with a similar meaning to a more formal one.

2 official: *I shall make a formal complaint to the hospital about the way I was treated.* •➤ opposite **informal** –**formally** /-məli/ adv

formality /fɔːˈmæləti/ noun *(pl* **formalities***)* **1** [C] an action that is necessary according to custom or law: *There are certain formalities to attend to before we can give you a visa.*

> ➤ If an action is **just a formality**, we mean that people think that it is necessary according to custom or law but that it has no real importance or effect otherwise.

2 [U] careful attention to rules of language and behaviour

format[1] /ˈfɔːmæt/ noun [C] the shape of sth or the way it is arranged or produced: *It's the same book but in a different format.*

format[2] /ˈfɔːmæt/ verb [T] (**formatting**; **formatted**) **1** *(computing)* to prepare a computer disk so that data can be recorded on it: *to format a disk* **2** to arrange text on a page or a screen: *to format a letter*

formation /fɔːˈmeɪʃn/ noun **1** [U] the act of making or developing sth: *the formation of a new government* **2** [C,U] a number of people or things in a particular shape or pattern: *rock formations* • *A number of planes flew over in formation.* • *formation dancing*

formative /ˈfɔːmətɪv/ adj having an important and lasting influence (on sb's character and opinions): *A child's early years are thought to be the most formative ones.*

★**former** /ˈfɔːmə/ adj (only *before* a noun) of an earlier time; belonging to the past: *George Bush, the former American President* • *In former times people often had larger families.*

★**the former** /ˈfɔːmə/ noun [sing] the first (of two people or things just mentioned): *Of the two hospitals in the town – the General and the Royal – the former* (= the General) *has the better reputation.* •➤ Look at **the latter.**

★**formerly** /ˈfɔːməli/ adv in the past; before now: *the country of Myanmar (formerly Burma)* • *The hotel was formerly a castle.*

> ➤ **Used to be** is a more common way of saying **was formerly**: *The hotel used to be a castle.*

formidable /ˈfɔːmɪdəbl/ adj **1** causing you to be quite frightened: *His mother is a rather formidable lady.* **2** difficult to deal with; needing a lot of effort: *Reforming the education system will be a formidable task.*

formula /ˈfɔːmjələ/ noun [C] (*pl* **formulas** or **formulae** /-liː/) **1** *(technical)* a group of signs, letters or numbers used in science or mathematics to express a general law or fact: *What is the formula for converting miles to kilometres?* **2** a list of (often chemical) substances used for making sth; the instructions for making sth: *The formula for the new vaccine has not yet been made public.* **3** a formula

for (doing) sth a plan of how to get or do sth: *What is her formula for success?* • *Unfortunately, there's no magic formula for a perfect marriage.*

formulate /ˈfɔːmjəleɪt/ verb [T] **1** to prepare and organize a plan or ideas for doing sth: *to formulate a plan* **2** to express sth (clearly and exactly): *She struggled to formulate a simple answer to his question.*

fort /fɔːt/ noun [C] a strong building that is used for military defence

forth /fɔːθ/ adv

> IDIOMS **and so forth** and other things like those just mentioned: *The sort of job that you'll be doing is taking messages, making tea and so forth.*

back and forth → BACK[3]

forthcoming /ˌfɔːθˈkʌmɪŋ/ adj **1** that will happen or appear in the near future: *Look in the local paper for a list of forthcoming events.* **2** (not before a noun) offered or given: *If no money is forthcoming, we shall not be able to continue the project.* **3** (not before a noun) (used about a person) ready to be helpful, give information, etc: *Kate isn't very forthcoming about her previous job, so I don't know what she did exactly.*

forthright /ˈfɔːθraɪt/ adj saying exactly what you think in a clear and direct way

★**fortieth** /ˈfɔːtiəθ/ pron, determiner, adv 40th •➤ Look at the examples at **sixth**[1].

fortification /ˌfɔːtɪfɪˈkeɪʃn/ noun [C, usually pl] walls, towers, etc, built especially in the past to protect a place against attack

fortify /ˈfɔːtɪfaɪ/ verb [T] (*pres part* **fortifying***; 3rd pers sing pres* **fortifies***; pt, pp* **fortified**) to make a place stronger and ready for an attack: *to fortify a city*

fortnight /ˈfɔːtnaɪt/ noun [C, usually sing] *(Brit)* two weeks: *We're going on holiday for a fortnight.* • *School finishes in a fortnight/in a fortnight's time* (= two weeks from now).

fortnightly /ˈfɔːtnaɪtli/ adj, adv (happening or appearing) once every two weeks: *This magazine is published fortnightly.*

fortress /ˈfɔːtrəs/ noun [C] a castle or other large strong building that it is not easy to attack

fortunate /ˈfɔːtʃənət/ adj lucky: *It was fortunate that he was at home when you phoned.* •➤ opposite **unfortunate**

★**fortunately** /ˈfɔːtʃənətli/ adv by good luck; luckily: *Fortunately, the traffic wasn't too bad so I managed to get to the meeting on time.*

★**fortune** /ˈfɔːtʃuːn/ noun **1** [C,U] a very large amount of money: *I always spend a fortune on presents at Christmas.* • *She went to Hollywood in search of fame and fortune.* **2** [U] chance or the power that affects what happens in a person's life; luck: *Fortune was not on our side that day* (= we were unlucky). •➤ synonym **fate 3** [C, usually pl] the things (both good and bad) that happen to a person, family, country, etc: *The country's fortunes depend on its industry being successful.* **4** [C] what is going to happen to a person in the future: *Show me your hand and I'll try to tell* *your fortune.* ••➤ synonym **fate** or **destiny**

IDIOM **cost the earth/a fortune** → **COST²**

'**fortune teller** noun [C] a person who tells people what will happen to them in the future

★**forty** /'fɔːti/ number 40

➤ For examples of how to use numbers in sentences, look at **sixty**.

IDIOM **forty winks** (*informal*) a short sleep, especially during the day

forum /'fɔːrəm/ noun [C] a forum (for sth) a place or meeting where people can exchange and discuss ideas: *Television is now an important forum for political debate.*

★**forward¹** /'fɔːwəd/ adv **1** (also **forwards**) in the direction that is in front of you; towards the front, end or future: *Keep going forward and try not to look back.* ••➤ opposite **back** or **backward(s) 2** in the direction of progress; ahead: *The new form of treatment is a big step forward in the fight against Aids.*

➤ **Forward** is used after many verbs, for example **bring**, **come**, **look**, **put**. For the meaning of the expressions look at the verb entries.

IDIOMS **backward(s) and forward(s)** → **BACKWARDS**

put the clock/clocks forward/back → **CLOCK¹**

★**forward²** /'fɔːwəd/ adj **1** (only *before* a noun) towards the front or future: *forward planning* **2** having developed earlier than is normal or expected; advanced ••➤ opposite **backward 3** behaving towards sb in a way that is too confident or too informal: *I hope you don't think I'm being too forward, asking you so many questions.*

forward³ /'fɔːwəd/ verb [T] **1** to send a letter, etc received at one address to a new address: *The post office is forwarding all our mail.* **2** to help to improve sth or to make sth progress: *I'm trying to forward my career in publishing.*

forward⁴ /'fɔːwəd/ noun [C] an attacking player in a sport such as football

'**forwarding address** noun [C] a new address to which letters, etc should be sent: *The previous owners didn't leave a forwarding address.*

'**forward-looking** adj thinking about or planning for the future; having modern ideas

forwent *past tense* of **FORGO**

fossil /'fɒsl/ noun [C] (part of) an animal or plant that lived thousands of years ago which has turned into rock

foster /'fɒstə/ verb [T] **1** (*especially Brit*) to take a child who needs a home into your family and to care for him/her without becoming the legal parent: *to foster a homeless child*

➤ The people who do this are **foster-parents**. The child is a **foster-child**. Look at **adopt**.

2 to help or encourage the development of sth (especially feelings or ideas): *to foster sb's friendship/trust*

fought *past tense, past participle* of **FIGHT¹**

foul¹ /faʊl/ adj **1** that smells or tastes disgusting: *a foul-smelling cigar* • *This coffee tastes foul!* **2** (*especially Brit*) very bad or unpleasant: *Careful what you say – he's in a foul temper/mood.* • *The foul weather prevented our plane from taking off.* **3** (used about language) very rude; full of swearing: *foul language*

IDIOM **fall foul of sb/sth** to get in trouble with sb/sth because you have done sth wrong: *At sixteen she fell foul of the law for the first time.*

foul² /faʊl/ verb **1** [I,T] (used in sports) to attack another player in a way that is not allowed: *Shearer was fouled inside the box and the referee awarded his team a penalty.* **2** [T] to make sth dirty (with rubbish, waste, etc): *Dogs must not foul the pavement.*

PHRASAL VERB **foul sth up** (*spoken*) to spoil sth: *The delay on the train fouled up my plans for the evening.*

foul³ /faʊl/ noun [C] (used in sports) an action that is against the rules: *He was sent off for a foul on the goalkeeper.*

,**foul 'play** noun [U] **1** violence or crime that causes sb's death: *The police suspect foul play.* **2** action that is against the rules of a sport

found¹ *past tense, past participle* of **FIND¹**

found² /faʊnd/ verb [T] **1** to start an organization, institution, etc: *This museum was founded in 1683.* **2** to be the first to start building and living in a town or country: *Liberia was founded by freed American slaves.* **3** **found sth (on sth)** (usually passive) to base sth on sth: *The book was founded on real life.*

★**foundation** /faʊn'deɪʃn/ noun **1 foundations** [pl] a layer of bricks, etc under the surface of the ground that forms the solid base of a building **2** [C,U] the idea, principle, or fact on which sth is based: *This coursebook aims to give students a solid foundation in grammar.* • *That rumour is completely without foundation* (= it is not true). **3** [C] an organization that provides money for a special purpose: *The British Heart Foundation* **4** [U] the act of starting a new institution or organization

founder /'faʊndə/ noun [C] a person who starts a new institution or organization

,**founder-'member** noun [C] one of the original members of a club, organization, etc

foundry /'faʊndri/ noun [C] (*pl* **foundries**) a place where metal or glass is melted and shaped into objects

★**fountain** /'faʊntən/ noun [C] **1** a decoration (in a garden or in a square in a town) that sends a flow of water into the air; the water that comes out of a fountain ••➤ picture on page C8 **2** a strong flow of liquid or another substance that is forced into the air: *a fountain of blood/sparks* **3** a person or thing that provides a large amount of sth: *Ed's a fountain of information on football.*

'**fountain pen** noun [C] a type of pen that you fill with ink

★**four** /fɔː/ number **1** 4

[C] **countable**, a noun with a plural form: *one book, two books*   [U] **uncountable**, a noun with no plural form: *some sugar*

➤ For examples of how to use numbers in sentences, look at **six**.

2 four- (in compounds) having four of the thing mentioned: *four-legged animals*

IDIOM **on all fours** with your hands and knees on the ground; crawling: *The children went through the tunnel on all fours.*

four-letter 'word **noun** [C] a swear word that shocks or offends people (often with four letters)

★fourteen /ˌfɔːˈtiːn/ **number** 14

➤ For examples of how to use numbers in sentences, look at **six**.

★fourteenth /ˌfɔːˈtiːnθ/ **pron, determiner, adv** 14th

★fourth /fɔːθ/ **pron, determiner, adv** 4th

➤ For ¼ we use the word **quarter**: *a quarter of an hour* (= fifteen minutes)

four-wheel 'drive **adj** (used about a vehicle) having an engine that turns all four wheels

fowl /faʊl/ **noun** [C] (*pl* **fowl** or **fowls**) a bird, especially a chicken, that is kept on a farm

fox

★fox /fɒks/ **noun** [C] a wild animal like a small dog with reddish fur, a pointed nose and a thick tail

➤ A fox is often described as **sly** or **cunning**. A female fox is a **vixen**, a young fox is a **cub**.

foyer /ˈfɔɪeɪ/ **noun** [C] an entrance hall in a cinema, theatre, hotel, etc where people can meet or wait

fraction /ˈfrækʃn/ **noun** [C] **1** a small part or amount: *For a fraction of a second I thought the car was going to crash.* **2** a division of a number: *½ and ¼ are fractions.*

fractionally /ˈfrækʃənəli/ **adv** to a very small degree; slightly: *fractionally faster/ taller/heavier*

fracture /ˈfræktʃə/ **noun** [C,U] a break in a bone or other hard material –**fracture** **verb** [I,T]: *She fell and fractured her ankle.* ● *A water pipe fractured and flooded the bathroom.*

fragile /ˈfrædʒaɪl/ **adj** easily damaged or broken: *This bowl is very fragile. Please handle it carefully.*

fragment¹ /ˈfrægmənt/ **noun** [C] a small piece that has broken off or that comes from sth larger: *The builders found fragments of Roman pottery on the site.* ● *I heard only a fragment of their conversation.*

fragment² /fræɡˈment/ **verb** [I,T] (*formal*) to break (sth) into small pieces: *The country is becoming increasingly fragmented by civil war.*

fragrance /ˈfreɪɡrəns/ **noun** [C,U] a pleasant smell

fragrant /ˈfreɪɡrənt/ **adj** having a pleasant smell

frail /freɪl/ **adj** weak or not healthy: *My aunt is still very frail after her accident.*

frailty /ˈfreɪlti/ **noun** [C,U] (*pl* **frailties**) weakness of a person's body or character

★frame¹ /freɪm/ **noun** [C] **1** a border of wood or metal that goes around the outside of a door, picture, window, etc: *a window frame* **2** the basic strong structure of a piece of furniture, building, vehicle, etc which gives it its shape: *the frame of a bicycle/an aircraft* •➤ picture on page S9 **3** [usually pl] a structure made of plastic or metal that holds the two pieces of glass (**lenses**) in a pair of glasses •➤ picture at **glasses** **4** [usually sing] the basic shape of a human or animal body: *He has a large frame but he's not fat.*

IDIOM **frame of mind** the particular state or condition of your feelings; mood: *I'm not in the right frame of mind for a party. I'd prefer to be on my own.*

frame² /freɪm/ **verb** [T] **1** to put a border around sth (especially a picture or photograph): *Let's have this photograph framed.* **2** (usually passive) to give false evidence against sb in order to make him/her seem guilty of a crime: *The man claimed that he had been framed by the police.* **3** (*formal*) to express sth in a particular way: *The question was very carefully framed.*

framework /ˈfreɪmwɜːk/ **noun** [C] **1** the basic structure of sth that gives it shape and strength: *A greenhouse is made of glass panels fixed in a metal framework.* ● (*figurative*) *the basic framework of society* **2** a system of rules or ideas which help you decide what to do: *The plan may be changed but it will provide a framework on which we can build.*

franc /fræŋk/ **noun** [C] the unit of money that is used in France, Belgium, Switzerland and several other countries

franchise /ˈfræntʃaɪz/ **noun** **1** [C,U] official permission to sell a company's goods or services in a particular area: *They have the franchise to sell this product in Cyprus.* ● *Most fast-food restaurants are operated under franchise.* **2** [U] (*formal*) the right to vote in elections

frank /fræŋk/ **adj** showing your thoughts and feelings clearly; saying what you mean: *To be perfectly frank with you, I don't think you'll pass your driving test.* –**frankly** **adv**: *Please tell me frankly what you think about my idea.* –**frankness** **noun** [U]

frankfurter /ˈfræŋkfɜːtə/ (*US also* **wiener**) **noun** [C] a type of small smoked sausage

frantic /ˈfræntɪk/ **adj 1** extremely worried or frightened: *The mother went frantic when she couldn't find her child.* ● *frantic cries for help* **2** very busy or done in a hurry: *a frantic search for the keys* ● *We're not busy at work*

now, but things get frantic at Christmas.
–**frantically** /-kli/ **adv**

fraternal /frə'tɜːnl/ **adj** (*formal*) connected with the relationship that exists between brothers; like a brother: *fraternal love/ rivalry*

fraternity /frə'tɜːnəti/ **noun** (*pl* **fraternities**) **1** [U] the feeling of friendship and support between people in the same group **2** [C] a group of people who share the same work or interests: *the medical fraternity*

fraud /frɔːd/ **noun 1** [C,U] (an act of) cheating sb in order to get money, often illegally: *The accountant was sent to prison for fraud.* • *Massive amounts of money are lost every year in credit card frauds.* **2** [C] a person who tricks sb by pretending to be sb else

fraudulent /'frɔːdjələnt/ **adj** (*formal*) done in order to cheat sb; dishonest: *the fraudulent use of stolen cheques*

fraught /frɔːt/ **adj 1** fraught with sth filled with sth unpleasant: *a situation fraught with danger/difficulty* **2** (used about people) worried and nervous; (used about a situation) very busy so that people become nervous: *Things are usually fraught at work on Mondays.*

fray /freɪ/ **verb** [I,T] **1** if cloth, etc frays or becomes frayed, some of the threads at the end start to come apart: *This shirt is beginning to fray at the cuffs.* • *a frayed rope* **2** if a person's nerves, etc fray or become frayed, he/she starts to get annoyed: *Tempers began to fray towards the end of the match.*

freak[1] /friːk/ **noun** [C] **1** (*informal*) a person who has a very strong interest in sth: *a fitness/computer freak* •➤ synonym **fanatic 2** a very unusual and strange event, person, animal, etc: *a freak accident/storm/result* • *The other kids think Ally's a freak because she doesn't watch TV.*

freak[2] /friːk/ **verb** [I,T] (*informal*) freak (sb) (out) to react very strongly to sth that makes you feel shocked, frightened, upset, etc: *She freaked out when she heard the news.* • *The film 'Psycho' really freaked me out.*

freckle /'frekl/ **noun** [C,usually pl] a small brown spot on your skin: *A lot of people with red hair have got freckles.* •➤ Look at **mole**. –**freckled adj**

★**free**[1] /friː/ **adj 1** not in prison, in a cage, etc; not held or controlled: *The government set Mandela free in 1989.* • *There is nowhere around here where dogs can run free.* **2** free (to do sth) not controlled by the government, rules, etc: *There is free movement of people across the border.* • *free speech/press* **3** costing nothing: *Admission to the museum is free/ free of charge.* • *Children under five usually travel free on trains.* **4** not busy or being used: *I'm afraid Mr Spencer is not free this afternoon.* • *I don't get much free time.* • *Is this seat free?* **5** free from/of sth not having sth dangerous, unpleasant, etc: *free of worries/responsibility* • *free from pain*

IDIOMS **feel free** → **FEEL**[1]

free and easy informal or relaxed:*The atmosphere in our office is very free and easy.*

get, have, etc a free hand to get, have, etc permission to make your own decisions about sth

of your own free will because you want to, not because sb forces you

★**free**[2] /friː/ **verb** [T] **1** free sb/sth (from sth) to let sb/sth leave or escape from a place where he/she/it is held: *to free a prisoner* • *The protesters freed the animals from their cages.* **2** free sb/sth of/from sth to take away sth that is unpleasant from sb: *The medicine freed her from pain for a few hours.* **3** free sb/sth (up) for sth; free sb/sth (up) to do sth to make sth available so that it can be used; to put sb in a position in which he/she can do sth: *If I cancel my trip, that will free me to see you on Friday.*

free 'agent noun [C] a person who can do what he/she wants because nobody else has the right to tell him/her what to do

★**freedom** /'friːdəm/ **noun 1** [U] the state of not being held prisoner or controlled by sb else: *The opposition leader was given his freedom after 25 years.* **2** [C,U] the right or ability to do or say what you want: *You have the freedom to come and go as you please.* • *freedom of speech* • *the rights and freedoms of the individual* •➤ Look at **liberty**. **3** [U] freedom from sth the state of not being affected by sth unpleasant: *freedom from fear/hunger/pain* **4** [U] the freedom of sth the right to use sth without restriction: *You can have the freedom of the ground floor, but please don't go upstairs.*

'freedom fighter noun [C] a person who belongs to a group that uses violence to try to remove a government from power

free 'enterprise noun [U] the operation of trade and business without government control

freehand /'friːhænd/ **adj, adv** (used about a drawing) done by hand, without the help of any instruments: *a freehand sketch* • *to draw freehand*

free 'kick noun [C] (in football or rugby) a situation in which a player of one team is allowed to kick the ball because a member of the other team has broken a rule

freelance /'friːlɑːns/ **adj, adv** earning money by selling your services or work to different organizations rather than being employed by a single company: *a freelance journalist* • *She works freelance.* –**freelance** (also **freelancer**) **noun** [C] –**freelance verb** [I]: *I left my job because I can earn more by freelancing.*

freely /'friːli/ **adv 1** in a way that is not controlled or limited: *He is the country's first freely elected president for 40 years.* **2** without trying to avoid the truth even though it might be embarrassing; in an honest way: *I freely admit that I made a mistake.*

Freemason /'friːmeɪsn/ (also **mason**) **noun** [C] a person, usually a man, who belongs to an international secret society whose members help each other and who recognize each other by secret signs

,free-'range adj (used about farm birds or their eggs) kept or produced in a place where birds can move around freely: *free-range hens/turkeys* ● *free-range eggs* ••➤ Look at **battery**.

,free 'speech noun [U] the right to express any opinion in public

freeway /'fri:weɪ/ (*US*) = **MOTORWAY**

*freeze¹ /fri:z/ verb (*pt* froze /frəʊz/; *pp* frozen /'frəʊzn/) 1 [I,T] to become hard (and often change into ice) because of extreme cold; to make sth do this: *Water freezes at 0° Celsius.* ● *The ground was frozen solid for most of the winter.* ● *frozen peas/fish/food* 2 [I] used with 'it' to describe extremely cold weather when water turns into ice: *I think it's going to freeze tonight.* 3 [I,T] to be very cold or to die from cold: *It was so cold on the mountain that we thought we would freeze to death.* ● *Turn the heater up a bit – I'm frozen stiff.* 4 [I] to stop moving suddenly and completely because you are frightened or in danger: *The terrible scream made her freeze with terror.* ● *Suddenly the man pulled out a gun and shouted 'Freeze!'* 5 [T] to keep the money you earn, prices, etc at a fixed level for a certain period of time: *Spending on defence has been frozen for one year.*

freeze² /fri:z/ noun [C] 1 a period of weather when the temperature stays below 0°C (freezing point) 2 the fixing of the money you earn, prices, etc at one level for a certain period of time

freezer /'fri:zə/ (also ,deep 'freeze) noun [C] a large box or cupboard in which you can store food for a long time at a temperature below 0°Celsius (freezing point) so that it stays frozen ••➤ Look at **fridge**. ••➤ picture on page C7

freezing¹ /'fri:zɪŋ/ adj (*informal*) very cold: *Can we turn the central heating on? I'm freezing.* ● *Put a coat on, it's absolutely freezing outside.*

freezing² /'fri:zɪŋ/ (also 'freezing point) noun [U] the temperature at which water freezes: *Last night the temperature fell to six degrees below freezing.*

freight /freɪt/ noun [U] goods that are carried from one place to another by ship, lorry, etc; the system for carrying goods in this way: *Your order will be sent by air freight.* ● *a freight train*

freighter /'freɪtə/ noun [C] a ship or an aircraft that carries only goods and not passengers

,French 'window (*US* ,French 'door) noun [C] one of a pair of glass doors that open onto a garden or balcony

frenzied /'frenzid/ adj that is wild and out of control: *a frenzied attack* ● *frenzied activity*

frenzy /'frenzi/ noun [sing,U] a state of great emotion or activity that is not under control: *There's no need to get in a frenzy – you've got until Friday to finish your essay.* ● *I could hear a frenzy of activity in the kitchen.*

frequency /'fri:kwənsi/ noun (*pl* frequencies) 1 [U] the number of times sth happens in a particular period: *Fatal accidents have decreased in frequency in recent years.* 2 [U] the fact that sth happens often: *The frequency of child deaths from cancer near the nuclear power station is being investigated.* 3 [C,U] the rate at which a sound wave or radio wave moves up and down (vibrates): *high-frequency/low-frequency sounds*

*frequent¹ /'fri:kwənt/ adj happening often: *His visits became less frequent.* ••➤ opposite **infrequent** –frequently adv

frequent² /fri'kwent/ verb [T] (*formal*) to go to a place often: *He spent most of his evenings in Paris frequenting bars and clubs.*

*fresh /freʃ/ adj 1 (used especially about food) produced or picked very recently; not frozen or in a tin: *fresh bread/fruit/flowers* ••➤ Look at **stale**. 2 left somewhere or experienced recently: *fresh blood/footprints* ● *Write a few notes while the lecture is still fresh in your mind.* 3 new and different: *They have decided to make a fresh start in a different town.* ● *I'm sure he'll have some fresh ideas on the subject.* 4 (used about water) without salt; not sea water 5 pleasantly clean or bright: *Open the window and let some fresh air in.* 6 not tired: *I'll think about the problem again in the morning when I'm fresh.* 7 fresh from/out of sth having just finished sth: *Life isn't easy for a young teacher fresh from university.* –freshly adv: *freshly baked bread* –freshness noun [U]

IDIOM break fresh/new ground → **GROUND¹**

freshen /'freʃn/ verb [T] freshen sth (up) to make sth cleaner or brighter: *Some new curtains and wallpaper would freshen up this room.*

PHRASAL VERB freshen up to wash and make yourself clean and tidy

fresher /'freʃə/ noun [C] (*Brit*) a student who is in his/her first year at university, college, etc

freshman /'freʃmən/ noun [C] (*pl* -men /-mən/) (*US*) a student who is in his/her first year at college, high school, university, etc

fret¹ /fret/ verb [I] (fretting; fretted) fret (about/at/over sth) to be worried and unhappy about sth: *I was awake for hours fretting about my exams.*

fret² /fret/ noun [C] one of the bars across the long thin part of a guitar, etc that show you where to put your fingers to produce a particular sound ••➤ picture at **music**

Fri abbr Friday: *Fri 27 May*

friction /'frɪkʃn/ noun [U] 1 the rubbing of one surface or thing against another: *You have to put oil in the engine to reduce friction between the moving parts.* 2 friction (between A and B) disagreement between people or groups: *There is a lot of friction between the older and younger members of staff.*

*Friday /'fraɪdeɪ; -di/ noun [C,U] (*abbr* Fri) the day of the week after Thursday ••➤ note on next page

➤ Days of the week are always written with a capital letter. For examples of how to use the days of the week in sentences, look at **Monday**.

★**fridge** /frɪdʒ/ (also *formal* **refrigerator**, *US* **icebox**) noun [C] a metal container with a door in which food, etc is kept cold (but not frozen) so that it stays fresh ••➤ Look at **freezer**. ••➤ picture on page C7

★**friend** /frend/ noun [C] **1** a person that you know and like (not a member of your family), and who likes you: *Trevor and I are old friends. We were at school together.* ● *We're only inviting close friends and relatives to the wedding.* ● *Helen's my best friend.* ● *A friend of mine told me about this restaurant.* ● *One of my friends told me about this restaurant.* ••➤ Look at **boyfriend**, **girlfriend** and **penfriend**. **2** a friend of/to sth a person who supports an organization, a charity, etc, especially by giving money; a person who supports a particular idea, etc: *the Friends of the Churchill Hospital*

IDIOMS **be/make friends (with sb)** to be/become a friend (of sb): *Tony is rather shy and finds it hard to make friends.*

a false friend → **FALSE**

★**friendly¹** /'frendli/ adj (**friendlier**; **friendliest**) **1** friendly (to/toward(s) sb) behaving in a kind and open way: *Everyone here has been very friendly towards us.* **2** showing kindness in a way that makes people feel happy and relaxed: *a friendly smile/atmosphere* ••➤ opposite for senses 1 and 2 **unfriendly 3** friendly with sb treating sb as a friend: *Nick's become quite friendly with the boy next door.* ● *Are you on friendly terms with your neighbours?* **4** (in compounds) helpful to sb/sth; not harmful to sth: *Our computer is extremely user-friendly.* ● *ozone-friendly sprays* **5** in which the people, teams, etc taking part are not competing seriously: *a friendly argument* ● *I've organized a friendly match against my brother's team.* –**friendliness** noun [U]

friendly² /'frendli/ noun [C] a sports match that is not part of a serious competition

★**friendship** /'frendʃɪp/ noun **1** [C] a friendship (with sb); a friendship (between A and B) a relationship between people who are friends: *a close/lasting/lifelong friendship* **2** [U] the state of being friends: *Our relationship is based on friendship, not love.*

fright /fraɪt/ noun [C,U] a sudden feeling of fear or shock: *I hope I didn't give you a fright when I shouted.* ● *The child cried out in fright.*

★**frighten** /'fraɪtn/ verb [T] to make sb/sth afraid or shocked: *That programme about crime really frightened me.*

PHRASAL VERB **frighten sb/sth away/off** to cause a person or animal to go away by frightening him/her/it: *Walk quietly so that you don't frighten the birds away.*

★**frightened** /'fraɪtnd/ adj **1** full of fear or worry: *Frightened children were calling for their mothers.* ● *I was frightened that they*

would think that I was rude. **2** frightened o sb/sth afraid of a particular person, thing o situation: *When I was young I was frightened of spiders.* ••➤ Look at the note at **afraid**.

★**frightening** /'fraɪtnɪŋ/ adj making you fee afraid or shocked: *a frightening experience* ● *It's frightening that time passes so quickly.*

frightful /'fraɪtfl/ adj (*old-fashioned*) **1** very bad or unpleasant: *The weather this summer has been frightful.* **2** (used for emphasizing sth) very bad or great: *We're in a frightfu rush.*

frightfully /'fraɪtfəli/ adv (*old-fashioned*) very: *I'm frightfully sorry.*

frill /frɪl/ noun [C] **1** a decoration for the edge of a dress, shirt, etc which is made by form ing many folds in a narrow piece of cloth **2** [usually pl] something that is added for dec oration that you feel is not necessary: *We just want a plain simple meal – no frills.* –**frilly** adj *a frilly dress*

fringe¹ /frɪndʒ/ noun [C] **1** (*US* **bangs** [pl]) the part of your hair that is cut so that it hangs over your forehead: *Your hair looks better with a fringe.* ••➤ picture at **hair 2** a border for decoration on a piece of clothing, etc that is made of lots of hanging threads **3** (*Brit*) the outer edge of an area or a group that is a long way from the centre or from what is usual: *Some people on the fringes of the socialist party are opposed to the policy on Europe.*

fringe² /frɪndʒ/ verb

IDIOM **be fringed with sth** to have sth as a border or around the edge: *The lake was fringed with pine trees.*

'**fringe benefit** noun [C,usually pl] an extra thing that is given to an employee in addition to the money he/she earns: *The fringe bene fits of this job include a car and free health insurance.* ••➤ A more informal word is **perk**.

frisk /frɪsk/ verb **1** [T] to pass your hands over sb's body in order to search for hidden weapons, drugs, etc **2** [I] (used about an ani mal or child) to play and jump about happily and with a lot of energy

frisky /'frɪski/ adj full of life and wanting to play

fritter /'frɪtə/ verb

PHRASAL VERB **fritter sth away (on sth)** to waste time or money on things that are not important

frivolity /frɪ'vɒləti/ noun [U] silly behaviour (especially when you should be serious)

frivolous /'frɪvələs/ adj not serious; silly

frizzy /'frɪzi/ adj (used about hair) with a lot of very small tight curls

fro /frəʊ/ adv

IDIOM **to and fro** → **TO**

frog /frɒg/ noun [C] a small animal with smooth skin and long back legs that it uses for jumping. Frogs live in or near water.

frogman /'frɒgmən/ noun [C] (*pl* -**men** /-mən/) a person whose job is to work under the surface of water wearing special rubber clothes and using breathing equipment: *Police frogmen searched the river.*

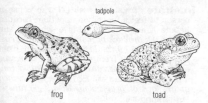

tadpole

frog   toad

from /frəm; *strong form* frɒm/ **prep 1** show-ing the place, direction or time that sb/sth starts or started: *She comes home from work at 7 o'clock.* ● *a cold wind from the east* ● *Water was dripping from the tap.* ● *Peter's on holiday from next Friday.* ● *The supermar-ket is open* **from** *8am* **till** *8pm every day.* **2** showing the person who sent or gave sth: *I borrowed this jacket from my sister.* ● *a phone call from my father* **3** showing the origin of sb/sth: *'Where do you come from?' 'I'm from Australia.'* ● *cheeses from France and Italy* ● *quotations from Shakespeare* **4** showing the material which is used to make sth: *Paper is* **made from** *wood.* ● *This sauce is made from cream and wine.*

> **Made of** tells us the material the object actually consists of: *a table made of wood* ● *a house made of bricks*

5 showing the distance between two places: *The house is five miles from the town centre.* ● *I work not far from here.* **6** showing the point at which a series of prices, figures, etc, start: *Our prices start from £2.50 a bottle.* ● *Tickets cost from £3 to £11.* **7** showing the state of sb/sth before a change: *The time of the meeting has been changed* **from** *7* **to** *8 o'clock.* ● *The article was translated* **from** *Russian* **into** *English.* ● *Things have gone* **from bad to worse.** **8** showing that sb/sth is taken away, removed or separated from sb/sth else: *Children don't like being separated from their parents for a long period.* ● *(in mathematics) 8 from 12 leaves 4.* **9** showing sth that you want to avoid: *There was no shelter from the wind.* ● *This game will stop you from getting bored.* **10** showing the cause of sth: *People in the camps are suffering from hunger and cold.* **11** showing the reason for making a judgement or forming an opinion: *You can tell quite a lot from a person's hand-writing.* **12** showing the difference between two people, places or things: *Can you tell margarine from butter?* ● *Is Portuguese very different from Spanish?*

IDIOM **from…on** starting at a particular time and continuing for ever: *She never spoke to him again from that day on.* ● *From now on you must earn your own living.*

★front¹ /frʌnt/ **noun 1 the front** [C, usually sing] the side or surface of sth/sb that faces forward: *a dress with buttons down the front* ● *the front of a building* (= the front wall) ● *a card with flowers* **on the front** ● *She slipped on the stairs and spilt coffee all down her front.* **2 the front** [C, usually sing] the most

forward part of sth; the area that is just outside of or before sb/sth: *Young children should not travel* **in the front of** *the car.* ● *There is a small garden* **at the front of** *the house.*

> **On the front of** means 'on the front surface of sth': *The number is shown on the front of the bus.* **In front (of sth)** means 'further forward than another person or thing'; before sb/sth else: *A car has stopped in front of the bus.* ● *There were three people in front of me in the queue.* **At/In the front (of sth)** means 'in the most forward part inside sth': *The driver sits at the front of the bus.* Look at these sentences too: *The teacher usually stands in front of the class.* ● *The noisy children were asked to sit at the front of the class* (= in the front seats).

3 [C] a particular area of activity: *Things are difficult* **on the** *domestic/political/economic* **front** *at the moment.* ● *Progress has been made* **on all fronts.** **4 the front** [sing] the line or area where fighting takes place in a war: *to be sent to the front* **5** [sing] a way of behaving that hides your true feelings: *His brave words were just a front. He was really feeling very nervous.* **6** [C] a line or area where warm air and cold air meet: *A* **cold front** *is moving in from the north.*

IDIOMS **back to front** → **BACK¹**
in front further forward than sb/sth; ahead: *Some of the children ran on in front.* ● *After three laps the Kenyan runner was in front.*
in front of sb/sth 1 in a position further forward than but close to sb/sth: *The bus stops right in front of our house.* ● *Don't stand in front of the television.* ● *The book was open in front of her on the desk.* ●➤ **In front of** does not mean the same as **opposite.** ●➤ picture at **opposite 2** if you do sth in front of sb, you do it when that person is there in the same room or place as you: *I couldn't talk about that in front of my parents.*
up front (*informal*) as payment before sth is done: *I want half the money up front and half when the job is finished.*

front² /frʌnt/ **adj** (only *before* a noun) of or at the front (1,2): *the front door/garden/room* ● *sit in the front row* ● *front teeth*

frontal /ˈfrʌntl/ **adj** (only *before* a noun) from the front: *a frontal attack*

frontier /ˈfrʌntɪə/ **noun 1** [C] the frontier (between A and B) the line where one coun-try joins another; border: *the end of frontier controls in Europe.* ●➤ Look at the note at **border.** **2 the frontiers** [pl] the limit between what we do and do not know: *Scien-tific research is constantly* **pushing back the frontiers** *of our knowledge about the world.*

front-ˈpage **adj** interesting or important enough to appear on the front page of a news-paper: *front-page news/headlines*

★frost¹ /frɒst/ **noun** [C,U] the weather condi-tion when the temperature falls below 0°Celsius (freezing point) and a thin layer of ice forms on the ground and other surfaces, especially at night: *There was a* **hard**

frost last night. • *It will be a chilly night with some **ground frost**.*

frost² /frɒst/ **verb** [T] (*especially US*) = **ICE²**
PHRASAL VERB **frost over/up** to become covered with a thin layer of ice: *The window has frosted over/up.* •➤ Look at **defrost**.

frostbite /'frɒstbaɪt/ **noun** [U] a serious medical condition of the fingers, toes, etc that is caused by very low temperatures: *All the climbers were suffering from frostbite.*

frosted /'frɒstɪd/ **adj** (used about glass or a window) with a special surface so you cannot see through it

frosting /'frɒstɪŋ/ (*especially US*) = **ICING**

frosty /'frɒsti/ **adj** **1** very cold, with frost: *a cold and frosty morning* **2** cold and unfriendly: *a frosty welcome*

froth¹ /frɒθ/ **noun** [U] a mass of small white bubbles on the top of a liquid, etc –**frothy adj**: *frothy beer* • *a frothy cappuccino*

froth² /frɒθ/ **verb** [I] to have or produce a mass of white bubbles: *The mad dog was frothing at the mouth.*

frown /fraʊn/ **verb** [I] to show you are angry, serious, etc by making lines appear on your forehead above your nose –**frown noun** [C]
PHRASAL VERB **frown on/upon sth** to disapprove of sth: *Smoking is very much frowned upon these days.*

froze *past tense of* **FREEZE¹**

frozen¹ *past participle of* **FREEZE¹**

frozen² /'frəʊzn/ **adj** **1** (used about food) stored at a low temperature in order to keep it for a long time: *frozen meat/vegetables* **2** (*informal*) (used about people and parts of the body) very cold: *My feet are frozen!* • *I was frozen stiff.* •➤ synonym **freezing** **3** (used about water) with a layer of ice on the surface: *The pond is frozen. Let's go skating.*

★**fruit** /fruːt/ **noun** **1** [C,U] the part of a plant or tree that contains seeds and that we eat: *Try and eat more **fresh fruit** and vegetables.* • *Marmalade is made with **citrus fruit** (=* oranges, lemons, grapefruit, etc). • *fruit juice*

➤ When we say 'a fruit' we mean 'a type of fruit': *Most big supermarkets sell all sorts of tropical fruits.* When talking about an individual piece of fruit we usually use the name of the fruit: *Would you like an apple?* or we use the uncountable form: *Would you like some fruit?*

2 [C] the part of any plant in which the seed is formed **3** [pl] **the fruits (of sth)** a good result or success from work that you have done: *It will be years before we see the fruits of this research.*
IDIOM **bear fruit** → **BEAR²**

fruitful /'fruːtfl/ **adj** producing good results; useful: *fruitful discussions*

fruition /fruˈɪʃn/ **noun** [U] (*formal*) the time when a plan, etc starts to be successful: *After months of hard work, our efforts were **coming to fruition**.*

fruitless /'fruːtləs/ **adj** producing poor or no results; not successful: *a fruitless search*

frustrate /frʌˈstreɪt/ **verb** [T] **1** to cause a person to feel annoyed or impatient because he/she cannot do or achieve what he/she wants: *It's the lack of money that really frustrates him.* **2** (*formal*) to prevent sb from doing sth or sth from happening: *The rescue work has been frustrated by bad weather conditions.* –**frustrated adj**: *He felt very frustrated at his lack of progress in learning Chinese.* –**frustrating adj**

frustration /frʌˈstreɪʃn/ **noun** [C,U] a feeling of anger because you cannot get what you want; sth that causes you to feel like this: *He felt anger and frustration at no longer being able to see very well.* • *Every job has its frustrations.*

★**fry¹** /fraɪ/ **verb** [I,T] (*pres part **frying**; 3rd pers sing pres **fries**; pt, pp **fried** /fraɪd/*) to cook sth or to be cooked in hot fat or oil: *to fry an egg* • *a fried egg* • *I could smell bacon frying in the kitchen.* •➤ Look at the note at **cook**.

fry² /fraɪ/ (*US* **French 'fry**) **noun** [C] (*pl* **fries**) a long thin piece of potato fried in oil

'frying pan (*US* **frypan**) **noun** [C] a flat pan with a long handle that is used for frying food •➤ picture at **pan**

ft **abbr** foot, feet; a measure of length, about 30.5 cm: *a room 10 ft by 6 ft*

★**fuel¹** /'fjuːəl/ **noun** **1** [U] material that is burned to produce heat or power **2** [C] a type of fuel: *I think gas is the best fuel for central heating.*

fuel² /'fjuːəl/ **verb** [T] (**fuelling**; **fuelled**; (*US*) **fueling**; **fueled**) to make sb feel an emotion more strongly: *Her interest in the Spanish language was fuelled by a visit to Spain.*

fugitive /'fjuːdʒətɪv/ **noun** [C] a person who is running away or escaping (for example from the police) •➤ Look at **refugee**.

fulfil (*US* **fulfill**) /fʊlˈfɪl/ **verb** [T] (**fulfilling**; **fulfilled**) **1** to make sth that you wish for happen; to achieve a goal: *He finally fulfilled his childhood dream of becoming a doctor.* • *to fulfil your ambition/potential* **2** to do or have everything that you should or that is necessary: *to fulfil a duty/obligation/promise/need* • *The conditions of entry to university in this country are quite difficult to fulfil.* **3** to have a particular role or purpose: *Italy fulfils a very important role within the European Union.* **4** to make sb feel completely happy and satisfied: *I need a job that really fulfils me.* –**fulfilled adj**: *When I had my baby I felt totally fulfilled.* –**fulfilling adj**: *I found working abroad a very fulfilling experience.*

fulfilment /fʊlˈfɪlmənt/ (*US* **fulfillment**) **noun** [U] the act of achieving a goal; the feeling of satisfaction that you have when you have done sth: *the fulfilment of your dreams/hopes/ambitions* • *to find personal/emotional fulfilment*

★**full¹** /fʊl/ **adj** **1** holding or containing as much or as many as possible: *The bin needs emptying. It's **full up** (=* completely full). • *a full bottle* • *The bus was full so we had to wait for the next one.* • (*figurative*) *We need a good night's sleep because we've got a full (=* busy) *day tomorrow.* **2** full of sb/sth containing a lot of sb/sth: *The room was full of people.* ● *His work was full of mistakes.* ● *The children are full of energy.* **3** full (up) having had enough to eat and drink: *No more, thank you. I'm full (up).* **4** (only *before* a noun) complete; not leaving anything out: *I should like* **a full report** *on the accident, please.* ● *Full details of today's TV programmes are on page 20.* ● *He took* **full responsibility** *for what had happened.* ● *Please give your* **full name and address.** **5** (only *before* a noun) the highest or greatest possible: *She got* **full marks** *in her French exam.* ● *The train was travelling* **at full speed.** **6** full of sb/sth/yourself thinking or talking a lot about sb/sth/yourself: *When she got back from holiday she was full of everything they had seen.* ● *He's* **full of himself** (= thinks that he is very important) *since he got that new job.* **7** round in shape: *She's got quite a full figure.* ● *He's quite full in the face.* **8** (used about clothes) made with plenty of material: *a full skirt*

IDIOMS **at full stretch** working as hard as possible: *When the factory is operating at full stretch, it employs 800 people.*

full of beans/life with a lot of energy and enthusiasm: *They came back from holiday full of beans.*

have your hands full → HAND¹

in full with nothing missing; completely: *Your money will be refunded in full* (= you will get all your money back). ● *Please write your name in full.*

in full swing at the stage when there is the most activity: *When we arrived the party was already in full swing.*

in full view (of sb/sth) in a place where you can easily be seen: *In full view of the guards, he tried to escape over the prison wall.*

to the full as much as possible: *to enjoy life to the full*

full² /fʊl/ **adv** full in/on (sth) straight; directly: *John hit him full in the face.* ● *The two cars crashed full on.*

full-'blown **adj** fully developed: *to have full-blown Aids*

full 'board **noun** [U] (in a hotel, etc) including all meals ••➤ Look at **half board** and **bed and breakfast.**

full-'length **adj 1** (used about a picture, mirror, etc) showing a person from head to foot **2** not made shorter: *a full-length film* **3** (used about a dress, skirt, etc) reaching the feet

full 'moon **noun** [sing] the moon when it appears as a complete circle

full-'scale **adj** (only *before* a noun) **1** using everything or person that is available: *The police have started a full-scale murder investigation.* **2** (used about a plan, drawing, etc) of the same size as the original object: *a full-scale plan/model*

★full 'stop (*especially US* **period**) **noun** [C] a mark (.) that is used in writing to show the end of a sentence

full-'time **adj, adv** for a whole of the normal period of work: *He has a full-time job.* ● *He*

works full-time. ● *We employ 800 full-time staff.* ••➤ Look at **part-time.**

★fully /'fʊli/ **adv** completely; to the highest possible degree: *I'm fully aware of the problem.* ● *All our engineers are fully trained.*

fully-'fledged (*US also* **full-fledged**) **adj** completely trained or completely developed; mature: *Computer science is now a fully-fledged academic subject.*

fumble /'fʌmbl/ **verb** [I] to try to find or take hold of sth with your hands in a nervous or careless way: *'It must be here somewhere', she said, fumbling in her pocket for her key.*

fume /fjuːm/ **verb** [I] to be very angry about sth

fumes /fjuːmz/ **noun** [pl] smoke or gases that smell unpleasant and that can be dangerous to breathe in: *diesel/petrol/exhaust fumes*

★fun¹ /fʌn/ **noun** [U] pleasure and enjoyment; an activity or a person that gives you pleasure and enjoyment: *We had a lot of fun at the party last night.* ● *The party was great fun.* ● *Have fun!* (= enjoy yourself) ● *It's no fun having to get up at 4 o'clock every day.*

IDIOMS **(just) for fun/for the fun of it** (just) for amusement or pleasure; not seriously: *I don't need English for my work. I'm just learning it for fun.*

in fun as a joke: *It was said in fun. They didn't mean to upset you.*

make fun of sb/sth to laugh at sb/sth in an unkind way; to make other people do this: *The older children are always making fun of him because of his accent.*

poke fun at sb/sth → POKE

★fun² /fʌn/ **adj** amusing or enjoyable: *to have a fun time/day out* ● *Brett's a fun guy.*

➤ Be careful. **Funny** describes something or someone that makes you laugh or that is strange. It is not the same as **fun**: *Jane is fun* (= I enjoy being with her). ● *Jane is funny* (= she tells jokes and makes me laugh all the time/she is strange).

★function¹ /'fʌŋkʃn/ **noun** [C] **1** the purpose or special duty of a person or thing: *The function of the heart is to pump blood through the body.* ● *to perform/fulfil a function* **2** an important social event, ceremony, etc: *The princess attends hundreds of official functions every year.*

function² /'fʌŋkʃn/ **verb** [I] to work correctly; to be in action: *Only one engine was still functioning.* ••➤ synonym **operate**

functional /'fʌŋkʃənl/ **adj 1** practical and useful rather than attractive: *cheap functional furniture* **2** working; being used: *The system is now fully functional.*

'function key **noun** [C] one of the buttons (keys) on a computer which are used to perform a particular operation

★fund¹ /fʌnd/ **noun 1** [C] a sum of money that is collected for a particular purpose: *They contributed £30 to the disaster relief fund.* **2 funds** [pl] money that is available and can be spent: *The hospital is trying to raise funds for a new kidney machine.*

fund² /fʌnd/ verb [T] to provide a project, school, charity etc with money: *The Channel Tunnel is not funded by government money.*

fundamental /ˌfʌndəˈmentl/ adj basic and important; from which everything else develops: *There will be fundamental changes in the way the school is run.* ● *There is a fundamental difference between your opinion and mine.* –**fundamentally** /-təli/ adv: *The government's policy has changed fundamentally.*

fundamentals /ˌfʌndəˈmentlz/ noun [pl] basic facts or principles

'**fund-raiser** noun [C] a person whose job is to find ways of collecting money for a charity or an organization –**fund-raising** noun [U]: *fund-raising events*

★**funeral** /ˈfjuːnərəl/ noun [C] a ceremony (usually religious) for burying or burning a dead person: *The funeral will be held next week.*

> The body of the dead person is carried in a **coffin**, on which there are often **wreaths** of flowers. The coffin is buried in a **grave** or is burned (**cremated**).

'**funeral director** = **UNDERTAKER**

funfair /ˈfʌnfeə/ = **FAIR²**(1)

fungus /ˈfʌŋɡəs/ noun [C,U] (*pl* **fungi** /-gaɪ/ or **funguses**) a plant that is not green and does not have leaves or flowers (for example a mushroom), or that is like a wet powder and grows on old wood or food, walls, etc. Some fungi can be harmful. ●► Look at **mould** and **toadstool**. –**fungal** adj: *a fungal disease/infection/growth*

funnel /ˈfʌnl/ noun [C] **1** an object that is wide at the top and narrow at the bottom, used for pouring liquid, powder, etc into a small opening ●► picture at **kitchen 2** the metal chimney of a ship, engine, etc

funnily /ˈfʌnɪli; -əli/ adv in a strange or unusual way: *She's walking very funnily.*
IDIOM **funnily enough** used for expressing surprise at sth strange that has happened: *Funnily enough, my parents weren't at all cross about it.*

★**funny** /ˈfʌni/ adj (**funnier; funniest**) **1** that makes you smile or laugh: *a funny story* ● *He's an extremely funny person.* ● *That's the funniest thing I've heard in ages!* **2** strange or unusual; difficult to explain or understand: *Oh dear, the engine is making a funny noise.* ● *It's funny that they didn't phone to let us know they couldn't come.* ● *That's funny* – *he was here a moment ago and now he's gone.* ● *Can I sit down for a minute? I feel a bit funny* (= a bit ill). ●► Look at the note at **fun²**.

★**fur** /fɜː/ noun **1** [U] the soft thick hair that covers the bodies of some animals ●► picture on page C1 **2** [C,U] the skin and hair of an animal that is used for making clothes, etc; a piece of clothing that is made from this: *a fur coat*

furious /ˈfjʊəriəs/ adj **1** furious (with sb); furious (at sth) very angry: *He was furious with her for losing the car keys.* ● *He was furious at having to catch the train home.*

●► noun **fury 2** very strong; violent: *A furious row has broken out over the closing of the school.* –**furiously** adv
IDIOM **fast and furious** → **FAST¹**

furnace /ˈfɜːnɪs/ noun [C] a large, very hot, enclosed fire that is used for melting metal, burning rubbish, etc

furnish /ˈfɜːnɪʃ/ verb [T] to put furniture in a room, house, etc: *The room was comfortably furnished.* –**furnished** adj: *She's renting a furnished room in Birmingham.*

furnishings /ˈfɜːnɪʃɪŋz/ noun [pl] the furniture, carpets, curtains, etc in a room, house, etc

★**furniture** /ˈfɜːnɪtʃə/ noun [U] the things that can be moved, for example tables, chairs, beds, etc in a room, house or office: *modern/ antique/second-hand furniture* ● *garden/ office furniture*

> Be careful. 'Furniture' is an uncountable noun: *They only got married recently and they haven't got much furniture.* If we are talking about an individual item we must say 'a piece of furniture': *The only nice piece of furniture in the room was an antique desk.*

furrow /ˈfʌrəʊ/ noun [C] **1** a line in a field that is made for planting seeds in by a farming machine that turns the earth (**plough**) **2** a deep line in the skin on a person's face, especially on the forehead ●► Look at **wrinkle**.

furry /ˈfɜːri/ adj having fur: *a small furry animal*

★**further¹** /ˈfɜːðə/ adj, adv **1** more; to a greater degree: *Are there any further questions?* ● *Please let us know if you require any further information.* ● *I have nothing further to say on the subject.* ● *The museum is closed until further notice* (= until another announcement is made). ● *Can I have time to consider the matter further?* **2** (the comparative of *far*) at or to a greater distance in time or space: *It's not safe to go any further.* ● *I can't remember any further back than 1970.*

> **Further** and **farther** can both be used when you are talking about distance: *Bristol is further/farther from London than Oxford is.* ● *I jumped further/farther than you did.* In other senses only **further** can be used: *We need a further week to finish the job.*
IDIOM **further afield** → **FAR²**

further² /ˈfɜːðə/ verb [T] (*formal*) to help sth to develop or be successful: *to further the cause of peace*

,**further edu'cation** noun [U] (*abbr* **FE**) (*Brit*) education for people who have left school (but not at a university) ●► Look at **higher education**.

furthermore /ˌfɜːðəˈmɔː/ adv also; in addition

★**furthest** /ˈfɜːðɪst/ *superlative* of **FAR**

furtive /ˈfɜːtɪv/ adj secret, acting as though you are trying to hide sth because you feel guilty: *a furtive glance at the letter* –**furtively** adv

fury /ˈfjʊəri/ noun [U] very great anger: *She was speechless with fury.* •➤ adjective **furious**

fuse¹ /fjuːz/ noun [C] **1** a small piece of wire in an electrical system, machine, etc that melts and breaks if there is too much power. This stops the flow of electricity and prevents fire or damage: *A fuse has blown – that's why the house is in darkness.* • *That plug needs a 15 amp fuse.* **2** a piece of rope, string, etc or a device that is used to make a bomb, etc explode at a particular time

fuse² /fjuːz/ verb [I,T] **1** (used about two things) to join together to become one; to make two things do this: *As they heal, the bones will fuse together.* • *The two companies have been fused into one large organization.* **2** to stop working because a fuse¹(1) has melted; to make a piece of electrical equipment do this: *The lights have fused.* • *I've fused the lights.*

fuselage /ˈfjuːzəlɑːʒ/ noun [C] the main part of a plane (not the engines, wings or tail)

fusion /ˈfjuːʒn/ noun [U,sing] the process or the result of joining different things together to form one: *the fusion of two political systems*

fuss¹ /fʌs/ noun [sing,U] a time when people behave in an excited, a nervous or an angry way, especially about sth unimportant: *The waiter didn't make a fuss when I spilt my drink.* • *What's all the fuss about?*

IDIOMS **make/kick up a fuss (about/over sth)** to complain strongly

make a fuss of/over sb/sth to pay a lot of attention to sb/sth: *My grandmother used to make a big fuss of me when she visited.*

fuss² /fʌs/ verb [I] **1** to be worried or excited about small things: *Stop fussing. We're not going to be late.* **2 fuss (over sb/sth)** to pay too much attention to sb/sth: *Stop fussing over all the details.*

IDIOM **not be fussed (about sb/sth)** (*Brit spoken*) to not care very much: *'Where do you want to go for lunch?' 'I'm not fussed.'*

fussy /ˈfʌsi/ adj **1 fussy (about sth)** (used about people) giving too much attention to small details and therefore difficult to please: *He is very fussy about food* (= there are many things which he does not eat). •➤ Look at **particular** and **picky**. **2** having too much detail or decoration: *I don't like that pattern. It's too fussy.*

futile /ˈfjuːtaɪl/ adj (used about an action) having no success; useless: *They made a last futile attempt to make him change his mind.* —**futility** noun [U]

★ **future** /ˈfjuːtʃə/ noun **1 the future** [sing] the time that will come after the present: *Who knows what will happen in the future?* • *in the near/distant future* (= soon/not soon) **2** [C] what will happen to sb/sth in the time after the present: *Our children's futures depend on a good education.* • *The company's future does not look very hopeful.* **3** [U] the possibility of being successful: *I could see no future in this country so I left to work abroad.* **4 the future (tense)** [sing] (*grammar*) the

tense of a verb that expresses what will happen after the present

➤ For more information about the future tense, look at the **Quick Grammar Reference** section at the back of this dictionary.

–**future** adj (only *before* a noun): *She met her future husband when she was still at school.* • *You can keep that book for future reference* (= to look at again later).

IDIOM **in future** from now on: *Please try to be more careful in future.*

fuzzy /ˈfʌzi/ adj not clear: *The photo was a bit fuzzy but I could just make out my mother on it.*

·······································

G

g

·······································

G, g¹ /dʒiː/ noun [C] (*pl* **G's**; **g's**) the seventh letter of the English alphabet: *'Girl' begins with (a) 'G'.*

g² abbr gram(s)

gable /ˈɡeɪbl/ noun [C] the pointed part at the top of an outside wall of a house between two parts of the roof

gadget /ˈɡædʒɪt/ noun [C] (*informal*) a small device, tool or machine that has a particular but usually unimportant purpose: *This car has all the latest gadgets.*

Gaelic /ˈɡeɪlɪk; ˈɡælɪk/ adj, noun [U] (of) the Celtic language and the culture of Ireland or Scotland

gag¹ /ɡæɡ/ noun [C] **1** a piece of cloth, etc that is put in or over sb's mouth in order to stop him/her from talking **2** a joke

gag² /ɡæɡ/ verb [T] (**gagging**; **gagged**) to put a gag in or over sb's mouth

gage (*US*) = **GAUGE¹**

★ **gain¹** /ɡeɪn/ verb **1** [T] to obtain or win sth, especially sth that you need or want: *They managed to gain access to secret information.* • *The country gained its independence ten years ago.* **2** [T] to gradually get more of sth: *The train was gaining speed.* • *to gain weight/confidence* •➤ opposite **lose 3** [I] **gain (sth) (by/from sth/doing sth)** to get an advantage: *I've got nothing to gain by staying in this job.* •➤ opposite **lose**

IDIOM **gain ground** to make progress; to become stronger or more popular

PHRASAL VERBS **gain in sth** to gradually get more of sth: *He's gained in confidence in the past year.*

gain on sb/sth to get closer to sb/sth that you are trying to catch: *I saw the other runners were gaining on me so I increased my pace.*

★ **gain²** /ɡeɪn/ noun [C,U] an increase, improvement or advantage in sth: *We hope to make a gain* (= more money) *when we sell our house.* • *a gain in weight of one kilo*

gait /geɪt/ noun [sing] the way that sb/sth walks

gala /'gɑːlə/ noun [C] a special social or sporting occasion: *a swimming gala*

galaxy /'gæləksi/ noun [C] (pl **galaxies**) a large group of stars and planets in space

gale /geɪl/ noun [C] a very strong wind: *Several trees blew down in the gale.* ••➤ Look at the note at **storm**.

gall abbr gallon(s)

gallant /'gælənt/ adj (*formal*) **1** showing courage in a difficult situation: *gallant men/ soldiers/heroes* ● *He made a gallant attempt to speak French, but nobody could understand him.* ••➤ synonym **brave 2** (used about men) polite to and showing respect for women

gallantry /'gæləntri/ noun [C,U] (pl **gallantries**) **1** courage, especially in battle **2** polite behaviour towards women by men

gallery /'gæləri/ noun [C] (pl **galleries**) **1** a building or room where works of art are shown to the public: *an art gallery* **2** an upstairs area at the back or sides of a large hall or theatre where people can sit

gallon /'gælən/ noun [C] (*abbr* **gall**) a measure of liquid; 4·5 litres ••➤ There are 8 **pints** in a gallon.

➤ An American gallon is the same as 3·8 litres.

gallop /'gæləp/ verb [I] (used about a horse or a rider) to go at the fastest speed ••➤ Look at **canter** and **trot**. –**gallop** noun [sing]

gallows /'gæləʊz/ noun [C] (pl **gallows**) a wooden frame used in the past for killing people by hanging

galore /gə'lɔː/ adv (only after a noun) in large numbers or amounts

gamble[1] /'gæmbl/ verb [I,T] **gamble (sth) (on sth)** to bet money on the result of a card game, horse race, etc: *to gamble on horses* ● *She gambled all her money on the last race.* ••➤ synonym **bet** –**gambler** noun [C]: *He's a compulsive gambler.* –**gambling** noun [U]

PHRASAL VERB **gamble on sth/on doing sth** to act in the hope that sth will happen although it may not: *I wouldn't gamble on the weather staying fine.*

gamble[2] /'gæmbl/ noun [C] something you do that is a risk: *Setting up this business was a bit of a gamble, but it paid off* (= was successful) *in the end.*

★**game**[1] /geɪm/ noun **1** [C] a game (of sth) a form of play or sport with rules; a time when you play it: *Shall we play a game?* ● *Let's have a game of chess.* ● *a game of football/ rugby/tennis* ● *'Monopoly' is a very popular board game.* ● *Tonight's game is between Holland and Italy.* ● *The game ended in a draw.* **2** [C] an activity that you do to have fun: *Some children were playing a game of cowboys and Indians.* **3** [C] how well sb plays a sport: *My new racket has really improved my game.* **4** **games** [pl] an important sports competition: *Where were the last Olympic Games held?* **5** [C] (*informal*) a secret plan or trick: *Stop playing games with me and tell me where you've hidden my bag.* **6** [U] wild animals or birds that are killed for sport or food: *big game* (= lions, tigers, etc)

IDIOM **give the game away** to tell a person sth that you are trying to keep secret: *It was the expression on her face that gave the game away.*

game[2] /geɪm/ adj (used about a person) ready to try sth new, unusual, difficult, etc: *I've never been sailing before but I'm game to try.*

gamekeeper /'geɪmkiːpə/ noun [C] a person who is responsible for private land where people hunt animals and birds

gander /'gændə/ noun [C] a male bird (**goose**)

gang[1] /gæŋ/ noun [C,with sing or pl verb] **1** an organized group of criminals **2** a group of young people who cause trouble, fight other groups, etc: *The woman was robbed by a gang of youths.* ● *gang warfare/violence* **3** (*informal*) a group of friends who meet regularly

gang[2] /gæŋ/ verb

PHRASAL VERB **gang up on sb** (*informal*) to join together with other people in order to act against sb: *She's upset because she says the other kids are ganging up on her.*

gangrene /'gæŋgriːn/ noun [U] the death of a part of the body because the blood supply to it has been stopped as a result of disease or injury –**gangrenous** /'gæŋgrɪnəs/ adj

gangster /'gæŋstə/ noun [C] a member of a group of criminals

gangway /'gæŋweɪ/ noun [C] **1** a passage between rows of seats in a cinema, an aircraft, etc **2** a bridge that people use for getting on or off a ship

gaol, gaoler (*Brit*) = **JAIL**, **JAILER**

★**gap** /gæp/ noun [C] **1** a gap (in/between sth) an empty space in sth or between two things: *The sheep got out through a gap in the fence.* **2** a period of time when sth stops, or between two events: *I returned to teaching after a gap of about five years.* ● *a gap in the conversation* **3** a difference between people or their ideas: *The gap between the rich and the poor is getting wider.* **4** a part of sth that is missing: *In this exercise you have to fill* (*in*) *the gaps in the sentences.* ● *I think our new product should fill a gap in the market.*

IDIOM **bridge a/the gap** ➙ **BRIDGE**[2]

gape /geɪp/ verb [I] **1** gape (at sb/sth) to stare at sb/sth with your mouth open: *We gaped in astonishment when we saw what Amy was wearing.* **2** gape (open) to be or become wide open: *a gaping hole/wound*

★**garage** /'gærɑːʒ; 'gærɪdʒ/ noun [C] **1** a small building where a car, etc is kept: *The house has a double garage* (= with space for two cars). **2** a place where vehicles are repaired and/or petrol is sold: *a garage mechanic* ••➤ Look at **petrol station**.

garbage /'gɑːbɪdʒ/ (*especially US*) = **RUBBISH**

garbage can (*US*) = **DUSTBIN**

garbled /'gɑːbld/ adj (used about a message, story, etc) difficult to understand because it is not clear

garden equipment

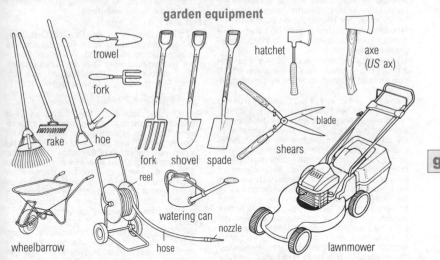

trowel

fork

rake

hoe

reel

fork shovel spade

wheelbarrow

hose

watering can

nozzle

hatchet

axe
(US ax)

blade

shears

lawnmower

★**garden**¹ /'gɑːdn/ noun [C] **1** (*US* **yard**) a piece of land next to a house where flowers and vegetables can be grown, usually with a piece of grass (**lawn**): *the back/front garden* ● *garden flowers* ● *garden chairs* (= for using in the garden) •➤ picture on page C7 •➤ Look at the note at **yard**. **2 gardens** [pl] a public park

garden² /'gɑːdn/ verb [I] to work in a garden: *She's been gardening all afternoon.*

'**garden centre** noun [C] a place where plants, seeds, garden equipment, etc are sold

gardener /'gɑːdnə/ noun [C] a person who works in a garden as a job or for pleasure

gardening /'gɑːdnɪŋ/ noun [U] looking after a garden: *I'm going to do some gardening this afternoon.* ● *gardening tools/gloves*

'**garden party** noun [C] a formal social event that takes place outside usually in a large garden in summer

gargle /'gɑːgl/ verb [I] to wash your throat with a liquid (which you do not swallow)

garish /'geərɪʃ/ adj very bright or decorated and therefore unpleasant •➤ synonym **gaudy**

garlic /'gɑːlɪk/ noun [U] a plant with a strong taste and smell that looks like a small onion and is used in cooking: *Chop two cloves of garlic and fry in oil.* •➤ picture on page C3

garment /'gɑːmənt/ noun [C] (*formal*) one piece of clothing. •➤ Look at **clothes**.

garnish /'gɑːnɪʃ/ verb [T] to decorate a dish of food with a small amount of another food: *Garnish the soup with a little parsley before serving.* –garnish noun [U,C]

garrison /'gærɪsn/ noun [C] a group of soldiers who are living in and guarding a town or building

★**gas**¹ /gæs/ noun (*pl* **gases**: *US also* **gasses**) **1** [C,U] a substance like air that is not a solid or a liquid: *Hydrogen and oxygen are gases.*

2 [U] a particular type of gas or mixture of gases that is used for heating or cooking: *a gas cooker* **3** [U] (*US*) = **PETROL**

gas² /gæs/ verb [T] (**gassing; gassed**) to poison or kill sb with gas

'**gas chamber** noun [C] a room that can be filled with poisonous gas in order to kill animals or people

gash /gæʃ/ noun [C] a long deep cut or wound: *He had a nasty gash in his arm.* –gash verb [T]

'**gas mask** noun [C] an piece of equipment that is worn over the face to protect against poisonous gas

'**gas meter** noun [C] an instrument that measures the amount of gas that you use in your home

gasoline /'gæsəliːn/ (*also* **gas**) (*US*) = **PETROL**

gasp /gɑːsp/ verb **1** [I] gasp (at sth) to take a sudden loud breath with your mouth open, usually because you are surprised or in pain: *She gasped in surprise as she read the letter.* **2** [I] to have difficulty breathing: *I pulled the boy out of the pool and he lay there gasping for breath.* –gasp noun [C]: *to give a gasp of surprise/pain/horror*

'**gas station** (*US*) = **PETROL STATION**

gastronomic /ˌgæstrə'nɒmɪk/ adj connected with good food

★**gate** /geɪt/ noun [C] **1** the part of a fence, wall, etc like a door that can be opened to let people or vehicles through: *Please keep the garden gate closed.* •➤ picture on page C7 **2** (also **gateway**) the space in a wall, fence, etc where the gate is: *Drive through the gates and you'll find the car park on the right.* **3** the place at an airport where you get on or off a plane: *Swissair Flight 139 to Geneva is now boarding at gate 16.*

gateau /'gætəʊ/ noun [C] (*pl* **gateaux**) a large cake that is usually decorated with cream, fruit, etc ••➤ picture on page C4

gatecrash /'geɪtkræʃ/ verb [I,T] to go to a private party without being invited –**gatecrasher** noun [C]

gateway /'geɪtweɪ/ noun [C] **1** = **GATE**(2) **2** [sing] **the gateway to sth** the place which you must go through in order to get to somewhere else

★**gather** /'gæðə/ verb **1** [I,T] gather (round) (sb/sth); gather sb/sth (round) (sb/sth) (used about people) to come or be brought together in a group: *A crowd soon gathered at the scene of the accident.* • *We all gathered round and listened to what the guide was saying.* **2** [T] gather sth (together/up) to bring many things together: *He gathered up all his papers and put them away.* • *They have gathered together a lot of information on the subject.* **3** [T] (*formal*) to pick wild flowers, fruit, etc from a wide area: *to gather mushrooms* **4** [T] to understand or find out sth (from sb/sth): *I gather from your letter that you have several years' experience of this kind of work.* • *'She's been very ill recently.' 'So I gather.'* **5** [I,T] to gradually become greater; to increase: *I gathered speed as I cycled down the hill.*

gathering /'gæðərɪŋ/ noun [C] a time when people come together; a meeting: *a family gathering*

gaudy /'gɔːdi/ adj very bright or decorated and therefore unpleasant ••➤ synonym **garish**

gauge¹ (*US also* **gage**) /geɪdʒ/ noun [C] **1** an instrument for measuring the amount of sth: *a fuel/temperature/pressure gauge* **2** (*technical*) a measurement of the width of sth or of the distance between two things: *a narrow-gauge railway* **3** a gauge (of sth) a fact that you can use to judge a situation, sb's feelings, etc

gauge² /geɪdʒ/ verb [T] **1** to make a judgement or to calculate sth by guessing: *It was difficult to gauge the mood of the audience.* **2** to measure sth accurately using a special instrument

gaunt /gɔːnt/ adj (used about a person) very thin because of hunger, illness, etc

gauze /gɔːz/ noun [U] a thin material like a net, that is used for covering an area of skin that you have hurt or cut

gave *past tense of* **GIVE¹**

gawp /gɔːp/ verb [I] (*informal*) gawp (at sb/sth) to look or stare in a stupid way: *Lots of drivers slowed down to gawp at the accident.*

gay¹ /geɪ/ adj **1** sexually attracted to people of the same sex; homosexual: *the gay community of New York* • *a gay bar/club* (= for gay people) ••➤ noun **gayness** ••➤ Look at **lesbian**. **2** (*old-fashioned*) happy and full of fun ••➤ noun **gaiety**

gay² /geɪ/ noun [C] a person, especially a man, who is sexually attracted to people of the same sex; a homosexual ••➤ Look at **lesbian**.

gaze /geɪz/ verb [I] to look steadily for a long time: *She sat at the window gazing dreamily into space.* –**gaze** noun [sing]

GB abbr Great Britain

GCSE /ˌdʒiː siː es 'iː/ abbr General Certificate of Secondary Education; an examination that schoolchildren in England, Wales and Northern Ireland take when they are about sixteen. They often take GCSEs in five or more subjects. For Scottish examinations, look at SCE.

➤ Compare A level.

★**gear¹** /gɪə/ noun **1** [C] the machinery in a vehicle that turns engine power into a movement forwards or backwards: *Most cars have four or five forward gears and a reverse.* **2** [U] a particular position of the gears in a vehicle: *first/second/top/reverse gear* • *to change gear* **3** [U] equipment or clothing that you need for a particular activity, etc: *camping/fishing/sports gear* **4** [sing] an instrument or part of a machine that is used for a particular purpose: *the landing gear of an aeroplane*

gear² /gɪə/ verb

PHRASAL VERBS **gear sth to/towards sb/sth** (often passive) to make sth suitable for a particular purpose or person: *There is a special course geared towards the older learner.* **gear up (for sb/sth); gear sb/sth up (for sb/sth)** to get ready or to make sb/sth ready

gearbox /'gɪəbɒks/ noun [C] the metal case that contains the gears¹(1) of a car, etc

'**gear lever** (*US* '**gearshift**) noun [C] a stick that is used for changing gear¹(2) in a car, etc ••➤ picture on page S9

gee /dʒiː/ interj (*US*) used for expressing surprise, pleasure, etc

geese *plural of* **GOOSE**

gel /dʒel/ noun [C,U] (often in compounds) a thick substance that is between a liquid and a solid: *hair gel* • *shower gel*

gelignite /'dʒelɪgnaɪt/ noun [U] a substance that is used for making explosions

gem /dʒem/ noun [C] **1** a jewel or precious stone **2** a person or thing that is especially good

Gemini /'dʒemɪnaɪ/ noun [C,U] the third sign of the zodiac, the Twins

Gen abbr General; an officer in the British and US armies

gender /'dʒendə/ noun [C,U] **1** (*formal*) the fact of being male or female ••➤ synonym **sex** **2** (*grammar*) (in some languages) the division of nouns, pronouns, etc into different classes (**masculine**, **feminine** and **neuter**); one of these three types

gene /dʒiːn/ noun [C] a unit of information inside a cell which controls what a living thing will be like. Genes are passed from parents to children. ••➤ Look at **genetics**.

★**general¹** /'dʒenrəl/ adj **1** affecting all or most people, places, things, etc: *Fridges were once a luxury, but now they are in general use.* • *That is a matter of general interest.* • *the general public* (= most ordinary people) **2** (only *before* a noun) referring to or describing the main part of sth, not the details: *Your general health is very good.* ● *The introduction gives you a general idea of what the book is about.* ● *As a general rule, the most common verbs in English tend to be irregular.* **3** not limited to one subject or area of study; not specialized: *Children need a good general education.* ● *The quiz tests your general knowledge.* ● *a general hospital* **4** (often in compounds) with responsibility for the whole of an organization: *a general manager* IDIOM **in general 1** in most cases; usually: *In general, standards of hygiene are good.* **2** as a whole: *I'm interested in Spanish history in general, and the civil war in particular.*

general² /'dʒenrəl/ **noun** [C] (*abbr* **Gen**) an army officer in a very high position

general e'lection noun [C] an election in which all the people of a country vote to choose a government ●◆ Look at **by-election**.

generalization (also **-isation**) /ˌdʒenrəlaɪ'zeɪʃn/ **noun** [C,U] a general statement that is based on only a few facts or examples; the act of making such a statement: *You can't make sweeping generalizations about French people if you've only been there for a day!*

generalize (also **-ise**) /'dʒenrəlaɪz/ **verb** [I] generalize (about sth) to form an opinion or make a statement using only a small amount of information instead of looking at the details: *You can't generalize about English food from only two meals.*

★**generally** /'dʒenrəli/ **adv 1** by or to most people: *He is generally considered to be a good doctor.* **2** usually: *She generally cycles to work.* **3** without discussing the details of sth: *Generally speaking, houses in America are bigger than houses in this country.*

generate /'dʒenəreɪt/ **verb** [T] to produce or create sth: *to generate heat/power/electricity*

★**generation** /ˌdʒenə'reɪʃn/ **noun 1** [C] all the people in a family, group or country who were born at about the same time: *We should look after the planet for future generations.* ● *This photograph shows three generations of my family* (= children, parents and grandparents).

> **Generation** is used in the singular with either a singular or plural verb: *The younger generation only seem/seems to be interested in money.*

2 [C] the average time that children take to grow up and have children of their own, usually considered to be about 25-30 years: *A generation ago foreign travel was still only possible for a few people.* **3** [U] the production of sth, especially heat, power, etc

the ˌgene'ration gap noun [sing] the difference in behaviour, and the lack of understanding, between young people and older people

generator /'dʒenəreɪtə/ **noun** [C] a machine that produces electricity

generosity /ˌdʒenə'rɒsəti/ **noun** [U] the quality of being generous

★**generous** /'dʒenərəs/ **adj 1** happy to give more money, help, etc than is usual or expected: *It was very generous of your parents to lend us all that money.* **2** larger than usual: *a generous helping of pasta* –**generously adv**: *People gave very generously to our appeal for the homeless.*

genetic /dʒə'netɪk/ **adj** connected with the units in the cells of living things (**genes**) that control what a person or plant is like, or with the study of genes (**genetics**): *The disease is caused by a genetic defect.* –**genetically** /-kli/ **adv**

geˌneticallyˌ'modified adj (*abbr* **GM**) (used about food, plants, etc) that has been grown from cells whose units of information (**genes**) have been changed artificially

geˌnetic engiˈneering noun [U] the science of changing the way a human, animal or plant develops by changing the information in its genes

genetics /dʒə'netɪks/ **noun** [U] the scientific study of the way that the development of living things is controlled by qualities that have been passed on from parents to children ●◆ Look at **gene**.

genial /'dʒiːniəl/ **adj** (used about a person) pleasant and friendly

genitals /'dʒenɪtlz/ (also **genitalia** /ˌdʒenɪ'teɪliə/) **noun** [pl] (*formal*) the parts of a person's sex organs that are outside the body –**genital** /'dʒenɪtl/ **adj**

genius /'dʒiːniəs/ **noun 1** [U] very great and unusual ability: *Her idea was a stroke of genius.* **2** [C] a person who has very great and unusual ability, especially in a particular subject: *Einstein was a mathematical genius.* ●◆ Look at **prodigy**. **3** [sing] a genius for (doing) sth a very good natural skill or ability

genocide /'dʒenəsaɪd/ **noun** [U] the murder of all the people of a particular race, religion, etc

gent /dʒent/ (*informal*) = **GENTLEMAN**

genteel /dʒen'tiːl/ **adj** behaving in a very polite and quiet way, often in order to make people think that you are from a high social class –**gentility** /dʒen'tɪləti/ **noun** [U]

★**gentle** /'dʒentl/ **adj 1** (used about people) kind and calm; touching or treating people or things in a careful way so that they are not hurt: *'I'll try and be as gentle as I can,' said the dentist.* **2** not strong, violent or extreme: *gentle exercise* ● *a gentle slope/curve* –**gentleness** /'dʒentlnəs/ **noun** [U] –**gently** /'dʒentli/ **adv**

gentleman /'dʒentlmən/ **noun** [C] (*pl* **-men** /-mən/) **1** a man who is polite and who behaves well towards other people: *Everyone likes and respects Joe because he's a real gentleman.* **2** (*formal*) used when speaking to or about a man or men in a polite way: *Ladies and gentlemen* (= at the beginning of a speech) ● *Mrs Flinn, there is a gentleman here to see you.* **3** (*old-fashioned*) a rich man with a high social position

g

the 'Gents noun [sing] (*Brit informal*) a public toilet for men ·•➤ Look at the note at **toilet**.

★genuine /'dʒenjuɪn/ adj **1** real; true: *He thought that he had bought a genuine Rolex watch but it was a cheap fake.* ·•➤ Look at **imitation**. **2** sincere and honest; that can be trusted –**genuinely** adv

geographer /dʒi'ɒɡrəfə/ noun [C] an expert in geography or a student of geography

★geography /dʒi'ɒɡrəfi/ noun [U] **1** the study of the world's surface, physical qualities, climate, population, products, etc: *human/physical/economic geography* **2** the physical arrangement of a place: *We're studying the geography of Asia.* –**geographical** /ˌdʒiːə'ɡræfɪkl/ adj –**geographically** /-kli/ adv

geologist /dʒi'ɒlədʒɪst/ noun [C] an expert in geology or a student of geology

geology /dʒi'ɒlədʒi/ noun [U] the study of rocks and of the way they are formed –**geological** /ˌdʒiːə'lɒdʒɪkl/ adj

geometric /ˌdʒiːə'metrɪk/ (also **geometrical** /-ɪkl/) adj **1** of geometry **2** consisting of regular shapes and lines: *a geometric design/pattern* –**geometrically** /-kli/ adv

geometry /dʒi'ɒmətri/ noun [U] the study in mathematics of lines, shapes, curves, etc

geothermal /ˌdʒiə'θɜːml/ adj connected with the natural heat of rock deep in the ground: *geothermal energy*

geriatrics /ˌdʒeri'ætrɪks/ noun [U] the medical care of old people –**geriatric** adj

germ /dʒɜːm/ noun **1** [C] a very small living thing that causes disease ·•➤ Look at **bacteria** and **virus**. **2** [sing] **the germ of sth** the beginning of sth that may develop: *the germ of an idea*

German measles /ˌdʒɜːmən 'miːzlz/ (also **rubella**) noun [U] a mild disease that causes red spots all over the body. It may damage a baby if the mother catches it when she is pregnant.

germinate /'dʒɜːmɪneɪt/ verb [I,T] (used about a seed) to start growing; to cause a seed to do this –**germination** /ˌdʒɜːmɪ'neɪʃn/ noun [U]

gerund /'dʒerənd/ noun [C] (*grammar*) a noun, ending in -ing, that has been made from a verb: *In the sentence 'His hobby is collecting stamps', 'collecting' is a gerund.*

gesticulate /dʒe'stɪkjəleɪt/ verb [I] to make movements with your hands and arms in order to express sth

gesture¹ /'dʒestʃə/ noun [C] **1** a movement of the hand, head, etc that expresses sth: *I saw the boy **make a rude gesture** at the policeman before running off.* **2** something that you do that shows other people what you think or feel

gesture² /'dʒestʃə/ verb [I,T] to point at sth, to make a sign to sb: *She asked them to leave and gestured towards the door.*

★get /ɡet/ verb (*pres part* **getting**; *pt* **got** /ɡɒt/; *pp* **got**: *US* **gotten** /'ɡɒtn/) **1** [T] (no passive) to receive, obtain or buy sth: *I got a letter from my sister.* ● *Did you get a present for your mother?* ● *Did you get your mother a present?* ● *She got a job in a travel agency.* ● *Louise got 75% in the maths exam.* ● *I'll come if I can get time off work.* ● *How much did you get for your old car* (= when you sold it)*?* ● *to get a shock/surprise* **2** [T] **have/has got sth** to have sth: *I've got a lot to do today.* ● *Lee's got blond hair.* ● *Have you got a spare pen?* **3** [T] (no passive) to go to a place and bring sth back; fetch: **Go and get** *me a pen, please.* ● *Sam's gone to get his mother from the station.* **4** [I] to become; to reach a particular state or condition; to make sb/sth be in a particular state or condition: *It's getting dark.* ● *to get angry/bored/hungry/fat* ● *I can't **get used to** my new bed.* ● *to get dressed* ● *When did you **get married**?* ● *to get pregnant* ● *Just give me five minutes to get ready.* ● *He's always **getting into trouble** with the police.* ● *She's shy, but she's great fun once you **get to know** her.* **5** [I] to arrive at or reach a place: *We should get to London at about ten.* ● *Can you tell me how to get to the hospital?* ● *What time do you usually get home?* ● *I got half way up the mountain then gave up.* ● *How far have you got with your book?* ·•➤ Look at **get in**, **on**, etc. **6** [I,T] to move or go somewhere; to move or put sth somewhere: *I can't swim so I couldn't get across the river.* ● *My grandmother's 92 and she doesn't get out of the house much.* ● *I couldn't get the piano upstairs.* ● *My foot was swollen and I couldn't get my shoe off.* **7** [I] used instead of 'be' in the passive: *She got bitten by a dog.* ● *Don't leave your wallet on the table or it'll get stolen.* **8** [T] **get sth done**, **mended**, **etc** to cause sth to be done, mended, etc: *Let's get this work done, then we can go out.* ● *I'm going to **get my hair cut**.* **9** [T] **get sb/sth to do sth** to make or persuade sb/sth to do sth: *I got him to agree to the plan.* ● *I can't get the television to work.* **10** [T] to catch or have an illness, pain, etc: *I think I'm getting a cold.* ● *He gets really bad headaches.* **11** [T] to use a form of transport: *Shall we walk or get the bus?* **12** [I] to hit, hold or catch sb/sth: *He got me by the throat and threatened to kill me.* ● *A boy threw a stone at me but he didn't get me.* **13** [T] to hear or understand sth: *I'm sorry, I didn't get that. Could you repeat it?* ● *Did you get that joke that Karen told?* **14** [T] **get (sb) sth; get sth (for sb)** to prepare food: *Can I get you anything to eat?* ● *Joe's in the kitchen getting breakfast for everyone.* **15** [I] **get to do sth** to have the chance to do sth *Did you get to try the new computer?* **16** [I] (used with verbs in the -ing form) to start doing sth: *We don't have much time so we'd better get working.* ● *I got talking to a woman on the bus.* ● *We'd better get going if we don't want to be late.*

IDIOM **get somewhere/nowhere (with sb/sth)** to make/not make progress: *I'm getting nowhere with my research.*

> For other idioms containing **get**, look at the noun and adjective entries, for example for **get rid of** look at **rid**.

PHRASAL VERBS **get about/around** to move or travel from place to place: *My grandmother needs a stick to get around these days.*

get about/around/round (used about news, a story, etc) to become known by many people: *The rumour got around that Freddie wore a wig.*

get sth across (to sb) to succeed in making people understand sth: *The party failed to get its policies across to the voters.*

get ahead to progress and be successful in sth, especially a career

get along 1 (*spoken*) (usually used in the continuous tenses) to leave a place: *I'd love to stay, but I should be getting along now.* **2** → GET ON

get around 1 → GET ABOUT/AROUND **2** → GET ABOUT/AROUND/ROUND

get around sb → GET ROUND/AROUND SB

get around sth → GET ROUND/AROUND STH

get around to sth/doing sth → GET ROUND/AROUND TO STH/DOING STH

get at sb to criticize sb a lot: *The teacher's always getting at me about my spelling.*

get at sb/sth to be able to reach sth; to have sth available for immediate use: *The files are locked away and I can't get at them.*

get at sth (only used in the continuous tenses) to try to say sth without saying it in a direct way; to suggest: *I'm not quite sure what you're getting at – am I doing something wrong?*

get away (from...) to succeed in leaving or escaping from sb or a place: *He kept talking to me and I couldn't get away from him.* ● *The thieves got away in a stolen car.*

get away with sth/doing sth to do sth bad and not be punished for it: *He lied but he got away with it.*

get away with murder → MURDER

get back to return to the place where you live or work: *When did you get back from Italy?*

get sth back to be given sth that you had lost or lent: *Can I borrow this book? You'll get it back next week, I promise.*

get back to sb to speak to, write to or telephone sb later, especially in order to give an answer: *I'll get back to you on prices when I've got some more information.*

get back to sth to return to doing sth or talking about sth: *I woke up early and couldn't get back to sleep.* ● *Let's get back to the point you raised earlier.*

get behind (with sth) to fail to do, pay sth, etc on time, and so have more to do, pay, etc the next time: *to get behind with your work/rent*

get by (on/in/with sth) to manage to live or do sth with difficulty: *It's very hard to get by on such a low income.* ● *My Italian is good and I can get by in Spanish.*

get sb down to make sb unhappy

get down to sth/doing sth to start working on sth: *We'd better stop chatting and get down to work.* ● *I must get down to answering these letters.*

get in to reach a place: *What time does your train get in?*

get in; get into sth 1 to climb into a car: *We all got in and Tim drove off.* **2** to be elected to a political position

get sb in to call sb to your house to do a job: *We had to get a plumber in to fix the pipes.*

get sth in 1 to collect or bring sth inside; to buy a supply of sth: *It's going to rain – I'd better get the washing in from outside.* **2** to manage to find an opportunity to say or do sth: *He talked all the time and I couldn't get a word in.*

get in on sth to become involved in an activity

get into sb (*informal*) (used about a feeling or attitude) to start affecting sb strongly, causing him/her to behave in an unusual way: *I wonder what's got into him – he isn't usually unfriendly.*

get into sth 1 to put on a piece of clothing with difficulty: *I've put on so much weight I can't get into my trousers.* **2** to start a particular activity; to become involved in sth: *How did you first get into the music business?* ● *She has got into the habit of turning up late.* ● *We got into an argument about politics.* **3** to become more interested in or familiar with sth: *I've been getting into yoga recently.* ● *It's taking me a while to get into my new job.*

get off (sb/sth) used especially to tell sb to stop touching you/sb/sth: *Get off (me) or I'll call the police!* ● *Get off that money, it's mine!*

get off (sth) 1 to leave a bus, train, etc; to climb down from a bicycle, horse, etc **2** to leave work with permission at a particular time: *I might be able to get off early today.*

get off (with sth) to be lucky to receive no serious injuries or punishment: *to get off with just a warning*

get on 1 to progress or become successful in life, in a career, etc **2** to be getting old: *He's getting on – he's over 70, I'm sure.* **3** to be getting late: *Time's getting on – we don't want to be late.*

> Senses **2** and **3** are only used in the continuous tenses.

get on/along to have a particular amount of success: *How are you getting on in your course?* ● *'How did you get on at your interview?' 'I got the job!'*

get on/onto sth to climb onto a bus, train, bicycle, horse, etc: *I got on just as the train was about to leave.*

get on for (only used in the continuous tenses) to be getting near to a certain time or age: *I'm not sure how old he is but he must be getting on for 50.*

get on to sb (about sth) to speak or write to sb about a particular matter

get on/along with sb; get on/along (together) to have a friendly relationship with sb: *Do you get on well with your colleagues?* ● *We're not close friends but we get on together quite well.*

ð **then** | s **so** | z **zoo** | ʃ **she** | ʒ **vision** | h **how** | m **man** | n **no** | ŋ **sing** | l **leg** | r **red** | j **yes** | w **wet**

get on/along with sth to make progress with sth that you are doing: *How are you getting on with that essay?*

get on with sth to continue doing sth, especially after an interruption: *Stop talking and get on with your work!*

get out (used about a piece of information) to become known, after being secret until now

get sth out (of sth) to take sth from its container: *I got my keys out of my bag.*

get out of sth/doing sth to avoid a duty or doing sth that you have said you will do

get sth out of sb to persuade or force sb to give you sth: *His parents finally got the truth out of him.*

get sth out of sb/sth to gain sth from sb/sth: *I get a lot of pleasure out of music.*

get over sth 1 to deal with a problem successfully: *We'll have to get over the problem of finding somewhere to live first.* **2** to feel normal again after being ill or having an unpleasant experience: *He still hasn't got over his wife's death.*

get sth over with (*informal*) to do and complete sth unpleasant that has to be done: *I'll be glad to get my visit to the dentist's over with.*

get round → **GET ABOUT/AROUND/ROUND**

get round/around sb (*informal*) to persuade sb to do sth or agree with sth: *My father says he won't lend me the money but I think I can get round him.*

get round/around sth to find a way of avoiding or dealing with a problem

get round/around to sth/doing sth to find the time to do sth, after a delay: *I've been meaning to reply to that letter for ages but I haven't got round to it yet.*

get through sth to use or complete a certain amount or number of sth: *I got through a lot of money at the weekend.* ● *I got through an enormous amount of work today.*

get (sb) through (sth) to manage to complete sth difficult or unpleasant; to help sb to do this: *She got through her final exams easily.*

get through (to sb) 1 to succeed in making sb understand sth: *They couldn't get through to him that he was completely wrong.* **2** to succeed in speaking to sb on the telephone: *I couldn't get through to them because their phone was engaged all day.*

get to sb (*informal*) to affect sb in a bad way: *Public criticism is beginning to get to the team manager.*

get sb/sth together to collect people or things in one place: *I'll just get my things together and then we'll go.*

get together (with sb) to meet socially or in order to discuss or do sth: *Let's get together and talk about it.*

get up to stand up: *He got up to let an elderly woman sit down.*

get (sb) up to get out of bed or make sb get out of bed: *What time do you have to get up in the morning?* ● *Could you get me up at 6 tomorrow?*

get up to sth 1 to reach a particular point or stage in sth: *We've got up to the last section of*

our grammar book. **2** to be busy with sth, especially sth secret or bad: *I wonder what the children are getting up to?*

getaway /'getəweɪ/ **noun** [C] an escape (after a crime): *to **make a getaway*** ● *a getaway car/driver*

'get-together noun [C] (*informal*) an informal social meeting or party: *We're going to have a get-together on Saturday evening.*

ghastly /'gɑːstli/ **adj** extremely unpleasant or bad: *a ghastly accident*

ghetto /'getəʊ/ **noun** [C] (*pl* **ghettoes**) a part of a town where many people of the same race, religion, etc live in poor conditions

★**ghost** /gəʊst/ **noun** [C] the spirit of a dead person that is seen or heard by sb who is still living: *I don't believe in ghosts.* ● *a ghost story* ⇢ Look at **spectre**.

ghostly /'gəʊstli/ **adj** looking or sounding like a ghost; full of ghosts: *ghostly noises*

'ghost town noun [C] a town whose inhabitants have all left

ghostwriter /'gəʊstraɪtə/ **noun** [C] a person who writes a book, etc for a famous person (whose name appears as the author)

★**giant** /'dʒaɪənt/ **noun** [C] **1** an extremely large, strong person **2** something that is very large: *the multinational oil giants* (= very large companies) –**giant adj**: *a giant new shopping centre*

gibberish /'dʒɪbərɪʃ/ **noun** [U] words that have no meaning or that are impossible to understand: *I was so nervous in my interview I just spoke gibberish.*

giddy /'gɪdi/ **adj** having the feeling that everything is going round and that you are going to fall; dizzy: *I feel giddy. I must sit down.*

★**gift** /gɪft/ **noun** [C] **1** something that you give to sb; a present: *This watch was a gift from my mother.* ● *This week's magazine contains a **free gift** of some make-up.* ● *The company **made a gift of** a computer to a local school.* ⇢ Look at the note at **present**. **2 a gift (for sth/doing sth)** natural ability

gifted /'gɪftɪd/ **adj** having natural ability or great intelligence

gig /gɪg/ **noun** [C] (*informal*) an event where a musician or band is paid to perform: *The band are doing gigs all around the country.*

gigantic /dʒaɪˈgæntɪk/ **adj** extremely big

giggle /'gɪgl/ **verb** [I] to laugh in a silly way that you can't control, because you are amused or nervous –**giggle noun** [C]: *I've got the giggles* (= I can't stop laughing).

gill /gɪl/ **noun** [C, usually pl] one of the parts on the side of a fish's head that it breathes through ⇢ picture on page C1

gilt /gɪlt/ **noun** [U] a thin covering of gold

gimmick /'gɪmɪk/ **noun** [C] an idea for attracting customers or persuading people to buy sth: *New magazines often use free gifts or other gimmicks to get people to buy them.*

gin /dʒɪn/ **noun** [C,U] a strong, colourless alcoholic drink

ginger /'dʒɪndʒə/ **noun** [U], **adj 1** a root that

tastes hot and is used in cooking: *ground ginger* • *ginger biscuits* **2** (of) a light brownish-orange colour: *ginger hair*

ˌginger 'ale *noun* [U] a drink that does not contain alcohol and is flavoured with a spice (ginger)

➤ **Ginger beer** is similar but has a little alcohol in it.

gingerly /ˈdʒɪndʒəli/ *adv* very slowly and carefully so as not to cause harm, make a noise, etc: *I removed the bandage very gingerly and looked at the cut.*

gipsy = GYPSY

giraffe /dʒəˈrɑːf/ *noun* [C] (*pl* **giraffe** or **giraffes**) a large African animal with a very long neck and legs and big dark spots on its skin

girder /ˈɡɜːdə/ *noun* [C] a long, heavy piece of iron or steel that is used in the building of bridges, large buildings, etc

★**girl** /ɡɜːl/ *noun* [C] **1** a female child: *Is the baby a boy or a girl?* • *There are more boys than girls in the class.* **2** a daughter: *They have two boys and a girl.* **3** a young woman: *He was eighteen before he became interested in girls.* • *The girl at the cash desk was very helpful.* **4 girls** [pl] a woman's female friends of any age: *a night out with the girls*

★**girlfriend** /ˈɡɜːlfrend/ *noun* [C] **1** a girl or woman with whom sb has a romantic and/or sexual relationship: *Have you got a girlfriend?* **2** (*especially US*) a girl or woman's female friend

Girl 'Guide (*old-fashioned*) = GUIDE¹(5)

girlhood /ˈɡɜːlhʊd/ *noun* [U] the time when sb is a girl (1)

girlish /ˈɡɜːlɪʃ/ *adj* looking, sounding or behaving like a girl: *a girlish figure/giggle*

giro /ˈdʒaɪrəʊ/ *noun* (*pl* **giros**) (*Brit*) **1** [U] a system for moving money from one bank, etc to another **2** [C] a cheque that the government pays to people who are unemployed or cannot work

gist /dʒɪst/ *noun* **the gist (of sth)** [sing] the general meaning of sth rather than all the details: *I know a little Spanish so I was able to get the gist of what he said.*

★**give¹** /ɡɪv/ *verb* (*pt* **gave** /ɡeɪv/; *pp* **given** /ˈɡɪvn/) **1** [T] **give sb sth; give sth to sb** to let sb have sth, especially sth that he/she wants or needs: *I gave Jackie a book for her birthday.* • *Give me that book a minute – I just want to check something.* • *I gave my bag to my friend to look after.* • *I'll give you my telephone number.* • *The doctor gave me this cream for my skin.* • *He was thirsty so I gave him a drink.* • *Just phone and I'll give you all the help you need.* **2** [T] **give sb sth; give sth to sb** to make sb have sth, especially sth he/she does not want: *Mr Johns gives us too much homework.* • *Playing chess gives me a headache.* **3** [T] to make sb have a particular feeling, idea, etc: *Swimming always gives me a good appetite.* • *to give sb a surprise/shock/ fright* • *What gives you the idea that he was lying?* **4** [T] **give (sb) sth; give sth to sb** to

let sb have your opinion, decision, judgement, etc: *Can you give me some advice?* • *My boss has given me permission to leave early.* • *The judge gave him five years in prison.* **5** [T] **give sb sth; give sth to sb** to speak to people in a formal situation: *to give a speech/ talk/lecture* • *The officer was called to give evidence in court.* • *Sarah's going to give me a cooking lesson.* **6** [T] **give (sb) sth for sth; give (sb) sth (to do sth)** to pay in order to have sth: *How much did you give him for fixing the car?* • (*figurative*) *I'd give anything* (= I would love) *to be able to sing like that.* **7** [T] to spend time dealing with sb/sth: *We need to give some thought to this matter urgently.* **8** [T] **give (sb/sth) sth** to do sth to sb/sth; to make a particular sound or movement: *to give sb a kiss/push/hug/bite* • *to give sth a clean/wash/polish* • *Give me a call when you get home.* • *She opened the door and gave a shout of horror.* **9** [T] to perform or organize sth for people: *The company gave a party to celebrate its 50th anniversary.* **10** [I] to bend or stretch under pressure: *The branch began to give under my weight.*

IDIOMS **not care/give a damn (about sb/sth)**
➜ DAMN³

give or take more or less the number mentioned: *It took us two hours to get here, give or take five minutes.*

➤ For other idioms containing **give**, look at the entries for the nouns, adjectives, etc, for example **give way** is at **way**.

PHRASAL VERBS **give sth away** to give sth to sb without wanting money in return: *When she got older she gave all her toys away.* • *We are giving away a free CD with this month's issue.*
give sth/sb away to show or tell the truth about sth/sb which was secret: *He smiled politely and didn't give away his real feelings.*
give (sth) back to return sth to the person that you took or borrowed it from: *I lent him some books months ago and he still hasn't given them back to me.*
give sth in to give sth to the person who is collecting it: *I've got to give this essay in to my teacher by Friday.*
give in (to sb/sth) to stop fighting against sb/sth; to accept that you have been defeated
give sth off to send sth (for example smoke, a smell, heat, etc) out into the air: *Cars give off poisonous fumes.*
give out (used about a machine, etc) to stop working: *His heart gave out and he died.*
give sth out to give one of sth to each person: *Could you give out these books to the class, please?*
give up to stop trying to do sth; to accept that you cannot do sth: *They gave up once the other team had scored their third goal.* • *I give up. What's the answer?*
give sb up; give up on sb to stop expecting sb to arrive, succeed, improve, etc: *When he was four hours late, I gave him up.* • *Her work was so poor that all her teachers gave up on her.*
give sth up; give up doing sth to stop doing

g

or having sth that you did or had regularly before: *I've tried many times to give up smoking.* ● *Don't give up hope. Things are bound to improve.*

give yourself/sb up (to sb) to go to the police when they are trying to catch you; to tell the police where sb is

give sth up (to sb) to give sth to sb who needs or asks for it: *He gave up his seat on the bus to an elderly woman.*

give² /gɪv/ **noun** [U] the quality of being able to bend or stretch a little

◼️IDIOM **give and take** a situation in which two people, groups, etc, respect each others' rights and needs: *There has to be some give and take for a marriage to succeed.*

giveaway /'gɪvəweɪ/ **noun** [C] (*informal*) **1** a thing that is included free when you buy sth: *There's usually some giveaway with that magazine.* **2** something that makes you guess the truth about sb/sth: *She said she didn't know about the money but her face was a* **dead giveaway**.

given¹ /'gɪvn/ **adj** (only *before* a noun) already stated or decided: *At any given time, up to 200 people are using the library.*

given² /'gɪvn/ **prep** considering sth: *Given that you had very little help, I think you did very well.*

'**given name** (*especially US*) = **FIRST NAME**
••➤ Look at the note at **name**.

glacier /'glæsiə/ **noun** [C] a mass of ice that moves slowly down a valley

★**glad** /glæd/ **adj 1** (not before a noun) glad (about sth); glad to do sth/that... happy; pleased: *Are you glad about your new job?* ● *I'm glad to hear he's feeling better.* ● *I'm glad (that) he's feeling better.* ● *I'll be glad when these exams are over.*

> ➤ You are usually **glad** or **pleased** about a particular event or situation. **Happy** is used for describing a state, condition of mind, etc and it can also be used before the noun it describes: *This kind of music always makes me feel happy.* ● *She's such a happy child – she's always laughing.*

2 glad (of sth); glad (if...) grateful for sth: *If you are free, I'd be glad of some help.* ● *I'd be glad if you could help me.* –**gladness** **noun** [U]

gladiator /'glædieɪtə/ **noun** [C] (in ancient Rome) a man who fought against another man or a wild animal in a public show

gladly /'glædli/ **adv** used for politely agreeing to a request or accepting an invitation: *'Could you help me carry these bags?' 'Gladly.'* ● *She gladly accepted the invitation to stay the night.*

glamorize (also **-ise**) /'glæməraɪz/ **verb** [T] to make sth appear more attractive or exciting than it really is: *Television tends to glamorize violence.*

glamour (*US also* **glamor**) /'glæmə/ **noun** [U] the quality of seeming to be more exciting or attractive than ordinary things or people: *Young people are often attracted by the glamour of city life.* –**glamorous** /-mərəs/ **adj**: *the*

glamorous world of show business –**glamorously adv**

glance¹ /glɑːns/ **verb** [I] to look quickly at sb/sth: *She glanced round the room to see if they were there.* ● *He glanced at her and smiled.* ● *The receptionist glanced down the list of names.*

◼️PHRASAL VERB **glance off (sth)** to hit sth at an angle and move off again in another direction: *The ball glanced off his knee and into the net.*

glance² /glɑːns/ **noun** [C] a quick look: *to take/have a glance at the newspaper headlines*

◼️IDIOMS **at a (single) glance** with one look: *I could tell at a glance that something was wrong.*

at first glance/sight → **FIRST¹**

gland /glænd/ **noun** [C] any of the small parts (organs) inside your body that produce chemical substances for your body to use: *sweat glands*

glare¹ /gleə/ **verb** [I] **1** glare (at sb/sth) to look at sb in a very angry way **2** to shine with strong light that hurts your eyes

glare² /gleə/ **noun 1** [U] strong light that hurts your eyes: *the glare of the sun/a car's headlights* **2** [C] a very angry look

glaring /'gleərɪŋ/ **adj 1** very easy to see; shocking: *a glaring mistake/injustice* **2** (used about a light) too strong and bright **3** angry: *glaring eyes* –**glaringly adv**: *a* **glaringly obvious mistake**

★**glass** /glɑːs/ **noun 1** [U] a hard substance that you can usually see through that is used for making windows, bottles, etc: *He cut himself on broken glass.* ● *a sheet/pane of glass* ● *a glass jar/dish/vase* **2** [C] a drinking container made of glass; the amount of liquid it contains: *a wine glass* ● *a brandy glass* ● *Could I have a glass of water, please?* ••➤ *picture at* **cup**

glasses

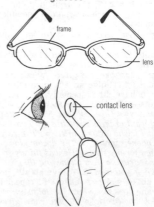

frame

lens

contact lens

★**glasses** /'glɑːsɪz/ (also **spectacles** or **specs**; *US also* **eyeglasses**) **noun** [pl] two pieces of glass or plastic (lenses) in a frame that a person wears in front of his/her eyes

---

in order to be able to see better: *My sister has to **wear** glasses.* ● *I need a new **pair** of glasses.* ● *I need some new glasses.* ● *reading glasses* ● *dark glasses/sunglasses*

glass 'fibre = FIBREGLASS

glasshouse /'glɑːshaʊs/ = GREENHOUSE

glassy /'glɑːsi/ *adj* **1** looking like glass **2** (used about the eyes) showing no interest or expression

glaze¹ /gleɪz/ *verb* [T] **1** to fit a sheet of glass into a window, etc ·➔ Look at **double-glazing**. **2 glaze sth (with sth)** to cover a pot, brick, pie, etc with a shiny transparent substance (before it is put into an oven)
PHRASAL VERB **glaze over** (used about the eyes) to show no interest or expression

glaze² /gleɪz/ *noun* [C,U] (a substance that gives) a shiny transparent surface on a pot, brick, pie, etc

glazed /gleɪzd/ *adj* (used about the eyes, etc) showing no interest or expression

glazier /'gleɪziə/ *noun* [C] a person whose job is to fit glass into windows, etc

gleam /gliːm/ *noun* [C, usually sing] **1** a soft light that shines for a short time: *the gleam of moonlight on the water* **2** a sudden expression of an emotion in sb's eyes: *I saw a gleam of amusement in his eyes.* **3** a small amount of sth: *a faint gleam of hope* –**gleam** *verb*: *gleaming white teeth* ● *Their eyes gleamed with enthusiasm.*

glee /gliː/ *noun* [U] a feeling of happiness, usually because sth good has happened to you or sth bad has happened to sb else: *She couldn't hide her glee when her rival came last in the race.* –**gleeful** /-fl/ *adj* –**gleefully** /-fəli/ *adv*

glen /glen/ *noun* [C] a deep, narrow valley, especially in Scotland or Ireland

glib /glɪb/ *adj* using words in a way that is clever and quick, but not sincere: *a glib salesman/politician* ● *a glib answer/excuse* –**glibly** *adv* –**glibness** *noun* [U]

glide /glaɪd/ *verb* [I] **1** to move smoothly without noise or effort: *The dancers glided across the floor.* **2** to fly in a glider: *I've always wanted to go gliding.*

glider /'glaɪdə/ *noun* [C] a light aircraft without an engine that flies using air currents ·➔ Look at **hang-glider**. ·➔ picture at **parachute** –**gliding** *noun* [U]: *to go gliding*

glimmer /'glɪmə/ *noun* [C] **1** a weak light that is not steady: *I could see a faint glimmer of light in one of the windows.* **2** a small sign of sth: *a glimmer of hope* –**glimmer** *verb* [I]

glimpse /glɪmps/ *noun* [C] **1** a glimpse (at/of sth) a very quick and not complete view of sb/sth: *I just managed to **catch a glimpse of** the fox's tail as it ran down a hole.* **2** a glimpse (into/of sth) a short experience of sth that helps you understand it: *The programme gives us an interesting glimpse into the life of the cheetah.* –**glimpse** *verb* [T]

glint /glɪnt/ *verb* [I] to shine with small bright flashes of light: *His eyes glinted at the thought of all that money.* –**glint** *noun* [C]

glisten /'glɪsn/ *verb* [I] (used about wet surfaces) to shine: *Her eyes glistened with tears.* ● *Tears glistened in her eyes.*

glitter /'glɪtə/ *noun* [U] **1** a shiny appearance consisting of many small flashes of light: *the glitter of jewellery* **2** the exciting quality that sth appears to have: *the glitter of a career in show business* **3** very small, shiny pieces of thin metal or paper, used as a decoration: *The children decorated their pictures with glitter.* –**glitter** *verb* [I]

glittering /'glɪtərɪŋ/ *adj* **1** very impressive or successful: *a glittering career/performance* **2** shining brightly with many small flashes of light

gloat /gləʊt/ *verb* [I] **gloat (about/over sth)** to feel or express happiness in an unpleasant way because sth good has happened to you or sth bad has happened to sb else

global /'gləʊbl/ *adj* **1** affecting the whole world: *the global effects of pollution* **2** considering or including all parts: *We must take a global view of the problem.* –**globally** /-bəli/ *adv*

the ,global 'village *noun* [sing] the world considered as a single community linked by computers, telephones, etc

,global 'warming *noun* [sing] the increase in the temperature of the earth's atmosphere, caused by the increase of certain gases ·➔ Look at **greenhouse effect**.

globe /gləʊb/ *noun* **1 the globe** [sing] the earth: *to travel all over the globe* **2** [C] a round object with a map of the world on it **3** [C] any object shaped like a ball

,globe 'artichoke = ARTICHOKE

globetrotter /'gləʊbtrɒtə/ *noun* [C] (*informal*) a person who travels to many countries

globule /'glɒbjuːl/ *noun* [C] a small drop or ball of a liquid: *There were globules of fat in the soup.*

gloom /gluːm/ *noun* [U] **1** a feeling of being sad and without hope: *The news brought deep gloom to the village.* **2** almost total darkness

gloomy /'gluːmi/ *adj* (**gloomier**; **gloomiest**) **1** dark in way that makes you feel sad: *This dark paint makes the room very gloomy.* **2** sad and without much hope: *Don't be so gloomy – cheer up!* –**gloomily** *adv* –**gloominess** *noun* [U]

glorified /'glɔːrɪfaɪd/ *adj* (only *before* a noun) described in a way that makes sb/sth seem better, bigger, more important, etc than he/she/it really is

glorify /'glɔːrɪfaɪ/ *verb* [T] (*pres part* **glorifying**; *3rd pers sing pres* **glorifies**; *pt, pp* **glorified**) to make sb/sth appear better or more important than he/she/it really is: *His biography does not attempt to glorify his early career.*

glorious /'glɔːriəs/ *adj* **1** having or deserving fame or success: *a glorious victory* **2** wonderful; splendid: *a glorious day/view* –**gloriously** *adv*

glory¹ /'glɔːri/ *noun* [U] **1** fame or honour that you get for achieving sth: *The winning team*

g

was welcomed home in a blaze of glory.
2 great beauty

glory² /ˈɡlɔːri/ **verb** (*pres part* **glorying**; *3rd pers sing pres* **glories**; *pt, pp* **gloried**)
PHRASAL VERB **glory in sth** to take (too much) pleasure or pride in sth: *He gloried in his sporting successes.*

gloss¹ /ɡlɒs/ **noun** [U,sing] (a substance that gives sth) a smooth, shiny surface: *gloss paint • gloss photographs* •➤ Look at **matt**.

gloss² /ɡlɒs/ **verb**
PHRASAL VERB **gloss over sth** to avoid talking about a problem, mistake, etc in detail

glossary /ˈɡlɒsəri/ **noun** [C] (*pl* **glossaries**) a list of special or unusual words and their meanings, usually at the end of a text or book

glossy /ˈɡlɒsi/ **adj** (**glossier**, **glossiest**) smooth and shiny: *glossy hair • a glossy magazine* (= printed on shiny paper)

★**glove** /ɡlʌv/ **noun** [C] a piece of clothing that covers your hand and has five separate parts for the fingers: *I need a new pair of gloves for the winter. • leather/woollen/rubber gloves* •➤ Look at **mitten**. •➤ picture on page C6

★**glow** /ɡləʊ/ **verb** [I] **1** to produce light and/or heat without smoke or flames: *A cigarette glowed in the dark.* **2 glow (with sth)** to be warm or red because of excitement, exercise, etc: *to glow with health/enthusiasm/pride* –**glow noun** [sing]: *the glow of the sky at sunset*

glower /ˈɡlaʊə/ **verb** [I] **glower (at sb/sth)** to look angrily (at sb/sth)

glowing /ˈɡləʊɪŋ/ **adj** saying that sb/sth is very good: *His teacher wrote a glowing report about his work.* –**glowingly adv**

glucose /ˈɡluːkəʊs/ **noun** [U] a type of sugar that is found in fruit

★**glue¹** /ɡluː/ **noun** [U] a thick sticky liquid that is used for joining things together: *You can make glue from flour and water. • Stick the photo in with glue.*

glue² /ɡluː/ **verb** [T] (*pres part* **gluing**) **glue A (to/onto B)**; **glue A and B (together)** to join a thing or things together with glue: *Do you think you can glue the handle back onto the teapot?*
IDIOM **glued to sth** (*informal*) giving all your attention to sth and not wanting to leave it: *He just sits there every evening glued to the television.*

glum /ɡlʌm/ **adj** sad and quiet –**glumly adv**

glut /ɡlʌt/ **noun** [C,usually sing] more of sth than is needed: *The glut of coffee has forced down the price.*

glutton /ˈɡlʌtn/ **noun** [C] **1** a person who eats too much **2** (*informal*) **a glutton for sth** a person who enjoys having or doing sth difficult, unpleasant, etc: *She's a glutton for hard work – she never stops.*

gluttony /ˈɡlʌtəni/ **noun** [U] the habit of eating and drinking too much

GM /ˌdʒiː ˈem/ **abbr** genetically modified

GMT /ˌdʒiː em ˈtiː/ **abbr** Greenwich Mean Time; the time system that is used in Britain during the winter and for calculating the time in other parts of the world

gnarled /nɑːld/ **adj** rough and having grown

into a strange shape, because of old age or hard work: *The old man had gnarled fingers.*
• *a gnarled oak tree*

gnash /næʃ/ **verb**
IDIOM **gnash your teeth** to feel very angry and upset about sth

gnat /næt/ **noun** [C] a type of very small fly that bites •➤ synonym **midge**

gnaw /nɔː/ **verb 1** [I,T] **gnaw (away) (at/on)** sth to bite a bone, etc many times with your back teeth **2** [I] **gnaw (away) at sb** to make sb feel worried or frightened over a long period of time: *Fear of the future gnawed away at her all the time.*

gnome /nəʊm/ **noun** [C] (in children's stories, etc) a little old man with a beard and a pointed hat who lives under the ground

★**go¹** /ɡəʊ/ **verb** [I] (*pres part* **going**; *3rd pers sing pres* **goes** /ɡəʊz/; *pt* **went** /went/; *pp* **gone** /ɡɒn/) **1** to move or travel from one place to another: *She always goes home by bus.* • *We're going to London tomorrow.* • *He went to the cinema yesterday.* • *We've still got fifty miles to go.* • *How fast does this car go?* • *I threw the ball and the dog went running after it.*

➤ **Been** is used as the past participle of **go** when somebody has travelled to a place and has returned. **Gone** means that somebody has travelled to a place but has not yet returned: *I've just been to Berlin. I got back this morning.* • *John's gone to Peru. He'll be back in two weeks.*

2 to travel to a place to take part in an activity or do sth: *Are you going to Dave's party?* • *Shall we go swimming this afternoon?* • *to go for a swim/drive/drink/walk/meal* • *We went on a school trip to a museum.* • *They've gone on holiday.* • *We went to watch the match.* • *I'll go and make the tea.* **3** to belong to or stay in an institution: *Which school do you go to?* • *to go to hospital/prison/college/university* **4** to leave a place: *I have to go now. It's nearly 4 o'clock.* • *What time does the train go?* **5** to lead to or reach a place or time: *Where does this road go to?* **6** to be put or to fit in a particular place: *Where does this vase go?* • *My clothes won't all go in one suitcase.* **7** to happen in a particular way; to develop: *How's the new job going?* **8** to become; to reach a particular state: *Her hair is going grey.* • *to go blind/deaf/bald/senile/mad* • *The baby has gone to sleep.* **9** to stay in the state mentioned: *Many mistakes go unnoticed.* **10** to be removed, lost; used, etc; to disappear: *Has your headache gone yet?* • *I like the furniture, but that carpet will have to go.* • *About half my salary goes on rent.* • *Jeans will never go out of fashion.* **11** to work correctly: *This clock doesn't go.* • *Is your car going at the moment?* **12** to become worse or stop working correctly: *The brakes on the car have gone.* • *His sight/voice/mind has gone.* **13** **go (with sth)**; **go (together)** to look or taste good with sth else: *This sauce goes well with rice or pasta.* • *These two colours don't really go.* **14** to have certain words or a

---

certain tune: *How does that song go?* **15** (used about time) to pass: *The last hour went very slowly.* **16** to start an activity: *Everybody ready to sing? Let's go!* **17** to make a sound: *The bell went early today.* • *Cats go 'miaow'.* **18** (*spoken, informal*) used in the present tense for saying what a person said: *I said, 'How are you, Jim?' and he goes, 'It's none of your business!'* **19** (*informal*) (only used in the continuous tenses) to be available: *Are there any jobs going in your department?* **20** (*informal*) used for saying that you do not want sb to do sth bad or stupid: *You can borrow my bike again, but don't go breaking it this time!* • *I hope John doesn't go and tell everyone about our plan.*

IDIOMS **as people, things, etc go** compared to the average person or thing: *As Chinese restaurants go, it wasn't bad.*

be going to do sth 1 used for showing what you plan to do in the future: *We're going to sell our car.* **2** used for saying that you think sth will happen: *It's going to rain soon.* • *Oh no! He's going to fall!*

go all out for sth; go all out to do sth to make a great effort to do sth

go for it (*informal*) to do sth after not being sure about it: *'Do you think we should buy it?' 'Yeah, let's go for it!'*

have a lot going for you to have many advantages

Here goes! said just before you start to do sth difficult or exciting

to go that is/are left before sth ends: *How long (is there) to go before the end of the lesson?*

➤ For other idioms containing **go**, look at the entries for nouns, adjectives, etc, for example **go astray** is at **astray**.

PHRASAL VERBS **go about** → **GO ROUND/AROUND/ABOUT**

go about sth/doing sth to start trying to do sth difficult: *I wouldn't have any idea how to go about building a house.*

go about with sb → **GO ROUND/AROUND/ABOUT WITH SB**

go after sb/sth to try to catch or get sb/sth: *I went after the boy who stole my wallet but he was too fast for me.*

go against sb to not be in sb's favour or not be to sb's advantage: *The referee's decision went against him.*

go against sb/sth to do sth that sb/sth says you should not do: *She went against her parents' wishes and married him.*

go ahead 1 to take place after being delayed or in doubt: *Although several members were missing, the meeting went ahead without them.* **2** to travel in front of other people in your group and arrive before them: *I'll go ahead and tell them you're coming.*

go ahead (with sth) to do sth after not being sure that it was possible: *We decided to go ahead with the match in spite of the heavy rain.* • *'Can I take this chair?' 'Sure, go ahead.'*

go along to continue; to progress: *The course gets more difficult as you go along.*

go along with sb/sth to agree with sb/sth; to do what sb else has decided: *I'm happy to go along with whatever you suggest.*

go around → **GO ROUND/AROUND/ABOUT**

go around with sb → **GO ROUND/AROUND/ABOUT WITH SB**

go away 1 to disappear or leave: *I've got a headache that just won't go away.* • *Just go away and leave me alone!* **2** to leave the place where you live for at least one night: *We're going away to the coast this weekend.*

go back (to sth) 1 to return to a place: *It's a wonderful city and I'd like to go back there one day.* **2** to return to an earlier matter or situation: *Let's go back to the subject we were discussing a few minutes ago.* **3** to have its origins in an earlier period of time: *A lot of the buildings in the village go back to the fifteenth century.*

go back on sth to break a promise, an agreement, etc: *I promised to help them and I can't go back on my word.*

go back to sth/doing sth to start doing again sth that you had stopped doing: *When the children got a bit older she went back to full-time work.*

go by 1 (used about time) to pass: *As time went by, her confidence grew.* **2** to pass a place: *She stood at the window watching people go by.*

go by sth to use particular information, rules, etc to help you decide your actions or opinions: *You can't go by the railway time-tables – the trains are very unreliable.*

go down 1 (used about a ship, etc) to sink **2** (used about the sun) to disappear from the sky **3** to become lower in price, level, etc; to fall: *The number of people out of work went down last month.*

go down (with sb) (used with adverbs, especially 'well' or 'badly' or in questions beginning with 'how') to be received in a particular way by sb: *The film went down well with the critics.*

go down with sth to catch an illness; to become ill with sth

go for sb to attack sb

go for sb/sth 1 to be true for a particular person or thing: *We've got financial problems but I suppose the same goes for a great many people.* **2** to choose sb/sth: *I think I'll go for the roast chicken.*

go in (used about the sun) to disappear behind a cloud

go in for sth to enter or take part in an exam or competition

go in for sth/doing sth to do or have sth as a hobby or interest

go into sth 1 to hit sth while travelling in/on a vehicle: *I couldn't stop in time and went into the back of the car in front.* **2** to start working in a certain type of job: *When she left school she went into nursing.* **3** to look at or describe sth in detail: *I haven't got time to go into all the details now.*

go off 1 to explode: *A bomb has gone off in the city centre.* **2** to make a sudden loud noise:

g

I woke up when my alarm clock went off.
3 (used about lights, heating, etc) to stop working: *There was a power cut and all the lights went off.* **4** (used about food and drink) to become too old to eat or drink; to go bad **5** to become worse in quality: *I used to like that band but they've gone off recently.*

go off sb/sth to stop liking or being interested in sb/sth: *I went off spicy food after I was ill last year.*

go off (with sb) to leave with sb: *I don't know where Sid is – he went off with some girls an hour ago.*

go off with sth to take sth that belongs to sb else

go on 1 (used about lights, heating, etc) to start working: *I saw the lights go on in the house opposite.* **2** (used about time) to pass: *As time went on, she became more and more successful.* **3** (used especially in the continuous tenses) to happen or take place: *Can anybody tell me what's going on here?* **4** (used about a situation) to continue without changing: *This is a difficult period but it won't go on forever.* **5** to continue speaking after stopping for a moment: *Go on. What happened next?* **6** used for encouraging sb to do sth: *Oh go on, let me borrow your car. I'll bring it back in an hour.*

go on sth to use sth as information so that you can understand a situation: *There were no witnesses to the crime, so the police had very little to go on.*

go on (about sb/sth) to talk about sb/sth for a long time in a boring or annoying way: *She went on and on about the people she works with.*

go/be on (at sb) (about sth) to keep complaining about sth: *She's always (going) on at me to mend the roof.*

go on (doing sth) to continue doing sth without stopping or changing: *We don't want to go on living here for the rest of our lives.*

go on (with sth) to continue doing sth, perhaps after a pause or break: *She ignored me and went on with her meal.*

go on to do sth to do sth after completing sth else

go out 1 to leave the place where you live or work for a short time, returning on the same day: *Let's go out for a meal tonight* (= to a restaurant). • *I'm just going out for a walk, I won't be long.* **2** to stop shining or burning: *Suddenly all the lights went out.* **3** to stop being fashionable or in use: *That kind of music went out in the seventies.* **4** (used about the sea) to move away from the land: *Is the tide coming in or going out?* •➤ synonym **ebb** •➤ Look at **tide**¹.

go out (with sb); go out (together) to spend time regularly with sb, having a romantic and/or sexual relationship: *Is Fiona going out with anyone?* • *They went out together for five years before they got married.*

go over sth to look at, think about or discuss sth carefully from beginning to end: *Go over your work before you hand it in.*

go over to sth to change to a different side, system, habit, etc

go round (used especially after 'enough') to be shared among all the people: *In this area, there aren't enough jobs to go round.*

go round/around/about (used about a story, an illness, etc) to pass from person to person: *There's a rumour going round that he's going to resign.* • *There's a virus going round at work.*

go round (to…) to visit sb's home, usually a short distance away: *I'm going round to Jo's for dinner tonight.*

go round/around/about with sb to spend time and go to places regularly with sb: *Her parents don't like the people she has started going round with.*

go through to be completed successfully: *The deal went through as agreed.*

go through sth 1 to look in or at sth carefully, especially in order to find sth: *I went through all my pockets but I couldn't find my wallet.* **2** to look at, think about or discuss sth carefully from beginning to end: *We'll start the lesson by going through your homework.* **3** to have an unpleasant experience: *I'd hate to go through such a terrible ordeal again.*

go through with sth to do sth unpleasant or difficult that you have decided, agreed or threatened to do: *Do you think she'll go through with her threat to leave him?*

go together (used about two or more things) **1** to belong to the same set or group **2** to look or taste good together

go towards sth to be used as part of the payment for sth: *The money I was given for my birthday went towards my new bike.*

go under 1 to sink below the surface of some water **2** (*informal*) (used about a company) to fail and close: *A lot of firms are going under in the recession.*

go up 1 to become higher in price, level, amount, etc; to rise: *The birth rate has gone up by 10%.* **2** to start burning suddenly and strongly: *The car crashed into a wall and went up in flames.* **3** to be built

go with sth 1 to be included with sth; to happen as a result of sth: *Pressure goes with the job.* **2** to look or taste good with sth else: *What colour carpet would go with the walls?*

go without (sth) to choose or be forced to not have sth: *They went without sleep night after night while the baby was ill.*

go² /gəʊ/ *noun* (*pl* **goes** /gəʊz/) **1** [C] a turn to play in a game, etc: *Whose go is it?* • *Hurry up – it's your go.* •➤ synonym **turn 2** [C] (*informal*) **a go (at sth/doing sth)** an occasion when you try to do sth; an attempt: *Shall I have a go at fixing it for you?* • *I've never played this game before, but I'll give it a go.* • *Andrew passed his driving test first go.*

IDIOMS **be on the go** (*informal*) to be very active or busy: *I'm exhausted. I've been on the go all day.*

have a go at sb (*informal*) to criticize sb/sth: *Dad's always having a go at me about my hair.*

make a go of sth (*informal*) to be successful at sth

goad /gəʊd/ **verb** [T] **goad sb/sth (into sth/ doing sth)** to cause sb to do sth by making him/her angry

'go-ahead¹ **noun** [sing] **the go-ahead (for sth)** permission to do sth: *It looks like the council are going to **give** us **the go-ahead** for the new building.*

'go-ahead² **adj** enthusiastic to try new ways of doing things

★**goal** /gəʊl/ **noun** [C] **1** (in football, rugby, hockey, etc) the area between two posts into which the ball must be kicked, hit, etc for a point or points to be scored: *He crossed the ball in front of the goal.* **2** a point that is scored when the ball goes into the goal: *Everton won by three goals to two.* • *to score a goal* **3** your purpose or aim: *This year I should **achieve** my **goal** of visiting all the capital cities of Europe.*

goalkeeper /'gəʊlkiːpə/ (also *informal* **goalie** /'gəʊli/ or **keeper**) **noun** [C] (in football, hockey, etc) the player who stands in front of the goal(1) and tries to stop the other team from scoring: *The goalkeeper made a magnificent save.*

goalless /'gəʊlləs/ **adj** with no goals scored: *a goalless draw* • *The match finished goalless.*

goalpost /'gəʊlpəʊst/ **noun** [C] (in football, hockey, etc) one of the two posts that form the sides of a goal. They are joined together by a bar (**the crossbar**).

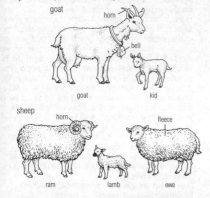

goat

horn

bell

goat   kid

sheep

horn   fleece

ram   lamb   ewe

goat /gəʊt/ **noun** [C] a small animal with horns which lives in mountain areas or is kept on farms for its milk and meat

goatee /gəʊˈtiː/ **noun** [C] a small pointed beard on a man's chin •► picture at **hair**

gobble /'gɒbl/ **verb** [I,T] (*informal*) **gobble sth (up/down)** to eat quickly and noisily

gobbledegook (also **gobbledygook**) /'gɒbldɪguːk/ **noun** [U] (*informal*) complicated language that is hard to understand

'go-between **noun** [C] a person who takes messages between two people or groups

goblin /'gɒblɪn/ **noun** [C] (in stories) a small ugly creature who tricks people

gobsmacked /'gɒbsmækt/ **adj** (*informal*) so surprised that you cannot speak; speechless

★**god** /gɒd/ **noun 1** [sing] **God** (not used with *the*) the being or spirit in Christianity, Islam and Judaism who people pray to and who people believe created the universe: *Do you believe in God?* • *Muslims worship God in a mosque.* **2** (*fem* **goddess**) [sing] a being or spirit that people believe has power over a particular part of nature or that represents a particular quality: *Mars was the Roman god of war and Venus was the goddess of love.*

> ► 'God' is used in a number of expressions. Some people think that it is wrong to use God's name in this way. *Oh my God!* expresses surprise or shock: *Oh my God! I've won the lottery!* We use *thank God* when we are happy and relieved about something: *Thank God you've arrived – I was beginning to think you'd had an accident.* We use *'for God's sake'* when we are asking somebody to do something and want to sound more urgent or when we are angry with somebody: *For God's sake, shut up!*

godchild /'gɒdtʃaɪld/ (also **'god-daughter**; **godson**) **noun** [C] a child who a chosen friend of the family (**godmother** or **godfather**) promises to help and to make sure is educated as a Christian

goddess /'gɒdes/ **noun** [C] a female god

godfather /'gɒdfɑːðə/ (also **godmother**; **godparent**) **noun** [C] a person chosen by a child's family who promises to help the child and to make sure he/she is educated as a Christian

godforsaken /'gɒdfəseɪkən/ **adj** (used about a place) not interesting or attractive in any way

godsend /'gɒdsend/ **noun** [C] something unexpected that is very useful because it comes just when it is needed

goggles /'gɒglz/ **noun** [pl] special glasses that you wear to protect your eyes from water, wind, dust, etc •► Look at **mask**. •► picture at **ski**

going¹ /'gəʊɪŋ/ **noun 1** [sing] (*formal*) the act of leaving a place; departure: *We were all saddened by his going.* **2** [U] the rate or speed of travel, progress, etc: *Three children in four years? That's **not bad going**!* **3** [U] how difficult it is to make progress: *The path up the mountain was **rough going**.* • *It'll be **hard going** if we need to finish this by Friday!*

IDIOM **get out, go, leave, etc while the going is good** to leave a place or stop doing sth while it is still easy to do so

going² /'gəʊɪŋ/ **adj**

IDIOMS **a going concern** a successful business

the going rate (for sth) the usual cost (of sth): *What's the going rate for an office cleaner?*

,going-'over **noun** [sing] (*informal*) **1** a very careful examination of sth: *Give the car a* *good going-over* before deciding to buy it. **2** a serious physical attack on sb

goings-'on noun [pl] (*informal*) unusual things that are happening

go-kart /'gəʊ kɑːt/ noun [C] a vehicle like a very small car with no roof or doors, used for racing

★**gold** /gəʊld/ noun **1** [U] (*symbol* **Au**) a precious yellow metal that is used for making coins, jewellery, etc: *Is your bracelet made of solid gold?* • *22 carat gold* • *a gold chain/ring/watch* **2** [C] = **GOLD MEDAL** –**gold** adj: *The invitation was written in gold letters.* •➤ Look at **golden**.

IDIOMS (as) good as gold → **GOOD**[1]

have a heart of gold → **HEART**

★**golden** /'gəʊldən/ adj **1** made of gold or bright yellow in colour like gold: *a golden crown* • *golden hair/sand* **2** best, most important, favourite, etc: *The golden rule is 'Keep your eye on the ball'.* • *a golden opportunity* **3** celebrating the 50th anniversary of sth: *The couple celebrated their golden wedding last year.* •➤ Look at **silver** and **diamond**.

IDIOM the golden rule (of sth) → **RULE**[1](2)

goldfish /'gəʊldfɪʃ/ noun [C] (*pl* **goldfish**) a small orange fish, often kept as a pet in a bowl or a small pool in the garden (**pond**)

gold 'medal (also **gold**) noun [C] the prize for first place in a sports competition: *How many gold medals did we win in the 2000 Olympics?* •➤ Look at **silver medal** and **bronze medal**.

gold 'medallist noun [C] the winner of a gold medal

'gold mine noun [C] **1** a place where gold is taken from the ground **2** a gold mine (of sth) a place, person or thing that provides a lot of sth: *This web site is a gold mine of information.*

★**golf** /gɒlf/ noun [U] a game that is played outdoors on a large area of grass (**golf course**) and in which you use a stick (**golf club**) to hit a small hard ball (**golf ball**) into a series of holes (usually 18): *to play a round of golf*

golfer /'gɒlfə/ noun [C] a person who plays golf

golly /'gɒli/ interj (*informal*) used for expressing surprise

gone[1] *past participle* of **GO**[1]

gone[2] /gɒn/ adj (not before a noun) not present any longer; completely used or finished: *He stood at the door for a moment, and then he was gone.* • *Can I have some more ice cream please or is it all gone?*

➤ *Gone* meaning 'disappeared' or 'finished' is used with the verb *be*, as in the examples above. When we are thinking about where something has disappeared to, we use *have*: *Nobody knows where John has gone.*

gone[3] /gɒn/ prep later than: *Hurry up! It's gone six already!*

gonna /'gɒnə/ (*informal*) a way of writing 'going to' to show that sb is speaking in an informal way

➤ Do not write 'gonna' yourself (unless you are copying somebody's accent) because it might be marked as a mistake. **Wanna** (= want to) and **gotta** (= got to) are similar.

goo /guː/ noun [U] (*informal*) a sticky wet substance –**gooey** /'guːi/ adj

★**good**[1] /gʊd/ adj (**better** /'betə/, **best** /best/) **1** of a high quality or standard: *a good book/film/actor* • *That's a really good idea!* • *The hotel was quite/pretty good, but not fantastic.* **2** good at sth; good with sb/sth able to do sth or deal with sb/sth well: *Jane's really good at science subjects but she's no good at languages.* • *He's very good with children.* • *Are you any good at drawing?* **3** pleasant or enjoyable: *It's good to be home again.* • *good news/weather* • *Have a good time at the party!* **4** morally right or well behaved: *She was a very good person – she spent her whole life trying to help other people.* • *Were the children good while we were out?* **5** good (to sb); good of sb (to do sth) kind; helpful: *They were good to me when I was ill.* • *It was good of you to come.* **6** good (for sb/sth) having a positive effect on sb/sth's health or condition: *Green vegetables are very good for you.* • *This cream is good for burns.* **7** good (for sb/sth) suitable or convenient: *This beach is very good for surfing.* • *I think Paul would be a good person for the job.* • *'When shall we meet?' 'Thursday would be a good day for me.'* **8** (used about a reason, etc) acceptable and easy to understand: *a good excuse/explanation/reason* • *She has good reason to be pleased – she's just been promoted.* **9** good (for sth) that can be used or can provide sth: *I've only got one good pair of shoes.* • *This ticket's good for another three days.* **10** a good... more, larger, etc than is usual or expected: *a good many/a good few people* (= a lot of people) • *a good distance* (= a long way) • *a good* (= at least) *ten minutes/a good three miles* • *Take a good* (= long and careful) *look at this photograph.* • *What you need is a good rest.* • *Give the fruit a good wash before you eat it.* **11** used when you are pleased about sth: *'Lisa's invited us to dinner next week.' 'Oh, good!'*

IDIOMS a good/great many → **MANY**

as good as almost; virtually: *The project is as good as finished.*

(as) good as gold very well-behaved

be in/for a good cause → **CAUSE**[1]

in good faith → **FAITH**

good for you, him, her, etc (*informal*) used to show that you are pleased that sb has done sth clever: *'I passed my driving test!' 'Well done! Good for you!'*

for good measure → **MEASURE**[2]

so far so good → **FAR**[2]

good[2] /gʊd/ noun [U] **1** behaviour that is morally right or acceptable: *the difference between good and evil* • *I'm sure there's some good in everybody.* **2** something that will help sb/sth; advantage: *She did it for the good of her country.* • *I know you don't want to go into hospital, but it's for your own good.*

• *What's the good of learning French if you have no chance of using it?* ••➤ Look also at the entry for **goods**.

IDIOMS **be no good (doing sth)** to be of no use or value: *It's no good standing here in the cold. Let's go home.* • *This sweater isn't any good. It's too small.*

do you good to help or be useful to you: *It'll do you good to meet some new people.*

for good for ever: *I hope they've gone for good this time!*

not much good (*informal*) bad or not useful: *'How was the party?' 'Not much good.'*

a/the world of good → **WORLD**

★ **goodbye** /,gʊd'baɪ/ **interj** said when sb goes or you go: *We said goodbye to Steven at the airport.* –**goodbye noun** [C]: *We said our goodbyes and left.*

,**Good 'Friday noun** [C] the Friday before Easter when Christians remember the death of Christ

,**good-'humoured adj** pleasant and friendly

goodies /'gʊdiz/ **noun** [pl] (*informal*) exciting things that are provided or given: *There were lots of cakes and other goodies on the table.*

,**good-'looking adj** (usually used about a person) attractive ••➤ Look at the note at **beautiful**.

,**good-'natured adj** friendly or kind

goodness /'gʊdnəs/ **noun** [U] **1** the quality of being good ••➤ synonym **virtue 2** the part of sth that has a good effect, especially on sb/sth's health: *Wholemeal bread has more goodness in it than white.*

➤ 'Goodness' is used in a number of expressions. We say *Goodness (me)!* to show that we are surprised. *Thank goodness* expresses happiness and relief: *Thank goodness it's stopped raining!* We say *For goodness' sake* when we are asking somebody to do something and want to sound more urgent or when we are angry with somebody: *For goodness' sake, hurry up!*

★ **goods** /gʊdz/ **noun** [pl] **1** things that are for sale: *a wide range of consumer goods* • *electrical goods* • *stolen goods* **2** (*especially US* **freight**) things that are carried by train or lorry: *a goods train* • *a heavy goods vehicle* (= *HGV*)

IDIOM **come up with/deliver the goods** (*informal*) to do what you have promised to do

,**good 'sense noun** [U] good judgement or intelligence: *He had the good sense to refuse the offer.*

goodwill /,gʊd'wɪl/ **noun** [U] friendly, helpful feelings towards other people: *The visit was designed to promote friendship and goodwill.*

goody (also **goodie**) /'gʊdi/ **noun** [C] (*pl* **goodies**) (*informal*) a good person in a film, book, etc ••➤ opposite **baddy**

'**goody-goody noun** [C] a person who always behaves well so that other people have a good opinion of him/her ••➤ If you call somebody a goody-goody it usually means that you do not like him/her.

gooey /'guːi/ **adj** (*informal*) soft and sticky: *gooey cakes*

goof /guːf/ **verb** [I] (*especially US informal*) to make a silly mistake

goose /guːs/ **noun** [C] (*pl* **geese** /giːs/) a large white bird that is like a duck, but bigger. Geese are kept on farms for their meat and eggs.

➤ A male goose is called a **gander** and a young goose is a **gosling**.

••➤ picture at **duck**

gooseberry /'gʊzbəri/ **noun** [C] (*pl* **gooseberries**) a small green fruit that is covered in small hairs and has a sour taste ••➤ picture on page C3

IDIOM **play gooseberry** to be present when two lovers want to be alone

'**goose pimples** (also **goosebumps** /'guːsbʌmps/) **noun** [pl] small points or lumps which appear on your skin because you are cold or frightened

gore[1] /gɔː/ **noun** [U] thick blood that comes from a wound ••➤ adjective **gory**

gore[2] /gɔː/ **verb** [T] (used about an animal) to wound sb with a horn, etc: *She was gored to death by a bull.*

gorge[1] /gɔːdʒ/ **noun** [C] a narrow valley with steep sides and a river running through it

gorge[2] /gɔːdʒ/ **verb** [I,T] **gorge (yourself) (on/with sth)** to eat a lot of food

gorgeous /'gɔːdʒəs/ **adj** (*informal*) extremely pleasant or attractive: *What gorgeous weather!* • *You look gorgeous in that dress.* –**gorgeously adv**

gorilla /gə'rɪlə/ **noun** [C] a large black African animal like a monkey (**ape**)

gory /'gɔːri/ **adj** full of violence and blood: *a gory film*

gosh /gɒʃ/ **interj** (*informal*) used for expressing surprise, shock, etc

gosling /'gɒzlɪŋ/ **noun** [C] a young bird (**goose**)

gospel /'gɒspl/ **noun 1 Gospel** [sing] one of the four books in the Bible that describe the life and teachings of Jesus Christ: *St Matthew's/Mark's/Luke's/John's Gospel* **2** (also **gospel truth**) [U] the truth: *You can't take what he says as gospel.* **3** (also **gospel music**) [U] a style of religious music that is especially popular among black American Christians

gossip /'gɒsɪp/ **noun 1** [U] informal talk about other people and their private lives, that is often unkind or not true: *Matt phoned me up to tell me the latest gossip.* **2** [C] an informal conversation (including gossip): *The two neighbours were having a good gossip over the fence.* **3** [C] a person who enjoys talking about other people's private lives –**gossip verb** [I]

'**gossip column noun** [C] a part of a newspaper or magazine where you can read about the private lives of famous people

got *past tense, past participle* of **GET**

gotta /'gɒtə/ (*US informal*) a way of writing

'got to' or 'got a' to show that sb is speaking in an informal way

➤ Do not write 'gotta' yourself (unless you are copying somebody's accent) because it might be marked as a mistake. **Gonna** and **wanna** are similar: *I gotta go* (= I have got to go). ● *Gotta* (= have you got a) *minute?*

gotten *(US) past participle of* **GET**

gouge /gaʊdʒ/ **verb** [T] to make a hole in a surface using a sharp object in a rough way

PHRASAL VERB **gouge sth out** to remove or form sth by digging into a surface.

gourmet /'gʊəmeɪ/ **noun** [C] a person who enjoys food and knows a lot about it

★**govern** /'gʌvn/ **verb 1** [I,T] to rule or control the public affairs of a country, city, etc: *Britain is governed by the Prime Minister and the Cabinet.* **2** [T] (often passive) to influence or control sb/sth: *Our decision will be governed by the amount of money we have to spend.*

★**government** /'gʌvənmənt/ **noun 1** [C] (often **the Government**) the group of people who rule or control a country: *He has resigned from the Government.* ● *The foreign governments involved are meeting in Geneva.* ● *government policy/money/ministers* ··➤ In the singular **government** may be followed by a singular or plural verb. We use a singular verb when we are thinking of the government as one single unit: *The Government welcomes the proposal.* We use a plural verb when we are thinking about all the individual members of the government: *The Government are still discussing the problem.*

➤ Different types of government are: *communist, conservative, democratic, liberal, reactionary, socialist,* etc. A country or state may also have a *military, provisional, central* or *federal, coalition,* etc government. Look at **local government** and **opposition**.

2 [U] the activity or method of controlling a country: *weak/strong/corrupt government* ● *Which party is in government?* –govern-mental /ˌgʌvn'mentl/ **adj**: *a governmental department* ● *different governmental systems*

governor /'gʌvənə/ **noun** [C] **1** a person who rules or controls a region or state (especially in the US): *the Governor of New York State* **2** the leader or member of a group of people who control an organization: *the governor of the Bank of England* ● *school governors*

gown /gaʊn/ **noun** [C] **1** a long formal dress for a special occasion: *a ball gown* **2** a long loose piece of clothing that is worn by judges, doctors performing operations, etc

GP /ˌdʒiː'piː/ **abbr** general practitioner; a doctor who treats all types of illnesses and works in a practice in a town or village, not in a hospital

★**grab** /græb/ **verb** (**grabbing**; **grabbed**) **1** [I,T] **grab sth (from sb)** to take sth with a sudden movement: *Helen grabbed the toy car from her little brother.* ● *Grab hold of his arm in case he tries to run!* ● *Someone had arrived before us and grabbed all the seats.* ● *(figurative) He grabbed the opportunity of a*

free trip to America. ● *(figurative) I'll try to grab the waitress's attention.* ··➤ Look at **snatch. 2** [I] **grab at/for sth** to try to get or catch sb/sth: *Jonathan grabbed at the ball but missed.* **3** [T] to do sth quickly because you are in a hurry: *I'll just grab something to eat and then we'll go.* –grab /græb/ **noun** [C]: *She made a grab for the boy but she couldn't stop him falling.*

grace /greɪs/ **noun** [U] **1** the ability to move in a smooth and controlled way **2** extra time that is allowed for sth **3** a short prayer of thanks to God before or after a meal: *to say grace*

IDIOMS **sb's fall from grace** a situation in which sb loses the respect that people had for him/her by doing sth wrong or immoral

have the grace to do sth to be polite enough to do sth

with good grace in a pleasant and reasonable way, without complaining: *He accepted the refusal with good grace.*

graceful /'greɪsfl/ **adj** having a smooth, attractive movement or form: *a graceful dancer* ● *graceful curves* ··➤ Look at **gracious**. Its meaning is different. –gracefully /-fəli/ **adv**: *The goalkeeper rose gracefully to catch the ball.* ● *She accepted the decision gracefully* (= without showing her disappointment). –gracefulness **noun** [U]

graceless /'greɪsləs/ **adj 1** not knowing how to be polite to people **2** (used about a movement or a shape) ugly and not elegant –gracelessly **adv**

gracious /'greɪʃəs/ **adj 1** (used about a person or his/her behaviour) kind, polite and generous: *a gracious smile* **2** (only *before* a noun) showing the easy comfortable way of life that rich people can have: *gracious living* ··➤ Look at **graceful**. Its meaning is different. IDIOM **good gracious!** used for expressing surprise: *Good gracious! Is that the time?* –graciously **adv** –graciousness **noun** [U]

grade¹ /greɪd/ **noun** [C] **1** the quality or the level of ability, importance, etc that sb/sth has: *Which grade of petrol do you need?* ● *We need to use high-grade materials for this job.* **2** a mark that is given for school work, etc or in an exam: *He got good/poor grades this term.* ● *Very few students pass the exam with a grade A.* **3** *(US)* a class or classes in a school in which all the children are the same age: *My daughter is in the third grade.* IDIOM **make the grade** *(informal)* to reach the expected standard; to succeed: *She wanted to be a professional tennis player, but she didn't make the grade.*

grade² /greɪd/ **verb** [T] (often passive) to put things or people into groups according to their quality, size, ability, size, etc: *I've graded their work from 1 to 10.* ● *Eggs are graded by size.*

gradient /'greɪdiənt/ **noun** [C] the degree at which a road, etc goes up or down: *The hill has a gradient of 1 in 4* (= 25%). ● *a steep gradient*

★**gradual** /'grædʒuəl/ **adj** happening slowly or over a long period of time; not sudden: *There has been a gradual increase in the number of people without jobs.* –**gradually adv**: *After the war life gradually got back to normal.*

graduate¹ /'grædʒuət/ **noun** [C] **1** a graduate (in sth) a person who has a first degree from a university, etc: *a law graduate/a graduate in law* • *a graduate of London University/a London University graduate* ·➤ Look at **postgraduate**, **undergraduate**, **bachelor** and **student**. **2** (*US*) a person who has completed a course at a school, college, etc: *a high-school graduate*

graduate² /'grædʒueɪt/ **verb** [I] **1** graduate (in sth) (from sth) to get a (first) degree from a university, etc: *She graduated in History from Cambridge University.* **2** (*US*) graduate (from sth) to complete a course at a school, college, etc **3** graduate (from sth) to sth to change (from sth) to sth more difficult, important, expensive, etc: *She's graduated from being a classroom assistant to teaching.*

graduation /ˌgrædʒuˈeɪʃn/ **noun 1** [U] the act of successfully completing a university degree or (in the US) studies at a high school **2** [sing] a ceremony in which certificates are given to people who have graduated

graffiti /grə'fiːti/ **noun** [U,pl] pictures or writing on a wall, etc in a public place: *The wall was covered with graffiti.*

graft /grɑːft/ **noun** [C] **1** a piece of a living plant that is fixed onto another plant so that it will grow **2** a piece of living skin, bone, etc that is fixed onto a damaged part of a body in an operation: *a skin graft* –**graft verb** [T] graft sth onto sth: *Skin from his leg was grafted onto the burnt area of his face.* ·➤ Look at **transplant**.

★**grain** /greɪn/ **noun 1** [U,C] the seeds of wheat, rice, etc: *The US is a major producer of grain.* • *grain exports* • *a few grains of rice* **2** [C] a grain of sth a very small piece of sth: *a grain of sand/salt/sugar* • (*figurative*) *There isn't a grain of truth in the rumour.* **3** [U] the natural pattern of lines that can be seen or felt in wood, rock, stone, etc: *to cut a piece of wood along/across the grain* —IDIOM (be/go) against the grain to be different from what is usual or natural

★**gram** (also **gramme**) /græm/ **noun** [C] (*abbr* g) a measure of weight. There are 1000 grams in a kilogram.

★**grammar** /'græmə/ **noun 1** [U] the rules of a language, for example for forming words or joining words together in sentences: *Russian grammar can be difficult for foreign learners.* **2** [U] the way in which sb uses the rules of a language: *You have a good vocabulary, but your grammar needs improvement.* **3** [C] a book that describes and explains the rules of a language: *a French grammar*

'**grammar school noun** [C] (in Britain, especially in the past) a type of secondary school for children from 11-18 who are good at academic subjects

grammatical /grə'mætɪkl/ **adj 1** connected with grammar: *the grammatical rules for forming plurals* **2** following the rules of a language: *The sentence is not grammatical.* –**grammatically** /-kli/ **adv**

gramme = GRAM

gran /græn/ (*Brit informal*) = GRANDMOTHER

★**grand¹** /grænd/ **adj 1** impressive and large or important (also used in names): *Our house isn't very grand, but it has a big garden.* • *She thinks she's very grand because she drives a Porsche.* • *the Grand Canyon* • *the Grand Hotel* ·➤ noun **grandeur 2** used before a noun to show a family relationship **3** (*informal*) very good or pleasant: *You've done a grand job!* –**grandly adv** –**grandness noun** [U]

grand² /grænd/ **noun** [C] (*pl* **grand**) (*slang*) 1000 pounds or dollars

grandad /'grændæd/ (*Brit informal*) = GRANDFATHER

grandchild /'græntʃaɪld/ (also **granddaughter**; **grandson**) **noun** [C] the daughter or son of your child

grandeur /'grændʒə/ **noun** [U] (*formal*) **1** the quality of being large and impressive: *the grandeur of the Swiss Alps* **2** the feeling of being important

'**grandfather clock noun** [C] a clock that stands on the floor in a tall wooden case

grandiose /'grændiəus/ **adj** bigger or more complicated than necessary

grandma /'grænmɑː/ (*informal*) = GRANDMOTHER

grandpa /'grænpɑː/ (*informal*) = GRANDFATHER

grandparent /'grænpeərənt/ (also **grandmother**; **grandfather**) **noun** [C] the mother or father of one of your parents: *This is a picture of two of my great-grandparents* (= the parents of one of my grandparents).

➤ If you need to make it clear which grandparent you are talking about you can say: *My maternal/paternal grandfather* or *my mother's/father's father*.

,**grand pi'ano noun** [C] a large flat piano (with horizontal strings)

,**grand 'slam noun** [C] winning all the important matches or competitions in a particular sport, for example tennis or rugby

grandstand /'grænstænd/ **noun** [C] rows of seats, usually covered by a roof, from which you get a good view of a sports competition, etc

,**grand 'total noun** [C] the amount that you get when you add several totals together

granite /'grænɪt/ **noun** [U] a hard grey rock

granny /'græni/ (*pl* **grannies**) (*informal*) = GRANDMOTHER

grant¹ /grɑːnt/ **verb** [T] **1** (*formal*) to (officially) give sb what he/she has asked for: *He was granted permission to leave early.* **2** to agree (that sth is true): *I grant you that New York is an interesting place but I still wouldn't want to live there.* —IDIOMS take sb/sth for granted to be so used

g

to sb/sth that you forget his/her/its true value and are not grateful: *In developed countries we take running water for granted.*

take sth for granted to accept sth as being true: *We can take it for granted that the new students will have at least an elementary knowledge of English.*

grant² /grɑːnt/ **noun** [C] money that is given by the government, etc for a particular purpose: *a student grant* (= to help pay for university education) ● *to apply for/be awarded a grant*

granted /'grɑːntɪd/ **adv** used for saying that sth is true, before you make a comment about it: *'We've never had any problems before.' 'Granted, but this year there are 200 more people coming.'*

granule /'grænjuːl/ **noun** [C] a small hard piece of sth: *instant coffee granules*

★**grape** /greɪp/ **noun** [C] a green or purple berry that grows in bunches on a climbing plant (a vine) and that is used for making wine: *a bunch of grapes* ·➤ picture on page C3

> ➤ Green grapes are usually called 'white' and purple grapes are usually called 'black'. Grapes that have been dried are called **raisins**, **currants** or **sultanas**.

IDIOM   sour grapes → **SOUR**

grapefruit /'greɪpfruːt/ **noun** [C] (*pl* **grapefruit** or **grapefruits**) a large round yellow fruit with a thick skin and a sour taste

the grapevine /'greɪpvaɪn/ **noun** [sing] the way that news is passed from one person to another: *I heard **on/through the grapevine** that you're moving.*

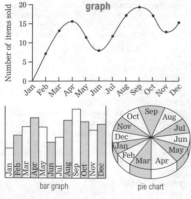

bar graph   pie chart

graph /grɑːf/ **noun** [C] a diagram in which a line or a curve shows the relationship between two quantities, measurements, etc: *a graph showing/to show the number of cars sold each month*

graphic /'græfɪk/ **adj 1** (only *before* a noun) connected with drawings, diagrams, etc: *graphic design* ● *a graphic artist* **2** (used about descriptions) clear and giving a lot of detail, especially about sth unpleasant: *She*

described the accident in graphic detail. –**graphically** /-kli/ **adv**

graphics /'græfɪks/ **noun** [pl] the production of drawings, diagrams, etc: *computer graphics*

grapple /'græpl/ **verb** [I] **grapple (with sb)** to get hold of sb and fight with or try to control him/her

★**grasp¹** /grɑːsp/ **verb** [T] **1** to take hold of sb/sth suddenly and firmly: *Lisa grasped the child firmly by the hand before crossing the road.* ● (*figurative*) *to grasp an opportunity/a chance* **2** to understand sth completely: *I don't think you've grasped how serious the situation is.*

PHRASAL VERB   **grasp at sth** to try to take hold of sth

grasp² /grɑːsp/ **noun** [sing,U] **1** a firm hold of sb/sth: *Get a good grasp on the rope before pulling yourself up.* ● *I grabbed the boy, but he slipped from my grasp.* **2** a person's understanding of a subject or of difficult facts: *He has **a good grasp of** English grammar.* **3** the ability to get or achieve sth: *Finally their dream was **within** their grasp.*

grasping /'grɑːspɪŋ/ **adj** wanting very much to have a lot more money, power, etc

★**grass** /grɑːs/ **noun 1** [U] the common green plant with thin leaves which covers fields and parts of gardens. Cows, sheep, horses, etc eat grass: *Don't walk on the grass.* ● *I must cut the grass at the weekend.* ● *a blade* (= one leaf) *of grass*

> ➤ An area of grass in a garden is called a **lawn**.

2 [C] one type of grass: *an arrangement of dried flowers and grasses*

grasshopper /'grɑːshɒpə/ **noun** [C] an insect that lives in long grass or trees and that can jump high in the air. Grasshoppers make loud noises. ·➤ picture at **insect**

grass 'roots noun [pl] the ordinary people in an organization, not those who make decisions: *the grass roots of the party*

grassy /'grɑːsi/ **adj** covered with grass

grate¹ /greɪt/ **verb 1** [T] to rub food into small pieces using a metal tool (a grater): *grated cheese/carrot* **2** [I] **grate (on sb)** to annoy or irritate **3** [I] **grate (against/on sth)** to make a sharp unpleasant sound (when two metal surfaces rub against each other)

grate² /greɪt/ **noun** [C] the metal frame that holds the wood, coal, etc in the space at the bottom of the chimney where you make a fire (fireplace) ·➤ picture at **fireplace**

★**grateful** /'greɪtfl/ **adj grateful (to sb) (for sth)**; **grateful (that...)** feeling or showing thanks (to sb): *We are very grateful to you for all the help you have given us.* ● *He was very grateful that you did as he asked.* ·➤ opposite **ungrateful** ·➤ noun **gratitude** –**gratefully** /-fəli/ **adv**

grater /'greɪtə/ **noun** [C] a kitchen tool that is used for cutting food (for example cheese) into small pieces by rubbing it across its rough surface ·➤ picture at **kitchen**

gratify /ˈɡrætɪfaɪ/ **verb** [T] (*pres part* **gratify-ing**; *3rd pers sing pres* **gratifies**; *pt, pp* **gratified**) (usually passive) (*formal*) to give sb pleasure and satisfaction –**gratifying** adj

grating /ˈɡreɪtɪŋ/ **noun** [C] a frame made of metal bars that is fixed over a hole in the road, a window, etc

gratitude /ˈɡrætɪtjuːd/ **noun** [U] **gratitude (to sb) (for sth)** the feeling of being grateful or of wanting to give your thanks to sb ••➤ opposite **ingratitude**

grave¹ /ɡreɪv/ **noun** [C] the place where a dead body is buried: *I put some flowers on my grandmother's grave.* ••➤ Look at **tomb**.
IDIOM **have one foot in the grave** → **FOOT¹**

grave² /ɡreɪv/ **adj** (*formal*) **1** bad or serious: *These events could have grave consequences for us all.* ● *The children were in grave danger.* **2** (used about people) sad or serious ••➤ **Serious** is much more common for both senses. –**gravely** adv: *gravely ill*

gravel /ˈɡrævl/ **noun** [U] very small stones that are used for making roads, paths, etc

gravestone /ˈɡreɪvstəʊn/ **noun** [C] a stone in the ground that shows the name, dates, etc of the dead person who is buried there ••➤ Look at **headstone** and **tombstone**.

graveyard /ˈɡreɪvjɑːd/ **noun** [C] an area of land next to a church where dead people are buried ••➤ Look at **cemetery** and **churchyard**.

gravity /ˈɡrævəti/ **noun** [U] **1** the natural force that makes things fall to the ground when you drop them: *the force of gravity* **2** (*formal*) importance; seriousness
➤ **Seriousness** is a more common word.
••➤ adjective **grave**

gravy /ˈɡreɪvi/ **noun** [U] a thin sauce that is made from the juices that come out of meat while it is cooking ••➤ Look at **sauce**.

gray (*especially US*) = **GREY**

graze¹ /ɡreɪz/ **verb** [T] **1** (used about cows, sheep, etc) to eat grass (that is growing in a field): *There were cows grazing by the river.* **2** to break the surface of your skin by rubbing it against sth rough: *The child fell and grazed her knee.* **3** to pass sth and touch it lightly: *The bullet grazed his shoulder.*

graze² /ɡreɪz/ **noun** [C] a slight injury where the surface of the skin has been broken by rubbing it against sth rough

grease¹ /ɡriːs/ **noun** [U] **1** a thick substance containing oil used, for example, to make engines run smoothly: *engine grease* **2** animal fat that has been softened by cooking: *You'll need very hot water to get all the grease off those pans.*

grease² /ɡriːs/ **verb** [T] to rub grease or fat on or in sth: *Grease the tin thoroughly to stop the cake from sticking.*

greasy /ˈɡriːsi/ **adj** covered with or containing a lot of grease: *greasy skin/hair* ● *greasy food*

★**great¹** /ɡreɪt/ **adj 1** large in amount, degree, size, etc; a lot of: *We had great difficulty in* solving the problem. ● *The party was a great success.* **2** particularly important; of unusually high quality: *Einstein was perhaps the greatest scientist of the century.* ••➤ Look at the note at **big**. **3** (*informal*) good; wonderful: *We had a great time in Paris.* ● *It's great to see you again.* **4** (*informal*) (used to emphasize adjectives of size, quantity, etc) very; very good: *There was a great big dog in the garden.* ● *They were great friends.* **5 great-** used before a noun to show a family relationship

➤ **Great-** can be added to other words for family members to show another generation: *your **great-aunt** (= the aunt of your mother or father)* ● *your **great-grandchild** (= the son or daughter of one of your grand-children)* ● *your **great-grandparents** (= the parents of your grandparents)* ● *your **great-great-grandfather** (= the grandfather of one of your grandparents).*

–**greatness** noun [U]
IDIOMS **go to great lengths** → **LENGTH**
a good/great deal → **DEAL²**
a good/great many → **MANY**

great² /ɡreɪt/ **noun** [C, usually pl] (*informal*) a person or thing of special ability or importance: *That film is one of the all-time greats.*

Great 'Britain (also **Britain**) (*abbr* **GB**) England, Wales and Scotland ••➤ Look at the note at **United Kingdom**.

greatly /ˈɡreɪtli/ **adv** very much

★**greed** /ɡriːd/ **noun** [U] **greed (for sth)** a desire for more food, money, power, etc than you really need

greedy /ˈɡriːdi/ **adj** (**greedier**; **greediest**) **greedy (for sth)** wanting more food, money, power, etc than you really need: *Don't be so greedy – you've had three pieces of cake already.* –**greedily** adv –**greediness** noun [U]

★**green¹** /ɡriːn/ **adj 1** having the colour of grass or leaves: *dark/light/pale green* **2** connected with protecting the environment or the natural world: *the Green party* ● *green products* (= that do not damage the environment) **3** (*informal*) (used about a person) with little experience of life or a particular job **4** jealous (wanting to have what sb else has got): *He was green with envy when he saw his neighbour's new car.* **5** (used about the skin) a strange, pale colour (because you feel sick): *At the sight of all the blood he turned green and fainted.*
IDIOMS **give sb/get the green light** (*informal*) to give sb/get permission to do sth
have green fingers; (*US*) **have a green thumb** (*informal*) to have the ability to make plants grow well

★**green²** /ɡriːn/ **noun 1** [C,U] the colour of grass or leaves: *They were dressed in green.* ● *The room was decorated in greens and blues.* **2 greens** [pl] green vegetables that are usually eaten cooked: *To have a healthy complexion you should eat more greens.* **3** [C] (*Brit*) an area of grass in the centre of a village **4** [C] a flat area of very short grass used in games such as golf **5 Green** [C] a member of a green political party

,green 'belt noun [C,U] (*Brit*) an area of open land around a city where building is not allowed

'green card noun [C] a document that allows sb from another country to live and work in the US

greenery /'gri:nəri/ noun [U] attractive green leaves and plants

greengrocer /'gri:ngrəʊsə/ noun (*Brit*) 1 [C] a person who has a shop that sells fruit and vegetables •➤ Look at grocer. 2 the greengrocer's [sing] a shop that sells fruit and vegetables

greenhouse /'gri:nhaʊs/ (also glass-house) noun [C] a building made of glass in which plants are grown •➤ picture on page C7. Look at hothouse.

the 'greenhouse effect noun [sing] the warming of the earth's atmosphere as a result of harmful gases, etc in the air •➤ Look at global warming.

greenish /'gri:nɪʃ/ adj slightly green

,green 'pepper noun [C] → PEPPER¹(2) •➤ picture on page C3

greet /gri:t/ verb [T] 1 greet sb (with sth) to welcome sb when you meet him/her; to say hello to sb: *He greeted me with a friendly smile.* • (*figurative*) *As we entered the house we were greeted by the smell of cooking.* 2 greet sb/sth (as/with) sth to react to sb or receive sth in a particular way: *The news was greeted with a loud cheer.*

greeting /'gri:tɪŋ/ noun [C] the first words you say when you meet sb or write to him/her: *'Hello' and 'Hi' are informal greetings.*

gregarious /grɪ'geəriəs/ adj liking to be with other people; sociable

grenade /grə'neɪd/ noun [C] a small bomb that is thrown by hand or fired from a gun

grew past tense of GROW

★grey¹ (*especially US* gray) /greɪ/ adj 1 having the colour between black and white: *dark/light/pale grey* • *He was wearing a grey suit.* 2 having grey hair: *He's going grey.* 3 (used about the weather) full of cloud; not bright: *grey skies* • *a grey day* 4 boring and sad; without interest or variety

grey² /greɪ/ (*especially US* gray) noun [C,U] the colour between black and white: *dressed in grey*

greyhound /'greɪhaʊnd/ noun [C] a large thin dog that can run very fast and that is used for racing: *greyhound racing*

greyish /'greɪɪʃ/ (*especially US* grayish) adj slightly grey

grid /grɪd/ noun [C] 1 a pattern of straight lines that cross each other to form squares: *She drew a grid to show how the students had scored in each part of the test.* 2 a frame of parallel metal or wooden bars, usually covering a hole in sth 3 a system of squares that are drawn on a map so that the position of any place can be described or found: *a grid reference* 4 the system of electricity wires, etc

taking power to all parts of a country: *the National Grid*

gridlock /'grɪdlɒk/ noun [U,C] a situation in which there are so many cars in the streets of a town that the traffic cannot move at all –gridlocked adj

grief /gri:f/ noun [U] great sadness (especially because of the death of sb you love)

IDIOM good grief (*spoken*) used for expressing surprise or shock: *Good grief! Whatever happened to you?*

grievance /'gri:vəns/ noun [C] a grievance (against sb) something that you think is unfair and that you want to complain or protest about

grieve /gri:v/ verb 1 [I] grieve (for sb) to feel great sadness (especially about the death of sb you love) 2 [T] (*formal*) to cause unhappiness

★grill¹ /grɪl/ noun [C] 1 a part of a cooker where the food is cooked by heat from above 2 a metal frame that you put food on to cook over an open fire 3 →GRILLE

★grill² /grɪl/ verb 1 (*especially US* broil) [I,T] to cook under a grill: *grilled steak/chicken/fish* 2 [T] (*informal*) grill sb (about sth) to question sb for a long time

grille /grɪl/ (also grill) noun [C] a metal frame that is placed over a window, a piece of machinery, etc

grim /grɪm/ adj (grimmer; grimmest) 1 (used about a person) very serious; not smiling 2 (used about a situation, news, etc) unpleasant or worrying: *The news is grim, I'm afraid.* 3 (used about a place) unpleasant to look at; not attractive: *a grim block of flats* 4 (*Brit informal*) feeling ill: *I was feeling grim yesterday but I managed to get to work.* –grimly adv

grimace /'grɪməs; *or* grɪ'meɪs/ noun [C] an ugly expression on your face that shows that you are angry, disgusted or that sth is hurting you: *a grimace of pain* –grimace verb [I]: *She grimaced with pain.*

grime /graɪm/ noun [U] a thick layer of dirt

grimy /'graɪmi/ adj very dirty

grin /grɪn/ noun [I] (grinning; grinned) grin (at sb) to give a broad smile (so that you show your teeth): *She grinned at me as she came into the room.* –grin noun [C]

grind¹ /graɪnd/ verb [T] (*pt, pp* ground /graʊnd/) 1 grind sth (down/up); grind sth (to/into sth) to press and break sth into very small pieces or into a powder between two hard surfaces or in a special machine: *Wheat is ground into flour.* • *ground pepper/coffee* 2 to make sth sharp or smooth by rubbing it on a rough hard surface: *to grind a knife on a stone* 3 grind sth in/into sth to press or rub sth into a surface: *He ground his cigarette into the ashtray.* 4 to rub sth together or make sth rub together, often producing an unpleasant noise: *Some people grind their teeth while they're asleep.*

IDIOM grind to a halt/standstill to stop slowly

grind² /graɪnd/ noun [sing] (*informal*) an activity that is tiring and boring and that takes a lot of time: *the **daily grind** of working life*

grinder /ˈgraɪndə/ **noun** [C] a machine for grinding: *a coffee grinder*

grip¹ /grɪp/ **verb** [I,T] (**gripping**; **gripped**) **1** to hold sb/sth tightly: *She gripped my arm in fear.* **2** to interest sb very much; to hold sb's attention: *The book grips you from start to finish.* ••➤ adjective **gripping**

grip² /grɪp/ **noun 1** [sing] a grip (on sb/sth) a firm hold (on sb/sth): *I relaxed my grip and he ran away.* ● *The climber slipped and lost her grip.* ● (*figurative*) *The teacher kept a firm grip on the class.* **2** [sing] a grip (on sth) an understanding of sth **3** [C] the person whose job it is to move the cameras while a film is being made

IDIOMS **come/get to grips with sth** to start to understand and deal with a problem

get/keep/take a grip/hold (on yourself) (*informal*) to try to behave in a calmer or more sensible way; to control yourself

in the grip of sth experiencing sth unpleasant that cannot be stopped: *a country in the grip of recession*

gripe /graɪp/ **noun** [C] (*informal*) a complaint about sb/sth –**gripe verb** [I]

gripping /ˈgrɪpɪŋ/ **adj** exciting; holding your attention: *a gripping film/book*

grisly /ˈgrɪzli/ **adj** (used for describing sth that is concerned with death or violence) terrible; horrible: *a grisly crime/death/murder* ••➤ Look at **gruesome**. It is similar in meaning.

gristle /ˈgrɪsl/ **noun** [U] a hard substance in a piece of meat that is unpleasant to eat –**gristly adj**

grit¹ /grɪt/ **noun** [U] **1** small pieces of stone or sand: *I've got some grit/a piece of grit in my shoe.* **2** (*informal*) courage; determination that makes it possible for sb to continue doing sth difficult or unpleasant

grit² /grɪt/ **verb** [T] (**gritting**; **gritted**) to spread small pieces of stone and sand on a road that is covered with ice

IDIOM **grit your teeth 1** to bite your teeth tightly together: *She gritted her teeth against the pain as the doctor examined her injured foot.* **2** to use your courage or determination in a difficult situation

groan /grəʊn/ **verb** [I] groan (at/with sth) to make a deep sad sound because you are in pain, or to show that you are unhappy about sth: *He groaned with pain.* ● *All the students were **moaning and groaning** (= complaining) about the amount of work they had to do.* –**groan noun** [C]

grocer /ˈgrəʊsə/ **noun 1** [C] a person who has a shop that sells food and other things for the home ••➤ Look at **greengrocer**. **2 the grocer's** [sing] a shop that sells food and other things for the home

groceries /ˈgrəʊsəriz/ **noun** [pl] food, etc that is sold by a grocer or in a larger food shop (**supermarket**): *Can you help me unload the groceries from the car, please?*

groggy /ˈgrɒgi/ **adj** (*informal*) weak and

unable to walk steadily because you feel ill, have not had enough sleep, etc: *She felt a bit groggy when she came round from the operation.*

groin /grɔɪn/ **noun** [C] the front part of your body where it joins your legs

groom¹ /gruːm/ **noun** [C] **1** = **BRIDEGROOM 2** a person who looks after horses, especially by cleaning and brushing them

groom² /gruːm/ **verb** [T] **1** to clean or look after an animal by brushing, etc: *to groom a horse/dog/cat* **2 groom sb (for/as sth)** (usually passive) to choose and prepare sb for a particular career or job

groove /gruːv/ **noun** [C] a long deep line that is cut in the surface of sth

grope /grəʊp/ **verb** [I,T] **1 grope (about/around) (for sth)** to search for sth or find your way using your hands because you cannot see: *He groped around for the light switch.* **2** (*informal*) to touch sb sexually, especially when he/she does not want you to

gross /grəʊs/ **adj 1** (only *before* a noun) being the total amount before anything is taken away: *gross income* (= before tax, etc is taken away) ••➤ opposite **net 2** (*formal*) (only *before* a noun) very great or serious: *gross indecency/negligence/misconduct* **3** very rude and unpleasant **4** very fat and ugly

grossly /ˈgrəʊsli/ **adv** very: *That is grossly unfair.*

grotesque /grəʊˈtesk/ **adj** strange or ugly in a way that is not natural

grotty /ˈgrɒti/ **adj** (*Brit informal*) unpleasant; of poor quality: *She lives in a grotty flat.*

★**ground¹** /graʊnd/ **noun 1 the ground** [sing] the solid surface of the earth: *We sat on the ground to eat our picnic.* ● *He slipped off the ladder and fell to the ground.* ● *waste ground* (= that is not being used) **2** [U] an area or type of soil: *solid/marshy/stony ground*

> The **Earth** is the name of the planet where we live. **Land** is the opposite of sea: *The sailors sighted land./The astronauts returned to Earth.* **Land** is also something that you can buy or sell: *The price of land in Tokyo is extremely high.* When you are outside, the surface under your feet is called **the ground**. When you are inside it is called **the floor**: *Don't sit on the ground. You'll get wet.* ● *Don't sit on the floor. I'll get another chair.* Plants grow in **earth** or **soil**.

3 [C] a piece of land that is used for a particular purpose: *a sports ground* ● *a playground* **4 grounds** [pl] land or gardens surrounding a large building: *the grounds of the palace* **5** [U] an area of interest, study, discussion, etc: *The lecture went over the **same old ground** /covered a lot of new ground.* ● *to be on dangerous ground* (= saying sth likely to cause anger) **6** [C, usually pl] **grounds (for sth/doing sth)** a reason for sth: *She retired on medical grounds.* ● *grounds for divorce* **7** (*US*) = **EARTH¹**(4)

IDIOMS **above/below ground** above/below the surface of the earth

g

g

break fresh/new ground to make a discovery or introduce a new method or activity

gain ground → GAIN¹

get off the ground (used about a business, project, etc) to make a successful start

hold/keep/stand your ground to refuse to change your opinion or to be influenced by pressure from other people

thin on the ground difficult to find; not common: *Jobs for people with my skills are fairly thin on the ground these days.*

ground² /graʊnd/ **verb** [T] **1** (usually passive) to force an aircraft, etc to stay on the ground: *to be grounded by fog* **2** (usually passive) to punish a child by not allowing them to go out with their friends for a period of time **3** (*especially US*) = EARTH²

ground³ *past tense, past participle* of **GRIND¹**: *ground almonds*

,**ground 'beef** (*US*) = MINCE

'**ground crew** (also '**ground staff**) **noun** [C,U] the people in an airport whose job it is to look after an aircraft while it is on the ground

,**ground 'floor** (*US* ,**first 'floor**) **noun** [C] the floor of a building that is at ground level: *a ground-floor flat* ∙→ Look at the note at **floor**.

grounding /'graʊndɪŋ/ **noun** [sing] a grounding (in sth) the teaching of the basic facts or principles of a subject: *This book provides a good grounding in English grammar.*

groundless /'graʊndləs/ **adj** having no reason or cause: *Our fears were groundless.*

groundwork /'graʊndwɜːk/ **noun** [U] work that is done in preparation for further work or study

★**group¹** /gruːp/ **noun** [C] **1** [with sing or pl verb] a number of people or things that are together in the same place or that are connected in some way: *Our discussion group is/are meeting this week.* ● *A group of us are planning to meet for lunch.* ● *Students were standing in groups waiting for their exam results.* ● *He is in the 40-50 age group.* ● *people of many different social groups* ● *a pressure group* (= a political group that tries to influence the government) ● *Which blood group* (for example A, O, etc) *do you belong to?* ● *Divide the class into groups.* ∙→ Group can be used in the singular with either a singular or plural verb. If you are thinking of the members of the group as several individuals who have come together, a plural verb is more common. **2** (used in business) a number of companies that are owned by the same person or organization **3** (*old-fashioned*) a number of people who play music together: *a pop group* ∙→ Look at **band**.

group² /gruːp/ **verb** [I,T] group (sb/sth) (around/round sb/sth); group (sb/sth) (together) to put sb/sth or to form into one or more groups: *Group these words according to their meaning.*

grouse /graʊs/ **noun** [C] (*pl* grouse) a fat brown bird with feathers on its legs that is shot for sport

grovel /'grɒvl/ **verb** [I] (**grovelling**; **grovelled**; *US* **groveling**; **groveled**) **1** grovel (to sb) (for sth) to try too hard to please sb who is more important than you or who can give you sth that you want: *to grovel for forgiveness* **2** grovel (around/about) (for sth) to move around on your hands and knees (usually when you are looking for sth) –**grovelling adj**: *I wrote a grovelling letter to my bank manager.*

★**grow** /grəʊ/ **verb** (*pt* grew /gruː/; *pp* grown /grəʊn/) **1** [I] grow (in sth) to increase in size or number; to develop into an adult form: *a growing child* ● *She's growing in confidence all the time.* ● *You must invest if you want your business to grow.* ● *Plants grow from seeds.* ● *Kittens soon grow into cats.* **2** [I,T] (used about plants) to exist and develop in a particular place; to make plants grow by giving them water, etc: *Palm trees don't grow in cold climates.* ● *We grow vegetables in our garden.* **3** [T] to allow your hair or nails to grow: *Claire's growing her hair long.* ● *to grow a beard/moustache* **4** [I] to gradually change from one state to another; to become: *It began to grow dark.* ● *to grow older/wiser/taller/bigger* ● *The teacher was growing more and more impatient.*

➤ **Get** is less formal.

PHRASAL VERBS **grow into sth 1** to gradually develop into a particular type of person: *She has grown into a very attractive young woman.* **2** to become big enough to fit into clothes, etc: *The coat is too big for him, but he will soon grow into it.*

grow on sb to become more pleasing: *I didn't like ginger at first, but it's a taste that grows on you.*

grow out of sth to become too big or too old for sth: *She's grown out of that dress I made her last year.*

grow (sth) out (used about hairstyles, etc) to disappear gradually as your hair grows; to allow your hair to grow in order to change the style

grow up **1** to develop into an adult; to mature: *What do you want to be when you grow up?* (= what job do you want to do later?) ● *She grew up* (= spent her childhood) *in Spain.* **2** (used about a feeling, etc) to develop or become strong: *A close friendship has grown up between them.*

growing /'grəʊɪŋ/ **adj** increasing: *A growing number of people are becoming vegetarian these days.*

growl /graʊl/ **verb** [I] growl (at sb/sth) (used about dogs and other animals) to make a low noise in the throat to show anger or to give a warning –**growl noun** [C]

grown /grəʊn/ **adj** physically an adult: *a fully-grown elephant*

,**grown-'up¹ adj** physically or mentally adult; mature: *She's very grown-up for her age.*

'**grown-up² noun** [C] an adult person

★**growth** /grəʊθ/ **noun 1** [U] the process of growing and developing: *A good diet is very* *important for children's growth.* • *a growth industry* (= one that is growing) **2** [U,sing] an increase (in sth): *population growth* [sing] **3** [C] a lump caused by a disease that grows in a person's or an animal's body: *a cancerous growth* **4** [U] something that has grown: *several days' growth of beard*

grub /grʌb/ **noun 1** [C] the first form that an insect takes when it comes out of the egg. Grubs are short fat and white. ••➤ picture at **insect 2** [U] (*informal*) food

grubby /'grʌbi/ **adj** (**grubbier; grubbiest**) (*informal*) dirty after being used and not washed

grudge¹ /grʌdʒ/ **noun** [C] **a grudge (against sb)** unfriendly feelings towards sb, because you are angry about what has happened in the past: *to bear a grudge against sb*

grudge² /grʌdʒ/ **verb** [T] **grudge sb sth; grudge doing sth** to be unhappy that sb has sth or that you have to do sth: *I don't grudge him his success – he deserves it.* • *I grudge having to pay so much tax.* ••➤ Look at **begrudge**.

grudging /'grʌdʒɪŋ/ **adj** given or done although you do not want to: *grudging thanks* **–grudgingly adv**

gruelling (*US* **grueling**) /'gruəlɪŋ/ **adj** very tiring and long: *a gruelling nine-hour march*

gruesome /'gru:səm/ **adj** (used about sth concerned with death or injury) very unpleasant or shocking ••➤ Look at **grisly**. It is similar in meaning.

gruff /grʌf/ **adj** (used about a person or a voice) rough and unfriendly **–gruffly adv**

grumble /'grʌmbl/ **verb** [I] to complain in a bad-tempered way; to keep saying that you do not like sth: *The students were always grumbling about the standard of the food.*

➤ People usually **grumble** or **moan** when something is not as good as they expect. If they want to take positive action they **complain** to somebody in authority.

–grumble noun [C]

grumpy /'grʌmpi/ **adj** (*informal*) bad-tempered **–grumpily adv**

grunt /grʌnt/ **verb** [I,T] to make a short low sound in the throat. People grunt when they do not like sth or are not interested and do not want to talk: *I tried to find out her opinion but she just grunted when I asked her.* **–grunt noun** [C]

★**guarantee¹** /ˌgærən'ti:/ **noun** [C,U] **1** a firm promise that sth will be done or that sth will happen: *The refugees are demanding guarantees about their safety before they return home.* **2** a written promise by a company that it will repair or replace sth if it breaks in a certain period of time: *The watch comes with a year's guarantee.* • *Is the computer still under guarantee?* ••➤ Look at **warranty**. **3** something that makes sth else certain to happen: *Without a reservation there's no guarantee that you'll get a seat on the train.*

guarantee² /ˌgærən'ti:/ **verb** [T] **1** to promise that sth will be done or will happen: *They have guaranteed delivery within one week.*

2 to give a written promise to repair or replace a product if anything is wrong with it: *This washing machine is guaranteed for three years.* **3** to make sth certain to happen: *Tonight's win guarantees the team a place in the final.*

★**guard¹** /gɑ:d/ **noun 1** [C] a person who protects a place or people, or who stops prisoners from escaping: *a security guard* ••➤ Look at **warder** and **bodyguard**. **2** [U] the state of being ready to prevent attack or danger: *Soldiers keep guard at the gate.* • *Who is on guard?* • *The prisoner arrived under armed guard.* • *a guard dog* **3** [sing,with sing or pl verb] a group of soldiers, police officers, etc who protect sb/sth: *The president always travels with an armed guard.* **4** [C] (often in compounds) something that covers sth dangerous or protects sth: *a fireguard* • *a mudguard* (= over the wheel of a bicycle) **5** (*US* **conductor**) [C] a person who is in charge of a train but does not drive it **6** [U] a position that you take to defend yourself, especially in sports such as boxing

IDIOM off/on (your) guard not ready/ready for an attack, surprise, mistake, etc: *The question caught me off (my) guard and I didn't know what to say.*

★**guard²** /gɑ:d/ **verb** [T] **1** to keep sb/sth safe from other people; protect: *The building was guarded by men with dogs.* • (*figurative*) *a closely guarded secret* **2** to be ready to stop prisoners from escaping

PHRASAL VERB guard against sth to try to prevent sth or stop sth happening

guarded /'gɑ:dɪd/ **adj** (used about an answer, statement, etc) careful; not giving much information or showing what you feel ••➤ opposite **unguarded** **–guardedly adv**

guardian /'gɑ:diən/ **noun** [C] **1** a person or institution that guards or protects sth: *The police are the guardians of law and order.* **2** a person who is legally responsible for the care of another person, especially of a child whose parents are dead

guerrilla (also **guerilla**) /gə'rɪlə/ **noun** [C] a member of a small military group who are not part of an official army and who make surprise attacks on the enemy

★**guess¹** /ges/ **verb 1** [I,T] **guess (at sth)** to try and give an answer or make a judgement about sth without being sure of all the facts: *I'd guess that he's about 45.* • *If you're not sure of an answer, guess.* • *We can only guess at her reasons for leaving.* **2** [I,T] to give the correct answer when you are not sure about it; to guess correctly: *Can you guess my age?* • *You'll never guess what Adam just told me!* • *Did I guess right?* **3** [T] (*especially US informal*) to imagine that sth is probably true or likely; to suppose: *I guess you're tired after your long journey.* **4** [T] used to show that you are going to say sth surprising or exciting: *Guess what! I'm getting married!*

★**guess²** /ges/ **noun** [C] an effort you make to imagine a possible answer or give an opinion when you cannot be sure if you are right:

If you don't know the answer, then **have a guess!** • *I don't know how far it is, but* **at a guess** *I'd say about 50 miles.* • *I'd say it'll take about four hours, but that's just* **a rough guess.**

IDIOMS **anybody's/anyone's guess** something that nobody can be certain about: *What's going to happen next is anybody's guess.*

your guess is as good as mine I don't know: *'Where's Ron?' 'Your guess is as good as mine.'*

guesswork /'gesw3:k/ **noun** [U] an act of guessing: *I arrived at the answer by pure* **guesswork.**

★**guest** /gest/ **noun** [C] **1** a person who is invited to a place or to a special event: *wedding guests* • *Who is the guest speaker at the conference?* **2** a person who is staying at a hotel, etc: *This hotel has accommodation for 500 guests.*

IDIOM **be my guest** (*informal*) used to give sb permission to do sth that he/she has asked to do: *'Do you mind if I have a look at your newspaper?' 'Be my guest!'*

'**guest house** **noun** [C] a small hotel, sometimes in a private house

guidance /'gaɪdns/ **noun** [U] guidance (on sth) help or advice: *The centre offers guidance for unemployed people on how to find work.*

★**guide¹** /gaɪd/ **noun** [C] **1** a book, magazine, etc that gives information or help on a subject: *Your Guide to Using the Internet* • *Have we got a TV guide for this week?* **2** (also **guidebook**) a book that gives information about a place for travellers and tourists: *The guide says that it was built 500 years ago.* **3** a person who shows tourists or travellers where to go: *She works as a* **tour guide** *in Venice.* **4** something that helps you to judge or plan sth: *As a rough guide, use twice as much water as rice.* **5 Guide** a member of an organization (**the Guides**) that teaches girls practical skills and organizes activities such as camping

➤ The similar organization for boys is **the Scouts**.

★**guide²** /gaɪd/ **verb** [T] **1** to help a person or a group of people to find the way to a place; to show sb a place that you know well: *He guided us through the busy streets to our hotel.* •➤ Look at the note at **lead**. **2** to have an influence on sb/sth: *I was guided by your advice.* **3** to help sb deal with sth difficult or complicated: *The manual will guide you through every step of the procedure.* **4** to carefully move sb/sth or to help sb/sth to move in a particular direction: *A crane lifted the piano and two men carefully guided it through the window.*

guided /'gaɪdɪd/ **adj** led by a guide: *a guided tour/walk*

guideline /'gaɪdlaɪn/ **noun** [C] **1** [usually pl] official advice or rules on how to do sth **2** something that can be used to help you make a decision or form an opinion: *These figures are a useful guideline when buying a house.*

guillotine /'gɪləti:n/ **noun** [C] **1** a machine used for cutting paper **2** a machine that was used in France in the past for cutting people's heads off –**guillotine** **verb** [T]

★**guilt** /gɪlt/ **noun** [U] **1** guilt (about/at sth) the bad feeling that you have when you know that you have done sth wrong: *I sometimes feel guilt about not spending more time with my children.* **2** the fact of having broken a law: *We took his refusal to answer questions as an admission of guilt.* •➤ opposite **innocence** **3** the responsibility for doing sth wrong or for sth bad that has happened; the blame for sth: *It's difficult to say whether the guilt lies with the parents or the children.*

guilty /'gɪlti/ **adj** **1** guilty (of sth) having broken a law; being responsible for doing sth wrong: *She* **pleaded guilty/not guilty** *to the crime.* • *to be guilty of murder* • *The jury* **found** *him* **guilty** *of fraud.* •➤ opposite **innocent 2** guilty (about sth) having an unpleasant feeling because you have done sth bad: *I feel really guilty about lying to Sam.* • *It's hard to sleep with* **a guilty conscience.** –**guiltily adv**

guinea pig /'gɪni pɪg/ **noun** [C] **1** a small animal with no tail that is often kept as a pet **2** a person who is used in an experiment: *I volunteered to act as a guinea pig in their research into dreams.*

guise /gaɪz/ **noun** [C] a way in which sb/sth appears, which is often different from usual or hides the truth: *The President was at the meeting* **in his guise as** *chairman of the charity.* • *His speech presented racist ideas* **under the guise of** *nationalism.*

★**guitar** /gɪ'tɑː/ **noun** [C] a type of musical instrument with strings that you play with your fingers or with a piece of plastic (a **plectrum**) •➤ Look at the note at **piano**. •➤ picture at **music**

guitarist /gɪ'tɑːrɪst/ **noun** [C] a person who plays the guitar

gulf /gʌlf/ **noun** **1** [C] a part of the sea that is almost surrounded by land: *the Gulf of Mexico* **2 the Gulf** [sing] the Persian Gulf **3** [C] an important or serious difference between people in the way they live, think or feel: *the gulf between rich and poor*

gull /gʌl/ (also **seagull**) **noun** [C] a white or grey seabird that makes a loud noise

gullible /'gʌləbl/ **adj** (used about a person) believing and trusting people too easily, and therefore easily tricked

gulp¹ /gʌlp/ **verb** **1** [I,T] gulp sth (down); gulp (for) sth to swallow large amounts of food, drink, etc quickly: *He gulped down his breakfast and went out.* • *She finally came to the surface, desperately gulping (for) air.* **2** [I] to make a swallowing movement because you are afraid, surprised, etc

gulp² /gʌlp/ *noun* [C] **1** the action of breathing in or swallowing sth: *I drank my coffee in one gulp and ran out of the door.* **2** a gulp (of sth) the amount that you swallow when you gulp

gum /gʌm/ *noun* **1** [C] either of the firm pink parts of your mouth that hold your teeth ⋯➤ picture on page C5 **2** [U] a substance that you use to stick things together (especially pieces of paper) **3** = CHEWING GUM ⋯➤ Look at **bubblegum**.

★**gun¹** /gʌn/ *noun* [C] **1** a weapon that is used for shooting: *The robber held a gun to the bank manager's head.*

> ➤ Verbs often used with 'gun' are **load**, **unload**, **point**, **aim**, **fire**. Different types of gun include a **machine gun**, **pistol**, **revolver**, **rifle**, **shotgun**.

2 a tool that uses pressure to send out a substance or an object: *a grease gun* ● *a staple gun*
IDIOM **jump the gun** → **JUMP¹**

gun² /gʌn/ *verb* [T] (**gunning**; **gunned**)
PHRASAL VERB **gun sb down** (*informal*) to shoot and kill or seriously injure sb

gunboat /'gʌnbəʊt/ *noun* [C] a small ship used in war that carries heavy guns

gunfire /'gʌnfaɪə/ *noun* [U] the repeated firing of guns: *We could hear gunfire.*

gunman /'gʌnmən/ *noun* [C] (*pl* -men /-mən/) a man who uses a gun to rob or kill people

gunpoint /'gʌnpɔɪnt/ *noun*
IDIOM **at gunpoint** threatening to shoot sb: *He held the hostages at gunpoint.*

gunpowder /'gʌnpaʊdə/ *noun* [U] an explosive powder that is used in guns, etc

gunshot /'gʌnʃɒt/ *noun* [C] the firing of a gun or the sound that it makes

gurgle /'gɜːgl/ *verb* [I] **1** to make a sound like water flowing quickly through a narrow space: *a gurgling stream* **2** if a baby gurgles, it makes a noise in its throat because it is happy –**gurgle** *noun* [C]

guru /'gʊruː/ *noun* [C] **1** a spiritual leader or teacher in the Hindu religion **2** somebody whose opinions you admire and respect, and whose ideas you follow: *a management/fashion guru*

gush /gʌʃ/ *verb* **1** [I] gush (out of/from/into sth); gush out/in (used about a liquid) to flow out suddenly and in great quantities: *Blood gushed from the wound.* ● *I turned the tap on and water gushed out.* **2** [T] (used about a container/vehicle, etc) to produce large amounts of a liquid: *The broken pipe was gushing water all over the road.* **3** [I,T] to express pleasure or admiration too much so that it doesn't sound sincere –**gush** *noun* [C]: *a sudden gush of water*

gust /gʌst/ *noun* [C] a sudden strong wind –**gust** *verb* [I]

gusto /'gʌstəʊ/ *noun*
IDIOM **with gusto** with great enthusiasm

gut¹ /gʌt/ *noun* **1** [C] the tube in your body that food passes through when it leaves your stomach ⋯➤ Look at **intestine** which is a more technical word. **2 guts** [pl] the organs in and around the stomach, especially of an animal **3 guts** [pl] (*informal*) courage and determination: *It takes guts to admit that you are wrong.* ● *I don't have the guts to tell my boss what he's doing wrong.* **4** [C] a person's fat stomach
IDIOM **work/sweat your guts out** to work extremely hard

gut² /gʌt/ *verb* [T] (**gutting**; **gutted**) **1** to remove the organs from inside an animal, fish, etc **2** to destroy the inside of a building: *The warehouse was gutted by fire.*

gut³ /gʌt/ *adj* (only *before* a noun) based on emotion or feeling rather than on reason: *a gut feeling/reaction*

gutter /'gʌtə/ *noun* [C] **1** a long piece of metal or plastic with a curved bottom that is fixed to the edge of a roof to carry away the water when it rains ⋯➤ picture on page C7 **2** a lower part at the edge of a road along which the water flows away when it rains **3** the very lowest level of society: *She rose from the gutter to become a great star.*

guy /gaɪ/ *noun* **1** [C] (*informal*) a man or a boy: *He's a nice guy.* **2 guys** [pl] (*informal*) used when speaking to a group of men and women: *What do you guys want to eat?* **3** [sing] (*Brit*) a model of a man that is burned on 5 November in memory of Guy Fawkes ⋯➤ Look at **Bonfire Night**.

guzzle /'gʌzl/ *verb* [I,T] (*informal*) to eat or drink too fast and too much

gym /dʒɪm/ *noun* **1** (also *formal* **gymnasium**) [C] a large room or a building with equipment for doing physical exercise: *I work out at the gym twice a week.* **2** [U] = GYMNASTICS: *gym shoes*

gymnasium /dʒɪm'neɪziəm/ *noun* [C] (*pl* **gymnasiums** or **gymnasia** /-zɪə/) = GYM(1)

gymnast /'dʒɪmnæst/ *noun* [C] a person who does gymnastics

gymnastics /dʒɪm'næstɪks/ (also **gym**) *noun* [U] physical exercises that are done indoors, often using special equipment such as bars and ropes: *I did gymnastics at school.*

gynaecology (*US* **gynecology**) /,gaɪnə-'kɒlədʒi/ *noun* [U] the study and treatment of the diseases and medical problems of women –**gynaecological** (*US* **gyne-**) /,gaɪnəkə-'lɒdʒɪkl/ *adj* –**gynaecologist** (*US* **gyne-**) /,gaɪnə'kɒlədʒɪst/ *noun* [C]

gypsy (also **gipsy**) /'dʒɪpsi/ *noun* [C] (*pl* **gypsies**) a member of a race of people who traditionally spend their lives travelling around from place to place, living in homes with wheels (caravans) ⋯➤ Look at **traveller**.

g

H, h /eɪtʃ/ **noun** [C] (*pl* **H's**; **h's**) the eighth letter of the English alphabet: *'Hat' begins with (an) 'H'.*

ha¹ /hɑː/ **interj 1** used for showing that you are surprised or pleased: *Ha! I knew he was hiding something!* **2 ha! ha!** used in written language to show that sb is laughing

ha² *abbr* hectare(s)

★**habit** /'hæbɪt/ **noun 1** [C] **a/the habit (of doing sth)** something that you do often and almost without thinking, that is hard to stop doing: *I'm trying to get into the habit of hanging up my clothes every night.* ● *Once you start smoking it's hard to break the habit.* •➤ adjective **habitual**

> ➤ A **habit** is usually something that is done by one person. A **custom** is something that is done by a group, community or nation: *the custom of giving presents at Christmas*

2 [U] usual behaviour: *I think I only smoke out of habit now – I don't really enjoy it.*
IDIOMS **force of habit** → **FORCE**¹
kick the habit → **KICK**¹

habitable /'hæbɪtəbl/ **adj** (used about buildings) suitable to be lived in •➤ opposite **uninhabitable**

habitat /'hæbɪtæt/ **noun** [C] the natural home of a plant or an animal: *I've seen wolves in the zoo, but not in their natural habitat.*

habitation /ˌhæbɪ'teɪʃn/ **noun** [U] (*formal*) living in a place

habitual /hə'bɪtʃuəl/ **adj 1** doing sth very often: *a habitual liar* **2** which you always have or do; usual: *He had his habitual cigarette after lunch.* –**habitually** /-tʃuəli/ **adv**

hack /hæk/ **verb** [I,T] **1 hack (away) (at) sth** to cut sth in a rough way with a tool such as a large knife: *He hacked at the branch of the tree until it fell.* **2** (*informal*) **hack (into) (sth)** to use a computer to look at and/or change information that is stored on another computer without permission

hacker /'hækə/ **noun** [C] (*informal*) a person who uses a computer to look at and/or change information on another computer without permission

had¹ /hæd; həd/ *past tense, past participle* of **HAVE**

had² /hæd/ **adj**
IDIOM **be had** (*informal*) to be tricked: *I've been had. This watch I bought doesn't work.*

hadn't *short for* **HAD NOT**

haemophilia (*US* **hemophilia**) /ˌhiːmə'fɪliə/ **noun** [U] a disease that causes a person to bleed a lot even from very small injuries because the blood does not stop flowing (**clot**)

haemophiliac (*US* **hemophiliac**) /ˌhiːmə'fɪliæk/ **noun** [C] a person who suffers from haemophilia

haemorrhage (*US* **hemorrhage**) /'hemərɪdʒ/ **noun** [C,U] a lot of bleeding inside the body –**haemorrhage verb** [I]

haemorrhoids (*especially US* **hemorrhoids**) /'hemərɔɪdz/ (*also* **piles**) **noun** [pl] a medical condition in which the tubes that carry blood (**veins**) to the opening where waste food leaves the body (**the anus**) swell and become painful

haggard /'hægəd/ **adj** (used about a person) looking tired or worried

haggle /'hægl/ **verb** [I] **haggle (with sb) (over/about sth)** to argue with sb until you reach an agreement, especially about the price of sth: *In the market, some tourists were haggling over the price of a carpet.*

hail¹ /heɪl/ **verb 1** [T] **hail sb/sth as sth** to say in public that sb/sth is very good or very special: *The book was hailed as a masterpiece.* **2** [T] to call or wave to sb/sth: *to hail a taxi* **3** [I] when it hails, small balls of ice fall from the sky like rain •➤ Look at the note at **weather**.

hail² /heɪl/ **noun 1** [U] small balls of ice (**hailstones**) that fall from the sky like rain **2** [sing] **a hail of sth** a large amount of sth that is aimed at sb in order to harm him/her: *a hail of bullets/stones/abuse*

★**hair** /heə/ **noun 1** [U,C] the mass of long thin things that grow on the head and body of people and animals; one of these things: *He has got short black hair.* ● *Dave's losing his hair* (= going bald). ● *The dog left hairs all over the furniture.* **2 -haired adj** (used in compounds) having the type of hair mentioned: *a dark-haired woman* ● *a long-haired dog*

> ➤ Some special words for the colour of hair are: **auburn**, **blond**, **fair**, **ginger** and **red**. In order to look after or style your hair you **brush**, **comb**, **wash** (or **shampoo**) it and then **blow-dry** it. You can **part** it (or have **a parting**) in the middle or on one side. When you go to the **hairdresser's** you can have your hair **cut** or **permed**.

3 a thing that looks like a very thin thread that grows on the surface of some plants: *The leaves and stem are covered in fine hairs.*
IDIOMS **keep your hair on** (*spoken*) (used to tell sb to stop shouting and become less angry) calm down
let your hair down (*informal*) to relax and enjoy yourself after being formal
make sb's hair stand on end to frighten or shock sb
not turn a hair to not show any reaction to sth that many people would find surprising or shocking
split hairs → **SPLIT**¹

hairbrush /'heəbrʌʃ/ **noun** [C] a brush that you use on your hair •➤ picture at **brush**

haircut /'heəkʌt/ **noun** [C] **1** the act of sb cutting your hair: *You need (to have) a*

hair

straight hair

wavy hair

curly hair

He is bald.

moustache

He has receding hair

He has a bald patch

He has long straight hair

He has dreadlocks

parting

goatee

beard

ponytail

bristles/
stubble

dreadlocks

pigtails (*US* braids)

plait (*US* braid)

bunches

bun

pigtail

bunch

fringe
(*US* bangs)

haircut **2** the style in which your hair has been cut: *That haircut really suits you.*

hairdo /ˈheədu:/ (*informal*) = **HAIRSTYLE**

hairdresser /ˈheədresə/ **noun 1** [C] a person whose job is to cut, shape, colour, etc hair

➤ A **barber** is a male hairdresser who only cuts men's hair.

2 the hairdresser's [sing] the place where you go to have your hair cut

hairdryer (also **hairdrier**) /ˈheədraɪə/ **noun** [C] a machine that dries hair by blowing hot air through it

hairgrip /ˈheəgrɪp/ **noun** [C] a U-shaped pin that is used for holding the hair in place

hairless /ˈheələs/ **adj** without hair ·➤ Look at **bald**.

hairline[1] /ˈheəlaɪn/ **noun** [C] the place on a person's forehead where his/her hair starts growing

hairline[2] /ˈheəlaɪn/ **adj** (used about a crack in sth) very thin: *a hairline fracture of the leg*

hairpin bend /ˌheəpɪn ˈbend/ **noun** [C] (*Brit*) a very sharp bend in a road, especially a mountain road

hair-raising **adj** that makes you very frightened: *a hair-raising experience*

hairspray /ˈheəspreɪ/ **noun** [U,C] a substance

you spray onto your hair to hold it in place
·➤ synonym **lacquer**

hairstyle /ˈheəstaɪl/ (also *informal* **hairdo**) **noun** [C] the style in which your hair has been cut or arranged

hairstylist /ˈheəstaɪlɪst/ (also **stylist**) **noun** [C] a person whose job it is to cut and shape sb's hair

hairy /ˈheəri/ **adj** (**hairier**; **hairiest**) **1** having a lot of hair **2** (*slang*) dangerous or worrying

haj (also **hajj**) /hædʒ/ **noun** [sing] a journey (**pilgrimage**) which many Muslims make to their most important religious place (**Mecca**)

halal /ˈhælæl/ **adj** (only *before* a noun) (used about meat) from an animal that has been killed according to Muslim law

★**half**[1] /hɑːf/ **determiner, noun** [C] (*pl* **halves** /hɑːvz/) one of two equal parts of sth: *three and a half kilos of potatoes* ● *Two halves make a whole.* ● *half an hour* ● *an hour and a half* ● *The second half of the book is more exciting.* ● *Giggs scored in the first half* (= of a match). ● *Half of this money is yours.* ● *Half the people in the office leave at 5.* ·➤ verb **halve**

IDIOMS **break, cut, etc sth in half** to break, etc sth into two parts

---

[I] **intransitive**, a verb which has no object: *He laughed.*   [T] **transitive**, a verb which has an object: *He ate an apple.*

go **half and half**/go **halves** with sb (*Brit*) to share the cost of sth with sb

do **nothing/not do anything by halves** to do whatever you do completely and properly

★**half²** /hɑːf/ *adv* not completely; to the extent of half: ***half full*** ● *The hotel was only **half** finished.* ● *He's **half** German* (= one of his parents is German).

[IDIOMS] **half past...** (in time) thirty minutes past an hour: *half past six* (= 6.30) ••➤ In spoken British English people also say **half six** to mean 6.30.

not half as much, many, good, bad, etc much less: *This episode wasn't half as good as the last.*

,half-'baked *adj* (*informal*) not well-planned or considered: *a half-baked idea/scheme*

,half 'board *noun* [U] (*Brit*) a price for a room in a hotel, etc, which includes breakfast and an evening meal ••➤ Look at **full board** and **bed and breakfast**.

'half-brother (also 'half-sister) *noun* [C] a brother with whom you share one parent

➤ Compare **stepbrother**.

,half-'hearted *adj* without interest or enthusiasm –half-heartedly *adv*

'half-sister *noun* [C] a sister with whom you share one parent

➤ Compare **stepsister**.

,half-'term *noun* [C] (*Brit*) a holiday of one week in the middle of a three-month period of school (**term**)

,half-'time *noun* [U] (in sport) the period of time between the two halves of a match

halfway /ˌhɑːf'weɪ/ *adj, adv* at an equal distance between two places; in the middle of a period of time: *They have a break halfway through the morning.* ••➤ synonym **midway**

★**hall** /hɔːl/ *noun* [C] **1** (also **hallway**) a room or passage that is just inside the front entrance of a house or public building: *There is a public telephone in the **entrance hall** of this building.* ••➤ picture on page C7 **2** a building or large room in which meetings, concerts, dances, etc can be held: *a concert hall* ••➤ Look at **town hall**.

hallmark /'hɔːlmɑːk/ *noun* [C] **1** a characteristic that is typical of sb: *The ability to motivate students is the hallmark of a good teacher.* **2** a mark that is put on objects made of valuable metals, giving information about the quality of the metal and when and where the object was made

hallo = HELLO

,hall of 'residence *noun* [C] (*pl* **halls of residence**) (*US* **dormitory**) (in colleges, universities, etc) a building where students live

Hallowe'en /ˌhæləʊ'iːn/ *noun* [sing] (also **Halloween**) the night of October 31st (before All Saints' Day)

➤ Hallowe'en is the time when people say that witches and ghosts appear. Children now dress up as witches, etc and play tricks on people. In the US they go to people's houses and say '**trick or treat**' and the people give them sweets.

hallucination /həˌluːsɪ'neɪʃn/ *noun* [C,U] seeing or hearing sth that is not really there (because you are ill or have taken a drug)

halo /'heɪləʊ/ *noun* [C] (*pl* **halos** or **haloes**) the circle of light that is drawn around the head of an important religious person in a painting

halt /hɔːlt/ *noun* [sing] a stop (that does not last very long): *Work came to a halt when the machine broke down.* –halt *verb* (*formal*): *An accident halted the traffic in the town centre for half an hour.*

[IDIOM] **grind to a halt/standstill** → GRIND¹

halve /hɑːv/ *verb* **1** [I,T] to reduce by a half; to make sth reduce by a half: *Shares in the company have halved in value.* ● *We aim to halve the number of people on our waiting list in the next six months.* **2** [T] to divide sth into two equal parts: *First halve the peach and then remove the stone.*

ham /hæm/ *noun* [U] meat from a pig's back leg that has been smoked, etc (**cured**) to keep it fresh ••➤ Look at **bacon** and **pork** and at the note at **meat**.

hamburger /'hæmbɜːgə/ *noun* **1** (also **burger**) [C] meat that has been cut up small and pressed into a flat round shape. Hamburgers are often eaten in a bread roll. ••➤ picture on page C4. Look at **beefburger**. **2** [U] (*US*) = MINCE

hamlet /'hæmlət/ *noun* [C] a very small village

★**hammer¹** /'hæmə/ *noun* [C] a tool with a heavy metal head that is used for hitting nails, etc ••➤ picture at **tool**

hammer² /'hæmə/ *verb* **1** [I,T] **hammer sth** (**in/into/onto sth**) to hit with a hammer: *She hammered the nail into the wall.* **2** [I] to hit sth several times, making a loud noise: *He hammered on the door until somebody opened it.*

[IDIOMS] **hammer sth into sb** to force sb to remember sth by repeating it many times

hammer sth out to succeed in making a plan or agreement after a lot of discussion

hammering /'hæmərɪŋ/ *noun* **1** [U] the noise that is made by sb using a hammer or by sb hitting sth many times **2** [C] (*Brit informal*) a very bad defeat

hammock /'hæmək/ *noun* [C] a bed, made of strong cloth (**canvas**) or rope, which is hung up between two trees or poles.

hamper¹ /'hæmpə/ *verb* [T] (usually passive) to make sth difficult: *The building work was hampered by bad weather.*

hamper² /'hæmpə/ *noun* [C] a large basket with a lid that is used for carrying food

hamster /'hæmstə/ *noun* [C] a small animal that is kept as a pet. Hamsters are like small rats but are fatter and do not have a tail. They store food in the sides of their mouths.

★**hand¹** /hænd/ *noun* **1** [C] the part of your body at the end of your arm which has five fingers: *He took the child **by the hand**.* ● *She* *was on her hands and knees* (= crawling on the floor) *looking for an earring.* •➤ picture on page C5 **2 a hand** [sing] (*informal*) some help: *I'll give you a hand with the washing up.* ● *Do you want/need a hand?* **3** [C] the part of a clock or watch that points to the numbers: *the hour/minute/second hand* •➤ picture at **clock 4** [C] a person who does physical work on a farm, in a factory etc: *farmhands* **5** [C] the set of playing cards that sb has been given in a game of cards: *have a good/bad hand* **6 -handed** *adj* (used in compounds) having, using or made for the type of hand(s) mentioned: *heavy-handed* (= clumsy and careless) ● *right-handed/left-handed*

IDIOMS **(close/near) at hand** (*formal*) near in space or time: *Help is close at hand.*

be an old hand (at sth) ➔ **OLD**

by hand 1 done by a person and not by machine: *I had to do all the sewing by hand.* **2** not by post: *The letter was delivered by hand.*

catch sb red-handed ➔ **CATCH¹**

change hands ➔ **CHANGE¹**

a firm hand ➔ **FIRM¹**

(at) first hand (used about information that you have received) from sb who was closely involved: *Did you get this information first hand?* •➤ Look at **second-hand**.

get, have etc a free hand ➔ **FREE¹**

get, etc the upper hand ➔ **UPPER**

get/lay your hands on sb/sth 1 to find or obtain sth: *I need to get my hands on a good computer.* **2** (*informal*) to catch sb: *Just wait till I get my hands on that boy!*

give sb a big hand to hit your hands together to show approval, enthusiasm, etc: *The audience gave the girl a big hand when she finished her song.*

hand in hand 1 holding each other's hands: *The couple walked hand in hand along the beach.* **2** usually happening together; closely connected: *Drought and famine usually go hand in hand.*

your hands are tied to not be in a position to do as you would like because of rules, promises, etc

hands off (sb/sth) (*informal*) used for ordering sb not to touch sth

hands up 1 used in a school, etc for asking people to lift one hand and give an answer: *Hands up, who'd like to go on the trip this afternoon?* **2** used by a person with a gun to tell other people to put their hands in the air

have a hand in sth to take part in or share sth: *Even members of staff had a hand in painting and decorating the new office.*

have sb eating out of your hand ➔ **EAT**

have your hands full to be very busy so that you cannot do anything else

a helping hand ➔ **HELP¹**

hold sb's hand to give sb support in a difficult situation: *I'll come to the dentist's with you to hold your hand.*

hold hands (with sb) (used about two people) to hold each other's hands

in hand 1 being dealt with at the moment; under control: *The situation is in hand.*

•➤ opposite **out of hand 2** (used about money, etc) not yet used: *If you have time in hand at the end of the exam, check what you have written.*

in safe hands ➔ **SAFE¹**

in your hands in your possession, control or care: *The matter is in the hands of a solicitor.*

keep your hand in to do an activity from time to time so that you do not forget how to do it or lose the skill: *I play tennis from time to time just to keep my hand in.*

lend (sb) a hand/lend a hand (to sb) ➔ **LEND**

off your hands not your responsibility any more

on hand available to help or to be used: *There is always an adult on hand to help when the children are playing outside.*

on your hands being your responsibility: *We seem to have a problem on our hands.*

on the one hand...on the other (hand) used for showing opposite points of view: *On the one hand, of course, cars are very useful. On the other hand, they cause a huge amount of pollution.*

(get/be) out of hand not under control: *Violence at football matches is getting out of hand.* •➤ opposite **in hand**

out of your hands not in your control; not your responsibility: *I can't help you, I'm afraid. The matter is out of my hands.*

shake sb's hand/shake hands (with sb)/ shake sb by the hand ➔ **SHAKE¹**

to hand near or close to you: *I'm afraid I haven't got my diary to hand.*

try your hand at sth ➔ **TRY¹**

turn your hand to sth to have the ability to do sth: *She can turn her hand to all sorts of jobs.*

wash your hands of sb/sth ➔ **WASH¹**

with your bare hands ➔ **BARE**

★**hand²** /hænd/ *verb* [T] **hand sb sth; hand sth to sb** to give or pass sth to sb

IDIOM **have (got) to hand it to sb** used to show admiration and approval of sb's work or efforts: *You've got to hand it to Rita – she's a great cook.*

PHRASAL VERBS **hand sth back (to sb)** to give or return sth to the person who owns it or to where it belongs

hand sth down (to sb) 1 to pass customs, traditions, etc from older people to younger ones **2** to pass clothes, toys, etc from older children to younger ones in the family

hand sth in (to sb) to give sth to sb in authority: *I found a wallet and handed it in to the police.*

hand sth on (to sb) to send or give sth to another person: *When you have read the article, please hand it on to another student.*

hand sth out (to sb) to give sth to many people in a group: *Food was handed out to the starving people.*

hand (sth) over (to sb) to give sb else your position of power or the responsibility for sth: *She resigned as chairperson and handed over to one of her younger colleagues.*

hand (sb) over to sb (used at a meeting or on

the television, radio, telephone, etc) to let sb speak or listen to another person

hand sb/sth over (to sb) to give sb/sth (to sb): *People were tricked into handing over large sums of money.*

hand sth round to offer to pass sth, especially food and drinks, to all the people in a group

handbag /'hændbæg/ (*US* **purse**) **noun** [C] a small bag in which women carry money, keys, etc •➤ synonym **shoulder bag** •➤ picture at **bag**

handbook /'hændbʊk/ **noun** [C] a small book that gives instructions on how to use sth or advice and information about a particular subject

handbrake /'hændbreɪk/ (*US* **e'mergency brake**; **'parking brake**) **noun** [C] a device that is operated by hand to stop a car from moving when it is parked •➤ picture on page S9

handcuffs /'hændkʌfs/ (also **cuffs**) **noun** [pl] a pair of metal rings that are joined together by a chain and put around the wrists of prisoners

handful /'hændfʊl/ **noun 1** [C] a handful (of sth) as much or as many of sth as you can hold in one hand: *a handful of sand* **2** [sing] a small number (of sb/sth): *Only a handful of people came to the meeting.* **3 a handful** [sing] (*informal*) a person or an animal that is difficult to control: *The little girl is quite a handful.*

handgun /'hændgʌn/ **noun** [C] a small gun that you can hold and fire with one hand

handicap¹ /'hændikæp/ **noun 1** [C] something that makes doing sth more difficult; a disadvantage: *Not speaking French is going to be a bit of a handicap in my new job.* **2** a disadvantage that is given to a strong competitor in a sports event, etc so that the other competitors have more chance **3** (*old-fashioned*) = **DISABILITY** •➤ Many people now find this word offensive.

handicap² /'hændikæp/ **verb** [T] (**handicapping**; **handicapped**) (usually passive) to give or be a disadvantage to sb: *They were handicapped by their lack of education.*

handicapped /'hændikæpt/ **adj** (*old-fashioned*) = **DISABLED** •➤ Many people now find this word offensive.

handicraft /'hændikrɑːft/ **noun 1** [C] an activity that needs skill with the hands as well as artistic ability, for example sewing **2 handicrafts** [pl] the objects that are produced by this activity

handiwork /'hændiwɜːk/ **noun** [U] **1** a thing that you have made or done, especially using your artistic skill: *She put the dress on and stood back to admire her handiwork.* **2** a thing done by a particular person or group, especially sth bad

handkerchief /'hæŋkətʃɪf; -tʃiːf/ **noun** [C] (*pl* **handkerchiefs** or **handkerchieves** /-tʃiːvz/) a square piece of cloth or soft thin paper that you use for clearing your nose •➤ A more informal word is **hanky** or **hankie**. A handkerchief that is made of soft thin

paper is also called a **paper handkerchief** or a **tissue**.

★**handle¹** /'hændl/ **verb** [T] **1** to touch or hold sth with your hand(s): *Wash your hands before you handle food.* **2** to deal with or to control sb/sth: *This port handles 100 million tons of cargo each year.* • *I have a problem at work and I don't really know how to handle it.* –**handler** **noun** [C]: *baggage/dog/food handlers*

handles

handle
handle

handle

knobs

knob
VOLUME
knob

knob

buttons

5
4
3
2
1
G

button

buttons
buttons

★**handle²** /'hændl/ **noun** [C] a part of sth that is used for holding or opening it: *She turned the handle and opened the door.*
  IDIOM **fly off the handle** → **FLY¹**

handlebar /'hændlbɑː/ **noun** [C, usually pl] the metal bar at the front of a bicycle that you hold when you are riding it •➤ picture on page S9

'hand luggage (*US* **'carry-on bag**) **noun** [U] a small bag, etc that you can keep with you on a plane

handmade /ˌhænd'meɪd/ **adj** made by hand and of very good quality, not by machine

handout /'hændaʊt/ **noun** [C] **1** food, money, etc to people who need it badly **2** a free document that is given to a lot of people, to advertise sth or explain sth, for example in a class

handpicked /ˌhænd'pɪkt/ **adj** chosen carefully or personally

handrail /'hændreɪl/ **noun** [C] a long narrow wooden or metal bar at the side of some steps, a bath, etc that you hold for support or balance

handset = **RECEIVER**(1)

handshake /'hændʃeɪk/ **noun** [C] the action of shaking sb's right hand with your own when you meet him/her

★**handsome** /'hænsəm/ **adj 1** (used about a man) attractive ••➤ Look at the note at **beautiful. 2** (used about money, an offer, etc) large or generous: *a handsome profit* –**handsomely adv**: *Her efforts were handsomely rewarded.*

hands-'on adj learnt by doing sth yourself, not watching sb else do it; practical: *She needs some hands-on computer experience.*

handwriting /'hændraɪtɪŋ/ **noun** [U] a person's style of writing by hand

handwritten /ˌhænd'rɪtn/ **adj** written by hand, not typed or printed

handy /'hændi/ **adj (handier; handiest) 1** useful; easy to use: *a handy tip • a handy gadget* **2** handy (for sth/doing sth) within easy reach of sth; nearby: *Always keep a first-aid kit handy for emergencies.* **3** skilful in using your hands or tools to make or repair things: *James is very handy around the house.* IDIOM **come in handy** to be useful at some time: *Don't throw that box away. It may come in handy.*

handyman /'hændimæn/ **noun** [sing] a person who is clever at making or repairing things, especially around the house

★**hang¹** /hæŋ/ **verb** (*pt, pp* **hung** /hʌŋ/) ••➤ The past tense and past participle **hanged** is only used in sense 2. **1** [I,T] to fasten sth or be fastened at the top so that the lower part is free or loose: *Hang your coat on the hook. • I left the washing hanging on the line all day. • A cigarette hung from his lips.* **2** [T] to kill sb/yourself by putting a rope around the neck and allowing the body to drop downwards: *He was hanged for murder.* **3** [I] hang (above/over sb/sth) to stay in the air in a way that is unpleasant or threatening: *Smog hung in the air over the city.* IDIOMS **be/get hung up (about/on sb/sth)** to think about sb/sth all the time in a way that is not healthy or good: *She's really hung up about her parents' divorce.*

hang (on) in there (*spoken*) to have courage and keep trying, even though a situation is difficult: *The worst part is over now. Just hang on in there and be patient.*

PHRASAL VERBS **hang about/around** (*informal*) to stay in or near a place not doing very much

hang back 1 to not want to do or say sth, often because you are shy or not sure of yourself **2** to stay in a place after other people have left it

hang on 1 to wait for a short time: *Hang on a minute. I'm nearly ready.* **2** to hold sth tightly: *Hang on, don't let go!*

hang on sth to depend on sth

hang on to sth 1 (*informal*) to keep sth: *Let's hang on to the car for another year.* **2** to hold sth tightly: *He hung on to the child's hand as they crossed the street.*

hang sth out to put washing, etc on a clothes line so that it can dry

hang over sb to be present or about to happen in a way which is unpleasant or threatening: *This essay has been hanging over me for days.*

hang sth up to put sth on a nail, hook, etc: *Hang your coat up over there.*

hang up to end a telephone conversation and put the telephone down

hang up on sb (*informal*) to end a telephone conversation without saying goodbye because you are angry

hang² /hæŋ/ **noun** IDIOM **get the hang of (doing) sth** (*informal*) to learn how to use or do sth: *It took me a long time to get the hang of my new computer.*

hangar /'hæŋə/ **noun** [C] a big building where planes are kept

hanger /'hæŋə/ (also **coat hanger, clothes-hanger**) **noun** [C] a metal, plastic or wooden object with a hook that is used for hanging up clothes in a cupboard ••➤ picture at **hook**

hanger-on /ˌhæŋər 'ɒn/ **noun** [C] (*pl* **hangers-on**) a person who tries to be friendly with sb who is rich or important

'hang-glider noun [C] a type of frame covered with cloth, which a person holds and flies through the air with as a sport ••➤ Look at **glider**. ••➤ picture at **parachute** –**hang-gliding noun** [U]

hanging /'hæŋɪŋ/ **noun** [C,U] death as a form of punishment for a crime, caused by putting rope around a person's neck and letting the body drop downwards

hangman /'hæŋmən/ **noun** [sing] **1** a person whose job is to kill criminals as a form of punishment by hanging them with a rope **2** a word game where the aim is to guess all the letters of a word before a picture of a person hanging is completed

hangover /'hæŋəʊvə/ **noun** [C] pain in your head and a sick feeling that you have if you have drunk too much alcohol the night before

'hang-up noun [C] (*slang*) a hang-up (about sb/sth) an emotional problem about sth that makes you embarrassed or worried: *He has a real hang-up about his height.*

hanker /'hæŋkə/ **verb** [I] hanker after/for sth to want sth very much (often sth that you cannot easily have)

hanky (also **hankie**) /'hæŋki/ **noun** [C] (*pl* **hankies**) (*informal*) ➔ **HANDKERCHIEF**

haphazard /hæp'hæzəd/ **adj** with no particular order or plan; badly organized –**haphazardly adv**

★**happen** /'hæpən/ **verb** [I] **1** (of an event or situation) to take place, usually without being planned first: *Can you describe to the police what happened after you left the party? • How did the accident happen?*

> **Happen** and **occur** are usually used for events that are not planned. **Occur** is more formal than **happen. Take place** suggests that an event is planned: *The wedding took place on Saturday June 13th.*

2 happen to sb/sth to be what sb/sth experiences: *What do you think has happened to Julie? She should have been here an hour ago.* ● *What will happen to the business when your father retires?* **3 happen to do sth** to do sth by chance: *I happened to meet him in London yesterday.*

IDIOMS **as it happens/happened** (used when you are adding to what you have said) actually: *As it happens, I did remember to bring the book you wanted.*

it (just) so happens → so¹

happening /'hæpənɪŋ/ **noun** [C, usually pl] a thing that happens; an event (that is usually strange or difficult to explain): *Strange happenings have been reported in that old hotel.*

> A **happening** is usually something that happens by chance. An **event** is usually something that is planned and is often special or important.

happily /'hæpɪli/ **adv 1** in a happy way: *I would happily give up my job if I didn't need the money.* **2** it is lucky that; fortunately: *The police found my handbag and, happily, nothing had been stolen.*

★**happy** /'hæpi/ **adj (happier; happiest) 1 happy (to do sth); happy for sb; happy that…** feeling or showing pleasure; pleased: *I was really happy to see Mark again yesterday.* ● *You look very happy today.* ● *Congratulations! I'm very happy for you.* ••➤ opposite **unhappy** or **sad**. Look at the note at **glad. 2** giving or causing pleasure: *a happy marriage/memory/childhood* ● *The film is sad but it has a **happy ending**.* **3 happy (with/about sb/sth)** satisfied that sth is good and right; not worried: *I'm not very happy with what you've done.* ● *She doesn't feel happy about the salary she's been offered.* **3** (not before a noun) **happy to do sth** ready to do sth; pleased: *I'll be happy to see you any day next week.* **4 Happy** used to wish sb an enjoyable time: *Happy Birthday!* **5** (only *before* a noun) lucky; fortunate: *a happy coincidence.* ••➤ opposite **unhappy** –happiness **noun** [U]

,**happy-go-'lucky adj** not caring or worried about life and the future

'**happy hour noun** [usually sing] a time, usually in the evening, when a pub or bar sells alcoholic drinks at lower prices than usual

harass /'hærəs; hə'ræs/ **verb** [T] to annoy or worry sb by doing unpleasant things to him/her, especially over a long time: *The court ordered him to stop harassing his ex-wife.* –harassment **noun** [U]: *She accused her boss of sexual harassment.*

harassed /'hærəst; hə'ræst/ **adj** tired and worried because you have too much to do

harbour¹ (*US* **harbor**) /'hɑːbə/ **noun** [C,U] a place on the coast where ships can be tied up (moored) and protected from the sea and bad weather ••➤ picture on page C8

harbour² (*US* **harbor**) /'hɑːbə/ **verb** [T] **1** to keep feelings or thoughts secret in your mind for a long time: *She began to **harbour doubts** about the decision.* **2** to hide or protect sb/sth that is bad: *They were accused of harbouring terrorists.*

★**hard¹** /hɑːd/ **adj 1** not soft to touch; not easy to break or bend: *The bed was so hard that I couldn't sleep.* ● *Diamonds are the hardest known mineral.* ••➤ opposite **soft 2 hard (for sb) (to do sth)** difficult to do or understand; not easy: *The first question in the exam was very hard.* ● *This book is hard to understand./It is a hard book to understand.* ● *It's hard for young people to find good jobs nowadays.* ● *I find his attitude very hard to take* (= difficult to accept). ••➤ opposite **easy 3** needing or using a lot of physical strength or mental effort: *It's a hard climb to the top of the hill.* ● *Hard work is said to be good for you.* ● *He's a hard worker.* **4** (used about a person) not feeling or showing kindness or pity; not gentle: *You have to be hard to succeed in business.* ••➤ opposite **soft** or **lenient 5** (used about conditions) unpleasant or unhappy; full of difficulty: *He had a hard time when his parents died.* ● *to have a hard day/life/childhood* **6** (used about the weather) very cold: *The forecast is for a hard winter/frost.* ••➤ opposite **mild 7** (used about water) containing particular minerals so that soap does not make many bubbles: *We live in a **hard water** area.* ••➤ opposite **soft** –hardness **noun** [U]

IDIOMS **a hard act to follow** a person or a thing that is difficult to do better than

be hard at it to be working very hard doing sth

be hard on sb/sth 1 to treat sb/sth in a harsh way or to make things difficult: *Don't be too hard on her – she's only a child.* **2** to be unfair to sb: *Moving the office to the country is a bit hard on the people who haven't got a car.*

give sb a hard time (*informal*) to make a situation unpleasant, embarrassing or difficult for sb

hard and fast (used about rules, etc) that cannot be changed: *There are no hard and fast rules about this.*

hard facts information that is true, not just people's opinions

hard luck → LUCK

hard of hearing unable to hear well

hard to swallow difficult to believe

have a hard job doing/to do sth; have a hard time doing sth to do sth with great difficulty

learn the hard way → LEARN

no hard feelings (*spoken*) used to tell sb you do not feel angry after an argument, etc: *'No hard feelings, I hope,' he said, offering me his hand.*

the hard way through having unpleasant or difficult experiences, rather than learning from what you are told: *She won't listen to my advice so she'll just have to learn the hard way.*

take a hard line (on sth) to deal with sth in a very serious way that you will not allow anyone to change: *The government has taken a hard line on people who drink and drive.*

★ hard² /hɑːd/ adv **1** with great effort, energy or attention: *He worked hard all his life.* ● *You'll have to try a bit harder than that.* **2** with great force; heavily: *It was raining/snowing hard.* ● *He hit her hard across the face.*

IDIOMS **be hard up (for sth)** to have too few or too little of sth, especially money

be hard pressed/pushed/put to do sth to find sth very difficult to do: *He was hard pressed to explain his wife's sudden disappearance.*

die hard → **DIE**

hard done by (*Brit*) not fairly treated: *He felt very hard done by when he wasn't chosen for the team.*

hardback /'hɑːdbæk/ noun [C] a book that has a hard rigid cover: *This book is only available in hardback.* ••➤ Look at **paperback**.

,hard-'boiled adj (used about an egg) boiled until it is solid inside

,hard 'core noun [sing,with sing or pl verb] the members of a group who are the most active

,hard 'currency noun [U] money belonging to a particular country that is easy to exchange and not likely to fall in value

,hard 'disk noun [C] a piece of hard plastic that is fixed inside a computer and is used for storing data and programs permanently ••➤ Look at **floppy disk**.

,hard 'drug noun [C,usually pl] a powerful and illegal drug that some people take for pleasure and may become dependent on (addicted): *Heroin and cocaine are hard drugs.*

➤ Compare **soft**.

harden /'hɑːdn/ verb **1** [I,T] to become or to make sth hard or less likely to change: *The concrete will harden in 24 hours.* ● *The firm has hardened its attitude on this question.* **2** [T] (usually passive) **harden sb (to sth/doing sth)** to make sb less kind or less easily shocked: *a hardened reporter/criminal* ● *Police officers get hardened to seeing dead bodies.* **3** [I] (used about a person's face, voice, etc) to become serious and unfriendly

,hard-'headed adj determined and not allowing yourself to be influenced by emotions: *a hard-headed businessman*

,hard-'hearted adj not kind to other people and not considering their feelings ••➤ opposite **soft-hearted**

,hard-'hitting adj that talks about or criticizes sb/sth in an honest and very direct way: *a hard-hitting campaign/speech/report*

★ hardly /'hɑːdli/ adv **1** almost no; almost not; almost none: *There's hardly any coffee left.* ● *We hardly ever go out nowadays.* ● *I hardly spoke any English when I first came here.* ••➤ Look at **almost**. **2** used especially after 'can' and 'could' and before the main verb to emphasize that sth is difficult to do: *Speak up – I can hardly hear you.* **3** (used to say that sth has just begun, happened, etc) only just: *She'd hardly gone to sleep than it was time to get up again.*

➤ Note that if 'hardly' is at the beginning of a sentence, the verb follows immediately. This use is found in formal writing: *Hardly had she gone to sleep than it was time to get up again.*

4 (used to suggest that sth is unlikely or unreasonable) not really: *You can hardly expect me to believe that excuse!* ••➤ Look at **barely** and **scarcely**.

,hard-'nosed adj not affected by feelings or emotions when trying to get what you want: *hard-nosed journalists/politicians*

hardship /'hɑːdʃɪp/ noun [C,U] the fact of not having enough money, food, etc: *This new tax is going to cause a lot of hardship.*

,hard 'shoulder (*US* shoulder) noun [C] a narrow section of road at the side of a motorway where cars are allowed to stop in an emergency

hardware /'hɑːdweə/ noun [U] **1** the machinery of a computer, not the programmes written for it ••➤ Look at **software**. **2** tools and equipment that are used in the house and garden: *a hardware shop*

,hard-'wearing adj (*Brit*) (used about materials, clothes, etc) strong and able to last for a long time

,hard-'working adj working with effort and energy: *a hard-working man*

hardy /'hɑːdi/ adj (**hardier**; **hardiest**) strong and able to survive difficult conditions and bad weather: *a hardy plant*

hare /heə/ noun [C] an animal like a rabbit but bigger with longer ears and legs ••➤ picture at **rabbit**

harem /'hɑːriːm/ noun [C] a number of women living with one man, especially in Muslim societies. The part of the building the women live in is also called a harem.

★ harm¹ /hɑːm/ noun [U] damage or injury: *Peter ate some of those berries but they didn't do him any harm.* ● *Experienced staff watch over the children to make sure they don't come to any harm.*

IDIOMS **no harm done** (*informal*) used to tell sb that he/she has not caused any damage or injury: *'Sorry about what I said to you last night.' 'That's all right, Jack, no harm done!'*

out of harm's way in a safe place: *Put the medicine out of harm's way where the children can't reach it.*

there is no harm in doing sth; it does no harm (for sb) to do sth there's nothing wrong in doing sth (and sth good may result): *I'm sure he'll say no, but there's no harm in asking.*

harm² /hɑːm/ verb [T] to cause injury or damage; hurt: *Too much sunshine can harm your skin.*

★ harmful /'hɑːmfl/ adj **harmful (to sb/sth)** causing harm: *Traffic fumes are harmful to the environment.*

★ harmless /'hɑːmləs/ adj **1** not able or not likely to cause damage or injury; safe: *You* *needn't be frightened – these insects are completely harmless.* **2** not likely to upset people: *The children can watch that film – it's quite harmless.* –**harmlessly** *adv*

harmonica /hɑːˈmɒnɪkə/ (also **mouth organ**) *noun* [C] a small musical instrument that you play by moving it across your lips while you are blowing ••➤ picture at **music**

harmonious /hɑːˈməʊniəs/ *adj* **1** friendly, peaceful and without disagreement **2** (used about musical notes, colours, etc) producing a pleasant effect when heard or seen together –**harmoniously** *adv*

harmonize (also **-ise**) /ˈhɑːmənaɪz/ *verb* [I] **1** harmonize (with sth) (used about two or more things) to produce a pleasant effect when seen, heard, etc together **2** harmonize (with sb/sth) to sing or play music that sounds good combined with the main tune –**harmonization** (also **-isation**) /ˌhɑːmənaɪˈzeɪʃn/ *noun* [U]

harmony /ˈhɑːməni/ *noun* (*pl* **harmonies**) **1** [U] a state of agreement or of peaceful existence together: *We need to live more in harmony with our environment.* **2** [C,U] a pleasing combination of musical notes, colours, etc: *There are some beautiful harmonies in that music.*

harness¹ /ˈhɑːnɪs/ *noun* [C] **1** a set of leather straps that is put around a horse's neck and body so that it can pull sth **2** a set of straps for fastening sth to a person's body or for stopping sb from moving around, falling, etc: *a safety harness*

harness² /ˈhɑːnɪs/ *verb* [T] **1** harness sth (to sth) to put a harness on a horse, etc or to tie a horse, etc to sth using a harness: *Two ponies were harnessed to the cart.* **2** to control the energy of sth in order to produce power or to achieve sth: *to harness the sun's rays as a source of energy*

harp /hɑːp/ *noun* [C] a large musical instrument which has many strings stretching from the top to the bottom of a frame. You play the harp with your fingers. ••➤ picture at **music** –**harpist** *noun* [C]

harpoon /hɑːˈpuːn/ *noun* [C] a long thin weapon with a sharp pointed end and a rope tied to it that is used to catch large sea animals (**whales**) –**harpoon** *verb* [T]

harrowing /ˈhærəʊɪŋ/ *adj* making people feel very sad or upset: *The programme showed harrowing scenes of the victims of the war.*

harsh /hɑːʃ/ *adj* **1** very strict and unkind: *a harsh punishment/criticism* • *The judge had some harsh words for the journalist's behaviour.* **2** unpleasant and difficult to live in, look at, listen to, etc: *She grew up in the harsh environment of New York City.* • *a harsh light/voice* **3** too strong or rough and likely to damage sth: *This soap is too harsh for a baby's skin.* –**harshly** *adv* –**harshness** *noun* [U]

harvest /ˈhɑːvɪst/ *noun* **1** [C,U] the time of year when the grain, fruit, etc is collected on a farm; the act of collecting the grain, fruit,

etc: *Farmers always need extra help with the harvest.* **2** [C] the amount of grain, fruit, etc that is collected: *This year's wheat harvest was very poor.* –**harvest** *verb* [I,T] ••➤ Look at **combine harvester**.

has /həz; *strong form* hæz/ ➔ **HAVE**

'has-been *noun* [C] (*informal*) a person or thing that is no longer as famous, successful or important as before

hash /hæʃ/ *noun* [U] **1** a hot dish of meat mixed together with potato and fried **2** = **HASHISH**

[IDIOM] **make a hash of sth** (*informal*) to do sth badly

hashish /ˈhæʃiːʃ/ (also **hash**) *noun* [U] a drug made from a plant (**hemp**) that some people smoke for pleasure and which is illegal in many countries

hasn't *short for* **HAS NOT**

hassle¹ /ˈhæsl/ *noun* (*informal*) **1** [C,U] a thing or situation that is annoying because it is complicated or involves a lot of effort: *It's going to be a hassle having to change trains with all this luggage.* **2** [U] disagreeing or arguing: *I've decided what to do – please don't give me any hassle about it.*

hassle² /ˈhæsl/ *verb* [T] to annoy sb, especially by asking him/her to do sth many times: *I wish he'd stop hassling me about decorating the house.*

haste /heɪst/ *noun* [U] speed in doing sth, especially because you do not have enough time: *It was obvious that the letter had been written in haste.*

hasten /ˈheɪsn/ *verb* (*formal*) **1** [I] hasten to do sth to be quick to do or say sth: *She hastened to apologize.* **2** [T] to make sth happen or be done earlier or more quickly

hasty /ˈheɪsti/ *adj* **1** said or done too quickly: *He said a hasty 'goodbye' and left.* **2** hasty (in doing sth/to do sth) (used about a person) acting or deciding sth too quickly or without enough thought: *Maybe I was too hasty in rejecting her for the job.* –**hastily** *adv*

★**hat** /hæt/ *noun* [C] a covering that you wear on your head, usually when you are outside: *to wear a hat*

[IDIOM] **at the drop of a hat** ➔ **DROP²**

hatch¹ /hætʃ/ *verb* **1** [I] hatch (out) (used about a baby bird, insect, fish, etc) to come out of an egg **2** [I,T] to make a baby bird, etc come out of an egg: *How long do these eggs take to hatch?* **3** [T] hatch sth (up) to think of a plan (usually to do sth bad): *He hatched a plan to avoid paying any income tax.*

hatch² /hætʃ/ *noun* [C] **1** an opening in the floor of a ship (**the deck**) through which cargo is lowered **2** an opening in the wall between a kitchen and another room that is used for passing food through **3** the door in a plane or spacecraft

hatchback /ˈhætʃbæk/ *noun* [C] a car with a large door at the back that opens upwards ••➤ picture at **car**

hatchet /ˈhætʃɪt/ *noun* [C] a tool with a short handle and a heavy metal head with a sharp

hats

woolly hat

crown

brim

bowler hat

top hat

peak (*US* bill)

baseball cap

cap

crash helmet

visor

sun hat

ribbon

hard hat

beret

edge used for cutting wood ·→ picture at **garden**

★**hate**¹ /heɪt/ **verb** [T] **1** to have a very strong feeling of not liking sb/sth at all: *I hate grapefruit.* • *I hate it when it's raining like this.* • *I hate to see the countryside spoilt.* • *He hates driving at night.* ·→ Look at **detest** and **loathe**. They express an even stronger feeling. **2** used as a polite way of introducing sth that you would prefer not to have to say: *I hate to bother you, but did you pick up my keys by mistake?*

hate² /heɪt/ **noun 1** [U] a very strong feeling of not liking sb/sth at all; hatred: *Do you feel any hate towards the kidnappers?* **2** [C] a thing that you do not like at all: *Plastic flowers are one of my pet hates* (= the things that I particularly dislike).

hateful /'heɪtfl/ **adj** hateful (to sb) extremely unpleasant; horrible: *It was a hateful thing to say.*

hatred /'heɪtrɪd/ **noun** [U] hatred (for/of sb/sth) a very strong feeling of not liking sb/sth; hate

'**hat-trick noun** [C] three points, goals, etc scored by one player in the same game; three successes achieved by one person: *to score a hat-trick*

haughty /'hɔːti/ **adj** proud, and thinking that you are better than other people: *She gave me a haughty look and walked away.* –**haughtily adv**

haul¹ /hɔːl/ **verb** [T] to pull sth with a lot of effort or difficulty: *A lorry hauled the car out of the mud.*

haul² /hɔːl/ **noun 1** [C, usually sing] a haul (of sth) a large amount of sth that has been stolen, caught, collected, etc: *The fishermen came back with a good haul of fish.* **2** [sing] a distance to be travelled: *It seemed a long haul back home at night.*

haulage /'hɔːlɪdʒ/ **noun** [U] (*Brit*) the transport of goods by road, rail, etc; the money charged for this

haunt¹ /hɔːnt/ **verb** [T] **1** (often passive) (used about a ghost of a dead person) to appear in a place regularly: *The house is said to be haunted.* **2** (used about sth unpleasant or sad) to be always in your mind: *His unhappy face has haunted me for years.*

haunt² /hɔːnt/ **noun** [C] a place that you visit regularly: *This cafe has always been a favourite haunt of mine.*

haunting /'hɔːntɪŋ/ **adj** having a quality that stays in your mind: *a haunting song*

★**have**¹ /həv; strong form hæv/ **auxiliary verb** used for forming the perfect tenses ·→ Look at the **Quick Grammar Reference** section at the back of this dictionary.

★**have**² /hæv/ **verb** [T] **1** (*Brit also* **have got**) (not used in the continuous tenses) to own or to hold sth; to possess: *I've got a new camera.* • *The flat has two bedrooms.* • *He's got short dark hair.* • *to have patience/enthusiasm/ skill* • *Have you got any brothers and sisters?* • *Do you have time to check my work?* **2** used

present tense	past tense
I **have** (I've)	I **had** (I'd)
you **have** (you've)	you **had** (you'd)
he/she/it **has**	he/she/it **had**
(he's/she's/it's)	(he'd/she'd/it'd)
we **have** (we've)	we **had** (we'd)
you **have** (you've)	you **had** (you'd)
they **have** (they've)	they **had** (they'd)
past participle	had
present participle	having
negative short forms	**haven't, hasn't,**
	hadn't

with many nouns to talk about doing sth: *What time do you have breakfast?* ● *to have a drink/something to eat* ● *I'll just have a shower then we'll go.* ● *to have an argument/talk/chat* **3** to experience sth: *to have fun* ● *to have problems/difficulties* ● *to have an idea/an impression/a feeling* ● *to have an accident* ● *She had her bag stolen on the underground.* **4** (also **have got**) (not used in the continuous tenses) to be ill with sth: *She's got a bad cold.* ● *to have flu/a headache/cancer/Aids* **5 have sth done** to arrange for sb to do sth: *I have my hair cut every six weeks.* ● *You should have your eyes tested.* **6** (also **have got**) to have a particular duty or plan: *Do you have any homework tonight?* ● *I've got a few things to do this morning, but I'm free later.* **7** (also **have got**) (not used in the continuous tenses) to hold sb/sth; to keep sth in a particular place: *The dog had me by the leg.* ● *We've got our TV up on a shelf.* **8** to cause sb/sth to do sth or to be in a particular state: *The music soon had everyone dancing.* ● *I'll have dinner ready when you get home.* **9** to look after or entertain sb: *We're having some people to dinner tomorrow.*

IDIOM **have had it** used about things that are completely broken, or dead: *This television has had it. We'll have to buy a new one.*

➤ For other idioms containing **have**, look at the entries for the nouns, adjectives, etc, for example **not have a clue** is at **clue**.

PHRASAL VERBS **have sb on** to trick sb as a joke: *Don't listen to what Jimmy says – he's only having you on.*

have (got) sth on 1 to be wearing sth: *She's got a green jumper on.* **2** (*informal*) to have an arrangement to do sth: *I've got a lot on this week* (= I'm very busy).

have sth out to allow part of your body to be removed: *to have a tooth/your appendix out*

haven /'heɪvn/ *noun* [C] a haven (of sth); a haven (for sb/sth) a place where people or animals can be safe and rest: *The lake is a haven for water birds.*

➤ A **tax haven** is a country where income tax is low.

★**have to** /'hæv tə; 'hæf tə; *strong form and before vowels* 'hæv tuː; 'hæf tuː/ (also **have got to**) **modal verb** used for saying that sb must do sth or that sth must happen: *I usually have to work on Saturday mornings.* ● *Do*

you have to have a visa to go to America? ● *She's got to go to the bank this afternoon.* ● *We don't have to* (= it's not necessary to) *go to the party if you don't want to* ● *We had to do lots of boring exercises.*

➤ For more information about modal verbs, look at the **Quick Grammar Reference** section at the back of this dictionary.

havoc /'hævək/ *noun* [U] a situation in which there is a lot of damage or confusion: *The rail strikes will **cause havoc** all over the country.*

hawk /hɔːk/ *noun* [C] a type of large bird that catches and eats small animals and birds. Hawks can see very well.

➤ Hawks are a type of **bird of prey**.

hay /heɪ/ *noun* [U] grass that has been cut and dried for use as animal food

'hay fever *noun* [U] an illness that affects the eyes, nose and throat and is caused by breathing in the powder (**pollen**) produced by some plants

haywire /'heɪwaɪə/ *adj*
IDIOM **be/go haywire** (*informal*) to be or become out of control: *I can't do any work because the computer's gone haywire.*

hazard[1] /'hæzəd/ *noun* [C] a danger or risk: *Smoking is a serious health hazard.*

hazard[2] /'hæzəd/ *verb* [T] to make a guess or to suggest sth even though you know it may be wrong: *I don't know what he paid for the house but I could **hazard a guess**.*

hazardous /'hæzədəs/ *adj* dangerous; risky

haze /heɪz/ *noun* [C,U] **1** air that is difficult to see through because of heat, dust or smoke ·➤ Look at the note at **fog**. **2** a mental state in which you cannot think clearly

hazel[1] /'heɪzl/ *noun* [C] a small tree or bush that produces nuts

hazel[2] /'heɪzl/ *adj* (used especially about eyes) light brown in colour

hazelnut /'heɪzlnʌt/ *noun* [C] a small nut that we eat ·➤ picture at **nut**

hazy /'heɪzi/ *adj* **1** not clear, especially because of heat: *The fields were hazy in the early morning sun.* **2** difficult to remember or understand clearly: *a hazy memory* **3** (used about a person) uncertain, not expressing things clearly: *She's a bit hazy about the details of the trip.*

★**he**[1] /hiː/ *pron* (the subject of a verb) the male person mentioned earlier: *I spoke to John before he left.* ● *Look at that little boy – he's going to fall in!*

➤ If you want to refer to a person who could be either male or female, there are several ways to do this: **He or she, him or her,** and in writing **he/she** or **s/he** can be used: *If you are not sure, ask your doctor. He/she can give you further information.* In informal language you can use **they, them** or **their**: *Everybody knows what they want.* ● *When somebody asks me a question I always try to give them a quick answer.* Or the sentence can be made plural: *A baby cries when s/he is tired* becomes: *Babies cry when they are tired.*

he² /hi:/ **noun** [sing] a male animal: *Is your cat a he or a she?*

★**head**¹ /hed/ **noun** [C] **1** the part of your body above your neck: *She turned her head to look at him.* •➤ picture on page C5 **2** **-headed** (used to form compound adjectives) having the type of head mentioned: *a bald-headed man* **3** a person's mind, brain or mental ability: *Use your head!* (= think!) • *A horrible thought entered my head.* **4** the top, front or most important part: *to sit at the head of the table* • *the head of a nail* • *the head of the queue* **5** the person in charge of a group of people: *the head of the family* • *Several heads of state* (= official leaders of countries) *attended the funeral.* • *the head waiter* **6** (also **head teacher**) the teacher in charge of a school: *Who is going to be the new head?* **7 heads** the side of a coin with the head of a person on it: *Heads or tails? Heads I go first, tails you do.*

IDIOMS a/per head for each person: *How much will the meal cost a head?*

bite sb's head off → BITE¹

come to a head; bring sth to a head if a situation comes to a head or if you bring it to a head, it suddenly becomes very bad and you have to deal with it immediately

do sb's head in (*Brit informal*) to make sb upset and confused

get sth into your head; put sth into sb's head to start or to make sb start believing or thinking sth: *Barry's got it into his head that glasses would make him more attractive.*

go to sb's head 1 to make sb too proud: *If you keep telling him how clever he is, it will go to his head!* **2** to make sb drunk: *Wine always goes straight to my head.*

have a head for sth to be able to deal with sth easily: *You need a good head for heights if you live on the top floor!* • *to have a head for business/figures*

head first 1 with your head before the rest of your body: *Don't go down the slide head first.* **2** too quickly or suddenly: *Don't rush head first into a decision.*

head over heels (in love) loving sb very much; madly: *Jane's fallen head over heels in love with her new boss.*

hit the nail on the head → HIT¹

keep your head to stay calm

keep your head above water to just manage to survive in a difficult situation, especially one in which you do not have enough money

keep your head down to try not to be noticed

laugh, scream, etc your head off to laugh, shout, etc very loudly and for a long time

lose your head → LOSE

make head or tail of sth to understand sth: *I can't make head or tail of this exercise.*

off the top of your head → TOP¹

out of/off your head (*informal*) crazy, often because of the effects of drugs or alcohol

put/get your heads together to make a plan with sb

a roof over your head → ROOF

shake your head → SHAKE¹

take it into your head to do sth to suddenly

decide to do sth that other people consider strange: *I don't know why Kevin took it into his head to enter that marathon!*

★**head**² /hed/ **verb 1** [I] to move in the direction mentioned: *The ship headed towards the harbour.* • *Where are you heading?* **2** [T] to be in charge of or to lead sth **3** [T] to be at the front of a line, top of a list, etc **4** [T] (often passive) to give a title at the top of a piece of writing: *The report was headed 'The State of the Market'.* **5** [T] (in football) to hit the ball with your head

PHRASAL VERB head for to move towards a place: *It's getting late – I think it's time to head for home.*

★**headache** /'hedeɪk/ **noun** [C] **1** a pain in your head: *I've got a splitting* (= very bad) *headache.* •➤ Look at the note at **ache**. **2** a person or thing that causes worry or difficulty: *Paying the bills is a constant headache.*

heading /'hedɪŋ/ **noun** [C] the words written as a title at the top of a page or a piece of writing: *I've grouped our ideas under three main headings.*

headland /'hedlənd; -lænd/ **noun** [C] a narrow piece of land that sticks out into the sea

headlight /'hedlaɪt/ (also **headlamp** /'hedlæmp/) **noun** [C] one of the two large bright lights at the front of a vehicle

headline /'hedlaɪn/ **noun 1** [C] the title of a newspaper article printed in large letters above the story **2 the headlines** [pl] the main items of news read on television or radio

headlong /'hedlɒŋ/ **adv, adj 1** with your head before the rest of your body: *I tripped and fell headlong into the road.* **2** too quickly; without enough thought: *He rushed headlong into buying the business.*

head-'on **adj, adv** with the front of one car, etc hitting the front of another: *a head-on crash*

headphones /'hedfəʊnz/ **noun** [pl] a piece of equipment worn over the ears that makes it possible to listen to music, the radio, etc without other people hearing it

headquarters /ˌhed'kwɔːtəz/ **noun** [pl, with sing or pl verb] (*abbr* **HQ**) the place from where an organization is controlled; the people who work there: *Where is/are the firm's headquarters?*

headset /'hedset/ **noun** [C] a piece of equipment that you wear on your head that includes a device for listening (**headphones**) and/or a device for speaking into (a **microphone**): *The pilot was talking into his headset.*

head 'start **noun** [sing] an advantage that you have from the beginning of a race or competition

➤ Compare **start**²(4).

headstone /'hedstəʊn/ **noun** [C] a large stone with writing on, used to mark where a dead person is buried •➤ Look also at **gravestone** and **tombstone**.

h

headstrong /'hedstrɒŋ/ **adj** doing what you want, without listening to advice from other people

,head 'teacher = HEAD¹(6)

headway /'hedweɪ/ **noun**
IDIOM make headway to go forward or make progress in a difficult situation

heal /hiːl/ **verb** [I,T] heal (over/up) to become healthy again; to make sth healthy again: *The cut will heal up in a few days.* ● (*figurative*) *Nothing he said could heal the damage done to their relationship.*

★**health** /helθ/ **noun** [U] **1** the condition of a person's body or mind: *Fresh fruit and vegetables are good for your health.* ● *in good/ poor health* ● (*figurative*) *the health of your marriage/finances* **2** the state of being well and free from illness: *As long as you have your health, nothing else matters.* **3** the work of providing medical care: *health and safety regulations*

'**health centre** **noun** [C] a building where a group of doctors see their patients

'**health food** **noun** [C,U] natural food that many people think is especially good for your health because it has been made or grown without adding chemicals

the '**health service** **noun** [C] the organization of the medical services of a country ●▸ Look at the National Health Service.

★**healthy** /'helθi/ **adj** (**healthier; healthiest**) **1** not often ill; strong and well: *a healthy child/animal/plant* **2** showing good health (of body or mind): *healthy skin and hair* **3** helping to produce good health: *a healthy climate/ diet/lifestyle* **4** normal and sensible: *There was plenty of healthy competition between the brothers.* ●▸ opposite for all senses **unhealthy** –**healthily adv**

heap¹ /hiːp/ **noun** [C] **1** a heap (of sth) an untidy pile of sth: *a heap of books/papers* ● *All his clothes are in a heap on the floor!* ●▸ Look at the note at pile. **2** (*informal*) a heap (of sth); heaps (of sth) a large number or amount; plenty: *I've got a heap of work to do.* ● *There's heaps of time before the train leaves.*
IDIOM heaps better, more, older, etc (*informal*) much better, etc

heap² /hiːp/ **verb** [T] **1** heap sth (up) to put things in a pile: *I'm going to heap all the leaves up over there.* ● *Add six heaped tablespoons of flour* (= in a recipe). **2** heap A on/onto B; heap B with A to put a large amount of sth on sth/sb: *He heaped food onto his plate.* ● *The press heaped the team with praise.*

★**hear** /hɪə/ **verb** (*pt, pp* heard /hɜːd/) **1** [I,T] (not used in the continuous tenses) to receive sounds with your ears: *Can you speak a little louder – I can't hear very well.* ● *I didn't hear you go out this morning.* ● *Did you hear what I said?*

➤ Compare hear and listen. Often, hear means to receive a sound without necessarily trying to; to listen is to make a conscious or active effort to hear something: *I*

always wake up when I hear the milkman come. ● *I love listening to music in the evening.* ● *Listen – I've got something to tell you.* Sometimes, **hear** can have a similar meaning to 'listen to': *We'd better hear what they have to say.*

2 [T] (not used in the continuous tenses) to be told or informed about sth: *I hear that you've been offered a job in Canada.* ● *I passed my test!' 'So I've heard – well done!'* ● *I was sorry to hear about your mum's illness.*

➤ Although this verb is not used in the continuous tenses, it is common to see the present participle (= -ing form): *Not hearing what he'd said over the roar of the machines, she just nodded in reply.*

3 [T] (used about a judge, a court, etc) to listen to the evidence in a trial in order to make a decision about it: *Your case will be heard this afternoon.*
IDIOMS hear! hear! used for showing that you agree with what sb has just said, especially in a meeting
won't/wouldn't hear of sth to refuse to allow sth: *I wanted to go to art school but my parents wouldn't hear of it.*
PHRASAL VERBS hear from sb to receive a letter, telephone call, etc from sb
hear of sb/sth to know that sb/sth exists because you have heard him/her/it mentioned: *Have you heard of the Bermuda Triangle?*

hearing /'hɪərɪŋ/ **noun 1** [U] the ability to hear: *Her hearing isn't very good so you need to speak louder.* **2** [sing] a time when evidence is given to a judge in a court of law: *a court/ disciplinary hearing* **3** [sing] a chance to give your opinion or explain your position: *to get/ give sb a fair hearing*
IDIOMS hard of hearing → HARD¹
in/within sb's hearing near enough to sb so that he/she can hear what is being said

'**hearing aid** **noun** [C] a small device for people who cannot hear well that fits inside the ear and makes sounds louder

hearsay /'hɪəseɪ/ **noun** [U] things you have heard another person or other people say, which may or may not be true

hearse /hɜːs/ **noun** [C] a large, black car used for carrying a dead person to his/her funeral

★**heart** /hɑːt/ **noun 1** [C] the organ inside your chest that sends blood round your body: *When you exercise your heart beats faster.* ● *heart disease/failure* ●▸ picture on page C5 **2** [C] the centre of a person's feelings and emotions: *She has a kind heart* (= she is kind and gentle). ● *They say he died of a broken heart* (= unhappiness caused by sb he loved). **3** -hearted (used to form compound adjectives) having the type of feelings or character mentioned: *kind-hearted* ● *cold-hearted* **4** [sing] the heart (of sth) the most central or important part of sth; the middle: *Rare plants can be found in the heart of the forest.* ● *Let's get straight to the heart of the matter.* **5** [C] a symbol that is shaped like a heart, often red or pink and used to show love: *He sent her a card with a big red heart on it.* **6 hearts** [pl] the group (**suit**) of playing cards with red shapes like hearts (5) on them: *the queen of hearts* •➤ Look at the note and picture at **card. 7** [C] one of the cards from this suit: *Play a heart, if you've got one.*

IDIOMS **after your own heart** (used about people) similar to yourself or of the type you like best

at heart really; in fact: *My father seems strict but he's a very kind man at heart.*

break sb's heart to make sb very sad

by heart by remembering exactly; from memory: *Learning lists of words off by heart isn't a good way to increase your vocabulary.*

a change of heart → CHANGE²

close/dear/near to sb's heart having a lot of importance and interest for sb: *a subject that is very dear to my heart*

cross my heart → CROSS²

from the (bottom of your) heart in a way that is true and sincere: *I mean what I said from the bottom of my heart.*

have a heart of gold to be a very kind person

have/with sb's (best) interests at heart → INTEREST¹

heart and soul with a lot of energy and enthusiasm

your heart is not in sth used to say that you are not very interested in or enthusiastic about sth

your heart sinks to suddenly feel disappointed or sad: *When I saw the queues of people in front of me my heart sank.*

in your heart (of hearts) used to say that you know that sth is true although you do not want to admit or believe it: *She knew in her heart of hearts that she was making the wrong decision.*

lose heart → LOSE

not have the heart (to do sth) to be unable to do sth unkind: *I didn't have the heart to say no.*

pour your heart out (to sb) → POUR

set your heart on sth; have your heart set on sth to decide you want sth very much; to be determined to do or have sth

take heart (from sth) to begin to feel positive and hopeful about sth

take sth to heart to be deeply affected or upset by sth

to your heart's content as much as you want

with all your heart; with your whole heart completely: *I hope with all my heart that things work out for you.*

young at heart → YOUNG¹

heartache /ˈhɑːteɪk/ **noun** [U] great sadness or worry

'heart attack noun [C] a sudden serious illness when the heart stops working correctly, sometimes causing death: *She's had a heart attack.*

heartbeat /ˈhɑːtbiːt/ **noun** [C] the regular movement or sound of the heart as it sends blood round the body

heartbreak /ˈhɑːtbreɪk/ **noun** [U] very great sadness

heartbreaking /ˈhɑːtbreɪkɪŋ/ **adj** making you feel very sad

heartbroken /ˈhɑːtbrəʊkən/ (also ˌbroken-ˈhearted) **adj** extremely sad because of sth that has happened: *Mary was heartbroken when John left her.*

hearten /ˈhɑːtn/ **verb** [T] (usually passive) to encourage sb; to make sb feel happier •➤ opposite **dishearten**

heartening /ˈhɑːtnɪŋ/ **adj** making you feel more hopeful; encouraging •➤ opposite **disheartening**

heartfelt /ˈhɑːtfelt/ **adj** deeply felt; sincere: *a heartfelt apology*

hearth /hɑːθ/ **noun** [C] the place where you have an open fire in the house or the area in front of it •➤ picture at **fireplace**

heartily /ˈhɑːtɪli/ **adv 1** with obvious enthusiasm and enjoyment: *He joined in heartily with the singing.* **2** very much; completely

heartland /ˈhɑːtlænd/ **noun** [C] the most central or important part of a country, area, etc: *Germany's industrial heartland*

heartless /ˈhɑːtləs/ **adj** unkind; cruel –**heartlessly adv** –**heartlessness noun** [U]

'heart-rending adj making you feel very sad: *The mother of the missing boy made a heart-rending appeal on television.*

ˌheart-to-ˈheart noun [C] a conversation in which you say exactly what you really feel or think: *John's teacher had a heart-to-heart with him to find out what was worrying him.*

hearty /ˈhɑːti/ **adj 1** showing warm and friendly feelings: *a hearty welcome* **2** loud, happy and full of energy: *a hearty laugh* **3** large; making you feel full: *a hearty appetite* **4** showing that you feel strongly about sth: *He nodded his head in hearty agreement.*

★**heat¹** /hiːt/ **noun 1** [U] the feeling of sth hot: *This fire doesn't give out much heat.* **2** [sing] (often with *the*) hot weather: *I like the English climate because I can't stand the heat.* **3** [sing] a thing that produces heat: *Remove the pan from the heat* (= the hot part of the cooker). **4** [U] a state or time of anger or excitement: *In the heat of the moment, she threatened to resign.* **5** [C] one of the first parts of a race or competition. The winners of the heats compete against other winners until the final result is decided.

IDIOM **be on heat** (used about some female animals) to be ready to have sex because it is the right time of the year

★**heat²** /hiːt/ **verb** [I,T] heat (sth) (up) to become or to make sth hot or warm: *Wait for the oven to heat up before you put the pie in.* • *The meal is already cooked but it will need heating up.*

heated /ˈhiːtɪd/ **adj** (used about a person or discussion) angry or excited: *a heated argument/debate* –**heatedly adv**

heater /ˈhiːtə/ **noun** [C] a machine used for making water or the air in a room, car, etc hotter: *an electric/gas heater* • *a water heater*

h

[I] **intransitive**, a verb which has no object: *He laughed.*   [T] **transitive**, a verb which has an object: *He ate an apple.*

heath /hi:θ/ **noun** [C] an area of open land that is not used for farming and that is often covered with rough grass and other wild plants

heather /'heðə/ **noun** [U] a low wild plant that grows especially on hills and land that is not farmed and has small purple, pink or white flowers

heating /'hi:tɪŋ/ **noun** [U] a system for making rooms and buildings warm: *Our heating goes off at 10 pm and comes on again in the morning.* ••➤ Look at **central heating**.

heatwave /'hi:tweɪv/ **noun** [C] a period of unusually hot weather

heave¹ /hi:v/ **verb 1** [I,T] to lift, pull or throw sb/sth heavy with one big effort: *Take hold of this rope and heave!* • *We heaved the cupboard up the stairs.* **2** [I] heave (with sth) to move up and down or in and out in a heavy but regular way: *His chest was heaving with the effort of carrying the cooker.* **3** [I] to experience the tight feeling you get in your stomach when you are just about to vomit: *The sight of all that blood made her stomach heave.*

   IDIOM heave a sigh to breathe out slowly and loudly: *He heaved a sigh of relief when he heard the good news.*

heave² /hi:v/ **noun** [C,U] a strong pull, push, throw, etc

heaven /'hevn/ **noun 1** [sing] the place where, in some religions, it is believed that God lives and where good people go when they die: *to go to/be in heaven* ••➤ Look at **hell**.

> ➤ **Heaven** is used in some expressions instead of the word **God**, which some people consider offensive. ••➤ Look at the note at **God**.

2 [U,C] a place or a situation in which you are very happy: *It was heaven being away from work for a week.* **3 the heavens** [pl] (used in poetry and literature) the sky

heavenly /'hevnli/ **adj 1** (only *before* a noun) connected with heaven or the sky: *heavenly bodies* (= the sun, moon, stars, etc) **2** (*informal*) very pleasant; wonderful

★**heavy** /'hevi/ **adj (heavier; heaviest) 1** weighing a lot; difficult to lift or move: *This box is too heavy for me to carry.* **2** used when asking or stating how much sb/sth weighs: *How heavy is your suitcase?* **3** larger, stronger or more than usual: *heavy rain* • *heavy traffic* • *a heavy smoker/drinker* (= a person who smokes/drinks a lot) **3** *The sound of his heavy* (= loud and deep) *breathing told her that he was asleep.* • *a heavy sleeper* (= sb who is difficult to wake) • *a heavy meal* **4** serious, difficult or boring: *His latest novel makes heavy reading.* • *Things got a bit heavy when she started talking about her failed marriage.* **5** full of hard work; (too) busy: *a heavy day/schedule/timetable* **6** (used about a material or substance) solid or thick: *heavy soil* • *a heavy coat* ••➤ opposite for all

senses **light** –**heavily adv** –**heaviness noun** [U]

   IDIOM make heavy weather of sth to make sth seem more difficult than it really is

,**heavy-'duty adj** not easily damaged and therefore suitable for regular use or for hard physical work: *a heavy-duty carpet/tyre*

,**heavy-'handed adj 1** not showing much understanding of other people's feelings: *a heavy-handed approach* **2** using unnecessary force: *heavy-handed police methods*

,**heavy 'industry noun** [C,U] industry that uses large machinery to produce metal, coal, vehicles, etc

,**heavy 'metal noun** [U] a style of very loud rock music that is played on electric instruments

heavyweight /'heviweɪt/ **noun** [C] a person who is in the heaviest weight group in certain fighting sports: *the world heavyweight boxing champion*

heckle /'hekl/ **verb** [I,T] to interrupt a speaker at a public meeting with difficult questions or rude comments –**heckler noun** [C]

hectare /'hekteə/ **noun** [C] (*abbr* **ha**) a measurement of land; 10000 square metres

hectic /'hektɪk/ **adj** very busy with of a lot of things that you have to do quickly –**hectically** /-kli/ **adv**

he'd /hi:d/ *short for* **HE HAD; HE WOULD**

★**hedge¹** /hedʒ/ **noun** [C] a row of bushes or trees planted close together at the edge of a garden or field to separate one piece of land from another ••➤ picture on page C7

hedge² /hedʒ/ **verb** [I] to avoid giving a direct answer to a question

   IDIOM hedge your bets to protect yourself against losing or making a mistake by supporting more than one person or opinion

hedgehog /'hedʒhɒg/ **noun** [C] a small brown animal covered with sharp needles (prickles)

hedgehog

prickle

hedgerow /'hedʒrəʊ/ **noun** [C] a row of bushes, etc especially at the side of a country road or around a field

heed¹ /hi:d/ **verb** [T] (*formal*) to pay attention to advice, a warning, etc

heed² /hi:d/ **noun** (*formal*)

   IDIOM take heed (of sb/sth); pay heed (to sb/sth) to pay careful attention to what sb says: *You should take heed of your doctor's advice.*

★**heel¹** /hi:l/ **noun** [C] **1** the back part of your foot ••➤ picture on page C5 **2** the part of a sock, etc that covers your heel **3** the higher part of a shoe under the heel of your foot: *High heels* (= shoes with high heels) *are not practical for long walks.* ••➤ picture at **shoe** **4 -heeled** having the type of heel mentioned: *high-heeled/low-heeled shoes*

   IDIOMS dig your heels in ➤ **DIG¹**
head over heels ➤ **HEAD¹**

heel² /hiːl/ **verb** [T] to repair the heel of a shoe

hefty /'hefti/ **adj** (*informal*) big and strong or heavy: *a hefty young man*

★**height** /haɪt/ **noun 1** [C,U] the measurement from the bottom to the top of a person or thing: *The nurse is going to check your height and weight.* ● *We need a fence that's about two metres in height.* ••➤ Look at the note at **tall**. ••➤ picture at **length 2** [U] the fact that sb/sth is tall or high: *He looks older than he is because of his height.* **3** [C,U] the distance that sth is above the ground: *We are now flying at a height of 10000 metres.*

➤ An aeroplane **gains** or **loses** height. When talking about aeroplanes a more formal word for height is **altitude**.

4 [C,usually pl] a high place or area: *I can't go up there. I'm afraid of heights.* **5** [U] the strongest or most important part of sth: *the height of summer*

heighten /'haɪtn/ **verb** [I,T] to become or to make sth greater or stronger: *I'm using yellow paint to heighten the sunny effect of the room.*

heir /eə/ **noun** [C] heir (to sth) the person with the legal right to receive (inherit) money, property or a title when the owner dies: *He's the heir to a large fortune.*

➤ A female heir is often called an **heiress**.

heirloom /'eəluːm/ **noun** [C] something valuable that has belonged to the same family for many years

held *past tense, past participle* of **HOLD¹**

★**helicopter** /'helɪkɒptə/ (also *informal* **chopper**) **noun** [C] a small aircraft that can go straight up into the air. Helicopters have long thin metal parts on top that go round

he'll /hiːl/ *short for* **HE WILL**

hell /hel/ **noun 1** [sing] the place where, in some religions, it is believed that the Devil lives and where bad people go to when they die: *to go to/be in hell* ••➤ Look at **heaven**. **2** [C,U] (*informal*) a situation or place that is very unpleasant or painful: *He went through hell when his wife left him.* ••➤ Be careful! Some people find the following senses of 'hell' and the idioms offensive. **3** [U] (*slang*) used as a swear word to show anger: *Oh hell, I've forgotten my money!* **4 the hell** (*slang*) used as a swear word in questions to show anger or surprise: *Why the hell didn't you tell me this before?*

IDIOMS **a/one hell of a...** (*informal*) used to make an expression stronger or to mean 'very': *He got into a hell of a fight* (= a terrible fight).

all hell broke loose (*informal*) there was suddenly a lot of noise and confusion

(just) for the hell of it (*informal*) for fun

give sb hell (*informal*) to speak to sb very angrily or to be very strict with sb

like hell (*informal*) very much; with a lot of effort: *I'm working like hell at the moment.*

hellish /'helɪʃ/ **adj** terrible; awful: *a hellish experience*

★**hello** (*Brit also* **hallo**) /hə'ləʊ/ **interj** used when you meet sb, for attracting sb's attention or when you are using the telephone

helm /helm/ **noun** [C] the part of a boat or ship that is used to guide it. The helm can be a handle or a wheel.

IDIOM **at the helm** in charge of an organization, group of people, etc

helmet /'helmɪt/ **noun** [C] a type of hard hat that you wear to protect your head: *a crash helmet* ••➤ picture on page S2

★**help¹** /help/ **verb 1** [I,T] help (sb) (with sth); help (sb) (to) do sth; help sb (across, over, out of, into, etc) to do sth for sb in order to be useful or to make sth easier for him/her: *Can I help?* ● *Could you help me with the cooking?* ● *I helped her to organize the day.* ● *My son's helping in our shop at the moment.* ● *She helped her grandmother up the stairs* (= supported her as she climbed the stairs). **2** [I,T] to make sth better or easier: *If you apologize to him it might help.* ● *This medicine should help your headache.* **3** [T] help yourself (to sth) to take sth (especially food and drink) that is offered to you: *'Can I borrow your pen?' 'Yes, help yourself.'* **4** [T] help yourself to sth to take sth without asking permission; to steal **5** [I] (*spoken*) used to get sb's attention when you are in danger or difficulty: *Help! I'm going to fall!*

IDIOMS **can/can't/couldn't help sth** be able/ not be able to stop or avoid doing sth: *It was so funny I couldn't help laughing.* ● *I just couldn't help myself – I had to laugh.*

a helping hand some help: *My neighbour is always ready to give me a helping hand.*

PHRASAL VERB **help (sb) out** to help sb in a difficult situation; to give money to help sb

★**help²** /help/ **noun 1** [U] help (with sth) the act of helping: *Do you need any help with that?* ● *This map isn't much help.* ● *She stopped smoking with the help of her family and friends.* ● *'Run and get help – my son's fallen in the river!'* **2** [sing] a help (to sb) a person or thing that helps: *Your directions were a great help – we found the place easily.*

helper /'helpə/ **noun** [C] a person who helps (especially with work)

★**helpful** /'helpfl/ **adj** giving help: *helpful advice* –**helpfully** adv –**helpfulness** noun [U]

helping /'helpɪŋ/ **noun** [C] the amount of food that is put on a plate at one time: *After two helpings of pasta, I couldn't eat any more.* ••➤ Look at **portion**.

helpless /'helpləs/ **adj** unable to take care of yourself or do things without the help of other people: *a helpless baby* –**helplessly** adv: *They watched helplessly as their house went up in flames.* –**helplessness** noun [U]

hem¹ /hem/ **noun** [C] the edge at the bottom of a piece of cloth (especially on a skirt, dress or trousers) that has been turned up and sewn ••➤ picture on page C6

hem² /hem/ **verb** [T] (**hemming**; **hemmed**) to turn up and sew the bottom of a piece of clothing or cloth

PHRASAL VERB **hem sb in** to surround sb a

h

prevent him/her from moving away: *We were hemmed in by the crowd and could not leave.*

hemisphere /'hemɪsfɪə/ **noun** [C] **1** one half of the earth: *the northern/southern/eastern/western hemisphere* ••➤ picture at **earth 2** the shape of half a ball; half a sphere

hemophilia, hemophiliac (*US*) = HAEMOPHILIA, HAEMOPHILIAC

hemorrhage (*US*) = HAEMORRHAGE

hemorrhoids (*US*) = HAEMORRHOIDS

hemp /hemp/ **noun** [U] a plant that is used for making rope and rough cloth and for producing an illegal drug (cannabis)

★**hen** /hen/ **noun** [C] **1** a female bird that is kept for its eggs or its meat ••➤ Look at the note and picture at **chicken**. **2** the female of any type of bird: *a hen pheasant*

> The male bird is a **cock**.

hence /hens/ **adv** (*formal*) for this reason: *I've got some news to tell you – hence the letter.*

henceforth /ˌhens'fɔːθ/ (also **henceforward** /ˌhens'fɔːwəd/) **adv** (*written*) from now on; in future

henchman /'hentʃmən/ **noun** [C] (*pl* **-men** /-mən/) a person who is employed by sb to protect him/her and who may do things that are illegal or violent

'**hen party** (also '**hen night**) **noun** [sing] a party that a woman who is getting married soon has with her female friends ••➤ Look at **stag night**.

henpecked /'henpekt/ **adj** used to describe a husband who always does what his wife tells him to do

hepatitis /ˌhepə'taɪtɪs/ **noun** [U] a serious disease of one of the body's main organs (liver)

★**her¹** /hɜː/ **pron** (the object of a verb or preposition) the female person that was mentioned earlier: *He told Sue that he loved her.* • *I've got a letter for your mother. Could you give it to her, please?* ••➤ Look at **she** and the note at **he**.

★**her²** /hɜː/ **determiner** of or belonging to the female person mentioned earlier: *That's her book. She left it there this morning.* • *Fiona has broken her leg.* ••➤ Look at **hers**.

herald /'herəld/ **verb** [T] (*written*) to be a sign that sb/sth is going to happen soon: *The minister's speech heralded a change of policy.*

herb /hɜːb/ **noun** [C] a plant whose leaves, seeds, etc are used in medicine or in cooking: *Add some herbs, such as rosemary and thyme.* ••➤ Look at **spice**.

herbal /'hɜːbl/ **adj** made of or using herbs: *herbal medicine/remedies*

herd¹ /hɜːd/ **noun** [C] a large number of animals that live and feed together: *a herd of cattle/deer/elephants* ••➤ Look at **flock**.

herd² /hɜːd/ **verb** [T] to move people or animals somewhere together in a group: *The prisoners were herded onto the train.*

★**here¹** /hɪə/ **adv 1** (after a verb or a preposition) in, at or to the place where you are or which you are pointing to: *Come* (*over*)

here. • *The school is a mile from here.* • *Please sign here.* **2** used at the beginning of a sentence to introduce or draw attention to sb/sth: *Here is the nine o'clock news.* • *Here comes the bus.* • *Here we are* (= we've arrived).

> Note the word order in the last example. We say: *Here are the children* but with a pronoun we say: *Here they are.* Note also the expression: **Here you are** which is used when we are giving something to somebody: *Here you are – this is that book I was talking about.*

3 (used for emphasizing a noun): *I think you'll find this book here very useful.* **4** at this point in a discussion or a piece of writing: *Here the speaker stopped and looked around the room.*

IDIOMS **here and there** in various places

here goes (*informal*) used to say that you are about to do sth exciting, dangerous, etc: *I've never done a backward dive before, but here goes!*

here's to sb/sth used for wishing for the health, success, etc of sb/sth while holding a drink: *Here's to a great holiday!*

neither here nor there not important: *My opinion is neither here nor there. If you like the dress then buy it.*

here² /hɪə/ **interj** used for attracting sb's attention, when offering help or when giving sth to sb: *Here, let me help!*

hereabouts /ˌhɪərə'baʊts/ (*US* **hereabout**) **adv** around or near here

hereafter /ˌhɪər'ɑːftə/ **adv** (*written*) (used in legal documents, etc) from now on

hereditary /hə'redɪtri/ **adj** passed on from parent to child: *a hereditary disease*

heredity /hə'redəti/ **noun** [U] the process by which physical or mental qualities pass from parent to child

heresy /'herəsi/ **noun** [C,U] (*pl* **heresies**) a (religious) opinion or belief that is different from what is generally accepted to be true

heretic /'herətɪk/ **noun** [C] a person whose religious beliefs are believed to be wrong or evil –**heretical** /hə'retɪkl/ **adj**

heritage /'herɪtɪdʒ/ **noun** [C,usually sing] the traditions, qualities and culture of a country that have existed for a long time and that have great importance for the country

hermit /'hɜːmɪt/ **noun** [C] a person who prefers to live alone, without contact with other people

hernia /'hɜːniə/ (also **rupture**) **noun** [C,U] the medical condition in which an organ inside the body, for example the stomach, pushes through the wall of muscle which surrounds it

★**hero** /'hɪərəʊ/ **noun** [C] (*pl* **heroes**) **1** a person who is admired, especially for having done sth difficult or good: *The team were given a hero's welcome on their return home.* **2** the most important male character in a book, play, film, etc: *The hero of the film is a little boy.* ••➤ Look also at **heroine** and **villain**.

heroic /hə'rəʊɪk/ **adj** (used about people or their actions) having a lot of courage: *a heroic effort* –**heroically** /-kli/ **adv**

heroin /'herəʊɪn/ **noun** [U] a powerful illegal drug that some people take for pleasure and then cannot stop taking

heroine /'herəʊɪn/ **noun** [C] **1** a woman who is admired, especially for having done sth difficult or good **2** the most important female character in a book, play, film, etc •➤ Look also at **hero**.

heroism /'herəʊɪzəm/ **noun** [U] great courage

herring /'herɪŋ/ **noun** [C,U] (*pl* **herring** or **herrings**) a fish that swims in large groups (**shoals**) in cold seas and is used for food
IDIOM a red herring → RED

hers /hɜːz/ **pron** of or belonging to her: *I didn't have a pen but Helen lent me hers.*

★**herself** /hɜː'self/ **pron 1** used when the female who does an action is also affected by it: *She hurt herself quite badly when she fell downstairs.* • *Irene looked at herself in the mirror.* **2** used to emphasize the female who did the action: *She told me the news herself.* • *Has Rosy done this herself?* (= or did sb else do it for her?)
IDIOMS **(all) by herself 1** alone: *She lives by herself.* •➤ Look at the note at **alone**. **2** without help: *I don't think she needs any help – she can change a tyre by herself.*
(all) to herself without having to share: *Julie has the bedroom to herself now her sister's left home.*

he's *short for* HE IS, HE HAS

hesitant /'hezɪtənt/ **adj** **hesitant (to do/about doing sth)** slow to speak or act because you are not sure if you should or not: *I'm very hesitant about criticizing him too much.* –**hesitancy** /-ənsi/ **noun** [U] –**hesitantly adv**

★**hesitate** /'hezɪteɪt/ **verb** [I] **1** hesitate (about/over sth) to pause before you do sth or before you take a decision, usually because you are uncertain or worried: *He hesitated before going into the room.* • *She's still hesitating about whether to accept the job or not.* **2** hesitate (to do sth) to not want to do sth because you are not sure that it is right: *Don't hesitate to phone if you have any problems.* –**hesitation** /ˌhezɪ'teɪʃn/ **noun** [C,U]: *She agreed without a moment's hesitation.*

heterosexual /ˌhetərə'sekʃuəl/ **adj** sexually attracted to a person of the opposite sex •➤ Look at **bisexual** and **homosexual**. –**heterosexual noun** [C]

het up /ˌhet 'ʌp/ **adj** (*informal*) (not before a noun) **het up (about/over sth)** worried or excited about sth

hexagon /'heksəgən/ **noun** [C] a shape with six sides –**hexagonal** /heks'ægənl/ **adj**

hey /heɪ/ **interj** (*informal*) used to attract sb's attention or to show that you are surprised or interested: *Hey, what are you doing?*
IDIOM **hey presto** people sometimes say 'hey presto' when they have done sth so quickly that it seems like magic

heyday /'heɪdeɪ/ **noun** [sing] the period when

sb/sth was most powerful, successful, rich, etc

HGV /ˌeɪtʃ dʒiː 'viː/ **abbr** (*Brit*) heavy goods vehicle, such as a lorry

hi /haɪ/ **interj** (*informal*) an informal word used when you meet sb you know well; hello

hibernate /'haɪbəneɪt/ **verb** [I] (used about animals) to spend the winter in a state like deep sleep –**hibernation** /ˌhaɪbə'neɪʃn/ **noun** [U]

hiccup (also **hiccough**) /'hɪkʌp/ **noun 1** [C] a sudden, usually repeated sound that is made in the throat and that you cannot control **2** (the) hiccups [pl] a series of hiccups: *Don't eat so fast or you'll get hiccups!* • *If you have the hiccups, try holding your breath.* **3** [C] a small problem or difficulty: *There's been a slight hiccup in our holiday arrangements but I've got it sorted out now.* –**hiccup** (also **hiccough**) **verb** [I]

★**hide¹** /haɪd/ **verb** (*pt* **hid** /hɪd/; *pp* **hidden** /'hɪdn/) **1** [T] to put or keep sb/sth in a place where he/she/it cannot be seen; to cover sth so that it cannot be seen: *Where shall I hide the money?* • *You couldn't see Bill in the photo – he was hidden behind John.* **2** [I] to be or go in a place where you cannot be seen or found: *Quick, run and hide!* • *The child was hiding under the bed.* **3** [T] hide sth (from sb) to keep sth secret, especially your feelings: *She tried to hide her disappointment from them.*

hide² /haɪd/ **noun 1** [C,U] the skin of an animal that will be used for making leather, etc **2** [C] a place from which people can watch wild animals, birds, etc without being seen

hide-and-'seek noun [U] a children's game in which one person hides and the others try to find him/her

hideous /'hɪdiəs/ **adj** very ugly or unpleasant: *a hideous sight* • *a hideous crime* –**hideously adv**

hiding /'haɪdɪŋ/ **noun** [C] **1** the state of being hidden: *The escaped prisoners are believed to be in hiding somewhere in London.* • *to go into hiding* **2** (*informal*) a punishment involving being hit hard many times: *You deserve a good hiding for what you've done.*

hierarchy /'haɪərɑːki/ **noun** [C] (*pl* **hierarchies**) a system or organization that has many levels from the lowest to the highest –**hierarchical** /ˌhaɪə'rɑːkɪkl/ **adj**

hieroglyphics /ˌhaɪərə'glɪfɪks/ **noun** [pl] the system of writing that was used in ancient Egypt in which a small picture represents a word or sound

hi-fi /'haɪ faɪ/ **noun** [C] equipment for playing recorded music that produces high quality sound –**hi-fi adj**: *a hi-fi system*

higgledy-piggledy /ˌhɪgldi 'pɪgldi/ **adv, adj** (*informal*) not in any order; mixed up together

★**high¹** /haɪ/ **adj 1** (used about things) having a large distance between the bottom and the top: *high cliffs* • *What's the highest mountain in the world?* • *high heels* (= on shoes) • *The garden wall was so high that we couldn't see over it.* •➤ opposite **low** •➤ **noun** height

h

••➤ Look at the note at **tall**. **2** having a particular height: *The hedge is one metre high.* • *knee-high boots* **3** at a level which is a long way from the ground, or from sea level: *a high shelf* • *The castle was built on high ground.* ••➤ opposite **low 4** above the usual or normal level or amount: *high prices* • *at high speed* • *a high level of unemployment* • *He's got a high temperature.* • *Oranges are high in vitamin C.* ••➤ opposite **low 5** better than what is usual: *high-quality goods* • *Her work is of a very high standard.* • *He has a high opinion of you.* ••➤ opposite **low 6** having an important position: *Sam only joined the company three years ago, but she's already quite high up.* **7** morally good: *high ideals* **8** (used about a sound or voice) not deep or low: *Dogs can hear very high sounds.* • *Women usually have higher voices than men.* ••➤ opposite **low 9** (*informal*) high (on sth) under the influence of drugs, alcohol, etc **10** (used about a gear in a car) that allows a faster speed ••➤ opposite **low**

IDIOM **be left high and dry** to be left without help in a difficult situation

★**high²** /haɪ/ **adv 1** at or to a high position or level: *The sun was high in the sky.* • *I can't jump any higher.* • *The plane flew high overhead.* ••➤ noun **height 2** (used about a sound) at a high level: *How high can you sing?* ••➤ opposite **low**

IDIOMS **high and low** everywhere: *We've searched high and low for the keys.*
run high (used about the feelings of a group of people) to be especially strong: *Emotions are running high in the neighbourhood where the murders took place.*

★**high³** /haɪ/ **noun** [C] **1** a high level or point: *Profits reached an all-time high last year.* **2** an area of high air pressure **3** (*informal*) a feeling of great pleasure or happiness that sb gets from doing sth exciting or being successful: *He was on a high after passing all his exams.* • *She talked about the highs and lows of her career.* **4** (*informal*) a feeling of great pleasure or happiness that may be caused by a drug, alcohol, etc ••➤ opposite for all senses **low**

IDIOM **on high** (*formal*) (in) a high place, the sky or heaven: *The order came from on high.*

highbrow /ˈhaɪbraʊ/ **adj** interested in or concerned with matters that many people would find too serious to be interesting: *highbrow newspapers/television programmes*

high-class adj of especially good quality: *a high-class restaurant*

High ˈCourt noun [C] the most important court of law in some countries

higher eduˈcation noun [U] education and training at a college or university, especially to degree level ••➤ Look at **further education**.

high jump noun [sing] the sport in which people try to jump over a bar in order to find out who can jump the highest ••➤ Look at **long jump**.

highland /ˈhaɪlənd/ **adj 1** in or connected

with an area of land that has mountains: *highland streams* ••➤ Look at **lowland**. **2** [pl] in or connected with the part of Scotland where there are mountains (the Highlands)

high-ˈlevel adj involving important people: *high-level talks*

highlight¹ /ˈhaɪlaɪt/ **verb** [T] **1** to emphasize sth so that people give it special attention: *The report highlighted the need for improved safety at football grounds.* **2** to mark part of a text with a different colour, etc so that people give it more attention

highlight² /ˈhaɪlaɪt/ **noun 1** [C] the best or most interesting part of sth: *The highlights of the match will be shown on TV tonight.* **2 highlights** [pl] areas of lighter colour that are put in a person's hair

★**highly** /ˈhaɪli/ **adv 1** to a high degree; very: *highly trained/educated/developed* • *a highly paid job* • *It's highly unlikely that anyone will complain.* **2** with admiration: *I think very highly of your work.*

highly ˈstrung adj nervous and easily upset

Highness /ˈhaɪnəs/ **noun** [C] **your/his/her Highness** a title used when speaking about or to a member of a royal family

high-ˈpowered adj 1 (used about things) having great power: *a high-powered engine* **2** (used about people) important and successful: *high-powered executives*

high-ˈrise adj (only *before* a noun) (used about a building) very tall and having a lot of floors

high school noun [C,U] a school for children who are about 13-18 years old

high street noun [C] (*Brit*) (often used in names) the main street of a town: *The Post Office is in the High Street.*

high-tech (also **hi-tech**) /ˈhaɪ tek/ **adj** using the most modern methods and machines, especially electronic ones: *high-tech industries/hospitals*

high ˈtide noun [U] the time when the sea comes furthest onto the land ••➤ opposite **low tide**

highway /ˈhaɪweɪ/ **noun** [C] (*especially US*) a main road (between towns) ••➤ Look at the note at **road**.

hijack /ˈhaɪdʒæk/ **verb** [T] **1** to take control of a plane, etc by force, usually for political reasons: *The plane was hijacked on its flight to Sydney.* ••➤ Look at **kidnap**. **2** to take control of a meeting, an event, etc in order to force people to pay attention to sth: *The peace rally was hijacked by right-wing extremists.* –**hijack noun** [C]: *The hijack was ended by armed police.* –**hijacker noun** [C] –**hijacking noun** [C,U]

hike /haɪk/ **noun** [C] a long walk in the country: *We went on a ten-mile hike at the weekend.* –**hike verb** [I] ••➤ **Go hiking** is used when you are talking about spending time hiking: *They went hiking in Wales for their holiday.* –**hiker noun** [C] ••➤ picture on page C8

hilarious /hɪˈleəriəs/ **adj** extremely funny –**hilariously adv**

hilarity /hɪˈlærəti/ noun [U] great amusement or loud laughter

★**hill** /hɪl/ noun [C] a high area of land that is not as high as a mountain: *There was a wonderful view from the top of the hill.* •➤ Look at **uphill** and **downhill**.

hillside /ˈhɪlsaɪd/ noun [C] the side of a hill

hilltop /ˈhɪltɒp/ noun [C] the top of a hill

hilly /ˈhɪli/ adj having a lot of hills: *The country's very hilly around here.*

hilt /hɪlt/ noun [C] the handle of a knife or a similar weapon (**sword**)

[IDIOM] **to the hilt** to a high degree; completely: *I'll defend you to the hilt.*

★**him** /hɪm/ pron (the object of a verb or preposition) the male person who was mentioned earlier: *Helen told Ian that she loved him.* • *I've got a letter for your father – can you give it to him, please?* •➤ Look at the note at **he**.

★**himself** /hɪmˈself/ pron **1** used when the male who does an action is also affected by it: *He cut himself when he was shaving.* • *John looked at himself in the mirror.* **2** used to emphasize the male who did the action: *He told me the news himself.* • *Did he write this himself?* (= or did sb else do it for him?)

[IDIOMS] **(all) by himself 1** alone: *He lives by himself.* •➤ Look at the note at **alone**. **2** without help: *He should be able to cook a meal by himself.*

(all) to himself without having to share: *Charlie has the bedroom to himself now his brother's left home.*

hind /haɪnd/ adj (used about an animal's legs, etc) at the back

➤ We also say **back legs**. The legs at the front are the **front legs** or **forelegs**. •➤ picture on page C1

hinder /ˈhɪndə/ verb [T] to make it more difficult for sb/sth to do sth: *A lot of scientific work is hindered by lack of money.*

hindrance /ˈhɪndrəns/ noun [C] a person or thing that makes it difficult for you to do sth

hindsight /ˈhaɪndsaɪt/ noun [U] the understanding that you have of a situation only after it has happened: *With hindsight, I wouldn't have lent him the money.* •➤ Look at **foresight**.

Hindu /ˈhɪnduː; ˌhɪnˈduː/ noun [C] a person whose religion is Hinduism –**Hindu** adj: *Hindu beliefs*

Hinduism /ˈhɪnduːɪzəm/ noun [U] the main religion of India. Hindus believe in many gods and that, after death, people will return to life in a different form.

hinge

hinge¹ /hɪndʒ/ noun [C] a piece of metal that joins two sides of a box, door, etc together and allows it to be opened or closed

hinge² /hɪndʒ/ verb

[PHRASAL VERB] **hinge on sth** to depend on sth: *The future of the project hinges on the meeting today.*

hint¹ /hɪnt/ noun [C] **1** something that you suggest in an indirect way: *If you keep mentioning parties, maybe they'll **take the hint** and invite you.* **2** sth that suggests what will happen in the future: *The first half of the match **gave** no **hint** of the excitement to come.* **3** a small amount of sth: *There was a hint of sadness in his voice.* **4** a piece of advice or information: *helpful hints*

hint² /hɪnt/ verb [I,T] hint (at sth); hint that... to suggest sth in an indirect way: *They only hinted at their great disappointment.* • *He hinted that he might be moving to Greece.*

★**hip¹** /hɪp/ noun [C] the part of the side of your body above your legs and below your waist: *He stood there angrily with his hands on his hips.* •➤ picture on page C5

hip² /hɪp/ interj

[IDIOM] **hip, hip, hurray/hurrah** shouted three times when a group wants to show that it is pleased with sb or with sth that has happened

hippie (also **hippy**) /ˈhɪpi/ noun [C] (pl **hippies**) a person who rejects the usual values and way of life of western society. Especially in the 1960s, hippies showed that they were different by wearing colourful clothes, having long hair and taking drugs.

hippopotamus /ˌhɪpəˈpɒtəməs/ noun [C] (pl **hippopotamuses** /-sɪz/ or **hippopotami** /-maɪ/) (also informal **hippo** /ˈhɪpəʊ/) a large African animal with a large head and short legs that lives in or near rivers

★**hire¹** /ˈhaɪə/ verb [T] **1** (US **rent**) hire sth (from sb) to have the use of sth for a short time by paying for it

➤ In British English, you **hire** something for a short time: *We hired a car for the day.* You **rent** something if the period of time is longer: *to rent a house/flat/television.* In US English **rent** is used in both situations.

2 to give sb a job for a short time: *We'll have to hire somebody to mend the roof.*

➤ In US English **hire** is also used for talking about permanent jobs: *We just hired a new secretary.*

3 (US **rent**) hire sth (out) (to sb) to allow sb to use sth for a short fixed period in exchange for money: *We hire (out) our vans by the day.* •➤ In British English, **rent** or **let** is used if the period of time is longer: *Mrs Higgs rents out rooms to students.* • *We let our house while we were in France for a year.*

hire² /ˈhaɪə/ noun [U] the act of paying to use sth for a short time: *Car hire is expensive in this country.* • *do you have bicycles **for hire**?*

hire 'purchase noun [U] (Brit) (abbr **HP**) a way of buying goods. You do not pay the full price immediately but make regular small payments (**instalments**) until the full amount is paid: *We're buying the video on hire purchase.*

[I] **intransitive**, a verb which has no object: *He laughed.*   [T] **transitive**, a verb which has an object: *He ate an apple.*

h

★ **his** /hɪz/ **determiner, pron** of or belonging to the male person that was mentioned earlier: *Matthew has hurt his shoulder.* • *This is my book so that one must be his.* ••➤ Look at the note at **he**.

hiss /hɪs/ **verb 1** [I,T] to make a sound like a very long 's' to show that you are angry or do not like sth: *The cat hissed at me.* • *The speech was hissed and booed.* **2** [T] to say sth in an angry hissing voice: *'Stay away from me!' she hissed.* –**hiss noun** [C]

historian /hɪˈstɔːriən/ **noun** [C] a person who studies or who is an expert in history

historic /hɪˈstɒrɪk/ **adj** famous or important in history: *The ending of apartheid was a historic event.*

★ **historical** /hɪˈstɒrɪkl/ **adj** that really lived or happened; connected with real people or events in the past: *historical events/records* • *This house has great historical interest.* –**historically** /-kli/ **adv**

★ **history** /ˈhɪstri/ **noun** (*pl* **histories**) **1** [U] the events of the past: *an important moment in history* ••➤ Look at **natural history**. **2** [C, usually sing] the series of events or facts that is connected with sb/sth: *He has a history of violence.* • *a patient's medical history* **3** [U] the study of past events: *She has a degree in history.* • *History was my favourite subject at school.* **4** [C] a written description of past events: *a new history of Europe*

> **History** is something true that really happened. A **story** is a description of a series of events that may or may not have happened.

IDIOMS **go down in/make history** to be or do sth so important that it will be recorded in history: *She made history by becoming the first woman President.*
the rest is history used when you are telling a story to say that you are not going to tell the end of the story, because everyone knows it already

★ **hit¹** /hɪt/ **verb** [T] (*pres part* **hitting**; *pt, pp* **hit**) **1** to make sudden, violent contact with sb/sth: *The bus left the road and hit a tree.* • *to hit somebody in the eye/across the face/on the nose*

> **Strike** is a more formal word than **hit**. **Beat** means to hit many times: *He was badly beaten in the attack.*

2 hit sth (on/against sth) to knock a part of your body, etc against sth: *Peter hit his head on the low beam.* **3** to have a bad or unpleasant effect on sb/sth: *Inner city areas have been badly hit by unemployment.* • *Her father's death has hit her very hard.* **4** to experience sth unpleasant or difficult: *Things were going really well until we hit this problem.* **5** to reach a place or a level: *If you follow this road you should hit the motorway in about ten minutes.* • *The price of oil hit a new high yesterday.* **6** to suddenly come into sb's mind; to make sb realize or understand sth: *I thought I recognized the man's face and then*

it hit me – he was my old maths teacher!
IDIOMS **hit it off (with sb)** (*informal*) to like sb when you first meet him/her: *When I first met Tony's parents, we didn't really hit it off.*
hit the nail on the head to say sth that is exactly right
hit the jackpot to win a lot of money or have a big success
PHRASAL VERBS **hit back (at sb/sth)** to attack (with words) sb who has attacked you: *The Prime Minister hit back at his critics.*
hit on sth to suddenly find sth by chance: *I finally hit on a solution to the problem.*
hit out (at sb/sth) to attack sb/sth: *The man hit out at the policeman.*

★ **hit²** /hɪt/ **noun** [C] **1** the act of hitting sth: *The ship took a direct hit and sank.* • *She gave her brother a hard hit on the head.* ••➤ Look at **miss**. **2** a person or thing that is very popular or successful: *The record was a big hit.* **3** (*computing*) a result of a search on a computer, especially on the Internet
IDIOM **make a hit (with sb)** (*informal*) to make a good impression on sb: *The new teacher seems to have made a hit with the girls.*

hit-and-ˈmiss (also **hit-or-ˈmiss**) **adj** (*informal*) not well organized; careless: *This method is a bit hit-or-miss, but it usually works.*

hit-and-ˈrun adj (used about a road accident) caused by a driver who does not stop to help

hitch¹ /hɪtʃ/ **verb 1** [I,T] (*informal*) to travel by waiting by the side of a road and holding out your hand or a sign until a driver stops and takes you in the direction you want to go: *I managed to hitch to Paris in just six hours.* • *We missed the bus so we had to hitch a lift.* ••➤ Look at **hitchhike**. **2** [T] to fasten sth to sth else: *to hitch a trailer to the back of a car*

hitch² /hɪtʃ/ **noun** [C] a small problem or difficulty: *a technical hitch*

hitchhike /ˈhɪtʃhaɪk/ (also *informal* **hitch**) **verb** [I] to travel by waiting by the side of a road and holding out your hand or a sign until a driver stops and takes you in the direction you want to go: *He hitchhiked across Europe.*

> **Hitchhike** is usually used to talk about travelling long distances in this way for pleasure. **Hitch** can be used to mean the same, but it is also used to talk about travelling short distances in this way, for example because your car has broken down or you have missed a bus. **Hitch** can also be used transitively: *I hitched a lift/ride to the nearest petrol station.* **Thumb a lift** means the same.

–**hitchhiker noun** [C]

hi-tech = HIGH-TECH

hitherto /ˌhɪðəˈtuː/ **adv** (*formal*) until now

HIV /ˌeɪtʃ aɪ ˈviː/ **abbr** human immunodeficiency virus; the virus that is believed to cause AIDS

hive /haɪv/ = BEEHIVE

hiya /ˈhaɪjə/ **interj** (*informal*) an informal word used when you meet sb you know well; hello

HM **abbr** His/Her Majesty's: *HMS* (= Her Majesty's Ship) *Invincible*

hm **interj** (used when you are not sure or when you are thinking about sth)

hoard¹ /hɔːd/ **noun** [C] a store (often secret) of money, food etc

hoard² /hɔːd/ **verb** [I,T] hoard (sth) (up) to collect and store large quantities of sth (often secretly)

hoarding /ˈhɔːdɪŋ/ (*Brit*) = BILLBOARD

hoarse /hɔːs/ **adj** (used about a person or his/her voice) sounding rough and quiet, especially because of a sore throat: *a hoarse whisper* –**hoarsely adv**

hoax /həʊks/ **noun** [C] a trick to make people believe sth that is not true, especially sth unpleasant: *The fire brigade answered the call, but found that it was a hoax.*

hob /hɒb/ (*US* **stovetop**) **noun** [C] the surface on the top of a cooker that is used for boiling, frying, etc

hobble /ˈhɒbl/ **verb** [I] to walk with difficulty because your feet or legs are hurt: *He hobbled home on his twisted ankle.*

✷**hobby** /ˈhɒbi/ **noun** [C] (*pl* **hobbies**) something that you do regularly for pleasure in your free time: *Barry's hobbies are stamp-collecting and surfing the net.* •➤ synonym **pastime**

hockey /ˈhɒki/ **noun** [U] **1** a game that is played on a field (**pitch**) by two teams of eleven players who try to hit a small hard ball into a goal with a curved wooden stick (**hockey stick**)

> ➤ In the US hockey is usually called **field hockey** to show that it is not **ice hockey**.

2 (*US*) = ICE HOCKEY

hoe /həʊ/ **noun** [C] a garden tool with a long handle that is used for turning the soil and for removing plants that you do not want •➤ picture at **garden**

hog¹ /hɒg/ **noun** [C] a male pig that is kept for its meat

IDIOM **go the whole hog** (*informal*) to do sth as completely as possible: *Instead of getting a taxi, why not go the whole hog and hire a limousine for the evening?*

hog² /hɒg/ **verb** [T] (**hogging**; **hogged**) (*informal*) to take or keep too much or all of sth for yourself: *The red car was hogging the middle of the road so no one could overtake.*

Hogmanay /ˈhɒgməneɪ/ **noun** [C] the Scottish name for New Year's Eve (31 December) and the celebrations that take place then

hoist /hɔɪst/ **verb** [T] to lift or pull sth up, often by using ropes, etc: *to hoist a flag/sail*

✷**hold¹** /həʊld/ **verb** (*pt, pp* **held** /held/) **1** [T] to take sb/sth and keep him/her/it in your hand, etc: *He held a gun in his hand.* • *The woman was holding a baby in her arms.* • *Hold my hand. This is a busy road.*

•➤ picture on page S8 **2** [T] to keep sth in a certain position: *Hold your head up straight.* • *Hold the camera still or you'll spoil the picture.* • *These two screws hold the shelf in place.* **3** [T] to take the weight of sb/sth: *Are you sure that branch is strong enough to hold you?* **4** [T] to organize an event; to have a meeting, an election, a concert, etc: *They're holding a party for his fortieth birthday.* • *The Olympic Games are held every four years.* **5** [I] to stay the same: *I hope this weather holds till the weekend.* • *What I said still holds – nothing has changed.* **6** [I,T] to contain or have space for a particular amount: *The car holds five people.* • *How much does this bottle hold?* **7** [T] to keep a person in a position or place by force: *The terrorists are* **holding** *three men* **hostage.** • *A man is being held at the police station.* **8** [T] to have sth, usually in an official way: *Does she* **hold** *a British passport?* • *She holds the world record in the 100 metres.* **9** [T] to have an opinion, etc: *They* **hold the view** *that we shouldn't spend any more money.* **10** [T] to believe that sth is true about a person: *I* **hold** *the parents* **responsible** *for the child's behaviour.* **11** [I,T] (used when you are telephoning) to wait until the person you are calling is ready: *I'm afraid his phone is engaged. Will you* **hold the line?** **12** [T] to have a conversation: *It's impossible to* **hold a conversation** *with all this noise.*

IDIOM **Hold it!** (*spoken*) Stop! Don't move!

> ➤ For other idioms containing **hold**, look at the entries for the nouns, adjectives, etc. For example **hold your own** is at **own**.

PHRASAL VERBS **hold sth against sb** to not forgive sb because of sth he/she has done

hold sb/sth back 1 to prevent sb from making progress **2** to prevent sb/sth from moving forward: *The police tried to hold the crowd back.*

hold sth back 1 to refuse to give some of the information that you have: *The police are sure that she is holding something back. She knows much more than she is saying.* **2** to control an emotion and stop yourself from showing what you really feel: *He fought to hold back tears of anger and frustration.*

hold off (sth/doing sth) to delay sth

hold on 1 to wait or stop for a moment: *Hold on. I'll be with you in a minute.* **2** to manage in a difficult or dangerous situation: *They managed to hold on until a rescue party arrived.*

hold onto sb/sth to hold sb/sth tightly: *The child held on to his mother; he didn't want her to go.*

hold onto sth to keep sth; to not give or sell sth: *They've offered me a lot of money for this painting, but I'm going to hold onto it.*

hold out to last (in a difficult situation): *How long will our supply of water hold out?*

hold sth out to offer sth by moving it towards sb in your hand: *He held out a carrot to the horse.*

hold out for sth (*informal*) to cause a delay

while you continue to ask for sth: *Union members are holding out for a better pay offer.*
hold sb/sth up to make sb/sth late; to cause a delay: *We were held up by the traffic.*
hold up sth to rob a bank, shop, vehicle, etc using a gun

hold² /həʊld/ *noun* **1** [C] the act or manner of having sb/sth in your hand(s): *to have a firm hold on the rope* ● *judo/wrestling holds* **2** [sing] a hold (on/over sb/sth) influence or control: *The new government has strengthened its hold on the country.* **3** [C] the part of a ship or an aircraft where cargo is carried
IDIOMS **catch, get, grab, take, etc hold (of sb/sth)** **1** to take sb/sth in your hands: *I managed to catch hold of the dog before it ran out into the road.* **2** to take control of sb/sth; to start to have an effect on sb/sth: *Mass hysteria seemed to have taken hold of the crowd.*
get hold of sb to find sb or make contact with sb: *I've been trying to get hold of the complaints department all morning.*
get hold of sth to find sth that will be useful: *I must try and get hold of a good second-hand bicycle.*

holdall /ˈhəʊldɔːl/ *noun* [C] a large bag that is used for carrying clothes, etc when you are travelling ••➤ picture at **bag**

holder /ˈhəʊldə/ *noun* [C] (often in compound nouns) **1** a person who has or holds sth: *a season ticket holder* ● *the world record holder in the 100 metres* ● *holders of European passports* **2** something that contains or holds sth: *a toothbrush holder*

'hold-up *noun* [C] **1** a delay: *'What's the hold-up?' 'There's been an accident ahead of us.'* **2** the act of robbing a bank, etc using a gun: *The gang have carried out three hold-ups of high street banks.*

★**hole** /həʊl/ *noun* **1** [C] an opening; an empty space in sth solid: *The pavement is full of holes.* ● *There are holes in my socks.* ● *I've got a hole in my tooth.* **2** [C] the place where an animal lives in the ground or in a tree: *a mouse hole* **3** [C] (in golf) the hole in the ground that you must hit the ball into. Each section of the land where you play (golf course) is also called a hole: *an eighteen-hole golf course*

★**holiday** /ˈhɒlədeɪ/ *noun* **1** (*US* **vacation**) [C,U] a period of rest from work or school (often when you go and stay away from home): *We're going to Italy for our summer holidays this year.* ● *How much holiday do you get a year in your new job?* ● *Mr Philips isn't here this week. He's away on holiday.* ● *I'm going to take a week's holiday in May and spend it at home.* ● *the school/Christmas/Easter/summer holidays*

➤ **Leave** is time when you do not go to work for a special reason: *sick leave* ● *maternity leave* (= when you are having a baby) ● *unpaid leave*

2 [C] a day of rest when people do not go to work, school, etc often for religious or national celebrations: *Next Monday is a holiday.* ● *New Year's Day is a bank/public*

holiday in Britain.
➤ **Holiday** in this sense is used in both British and US English. A day when you choose not go to work is also called a **day off**: *I'm having two days off next week when we move house.*

'holiday camp *noun* [C] (*Brit*) a place that provides a place to stay and organized entertainment for people on holiday

holidaymaker /ˈhɒlədeɪmeɪkə; -dɪmeɪ-/ *noun* [C] (*Brit*) a person who is away from home on holiday

★**hollow¹** /ˈhɒləʊ/ *adj* **1** with a hole or empty space inside: *a hollow tree* **2** (used about parts of the face) sinking deep into the face: *hollow cheeks* ● *hollow-eyed* **3** not sincere: *a hollow laugh/voice* ● *hollow promises/threats* **4** (used about a sound) seeming to come from a hollow place: *hollow footsteps*

hollow² /ˈhɒləʊ/ *verb*
PHRASAL VERB **hollow sth out** to take out the inside part of sth

hollow³ /ˈhɒləʊ/ *noun* [C] an area that is lower than the land around it

holly /ˈhɒli/ *noun* [U] a plant that has shiny dark green leaves with sharp points and red berries in the winter. It is often used as a Christmas decoration.

holocaust /ˈhɒləkɔːst/ *noun* [C] a situation where a great many things are destroyed and a great many people die: *a nuclear holocaust*

hologram /ˈhɒləɡræm/ *noun* [C] an image or picture which appears to stand out from the flat surface it is on when light falls on it

holster /ˈhəʊlstə/ *noun* [C] a leather case for a gun that is fixed to a belt or worn under the arm

★**holy** /ˈhəʊli/ *adj* (**holier, holiest**) **1** connected with God or with religion and therefore very special or important: *the Holy Bible* ● *holy water* ● *The Koran is the holy book of Islam.* **2** (used about a person) serving God; pure —**holiness** *noun* [U]

homage /ˈhɒmɪdʒ/ *noun* [U,C, usually sing] (*formal*) **homage (to sb/sth)** something that is said or done to show respect publicly for sb: *Thousands came to pay/do homage to the dead leader.*

★**home¹** /həʊm/ *noun* **1** [C,U] the place where you live or where you feel that you belong: *She left home* (= left her parents' house and began an independent life) *at the age of 21.* ● *Children from broken homes* (= whose parents are divorced) *sometimes have learning difficulties.* ● *That old house would make an ideal family home.* ••➤ Look at the note at **house**.

➤ Be careful. The preposition *to* is not used before 'home': *It's time to go home.* ● *She's usually tired when she gets/arrives home.* If you want to talk about somebody else's home you have to say: *at Jane and Andy's* or: *at Jane and Andy's place/house.*

2 [C] a place that provides care for a particular type of person or for animals: *a children's* *home* (= for children who have no parents to look after them) ● *an old people's home* **3** [sing] **the home of sth** the place where sth began: *Greece is said to be the home of democracy.*

IDIOMS **at home 1** in your house, flat, etc: *Is anybody at home?* ● *Tomorrow we're staying at home all day.*

➤ In US English **home** is often used without the preposition *at*: *Is anybody home?*

2 comfortable, as if you were in your own home: *Please make yourself at home.* ● *I felt quite at home on the ship.* **3** (used in sport) played in the town to which the team belongs: *Manchester City are playing at home on Saturday.*

romp home/to victory → ROMP

★home² /həʊm/ *adj* (only *before* a noun) **1** connected with home: *home cooking* ● *your home address/town* ● *a happy home life* (= with your family) **2** (*especially Brit*) connected with your own country, not with a foreign country: *The Home Secretary is responsible for home affairs.* **3** (used in sport) connected with a team's own sports ground: *The home team has a lot of support.* ● *a home game* ●➤ opposite **away**

★home³ /həʊm/ *adv* at, in or to your home or home country: *We must be getting home soon.* ● *She'll be flying home for New Year.*

IDIOMS **bring sth home to sb** to make sb understand sth fully

drive sth home (to sb) → DRIVE¹

home⁴ /həʊm/ *verb*

PHRASAL VERB **home in on sb/sth** to move towards sb/sth: *The police homed in on the house where the thieves were hiding.*

homecoming /'həʊmkʌmɪŋ/ *noun* [C,U] the act of returning home, especially when you have been away for a long time

home-'grown *adj* (used about fruit and vegetables) grown in your own garden

homeland /'həʊmlænd/ *noun* [C] the country where you were born or that your parents came from, or to which you feel you belong

homeless /'həʊmləs/ *adj* **1** having no home **2 the homeless** *noun* [pl] people who have no home –**homelessness** *noun* [U]

homely /'həʊmli/ *adj* (*Brit*) (used about a place) simple but also pleasant or welcoming

home-'made *adj* made at home; not bought in a shop: *home-made cakes*

the 'Home Office *noun* [sing] (*Brit*) the department of the British Government that is responsible for the law, police and prisons within Britain and for decisions about who can enter the country

homeopath (also **homoeopath**) /'həʊmɪəpæθ/ *noun* [C] a person who treats sick people using homoeopathy

homeopathy (also **homoeopathy**) /,həʊmi'ɒpəθi/ *noun* [U] the treatment of a disease by giving very small amounts of a drug that would cause the disease if given in large amounts –**homeopathic** (also **homoeopathic**) /həʊmɪə'pæθɪk/ *adj*: *homeopathic medicine*

'home page *noun* [C] (*computing*) the first of a number of pages of information on the Internet that belongs to a person or an organization. A home page contains connections to other pages of information.

the ,Home 'Secretary *noun* [C] (*Brit*) a politician in the British Government (minister) who is in charge of the Home Office ●➤ Look at **the Foreign Secretary**.

homesick /'həʊmsɪk/ *adj* **homesick (for sb/ sth)** sad because you are away from home and you miss it: *She was very homesick for Canada.* –**homesickness** *noun* [U]

homeward /'həʊmwəd/ *adj, adv* going towards home: *the homeward journey* ● *to travel homeward*

★homework /'həʊmwɜːk/ *noun* [U] the written work that teachers give to students to do away from school: *Have we got any homework?* ● *We've got a translation to do for homework.*

➤ Note that **homework** is uncountable, so you cannot use it in the plural. If you want to talk about a single unit, you have to say **a piece of homework**.

●➤ Look at the note at **housework**.

homicidal /,hɒmɪ'saɪdl/ *adj* likely to murder sb: *a homicidal maniac*

homicide /'hɒmɪsaɪd/ *noun* [C,U] (*especially US*) the illegal killing of one person by another; murder

homonym /'hɒmənɪm/ *noun* [C] (*grammar*) a word that is spelt and pronounced like another word but that has a different meaning

homophone /'hɒməfəʊn/ *noun* [C] (*grammar*) a word that is pronounced the same as another word but that has a different spelling and meaning: *'Flower' and 'flour' are homophones.*

homosexual /,həʊmə'sekʃuəl; ,hɒm-/ *adj* sexually attracted to people of the same sex ●➤ Look at **heterosexual**, **bisexual**, **gay** and **lesbian**. –**homosexual** *noun* [C] –**homosexuality** /,həʊmə,sekʃu'æləti; ,hɒm-/ *noun* [U]

Hon *abbr* **1** Honorary; used to show that sb holds a position without being paid for it: *Hon President* **2** Honourable: a title for Members of Parliament and some high officials

★honest /'ɒnɪst/ *adj* **1** (used about a person) telling the truth; not deceiving people or stealing: *Just be honest – do you like this skirt or not?* ● *To be honest, I don't think that's a very good idea.* **2** showing honest qualities: *an honest face* ● *I'd like your honest opinion, please.* ●➤ opposite for both senses **dishonest** –**honesty** *noun* [U] ●➤ opposite **dishonesty**

honestly /'ɒnɪstli/ *adv* **1** in an honest way: *He tried to answer the lawyer's questions honestly.* **2** used for emphasizing that what you are saying is true: *I honestly don't know where she has gone.* **3** used for expressing disapproval: *Honestly! What a mess!*

honey /'hʌni/ *noun* [U] the sweet sticky substance that is made by bees and that people eat ●➤ picture on page C4

➤ **Honey** is also another word for **darling** (used especially in the US).

honeycomb

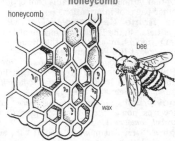

honeycomb

bee

wax

honeycomb /'hʌnikəʊm/ **noun** [C,U] a structure of holes (**cells**) with six sides, in which bees keep their eggs and the substance they produce (**honey**)

honeymoon /'hʌnimu:n/ **noun** [C] a holiday that is taken by a man and a woman who have just got married: *We had our first argument while we were* **on our honeymoon**.

honk /hɒŋk/ **verb** [I,T] to sound the horn of a car; to make this sound

honorary /'ɒnərəri/ **adj 1** given as an honour (without the person needing the usual certificates, etc): *to be awarded an honorary degree* **2** (often **Honorary**) (*abbr* Hon) not paid: *He is the Honorary President.*

honour¹ (*US* honor) /'ɒnə/ **noun 1** [U] the respect from other people that a person, country, etc gets because of high standards of behaviour and moral character: *the guest of honour* (= the most important one) ••➤ Look at **dishonour**. **2** [sing] (*formal*) something that gives pride or pleasure: *It was a great honour to be asked to speak at the conference.* **3** [U] the quality of doing what is morally right: *I give you my word of honour.* **4** **Honours** [pl] the four highest marks you can be given in Bachelor degrees

IDIOM **in honour of sb/sth; in sb/sth's honour** out of respect for sb/sth: *A party was given in honour of the guests from Bonn.*

honour² (*US* honor) /'ɒnə/ **verb** [T] **1** honour sb/sth (with sth) to show great (public) respect for sb/sth or to give sb pride or pleasure: *I am very honoured by the confidence you have shown in me.* **2** to do what you have agreed or promised

honourable (*US* honorable) /'ɒnərəbl/ **adj 1** acting in a way that makes people respect you; having or showing honour ••➤ opposite **dishonourable 2 the Honourable** (*abbr* **the Hon**) a title that is given to some high officials and to Members of Parliament when they are speaking to each other –**honourably** /-əbli/ **adv**

Hons /ɒnz/ **abbr** Honours (in Bachelor degrees): *John North BSc* (*Hons*)

hood /hʊd/ **noun** [C] **1** the part of a coat, etc that you pull up to cover your head and neck in bad weather **2** (*especially Brit*) a soft cover

for a car that has no roof, or a folding cover on transport for a baby (**a pram**) that can be folded down **3** (*US*) = **BONNET**(1)

hoof /hu:f/ **noun** [C] (*pl* **hoofs** or **hooves** /hu:vz/) the hard part of the foot of horses and some other animals ••➤ Look at **paw** picture at **horse**

hooks   hanger

★**hook¹** /hʊk/ **noun** [C] **1** a curved piece of metal, plastic, etc that is used for hanging sth on or for catching fish: *Put your coat on the hook over there.* • *a fish-hook* **2** (used in boxing) a way of hitting sb that is done with the arm bent: *a right hook* (= with the right arm)

IDIOMS **off the hook** (used about the top part of a telephone) not in position, so that telephone calls cannot be received

get/let sb off the hook (*informal*) to free yourself or sb else from a difficult situation or punishment: *My father paid the money I owed and got me off the hook.*

hook² /hʊk/ **verb 1** [I,T] to fasten or catch sth with a hook or sth in the shape of a hook; to be fastened in this way: *We hooked the trailer to the back of the car.* • *The curtain simply hooks onto the rail.* **2** [T] to put sth through a hole in sth else: *Hook the rope through your belt.*

PHRASAL VERB **hook (sth) up (to sth)** to connect sb/sth to a piece of electronic equipment or to a power supply

hook and 'eye **noun** [C] a thing that is used for fastening clothes ••➤ picture at **button**

hooked /hʊkt/ **adj 1** shaped like a hook: *a hooked nose* **2** (not before a noun) (*informal*) **hooked (on sth)** dependent on sth bad, especially drugs: *to be hooked on gambling* ••➤ synonym **addicted 3** (not before a noun) (*informal*) **hooked (on sth)** enjoying sth very much, so that you want to do it, see it, etc as much as possible: *Suzi is hooked on computer games.*

hooligan /'hu:lɪgən/ **noun** [C] a person who behaves in a violent and aggressive way in public places: *football hooligans* ••➤ Look at **lout** and **yob**. –**hooliganism** /-ɪzəm/ **noun** [U]

hoop /hu:p/ **noun** [C] a large metal or plastic ring

hooray = **HURRAY**

hoot¹ /hu:t/ **noun 1** [C] (*especially Brit*) a short loud laugh or shout: *hoots of laughter* **2** [sing] (*spoken*) a situation or a person that is very funny: *Bob is a real hoot!* **3** [C] the loud sound that is made by the horn of a vehicle **4** [C] the cry of a particular bird (an owl)

hoot² /hu:t/ **verb** [I,T] to sound the horn of a car or to make a loud noise: *The driver hooted* (*his horn*) *at the dog but it wouldn't move.* • *They hooted with laughter at the suggestion.*

hoover /ˈhuːvə/ verb [I,T] (*Brit*) to clean a carpet, etc with a machine that sucks up the dirt: *This carpet needs hoovering.* •▸ synonym **vacuum** –Hoover™ noun [C] •▸ synonym **vacuum cleaner**

hooves /huːvz/ *plural* of **HOOF**

hop/jump/bounce

jumping

hopping

bouncing

hop¹ /hɒp/ verb [I] (**hopping**; **hopped**) **1** (used about a person) to jump on one leg: *I had twisted my ankle so badly I had to hop all the way back to the car.* **2** (used about an animal or bird) to jump with both or all feet together **3** hop (from sth to sth) to change quickly from one activity or subject to another

IDIOM **hop it!** (*slang*) Go away!

PHRASAL VERBS **hop in/into sth; hop out/out of sth** (*informal*) to get in or out of a car, etc (quickly)

hop on/onto sth; hop off sth (*informal*) to get onto/off a bus, etc (quickly)

hop² /hɒp/ noun **1** [C] a short jump by a person on one leg or by a bird or animal with its feet together **2** [C] a tall climbing plant with flowers **3** hops [pl] the flowers of this plant that are used in making beer

★**hope¹** /həʊp/ verb [I,T] hope that...; hope to do sth; hope (for sth) to want sth to happen or be true: *'Is it raining?' 'I hope not. I haven't got a coat with me.'* • *'Are you coming to London with us?' 'I'm not sure yet but I hope so.'* • *I hope that you feel better soon.* • *Hoping to hear from you soon* (= at the end of a letter).

★**hope²** /həʊp/ noun **1** [C,U] (a) hope (of/for sth); (a) hope of doing sth; (a) hope that... the feeling of wanting sth to happen and thinking that it will: *What hope is there for the future?* • *There is no hope of finding anybody else alive.* • *David has **high hopes** of becoming a jockey* (= is very confident about it). • *She never **gave up hope** that a cure for the disease would be found.* **2** [sing] a person, a thing or a situation that will help you get what you want: *Please can you help me? You're my **last hope**.*

IDIOMS **dash sb's hopes (of sth/of doing sth)** → **DASH²**

in the hope of sth/that... because you want sth to happen: *I came here in the hope that we could talk privately.*

pin (all) your hopes on sb/sth → **PIN²**

a ray of hope → **RAY**

hopeful /ˈhəʊpfl/ adj **1** hopeful (about sth); hopeful that... believing that sth that you want will happen: *He's very hopeful about the success of the business.* • *The ministers seem hopeful that an agreement will be reached.* **2** making you think that sth good will happen: *a hopeful sign*

hopefully /ˈhəʊpfəli/ adv **1** (*informal*) I/We hope; if everything happens as planned: *Hopefully, we'll be finished by six o'clock.* **2** hoping that what you want will happen: *She smiled hopefully at me, waiting for my answer.*

hopeless /ˈhəʊpləs/ adj **1** giving no hope that sth/sb will be successful or get better: *It's hopeless. There is nothing we can do.* **2** (*informal*) hopeless (at sth) (*especially Brit*) (used about a person) often doing things wrong; very bad at doing sth: *I'm absolutely hopeless at tennis.* –hopelessly adv: *They were hopelessly lost.* –hopelessness noun [U]

horde /hɔːd/ noun [C] a very large number of people

horizon /həˈraɪzn/ noun **1** [sing] the line where the earth and sky appear to meet: *The ship appeared on/disappeared over the horizon.* **2** horizons [pl] the limits of your knowledge or experience: *Foreign travel is a good way of expanding your horizons.*

IDIOM **on the horizon** likely to happen soon: *There are further job cuts on the horizon.*

★**horizontal** /ˌhɒrɪˈzɒntl/ adj going from side to side, not up and down; flat or level: *The gymnasts were exercising on the horizontal bars.*

➤ Compare **vertical** and **perpendicular**.

•▸ picture at **line** –horizontally /-təli/ adv

hormone /ˈhɔːməʊn/ noun [C] a substance in your body that influences growth and development

★**horn** /hɔːn/ noun [C] **1** one of the hard pointed things that some animals have on their heads •▸ picture at **cow** •▸ picture at **goat** **2** the thing in a car, etc that gives a loud warning sound: *Don't sound your horn late at night.* •▸ picture on page S9 **3** one of the family of metal musical instruments that you play by blowing into them: *the French horn* •▸ Look at the note at **piano**. •▸ picture at **music**

horoscope /ˈhɒrəskəʊp/ noun [C] (also **stars** [pl]) a statement about what is going to happen to a person in the future, based on the position of the stars and planets when he/she was born: *What does my horoscope for next week say?* •▸ Look at **astrology** and **zodiac**.

horrendous /hɒˈrendəs/ adj (*informal*) very bad or unpleasant: *The queues were absolutely horrendous.* –horrendously adv

★**horrible** /ˈhɒrəbl/ adj **1** (*informal*) bad or unpleasant: *This coffee tastes horrible!* • *Don't be so horrible!* (= unkind) • *I've got **a horrible feeling** that I've forgotten something.* •▸ synonym **horrid** **2** shocking and/or frightening: *a horrible murder/death/nightmare* –horribly /-əbli/ adv

h

horrid /'hɒrɪd/ **adj** (*informal*) very unpleasant or unkind: *horrid weather* ● *I'm sorry that I was so horrid last night.* •➤ synonym **horrible**

horrific /hə'rɪfɪk/ **adj 1** extremely bad and shocking or frightening: *a horrific murder/ accident/attack* **2** (*informal*) very bad or unpleasant –**horrifically** /-kli/ **adv**: *horrifically expensive*

horrify /'hɒrɪfaɪ/ **verb** [T] (*pres part* **horrifying**; *3rd pers sing pres* **horrifies**; *pt, pp* **horrified**) to make sb feel extremely shocked, disgusted or frightened –**horrifying adj**

horror /'hɒrə/ **noun 1** [U,sing] a feeling of great fear or shock: *They watched in horror as the building collapsed.* **2** [C] something that makes you feel frightened or shocked: *a horror film/story*

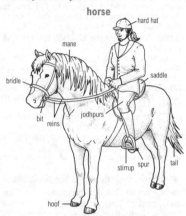

horse

hard hat
mane
saddle
bridle
bit
reins
jodhpurs
stirrup
spur
tail
hoof

★**horse** /hɔːs/ **noun 1** [C] a large animal that is used for riding on or for pulling or carrying heavy loads
  ➤ A male horse is a **stallion**, a female horse is a **mare** and a young horse is a **foal**.
2 the horses [pl] (*informal*) horse racing
  IDIOM **on horseback** sitting on a horse
  ➤ Police on horseback are called **mounted police**.

horse 'chestnut noun [C] **1** a large tree that has leaves divided into seven sections and pink or white flowers **2** (also *informal* **conker**) the nut from this tree

horseman /'hɔːsmən/ **noun** [C] (*pl* -**men** /-mən/) a man who rides a horse well: *an experienced horseman*

horsepower /'hɔːspaʊə/ **noun** [C] (*pl* **horsepower**) (*abbr* **hp**) a measurement of the power of an engine

horse racing (also **racing**) **noun** [U] the sport in which a person (**jockey**) rides a horse in a race to win money
  ➤ Horse racing takes place at a **racecourse**. People often **bet** on the results of horse races.

horseshoe /'hɔːsʃuː/ (also **shoe**) **noun** [C] a U-shaped piece of metal that is fixed to the bottom of a horse's foot (**hoof**). Some people believe that horseshoes bring good luck.

horsewoman /'hɔːswʊmən/ **noun** [C] (*pl* -**women** /-wɪmɪn/) a woman who rides a horse well

horticulture /'hɔːtɪkʌltʃə/ **noun** [U] the study or practice of growing flowers, fruit and vegetables –**horticultural** /ˌhɔːtɪ'kʌltʃərəl/ **adj**

hose /həʊz/ (also **hosepipe** /'həʊzpaɪp/) **noun** [C,U] a long rubber or plastic tube that water can flow through •➤ picture at **garden**

hospice /'hɒspɪs/ **noun** [C] a special hospital where people who are dying are cared for

hospitable /hɒ'spɪtəbl; 'hɒspɪtəbl/ **adj** (used about a person) friendly and kind to visitors •➤ opposite **inhospitable**

★**hospital** /'hɒspɪtl/ **noun** [C] a place where ill or injured people are treated: *He was rushed to hospital in an ambulance.* ● *to be admitted to/discharged from hospital* ● *a psychiatric/ mental hospital*

  ➤ If a person goes **to hospital** or is **in hospital** (without 'the'), he/she is a patient receiving treatment there: *His mother's in hospital.* ● *She cut her hand and had to go to hospital.* 'The hospital' refers to one particular hospital, or indicates that the person is only visiting the building temporarily: *He went to the hospital to visit Muriel.*
  A person who is being treated in a hospital by **doctors** and **nurses** is a **patient**. If you have an accident you are taken first to the **casualty** department (*US* **emergency room**).

hospitality /ˌhɒspɪ'tæləti/ **noun** [U] looking after guests and being friendly and welcoming towards them

★**host** /həʊst/ **noun** [C] **1** a person who invites guests to his/her house, etc and provides them with food, drink, etc: *It's polite to write a thank-you letter to your host.* •➤ Look at **hostess**. **2** a person who introduces a television or radio show and talks to the guests **3** **a host of sth** a large number of people or things –**host verb** [T]: *The city is aiming to host the Olympic Games in ten years' time.*

★**hostage** /'hɒstɪdʒ/ **noun** [C] a person who is caught and kept prisoner. A hostage may be killed or injured if the person or group who is holding him/her does not get what it is asking for: *The robbers tried to take the staff hostage.* ● *The hijackers say they will hold the passengers hostage until their demands are met.* •➤ Look at **ransom**.

hostel /'hɒstl/ **noun** [C] **1** a place like a cheap hotel where people can stay when they are living away from home: *a youth hostel* ● *a student hostel* **2** a building where people who have no home can stay for a short time

hostess /'həʊstəs; -es/ **noun** [C] **1** a woman who invites guests to her house, etc and provides them with food, drink, etc •➤ Look at **host**. **2** a woman who introduces a television or radio show and talks to the guests **3** =**AIR HOSTESS**

hostile /'hɒstaɪl/ *adj* hostile (to/towards sb/ sth) having very strong feelings against sb/ sth: *a hostile crowd* • *They are very hostile to any change.*

hostility /hɒ'stɪləti/ *noun* **1** [U] hostility (to/ towards sth) very strong feelings against sb/ sth: *She didn't say anything but I could sense her hostility.* **2 hostilities** [pl] fighting in a war

★**hot**[1] /hɒt/ *adj* (**hotter**; **hottest**) **1** having a high temperature: *Can I open the window? I'm really hot.* • *It was **boiling hot** on the beach.* • *a hot meal* • *Don't touch the plates – they're **red hot**!*

➤ You can describe the temperature of sth as **freezing (cold), cold, cool, tepid** (used about water), **warm, hot** or **boiling (hot)**. Look also at the note at **cold**[1].

2 (used about food) causing a burning feeling in your mouth; spicy: *hot curry* **3** (*informal*) difficult or dangerous to deal with: *The defenders found the Italian strikers **too hot to handle**.* **4** (*informal*) exciting and popular: *This band is **hot stuff**!*

IDIOM in hot pursuit following sb who is moving fast

hot[2] /hɒt/ *verb* (**hotting**; **hotted**)

PHRASAL VERB hot up (*Brit informal*) to become more exciting: *The election campaign has really hotted up in the past few days.*

hot-'air balloon = **BALLOON**(2)

'**hot dog** *noun* [C] a hot sausage in a soft bread roll •➤ picture on page C4

★**hotel** /həʊ'tel/ *noun* [C] a place where you pay to stay when you are on holiday or travelling: *to stay in/at a hotel* • *I've booked a double room at the Grand Hotel.* • *a two-star hotel*

➤ You book a **double, single** or **twin-bedded** room at a hotel. When you arrive you **check in** or **register** and when you leave you **check out**.

hotelier /həʊ'teliə; -lieɪ/ *noun* [C] a person who owns or manages a hotel

hothouse /'hɒthaʊs/ *noun* [C] a heated glass building where plants are grown •➤ Look at **greenhouse**.

hotline /'hɒtlaɪn/ *noun* [C] a direct telephone line to a business or organization

hotly /'hɒtli/ *adv* **1** in an angry or excited way: *They hotly denied the newspaper reports.* **2** closely and with determination: *The dog ran off, hotly pursued by its owner.*

'**hot-'water bottle** *noun* [C] a rubber container that is filled with hot water and put in a bed to warm it

hound[1] /haʊnd/ *noun* [C] a type of dog that is used for hunting or racing: *a foxhound*

hound[2] /haʊnd/ *verb* [T] to follow and disturb sb: *Many famous people complain of being hounded by the press.*

★**hour** /'aʊə/ *noun* **1** [C] a period of 60 minutes: *He studies for three hours most evenings.* • *The programme lasts about half an hour.* • *I'm going shopping now. I'll be back in about an hour.* • *In two hours' time I'll be having lunch.* • *a four-hour journey* • *Japan is eight hours ahead of the UK.* • *I get paid **by the hour**.* • *How much do you get paid **per/an hour**?* **2** [C] the distance that you can travel in about 60 minutes: *London is only two hours away.* **3 hours** [pl] the period of time when sb is working or a shop, etc is open: *Employees are demanding shorter **working hours**.* **4** [C] a period of about an hour when sth particular happens: *I'm going shopping in my **lunch hour**.* • *The traffic is very bad in the **rush hour**.* **5 the hour** [sing] the time when a new hour starts (= 1 o'clock, 2 o'clock, etc): *Buses are **on the hour** and at twenty past the hour.* **6 hours** [pl] a long time: *He went on speaking **for hours** and hours.*

IDIOMS at/till all hours at/until any time: *She stays out till all hours (= very late).*
the early hours → EARLY

hourly /'aʊəli/ *adj, adv* **1** done, happening, etc every hour: *an hourly news bulletin* • *Trains are hourly.* **2** for one hour: *What is your hourly rate of pay?*

★**house**[1] /haʊs/ *noun* [C] (*pl* **houses** /'haʊzɪz/) **1** a building that is made for people to live in: *Is yours a four-bedroomed or a three-bedroomed house?* •➤ Look at **bungalow, cottage** and **flat**. Your **home** is the place where you live, even if it is not a house: *Let's go home to my flat.* Your home is also the place where you feel that you belong. A house is just a building: *We've only just moved into our new house and it doesn't feel like home yet.*

➤ You can **build, do up, redecorate** or **extend** a house. You may **rent** a house from somebody or **let** it out to somebody else. If you want to **move house** you go to an **estate agent**.

2 [usually sing] all the people who live in one house: *Don't shout. You'll wake the whole house up.* **3** a building that is used for a particular purpose: *a warehouse* **4** a large firm involved in a particular kind of business: *a fashion/publishing house* **5** a restaurant, usually that sells one particular type of food: *a curry/spaghetti house* • *house wine* (= the cheapest wine on a restaurant's menu) **6 House** a group of people who meet to make a country's laws: *the House of Commons* • *the Houses of Parliament* •➤ Look at the note at **Parliament**. **7** [usually sing] the audience at a theatre or cinema, or the area where they sit: *There was a full house for the play this evening.*

IDIOMS move house → MOVE[1]
on the house paid for by the pub, restaurant, etc that you are visiting; free: *Your first drink is on the house.*
get on/along like a house on fire to immediately become good friends with sb

house[2] /haʊz/ *verb* [T] **1** to provide sb with a

h

place to live: *The Council must house home-less families.* **2** to contain or keep sth: *Her office is housed in a separate building.*

houseboat /'haʊsbəʊt/ **noun** [C] a boat on a river, etc where sb lives and which usually stays in one place

housebound /'haʊsbaʊnd/ **adj** unable to leave your house because you are old or ill

household /'haʊshəʊld/ **noun** [C] all the people who live in one house and the work, money, organization, etc that is needed to look after them: *household expenses*

householder /'haʊshəʊldə/ **noun** [C] a person who rents or owns a house

housekeeper /'haʊskiːpə/ **noun** [C] a person who is paid to look after sb else's house and organize the work in it

housekeeping /'haʊskiːpɪŋ/ **noun** [U] **1** the work involved in looking after a house **2** the money that you need to manage a house

the ,House of 'Commons noun [sing] the group of people (**Members of Parliament**) who are elected to make new laws in Britain

the ,House of 'Lords noun [sing] the group of people (who are not elected) who meet to discuss the laws that have been suggested by the House of Commons

the ,House of ,Repre'sentatives noun [sing] the group of people who are elected to make new laws in the US •➤ Look at **Congress** and **the Senate**.

'house-proud adj paying great attention to the care, cleaning, etc of your house

,house-to-'house adj going to each house: *The police are making house-to-house enquiries.*

'house-warming noun [C] a party that you have when you have just moved into a new home

housewife /'haʊswaɪf/ **noun** [C] (*pl* **housewives**) a woman who does not have a job outside the home and who spends her time cleaning the house, cooking, looking after her family, etc

➤ A man who does this is called a **house husband**.

★**housework** /'haʊswɜːk/ **noun** [U] the work that is needed to keep a house clean and tidy

➤ Be careful. The word for work that is given to pupils by teachers to be done out of school hours is **homework**.

housing /'haʊzɪŋ/ **noun** [U] houses, flats, etc for people to live in

'housing estate noun [C] an area where there are a large number of similar houses that were built at the same time

hover /'hɒvə/ **verb** [I] **1** (used about a bird, etc) to stay in the air in one place **2** (used about a person) to wait near sb/sth: *He hovered nervously outside the office.*

hovercraft /'hɒvəkrɑːft/ **noun** [C] (*pl* **hovercraft**) a type of boat that moves over land or water on a cushion of air

★**how** /haʊ/ **adv, conj 1** (often used in questions) in what way: *How do you spell your

name?* ● *Can you show me how to use this machine?* ● *I can't remember how to get there* **2** used when you are asking about sb's health or feelings: *'How is your mother?' 'She's much better, thank you.'* ● *How are you feeling today?* ● *How do you feel about your son joining the army?*

➤ You use 'how' only when you are asking about a person's health. When you are asking about a person's character or appearance you say **what ... like**?: *'What is your mother like?' 'Well, she's much taller than me and she's got dark hair.'*

3 used when you are asking about sb's opinion of a thing or a situation: *How was the weather?* ● *How is your meal?* ● *How did the interview go?* **4** used in questions when you are asking about the degree, amount, age, etc of sb/sth: *How old are you?* ● *How much is that?* **5** used for expressing surprise, pleasure, etc: *She's gone. How strange!* ● *I can't believe how expensive it is!*

IDIOMS **how/what about...?** ➜ **ABOUT²**

how come? ➜ **COME**

how do you do? (*formal*) used when meeting sb for the first time

➤ Be careful. **How are you?** and **How do you do?** are answered differently: *'How do you do?'* is answered with the same words: *'How do you do?'* The answer to: *'How are you?'* depends on how you are feeling: *'I'm fine.'/'Very well.'/'Much better.'*

★**however** /haʊ'evə/ **adv, conj 1** (*formal*) (used for adding a comment to what you have just said) although sth is true: *Sales are poor this month. There may, however, be an increase before Christmas.* **2** (used in questions for expressing surprise) in what way; how: *However did you manage to find me here?*

➤ When you use only **how** in a question like this there is not such a feeling of surprise.

3 in whatever way: *However I sat I couldn't get comfortable.* ● *You can dress however you like.* **4** (before an adjective or adverb) to whatever degree: *He won't wear a hat however cold it is.* ● *You can't catch her however fast you run.*

howl /haʊl/ **verb** [I] to make a long loud sound: *I couldn't sleep because there was a dog howling all night.* ● *The wind howled around the house.* –**howl noun** [C]

hp /ˌeɪtʃ 'piː/ **abbr 1** (used about an engine) horsepower **2 HP** (*Brit*) hire purchase

HQ /ˌeɪtʃ 'kjuː/ **abbr** headquarters

hr (*pl* **hrs**) **abbr** hour: *3 hrs 15 min*

hub /hʌb/ **noun** [usually sing] **1 the hub (of sth)** the central and most important part of a place or an activity: *the commercial hub of the city* **2** the central part of a wheel

hubbub /'hʌbʌb/ **noun** [sing,U] **1** the noise made by a lot of people talking at the same time: *I couldn't hear the announcement over the hubbub.* **2** a situation in which there is a lot of noise, excitement and activity: *the hub-bub of city life*

huddle¹ /'hʌdl/ **verb** [I] **huddle (up) (together)** **1** to get close to other people because you are cold or frightened: *The campers huddled together around the fire.* **2** to make your body as small as possible because you are cold or frightened: *She huddled up in her sleeping bag and tried to get some sleep.* –**huddled adj**: *We found the children lying huddled together on the ground.*

huddle² /'hʌdl/ **noun** [C] a small group of people or things that are close together: *They all stood in a huddle, laughing and chatting.*

huff /hʌf/ **noun** [C]

IDIOM **in a huff** (*informal*) in a bad mood because sb has annoyed or upset you: *Did you see Stan go off in a huff when he wasn't chosen for the team?*

hug /hʌg/ **verb** [T] (**hugging; hugged**) **1** to put your arms around sb, especially to show that you love him/her: *He hugged his mother and sisters and got on the train.* **2** to hold sth close to your body: *She hugged the parcel to her chest as she ran.* **3** (used about a ship, car, road, etc) to stay close to sth: *to hug the coast* –**hug noun** [C]: *Noel's crying – I'll go and give him a hug.*

★**huge** /hju:dʒ/ **adj** very big: *a huge amount/quantity/sum/number* ● *a huge building* ● *The film was a huge success.* –**hugely adv**: *hugely successful/popular/expensive*

huh /hʌ/ **interj** (*informal*) used for expressing anger, surprise, etc or for asking a question: *They've gone away, huh? They didn't tell me.*

hull /hʌl/ **noun** [C] the body of a ship

hullabaloo /ˌhʌləbə'lu:/ **noun** [sing] a lot of loud noise, for example made by people shouting

hum /hʌm/ **verb** (**humming; hummed**) **1** [I] to make a continuous low noise: *The machine began to hum as I switched it on.* **2** [I,T] to sing with your lips closed: *You can hum the tune if you don't know the words.* –**hum noun** [sing]: *the hum of machinery/distant traffic*

★**human¹** /'hju:mən/ **adj** connected with people, not with animals, machines or gods; typical of people: *the human body* ● *The disaster was caused by human error.* –**humanly adv**: *They did all that was humanly possible to rescue him* (= everything that a human being could possibly do).

human² /'hju:mən/ (also ˌhuman 'being) **noun** [C] a person

humane /hju:'meɪn/ **adj** having or showing kindness or understanding, especially to a person or animal that is suffering: *Zoo animals must be kept in humane conditions.* ●→ opposite **inhumane** –**humanely adv**

humanitarian /hju:ˌmænɪ'teəriən/ **adj** concerned with trying to make people's lives better and reduce suffering: *Many countries have sent humanitarian aid to the earthquake victims.*

humanity /hju:'mænəti/ **noun** [U] **1** all the people in the world, thought of as a group: *crimes against humanity* ●→ synonym **the**

human race 2 the quality of being kind and understanding: *The prisoners were treated with humanity.* ●→ opposite **inhumanity**

ˌhuman 'nature **noun** [U] feelings, behaviour, etc that all people have in common

the ˌhuman 'race noun [sing] all the people in the world, thought of as a group ●→ synonym **humanity**

ˌhuman 'rights **noun** [pl] the basic freedoms that all people should have, for example the right to say what you think, to travel freely, etc

humble¹ /'hʌmbl/ **adj 1** not thinking that you are better or more important than other people; not proud: *He became very rich and famous but he always remained a very humble man.* ●→ noun **humility** ●→ Look at **modest**. **2** not special or important: *She comes from a humble background.* –**humbly** /'hʌmbli/ **adv**: *He apologized very humbly for his behaviour.*

humble² /'hʌmbl/ **verb** [T] to make sb feel that he/she is not as good or important as he/she thought

humid /'hju:mɪd/ **adj** (used about the air or climate) containing a lot of water; damp: *Hong Kong is hot and humid in summer.* –**humidity noun** [U]

humiliate /hju:'mɪlieɪt/ **verb** [T] to make sb feel very embarrassed: *I felt humiliated when the teacher laughed at my work.* –**humiliating adj**: *a humiliating defeat* –**humiliation** /hju:ˌmɪli'eɪʃn/ **noun** [C,U]

humility /hju:'mɪləti/ **noun** [U] the quality of not thinking that you are better than other people ●→ adjective **humble**

humorous /'hju:mərəs/ **adj** amusing or funny –**humorously adv**

★**humour¹** (*US* **humor**) /'hju:mə/ **noun** [U] **1** the funny or amusing qualities of sb/sth: *It is sometimes hard to understand the humour* (= the jokes) *of another country.* **2** being able to see when sth is funny and to laugh at things: *Rose has a good sense of humour.* **3 -humoured** (*US* **-humored**) (used to form compound adjectives) having or showing a particular mood: *good-humoured*

humour² (*US* **humor**) /'hju:mə/ **verb** [T] to keep sb happy by doing what he/she wants

humourless /'hju:mələs/ (*US* **humorless**) **adj** having no sense of fun; serious

hump /hʌmp/ **noun** [C] a large round lump, for example on the back of an animal who lives in the desert (**camel**) ●→ picture at **camel**

hunch¹ /hʌntʃ/ **noun** [C] (*informal*) a thought or an idea that is based on a feeling rather than on facts or information: *I'm not sure, but I've got a hunch that she's got a new job.*

hunch² /hʌntʃ/ **verb** [I,T] to bend your back and shoulders forward into a round shape

hunchback /'hʌntʃbæk/ **noun** [C] a person with a back that has a round lump on it

★**hundred** /'hʌndrəd/ **number 1** (*pl* **hundred**) 100: *two hundred* ● *There were a/one hundred people in the room.* ● *She's a hundred today.*

➤ Note that when we are saying a number, for example 1,420, we put 'and' after the word **hundred**: *one thousand four hundred and twenty*.
For examples of how to use numbers in sentences, look at **six**.

2 hundreds (*informal*) a lot; a large amount: *I've got hundreds of things to do today.*

➤ For more information about numbers look at the special section on numbers at the back of this dictionary.

hundredth¹ /'hʌndrədθ/ **noun** [C] the fraction ¹⁄₁₀₀; one of a hundred equal parts of sth
hundredth² /'hʌndrədθ/ **pron, determiner, adv** 100th •➤ Look at the examples at **sixth¹**.
hundredweight /'hʌndrədweɪt/ **noun** [C] (*abbr* **cwt**) a measurement of weight

➤ For more information about weights look at the special section on numbers at the back of this dictionary.

hung *past tense, past participle* of **HANG¹**

★ **hunger¹** /'hʌŋgə/ **noun 1** [U] the state of not having enough food to eat, especially when this causes illness or death: *In the Third World many people die of hunger each year.* •➤ Look at **thirst**. **2** [U] the feeling caused by a need to eat: *Hunger is one reason why babies cry.*

➤ Be careful. You cannot say *I have hunger* in English. You must say: *I am hungry.*

3 [sing] hunger (for sth) a strong desire for sth: *a hunger for knowledge/fame/success*
hunger² /'hʌŋgə/ **verb** (*formal*)
PHRASAL VERB hunger for/after sth to have a strong desire for sth
'**hunger strike noun** [C,U] a time when sb (especially a prisoner) refuses to eat because he/she is protesting about sth: *to be/go on hunger strike*

★ **hungry** /'hʌŋgri/ **adj** (**hungrier**; **hungriest**) **1** wanting to eat: *I'm hungry. Let's eat soon.*
• *There were hungry children begging for food in the streets.* •➤ Look at **thirsty**. **2** hungry for sth wanting sth very much: *I'm hungry for some excitement tonight.* –**hungrily adv**
IDIOM go hungry to not have any food
hunk /hʌŋk/ **noun** [C] **1** a large piece of sth: *a hunk of bread/cheese/meat* **2** (*informal*) a man who is big, strong and attractive

★ **hunt¹** /hʌnt/ **verb** [I,T] **1** to run after wild animals, etc in order to catch or kill them either for sport or for food: *Owls hunt at night.* • *Are tigers still hunted in India?* •➤ We often use the expression **go hunting** when we are talking about people spending time hunting. **2** hunt (for) (sb/sth) to try to find sb/sth: *The police are still hunting the murderer.*
hunt² /hʌnt/ **noun** [C] **1** the act of hunting wild animals, etc: *a fox-hunt* **2** [usually sing] a hunt (for sb/sth) the act of looking for sb/sth that is difficult to find: *The police have launched a hunt for the missing child.*
hunter /'hʌntə/ **noun** [C] a person that hunts

wild animals for food or sport; an animal that hunts its food
hunting /'hʌntɪŋ/ **noun** [U] the act of following and killing wild animals or birds as a sport or for food •➤ Look at **shoot**.
hurdle¹ /'hɜːdl/ **noun 1** [C] a type of light fence that a person or a horse jumps over in a race: *to clear a hurdle* (= to jump over it successfully) **2 hurdles** [pl] a race in which runners or horses have to jump over hurdles: *the 200 metres hurdles* **3** [C] a problem or difficulty that you must solve or deal with before you can achieve sth
hurdle² /'hɜːdl/ **verb** [I,T] hurdle (over sth) to jump over sth while you are running
hurl /hɜːl/ **verb** [T] to throw sth with great force
hurray (also **hooray**) /hʊ'reɪ/ (also **hurrah** /hə'rɑː/) **interj** used for expressing great pleasure, approval, etc: *Hurray! We've won!*
IDIOM hip, hip, hurray/hurrah ➔ **HIP²**
hurricane /'hʌrɪkeɪn; -kən/ **noun** [C] a violent storm with very strong winds •➤ Look at the note at **storm**.
hurried /'hʌrid/ **adj** done (too) quickly: *a hurried meal* –**hurriedly adv**

★ **hurry¹** /'hʌri/ **noun** [U] the need or wish to do sth quickly: *Take your time. There's* **no** *hurry.*
IDIOMS in a hurry quickly: *She got up late and left in a hurry.*
in a hurry (to do sth) wanting to do sth soon; impatient: *They are in a hurry to get the job done before the winter.*
in no hurry (to do sth); not in any hurry (to do sth) **1** not needing or wishing to do sth quickly: *We weren't in any hurry so we stopped to admire the view.* **2** not wanting to do sth: *I am in no hurry to repeat that experience.*

★ **hurry²** /'hʌri/ **verb** (*pres part* **hurrying**; *3rd pers sing pres* **hurries**; *pt, pp* **hurried**) **1** [I] to move or do sth quickly because there is not much time: *Don't hurry. There's plenty of time.* • *They hurried back home after school.*
• *Several people hurried to help.* **2** hurry (into sth/doing sth) [T] to cause sb/sth to do sth, or sth to happen more quickly: *Don't hurry me. I'm going as fast as I can.* • *He was hurried into a decision.* **3** (usually passive) to do sth too quickly
PHRASAL VERB hurry up (with sth) (*informal*) to move or do sth more quickly: *Hurry up or we'll miss the train.*

★ **hurt** /hɜːt/ **verb** (*pt, pp* **hurt**) **1** [T,I] to cause sb/yourself physical pain or injury: *Did he hurt himself?* • *I fell and hurt my arm.* • *No one was seriously hurt in the accident.* • *These shoes hurt; they're too tight.*

➤ Compare **hurt, injure** and **wound**. A person may be **wounded** by a knife, sword, gun, etc, usually as a result of fighting: *a wounded soldier.* People are usually **injured** in an accident: *Five people were killed in the crash and twelve others were injured.* **Hurt** and **injured** are similar in meaning but **hurt** is more often used when the damage is

not very great: *I hurt my leg when I fell off my bike.*
2 [I] to feel painful: *My leg hurts.* ● *It hurts when I lift my leg.* ● *Where exactly does it hurt?* **3** [T] to make sb unhappy; to upset sb: *His unkind remarks hurt her deeply.* ● *I didn't want to* **hurt** *his* **feelings.**
[IDIOM] **it won't/wouldn't hurt (sb/sth) (to do sth)** (*informal*) used to say that sb should do sth: *It wouldn't hurt you to help with the housework occasionally.*

*★ **hurt²** /hɜːt/ adj* **1** injured physically: *None of the passengers were* **badly/seriously hurt.** **2** upset and offended by sth that sb has said or done: *She was* **deeply hurt** *that she had not been invited to the party.*

hurt³ /hɜːt/ *noun* [U] a feeling of unhappiness because sb has been unkind or unfair to you: *There was hurt and real anger in her voice.*

hurtful /'hɜːtfl/ *adj* **hurtful (to sb)** unkind; making sb feel upset and offended

hurtle /'hɜːtl/ *verb* [I] to move with great speed, perhaps causing danger: *The lorry came hurtling towards us.*

*★ **husband** /'hʌzbənd/ *noun* [C] a man that a woman is married to: *Her ex-husband sees the children once a month.*

hush¹ /hʌʃ/ *verb* [I] (*spoken*) used to tell sb to be quiet, to stop talking or crying: *Hush now and try to sleep.*
[PHRASAL VERB] **hush sth up** to hide information to stop people knowing about sth; to keep sth secret

hush² /hʌʃ/ *noun* [sing] silence

hush-'hush *adj* (*informal*) very secret

husky¹ /'hʌski/ *adj* (used about a person's voice) sounding rough and quiet as if your throat were dry

husky² /'hʌski/ *noun* [C] (*pl* **huskies**) a strong dog with thick fur that is used in teams for pulling heavy loads over snow

hustle /'hʌsl/ *verb* [T] to push or move sb in a way that is not gentle

hut /hʌt/ *noun* [C] a small building with one room, usually made of wood or metal: *a wooden/mud hut*

hutch /hʌtʃ/ *noun* [C] a wooden box with a front made of wire, that is used for keeping rabbits or other small animals

hydrant /'haɪdrənt/ *noun* [C] a pipe in a street from which water can be taken for stopping fires, cleaning the streets, etc

hydraulic /haɪ'drɔːlɪk/ *adj* operated by water or another liquid moving through pipes, etc under pressure: *hydraulic brakes*

hydroelectric /ˌhaɪdrəʊ'lektrɪk/ *adj* using the power of water to produce electricity; produced by the power of water: *a hydroelectric dam* ● *hydroelectric power*

hydrogen /'haɪdrədʒən/ *noun* [U] (*symbol* **H**) a light colourless gas. Hydrogen and another gas (oxygen) form water (H_2O).

hygiene /'haɪdʒiːn/ *noun* [U] (the rules of) keeping yourself and things around you clean, in order to prevent disease: *High standards of hygiene are essential when you are preparing food.* ● *personal hygiene*

hygienic /haɪ'dʒiːnɪk/ *adj* clean, without the bacteria that cause disease: *hygienic conditions* –**hygienically** /-kli/ *adv*

hymn /hɪm/ *noun* [C] a religious song that Christians sing together in church, etc

hype¹ /haɪp/ *noun* [U] advertisements that tell you how good and important a new product, film, etc is: *Don't believe all the hype – the book is rubbish!*

hype² /haɪp/ *verb* [T] **hype sth (up)** to exaggerate how good or important sth is: *His much-hyped new movie is released next week.*

hypermarket /'haɪpəmɑːkɪt/ *noun* [C] (*Brit*) a very large shop that is usually situated outside a town and sells a wide variety of goods

hyphen /'haɪfn/ *noun* [C] the mark (-) used for joining two words together (for example *left-handed, red-hot*) or to show that a word has been divided and continues on the next line ●●▸ Look at **dash**.

hyphenate /'haɪfəneɪt/ *verb* [T] to join two words together with a hyphen –**hyphenation** /ˌhaɪfə'neɪʃn/ *noun* [U]

hypnosis /hɪp'nəʊsɪs/ *noun* [U] (the producing of) an unconscious state where sb's mind and actions can be controlled by another person: *She was questioned* **under hypnosis.**

hypnotize (also **-ise**) /'hɪpnətaɪz/ *verb* [T] to put sb into an unconscious state where the person's mind and actions can be controlled –**hypnotic** /hɪp'nɒtɪk/ –**hypnotism** /'hɪpnətɪzəm/ *noun* [U] –**hypnotist** /'hɪpnətɪst/ *noun* [C]

hypochondriac /ˌhaɪpə'kɒndriæk/ *noun* [C] a person who is always worried about his/her health and believes he/she is ill, even when there is nothing wrong

hypocrisy /hɪ'pɒkrəsi/ *noun* [U] behaviour in which sb pretends to have moral standards or opinions that he/she does not really have

hypocrite /'hɪpəkrɪt/ *noun* [C] a person who pretends to have moral standards or opinions which he/she does not really have. Hypocrites say one thing and do another: *What a hypocrite! She says she's against the hunting of animals but she's wearing a fur coat.* –**hypocritical** /ˌhɪpə'krɪtɪkl/ *adj* –**hypocritically** /-kli/ *adv*

hypodermic /ˌhaɪpə'dɜːmɪk/ *adj* a medical instrument with a long needle that is used for putting drugs under the skin (giving an injection): *a hypodermic needle/syringe*

hypothesis /haɪ'pɒθəsɪs/ *noun* [C] (*pl* **hypotheses** /-siːz/) an idea that is suggested as the possible explanation for sth but has not yet been found to be true or correct

hypothetical /ˌhaɪpə'θetɪkl/ *adj* based on situations that have not yet happened, not on facts: *That's a hypothetical question because we don't know what the situation will be next year.* –**hypothetically** /-kli/ *adv*

[h]

[I] **intransitive**, a verb which has no object: *He laughed.*   [T] **transitive**, a verb which has an object: *He ate an apple.*

hysteria /hɪ'stɪəriə/ **noun** [U] a state in which a person or a group of people cannot control their emotions, for example cannot stop laughing, crying, shouting, etc: *mass hysteria*

hysterical /hɪ'sterɪkl/ **adj 1** very excited and unable to control your emotions: *hysterical laughter* ● *She was hysterical with grief.* **2** (*informal*) very funny –**hysterically** /-kli/ **adv**

hysterics /hɪ'sterɪks/ **noun** [pl] **1** an expression of extreme fear, excitement or anger that makes sb lose control of his/her emotions: *She **went into hysterics** when they told her the news.* ● (*informal*) *My father would **have hysterics** (= be furious) if he knew I was going out with you.* **2** (*informal*) laughter that you cannot control: *The comedian had the audience **in hysterics**.*

Hz /hɜːts/ **abbr** hertz; (used in radio) a measure of frequency, one cycle per second

....

I i

....

I, i[1] /aɪ/ **noun** [C] (*pl* **I's; i's**) the ninth letter of the English alphabet: *'Island' begins with (an) 'I'.*

★**I**[2] /aɪ/ **pron** (the subject of a verb) the person who is speaking or writing: *I phoned and said that I was busy.* ● *I'm not going to fall, am I?*

★**ice**[1] /aɪs/ **noun** [U] water that has frozen and become solid: *Do you want ice in your orange juice?* ● *I slipped on a patch of ice.* ● *black ice* (= ice on roads, that cannot be seen easily)

　IDIOMS　**break the ice** to say or do sth that makes people feel more relaxed, especially at the beginning of a party or meeting: *She smiled to break the ice.*

　cut no ice (with sb) to have no influence or effect on sb: *His excuses cut no ice with me.*

　on ice 1 (used about wine, etc) kept cold by being surrounded by ice **2** (used about a plan, etc) waiting to be dealt with later; delayed: *We've had to put our plans to go to Australia on ice for the time being.*

ice[2] /aɪs/ (*especially US* **frost**) **verb** [T] to decorate a cake by covering it with a mixture of sugar, butter, chocolate, etc ••➤ Look at **icing**.

　PHRASAL VERB　**ice (sth) over/up** to cover sth or become covered with ice: *The windscreen of the car had iced over in the night.*

iceberg /'aɪsbɜːɡ/ **noun** [C] a very large block of ice that floats in the sea

　IDIOM　**the tip of the iceberg** → **TIP**[1]

icebox /'aɪsbɒks/ (*US*) = **FRIDGE**

ice-'cold adj very cold: *ice-cold beer* ● *Your hands are ice-cold.*

ice 'cream noun 1 [U] a frozen sweet food that is made from cream ••➤ picture on page

C4 **2** [C] an amount of ice cream that is served to sb, often in a special container (a cone): *a strawberry ice cream*

'ice cube noun [C] a small block of ice that you put in a drink to make it cold

iced /aɪst/ **adj** (used about drinks) very cold: *iced tea*

'ice hockey (*US* **hockey**) **noun** [U] a game that is played on ice by two teams who try to hit a small flat rubber object (a puck) into a goal with long wooden sticks

,ice 'lolly noun [C] (*pl* **ice lollies**) (*US* **Popsicle**) a piece of flavoured ice on a stick ••➤ Look at **lollipop**.

'ice rink = **SKATING RINK**

'ice-skate = **SKATE**[2]

'ice skating = **SKATING**(1)

icicle /'aɪsɪkl/ **noun** [C] a pointed piece of ice that is formed by water freezing as it falls or runs down from sth

icing /'aɪsɪŋ/ (*US* **frosting**) **noun** [U] a sweet mixture of sugar and water, milk, butter, etc that is used for decorating cakes ••➤ picture at **cake**

icon /'aɪkɒn/ **noun** [C] **1** (*computing*) a small picture or symbol on a computer screen that represents a program: *Click on the printer icon with the mouse.* ••➤ picture on page S7 **2** a person or thing that is considered to be a symbol of sth: *Madonna and other pop icons of the 1980s* **3** (also **ikon**) a picture or figure of an important religious person, used by some types of Christians

icy /'aɪsi/ **adj 1** very cold: *icy winds/water/weather* **2** covered with ice: *icy roads*

I'd /aɪd/ **short for** **I HAD, I WOULD**

ID /,aɪ 'diː/ **abbr** (*informal*) identification; identity: *an ID card*

Id = **EID**

★**idea** /aɪ'dɪə/ **noun 1** [C] **an idea (for sth); an idea (of sth/of doing sth)** a plan, thought or suggestion, especially about what to do in a particular situation: *That's a good idea!* ● *He's got **an idea** for a new play.* ● *I had the **bright idea** of getting Jane to help me with my homework.* ● *Has anyone got **any ideas** of how to tackle this problem?* ● *It was your idea to invite so many people to the party.* **2** [sing] **an idea (of sth)** a picture or impression in your mind: *You have **no idea** (= you can't imagine) how difficult it was to find a time that suited everybody.* ● *The programme **gave a good idea** of what life was like before the war.* ● *Staying in to watch the football on TV is not my idea of a good time.* **3** [C] an idea (about sth) an opinion or belief: *She has her own ideas about how to bring up her children.* **4 the idea** [sing] **the idea (of sth/of doing sth)** the aim or purpose of sth: *The idea of the course is to teach the basics of car maintenance.*

　IDIOMS　**get the idea** to understand the aim or purpose of sth: *Right! I think I've got the idea now.*

　get the idea that... to get the feeling or impression that...: *Where did you get the idea*

that I was paying for this meal?
have an idea that... to have a feeling or think that...: *I'm not sure but I have an idea that they've gone on holiday.*
not have the faintest/foggiest (idea) → **FAINT**[1]

*★**ideal**[1] /aɪˈdiːəl/ **adj** ideal (for sb/sth) the best possible; perfect: *She's the ideal candidate for the job.* ● **In an ideal world** there would be no poverty. ● *It would be an **ideal opportunity** for you to practise your Spanish.*

ideal[2] /aɪˈdiːəl/ **noun** [C] **1** an idea or principle that seems perfect to you and that you want to achieve: *She finds it hard to live up to her parents' high ideals.* ● *political/moral/ social ideals* **2** [usually sing] an ideal (of sth) a perfect example of a person or thing: *It's my ideal of what a family home should be.*

idealism /aɪˈdiːəlɪzəm/ **noun** [U] the belief that a perfect life, situation, etc can be achieved, even when this is not very likely: *Young people are usually full of idealism.* ••▸ Look at **realism**. –**idealist** **noun** [C]: *Most people are idealists when they are young.* –**idealistic** /ˌaɪdɪəˈlɪstɪk/ **adj**

idealize (also **-ise**) /aɪˈdɪəlaɪz/ **verb** [T] to imagine or show sb/sth as being better than he/she/it really is: *Old people often idealize the past.*

ideally /aɪˈdiːəli/ **adv 1** perfectly: *They are ideally suited to each other.* **2** in an ideal situation: *Ideally, no class should be larger than 25.*

identical /aɪˈdentɪkl/ **adj 1** identical (to/ with sb/sth) exactly the same as; similar in every detail: *I can't see any difference between these two pens – they look identical to me.* ● *That watch is identical to the one I lost yesterday.* **2 the identical** (only *before* a noun) the same: *This is the identical room we stayed in last year.* –**identically** /-kli/ **adv**

i,dentical 'twin noun [C] one of two children born at the same time from the same mother, and who are of the same sex and look very similar.

*★**identification** /aɪˌdentɪfɪˈkeɪʃn/ **noun** [U,C] **1** the process of showing, recognizing or giving proof of who or what sb/sth is: *The identification of the bodies of those killed in the explosion was very difficult.* **2** (*abbr* **ID**) [U] an official paper, document, etc that is proof of who you are: *Do you have any identification?* **3** identification (with sb/sth) a strong feeling of understanding or sharing the same feelings as sb/sth: *children's identification with TV heroes*

*★**identify** /aɪˈdentɪfaɪ/ **verb** [T] (*pres part* **identifying**; *3rd pers sing pres* **identifies**; *pt, pp* **identified**) identify sb/sth (as sb/sth) to recognize or be able to say who or what sb/sth is: *The police need someone to identify the body.* ● *We must identify the cause of the problem before we look for solutions.*
[PHRASAL VERBS] **identify sth with sth** to think or say that sth is the same as sth else: *You can't identify nationalism with fascism.*
identify with sb to feel that you understand and share what sb else is feeling: *I found it*

hard to identify with the woman in the film.
identify (yourself) with sb/sth to support or be closely connected with sb/sth: *She became identified with the new political party.*

*★**identity** /aɪˈdentəti/ **noun** [C,U] (*pl* **identities**) who or what a person or a thing is: *There are few clues to the identity of the killer.* ● *The region has its own **cultural identity**.* ● *The arrest was a case of mistaken identity* (= the wrong person was arrested).

i'dentity card (also **ID card**) **noun** [C] a card with your name, photograph, etc that is proof of who you are

ideology /ˌaɪdiˈɒlədʒi/ **noun** [C,U] (*pl* **ideologies**) a set of ideas which form the basis for a political or economic system: *Marxist ideology* –**ideological** /ˌaɪdiəˈlɒdʒɪkl/ **adj**

idiom /ˈɪdiəm/ **noun** [C] an expression whose meaning is different from the meanings of the individual words in it: *The idiom 'bring sth home to sb' means 'make sb understand sth'.*

idiomatic /ˌɪdiəˈmætɪk/ **adj 1** using language that contains expressions that are natural to a native speaker: *He speaks good idiomatic English.* **2** containing an idiom: *an idiomatic expression*

idiot /ˈɪdiət/ **noun** [C] (*informal*) a very stupid person: *I was an idiot to forget my passport.* –**idiotic** /ˌɪdiˈɒtɪk/ **adj** –**idiotically** /-kli/ **adv**

idle /ˈaɪdl/ **adj 1** not wanting to work hard; lazy: *He has the ability to succeed but he is just **bone** (= very) **idle**.* **2** not doing anything; not being used: *She can't bear to be idle.* ● *The factory **stood idle** while the machines were being repaired.* **3** (only *before* a noun) not to be taken seriously because it will not have any result: *an idle promise/threat* ● *idle chatter/curiosity* –**idleness noun** [U] –**idly** /ˈaɪdli/ **adv**

idol /ˈaɪdl/ **noun** [C] **1** a person (such as a film star or pop musician) who is admired or loved: *a pop/football/teen/screen idol* **2** a statue that people treat as a god

idolize (also **-ise**) /ˈaɪdəlaɪz/ **verb** [T] to love or admire sb very much or too much: *He is an only child and his parents idolize him.*

idyllic /ɪˈdɪlɪk/ **adj** very pleasant and peaceful; perfect: *an idyllic holiday*

ie /ˌaɪ ˈiː/ **abbr** that is; in other words: *deciduous trees, ie those which lose their leaves in autumn*

*★**if** /ɪf/ **conj 1** used in sentences in which one thing only happens or is true when another thing happens or is true: *If you see him, give him this letter.* ● *We won't go to the beach if it rains.* ● *If I had more time, I would learn another language.* ● *I might see her tomorrow. If not, I'll see her at the weekend.* **2** when; every time: *If I try to phone her she just hangs up.* ● *If metal gets hot it expands.* **3** used after verbs such as 'ask', 'know', 'remember': *They asked if we would like to go too.* ● *I can't remember if I posted the letter or not.* ••▸ Look at the note at **whether**. **4** used when you are asking sb to do sth or suggesting sth politely: *If you could just come this way, sir.* ● *If I*

might suggest something...

IDIOMS **as if → AS**

even if → EVEN²

if I were you used when you are giving sb advice: *If I were you, I'd leave now.*

if it wasn't/weren't for sb/sth if a particular person or situation did not exist or was not there; without sb/sth: *If it wasn't for him, I wouldn't stay in this country.*

if only used for expressing a strong wish: *If only I could drive.* ● *If only he'd write.*

igloo /'ɪgluː/ **noun** [C] (*pl* **igloos**) a small house that is built from blocks of hard snow

ignite /ɪg'naɪt/ **verb** [I,T] (*formal*) to start burning or to make sth start burning: *A spark from the engine ignited the petrol.*

ignition /ɪg'nɪʃn/ **noun 1** [C] the electrical system that starts the engine of a car: *to turn the ignition on/off* ● *First of all, put the key in the ignition.* **2** [U] the action of starting to burn or making sth start to burn

ignominious /ˌɪgnə'mɪniəs/ **adj** (*formal*) making you feel embarrassed: *The team suffered an ignominious defeat.* –**ignominiously adv**

ignorance /'ɪgnərəns/ **noun** [U] ignorance (**of/about sth**) a lack of information or knowledge: *The workers were in complete ignorance of the management's plans.*

ignorant /'ɪgnərənt/ **adj 1** ignorant (**of/ about sth**) not knowing about sth: *Many people are ignorant of their rights.* **2** (*informal*) having or showing bad manners: *an ignorant person/remark*

⋆**ignore** /ɪg'nɔː/ **verb** [T] to pay no attention to sb/sth: *I said hello to Debbie but she totally ignored me* (= acted as though she hadn't seen me). ● *Alison ignored her doctor's advice about drinking and smoking less.*

> Be careful. **Ignore** and **be ignorant** are different in meaning.

ikon = **ICON**(3)

I'll /aɪl/ *short for* **I WILL, I SHALL**

⋆**ill¹** /ɪl/ **adj 1** (*US* **sick**) (not before a noun) not in good health; not well: *I can't drink milk because it makes me feel ill.* ● *My mother was taken ill suddenly last week.* ● *My grandfather is seriously ill in hospital.* ●⋆ Look at the note at **sick**. **2** (only *before* a noun) bad or harmful: *He resigned because of ill health.* ● *I'm glad to say I suffered no ill effects from all that rich food.* ●⋆ noun **illness**

ill² /ɪl/ **adv 1** (often in compounds) badly or wrongly: *You would be ill-advised to drive until you have fully recovered.* **2** only with difficulty; not easily: *They could ill afford the extra money for better heating.*

IDIOMS **augur well/ill for sb/sth → AUGUR**

bode well/ill (for sb/sth) → BODE

⋆**illegal** /ɪ'liːgl/ **adj** not allowed by the law: *It is illegal to own a gun without a special licence.* ● *illegal drugs/immigrants/activities* ●⋆ opposite **legal** –**illegally** /-gəli/ **adv**

illegible /ɪ'ledʒəbl/ **adj** difficult or impossible to read: *Your handwriting is quite*

illegible. ●⋆ opposite **legible** –**illegibly** /-əbli/ **adv**

illegitimate /ˌɪlə'dʒɪtəmət/ **adj 1** (*old-fashioned*) (used about a child) born to parents who are not married to each other **2** not allowed by law; against the rules: *the illegitimate use of company money* ●⋆ opposite **legitimate** –**illegitimacy** /ˌɪlə'dʒɪtəməsi/ **noun** [U]

,**ill·'fated adj** not lucky: *the ill-fated ship, the Titanic*

illicit /ɪ'lɪsɪt/ **adj** (used about an activity or substance) not allowed by law or by the rules of society: *the illicit trade in ivory* ● *They were having an illicit affair.*

illiterate /ɪ'lɪtərət/ **adj 1** not able to read or write ●⋆ opposite **literate 2** (used about a piece of writing) very badly written **3** not knowing much about a particular subject: *computer illiterate* –**illiteracy** /ɪ'lɪtərəsi/ **noun** [U]: *adult illiteracy* ●⋆ opposite **literacy**

⋆**illness** /'ɪlnəs/ **noun 1** [U] the state of being physically or mentally ill: *He's missed a lot of school through illness.* ● *There is a history of mental illness in the family.* **2** [C] a type or period of physical or mental ill health: *minor/serious/childhood illnesses* ● *My dad is just getting over his illness.* ●⋆ adjective **ill** ●⋆ Look at the note at **disease**.

illogical /ɪ'lɒdʒɪkl/ **adj** not sensible or reasonable: *It seems illogical to me to pay somebody to do work that you could do yourself.* ●⋆ opposite **logical** –**illogicality** /ɪˌlɒdʒɪ-'kæləti/ **noun** [C,U] (*pl* **illogicalities**) –**illogically adv**

,**ill·'treat verb** [T] to treat sb/sth badly or in an unkind way: *This cat has been ill-treated.* –**ill·'treatment noun** [U]

illuminate /ɪ'luːmɪneɪt/ **verb** [T] (*formal*) **1** to shine light on sth or to decorate sth with lights: *The palace was illuminated by spotlights.* **2** to explain sth or make sth clear

illuminating /ɪ'luːmɪneɪtɪŋ/ **adj** helping to explain sth or make sth clear: *an illuminating discussion*

illumination /ɪˌluːmɪ'neɪʃn/ **noun 1** [U,C] light or the place where a light comes from: *These big windows give good illumination.* **2 illuminations** [pl] (*Brit*) bright colourful lights that are used for decorating a street, town, etc

illusion /ɪ'luːʒn/ **noun 1** [C,U] a false idea, belief or impression: *I have no illusions about the situation – I know it's serious.* ● *I think Peter's under the illusion that he will be the new director.* **2** [C] something that your eyes tell you is there or is true but in fact is not: *That line looks longer, but in fact they're the same length. It's an optical illusion.*

illusory /ɪ'luːsəri/ **adj** (*formal*) not real, although seeming to be: *The profits they had hoped for proved to be illusory.*

⋆**illustrate** /'ɪləstreɪt/ **verb** [T] **1** to explain or make sth clear by using examples, pictures or diagrams: *These statistics illustrate the point that I was making very well.* **2** to add

illustration 341 immensely

pictures, diagrams, etc to a book or magazine: *Most cookery books are illustrated.*

illustration /ˌɪlə'streɪʃn/ **noun 1** [C] a drawing, diagram or picture in a book or magazine: *colour illustrations* **2** [U] the activity or art of illustrating **3** [C] an example that makes a point or an idea clear: *Can you give me an illustration of what you mean?*

illustrious /ɪ'lʌstriəs/ **adj** (*formal*) famous and successful

I'm /aɪm/ *short for* I AM

∗**image** /'ɪmɪdʒ/ **noun** [C] **1** the general impression that a person or organization gives to the public: *When you meet him, he's very different from his public image.* **2** a mental picture or idea of sb/sth: *I have an image of my childhood as always sunny and happy.* **3** a picture or description that appears in a book, film or painting: *horrific images of war* **4** a copy or picture of sb/sth seen in a mirror, through a camera, on television, computer, etc: *A perfect image of the building was reflected in the lake.* • (*figurative*) *He's the* (**spitting**) *image of his father* (= he looks exactly like him).

imagery /'ɪmɪdʒəri/ **noun** [U] language that produces pictures in the minds of the people reading or listening: *poetic imagery*

imaginable /ɪ'mædʒɪnəbl/ **adj** that you can imagine: *Sophie made all the excuses imaginable when she was caught stealing.* • *His house was equipped with every imaginable luxury.*

∗**imaginary** /ɪ'mædʒɪnəri/ **adj** existing only in the mind; not real: *Many children have imaginary friends.*

∗**imagination** /ɪˌmædʒɪ'neɪʃn/ **noun 1** [U,C] the ability to create mental pictures or new ideas: *He has a lively imagination.* • *She's very clever but she doesn't* **have** *much imagination.*

> **Imagination** is a creative quality that a person has. **Fantasy** refers to thoughts, stories, etc that are not related to reality.

2 [C] the part of the mind that uses this ability: *If you* **use** *your imagination, you should be able to guess the answer.* –imaginatively **adv**

imaginative /ɪ'mædʒɪnətɪv/ **adj** having or showing imagination: *She's always full of imaginative ideas.*

∗**imagine** /ɪ'mædʒɪn/ **verb** [T] **1** imagine that...; imagine sb/sth (doing/as sth) to form a picture or idea in your mind of what sth/sb might be like: *Imagine that you're lying on a beach.* • *It's not easy to imagine your brother as a doctor.* • *I can't imagine myself cycling 20 miles a day.* **2** to see, hear or think sth that is not true or does not exist: *She's always imagining that she's ill but she's fine really.* • *I thought I heard someone downstairs, but I must have been imagining things.* **3** to think that sth is probably true; to suppose: *I imagine he'll be coming by car.*

imbalance /ɪm'bæləns/ **noun** [C] an imbalance (between A and B); an imbalance

(in/of sth) a difference; not being equal: *an imbalance in the numbers of men and women teachers*

imbecile /'ɪmbəsiːl/ **noun** [C] a stupid person; an idiot

IMF /ˌaɪ em 'ef/ **abbr** the International Monetary Fund

imitate /'ɪmɪteɪt/ **verb** [T] **1** to copy the behaviour of sb/sth: *Small children learn by imitating their parents.* **2** to copy the speech or actions of sb/sth, often in order to make people laugh: *She could imitate her mother perfectly.*

imitation /ˌɪmɪ'teɪʃn/ **noun 1** [C] a copy of sth real: *Some artificial flowers are good imitations of real ones.* •➤ Look at **genuine**. **2** [U] the act of copying sb/sth: *Good pronunciation of a language is best learnt by imitation.* **3** [C] the act of copying the way sb talks and behaves, especially in order to make people laugh: *Can you* **do** *any imitations of politicians?*

immaculate /ɪ'mækjələt/ **adj 1** perfectly clean and tidy: *immaculate white shirts* **2** without any mistakes; perfect: *His performance of 'Romeo' was immaculate.* –immaculately **adv**

immaterial /ˌɪmə'tɪəriəl/ **adj** immaterial (to sb/sth) not important: *It's immaterial to me whether we go today or tomorrow.*

immature /ˌɪmə'tjʊə/ **adj 1** not fully grown or developed; not mature: *an immature body* **2** (used about a person) behaving in a way that is not sensible and is typical of people who are much younger: *I think he's too immature to take his work seriously.* •➤ opposite **mature**

immediacy /ɪ'miːdiəsi/ **noun** [U] the quality of being available or seeming to happen close to you and without delay: *Letters do not have the same immediacy as e-mail.*

∗**immediate** /ɪ'miːdiət/ **adj 1** happening or done without delay: *I'd like an immediate answer to my proposal.* • *The government responded with immediate action.* **2** (only *before* a noun) existing now and needing urgent attention: *Tell me what your immediate needs are.* **3** (only *before* a noun) nearest in time, position or relationship: *They won't make any changes in the immediate future.* • *He has left most of his money to his immediate family* (= parents, children, brothers and sisters).

immediately /ɪ'miːdiətli/ **adv, conj 1** at once; without delay: *Can you come home immediately after work?* • *I couldn't immediately see what he meant.* **2** very closely; directly: *He wasn't immediately involved in the crime.* **3** nearest in time or position: *Who's the girl immediately in front of Simon?* • *What did you do immediately after the war?* **4** (*Brit*) as soon as: *I opened the letter immediately I got home.*

immense /ɪ'mens/ **adj** very big or great: *immense difficulties/importance/power* • *She gets immense pleasure from her garden.*

immensely /ɪ'mensli/ **adv** extremely; very

much: *immensely enjoyable* ● *'Did you enjoy the party?' 'Yes, immensely.'*

immensity /ɪˈmensəti/ **noun** [U] an extremely large size: *the immensity of the universe*

immerse /ɪˈmɜːs/ **verb** [T] **1** immerse sth (in sth) to put sth into a liquid so that it is covered: *Make sure the spaghetti is fully immersed in the boiling water.* **2** immerse yourself (in sth) to involve yourself completely in sth so that you give it all your attention: *Rachel's usually immersed in a book.*

★**immigrant** /ˈɪmɪɡrənt/ **noun** [C] a person who has come into a foreign country to live there permanently: *The government plans to tighten controls to prevent illegal immigrants.* ● *London has a high immigrant population.*

> Great Britain has many immigrant communities which make it a **multicultural society**. Groups of immigrants or children of immigrants who share a common cultural tradition form an **ethnic minority**.

★**immigration** /ˌɪmɪˈɡreɪʃn/ **noun** [U] **1** the process of coming to live permanently in a country that is not your own; the number of people who do this: *There are greater controls on immigration than there used to be.* **2** (also **immigration control**) the control point at an airport, port, etc where the official documents of people who want to come into a country are checked: *When you leave the plane you have to go through customs and immigration.* ●► There is a verb 'immigrate' but it is very rarely used. We normally use the expression 'be an immigrant' or the verb 'emigrate' which is used in connection with the place that somebody has come from: *My parents emigrated to this country from Jamaica.* ●► Look at **emigrate**, **emigrant** and **emigration**.

imminent /ˈɪmɪnənt/ **adj** (usually used about sth unpleasant) almost certain to happen very soon: *Heavy rainfall means that flooding is imminent.* –**imminently adv**

immobile /ɪˈməʊbaɪl/ **adj** not moving or not able to move: *The hunter stood immobile until the lion had passed.* ●► opposite **mobile** –**immobility** /ˌɪməˈbɪləti/ **noun** [U]

immobilize (also **-ise**) /ɪˈməʊbəlaɪz/ **verb** [T] to prevent sb/sth from moving or working normally: *The railways have been completely immobilized by the strike.* ● *This device immobilizes the car to prevent it being stolen.* ●► opposite **mobilize**

immobilizer (also **-iser**) /ɪˈməʊbəlaɪzə/ a device in a vehicle that prevents thieves from starting the engine when the vehicle is parked

immoral /ɪˈmɒrəl/ (used about people or their behaviour) considered wrong or not honest by most people: *It's immoral to steal.* ●► opposite **moral**. Look at **amoral**, it has a different meaning. –**immorality** /ˌɪməˈræləti/

noun [U] ●► opposite **morality** –**immorally** /-rəli/ **adv**

immortal /ɪˈmɔːtl/ **adj** living or lasting for ever: *Nobody is immortal – we all have to die some time.* ●► opposite **mortal** –**immortality** /ˌɪmɔːˈtæləti/ **noun** [U]

immortalize (also **-ise**) /ɪˈmɔːtəlaɪz/ **verb** [T] to give lasting fame to sb/sth: *He immortalized their relationship in a poem.*

immune /ɪˈmjuːn/ **adj 1** immune (to sth) having natural protection against a certain disease or illness: *You should be immune to measles if you've had it already.* **2** immune (to sth) not affected by sth: *You can say what you like – I'm immune to criticism.* **3** immune (from sth) protected from a danger or punishment: *Young children are immune from prosecution.*

immunity /ɪˈmjuːnəti/ **noun** [U] the ability to avoid or not be affected by disease, criticism, punishment by law, etc: *In many countries people have no immunity to diseases like measles.* ● *Ambassadors to other countries receive diplomatic immunity* (= protection from prosecution, etc).

immunize (also **-ise**) /ˈɪmjʊnaɪz/ **verb** [T] to make sb immune to a disease, usually by putting a substance (vaccine) into his/her body: *Before visiting certain countries you will need to be immunized against cholera.* ●► Inoculate and vaccinate have similar meanings. –**immunization** (also **-isation**) /ˌɪmjʊnaɪˈzeɪʃn/ **noun** [C,U]

imp /ɪmp/ **noun** [C] (in stories) a small creature like a little devil

★**impact** /ˈɪmpækt/ **noun 1** [C,usually sing] an impact (on/upon sb/sth) an effect or impression: *I hope this anti-smoking campaign will make/have an impact on young people.* **2** [U] the action or force of one object hitting another: *The impact of the crash threw the passengers out of their seats.* ● *The bomb exploded on impact.*

impair /ɪmˈpeə/ **verb** [T] to damage sth or make it weaker: *Ear infections can result in impaired hearing.*

impale /ɪmˈpeɪl/ **verb** [T] impale sb/sth (on sth) to push a sharp pointed object through sb/sth: *The boy fell out of the tree and impaled his leg on some railings.*

impart /ɪmˈpɑːt/ **verb** [T] (*formal*) **1** impart sth (to sb) pass information, knowledge, etc to other people: *He rushed home eager to impart the good news.* **2** impart sth (to sth) to give a certain quality to sth: *The low lighting imparted a romantic atmosphere to the room.*

impartial /ɪmˈpɑːʃl/ **adj** not supporting one person or group more than another; fair: *The referee must be impartial.* –**impartiality** /ˌɪmˌpɑːʃiˈæləti/ **noun** [U] ●► opposite **partiality** –**impartially adv**

impassable /ɪmˈpɑːsəbl/ **adj** (used about a road, etc) impossible to travel on because it is blocked: *Flooding and fallen trees have made many roads impassable.* ●► opposite **passable**

impassive /ɪmˈpæsɪv/ **adj** (used about a

person) showing no emotion or reaction –**impassively** adv

impatient /ɪmˈpeɪʃnt/ adj **1** impatient (at sth/with sb) not able to stay calm and wait for sb/sth; easily annoyed by sb/sth that seems slow: *The passengers are getting impatient at the delay.* • *It's no good being impatient with small children.* ••➤ opposite **patient 2** impatient for/to do sth wanting sth to happen soon: *By the time they are sixteen many young people are impatient to leave school.* –**impatience** noun [U]: *He began to explain for the third time with growing impatience.* –**impatiently** adv

impeccable /ɪmˈpekəbl/ adj without any mistakes or faults; perfect: *impeccable behaviour* • *His accent is impeccable.* –**impeccably** /-bli/ adv

impede /ɪmˈpiːd/ verb [T] (*formal*) to make it difficult for sb/sth to move or go forward: *The completion of the new motorway has been impeded by bad weather conditions.*

impediment /ɪmˈpedɪmənt/ noun [C] (*formal*) **1** an impediment (to sth) something that makes it difficult for a person or thing to move or progress: *The high rate of tax will be a major impediment to new businesses.* **2** something that makes speaking difficult: *a speech impediment*

impending /ɪmˈpendɪŋ/ adj (only *before* a noun) (usually used about sth bad) that will happen soon: *There was a feeling of impending disaster in the air.*

impenetrable /ɪmˈpenɪtrəbl/ adj **1** impossible to enter or go through: *The jungle was impenetrable.* **2** impossible to understand: *an impenetrable mystery*

imperative¹ /ɪmˈperətɪv/ adj very important or urgent: *It's imperative that you see a doctor immediately.*

the imperative² /ɪmˈperətɪv/ noun [C] (*grammar*) the form of the verb that is used for giving orders: *In 'Shut the door!' the verb is in the imperative.*

imperceptible /ˌɪmpəˈseptəbl/ adj too small to be seen or noticed: *The difference between the original painting and the copy was almost imperceptible.* ••➤ opposite **perceptible** –**imperceptibly** /-əbli/ adv: *Almost imperceptibly winter was turning into spring.*

imperfect¹ /ɪmˈpɜːfɪkt/ adj with mistakes or faults: *This is a very imperfect system.* ••➤ opposite **perfect** –**imperfectly** adv

the imperfect² /ɪmˈpɜːfɪkt/ noun [U] (*grammar*) used for expressing action in the past that is not completed: *In 'I was having a bath', the verb is in the imperfect.*

➤ It is more usual to call this tense the **past continuous** or **past progressive**.

imperial /ɪmˈpɪəriəl/ adj **1** connected with an empire or its ruler: *the imperial palace* **2** belonging to a system of weighing and measuring that, in the past, was used for all goods in the United Kingdom and is still used for some ••➤ Look at **metric** and at **inch**, **foot**, **yard**, **ounce**, **pound**, **pint** and **gallon**.

imperialism /ɪmˈpɪəriəlɪzəm/ noun [U] a political system in which a rich and powerful country controls other countries (colonies) which are not as rich and powerful as itself –**imperialist** noun [C]

impersonal /ɪmˈpɜːsənl/ adj **1** not showing friendly human feelings; cold in feeling or atmosphere: *The hotel room was very impersonal.* **2** not referring to any particular person: *Can we try to keep the discussion as impersonal as possible, please?*

impersonate /ɪmˈpɜːsəneɪt/ verb [T] to copy the behaviour and way of speaking of a person or to pretend to be a different person: *a comedian who impersonates politicians* –**impersonation** /ɪmˌpɜːsəˈneɪʃn/ noun [C,U] –**impersonator** noun [C]

impertinent /ɪmˈpɜːtɪnənt/ adj (*formal*) not showing respect; rude: *I do apologize. It was impertinent of my daughter to speak to you like that.* ••➤ The opposite is NOT **pertinent**. It is **polite** or **respectful**. –**impertinence** noun [U] –**impertinently** adv

imperturbable /ˌɪmpəˈtɜːbəbl/ adj (*formal*) not easily worried by a difficult situation

impervious /ɪmˈpɜːviəs/ adj impervious (to sth) **1** not affected or influenced by sth: *She was impervious to criticism.* **2** not allowing water, etc to pass through

impetuous /ɪmˈpetʃuəs/ adj acting or done quickly and without thinking: *Her impetuous behaviour often got her into trouble.* ••➤ A more common word is **impulsive**. –**impetuously** adv

impetus /ˈɪmpɪtəs/ noun [U, sing] (an) impetus (for sth); (an) impetus (to do sth) something that encourages sth else to happen: *This scandal provided the main impetus for changes in the rules.* • *I need fresh impetus to start working on this essay again.*

impinge /ɪmˈpɪndʒ/ verb [I] (*formal*) impinge on/upon sth to have a noticeable effect on sth, especially a bad one: *I'm not going to let my job impinge on my home life.*

implant /ɪmˈplɑːnt/ noun [C] something that is put into a part of the body in a medical operation, often in order to make it bigger or a different shape

implausible /ɪmˈplɔːzəbl/ adj not easy to believe: *an implausible excuse* ••➤ opposite **plausible**

implement¹ /ˈɪmplɪmənt/ noun [C] a tool or instrument (especially for work outdoors): *farm implements* ••➤ Look at the note at **tool**.

implement² /ˈɪmplɪment/ verb [T] to start using a plan, system, etc: *Some teachers are finding it difficult to implement the government's educational reforms.* –**implementation** /ˌɪmplɪmenˈteɪʃn/ noun [U]

implicate /ˈɪmplɪkeɪt/ verb [T] implicate sb (in sth) to show that sb is involved in sth unpleasant, especially a crime: *A well-known politician was implicated in the scandal.*

implication /ˌɪmplɪˈkeɪʃn/ noun **1** [C,usually pl] implications (for/of sth) the effect that sth will have on sth else in the future: *The new law will have serious implications for* *our work.* **2** [C,U] something that is suggested or said indirectly: *The implication of what she said was that we had made a bad mistake.* •➤ verb **imply 3** [U] **implication (in sth)** the fact of being involved, or of involving sb, in sth unpleasant, especially a crime: *The player's implication in this scandal could effect his career.* •➤ verb **implicate**

implicit /ɪm'plɪsɪt/ adj **1** not expressed in a direct way but understood by the people involved: *We had an implicit agreement that we would support each other.* •➤ Look at **explicit. 2** complete; total: *I have implicit faith in your ability to do the job.* –**implicitly** adv

implore /ɪm'plɔː/ verb [T] (*formal*) to ask sb with great emotion to do sth, because you are in a very serious situation: *She implored him not to leave her alone.* •➤ synonym **beg**

imply /ɪm'plaɪ/ verb [T] (*pres part* **implying**; *3rd pers sing pres* **implies**; *pt, pp* **implied**) to suggest sth in an indirect way or without actually saying it: *He didn't say so – but he implied that I was lying.* •➤ noun **implication**

impolite /ˌɪmpə'laɪt/ adj rude: *I think it was impolite of him to ask you to leave.* •➤ opposite **polite** –**impolitely** adv

★**import**¹ /'ɪmpɔːt/ noun **1** [C,usually pl] a product or service that is brought into one country from another: *What are your country's major imports?* •➤ opposite **export 2** [U] (also **importation**) the act of bringing goods or services into a country: *new controls on the import of certain goods from abroad*

★**import**² /ɪm'pɔːt/ verb [I,T] **1** **import sth (from...)** to buy goods, etc from a foreign country and bring them into your own country: *imported goods* ● *Britain imports wine from France/Italy/Spain.* ● (*figurative*) *We need to import some extra help from somewhere.* •➤ opposite **export 2** (*computing*) to move information onto a program from another program –**importer** noun [C] •➤ opposite **exporter**

★**importance** /ɪm'pɔːtns/ noun [U] the quality of being important: *The decision was of great importance to the future of the business.*

★**important** /ɪm'pɔːtnt/ adj **1** **important (to sb)**; **important (for sb/sth) (to do sth)**; **important that...** having great value or influence; very necessary: *an important meeting/decision/factor* ● *This job is very important to me.* ● *It's important not to be late.* ● *It's important for people to see the results of what they do.* ● *It was important to me that you were there.* **2** (used about a person) having great influence or authority: *He was one of the most important writers of his time.* –**importantly** adv

importation /ˌɪmpɔː'teɪʃn/ = **IMPORT**¹(2)

impose /ɪm'pəʊz/ verb **1** [T] **impose sth (on/upon sb/sth)** to make a law, rule, opinion, etc be accepted by using your power or authority: *A new tax will be imposed on cigarettes.* ● *Parents should try not to impose their own ideas on their children.* **2** [I] **impose (on/**

upon sb/sth) to ask or expect sb to do sth that may cause extra work or trouble: *I hate to impose on you but can you lend me some money?* –**imposition** /ˌɪmpə'zɪʃn/ noun [U,C] *the imposition of military rule*

imposing /ɪm'pəʊzɪŋ/ adj big and important; impressive: *They lived in a large, imposing house near the park.*

★**impossible** /ɪm'pɒsəbl/ adj **1** not able to be done or to happen: *It's impossible for me to be there before 12.* ● *I find it almost impossible to get up in the morning!* ● *That's impossible!* (= I don't believe it!) **2** very difficult to deal with or control: *This is an impossible situation.* ● *He's always been an impossible child.* •➤ opposite **possible** –**the impossible** noun [sing]: *Don't attempt the impossible!* –**impossibility** /ɪmˌpɒsə'bɪləti/ noun [C,U] (*pl* **impossibilities**) *What you are suggesting is a complete impossibility!*

impossibly /ɪm'pɒsəbli/ adv extremely: *impossibly complicated*

impostor /ɪm'pɒstə/ noun [C] a person who pretends to be sb else in order to trick other people

impotent /'ɪmpətənt/ adj **1** without enough power to influence a situation or to change things **2** (*medical*) (used about men) not capable of having sex –**impotence** noun [U]

impoverish /ɪm'pɒvərɪʃ/ verb [T] (*formal*) to make sb/sth poor or lower in quality •➤ opposite **enrich**

impractical /ɪm'præktɪkl/ adj **1** not sensible or realistic: *It would be impractical to take our bikes on the train.* **2** (used about a person) not good at doing ordinary things that involve using your hands; not good at organizing or planning things: *He's clever but completely impractical.* •➤ opposite **practical**

imprecise /ˌɪmprɪ'saɪs/ adj not clear or exact: *imprecise instructions* •➤ opposite **precise**

★**impress** /ɪm'pres/ verb [T] **1** **impress sb (with sth)**; **impress sb that...** to make sb feel admiration and respect: *She's always trying to impress people with her new clothes.* ● *It impressed me that he understood immediately what I meant.* **2** (*formal*) **impress sth on/upon sb** to make the importance of sth very clear to sb: *I wish you could impress on John that he must pass these exams.*

★**impression** /ɪm'preʃn/ noun [C] **1** an idea, a feeling or an opinion that you get about sb/sth: *What's your first impression of the new director?* ● *I'm not sure but I have/get the impression that Jane's rather unhappy.* ● *I was under the impression* (= I believed, but I was wrong) *that you were married.* **2** the effect that a person or thing produces on sb else: *She gives the impression of being older than she really is.* ● *Do you think I made a good impression on your parents?* **3** an amusing copy of the way a person acts or speaks; an imitation: *My brother can do a good impression of the Prime Minister.* **4** a mark that is left when an object has been pressed hard into a surface

impressionable /ɪmˈpreʃənəbl/ **adj** easy to influence: *Sixteen is a very impressionable age.*

*★***impressive** /ɪmˈpresɪv/ **adj** causing a feeling of admiration and respect because of the importance, size, quality, etc of sth: *an impressive building/speech* ● *The way he handled the situation was most impressive.*

imprint /ɪmˈprɪnt/ **noun** [C] a mark made by pressing an object on a surface: *the imprint of a foot in the sand*

imprison /ɪmˈprɪzn/ **verb** [T] (often passive) to put or keep in prison: *He was imprisoned for armed robbery.* –**imprisonment noun** [U]: *She was sentenced to five years' imprisonment.*

improbable /ɪmˈprɒbəbl/ **adj** not likely to be true or to happen: *an improbable explanation* ● *It is highly improbable that she will arrive tonight.* ••➤ synonym **unlikely** ••➤ opposite **probable** –**improbability** /ɪm-ˌprɒbəˈbɪləti/ **noun** [U] –**improbably** /-əbli/ **adv**

impromptu /ɪmˈprɒmptjuː/ **adj** (done) without being prepared or organized: *an impromptu party*

improper /ɪmˈprɒpə/ **adj 1** illegal or dishonest: *It seems that she had been involved in improper business deals.* **2** not suitable for the situation; rude in a sexual way: *It would be improper to say anything else at this stage.* ● *He lost his job for making improper suggestions to several of the women.* ••➤ opposite **proper** –**improperly adv** ••➤ opposite **properly**

impropriety /ˌɪmprəˈpraɪəti/ **noun** [U,C] (*pl* **improprieties**) (*formal*) behaviour or actions that are morally wrong or not appropriate: *She was unaware of the impropriety of her remark.*

*★***improve** /ɪmˈpruːv/ **verb** [I,T] to become or to make sth better: *Your work has greatly improved.* ● *I hope the weather will improve later on.* ● *Your vocabulary is excellent but you could improve your pronunciation.*
PHRASAL VERB **improve on/upon sth** to produce sth that is better than sth else: *Nobody will be able to improve on that score* (= nobody will be able to make a higher score).

*★***improvement** /ɪmˈpruːvmənt/ **noun** [C,U] (an) improvement (on/in sth) (a) change which makes the quality or condition of sb/sth better: *Your written work is in need of some improvement.*

➤ We use **improvement in** to talk about something that has got better than it was before: *There's been a considerable improvement in your mother's condition.* **Improvement on** is used when we are comparing two things and one is better than the other: *These marks are an improvement on your previous ones.*

improvise /ˈɪmprəvaɪz/ **verb** [I,T] **1** to make, do, or manage sth without preparation, using what you have: *If you're short of teachers today you'll just have to improvise* (= manage somehow with the people that you've got).

2 to play music, speak or act using your imagination instead of written or remembered material: *It was obvious that the actor had forgotten his lines and was trying to improvise.* –**improvisation** /ˌɪmprəvaɪˈzeɪʃn/ **noun** [C,U]

impudent /ˈɪmpjədənt/ **adj** (*formal*) very rude; lacking respect and not polite ••➤ A more informal word is **cheeky**. –**impudently adv** –**impudence noun** [U]

impulse /ˈɪmpʌls/ **noun** [C] **1** [usually sing] an impulse (to do sth) a sudden desire to do sth without thinking about the results: *She felt a terrible impulse to rush out of the house and never come back.* **2** (*technical*) a force or movement of energy that causes a reaction: *nerve/electrical impulses*
IDIOM **on (an) impulse** without thinking or planning and not considering the results: *When I saw the child fall in the water, I just acted on impulse and jumped in after her.*

impulsive /ɪmˈpʌlsɪv/ **adj** likely to act suddenly and without thinking; done without careful thought: *an impulsive character* –**impulsively adv** –**impulsiveness noun** [U]

impure /ɪmˈpjʊə/ **adj 1** not pure or clean; consisting of more than one substance mixed together (and therefore not of good quality): *impure metals* **2** (*old-fashioned*) (used about thoughts and actions connected with sex) not moral; bad ••➤ opposite **pure**

impurity /ɪmˈpjʊərəti/ **noun** (*pl* **impurities**) **1** [C,usually pl] a substance that is present in small amounts in another substance, making it dirty or of poor quality: *People are being advised to boil their water because certain impurities have been found in it.* **2** [U] (*old-fashioned*) the state of being morally bad ••➤ Look at **purity**.

in abbr inch(es)

*★***in¹** /ɪn/ **adv, prep**
➤ For special uses with many nouns, for example in **time**, look at the noun entries. For special uses with many verbs, for example **give in**, look at the verb entries.

1 (used to show place) inside or to a position inside a particular area or object: *a country in Africa* ● *an island in the Pacific* ● *in a box* ● *I read about it in the newspaper.* ● *He lay in bed.* ● *She put the keys in her pocket.* ● *His wife's in hospital.* ● *She opened the door and went in.* ● *My suitcase is full. I can't get any more in.* ● *When does the train get in* (= to the station)? **2** at home or at work: *I phoned him last night but he wasn't in.* ● *She won't be in till late today.* **3** (showing time) during a period of time: *My birthday is in August.* ● *in spring/summer/autumn/winter* ● *He was born in 1980.* ● *You could walk there in about an hour* (= it would take that long to walk there). **4** (showing time) after a period of time: *I'll be finished in ten minutes.* **5** wearing sth: *They were all dressed in black for the funeral.* ● *I've never seen you in a suit before.* ● *a woman in a yellow dress* **6** showing the condition or state of sb/sth: *My father is in poor health.* ● *This room is in a mess!*

● *Richard's* **in** *love.* ● *He's* **in** *his mid-thirties.* **7** showing sb's job or the activity sb is involved in: *He's got a good job* **in** *advertising.* ● *All her family are* **in** *politics* (= they are politicians). ● *He's* **in** *the army.* **8** contained in; forming the whole or part of sth: *There are 31 days* **in** *January.* ● *What's* **in** *this casserole?* **9** used for saying how things are arranged: *We sat* **in** *a circle.* ● *She had her hair* **in** *plaits.* **10** used for saying how sth is written or expressed: *Please write* **in** *pen.* ● *They were talking* **in** *Italian/French/Polish.* ● *to work* **in** *groups/teams* **11** used with feelings: *I watched* **in** *horror as the plane crashed to the ground.* ● *He was in such a rage I didn't dare to go near him.* **12** used for giving the rate of sth and for talking about numbers: *One family* **in** *ten owns a dishwasher.* **13** received by sb official: *Entries should* **be in** *by 20 March.* ● *All applications must* **be in** *by Friday.* **14** (used about the sea) at the highest point, when the water is closest to the land: *The tide's coming* **in.**

[IDIOMS] **be in for it/sth** to be going to experience sth unpleasant: *He'll* **be in for** *a shock when he gets the bill.* ● *You'll* **be in for it** *when Mum sees what you've done.*

be/get in on sth to be included or involved in sth: *I'd like to* **be in on** *the new project.*

have (got) it in for sb (*informal*) to be unpleasant to sb because he/she has done sth to upset you: *The boss has had it* **in for** *me ever since I asked to be considered for the new post.*

in² /ɪn/ noun

[IDIOM] **the ins and outs (of sth)** the details and difficulties (involved in sth): *Will somebody explain the* **ins and outs** *of the situation to me?*

in³ /ɪn/ adj (*informal*) fashionable at the moment: *the* **in** *place to go* ● *The colour grey is very* **in** *this season.*

inability /ˌɪnə'bɪləti/ noun [sing] inability (to do sth) lack of ability, power or skill: *He has a complete inability to listen to other people's opinions.* ••➤ adjective **unable**

inaccessible /ˌɪnæk'sesəbl/ adj very difficult or impossible to reach or contact: *That beach is inaccessible by car.* ••➤ opposite **accessible** –**inaccessibility** /ˌɪnækˌsesə'bɪləti/ noun [U]

inaccurate /ɪn'ækjərət/ adj not correct or accurate; with mistakes: *an inaccurate report/ description/statement* ••➤ opposite **accurate** –**inaccuracy** /ɪn'ækjərəsi/ noun [C,U] (*pl* **inaccuracies**): *There are always some inaccuracies in newspaper reports.* ••➤ opposite **accuracy**

inaction /ɪn'ækʃn/ noun [U] doing nothing; lack of action: *The crisis was blamed on the government's earlier inaction.* ••➤ opposite **action**

inactive /ɪn'æktɪv/ adj doing nothing; not active: *The virus remains inactive in the body.* ••➤ opposite **active** –**inactivity** /ˌɪnæk'tɪvəti/ noun [U] ••➤ opposite **activity**

inadequate /ɪn'ædɪkwət/ adj **1** inadequate (for sth/to do sth) not enough; not good enough: *the problem of inadequate housing* **2** (used about a person) not able to deal with a problem or situation; not confident: *There was so much to learn in the new job that for a while I felt totally inadequate.* ••➤ opposite **adequate** –**inadequately** adv –**inadequacy** /ɪn'ædɪkwəsi/ noun [C,U] (*pl* **inadequacies**): *his inadequacy as a parent*

inadvertent /ˌɪnəd'vɜːtənt/ adj (used about actions) done without thinking, not on purpose ••➤ opposite **intentional** or **deliberate** –**inadvertently** adv: *She had inadvertently left the letter where he could find it.*

inadvisable /ˌɪnəd'vaɪzəbl/ adj not sensible, not showing good judgement: *It is inadvisable to go swimming when you have a cold.* ••➤ opposite **advisable**

inane /ɪ'neɪn/ adj without any meaning; silly: *an inane remark* –**inanely** adv

inappropriate /ˌɪnə'prəʊpriət/ adj not suitable: *Isn't that dress rather inappropriate for the occasion?* ••➤ opposite **appropriate**

inarticulate /ˌɪnɑː'tɪkjələt/ adj **1** (used about a person) not able to express ideas and feelings clearly **2** (used about speech) not clear or well expressed ••➤ opposite **articulate** –**inarticulately** adv

inasmuch as /ˌɪnəz'mʌtʃ əz/ conj (*formal*) because of the fact that: *We felt sorry for the boys inasmuch as they had not realized that what they were doing was wrong.*

inattention /ˌɪnə'tenʃn/ noun [U] lack of attention: *a moment of inattention* ••➤ opposite **attention**

inattentive /ˌɪnə'tentɪv/ adj not paying attention: *One inattentive student can disturb the whole class.* ••➤ opposite **attentive**

inaudible /ɪn'ɔːdəbl/ adj not loud enough to be heard ••➤ opposite **audible** –**inaudibly** /-bli/ adv

inaugurate /ɪ'nɔːgjəreɪt/ verb [T] **1** to introduce a new official, leader, etc at a special formal ceremony: *He will be inaugurated as President next month.* **2** to start, introduce or open sth new (often at a special formal ceremony) –**inaugural** /ɪ'nɔːgjərəl/ adj (only *before* a noun): *the President's inaugural speech* –**inauguration** /ɪˌnɔːgjə'reɪʃn/ noun [C,U]

inauspicious /ˌɪnɔː'spɪʃəs/ adj (*formal*) showing signs that the future will not be good or successful: *an inauspicious start* ••➤ opposite **auspicious**

Inc (also **inc**) /ɪŋk/ abbr (*US*) Incorporated: *Manhattan Drugstores Inc*

incalculable /ɪn'kælkjələbl/ adj very great; too great to calculate: *an incalculable risk*

incapable /ɪn'keɪpəbl/ adj **1** incapable of sth/doing sth not able to do sth: *She is incapable of hard work/working hard.* ● *He's quite incapable of unkindness* (= too nice to be unkind). **2** not able to do, manage or organize anything well: *As a doctor, she's totally incapable.* ••➤ opposite **capable**

incapacitate /ˌɪnkə'pæsɪteɪt/ verb [T] to

make sb unable to do sth: *They were completely incapacitated by the heat in Spain.*

incarnation /ˌɪnkɑːˈneɪʃn/ **noun** [C] **1** a period of life on earth in a particular form: *He believes he was a prince in a previous incarnation.* **2** the incarnation of sth (a person that is) a perfect example of a particular quality: *She is the incarnation of goodness.* ••► Look at **reincarnation**.

incendiary /ɪnˈsendiəri/ **adj** that causes a fire: *an incendiary bomb/device*

incense /ˈɪnsens/ **noun** [U] a substance that produces a sweet smell when burnt, used especially in religious ceremonies

incensed /ɪnˈsenst/ **adj** incensed (by/at sth) very angry; furious

incentive /ɪnˈsentɪv/ **noun** [C,U] (an) incentive (for/to sb/sth) (to do sth) something that encourages you (to do sth): *There's no incentive for young people to do well at school because there aren't any jobs when they leave.*

incessant /ɪnˈsesnt/ **adj** never stopping (and usually annoying): *incessant rain/noise/ chatter* ••► Look at **continual**. –**incessantly adv**

incest /ˈɪnsest/ **noun** [U] illegal sex between members of the same family, for example brother and sister

incestuous /ɪnˈsestjuəs/ **adj** **1** involving illegal sex between members of the same family: *an incestuous relationship* **2** (used about a group of people and their relationships with each other) too close; not open to anyone outside the group: *Life in a small community can be very incestuous.*

★**inch**[1] /ɪntʃ/ **noun** [C] (*abbr* in) a measure of length; 2·54 centimetres. There are 12 inches in a foot: *He's 5 foot 10 inches tall.* • *Three inches of rain fell last night.*

inch[2] /ɪntʃ/ **verb** [I,T] inch forward, past, through, etc to move slowly and carefully in the direction mentioned: *He inched (his way) forward along the cliff edge.*

incidence /ˈɪnsɪdəns/ **noun** [sing] (*formal*) incidence of sth the number of times sth (usually unpleasant) happens; the rate of sth: *a high incidence of crime/disease/unemployment*

★**incident** /ˈɪnsɪdənt/ **noun** [C] (*formal*) something that happens (especially sth unusual or unpleasant): *There were a number of incidents after the football match.* • *a diplomatic incident* (= a dangerous or unpleasant situation between countries)

incidental /ˌɪnsɪˈdentl/ **adj** incidental (to sth) happening as part of sth more important: *The book contains various themes that are incidental to the main plot.*

incidentally /ˌɪnsɪˈdentəli/ **adv** used to introduce extra news, information, etc that the speaker has just thought of: *Incidentally, that new restaurant you told me about is excellent.* ••► Another way of saying 'incidentally' is **by the way**.

incinerate /ɪnˈsɪnəreɪt/ **verb** [T] (*formal*) to destroy sth completely by burning

incinerator /ɪnˈsɪnəreɪtə/ **noun** [C] a container or machine for burning rubbish, etc

incision /ɪnˈsɪʒn/ **noun** [C] (*formal*) a cut carefully made into sth (especially into a person's body as part of a medical operation)

incite /ɪnˈsaɪt/ **verb** [T] incite sb (to sth) to encourage sb to do sth by making him/her very angry or excited: *He was accused of inciting the crowd to violence.* –**incitement noun** [C,U]: *He was guilty of incitement to violence.*

incl *abbr* including; inclusive: *total £59.00 incl tax*

inclination /ˌɪnklɪˈneɪʃn/ **noun** [C,U] inclination (to do sth); inclination (towards/for sth) a feeling that makes sb want to behave in a particular way: *He did not show **the slightest inclination** to help.* • *She had no inclination for a career in teaching.*

incline[1] /ɪnˈklaɪn/ **verb** **1** [I] (*formal*) incline to/towards sth to want to behave in a particular way or make a particular choice: *I don't know what to choose, but I'm inclining towards the fish.* **2** [T] (*formal*) to bend (your head) forward: *They sat round the table, heads inclined, deep in discussion.* **3** [I] incline towards sth to be at an angle in a particular direction: *The land inclines towards the shore.*

incline[2] /ˈɪnklaɪn/ **noun** [C] (*formal*) a slight hill; a slope: *a steep/slight incline*

inclined /ɪnˈklaɪnd/ **adj** **1** inclined (to do sth) (not before a noun) wanting to behave in a particular way: *I know Amir well so I'm **inclined to believe** what he says.* **2** inclined to do sth likely to do sth: *She's inclined to change her mind very easily.* **3** having a natural ability in the subject mentioned: *to be musically inclined*

★**include** /ɪnˈkluːd/ **verb** [T] (not used in the continuous tenses) **1** to have as one part; to contain (among other things): *The price of the holiday includes the flight, the hotel and car-hire.* • *The crew included one woman.* ••► Look at the note at **contain**. ••► opposite **exclude 2** include sb/sth (as/in/on sth) to make sb/sth part (of another group, etc): *The children immediately included the new girl in their games.* • *Everyone was disappointed, myself included.* –**inclusion** /ɪnˈkluːʒn/ **noun** [U]: *The inclusion of all that violence in the film was unnecessary.*

including /ɪnˈkluːdɪŋ/ **prep** having as a part: *It costs $17.99, including postage and packing.* ••► opposite **excluding**

inclusive /ɪnˈkluːsɪv/ **adj** **1** inclusive (of sth) (used about a price, etc) including or containing everything; including the thing mentioned: *Is that an inclusive price or are there some extras?* • *The rent is inclusive of electricity.* **2** (only *after* a noun) including the dates, numbers, etc mentioned: *You are booked at the hotel from Monday to Friday inclusive* (= including Monday and Friday).

➤ When talking about time **through** is often used in US English instead of **inclusive**: *We'll be away from Friday through Sunday.*

incognito /ˌɪnkɒgˈniːtəʊ/ adv hiding your real name and identity (especially if you are famous and do not want to be recognized): *to travel incognito*

incoherent /ˌɪnkəʊˈhɪərənt/ adj not clear or easy to understand; not saying sth clearly ••➤ opposite **coherent** –**incoherence** noun [U] –**incoherently** adv

★ **income** /ˈɪnkʌm; -kəm/ noun [C,U] the money you receive regularly as payment for your work or as interest on money you have saved, etc: *It's often difficult for a family to live on one income.*

➤ We talk about a **monthly** or an **annual** income. An income may be **high** or **low**. Your **gross** income is the amount you earn before paying tax. Your **net** income is your income after tax. Look at the note at **pay²**.

'**income tax** noun [U] the amount of money you pay to the government according to how much you earn

incoming /ˈɪnkʌmɪŋ/ adj (only *before* a noun) **1** arriving or being received: *incoming flights/passengers* • *incoming telephone calls* **2** new; recently elected: *the incoming government*

incomparable /ɪnˈkɒmprəbl/ adj so good or great that it does not have an equal: *incomparable beauty* ••➤ verb **compare**

incompatible /ˌɪnkəmˈpætəbl/ adj incompatible with sb/sth very different and therefore not able to live or work happily with sb or exist with sth: *The working hours of the job are incompatible with family life.* ••➤ opposite **compatible** –**incompatibility** /ˌɪnkəmˌpætəˈbɪləti/ noun [C,U] (pl **incompatibilities**)

incompetent /ɪnˈkɒmpɪtənt/ adj lacking the necessary skill to do sth well: *He is completely incompetent at his job.* • *an incompetent teacher/manager* ••➤ opposite **competent** –**incompetent** noun [C]: *She's a total incompetent at basketball.* –**incompetence** noun [U] –**incompetently** adv

incomplete /ˌɪnkəmˈpliːt/ adj having a part or parts missing; not total: *Unfortunately the jigsaw puzzle was incomplete.* ••➤ opposite **complete** –**incompletely** adv

incomprehensible /ɪnˌkɒmprɪˈhensəbl/ adj impossible to understand: *an incomprehensible explanation* • *Her attitude is incomprehensible to the rest of the committee.* ••➤ opposite **comprehensible** or **understandable** –**incomprehension** /ɪnˌkɒmprɪˈhenʃn/ noun [U]

inconceivable /ˌɪnkənˈsiːvəbl/ adj impossible or very difficult to believe or imagine: *It's inconceivable that he would have stolen anything.* ••➤ opposite **conceivable**

inconclusive /ˌɪnkənˈkluːsɪv/ adj not leading to a definite decision or result: *an inconclusive discussion* • *inconclusive evidence* (= that doesn't prove anything) ••➤ opposite **conclusive** –**inconclusively** adv

incongruous /ɪnˈkɒŋgruəs/ adj strange and out of place; not suitable in a particular situation: *That huge table looks rather incongruous in such a small room.* –**incongruously** adv –**incongruity** /ˌɪnkɒnˈgruːəti/ noun [U]

inconsiderate /ˌɪnkənˈsɪdərət/ adj (used about a person) not thinking or caring about the feelings, or needs of other people: *It was inconsiderate of you not to offer her a lift.* ••➤ synonym **thoughtless** ••➤ opposite **considerate** –**inconsiderately** adv –**inconsiderateness** noun [U]

inconsistent /ˌɪnkənˈsɪstənt/ adj **1** inconsistent (with sth) (used about statements, facts, etc) not the same as sth else; not matching, so that one thing must be wrong or not true: *The witnesses' accounts of the event are inconsistent.* • *These new facts are inconsistent with the earlier information.* **2** (used about a person) likely to change (in attitude, behaviour, etc) so that you cannot depend on him/her: *She's so inconsistent – sometimes her work is good and sometimes it's really awful.* ••➤ opposite **consistent** –**inconsistency** /-ənsi/ noun [C,U] (pl **inconsistencies**): *There were a few inconsistencies in her argument.* ••➤ opposite **consistency** –**inconsistently** adv

inconspicuous /ˌɪnkənˈspɪkjuəs/ adv not easily noticed: *I tried to make myself as inconspicuous as possible so that no one would ask me a question.* ••➤ opposite **conspicuous** –**inconspicuously** adv

incontinent /ɪnˈkɒntɪnənt/ adj unable to control the passing of waste (urine and faeces) from the body –**incontinence** noun [U]

inconvenience /ˌɪnkənˈviːniəns/ noun [U,C] trouble or difficulty, especially when it effects sth that you need to do; a person or thing that causes this: *We apologize for any inconvenience caused by the delays.* –**inconvenience** verb [T]

inconvenient /ˌɪnkənˈviːniənt/ adj causing trouble or difficulty, especially when it effects sth that you need to do: *It's a bit inconvenient at the moment – could you phone again later?* ••➤ opposite **convenient** –**inconveniently** adv

incorporate /ɪnˈkɔːpəreɪt/ verb [T] incorporate sth (in/into/within sth) to make sth a part of sth else; to have sth as a part: *I'd like you to incorporate this information into your report.* ••➤ synonym **include** –**incorporation** /ɪnˌkɔːpəˈreɪʃn/ noun [U]

incorporated /ɪnˈkɔːpəreɪtɪd/ adj (abbr **Inc**) (following the name of a company) formed into a legal organization (corporation)

incorrect /ˌɪnkəˈrekt/ adj not right or true: *Incorrect answers should be marked with a cross.* ••➤ opposite **correct** –**incorrectly** adv

incorrigible /ɪnˈkɒrɪdʒəbl/ adj (used about a person or his/her behaviour) very bad; too bad to be corrected or improved: *an incorrigible liar*

★ **increase¹** /ɪnˈkriːs/ verb [I,T] increase (sth) (from A) (to B); increase (sth) (by sth) to become or to make sth larger in number or amount: *The rate of inflation has increased by*

[C] **countable**, a noun with a plural form: *one book, two books*   [U] **uncountable**, a noun with no plural form: *some sugar*

1% to 7%. ● *My employer would like me to increase my hours of work from 25 to 30.* ● *She increased her speed to overtake the lorry.* ●➤ opposite **decrease** or **reduce**

★**increase²** /'ɪnkriːs/ **noun** [C,U] **(an) increase (in sth)** a rise in the number, amount or level of sth: *There has been a **sharp increase** of nearly 50% on last year's figures.* ● *Doctors expect some further increase in the spread of the disease.* ● *They are demanding a large wage increase.* ●➤ opposite **decrease** or **reduction**

[IDIOM] **on the increase** becoming larger or more frequent; increasing: *Attacks by dogs on children are on the increase.*

increasingly /ɪn'kriːsɪŋli/ **adv** more and more: *It's becoming increasingly difficult/important/dangerous to stay here.*

incredible /ɪn'kredəbl/ **adj 1** impossible or very difficult to believe: *I found his account of the event incredible.* ●➤ opposite **credible** Look at **unbelievable**. **2** *(informal)* extremely good or big: *He earns an incredible salary.* –**incredibly** **adv**: *We have had some incredibly strong winds recently.*

incriminate /ɪn'krɪmɪneɪt/ **verb** [T] to provide evidence that sb is guilty of a crime: *The police searched the house but found nothing to incriminate the man.*

incubate /'ɪŋkjubeɪt/ **verb** [I,T] **1** to keep an egg at the right temperature so that it can develop and produce a bird (**hatch**) **2** (used about a disease) to develop without showing signs; (used about a person or an animal) to carry a disease without showing signs: *Some viruses take weeks to incubate.*

incubation /ˌɪŋkju'beɪʃn/ **noun 1** [U] the process of incubating eggs **2** [C] (also ,**incu-'bation period**) the period between catching a disease and the time when signs of it (**symptoms**) appear

incubator /'ɪŋkjubeɪtə/ **noun** [C] **1** a heated machine used in hospitals for keeping small or weak babies alive **2** a heated machine for keeping eggs warm until they break open (**hatch**)

incur /ɪn'kɜː/ **verb** [T] (**incurred**; **incurring**) *(formal)* to suffer the unpleasant results of a situation that you have caused: *to incur debts/sb's anger*

incurable /ɪn'kjʊərəbl/ **adj** that cannot be cured or made better: *an incurable disease* ●➤ opposite **curable** –**incurably** /-əbli/ **adv**: *incurably ill*

indebted /ɪn'detɪd/ **adj indebted (to sb) (for sth)** very grateful to sb: *I am deeply indebted to my family and friends for all their help.*

indecent /ɪn'diːsnt/ **adj** shocking to many people in society, especially because sth involves sex or the body: *indecent photos/behaviour/language* ● *You can't wear those tiny swimming trunks – they're indecent!* ●➤ opposite **decent** –**indecency** /-nsi/ **noun** [U,sing] –**indecently** **adv**

indecision /ˌɪndɪ'sɪʒn/ (also **indecisiveness**) **noun** [U] the state of being unable to

decide: *This indecision about the future is really worrying me.*

indecisive /ˌɪndɪ'saɪsɪv/ **adj** not able to make decisions easily ●➤ opposite **decisive** –**indecisively** **adv**

★**indeed** /ɪn'diːd/ **adv 1** (used for emphasizing a positive statement or answer) really; certainly: *'Have you had a good holiday?' 'We have indeed.'* **2** used after 'very' with an adjective or adverb to emphasize the quality mentioned: *Thank you very much indeed.* ● *She's very happy indeed.* **3** (used for adding information to a statement) in fact: *It's important that you come at once. Indeed, it's essential.* **4** used for showing interest, surprise, anger, etc: *'They were talking about you last night.' 'Were they indeed!'*

indefensible /ˌɪndɪ'fensəbl/ **adj** (used about behaviour, etc) completely wrong; that cannot be defended or excused

indefinable /ˌɪndɪ'faɪnəbl/ **adj** difficult or impossible to describe: *There was an indefinable atmosphere of hostility.* –**indefinably** /-əbli/ **adv**

indefinite /ɪn'defnət/ **adj** not fixed or clear: *Our plans are still rather indefinite.* ●➤ opposite **definite**

the in,definite 'article **noun** [C] *(grammar)* the name used for the words *a* and *an* ●➤ Look at **the definite article**.

➤ For more information about the indefinite article, look at the **Quick Grammar Reference** at the back of this dictionary.

indefinitely /ɪn'defnətli/ **adv** for a period of time that has no fixed end: *The meeting was postponed indefinitely.*

indelible /ɪn'deləbl/ **adj** that cannot be removed or washed out: *indelible ink* ● *(figurative)* *The experience made an indelible impression on me.* –**indelibly** /-əbli/ **adv**

indent /ɪn'dent/ **verb** [I,T] to start a line of writing further from the left-hand side of the page than the other lines

★**independence** /ˌɪndɪ'pendəns/ **noun** [U] **independence (from sb/sth)** (used about a person, country, etc) the state of being free and not controlled by another person, country, etc: *In 1947 India achieved independence from Britain.* ● *financial independence*

➤ On **Independence Day** (4 July) Americans celebrate the day in 1776 when America declared itself independent from Britain.

★**independent** /ˌɪndɪ'pendənt/ **adj 1** independent (of/from sb/sth) free from and not controlled by another person, country, etc: *Many former colonies are now independent nations.* ● *independent schools/television* (= not supported by government money) **2** independent (of/from sb/sth) not needing or wanting help: *I got a part-time job because I wanted to be financially independent from my parents.* ●➤ opposite **dependent 3** not influenced by or connected with sb/sth: *Complaints against the police should be investigated by an independent body.* ● *Two* *independent opinion polls have obtained similar results.* –**independently** *adv* independently (of sb/sth): *Scientists working independently of each other have had very similar results in their experiments.*

indescribable /ˌɪndɪˈskraɪbəbl/ *adj* too good or bad to be described: *indescribable poverty/luxury/noise* –**indescribably** /-əbli/ *adv*

indestructible /ˌɪndɪˈstrʌktəbl/ *adj* that cannot be easily damaged or destroyed

★**index** /ˈɪndeks/ *noun* [C] (*pl* **indexes**) **1** a list in order from A to Z, usually at the end of a book, of the names or subjects that are referred to in the book: *If you want to find all the references to London, look it up in the index.* **2** (also **card index**) a list in order from A to Z of names, books, subjects, etc written on a series of cards (**index cards**) **3** (*pl* **indexes** or **indices**) a way of showing how the price, value, rate, etc of sth has changed: *the cost-of-living index* –**index** *verb* [T]: *The books in the library are indexed by subject and title.*

index finger *noun* [C] the finger next to your thumb that you use for pointing ••➤ synonym **forefinger**

★**Indian** /ˈɪndiən/ *noun* [C], *adj* **1** (a person) from the Republic of India: *Indian food is hot and spicy.* **2** = **NATIVE AMERICAN**: *The Sioux were a famous Indian tribe.* ••➤ Look at **West Indian**.

★**indicate** /ˈɪndɪkeɪt/ *verb* **1** [T] to show that sth is probably true or exists: *Recent research indicates that children are getting too little exercise.* **2** [T] to say sth in an indirect way: *The spokesman indicated that an agreement was likely soon.* **3** [T] to make sb notice sth, especially by pointing to it: *The receptionist indicated where I should sign.* ● *The boy seemed to be indicating that I should follow him.* **4** [I,T] to signal that your car, etc is going to turn: *The lorry indicated left but turned right.*

indication /ˌɪndɪˈkeɪʃn/ *noun* [C,U] an indication (of sth/doing sth); an indication that… something that shows sth; a sign: *There was no indication of a struggle.* ● *There is every indication that he will make a full recovery.*

indicative /ɪnˈdɪkətɪv/ *adj* (*formal*) being or giving a sign of sth: *Is the unusual weather indicative of climatic changes?*

indicator /ˈɪndɪkeɪtə/ *noun* [C] **1** something that gives information or shows sth; a sign: *The indicator showed that we had plenty of petrol.* ● *The unemployment rate is a reliable indicator of economic health.* **2** (*US* **turn signal**) the flashing light on a car, etc that shows that it is going to turn right or left ••➤ picture on page S9

indices /ˈɪndɪsiːz/ *plural of* **INDEX**(3)

indictment /ɪnˈdaɪtmənt/ *noun* [C] **1** a written paper that officially accuses sb of a crime **2** an indictment (of sth) something that shows how bad sth is: *The fact that many*

children leave school with no qualifications is an indictment of our education system.

indifference /ɪnˈdɪfrəns/ *noun* [U] indifference (to sb/sth) a lack of interest or feeling towards sb/sth: *He has always shown indifference to the needs of others.*

indifferent /ɪnˈdɪfrənt/ *adj* **1** indifferent (to sb/sth) not interested in or caring about sb/sth: *The manager of the shop seemed indifferent to our complaints.* **2** not very good: *The standard of football in the World Cup was rather indifferent.* –**indifferently** *adv*

indigenous /ɪnˈdɪdʒənəs/ *adj* (used about people, animals or plants) living or growing in the place where they are from originally

indigestible /ˌɪndɪˈdʒestəbl/ *adj* (used about food) difficult or impossible for the stomach to deal with

indigestion /ˌɪndɪˈdʒestʃən/ *noun* [U] pain in the stomach that is caused by difficulty in dealing with food: *Peppers give me indigestion.*

indignant /ɪnˈdɪgnənt/ *adj* indignant (with sb) (about/at sth); indignant that… shocked or angry because sb has said or done sth that you do not like and do not agree with: *They were indignant that they had to pay more for worse services.* –**indignantly** *adv*

indignation /ˌɪndɪgˈneɪʃn/ *noun* [U] indignation (at/about sth); indignation that… shock and anger: *commuters' indignation at the rise in fares*

indirect /ˌɪndəˈrekt; -daɪˈr-/ *adj* **1** not being the direct cause of sth; not having a direct connection with sth: *an indirect result* **2** that avoids saying sth in an obvious way: *She gave only an indirect answer to my question.* **3** not going in a straight line or using the shortest route: *We came the indirect route to avoid driving through London.* ••➤ opposite **direct** –**indirectly** *adv* ••➤ opposite **directly** –**indirectness** *noun* [U]

indirect 'object *noun* [C] (*grammar*) a person or thing that an action is done to or for: *In the sentence, 'I wrote him a letter', 'him' is the indirect object.* ••➤ Look at **direct object**.

➤ For more information about indirect objects, look at the **Quick Grammar Reference** at the back of this dictionary.

indirect 'speech (also **re'ported speech**) *noun* [U] (*grammar*) reporting what sb has said, not using the actual words

➤ Hadi's words were: *'I'll phone again later.'* In indirect speech this becomes: *Hadi said that he would phone again later.*

••➤ Look at **direct speech**.

➤ For more information about indirect speech, look at the **Quick Grammar Reference** at the back of this dictionary.

indiscreet /ˌɪndɪˈskriːt/ *adj* not careful or polite in what you say or do ••➤ opposite **discreet** –**indiscreetly** *adv*

indiscretion /ˌɪndɪˈskreʃn/ *noun* [C,U] behaviour that is not careful or polite, and that might cause embarrassment or offence

indiscriminate /ˌɪndɪˈskrɪmɪnət/ **adj** done or acting without making sensible judgement or caring about the possible harmful effects: *He's indiscriminate in his choice of friends.* –indiscriminately **adv**

indispensable /ˌɪndɪˈspensəbl/ **adj** very important, so that it is not possible to be without it: *A car is indispensable nowadays if you live in the country.* ••➤ synonym **essential** ••➤ opposite **dispensable**

indisputable /ˌɪndɪˈspjuːtəbl/ **adj** definitely true; that cannot be shown to be wrong

indistinct /ˌɪndɪˈstɪŋkt/ **adj** not clear: *indistinct figures/sounds/memories* ••➤ opposite **distinct** –indistinctly **adv**

indistinguishable /ˌɪndɪˈstɪŋgwɪʃəbl/ **adj** indistinguishable (from sth) appearing to be the same: *From a distance the two colours are indistinguishable.* ••➤ opposite **distinguishable**

★**individual¹** /ˌɪndɪˈvɪdʒuəl/ **adj 1** (only *before* a noun) considered separately rather than as part of a group: *Each individual animal is weighed and measured before being set free.* **2** for or from one person: *an individual portion of butter* • *Children need individual attention when they are learning to read.* **3** typical of one person in a way that is different from other people: *I like her individual style of dressing.*

individual² /ˌɪndɪˈvɪdʒuəl/ **noun** [C] **1** one person, considered separately from others or a group: *Are the needs of society more important than the rights of the individual?* **2** (*informal*) a person of the type that is mentioned: *She's a strange individual.*

individuality /ˌɪndɪˌvɪdʒuˈæləti/ **noun** [U] the qualities that make sb/sth different from other people or things: *Young people often try to express their individuality by the way they dress.*

individually /ˌɪndɪˈvɪdʒuəli/ **adv** separately; one by one: *The teacher talked to each member of the class individually.*

indivisible /ˌɪndɪˈvɪzəbl/ **adj** that cannot be divided or split into smaller pieces

indoctrinate /ɪnˈdɒktrɪneɪt/ **verb** [T] to force sb to accept particular beliefs without considering others: *For 20 years the people have been indoctrinated by the government.* –indoctrination /ɪnˌdɒktrɪˈneɪʃn/ **noun** [U]

★**indoor** /ˈɪndɔː/ **adj** (only *before* a noun) done or used inside a building: *indoor games* • *an indoor swimming pool* ••➤ opposite **outdoor**

★**indoors** /ˌɪnˈdɔːz/ **adv** in or into a building: *Let's go indoors.* • *Oh dear! I've left my sunglasses indoors.* ••➤ opposite **outdoors** or **out of doors**

induce /ɪnˈdjuːs/ **verb** [T] (*formal*) **1** to make or persuade sb to do sth: *Nothing could induce him to change his mind.* **2** to cause or produce: *drugs that induce sleep*

inducement /ɪnˈdjuːsmənt/ **noun** [C,U] something that is offered to sb to make him/her do sth: *The player was offered a car as an inducement to join the club.*

induction /ɪnˈdʌkʃn/ **noun** [U,C] the process of introducing sb to a new job, skill, organization, etc; an event at which this takes place: *an induction day for new students*

indulge /ɪnˈdʌldʒ/ **verb 1** [I,T] indulge (yourself) (in sth) to allow yourself to have or do sth for pleasure: *I'm going to indulge myself and go shopping for some new clothes.* • *Maria never indulges in gossip.* **2** [T] to give sb/sth what he/she/it wants or needs: *You shouldn't indulge that child. It will make him very selfish.* • *At the weekends he indulges his passion for fishing.*

indulgence /ɪnˈdʌldʒəns/ **noun 1** [U] the state of having or doing whatever you want: *to lead a life of indulgence* • *Over-indulgence in chocolate makes you fat.* **2** [C] something that you have or do because it gives you pleasure: *A cigar after dinner is my only indulgence.*

indulgent /ɪnˈdʌldʒənt/ **adj** allowing sb to have or do whatever he/she wants: *indulgent parents* –indulgently **adv**

★**industrial** /ɪnˈdʌstriəl/ **adj 1** (only *before* a noun) connected with industry: *industrial development* • *industrial workers* **2** having a lot of factories, etc: *an industrial region/country/town*

in,dustrial 'action **noun** [U] action that workers take, especially stopping work, in order to protest about sth to their employers; a strike: *to threaten (to take) industrial action*

industrialist /ɪnˈdʌstriəlɪst/ **noun** [C] a person who owns or manages a large industrial company

industrialize (also **-ise**) /ɪnˈdʌstriəlaɪz/ **verb** [I,T] to develop industries in a country: *Japan industrialized rapidly in the late nineteenth century.* –industrialization (also -isation) /-eɪʃn/ **noun** [U]

industrious /ɪnˈdʌstriəs/ **adj** always working hard

★**industry** /ˈɪndəstri/ **noun** (*pl* **industries**) **1** [U] the production of goods in factories: *Is British industry being threatened by foreign imports?* • *heavy/light industry* **2** [C] the people and activities involved in producing sth, providing a service, etc: *the tourist/catering/entertainment industry*

inedible /ɪnˈedəbl/ **adj** (*formal*) not suitable to be eaten: *an inedible plant* ••➤ opposite **edible**

ineffective /ˌɪnɪˈfektɪv/ **adj** not producing the effect or result that you want ••➤ opposite **effective**

inefficient /ˌɪnɪˈfɪʃnt/ **adj** not working or producing results in the best way, so that time or money is wasted: *Our heating system is very old and extremely inefficient.* • *an inefficient secretary* ••➤ opposite **efficient** –inefficiency /-ənsi/ **noun** [U] –inefficiently **adv**

ineligible /ɪnˈelɪdʒəbl/ **adj** ineligible (for/to do sth) without the necessary certificates, etc to do or get sth: *She was ineligible for the job because she wasn't a German citizen.*

••➤ opposite **eligible** –**ineligibility** /ˌɪnˌelɪdʒə-ˈbɪləti/ **noun** [U]

inept /ɪˈnept/ **adj inept (at sth)** not able to do sth well: *She is totally inept at dealing with people.* ••➤ opposite **adept**

inequality /ˌɪnɪˈkwɒləti/ **noun** [C,U] (*pl* **inequalities**) (a) difference between groups in society because one has more money, advantages, etc than the other: *There will be problems as long as inequality between the races exists.* ••➤ opposite **equality**

inert /ɪˈnɜːt/ **adj** not able to move or act

inertia /ɪˈnɜːʃə/ **noun** [U] **1** a lack of energy; an inability to move or change **2** the physical force that keeps things where they are or keeps them moving in the direction they are travelling

inescapable /ˌɪnɪˈskeɪpəbl/ **adj** (*formal*) that cannot be avoided: *an inescapable conclusion*

inevitable /ɪnˈevɪtəbl/ **adj** that cannot be avoided or prevented from happening: *With more cars on the road, traffic jams are inevitable.* –**the inevitable noun** [sing]: *They fought to save the firm from closure, but eventually had to accept the inevitable.* –**inevitability** /ɪnˌevɪtəˈbɪləti/ **noun** [U] –**inevitably** /-əbli/ **adv**

inexcusable /ˌɪnɪkˈskjuːzəbl/ **adj** that cannot be allowed or forgiven: *Their behaviour was quite inexcusable.* ••➤ opposite **excusable**

inexhaustible /ˌɪnɪɡˈzɔːstəbl/ **adj** that cannot be finished or used up completely: *Our energy supplies are not inexhaustible.*

inexpensive /ˌɪnɪkˈspensɪv/ **adj** low in price: *an inexpensive camping holiday* ••➤ synonym **cheap** ••➤ opposite **expensive** –**inexpensively adv**

inexperience /ˌɪnɪkˈspɪəriəns/ **noun** [U] not knowing how to do sth because you have not done it before: *The mistakes were all due to inexperience.* ••➤ opposite **experience** –**inexperienced adj**: *He's too young and inexperienced to be given such responsibility.*

inexplicable /ˌɪnɪkˈsplɪkəbl/ **adj** that cannot be explained: *Her sudden disappearance is quite inexplicable.* ••➤ opposite **explicable** –**inexplicably** /-əbli/ **adv**

infallible /ɪnˈfæləbl/ **adj 1** (used about a person) never making mistakes or being wrong: *Even the most careful typist is not infallible.* **2** always doing what you want it to do; never failing: *No computer is infallible.* ••➤ opposite **fallible** –**infallibility** /ɪnˌfæləˈbɪləti/ **noun** [U]

infamous /ˈɪnfəməs/ **adj infamous (for sth)** famous for being bad: *The area is infamous for drugs and crime.* ••➤ synonym **notorious**. Look at **famous**.

infancy /ˈɪnfənsi/ **noun** [U] the time when you are a baby or young child: (*figurative*) *Research in this field is still in its infancy.*

infant /ˈɪnfənt/ **noun** [C] a baby or very young child: *There is a high rate of infant mortality* (= many children die when they are still babies). ● *Mrs Davies teaches infants* (= children aged between four and seven).

➤ **Baby**, **toddler** and **child** are more common in spoken or informal English.

infantile /ˈɪnfəntaɪl/ **adj** (of behaviour) typical of, or connected with, a baby or very young child and therefore not appropriate for adults or older children: *infantile jokes*

infantry /ˈɪnfəntri/ **noun** [U, with sing or pl verb] soldiers who fight on foot: *The infantry was/were supported by heavy gunfire.*

'infant school noun [C] a school for children between the ages of four and seven

infatuated /ɪnˈfætʃueɪtɪd/ **adj infatuated (with sb/sth)** having a very strong feeling of love or attraction for sb/sth that usually does not last long and makes you unable to think about anything else: *The young girl was infatuated with one of her teachers.* –**infatuation** /ɪnˌfætʃuˈeɪʃn/ **noun** [C,U]

★**infect** /ɪnˈfekt/ **verb** [T] **1 infect sb/sth (with sth)** (usually passive) to cause sb/sth to have a disease or illness: *We must clean the wound before it becomes infected.* ● *Many thousands of people have been infected with the virus.* **2** to make people share a particular feeling or emotion: *Paul's happiness infected the whole family.*

★**infection** /ɪnˈfekʃn/ **noun 1** [U] the act of becoming or making sb ill: *A dirty water supply can be a source of infection.* ● *There is a danger of infection.* **2** [C] a disease or illness that is caused by harmful bacteria, etc and affects one part of your body: *She is suffering from a chest infection.* ● *an ear infection*

➤ Infections can be caused by **bacteria** or **viruses**. An informal word for these is **germs**.

★**infectious** /ɪnˈfekʃəs/ **adj** (used about a disease, illness, etc) that can be easily passed on to another person: *Flu is very infectious.* ● (*figurative*) *infectious laughter*

➤ Infectious diseases are usually passed by the air that we breathe. **Contagious** diseases are passed by touch.

infer /ɪnˈfɜː/ **verb** [T] (**inferring**; **inferred**) **infer sth (from sth)** to form an opinion or decide that sth is true from the information you have: *I inferred from our conversation that he was unhappy with his job.* –**inference noun** [C]

inferior /ɪnˈfɪəriə/ **adj inferior (to sb/sth)** low or lower in social position, importance, quality, etc: *This material is obviously inferior to that one.* ● *Don't let people make you feel inferior.* ••➤ opposite **superior** –**inferior noun** [C]: *She always treats me as her intellectual inferior.* –**inferiority** /ɪnˌfɪəriˈɒrəti/ **noun** [U]

inferi'ority complex noun [C] the state of feeling less important, clever, successful, etc than other people

infertile /ɪnˈfɜːtaɪl/ **adj 1** (used about a person or animal) not able to have babies or produce young **2** (used about land) not able to grow strong healthy plants ••➤ opposite

fertile –infertility /ˌɪnfɜːˈtɪləti/ **noun** [U]: *infertility treatment* ••➤ opposite **fertility**

infested /ɪnˈfestɪd/ **adj infested (with sth)** (used about a place) with large numbers of unpleasant animals or insects in it: *The warehouse was infested with rats.*

infidelity /ˌɪnfɪˈdeləti/ **noun** [U,C] (*pl* **infidelities**) the act of not being faithful to your wife or husband by having a sexual relationship with sb else ••➤ A less formal word is **unfaithfulness**.

infiltrate /ˈɪnfɪltreɪt/ **verb** [T] to enter an organization, etc secretly so that you can find out what it is doing: *The police managed to infiltrate the gang of terrorists.* –infiltration /-eɪʃn/ **noun** [C,U] –infiltrator **noun** [C]

infinite /ˈɪnfɪnət/ **adj 1** very great: *You need infinite patience for this job.* **2** without limits; that never ends: *Supplies of oil are not infinite.* ••➤ opposite **finite**

infinitely /ˈɪnfɪnətli/ **adv** very much: *Compact discs sound infinitely better than audio cassettes.*

infinitive /ɪnˈfɪnətɪv/ **noun** [C] (*grammar*) the basic form of a verb

➤ In English the infinitive can be used either with or without *to* depending on what comes before it: *He can sing.* • *He wants to sing.*

infinity /ɪnˈfɪnəti/ **noun 1** [U] space or time without end: (*figurative*) *The ocean seemed to stretch over the horizon into infinity.* **2** [U,C] (*symbol* ∞) (in mathematics) the number that is larger than any other that you can think of

infirmary /ɪnˈfɜːməri/ **noun** [C] (*pl* **infirmaries**) (used mainly in names) a hospital: *The Manchester Royal Infirmary*

inflamed /ɪnˈfleɪmd/ **adj** (used about a part of the body) red and swollen or painful because of an infection or injury

inflammable /ɪnˈflæməbl/ **adj** that burns easily: *Petrol is highly inflammable.* ••➤ Look at **flammable**. It has the same meaning but is less common. ••➤ opposite **non-flammable**

inflammation /ˌɪnfləˈmeɪʃn/ **noun** [C,U] a condition in which a part of the body becomes red, sore and swollen because of infection or injury

inflatable /ɪnˈfleɪtəbl/ **adj** that can or must be filled with air: *an inflatable dinghy/mattress*

inflate /ɪnˈfleɪt/ **verb** [I,T] (*formal*) to fill sth with air; to become filled with air ••➤ A less formal word is **blow up**. ••➤ opposite **deflate**

★**inflation** /ɪnˈfleɪʃn/ **noun** [U] a general rise in prices; the rate at which prices rise: *the inflation rate/rate of inflation* • *Inflation now stands at 3%.*

inflection (also **inflexion**) /ɪnˈflekʃn/ **noun** [C,U] **1** (*grammar*) a change in the form of a word, especially its ending, that changes its function in the grammar of the language, for example – *ed*, – *est* **2** the rise and fall of your voice when you are talking ••➤ synonym **intonation**

inflexible /ɪnˈfleksəbl/ **adj 1** that cannot be changed or made more suitable for a particular situation; rigid: *He has a very inflexible attitude to change.* **2** (used about a material) not able to bend or be bent easily ••➤ opposite **flexible** –inflexibly /-əbli/ **adv** –inflexibility /ɪnˌfleksəˈbɪləti/ **noun** [U]

inflict /ɪnˈflɪkt/ **verb** [T] **inflict sth (on sb)** to force sb to have sth unpleasant or that he/she does not want: *Don't inflict your problems on me – I've got enough of my own.*

'**in-flight adj** (only *before* a noun) happening or provided during a journey in a plane: *in-flight entertainment*

★**influence**[1] /ˈɪnfluəns/ **noun 1** [U,C] (an) **influence (on/upon sb/sth)** the power to affect, change or control sb/sth: *Television can have a strong influence on children.* • *Nobody should drive while they are **under the influence** of alcohol.* **2** [C] an **influence (on sb/sth)** a person or thing that affects or changes sb/sth: *His new girlfriend has been a good influence on him.* • *cultural/environmental influences*

influence[2] /ˈɪnfluəns/ **verb** [T] to have an effect on or power over sb/sth so that he/she/it changes: *You must decide for yourself. Don't let anyone else influence you.* • *Her style of painting has been influenced by Japanese art.*

➤ **Affect** and **influence** are often very similar in meaning. **Affect** is usually used when the change is physical and **influence** is more often used to describe a change of opinion or attitude: *Drinking alcohol can affect your ability to drive.* • *TV advertisements have influenced my attitude towards the homeless.*

influential /ˌɪnfluˈenʃl/ **adj influential (in sth/in doing sth)** having power or influence: *an influential politician* • *He was influential in getting the hostages set free.*

influenza /ˌɪnfluˈenzə/ (*formal*) = **FLU**

influx /ˈɪnflʌks/ **noun** [C, usually sing] an **influx (of sb/sth) (into…)** large numbers of people or things arriving suddenly: *the summer influx of visitors from abroad*

★**inform** /ɪnˈfɔːm/ **verb** [T] **inform sb (of/about sth)** to give sb information (about sth), especially in an official way: *You should inform the police of the accident.* • *Do **keep** me **informed** of any changes.*

PHRASAL VERB **inform on sb** to give information to the police, etc about what sb has done wrong: *The wife of the killer informed on her husband.*

★**informal** /ɪnˈfɔːml/ **adj** relaxed and friendly or suitable for a relaxed occasion: *Don't get dressed up for the party – it'll be very informal.* • *The two leaders had informal discussions before the conference began.* ••➤ opposite **formal** ••➤ Some words and expressions in this dictionary are described as *(informal)*. This means that you can use them when you are speaking to friends or people that you know well but that you should not use them in written work, official letters, etc. –infor-mality /ˌɪnfɔː'mælɪti/ **noun** [U]: *an atmosphere of informality* –informally **adv**: *I was told informally* (= unofficially) *that our plans had been accepted.*

informant /ɪn'fɔːmənt/ **noun** [C] a person who gives secret knowledge or information about sb/sth to the police or a newspaper: *The journalist refused to name his informant.* ••➤ Look at **informer**.

★**information** /ˌɪnfə'meɪʃn/ **noun** [U] informa-tion (on/about sb/sth) knowledge or facts: *For further information please send for our fact sheet.* ● *Can you give me some informa-tion about evening classes in Italian, please?*

➤ The word **information** is uncountable so you CANNOT say: *I need an information.* You can, however, talk about **a bit** or **piece of information**.

infor,mation tech'nology noun [U] (*abbr* **IT**) (*computing*) the study or use of electronic equipment, especially computers, for collect-ing, storing and sending out information

informative /ɪn'fɔːmətɪv/ **adj** giving useful knowledge or information

informed /ɪn'fɔːmd/ **adj** having knowledge or information about sth: *Consumers cannot make informed choices unless they are told all the facts.*

informer /ɪn'fɔːmə/ **noun** [C] a criminal who gives the police information about other criminals ••➤ Look at **informant**.

infrequent /ɪn'friːkwənt/ **adj** not happening often ••➤ opposite **frequent** –infrequently **adv**

infringe /ɪn'frɪndʒ/ **verb** (*formal*) **1** [T] to break a rule, law, agreement, etc: *The mater-ial can be copied without infringing copyright.* **2** [I] infringe on/upon sth to reduce or limit sb's rights, freedom, etc: *She refused to answer questions that infringed on her private affairs.* –infringement **noun** [C,U]

infuriate /ɪn'fjʊərieɪt/ **verb** [T] to make sb very angry –infuriating **adj**: *an infuriating habit* –infuriatingly **adv**

ingenious /ɪn'dʒiːniəs/ **adj 1** (used about a thing or an idea) made or planned in a clever way: *an ingenious plan for making lots of money* ● *an ingenious device/experiment/ invention* **2** (used about a person) full of new ideas and clever at finding solutions to prob-lems or at inventing things –ingeniously **adv** –ingenuity /ˌɪndʒə'njuːəti/ **noun** [U]

ingrained /ɪn'greɪnd/ **adj** ingrained (in sb/ sth) (used about a habit, an attitude, etc) that has existed for a long time and is therefore difficult to change: *ingrained prejudices/ beliefs*

ingratiate /ɪn'greɪʃieɪt/ **verb** [T] (*formal*) ingratiate yourself (with sb) to make your-self liked by doing or saying things that will please people, especially people who might be useful to you: *He was always trying to ingrati-ate himself with his teachers.* –ingratiating **adj**: *an ingratiating smile* –ingratiatingly **adv**

ingratitude /ɪn'grætɪtjuːd/ **noun** [U] (*formal*) the state of not showing or feeling

thanks for sth that has been done for you; not being grateful ••➤ A less formal word is **ungratefulness**. ••➤ opposite **gratitude**

ingredient /ɪn'griːdiənt/ **noun** [C] **1** one of the items of food you need to make sth to eat: *Mix all the ingredients together in a bowl.* **2** one of the qualities necessary to make sth successful: *The film has all the ingredients of success.*

★**inhabit** /ɪn'hæbɪt/ **verb** [T] to live in a place: *Are the Aran Islands still inhabited* (= do people live there)?

inhabitant /ɪn'hæbɪtənt/ **noun** [C,usually pl] a person or animal that lives in a place: *The local inhabitants protested at the plans for a new motorway.* ••➤ When you want to know how many people live in a particular place, you say: *What is the population of...?* NOT: *How many inhabitants are there in...?* How-ever, when you answer this question you can say: *The population is 10000.* OR: *It has 10000 inhabitants.*

inhale /ɪn'heɪl/ **verb** [I,T] to breathe in: *Be careful not to inhale the fumes from the paint.* ••➤ opposite **exhale**

inherent /ɪn'hɪərənt/ **adj** inherent (in sb/ sth) that is a basic or permanent part of sb/sth and that cannot be removed: *The risk of collapse is inherent in any business.* –inherently **adv**: *No matter how safe we make them, cars are inherently dangerous.*

inherit /ɪn'herɪt/ **verb** [T] inherit sth (from sb) **1** to receive property, money, etc from sb who has died: *I inherited quite a lot of money from my mother. She left me $12000 when she died.*

➤ The person who inherits from sb is that person's **heir**.

2 to receive a quality, characteristic, etc from your parents or family: *She has inherited her father's gift for languages.*

inheritance /ɪn'herɪtəns/ **noun** [C,U] the act of inheriting; the money, property, etc that you inherit: *inheritance tax*

inhibit /ɪn'hɪbɪt/ **verb** [T] **1** to prevent sth or make sth happen more slowly: *a drug to inhibit the growth of tumours* **2** inhibit sb (from sth/from doing sth) to make sb ner-vous and embarrassed so that he/she is unable to do sth: *The fact that her boss was there inhibited her from saying what she really felt.* –inhibited **adj**: *The young man felt shy and inhibited in the roomful of women.* ••➤ opposite **uninhibited**

inhibition /ˌɪnhɪ'bɪʃn; ˌɪnɪ'b-/ **noun** [C,U] a shy or nervous feeling that stops you from saying or doing what you really want: *After the first day of the course, people started to lose their inhibitions.*

inhospitable /ˌɪnhɒ'spɪtəbl/ **adj 1** (used about a place) not pleasant to live in, espe-cially because of the weather: *the inhospit-able Arctic regions* **2** (used about a person) not friendly or welcoming to guests ••➤ oppos-ite **hospitable**

inhuman /ɪn'hjuːmən/ **adj 1** very cruel and

without pity: *inhuman treatment/conditions*
2 not seeming to be human and therefore
frightening: *an inhuman noise*

inhumane /ˌɪnhjuːˈmeɪn/ *adj* very cruel; not
caring if people or animals suffer: *the inhumane conditions in which animals are kept on
some large farms* ••➤ opposite **humane**

inhumanity /ˌɪnhjuːˈmænəti/ *noun* [U] very
cruel behaviour: *The twentieth century is full
of examples of man's inhumanity to man.*
••➤ opposite **humanity**

★**initial¹** /ɪˈnɪʃl/ *adj* (only *before* a noun) happening at the beginning; first: *My initial reaction was to refuse, but I later changed my
mind.* ● *the initial stages of our survey*

★**initial²** /ɪˈnɪʃl/ *noun* [C, usually pl] the first
letter of a name: *Alison Elizabeth Waters'
initials are A.E.W.*

initial³ /ɪˈnɪʃl/ *verb* [T] (**initialling**; **initialled**; *US* **initialing**; **initialed**) to mark or
sign sth with your initials: *Any changes made
when writing a cheque should be initialled by
you.*

initially /ɪˈnɪʃəli/ *adv* at the beginning; at
first: *I liked the job initially but it soon got
quite boring.*

initiate /ɪˈnɪʃieɪt/ *verb* [T] **1** (*formal*) to start
sth: *to initiate peace talks* **2** initiate sb (into
sth) to explain sth to sb or make him/her
experience sth for the first time: *I wasn't
initiated into the joys of skiing until I was 30.*
3 initiate sb (into sth) to bring sb into a
group by means of a special ceremony: *to
initiate sb into a secret society* –initiation
/-eɪʃn/ *noun* [U]: *All the new students had to go
through a strange **initiation ceremony**.*

★**initiative** /ɪˈnɪʃətɪv/ *noun* **1** [C] official
action that is taken to solve a problem or
improve a situation: *a new government initiative to help people start small businesses* **2** [U]
the ability to see and do what is necessary
without waiting for sb to tell you: *Don't keep
asking me how to do it. Use your initiative.*
3 the initiative [sing] the stronger position
because you have done sth first; the advantage: *The enemy forces have **lost the initiative**.*
 IDIOMS **on your own initiative** without being
told by sb else what to do
take the initiative to be first to act to influence a situation: *Let's take the initiative and
start organizing things now.*

★**inject** /ɪnˈdʒekt/ *verb* [T] **1** to put a drug
under the skin of person's or an animal's
body with a needle (**syringe**) **2** inject sth
(into sth) to add sth: *They injected a lot of
money into the business.*

★**injection** /ɪnˈdʒekʃn/ *noun* **1** [C,U] (an)
injection (of sth) (into sb/sth) the act of
putting a drug or substance under the skin of
a person's or an animal's body with a needle
(a **syringe**): *to give sb an injection* ● *a tetanus
injection* ● *An anaesthetic was administered
by injection.* ••➤ synonym **jab 2** [C] a large
amount of sth that is added to sth to help it:
*The theatre needs a huge **cash injection** if it*

is to stay open. **3** [U,C] the act of forcing
liquid into sth: *fuel injection*

injunction /ɪnˈdʒʌŋkʃn/ *noun* [C] an injunction (against sb) an official order from a
court of law to do/not do sth: *A court injunction prevented the programme from being
shown on TV.*

★**injure** /ˈɪndʒə/ *verb* [T] to harm or hurt yourself or sb else physically, especially in an
accident: *The goalkeeper seriously injured
himself when he hit the goalpost.* ● *She fell
and injured her back.* ••➤ Look at the note at
hurt.

★**injured** /ˈɪndʒəd/ *adj* **1** physically or mentally hurt: *an injured arm/leg* ● *injured pride*
2 the injured *noun* [pl] people who have been
hurt: *The injured were rushed to hospital.*

★**injury** /ˈɪndʒəri/ *noun* [C,U] (*pl* **injuries**)
injury (to sb/sth) harm done to a person's or
an animal's body, especially in an accident:
*They escaped from the accident with only
minor injuries.* ● *Injury to the head can be
extremely dangerous.*

'**injury time** *noun* [U] (*Brit*) time that is
added to the end of a rugby, football, etc
match when there has been time lost because
of injuries to players

injustice /ɪnˈdʒʌstɪs/ *noun* [U,C] the fact of a
situation being unfair; an unfair act: *racial/
social injustice* ● *People are protesting about
the injustice of the new tax.*
 IDIOM **do sb an injustice** to judge sb unfairly:
I'm afraid I've done you both an injustice.

★**ink** /ɪŋk/ *noun* [U,C] coloured liquid that is
used for writing, drawing, etc: *Please write in
ink, not pencil.*

inkling /ˈɪŋklɪŋ/ *noun* [usually sing] an inkling (of sth/that…) a slight feeling (about
sth): *I had an inkling that something was
wrong.*

inky /ˈɪŋki/ *adj* made black with ink; very
dark: *inky fingers* ● *an inky night sky*

inland /ˌɪnˈlænd/ *adj*, *adv* away from the coast
or borders of a country: *The village lies
twenty miles inland.* ● *Goods are carried
inland along narrow mountain roads.*

ˌInland ˈRevenue *noun* [sing] (*Brit*) the government department that collects taxes

'**in-laws** *noun* [pl] (*informal*) your husband's
or wife's mother and father or other relations: *My in-laws are coming to lunch on Sunday.*

inmate /ˈɪnmeɪt/ *noun* [C] one of the people
living in an institution such as a prison

inn /ɪn/ *noun* [C] (*Brit*) a small hotel or old pub
usually in the country

innate /ɪˈneɪt/ *adj* (used about an ability or
quality) that you have when you are born:
the innate ability to learn

★**inner** /ˈɪnə/ *adj* (only *before* a noun) **1** (of the)
inside; towards or close to the centre of a
place: *The inner ear is very delicate.* ● *an
inner courtyard* ••➤ opposite **outer 2** (used
about a feeling, etc) that you do not express
or show to other people; private: *Everyone
has inner doubts.*

,inner 'city noun [C] the poor parts of a large city, near the centre, that often have a lot of social problems –**inner-city** adj (only *before* a noun): *Inner-city schools often have difficulty in attracting good teachers.*

innermost /'ɪnəməʊst/ adj (only *before* a noun) **1** (used about a feeling or thought) most secret or private: *She never told anyone her innermost thoughts.* **2** nearest to the centre or inside of sth: *the innermost shrine of the temple*

innings /'ɪnɪŋz/ noun [C] (*pl* **innings**) a period of time in a game of cricket when it is the turn of one player or team to hit the ball (to bat)

★**innocence** /'ɪnəsns/ noun [U] **1** the fact of not being guilty of a crime, etc: *The accused man protested his innocence throughout his trial.* ••➤ opposite **guilt** **2** lack of knowledge and experience of the world, especially of bad things: *the innocence of childhood*

★**innocent** /'ɪnəsnt/ adj **1** innocent (of sth) not having done wrong: *An innocent man was arrested by mistake.* • *to be innocent of a crime* ••➤ synonym **blameless** ••➤ opposite **guilty** **2** (only *before* a noun) being hurt or killed in a crime, war, etc although not involved in it in any way: *innocent victims of a bomb blast* • *an innocent bystander* **3** not wanting to cause harm or upset sb, although it does: *He got very aggressive when I asked an innocent question about his past life.* **4** not knowing the bad things in life; believing everything you are told: *She was so innocent as to believe that politicians never lie.* ••➤ synonym **naive** –**innocently** adv: *'What are you doing here?' she asked innocently* (= pretending she did not know the answer).

innocuous /ɪ'nɒkjuəs/ adj (*formal*) not meant to cause harm or upset sb: *I made an innocuous remark about teachers and she got really angry.* ••➤ synonym **harmless** –**innocuously** adv

innovate /'ɪnəveɪt/ verb [I] to create new things, ideas or ways of doing sth –**innovation** /ˌɪnə'veɪʃn/ noun [C,U] (an) innovation (in sth): *technological innovations in industry* –**innovative** /'ɪnəvətɪv; 'ɪnəveɪtɪv/ adj: *innovative methods/designs/products* –**innovator** noun [C]

innuendo /ˌɪnju'endəʊ/ noun [C,U] (*pl* **innu-endoes** or **innuendos**) an indirect way of talking about sb/sth, usually suggesting sth bad or rude: *His speech was full of sexual innuendo.*

innumerable /ɪ'nju:mərəbl/ adj too many to be counted

inoculate /ɪ'nɒkjuleɪt/ verb [T] inoculate sb (against sth) to protect a person or animal from a disease by giving him/her/it a mild form of the disease with a needle which is put under the skin (an injection): *The children have been inoculated against tetanus.* ••➤ **Immunize** and **vaccinate** have similar meanings. –**inoculation** /-eɪʃn/ noun [C,U]

inoffensive /ˌɪnə'fensɪv/ adj not likely to offend or upset sb; harmless ••➤ opposite **offensive**

inordinate /ɪn'ɔ:dɪnət/ adj (*formal*) much greater than usual or expected: *They spent an inordinate amount of time and money on the production.* –**inordinately** adv

inorganic /ˌɪnɔ:'gænɪk/ adj not made of or coming from living things: *Rocks and metals are inorganic substances.* ••➤ opposite **organic**

input¹ /'ɪnpʊt/ noun **1** [C,U] input (of sth) (into/to sth) what you put into sth to make it successful: *We need some input from teachers into this book.* **2** [U] the act of putting information into a computer: *The computer break-down means we have lost the whole day's input.* ••➤ Look at **output**.

input² /'ɪnpʊt/ verb [T] (*pres part* **inputting**; *pt, pp* **input** or **inputted**) to put information into a computer

inquest /'ɪŋkwest/ noun [C] an official inquiry to find out how sb died: *to hold an inquest*

inquire, inquirer, inquiring, inquiry = **ENQUIRE, ENQUIRER, ENQUIRING, ENQUIRY**

inquisitive /ɪn'kwɪzətɪv/ adj **1** too interested in finding out about what other people are doing: *Don't be so inquisitive. It's none of your business.* **2** interested in finding out about many different things: *You need an inquisitive mind to be a scientist.* –**inquisitively** adv –**inquisitiveness** noun [U]

insane /ɪn'seɪn/ adj **1** crazy or mentally ill **2** not showing sensible judgement: *You must be insane to leave your job before you've found another one.* ••➤ Look at the note at **mad**. –**insanely** adv: *insanely jealous* –**insanity** /ɪn'sænəti/ noun [U]

insanitary /ɪn'sænətri/ adj (*formal*) dirty and likely to cause disease: *The restaurant was closed because of the insanitary conditions of the kitchen.* ••➤ Look at **sanitary**.

insatiable /ɪn'seɪʃəbl/ adj that cannot be satisfied; very great: *an insatiable desire for knowledge* • *an insatiable appetite*

inscribe /ɪn'skraɪb/ verb [T] (*formal*) inscribe A (on/in B); inscribe B (with A) to write or cut (carve) words on sth: *The names of all the previous champions are inscribed on the cup.* • *The book was inscribed with the author's name.*

inscription /ɪn'skrɪpʃn/ noun [C] words that are written or cut on sth: *There was a Latin inscription on the tombstone.*

★**insect** /'ɪnsekt/ noun [C] a small animal with six legs, two pairs of wings and a body which is divided into three parts: *Ants, flies, beetles, butterflies and mosquitoes are all insects.* • *an insect bite/sting* ••➤ picture on page C1

> Some other small animals, for example spiders, are often also called insects although this is technically incorrect.

insecticide /ɪn'sektɪsaɪd/ noun [C,U] a substance that is used for killing insects ••➤ Look at **pesticide**.

insecure /ˌɪnsɪ'kjʊə/ adj **1** insecure (about

insects

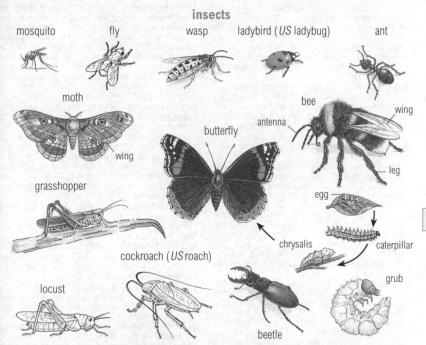

mosquito fly wasp ladybird (*US* ladybug) ant

moth bee wing

antenna

butterfly

leg

grasshopper

egg

chrysalis caterpillar

cockroach (*US* roach)

grub

locust

beetle

sb/sth) not confident about yourself or your relationships with other people: *Many teenagers are insecure about their appearance.* **2** not safe or protected: *This ladder feels a bit insecure.* ● *The future of the company looks very insecure.* ••➤ opposite **secure** –**insecurely adv** –**insecurity noun** [U]: *Their aggressive behaviour is really a sign of insecurity.* ••➤ opposite **security**

insensitive /ɪnˈsensətɪv/ **adj insensitive (to sth) 1** not knowing or caring how another person feels and therefore likely to hurt or upset him/her: *Some insensitive reporters tried to interview the families of the accident victims.* ● *an insensitive remark* **2 insensitive (to sth)** not able to feel or react to sth: *insensitive to pain/cold/criticism* ••➤ opposite **sensitive** –**insensitively adv** –**insensitivity** /ɪnˌsensəˈtɪvəti/ **noun** [U]

inseparable /ɪnˈseprəbl/ **adj** that cannot be separated from sb/sth: *inseparable friends* ••➤ opposite **separable**

insert /ɪnˈsɜːt/ **verb** [T] (*formal*) to put sth into sth or between two things: *I decided to insert an extra paragraph in the text.* –**insertion noun** [C,U]

inshore /ˌɪnˈʃɔː/ **adj, adv** in or towards the part of the sea that is close to the land: *inshore fishermen* ● *Sharks don't often come inshore.*

★ **inside¹** /ɪnˈsaɪd/ **prep, adj, adv 1** in, on or to the inner part or surface of sth: *Is there any-*

thing inside the box? ● *It's safer to be inside the house in a thunderstorm.* ● *We'd better stay inside until the rain stops.* ● *It's getting cold. Let's go inside.* ● *the inside pages of a newspaper* **2** (*formal*) (used about time) in less than; within: *Your photos will be ready inside an hour.* **3** (used about information, etc) told secretly by sb who belongs to a group, organization, etc: *The robbers seemed to have had some inside information about the bank's security system.* **4** (*slang*) in prison

★ **inside²** /ɪnˈsaɪd/ **noun 1** [C] the inner part or surface of sth: *The door was locked from the inside.* ● *There's a label somewhere on the inside.* **2 insides** [pl] (*informal*) the organs inside the body: *The coffee warmed his insides.*

IDIOM **inside out 1** with the inner surface on the outside: *You've got your jumper on inside out.* ••➤ picture at **back 2** very well, in great detail: *She knows these streets inside out.*

insider /ɪnˈsaɪdə/ **noun** [C] a person who knows a lot about a group or an organization because he/she is a part of it: *The book gives us an insider's view of how government works.*

insight /ˈɪnsaɪt/ **noun** [C,U] **(an) insight (into sth)** an understanding of what sb/sth is like: *The book gives a good insight into the lives of the poor.*

insignificant /ˌɪnsɪɡˈnɪfɪkənt/ **adj** of little value or importance: *an insignificant detail* ● *Working in such a big company made her*

feel insignificant. –**insignificance noun** [U]
–**insignificantly adv**

insincere /ˌɪnsɪn'sɪə/ **adj** saying or doing sth that you do not really believe: *His apology sounded insincere.* ● *an insincere smile* ••➤ opposite **sincere** –**insincerely adv** –**insincerity** /ˌɪnsɪn'serəti/ **noun** [U] ••➤ opposite **sincerity**

insinuate /ɪn'sɪnjueɪt/ **verb** [T] to suggest sth unpleasant in an indirect way: *She seemed to be insinuating that our work was below standard.* –**insinuation** /ɪn,sɪnju'eɪʃn/ **noun** /ɪn,sɪnjuiʃn/ '[C,U]: *to make insinuations about sb's honesty*

insipid /ɪn'sɪpɪd/ **adj** having too little taste, flavour or colour

★**insist** /ɪn'sɪst/ **verb** [I] **1** insist (on sth/doing sth); insist that... to say strongly that you must have or do sth, or that sb else must do sth: *He always insists on the best.* ● *Dan insisted on coming too.* ● *My parents insist that I come home by taxi.* ● *'Have another drink.' 'Oh all right, if you insist.'* **2** insist (on sth); insist that... to say firmly that sth is true (when sb does not believe you): *She insisted on her innocence.* ● *James insisted that the accident wasn't his fault.* –**insistence noun** [U]

insistent /ɪn'sɪstənt/ **adj 1** insistent (on sth/doing sth); insistent that... saying strongly that you must have or do sth, or that sb else must do sth: *Doctors are insistent on the need to do more exercise.* ● *She was most insistent that we should all be there.* **2** continuing for a long time in a way that cannot be ignored: *the insistent ringing of the telephone* –**insistently adv**

insolent /'ɪnsələnt/ **adj** (*formal*) lacking respect; rude: *insolent behaviour* –**insolence noun** [U] –**insolently adv**

insoluble /ɪn'sɒljəbl/ **adj 1** that cannot be explained or solved: *We faced almost insoluble problems.* **2** that cannot be dissolved in a liquid ••➤ opposite **soluble**

insomnia /ɪn'sɒmniə/ **noun** [U] inability to sleep: *Do you ever suffer from insomnia?* ••➤ Look at **sleepless**.

insomniac /ɪn'sɒmniæk/ **noun** [C] a person who cannot sleep

★**inspect** /ɪn'spekt/ **verb** [T] **1** inspect sb/sth (for sth) to look at sth closely or in great detail: *The detective inspected the room for fingerprints.* **2** to make an official visit to make sure that rules are being obeyed, work is being done properly, etc: *All food shops should be inspected regularly.* –**inspection noun** [C,U]: *The fire prevention service will carry out an inspection of the building next week.* ● *On inspection, the passport turned out to be false.*

★**inspector** /ɪn'spektə/ **noun** [C] **1** an official who visits schools, factories, etc to make sure that rules are being obeyed, work is being done properly, etc: *a health and safety inspector* **2** (*Brit*) a police officer with quite an important position **3** a person whose job is to check passengers' tickets on buses or trains

inspiration /ˌɪnspə'reɪʃn/ **noun 1** [C,U] an inspiration (to/for sb); inspiration (to do/for sth) a feeling, person or thing that makes you want to do sth or gives you exciting new ideas: *The beauty of the mountains was a great source of inspiration to the writer.* ● *What gave you the inspiration to become a dancer?* **2** [C] (*informal*) a sudden good idea: *I've had an inspiration – why don't we go to that new club?*

inspire /ɪn'spaɪə/ **verb** [T] **1** inspire sth; inspire sb (to do sth) to make sb want to do or create sth: *Nelson Mandela's autobiography inspired her to go into politics.* ● *The attack was inspired by racial hatred.* **2** inspire sb (with sth); inspire sth (in sb) to make sb feel, think, etc sth: *to be inspired with enthusiasm* ● *The guide's nervous manner did not inspire much confidence in us.* –**inspiring adj**: *an inspiring speech.*

inspired /ɪn'spaɪəd/ **adj** influenced or helped by a particular feeling, thing or person: *The pianist gave an inspired performance.* ● *a politically inspired killing*

instability /ˌɪnstə'bɪləti/ **noun** [U] the state of being likely to change: *There are growing signs of political instability.* ••➤ adjective **unstable** ••➤ opposite **stability**

★**install** (*US also* instal) /ɪn'stɔːl/ **verb** [T] **1** to put a piece of equipment, etc in place so that it is ready to be used: *We are waiting to have our new washing machine installed.* ● *to install a computer system* ••➤ synonym **put in** **2** install sb (as sth) to put sb/sth or yourself in a position or place: *He was installed as President yesterday.* –**installation** /ˌɪnstə-'leɪʃn/ **noun** [C,U]: *a military/nuclear installation* ● *the installation of a new chairman*

instalment (*US* **installment**) /ɪn'stɔːl-mənt/ **noun** [C] **1** one of the regular payments that you make for sth until you have paid the full amount: *to pay for sth in instalments* **2** one part of a story that is shown or published as a series: *Don't miss next week's exciting instalment.*

★**instance** /'ɪnstəns/ **noun** [C] an instance (of sth) an example or case (of sth): *There have been several instances of racial attacks in the area.* ● *In most instances the drug has no side effects.*

IDIOM **for instance** for example: *There are several interesting places to visit around here – Warwick, for instance.*

★**instant**[1] /'ɪnstənt/ **adj 1** happening suddenly or immediately: *The film was an instant success.* **2** (used about food) that can be prepared quickly and easily, usually by adding hot water: *instant coffee*

instant[2] /'ɪnstənt/ **noun** [usually sing] **1** a very short period of time: *Alex thought for an instant and then agreed.* **2** a particular point in time: *At that instant I realized I had been tricked.* ● *Stop doing that this instant!* (= now)

instantaneous /ˌɪnstən'teɪniəs/ **adj** happening immediately or extremely quickly –**instantaneously adv**

instantly /'ɪnstəntli/ **adv** without delay; immediately: *I asked him a question and he replied instantly.*

★**instead** /ɪn'sted/ **adv, prep** instead (of sb/ sth/doing sth) in the place of sb/sth: *I couldn't go so my husband went instead.* ● *You should play football instead of just watching it on TV.* ● *Instead of 7.30 could I come at 8.00?*

instigate /'ɪnstɪgeɪt/ **verb** [T] (*formal*) to make sth start to happen –instigation /,ɪnstɪ'geɪʃn/ **noun** [U]

instil (*US* **instill**) /ɪn'stɪl/ **verb** [T] (**instilling**; **instilled**) instil sth (in/into sb) to make sb think or feel sth: *Parents should try to instil a sense of responsibility into their children.*

instinct /'ɪnstɪŋkt/ **noun** [C,U] the natural force that causes a person or animal to behave in a particular way without thinking or learning about it: *Birds learn to fly by instinct.* ● *In a situation like that you don't have time to think – you just act on instinct.* –instinctive /ɪn'stɪŋktɪv/ **adj**: *Your instinctive reaction is to run from danger.* –instinctively **adv**

★**institute**[1] /'ɪnstɪtju:t/ **noun** [C] an organization that has a particular purpose; the building used by this organization: *the Institute of Science and Technology* ● *institutes of higher education*

institute[2] /'ɪnstɪtju:t/ **verb** [T] (*formal*) to introduce a system, policy, etc, or start a process: *The government has instituted a new scheme for youth training.*

★**institution** /,ɪnstɪ'tju:ʃn/ **noun 1** [C] a large, important organization that has a particular purpose, such as a bank, a university, etc: *the financial institutions in the City of London* **2** [C] a building where certain people with special needs live and are looked after: *a mental institution* (= a hospital for the mentally ill) ● *She's been in institutions all her life.* **3** [C] a social custom or habit that has existed for a long time: *the institution of marriage* **4** [U] the act of introducing a system, policy, etc, or starting a process: *the institution of new safety procedures*

institutional /,ɪnstɪ'tju:ʃənl/ **adj** connected with an institution: *The old lady is in need of institutional care.*

★**instruct** /ɪn'strʌkt/ **verb** [T] **1** instruct sb (to do sth) to give an order to sb; to tell sb to do sth: *The soldiers were instructed to shoot above the heads of the crowd.* **2** (*formal*) instruct sb (in sth) to teach sb sth: *Children must be instructed in road safety before they are allowed to ride a bike on the road.*

★**instruction** /ɪn'strʌkʃn/ **noun 1 instructions** [pl] detailed information on how you should use sth, do sth, etc: *Read the instructions on the back of the packet carefully.* ● *You should always follow the instructions.* **2** [C] an instruction (to do sth) an order that tells you what to do or how to do sth: *The guard was under strict instructions not to let anyone in or out.* **3** [U] instruction (in sth) the

act of teaching sth to sb: *The staff need instruction in the use of computers.*

instructive /ɪn'strʌktɪv/ **adj** giving useful information –instructively **adv**

instructor /ɪn'strʌktə/ **noun** [C] a person whose job is to teach a practical skill or sport: *a driving/fitness/golf instructor*

★**instrument** /'ɪnstrəmənt/ **noun** [C] **1** a tool that is used for doing a particular job or task: *surgical/optical/precision instruments* ••➤ Look at the note at **tool**. **2** something that is used for playing music: *'What instrument do you play?' 'The violin.'*

➤ **Musical instruments** may be **stringed** (*violins, guitars, etc*), **brass** (*horns, trumpets, etc*), **woodwind** (*flutes, clarinets, etc*) or **keyboard** (*piano, organ, synthesizer, etc*). **Percussion** instruments include *drums* and *cymbals.*

3 something that is used for measuring speed, distance, temperature, etc in a car, plane or ship: *the instrument panel of a plane* **4** something that sb uses in order to achieve sth: *The press should be more than an instrument of the government.*

★**instrumental** /,ɪnstrə'mentl/ **adj 1** instrumental in doing sth helping to make sth happen: *She was instrumental in getting him the job.* **2** for musical instruments without voices: *instrumental music*

insubordinate /,ɪnsə'bɔ:dɪnət/ **adj** (*formal*) (used about a person or behaviour) not obeying rules or orders –insubordination /,ɪnsə,bɔ:dɪ'neɪʃn/ **noun** [C,U]: *He was dismissed from the army for insubordination.*

insubstantial /,ɪnsəb'stænʃl/ **adj** not large, solid or strong: *a hut built of insubstantial materials* ••➤ opposite **substantial**

insufferable /ɪn'sʌfrəbl/ **adj** (*formal*) (used about a person or behaviour) extremely unpleasant or annoying

insufficient /,ɪnsə'fɪʃnt/ **adj** insufficient (for sth/to do sth) not enough: *The students complained that they were given insufficient time for the test.* ••➤ opposite **sufficient** –insufficiently **adv**

insular /'ɪnsjələ/ **adj** not interested in or able to accept new people or different ideas ••➤ synonym **narrow-minded** –insularity /,ɪnsjə'lærəti/ **noun** [U]

insulate /'ɪnsjuleɪt/ **verb** [T] insulate sth (against/from sth) to protect sth with a material that prevents electricity, heat or sound from passing through: *The walls are insulated against noise.* ● (*figurative*) *This industry has been insulated from the effects of competition.* –insulation /,ɪnsju'leɪʃn/ **noun** [U]

★**insult**[1] /ɪn'sʌlt/ **verb** [T] to speak or act rudely to sb: *I felt very insulted when I didn't even get an answer to my letter.* ● *He was thrown out of the hotel for insulting the manager.*

insult[2] /'ɪnsʌlt/ **noun** [C] a rude remark or action: *The drivers were standing in the road yelling insults at each other.*

insulting /ɪn'sʌltɪŋ/ **adj** insulting (to sb/sth)

i

making sb feel offended: *insulting behaviour/ remarks* ● *That poster is insulting to women.*

insuperable /ɪnˈsuːpərəbl/ *adj* (*formal*) (used about a problem, etc) impossible to solve

★**insurance** /ɪnˈʃɔːrəns/ *noun* **1** [U] insurance (against sth) an arrangement with a company in which you pay them regular amounts of money and they agree to pay the costs if, for example, you die or are ill, or if you lose or damage sth: *Builders should always have insurance against personal injury.*

➤ We take out an insurance policy. An insurance premium is the regular amount you pay to the insurance company. We can take out life, health, car, travel and household insurance.

2 [U] the business of providing insurance: *He works in insurance.* **3** [U,sing] (an) insurance (against sth) something you do to protect yourself (against sth unpleasant): *Many people take vitamin pills as an insurance against illness.*

★**insure** /ɪnˈʃɔː/ *verb* [T] **1** insure yourself/sth (against/for sth) to buy or to provide insurance: *They insured the painting for £10000 against damage or theft.* **2** (*US*) = **ENSURE**

insurmountable /ˌɪnsəˈmaʊntəbl/ *adj* (*formal*) (used about a problem, etc) impossible to solve ●➤ Look at **surmountable**.

insurrection /ˌɪnsəˈrekʃn/ *noun* [C,U] (*formal*) violent action against the rulers of a country or the government

intact /ɪnˈtækt/ *adj* (not before a noun) complete; not damaged: *Very few of the buildings remain intact following the earthquake.*

intake /ˈɪnteɪk/ *noun* [C, usually sing] **1** the amount of food, drink, etc that you take into your body: *The doctor told me to cut down my alcohol intake.* **2** the (number of) people who enter an organization or institution during a certain period: *This year's intake of students is down 10%.* **3** the act of taking sth into your body, especially breath

intangible /ɪnˈtændʒəbl/ *adj* difficult to describe, understand or measure: *The benefits of good customer relations are intangible.* ●➤ opposite **tangible**

integral /ˈɪntɪɡrəl/ *adj* **1** integral (to sth) necessary in order to make sth complete: *Spending a year in France is an integral part of the university course.* **2** including sth as a part: *The car has an integral CD player.*

integrate /ˈɪntɪɡreɪt/ *verb* **1** [T] integrate sth (into sth); integrate A and B/integrate A with B to join things so that they become one thing or work together: *The two small schools were integrated into one large one.* ● *These programmes will integrate with your existing software.* **2** [I,T] integrate (sb) (into/with sth) to join in and become part of a group or community, or to make sb do this: *It took Amir a while to integrate into his new school.* ●➤ Look at **segregate**. –integration /ˌɪntɪˈɡreɪʃn/

noun [U]: *racial integration* ●➤ Look at **segregation**.

integrity /ɪnˈteɡrəti/ *noun* [U] the quality of being honest and having strong moral principles: *He's a person of great integrity who will say exactly what he thinks.*

intellect /ˈɪntəlekt/ *noun* **1** [U] the power of the mind to think and to learn: *a woman of considerable intellect* **2** [C] an extremely intelligent person: *He was one of the most brilliant intellects of his time.*

★**intellectual**¹ /ˌɪntəˈlektʃuəl/ *adj* **1** (only before a noun) connected with a person's ability to think logically and to understand things: *The boy's intellectual development was very advanced for his age.* **2** (used about a person) enjoying activities in which you have to think deeply about sth –intellectually *adv*

intellectual² /ˌɪntəˈlektʃuəl/ *noun* [C] a person who enjoys thinking deeply about things

★**intelligence** /ɪnˈtelɪdʒəns/ *noun* [U] **1** the ability to understand, learn and think: *a person of normal intelligence* ● *an intelligence test* **2** important information about an enemy country: *to receive intelligence about sb*

★**intelligent** /ɪnˈtelɪdʒənt/ *adj* having or showing the ability to understand, learn and think; clever: *All their children are very intelligent.* ● *an intelligent question* –intelligently *adv*

intelligible /ɪnˈtelɪdʒəbl/ *adj* (used especially about speech or writing) possible or easy to understand ●➤ opposite **unintelligible**

★**intend** /ɪnˈtend/ *verb* [T] **1** intend to do sth/ doing sth to plan or mean to do sth: *I'm afraid I spent more money than I had intended.* ● *I certainly don't intend to wait here all day!* ● *They had intended staying in Wales for two weeks but the weather was so bad that they left after one.* ●➤ noun **intention 2** intend sth for sb/sth; intend sb to do sth to plan, mean or make sth for a particular person or purpose: *You shouldn't have read that letter – it wasn't intended for you.* ● *I didn't intend you to have all the work.*

★**intense** /ɪnˈtens/ *adj* very great, strong or serious: *intense heat/cold/pressure* ● *intense anger/interest/desire* –intensely *adv*: *They obviously dislike each other intensely.* –intensity /-səti/ *noun* [U]: *I wasn't prepared for the intensity of his reaction to the news.*

intensify /ɪnˈtensɪfaɪ/ *verb* [I,T] (*pres part* **intensifying**; *3rd pers sing pres* **intensifies**; *pt, pp* **intensified**) to become or to make sth greater or stronger: *The government has intensified its anti-smoking campaign.* ● *Fighting in the region has intensified.* –intensification /ɪnˌtensɪfɪˈkeɪʃn/ *noun* [U]

intensive /ɪnˈtensɪv/ *adj* **1** involving a lot of work or care in a short period of time: *an intensive investigation/course* **2** (used about methods of farming) aimed at producing as much food as possible from the land or money available: *intensive agriculture* –intensively *adv*

in,tensive 'care noun [U] special care in hospital for patients who are very seriously ill or injured; the department that gives this care: *She was in intensive care for a week after the crash.*

intent[1] /ɪn'tent/ adj **1** intent (on/upon sth) showing great attention: *She was so intent upon her work that she didn't hear me come in.* **2** intent on/upon sth/doing sth determined to do sth: *He's always been intent on making a lot of money.* –intently adv

intent[2] /ɪn'tent/ noun [U] (*formal*) what sb intends to do; intention: *He was charged with possession of a gun with intent to commit a robbery.* ● *to do sth with evil/good intent*

IDIOM **to/for all intents and purposes** in effect, even if not completely true: *When they scored their fourth goal the match was, to all intents and purposes, over.*

★**intention** /ɪn'tenʃn/ noun [C,U] (an) intention (of doing sth/to do sth) what sb intends or means to do; a plan or purpose: *Our intention was to leave early in the morning.* ● *I have no intention of staying indoors on a nice sunny day like this.* ● *I borrowed the money with the intention of paying it back the next day.*

★**intentional** /ɪn'tenʃənl/ adj done on purpose, not by chance: *I'm sorry I took your jacket – it wasn't intentional!* •➤ synonym **deliberate** •➤ opposite **unintentional** or **inadvertent** –intentionally /-ʃənəli/ adv: *I can't believe the boys broke the window intentionally.*

interact /ˌɪntər'ækt/ verb [I] **1** interact (with sb) (used about people) to communicate or mix with sb, especially while you work, play or spend time together: *He is studying the way children interact with each other at different ages.* **2** (of two things) to have an effect on each other –interaction noun [U,C] interaction (between/with sb/sth): *There is a need for greater interaction between the two departments.*

interactive /ˌɪntər'æktɪv/ adj **1** that involves people working together and having an influence on each other: *interactive language-learning techniques* **2** (*computing*) involving direct communication both ways, between the computer and the person using it: *interactive computer games*

intercept /ˌɪntə'sept/ verb [T] to stop or catch sb/sth that is moving from one place to another: *Detectives intercepted him at the airport.* –interception noun [U,C]

interchangeable /ˌɪntə'tʃeɪndʒəbl/ adj interchangeable (with sth) able to be used in place of each other without making any difference to the way sth works: *Are these two words interchangeable* (= do they have the same meaning)? –interchangeably /-əbli/ adv

intercom /'ɪntəkɒm/ noun [C] a system of communication by radio or telephone inside an office, plane, etc; the device you press or switch on to start using this system

interconnect /ˌɪntəkə'nekt/ verb [I,T] interconnect (A) (with B); interconnect A and B to connect similar things; to be connected to similar things: *electronic networks which interconnect thousands of computers around the world*

intercontinental /ˌɪntəˌkɒntɪ'nentl/ adj between continents: *intercontinental flights*

intercourse /'ɪntəkɔːs/ = **sex**(3)

interdependent /ˌɪntədɪ'pendənt/ adj depending on each other: *Exercise and good health are generally interdependent.* ● *interdependent economies/organizations* –interdependence noun [U]

★**interest**[1] /'ɪntrəst/ noun **1** [U,sing] an interest (in sb/sth) a desire to learn or hear more about sb/sth or to be involved with sb/sth: *She's begun to show a great interest in politics.* ● *I wish he'd take more interest in his children.* ● *Don't lose interest now!* **2** [U] the quality that makes sth interesting: *I thought this article might be of interest to you.* ● *Computers hold no interest for me.* ● *places of historical interest* **3** [C, usually pl] something that you enjoy doing or learning about: *What are your interests and hobbies?* **4** [U] interest (on sth) the money that you pay for borrowing money from a bank, etc or the money that you earn when you keep money in a bank, etc: *We pay 6% interest on our mortgage at the moment.* ● *The interest rate has never been so high/low.* ● *Some companies offer interest-free loans.*

IDIOMS **have/with sb's interests at heart** to want sb to be happy and successful, even though your actions may not show it: *Don't be angry with your father – you know he has your best interests at heart.*

in sb's interest(s) to sb's advantage: *Using lead-free petrol is in the public interest.*

in the interest(s) of sth in order to achieve or protect sth: *In the interest(s) of safety, please fasten your seat belts.*

★**interest**[2] /'ɪntrəst/ verb [T] to make sb want to learn or hear more about sth or to become involved in sth: *It might interest you to know that I didn't accept the job.* ● *The subject of the talk was one that interests me greatly.*

PHRASAL VERB **interest sb in sth** to persuade sb to buy, have, do sth: *Can I interest you in our new brochure?*

★**interested** /'ɪntrəstɪd/ adj **1** (not before a noun) interested (in sth/sb); interested in doing sth; interested to do sth wanting to know or hear more about sth/sb; enjoying or liking sth/sb: *They weren't interested in my news at all!* ● *I'm really not interested in going to university.* ● *I was interested to hear that you've got a new job. Where is it?* •➤ opposite **uninterested**

➤ If you like what you are doing, and want to know or hear more, then you are **interested** in it. The person or thing that makes you feel like this is **interesting**.

2 (only *before* a noun) involved in or affected by sth; in a position to gain from sth: *As an interested party* (= a person directly involved)*, I was not allowed to vote.* •➤ opposite **disinterested**

i

★**interesting** /'ɪntrəstɪŋ; -trest-/ adj interesting (to do sth); interesting that... enjoyable and entertaining; holding your attention: *an interesting person/book/idea/job* • *It's always interesting to hear about the customs of other societies.* • *It's interesting that Luisa chose Peru for a holiday.* –interestingly adv

★**interfere** /ˌɪntə'fɪə/ verb [I] **1** interfere (in sth) to get involved in a situation which does not involve you and where you are not wanted: *You shouldn't interfere in your children's lives – let them make their own decisions.* **2** interfere (with sb/sth) to prevent sth from succeeding or to slow down the progress that sb/sth makes: *Every time the telephone rings it interferes with my work.* • *She never lets her private life interfere with her career.* **3** interfere (with sth) to touch or change sth without permission: *Many people feel that scientists shouldn't interfere with nature.* –interfering adj

interference /ˌɪntə'fɪərəns/ noun [U] **1** interference (in sth) the act of getting involved in a situation that does not involve you and where you are not wanted: *I left home because I couldn't stand my parents' interference in my affairs.* **2** extra noise (because of other signals or bad weather) that prevents you from receiving radio, television or telephone signals clearly

interim[1] /'ɪntərɪm/ adj (only *before* a noun) not final or lasting; temporary until sb/sth more permanent is found: *an interim arrangement* • *The deputy head teacher took over in the interim period until a replacement could be found.*

interim[2] /'ɪntərɪm/ noun
IDIOM in the interim in the time between two things happening; until a particular event happens

★**interior** /ɪn'tɪəriə/ noun **1** [C, usually sing] the inside part of sth: *I'd love to see the interior of the castle.* • *interior walls* ••► opposite **exterior 2 the interior** [sing] the central part of a country or continent that is a long way from the coast **3 the Interior** [sing] a country's own news and affairs that do not involve other countries: *the Department of the Interior*

in,terior de'sign noun [U] the art or job of choosing colours, furniture, carpets, etc to decorate the inside of a house –interior designer noun [C]

interjection /ˌɪntə'dʒekʃn/ noun [C] (*grammar*) a word or phrase that is used to express surprise, pain, pleasure, etc (for example Oh!, Hurray! or Wow!) ••► synonym **exclamation**

interlude /'ɪntəlu:d/ noun [C] a period of time between two events or activities: *They finally met again after an interlude of 20 years.* ••► Look at the note at **interval**.

intermarry /ˌɪntə'mæri/ verb (*pres part* **intermarrying**; *3rd pers sing pres* **intermarries**; *pt, pp* **intermarried**) [I] to marry sb from a different religion, culture, country, etc –intermarriage /ˌɪntə'mærɪdʒ/ noun [U]

intermediary /ˌɪntə'mi:diəri/ noun [C] (*pl* **intermediaries**) an intermediary (between A and B) a person or an organization that helps two people or groups to reach an agreement, by being a means of communication between them

★**intermediate** /ˌɪntə'mi:diət/ adj **1** situated between two things in position, level, etc: *an intermediate step/stage in a process* **2** having more than a basic knowledge of sth but not yet advanced; suitable for sb who is at this level: *an intermediate student/book/level*

interminable /ɪn'tɜ:mɪnəbl/ adj lasting for a very long time and therefore boring or annoying: *an interminable delay/wait/speech* ••► synonym **endless** –interminably /-əbli/ adv

intermission /ˌɪntə'mɪʃn/ noun [C] (*especially US*) a short period of time separating the parts of a film, play, etc ••► Look at the note at **interval**.

intermittent /ˌɪntə'mɪtənt/ adj stopping for a short time and then starting again several times: *There will be intermittent showers.* –intermittently adv

intern /ɪn'tɜ:n/ verb [T] (*formal*) intern sb (in sth) (usually passive) to keep sb in prison for political reasons, especially during a war –internment noun [U]

★**internal** /ɪn'tɜ:nl/ adj **1** (only *before* a noun) of or on the inside (of a place, person or object): *He was rushed to hospital with internal injuries.* **2** happening or existing inside a particular organization: *an internal exam* (= one arranged and marked inside a particular school or college) • *an internal police inquiry* **3** (used about political or economic affairs) inside a country; not abroad: *a country's internal affairs/trade/markets* • *an internal flight* ••► opposite **external** –internally /-nəli/ adv: *This medicine is not to be taken internally* (= not swallowed).

★**international** /ˌɪntə'næʃnəl/ adj involving two or more countries: *an international agreement/flight/football match* • *international trade/law/sport* ••► Look at **local**, **national** and **regional**. –internationally /-nəli/ adv

★**the Internet** /'ɪntənet/ (also **the Net**) noun [sing] (*computing*) the international system of computers that makes it possible for you to see information from all around the world on your computer and to send information to other computers: *I read about it on the Internet.*

➤ Compare **intranet**.

★**interpret** /ɪn'tɜ:prɪt/ verb **1** [T] interpret sth (as sth) to explain or understand the meaning of sth: *Your silence could be interpreted as arrogance.* • *How would you interpret this part of the poem?* ••► opposite **misinterpret 2** [I] interpret (for sb) to translate what sb is saying into another language as you hear it: *He can't speak much English so he'll need somebody to interpret for him.*

interpretation /ɪnˌtɜ:prɪ'teɪʃn/ noun [C,U]

1 an explanation or understanding of sth: *What's your interpretation of these statistics?* • *What he meant by that remark is* **open to interpretation** (= it can be explained in different ways). **2** the way an actor or musician chooses to perform or understand a character or piece of music: *a modern interpretation of 'Hamlet'*

interpreter /ɪnˈtɜːprɪtə/ **noun** [C] a person whose job is to translate what sb is saying immediately into another language: *The president spoke through an interpreter.* •➤ Look at **translator**.

interrelate /ˌɪntərɪˈleɪt/ **verb** [I,T] (usually passive) (*formal*) (used about two or more things) to connect or be connected very closely so that each has an effect on the other –**interrelated** adj

interrogate /ɪnˈterəgeɪt/ **verb** [T] **interrogate sb (about sth)** to ask sb a lot of questions over a long period of time, especially in an aggressive way: *The prisoner was interrogated for six hours.* –**interrogator** noun [C] –**interrogation** /ɪnˌterəˈgeɪʃn/ **noun** [C,U]: *The prisoner broke down under interrogation and confessed.*

interrogative[1]   /ˌɪntəˈrɒgətɪv/   adj **1** (*formal*) asking a question; having the form of a question: *an interrogative tone/ gesture/remark* **2** (*grammar*) used in questions: *an interrogative sentence/pronoun/ determiner/adverb*

interrogative[2]   /ˌɪntəˈrɒgətɪv/   **noun** [C] (*grammar*) a question word: *'Who', 'what' and 'where' are interrogatives.*

★**interrupt** /ˌɪntəˈrʌpt/ **verb 1** [I,T] **interrupt (sb/sth) (with sth)** to say or do sth that makes sb stop what he/she is saying or doing: *He kept interrupting me with silly questions.* **2** [T] to stop the progress of sth for a short time: *The programme was interrupted by an important news flash.*

interruption /ˌɪntəˈrʌpʃn/ **noun** [U,C] the act of interrupting sb/sth; the person or thing that interrupts sb/sth: *I need to work for a few hours without interruption.* • *I've had so many interruptions this morning that I've done nothing!*

intersect /ˌɪntəˈsekt/ **verb** [I,T] (used about roads, lines, etc) to meet or cross each other: *The lines intersect at right angles.*

intersection /ˌɪntəˈsekʃn/ **noun** [C] the place where two or more roads, lines, etc meet or cross each other

intersperse /ˌɪntəˈspɜːs/ **verb** [T] (usually passive) to put things at various points in sth: *He interspersed his speech with jokes.*

intertwine /ˌɪntəˈtwaɪn/ **verb** [I,T] if two things intertwine or if you intertwine them, they become very closely connected and difficult to separate: *His interests in business and politics were closely intertwined.*

★**interval** /ˈɪntəvl/ **noun** [C] **1** a period of time between two events: *There was a long interval between sending the letter and getting a reply.* **2** a short break separating the different parts of a play, film, concert, etc **3** [usually pl] a short period during which sth different

happens from what is happening for the rest of the time: *There'll be a few* **sunny intervals** *between the showers today.*

> Some words that have a similar meaning to interval are **intermission**, **break**, **recess**, **interlude** and **pause**. In British English we use **interval** for a break in a performance. The US word is **intermission**. A **break** is especially used in connection with periods of work or study, for example **a lunch/tea break** in an office, factory or school: *The children play outside in the breaks at school.* • *You've worked so hard you've earned a break.* In US English a break at school is called **(a) recess**. In British English **recess** is a longer period of time when work or business stops, especially in Parliament or the law courts: *Parliament is in recess.* • *the summer recess.* An **interlude** is a short period of time that passes between two events, during which something different happens: *a peaceful interlude in the fighting* and a **pause** is a short temporary stop in action or speech: *After a moment's pause, she answered.*

IDIOM **at intervals** with time or spaces between: *I write home* **at regular intervals.** • *Plant the trees at two-metre intervals.*

intervene /ˌɪntəˈviːn/ **verb** [I] **1 intervene (in sth)** to act in a way that prevents sth happening or influences the result of sth: *She would have died if the neighbours hadn't intervened.* • *to intervene in a dispute* **2** to interrupt sb who is speaking in order to say sth **3** (used about events, etc) to happen in a way that delays sth or stops it from happening: *If no further problems intervene we should be able to finish in time.* –**intervention** /ˌɪntəˈvenʃn/ **noun** [U,C] **intervention (in sth)**: *military intervention in the crisis*

intervening /ˌɪntəˈviːnɪŋ/ **adj** (only *before* a noun) coming or existing between two events, dates, objects, etc: *the intervening years/days/months*

★**interview**[1] /ˈɪntəvjuː/ **noun** [C] **1** an **interview (for sth)** a meeting at which sb is asked questions to find out if he/she is suitable for a job, course of study, etc: *to attend an interview* **2** an **interview (with sb)** a meeting at which a journalist asks sb questions in order to find out his/her opinion, etc: *There was an interview with the Prime Minister on television last night.* • *The actress refused to* **give an interview** (= answer questions).

★**interview**[2] /ˈɪntəvjuː/ **verb** [T] **1 interview sb (for sth)** to ask sb questions to find out if he/she is suitable for a job, course of study, etc: *How many applicants did you interview for the job?* **2 interview sb (about sth)** to ask sb questions about his/her opinions, private life, etc especially on the radio or television or for a newspaper, magazine, etc **3 interview sb (about sth)** to ask sb questions at a private meeting: *The police are waiting to interview the injured girl.*

interviewee /ˌɪntəvjuːˈiː/ **noun** [C] a person who is questioned in an interview

interviewer /'ɪntəvjuːə/ noun [C] a person who asks the questions in an interview

intestine /ɪn'testɪn/ noun [C,usually pl] the tube in your body that carries food away from your stomach to the place where it leaves your body ••> **Gut** is a less formal word. ••> picture on page C5 –intestinal /ɪn'testɪnl; ˌɪnte'staɪnl/ adj

intimacy /'ɪntɪməsi/ noun [U] the state of having a close personal relationship with sb: *Their intimacy grew over the years.*

intimate /'ɪntɪmət/ adj **1** (used about people) having a very close relationship: *They're intimate friends.* **2** very private and personal: *They told each other their most intimate thoughts and secrets.* **3** (used about a place, an atmosphere, etc) quiet and friendly: *I know an intimate little restaurant we could go to.* **4** very detailed: *He's lived here all his life and has an intimate knowledge of the area.* –intimately adv

intimidate /ɪn'tɪmɪdeɪt/ verb [T] intimidate sb (into sth/doing sth) to frighten or threaten sb, often in order to make him/her do sth: *She refused to be intimidated by their threats.* –intimidating adj: *The teacher had rather an intimidating manner.* –intimidation /ɪnˌtɪmɪ'deɪʃn/ noun [U]: *The rebel troops controlled the area by intimidation.*

★**into** /'ɪntə; *before vowels* 'ɪntə; 'ɪntuː/ prep **1** moving to a position inside or in sth: *Come into the house.* ● *I'm going into town.* ••> opposite **out of** (1) **2** in the direction of sth: *Please speak into the microphone.* ● *At this point we were driving into the sun and had to shade our eyes.* **3** to a point at which you hit sth: *I backed the car into a wall.* ● *She walked into a glass door.* **4** showing a change from one thing to another: *We're turning the spare room into a study.* ● *She changed into her jeans.* ● *Translate the passage into German.* **5** concerning or involving sth: *an inquiry into safety procedures* **6** used when you are talking about dividing numbers: *7 into 28 goes 4 times*

IDIOM be into sth (*spoken*) to be very interested in sth, for example as a hobby: *I'm really into canoeing.*

intolerable /ɪn'tɒlərəbl/ adj too bad, unpleasant or difficult to bear or accept: *The living conditions were intolerable.* ● *intolerable pain* ••> synonym **unbearable** ••> opposite **tolerable** ••> verb **tolerate** –intolerably /-əbli/ adv

intolerant /ɪn'tɒlərənt/ adj intolerant (of sb/sth) not able to accept behaviour or opinions that are different from your own; finding sb/sth too unpleasant to bear: *She's very intolerant of young children.* ••> opposite **tolerant** –intolerance noun [U] ••> opposite **tolerance** –intolerantly adv

intonation /ˌɪntə'neɪʃn/ noun [C,U] the rise and fall of your voice while you are speaking ••> synonym **inflection**

intoxicated /ɪn'tɒksɪkeɪtɪd/ adj (*formal*)

1 having had too much alcohol to drink; drunk **2** very excited and happy: *She was intoxicated by her success.* –intoxication /ɪnˌtɒksɪ'keɪʃn/ noun [U]

intranet /'ɪntrənet/ noun [C] (*computing*) a system of computers inside an organization that makes it possible for people who work there to look at the same information and to send information to each other

> Compare **the Internet**.

intransitive /ɪn'trænsətɪv/ adj (*grammar*) (used about a verb) used without an object ••> opposite **transitive**

> Intransitive verbs are marked [I] in this dictionary. For more information about intransitive verbs, look at the **Quick Grammar Reference** section.

–intransitively adv

intrepid /ɪn'trepɪd/ adj without any fear of danger: *an intrepid climber*

intricacy /'ɪntrɪkəsi/ noun **1** intricacies [pl] the intricacies of sth the complicated parts or details of sth: *It's difficult to understand all the intricacies of the situation.* **2** [U] the quality of having complicated parts, details or patterns

intricate /'ɪntrɪkət/ adj having many small parts or details put together in a complicated way: *an intricate pattern* ● *The story has an intricate plot.* –intricately adv

intrigue¹ /ɪn'triːg/ verb [T] to make sb very interested and wanting to know more: *I was intrigued by the way he seemed to know all about us already.* –intriguing adj: *an intriguing story*

intrigue² /'ɪntriːg/ noun [C,U] secret plans to do sth, especially sth bad: *The film is about political intrigues against the government.* ● *His new novel is full of intrigue and suspense.*

intrinsic /ɪn'trɪnzɪk/ adj (only *before* a noun) belonging to sth as part of its nature; basic: *The object is of no intrinsic value* (= the material it is made of is not worth anything). –intrinsically /-kli/ adv

★**introduce** /ˌɪntrə'djuːs/ verb [T] **1** introduce sth (in/into sth) to bring in sth new, use sth, or take sth to a place for the first time: *The new law was introduced in 1991.* ● *The company is introducing a new range of cars this summer.* ● *Goats were first introduced to the island in the 17th century.* **2** introduce sb (to sb) to tell two or more people who have not met before what each others' names are: *'Who's that girl over there?' 'Come with me and I'll introduce you to her.'* **3** introduce yourself (to sb) to tell sb you have met for the first time what your name is: *He just walked over and introduced himself to me.* **4** introduce sb to sth to make sb begin to learn about sth or do sth for the first time: *This pamphlet will introduce you to the basic aims of our society.* **5** to be the first or main speaker on a radio or television programme telling the audience who is going to speak, perform, etc: *May I introduce my first guest on* *the show tonight...*

➤ In Britain there are a number of different ways of introducing one person to another, depending on the occasion. In a formal introduction, we use a person's title followed by the surname. In an informal situation, or when introducing children, we use first names. In both formal and informal introductions we say 'this is', when referring to the people we are introducing, not 'he/she is' (*informal*): *'John, meet Mary.'* ● (*informal*): *'Mrs Smith, this is my daughter, Jane.'* ● (*formal*): *'May I introduce you. Dr Waters, this is Mr Jones. Mr Jones, Dr Waters.'* An informal response to an introduction is 'Hello' or 'Nice to meet you.' A formal response is 'How do you do?' The other person also replies: 'How do you do?' When people are introduced they often shake hands.

★**introduction** /ˌɪntrə'dʌkʃn/ **noun 1** [U] introduction of sth (into sth) the action of bringing in sth new; using sth or taking sth to a place for the first time: *the introduction of computers into the classroom* **2** [C, usually pl] the act of telling two or more people each others' names for the first time: *I think I'll get my husband to make/do the introductions – he's better at remembering names!* **3** [C] the first part of a book, a piece of written work or a talk which gives a general idea of what is going to follow **4** [C] an introduction (to sth) a book for people who are beginning to study a subject: *'An Introduction to English Grammar'* **5** [sing] an introduction to sth first experience of sth: *My first job – in a factory – was not a pleasant introduction to work.*

introductory /ˌɪntrə'dʌktəri/ **adj 1** happening or said at the beginning in order to give a general idea of what will follow: *an introductory speech/chapter/remark* **2** a first experience of a subject or activity: *introductory courses*

introvert /'ɪntrəvɜːt/ **noun** [C] a quiet, shy person who prefers to be alone than with other people ⋯➤ opposite **extrovert** –**introverted adj**

intrude /ɪn'truːd/ **verb** [I] intrude on/upon sb/sth to enter a place or situation without permission or when you are not wanted: *I'm sorry to intrude on your Sunday lunch but...*

intruder /ɪn'truːdə/ **noun** [C] a person who enters a place without permission and often secretly

intrusion /ɪn'truːʒn/ **noun** [C,U] (an) intrusion (on/upon/into sth) something that disturbs you or your life when you want to be private: *This was another example of press intrusion into the affairs of the royals.* –**intrusive** /ɪn'truːsɪv/ **adj**

intuition /ˌɪntjuː'ɪʃn/ **noun** [C,U] the feeling or understanding that makes you believe or know sth is true without being able to explain why: *She knew, by intuition, about his illness although he never mentioned it.*

–**intuitive** /ɪn'tjuːɪtɪv/ **adj** –**intuitively adv**: *Intuitively, she knew that he was lying.*

Inuit /'ɪnuːt/ **noun** [C] (*pl* **Inuit** or **Inuits**) (a member of) the race of people from northern Canada and parts of Alaska, Greenland, and eastern Siberia –**Inuit adj**

inundate /'ɪnʌndeɪt/ **verb** [T] (usually passive) **1** inundate sb (with sth) to give or send sb so many things that he/she cannot deal with them all: *We were inundated with applications for the job.* ⋯➤ synonym **swamp** **2** (*formal*) to cover an area of land with water: *After the heavy rains the fields were inundated.* ⋯➤ A less formal word is **flood**.

invade /ɪn'veɪd/ **verb 1** [I,T] to enter a country with an army in order to attack and take control of it: *When did the Romans invade Britain?* **2** [T] to enter in large numbers, often where sb/sth is not wanted: *The whole area has been invaded by tourists.* ⋯➤ noun **invasion** –**invader noun** [C]

invalid[1] /ɪn'vælɪd/ **adj 1** not legally or officially acceptable: *I'm afraid your passport is invalid.* **2** not correct according to reason; not based on all the facts: *an invalid argument* **3** (*computing*) (used about an instruction, etc) of a type that the computer cannot recognize: *an invalid command* ⋯➤ opposite **valid**

invalid[2] /'ɪnvəlɪd/ **noun** [C] a person who has been very ill for a long time and needs to be looked after

invaluable /ɪn'væljuəbl/ **adj** invaluable (to/for sb/sth) extremely useful: *invaluable help/information/support* ⋯➤ Be careful. Invaluable is not the opposite of valuable. The opposite of valuable is **valueless** or **worthless**.

invariable /ɪn'veəriəbl/ **adj** not changing

invariably /ɪn'veəriəbli/ **adv** almost always: *She invariably arrives late.*

★**invasion** /ɪn'veɪʒn/ **noun 1** [C,U] the action of entering another country with your army in order to take control of it: *the threat of invasion* **2** [C] the action of entering a place where you are not wanted and disturbing sb: *Such questions are an invasion of privacy.* ⋯➤ verb **invade**

★**invent** /ɪn'vent/ **verb** [T] **1** to think of or make sth for the first time: *When was the camera invented?* **2** to say or describe sth that is not true: *I realized that he had invented the whole story.* –**invention noun** [C]

★**invention** /ɪn'venʃn/ **noun 1** [C] a thing that has been made or designed by sb for the first time: *The microwave oven is a very useful invention.* **2** [U] the action or process of making or designing sth for the first time: *Books had to be written by hand before the invention of printing.* **3** [C,U] telling a story or giving an excuse that is not true: *It was obvious that his story about being robbed was (an) invention.*

inventive /ɪn'ventɪv/ **adj** having clever and original ideas –**inventiveness noun** [U]

inventory /'ɪnvəntri/ **noun** [C] (*pl* **inventories**) a detailed list, for example of all the furniture in a house: *The landlord is coming to **make an inventory** of the contents of the flat.*

invert /ɪnˈvɜːt/ *verb* [T] (*formal*) to put sth in the opposite order or position to the way it usually is: *What you see in a mirror is an inverted image of yourself.*

in,verted 'commas (*Brit*) = QUOTATION MARKS: *to put sth in inverted commas*

★**invest** /ɪnˈvest/ *verb* [I,T] **invest (sth) (in sth) 1** to put money into a bank, business, property, etc in the hope that you will make a profit: *Many firms have invested heavily in this project.* ● *I've invested all my money in the company.* **2** to spend money, time or energy on sth that you think is good or useful: *I'm thinking of investing in a computer.* ● *You have to invest a lot of time if you really want to learn a language well.* –**investor** *noun* [C]

★**investigate** /ɪnˈvestɪɡeɪt/ *verb* [I,T] to try to find out all the facts about sth: *A murder was reported and the police were sent to investigate.* ● *A group of experts are investigating the cause of the crash.* –**investigator** *noun* [C]

★**investigation** /ɪnˌvestɪˈɡeɪʃn/ *noun* [C,U] **(an) investigation (into sth)**: *The airlines are going to **carry out an investigation** into security procedures at airports.* ● *The matter is still **under investigation**.*

investigative /ɪnˈvestɪɡətɪv/ *adj* trying to find out all the facts about sb/sth: *investigative journalism*

investment /ɪnˈvestmənt/ *noun* **1** [U,C] **(an) investment (in sth)** the act of putting money in a bank, business, property, etc; the amount of money that you put in: *investment in local industry* ● *The company will have to **make an enormous investment** to computerize production.* **2** [C] (*informal*) a thing that you have bought: *This coat has been a good investment – I've worn it for three years.*

invigilate /ɪnˈvɪdʒɪleɪt/ *verb* [I,T] (*Brit*) to watch the people taking an exam to make sure that nobody is cheating –**invigilator** *noun* [C]

invigorate /ɪnˈvɪɡəreɪt/ *verb* [I,T] to make sb feel healthy, fresh and full of energy: *I felt invigorated after my run.* –**invigorating** *adj*

invincible /ɪnˈvɪnsəbl/ *adj* too strong or powerful to be defeated

invisible /ɪnˈvɪzəbl/ *adj* **invisible (to sb/sth)** that cannot be seen: *bacteria that are invisible to the naked eye* ••➤ opposite **visible** –**invisibility** /ɪnˌvɪzəˈbɪləti/ *noun* [U] –**invisibly** *adv*

invitation /ˌɪnvɪˈteɪʃn/ *noun* **1** [U] the act of inviting sb or being invited: *Entry is by invitation only.* ● *a letter of invitation* **2** [C] an **invitation to sb/sth (to sth/to do sth)** a written or spoken request to go somewhere or do sth: *Did you get an invitation to the conference?* ● *a wedding invitation* ••➤ You may **accept** an invitation, or you may **turn it down** or **decline** it.

★**invite** /ɪnˈvaɪt/ *verb* [T] **1 invite sb (to/for sth)** to ask sb to come somewhere or to do sth: *We invited all the family to the wedding.* ● *Successful applicants will be invited for interview next week.* **2** to make sth unpleasant likely to happen: *You're inviting trouble if you carry so much money around.*

PHRASAL VERBS **invite sb back 1** to ask sb to return with you to your home: *Shall we invite the others back for coffee after the meeting?* **2** to ask sb to come to your home a second time, or after you have been a guest at his/ her home

invite sb in to ask sb to come into your home

invite sb out to ask sb to go out somewhere with you: *We've been invited out to lunch by the neighbours.*

invite sb over/round (*informal*) to ask sb to come to your home: *I've invited Mohamed and his family round for lunch on Sunday.*

➤ Note that **ask** can be used instead of invite in all senses.

inviting /ɪnˈvaɪtɪŋ/ *adj* attractive and pleasant: *The smell of cooking was very inviting.*

invoice /ˈɪnvɔɪs/ *noun* [C] an official paper that lists goods or services that you have received and says how much you have to pay for them

involuntary /ɪnˈvɒləntri/ *adj* done without wanting or meaning to: *She gave an involuntary gasp of pain as the doctor inserted the needle.* ••➤ opposite **voluntary** or **deliberate** –**involuntarily** /ɪnˈvɒləntrəli/ *adv*

★**involve** /ɪnˈvɒlv/ *verb* [T] **1** (not used in the continuous tenses) to make sth necessary: *The job involves a lot of travelling.* **2** (not used in the continuous tenses) if a situation, an event or an activity involves sb/sth, he/ she/it takes part in it: *The story involves a woman who went on holiday with her child.* ● *More than 100 people were involved in the project.*

➤ Although this verb is not used in the continuous tenses, it is common to see the present participle (= *-ing* form): *There was a serious accident involving a stolen car.*

3 involve sb/sth in (doing) sth to cause sb/ sth to take part in or be concerned with sth: *Please don't involve me in your family arguments.* –**involvement** *noun* [C,U]: *The men deny any involvement in the robbery.*

involved /ɪnˈvɒlvd/ *adj* **1** difficult to understand; complicated: *The book has a very involved plot.* **2** (not before a noun) **involved (in sth)** closely connected with sth; taking an active part in sth: *I'm very involved in local politics.* **3** (not before a noun) **involved (with sb)** having a sexual relationship with sb: *She is involved with an older man.*

inward /ˈɪnwəd/ *adv, adj* **1** (also **inwards**) towards the inside or centre: *Stand in a circle facing inwards.* **2** inside your mind, not shown to other people: *my inward feelings* ••➤ opposite **outward**

inwardly /ˈɪnwədli/ *adv* in your mind; secretly: *He was inwardly relieved that they could not come.*

iodine /ˈaɪədiːn/ *noun* [U] a dark-coloured

substance that is found in sea water. A purple liquid containing iodine is sometimes used to clean cuts in your skin.

IOU /,aɪ əʊ 'ju:/ **abbr** I owe you; a piece of paper that you sign showing that you owe sb some money

IPA /,aɪ pi: 'eɪ/ **abbr** the International Phonetic Alphabet

IQ /,aɪ 'kju:/ **abbr** a measure of how intelligent sb is: *have a high/low IQ* ● *an IQ of 120*

IRA /,aɪ ɑːr 'eɪ/ **abbr** the Irish Republican Army

irate /aɪ'reɪt/ **adj** (*formal*) very angry

iris /'aɪrɪs/ **noun** [C] the coloured part of your eye

★**Irish** /'aɪrɪʃ/ **adj** from Ireland ••> Look at the section on geographical names at the back of this dictionary.

★**iron¹** /'aɪən/ **noun 1** [U] (*symbol* **Fe**) a hard strong metal that is used for making steel and is found in small quantities in food and in blood: *an iron bar* ● *iron ore* ● *The doctor gave me iron tablets.* ● (*figurative*) *The general has an iron* (= very strong) *will.* **2** [C] an electrical instrument with a flat bottom that is heated and used to smooth clothes after you have washed and dried them: *a steam iron*

iron

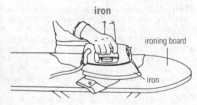

ironing board

iron

★**iron²** /'aɪən/ **verb** [I,T] to use an iron to make clothes, etc smooth: *Could you iron this dress for me?* ••> **Do the ironing** is often used instead of iron: *I usually do the ironing on Sunday.*

PHRASAL VERB **iron sth out** to get rid of any problems or difficulties that are affecting sth

ironic /aɪ'rɒnɪk/ (also **ironical** /aɪ'rɒnɪkl/) **adj 1** meaning the opposite of what you say: *Jeff sometimes offends people with his ironic sense of humour.* ••> Look at **sarcastic**. **2** (used about a situation) strange or amusing because it is unusual or unexpected: *It is ironic that the busiest people are often the most willing to help.* –**ironically** /-kli/ **adv**

ironing /'aɪənɪŋ/ **noun** [U] clothes, etc that need ironing or that have just been ironed: *a large pile of ironing* ••> Look at the note at **iron**.

'**ironing board noun** [C] a special table that is used for putting clothes on when we are making them smooth with an iron ••> picture at **iron**

irony /'aɪrəni/ **noun** (*pl* **ironies**) **1** [C,U] an unusual or unexpected part of a situation, etc that seems strange or amusing: *The irony was that he was killed in a car accident soon after the end of the war.* **2** [U] a way of

speaking that shows you are joking or that you mean the opposite of what you say: *'The English are such good cooks', he said with heavy irony.*

irrational /ɪ'ræʃənl/ **adj** not based on reason or clear thought: *an irrational fear of spiders* –**irrationality** /ɪ,ræʃə'næləti/ **noun** [U] –**irrationally** /-nəli/ **adv**

irreconcilable /ɪ,rekən'saɪləbl/ **adj** (*formal*) (used about people or their ideas and beliefs) so different that they cannot be made to agree –**irreconcilably** /-əbli/ **adv**

★**irregular** /ɪ'regjələ/ **adj 1** not having a shape or pattern that we recognize or can predict: *an irregular shape* **2** happening at times that you cannot predict: *His visits became more and more irregular.* **3** not allowed according to the rules or social customs: *It is highly irregular for a doctor to give information about patients without their permission.* **4** (*grammar*) not following the usual rules of grammar: *'Caught' is an irregular past tense form.* ••> opposite for senses 1, 2 and 4 **regular** –**irregularity** /ɪ,regjə'lærəti/ **noun** [C,U] (*pl* **irregularities**) –**irregularly adv**

irrelevancy /ɪ'reləvənsi/ **noun** [C] (*pl* **irrelevancies**) something that is not important because it is not connected with sth else

irrelevant /ɪ'reləvənt/ **adj** not connected with sth or important to it: *That's completely irrelevant to the subject under discussion.* ••> opposite **relevant** –**irrelevance noun** [U,C] –**irrelevantly adv**

irreparable /ɪ'repərəbl/ **adj** that cannot be repaired: *Irreparable damage has been done to the forests of Eastern Europe.* –**irreparably adv**

irreplaceable /,ɪrɪ'pleɪsəbl/ **adj** (used about sth very valuable or special) that cannot be replaced ••> opposite **replaceable**

irrepressible /,ɪrɪ'presəbl/ **adj** full of life and energy: *young people full of irrepressible good humour* –**irrepressibly** /-əbli/ **adv**

irresistible /,ɪrɪ'zɪstəbl/ **adj 1** so strong that it cannot be stopped or prevented: *an irresistible urge to laugh* **2** irresistible (to sb) very attractive: *He seems to think he's irresistible to women.* ••> verb **resist** –**irresistibly** /-əbli/ **adv**

irrespective of /,ɪrɪ'spektɪv əv/ **prep** not affected by: *Anybody can take part in the competition, irrespective of age.*

irresponsible /,ɪrɪ'spɒnsəbl/ **adj** not thinking about the effect your actions will have; not sensible: *It is irresponsible to let small children go out alone.* ••> opposite **responsible** –**irresponsibility** /,ɪrɪ,spɒnsə'bɪləti/ **noun** [U] –**irresponsibly** /-əbli/ **adv**

irreverent /ɪ'revərənt/ **adj** not feeling or showing respect: *This comedy takes an irreverent look at the world of politics.* –**irreverence noun** [U] –**irreverently adv**

irreversible /,ɪrɪ'vɜːsəbl/ **adj** that cannot be stopped or changed: *The disease can do irreversible damage to the body.* –**irreversibly adv**

irritable /'ɪrɪtəbl/ **adj** becoming angry easily:

i

to be/feel/get irritable –**irritability** /ˌɪrɪtə-'bɪləti/ **noun** [U] –**irritably** /-əbli/ **adv**

irritate /'ɪrɪteɪt/ **verb** [T] **1** to make sb angry; to annoy: *It really irritates me the way he keeps repeating himself.* **2** to cause a part of the body to be painful or sore: *I don't use soap because it irritates my skin.* –**irritation** /ˌɪrɪ'teɪʃn/ **noun** [C,U]

is → BE

★**Islam** /ɪz'lɑːm/ **noun** [U] the religion of Muslim people. Islam teaches that there is only one God and that Muhammad is His Prophet. –**Islamic adj**: *Islamic law*

★**island** /'aɪlənd/ **noun** [C] **1** a piece of land that is surrounded by water: *the Greek islands* **2** = TRAFFIC ISLAND

islander /'aɪləndə/ **noun** [C] a person who lives on a small island

isle /aɪl/ **noun** [C] an island: *the Isle of Wight* ● *the British Isles* •➤ Isle is most commonly used in names.

isn't *short for* IS NOT

isolate /'aɪsəleɪt/ **verb** [T] **isolate sb/sth (from sb/sth)** to put or keep sb/sth separate from other people or things: *Some farms were isolated by the heavy snowfalls.* ● *We need to isolate all the animals with the disease so that the others don't catch it.*

isolated /'aɪsəleɪtɪd/ **adj 1 isolated (from sb/sth)** alone or apart from other people or things: *an isolated village deep in the country-side* ● *I was kept isolated from the other patients.* **2** not connected with others; happening once: *Is this an isolated case or part of a general pattern?*

isolation /ˌaɪsə'leɪʃn/ **noun** [U] **isolation (from sb/sth)** the state of being separate and alone; the act of separating sb/sth: *He lived in complete isolation from the outside world.* ● *In isolation each problem does not seem bad, but together they are quite daunting.*

➤ Compare **loneliness** and **solitude**.

★**issue¹** /'ɪʃuː; 'ɪsjuː/ **noun 1** [C] a problem or subject for discussion: *I want to raise the issue of overtime pay at the meeting.* ● *The government cannot avoid the issue of homelessness any longer.* **2** [C] one in a series of things that are published or produced: *Do you have last week's issue of this magazine?* **3** [U] the act of publishing or giving sth to people: *the issue of blankets to the refugees* IDIOM **make an issue (out) of sth** to give too much importance to a small problem: *OK, we disagree on this but let's not make an issue of it.*

issue² /'ɪʃuː; 'ɪsjuː/ **verb 1** [T] to print and supply sth: *to issue a magazine/newsletter* **2** [T] to give or say sth to sb officially: *The new employees were issued with uniforms.* ● *to issue a visa* ● *The police will issue a statement later today.* **3** [I] (*formal*) to come or go out: *An angry voice issued from the loudspeaker.*

IT /ˌaɪ 'tiː/ **abbr** (*computing*) Information Technology

★**it** /ɪt/ **pron 1** (used as the subject or object of a verb, or after a preposition) the animal or thing mentioned earlier: *Look at that car. It's going much too fast.* ● *The children went up to the dog and patted it.* •➤ It can also refer to a baby whose sex you do not know: *Is it a boy or a girl?* **2** used for identifying a person: *It's your Mum on the phone.* ● *'Who's that?' 'It's the postman.'* ● *It's me!* ● *It's him!* **3** used in the position of the subject or object of a verb when the real subject or object is at the end of the sentence: *It's hard for them to talk about their problems.* ● *I think it doesn't really matter what time we arrive.* **4** used in the position of the subject of a verb when you are talking about time, the date, distance, the weather, etc: *It's nearly half past eight.* ● *It's Tuesday today.* ● *It's about 100 kilometres from London.* ● *It was very cold at the weekend.* ● *It's raining.* **5** used when you are talking about a situation: *It gets very crowded here in the summer.* ● *I'll come at 7 o'clock if it's convenient.* ● *It's a pity they can't come to the party.* **6** used for emphasizing a part of a sentence: *It was Jerry who said it, not me.* ● *It's your health I'm worried about, not the cost.*
IDIOM **that/this is it 1** that/this is the answer: *That's it! You've solved the puzzle!* **2** that/this is the end: *That's it, I've had enough! I'm going home!*

italics /ɪ'tælɪks/ **noun** [pl] a type of writing or printing in which the letters do not stand straight up: *All the example sentences in the dictionary are printed in italics.* –**italic adj**

itch /ɪtʃ/ **noun** [C] the feeling on your skin that makes you want to rub or scratch it: *I've got an itch on my back.* –**itch verb** [I]: *My nose is itching.* –**itchy adj**: *This shirt is itchy.* ● *My skin is all itchy.*

it'd /'ɪtəd/ *short for* IT HAD, IT WOULD

★**item** /'aɪtəm/ **noun** [C] **1** one single thing on a list or in a collection: *Some items arrived too late to be included in the catalogue.* ● *What is the first item on the agenda?* **2** one single article or object: *Can I pay for each item separately?* ● *an item of clothing* **3** a single piece of news: *There was an interesting item about Spain in yesterday's news.*

itemize (also **-ise**) /'aɪtəmaɪz/ **verb** [T] to make a list of all the separate items in sth: *an itemized telephone bill*

itinerant /aɪ'tɪnərənt/ **adj** (only *before* a noun) travelling from place to place: *an itinerant circus family*

itinerary /aɪ'tɪnərəri/ **noun** [C] (*pl* **itineraries**) a plan of a journey, including the route and the places that you will visit

it'll /'ɪtl/ *short for* IT WILL

it's /ɪts/ *short for* IT IS, IT HAS

➤ Be careful. **It's** is a short way of saying *it is* or *it has*. **Its** means 'belonging to it': *The bird has broken its wing.*

★**its** /ɪts/ **determiner** of or belonging to a thing: *The club held its Annual General Meeting last night.* •➤ Look at the note at **it's**.

★**itself** /ɪt'self/ **pron 1** used when the animal or thing that does an action is also affected by it: *The cat was washing itself.* ● *The company has got itself into financial difficulties.* **2** used to emphasize sth: *The building itself is beautiful, but it's in a very ugly part of town.*

IDIOM **(all) by itself 1** without being controlled by a person; automatically: *The central heating comes on by itself before we get up.* **2** alone: *The house stood all by itself on the hillside.* •➤ Look at the note at **alone**.

ITV /ˌaɪ tiː ˈviː/ *abbr* (*Brit*) Independent Television; the group of television companies that are paid for by advertising: *watch a film on ITV*

I've /aɪv/ *short for* I HAVE

ivory /ˈaɪvəri/ *noun* [U] the hard white substance that the long teeth (**tusks**) of an elephant are made of

ivy /ˈaɪvi/ *noun* [U] a climbing plant that has dark leaves with three or five points •➤ picture on page C2

J, j /dʒeɪ/ *noun* [C] (*pl* **J's**; **j's**) the tenth letter of the English alphabet: *'Jam' begins with (a) 'J'.*

jab¹ /dʒæb/ *verb* [I,T] jab sb/sth (with sth); jab sth into sb/sth to push at sb/sth with a sudden, rough movement, usually with sth sharp: *She jabbed me in the ribs with her elbow.* ● *The robber jabbed a gun into my back and ordered me to move.*

jab² /dʒæb/ *noun* [C] **1** a sudden rough push with sth sharp: *He **gave** me **a** jab in the ribs with the stick.* **2** (*informal*) the action of putting a drug, etc under sb's skin with a needle: *I'm going to the doctor's to **have a** flu **jab** today.* •➤ synonym **injection**

jack¹ /dʒæk/ *noun* [C] **1** a piece of equipment for lifting a car, etc off the ground, for example in order to change its wheel **2** the card between the ten and the queen in a pack of cards •➤ Look at the note and picture at **card**.

jack² /dʒæk/ *verb*
PHRASAL VERBS **jack** sth **in** (*slang*) to stop doing sth: *Jerry got fed up with his job and jacked it in.*
jack sth **up** to lift a car, etc using a jack: *We jacked the car up to change the wheel.*

★jacket /ˈdʒækɪt/ *noun* [C] a short coat with sleeves: *Do you have to wear a jacket and tie to work?* •➤ picture on page C6 •➤ Look at **life jacket**.

jacket po'tato *noun* [C] a potato that is cooked in the oven in its skin

jackknife /ˈdʒæknaɪf/ *verb* [I] (used about a lorry that is in two parts) to go out of control and bend suddenly in a dangerous way

the jackpot /ˈdʒækpɒt/ *noun* [C] the largest money prize that you can win in a game
IDIOM **hit the jackpot** → HIT¹

Jacuzzi™ /dʒəˈkuːzi/ *noun* [C] a special bath in which powerful movements of air make bubbles in the water

jaded /ˈdʒeɪdɪd/ *adj* tired and bored after doing the same thing for a long time without a break

jagged /ˈdʒægɪd/ *adj* rough with sharp points: *jagged rocks*

jaguar /ˈdʒægjuə/ *noun* [C] a large wild cat with black spots that comes from Central and South America •➤ picture at **lion**

jail¹ /dʒeɪl/ *noun* [C,U] (a) prison: *She was sent to jail for ten years.* •➤ Look at the note at **prison**.

jail² /dʒeɪl/ *verb* [T] to put sb in prison: *She was jailed for ten years.*

jailer /ˈdʒeɪlə/ *noun* [C] (*old-fashioned*) a person whose job is to guard prisoners

★jam¹ /dʒæm/ *noun* **1** [U] (*especially US* **jelly**) a sweet substance that you spread on bread, made by boiling fruit and sugar together: *a jar of raspberry jam* •➤ picture at **container**

➤ Note that jam made from oranges or lemons is called **marmalade**.

2 [C] a situation in which you cannot move because there are too many people or vehicles: *a traffic jam* **3** [C] (*informal*) a difficult situation: *We're in a bit of a jam without our passports or travel documents.*

jam² /dʒæm/ *verb* (**jamming**; **jammed**) **1** [T] jam sb/sth in, under, between, etc sth to push or force sb/sth into a place where there is not much room: *She managed to jam everything into her suitcase.* **2** [I,T] jam (sth) (up) to become or to make sth unable to move or work: *Something is jamming (up) the machine.* ● *The paper keeps jamming in the photocopier.* ● *I can't open the door. The lock has jammed.* **3** [T] jam sth (up) (with sb/sth) (usually passive) to fill sth with too many people or things: *The cupboard was **jammed full** of old newspapers and magazines.* ● *The suitcase was **jam-packed with** (= completely full of) designer clothes.* ● *The switchboard was jammed with calls from unhappy customers.* **4** [T] to send out signals in order to stop radio programmes, etc from being received or heard clearly
PHRASAL VERB **jam on the brakes/jam the brakes on** to stop a car suddenly by pushing hard on the controls (**brakes**) with your feet

Jan *abbr* January: *1 Jan 1993*

jangle /ˈdʒæŋgl/ *verb* [I,T] to make a noise like metal hitting against metal; to move sth so that it makes this noise: *The baby smiles if you jangle your keys.* ─**jangle** *noun* [U]

janitor /ˈdʒænɪtə/ (*US*) = CARETAKER

★January /ˈdʒænjuəri/ *noun* [U,C] (*abbr* **Jan**) the first month of the year, coming after December: *We're going skiing **in January**.* ● *last/next January* ● *We first met **on January 31st, 1989**.* ● *Christine's birthday is (on) January 17.* ● *Our wedding anniversary is at*

j

the end of January. • January mornings can be very dark in Britain. ••➤ We say 'on January the seventeenth' or 'on the seventeenth of January' or, in US English, 'January seventeenth'. In both British and US English, the months of the year are always written with a capital letter.

★ **jar¹** /dʒɑː/ **noun** [C] **1** a container with a lid, usually made of glass and used for keeping food, etc in: *a jam jar • a large storage jar for flour* **2** the food that a jar contains: *a jar of honey/jam/coffee*

jar² /dʒɑː/ **verb** (**jarring**; **jarred**) **1** [T] to hurt or damage sth as a result of a sharp knock: *He fell and jarred his back.* **2** [I] **jar (on sb/sth)** to have an unpleasant or annoying effect: *The dripping tap jarred on my nerves.*

jargon /ˈdʒɑːgən/ **noun** [U] special or technical words that are used by a particular group of people in a particular profession and that other people do not understand: *medical/scientific/legal/computer jargon*

jaundice /ˈdʒɔːndɪs/ **noun** [U] a disease that makes your skin and eyes yellow

javelin /ˈdʒævlɪn/ **noun 1** [C] a long stick with a pointed end that is thrown in sports competitions **2 the javelin** [sing] the event or sport of throwing the javelin as far as possible

jaw /dʒɔː/ **noun 1** [C] either of the two bones in your face that contain your teeth: *the lower/upper jaw* ••➤ picture on page C5 **2 jaws** [pl] the mouth (especially of a wild animal): *The lion came towards him with its jaws open.*

★ **jazz¹** /dʒæz/ **noun** [U] a style of music with a strong rhythm, originally of African American origin: *modern/traditional jazz* ••➤ Look at **classical**, **pop** and **rock**.

jazz² /dʒæz/ **verb**
PHRASAL VERB **jazz sth up** (*informal*) to make sth brighter, more interesting or exciting

★ **jealous** /ˈdʒeləs/ **adj 1** feeling upset or angry because you think that sb you like or love is showing interest in sb else: *Tim seems to get jealous whenever Sue speaks to another boy!* **2 jealous (of sb/sth)** feeling angry or sad because you want to be like sb else or because you want what sb else has: *He's always been jealous of his older brother. • I'm very jealous of your new car – how much did it cost?* ••➤ synonym **envious** –**jealously** adv –**jealousy** noun [C,U] (*pl* **jealousies**)

★ **jeans** /dʒiːnz/ **noun** [pl] trousers made of strong, usually blue, cotton cloth (**denim**): *These jeans are a bit too tight. • a pair of jeans*

Jeep™ /dʒiːp/ **noun** [C] a small, strong vehicle suitable for travelling over rough ground

jeer /dʒɪə/ **verb** [I,T] **jeer (at) sb/sth** to laugh or shout rude comments at sb/sth to show your lack of respect for him/her/it: *The spectators booed and jeered at the losing team.* –**jeer** noun [C,usually pl]: *The Prime Minister was greeted with jeers in the House of Commons today.*

jelly /ˈdʒeli/ **noun** (*pl* **jellies**) (*US* **Jell-O**™) **1** [C,U] a soft, solid brightly-coloured food that shakes when it is moved. Jelly is made from sugar and fruit juice and is eaten cold at the end of a meal, especially by children **2** [U] (*especially US*) a type of jam that does not contain any solid pieces of fruit
IDIOMS **be/feel like jelly** (used especially about the legs or knees) to feel weak because you are nervous, afraid, etc: *My legs felt like jelly before the exam.*
turn to jelly (used about the legs and knees) to suddenly become weak because of fear

jellyfish

jellyfish /ˈdʒelifɪʃ/ **noun** [C] (*pl* **jellyfish**) a sea animal with a soft colourless body and long thin parts that can sting you.

jeopardize (also **-ise**) /ˈdʒepədaɪz/ **verb** [T] to do sth that may damage sth or put it at risk: *He would never do anything to jeopardize his career.*

jeopardy /ˈdʒepədi/ **noun**
IDIOM **in jeopardy** in a dangerous position and likely to be lost or harmed: *The future of the factory and 15,000 jobs are in jeopardy.*

jerk¹ /dʒɜːk/ **verb** [I,T] to move or make sb/sth move with a sudden sharp movement: *She jerked the door open. • His head jerked back as the car suddenly set off.* –**jerky** adj –**jerkily** adv

jerk² /dʒɜːk/ **noun** [C] **1** a sudden sharp movement **2** (*especially US slang*) a stupid or annoying person

jersey /ˈdʒɜːzi/ **noun 1** [C] a piece of clothing made of wool that you wear over a shirt ••➤ **Jersey**, **jumper**, **pullover** and **sweater** are all words for the same piece of clothing. **2** [U] a soft thin material made of cotton or wool that is used for making clothes

Jesus /ˈdʒiːzəs/ = **CHRIST**

★ **jet** /dʒet/ **noun** [C] **1** a fast modern aeroplane **2** a fast, thin current of water, gas, etc coming out of a small hole

jet-ˈblack adj very dark black in colour

ˈjet engine noun [C] a powerful engine that makes planes fly by pushing out a current of hot air and gases at the back

ˈjet lag noun [U] the tired feeling that people often have after a long journey in a plane to a place where the local time is different –**ˈjet-lagged** adj

the ˈjet set noun [sing] the group of rich, successful and fashionable people (especially those who travel around the world a lot)

jetty /ˈdʒeti/ **noun** [C] (*pl* **jetties**) (*US* **dock**) a stone wall or wooden platform built out into the sea or a river where boats are tied and where people can get on and off them ••➤ synonym **landing stage** ••➤ picture on page C8

★**Jew** /dʒuː/ **noun** [C] a person whose family was originally from the ancient land of Israel or whose religion is Judaism –**Jewish adj**

★**jewel** /'dʒuːəl/ **noun 1** [C] a valuable stone (for example a diamond) **2** [pl] a piece of jewellery or an object that contains precious stones

jeweller (*US* **jeweler**) /'dʒuːələ/ **noun 1** [C] a person whose job is to buy, sell, make or repair jewellery and watches **2 the jeweller's** [sing] a shop where jewellery and watches are made, sold and repaired

jewellery

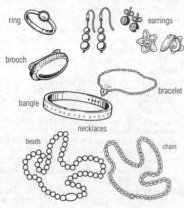

ring
earrings
brooch
bracelet
bangle
necklaces
beads
chain

jewellery (*US* **jewelry**) /'dʒuːəlri/ **noun** [U] objects such as rings, etc that are worn as personal decoration: *a piece of jewellery*

jig¹ /dʒɪg/ **noun** [C] a type of quick dance with jumping movements; the music for this dance

jig² /dʒɪg/ **verb** [I] (**jigging**; **jigged**) jig about/around to move about in an excited or impatient way

jiggle /'dʒɪgl/ **verb** [T] (*informal*) to move sth quickly from side to side: *She jiggled her car keys to try to distract the baby.*

jigsaw /'dʒɪgsɔː/ (also '**jigsaw puzzle**) **noun** [C] a picture on cardboard or wood that is cut into small pieces and has to be fitted together again ••➤ picture on page S2

jingle¹ /'dʒɪŋgl/ **noun 1** [sing] a ringing sound like small bells, made by metal objects gently hitting each other: *the jingle of coins* **2** [C] a short simple tune or song that is easy to remember and is used in advertising on television or radio

jingle² /'dʒɪŋgl/ **verb** [I,T] to make or cause sth to make a pleasant gentle sound like small bells ringing: *She jingled the coins in her pocket.*

jinx /dʒɪŋks/ **noun** [C,usually sing] (*informal*) bad luck; a person or thing that people believe brings bad luck to sb/sth –**jinx verb** [T]

–**jinxed adj**: *After my third accident in a month, I began to think I was jinxed.*

the jitters /'dʒɪtəz/ **noun** [pl] (*informal*) feelings of fear or worry, especially before an important event or before having to do sth difficult: *Just thinking about the exam* **gives me the jitters!**

jittery /'dʒɪtəri/ **adj** (*informal*) nervous or worried

Jnr (also **Jr**) /'dʒuːnɪə/ **abbr** (*especially US*) Junior: *Samuel P Carson, Jnr*

★**job** /dʒɒb/ **noun** [C] **1** the work that you do regularly to earn money: *She took/got a job as a waitress.* ● *A lot of people will* **lose** *their* **jobs** *if the factory closes.*

➤ We **look for**, **apply for** or **find** a job. A job can be **well-paid/highly-paid** or **badly-paid/low-paid**. A job can be **full-time** or **part-time**, **permanent** or **temporary**. **Job sharing** is becoming popular with people who want to work part-time.

••➤ Look at the note at **work¹**. **2** a task or a piece of work: *I always have a lot of jobs to do in the house at weekends.* ● *The garage has* **done a good/bad job** *on our car.* **3** [usually sing] a duty or responsibility: *It's not his job to tell us what we can and can't do.*

IDIOMS **do the job/trick** (*informal*) to get the result that is wanted: *This extra strong glue should do the job.*

have a hard job to do sth/doing sth ➔ **HARD¹**

it's a good job (*spoken*) it is a good or lucky thing: *It's a good job you reminded me – I had completely forgotten!*

just the job/ticket (*informal*) exactly what is needed in a particular situation: *This dress will be just the job for Helen's party.*

make a bad, good, etc job of sth to do sth badly, well, etc

make the best of a bad job ➔ **BEST³**

out of a job without paid work ••➤ A more formal word is **unemployed**.

jobless /'dʒɒbləs/ **adj 1** (usually used about large numbers of people) without paid work ••➤ synonym **unemployed 2 the jobless noun** [pl] people without paid work –**joblessness noun** [U] ••➤ synonym **unemployment**

jockey /'dʒɒki/ **noun** [C] a person who rides horses in races, especially as a profession ••➤ Look at **DJ**.

jodhpurs /'dʒɒdpəz/ **noun** [pl] special trousers that you wear for riding a horse ••➤ picture at **horse**

jog¹ /dʒɒg/ **verb** (**jogging**; **jogged**) **1** [I] to run slowly, especially as a form of exercise ••➤ When we talk about jogging for pleasure or exercise, it is more usual to say **go jogging**: *I go jogging most evenings.* **2** [T] to push or knock sb/sth slightly: *He jogged my arm and I spilled the milk.*

IDIOM **jog sb's memory** to say or do sth that makes sb remember sth

jog² /dʒɒg/ **noun** [sing] **1** a slow run as a form of exercise: *She goes for a jog before breakfast.* **2** a slight push or knock

jogger /'dʒɒgə/ *noun* [C] a person who goes jogging for exercise

★**join**¹ /dʒɔɪn/ *verb* **1** [T] join A to B; join A and B (together) to fasten or connect one thing to another: *The Channel Tunnel joins Britain to Europe.* ● *The two pieces of wood had been carefully joined together.* ● *We've knocked down the wall and joined the two rooms into one.* **2** [I,T] join (up) (with sb/sth) to meet or unite (with sb/sth) to form one thing or group: *Do the two rivers join (up) at any point?* ● *Where does this road join the motorway?* ● *Would you like to join us for a drink?* **3** [T] to become a member of a club or organization: *I've joined an aerobics class.* ● *He joined the company three months ago.* **4** [T] to take your place in sth or to take part in sth: *We'd better go and join the queue if we want to see the film.* ● *Come downstairs and join the party.* **5** [I,T] join (with) sb in sth/in doing sth/to do sth; join together in doing sth/to do sth to take part with sb (often in doing sth for sb else): *Everybody here joins me in wishing you the best of luck in your new job.* ● *The whole school joined together to sing the school song.*
IDIOM join forces (with sb) → FORCE¹
PHRASAL VERBS join in (sth/doing sth) to take part in an activity: *Everyone started singing but Frank refused to join in.*
join up to become a member of the army, navy or air force

join² /dʒɔɪn/ *noun* [C] a place where two things are fixed or connected: *He glued the handle back on so cleverly that you couldn't see the join.*

joiner /'dʒɔɪnə/ *noun* [C] a person who makes the wooden parts of a building •→ Look at **carpenter**.

★**joint**¹ /dʒɔɪnt/ *noun* [C] **1** a part of the body where two bones fit together and are able to bend **2** the place where two or more things are fastened or connected together, especially to form a corner **3** a large piece of meat that you cook whole in the oven: *a joint of lamb*

★**joint**² /dʒɔɪnt/ *adj* (only *before* a noun) shared or owned by two or more people: *Have you and your husband got a joint account?* (= a shared bank account) ● *a joint decision* –**jointly** *adv*

★**joke**¹ /dʒəʊk/ *noun* **1** [C] something said or done to make you laugh, especially a funny story: *to tell/crack jokes* ● *a dirty joke* (= about sex) ● *I'm sorry, I didn't get the joke* (= understand it).
➤ A **practical joke** is something you do to make a person look silly, not a joke that you tell.
2 [sing] a ridiculous person, thing or situation: *The salary he was offered was a joke!*
IDIOMS play a joke/trick on sb to trick sb in order to amuse yourself or other people
see the joke to understand what is funny about a joke or trick
take a joke to be able to laugh at a joke against yourself: *The trouble with Pete is he can't take a joke.*

joke² /dʒəʊk/ *verb* [I] **1** joke (with sb) (about sth) to say sth to make people laugh; to tell a funny story: *She spent the evening laughing and joking with her old friends.* **2** to say sth that is not true because you think it is funny: *I never joke about religion.* ● *Don't get upset. I was only joking!*
IDIOM you must be joking; you're joking (*spoken*) (used to express great surprise) you cannot be serious

joker /'dʒəʊkə/ *noun* [C] **1** a person who likes to tell jokes or play tricks **2** an extra card which can be used instead of any other one in some card games •→ picture at **card**

jolly /'dʒɒli/ *adj* happy

jolt¹ /dʒəʊlt/ *verb* [I,T] to move or make sb/sth move in a sudden rough way: *The lorry jolted along the bumpy track.* ● *The crash jolted all the passengers forward.*

jolt² /dʒəʊlt/ *noun* [usually sing] **1** a sudden movement: *The train stopped with a jolt.* **2** a sudden surprise or shock: *His sudden anger gave her quite a jolt.*

jostle /'dʒɒsl/ *verb* [I,T] to push hard against sb in a crowd

jot /dʒɒt/ *verb* (**jotting; jotted**)
PHRASAL VERB jot sth down to make a quick short note of sth: *Let me jot down your address.*

journal /'dʒɜːnl/ *noun* [C] **1** a newspaper or a magazine, especially one in which all the articles are about a particular subject or profession: *a medical/scientific journal* **2** a written account of what you have done each day: *Have you read his journal of the years he spent in India?* •→ Look at **diary**.

journalism /'dʒɜːnəlɪzəm/ *noun* [U] the profession of collecting and writing about news in newspapers and magazines or talking about it on the television or radio

★**journalist** /'dʒɜːnəlɪst/ *noun* [C] a person whose job is to collect and write about news in newspapers and magazines or to talk about it on the television or radio •→ Look at **reporter**.

★**journey** /'dʒɜːni/ *noun* [C] the act of travelling from one place to another, usually on land: *Did you have a good journey?* ● *a two-hour journey* ● *The journey to work takes me forty-five minutes.* ● *We'll have to break the journey* (= stop for a rest).
➤ A journey can include both air and sea travel but to refer specifically to a journey by air we say a **flight** and by sea we say a **voyage** or if it is for pleasure we say a **cruise**.
•→ Look at the note at **travel**.

jovial /'dʒəʊviəl/ *adj* (used about a person) happy and friendly

joy /dʒɔɪ/ *noun* **1** [U] a feeling of great happiness: *We'd like to wish you joy and success in your life together.* **2** [C] a person or thing that gives you great pleasure: *the joys of fatherhood* ● *That class is a joy to teach.* **3** [U] (*Brit informal*) (used in questions and negative sentences) success or satisfaction: *'I asked* *again if we could have seats with more leg-room but got no joy from the check-in clerk.'*

IDIOMS **jump for joy** → **JUMP¹**

sb's pride and joy → **PRIDE¹**

joyful /ˈdʒɔɪfl/ *adj* very happy: *a joyful occasion* –**joyfully** /-fəli/ *adv* –**joyfulness** *noun* [U]

joyless /ˈdʒɔɪləs/ *adj* unhappy: *a joyless marriage*

joyriding /ˈdʒɔraɪdɪŋ/ *noun* [U] the crime of stealing a car and driving it for pleasure, usually in a fast and dangerous way –**joyrider** *noun* [C] –**joyride** *noun* [C]

joystick /ˈdʒɔɪstɪk/ *noun* [C] a handle used for controlling movement on a computer, aircraft, etc

JP /ˌdʒeɪ ˈpiː/ *abbr* Justice of the Peace

Jr *abbr* = **JNR**

jubilant /ˈdʒuːbɪlənt/ *adj* (*formal*) extremely happy, especially because of a success: *The football fans were jubilant at their team's victory in the cup.*

jubilation /ˌdʒuːbɪˈleɪʃn/ *noun* [U] (*formal*) great happiness because of a success

jubilee /ˈdʒuːbɪliː/ *noun* [C] a special anniversary of an event that took place a certain number of years ago, and the celebrations that go with it: *It's the company's **golden jubilee** this year* (= it is fifty years since it was started).

> There is also a **silver** jubilee (25 years) and a **diamond** jubilee (60 years).

Judaism /ˈdʒuːdeɪɪzəm/ *noun* [U] the religion of the Jewish people

★**judge¹** /dʒʌdʒ/ *noun* [C] **1** a person in a court of law whose job is to decide how criminals should be punished and to make legal decisions: *The judge sentenced the man to three years in prison.* **2** a person who decides who has won a competition: *a panel of judges* **3** [usually sing] **a judge of sth** a person who has the ability or knowledge to give an opinion about sth: *You're a good judge of character – what do you think of him?*

★**judge²** /dʒʌdʒ/ *verb* **1** [I,T] to form or give an opinion about sb/sth based on the information you have: *Judging by/from what he said, his work is going well.* ● *It's difficult to judge how long the project will take.* ● *The party was judged a great success by everybody.* **2** [T] to decide the result or winner of a competition: *The head teacher will judge the competition.* **3** [T] to form an opinion about sb/sth, especially when you disapprove of him/her/it: *Don't judge him too harshly – he's had a difficult time.* **4** [I,T] to decide if sb is guilty or innocent in a court of law

★**judgement** (also **judgment**) /ˈdʒʌdʒmənt/ *noun* **1** [U] the ability to form opinions or to make sensible decisions: *He always shows excellent judgement in his choice of staff.* ● *to have good/poor/sound judgement* **2** [C,U] an opinion formed after carefully considering the information you have: *What, in your judgement, would be the best course of action?* **3** **judgment** [C] an official decision made by

a judge or a court of law: *The man collapsed when the judgment was read out in court.*

judicial /dʒuˈdɪʃl/ *adj* connected with a court of law, a judge or a legal judgment: *the judicial system*

judicious /dʒuˈdɪʃəs/ *adj* (used about a decision or an action) sensible and carefully considered; showing good judgement –**judiciously** *adv*

judo /ˈdʒuːdəʊ/ *noun* [U] a sport from Asia in which two people fight and try to throw each other to the ground ••> Look at **martial arts**.

jug (*US* pitcher)   pitcher   carafe

jug /dʒʌg/ (*US* **pitcher**) *noun* [C] a container with a handle used for holding or pouring liquids: *a milk jug* ● *a jug of water*

juggle /ˈdʒʌgl/ *verb* [I,T] **1 juggle (with sth)** to keep three or more objects such as balls in the air at the same time by throwing them one at a time and catching them quickly **2 juggle sth (with sth)** to try to deal with two or more important jobs or activities at the same time

juggler /ˈdʒʌglə/ *noun* [C] a person who juggles to entertain people

★**juice** /dʒuːs/ *noun* [C,U] **1** the liquid that comes from fruit and vegetables: *carrot/grapefruit/lemon juice* ● *I'll have an orange juice, please.* ••> picture on page C4 **2** the liquid that comes from a piece of meat when it is cooked: *You can use the juices of the meat to make gravy.* **3** the liquid in your stomach or another part of your body that deals with the food you eat: *gastric/digestive juices*

juicy /ˈdʒuːsi/ *adj* (**juicier**; **juiciest**) **1** containing a lot of juice: *juicy oranges* **2** (*informal*) (used about information) interesting because it is shocking: *juicy gossip*

jukebox /ˈdʒuːkbɒks/ *noun* [C] a machine in a cafe or bar, that plays music when money is put in

Jul *abbr* July: *4 Jul 1999*

★**July** /dʒuˈlaɪ/ *noun* [U,C] (*abbr* **Jul**) the seventh month of the year, coming after June

> To see how the months are used in sentences, look at the examples and the note at **January**.

jumble¹ /ˈdʒʌmbl/ *verb* [T] (usually passive) **jumble sth (up/together)** to mix things together in a confused and untidy way: *I must sort my clothes out – they're all jumbled up in the drawer.*

jumble² /ˈdʒʌmbl/ *noun* **1** [sing] an untidy group of things; a mess: *a jumble of papers/ideas* **2** [U] (*Brit*) a collection of old things for

j

a jumble sale: *Have you got any jumble you don't want?*

'jumble sale (*US* **'rummage sale**) *noun* [C] a sale of old things that people do not want any more. Clubs, churches, schools and other organizations hold jumble sales to get money.

jumbo¹ /'dʒʌmbəʊ/ *adj* (*informal*) (only *before* a noun) very large

jumbo² /'dʒʌmbəʊ/ *noun* [C] (*pl* **jumbos**) (also **jumbo 'jet**) a very large aircraft that can carry several hundred passengers

★**jump**¹ /dʒʌmp/ *verb* **1** [I] to move quickly into the air by pushing yourself up with your legs and feet, or by stepping off a high place: *to jump into the air/off a bridge/onto a chair* ● *How high can you jump?* ● *Jump up and down to keep warm.* ·➤ picture at **hop 2** [I] to move quickly and suddenly: *The telephone rang and she jumped up to answer it.* ● *A taxi stopped and we jumped in.* **3** [T] to get over sth by jumping: *The dog jumped the fence and ran off down the road.* **4** [I] to make a sudden movement because of surprise or fear: *'Oh, it's only you – you made me jump,' he said.* **5** [I] jump (from sth) to sth; jump (by) (sth) to increase suddenly by a very large amount: *His salary jumped from £20000 to £28000 last year.* ● *Prices jumped (by) 50% in the summer.* **6** [I] jump (from sth) to sth to go suddenly from one point in a series, a story, etc to another: *The book kept jumping from the present to the past.*

IDIOMS climb/jump on the bandwagon →BANDWAGON

jump for joy to be extremely happy about sth
jump the gun to do sth too soon, before the proper time
jump the queue to go to the front of a line of people (**queue**) without waiting for your turn
jump to conclusions to decide that sth is true without thinking about it carefully enough

PHRASAL VERB **jump at sth** to accept an opportunity, offer, etc with enthusiasm: *Of course I jumped at the chance to work in New York for a year.*

★**jump**² /dʒʌmp/ *noun* [C] **1** an act of jumping: *With a huge jump the horse cleared the hedge.* ● *to do a parachute jump* ·➤ Look at **high jump** and **long jump**. **2** a jump (in sth) a sudden increase in amount, price or value **3** a thing to be jumped over: *The horse fell at the first jump.*

jumper /'dʒʌmpə/ *noun* [C] **1** (*Brit*) a piece of clothing with sleeves, usually made of wool, that you wear on the top part of your body ·➤ Look at the note at **sweater**. **2** a person or animal that jumps

jumpy /'dʒʌmpi/ *adj* (*informal*) nervous or worried: *I always get a bit jumpy if I'm travelling by air.*

Jun *abbr* June: *10 Jun 1999*

junction /'dʒʌŋkʃn/ *noun* [C] a place where roads, railway lines, etc meet

★**June** /dʒuːn/ *noun* [U,C] (*abbr* **Jun**) the sixth month of the year, coming after May

➤ To see how the months are used in sentences, look at the examples and the note at **January**.

jungle /'dʒʌŋgl/ *noun* [C,U] a thick forest in a hot tropical country: *the jungles of Africa and South America* ·➤ Look at the note at **forest**.

junior¹ /'dʒuːniə/ *adj* **1** junior (to sb) having a low or lower position (than sb) in an organization, etc: *a junior officer/doctor/employee* ● *A lieutenant is junior to a captain in the army.* **2 Junior** (*abbr* **Jnr, Jr**) (*especially US*) used after the name of a son who has the same first name as his father: *Sammy Davis, Junior* **3** (*Brit*) of or for children below a particular age: *the junior athletics championships* ·➤ Look at **senior**¹.

junior² /'dʒuːniə/ *noun* **1** [C] a person who has a low position in an organization, etc **2** [sing] (with *his, her, your,* etc) a person who is younger than sb else by the number of years mentioned: *She's two years his junior/ his junior by two years.* **3** [C] (*Brit*) a child who goes to junior school: *The juniors are having an outing to a museum today.* ·➤ Look at **senior**².

'junior school *noun* [C] a school for children aged between seven and eleven

junk /dʒʌŋk/ *noun* [U] (*informal*) things that are old or useless or do not have much value: *There's an awful lot of junk up in the attic.*

'junk food *noun* [U] (*informal*) food that is not very good for you but that is ready to eat or quick to prepare

junta /'dʒʌntə/ *noun* [C,with sing or pl verb] a group, especially of military officers, who rule a country by force

Jupiter /'dʒuːpɪtə/ *noun* [sing] the planet that is fifth in order from the sun

jurisdiction /,dʒʊərɪs'dɪkʃn/ *noun* [U] legal power or authority; the area in which this power can be used: *That question is outside the jurisdiction of this council.*

juror /'dʒʊərə/ *noun* [C] a member of a jury

★**jury** /'dʒʊəri/ *noun* [C,with sing or pl verb] (*pl* **juries**) **1** a group of members of the public in a court of law who listen to the facts about a crime and decide if sb is guilty or not guilty: *Has/have the jury reached a verdict?* **2** a group of people who decide who is the winner in a competition: *The jury is/are about to announce the winners.*

★**just**¹ /dʒʌst/ *adv* **1** a very short time before: *She's just been to the shops.* ● *He'd just returned from France when I saw him.* ● *They came here just before Easter.* **2** at exactly this/ that moment, or immediately after: *He was just about to break the window when he noticed a policeman.* ● *I was just going to phone my mother when she arrived.* ● *Just as I was beginning to enjoy myself, John said it was time to go.* ● *Just then the door opened.* **3** exactly: *It's just eight o'clock.* ● *That's just what I meant.* ● *You're just as clever as he is.* ● *The room was too hot before, but now it's just right.* ● *He looks just like his father.* ● *My arm hurts just here.* **4** only: *She's just a*

child. • *Just a minute! I'm nearly ready.*
5 almost not; hardly: *I could **only just** hear what she was saying.* • *We got to the station **just in time.*** **6** (often with the imperative) used for getting attention or to emphasize what you are saying: *Just let me speak for a moment, will you?* • *I just don't want to go to the party.* **7** used with *might, may* or *could* to express a slight possibility: *This might just/ just might be the most important decision of your life.* **8** really; absolutely: *The whole day was just fantastic!*

IDIOMS **all/just the same** → **SAME**

it is just as well (that...) it is a good thing: *It's just as well you remembered to bring your umbrella!* •➤ Look also at **(just) as well (to do sth)** at **well**.

just about almost or approximately: *I've just about finished.* • *Karen's plane should be taking off just about now.*

just in case in order to be completely prepared or safe: *It might be hot in France – take your shorts just in case.*

just now 1 at this exact moment or during this exact period: *I can't come with you just now – can you wait 20 minutes?* **2** a very short time ago: *I saw Tony just now.*

just so exactly right

not just yet not now, but probably quite soon

just² /dʒʌst/ **adj** fair and right; reasonable: *I don't think that was a very just decision.* –**justly adv**

★**justice** /'dʒʌstɪs/ **noun 1** [U] the fair treatment of people: *a struggle for justice* **2** [U] the quality of being fair or reasonable: *Everybody realized the justice of what he was saying.* **3** [U] the law and the way it is used: *the criminal justice system* **4** [C] (*US*) a judge in a court of law

IDIOMS **do justice to sb/sth; do sb/sth justice** to treat sb/sth fairly or to show the real quality of sb/sth: *I don't like him, but to do him justice, he's a very clever man.* • *The photograph doesn't do her justice – she's actually very pretty.*

a miscarriage of justice → **MISCARRIAGE**

Justice of the 'Peace (*abbr* **JP**) **noun** [C] a person who judges less serious cases in a court of law in Britain

justifiable /ˌdʒʌstɪ'faɪəbl/ **adj** that you can accept because there is a good reason for it: *His action was entirely justifiable.* –**justifiably** /'dʒʌstɪfaɪəbli; ˌdʒʌstɪ'faɪəbli/ **adv**

justification /ˌdʒʌstɪfɪ'keɪʃn/ **noun** [C,U] (a) justification (for sth/doing sth) (a) good reason: *I can't see any justification for cutting his salary.*

★**justify** /'dʒʌstɪfaɪ/ **verb** [T] (*pres part* **justifying**; *3rd pers sing pres* **justifies**; *pt, pp* **justified**) to give or be a good reason for sth: *Can you justify your decision?*

jut /dʒʌt/ **verb** [I] (**jutting**; **jutted**) **jut (out)** (**from/into/over sth**) to stick out further than the surrounding surface, objects, etc: *rocks that jut out into the sea*

juvenile /'dʒuːvənaɪl/ **adj 1** (*formal*) of, for or involving young people who are not yet adults: *juvenile crime* **2** behaving like sb of a younger age; childish: *He's twenty but he is still quite juvenile.* –**juvenile noun** [C]

juvenile de'linquent noun [C] a young person who is guilty of committing a crime

juxtapose /ˌdʒʌkstə'pəʊz/ **verb** [T] (*formal*) to put two people, things, etc very close together, especially in order to show how they are different: *The artist achieves a special effect by juxtaposing light and dark.* –**juxtaposition** /ˌdʒʌkstəpə'zɪʃn/ **noun** [U]

K k

K, k¹ /keɪ/ **noun** [C] (*pl* **K's**; **k's**) the eleventh letter of the English alphabet: *'Kate' begins with (a) 'K'.*

K² /keɪ/ **abbr** (*informal*) one thousand: *She earns 22K (=£22 000) a year.*

k

kaleidoscope /kə'laɪdəskəʊp/ **noun** [C] **1** a large number of different things **2** a toy that consists of a tube containing mirrors and small pieces of coloured glass. When you look into one end of the tube and turn it, you see changing patterns of colours.

kangaroo

kangaroo /ˌkæŋgə-'ruː/ **noun** [C] (*pl* **kangaroos**) an Australian animal that moves by jumping on its strong back legs and that carries its young in a pocket of skin (a pouch) on its stomach

karaoke /ˌkæri'əʊki/ **noun** [U] a type of entertainment in which a machine plays only the music of popular songs so that people can sing the words themselves

karat (*US*) = **CARAT**

karate /kə'rɑːti/ **noun** [U] a style of fighting originally from Japan in which the hands and feet are used as weapons •➤ Look at **martial arts**.

kart /kɑːt/ **noun** [C] = **GO-KART**

kayak /'kaɪæk/ **noun** [C] a light narrow boat (a canoe) for one person, that you move using with a stick with a flat part at each end (a paddle) •➤ picture at **boat**

kebab /kɪ'bæb/ **noun** [C] small pieces of meat, vegetables, etc that are cooked on a stick (a skewer) •➤ picture on page C4

keel¹ /kiːl/ **noun** [C] a long piece of wood or metal on the bottom of a boat that stops it falling over sideways in the water

keel² /kiːl/ **verb**

PHRASAL VERB **keel over** to fall over

★**keen** /kiːn/ **adj 1 keen (to do sth/that...)** very interested in sth; wanting to do sth: *They are both keen gardeners.* ● *I failed the first time but I'm keen to try again.* ● *She was keen that we should all be there.* **2** (used about one of the senses, a feeling, etc) good or strong: *Foxes have a keen sense of smell.*

IDIOM **keen on sb/sth** very interested in or having a strong desire for sb/sth: *He's very keen on jazz.* –**keenly adv** –**keenness noun** [U]

★**keep¹** /kiːp/ **verb** (*pt, pp* **kept** /kept/) **1** [I] to continue to be in a particular state or position: *You must keep warm.* ● *That child can't keep still.* ● *I still keep in touch with my old school friends.* **2** [T] to make sb/sth stay in a particular state, place or condition: *Please keep this door closed.* ● *He kept his hands in his pockets.* ● *I'm sorry to keep you waiting.* **3** [T] to continue to have sth; to save sth for sb: *You can keep that book – I don't need it any more.* ● *Can I keep the car until next week?* ● *Can you keep my seat for me till I get back?* **4** [T] to have sth in a particular place: *Where do you keep the matches?* ● *Keep your passport in a safe place.* **5** [T] **keep doing sth** to continue doing sth or to repeat an action many times: *Keep going until you get to the church and then turn left.* ● *She keeps asking me silly questions.* **6** [T] to do what you promised or arranged: *Can you keep a promise?* ● *She didn't keep her appointment at the dentist's.* ● *to keep a secret* (= not tell it to anyone) **7** [T] to write down sth that you want to remember: *Keep a record of how much you spend.* ● *to keep a diary* **8** [I] (used about food) to stay fresh: *Drink up all the milk – it won't keep in this weather.* **9** [T] to support sb with your money: *You can't keep a family on the money I earn.* **10** [T] to have and look after animals: *They keep ducks on their farm.* **11** [T] to delay sb/sth; to prevent sb from leaving: *Where's the doctor? What's keeping him?*

IDIOM **keep it up** to continue doing sth as well as you are doing it now

➤ For other expressions using **keep**, look at the entries for the nouns and adjectives, for example **keep count** is at **count**.

PHRASAL VERBS **keep at it/sth** to continue to work on/at sth: *Keep at it – we should be finished soon.*

keep away from sb/sth to not go near sb/sth: *Keep away from the town centre this weekend.*

keep sb/sth back to prevent sb/sth from moving forwards: *The police tried to keep the crowd back.*

keep sth back (from sb) to refuse to tell sb sth: *I know he's keeping something back; he knows much more than he says.*

keep sth down to make sth stay at a low level, to stop sth increasing: *Keep your voice down.*

keep sb from sth/from doing sth to prevent sb from doing sth

keep sth from sb to refuse to tell sb sth

keep your mouth shut → MOUTH¹

keep off sth to not go near or on sth: *Keep off the grass!*

keep sth off (sb/sth) to stop sth touching or going on sb/sth: *I'm trying to keep the flies off the food.*

keep on (doing sth) to continue doing sth or to repeat an action many times, especially in an annoying way: *He keeps on interrupting me.*

keep on (at sb) (about sb/sth) to continue talking to sb in an annoying or complaining way: *She kept on at me about my homework until I did it.*

keep (sb/sth) out (of sth) to not enter sth; to stop sb/sth entering sth: *They put up a fence to keep people out of their garden.*

keep to sth to not leave sth; to do sth in the usual, agreed or expected way: *Keep to the path!* ● *He didn't keep to our agreement.*

keep sth to/at sth to not allow sth to rise above a particular level: *We're trying to keep costs to a minimum.*

keep sth up 1 to prevent sth from falling down **2** to make sth stay at a high level: *We want to keep up standards of education.* **3** to continue doing sth

keep up (with sb) to move at the same speed as sb: *Can't you walk a bit slower? I can't keep up.*

keep up (with sth) to know about what is happening: *You have to read the latest magazines if you want to keep up.*

keep² /kiːp/ **noun** [U] food and other things that you need in your daily life

IDIOM **for keeps** (*informal*) for always: *Take it. It's yours for keeps.*

keeper /ˈkiːpə/ **noun** [C] **1** a person who guards or looks after sth: *a zookeeper* **2** (*informal*) = GOALKEEPER

keeping /ˈkiːpɪŋ/ **noun**

IDIOM **in/out of keeping (with sth) 1** that does/does not look good with sth: *That modern table is out of keeping with the style of the room.* **2** in/not in agreement with a rule, belief, etc: *The Council's decision is in keeping with government policy.*

keg /keg/ **noun** [C] a round metal or wooden container, used especially for storing beer

kennel /ˈkenl/ **noun** [C] a small house for a dog

kept *past tense, past participle* of KEEP¹

kerb (*especially US* **curb**) /kɜːb/ **noun** [C] the edge of the path (the pavement) along the sides of a road: *They stood on the kerb waiting to cross the road.*

kerosene /ˈkerəsiːn/ (*US*) = PARAFFIN

ketchup /ˈketʃəp/ **noun** [U] a cold sauce made from soft red fruit (tomatoes) that is eaten with hot or cold food

kettle /ˈketl/ **noun** [C] a container with a lid, used for boiling water: *an electric kettle*

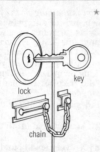

key

lock

chain

★key¹ /kiː/ **noun** [C]
1 a metal object that is used for locking a door, starting a car, etc: *Have you seen my car keys anywhere?* • *We need a spare key to the front door.* • *a bunch of keys* **2** [usually sing] the key (to sth) something that helps you achieve or understand sth: *A good education is the key to success.* **3** one of the parts of a piano, computer, etc that you press with your fingers to make it work ••➤ picture at **music** and on page S7 **4** a set of musical notes that is based on one particular note: *The concerto is in the key of A minor.* **5** a set of answers to exercises or problems: *an answer key* **6** a list of the symbols and signs used in a map or book, showing what they mean
IDIOM **under lock and key** → LOCK²

key² /kiː/ **verb** [T] key sth (in) to put information into a computer or give it an instruction by typing: *Have you keyed that report yet?* • *First, key in your password.*

key³ /kiː/ **adj** (only *before* a noun) very important: *Tourism is a key industry in Spain.*

keyboard /ˈkiːbɔːd/ **noun** [C] **1** the set of keys on a piano, computer, etc ••➤ picture on page S7 **2** an electrical musical instrument like a small piano ••➤ Look at the note at **piano.**

keyhole /ˈkiːhəʊl/ **noun** [C] the hole in a lock where you put the key

keyring /ˈkiːrɪŋ/ **noun** [C] a ring on which you keep keys

keyword /ˈkiːwɜːd/ **noun** [C] **1** a word that tells you about the main idea or subject of sth: *When you're studying a language, the keyword is patience.* **2** a word or phrase that is used to give an instruction to a computer

kg abbr kilogram(s): *weight 10kg*

khaki /ˈkɑːki/ **adj, noun** [U] (of) a pale brownish-yellow or brownish-green colour: *The khaki uniforms of the desert soldiers.*

kHz /ˈkɪləhɜːts/ **abbr** kilohertz; (used in radio) a measure of frequency

★kick¹ /kɪk/ **verb 1** [T] to hit or move sb/sth with your foot: *He kicked the ball wide of the net.* • *The police kicked the door down.* **2** [I,T] to move your foot or feet: *You must kick harder if you want to swim faster.*
IDIOMS **kick the habit** to stop doing sth harmful that you have done for a long time
kick yourself to be annoyed with yourself because you have done sth stupid, missed an opportunity, etc
make, kick up, etc a fuss → FUSS¹
PHRASAL VERBS **kick off** to start a game of football

kick sb out (of sth) (*informal*) to force sb to leave a place: *to be kicked out of university*

★kick² /kɪk/ **noun** [C] **1** an act of kicking: *She gave the door a kick and it closed.* **2** (*informal*) a feeling of great pleasure, excitement, etc: *He seems to get a real kick out of driving fast.*

ˈkick-off noun [C] the start of a game of football: *The kick-off is at 2.30.*

★kid¹ /kɪd/ **noun** [C] **1** (*informal*) a child or young person: *How are your kids?* **2** kid brother/sister (*especially US informal*) younger brother/sister **3** a young animal (goat) or its skin ••➤ picture at **goat**

kid² /kɪd/ **verb** [I,T] (**kidding; kidded**) (*informal*) to trick yourself by saying sth that is not true; to make a joke about sth: *I didn't mean it. I was only kidding.*

kiddy (also **kiddie**) /ˈkɪdi/ **noun** [C] (*pl* **kiddies**) (*informal*) a child

kidnap /ˈkɪdnæp/ **verb** [T] (**kidnapping; kidnapped**) to take sb away by force and demand money for his/her safe return: *The child was kidnapped and £50000 ransom was demanded for her release.* ••➤ Look at **hijack.** –**kidnapper noun** [C]: *The kidnappers demanded £50000.* –**kidnapping noun** [C,U]

kidney /ˈkɪdni/ **noun 1** [C] one of the two parts of your body that separate waste liquid from your blood ••➤ picture on page C5 **2** [U,C] the kidneys of an animal when they are cooked and eaten as food: *steak and kidney pie*

★kill /kɪl/ **verb 1** [I,T] to make sb/sth die: *Smoking kills.* • *She was killed instantly in the crash.*

> **Murder** means to kill a person on purpose: *This was no accident. The old lady was murdered.* **Assassinate** means to kill for political reasons: *President Kennedy was assassinated.* **Slaughter** and **massacre** mean to kill a large number of people: *Hundreds of people were massacred when the army opened fire on the crowd.* **Slaughter** is also used of killing an animal for food.

2 [T] (*informal*) to cause sb pain; to hurt: *My feet are killing me.* **3** [T] to cause sth to end or fail: *The minister's opposition killed the idea stone dead.* **4** [T] (*spoken*) to be very angry with sb: *My mum will kill me when she sees this mess.* **5** [T] (*informal*) kill yourself/sb to make yourself/sb laugh a lot: *We were killing ourselves laughing.*
IDIOMS **kill time, an hour, etc** to spend time doing sth that is not interesting or important while you are waiting for sth else to happen
kill two birds with one stone to do one thing which will achieve two results
PHRASAL VERB **kill sth off** to cause sth to die or to not exist any more

kill² /kɪl/ **noun** [sing] **1** the act of killing: *Lions often make a kill in the evening.* **2** an animal or animals that have been killed: *The eagle took the kill back to its young.*

killer /ˈkɪlə/ **noun** [C] a person, animal or

thing that kills: *a killer disease* ● *He's a dangerous killer who may strike again.*

killing /'kılıŋ/ **noun** [C] act of killing a person on purpose; a murder: *There have been a number of brutal killings in the area recently.*

IDIOM **make a killing** to make a large profit quickly

★**kilo** /'kiːləʊ/ (also **kilogram**; **kilogramme** /'kıləgræm/) **noun** [C] (*pl* **kilos**) (*abbr* **kg**) a measure of weight; 1000 grams

★**kilometre** (*US* **kilometer**) /'kıləmiːtə; kɪ'lɒmɪtə/ **noun** [C] (*abbr* **km**) a measure of length; 1000 metres

kilt /kɪlt/ **noun** [C] a skirt with many folds (**pleats**) that is worn by men as part of the national dress of Scotland

kin /kın/ → NEXT OF KIN

★**kind¹** /kaınd/ **noun** [C] a group whose members all have the same qualities: *The concert attracted people of all kinds.* ● *The concert attracted all kinds of people.* ● *What kind of car have you got?* ● *Many kinds of plant and animal are being lost every year.* ● *In the evenings I listen to music, write letters, that kind of thing.* ••➤ synonym **sort** or **type**

> ➤ Remember that *kind* is countable, so you CANNOT say: *Those kind of dogs are really dangerous* or: *I like all kind of music.* You should say: *That kind of dog is really dangerous./Those kinds of dogs are really dangerous.* and: *I like all kinds of music. Kinds of* may be followed by a singular noun or a plural noun: *There are so many kinds of camera/cameras on the market that it's hard to know which is best.*

IDIOMS **a kind of** (*informal*) used for describing sth in a way that is not very clear: *I had a kind of feeling that something would go wrong.* ● *There's a funny kind of smell in here.*

kind of (*informal*) slightly; a little bit: *I'm kind of worried about the interview.*

of a kind 1 the same: *The friends were two of a kind – very similar in so many ways.* **2** of poor quality

★**kind²** /kaınd/ **adj** **kind (to sb)**; **kind (of sb) (to do sth)** caring about others; friendly and generous: *Everyone's been so kind to us since we came here!* ● *It was kind of you to offer, but I don't need any help.* ••➤ opposite **unkind**

kindergarten /'kındəgɑːtn/ **noun** [C] a school for very young children, aged from about 3 to 5 ••➤ Look at **nursery school**.

kind-'hearted **adj** kind and generous

kindly /'kaındli/ **adv, adj 1** in a kind way: *The nurse smiled kindly.* **2** (used for asking sb to do sth) please: *Would you kindly wait a moment?* **3** kind and friendly

kindness /'kaındnəs/ **noun** [C,U] the quality of being kind; a kind act: *Thank you very much for all your kindness.*

★**king** /kıŋ/ **noun** [C] **1** (the title of) a man who rules a country. A king is usually the son or close relative of the former ruler: *The new king was crowned yesterday in Westminster Abbey.* ● *King Edward VII* (= the seventh)

● (*figurative*) *The lion is the king of the jungle.* ••➤ Look at **queen**, **prince** and **princess**. **2** one of the four playing cards in a pack with a picture of a king: *the king of spades* ••➤ Look at the note and picture at **card**.

kingdom /'kıŋdəm/ **noun** [C] **1** a country that is ruled by a king or queen: *the United Kingdom* **2** one of the parts of the natural world: *the animal kingdom*

'**king-size** (also '**king-sized**) **adj** bigger than usual: *a king-size bed*

kink /kıŋk/ **noun** [C] a turn or bend in sth that should be straight

kiosk /'kiːɒsk/ **noun** [C] a very small building in the street where newspapers, sweets, cigarettes, etc are sold ••➤ picture on page C8

kip /kıp/ **verb** [I] (**kipping**; **kipped**) (*Brit slang*) to sleep: *You could kip on the sofa if you like.* –**kip noun** [sing,U]: *I'm going to have a kip.* ● *I didn't get much kip last night.*

kipper /'kıpə/ **noun** [C] a type of fish that has been kept for a long time in salt, and then smoked

★**kiss** /kıs/ **verb** [I,T] to touch sb with your lips to show love or friendship: *He kissed her on the cheek.* ● *They kissed each other goodbye.* –**kiss noun** [C]: *a kiss on the lips/cheek*

kit¹ /kıt/ **noun 1** [C,U] a set of tools, equipment or clothes that you need for a particular purpose, sport or activity: *a tool kit* ● *a drum kit* ● *football/gym kit* **2** [C] a set of parts that you buy and put together in order to make sth: *a kit for a model aeroplane*

kit² /kıt/ **verb** (**kitting**; **kitted**)

PHRASAL VERB **kit sb/yourself out/up (in/with sth)** to give sb all the necessary clothes, equipment, tools, etc for sth

★**kitchen** /'kıtʃın/ **noun** [C] a room where food is prepared and cooked: *We usually eat in the kitchen.* ••➤ picture on next page

kite /kaıt/ **noun** [C] a toy which consists of a light frame covered with paper or cloth. Kites are flown in the wind on the end of a long piece of string: *to fly a kite*

kitten /'kıtn/ **noun** [C] a young cat

kitty /'kıti/ **noun** [C] (*pl* **kitties**) **1** a sum of money that is collected from a group of people and used for a particular purpose: *All the students in the flat put £5 a week into the kitty.* **2** (*spoken*) a way of calling or referring to a cat

kiwi /'kiːwiː/ **noun** [C] (*pl* **kiwis**) **1** a New Zealand bird with a long beak and short wings that cannot fly **2** (also '**kiwi fruit**) a fruit with brown skin that is green inside with black seeds ••➤ picture on page C3

km **abbr** kilometre(s)

knack /næk/ **noun** [sing] (*informal*) **knack (of/for doing sth)** skill or ability to do sth (difficult) that you have naturally or you can learn: *Knitting isn't difficult once you've got the knack of it.*

knead /niːd/ **verb** [T] to press and squeeze a mixture of flour and water (**dough**) with your hands in order to make bread, etc

---

[C] **countable**, a noun with a plural form: *one book, two books*   [U] **uncountable**, a noun with no plural form: *some sugar*

kitchen utensils

rolling pin

sieve

grater

peeler

colander

whisk

funnel

tongs

chopping board

knives

spatula ladle

spoons

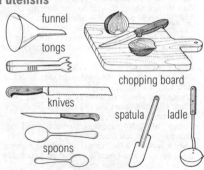

★**knee** /ni:/ **noun** [C] **1** the place where your leg bends in the middle: *Angie fell and grazed her knee.* ● *She was on her hands and knees on the floor looking for her earrings.* ● *Come and sit on my knee.* •➤ picture on page C5 **2** the part of a pair of trousers, etc that covers the knee: *There's a hole in the knee of those jeans.*

kneecap /'ni:kæp/ **noun** [C] the bone that covers the front of the knee •➤ picture on page C5

'**knee-deep adj, adv** up to your knees: *The water was knee-deep in places.*

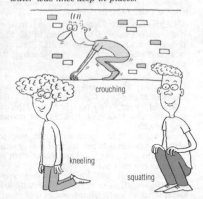

crouching

kneeling

squatting

★**kneel** /ni:l/ **verb** [I] (*pt, pp* **knelt** /nelt/ or **kneeled**) kneel (**down**) to rest on one or both knees: *She knelt down to talk to the child.*

knew *past tense of* **KNOW¹**

knickers /'nɪkəz/ (*especially US* **panties**) **noun** [pl] a piece of underwear for women that covers the area between the waist and the top of the legs •➤ Note that you say *a pair of knickers.*

★**knife¹** /naɪf/ **noun** [C] (*pl* **knives** /naɪvz/) a sharp flat piece of metal (**a blade**) with a handle. A knife is used for cutting things or as a weapon: *The carving knife is very blunt/ sharp.* ● *a knife and fork* ● *a penknife/pocket knife/flick knife* •➤ picture above

knife² /naɪf/ **verb** [T] to deliberately injure sb with a knife •➤ synonym **stab**

knight /naɪt/ **noun** [C] **1** a man who has been given a title of honour by a king or queen for good work he has done and who can use *Sir* in front of his name **2** a soldier of a high level who fought on a horse in the Middle Ages –**knighthood** /'naɪthʊd/ **noun** [C,U]

knit sew

stitches

knitting needle

wool

needle

cotton

stitches

reel of cotton

★**knit** /nɪt/ **verb** [I,T] (**knitting; knitted**) or (*US pt, pp* **knit**) **1** to make sth (for example an article of clothing) with wool using two long needles or a special machine: *I'm knitting a sweater for my nephew.* •➤ Look at **crochet**. **2 knit** (only used in this form) joined closely together: *a closely/tightly knit village community* –**knitting noun** [U]: *I usually do some knitting while I'm watching TV.*

'**knitting needle** = **NEEDLE**(2)

knitwear /'nɪtweə/ **noun** [U] articles of clothing that have been knitted: *the knitwear department*

knob /nɒb/ **noun** [C] **1** a round switch on a machine (for example a television) that you press or turn: *the volume control knob* **2** a round handle on a door, drawer, etc •➤ picture at **handle**

★**knock¹** /nɒk/ **verb 1** [I] knock (at/on sth) to make a noise by hitting sth firmly with your hand: *Someone is knocking at the door.* ● *I knocked on the window but she didn't hear me.* **2** [T] knock sth (on/against sth) to hit sb/sth hard, often by accident: *He knocked the vase onto the floor.* ● *Be careful not to knock*

k

[I] **intransitive**, a verb which has no object: *He laughed.*   [T] **transitive**, a verb which has an object: *He ate an apple.*

your head on the shelf when you get up. ● *to knock sb unconscious* **3** [T] (*informal*) to say bad things about sb/sth; to criticize sb/sth

IDIOM **knock on wood** → **WOOD**

PHRASAL VERBS **knock about/around** (*informal*) to be in a place; to travel and live in various places: *Is last week's newspaper still knocking about?*

knock sb down to hit sb causing him/her to fall to the ground: *The old lady was knocked down by a cyclist.*

knock sth down to destroy a building, etc: *They knocked down the old factory because it was unsafe.*

knock off (sth) (*spoken*) to stop working: *What time do you knock off?*

knock sth off 1 (*informal*) to reduce a price by a certain amount: *He agreed to knock £10 off the price.* **2** (*slang*) to steal sth

knock sb out 1 to hit sb so that he/she becomes unconscious or cannot get up again for a while: *The punch on the nose knocked him out.* **2** (used about a drug, alcohol, etc) to cause sb to sleep

knock sb out (of sth) to beat a person or team in a competition so that they do not play any more games in it: *Belgium was knocked out of the European Cup by France.*

knock sb/sth over to cause sb/sth to fall over: *Be careful not to knock over the drinks.*

★**knock²** /nɒk/ **noun** [C] a sharp hit from sth hard or the sound it makes: *a nasty knock on the head* ● *I thought I heard a knock at the door.* ● (*figurative*) *She has suffered some hard knocks* (= bad experiences) *in her life.*

knocker /'nɒkə/ **noun** [C] a piece of metal fixed to the outside of a door that you hit against the door to attract attention

'**knock-on** **adj** (*especially Brit*) causing other events to happen one after the other: *An increase in the price of oil has a knock-on effect on other fuels.*

knockout /'nɒkaʊt/ **noun** [C] **1** a hard hit that causes sb to become unconscious or to be unable to get up again for a while **2** (*especially Brit*) (only *before* a noun) a competition in which the winner of each game goes on to the next part but the person who loses plays no more games

★**knot¹** /nɒt/ **noun** [C] **1** a place where two ends or pieces of rope, string, etc have been tied together: *to tie/untie a knot* ••➤ picture at **loop 2** a measure of the speed of a ship; approximately 1.8 kilometres per hour

knot² /nɒt/ **verb** [T] (**knotting; knotted**) to fasten sth together with a knot

★**know¹** /nəʊ/ **verb** (*pt* **knew** /njuː/; *pp* **known** /nəʊn/) (not used in the continuous tenses) **1** [I,T] **know (about sth); know that…** to have knowledge or information in your mind: *I don't know much about sport.* ● *Do you know where this bus stops?* ● *Do you know their telephone number?* ● *'You've got a flat tyre.' 'I know.'* ● *Do you know the way to the restaurant?* ● *Knowing Katie, she'll be out with her friends.* **2** [T] to be familiar with a person or a place; to have met sb or been

somewhere before: *We've known each other for years.* ● *I don't know this part of London well.*

➤ The first time sb introduces you to sb or you see and talk to sb we use the verb **meet**: *Peter and I met at university in 1997.* After meeting sb, as you gradually become friends, we use **get to know sb**: *Kevin's wife seems very interesting. I'd like to get to know her better.* To talk about places that you go to for the first time, we use **see** or **visit**: *I'd love to go to the States and see/visit San Francisco and New York.*

3 [T,I] to feel certain; to be sure of sth: *I just know you'll pass the exam!* ● **As far as I know** (= I think it is true but I am not absolutely sure)*, the meeting is next Monday afternoon.* **4** [T] (only in the past and perfect tenses) to have seen, heard, or experienced sth: *I've known him go a whole day without eating.* ● *It's been known to snow in June.* **5** [T] (often passive) **know sb/sth as sth** to give sth a particular name; to recognize sb/sth as sth: *Istanbul was previously known as Constantinople.* **6** [T] **know how to do sth** to have learned sth and be able to do it: *Do you know how to use a computer?*

➤ Be careful. In front of a verb you must use **how to**; you CANNOT say: *I know use a computer.*

7 [T] to have personal experience of sth: *Many people in western countries don't know what it's like to be hungry.*

➤ Although this verb is not used in the continuous tenses, it is common to use the present participle (= -*ing* form): *Knowing how he'd react if he ever found out about it, she kept quiet.*

IDIOMS **God/goodness/Heaven knows 1** I don't know: *They've ordered a new car but goodness knows how they're going to pay for it.* **2** used for emphasizing sth: *I hope I get an answer soon. Goodness knows, I've waited long enough.*

know better (than that/than to do sth) to have enough sense to realize that you should not do sth: *I thought you knew better than to go out in the rain with no coat on.*

know sth inside out/like the back of your hand (*informal*) to be very familiar with sth

know what you are talking about (*informal*) to have knowledge of sth from your own experience: *I've lived in London so I know what I'm talking about.*

know what's what (*informal*) to have all the important information about sth; to fully understand sth

let sb know to tell sb; to inform sb about sth: *Could you let me know what time you're arriving?*

you know used when the speaker is thinking of what to say next, or to remind sb of sth: *Well, you know, it's rather difficult to explain.* ● *I've just met Marta. You know – Jim's ex-wife.*

you never know (*spoken*) you cannot be

certain: *Keep those empty boxes. You never know, they might come in handy one day.*

PHRASAL VERB **know of sb/sth** to have information about or experience of sb/sth: *Do you know of any pubs around here that serve food?*

know² /nəʊ/ **noun**

IDIOM **in the know** (*informal*) having information that other people do not

'know-all (*US* **'know-it-all**) **noun** [C] an annoying person who behaves as if he/she knows everything

'know-how noun [U] (*informal*) practical knowledge of or skill in sth

knowing /'nəʊɪŋ/ **adj** showing that you know about sth that is thought to be secret: *a knowing look*

knowingly /'nəʊɪŋli/ **adv 1** on purpose; deliberately: *I've never knowingly lied to you.* **2** in a way that shows that you know about sth that is thought to be secret: *He smiled knowingly at her.*

★**knowledge** /'nɒlɪdʒ/ **noun 1** [U,sing] knowledge (of/about sth) information, understanding and skills that you have gained through learning or experience: *I have* ***a working knowledge*** *of French* (= enough to be able to make myself understood). **2** [U] the state of knowing about a particular fact or situation: ***To my knowledge*** (= from the information I have, although I may not know everything) *they are still living there.* • *She did it **without my knowledge*** (= I did not know about it).

IDIOM **be common/public knowledge** to be sth that everyone knows

knowledgeable /'nɒlɪdʒəbl/ **adj** having a lot of knowledge: *She's very knowledgeable about history.* –**knowledgeably** /-əbli/ **adv**

knuckle /'nʌkl/ **noun** [C] the bones where your fingers join the rest of your hand ••► picture on page C5

koala /kəʊ'ɑːlə/ **noun** [C] an Australian animal with thick grey fur that lives in trees and looks like a small bear

the Koran (also **Quran, Qur'an**) /kə'rɑːn/ **noun** [sing] the most important book in the Islamic religion

kosher /'kəʊʃə/ **adj** (used about food) prepared according to the rules of Jewish law

kph /ˌkeɪ piː 'eɪtʃ/ **abbr** kilometres per hour

kung fu /ˌkʌŋ'fuː/ **noun** [U] a Chinese style of fighting using the feet and hands as weapons ••► Look at **martial arts**.

kW (also **kw**) /'kɪləwɒt/ **abbr** kilowatt(s): *a 2kw electric heater*

L, l¹ /el/ **noun** [C] (*pl* **L's; l's**) the twelfth letter of the English alphabet: *'Lake' begins with (an) 'L'.*

l² **abbr 1 l** litre(s) **2** (*Brit*) **L** (on a sign on a car) learner-driver **3 L** large (size)

Lab abbr (in British politics) Labour

label   price tag

ticket

★**label¹** /'leɪbl/ **noun** [C] **1** a piece of paper, etc that is fixed to sth and which gives information about it: *There is a list of all the ingredients on the label.* **2 record label** a company that produces and sells records, CDs, etc

label² /'leɪbl/ **verb** [T] (**labelling**; **labelled**; *US* **labeling**; **labeled**) **1** (usually passive) to fix a label or write information on sth **2** label sb/sth (as) sth to describe sb/sth in a particular way, especially unfairly

★**laboratory** /lə'bɒrətri/ **noun** [C] (*pl* **laboratories**) (also *informal* **lab**) a room or building that is used for scientific research, testing, experiments, etc or for teaching about science: *The blood samples were sent to the laboratory for analysis.* • *a physics laboratory* ••► Look at **language laboratory**.

laborious /lə'bɔːriəs/ **adj** needing a lot of time and effort: *a laborious task/process/job* –**laboriously adv**

labour¹ (*US* **labor**) /'leɪbə/ **noun 1** [U] work, usually of a hard, physical kind: *manual labour* (= work using your hands) **2** [U] workers, when thought of as a group: *There is a shortage of skilled labour.* **3** [U,C,usually sing] the process of giving birth to a baby: *She **went into labour** in the early hours of this morning.* • *She was **in labour** for ten hours.*

labour² (*US* **labor**) /'leɪbə/ **verb** [I] **1** labour (away) to work hard at sth: *She laboured on her book for two years.* **2** to move or do sth with difficulty and effort

laboured (*US* **labored**) /'leɪbəd/ **adj** done slowly or with difficulty: *laboured breathing*

labourer (*US* **laborer**) /'leɪbərə/ **noun** [C] a person whose job involves hard physical work: *unskilled/farm labourers*

the 'Labour Party (also **Labour**) **noun** [sing,with sing or pl verb] one of the main political parties in Britain. The Labour Party supports the interests of working people: *He has always voted Labour.* • *a Labour MP*

ð **then** | s **so** | z **zoo** | ʃ **she** | ʒ **vision** | h **how** | m **man** | n **no** | ŋ **sing** | l **leg** | r **red** | j **yes** | w **wet**

••➤ Look at **the Conservative Party** and the **Liberal Democrats**.

'labour-saving adj reducing the amount of work needed to do sth: *labour-saving devices such as washing machines and dishwashers*

labyrinth /'læbərɪnθ/ noun [C] a complicated set of paths and passages, through which it is difficult to find your way: *a labyrinth of corridors* ••➤ synonym **maze**

lace

lace collar

lace¹ /leɪs/ noun
1 [U] cloth that is made of very thin threads sewn in patterns with small holes in between: *lace curtains* ● *a collar made of lace* ••➤ adjective **lacy**
2 [C] a string that is used for tying a shoe: *Your shoelace is undone.* ● *Do up your laces or you'll trip over them.* ••➤ picture at **shoe**

lace² /leɪs/ verb [I,T] **lace (sth) (up)** to tie or fasten sth with a lace¹(2): *She was sitting on the end of the bed lacing up her boots.* –**lace-up** adj, noun [C]: *lace-up boots/shoes*

lack¹ /læk/ noun [U] **lack (of sth)** the state of not having sth or not having enough of sth: *A lack of food forced many people to leave their homes.*

★**lack²** /læk/ verb [T] to have none or not enough of sth: *She seems to lack the will to succeed.*

lacking /'lækɪŋ/ adj (not before a noun) **1 lacking in sth** not having enough of sth: *He's certainly not lacking in intelligence.* **2** not present or available: *I feel there is something lacking in my life.*

lacklustre /'læklʌstə/ adj not interesting or exciting; dull: *a lacklustre performance*

laconic /lə'kɒnɪk/ adj (formal) using only a few words to say sth –**laconically** /-kli/ adv

lacquer /'lækə/ noun [U] **1** a type of transparent paint that is put on wood, metal, etc to give it a hard, shiny surface **2** (old-fashioned) a liquid that you put on your hair to keep it in place ••➤ synonym **hairspray**

lacy /'leɪsi/ adj made of or looking like material made of thin threads with small holes to form a pattern (**lace**)

lad /læd/ noun [C] (informal) a boy or young man: *School has changed since I was a lad.*

ladder

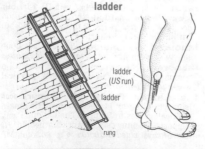

ladder
(US run)

ladder

rung

★**ladder** /'lædə/ noun [C] **1** a piece of equipment that is used for climbing up sth. A ladder consists of two long pieces of metal, wood or rope with steps fixed between them: (figurative) *to climb the ladder of success* ••➤ Look at **stepladder**. **2** (US run) a long hole in the thin pieces of clothing that women wear to cover their legs (**tights** or **stockings**), where the threads have broken: *Oh no! I've got a ladder in my tights.* –**ladder** verb [T]

laden /'leɪdn/ adj **laden (with sth)** (not before a noun) having or carrying a lot of sth: *The travellers were laden down with luggage.* ● *The orange trees were laden with fruit.*

the 'Ladies noun [sing] (Brit informal) a public toilet for women ••➤ Look at the note at **toilet**.

ladle¹ /'leɪdl/ noun [C] a large deep spoon with a long handle, used especially for serving soup ••➤ picture at **kitchen**

ladle² /'leɪdl/ verb [T] to serve food with a ladle

★**lady** /'leɪdi/ noun [C] (pl ladies) **1** a polite way of saying 'woman', especially when you are referring to an older woman: *The old lady next door lives alone.* **2** (formal) used when speaking to or about a woman or women in a polite way: *Ladies and gentlemen!* (= at the beginning of a speech) ● *Mrs Flinn, there's a lady here to see you.* **3** a title that is used before the name of a woman who has a high social position: *Lady Elizabeth Groves* ••➤ Look at **Lord**.

ladybird /'leɪdibɜːd/ (US **ladybug** /'leɪdibʌɡ/) noun [C] a small insect that is red or yellow with black spots ••➤ picture at **insect**

lag¹ /læɡ/ verb [I] (**lagging; lagged**) **lag (behind) (sb/sth)** to move or develop more slowly than sb/sth: *James has missed a lot of classes and is lagging behind the others at school.*

lag² /læɡ/ (also **time lag**) noun [C] a period of time between two events; a delay ••➤ Look at **jet lag**.

lager /'lɑːɡə/ noun [C,U] (Brit) a type of light beer that is a gold colour: *Three pints of lager, please.*

lagoon /lə'ɡuːn/ noun [C] a lake of salt water that is separated from the sea by sand or rock

laid past tense, past participle of **LAY¹**

laid-back /ˌleɪd 'bæk/ adj (informal) calm and relaxed; seeming not to worry about anything

lain past participle of **LIE²**

★**lake** /leɪk/ noun [C] a large area of water that is surrounded by land: *They've gone sailing on the lake.* ● *We all swam in the lake.* ● *Lake Constance*

➤ A **pond** is smaller than a lake.

••➤ picture on page C8

★**lamb** /læm/ noun **1** [C] a young sheep ••➤ Look at the note at **sheep**. ••➤ picture at **goat 2** [U] the meat of a young sheep: *lamb chops* ••➤ Look at the note at **meat**.

lame /leɪm/ adj **1** (used mainly about

animals) not able to walk properly because of an injury to the leg or foot: *The horse is lame and cannot work.*

> ➤ **Lame** is not often used nowadays about a person. The verb and noun **limp** are more often used: *He's got a limp.* • *You're limping. Have you hurt your leg?*

2 (used about an excuse, argument, etc) not easily believed; weak

lament /lə'ment/ **noun** [C] (*formal*) a song, poem or other expression of sadness for sb who has died or for sth that has ended ▸**lament verb** [I,T]

laminated /'læmɪneɪtɪd/ **adj 1** (used about wood, plastic, etc) made by sticking several thin layers together: *laminated glass* **2** covered with thin transparent plastic for protection

★**lamp** /læmp/ **noun** [C] a device that uses electricity, gas or oil to produce light: *a street lamp* • *a table/desk/bicycle lamp* • *a sunlamp* •➤ picture at **light** and on page S9

lamp post noun [C] a tall pole at the side of the road with a light on the top

lampshade /'læmpʃeɪd/ **noun** [C] a cover for a lamp that makes it look more attractive and makes the light softer •➤ picture at **light**

★**land**¹ /lænd/ **noun 1** [U] the solid part of the surface of the earth (= not sea): *Penguins can't move very fast on land.* •➤ Look at the note at **ground.** •➤ opposite **sea 2** [U] an area of ground: *The land rose to the east.* • *She owns 500 acres of land in Scotland.* **3** [U] ground, soil or earth of a particular kind: *The land is rich and fertile.* • *arid/ barren land* • *arable/agricultural/industrial land* **4** [C] (*written*) a country or region: *She died far from her native land.* • *to travel to distant lands* •➤ Look at the note at **country.**

★**land**² /lænd/ **verb 1** [I,T] to come down from the air or to bring sth down to the ground: *The bird landed on the roof.* • *He fell off the ladder and landed on his back.* • *The pilot landed the aeroplane safely.* • *His flight is due to land at 3 o'clock.* •➤ picture at **take off 2** [I,T] to go onto land or put sth onto land from a ship **3** [T] to succeed in getting sth, especially sth that a lot of people want: *The company has just landed a million-dollar contract.*

> IDIOM **fall/land on your feet → FOOT**¹
> PHRASAL VERBS **land up (in...)** (*Brit informal*) to finish in a certain position or situation: *He landed up in a prison cell for the night.*
> **land sb with sth/sth** (*informal*) to give sb sth unpleasant to do, especially because no one else wants to do it

landfill /'lændfɪl/ **noun 1** [C,U] an area of land where large amounts of waste material are buried **2** [U] waste material that will be buried; the burying of waste material

★**landing** /'lændɪŋ/ **noun** [C] **1** the action of coming down onto the ground (in an aircraft): *The plane made an **emergency landing** in a field.* • *a crash landing* • *a safe landing* •➤ opposite **take-off 2** the area at

the top of a staircase in a house, or between one staircase and another in a large building •➤ picture on page C7

landing card noun [C] a form on which you have to write details about yourself when flying to a foreign country

landing stage (*US* **dock**) **noun** [C] a wooden platform built out into the sea or a river where boats are tied and where people can get on or off them •➤ synonym **jetty**

landing strip = AIRSTRIP

landlady /'lændleɪdi/ **noun** [C] (*pl* **landladies**) **1** a woman who rents a house or room to people for money **2** a woman who owns or manages a pub, small hotel, etc

landlord /'lændlɔːd/ **noun** [C] **1** a person who rents a house or room to people for money **2** a person who owns or manages a pub, small hotel, etc

landmark /'lændmɑːk/ **noun** [C] **1** an object (often a building) that can be seen easily from a distance and will help you to recognize where you are: *Big Ben is one of the landmarks on London's skyline.* **2** a landmark (in sth) an important stage or change in the development of sth

landscape¹ /'lændskeɪp/ **noun 1** [C,usually sing] everything you can see when you look across a large area of land: *an urban/industrial landscape* •➤ Look at the note at **scenery. 2** [C,U] a picture or a painting that shows a view of the countryside; this style of painting

landscape² /'lændskeɪp/ **verb** [T] to improve the appearance of an area of land by changing its design and planting trees, flowers, etc

landslide /'lændslaɪd/ **noun** [C] **1** the sudden fall of a mass of earth, rocks, etc down the side of a mountain: *Part of the railway line was buried beneath a landslide.* **2** a great victory for one person or one political party in an election

lane /leɪn/ **noun** [C] **1** a narrow road in the country: *We found a route through country lanes to avoid the traffic jam on the main road.* **2** used in the names of roads: *Crossley Lane* **3** a section of a wide road that is marked by painted white lines to keep lines of traffic separate: *a four-lane motorway* • *the inside/middle/fast/outside lane* **4** a section of a sports track, swimming pool, etc for one person to go along: *The British athlete is in lane two.* **5** a route or path that is regularly used by ships or aircraft

★**language** /'læŋgwɪdʒ/ **noun 1** [C] the system of communication in speech and writing that is used by people of a particular country: *How many languages can you speak?* • *They fell in love in spite of the language barrier* (= being unable to speak or understand each other's native language). • *What is your first language* (= your mother tongue)? **2** [U] the system of sounds and writing that human beings use to express their thoughts, ideas and feelings: *written/spoken language* **3** [U] words of a particular type or words that are used by a particular person or group: *bad* (= rude) *language* • *legal language* • *the language of Shakespeare* **4** [U] any system of signs, symbols, movements, etc that is used to express sth: *sign language* (= using your hands, not speaking) ••> Look at **body language**. **5** [C,U] (*computing*) a system of symbols and rules that is used to operate a computer

ˈlanguage laboratory noun [C] a room in a school or college that contains special equipment to help students to learn foreign languages by listening to tapes, watching videos, recording themselves, etc

lanky /ˈlæŋki/ adj (used about a person) very tall and thin

lantern /ˈlæntən/ noun [C] a type of light that can be carried with a metal frame, glass sides and a light or candle inside

lap¹ /læp/ noun [C] **1** the flat area that is formed by the upper part of your legs when you are sitting down: *The child sat quietly on his mother's lap.* **2** one journey around a running track, etc: *There are three more laps to go in the race.* **3** one part of a long journey

lap² /læp/ verb (**lapping**; **lapped**) **1** [I] (used about water) to make gentle sounds as it moves against sth: *The waves lapped against the side of the boat.* **2** [T] lap sth (up) (usually used about an animal) to drink sth using the tongue: *The cat lapped up the cream.* **3** [T] to pass another competitor in a race who has been round the track fewer times than you

PHRASAL VERB **lap sth up** (*informal*) to accept sth with great enjoyment without stopping to think if it is good, true, etc

lapel /ləˈpel/ noun [C] one of the two parts of the front of a coat or jacket that are folded back

lapse¹ /læps/ noun [C] **1** a short time when you cannot remember sth or you are not thinking about what you are doing: *a lapse of memory* • *The crash was the result of a temporary lapse in concentration.* **2** a period of time between two things that happen: *She returned to work after a lapse of ten years bringing up her family.* ••> Look at the verb **elapse**. **3** a piece of bad behaviour from sb who usually behaves well

lapse² /læps/ verb [I] **1** (used about a contract, an agreement, etc) to finish or stop, often by accident: *My membership has lapsed because I forgot to renew it.* **2** to become weaker or stop for a short time: *My concentration lapsed during the last part of the exam.*

PHRASAL VERB **lapse into sth** to gradually pass into a worse or less active state or condition; to start speaking or behaving in a less acceptable way: *to lapse into silence/a coma*

laptop /ˈlæptɒp/ noun [C] a small computer that is easy to carry and that can use batteries for power ••> Look at **desktop**.

larder /ˈlɑːdə/ noun [C] a large cupboard or small room that is used for storing food ••> synonym **pantry**

★**large** /lɑːdʒ/ adj greater in size, amount, etc than usual; big: *a large area/house/family/ appetite* • *a large number of people* • *I'd like a large coffee, please.* • *We have this shirt in small, medium or large.* ••> Look at the note at **big**.

IDIOMS **at large 1** as a whole; in general: *He is well known to scientists but not to the public at large.* **2** (used about a criminal, animal, etc) not caught; free

by and large mostly; in general: *By and large the school is very efficient.*

largely /ˈlɑːdʒli/ adv mostly: *His success was largely due to hard work.*

ˈlarge-scale adj happening over a large area or affecting a lot of people: *large-scale production/unemployment*

laryngitis /ˌlærɪnˈdʒaɪtɪs/ noun [U] a mild illness of the throat that makes it difficult to speak

laser /ˈleɪzə/ noun [C] a device that produces a controlled ray of very powerful light that can be used as a tool

lash¹ /læʃ/ verb **1** [I,T] (used especially about wind, rain and storms) to hit sth with great force: *The rain lashed against the windows.* **2** [T] to hit sb with a piece of rope, leather, etc; to move sth like a piece of rope, leather, etc violently **3** [T] lash A to B; lash A and B together to tie two things together firmly with rope, etc: *The two boats were lashed together.*

PHRASAL VERB **lash out (at/against sb/sth)** to suddenly attack sb/sth (with words or by hitting him/her/it): *The actor lashed out at a photographer outside his house.*

lash² /læʃ/ noun [C] **1** = EYELASH **2** a hit with a long piece of rope, leather, etc (a whip)

lass /læs/ (also **lassie** /ˈlæsi/) noun [C] (*informal*) a girl or young woman

➤ **Lass** is most commonly used in Scotland and the North of England.

lasso /læˈsuː/ noun [C] (*pl* **lassos** or **lassoes**) a long rope tied in a circle at one end that is used for catching cows and horses –**lasso** verb [T]

★**last¹** /lɑːst/ determiner, adj, adv, noun [C] **1** at the end; after all the others: *December is the last month of the year.* • *Would the last person to leave please turn off the lights?* • *Our house is the last one on the left.* • *She lived alone for the last years of her life.* • *The British athlete came in last.* • *Her name is last on the list.* • *Alex was the last to arrive.* **2** used about a time, period, event, etc in the past that is nearest to the present: *last night/week/Saturday/summer* • *We have been working on the book for the last six months.* • *The last time I saw her was in London.* • *We'll win this time, because they beat us last time.* • *When did you last have your eyes checked?* • *When I saw her last she seemed very happy.*

➤ **The latest** means 'most recent' or 'new'. **The last** means the one before the present one: *His last novel was a huge success, but the latest one is much less popular.*

3 final: *This is my last chance to take the exam.* ● *Alison's retiring – tomorrow is her last day at work.* ● *We finished **the last of the** bread at breakfast so we'd better get some more.* **4** (only *before* a noun) not expected or not suitable: *He's the last person I thought would get the job.* —**lastly** adv: *Lastly, I would like to thank the band who played this evening.* ••▶ synonym **finally**

IDIOMS **the last/next but one, two, etc** one, two, etc away from the last/next: *I live in the next house but one on the right.* ● *X is the last letter but two of the alphabet* (= the third letter from the end).

at (long) last in the end; finally: *After months of separation they were together at last.*

first/last thing → THING

have the last laugh to be the person, team, etc who is successful in the end

have, etc the last word to be the person who makes the final decision or the final comment

in the last resort; (as) a last resort when everything else has failed; the person or thing that helps when everything else has failed: *In the last resort my grandad could play in the match.*

last but not least (used before the final item in a list) just as important as all the other items

a last-ditch attempt a final effort to avoid sth unpleasant or dangerous

the last/final straw → STRAW

the last minute/moment the final minute/ moment before sth happens: *We arrived at the last minute to catch the train.* ● *a last-minute change of plan*

★**last²** /lɑːst/ **verb** (not used in the continuous tenses) **1** [T] to continue for a period of time: *The exam lasts three hours.* ● *How long does a cricket match last?* ● *The flight seemed to last forever.* **2** [I,T] to continue to be good or to function: *Do you think this weather will last till the weekend?* ● *It's only a cheap radio but it'll probably last a year or so.* **3** [I,T] to be enough for what sb needs: *This money won't last me till the end of the month.*

➤ Although this verb is not used in the continuous tenses, it is common to see the present participle (= -*ing* form): *An earthquake lasting approximately 20 seconds struck the city last night.*

lasting /'lɑːstɪŋ/ **adj** continuing for a long time: *The museum left a lasting impression on me.*

'**last name** = SURNAME ••▶ Look at the note at **name**.

latch¹ /lætʃ/ **noun** [C] **1** a small metal bar that is used for fastening a door or a gate. You have to lift the latch in order to open the door. **2** a type of lock for a door that you open with a key from the outside

latch² /lætʃ/ **verb**

PHRASAL VERB **latch on (to sth)** (*informal*) to understand sth: *It took them a while to latch on to what she was talking about.*

★**late** /leɪt/ **adj, adv** **1** near the end of a period of time: *in the late afternoon/summer/twentieth century* ● *in the late morning* ● *His mother's in her late fifties* (= between 55 and 60). ● *in late May/late in May* ● *We got back home late in the evening.* **2** after the usual or expected time: *I'm sorry I'm late.* ● *She was ten minutes late for school.* ● *The ambulance arrived too late to save him.* ● *to be late with the rent* ● *The buses are running late today.* ● *to stay up late* **3** near the end of the day: *It's getting late – let's go home.* **4** (only *before* a noun) no longer alive; dead: *his late wife*

IDIOMS **an early/a late night** → NIGHT

later on at a later time: *Later on you'll probably wish that you'd worked harder at school.* ● *Bye – I'll see you a bit later on.*

sooner or later → SOON

latecomer /'leɪtkʌmə/ **noun** [C] a person who arrives or starts sth late

★**lately** /'leɪtli/ **adv** in the period of time up until now; recently: *What have you been doing lately?* ● *Hasn't the weather been dreadful lately?*

★**latest** /'leɪtɪst/ **adj** very recent or new: *the latest fashions* ● *the latest news* ● *the terrorists' latest attack on the town* ••▶ Look at the note at **last¹**.

the latest **noun** [sing] (*informal*) the most recent or the newest thing or piece of news: *This is the very latest in computer technology.* ● *This is the latest in a series of attacks by this terrorist group.*

IDIOM **at the latest** no later than the time or the date mentioned: *You need to hand your projects in by Friday at the latest.*

lather /'lɑːðə/ **noun** [U] a white mass of bubbles that are produced when you mix soap with water

Latin /'lætɪn/ **noun** [U] the language that was used in ancient Rome —**Latin** adj: *Latin poetry* ● *Spanish, Italian and other Latin languages* (= that developed from Latin)

,**Latin A'merican** **noun** [C], **adj** (a person who comes from Latin America (the parts of Central and South America where Spanish or Portuguese is spoken): *Latin American music*

latitude /'lætɪtjuːd/ **noun** [U] the distance of a place north or south of the line that we imagine around the middle of the earth (the equator)

➤ Latitude is measured in **degrees**. Look at **longitude**.

••▶ picture at **earth**

latter /'lætə/ **adj** (*formal*) (only *before* a noun) nearer to the end of a period of time; later: *Interest rates should fall in the latter half of the year.* —**latterly** adv

the latter **noun** [sing], **pron** the second (of two people or things that are mentioned): *The options were History and Geography. I chose the latter.*

➤ The first of two people or things that are mentioned is **the former**.

★**laugh¹** /lɑːf/ **verb** [I] to make the sounds that show you are happy or amused: *His jokes* *always make me laugh.* ● *to laugh out loud*

IDIOM **die laughing** → DIE

PHRASAL VERB **laugh at sb/sth 1** to show, by laughing, that you think sb/sth is funny: *The children laughed at the clown.* **2** to show that you think sb is ridiculous: *Don't laugh at him. He can't help the way he speaks.*

laugh² /lɑːf/ **noun** [C] **1** the sound or act of laughing: *Her jokes got a lot of laughs.* ● *We all had a good laugh at what he'd written.* **2** (*informal*) a person or thing that is amusing

IDIOMS **for a laugh** as a joke
have the last laugh → LAST¹

laughable /'lɑːfəbl/ **adj** deserving to be laughed at; of very poor quality; ridiculous

laughing stock noun [C] a person or thing that other people laugh at or make fun of (in an unpleasant way)

laughter /'lɑːftə/ **noun** [U] the sound or act of laughing: *Everyone roared with laughter.*

launch¹ /lɔːntʃ/ **verb** [T] **1** to send a ship into the water or a spacecraft into the sky **2** to start sth new or to show sth for the first time: *to launch a new product onto the market*

launch² /lɔːntʃ/ **noun** [C] **1** [usually sing] the act of launching a ship, spacecraft, new product, etc **2** a large motor boat

launderette /lɔːn'dret/ (*US* **Laundromat** /'lɔːndrəmæt/) **noun** [C] a type of shop where you pay to wash and dry your clothes in machines

laundry /'lɔːndri/ **noun** (*pl* **laundries**) **1** [U] clothes, etc that need washing or that are being washed: *dirty laundry*

> It is more usual to talk about doing **the washing** than 'the laundry'.

2 [C] a business where you send sheets, clothes, etc to be washed and dried

lava /'lɑːvə/ **noun** [U] hot liquid rock that comes out of a mountain with an opening in the top (**volcano**) ●➤ picture at **volcano**

lavatory /'lævətri/ **noun** [C] (*pl* **lavatories**) (*formal*) **1** a toilet **2** a room that contains a toilet, a place to wash your hands, etc: *Where's the ladies' lavatory, please?* ●➤ Look at the note at **toilet**.

lavender /'lævəndə/ **noun** [U] a garden plant with purple flowers that smells very pleasant

lavish¹ /'lævɪʃ/ **adj 1** giving or spending a large amount of money: *She was always very lavish with her presents.* **2** large in amount or number: *a lavish meal*

lavish² /'lævɪʃ/ **verb**
PHRASAL VERB **lavish sth on sb/sth** to give sth generously or in large quantities to sb

★**law** /lɔː/ **noun 1** [C] an official rule of a country or state that says what people may or may not do: *There's a new law about wearing seat belts in the back of cars.* **2 the law** [U] all the laws in a country or state: *Stealing is* ***against the law.*** ● *to break the law* ● *to obey the law* ●➤ Look at **legal**. **3** [U] the law as a subject of study or as a profession: *She is studying law.* ● *My brother works for* ***a law firm*** *in Brighton.* ●➤ Look at **legal**. **4** [C] (in

science) a statement of what always happens in certain situations or conditions: *the laws of mathematics/gravity*

IDIOM **law and order** a situation in which the law is obeyed

law-abiding adj (used about a person) obeying the law: *law-abiding citizens*

lawbreaker /'lɔːbreɪkə/ **noun** [C] a person who does not obey the law; a criminal

law court (also **court of 'law**) **noun** [C] a place where legal cases are decided by a judge and often by twelve members of the public (**a jury**)

> A **case** is **tried** in a law court. Look also at **defence**, **prosecution** and **witness**.

lawful /'lɔːfl/ **adj** allowed or recognized by law: *We shall use all lawful means to obtain our demands.* ●➤ Look at **legal** and **legitimate**.

lawless /'lɔːləs/ **adj** (used about a person or his/her actions) breaking the law –**lawlessness noun** [U]

lawn /lɔːn/ **noun** [C,U] an area of grass in a garden or park that is regularly cut ●➤ picture on page C7

lawnmower /'lɔːnməʊə/ **noun** [C] a machine that is used for cutting the grass in a garden ●➤ picture at **garden**

lawsuit /'lɔːsuːt/ **noun** [C] a legal argument in a court of law that is between two people or groups and not between the police and a criminal

★**lawyer** /'lɔːjə/ **noun** [C] a person who has a certificate in law: *to consult a lawyer*

> A **solicitor** is a lawyer who gives legal advice, prepares legal documents, arranges the buying or selling of land, etc. A **barrister** is a lawyer who speaks for you in a court of law. The American term is **attorney**.

lax /læks/ **adj** not having high standards; not strict: *Their security checks are rather lax.*

★**lay¹** /leɪ/ **verb** [T] (*pt, pp* **laid** /leɪd/) **1** to put sb/sth carefully in a particular position or on a surface: *She laid a sheet over the dead body.* ● *He laid the child gently down on her bed.* ● *'Don't worry,' she said, laying her hand on my shoulder.* **2** to put sth in the correct position for a particular purpose: *They're laying new electricity cables in our street.* **3** to prepare sth for use: *The police have laid a trap for him and I think they'll catch him this time.* ● *Can you lay the table please* (= put the knives, forks, plates, etc on it)? **4** to produce eggs: *Hens lay eggs.* **5** (used with some nouns to give a similar meaning to a verb) to put: *They laid all the blame on him* (= they blamed him). ● *to lay emphasis on sth* (= emphasize it)

PHRASAL VERBS **lay sth down** to give sth as a rule: *It's all laid down in the rules of the club.*
lay off (sb) (*informal*) to stop annoying sb: *Can't you lay off me for a bit?*
lay sb off to stop giving work to sb: *They've laid off 500 workers at the car factory.*
lay sth on (*informal*) to provide sth: *They're*

laying on a trip to London for everybody.

lay sth out 1 to spread out a number of things so that you can see them easily or so that they look nice: *All the food was laid out on a table in the garden.* **2** to arrange sth in a planned way

lay² /leɪ/ **adj** (only *before* a noun) **1** (used about a religious teacher) who has not been officially trained as a priest: *a lay preacher* **2** without special training in or knowledge of a particular subject

★**lay³** *past tense* of LIE²

layabout /'leɪəbaʊt/ **noun** [C] (*Brit informal*) a person who is lazy and does not do much work

ˈ**lay-by** (*US* ˈ**rest stop**) **noun** [C] (*pl* **lay-bys**) an area at the side of a road where vehicles can stop for a short time

★**layer** /'leɪə/ **noun** [C]
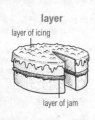
layer

layer of icing

layer of jam

a thickness or quantity of sth that is on sth else or between other things: *A thin layer of dust covered everything in the room.* • *It's very cold. You'll need several layers of clothing.* • *the top/bottom layer* • *the inner/outer layer*

layman /'leɪmən/ **noun** [C] (*pl* **-men** /-mən/) a person who does not have special training in or knowledge of a particular subject: *a medical reference book for the layman*

laze /leɪz/ **verb** [I] **laze (about/around)** to do very little; to rest or relax

★**lazy** /'leɪzi/ **adj** (**lazier**; **laziest**) **1** (used about a person) not wanting to work: *Don't be lazy. Come and give me a hand.* **2** moving slowly or without much energy: *a lazy smile* **3** making you feel that you do not want to do very much: *a lazy summer's afternoon* –**lazily adv** –**laziness noun** [U]

lb *abbr* pound(s); a measurement of weight

lead¹ /liːd/ **verb** (*pt, pp* **led** /led/) **1** [T] to go with or in front of a person or animal to show the way or to make him/her/it go in the right direction: *The teacher led the children out of the hall and back to the classroom.* • *She led the horse into its stable.* • *The receptionist led the way to the boardroom.* • *to lead sb by the hand*

➤ You usually **guide** a tourist or somebody who needs special help: *to guide visitors around Oxford* • *He guided the blind woman to her seat.* If you **direct** somebody, you explain with words how to get somewhere: *Could you direct me to the nearest Post Office, please?*

2 [I] (used about a road or path) to go to a place: *I don't think this path leads anywhere.* **3** [I] **lead to sth** to have sth as a result: *Eating too much sugar can lead to all sorts of health problems.* **4** [T] **lead sb to do sth** to influence what sb does or thinks: *He led me to*

believe he really meant what he said. **5** [T] to have a particular type of life: *They lead a very busy life.* • *to lead a life of crime* **6** [I,T] to be winning or in first place in front of sb: *Hingis is leading by two games to love.* • *Hingis is leading Williams by two games to love.* **7** [I,T] to be in control or the leader of sth: *Who is going to lead the discussion?*

IDIOM **lead sb astray** to make sb start behaving or thinking in the wrong way

PHRASAL VERB **lead up to sth** to be an introduction to or cause of sth

lead² /liːd/ **noun 1 the lead** [sing] the first place or position in front of other people or organizations: *The French athlete has gone into the lead.* • *Who is in the lead?* • *Britain has taken the lead in developing computer software for that market.* **2** [sing] the distance or amount by which sb/sth is in front of another person or thing: *The company has a lead of several years in the development of the new technology.* **3** [C] the main part in a play, show or other situation: *Who's playing the lead in the new film?* • *Jill played a lead role in getting the company back into profit.* **4** [C] a piece of information that may help to give the answer to a problem: *The police are following all possible leads to track down the killer.* **5** [C] a long chain or piece of leather that is connected to the collar around a dog's neck and used for keeping the dog under control: *All dogs must be kept on a lead.* **6** [C] a piece of wire that carries electricity to a piece of equipment •➤ picture at **cable**

IDIOM **follow sb's example/lead** → FOLLOW

lead³ /led/ **noun 1** [U] (*symbol* **Pb**) a soft heavy grey metal. Lead is used in pipes, roofs, etc. **2** [C,U] the black substance inside a pencil that makes a mark when you write

★**leader** /'liːdə/ **noun** [C] **1** a person who is a manager or in charge of sth: *a weak/strong leader* • *She is a natural leader* (= she knows how to tell other people what to do). **2** the person or thing that is best or in first place: *The leader has just finished the third lap.* • *The new shampoo soon became a market leader.*

leadership /'liːdəʃɪp/ **noun 1** [U] the state or position of being a manager or the person in charge: *Who will take over the leadership of the party?* **2** [U] the qualities that a leader should have: *She's got good leadership skills.* **3** [C,with sing or pl verb] the people who are in charge of a country, organization, etc

leading /'liːdɪŋ/ **adj 1** best or most important: *He's one of the leading experts in this field.* • *She played a leading role in getting the business started.* **2** that tries to make sb give a particular answer: *The lawyer was warned not to ask the witness leading questions.*

ˈ**lead story noun** [C] the most important piece of news in a newspaper or on a news programme

★**leaf¹** /liːf/ **noun** [C] (*pl* **leaves** /liːvz/) one of the thin, flat, usually green parts of a plant or

tree: *The trees lose their leaves in autumn.*
••➤ picture on pages C2 and C3

leaf² /liːf/ **verb**
PHRASAL VERB **leaf through sth** to turn the pages of a book, etc quickly and without looking at them carefully

★**leaflet** /'liːflət/ **noun** [C] a printed piece of paper that gives information about sth. Leaflets are usually given free of charge: *I picked up a leaflet advertising a new club.*

leafy /'liːfi/ **adj 1** having many leaves: *a leafy bush* **2** (used about a place) with many trees

league /liːg/ **noun** [C] **1** a group of sports clubs that compete with each other for a prize: *the football league* ● *Which team is top of the league at the moment?* ••➤ Look at **rugby league**. **2** a group of people, countries, etc that join together for a particular purpose: *the League of Nations* **3** a level of quality, ability, etc: *He is so much better than the others. They're just not in the same league.*
IDIOM **in league (with sb)** having a secret agreement (with sb)

★**leak¹** /liːk/ **verb 1** [I,T] to allow liquid or gas to get through a hole or crack: *The boat was leaking badly.* **2** [I] (used about liquid or gas) to get out through a hole or crack: *Water is leaking in through the roof.* **3** [T] **leak sth (to sb)** to give secret information to sb: *The committee's findings were leaked to the press before the report was published.*
PHRASAL VERB **leak out** (used about secret information) to become known

★**leak²** /liːk/ **noun** [C] **1** a small hole or crack which liquid or gas can get through: *There's a leak in the pipe.* ● *The roof has sprung a leak.* **2** the liquid or gas that gets through a hole: *a gas leak* **3** the act of giving away information that should be kept secret —**leaky** **adj**

leakage /'liːkɪdʒ/ **noun** [C,U] the action of coming out of a hole or crack; the liquid or gas that comes out: *a leakage of dangerous chemicals*

lean

She is leaning against a tree.

He is leaning out of a window.

★**lean¹** /liːn/ **verb** (*pt, pp* **leant** /lent/ or **leaned** /liːnd/) **1** [I] to move the top part of your body and head forwards, backwards or to the side: *He leaned across the table to pick up the phone.* ● *She leaned out of the window and waved.* ● *Just lean back and relax.* **2** [I]

to be in a position that is not straight or upright: *That wardrobe leans to the right.* **3** [I,T] **lean (sth) against/on sth** to rest against sth so that it gives support; to put sth in this position: *She had to stop and lean on the gate.* ● *Please don't lean bicycles against this window.*

lean² /liːn/ **adj 1** (used about a person or animal) thin and in good health **2** (used about meat) having little or no fat **3** not producing much: *a lean harvest*

leap¹ /liːp/ **verb** [I] (*pt, pp* **leapt** /lept/ or **leaped** /liːpt/) **1** to jump high or a long way: *The horse leapt over the wall.* ● *A fish suddenly leapt out of the water.* ● *We all leapt into the air when they scored the goal.* ● (*figurative*) *Share prices leapt to a record high yesterday.* **2** to move quickly: *I looked at the clock and leapt out of bed.* ● *She leapt back when the pan caught fire.*
PHRASAL VERB **leap at sth** to accept a chance or offer with enthusiasm: *She leapt at the chance to work in television.*

leap² /liːp/ **noun** [C] **1** a big jump: *He took a flying leap at the wall but didn't get over it.* ● (*figurative*) *My heart gave a leap when I heard the news.* **2** a sudden large change or increase in sth: *The development of penicillin was a great leap forward in the field of medicine.*

leapfrog /'liːpfrɒg/ **noun** [U] a children's game in which one person bends over and another person jumps over his/her back

leap year noun [C] one year in every four, in which February has 29 days instead of 28

★**learn** /lɜːn/ **verb** (*pt, pp* **learnt** /lɜːnt/ or **learned** /lɜːnd/) **1** [I,T] **learn (sth) (from sb/sth)** to get knowledge, a skill, etc (from sb/sth): *I'm not very good at driving yet – I'm still learning.* ● *We're learning about China at school.* ● *Debbie is learning to play the piano.* ● *to learn a foreign language/a musical instrument* ● *Where did you learn how to swim?* **2** [I] **learn (of/about) sth** to get some information about sth; to find out: *I was sorry to learn about your father's death.* **3** [T] to study sth so that you can repeat it from memory **4** [I] to understand or realize: *We should have learned by now that we can't rely on her.* ● *It's important to learn from your mistakes.*
IDIOMS **learn the hard way** to understand or realize sth by having an unpleasant experience rather than by being told
learn your lesson to understand what you must do/not do in the future because you have had an unpleasant experience

learned /'lɜːnɪd/ **adj** having a lot of knowledge from studying; for people who have a lot of knowledge

learner /'lɜːnə/ **noun** [C] a person who is learning: *a learner driver* ● *books for young learners*

learning /'lɜːnɪŋ/ **noun** [U] **1** the process of learning sth: *new methods of language learning* **2** knowledge that you get from studying

lease /liːs/ **noun** [C] a legal agreement that

allows you to use a building or land for a fixed period of time in return for rent: *The lease on the flat runs out/expires next year.* –**lease** verb [T]: *They lease the land from a local farmer.* ● *Part of the building is leased out to tenants.*

least /liːst/ determiner, pron, adv **1** (used as the superlative of *little*) smallest in size, amount, degree, etc: *He's got the least experience of all of us.* ● *You've done the most work, and I'm afraid John has done the least.* **2** less than anyone/anything else; less than at any other time: *He's the person who needs help least.* ● *I bought the least expensive tickets.* ● *My uncle always appears when we're least expecting him.* ••➤ opposite **most**

IDIOMS **at least 1** not less than, and probably more: *It'll take us at least two hours to get there.* ● *You could at least say you're sorry!* **2** even if other things are wrong: *It may not be beautiful but at least it's cheap.* **3** used for correcting sth that you have just said: *I saw him – at least I think I saw him.*

at the (very) least not less and probably much more: *It'll take six months to build at the very least.*

least of all especially not: *Nobody should be worried, least of all you.*

not in the least (bit) not at all: *It doesn't matter in the least.* ● *I'm not in the least bit worried.*

last but not least ➔ **LAST**[1]

to say the least used to say that sth is in fact much worse, more serious, etc than you are saying: *Adam's going to be annoyed, to say the least, when he sees his car.*

leather /ˈleðə/ noun [U] the skin of animals which has been specially treated. Leather is used to make shoes, bags, coats, etc: *a leather jacket*

leave[1] /liːv/ verb (pt, pp **left** /left/) **1** [I,T] to go away from sb/sth: *We should leave now if we're going to get there by eight o'clock.* ● *I felt sick in class so I left the room.* ● *At what age do most people leave school in your country?* ● *Barry left his wife for another woman.*

➤ Notice that if you leave sb/sth it may be permanently or just for a short time: *He leaves the house at 8.00 every morning.* ● *He left New York and went to live in Canada.* **Depart** is a more formal word and is used about boats, trains, aeroplanes, etc: *The 6.15 train for Bath departs from Platform 3.*

2 [T] to cause or allow sb/sth to stay in a particular place or condition; to not deal with sth: *Leave the door open, please.* ● *Don't leave the iron on when you are not using it.* ● *Why do you always leave your homework till the last minute?* **3** [T] **leave sth (behind)** to forget to bring sth with you: *I'm afraid I've left my homework at home. Can I give it to you tomorrow?* ● *I can't find my glasses. Maybe I left them behind at work.* **4** [T] to make sth happen or stay as a result: *Don't put that cup on the table. It'll leave a mark.* **5** [T] to not use sth: *Leave some milk for me, please.* **6** [T] to put sth somewhere: *Val left a message on her*

answerphone. ● *I left him a note.* **7** [T] to give sth to sb when you die: *In his will he left everything to his three sons.* **8** [T] to give the care or responsibility for sb/sth to another person: *I'll leave it to you to organize all the food.*

IDIOMS **leave sb/sth alone** to not touch, annoy or speak to sb/sth

leave go (of sth) to stop touching or holding sth: *Will you please leave go of my arm.*

be left high and dry ➔ **HIGH**[1]

leave sb in the lurch to leave sb without help in a difficult situation

leave sth on one side ➔ **SIDE**[1]

PHRASAL VERB **leave sb/sth out (of sth)** to not include sb/sth: *This doesn't make sense. I think the typist has left out a line.*

leave[2] /liːv/ noun [U] a period of time when you do not go to work: *Diplomats working abroad usually get a month's home leave each year.* ● *annual leave* ● *sick leave* ● *Molly's not working – she's on maternity leave.* ••➤ Look at the note at **holiday**.

leaves plural of **LEAF**[1]

lecture /ˈlektʃə/ noun [C] **1** a lecture (on/about sth) a talk that is given to a group of people to teach them about a particular subject, especially as part of a university course: *The college has asked a journalist to come and give a lecture on the media.* ● *a course of lectures* **2** a serious talk to sb that explains what he/she has done wrong or how he/she should behave: *We got a lecture from a policemen about playing near the railway.* –**lecture** verb: *Alex lectures in European studies at London University.* ● *The policeman lectured the boys about playing ball games in the road.*

lecturer /ˈlektʃərə/ noun [C] a person who gives talks to teach people about a subject, especially as a job in a university

led past tense, past participle of **LEAD**[1]

ledge /ledʒ/ noun [C] a narrow shelf underneath a window, or a narrow piece of rock that sticks out on the side of a cliff or mountain

leek /liːk/ noun [C] a long thin vegetable that is white at one end with thin green leaves ••➤ picture on page C3

left[1] *past tense, past participle of* **LEAVE**[1]

left[2] /left/ adj **1** on the side where your heart is in the body: *I've broken my left arm.* ••➤ opposite **right 2** still available after everything else has been taken or used: *Is there any bread left?* ● *How much time do we have left?* ● *If there's any money left over, we'll have a cup of coffee.*

left[3] /left/ adv to or towards the left: *Turn left just past the Post Office.* ••➤ opposite **right**

left[4] /left/ noun **1** [U] the left side: *In Britain we drive on the left.* ● *Our house is just to/on the left of that tall building.* ● *If you look to your left you'll see some of the city's most famous landmarks.* ••➤ opposite **right 2 the Left** [with sing or pl verb] political parties or groups that support a particular set of ideas and beliefs (socialism)

'left-hand adj (only *before* a noun) of or on the left: *the left-hand side of the road* ● *a left-hand drive car*

,left-'handed adj, adv **1** using the left hand rather than the right hand: *Are you left-handed?* ● *I write left-handed.* **2** made for left-handed people to use: *left-handed scissors*

,left-'luggage office (*Brit*) (*US* **'baggage room**) noun [C] the place at a railway station, etc where you can leave your luggage for a short time

leftovers /'leftəʊvəz/ noun [pl] food that has not been eaten when a meal has finished

,left 'wing noun [sing] **1** [with sing or pl verb] the members of a political party, group, etc that want more social change than the others in their party: *the left wing of the Labour Party* **2** the left side of the field in some team sports: *He plays on the left wing for Ajax.* –left-wing adj ● ► opposite **right-wing**

★**leg** /leg/ noun [C] **1** one of the parts of the body on which a person or animal stands or walks: *A spider has eight legs.* ● *She sat down and crossed her legs.* ● ► picture at **insect** **2** one of the parts of a chair, table etc on which it stands: *the leg of a chair/table* ● *a chair/table leg* **3** the part of a pair of trousers, shorts, etc that covers the leg: *There's a hole in the leg of my trousers/my trouser leg.* **4** one part or section of a journey, competition, etc: *The band are in Germany on the first leg of their world tour.*

[IDIOMS] **pull sb's leg** → **PULL¹**
stretch your legs → **STRETCH¹**

legacy /'legəsi/ noun [C] (*pl* **legacies**) money or property that is given to you after sb dies, because he/she wanted you to have it: *He received a large legacy from his grandmother.*

★**legal** /'li:gl/ adj **1** (only *before* a noun) using or connected with the law: *legal advice* ● *to take legal action against sb* ● *the legal profession* **2** allowed by law: *It is not legal to own a gun without a licence.* ● ► opposite **illegal** ● ► Look at **lawful** and **legitimate**. –legally /'li:gəli/ adv: *Schools are legally responsible for the safety of their pupils.*

legality /li:'gæləti/ noun [U] the state of being legal

legalize (also **-ise**) /'li:gəlaɪz/ verb [T] to make sth legal

legend /'ledʒənd/ noun **1** [C] an old story that may or may not be true: *the legend of Robin Hood* **2** [U] such stories when they are grouped together: *According to legend, Robin Hood lived in Sherwood Forest.* **3** [C] a famous person or event: *a movie/jazz/baseball legend* –legendary /'ledʒəndri/ adj: *the legendary heroes of Greek myths* ● *Michael Jordan, the legendary basketball star*

leggings /'legɪŋz/ noun [pl] a piece of women's clothing that fits tightly over both legs from the waist to the feet, like a very thin pair of trousers ● ► picture on page C6

legible /'ledʒəbl/ adj that is clear enough to be read easily: *His writing is so small that it's barely legible.* ● ► opposite **illegible**. Look at

readable. –legibility /,ledʒə'bɪləti/ noun [U] –legibly /-əbli/ adv

legislate /'ledʒɪsleɪt/ verb [I] legislate (for/ against sth) to make a law or laws

legislation /,ledʒɪs'leɪʃn/ noun [U] **1** a group of laws: *The government is introducing new legislation to help small businesses.* **2** the process of making laws

legitimate /lɪ'dʒɪtɪmət/ adj **1** reasonable or acceptable: *a legitimate excuse/question/concern* **2** allowed by law: *Could he earn so much from legitimate business activities?* ● ► Look at **lawful** and **legal**. **3** (*old-fashioned*) (used about a child) having parents who are married to each other ● ► opposite **illegitimate** –legitimately adv

leisure /'leʒə/ noun [U] the time when you do not have to work; spare time: *Shorter working hours mean that people have more leisure.* ● *leisure activities*

[IDIOM] **at your leisure** (*formal*) when you have free time: *Look through the catalogue at your leisure and then order by telephone.*

'leisure centre noun [C] a public building where you can do sports and other activities in your free time

leisurely /'leʒəli/ adj without hurry: *a leisurely Sunday breakfast* ● *I always cycle at a leisurely pace.*

★**lemon** /'lemən/ noun [C,U] a yellow fruit with sour juice that is used for giving flavour to food and drink: *a slice of lemon* ● *Add the juice of 2 lemons.* ● ► picture on page C3

lemonade /,lemə'neɪd/ noun [C,U] **1** (*Brit*) a colourless sweet drink with a lot of bubbles in it **2** a drink that is made from fresh lemon juice, sugar and water

★**lend** /lend/ verb [T] (*pt, pp* **lent** /lent/) **1** lend sb sth; lend sth to sb to allow sb to use sth for a short time or to give sb money that must be paid back after a certain period of time: *Could you lend me £10 until Friday?* ● *He lent me his bicycle.* ● *He lent his bicycle to me.* ● ► opposite **borrow** ● ► picture at **borrow**

> If a bank, etc lends you money you must **pay** it **back/ repay** it over a fixed period of time with extra payments (called **interest**).

2 (*formal*) lend sth (to sth) to give or add sth: *to lend advice/support* ● *This evidence lends weight to our theory.*

[IDIOM] **lend (sb) a hand/lend a hand (to sb)** to help sb

[PHRASAL VERB] **lend itself to sth** to be suitable for sth

lender /'lendə/ noun [C] a person or organization that lends sth, especially money

★**length** /leŋθ/ noun **1** [U,C] the size of sth from one end to the other; how long sth is: *to measure the length of a room* ● *It took an hour to walk the length of Oxford Street.* ● *The tiny insect is only one millimetre in length.* ● *This snake can grow to a length of two metres.* ● ► Look at **width** and **breadth**.

depth / length / width / depth / height

2 [U] the amount of time that sth lasts: *Many people complained about the length of time they had to wait.* ● *the length of a class/speech/film* **3** [U] the number of pages in a book, a letter, etc **4** [C] the distance from one end of a swimming pool to the other: *I can swim a length in thirty seconds.* **5** [C] a piece of sth long and thin: *a length of material/rope/string*

IDIOMS **at length** for a long time or in great detail: *We discussed the matter at great length.*

go to great lengths to make more effort than usual in order to achieve sth: *I went to great lengths to find this book for you.*

the length and breadth of sth to or in all parts of sth: *They travelled the length and breadth of India.*

lengthen /ˈleŋθən/ **verb** [I,T] to become longer or to make sth longer

lengthways /ˈleŋθweɪz/ (also **lengthwise** /ˈleŋθwaɪz/) **adv** in a direction from one end to the other of sth: *Fold the paper lengthwise.*

lengthy /ˈleŋθi/ **adj** very long

lenient /ˈliːniənt/ **adj** (used about a punishment or person who punishes) not as strict as expected –**lenience** (also **leniency** /-ənsi/) **noun** [U] –**leniently adv**

lens /lenz/ **noun** [C] (*pl* **lenses**) **1** a curved piece of glass that makes things look bigger, clearer, etc when you look through it

➤ Some people wear **contact lenses** to help them see better. You may use a **zoom** or **telephoto lens** on your camera.

•➤ picture at **camera** **2** = **CONTACT LENS**
•➤ picture at **glasses**

lent¹ *past tense, past participle* of **LEND**

Lent² /lent/ **noun** [U] a period of 40 days starting in February or March, when some Christians stop doing or eating certain things for religious reasons: *I'm giving up smoking for Lent.*

lentil /ˈlentl/ **noun** [C] a small brown, orange or green seed that can be dried and used in cooking: *lentil soup/stew*

Leo /ˈliːəʊ/ **noun** [C,U] the fifth sign of the zodiac, the Lion

leopard /ˈlepəd/ **noun** [C] a large wild animal of the cat family that has yellow fur with dark spots. Leopards live in Africa and Southern Asia.

➤ A female leopard is called a **leopardess** and a baby is called a **cub**.

•➤ picture at **lion**

leotard /ˈliːətɑːd/ **noun** [C] a piece of clothing that fits the body tightly from the neck down to the tops of the legs. Leotards are worn by dancers or women doing certain sports.

leper /ˈlepə/ **noun** [C] a person who has leprosy

leprosy /ˈleprəsi/ **noun** [U] a serious infectious disease that affects the skin, nerves, etc and can cause parts of the body to fall off

lesbian /ˈlezbiən/ **noun** [C] a woman who is sexually attracted to other women –**lesbian adj**: *a lesbian relationship* –**lesbianism noun** [U] •➤ Look at **gay** and **homosexual**.

★**less¹** /les/ **determiner, pron, adv** **1** (used with uncountable nouns) a smaller amount (of): *It took less time than I thought.* ● *I'm too fat – I must try to eat less.* ● *It's not far – it'll take less than an hour to get there.*

➤ Some people use **less** with plural nouns: *less cars*, but **fewer** is the form which is still considered to be correct: *fewer cars.*

2 not so much (as): *He's less intelligent than his brother.* ● *It rains less in London than in Manchester.* ● *People work less well when they're tired.* •➤ opposite **more**

IDIOMS **less and less** becoming smaller and smaller in amount or degree

more or less → **MORE²**

less² /les/ **prep** taking a certain number or amount away; minus: *You'll earn £10 an hour, less tax.*

lessen /ˈlesn/ **verb** [I,T] to become less; to make sth less

lesser /ˈlesə/ **adj, adv** (only *before* a noun) not as great/much as: *He is guilty and so, to a lesser extent, is his wife.* ● *a lesser-known artist*

IDIOM **the lesser of two evils** the better of two bad things

★**lesson** /ˈlesn/ **noun** [C] **1** a period of time when you learn or teach sth: *She gives piano lessons.* ● *I want to take extra lessons in English conversation.* ● *a driving lesson* **2** something that is intended to be or should be learnt: *I hope we can learn some lessons from this disaster.*

IDIOMS **learn your lesson** → **LEARN**

teach sb a lesson → **TEACH**

★**let** /let/ **verb** [T] (*pres part* **letting**; *pt, pp* **let**) **1** let sb/sth do sth to allow sb/sth to do sth; to make sb/sth able to do sth: *My parents let me stay out till 11 o'clock.* ● *I wanted to borrow Dave's bike but he wouldn't let me.* ● *This ticket lets you travel anywhere in the city for a day.*

➤ You cannot use **let** in the passive here. You must use **allow** or **permit** and **to**: *They let him take the exam again.* ● *He was allowed to take the exam again.* Look at the note at **allow**.

2 to allow sth to happen: *He's let the dinner burn again!* ● *Don't let the fire go out.* **3** used for offering help to sb: *Let me help you carry your bags.* **4** to allow sb/sth to go somewhere: *Open the windows and let some fresh air in.* ● *She was let out of prison yesterday.* **5** used for making suggestions about what you and other people can do: *'Let's go to the cinema tonight.' 'Yes, let's.'*

➤ The negative is **let's not** or (in British English only) **don't let's**: *Let's not/Don't let's go to that awful restaurant again.*

[I] **intransitive**, a verb which has no object: *He laughed.*   [T] **transitive**, a verb which has an object: *He ate an apple.*

6 let sth (out) (to sb) to allow sb to use a building, room, etc in return for rent: *They let out two rooms to students.* ● *There's a flat to let in our block.* ••➤ Look at the note at **hire**.

IDIOMS **let alone** and certainly not: *We haven't decided where we're going yet, let alone booked the tickets.*

let sb/sth go; let go of sb/sth to stop holding sb/sth: *Let me go. You're hurting me!* ● *Hold the rope and don't let go of it.*

let sb know to give sb a piece of information; to tell sb: *I'll phone you to let you know what time we'll be arriving.*

let me see; let's see used when you are thinking or trying to remember sth: *Where did I put the car keys? Let's see. I think I left them by the telephone.*

let sth slip to accidentally say sth that you should keep secret

let's say for example: *You could work two mornings a week, let's say Tuesday and Friday.*

let yourself go 1 to relax without worrying what other people think: *After work I like to go out with friends and let myself go.* **2** to allow yourself to become untidy, dirty, etc

PHRASAL VERBS **let sb down** to not do sth that you promised to do for sb; to disappoint sb: *Rob really let me down when he didn't finish the work on time.*

let on (about sth) (to sb) to tell sb a secret: *He didn't let on how much he'd paid for the vase.*

let sb off to not punish sb, or to give sb a lesser punishment than expected: *He expected to go to prison but they let him off with a fine.*

let sth out to make a sound with your voice: *to let out a scream/sigh/groan/yell*

lethal /ˈliːθl/ *adj* that can cause death or great damage: *a lethal weapon/drug* –**lethally** /ˈliːθəli/ *adv*

lethargy /ˈleθədʒi/ *noun* [U] the feeling of being very tired and not having any energy –**lethargic** /ləˈθɑːdʒɪk/ *adj*

★**letter** /ˈletə/ *noun* [C] **1** a written or printed message that you send to sb: *I got a letter from Matthew this morning.* ● *I'm writing a **thank-you** letter to my uncle for the flowers he sent.*

➤ When you have written a letter you put it in an **envelope**, **address** it, **put/stick** a **stamp** on it and then **post** (*US* **mail**) it. You may **forward** a letter to a person who has moved away.

2 a written or printed sign that represents a sound in a language: *'Z' is the last letter of the English alphabet.*

➤ Letters may be written or printed as **capitals** or **small** letters: *Is 'east' written with a capital or a small 'e'?*

'**letter box** *noun* [C] **1** a hole in a door or wall for putting letters, etc through **2** (*US* **mailbox**) a small box near the main door of a building or by the road in which letters are left for the owner to collect **3** = **POSTBOX**

lettuce /ˈletɪs/ *noun* [C,U] a plant with large green leaves which are eaten cold in salads: *a lettuce leaf* •➤ picture on page C3

leukaemia (*US* **leukemia**) /luːˈkiːmɪə/ *noun* [U] a serious disease of the blood which often results in death

★**level**[1] /ˈlevl/ *noun* [C] **1** the amount, size or number of sth (compared to sth else): *a low level of unemployment* ● *high stress/pollution levels* **2** the height, position, standard, etc of sth: *He used to play tennis at a high level.* ● *an intermediate-level student* ● *top-level discussions* **3** a way of considering sth: *on a spiritual/personal/professional level* **4** a flat surface or layer: *a multi-level shopping centre*

★**level**[2] /ˈlevl/ *adj* **1** with no part higher than any other; flat: *Make sure the shelves are level before you fix them in position.* ● *Put the tent up on level ground.* ● *a level teaspoon of sugar* **2** level (with sb/sth) at the same height, standard or position: *The boy's head was level with his father's shoulder.* ● *The teams are level on 34 points.*

IDIOM **a level playing field** a situation in which everyone has an equal chance of success

level[3] /ˈlevl/ *verb* [T] (**levelling; levelled;** *US* **leveling; leveled**) to make sth flat, equal or level: *The ground needs levelling before we lay the patio.* ● *Juventus levelled the score with a late goal.* ● *Many buildings were levelled* (= destroyed) *in the earthquake.*

PHRASAL VERBS **level sth at sb/sth** to aim sth at sb/sth: *They levelled serious criticisms at the standard of teaching.*

level off/out to become flat, equal or level

,**level 'crossing** (*US* ,**railroad crossing**) *noun* [C] a place where a railway crosses the surface of a road

,**level-'headed** *adj* calm and sensible; able to make good decisions in a difficult situation

lever /ˈliːvə/ *noun* [C] **1** a handle that you pull or push in order to make a machine, etc work: *Pull the lever towards you.* ● *the gear lever in a car* **2** a bar or tool that is used to lift or open sth when you put pressure or force on one end: *You need to get the tyre off with a lever.* –**lever** *verb* [T]: *The police had to lever the door open.*

leverage /ˈliːvərɪdʒ/ *noun* [U] the act of using a lever to lift or open sth; the force needed to do this

levy /ˈlevi/ *verb* [T] (*pt, pp* **levied**) (*written*) **levy sth (on sb)** to officially demand and collect money, etc: *to levy a tax/fine*

liability /ˌlaɪəˈbɪləti/ *noun* (*pl* **liabilities**) **1** [U] liability (for sth) the state of being responsible for sth: *The company cannot accept liability for damage to cars in this car park.* **2** [C] (*informal*) a person or thing that can cause a lot of problems, cost a lot of money, etc

liable /ˈlaɪəbl/ *adj* (not before a noun) **1 liable to do sth** likely to do sth: *We're all liable to have accidents when we are very tired.* **2 liable to sth** likely to have or suffer from sth: *The area is liable to floods.* **3** liable (for sth) (in law) responsible for sth

liaise /li'eɪz/ **verb** [I] liaise (with sb/sth) to work closely with a person, group, etc and give him/her/it regular information about what you are doing

liaison /li'eɪzn/ **noun 1** [U,sing] liaison (between A and B) communication between two or more people or groups that work together **2** [C] a secret sexual relationship

liar /'laɪə/ **noun** [C] a person who does not tell the truth: *She called me a liar.* •➤ Look at the verb and noun **lie**.

Lib Dem /ˌlɪb 'dem/ **abbr** (in British politics) Liberal Democrat

libel /'laɪbl/ **noun** [C,U] the act of printing a statement about sb that is not true and would give people a bad opinion of him/her: *The singer is suing the newspaper for libel.* –**libel verb** [T] (**libelling**; **libelled**; *US* **libeling**; **libeled**): *The actor claims he was libelled in the magazine article.*

liberal /'lɪbərəl/ **adj 1** accepting different opinions or kinds of behaviour; tolerant: *He has very liberal parents.* **2** (in politics) believing in or based on principles of commercial freedom, freedom of choice, and avoiding extreme social and political change: *liberal policies/politicians* **3** not strictly limited in amount or variety –**liberal noun** [C]: *He's always considered himself a liberal.* –**liberalism** /-ɪzəm/ **noun** [U]

the ˌLiberal 'Democrats noun [pl] a political party in Britain that represents views that are not extreme

liberally /'lɪbrəli/ **adv** freely or in large amounts

liberate /'lɪbəreɪt/ **verb** [T] liberate sb/sth (from sth) to allow sb/sth to be free: *France was liberated in 1945.* –**liberation** /ˌlɪbə'reɪʃn/ **noun** [U]

liberated /'lɪbəreɪtɪd/ **adj** free from the restrictions of traditional opinions or ways of behaving

liberty /'lɪbəti/ **noun** [C,U] (*pl* **liberties**) the freedom to go where you want, do what you want, etc: *We must defend our civil liberties at all costs.* •➤ Look at **freedom**.
IDIOM at liberty (to do sth) free or allowed to do sth: *You are at liberty to leave when you wish.*

Libra /'liːbrə/ **noun** [C,U] the seventh sign of the zodiac, the Scales

librarian /laɪ'breəriən/ **noun** [C] a person who works in or is in charge of a library

★**library** /'laɪbrəri; 'laɪbri/ **noun** [C] (*pl* **libraries**) **1** a room or building that contains a collection of books, etc that can be looked at or borrowed: *My library books are due back tomorrow.* •➤ Look at **bookshop**. **2** a private collection of books, etc

lice *plural of* **LOUSE**

★**licence** (*US* **license**) /'laɪsns/ **noun 1** [C] a licence (for sth/to do sth) an official paper that shows that you are allowed to do or have sth: *Do you have a licence for this gun?* ● *The shop*

has applied for a licence to sell alcoholic drinks. •➤ Look at **driving licence**. **2** [U] (*formal*) licence (to do sth) permission or freedom to do sth: *The soldiers were given licence to kill if they were attacked.*

'licence plate (*US* **license plate**) = **NUMBER PLATE**

license[1] /'laɪsns/ **verb** [T] to give official permission for sth: *Is that gun licensed?*

license[2] (*US*) = **LICENCE**

licensee /ˌlaɪsn'siː/ **noun** [C] a person who has a licence to sell alcoholic drinks

'licensing laws noun [pl] (*Brit*) the laws that control when and where alcoholic drinks can be sold

lick/bite/swallow

licking   biting   swallowing

★**lick** /lɪk/ **verb** [T] to move your tongue across sth: *The child licked the spoon clean.* ● *I licked the envelope and stuck it down.* –**lick noun** [C]

licorice = **LIQUORICE**

★**lid** /lɪd/ **noun** [C] **1** the top part of a box, pot, etc that can be lifted up or taken off •➤ picture at **container** and **pan 2** = **EYELID**

★**lie**[1] /laɪ/ **verb** [I] (*pres part* **lying**; *pt, pp* **lied**) lie (to sb) (about sth) to say or write sth that you know is not true: *He lied about his age in order to join the army.* ● *How could you lie to me?!* –**lie noun** [C]: *to tell a lie* ● *That story about his mother being ill was just* ***a pack of lies***.

➤ You tell a **white lie** in order not to hurt sb's feelings. Look at **liar** and **fib**.

★**lie**[2] /laɪ/ **verb** [I] (*pres part* **lying**; *pt* **lay** /leɪ/; *pp* **lain** /leɪn/) **1** to be in or move into in a flat or horizontal position (so that you are not standing or sitting): *He lay on the sofa and went to sleep.* ● *to lie on your back/side/front* ● *The book lay open in front of her.*

➤ Remember that **lie** cannot be used with an object. If you put an object in a flat position you **lay** it down.

2 to be or stay in a certain state or position: *Snow lay thick on the ground.* ● *The hills lie to the north of the town.* ● *They are young and their whole lives lie ***ahead*** of them.* **3** lie (in sth) to exist or to be found somewhere: *The problem lies in deciding when to stop.*
IDIOMS lie in wait (for sb) to hide somewhere waiting to attack, surprise or catch sb
lie low to try not to attract attention to yourself
PHRASAL VERBS lie about/around to relax and do nothing
lie back to relax and do nothing while sb else works, etc
lie behind sth to be the real hidden reason

for sth: *We may never know what lay behind his decision to resign.*

lie down (used about a person) to be in or move into a flat or horizontal position so that you can rest

➤ Note the related expression **have a lie-down**.

lie in (*informal*) to stay in bed later than usual because you do not have to get up

➤ Note the related expression **have a lie-in**. Compare **oversleep**.

lie with sb (*informal*) to be sb's responsibility to do sth

'lie detector noun [C] a piece of equipment that can show if a person is telling the truth or not

Lieut (also **Lt**) abbr Lieutenant

lieutenant /lef'tenənt/ noun [C] an officer at a middle level in the army, navy or air force

★ **life** /laɪf/ noun (*pl* **lives** /laɪvz/) **1** [U] the quality that people, animals or plants have when they are not dead: *Do you believe in life after death?* • *to bring sb/come back to life* **2** [U] living things: *Life on earth began in a very simple form.* • *No life was found on the moon.* • *There was no sign of life in the deserted house.* • *plant life* **3** [C,U] the state of being alive as a human being: *Would you **risk** your **life** to protect your property?* • *Doctors fought all night to **save** her **life**.* **4** [C,U] the period during which sb/sth is alive or exists: *I've lived in this town **all** my **life**.* • *I spent my early life in London.* • *to have a short/long/ exciting life* **5** [U] the things that you may experience while you are alive: *Life can be hard for a single parent.* • *I'm not happy with the situation, but I suppose **that's life**.* **6** [C,U] a way of living: *They went to America to **start a new life**.* • *They **lead** a busy life.* • *married life* **7** [U] energy; activity: *Young children are **full of life**.* • *These streets **come to life** in the evenings.* **8** [U] something that really exists and is not just a story, a picture, etc: *I wonder what that actor's like **in real life**.* • *Do you draw people **from life** or from photographs?*

IDIOMS **a fact of life** → FACT
the facts of life → FACT
full of beans/life → FULL¹
get a life (*spoken*) used to tell sb to stop being boring and do sth more interesting
lose your life → LOSE
a matter of life and/or death → MATTER¹
take your (own) life to kill yourself
a walk of life → WALK²
a/sb's way of life → WAY¹
have the time of your life → TIME¹

,life-and-'death (also **,life-or-'death**) adj (only *before* a noun) very serious or dangerous: *a life-and-death struggle/matter/decision*

lifebelt /'laɪfbelt/ (also **lifebuoy** /'laɪfbɔɪ/) noun [C] (*Brit*) a ring that is made from light material which will float. A lifebelt is thrown to a person who has fallen into water to stop him/her from sinking.

lifeboat /'laɪfbəʊt/ noun [C] **1** a small boat that is carried on a large ship and that is used to escape from the ship if it is in danger of sinking **2** a special boat that is used for rescuing people who are in danger at sea

'life cycle noun [C] the series of forms into which a living thing changes as it develops

'life expectancy noun [C,U] (*pl* **life expectancies**) the number of years that a person is likely to live

lifeguard /'laɪfgɑːd/ noun [C] a person at a beach or swimming pool whose job is to rescue people who are in difficulty in the water

'life jacket noun [C] a plastic or rubber jacket without sleeves that can be filled with air. A life jacket is used to make sb float if he/she falls into water. •➤ picture at **boat**

lifeless /'laɪfləs/ adj **1** dead or appearing to be dead **2** without energy or interest; dull

lifelike /'laɪflaɪk/ adj looking like a real person or thing: *The flowers are made of silk but they are very lifelike.*

lifeline /'laɪflaɪn/ noun [C] something that is very important for sb and that he/she depends on: *For many old people their telephone is a lifeline.*

lifelong /'laɪflɒŋ/ adj (only *before* a noun) for all of your life: *a lifelong friend*

'life-size(d) adj of the same size as the real person or thing: *a life-sized statue*

lifespan /'laɪfspæn/ noun [C] the length of time that sth is likely to live, work, last, etc: *A mosquito has a lifespan of only a few days.*

'life story noun [C] (*pl* **life stories**) the story of sb's life

lifestyle /'laɪfstaɪl/ noun [C] the way that you live

lifetime /'laɪftaɪm/ noun [C] the period of time that sb is alive

★ **lift¹** /lɪft/ verb **1** [T] lift sb/sth (up) to move sb/sth to a higher level or position: *He lifted the child up onto his shoulders.* • *Lift your arm very gently and see if it hurts.* • *It took two men to lift the piano.* **2** [T] to move sb/sth from one place or position to another: *She lifted the suitcase down from the rack.* **3** [T] to end or remove a rule, law, etc: *The ban on public meetings has been lifted.* **4** [I,T] to become or make sb happier: *The news lifted our spirits.* **5** [I] (used about clouds, fog, etc) to rise up or disappear: *The mist lifted towards the end of the morning.* **6** [T] (*informal*) lift sth (from sb/sth) to steal or copy sth: *Most of his essay was lifted straight from the textbook.* •➤ Look at **shoplifting**.

PHRASAL VERB **lift off** (used about a spacecraft) to rise straight up from the ground

lift² /lɪft/ noun **1** (*US* **elevator**) [C] a machine in a large building that is used for carrying people or goods from one floor to another: *It's on the third floor so we'd better **take the lift**.* **2** [C] a free ride in a car, etc: *Can you **give me a lift** to the station, please?* • *I got a lift from a passing car.* **3** [sing] (*informal*) a feeling of being happier or more confident than before: *Her words of encouragement **gave** the whole team **a lift**.* **4** [sing] the action of moving or being moved to a higher position

IDIOM **thumb a lift** ➔ THUMB²

'**lift-off** noun [C] the start of the flight of a spacecraft when it leaves the ground

ligament /'lɪgəmənt/ noun [C] a strong band in a person's or animal's body that holds the bones, etc together

lights

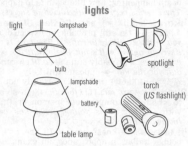

light   lampshade   spotlight   bulb   lampshade   torch (US flashlight)   battery   table lamp

★**light¹** /laɪt/ noun **1** [U,C] the energy from the sun, a lamp, etc that allows you to see things: *a beam/ray of light* • *The light was too dim for us to read by.* • *Strong light is bad for the eyes.* • *We could see strange lights in the sky.*

➤ You may see things by **sunlight**, **moonlight**, **firelight**, **candlelight** or **lamplight**.

2 [C] something that produces light, for example an electric lamp: *Suddenly all the lights went out/came on.* • *the lights of the city in the distance* • *If the lights* (= traffic lights) *are red, stop!* • *That car hasn't got its lights on.*

➤ A light may be **on** or **off**. You **put**, **switch** or **turn** a light **on**, **off** or **out**: *Shall I put the light on? It's getting dark in here.* • *Please turn the lights out before you leave.*

3 [C] something, for example a match, that can be used to light a cigarette, start a fire, etc: *Have you got a light?*

IDIOMS **bring sth/come to light** to make sth known or to become known

cast light on sth ➔ CAST¹

give sb/get the green light ➔ GREEN¹

in a good, bad, etc light (used about the way that sth is seen or described by other people) well, badly, etc: *The newspapers often portray his behaviour in a bad light.*

in the light of because of; considering

set light to sth to cause sth to start burning

shed light on sth ➔ SHED²

★**light²** /laɪt/ adj **1** not of great weight: *Carry this bag – it's the lightest.* • *I've lost weight – I'm five kilos lighter than I used to be.* • *light clothes* (= for summer) •➤ opposite **heavy 2** having a lot of light: *In summer it's still light at 10 o'clock.* • *a light room* •➤ opposite **dark 3** (used about a colour) pale: *a light-blue sweater* •➤ opposite **dark 4** not great in amount, degree, etc: *Traffic in London is light on a Sunday.* • *a light prison sentence* • *a light wind* • *a light breakfast* **5** not using much force; gentle: *a light touch on the shoulder* **6** not hard or tiring: *light exercise* • *light*

entertainment/reading **7** (used about sleep) not deep: *I'm a light sleeper, so the slightest noise wakes me.* –**lightness** noun [U]

★**light³** /laɪt/ verb (*pt, pp* **lit** or **lighted**) **1** [I,T] to begin or to make sth begin to burn: *The gas cooker won't light.* • *to light a fire*

➤ **Lighted** is usually used as an adjective before a noun. **Lit** is used as the past participle of the verb: *Candles were lit in memory of the dead.* • *The church was full of lighted candles.*

2 [T] to give light to sth: *The street is well/badly lit at night.* • *We only had a small torch to light our way.*

PHRASAL VERB **light (sth) up 1** to make sth bright with light: *The fireworks lit up the whole sky.* **2** (used about sb's face, eyes, etc) to become bright with happiness or excitement **3** to start smoking a cigarette

light⁴ /laɪt/ adv without much luggage: *I always travel light.*

'**light bulb** = BULB(1)

lighten /'laɪtn/ verb [I,T] **1** to become lighter in weight or to make sth lighter **2** to become or to make sth brighter

lighter /'laɪtə/ = CIGARETTE LIGHTER

,**light-'headed** adj feeling slightly ill and not in control of your thoughts and movements

,**light-'hearted** adj **1** intended to be funny and enjoyable **2** happy and without problems

lighthouse /'laɪthaʊs/ noun [C] a tall building with a light at the top to warn and guide ships near the coast

lighting /'laɪtɪŋ/ noun [U] the quality or type of lights used in a room, building, etc

lightly /'laɪtli/ adv **1** gently; with very little force: *He touched her lightly on the arm.* **2** only a little; not much: *lightly cooked/spiced/whisked* **3** not seriously; without serious thought: *We do not take our customers' complaints lightly.*

IDIOM **get off/be let off lightly** to avoid serious punishment or trouble

lightning¹ /'laɪtnɪŋ/ noun [U] a bright flash of light that appears in the sky during a storm: *The tree was **struck by lightning** and burst into flames.* • *a flash of lightning*

➤ Lightning is usually followed by a noise called **thunder**.

lightning² /'laɪtnɪŋ/ adj (only *before* a noun) very quick or sudden: *a lightning attack*

lightweight /'laɪtweɪt/ noun [C], adj **1** a person who is in one of the lightest weight groups in certain fighting sports: *a lightweight boxing champion* **2** (a thing) weighing less than usual: *a lightweight suit for the summer*

likable = LIKEABLE

★**like¹** /laɪk/ verb [T] **1** like sb/sth; like doing sth; like to do sth; like sb about sb/sth to find sb/sth pleasant; to enjoy sth: *He's nice. I like him a lot.* • *Do you like their new flat?* • *How do you like John's new girlfriend?* • *I like my coffee strong.* • *I like playing tennis.*

● *I like to go to the cinema on Thursdays.*
● *What is it you like about Sarah so much?*
● *She didn't like it when I shouted at her.* ● *I don't like her borrowing my things without asking.* ● *The job seems strange at first, but you'll **get to like** it.* ● *I don't **like the look/sound/idea/thought** of that.* ••➤ opposite **dislike**

➤ When **like** means 'have the habit of...' or 'think it's a good thing to...', it is followed by the infinitive: *I like to get up early so that I can go for a run before breakfast.*

2 to want: *Do what you like. I don't care.* ● *We can go whenever you like.* ● *I didn't like to disturb you while you were eating.*

➤ **Would like** is a more polite way to say 'want': *Would you like something to eat?* ● *I'd like to speak to the manager.* ● *We'd like you to come to dinner on Sunday.* ● *How would you like to come to Scotland with us?* **Would like** is always followed by the infinitive, never by the – *ing* form.

IDIOMS **if you like** used for agreeing with sb or suggesting sth in a polite way: *'Shall we stop for a rest?' 'Yes, if you like.'*
I like that! (*Brit informal*) used for saying that sth is not true or not fair
like the look/sound of sb/sth to have a good impression of sb/sth after seeing or hearing about him/her/it

★**like²** /laɪk/ **prep, conj 1** similar to sb/sth: *You look very/just/exactly **like** your father.* ● *Those two singers **sound like** cats!* ● *Your house is **nothing like** how I imagined it.*

➤ If you want somebody to give a description of something you ask: **'What's he/she/it like?'**: *Tell me about your town. What's it like?* ● *'What's your brother like?' 'He's tall and fair, and quite serious.'* ● *What was it like being interviewed on TV?*

2 (in compounds) in the manner of; similar to: *childlike innocence/simplicity* ● *a very lifelike statue* **3** in the same way as sb/sth: *Stop behaving like children.* ● *That's not right. Do it like this.* ● *She can't draw like her sister can.* **4** for example; such as: *They enjoy most team games, like football and rugby.* **5** typical of a particular person: *It was just like Maria to be late.* **6** (*informal*) as if: *She behaves like she owns the place.* **7** (*slang*) (used before saying what sb said, how sb felt, etc): *When I saw the colour of my hair I was like 'Wow, I can't believe it!'*

IDIOMS **like anything** (*spoken*) very much, fast, hard, etc: *We had to pedal like anything to get up the hill.*
nothing like → **NOTHING**
something like about; approximately: *The cathedral took something like 200 years to build.*
that's more like it (used to say that sth is better than before): *The sun's coming out now – that's more like it!*

like³ /laɪk/ **noun 1** [sing] a person or thing that is similar to sb/sth else: *I enjoy going round castles, old churches **and the like**.*

● *She was a great singer, and we may never see her like/the like of her again.* **2 likes** [pl] things that you like: *Tell me about some of your **likes and dislikes**.* –**like adj** (*formal*)

likeable (also **likable**) /ˈlaɪkəbl/ **adj** (used about a person) easy to like; pleasant

likelihood /ˈlaɪklihʊd/ **noun** [U] the chance of sth happening; how likely sth is to happen: *There seems very little likelihood of success.*

★**likely** /ˈlaɪkli/ **adj, adv** (**likelier; likeliest**)
1 likely (to do sth) probable or expected: *Do you think it's likely to rain?* ● *The boss is not likely to agree.* ● *It's not likely that the boss will agree.* **2** probably suitable: *a likely candidate for the job* ••➤ opposite **unlikely**

IDIOM **not likely!** (*informal*) certainly not

liken /ˈlaɪkən/ **verb** [T] (*formal*) **liken sb/sth to sb/sth** to compare one person or thing with another: *This young artist has been likened to Picasso.*

likeness /ˈlaɪknəs/ **noun** [C,U] the fact of being similar in appearance; an example of this: *The witness's drawing turned out to be **a good likeness** of the attacker.*

likewise /ˈlaɪkwaɪz/ **adv** (*formal*) the same; in a similar way: *I intend to send a letter of apology and suggest that you do likewise.*

liking /ˈlaɪkɪŋ/ **noun** [sing] **a liking (for sb/sth)** the feeling that you like sb/sth: *I have a liking for spicy food.*

IDIOM **too...for your liking** that you do not like because he/she/it has too much of a particular quality: *The music was a bit too loud for my liking.*

lilac /ˈlaɪlək/ **noun** [C,U], **adj 1** a tree or large bush that has large purple or white flowers in spring **2** (of) a pale purple colour

lilo (also **Li-lo**™) /ˈlaɪləʊ/ **noun** [C] (*pl* **lilos**) (*Brit*) a plastic or rubber bed that you fill with air when you want to use it. A Lilo is used on the beach or for camping. ••➤ picture on page C8

lily /ˈlɪli/ **noun** [C] (*pl* **lilies**) a type of plant that has large white or coloured flowers in the shape of a bell ••➤ picture on page C2

limb /lɪm/ **noun** [C] **1** a leg or an arm of a person **2** one of the main branches of a tree
IDIOM **out on a limb** without the support of other people

lime /laɪm/ **noun 1** [C] a fruit that looks like a small green lemon ••➤ picture on page C3 **2** [U] (also **lime ˈgreen**) a yellowish-green colour **3** [U] a white substance that is used for making cement and also for adding to soil to improve its quality

the limelight /ˈlaɪmlaɪt/ **noun** [U] the centre of public attention: *to be in/out of the limelight*

★**limit¹** /ˈlɪmɪt/ **noun** [C] **1** the greatest or smallest amount of sth that is allowed or possible: *a speed/age/time limit* ● *He was fined for exceeding the speed limit.* ● *There's a limit to the amount of time I'm prepared to spend on this.* **2** the outside edge of a place or area: *the city limits* ● *Lorries are not allowed within a two-mile limit of the town centre.*
IDIOMS **off limits** (*US*) = **OUT OF BOUNDS**

within limits only up to a reasonable point or amount

★**limit²** /'lɪmɪt/ **verb** [T] **limit sb/sth (to sth)** to keep sb/sth within or below a certain amount, size, degree or area: *In China families are limited to just one child.*

limitation /ˌlɪmɪ'teɪʃn/ **noun 1** [C,U] **(a)** limitation (on sth) the act of limiting or controlling sth; a condition that puts a limit on sth: *There are no limitations on what we can do.* **2** [pl] **limitations** things that you cannot do: *It is important to know your own limitations.*

limited /'lɪmɪtɪd/ **adj** small or restricted in number, amount, etc: *Book early because there are only a limited number of seats available.* •▸ opposite **unlimited**

ˌ**limited 'company** **noun** [C] (*abbr* **Ltd**) a company whose owners only have to pay a limited amount of its debts if it fails

limousine /'lɪməziːn; ˌlɪmə'ziːn/ (also *informal* **limo** /'lɪməʊ/) **noun** [C] a large expensive car that usually has a sheet of glass between the driver and the passengers in the back

limp¹ /lɪmp/ **verb** [I] to walk with difficulty because you have hurt your leg or foot: *The goalkeeper limped off the field with a twisted ankle.* –**limp noun** [sing]: *to walk with a limp*

limp² /lɪmp/ **adj** not firm or strong: *You should put those flowers in water before they go limp.*

lines

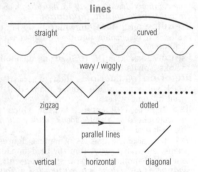

straight   curved

wavy / wiggly

zigzag   dotted

parallel lines

vertical   horizontal   diagonal

★**line¹** /laɪn/ **noun 1** [C] a long thin mark on the surface of sth or on the ground: *to draw a line* • *a straight/wiggly/dotted line* • *The old lady had lines on her forehead.* • *The ball was definitely over the line.* • *the finishing line of a race* **2** [C] a row of people, things, words on a page, etc: *There was a long line of people waiting at the Post Office.* • *Start each paragraph on a new line.* **3** [C] a border or limit between one place or thing and another: *to cross state lines* • *There's a thin line between showing interest and being nosy.* **4** [C,usually sing] a direction or course of movement, thought or action: *He was so drunk he couldn't walk **in a straight line**.* • *The answer's not quite correct, but you're **on the right lines**.* • *The two countries' economies are developing **along** similar **lines**.* **5** [C] a piece of rope or string: *Hang out the*

clothes on the (washing) line, please. • a fishing line **6** [C] a telephone or electricity wire or connection: *I'm sorry – the line is engaged. Can you try again later?* • *I'll just check for you. Can you **hold the line** (= wait)?* **7** [C] a section of railway track **8 lines** [pl] the words that are spoken by an actor in a play, etc **9** [C] a company that provides transport by air, ship, etc: *an airline* **10** [sing] one type of goods in a shop, etc **11** [C] the place where an army is fighting: *There's renewed fighting on **the front line**.* **12** [C] a series of people in a family, things or events that follow one another in time: *He comes from **a long line of** musicians.* **13** [C] something that you do as a job, do well, or enjoy doing: *What **line of business/work** are you in?*

▌IDIOMS▐ **draw the line at sth/doing sth** → **DRAW¹**

drop sb a line → **DROP¹**

in line for sth likely to get sth: *You could be in line for promotion if you keep working like this.*

in line with sth similar to sth; in agreement with sth: *These changes will bring the industry in line with the new laws.*

on line connected to or available on a computer system

somewhere along/down the line at some time; sooner or later

take a hard line (on sth) → **HARD¹**

toe the (party) line → **TOE²**

line² /laɪn/ **verb** [T] **1** (often passive) to cover the inside surface of sth with a different material **2** to form lines or rows along sth: *Crowds lined the streets to watch the race.*

▌PHRASAL VERBS▐ **line up (for sth)** (*US*) to form a line of people; to queue

line sth up (*informal*) to arrange or organize sth: *She lined the bottles up on the shelf.*

lined /laɪnd/ **adj 1** covered in lines: *a face lined with age* • *lined paper* **2 -lined** (used in compounds) having the object mentioned all along the side(s); having the inside surface covered with the material mentioned: *a tree-lined avenue* • *fur-lined boots*

linen /'lɪnɪn/ **noun** [U] **1** a type of strong cloth that is made from a natural substance (flax) **2** sheets and other cloth coverings used in the house on a bed, table, etc: *bedlinen*

liner /'laɪnə/ **noun** [C] **1** a large ship that carries people, etc long distances **2** something that is put inside sth else to keep it clean or protect it. A liner is usually thrown away after it has been used: *a dustbin liner*

linger /'lɪŋgə/ **verb** [I] **linger (on)** to stay somewhere or do sth for longer than usual: *His eyes lingered on the money in her bag.*

lingerie /'lænʒəri/ **noun** [U] (used in shops, etc) women's underwear

linguist /'lɪŋgwɪst/ **noun** [C] a person who is good at learning foreign languages; a person who studies or teaches language(s)

linguistic /lɪŋ'gwɪstɪk/ **adj** connected with language or the study of language

linguistics /lɪŋ'gwɪstɪks/ noun [U] the scientific study of language

lining /'laɪnɪŋ/ noun [C,U] material that covers the inside surface of sth: *I've torn the lining of my coat.*
> IDIOM **every cloud has a silver lining** → **CLOUD¹**

★**link¹** /lɪŋk/ noun [C] **1** a link (between A and B); a link (with sb/sth) a connection or relationship between two or more people or things: *There is a strong link between smoking and heart disease.* **2** one ring of a chain •➤ picture at **padlock 3** a means of travelling or communicating between two places: *To visit similar web sites to this one, click on the links at the bottom of the page.*

link² /lɪŋk/ verb [T] link A to/with B; link A and B (together) to make a connection between two or more people or things: *The new bridge will link the island to the mainland.* • *The computers are linked together in a network.*
> PHRASAL VERB **link up (with sb/sth)** to join together (with sb/sth): *All our branches are linked up by computer.*

'link-up noun [C] the joining together or connection of two or more things

linoleum /lɪ'nəʊliəm/ (also *informal* **lino** /'laɪnəʊ/) noun [U] a type of plastic covering for floors

lioness
cub
mane
lion
tiger
leopard
panther
jaguar
cheetah

★**lion** /'laɪən/ noun [C] a large animal of the cat family that lives in Africa and parts of southern Asia. Male lions have a large amount of hair around their head and neck (**a mane**).

> A female lion is called a **lioness** and a young lion is called a **cub**. The noise a lion makes is a **roar**.

★**lip** /lɪp/ noun [C] **1** either of the two soft edges at the opening of your mouth: *to kiss sb on the lips* •➤ picture on page C5

> You have a **top/upper** lip and a **bottom/lower** lip.

2 -lipped (used to form compound adjectives) having the type of lips mentioned: *thin-lipped* **3** the edge of a cup or sth that is shaped like a cup
> IDIOM **purse your lips** → **PURSE²**

'lip-read verb [I,T] (*pt, pp* **lip-read** /-red/) to understand what sb is saying by looking at the movements of his/her lips

lipstick /'lɪpstɪk/ noun [C,U] a substance that is used for giving colour to your lips: *to put on some lipstick* • *a new lipstick*

liqueur /lɪ'kjʊə/ noun [U] a strong sweet alcoholic drink that is often drunk in small quantities after a meal

★**liquid** /'lɪkwɪd/ noun [C,U] a substance, for example water, that is not solid or a gas and that can flow or be poured –**liquid** adj

liquidate /'lɪkwɪdeɪt/ verb [T] **1** to close a business because it has no money left **2** to destroy or remove sb/sth that causes problems –**liquidation** /ˌlɪkwɪ'deɪʃn/ noun [U]: *If the company doesn't receive a big order soon, it will have to go into liquidation.*

liquidize (also **-ise**) /'lɪkwɪdaɪz/ verb [T] to cause sth to become liquid –**liquidizer** (also **liquidiser**) = **BLENDER**

liquor /'lɪkə/ noun [U] (*US*) strong alcoholic drinks; spirits

liquorice (*US* **licorice**) /'lɪkərɪʃ/ noun [U] a black substance, made from a plant, that is used in some sweets

lisp /lɪsp/ noun [C] a speech fault in which 's' is pronounced as 'th': *He speaks with a slight lisp.* –**lisp** verb [I,T]

★**list** /lɪst/ noun [C] a series of names, figures, items, etc that are written, printed or said one after another: *a checklist of everything that needs to be done* • *a waiting list* • *Your name is third on the list.* –**list** verb [T]: *to list items in alphabetical order*

★**listen** /'lɪsn/ verb [I] **1** listen (to sb/sth) to pay attention to sb/sth in order to hear him/her/it: *Now please listen carefully to what I have to say.* • *to listen to music/the radio* •➤ Look at the note at **hear**. **2** listen to sb/sth to take notice of or believe what sb says: *You should listen to your parents' advice.* –**listen** noun [sing] (*informal*): *Have a listen and see if you can hear anything.*
> PHRASAL VERBS **listen (out) for sth** to wait to hear sth: *to listen (out) for a knock on the door* **listen in (on/to sth)** to listen to sb else's private conversation: *Have you been listening in on my phone calls?*

listener /'lɪsənə/ noun [C] a person who listens: *When I'm unhappy I always phone Charlie – he's such a good listener.* • *The new radio* *show has attracted a record number of listeners.*

listless /'lɪstləs/ **adj** tired and without energy –**listlessly adv**

lit *past tense, past participle of* **LIGHT**[3]

liter (*US*) = **LITRE**

literacy /'lɪtərəsi/ **noun** [U] the ability to read and write ••► opposite **illiteracy**

literal /'lɪtərəl/ **adj 1** (used about the meaning of a word or phrase) original or basic: *The adjective 'big-headed' is hardly ever used in its literal sense.* ••► Look at **figurative** and **metaphor. 2** (used when translating, etc) dealing with each word separately without looking at the general meaning

literally /'lɪtərəli/ **adv 1** according to the basic or original meaning of the word, etc: *You can't translate these idioms literally.* **2** (*informal*) used for emphasizing sth: *We were literally frozen to death* (= we were very cold).

literary /'lɪtərəri/ **adj** of or concerned with literature: *literary criticism • a literary journal*

literate /'lɪtərət/ **adj 1** able to read and write ••► opposite is **illiterate** ••► noun **literacy** ••► Look at **numerate. 2** well-educated

literature /'lɪtrətʃə/ **noun** [U] **1** writing that is considered to be a work of art. Literature includes novels, plays and poetry: *French literature* **2** literature (on sth) printed material about a particular subject

litre (*US* **liter**) /'liːtə/ **noun** [C] (*abbr* l) a measure of liquid: *ten litres of petrol • a litre bottle of wine*

litter /'lɪtə/ **noun 1** [U] pieces of paper, rubbish, etc that are left in a public place ••► picture at **bin 2** [C] all the young animals that are born to one mother at the same time: *a litter of six puppies* –**litter verb** [T]: *The streets were littered with rubbish.*

'litter bin noun [C] a container to put rubbish in, in the street or a public building ••► picture at **bin**

★ **little**[1] /'lɪtl/ **adj 1** not big; small: *a little bag of sweets • Do you want the big one or the little one? • a little mistake/problem*

> **Little** is often used with another adjective: *a little old lady • a cute little kitten • What a funny little shop!* ••► Look at the note at **small**.

2 (used about distance or time) short: *Do you mind waiting a little while? • We only live a little way from here. • It's only a little further.* **3** young: *a little girl/boy • my little brother • I was very naughty when I was little.*

little[2] /'lɪtl/ **adv, pron, determiner 1** (also as a noun after *the*) not much or not enough: *I slept very little last night. • a little-known author • They have very little money. • There is little hope that she will recover.* ••► Look at **less** and **least. 2 a little** a small amount of sth: *I like a little sugar in my tea. • Could I*

have a little help, please?

[IDIOM] **little by little** slowly: *After the accident her strength returned little by little.*

a little /ə 'lɪtl/ **adv, pron 1** rather; to a small degree: *This skirt is a little too tight.*

> **A little bit** or **a bit** is often used instead of 'a little': *I was feeling a little bit tired so I decided not to go out.*

2 a small amount: *'Is there any butter left?' 'Yes, just a little.'*

★ **live**[1] /lɪv/ **verb 1** [I] to have your home in a particular place: *Where do you live? • He still lives with his parents.* **2** [I] to be or stay alive: *She hasn't got long to live. • to live to a great age* **3** [I,T] to pass or spend your life in a certain way: *to live a quiet life • to live in comfort/poverty* **4** [I] to enjoy all the opportunities of life fully: *I want to live a bit before settling down and getting married.*

[IDIOM] **live/sleep rough** → **ROUGH**[3]

[PHRASAL VERBS] **live by sth** to follow a particular belief or set of principles

live by doing sth to get the money, food, etc you need by doing a particular activity: *They live by hunting and fishing.*

live for sb/sth to consider sb/sth to be the most important thing in your life: *He felt he had nothing to live for after his wife died.*

not live sth down to be unable to make people forget sth bad or embarrassing that you have done

live it up to enjoy yourself in an exciting way, usually spending a lot of money

live off sb/sth to depend on sb/sth in order to live: *Barry lives off tinned food. • She could easily get a job but she still lives off her parents.*

live on to continue to live or exist: *Mozart is dead but his music lives on.*

live on sth 1 to have sth as your only food: *to live on bread and water* **2** to manage to buy what you need to live: *I don't know how they live on so little money!*

live out sth 1 to actually do sth that you only imagined doing before: *to live out your dreams/fantasies* **2** to spend the rest of your life in a particular way

live through sth to survive an unpleasant experience: *She lived through two wars.*

live together to live in the same house, etc as sb and have a sexual relationship with him/her

live up to sth to be as good as expected: *Children sometimes find it hard to live up to their parents' expectations.*

live with sb = **LIVE TOGETHER**

live with sth to accept sth unpleasant that you cannot change: *It can be hard to live with the fact that you are getting older.*

★ **live**[2] /laɪv/ **adj, adv 1** having life; not dead: *Have you ever touched a real live snake?* **2** (used about a radio or television programme) seen or heard as it is happening: *live coverage of the Olympic Games • This programme is coming live from Wembley Stadium. • to go out live on TV* **3** performed or performing for an audience: *That pub has* *live music on Saturdays.* **4** (used about a bomb, bullet, etc) that has not yet exploded **5** (used about a wire, etc) carrying electricity

livelihood /'laɪvlihʊd/ **noun** [C,usually sing] the way that you earn money: *to lose your livelihood*

★ **lively** /'laɪvli/ **adj** (**livelier**; **liveliest**) full of energy, interest, excitement, etc: *lively children* • *The town is quite lively at night.*

liven /'laɪvn/ **verb**

PHRASAL VERB **liven (sb/sth) up** to become or make sb/sth become more interesting and exciting: *Once the band began to play the party livened up.*

liver /'lɪvə/ **noun 1** [C] the part of your body that cleans your blood •➤ picture on page C5 **2** [U] the liver of an animal when it is cooked and eaten as food: *fried liver and onions*

lives *plural of* LIFE

livestock /'laɪvstɒk/ **noun** [U] animals that are kept on a farm, such as cows, pigs, sheep, etc

living¹ /'lɪvɪŋ/ **adj 1** alive now: *He has no living relatives.* •➤ Look at the note at **alive**. **2** still used or practised now: *living languages/traditions* •➤ opposite **dead**

living² /'lɪvɪŋ/ **noun 1** [C,usually sing] money to buy things that you need in life: *What do you do for a living?* **2** [U] your way or quality of life: *The cost of living has risen in recent years.* • *The standard of living is very high in that country.*

'living room (*especially Brit* **'sitting room**) **noun** [C] the room in a house where people sit, relax, watch TV, etc together

lizard

lizard /'lɪzəd/ **noun** [C] a small animal with four legs, dry skin and a long tail

load¹ /ləʊd/ **noun** [C] **1** something (heavy) that is being or is waiting to be carried: *a truck carrying a load of sand* **2** (often in compounds) the quantity of sth that can be carried: *bus loads of tourists* **3 loads (of sth)** [pl] (*informal*) a lot (of sth): *There are loads of things to do in London in the evenings.*

IDIOM **a load of rubbish, etc** (*informal*) nonsense

load² /ləʊd/ **verb 1** [I,T] **load (sth/sb) (up) (with sth); load (sth/sb) (into/onto sth)** to put a large quantity of sth into or onto sb/ sth: *They loaded the plane (up) with supplies.* • *Load the washing into the machine.* **2** [I] to receive a load: *The ship is still loading.* **3** [T] to put a program or disk into a computer: *First, switch on the machine and load the disk.* **4** [T] to put sth into a machine, a weapon, etc so that it can be used: *to load film into a camera* • *to load a gun* •➤ opposite **unload**

loaded /'ləʊdɪd/ **adj 1 loaded (with sth)** carrying a load; full and heavy **2** (used especially about a gun or a camera) containing a

bullet, a film, etc **3** giving an advantage: *The system is loaded in their favour.* **4** (*informal*) (not before a noun) having a lot of money; rich

loaf /ləʊf/ **noun** [C] (*pl* **loaves** /ləʊvz/) bread baked in one piece: *a loaf of bread* •➤ picture at **bread**

loan /ləʊn/ **noun 1** [C] money, etc that sb/sth lends you: *to take out a bank loan* • *to pay off a loan* **2** [U] the act of lending sth or the state of being lent: *The books are on loan from the library.* –**loan verb** [T] (*formal*) loan sth (to sb)

➤ In US English **loan** is less formal and more common.

loathe /ləʊð/ **verb** [T] (not used in the continuous tenses) to hate sb/sth

➤ Although this verb is not used in the continuous tenses, it is common to see the present participle (= *-ing* form): *Loathing the thought of having to apologize, she knocked on his door.*

–**loathsome** /-səm/ **adj** –**loathing noun** [U]

loaves *plural of* LOAF

lob /lɒb/ **verb** [I,T] (**lobbing**; **lobbed**) (*sport*) to hit, kick or throw a ball high into the air so that it lands behind your opponent –**lob noun** [C]

lobby¹ /'lɒbi/ **noun** [C] (*pl* **lobbies**) **1** the area that is just inside a large building where people can meet and wait: *a hotel lobby* **2** [with sing or pl verb] a group of people who try to influence politicians to do or not do sth: *the anti-smoking lobby*

lobby² /'lɒbi/ **verb** [I,T] (*pres part* **lobbying**; *3rd pers sing pres* **lobbies**; *pt, pp* **lobbied**) to try to influence a politician or the government to do or not do sth

lobe /ləʊb/ **noun** [C] **1** = EAR LOBE **2** one part of an organ of the body, especially the brain or lungs

lobster /'lɒbstə/ **noun 1** [C] a large shellfish that has eight legs. A lobster is bluish-black but it turns red when it is cooked. •➤ picture at **shellfish 2** [U] a cooked lobster eaten as food

★ **local¹** /'ləʊkl/ **adj** of a particular place (near you): *local newspapers/radio* • *the local doctor/policeman/butcher* •➤ Look at **international**, **national** and **regional**. –**locally adv**: *I do most of my shopping locally.*

local² /'ləʊkl/ **noun** [C] **1** [usually pl] a person who lives in a particular place: *The locals seem very friendly.* **2** (*Brit informal*) a pub that is near your home where you often go to drink

localize (also **-ise**) /'ləʊkəlaɪz/ **verb** [T] to limit sth to a particular place or area

'local time noun [U] the time at a particular place in the world: *We arrive in Singapore at 2 o'clock in the afternoon, local time.*

locate /ləʊ'keɪt/ **verb** [T] **1** to find the exact position of sb/sth: *The damaged ship has been located two miles off the coast.* **2** to put or build sth in a particular place –**located adj**: *Where exactly is your office located?*

location /ləʊˈkeɪʃn/ *noun* **1** [C] a place or position: *Several locations have been suggested for the new office block.* **2** [U] the action of finding where sb/sth is

IDIOM **on location** (used about a film, television programme, etc) made in a suitable place outside the building where films, etc are usually made (a studio): *The series was filmed on location in Thailand.*

loch /lɒk/ *noun* [C] the Scottish word for a lake: *the Loch Ness monster*

lock¹ /lɒk/ *verb* **1** [I,T] to close or fasten (sth) so that it can only be opened with a key: *Have you locked the car?* ● *The door won't lock.* •➤ opposite **unlock** **2** [T] to put sb/sth in a safe place and lock it: *Lock your passport in a safe place.* **3** [T] **be locked in sth** to be involved in an angry argument, etc with sth, or to be holding sb very tightly: *The two sides were locked in a bitter dispute.* ● *They were locked in a passionate embrace.*

PHRASAL VERBS **lock sth away** to keep sth in a safe or secret place that is locked

lock sb in/out to lock a door so that a person cannot get in/out: *I locked myself out of the house and had to climb in through the window.*

lock (sth) up to lock all the doors, windows, etc of a building: *Make sure that you lock up before you leave.*

lock sb up to put sb in prison

lock² /lɒk/ *noun* [C] **1** something that is used for fastening a door, lid, etc so that you need a key to open it again: *to turn the key in the lock* •➤ Look at **padlock**. •➤ picture at **key** **2** a part of a river or a canal where the level of water changes. Locks have gates at each end and are used to allow boats to move to a higher or lower part of the canal or river.

IDIOMS **pick a lock → PICK¹**

under lock and key in a locked place

locker /ˈlɒkə/ *noun* [C] a small cupboard that can be locked in a school or sports centre, where you can leave your clothes, books, etc

locket /ˈlɒkɪt/ *noun* [C] a piece of jewellery that you wear on a chain around your neck and which opens so that you can put a picture, etc inside

locksmith /ˈlɒksmɪθ/ *noun* [C] a person who makes and repairs locks

locomotive /ˌləʊkəˈməʊtɪv/ = ENGINE(2)

locust /ˈləʊkəst/ *noun* [C] a flying insect from Africa and Asia that moves in very large groups, eating and destroying large quantities of plants •➤ picture at **insect**

lodge¹ /lɒdʒ/ *verb* **1** [I] to pay to live in sb's house with him/her: *He lodged with a family for his first term at university.* **2** [I,T] to become firmly fixed or to make sth do this **3** [T] (*formal*) to make an official statement complaining about sth

lodge² /lɒdʒ/ *noun* [C] **1** a room at the entrance to a large building such as a college or factory **2** a small house in the country

lodger /ˈlɒdʒə/ *noun* [C] a person who pays rent to live in a house as a member of the family •➤ Look at **boarder**.

lodging /ˈlɒdʒɪŋ/ *noun* **1** [C,U] a place where you can stay: *The family offered full board and lodging* (= a room and all meals) *in exchange for English lessons.* **2** (*old-fashioned*) **lodgings** [pl] a room or rooms in sb's house where you can pay to stay

loft /lɒft/ *noun* [C] the room or space under the roof of a house or other building •➤ Look at **attic**.

log¹ /lɒg/ *noun* [C] **1** a thick piece of wood that has fallen or been cut from a tree **2** (also **logbook**) the official written record of a ship's or an aircraft's journey: *to keep a log*

log² /lɒg/ *verb* [T] (**logging; logged**) to keep an official written record of sth

PHRASAL VERBS **log in/on** to perform the actions that allow you to start using a computer system: *You need to key in your password to log on.*

log off/out to perform the actions that allow you to finish using a computer system

logarithm /ˈlɒgərɪðəm/ (also *informal* **log**) *noun* [C] one of a series of numbers arranged in lists (tables) that allow you to solve problems in mathematics by adding or subtracting numbers instead of multiplying or dividing

loggerheads /ˈlɒgəhedz/ *noun*

IDIOM **at loggerheads (with sb)** strongly disagreeing (with sb)

logic /ˈlɒdʒɪk/ *noun* [U] **1** a sensible reason or way of thinking: *There is no logic in your argument.* **2** the science of using reason

logical /ˈlɒdʒɪkl/ *adj* **1** seeming natural, reasonable or sensible: *As I see it, there is only one logical conclusion.* •➤ opposite **illogical** **2** thinking in a sensible way: *a logical mind* –**logically** /-kli/ *adv*

logo /ˈləʊgəʊ/ *noun* [C] (*pl* **logos**) a printed symbol or design that a company or an organization uses as its special sign: *the company/brand logo*

loiter /ˈlɔɪtə/ *verb* [I] to stand or walk around somewhere for no obvious reason

lollipop /ˈlɒlipɒp/ (also **lolly**) *noun* [C] a sweet on a stick •➤ Look at **ice lolly**.

lone /ləʊn/ *adj* (only *before* a noun) **1** without any other people; alone: *a lone swimmer* •➤ synonym **solitary** **2** (used about a parent) single; without a partner: *a support group for lone parents*

★**lonely** /ˈləʊnli/ *adj* (**lonelier; loneliest**) **1** unhappy because you are not with other people: *to feel sad and lonely* **2** (used about a situation or a period of time) sad and spent alone **3** (only *before* a noun) far from other people and places where people live •➤ Look at the note at **alone**. –**loneliness** *noun* [U]

➤ Compare **solitude** and **isolation**.

loner /ˈləʊnə/ *noun* [C] (*informal*) a person who prefers being alone to being with other people

lonesome /ˈləʊnsəm/ *adj* (*US*) lonely or making you feel lonely •➤ Look at the note at **alone**.

★**long¹** /lɒŋ/ adj (**longer** /-ŋgə/, **longest** /-ŋgɪst/) measuring a large amount in distance or time: *She has lovely long hair.* • *We had to wait a long time.* • *a very long journey/book/corridor* • *I walked a long way today.* • *Nurses work very long hours.* ⁕➤ noun **length**

> **Long** is also used when you are asking for or giving information about how much something measures in length, distance or time: *How long is the film?* • *The insect was only 2 millimetres long.* • *a five-mile-long traffic jam*

⁕➤ opposite **short** –**long** noun [U]: *I'm sorry I haven't written to you for so long.* • *This shouldn't take long.*

[IDIOMS] **a long shot** a person or thing that probably will not succeed, win, etc
at (long) last → **LAST¹**
at the longest not longer than the stated time: *It will take a week at the longest.*
go a long way (used about money, food, etc) to be used for buying a lot of things, feeding a lot of people, etc
have a long way to go to need to make a lot more progress before sth can be achieved
in the long run after a long time; in the end
in the long/short term → **TERM¹**

★**long²** /lɒŋ/ adv (**longer** /-ŋgə/, **longest** /-ŋgɪst/) **1** for a long time: *She didn't stay long.* • *You shouldn't have to wait long.* • *I hope we don't have to wait much longer.* • *They won't be gone for long.* • *Just wait here – I won't be long.* • *'How long will it take to get there?' 'Not long.'*

> **Long** and **a long time** are both used as expressions of time. In positive sentences **a long time** is usually used: *They stood there for a long time.* **Long** is only used in positive sentences with another adverb, for example 'too', 'enough', 'ago', etc: *We lived here long ago.* • *I've put up with this noise long enough. I'm going to make a complaint.* Both **long** and **a long time** can be used in questions: *Were you away long/a long time?* In negative sentences there is sometimes a difference in meaning between **long** and **a long time**: *I haven't been here long* (= I arrived only a short time ago). • *I haven't been here for a long time* (= it is a long time since I was last here).

2 a long time before or after a particular time or event: *We got married long before we moved here.* • *Don't worry – they'll be here before long.* • *All that happened long ago.* **3** for the whole of the time that is mentioned: *The baby cried all night long.*

[IDIOMS] **as/so long as** on condition that; provided (that): *As long as no problems arise we should get the job finished by Friday.*
no/not any longer not any more: *They no longer live here.* • *They don't live here any longer.*

long³ /lɒŋ/ verb [I] **long for sth; long (for sb) to do sth** to want sth very much, especially sth that is not likely: *She longed to return to*

Greece. –**longing** noun [C,U]: *a longing fo peace* –**longingly** adv

long-'distance adj, adv (used about trave or communication) between places that ar far from each other: *to phone long-distance*

'**long-haul** adj (only *before* a noun) connecte with the transport of people or goods ove long distances: *a long-haul flight*

longitude /'lɒndʒɪtjuːd; 'lɒŋgɪ-/ noun [U] th distance of a place east or west of a line fro the North Pole to the South Pole that passe through Greenwich in London. Longitude i measured in degrees. ⁕➤ Look at **latitude** ⁕➤ picture at **earth**

'**long jump** noun [sing] the sport in which people try to jump as far as possible ⁕➤ Look at **high jump**.

long-'life adj made to last for a long time: *long-life battery* • *long-life milk*

long-'lived adj that has lived or lasted for a long time: *a long-lived dispute*

'**long-range** adj **1** of or for a long period o time starting from the present: *the long-range weather forecast* **2** that can go or be sent over long distances: *long-range nuclear missiles*

long-'sighted (US **far-'sighted**) adj able to see things clearly only when they are quite far away ⁕➤ opposite **short-sighted** (US **near-sighted**)

long-'standing adj that has lasted for a long time: *a long-standing arrangement*

long-'suffering adj (used about a person) having a lot of troubles but not complaining

long-'term adj of or for a long period of time: *long-term planning*

long-'winded adj (used about sth that is written or spoken) boring because it is too long

loo /luː/ noun [C] (*pl* **loos**) (*Brit informal*) toilet ⁕➤ Look at the note at **toilet**.

★**look¹** /lʊk/ verb **1** [I,T] **look (at sth)** to turn your eyes in a particular direction (in order to pay attention to sb/sth): *Sorry, I wasn't looking. Can you show me again?* • *Look carefully at this picture.* • *to look out of the window* • *She blushed and looked away.* • *Look who's come to see us.* • *Look where you're going!*

> You can **see** something without paying attention to it: *I saw a girl riding past on a horse.* If you **look** at something you pay attention to it: *Look carefully. Can you see anything strange?*

2 [I] **look (for sb/sth)** to try to find (sb/sth): *We've been looking for you everywhere. Where have you been?* • *to look for work* • *'I can't find my shoes.' 'Have you looked under the bed?'* **3** [I] **look (like sb/sth) (to sb); look (to sb) as if.../as though...** to seem or appear: *You look very smart in that shirt.* • *to look tired/ill/sad/well/happy* • *The boy looks like his father.* • *That film looks good – I might go and see it.* • *You look (to me) as if/as though you need some sleep.* **4** [I] used for asking sb to listen to what you are saying: *Look, Will, I know you are busy but could you give me a*

Study pages

Vocabulary pages

Study notes

Sports and hobbies

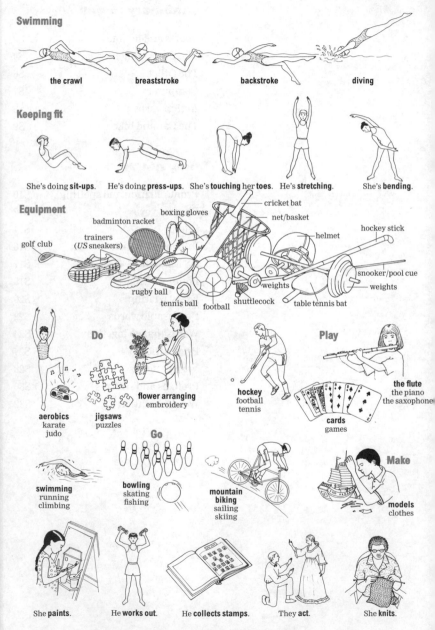

Swimming

the crawl   breaststroke   backstroke   diving

Keeping fit

She's doing **sit-ups**.   He's doing **press-ups**.   She's **touching** her **toes**.   He's **stretching**.   She's **bending**.

Equipment

cricket bat
net/basket
boxing gloves
badminton racket
helmet
hockey stick
trainers (*US* sneakers)
golf club
snooker/pool cue
weights
weights
rugby ball
tennis ball   football   shuttlecock   table tennis bat

Do

aerobics
karate
judo

jigsaws
puzzles

flower arranging
embroidery

hockey
football
tennis

Play

the flute
the piano
the saxophone

cards
games

Go

swimming
running
climbing

bowling
skating
fishing

mountain biking
sailing
skiing

Make

models
clothes

She **paints**.   He **works out**.   He **collects stamps**.   They **act**.   She **knits**.

Sports and hobbies

Look at the pictures opposite and notice the verbs that we use to talk about doing different sports and hobbies.

We say:
She *does* aerobics/karate/puzzles/embroidery.
I *make* models/clothes.
He *plays* football/tennis/cards/the flute.
We *go* swimming/bowling/mountain biking.

Note that '**go**' is usually used with words ending in **-ing**.

With some sports and hobbies we <u>do not</u> use any other verb.
He paints.   She acts.   I collect stamps.   They work out twice a week.

Exercise 1

Look at the following words in your dictionary and put them in the table below.

golf   gymnastics   netball   athletics   climb   models
clothes   sew   chess   the piano   snooker   crosswords
badminton   hike   judo   darts   squash   cycle
windsurf   draw

play	do	go + -ing	make	no other verb

Exercise 2

Look at the pictures opposite and the entries for the words in bold, then fill in the blanks with the correct pieces of sports equipment.

1 I'm going to play **badminton** so I'll need my _____ and a _____.
2 Can I borrow your _____? I'm playing **golf** this afternoon.
3 Bob couldn't play **tennis** because he forgot his _____.
4 In **hockey** you are not allowed to raise your _____ above shoulder height.
5 **American football** can be dangerous so the players wear pads and a _____.
6 After running the marathon I needed a new pair of _____.
7 You use a _____ to play **snooker** or **pool**.
8 In **cricket**, the bowler bowls the ball and you have to hit it with a _____.
9 When you go **horse** riding, it's best to wear special trousers called _____.
10 You score points in **basketball** by throwing a ball through a _____.

The Environment

Our growing need for food, goods and energy has had many harmful effects on the environment.

Gases produced by cars, power stations and factories cause **acid rain**①, which kills trees and fish and damages buildings. By using more **environmentally-friendly forms of transport**②, we help reduce this form of pollution.

A layer of carbon dioxide and other gases traps heat and keeps the earth at the right temperature. This is called **the greenhouse effect**③. By burning **fossil fuels** (oil, coal, petrol, etc) we are producing too much carbon dioxide, which is causing temperatures to rise gradually. This **global warming**④ could lead to dramatic changes in climate.

A layer of a gas called ozone protects the earth from harmful ultraviolet radiation. Certain chemicals used in industry, such as **CFCs**, have caused a hole to develop in **the ozone layer**⑤. The increased levels of ultraviolet radiation damage plants and sea life, and increase the risk of skin cancer.

Most of the energy we use to heat and light buildings, run machines, etc is made by burning fossil fuels. These will eventually run out, so we need to use more **alternative sources of energy**⑥, such as **wind** and **solar power**, that are renewable and do not pollute the air. We should also avoid wasting energy by using less electricity and water and insulating our houses.

We are destroying our forests, which produce oxygen and provide habitats for animals and birds. **Deforestation**⑦ also allows rain to wash away the soil, making the land useless for growing things.

We pollute water by dumping waste⑧ from factories and houses, and by accidentally spilling chemicals and oil. **Chemical fertilizers**⑨ damage rivers and lakes by causing a layer of tiny plants, called algae, to cover the surface of the water⑩. **Organic farming**⑪ does not harm the water supply.

Burying rubbish in **landfills**⑫ can let harmful chemicals leak through the ground into rivers, and it uses a lot of land. Burning rubbish⑬ adds to global warming. By sorting our rubbish for **recycling**⑭, we can cut down on waste.

S5

harmful　　　helpful

The Office

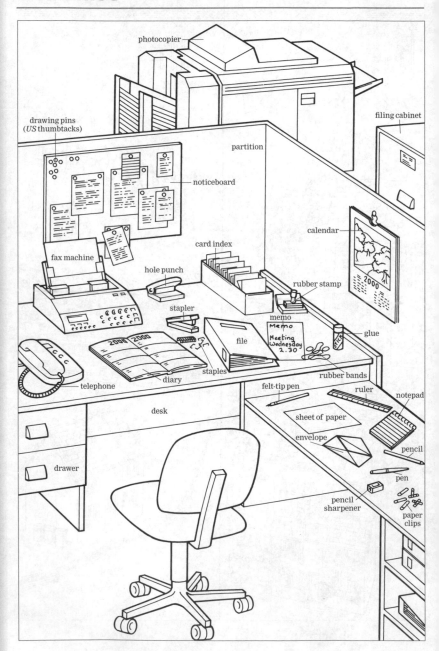

Computers

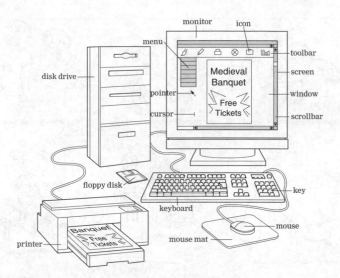

A computer can store and process information. This information is called data and can be words, numbers or graphics (pictures/images). To process data, the computer uses a program, which is a set of instructions stored on the computer's hard drive.

To input data, you can enter it using the keyboard. If you want to store this data, you save it in the computer's memory or onto a floppy disk. Large amounts of information, such as books, can be stored on a CD-ROM.

On the screen, icons (special symbols), which are arranged in a row on a toolbar or on the desktop, and menus show you what programs and data are stored on the computer and what jobs the computer can do. You use the mouse to click on an icon and tell the computer what job you want it to do and to move to the part of the screen you want to work on. A small marker called a cursor shows your position on the screen.

Computers can be connected to other computers to form a network. This allows different people to have access to the same information and to communicate with each other using e-mail (electronic mail). To communicate with someone using e-mail, you send your message to their e-mail address. For example, john.jones@aol.com is a typical e-mail address. To say this address, you say 'John dot Jones at A O L dot com'.

The Internet or the Net is an enormous network that covers the world. People who want to make information available to the whole world can pay for their own space on the Internet. This is called a web site. The Web or the World Wide Web (WWW) is the system which lets you download (look at) information on the Internet. You can enter a subject and find all the web sites that have information about it. This is called surfing the Net. Online services are ones that are available on the Internet.

Action verbs

The Car and bike

Car

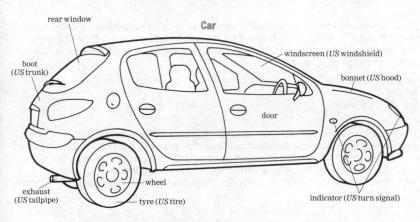

rear window

windscreen (*US* windshield)

boot (*US* trunk)

bonnet (*US* hood)

door

exhaust (*US* tailpipe)

wheel

tyre (*US* tire)

indicator (*US* turn signal)

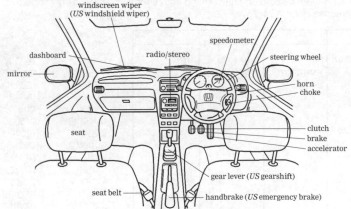

windscreen wiper (*US* windshield wiper)

speedometer

dashboard

radio/stereo

steering wheel

mirror

horn

choke

seat

clutch

brake

accelerator

gear lever (*US* gearshift)

seat belt

handbrake (*US* emergency brake)

Bike

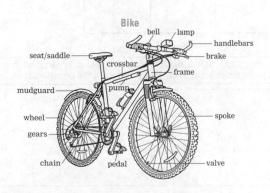

bell

lamp

handlebars

seat/saddle

brake

crossbar

frame

mudguard

pump

wheel

spoke

gears

chain

pedal

valve

Pronunciation and spelling

In many languages, when you see a word written, you immediately know how to pronounce it. In English, however, the same letters can sometimes be pronounced in several different ways. Look, for example, how the letters -ei- are pronounced in these words:

receive	/rɪ'siːv/		their	/ðeə/
height	/haɪt/		foreign	/'fɒrən/
weight	/weɪt/		leisure	/'leʒə/
weird	wɪəd/			

Here are four vowel sounds that can have various different spellings. Use your dictionary to look up the pronunciation of the words in the list. Write each word under the vowel sound that it contains, or that the underlined part of the word contains. For example, the pronunciation of mountain is /'maʊntɪn/, so you would write it in the I column, and other is pronounced /'ʌðə/ so you would write it in the ʌ column.

The sound ə is the most common vowel sound in English. It is pronounced softly, with the mouth relaxed and not forming any particular shape. ə only occurs in unstressed syllables.

ə	I	ʌ	3:
ago, father	sit *mountain*	cup *other*	turn

bird   money
biscuit   mountain ✓
blood   moustache
busy   nurse
certain   one
chocolate   orange
control   other ✓
country   package
earth   packet
expert   pleasure
famous   pretty
heard   woman
journey   women
language   won
married   work
minute (noun)

Here are some more words that do not look like they sound. Look up each word in your dictionary and write the missing symbol or symbols in the pronunciation.

beard	/b__d/	fruit	/fr__t/	restaurant	/'restr__nt/
beautiful	/'bj__tɪfl/	government	/'g__vənm__nt/	sausage	/'s__s__dʒ/
break	/br__k/	guide	/g__d/	sew	/s__/
breakfast	/'br__kf__st/	heart	/h__t/	stomach	/'st__m__k/
comfortable	/'k__mft__bl/	iron	/'aɪ__n/	suit	/s__t/
cupboard	/'k__b__d/	naked	/'n__k__d/	tired	/'taɪ__d/
friend	/fr__nd/	queue	/kj__/	vegetable	/'vedʒt__bl/

Pronunciation and spelling

These words all have a silent consonant.

B climb, comb, debt, doubt, dumb, lamb, thumb **C** fascinating, muscle, science, yacht **D** handkerchief, Wednesday **G** champagne, foreign, sign **H** exhausted, honest, hour, yoghurt **K** knee, knife, knob, knock, know **L** calm, could, should, would, half, palm, salmon, talk, walk, **N** autumn **P** psychiatrist, psychology, receipt **R** iron **S** island **T** ballet, castle, duvet, fasten, listen, often, whistle **W** answer, who, whose, write, wrong

---

These words can be difficult to spell. The part of each word that usually causes problems is in bold.

acco**mm**odation	jewe**ll**ery
add**r**ess	mille**nn**ium
al**r**ight (*but* all right)	**opp**osite
	po**ss**e**ss**ion
a**ss**ociation	pract**ise** (verb)
ca**ss**ette	pract**ice** (noun)
cigare**tt**e	(a TV) pro**gramme**
comme**r**cial	(US pro**gram**)
commi**tt**ee	(a computer)
defini**te**ly	pro**gram**
disa**pp**ointed	reco**mm**end
emba**rr**a**ss**ed	se**p**arate
exa**gg**erate	su**cc**e**ss**ful
e**xc**ellent	unne**c**e**ss**ary
i**mm**ediately	un**til** (*but* ti**ll**)
inde**p**endent	woo**ll**en

Here is one spelling rule that is worth learning! The sound /iː/ is often spelled **ie**, as in *piece* and *believe*. After the letter **c**, however, this is written **ei**, as in *receive*, *ceiling* and *receipt*. **Remember the rhyme:**

i before e except after c

(Two common exceptions are *seize* and *weird*.)

---

gh
In which of the words below
is the **gh** silent?
is the **gh** pronounced as /f/ ?
is the **gh** pronounced as /g/ ?

_____	_____	_____
ghetto	cough	night
although	ghost	daughter
higher	rough	enough
thorough	tough	

Double consonants
Some words double their final consonant when an ending such as **–ing**, **–ed**, **–er**, **–able**, etc is added, usually in order to show that the vowel that comes before is short. Fill the gaps in these sentences with the words on the left, doubling the final consonant where necessary.

fat	The baby's getting ____er every day.	big	As usual, the boss got the ____est pay rise.
hope	I'm ____ing to go to India next year.		
stop	I ____ed to look at the map.	refer	Whose mistake was he ____ing to?
write	I'm ____ing to thank you for all your help.	prefer	A boring job is ____able to no job.
write	Have you ever ____en to a newspaper?	kidnap	The boy is believed to have been ____ed.
win	We've got no chance of ____ing.	beat	We were ____en 4–0 in the final.
whine	The dog was ____ing outside the door.	equal	Her last jump ____ed the world record.
open	I cut my thumb while ____ing a tin.	offer	Are you ____ing to pay?
listen	You're not ____ing to me!	happen	What ____ed to my newspaper?
plan	I had ____ed to study but I fell asleep.	develop	She died after ____ing an infection.
visit	Have you ____ed him in hospital yet?		

Phrasal verbs

In this dictionary you can find the phrasal verbs at the end of the entry for the verb in the section marked PHRASAL VERBS . They are arranged alphabetically according to the particle (away, back, up, etc).

Which particle?

Some particles have a particular meaning that they keep when they are used with various different verbs, for example *back*, *on* and *off*.

Look at these sentences:

I'll **call** you **back** later.
She wrote to him but he didn't **write back**.
Go on. I want to know what happens next!
They liked the hotel so much that they **stayed on** for an extra week.
When I picked up the mug the handle **came off**.
I didn't pay the bill and now my phone's been **cut off**.

Now match the particles with their meanings.

back	separate, no longer attached
on	in return
off	continuing

Fill in the missing particle (*back*, *on*, or *off*) in these sentences.

1 I lent that book to George last week, but he hasn't given it _____ yet.
2 The police have sealed _____ the street where the attack took place.
3 When you've finished with the book please pass it _____ to the next student.
4 Louis got into trouble for answering his teacher _____ when she told him off in class.
5 Although it was very late we decided to push _____ to the next village.
6 The road branches _____ to the left a little way up ahead.

Formal to informal language

We use phrasal verbs all the time when we are speaking or writing in English. Often phrasal verbs can be replaced by another single-word verb with the same meaning, but these verbs usually sound a lot more formal. Compare these two sentences:

The fire fighters took four hours to **extinguish** the blaze.
I **put out** the fire with some water.

Replace the words in bold with a phrasal verb formed from the verb in brackets. (Remember that you may need to change the tense or the form of the verb). The first one has been done for you.

1 Shall we continue after lunch? (*carry*) *Shall we **carry on** after lunch?*
2 Tell the boss exactly what you think. Don't worry – I'll support you. (back)
3 You'll never guess who I met in the street just now! (bump)

Phrasal verbs

4 I'm trying to **reduce** the amount of coffee I drink each day. (cut)
5 I'll have to **postpone** the meeting until next week. (put)
6 The flight is at 8.00 so we'll have to **leave** very early for the airport. (set)
7 I think the baby really **resembles** his mother. (take)
8 I was so pleased when my dad finally **stopped** smoking. (give)
9 It's amazing how some people manage to **raise** their children alone. (bring)
10 Have we got time to **visit** Elena on the way home? (drop)

Opposites

Often you can find phrasal verbs that have opposite meanings to each other. It may help you to remember them if you learn them together.

Match up the following sentences into pairs with opposite meanings, then write the pairs in the spaces below.

1 It was getting dark so I **turned on** the light.
2 Don't leave your bag on the floor like that – **pick** it **up**!
3 It's cold – **put** your coat **on**.
4 I bought Jon a present to **cheer** him **up**.
5 You should **check in** at reception as soon as you arrive.
6 I **pulled over** at the side of the road to look at the map.
7 I tried to learn the guitar but **packed** it **in** after a few weeks.
8 My dad is coming to **pick** me **up** at ten.
9 A 10% service charge is **added on** to the bill.
10 I'm so tired. I can't wait to get home and **sit down**.

a I can **drop** you **off** on my way home if you like.
b You have to **check out** of the hotel before midday.
c **Take off** that silly hat!
d I've decided to **take up** aerobics.
e Did you see that? That driver **pulled out** right in front of me.
f Don't forget to **turn off** the TV before you go to bed.
g We all **stood up** when the head teacher came into the classroom.
h What's thirty-one **take away** fourteen?
i He **put** the baby **down** gently on the bed.
j Don't let the exams **get** you **down**.

turn sth on _____   pick sth up _____
put sth on _____   cheer sb up _____
check in _____   pull over _____
pack sth in _____   pick sb up _____
add sth on _____   sit down _____

Idioms

An idiom is a particular combination of words, which has a special meaning that is difficult to guess, even if you know the meanings of the individual words in it. In order to find an idiom in this dictionary, you need to choose the first most important word in it (ignoring words like 'off' and 'the'). You will find the idiom in the idioms section, marked IDIOMS. If you do not find the meaning there, there will be a cross reference telling you where to go in the dictionary to find it.

Exercise 1

Match the sentences to the pictures and then fill in the blanks with the parts of the body from the list. You may use each word only once.

eye eyes nose chest head head back mind heart arm heels feet

a Doctor, there's something I need to get off my _____ .
b I don't know what's wrong with the boss today. I only asked a question and she bit my _____ off!
c We weren't really arguing until Basil came along and decided to stick his _____ in.
d I can't possibly meet you for lunch today. I'm up to my _____ in work at the moment.
e As she walked up the aisle towards Barry, Linda started to get cold _____ .
f When John left me for another woman, he broke my _____ .
g I have to sit near the water's edge so I can keep an _____ on Emma.
h Oh all right, I'll come and watch it with you. You've twisted my _____ .
i I fell _____ over _____ in love with her the moment I saw her, but she doesn't want to know me.
j As I walked away, I could hear them whispering about me behind my _____ .
k He was in the shop for ages because he couldn't make up his _____ which T-shirt to buy.

Exercise 2

Replace the word or phrase in bold in sentences 1–10 with one of the idioms from the list below, changing verb forms, pronouns, etc as necessary.

for example It **would make me very sad** if anything happened to my cat.
It **would break my heart** if anything happened to my cat.

have/get cold feet   head over heels in love   behind sb's back
twist sb's arm   break sb's heart   keep an eye on sb/sth
poke/stick your nose in(to sth)   get sth off your chest   bite sb's head off
be up to your eyes in sth   make up your mind

1 Could you **watch** my bags for me while I go into the shop, please?
2 The way we bring up the children is our business. I don't want your mother **interfering**!
3 Mark and Emma are both still **crazy about each other** even after five years.
4 He was going to report it to the police, but at the last minute he **felt too scared** and decided to keep quiet.
5 Why not tell him how you feel? It might do you good to **talk about it**.
6 Fran says she's too busy to come to the party tonight. See if you can **persuade her**.
7 You'll just have to **decide** which one you want. I'm not waiting any longer!
8 When I asked him what he wanted to eat, he **just shouted at me**.
9 It's not fair of us to discuss Jo's work **without her knowing about it**.
10 We're so busy because we've just moved house and we **have got loads** of boxes that need unpacking

Idioms

Informal English

Types of people

a babe	a wally	an anorak	a spoilsport	a twit
a prat	a yob	a sucker	a loony	a pain
a wet blanket	a psycho	a big mouth	a big-head	a swot
a wimp	a crook	a doormat	a creep	a layabout
a loner	a lunatic	a moron	a globetrotter	a pest
a has-been	a pushover	a hunk	a scream	a slob
a trainspotter				

Match the person with the description. Sometimes there is more than one possible answer and the number in brackets tells you how many words match the description. Use each word once.

What kind of a person...?

1 is stupid? (**4**)
2 does not allow others to enjoy themselves? (**2**)
3 believes everything other people say?
4 is easy to persuade? (**2**)
5 tries to impress people in authority to get something he/she wants?
6 is lazy and untidy? (**2**)
7 is good-looking? (**2**)
8 is very funny and makes you laugh?
9 studies too much?
10 is weak and too afraid to do anything?
11 is crazy or mad? (**3**)
12 is dishonest?
13 travels a lot?
14 is annoying? (**2**)
15 does not like other people's company?
16 knows a lot of boring facts? (**2**)
17 cannot keep a secret?
18 has a high opinion of himself/herself?
19 is aggressive and unpleasant?
20 is not as famous or successful as he/she once was?

Informal to formal English

Change the text from informal to formal English by substituting the phrases in **bold** with a phrase from the list (a–q).

These days, I'm so **broke** that I've had to move out of my flat. I'm £3,000 **in the red** and I had to find a way of **getting** my bank manager **off my back**. Still, **looking on the bright side**, at least I don't have to **fork out** much for rent now because a **mate** of mine is letting me stay at his **place** until things start to **look up**. The only thing is, he and his girlfriend are **going through a bad patch** and their rows are driving me **round the bend**. The last one was about where they should go on holiday. I mean, James is OK, but he's a bit of **a doormat** and **at the end of the day** Claire always **gets her own way**, so what's the point of him **digging his heels in** about where they go on holiday? I'm probably making the atmosphere worse by **playing gooseberry**, which must **be hard on** them. I suppose I should **get my act together** and find a job.

a **overdrawn**
b **mad**
c **poor**
d **a weak person**
e **improve**
f **house**
g **taking an optimistic view**
h **having problems**
i **pay**
j **stopping sb annoying me**
k **the most important thing is**
l **refusing to change his mind**
m **gets what she wants**
n **organize myself properly**
o **being there when the couple want to be alone**
p **make things difficult for**
q **friend**

This dictionary gives you a lot of information about differences in vocabulary and spelling between British and US English. If you look up the word **holiday** you will see that the US equivalent is given in brackets (*US* **vacation**). Often the same word is used in both British and US English, but with different meanings. Look at the entry for purse. First you will find the British meaning and then its meaning in US English (*US* = **HANDBAG**).

Exercise 1

Complete the balloons with the British or US equivalents for the words given. In the first one you are given the British words and in the second you are given the US English words.

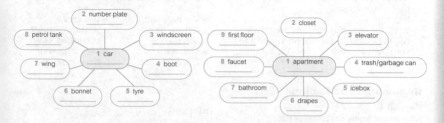

Exercise 2

Below are directions for getting to Alex's house written in British English. Change the words in **bold** so that his friend from New York can find his way there.

As soon as you leave **the motorway**, you'll see **a petrol station** on your right and the entrance to **the casualty department** of the city hospital ahead of you. Turn left here, go past **the cinema**, and carry on until you see a big **car park** on the corner opposite **the chemist's** and **an off-licence**. Park here, cross the street and my **flat** is just in front of you. If you decide not to drive, there's **a tube station** next to the hospital. As you come out onto **the pavement**, turn right and I am just 100 yards away on the same side of the street.

Spelling

In many cases the same words are used in British and US English, but they are spelled differently. Here are the most common differences:

	British	US	British	US
a	trave**ll**ed	trave**l**ed	cance**ll**ing	cance**l**ing
b	met**re**	met**er**	cent**re**	cent**er**
c	col**our**	col**or**	hon**our**	hon**or**
d	def**ence**	def**ense**	lic**ence**	lic**ense**
e	dial**ogue**	dial**og**	catal**ogue**	catal**og**

Letter writing

The Layout of a letter

Formal letter
▶ **never** write your name at the top of a letter
▶ write your own address on the right-hand side **and** write the address and name or position of the person you are writing to below that on the left-hand side
▶ write the date in full underneath your own address

Informal letter
▶ **never** write your name at the top of a letter
▶ write your own address above the date but **not** the address of the person you are writing to
▶ the date can be abbreviated and goes under your address

Beginnings and Endings

Formal 1
(you **do not know** the name of the person)

Dear Sir or Madam,
Yours faithfully,
Gwen Hollis

Formal 2
(you **know** the name of the person)

Dear Ms/Mr Marzec,
Yours sincerely,
Gwen Hollis

Style

In formal letters you...
▶ use Sir or Madam, or the person's title + surname
▶ use the passive
▶ do not use contractions or abbreviations
▶ use single-word verbs, formal linking words and phrases
▶ use long sentences, impersonal style
▶ sign with your full name and print it afterwards

In informal letters you...
▶ use first names only
▶ use I/we
▶ can use contractions and abbreviations
▶ can use phrasal verbs, idioms and colloquial language
▶ use short sentences, omit pronouns, etc
▶ sign with your first name only

Informal
Dear Jania,
Yours/Love from/Best Wishes
Gwen

Paragraphing

You use **paragraphs** to organize the information in your letter.

1st Your reason for writing the letter
2nd Dates, facts and further details
3rd A request for action, information, etc
4th Ending/conclusion

Important phrases

All the phrases below can be found in formal or informal letters. Match the formal phrase on the left with its informal equivalent on the right.

Formal
1 I would be grateful if you could …
2 I look forward to hearing from you
3 I am writing to …
4 I regret to inform you …
5 You will be informed of …
6 I enclose a cheque for …
7 I would be happy to attend an interview
8 at your convenience
9 Further to my letter of September 8th …
10 Please do not hesitate to contact me should you require any further information
11 Please give my regards to …

Informal
a I'd love to come and see you
b We'll let you know about …
c Hope you got my last letter
d Do you think you could …?
e Just a note to say …
f Write back soon/Keep in touch
g when you can make it
h I'm really sorry to say …
i Give my love to …
j Here's the money for …
k Just give me a ring if you need to know anything else

Letter writing

Informal and formal letters

10, Park Road,
Birmingham,
B15 4BU.

3/6/00

Dear Morag,

Sorry I haven't been in touch for ages but I hope you're all well.
I'm actually writing to ask you a favour.

On July 16th, I'm coming to Scotland with 5 of my students here, who are really keen to visit as much of Britain as possible. I thought it would be really nice if we could all stay in your B&B in Nairn for a few nights. I'm sure they'd appreciate your huge breakfasts and general hospitality! We'd come for 3 nights from 17th to 19th July, and we'd need something like two single and two twin-bedded rooms (the latter preferably with en-suite bathrooms). Can you let me know if you can fit us in, and how much you charge now?

I really hope to see you soon. Write back or ring me asap so I can book the trip. Could you also tell me how much deposit you'd need? Thanks a lot. Give my love to Duncan and the kids.

Love from

Alison

PS I'm getting one of the students to write a formal letter to you as well, to give her a chance to practise her letter writing.

Here is the formal letter, written by Alison's student. Fill in the blue lines with a suitable word or phrase for a letter of this type, and fill in the numbered gaps in the text with appropriate forms of the verbs given below.

**plan   require   enquire
reserve   recommend**

10, Park Road,
Birmingham,
B15 4BU

_____

Mrs M. Maclennan,
12 St Helen's Road,
Nairn IV12 4EZ

_____

Your guest house 1 _____ to us by our English teacher, and I am writing 2 _____ whether you have any rooms available this July.

There are six of us in the group: five students and our teacher. We 3 _____ a trip to Scotland this summer and would be interested in 4 _____ two twin-bedded rooms and two single rooms for three nights, from July 17th to July 19th.

If you should have rooms available for those dates, _____ tell me the price of bed and breakfast per person and whether any of the rooms have en-suite bathrooms. I would also need to know whether a deposit 5 _____ in advance.

_____

Sandra Garcia

Essay writing

When you write an essay, you need to be able to express your ideas in a clearly organized and formal way. These pages show an example of how a typical 'advantages and disadvantages' essay can be constructed, and provide practice using linking words and punctuation.

Write your essay in paragraphs. Each paragraph should contain one main idea. The four paragraphs in this essay are:

1 introduction
2 advantages
3 disadvantages
4 conclusion

Before you start writing, note down briefly what you will say in each paragraph.

Discuss the advantages and disadvantages of having a car.

Nowadays, as roads are becoming more and more crowded, people are considering both the advantages and the disadvantages of having a car before they buy one.

The main advantage of the car is that it gives the freedom to travel when and where you want, without being limited to fixed routes and timetables. *What is more*, you can carry several passengers and as much luggage as you like, at no extra cost. *In addition to this*, you can travel in comfort in a car, with a seat to yourself and the possibility of comforts such as a music system and air conditioning.

On the other hand, owning a car is very expensive. As well as the price of the car, the cost of tax, insurance, petrol and repairs must also be considered before buying. *Moreover*, the increase in traffic means that drivers are spending more and more time stuck in traffic jams. Perhaps the major disadvantage of cars in general is the huge damage that they do to human life and to the environment, and all motorists must accept that they are making a small contribution to this.

To sum up, provided you have access to an efficient public transport system, then buying and running your own car could be considered an expensive luxury.

In the introduction, say briefly why the question is important or interesting.

Make the essay as balanced as possible. In this case, that means mentioning about the same number of advantages and disadvantages.

It is usual to leave about five spaces to show that you are starting a new paragraph.

In the conclusion you can give your personal opinion on the subject

Join your ideas together using formal linking words such as the ones in *bold* here.

Photocopiable © Oxford University Press

Essay writing

Punctuation

- A **full stop** shows the end of a sentence, and is also often used after initials and abbreviations: *The mini was designed by A.C.Issigonis.*
- A **comma** shows a short pause that separates parts of a sentence *Only buses, taxis and bicycles can use this street.* ● *The new road was supposed to reduce traffic jams, but they are even worse now.* It is also used to separate spoken words from the rest of the sentence: *'I'll drive,' said Linda.*
- **' '** *or* **" "** **Inverted commas** are used to show words that are spoken and around titles of books, films etc. They are also used around a nickname or a description that is often used for a person, place or thing: *The car was nicknamed 'the Beetle' because of its shape.* ● *A witness described the crash as 'horrific'.*
- **( )** **Brackets** are used when the writer adds information, an explanation, a comment, etc to something in the text. The text would still make sense if the information in brackets was removed: *The car is about nine feet (almost three metres) long.*
- **–** A **dash** is used when an additional comment or information is added to a sentence: *I don't often drive long distances – hardly ever, in fact.*
- **-** A **hyphen** is used in many cases where two words have been joined together to form one, and it is also used to separate long words that will not fit on one line. There are complicated rules about where you can divide words, and so it is safer to start the word on the next line: *anti-road protesters*
- **:** A **colon** tells the reader that something is coming next, for example a list: *Check the following things before a journey: fuel, tyre pressure, oil and water.*

Each of the following sentences has one mistake. Correct the mistake and add punctuation.

example: on other hand some say that lower speed limits would not reduce accidents.
On the other hand, some say that lower speed limits would not reduce accidents.

1 despite thousands die on the roads every year little is being done to improve safety

2 firstly of all limits should be imposed on the power of car engines

3 there are three mainly causes of accidents excessive speed carelessness and alcohol

4 in the whole results have been poor in fact the transport minister called them disastrous

5 because the number of fatal accidents the road is called the motorway of death

6 car manufacturers are reluctant to accept this how ever

7 stricter laws on drink driving have not led to fewer deaths too

8 all though there are heavy fines for speeding many drivers still take the risk

Confusable words

Exercise 1

In each sentence, only one of the words in bold is right for the context. Underline the correct word and use your dictionary to find out why the other words are not appropriate.

Example: Our trip to London was **funny/<u>fun</u>**. (funny = that makes you laugh/fun = enjoyable)

1 We had a great **landscape/scenery/view** from our hotel window.
2 The doctor gave me a **receipt/recipe/prescription** for some antibiotics.
3 You shouldn't take what he says seriously. You're just too **sensitive/sensible**
4 I've met a lot of **nice/sympathetic** people during my stay here.
5 Her grandmother is **died/dead/death**.
6 She works **like/as** a receptionist in a big hotel.
7 I lived there **during/since/for** ten years and came back to the UK five years **since/ago/for**.
8 She has a good **job/work** in Brussels.
9 The band are **actually/currently** touring in the US and won't be back until early autumn.
10 She lives on her own and says she never gets **alone/lonely**

Exercise 2

-ing or -ed adjectives?

Some adjectives have two forms depending on whether a person is **being affected by sth** (eg: *I was frightened by the look in his eye*) or whether a person or thing is **having an effect on sb/sth** (eg: *He is very frightening when he's angry*). Remember that a thing can *only* be described with the -ing form (eg: *the book is interesting*) because a thing cannot be affected by anything. Only *people* can be described by both -ing and -ed adjectives.

Fill in the blanks with the correct form of the adjective. The verb from which the adjective is formed is given in brackets.

Example: People who talk about football all the time are **boring** (**bore**).

1 The scenery in the Swiss Alps is absolutely _____ (**amaze**).
2 When she realized what a fool she'd made of herself, she felt terribly _____ (**embarrass**).
3 Don't go to that restaurant – the food is _____ (**revolt**).
4 The film was so _____ (**move**) that I cried at the end.
5 Looking after children all day long is very _____ (**tire**). By the evening, I'm completely _____ (**exhaust**).

Confusable words

Right or wrong?
Where necessary, change the form of the adjective(s) in each sentence. Mark any that are correct with a tick (✓) and any that are wrong with a cross (✗).

Example: That boy is really **annoyed** – he is always losing things. ✗ **annoying**

6 I've heard some **worried** news about possible redundancies at work.
7 After a **relaxed** bath, she felt **refreshing**.
8 The theme park was rather **disappointing**. There was only one ride which the children thought was really **frightened**.
9 My job is **challenging** and I generally enjoy it, but it has its **bored** moments, too.
10 Some of the students' exam results were **disappointed**, but on the whole, I'm quite **satisfying** with their progress.

Exercise 3

Complete the following sentences by choosing the correct verb from each pair in **bold**. Remember to put the verbs in the appropriate tenses.

1 My father _____ me to drive when I was 17. (**teach/learn**)
2 I got in the taxi and asked the driver to _____ me to the airport. (**bring/take**)
3 Hurry up or we'll _____ the bus! (**miss/lose**)
4 She's only in her forties, but with her grey hair, she _____ seventy. (**seem/look**)
5 Several buildings were badly _____ in the blast, but luckily no one was _____. (**damage/hurt**)
6 I _____ my towel on the sand, _____ down on it and went to sleep. (**lie/lay**)
7 The thief _____ my wallet. (**rob/steal**)
8 I'm afraid I _____ my books at home this morning. (**forget/leave**)
9 Could you _____ me how to get to the post office, please? (**tell/say**)
10 _____ your hand if you know the answer. (**rise/raise**)
11 Could you _____ me some money? (**lend/borrow**)
12 When you come to class tomorrow, _____ your dictionaries. (**bring/take**)
13 _____ bald is a sure sign that you are _____ old. (**get/go**)
14 Could you _____ how to do this exercise? (**tell/explain**)
15 Don't _____ time queuing to go up the tower. The view from the top isn't worth it. (**waste/lose**)
16 The price of oil _____ dramatically in the seventies. (**rise/raise**)
17 The old lady was beaten and _____. (**rob/steal**)
18 From what I could hear, the couple _____ to be having an argument about money. (**seem/look**)
19 I _____ in the north of the country and moved south in my early twenties. (**grow/grow up**)
20 The prisoner _____ escape by digging a tunnel. (**can/manage to**)

Words that go together

Certain pairs or groups of words occur together very frequently. These pairs or groups of words are called collocations. Look at the entry for the noun work to see how this dictionary shows you the most common collocations in bold. The more collocations like this that you use, the more natural your English will sound. As you study English, collect collocations that you like or that you think are useful.

work² /wɜːk/ **noun** [U] **1** the job that you do, especially in order to earn money; the place where you do your job: *It is very difficult to **find work** in this city.* ● *He's been **out of work** (= without a job) for six months.* ● *When do you **start work**?* ● *I'll ask if I can **leave work** early today.* ● *I **go to work** at 8 o'clock.* **2** something that requires physical or mental effort that you do in order to achieve sth: *Her success is due to sheer **hard work**.* ● *We hope to **start work on** the project next week.*

Exercise 1

Which adverb?

Match each adjective or verb with an adverb that makes it stronger (you can use an adverb more than once):

boiling	ill	drink	heavily
highly	hurt	fail	sick
gravely	hot	frozen	miserably
bitterly	disappointed	worried	stiff
badly	obvious	sleep	soundly
glaringly	unlikely	bored	
	cold		

Exercise 2

Which adjective?

Choose an adjective to go with the noun in each sentence:

1 The latest figures show a _____ increase in crime.   minute /maɪˈnjuːt/
2 I've know idea how much it costs – this is just a _____ guess.   wild
3 He explained in _____ detail how the photocopier worked.   heavy
4 It was by _____ luck that I knew the answer to every question.   full
5 He'll face a _____ fine if he's found guilty of speeding.   sharp
6 There is _____ competition to get a place in that university.   fierce
7 She accepted _____ responsibility for the mistake.   sheer

Words that go together

Exercise 3

Which verb?

Choose a verb to go with the noun in each sentence:

1 He promised me he would come, but he ___*broke*___ his promise.   catch
2 The sun was so hot that the grass _____ fire.   form
3 People who arrived early _____ a queue at the door.   ~~break~~
4 She _____ her ambition of becoming world champion.   draw
5 How do you _____ the difference between the male bird and the female?   tell
6 He _____ suicide at the age of 35.   drive
7 His singing in the shower _____ me crazy!   commit
8 _____ the curtains if there's too much sunlight.   achieve

Expressions with make, do and other common verbs

The only way to learn these is to collect them and keep practising them, but there are just a few points that can help you decide which verb to use:

Do is often used for tasks and duties that you **have to do** and that are not creative, or in expressions with the words **thing**, **nothing**, **anything**, etc:

do the cleaning	do something wrong
do an exam	do things your own way
do a job	nothing to do

Make is often used when sth is produced by you, using your **skills**, your **mind** or your **words**:

make dinner	make a decision	make a comment
make a movie	make a judgement	make an excuse
make a model	make a guess	make a suggestion
(But **do** a painting)		make a promise

Give, too, is used in many expressions connected with **words**. It is also used in expressions that describe **physical actions**:

give (sb) advice	give sth a kick/a twist/a push
give (sb) your word	give sb a slap/a kiss/a hug
give a reason	
give a lecture	
give evidence	

Words that go together

Complete each of the following sentences with the verb **make, do, give, have** or **take**:

1 He couldn't _____ a good explanation why he was late.
2 Are you _____ anything next Sunday?
3 Did anyone _____ a comment about the food?
4 We are going to have some difficult choices to _____.
5 You should _____ some stretching before you run.
6 I think Barry's _____ an argument with his mother.
7 My brother doesn't like _____ risks.
8 He _____ his friend a friendly punch on the arm.
9 Shall we _____ a five-minute break?
10 I _____ a short cut through the woods.
11 Are you _____ a party on your birthday?
12 She _____ her word that she'd keep my secret.
13 I always _____ a lot of photos on holiday.
14 I told him to slow down but he _____ no notice.
15 Have you _____ any plans for next year?
16 I'll _____ you a call later.
17 I'm just going to _____ a phone call.
18 You can _____ a lot of money working with computers.
19 Those boys have just come here to _____ trouble.
20 People kept _____ jokes about her hair.

Keep a section of your vocabulary book just for collecting collocations. Try keeping two lists: expressions that you think have a good or positive meaning, and ones that you think have a bad or negative meaning. Deciding which list to write a collocation in will help you remember it.
  Where would you write 'take a risk'?

Prepositions

Knowing which preposition to use can be a problem, as often it does not seem logical. Make your own lists, like the ones below, of uses of prepositions that you think are useful. Put each list in a place where you can see it every day and it will help you to remember.

	in	on	at
where	**in** a queue **in** France/Rome **in** the street	**on** the first floor **on** the list **on** the street	**at** the top/the bottom **at** the cinema/the station **at** work/school
when	**in** the morning **in** two weeks *in 2001*	**on** Friday/my birthday **on** time	**at** 3 o'clock **at** the weekend **at** first
how	**in** the car/a taxi **in** a hurry **in** English	**on** your own	**at** your first attempt one **at** a time
idioms	**in** general **in** theory/in practice	**on** paper **on** the whole *on a diet*	
after verbs, nouns and adjectives	I'm not interested **in** politics.	He had a bet **on** the race.	I was surprised **at** his reaction. Stop laughing **at** me!

Complete each expression with **in**, **on** or **at**, and put it in the box where you think it best belongs (some expressions could go in more than one box).

in 2001	____ the moment	____ your own pace
on a diet	____ the newspaper	____ the bus/your bike
____ summer/July	____ the phone	____ the left
____ holiday	____ night	____ TV/video/the radio
____ times	____ a trip	____ the front/the back
____ the middle	____ random	____ the mountains
____ New Year/Christmas	____ a strange way	____ the way here
____ the seaside	____ the same time	

I was covered ____ mud.
She's hopeless ____ maths.
He smiled ____ her.
I'd like some information ____ museums.

Do you believe ____ ghosts?
I can't concentrate ____ my work.
Everything depends ____ this exam.

Verb patterns

He promised **to write** me a letter.
She suggested **taking** regular exercise.
I thanked them **for looking after** me.
He let me **borrow** his car for the day.

> **promise** /'prɒmɪs/ **verb** [U] **1** [I,T] promise (to do sth); promise (sb) that… to say definitely that you will do or not do sth or that sth will happen: *She promises to be back before 5.00…*

When one verb is followed by another, you need to know what form the second verb should take. Look at the entry for **promise** to see how this information is shown. Every time you learn a new verb, write it down with the pattern that it uses. You will soon come to know which pattern looks or sounds right.

The meaning of the verb can sometimes make one pattern more likely than another. The following points can help you to make a good guess:

Many verbs that suggest that **an action will follow**, or will be completed successfully, are followed by **to** do:

agree to do sth	**ask (sb)** to do sth
offer to do sth	**want (sb)** to do sth
decide to do sth	**would like (sb)** to do sth
intend to do sth	**need (sb)** to do sth
plan to do sth	**expect (sb)** to do sth
hope to do sth	**help (sb)** to do sth
try to do sth	**wait (for sb)** to do sth
(or **try** doing sth)	**tell sb** to do sth
manage to do sth	**advise sb** to do sth
(**can**) **afford** to do sth	**encourage sb** to do sth
remember to do sth	**enable sb** to do sth
volunteer to do sth	**allow sb** to do sth
	persuade sb to do sth
	remind sb to do sth
	teach sb to do sth
	get sb to do sth

But note these verbs, which have a similar meaning but a different pattern:

consider doing sth	**make sb do sth**
think about doing sth	**let sb do sth**
suggest doing sth	**look forward to doing sth**
recommend doing sth	**succeed in doing sth**

Several verbs that suggest that **an action is unlikely to follow**, or to be completed successfully, are followed by an **-ing** form, sometimes with a preposition too:

avoid doing sth	**save sb (from)** doing sth
put sb off doing sth	**prevent sb from** doing sth
resist doing sth	**dissuade sb from** doing sth
advise sb against doing sth	
(or **advise sb** not to do sth)	

But note these verbs:
forget to do sth **fail to do sth** **refuse to do sth**

Verb patterns

Several verbs that refer to past events or actions are followed by an -ing form, sometimes with a preposition:

remember doing sth	regret doing sth
miss doing sth	admit doing sth
celebrate doing sth	thank sb for doing sth

Verbs that refer to starting, stopping or continuing are often followed by an -ing form:

start doing sth	begin doing sth
continue doing sth	put off doing sth
finish doing sth	carry on doing sth
go on doing sth	

Note: You can also say start to do sth   begin to do sth   continue to do sth

---

Verbs meaning like and dislike are usually followed by an -ing form:

like doing sth	love doing sth
prefer doing sth	hate doing sth
dread doing sth	

Note: You can also say
like to do sth   prefer to do sth   hate to do sth

Look at the entries for these verbs to see the slight difference in meaning that this pattern gives.

Now complete these sentences

1 She denied _____ the purse.	steal
2 I tried to stop the man _____ the dog.	hit
3 The dog has learnt _____ the door.	open
4 I can't stand _____ animals in pain.	see
5 I've arranged _____ him tomorrow.	meet
6 I attempted _____ in French.	speak
7 I'll never forget _____ him for the first time.	meet
8 My dad discouraged me from _____ the army.	join
9 I really enjoy _____ crosswords.	do
10 He apologized for ____ ____ late.	be

Here are some more common verbs and their patterns:

seem to do sth	**risk doing sth**
claim to do sth	**imagine doing sth**
dare (to) do sth	**practise doing sth**
pretend to do sth	**end up doing sth**
tend to do sth	**spend time doing sth**
deserve to do sth	**involve doing sth**

see/hear/watch/etc sb do sth
or   **see/hear/watch/etc sb doing sth**

Note that you use the first pattern, with do, when you see/hear/etc an action or activity from start to finish; you use doing when you see/hear/etc only part of the action or activity.

Prefixes and suffixes

Prefixes

a- not: **atypical**

ante- before: **antenatal** (= before birth)

anti- against: **anti-American, antisocial**

auto- self: **autobiography** (the story of the writer's own life)

bi- two: **bicycle, bilingual** (using two languages), **bimonthly** (twice a month or every two months)

cent-, centi- hundred: **centenary** (= the hundredth anniversary), **centimetre** (= one hundredth of a metre)

circum- around: **circumnavigate** (= sail around)

co- with; together: **co-pilot, coexist, cooperation**

con- with; together: **context** (the words or sentences that come before and after a particular word or sentence)

contra- against; opposite: **contradict** (say the opposite)

counter- against; opposite: **counterrevolution, counterproductive** (producing the opposite of the desired effect)

de- taking sth away; the opposite: **defrost** (removing the layers of ice from a fridge, etc), **decentralize**

deca- ten: **decathlon** (a competition involving ten different sports)

deci- one tenth: **decilitre**

dis- reverse or opposite: **displeasure, disembark, discomfort**

ex- former: **ex-wife, ex-president**

extra- 1 very; more than usual: **extra-thin, extra-special** 2 outside; beyond: **extraordinary, extraterrestrial** (coming from somewhere beyond the earth)

fore- 1 before; in advance: **foreword** (= at the beginning of a book) 2 front: **foreground** (= the front part of a picture), forehead

hexa- six; **hexagon** (a shape with six sides)

in- il-, im-, ir- not: **incorrect, invalid, illegal, illegible, immoral, impatient, impossible, irregular, irrelevant**

inter- between; from one to another: **international, interracial**

kilo- thousand: **kilogram, kilowatt**

maxi- most; very large: **maximum**

mega- million; very large: **megabyte, megabucks** (= a lot of money)

micro- very small: **microchip**

mid- in the middle of: **mid-afternoon, midair**

milli- thousandth: **millisecond, millimetre**

mini- small: **miniskirt, mini-series**

mis- bad or wrong; not: **misbehave, miscalculate, misunderstand**

mono- one; single: **monolingual** (= using one language), **monorail**

multi- many: **multinational** (= involving many countries)

non- not: **non-alcoholic, nonsense, non-smoker, non-stop**

nona- nine: **nonagon** (a shape with nine sides)

octa- eight: **octagon** (a shape with eight sides)

out- more; to a greater degree: **outdo, outrun** (= run faster or better than sb)

over- more than normal; too much: **overeat, oversleep** (= sleep too long)

penta- five; **pentagon** (a shape with five sides), **pentathlon** (a competition involving five different sports)

post- after: **post-war**

pre- before: **prepay, preview**

pro- for; in favour of: **pro-democracy, pro-hunting**

quad- four: **quadruple** (= multiply by four), **quadruplet** (= one of four babies born at the same time)

re- again: **rewrite, rebuild**

semi- half: **semicircle, semiconscious**

septa- seven: **septagon** (a shape with seven sides)

sub- 1 below; less than: **subzero** 2 under: **subway, subtitles** (= translations under the pictures of a film)

super- extremely; more than: **superhuman** (= having greater power than humans normally have), **supersonic** (= faster than the speed of sound)

tele- far; over a long distance: **telecommunications, telephoto lens**

trans- across; through: **transatlantic, transcontinental**

tri- three: **triangle, tricycle**

ultra- extremely; beyond a certain limit: **ultramodern**

un- not; opposite; taking sth away: **uncertain, uncomfortable, unsure, undo, undress**

uni- one; single: **uniform** (= having the same form)

Prefixes and suffixes

Suffixes

-able, -ible,-ble (to make adjectives) possible to: **acceptable, noticeable, convertible, divisible** (= possible to divide), **irresistible** (= that you cannot resist)

-age (to make nouns) a process or state: **storage, shortage**

-al (to make adjectives) connected with: **experimental, accidental, environmental**

-ance, -ence, -ancy, -ency (to make nouns) an action. process or state: **appearance, performance,existence, intelligence, pregnancy, efficiency**

-ant,-ent (to make nouns) a person who does sth: **assistant, immigrant, student**

-ation (to make nouns) a state or action: **examination, imagination, organization**

-ble → -able

-ed (to make adjectives) having a particular state or quality: **bored, patterned**

-ee (to make nouns) a person to whom sth is done: **employee** (= sb who is employed), **trainee** (= sb who is being trained)

-en (to make verbs) to give sth a particular quality; to make sth more ~: **shorten, widen, blacken, sharpen, loosen,** (but note: **lengthen**)

-ence (-ency) → -ance

-ent → -ant

-er (to make nouns) a person who does sth: **rider, painter, banker, driver, teacher**

-ese (to make adjectives) from a place: **Japanese, Chinese, Viennese**

-ess (to make nouns) a woman who does sth as a job: **waitress, actress**

-ful (to make adjectives) having a particular quality: **helpful, useful, beautiful**

-hood (to make nouns) 1 a state, often during a particular period of time: **childhood, motherhood** 2 a group with sth in common: **sisterhood, neighbourhood**

-ian (to make nouns) a person who does sth as a job or hobby: **historian, comedian, politician**

-ible → -able

-ical (to make adjectives from nouns ending in -y or -ics) connected with: **economical, mathematical, physical**

-ify (to make verbs) to produce a state or quality: **beautify, simplify, purify**

-ing (to make adjectives) producing a particular state or effect: **interesting**

-ish (to make adjectives) 1 describing nationality or language: **English, Swedish, Polish** 2 like sth: **babyish, foolish** 3 fairly, sort of: **longish, youngish, brownish**

-ist (to make nouns) 1 a person who has studied sth or does sth as a job: **artist, scientist, economist** = 2 a person who believes in sth or belongs to a particular group: **capitalist, pacifist, feminist**

-ion (to make nouns) a state or process: **action, connection, exhibition**

-ive (to make adjectives) having a particular quality: **attractive, effective**

-ize, -ise (to make verbs) producing a particular state: **magnetize, standardize, modernize, generalize**

-less (to make adjectives) not having sth: **hopeless, friendless**

-like (to make adjectives) similar to: **childlike**

-ly (to make adverbs) in a particular way: **badly, beautifully, completely**

-ment (to make nouns) a state, action or quality: **development, arrangement, excitement, achievement**

-ness (to make nouns) a state or quality: **kindness, happiness, weakness**

-ology (to make nouns) the study of a subject: **biology, psychology, zoology**

-or (to make nouns) a person who does sth, often as a job: **actor, conductor, sailor**

-ous (to make adjectives) having a particular quality: **dangerous, religious, ambitious**

-ship (to make nouns) showing status: **friendship, membership, citizenship**

-ward, -wards (to make adverbs) in a particular direction: **backward, upwards**

-wise (to make adverbs) in a particular way: **clockwise, edgewise**

-y (to make adjectives) having the quality of the thing mentioned: **cloudy, rainy, fatty, thirsty**

Word formation

What do you do when you find a new word in English? Before you reach for your dictionary, do you try to work out what it means? Often long words are made from shorter words that you know combined with a few letters at the beginning (a prefix) or a few letters at the end (a suffix). Prefixes generally alter the meaning of a word and suffixes change its part of speech (whether it is a noun, a verb, an adjective or an adverb). You can find a full list of all prefix and suffixes with their meanings and use on the previous two pages.

Exercise 1

Put these prefixes in numerical order from the smallest to the largest:
nona- bi- cent- penta- kilo- hexa- quad- mono- octa- deca- tri- septa-

Exercise 2

Use either a prefix or a suffix to form the opposites of the following words:

legible	responsible	obedient	typical
attractive	patient	useless	alcoholic
harmful	relevant	comfortable	successful

Exercise 3

Using the prefixes and suffixes below, change the words in bold to complete these sentences:

-ally -ment -ify extra- trans- -ous -ward -able il- -ish
1 Simpler language would make this report more _____. **read**
2 What do people in your country _____ eat at Christmas? **tradition**
3 Have you got this shirt in an _____? This one's not big enough. **large**
4 When I mixed all the paints together I got a _____ colour. **brown**
5 It's _____ to sell cigarettes to children under 16. **legal**
6 I think you should _____ these instructions – they're too complicated. **simple**
7 Passing your driving test first time was quite an _____. **achieve**
8 When is the next _____ flight from London to New York? **Atlantic**
9 Don't eat those berries – they're _____. **poison**
10 Travel _____ for about eight miles until you reach a junction. **north**

Exercise 4

Make as many words as possible out of the following by adding different prefixes and suffixes:

1 **beauty**   6 **excite**
2 **please**   7 **responsible**
3 **sense**   8 **rely**
4 **patient**   9 **behave**
5 **collect**   10 **real**

hand? **5** [I] to face a particular direction: *This room looks south so it gets the sun.* **6** [I] **look to do sth** to aim to do sth: *We are looking to double our profits over the next five years.*

IDIOMS **look bad; not look good** to be considered bad manners: *It'll look bad if we get there an hour late.*

look good to seem to be encouraging: *This year's sales figures are looking good.*

look sb in the eye to look straight at sb without feeling embarrassed or afraid

(not) look yourself to (not) look as well or healthy as usual

look on the bright side (of sth) to think only about the good side of a bad situation and be happy and hopeful

never/not look back to become and continue being successful

PHRASAL VERBS **look after sb/sth/yourself** to be responsible for or take care of sb/sth/yourself: *I want to go back to work if I can find somebody to look after the children.* • *The old lady's son looked after all her financial affairs.*

look ahead to think about or plan for the future

look at sth 1 to examine or study sth: *My tooth aches. I think a dentist should look at it.* • *The government is looking at ways of reducing unemployment.* **2** to read sth: *Could I look at the newspaper when you've finished with it?* **3** to consider sth: *Different races and nationalities look at life differently.*

look back (on sth) to think about sth in your past

look down on sb/sth to think that you are better than sb/sth

look forward to sth/doing sth to wait with pleasure for sth to happen: *I'm really looking forward to the weekend.*

look into sth to study or try to find out sth: *A committee was set up to look into the causes of the accident.*

look on to watch sth happening without taking any action: *All we could do was look on as the house burned.*

look on sb/sth as sth; look on sb with sth to think of sb/sth in a particular way: *They seem to look on me as someone who can advise them.*

look out to be careful or to pay attention to sth dangerous: *Look out! There's a bike coming.*

look out (for sb/sth) to pay attention in order to see, find or avoid sb/sth: *Look out for thieves!*

look round 1 to turn your head in order to see sb/sth **2** to look at many things (before buying sth): *She looked round but couldn't find anything she liked.*

look round sth to walk around a place looking at things: *to look round a town/shop/museum*

look through sth to read sth quickly

look to sb for sth; look to sb to do sth to expect sb to do or to provide sth: *He always looked to his father for advice.*

look up 1 to move your eyes upwards to look

at sb/sth: *She looked up and smiled.* **2** (*informal*) to improve: *Business is looking up.*

look sth up to search for information in a book: *to look up a word in a dictionary*

look up to sb to respect and admire sb

★**look²** /lʊk/ **noun 1** [C] the act of looking: *Have a look at this article.* • *Take a close look at the contract before you sign it.* **2** [C, usually sing] **a look (for sb/sth)** a search: *I'll have a good look for that book later.* **3** [C] the expression on sb's face: *He had a worried look on his face.* **4 looks** [pl] a person's appearance: *He's lucky – he's got good looks and intelligence.* **5** [C] a fashion or style: *The shop has a new look to appeal to younger customers.*

IDIOMS **by/from the look of sb/sth** judging by the appearance of sb/sth: *It's going to be a fine day by the look of it.*

like the look/sound of sb/sth → **LIKE¹**

'look-in noun

IDIOM **(not) give sb a look-in; (not) get/have a look-in** (*informal*) to (not) give sb, or to (not) have a chance to do sth

-looking /'lʊkɪŋ/ (used to form compound adjectives) having the appearance mentioned: *an odd-looking building* • *He's very good-looking.*

lookout /'lʊkaʊt/ **noun** [C] (a person who has) the responsibility of watching to see if danger is coming; the place this person watches from: *One of the gang acted as lookout.*

IDIOM **be on the lookout for sb/sth; keep a lookout for sb/sth** to pay attention in order to see, find or avoid sb/sth

loom¹ /luːm/ **noun** [C] a machine that is used for making cloth (**weaving**) by passing pieces of thread across and under other pieces

loom² /luːm/ **verb** [I] **loom (up)** to appear as a shape that is not clear and in a way that seems frightening: *The mountain loomed (up) in the distance.*

loony /'luːni/ **noun** [C] (*pl* **loonies**) (*slang*) a person who is crazy –**loony adj**: *I'm tired of listening to his loony plans.*

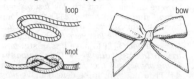

loop   bow

knot

loop /luːp/ **noun** [C] a curved or round shape made by a line curving round and joining or crossing itself: *a loop in a rope* • *The road goes around the lake in a loop.* •✲ picture at **coil** –**loop verb** [I,T]: *He was trying to loop a rope over the horse's head.*

loophole /'luːphəʊl/ **noun** [C] a way of avoiding sth because the words of a rule or law are badly chosen

★**loose¹** /luːs/ **adj 1** not tied up or shut in sth; free: *The horse managed to get loose and escape.* • *I take the dog to the woods and let* him **loose**. • *She wore her long hair loose.* **2** not firmly fixed: *a loose tooth* • *The saucepan handle is a bit loose so be careful.* **3** not contained in sth or joined together: *loose change* (= coins) • *some loose sheets of paper* **4** not fitting closely; not tight: *These trousers don't fit. They're much too loose round the waist.* •➤ opposite **tight** **5** not completely accurate or the same as sth: *a loose translation—loosely* **adv**: *The film is loosely based on the life of Beethoven.*

IDIOMS **all hell broke loose →** HELL

at a loose end having nothing to do and feeling bored

loose² /luːs/ **noun**

IDIOM **on the loose** escaped and dangerous: *a lion on the loose from a zoo*

loose-'leaf **adj** (used about a book, file, etc) with pages that can be removed or added separately

loosen /'luːsn/ **verb** [I,T] to become or make sth less tight: *to loosen your tie/belt* • *Don't loosen your grip on the rope or you'll fall.*

PHRASAL VERB **loosen (sb/sth) up** to relax or move more easily: *These exercises will help you to loosen up.*

loot /luːt/ **verb** [I,T] to steal things during a war or period of fighting

lop /lɒp/ **verb** [T] (**lopping**; **lopped**) to cut branches off a tree

PHRASAL VERB **lop sth off/away** to cut sth off/away

lopsided /ˌlɒp'saɪdɪd/ **adj** with one side lower or smaller than the other: *a lopsided smile*

lord /lɔːd/ **noun** [C] **1** a man with a very high position in society: *the Lord Mayor of London* • *Lord and Lady Derby* **2 the Lord** [sing] 'God; Christ **3 the Lords** [with sing or pl verb] (*Brit*) (members of) the House of Lords: *The Lords has/have voted against the bill.*

★**lorry** /'lɒri/ (*Brit*) **noun** [C] (*pl* **lorries**) (*especially US* **truck**) a large strong motor vehicle that is used for carrying goods by road •➤ picture at **vehicle**

★**lose** /luːz/ **verb** (*pt, pp* **lost** /lɒst/) **1** [T] to become unable to find sth: *I've lost my purse. I can't find it anywhere.* **2** [T] to no longer have sb/sth: *She lost a leg in the accident.* • *He lost his wife last year* (= she died). • *to lose your job* **3** [T] to have less of sth: *to lose weight/interest/patience* • *The company is losing money all the time.* •➤ opposite **gain** **4** [I,T] to not win; to be defeated: *We played well but we lost 2-1.* • *to lose a court case/an argument* • *Parma lost to Milan in the final.* **5** [T] to waste time, a chance, etc: *Hurry up! There's **no time to lose**.* **6** [I,T] to become poorer (as a result of sth): *The company lost on the deal.* **7** [T] (*informal*) to cause sb not to understand sth: *You've totally lost me! Please explain again.*

IDIOMS **keep/lose your cool →** COOL³
keep/lose count (of sth) → COUNT²
keep/lose your temper → TEMPER
keep/lose track of sb/sth → TRACK¹
lose your bearings to become confused about where you are

lose face to lose the respect of other people

lose it (*spoken*) to go crazy or suddenly become unable to control your emotions

lose your head to become confused or very excited

lose heart to stop believing that you will be successful in sth you are trying to do

lose your life to be killed

lose sight of sb/sth to no longer be able to see sb/sth: *We eventually lost sight of the animal in some trees.* • (*figurative*) *We mustn't lose sight of our original aim.*

lose your touch to lose a special skill or ability

lose touch (with sb/sth) to no longer have contact (with sb/sth): *I've lost touch with a lot of my old school friends.*

a losing battle a competition, fight, etc in which it seems that you will fail to be successful

win/lose the toss → TOSS

PHRASAL VERB **lose out (on sth/to sb)** (*informal*) to be at a disadvantage: *If a teacher pays too much attention to the bright students, the others lose out.*

loser /'luːzə/ **noun** [C] **1** a person who is defeated: *He is a bad loser. He always gets angry if I beat him.* **2** a person who is never successful **3** a person who suffers because of a particular situation, decision, etc

★**loss** /lɒs/ **noun** **1** [C,U] (a) loss (of sth) the state of no longer having sth or not having as much as before; the act of losing sth: *loss of blood/sleep* • *weight/hair loss* • *Have you reported the loss of your wallet?* • *The plane crashed with great loss of life.* **2** [C] a loss (of sth) the amount of money which is lost by a business: *The firm made a loss of £5 million.* •➤ Look at **profit. 3** [C] a loss (to sb) the disadvantage that is caused when sb/sth leaves or is taken away; the person or thing that causes this disadvantage: *If she leaves, it/she will be a big loss to the school.*

IDIOMS **at a loss** not knowing what to do or say

cut your losses to stop wasting time or money on sth that is not successful

lost¹ *past tense, past participle of* LOSE

★**lost²** /lɒst/ **adj 1** unable to find your way; not knowing where you are: *This isn't the right road – we're completely lost!* • *If you get lost, stop and ask someone the way.* **2** that cannot be found or that no longer exists: *The letter must have got lost in the post.* **3** unable to deal with a situation or to understand sth: *Sorry, I'm lost. Could you explain the last part again?* **4** lost on sb not noticed or understood by sb: *The humour of the situation was completely lost on Joe.*

IDIOMS **get lost** (*slang*) used to rudely tell sb to go away

a lost cause a goal or an aim that cannot be achieved

lost for words not knowing what to say

lost 'property **noun** [U] things that people have lost or left in a public place and that are kept in a special office for the owners to collect

★**lot¹** /lɒt/ **noun 1** [C] **a lot (of sth); lots (of sth)** a large amount or number of things or people: *Sit here – there's lots of room.* ● *There seem to be quite a lot of new shops opening.* ● *An awful lot of* (= very many) *people will be disappointed if the concert is cancelled.* ● *I've got a lot to do today.*

➤ In negative statements and questions, **much** and **many** are more usual: *A lot of girls go to dancing classes, but not many boys.* ● *'How much would a car like that cost?' 'A lot!'*

2 [sing,with sing or pl verb] (*informal*) all of sth; the whole of a group of things or people: *When we opened the bag of potatoes the whole lot was/were bad.* ● *The manager has just sacked the lot of them!* ● *Just one more suitcase and that's the lot!* ● *'How many of these books shall we take?' 'The lot.'* ● *You count those kids and I'll count this lot.*

IDIOM **draw lots →** DRAW¹

★**lot²** /lɒt/ **adv** (*informal*) **1 a lot; lots** (before adjectives and adverbs) very much: *a lot bigger/better/faster* ● *They see lots more of each other than before.* **2 a lot** very much or often: *Thanks a lot – that's very kind.* ● *It generally rains a lot at this time of year.*

a lot of /ə 'lɒt əv/ (also *informal* **lots of** /'lɒts əv/) **determiner** a large amount or number of (sb/sth): *There's been a lot of rain this year.* ● *Lots of love, Billy* (= an informal ending for a letter). ● *There were a lot of people at the meeting.*

lotion /'ləʊʃn/ **noun** [C,U] liquid that you use on your hair or skin: *suntan lotion*

lottery /'lɒtəri/ **noun** [C] (*pl* **lotteries**) a way of making money for the government, for charity, etc by selling tickets with numbers on them and giving prizes to the people who have bought certain numbers which are chosen by chance

★**loud** /laʊd/ **adj, adv 1** making a lot of noise; not quiet: *Can you turn the television down, it's too loud.* ● *Could you speak a bit louder – the people at the back can't hear.* ●➤ opposite **quiet** or **soft**

➤ **Loud** is usually used to describe the sound itself or the thing producing the sound: *a loud noise/bang* ● *loud music* **Noisy** is used to describe a person, animal, place, event, etc that is very or too loud: *a noisy road/party/engine/child*

2 (used about clothes or colours) too bright: *a loud shirt* –**loudly** adv –**loudness** noun [U]

IDIOM **out loud** so that people can hear it: *Shall I read this bit out loud to you?*

loudspeaker /ˌlaʊd'spiːkə/ **noun** [C] **1** (also **speaker**) the part of a radio, CD player, etc which the sound comes out of **2** a piece of electrical equipment for speaking, playing music, etc to a lot of people

lounge¹ /laʊndʒ/ **noun** [C] **1** a comfortable room in a house or hotel where you can sit and relax ●➤ picture on page C7 **2** the part of

an airport where passengers wait: *the departure lounge*

lounge² /laʊndʒ/ **verb** [I] **lounge (about/around)** to sit, stand or lie in a lazy way

louse /laʊs/ **noun** [C] (*pl* **lice** /laɪs/) a small insect that lives on the bodies of animals and people

lousy /'laʊzi/ **adj** (*informal*) very bad: *We had lousy weather on holiday.*

lout /laʊt/ **noun** [C] a young man who behaves in a rude, rough or stupid way ●➤ Look at **hooligan** and **yob**.

lovable (also **loveable**) /'lʌvəbl/ **adj** having a personality or appearance that is easy to love: *a lovable little boy*

★**love¹** /lʌv/ **noun 1** [U] a strong feeling that you have when you like sb/sth very much: *a mother's love for her children* ● *to fall in love with sb* ● *It was love at first sight. They got married two months after they met!* ● *He's madly in love with her.* ● *a love song/story* **2** [U,sing] a strong feeling of interest in or enjoyment of sth: *a love of adventure/nature/sport* **3** [C] a person, a thing or an activity that you like very much: *His great love was always music.* ● *Who was your first love?* **4** [C] (*Brit informal*) used as a friendly way of speaking to sb, often sb you do not know: *'Hello, love. What can I do for you?'*

➤ Often written **luv**.

5 [U] (used in tennis) a score of zero: *The score is forty-love.*

IDIOMS **give/send sb your love** to give/send sb a friendly message: *Give Maria my love when you next see her.*
(lots of) love (from) used at the end of a letter to a friend or a member of your family: *See you soon. Love, Jim*
make love (to sb) to have sex

★**love²** /lʌv/ **verb** [T] **1** to like sb/sth in the strongest possible way: *I split up from my girlfriend last year, but I still love her.* ● *She loves her children.* **2** to like or enjoy sth very much: *I love the summer!* ● *I really love swimming in the sea.* ● *'What do you think of this music?' 'I love it!'* **3 would love sth/to do sth** used to say that you would very much like sth/to do sth: *'Would you like to come?' 'I'd love to.'* ● *'What about a drink?' 'I'd love one.'* ● *We'd love you to come and stay with us.*

love affair noun [C] **1** a usually sexual relationship between two people who love each other but are not married: *She had a love affair with her tennis coach.* **2** a great enthusiasm for sth

★**lovely** /'lʌvli/ **adj** (**lovelier**; **loveliest**) **1** beautiful or attractive: *a lovely room/voice/expression* ● *You look lovely with your hair short.* **2** enjoyable or pleasant; very nice: *We had a lovely holiday.* –**loveliness** noun [U]

IDIOM **lovely and warm, peaceful, fresh, etc** used for emphasizing how good sth is because of the quality mentioned: *These blankets are lovely and soft.*

★**lover** /'lʌvə/ **noun** [C] **1** a partner in a sexual relationship with sb who he/she is not married to: *He discovered that his wife had a lover.* • *The park was full of young lovers holding hands.* **2** a person who likes or enjoys the thing mentioned: *a music lover* • *an animal lover*

loving /'lʌvɪŋ/ **adj 1** feeling or showing love or care: *She's very loving towards her brother.* **2** (in compound adjectives) **-loving** loving the thing or activity mentioned: *a fun-loving girl* –**lovingly** **adv**

★**low**[1] /ləʊ/ **adj, adv 1** close to the ground or to the bottom of sth: *Hang that picture a bit higher, it's much too low!* • *That plane is flying very low.* **2** below the usual or normal level or amount: *Temperatures were very low last winter.* • *The price of fruit is lower in the summer.* • *low wages* • *low-fat yoghurt* **3** below what is normal or acceptable in quality, importance or development: *a low standard of living* • *low status* **4** (used about a sound or voice) deep or quiet: *His voice is already lower than his father's.* • *A group of people in the library were speaking in low voices.* **5** not happy and lacking energy: *He's been **feeling** a bit **low** since his illness.* **6** (used about a light, an oven, etc) made to produce only a little light or heat: *Cook the rice on a low heat for 20 minutes.* • *The low lighting adds to the restaurant's atmosphere.* **7** (used about a gear in a car) that allows a slower speed ••➤ opposite for all senses **high**

IDIOMS **high and low** → **HIGH**[2]

lie low → **LIE**[2]

run low (on sth) to start have less of sth than you need; to start to be less than is needed: *We're running low on coffee – shall I go and buy some?*

low[2] /ləʊ/ **noun** [C] a low point, level, figure, etc: *Unemployment has fallen to a new low.* ••➤ opposite **high**

'low-down **noun** [sing] (*informal*)

IDIOM **give sb/get the low-down (on sb/sth)** to tell sb/be told the true facts or secret information (about sb/sth)

lower[1] /'ləʊə/ **adj** below sth or at the bottom of sth: *She bit her lower lip.* • *the lower deck of a ship* ••➤ opposite **upper**

★**lower**[2] /'ləʊə/ **verb** [T] **1** to make or let sb/sth go down: *They lowered the boat into the water.* • *to lower your head/eyes* **2** to make sth less in amount, quality, etc: *The virus lowers resistance to other diseases.* • *Could you lower your voice slightly? I'm trying to sleep.* ••➤ opposite **raise**

lower 'case **noun** [U] letters that are written or printed in their small form; not in capital letters: *The text is all in lower case.* • *lower-case letters* ••➤ opposite **upper case**

low-'key **adj** quiet and not wanting to attract a lot of attention: *The wedding will be very low-key. We're only inviting ten people.*

lowland /'ləʊlənd/ **noun** [C, usually pl] a flat area of land at about sea level: *the lowlands near the coast* • *lowland areas*

low-'lying **adj** (used about land) near to sea level; not high

low 'tide **noun** [U] the time when the sea is at its lowest level: *At low tide you can walk out to the island.* ••➤ opposite **high tide**

loyal /'lɔɪəl/ **adj** (used about a person) not changing in your friendship or beliefs: *a loyal friend/supporter* ••➤ synonym **faithful** ••➤ opposite **disloyal** –**loyally** **adv** –**loyalty** /'lɔɪəlti/ **noun** [C,U] (*pl* **loyalties**)

lozenge /'lɒzɪndʒ/ **noun** [C] a sweet that you suck if you have a cough or a sore throat

L-plate /'el pleɪt/ **noun** [C] a sign with a large red letter L (for 'learner') on it, that you fix to a car to show that the driver is learning to drive

Ltd /'lɪmətɪd/ **abbr** (*Brit*) (used about private companies) Limited: *Pierce and Co Ltd*

lubricant /'lu:brɪkənt/ **noun** [C,U] a substance, for example oil, that makes the parts of a machine work easily and smoothly

lubricate /'lu:brɪkeɪt/ **verb** [T] to put oil, etc onto or into sth so that it works smoothly –**lubrication** /ˌlu:brɪ'keɪʃn/ **noun** [U]

lucid /'lu:sɪd/ **adj** (*formal*) **1** (used about sth that is said or written) clear and easy to understand: *a lucid style/description* **2** (used about a person's mind) not confused; clear and normal –**lucidly** **adv** –**lucidity** /lu:'sɪdəti/ **noun** [U]

★**luck** /lʌk/ **noun** [U] **1** success or good things that happen by chance: *We'd like to wish you lots of luck in your new career.* • *He says this necklace will bring you luck.* • *I could hardly believe my luck when they offered me the job.* • *With a bit of luck, we'll finish this job today.* **2** chance; the force that people believe makes things happen: *There's no skill in this game – it's all luck.* • *to have good/bad luck*

IDIOMS **bad luck!; hard luck!** used to show pity for sb: *'Bad luck. Maybe you'll win next time.'*

be in/out of luck to be lucky/to not be lucky: *I was in luck – they had one ticket left!*

good luck (to sb) used to wish that sb is successful: *Good luck! I'm sure you'll get the job.*

worse luck → **WORSE**

★**lucky** /'lʌki/ **adj** (**luckier; luckiest**) **1** (used about a person) having good luck: *He's lucky to be alive after an accident like that.* • *With so much unemployment, I **count myself lucky** that I've got a job.* • *'I'm off on holiday next week.' 'Lucky you!'* **2** (used about a situation, event, etc) having a good result: *It's lucky I got here before the rain started.* • *a lucky escape* **3** (used about a thing) bringing success or good luck: *a lucky number* • *It was not my lucky day.* ••➤ opposite **unlucky** –**luckily** **adv**: *Luckily, I remembered to bring some money.*

IDIOM **you'll be lucky** used to tell sb that sth they are expecting will probably not happen: *You're looking for a good English restaurant? You'll be lucky!*

lucrative /'lu:krətɪv/ **adj** (*formal*) allowing

sb to earn a lot of money: *a lucrative contract/business*

ludicrous /'lu:dɪkrəs/ adj very silly; ridiculous: *What a ludicrous idea!* –ludicrously adv

lug /lʌg/ verb [T] (**lugging; lugged**) (*informal*) to carry or pull sth very heavy with great difficulty

★**luggage** /'lʌgɪdʒ/ noun [U] bags, suitcases, etc used for carrying a person's clothes and things on a journey: *'How much luggage are you taking with you?' 'Only one suitcase.'* ● *You're only allowed one piece of hand luggage* (= a bag that you carry with you on the plane). •▸ synonym **baggage**

'**luggage rack** noun [C] a shelf above the seats in a train or bus for putting your bags, etc on

lukewarm /ˌlu:k'wɔ:m/ adj **1** (used about liquids) only slightly warm **2** lukewarm (about sb/sth) not showing much interest; not keen

lull[1] /lʌl/ noun [C,usually sing] a lull (in sth) a short period of quiet between times of activity

lull[2] /lʌl/ verb [T] **1** to make sb relaxed and calm: *She sang a song to lull the children to sleep.* **2** lull sb into sth to make sb feel safe, and not expecting anything bad to happen: *Our first success lulled us into a false sense of security.*

lullaby /'lʌləbaɪ/ noun [C] (*pl* **lullabies**) a gentle song that you sing to help a child to go to sleep

lumber[1] /'lʌmbə/ (*especially US*) = **TIMBER**(1)

lumber[2] /'lʌmbə/ verb **1** [I] to move in a slow, heavy way: *A family of elephants lumbered past.* **2** [T] (*informal*) lumber sb (with sb/sth) (usually passive) to give sb a responsibility or job that he/she does not want

luminous /'lu:mɪnəs/ adj that shines in the dark: *a luminous watch*

★**lump**[1] /lʌmp/ noun [C] **1** a piece of sth solid of any size or shape: *a lump of coal/cheese/wood* ● *The sauce was full of lumps.* **2** a swelling under the skin: *You'll have a bit of a lump on your head where you banged it.* •▸ picture at **bump**

IDIOM have/feel a lump in your throat to feel pressure in your throat because you are about to cry

lump[2] /lʌmp/ verb [T] lump A and B together; lump A (in) with B to put or consider different people or things together in the same group

IDIOM lump it (*informal*) to accept sth unpleasant because you have no choice: *That's the deal – like it or lump it.*

'**lump sum** noun [C] an amount of money paid all at once rather than in several smaller amounts

lumpy /'lʌmpi/ adj full of or covered with lumps: *This bed is very lumpy.* •▸ opposite **smooth**

lunacy /'lu:nəsi/ noun [U] very stupid behaviour; madness: *It was lunacy to drive so fast in that terrible weather.*

lunar /'lu:nə/ adj (usually before a noun) connected with the moon: *a lunar spacecraft/eclipse/landscape*

lunatic[1] /'lu:nətɪk/ noun [C] (*informal*) a person who behaves in a stupid way doing crazy and often dangerous things •▸ synonym **madman**

lunatic[2] /'lu:nətɪk/ adj stupid; crazy: *a lunatic idea*

★**lunch** /lʌntʃ/ noun [C,U] a meal that you have in the middle of the day: *Hot and cold lunches are served between 12 and 2.* ● *What would you like for lunch?*

▸ You can take a **packed lunch** or a **picnic lunch** if you're out for the day. If you're working you might have a **business lunch** or a **working lunch** (= working at the same time as having lunch). For children at school lunch is usually called **school dinner**.

–lunch verb [I] (*formal*)

'**lunch hour** noun [C,usually sing] the time around the middle of the day when you stop work or school to have lunch: *I went to the shops in my lunch hour.*

lunchtime /'lʌntʃtaɪm/ noun [C,U] the time around the middle of the day when lunch is eaten: *I'll meet you at lunchtime.*

★**lung** /lʌŋ/ noun [C] one of the two organs of your body that are inside your chest and are used for breathing •▸ picture on page C5

lunge /lʌndʒ/ noun [C,usually sing] a lunge (at sb); a lunge (for sb/sth) a sudden powerful forward movement of the body, especially when trying to attack sb/sth: *She made a lunge for the ball.* –lunge verb [I]: *He lunged towards me with a knife.*

lurch /lɜ:tʃ/ noun [C,usually sing] a sudden movement forward or to one side –lurch verb [I]

IDIOM leave sb in the lurch → **LEAVE**[1]

lure[1] /lʊə/ verb [T] to persuade or trick sb to go somewhere or do sth, usually by offering him/her sth nice: *Young people are lured to the city by the prospect of a job and money.*

lure[2] /lʊə/ noun [C] the attractive qualities of sth: *the lure of money/fame/adventure*

lurid /'lʊərɪd; 'ljʊər-/ adj **1** having colours that are too bright, in a way that is not attractive: *a lurid purple and orange dress* **2** (used about a story or a piece of writing) deliberately shocking, especially because of violent or unpleasant detail –luridly adv

lurk /lɜ:k/ verb [I] to wait somewhere secretly especially in order to do sth bad or illegal: *I thought I saw somebody lurking among the trees.*

luscious /'lʌʃəs/ adj (used about food) tasting very good: *luscious fruit*

lush /lʌʃ/ adj (used about plants or gardens) growing very thickly and well

lust[1] /lʌst/ noun **1** [U] lust (for sb) strong sexual desire **2** [C,U] (a) lust (for sth) (a) very strong desire to have or get sth: *a lust for power* ● *(a) lust for life* (= enjoyment of life)

lust² /lʌst/ **verb** [I] lust (after sb); lust (after/ for sth) to feel a very strong desire for sb/ sth: *to lust for power/success/fame*

lustful /'lʌstfl/ **adj** full of sexual desire: *lustful thoughts* –**lustfully** /-fəli/ **adv**

luxurious /lʌg'ʒʊəriəs/ **adj** very comfortable; full of expensive and beautiful things: *a luxurious hotel* –**luxuriously adv**

luxury /'lʌkʃəri/ **noun** (*pl* **luxuries**) **1** [U] the enjoyment of expensive and beautiful things; great comfort and pleasure: *They are said to be living in luxury in Barbados.* ● *to lead a life of luxury* ● *a luxury hotel/car/yacht* **2** [C] something that is enjoyable and expensive that you do not really need: *luxury goods, such as wine and chocolates* **3** [U,sing] a pleasure which you do not often have: *It was (an) absolute luxury to do nothing all weekend.*

lynch /lɪntʃ/ **verb** [T] (used about a crowd of people) to kill sb, usually by hanging, who is thought to be guilty of a crime without a legal trial in a court of law

lyric /'lɪrɪk/ **adj** (used about poetry) expressing personal feelings and thoughts: *lyric poems*

lyrical /'lɪrɪkl/ **adj** like a song or a poem, expressing strong personal feelings

lyrics /'lɪrɪks/ **noun** [pl] the words of a song

···

M m

···

M, m¹ /em/ **noun** [C] (*pl* **M's; m's**) the thirteenth letter of the English alphabet: *'Miranda' begins with (an) 'M'.*

M² *abbr* **1** (also **med**) medium (size) **2** /em/ (*Brit*) motorway: *heavy traffic on the M25* **3 m** metre(s): *a 500m race* **4 m** million(s): *population 10m*

MA /ˌem 'eɪ/ **abbr** Master of Arts; a second degree that you receive when you complete a more advanced course or piece of research in an arts subject at university or college ··➤ Look at **BA** and **MSc**.

mac /mæk/ (also **mackintosh** /'mækɪntɒʃ/) **noun** [C] (*especially Brit*) a coat that is made to keep out the rain

macabre /məˈkɑːbrə/ **adj** unpleasant and frightening because it is connected with death: *a macabre tale/joke/ritual*

macaroni /ˌmækəˈrəʊni/ **noun** [U] a type of Italian food made from dried flour and water (pasta) in the shape of short tubes

★**machine** /məˈʃiːn/ **noun** [C] (often in compounds) a piece of equipment with moving parts that is designed to do a particular job. A machine usually needs electricity, gas, steam, etc in order to work: *a washing/sewing/knitting machine* ● *a machine for making pasta* ··➤ Look at the note at **tool**.

ma'chine gun noun [C] a gun that fires bullets very quickly and continuously

machinery /məˈʃiːnəri/ **noun** [U] machines in general, especially large ones; the moving parts of a machine: *farm/agricultural/industrial machinery*

macho /'mætʃəʊ/ **adj** (*informal*) (used about a man or his behaviour) having typically male qualities like strength and courage, but using them in an aggressive way: *He's too macho to ever admit he was wrong and apologize.*

mackintosh = **MAC**

★**mad** /mæd/ **adj 1** having a mind that does not work normally; mentally ill

➤ It is not usual nowadays to use **mad** or **insane** to describe a person who is not mentally normal. We use the expression **mentally ill**.

2 (*Brit*) not at all sensible; crazy: *You must be mad to drive in this weather.* **3** (not before a noun) mad (at/with sb) (about sth) very angry: *His laziness drives me mad!* ● (*especially US*) *Don't get/go mad at him. He didn't mean to do it.* **4** (*informal*) mad about/on sb/sth liking sb/sth very much: *He's mad or computer games at the moment.* ● *Steve's mad about Jane.* **5** not controlled; wild or very excited: *The audience was cheering and clapping like mad* (= very hard). ● *When DiCaprio appeared on the hotel balcony his fans went mad.*

madam /'mædəm/ **noun** [sing] **1** (*formal*) used as a polite way of speaking to a woman especially to a customer in a shop or restaurant: *Can I help you, madam?* ··➤ Look at **sir** **2 Madam** used for beginning a formal letter to a woman when you do not know her name: *Dear Madam, I am writing in reply...*

mad 'cow disease = **BSE**

maddening /'mædnɪŋ/ **adj** that makes you very angry or annoyed: *She has some really maddening habits.* –**maddeningly adv**

made *past tense, past participle* of **MAKE¹**

IDIOM **made to measure** → **MEASURE²**

madly /'mædli/ **adv 1** in a wild or crazy way: *They were rushing about madly.* **2** (*informal*) very; extremely: *They're madly in love.*

madman /'mædmən/ **noun** [C] (*pl* **madmen** /-mən; -men/) a person who behaves in a wild or crazy way ··➤ synonym **lunatic**

madness /'mædnəs/ **noun** [U] crazy or stupid behaviour that could be dangerous: *It would be madness to take a boat out in such rough weather.*

★**magazine** /ˌmægəˈziːn/ (also *informal* **mag** /mæg/) **noun** [C] a type of large thin book with a paper cover that you can buy every week or month containing articles, photographs, etc often on a particular topic: *a woman's/computer/gardening magazine*

maggot /'mægət/ **noun** [C] a young insect before it grows wings and legs and becomes a fly ··➤ picture at **worm**

★**magic¹** /'mædʒɪk/ **noun** [U] **1** a secret power that some people believe can make strange or impossible things happen by saying special words or doing special things ••➤ Look at **black magic. 2** the art of doing tricks that seem impossible in order to entertain people **3** a special quality that makes sth seem wonderful: *I'll never forget the magic of that moment.*

magic² /'mædʒɪk/ **adj 1** used in or using magic: *a magic spell/potion/charm/trick* ● *There is no magic formula for passing exams – just hard work.* **2** having a special quality that makes sth seem wonderful: *Respect is the magic ingredient in our relationship.* –**magically** /-kli/ **adv**

magical /'mædʒɪkl/ **adj 1** that seems to use magic: *a herb with magical powers to heal* **2** wonderful and exciting: *Our holiday was absolutely magical.*

magician /mə'dʒɪʃn/ **noun** [C] **1** a person who performs magic tricks to entertain people ••➤ Look at **conjuror. 2** (in stories) a man who has magic powers ••➤ Look at **wizard.**

magistrate /'mædʒɪstreɪt/ **noun** [C] an official who acts as a judge in cases involving less serious crimes

magnanimous /mæg'nænɪməs/ **adj** kind, generous and forgiving (especially towards an enemy or a competitor that you have beaten)

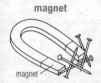
magnet

magnet /'mægnət/ **noun** [C] a piece of iron, steel, etc that can attract and pick up other metal objects

magnetic /mæg'netɪk/ **adj 1** having the ability to attract metal objects: *magnetic fields* ● *a magnetic tape/disk* (= containing electronic information which can be read by a computer or other machine) **2** having a quality that strongly attracts people: *a magnetic personality* –**magnetism** /'mægnətɪzəm/ **noun** [U]: *Nobody could resist his magnetism.*

magnificent /mæg'nɪfɪsnt/ **adj** extremely impressive and attractive: *What a magnificent castle!* –**magnificently adv** –**magnificence noun** [U]

magnify

magnifying glass

magnify /'mægnɪfaɪ/ **verb** [T] (*pres part* **magnifying**; *3rd pers sing pres* **magnifies**; *pt, pp* **magnified**) **1** to make sth look bigger than it is, usually using a special piece of equipment: *to magnify sth under a microscope* **2** to make sth seem more important than it

really is: *to magnify a problem* –**magnification** /,mægnɪfɪ'keɪʃn/ **noun** [U]

magnifying glass noun [C] a round piece of glass, usually with a handle, that is used for making things look bigger than they are ••➤ picture at **magnify**

magnitude /'mægnɪtjuːd/ **noun** [U] the great size or importance of sth

mahogany /mə'hɒgəni/ **noun** [U] hard dark reddish-brown wood (from a tropical tree) that is used for making furniture

maid /meɪd/ **noun** [C] a woman whose job is to clean in a hotel or large house ••➤ Look at **chambermaid.**

maiden name /'meɪdn neɪm/ **noun** [C] a woman's family name before marriage ••➤ Look at **née.**

maiden voyage /,meɪdn 'vɔɪɪdʒ/ **noun** [C] the first journey of a new ship

★**mail** /meɪl/ (*Brit also* **post**) **noun** [U] **1** the system for collecting and sending letters and packages: *to send a parcel by airmail/surface mail* **2** the letters, etc that you receive: *junk mail* (= letters, usually advertising sth, that are sent to people although they have not asked for them) ••➤ Look at the note at **post. 3** (*especially US*) = **E-MAIL** –**mail verb** [T] (*especially US*)

mailbox /'meɪlbɒks/ **noun** [C] **1** (*US*) = **LETTER BOX**(2) **2** (*US*) = **POSTBOX 3** a computer program that receives and stores electronic messages (e-mail)

mailing list noun [C] a list of the names and addresses of people to whom advertising material or information is regularly sent by a business or an organization

mailman /'meɪlmæn/ (*pl* **-men** /-mən/) (*US*) = **POSTMAN**

mail order noun [U] a method of shopping. You choose what you want from a special book (a catalogue) and the goods are then sent to you by post.

maim /meɪm/ **verb** [T] to hurt sb so badly that part of his/her body can no longer be used

★**main¹** /meɪn/ **adj** (only *before* a noun) most important; chief: *My main reason for wanting to learn English is to get a better job.* ● *a busy main road* ● *He doesn't earn very much but he's happy, and that's **the main thing.***

IDIOM **in the main** (*formal*) generally; mostly: *We found English people very friendly in the main.*

main² /meɪn/ **noun 1** [C] a large pipe or wire that carries water, gas or electricity between buildings: *The water main has burst.* **2 the mains** [pl] (*Brit*) the place where the supply of gas, water or electricity to a building starts; the system of providing these services to a building: *Turn the water off at the mains.* ● *mains gas/water/electricity*

mainland /'meɪnlænd/ **noun** [sing] the main part of a country or continent, not including the islands around it: *mainland Greece*

mainly /'meɪnli/ **adv** mostly: *The students here are mainly from Japan.*

m

[I] intransitive, a verb which has no object: *He laughed.*   **[T] transitive**, a verb which has an object: *He ate an apple.*

mainstay /ˈmeɪnsteɪ/ **noun** [C] a person or thing that is the most important part of sth, which makes it possible for it to exist or to be successful: *Cocoa is the mainstay of the country's economy.*

mainstream /ˈmeɪnstriːm/ **noun** [sing] the ideas and opinions that are considered normal because they are shared by most people; the people who hold these opinions and beliefs: *The Green Party is not in the mainstream of British politics.*

★**maintain** /meɪnˈteɪn/ **verb** [T] **1** to make sth continue at the same level, standard, etc: *We need to maintain the quality of our goods but not increase the price.* ● *to maintain law and order* **2** to keep sth in good condition by checking and repairing it regularly: *to maintain a road/building/machine* ● *The house is large and expensive to maintain.* **3** to keep saying that sth is true even when others disagree or do not believe it: *I still maintain that I was right to sack him.* ● *She has always maintained her innocence.* **4** to support sb with your own money: *He has to maintain two children from his previous marriage.*

maintenance /ˈmeɪntənəns/ **noun** [U] **1** keeping sth in good condition: *This house needs a lot of maintenance.* ● *car maintenance* **2** (*Brit*) money that sb must pay regularly to a former wife, husband or partner especially when they have had children together: *He has to pay maintenance to his ex-wife.*

maisonette /ˌmeɪzəˈnet/ **noun** [C] (*Brit*) a flat/apartment on two floors that is part of a larger building

maize /meɪz/ (*US* **corn**) **noun** [U] a tall plant that produces yellow grains in a large mass (a cob)

> The yellow grains from maize that we eat as a vegetable are called **sweet corn**.

••► picture at **cereal**

majestic /məˈdʒestɪk/ **adj** impressive because of its size or beauty: *a majestic mountain landscape* –**majestically** /-kli/ **adv**

majesty /ˈmædʒəsti/ **noun** (*pl* **majesties**) **1** [U] the impressive and attractive quality that sth has: *the splendour and majesty of the palace and its gardens* **2** **His/Her/Your Majesty** [C] (*formal*) used when speaking to or about a royal person: *Her Majesty the Queen*

★**major¹** /ˈmeɪdʒə/ **adj 1** (only *before* a noun) very large, important or serious: *The patient needs major heart surgery.* ● *There haven't been any major problems.* ••► opposite **minor** **2** of one of the two types of key¹(4) in which music is usually written: *the key of D major* ••► Look at **minor**.

major² /ˈmeɪdʒə/ **noun 1** (*abbr* **Maj**) [C] an officer of a middle level in the army or the US air force **2** [C] (*US*) the main subject or course of a student at college or university; the student who studies it: *Her major is French.* **3** [U] (used in music) a type of key¹(4) or scale: *a change from major to minor*

major³ /ˈmeɪdʒə/ **verb**
▐PHRASAL VERB▐ **major in sth** (*US*) to study sth as your main subject at college or university

major 'general noun [C] an officer of a high level in the army

★**majority** /məˈdʒɒrəti/ **noun** (*pl* **majorities**) **1** [sing, with sing or pl verb] **majority (of sb/sth)** the largest number or part of a group of people or things: *The majority of students in the class come/comes from Japan.* ● *This treatment is not available in the vast majority of hospitals.* ••► opposite **minority** **2** [C usually sing] **majority (over sb)** (in an election) the difference in the number of votes for the person/party who came first and the person/party who came second: *He was elected by/with a majority of almost 5000 votes.*

➤ If you have an **overall majority** you got more votes than all the other people/parties added together.

▐IDIOM▐ **be in the/a majority** to form the largest number or part of sth: *Women are in the majority in the teaching profession.*

★**make¹** /meɪk/ **verb** [T] (*pt, pp* **made** /meɪd/) **1** to produce or create sth: *to make bread* ● *This model is made of steel, and that one is made out of used matches.* ● *Cheese is made from milk.* ● *Those cars are made in Slovakia.* ● *Shall I make you a sandwich/make a sandwich for you?* ● *to make a hole in sth* ● *to make a law/rule* ● *to make a movie* **2** (used with nouns) to perform a certain action: *to make a mistake/noise* ● *to make a guess/comment/statement/suggestion* ● *to make progress* ● *I've made an appointment to see the doctor.*

➤ Often there is a verb with a similar form, for example **decide** = **make a decision**. If you use 'make' + noun, you can use an adjective with it: *He made the right decision.* ● *They made a generous offer.*

3 to cause a particular effect, feeling, situation, etc: *The film made me cry.* ● *Flying makes him nervous.* ● *Her remarks made the situation worse.* ● *I'll make it clear to him that we won't pay.* ● *Make sure you lock the car.* ● *You don't need to know much of a language to make yourself understood.* ● *to make trouble/a mess/a noise* **4** to force sb/sth to do sth: *You can't make her come with us if she doesn't want to.* ● *They made him wait at the police station all day.*

➤ In the passive we must use **to**: *He was made to wait at the police station.*

5 used with money, numbers and time: *How much do you think he makes* (= earns) *a month?* ● *to make a lot of money* ● *5 and 7 make 12.* ● *'What's the time?' 'I make it 6.45.'* **6** to make sb/sth become sth; to have the right qualities to become sth: *She was made* (= given the job of) *President.* ● *You can borrow some money this time, but don't make a habit of it.* ● *Karen explains things very clearly – she'd make a good teacher.* **7** to become sth; to achieve sth: *I'm hoping to make head of the department by the time I'm* *thirty.* **8** to manage to reach a place or go somewhere: *We should make Bristol by about 10.* ● *I can't make the meeting next week.*

IDIOMS **make do with sth** to use sth that is not good enough because nothing better is available: *If we can't get limes, we'll have to make do with lemons.*

make it to manage to do sth; to succeed: *She'll never make it as an actress.* ● *He's badly injured – it looks like he might not make it* (= survive).

make the most of sth to get as much pleasure, profit, etc as possible from sth: *You won't get another chance – make the most of it!*

> For other expressions with **make**, look at the noun and adjective entries, for example, for **make amends** look at **amends**.

PHRASAL VERBS **make for sb/sth** to move towards sb/sth

make for sth to help or allow sth to happen: *Arguing all the time doesn't make for a happy marriage.*

be made for sb/each other to be well suited to sb/each other: *Jim and Alice seem made for each other.*

make sb/sth into sb/sth to change sb/sth into sb/sth: *She made her spare room into an office.*

make sth of sb/sth to understand the meaning or nature of sb/sth: *What do you make of Colin's letter?*

make off (with sth) (*informal*) to leave or escape in a hurry, for example after stealing sth: *Someone's made off with my wallet!*

make sb/sth out 1 to understand sb/sth: *I just can't make him out.* **2** to be able to see or hear sb/sth; to manage to read sth: *I could just make out her signature.*

make out that…; make yourself out to be sth to say that sth is true and try to make people believe it: *He made out that he was a millionaire.* ● *She's not as clever as she makes herself out to be.*

make (yourself/sb) up to put powder, colour, etc on your/sb's face to make it look attractive

make sth up 1 to form sth: *the different groups that make up our society* **2** to invent sth, often sth that is not true: *to make up an excuse* **3** to make a number or an amount complete; to replace sth that has been lost: *We need one more person to make up our team.*

make up for sth to do sth that corrects a bad situation: *Her enthusiasm makes up for her lack of experience.*

make it up to sb (*informal*) to do sth that shows that you are sorry for what you have done to sb or that you are grateful for what he/she has done for you: *You've done me a big favour. How can I make it up to you?*

make (it) up (with sb) to become friends again after an argument: *Has she made it up with him yet?*

★**make²** /meɪk/ *noun* [C] the name of the company that produces sth: *'What make is your television?' 'It's a Sony.'*

IDIOM **on the make** always trying to make money for yourself, especially in a dishonest way: *The country is being ruined by politicians on the make.*

¹make-believe *noun* [U] things that sb imagines or invents that are not real

★**maker** /'meɪkə/ *noun* [C] a person, company or machine that makes sth: *a film-maker* ● *If it doesn't work, send it back to the maker.* ● *an ice cream maker*

makeshift /'meɪkʃɪft/ *adj* made to be used for only a short time until there is sth better: *makeshift shelters out of old cardboard boxes*

¹make-up *noun* **1** [U] powder, cream, etc that you put on your face to make yourself more attractive. Actors use make-up to change their appearance when they are acting: *to put on/take off make-up* ••> Look at **cosmetic¹**. ••> *verb* **make (yourself/sb) up 2** [sing] a person's character: *He can't help his temper. It's part of his make-up.*

making /'meɪkɪŋ/ *noun* [sing] the act of doing or producing sth; the process of being made: *breadmaking* ● *This movie has been three years in the making.*

IDIOMS **be the making of sb** to be the reason that sb is successful: *University was the making of Gina.*

have the makings of sth to have the necessary qualities for sth: *The book has the makings of a good film.*

maladjusted /ˌmælə'dʒʌstɪd/ *adj* (used about a person) not able to behave well with other people

malaria /mə'leəriə/ *noun* [U] a serious disease in hot countries that you get from the bite of a small flying insect (a **mosquito**)

★**male** /meɪl/ *adj* belonging to the sex that does not give birth to babies or produce eggs: *a male goat* ● *a male model/nurse* ••> Look at **masculine** and the note at **female**. –**male** *noun* [C] a male person or animal

malice /'mælɪs/ *noun* [U] a wish to hurt other people –**malicious** /mə'lɪʃəs/ *adj* –**maliciously** *adv*

malignant /mə'lɪɡnənt/ *adj* (used about a disease (**cancer**) that spreads in the body, or a growing mass (a **tumour**) caused by disease) likely to cause death if not controlled: *He has a malignant brain tumour.* ••> opposite **benign**

mall /mæl; mɔːl/ = **SHOPPING CENTRE**

mallet /'mælɪt/ *noun* [C] a heavy wooden hammer ••> picture at **tool**

malnutrition /ˌmælnjuː'trɪʃn/ *noun* [U] bad health that is the result of not having enough food or enough of the right kind of food –**malnourished** /ˌmæl'nʌrɪʃt/ *adj*: *The children were badly malnourished.*

malt /mɔːlt/ *noun* [U] grain that is used for making beer and a strong alcoholic drink (**whisky**)

maltreat /ˌmæl'triːt/ *verb* [T] (*formal*) to treat a person or animal in a cruel or unkind way –**maltreatment** *noun* [U]

mammal /'mæml/ *noun* [C] an animal of the type that gives birth to live babies, not eggs, and feeds its young on milk from its own body: *Whales, dogs and humans are mammals.*

mammoth /'mæməθ/ *adj* very big

★**man**¹ /mæn/ *noun* (*pl* **men** /men/) **1** [C] an adult male person **2** [C] a person of either sex, male or female: *All men are equal.* ● *No man could survive long in such conditions.* **3** [U] the human race; human beings: *Early man lived by hunting.* ● *the damage man has caused to the environment* **4** [C] (often in compounds) a man who comes from a particular place; a man who has a particular job or interest: *a Frenchman* ● *a businessman* ● *sportsmen and women*

IDIOMS the man in the street (*Brit*) an ordinary man or woman

the odd man/one out → ODD

man² /mæn/ *verb* [T] (**manning**; **manned**) to operate sth or to provide people to operate sth: *The telephones are manned 24 hours a day.*

★**manage** /'mænɪdʒ/ *verb* **1** [I,T] (often with *can* or *could*) to succeed in doing or dealing with sth difficult; to be able to do sth: *However did you manage to find us here?* ● *I can't manage this suitcase. It's too heavy.* ● *Paula can't manage next Tuesday* (= she can't come then) *so we'll meet another day.* **2** [T] to be in charge or control of sth: *She manages a small advertising business.* ● *You need to manage your time more efficiently.* **3** [I] manage (without/with sb/sth); manage (on sth) to deal with a difficult situation; to continue in spite of difficulties: *My grandmother couldn't manage without her neighbours.* ● *Can you manage with just one assistant?* ● *It's hard for a family to manage on just one income.*

manageable /'mænɪdʒəbl/ *adj* not too big or too difficult to deal with

★**management** /'mænɪdʒmənt/ *noun* **1** [U] the control or organization of sth: *Good classroom management is vital with large groups of children.* **2** [C,U] the people who control a business or company: *The hotel is now under new management.*

➤ In the singular, **management** can be used with a singular or plural verb: *The management is/are considering making some workers redundant.*

★**manager** /'mænɪdʒə/ *noun* [C] **1** a man or woman who controls an organization or part of an organization: *a bank manager* **2** a person who looks after the business affairs of a singer, actor, etc **3** a person who is in charge of a sports team: *the England manager*

manageress /ˌmænɪdʒə'res/ *noun* [C] the woman who is in charge of a shop or restaurant

managerial /ˌmænə'dʒɪəriəl/ *adj* connected with the work of a manager: *Do you have any managerial experience?*

‚**managing di'rector** *noun* [C] a person who controls a business or company

mandarin /'mændərɪn/ *noun* [C] a type of small orange

mandate /'mændeɪt/ *noun* [usually sing] the power that is officially given to a group of people to do sth, especially after they have won an election: *The union leaders had a clear mandate from their members to call a strike.*

mandatory /'mændətəri; mæn'deɪtəri/ *ad (formal)* that you must do, have, obey etc: *The crime carries a mandatory life sentence.* •➤ synonym **obligatory** •➤ opposite **optional**

mane /meɪn/ *noun* [C] the long hair on the neck of a horse or male lion ••➤ picture a horse and lion

maneuver (*US*) = MANOEUVRE

mangle /'mæŋgl/ *verb* [T] (usually passive) to damage sth so badly that it is difficult to see what it looked like originally: *The motorway was covered with the mangled wreckage of cars.*

mango /'mæŋgəʊ/ *noun* [C] (*pl* **mangoes** or **mangos**) a tropical fruit that has a yellow and red skin and is yellow inside ••➤ picture on page C3

manhole /'mænhəʊl/ *noun* [C] a hole in the street with a lid over it through which sb can go to look at the pipes, wires, etc that are underground

manhood /'mænhʊd/ *noun* [U] the state of being a man rather than a boy

mania /'meɪniə/ *noun* **1** [C] (*informal*) a great enthusiasm for sth: *World Cup mania is sweeping the country.* **2** [U] a serious mental illness that may cause sb to be very excited or violent

maniac /'meɪniæk/ *noun* [C] **1** a person who behaves in a wild and stupid way: *to drive like a maniac* **2** a person who has a stronger love of sth than is normal: *a football/sex maniac*

manic /'mænɪk/ *adj* **1** full of nervous energy or excited activity: *His behaviour became more manic as he began to feel stressed.* **2** (*medical*) connected with mania(2)

manicure /'mænɪkjʊə/ *noun* [C,U] treatment to make your hands and fingernails look attractive

manifest /'mænɪfest/ *verb* [I,T] (*formal*) **manifest (sth/itself) (in/as sth)** to show sth or to be shown clearly: *Mental illness can manifest itself in many forms.* –manifest *adj*: *manifest failure/anger*

manifestation /ˌmænɪfe'steɪʃn/ *noun* [C,U] (*formal*) a sign that sth is happening

manifesto /ˌmænɪ'festəʊ/ *noun* [C] (*pl* **manifestos**) a written statement by a political party that explains what it hopes to do if it becomes the government in the future

manipulate /mə'nɪpjuleɪt/ *verb* [T] **1** to influence sb so that he/she does or thinks what you want: *Clever politicians know how to manipulate public opinion.* **2** to use, move or control sth with skill: *The doctor manipulated the bone back into place.* –manipulation /məˌnɪpju'leɪʃn/ *noun* [C,U]

mankind /mæn'kaɪnd/ *noun* [U] all the people in the world: *A nuclear war would be a* *threat to all mankind.* ·➤ Look at the note at **man**.

manly /'mænli/ **adj** typical of or suitable for a man: *a deep manly voice* –**manliness noun** [U]

,**man-'made adj** made by people, not formed in a natural way; artificial: *man-made fabrics such as nylon and polyester*

★**manner** /'mænə/ **noun 1** [sing] the way that you do sth or that sth happens: *Stop arguing! Let's try to act in a civilized manner.* **2** [sing] the way that sb behaves towards other people: *to have an aggressive/a relaxed/a professional manner* **3 manners** [pl] a way of behaving that is considered acceptable in your country or culture: *In some countries it is bad manners to show the soles of your feet.* ● *Their children have no manners.*
IDIOM **all manner of...** every kind of...: *You meet all manner of people in my job.*

mannerism /'mænərɪzəm/ **noun** [C] sb's particular way of speaking or a particular movement he/she often does

manoeuvre¹ (*US* **maneuver**) /mə'nu:və/ **noun 1** [C] a movement that needs care or skill: *Parking the car in such a small space would be a tricky manoeuvre.* **2** [C,U] something clever that you do in order to win sth, trick sb, etc: *political manoeuvre(s)* **3 manoeuvres** [pl] a way of training soldiers when large numbers of them practise fighting in battles

manoeuvre² (*US* **maneuver**) /mə'nu:və/ **verb** [I,T] to move (sth) to a different position using skill: *The driver was manoeuvring his lorry into a narrow gateway.*

manor /'mænə/ (also '**manor house**) **noun** [C] a large house in the country that has land around it

manpower /'mænpaʊə/ **noun** [U] the people that you need to do a particular job: *There is a shortage of skilled manpower in the computer industry.*

mansion /'mænʃn/ **noun** [C] a very large house

manslaughter /'mænslɔ:tə/ **noun** [U] the crime of killing sb without intending to do so ·➤ Look at **murder**.

mantelpiece /'mæntlpi:s/ **noun** [C] a narrow shelf above the space in a room where a fire goes ·➤ picture at **fireplace**

manual¹ /'mænjuəl/ **adj** using your hands; operated by hand: *Office work can sometimes be more tiring than manual work.* ● *a skilled manual worker* ● *Does your car have a manual or an automatic gearbox?* –**manually adv**

manual² /'mænjuəl/ **noun** [C] a book that explains how to do or operate sth: *a training manual* ● *a car manual*

★**manufacture** /,mænju'fæktʃə/ **verb** [T] to make sth in large quantities using machines: *a local factory that manufactures furniture* ● *manufacturing industries* ·➤ synonym **produce** –**manufacture noun** [U]: *The manufacture of chemical weapons should be illegal.*

manufacturer /,mænju'fæktʃərə/ **noun** [C] a person or company that makes sth: *a car manufacturer*

manure /mə'njʊə/ **noun** [U] the waste matter from animals that is put on the ground in order to make plants grow better ·➤ Look at **fertilizer**.

manuscript /'mænjuskrɪpt/ **noun** [C] **1** a copy of a book, piece of music, etc before it has been printed **2** a very old book or document that was written by hand

★**many** /'meni/ **determiner, pron** (used with plural nouns or verbs) **1** a large number of people or things: *Have you made many friends at school yet?* ● *Not many of my friends smoke.* ● *Many of the mistakes were just careless.* ● *There are too many mistakes in this essay.*

➤ **Many** in positive sentences sounds quite formal: *Many schools teach computing nowadays.* When speaking or writing informally we usually use **a lot of**: *A lot of schools teach computing nowadays.* In negative sentences and questions, however, **many** can always be used without sounding formal: *I don't know many cheap places to eat.* ● *Are there many hotels in this town?*

2 used to ask about the number of people or things, or to refer to a known number: *How many children have you got?* ● *How many came to the meeting?* ● *I don't work as many hours as you.* ● *There are half/twice as many boys as girls in the class.* **3** (used to form compound adjectives) having a lot of the thing mentioned: *a many-sided shape* **4 many a** (used with a singular noun and verb) a large number of: *I've heard him say that many a time.*
IDIOM **a good/great many** very many

Maori /'maʊri/ **noun** [C] (*pl* **Maori** or **Maoris**) a member of the race of people who were the original inhabitants of New Zealand –**Maori adj**

★**map** /mæp/ **noun** [C] a drawing or plan of (part of) the surface of the earth that shows countries, rivers, mountains, roads, etc: *a map of the world* ● *a road/street map* ● *I can't find Cambridge on the map.* ● *to read a map*

➤ A book of maps is called an **atlas**.

–**map verb** [T] (**mapping**; **mapped**): *The region is so remote it has not yet been mapped.*

maple /'meɪpl/ **noun** [C] a tree that has leaves with five points and that produces a very sweet liquid that you can eat: *maple syrup*

Mar abbr March: *17 March 1956*

marathon /'mærəθən/ **noun** [C] **1** a long-distance running race, in which people run about 42 kilometres or 26 miles **2** an activity that lasts much longer than expected: *The interview was a real marathon.*

marble /'mɑ:bl/ **noun 1** [U] a hard attractive stone that is used to make statues and parts of buildings: *a marble statue* **2** [C] a small ball of coloured glass that children play with **3 marbles** [pl] the children's game that you play by rolling marbles along the ground trying to hit other marbles

★**March**[1] /mɑːtʃ/ **noun** [U,C] (*abbr* **Mar**) the third month of the year, coming after February

> ➤ To see how the months are used in sentences, look at the examples and the note at **January**.

★**march**[2] /mɑːtʃ/ **verb 1** [I] to walk with regular steps (like a soldier): *The President saluted as the troops marched past.* **2** [I] to walk in a determined way: *She marched up to the manager and demanded an apology.* **3** [T] to make sb walk or march somewhere: *The prisoner was marched away.* **4** [I] to walk in a large group to protest about sth: *The demonstrators marched through the centre of town.*

★**march**[3] /mɑːtʃ/ **noun** [C] **1** an organized walk by a large group of people who are protesting about sth: *a peace march* •➤ Look at **demonstration. 2** a journey made by marching: *The soldiers were tired after their long march.*

mare /meə/ **noun** [C] a female horse •➤ Look at the note at **horse**.

margarine /ˌmɑːdʒəˈriːn/ **noun** [U] a food that is similar to butter, made of animal or vegetable fats •➤ picture on page C4

margin /ˈmɑːdʒɪn/ **noun 1** [C] the empty space at the side of a page in a book, etc **2** [C] the amount of space, time, votes, etc by which you win sth: *He won by a wide/narrow/comfortable margin.* **3** [C] the amount of profit that a company makes on sth **4** [C] the area around the edge of sth: *the margins of the Pacific Ocean* **5** [U] an amount of space, time, etc that is more than you need: *It is a complex operation with little margin for error.*

marginal /ˈmɑːdʒɪnl/ **adj** small in size or importance: *The differences are marginal.* –**marginally adv**: *In most cases costs will increase only marginally.*

marijuana /ˌmærɪˈwɑːnə/ **noun** [U] a drug that is smoked and is illegal in many countries

marina /məˈriːnə/ **noun** [C] a small area of water (a harbour) designed for pleasure boats

marine[1] /məˈriːn/ **adj 1** connected with the sea: *the study of marine life* **2** connected with ships or sailing: *marine insurance*

marine[2] /məˈriːn/ **noun** [C] a soldier who has been trained to fight on land or at sea

marital /ˈmærɪtl/ **adj** (only *before* a noun) connected with marriage: *marital problems*

marital 'status noun [U] (*written*) (used on official documents) if you are married, single, divorced, etc

maritime /ˈmærɪtaɪm/ **adj** connected with the sea or ships

★**mark**[1] /mɑːk/ **noun** [C] **1** a spot or line that spoils the appearance of sth: *There's a dirty mark on the front of your shirt.* • *If you put a hot cup down on the table it will leave a mark.* •➤ Look at **birthmark.** •➤ picture at **blob 2** something that shows who or what sb/sth is, especially by making him/her/it different from others: *My horse is the one with*

the white mark on its face. **3** a written or printed symbol that is a sign of sth: *a question/punctuation/exclamation mark* **4** a sign of a quality or feeling: *They stood in silence for two minutes as **a mark of respect**.* **5** a number or letter you get for school work that tells you how good your work was: *She got very good marks in the exam.* • *The **pass mark** is 60 out of 100.* • *to get full marks* (= everything correct) **6** the level or point that sth/sb has reached: *The race is almost at the half-way mark.* **7** an effect that people notice and will remember: *The time he spent in prison **left** its **mark on** him.* • *He was only eighteen when he first **made** his **mark** in politics.* **8** a particular model or type of sth: *the new SL 53 Mark III* •➤ Be careful. You cannot use **mark** to talk about the product itself, or the company that makes it. Use **brand** or **make** instead: *What make is your car?* • *What brand of coffee do you buy?* **9** (*formal*) a person or an object towards which sth is directed; a target: *the arrow hit/missed its mark* • *His judgement of the situation is **wide of the mark*** (= wrong). **10** the unit of money in Germany

IDIOMS **on your marks, get set, go!** used at the start of a sports race

quick, slow, etc off the mark quick, slow, etc in reacting to a situation

★**mark**[2] /mɑːk/ **verb** [T] **1** to put a sign on sth: *We marked the price on all items in the sale.* • *I'll mark all the boxes I want you to move.* **2** to spoil the appearance of sth by making a mark on it: *The white walls were dirty and marked.* **3** to show where sth is or where sth happened: *The route is marked in red.* • *Flowers mark the spot where he died.* **4** to celebrate or officially remember an important event: *The ceremony marked the fiftieth anniversary of the opening of the school.* **5** to be a sign that sth new is going to happen: *This decision marks a change in government policy.* **6** to look at sb's school, etc work, show where there are mistakes and give it a number or letter to show how good it is: *Why did you mark that answer wrong?* • *He has 100 exam papers to mark.* **7** (in sport) to stay close to a player of the opposite team so that he/she cannot play easily

PHRASAL VERBS **mark sb/sth down as/for sth** to decide that sb/sth is of a particular type or suitable for a particular use: *From the first day of school, the teachers marked Fred down as a troublemaker.*

mark sth out to draw lines to show the position of sth: *Spaces for each car were marked out in the car park.*

mark sth up/down to increase/decrease the price of sth that you are selling: *All goods have been marked down by 15%.*

marked /mɑːkt/ **adj** clear; noticeable: *There has been a marked increase in vandalism in recent years.*

marker /ˈmɑːkə/ **noun** [C] something that shows the position of sth: *I've highlighted the important sentences with a marker pen.*

★ **market**[1] /'mɑːkɪt/ noun 1 [C] a place where people go to buy and sell things: *a market stall/trader/town* ⇒ *a cattle/fish/meat market* •◆ picture on page C8 •◆ Look at **flea market**, **hypermarket** and **supermarket**. 2 [C] business or commercial activity; the amount of trade in a particular type of goods: *The company currently has a 10% share of the market.* ● *the property/job market* 3 [C,U] a country, an area or a group of people that buys sth; the number of people who buy sth: *The company is hoping to expand into the European Market.* ● *There's no market for very large cars when petrol is so expensive.* •◆ Look at **black market** and **stock market**.
IDIOM **on the market** available to buy: *This is one of the best cameras on the market.*

market[2] /'mɑːkɪt/ verb [T] to sell sth with the help of advertising

marketable /'mɑːkɪtəbl/ adj that can be sold easily because people want it

marketing /'mɑːkɪtɪŋ/ noun [U] the activity of showing and advertising a company's products in the best possible way: *Effective marketing will lead to increased sales.* ● *the marketing department*

market place noun 1 **the market place** [sing] the activity of competing with other companies to buy and sell goods, services, etc 2 [C] the place in a town where a market is held

market re'search noun [U] the study of what people want to buy and why: *to carry out/do market research*

marking /'mɑːkɪŋ/ noun [C, usually pl] shapes, lines and patterns of colour on an animal or a bird, or painted on a road, vehicle, etc

marksman /'mɑːksmən/ noun [C] (*pl* -**men** /-mən/) a person who can shoot very well with a gun

marmalade /'mɑːməleɪd/ noun [U] a type of jam that is made from oranges or lemons •◆ picture on page C4

maroon /mə'ruːn/ adj, noun [U] (of) a dark brownish-red colour

marooned /mə'ruːnd/ adj in a place that you cannot leave: *The sailors were marooned on a desert island.*

marquee /mɑː'kiː/ noun [C] a very large tent that is used for parties, shows, etc

★ **marriage** /'mærɪdʒ/ noun 1 [C,U] the state of being husband and wife: *They are getting divorced after five years of marriage.* ● *a happy marriage* 2 [C] a wedding ceremony: *The marriage took place at a registry office in Birmingham.* •◆ Look at the note at **wedding**. •◆ verb get married (to sb) or **marry** (sb)

★ **married** /'mærɪd/ adj 1 married (to sb) having a husband or wife: *a married man/woman/couple* ● *Sasha's married to Mark.* ● *They're planning to get married in summer.* •◆ opposite **unmarried** or **single** 2 (only *before* a noun) connected with marriage: *How do you like married life?*

marrow /'mærəʊ/ noun 1 [C,U] a large vegetable with green skin that is white inside •◆ picture on page C3 2 = **BONE MARROW**

★ **marry** /'mæri/ verb (*pres part* **marrying**; *3rd pers sing pres* **marries**; *pt*, *pp* **married**) 1 [I,T] to take sb as your husband or wife: *They married when they were very young.* ● *When did Rick ask you to marry him?*

▶ **Get married (to sb)** is more commonly used than **marry**: *When are Sue and Ian getting married?* ● *They got married in 1997.*

2 [T] to join two people together as husband and wife: *We asked the local vicar to marry us.* •◆ noun marriage

Mars /mɑːz/ noun [sing] the red planet, that is fourth in order from the sun •◆ Look at Martian.

marsh /mɑːʃ/ noun [C,U] an area of soft wet land –**marshy** adj

marshal /'mɑːʃl/ noun [C] 1 a person who helps to organize or control a large public event: *Marshals are directing traffic in the car park.* 2 (*US*) an officer of a high level in the police or fire department or in a court of law

martial /'mɑːʃl/ adj (*formal*) connected with war

martial 'arts noun [pl] fighting sports such as karate or judo, in which you use your hands and feet as weapons

Martian /'mɑːʃn/ noun [C] (in stories) a creature that comes from the planet Mars

martyr /'mɑːtə/ noun [C] 1 a person who is killed because of what he/she believes 2 a person who tries to make people feel sorry for him/her: *Don't be such a martyr! You don't have to do all the housework.* –**martyrdom** /'mɑːtədəm/ noun [U]

marvel /'mɑːvl/ noun [C] a person or thing that is wonderful or that surprises you: *the marvels of modern technology* –**marvel** verb [I] (**marvelling**; **marvelled**; *US* **marveling**; **marveled**) (*formal*) **marvel (at sth)**: *We marvelled at how much they had managed to do.*

marvellous (*US* **marvelous**) /'mɑːvələs/ adj very good; wonderful: *a marvellous opportunity* –**marvellously** (*US* **marvelously**) adv

Marxism /'mɑːksɪzəm/ noun [U] the political and economic thought of Karl Marx •◆ Look at **communism**, **socialism** and **capitalism**. –**Marxist** noun [C], adj: *Marxist ideology*

marzipan /'mɑːzɪpæn/ noun [U] a food that is made of sugar, egg and nuts (**almonds**). Marzipan is used to make sweets or to put on cakes.

masc abbr masculine

mascara /mæ'skɑːrə/ noun [U] a beauty product that is used to make the hairs around your eyes (**eyelashes**) dark and attractive

mascot /'mæskət; -skɒt/ noun [C] a person, animal or thing that is thought to bring good luck

masculine /'mæskjəlɪn/ adj with the qualities that people think are typical of men: *a deep, masculine voice* ● *Her short hair makes her look quite masculine.* •◆ Look at **male**,

m

manly, and at **feminine** and at the note at **female**.

> In English grammar **masculine** words refer to male people or animals: *'He' is a masculine pronoun*. In some other languages all nouns are given a gender; **masculine**, **feminine** or **neuter**.

–**masculinity** /ˌmæskjuˈlɪnəti/ **noun** [U]

mash /mæʃ/ **verb** [T] to mix or crush sth until it is soft: *mashed potatoes*

mask¹ /mɑːsk/ **noun** [C] something that you wear that covers your face or part of your face. People wear masks in order to hide or protect their faces or to make themselves look different. •➤ Look at **gas mask** and **goggles**.

mask² /mɑːsk/ **verb** [T] **1** to cover or hide your face with a mask: *a masked gunman* **2** to hide a feeling, smell, fact, etc: *He masked his anger with a smile*.

masochism /ˈmæsəkɪzəm/ **noun** [U] the enjoyment of pain, or of what most people would find unpleasant: *He swims in the sea even in winter – that's sheer masochism!* •➤ Look at **sadism**. –**masochist** /-kɪst/ **noun** [C] –**masochistic** /ˌmæsəˈkɪstɪk/ **adj**

mason /ˈmeɪsn/ **noun** [C] **1** a person who makes things from stone **2** = **FREEMASON**

masonry /ˈmeɪsənri/ **noun** [U] the parts of a building that are made of stone

masquerade /ˌmæskəˈreɪd, ˌmɑːsk-/ **noun** [C] a way of behaving that hides the truth or sb's true feelings –**masquerade verb** [I] masquerade as sth: *Two people, masquerading as doctors, knocked at the door and asked to see the child*.

★**mass¹** /mæs/ **noun 1** [C] a mass (of sth) a large amount or number of sth: *a dense mass of smoke* • (*informal*) *There were masses of people at the market today*. **2 the masses** [pl] ordinary people when considered as a political group **3** [U] (in physics) the quantity of material that sth contains **4 Mass** [C,U] the ceremony in some Christian churches when people eat bread and drink wine in order to remember the last meal that Christ had before he died: *to go to Mass*

mass² /mæs/ **adj** (only *before* a noun) involving a large number of people or things: *a mass murderer*

mass³ /mæs/ **verb** [I,T] to come together or bring people or things together in large numbers: *The students massed in the square*.

massacre /ˈmæsəkə/ **noun** [C] the killing of a large number of people or animals –**massacre verb** [T] •➤ Look at the note at **kill**.

massage /ˈmæsɑːʒ/ **noun** [C,U] the act of rubbing and pressing sb's body in order to reduce pain or to help him/her relax: *to give sb a massage* –**massage verb** [T]

massive /ˈmæsɪv/ **adj** very big; huge: *a massive increase in prices*

ˌ**mass ˈmedia noun** [pl] newspapers, television and radio that reach a large number of people

ˌ**mass-proˈduce** **verb** [T] to make large numbers of similar things by machine in a factory: *mass-produced goods* –**mass production noun** [U]

mast /mɑːst/ **noun** [C] **1** a tall wooden or metal pole for a flag, a ship's sails, etc **2** a tall pole that is used for sending out radio or television signals

master¹ /ˈmɑːstə/ **noun** [C] **1** a person who has great skill at doing sth: *a master builder* • *an exhibition of work by French masters* (= painters) **2** (*old-fashioned*) a male teacher (usually in a private school): *the chemistry master* **3** a film or tape from which copies can be made

master² /ˈmɑːstə/ **verb** [T] **1** to learn how to do sth well: *It takes a long time to master a foreign language*. **2** to control sth: *to master a situation*

mastermind /ˈmɑːstəmaɪnd/ **noun** [C] a very clever person who has planned or organized sth: *The mastermind behind the robbery was never caught*. –**mastermind verb** [T]: *The police failed to catch the man who masterminded the robbery*.

masterpiece /ˈmɑːstəpiːs/ **noun** [C] a work of art, music, literature, etc that is of the highest quality

Master's degree (also **Master's**) **noun** [C] a second or higher university degree. You usually get a Master's degree by studying for one or two years after your first degree: *Master of Arts* (*MA*) • *Master of Science* (*MSc*) •➤ Look at **Bachelor's degree**.

mastery /ˈmɑːstəri/ **noun** [U] **1** mastery (of sth) great skill at doing sth: *His mastery of the violin was quite exceptional for a child*. **2** mastery (of/over sb/sth) control over sb/sth: *The battle was fought for mastery of the seas*.

masturbate /ˈmæstəbeɪt/ **verb** [I,T] to make yourself or sb else feel sexually excited by touching and rubbing the sex organs –**masturbation** /ˌmæstəˈbeɪʃn/ **noun** [U]

mat /mæt/ **noun** [C] **1** a piece of carpet or other thick material that you put on the floor: *a doormat* •➤ Look at **rug**. **2** a small piece of material that you put under sth on a table: *a table mat* • *a beer mat* • *a mouse mat* •➤ picture on page S7

★**match¹** /mætʃ/ **noun 1** [C] a small stick of wood, cardboard, etc that you use for starting a fire, lighting a cigarette, etc: *to light/strike a match* • *a box of matches* **2** [C] an organized game or sports event: *a tennis/football match* **3** [sing] a match for sb; sb's match a person or thing that is as good as or better than sb/sth else: *Charo is no match for her mother when it comes to cooking* (= she doesn't cook as well as her mother). • *I think you've met your match in Dave – you won't beat him*. **4** [sing] a match (for sb/sth) something that looks good with sth else: *Those shoes aren't a very good match with your dress*.

★**match²** /mætʃ/ **verb 1** [I,T] to have the same colour or pattern as sth else; to look good with sth else: *That shirt doesn't match your*

jacket. • *Your shirt and jacket don't match.*
2 [T] to find sb/sth that is like or suitable for sb/sth else: *The agency tries to match single people with suitable partners.* **3** [T] to be as good as or better than sb/sth else: *The two teams are very evenly matched.* • *Taiwan produces the goods at a price that Europe cannot match.*

PHRASAL VERBS **match up** to be the same: *The statements of the two witnesses don't match up.*

match sth up (with sth) to fit or put sth together (with sth else): *What you have to do is match up each star with his or her pet.*

match up to sb/sth to be as good as sb/sth: *The film didn't match up to my expectations*

matchbox /'mætʃbɒks/ **noun** [C] a small box for matches •➤ picture at **container**

matchstick /'mætʃstɪk/ **noun** [C] the thin wooden part of a match

mate¹ /meɪt/ **noun** [C] **1** (*informal*) a friend or sb you live, work or do an activity with: *He's an old mate of mine.* • *a flatmate/classmate/team-mate/playmate* **2** (*Brit slang*) used when speaking to a man: *Can you give me a hand, mate?* **3** one of a male and female pair of animals, birds, etc: *The female sits on the eggs while her mate hunts for food.* **4** an officer on a ship

mate² /meɪt/ **verb 1** [I] (used about animals and birds) to have sex and produce young: *Pandas rarely mate in zoos.* **2** [T] to bring two animals together so that they can mate •➤ synonym **breed**

★**material¹** /mə'tɪəriəl/ **noun 1** [C,U] a substance that can be used for making or doing sth: *raw materials* • *writing/teaching/building materials* • *This new material is strong but it is also very light.* **2** [C,U] cloth (for making clothes, etc): *Is there enough material for a dress?* **3** [U] facts or information that you collect before you write a book, article, etc

material² /mə'tɪəriəl/ **adj 1** connected with real or physical things rather than the spirit or emotions: *We should not value material comforts too highly.* •➤ Look at **spiritual**. **2** important and needing to be considered: *material evidence* •➤ This word is not common but look at **immaterial**. –**materially** adv

materialism /mə'tɪəriəlɪzəm/ **noun** [U] the belief that money and possessions are the most important things in life –**materialist** /-lɪst/ **noun** [C] –**materialistic** /mə,tɪəriə'lɪstɪk/ **adj**

materialize (also **-ise**) /mə'tɪərɪəlaɪz/ **verb** [I] to become real; to happen: *The pay rise that they had promised never materialized.*

maternal /mə'tɜːnl/ **adj 1** behaving as a mother would behave; connected with being a mother: *maternal love/instincts* **2** (only *before* a noun) related through your mother's side of the family: *your maternal grandfather* •➤ Look at **paternal**.

maternity /mə'tɜːnəti/ **adj** connected with women who are going to have or have just had a baby: *maternity clothes* • *the hospital's maternity ward* •➤ Look at **paternity**.

mathematician /,mæθəmə'tɪʃn/ **noun** [C] a person who studies or is an expert in mathematics

★**mathematics** /,mæθə'mætɪks/ **noun** [U] the science or study of numbers, quantities or shapes

➤ The British abbreviation is **maths**, the US is **math**: *Maths is my favourite subject.*

•➤ Look also at **arithmetic**, **algebra** and **geometry**. –**mathematical** /,mæθə'mætɪkl/ **adj**: *mathematical calculations* –**mathematically** /-kli/ **adv**

matinée /'mætneɪ/ **noun** [C] an afternoon performance of a play, film, etc

matrimony /'mætrɪməni/ **noun** [U] (*formal*) the state of being married –**matrimonial** /,mætrɪ'məʊniəl/ **adj**

matron /'meɪtrən/ **noun** [C] **1** (*old-fashioned*) a nurse who is in charge of the other nurses in a hospital •➤ **Senior nursing officer** is now usually used instead. **2** a woman who works as a nurse in a school

matt (*US also* **matte**) /mæt/ **adj** not shiny: *This paint gives a matt finish.* •➤ Look at **gloss**.

matted /'mætɪd/ **adj** (used especially about hair) forming a thick mass, especially because it is wet and/or dirty

★**matter¹** /'mætə/ **noun 1** [C] a subject or situation that you must think about and give your attention to: *It's a personal matter and I don't want to discuss it with you.* • *Finding a job will be no easy matter.* • *to simplify/complicate matters* **2** [sing] the matter (with sb/sth) the reason sb/sth has a problem or is not good: *She looks sad. What's the matter with her?* • *There seems to be something the matter with the car.* • *Eat that food! There's nothing the matter with it.* **3** [U] all physical substances; a substance of a particular kind: *reading matter* **4** [U] the contents of a book, film, etc: *I don't think the subject matter of this programme is suitable for children.*

IDIOMS **a matter of hours, miles, etc** used to say that sth is not very long, far, expensive, etc: *The fight lasted a matter of seconds.*

a matter of life and/or death extremely urgent and important

another/a different matter something much more serious, difficult, etc: *I can speak a little Japanese, but reading it is quite another matter.*

as a matter of fact to tell the truth; in reality: *I like him very much, as a matter of fact.*

for that matter in addition; now that I think about it: *Mick is really fed up with his course. I am too, for that matter.*

to make matters/things worse → **WORSE**

a matter of course something that you always do; the usual thing to do: *Goods leaving the factory are checked as a matter of course.*

a matter of opinion a subject on which people do not agree: *'I think the government is doing*

a good job.' 'That's a matter of opinion.'
(be) a matter of sth/doing sth a situation in which sth is needed: *Learning a language is largely a matter of practice.*
no matter who, what, where, etc whoever, whatever, wherever, etc: *They never listen no matter what you say.*

★**matter²** /'mætə/ verb [I] matter (to sb) (not used in the continuous tenses) to be important: *It doesn't really matter how much it costs.* ● *Nobody's hurt, and that's all that matters.* ● *Some things matter more than others.* ● *It doesn't matter to me what he does in his free time.*

,matter-of-'fact adj said or done without showing any emotion, especially when it would seem more normal to express your feelings: *He was very matter-of-fact about his illness.*

mattress /'mætrəs/ noun [C] a large soft thing that you lie on to sleep, usually put on a bed ••➤ picture at **bed**

mature /mə'tʃʊə/ adj **1** fully grown or fully developed: *a mature tree/bird/animal* **2** behaving in a sensible adult way: *Is she mature enough for such responsibility?* ••➤ opposite **immature** –mature verb [I]: *He matured a lot during his two years at college.* –maturity /mə'tʃʊərəti/ noun [U]

maul /mɔːl/ verb [T] (usually used about a wild animal) to attack and injure sb

mauve /məʊv/ adj, noun [U] (of) a pale purple colour

max /mæks/ abbr maximum: *max temp 21°C*

maxim /'mæksɪm/ noun [C] a few words that express a rule for good or sensible behaviour: *Our maxim is: 'If a job's worth doing, it's worth doing well.'*

maximize (also -ise) /'mæksɪmaɪz/ verb [T] to increase sth as much as possible: *to maximize profits* ••➤ opposite **minimize**

★**maximum** /'mæksɪməm/ noun [sing] (abbr **max**) the greatest amount or level of sth that is possible, allowed, etc: *The bus can carry a maximum of 40 people.* ● *That is the maximum we can afford.* ••➤ opposite **minimum** –maximum adj (only *before* a noun): *a maximum speed of 120 miles per hour*

★**May¹** /meɪ/ noun [U,C] the fifth month of the year, coming after April

➤ To see how the months are used in sentences, look at the examples and the note at **January**.

★**may²** /meɪ/ modal verb (negative **may not**) **1** used for saying that sth is possible: *'Where's Sue?' 'She may be in the garden.'* ● *You may be right.* ● *I may be going to China next year.* ● *They may have forgotten the meeting.* **2** used as a polite way of asking for and giving permission: *May I use your phone?* ● *You may not take photographs in the museum.* **3** used for contrasting two facts: *He may be very clever but he can't do anything practical.* **4** (formal) used for expressing wishes and hopes: *May you both be very happy.*

➤ For more information about modal verbs, look at the **Quick Grammar Reference** section at the back of this dictionary.

IDIOM may/might as well (do sth) → **WELL¹**

★**maybe** /'meɪbi/ adv perhaps; possibly: *'Are you going to come?' 'Maybe.'* ● *There were three, maybe four armed men.* ● *Maybe I'll accept the invitation and maybe I won't.* ••➤ Look at the note at **perhaps**.

'**May Day** noun [C] 1st May

➤ **May Day** is traditionally celebrated as a spring festival and in some countries as a holiday in honour of working people

mayonnaise /,meɪə'neɪz/ noun [U] a cold thick pale yellow sauce made with eggs and oil

mayor /meə/ noun [C] a person who is elected to be the leader of the group of people (a council) who manage the affairs of a town or city

mayoress /meə'res/ noun [C] a woman mayor, or a woman who is married to or helps a mayor

maze /meɪz/ noun [C] a system of paths which is designed to confuse you so that it is difficult to find your way out: (figurative) *a maze of winding streets* ••➤ synonym **labyrinth**

MBA /,em bi: 'eɪ/ abbr Master of Business Administration; an advanced university degree in business

MD /,em 'di:/ abbr Doctor of Medicine

★**me** /mi:/ pron (used as an object) the person who is speaking or writing: *He telephoned me yesterday.* ● *She wrote to me last week.* ● *Hello, is that Frank? It's me, Sadiq.*

meadow /'medəʊ/ noun [C] a field of grass

meagre (US **meager**) /'mi:gə/ adj too small in amount: *a meagre salary*

★**meal** /mi:l/ noun [C] the time when you eat or the food that is eaten at that time: *Shall we go out for a meal on Friday?* ● *a heavy/light meal*

➤ The main meals of the day are **breakfast**, **lunch** and **dinner**. **Tea** and **supper** are usually smaller meals (but look at the note at **dinner**). Something small that you eat between meals is a **snack**.

IDIOM a square meal → **SQUARE²**

mealtime /'mi:ltaɪm/ noun [C] the time at which a meal is usually eaten

★**mean¹** /mi:n/ verb [T] (pt, pp **meant** /ment/) **1** (not used in the continuous tenses) to express, show or have as a meaning: *What does this word mean?* ● *The bell means that the lesson has ended.* ● *Does the name 'Michael Potter' mean anything to you?*

➤ Although this verb is not used in the continuous tenses, it is common to see the present participle (= -ing form): *The weather during filming was terrible, meaning that several scenes had to be reshot later.*

2 to want or intend to say sth; to refer to sb/sth: *Well, she said 'yes' but I think she*

really meant 'no'. ● *What do you mean by 'a lot of money'?* ● *I only meant that I couldn't come tomorrow – any other day would be fine.* ● *I see what you mean, but I'm afraid it's not possible.*

> Note that **mean** cannot be used with the meaning 'to have the opinion that'. We say: *I think that...* or *In my opinion...: I think that she'd be silly to buy that car.*
> **I mean** is often used in conversation when you want to explain something you have just said or to add more information: *What a terrible summer – I mean it's rained almost all the time.* **I mean** is also used to correct something you have just said: *We went there on Tuesday, I mean Thursday.*

3 (often passive) mean (sb) to do sth; mean sth (as/for sth/sb); mean sb/sth to be sth to intend sth; to be supposed to be/do sth: *I'm sure she didn't mean to upset you.* ● *She meant the present to be for both of us.* ● *I didn't mean you to cook the whole meal!* ● *It was only meant as a joke.* ● *What's this picture meant to be?* **4** to make sth likely; to cause: *The shortage of teachers means that classes are larger.* **5** mean sth (to sb) to be important to sb: *This job means a lot to me.* ● *Money means nothing to her.* **6** to be serious or sincere about sth: *He said he loved me but I don't think he meant it!*

IDIOMS **be meant to be sth** to be considered or said to be sth: *That restaurant is meant to be excellent.*

mean well to want to be kind and helpful but usually without success: *My mother means well but I wish she'd stop treating me like a child.*

★**mean²** /miːn/ *adj* **1** mean (with sth) wanting to keep money, etc for yourself rather than let other people have it: *It's no good asking him for any money – he's much too mean.* ● *They're mean with the food in the canteen.* **2** mean (to sb) (used about people or their behaviour) unkind: *It was mean of him not to invite you too.* **3** (only *before* a noun) average: *What is the mean annual temperature in California?* –**meanness** noun [U]

meander /mi'ændə/ *verb* [I] **1** (used about a river, road, etc) to have a lot of curves and bends **2** (used about a person or animal) to walk or travel slowly or without any definite direction

★**meaning** /'miːnɪŋ/ *noun* **1** [C,U] the thing or idea that sth represents; what sb is trying to communicate: *This word has two different meanings in English.* ● *What do you think the meaning is of the last line of the poem?* **2** [U] the purpose or importance of an experience: *With his child dead there seemed to be no meaning in life.*

meaningful /'miːnɪŋfl/ *adj* **1** useful, important or interesting: *Most people need a meaningful relationship with another person.* **2** (used about a look, expression, etc) trying to express a certain feeling or idea: *They kept giving each other meaningful glances across the table.* –**meaningfully** /-fəli/ *adv*

meaningless /'miːnɪŋləs/ *adj* without meaning, reason or sense: *The figures are meaningless if we have nothing to compare them with.*

★**means** /miːnz/ *noun* **1** [C] (*pl* means) a means (of doing sth) a method of doing sth: *Do you have any means of transport* (= a car, bicycle, etc)? ● *Is there any means of contacting your husband?* **2** [pl] (*formal*) all the money that sb has: *This car is beyond the means of most people.*

IDIOMS **by all means** used to say that you are happy for sb to have or do sth: *'Can I borrow your newspaper?' 'By all means.'*

by means of by using: *We got out of the hotel by means of the fire escape.*

by no means; not by any means (used to emphasize sth) not at all: *I'm by no means sure that this is the right thing to do.*

a means to an end an action or thing that is not important in itself but is a way of achieving sth else: *I don't enjoy my job, but it's a means to an end.*

meant *past tense, past participle* of **MEAN¹**

meantime /'miːntaɪm/ *noun*

IDIOM **in the meantime** in the time between two things happening: *Our house isn't finished so in the meantime we're living with my mother.*

★**meanwhile** /'miːnwaɪl/ *adv* during the same time or during the time between two things happening: *Peter was at home studying. Omar, meanwhile, was out with his friends.*

measles /'miːzlz/ *noun* [U] a common infectious disease, especially among children, in which your body feels hot and your skin is covered in small red spots

> **Measles** looks like a plural noun but it is used with a singular verb: *In many countries measles is a very dangerous disease.*

measly /'miːzli/ *adj* (*informal*) much too small in size, amount or value: *All that work for this measly amount of money!*

★**measure¹** /'meʒə/ *verb* **1** [I,T] to find the size, weight, quantity, etc of sb/sth in standard units by using an instrument: *to measure the height/width/length/depth of sth* ● *Could you measure the table to see if it will fit into our room?* **2** [T] to be a certain height, width, length, etc: *The room measures five metres across.* **3** [T] measure sth (against sth) to judge the value or effect of sth: *Our sales do not look good when measured against those of our competitors.*

PHRASAL VERB **measure up (to sth)** to be as good as you need to be or as sb expects you to be: *Did the holiday measure up to your expectations?*

★**measure²** /'meʒə/ *noun* **1** [C, usually pl] an action that is done for a special reason: *The government is to take new measures to reduce inflation.* ● *As a temporary measure, the road will have to be closed.* **2** [sing] (*formal*) a/some measure of sth a certain amount of sth; some: *The play achieved a measure of* *success.* **3** [sing] a way of understanding or judging sth: *The school's popularity is a measure of the teachers' success.* **4** [C] a way of describing the size, amount, etc of sth: *A metre is a measure of length.* •➤ Look at **tape measure**.

[IDIOMS] **for good measure** in addition to sth, especially to make sure that there is enough: *He made a few extra sandwiches for good measure.*

made to measure specially made or perfectly suitable for a particular person, use, etc: *I'm getting a suit made to measure for the wedding.*

measurement /'meʒəmənt/ **noun 1** [C] a size, amount, etc that is found by measuring: *What are the exact measurements of the room?* (= how wide, long, etc is it?) **2** [U] the act or process of measuring sth

★ **meat** /miːt/ **noun** [U] the parts of animals or birds that people eat: *She doesn't eat meat – she's a vegetarian.* • **meat-eating animals**

> Some types of meat have different names from the animals they come from. We get **pork**, **ham** or **bacon** from a pig, **beef** from a cow and **veal** from a calf. **Mutton** comes from a sheep, but we get **lamb** from a lamb. For birds and fish there is not a different word. We often call beef, mutton and lamb **red meat**. The meat from birds is called **white meat**. We can **fry**, **grill**, **roast** or **stew** meat. We **carve** a **joint** of meat. Meat can be described as **tough** or **tender**, **lean** or **fatty**. Uncooked meat is **raw**.

meaty /'miːti/ **adj 1** like meat, or containing a lot of meat: *meaty sausages* **2** large and fat: *meaty tomatoes* **3** containing a lot of important or good ideas: *a meaty topic for discussion*

Mecca /'mekə/ **noun 1** [sing] the city in Saudi Arabia where Muhammad was born, which is the centre of Islam **2 mecca** [C, usually sing] a place that many people wish to visit because of a particular interest: *Italy is a mecca for art lovers.*

mechanic /mə'kænɪk/ **noun 1** [C] a person whose job is to repair and work with machines: *a car mechanic* **2 mechanics** [U] the science of how machines work **3 the mechanics** [pl] the way in which sth works or is done: *Don't ask me – I don't understand the mechanics of the legal system.*

★ **mechanical** /mə'kænɪkl/ **adj 1** connected with or produced by machines: *a mechanical pump* • *mechanical engineering* • *mechanical problems* **2** (used about a person's behaviour) done like a machine as if you are not thinking about what you are doing: *He played the piano in a dull and mechanical way.* –**mechanically** /-kli/ **adv**

mechanism /'mekənɪzəm/ **noun** [C] **1** a set of moving parts in a machine that does a certain task: *Our car has an automatic locking mechanism.* **2** the way in which sth works or is done: *I'm afraid there is no mechanism for dealing with your complaint.*

mechanize (also **-ise**) /'mekənaɪz/ **verb** [I,T]

to use machines instead of people to do work: *We have mechanized the entire production process.* –**mechanization** (also **-isation**) /ˌmekənaɪ'zeɪʃn/ **noun** [U]

the Med (*informal*) = **THE MEDITERRANEAN**

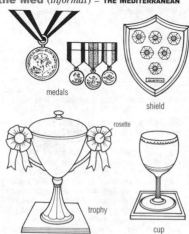

medals

shield

rosette

trophy

cup

medal /'medl/ **noun** [C] a small flat piece of metal, usually with a design and words on it, which is given to sb who has shown courage or as a prize in a sporting event: *to win a gold/silver/bronze medal in the Olympics*

medallion /mə'dæliən/ **noun** [C] a small round piece of metal on a chain which is worn as jewellery around the neck

medallist (*US* **medalist**) /'medəlɪst/ **noun** [C] a person who has won a medal, especially in sport: *an Olympic gold medallist*

meddle /'medl/ **verb** [I] **meddle (in/with sth)** to take too much interest in sb's private affairs or to touch sth that does not belong to you: *She criticized her mother for meddling in her private life.*

★ **media** /'miːdiə/ **noun** [pl] television, radio and newspapers used as a means of communication: *The reports in the media have been greatly exaggerated.* •➤ Look at **mass media** and the **press**.

> Sometimes **media** is used with a singular verb, although it is a plural noun: *The media always take/takes a great interest in the Royal family.*

mediaeval = **MEDIEVAL**

mediate /'miːdieɪt/ **verb** [I,T] **mediate (in sth) (between A and B)** to try to end a disagreement between two or more people or groups: *As a supervisor she had to mediate between her colleagues and the management.* –**mediation** /ˌmiːdi'eɪʃn/ **noun** [U] –**mediator noun** [C]

★ **medical¹** /'medɪkl/ **adj** connected with medicine and the treatment of illness: *medical treatment/care* • *the medical profession*

medical² /'medɪkl/ **noun** [C] an examination

m

of your body by a doctor to check your state of health: *to have a medical*

medication /ˌmedɪˈkeɪʃn/ *noun* [C,U] (*especially US*) medicine that a doctor has given to you: *Are you on any medication?*

medicinal /məˈdɪsɪnl/ *adj* useful for curing illness or infection: *medicinal plants*

★**medicine** /ˈmedsn/ *noun* **1** [U] the science of preventing and treating illness: *to study medicine* **2** [C,U] a substance, especially a liquid, that you take in order to cure an illness: *Take this medicine three times a day.* • *cough medicine* ◦➤ picture at **bandage**

medieval (also **mediaeval**) /ˌmedɪˈiːvl/ *adj* connected with the period in history between about 1100 and 1500 AD (**the Middle Ages**)

mediocre /ˌmiːdiˈəʊkə/ *adj* of not very high quality: *a mediocre performance* –**mediocrity** /ˌmiːdiˈɒkrəti/ *noun* [U]

meditate /ˈmedɪteɪt/ *verb* [I,T] **meditate (on/ upon sth)** to think carefully and deeply, especially for religious reasons or to make your mind calm: *I've been meditating on what you said last week.* –**meditation** /ˌmedɪˈteɪʃn/ *noun* [U]

the Mediterranean /ˌmedɪtəˈreɪniən/ (also *informal* **the Med**) *noun* [sing], *adj* (of) the Mediterranean Sea or the countries around it: *Mediterranean cookery*

★**medium¹** /ˈmiːdiəm/ *adj* **1** in the middle between two sizes, lengths, temperatures, etc; average: *She was of medium height.* • *Would you like the small, medium or large packet?* • *a medium-sized car/town/dog* **2** (used about meat) cooked until it is brown all the way through

➤ Compare **rare** and **well done**.

medium² /ˈmiːdiəm/ *noun* **1** [C] (*pl* **media** or **mediums**) a means you can use to express or communicate sth: *English is the medium of instruction in the school.* ◦➤ Look at **media** and **mass media**. **2** [C,U] medium size: *Have you got this shirt in (a) medium?* **3** [C] (*pl* **mediums**) a person who says that he/she can speak to the spirits of dead people

medley /ˈmedli/ *noun* [C] **1** a piece of music consisting of several tunes or songs played one after the other without a break **2** a mixture of different things: *a medley of styles/ flavours*

meek /miːk/ *adj* (used about people) quiet, and doing what other people say without asking questions –**meekly** *adv* –**meekness** *noun* [U]

★**meet** /miːt/ *verb* (*pt, pp* **met** /met/) **1** [I,T] to come together by chance or because you have arranged it: *I just met Kareem on the train.* • *What time shall we meet for lunch?* **2** [I,T] to see and know sb for the first time: *Where did you first meet your husband?* • *Have you two met before?* **3** [T] to go to a place and wait for sb/sth to arrive: *I'll come and meet you at the station.* **4** [I,T] to play, fight, etc together as opponents in a sports competition: *These two teams met in last year's final.* • *Yamada will meet Suzuki in the second round.* **5** [T] to

experience sth, often sth unpleasant: *We will never know how he met his death.* **6** [I,T] to touch, join or make contact with: *The two roads meet not far from here.* • *His eyes met hers.* **7** [T] to be enough for sth; to be able to deal with sth: *The money that I earn is enough to meet our basic needs.* • *to meet a challenge*

IDIOMS **make ends meet** → **END¹**

there is more to sb/sth than meets the eye sb/sth is more interesting or complicated than he/she/it seems: *Do you think there's more to their relationship than meets the eye?*

PHRASAL VERBS **meet up (with sb)** to meet sb, especially after a period of being apart: *I have a few things I need to do now, but let's meet up later.*

meet with sb (*especially US*) to meet sb, especially for discussion: *The President met with his advisers early this morning.*

meet with sth to get a particular answer, reaction or result: *to meet with success/failure/opposition*

★**meeting** /ˈmiːtɪŋ/ *noun* **1** [C] an organized occasion when a number of people come together in order to discuss or decide sth: *The group hold regular meetings all year.* • *We need to have a meeting to discuss these matters.*

➤ We **call**, **arrange** or **organize** a meeting. We can also **cancel** or **postpone** a meeting.

2 [sing] the people at a meeting: *The meeting was in favour of the new proposals.* **3** [C] the coming together of two or more people: *Christmas is a time of family meetings and reunions.*

megaphone /ˈmegəfəʊn/ *noun* [C] a piece of equipment that you speak through to make your voice sound louder when speaking to a crowd

melancholy /ˈmelənkəli; -kɒli/ *noun* [U] (*formal*) a feeling of sadness which lasts for a long time –**melancholy** *adj*

mellow /ˈmeləʊ/ *adj* **1** (used about colours or sounds) soft and pleasant **2** (used about people) calm and relaxed: *My dad's grown mellower as he's got older.* –**mellow** *verb* [I,T]: *Experience had mellowed her views about many things.*

melodrama /ˈmelədrɑːmə/ *noun* [C,U] a story, play or film in which a lot of exciting things happen and in which people's emotions are stronger than in real life

melodramatic /ˌmelədrəˈmætɪk/ *adj* (used about a person's behaviour) making things seem more exciting or serious than they really are: *Don't be so melodramatic, Simon – of course you're not going to die!*

melody /ˈmelədi/ *noun* [C] (*pl* **melodies**) a song or tune; the main tune of a piece of music

melon /ˈmelən/ *noun* [C,U] a large roundish fruit with a thick yellow or green skin and a lot of seeds ◦➤ picture on page C3

★**melt** /melt/ *verb* **1** [I,T] to change or make sth change from a solid to a liquid by means of heat: *When we got up in the morning the snow*

m

had melted. ● *First melt the butter in a sauce-pan.* •➤ Look at **thaw. 2** [I] (used about sb's feelings, etc) to become softer or less strong: *My heart melted when I saw the baby.*

PHRASAL VERBS **melt away** to disappear: *The crowd slowly melted away when the speaker had finished.*

melt sth down to heat a metal or glass object until it becomes liquid

'melting pot *noun* [C] a place where a lot of different cultures, ideas, etc come together: *New York is a melting pot of different cultures.*

★**member** /'membə/ *noun* [C] a person, animal or thing that belongs to a group, club, organization, etc: *All the members of the family were there.* ● *to become a member of a club* ● *a member of staff*

,**Member of 'Parliament** *noun* [C] (*abbr* **MP**) a person who has been elected to represent people from a particular area in Parliament: *the MP for Oxford East*

membership /'membəʃɪp/ *noun* **1** [U] the state of being a member of a group, organization, etc: *To **apply for membership**, please fill in the enclosed form.* ● *a membership card/fee* **2** [C,U] the people who belong to a group, organization, etc: *Membership has fallen in the past year* (= the number of members).

membrane /'membreɪn/ *noun* [C] a thin skin which covers certain parts of a person's or an animal's body

memento /mə'mentəʊ/ *noun* [C] (*pl* **mementoes; mementos**) something that you keep to remind you of sb/sth

memo /'meməʊ/ *noun* [C] (*pl* **memos**) (also *formal* **memorandum**) a note sent from one person or office to another within an organization •➤ picture on page S6

memoirs /'memwɑːz/ *noun* [pl] a person's written account of his/her own life and experiences; autobiography

memorabilia /ˌmemərə'bɪliə/ *noun* [U] things that people buy because they are connected with a famous person, event, etc: *Beatles/Titanic/war memorabilia*

memorable /'memərəbl/ *adj* worth remembering or easy to remember: *The concert was a memorable experience.* –**memorably** *adv*

memorandum /ˌmemə'rændəm/ (*pl* **memoranda** /-də/) (*formal*) = **MEMO**

memorial /mə'mɔːriəl/ *noun* [C] a memorial (to sb/sth) something that is built or done to remind people of an event or a person: *a memorial to the victims of the bombing* ● *a war memorial* ● *a memorial service*

memorize (also **-ise**) /'meməraɪz/ *verb* [T] to learn sth so that you can remember it exactly: *Actors have to memorize their lines.*

★**memory** /'meməri/ *noun* (*pl* **memories**) **1** [C] a person's ability to remember things: *to have a good/bad memory* ● *The drug can affect your short-term memory.* **2** [C,U] the part of your mind in which you store things that you remember: *That day remained firmly in my **memory** for the rest of my life.* ● *Are you going to do your speech from mem-*

ory, or are you going to use notes? **3** [C] something that you remember: *That is one of my happiest memories.* ● *childhood memories* **4** [C,U] the part of a computer where information is stored: *This computer has a 640k memory/640k of memory.*

IDIOMS **in memory of sb** in order to remind people of sb who has died: *A service was held in memory of the dead.*

jog sb's memory → **JOG¹**

refresh your memory → **REFRESH**

men *plural* of **MAN¹**

menace /'menəs/ *noun* **1** [C] a menace (to sb/sth) a danger or threat: *The new road is a menace to everyone's safety.* **2** [U] a quality, feeling, etc that is threatening or frightening: *He spoke with menace in his voice.* **3** [C] a person or thing that causes trouble –**menace** *verb* [T] –**menacing** *adj*

★**mend¹** /mend/ *verb* [T] to repair sth that is damaged or broken: *Can you mend the hole in this jumper for me?* •➤ synonym **repair**

mend² /mend/

IDIOM **be on the mend** (*informal*) to be getting better after an illness or injury: *She's been in bed for a week but she's on the mend now.*

menial /'miːniəl/ *adj* (used about work) not skilled or important: *a menial job*

meningitis /ˌmenɪn'dʒaɪtɪs/ *noun* [U] a dangerous illness which affects the brain and the inside of the bones in your back (the spinal cord)

the menopause /'menəpɔːz/ *noun* [sing] the time when a woman stops losing blood once a month (menstruating) and can no longer have children. This usually happens around the age of 50.

menstruate /'menstrueɪt/ *verb* [I] (*formal*) (used about women) to lose blood once a month from the part of the body where a baby would develop (the womb) •➤ A less formal way of saying this is to **have a period**. –**menstruation** /ˌmenstru'eɪʃn/ *noun* [U]

★**mental** /'mentl/ *adj* (only *before* a noun) **1** of or in the mind; involving the process of thinking: *It's fascinating to watch a child's mental development.* ● *mental arithmetic* (= calculations done in your head) **2** connected with illness of the mind: *a mental illness/hospital* –**mentally** /'mentəli/ *adv*: *She's mentally ill.*

mentality /men'tæləti/ *noun* [C] (*pl* **mentalities**) a type of mind or way of thinking: *I just can't understand his mentality!* ● *the criminal mentality*

★**mention** /'menʃn/ *verb* [T] to say or write sth about sb/sth without giving much information: *He mentioned (to me) that he might be late.* ● *Did she mention what time the film starts?*

IDIOMS **don't mention it** used as a polite reply when sb thanks you for sth: *'Thank you for all your help.' 'Don't mention it.'*

not to mention (used to emphasize sth) and also; as well as: *This is a great habitat for* *birds, not to mention other wildlife.* –mention **noun** [C,U]: *It was odd that there wasn't even a mention of the riots in the newspaper.*

★**menu** /'menjuː/ **noun** [C] **1** a list of the food that you can choose at a restaurant: *I hope there's soup on the menu.* ● *They do a special lunchtime menu here.* **2** a list of choices in a computer program which is shown on the screen: *a pull-down menu* ••➤ picture on page S7

MEP /ˌem iː 'piː/ **abbr** Member of the European parliament

mercenary[1] /'mɜːsənəri/ **adj** interested only in making money: *His motives are entirely mercenary.*

mercenary[2] /'mɜːsənəri/ **noun** [C] (*pl* **mercenaries**) a soldier who fights for any group or country that will pay him/her

merchandise /'mɜːtʃəndaɪz/ **noun** [U] (*formal*) goods that are for sale

merchant /'mɜːtʃənt/ **noun** [C] a person whose job is to buy and sell goods, usually of one particular type, in large amounts

the ˌmerchant 'navy noun [C,with sing or pl verb] a country's commercial ships and the people who work on them

merciful /'mɜːsɪfl/ **adj** feeling or showing mercy: *His death was a merciful release from pain.* –mercifully /-fəli/ **adv**

merciless /'mɜːsɪləs/ **adj** showing no mercy –mercilessly **adv**

Mercury[1] /'mɜːkjəri/ **noun** [sing] the planet that is nearest to the sun

mercury[2] /'mɜːkjəri/ **noun** [U] (*symbol* **Hg**) a heavy silver-coloured metal that is usually in liquid form. Mercury is used in instruments that measure temperature (thermometers).

★**mercy** /'mɜːsi/ **noun** [U] kindness shown by sb/sth who has the power to make sb suffer: *The rebels were shown no mercy. They were taken out and shot.*

IDIOM **at the mercy of sb/sth** having no power against sb/sth that is strong: *The climbers spent the night on the mountain at the mercy of the wind and rain.*

★**mere** /mɪə/ **adj** (only *before* a noun) **1** (used for emphasizing how small or unimportant sth is) nothing more than: *90% of the country's land is owned by a mere 2% of the population.* **2** used to say that just the fact that sb/sth is present in a situation is enough to have an influence: *The mere thought of giving a speech in public makes me feel sick.*

IDIOM **the merest** even a very small amount of sth: *The merest smell of the fish market made her feel ill.*

merely /'mɪəli/ **adv** (*formal*) only; just: *I don't want to place an order. I am merely making an enquiry.*

merge /mɜːdʒ/ **verb 1** [I] **merge (with/into sth); merge (together)** to become part of sth larger: *Three small companies merged into one large one.* ● *This stream merges with the river a few miles downstream.* **2** [T] to join things together so that they become one: *We have merged the two classes into one.*

merger /'mɜːdʒə/ **noun** [C,U] a merger (with sb/sth); a merger (between/of A and B) the act of joining two or more companies together

meridian /mə'rɪdiən/ **noun** [C] a line that we imagine on the surface of the earth that joins the North Pole to the South Pole and passes through a particular place: *the Greenwich meridian* ••➤ Look at **longitude**.

meringue /mə'ræŋ/ **noun** [C,U] a mixture of sugar and egg whites that is cooked in the oven; a cake made from this

merit[1] /'merɪt/ **noun 1** [U] the quality of being good: *There is a lot of merit in her ideas.* ● *He got the job* **on merit***, not because he's the manager's son.* **2** [C,usually pl] an advantage or a good quality of sb/sth: *Each case must be judged separately on its own merits* (= not according to general principles).

merit[2] /'merɪt/ **verb** [T] (*formal*) to be good enough for sth; to deserve: *This suggestion merits further discussion.*

mermaid /'mɜːmeɪd/ **noun** [C] (in stories) a woman who has the tail of a fish instead of legs and who lives in the sea

merriment /'merɪmənt/ **noun** [U] laughter and enjoyment

merry /'meri/ **adj** (**merrier; merriest**) **1** happy: *merry laughter* ● **Merry Christmas** (= used to say you hope sb has a happy holiday) **2** (*informal*) slightly drunk –merrily **adv**

'merry-go-round (*Brit* **roundabout** *US* **carousel**) **noun** [C] a big round platform that turns round and round and has model animals, etc on it for children to ride on

mesh /meʃ/ **noun** [C,U] material that is like a net (= made of plastic, wire or rope threads with holes in between): *a fence made of wire mesh*

mesmerize (also **-ise**) /'mezməraɪz/ **verb** [T] to hold sb's attention completely: *The audience seemed to be mesmerized by the speaker's voice.*

★**mess**[1] /mes/ **noun 1** [C,usually sing] the state of being dirty or untidy; a person or thing that is dirty or untidy: *The kitchen's* **in a** *terrible* **mess***!* ● *My hair is a mess.* ● *You can paint the door, but don't* **make a mess***!* **2** [sing] the state of having problems or troubles: *The company is* **in a** *financial* **mess***.* ● *to* **make a mess** *of your life*

mess[2] /mes/ **verb** [T] (*US informal*) to make sth dirty or untidy: *Don't mess your hands.*

PHRASAL VERBS **mess about/around 1** to behave in a silly and annoying way **2** to spend your time in a relaxed way without any real purpose: *We spent Sunday just messing around at home.*

mess sb about/around to treat sb in a way that is not fair or reasonable, for example by changing your plans without telling him/her **mess about/around with sth** to touch or use sth in a careless way: *It is dangerous to mess about with fireworks.*

mess sth up 1 to make sth dirty or untidy **2** to do sth badly or spoil sth: *I really messed*

up the last question in the exam.
mess with sb/sth to deal or behave with sb/sth in a way that you should not: *You shouldn't mess with people's feelings.*

★**message** /'mesɪdʒ/ **noun 1** [C] a written or spoken piece of information that you send to or leave for a person when you cannot speak to him/her: *Mr Khan is not here at the moment. Can I* **take a message***?* • *Could you* **give a message** *to Jake, please?* • *If he's not in I'll* **leave a message** *on his answering machine.* **2** [sing] an important idea that a book, speech, etc is trying to communicate: *It was a funny film but it also had a serious message.* • *The advertising campaign is trying to* **get the message across** *that smoking kills.*
IDIOM **get the message** (*informal*) to understand what sb means even if it is not clearly stated: *He finally got the message and went home.*

messenger /'mesɪndʒə/ **noun** [C] a person who carries a message

Messiah (also **messiah**) /mɪ'saɪə/ **noun** [C] a person, for example Jesus Christ, who is expected to come and save the world

messy /'mesi/ **adj** (**messier**; **messiest**) **1** dirty or untidy: *a messy room* **2** that makes sb/sth dirty: *Painting the ceiling is a messy job.* **3** having or causing problems or trouble: *a messy divorce*

met *past tense of* **MEET**

★**metal** /'metl/ **noun** [C,U] a type of solid substance that is usually hard and shiny and that heat and electricity can travel through: *metals such as tin, iron, gold and steel* • *to recycle scrap metal* • *a metal bar/pipe*

metallic /mə'tælɪk/ **adj** looking like metal or making a noise like one piece of metal hitting another: *a metallic blue car* • *harsh metallic sounds*

metamorphosis /ˌmetə'mɔːfəsɪs/ **noun** [C] (*pl* **metamorphoses** /-əsiːz/) (*formal*) a complete change of form (as part of natural development): *the metamorphosis of a tadpole into a frog*

metaphor /'metəfə/ **noun** [C,U] a word or phrase that is used in an imaginative way to show that sb/sth has the same qualities as another thing. 'Her words were a knife in his heart' is a metaphor. •➤ Look at **figurative** and **literal**. –**metaphorical** /ˌmetə'fɒrɪkl/ **adj** –**metaphorically** /-kli/ **adv**

meteor /'miːtiə; -iɔː/ **noun** [C] a small piece of rock, etc in space. When a meteor enters the earth's atmosphere it makes a bright line in the night sky.

meteoric /ˌmiːti'ɒrɪk/ **adj** very fast or successful: *a meteoric rise to fame*

meteorologist /ˌmiːtiə'rɒlədʒɪst/ **noun** [C] a person who studies the weather

meteorology /ˌmiːtiə'rɒlədʒi/ **noun** [U] the study of the weather and climate –**meteorological** /ˌmiːtiərə'lɒdʒɪkl/ **adj**

meter /'miːtə/ **noun** [C] **1** a piece of equipment that measures the amount of gas, water, electricity, etc you have used: *a parking*

meter 2 (*US*) = **METRE** –**meter verb** [T]: *Is your water metered?*

★**method** /'meθəd/ **noun** [C] a way of doing sth: *What method of payment do you prefer? Cash, cheque or credit card?* • *modern teaching methods*

methodical /mə'θɒdɪkl/ **adj** having or using a well-organized and careful way of doing sth: *Paul is a very methodical worker.* –**methodically** /-kli/ **adv**

methodology /ˌmeθə'dɒlədʒi/ (*pl* **methodologies**) **noun** [C,U] a way of doing sth based on particular principles and methods: *language teaching methodologies* –**methodological** /ˌmeθədə'lɒdʒɪkl/ **adj**

meticulous /mə'tɪkjələs/ **adj** giving or showing great attention to detail; very careful –**meticulously adv**

★**metre** (*US* **meter**) /'miːtə/ **noun** [C] (*abbr* **m**) a measure of length; 100 centimetres: *a two-metre high wall* • *Who won the 100 metres?*

metric /'metrɪk/ **adj** using the system of measurement that is based on metres, grams, litres, etc (**the metric system**) •➤ Look at **imperial**.

metropolis /mə'trɒpəlɪs/ **noun** [C] a very large city –**metropolitan** /ˌmetrə'pɒlɪtən/ **adj**

mg *abbr* milligram(s)

MHz /'megəhɜːts/ *abbr* megahertz; (used in radio) a measure of frequency

miaow /mi'aʊ/ **noun** [C] the sound that a cat makes –**miaow verb** [I] •➤ Look at **purr**.

mice *plural of* **MOUSE**

microchip /'maɪkrəʊtʃɪp/ (also **chip**) **noun** [C] a very small piece of a special material (**silicon**) that is used inside a computer, etc to make it work

microcosm /'maɪkrəʊkɒzəm/ **noun** [C] a **microcosm (of sth)** something that is a small example of sth larger: *Our little village is a microcosm of society as a whole.*

microphone /'maɪkrəfəʊn/ (also *informal* **mike**) **noun** [C] a piece of electrical equipment that is used for making sounds louder or for recording them

microscope /'maɪkrəskəʊp/ **noun** [C] a piece of equipment that makes very small objects look big enough for you to be able to see them: *to examine sth under a microscope*

microscopic /ˌmaɪkrə'skɒpɪk/ **adj** too small to be seen without a microscope

microwave /'maɪkrəweɪv/ **noun** [C] **1** a short electric wave that is used for sending radio messages and for cooking food **2** (also ˌmicrowave 'oven) a type of oven that cooks or heats food very quickly using microwaves

mid /mɪd/ **adj** (only *before* a noun) **1** the middle of: *I'm away from mid June.* • *the mid 1990s* **2 mid-** (used to form compound adjectives) in the middle of: *a mid-air collision*

★**midday** /ˌmɪd'deɪ/ **noun** [U] at or around twelve o'clock in the middle of the day; noon: *We arranged to meet at midday.* • *the heat of the midday sun* •➤ Look at **midnight**.

★**middle¹** /'mɪdl/ **noun 1** [sing] the middle (of sth) the part, point or position that is at about the same distance from the two ends or sides of sth: *the white line **in the middle** of the road* ● *Here's a photo of me with my two brothers. I'm the one **in the middle**.*

➤ **Centre** and **middle** are often very similar in meaning, but centre is used when you mean the exact middle of something: *How do you find the centre of a circle?* ● *There was a large table in the middle of the room.* ● *The bee stung me **right in the middle** of my back.* When you are talking about a period of time only **middle** may be used: *in the middle of the night* ● *the middle of July*

2 [C] (*informal*) your waist: *I want to lose weight around my middle.*

IDIOMS **be in the middle of sth/doing sth** to be busy doing sth: *Can you call back in five minutes – I'm in the middle of feeding the baby.*

in the middle of nowhere a long way from any town

middle² /'mɪdl/ **adj** (only *before* a noun) in the middle: *I wear my ring on my middle finger.*

,**middle 'age** **noun** [U] the time when you are about 40 to 60 years old: *in late middle age* –,**middle-'aged** **adj**: *a middle-aged man*

the ,Middle 'Ages **noun** [pl] the period of European history from about 1100 to 1500 AD

the ,Middle 'East **noun** [sing] the part of the world between Egypt and Pakistan

middleman /'mɪdlmæn/ **noun** [C] (*pl* **-men** /-men/) **1** a person or company who buys goods from the company that makes them and then sells them to sb else **2** a person who helps to arrange things between two people who do not want to meet each other

'**middle school** **noun** [C] (*Brit*) a school for children aged between nine and thirteen

midge /mɪdʒ/ **noun** [C] a very small flying insect that can bite people ••➤ synonym **gnat**

midget /'mɪdʒɪt/ **noun** [C] a very small person ••➤ Be careful. Some people find this word offensive.

the Midlands /'mɪdləndz/ **noun** [sing, with sing or pl verb] the central part of England around Birmingham and Nottingham

★**midnight** /'mɪdnaɪt/ **noun** [U] twelve o'clock at night: *They left the party **at midnight**.* ● *The clock struck midnight.* ••➤ Look at **midday**.

midriff /'mɪdrɪf/ **noun** [C] the part of your body between your chest and your waist

midst /mɪdst/ **noun** [U] the middle of sth; among a group of people or things: *The country is **in the midst of** a recession.* ● *They realized with a shock that there was an enemy **in their midst**.*

midway /,mɪd'weɪ/ **adj, adv** in the middle of a period of time or between two places: *The village lies midway between two large towns.* ••➤ synonym **halfway**

midweek /,mɪd'wiːk/ **noun** [U] the middle of the week (= Tuesday, Wednesday and Thursday) –midweek **adv**: *If you travel midweek it will be less crowded.*

the Midwest /,mɪd'west/ **noun** [sing] the northern central part of the US

midwife /'mɪdwaɪf/ **noun** [C] (*pl* **midwives** /-waɪvz/) a person who has been trained to help women give birth to babies

★**might¹** /maɪt/ **modal verb** (*negative* **might not**; *short form* **mightn't** /'maɪtnt/) **1** used for saying that sth is possible: *'Where's Vinay?' 'He might be upstairs.'* ● *I think I might have forgotten the tickets.* ● *She might not come if she's very busy.* **2** (*Brit formal*) used to ask for sth or suggest sth very politely: *I wonder if I might go home half an hour early today?* **3** used as the form of 'may' when you report what sb has said: *He said he might be late* (= his words were, 'I may be late').

➤ For more information about modal verbs, look at the **Quick Grammar Reference** section at the back of this dictionary.

IDIOMS **may/might as well (do sth)** ➔ **WELL¹**

you, etc might do sth used when you are angry to say what sb could or should have done: *They might at least have phoned if they're not coming.*

I might have known used for saying that you are not surprised that sth has happened: *I might have known he wouldn't help.*

might² /maɪt/ **noun** [U] (*formal*) great strength or power: *I pushed **with all my might**, but the rock did not move.*

mighty¹ /'maɪti/ **adj** (**mightier**; **mightiest**) very strong or powerful

mighty² /'maɪti/ **adv** (*US informal*) very: *That's mighty kind of you.*

migraine /'miːɡreɪn/ **noun** [C,U] very bad pain in your head that makes you feel sick; a severe headache

migrant /'maɪɡrənt/ **noun** [C] a person who goes from place to place looking for work

migrate /maɪ'ɡreɪt/ **verb** [I] **1** (used about animals and birds) to travel from one part of the world to another at the same time every year **2** (used about a large number of people) to go and live and work in another place: *Many country people were forced to migrate to the cities to look for work.* ••➤ Look at **emigrate**. –**migration** /maɪ'ɡreɪʃn/ **noun** [C,U]

mike /maɪk/ (*informal*) = **MICROPHONE**

milage = **MILEAGE**

★**mild** /maɪld/ **adj 1** not strong; not very bad: *a mild soap* ● *a mild winter* ● *a mild punishment* **2** (used about food) not having a strong taste: *mild cheese* **3** kind and gentle: *He's a very mild man – you never see him get angry.* ••➤ opposite **hard** –**mildness** **noun** [U]

mildly /'maɪldli/ **adv 1** not very; slightly: *mildly surprised* **2** in a gentle way

★**mile** /maɪl/ **noun 1** [C] a measure of length; 1·6 kilometres. There are 1760 yards in a mile: *The nearest beach is seven miles away.* ● *It's a seven-mile drive to the beach.* **2** [C] a lot: *He missed the target by a mile.* ● *I'm feeling miles better this morning.* **3 miles** [pl]

m

a long way: *How much further is it? We've walked miles already.* ● *From the top of the hill you can see for miles.*

IDIOM see, hear, tell, spot, etc sb/sth a mile off (*informal*) used to say that sb/sth is very obvious: *He's lying – you can tell that a mile off.*

mileage (also **milage**) /'maɪlɪdʒ/ noun **1** [C,U] the distance that has been travelled, measured in miles: *The car is five years old but it has a low mileage.* **2** [U] (*informal*) the amount of use that you get from sth: *The newspapers got a lot of mileage out of the scandal.*

milestone /'maɪlstəʊn/ noun [C] a very important event: *The concert was a milestone in the band's history.*

militant /'mɪlɪtənt/ adj ready to use force or strong pressure to get what you want: *The workers were in a very militant mood.* –militant noun [C] –militancy /-ənsi/ noun [U]

★ **military** /'mɪlətri/ adj (only *before* a noun) connected with soldiers or the army, navy, etc: *All men in that country have to do two years' military service.* ● *to take military action*

militia /mə'lɪʃə/ noun [C,with sing or pl verb] a group of people who are not professional soldiers but who have had military training

★ **milk**¹ /mɪlk/ noun [U] **1** a white liquid that is produced by women and female animals to feed their babies. People drink the milk of some animals and use it to make butter and cheese: *skimmed/long-life/low-fat milk* ● *a bottle/carton of milk* **2** the juice of some plants or trees that looks like milk: *coconut milk*

milk² /mɪlk/ verb **1** [I,T] to take milk from a cow, goat, etc **2** [T] to get as much money, advantage, etc for yourself from sb/sth as you can, without caring about others

milkman /'mɪlkmən/ noun [C] (*pl* -men /-mən; -men/) a person who takes milk to people's houses every day

milkshake /'mɪlkʃeɪk/ noun [C,U] a drink made of milk with an added flavour of fruit or chocolate •➤ picture on page C4

milky /'mɪlki/ adj like milk, or made with milk: *milky white skin* ● *milky coffee*

mill¹ /mɪl/ noun [C] **1** a factory that is used for making certain kinds of material: *a cotton/paper/steel mill* **2** a building that contains a large machine that was used in the past for making grain into flour: *a windmill* **3** a kitchen tool that is used for making sth into powder: *a pepper mill*

mill² /mɪl/ verb [T] to produce sth in a mill

PHRASAL VERB mill about/around (*informal*) (used about a large number of people or animals) to move around in a place with no real purpose

millennium /mɪ'leniəm/ noun [C] (*pl* millennia /-niə/ or millenniums) a period of 1000 years: *We are at the start of the new millennium.*

millet /'mɪlɪt/ noun [U] a plant with a lot of

small seeds that are used as food for people and birds •➤ picture at **cereal**

milligram (also **milligramme**) /'mɪlɪgræm/ noun [C] (*abbr* mg) a measure of weight. There are 1000 milligrams in a gram.

millilitre (*US* **milliliter**) /'mɪlɪliːtə/ noun [C] (*abbr* ml) a measure of liquid. There are 1000 millilitres in a litre.

millimetre (*US* **millimeter**) /'mɪlɪmiːtə/ noun [C] (*abbr* mm) a measure of length. There are 1000 millimetres in a metre.

millinery /'mɪlɪnəri/ noun [U] the business of making or selling women's hats

★ **million** /'mɪljən/ number **1** 1000000: *Nearly 60 million people live in Britain.* ● *Millions of people are at risk from the disease.*

➤ Notice that you use million without s when talking about more than one million: *six million people.* For examples of how to use numbers in sentences, look at **six**.

2 a million; millions (of) (*informal*) a very large amount: *I still have a million things to do.* ● *There are millions of reasons why you shouldn't go.*

➤ For more information about numbers look at the special section on numbers at the back of this dictionary.

millionaire /ˌmɪljə'neə/ noun [C] a person who has a million pounds, dollars, etc; a very rich person

millionth¹ /'mɪljənθ/ pron, determiner 1000000th

millionth² /'mɪljənθ/ noun [C] one of a million equal parts of sth: *a millionth of a second*

mime /maɪm/ (*US* **pantomime**) noun [U,C] the use of movements of your hands and body and the expression on your face to tell a story or to act sth without speaking; a performance using this method of acting: *The performance consisted of dance, music and mime.* –mime verb [I,T]

mimic¹ /'mɪmɪk/ verb [T] (*pres part* mimicking; *pt, pp* mimicked) to copy sb's behaviour, movements, voice, etc in an amusing way: *She's always mimicking the teachers.*

mimic² /'mɪmɪk/ noun [C] a person who can copy sb's behaviour, movements, voice, etc in an amusing way –mimicry /'mɪmɪkri/ noun [U]

min abbr **1** minimum: *min temp tomorrow 2°* **2** minute(s): *fastest time: 6 min*

mince /mɪns/ (*Brit*) (*US* **ground 'beef; hamburger**) noun [U] meat that has been cut into very small pieces with a special machine –mince verb [T]

mince 'pie noun [C] a small round cake with a mixture of dried fruit, sugar, etc (mincemeat) inside, traditionally eaten in Britain at Christmas time

★ **mind**¹ /maɪnd/ noun [C,U] the part of your brain that thinks and remembers; your thoughts, feelings and intelligence: *He has a brilliant mind.* ● *Not everybody has the right*

m

sort of mind for this work.

IDIOMS **at/in the back of your mind** → BACK¹

be in two minds (about sth/doing sth)) to not feel sure of sth: *I'm in two minds about leaving Will alone in the house while we're away.*

be/go out of your mind (*informal*) to be or become crazy or very worried: *I was going out of my mind when Tina didn't come home on time.*

bear in mind (that); bear/keep sb/sth in mind to remember or consider (that); to remember sb/sth: *We'll bear/keep your suggestion in mind for the future.*

bring/call sb/sth to mind to be reminded of sb/sth; to remember sb/sth

cast your mind back → CAST¹

change your mind → CHANGE¹

come/spring to mind if sth comes/springs to mind, you suddenly remember or think of it

cross your mind → CROSS²

ease sb's mind → EASE²

frame of mind → FRAME¹

give sb a piece of your mind → PIECE¹

go clean out of your mind → CLEAN³

have/keep an open mind → OPEN¹

have sb/sth in mind (for sth) to be considering sb/sth as suitable for sth; to have a plan: *Who do you have in mind for the job?*

keep your mind on sth to continue to pay attention to sth: *Keep your mind on the road while you're driving!*

make up your mind to decide: *I can't make up my mind which sweater to buy.*

on your mind worrying you: *Don't bother her with that. She's got enough on her mind already.*

prey on sb's mind → PREY²

put/set sb's mind at rest to make sb stop worrying: *The results of the blood test set his mind at rest.*

slip your mind → SLIP¹

speak your mind → SPEAK

state of mind → STATE¹

take sb's mind off sth to help sb not to think or worry about sth

to my mind in my opinion: *To my mind, this is a complete waste of time!*

★ **mind²** /maɪnd/ *verb* **1** [I,T] (especially in questions, answers, and negative sentences) to feel annoyed, upset or uncomfortable about sth/sb: *I'm sure Simon won't mind if you don't invite him.* • *I don't mind what you do – it's your decision.* • *Do you mind having to travel so far to work every day?* • *Are you sure your parents won't mind me coming?* • *'Would you like tea or coffee?' 'I don't mind.'* (= I'm happy to have either) • *I wouldn't mind a break right now* (= I would like one). **2** [T] (used in a question as a polite way of asking sb to do sth or for permission to do sth) could you...?; may I...?: *Would you mind closing the window for me?* • *Do you mind driving? I'm feeling rather tired.* **3** [T] used to tell sb to be careful of sth or to pay attention to sth/sb: *It's a very low doorway so mind your head.* • *Mind that step!* • *Don't mind me! I won't disturb you.* **4** [T] (*especially Brit*)

to look after or watch sb/sth for a short time: *Could you mind my bag while I go and get us some drinks?*

IDIOMS **mind you** used for attracting attention to a point you are making or for giving more information: *Paul seems very tired. Mind you, he has been working very hard recently.*

mind your own business to pay attention to your own affairs, not other people's: *Stop asking me personal questions and mind your own business!*

never mind don't worry; it doesn't matter: *'I forgot to post your letter.' 'Never mind, I'll do it later.'*

PHRASAL VERB **mind out** (*informal*) Get out of the way!: *Mind out! There's a car coming.*

'mind-boggling *adj* (*informal*) difficult to imagine, understand or believe: *Mind-boggling amounts of money were being discussed.*

-minded /'maɪndɪd/ *adj* (used to form compound adjectives) **1** having the type of mind mentioned: *a strong-minded/open-minded/narrow-minded person* **2** interested in the thing mentioned: *money-minded*

minder /'maɪndə/ *noun* [C] a person whose job is to look after and protect sb/sth: *My son goes to a childminder so that I can work part-time.*

mindless /'maɪndləs/ *adj* **1** done or acting without thought and for no particular reason: *mindless violence* **2** not needing thought or intelligence: *a mindless and repetitive task*

★ **mine¹** /maɪn/ *pron* of or belonging to me: *'Whose is this jacket?' 'It's mine.'* • *Don't take your car – you can come in mine.* • *May I introduce a friend of mine* (= one of my friends)? ••► Look at **my**.

★ **mine²** /maɪn/ *noun* [C] **1** a deep hole, or a system of passages under the ground where minerals such as coal, tin, gold, etc are dug: *a coal/salt/gold mine* ••► Look at **quarry**. **2** a bomb that is hidden under the ground or under water and explodes when sb/sth touches it: *The car went over a mine and blew up.*

mine³ /maɪn/ *verb* **1** [I,T] to dig in the ground for minerals such as coal, tin, gold, etc: *Diamonds are mined in South Africa.* ••► Look at **mining**. **2** [T] to put mines²(2) in an area of land or sea

minefield /'maɪnfiːld/ *noun* [C] **1** an area of land or sea where mines²(2) have been hidden **2** a situation that is full of hidden dangers or difficulties: *a political minefield*

★ **miner** /'maɪnə/ *noun* [C] a person whose job is to work in a mine²(1) to get coal, salt, tin, etc

★ **mineral** /'mɪnərəl/ *noun* [C] a natural substance such as coal, salt, oil, etc, especially one that is found in the ground. Some minerals are also present in food and drink and are very important for good health: *a country rich in minerals* • *the recommended daily intake of vitamins and minerals*

'mineral water *noun* [U] water that comes straight from a place in the ground (a spring), which contains minerals or gases and is thought to be good for your health •➤ picture on page C4

mingle /'mɪŋgl/ verb [I,T] mingle A and B (together); mingle (A) (with B) to mix with other things or people: *The colours slowly mingled together to make a muddy brown.* • *His excitement was mingled with fear.* • *to mingle with the rich and famous*

mini- /'mɪni/ (used to form compound nouns) very small: *a miniskirt* • *minigolf*

miniature /'mɪnətʃə/ noun [C] a small copy of sth which is much larger: *a miniature camera*

IDIOM in miniature exactly the same as sb/sth else but in a very small form

minibus /'mɪnibʌs/ noun [C] (*especially Brit*) a small bus, usually for no more than 12 people

minimal /'mɪnɪməl/ adj very small in amount, size or level; as little as possible: *The project must be carried out at minimal cost.*

minimize (also **-ise**) /'mɪnɪmaɪz/ verb [T] **1** to make sth as small as possible (in amount or level): *We shall try to minimize the risks to the public.* **2** to try to make sth seem less important than it really is **3** (*computing*) to make sth small on a computer screen •➤ opposite **maximize**

★ **minimum¹** /'mɪnɪməm/ noun [sing] the smallest amount or level that is possible or allowed: *I need a minimum of seven hours' sleep.* • *We will try and keep the cost of the tickets to a minimum.* •➤ opposite **maximum**

★ **minimum²** /'mɪnɪməm/ adj (only *before* a noun) the smallest possible or allowed; extremely small: *to introduce a national minimum wage* (= the lowest wage that an employer is legally allowed to pay) •➤ opposite **maximum** –minimum adv: *We'll need £200 minimum for expenses.*

mining /'maɪnɪŋ/ noun [U] (often used to form compound nouns) the process or industry of getting minerals, metals, etc out of the ground by digging: *coal/tin/gold mining*

★ **minister** /'mɪnɪstə/ noun [C] **1** Minister (*US* **Secretary**) a member of the government, often the head of a government department: *the Minister for Trade and Industry* •➤ Look at **Prime Minister** and **Cabinet Minister**. **2** a priest in some Protestant churches •➤ Look at **vicar**.

ministerial /ˌmɪnɪ'stɪəriəl/ adj connected with a government minister or department

★ **ministry** /'mɪnɪstri/ noun [C] (pl **ministries**) (also **department**) a government department that has a particular area of responsibility: *the Ministry of Defence* •➤ **Department** is the only word used in US English.

mink /mɪŋk/ noun [C] a small wild animal that is kept for its thick brown fur which is used to make expensive coats

★ **minor¹** /'maɪnə/ adj **1** not very big, serious or important (when compared with others): *It's only a minor problem. Don't worry.* • *She's*

gone into hospital for a *minor operation.* •➤ opposite **major 2** of one of the two types of key¹(4) in which music is usually written: *a symphony in F minor* •➤ Look at **major**.

minor² /'maɪnə/ noun [C] (used in law) a person who is not legally an adult

➤ In Britain you are a minor until you are eighteen when you **come of age**.

★ **minority** /maɪ'nɒrəti/ noun [C] (pl **minorities**) **1** [usually sing, with sing or pl verb] the smaller number or part of a group; less than half: *Only a minority of teenagers become/becomes involved in crime.* •➤ opposite **majority 2** a small group of people who are of a different race or religion to most of the people in the community or country where they live: *Schools in Britain need to do more to help children of ethnic/racial minorities.* IDIOM be in a/the minority to be the smaller of two groups: *Men are in the minority in the teaching profession.* •➤ Look at **in a/the majority**.

mint /mɪnt/ noun **1** [U] a type of plant (a herb) whose leaves are used to give flavour to food, drinks, toothpaste, etc: *lamb with mint sauce* **2** [C] a type of sweet with a strong fresh flavour **3** [sing] the place where money in the form of coins and notes is made by the government –mint verb [T]: *freshly minted coins*

minus¹ /'maɪnəs/ prep **1** (used in sums) less; subtract; take away: *Six minus two is four (6 – 2 = 4).* •➤ opposite **plus 2** (used about a number) below zero: *The temperature will fall to minus 10.* **3** (*informal*) without sth that was there before: *We're going to be minus a car for a while.*

minus² /'maɪnəs/ noun [C] **1** (also '**minus sign**) (*symbol* –) the symbol which is used in mathematics to show that a number is below zero or that you should subtract the second number from the first **2** (also '**minus point**) (*informal*) a negative quality; a disadvantage: *Let's consider the pluses and minuses of moving out of the city.* •➤ opposite **plus**

minus³ /'maɪnəs/ adj **1** (used in mathematics) lower than zero: *a minus figure* **2** (used in a system of grades given for school work) slightly lower than: *I got A minus (A–) for my essay.* •➤ opposite **plus**

minuscule /'mɪnəskju:l/ adj extremely small

★ **minute¹** /'mɪnɪt/ noun **1** [C] (*abbr* min) one of the 60 parts that make up one hour; 60 seconds: *It's twelve minutes to nine.* • He telephoned ten minutes ago. • *The programme lasts for about fifty minutes.* **2** [sing] (*spoken*) a very short time; a moment: *Just/Wait a minute* (= wait)! *You've forgotten your notes.* • *Have you got a minute? – I'd like to talk to you.* **3 the minutes** [pl] a written record of what is said and decided at a meeting IDIOMS (at) any minute/moment (now) (*informal*) very soon: *The plane should be landing any minute now.* in a minute very soon: *I'll be with you in a*

minute.
the last minute/moment → **LAST**¹(1)
the minute/moment (that) as soon as: *I'll tell him you rang the minute (that) he gets here.*
this minute immediately; now: *I don't know what I'm going to do yet – I've just this minute found out.*
up to the minute (*informal*) having the most recent information: *For up to the minute information on flight times, phone this number...*

minute² /maɪˈnjuːt/ **adj** (*superl* **minutest**) (no comparative) **1** very small: *I couldn't read his writing. It was minute!* **2** very exact or accurate: *She was able to describe the man in minute/the minutest detail.*

miracle /ˈmɪrəkl/ **noun 1** [C] a wonderful event that seems impossible and that is believed to be caused by God or a god **2** [sing] a lucky thing that happens that you did not expect or think was possible: *It's a miracle (that) nobody was killed in the crash.*

IDIOM work/perform miracles to achieve very good results: *The new diet and exercise programme have worked miracles for her.*

miraculous /mɪˈrækjələs/ **adj** completely unexpected and very lucky: *She's made a miraculous recovery.* –**miraculously adv**

mirage /ˈmɪrɑːʒ; mɪˈrɑːʒ/ **noun** [C] something that you think you see in very hot weather, for example water in a desert, but which does not really exist

★**mirror** /ˈmɪrə/ **noun** [C] a piece of special flat glass that you can look into in order to see yourself or what is behind you: *to look in the mirror* • *a rear-view mirror* (= in a car, so that the driver can see what is behind)

➤ A mirror **reflects** images. What you see in a mirror is a **reflection**.

•➤ picture at **motorbike** and on page S9 –**mirror verb** [T]: *The trees were mirrored in the lake.*

mirth /mɜːθ/ **noun** [U] (*written*) amusement or laughter

misapprehension /ˌmɪsæprɪˈhenʃn/ **noun** [U,C] (*formal*) to have the wrong idea about sth or to believe sth is true when it is not: *I was under the misapprehension that this course was for beginners.*

misbehave /ˌmɪsbɪˈheɪv/ **verb** [I] to behave badly •➤ opposite **behave** –**misbehaviour** (*US* **misbehavior**) /ˌmɪsbɪˈheɪvɪə/ **noun** [U]

misc abbr miscellaneous

miscalculate /ˌmɪsˈkælkjuleɪt/ **verb** [I,T] to make a mistake in calculating or judging a situation, an amount, etc: *The driver totally miscalculated the speed at which the other car was travelling.* –**miscalculation** /ˌmɪskælkjuˈleɪʃn/ **noun** [C,U]

miscarriage /ˈmɪskærɪdʒ/ **noun** [C,U] (*medical*) giving birth to a baby a long time before it is ready to be born, with the result that it cannot live

➤ Compare **abortion**.

IDIOM a miscarriage of justice an occasion when sb is punished for a crime that he/she

did not do

miscarry /mɪsˈkæri/ **verb** [I] (*pres part* **miscarrying**; *3rd pers sing pres* **miscarries**; *pt, pp* **miscarried**) to give birth to a baby before it is ready to be born, with the result that it cannot live

miscellaneous /ˌmɪsəˈleɪniəs/ **adj** (*abbr* **misc**) consisting of many different types or things: *a box of miscellaneous items for sale*

mischief /ˈmɪstʃɪf/ **noun** [U] bad behaviour (usually of children) that is not very serious: *The children in Class 9 are always getting into mischief.*

mischievous /ˈmɪstʃɪvəs/ **adj** (usually used about children) liking to behave badly and embarrassing or annoying people –**mischievously adv**

misconception /ˌmɪskənˈsepʃn/ **noun** [C] a wrong idea or understanding of sth: *It is a popular misconception* (= many people wrongly believe) *that people need meat to be healthy.*

misconduct /ˌmɪsˈkɒndʌkt/ **noun** [U] (*formal*) unacceptable behaviour, especially by a professional person: *The doctor was dismissed for gross* (= very serious) *misconduct.*

misconstrue /ˌmɪskənˈstruː/ **verb** [T] (*formal*) misconstrue sth (as sth) to understand sb's words or actions wrongly •➤ Look at **construe**.

misdemeanour (*US* **misdemeanor**) /ˌmɪsdɪˈmiːnə/ **noun** [C] something slightly bad or wrong that a person does; a crime that is not very serious

miser /ˈmaɪzə/ **noun** [C] a person who loves having a lot of money but hates spending it –**miserly adj**

★**miserable** /ˈmɪzrəbl/ **adj 1** very unhappy: *Oh dear, you look miserable. What's wrong?* **2** unpleasant; making you feel unhappy: *What miserable weather!* (= grey, cold and wet) •➤ synonym **dismal 3** too small or of bad quality: *I was offered a miserable salary so I didn't take the job.* –**miserably** /-əbli/ **adv**: *I stared miserably out of the window.* • *He failed miserably as an actor.*

★**misery** /ˈmɪzəri/ **noun** [U,C] (*pl* **miseries**) great unhappiness or suffering: *I couldn't bear to see him in such misery.* • *the miseries of war*

IDIOMS put sb out of his/her misery (*informal*) to stop sb worrying about sth by telling the person what he/she wants to know: *Put me put of my misery – did I pass or not?*
put sth out of its misery to kill an animal because it has an illness or injury that cannot be treated

misfire /ˌmɪsˈfaɪə/ **verb** [I] to fail to have the intended result or effect: *The plan misfired.*

misfit /ˈmɪsfɪt/ **noun** [C] a person who not is accepted by other people, especially because his/her behaviour or ideas are very different

misfortune /ˌmɪsˈfɔːtʃuːn/ **noun** [C,U] (*formal*) (an event, accident, etc that brings) bad luck or disaster: *I hope I don't ever have the misfortune to meet him again.*

m

misgiving /ˌmɪsˈɡɪvɪŋ/ **noun** [C,U] a feeling of doubt, worry or suspicion: *I had serious misgivings about leaving him on his own.*

misguided /ˌmɪsˈɡaɪdɪd/ **adj** wrong because you have understood or judged a situation badly: *She only moved the victim in a misguided effort to help.*

mishap /ˈmɪshæp/ **noun** [C,U] a small accident or piece of bad luck that does not have serious results: *to have a slight mishap*

misinform /ˌmɪsɪnˈfɔːm/ **verb** [T] (*formal*) to give sb the wrong information: *I think you've been misinformed – no one is going to lose their job.*

misinterpret /ˌmɪsɪnˈtɜːprɪt/ **verb** [T] misinterpret sth (as sth) to understand sth wrongly: *His comments were misinterpreted as a criticism of the project.* •➤ opposite **interpret** –**misinterpretation** /ˌmɪsɪntɜːprɪˈteɪʃn/ **noun** [C,U]: *Parts of the speech were **open to misinterpretation*** (= easy to understand wrongly).

misjudge /ˌmɪsˈdʒʌdʒ/ **verb** [T] **1** to form a wrong opinion of sb/sth, usually in a way which is unfair to him/her/it **2** to guess time, distance, etc wrongly: *He completely misjudged the speed of the other car and almost crashed.* –**misjudgement** (also **misjudgment**) **noun** [C,U]

mislay /ˌmɪsˈleɪ/ **verb** [T] (*pres part* **mislaying**; *3rd pers sing pres* **mislays**; *pt, pp* **mislaid** /-ˈleɪd/) to lose sth, usually for a short time, because you cannot remember where you put it

mislead /ˌmɪsˈliːd/ **verb** [T] (*pt, pp* **misled** /-ˈled/) to make sb have the wrong idea or opinion about sb/sth –**misleading adj**: *a misleading advertisement*

mismanage /ˌmɪsˈmænɪdʒ/ **verb** [T] to manage or organize sth badly –**mismanagement noun** [U]

misplaced /ˌmɪsˈpleɪst/ **adj** given to sb/sth that is not suitable or good enough to have it: *misplaced loyalty*

misprint /ˈmɪsprɪnt/ **noun** [C] a mistake in printing or typing

mispronounce /ˌmɪsprəˈnaʊns/ **verb** [T] to say a word or letter wrongly: *People always mispronounce my surname.* –**mispronunciation** /ˌmɪsprəˌnʌnsiˈeɪʃn/ **noun** [C,U]

misread /ˌmɪsˈriːd/ **verb** [T] (*pt, pp* **misread** /-ˈred/) misread sth (as sth) to read or understand sth wrongly: *He misread my silence as a refusal.*

misrepresent /ˌmɪsreprɪˈzent/ **verb** [T] (usually passive) to give a wrong description of sb/sth: *In the newspaper article they were misrepresented as uncaring parents.* –**misrepresentation** /ˌmɪsˌreprɪzenˈteɪʃn/ **noun** [C,U]

★**Miss¹** /mɪs/ used as a title before the family name of a young woman or a woman who is not married

> **Miss, Mrs, Ms** and **Mr** are all titles that we use in front of a person's family name, NOT his/her first name, unless it is included with the family name: *Is there a Miss (Tamsin) Hudson here?* NOT *Miss Tamsin* • *'Dear Miss Harris,' the letter began.*

★**miss²** /mɪs/ **verb 1** [I,T] to fail to hit, catch, etc sth: *She tried to catch the ball but she missed.* • *The bullet narrowly missed his heart.* **2** [T] to not see, hear, understand, etc sb/sth: *The house is on the corner so **you can't miss it**.* • *They completely **missed the point** of what I was saying.* • *My Mum will know there's something wrong. She **doesn't miss much**.* **3** [T] to arrive too late for sth or to fail to go to or do sth: *Hurry up or you'll miss the plane!* • *Of course I'm coming to your wedding. I **wouldn't miss it for the world*** (= used to emphasize that you really want to do sth). **4** [T] to feel sad because sb is not with you any more, or because you have not got or cannot do sth that you once had or did: *I'll miss you terribly when you go away.* • *What did you miss most when you lived abroad?* **5** [T] to notice that sb/sth is not where he/she/it should be: *When did you first miss your handbag?* **6** [T] to avoid sth unpleasant: *If we leave now, we'll miss the rush-hour traffic.*

PHRASAL VERBS **miss sb/sth out** to not include sb/sth: *You've missed out several important points in your report.*

miss out (on sth) to not have a chance to have or do sth: *You'll miss out on all the fun if you stay at home.*

miss³ /mɪs/ **noun** [C] a failure to hit, catch or reach sth: *After several misses he finally managed to hit the target.*

IDIOMS **give sth a miss** (*especially Brit informal*) to decide not to do or have sth: *I think I'll give aerobics a miss tonight.*

a near miss → NEAR¹

missile /ˈmɪsaɪl/ **noun** [C] **1** a powerful exploding weapon that can be sent long distances through the air: *nuclear missiles* **2** an object or weapon that is fired from a gun or thrown in order to hurt sb or damage sth: *The rioters threw missiles such as bottles and stones.*

missing /ˈmɪsɪŋ/ **adj 1** lost, or not in the right or usual place: *a missing person* • *Two files have **gone missing** from my office.* **2** (used about a person) not present after a battle, an accident, etc but not known to have been killed: *Many soldiers were listed as **missing in action**.* **3** not included, often when it should have been: *Fill in the missing words in the text.*

mission /ˈmɪʃn/ **noun** [C] **1** an important official job that sb is sent somewhere to do, especially to another country: *Your mission is to send back information about the enemy's movements.* **2** a group of people who are sent to a foreign country to perform a special task: *a British trade mission to China* **3** a special journey made by a spacecraft or military aircraft: *a mission to the moon* **4** a place where people are taught about the Christian religion, given medical help, etc by people who are sent from another country to do this (**missionaries**) **5** a particular task which you feel it is your duty to do: *Her work with the poor was more than just a job – it was her mission in life.*

missionary /'mɪʃənri/ noun [C] (*pl missionaries*) a person who is sent to a foreign country to teach about the Christian religion

misspell /ˌmɪs'spel/ verb [T] (*pt, pp misspelled* or *misspelt* /-'spelt/) to spell sth wrongly

★**mist¹** /mɪst/ noun [C,U] a cloud made of very small drops of water in the air just above the ground, that makes it difficult to see: *The fields were covered in mist.* • Look at the notes at **fog** and **weather**. –**misty** adj: *a misty morning* •➤ Look at **foggy**.

mist² /mɪst/ verb

PHRASAL VERB mist (sth) up/over to cover or be covered with very small drops of water that make it difficult to see: *My glasses keep misting up.*

★**mistake¹** /mɪ'steɪk/ noun [C] something that you think or do that is wrong: *Try not to make any mistakes in your essays.* • *a spelling mistake* • *It was a big mistake to trust her.* • *I made the mistake of giving him my address.*

IDIOM **by mistake** as a result of being careless: *The terrorists shot the wrong man by mistake.*

➤ **Error** is more formal than **mistake**: *a computing error.* **Fault** indicates who is responsible for sth bad: *The accident wasn't my fault. The other driver pulled out in front of me.* **Fault** is also used to describe a problem or weakness that sb/sth has: *a technical fault*

★**mistake²** /mɪ'steɪk/ verb [T] (*pt mistook* /mɪ'stʊk/; *pp mistaken* /mɪ'steɪkən/) **1** mistake A for B to think wrongly that sb/sth is sb/sth else: *I'm sorry, I mistook you for a friend of mine.* **2** to be wrong about sth: *I think you've mistaken my meaning.*

mistaken /mɪ'steɪkən/ adj wrong; not correct: *a case of mistaken identity* • *a mistaken belief/idea* –**mistakenly** adv

mister → **Mr**

mistletoe /'mɪsltəʊ/ noun [U] a plant with white berries and green leaves. Mistletoe grows on trees.

➤ Mistletoe is used as a decoration inside houses in Britain at Christmas time. There is a tradition of kissing people 'under the mistletoe'.

mistook *past tense* of **MISTAKE²**

mistreat /ˌmɪs'triːt/ verb [T] to be cruel to a person or animal: *The owner of the zoo was accused of mistreating the animals.* –**mistreatment** noun [U]

mistress /'mɪstrəs/ noun [C] (*old-fashioned*) a married man's secret lover

mistrust /ˌmɪs'trʌst/ verb [T] to have no confidence in sb/sth because you think he/she/it

may be harmful: *I always mistrust politicians who smile too much.* –**mistrust** noun [U,sing]: *She has a deep mistrust of strangers.* •➤ Look at **distrust**.

misty /'mɪsti/ → **MIST¹**

misunderstand /ˌmɪsʌndə'stænd/ verb [T] (*pt, pp misunderstood* /-'stʊd/) to understand sb/sth wrongly: *I misunderstood the instructions and answered too many questions.*

misunderstanding /ˌmɪsʌndə'stændɪŋ/ noun **1** [C,U] a situation in which sb/sth is not understood correctly: *The contract is written in both languages to avoid any misunderstanding.* **2** [C] a disagreement or an argument

misuse /ˌmɪs'juːz/ verb [T] to use sth in the wrong way or for the wrong purpose: *These chemicals can be dangerous if misused.* –**misuse** /ˌmɪs'juːs/ noun [C,U]

mitigate /'mɪtɪgeɪt/ verb [T] (*formal*) to make sth less serious, painful, unpleasant, etc –**mitigating** adj: *Because of the mitigating circumstances* (= that made the crime seem less bad) *the judge gave her a lighter sentence.*

mitten /'mɪtn/ noun [C] a type of glove that has one part for the thumb and another part for all four fingers •➤ picture on page C6. Look at **glove**.

★**mix¹** /mɪks/ verb **1** [I,T] mix (A) (with B); mix (A and B) (together) if two or more substances mix or if you mix them, they combine to form a new substance: *Oil and water don't mix.* • *Mix all the ingredients together in a bowl.* • *to mix cement* (= to make cement by mixing other substances) **2** [I] mix (with sb) to be with and talk to other people: *He mixes with all types of people at work.*

IDIOM **be/get mixed up in sth** (*informal*) to be/become involved in sth bad or unpleasant

PHRASAL VERBS **mix sth up** to put something in the wrong order: *He was so nervous that he dropped his speech and got the pages all mixed up.*

mix sb/sth up (with sb/sth) to confuse sb/sth with sb/sth else: *I always get him mixed up with his brother.*

mix² /mɪks/ noun **1** [C,usually sing] a group of different types of people or things: *We need a good racial mix in the police force.* **2** [C,U] a special powder that contains all the substances needed to make sth. You add water or another liquid to this powder: *cake mix*

★**mixed** /mɪkst/ adj **1** being both good and bad: *I have mixed feelings about leaving my job.* **2** made or consisting of different types of person or thing: *Was your school mixed or single-sex?* • *a mixed salad*

mixed marriage noun [C] a marriage between people of different races or religions

mixed-up adj (*informal*) confused because of emotional problems: *He has been very mixed-up since his parents' divorce.*

blender

mixer

blender
(*Brit also* liquidizer)

food processor

mixer /'mɪksə/ **noun** [C] a machine that is used for mixing sth: *a food/cement mixer*

★mixture /'mɪkstʃə/ **noun 1** [sing] a combination of different things: *Monkeys eat a mixture of leaves and fruit.* **2** [C,U] a substance that is made by mixing other substances together: *cake mixture • a mixture of eggs, flour and milk*

'mix-up noun [C] (*informal*) a mistake in the planning or organization of sth: *There was a mix-up and we were given the wrong ticket.*

ml abbr millilitre(s): *contents 75ml*

mm abbr millimetre(s): *a 35mm camera*

moan /məʊn/ **verb** [I] **1** to make a low sound because you are in pain, very sad, etc: *to moan with pain* **2** (*informal*) to keep saying what is wrong about sth; to complain: *The English are always moaning about the weather.* –**moan noun** [C]

mob¹ /mɒb/ **noun** [C,with sing or pl verb] a large crowd of people that may become violent or cause trouble

mob² /mɒb/ **verb** [T] (**mobbing; mobbed**) to form a large crowd around sb, for example in order to see or touch him/her: *The band was mobbed by fans as they left the hotel.*

mobile¹ /'məʊbaɪl/ **adj** able to move or be moved easily: *My daughter is much more mobile now she has her own car.* •➤ opposite **immobile** –**mobility** /məʊˈbɪləti/ **noun** [U]

mobile² /'məʊbaɪl/ **noun** [C] **1** a decoration that you hang from the ceiling and that that moves when the air around it moves **2** = MOBILE PHONE

'mobile phone (also **mobile; cellphone**) **noun** [C] a telephone that you can carry around with you •➤ picture at **telephone**

mobilize (also **-ise**) /'məʊbɪlaɪz/ **verb 1** [T] to organize people or things to do sth: *They mobilized the local residents to oppose the new development.* **2** [I,T] (used about the army, navy, etc) to get ready for war •➤ opposite **immobilize**

mock¹ /mɒk/ **verb** [I,T] (*formal*) to laugh at sb/sth in an unkind way or to make other people laugh at him/her

➤ **Laugh at** and **make fun of** are less formal and more common.

mock² /mɒk/ **adj** (only *before* a noun) not real or genuine: *He held up his hands in mock surprise.* • *a mock* (= practice) *exam*

mock³ /mɒk/ **noun** [usually pl] (in Britain) a practice exam that you do before the official one

'mock-up noun [C] a model of sth that shows what it will look like or how it will work

modal /'məʊdl/ (also **'modal verb**) **noun** [C] (*grammar*) a verb, for example 'might', 'can' or 'must' that is used with another verb for expressing possibility, permission, intention, etc

➤ For more information about modal verbs, look at the **Quick Grammar Reference** section at the back of this dictionary.

mode /məʊd/ **noun** [C] **1** a type of sth or way of doing sth: *a mode of transport/life* **2** one of the ways in which a machine can work: *Switch the camera to automatic mode.*

★model¹ /'mɒdl/ **noun** [C] **1** a copy of sth that is usually smaller than the real thing: *a model aeroplane* **2** one of the machines, vehicles, etc that is made by a particular company: *The latest models are on display at the show.* **3** a person or thing that is a good example to copy: *a model student • Children often use older brothers or sisters as role models* (= copy the way they behave). **4** a person who is employed to wear clothes at a fashion show or for magazine photographs **5** a person who is painted, drawn or photographed by an artist

★model² /'mɒdl/ **verb** (**modelling; modelled**: *US* **modeling; modeled**) **1** [T] model sth/yourself on sb/sth to make sth/yourself similar to sth/sb else: *The house is modelled on a Roman villa.* **2** [I,T] to wear and show clothes at a fashion show or for photographs: *to model swimsuits* **3** [I,T] to make a model of sth: *This clay is difficult to model.*

modelling (*US* **modeling**) /'mɒdlɪŋ/ **noun** [U] the work of a fashion model

modem /'məʊdem/ **noun** [C] a piece of equipment that connects two or more computers together by means of a telephone line so that information can go from one to the other

★moderate¹ /'mɒdərət/ **adj 1** being, having, using, etc neither too much nor too little of sth: *a moderate speed • We've had a moderate amount of success.* **2** having or showing opinions, especially about politics, that are not extreme: *moderate policies/views* •➤ Look at **extreme** and **radical**. –**moderately adv**: *His career has been moderately successful.*

moderate² /'mɒdəreɪt/ **verb** [I,T] to become or to make sth less strong or extreme: *The union moderated its original demands.*

moderate³ /'mɒdərət/ **noun** [C] a person

m

whose opinions, especially about politics, are not extreme ••➤ Look at **extremist**.

moderation /ˌmɒdə'reɪʃn/ **noun** [U] the quality of being reasonable and not being extreme: *Alcohol can harm unborn babies even if it's taken in moderation.*

★**modern** /'mɒdn/ **adj 1** of the present or recent times: *Pollution is one of the major problems in the modern world.* **2** (used about styles of art, music, etc) new and different from traditional styles: *modern jazz/architecture* **3** with all the newest methods, equipment, designs, etc; up-to-date: *It is one of the most modern hospitals in the country.* ••➤ Look at **old-fashioned**.

modernize (also **-ise**) /'mɒdənaɪz/ **verb** [T] to make sth suitable for use today using new methods, styles, etc –modernization (also -isation) /ˌmɒdənaɪ'zeɪʃn/ **noun** [U]: *The house is large but is in need of modernization.*

ˌmodern ˈlanguages **noun** [pl] languages that are spoken now

modest /'mɒdɪst/ **adj 1** not talking too much about your own abilities, good qualities, etc: *She got the best results in the exam but she was too modest to tell anyone.* ••➤ Look at **humble** and **proud**. **2** not very large: *a modest pay increase* **3** (used about a woman's clothes) not showing much of the body –modesty **noun** [U] –modestly **adv**

modify /'mɒdɪfaɪ/ **verb** [T] (*pres part* **modifying**; *3rd pers sing pres* **modifies**; *pt, pp* **modified**) to change sth slightly: *We shall need to modify the existing plan.* –modification /ˌmɒdɪfɪ'keɪʃn/ **noun** [C,U]

module /'mɒdjuːl/ **noun** [C] a unit that forms part of sth bigger: *You must complete three modules* (= courses that you study) *in your first year.*

mohair /'məʊheə/ **noun** [U] very soft wool that comes from a certain type of animal (a goat)

moist /mɔɪst/ **adj** slightly wet; damp: *Her eyes were moist with tears.* ● *Keep the soil moist or the plant will die.* ••➤ Look at the note at **wet**. –moisten /'mɔɪsn/ **verb** [I,T]

moisture /'mɔɪstʃə/ **noun** [U] water in small drops on a surface, in the air, etc

molar /'məʊlə/ **noun** [C] one of the large teeth at the back of your mouth

mold (*US*) = **MOULD**

moldy (*US*) = **MOULDY**

mole /məʊl/ **noun** [C] **1** a small dark spot on a person's skin that never goes away ••➤ Look at **freckle**. **2** a small animal with dark fur that lives underground and is almost blind **3** (*informal*) a person who works in one organization and gives secret information to another organization; a spy

molecule /'mɒlɪkjuːl/ **noun** [C] the smallest unit into which a substance can be divided without changing its chemical nature ••➤ Look at **atom**.

molest /mə'lest/ **verb** [T] to attack sb, especially a child, in a sexual way

molt (*US*) = **MOULT**

molten /'məʊltən/ **adj** (used about metal or rock) made liquid by very great heat

mom (*US*) = **MUM**

★**moment** /'məʊmənt/ **noun 1** [C] a very short period of time: *One moment, please* (= please wait). ● *Joe left just a few moments ago.* **2** [sing] a particular point in time: *Just at that moment my mother arrived.* ● *the moment of birth/death*

IDIOMS **(at) any minute/moment (now)** ➔ **MINUTE**[1]

at the moment now: *I'm afraid she's busy at the moment. Can I take a message?*

for the moment/present for a short time; for now: *I'm not very happy at work but I'll stay there for the moment.*

in a moment very soon: *Just wait here. I'll be back in a moment.*

the last minute/moment ➔ **LAST**[1]
the minute/moment (that) ➔ **MINUTE**[1]
on the spur of the moment ➔ **SPUR**[1]

momentary /'məʊməntri/ **adj** lasting for a very short time: *a momentary lack of concentration* –momentarily /'məʊməntrəli/ **adv**

momentous /mə'mentəs/ **adj** very important: *a momentous decision/event/change*

momentum /mə'mentəm/ **noun** [U] the ability to keep increasing or developing; the force that makes sth move faster and faster: *The environmental movement is gathering momentum.*

mommy (*US*) = **MUMMY**(1)

Mon **abbr** Monday: *Mon 6 June*

monarch /'mɒnək/ **noun** [C] a king or queen

monarchy /'mɒnəki/ **noun** (*pl* **monarchies**) **1** [sing,U] the system of government or rule by a king or queen **2** [C] a country that is governed by a king or queen ••➤ Look at **republic**.

monastery /'mɒnəstri/ **noun** [C] (*pl* **monasteries**) a place where men (**monks**) live in a religious community ••➤ Look at **convent**.

★**Monday** /'mʌndeɪ, -di/ **noun** [C,U] (*abbr* **Mon**) the day of the week after Sunday: *I'm going to see her on Monday.* ● (*informal*) *I'll see you Monday.* ● *I finish work a bit later on Mondays/on a Monday.* ● *Monday morning/afternoon/evening/night* ● *last/next Monday* ● *a week on Monday/Monday week* (= not next Monday, but the Monday after that) ● *The museum is open Monday to Friday, 10 till 4.30.* ● *Did you see that article about Italy in Monday's paper?*

➤ Days of the week are always written with a capital letter.

monetary /'mʌnɪtri/ **adj** connected with money: *the government's monetary policy*

m

money

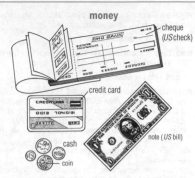

cheque (US check)

credit card

cash

note (US bill)

coin

★money /'mʌni/ **noun** [U] the means of paying for sth or buying sth (= coins or notes): *Will you **earn** more **money** in your new job?* ● *The new road will **cost** a lot of **money**.* ● *If we do the work ourselves we will **save money**.* ● *The government **make** a huge amount of **money** out of tobacco tax.* ··➤ Look also at **pocket money**.

IDIOMS **be rolling in money/in it** ➔ ROLL²

get your money's worth to get full value for the money you have spent

mongrel /'mʌŋgrəl/ **noun** [C] a dog that has parents of different types (**breeds**) ··➤ Look at **pedigree**.

monitor¹ /'mɒnɪtə/ **noun** [C] **1** a machine that shows information or pictures on a screen like a television ··➤ picture on page S7 **2** a machine that records or checks sth: *A monitor checks the baby's heartbeat.*

monitor² /'mɒnɪtə/ **verb** [T] to check, record or test sth regularly for a period of time: *Pollution levels in the lake are closely monitored.*

monk /mʌŋk/ **noun** [C] a member of a religious group of men who live in a special building (**monastery**) and do not get married or have possessions ··➤ Look at **nun**.

★monkey /'mʌŋki/ **noun** [C] an animal with a long tail that lives in hot countries and can climb trees ··➤ Look at **ape**. **Chimpanzees** and **gorillas** are apes, although people sometimes call them monkeys.

IDIOM **monkey business** silly or dishonest behaviour

mono /'mɒnəʊ/ **adj** (used about recorded music or a system for playing it) having the sound coming from one direction only ··➤ Look at **stereo**.

monolingual /ˌmɒnə'lɪŋgwəl/ **adj** using only one language: *This is a monolingual dictionary.* ··➤ Look at **bilingual**.

monologue (*US also* **monolog**) /'mɒnəlɒg/ **noun** [C] a long speech by one person, for example in a play

monopolize (*also* **-ise**) /mə'nɒpəlaɪz/ **verb** [T] to control sth so that other people cannot share it: *She completely monopolized the conversation. I couldn't get a word in.*

monopoly /mə'nɒpəli/ **noun** [C] (*pl* **monopolies**) a monopoly (**on/in sth**) **1** the control of an industry or service by only one company; a type of goods or a service that is controlled in this way: *The company has a monopoly on broadcasting international football.* **2** the complete control, possession or use of sth; something that belongs to only one person or group and is not shared

monorail /'mɒnəʊreɪl/ **noun** [C] a railway in which the train runs on a single track, usually high above the ground

monosyllable /'mɒnəsɪləbl/ **noun** [C] a short word, such as 'leg', that has only one syllable

monotonous /mə'nɒtənəs/ **adj** never changing and therefore boring: *monotonous work* ● *a monotonous voice* –**monotonously adv**

monotony /mə'nɒtəni/ **noun** [U] the state of being always the same and therefore boring: *the monotony of working on a production line*

monsoon /ˌmɒn'suːn/ **noun** [C] the season when it rains a lot in Southern Asia; the rain that falls during this period

monster /'mɒnstə/ **noun** [C] (in stories) a creature that is large, ugly and frightening: (*figurative*) *The murderer was described as a dangerous monster.*

monstrosity /mɒn'strɒsəti/ **noun** [C] (*pl* **monstrosities**) something that is very large and ugly, especially a building

monstrous /'mɒnstrəs/ **adj** **1** that people think is shocking and unacceptable because it is morally wrong or unfair: *It's monstrous that she earns less than he does for the same job!* **2** very large (and often ugly or frightening): *a monstrous spider/wave*

★month /mʌnθ/ **noun** [C] **1** one of the twelve periods of time into which the year is divided: *They are starting work next month.* ● *Have you seen this month's 'Vogue'?* **2** the period of about four weeks from a certain date in one month to the same date in the next, for example 13 May to 13 June; a calendar month: *'How long will you be away?' 'For about a month.'* ● *a six-month course*

monthly¹ /'mʌnθli/ **adj, adv** (happening or produced) once every month: *a monthly meeting/magazine/visit* ● *Are you paid weekly or monthly?*

monthly² /'mʌnθli/ **noun** [C] (*pl* **monthlies**) a magazine that is published once a month

monument /'mɒnjumənt/ **noun** [C] a monument (**to sb/sth**) **1** a building or statue that is built to remind people of a famous person or event ··➤ picture at **column 2** an old building or other place that is of historical importance

monumental /ˌmɒnju'mentl/ **adj** (only *before* a noun) very great, large or important: *a monumental success/task/achievement*

moo /muː/ **noun** [C] the sound that a cow makes –**moo verb** [I]

★mood /muːd/ **noun 1** [C,U] the way that you are feeling at a particular time: *to be in a bad/good mood* (= to feel angry/happy) ● *Turn that music down a bit – I'm not **in the mood for** it.* **2** [C] a time when you are angry or bad-tempered: *Debby's in one of her moods again.* ••➤ synonym **temper 3** [sing] the way that a group of people feel about sth: *The mood of the crowd suddenly changed and violence broke out.*

moody /'muːdi/ **adj 1** often changing moods in a way that people cannot predict: *You never know where you are with Andy because he's so moody.* **2** bad-tempered or unhappy, often for no particular reason –**moodily** *adv* –**moodiness** *noun* [U]

★**moon** /muːn/ *noun* **1 the moon** [sing] the object that shines in the sky at night and that moves round the earth once every 28 days

➤ The moon as it appears at its different stages, can be called a **new moon**, a **full moon**, a **half-moon** or a **crescent moon**.

••➤ *adjective* **lunar 2** [C] an object like the moon that moves around another planet: *How many moons does Neptune have?*
IDIOMS **once in a blue moon** → ONCE
over the moon (*especially Brit informal*) extremely happy and excited about sth

moonlight /'muːnlaɪt/ *noun* [U] light that comes from the moon: *The lake looked beautiful in the moonlight.*

moonlit /'muːnlɪt/ *adj* lit by the moon

moor¹ /mɔː/ (also **moorland** /'mɔːlənd/) *noun* [C,U] a wild open area of high land that is covered with grass and other low plants (**heather**): *We walked across the moors.* ••➤ Look at **heath**.

moor² /mɔː/ *verb* [I,T] **moor (sth to sth)** to fasten a boat to the land or to an object in the water with a rope or chain

mooring /'mɔːrɪŋ/ *noun* [C,usually pl] a place where a boat is tied; the ropes, chains, etc used to fasten a boat

moose /muːs/ (*especially US*) = ELK

mop¹ /mɒp/ *noun* [C] a tool for washing floors that consists of a long stick with thick strings, pieces of cloth or a sponge on the end ••➤ picture at **bucket**

mop² /mɒp/ *verb* [T] (**mopping; mopped**) **1** to clean a floor with water and a mop **2** to remove liquid from sth using a dry cloth: *to mop your forehead with a handkerchief*
PHRASAL VERB **mop sth up** to get rid of liquid from a surface with a mop or dry cloth: *Mop up that tea you've spilt or it'll leave a stain!*

mope /məʊp/ *verb* [I] **mope (about/around)** to spend your time doing nothing and feeling sorry for yourself because you are unhappy: *Moping around the house all day won't make the situation any better.*

moped /'məʊped/ *noun* [C] a type of small, not very powerful motorbike ••➤ picture at **motorbike**

★**moral**¹ /'mɒrəl/ *adj* **1** (only *before* a noun) concerned with what is right and wrong: *Some people refuse to eat meat on moral grounds* (= because they believe it to be wrong). • *a moral dilemma/issue/question* **2** having a high standard of behaviour that is considered good and right by most people: *She has always led a very moral life.*

➤ opposite **immoral**. Compare **amoral**, it has a different meaning.

IDIOM **moral support** help or encouragement that you give to sb who is nervous or worried: *I went to the dentist's with him just to give him some moral support.*

★**moral**² /'mɒrəl/ *noun* **1 morals** [pl] standards of good behaviour: *These people appear to have no morals.* **2** [C] a lesson in the right way to behave that can be learnt from a story or an experience: *The moral of the play is that friendship is more important than money.*

morale /mə'rɑːl/ *noun* [U] how happy, sad, confident, etc that a group of people feels at a particular time: *The team's morale was low/ high before the match* (= they felt worried/ confident). • *to boost/raise/improve morale*

★**morality** /mə'ræləti/ *noun* [U] principles concerning what is good and bad or right and wrong behaviour: *a debate about the morality of abortion* ••➤ opposite **immorality**

moralize (also **-ise**) /'mɒrəlaɪz/ *verb* [I] **moralize (about/on sth)** to tell other people what the right or wrong way to behave is

morally /'mɒrəli/ *adv* connected with standards of what is right or wrong

morbid /'mɔːbɪd/ *adj* showing interest in unpleasant things, for example disease and death

★**more**¹ /mɔː/ *determiner, pron* a larger number or amount of people or things; sth extra as well as what you have: *There were more people than I expected.* • *We had more time than we thought.* • *There's room for three more people.* • *I couldn't eat any more.* • *I can't stand much more of this.* • *Tell me more about your job.* ••➤ opposite **less** or **fewer**
IDIOMS **more and more** an increasing amount or number: *There are more and more cars on the road.*
what's more (used for adding another fact) also; in addition: *The hotel was awful and what's more it was miles from the beach.*

★**more**² /mɔː/ *adv* **1** (used to form the comparative of many adjectives and adverbs): *She was far/much more intelligent than her sister.* • *a course for more advanced students* • *Please write more carefully.* ••➤ opposite **less 2** to a greater degree than usual or than sth else: *I like him far/much more than his wife.* ••➤ opposite **less**
IDIOMS **not any more** not any longer: *She doesn't live here any more.*
more or less approximately; almost: *We are more or less the same age.*

moreover /mɔːr'əʊvə/ *adv* (*written*) (used for adding another fact) also; in addition: *This firm did the work very well. Moreover, the cost was not too high.*

morgue /mɔːg/ *noun* [C] a building where dead bodies are kept until they are buried or burned ••➤ Look at **mortuary**.

★**morning** /'mɔːnɪŋ/ *noun* [C,U] **1** the early part of the day between the time when the sun rises and midday: *Pat's going to London tomorrow morning.* • *Bye, see you in the* *morning* (= tomorrow morning). • *I've been studying hard **all morning**.* • *Dave makes breakfast **every morning**.* • *She only works **in the mornings**.* **2** the part of the night that is after midnight: *I was woken by a strange noise in the **the early hours of the morning**.* • *He didn't come home until three **in the morning**.*

➤ When you use the adjectives *early* or *late* before 'morning', 'afternoon' or 'evening' you must use the preposition *in*: *The accident happened in the early morning.* • *We arrived in the late afternoon.* With other adjectives, use *on*: *School starts on Monday morning.* • *They set out on a cold, windy afternoon.* No preposition is used before *this, tomorrow, yesterday*: *Let's go swimming this morning.* • *I'll phone Liz tomorrow evening.* • *What did you do yesterday afternoon?*

IDIOM **Good morning** (*formal*) used when you see sb for the first time in the morning ⇢ In a less formal situation we just say **Morning**: *Morning Kay, how are you today?*

moron /'mɔːrɒn/ *noun* [C] (*informal*) a rude way of referring to sb who you think is very stupid: *Stop treating me like a moron!* –**moronic** /məˈrɒnɪk/ *adj*

morose /məˈrəʊs/ *adj* bad-tempered, and not saying much to other people

morphine /'mɔːfiːn/ *noun* [U] a powerful drug that is used for reducing pain

morsel /'mɔːsl/ *noun* [C] a very small piece of sth, usually food

mortal¹ /'mɔːtl/ *adj* **1** that cannot live for ever and must die: *We are all mortal.* ⇢ opposite **immortal 2** (*written*) that will result in death: *a mortal wound/blow* • *to be in mortal danger* ⇢ Look at **fatal**, it has a similar meaning. **3** very great or extreme: *They were in mortal fear of the enemy.* –**mortally** /-təli/ *adv*

mortal² /'mɔːtl/ *noun* [C] (*formal*) a human being

mortality /mɔːˈtæləti/ *noun* [U] **1** the number of deaths in one period of time or in one place: *Infant mortality is high in the region.* **2** the fact that nobody can live forever: *He didn't like to think about his own mortality.*

mortar /'mɔːtə/ *noun* **1** [U] a mixture of cement, sand and water used in building for holding bricks and stones together **2** [C] a type of heavy gun that fires a type of bomb high into the air **3** [C] a small heavy bowl used for crushing some foods into powder using a special object (a pestle)

mortgage /'mɔːgɪdʒ/ *noun* [C] money that you borrow in order to buy a house or flat: *We took out a £40000 mortgage.*

➤ You usually borrow money from a **bank** or a **building society**, who decide what **rate of interest** you must pay on the **loan**.

mortician /mɔːˈtɪʃn/ *noun* (*US*) = **UNDERTAKER**

mortuary /'mɔːtʃəri/ *noun* [C] (*pl* **mortuaries**) a room, usually in a hospital, where dead bodies are kept before they are buried or burned ⇢ Look at **morgue**.

mosaic /məʊˈzeɪɪk/ *noun* [C,U] a picture or pattern that is made by placing together small coloured stones, pieces of glass, etc

Moslem = **MUSLIM**

mosque /mɒsk/ *noun* [C] a building where Muslims meet and pray

mosquito /məˈskiːtəʊ; mɒs-/ *noun* [C] (*pl* **mosquitoes**) a small flying insect that lives in hot countries and bites people or animals to drink their blood. Some types of mosquito spread a very serious disease (malaria). ⇢ picture at **insect**

moss /mɒs/ *noun* [C,U] a small soft green plant, with no flowers, that grows in wet places, especially on rocks or trees ⇢ picture on page C2 –**mossy** *adj*

★**most¹** /məʊst/ *determiner, pron* **1** (used as the superlative of *many* and *much*) greatest in number or amount: *Who got the most points?* • *The children had the most fun.* • *We all worked hard but I did the most.* ⇢ opposites **least** or **fewest 2** nearly all of a group of people or things: *Most people in this country have a television.* • *I like most Italian food.*

➤ When **most** is followed by a noun which has **the, this, my**, etc before it, we must use **most of**: *Most of my friends were able to come to the wedding.* • *It rained most of the time we were in Ireland.*

IDIOMS **at (the) most** not more than a certain number, and probably less: *There were 20 people there, at the most.*
make the most of sth → **MAKE¹**

★**most²** /məʊst/ *adv* **1** (used to form the superlative of many adjectives and adverbs): *It's the most beautiful house I've ever seen.* • *I work most efficiently in the morning.* ⇢ opposite **least 2** more than anybody/anything else: *What do you miss most when you're abroad?* ⇢ opposite **least 3** (*formal*) very: *We heard a most interesting talk about Japan.*

mostly /'məʊstli/ *adv* in almost every case; almost all the time: *Our students come mostly from Japan.*

MOT /ˌem əʊ ˈtiː/ *abbr* (also **MOT test**) a test to make sure that vehicles over a certain age are safe to drive: *My car failed its MOT.*

motel /məʊˈtel/ *noun* [C] a hotel near a main road for people who are travelling by car

moth /mɒθ/ *noun* [C] an insect with a hairy body that usually flies at night. Some moths eat cloth and leave small holes in your clothes. ⇢ picture at **insect**

mothball /'mɒθbɔːl/ *noun* [C] a small ball made of a chemical substance that protects clothes in cupboards from moths

★**mother¹** /'mʌðə/ *noun* [C] the female parent of a person or an animal ⇢ Look at **mum, mummy** and **stepmother**.

mother² /ˈmʌðə/ **verb** [T] to look after sb as a mother does: *Stop mothering me – I can look after myself!*

motherhood /ˈmʌðəhʊd/ **noun** [U] the state of being a mother

ˈmother-in-law **noun** [C] (*pl* **mothers-in-law**) the mother of your husband or wife

motherland /ˈmʌðəlænd/ **noun** [C] (*formal*) the country where you or your family were born and which you feel a strong emotional connection with

motherly /ˈmʌðəli/ **adj** having the qualities of a good mother: *motherly love/instincts/advice*

ˈmother tongue **noun** [C] the first language that you learned to speak as a child

motif /məʊˈtiːf/ **noun** [C] a picture or pattern on sth

motion¹ /ˈməʊʃn/ **noun 1** [U] movement or a way of moving: *The motion of the ship made us all feel sick.* • *Pull the lever to* **set** *the machine in motion* (= make it start moving). ••➤ Look at **slow motion**. **2** [C] a formal suggestion at a meeting that you discuss and vote on: *The motion was carried/rejected by a majority of eight votes.*

motion² /ˈməʊʃn/ **verb** [I,T] **motion to sb (to do sth)**; **motion (for) sb (to do sth)** to make a movement, usually with your hand, that tells sb what to do: *I motioned to the waiter.* • *The manager motioned for me to sit down.*

motionless /ˈməʊʃnləs/ **adj** not moving

motivate /ˈməʊtɪveɪt/ **verb** [T] **1** (usually passive) to cause sb to act in a particular way: *Her reaction was motivated by fear.* **2** to make sb want to do sth, especially sth that involves hard work and effort: *Our new teacher certainly knows how to motivate his classes.* • *I just can't motivate myself to do anything this morning.* –**motivated adj:** *highly motivated students* –**motivation** /ˌməʊtɪˈveɪʃn/ **noun** [C,U]: *He's clever enough, but he lacks motivation.*

motive /ˈməʊtɪv/ **noun** [C,U] **(a) motive (for sth/doing sth)** a reason for doing sth, often sth bad: *The police couldn't discover a motive for the murder.*

★**motor¹** /ˈməʊtə/ **noun** [C] a device that uses petrol, gas, electricity, etc to produce movement and makes a machine, etc work: *The washing machine doesn't work. I think something is wrong with the motor.*

> **Engine**, not **motor**, is usually used in connection with cars and motorbikes. Cars are, in fact, sometimes formally referred to as **motor cars**.

motor² /ˈməʊtə/ **adj** (only *before* a noun) **1** having or using the power of an engine or a motor: *a motor vehicle* **2** (*especially Brit*) connected with vehicles that have engines, especially cars: *the motor industry* • *motor racing*

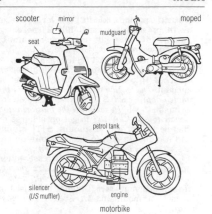

scooter   mirror   mudguard   moped
seat
petrol tank
silencer (*US* muffler)   engine
motorbike

motorbike /ˈməʊtəbaɪk/ (also *formal* **motorcycle**) **noun** [C] a vehicle that has two wheels and an engine

ˈmotor boat **noun** [C] a small fast boat that has a motor

ˈmotor car (*Brit formal*) = **CAR**(1)

motorcycle /ˈməʊtəsaɪkl/ (*formal*) = **MOTORBIKE**

motorcyclist /ˈməʊtəsaɪklɪst/ **noun** [C] a person who rides a motorbike

motoring /ˈməʊtərɪŋ/ **noun** [U] driving in a car: *a motoring holiday*

motorist /ˈməʊtərɪst/ **noun** [C] a person who drives a car ••➤ Look at **pedestrian**.

motorized (also **-ised**) /ˈməʊtəraɪzd/ **adj** (only *before* a noun) that has an engine: *a motorized wheelchair*

motorway /ˈməʊtəweɪ/ (*US* **expressway; freeway**) **noun** [C] a wide road connecting cities that is specially built for fast traffic

motto /ˈmɒtəʊ/ **noun** [C] (*pl* **mottoes** or **mottos**) a short sentence or phrase that expresses the aims and beliefs of a person, a group, an organization, etc: *'Live and let live' that's my motto.*

mould¹ (*US* **mold**) /məʊld/ **noun 1** [C] a container that you pour a liquid or substance into. The liquid then becomes solid (**sets**) in the same shape as the container, for example after it has cooled or cooked. **2** [C, usually sing] a particular type: *She doesn't fit into the usual mould of sales directors.* **3** [U] a soft green or black substance like fur (**fungus**) that grows in wet places or on old food –**mouldy** (*US* **moldy**) **adj:** *The cheese had gone mouldy.*

mould² (*US* **mold**) /məʊld/ **verb** [T] **mould A (into B)**; **mould B (from/out of A)** to make sth into a particular shape or form by pressing it or by putting it into a mould¹(1): *First mould the dough into a ball.* • *a bowl moulded from clay*

moult (*US* **molt**) /məʊlt/ **verb** [I] (used about an animal or a bird) to lose hairs or feathers before growing new ones

mound /maʊnd/ noun [C] **1** a large pile of earth or stones; a small hill **2** (*spoken*) a **mound (of sth)** a pile or a large amount of sth: *I've got a mound of work to do.*

★**mount¹** /maʊnt/ verb **1** [T] to organize sth: *to mount a protest/a campaign/an exhibition/an attack* **2** [I] to increase gradually in level or amount: *The tension mounted as the end of the match approached.* **3** [T] (*written*) to go up sth or up on to sth: *He mounted the platform and began to speak.* **4** [I,T] to get on a horse or bicycle ••➤ opposite **dismount 5** [T] **mount sth (on/onto/in sth)** to fix sth firmly on sth else: *The gas boiler was mounted on the wall.*

IDIOM **mount up** to increase (often more than you want): *When you're buying food for six people the cost soon mounts up.*

mount² /maʊnt/ noun [C] (*abbr* **Mt**) (used in names) a mountain: *Mt Everest/Vesuvius/ Fuji*

★**mountain** /'maʊntən/ noun [C] **1** a very high hill: *Which is the highest mountain in the world?* ● *mountain roads/scenery/villages* ● *a mountain range* ••➤ picture on page C8 **2** a **mountain (of sth)** a large amount of sth: *I've got a mountain of work to do.*

'**mountain bike** noun [C] a bicycle with a strong frame, wide tyres and many different speeds (gears) designed for riding on rough ground ••➤ We usually use **go mountain biking** to talk about riding a mountain bike for pleasure.

mountaineering /ˌmaʊntə'nɪərɪŋ/ noun [U] the sport of climbing mountains —**mountaineer** /-'nɪə/ noun [C]

mountainous /'maʊntənəs/ adj **1** having many mountains: *a mountainous region* **2** very large in size or amount: *The mountainous waves made sailing impossible.*

mountainside /'maʊntənsaɪd/ noun [C] the land on the side of a mountain

mounted /'maʊntɪd/ adj riding a horse: *mounted police*

mounting /'maʊntɪŋ/ adj (only *before* a noun) increasing: *mounting unemployment/ tension*

mourn /mɔːn/ verb [I,T] **mourn (for/over) sb/ sth** to feel and show great sadness, especially because sb has died: *She is still mourning (for) her child.* —**mourning** noun [U]: *He wore a black armband to show he was in mourning.*

mourner /'mɔːnə/ noun [C] a person who goes to a funeral as a friend or relative of the person who has died

mournful /'mɔːnfl/ adj (*written*) very sad: *a mournful song* —**mournfully** /-fəli/ adv

★**mouse** /maʊs/ noun [C] (*pl* **mice** /maɪs/) **1** a very small animal with fur and a long thin tail

> **Mice**, like **rats**, **hamsters**, etc are members of the **rodent** family.

2 a piece of equipment, connected to a computer, for moving around the screen and entering commands without touching the keys: *Use the mouse to drag the icon to a new position.* ••➤ picture on page S7

★**moustache** (*US* **mustache**) /mə'stɑːʃ/ noun [C] hair that grows on a man's top lip, between the mouth and nose ••➤ picture at **hair**

★**mouth¹** /maʊθ/ noun [C] (*pl* **mouths** /maʊðz/) **1** the part of your face that you use for eating and speaking: *to open/close your mouth* ••➤ picture on page C5 **2** -**mouthed** /-maʊðd/ (used to form compound adjectives) having a particular type of mouth or a particular way of speaking: *We stared open-mouthed in surprise.* ● *He's a loud-mouthed bully.* **3** the place where a river enters the sea

IDIOM **keep your mouth shut** (*informal*) to not say sth to sb because it is a secret or because it will upset or annoy him/her

mouth² /maʊð/ verb [I,T] to move your mouth as if you were speaking but without making any sound: *Vinay was outside the window, mouthing something to us.*

mouthful /'maʊθfl/ noun **1** [C] the amount of food or drink that you can put in your mouth at one time **2** [sing] a word or phrase that is long or difficult to say: *Her name is a bit of a mouthful.*

'**mouth organ** = HARMONICA

mouthpiece /'maʊθpiːs/ noun [C] **1** the part of a telephone, musical instrument, etc that you put in or near your mouth **2** a person, newspaper, etc that a particular group uses to express its opinions: *Pravda was the mouthpiece of the Soviet government.*

'**mouth-watering** adj (used about food) that looks or smells very good

movable /'muːvəbl/ adj that can be moved ••➤ opposite **fixed** ••➤ Look at **portable** and **mobile**.

★**move¹** /muːv/ verb **1** [I,T] to change position or to put sth in a different position: *Please move your car. It's blocking the road.* ● *The station is so crowded you* **can hardly move.** ● *The meeting has been moved to Thursday.* **2** [I,T] **move along, down, over, up, etc** to move (sth) further in a particular direction in order to make space for sb/sth else: *If we move up a bit, Rob can sit here too.* ● *Move your head down – I can't see the screen.* **3** [I,T] to change the place where you live, work, study, etc: *Our neighbours are moving to York next week.* ● *to* **move house** ● *Yuka's moved down to the beginners' class.* **4** [I] **move (on/ ahead)** to make progress: *When the new team of builders arrived things started moving very quickly.* **5** [I] to take action: *Unless we move quickly lives will be lost.* **6** [T] to cause sb to have strong feelings, especially of sadness: *Many people were* **moved to tears** *by reports of the massacre.*

IDIOMS **get moving** to go, leave or do sth quickly

get sth moving to cause sth to make progress

PHRASAL VERBS **move in (with sb)** to start living in a new house (with sb)

move on (to sth) to start doing or discussing sth new

move off (used about a vehicle) to start a

journey; to leave

move out to leave your old home

★ **move²** /muːv/ **noun** [C] **1** a change of place or position: *She was watching every move I made.* **2** a change in the place where you live or work: *a move to a bigger house* **3** action that you take because you want to achieve a particular result: *Both sides want to negotiate but neither is prepared to make the first move.* ● *Asking him to help me was a good move.* **4** (in chess and other games) a change in the position of a piece: *It's your move.*

IDIOMS **be on the move** to be going somewhere: *We've been on the move for four hours so we should stop for a rest.*

get a move on (*informal*) to hurry: *I'm late. I'll have to get a move on.*

make a move to start to go somewhere: *It's time to go home. Let's make a move.*

★ **movement** /ˈmuːvmənt/ **noun** **1** [C,U] an act of moving: *The dancer's movements were smooth and controlled.* ● *The seat belt doesn't allow much freedom of movement.* ● *I could see some movement* (= sb/sth moving) *in the trees.* **2** [C,U] an act of moving or being moved from one place to another: *the slow movement of the clouds across the sky* **3** [C, usually sing] **a movement (away from/ towards sth)** a general change in the way people think or behave: *There's been a movement away from the materialism of the 1980s.* **4 movements** [pl] a person's actions or plans during a period of time: *Detectives have been watching the man's movements for several weeks.* **5** [C] a group of people who have the same aims or ideas: *I support the Animal Rights movement.* **6** [C] one of the main parts of a long piece of music

★ **movie** /ˈmuːvi/ **noun** (*especially US*) **1** = FILM¹ (1): *Shall we go and see a movie?* ● *a science fiction/horror movie* ● *a movie director/star* ● *a movie theater* (= cinema) **2 the movies** [pl] = CINEMA: *Let's go to the movies.*

moving /ˈmuːvɪŋ/ **adj** **1** causing strong feelings, especially of sadness: *a deeply moving speech/story* **2** that moves: *It's a computerized machine with few moving parts.*

mow /məʊ/ **verb** [I,T] (*pt* **mowed**; *pp* **mown** /məʊn/ or **mowed**) to cut grass using a machine (a **mower**): *to mow the lawn*

PHRASAL VERB **mow sb down** to kill sb with a gun or a car

mower /ˈməʊə/ **noun** [C] a machine for cutting grass: *a lawnmower* ● *an electric mower*

MP /ˌem ˈpiː/ **abbr** (*especially Brit*) Member of Parliament

mpg /ˌem piː ˈdʒiː/ **abbr** miles per gallon: *This car does 40 mpg* (= *you can drive 40 miles on one gallon of petrol*).

mph /ˌem piː ˈeɪtʃ/ **abbr** miles per hour: *a 70 mph speed limit*

★ **Mr** /ˈmɪstə/ used as a title before the name of a man: *Mr (Matthew) Botham* ••➤ Look at the note at **Miss**.

★ **Mrs** /ˈmɪsɪz/ used as a title before the name of a married woman: *Mrs (Sylvia) Allen* ••➤ Look at the note at **Miss**.

MS /ˌem ˈes/ **abbr** multiple sclerosis

★ **Ms** /mɪz; məz/ used as a title before the family name of a woman who may or may not be married: *Ms (Donna) Hackett*

➤ Some women prefer the title **Ms** to **Mrs** or **Miss**. We can also use it if we do not know whether or not a woman is married. Look also at the note at **Miss**.

MSc /ˌem es ˈsiː/ **abbr** Master of Science: a second degree that you receive when you complete a more advanced course or piece of research in a science subject at university or college ••➤ Look at **BSc** and **MA**.

Mt **abbr** Mount: *Mt Everest*

mth (*US* **mo**) (*pl* **mths**; *US* **mos**) **abbr** month: *6 mths old*

★ **much** /mʌtʃ/ **determiner, pron, adv** **1** (used with uncountable nouns, mainly in negative sentences and questions, or after *as, how, so, too*) a large amount of sth: *I haven't got much money.* ● *Did she say much?* ● *You've given me too much food.* ● *How much time have you got?* ● *I can't carry that much!* ● *Eat as much as you can.*

➤ In statements we usually use **a lot of** NOT **much**: *I've got a lot of experience.*

2 to a great degree: *I don't like her very much.* ● *Do you see Sashi much?* (= very often) ● *Do you see much of Sashi?* ● *much taller/prettier/ harder* ● *much more interesting/unusual* ● *much more quickly/happily* ● *You ate much more than me.* **3** (with past participles used as adjectives) very: *She was much loved by all her friends.*

➤ Compare: *She was **very** popular.*

IDIOMS **much the same** very similar: *Softball is much the same as baseball.*

nothing much ➔ NOTHING

not much good (at sth) not skilled (at sth): *I'm not much good at singing.*

not much of a… not a good…: *She's not much of a cook.*

not up to much ➔ UP

muck¹ /mʌk/ **noun** [U] **1** the waste from farm animals, used to make plants grow better ••➤ A more common word is **manure**. **2** (*informal*) dirt or mud

muck² /mʌk/ **verb** (*informal*)

PHRASAL VERBS **muck about/around** to behave in a silly way or to waste time: *Stop mucking around and come and help me!*

muck sth up to do sth badly; to spoil sth: *I was so nervous that I completely mucked up my interview.*

mucus /ˈmjuːkəs/ **noun** [U] (*formal*) a sticky substance that is produced in some parts of the body, especially the nose

★ **mud** /mʌd/ **noun** [U] soft, wet earth: *He came home from the football match covered in mud.*

muddle /ˈmʌdl/ **verb** [T] **1 muddle sth (up)** to put things in the wrong place or order or to make them untidy: *Try not to get those papers muddled up.* **2 muddle sb (up)** to confuse sb: *I do my homework and schoolwork*

m

[I] **intransitive**, a verb which has no object: *He laughed.*   [T] **transitive**, a verb which has an object: *He ate an apple.*

in separate books so that I don't get muddled up. –muddle noun [C,U]: *If you get in a muddle, I'll help you.* –muddled adj

muddy /'mʌdi/ adj full of or covered in mud: *muddy boots* • *It's very muddy down by the river.*

mudguard /'mʌdgɑːd/ noun [C] a curved cover over the wheel of a bicycle or motorbike •► picture at **motorbike** and on page S9

muesli /'mjuːzli/ noun [U] food made of grains, nuts, dried fruit, etc that you eat with milk for breakfast

muffin /'mʌfɪn/ noun [C] **1** (*US* English muffin) a type of bread roll often eaten hot with butter **2** a type of small cake •► picture at **cake**

muffle /'mʌfl/ verb [T] to make a sound quieter and more difficult to hear: *He put his hand over his mouth to muffle his laughter.* –muffled adj: *I heard muffled voices outside.*

mug¹ /mʌg/ noun [C] **1** a large cup with straight sides and a handle: *a coffee mug* • *a mug of tea* •► picture at **cup 2** (*informal*) a person who seems stupid

mug² /mʌg/ verb [T] (**mugging**; **mugged**) to attack and rob sb in the street: *Keep your wallet out of sight or you'll get mugged.* –mugger noun [C] •► Look at the note at **thief.** –mugging noun [C,U]: *The mugging took place around midnight.*

muggy /'mʌgi/ adj (used about the weather) warm and slightly wet in an unpleasant way (**humid**)

mule /mjuːl/ noun [C] an animal that is used for carrying heavy loads and whose parents are a horse and another animal (a donkey)

mull /mʌl/ verb

PHRASAL VERB **mull sth over** to think about sth carefully and for a long time: *Don't ask me for a decision right now. I'll have to mull it over.*

multicultural /ˌmʌlti'kʌltʃərəl/ adj for or including people of many different races, languages, religions and traditions: *a multicultural society*

multilateral /ˌmʌlti'lætərəl/ adj involving more than two groups of people, countries, etc: *a multilateral agreement* •► Look at **unilateral.**

multimedia /ˌmʌlti'miːdiə/ adj (only *before* a noun) (*computing*) using sound, pictures and film in addition to text on a screen: *multimedia systems/products*

multinational /ˌmʌlti'næʃnəl/ adj existing in or involving many countries: *multinational companies* –multinational noun [C]: *The company is owned by Ford, the US multinational.*

multiple¹ /'mʌltɪpl/ adj involving many people or things or having many parts: *Three drivers died in a multiple pile-up on the motorway.*

multiple² /'mʌltɪpl/ noun [C] a number that contains another number an exact number of times: *12, 18 and 24 are multiples of 6.*

multiple-'choice adj (used about exam questions) showing several different answers from which you have to choose the right one

multiple sclerosis /ˌmʌltɪpl sklə'rəʊsɪs/ noun [U] (*abbr* **MS**) a serious disease which causes you to slowly lose control of your body and become less able to move

★**multiply** /'mʌltɪplaɪ/ verb (*pres part* **multiplying**; *3rd pers sing pres* **multiplies**; *pt, pp* **multiplied**) **1** [I,T] multiply A by B to increase a number by the number of times mentioned: *2 multiplied by 4 makes 8* (2 x 4 = 8) •► opposite **divide 2** [I,T] to increase or make sth increase by a very large amount: *We've multiplied our profits over the last two years.* –multiplication /ˌmʌltɪplɪ'keɪʃn/ noun [U] •► Look at **division**, **addition** and **subtraction.**

multi-purpose /ˌmʌlti 'pɜːpəs/ adj that can be used for several different purposes: *a multi-purpose tool/machine*

multitude /'mʌltɪtjuːd/ noun [C] (*formal*) a very large number of people or things

mum /mʌm/ (*US* **mom** /mɒm/) noun [C] (*informal*) mother: *Is that your mum?* • *Can I have a drink, Mum?* •► Look at **mummy.**

mumble /'mʌmbl/ verb [I,T] to speak quietly without opening your mouth properly, so that people cannot hear the words: *I can't hear if you mumble.* •► Look at **mutter.**

★**mummy** /'mʌmi/ noun [C] (*pl* **mummies**) **1** (*US* **mommy** /'mɒmi/) (*informal*) (used by or to children) mother: *Here comes your mummy now.* **2** the dead body of a person or animal which has been kept by rubbing it with special oils and covering it in cloth

mumps /mʌmps/ noun [U] an infectious disease, especially of children, that causes the neck to swell: *to have/catch (the) mumps*

munch /mʌntʃ/ verb [I,T] munch (on sth) to bite and eat sth noisily: *He sat there munching (on) an apple.*

mundane /mʌn'deɪn/ adj ordinary; not interesting or exciting: *a mundane job*

municipal /mjuː'nɪsɪpl/ adj connected with a town or city that has its own local government: *municipal buildings* (= the town hall, public library, etc)

munitions /mjuː'nɪʃnz/ noun [pl] military supplies, especially bombs and guns

mural /'mjʊərəl/ noun [C] a large picture painted on a wall

★**murder** /'mɜːdə/ noun **1** [C,U] the crime of killing a person illegally and on purpose: *to commit murder* • *a vicious murder* • *the murder victim/weapon* •► Look at **manslaughter. 2** [U] (*informal*) a very difficult or unpleasant experience: *It's murder trying to work when it's as hot as this.*

IDIOM **get away with murder** to do whatever you want without being stopped or punished: *He lets his students get away with murder.* –murder verb [I,T] •► Look at the note at **kill.** –murderer noun [C]

murderous /'mɜːdərəs/ adj intending or likely to murder

murky /'mɜːki/ adj dark and unpleasant or dirty: *The water in the river looked very*

musical instruments

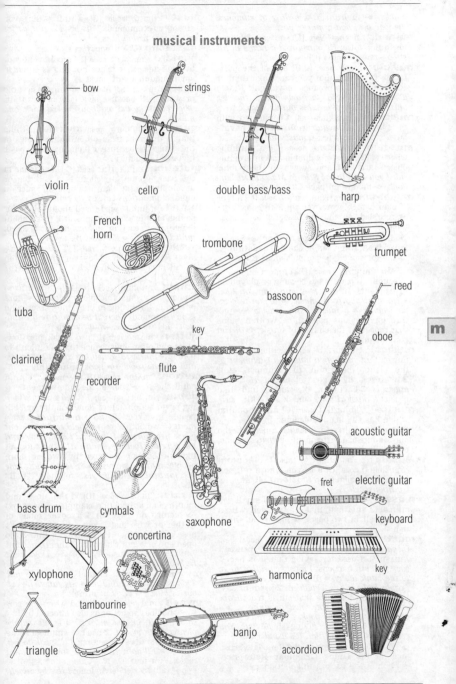

m

murky. ● (*figurative*) *According to rumours, the new boss had a murky past.*

murmur /'mɜːmə/ **verb** [I,T] to say sth in a low quiet voice: *He murmured a name in his sleep.* —**murmur noun** [C]

★**muscle** /'mʌsl/ **noun** [C,U] one of the parts inside your body that you can make tight or relax in order to produce movement: *Riding a bicycle is good for developing the leg muscles.* ● *Lifting weights builds muscle.*

muscular /'mʌskjələ/ **adj 1** connected with the muscles: *muscular pain/tissue* **2** having large strong muscles: *a muscular body*

★**museum** /mju'zɪəm/ **noun** [C] a building where collections of valuable and interesting objects are kept and shown to the public: *Have you been to the Science Museum in London?* ●➤ picture on page C8

mushroom /'mʌʃrʊm; -ruːm/ **noun** [C] a type of plant which grows very quickly, has a flat or rounded top and can be eaten as a vegetable

➤ A mushroom is a type of **fungus**. Some, but not all, **fungi** can be eaten. **Toadstool** is name for some types of poisonous fungi.

★**music** /'mjuːzɪk/ **noun** [U] **1** an arrangement of sounds in patterns to be sung or played on instruments: *What sort of music do you like?* ● *classical/pop/rock music* ● *to write/compose music* ● *a music lesson/teacher* ●➤ picture on previous page **2** the written signs that represent the sounds of music: *Can you read music?*

★**musical¹** /'mjuːzɪkl/ **adj 1** connected with music: *Can you play a musical instrument (=* the piano, the violin, the trumpet, etc*)?* **2** interested in or good at music: *He's very musical.* **3** having a pleasant sound like music: *a musical voice* —**musically** /-kli/ **adv**

musical² /'mjuːzɪkl/ **noun** [C] a play or film which has singing and dancing in it

★**musician** /mju'zɪʃn/ **noun** [C] a person who plays a musical instrument or writes music, especially as a job

★**Muslim** /'mʊzlɪm/ (also **Moslem** /'mɒzləm/) **noun** [C] a person whose religion is Islam —**Muslim** (also **Moslem**) **adj**: *Muslim traditions/beliefs*

mussel /'mʌsl/ **noun** [C] a type of small sea animal (a **shellfish**) that can be eaten, with a black shell in two parts ●➤ picture at **shellfish**

★**must¹** /məst/; *strong form* mʌst/ **modal verb** (*negative* **must not**; *short form* **mustn't** /'mʌsnt/) **1** used for saying that it is necessary that sth happens: *I must remember to go to the bank today.* ● *You mustn't take photographs in here. It's forbidden.* **2** used for saying that you feel sure that sth is true: *Have something to eat. You must be hungry.* ● *I can't find my cheque book. I must have left it at home.* **3** used for giving sb advice: *You really must see that film. It's wonderful.*

➤ For more information about modal verbs, look at the **Quick Grammar Reference** section at the back of this dictionary.

must² /məst/ **noun** [C] a thing that you strongly recommend: *This book is a must for all science fiction fans.*

mustache (*US*) = **MOUSTACHE**

mustard /'mʌstəd/ **noun** [U] a cold yellow or brown sauce that tastes hot and is eaten in small amounts with meat

musty /'mʌsti/ **adj** having an unpleasant old or wet smell because of a lack of fresh air: *The rooms in the old house were dark and musty.*

mutant /'mjuːtənt/ **noun** [C] a living thing that is different from other living things of the same type because of a change in its basic (genetic) structure

mutation /mju'teɪʃn/ **noun** [C,U] a change in the basic (genetic) structure of a living or developing thing; an example of such a change: *mutations caused by radiation*

muted /'mjuːtɪd/ **adj 1** (used about colours or sounds) not bright or loud; soft **2** (used about a feeling or reaction) not strongly expressed: *muted criticism* ● *a muted response*

mutilate /'mjuːtɪleɪt/ **verb** [T] (usually passive) to damage sb's body very badly, often by cutting off parts —**mutilation** /,mjuːtɪ'leɪʃn/ **noun** [C,U]

mutiny /'mjuːtəni/ **noun** [C,U] (*pl* **mutinies**) an act of a group of people, especially sailors or soldiers, refusing to obey the person who is in command: *There'll be a mutiny if conditions don't improve.* —**mutiny verb** [I]

mutter /'mʌtə/ **verb** [I,T] to speak in a low, quiet and often angry voice that is difficult to hear: *He muttered something about being late and left the room.* ●➤ Look at **mumble**.

mutton /'mʌtn/ **noun** [U] the meat from an adult sheep ●➤ Look at the note at **meat**.

mutual /'mjuːtʃuəl/ **adj 1** (used about a feeling or an action) felt or done equally by both people involved: *We have **a mutual agreement** (=* we both agree*) to help each other out when necessary.* ● *I just can't stand her and I'm sure **the feeling is mutual** (=* she doesn't like me either*).* **2** shared by two or more people: *mutual interests* ● *It seems that Jane is **a mutual friend** of ours.* —**mutually** /-uəli/ **adv**

muzzle /'mʌzl/ **noun** [C] **1** the nose and mouth of an animal (for example a dog or fox) ●➤ picture on page C1 **2** a cover made of leather or wire that is put over an animal's nose and mouth so that it cannot bite **3** the open end of a gun where the bullets come out —**muzzle verb** [T] (usually passive): *Dogs must be kept muzzled.*

★**my** /maɪ/ **determiner** of or belonging to me: *This is my husband, Jim.* ● *My favourite colour is blue.* ●➤ Look at **mine¹**.

★**myself** /maɪ'self/ **pron 1** used when the person who does an action is also affected by it: *I saw myself in the mirror.* ● *I felt rather pleased with myself.* **2** used to emphasize the person who does the action: *I'll speak to her myself.* ● *I'll do it myself (=* if you don't want to do it for me*).*

IDIOM **(all) by myself 1** alone: *I live by myself.*

•➤ Look at the note at **alone**. **2** without help: *I painted the house all by myself.*

mysterious /mɪˈstɪəriəs/ *adj* **1** that you do not understand or cannot explain; strange: *Several people reported seeing mysterious lights in the sky.* **2** (used about a person) keeping sth secret or refusing to explain sth: *They're being very mysterious about where they're going this evening.* –**mysteriously** *adv*

mystery /ˈmɪstri/ *noun* (*pl* **mysteries**) **1** [C] a thing that you cannot understand or explain: *The cause of the accident is a complete mystery.* • *It's a mystery to me what my daughter sees in her boyfriend.* **2** [U] the quality of being strange and secret and full of things that are difficult to explain: *There's a lot of mystery surrounding this case.* **3** [C] a story, film or play in which crimes or strange events are only explained at the end

mystic /ˈmɪstɪk/ *noun* [C] a person who spends his/her life developing his/her spirit and communicating with God or a god

mystical /ˈmɪstɪkl/ (also **mystic** /ˈmɪstɪk/) *adj* connected with the spirit; strange and wonderful: *Watching the sun set over the island was an almost mystical experience.*

mysticism /ˈmɪstɪsɪzəm/ *noun* [U] the belief that you can reach complete truth and knowledge of God or gods by prayer, thought and development of the spirit: *Eastern mysticism*

mystify /ˈmɪstɪfaɪ/ *verb* [T] (*pres part* **mystifying**; *3rd pers sing pres* **mystifies**; *pt, pp* **mystified**) to make sb confused because he/she cannot understand sth: *I was mystified by the strange note he'd left behind.*

myth /mɪθ/ *noun* [C] **1** a story from past times, especially one about gods and men of courage. Myths often explain natural or historical events. **2** an idea or story which many people believe but that does not exist or is false: *The idea that money makes you happy is a myth.*

mythical /ˈmɪθɪkl/ *adj* **1** existing only in myths(1): *mythical beasts/heroes* **2** not real or true; existing only in the imagination

mythology /mɪˈθɒlədʒi/ *noun* [U] very old stories and the beliefs contained in them: *Greek and Roman mythology*

Nn

N, n ¹ /en/ *noun* [C] (*pl* **N's** or **n's**) the fourteenth letter of the English alphabet: *'Nicholas' begins with (an) 'N'.*

N² (*US* **No**) *abbr* north(ern): *N Yorkshire*

nag /næg/ *verb* (**nagging**; **nagged**) **1** [I,T] nag (at) sb to continuously complain to sb about his/her behaviour or to ask him/her to do sth many times: *My parents are always nagging (at) me to work harder.* **2** [T] to worry or irritate sb continuously: *a nagging doubt/headache*

nail /neɪl/ *noun* [C] **1** the thin hard layer that covers the ends of your fingers and toes: *fingernails/toenails* •➤ picture on page C5 **2** a small thin piece of metal that is used for holding pieces of wood together, hanging pictures on, etc: *to hammer in a nail* •➤ picture at **bolt** and **tool** –**nail** *verb* [T]

IDIOM **hit the nail on the head** → **HIT**¹

PHRASAL VERB **nail sb down (to sth)** to make a person say clearly what he/she wants or intends to do: *She says she'll visit us in the summer but I can't nail her down to a definite date.*

'nail brush *noun* [C] a small brush for cleaning your fingernails •➤ picture at **brush**

'nail file *noun* [C] a small metal tool with a rough surface that you use for shaping your nails

'nail polish (*Brit* **'nail varnish**) *noun* [U] a liquid that people paint on their nails to give them colour

naive (also **naïve**) /naɪˈiːv/ *adj* without enough experience of life and too ready to believe or trust other people: *I was too naive to realize what was happening.* • *a naive remark/question/view* •➤ synonym **innocent** –**naively** (also **naïvely**) *adv*: *She naively accepted the first price he offered.* –**naivety** (also **naïvety** /naɪˈiːvəti/) *noun* [U]

naked /ˈneɪkɪd/ *adj* **1** not wearing any clothes: *He came to the door naked except for a towel.* • *naked shoulders/arms* •➤ Look at **bare** and **nude**. **2** (only *before* a noun) (used about sth that is usually covered) not covered: *a naked flame/bulb/light* **3** (only *before* a noun) clearly shown or expressed in a way that is often shocking: *naked aggression/ambition/fear*

IDIOM **the naked eye** the normal power of your eyes without the help of glasses, a machine, etc: *Bacteria are too small to be seen with the naked eye.*

name¹ /neɪm/ *noun* **1** [C] a word or words by which sb/sth is known: *What's your name, please?* • *Do you know the name of this flower?* **2** [sing] an opinion that people have of a person or thing: *That area of London has rather a bad name.* •➤ synonym **reputation** **3** [C] a famous person: *All the big names in show business were invited to the party.*

IDIOMS **by name** using the name of sb/sth: *It's a big school but the head teacher knows all the children by name.*

call sb names → **CALL**¹

in the name of sb; in sb's name for sb/sth; officially belonging to sb: *The contract is in my name.*

in the name of sth used to give a reason or excuse for an action, even when what you are doing might be wrong: *They acted in the name of democracy.*

make a name for yourself; make your name to become well known and respected: *She made a name for herself as a journalist.*

> Your **first name** (*US* often **given name**) is the name your parents choose for you when you are born. In Christian countries this is sometimes called your **Christian name**. Your parents may give you another name after your first name, called your **middle name**, which you rarely use except on formal, official documents where both names are referred to as your **forenames**. **Surname** is the word usually used for your **family name** which you are born with. When a woman marries she may change her surname to be the same as her husband's. Her surname before marriage is then called her **maiden name**.

name² /neɪm/ **verb** [T] **1** name sb/sth (after sb) to give sb/sth a name: *Columbia was named after Christopher Columbus.*

> When you are talking about being known by a particular name **be called** is used: *Their youngest is called Mark.*

2 to say what the name of sb/sth is: *The journalist refused to name the person who had given her the information.* ● *Can you name all the planets?* **3** to state sth exactly: *Name your price – we'll pay it!*

nameless /'neɪmləs/ **adj 1** without a name or with a name that you do not know **2** whose name is kept a secret: *a well-known public figure who shall remain nameless*

namely /'neɪmli/ **adv** (used for giving more detail about what you are saying) that is to say: *There is only one person who can overrule the death sentence, namely the President.*

namesake /'neɪmseɪk/ **noun** [C] a person who has the same name as another

nanny /'næni/ **noun** [C] (*pl* **nannies**) (*Brit*) a woman whose job is to look after a family's children and who usually lives in the family home

nap /næp/ **noun** [C] a short sleep that you have during the day ••► Look at **snooze**. –**nap verb** [I] (**napping; napped**)

nape /neɪp/ **noun** [sing] the back part of your neck

napkin /'næpkɪn/ **noun** [C] a piece of cloth or paper that you use when you are eating to protect your clothes or for cleaning your hands and mouth: *a paper napkin* ••► synonym **serviette**

nappy /'næpi/ **noun** [C] (*pl* **nappies**) (*US* **diaper**) a piece of soft thick cloth or paper that a baby or very young child wears around its bottom and between its legs: *Does his nappy need changing?* ● *disposable nappies* (= that you throw away when they have been used)

narcotic /nɑː'kɒtɪk/ **noun** [C] **1** a powerful illegal drug that affects your mind in a harmful way **2** a substance or drug that relaxes you, stops pain, or makes you sleep –**narcotic adj**

narrate /nə'reɪt/ **verb** [T] (*formal*) to tell a story –**narration** /nə'reɪʃn/ **noun** [C,U]

narrative /'nærətɪv/ **noun** (*formal*) **1** [C] the description of events in a story **2** [U] the process or skill of telling a story

narrator /nə'reɪtə/ **noun** [C] the person who tells a story or explains what is happening in a play, film, etc

★**narrow** /'nærəʊ/ **adj 1** having only a short distance from side to side: *The bridge is too narrow for two cars to pass.* ••► opposite **wide** or **broad 2** not large: *a narrow circle of friends* **3** by a small amount: *That was a very narrow escape. You were lucky.* ● *a narrow defeat/victory* –narrow **verb** [I,T]: *The road narrows in 50 metres.* –**narrowness noun** [U]

PHRASAL VERB **narrow sth down** to make a list of things smaller: *The police have narrowed down their list of suspects to three.*

narrowly /'nærəʊli/ **adv** only by a small amount

narrow-'minded adj not wanting to accept new ideas or the opinions of other people if they are not the same as your own ••► synonym **insular** ••► opposite **broad-minded**

nasal /'neɪzl/ **adj 1** of or for the nose **2** produced partly through the nose: *a nasal voice*

★**nasty** /'nɑːsti/ **adj** (**nastier; nastiest**) very bad or unpleasant: *a nasty accident* ● *I had a nasty feeling he would follow me.* ● *When she was asked to leave she got/turned nasty.* ● *a nasty bend in the road* ● *What's that nasty smell in this cupboard?* –**nastily adv** –**nastiness noun** [U]

nation /'neɪʃn/ **noun** [C] a country or all the people in a country: *a summit of the leaders of seven nations*

★**national**¹ /'næʃnəl/ **adj** connected with all of a country; typical of a particular country: *Here is today's national and international news.* ● *a national newspaper* ••► Look at **international, regional** and **local**. –**nationally adv**

national² /'næʃnəl/ **noun** [C, usually pl] (*formal*) a citizen of a particular country

national 'anthem noun [C] the official song of a country that is played at public events

the National 'Health Service noun [sing] (*abbr* **NHS**) (*Brit*) the system that provides free or cheap medical care for everyone in Britain and that is paid for by taxes ••► Look at **health service**.

National In'surance noun [U] (*abbr* **NI**) (*Brit*) the system of payments that have to be made by employers and employees to the government to help people who are ill, unemployed, old, etc: *to pay National Insurance contributions*

nationalism /'næʃnəlɪzəm/ **noun** [U] **1** the desire of a group of people who share the same race, culture, language, etc to form an independent country **2** a feeling of love or pride for your own country; a feeling that your country is better than any other

nationalist /'næʃnəlɪst/ **noun** [C] a person who wants his/her country or region to become independent: *a Welsh nationalist*

nationalistic /ˌnæʃnə'lɪstɪk/ **adj** having

strong feelings of love for or pride in your own country so that you think it is better than any other ·➤ **Nationalistic** is usually used in a critical way, meaning that a person's feelings of pride are too strong.

★**nationality** /ˌnæʃəˈnæləti/ noun [C,U] (pl **nationalities**) the state of being legally a citizen of a particular nation or country: *to have French nationality* • *students of many nationalities* • *to have **dual nationality*** (= of two countries)

nationalize (also **-ise**) /ˈnæʃnəlaɪz/ verb [T] to put a company or organization under the control of the government ·➤ opposite **privatize** –nationalization (also **nationalisation**) /ˌnæʃnəlaɪˈzeɪʃn/ noun [U]

ˌnational ˈpark noun [C] a large area of beautiful land that is protected by the government so that the public can enjoy it

nationwide /ˌneɪʃnˈwaɪd/ adj, adv over the whole of a country: *The police launched a nationwide hunt for the killer.*

native¹ /ˈneɪtɪv/ adj **1** (only *before* a noun) connected with the place where you were born or where you have always lived: *your native language/country/city* • *native Londoners* **2** (only *before* a noun) connected with the people who originally lived in a country before other people, especially white people, came to live there: *native art/dance* ·➤ Be careful. This sense of **native** is sometimes considered offensive **3** native (to...) (used about an animal or plant) living or growing naturally in a particular place: *This plant is native to South America.* • *a native species/ habitat*

native² /ˈneɪtɪv/ noun [C] **1** a person who was born in a particular place: *a native of New York* **2** [usually pl] (*old-fashioned*) the people who were living in Africa, America, etc originally, before the Europeans arrived there ·➤ Be careful. This sense of **native** is now considered offensive.

ˌNative Aˈmerican (also **American Indian**) adj, noun [C] (of) a member of the race of people who were the original inhabitants of America

ˌnative ˈspeaker noun [C] a person who speaks a language as his/her first language and has not learned it as a foreign language: *All our Spanish teachers are native speakers.*

NATO (also **Nato**) /ˈneɪtəʊ/ abbr North Atlantic Treaty Organization; a group of European countries, Canada and the US, who agree to give each other military help if necessary

★**natural** /ˈnætʃrəl/ adj **1** (only *before* a noun) existing in nature; not made or caused by human beings: *I prefer to see animals in their natural habitat rather than in zoos.* • *Britain's natural resources include coal, oil and gas.* • *She died of natural causes* (= of old age or illness). ·➤ opposite **man-made 2** usual or normal: *It's natural to feel nervous before an interview.* ·➤ opposite **unnatural 3** that you had from birth or that was easy for you to learn: *a natural gift for languages*

4 (only *before* a noun) (used about parents or their children) related by blood: *She's his stepmother not his natural mother.*

ˌnatural ˈhistory noun [U] the study of plants and animals

naturalist /ˈnætʃrəlɪst/ noun [C] a person who studies plants and animals

naturalize (also **-ise**) /ˈnætʃrəlaɪz/ verb [T] (usually passive) to make sb a citizen of a country where he/she was not born –naturalization (also **-isation**) /ˌnætʃrəlaɪˈzeɪʃn/ noun [U]

naturally /ˈnætʃrəli/ adv **1** of course; as you would expect: *The team was naturally upset about its defeat.* **2** in a natural way; not forced or made artificially: *naturally wavy hair* • *Vera is naturally a very cheerful person.* **3** in a way that is relaxed and normal: *Don't try and impress people. Just act naturally.*

★**nature** /ˈneɪtʃə/ noun **1** [U] all the plants, animals, etc in the universe and all the things that happen in it that are not made or caused by people: *the forces of nature* (for example volcanoes, hurricanes, etc) • *the wonders/beauties of nature* **2** [C,U] the qualities or character of a person or thing: *He's basically honest by nature.* • *It's not in his nature to be unkind.* • *It's human nature never to be completely satisfied.* **3** [sing] a type or sort of sth: *I'm not very interested in things of that nature.* • *books of a scientific nature* **4** -natured (used to form compound adjectives) having a particular quality or type of character: *a kind-natured man*

IDIOM second nature → SECOND¹

naughty /ˈnɔːti/ adj (*especially Brit*) (used when you are talking to or about a child) badly-behaved; not obeying: *It was very naughty of you to wander off on your own.* –naughtily adv –naughtiness noun [U]

nausea /ˈnɔːziə/ noun [U] the feeling that you are going to vomit (= bring up food from your stomach) ·➤ Look at **sick**(2).

nauseate /ˈnɔːzieɪt/ verb [T] to cause sb to feel sick or disgusted –nauseating adj

nautical /ˈnɔːtɪkl/ adj connected with ships, sailors or sailing

naval /ˈneɪvl/ adj connected with the navy: *a naval base/officer/battle*

navel /ˈneɪvl/ (also *informal* ˈbelly button) noun [C] the small hole or lump in the middle of your stomach

navigable /ˈnævɪɡəbl/ adj (used about a river or narrow area of sea) that boats can sail along

navigate /ˈnævɪɡeɪt/ verb **1** [I] to use a map, etc to find your way to somewhere: *If you drive, I'll navigate.* **2** [T] (*written*) to sail a boat along a river or across a sea –navigator noun [C] –navigation /ˌnævɪˈɡeɪʃn/ noun [U]

★**navy** /ˈneɪvi/ noun [C] (pl **navies**) the part of a country's armed forces that fights at sea in times of war: *to join the navy* • *Their son is in the Navy.* ·➤ When it is used in the singular **Navy** can take either a singular or a plural verb: *The Navy is/are introducing a*

n

new warship this year. Look at **army**, **air force** and **merchant navy**. ⇥ adjective **naval**

ˌnavy ˈblue (also **navy**) adj, noun [U] (of) a very dark blue colour

NB (also **nb**) /ˌen ˈbiː/ abbr (used before a written note) take special notice of: *NB There is an extra charge for reservations*

NE abbr north-east: *NE Scotland*

★**near¹** /nɪə/ adj, adv, prep **1** not far away in time or distance; close: *Let's walk to the library. It's quite near.* ● *We're hoping to move to Wales in the near future* (= very soon). ● *Where's the nearest Post Office?* ● *The day of the interview was getting nearer.*

> **Close** and **near** are often the same in meaning but in some phrases only one of them may be used: *a close friend/relative* ● *the near future* ● *a close contest.* Look at the note at **next**.

2 near- (used to form compound adjectives) almost: *a near-perfect performance*

IDIOMS **close/dear/near to sb's heart → HEART**

or near(est) offer; ono (used when you are selling sth or an amount that is less than but near the amount that you have asked for: *Motorbike for sale. £750 ono.*

a near miss a situation where sth nearly hits you or where sth bad nearly happens: *The bullet flew past his ear. It was a very near miss.*

nowhere near far from: *We've sold nowhere near enough tickets to make a profit.*

near² /nɪə/ verb [T,I] to get closer to sth in time or distance: *At last we were nearing the end of the project.*

nearby /ˌnɪəˈbaɪ/ adj, adv not far away in distance: *A new restaurant has opened nearby.* ● *We went out to a nearby restaurant.*

> Notice that **nearby** as an adjective is only used before the noun. **Near** cannot be used before a noun in this way: *We went out to a nearby restaurant.* ● *The restaurant we went to is quite near.*

★**nearly** /ˈnɪəli/ adv almost; not completely or exactly: *It's nearly five years since I've seen him.* ● *Linda was so badly hurt she very nearly died.* ● *It's not far now. We're nearly there.*

IDIOM **not nearly** much less than; not at all: *It's not nearly as warm as it was yesterday.*

ˌnear-ˈsighted (*US*) = **SHORT-SIGHTED**(1)

neat /niːt/ adj **1** arranged or done carefully; tidy and in order: *Please keep your room neat and tidy.* ● *neat rows of figures* **2** (used about a person) liking to keep things tidy and in order: *The new secretary was very neat and efficient.* **3** simple but clever: *a neat solution/explanation/idea/trick* **4** (*US spoken*) good; nice: *That's a really neat car!* **5** (*US* **straight**) (used about an alcoholic drink) on its own, without ice, water or any other liquid: *a neat whisky* –**neatly** adv: *neatly folded clothes* –**neatness** noun [U]

★**necessarily** /ˈnesəsərəli; ˌnesəˈserəli/ adv used to say that sth cannot be avoided or has

to happen: *The number of tickets available is necessarily limited.*

IDIOM **not necessarily** used to say that sth might be true but is not definitely or always true

★**necessary** /ˈnesəsəri/ adj necessary (for sb/sth) (to do sth) that is needed for a purpose or a reason: *A good diet is necessary for a healthy life.* ● *It's not necessary for you all to come.* ● *If necessary I can take you to work that day.* ⇥ opposite **unnecessary**

necessitate /nəˈsesɪteɪt/ verb [T] (*formal*) to make sth necessary

necessity /nəˈsesəti/ noun (*pl* **necessities**) **1** [U] necessity (for sth/to do sth) the need for sth; the fact that sth must be done or must happen: *Is there any necessity for change?* ● *There's no necessity to write every single name down.* ● *They sold the car out of necessity* (= because they had to). **2** [C] something that you must have: *Clean water is an absolute necessity.*

★**neck** /nek/ noun **1** [C] the part of your body that joins your head to your shoulders: *She wrapped a scarf around her neck.* ● *Giraffes have long necks.* ⇥ picture on page C5 **2** [C] the part of a piece of clothing that goes round your neck: *a polo-neck/V-neck sweater* ● *The neck on this shirt is too tight.* ⇥ picture on page C6 **3** [C] the long narrow part of sth: *the neck of a bottle* **4** **-necked** (used to form compound adjectives) having the type of neck mentioned: *a round-necked sweater*

IDIOMS **by the scruff (of the/your neck) → SCRUFF**

neck and neck (with sb/sth) equal or level with sb in a race or competition

up to your neck in sth having a lot of sth to deal with: *We're up to our necks in work at the moment.*

necklace /ˈnekləs/ noun [C] a piece of jewellery that you wear around your neck ⇥ picture at **jewellery**

necktie /ˈnektaɪ/ (*US*) = **TIE¹**(1)

née /neɪ/ adj used in front of the family name that a woman had before she got married: *Louise Mitchell, née Greenan* ⇥ Look at **maiden name**.

★**need¹** /niːd/ verb [T] (not usually used in the continuous tenses) **1** need sb/sth (for sth/to do sth) if you need sth, you want it or must have it: *All living things need water.* ● *I need a new film for my camera.* ● *Does Roshni need any help?* ● *I need to find a doctor.* ● *I need you to go to the shop for me.* **2** to have to; to be obliged to: *Do we need to buy the tickets in advance?* ● *I need to ask some advice.* ● *You didn't need to bring any food but it was very kind of you.*

> Note that the question form of the main verb **need** is **do I need?**, etc and the past tense is **needed** (question form **did you need?**, etc; negative **didn't need**).

3 need (sth) doing if sth needs doing, it is necessary or must be done: *This jumper needs washing.* ● *He needed his eyes testing.*

> Although this verb is not usually used in the continuous tenses, it is common to see the present participle (= -*ing* form): *Patients needing emergency treatment will go to the top of the waiting list.*

★**need²** /niːd/ **modal verb**

> present tense **need** in all persons; negative **need not** (**needn't**), question form **need I?**, etc

(not used in the continuous tenses; used mainly in questions or negative sentences after *if* and *whether*, or with words like *hardly, only, never*) to have to; to be obliged to: *Need we pay the whole amount now?* ● *You needn't come to the meeting if you're too busy.* ● *I **hardly** need remind you* (= you already know) *that this is very serious.*

> When talking about the past, **needn't have** with a past participle shows that you *did* something but discovered after doing it that it was *not* necessary: *I needn't have gone to the hospital* (= I went but it wasn't necessary). **Didn't need to** with an infinitive usually means that you did *not* do sth because you *already* knew that it was not necessary: *I didn't need to go to the hospital* (= I didn't go because it wasn't necessary). For more information about modal verbs, look at the **Quick Grammar Reference** section at the back of this dictionary.

need³ /niːd/ **noun 1** [U,sing] **need (for sth); need (for sb/sth) to do sth** a situation in which you must have or do sth: *We are all in need of a rest.* ● *There is a growing need for new books in schools.* ● *There's no need for you to come if you don't want to.* ● *Do phone me if you feel the need to talk to someone.* **2** [C, usually pl] the things that you must have: *He doesn't earn enough to pay for his basic needs.* ● *Parents must consider their children's emotional as well as their physical needs.* **3** [U] the state of not having enough food, money or support: *a campaign to help families in need*

★**needle** /ˈniːdl/ **noun** [C] **1** a small thin piece of metal with a point at one end and a hole (an eye) at the other that is used for sewing: *to thread a needle with cotton* •► Look at **pins and needles. 2** (also **knitting needle**) one of two long thin pieces of metal or plastic with a point at one end that are used for knitting •► picture at **knit 3** the sharp metal part of a device (a syringe) that is used for putting drugs into sb's body and for taking blood out **4** a thin metal part on a scientific instrument that moves to point to the correct measurement or direction **5** the thin, hard pointed leaf of certain trees that stay green all year: *pine needles* •► picture on page C2

needless /ˈniːdləs/ **adj** that is not necessary and that you can easily avoid •► Look at **unnecessary,** it has a different meaning. –**needlessly adv**

needlework /ˈniːdlwɜːk/ **noun** [U] sth that you sew by hand, especially for decoration

needy /ˈniːdi/ **adj 1** not having enough money, food, clothes, etc **2 the needy noun** [pl] people who do not have enough money, food, clothes, etc

neg abbr negative

★**negative¹** /ˈnegətɪv/ **adj 1** bad or harmful: *The effects of the new rule have been rather negative.* **2** only thinking about the bad qualities of sb/sth: *I'm feeling very negative about my job – in fact I'm thinking about leaving.* ● *If you go into the match with a negative attitude, you'll never win.* **3** (used about a word, phrase or sentence) meaning 'no' or 'not': *a negative sentence* ● *His reply was negative/He gave a negative reply* (= he said 'no'). •► opposite **affirmative 4** (used about a medical or scientific test) showing that sth has not happened or has not been found: *The results of the pregnancy test were negative.* **5** (used about a number) less than zero •► opposite for senses 1, 2, 4 and 5 **positive** –**negatively adv**

negative² /ˈnegətɪv/ **noun** [C] **1** a word, phrase or sentence that says or means 'no' or 'not': *Aisha answered in the negative* (= she said no). ● *'Never', neither' and 'nobody' are all negatives.* •► opposite **affirmative 2** a piece of film from which we can make a photograph. The light areas of a negative are dark on the final photograph and the dark areas are light.

neglect /nɪˈɡlekt/ **verb 1** [T] to give too little or no attention or care to sb/sth: *Don't neglect your health.* ● *The old house had stood neglected for years.* **2 neglect to do sth** to fail or forget to do sth: *He neglected to mention that he had spent time in prison.* –**neglect noun** [U]: *The garden was like a jungle after years of neglect.* –**neglected adj**: *neglected children*

negligence /ˈneglɪdʒəns/ **noun** [U] not being careful enough; lack of care: *The accident was a result of negligence.* –**negligent** /ˈneglɪdʒənt/ **adj** –**negligently adv**

negligible /ˈneglɪdʒəbl/ **adj** very small and therefore not important

negotiable /nɪˈɡəʊʃiəbl/ **adj** that can be decided or changed by discussion: *The price is not negotiable/non-negotiable.*

negotiate /nɪˈɡəʊʃieɪt/ **verb 1** [I] **negotiate (with sb) (for/about sth)** to talk to sb in order to decide or agree about sth: *The unions are still negotiating with management about this year's pay claim.* **2** [T] to decide or agree sth by talking about it: *to negotiate an agreement/a deal/a settlement* **3** [T] to get over, past or through sth difficult: *To escape, prisoners would have to negotiate a five-metre wall.* –**negotiator noun** [C]

negotiation /nɪˌɡəʊʃiˈeɪʃn/ **noun** [pl,U] discussions at which people try to decide or agree sth: *to enter into/break off negotiations* ● *The pay rise is still under negotiation.*

neigh /neɪ/ **noun** [C] the long high sound that a horse makes –**neigh verb** [I]

★**neighbour** (*US* **neighbor**) /ˈneɪbə/ **noun** [C] **1** a person who lives near you: *My neighbours are very friendly.* ● *our next-door neighbours* **2** a person or thing that is near

n

or next to another: *Britain's nearest neighbour is France.* ● *Try not to look at what your neighbour is writing.*

neighbourhood (*US* **neighborhood**) /'neɪbəhʊd/ noun [C] a particular part of a town and the people who live there: *a friendly neighbourhood*

neighbouring (*US* **neighboring**) /'neɪbərɪŋ/ adj (only *before* a noun) near or next to: *Farmers from neighbouring villages come into town each week for the market.*

neighbourly (*US* **neighborly**) /'neɪbəli/ adj friendly and helpful

★**neither** /'naɪðə; 'niːðə/ determiner, pron, adv **1** (used about two people or things) not one and not the other: *Neither team played very well.* ● *Neither of the teams played very well.* ● *'Would you like tea or juice?' 'Neither, thank you. I'm not thirsty.'*

➤ Notice that **neither** is followed by a singular noun and verb: *Neither day was suitable.* The noun or pronoun that follows **neither of** is in the plural but the verb may be singular or plural: *Neither of the days is/are suitable.*

2 also not; not either: *I don't eat meat and neither does Carlos.* ● *'I don't like fish.' 'Neither do I.'* ● (*informal*) *'I don't like fish.' 'Me neither.'*

➤ In this sense **nor** can be used in the same way: *'I don't like fish.' 'Nor do I.'* Notice that when you use **not...either** the order of words is different: *I don't eat meat and Carlos doesn't either.* ● *'I haven't seen that film.' 'I haven't either.'*

3 neither...nor not...and not: *Neither Carlos nor I eat meat.*

➤ **Neither...nor** can be used with a singular or a plural verb: *Neither Stella nor Meena was/were at the meeting.*

neon /'niːɒn/ noun [U] (*symbol* **Ne**) a type of gas that is used for making bright lights and signs

★**nephew** /'nefjuː; 'nevjuː/ noun [C] the son of your brother or sister, or the son of your husband's or wife's brother or sister ●➤ Look at **niece**.

Neptune /'neptjuːn/ noun [sing] the planet that is eighth in order from the sun

nerd /nɜːd/ noun [C] a person who is not fashionable and has a boring hobby –**nerdy** adj

★**nerve** /nɜːv/ noun **1** [C] one of the long thin threads in your body that carry feelings or other messages to and from your brain **2 nerves** [pl] worried, nervous feelings: *Breathing deeply should help to calm/steady your nerves.* ● *I was a bag of nerves before my interview.* **3** [U] the courage that you need to do sth difficult or dangerous: *Racing drivers need a lot of nerve.* ● *He didn't have the nerve to ask Maria to go out with him.* ● *Some pilots lose their nerve and can't fly any more.* **4** [sing] a way of behaving that people think is not acceptable: *You've got a*

nerve, calling me lazy!

IDIOM **get on sb's nerves** (*informal*) to annoy sb or make sb angry

'nerve-racking adj making you very nervous or worried

★**nervous** /'nɜːvəs/ adj **1 nervous (about/of sth/doing sth)** worried or afraid: *I'm a bit nervous about travelling on my own.* ● *I always get nervous just before a match.* ● *a nervous laugh/smile/voice* ● *She was nervous of giving the wrong answer.* **2** connected with the nerves of the body: *a nervous disorder* –**nervously** adv –**nervousness** noun [U]

,nervous 'breakdown (also **breakdown**) noun [C] a time when sb suddenly becomes so unhappy that he/she cannot continue living and working normally: *to have a nervous breakdown*

the 'nervous system noun [C] your brain and all the nerves in your body

★**nest** /nest/ noun [C] **1** a structure that a bird builds to keep its eggs and babies in ●➤ picture on page C1 **2** the home of certain animals or insects: *a wasps' nest* –**nest** verb [I]

nestle /'nesl/ verb [I,T] to be or go into a position where you are comfortable, protected or hidden: *The baby nestled her head on her mother's shoulder.*

★**net¹** /net/ noun **1** [U] material that has large, often square, spaces between the threads **2** [C] a piece of net that is used for a particular purpose: *a tennis/fishing/mosquito net* ●➤ Look at **safety net**. **3 the net** [sing] = **THE INTERNET**

IDIOM **surf the net** → **SURF²**

net² /net/ verb [T] (**netting**; **netted**) **1** to catch sth with a net; to kick a ball into a net **2** to gain sth as a profit

net³ (also **nett**) /net/ adj **net (of sth)** (used about a number or amount) from which nothing more needs to be taken away: *I earn about £15000 net* (= after tax, etc has been paid) ● *The net weight of the jam is 350g* (= not including the jar). ● *a net profit* ●➤ opposite **gross**

netball /'netbɔːl/ noun [U] a game that is played by two teams of seven players, usually women. Players score by throwing the ball through a high net hanging from a ring.

netting /'netɪŋ/ noun [U] material that is made of long pieces of string, thread, wire, etc that are tied together with spaces between them

nettle /'netl/ noun [C] a wild plant with hairy leaves. Some nettles make your skin red and painful if you touch them.

★**network** /'netwɜːk/ noun [C] **1** a system of roads, railway lines, nerves, etc that are connected to each other: *an underground railway network* **2** a group of people or companies that work closely together: *We have a network of agents who sell our goods all over the country.* **3** a number of computers that are connected together so that information can be shared **4** a group of television or radio companies that are connected and that send out the same programmes at the same time in different parts of a country

neurosis /njʊəˈrəʊsɪs/ **noun** [C] (*pl* **neuroses** /-əʊsiːz/) (*medical*) a mental illness that causes strong feelings of fear and worry

neurotic /njʊəˈrɒtɪk/ **adj 1** worried about things in a way that is not normal **2** (*medical*) suffering from a neurosis

neuter¹ /ˈnjuːtə/ **adj** (used about a word in some languages) not masculine or feminine according to the rules of grammar

neuter² /ˈnjuːtə/ **verb** [T] to remove the sexual parts of an animal •➤ Look at **castrate**.

neutral¹ /ˈnjuːtrəl/ **adj 1** not supporting or belonging to either side in an argument, war, etc: *I don't take sides when my brothers argue – I **remain neutral**.* • *The two sides agreed to meet on neutral ground.* **2** having or showing no strong qualities, emotions or colour: *neutral colours* • *a neutral tone of voice*

neutral² /ˈnjuːtrəl; ˈnuːtrəl/ **noun** [U] the position of part of a vehicle (**the gears**), when no power is sent from the engine to the wheels

neutrality /njuːˈtræləti/ **noun** [U] the state of not supporting either side in an argument, war, etc

neutralize (also **-ise**) /njuːˈtrəlaɪz/ **verb** [T] to take away the effect of sth: *to neutralize a threat*

★**never** /ˈnevə/ **adv 1** at no time; not ever: *I've never been to Portugal.* • *He never ever eats meat.* • (*formal*) *Never before has such a high standard been achieved.* **2** used for emphasizing a negative statement: *I never realized she was so unhappy.* • *Roy never so much as looked at us* (= he didn't even look at us). • *'I got the job!' 'Never!'* (= expressing surprise)'
IDIOMS **never mind** → **MIND²**
you never know → **KNOW¹**

nevertheless /ˌnevəðəˈles/ **adv**, **conj** (*formal*) in spite of that: *It was a cold, rainy day. Nevertheless, more people came than we had expected.* •➤ synonym **nonetheless**

★**new** /njuː/ **adj 1** that has recently been built, made, discovered, etc: *a new design/film/hospital* • *a new method of treating mental illness* • *new evidence* •➤ opposite **old 2** different or changed from what was before: *I've just started reading a new book.* • *to make new friends* •➤ opposite **old 3** new (to sb) that you have not seen, learnt, etc before: *This type of machine is new to me.* • *to learn a new language* **4** new (to sth) having just started being or doing sth: *a new parent* • *She's new to the job and needs a lot of help.* • *a new member of the club* –**newness noun** [U]
IDIOM **break fresh/new ground** → **GROUND¹**

'New Age adj connected with a way of life that rejects modern Western values and is based on spiritual ideas and beliefs: *a New Age festival* • *New Age travellers* (= people in Britain who reject the values of modern society and travel from place to place living in their vehicles)

newborn /ˈnjuːbɔːn/ **adj** (used about a baby) that has been born very recently

newcomer /ˈnjuːkʌmə/ **noun** [C] a person who has just arrived in a place

newfangled /ˌnjuːˈfæŋgld/ **adj** new or modern in a way that the speaker does not like

newly /ˈnjuːli/ **adv** (usually before a past participle) recently: *the newly appointed Minister of Health*

'newly-wed noun [C,usually pl] a person who has recently got married

★**news** /njuːz/ **noun 1** [U] information about sth that has happened recently: *Write and tell me all your news.* • *Have you had any news from Nadia recently?* • *That's news to me* (= I didn't know that). • *News is coming in of a plane crash in Thailand.*

➤ **News** is an uncountable noun. If we are talking about an individual item we must say 'a piece of news': *We had two pieces of good news yesterday.*

2 the news [sing] a regular programme giving the latest news on the radio or television: *We always watch the nine o'clock news on television.* • *I heard about the accident **on the news**.*

IDIOM **break the news (to sb)** to be the first to tell sb about sth important that has happened

newsagent /ˈnjuːzeɪdʒənt/ (*US* **newsdealer**) **noun 1** [C] a person who owns or works in a shop that sells newspapers and magazines, etc **2** **the newsagent's** [sing] a shop that sells newspapers, magazines, etc

newsletter /ˈnjuːzletə/ **noun** [C] a printed report about a club or organization that is sent regularly to members and other people who may be interested

★**newspaper** /ˈnjuːzpeɪpə/ **noun 1** (also **paper**) [C] large folded pieces of paper printed with news, advertisements and articles on various subjects. Newspapers are printed and sold either every day or every week: *a daily/weekly/Sunday newspaper* • *a newspaper article* • *I read about it **in the newspaper**.* **2** (also **paper**) [C] an organization that produces a newspaper: *Which newspaper does he work for?* **3** [U] the paper on which newspapers are printed: *We wrapped the plates in newspaper so they would not get damaged.*

➤ **Journalists** and **reporters** collect news for newspapers. The **editor** decides what is printed. **Quality** newspapers deal with the news in a serious way. **Tabloids** are popular papers and are smaller in size with many more pictures and stories about famous people.

newsreader /ˈnjuːzriːdə/ (also **newscaster** /ˈnjuːzkɑːstə/) **noun** [C] a person who reads the news on the radio or television

'news-stand (*US*) = **BOOKSTALL**

new 'year (also **New Year**) **noun** [sing] the first few days of January: *Happy New Year!* • *We will get in touch in the new year.* • *New Year's Eve* (= 31 December) • *New Year's Day* (= 1 January)

★**next** /nekst/ **adj**, **adv 1** (usually with *the*) coming immediately after sth in order, space or time; closest: *The next bus leaves in twenty minutes.* • *The next name on the list is Paulo.*

> Compare **nearest** and **next**. **The next** means 'the following' in a series of events or places: *When is your next appointment?* • *Turn left at the next traffic lights.* **The nearest** means 'the closest' in time or place: *Where's the nearest supermarket?*

2 (used without *the* before days of the week, months, seasons, years, etc) the one immediately following the present one: *See you again next Monday.* • *Let's go camping next weekend.* • *next summer/next year/next Christmas* **3** after this or after that; then: *I wonder what will happen next.* • *I know Joe arrived first, but who came next?* • *It was ten years until I next saw her.* **4 the next noun** [sing] the person or thing that is next: *If we miss this train we'll have to wait two hours for the next.*

IDIOM last/next but one, two etc → LAST¹

next 'door adj, adv in or into the next house or building: *our **next-door neighbours*** • *Who lives next door?* • *The school is next door to an old people's home.*

next of 'kin noun [C] (*pl* **next of kin**) your closest living relative or relatives: *My husband is my next of kin.*

★**next to prep 1** at the side of sb/sth; beside: *He sat down next to Gita.* • *There's a public telephone next to the bus stop.* **2** in a position after sth: *Next to English my favourite subject is Maths.*

IDIOM next to nothing almost nothing: *We took plenty of money but we've got next to nothing left.*

NHS /ˌen eɪtʃ 'es/ **abbr** (*Brit*) National Health Service

nibble /'nɪbl/ **verb** [I,T] to eat sth by taking small bites: *The bread had been nibbled by mice.* –**nibble noun** [C]

★**nice** /naɪs/ **adj 1** pleasant, enjoyable or attractive: *a nice place/feeling/smile* • *I'm not eating this – it doesn't taste very nice.* • *It would be nice to spend more time at home.* • *'Hi, I'm Tony.' 'I'm Ray – nice to meet you.'* **2** nice (to sb); nice (of sb) (to do sth); nice (about sth) kind; friendly: *What a nice girl!* • *Everyone was very nice to me when I felt ill.* • *It was really nice of Donna to help us.* **3** (*informal*) used before adjectives and adverbs to emphasize how pleasant or suitable sth is: *It's nice and warm by the fire.* • *a nice long chat* –**nicely adv** –**niceness noun** [U]

niche /niːtʃ; niːʃ/ **noun** [C] **1** a job, position, etc that is suitable for you: *to find your niche in life* **2** (in business) an opportunity to sell a particular product to a particular group of people **3** a place in a wall that is further back, where a statue, etc can be put

nick¹ /nɪk/ **noun** [C] a small cut in sth
IDIOMS in good/bad nick (*Brit slang*) in a good/bad state or condition
in the nick of time only just in time

nick² /nɪk/ **verb** [T] **1** to make a very small cut in sb/sth **2** (*Brit slang*) to arrest sb **3** (*Brit slang*) to steal sth

nickel /'nɪkl/ **noun 1** [U] (*symbol* **Ni**) a hard silver-white metal that is often mixed with other metals **2** [C] an American or Canadian coin that is worth five cents

nickname /'nɪkneɪm/ **noun** [C] an informal name that is used instead of your real name, usually by your family or friends –**nickname verb** [T]

nicotine /'nɪkətiːn/ **noun** [U] the poisonous chemical substance in tobacco

★**niece** /niːs/ **noun** [C] the daughter of your brother or sister; the daughter of your husband's or wife's brother or sister ••➤ Look at **nephew**.

niggle /'nɪgl/ **verb 1** [I,T] niggle (at) sb to annoy or worry sb: *His untidy habits really niggled her.* **2** [I] niggle (about/over sth) to complain or argue about things that are not important

niggling /'nɪglɪŋ/ **adj** not very serious (but that does not go away): *niggling doubts* • *a niggling injury*

★**night** /naɪt/ **noun** [C,U] **1** the part of the day when it is dark and when most people sleep: *I had a strange dream last night.* • *The baby cried all night.* • *It's a long way home. Why don't you stay the night?* • *We will be away for a few nights.* **2** the time between late afternoon and when you go to bed: *Let's go out on Saturday night.* • *He doesn't get home until 8 o'clock at night.* • *I went out with Kate the other night* (= a few nights ago).

> Note the use of different prepositions with **night**. **At** is most common: *I'm not allowed out after 11 o'clock at night.* **By** is used about something that you usually do in the night-time: *These animals sleep by day and hunt by night.* **In/during** the night is usually used for the night that has just passed: *I woke up twice in the night.* **On** is used when you are talking about one particular night: *On the night of Saturday 30 June.* **Tonight** means the night or evening of today: *Where are you staying tonight?*

IDIOMS an early/a late night an evening when you go to bed earlier/later than usual
a night out an evening that you spend out of the house enjoying yourself
in the/at dead of night → DEAD²
good night said late in the evening, before you go home or before you go to sleep

nightclub /'naɪtklʌb/ **noun** [C] = CLUB¹(2)

nightdress /'naɪtdres/ (also *informal* **nightie** /'naɪti/) **noun** [C] a loose dress that a girl or woman wears in bed

nightingale /'naɪtɪŋgeɪl/ **noun** [C] a small brown bird that has a beautiful song

nightlife /'naɪtlaɪf/ **noun** [U] the entertainment that is available in the evenings in a particular place: *It's a small town with very little nightlife.*

nightly /'naɪtli/ **adj, adv** happening every night: *a nightly news bulletin*

nightmare /'naɪtmeə/ **noun** [C] **1** a frightening or unpleasant dream: *I had a terrible nightmare about being stuck in a lift last* *night.* **2** (*informal*) an experience that is very unpleasant or frightening: *Travelling in the rush hour can be a real nightmare.*

'night-time noun [U] the time when it is dark

nightwatchman /naɪt'wɒtʃmən/ **noun** [C] (*pl* **nightwatchmen** /-mən/) a person who guards a building at night

nil /nɪl/ **noun** [U] the number 0 (especially as the score in some games): *We won two-nil/by two goals to nil.* ••➤ Look at the note at **zero**.

nimble /'nɪmbl/ **adj** able to move quickly and lightly –**nimbly** /'nɪmbli/ **adv**

★**nine** /naɪn/ **number** 9

➤ For examples of how to use numbers in sentences, look at **six**.

IDIOM **nine to five** the hours that you work in most offices: *a nine-to-five job*

★**nineteen** /ˌnaɪn'tiːn/ **number** 19

➤ For examples of how to use numbers in sentences, look at **six**.

nineteenth /ˌnaɪn'tiːnθ/ **pron, determiner, adv** 19th ••➤ Look at the examples at **sixth**.

ninetieth /'naɪntiəθ/ **1 pron, determiner, adv** 90th ••➤ Look at the examples at **sixth**. **2 pron, noun** [C] one of ninety equal parts of sth

★**ninety** /'naɪnti/ **number** 90

➤ For examples of how to use numbers in sentences, look at **sixty**.

ninth[1] /naɪnθ/ **noun** [C] the fraction ⅑; one of nine equal parts of sth ••➤ Look at the examples at **sixth**.

ninth[2] /naɪnθ/ **pron, determiner, adv** 9th ••➤ Look at the examples at sixth.

nip /nɪp/ **verb** (**nipping; nipped**) **1** [I,T] to give sb/sth a quick bite or to quickly squeeze a piece of sb's skin between your thumb and finger: *She nipped him on the arm.* **2** [I] (*Brit spoken*) to go somewhere quickly and/or for a short time –**nip noun** [C]

IDIOM **nip sth in the bud** to stop sth bad before it develops or gets worse

nipple /'nɪpl/ **noun** [C] either of the two small dark circles on either side of your chest. A baby can suck milk from his/her mother's breast through the nipples.

nit /nɪt/ **noun** [C] the egg of a small insect that lives in the hair of people or animals

'nit-picking adj, noun [U] the habit of finding small mistakes in sb's work or paying too much attention to small, unimportant details

nitrogen /'naɪtrədʒən/ **noun** [U] (*symbol* **N**) a gas that has no colour, taste or smell. Nitrogen forms about 80% of the air around the earth.

the nitty-gritty /ˌnɪti'grɪti/ **noun** [sing] (*spoken*) the most important facts, not the small or unimportant details

★**no**[1] /nəʊ/ **determiner, adv 1** not any; not a: *I have no time to talk now.* ● *No visitors may enter without a ticket.* ● *He's no friend of mine.* ● *Alice is feeling no better this morning.* **2** used for saying that sth is not allowed: *No smoking.* ● *No flash photography.* ● *No parking.*

★**no**[2] /nəʊ/ **interj 1** used for giving a negative reply: *'Are you ready?' 'No, I'm not.'* ● *'Would you like something to eat?' 'No, thank you.'* ••➤ opposite **Yes, please** ● *'Can I borrow the car?' 'No, you can't.'*

➤ You can also use **no** when you want to agree with a negative statement: *'This programme's not very good.' 'No, you're right. It isn't.'*

••➤ opposite **yes 2** used for expressing surprise or shock: *'Mike's had an accident.' 'Oh, no!'*

No[3] (also **no**; *US symbol* #) (*pl* **Nos; nos**) **abbr** number: *No 10 Downing Street* ● *tel no 512364*

nobility /nəʊ'bɪləti/ **noun 1 the nobility** [sing, with sing or pl verb] the group of people who belong to the highest social class and have special titles such as (**Duke**) or (**Duchess**) ••➤ synonym **aristocracy 2** [U] (*formal*) the quality of having courage and honour

noble[1] /'nəʊbl/ **adj 1** honest; full of courage and care for others: *a noble leader* ● *noble ideas/actions* **2** belonging to the highest social class: *a man of noble birth* –**nobly** /'nəʊbli/ **adv**

noble[2] /'nəʊbl/ **noun** [C] (in past times) a person who belonged to the highest social class and had a special title ••➤ A more common word nowadays is a **peer**.

★**nobody**[1] /'nəʊbədi/ (also **no one** /'nəʊ wʌn/) **pron** no person; not anyone: *He screamed but nobody came to help him.* ● *No one else was around.* ● *There was nobody at home.*

➤ **None of**, not **nobody**, must be used before words like *the, his, her, those,* etc or before a pronoun: *None of my friends remembered my birthday.* ● *I've asked all my classmates but none of them are free.*

nobody[2] /'nəʊbədi/ **noun** [C] (*pl* **nobodies**) a person who is not important or famous: *She rose from being a nobody to a superstar.*

nocturnal /nɒk'tɜːnl/ **adj 1** (used about animals and birds) awake and active at night and asleep during the day: *Owls are nocturnal birds.* **2** (*written*) happening in the night: *a nocturnal adventure*

★**nod** /nɒd/ **verb** [I,T] (**nodding; nodded**) to move your head up and down as a way of saying 'yes' or as a sign to sb to do sth: *Everybody at the meeting nodded in agreement.* ● *Nod your head if you understand what I'm saying and shake it if you don't.* ••➤ picture on page S8 –**nod noun** [C]

PHRASAL VERB **nod off** (*informal*) to fall asleep for a short time

,no-'go area noun [sing] a place, especially part of a city, where it is very dangerous to go because there is a lot of violence or crime

★**noise** /nɔɪz/ **noun** [C,U] a sound, especially one that is loud or unpleasant: *Did you hear a noise downstairs?* ● *Try not to make a noise if you come home late.* ● *What an awful noise!* ● *Why is the engine making so much noise?*

n

[I] **intransitive**, a verb which has no object: *He laughed.* [T] **transitive**, a verb which has an object: *He ate an apple.*

noiseless /'nɔɪzləs/ adj making no sound
–**noiselessly** adv

★**noisy** /'nɔɪzi/ adj (**noisier; noisiest**) making a lot of or too much noise; full of noise: *The clock was so noisy that it kept me awake.* • *noisy children/traffic/crowds* • *The classroom was very noisy.* ••➤ Look at the note at **loud.** –**noisily** adv

nomad /'nəʊmæd/ noun [C] a member of a group of people (a tribe) that moves with its animals from place to place –**nomadic** adj

'**no-man's-land** noun [U,sing] an area of land between the borders of two countries or between two armies during a war and which is not controlled by either

nominal /'nɒmɪnl/ adj **1** being sth in name only but not in reality: *the nominal leader of the country* (= sb else is really in control) **2** (used about a price, sum of money, etc) very small; much less than normal: *Because we are friends he only charges me* **a nominal rent.**

nominate /'nɒmɪneɪt/ verb [T] **nominate sb/ sth (for/as sth)** to formally suggest that sb/ sth should be given a job, role, prize, etc: *I would like to nominate Bob Turner as chairman.* • *The novel has been nominated for the Booker prize.* • *You may nominate a representative to speak for you.* –**nomination** /,nɒmɪ'neɪʃn/ noun [C,U]

nominee /,nɒmɪ'niː/ noun [C] a person who is suggested for an important job, role, prize, etc

non- /nɒn/ (used to form compounds) not: *non-biodegradable* • *non-flammable*

,**non-aca'demic** adj connected with technical or practical subjects rather than subjects of interest to the mind

,**non-alco'holic** adj (used about drinks) not containing any alcohol: *non-alcoholic drinks*

nonchalant /'nɒnʃələnt/ adj not feeling or showing interest or excitement about sth –**nonchalance** noun [U] –**nonchalantly** adv

noncommittal /,nɒnkə'mɪtl/ adj not saying or showing exactly what your opinion is or which side of an argument you agree with

nonconformist /,nɒnkən'fɔːmɪst/ noun [C] a person who behaves or thinks differently from most other people in society ••➤ opposite **conformist** –**nonconformism** adj

nondescript /'nɒndɪskrɪpt/ adj not having any interesting or unusual qualities

★**none**[1] /nʌn/ (of a group of three or more): *They gave me a lot of information but none of it was very helpful.* • *I've got four brothers but none of them live/lives nearby.* • *'Have you brought any books to read?' 'No, none.'* • *I went to several shops but none had what I was looking for.*

➤ When we use **none of** with a plural noun, the verb can be singular or plural depending on the sense. If we mean 'not any one of sth', then we use a singular verb to emphasize this: *None of these trains goes to Birmingham.* If we mean 'not any of sth', then

we use a plural verb: *None of the children like spinach.* When we are talking about two people or things we use **neither** not **none**: *Neither of my brothers lives nearby.* Note the difference between **none** and **no. No** must go in front of a noun, but **none** replaces the noun: *I told him that I had* **no money** *left.* • *When he asked me how much money I had left, I told him that I had* **none.**

none[2] /nʌn/ adv

IDIOMS **none the wiser/worse** knowing no more than before; no worse than before: *We talked for a long time but I'm still* **none the wiser.**

none too happy, clean, pleased, etc (*informal*) not very happy, clean, pleased, etc

nonetheless /,nʌnðə'les/ adv (*written*) in spite of this fact: *It won't be easy but they're going to try nonetheless.* ••➤ synonym **nevertheless**

,**non-e'xistent** adj not existing or not available

,**non-'fiction** noun [U] writing that is about real people, events and facts: *You'll find biographies in the non-fiction section of the library.* ••➤ opposite **fiction**

nonplussed /,nɒn'plʌst/ adj confused; not able to understand

,**non-re'newable** adj (used about natural sources of energy such as gas or oil) that cannot be replaced after use

★**nonsense** /'nɒnsns/ noun [U] **1** ideas, statements or beliefs that you think are ridiculous or not true: *Don't* **talk nonsense!** • *It's nonsense to say you aren't good enough to go to university!* **2** silly or unacceptable behaviour: *The head teacher won't stand for any nonsense.*

nonsensical /nɒn'sensɪkl/ adj ridiculous; without meaning

,**non-'smoker** noun [C] a person who does not smoke cigarettes or cigars ••➤ opposite **smoker** –,**non-'smoking** adj: *Would you like a table in the smoking or the non-smoking section?*

,**non-'starter** noun [C] a person, plan or idea that has no chance of success

,**non-'stick** adj (used about a pan, etc) covered with a substance that prevents food from sticking to it

,**non-'stop** adj, adv without a stop or a rest: *a non-stop flight to Bombay* • *He talked non-stop for two hours about his holiday.*

,**non-'violence** noun [U] fighting for political or social change without using force, for example by not obeying laws –**non-violent** adj

noodle /'nuːdl/ noun [C,usually pl] long thin pieces of food made of flour, egg and water that are cooked in boiling water or used in soups

nook /nʊk/ noun [C] a small quiet place or corner (in a house, garden, etc)

IDIOM **every nook and cranny** (*informal*) every part of a place

★**noon** /nuːn/ **noun** [U] 12 o'clock in the middle of the day; midday: *At noon the sun is at its highest point in the sky.* •➤ Look at **midnight**.

ˈno one = NOBODY¹

noose /nuːs/ **noun** [C] a circle that is tied in the end of a rope and that gets smaller as one end of the rope is pulled

★**nor** /nɔː/ **conj, adv 1** neither...nor... and not: *I have neither the time nor the inclination to listen to his complaints again.* **2** (used before a positive verb to agree with sth negative that has just been said) also not; neither: *'I don't like football.' 'Nor do I.'* • *'We haven't been to America.' 'Nor have we.'* •➤ In this sense **neither** can be used in the same way: *'I won't be here tomorrow.' 'Nor/Neither will I.'* **3** (used after a negative statement to add some more information) also not: *Michael never forgot her birthday. Nor their wedding anniversary for that matter.*

norm /nɔːm/ **noun** [C] (often with *the*) a situation or way of behaving that is usual or expected

★**normal¹** /ˈnɔːml/ **adj** typical, usual or ordinary; what you expect: *I'll meet you at the normal time.* • *It's quite normal to feel angry in a situation like this.* •➤ opposite **abnormal**

★**normal²** /ˈnɔːml/ **noun** [U] the usual or average state, level or standard: *temperatures above/below normal* • *Things are **back to normal** at work now.*

normality /nɔːˈmæləti/ (*US* **normalcy** /ˈnɔːmlsi/) **noun** [U] the state of being normal

normalize (also **-ise**) /ˈnɔːməlaɪz/ **verb** [I,T] (*written*) to make sth become normal again or return to how it was before: *The two countries agreed to normalize relations* (= return to a normal, friendly relationship, for example after a disagreement or a war).

★**normally** /ˈnɔːməli/ **adv 1** usually: *I normally leave the house at 8 o'clock.* • *Normally he takes the bus.* **2** in the usual or ordinary way

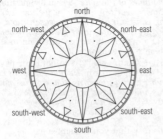

north

north-west

north-east

west

east

south-west

south-east

south

★**north¹** /nɔːθ/ **noun** [sing] (*abbr* **N**) (also **the north**) **1** the direction that is on your left when you watch the sun rise; one of the four main directions that we give names to (the points of the compass): *cold winds from the north* • *Which way is north?* • *I live to the north of* (= further north than) *Belfast.* **2** **the North** the northern part of any country, city, region or the world: *Houses are less expensive in the North of England than in the South.* • *I live in the north of Athens.* •➤ Look at **south**, **east** and **west**.

★**north²** /nɔːθ/ **adj, adv 1** (also **North**) (only before a noun) in the north: *The new offices will be in North London.* • *The north wing of the hospital was destroyed in a fire.* **2** to or towards the north: *We got onto the motorway going north instead of south.* • *The house faces north.* • *Is Leeds north of Manchester?* **3** (used about a wind) coming from the north

northbound /ˈnɔːθbaʊnd/ **adj** travelling or leading towards the north: *northbound traffic*

★**north-ˈeast¹** **noun** [sing] (*abbr* **NE**) (also **the North-East**) the direction or a region halfway between north and east •➤ picture at **north**

★**north-ˈeast²** **adj, adv** in, from or to the north-east of a place or country: *the north-east coast of Australia* • *If you look north-east you can see the sea.*

north-ˈeasterly **adj 1** towards the north-east: *in a north-easterly direction* **2** (used about a wind) coming from the north-east

north-ˈeastern **adj** (only before a noun) connected with the north-east of a place or country

north-ˈeastward(s) **adv** towards the north-east: *Follow the A619 north-eastward.*

northerly /ˈnɔːðəli/ **adj 1** to, towards or in the north: *Keep going in a northerly direction.* **2** (used about a wind) coming from the north

★**northern** (also **Northern**) /ˈnɔːðən/ **adj** of, in or from the north of a place: *She has a northern accent.* • *in northern Australia*

northerner (also **Northerner**) /ˈnɔːðənə/ **noun** [C] a person who was born in or who lives in the northern part of a country •➤ opposite **southerner**

northernmost /ˈnɔːðənməʊst/ **adj** furthest north: *the northernmost island of Japan*

the ˌNorth ˈPole **noun** [sing] the point on the Earth's surface which is furthest north •➤ picture at **earth**

northward /ˈnɔːθwəd/ (also **northwards**) **adv, adj** towards the north: *Continue northwards out of the city for about five miles.* • *in a northward direction*

★**north-ˈwest¹** **adj, adv** in, from or to the north-west of a place or country: *the north-west coast of Scotland* • *Our house faces north-west.*

★**north-ˈwest²** **noun** [sing] (*abbr* **NW**) (also **the North-West**) the direction or region halfway between north and west •➤ picture at **north**

north-ˈwesterly **adj 1** towards the north-west: *in a north-westerly direction* **2** (used about a wind) coming from the north-west

north-ˈwestern **adj** (only before a noun) connected with the north-west of a place or country

north-ˈwestward(s) **adv** towards the north-west: *Follow the A40 north-westward for ten miles.*

n

★**nose**[1] /nəʊz/ **noun** [C] **1** the part of your face, above your mouth, that is used for breathing and smelling ⋯➤ picture on page C5 **2 -nosed** (used to form compound adjectives) having the type of nose mentioned: *red-nosed* ● *big-nosed* **3** the front part of a plane, spacecraft, etc

IDIOMS **blow your nose** → **BLOW**[1]

follow your nose → **FOLLOW**

look down your nose at sb/sth (*especially Brit informal*) to think that you are better than sb else; to think that sth is not good enough for you

poke/stick your nose into sth (*spoken*) to be interested in or try to become involved in sth which does not concern you

turn your nose up at sth (*informal*) to refuse sth because you do not think it is good enough for you

nose[2] /nəʊz/ **verb** [I] (used about a vehicle) to move forward slowly and carefully

PHRASAL VERB **nose about/around** (*informal*) to look for sth, especially private information about sb

nosebleed /'nəʊzbliːd/ **noun** [C] a sudden flow of blood that comes from your nose

nosedive /'nəʊzdaɪv/ **noun** [C] a sudden sharp fall or drop: *Oil prices took a nosedive in the crisis.* –**nosedive verb** [I]

nostalgia /nɒ'stældʒə/ **noun** [U] a feeling of pleasure, mixed with sadness, when you think of happy times in the past: *She was suddenly filled with nostalgia for her university days.* –**nostalgic** /-dʒɪk/ **adj** –**nostalgically** /-dʒɪkli/ **adv**

nostril /'nɒstrəl/ **noun** [C] one of the two openings at the end of your nose that you breathe through ⋯➤ picture on page C5

nosy (also **nosey**) /'nəʊzi/ **adj** too interested in other people's personal affairs: *a nosy neighbour*

★**not** /nɒt/ **adv 1** used to form the negative with the verbs *be, do* and *have* (auxiliary verbs) and with verbs such as *can, must, will*, etc (modal verbs). *Not* is often pronounced or written *n't* in informal situations: *It's not/it isn't raining now.* ● *I cannot/can't see from here.* ● *He didn't invite me.* ● *Don't you like spaghetti?* ● *I hope she will not/won't be late.* ● *You're German, aren't you?* **2** used to give the following word or phrase a negative meaning: *He told me not to telephone.* ● *She accused me of not telling the truth.* ● *Not one person replied to my advertisement.* ● *It's not easy.* ● *He's not very tall.* **3** used to give a short negative reply: *'Do you think they'll get divorced?' 'I hope not.'* (= I hope that they will not.) ● *'Can I borrow £20?' 'Certainly not!'* ● *'Whose turn is it to do the shopping?' 'Not mine.'* **4** used with *or* to give a negative possibility: *Shall we tell her or not?* ● *I don't know if/whether he's telling the truth or not.*

IDIOMS **not at all 1** used as a way of replying when sb has thanked you: *'Thanks for the present.' 'Not at all, don't mention it.'* **2** used as a way of saying 'no' or 'definitely not': *'Do you mind if I come too?' 'Not at all.'* ● *The*

instructions are not at all clear.

not only... (but) also used for emphasizing the fact that there is something more to add: *They not only have two houses in London, they also have one in France.*

notable /'nəʊtəbl/ **adj** notable (for sth) interesting or important enough to receive attention: *The area is notable for its wildlife.*

notably /'nəʊtəbli/ **adv** used for giving an especially important example of what you are talking about: *Several politicians, most notably the Prime Minister and the Home Secretary, have given the proposal their full support.*

notch[1] /nɒtʃ/ **noun** [C] **1** a level on a scale of quality: *This meal is certainly a notch above the last one we had here.* **2** a cut in an edge or surface in the shape of a V or a circle, sometimes used to help you count sth ⋯➤ picture at **blob**

notch[2] /nɒtʃ/ **verb**

PHRASAL VERB **notch sth up** to score or achieve sth: *Lewis notched up his best ever time in the 100 metres.*

★**note**[1] /nəʊt/ **noun 1** [C] some words that you write down quickly to help you remember sth: *I'd better make a note of your name and address.* ● *Keep a note of who has paid and who hasn't.* ● *The lecturer advised the students to take notes while he was speaking.* **2** [C] a short letter: *This is just a note to thank you for having us to dinner.* ● *If Mark's not at home we'll leave a note for him.* ● *a sick note from your doctor* **3** [C] a short explanation or extra piece of information that is given at the back of a book, etc or at the bottom or side of a page: *See note 5, page 340.* ⋯➤ Look at **footnote**. **4** [C] (also **banknote**; *US* **bill**) a piece of paper money: *I'd like the money in £10 notes, please.* ⋯➤ picture at **money 5** [C] a single musical sound made by a voice or an instrument; a written sign that represents a musical sound: *I can only remember the first few notes of the song.* **6** [sing] something that shows a certain quality or feeling: *The meeting ended on a rather unpleasant note.*

IDIOMS **compare notes (with sb)** → **COMPARE**

take note (of sth) to pay attention to sth and be sure to remember it

note[2] /nəʊt/ **verb** [T] **1** to notice or pay careful attention to sth: *He noted a slight change in her attitude towards him.* ● *Please note that this office is closed on Tuesdays.* **2** to mention sth: *I'd like to note that the project has so far been extremely successful.*

PHRASAL VERB **note sth down** to write sth down so that you remember it

★**notebook** /'nəʊtbʊk/ **noun** [C] a small book in which you write things that you want to remember

noted /'nəʊtɪd/ **adj** (*formal*) noted (for/as sth) well-known; famous: *The hotel is noted for its food.*

notepad /'nəʊtpæd/ **noun** [C] some sheets of paper in a block that are used for writing things on ⋯➤ picture on page S6

notepaper /ˈnəʊtpeɪpə/ **noun** [U] paper that you write letters on

noteworthy /ˈnəʊtwɜːði/ **adj** interesting or important; that is worth noticing

★**nothing** /ˈnʌθɪŋ/ **pron** not anything; no thing: *There's nothing in this suitcase.* • *I'm bored – there's nothing to do here.* • *There was nothing else to say.* • *'What's the matter?' 'Oh, nothing.'* • *'Thank you so much for all your help.' 'It was nothing.'* • *The doctor said there's nothing wrong with me.* ••► Look at the note at **zero**.

IDIOMS **be/have nothing to do with sb/sth** to have no connection with sb/sth: *That question has nothing to do with what we're discussing.* • *Put my diary down – it's nothing to do with you.*

come to nothing → COME

for nothing 1 for no good reason or with no good result: *His hard work was all for nothing.* **2** for no payment; free: *Children under four are allowed in for nothing.*

nothing but only: *He does nothing but sit around watching TV all day.*

nothing like 1 not at all like: *She looks nothing like either of her parents.* **2** not at all; not nearly: *There's nothing like enough food for all of us.*

nothing much not a lot of sth; nothing of importance: *It's a nice town but there's nothing much to do in the evenings.* • *'What did you do at the weekend?' 'Nothing much.'*

(there's) nothing to it (it's) very easy: *You'll soon learn – there's nothing to it really.*

there is/was nothing (else) for it (but to do sth) there is/was no other action possible: *There was nothing for it but to resign.*

★**notice¹** /ˈnəʊtɪs/ **noun 1** [U] the act of paying attention to sth or knowing about sth: *The protests are finally making the government take notice.* • *Take no notice of what he said – he was just being silly.* • *Some people don't take any notice of* (= choose to ignore) *speed limits.* • *It has come to my notice that you have missed a lot of classes.* **2** [C] a piece of paper or a sign giving information, a warning, etc that is put where everyone can read it: *There's a notice on the board saying that the meeting has been cancelled.* • *The notice said 'No dogs allowed'.* **3** [U] a warning that sth is going to happen! *I can't produce a meal at such short notice!* • *I wish you'd give me more notice when you're going to be off work.* • *The swimming pool is closed until further notice* (= until we are told that it will open again).

★**notice²** /ˈnəʊtɪs/ **verb** [I,T] (not usually used in the continuous tenses) to see and become conscious of sth: *'What kind of car was the man driving?' 'I'm afraid I didn't notice.'* • *I noticed (that) he was carrying a black briefcase.* • *Did you notice which direction she went in?* • *We didn't notice him leave/him leaving.*

noticeable /ˈnəʊtɪsəbl/ **adj** easy to see or notice: *The scar from the accident was hardly noticeable.* –**noticeably** /-əbli/ **adv**

noticeboard /ˈnəʊtɪsbɔːd/ (*US* **bulletin board**) **noun** [C] a board on a wall for putting written information where everyone can read it ••► picture on page S6

notify /ˈnəʊtɪfaɪ/ **verb** [T] (*pres part* **notifying**; *3rd pers sing pres* **notifies**; *pt, pp* **notified**) **notify sb (of sth)** to inform sb about sth officially –**notification** /ˌnəʊtɪfɪˈkeɪʃn/ **noun** [C,U]

notion /ˈnəʊʃn/ **noun** [C] a notion (that.../of sth) something that you have in your mind; an idea: *I had a vague notion that I had seen her before.*

notional /ˈnəʊʃənl/ **adj** existing only in the mind; not based facts or reality

notoriety /ˌnəʊtəˈraɪəti/ **noun** [U] the state of being well-known for sth bad

notorious /nəʊˈtɔːriəs/ **adj** notorious (for/as sth) well-known for sth bad: *a notorious drug dealer* • *This road is notorious for the number of accidents on it.* ••► synonym **infamous** –**notoriously adv**

notwithstanding /ˌnɒtwɪθˈstændɪŋ/ **prep, adv** (*written*) in spite of sth

★**nought** /nɔːt/ (*especially US* **zero**) **noun** [C] the figure 0: *A million is written with six noughts.* • *We say 0.1 'nought point one'.*

noughts and crosses

IDIOM **noughts and crosses** a game for two players in which each person tries to win by writing three 0s or three Xs in a line.

★**noun** /naʊn/ **noun** [C] (*grammar*) a word that is the name of a thing, an idea, a place or a person: *'James', 'water', 'happiness' and 'France' are all nouns.* ••► Look at **countable** and **uncountable**.

nourish /ˈnʌrɪʃ/ **verb** [T] **1** to give sb/sth the right kind of food so that he/she/it can grow and be healthy **2** (*formal*) to allow a feeling, an idea, etc to grow stronger –**nourishment noun** [U]

Nov **abbr** November: *17 Nov 2001*

★**novel¹** /ˈnɒvl/ **noun** [C] a book that tells a story about people and events that are not real: *a romantic/historical/detective novel*

novel² /ˈnɒvl/ **adj** new and different: *That's a novel idea! Let's try it.*

novelist /ˈnɒvəlɪst/ **noun** [C] a person who writes novels

novelty /ˈnɒvlti/ **noun** (*pl* **novelties**) **1** [U] the quality of being new and different: *The novelty of her new job soon wore off.* **2** [C] something new and unusual: *It was quite a novelty not to have to get up early.* **3** [C] a small, cheap object that is sold as a toy or decoration

★**November** /nəʊˈvembə/ **noun** [U,C] (*abbr* **Nov**) the eleventh month of the year, coming after October

➤ To see how the months are used in sentences, look at the examples and the note at **January**.

novice /'nɒvɪs/ **noun** [C] a person who is new and without experience in a certain job, situation, etc; a beginner

★**now** /naʊ/ **adv, conj 1** (at) the present time: *We can't go for a walk now – it's raining.* • *Where are you living now?* • *From now on I'm going to work harder.* • *Up till now we haven't been able to afford a house of our own.* • *He will be on his way home by now.* • *I can manage for now but I might need some help later.* **2** immediately: *Go now before anyone sees you.* • *You must go to the doctor right now.* **3** used to introduce or to emphasize what you are saying, or while pausing to think: *Now listen to what he's saying.* • *What does he want now?* • *Now, let me think.*

➤ **Now then** is also used: *Now then, what was I saying?*

4 now (that)... because of the fact that: *Now (that) the children have left home we can move to a smaller house.*

IDIOMS any moment/second/minute/day (now) → ANY

(every) now and again/then from time to time; occasionally: *We see each other now and then, but not very often.*

just now → JUST¹

right now → RIGHT²

nowadays /'naʊədeɪz/ **adv** at the present time (when compared with the past): *I don't go to London much nowadays* (= but I did in the past). •➤ synonym **today**

★**nowhere** /'nəʊweə/ **adv** not in or to any place; not anywhere: *I'm afraid there's nowhere to stay in this village.* • *I don't like it here, but there's nowhere else for us to sit.*

IDIOMS get nowhere (with sth) to not make any progress with sth

in the middle of nowhere → MIDDLE¹

nowhere near → NEAR¹

noxious /'nɒkʃəs/ **adj** (*formal*) harmful or poisonous: *noxious gases*

nozzle /'nɒzl/ **noun** [C] a narrow tube that is put on the end of a pipe to control the liquid or gas coming out

nr abbr (used in addresses) near: *Masham, nr Ripon*

nuance /'njuːɑːns/ **noun** [C] a very small difference in meaning, feeling, sound, etc

★**nuclear** /'njuːkliə/ **adj 1** using, producing or resulting from the energy that is produced when the central part (**nucleus**) of an atom is split: *nuclear energy* • *a nuclear power station* • *nuclear war/weapons* •➤ Look at **atomic**. **2** connected with the nucleus of an atom: *nuclear physics*

nuclear re'actor (also **reactor**) **noun** [C] a very large machine that produces nuclear energy

nucleus /'njuːkliəs/ **noun** [C] (*pl* **nuclei** /-kliaɪ/) **1** the central part of an atom or of certain cells **2** the central or most important part of sth

nude¹ /njuːd/ **adj** not wearing any clothes •➤ Look at **bare** and **naked**. –**nudity** /'njuːdəti/ **noun** [U]: *This film contains scenes of nudity.*

nude² /njuːd/ **noun** [C] a picture or photograph of a person who is not wearing any clothes

IDIOM in the nude not wearing any clothes

nudge /nʌdʒ/ **verb** [T] to touch or push sb/sth with your elbow •➤ picture on page S8 –**nudge noun** [C]: *to give sb a nudge*

nuisance /'njuːsns/ **noun** [C] a person, thing or situation that annoys you or causes you trouble: *It's a nuisance having to queue for everything.*

numb /nʌm/ **adj** not able to feel anything; not able to move: *My fingers were numb with cold.* • *I'll give you an injection and the tooth will go numb.* –**numb verb** [T]: *We were numbed by the dreadful news.* –**numbness noun** [U]

★**number**¹ /'nʌmbə/ **noun 1** [C] a word or symbol that indicates a quantity: *Choose a number between ten and twenty.* • *2, 4, 6, etc are even numbers and 1, 3, 5, etc are odd numbers.* • *a three-figure number* (= from 100 to 999) **2** [C] a group of numbers that is used to identify sb/sth: *a telephone number* • *a code number* **3** [C,U] a number (of sth) a quantity of people or things: *a large number of visitors* • *We must reduce the number of accidents on the roads.* • *Pupils in the school have doubled in number in recent years.* • *There are a number of* (= several) *things I don't understand.* **4** [C] (*abbr* **No; no**) used before a number to show the position of sth in a series: *We live in Hazel Road, at number 21.* • *room No 347* **5** [C] a copy of a magazine, newspaper, etc: *Back numbers of 'New Scientist' are available from the publishers.* **6** [C] (*informal*) a song or dance

IDIOMS any number of very many: *There could be any number of reasons why she hasn't arrived yet.*

in round figures/numbers → ROUND¹

opposite number → OPPOSITE

number² /'nʌmbə/ **verb** [T] **1** to give a number to sth: *The houses are numbered from 1 to 52.* **2** used for saying how many people or things there are: *Our forces number 40 000.*

'number plate (*US* **license plate**) **noun** [C] the sign on the front and back of a vehicle that shows a particular combination of numbers and letters (the registration number)

numeral /'njuːmərəl/ **noun** [C] a sign or symbol that represents a quantity: *Roman numerals* (= I, II, III, IV, etc)

numerate /'njuːmərət/ **adj** having a good basic knowledge of mathematics •➤ Look at **literate**.

numerical /njuː'merɪkl/ **adj** of or shown by numbers: *to put sth in numerical order*

numerous /'njuːmərəs/ **adj** (*formal*) existing in large numbers; many

nun /nʌn/ **noun** [C] a member of a religious group of women who live together in a special building (a **convent**) away from other people •➤ Look at **monk**.

★**nurse**[1] /nɜːs/ noun [C] a person who is trained to look after sick or injured people: *a male nurse* • *a psychiatric nurse*

> A **community** or **district** nurse visits sick people in their homes to give them the care that they need. A **health visitor** is a nurse who gives help and advice to parents of babies and young children. A **midwife** helps women give birth.

nurse[2] /nɜːs/ verb [T] **1** to take care of sb who is sick or injured; to take care of an injury: *She nursed her mother back to health.* • *Ahmed is still nursing a back injury.* **2** to hold sb/sth in a loving way: *He nursed the child in his arms.* **3** (*formal*) to have a strong feeling or idea in your mind for a long time: *Tim had long nursed the hope that Sharon would marry him.* **4** to feed a baby or young animal with milk from the breast; to drink milk from the mother's breast

nursery /nɜːsəri/ noun [C] (*pl* **nurseries**) **1** a place where small children and babies are looked after so that their parents can go to work ••► Look at **crèche**. **2** a place where young plants are grown and sold

'nursery rhyme noun [C] a traditional poem or song for young children

'nursery school (also **playgroup**; **playschool**) noun [C] a school for children aged from three to five ••► Look at **kindergarten**.

nursing /nɜːsɪŋ/ noun [U] the job of being a nurse

'nursing home noun [C] a small private hospital, often for old people

nuts

almond
shell
brazil nut
hazelnut
walnut
peanut
cashew
pecan
chestnut

★**nut** /nʌt/ noun [C] **1** a dry fruit that consists of a hard shell with a seed inside. Many types of nut can be eaten **2** a small piece of metal with a round hole in the middle through which you screw a long round piece of metal (a **bolt**) to fasten things together ••► picture at **bolt**

nutcrackers /nʌtkrækəz/ noun [pl] a tool that you use for breaking open the shell of a nut

nutmeg /nʌtmeg/ noun [C,U] a type of hard seed that is often made into powder and used as a spice in cooking

nutrition /njuˈtrɪʃn/ noun [U] the food that you eat and the way that it affects your health: *Good nutrition is essential for children's growth.* –**nutritional** adj

nutritious /njuˈtrɪʃəs/ adj (used about a food) very good for you

nutshell /nʌtʃel/ noun
IDIOM **in a nutshell** using few words

nutty /nʌti/ adj containing or tasting of nuts

nuzzle /nʌzl/ verb [I,T] to press or rub sb/sth gently with the nose

NW abbr north-west(ern): *NW Australia*

nylon /naɪlɒn/ noun [U] a very strong man-made material that is used for making clothes, rope, brushes, etc

O, o /əʊ/ noun [C] (*pl* **O's; o's**) **1** the fifteenth letter of the English alphabet: *'Orange' begins with (an) 'O'.* **2** (used when you are speaking) zero: *My number is five O nine double four* (= 50944). ••► Look at the note at **zero**.

oak /əʊk/ noun **1** (also **'oak tree**) [C] a type of large tree with hard wood that is common in many northern parts of the world **2** [U] the wood from the oak tree: *a solid oak table*

> The fruit of the oak is an **acorn**.

OAP /ˌəʊ eɪ ˈpiː/ abbr (*Brit*) old-age pensioner

oar /ɔː/ noun [C] a long pole that is flat and wide at one end and that you use for moving a small boat through water (rowing) ••► Look at **paddle**.

oasis /əʊˈeɪsɪs/ noun [C] (*pl* **oases** /-siːz/) a place in the desert where there is water and where plants grow

oath /əʊθ/ noun [C] **1** a formal promise: *They have to swear/take an oath of loyalty.* **2** (*old-fashioned*) = SWEAR WORD
IDIOM **be on/under oath** to have made a formal promise to tell the truth in a court of law

oats /əʊts/ noun [pl] a type of grain that is used as food for people and animals ••► picture at **cereal**

obedient /əˈbiːdiənt/ adj obedient (to sb/sth) doing what you are told to do: *As a child he was always obedient to his parents.* ••► opposite **disobedient** –**obedience** noun [U] –**obediently** adv

obese /əʊˈbiːs/ adj (used about people) very fat, in a way that is not healthy –**obesity** /əʊˈbiːsəti/ noun [U]

★**obey** /əˈbeɪ/ verb [I,T] to do what you are told to do: *Soldiers are trained to obey orders.* ••► opposite **disobey**

obituary /əˈbɪtʃuəri/ noun [C] (*pl* **obituaries**) a piece of writing about a person's life that is printed in a newspaper soon after he/she has died

★**object**[1] /ˈɒbdʒɪkt/ noun [C] **1** a thing that can be seen and touched, but is not alive: *The*

o

shelves were filled with objects of all shapes and sizes. • *everyday/household objects* **2** an aim or purpose: *Making money is his sole object in life.* **3** the object of sth a person or thing that causes a feeling, interest, thought, etc: *the object of his desire/affections/interest* **4** (*grammar*) the noun or phrase describing the person or thing that is affected by the action of a verb

➤ In the sentences: *I sent a letter to Meera* • *I sent Meera a letter* 'a letter' is the **direct object** of the verb and 'Meera' is the **indirect object**.

•➤ Look at **subject**.

IDIOM **money, etc is no object** money, etc is not important or is no problem: *They always want the best. Expense is no object.*

object² /əbˈdʒekt/ **verb 1** [I] **object (to sb/ sth); object (to doing sth/to sb doing sth)** to not like or to be against sb/sth: *Many people object to the new tax.* • *I object to companies trying to sell me things over the phone.* **2** [T] to say a reason why you think sth is wrong: *'I think that's unfair,' he objected.* –**objector** **noun** [C]

objection /əbˈdʒekʃn/ **noun** [C] **an objection (to sb/sth); an objection (to doing sth/to sb doing sth)** a reason why you do not like or are against sb/sth: *We listed our objections to the proposed new road.* • *I have no objection to you using my desk while I'm away.*

objectionable /əbˈdʒekʃənəbl/ **adj** very unpleasant

objective¹ /əbˈdʒektɪv/ **noun** [C] something that you are trying to achieve; an aim: *Our objective is to finish by the end of the year.* • *to achieve your objective*

objective² /əbˈdʒektɪv/ **adj** not influenced by your own personal feelings; considering only facts: *Please try and give an objective report of what happened.* • *It's hard to be objective about your own family.* •➤ opposite **subjective** –**objectively adv:** *He is too upset to see things objectively.* –**objectivity** /ˌɒbdʒekˈtɪvəti/ **noun** [U]

obligation /ˌɒblɪˈɡeɪʃn/ **noun** [C,U] **(an) obligation (to sb) (to do sth)** the state of having to do sth because it is a law or duty, or because you have promised: *Unfortunately the shop is under no obligation to give you your money back.* • *We have an obligation to help people who are in need.* • *By refusing to examine the animal, the vet failed to fulfil his professional obligations.*

obligatory /əˈblɪɡətri/ **adj** (*formal*) that you must do: *It is obligatory to get insurance before you drive a car.* •➤ opposite **optional**

oblige /əˈblaɪdʒ/ **verb 1** [T] (usually passive) to force sb to do sth: *Parents are obliged by law to send their children to school.* • *Although I wasn't hungry, I felt obliged to eat the food they had made.* **2** [I,T] (*formal*) to do what sb asks; to be helpful: *If you ever need any help, I'd be happy to oblige.* –**obliged adj:** *Thanks for your help. I'm much obliged to*

you. –**obliging adj:** *I asked my neighbour for advice and he was very obliging.*

obliterate /əˈblɪtəreɪt/ **verb** [T] (*formal*) (often passive) to remove all signs of sth by destroying or covering it completely

oblivion /əˈblɪviən/ **noun** [U] **1** a state in which you do not realize what is happening around you, usually because you are unconscious or asleep: *I was in a state of complete oblivion.* **2** the state in which sb/sth has been forgotten and is no longer famous or important: *His work faded into oblivion after his death.*

oblivious /əˈblɪviəs/ **adj oblivious (to/of sb/ sth)** not noticing or realizing what is happening around you: *She was completely oblivious of all the trouble she had caused.*

oblong /ˈɒblɒŋ/ **adj, noun** [C] (of) a shape with two long sides and two short sides and four angles of 90° (**right angles**) •➤ synonym **rectangle**

obnoxious /əbˈnɒkʃəs/ **adj** extremely unpleasant, especially in a way that offends people

oboe /ˈəʊbəʊ/ **noun** [C] a musical instrument made of wood that you play by blowing through it •➤ Look at the note at **piano**. •➤ picture at **music**

obscene /əbˈsiːn/ **adj 1** connected with sex in a way that most people find disgusting and which causes offence: *obscene books/gestures/language* **2** very large in size or amount in a way that some people find unacceptable: *He earns an obscene amount of money.*

obscenity /əbˈsenəti/ **noun** (*pl* **obscenities**) **1** [C] sexual words or acts that shock people and cause offence: *He shouted a string of obscenities out of the car window.* **2** [U] sexual language or behaviour, especially in books, plays, etc which shocks people and causes offence

obscure¹ /əbˈskjʊə/ **adj 1** not well-known: *an obscure Spanish poet* **2** not easy to see or understand: *For some obscure reason, he decided to give up his well-paid job, to become a writer.* –**obscurity** /əbˈskjʊərəti/ **noun** [U]

obscure² /əbˈskjʊə/ **verb** [T] to make sth difficult to see or understand: *A high fence obscured our view.*

observance /əbˈzɜːvəns/ **noun** [U, sing] **observance (of sth)** the practice of obeying or following a law, custom, etc

observant /əbˈzɜːvənt/ **adj** good at noticing things around you: *An observant passer-by gave the police a full description of the men.*

observation /ˌɒbzəˈveɪʃn/ **noun 1** [U] the act of watching sb/sth carefully, especially to learn sth: *My research involves the observation of animals in their natural surroundings.* • *The patient is being kept under observation.* **2** [U] the ability to notice things: *Scientists need good powers of observation.* **3** [C] **an observation (about/on sth)** something that you say or write about sth: *He began by making a few general observations about the* *sales figures.* ••► Look at **remark** and **comment**. These words are more common.

observatory /əb'zɜ:vətri/ **noun** [C] (*pl* **observatories**) a building from which scientists can watch the stars, the weather, etc

★**observe** /əb'zɜ:v/ **verb** [T] **1** to watch sb/sth carefully, especially to learn more about him/her/it: *We observed the birds throughout the breeding season.* **2** (*formal*) to see or notice sb/sth: *A man and a woman were observed leaving by the back door.* **3** (*formal*) to make a comment: *'We're late,' she observed.* **4** (*formal*) to obey a law, rule, etc: *to observe the speed limit*

observer /əb'zɜ:və/ **noun** [C] **1** a person who watches sb/sth: *According to observers, the plane exploded shortly after take-off.* **2** a person who attends a meeting, lesson, etc to watch and listen but who does not take part

obsess /əb'ses/ **verb** [T] (usually passive) **be obsessed (about/with sb/sth)** to completely fill your mind so that you cannot think of anything else: *He became obsessed with getting his revenge.*

obsession /əb'seʃn/ **noun** **obsession (with sb/sth)** **1** [U] the state in which you can only think about one person or thing so that you cannot think of anything else: *the tabloid press's obsession with the sordid details of the affair* **2** [C] a person or thing that you think about too much

obsessive /əb'sesɪv/ **adj** thinking too much about one particular person or thing; behaving in a way that shows this: *He's obsessive about not being late.* • *obsessive cleanliness*

obsolete /'ɒbsəli:t/ **adj** no longer useful because sth better has been invented

obstacle /'ɒbstəkl/ **noun** [C] **an obstacle (to sth/doing sth)** something that makes it difficult for you to do sth or go somewhere: *Not speaking a foreign language was a major obstacle to her career.*

obstetrician /,ɒbstə'trɪʃn/ **noun** [C] a hospital doctor who looks after women who are pregnant

obstinate /'ɒbstɪnət/ **adj** refusing to change your opinions, way of behaving, etc when other people try to persuade you to: *an obstinate refusal to apologize* ••► synonym **stubborn** –**obstinacy** /'ɒbstɪnəsi/ **noun** [U] –**obstinately adv**

obstruct /əb'strʌkt/ **verb** [T] to stop sb/sth from happening or moving either by accident or deliberately: *Could you move on, please? You're obstructing the traffic if you park there.*

obstruction /əb'strʌkʃn/ **noun** **1** [U] the act of stopping sth from happening or moving **2** [C] a thing that stops sb/sth from moving or doing sth: *This car is causing an obstruction.*

obstructive /əb'strʌktɪv/ **adj** trying to stop sb/sth from moving or doing sth

★**obtain** /əb'teɪn/ **verb** [T] (*formal*) to get sth: *to obtain advice/information/permission*

obtainable /əb'teɪnəbl/ **adj** that you can get:

That make of vacuum cleaner is no longer obtainable.

★**obvious** /'ɒbviəs/ **adj obvious (to sb)** easily seen or understood; clear: *For obvious reasons, I'd prefer not to give my name.* • *His disappointment was obvious to everyone.* –**obviously adv**: *There has obviously been a mistake.*

★**occasion** /ə'keɪʒn/ **noun** **1** [C] a particular time when sth happens: *I have met Bill on two occasions.* **2** [C] a special event, ceremony, etc: *Their wedding was a memorable occasion.* **3** [sing] the suitable or right time (for sth): *I shall tell her what I think if the occasion arises* (= if I get the chance).

> You use **occasion** when you mean the time is right or suitable for something: *I saw them at the funeral, but it was not a suitable occasion for discussing holiday plans.* You use **opportunity** or **chance** when you mean that it is possible to do something: *I was only in Paris for one day and I didn't get the opportunity/chance to visit the Louvre.*

IDIOM **on occasion(s)** sometimes but not often

★**occasional** /ə'keɪʒənl/ **adj** done or happening from time to time but not very often: *We have the occasional argument but most of the time we get on.* –**occasionally** /-nəli/ **adv**: *We see each other occasionally.*

occult /'ɒkʌlt/ **adj** **1** (only *before* a noun) connected with magic powers and things that cannot be explained by reason or science **2 the occult** /ə'kʌlt/ **noun** [sing] magic powers, ceremonies, etc

occupant /'ɒkjəpənt/ **noun** [C] a person who is in a building, car, etc at a particular time

★**occupation** /,ɒkju'peɪʃn/ **noun** **1** [C] (*written*) a job or profession; the way in which you spend your time: *Please state your occupation on the form.* ••► Look at the note at **work**¹. **2** [U] the act of the army of one country taking control of another country; the period of time that this situation lasts: *the Roman occupation of Britain* **3** [U] the act of living in or using a room, building, etc

occupational /,ɒkju'peɪʃənl/ **adj** (only *before* a noun) connected with your work: *Accidents are an occupational hazard* (= a risk connected with a particular job) *on building sites.*

occupied /'ɒkjupaɪd/ **adj** **1** (not before a noun) being used by sb: *Is this seat occupied?* **2** busy doing sth: *Looking after the children keeps me fully occupied.* ••► Look at **preoccupied**. **3** (used about a country or a piece of land) under the control of another country

occupier /'ɒkjupaɪə/ **noun** [C] (*written*) a person who owns, lives in or uses a house, piece of land, etc

★**occupy** /'ɒkjupaɪ/ **verb** [T] (*pres part* **occupying**; *3rd pers sing pres* **occupies**; *pt, pp* **occupied**) **1** to fill a space or period of time: *The large table occupied most of the room.* ••► synonym **take up 2** (*formal*) to live in or

O

use a house, piece of land, etc **3** to take control of a building, country, etc by force **4 occupy sb/yourself** to keep sb/yourself busy

★ **occur** /əˈkɜː/ *verb* [I] (**occurring**; **occurred**) **1** (*formal*) to happen, especially in a way that has not been planned: *The accident occurred late last night.* ••➤ Look at the note at **happen**. **2** to exist or be found somewhere: *The virus occurs more frequently in children.* **3 occur to sb** (used about an idea or a thought) to come into your mind: *It never occurred to John that his wife might be unhappy.*

occurrence /əˈkʌrəns/ *noun* [C] something that happens or exists

★ **ocean** /ˈəʊʃn/ *noun* **1** [U] (*especially US*) the mass of salt water that covers most of the surface of the earth: *Two thirds of the earth's surface is covered by ocean.* **2** [C] (also **Ocean**) one of the five main areas into which the water is divided: *the Atlantic/Indian/Pacific Ocean* ••➤ Look at **sea**.
IDIOM **a drop in the ocean** → **DROP²**

★ **o'clock** /əˈklɒk/ *adv* used after the numbers one to twelve for saying what the time is: *Lunch is at twelve o'clock.*

➤ Be careful. **o'clock** can only be used with full hours: *We arranged to meet at 5 o'clock. It's 5.30 already and he's still not here.*

Oct *abbr* October: *13 Oct 1999*

octagon /ˈɒktəgən/ *noun* [C] a shape that has eight straight sides –**octagonal** /ɒkˈtægənl/ *adj*

octave /ˈɒktɪv/ *noun* [C] the set of eight musical notes that western music is based on

★ **October** /ɒkˈtəʊbə/ *noun* [U,C] (*abbr* **Oct**) the tenth month of the year, coming after September

➤ To see how the months are used in sentences, look at the examples and the note at **January**.

octopus
tentacle
squid

octopus /ˈɒktəpəs/ *noun* [C] (*pl* **octopuses**) a sea animal with a soft body and eight long arms (**tentacles**)

★ **odd** /ɒd/ *adj* **1** strange; unusual: *There's something odd about him.* ● *It's a bit odd that she didn't phone to say she couldn't come.* ••➤ synonym **peculiar 2 odd-** (used to form compound adjectives) strange or unusual in the way mentioned: *an odd-sounding name* **3** (only *before* a noun) not regular or fixed; happening sometimes: *He makes the odd mis-*

take, *but nothing very serious.* **4** (only *before* a noun) that is left after other similar things have been used: *He made the bookshelves out of a few odd bits of wood.* **5** not with the pair or set it belongs to; not matching: *You're wearing odd socks.* **6** (used about a number) that cannot be divided by two: *One, three, five and seven are all odd numbers.* ••➤ opposite **even 7** (usually used after a number) a little more than: *'How old do you think he is?' 'Well, he must be thirty-odd, I suppose.'* –**oddly** *adv*: *Oddly enough, the most expensive tickets sold fastest.* –**oddness** *noun* [U]
IDIOM **the odd man/one out** one that is different from all the others in a group: *Her brothers and sisters were much older than she was. She was always the odd one out.*

oddity /ˈɒdəti/ *noun* (*pl* **oddities**) [C] a person or thing that is unusual

,**odd 'jobs** *noun* [pl] small jobs or tasks of various types

oddment /ˈɒdmənt/ *noun* [C,usually pl] (*especially Brit*) a small piece of material, wood, etc that is left after the rest has been used

odds /ɒdz/ *noun* [pl] **the odds (on/against sth/sb)** the degree to which sth is likely to happen; the probability of sth happening: *The odds on him surviving are very slim* (= he will probably die). ● *The odds are against you* (= you are not likely to succeed). ● *The odds are in your favour* (= you are likely to succeed).
IDIOMS **against (all) the odds** happening although it seemed impossible
be at odds (with sb) (over sth) to disagree with sb about sth
be at odds (with sth) to be different from sth, when the two things should be the same
odds and ends (*Brit informal*) small things of little value or importance

odometer /əʊˈdɒmɪtə/ (*US*) = **MILOMETER**

odour (*US* **odor**) /ˈəʊdə/ *noun* [C] (*formal*) a smell (often an unpleasant one)

odourless (*US* **odorless**) /ˈəʊdələs/ *adj* without a smell

★ **of** /əv; *strong form* ɒv/ *prep* **1** belonging to, connected with, or part of sth/sb: *the roof of the house* ● *the result of the exam* ● *the back of the book* ● *the leader of the party* ● *a friend of mine* (= one of my friends) **2** made, done or produced by sb: *the poems of Milton* **3** used for saying what sb/sth is or what a thing contains or is made of: *a woman of intelligence* ● *the city of Paris* ● *a glass of milk* ● *a crowd of people* ● *It's made of silver.* ● *a feeling of anger* **4** showing sb/sth: *a map of York* ● *a photograph of my parents* **5** showing that sb/sth is part of a larger group: *some of the people* ● *three of the houses* **6** with measurements, directions and expressions of time and age: *a litre of milk* ● *the fourth of July* ● *a girl of 12* ● *an increase of 2.5%* ● *five miles north of Leeds* **7** indicating the reason for or cause of sth: *He died of pneumonia.* **8** with some adjectives: *I'm proud of you.* ● *She's jealous of her.* **9** with some verbs: *This perfume smells of roses.* ● *Think of a number.* ● *It reminds me of you.* **10** used after a noun describing an action to show either who did the action or who it happened to: *the arrival of the president* (= he arrives) ● *the murder of the president* (= he is murdered)

★ **off**¹ /ɒf/ *adv, prep*

> ➤ For special uses with many verbs, for example **go off**, look at the verb entries.

1 down or away from a place or a position on sth: *to fall off a ladder/motorbike/wall* ● *We got off the bus.* ● *I shouted to him but he just walked off.* ● *I must be off* (= I must leave here). *It's getting late.* ● *When are you off to Spain?* ● (*figurative*) *We've got off the subject.* **2** used with verbs that mean 'remove' or 'separate': *She took her coat off.* ● *He shook the rain off his umbrella.* ·➤ opposite **on 3** joined to and leading away from: *My road is off the Cowley Road.* **4** at some distance from sth: *The Isle of Wight is just off the south coast of England.* ● *Christmas is still a long way off* (= it is a long time till then). **5** (used about a machine, a light, etc) not connected, working or being used: *Please make sure the TV/light/ heating is off.* **6** not present at work, school, etc: *She's off work/off sick with a cold.* ● *I'm having a day off* (= a day's holiday) *next week.* **7** (used about a plan or arrangement) not going to happen; cancelled: *The meeting/ wedding/trip is off.* ·➤ opposite **on 8** cheaper; less by a certain amount: *cars with £400 off* ● *£400 off the price of a car* **9** not eating or using sth: *The baby's off his food.*

IDIOMS off and on; on and off sometimes; starting and stopping: *It rained on and off all day.*

off limits (*US*) forbidden; not to be entered by sb

off the top of your head → **TOP**¹

well/badly off having/not having a lot of money

off² /ɒf/ *adj* (not before a noun) **1** (used about food or drink) no longer fresh enough to eat or drink: *The milk's off.* **2** (*spoken*) unfriendly: *My neighbour was rather off with me today.*

offal /'ɒfl/ *noun* [U] the heart and other organs of an animal, used as food

'**off chance** *noun* [sing] a slight possibility: *She popped round on the off chance of finding him at home.*

'**off-day** *noun* [C] (*informal*) a day when things go badly or you do not work well: *Even the best players have off-days occasionally.*

★ **offence** (*US* **offense**) /ə'fens/ *noun* **1** [C] (*formal*) an offence (against sth) a crime; an illegal action: *to commit an offence* ● *a criminal/minor/serious/sexual offence* **2** [U] offence (to sb/sth) the act of upsetting or insulting sb: *I didn't mean to cause you any offence.*

IDIOM take offence (at sth) to feel upset or hurt by sb/sth

★ **offend** /ə'fend/ *verb* **1** [T] (often passive) to hurt sb's feelings; to upset sb: *I hope they won't be offended if I don't come.* ● *He felt offended that she hadn't written for so long.*

2 [I] (*formal*) to do sth illegal; to commit a crime

offender /ə'fendə/ *noun* [C] **1** (*formal*) a person who breaks the law or commits a crime: *Young offenders should not be sent to adult prisons.* ● *a first offender* (= sb who has committed a crime for the first time) **2** a person or thing that does sth wrong

offensive¹ /ə'fensɪv/ *adj* **1** offensive (to sb) unpleasant; insulting: *offensive behaviour/ language/remarks* ·➤ opposite **inoffensive 2** (*formal*) (only *before* a noun) used for or connected with attacking: *offensive weapons* ·➤ opposite **defensive** –**offensively** *adv*

offensive² /ə'fensɪv/ *noun* [C] a military attack

IDIOM be on the offensive to be the first to attack, rather than waiting for others to attack you

★ **offer**¹ /'ɒfə/ *verb* **1** [T] offer sth (to sb) (for sth); offer sb sth to ask if sb would like sth or to give sb the chance to have sth: *He offered his seat on the bus to an old lady.* ● *I've been offered a job in London.* ● *He offered (me) £2000 for the car and I accepted.* **2** [I] offer (to do sth) to say or show that you will do sth for sb if he/she wants: *I don't want to do it but I suppose I'll have to offer.* ● *My brother's offered to help me paint the house.* **3** [T] to make sth available or to provide the opportunity for sth: *The job offers plenty of opportunity for travel.*

★ **offer**² /'ɒfə/ *noun* [C] **1** an offer (of sth); an offer (to do sth) a statement offering to do sth or give sth to sb: *She accepted my offer of help.* ● *Thank you for your kind offer to help.*

> ➤ We can **make**, **accept**, **refuse**, **turn down** or **withdraw** an offer.

2 an offer (or sth) (for sth) an amount of money that you say you will give for sth: *They've made an offer for the house.* ● *We've turned down* (= refused) *an offer of £90000.* **3** a low price for sth in a shop, usually for a short time: *See below for details of our special holiday offer.*

IDIOMS on offer **1** for sale or available: *The college has a wide range of courses on offer.* **2** (*especially Brit*) for sale at a lower price than usual for a certain time: *This cheese is on offer until next week.*

or nearest offer; ono → **NEAR**¹

offering /'ɒfərɪŋ/ *noun* [C] something that is given or produced for other people to watch, enjoy, etc

offhand¹ /ˌɒf'hænd/ *adj* (used about behaviour) not showing any interest in sb/sth in a way that seems rude: *an offhand manner/voice*

offhand² /ˌɒf'hænd/ *adv* without having time to think; immediately: *I can't tell you what it's worth offhand.*

★ **office** /'ɒfɪs/ *noun* **1** [C] a room, set of rooms or a building where people work, usually sitting at desks: *I usually get to the office at about 9 o'clock.* ● *The firm's head office* (=

the main branch of the company) *is in Glasgow.* ● *Please phone again during* **office hours**.

➤ In the US doctors and dentists have **offices**. In Britain they have **surgeries**.

2 [C] (often used to form compound nouns) a room or building that is used for a particular purpose, especially for providing a service: *the tax/ticket/tourist office* ••➤ Look at **booking office**, **box office** and **post office**. **3 Office** [sing] a government department, including the people who work there and the work they do: *the Foreign/Home Office* **4** [U] an official position, often as part of a government or other organization: *The Labour party has been in office since 1997.*

'office block noun [C] a large building that contains offices, usually belonging to more than one company

★**officer** /'ɒfɪsə/ **noun** [C] **1** a person who is in a position of authority in the armed forces: *an army/air-force officer* **2** a person who is in a position of authority in the government or a large organization: *a prison/customs/welfare officer* **3** = POLICE OFFICER ••➤ Look at the note at **official²**.

★**official¹** /ə'fɪʃl/ **adj 1** (only *before* a noun) connected with the position of sb in authority: *official duties/responsibilities* **2** accepted and approved by the government or some other authority: *The scheme has not yet received official approval.* ● *The country's official language is Spanish.* **3** that is told to the public, but which may or may not be true: *The official reason for his resignation was that he wanted to spend more time with his family.* ••➤ opposite **unofficial**

official² /ə'fɪʃl/ **noun** [C] a person who has a position of authority: *The reception was attended by MPs and high-ranking officials.*

➤ An **office worker** is a person who works in an office, at a desk. An **official** is a person who has a position of responsibility in an organization, often the government: *senior government officials*. An **officer** is either a person who gives orders to others in the armed forces or the police force. However the word is sometimes used like **official**: *She's a tax officer in the Civil Service.*

officialdom /ə'fɪʃldəm/ **noun** [U] groups of people in positions of authority in large organizations who seem more interested in following the rules than in being helpful

officially /ə'fɪʃəli/ **adv 1** that is done publicly and by sb in a position of authority: *The new school was officially opened last week.* **2** according to a particular set of laws, rules, etc: *Officially we don't accept children under six, but we'll make an exception in this case.*

officious /ə'fɪʃəs/ **adj** too ready to tell other people what to do and use the power you have to give orders

offing /'ɒfɪŋ/ **noun**
IDIOM **in the offing** (*informal*) likely to appear or happen soon

'off-licence noun [C] (*US* **'liquor store**) a

shop which sells alcoholic drinks in bottles and cans

offload /,ɒf'ləʊd/ **verb** [T] (*informal*) **offload sth (on/onto sb)** to give away sth that you do not want to sb else: *It's nice to have someone you can offload your problems onto.*

,off-'peak adj, adv (only *before* a noun) available, used or done at a less popular or busy time: *an off-peak train ticket/bus-pass/phone call* ● *It's cheaper to travel off-peak.* ••➤ Look at **peak**.

,off-'putting adj (*especially Brit*) unpleasant in a way that stops you from liking sb/sth

offset /'ɒfset/ **verb** [T] (**offsetting**; *pt, pp* **offset**) to make the effect of sth less strong or noticeable: *The disadvantages of the scheme are more than offset by the advantages.*

offshoot /'ɒfʃuːt/ **noun** [C] a thing that develops from sth else, especially a small organization that develops from a larger one

offshore /,ɒf'ʃɔː/ **adj** in the sea but not very far from the land: *an offshore oil rig*

offside **adj 1** /,ɒf'saɪd/(used about a player in football) in a position that is not allowed by the rules of the game **2** /'ɒfsaɪd/(*Brit*) (used about a part of a vehicle) on the side that is furthest away from the edge of the road

offspring /'ɒfsprɪŋ/ **noun** [C] (*pl* **offspring**) (*formal*) a child or children; the young of an animal: *to produce/raise offspring*

,off-'white adj not pure white

★**often** /'ɒfn; 'ɒftən/ **adv 1** many times; frequently: *We often go swimming at the weekend.* ● *I'm sorry I didn't write very often.* ● *How often should you go to the dentist?* **2** in many cases; commonly: *Old houses are often damp.*
IDIOMS **every so often** sometimes; from time to time
more often than not usually

ogre /'əʊgə/ **noun** [C] **1** (in children's stories) a very large, cruel and frightening creature that eats people **2** a person who is unpleasant and frightening

★**Oh** /əʊ/ (also **O**) **interj** used for reacting to sth that sb has said, for emphasizing what you are saying, or when you are thinking of what to say next: *'I'm a teacher.' 'Oh? Where?'* ● *'Oh no!' she cried as she began to read the letter.*

★**oil** /ɔɪl/ **noun** [U] **1** a thick dark liquid that comes from under the ground and is used as a fuel or to make machines work smoothly **2** a thick liquid that comes from animals or plants and is used in cooking: *cooking/vegetable/sunflower/olive oil* –**oil verb** [T]

oilfield /'ɔɪlfiːld/ **noun** [C] an area where there is oil under the ground or under the sea

'oil painting noun [C] a picture that has been painted using paint made with oil

'oil rig (also **rig**) **noun** [C] a large platform in the sea with equipment for getting oil out from under the sea

'oil slick (also **slick**) **noun** [C] an area of oil that floats on the sea, usually after a ship carrying oil has crashed

'oil well (also **well**) **noun** [C] a hole that is made deep in the ground or under the sea in order to obtain oil

oily /'ɔɪli/ **adj** covered with oil or like oil: *oily food* • *Mechanics always have oily hands.*

ointment /'ɔɪntmənt/ **noun** [C,U] a smooth substance that you put on sore skin or on an injury to help it get better ••➤ picture at **bandage**

★**OK**¹ (also **okay**) /,əʊ'keɪ/ **adj, adv, interj** (*informal*) **1** all right; good or well enough: *'Did you have a nice day?' 'Well, it was OK, I suppose.'* • *Is it okay if I come at about 7?* **2** yes; all right: *'Do you want to come with us?' 'OK.'*

OK² (also **okay**) /,əʊ'keɪ/ **noun** [sing] agreement or permission: *As soon as my parents **give me the OK**, I'll come and stay with you.* –OK (also **okay**) (*3rd pers sing pres* **OK's**; *pres part* **OK'ing**; *pt, pp* **OK'd**) **verb** [T] **OK sth (with sb)**: *If you need time off, you have to OK it with your boss.*

★**old** /əʊld/ **adj 1** that has existed for a long time; connected with past times: *This house is quite old.* • *old ideas/traditions* • *In the old days, people generally had larger families than nowadays.* ••➤ opposite **new** or **modern 2** (used about people and animals) having lived a long time: *My mother wasn't very old when she died.* • *He's only 50 but he looks older.* • *to **get/grow** old* ••➤ opposite **young 3** (used with a period of time or with *how*) of a particular age: *That building is 500 years old.* • *The book is aimed at eight- to ten-year-olds.* • *How old are you?* ••➤ Look at the note at **age**¹.

> ➤ **Older** and **oldest** are the usual comparative and superlative forms of **old**: *My father's older than my mother.* • *I'm the oldest in the class.* **Elder** and **eldest** can be used when comparing the ages of people, especially members of a family. However they cannot be used with *than*.

4 the old noun [pl] old people ••➤ Look at **the elderly** and **the aged**. **5** having been used a lot: *I got rid of all my old clothes.* ••➤ opposite **new** ••➤ Look at **second-hand**. **6** (only *before* a noun) former; previous: *I earn more now than I did in my old job.* **7** (only *before* a noun) known for a long time: *She's a very old friend of mine. We knew each other at school.* **8** (only *before* a noun) (*informal*) used for emphasizing that sth has little importance or value: *I write any old rubbish in my diary.* IDIOM **be an old hand (at sth)** to be good at sth because you have done it often before

,old 'age noun [U] the part of your life when you are old: *He's enjoying life **in** his **old age**.* ••➤ Look at **youth**.

,old-age 'pension noun [U] money paid by the state to people above a certain age –**,old-age 'pensioner** (also **pensioner**) **noun** [C] (*abbr* **OAP**) ••➤ Nowadays the expression **senior citizen** is more common and acceptable.

,old-'fashioned adj 1 usual in the past but not now: *old-fashioned clothes/ideas* • *That word sounds a bit old-fashioned.* **2** (used about people) believing in old ideas, customs, etc: *My parents are quite old-fashioned about some things.* ••➤ Look at **modern** and **unfashionable**.

the ,Old 'Testament noun [sing] the first part of the Bible that tells the history of the Jewish people.

olive /'ɒlɪv/ **noun 1** [C] a small green or black fruit with a bitter taste, used for food and oil: *Fry the onions in a little olive oil.* ••➤ picture on page C3 **2** (also **,olive 'green**) [U], **adj** (of) a colour between yellow and green

the O,lympic 'Games (also **the Olympics**) /ə'lɪmpɪks/ **noun** [pl] an international sports competition which is organized every four years in a different country: *to win a medal at/in the Olympics* • *the Winter/Summer Olympics* –**Olympic adj** (only *before* a noun): *Who holds the Olympic record for the 1500 metres?*

ombudsman /'ɒmbʊdzmən; -mæn/ **noun** [sing] a government official who deals with complaints made by ordinary people against public organizations

omelette (also **omelet**) /'ɒmlɪt/ **noun** [C] a dish made of eggs that have been mixed together very fast (**beaten**) and fried ••➤ picture on page C4

omen /'əʊmən/ **noun** [C] a sign of sth that will happen in the future: *a good/bad omen for the future*

ominous /'ɒmɪnəs/ **adj** suggesting that sth bad is going to happen: *Those black clouds look ominous.*

omission /ə'mɪʃn/ **noun** [C,U] something that has not been included; the act of not including sb/sth: *There were several omissions on the list of names.*

omit /ə'mɪt/ **verb** [T] (**omitting**; **omitted**) **1** to not include sth; to leave sth out: *Several verses of the song can be omitted.* **2** (*formal*) **omit to do sth** to forget or choose not to do sth

★**on** /ɒn/ **adv, prep**

> ➤ For special uses with many verbs and nouns, for example **get on**, **on holiday**, see the verb and noun entries.

1 (also *formal* **upon**) supported by, fixed to or touching sth, especially a surface: *on the table/ceiling/wall* • *We sat on the beach/grass/floor.* • *She was carrying the baby on her back.* • *Write it down on a piece of paper.* • *The ball hit me on the head.* **2** in a place or position: *on a farm/housing estate/campsite* • *a house on the river/seafront/border* • *I live on the other side of town.* • *on the right/left* • *on the way to school* **4** used with ways of travelling and types of travel: *on the bus/train/plane* • *We came **on foot** (=* we walked*).* • *Eddie went past on his bike.* • *to go on a trip/journey/excursion*

> ➤ Note that we say **in the car**.

5 with expressions of time: *on August 19th* • *on Monday* • *on Christmas Day* • *on your* birthday **6** working; being used: *All the lights were on.* ● *Switch* the television *on*. **7** wearing sth; carrying sth in your pocket or bag: *What did she have on?* ● *to put your shoes/ coat/hat/make-up on* ● *I've got no money on me.* ● *You should carry ID on you at all times.* **8** about sth: *We've got a test on irregular verbs tomorrow.* ● *a talk/a book/an article on Japan* **9** happening or arranged to happen: *What's on at the cinema?* ● *Is the meeting still on, or has it been cancelled?* **10** using sth; by means of sth: *I was (talking) on the phone to Laura.* ● *I saw it on television.* ● *I cut my hand on some glass.* ● *Dave spends most evenings on the Internet.* **11** showing the thing or person that is affected by an action or is the object of an action: *Divorce can have a bad effect on children.* ● *He spends a lot on clothes.* ● *Don't waste your time on that.* **12** using drugs or medicine; using a particular kind of food or fuel: *to be on medication/ antibiotics/heroin* ● *Gorillas live on leaves and fruit.* ● *Does this car run on petrol or diesel?* **13** receiving a certain amount of money: *What will you be on* (= how much will you earn) *in your new job?* ● *He's been (living) on unemployment benefit since he lost his job.* **14** showing that sth continues: *The man shouted at us but we walked on.* ● *The speeches went on and on until everyone was bored.* **15** showing the reason for or basis for sth: *She doesn't eat meat on principle.* ● *The film is based on a true story.* **16** compared to: *Sales are up 10% on last year.* **17** immediately; soon after: *He telephoned her on his return from New York.* **18** paid for by sb: *The drinks are on me!*

IDIOMS from now/then on starting from this/ that time and continuing: *From then on she never smoked another cigarette.*

not on not acceptable: *No, you can't stay out that late. It's just not on.*

off and on; on and off → **OFF**[1]

be/go on at sb → **GO**[1]

★**once** /wʌns/ *adv, conj* **1** one time only; on one occasion: *I've only been to France once.* ● *once a week/month/year* ● *I visit them about once every six months.* **2** at some time in the past; formerly: *This house was once the village school.* **3** as soon as; when: *Once you've practised a bit you'll find that it's quite easy.*

IDIOMS all at once all at the same time or suddenly: *People began talking all at once.* ● *All at once she got up and left the room.*

at once **1** immediately; now: *Come here at once!* **2** at the same time: *I can't understand if you all speak at once.*

just this once; (just) for once on this occasion only: *Just this once, I'll help you with your homework.*

once again/more again, as before: *Spring will soon be here once again.*

once and for all now and for the last time: *You've got to make a decision once and for all.*

once in a blue moon (*informal*) very rarely; almost never

once in a while sometimes but not often

once more one more time: *Let's listen to that cassette once more, shall we?*

once upon a time (used at the beginning of a children's story) a long time ago; in the past: *Once upon a time there was a beautiful princess...*

oncoming /ˈɒnkʌmɪŋ/ *adj* (only *before* a noun) coming towards you: *oncoming traffic*

★**one**[1] /wʌn/ *pron, determiner, noun* [C] **1** 1:*There's only one biscuit left.* ● *The journey takes one hour.* ● *If you take one from ten it leaves nine.* ·▸ Look at **first**.

➢ For examples of how to use numbers in sentences, look at **six**.

2 (used when you are talking about a time in the past or future without actually saying when) a certain: *He came to see me one evening last week.* ● *We must go and visit them one day.* **3** used with *the other, another* or *other(s)* to make a contrast: *The twins are so alike that it's hard to tell one from the other.* **4** the one used for emphasizing that there is only one of sth: *She's the one person I trust.* ● *We can't all get in the one car.*

IDIOMS (all) in one all together or combined: *It's a phone and fax machine all in one.*

one after another/the other first one, then the next, etc: *One after another the winners went up to get their prizes.*

one at a time separately; individually: *I'll deal with the problems one at a time.*

one by one separately; individually: *One by one, people began to arrive at the meeting.*

one or two a few: *I've borrowed one or two new books from the library.*

★**one**[2] /wʌn/ *pron, noun* [C] **1** used instead of repeating a noun: *I think I'll have an apple. Would you like one?* **2** one of a member (of a certain group): *He's staying with one of his friends.* ● *One of the children is crying.*

➢ **One of** is always followed by a plural noun. The verb is singular because the subject is **one**: *One of our assistants is ill.* ● *One of the buses was late.*

3 used after *this, that, which* or after an adjective instead of a noun: *'Which dress do you like?' 'This one.'* ● *'Can I borrow some books of yours?' 'Yes. Which ones?'* ● *'This coat's a bit small. You need a bigger one.'* ● *That idea is a very good one.* **4** the one/ the ones used before a group of words that show which person or thing you are talking about: *My house is the one after the post office.* ● *If you find some questions difficult, leave out the ones you don't understand.* **5** (*formal*) used for referring to people in general, including the speaker or writer: *One must be sure of one's facts before criticizing other people.* ·▸ It is very formal to use **one** in this way. In everyday English it is usual to use **you**.

,one a'nother *pron* each other: *We exchanged news with one another.*

,one-'off *noun* [C], *adj* (*informal*) something that is made or that happens only once: *a one-off payment/opportunity*

oneself /wʌn'self/ *pron* **1** used when the person who does an action is also affected by it: *One can teach oneself to play the piano but it is easier to have lessons.* **2** used for emphasis: *One could easily arrange it all oneself.*

IDIOM **(all) by oneself 1** alone ••➤ Look at the note at **alone**. **2** without help

one-'sided *adj* **1** (used about an opinion, an argument, etc) showing only one point of view; not balanced: *Some newspapers give a very one-sided view of politics.* **2** (used about a relationship or a competition) not equal: *The match was very one-sided – we lost 12-1.*

one-to-'one (also **one-on-'one**) *adj, adv* between only two people: *one-to-one English lessons* (= one teacher to one student)

one-'way *adv, adj* **1** (used about roads) that you can only drive along in one direction: *a one-way street* **2** (used about a ticket) that you can use to travel somewhere but not back again: *a one-way ticket* ••➤ synonym **single** ••➤ opposite **return**

ongoing /'ɒngəʊɪŋ/ *adj* (only *before* a noun) continuing to exist now: *It's an ongoing problem.*

onion /'ʌnjən/ *noun* [C,U] a white or red vegetable with many layers. Onions are often used in cooking and have a strong smell that makes some people cry: *a kilo of onions* ● *onion soup* ••➤ picture on page C3

online /ˌɒn'laɪn/ *adj, adv* controlled by or connected to a computer or to the Internet: *an online ticket booking system* ● *I'm studying French online.*

onlooker /'ɒnlʊkə/ *noun* [C] a person who watches sth happening without taking part in it

only /'əʊnli/ *adj, adv, conj* (only *before* a noun) **1** with no others existing or present: *I was the only woman in the room.* ● *This is the only dress we have in your size.* **2** and no one or nothing else; no more than: *She only likes pop music.* ● *I've only asked a few friends to the party.* ● *It's only one o'clock.* **3** the most suitable or the best: *It's so cold that the only thing to do is to sit by the fire.*

➤ In written English **only** is usually placed *before* the word it refers to. In spoken English we can use stress to show which word it refers to and **only** does not have to change position: *I only kissed 'Jane* (= I kissed Jane and no one else). ● *I only 'kissed Jane* (= I kissed Jane but I didn't do anything else).

4 (*informal*) except that; but: *The film was very good, only it was a bit too long.*

IDIOMS **if only →** **IF**

not only…but also both…and: *He not only did the shopping but he also cooked the meal.*
only just 1 not long ago: *I've only just started this job.* **2** almost not; hardly: *We only just had enough money to pay for the meal.*

only 'child *noun* [C] a child who has no brothers or sisters

onset /'ɒnset/ *noun* [sing] the onset (of sth) the beginning (often of sth unpleasant): *the onset of winter/a headache*

onslaught /'ɒnslɔːt/ *noun* [C] an onslaught (on/against sb/sth) a violent or strong attack: *an onslaught on government policy*

onto (also **on to**) /'ɒntə; *before vowels* 'ɒntʌ/ *prep* to a position on sth: *The cat jumped onto the sofa.* ● *The bottle fell off the table onto the floor.* ● *The crowd ran onto the pitch.*

IDIOMS **be onto sb** (*informal*) to have found out about sth illegal that sb is doing: *The police were onto the car thieves.*
be onto sth to have some information, etc that could lead to an important discovery

onwards /'ɒnwədz/ (also **onward** /'ɒnwəd/) *adv* **1** from…onwards continuing from a particular time: *From September onwards it usually begins to get colder.* **2** (*formal*) forward: *The road stretched onwards into the distance.*

ooze /uːz/ *verb* ooze from/out of sth; ooze (with) sth [I,T] to flow slowly out or to allow sth to flow slowly out: *Blood was oozing from a cut on his head.* ● *The fruit was oozing with juice.*

op /ɒp/ (*spoken*) = **OPERATION**(1)

opaque /əʊ'peɪk/ *adj* **1** that you cannot see through: *opaque glass in the door* **2** (*formal*) difficult to understand; not clear ••➤ opposite **transparent**

OPEC /'əʊpek/ *abbr* Organization of Petroleum Exporting Countries

open¹ /'əʊpən/ *adj* **1** not closed or covered: *Don't leave the door open.* ● *an open window* ● *I can't get this bottle of wine open.* ● *She stared at me with her eyes wide open.* ● *The diary was lying open on her desk.* ● *The curtains were open so that we could see into the room.* ● *His shirt was open at the neck.* **2** open (to sb/sth); open (for sth) available for people to enter, visit, use, etc; not closed to the public: *The bank isn't open till 9.30.* ● *The new shopping centre will soon be open.* ● *The hotel damaged by the bomb is now open for business again.* ● *The competition is open to everyone.* ● *The gardens are open to the public* in the summer. ••➤ opposite **closed** or **shut 3** not keeping feelings and thoughts hidden: *Elena doesn't mind talking about her feelings – she's a very open person.* ● *He looked at him with open dislike.* **4** (only *before* a noun) (used about an area of land) away from towns and buildings; (used about an area of sea) at a distance from the land: *open country* **5** (not *before* a noun) not finally decided; still being considered: *Let's leave the details open.*

IDIOMS **have/keep an open mind (about/on sth)** to be ready to listen to or consider new ideas and suggestions
in the open air outside: *Somehow, food eaten in the open air tastes much better.*
keep an eye open/out (for sb/sth) → **EYE¹**
open to sth willing to receive sth: *I'm always open to suggestions.*
with your eyes open → **EYE¹**
with open arms in a friendly way that shows that you are pleased to see sb or have sth: *The unions welcomed the government's decision with open arms.*

★**open**² /'əʊpən/ *verb* **1** [I,T] to move sth or part of sth so that it is no longer closed; to move so as to be no longer closed: *This window won't open – it's stuck.* ● *The parachute failed to open and he was killed.* ● *The book opened at the very page I needed.* ● *Open the curtains, will you?* ● *to open your eyes/hand/ mouth* ● *to open a bag/letter/box* ••➤ opposite **close** or **shut 2** [I,T] to make it possible for people to enter a place: *Does that shop open on Sundays?* ● *The museum opens at 10.* ● *The company are opening two new branches soon.* ● *Police finally opened the road six hours after the accident.* ••➤ opposite **close** or **shut 3** [I,T] to start: *The chairman opened the meeting by welcoming everybody.* ● *I'd like to open a bank account.* ••➤ opposite **close 4** [T] (*computing*) to start a program or file so that you can use it on the screen

IDIOM **open fire (at/on sb/sth)** to start shooting: *He ordered his men to open fire.*

PHRASAL VERBS **open into/onto sth** to lead to another room, area or place: *This door opens onto the garden.*

open out to become wider

open up 1 to talk about what you feel and think **2** to open a door

open (sth) up 1 to become available or to make sth available: *When I left school all sorts of opportunities opened up for me.* **2** to start business: *The restaurant opened up last year.*

the open³ /'əʊpən/ *noun* [sing] outside or in the countryside: *After working in an office I like to be out in the open at weekends.*

IDIOM **bring sth out into the open; come out into the open** to make sth known publicly; to be known publicly: *I'm glad our secret has come out into the open at last.*

,**open-'air** *adj* not inside a building: *an open-air swimming pool*

'**open day** *noun* [C] a day when the public can visit a place that they cannot usually go into: *The hospital is having an open day next month.*

opener /'əʊpnə/ *noun* [C] (in compounds nouns) a thing that takes the lid, etc off sth: *a tin-opener* ● *a bottle-opener*

opening /'əʊpnɪŋ/ *noun* [C] **1** a space or hole that sb/sth can go through: *We were able to get through an opening in the hedge.* ••➤ picture at **tent 2** the beginning or first part of sth: *The film is famous for its dramatic opening.* **3** a ceremony to celebrate the first time a public building, road, etc is used: *the opening of the new hospital* **4** a job which is available: *We have an opening for a sales manager at the moment.* **5** a good opportunity: *I'm sure she'll be a great journalist – all she needs is an opening.* –**opening** *adj* (only *before* a noun): *the opening chapter of a book* ● *the opening ceremony of the Olympic Games*

openly /'əʊpənli/ *adv* honestly; not keeping anything secret: *I think you should discuss your feelings openly with each other.*

,**open-'minded** *adj* ready to consider new ideas and opinions

openness /'əʊpənnəs/ *noun* [U] the quality of being honest and ready to talk about your feelings

,**open-'plan** *adj* (used about a large area indoors) not divided into separate rooms: *an open-plan office*

the ,Open Uni'versity *noun* [sing] (*Brit*) a university whose students study mainly at home. Their work is sent to them by post and there are special television and radio programmes for them.

opera /'ɒprə/ *noun* [C,U] a play in which the actors (**opera singers**) sing the words to music; works of this kind performed as entertainment: *an opera by Wagner* ● *Do you like opera?* ● *a comic opera* ••➤ Look at **soap opera**.

'**opera house** *noun* [C] a theatre where operas are performed

★**operate** /'ɒpəreɪt/ *verb* **1** [I,T] to work, or to make sth work: *I don't understand how this machine operates.* ● *These switches here operate the central heating.* ••➤ synonym **function 2** [I,T] to do business; to manage sth: *The firm operates from its central office in Bristol.* **3** [I] to act or to have an effect: *Several factors were operating to our advantage.* **4** [I] operate (on sb/sth) (for sth) to cut open a person's body in hospital in order to deal with a part that is damaged, infected, etc: *The surgeon is going to operate on her in the morning* ● *He was operated on for appendicitis.*

operatic /,ɒpə'rætɪk/ *adj* connected with opera: *operatic music*

'**operating system** *noun* [C] a computer program that organizes a number of other programs at the same time

'**operating theatre** (also **theatre**) *noun* [C] a room in a hospital where operations are performed

★**operation** /,ɒpə'reɪʃn/ *noun* **1** [C] (also spoken **op**) the process of cutting open a patient's body in order to deal with a part inside: *He had an operation to remove his appendix.* **2** [C] an organized activity that involves many people doing different things: *A rescue operation was mounted to find the missing children.* **3** [C] a business or company involving many parts **4** [C] an act performed by a machine, especially a computer **5** [U] the way in which you make sth work: *The operation of these machines is extremely simple.*

IDIOM **be in operation; come into operation** to be/start working or having an effect: *The new tax system will come into operation in the spring.*

operational /,ɒpə'reɪʃənl/ *adj* **1** (usually *before* a noun) connected with the way a business, machine, system, etc works **2** (not usually before a noun) ready for use: *The new factory is now fully operational.* **3** (only *before* a noun) connected with military operations

operative /'ɒpərətɪv/ *adj* (*formal*) **1** working, able to be used; in use: *The new law will be operative from 1 May.* **2** connected with a medical operation

* **operator** /'ɒpəreɪtə/ *noun* [C] **1** a person whose job is to connect telephone calls, for the public or in a particular building: *Dial 100 for the operator.* • *a switchboard operator* **2** a person whose job is to work a particular machine or piece of equipment: *a computer operator* **3** a person or company that does certain types of business: *a tour operator*

* **opinion** /ə'pɪnjən/ *noun* **1** [C] an opinion (of sb/sth); an opinion (on/about sth) what you think about sb/sth: *She asked me for my opinion of her new hairstyle and I told her.* • *He has very strong opinions on almost everything.* • *In my opinion, you're making a terrible mistake.* **2** [U] what people in general think about sth: *Public opinion is in favour of a change in the law.*
IDIOMS be of the opinion that... (*formal*) to think or believe that...
have a good/high opinion of sb/sth; have a bad/low/poor opinion of sb/sth to think that sb/sth is good/bad
a matter of opinion → **MATTER¹**

o'pinion poll = **POLL¹**(1)

opium /'əʊpiəm/ *noun* [U] a powerful drug that is made from the seeds of a flower (poppy)

opp *abbr* opposite

* **opponent** /ə'pəʊnənt/ *noun* [C] **1** (in sport or competitions) a person who plays against sb: *They are the toughest opponents we've played against.* **2** an opponent (of sth) a person who disagrees with sb's actions, plans or beliefs and tries to stop or change them: *the President's political opponents*

* **opportunity** /ˌɒpə'tjuːnəti/ *noun* [C,U] (*pl* **opportunities**) an opportunity (for sth/to do sth) a chance to do sth that you would like to do; a situation or a time in which it is possible to do sth that you would like to do: *There will be plenty of opportunity for asking questions later.* • *I have a golden opportunity to go to America now that my sister lives there.* • *When we're finally alone, I'll take the opportunity to ask him a few personal questions.* • *I'll give Steve your message if I get the opportunity.* ••➤ Look at the note at **occasion**.

oppose /ə'pəʊz/ *verb* [T] to disagree with sb's beliefs, actions or plans and to try to change or stop them: *They opposed the plan to build a new road.*

opposed /ə'pəʊzd/ *adj* opposed to sth disagreeing with a plan, action, etc; believing that sth is wrong: *She has always been strongly opposed to experiments on animals.*
IDIOM as opposed to (used to emphasize the difference between two things) rather than; and not: *Your work will be judged by quality, as opposed to quantity.*

* **opposite** /'ɒpəzɪt/ *adj, adv, prep* **1** in a position on the other side of sb/sth; facing: *The old town and the new town are on opposite sides of the river.* • *You sit there and I'll sit opposite.*
➤ Sometimes **opposite** is used after a noun: *Write your answer in the space opposite.*

opposite   in front of

2 completely different: *I can't walk with you because I'm going in the opposite direction.* • *the opposite sex* (= the other sex) –opposite *noun* [C]: *'Hot' is the opposite of 'cold'.*
IDIOM your opposite number a person who does the same job or has the same position as you in a different company, organization, team, etc: *The Prime Minister met his Italian opposite number.*

* **opposition** /ˌɒpə'zɪʃn/ *noun* [U] **1** opposition (to sb/sth) the feeling of disagreeing with sth and the action of trying to change it: *He expressed strong opposition to the plan.* **2** the opposition [sing] the person or team who you compete against in sport, business, etc: *We need to find out what the opposition is doing.* **3** the Opposition [sing] the politicians or the political parties that are in Parliament but not in the government: *the leader of the Opposition* • *Opposition MPs* ••➤ In numbers **2** and **3**, **opposition** can be used with either a singular or a plural verb.

oppress /ə'pres/ *verb* [T] (usually passive) to treat a group of people in a cruel and unfair way by not allowing them the same freedom and rights as others –oppressed *adj*: *an oppressed minority* –oppression *noun* [U]: *a struggle against oppression*

oppressive /ə'presɪv/ *adj* **1** allowing no freedom; controlling by force **2** (used especially about heat or the atmosphere) causing you to feel very uncomfortable

opt /ɒpt/ *verb* [I] opt to do sth/for sth to choose or decide to do or have sth after thinking about it
PHRASAL VERB opt out (of sth) to choose not to take part in sth; to decide to stop being involved in sth

optical /'ɒptɪkl/ *adj* connected with the sense of sight: *optical instruments*

optical il'lusion *noun* [C] an image that tricks the eye and makes you think you can see sth that you cannot

optician /ɒp'tɪʃn/ *noun* [C] a person whose job is to test eyes, sell glasses, etc: *I have to go to the optician's* (= the shop) *for an eye test.*

optimism /'ɒptɪmɪzəm/ *noun* [U] the feeling that the future will be good or successful: *There is considerable optimism that the economy will improve.* ••➤ opposite **pessimism** –optimist *noun* [C]: *I am an optimist and I believe that the talks will be successful.* ••➤ opposite **pessimist**

optimistic /ˌɒptɪ'mɪstɪk/ *adj* optimistic (about sth/that...): *I've applied for the job but I'm not very optimistic that I'll get it.*

•➤ opposite **pessimistic** –**optimistically** /-kli/ **adv** •➤ opposite **pessimistically**

★**option** /'ɒpʃn/ **noun** [U,C] something that you can choose to do; the freedom to choose: *She looked carefully at all the options before deciding on a career.* ● *Students* **have the option** *of studying part-time or full-time.* ● *If you're late again, you will give us* **no option but to** *dismiss you.* •➤ synonym **choice**

optional /'ɒpʃənl/ **adj** that you can choose or not choose: *an optional subject at school* •➤ opposite **compulsory** or **obligatory**

★**or** /ɔ:/ **conj 1** used in a list of possibilities or choices: *Would you like to sit here or next to the window?* ● *Are you interested or not?* ● *For the main course, you can have lamb, beef or fish.* •➤ Look at **either...or**. **2** if not; otherwise: *Don't drive so fast or you'll have an accident!* •➤ **Or else** and **otherwise** can be used with this meaning. **3** (after a negative) and neither; and not: *She hasn't phoned or written to me for weeks.* ● *I've never been either to Italy or Spain.* •➤ Look at **neither ...nor**. **4** used between two numbers to show approximately how many: *I've been there five or six times.* **5** used before a word or phrase that explains or comments on what has been said before: *20% of the population, or one in five*

IDIOMS **or else** → **ELSE**

or so about: *You should feel better in three days or so.*

or something/somewhere (*spoken*) used for showing that you are not sure, cannot remember or do not know which thing or place: *She's a computer programmer or something.*

➤ Another phrase that shows that you are not sure is **...or other**: *He muttered something or other about having no time and disappeared.*

★**oral¹** /'ɔ:rəl/ **adj 1** spoken, not written: *an oral test* **2** concerning or using the mouth: *oral hygiene* •➤ Look at **aural**. –**orally adv**: *You can ask the questions orally or in writing.* ● *This medicine is taken orally* (= is swallowed).

oral² /'ɔ:rəl/ **noun** [C] a spoken exam: *I've got my German oral next week.*

★**orange¹** /'ɒrɪndʒ/ **noun 1** [C,U] (*Brit*) a round fruit with a thick skin that is divided into sections (**segments**) inside and is a colour between red and yellow: *orange juice/peel* ● *an orange tree* •➤ picture on page C3 **2** [U,C] a drink made from oranges or with the taste of oranges; a glass of this drink **3** [U,C] the colour of this fruit, between red and yellow

★**orange²** /'ɒrɪndʒ/ **adj** of the colour orange: *orange paint*

‚**orange 'squash noun** [C,U] (*Brit*) a drink made by adding water to an orange-flavoured liquid

orator /'ɒrətə/ **noun** [C] (*formal*) a person who is good at making public speeches

orbit /'ɔ:bɪt/ **noun** [C,U] a curved path taken

by a planet or another object as it moves around another planet, star, moon, etc –**orbit verb** [I,T]

orbital /'ɔ:bɪtl/ **adj 1** (used about a road) built around the outside of a city or town to reduce the amount of traffic travelling through the centre **2** connected with the orbit of a planet or another object in space –**orbital noun** [C,usually sing]

orchard /'ɔ:tʃəd/ **noun** [C] a piece of land on which fruit trees are grown: *a cherry orchard*

★**orchestra** /'ɔ:kɪstrə/ **noun** [C] a large group of musicians who play many different musical instruments together, led by one person (a **conductor**): *a symphony orchestra*

➤ An orchestra usually plays classical music. Pop music, jazz, etc are played by a **group** or **band**.

–**orchestral** /ɔ:'kestrəl/ **adj**

orchid /'ɔ:kɪd/ **noun** [C] a beautiful and sometimes rare type of plant that has flowers of unusual shapes and bright colours •➤ picture on page C2

ordeal /ɔ:'di:l; 'ɔ:di:l/ **noun** [C,usually sing] a very unpleasant or difficult experience

★**order¹** /'ɔ:də/ **noun 1** [U,sing] the way in which people or things are arranged in relation to each other: *a list of names in* **alphabetical order** ● *Try to put the things you have to do* **in order** *of importance.* ● *What's the order of events today?* **2** [U] an organized state, where everything is in its right place: *I really must* **put my notes in order**, *because I can never find what I'm looking for.* •➤ opposite **disorder 3** [C] an **order** (**for sb**) (**to do sth**) sth that you are told to do by sb in a position of authority: *In the army, you have to* **obey orders** *at all times.* ● *She* **gave the order** *for the work to be started.* **4** [U] the situation in which laws, rules, authority, etc are obeyed: *Following last week's riots, order has now been restored.* •➤ Look at **disorder**. **5** [C,U] an **order** (**for sth**) a request asking for sth to be made, supplied or sent: *The company has just received a major export order.* ● *The book I need is* **on order** (= they are waiting for it to arrive). **6** [C] a request for food or drinks in a hotel, restaurant, etc; the food or drinks you asked for: *Can I* **take your order** *now, sir?*

IDIOMS **in order to do sth** with the purpose or intention of doing sth; so that sth can be done: *We left early in order to avoid the traffic.*

in/into reverse order → **REVERSE³**

in working order (used about machines, etc) working properly, not broken

law and order → **LAW**

out of order 1 (used about a machine, etc) not working properly or not working at all: *I had to walk up to the tenth floor because the lift was out of order.* **2** (*informal*) (used about a person's behaviour) unacceptable, because it is rude, etc: *That comment was completely out of order!*

★**order²** /'ɔ:də/ **verb 1** [T] **order sb** (**to do sth**) to use your position of authority to tell sb to do sth or to say that sth must happen: *I'm not*

asking you to do your homework, I'm ordering you! • *The company was ordered to pay compensation to its former employees.* **2** [T] to ask for sth to be made, supplied or sent somewhere: *The shop didn't have the book I wanted so I ordered it.* **3** order (sb) (sth); order (sth) (for sb) [I,T] to ask for food or drinks in a restaurant, hotel, etc: *Are you ready to order yet, madam?* • *Can you order me a sandwich while I make a phone call?* • *Could you order a sandwich for me?*
PHRASAL VERB order sb about/around to keep telling sb what to do and how to do it: *Stop ordering me about! You're not my father.*

orderly¹ /'ɔːdəli/ **adj 1** arranged or organized in a tidy way: *an orderly office/desk* **2** well-behaved; peaceful ••➤ opposite **disorderly**

orderly² /'ɔːdəli/ **noun** [C] (*pl* **orderlies**) a worker in a hospital, usually doing jobs that do not need special training

ordinal /'ɔːdɪnl/ (also ˌordinal 'number) **noun** [C] a number that shows the order or position of sth in a series: *'First', 'second', and 'third' are ordinals.* ••➤ Look at **cardinal**.

ordinarily /'ɔːdnrəli/ **adv** usually; generally: *Ordinarily, I don't work as late as this.*

★**ordinary** /'ɔːdnri/ **adj** normal; not unusual or different from others: *It's interesting to see how ordinary people live in other countries.*
IDIOM out of the ordinary unusual; different from normal

ore /ɔː/ **noun** [C,U] rock or earth from which metal can be taken: *iron ore*

★**organ** /'ɔːgən/ **noun** [C] **1** one of the parts inside your body that have a particular function: ***vital organs*** (= those such as the heart and liver which help to keep you alive) • *sexual/reproductive organs* **2** a large musical instrument like a piano with pipes through which air is forced. Organs are often found in churches: *organ music* ••➤ Look at the note at **piano**. –**organist noun** [C]

organic /ɔː'gænɪk/ **adj 1** (used about food or farming methods) produced by or using natural materials, without artificial chemicals: *organic vegetables* • *organic farming* **2** produced by or existing in living things: *organic compounds/molecules* ••➤ opposite **inorganic** –**organically** /-kli/ **adv**: *organically grown/produced*

organism /'ɔːgənɪzəm/ **noun** [C] a living thing, especially one that is so small that you can only see it with a special instrument (a microscope)

★**organization** (also **-isation**) /ˌɔːgənaɪ-'zeɪʃn/ **noun 1** [C] a group of people who form a business, club, etc together in order to achieve a particular aim: *She works for a voluntary organization helping homeless people.* **2** [U] the activity of making preparations or arrangements for sth: *An enormous amount of organization went into the festival.* **3** [U] the way in which sth is organized, arranged or prepared ••➤ opposite **disorganization** –**organizational** (also **-isational**) /-ʃənl/ **adj**: *The job requires a high level of organizational ability.*

★**organize** (also **-ise**) /'ɔːgənaɪz/ **verb 1** [T] to plan or arrange an event, activity, etc: *The school organizes trips to various places of interest.* **2** [I,T] to put or arrange things into a system or logical order: *Can you decide what needs doing? I'm hopeless at organizing.* • *You need to organize your work more carefully.* –**organizer** (also **-iser**) [C]: *The organizers of the concert said that it had been a great success.*

organized (also **-ised**) /'ɔːgənaɪzd/ **adj 1** arranged or planned in the way mentioned: *a carefully/badly/well organized trip* **2** (used about a person) able to plan your work, life, etc well: *I wish I were as organized as you!* ••➤ opposite for sense 1 and 2 **disorganized 3** (only *before* a noun) involving a large number of people working together to do sth in a way that has been carefully planned: *an organized campaign against cruelty to animals* • *organized crime* (= done by a large group of professional criminals)

orgasm /'ɔːgæzəm/ **noun** [U,C] the point of greatest sexual pleasure: *to have an orgasm*

orgy /'ɔːdʒi/ **noun** [C] (*pl* **orgies**) **1** a party, involving a lot of eating, drinking and sexual activity **2** an orgy (of sth) a period of doing sth in a wild way, without control: *an orgy of destruction*

orient¹ /'ɔːriənt; 'ɒrient/ (*Brit also* **orientate** /'ɔːriənteɪt/) **verb** [T] orient yourself to find out where you are; to become familiar with a place ••➤ Look at **disorientate**.

the Orient² /'ɔːriənt/ **noun** [sing] (*formal*) the eastern part of the world, especially China and Japan

oriental /ˌɔːri'entl/ **adj** Oriental (*old-fashioned*) coming from or belonging to the East or Far East: *oriental languages* ••➤ Be careful. Many people find this word offensive now. It is better to say 'Asian'.

oriented /'ɔːrientɪd/ (also **orientated**) /'ɔːriənteɪtɪd/ **adj** for or interested in a particular type of person or thing: *Our products are male-oriented.* • *She's very career orientated.*

orienteering /ˌɔːriən'tɪərɪŋ/ **noun** [U] a sport in which you find your way across country on foot, using a map and an instrument that shows direction (a compass)

origin /'ɒrɪdʒɪn/ **noun** [C,U] (often used in the plural) the point from which sth starts; the cause of sth: *This particular tradition **has its origins in** Wales.* • *Many English words are of Latin origin.* **2** (often used in the plural) the country, race, culture, etc that a person comes from: *people of African origin*

★**original¹** /ə'rɪdʒənl/ **adj 1** (only *before* a noun) first; earliest (before any changes or developments): *The original meaning of this word is different from the meaning it has nowadays.* **2** new and interesting; different from others of its type: *There are no original ideas in his work.* **3** made or created first, before copies: *'Is that the original painting?' 'No, it's a copy.'*

o

---

original² /əˈrɪdʒənl/ **noun** [C] the first document, painting, etc that was made; not a copy: *Could you make a photocopy of my birth certificate and give the original back to me?*

originality /ə,rɪdʒəˈnæləti/ **noun** [U] the quality of being new and interesting

originally /əˈrɪdʒənəli/ **adv 1** in the beginning, before any changes or developments: *I'm from London originally, but I left there when I was very young.* **2** in a way or style that is new and different from any others: *She has a talent for expressing simple ideas originally.*

originate /əˈrɪdʒɪneɪt/ **verb** [I] (*formal*) to happen or appear for the first time in a particular place or situation

ornament /ˈɔːnəmənt/ **noun** [C] an object that you have because it is attractive, not because it is useful. Ornaments are used to decorate rooms, etc.

ornamental /,ɔːnəˈmentl/ **adj** made or put somewhere in order to look attractive, not for any practical use

ornate /ɔːˈneɪt/ **adj** covered with a lot of small complicated designs as decoration

ornithology /,ɔːnɪˈθɒlədʒi/ **noun** [U] the study of birds –**ornithologist** /-ɪst/ **noun** [C]

orphan /ˈɔːfn/ **noun** [C] a child whose parents are dead –**orphan verb** [T] (usually passive): *She was orphaned when she was three and went to live with her grandparents.*

orphanage /ˈɔːfənɪdʒ/ **noun** [C] a home for children whose parents are dead •➤ A more common word is **children's home.**

orthodox /ˈɔːθədɒks/ **adj 1** that most people believe, do or accept; usual: *orthodox opinions/methods* •➤ opposite **unorthodox 2** (in certain religions) closely following the old, traditional beliefs, ceremonies, etc: *an orthodox Jew* • *the Greek Orthodox Church*

ostentatious /,ɒstenˈteɪʃəs/ **adj 1** expensive or noticeable in a way that is intended to impress other people: *ostentatious gold jewellery* **2** behaving in a way that is intended to impress people with how rich or important you are –**ostentatiously adv**

ostracize (also **-ise**) /ˈɒstrəsaɪz/ **verb** [T] (*formal*) to refuse to allow sb to be a member of a social group; to refuse to meet or talk to sb

ostrich /ˈɒstrɪtʃ/ **noun** [C] a very large African bird with a long neck and long legs, which can run very fast but which cannot fly

★**other** /ˈʌðə/ **determiner, pron 1** in addition to or different from the one or ones that have already been mentioned: *I hadn't got any other plans that evening so I accepted their invitation.* • *If you're busy now, I'll come back some other time.* • *I like this jumper but not the colour. Have you got any others?* • *Some of my friends went to university, others didn't.* • *She doesn't care what other people think.*

➤ **Other** cannot be used after 'an'. Look at **another.**

2 (after *the, my, your, his, her,* etc with a singular noun) the second of two people or things, when the first has already been

mentioned: *I can only find one sock. Have you seen the other one?* **3** (after *the, my, your, his, her,* etc with a plural noun) the rest of a group or number of people or things: *Their youngest son still lives with them but their other children have left home.* • *I'll have to wear this shirt because all my others are dirty* • *Mick and I got a taxi there, the others walked.*

IDIOMS **every other** ➔ **EVERY**

in other words used for saying sth in a different way: *My boss said she would have to let me go. In other words, she sacked me.*

one after another/the other ➔ **ONE¹**

other than (usually after a negative) apart from; except (for): *The plane was a little late, but other than that the journey was fine.*

the other day/morning/week recently, not long ago: *An old friend rang me the other day.*

the other way round ➔ **ROUND²**

sb/sth/somewhere or other ➔ **OR**

★**otherwise** /ˈʌðəwaɪz/ **adv, conj 1** (used for stating what would happen if you do not do sth or if sth does not happen) if not: *You have to press the red button, otherwise it won't work.* **2** apart from that: *I'm a bit tired but otherwise I feel fine.* **3** in a different way to the way mentioned; differently

otter

tail

otter /ˈɒtə/ **noun** [C] a river animal with brown fur that eats fish

ouch /aʊtʃ/ (also **ow** /aʊ/) **interj** used when reacting to a sudden feeling of pain

★**ought to** /ˈɔːt tə/ *before vowels and in final position* /ˈɔːt tuː/ **modal verb** (*negative* **ought not to;** *short form* **oughtn't to** /ˈɔːtnt tə/ *before vowels and in final position* /ˈɔːtnt tuː/) **1** used to say what sb should do: *You ought to visit your parents more often.* • *She oughtn't to make private phone calls in work time.* • *He oughtn't to have been driving so fast.* **2** used to say what should happen or what you expect: *She ought to pass her test.* • *They ought to be here by now. They left at six.* • *There ought to be more buses in the rush hour.* **3** used for asking for and giving advice about what to do: *You ought to read this book. It's really interesting.*

➤ For more information about modal verbs, look at the **Quick Grammar Reference** section at the back of this dictionary.

ounce /aʊns/ **noun 1** [C] (*abbr* **oz**) a measure of weight; 28·35 grams. There are 16 ounces in a pound: *For this recipe you need four ounces of flour.* **2** [sing] **an ounce of sth** (usually in negative statements) a very small amount of sth: *He hasn't got an ounce of imagination.*

★ **our** /ɑː; 'aʊə/ **determiner** of or belonging to us: *Our house is at the bottom of the road.* • *This is our first visit to Britain.*

★ **ours** /ɑːz; 'aʊəz/ **pron** the one or ones belonging to us: *Their garden is quite nice but I prefer ours.*

★ **ourselves** /ɑː'selvz; ˌaʊə's-/ **pron 1** used when the people who do an action are also affected by it: *Let's forget all about work and just enjoy ourselves.* • *They asked us to wait so we sat down and made ourselves comfortable.* **2** used for emphasis: *Do you think we should paint the flat ourselves?* (= or should we ask sb else to do it for us?)

IDIOM **(all) by ourselves 1** alone: *Now that we're by ourselves, could I ask you a personal question?* •➤ Look at the note at **alone**. **2** without help: *We managed to move all our furniture into the new flat by ourselves.*

★ **out¹** /aʊt/ **adj, adv**

➤ For special uses with many verbs, for example **look out**, look at the verb entries.

1 away from the inside of a place: *He opened the drawer and took a fork out.* • *She opened the window and put her head out.* • *Can you show me the way out?* **2** not at home or in your place of work: *My manager was out when she called.* • *I'd love a night out – I'm bored of staying at home.* **3** a long distance away from a place, for example from land or your country: *The current is quite strong so don't swim too far out.* **4** (used about the sea) when the water is furthest away from the shore: *Don't swim when the tide is on the way out.* **5** used for showing that sth is no longer hidden: *I love the spring when all the flowers are out.* • *The secret's out now. There's no point pretending any more.* **6** made available to the public; published: *There'll be a lot of controversy when her book comes out next year.* **7** in a loud voice; clearly: *She cried out in pain.* **8** not in fashion: *Short skirts are out this season.* **9** (*spoken*) not possible or acceptable: *I'm afraid Friday is out. I've got a meeting that day.* **10** (used about a player in a game or sport) not allowed to continue playing: *If you get three answers wrong, you're out.* **11** (used about a ball, etc in a game or sport) not inside the playing area and therefore not allowed **12** (used when you are calculating sth) making or containing a mistake; wrong: *My guess was only out by a few centimetres.* **13** (used about a light or a fire) not on; not burning: *The lights are out. They must be in bed.* • *Once the fire was completely out, experts were sent in to inspect the damage.*

IDIOMS **be out for sth; be out to do sth** to try hard to get or do sth: *I'm not out for revenge.*
be/come out to tell family, friends, etc that you are a homosexual
out-and-out complete: *It was out-and-out war*

between us.
ˌout 'loud = ALOUD

out² /aʊt/ **verb** [T] to say publicly that sb is a homosexual, especially when he/she would rather keep it a secret: *The politician was eventually outed by a tabloid newspaper.*

the outback /'aʊtbæk/ **noun** [sing] the part of a country (especially Australia) which is a long way from the coast and towns, where few people live

outboard motor /ˌaʊtbɔːd 'məʊtə/ **noun** [C] an engine that can be fixed to a boat

outbreak /'aʊtbreɪk/ **noun** [C] the sudden start of sth unpleasant (especially a disease or violence): *an outbreak of cholera/fighting*

outburst /'aʊtbɜːst/ **noun** [C] a sudden expression of a strong feeling, especially anger: *Afterwards, she apologized for her outburst.*

outcast /'aʊtkɑːst/ **noun** [C] a person who is no longer accepted by society or by a group of people: *a social outcast*

outclass /ˌaʊt'klɑːs/ **verb** [T] (often passive) to be much better than sb/sth, especially in a game or competition

outcome /'aʊtkʌm/ **noun** [C] the result or effect of an action or an event

outcry /'aʊtkraɪ/ **noun** [C, usually sing] (*pl* **outcries**) a strong protest by a large number of people because they disagree with sth: *The public outcry forced the government to change its mind about the new tax.*

outdated /ˌaʊt'deɪtɪd/ **adj** not useful or common any more; old-fashioned: *A lot of the computer equipment is getting outdated.*

outdo /ˌaʊt'duː/ **verb** [T] (*pres part* **outdoing**; *3rd pers sing pres* **outdoes** /-'dʌz/; *pt* **outdid** /-'dɪd/; *pp* **outdone** /-'dʌn/) to do sth better than another person; to be more successful than sb else: *Not to be outdone* (= not wanting anyone else to do better), *she tried again.*

★ **outdoor** /'aʊtdɔː/ **adj** (only *before* a noun) happening, done, or used outside, not in a building: *an outdoor swimming pool* • *outdoor clothing/activities* •➤ opposite **indoor**

★ **outdoors** /ˌaʊt'dɔːz/ **adv** outside a building: *It's a very warm evening so why don't we eat outdoors?* •➤ synonym **out of doors** •➤ opposite **indoors** •➤ Look at **outside**.

★ **outer** /'aʊtə/ **adj** (only *before* a noun) **1** on the outside of sth: *the outer layer of skin on an onion* **2** far from the inside or the centre of sth: *the outer suburbs of a city* •➤ opposite **inner**

outermost /'aʊtəməʊst/ **adj** (only *before* a noun) furthest from the inside or centre; most distant •➤ opposite **innermost**

ˌouter 'space = SPACE¹(2)

outfit /'aʊtfɪt/ **noun** [C] a set of clothes that are worn together for a particular occasion or purpose: *I'm going to buy a whole new outfit for the party.*

outgoing /'aʊtgəʊɪŋ/ **adj 1** friendly and interested in other people and new experiences **2** (only *before* a noun) leaving a job or a place: *the outgoing president/government* ● *Put all the outgoing mail in a pile on that table.* ∙➤ opposite **incoming**

outgoings /'aʊtgəʊɪŋz/ **noun** [pl] (*Brit*) an amount of money that you spend regularly for example every week or month ∙➤ opposite **income**

outgrow /ˌaʊt'grəʊ/ **verb** [T] (*pt* **outgrew** /-'gruː/; *pp* **outgrown** /-'grəʊn/) to become too old or too big for sth

outing /'aʊtɪŋ/ **noun** [C] a short trip for pleasure: *to go on an outing to the zoo*

outlandish /aʊt'lændɪʃ/ **adj** very strange or unusual: *outlandish clothes*

outlast /aʊt'lɑːst/ **verb** [T] to continue to exist or to do sth for a longer time than sb/sth

outlaw¹ /'aʊtlɔː/ **verb** [T] to make sth illegal

outlaw² /'aʊtlɔː/ **noun** [C] (*old-fashioned*) (used in past times) a person who has done sth illegal and is hiding to avoid being caught

outlay /'aʊtleɪ/ **noun** [C,usually sing] **outlay (on sth)** money that is spent, especially in order to start a business or project

outlet /'aʊtlet/ **noun** [C] **an outlet (for sth) 1** a way of expressing and making good use of strong feelings, ideas or energy: *Gary found an outlet for his aggression in boxing.* **2** a shop, business, etc that sells goods made by a particular company or of a particular type: *fast food/retail outlets* **3** a pipe through which a gas or liquid can escape

★**outline¹** /'aʊtlaɪn/ **noun** [C] **1** a description of the most important facts or ideas about sth: *a brief outline of Indian history* **2** a line that shows the shape or outside edge of sb/sth: *She could see the outline of a person through the mist.*

outline² /'aʊtlaɪn/ **verb** [T] **outline sth (to sb)** to tell sb or give the most important facts or ideas about sth

outlive /ˌaʊt'lɪv/ **verb** [T] to live or exist longer than sb/sth

outlook /'aʊtlʊk/ **noun** [C] **1 an outlook (on sth)** your attitude to or feeling about life and the world: *an optimistic outlook on life* **2** outlook (for sth) what will probably happen: *The outlook for the economy is not good.*

outlying /'aʊtlaɪɪŋ/ **adj** (only *before* a noun) far from the centre of a town or city: *The bus service to the outlying villages is very poor.*

outmoded /ˌaʊt'məʊdɪd/ **adj** (only *before* a noun) no longer common or fashionable

outnumber /ˌaʊt'nʌmbə/ **verb** [T] (often passive) to be greater in number than an enemy, another team, etc: *The enemy troops outnumbered us by three to one.*

★**out of prep 1** used with verbs expressing movement away from the inside of sth: *She took her purse out of her bag.* ● *to get out of bed* ∙➤ opposite **into 2** away from or no longer in a place or situation: *He's out of the country on business.* ● *The doctors say she's out of danger.* **3** at a distance from a place: *We live a long way out of London.* **4** used for saying which feeling causes you to do sth: *I*

was only asking out of curiosity. **5** used for saying what you use to make sth else: *What is this knife made out of?* ● *to be made out of wood/metal/plastic/gold* **6** from among a number or set: *Nine out of ten people prefer this model.* **7** from; having sth as its source: *I copied the recipe out of a book.* ● *I paid for it out of the money I won on the lottery.* **8** used for saying that you no longer have sth: *to be out of milk/sugar/tea* ● *He's been out of work for months.* **9** used for saying that sth is not as it should be: *My notes are all out of order and I can't find the right page.*

be/feel out of it to feel lonely and unhappy because you are not included in sth *I don't speak French so I felt rather out of it at the meeting.*

out of bounds → **BOUNDS**

out of order → **ORDER¹**

out-of-work adj unable to find a job unemployed: *an out-of-work actor*

outpatient /'aʊtpeɪʃnt/ **noun** [C] a person who goes to a hospital for treatment but who does not stay there during the night

output /'aʊtpʊt/ **noun** [U,C] **1** the amount that a person or machine produces **2** the information that a computer produces ∙➤ Look at **input**.

outrage /'aʊtreɪdʒ/ **noun 1** [C] something that is very bad or wrong and that causes you to feel great anger: *It's an outrage that such poverty should exist in the 21st century.* **2** [U] great anger: *a feeling of outrage* –**outrage verb** [T]

outrageous /aʊt'reɪdʒəs/ **adj** that makes you very angry or shocked: *outrageous behaviour/prices* –**outrageously adv**

outright /aʊt'raɪt; 'aʊtraɪt/ **adj, adv 1** open and direct; openly and directly: *She told them outright what she thought about it.* **2** complete and clear; completely and clearly: *an outright victory* ● *to win outright* **3** not gradually; immediately: *They were able to buy the house outright.*

outset /'aʊtset/ **noun**

at/from the outset (of sth) at/from the beginning (of sth)

★**outside¹** /ˌaʊt'saɪd/ **adv, prep 1** in, at or to a place that is not in a room or not in a building: *Please wait outside for a few minutes.* ● *Leave your muddy boots outside the door.* ∙➤ Look at **outdoors** and **out of doors** (at the entry for **door**). **2** (*US also* **outside of**) not in: *You may do as you wish outside office hours.* ● *a small village just outside Stratford*

★**outside²** /'aʊtsaɪd/ **adj** (only *before* a noun) **1** of or on the outer side or surface of sth: *the outside walls of a building* **2** not part of the main building: *an outside toilet* **3** not connected with or belonging to a particular group or organization: *We can't do all the work by ourselves. We'll need outside help.* **4** (used about a chance or possibility) very small

the outside world people, places, activities, etc that are away from the area where you live and your own experience of life

★**outside**³ /ˌaʊt'saɪd/ noun 1 [C, usually sing] the outer side or surface of sth: *There is a list of all the ingredients on the outside of the packet.* 2 [sing] the area that is near or round a building, etc: *We've only seen the church from the outside.* 3 [sing] the part of a road, a track, etc that is away from the side that you usually drive on, run on, etc: *The other runners all overtook him on the outside.* ··➤ opposite for all senses **inside**

IDIOM **at the outside** at the most: *It will take us 3 days at the outside.*

outsider /ˌaʊt'saɪdə/ noun [C] 1 a person who is not accepted as a member of a particular group 2 a person or animal in a race or competition that is not expected to win ··➤ opposite **favourite**

outsize /'aʊtsaɪz/ adj (often used about clothes) larger than usual

outskirts /'aʊtskɜːts/ noun [pl] the parts of a town or city that are furthest from the centre: *They live **on the outskirts** of Athens.*

outspoken /aʊt'spəʊkən/ adj saying exactly what you think or feel although you may shock or upset other people: *Linda is very outspoken in her criticism.*

outstanding /aʊt'stændɪŋ/ adj 1 extremely good; excellent: *The results in the exams were outstanding.* 2 not yet paid, done or dealt with: *Some of the work is still outstanding.* ● *outstanding debts/issues*

outstandingly /aʊt'stændɪŋli/ adv extremely; very well: *outstandingly good/successful*

outstretched /ˌaʊt'stretʃt/ adj reaching as far as possible: *He came towards her with his arms outstretched.*

outward /'aʊtwəd/ adj (only *before* a noun) 1 on the outside: *Despite her cheerful outward appearance, she was in fact very unhappy.* 2 (used about a journey) going away from the place that you will return to later ··➤ opposite **return** 3 away from the centre or from a particular point: *outward movement/pressure* ··➤ opposite **inward** –**outwardly** adv: *He remained outwardly calm so as not to frighten the children.*

outwards /'aʊtwədz/ (*especially US* **outward**) adv towards the outside or away from the place where you are: *This door opens outwards.*

outweigh /ˌaʊt'weɪ/ verb [T] to be more in amount or importance than sth: *The advantages outweigh the disadvantages.*

outwit /ˌaʊt'wɪt/ verb [T] (**outwitting**; **outwitted**) to gain an advantage over sb by doing sth clever

★**oval** /'əʊvl/ adj, noun [C] shaped like an egg; a shape like that of an egg ··➤ picture at **shape**

ovary /'əʊvəri/ noun [C] (*pl* **ovaries**) one of the two parts of the female body that produce eggs

ovation /əʊ'veɪʃn/ noun [C] an enthusiastic reaction given by an audience when it likes sb/sth very much. The people in the audience make a noise with their hands (**clap**) and shout (**cheer**) and often stand up: *The dancers got **a standing ovation** at the end of the performance.*

★**oven** /'ʌvn/ noun [C] the part of a cooker that has a door. You put things inside an oven to cook them: *Cook in a hot oven for 50 minutes.* ● *a microwave oven*

➤ You **roast** or **bake** food in an oven.

★**over**¹ /'əʊvə/ adv, prep

➤ For special uses with many verbs, for example **get over sth**, look at the verb entries.

1 straight above sth, but not touching it: *There's a painting over the bookcase.* ● *We watched the plane fly over.* ··➤ Look at **above**. 2 covering sth: *He was holding a towel over the cut.* ● *She hung her coat over the back of the chair.* 3 across to the other side of sth: *The horse jumped over the fence.* ● *a bridge over the river* 4 on or to the other side: *The student turned the paper over and read the first question.* 5 down or sideways from an upright position: *He leaned over to speak to the woman next to him.* ● *I fell over in the street this morning.* 6 above or more than a number, price, etc: *She lived in Athens for over ten years.* ● *suitable for children aged 10 and over* 7 used for expressing distance: *He's over in America at the moment.* ● *Sit down over there.* ● *Come over here, please.* 8 not used; still remaining: *There are a lot of cakes **left over** from the party.* 9 (used with **all**) everywhere: *There was blood **all over the place**.* ● *I can't find my glasses. I've looked all over for them.* 10 used for saying that sth is repeated: *You'll have to start **all over again** (= from the beginning).* ● *She kept saying the same thing **over and over again**.* 11 about; on the subject of: *We quarrelled over money.* 12 during: *We met several times over the Christmas holiday.*

over² /'əʊvə/ adj 1 finished: *The exams are all over now.* 2 (used to form compound verbs, nouns, adjectives and adverbs) too; too much: *overexcited/overworked* ● *to overeat/overreact*

overall¹ /'əʊvərɔːl; ˌəʊvər'ɔːl/ adv, adj 1 including everything; total: *What will the overall cost of the work be?* 2 generally; when you consider everything: *Overall, I can say that we are pleased with the year's work.*

overall   aprons   overalls
                                 (US coveralls)

overall² /'əʊvərɔːl/ noun 1 [C] a piece of clothing like a coat and that you wear over your clothes to keep them clean when you are working 2 **overalls** (*US* **coveralls**) [pl] a piece of clothing that covers your legs and body (and sometimes your arms) and that you wear over your clothes to keep them clean when you are working

overawe /ˌəʊvərˈɔː/ **verb** [T] (usually passive) to impress sb so much that he/she feels nervous or frightened

overbalance /ˌəʊvəˈbæləns/ **verb** [I] to lose your balance and fall

overboard /ˈəʊvəbɔːd/ **adv** over the side of a boat or ship into the water

IDIOM **go overboard (on/about/for sb/sth)** to be too excited or enthusiastic about sb/sth

overcast /ˌəʊvəˈkɑːst/ **adj** (used about the sky) covered with cloud

overcharge /ˌəʊvəˈtʃɑːdʒ/ **verb** [I,T] to ask sb to pay too much money for sth: *The taxi driver overcharged me.* •➤ Look at **charge**.

overcoat /ˈəʊvəkəʊt/ **noun** [C] a long thick coat that you wear in cold weather

overcome /ˌəʊvəˈkʌm/ **verb** [T] (*pt* **overcame** /-ˈkeɪm/; *pp* **overcome**) **1** to manage to control or defeat sb/sth: *She tried hard to overcome her fear of flying.* **2** (usually passive) to be extremely strongly affected by sth

overcrowded /ˌəʊvəˈkraʊdɪd/ **adj** (used about a place) with too many people inside: *The trains are overcrowded on Friday evenings.*

overdo /ˌəʊvəˈduː/ **verb** [T] (*pt* **overdid** /-ˈdɪd/; *pp* **overdone** /-ˈdʌn/) **1** to use or do too much of sth **2** to cook sth too long: *The meat was overdone.*

IDIOM **overdo it/things** to work, etc too hard: *Exercise is fine but don't overdo it.*

overdose /ˈəʊvədəʊs/ **noun** [C] an amount of a drug or medicine that is too large and so is not safe: *to take an overdose* •➤ Look at **dose**.

overdraft /ˈəʊvədrɑːft/ **noun** [C] an amount of money that you have spent that is greater than the amount you have in your bank account; an arrangement that allows you to do this

overdrawn /ˌəʊvəˈdrɔːn/ **adj** having spent more money than you have in your bank account: *I checked my balance and discovered I was overdrawn.*

overdue /ˌəʊvəˈdjuː/ **adj** late in arriving, happening, being paid, returned, etc: *an overdue library book* • *Her baby is a week overdue.*

overestimate /ˌəʊvərˈestɪmeɪt/ **verb** [T] to guess that sb/sth is bigger, better, more important, etc than he/she/it really is: *I overestimated how much we could paint in a day.* •➤ opposite **underestimate**

overflow /ˌəʊvəˈfləʊ/ **verb 1** [I,T] overflow (with sth) to be so full that there is no more space: *The tap was left on and the bath overflowed.* • *The roads are overflowing with cars.* **2** [I] overflow (into sth) to be forced out of a place or a container that is too full: *The crowd overflowed into the street.*

overgrown /ˌəʊvəˈgrəʊn/ **adj** covered with plants that have grown too big and untidy

overhang /ˌəʊvəˈhæŋ/ **verb** [I,T] (*pt, pp*

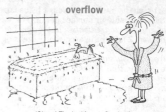

overflow

'Oh no! The bath's overflowing!'

overhung) to stick out above sth else: *The overhanging trees kept the sun off us.*

overhaul /ˌəʊvəˈhɔːl/ **verb** [T] to look at sth carefully and change or repair it if necessary to overhaul an engine –overhaul /ˈəʊvəhɔːl/ **noun** [C]

overhead /ˈəʊvəhed/ **adj, adv** above your head: *overhead electricity cables* • *A helicopter flew overhead.*

overheads /ˈəʊvəhedz/ **noun** [pl] money that a company must spend on things like heat, light, rent, etc

overhear /ˌəʊvəˈhɪə/ **verb** [T] (*pt, pp* **overheard** /-ˈhɜːd/) to hear what sb is saying by accident, when he/she is speaking to sb else and not to you

overjoyed /ˌəʊvəˈdʒɔɪd/ **adj** (not before a noun) overjoyed (at sth/to do sth) very happy

overland /ˈəʊvəlænd/ **adj** not by sea or by air: *an overland journey* –overland **adv**

overlap

overlapping tiles

overlap /ˌəʊvəˈlæp/ **verb** [I,T] (**overlapping**; **overlapped**) **1** when two things overlap, part of one covers part of the other: *Make sure that the two pieces of material overlap.* **2** to be partly the same as sth: *Our jobs overlap to some extent.* –overlap /ˈəʊvəlæp/ **noun** [C,U]

overleaf /ˌəʊvəˈliːf/ **adv** on the other side of the page: *Full details are given overleaf.*

overload /ˌəʊvəˈləʊd/ **verb** [T] **1** (often passive) to put too many people or things into or onto sth: *an overloaded vehicle* **2** overload sb (with sth) to give sb too much of sth: *to be overloaded with work/information* **3** to put too much electricity through sth: *If you use too many electrical appliances at one time you may overload the system.*

overlook /ˌəʊvəˈlʊk/ **verb** [T] **1** to fail to see or notice sth: *to overlook a spelling mistake* • *She felt that her opinion had been completely overlooked.* **2** to see sth wrong but decide to forget it: *I will overlook your behaviour this time but don't let it happen again.* **3** to have a view over sth: *My room overlooks the sea.*

overnight /ˌəʊvəˈnaɪt/ **adj, adv 1** for one night: *an overnight bag* • *We stayed overnight*

[C] **countable**, a noun with a plural form: *one book, two books*   [U] **uncountable**, a noun with no plural form: *some sugar*

in Hamburg. **2** (happening) very suddenly: *She became a star overnight.*

overpass /'əʊvəpɑːs/ (*US*) = **FLYOVER**

overpay /,əʊvə'peɪ/ **verb** [T] (*pt, pp* **overpaid**) (usually passive) to pay sb too much; to pay sb more than his/her job is worth •➤ opposite **underpay**

overpower /,əʊvə'paʊə/ **verb** [T] to be too strong for sb: *The fireman was overpowered by the heat and smoke.* –**overpowering adj**: *an overpowering smell*

overrate /,əʊvə'reɪt/ **verb** [T] (often passive) to think that sth/sb is better than he/she/it really is •➤ opposite **underrate**

override /,əʊvə'raɪd/ **verb** [T] (*pt* **overrode** /-'rəʊd/; *pp* **overridden** /-'rɪdn/) **1** to use your authority to reject sb's decision, order, etc: *They overrode my protest and continued with the meeting.* **2** to be more important than sth

overriding /,əʊvə'raɪdɪŋ/ **adj** (only *before* a noun) more important than anything else: *Our overriding concern is safety.*

overrule /,əʊvə'ruːl/ **verb** [T] to use your authority to change what sb else has already decided or done: *The Appeal Court overruled the judge's decision.*

overrun /,əʊvə'rʌn/ **verb** (*pt* **overran** /-'ræn/; *pp* **overrun** /'əʊvərʌn; ,əʊvə'rʌn/) **1** [T] (often passive) to spread all over an area in great numbers: *The city was overrun by rats.* **2** [I,T] to use more time or money than expected: *The meeting overran by 30 minutes.*

overseas /,əʊvə'siːz/ **adj** (only *before* a noun) **adv** in, to or from another country that you have to cross the sea to get to: *overseas students studying in Britain* ● *Frank has gone to live overseas.*

oversee /,əʊvə'siː/ **verb** [T] (*pt* **oversaw** /-'sɔː/; *pp* **overseen** /-'siːn/) to watch sth to make sure that it is done properly

overshadow /,əʊvə'ʃædəʊ/ **verb** [T] **1** to cause sb/sth to seem less important or successful: *Connor always seemed to be overshadowed by his sister.* **2** to cause sth to be less enjoyable

oversight /'əʊvəsaɪt/ **noun** [C,U] something that you do not notice or do (that you should have noticed or done)

oversimplify /,əʊvə'sɪmplɪfaɪ/ **verb** [I,T] (*pres part* **oversimplifying**; *3rd pers sing pres* **oversimplifies**; *pt, pp* **oversimplified**) to explain sth in such a simple way that its real meaning is lost

oversleep /,əʊvə'sliːp/ **verb** [I] (*pt, pp* **overslept** /-'slept/) to sleep longer than you should have done: *I overslept and was late for school.*

➤ Compare **lie in** and **sleep in**.

overstate /,əʊvə'steɪt/ **verb** [T] to say sth in a way that makes it seem more important than it really is •➤ opposite **understate**

★**overtake** /,əʊvə'teɪk/ **verb** [I,T] (*pt* **overtook** /-'tʊk/; *pp* **overtaken** /-'teɪkən/) to go past another person, car, etc because you are

moving faster: *The lorry overtook me on the bend.*

overthrow /,əʊvə'θrəʊ/ **verb** [T] (*pt* **overthrew** /-'θruː/; *pp* **overthrown** /-'θrəʊn/) to remove a leader or government from power, by using force –**overthrow** /'əʊvəθrəʊ/ **noun** [sing]

overtime /'əʊvətaɪm/ **noun** [U] time that you spend at work after your usual working hours; the money that you are paid for this: *Betty did ten hours overtime last week.* –**overtime adv**: *I have been working overtime for weeks.*

overtone /'əʊvətəʊn/ **noun** [C,usually pl] something that is suggested but not expressed in an obvious way: *Some people claimed there were racist overtones in the advertisement.*

overture /'əʊvətʃʊə; -tjʊə/ **noun 1** [C] a piece of music that is the introduction to a musical play (such as an opera or a ballet) **2** [C,usually pl] (*formal*) an act of being friendly towards sb, especially because you want to be friends, to start a business relationship, etc

overturn /,əʊvə'tɜːn/ **verb** [I,T] **1** to turn over so that the top is at the bottom: *The car overturned but the driver escaped unhurt.* **2** to officially decide that a decision is wrong and change it

overweight /,əʊvə'weɪt/ **adj** too heavy or fat: *I'm a bit overweight – I think I might go on a diet.* •➤ Look at the note at **fat**. •➤ opposite **underweight**

overwhelm /,əʊvə'welm/ **verb** [T] (usually passive) **1** to cause sb to feel such a strong emotion that he/she does not know how to react: *The new world champion was overwhelmed by all the publicity.* **2** to be so powerful, big, etc, that sb cannot deal with it: *He overwhelmed his opponent with his superb technique.* ● *The television company were overwhelmed by complaints.*

overwhelming /,əʊvə'welmɪŋ/ **adj** extremely great or strong: *Anna had an overwhelming desire to return home.* –**overwhelmingly adv**

overwork /,əʊvə'wɜːk/ **verb** [T] to make sb work too hard: *They are overworked and underpaid.* –**overwork** /'əʊvəwɜːk/ **noun** [U]

★**owe** /əʊ/ **verb** [T] **1** owe sth (to sb); owe sb for sth to have to pay money to sb for sth that he/she has done or given: *I owe Katrina a lot of money.* ● *I owe a lot of money to Katrina.* ● *I still owe you for that bread you bought yesterday.*

➤ The money, etc that you owe is a **debt**.

2 to feel that you should do sth for sb or give sth to sb, especially because he/she has done sth for you: *Claudia owes me an explanation.* ● *I owe you an apology.* **3** owe sth (to sb/sth) to have sth (for the reason given): *She said she owes her success to hard work and determination.*

owing /'əʊɪŋ/ **adj** (not before a noun) owing (to sb) not yet paid

'**owing to** prep because of: *The match was cancelled owing to bad weather.*

owl

owl /aʊl/ noun [C] a bird with large eyes that hunts small animals at night

★**own¹** /əʊn/ determiner, pron **1** used to emphasize that sth belongs to a particular person: *I saw him do it with my own eyes.* • *This is his own house.* • *This house is his own.* • *Rachel would like her own room/a room of her own.* **2** used to show that sth is done or made without help from another person: *The children are old enough to get their own breakfast.*
IDIOMS **come into your own** to have the opportunity to show your special qualities
hold your own (against sb/sth) to be as strong, good, etc as sb/sth else
(all) on your, etc own 1 alone: *John lives all on his own.* ·➤ Look at the note at **alone**. **2** without help: *I managed to repair the car all on my own.*
get/have your own back (on sb) (*informal*) to hurt sb who has hurt you

★**own²** /əʊn/ verb [T] to have sth belonging to you; possess: *We don't own the house. We just rent it.* • *a privately owned company*
PHRASAL VERB **own up (to sth)** (*informal*) to tell sb that you have done sth wrong: *None of the children owned up to breaking the window.* ·➤ Look at **confess**. It is more formal.

★**owner** /ˈəʊnə/ noun [C] a person who owns sth: *a house/dog owner*

ownership /ˈəʊnəʃɪp/ noun [U] the state of owning sth: *in private/public ownership*

ox /ɒks/ noun [C] (*pl* **oxen** /ˈɒksn/) a male cow that cannot produce young. Oxen were used in past times for pulling or carrying heavy loads. ·➤ Look at **bull**. ·➤ picture at **plough**

★**oxygen** /ˈɒksɪdʒən/ noun [U] (*symbol* **O**) a gas that you cannot see, taste or smell. Plants and animals cannot live without oxygen.

oyster /ˈɔɪstə/ noun [C] a shellfish that we eat. Some oysters produce precious jewels (pearls). ·➤ picture at **shellfish**

oz abbr ounce(s): *Add 4oz flour.*

ozone /ˈəʊzəʊn/ noun [U] a poisonous gas which is a form of another gas (oxygen)

,**ozone-'friendly** adj (used about cleaning products, etc) not containing chemicals that could harm the atmosphere (the ozone layer)

the 'ozone layer noun [sing] the layer of the gas (ozone) high up in the atmosphere that helps to protect the earth from the dangerous rays of the sun: *a hole in the ozone layer* ·➤ Look at **CFC**.

Pp

P, p¹ /piː/ noun [C] (*pl* **P's; p's**) the sixteenth letter of the English alphabet: *'Pencil' begins with (a) 'P'.*

p² abbr **1** (*pl* **pp**) page: *See p94.* • *pp 63-96* **2** (*Brit informal*) penny, pence: *a 27p stamp* **3** P (on a road sign) parking

PA¹ /ˌpiː ˈeɪ/ abbr, noun [C] (*especially Brit*) personal assistant; a person whose job is to type letters, answer the telephone, etc (a secretary) for just one manager

pa² /pəˈrænəm/ abbr per annum; in or for a year: *salary £15000 pa*

★**pace¹** /peɪs/ noun **1** [U,sing] pace (of sth) the speed at which you walk, run, etc or at which sth happens: *to run at a steady/gentle pace* • *I can't stand the pace of life in London.* • *Students are encouraged to work at their own pace* (= as fast or as slowly as they like). **2** [C] the distance that you move when you take one step: *Take two paces forward and then stop.*
IDIOMS **keep pace (with sb/sth)** to move or do sth at the same speed as sb/sth else; to change as quickly as sth else is changing: *Wages are not keeping pace with inflation.*
set the pace to move or do sth at the speed that others must follow: *Pinto set the pace for the first three miles.*

pace² /peɪs/ verb [I,T] to walk up and down in the same area many times, especially because you are nervous or angry

pacemaker /ˈpeɪsmeɪkə/ noun [C] **1** a machine that helps to make a person's heart beat regularly or more strongly **2** a person in a race who sets the speed that the others must follow

pacifier /ˈpæsɪfaɪə/ (*US*) = DUMMY(3)

pacifism /ˈpæsɪfɪzəm/ noun [U] the belief that all wars are wrong and that you should not fight in them –**pacifist** /-ɪst/ noun [C]

pacify /ˈpæsɪfaɪ/ verb [T] (*pres part* **pacifying**; *3rd pers sing pres* **pacifies**; *pt, pp* **pacified**) to make sb who is angry or upset be calm or quiet

★**pack¹** /pæk/ noun [C] **1** a set of things that are supplied together for a particular purpose: *an information pack* • *These batteries are sold in packs of four.* • (*figurative*) *Everything she told me was a pack of lies.* ·➤ Look at the entries for **package**, **packet** and **parcel**. **2** (*US*) = PACKET(1) **3** a bag that you carry on your back ·➤ synonym **rucksack** or **backpack 4** [with sing or pl verb] a group of wild animals that hunt together: *a pack of dogs/wolves* **5** a large group of similar people or things, especially one that you do not like or approve of: *a pack of journalists* **6** (*US*

deck) a complete set of playing cards •➤ Look at the note and picture at **card**.

★**pack**² /pæk/ *verb* **1** [I,T] to put your things into a suitcase, etc before you go away or go on holiday: *I'll have to pack my suitcase in the morning.* • *Have you packed your toothbrush?*

➤ The expression **do your packing** means the same.

•➤ opposite **unpack 2** [I,T] to put things into containers so they can be stored, transported or sold: *I packed all my books into boxes.* •➤ opposite **unpack 3** [T] (often passive) (*informal*) to fill with people or things until crowded or full: *The train was absolutely packed.* • *The book is packed with useful information.* • *People packed the pavements, waiting for the president to arrive.*

PHRASAL VERBS **pack sth in** (*informal*) to stop doing sth: *I've packed in my job.* • *I've had enough of you boys arguing – just pack it in, will you!*

pack sth in/into sth to do a lot in a short time: *They packed a lot into their three days in Rome.*

pack sth out (usually passive) to fill sth with people: *The bars are packed out every night.*

pack up (*informal*) **1** to finish working or doing sth: *There was nothing else to do so we packed up and went home.* **2** (used about a machine, engine, etc) to stop working: *My old car packed up last week so now I cycle to work.*

★**package** /'pækɪdʒ/ *noun* [C] **1** (*Brit*) something, or a number of things, covered in paper or in a box: *There's a large package on the table for you.* •➤ Look at the entries for **pack**, **packet** and **parcel**. **2** a number of things that must be bought or accepted together: *a word-processing package* • *a financial aid package* **3** (*US*) = **PARCEL** and **PACKET**(1) –**package** *verb* [T]: *Goods that are attractively packaged sell more quickly.*

‚package 'holiday (*US* 'package tour) *noun* [C] a holiday that is organized by a company for a fixed price that includes the cost of travel, hotels, etc

packaging /'pækɪdʒɪŋ/ *noun* [U] all the materials (boxes, bags, paper, etc) that are used to cover or protect goods before they are sold

‚packed 'lunch *noun* [C] food that you prepare at home and take with you to eat at work or school

packer /'pækə/ *noun* [C] a person, company or machine that puts goods, especially food, into boxes, plastic, paper, etc to be sold

★**packet** /'pækɪt/ *noun* **1** (*US* **pack**; **package**) [C] a small box, bag, etc in which things are packed to be sold in a shop: *a packet of sweets/biscuits/crisps* • *a cigarette packet* •➤ Look at the entries for **pack**, **package** and **parcel**. •➤ picture at **container 2** [sing] (*spoken*) a large amount of money: *That new kitchen must have cost them a packet.*

packing /'pækɪŋ/ *noun* [U] **1** the act of putting your clothes, possessions, etc into a boxes or cases in order to take or send them somewhere: *We're going on holiday tomorrow so I'll do my packing tonight.* **2** (*Brit*) soft material that you use to stop things from being damaged or broken when you are sending them somewhere: *The price of the book includes postage and packing.*

pact /pækt/ *noun* [C] a formal agreement between two or more people, groups or countries

★**pad**¹ /pæd/ *noun* [C] **1** a thick piece of soft material, used for cleaning or protecting sth or to make sth a different shape: *Remove eye make-up with cleanser and a cotton-wool pad.* • *a jacket with shoulder pads* **2** a number of pieces of paper that are fastened together at one end: *a notepad* **3** the place where a spacecraft takes off: *a launch pad* **4** the soft part on the bottom of the feet of some animals, for example dogs and cats •➤ picture on page C1

pad² /pæd/ *verb* (**padding**; **padded**) **1** [T] **pad sth (with sth)** (usually passive) to fill or cover sth with soft material in order to protect it, make it larger or more comfortable, etc: *I sent the photograph frame in a padded envelope.* **2** [I] **pad about, along, around, etc** to walk quietly, especially because you are not wearing shoes: *He got up and padded into the bathroom.*

PHRASAL VERB **pad sth out** to make a book, speech, etc longer by adding things that are not necessary

padding /'pædɪŋ/ *noun* [U] soft material that is put inside sth to protect it or to make it larger, more comfortable, etc

paddle¹ /'pædl/ *noun* [C] a short pole that is flat and wide at one or both ends and that you use for moving a small boat through water •➤ Look at **oar**. •➤ picture at **boat**

paddle² /'pædl/ *verb* **1** [I,T] to move a small boat through water using a short pole that is flat and wide at one or both ends: *We paddled down the river.* •➤ Look at **row**. **2** [I] to walk in water that is not very deep: *We paddled in the stream.* •➤ picture on page C8

paddock /'pædək/ *noun* [C] a small field where horses are kept

padlock

link

chain

padlock /'pædlɒk/ *noun* [C] a type of lock that you can use for fastening gates, bicycles, etc –**padlock** *verb* [T] **padlock sth (to sth)**: *I padlocked my bicycle to a post.*

paediatrician (*US* **pediatrician**) /ˌpiːdɪə'trɪʃn/ *noun* [C] a doctor who deals with the diseases of children

paediatrics (*US* **pediatrics**) /ˌpiːdi'ætrɪks/ *noun* [U] the area of medicine connected with the diseases of children –**paediatric** (*US* **pediatric**) *adj*

paella /paɪ'elə/ *noun* [U,C] a Spanish dish made with rice, meat, fish and vegetables

pagan /'peɪɡən/ *adj* having religious beliefs

p

that do not belong to any of the main religions –pagan noun [C]

★**page¹** /peɪdʒ/ noun [C] (*abbr* p) one or both sides of a piece of paper in a book, magazine, etc: *The letter was three pages long.* ● *Turn over the page.* ● *Turn to page 12 of your book.* ● *the front page of a newspaper*

page² /peɪdʒ/ verb [T] to call somebody by sending a message to a small machine (a pager) that they carry, or by calling their name publicly through a device fixed to the wall (a loudspeaker)

pageant /'pædʒənt/ noun [C] **1** a type of public entertainment at which people dress in clothes from past times and give outdoor performances of scenes from history **2** (*US*) a beauty competition for young women

pager /'peɪdʒə/ noun [C] a small machine that you carry, that makes a sound when somebody sends you a message ••➤ synonym **bleeper**

paid *past tense, past participle* of **PAY²**

ˈpaid-up adj (only *before* a noun) having paid all the money that you owe, for example to become a member of a club: *He's a fully paid-up member of Friends of the Earth.*

★**pain¹** /peɪn/ noun **1** [C,U] the unpleasant feeling that you have when a part of your body has been hurt or when you are ill: *to be in pain* ● *He screamed with pain.* ● *chest pains*

➤ We use **ache** for a long, continuous pain and **pain** for sudden, short, sharp periods of pain. Therefore we usually say: *I've got earache/backache/toothache/a headache* but: *He was admitted to hospital with pains in his chest.* For the use of 'a' or 'an' with **ache**, look at the note at **ache**.

2 [U] sadness that you feel because sth bad has happened: *the pain of losing a parent*
IDIOM **be a pain (in the neck)** (*spoken*) a person, thing or situation that makes you angry or annoyed

pain² /peɪn/ verb [T] (*formal*) to make sb feel sad or upset: *It pains me to think how much money we've wasted.*

pained /peɪnd/ adj showing that you are sad or upset: *a pained expression*

★**painful** /'peɪnfl/ adj **painful (for sb) (to do sth) 1** that causes pain or hurts: *A wasp sting can be very painful.* **2** making you feel upset or embarrassed: *The break-up of their marriage was very painful for the children.* –painfully /-fəli/ adv

painkiller /'peɪnkɪlə/ noun [C] a drug that is used for reducing pain

painless /'peɪnləs/ adj that does not cause pain: *The animals' death is quick and painless.* –painlessly adv

pains /peɪnz/ noun
IDIOM **be at/take (great) pains to do sth; take (great) pains (with/over sth)** to make a special effort to do sth well: *He was at pains to hide his true feelings.*

painstaking /'peɪnzteɪkɪŋ/ adj very careful and taking a long time: *The painstaking*

search of the wreckage gave us clues as to the cause of the crash. –painstakingly adv

★**paint¹** /peɪnt/ noun **1** [U] coloured liquid that you put onto a surface to decorate or protect it: *green/orange/yellow paint* ● *The door will need another coat of paint.* **2** [U] coloured liquid that you can use to make a picture: *oil paint* ● *watercolour paint* **3** paints [pl] a collection of tubes or blocks of paint that an artist uses for painting pictures

★**paint²** /peɪnt/ verb [I,T] **1** to put paint onto a surface or an object: *We painted the fence.* ● *The walls were painted pink.* **2** to make a picture of sb/sth using paints: *We painted some animals on the wall.*

paintbox /'peɪntbɒks/ noun [C] a box that contains blocks or tubes of paint of many colours

paintbrush /'peɪntbrʌʃ/ noun [C] a brush that you use for painting with ••➤ picture at **brush**

★**painter** /'peɪntə/ noun [C] **1** a person whose job is to paint buildings, walls, etc **2** a person who paints pictures

★**painting** /'peɪntɪŋ/ noun **1** [C] a picture that sb has painted: *a famous painting by Van Gogh*

➤ A **drawing** is similar to a painting, but is done using pencils, pens or crayons instead of paints.

2 [U] the act of painting pictures or buildings: *She studies Indian painting.*

paintwork /'peɪntwɜːk/ noun [U] a painted surface, especially on a vehicle

★**pair¹** /peə/ noun **1** [C] two things of the same type that are used or worn together: *a pair of shoes/gloves/earrings* **2** [C] a thing that consists of two parts that are joined together: *a pair of scissors/glasses/trousers* **3** [C, with pl verb] two people or animals that are doing sth together: *These boxers have fought several times, and tonight the pair meet again.*

➤ We use **couple** to refer to two people who are married or in a relationship together.

IDIOM **in pairs** two at a time: *These earrings are only sold in pairs.* ● *The students were working in pairs.*

pair² /peə/ verb
PHRASAL VERBS **pair (sb/sth) off (with sb)** to come together, especially to form a romantic relationship; to bring two people together for this purpose: *She's always trying to pair me off with her brother.*
pair up (with sb) to join together with another person or group to work, play a game, etc: *I paired up with another student and we did the project together.*

pajamas (*US*) = **PYJAMAS**

★**palace** /'pæləs/ noun [C] a large house that is or was the home of a king or queen

palate /'pælət/ noun [C] the top part of the inside of your mouth

★**pale** /peɪl/ adj **1** (used about a person or his/her face) having skin that is light in colour, often because of fear or illness: *She has a pale* complexion. ● *I felt myself go/turn pale with fear.* ·➤ noun pallor. Compare **pallid**. **2** not bright or strong in colour: *a pale yellow dress* ·➤ opposite **dark** –**pale** verb [I]

pall /pɔːl/ verb [I] to become less interesting or important: *After a few months, the excitement of his new job began to pall.*

pallid /ˈpælɪd/ adj (used about a person or his/her face) light in colour, especially because of illness: *His pallid complexion made him look unhealthy.*

➤ Compare **pale**.

pallor /ˈpælə/ noun [U] having pale skin because of illness or fear

palm¹ /pɑːm/ noun [C] **1** the flat, inner surface of your hand: *She held the coins tightly in the palm of her hand.* ·➤ picture on page C5 **2** (also **'palm tree**) noun [C] a tall straight type of tree that grows in hot countries. Palms have a lot of large leaves at the top but no branches. ·➤ picture on page C2

palm² /pɑːm/ verb
PHRASAL VERBS **palm sb off (with sth)** (*informal*) to persuade sb to believe sth that is not true in order to stop him/her asking questions or complaining
palm sth off (on sb) to persuade sb to accept sth that he/she does not want: *She's always palming off a worst jobs on her assistant.*

paltry /ˈpɔːltri/ adj too small to be considered important or useful: *paltry sum of money*

pamper /ˈpæmpə/ verb [T] to take care of sb very well and make him/her feel as comfortable as possible

pamphlet /ˈpæmflət/ noun [C] a very thin book with a paper cover containing information about a particular subject

pans

handle

frying pan (*US* frypan)   casserole

wok   saucepan

lid

★**pan** /pæn/ noun [C] a metal container with a handle or handles that is used for cooking food in; the contents of a pan: *Cook the spaghetti in a large pan of boiling water.*

pancake /ˈpænkeɪk/ noun [C] a type of very thin round cake that is made by frying a mixture of flour, milk and eggs (batter) ·➤ picture on page C4

'Pancake Day (also ˌShrove 'Tuesday) a Tuesday in February when people in Britain traditionally eat pancakes. Pancake Day is the day before the period of Lent begins.

panda
bamboo

panda /ˈpændə/ noun [C] a large black and white bear that comes from China

pandemonium /ˌpændəˈməʊniəm/ noun [U] a state of great noise and confusion

pander /ˈpændə/ verb
PHRASAL VERB **pander to sb/sth** to do or say exactly what sb wants especially when this is not reasonable: *He refuses to pander to his boss's demands.*

p and p abbr (*Brit*) postage and packing: *price: £29 incl p and p*

pane /peɪn/ noun [C] a piece of glass in a window, etc: *a windowpane* ·➤ picture on page C7

panel /ˈpænl/ noun **1** [C] a square or rectangular piece of wood, metal or glass that forms part of a door or wall **2** [C, with sing or pl verb] a group of people who give their advice or opinions about sth; a group of people who discuss topics of interest on television or radio: *a panel of judges* (= in a competition) ● *a panel game* (= a TV game show with two teams) **3** [C] a flat surface that contains the equipment for controlling a vehicle, machine, etc: *a control/display panel*

panellist (*US* panelist) /ˈpænəlɪst/ noun [C] a member of a panel(2)

pang /pæŋ/ noun [C, usually pl] a sudden strong feeling of emotional or physical pain: *a pang of jealousy* ● *hunger pangs*

★**panic** /ˈpænɪk/ noun [C,U] a sudden feeling of fear that cannot be controlled and stops you from thinking clearly: *People fled in panic as the fire spread.* ● *There was a mad panic when the alarm went off.* –**panic** verb [I] (**panicking**; **panicked**): *Stay calm and don't panic.*

'panic-stricken adj very frightened in a way that stops you from thinking clearly

panorama /ˌpænəˈrɑːmə/ noun [C] a view over a wide area of land –**panoramic** /ˌpænəˈræmɪk/ adj

pant /pænt/ verb [I] to breathe quickly, for example after running or because it is very hot –**pant** noun [C]

panther /ˈpænθə/ noun [C] a large wild animal of the cat family with black fur ·➤ picture at **lion**

panties /ˈpæntiz/ (*especially US*) = KNICKERS

pantomime /ˈpæntəmaɪm/ noun [C,U] **1** (also *informal* **panto** /ˈpæntəʊ/) (*Brit*) a type of play for children, with music, dancing and jokes, that is usually performed at Christmas. Pantomimes are based on traditional children's stories (fairy stories). **2** (*US*) = MIME

pantry /ˈpæntri/ noun [C] (*pl* **pantries**) a

p

small room where food is kept ⋯➤ synonym
larder

★**pants** /pænts/ **noun** [pl] **1** (*Brit*) = **UNDERPANTS**
2 (*US*) = **TROUSERS**

pantyhose /ˈpæntɪhəʊz/ (*US*) = **TIGHTS**

paparazzi /ˌpæpəˈrætsi/ **noun** [pl] photographers who follow famous people around in order to get pictures of them to sell to a newspaper or magazine

papaya /pəˈpaɪə/ (also **pawpaw** /ˈpɔːpɔː/) **noun** [C] a large tropical fruit which is sweet and orange inside and has small black seeds ⋯➤ picture on page C3

★**paper** /ˈpeɪpə/ **noun 1** [U] a material made in thin sheets that you use for writing or drawing on, covering things, etc: *a piece/sheet of paper* ● *a paper handkerchief*
➤ Types of paper include **filter paper**, **tissue paper**, **toilet paper** and **writing paper**.

2 = **NEWSPAPER**(1): *Where's today's paper?*
➤ You buy a paper at a **paper shop** or **newsagent's**.

3 papers [pl] important letters or pieces of paper that have information written on them: *The document you want is somewhere in the pile of papers on her desk.* **4** [C] the written questions or the written answers in an exam: *The history exam is divided into three papers.* **5** [C] a piece of writing on a particular subject that is written for specialists: *At the conference, the Professor presented a paper on Sri Lankan poetry.*
IDIOM **on paper 1** in writing: *I've had nothing on paper to say that I've been accepted.* **2** as an idea, but not in a real situation; in theory: *The scheme seems fine on paper, but would it work in practice?*

paperback /ˈpeɪpəbæk/ **noun** [C,U] a book that has a paper cover: *The novel is available in paperback.* ⋯➤ Look at **hardback**.

'**paper boy noun** [C] a boy who takes newspapers to people's houses

'**paper clip noun** [C] a small piece of bent wire that is used for holding pieces of paper together ⋯➤ picture on page S6

'**paper girl noun** [C] a girl who takes newspapers to people's houses

paperwork /ˈpeɪpəwɜːk/ **noun** [U] **1** the written work that is part of a job, such as writing letters and reports and filling in forms, etc: *I hate doing paperwork.* **2** documents that need to be prepared, collected, etc in order for a piece of business to be completed: *Some of the paperwork is missing from this file.*

paprika /ˈpæprɪkə/ **noun** [U] a red powder made from a sweet red pepper that you can use in cooking

par¹ /pɑː/ **noun** [U] (in golf) the standard number of times a player should hit the ball in order to complete a particular hole or series of holes
IDIOMS **below par** (*informal*) not as good as or as well as usual
on a par with sb/sth of an equal level, standard, etc to sb/sth else: *Is a teacher's salary on a par with a doctor's?*

par² (also **para**) **abbr** paragraph

parable /ˈpærəbl/ **noun** [C] a short story that teaches a lesson, especially one told by Jesus in the Bible

parabola /pəˈræbələ/ **noun** [C] a curve like the path of an object that is thrown through the air and falls back to earth

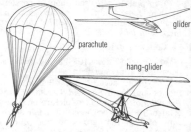
glider
parachute
hang-glider

parachute /ˈpærəʃuːt/ **noun** [C] a piece of equipment that opens and lets the person fall to the ground slowly when he/she jumps from a plane –**parachute verb** [I]

parade /pəˈreɪd/ **noun** [C] an occasion when a group of people stand or walk in a line so that people can look at them: *a military parade* ● *a fashion parade*

paradise /ˈpærədaɪs/ **noun 1 Paradise** [sing] (without *a* or *the*) the place where some people think that good people go after they die; heaven **2** [C] a perfect place: *This beach is a paradise for windsurfers.*

paradox /ˈpærədɒks/ **noun** [C] a situation or statement with two or more parts that seem strange or impossible together: *It's a paradox that some countries produce too much food while in other countries people are starving.* –**paradoxical** /ˌpærəˈdɒksɪkl/ **adj**

paraffin /ˈpærəfɪn/ (*US* **kerosene**) **noun** [U] a type of oil that is burned to produce heat or light

★**paragraph** /ˈpærəgrɑːf/ **noun** [C] a part of a piece of writing that consists of one or more sentences. A paragraph always starts on a new line.

★**parallel¹** /ˈpærəlel/ **adj**, **adv 1 parallel (to sth)** (used about two lines, etc) with the same distance between them for all their length: *parallel lines* ● *The railway runs parallel to the road.* ⋯➤ picture at **line 2** similar and happening at the same time: *The two brothers followed parallel careers in different companies.*

parallel² /ˈpærəlel/ **noun** [C,U] a person, thing or situation that is similar to another one in a different situation, place or time: *The government's huge election victory is without parallel this century.*

paralyse (*US* **paralyze**) /ˈpærəlaɪz/ **verb** [T] **1** to make a person unable to move his/her body or a part of it: *Miriam is paralysed from the waist down.* **2** to make sb/sth unable to work in a normal way –**paralysis**

p

/pə'rælǝsis/ noun: *The disease can cause paralysis or even death.* • *There has been complete paralysis of the railway system.*

paramedic /,pærǝ'medik/ noun [C] a person who has had special training in treating people who are hurt or ill, but who is not a doctor or nurse

paramilitary /,pærǝ'militri/ adj organized in the same way as, but not belonging to, an official army: *a paramilitary group*

paramount /'pærǝmaunt/ adj (*formal*) most important: *Safety is paramount in car design.*

paranoia /,pærǝ'nɔiǝ/ noun [U] **1** a type of mental illness in which you wrongly believe that other people want to harm you **2** (*informal*) a feeling of fear and suspicion of other people

paranoid /'pærǝnɔid/ adj wrongly believing that other people are trying to harm you or are saying bad things about you

paraphernalia /,pærǝfǝ'neiliǝ/ noun [U] a large number of different objects that you need for a particular purpose

paraphrase /'pærǝfreiz/ verb [T] to express sth again using different words so that it is easier to understand –**paraphrase** noun [C]

parasite /'pærǝsait/ noun [C] a plant or an animal that lives in or on another plant or animal and gets its food from it

parasol /'pærǝsɒl/ noun [C] an umbrella that you use to protect yourself from the sun •➤ picture on page C8

paratroops /'pærǝtruːps/ noun [pl] soldiers who are trained to jump from a plane with a piece of equipment on their backs that opens to help them fall slowly (a **parachute**)

★**parcel** /'pɑːsl/ (*US also* **package**) noun [C] something that is covered in brown paper and sent to sb •➤ Look at the entries for **pack**, **package** and **packet**.

parched /pɑːtʃt/ adj very hot and dry, or very thirsty: *Can I have a drink? I'm parched!*

★**pardon**[1] /'pɑːdn/ noun [C,U] an official decision not to punish sb for a crime

➤ **I beg your pardon** is a formal way of saying 'sorry': *Oh, I do beg your pardon. I had no idea this was your seat.* It can also be used when you want to ask somebody to repeat what he/she has said because you did not understand.

–**pardon** verb [T] **pardon sb (for sth/doing sth)**

pardon[2] /'pɑːdn/ (*also* ,**pardon 'me**) interj **1** used for asking sb to repeat what he/she has just said because you did not hear or understand it **2** used by some people to mean *sorry* or *excuse me*

★**parent** /'peǝrǝnt/ noun [C] **1** a person's mother or father

➤ A **single parent** is a mother or father who is bringing up his/her child or children alone, without the other parent. A **foster-parent** is a person who looks after a child who is not legally his/her own.

2 a company that owns smaller companies of the same type: *a parent company*

parental /pǝ'rentl/ adj (only *before* a noun) of a parent or parents: *parental support/advice*

parentheses /pǝ'renθǝsiːz/ (*especially US*) = **BRACKET**[1](1)

parenthood /'peǝrǝnthʊd/ noun [U] the state of being a parent

parish /'pæriʃ/ noun [C] an area or district which has its own church; the people who live in this area: *the parish church* –**parishioner** /pǝ'riʃǝnǝ/ noun [C]

★**park**[1] /pɑːk/ noun [C] **1** an open area in a town, often with grass or trees, where people can go to walk, play, etc: *Let's go for a walk in the park.* **2** (in compounds) a large area of land that is used for a special purpose: *a national park* • *a business park* • *a theme park*

★**park**[2] /pɑːk/ verb [I,T] to leave the vehicle that you are driving somewhere for period a time: *You can't park in the centre of town.* • *Somebody's parked their car in front of the exit.*

parking /'pɑːkiŋ/ noun [U] the action of leaving a car, lorry, etc somewhere for a time: *The sign said 'No Parking'.*

➤ A place where many cars can be parked and left is called a **car park**. A place where one car can be parked is called a **parking space**.

'**parking lot** (*US*) = **CAR PARK**

'**parking meter** noun [C] a metal post that you put coins into to pay for parking a car in the space beside it for a period of time

'**parking ticket** noun [C] a piece of paper that orders you to pay money (a **fine**) for parking your car where it is not allowed

★**parliament** /'pɑːlǝmǝnt/ noun [C] **1** the group of people who are elected to make and change the laws of a country •➤ When **parliament** is singular it can be used with either a singular or plural verb. **2 Parliament** [sing] the parliament of the United Kingdom: *a Member of Parliament (MP)*

➤ The UK Parliament consists of **the House of Lords**, whose members have been appointed rather than elected, and **the House of Commons**, whose members have been elected by the people to represent areas of the country (called **constituencies**).

parliamentary /,pɑːlǝ'mentri/ adj (only *before* a noun) connected with parliament

parody /'pærǝdi/ noun [C,U] (*pl* **parodies**) a piece of writing, speech or music that copies the style of sb/sth in a funny way: *a parody of a spy novel* –**parody** verb [T] (*pres part* **parodying**; *3rd pers sing pres* **parodies**; *pt, pp* **parodied**)

parole /pǝ'rǝul/ noun [U] permission that is given to a prisoner to leave prison early on the condition that he/she behaves well: *He's going to be released on parole.*

p

parrot /'pærət/ noun [C] a type of tropical bird with a curved beak and usually with very bright feathers. Parrots that are kept as pets can be trained to copy what people say.

'**parrot-fashion** adv without understanding the meaning of sth: *to learn sth parrot-fashion*

parsley /'pɑːsli/ noun [U] a plant (herb) with very small leaves that are used for adding taste to or decorating food

parsnip /'pɑːsnɪp/ noun [C] a long thin white vegetable, that grows under the ground •➤ picture on page C3

★**part**[1] /pɑːt/ noun **1** [C,U] (a) part (of sth) one of the pieces, areas, periods, things, etc that together with others forms the whole of sth; some, but not all of sth: *Which part of Spain do you come from?* ● *The film is good in parts.* ● *spare parts for a car* ● *a part of the body* ● *Part of the problem is lack of information.* ● *I enjoy being part of a team.* **2** [C] a role or character in a play, film, etc: *He played the part of Macbeth.* ● *I had a small part in the school play.* **3** parts [pl] a region or area: *Are you from these parts?* **4** [C] a section of a book, television series, etc: *You can see part two of this programme at the same time next week.* **5** [C] an amount or quantity (of a liquid or substance): *Use one part cleaning fluid to ten parts water.*

IDIOMS **the best/better part of sth** most of sth; more than half of sth, especially a period of time: *They've lived here for the best part of forty years.*

for the most part usually or mostly

for my, his, their, etc part speaking for myself, etc; personally

have/play a part (in sth) to be involved in sth

in part not completely: *The accident was, in part, the fault of the driver.*

on the part of sb/on sb's part made, done or felt by sb: *There is concern on the part of the teachers that class size will increase.* ● *I'm sorry. It was a mistake on my part.*

take part (in sth) to join with other people in an activity: *Everybody took part in the discussion.*

part[2] /pɑːt/ verb **1** [I,T] (*formal*) part (sb) (from sb) to leave or go away from sb; to separate people or things: *We exchanged telephone numbers when we parted.* ● *He hates being parted from his children for long.* **2** [I,T] to move apart; to make things or people move apart: *Her lips were slightly parted.* **3** [T] to separate the hair on the head with a comb so as to make a clear line: *She parts her hair in the middle.* •➤ Look at **parting**.

IDIOM **part company (with sb/sth)** to go different ways or to separate after being together

PHRASAL VERB **part with sth** to give or sell sth to sb: *When we went to live in Italy, we had to part with our horses.*

part[3] /pɑːt/ adv not completely one thing and not completely another: *She's part Russian and part Chinese.*

,**part ex'change** noun [U] a way of buying sth, such as a car, in which you give your old one as some of the payment for a more expensive one

partial /'pɑːʃl/ adj **1** not complete: *The project was only a partial success.* **2** (*old-fashioned*) partial to sb/sth liking sth very much: *He's very partial to ice cream.* –**partially** adv

partiality /,pɑːʃi'æləti/ noun [U] (*formal*) the unfair support of one person, team, etc above another: *The referee was accused of partiality towards the home team.* •➤ opposite **impartiality** •➤ Look at **impartial**.

participant /pɑː'tɪsɪpənt/ noun [C] a person who takes part in sth

participate /pɑː'tɪsɪpeɪt/ verb [I] participate (in sth) to take part or become involved in sth: *Students are encouraged to participate in sporting activities.* –**participation** /pɑː,tɪsɪ'peɪʃn/ noun [U]

participle /'pɑːtɪsɪpl; ,pɑː'tɪsɪpl/ noun [C] (*grammar*) a word that is formed from a verb and that ends in –*ing* (present participle) or –*ed*, –*en*, etc (past participle). Participles are used to form tenses of the verb, or as adjectives: *'Hurrying' and 'hurried' are the present and past participles of 'hurry'.*

particle /'pɑːtɪkl/ noun [C] **1** a very small piece; a bit: *dust particles* **2** (*grammar*) a small word that is not as important as a noun, verb or adjective: *In the phrasal verb 'break down', 'down' is an adverbial particle.*

★**particular** /pə'tɪkjələ/ adj **1** (only *before* a noun) used to emphasize that you are talking about one person, thing, time, etc and not about others: *Is there any particular dish you enjoy making?* **2** (only *before* a noun) greater than usual; special: *This article is of particular interest to me.* **3** connected with one person or thing and not with others: *Everybody has their own particular problems.* **4** particular (about/over sth) (not before a noun) difficult to please: *Some people are extremely particular about what they eat.* •➤ Look at **fussy**.

IDIOM **in particular** especially: *Is there anything in particular you'd like to do this weekend?*

★**particularly** /pə'tɪkjələli/ adv especially; more than usual or more than others: *I'm particularly interested in Indian history.* ● *The match was excellent, particularly the second half.*

particulars /pə'tɪkjələz/ noun [pl] (*formal*) facts or details about sb/sth: *The police took down all the particulars about the missing child.*

parting /'pɑːtɪŋ/ noun **1** [C,U] saying goodbye to, or being separated from, another person (usually for quite a long time) **2** [C] the line in a person's hair where it is divided in two with a comb: *a side/centre parting* •➤ Look at **part**. •➤ picture at **hair**

partition /pɑː'tɪʃn/ noun **1** [C] something that divides a room, office etc into two or more parts, especially a thin or temporary wall •➤ picture on page S6 **2** [U] the division of a country into two or more countries –**partition** verb [T]

partly /'pɑːtli/ *adv* not completely: *She was only partly responsible for the mistake.*

★**partner** /'pɑːtnə/ *noun* [C] **1** the person that you are married to or live with as if you are married **2** one of the people who own a business: *business partners* **3** a person that you are doing an activity with as a team, for example dancing or playing a game **4** a country or organization that has an agreement with another –**partner** *verb* [T]: *Hales partnered his brother in the doubles, and they won the gold medal.*

partnership /'pɑːtnəʃɪp/ *noun* **1** [U] the state of being a partner in business: *Simona went into partnership with her sister and opened a shop in Rome.* **2** [C] a relationship between two people, organizations, etc: *Marriage is a partnership for life.* **3** [C] a business owned by two or more people

,**part of 'speech** *noun* [C] (*grammar*) one of the groups that words are divided into, for example noun, verb, adjective, etc

,**part-'time** *adj, adv* for only a part of the working day or week: *She's got a part-time job.* •➤ Look at **full-time**.

★**party** /'pɑːti/ *noun* [C] (*pl* **parties**) **1** a social occasion to which people are invited in order to eat, drink and enjoy themselves: *When we've moved into our new house we're going to* **have a party.** • *a birthday/dinner party* **2** (also **Party**) a group of people who have the same political aims and ideas and who are trying to win elections to parliament, etc

➤ The two main political parties in Great Britain are the **Labour** Party (left-wing) and the **Conservative** (or **Tory**) Party (right-wing). There is also a centre party called the **Liberal Democrats** and some other smaller parties. In the United States the main political parties are the **Republicans** and the **Democrats**.

3 (often in compounds) a group of people who are working, travelling, etc together: *a party of tourists* **4** (*formal*) one of the people or groups of people involved in a legal case: *the guilty/innocent party* •➤ Look at **third party**.

★**pass¹** /pɑːs/ *verb* **1** [I,T] to move past or to the other side of sb/sth: *The street was crowded and the two buses couldn't pass.* • *I passed him in the street but he didn't say hello.* • *The number of children at the school has passed 500.*

➤ The past tense of **pass** is **passed** not **past** which is an adjective or a preposition: *The summer months passed slowly.* • *The past week was very hot.* • *Our house is just past the church.*

2 [I,T] **pass (sth) along, down, through, etc (sth)** to go or move, or make sth move, in the direction mentioned: *A plane passed overhead.* • *We'll have to pass the wire through the window.* **3** [T] **pass sth (to sb)** to give sth to sb: *Could you pass (me) the salt, please?* **4** [I,T] **pass (sth) (to sb)** (in some sports) to kick, hit or throw the ball to sb on your own

team **5** [I] (used about time) to go by: *At least a year has passed since I last saw them.* • *It was a long journey but the time passed very quickly.* **6** [T] to spend time, especially when you are bored or waiting for sth: *I'll have to think of something to do to* **pass the time** *in hospital.* **7** [I,T] to achieve the necessary standard in an exam, test, etc: *Good luck in the exam! I'm sure you'll pass.* •➤ opposite **fail** **8** [T] to test sb/sth and say that he/she/it is good enough: *The examiner passes most of the students.* **9** [T] to officially approve a law, etc by voting: *One of the functions of Parliament is to* **pass new laws.** **10** [T] **pass sth (on sb/sth)** to give an opinion, judgement, etc: *The judge passed sentence on the young man* (= said what his punishment would be). **11** [I] to be allowed or accepted: *I didn't like what they were saying but I* **let it pass.**

IDIOMS **pass the buck (to sb)** to make sb else responsible for a difficult situation

pass water (*formal*) to get rid of waste liquid from your body

PHRASAL VERBS **pass away** used as a polite way of saying 'die'

pass by (sb/sth) to go past: *I pass by your house on the way to work.*

pass sth down to give or teach sth to people who will live after you have died

pass for sb/sth to be accepted as sb/sth that he/she/it is not: *His mother looks so young she'd pass for his sister.*

pass sb/sth off (as sb/sth) to say that a person or a thing is sth that he/she/it is not: *He tried to pass the work off as his own.*

pass sth on (to sb) to give sth to sb else, especially after you have been given it or used it yourself: *Could you pass the message on to Mr Roberts?*

pass out to become unconscious; to faint •➤ opposite **come round/to**

★**pass²** /pɑːs/ *noun* [C] **1** a successful result in an exam: *The pass mark is 50%.* • *Grades A, B and C are passes.* •➤ opposite **fail** **2** an official piece of paper that gives you permission to enter or leave a building, travel on a bus or train, etc: *Show your student pass when you buy a ticket.* **3** the act of kicking, hitting or throwing the ball to sb on your own team in some sports **4** a road or way over or through mountains: *a mountain pass*

passable /'pɑːsəbl/ *adj* **1** good enough but not very good: *My French is not brilliant but it's passable.* **2** (not before a noun) (used about roads, rivers, etc) possible to use or cross; not blocked •➤ opposite **impassable**

★**passage** /'pæsɪdʒ/ *noun* **1** [C] (also **passageway**) a long, narrow way with walls on either side that connects one place with another: *a secret underground passage* **2** [C] a tube in your body which air, liquid, etc can pass through: *the nasal passages* **3** [C] a short part of a book, a speech or a piece of music: *The students were given a passage from the novel to study.* **4** [sing] the process of passing: *His painful memories faded with* **the passage of time.**

p

passenger /'pæsɪndʒə/ **noun** [C] a person who is travelling in a car, bus, train, plane, etc but who is not driving it or working on it

passer-'by **noun** [C] (*pl* passers-by) a person who is walking past sb/sth

passing[1] /'pɑːsɪŋ/ **adj** (only *before* a noun) **1** lasting for only a short time; brief: *a passing phase/thought/interest* **2** going past: *I stopped a passing car and asked for help.*

passing[2] /'pɑːsɪŋ/ **noun** [U] the process of going by: *the passing of time*

IDIOM **in passing** done or said quickly, while you are thinking or talking about sth else: *He mentioned the house in passing but he didn't give any details.*

passion /'pæʃn/ **noun 1** [C,U] (a) very strong feeling, especially of love, hate or anger: *He was a violent man, controlled by his passions.* **2** [sing] **a passion (for sb)** very strong sexual love or attraction: *His longed to tell Sashi of his passion for her.* **3** [sing] **a passion for sth** a very strong liking for or interest in sth: *He has a passion for history.*

passionate /'pæʃənət/ **adj 1** showing or caused by very strong feelings: *The President gave a passionate speech about crime.* **2** showing or feeling very strong love or sexual attraction: *a passionate kiss* –**passionately** **adv**: *He believes passionately in democracy.*

passive /'pæsɪv/ **adj 1** showing no reaction, feeling or interest; not active: *Some people prefer to play a passive role in meetings.* **2** used about the form of a verb or a sentence when the subject of the sentence is affected by the action of the verb: *In the sentence 'He was bitten by a dog', the verb is passive.* •▸ You can also say: 'The verb is in the passive'. Look at **active**. –**passively** **adv**

Passover /'pɑːsəʊvə/ **noun** [sing] the most important Jewish festival, which takes place in spring and lasts seven or eight days

passport /'pɑːspɔːt/ **noun** [C] **1** an official document that identifies you as a citizen of a particular country and that you have to show when you enter or leave a country

▸ You **apply for** or **renew** your passport at the **passport office**. This office **issues** new passports.

2 **a passport to sth** a thing that makes it possible to achieve sth: *a passport to success*

password /'pɑːswɜːd/ **noun** [C] **1** a secret word or phrase that you need to know in order to be allowed into a place **2** a series of letters or numbers that you must type into a computer or computer system in order to be able to use it: *Please enter your password.*

past[1] /pɑːst/ **adj 1** already gone; belonging to a time earlier than the present: *in past centuries/times* • *I'd rather forget some of my past mistakes.* **2** (only *before* a noun) just finished; last: *He's had to work very hard during the past year.*

past[2] /pɑːst/ **prep, adv 1** (used when telling the time) after; later than: *It's ten (minutes) past three.* • *It was past midnight when we got home.* **2** from one side to the other of

sb/sth; further than or on the other side of sb/sth: *He walked straight past me.* • *She looked right past me without realizing who I was.* **3** above or further than a certain point, limit or age: *Unemployment is now past the 2 million mark.* • *I'm so tired that I'm* **past caring** (= I don't care any more) *what we eat.*

IDIOMS **not put it past sb (to do sth)** (used with *would*) to think sb is capable of doing sth bad: *I wouldn't put it past him to do a thing like that.*

past it (*informal*) too old

past[3] /pɑːst/ **noun 1** **the past** [sing] the time that has gone by; the things that happened before now: *in the recent/distant past* • *The art of writing letters seems to be* **a thing of the past.** **2** [C] a person's life and career before now: *We know nothing about his past.* **3** **the past** (also **past tense**) [sing] (*grammar*) a form of a verb used to describe actions in the past: *The past (tense) of the verb 'come' is 'came'.*

▸ For more information about the past tenses, look at the **Quick Grammar Reference** at the back of this dictionary.

pasta /'pæstə/ **noun** [U] an Italian food made from flour, eggs and water, formed into different shapes, cooked, and usually served with a sauce

paste[1] /peɪst/ **noun 1** [C,U] a soft, wet mixture, usually made of a powder and a liquid and sometimes used for sticking things: *wallpaper paste* • *Mix the flour and milk into a paste.* **2** [U] (usually used in compound nouns) a soft mixture of food that you can spread onto bread, etc: *fish/chicken paste*

paste[2] /peɪst/ **verb** [T] **1** to stick sth to sth else using paste or a similar substance (glue): *He pasted the picture into his book.* **2** (*computing*) to copy or move text into a document from somewhere else: *This function allows you to* **cut and paste** *text.*

pastel /'pæstl/ **adj** (used about colours) pale; not strong

pasteurized (also **-ised**) /'pɑːstʃəraɪzd/ **adj** (used about milk or cream) free from bacteria because it has been heated and then cooled

pastime /'pɑːstaɪm/ **noun** [C] something that you enjoy doing when you are not working •▸ synonym **hobby**

pastoral /'pɑːstərəl/ **adj 1** (connected with the work of a priest or a teacher) giving help and advice on personal matters rather than on matters of religion or education **2** connected with country life

past par'ticiple → PARTICIPLE

past 'perfect (also **pluperfect**) **noun** [sing] (*grammar*) the tense of a verb that describes an action that was finished before another event happened

▸ For more information about the past perfect, look at the **Quick Grammar Reference** at the back of this dictionary.

pastry /'peɪstri/ **noun** (*pl* pastries) **1** [U] a mixture of flour, fat and water that is rolled out flat and cooked as a base or covering for pies, etc **2** [C] a small cake made with pastry

pasture /'pɑːstʃə/ **noun** [C,U] a field or land covered with grass, where cows, etc can feed

pasty /'pæsti/ **noun** [C] (*pl* **pasties**) (*Brit*) a small pie containing meat and/or vegetables

pat

pat¹ /pæt/ **verb** [T] (**patting**; **patted**) to touch sb/sth gently with a flat hand, especially as a sign of friendship, care, etc

pat² /pæt/ **noun** [C] a gentle friendly touch with a flat hand: *He gave her knee an affectionate pat.*

IDIOM **a pat on the back (for sth/doing sth)** approval for sth good that a person has done: *She deserves a pat on the back for all her hard work.*

pat³ /pæt/ **adj, adv** (only *before* a noun) (used about an answer, comment, etc) said in a quick or simple way that does not sound natural or realistic

patch¹ /pætʃ/ **noun** [C] **1** a patch (of sth) a part of a surface that is different in some way from the area around it: *Drive carefully. There are patches of ice on the roads.* • *a bald patch* **2** a piece of material that you use to cover a hole in clothes, etc: *I sewed patches on the knees of my jeans.* **3** a small piece of material that you wear over one eye, usually because the eye is damaged **4** a small piece of land, especially for growing vegetables or fruit: *a vegetable patch*

IDIOMS **go through a bad patch** (*especially Brit informal*) to experience a difficult or unhappy period of time

not a patch on sb/sth (*especially Brit informal*) not nearly as good as sb/sth: *Her new book isn't a patch on her others.*

patch² /pætʃ/ **verb** [T] to cover a hole in clothes, etc with a piece of material in order to repair it: *patched jeans*

PHRASAL VERB **patch sth up 1** to repair sth, especially in a temporary way by adding a new piece of material **2** to stop arguing with sb and to be friends again: *Have you tried to patch things up with her?*

patchwork /'pætʃwɜːk/ **noun** [U] a type of sewing in which small pieces of cloth of different colours and patterns are sewn together

patchy /'pætʃi/ **adj 1** existing or happening in some places but not others: *patchy fog/clouds/rain* **2** not complete; good in some parts but not in others: *My knowledge of German is rather patchy.*

pâté /'pæteɪ/ **noun** [U] food that is made by making meat, fish or vegetables into a smooth, thick mixture that is served cold and spread on bread, etc: *liver pâté*

patent¹ /'peɪtnt/ **adj** (*formal*) clear; obvious: *a patent lie* –**patently adv**

patent² /'peɪtnt; 'peɪtnt/ **noun** [C,U] the offi-

cial right to be the only person to make, use or sell a product or an invention; the document that proves this –**patent verb** [T]

,**patent 'leather noun** [U] a type of leather with a hard, shiny surface, used especially for making shoes and bags

paternal /pə'tɜːnl/ **adj** (only *before* a noun) **1** behaving as a father would behave; connected with being a father **2** related through the father's side of the family: *my paternal grandparents* •➤ Look at **maternal**.

paternity /pə'tɜːnəti/ **noun** [U] the fact of being the father of a child: *paternity leave* (= time that the father of a new baby is allowed to have away from work) •➤ Look at **maternity**.

★**path** /pɑːθ/ **noun** [C] **1** a way across a piece of land that is made by or used by people walking: *the garden path* •➤ picture on page C7

> **Pathway** is similar in meaning: *There was a narrow pathway leading down the cliff.* Look also at **footpath**.

2 the line along which sb/sth moves; the space in front of sb/sth as he/she/it moves: *the flight path of an aeroplane*

pathetic /pə'θetɪk/ **adj 1** causing you to feel pity or sadness: *the pathetic cries of the hungry children* **2** (*informal*) very bad, weak or useless: *What a pathetic performance! The team deserved to lose.* –**pathetically** /-kli/ **adv**

pathological /ˌpæθə'lɒdʒɪkl/ **adj 1** caused by feelings that you cannot control; not reasonable or sensible: *He's a pathological liar* (= he cannot stop lying). • *pathological fear/hatred/violence* **2** caused by or connected with disease or illness: *pathological depression* **3** (*medical*) connected with pathology –**pathologically** /-kli/ **adv**

pathologist /pə'θɒlədʒɪst/ **noun** [C] a doctor who is an expert in pathology, and examines dead bodies to find out why a person has died

pathology /pə'θɒlədʒi/ **noun** [U] (*medical*) the scientific study of diseases of the body

★**patience** /'peɪʃns/ **noun** [U] **1** patience (with sb/sth) the quality of being able to stay calm and not get angry, especially when there is a difficulty or you have to wait a long time: *I've got no patience with people who don't even try.* • *to lose patience with sb* •➤ opposite **impatience 2** (*US* **solitaire**) a card game for only one player

★**patient¹** /'peɪʃnt/ **adj** patient (with sb/sth) able to stay calm and not get angry, especially when there is a difficulty or you have to wait a long time: *She's very patient with young children.* •➤ opposite **impatient** –**patiently adv**: *to wait patiently*

★**patient²** /'peɪʃnt/ **noun** [C] a person who is receiving medical treatment: *a hospital patient* • *He's one of Dr Waters' patients.*

patio /'pætiəʊ/ **noun** [C] (*pl* **patios** /-əʊz/) a flat, hard area, usually behind a house, where people can sit, eat, etc outside •➤ Look at **balcony**, **verandah** and **terrace**. •➤ picture on page C7

patriot /'peɪtriət; 'pæt-/ **noun** [C] a person who loves his/her country and is ready to defend it against an enemy –patriotism /'peɪ-triətɪzəm; 'pæt-/ noun [U]

patriotic /ˌpeɪtri'ɒtɪk; ˌpæt-/ adj having or showing great love for your country –patriotically /-kli/ adv

patrol¹ /pə'trəʊl/ verb [I,T] (patrolling; patrolled) to go round an area, building, etc at regular times to make sure that it is safe and that nothing is wrong

patrol² /pə'trəʊl/ noun **1** [C,U] the act of going round an area, building, etc at regular times to make sure that it is safe and that nothing is wrong: *a police car on patrol in the area* **2** [C] a group of soldiers, vehicles, etc that patrol sth: *a naval/police patrol* • *a patrol car/boat*

patron /'peɪtrən/ noun [C] **1** a person who gives money and support to artists, writers and musicians: *a patron of the arts* **2** a famous person who supports an organization such as a charity and whose name is used in advertising it ••➤ Look at **sponsor**. **3** (*formal*) a person who uses a particular shop, theatre, restaurant, etc: *This car park is for patrons only.*

patronize (also **-ise**) /'pætrənaɪz/ verb [T] **1** to treat sb in a way that shows that you think you are better, more intelligent, experienced, etc than he/she is **2** (*formal*) to be a regular customer of a shop, restaurant, etc –patronizing (also -ising) adj: *I really hate that patronizing smile of hers.* –patronizingly (also -isingly) adv

ˌpatron 'saint noun [C] a religious being who is believed by Christians to protect a particular place or people doing a particular activity

patter /'pætə/ noun [sing] the sound of many quick light steps or knocks on a surface: *the patter of the children's feet on the stairs* –patter verb [I]

★**pattern** /'pætn/ noun [C] **1** the way in which sth happens, develops, or is done: *Her days all seemed to follow the same pattern.* • *changing patterns of behaviour/work/weather* **2** an arrangement of lines, shapes, colours, etc as a design: *a shirt with a floral pattern on it* ••➤ synonym **design 3** a design, a set of instructions or a shape to cut around that you use in order to make sth

patterned /'pætənd/ adj decorated with a pattern(2)

★**pause**¹ /pɔːz/ noun **1** [C] a pause (in sth) a short period of time during which sb stops talking or stops what he/she is doing: *He continued playing for twenty minutes without a pause.* ••➤ Look at the note at **interval**. **2** (also ˈpause button) [U] a control on a video player, etc that allows you to stop playing or recording for a short time: *Can you press pause to stop the tape while I go and make a cup of tea?*

pause² /pɔːz/ verb [I] pause (for sth) to stop talking or doing sth for a short time before continuing

pave /peɪv/ verb [T] pave sth (with sth) (often passive) to cover an area of ground with flat stones (paving stones) or bricks

pavement /'peɪvmənt/ (*US* sidewalk) noun [C] a hard flat area at the side of a road for people to walk on ••➤ picture at **roundabout**

pavilion /pə'vɪliən/ noun [C] (*Brit*) a building at a sports ground where players can change their clothes

ˈpaving stone noun [C] a flat piece of stone that is used for covering the ground ••➤ picture on page C7

★**paw**¹ /pɔː/ noun [C] the foot of animals such as dogs, cats, bears, etc ••➤ picture on page C1

paw² /pɔː/ verb [I,T] paw (at) sth (used about an animal) to touch or scratch sb/sth several times with a paw: *The dog pawed at my sleeve.*

pawn¹ /pɔːn/ noun [C] **1** (in the game of chess) one of the eight pieces that are of least value and importance **2** a person who is used or controlled by other more powerful people

pawn² /pɔːn/ verb [T] to leave a valuable object with a person who lends money, (a pawnbroker) in return for money. If you cannot pay back the money after a certain period, the object can be sold or kept.

pawnbroker /'pɔːnbrəʊkə/ noun [C] a person who lends money to people when they leave sth of value with him/her

★**pay**¹ /peɪ/ verb (*pt, pp* paid) **1** [I,T] pay (sb) (for sth); pay (sb) sth (for sth) to give sb money for work, goods, services, etc: *She is very well paid.* • *The work's finished but we haven't paid for it yet.* • *We paid the dealer £3000 for the car.* **2** [T] pay sth (to sb) to give the money that you owe for sth: *Have you paid her the rent yet?* • *to pay a bill/fine* **3** [I,T] to make a profit; to be worth doing: *It would pay you to get professional advice before making a decision.* **4** [I] pay (for sth) to suffer or be punished because of your beliefs or actions: *You'll pay for that remark!*

IDIOMS be paid in arrears → **ARREARS**

pay attention (to sb/sth) to listen carefully to or to take notice of sb/sth

pay sb a compliment; pay a compliment to sb to say that you like sth about sb

pay your respects (to sb) (*formal*) to visit sb as a sign of respect: *Hundreds came to pay their last respects to her* (= to go to sb's funeral).

pay tribute to sb/sth to say good things about sb/sth and show your respect for sb/sth

put paid to sth to destroy or finish sth: *The bad weather put paid to our picnic.*

PHRASAL VERBS pay sb back (to sb) to give money back to sb that you borrowed from him/her: *Can you lend me £5? I'll pay you back/I'll pay it back to you on Friday.*

pay sb back (for sth) to punish sb for making you or sb else suffer: *What a mean trick! I'll pay you back one day.*

pay off (*informal*) to be successful: *All her hard work has paid off! She passed her exam.*

pay sth off to pay all the money that you owe for sth: *to pay off a debt/mortgage*

pay up (*informal*) to pay the money that you

[C] **countable**, a noun with a plural form: *one book, two books*   [U] **uncountable**, a noun with no plural form: *some sugar*

owe: *If you don't pay up, we'll take you to court.*

★pay² /peɪ/ **noun** [U] money that you get regularly for work that you have done

> ➤ **Pay** is the general word for money that you get regularly for work that you have done. **Wages** are paid weekly or daily in cash. A **salary** is paid monthly, directly into a bank account. You pay a **fee** for professional services, for example to a doctor, lawyer, etc. **Payment** is money for work that you do once or not regularly. Your **income** is all the money you get regularly, both for work you have done, and as interest on money you have saved.

payable /ˈpeɪəbl/ **adj** that should or must be paid: *A 10% deposit is payable in advance.* • *Make the cheque payable to Pauline Nolan.*

payee /ˌpeɪˈiː/ **noun** [C] (*written*) a person that money, especially a cheque, is paid to

★payment /ˈpeɪmənt/ **noun** payment (for sth) **1** [U] the act of paying sb or of being paid: *I did the work last month but I haven't had any payment for it yet.* ••➤ Look at the note at **pay²**. **2** [C] an amount of money that you must pay: *They asked for a payment of £100 as a deposit.*

PC /ˌpiːˈsiː/ **noun** [C] **1** (*computing*) personal computer; a computer that is designed for one person to use at work or at home **2** = **POLICE CONSTABLE 3** adj = **POLITICALLY CORRECT**

PE /ˌpiːˈiː/ **abbr** physical education: *a PE lesson*

pea /piː/ **noun** [C] a small round green seed that is eaten as a vegetable. A number of peas grow together in a long thin case (a pod). ••➤ picture on page C3

★peace /piːs/ **noun** [U] **1** a situation or a period of time in which there is no war or violence in a country or area: *The two communities now manage to live in peace together.* • *A UN force has been sent in to keep the peace.* **2** the state of being calm or quiet: *He longed to escape from the city to the peace and quiet of the countryside.*

★peaceful /ˈpiːsfl/ **adj** **1** not wanting or involving war, violence or argument: *a peaceful protest/demonstration/solution* **2** calm and quiet: *a peaceful village* –**peacefully** /-fəli/ **adv**: *The siege ended peacefully.* –**peacefulness** **noun** [U]

peacetime /ˈpiːstaɪm/ **noun** [U] a period when a country is not at war

peach /piːtʃ/ **noun** **1** [C] a soft round fruit with orange-red skin. A peach is soft inside and has a large stone in its centre. ••➤ picture on page C3 **2** [U] a pinkish-orange colour

peacock /ˈpiːkɒk/ **noun** [C] a large bird with beautiful long blue and green tail feathers that it can lift up and spread out

peak¹ /piːk/ **noun** [C] **1** the point at which sth is the highest, best, strongest, etc: *a man at the peak of his career* **2** the pointed top of a mountain: *snow-covered peaks* ••➤ picture on

page C8 **3** the rigid front part of a cap that sticks out above your eyes ••➤ picture at **hat**

peak² /piːk/ **adj** (only *before* a noun) used to describe the highest level of sth, or a time when the greatest number of people are doing or using sth: *Summer is the peak period for most hotels.* • *The athletes are all in peak condition.* ••➤ Look at **off-peak**.

peak³ /piːk/ **verb** [I] to reach the highest point or value: *Sales peak just before Christmas.*

peal /piːl/ **noun** [C] the loud ringing of a bell or bells: (*figurative*) *peals of laughter* –**peal** **verb** [I]

peanut /ˈpiːnʌt/ (also **groundnut** /ˈɡraʊndnʌt/) **noun** **1** [C] a nut that grows under the ground that we eat ••➤ picture at **nut 2 pea-nuts** [pl] (*informal*) a very small amount of money: *We get paid peanuts for doing this job.*

pear /peə/ **noun** [C] a fruit that has a yellow or green skin and is white inside. Pears are thinner at the top than at the bottom. ••➤ picture on page C3

★pearl /pɜːl/ **noun** [C] a small, hard, round, white object that grows inside the shell of a type of shellfish (an oyster). Pearls are used to make jewellery: *pearl earrings*

peasant /ˈpeznt/ **noun** [C] (used especially in past times) a person who owns or rents a small piece of land on which he/she grows food and keeps animals in order to feed his/her family

> ➤ **Peasant** is considered offensive nowadays.

peat /piːt/ **noun** [U] a soft black or brown natural substance that is formed from dead plants just under the surface of the ground in cool, wet places. It can be burned as a fuel or put on the garden to make plants grow better.

pebble /ˈpebl/ **noun** [C] a smooth round stone that is found in or near water

pecan /ˈpiːkən/ **noun** [C] a type of nut that we eat ••➤ picture at **nut**

peck /pek/ **verb** [I,T] **1 peck (at) sth** (used about a bird) to eat or bite sth with its beak **2** (*informal*) to kiss sb quickly and lightly: *She pecked him on the cheek and then left.* –**peck** **noun** [C]

peckish /ˈpekɪʃ/ **adj** (*informal*) hungry

peculiar /pɪˈkjuːliə/ **adj** **1** unusual or strange: *There's a very peculiar smell in here.* ••➤ synonym **odd 2 peculiar to sb/sth** only belonging to one person or found in one place: *a species of bird peculiar to South East Asia*

peculiarity /pɪˌkjuːliˈærəti/ **noun** (*pl* peculi-arities) **1** [C] a strange or unusual characteristic, quality or habit: *There are some peculiarities in her behaviour.* **2** [C] a characteristic or a quality that only belongs to one particular person, thing or place: *the cultural peculiarities of the English* **3** [U] the quality of being strange or unusual

peculiarly /pɪˈkjuːliəli/ **adv** **1** in a strange

p

and unusual way: *Luke is behaving very peculiarly.* **2** especially; very: *Lilian's laugh can be peculiarly annoying.* **3** in a way that is especially typical of one person, thing or place: *a peculiarly French custom*

pedagogical /ˌpedə'gɒdʒɪkl/ **adj** connected with ways of teaching

pedal /'pedl/ **noun** [C] the part of a bicycle or other machine that you push with your foot in order to make it move or work ··➤ picture on page S9 –**pedal verb** [I,T] (**pedalling**; **pedalled**; *US* **pedaling**; **pedaled**): *She had to pedal hard to get up the hill.*

pedantic /pɪ'dæntɪk/ **adj** too worried about rules or details –**pedantically** /-kli/ **adv**

pedestal /'pedɪstl/ **noun** [C] the base on which a column, statue, etc stands

pedestrian /pə'destriən/ **noun** [C] a person who is walking in the street (not travelling in a vehicle) ··➤ Look at **motorist**.

pe,destrian 'crossing (*US* **crosswalk**) **noun** [C] a place for pedestrians to cross the road ··➤ Look at **zebra crossing**. ··➤ picture at **roundabout**

pediatrician (*US*) = **PAEDIATRICIAN**

pedigree¹ /'pedɪgri:/ **noun** [C] **1** an official record of the parents, grandfather, grandmother, etc from which an animal has been bred ··➤ Look at **mongrel**. **2** a person's family history, especially when this is impressive

pedigree² /'pedɪgri:/ **adj** (only *before* a noun) (used about an animal) of high quality because the parents, grandfather, grandmother, etc are all of the same breed and specially chosen

pee /pi:/ **verb** [I] (*informal*) to get rid of waste water from your body; urinate –**pee noun** [sing]

peek /pi:k/ **verb** [I] (*informal*) **peek (at sth)** to look at sth quickly and secretly because you should not be looking at it: *No peeking at your presents before your birthday!* –**peek noun** [sing]: *to have a quick peek*

peel¹ /pi:l/ **verb 1** [T] to take the skin off a fruit or vegetable: *Could you peel the potatoes, please?* **2** [I,T] **peel (sth) (off/away/back)** to come off or to take sth off a surface in one piece or in small pieces: *I peeled off the price label before handing her the book.*

IDIOM **keep your eyes peeled/skinned (for sb/sth)** ➔ **EYE¹**

peel² /pi:l/ **noun** [U] the skin of a fruit or vegetable: *apple/potato peel* ··➤ picture on page C3 ··➤ Look at **rind** and **skin**.

peeler /'pi:lə/ **noun** [C] a special knife for taking the skin off fruit and vegetables: *a potato peeler* ··➤ picture at **kitchen**

peep¹ /pi:p/ **verb** [I] **1** **peep (at sth)** to look at sth quickly and secretly, especially through a small opening **2** to be in a position where a small part of sb/sth can be seen: *The moon is peeping out from behind the clouds.*

peep² /pi:p/ **noun** [sing] (*informal*) **1** a quick look: *Have a peep in the bedroom and see if*

the baby is asleep. **2** a sound: *There hasn't been a peep out of the children for hours.*

peer¹ /pɪə/ **noun** [C] **1** a person who is of the same age or position in society as you: *Children hate to look stupid in front of their peers.* **2** (*Brit*) a member of the top level of society (**the nobility**)

peer² /pɪə/ **verb** [I] **peer (at sb/sth)** to look closely or carefully at sb/sth, for example because you cannot see very well: *He peered at the photo, but it was blurred.*

peerage /'pɪərɪdʒ/ **noun 1** [with sing or pl verb] all the peers¹(2) as a group **2** [C] the social position (**rank**) of a peer¹(2)

'peer group noun [C] a group of people who are all of the same age and social position

peeved /pi:vd/ **adj** (*informal*) quite angry or annoyed

peg¹ /peg/ **noun** [C] **1** a piece of wood, metal, etc on a wall or door that you hang your coat on **2** (also **tent peg**) a piece of metal that you push into the ground to keep one of the ropes of a tent in place ··➤ picture at **tent 3** (also **clothes peg**, *US* **clothes pin**) a type of small wooden or plastic object used for fastening wet clothes to a clothes line

peg² /peg/ **verb** [T] (**pegging**; **pegged**) **1** **peg sth (out)** to fix sth with a peg **2** **peg sth (at/to sth)** to fix or keep sth at a certain level: *Wage increases were pegged at 5%.*

pelican /'pelɪkən/ **noun** [C] a large bird that lives near water in warm countries. A pelican has a large beak that it uses for catching and holding fish.

pellet /'pelɪt/ **noun** [C] **1** a small hard ball of any substance, often of soft material that has become hard **2** a very small metal ball that is fired from a gun: *shotgun pellets*

pelt /pelt/ **verb 1** [T] to attack sb/sth by throwing things **2** [I] **pelt (down)** (used about rain) to fall very heavily: *It's absolutely pelting down.* **3** [I] (*informal*) to run very fast: *Some kids pelted past us.*

pelvis /'pelvɪs/ **noun** [C] (*pl* **pelvises**) the set of wide bones at the bottom of your back, to which your leg bones are joined ··➤ picture on page C5 –**pelvic** /'pelvɪk/ **adj**

★**pen** /pen/ **noun** [C] **1** an object that you use for writing in ink: *a ballpoint/felt-tip/ marker/fountain pen* **2** a small piece of ground with a fence around it that is used for keeping animals in

penal /'pi:nl/ **adj** (only *before* a noun) connected with punishment by law: *the penal system*

penalize (also **-ise**) /'pi:nəlaɪz/ **verb** [T] **1** to punish sb for breaking a law or rule **2** to cause sb to have a disadvantage: *Children should not be penalized because their parents cannot afford to pay.*

penalty /'penəlti/ **noun** [C] (*pl* **penalties**) **1** a punishment for breaking a law, rule or contract: *the death penalty* ● *What's the maximum penalty for smuggling drugs?* **2** a disadvantage or sth unpleasant that happens as the result of sth: *I didn't work hard enough*

*and I **paid the penalty**. I failed all my exams.*
3 (in sport) a punishment for one team and an advantage for the other team because a rule has been broken: *The referee awarded a penalty to the home team.*

the 'penalty area noun [C] the marked area in front of the goal in football

penance /'penəns/ noun [C,U] a punishment that you give yourself to show you are sorry for doing sth wrong

★**pence** plural of PENNY

★**pencil¹** /'pensl/ noun [C,U] an object that you use for writing or drawing. Pencils are usually made of wood and contain a thin stick of a black or coloured substance: *Bring a pencil and paper with you.* • *Write **in pencil**, not ink.*

pencil² /'pensl/ verb [T] (**pencilling; pencilled**; *US* **penciling; penciled**) to write or draw with a pencil
PHRASAL VERB **pencil sth/sb in** to write down the details of an arrangement that might have to be changed later: *Shall we pencil the next meeting in for the fourteenth?*

'pencil case noun [C] a small bag or box that you keep pens, pencils, etc in

'pencil sharpener noun [C] an instrument that you use for making pencils sharp •➤ picture on page S6

pendant /'pendənt/ noun [C] a small attractive object that you wear on a chain around your neck

pending /'pendɪŋ/ adj, prep (*formal*) **1** waiting to be done or decided: *The judge's decision is still pending.* **2** until sth happens: *He took over the leadership pending the elections.*

pendulum /'pendjələm/ noun [C] **1** a chain or stick with a heavy weight at the bottom that moves regularly from side to side to work a clock **2** a way of describing a situation that changes from one thing to its opposite: *Since last year's election, the pendulum of public opinion has swung against the government.*

penetrate /'penɪtreɪt/ verb [I,T] **1** to go through or into sth, especially when this is difficult: *The knife penetrated ten centimetres into his chest.* **2** to manage to understand sth difficult: *Scientists have still not penetrated the workings of the brain.* **3** to be understood or realized: *I was back at home when the meaning of her words finally penetrated.* –**penetration** /ˌpenɪ'treɪʃn/ noun [U]

penetrating /'penɪtreɪtɪŋ/ adj **1** (used about sb's eyes or of a way of looking) making you feel uncomfortable because it seems sb knows what you are thinking: *a penetrating look/stare/gaze* • *penetrating blue eyes* **2** showing that you have understood sth completely and quickly: *a penetrating question/comment* **3** that can be heard, felt, smelled, etc a long way away

penfriend /'penfrend/ (*especially US* **'pen pal**) noun [C] a person that you become friendly with by exchanging letters, often a person who you have never met

penguin

penguin /'peŋgwɪn/ noun [C] a black and white seabird that cannot fly and that lives in the Antarctic

penicillin /ˌpenɪ'sɪlɪn/ noun [U] a substance that is used as a medicine (an antibiotic) for preventing and treating diseases and infections caused by bacteria

peninsula /pə'nɪnsjələ/ noun [C] an area of land that is almost surrounded by water

penis /'piːnɪs/ noun [C] the male sex organ that is used for getting rid of waste liquid and having sex

penitent /'penɪtənt/ adj (*formal*) sorry for having done sth wrong

penitentiary /ˌpenɪ'tenʃəri/ noun [C] (*pl* **penitentiaries**) (*US*) a prison

penknife
blade

penknife /'pennaɪf/ noun [C] (*pl* **penknives**) a small knife with parts used for cutting (**blades**), opening bottles, etc that fold safely away when not being used

penniless /'peniləs/ adj having no money; poor

★**penny** /'peni/ noun [C] (*pl* **pence** /pens/ or **pennies**) **1** (*abbr* p) a small brown British coin. There are a hundred pence in a pound: *a fifty-pence piece/coin* **2** (*US*) a cent

★**pension** /'penʃn/ noun [C] money that is paid regularly by a government or company to sb who has stopped working (retired) because of old age or who cannot work because he/she is ill –**pensioner** = OLD-AGE PENSIONER

pentagon /'pentəgən/ noun **1** [C] a shape that has five straight and equal sides **2 the Pentagon** [sing] a large government building near Washington DC in the US that contains the main offices of the US military forces; the military officials who work there

pentathlon /pen'tæθlən/ noun [C] a sports competition in which you have to take part in five different events

penthouse /'penthaʊs/ noun [C] an expensive flat at the top of a tall building

pent-up /'pent ʌp/ adj (only *before* a noun) (used about feelings) that you hold inside and do not express: *pent-up anger*

penultimate /pen'ʌltɪmət/ adj (in a series) the one before the last one: *'Y' is the penultimate letter of the alphabet.*

★**people** /'piːpl/ noun **1** [pl] more than one person: *How many people are coming to the party?*

➤ Be careful. **People** is almost always used instead of the plural form **persons**. **Persons** is very formal and is usually used in legal

p

language: *Persons under the age of sixteen are not permitted to buy cigarettes.*

2 [C] (*pl* **peoples**) (*formal*) all the men, women and children who belong to a particular place or race: *The President addressed the American people.* • *the French-speaking peoples of the world* **3** [pl] men and women who work in a particular activity: *business/sports people* **4 the people** [pl] the ordinary citizens of a country: *The President is popular because he listens to the people.*

pepper¹ /'pepə/ **noun 1** [U] a black or white powder with a hot taste that is used for flavouring food: *salt and pepper* **2** [C] a green, red or yellow vegetable that is almost empty inside •➤ picture on page C3

pepper² /'pepə/ **verb** [T] **pepper sb/sth with sth** (usually passive) to hit sb/sth with a series of small objects, especially bullets: *The wall had been peppered with bullets.*

peppermint /'pepəmɪnt/ **noun 1** [U] a natural substance with a strong fresh flavour that is used in sweets and medicines **2** [C] (also **mint**) a sweet with a peppermint flavour •➤ Look at **spearmint**.

pep talk /'pep tɔːk/ **noun** [C] (*informal*) a speech that is given to encourage people or to make them work harder

★**per** /pə; *strong form* pɜː/ **prep** for each: *The speed limit is 110 kilometres per hour.* • *Rooms cost 60 dollars per person per night.*

perceive /pə'siːv/ **verb** [T] (*formal*) **1** to notice or realize sth: *Scientists failed to perceive how dangerous the level of pollution had become.* **2** to understand or think of sth in a particular way: *I perceived his comments as a criticism.* •➤ noun **perception**

★**per 'cent** (*US* **percent**) **adj, adv, noun** [C, with sing or pl verb] (*pl* **per cent**) (*symbol* **%**) in or of each hundred; one part in every hundred: *You get 10% off if you pay cash.* • *90% of the population owns a television.* • *The price of bread has gone up by 50 per cent in two years.*

percentage /pə'sentɪdʒ/ **noun** [C, with sing or pl verb] the number, amount, rate, etc of sth, expressed as if it is part of a total which is a hundred; a part or share of a whole: *What percentage of people voted in the last election?*

perceptible /pə'septəbl/ **adj** (*formal*) that can be seen or felt: *a barely perceptible change in colour* •➤ opposite **imperceptible** –**perceptibly** /-əbli/ **adv**

perception /pə'sepʃn/ **noun 1** [U] the ability to notice or understand sth **2** [C] a particular way of looking at or understanding sth; an opinion: *What is your perception of the situation?* •➤ verb **perceive**

perceptive /pə'septɪv/ **adj** (*formal*) quick to notice or understand things –**perceptively adv**

perch¹ /pɜːtʃ/ **verb 1** [I] (used about a bird) to sit on a branch, etc **2** [I,T] to sit or be put on the edge of sth: *The house was perched on the edge of a cliff.*

perch² /pɜːtʃ/ **noun** [C] a branch (or a bar in a cage) where a bird sits

percussion /pə'kʌʃn/ **noun** [U] drums and other instruments that you play by hitting them

perennial /pə'reniəl/ **adj** that happens often or that lasts for a long time: *a perennial problem*

★**perfect¹** /'pɜːfɪkt/ **adj 1** completely good; without faults or weaknesses: *The car is two years old but it is still in perfect condition.* •➤ opposite **imperfect 2** perfect (for sb/sth) exactly suitable or right: *Ken would be perfect for the job.* **3** (only *before* a noun) complete; total: *What he was saying made perfect sense to me.* • *a perfect stranger* **4** used to describe the tense of a verb that is formed with *has/have/had* and the past participle –**perfectly adv:** *He played the piece of music perfectly.*

perfect² /pə'fekt/ **verb** [T] to make sth perfect: *Vinay is spending a year in France to perfect his French.*

perfection /pə'fekʃn/ **noun** [U] the state of being perfect or without fault: *The steak was cooked to perfection.*

perfectionist /pə'fekʃənɪst/ **noun** [C] a person who always does things as well as he/she possibly can and who expects others to do the same

the 'perfect tense (also **the perfect**) **noun** [sing] (*grammar*) the tense of a verb that is formed with *has/have/had* and the past participle: *'I've finished' is in the present perfect tense.*

➤ For more information about the perfect tense, look at the **Quick Grammar Reference** section at the back of this dictionary.

perforate /'pɜːfəreɪt/ **verb** [T] to make a hole or holes in sth

perforation /ˌpɜːfə'reɪʃn/ **noun 1** [C] a series of small holes in paper, etc that make it easy for you to tear **2** [U] the action of making a hole or holes in sth

★**perform** /pə'fɔːm/ **verb 1** [T] (*formal*) to do a piece of work or sth that you have been ordered to do: *to perform an operation/an experiment/a task* **2** [I,T] to take part in a play or to sing, dance, etc in front of an audience: *She is currently performing at the National Theatre.* **3** [I] **perform (well/badly/poorly)** to work or function well or badly: *The company has not been performing well recently.*

> IDIOM **work/perform miracles** ➔ **MIRACLE**

★**performance** /pə'fɔːməns/ **noun 1** [C] the act of performing sth in front of an audience; something that you perform: *What time does the performance start?* **2** [C] the way a person performs in a play, concert, etc: *His moving performance in the film won him an Oscar.* **3** [C] the way in which you do sth, especially how successful you are: *The company's performance was disappointing last year.* **4** [U] (used about a machine, etc) the ability to work well: *This car has a high performance engine.* **5** [sing] (*formal*) the act or process of doing a task, an action, etc: *the performance of your duties*

performer /pə'fɔːmə/ *noun* [C] **1** a person who performs for an audience **2** a person or thing that behaves or works in the way mentioned: *Diana is a poor performer in exams.*

⋆**perfume** /'pɜːfjuːm/ *noun* [C,U] **1** (*Brit also* scent) a liquid with a sweet smell that you put on your body to make yourself smell nice: *Are you wearing perfume?* **2** a pleasant, often sweet, smell

⋆**perhaps** /pə'hæps; præps/ *adv* (used when you are not sure about sth) possibly; maybe: *Perhaps he's forgotten.* ● *She was, perhaps, one of the most famous writers of the time.*

➤ **Perhaps** and **maybe** are similar in meaning. They are often used to make what you are saying sound more polite: *Perhaps I could borrow your book, if you're not using it?* ● *Maybe I'd better explain...*

peril /'perəl/ *noun* (*written*) **1** [U] great danger: *A lack of trained nurses is putting patients' lives in peril.* **2** [C] sth that is very dangerous: *the perils of drug abuse* –**perilous** /'perələs/ *adj* ••➤ **Danger** and **dangerous** are more common words.

perimeter /pə'rɪmɪtə/ *noun* [C] the outside edge or limit of an area of land: *the perimeter fence of the army camp*

⋆**period** /'pɪəriəd/ *noun* [C] **1** a length of time: *The scheme will be introduced for a six-month trial period.* ● *Her son is going through a difficult period at the moment.* ● *What period of history are you most interested in?* **2** a lesson in school: *We have five periods of English a week.* **3** the time every month when a woman loses blood from her body **4** (*especially US*) = **FULL STOP**

periodic /,pɪəri'ɒdɪk/ (also **periodical** /-kl/) *adj* happening fairly regularly: *We have periodic meetings to check on progress.* –**periodically** /-kli/ *adv*: *All machines need to be checked periodically.*

periodical /,pɪəri'ɒdɪkl/ *noun* [C] (*formal*) a magazine that is produced regularly

perish /'perɪʃ/ *verb* [I] (*written*) to die or be destroyed: *Thousands perished in the war.*

perishable /'perɪʃəbl/ *adj* (used about food) that will go bad quickly ••➤ opposite **non-perishable**

perjury /'pɜːdʒəri/ *noun* [U] (*formal*) the act of telling a lie in a court of law –**perjure** /'pɜːdʒə/ *verb* [T] **perjure yourself**: *She admitted that she had perjured herself while giving evidence.*

perk¹ /pɜːk/ *verb*
PHRASAL VERB **perk (sb/sth) up** to become or make sb become happier and have more energy

perk² /pɜːk/ *noun* [C] (*informal*) something extra that you get from your employer in addition to money: *Travelling abroad is one of the perks of the job.*

perm /pɜːm/ *noun* [C] the treatment of hair with special chemicals in order to make it curly ••➤ Look at **wave**. –**perm** *verb* [T]: *She has had her hair permed.*

⋆**permanent** /'pɜːmənənt/ *adj* lasting for a long time or for ever; that will not change: *The accident left him with a permanent scar.* ● *Are you looking for a permanent or a temporary job?* –**permanence** *noun* [U] –**permanently** *adv*: *Has she left permanently?*

permissible /pə'mɪsəbl/ *adj* (*formal*) permissible (for sb) (to do sth) that is allowed by law or by a set of rules: *They have been exposed to radiation above the permissible level.*

⋆**permission** /pə'mɪʃn/ *noun* [U] permission (for sth); permission (for sb) (to do sth) the act of allowing sb to do sth, especially when this is done by sb in a position of authority: *I'm afraid you can't leave without permission.* ● *to ask/give permission for sth*

➤ Be careful. **Permission** is uncountable. A document that says that you are allowed to do something is a **permit**.

permissive /pə'mɪsɪv/ *adj* having, allowing or showing a lot of freedom that many people do not approve of, especially in sexual matters

⋆**permit¹** /pə'mɪt/ *verb* (**permitting**; **permitted**) **1** [T] (*formal*) to allow sb to do sth or to allow sth to happen: *You are not permitted to smoke in the hospital.* ● *His visa does not permit him to work.* ••➤ Look at the note at **allow**. **2** [I,T] to make sth possible: *Let's have a barbecue at the weekend, weather permitting.*

permit² /'pɜːmɪt/ *noun* [C] an official document that says that you are allowed to do sth, especially for a limited period of time: *Next month I'll have to apply for a new work permit.*

perpendicular /,pɜːpən'dɪkjələ/ *adj* **1** at an angle of 90° to sth: *Are the lines perpendicular to each other?*

➤ Compare **horizontal** and **vertical**.

2 pointing straight up; upright: *The path was almost perpendicular* (= it was very steep).

perpetual /pə'petʃuəl/ *adj* **1** continuing for a long period of time without stopping: *They lived in perpetual fear of losing their jobs.* **2** frequently repeated in a way which is annoying: *How can I work with these perpetual interruptions?* –**perpetually** /-tʃuəli/ *adv*

perpetuate /pə'petʃueɪt/ *verb* [T] (*formal*) to cause sth to continue for a long time: *to perpetuate an argument*

perplexed /pə'plekst/ *adj* not understanding sth; confused

persecute /'pɜːsɪkjuːt/ *verb* [T] **1** persecute sb (for sth) (often passive) to treat sb in a cruel and unfair way, especially because of race, religion or political beliefs **2** to deliberately annoy sb and make his/her life unpleasant –**persecution** /,pɜːsɪ'kjuːʃn/ *noun* [C,U]: *the persecution of minorities* –**persecutor** /'pɜːsɪkjuːtə/ *noun* [C]

persevere /,pɜːsɪ'vɪə/ *verb* [I] persevere (at/in/with sth) to continue trying to do or achieve sth that is difficult: *The treatment is painful but I'm going to persevere with it.* –**perseverance** *noun* [U]

p

persist /pəˈsɪst/ verb [I] **1** persist (in sth/ doing sth) to continue doing sth even though other people say that you are wrong or that you cannot do it: *If you persist in making so much noise, I shall call the police.* **2** to continue to exist: *If your symptoms persist you should consult your doctor.* –**persistence** noun [U]: *Finally her persistence was rewarded and she got what she wanted.*

persistent /pəˈsɪstənt/ adj **1** determined to continue doing sth even though people say that you are wrong or that you cannot do it: *Some salesmen can be very persistent.* **2** lasting for a long time or happening often: *a persistent cough* –**persistently** adv

★**person** /ˈpɜːsn/ noun [C] (*pl* people) **1** a man or woman; a human being: *I would like to speak to the person in charge.*

> ➤ In some very formal cases the plural of *person* can be **persons**. Look at the note at **people**.

2 -person (used to form compound nouns) a person doing the job mentioned: *a salesperson/spokesperson* **3** (*grammar*) one of the three types of pronoun in grammar. *I/we* are the first person, *you* is the second person and *he/she/it/they* are the third person.
> IDIOM **in person** seeing or speaking to sb face to face (not speaking on the telephone or writing a letter)

★**personal** /ˈpɜːsənl/ adj **1** (only *before* a noun) of or belonging to one particular person: *personal belongings* ● *Judges should not let their **personal feelings** influence their decisions.* **2** concerning your feelings, health or relationships with other people: *I should like to speak to you in private. I have something personal to discuss.* ● *Do you mind if I ask you a **personal question**?* **3** not connected with a person's job or official position: *Please keep personal phone calls to a minimum.* ● *I try not to let work interfere with my **personal life**.* **4** (only *before* a noun) done by a particular person rather than by sb who is acting for him/her: *The Prime Minister made a personal visit to the victims in hospital.* **5** (only *before* a noun) made or done for one particular person rather than for a large group of people or people in general: *We offer a personal service to all our customers.* **6** speaking about sb's appearance or character in an unpleasant or unfriendly way: *It started as a general discussion but then people started to **get personal** and an argument began.* **7** (only *before* a noun) connected with the body: *personal hygiene* ● *She's always worrying about her personal appearance.*¹

,**personal asˈsistant** = **PA**¹

,**personal comˈputer** = **PC**(1)

personality /ˌpɜːsəˈnæləti/ noun (*pl* personalities) **1** [C,U] the different qualities of a person's character that make him/her different from other people: *Joe has a kind personality.* **2** [U] the quality of having a strong, interesting and attractive character: *A good*

entertainer needs a lot of personality. **3** [C] a famous person (especially in sport, on television, etc): *a television personality*

personalize (also **-ise**) /ˈpɜːsənəlaɪz/ verb [T] to mark sth with the first letters of your name (**your initials**), etc to show that it belongs to you: *a car with a personalized number plate*

personally /ˈpɜːsənəli/ adv **1** used to show that you are expressing your own opinion: *Personally, I think that nurses deserve more money.* **2** done by you yourself, not by sb else acting for you: *I will deal with this matter personally.* **3** in a way that is connected with one particular person rather than a group of people: *I wasn't talking about you personally – I meant all teachers.* **4** in a way that is intended to offend: *Please don't **take it personally**, but I would just rather be alone this evening.* **5** in a way that is connected with sb's private life, rather than his/her job

,**personal ˈpronoun** noun [C] (*grammar*) any of the pronouns *I, me, she, her, he, him, we, us, you, they, them*

,**personal ˈstereo** noun [C] a small machine that plays CDs or cassettes that you can carry round with you and listen to through a wire which goes in each ear (**headphones**)

personify /pəˈsɒnɪfaɪ/ verb [T] (*pres part* personifying; *3rd pers sing pres* personifies; *pt, pp* personified) **1** to be an example in human form of a particular quality: *She is kindness personified.* **2** to describe an object or a feeling as if it were a person, for example in a poem –**personification** /pəˌsɒnɪfɪˈkeɪʃn/ noun [C,U]

personnel /ˌpɜːsəˈnel/ noun **1** [pl] the people who work for a large organization or one of the armed forces: *sales/medical/technical personnel* **2** (also **perˈsonnel department**) [U, with sing or pl verb] the department of a large company or organization that deals with employing and training people: *Personnel is/ are currently reviewing pay scales.*

perspective /pəˈspektɪv/ noun **1** [U] the ability to think about problems and decisions in a reasonable way without exaggerating them: *Hearing about others' experiences often helps to **put** your own problems **into perspective** (= makes them seem less important then you thought).* ● *Try to **keep** these issues **in perspective** (= do not exaggerate them).* **2** [C] your opinion or attitude towards sth: *Try and look at this from my perspective.* **3** [U] the art of drawing on a flat surface so that some objects appear to be farther away than others

perspire /pəˈspaɪə/ verb [I] (*formal*) to lose liquid through your skin when you are hot; to sweat –**perspiration** /ˌpɜːspəˈreɪʃn/ noun [U]
•➤ **Sweat** is a more common word.

★**persuade** /pəˈsweɪd/ verb [T] **1** persuade sb (to do sth); persuade sb (into sth/doing sth) to make sb do sth by giving him/her

p

good reasons: *It was difficult to persuade Louise to change her mind.* ● *We eventually persuaded Sanjay into coming with us.* ••▶ opposite **dissuade 2** (*formal*) **persuade sb that...**; **persuade sb (of sth)** to make sb believe sth: *She had persuaded herself that she was going to fail.* ● *The jury was not persuaded of her innocence.* ••▶ Look at **convince**.

persuasion /pəˈsweɪʒn/ *noun* **1** [U] the act of persuading sb to do sth or to believe sth: *It took a lot of persuasion to get Alan to agree.* **2** [C] (*formal*) a religious or political belief: *politicians of all persuasions*

persuasive /pəˈsweɪsɪv/ *adj* able to persuade sb to do or believe sth: *the persuasive power of advertising* –**persuasively** *adv* –**persuasiveness** *noun* [U]

pertinent /ˈpɜːtɪnənt/ *adj* (*formal*) closely connected with the subject being discussed: *to ask a pertinent question*

perturb /pəˈtɜːb/ *verb* [T] (*formal*) to make sb worried or upset –**perturbed** *adj*

pervade /pəˈveɪd/ *verb* [T] (*formal*) to spread through and be noticeable in every part of sth: *A sadness pervades most of her novels.*

pervasive /pəˈveɪsɪv/ *adj* that is present in all parts of sth: *a pervasive mood of pessimism*

perverse /pəˈvɜːs/ *adj* (*formal*) liking to behave in a way that is not acceptable or reasonable or that most people think is wrong: *Derek gets perverse pleasure from shocking his parents.* –**perversely** *adv* –**perversity** *noun* [U]

perversion /pəˈvɜːʃn/ *noun* [U,C] **1** sexual behaviour that is not considered normal or acceptable by most people **2** the action of changing sth from right to wrong or from good to bad: *That statement is a perversion of the truth.*

pervert[1] /pəˈvɜːt/ *verb* [T] **1** to change a system, process, etc in a bad way: *to pervert the course of justice* (= to deliberately prevent the police from finding out the truth about a crime) **2** to cause sb to think or behave in a way that is not moral or acceptable

pervert[2] /ˈpɜːvɜːt/ *noun* [C] a person whose sexual behaviour is not thought to be natural or normal by most people

pessimism /ˈpesɪmɪzəm/ *noun* [U] **pessimism (about/over sth)** the state of expecting or believing that bad things will happen and that sth will not be successful ••▶ opposite **optimism** –**pessimistic** /ˌpesɪˈmɪstɪk/ *adj* ••▶ opposite **optimistic** –**pessimistically** /-kli/ *adv* ••▶ opposite **optimistically**

pessimist /ˈpesɪmɪst/ *noun* [C] a person who always thinks that bad things will happen or that sth will be not be successful ••▶ opposite **optimist**

pest /pest/ *noun* [C] **1** an insect or animal that destroys plants, food, etc **2** (*informal*) a person or thing that annoys you: *That child is such a pest!*

pester /ˈpestə/ *verb* [T] **pester sb (for sth)**;

pester sb (to do sth) to annoy sb, for example by asking him/her sth many times: *to pester sb for money* ● *The kids kept pestering me to take them to the park.*

pesticide /ˈpestɪsaɪd/ *noun* [C,U] a chemical substance that is used for killing animals, especially insects, that eat food crops ••▶ Look at **insecticide**.

★**pet** /pet/ *noun* [C] **1** an animal or bird that you keep in your home for pleasure rather than for food or work: *a pet dog/cat/hamster* ● *a pet shop* (= where pets are sold) **2** a person who is treated as a favourite: *teacher's pet*

petal /ˈpetl/ *noun* [C] one of the thin soft coloured parts of a flower ••▶ picture on page C2

peter /ˈpiːtə/ *verb*
PHRASAL VERB **peter out** to slowly become smaller, quieter, etc and then stop

pet ˈhate *noun* [C] sth that you particularly do not like: *Filling in forms is one of my pet hates.*

petition /pəˈtɪʃn/ *noun* [C] a written document, signed by many people, that asks a government, etc to do or change sth: *More than 50 000 people signed the petition protesting about the new road.* –**petition** *verb* [I,T]

petrified /ˈpetrɪfaɪd/ *adj* very frightened

★**petrol** /ˈpetrəl/ (*US* **gas**; **gasoline**) *noun* [U] the liquid that is used as fuel for vehicles such as cars and motorbikes ••▶ Look at **diesel**.

petroleum /pəˈtrəʊliəm/ *noun* [U] mineral oil that is found under the ground or sea and is used to make petrol, plastic and other types of chemical substances

ˈpetrol station (*US* **gas station**) *noun* [C] a place where you can buy petrol and other things for your car ••▶ Look at **garage**.

petty /ˈpeti/ *adj* **1** small and unimportant: *He didn't want to get involved with the petty details.* ● *petty crime/theft* (= that is not very serious) **2** unkind or unpleasant to other people (for a reason that does not seem very important): *petty jealousy/revenge*

PG /ˌpiː ˈdʒiː/ *abbr* (*Brit*) (used about films in which there are scenes that are unsuitable for children) parental guidance

phantom /ˈfæntəm/ *noun* [C] **1** (*written*) the spirit of a dead person that is seen or heard by sb who is still living ••▶ **Ghost** is a more common word. **2** something that you think exists, but that is not real

pharmaceutical /ˌfɑːməˈsjuːtɪkl; -ˈsuː-/ *adj* connected with the production of medicines and drugs: *pharmaceutical companies*

pharmacist /ˈfɑːməsɪst/ = **CHEMIST**(1)

pharmacy /ˈfɑːməsi/ *noun* (*pl* **pharmacies**) **1** [C] a shop or part of a shop where medicines and drugs are prepared and sold

➤ A shop that sells medicine is also called **a chemist's** (**shop**) in British English or a **drugstore** in US English.

2 [U] the preparation of medicines and drugs

p

★**phase**[1] /feɪz/ *noun* [C] a stage in the development of sth: *Julie went through a difficult phase when she started school.*

phase[2] /feɪz/ *verb*

PHRASAL VERBS **phase sth in** to introduce or start using sth gradually in stages over a period of time: *The metric system was phased in over several years.*

phase sth out to stop using sth gradually in stages over a period of time: *The older machines are gradually being phased out and replaced by new ones.*

PhD /ˌpiː eɪtʃ 'diː/ *abbr* Doctor of Philosophy; an advanced university degree that you receive when you complete a piece of research into a special subject: *She has a PhD in History.*

pheasant /'feznt/ *noun* [C] (*pl* **pheasants** or **pheasant**) a type of bird with a long tail. The males have brightly coloured feathers. Pheasants are often shot for sport and eaten.

phenomenal /fə'nɒmɪnl/ *adj* very great or impressive: *phenomenal success* –**phenomenally** /-nəli/ *adv*

phenomenon /fə'nɒmɪnən/ *noun* [C] (*pl* **phenomena** /-mə/) a fact or an event in nature or society, especially one that is not fully understood: *Acid rain is not a natural phenomenon. It is caused by pollution.*

phew /fjuː/ *interj* a sound which you make to show that you are hot, tired or happy that sth bad did not happen or has finished: *Phew, it's hot!* ● *Phew, I'm glad that interview's over!*

philanthropist /fɪ'lænθrəpɪst/ *noun* [C] a rich person who helps the poor and those in need, especially by giving money

philosopher /fə'lɒsəfə/ *noun* [C] a person who has developed a set of ideas and beliefs about the meaning of life

philosophical /ˌfɪlə'sɒfɪkl/ (also **philosophic**) *adj* **1** of or concerning philosophy: *a philosophical debate* **2** philosophical (about sth) staying calm and not getting upset or worried about sth bad that happens: *He is quite philosophical about failing the exam and says he will try again next year.* –**philosophically** /-kli/ *adv*

★**philosophy** /fə'lɒsəfi/ *noun* (*pl* **philosophies**) **1** [U] the study of ideas and beliefs about the meaning of life **2** [C] a set of beliefs that tries to explain the meaning of life or give rules about how to behave: *Her philosophy is 'If a job's worth doing, it's worth doing well'.*

phlegm /flem/ *noun* [U] the thick substance that is produced in your nose and throat when you have a cold

phlegmatic /fleg'mætɪk/ *adj* (*formal*) not easily made angry or upset; calm

phobia /'fəʊbiə/ *noun* [C] (often used in compounds) a very strong fear or hatred that you cannot explain: *arachnophobia* (= fear of spiders)

★**phone** /fəʊn/ *noun* (*informal*) **1** [U] = **TELEPHONE**(1): *a phone conversation* ● *You can book the tickets over the/by phone.* **2** [C] = **TELEPHONE**(2): *The phone is ringing – could*

you answer it? –**phone** *verb* [I,T]: *Did anybody phone while I was out?* ● *Could you phone the restaurant and book a table?* ••➤ synonym **ring** or **call**

IDIOM **on the phone/telephone 1** using the telephone **2** having a telephone in your home: *I'll have to write to her because she's not on the phone.*

'**phone book** = **TELEPHONE DIRECTORY**

'**phone box** = **TELEPHONE BOX**

phonecard /'fəʊnkɑːd/ *noun* [C] a small plastic card that you can use to pay for calls in a public telephone box ••➤ picture at **telephone**

'**phone-in** *noun* [C] a radio or television programme during which you can ask a question or give your opinion by telephone

phonetic /fə'netɪk/ *adj* **1** connected with the sounds of human speech; using special symbols to represent these sounds: *the phonetic alphabet* **2** (used about spelling) having a close relationship with the sounds represented: *Spanish spelling is phonetic, unlike English spelling.* –**phonetically** /-kli/ *adv*

phonetics /fə'netɪks/ *noun* [U] the study of the sounds of human speech

phoney (*US* **phony**) /'fəʊni/ *adj* not real; false: *She spoke with a phoney Russian accent.* –**phoney** (*US* **phony**) *noun* [C]

★**photo** /'fəʊtəʊ/ *noun* [C] (*pl* **photos** /-təʊz/) (*informal*) = **PHOTOGRAPH**

photocopier /'fəʊtəʊkɒpiə/ *noun* [C] a machine that makes copies of documents by photographing them

photocopy /'fəʊtəʊkɒpi/ *noun* [C] (*pl* **photocopies**) a copy of a document, a page in a book, etc that is made by a special machine (a photocopier) ••➤ synonym **Xerox** ••➤ Look at **copy**. –**photocopy** *verb* [I,T] (*pres part* photocopying; *3rd pers sing pres* photocopies; *pt, pp* photocopied)

★**photograph** /'fəʊtəɡrɑːf/ (also **photo**) *noun* [C] a picture that is taken with a camera: *to take a photograph* ● *She looks younger in real life than she did in the photograph.* ••➤ Look at **negative** and **slide**. –**photograph** *verb* [T]

photographer /fə'tɒɡrəfə/ *noun* [C] a person who takes photographs ••➤ Look at **cameraman**.

photographic /ˌfəʊtə'ɡræfɪk/ *adj* connected with photographs or photography

photography /fə'tɒɡrəfi/ *noun* [U] the skill or process of taking photographs

phrasal verb /ˌfreɪzl 'vɜːb/ *noun* [C] (*grammar*) a verb that is combined with an adverb or a preposition to give a new meaning, such as 'look after' or 'put sb off' ••➤ Look at **verb**.

★**phrase**[1] /freɪz/ *noun* [C] (*grammar*) a group of words that are used together. A phrase does not contain a full verb: *'First of all' and 'a bar of chocolate' are phrases.* ••➤ Look at **sentence**.

phrase[2] /freɪz/ *verb* [T] to express sth in a particular way: *The statement was phrased so that it would offend no one.*

'**phrase book** noun [C] a book that gives common words and useful phrases in a foreign language. People often use phrase books when they travel to another country whose language they do not know.

★**physical** /'fɪzɪkl/ adj **1** connected with your body rather than your mind: *physical fitness/ strength/disabilities* **2** (only *before* a noun) connected with real things that you can touch, or with the laws of nature: *physical geography* (= the natural features on the face of the earth) **3** (only *before* a noun) connected with the study of natural forces (physics) and things that are not alive –physically /-kli/ adv: *to be physically fit* • *It will be physically impossible to get to London before ten.*

physician /fɪ'zɪʃn/ (*US formal*) = DOCTOR¹(1)

physicist /'fɪzɪsɪst/ noun [C] a person who studies or is an expert in physics

★**physics** /'fɪzɪks/ noun [U] the scientific study of natural forces such as light, sound, heat, electricity, pressure, etc

physiotherapist /ˌfɪziəʊ'θerəpɪst/ noun [C] a person who is trained to use physiotherapy

physiotherapy /ˌfɪziəʊ'θerəpi/ (*US* ˌphysical 'therapy) noun [U] the treatment of disease or injury by exercise, light, heat, rubbing the muscles (massage), etc

physique /fɪ'ziːk/ noun [C] the size and shape of a person's body: *a strong muscular physique*

pianist /'pɪənɪst/ noun [C] a person who plays the piano

★**piano** /pi'ænəʊ/ noun [C] (*pl* pianos /-nəʊz/) a large musical instrument that you play by pressing down black and white keys: *an upright piano* • *a grand piano*

➤ Note that we usually say 'play **the** piano, **the** violin, **the** guitar, etc': *I've been learning the piano for four years.* When talking about modern music such as jazz, rock, etc, 'play drums, guitar, etc' is more usual without the use of 'the': *He plays bass in a band.* • *This recording features Miles Davis on trumpet.*

★**pick**¹ /pɪk/ verb [T] **1** to choose sb/sth from a group of people or things: *I was upset not to be picked for the team.* • *Have I picked a bad time to visit?* **2** to take a flower, fruit or vegetable from the place where it is growing: *to pick flowers/grapes/cotton* **3** to remove a small piece or pieces of sth with your fingers: *Don't pick your nose!* • *She picked a hair off her jacket.* **4** pick your way across, over, through, etc sth to walk carefully, choosing the best places to put your feet

IDIOMS have a bone to pick with sb → BONE¹
pick a fight (with sb) to start a fight with sb deliberately
pick a lock to open a lock without using a key
pick and choose to choose only the things that you like or want very much
pick sb's pocket to steal money, etc from sb's pocket or bag

PHRASAL VERBS pick at sth **1** to eat only small

amounts of food because you are not hungry **2** to touch sth many times with your fingers
pick on sb to behave unfairly or in a cruel way towards sb
pick sb/sth out to choose or recognize sb/sth from a number of people or things; identify: *I immediately picked Jean out in the photo.*
pick up to become better; to improve
pick sb up to collect sb, in a car, etc: *We've ordered a taxi to pick us up at ten.*
pick sb/sth up **1** to take hold of and lift sb/ sth: *Lucy picked up the child and gave him a cuddle.* **2** to receive an electronic signal, sound or picture: *In the north of France you can pick up English television programmes.*
pick sth up **1** to learn sth without formal lessons: *Joe picked up a few words of Spanish on holiday.* **2** to get or find sth: *I picked up this book at the market.* **3** to go and get sth; to collect sth: *I have to pick up my jacket from the cleaner's.*

pick² /pɪk/ noun **1** [sing] the one that you choose; your choice: *You can have whichever cake you like.* **Take your pick. 2** [sing] the best of a group: *You can see the pick of the new films at this year's festival.* **3** (also pickaxe *US* pickax /'pɪkæks/) a tool that consists of a curved iron bar with sharp points at both ends, fixed onto a wooden handle. Picks are used for breaking stones or hard ground.

picket /'pɪkɪt/ noun [C] a worker or group of workers who stand outside the entrance to a building to protest about sth, especially in order to stop people entering a factory, etc during a strike –picket verb [I,T]

pickle /'pɪkl/ noun [C,U] food such as fruit or vegetables that is put in salt water or another liquid (vinegar) so that it can be kept for a long time –pickle verb [T]: *pickled onions*

pickpocket /'pɪkpɒkɪt/ noun [C] a person who steals things from other people's pockets or bags in public places

pickup /'pɪkʌp/ (also 'pickup truck) noun [C] a type of vehicle that has an open part with low sides at the back •➤ picture at vehicle

picky /'pɪki/ adj (*informal*) (used about a person) liking only certain things and difficult to please •➤ Look at fussy.

★**picnic** /'pɪknɪk/ noun [C] a meal that you take with you to eat outdoors: *We had a picnic on the beach.* –picnic verb [I] (*pres part* picnicking; *pt, pp* picnicked)

pictorial /pɪk'tɔːriəl/ adj expressed in pictures: *pictorial representations of objects*

★**picture**¹ /'pɪktʃə/ noun [C] **1** a painting, drawing or photograph: *Who painted the picture in the hall?* • *The teacher asked us to draw a picture of our families.* **2** an image on a television screen: *They showed pictures of the crash on the news.* **3** a description of sth that gives you a good idea of what it is like: *The police are trying to build up a picture of exactly what happened.*

picture² /'pɪktʃə/ verb [T] **1** picture sb/sth (as sth) to imagine sth in your mind: *I can't picture Ivan as a father.* **2** to make a picture of sb/sth: *She is pictured here with her parents.*

picturesque /ˌpɪktʃəˈresk/ **adj** (usually used about an old building or place) attractive: *a picturesque fishing village*

★**pie** /paɪ/ **noun** [C,U] a type of food consisting of fruit, meat or vegetables inside a pastry case: *apple pie ● meat pie* ••➤ picture on page C4

★**piece¹** /piːs/ **noun** [C] **1** an amount or example of sth: *a piece of paper ● a piece of furniture ● a good piece of work ● a piece of advice/information/news* **2** one of the parts that sth is made of: *We'll have to **take the** engine **to pieces** to find the problem.* **3** one of the parts into which sth breaks: *The plate fell to the floor and smashed **to pieces**. ● The vase lay **in pieces** on the floor.* **4** a piece (on/ about sb/sth) an article in a newspaper or magazine: *There's a good piece on China in today's paper.* **5** a single work of art, music, etc: *He played a piece by Chopin.* **6** one of the small objects that you use when you are playing games such as chess **7** a coin of the value mentioned: *a fifty-pence piece*

IDIOMS **bits and pieces → BIT¹**
give sb a piece of your mind to speak to sb angrily because of sth he/she has done
go to pieces to be no longer able to work or behave normally because of a difficult situation: *When his wife died he seemed to go to pieces.*
in one piece not broken or injured: *I've only been on a motorbike once, and I was just glad to get home in one piece.*
a piece of cake (*informal*) something that is very easy

piece² /piːs/ **verb**
PHRASAL VERB **piece sth together 1** to discover the truth about sth from different pieces of information: *Detectives are trying to piece together the last few days of the man's life.* **2** to put sth together from several pieces

piecemeal /ˈpiːsmiːl/ **adj, adv** done or happening a little at a time

'pie chart noun [C] a diagram consisting of a circle divided into parts to show the size of particular parts in relation to the whole ••➤ picture at **graph**

pier /pɪə/ **noun** [C] **1** a large wooden or metal structure that is built out into the sea from the shore. Boats can stop at piers so that people or goods can be taken on or off **2** (in Britain) a large wooden or metal structure that is built out into the sea in holiday towns, where people can walk ••➤ picture on page C8

pierce /pɪəs/ **verb** [T] **1** to make a hole in sth with a sharp point: *I'm going to **have my ears pierced**.* **2** [I,T] pierce (through/into) sth to manage to go through or into sth: *A scream pierced the air.*

piercing /ˈpɪəsɪŋ/ **adj 1** (used about the wind, pain, a loud noise, etc) strong and unpleasant **2** (used about sb's eyes or a look) seeming to know what you are thinking

piety /ˈpaɪəti/ **noun** [U] a way of behaving that shows a deep respect for God and religion ••➤ adjective **pious**

★**pig¹** /pɪg/ **noun** [C] **1** a fat pinkish animal with short legs and a short tail that is kept on farms for its meat (**pork**)

➤ A male pig is a **boar**, a female pig is a **sow** and a young pig is a **piglet**. When they make a noise, pigs **grunt** and piglets **squeal**. Look at the note at **meat**.

2 (*informal*) an unpleasant person or a person who eats too much

pig² /pɪg/ **verb** [T] (**pigging**; **pigged**) (*slang*) pig yourself to eat too much
PHRASAL VERB **pig out (on sth)** (*slang*) to eat too much of sth

pigeon /ˈpɪdʒɪn/ **noun** [C] a fat grey bird that often lives in towns

'pigeon-hole noun [C] one of a set of small open boxes that are used for putting papers or letters in

piggyback /ˈpɪgibæk/ **noun** [C] the way of carrying sb, especially a child, on your back: *to give sb a piggyback*

'piggy bank noun [C] a small box, often shaped like a pig, that children save money in

pig-'headed adj (*informal*) not prepared to change your mind or say that you are wrong ••➤ Look at **stubborn** and **obstinate**.

piglet /ˈpɪglət/ **noun** [C] a young pig

pigment /ˈpɪgmənt/ **noun** [C,U] a substance that gives colour to things: *The colour of your skin depends on the amount of pigment in it.*

pigsty /ˈpɪgstaɪ/ (also **sty** *US* **'pigpen) noun** [C] (*pl* **pigsties**) a small building where pigs are kept

pigtail /ˈpɪgteɪl/ (*US* **braid**) **noun** [C] hair that is tied together in one or two thick pieces made by putting (**plaiting**) three pieces of hair in and out of each other ••➤ picture at **hair**

★**pile¹** /paɪl/ **noun** [C] **1** a number of things lying on top of one another, or an amount of sth lying in a mass: *a pile of books/sand ● He put the coins in **neat piles**. ● She threw the clothes **in a pile** on the floor.*

➤ A **pile** may be tidy or untidy. A **heap** is untidy.

2 (usually plural) (*informal*) **piles of sth** a lot of sth: *I've got piles of work to do this evening.* **3 piles = HAEMORRHOIDS**

pile² /paɪl/ **verb** [T] **1** pile sth (up) to put things one on top of the other to form a pile: *We piled the boxes in the corner.* **2** pile A on(to) B; pile B with A to put a lot of sth on top of sth: *She piled the papers on the desk. ● The desk was piled with papers.*
PHRASAL VERBS **pile into, out of, off, etc sth** (*informal*) to go into, out of, off, etc sth quickly and all at the same time: *The children piled onto the bus.*
pile up (used about sth bad) to increase in quantity: *Our problems are really piling up.*

'pile-up noun [C] a crash that involves several cars, etc

pilgrim /'pɪlgrɪm/ **noun** [C] a person who travels a long way to visit a religious place

pilgrimage /'pɪlgrɪmɪdʒ/ **noun** [C,U] a long journey that a person makes to visit a religious place

pill /pɪl/ **noun 1** [C] a small round piece of medicine that you swallow: *Take one pill, three times a day after meals.* ● *a sleeping pill* •➤ Look at **tablet**. •➤ picture at **bandage 2 the pill** [sing] a pill that some women take regularly so that they do not become pregnant: *She is on the pill.*

pillar /'pɪlə/ **noun** [C] **1** a column of stone, wood or metal that is used for supporting part of a building **2** a person who has a strong character and is important to sb/sth: *Dave was a pillar of strength to his sister when she was ill.*

'pillar box **noun** [C] (in Britain) a tall round red box in a public place into which you can post letters, which are then collected by sb from the post office •➤ Look at **postbox** and **letter box**.

pillion /'pɪliən/ **noun** [C] a seat for a passenger behind the driver on a motorbike –**pillion** **adv**: *to ride pillion on a motorbike*

pillow /'pɪləʊ/ **noun** [C] a large cushion that you put under your head when you are in bed •➤ picture at **bed**

pillowcase /'pɪləʊkeɪs/ **noun** [C] a thin soft cover for a pillow

pilot¹ /'paɪlət/ **noun** [C] a person who flies an aircraft: *an airline pilot*

pilot² /'paɪlət/ **verb** [T] **1** to operate the controls of a vehicle, especially an aircraft or a boat: *to pilot a ship* **2** to lead sb/sth through a difficult situation: *The booklet pilots you through the process of starting your own business.* **3** to be the first to test sth that will be used by everyone: *The new exam is being piloted in schools in Italy.*

pilot³ /'paɪlət/ **adj** (only *before* a noun) done as an experiment or to test sth that will be used by everyone: *The pilot scheme will run for six months.*

pimple /'pɪmpl/ **noun** [C] a small spot on your skin

pin   drawing pin   safety pin
       (US thumbtack)

pin¹ /pɪn/ **noun** [C] **1** a short thin piece of metal with a round head at one end and a sharp point at the other. Pins are used for fastening together pieces of cloth, paper, etc. **2** a thin piece of wood or metal that is used for a particular purpose: *a hairpin* ● *a two-pin plug* •➤ picture at **plug**

pin² /pɪn/ **verb** [T] (**pinning; pinned**) **pin** sth **to/on** sth; **pin** sth **together 1** to fasten sth with a pin or pins: *Could you pin this notice on the board, please?* **2** pin sb/sth **against, to, under, etc** sth to make sb/sth unable to move by holding or pressing down on him/her/it: *He caught his brother and pinned him to the floor.* ● *He was pinned under the fallen tree.*

IDIOM **pin** (all) **your hopes on** sb/sth to believe completely that sb/sth will help you or will succeed

PHRASAL VERBS **pin** sb **down 1** to hold sb so he/she cannot move **2** to force sb to decide sth or to say exactly what he/she is going to do: *Can you pin her down to what time she'll be coming?*

pin sth **down** to describe or explain exactly what sth is

PIN³ /pɪn/ (also **PIN number**) **noun** [C,usually sing] personal identification number; a number given to you by your bank so that you can use a plastic card to take out money from a cash machine

pincer /'pɪnsə/ **noun 1 pincers** [pl] a tool made of two crossed pieces of metal that is used for holding things, pulling nails out of wood, etc **2** [C] one of the two sharp, curved front legs of some shellfish that are used for holding things •➤ picture at **shellfish**

pinch¹ /pɪntʃ/ **verb** [T] **1** to hold a piece of sb's skin tightly between your thumb and first finger, especially in order to hurt him/her: *Paul pinched his brother and made him cry.* •➤ picture on page S8 **2** to hold sth too tight, often causing pain: *I've got a pinched nerve in my neck.* **3** (*informal*) to steal: *Who's pinched my pen?*

pinch² /pɪntʃ/ **noun** [C] **1** the holding of sb's skin tightly between your finger and thumb: *She gave him a little pinch on the arm.* **2** the amount of sth that you can pick up with your thumb and first finger: *a pinch of salt*

IDIOMS **at a pinch** used to say that sth can be done if it is really necessary: *We really need three cars but we could manage with two at a pinch.*

take sth **with a pinch of salt** to think that sth is probably not true or accurate

pinched /pɪntʃt/ **adj** (used about sb's face) thin and pale because of illness or cold

pine¹ /paɪn/ **noun 1** [C] (also **'pine tree**) a tall tree that has thin sharp leaves (needles)

➤ Trees, like the pine, that do not lose their leaves in winter are called **evergreen**.

2 [U] the wood from pine trees (which is often used for making furniture): *a pine table*

pine² /paɪn/ **verb** [I] **pine (for** sb/sth) to be very unhappy because sb has died or gone away: *The dog sat outside, pining for its owner.*

pineapple /'paɪnæpl/ **noun** [C,U] a large sweet fruit that is yellow inside and has a thick brown skin with sharp points. Pineapples grow in hot countries. •➤ picture on page C3

ping /pɪŋ/ **noun** [C] a short high noise that is made by a small bell or by a metal object hitting against sth: *The lift went ping and the doors opened.* –**ping** **verb** [I]

'ping-pong (*informal*) = **TABLE TENNIS**

★**pink** /pɪŋk/ **adj, noun** [U] (of) a pale red colour

pinnacle /'pɪnəkl/ **noun** [C] **1** the most important or successful part of sth: *Celia is at the pinnacle of her career.* **2** a high pointed rock on a mountain

pinpoint /'pɪnpɔɪnt/ **verb** [T] **1** to find the exact position of sth: *to pinpoint a place on the map* **2** to describe or explain exactly what sth is: *First we have to pinpoint the cause of the failure.*

,**pins and 'needles noun** [pl] a strange, sometimes painful feeling that you get in a part of your body after it has been in one position for too long and when the blood is returning to it

★**pint** /paɪnt/ **noun** [C] **1** (*abbr* pt) a measure of liquid; 0·57 of a litre. There are 8 pints in a gallon: *a pint of milk* •➤ An American pint is 0·47 of a litre. **2** (*Brit informal*) a pint of beer

'**pin-up noun** [C] (*informal*) a picture of an attractive person, made to be put on a wall; a person who appears in these pictures

pioneer /ˌpaɪə'nɪə/ **noun** [C] **1** a pioneer (in/of sth) a person who is one of the first to develop an area of human knowledge, culture, etc: *Yuri Gagarin was one of the pioneers of space exploration.* **2** a person who is one of the first to go and live in a particular area: *the pioneers of the American West* –**pioneer verb** [I,T]: *a technique pioneered in the US*

pious /'paɪəs/ **adj** having or showing a deep belief in religion –**piously adv** •➤ noun **piety**

pip /pɪp/ **noun** [C] (*Brit*) the small seed of an apple, a lemon, an orange, etc •➤ picture on page C3

★**pipe**[1] /paɪp/ **noun** [C] **1** a tube that carries gas or liquid: *Waste water is carried away down the drainpipe.* **2** a tube with a small bowl at one end that is used for smoking tobacco: *to smoke a pipe* **3** a simple musical instrument that consists of a tube with holes in it. You blow into it to play it.

pipe[2] /paɪp/ **verb** [T] to carry liquid or gas in pipes: *Water is piped to all the houses in the village.*

PHRASAL VERB **pipe up** to suddenly say sth: *Suddenly Shirin piped up with a question.*

pipeline /'paɪplaɪn/ **noun** [C] a line of pipes that are used for carrying liquid or gas over a long distance

IDIOM **in the pipeline** being planned or prepared

piper /'paɪpə/ **noun** [C] a person who plays music on a pipe, or who plays a musical instrument that is typical in Scotland (the bagpipes)

piracy /'paɪrəsi/ **noun** [U] **1** the crime of attacking ships in order to steal from them **2** the illegal copying of books, video tapes, etc

pirate[1] /'paɪrət/ **noun** [C] **1** (usually in the past or in stories) a criminal who attacks ships in order to steal from them **2** a person who copies books, video tapes, computer programs, etc in order to sell them illegally

pirate[2] /'paɪrət/ **verb** [T] to make an illegal copy of a book, video tape, etc in order to sell it

Pisces /'paɪsi:z/ **noun** [C,U] the twelfth sign of the zodiac, the Fishes

pistol /'pɪstl/ **noun** [C] a small gun that you hold in one hand •➤ Look at the note at **gun**

piston /'pɪstən/ **noun** [C] a piece of metal in an engine, etc that fits tightly inside a tube (shaft). The piston is moved up and down inside the tube and causes other parts of the engine to move.

pit[1] /pɪt/ **noun 1** [C] a large hole that is made in the ground: *They dug a large pit to bury the dead animals.* **2** = COAL MINE **3** the pits [pl] the place on a motor racing track where cars stop for fuel, new tyres, etc during a race

IDIOM **be the pits** (*slang*) to be very bad: *The food in that restaurant is the pits!*

pit[2] /pɪt/ **verb** [T] (**pitting; pitted**) to make small holes in the surface of sth: *The front of the building was pitted with bullet marks.*

PHRASAL VERB **pit A against B** to test one person or thing against another in a fight or competition: *The two strongest teams were pitted against each other in the final.*

pitch[1] /pɪtʃ/ **noun 1** [C] (*Brit*) a special area of ground where you play certain sports: *a football/hockey/cricket pitch*

➤ Compare **court** and **field**.

2 [sing] the strength or level of feelings, activity, etc: *The children's excitement almost reached fever pitch.* **3** [U] how high or low a sound is, especially a musical note **4** [C] talk or arguments used by sb who is trying to sell sth or persuade sb to do sth: *a sales pitch* • *to make a pitch for sth*

pitch[2] /pɪtʃ/ **verb 1** [T] to set sth at a particular level: *The talk was pitched at people with far more experience than me.* • *a high-pitched voice* **2** [I,T] to throw sth/sb; to be thrown: *Doug pitched his can into the bushes.* **3** [T] to put up a tent or tents: *They pitched their tents in the valley.* **4** [T] **pitch sth (at sb)** to try to sell a product to a particular group of people or in a particular way: *This new breakfast cereal is being pitched at kids.*

PHRASAL VERB **pitch in** (*informal*) to join in and work together with other people: *Everybody pitched in to clear up the flood damage.*

,**pitch-'black adj** completely dark; with no light at all

pitcher /'pɪtʃə/ **noun** [C] **1** a large container for holding and pouring liquids •➤ picture at **jug 2** (in baseball) the player who throws (pitches) the ball to a player from the other team, who tries to hit it

piteous /'pɪtiəs/ **adj** (*formal*) that makes you feel pity or sadness –**piteously adv**

pitfall /'pɪtfɔːl/ **noun** [C] a danger or difficulty, especially one that is hidden or not obvious

pith /pɪθ/ **noun** [U] the white substance inside the skin of an orange, lemon, etc

pithy /'pɪθi/ **adj** expressed in a clear, direct way: *a pithy comment*

pitiful /'pɪtɪfl/ **adj** causing you to feel pity or

p

sadness: *the pitiful groans of the wounded soldiers* –**pitifully** /-fəli/ **adv**

pitiless /'pɪtiləs/ **adj** having or showing no pity for other people's suffering –**pitilessly** **adv**

★**pity¹** /'pɪti/ **noun 1** [U] a feeling of sadness that you have for sb/sth that is suffering or in trouble: *The situation is his fault so I don't feel any pity for him.* **2** [sing] something that makes you feel a little sad or disappointed: *'You're too late. Emily left five minutes ago.' 'Oh, what a pity!'* • *It's a pity that Bina couldn't come.*

⟨IDIOM⟩ **take pity on sb** to help sb who is suffering or in trouble because you feel sorry for him/her

pity² /'pɪti/ **verb** [T] (*pres part* **pitying**; *3rd pers sing pres* **pities**; *pt, pp* **pitied**) to feel pity or sadness for sb who is suffering or in trouble: *We shouldn't just pity these people; we must help them.*

pivot¹ /'pɪvət/ **noun** [C] **1** the central point on which sth turns or balances **2** the central or most important person or thing: *West Africa was the pivot of the cocoa trade.*

pivot² /'pɪvət/ **verb** [I] to turn or balance on a central point

pixie /'pɪksi/ **noun** [C] (in children's stories) a creature like a small person with pointed ears that has magic powers

pizza /'piːtsə/ **noun** [C,U] an Italian dish consisting of a flat round bread base with vegetables, cheese, meat, etc on top, which is cooked in an oven

pkt **abbr** packet

pl **abbr** (*grammar*) plural

placard   banner
WE WANT PEACE   STOP CRUELTY TO ANIMALS

placard /'plækɑːd/ **noun** [C] a large written or printed notice that is put in a public place or carried on a stick in a protest march

placate /plə'keɪt/ **verb** [T] to make sb feel less angry about sth

★**place¹** /pleɪs/ **noun** [C] **1** a particular position or area: *Show me the exact place where it happened.* • *This would be a good place to sit down and have a rest.* • *The wall was damaged in several places.* **2** a particular village, town, country, etc: *Which places did you go to in Italy?* • *Vienna is a very beautiful place.* **3** a building or area that is used for a particular purpose: *The square is a popular meeting place for young people.* • *The town is full of inexpensive eating places.* **4** a seat or position that can be used by sb/sth: *They went into the*

classroom and sat down in their places. • *Go on ahead and save me a place in the queue.*

➤ A **place** is a seat or position for sb/sth. A place where you can park your car is also called a **space**. You use **space** and **room** when you are talking about empty areas: *This piano takes up too much space.* • *There is enough room for three people in the back of the car.*

5 your position in society; your role: *I feel it is not my place to criticize my boss.* **6** an opportunity to study at a college, play for a team, etc: *Abina has got a place to study law at Hull.* • *Laila is now sure of a place on the team.* **7** the usual or correct position or occasion for sth: *The room was tidy. Everything had been put away in its place.* • *A funeral is not the place to discuss business.* **8** the position of a number after the decimal point: *Your answer should be correct to three decimal places.* **9** [sing] (*spoken*) a person's home: *Her parents have got a place on the coast.* **10** the position that you have at the end of a race, competition, etc: *Cara finished in second place.*

⟨IDIOMS⟩ **all over the place** everywhere

change/swap places (with sb) to take sb's seat, position, etc and let him/her have yours: *Let's change places so that you can look out of the window.*

fall/slot into place (used about sth that is complicated or difficult to understand) to become organized or clear in your mind: *After two weeks in my new job, everything suddenly started to fall into place.*

in my, your, etc place/shoes in my, your, etc situation or position: *If I were in your place I would wait a year before getting married.*

in place 1 in the correct or usual position: *Use tape to hold the picture in place.* **2** (used about plans or preparations) finished and ready to be used: *All the preparations for the trip are now in place.*

in place of sb/sth; in sb/sth's place instead of sb/sth

in the first, second, etc place (*informal*) used when you are giving a list of reasons for sth or explaining sth; firstly, secondly, etc

out of place 1 not suitable for a particular situation: *I felt very out of place among all those clever people.* **2** not in the correct or usual place

put sb in his/her place to show that sb is not as clever, important, etc as he/she believes: *It really put her in her place when she failed to qualify for the race.*

put yourself in sb's place to imagine that you are in the same situation as sb else: *Put yourself in Steve's place and you will realize how worried he must be.*

take place (used about a meeting, an event, etc) to happen: *The ceremony took place in glorious sunshine.*

★**place²** /pleɪs/ **verb** [T] **1** (*formal*) to put sth carefully or deliberately in a particular position: *The chairs had all been placed in neat rows.* • *The poster was placed where everyone*

p

could see it. **2** to put sb in a particular position or situation: *His behaviour placed me in a difficult situation.* • *to place sb in charge* • *Rhoda was placed third in the competition.* **3** used to express the attitude that sb has to sb/sth: *We placed our trust in you and you failed us.* • *The blame for the disaster was placed firmly on the company.* **4** (usually in negative statements) to recognize him/her/it: *Her face is familiar but I just can't place her.* **5** to give instructions about sth or to ask for sth to happen: *to place a bet on sth* • *to place an order for sth*

'**place name** noun [C] the name of a city, town, etc

placid /'plæsɪd/ adj (used about a person or an animal) calm and not easily excited –**placidly** adv

plague[1] /pleɪg/ noun **1** [C,U] any infectious disease that spreads quickly and kills many people **2** **the plague** [U] an infectious disease spread by rats that causes swellings on the body, a very high temperature and often results in death **3** [C] **a plague of sth** a large number of unpleasant animals or insects that come into an area at one time: *a plague of ants/locusts*

plague[2] /pleɪg/ verb [T] to cause sb/sth a lot of trouble: *The project was plagued by a series of disasters.*

plaice /pleɪs/ noun [C,U] (*pl* **plaice**) a type of flat sea fish that we eat

★**plain**[1] /pleɪn/ adj **1** easy to see, hear or understand; clear: *It was plain that he didn't want to talk about it.* • *She made it plain that she didn't want to see me again.* **2** (used about people, thoughts, actions, etc) saying what you think; direct and honest: *I'll be plain with you. I don't like the idea.* **3** simple in style; not decorated or complicated: *My father likes plain English cooking.* **4** (only *before* a noun) all one colour; without a pattern on it: *a plain blue jumper* **5** (used especially about a woman or girl) not beautiful or attractive: *She's a rather plain child.*

plain[2] /pleɪn/ noun [C] a large area of flat land with few trees

plain[3] /pleɪn/ adv (*spoken*) completely: *That's plain silly.*

'**plain clothes** adj (used about a police officer) in ordinary clothes; not uniform: *a plain-clothes detective*

,**plain 'flour** noun [U] flour that does not contain a powder (**baking powder**) which makes cakes, etc rise ••➤ Look at **self-raising flour**.

plainly /'pleɪnli/ adv **1** clearly: *He was plainly very upset.* **2** using simple words to say sth in a direct and honest way: *She told him plainly that he was not doing his job properly.* **3** in a simple way, without decoration: *She was plainly dressed and wore no make-up.*

plaintiff /'pleɪntɪf/ noun [C] a person who starts a legal action against sb in a court of law ••➤ Look at **defendant**.

plaintive /'pleɪntɪv/ adj sounding sad, especially in a weak complaining way –**plaintively** adv

plait /plæt/ (*US* **braid**) verb [T] to cross three or more long pieces of hair, rope, etc over and under each other to make one thick piece ••➤ picture at **hair** –**plait** noun [C]

★**plan**[1] /plæn/ noun **1** [C] **a plan (for sth/to do sth)** an idea or arrangement for doing or achieving sth in the future: *We usually make our holiday plans in January.* • *The firm has no plans to employ more people.* • *There has been a change of plan* – *we're meeting at the restaurant.* • *If everything goes according to plan* (= happens as we planned) *we should be home by midnight.* **2** [C] a detailed map of a building, town, etc: *a street plan of Berlin* **3** **plans** [pl] detailed drawings of a building, machine, road, etc that show its size, shape and measurements: *We're getting an architect to draw up some plans for a new kitchen.* **4** [C] a diagram that shows how sth is to be organized or arranged: *Before you start writing an essay, it's a good idea to make a brief plan.*

plan[2] /plæn/ verb (**planning**; **planned**) **1** [I,T] **plan (sth) (for sth)** to decide, organize or prepare for sth you want to do in the future: *to plan for the future* • *You need to plan your work more carefully.* **2** [I,T] **plan (on sth/doing sth)** to intend or expect to do sth: *I'm planning on having a holiday in July.* • *We plan to arrive at about 4 o'clock.* **3** [T] to make a diagram or a design of sth: *The new shopping centre is very badly planned.* –**planning** noun [U]: *The project requires careful planning.*

★**plane**[1] /pleɪn/ noun [C] **1** = **AEROPLANE**: *Has her plane landed yet?* **2** a tool used for making the surface of wood smooth by taking very thin pieces off it ••➤ picture at **tool** **3** (*technical*) a flat surface

plane[2] /pleɪn/ verb [T] to make the surface of a piece of wood flat and smooth using a plane[1](2)

★**planet** /'plænɪt/ noun **1** [C] a very large round object in space that moves around the sun or another star: *the planets of our solar system* **2** **the planet** [sing] the world we live in; the Earth, especially when talking about the environment

planetarium /,plænɪ'teəriəm/ noun [C] a building with a curved ceiling that represents the sky at night. It is used for showing the positions and movements of the planets and stars for education and entertainment.

plank /plæŋk/ noun [C] a long flat thin piece of wood that is used for building or making things

★**plant**[1] /plɑːnt/ noun **1** [C] a living thing that grows in the ground and usually has leaves, a long thin green central part (a **stem**) and roots: *a tomato plant* • *a plant pot* (= a container for plants) ••➤ picture on page C2 **2** [C] a very large factory: *a car plant* • *a nuclear reprocessing plant*

★**plant**² /plɑːnt/ **verb** [T] **1** to put plants, seeds, etc in the ground to grow: *Bulbs should be planted in the autumn.* **2** plant sth (with sth) to cover or supply a garden, area of land, etc with plants: *The field's been planted with wheat this year.* **3** to put yourself/sth firmly in a particular place or position: *He planted himself in the best seat.* **4** plant sth (on sb) to hide sth, especially sth illegal, in sb's clothing, property, etc in order to make him/her seem guilty of a crime: *The police think that terrorists may have planted the bomb.* ● *The women claimed that the drugs had been planted on them.*

plantation /plɑːnˈteɪʃn/ **noun** [C] **1** a large area of land, especially in a hot country, where tea, cotton, tobacco, etc are grown: *a coffee plantation* **2** an area of land where trees are grown to produce wood

plaque /plɑːk/ **noun 1** [C] a flat piece of stone or metal, usually with names and dates on it, that is fixed on a wall in memory of a famous person or event ●➤ picture at **column** **2** [U] a harmful substance that forms on your teeth

plaster¹ /ˈplɑːstə/ **noun 1** [U] a mixture of a special powder and water that becomes hard when it is dry. Plaster is put on walls and ceilings to form a smooth surface. **2** (also **sticking plaster**) [C] a small piece of sticky material that is used to cover a cut, etc on the body **3** [U] a white powder that is mixed with water and becomes hard when dry. It is used for putting round broken bones, etc until they get better: *When Alan broke his leg it was **in plaster** for six weeks.* ●➤ picture at **bandage**

plaster² /ˈplɑːstə/ **verb** [T] **1** to cover a wall, etc with plaster¹(1) to make the surface smooth **2** plaster sb/sth (in/with sth) to cover sb/sth with a large amount of sth: *He plastered his walls with posters.*

★**plastic**¹ /ˈplæstɪk/ **noun** [C,U] a light, strong material that is made with chemicals and is used for making many different sorts of objects

plastic² /ˈplæstɪk/ **adj** made of plastic: *plastic cups* ● *a plastic bag*

plastic 'surgery noun [U] a medical operation to repair or replace damaged skin or to improve the appearance of a person's face or body ●➤ Look at **facelift** and **surgery**.

★**plate** /pleɪt/ **noun 1** [C] a flat, usually round, dish for eating or serving food from: *a plastic/paper/china plate* ● *a plate of food*

➤ You eat your main course from a **dinner plate**. You may put bread, etc on a **side plate**. You eat cereal or a pudding from a **bowl**.

2 [C] a thin flat piece of metal or glass: *a steel/metal plate* **3** [C] a flat piece of metal with sth written on it: *The brass plate beside the door said 'Dr Waters'.* **4** [U] metal that has a thin covering of gold or silver: *gold/silver plate*

plateau /ˈplætəʊ/ **noun** [C] (*pl* **plateaus** /-təʊz/ or **plateaux** /-təʊ/) **1** a large high area of flat land **2** a state where there is little development or change: *House prices seem to have reached a plateau.*

plateful /ˈpleɪtfʊl/ **noun** [C] the amount of food that a plate(1) can hold

★**platform** /ˈplætfɔːm/ **noun** [C] **1** the place where you get on or off trains at a railway station: *Which platform does the train to York leave from?* **2** a flat surface, higher than the level of the floor or ground, on which public speakers or performers stand so that the audience can see them **3** [usually sing] the ideas and aims of a political party who want to be elected: *They fought the election on a platform of low taxes.*

platinum /ˈplætɪnəm/ **noun** [U] (*symbol* **Pt**) a silver-grey metal that is often used for making expensive jewellery: *a platinum wedding ring*

platonic /pləˈtɒnɪk/ **adj** (used about a relationship between two people) friendly but not sexual

platoon /pləˈtuːn/ **noun** [C] a small group of soldiers

plausible /ˈplɔːzəbl/ **adj** that you can believe; reasonable: *a plausible excuse* ●➤ opposite **implausible**

★**play**¹ /pleɪ/ **verb 1** [I] play (with sb/sth) to do sth to enjoy yourself; to have fun: *The children have been playing on the beach all day.* ● *Emma's found a new friend to play with.* **2** [I,T] to take part in a game or sport: *to play football/tennis/hockey* ● *I usually play against Bill.* ● *She played him at table tennis and won.* ● *Do you know how to play chess?* ● *Who's Brazil playing next in the World Cup?* **3** [I,T] play (sth) (on sth) to make music with a musical instrument: *to play the piano/guitar/trumpet* ● *My son's learning the piano. He plays very well.* ● *She played a few notes on the violin.* ●➤ Look at the note at **piano**. **4** [T] to turn on a video, tape, etc so that it produces sound: *Shall I play the CD for you again?* **5** [I,T] to act in a play, film, TV programme, etc; to act the role of sb: *Richard is going to play Romeo.*

➤ **Play a part, role**, etc is often used in a figurative way: *Britain has played an active part in the recent discussions.* ● *John played a key role in organizing the protest.*

6 [I] (*formal*) to move quickly and lightly: *Sunlight played on the surface of the sea.*

➤ For idioms containing **play**, look at the entries for the nouns, adjectives, etc, for example **play it by ear** is at **ear**.

PHRASAL VERBS **play at sth/being sth** to do sth with little interest or effort: *He's only playing at studying. He'd prefer to get a job now.* ● *What is that driver playing at* (= doing)?

play sth back (to sb) to turn on and watch or listen to a film, tape, etc that you have recorded: *Play that last scene back to me again.*

play sth down to make sth seem less important than it really is: *to play down a crisis*

play A off against B to make people compete

p

or argue with each other, especially for your own advantage: *I think she enjoys playing one friend off against another.*

play on sth to use and take advantage of sb's fears or weaknesses: *This advertising campaign plays on people's fears of illness.*

play (sb) up (*informal*) to cause sb trouble or pain: *The car always plays up in wet weather.*

★**play²** /pleɪ/ *noun* **1** [C] a piece of writing performed by actors in the theatre, or on television or radio: *Would you like to see a play while you're in London?* • *a radio/television play*

> Actors and actresses **rehearse** a play. A theatre company, drama group, etc **produces** a play. A play is usually acted on a **stage**.

2 [U] the playing of a game or sport: *Bad weather stopped play yesterday.*

> We **play** tennis, football, etc but we CANNOT say **a play** of tennis. We have **a game** of tennis.

3 [U] activity done for enjoyment only, especially by children: *Young children learn through play.* • *the happy sound of children at play* **4** [U] a control on a video or cassette player, etc that you press to start the tape running: *Put the video into the machine then press play.*

IDIOM **fair play** → FAIR¹

playboy /'pleɪbɔɪ/ *noun* [C] a rich man who spends his time enjoying himself

★**player** /'pleɪə/ *noun* [C] **1** a person who plays a game or sport: *a game for four players* • *She's an excellent tennis player.* **2** (used to form compound nouns) a machine on which you can listen to sound that has been recorded on CD, tape, etc: *a CD/cassette player* **3** a person who plays a musical instrument: *a piano player*

playful /'pleɪfl/ *adj* **1** done or said in fun; not serious: *a playful remark* **2** full of fun; wanting to play: *a playful puppy*

playground /'pleɪɡraʊnd/ *noun* [C] an area of land where children can play: *the school playground*

playgroup /'pleɪɡruːp/ (also **playschool** /'pleɪskuːl/) (*Brit*) = NURSERY SCHOOL

playhouse /'pleɪhaʊs/ *noun* **1** [sing] used in the name of some theatres: *the Liverpool Playhouse* **2** [C] a model of a house for children to play in

'**playing card** = CARD(4)

'**playing field** *noun* [C] a large field used for sports such as cricket and football

IDIOM **a level playing field** → LEVEL²

'**play-off** *noun* [C] a match between two teams or players who have equal scores to decide the winner: *They lost to Chicago in the play-offs.*

plaything /'pleɪθɪŋ/ *noun* [C] (*formal*) a toy

playtime /'pleɪtaɪm/ *noun* [C,U] a period of time between lessons when children at school can go outside to play

playwright /'pleɪraɪt/ *noun* [C] a person who

writes plays for the theatre, television or radio

PLC (also **plc**) /ˌpiː el 'siː/ *abbr* (*Brit*) Public Limited Company

plea /pliː/ *noun* [C] **1** (*formal*) a plea (for sth) an important and emotional request: *a plea for help* **2** a plea of sth a statement made by or for sb in a court of law: *a plea of guilty/not guilty*

plead /pliːd/ *verb* **1** [I] plead (with sb) (to do/for sth) to ask sb for sth in a very strong and serious way: *She pleaded with him not to leave her.* • *He pleaded for mercy.* **2** [T] to state in a court of law that you did or did not do a crime: *The defendant pleaded not guilty to the charge of theft.* **3** [I,T] plead (sth) (for sb/sth) (used especially about a lawyer in a court of law) to support sb's case: *He needs the very best lawyer to plead (his case) for him.* **4** [T] to give sth as an excuse or explanation for sth: *He pleaded family problems as the reason for his lack of concentration.*

★**pleasant** /'pleznt/ *adj* nice, enjoyable or friendly: *a pleasant evening/climate/place/view* • *a pleasant smile/voice/manner* •→ opposite **unpleasant** –**pleasantly** *adv*

★**please¹** /pliːz/ *interj* used as a polite way of asking for sth or telling sb to do sth: *Come in, please.* • *Please don't spend too much money.* • *Sit down, please.* • *Two cups of coffee, please.*

IDIOM **yes, please** used when you are accepting an offer of sth politely: *'Sugar?' 'Yes, please.'* •→ opposite **No, thank you**

★**please²** /pliːz/ *verb* **1** [I,T] to make sb happy; to satisfy: *There's just no pleasing some people* (= some people are impossible to please). **2** [I] (not used as the main verb in a sentence; used after words like *as, what, whatever, anything*, etc) to want; to choose: *You can't always do as you please.* • *She has so much money she can buy anything she pleases.*

IDIOM **please yourself** to be able to do whatever you want: *Without anyone else to cook for, I can please myself what I eat.*

★**pleased** /pliːzd/ *adj* (not before a noun) pleased (with sb/sth); pleased to do sth; pleased that… happy or satisfied about sth: *John seems very pleased with his new car.* • *Aren't you pleased to see me?* • *We're only too pleased* (= very happy) *to help.* • *I'm so pleased that you've decided to stay another week.* •→ Look at the note at **glad**. •→ opposite **displeased**

pleasing /'pliːzɪŋ/ *adj* giving you pleasure and satisfaction: *The exam results are very pleasing this year.* •→ opposite **displeasing**

pleasurable /'pleʒərəbl/ *adj* (*formal*) enjoyable: *a pleasurable experience*

★**pleasure** /'pleʒə/ *noun* **1** [U] the feeling of being happy or satisfied: *Parents get a lot of pleasure out of watching their children grow up.* • *It gives me great pleasure to introduce our next speaker.* **2** [U] enjoyment (rather than work): *What brings you to Paris – business or pleasure?* **3** [C] an event or activity, that you enjoy or that makes you happy: *It's* *been a pleasure to work with you.* • *'Thanks for your help.' 'It's a pleasure.'*

IDIOMS take (no) pleasure in sth/doing sth to enjoy/not enjoy (doing) sth

with pleasure used as a polite way of saying that you are happy to do sth: *'Could you give me a lift into town?' 'Yes, with pleasure.'*

pleat /pliːt/ **noun** [C] a permanent fold that is sewn or pressed into a piece of cloth: *a skirt with pleats at the front*

pledge /pledʒ/ **noun** [C] a pledge (to do sth) a formal promise or agreement –pledge **verb** [T] pledge (sth) (to sb/sth): *The Government has pledged £250000 to help the victims of the crash.*

plentiful /'plentɪfl/ **adj** available in large amounts or numbers: *Fruit is plentiful at this time of year.* ••➤ opposite **scarce**

★ **plenty** /'plenti/ **pron, adv 1** plenty (of sb/sth) as much or as many of sth as you need: *'Shall I get some more coffee?' 'No, we've still got plenty.'* • *There's still plenty of time to get there.* • *Have you brought plenty to drink?* **2** (before *more*) a lot: *There's plenty more ice cream.* **3** (*informal*) (with *big, long, tall,* etc followed by *enough*) easily: *'This shirt's too small.' 'Well, it looks plenty big enough to me.'*

pliable /'plaɪəbl/ (also **pliant** /'plaɪənt/) **adj 1** easy to bend or shape **2** (used about a person) easy to influence

pliers /'plaɪəz/ **noun** [pl] a tool made of two crossed pieces of metal with handles, that is used for holding things firmly and for cutting wire: *a pair of pliers* ••➤ picture at **tool**

plight /plaɪt/ **noun** [sing] (*formal*) a bad or difficult state or situation

plimsoll /'plɪmsəl/ (also **pump**, *US* **sneaker**) **noun** [C] a light shoe made of strong material (canvas) that is especially used for sports, etc: *a pair of plimsolls* ••➤ Look at **trainer**.

plod /plɒd/ **verb** [I] (**plodding**; **plodded**) plod (along/on) **1** to walk slowly and in a heavy or tired way: *We plodded on through the rain for nearly an hour.* **2** to make slow progress, especially with difficult or boring work: *I just plod on with my work and never seem to get anywhere.*

plonk¹ /plɒŋk/ **verb** [T] (*spoken*) **1** plonk sth (down) to put sth down on sth, especially noisily or carelessly: *Just plonk your bag down anywhere.* **2** plonk (yourself) (down) to sit down heavily and carelessly: *He just plonked himself down in front of the TV.*

plonk² /plɒŋk/ **noun** [U] (*Brit informal*) cheap wine: *Let's open a bottle of plonk!*

plop¹ /plɒp/ **noun** [usually sing] a sound like that of a small object dropping into water

plop² /plɒp/ **verb** [I] (**plopping**; **plopped**) to fall making a plopping noise: *The frog plopped back into the water.*

★ **plot¹** /plɒt/ **noun** [C] **1** the series of events which form the story of a novel, film, etc: *The play had a very weak plot.* • *I can't follow the plot of this novel.* **2** a plot (to do sth) a secret plan made by several people to do sth wrong or illegal: *a plot to kill the president* **3** a small

piece of land, used for a special purpose: *a plot of land*

plot² /plɒt/ **verb** (**plotting**; **plotted**) **1** [I,T] plot (with sb) (against sb) to make a secret plan to do something wrong or illegal: *They were accused of plotting against the government.* • *The terrorists had been plotting this campaign for years.* **2** [T] to mark sth on a map, diagram, etc: *to plot the figures on a graph*

plough

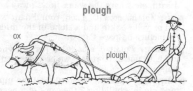

ox   plough

plough (*US* **plow**) /plaʊ/ **noun** [C] a large farm tool which is pulled by a vehicle (a tractor) or by an animal. A plough turns the soil over ready for seeds to be planted. ••➤ Look at **snowplough**. –plough **verb** (*figurative*): *The book was long and boring but I managed to plough through it* (= read it with difficulty).

ploy /plɔɪ/ **noun** [C] a ploy (to do sth) something that you say or do in order to get what you want or to persuade sb to do sth

pluck¹ /plʌk/ **verb** [T] **1** pluck sth/sb (from sth/out) to remove or take sth/sb from a place: *He plucked the letter from my hands.* **2** to pull the feathers out of a bird in order to prepare it for cooking **3** to make the strings of a musical instrument play notes by moving your fingers across them

IDIOM pluck up courage to try to get enough courage to do sth

PHRASAL VERB pluck at sth to pull sth gently several times

pluck² /plʌk/ **noun** [U] (*informal*) courage and determination –plucky **adj**

plugs

tap (*US* faucet)

socket   plug

pin   plug

wash basin (*also* basin)

plug¹ /plʌg/ **noun** [C] **1** a plastic or rubber object with two or three metal pins, which connects a piece of electrical equipment to the electricity supply **2** a round piece of rubber or plastic that you use to block the hole in a sink, bath, etc **3** a mention that sb makes of a new book, film, etc in order to encourage people to buy or see it

plug² /plʌg/ **verb** [T] (**plugging**; **plugged**) **1** to fill or block a hole with sth that fits

p

tightly into it: *He managed to plug the leak in the pipe.* **2** (*informal*) to say good things about a new book, film, etc in order to make people buy or see it: *They're really plugging that song on the radio at the moment.*

PHRASAL VERB **plug sth in** to connect a piece of electrical equipment to the electricity supply or to another piece of equipment: *Is the microphone plugged in?* •➤ opposite **unplug**

plughole /'plʌɡhəʊl/ **noun** [C] (*Brit*) a hole in a bath, etc where the water flows away

plum /plʌm/ **noun** [C] a soft, round fruit with red or yellow skin and a stone in the middle •➤ picture on page C3

plumber /'plʌmə/ **noun** [C] a person whose job is to put in or repair water pipes, baths, toilets, etc

plumbing /'plʌmɪŋ/ **noun** [U] **1** all the pipes, taps, etc in a building **2** the work of a person who puts in and repairs water pipes, taps, etc

plume /pluːm/ **noun** [C] **1** a quantity of smoke that rises in the air **2** a large feather or group of feathers, often worn as a decoration

plump¹ /plʌmp/ **adj** (used about a person or an animal) pleasantly fat: *the baby's plump cheeks*

plump² /plʌmp/ **verb**
PHRASAL VERBS **plump (yourself/sb/sth) down** to sit down or to put sb/sth down heavily: *She plumped herself down by the fire.*
plump for sb/sth (*Brit informal*) to choose or decide to have sb/sth: *I think I'll plump for the roast chicken, after all.*

plunder /'plʌndə/ **noun** [U] the action of stealing from people or places, especially during war or fighting; the goods that are stolen –**plunder** verb [I,T]

plunge¹ /plʌndʒ/ **verb 1** [I] plunge (into sth/ in) to jump, drop or fall suddenly and with force: *He ran to the river and plunged in.* • (*figurative*) *Share prices plunged overnight.* **2** [T] plunge sth in/into sth to push sth suddenly and with force into sth: *He plunged the knife into the table in anger.* **3** [T] to cause sb/sth to suddenly be in the state mentioned: *The country has been plunged into chaos by the floods.* **4** [I] plunge into sth to start doing sth with energy and enthusiasm: *Think carefully before you plunge into buying a house.*

plunge² /plʌndʒ/ **noun** [C] a sudden jump, drop or fall: *I slipped and took a plunge in the river.* • *the plunge in house prices*
IDIOM **take the plunge** to decide to do sth difficult after thinking about it for quite a long time: *After going out together for five years, they took the plunge and got married.*

pluperfect /ˌpluːˈpɜːfɪkt/ = **PAST PERFECT**

★**plural** /'plʊərəl/ **noun** [C] (*grammar*) the form of a noun, verb, etc which refers to more than one person or thing: *The plural of 'boat' is 'boats'.* • *The verb should be in the plural.* –**plural** adj •➤ Look at **singular**.

★**plus**¹ /plʌs/ **prep 1** and; added to: *Two plus two is four (2 + 2 = 4).* •➤ opposite **minus 2** in

addition to; and also: *You have to work five days a week plus every other weekend.*

plus² /plʌs/ **noun** [C] **1** the sign (+) •➤ opposite **minus 2** an advantage of a situation

plus³ /plʌs/ **adj** (only *after* a noun) **1** or more: *I'd say there were 30000 plus at the match.* **2** (used for marking work done by students) slightly above: *I got a B plus (= B+) for my homework.* •➤ opposite **minus**

plush /plʌʃ/ **adj** comfortable and expensive: *a plush hotel*

Pluto /'pluːtəʊ/ **noun** [sing] the planet that is furthest from the sun

ply /plaɪ/ **verb** (*pres part* **plying**; *3rd pers sing pres* **plies**; *pt, pp* **plied**) [I,T] to try to sell services or goods to people, especially on the street: *Boat owners were plying their trade to passing tourists.* • *to ply for business*
PHRASAL VERB **ply sb with sth** to keep giving sb food and drink, or asking sb questions: *They plied us with food from the moment we arrived.*

plywood /'plaɪwʊd/ **noun** [U] board made by sticking several thin layers of wood together

★**pm** (*US* **PM**) /ˌpiː ˈem/ **abbr** after midday: *2 pm* (= 2 o'clock in the afternoon) • *11.30pm* (= 11.30 in the evening)

pneumonia /njuːˈməʊniə/ **noun** [U] a serious illness of the lungs which makes breathing difficult

PO /ˌpiː ˈəʊ/ **abbr** (used in compound nouns) Post Office: *a PO box*

poach /pəʊtʃ/ **verb** [T] **1** to cook food (especially fish or eggs) gently in a small amount of liquid: *poached eggs* **2** to hunt animals illegally on sb else's land: *The men were caught poaching elephants.* **3** to take an idea from sb else and use it as though it is your own **4** to take members of staff from another company in an unfair way

poacher /'pəʊtʃə/ **noun** [C] a person who hunts animals illegally on sb else's land

PO box /ˌpiː ˈəʊ bɒks/ **noun** [C] a place in a post office where letters, packages, etc are kept until they are collected by the person they were sent to: *The address is PO Box 4287, Nairobi, Kenya.*

★**pocket**¹ /'pɒkɪt/ **noun** [C] **1** a piece of material like a small bag that is sewn inside or on a piece of clothing and is used for carrying things in: *He always walks with his hands in his trouser pockets.* • *a pocket dictionary/calculator* (= one small enough to fit in your pocket) •➤ picture on page C6 **2** a small bag or container that is fixed to the inside of a car door, suitcase, etc and used for putting things in: *There are safety instructions in the pocket of the seat in front of you.* •➤ picture at **bag 3** used to talk about the amount of money that you have to spend: *They sell cars to suit every pocket.* • *The school couldn't afford a CD player, so the teacher bought one out of his own pocket.* **4** a small area or group that is different from its surroundings: *a pocket of warm air*
IDIOM **pick sb's pocket** → **PICK**¹

pocket² /'pɒkɪt/ **verb** [T] **1** to put sth in your

pocket: *He took the letter and pocketed it quickly.* **2** to steal or win money

'pocket money (*US* **allowance**) *noun* [U] an amount of money that parents give a child to spend, usually every week

pod /pɒd/ *noun* [C] the long, green part of some plants, such as peas and beans, that contains the seeds ••➤ picture on page C3

podium /'pəʊdiəm/ *noun* [C] a small platform for a speaker, a performer, etc to stand on

★**poem** /'pəʊɪm/ *noun* [C] a piece of writing arranged in short lines. Poems try to express thoughts and feelings with the help of sound and rhythm.

★**poet** /'pəʊɪt/ *noun* [C] a person who writes poems

poetic /pəʊ'etɪk/ (also **poetical** /-ɪkl/) *adj* connected with poets or like a poem –**poetically** /-kli/ *adv*

★**poetry** /'pəʊətri/ *noun* [U] a collection of poems; poems in general: *Shakespeare's poetry and plays* ● *Do you like poetry?*

➤ Compare **prose**.

poignant /'pɔɪnjənt/ *adj* causing sadness or pity: *a poignant memory* –**poignancy** /-jənsi/ *noun* [U] –**poignantly** *adv*

★**point¹** /pɔɪnt/ *noun* **1** [C] a particular fact, idea or opinion that sb expresses: *You make some interesting points in your essay.* ● *I see your point but I don't agree with you.*

➤ We can **bring up**, **raise**, **make**, **argue**, **emphasize** and **illustrate** a point.

2 the point [sing] the most important part of what is being said; the main piece of information: *It makes no difference how much it costs – the point is we don't have any money! ● She always talks and talks and takes ages to get to the point.* **3** [C] an important idea or thought that needs to be considered: *'Have you checked what time the last bus back is?' 'That's a point – no I haven't.'* **4** [C] a detail, characteristic or quality of sb/sth: *Make a list of your strong points and your weak points* (= good and bad qualities). **5** [sing] the point (of/in sth/doing sth) the meaning, reason or purpose of sth: *She's said no, so what's the point of telephoning her again? ● There's no point in talking to my parents – they never listen.* **6** [C] (often in compounds) a particular place, position or moment: *The library is a good starting point for that sort of information. ● He has reached the high point of his career. ● the boiling/freezing point of water ● He waved to the crowd and it was at that point that the shot was fired. ● At one point I thought I was going to laugh.* **7** [C] the thin sharp end of sth: *the point of a pin/needle/pencil* **8** [C] a small round dot used when writing parts of numbers: *She ran the race in 11·2 (eleven point two) seconds.* **9** [C] a single mark in some games, sports, etc that you add to others to get the score: *to score a point ● Rios needs two more points to win the match.* **10** [C] a unit of measurement for certain things: *The value of the dollar has fallen*

by a few points.

IDIOMS **be on the point of doing sth** just going to do sth: *I was on the point of going out when the phone rang.*

beside the point ➔ **BESIDE**

have your, etc (good) points to have some good qualities: *Bill has his good points, but he's very unreliable.*

make a point of doing sth to make sure you do sth because it is important or necessary: *I made a point of locking all the doors and windows before leaving the house.*

point of view a way of looking at a situation; an opinion: *From my point of view it would be better to wait a little longer.* ••➤ synonym **viewpoint** or **standpoint**

➤ Do not confuse **from my point of view** with **in my opinion**. The first means 'from my position in life' (= as a woman, business person, teacher, etc). The second means 'I think': *From an advertiser's point of view, television is a wonderful medium.* ● *In my opinion people watch too much television.*

prove your/the case/point ➔ **PROVE**

a sore point ➔ **SORE¹**

sb's strong point ➔ **STRONG**

take sb's point to understand and accept what sb is saying

to the point connected with what is being discussed; relevant: *His speech was short and to the point.*

up to a point partly: *I agree with you up to a point.*

★**point²** /pɔɪnt/ *verb* **1** [I] point (at/to sb/sth) to show where sth is or to draw attention to sth using your finger, a stick, etc: *'I'll have that one,' she said, pointing to a chocolate cake.* **2** [I,T] point (sth) (at/towards sb/sth) to aim (sth) in the direction of sb/sth: *She pointed the gun at the target and fired.* **3** [I] to face in a particular direction or to show that sth is in a particular direction: *The sign pointed towards the motorway. ● Turn round until you're pointing north.* **4** [I] point to sth to show that sth is likely to exist, happen or be true: *Research points to a connection between diet and cancer.*

PHRASAL VERB **point sth out (to sb)** to make sb look at sth; to make sth clear to sb: *The guide pointed out all the places of interest to us on the way.* ● *I'd like to point out that we haven't got much time left.*

point-'blank *adj*, *adv* **1** (used about a shot) from a very close position: *He was shot in the leg at point-blank range.* **2** (used about sth that is said) very direct and not polite; not allowing any discussion: *He told her point-blank to get out of the house and never come back.*

pointed /'pɔɪntɪd/ *adj* **1** having a sharp end: *a pointed stick/nose* **2** (used about sth that is said) critical of sb in an indirect way: *She made a pointed comment about people who are always late.* –**pointedly** *adv*

pointer /'pɔɪntə/ *noun* [C] **1** a piece of helpful advice or information: *Could you give me*

[I] **intransitive**, a verb which has no object: *He laughed.*   [T] **transitive**, a verb which has an object: *He ate an apple.*

some pointers on how best to tackle the problem? **2** a small arrow on a computer screen that you move by moving the mouse ••➤ picture on page S7 **3** a stick that is used to point to things on a map, etc

pointless /'pɔɪntləs/ **adj** without any use or purpose: *It's pointless to try and make him agree.* –**pointlessly adv** –**pointlessness noun** [U]

poise /pɔɪz/ **noun** [U] a calm, confident way of behaving

poised /pɔɪzd/ **adj 1** not moving but ready to move: *'Shall I call the doctor or not?' he asked, his hand poised above the telephone.* **2** poised (to do sth) ready to act; about to do sth: *The government is poised to take action if the crisis continues.* **3** calm and confident

★**poison¹** /'pɔɪzn/ **noun** [C,U] a substance that kills or harms you if you eat or drink it: *rat poison* • *poison gas*

poison² /'pɔɪzn/ **verb** [T] **1** to kill, harm or damage sb/sth with poison **2** to put poison in sth: *The cup of coffee had been poisoned.* **3** to spoil or ruin sth: *The quarrel had poisoned their relationship.* –**poisoned adj:** *a poisoned drink*

poisoning /'pɔɪzənɪŋ/ **noun** [U] the giving or taking of poison or a dangerous substance: *He got food poisoning from eating fish that wasn't fresh.*

poisonous /'pɔɪzənəs/ **adj 1** causing death or illness if you eat or drink it **2** (used about animals, etc) producing and using poison to attack its enemies: *He was bitten by a poisonous snake.* **3** very unpleasant and intended to upset sb: *She wrote him a poisonous letter criticizing his behaviour.*

poke /pəʊk/ **verb 1** [T] to push sb/sth with a finger, stick or other long, thin object: *Be careful you don't poke yourself in the eye with that stick!* **2** [I,T] poke (sth) into, through, out of, down, etc sth to push sth quickly into sth or in a certain direction: *He poked the stick down the hole to see how deep it was.* • *A child's head poked up from behind the wall.* ••➤ picture on page S8 –**poke noun** [C]

IDIOMS **poke fun at sb/sth** to make jokes about sb/sth, often in an unkind way

poke/stick your nose into sth ➔ NOSE¹

poker /'pəʊkə/ **noun 1** [U] a type of card game usually played to win money **2** [C] a metal stick for moving the coal or wood in a fire ••➤ picture at **fireplace**

poky /'pəʊki/ **adj** (*Brit informal*) (used about a house, room, etc) too small: *a poky little office*

polar /'pəʊlə/ **adj** (only *before* a noun) of or near the North or South Pole: *the polar regions*

polar bear noun [C] a large white bear that lives in the area near the North Pole

★**pole** /pəʊl/ **noun** [C] **1** a long, thin piece of wood or metal, used especially to hold sth up: *a flagpole* • *a tent pole* ••➤ picture at **ski** **2** either of the two points at the exact top and bottom of the earth: *the North/South Pole* ••➤ picture at **earth**

the ꞌpole vault noun [C] the sport of jumping over a high bar with the help of a long pole

★**police¹** /pə'liːs/ **noun** [pl] the official organization whose job is to make sure that people obey the law, and to prevent and solve crime: *Dial 999 if you need to call the police.* • *a police car* • *Kamal wants to join the police force when he finishes school.* • *the local police station*

➤ **Police** is a plural noun, always used with a plural verb. You cannot say 'a police' meaning one man or woman. When we are talking about the organization, we always use the: *There were over 100 police on duty.* • *The police are investigating the murder.*

police² /pə'liːs/ **verb** [T] to keep control in a place by using the police or a similar official group: *The cost of policing football games is extremely high.*

po꞉lice Ꞌconstable (also **constable**) **noun** [C] (*Brit*) (*abbr* **PC**) a police officer of the lowest rank

poꞋlice officer (also **officer**) **noun** [C] a member of the police

★**policy** /'pɒləsi/ **noun** [C,U] (*pl* **policies**) **1** policy (on sth) a plan of action agreed or chosen by a government, a company, etc: *Labour has a new set of policies on health.* • *It is company policy not to allow smoking in meetings.* **2** a way of behaving that you think is best in a particular situation: *It's my policy only to do business with people I like.* **3** a document that shows an agreement that you have made with an insurance company: *an insurance policy*

polio /'pəʊliəʊ/ **noun** [U] a serious disease which can cause you to lose the power in certain muscles

polish¹ /'pɒlɪʃ/ **verb** [T] to make sth shine by rubbing it and often by putting a special cream or liquid on it: *to polish your shoes/a table*

PHRASAL VERB **polish sth off** (*informal*) to finish sth quickly: *The two of them polished off a whole chicken for dinner!*

polish² /'pɒlɪʃ/ **noun 1** [U] a cream, liquid, etc that you put on sth to clean it and make it shine: *a tin of shoe polish* ••➤ picture at **bucket 2** [sing] the action of polishing sth: *I'll give the glasses a polish before the guests arrive.*

polished /'pɒlɪʃt/ **adj 1** shiny because of polishing: *polished wood floors* **2** (used about a performance, etc) of a high standard: *Most of the actors gave a polished performance.*

★**polite** /pə'laɪt/ **adj** having good manners and showing respect for others: *The assistants in that shop are always very helpful and polite.* • *He gave me a polite smile.* ••➤ opposite **impolite** or **impertinent** –**politely adv** –**politeness noun** [U]

★**political** /pə'lɪtɪkl/ **adj 1** connected with politics and government: *a political leader/ debate/party* • *She has very strong political opinions.* **2** (used about people) interested in politics **3** concerned with the competition for power inside an organization: *I suspect he was dismissed for political reasons.* –politic-ally **adv**: *Politically he's fairly right wing.*

po,litical a'sylum noun [U] protection given by a state to a person who has left his/her own country for political reasons

po,litically cor'rect adj (*abbr* **PC**) used to describe language or behaviour that care-fully avoids offending particular groups of people –po,litical cor'rectness **noun** [U]

★**politician** /,pɒlə'tɪʃn/ **noun** [C] a person whose job is in politics, especially one who is a member of parliament or of the govern-ment: *Politicians of all parties supported the war.*

★**politics** /'pɒlətɪks/ **noun 1** [U,with sing or pl verb] the work and ideas that are connected with governing a country, a town, etc: *to go into politics.* ● *Politics has/have never been of great interest to me.* **2** [pl] a person's political opinions and beliefs: *His politics are extreme.* **3** matters concerned with competition for power between people in an organization: *I never get involved in office politics.* **4** (*US* **Pol,l-itical 'Science**) [U] the scientific study of government: *a degree in Politics*

poll[1] /pəʊl/ **noun** [C] **1** (also **opinion poll**) a way of finding out public opinion by asking a number of people their views on sth: *This was voted best drama series in a viewers' poll.* **2** the process of voting in a political election; the number of votes given: *The country will go to the polls* (= vote) *in June.*

poll[2] /pəʊl/ **verb** [T] **1** to receive a certain number of votes in an election: *The Liberal Democrat candidate polled over 3 000 votes.* **2** to ask members of the public their opinion on a subject: *Of those polled, only 20 per cent were in favour of changing the law.*

pollen /'pɒlən/ **noun** [U] a fine, usually yel-low, powder which is formed in flowers. It makes other flowers of the same type produce seeds when it is carried to them by the wind, insects, etc. ••► picture on page C2

polling /'pəʊlɪŋ/ **noun** [U] the process of vot-ing in an election

pollutant /pə'luːtənt/ **noun** [C] a substance that pollutes air, rivers, etc

★**pollute** /pə'luːt/ **verb** [T] to make air, rivers, etc dirty and dangerous: *Traffic fumes are polluting our cities.* ● *The beach has been pol-luted with oil.*

★**pollution** /pə'luːʃn/ **noun** [U] **1** the action of making the air, water, etc dirty and danger-ous: *Major steps are being taken to control the pollution of beaches.* **2** substances that pol-lute: *The rivers are full of pollution.*

polo /'pəʊləʊ/ **noun** [U] a game for two teams of horses and riders. The players try to score goals by hitting a ball with long wooden ham-mers.

'**polo neck noun** [C] a high collar on a piece of clothing that is rolled over and that covers most of your neck; a piece of clothing with this type of collar ••► picture on page C6

polyester /,pɒli'estə/ **noun** [U] an artificial material that is used for making clothes, etc

polystyrene /,pɒli'staɪriːn/ **noun** [U] a light firm plastic substance that is used for pack-ing things so that they do not get broken

polythene /'pɒlɪθiːn/ (*US* **polyethylene**) **noun** [U] a type of very thin plastic material often used to make bags for food, etc or to keep things dry

pomp /pɒmp/ **noun** [U] the impressive nature of a large official occasion or ceremony

pompous /'pɒmpəs/ **adj** showing that you think you are more important than other people, for example by using long words that sound impressive ••► This word is used in a critical way.

pond /pɒnd/ **noun** [C] an area of water that is smaller than a lake ••► picture on page C7

➤ A **lake** is usually big enough to sail on: *Lake Como.* A **pond** may be big enough for animals to drink from or may be a very small area of water in a garden: *We have a fish pond in our garden.* A **pool** is a much smaller area of water: *When the tide went out, pools of water were left among the rocks.* An artificial pool, however, can be larger: *a swimming pool.* A **puddle** is a small pool of water made by the rain.

ponder /'pɒndə/ **verb** [I,T] ponder (on/over sth) to think about sth carefully or for a long time: *The teacher gave us a question to ponder over before the next class.*

pong /pɒŋ/ **noun** [C] (*Brit slang*) a strong unpleasant smell –pong **verb** [I]

pony /'pəʊni/ **noun** [C] (*pl* **ponies**) a small horse

ponytail /'pəʊniteɪl/ **noun** [C] long hair that is tied at the back of the head and that hangs down in one piece ••► picture at **hair**

'**pony-trekking** (*US* '**trail riding**) **noun** [U] the activity of riding horses for pleasure in the country

poodle /'puːdl/ **noun** [C] a type of dog with thick curly fur that is sometimes cut into a special pattern

pooh /puː/ **interj** (*Brit informal*) said when you smell sth unpleasant

pool

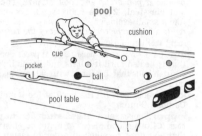

★**pool**[1] /puːl/ **noun 1** [C] a pool (of sth) a small amount of liquid lying on a surface: *There's a huge pool of water on the kitchen floor.* ••► Look at the note at **pond**. **2** [C] a small area of light: *a pool of light* **3** [C] = **SWIMMING POOL**: *He swam ten lengths of the pool.* **4** [C] a quantity of money, goods, etc that is shared between a group of people: *There is a pool of cars that anyone in the company can use.* **5** [U] a game that is played on a table with 16 coloured and numbered balls. Two players try to hit these balls into holes in the table (**pockets**) with long thin sticks (**cues**). •➤ Look at **billiards** and **snooker**. **6 the pools** [pl] = **FOOTBALL POOLS**

pool² /puːl/ **verb** [T] to collect money, ideas, etc together from a number of people: *If we pool our ideas we should come up with a good plan.*

★**poor** /pɔː/ **adj 1** not having enough money to have a comfortable life: *The family was too poor to buy new clothes.* • *Richer countries could do more to help poorer countries.* •➤ opposite **rich 2 the poor noun** [pl] people who do not have enough money to have a comfortable life **3** of low quality or in a bad condition: *Paul is in very poor health.* • *The industry has a poor safety record.* **4** used when you are showing that you feel sorry for somebody: *Poor Dan! He's very upset!*

poorly¹ /ˈpɔːli/ **adv** not well; badly: *a poorly paid job*

poorly² /ˈpɔːli/ **adj** (*Brit informal*) not well; ill: *I'm feeling a bit poorly.*

pop¹ /pɒp/ **verb** (**popping; popped**) **1** [I,T] to make a short sudden sound like a small explosion; to cause sth to do this: *The balloon popped.* • *He popped the balloon.* **2** [I] **pop across, down, out,** etc to come or go somewhere quickly or suddenly: *I'm just popping out to the shops.* **3** [T] **pop sth in, into,** etc **sth** to put or take sth somewhere quickly or suddenly: *She popped the note into her bag.*
PHRASAL VERBS **pop in** to make a quick visit: *Why don't you pop in for a cup of tea?*
pop out to come out (of sth) suddenly or quickly: *Her eyes nearly popped out of her head in surprise.*
pop up (*informal*) to appear or happen when you are not expecting it

★**pop**² /pɒp/ **noun 1** [U] (also '**pop music**) modern music that is most popular among young people: *a pop group* •➤ Look at **jazz, rock** and **classical**. **2** [C] a short sudden sound like a small explosion: *There was a loud pop as the champagne cork came out of the bottle.*

pop³ **abbr** population: *pop 12m*

popcorn /ˈpɒpkɔːn/ **noun** [U] a type of corn that is heated until it bursts and forms light whitish balls that are eaten with salt or sugar on them

★**pope** /pəʊp/ **noun** [C] the head of the Roman Catholic Church

popper /ˈpɒpə/ (also '**press stud**; *US* **snap**) **noun** [C] two round pieces of metal or plastic that you press together in order to fasten a piece of clothing •➤ picture at **button**

poppy /ˈpɒpi/ **noun** [C] (*pl* **poppies**) a bright red wild flower that has small black seeds •➤ picture on page C2

Popsicle™ /ˈpɒpsɪkl/ **noun** [C] (*US*) = **ICE LOLLY**

★**popular** /ˈpɒpjələ/ **adj 1** popular (**with sb**) liked by many people or by most people in a group: *a popular holiday resort* • *He's always been very popular with his pupils.* •➤ opposite **unpopular 2** made for the tastes and knowledge of ordinary people: *The popular newspapers seem more interested in scandal than news.* **3** (only *before* a noun) of or for a lot of people: *The programme is being repeated by popular demand.*

popularity /ˌpɒpjuˈlærəti/ **noun** [U] the quality or state of being liked by many people: *The band's popularity is growing.*

popularize (also **-ise**) /ˈpɒpjʊləraɪz/ **verb** [T] to make a lot of or most people like sth: *The film did a lot to popularize her novels.*

popularly /ˈpɒpjʊləli/ **adv** by many people; generally: *The Conservatives are popularly known as the Tories.*

populate /ˈpɒpjuleɪt/ **verb** [T] (usually passive) to fill a particular area with people: *Parts of the country are very thinly populated.*

★**population** /ˌpɒpjuˈleɪʃn/ **noun 1** [C,U] the number of people who live in a particular area, city or country: *What is the population of your country?* • *an increase/a fall in population* **2** [C] all the people who live in a particular place or all the people or animals of a particular type that live somewhere: *the local population* • *the male/female population* • *The prison population has increased in recent years.*

porcelain /ˈpɔːsəlɪn/ **noun** [U] a hard white substance that is used for making expensive cups, plates, etc

porch /pɔːtʃ/ **noun** [C] **1** (*Brit*) a small covered area at the entrance to a house or church **2** (*US*) = **VERANDA**

pore¹ /pɔː/ **noun** [C] one of the small holes in your skin through which sweat can pass

pore² /pɔː/ **verb**
PHRASAL VERB **pore over sth** to study or read sth very carefully

pork /pɔːk/ **noun** [U] meat from a pig •➤ Look at **bacon** and **ham** and at the note at **meat**.

pornography /pɔːˈnɒɡrəfi/ (also *informal* **porn** /pɔːn/) **noun** [U] books, magazines, films, etc that describe or show sexual acts in order to cause sexual excitement –**pornographic** /ˌpɔːnəˈɡræfɪk/ **adj**

porpoise /ˈpɔːpəs/ **noun** [C] a sea animal with a pointed nose that lives in groups. Porpoises are similar to another sea animal (a **dolphin**).

porridge /ˈpɒrɪdʒ/ **noun** [U] a soft, thick white food that is made from a type of grain (**oats**) boiled with milk or water and eaten hot

★**port** /pɔːt/ **noun 1** [C,U] an area where ships stop to let goods and passengers on and off: *a fishing port* • *The damaged ship reached port safely.* **2** [C] a town or city that has a large area of water where ships load cargo, etc: *Hamburg is a major port.* **3** [U] a strong sweet red wine **4** [U] the side of a ship that is on your left when you are facing towards the front of the ship ••➤ opposite **starboard**

portable /'pɔːtəbl/ **adj** that can be moved or carried easily: *a portable television* ••➤ Look at **movable** and **mobile**.

porter /'pɔːtə/ **noun** [C] **1** a person whose job is to carry suitcases, etc at a railway station, airport, etc **2** a person whose job is to be in charge of the entrance of a hotel or other large building

porthole /'pɔːthəʊl/ **noun** [C] a small round window in a ship

portion /'pɔːʃn/ **noun** [C] **a portion (of sth) 1** a part or share of sth: *What portion of your salary goes on tax?* ● *We must both accept a portion of the blame.* **2** an amount of food for one person (especially in a restaurant): *Could we have two extra portions of chips, please?* ••➤ Look at **helping**.

portrait /'pɔːtreɪt/ **noun** [C] **1** a picture, painting or photograph of a person: *to paint sb's portrait* **2** a description of sb/sth in words

portray /pɔː'treɪ/ **verb** [T] **1** to show sb/sth in a picture; to describe sb/sth in a piece of writing: *Zola portrayed life in 19th-century France.* **2** portray sb/sth as sth to describe sb/sth in a particular way: *In many of his novels life is portrayed as being hard.* **3** to act the part of sb in a play or film: *In this film she portrays a very old woman.* –portrayal /pɔː'treɪəl/ **noun** [C]

pose[1] /pəʊz/ **verb 1** [T] to create or give sb sth that he/she has to deal with: *to pose a problem/threat/challenge/risk* ● *to pose* (= ask) *a question* **2** [I] to sit or stand in a particular position for a painting, photograph, etc: *After the wedding we all posed for photographs.* **3** [I] pose as sb/sth to pretend to be sb/sth: *The robbers got into the house by posing as telephone engineers.* **4** [I] to behave in a way that is intended to impress people who see you: *They hardly swam at all. They just sat posing at the side of the pool.*

pose[2] /pəʊz/ **noun** [C] **1** a position in which sb stands, sits, etc especially in order to be painted or photographed **2** a way of behaving that is intended to impress people who see you

posh /pɒʃ/ **adj** (*informal*) **1** fashionable and expensive: *We went for a meal in a really posh hotel.* **2** (*Brit*) (used about people) belonging to or typical of a high social class

★**position**[1] /pə'zɪʃn/ **noun 1** [C,U] the place where sb/sth is or should be: *Are you happy with the position of the chairs?* ● *All the dancers were in position waiting for the music to begin.* **2** [C,U] the way in which sb/sth sits or stands, or the direction that sth is pointing in: *My leg hurts when I change position.* ● *Turn the switch to the off position.* **3** [C, usually sing] the state or situation that sb/sth is in: *I'm in a very difficult position.* ● *I'm sorry, I'm not in a position to help you financially.* **4** [C] a position (on sth) what you think about sth; your opinion: *What is your*

position on smoking? **5** [C,U] the place or level of a person, company, team, etc compared to others: *the position of women in society* ● *Max finished the race in second position.* ● *Wealth and position are very important to some people.* **6** [C] a job: *There have been over a hundred applications for the position of Sales Manager.* ••➤ synonym **post 7** [C] the part you play in a team game: *Danny can play any position except goalkeeper.*

position[2] /pə'zɪʃn/ **verb** [T] to put sb/sth in a particular place or position: *Mary positioned herself near the door so she could get out quickly.*

★**positive** /'pɒzətɪv/ **adj 1** thinking or talking mainly about the good things in a situation, in a way that makes you or sb else feel hopeful and confident: *Their reaction to my idea was generally positive.* ● *I feel very positive about our team's chances this season.* ● *Positive thinking will help you to succeed.* ••➤ opposite **negative 2** positive (about sth/ that…) certain; sure: *Are you positive that this is the woman you saw?* **3** clear; definite: *There is no positive evidence that he is guilty.* ● *to take positive action* **4** (used about a medical or scientific test) showing that sth has happened or is present: *The result of the pregnancy test was positive.* ● *Two athletes tested positive for steroids.* ••➤ opposite **negative 5** (used about a number) more than zero ••➤ opposite **negative**

positively /'pɒzətɪvli/ **adv 1** with no doubt; firmly: *I was positively convinced that I was doing the right thing.* **2** in a way that shows you are thinking about the good things in a situation, not the bad: *Thinking positively helps many people deal with stress.* **3** (used about a person's way of speaking or acting) in a confident and hopeful way: *The team played cautiously for the first ten minutes, then continued more positively.* **4** (*informal*) (used for emphasizing sth) really; extremely: *He wasn't just annoyed – he was positively furious!*

★**possess** /pə'zes/ **verb** [T] (not used in the continuous tenses) **1** (*formal*) to have or own sth: *They lost everything they possessed in the fire.* ● *Paola possesses a natural ability to make people laugh.* **2** to influence sb or to make sb do sth: *What possessed you to say a thing like that!*

➤ Although this verb is not used in the continuous tenses, it is common to see the present participle (= -*ing* form): *Any student possessing the necessary qualifications will be considered for the course.*

★**possession** /pə'zeʃn/ **noun 1** [U] the state of having or owning sth: *The gang were caught in possession of stolen goods.* ● *Enemy forces managed to take possession of the town.* **2** [C, usually pl] something that you have or own: *Bud packed all his possessions and left.*

possessive /pə'zesɪv/ **adj 1** possessive (of/about sb/sth) not wanting to share sb/ sth: *Dan is so possessive with his toys – he won't let other children play with them.*

p

2 (*grammar*) used to describe words that show who or what a person or thing belongs to: *'My', 'your' and 'his' are possessive adjectives.* ● *'Mine', 'yours' and 'his' are possessive pronouns.*

possessor /pə'zesə/ **noun** [C] a person who has or owns sth

★**possibility** /ˌpɒsə'bɪləti/ **noun** (*pl* **possibilities**) **1** [U,C] (a) possibility (of sth/doing sth); (a) possibility that... the fact that sth might exist or happen, but is not likely to: *There's not much possibility of the letter reaching you before Saturday.* ● *There is **a strong possibility** that the fire was started deliberately.* **2** [C] one of the different things that you can do in a particular situation or in order to achieve sth: *There is a wide range of possibilities open to us.*

★**possible** /'pɒsəbl/ **adj 1** that can happen or be done: *I'll phone you back **as soon as possible**.* ● *Could you give me your answer today, if possible?* ● *The doctors did **everything possible** to save his life.* ● *You were warned of all the possible dangers.* ●➤ opposite **impossible 2** that may be suitable or acceptable: *There are four possible candidates for the job.* ●➤ Look at **probable**. **3** used after adjectives to emphasize that sth is the best, worst, etc of its type: *Alone and with no job or money, I was in the worst possible situation.*

possibly /'pɒsəbli/ **adv 1** perhaps; maybe: *'Will you be free on Sunday?' 'Possibly.'* **2** (used for emphasizing sth) according to what is possible: *I will leave as soon as I possibly can.*

★**post**[1] /pəʊst/ **noun 1** (*especially US* **mail**) [U] the system or organization for collecting and dealing with letters, packages, etc: *The document is too valuable to send by post.* ● *If you hurry you might **catch the post** (= post it before everything is collected).* **2** (*US* **mail**) [U] letters, packages, etc that are collected or brought to your house: *Has the post come yet this morning?* ● *There wasn't any post for you.* **3** [C] a job: *The post was advertised in the local newspaper.* ●➤ synonym **position 4** [C] a place where sb is on duty or is guarding sth: *The soldiers had to remain at their posts all night.* **5** [C] an upright piece of metal or wood that is put in the ground to mark a position or to support sth: *a goal post* ● *Can you see a signpost anywhere?*

IDIOM **by return (of post)** → **RETURN**[2]

★**post**[2] /pəʊst/ **verb** [T] **1** (*especially US* **mail**) to send a letter, package, etc by post: *This letter was posted in Edinburgh yesterday.*

➤ Post (noun and verb) is more commonly used in British English and **mail** in US English. However, British English also uses the noun **mail** quite often. The official name of the Post Office organization is the **Royal Mail**. Note too, that the expressions **airmail** and **surface mail**. When we order goods in a letter, we use a **mail-order** service.

2 to send sb to go and work somewhere: *After two years in London, Rosa was posted to the Tokyo office.* **3** to put sb on guard or on duty

in a particular place: *Policemen were posted outside the building.* **4** (*formal*) (often passive) to put a notice where everyone can see it: *The exam results will be posted on the main noticeboard.*

postage /'pəʊstɪdʒ/ **noun** [U] the amount that you must pay to send a letter, package etc

'**postage stamp** = **STAMP**[1](1)

★**postal** /'pəʊstl/ **adj** connected with the sending and collecting of letters, packages, etc

'**postal order noun** [C] a piece of paper that you can buy at a post office that represents a certain amount of money. A postal order is a safe way of sending money by post.

postbox /'pəʊstbɒks/ (also '**letter box**, *US* **mailbox**) **noun** [C] a box in a public place where you put letters, etc that you want to send ●➤ Look at **pillar box**.

postcard /'pəʊstkɑːd/ **noun** [C] a card that you write a message on and send to sb. Postcards have a picture on one side and are usually sent without an envelope.

postcode /'pəʊstkəʊd/ (*US* **ZIP code**) **noun** [C] a group of letters and/or numbers that you put at the end of an address

★**poster** /'pəʊstə/ **noun** [C] **1** a large printed picture or a notice in a public place, often used to advertise sth **2** a large picture printed on paper that is put on a wall for decoration

posterity /pɒ'sterəti/ **noun** [U] the future and the people who will be alive then: *We should look after our environment for the sake of posterity.*

postgraduate /ˌpəʊst'grædʒuət/ **noun** [C] a person who is doing further studies at a university after taking his/her first degree ●➤ Look at **graduate** and **undergraduate**.

posthumous /'pɒstjʊməs/ **adj** given or happening after sb has died: *a posthumous medal for bravery* –**posthumously adv**

posting /'pəʊstɪŋ/ **noun** [C] a job in another country that you are sent to do by your employer

postman /'pəʊstmən/ (*US* **mailman**) **noun** [C] (*pl* **-men** /-mən/) a person whose job is to collect letters, packages, etc and take them to people's houses

postmark /'pəʊstmɑːk/ **noun** [C] an official mark over a stamp on a letter, package, etc that says when and where it was posted

post-mortem /ˌpəʊst 'mɔːtəm/ **noun** [C] a medical examination of a dead body to find out how the person died

post-natal /ˌpəʊst 'neɪtl/ **adj** (only *before* a noun) connected with the period after the birth of a baby ●➤ opposite **antenatal**

'**post office noun** [C] **1** a place where you can buy stamps, post packages, etc **2 the Post Office** the national organization that is responsible for collecting and dealing with letters, packages, etc

postpone /pə'spəʊn/ **verb** [T] to arrange that sth will happen at a later time than the time you had planned; to delay: *The match was*

postponed because of water on the pitch.
•→ Look at **cancel**. –**postponement noun** [C,U]

postscript /ˈpəʊstskrɪpt/ **noun** [C] an extra message or extra information that is added at the end of a letter, note, etc •→ Look at **PS**.

posture /ˈpɒstʃə/ **noun** [C,U] the way that a person sits, stands, walks, etc: *Poor posture can lead to backache.*

postwar /ˌpəʊstˈwɔː/ **adj** existing or happening in the period after the end of a war, especially the Second World War

★ **pot**[1] /pɒt/ **noun** [C] **1** a round container that is used for cooking food in **2** a container that you use for a particular purpose: *a flowerpot* ● *a pot of paint* **3** the amount that a pot contains: *We drank two pots of tea.*

pot[2] /pɒt/ **verb** [T] (**potting**; **potted**) **1** to put a plant into a pot filled with soil **2** to hit a ball into one of the pockets in the table in the game of (**pool**, **billiards** or **snooker**): *He potted the black ball into the corner pocket.*

★ **potato** /pəˈteɪtəʊ/ **noun** [C,U] (*pl* **potatoes**) a round vegetable that grows under the ground with a brown, yellow or red skin. Potatoes are white or yellow inside: *mashed potato* ● *to peel potatoes* •→ picture on page C3

potato ˈcrisp (*US* **poˈtato chip**) = **CRISP**[2]

potent /ˈpəʊtnt/ **adj** strong or powerful: *a potent drug/drink* –**potency** /-nsi/ **noun** [U]

★ **potential**[1] /pəˈtenʃl/ **adj** (only *before* a noun) that may possibly become sth, happen, be used, etc: *Wind power is a potential source of energy.* ● *potential customers* –**potentially** /-ʃəli/ **adv**

potential[2] /pəˈtenʃl/ **noun** [U] the qualities or abilities that sb/sth has but that may not be fully developed yet: *That boy has great potential as an athlete.*

pothole /ˈpɒthəʊl/ **noun** [C] **1** a hole in the surface of a road that is formed by traffic and bad weather **2** a deep hole in rock that is formed by water over thousands of years and often leads to underground rooms (**caves**)

potholing /ˈpɒthəʊlɪŋ/ **noun** [U] the sport of climbing down inside potholes(2), walking through underground tunnels, etc: *to go potholing*

ˈ**pot plant noun** [C] (*Brit*) a plant that you keep indoors

potter[1] /ˈpɒtə/ (*US* **putter** /ˈpʌtə/) **verb** [I] **potter (about/around)** to spend your time doing small jobs or things that you enjoy without hurrying: *Grandpa spends most of the day pottering in the garden.*

potter[2] /ˈpɒtə/ **noun** [C] a person who makes pots, dishes, etc (**pottery**) from baked clay

pottery /ˈpɒtəri/ **noun** (*pl* **potteries**) **1** [U] pots, dishes, etc that are made from baked clay **2** [U] the activity or skill of making dishes, etc from clay: *a pottery class* **3** [C] a place where clay pots and dishes are made

potty[1] /ˈpɒti/ **adj** (*Brit informal*) **1** crazy or silly **2 potty about sb/sth** liking sb/sth very much: *Penny's potty about Mark.*

potty[2] /ˈpɒti/ **noun** [C] (*pl* **potties**) a plastic bowl that young children use when they are too small to use a toilet

pouch /paʊtʃ/ **noun** [C] **1** a small leather bag **2** a pocket of skin on the stomach of some female animals, for example kangaroos, in which they carry their babies

poultry /ˈpəʊltri/ **noun 1** [pl] birds, for example chickens, ducks, etc that are kept for their eggs or their meat **2** [U] the meat from these birds: *Eat plenty of fish and poultry.*

pounce /paʊns/ **verb** [I] **pounce (on sb/sth)** to attack sb/sth by jumping suddenly on him/her/it: (*figurative*) *He was quick to pounce on any mistakes I made.*

★ **pound**[1] /paʊnd/ **noun 1** [C] (also ˌ**pound** ˈ**sterling**) (*symbol* **£**) the unit of money in Britain; one hundred pence (100p): *Melissa earns £16000 a year.* ● *Can you change a ten-pound note?* ● *a pound coin* **2** [sing] **the pound** the value of the British pound on international money markets: *The pound has fallen against the dollar.* ● *How many yen are there to the pound?* **3** [C] (*abbr* **lb**) a measurement of weight; equal to 0·454 of a kilogram: *The carrots cost 30p a pound.* ● *Half a pound of mushrooms, please.*

➤ For more information about measurements look at the special section on numbers at the back of this dictionary.

pound[2] /paʊnd/ **verb 1** [I] **pound (at/against/on sth)** to hit sth hard many times making a lot of noise: *She pounded on the door with her fists.* **2** [I] **pound along, down, up, etc** to walk with heavy, noisy steps in a particular direction: *Jason went pounding up the stairs three at a time.* **3** [I] (used about your heart, blood, etc) to beat quickly and loudly: *Her heart was pounding with fear.* **4** [T] to hit sth many times to break it into smaller pieces

★ **pour** /pɔː/ **verb 1** [T] to make a liquid or other substance flow steadily out of or into a container: *Pour the sugar into a bowl.* **2** [I] (used about a liquid, smoke, light, etc) to flow out of or into sth quickly and steadily, and in large quantities: *Tears were pouring down her cheeks.* ● *She opened the curtains and sunlight poured into the room.* **3** [T] **pour sth (out)** to serve a drink to sb by letting it flow from a container into a cup or glass: *Have you poured out the tea?* **4** [I] **pour (down) (with rain)** to rain heavily: *The rain poured down all day long.* ● *I'm not going out. It's pouring with rain.* **5** [I] to come or go somewhere continuously in large numbers: *People were pouring out of the station.*

IDIOM **pour your heart out (to sb)** to tell sb all your personal problems, feelings, etc

PHRASAL VERB **pour sth out** to speak freely about what you think or feel about sth that has happened to you: *to pour out all your troubles*

pout /paʊt/ **verb** [I] to push your lips, or your bottom lip, forward to show that you are annoyed about sth or to look sexually attractive –**pout noun** [C]

[I] **intransitive**, a verb which has no object: *He laughed.*   [T] **transitive**, a verb which has an object: *He ate an apple.*

★**poverty** /'pɒvəti/ **noun** [U] the state of being poor: *There are millions of people in this country who are living in poverty.*

poverty-stricken /'pɒvəti strɪkn/ **adj** very poor

★**powder** /'paʊdə/ **noun** [U,C] a dry substance that is in the form of very small grains: *washing powder* ● *Grind the spices into a fine powder.* –**powder verb** [T]

powdered /'paʊdəd/ **adj** (used about a substance that is usually liquid) dried and made into powder: *powdered milk/soup*

★**power**[1] /'paʊə/ **noun 1** [U] power (over sb/ sth); power (to do sth) the ability to control people or things or to do sth: *The aim is to give people more power over their own lives.* ● *to have sb in your power* ● *It's not in my power* (= I am unable) *to help you.* **2** [U] political control of a country or area: *When did this government come to power?* ● *to take/seize power* **3** [C] the power (to do sth) the right or authority to do sth: *Do the police have the power to stop cars without good reason?* **4** [C] a country with a lot of influence in world affairs or that has great military strength: *Britain is no longer a world power.* ● *a military/economic power* **5** powers [pl] a particular ability of the body or mind: *He has great powers of observation.* ● *She had to use all her powers of persuasion on him.* **6** [U] the energy or strength that sb/sth has: *The ship was helpless against the power of the storm.* ● *I've lost all power in my right arm.* **7** [U] energy that can be collected and used for operating machines, making electricity, etc: *nuclear/wind/solar power* ● *This car has power steering.*

power[2] /'paʊə/ **verb** [T] to supply energy to sth to make it work: *What powers the motor in this machine?* –**powered adj**: *a solar-powered calculator* ● *a high-powered engine*

'**power cut noun** [C] a time when the supply of electricity stops, for example during a storm

★**powerful** /'paʊəfl/ **adj 1** having a lot of control or influence over other people: *a powerful nation* ● *He's one of the most powerful directors in Hollywood.* **2** having great strength or force: *a powerful car/engine/telescope* ● *a powerful swimmer* **3** having a strong effect on your mind or body: *The Prime Minister made a powerful speech.* ● *a powerful drug* –**powerfully** /-fəli/ **adv**

powerless /'paʊələs/ **adj 1** without strength, influence or control **2** powerless to do sth completely unable to do sth: *I stood and watched him struggle, powerless to help.*

'**power point** (*Brit*) = **socket**(1)

'**power station** (*US* '**power plant**) **noun** [C] a place where electricity is made (generated)

pp abbr 1 pages **2** (before a signature) on behalf of: *pp J Symonds* (= signed, for example, by a secretary in sb's absence)

PR /ˌpi: 'ɑː/ **abbr 1** public relations **2** proportional representation

practicable /'præktɪkəbl/ **adj** (used about an idea, a plan or a suggestion) able to be done successfully: *The scheme is just not practicable.* ●➤ opposite **impracticable**

★**practical**[1] /'præktɪkl/ **adj 1** concerned with actually doing sth rather than with ideas or thought: *Have you got any practical experience of working on a farm?* ●➤ Look at **theoretical**. **2** that is likely to succeed; right or sensible: *We need to find a practical solution to the problem.* **3** very suitable for a particular purpose; useful: *a practical little car, ideal for the city* **4** (used about people) making sensible decisions and good at dealing with problems: *We must be practical. It's no good buying a house we cannot afford.* ●➤ opposite for senses **2**, **3** and **4** **impractical 5** (used about a person) good at making and repairing things: *Brett's very practical and has made a lot of improvements to their new house.*

practical[2] /'præktɪkl/ **noun** [C] (*Brit*) a lesson or exam where you do or make sth rather than just writing: *He passed the theory paper but failed the practical.*

practicality /ˌpræktɪ'kæləti/ (*pl* **practicalities**) **noun 1** [U] the quality of being suitable and realistic, or likely to succeed: *I am not convinced of the practicality of the scheme.* **2** practicalities [pl] the real facts rather than ideas or thoughts: *Let's look at the practicalities of the situation.*

ˌ**practical** '**joke noun** [C] a trick that you play on sb that makes him/her look silly and makes other people laugh

practically /'præktɪkli/ **adv 1** (*spoken*) almost; very nearly: *My essay is practically finished now.* **2** in a realistic or sensible way

★**practice** /'præktɪs/ **noun 1** [U] action rather than ideas or thought: *Your suggestion sounds fine in theory, but would it work in practice?* ● *I can't wait to put what I've learnt into practice.* **2** [C,U] (*formal*) the usual or expected way of doing sth in a particular organization or situation; a habit or custom: *It is standard practice not to pay bills until the end of the month.* **3** [C,U] (a period of) doing an activity many times or training regularly so that you become good at it: *piano/football practice* ● *His accent should improve with practice.* **4** [U] the work of a doctor or lawyer: *Dr Roberts doesn't work in a hospital. He's in general practice* (= he's a family doctor). **5** [C] the business of a doctor, dentist or lawyer: *a successful medical/dental practice*

IDIOMS be/get out of practice to find it difficult to do sth because you have not done it for a long time: *I'm not playing very well at the moment. I'm really out of practice.*

in practice in reality

★**practise** (*US* practice) /'præktɪs/ **verb** [I,T] **1** to do an activity or train regularly so that you become very good at sth: *If you want to play a musical instrument well, you must practise every day.* ● *He always wants to practise his English on me.* **2** to do sth or take part in sth regularly or publicly: *a practising Catholic/Jew/Muslim* **3** practise (sth/as sth) to work as a doctor or lawyer: *She's practising as a barrister in Leeds.* ● *He was banned from practising medicine.*

practised (*US* **practiced**) /'præktɪst/ adj practised (in sth) very good at sth, because you have done it a lot or often: *He was practised in the art of inventing excuses.*

practitioner /præk'tɪʃənə/ noun [C] (*formal*) a person who works as a doctor, dentist or lawyer ·► Look at **GP**.

pragmatic /præg'mætɪk/ adj dealing with problems in a practical way rather than by following ideas or principles

prairie /'preəri/ noun [C] a very large area of flat land covered in grass with few trees (especially in North America)

★**praise¹** /preɪz/ verb [T] praise sb/sth (for sth) to say that sb/sth is good and should be admired: *The fireman was praised for his courage.*

★**praise²** /preɪz/ noun [U] what you say when you are expressing admiration for sb/sth: *The survivors were full of praise for the paramedics.*

praiseworthy /'preɪzwɜːði/ adj that should be admired and recognized as good

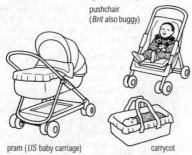

pushchair (*Brit also* buggy)

pram (*US* baby carriage)   carrycot

pram /præm/ (*US* **'baby carriage**) noun [C] a small vehicle on four wheels for a young baby, pushed by a person on foot

prance /prɑːns/ verb [I] to move about with quick, high steps, often because you feel proud or pleased with yourself

prat /præt/ noun [C] (*Brit slang*) a stupid person: *What a prat!*

prawn /prɔːn/ (*US* **shrimp**) noun [C] a small shellfish that we eat and becomes pink when cooked ·► Look at **shrimp**. ·► picture at **shellfish**

★**pray** /preɪ/ verb [I,T] pray (to sb) (for sb/sth) to speak to God or a god in order to give thanks or to ask for help: *They knelt down and prayed for peace.*

★**prayer** /preə/ noun 1 [C] a prayer (for sb/sth) the words that you use when you speak to God or a god: *Let's say a prayer for all the people who are ill.* ● *a prayer book* 2 [U] the act of speaking to God or a god: *to kneel in prayer*

preach /priːtʃ/ verb 1 [I,T] to give a talk (a sermon) on a religious subject, especially in

a church 2 [T] to say that sth is good and persuade other people to accept it: *I always preach caution in situations like this.* 3 [I] to give sb advice on morals and how to behave in a way which he/she finds boring or annoying: *I'm sorry, I didn't mean to preach.*

preacher /'priːtʃə/ noun [C] a person who gives religious talks (sermons), for example in a church

precarious /prɪ'keəriəs/ adj not safe or certain; dangerous: *Working on the roof of that building looks very precarious.* –**precariously** adv

precaution /prɪ'kɔːʃn/ noun [C] a precaution (against sth) something that you do now in order to avoid danger or problems in the future: *You should always take the precaution of locking your valuables in the hotel safe.* ● *precautions against fire/theft* –**precautionary** /prɪ'kɔːʃənəri/ adj

precede /prɪ'siːd/ verb [I,T] (*written*) to happen, come or go before sb/sth: *Look at the table on the preceding page.*

precedence /'presɪdəns/ noun [U] precedence (over sb/sth) the right that sb/sth has to come before sb/sth else because he/she/it is more important: *In business, making a profit seems to take precedence over everything else.*

precedent /'presɪdənt/ noun [C,U] an official action or decision that has happened in the past and that is considered as an example or rule to follow in the same situation later: *We don't want to set a precedent by allowing one person to come in late or they'll all want to do it.* ● *Such protests are without precedent in recent history.* ·► Look at **unprecedented**.

precinct /'priːsɪŋkt/ noun 1 [C] (*Brit*) a special area of shops in a town where cars are not allowed: *a shopping precinct* 2 [C] (*US*) a part of a town that has its own police station 3 **precincts** [pl] (*formal*) the area near or around a building: *the hospital and its precincts*

★**precious** /'preʃəs/ adj 1 of great value (usually because it is rare or difficult to find): *In overcrowded Hong Kong, every small piece of land is precious.* 2 loved very much: *The painting was very precious to her.*

precious 'metal noun [C] a metal which is very rare and valuable and often used in jewellery: *Gold and silver are precious metals.*

precious 'stone (also **stone**) noun [C] a stone which is very rare and valuable and often used in jewellery: *diamonds and other precious stones*

precipice /'presəpɪs/ noun [C] a very steep side of a high mountain or cliff

précis /'preɪsi/ noun [C,U] (*pl* **précis** /'preɪsiːz/*) a short version of a speech or written text that contains only the most important points: *Jim gave us a précis of the main points.* ·► synonym **summary**

★**precise** /prɪ'saɪs/ adj 1 clear and accurate: *precise details/instructions/measurements* ● *He's in his forties – well, forty-four, to be precise.* ● *She couldn't be very precise about* *what her attacker was wearing.* ∙➤ opposite **imprecise 2** (only *before* a noun) exact; particular: *I'm sorry. I can't come just at this precise moment.* **3** (used about a person) taking care to get small details right: *He's very precise about his work.*

★ **precisely** /prɪ'saɪsli/ **adv 1** exactly: *The time is 10.03 precisely.* ∙➤ synonym **exactly 2** used to emphasize that sth is very true or obvious: *It's precisely because I care about you that I got so angry when you stayed out late.* **3** (*spoken*) (used for agreeing with a statement) yes, that is right: *'So, if we don't book now, we probably won't get a flight?' 'Precisely.'*

precision /prɪ'sɪʒn/ (also **preciseness**) **noun** [U] the quality of being clear or exact: *The plans were drawn with great precision.*

precocious /prɪ'kəʊʃəs/ **adj** (used about children) having developed certain abilities and ways of behaving at a much younger age than usual: *a precocious child who starting her acting career at the age of five* ∙➤ This word is often used in a critical way.

preconceived /ˌpriːkən'siːvd/ **adj** (only *before* a noun) (used about an idea or opinion) formed before you have enough information or experience

preconception /ˌpriːkən'sepʃn/ **noun** [C] an idea or opinion that you have formed about sb/sth before you have enough information or experience

predator /'predətə/ **noun** [C] an animal that kills and eats other animals

predecessor /'priːdɪsesə/ **noun** [C] **1** the person who was in the job or position before the person who is in it now: *The new head teacher is much better than her predecessor.* **2** a thing such as a machine, that has been followed or replaced by sth else: *This computer has a larger memory than its predecessors.* ∙➤ Look at **successor**.

predicament /prɪ'dɪkəmənt/ **noun** [C] an unpleasant and difficult situation that is hard to get out of

predicative /prɪ'dɪkətɪv/ **adj** (*grammar*) (used about an adjective) not used before a noun: *You cannot say 'an asleep child' because 'asleep' is a predicative adjective.* ∙➤ An adjective that *can* be used before a noun is called **attributive**. Many adjectives, for example 'big', can be either predicative or attributive: *The house is big.* ● *It's a big house.* –**predicatively adv**

★ **predict** /prɪ'dɪkt/ **verb** [T] to say that sth will happen in the future: *Scientists still cannot predict exactly when earthquakes will happen.*

predictable /prɪ'dɪktəbl/ **adj 1** that was or could be expected to happen: *The match had a predictable result.* **2** (used about a person) always behaving in a way that you would expect and therefore rather boring: *I knew you were going to say that – you're so predictable.* –**predictably adv**

prediction /prɪ'dɪkʃn/ **noun** [C,U] saying what will happen; what sb thinks will hap-

pen: *The exam results confirmed my predictions.*

predominance /prɪ'dɒmɪnəns/ [sing] the state of being more important or greater in number than other people or things: *There is a predominance of Japanese tourists in Hawaii.*

predominant /prɪ'dɒmɪnənt/ **adj** most noticeable, powerful or important: *The predominant colour was blue.*

predominantly /prɪ'dɒmɪnəntli/ **adv** mostly; mainly: *The population of the island is predominantly Spanish.*

predominate /prɪ'dɒmɪneɪt/ **verb** [I] (*formal*) predominate (over sb/sth) to be most important or greatest in number: *Private interest was not allowed to predominate over public good.*

preface /'prefəs/ **noun** [C] a written introduction to a book that explains what it is about or why it was written

prefect /'priːfekt/ **noun** [C] (*Brit*) an older girl or boy in a school who has special duties and responsibilities. Prefects often help to make sure that the younger schoolchildren behave properly.

★ **prefer** /prɪ'fɜː/ **verb** [T] (**preferring**; **preferred**) prefer sth (to sth); prefer to do sth; prefer doing sth (not used in the continuous tenses) to choose sth rather than sth else; to like sth better: *Would you prefer tea or coffee?* ● *Marianne prefers not to walk home on her own at night.* ● *My parents would prefer me to study law at university.*

➤ Notice the different ways that **prefer** can be used: *Helen **prefers going** by train to flying* (= generally or usually). ● *Helen **would prefer to go** by train rather than (to) fly* (= on this occasion).

∙➤ **Prefer** is generally rather formal. Instead of: *Would you prefer tea or coffee?* we can say: *Would you rather have tea or coffee?* Instead of: *I prefer skating to skiing* we can say: *I like skating better than skiing.*

➤ Although this verb is not used in the continuous tenses, it is common to see the present participle (= -ing form): *Their elder son had gone to work in London, preferring not to join the family firm.*

preferable /'prefrəbl/ **adj** preferable (to sth/doing sth) better or more suitable: *Going anywhere is preferable to staying at home for the weekend.*

preferably /'prefrəbli/ **adv** used to show which person or thing would be better or preferred, if you are given a choice: *Give me a ring tonight – preferably after 7 o'clock.*

preference /'prefrəns/ **noun 1** [sing,U] preference (for sth) an interest in or desire for one thing more than another: *What you wear is entirely a matter of personal preference.* ● *Please list your choices in order of preference* (= put the things you want most first on the list). **2** [U] special treatment that you give to one person or group rather than to others:

When allocating accommodation, we will give preference to families with young children.

preferential /ˌprefəˈrenʃl/ adj (only *before* a noun) giving or showing special treatment to one person or group rather than to others: *I don't see why he should get **preferential treatment** – I've worked here just as long as he has!*

prefix /ˈpriːfɪks/ noun [C] (*grammar*) a letter or group of letters that you put at the beginning of a word to change its meaning ••➤ Look at **suffix**.

pregnancy /ˈpregnənsi/ noun (*pl* **pregnancies**) [U,C] the state of being pregnant

*★**pregnant** /ˈpregnənt/ adj (used about a woman or female animal) having a baby developing in her body: *Liz is five months pregnant. • to get pregnant* ••➤ It is also possible to say: *Liz is expecting a baby* or: *Liz is going to have a baby.*

prehistoric /ˌpriːhɪˈstɒrɪk/ adj from the time in history before events were written down

*★**prejudice¹** /ˈpredʒudɪs/ noun [C,U] prejudice (against sb/sth) a strong unreasonable feeling of not liking or trusting sb/sth, especially when it is based on his/her/its race, religion or sex: *a victim of **racial prejudice***

prejudice² /ˈpredʒudɪs/ verb [T] 1 prejudice sb (against sb/sth) to influence sb so that he/she has an unreasonable or unfair opinion about sb/sth: *The newspaper stories had prejudiced the jury against him.* 2 to have a harmful effect on sb/sth: *Continuing to live with her violent father may prejudice the child's welfare.*

prejudiced /ˈpredʒudɪst/ adj not liking or trusting sb/sth for no other reason than his/her/its race, religion or sex

preliminary¹ /prɪˈlɪmɪnəri/ adj coming or happening before sth else that is more important: *After a few preliminary remarks the discussions began.*

preliminary² /prɪˈlɪmɪnəri/ noun [C,usually pl] (*pl* **preliminaries**) an action or event that is done before and in preparation for another event: *Once the preliminaries are over, we can get down to business.*

prelude /ˈpreljuːd/ noun [C] 1 a short piece of music, especially an introduction to a longer piece 2 (*written*) prelude (to sth) an action or event that happens before sth else or that forms an introduction to sth

premature /ˈpremətʃʊə/ adj 1 happening before the normal or expected time: *Her baby was premature* (= born before the expected time). 2 acting or happening too soon: *I think our decision was premature. We should have thought about it for longer.* –prematurely adv

premeditated /ˌpriːˈmedɪteɪtɪd/ adj (used about a crime) planned in advance

premier¹ /ˈpremiə/ adj (only *before* a noun) most important; best: *a premier chef • the Premier Division* (= in football)

premier² /ˈpremiə/ noun [C] (used especially in newspapers) the leader of the government of a country (prime minister)

première /ˈpremieə/ noun [C] the first public performance of a play, film, etc

premises /ˈpremɪsɪz/ noun [pl] the building and the land that around it that a business owns or uses: *Smoking is not allowed **on the premises**.*

premium /ˈpriːmiəm/ noun [C] 1 an amount of money that you pay regularly to a company for insurance against accidents, damage, etc: *a monthly premium of £25* 2 an extra payment: *You must pay a premium for express delivery.*

premonition /ˌpriːməˈnɪʃn; ˌprem-/ noun [C] a premonition (of sth) a feeling that sth unpleasant is going to happen in the future: *a premonition of disaster*

preoccupation /priˌɒkjuˈpeɪʃn/ noun [U,C] preoccupation (with sth) the state of thinking and/or worrying continuously about sth: *She was irritated by his preoccupation with money.*

preoccupied /priˈɒkjupaɪd/ adj preoccupied (with sth) not paying attention to sb/sth because you are thinking or worrying about sb/sth else: *Sarah is very preoccupied with her work at present.* ••➤ Look at **occupied**.

preoccupy /priˈɒkjupaɪ/ verb [T] (*pres part* preoccupying; *3rd pers sing pres* preoccupies; *pt, pp* preoccupied) to fill sb's mind so that he/she does not think about anything else; to worry

*★**preparation** /ˌprepəˈreɪʃn/ noun 1 [U] getting sb/sth ready: *The team has been training hard **in preparation for** the big game. • exam preparation* 2 [C,usually pl] preparation (for sth/to do sth) something that you do to get ready for sth: *We started to **make preparations** for the wedding six months ago.*

preparatory /prɪˈpærətri/ adj done in order to get ready for sth

preˈparatory school (also ˈprep school) noun [C] 1 (*Brit*) a private school for children aged between seven and thirteen 2 (*US*) a private school that prepares students for college or university

*★**prepare** /prɪˈpeə/ verb [I,T] prepare (sb/sth) (for sb/sth) to get ready or to make sb/sth ready: *Bo helped me prepare for the exam. • The course prepares foreign students for studying at university. • to prepare a meal*
IDIOMS **be prepared for sth** to be ready for sth difficult or unpleasant
be prepared to do sth to be ready and happy to do sth: *I am not prepared to stay here and be insulted.*

preposition /ˌprepəˈzɪʃn/ noun [C] a word or phrase that is used before a noun or pronoun to show place, time, direction, etc: *'In', 'for', 'to' and 'out of' are all prepositions.*

preposterous /prɪˈpɒstərəs/ adj silly; ridiculous; not to be taken seriously

p

prerequisite /ˌpriːˈrekwəzɪt/ noun [C] a prerequisite (for/of sth) something that is necessary for sth to happen or exist: *Is a good education a prerequisite of success?*

prerogative /prɪˈrɒɡətɪv/ noun [C] a special right that sb/sth has: *It is the Prime Minister's prerogative to fix the date of the election.*

Pres abbr President

prescribe /prɪˈskraɪb/ verb [T] **1** to say what medicine or treatment sb should have: *Can you prescribe something for my cough please, doctor?* **2** (*formal*) (used about a person or an organization with authority) to say that sth must be done: *The law prescribes that the document must be signed in the presence of two witnesses.*

prescription /prɪˈskrɪpʃn/ noun [C,U] a paper on which a doctor has written the name of the medicine that you need. You take your prescription to a shop (the chemist's) and get the medicine there: *a prescription for sleeping pills* ● *Some medicines are only available on prescription* (= with a prescription from a doctor).

presence /ˈprezns/ noun **1** [U] the fact of being in a particular place: *He apologized to her in the presence of the whole family.* ● *an experiment to test for the presence of oxygen* •➤ opposite **absence 2** [sing] a number of soldiers or police officers who are in a place for a special reason: *There was a huge police presence at the demonstration.*

★**present**[1] /ˈpreznt/ adj **1** (only *before* a noun) existing or happening now: *We hope to overcome our present difficulties very soon.* **2** (not *before* a noun) being in a particular place: *There were 200 people present at the meeting.* •➤ opposite **absent**

IDIOM **the present day** modern times: *In some countries traditional methods of farming have survived to the present day.*

★**present**[2] /ˈpreznt/ noun **1** [C] something that you give to sb or receive from sb; a gift: *a birthday/wedding/leaving/Christmas present*

➤ **Gift** is more formal and is often used in shops, catalogues, etc.

2 (usually **the present**) [sing] the time now: *We live in the present but we must learn from the past.* ● *I'm rather busy at present. Can I call you back later?* **3 the present** [sing] = **THE PRESENT TENSE**

IDIOM **for the moment/present → MOMENT**

present[3] /prɪˈzent/ verb [T] **1** present sb with sth; present sth (to sb) to give sth to sb, especially at a formal ceremony: *All the dancers were presented with flowers.* ● *Flowers were presented to all the dancers.* **2** present sth (to sb) to show sth that you have prepared to people: *Good teachers try to present their material in an interesting way.* **3** present sb with sth; present sth (to sb) to give sb sth that has to be dealt with: *Learning English presented no problem to him.* ● *The manager presented us with a bill for the broken chair.* **4** to introduce a television or radio programme **5** to show a play, etc to the

public: *The Theatre Royal is presenting a new production of 'Ghosts'.* **6** present sb (to sb) to introduce sb to a person in a formal ceremony: *The teams were presented to the President before the game.*

presentable /prɪˈzentəbl/ adj good enough to be seen by people you do not know well

presentation /ˌprezn̩ˈteɪʃn/ noun **1** [C,U] the act of giving or showing sth to sb: *The head will now make a presentation to the winners of the competition.* **2** [U] the way in which sth is shown, explained, offered, etc to people: *Untidy presentation of your work may lose you marks.* **3** [C] a meeting at which sth is shown or explained to a group of people: *Each student has to give a short presentation on a subject of his/her choice.* **4** [C] a formal ceremony at which a prize, etc is given to sb

presenter /prɪˈzentə/ noun [C] a person who introduces a television or radio programme

presently /ˈprezntli/ adv **1** soon; shortly: *I'll be finished presently.* **2** (*written*) after a short time: *Presently I heard the car door shut.* **3** (*especially US*) now; currently: *The management are presently discussing the matter.*

➤ Notice that when **presently** means 'soon' it usually comes at the end of the sentence and when it means 'after a short time' it usually comes at the beginning of the sentence. When **presently** means 'now' it goes with the verb.

present ˈparticiple noun [C] (*grammar*) the form of the verb that ends in *–ing*

the present ˈperfect noun [sing] (*grammar*) the form of a verb that expresses an action done in a time period from the past to the present, formed with the present tense of *have* and the past participle of the verb: *'I've finished', 'She hasn't arrived' and 'I've been studying'* are all **in the present perfect**.

➤ For more information about the use of tenses look at the **Quick Grammar Reference** section at the back of this dictionary.

the ˈpresent ˈtense (also **the present**) noun [C] (*grammar*) the tense of the verb that you use when you are talking about what is happening or what exists now

preservative /prɪˈzɜːvətɪv/ noun [C,U] a substance that is used for keeping food, etc in good condition

★**preserve** /prɪˈzɜːv/ verb [T] to keep sth safe or in good condition: *They've managed to preserve most of the wall paintings in the caves.* –preservation /ˌprezəˈveɪʃn/ noun [U]

preside /prɪˈzaɪd/ verb [I] to be in charge of a discussion, meeting, etc

PHRASAL VERB **preside over sth** to be in control of or responsible for sth

presidency /ˈprezɪdənsi/ noun (*pl* presidencies) **1 the presidency** [sing] the position of being president **2** [C] the period of time that sb is president

★**president** /ˈprezɪdənt/ noun [C] **1** (also **President**) the leader of a republic: *the President of France* ● *the US President* **2** the person with the highest position in some

---

[C] **countable**, a noun with a plural form: *one book, two books*   [U] **uncountable**, a noun with no plural form: *some sugar*

organizations –**presidential** /ˌprezɪ'denʃl/ **adj**: *presidential elections*

★**press**[1] /pres/ **noun 1** (usually **the press**) [sing, with sing or pl verb] newspapers and the journalists who work for them: *The story has been reported on TV and in the press.* ● *the local/national press* ● *The press support/supports government policy.* **2** [sing,U] what or the amount that is written about sb/sth in newspapers: *This company has had a bad press recently.* ● *The strike got very little press.* **3** [C,U] a machine for printing books, newspapers, etc; the process of printing them: *All details were correct at the time of going to press.* **4** [C] a business that prints books, etc: *Oxford University Press* **5** [C] an act of pushing sth firmly: *Give that button a press and see what happens.*

★**press**[2] /pres/ **verb 1** [I,T] to push sth firmly: *Just press that button and the door will open.* ● *He pressed the lid firmly shut.* **2** [T] to put weight onto sth, for example in order to get juice out of it: *to press grapes* ••➤ picture at **squeeze 3** [T] to make a piece of clothing smooth by using an iron: *This shirt needs pressing.* **4** [T] to hold sb/sth firmly in a loving way: *She pressed the photo to her chest.* **5** [I] press across, against, around, etc (sth) (used about people) to move in a particular direction by pushing: *The crowd pressed against the wall of policemen.* **6** [I,T] press (sb) (for sth/to do sth) to try to persuade or force sb to do sth: *I pressed them to stay for dinner.* ● *to press sb for an answer* **7** [T] to express or repeat sth in an urgent way: *I don't want to press the point, but you still owe me money.*

IDIOMS **be hard pressed/pushed/put to do sth** → **HARD**[2]

be pressed for sth to not have enough of sth: *I must hurry. I'm really pressed for time.*

bring/press charges (against sb) → **CHARGE**[1]

PHRASAL VERB **press ahead/forward/on (with sth)** to continue doing sth even though it is difficult or hard work: *They pressed on with the building work in spite of the bad weather.*

'**press conference noun** [C] a meeting when a famous or important person answers questions from newspaper and television journalists: *to hold a press conference*

pressing /'presɪŋ/ **adj** that must be dealt with immediately; urgent

'**press stud noun** [C] → **POPPER**

'**press-up** (*US* '**push-up**) **noun** [C] a type of exercise in which you lie on your front on the floor and push your body up with your arms: *I do 50 press-ups every morning.* ••➤ picture on page S2

★**pressure** /'preʃə/ **noun 1** [U] the force that is produced when you press on or against sth: *Apply pressure to the cut and it will stop bleeding.* ● *The pressure of the water caused the dam to crack.* **2** [C,U] the force that a gas or liquid has when it is contained inside sth: *high/low blood pressure* ● *You should check your tyre pressures regularly.* **3** [C,U] worries or difficulties that you have because you

have too much to deal with; stress: *financial pressures* ● *I find it difficult to cope with pressure at work.*

IDIOMS **put pressure on sb (to do sth)** to force sb to do sth: *The press is putting pressure on him to resign.*

under pressure 1 being forced to do sth: *Anna was under pressure from her parents to leave school and get a job.* **2** worried or in difficulty because you have too much to deal with: *I perform poorly under pressure, so I hate exams.* **3** (used about liquid or gas) contained inside sth or sent somewhere using force: *Water is forced out through the hose under pressure.* –**pressure verb** [T] = **PRESSURIZE**

'**pressure group noun** [C, with sing or pl verb] a group of people who are trying to influence what a government or other organization does

pressurize (also **-ise**) /'preʃəraɪz/ (also **pressure**) **verb** [T] pressurize sb (into sth/doing sth) to use force or influence to make sb do sth: *Some workers were pressurized into taking early retirement.*

pressurized (also **-ised**) /'preʃəraɪzd/ **adj** (used about air in an aircraft) kept at the pressure at which people can breathe

prestige /pre'stiːʒ/ **noun** [U] the respect and admiration that people feel for a person because he/she has a high social position or has been very successful: *Nursing isn't a high prestige job.* –**prestigious** /pre'stɪdʒəs/ **adj**: *a prestigious prize/school/job*

presumably /prɪ'zjuːməbli/ **adv** I imagine; I suppose: *Presumably this rain means the match will be cancelled?*

presume /prɪ'zjuːm/ **verb** [T] to think that sth is true even if you do not know for sure; to suppose: *The house looks empty so I presume they are away on holiday.* –**presumption** /prɪ'zʌmpʃn/ **noun** [C]

presumptuous /prɪ'zʌmptʃuəs/ **adj** confident that sth will happen or that sb will do sth without making sure first, in a way that annoys people: *It was very presumptuous of him to say that I would help without asking me first.*

pretence (*US* **pretense**) /prɪ'tens/ **noun** [U, sing] an action that makes people believe sth that is not true: *She was unable to keep up the pretence that she loved him.*

IDIOM **on/under false pretences** → **FALSE**

★**pretend** /prɪ'tend/ **verb** [I,T] **1** to behave in a particular way in order to make other people believe sth that is not true: *You can't just pretend that the problem doesn't exist.* ● *Paul's not really asleep. He's just pretending.* **2** (used especially about children) to imagine that sth is true as part of a game: *The kids were under the bed pretending to be snakes.*

pretentious /prɪ'tenʃəs/ **adj** trying to appear more serious or important than you really are: *I think it sounds pretentious to use a lot of foreign words.*

pretext /'priːtekst/ **noun** [C] a reason that

p

you give for doing sth that is not the real reason: *Tariq left **on the pretext of** having an appointment at the dentist's.*

★**pretty**¹ /'prɪti/ adj (**prettier**; **prettiest**) attractive and pleasant to look at or hear: *a pretty girl/smile/dress/garden/name*

➤ **Pretty** is not normally used to describe men or boys. **Good-looking** can be used for all people, and **handsome** is usually used for men. Look also at the note at **beautiful**.

–**prettily** adv: *The room is prettily decorated.*
–**prettiness** noun [U]

★**pretty**² /'prɪti/ adv (*informal*) quite; fairly: *The film was pretty good but not fantastic.* ● *I'm pretty certain that Alex will agree.* ••➤ Look at the note at **rather**.

IDIOM **pretty much/nearly/well** almost; very nearly: *I won't be long. I've pretty well finished.*

prevail /prɪ'veɪl/ verb [I] **1** to exist or be common in a particular place or at a particular time: *In some remote areas traditional methods of farming still prevail.* **2** (*formal*) **prevail (against/over sb/sth)** to win or be accepted, especially after a fight or discussion: *In the end justice prevailed and the men were set free.*

prevailing /prɪ'veɪlɪŋ/ adj (only *before* a noun) **1** existing or most common at a particular time: *the prevailing climate of opinion* **2** (used about the wind) most common in a particular area: *The prevailing wind is from the south-west.*

prevalent /'prevələnt/ adj (*formal*) most common in a particular place at a particular time: *The prevalent atmosphere was one of fear.*

★**prevent** /prɪ'vent/ verb [T] **prevent sb/sth (from) (doing sth)** to stop sth happening or to stop sb doing sth: *This accident could have been prevented.* ● *Her parents tried to prevent her from going to live with her boyfriend.* ••➤ **Prevent** is more formal than **stop**.
–**prevention** noun [U]: *accident/crime prevention*

preventable /prɪ'ventəbl/ adj that can be prevented: *Many accidents are preventable.*

preventive /prɪ'ventɪv/ (also **preventative** /prɪ'ventətɪv/) adj intended to stop or prevent sth from happening: *preventative medicine*

preview /'priːvjuː/ noun [C] a chance to see a play, film, etc before it is shown to the general public

★**previous** /'priːviəs/ adj coming or happening before or earlier: *Do you have previous experience of this type of work?* –**previously** adv: *Before I moved to Spain I had previously worked in Italy.*

prey¹ /preɪ/ noun [U] an animal or bird that is killed and eaten by another animal or bird: *The eagle is a bird of prey* (= it kills and eats other birds or small animals).

prey² /preɪ/ verb
IDIOM **prey on sb's mind** to cause sb to worry or think about sth: *The thought that he was*

responsible for the accident preyed on the train driver's mind.

PHRASAL VERB **prey on sth** (used about an animal or bird) to kill and eat other animals or birds: *Owls prey on mice and other small animals.*

★**price**¹ /praɪs/ noun **1** [C] the amount of money that you must pay in order to buy sth: *What's the price of petrol now?* ● *We can't afford to buy the car at that price.* ● *There's no price on* (= written on) *this jar of coffee.*

➤ A **charge** is the amount of money that you must pay for using something: *Is there a charge for parking here?* ● *admission charges.* You use **cost** when you are talking about paying for services or about prices in general without mentioning an actual sum of money: *The cost of electricity is going up.* ● *the cost of living.* The **price** of something is the amount of money that you must pay in order to buy it.
A shop may **raise/increase**, **reduce/bring down** or **freeze** its prices. The prices **rise/go up** or **fall/go down**.

2 unpleasant things that you have to experience in order to achieve sth or as a result of sth: *Sleepless nights are a small price to pay for having a baby.*

IDIOMS **at a price** costing a lot of money or involving sth unpleasant: *He'll help you get a job – at a price.*
at any price even if the cost is very high or if it will have unpleasant results: *Richard was determined to succeed at any price.*
not at any price never; under no circumstances

price² /praɪs/ verb [T] to fix the price of sth or to write the price on sth: *The books were all priced at between £5 and £10.*

priceless /'praɪsləs/ adj of very great value: *priceless jewels and antiques* ••➤ Look at **worthless**, **valuable** and **invaluable**.

'**price list** noun [C] a list of the prices of the goods that are on sale

pricey /'praɪsi/ adj (*informal*) expensive

prick¹ /prɪk/ verb [T] to make a small hole in sth or to cause sb pain with a sharp point: *She pricked her finger on a needle.*
IDIOM **prick up your ears** (used about an animal) to hold up the ears in order to listen carefully to sth: (*figurative*) *Mike pricked up his ears when he heard Emma's name mentioned.*

prick² /prɪk/ noun [C] the sudden pain that you feel when sth sharp goes into your skin

prickle¹ /'prɪkl/ noun [C] one of the sharp points on some plants and animals: *Hedgehogs are covered in prickles.* ••➤ Look at **spine**. ••➤ picture at **hedgehog**

prickle² /'prɪkl/ verb [I] to have or make sb/sth have an uncomfortable feeling on the skin: *I don't like that shirt – it prickles.* ● *His skin prickled with fear.*

prickly /'prɪkli/ adj **1** covered with sharp points: *a prickly bush* **2** causing an uncomfortable feeling on the skin: *That T-shirt* *makes my skin go all prickly.* **3** (*informal*) (used about a person) easily made angry: *Don't mention his accident – he's a bit prickly about it.*

⋆**pride¹** /praɪd/ **noun 1** [U,sing] **pride (in sth/ doing sth)** the feeling of pleasure that you have when you or people who are close to you do sth good or own sth good: *I take a great pride in my work.* ● *Her parents watched with pride as Milena went up to collect her prize.* ● *You should feel pride in your achievement.* ••➤ adjective **proud 2** [U] the respect that you have for yourself: *You'll hurt his pride if you refuse to accept the present.* **3** [U] the feeling that you are better than other people **4** [sing] the pride of sth/sb a person or thing that is very important to or of great value to sth/sb: *The new stadium was the pride of the whole town.*

◼◼◼ **sb's pride and joy** a thing or person that gives sb great pleasure or satisfaction

pride² /praɪd/ **verb**
◼◼◼ **pride yourself on sth/doing sth** to feel pleased about sth good or clever that you can do: *Fabio prides himself on his ability to cook.*

⋆**priest** /priːst/ **noun** [C] a person who performs religious ceremonies in some religions

➤ In some religions a female priest is called a **priestess**.

prim /prɪm/ **adj** (used about a person) always behaving in a careful or formal way and easily shocked by anything that is rude –primly **adv**

primarily /'praɪmərəli; praɪ'merəli/ **adv** more than anything else; mainly: *The course is aimed primarily at beginners.*

⋆**primary¹** /'praɪməri/ **adj 1** most important; main: *Smoking is one of the primary causes of lung cancer.* **2** connected with the education of children between about five and eleven years old: *Their children are at primary school.*

primary² /'praɪməri/ (also **primary e'lection**) **noun** [C] (*pl* **primaries**) (*US*) an election in which a political party chooses the person who will represent the party (the candidate) in a later important election, such as for president

primary 'colour noun [C] any of the colours red, yellow or blue. You can make any other colour by mixing primary colours in different ways.

prime¹ /praɪm/ **adj** (only *before* a noun) **1** main; the first example of sth that sb would think of or choose: *She is a prime candidate as the next team captain.* **2** of very good quality; best: *prime pieces of beef* **3** having all the typical qualities: *That's a prime example of what I was talking about.*

prime² /praɪm/ **noun** [sing] the time when sb is strongest, most beautiful, most successful, etc: *Several of the team are past their prime.* ● *In his prime, he was a fine actor.* ● *to be in the prime of life*

prime³ /praɪm/ **verb** [T] **prime sb (for/with**

sth) to give sb information in order to prepare him/her for sth: *The politician had been well primed with all the facts before the interview.*

prime 'minister noun [C] (*abbr* **PM**) the leader of the government in some countries, for example Britain ••➤ Look at **minister**.

primitive /'prɪmətɪv/ **adj 1** very simple and not developed: *The washing facilities in the camp were very primitive.* **2** (only *before* a noun) connected with a very early stage in the development of humans or animals: *Primitive man lived in caves and hunted wild animals.*

primrose /'prɪmrəʊz/ **noun** [C] a yellow spring flower ••➤ picture on page C2

⋆**prince** /prɪns/ **noun** [C] **1** a son or other close male relative of a king or queen **2** the male ruler of a small country

⋆**princess** /ˌprɪn'ses/ **noun** [C] **1** a daughter or other close female relative of a king or queen **2** the wife of a prince

⋆**principal¹** /'prɪnsəpl/ **adj** (only *before* a noun) most important; main: *the principal characters in a play* –**principally** /-pli/ **adv**: *Our products are designed principally for the European market.*

principal² /'prɪnsəpl/ **noun** [C] the head of some schools, colleges, etc

⋆**principle** /'prɪnsəpl/ **noun 1** [C,U] a rule for good behaviour, based on what a person believes is right: *He doesn't eat meat on principle.* ● *She refuses to wear fur. It's a matter of principle with her.* **2** [C] a basic general law, rule or idea: *The system works on the principle that heat rises.* ● *The course teaches the basic principles of car maintenance.*

◼◼◼ **in principle** in general, but possibly not in detail: *His proposal sounds fine in principle, but there are a few points I'm not happy about.*

⋆**print¹** /prɪnt/ **verb 1** [T] to put words, pictures, etc onto paper by using a special machine: *How much did it cost to print the posters?* **2** [I,T] to produce books, newspapers, etc in this way: *50000 copies of the textbook were printed.* **3** [T] to include sth in a book, newspaper, etc: *The newspaper should not have printed the photographs of the crash.* **4** [T] to make a photograph from a piece of negative film **5** [I,T] to write with letters that are not joined together: *Please print your name clearly at the top of the paper.* **6** [T] to put a pattern onto cloth, paper, etc
◼◼◼ **print (sth) out** to print information from a computer onto paper: *I'll just print out this file.* –**printing noun** [U]

⋆**print²** /prɪnt/ **noun 1** [U] the letters, words, etc in a book, newspaper, etc: *The print is too small for me to read without my glasses.* **2** [U] used to refer to the business of producing newspapers, books, etc: *the print unions/ workers* **3** [C] a mark that is made by sth pressing onto sth else: *The police are searching the room for fingerprints.* ● *footprints in the snow* **4** [C] a picture that was made by printing **5** [C] a photograph (when it has been printed from a negative): *I ordered an extra set of prints for my friends.*

IDIOMS **in print 1** (used about a book) still available from the company that published it **2** (used about a person's work) published in a book, newspaper, etc

out of print (used about a book) no longer available from the company that published it; not being printed any more

printer /'prɪntə/ *noun* [C] **1** a person or company that prints books, newspapers, etc **2** a machine that prints out information from a computer onto paper: *a laser printer* ••➤ picture on page S7

'**printing press** (also **press**) *noun* [C] a machine that is used for printing books, newspapers, etc

printout /'prɪntaʊt/ *noun* [C,U] information from a computer that is printed onto paper

prior /'praɪə/ *adj* (only *before* a noun) coming before or earlier

★**priority** /praɪ'ɒrəti/ *noun* (*pl* **priorities**) **1** [U] **priority (over sb/sth)** the state of being more important than sb/sth or of coming before sb/sth else: *We give priority to families with small children.* ● *Emergency cases take priority over other patients in hospital.* **2** [C] something that is most important or that you must do before anything else: *Our top priority is to get food and water to the refugee camps.* ● *I'll make it my priority to sort out your problem.*

'**prior to** *prep* (*formal*) before: *Passengers are asked to report to the check-in desk prior to departure.*

prise /praɪz/ (*especially US* **prize**, **pry**) *verb* [T] prise sth off, apart, open, etc to use force to open sth, remove a lid, etc: *He prised the door open with an iron bar.*

★**prison** /'prɪzn/ (also **jail**) *noun* [C,U] a building where criminals are kept as a punishment: *The terrorists were sent to prison for twenty-five years.* ● *He will be released from prison next month.* ••➤ Look at **imprison** and **jail**.

> If a person goes **to prison** or is **in prison** (without '**the**'), he/she has to stay there as a prisoner: *He was sent to prison for two years.* 'The prison' refers to a particular prison, or indicates that a person is only visiting the building temporarily: *The politician visited the prison and said that conditions were poor.*

★**prisoner** /'prɪzənə/ *noun* [C] a person who is being kept in prison: *a political prisoner*

,**prisoner of 'war** *noun* [C] a soldier, etc who is caught by the enemy during a war and who is kept in prison until the end of the war

privacy /'prɪvəsi/ *noun* [U] **1** the state of being alone and not watched or disturbed by other people: *There is not much privacy in large hospital wards.* **2** the state of being free from the attention of the public: *The actress*

claimed that the photographs were an invasion of privacy.

★**private¹** /'praɪvət/ *adj* **1** belonging to or intended for one particular person or group and not to be shared by others: *This is private property. You may not park here.* ● *a private letter/conversation* **2** not connected with work or business: *He never discusses his private life with his colleagues at work.* **3** owned, done or organized by a person or company, and not by the government: *a private hospital/school* (= you pay to go there) ● *a private detective* (= one who is not in the police) ••➤ Look at **public**. **4** with no one else present: *I would like a private interview with the personnel manager.* **5** not wanting to share thoughts and feelings with other people: *He's a very private person.* **6** (used about classes, lessons, etc) given by a teacher to one student or a small group for payment: *Claire gives private English lessons at her house.* –**privately** *adv*

private² /'praɪvət/ *noun* [C] a soldier of the lowest level

IDIOM **in private** with no one else present: *May I speak to you in private?*

privatize (also **-ise**) /'praɪvɪtaɪz/ *verb* [T] to sell a business or an industry that was owned by the government to a private company: *The water industry has been privatized.* ••➤ opposite **nationalize** –**privatization** (also **-isation**) /,praɪvɪtaɪ'zeɪʃn/ *noun* [U]

★**privilege** /'prɪvəlɪdʒ/ *noun* **1** [C,U] a special right or advantage that only one person or group has: *Prisoners who behave well enjoy special privileges.* **2** [sing] a special advantage or opportunity that gives you great pleasure: *It was a great privilege to hear her sing.*

privileged /'prɪvəlɪdʒd/ *adj* having an advantage or opportunity that most people do not have: *Only a privileged few are allowed to enter this room.* ● *I feel very privileged to be playing for the national team.* ••➤ opposite **underprivileged**

★**prize¹** /praɪz/ *noun* [C] something of value that is given to sb who is successful in a race, competition, game, etc: *She won first prize in the competition.* ● *a prize-winning novel*

prize² /praɪz/ *adj* (only *before* a noun) winning, or good enough to win, a prize: *a prize flower display*

prize³ /praɪz/ *verb* [T] to consider sth to be very valuable: *This picture is one of my most prized possessions.*

prize⁴ /praɪz/ (*especially US*) = **PRISE**

pro /prəʊ/ *noun* [C] (*pl* **pros**) (*informal*) **1** a person who plays or teaches a sport for money: *a golf pro* **2** a person who has a lot of skill and experience ••➤ synonym **professional**

IDIOM **the pros and cons** the reasons for and against doing sth: *We should consider all the pros and cons before reaching a decision.*

probability /,prɒbə'bɪləti/ *noun* (*pl* **probabilities**) **1** [U,sing] how likely sth is to happen: *At that time there seemed little* *probability of success*. **2** [C] something that is likely to happen: *Closure of the factory now seems a probability*.

★**probable** /'prɒbəbl/ **adj** that you expect to happen or to be true; likely

> ➤ Notice that **probable** and **likely** mean the same but are used differently: *It's probable that he will be late.* ● *He is likely to be late.*

•➤ opposite **improbable** ••➤ Look at **possible**.

probably /'prɒbəbli/ **adv** almost certainly: *I will phone next week, probably on Wednesday*.

probation /prə'beɪʃn/ **noun** [U] **1** a system that allows sb who has committed a crime not to go to prison if he/she goes to see to an official (a **probation officer**) regularly for a fixed period of time: *Jamie is on probation for two years*. **2** a period of time at the start of a new job when you are tested to see if you are suitable: *a three-month probation period*

probe¹ /prəʊb/ **verb** [I,T] **1** probe (into sth) to ask questions in order to find out secret or hidden information: *The newspapers are now probing into the President's past.* **2** to examine or look for sth, especially with a long thin instrument: *The doctor probed the cut for pieces of broken glass*. –probing **adj**: *to ask probing questions*

probe² /prəʊb/ **noun** [C] **1** the process of asking questions, collecting facts, etc in order to find out hidden information about sth: *a police probe into illegal financial dealing* **2** a long thin tool that you use for examining sth that is difficult to reach, especially a part of the body

★**problem** /'prɒbləm/ **noun** [C] **1** a thing that is difficult to deal with or to understand: *social/family/financial/technical problems* ● *You won't solve the problem if you ignore it.* ● *The company will face problems from unions if it sacks workers.* ● *It's going to cause problems if Donna brings her husband.* ● *I can't play because I've got a problem with my knee.* ● *'Can you fix this for me?' 'No problem.'* ● *It's a great painting – the problem is I've got nowhere to put it.* **2** a question that you have to solve by thinking about it: *a maths/logic problem*

★**procedure** /prə'siːdʒə/ **noun** [C,U] the usual or correct way for doing sth: *What's the procedure for making a complaint?*

★**proceed** /prə'siːd; prəʊ-/ **verb** [I] **1** (*formal*) to continue doing sth; to continue being done: *The building work was proceeding according to schedule.* **2** (*formal*) proceed (with sth/to do sth) to start doing the next thing after finishing the last one: *Once he had calmed down he proceeded to tell us what had happened.*

proceedings /prə'siːdɪŋz/ **noun** [pl] **1** proceedings (against sb/for sth) legal action: *to start divorce proceedings* **2** events that happen, especially at a formal meeting, ceremony, etc: *The proceedings were interrupted by demonstrators.*

proceeds /'prəʊsiːdz/ **noun** [pl] proceeds (of/from sth) money that you get when you sell sth: *The proceeds from the sale will go to charity.*

★**process¹** /'prəʊses/ **noun** [C] **1** a series of actions that you do for a particular purpose: *We've just begun the complicated process of selling the house.* **2** a series of changes that happen naturally: *Mistakes are part of the learning process.*

IDIOMS **in the process** while you are doing sth else: *We washed the dog yesterday – and we all got very wet in the process.*

in the process of sth/doing sth in the middle of doing sth: *They are in the process of moving house.*

process² /'prəʊses/ **verb** [T] **1** to treat sth, for example with chemicals, in order to keep it, change it, etc: *Cheese is processed so that it lasts longer.* ● *I sent two rolls of film away to be processed.* **2** to deal with information, for example on a computer: *It will take about ten days to process your application.*

procession /prə'seʃn/ **noun** [C,U] a number of people, vehicles, etc that move slowly in a line, especially as part of a ceremony: *to walk in procession* ● *a funeral procession*

processor /'prəʊsesə/ **noun** [C] a machine that changes food or information into a suitable form: *Mix the ingredients in a food processor.* ● *a word processor*

proclaim /prə'kleɪm/ **verb** [T] (*written*) to make sth known officially or publicly: *The day was proclaimed a national holiday.* –proclamation /ˌprɒkləˈmeɪʃn/ **noun** [C,U]: *to make a proclamation of war*

procure /prə'kjʊə/ **verb** [T] (*written*) procure sth (for sb) to obtain sth, especially with difficulty: *I managed to procure two tickets for the match.*

prod /prɒd/ **verb** [I,T] (**prodding; prodded**) to push or press sb/sth with your finger or a pointed object: (*figurative*) *Ruth works quite hard but she does need prodding occasionally.* ••➤ picture on page S8 –prod **noun** [C]: *to give the fire a prod with a stick* –prodding **noun** [U]

prodigious /prə'dɪdʒəs/ **adj** very large or powerful and surprising: *He seemed to have a prodigious amount of energy.*

prodigy /'prɒdədʒi/ **noun** [C] (*pl* prodigies) a child who is unusually good at sth: *Mozart was a child prodigy.* ••➤ Look at **genius**.

★**produce¹** /prə'djuːs/ **verb** [T] **1** to make sth to be sold, especially in large quantities: *The factory produces 20000 cars a year.* ••➤ synonym **manufacture** **2** to grow or make sth by a natural process: *This region produces most of the country's wheat.* ● (*figurative*) *He's the greatest athlete this country has produced.* **3** to create sth using skill: *The children have produced some beautiful pictures for the exhibition.* **4** to cause a particular effect or result: *Her remarks produced roars of laughter.* **5** to show sth so that sb else can look at or examine it: *to produce evidence in court* **6** to be in charge of preparing a film, play, etc so that it can be shown to the public: *She is*

p

producing 'Romeo and Juliet' at the local theatre.

produce² /'prɒdjuːs/ **noun** [U] food, etc that is grown on a farm and sold: *fresh farm produce.* ··➤ Look at the note at **production**.

producer /prə'djuːsə/ **noun** [C] **1** a person, company or country that makes or grows sth: *Brazil is a major producer of coffee.* **2** a person who deals with the business side of organizing a play, film, etc **3** a person who arranges for sb to make a programme for TV or radio, or a record

★ **product** /'prɒdʌkt/ **noun** [C] **1** something that is made in a factory or that is formed naturally: *dairy/meat/pharmaceutical/software products* • *Carbon dioxide is one of the waste products of this process.* ··➤ Look at the note at **production**. **2** product of sth the result of sth: *The industry's problems are the product of government policy.*

★ **production** /prə'dʌkʃn/ **noun 1** [U] the making or growing of sth, especially in large quantities: *The latest model will be in production from April.* • *This farm specializes in the production of organic vegetables.* • *mass production* **2** [U] the amount of sth that is made or grown: *a rise/fall in production* • *a high level of production* **3** [C] a play, film or programme that has been made for the public

➤ Notice that **produce** (noun) means food, etc that comes from a farm and a **product** is something that was made in a factory. A **production** is a play, film, etc: *The label on the bottle says 'Produce of Italy'.* • *The company's main products are plastic toys.* • *the Bolshoi Ballet's production of Swan Lake*

IDIOM **on production of sth** when you show sth: *You can get a ten per cent discount on production of your membership card.*

productive /prə'dʌktɪv/ **adj 1** that makes or grows sth, especially in large quantities: *The company wants to sell off its less\productive factories.* **2** useful (because results come from it): *a productive discussion* –**productivity** /ˌprɒdʌk'tɪvəti/ **noun** [U]

profess /prə'fes/ **verb** [T] (*formal*) **1** to say that sth is true or correct, even when it is not: *Marianne professed to know nothing at all about it, but I did not believe her.* **2** to state honestly that you have a particular belief, feeling, etc: *He professed his hatred of war.*

★ **profession** /prə'feʃn/ **noun** [C] **1** a job that needs a high level of training and/or education: *the medical/legal/teaching profession* • *She's thinking of entering the nursing profession.* ··➤ Look at the note at **work¹**. **2** the...profession [with sing or pl verb] all the people who work in a particular profession: *The legal profession is/are trying to resist the reforms.*

IDIOM **by profession** as your job: *George is an accountant by profession.*

★ **professional¹** /prə'feʃənl/ **adj 1** (only *before* a noun) connected with a job that

needs a high level of training and/or education: *Get professional advice from your lawyer before you take any action.* **2** doing sth in a way that shows skill, training or care: *The police are trained to deal with every situation in a calm and professional manner.* • *Her application was neatly typed and looked very professional.* ··➤ opposite **unprofessional 3** doing a sport, etc as a job or for money; (used about a sport, etc) done by people who are paid: *He's planning to turn professional after the Olympics.* • *professional football* ··➤ opposite **amateur**

★ **professional²** /prə'feʃənl/ **noun** [C] **1** a person who works in a job that needs a high level of training and/or education **2** (also *informal* **pro**) a person who plays or teaches a sport, etc for money **3** (also *informal* **pro**) a person who has a lot of skill and experience

professionalism /prə'feʃənəlɪzəm/ **noun** [U] a way of doing a job that shows great skill and experience: *We were impressed by the professionalism of the staff.*

professionally /prə'feʃənəli/ **adv 1** in a way that shows great skill and experience **2** for money; by a professional person: *Rob plays the saxophone professionally.*

★ **professor** /prə'fesə/ **noun** [C] (*abbr* **Prof**) **1** a university teacher of the highest level: *She's professor of English at Bristol University.* **2** (*US*) a teacher at a college or university

proficient /prə'fɪʃnt/ **adj** proficient (in/at sth/doing sth) able to do a particular thing well; skilled: *We are looking for someone who is proficient in French.* –**proficiency** **noun** [U] proficiency (in sth/doing sth): *a certificate of proficiency in English*

profile /'prəʊfaɪl/ **noun** [C] **1** a person's face or head seen from the side, not the front: *I did a sketch of him in profile.* **2** a short description of sb/sth that gives useful information: *We're building up a profile of our average customer.*

IDIOM **a high/low profile** a way of behaving that does/does not attract other people's attention: *I don't know much about the subject – I'm going to keep a low profile at the meeting tomorrow.*

★ **profit¹** /'prɒfɪt/ **noun** [C,U] the money that you make when you sell sth for more than it cost you: *Did you make a profit on your house when you sold it?* • *I'm hoping to sell my shares at a profit.* ··➤ Look at **loss**.

profit² /'prɒfɪt/ **verb** [I,T] (*formal*) profit (from/by sth) to get an advantage from sth; to give sb an advantage: *Who will profit most from the tax reforms?*

profitable /'prɒfɪtəbl/ **adj 1** that makes money: *a profitable business* **2** helpful or useful: *We had a very profitable discussion yesterday.* –**profitably adv**: *to spend your time profitably* –**profitability** /ˌprɒfɪtə'bɪləti/ **noun** [U]

profound /prə'faʊnd/ **adj 1** very great; that you feel very strongly: *The experience had a profound influence on her.* **2** needing or showing a lot of knowledge or thought: *He's always making profound statements about the meaning of life.* –**profoundly** adv: *I was profoundly relieved to hear the news.*

profuse /prə'fju:s/ adj (*formal*) given or produced in great quantity: *profuse apologies* –**profusely** adv: *She apologized profusely for being late.*

★**program**¹ /'prəʊgræm/ noun [C] **1** a set of instructions that you give to a computer so that it will do a particular task: *to write a program*

➤ When we are talking about computers both the US and the British spelling is **program**. For every other meaning the British spelling is **programme** and the US spelling is **program**.

2 (*US*) = PROGRAMME¹

★**program**² /'prəʊgræm/ verb [T] (**program-ming**; **programmed**) to give a set of instructions to a computer

★**programme**¹ (*US* **program**) /'prəʊgræm/ noun [C] **1** a show or other item that is sent out on the radio or television: *a TV/radio programme* ● *We've just missed an interesting programme on elephants.* **2** a plan of things to do; a scheme: *What's (on) your programme today?* (= what are you going to do today?) ● *The leaflet outlines the government's programme of educational reforms.* **3** a little book or piece of paper which you get at a concert, a sports event, etc that gives you information about what you are going to see

programme² /'prəʊgræm/ (*US* **program**) verb [T] (**programming**; **programmed**: *US also* **programing**; **programed**) **1** to plan for sth to happen at a particular time: *The road is programmed for completion next May.* **2** to make sb/sth work or act automatically in a particular way: *The lights are programmed to come on as soon as it gets dark.*

programmer /'prəʊgræmə/ noun [C] a person whose job is to write programs for a computer

★**progress**¹ /'prəʊgres/ noun [U] **1** movement forwards or towards achieving sth: *Anna's making progress at school.* ● *to make slow/steady/rapid/good progress* **2** change or improvement in society: *scientific progress*
IDIOM **in progress** happening now: *Silence! Examination in progress.*

progress² /prə'gres/ verb [I] **1** to become better; to develop (well): *Medical knowledge has progressed rapidly in the last twenty years.* **2** to move forward; to continue: *I got more and more tired as the evening progressed.*

progression /prə'greʃn/ noun [C,U] (**a**) progression (from sth) (to sth) movement forward or a development from one stage to another: *You've made the progression from beginner to intermediate level.*

progressive /prə'gresɪv/ adj **1** using modern methods and ideas: *a progressive school* **2** happening or developing steadily: *a progressive reduction in the number of staff*

progressively /prə'gresɪvli/ adv steadily; a little at a time: *The situation became progressively worse.*

the pro‚**gressive** '**tense** noun [sing] (*grammar*) = THE CONTINUOUS TENSE

prohibit /prə'hɪbɪt/ verb [T] (*formal*) **prohibit sb/sth (from doing sth)** to say that sth is not allowed by law; to forbid: *English law prohibits children under 16 from buying cigarettes.*

prohibition /‚prəʊɪ'bɪʃn/ noun **1** [C] (*formal*) **a prohibition (on/against sth)** a law or rule that forbids sth: *There is a prohibition on the carrying of knives.* **2** [U] the action of stopping sth being done or used, especially by law: *the prohibition of alcohol in the 1920s*

prohibitive /prə'hɪbətɪv/ adj (used about a price or cost) so high that it prevents people from buying sth or doing sth: *The price of houses in the centre of town is prohibitive.* –**prohibitively** adv

★**project**¹ /'prɒdʒekt/ noun [C] **1** a piece of work, often involving many people, that is planned and organized carefully: *a major project to reduce pollution in our rivers* **2** a piece of school work in which the student has to collect information about a certain subject and then write about it: *Our group chose to do a project on rainforests.*

project² /prə'dʒekt/ verb **1** [T] (usually passive) to plan sth that will happen in the future: *the band's projected world tour* **2** [T] (usually passive) to guess or calculate the size, cost or amount of sth: *a projected increase of 10%* **3** [T] **project sth (on/onto sth)** to make light, a picture from a film, etc appear on a flat surface or screen **4** [T] to show or represent sb/sth/yourself in a certain way: *The government is trying to project a more caring image.* **5** [I] (*formal*) to stick out: *The balcony projects one metre out from the wall.* **6** [T] to send or throw sth upwards or away from you: *Actors have to learn to project their voice.*

projection /prə'dʒekʃn/ noun **1** [C] a guess about a future amount, situation, etc based on the present situation: *sales projections for the next five years* **2** [U] the act of making light, a picture from a film, etc appear on a surface

projector /prə'dʒektə/ noun [C] a piece of equipment that projects pictures or films onto a screen or wall: *a film/slide/overhead projector*

proliferate /prə'lɪfəreɪt/ verb [I] (*formal*) to increase quickly in number –**proliferation** /prə‚lɪfə'reɪʃn/ noun [U]

prolific /prə'lɪfɪk/ adj (used especially about a writer, artist, etc) producing a lot: *a prolific goal scorer*

prologue /'prəʊlɒg/ noun [C] a piece of writing or a speech that introduces a play, poem, etc •➤ Look at **epilogue**.

prolong /prə'lɒŋ/ verb [T] to make sth last longer

prolonged /prə'lɒŋd/ adj continuing for a

p

long time: *There was a prolonged silence before anybody spoke.*

prom /prɒm/ **noun** [C] **1** =PROMENADE **2** (*US*) a formal dance that is held by a high school class at the end of a school year

promenade /ˌprɒmə'nɑːd/ (also **prom**) **noun** [C] a wide path where people walk beside the sea in a town on the coast ••➤ picture on page C8

prominent /'prɒmɪnənt/ **adj 1** important or famous: *a prominent political figure* **2** noticeable; easy to see: *The church is the most prominent feature of the village.* –**prominence noun** [U]: *The newspaper gave the affair great prominence.* –**prominently adv**

promiscuous /prə'mɪskjuəs/ **adj** having sexual relations with many people –**promiscuity** /ˌprɒmɪ'skjuːəti/ **noun** [U]

★**promise¹** /'prɒmɪs/ **verb 1** [I,T] promise (to do sth); promise (sb) that… to say definitely that you will do or not do sth or that sth will happen: *She promised (me) that she would write every week.* ● *She promised not to forget to write.* **2** [T] promise sth (to sb); promise sb sth to say definitely that you will give sth to sb: *Can you promise your support?* ● *My dad has promised me a bicycle.* ● *You have to give him the money if you promised it to him.* **3** [T] to show signs of sth, so that you expect it to happen: *It promises to be an exciting occasion.*

★**promise²** /'prɒmɪs/ **noun 1** [C] a promise (to do sth/that…) a written or spoken statement or agreement that you will or will not do sth: *I want you to **make a promise** that you won't do that again.* ● *Make sure you **keep** your **promise** to always do your homework.* ● *You should never **break** a promise.* ● *I **give** you my **promise** that I won't tell anyone.* **2** [U] signs that you will be able to do sth well or be successful: *He **showed** great **promise** as a musician.*

promising /'prɒmɪsɪŋ/ **adj** showing signs of being very good or successful: *a promising young writer*

promote /prə'məʊt/ **verb** [T] **1** to encourage sth; to help sth to happen or develop: *to promote good relations between countries* **2** promote sth (as sth) to advertise sth in order to increase its sales or make it popular: *The new face cream is being promoted as a miracle cure for wrinkles.* **3** promote sb (from sth) (to sth) (often passive) to give sb a higher position or more important job: *He's been promoted from assistant manager to manager.*

promoter /prə'məʊtə/ **noun** [C] a person who organizes or provides the money for an event

★**promotion** /prə'məʊʃn/ **noun 1** promotion (to sth) [C,U] a move to a higher position or more important job: *The new job is a promotion for her.* **2** [U,C] things that you do in order to advertise a product and increase its sales: *It's all part of a special promotion of the new book.* **3** [U] (*formal*) promotion (of sth) the activity of trying to make sth develop or become accepted by people: *We need to work*

on the promotion of health, not the treatment of disease.

★**prompt¹** /prɒmpt/ **adj 1** immediate; done without delay: *We need a prompt decision on this matter.* **2** prompt (in doing sth/to do sth) (not before a noun) (used about a person) quick; acting without delay: *We are always prompt in paying our bills.* ● *She was prompt to point out my mistake.*

prompt² /prɒmpt/ **verb 1** [T] to cause sth to happen; to make sb decide to do sth: *What prompted you to give up your job?* **2** [I,T] to encourage sb to speak by asking questions or to remind an actor of his/her words in a play: *The speaker had to be prompted several times.* –**prompting noun** [U]: *He apologized without any prompting.*

prompt³ /prɒmpt/ **noun** [C] **1** a word or words said to an actor to remind him/her of what to say next: *When she forgot her lines I had to give her a prompt.* **2** (*computing*) a sign on a computer screen that shows that the computer has finished what it was doing and is ready for more instructions: *Wait for the prompt to come up then type in your password.*

promptly /'prɒmptli/ **adv 1** immediately; without delay: *I invited her to dinner and she promptly accepted.* **2** (also **prompt**) at exactly the time that you have arranged; punctually: *We arrived promptly at 12 o'clock.* ● *I'll pick you up at 7 o'clock prompt.*

prone /prəʊn/ **adj** prone to sth/to do sth likely to suffer from sth or to do sth bad: *prone to infection/injury/heart attacks* ● *Working without a break makes you more prone to error.* ● *to be **accident-prone** (= to have a lot of accidents)*

prong /prɒŋ/ **noun** [C] **1** each of the two or more long pointed parts of a fork **2** each of the separate parts of an attack, argument, etc that sb uses to achieve sth **3** -**pronged** (used to form compound adjectives) having the number or type of prongs mentioned: *a three-pronged attack*

pronoun /'prəʊnaʊn/ **noun** [C] (*grammar*) a word that is used in place of a noun or a phrase that contains a noun: *'He', 'it', 'hers', 'me', 'them', etc are all pronouns.* ••➤ Look also at **personal pronoun**.

★**pronounce** /prə'naʊns/ **verb 1** [T] to make the sound of a word or letter in a particular way: *You don't pronounce the 'b' at the end of 'comb'.* ● *How do you pronounce your surname?* ••➤ noun pronunciation **2** [T] (*formal*) to say or give sth formally, officially or publicly: *The judge will pronounce sentence today.* **3** [I,T] (*formal*) pronounce (on sth) to give your opinion on sth, especially formally: *The play was pronounced 'brilliant' by all the critics.*

pronounced /prə'naʊnst/ **adj** very noticeable; obvious: *His English is excellent although he speaks with a pronounced French accent.*

p

★**pronunciation** /prəˌnʌnsiˈeɪʃn/ **noun**
1 [U,C] the way in which a language or a particular word or sound is said: *American pronunciation* ◦➤ verb **pronounce 2** [U] a person's way of speaking a language: *His grammar is good but his pronunciation is awful!*

★**proof**¹ /pruːf/ **noun 1** [U] proof (of sth); proof that... information, documents, etc which show that sth is true: *'We need some **proof of identity**,' the shop assistant said.* ◦ *You've got no proof that John took the money.* ◦➤ verb **prove 2** [C, usually pl] (*technical*) a first copy of printed matter that is produced so that mistakes can be corrected

-proof² /pruːf/ **adj** (used to form compound adjectives) able to protect against the thing mentioned: *a soundproof room* ◦ *a waterproof/windproof jacket* ◦ *bulletproof glass*

prop¹ /prɒp/ **verb** [T] (**propping**; **propped**) to support sb/sth or keep sb/sth in position by putting him/her/it against or on sth: *I'll use this book to prop the window open.* ◦ *He propped his bicycle against the wall.*
PHRASAL VERB **prop sth up** to support sth that would otherwise fall

prop² /prɒp/ **noun** [C] **1** a stick or other object that you use to support sth or to keep sth in position: *Rescuers used props to stop the roof of the tunnel collapsing.* **2** [usually pl] an object that is used in a play, film, etc: *He's responsible for all the stage props, machinery and lighting.*

propaganda /ˌprɒpəˈɡændə/ **noun** [U] information and ideas that may be false or exaggerated, which are used to gain support for a political leader, party, etc: *political propaganda*

propel /prəˈpel/ **verb** [T] (**propelling**; **propelled**) to move, drive or push sb/sth forward or in a particular direction

propeller /prəˈpelə/ **noun** [C] a device with several flat metal parts (blades) which turn round very fast in order to make a ship or a plane move

★**proper** /ˈprɒpə/ **adj 1** (*especially Brit*) (only *before* a noun) right, suitable or correct: *If you're going skiing you must have the proper clothes.* ◦ *I've got to get these pieces of paper in the proper order.* **2** (only *before* a noun) that you consider to be real or good enough: *I didn't see much of the flat yesterday. I'm going to go today and have a proper look.* **3** (*formal*) socially and morally acceptable: *I think it would be only proper for you to apologize.* ◦➤ opposite **improper 4** (only *after* a noun) real or main: *We travelled through miles of suburbs before we got to the city proper.*

properly /ˈprɒpəli/ **adv 1** (*especially Brit*) correctly; in an acceptable way: *The teacher said I hadn't done my homework properly.* ◦ *These shoes don't fit properly.* **2** in a way that is socially and morally acceptable; politely: *If you two children can't behave properly then we'll have to go home.* ◦➤ opposite **improperly**

ˈ**proper name** (also ˈ**proper noun**) **noun** [C]

(*grammar*) a word which is the name of a particular person or place and begins with a large letter (a capital letter): *'Mary' and 'Rome' are proper names.*

★**property** /ˈprɒpəti/ **noun** (*pl* **properties**)
1 [U] a thing or things that belong to sb: *The sack contained **stolen property**.* ◦ *Is this bag your property?* ◦ *This file is government property.* ◦➤ Look at **lost property**. **2** [U] land and buildings: *Property prices vary enormously from area to area.* **3** [C] one building and the land around it: *There are a lot of empty properties in the area.* **4** [C, usually pl] (*formal*) a special quality or characteristic that a substance, etc has: *Some plants have healing properties.*

prophecy /ˈprɒfəsi/ **noun** [C] (*pl* **prophecies**) a statement about what is going to happen in the future: *to fulfil a prophecy* (= to make it come true)

prophesy /ˈprɒfəsaɪ/ **verb** [T] (*pres part* **prophesying**; *3rd pers sing pres* **prophesies**; *pt, pp* **prophesied**) to say what you think will happen in the future: *to prophesy disaster/war*

prophet /ˈprɒfɪt/ **noun** [C] **1** (also **Prophet**) (in the Christian, Jewish and Muslim religions) a person who is sent by God to teach the people and give them messages from God **2** a person who tells what will happen in the future –**prophetic adj**

★**proportion** /prəˈpɔːʃn/ **noun 1** [C] a part or share of a whole: *A large proportion of the earth's surface is covered by sea.* **2** [U] proportion (of sth to sth) the relationship between the size or amount of two things: *The proportion of men to women in the college has changed dramatically over the years.* **3** **proportions** [pl] the size or shape of sth: *a room of odd proportions* ◦ *Political unrest is reaching alarming proportions.*

IDIOMS **in proportion** the right size in relation to other things: *to draw sth in proportion* ◦ *She's so upset that it's hard for her to keep the problem in proportion* (= to her it seems more important or serious than it really is). **in proportion to sth 1** by the same amount or number as sth else; relative to: *Salaries have not risen in proportion to inflation.* **2** compared with: *In proportion to the number of students as a whole, there are very few women.* **out of proportion (to sth) 1** too big, small, etc in relation to other things **2** too great, serious, important, etc in relation to sth: *His reaction was completely out of proportion to the situation.*

proportional /prəˈpɔːʃənl/ **adj** proportional (to sth) of the right size, amount or degree compared with sth else: *Salary is proportional to years of experience.*

proˌportional ˌrepresenˈtation noun [U] (*abbr* PR) a system that gives each political party in an election a number of representatives in parliament in direct relation to the number of votes its candidates receive ◦➤ Look at **representation**.

p

★**proposal** /prə'pəʊzl/ noun [C] **1** a proposal (for/to do sth); a proposal that... a plan that is formally suggested: *a new proposal for raising money* ● *a proposal to build more student accommodation* ● *May I make a proposal that we all give an equal amount?* **2** an act of formally asking sb to marry you

★**propose** /prə'pəʊz/ verb **1** [T] to formally suggest sth as a possible plan or action: *At the meeting a new advertising campaign was proposed.* **2** [T] to intend to do sth; to have sth as a plan: *What do you propose to do now?* **3** [I,T] propose (to sb) to ask sb to marry you: *to propose marriage* **4** [T] propose sb for/as sth to suggest sb for an official position: *I'd like to propose Anna Marsland as Chairperson.*

proposition /ˌprɒpə'zɪʃn/ noun [C] **1** an idea, a plan or an offer, especially in business; a suggestion: *A month's holiday in Spain is an attractive proposition.* **2** an idea or opinion that sb expresses about sth: *That's a very interesting proposition. But can you prove it?*

proprietor /prə'praɪətə/ noun [C] (fem **proprietress** /prə'praɪətrəs/) the owner of a business, a hotel, etc

prose /prəʊz/ noun [U] written or spoken language that is not poetry: *to write in prose*
➤ Compare **poetry**.

prosecute /'prɒsɪkjuːt/ verb [I,T] prosecute sb (for sth) to officially charge sb with a crime and try show that he/she is guilty, in a court of law: *the prosecuting counsel/lawyer/attorney* ● *He was prosecuted for theft.*
•➤ Look at **defend**.

prosecution /ˌprɒsɪ'kjuːʃn/ noun **1** [U,C] the process of officially charging sb with a crime and of trying to show that he/she is guilty, in a court of law: *to bring a prosecution against sb* ● *Failure to pay your parking fine will result in prosecution.* **2 the prosecution** [sing,with sing or pl verb] a person or group of people who try to show that sb is guilty of a crime in a court of law: *The prosecution claim/claims that Lloyd was driving at 100 miles per hour.* •➤ Look at **defence**.

prospect /'prɒspekt/ noun **1** [U,sing] prospect (of sth/of doing sth) the possibility that sth will happen: *There's little prospect of better weather before next week.* **2** [sing] prospect (of sth/of doing sth) a thought about what may or will happen in the future: *The prospect of becoming a father filled James with horror.* **3 prospects** [pl] chances of being successful in the future: *good job/career/promotion prospects*

prospective /prə'spektɪv/ adj likely to be or to happen; possible: *prospective changes in the law*

prospectus /prə'spektəs/ noun [C] a small book which gives information about a school or college in order to advertise it

prosper /'prɒspə/ verb [I] to develop in a successful way; to be successful, especially with money

prosperity /prɒ'sperəti/ noun [U] the state of being successful, especially with money: *Tourism has brought prosperity to many parts of Spain.*

prosperous /'prɒspərəs/ adj rich and successful

prostitute /'prɒstɪtjuːt/ noun [C] a person, especially a woman, who earns money by having sex with people

prostitution /ˌprɒstɪ'tjuːʃn/ noun [U] working as a prostitute

prostrate /prɒ'streɪt/ adj lying flat on the ground, facing downwards

★**protect** /prə'tekt/ verb [T] protect sb/sth (against/from sth) to keep sb/sth safe; to defend sb/sth: *Parents try to protect their children from danger as far as possible.* ● *Bats are a protected species* (= they must not be killed).

★**protection** /prə'tekʃn/ noun [U] protection (against/from sth) the act of keeping sb/sth safe so that he/she/it is not harmed or damaged: *Vaccination gives protection against diseases.* ● *After the attack he was put under police protection.*

protective /prə'tektɪv/ adj **1** (only before a noun) that prevents sb/sth from being damaged or harmed: *In certain jobs workers need to wear protective clothing.* **2** protective (of/towards sb/sth) wanting to keep sb/sth safe: *Female animals are very protective of their young.*

protector /prə'tektə/ noun [C] a person who protects sb/sth

protein /'prəʊtiːn/ noun [C,U] a substance found in food such as meat, fish, eggs and beans. It is important for helping people and animals to grow and be healthy.

★**protest¹** /'prəʊtest/ noun [U,C] protest (against sth) a statement or action that shows that you do not like or approve of sth: *He resigned in protest against the decision.* ● *The union organized a protest against the redundancies.*

IDIOM **under protest** not happily and after expressing disagreement: *Fiona agreed to pay in the end but only under protest.*

★**protest²** /prə'test/ verb **1** [I,T] protest (about/against/at sth) to say or show that you do not approve of or agree with sth, especially publicly: *Students have been protesting against the government's decision.*

➤ In US English **protest** is used without a preposition: *They protested the government's handling of the situation.*

2 [T] to say sth firmly, especially when others do not believe you: *She has always protested her innocence.* •➤ **Protest** is stronger and usually used about more serious things than **complain**. You **protest** about something that you feel is not right or fair, you **complain** about the quality of something or about a less serious action: *to protest about a new tax* ● *to complain about the poor weather.* –protester noun [C]: *Protesters blocked the road outside the factory.*

★**Protestant** /'prɒtɪstənt/ **noun** [C] a member of the Christian church that separated from the Catholic church in the 16th century –Protestant **adj**: *a Protestant church* ••► Look at **Roman Catholic**.

prototype /'prəʊtətaɪp/ **noun** [C] the first model or design of sth from which other forms will be developed

protrude /prə'truːd/ **verb** [I] protrude (from sth) to stick out from a place or surface: *protruding eyes/teeth*

★**proud** /praʊd/ **adj** **1** proud (of sb/sth); proud to do sth/that... feeling pleased and satisfied about sth that you own or have done: *They are very proud of their new house.* ● *I feel very proud to be part of such a successful organization.* ● *You should feel very proud that you have been chosen.* **2** feeling that you are better and more important than other people: *Now she's at university she'll be much too proud to talk to us!* **3** having respect for yourself and not wanting to lose the respect of others: *He was too proud to ask for help.* ••► noun pride –**proudly** **adv**: *'I did all the work myself,' he said proudly.*

★**prove** /pruːv/ **verb** (*pp* proved; *US* proven) **1** [T] prove sth (to sb) to use facts and evidence to show that sth is true: *It will be difficult to prove that she was lying.* ● *She tried to prove her innocence to the court.* ● *He felt he needed to prove a point* (= show other people that he was right). ••► noun proof **2** [I] to show a particular quality over a period of time: *The job proved more difficult than we'd expected.* **3** [T] prove yourself (to sb) to show other people how good you are at doing sth and/or that you are capable of doing sth: *He constantly feels that he has to prove himself to others.*

proven /'pruːvn; 'pruːvn/ **adj** that has been shown to be true: *a proven fact*

proverb /'prɒvɜːb/ **noun** [C] a short well-known sentence or phrase that gives advice or says that sth is generally true in life: *'Too many cooks spoil the broth,' is a proverb.* ••► Look at **saying**.

★**provide** /prə'vaɪd/ **verb** [T] provide sb (with sth); provide sth (for sb) to give sth to sb or make sth available for sb to use; to supply sth: *This book will provide you with all the information you need.* ● *We are able to provide accommodation for two students.* ••► noun provision

PHRASAL VERBS provide for sb to give sb all that he/she needs to live, for example food and clothing: *Robin has four children to provide for.*

provide for sth to make preparations to deal with sth that might happen in the future: *We did not provide for such a large increase in prices.*

★**provided** /prə'vaɪdɪd/ (also **providing**) **conj** provided/providing (that) only if; on condition that: *She agreed to go and work abroad provided (that) her family could go with her.*

★**province** /'prɒvɪns/ **noun** **1** [C] one of the main parts into which some countries are divided with its own local government: *Canada has ten provinces.*

➤ Compare **county** and **state**.

2 the provinces [pl] (*Brit*) the part of a country that is outside the most important city (the capital)

provincial /prə'vɪnʃl/ **adj** **1** (only *before* a noun) connected with one of the large areas that some countries are divided into: *provincial governments/elections* **2** connected with the parts of a country that do not include its most important city: *a provincial town/newspaper* **3** (used about a person or his/her ideas) not wanting to consider new or different ideas or fashions: *provincial attitudes*

★**provision** /prə'vɪʒn/ **noun 1** [U] the giving or supplying of sth to sb or making sth available for sb to use: *The council is responsible for the provision of education and social services.* **2** [U] provision for sb/sth preparations that you make to deal with sth that might happen in the future: *She made provision for* (= planned for the financial future of) *the children in the event of her death.* **3** provisions [pl] (*formal*) supplies of food and drink, especially for a long journey ••► verb provide

provisional /prə'vɪʒənl/ **adj** only for the present time, that is likely to be changed in the future: *The provisional date for the next meeting is 18 November.* ● *a provisional driving licence* (= that you use when you are learning to drive) –**provisionally** /-nəli/ **adv**: *I've only repaired the bike provisionally – we'll have to do it properly later.*

provocation /ˌprɒvə'keɪʃn/ **noun** [U,C] doing or saying sth deliberately to try to make sb angry or upset; sth that is said or done to cause this: *You should never hit children, even under extreme provocation.* ••► verb provoke

provocative /prə'vɒkətɪv/ **adj** **1** intended to make sb angry or upset or to cause an argument: *He made a provocative remark about a woman's place being in the home.* **2** intended to cause sexual excitement –provocatively **adv**

provoke /prə'vəʊk/ **verb** [T] **1** to cause a particular feeling or reaction: *an article intended to provoke discussion* **2** provoke sb (into sth/into doing sth) to say or do sth that you know will make a person angry or upset: *The lawyer claimed his client was provoked into acts of violence.* ••► noun provocation

prow /praʊ/ **noun** [C] the front part of a ship or boat ••► The back of a ship is the **stern**.

prowess /'praʊəs/ **noun** [U] (*formal*) great skill at doing sth: *academic/sporting prowess*

prowl /praʊl/ **verb** [I,T] prowl (about/around) (used about an animal that is hunting or a person who is waiting for a chance to steal sth or do sth bad) to move around an area quietly so that you are not seen or heard: *I could hear someone prowling around outside so I called the police.* ••► A person or animal that is prowling is **on the prowl**.

p

–**prowler** noun [C]: *The police arrested a prowler outside the hospital.*

proximity /prɒkˈsɪməti/ noun [U] (*formal*) proximity (of sb/sth) (to sb/sth) the state of being near to sb/sth in distance or time: *An advantage is the proximity of the new offices to the airport.*

proxy /ˈprɒksi/ noun [U] the authority that you give to sb to act for you if you cannot do sth yourself: *to vote by proxy*

prude /pruːd/ noun [C] a person who is easily shocked by anything connected with sex –**prudish** adj

prudent /ˈpruːdnt/ adj (*formal*) sensible and careful when making judgements and decisions; avoiding unnecessary risks: *It would be prudent to get some more advice before you invest your money.* •➤ opposite **imprudent** –**prudence** noun [U] –**prudently** adv

prune¹ /pruːn/ noun [C] a dried fruit (**plum**)

prune² /pruːn/ verb [T] to cut branches or parts of branches off a tree or bush in order to make it a better shape

pry /praɪ/ verb (*pres part* **prying**; *3rd pers sing pres* **pries**; *pt, pp* **pried**) **1** [I] pry (into sth) to try to find out about other people's private affairs: *I'm sick of you prying into my personal life.* **2** [T] (*especially US*) = **PRISE**

PS (also **ps**) /ˌpiː ˈes/ abbr (used for adding sth to the end of a letter) postscript: *Love Tessa. PS I'll bring the car.*

pseudonym /ˈsuːdənɪm; ˈsjuː-/ noun [C] a name used by sb, especially a writer, instead of his/her real name

psych /saɪk/ verb
PHRASAL VERB **psych yourself up** (*informal*) to prepare yourself in your mind for sth difficult: *I've got to psych myself up for this interview.*

psyche /ˈsaɪki/ noun [C] (*formal*) the mind; your deepest feelings and attitudes: *the human/female/national psyche*

psychedelic /ˌsaɪkəˈdelɪk/ adj (used about art, music, clothes, etc) having bright colours or patterns or strange sounds

psychiatrist /saɪˈkaɪətrɪst/ noun [C] a doctor who is trained to treat people with mental illness

psychiatry /saɪˈkaɪətri/ noun [U] the study and treatment of mental illness

➤ Compare **psychology**.

–**psychiatric** /ˌsaɪkiˈætrɪk/ adj: *a psychiatric hospital/unit/nurse*

psychic /ˈsaɪkɪk/ adj (used about a person or his/her mind) having unusual powers that cannot be explained, for example knowing what sb else is thinking or being able to see into the future

psychoanalysis /ˌsaɪkəʊəˈnæləsɪs/ (also **analysis**) noun [U] a method of treating sb with a mental illness by asking about his/her past experiences, feelings, dreams, etc in order to find out what is making him/her ill

–**psychoanalyse** (*US* -**lyze**) /ˌsaɪkəʊˈænəlaɪz/ verb [T]

psychoanalyst /ˌsaɪkəʊˈænəlɪst/ noun [C] a person who treats sb with a mental illness by using psychoanalysis

psychological /ˌsaɪkəˈlɒdʒɪkl/ adj **1** connected with the mind or the way that it works: *Has her ordeal caused her long-term psychological damage?* **2** connected with the study of the mind and the way people behave (**psychology**) –**psychologically** /-kli/ adv: *Psychologically, it was a bad time to be starting a new job.*

psychologist /saɪˈkɒlədʒɪst/ noun [C] a scientist who studies the mind and the way that people behave

psychology /saɪˈkɒlədʒi/ noun **1** [U] the scientific study of the mind and the way that people behave: *child psychology*

➤ Compare **psychiatry**.

2 [sing] the type of mind that a person or group of people has: *If we understood the psychology of the killer we would have a better chance of catching him.*

psychopath /ˈsaɪkəpæθ/ (also *spoken* **psycho**) noun [C] a person who has a serious mental illness that may cause him/her to hurt or kill other people

psychosis /saɪˈkəʊsɪs/ noun [C,U] (*pl* **psychoses**) a very serious mental illness that affects your whole personality –**psychotic** /saɪˈkɒtɪk/ adj, noun [C]: *a psychotic patient/individual*

psychotherapy /ˌsaɪkəʊˈθerəpi/ noun [U] the treatment of mental illness by discussing sb's problems rather than by giving him/her drugs

pt (*pl* **pts**) abbr **1** pint: *2 pts milk* **2** (in a game or competition) point: *Laura 5pts, Arthur 4pts*

PTO (also **pto**) /ˌpiː tiː ˈəʊ/ abbr (at the bottom of a page) please turn over

★**pub** /pʌb/ (also *formal* **public house**) noun [C] (*Brit*) a place where people go to buy and drink alcohol and that also often serves food

puberty /ˈpjuːbəti/ noun [U] the time when a child's body is changing and becoming physically like that of an adult: *to reach puberty*

pubic /ˈpjuːbɪk/ adj of the area around the sexual organs: *pubic hair*

★**public**¹ /ˈpʌblɪk/ adj **1** (only *before* a noun) connected with ordinary people in general, not those who have an important position in society: *Public opinion was in favour of the war.* ● *How much public support is there for the government's policy?* **2** provided for the use of people in general; not private: *a public library/telephone* ● *public spending* (= money that the government spends on education, health care, etc) **3** known by many people: *We're going to make the news public soon.* •➤ Look at **private**. –**publicly** /-kli/ adv: *The company refused to admit publicly that it had* *acted wrongly.*

IDIOMS **be common/public knowledge** → **KNOWLEDGE**

go public 1 to tell people about sth that is a secret: *The sacked employee went public with his stories of corruption inside the company.* **2** (used about a company) to start selling shares to the public

in the public eye often appearing on television, in magazines, etc

★ **public²** /'pʌblɪk/ *noun* [sing, with sing or pl verb] **1 the public** people in general: *The university swimming pool is open to the public in the evenings.* ● *The police have asked for help from members of the public.* ● *The public is/are generally in favour of the new law.* **2** a group of people who are all interested in sth or who have sth in common: *the travelling public*

IDIOM **in public** when other people are present: *This is the first time that Miss Potter has spoken about her experience in public.*

publican /'pʌblɪkən/ *noun* [C] a person who owns or manages a pub

★ **publication** /ˌpʌblɪ'keɪʃn/ *noun* **1** [U] the act of printing a book, magazine, etc and making it available to the public: *His latest book has just been accepted for publication.* **2** [C] a book, magazine, etc that has been published **3** [U] the action of making sth known to the public: *the publication of exam results*

ˌpublic 'company (also ˌpublic ˌlimited 'company) *noun* [C] (*Brit*) (*abbr* **plc**) a large company that sells shares in itself to the public

ˌpublic con'venience *noun* [C] (*Brit*) a toilet in a public place that anyone can use

ˌpublic 'house (*formal*) = **PUB**

publicity /pʌb'lɪsəti/ *noun* [U] **1** notice or attention from the newspapers, television, etc: *to seek/avoid publicity* **2** the business of attracting people's attention to sth/sb; advertising: *There has been a lot of publicity for this film.*

publicize (also **-ise**) /'pʌblɪsaɪz/ *verb* [T] to attract people's attention to sth: *The event has been well publicized and should attract a lot of people.*

ˌpublic re'lations *noun* (*abbr* **PR**) **1** [pl] the state of the relationship between an organization and the public: *Giving money to local charities is good for public relations.* **2** [U] the job of making a company, organization, etc popular with the public: *a Public Relations Officer*

ˌpublic 'school *noun* [C] **1** (in Britain, especially in England) a private school for children aged between 13 and 18. Parents have to pay to send their children to one of these schools. Many of the children at public schools live (board) there while they are studying. **2** (in the US, Australia, Scotland and other countries) a local school that any child can go to that provides free education

ˌpublic-'spirited *adj* always ready to help other people and the public in general

ˌpublic 'transport *noun* [U] (the system of) buses, trains, etc that run according to a series of planned times and that anyone can use: *to travel by/on public transport*

★ **publish** /'pʌblɪʃ/ *verb* **1** [I,T] to prepare and print a book, magazine, etc and make it available to the public: *This dictionary was published by Oxford University Press.* **2** [T] (used about a writer, etc) to have your work put in a book, magazine, etc: *Dr Wreth has published several articles on the subject.* **3** [T] to make sth known to the public: *Large companies must publish their accounts every year.*

publisher /'pʌblɪʃə/ *noun* [C] a person or company that publishes books, magazines, etc

publishing /'pʌblɪʃɪŋ/ *noun* [U] the business of preparing books, magazines, etc to be printed and sold: *She's aiming for a career in publishing.*

★ **pudding** /'pʊdɪŋ/ *noun* [C,U] (*Brit*) **1** any sweet food that is eaten at the end of a meal: *What's for pudding today?* ••➤ **Dessert** is more formal. ••➤ Look at **sweet**. **2** a type of sweet food that is made from bread, flour or rice with eggs, milk, etc: *rice pudding*

puddle /'pʌdl/ *noun* [C] a small pool of water or other liquid, especially rain, that has formed on the ground ••➤ Look at the note at **pond**.

puff¹ /pʌf/ *verb* **1** [I,T] (used about air, smoke, wind, etc) to blow or come out in clouds: *Smoke was puffing out of the chimney.* **2** [I,T] to smoke a cigarette, pipe etc: *to puff on a cigarette* **3** [I] to breathe loudly or quickly, for example when you are running: *He was puffing hard as he ran up the hill.* **4** [I] **puff along, in, out, up,** etc to move in a particular direction with loud breaths or small clouds of smoke: *The train puffed into the station.*

PHRASAL VERBS **puff sth out/up** to cause sth to become larger by filling it with air: *The trumpet player was puffing out his cheeks.*

puff up (used about part of the body) to become swollen: *Her arm puffed up when she was stung by a wasp.*

puff² /pʌf/ *noun* [C] **1** a small amount of air, smoke, wind, etc that is blown or sent out: *a puff of smoke* **2** one breath that you take when you are smoking a cigarette or pipe: *to take/have a puff on a cigarette*

puffed /pʌft/ (also ˌpuffed 'out) *adj* finding it difficult to breathe, for example because you have been running

puffin /'pʌfɪn/ *noun* [C] a North Atlantic seabird with a large brightly-coloured beak

puffy /'pʌfi/ *adj* (used about a part of a person's body) looking soft and swollen: *Your eyes look a bit puffy. Have you been crying?*

puke /pjuːk/ *verb* [I,T] (*slang*) to be sick; to vomit –**puke** *noun* [U]

p

pull/push/drag

pull

push

drag

waved as the bus *pulled away*.

pull sth down to destroy a building

pull in (to sth); **pull into sth 1** (used about a train) to enter a station **2** (used about a car, etc) to move to the side of the road and stop

pull sth off (*informal*) to succeed in sth: *to pull off a business deal*

pull out (used about a car, etc) to move away from the side of the road: *I braked as a car suddenly pulled out in front of me.*

pull out (of sth) (used about a train) to leave a station

pull (sb/sth) out (of sth) (to cause sb/sth) to leave sth: *The Americans have pulled their forces out of the area.* ● *We've pulled out of the deal.*

pull sth out to take sth out of a place suddenly or with force: *She walked into the bank and pulled out a gun.*

pull over (used about a vehicle or its driver) to slow down and move to the side of the road: *I pulled over to let the ambulance past.*

pull through (sth) to survive a dangerous illness or a difficult time

pull together to do sth or work together with other people in an organized way and without fighting

pull yourself together to control your feelings and behave in a calm way: *Pull yourself together and stop crying.*

pull up (to cause a car, etc) to stop

★**pull¹** /pʊl/ **verb 1** [I,T] to use force to move sb/sth towards yourself: *I pulled on the rope to make sure that it was secure.* ● *to pull the trigger of a gun* ● *I felt someone pull at my sleeve and turned round.* ● *They managed to pull the child out of the water just in time.* **2** [T] **pull sth on, out, up, down, etc** to move sth in the direction that is described: *She pulled her sweater on/She pulled on her sweater.* ● *He pulled up his trousers/He pulled his trousers up.* ● *I switched off the TV and pulled out the plug.* **3** [T] to hold or be fastened to sth and move it along behind you in the direction that you are going: *That cart is too heavy for one horse to pull.* **4** [I,T] to move your body or a part of your body away with force: *She pulled away as he tried to kiss her.* ● *I pulled back my fingers just as the door slammed.* **5** [T] to damage a muscle, etc by using too much force: *I've pulled a muscle in my thigh.*

IDIOMS **make/pull faces/a face (at sb)** → FACE¹

pull sb's leg (*informal*) to play a joke on sb by trying to make him/her believe sth that is not true

pull out all the stops (*informal*) to make the greatest possible effort to achieve sth

pull your punches (*informal*) (usually used in negative sentences) to be careful what you say or do in order not to shock or upset anyone: *The film pulls no punches in its portrayal of urban violence.*

pull strings to use your influence to gain an advantage

pull your weight to do your fair share of the work

PHRASAL VERBS **pull away (from sb/sth)** to start moving forward, leaving sb/sth behind: *We*

pull² /pʊl/ **noun 1** [C] **a pull (at/on sth)** the action of moving sb/sth towards you using force: *I gave a pull on the rope to check it was secure.* **2** [sing] a physical force or an attraction that makes sb/sth move in a particular direction: *the earth's gravitational pull* ● *He couldn't resist the pull of the city.* **3** [sing] the act of taking a breath of smoke from a cigarette

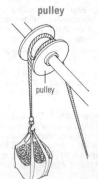

pulley

pulley

pulley /'pʊli/ **noun** [C] a piece of equipment, consisting of a wheel and a rope, that is used for lifting heavy things

pullover /'pʊləʊvə/ **noun** [C] a knitted woollen piece of clothing for the upper part of the body, with long sleeves and no buttons ••➤ Look at the note at **sweater**.

pulp /pʌlp/ **noun 1** [sing,U] a soft substance that is made especially by crushing sth: *Mash the beans to a pulp.* **2** [U] the soft inner part of some fruits or vegetables

pulsate /pʌl'seɪt/ **verb** [I] to move or shake with strong regular movements: *a pulsating rhythm*

pulse¹ /pʌls/ **noun 1** [C,usually sing] the regular beating in your body as blood is pushed around it by your heart. You can feel your pulse at your wrist, neck, etc: *Your pulse rate increases after exercise.* ● *to feel/take sb's pulse* (= to count how many times it beats in one minute) **2 pulses** [pl] The seeds of some plants such as beans and peas that are cooked and eaten as food

pulse² /pʌls/ **verb** [I] to move with strong regular movements

★**pump¹** /pʌmp/ **verb 1** [T] to force a gas or liquid to go in a particular direction: *Your heart pumps blood around your body.* **2** [I] (used about a liquid) to flow in a particular direction as if forced by a pump: *Blood was pumping out of the wound.* **3** [I,T] to be moved or to move sth very quickly up and down or in and out: *He pumped his arms up and down to keep warm.*

PHRASAL VERBS **pump sth into sth/sb** to put a lot of sth into sth/sb: *He pumped all his savings into the business.*

pump sth up to fill sth with air, for example by using a pump: *to pump up a car tyre*

pump² /pʌmp/ **noun** [C] **1** a machine that is used for forcing a gas or liquid in a particular direction: *Have you got a bicycle pump?* ● *a petrol pump* ••➤ picture on page S9 **2** [usually pl] a flat woman's shoe with no fastening: *ballet pumps*

pumpkin /'pʌmpkɪn/ **noun** [C,U] a very large round fruit with thick orange-coloured skin that is cooked and eaten as a vegetable ••➤ picture on page C3

pun /pʌn/ **noun** [C] an amusing use of a word that can have two meanings or of different words that sound the same

punch¹ /pʌntʃ/ **verb** [T] **1 punch sb (in/on sth)** to hit sb/sth hard with your closed hand (fist): *to punch sb on the nose* ● *He punched the air when he heard the good news.* ••➤ picture on page S8 **2** to make a hole in sth with a special tool (a punch): *He punched a hole in the ticket.*

punch² /pʌntʃ/ **noun 1** [C] a hard hit with your closed hand (fist) **2** [C] a machine or tool that you use for making holes in sth: *a ticket punch* ● *a hole punch* ••➤ picture on page S6 **3** [U] a drink made from wine, fruit juice and sugar

IDIOM **pull your punches** → PULL¹

punchline /'pʌntʃlaɪn/ **noun** [C] the last and most important words of a joke or story

'punch-up noun [C] (*Brit informal*) a fight in which people hit each other

★**punctual** /'pʌŋktʃuəl/ **adj** doing sth or happening at the right time; not late: *It is important to be punctual for your classes.*

➤ We say the train, bus, etc was **on time** not punctual.

–**punctuality** /ˌpʌŋktʃu'ælɪti/ **noun** [U]: *Japanese trains are famous for their punctuality.* –**punctually adv**

punctuate /'pʌŋktʃueɪt/ **verb 1** [T] punctuate sth (with sth) to interrupt sth many times: *Her speech was punctuated with bursts of applause.* **2** [I,T] to divide writing into sentences and phrases by adding full stops, question marks, etc

punctuation /ˌpʌŋktʃu'eɪʃn/ **noun** [U] the marks used for dividing writing into sentences and phrases: *Punctuation marks include full stops, commas and question marks.*

puncture /'pʌŋktʃə/ **noun** [C] a small hole made by a sharp point, especially in a bicycle or car tyre –**puncture verb** [I,T]

pungent /'pʌndʒənt/ **adj** (used about a smell) very strong

★**punish** /'pʌnɪʃ/ **verb** [T] punish sb (for sth/ for doing sth) to make sb suffer because he/she has done sth bad or wrong: *The children were severely punished for telling lies.*

punishable /'pʌnɪʃəbl/ **adj** punishable (by sth) (used about a crime, etc) that you can be punished for doing: *a punishable offence* ● *In some countries drug smuggling is punishable by death.*

punishing /'pʌnɪʃɪŋ/ **adj** that makes you very tired or weak: *The Prime Minister had a punishing schedule, visiting five countries in five days.*

★**punishment** /'pʌnɪʃmənt/ **noun** [C,U] the action or way of punishing sb: *He was excluded from school for a week as a punishment.* ● *capital punishment* (= punishment by death)

punitive /'pjuːnətɪv/ **adj** (*formal*) **1** intended as a punishment: *to take punitive measures against sb* **2** very harsh and that people find difficult to pay: *punitive taxation*

punk /pʌŋk/ **noun 1** [U] a type of loud music that was popular in Britain in the late 1970s and early 1980s. Punk deliberately tried to offend people with traditional views and behaviour. **2** [C] a person who likes punk music and often has brightly-coloured hair and unusual clothes

puny /'pjuːni/ **adj** very small and weak

pup /pʌp/ **noun** [C] **1** =PUPPY **2** the young of some animals, for example seals

★**pupil** /'pjuːpl/ **noun** [C] **1** a child in school: *There are 28 pupils in my class.* **2** a person who is taught artistic, musical, etc skills by an expert: *He was a pupil of Liszt.*

➤ Compare **student**.

3 the round black hole in the middle of your eye

puppet /'pʌpɪt/ **noun** [C] **1** a model of a person or animal that you can move by pulling the strings which are tied to it or by putting your hand inside it and moving your fingers **2** a person or organization that is controlled by sb else: *The occupying forces set up a puppet government.*

puppy /'pʌpi/ (also **pup**) **noun** [C] (*pl* **puppies**) a young dog

purchase /'pɜːtʃəs/ **noun** (*formal*) **1** [U] the action of buying sth: *to take out a loan for the purchase of a car* **2** [C] something that you buy: *These shoes were a poor purchase – they're falling apart already.* ● *to make a purchase* –**purchase verb** [T]: *Many employees* *have the opportunity to purchase shares in the company they work for.*

purchaser /'pɜːtʃəsə/ **noun** [C] (*formal*) a person who buys sth: *The purchaser of the house agrees to pay a deposit of 10%.* ••➤ Look at **vendor**.

★**pure** /pjʊə/ **adj 1** not mixed with anything else: *pure orange juice/silk/alcohol* **2** clean and not containing any harmful substances: *pure air/water* ••➤ opposite **impure 3** (only *before* a noun) complete and total: *We met by pure chance.* **4** (used about a sound, colour or light) very clear; perfect: *She was dressed in pure white.* **5** (only *before* a noun) (used about an area of learning) concerned only with increasing your knowledge rather than having practical uses: *pure mathematics* ••➤ opposite **applied 6** not doing or knowing anything evil or anything that is connected with sex: *a young girl still pure in mind and body* ••➤ opposite **impure**

purée /'pjʊəreɪ/ **noun** [C,U] a food that you make by cooking a fruit or vegetable and then pressing and mixing it until it is smooth and liquid: *apple/tomato purée*

purely /'pjʊəli/ **adv** only or completely: *It's not purely a question of money.*

purge /pɜːdʒ/ **verb** [T] **purge sth (of sb)**; **purge sb (from sth)** to remove people that you do not want from a political party or other organization –purge **noun** [C]: *The General carried out a purge of his political enemies.*

purify /'pjʊərɪfaɪ/ **verb** [T] (*pres part* **purifying**; *3rd pers sing pres* **purifies**; *pt, pp* **purified**) to remove dirty or harmful substances from sth: *purified water*

puritan /'pjʊərɪtən/ **noun** [C] a person who thinks that it is wrong to enjoy yourself –puritan (also **puritanical** /ˌpjʊərɪ'tænɪkl/) **adj**: *a puritan attitude to life*

purity /'pjʊərəti/ **noun** [U] the state of being pure: *to test the purity of the air* ••➤ Look at **impurity**.

★**purple** /'pɜːpl/ **adj, noun** [U] (of) a reddish-blue colour: *His face was purple with rage.*

★**purpose** /'pɜːpəs/ **noun 1** [C] the aim or intention of sth: *The main purpose of this meeting is to decide what we should do next.* • *You may only use the telephone for business purposes.* **2 purposes** [pl] what is needed in a particular situation: *For the purposes of this demonstration, I will use model cars.* **3** [U] a meaning or reason that is important to you: *A good leader inspires people with a sense of purpose.* **4** [U] the ability to plan sth and work hard to achieve it: *I was impressed by his strength of purpose.*

| IDIOMS | **to/for all intents and purposes** → INTENT²

on purpose not by accident; with a particular intention: *'You've torn a page out of my book!' 'I'm sorry, I didn't do it on purpose.'* ••➤ synonym **deliberately**

purposeful /'pɜːpəsfl/ **adj** having a definite aim or plan: *Greg strode off down the street looking purposeful.* –purposefully /-fəli/ **adv**

purposely /'pɜːpəsli/ **adv** with a particular intention: *I purposely waited till everyone had gone so that I could speak to you in private.* ••➤ synonym **deliberately**

purr /pɜː/ **verb** [I] (used about a cat) to make a continuous low sound that shows pleasure ••➤ Look at **miaow**.

★**purse¹** /pɜːs/ **noun** [C] **1** a small bag made of leather, etc, for carrying coins and often also paper money, used especially by women ••➤ Look at **wallet**. **2** (*US*) = **HANDBAG** ••➤ picture at **bag**

purse² /pɜːs/ **verb**

| IDIOM | **purse your lips** to press your lips together to show that you do not like sth

★**pursue** /pə'sjuː/ **verb** [T] (*formal*) **1** to follow sb/sth in order to catch him/her/it: *The robber ran off pursued by two policemen.* ••➤ **Pursue** is more formal than **chase**. **2** to try to achieve sth or to continue to do sth over a period of time: *to pursue a career in banking* • *She didn't seem to want to pursue the discussion so I changed the subject.*

pursuer /pə'sjuːə/ **noun** [C] a person who is following and trying to catch sb/sth

pursuit /pə'sjuːt/ **noun 1** [U] the action of trying to achieve or get sth: *the pursuit of pleasure* **2** [C] an activity that you do either for work or for pleasure: *outdoor/leisure pursuits*

| IDIOMS | **in hot pursuit** → HOT¹

in pursuit (of sb/sth) trying to catch or get sb/sth: *He neglected his family in pursuit of his own personal ambitions.*

pus /pʌs/ **noun** [U] a thick yellowish liquid that may form in a part of your body that has been hurt

★**push¹** /pʊʃ/ **verb 1** [I,T] to use force to move sb/sth forward or away from you: *She pushed him into the water.* • *to push a pram* • *She pushed the door shut with her foot.* ••➤ picture at **pull 2** [I,T] to move forward by pushing sb/sth: *John pushed his way through the crowd.* • *to push past sb* • *People were pushing and shoving to try to get to the front.* **3** [I,T] to press a switch, button, etc, for example in order to start a machine: *Push the red button if you want the bus to stop.* **4** [T] **push sb (to do sth/into doing sth)**; **push sb (for sth)** to try to make sb do sth that he/she does not want to do: *My friend pushed me into entering the competition.* • *Ella will not work hard unless you push her.* **5** [T] (*informal*) to try to make sth seem attractive, for example so that people will buy it: *They are launching a major publicity campaign to push their new product.*

| IDIOMS | **be hard pressed/pushed/put to do sth** → HARD²

be pushed for sth (*informal*) to not have enough of sth: *Hurry up. We're really pushed for time.*

| PHRASAL VERBS | **push sb about/around** to give orders to sb in a rude and unpleasant way: *Don't let your boss push you around.*

push ahead/forward (with sth) to continue with sth

push for sth to try hard to get sth: *Jim is pushing for a pay rise.*

push in to join a line of people waiting for sth by standing in front of others who were there before you

push on to continue a journey: *Although it was getting dark, we decided to push on.*

push sb/sth over to make sb/sth fall down by pushing him/her/it

*push² /pʊʃ/ noun [C] an act of pushing: *Can you help me give the car a push to get it started?* • *The car windows opened at the push of a button.*

IDIOMS at a push (*informal*) if it is really necessary (but only with difficulty): *We can get ten people round the table at a push.*

give sb the push to tell sb you no longer want him/her in a relationship, or in a job

'push-button adj (only *before* a noun) (used about a machine, etc) that you work by pressing a button: *a radio with push-button controls*

pushchair /'pʊʃtʃeə/ (*Brit also* buggy) noun [C] a chair on wheels that you use for pushing a young child in ••▸ picture at pram

pusher /'pʊʃə/ noun [C] a person who sells illegal drugs

pushover /'pʊʃəʊvə/ noun [C] (*informal*) 1 something that is easy to do or win 2 a person who is easy to persuade to do sth

'push-up (*US*) = PRESS-UP

pushy /'pʊʃi/ adj (*informal*) (used about a person) trying hard to get what you want, in a way that seems rude: *You need to be pushy to be successful in show business.*

*put /pʊt/ verb [T] (*pres part* putting; *pt, pp* put) 1 to move sb/sth into a particular place or position: *She put the book on the table.* • *Did you put sugar in my tea?* • *When do you put the children to bed?* 2 to fix sth to or in sth else: *Can you put (= sew) a button on this shirt?* • *We're going to put a picture on this wall.* 3 to write sth: *12.30 on Friday? I'll put it in my diary.* • *What did you put for question 2?* 4 put sb/sth in/into sth to bring sb/sth into the state or condition mentioned: *This sort of weather always puts me in a bad mood.* • *I was put in charge of the project.* • *It was time to put our ideas into practice.* 5 to make sb/sth feel sth or be affected by sth: *This will put pressure on them to finish the job quickly.* • *Don't put the blame on me!* • *The new teacher soon put a stop to cheating in tests.* 6 to give or fix a particular value or importance to sb/sth: *We'll have to put a limit on how much we spend.* • *I'd put him in my top five favourite writers.* 7 to say or express sth: *I don't know exactly how to put this, but...* • *To put it another way, you're sacked.* • *Put simply, he just wasn't good enough.*

IDIOMS put it to sb that... (*formal*) to suggest to sb that sth is true: *I put it to you that this man is innocent.*

put together (used after a noun or nouns referring to a group of people or things) combined; in total: *You got more presents than the rest of the family put together.*

➤ For other idioms containing put, look at the entries for the nouns, adjectives, etc, for example put an end to sth is at end.

PHRASAL VERBS put sth/yourself across/over to say what you want to say clearly, so that people can understand it: *He didn't put his ideas across very well at the meeting.*

put sth aside 1 to save sth, especially money, to use later 2 to ignore or forget sth: *We agreed to put aside our differences and work together.*

put sb away (*informal*) to send sb to prison

put sth away 1 to put sth where you usually keep it because you have finished using it: *Put the tools away if you've finished with them.* 2 to save money to spend later

put sth back 1 to return sth to its place: *to put books back on the shelf* 2 to move sth to a later time: *The meeting's been put back until next week.* ••▸ opposite bring sth forward 3 to change the time shown on a clock to an earlier time: *We have to put the clocks back tonight.* ••▸ opposite put sth forward

put sb/sth before/above sb/sth to treat sb/sth as more important than sb/sth else: *He puts his children before anything else.*

put sth by to save money to use later: *Her grandparents had put some money by for her wedding.*

put sb down 1 (*informal*) to say things to make sb seem stupid or foolish: *He's always putting his wife down.* 2 to put a baby to bed

put sth down 1 to stop holding sth and put it on the floor, a table, etc: *The policeman persuaded him to put the gun down.* 2 to write sth: *I'll put that down in my diary.* 3 to pay part of the cost of sth: *We put down a 10% deposit on a car.* 4 (used about a government, an army or the police) to stop sth by force: *to put down a rebellion* 5 to kill an animal because it is old, sick or dangerous: *The dog was put down after it attacked a child.*

put sth down to sth to believe that sth is caused by sth: *I put his bad exam results down to laziness rather than a lack of ability.*

put yourself/sb forward to suggest that you or another person should be considered for a job, etc: *His name was put forward for the position of chairman.*

put sth forward 1 to change the time shown on a clock to a later time: *We put the clocks forward in spring.* ••▸ opposite put sth back 2 to suggest sth: *She put forward a plan to help the homeless.*

put sth in 1 to fix equipment or furniture in position so that it can be used: *We're having a shower put in.* ••▸ synonym install 2 to include a piece of information, etc in sth that you write: *In your letter, you forgot to put in the time your plane would arrive.* 3 to ask for sth officially: *to put in an invoice/request*

put sth in; put sth into sth/into doing sth to spend time, etc on sth: *She puts all her time and energy into her business.*

put sb off (sb/sth/doing sth) 1 to make sb not like sb/sth or not want to do sth: *The accident*

p

put me off driving for a long time. **2** to say to a person that you can no longer do what you had agreed: *They were coming to stay last weekend but I had to put them off at the last moment.* **3** to make sb unable to give his/her attention to sth: *Don't stare at me – you're putting me off!*

put sth off to turn or switch a light off: *She put off the light and went to sleep.*

put sth off; put off doing sth to move sth to a later time; to delay doing sth: *She put off writing her essay until the last minute.*

put sth on **1** to dress yourself in sth: *Put on your coat!* • *I'll have to put my glasses on.* **2** to cover an area of your skin with sth: *You'd better put some sun cream on.* **3** to switch on a piece of electrical equipment: *It's too early to put the lights on yet.* **4** to make a tape, a CD, etc begin to play: *Let's put some music on.* **5** to become fatter or heavier: *I put on weight very easily.* ••➤ opposite **lose** **6** to organize or prepare sth for people to see or use: *The school is putting on 'Macbeth'.* • *They put on extra trains in the summer.* **7** to pretend to be feeling sth; to pretend to have sth: *He's not angry with you really: he's just putting it on.*

put sth on sth **1** to add an amount of money, etc to the cost or value of sth: *The government want to put more tax on the price of a packet of cigarettes.* **2** to bet money on sth: *He put all his money on a horse.* ••➤ synonym **bet**

put sb out **1** to give sb trouble or extra work: *He put his hosts out by arriving very late.* **2** to make sb upset or angry: *I was quite put out by their selfish behaviour.*

put sth out **1** to make sth stop burning: *to put out a fire* ••➤ synonym **extinguish** **2** to switch off a piece of electrical equipment: *They put out the lights and locked the door.* **3** to take sth out of your house and leave it: *to put the rubbish out* **4** to give or tell the public sth, often on the television or radio or in newspapers: *The police put out a warning about the escaped prisoner.*

put yourself out (*informal*) to do sth for sb, even though it brings you trouble or extra work: *'I'll give you a lift home.' 'I don't want to put yourself out. I'll take a taxi.'*

put sth/yourself over ➔ **PUT STH/YOURSELF ACROSS/OVER**

put sb through sth to make sb experience sth unpleasant

put sb/sth through to make a telephone connection that allows sb to speak to sb: *Could you put me through to Jeanne, please?*

put sth to sb to suggest sth to sb; to ask sb sth: *I put the question to her.*

put sth together to build or repair sth by joining its parts together: *The furniture comes with instructions on how to put it together.*

put sth towards sth to give money to pay part of the cost of sth: *We all put a pound towards a leaving present for Joe.*

put sb up to give sb food and a place to stay: *She had missed the last train home, so I offered to put her up for the night.*

put sth up **1** to lift or hold sth up: *Put your*

hand up if you know the answer.* **2** to build sth: *to put up a fence/tent* **3** to fix sth to a wall, etc so that everyone can see it: *to put up a notice* **4** to increase sth: *Some shops put up their prices just before Christmas.*

put up sth to try to stop sb attacking you: *The old lady put up a struggle against her attacker.*

put up with sb/sth to suffer sb/sth unpleasant and not complain about it: *I don't know how they put up with this noise.*

putt /pʌt/ **verb** [I,T] (used in golf) to hit the ball gently when it is near the hole

putty /'pʌti/ **noun** [U] a soft substance that is used for fixing glass into windows that becomes hard when dry

puzzle¹ /'pʌzl/ **noun** [C] **1** [usually sing] something that is difficult to understand or explain; a mystery: *The reasons for his actions have remained a puzzle to historians.* **2** a game or toy that makes you think a lot: *a crossword/jigsaw puzzle* • *I like to do puzzles.*

puzzle² /'pʌzl/ **verb** **1** [T] to make sb feel confused because he/she does not understand sth: *Her strange illness puzzled all the experts.* **2** [I] puzzle over sth to think hard about sth in order to understand or explain it: *to puzzle over a mathematical problem*

PHRASAL VERB **puzzle sth out** to find the answer to sth by thinking hard: *The letter was in Italian and it took us an hour to puzzle out what it said.*

puzzled /'pʌzld/ **adj** not able to understand or explain sth: *a puzzled expression*

★**pyjamas** (*US* **pajamas**) /pə'dʒɑːməz/ **noun** [pl] loose trousers and a loose jacket or T-shirt that you wear in bed ••➤ Notice that you use **pyjama** (without an 's') before another noun: *pyjama trousers*

pylon /'paɪlən/ **noun** [C] a tall metal tower that supports heavy electrical wires

pyramid /'pɪrəmɪd/ **noun** [C] a shape with a flat base and three or four sides in the shape of triangles ••➤ picture at **cube**

python /'paɪθən/ **noun** [C] a large snake that kills animals by squeezing them very hard

Q, q¹ /kjuː/ **noun** [C] (*pl* **Q's**; **q's** /kjuːz/) the seventeenth letter of the English alphabet: *'Queen' begins with (a) 'Q'.*

Q² *abbr* question: *Qs 1-5 are compulsory.*

qt *abbr* quart(s)

quack /kwæk/ **noun** [C] the sound that a duck makes –**quack verb** [I]

quadrangle /'kwɒdræŋgl/ (also **quad**) **noun** [C] a square open area with buildings round it in a school, college, etc

quadruple /'kwɒdrʊpl/ verb [I,T] to multiply or be multiplied by four

quaint /kweɪnt/ adj attractive or unusual because it seems to belong to the past

quake /kweɪk/ verb [I] (used about a person) to shake: *to quake with fear* –quake noun [C] (*informal*) = **EARTHQUAKE**

*★**qualification** /ˌkwɒlɪfɪˈkeɪʃn/ noun **1** [C] an exam that you have passed or a course of study that you have completed: *to have a teaching/nursing qualification* ● *She left school at 16 with no formal qualifications.* **2** [C] a skill or quality that you need to do a particular job: *Is there a height qualification for the police force?* **3** [C,U] something that limits the meaning of a general statement or makes it weaker: *I can recommend him for the job without qualification.* ● *She accepted the proposal with only a few qualifications.* **4** [U] the fact of doing what is necessary in order to be able to do a job, play in a competition, etc

qualified /'kwɒlɪfaɪd/ adj **1** qualified (for sth/to do sth) having passed an exam or having the knowledge, experience, etc in order to be able to do sth: *Edward is well qualified for this job.* ● *a fully qualified doctor* ● *I don't feel qualified to comment – I know nothing about the subject.* **2** not complete; limited: *My boss gave only qualified approval to the plan.* •► opposite **unqualified**

*★**qualify** /'kwɒlɪfaɪ/ verb (pres part qualifying; 3rd pers sing pres qualifies; pt, pp qualified) **1** [I] qualify (as sth) to pass the examination that is necessary to do a particular job; to have the qualities that are necessary for sth: *It takes five years to qualify as a vet.* ● *A cup of coffee and a sandwich doesn't really qualify as a meal.* **2** [I,T] qualify (sb) (for sth/to do sth) to have or give sb the right to have or do sth: *How many years must you work to qualify for a pension?* ● *This exam will qualify me to teach music.* **3** [I] qualify (for sth) to win the right to enter a competition or continue to the next part: *Our team has qualified for the final.* **4** [T] to limit the meaning of a general statement or make it weaker

*★**quality** /'kwɒləti/ noun (pl qualities) **1** [U, sing] how good or bad sth is: *This paper isn't very good quality.* ● *to be of good/poor/top quality* ● *goods of a high quality* ● *high-quality goods* ● *the quality of life in our cities* **2** [U] a high standard or level: *Aim for quality rather than quantity in your writing.* **3** [C] something that is typical of a person or thing: *Vicky has all the qualities of a good manager.*

qualm /kwɑːm/ noun [C,usually pl] a feeling of doubt or worry that what you are doing may not be morally right: *I don't have any qualms about asking them to lend us some money.*

quandary /'kwɒndəri/ noun [C,usually sing] a state of not being able to decide what to do; a difficult situation: *I'm in a quandary – should I ask her or not?*

*★**quantity** /'kwɒntəti/ noun (pl quantities) [C,U] **1** a number or an amount of sth: *Add a small quantity of salt.* ● *It's cheaper to buy goods in large quantities.* **2** a large number or amount of sth: *It's cheaper to buy goods in quantity.*

◾️IDIOM◾️ an unknown quantity → **UNKNOWN**[1]

quarantine /'kwɒrəntiːn/ noun [U] a period of time when a person or animal that has or may have an infectious disease must be kept away from other people or animals

*★**quarrel**[1] /'kwɒrəl/ noun [C] **1** a quarrel (about/over sth) an angry argument or disagreement: *We sometimes have a quarrel about who should do the washing-up.* •► Look at **argument** and **fight**[2](3). **2** a quarrel with sb/sth a reason for complaining about or disagreeing with sb/sth: *I have no quarrel with what has just been said.*

*★**quarrel**[2] /'kwɒrəl/ verb [I] (quarrelling; quarrelled: *US* quarreling; quarreled) **1** quarrel (with sb) (about/over sth) to have an angry argument or disagreement: *The children are always quarrelling!* ● *I don't want to quarrel with you about it.* •► Look at **argue** and **fight**[1](4). **2** quarrel with sth to disagree with sth

quarry[1] /'kwɒri/ noun (pl quarries) **1** [C] a place where sand, stone, etc is dug out of the ground •► Look at **mine**. **2** [sing] a person or animal that is being hunted

quarry[2] /'kwɒri/ verb [I,T] (pres part quarrying; 3rd pers sing pres quarries; pt, pp quarried) to dig, stone, sand, etc out of the ground: *to quarry for marble*

quart /kwɔːt/ noun [C] (abbr qt) a measure of liquid; 1·14 litres. There are 2 pints in a quart.

> An American quart is 0·94 of a litre.

*★**quarter** /'kwɔːtə/ noun **1** [C] one of four equal parts of sth: *The programme lasts for three quarters of an hour.* ● *a mile and a quarter* ● *to cut an apple into quarters* **2** [sing] fifteen minutes before or after every hour: *I'll meet you at (a) quarter past six.* ● *It's (a) quarter to three.*

> In US English you say '(a) quarter **after**' and '(a) quarter **of**': *I'll meet you at (a) quarter after six.* ● *It's a quarter of three.*

3 [C] a period of three months: *You get a gas bill every quarter.* **4** [C] a part of a town, especially a part where a particular group of people live: *the Chinese quarter of the city* **5** [C] a person or group of people who may give help or information or who have certain opinions **6** [C] (in the US or Canada) a coin that is worth 25 cents (¼ dollar) **7** quarters [pl] a place that is provided for people, especially soldiers, to live in **8** [C] four ounces of sth; ¼ of a pound: *a quarter of mushrooms*

◾️IDIOM◾️ at close quarters → **CLOSE**[3]

quarter-'final noun [C] one of the four matches between the eight players or teams left in a competition •► Look at **semi-final**.

quarterly /'kwɔːtəli/ adj, adv (produced or happening) once every three months: *a quarterly magazine*

quartet /kwɔːˈtet/ noun [C] **1** four people who

---

sing or play music together **2** a piece of music for four people to sing or play together

quartz /kwɔːts/ *noun* [U] a type of hard rock that is used in making very accurate clocks or watches

quash /kwɒʃ/ *verb* [T] (*formal*) **1** to say that an official decision is no longer true or legal **2** to stop or defeat sth by force: *to quash a rebellion*

quay /kiː/ *noun* [C] a platform where goods and passengers are loaded on and off boats

quayside /ˈkiːsaɪd/ *noun* [sing] the area of land that is near a quay

★**queen** /kwiːn/ *noun* [C] **1** (also **Queen**) the female ruler of a country: *Queen Elizabeth II* (= the second) •➤ Look at **king**, **prince** and **princess**. **2** (also **Queen**) the wife of a king **3** the largest and most important female in a group of insects: *the queen bee* **4** one of the four playing cards in a pack with a picture of a queen: *the queen of hearts* •➤ Look at the note and picture at **card**. **5** (in chess) the most powerful piece, that can move any distance and in all directions

quell /kwel/ *verb* [T] (*formal*) to end sth

quench /kwentʃ/ *verb* [T] to satisfy your feeling of thirst by drinking liquid: *He drank some juice to quench his thirst.*

query /ˈkwɪəri/ *noun* [C] (*pl* **queries**) a question, especially one asking for information or expressing a doubt about sth: *Does anyone have any queries?* –**query** *verb* [T] (*pres part* querying; *3rd pers sing pres* queries; *pt, pp* queried): *We queried the bill but were told it was correct.*

quest /kwest/ *noun* [C] (*formal*) a long search for sth that is difficult to find: *the quest for happiness/knowledge/truth*

★**question**¹ /ˈkwestʃən/ *noun* **1** [C] a question (about/on sth) a sentence or phrase that asks for an answer: *Put up your hand if you want to ask a question.* • *In the examination, you must answer five questions in one hour.* • *What's the answer to Question 5?* **2** [C] a problem or difficulty that needs to be discussed or dealt with: *The resignations raise the question of who will take over.* • *The question is, how are we going to raise the money?* **3** [U] doubt or uncertainty: *There is no question about Brenda's enthusiasm for the job.* • *His honesty is beyond question.* • *The results of the report were accepted without question.*

IDIOMS (be) a question of sth/of doing sth a situation in which sth is needed: *It's not difficult – it's just a question of finding the time to do it.*

in question that is being considered or talked about: *The lawyer asked where she was on the night in question.*

no question of no possibility of: *There is no question of him leaving hospital yet.*

out of the question impossible: *A new car is out of the question. It's just too expensive.*

★**question**² /ˈkwestʃən/ *verb* [T] **1** question sb (about/on sth) to ask sb a question or questions: *the police questioned him for sev-*

eral hours. **2** to express or feel doubt about sth: *She told me she was from the council so I didn't question her right to be there.* • *to question sb's sincerity/honesty*

questionable /ˈkwestʃənəbl/ *adj* **1** that you have doubts about; not certain: *It's questionable whether we'll be able to finish in time* **2** likely to be dishonest or morally wrong: *questionable motives* ••➤ opposite **unquestionable**

ˈ**question mark** *noun* [C] the sign (?) that you use when you write a question

questionnaire /ˌkwestʃəˈneə/ *noun* [C] a list of questions that are answered by many people. A questionnaire is used to collect information about a particular subject: *to complete/fill in a questionnaire*

ˈ**question tag** (also **tag**) *noun* [C] a short phrase such as 'isn't it?' or 'did you?' at the end of a sentence that changes it into a question and is often used to ask sb to agree with you

★**queue** /kjuː/ (*US* **line**) *noun* [C] a line of people, cars, etc that are waiting for sth or to do sth: *We had to wait in a queue for hours to get tickets.* • *to join the end of a queue* • *We were told to form a queue outside the doors.* –**queue** *verb* [I] queue (up) (for sth): *to queue for a bus*

IDIOM jump the queue → **JUMP**¹

quiche /kiːʃ/ *noun* [C,U] a type of food made of pastry filled with a mixture of eggs and milk with cheese, onion, etc and cooked in the oven. You can eat quiche hot or cold ••➤ picture on page C4

★**quick**¹ /kwɪk/ *adj* **1** done with speed; taking or lasting a short time: *May I make a quick telephone call?* • *This dish is quick and easy to make.* • *His quick thinking saved her life* • *We need to make a quick decision.* **2** quick (to do sth) doing sth at speed or in a short time: *It's quicker to travel by train.* • *Nicola is a quick worker.* • *She was quick to point out all the mistakes I had made.*

➤ **Fast** is more often used for describing a person or thing that moves or can move at great speed: *a fast horse/car/runner.* **Quick** is more often used for describing sth that is done in a short time: *a quick decision/visit.*

3 used to form compound adjectives: *quick-thinking* • *quick-drying paint*

IDIOMS (as) quick as a flash very quickly: *Quick as a flash, he grabbed my money and ran.*

quick/slow on the uptake → **UPTAKE**

quick² /kwɪk/ *adv* (*informal*) quickly: *Come over here quick!*

★**quickly** /ˈkwɪkli/ *adv* fast; in a short time: *He quickly undressed and got into bed.* • *I'd like you to get here as quickly as possible.*

quid /kwɪd/ *noun* [C] (*pl* **quid**) (*Brit informal*) a pound (in money); £1: *Can you lend me a couple of quid until tomorrow?*

★**quiet**¹ /ˈkwaɪət/ *adj* **1** with very little or no noise: *Be quiet!* • *His voice was quiet but firm.* • *Go into the library if you want to work. It's*

q

much quieter in there. ·→ opposite **loud**
2 without much activity or many people: *The
streets are very quiet on Sundays.* ● *Business
is quiet at this time of year.* ● *a quiet country
village* ● *We lead a quiet life.* **3** (used about a
person) not talking very much: *You're very
quiet today. Is anything wrong?* ● *He's very
quiet and shy.* –quietly **adv**: *Try and shut the
door quietly!* –quietness **noun** [U]
IDIOM **keep quiet about sth; keep sth quiet** to
say nothing about sth: *Would you keep quiet
about me leaving until I've told the boss?*

quiet² /ˈkwaɪət/ **noun** [U] the state of being
calm and without much noise or activity: *the
peace and quiet of the countryside*
IDIOM **on the quiet** secretly: *She's given up
smoking but she still has an occasional cigarette on the quiet.*

quieten /ˈkwaɪətn/ **verb** [T] to make sb/sth
quiet
PHRASAL VERB **quieten (sb/sth) down** to
become quiet or to make sb/sth quiet: *When
you've quietened down, I'll tell you what happened.*

quilt /kwɪlt/ **noun** [C] a cover for a bed that
has a thick warm material, for example feathers, inside it ·→ Look at **duvet**.

quintet /kwɪnˈtet/ **noun** [C] **1** a group of five
people who sing or play music together **2** a
piece of music for five people to sing or play
together

quirk /kwɜːk/ **noun** [C] **1** an aspect of sb's
character or behaviour that is strange: *You'll
soon get used to the boss's little quirks.* **2** a
strange thing that happens by chance: *By a
strange quirk of fate they met again several
years later.* –quirky **adj**: *Some people don't like
his quirky sense of humour.*

quit /kwɪt/ **verb** (*pres part* **quitting**; *pt, pp*
quit) **1** [I,T] **quit (as sth)** to leave a job, etc or
to go away from a place: *She quit as manager
of the volleyball team.* **2** [T] (*especially US
informal*) to stop doing sth: *to quit smoking*
3 [I,T] (*computing*) to close a computer program

★ **quite** /kwaɪt/ **adv 1** not very; to a certain
degree; rather: *The film's quite good.* ● *It's
quite a good film.* ● *I quite enjoy cooking.*
● *They had to wait quite a long time.* ● *It's
quite cold today.* ● *We still meet up quite often.*
·→ Look at the note at **rather**. **2** (used for
emphasizing sth) completely; very: *Are you
quite sure you don't mind?* ● *I quite agree –
you're quite right.* ● *To my surprise, the room
was quite empty.* **3** used for showing that you
agree with or understand sth
IDIOMS **not quite** used for showing that there
is almost enough of sth, or that it is almost
suitable: *There's not quite enough bread for
breakfast.* ● *These shoes don't quite fit.*
quite a used for showing that sth is unusual:
It's quite a climb to the top of the hill.
quite a few; quite a lot (of) a fairly large
amount or number: *We've received quite a few
enquiries.*
quite enough used for emphasizing that no

more of sth is wanted or needed: *I've had
quite enough of listening to you two arguing!*
● *That's quite enough wine, thanks.*

quits /kwɪts/ **adj**
IDIOM **be quits (with sb)** (*informal*) if two
people are quits, it means that neither of
them owes the other anything: *You buy me a
drink and then we're quits.*

quiver /ˈkwɪvə/ **verb** [I] to shake slightly;
tremble: *to quiver with rage/excitement/fear*

quiz¹ /kwɪz/ **noun** [C] (*pl* **quizzes**) a game or
competition in which you have to answer
questions: *a quiz programme on TV* ● *a general knowledge quiz*

quiz² /kwɪz/ (*3rd pers sing pres* **quizzes**;
pres part **quizzing**; *pt* **quizzed**) **verb** [T] to
ask sb a lot of questions in order to get
information

quizzical /ˈkwɪzɪkl/ **adj** (used about a look,
smile, etc) seeming to ask a question
–quizzically /-kli/ **adv**

quorum /ˈkwɔːrəm/ **noun** [sing] the smallest
number of people that must be at a meeting
before it can make official decisions

quota /ˈkwəʊtə/ **noun** [C] the number or
amount of sth that is allowed or that you
must do: *We have a fixed quota of work to get
through each day.*

quotation /kwəʊˈteɪʃn/ (also *informal*
quote) **noun** [C] **1** a phrase from a book,
speech, play, etc, that sb repeats because it is
interesting or useful: *a quotation from
Shakespeare* **2** a statement that says how
much a piece of work will probably cost: *You
should get quotations from three different
builders.* ·→ Look at **estimate**.

quoˈtation marks (also *informal* **quotes**
Brit also **inverted commas**) **noun** [pl] the
signs ('...') or ("...") that you put around a
word, a sentence, etc to show that it is what
sb said or wrote, or that it is a title or that you
are using it in a special way

quote /kwəʊt/ **verb 1** [I,T] **quote (sth) (from
sb/sth)** to repeat exactly sth that sb else has
said or written before: *The minister asked the
newspaper not to quote him.* **2** [T] to give sth
as an example to support what you are saying **3** [T] to say what the cost of a piece of
work, etc will probably be

··

Rr

··

R, r¹ /ɑː/ **noun** [C] (*pl* **R's; r's**) the eighteenth
letter of the English alphabet: *'Rabbit' begins
with an 'R'.*

R² **abbr** river: *R Thames*

rabbi /ˈræbaɪ/ **noun** [C] (*pl* **rabbis**) a Jewish
religious leader and teacher of Jewish law

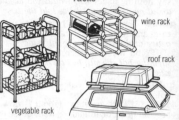

hare

rabbit

★**rabbit** /'ræbɪt/ **noun** [C] a small animal with long ears: *a wild rabbit* • *a rabbit hutch* (= a cage for rabbits)

> ➤ The children's word for a rabbit is **bunny**.

rabble /'ræbl/ **noun** [C] a noisy crowd of people who are or may become violent

rabies /'reɪbiːz/ **noun** [U] a very dangerous disease that a person can get if he/she is bitten by an animal that has the disease

RAC /ˌɑːr eɪ 'siː/ **abbr** (*Brit*) the Royal Automobile Club; an organization for motorists. If you are a member of the RAC and your car breaks down, you can phone them and they will send sb to help you.

★**race**[1] /reɪs/ **noun 1** [C] a race (against/with sb/sth); a race for sth/to do sth a competition between people, animals, cars etc to see which is the fastest or to see which can achieve sth first: *to run/win/lose a race* • *to come first/second/last in a race* • *the race for the presidency* • *the race to find a cure for Aids* • *Rescuing victims of the earthquake is now a race against time.* **2 the races** [pl] (*Brit*) an occasion when a number of horse races are held in one place

> ➤ In Britain going to horse races and dog races is very popular. People often **bet** with a **bookie** on the result of a race.

3 [C,U] one of the groups into which people can be divided according to the colour of their skin, their hair type, the shape of their face, etc ••➤ Look at **human race**. **4** [C] a group of people who have the same language, customs, history, etc

IDIOM **the rat race** ➔ **RAT**

★**race**[2] /reɪs/ **verb 1** [I,T] race (against/with) (sb/sth) to have a competition with sb/sth to find out who is the fastest or to see who can do sth first: *I'll race you home.* **2** [I,T] to go very fast or to move sb/sth very fast: *We raced up the stairs.* • *The child had to be raced to hospital.* **3** [T] to make an animal or a vehicle take part in a race

racecourse /'reɪskɔːs/ (*US* **racetrack**) **noun** [C] a place where horse races take place

racehorse /'reɪshɔːs/ **noun** [C] a horse that is trained to run in races

‚**race re'lations noun** [pl] the relations between people of different races who live in the same town, area, etc

racial /'reɪʃl/ **adj** connected with people's race; happening between people of different races: *racial tension/discrimination* –**racially** /-ʃəli/ **adv**: *a racially mixed school*

★**racing** /'reɪsɪŋ/ **noun** [U] **1** = HORSE RACIN **2** the sport of taking part in races: *moto racing* • *a racing driver/car*

racism /'reɪsɪzəm/ **noun** [U] the belief tha some races of people are better than others unfair ways of treating people that show thi belief: *to take measures to combat racisn* –**racist** /'reɪsɪst/ **noun** [C], **adj**: *He's a racis* • *racist beliefs/views/remarks*

racks

wine rack

roof rack

vegetable rack

rack[1] /ræk/ **noun** [C] (often in compounds) a piece of equipment, usually made of bars that you can put things in or on: *I got on the train and put my bags up in the luggage rack* • *We need a roof rack on the car for all thi luggage.*

IDIOM **go to rack and ruin** to be in or get into a bad state because of a lack of care

rack[2] /ræk/ **verb**

IDIOM **rack your brains** to try hard to think o sth or remember sth

racket /'rækɪt/ **noun 1** [sing] (*informal*) a loud noise: *Stop making that terrible racket* **2** [C] an illegal way of making money: *c drugs racket* **3** (also **racquet**) [C] a piece o sports equipment that you use to hit the bal with in sports such as tennis and badmintor

> ➤ Rackets are different from **bats** because they have **strings**.

••➤ picture on page S2

radar /'reɪdɑː/ **noun** [U] a system that uses radio waves for finding the position of moving objects, for example ships and planes *This plane is hard to detect by radar.*

radiant /'reɪdiənt/ **adj 1** showing great happiness: *a radiant smile* **2** sending out light or heat: *the radiant heat/energy of the sun*

radiate /'reɪdieɪt/ **verb 1** [T] (used about people) to clearly show a particular quality or emotion in your appearance or behaviour: *She radiated self-confidence in the interview.* **2** [T] to send out light or heat **3** [I] to go out in all directions from a central point: *Narrow streets radiate from the village square.*

radiation /ˌreɪdi'eɪʃn/ **noun** [U] **1** powerful and very dangerous rays that are sent out from certain substances. You cannot see or feel radiation but it can cause serious illness or death ••➤ Look at **radioactive**. **2** heat, light or energy that is sent out from sth: *ultraviolet radiation*

radiator /'reɪdieɪtə/ **noun** [C] **1** a piece of equipment that is usually fixed to the wall and is used for heating a room. Radiators are made of metal and filled with hot water. •➤ picture on page C7 **2** a piece of equipment that is used for keeping a car engine cool

radical[1] /'rædɪkl/ **adj 1** (used about changes in sth) very great; complete: *The tax system needs radical reform.* • *radical change* **2** wanting great social or political change: *to have radical views* •➤ Look at **moderate**[1](2) and **extreme**[3]. –**radically** /-kli/ **adv**: *The First World War radically altered the political map of Europe.*

radical[2] /'rædɪkl/ **noun** [C] a person who wants great social or political change •➤ Look at **moderate**[3] and **extremist**.

radio /'reɪdiəʊ/ **noun** (*pl* **radios**) **1** (often **the radio**) [U,sing] the activity of sending out programmes for people to listen to on their radios: *I always listen to the radio in the car.* • *I heard an interesting report on the radio this morning.* • *a radio station/programme* • *national/local radio* **2** [C] a piece of equipment that is used for receiving and/or sending radio messages or programmes (on a ship, plane, etc or in your house)

> ➤ You may **put**, **switch** or **turn** a radio **on** or **off**. You may also **turn** it **up** or **down** to make it louder or quieter.

•➤ picture on page S9 **3** [U] the sending or receiving of messages through the air by electrical signals: *to keep in radio contact* • *radio signals/waves* –**radio** verb [I,T] (*pt, pp* **radioed**)

radioactive /,reɪdiəʊ'æktɪv/ **adj** sending out powerful and very dangerous rays that are produced when atoms are broken up. These rays cannot be seen or felt but can cause serious illness or death: *the problem of the disposal of radioactive waste from power stations* •➤ Look at **radiation**. –**radioactivity** /,reɪdiəʊæk'tɪvəti/ **noun** [U]

radiographer /,reɪdi'ɒɡrəfə/ **noun** [C] a person who is trained to take pictures of your bones, etc (X-rays) in a hospital or to use them for the treatment of certain illnesses

radish /'rædɪʃ/ **noun** [C] a small red vegetable that is white inside with a strong taste. You eat radishes in salads. •➤ picture on page C3

radius /'reɪdiəs/ **noun** [C] (*pl* **radii**) /-dɪaɪ/ **1** the distance from the centre of a circle to the outside edge •➤ Look at **diameter** and **circumference**. •➤ picture at **circle 2** a circular area that is measured from a point in its centre: *The wreckage of the plane was scattered over a radius of several miles.*

RAF /,ɑːr eɪ 'ef; ræf/ **abbr** (*Brit*) the Royal Air Force

raffle /'ræfl/ **noun** [C] a way of making money for a charity or a project by selling tickets with numbers on them. Later some numbers are chosen and the tickets with these numbers win prizes.

raft /rɑːft/ **noun** [C] a flat structure made of pieces of wood tied together and used as a boat or a floating platform

rafter /'rɑːftə/ **noun** [C] one of the long pieces of wood that support a roof

rag /ræɡ/ **noun 1** [C,U] a small piece of old cloth that you use for cleaning **2 rags** [pl] clothes that are very old and torn

rage[1] /reɪdʒ/ **noun** [C,U] a feeling of violent anger that is difficult to control: *He was trembling with rage.* • *to fly into a rage*

rage[2] /reɪdʒ/ **verb** [I] **1 rage** (at/against/ about sb/sth) to show great anger about sth, especially by shouting: *He raged against the injustice of it all.* **2** (used about a battle, disease, storm, etc) to continue with great force: *The battle raged for several days.* –**raging** adj (only *before* a noun): *a raging headache*

ragged /'ræɡɪd/ **adj 1** (used about clothes) old and torn **2** not straight; untidy: *a ragged edge/coastline*

raid /reɪd/ **noun** [C] a **raid** (on sth) **1** a short surprise attack on an enemy by soldiers, ships or aircraft: *an air raid* **2** a surprise visit by the police looking for criminals or illegal goods **3** a surprise attack on a building in order to steal sth: *a bank raid* –**raid** verb [T]: *Police raided the club at dawn this morning.*

rail /reɪl/ **noun 1** [C] a wooden or metal bar fixed to a wall, which you can hang things on: *a towel/curtain/picture rail* •➤ picture on page C7 **2** [C] a bar which you can hold to stop you from falling (on stairs, from a building, etc) **3** [C, usually pl] each of the two metal bars that form the track that trains run on **4** [U] the railway system; trains as a means of transport: *rail travel/services/fares*

railcard /'reɪlkɑːd/ **noun** [C] (*Brit*) a special card that allows you to buy train tickets at a lower price if you are an old person, student, etc

railing /'reɪlɪŋ/ **noun** [C, usually pl] a fence (around a park, garden, etc) that is made of metal bars

railway /'reɪlweɪ/ (*US* **railroad**) **noun** [C] **1** (*Brit* **railway line**) the metal lines on which trains travel between one place and another **2** the whole system of tracks, the trains and the organization and people needed to operate them: *He works on the railways.* • *a railway engine/company*

'railway station = **STATION**[1](1)

rain[1] /reɪn/ **noun 1** [U] the water that falls from the sky: *Take your umbrella, it looks like rain* (= as if it is going to rain). • *It's pouring with rain* (= the rain is very heavy). •➤ Look at **shower** (3) and **acid rain** and the note at **weather**. **2 rains** [pl] (in tropical countries) the time of the year when there is a lot of rain

IDIOM **(as) right as rain** → **RIGHT**[1]

rain[2] /reɪn/ **verb 1** [I] (used with *it*) to fall as rain: *Oh no! It's raining again!* • *Is it raining hard?* • *We'll go out when it stops raining.* **2** [I,T] **rain** (sth) (down) (on sb/sth) to fall or make sth fall on sb/sth in large quantities: *Bombs rained down on the city.*

PHRASAL VERB **be rained off** to be cancelled or

r

to have to stop because it is raining: *The tennis was rained off.*

rainbow /'reɪnbəʊ/ noun [C] an arch of many colours that sometimes appears in the sky when the sun shines through rain

'rain check noun (*especially US*)

IDIOM **take a rain check on sth** (*spoken*) to refuse an invitation or offer but say that you might accept it later

raincoat /'reɪnkəʊt/ noun [C] a long light coat which keeps you dry in the rain

raindrop /'reɪndrɒp/ noun [C] a single drop of rain

rainfall /'reɪnfɔːl/ noun [U,sing] the total amount of rain that falls in a particular place during a month, year, etc

rainforest /'reɪnfɒrɪst/ noun [C] a thick forest in tropical parts of the world that have a lot of rain: *the Amazon rainforest*

rainy /'reɪni/ adj having or bringing a lot of rain: *a rainy day • the rainy season*

IDIOM **keep/save sth for a rainy day** to save sth, especially money, for a time when you really need it

★**raise** /reɪz/ verb [T] **1** to lift sth up: *If you want to leave the room raise your hand. • He raised himself up on one elbow.* **2 raise sth (to sth)** to increase the level of sth or to make sth better or stronger: *to raise taxes/salaries/prices • The hotel needs to raise its standards. • There's no need to raise your voice* (= speak loudly or angrily). •➤ opposite for senses 1 and 2 **lower 3** to get money from people for a particular purpose: *We are doing a sponsored walk to raise money for charity. • a fund-raising event* **4** to introduce a subject that needs to be talked about or dealt with: *I would like to raise the subject of money. • This raises the question of why nothing was done before.* **5** to cause a particular reaction or emotion: *The neighbours raised the alarm* (= told everybody there was a fire/an emergency) *when they saw smoke coming out of the window. • to raise hopes/fears/suspicions in people's minds* **6** to look after a child or an animal until he/she is an adult: *You can't raise a family on what I earn.* •➤ Look at **bring sb up. 7** to breed animals or grow a particular plant for a specific purpose

IDIOM **raise your eyebrows** to show that you are surprised or that you do not approve of sth

raisin /'reɪzn/ noun [C] a dried grape, used in cakes, etc •➤ Look at **sultana.**

rake /reɪk/ noun [C] a garden tool with a long handle and a row of metal teeth, used for collecting leaves or making the earth smooth •➤ picture at **garden** –rake verb [T]: *to rake up the leaves*

PHRASAL VERBS **rake sth in** (*informal*) to earn a lot of money, especially when it is done easily: *She's been raking it in since she got promoted.*

rake sth up to start talking about sth that it would be better to forget: *Don't rake up all those old stories again.*

rally[1] /'ræli/ noun [C] (*pl* **rallies**) **1** a large public meeting, especially one held to support a political idea: *a peace rally* **2** (*Brit*) race for cars or motorbikes on public road **3** (used in tennis and similar sports) a series of hits of the ball before a point is won

rally[2] /'ræli/ verb (*pres part* **rallying**; *3rd pers sing pres* **rallies**; *pt, pp* **rallied**) **1** (**I**) **rally (sb/sth) (around/behind/to sb)** to come together or to bring people together in order to help or support sb/sth: *The cabinet rallied behind the Prime Minister.* **2** (I) to get stronger, healthier, etc after an illness or a period of weakness: *He never really rallied after the operation.*

PHRASAL VERB **rally round** to come together to help sb: *When I was in trouble my family all rallied round.*

ram[1] /ræm/ noun [C] a male sheep •➤ Look at the note at **sheep.** •➤ picture at **goat**

ram[2] /ræm/ verb [T] (**ramming**; **rammed**) to crash into sth or push sth with great force

Ramadan /'ræmədæn; ˌræmə'dæn/ noun [sing] a period of a month when, for religious reasons, Muslims do not eat anything from early morning until the sun goes down in the evening •➤ Look at **Eid.**

ramble[1] /'ræmbl/ verb [I] **1** to walk in the countryside for pleasure: *to go rambling* **2 ramble (on) (about sth)** to talk for a long time in a confused way: *Halfway through his speech he began to ramble.*

ramble[2] /'ræmbl/ noun [C] a long, organized walk in the country for pleasure

rambling /'ræmblɪŋ/ adj **1** (used about speech or writing) very long and confused **2** (used about a building) spreading in many directions: *a rambling old house in the country*

ramp /ræmp/ noun [C] a path going up or down which you can use instead of steps or stairs to get from one place to a higher or lower place: *There are ramps at both entrances for wheelchair access.*

rampage[1] /ræm'peɪdʒ/ verb [I] to move through a place in a violent group, usually breaking things and attacking people: *The football fans rampaged through the town.*

rampage[2] /'ræmpeɪdʒ/ noun

IDIOM **be/go on the rampage** to move through a place in a violent group, usually breaking things and attacking people

rampant /'ræmpənt/ adj (used about sth bad) existing or spreading everywhere in a way that is very difficult to control: *Car theft is rampant in this town.*

ramshackle /'ræmʃækl/ adj (usually used about a building) old and needing repair

ran *past tense of* **RUN**[1]

ranch /rɑːntʃ/ noun [C] a large farm, especially in the US or Australia, where cows, horses, sheep, etc are kept

random /'rændəm/ adj chosen by chance: *For the opinion poll they interviewed a random selection of people in the street.*

−randomly adv

IDIOM **at random** without thinking or deciding in advance what is going to happen: *The competitors were chosen at random from the audience.*

randy /'rændi/ adj (*Brit informal*) sexually excited

rang past tense of **RING²**

★**range¹** /reɪndʒ/ noun **1** [C, usually sing] a **range (of sth)** a variety of things that belong to the same group: *The course will cover a whole range of topics.* ● *This shop has a very wide range of clothes.* **2** [C] the limits between which sth can vary: *That car is outside my price range.* ● *I don't think this game is suitable for all age ranges.* **3** [C,U] the distance that it is possible for sb/sth to travel, see, hear, etc: *Keep out of range of the guns.* ● *The gunman shot the policeman at close range.* ● *They can pick up signals at a range of 400 metres.* **4** [C] a line of mountains or hills

range² /reɪndʒ/ verb [I] **1 range between A and B; range from A to B** to vary between two amounts, sizes, etc, including all those between them: *The ages of the students range from 15 to 50.* **2 range (from A to B)** to include a variety of things in addition to those mentioned

★**rank¹** /ræŋk/ noun **1** [C,U] the position, especially a high position, that sb has in an organization such as the army, or in society: *General is one of the highest ranks in the army.* ● *She's much higher in rank than I am.* **2** [C] a group or line of things or people: *a taxi rank* **3 the ranks** [pl] the ordinary soldiers in the army; the members of any large group: *At the age of 43, he was forced to join the ranks of the unemployed.*

IDIOM **the rank and file** the ordinary soldiers in the army; the ordinary members of an organization

rank² /ræŋk/ verb [I,T] **rank (sb/sth) (as sth)** (not used in the continuous tenses) to give sb/sth a particular position on a scale according to importance, quality, success, etc; to have a position of this kind: *She's ranked as one of the world's top players.* ● *a high-ranking police officer*

ransom /'rænsəm/ noun [C,U] the money that you must pay to free sb who has been captured illegally and who is being kept as a prisoner: *The kidnappers demanded a ransom of $500000 for the boy's release.*

IDIOM **hold sb to ransom** to keep sb as a prisoner and say that you will not free him/her until you have received a certain amount of money ••➤ Look at **hostage**.

rap¹ /ræp/ noun **1** [C] a quick, sharp hit or knock on a door, window, etc: *There was a sharp rap on the door.* **2** [C,U] a style or a piece of music with a fast strong rhythm, in which the words are spoken fast, not sung

rap² /ræp/ verb (**rapping**; **rapped**) **1** [I,T] to hit a hard object or surface several times quickly and lightly, making a noise: *She rapped angrily on/at the door.* **2** [T] (*infor-*

mal) (used mainly in newspaper headlines) to criticize sb strongly: *Minister raps police over rise in crime.* **3** [I] to speak the words of a song (a rap) that has music with a very fast strong rhythm

rape¹ /reɪp/ verb [T] to force a person to have sex when he/she does not want to, using threats or violence

rape² /reɪp/ noun **1** [U,C] the crime of forcing sb to have sex when he/she does not want to: *to commit rape* **2** [sing] (*written*) **the rape (of sth)** the destruction of sth beautiful

rapid /'ræpɪd/ adj happening very quickly or moving with great speed: *She made rapid progress and was soon the best in the class.* −**rapidity** noun (*formal*): *The rapidity of change has astonished most people.* −**rapidly** adv

rapids /'ræpɪdz/ noun [pl] a part of a river where the water flows very fast over rocks

rapist /'reɪpɪst/ noun [C] a person who forces sb to have sex when he/she does not want to

rapture /'ræptʃə/ noun [U] a feeling of extreme happiness

IDIOM **go into raptures (about/over sb/sth)** to feel and show that you think that sb/sth is very good: *I didn't like the film much but my boyfriend went into raptures about it.*

★**rare** /reə/ adj **1 rare (for sb/sth to do sth); rare (to do sth)** not often seen, happening, etc very often: *a rare bird/flower/plant* **2** (used about meat) not cooked for very long so that the inside is still red: *a rare steak*

➤ Compare **medium** and **well done**.

−**rarely** adv: *People rarely live to be over 100 years old.*

raring /'reərɪŋ/ adj **raring to do sth** wanting to start doing sth very much: *They were raring to try out the new computer.*

rarity /'reərəti/ noun (*pl* **rarities**) **1** [C] a thing or a person that is unusual and is therefore often valuable or interesting: *Women lorry drivers are still quite a rarity.* **2** [U] the quality of being rare: *The rarity of this stamp increases its value a lot.*

rash¹ /ræʃ/ noun **1** [C, usually sing] an area of small red spots that appear on your skin when you are ill or have a reaction to sth: *He came out in a rash where the plant had touched him.* **2** [sing] **a rash (of sth)** a series of unpleasant events of the same kind happening close together

rash² /ræʃ/ adj (used about people) doing things that might be dangerous or bad without thinking about the possible results first; (used about actions) done in this way: *a rash decision/promise* −**rashly** adv

rasher /'ræʃə/ noun [C] (*Brit*) a slice of meat (bacon) from a pig

raspberry /'rɑːzbəri/ noun [C] (*pl* **raspberries**) a small, soft, red fruit which grows on bushes: *raspberry jam* ••➤ picture on page C3

★**rat** /ræt/ noun [C] an animal like a large mouse

r

➤ Rats belong to the family of animals that are called **rodents**.

IDIOM **rat race** the way of life in which everyone is only interested in being better or more successful than everyone else

★**rate¹** /reɪt/ *noun* [C] **1** a measurement of the speed at which sth happens or the number of times sth happens or exists during a particular period: *The birth rate* (= the number of children born each year) *is falling.* ● *The population is increasing at the rate of less than 0.5% a year.* ● *an exchange rate of one pound to ten francs* **2** a fixed amount of money that sth costs or that sb is paid: *The basic rate of pay is £10 an hour.* ● *We offer special reduced rates for students.* ●➤ Look at **first-rate** and **second-rate**.

IDIOMS **at any rate** (*spoken*) **1** used when you are giving more exact information about sth: *He said that they would be here by ten. At any rate, I think that's what he said.* **2** whatever else might happen: *Well, that's one good piece of news at any rate.*

the going rate (for sth) → GOING²

rate² /reɪt/ *verb* [T] (not used in the continuous tenses) **1** (usually passive) to say how good you think sb/sth is: *She's rated among the best tennis players of all time.* **2** to be good, important, etc enough to be treated in a particular way: *The accident wasn't very serious – it didn't rate a mention in the local newspaper.*

★**rather** /ˈrɑːðə/ *adv* quite; to some extent: *It was a rather nice day.* ● *It was rather a nice day.* ● *It cost rather a lot of money.* ● *I was rather hoping that you'd be free on Friday.*

➤ **Fairly**, **quite**, **rather** and **pretty** can all mean 'not very'. **Fairly** is the weakest. **Rather** and **pretty** (informal) are the strongest. **Fairly** and **quite** are mostly used with words that are positive: *The room was fairly tidy.* **Rather** is used when you are criticizing sth: *This room's rather untidy.* If you use **rather** with a positive word, it sounds as if you are surprised and pleased: *The new teacher is actually rather nice, though he doesn't look very friendly.*

IDIOMS **or rather** used as a way of correcting sth you have said, or making it more exact: *She lives in London, or rather she lives in a suburb of London.*

rather than instead of; in place of: *I think I'll just have a sandwich rather than a full meal.*

would rather... (than) would prefer to: *I'd rather go to the cinema than watch television.*

rating /ˈreɪtɪŋ/ *noun* [C] **1** a measurement of how popular, important, good, etc sth is **2** (usually **the ratings**) a set of figures showing the number of people who watch a particular television programme, etc, used to show how popular the programme is

ratio /ˈreɪʃiəʊ/ *noun* [C] **ratio (of A to B)** the relation between two numbers which shows how much bigger one quantity is than another: *The ratio of boys to girls in this class*

is three to one (= there are three times as many boys as girls).

ration /ˈræʃn/ *noun* [C] a limited amount of food, petrol, etc that you are allowed to have when there is not enough for everyone to have as much as he/she wants –**ration** *verb* [T]: *In the desert water is strictly rationed* –**rationing** *noun* [U]

rational /ˈræʃnəl/ *adj* **1** (used about a person) able to use logical thought to make decisions rather than emotions ••➤ opposite **irrational 2** based on reason; sensible or logical: *There must be a rational explanation for why he's behaving like this.* –**rationally** *adv*

rationalize (also **-ise**) /ˈræʃnəlaɪz/ *verb* **1** [I,T] to find reasons that explain why you have done sth (perhaps because you do not like the real reason) **2** [T] to make a business or a system better organized –**rationalization** (also **rationalisation**) /ˌræʃnəlaɪˈzeɪʃn/ *noun* [C,U]

rattle¹ /ˈrætl/ *verb* **1** [I,T] to make a noise like hard things hitting each other or to shake sth so that it makes this noise: *The windows were rattling all night in the wind.* ● *He rattled the money in the tin.* **2** [T] (*informal*) to make sb suddenly become worried: *The news of his arrival really rattled her.*

PHRASAL VERB **rattle sth off** to say a list of things you have learned very quickly: *She rattled off the names of every player in the team.*

rattle² /ˈrætl/ *noun* [C] **1** a toy that a baby can shake to make a noise **2** a noise made by hard things hitting each other

raucous /ˈrɔːkəs/ *adj* (used about people's voices) loud and unpleasant: *raucous laughter*

ravage /ˈrævɪdʒ/ *verb* [T] to damage sth very badly; to destroy sth: *The forests were ravaged by the winter storms.*

rave¹ /reɪv/ *verb* [I] **1** (*informal*) **rave (about sb/sth)** to say very good things about sb/sth: *Everyone's raving about her latest record!* **2** to speak angrily or wildly

rave² /reɪv/ *noun* [C] (*Brit*) a large party held outside or in an empty building, at which people dance to electronic music

raven /ˈreɪvn/ *noun* [C] a large black bird that has an unpleasant voice

ravenous /ˈrævənəs/ *adj* very hungry –**ravenously** *adv*

ˌrave reˈview *noun* [C] an article in a newspaper, etc that says very good things about a new book, film, play, etc

ravine /rəˈviːn/ *noun* [C] a narrow deep valley with steep sides

raving /ˈreɪvɪŋ/ *adj*, *adv* (*informal*) used to emphasize a particular state or quality: *Have you gone raving mad?*

★**raw** /rɔː/ *adj* **1** not cooked: *Raw vegetables are good for your teeth.* **2** in the natural state; not yet made into anything: *raw materials* (= that are used to make things in factories, etc) **3** used about an injury where the skin has come off from being rubbed

ray /reɪ/ *noun* [C] a line of light, heat or energy: *the sun's rays* ● *ultraviolet rays* ••➤ Look at **X-ray**.

  IDIOM **a ray of hope** a small chance that things will get better

★**razor** /'reɪzə/ *noun* [C] a sharp instrument which people use to cut off the hair from their skin (**shave**): *an electric razor* ● *a disposable razor*

'razor blade *noun* [C] the thin sharp piece of metal that you put in a razor

Rd *abbr* road: *21 Hazel Rd*

★**reach¹** /riːtʃ/ *verb* **1** [T] to arrive at a place or condition that you have been going towards: *We won't reach Dover before 12.* ● *The two sides hope to reach an agreement sometime today.* ● *Sometimes the temperature reaches 45°C.* ● *The team reached the semifinal last year.* ● *to reach a decision/conclusion/compromise* **2** [I,T] reach (out) (for sb/ sth); reach (sth) (down) to stretch out your arm to try and touch or get sth: *The child reached for her mother.* ● *She reached into her bag for her purse.* **3** [I,T] to be able to touch sth: *Can you get me that book off the top shelf? I can't reach.* ● *He couldn't reach the light switch.* ● *I need a longer ladder. This one won't reach.* **4** [T] to communicate with sb, especially by telephone; contact: *You can reach me at this number.*

reach² /riːtʃ/ *noun* [U] the distance that you can stretch your arm

  IDIOMS **beyond/out of (sb's) reach 1** outside the distance that you can stretch your arm: *Keep this medicine out of the reach of children.* **2** not able to be got or done by sb: *A job like that is completely beyond his reach.*

within (sb's) reach 1 inside the distance that you can stretch your arm **2** able to be achieved by sb: *We were one goal ahead with ten minutes left and so could sense that victory was within our reach.*

within (easy) reach of sth not far from sth

★**react** /ri'ækt/ *verb* [I] **1** react (to sth) (by doing sth) to do or say sth because of sth that has happened or been said: *He reacted to the news by jumping up and down and shouting.* ● *The players reacted angrily to the decision.* **2** react (to sth) to become ill after eating, breathing, etc a particular substance **3** react (with sth/together) (used about a chemical substance) to change after coming into contact with another substance

  PHRASAL VERB **react against sb/sth** to behave or talk in a way that shows that you do not like the influence of sb/sth (for example authority, your family, etc)

★**reaction** /ri'ækʃn/ *noun* **1** [C,U] (a) reaction (to sb/sth) something that you do or say because of sth that has happened: *Could we have your reaction to the latest news, Prime Minister?* ● *I shook him to try and wake him up but there was no reaction.* **2** [C,U] (a) reaction (against sb/sth) behaviour that shows that you do not like the influence of sb/sth (for example authority, your family, etc) **3** [C] a reaction (to sth) a bad effect that

your body experiences because of sth that you have eaten, touched or breathed: *She had an allergic reaction to something in the food.* **4** [C, usually pl] the physical ability to act quickly when sth happens: *If the other driver's reactions hadn't been so good, there would have been an accident.* **5** [C,U] (technical) a chemical change produced by two or more substances coming into contact with each other

reactionary /ri'ækʃənri/ *noun* [C] (*pl* **reactionaries**) a person who tries to prevent political or social change –**reactionary** *adj*: *reactionary views/politics/groups*

reactor /ri'æktə/ = **NUCLEAR REACTOR**

★**read¹** /riːd/ *verb* (*pt, pp* **read** /red/) **1** [I,T] to look at words or symbols and understand them: *He never learnt to read and write.* ● *Have you read any good books lately?* ● *Can you read music?* **2** [I,T] read (sb) (sth); read sth (to sb) to say written words to sb: *My father used to read me stories when I was a child.* ● *I hate reading out loud.* **3** [T] to be able to understand sth from what you can see: *A man came to read the gas meter.* ● *Profoundly deaf people train to read lips.* ● *I've no idea what he'll say – I can't read his mind!* **4** [T] to show words or a sign of sth: *The sign read 'Keep Left'.* **5** [T] (*formal*) to study a subject at university: *She read Modern Languages at Cambridge.*

  PHRASAL VERBS **read sth into sth** to think that there is a meaning in sth that may not really be there

read on to continue reading; to read the next part of sth

read sth out to read sth to other people

read sth through to read sth to check details or to look for mistakes: *I read my essay through a few times before handing it in.*

read up on sth to find out everything you can about a subject

read² /riːd/ *noun* [sing] (*informal*) a period or the action of reading: *Her detective novels are usually a good read.*

readable /'riːdəbl/ *adj* **1** able to be read: *machine-readable data* ••➤ Look at **legible**. **2** easy or interesting to read

★**reader** /'riːdə/ *noun* [C] **1** a person who reads sth (a particular newspaper, magazine, type of book, etc): *She's an avid reader of science fiction.* **2** (with an adjective) a person who reads in a particular way: *a fast/slow reader* **3** a book for practising reading

readership /'riːdəʃɪp/ *noun* [sing] the number of people who regularly read a particular newspaper, magazine, etc: *The newspaper has a readership of 200000.*

readily /'redɪli/ *adv* **1** easily, without difficulty: *Most vegetables are readily available at this time of year.* **2** without pausing; without being forced: *He readily admitted that he was wrong.*

readiness /'redɪnəs/ *noun* [U] **1** readiness (for sth) the state of being ready or prepared **2** readiness (to do sth) the state of being

r

prepared to do sth without arguing or complaining: *The bank have indicated their readiness to lend him the money.*

★**reading** /'riːdɪŋ/ **noun** [U] **1** what you do when you read: *I haven't had time to do much reading lately.* ● *Her hobbies include painting and reading.* **2** books, articles, etc that are intended to be read: *The information office gave me a pile of **reading matter** to take away.* **3** the particular way in which sb understands sth: *What's your reading of the situation?* **4** the number or measurement that is shown on an instrument: *a reading of 20°*

readjust /ˌriːə'dʒʌst/ **verb 1** [I] readjust (to sth) to get used to a different or new situation: *After her divorce, it took her a long time to readjust to being single again.* **2** [T] to change or move sth slightly –readjustment **noun** [C,U]

★**ready** /'redi/ **adj 1** ready (for sb/sth); ready (to do sth) prepared and able to do sth or to be used: *The car will be ready for you to collect on Friday.* ● *He isn't ready to take his driving test – he hasn't had enough lessons.* ● *I'm meeting him at 7, so I don't have long to **get ready**.* ● *I'll go and **get the dinner ready**.* ● *Have your money **ready** before you get on the bus.* **2** ready to do sth; ready (with/for sth) prepared and happy to do sth: *You know me – I'm always ready to help.* ● *Charlie's always ready with advice.* ● *The men were angry and ready for a fight.* ● *I know it's early, but I'm **ready for bed**.* **3** adv (used to form compound adjectives) that has already been made or done; not done especially for you: *ready-cooked food* ● *There are no **ready-made** answers to this problem – we'll have to find our own solution.*

★**real¹** /rɪəl/ **adj 1** actually existing, not imagined: *The film is based on real life.* ● *This isn't a real word, I made it up.* ● *We have a real chance of winning.* ● *Closure of the factory is a very real danger.* **2** actually true; not only what people think is true: *The name he gave to the police wasn't his real name.* **3** (only *before* a noun) having all, not just some, of the qualities necessary to really be sth: *She was my first real girlfriend.* **4** natural, not false or artificial: *This shirt is real silk.* **5** (only *before* a noun) (used to emphasize a state, feeling or quality) strong or big: *Money is a real problem for us at the moment.* ● *He made a real effort to be polite.*

IDIOMS **for real** genuine or serious: *Her tears weren't for real.* ● *Was he for real when he offered you the job?*
the real thing something genuine, not a copy: *This painting is just a copy. The real thing is in a gallery.* ● *She's had boyfriends before but this time she says it's the real thing* (= real love).

real² /rɪəl/ **adv** (*US informal*) very; really

'real estate noun [U] property in the form of land and buildings

'real estate agent (*US*) = **ESTATE AGENT**

realism /'rɪəlɪzəm/ **noun** [U] **1** behaviour that shows that you accept the facts of a

situation and are not influenced by your feelings ●► Look at **idealism**. **2** (in art, literature, etc) showing things as they really are

realist /'rɪəlɪst/ **noun** [C] **1** a person who accepts the facts of a situation, and does not try to pretend that it is different: *I'm a realist – I don't expect the impossible.* **2** an artist or writer who shows things as they really are

realistic /ˌrɪə'lɪstɪk/ **adj 1** sensible and understanding what it is possible to achieve in a particular situation: *We have to be realistic about our chances of winning.* **2** showing things as they really are: *a realistic drawing/ description* **3** not real but appearing to be real: *The monsters in the film were very realistic.* –realistically /ˌrɪə-; ˌriːə'lɪstɪkli/ **adv**

★**reality** /ri'æləti/ **noun** (*pl* **realities**) **1** [U] the way life really is, not the way it may appear to be or how you would like it to be: *I enjoyed my holiday, but now it's back to reality.* ● *We have to **face reality** and accept that we've failed.* **2** [C] a thing that is actually experienced, not just imagined: *Films portray war as heroic and exciting, but the reality is very different.*

IDIOM **in reality** in fact, really (not the way sth appears or has been described): *People say this is an exciting city but in reality it's rather boring.*

★**realize** (also **-ise**) /'rɪəlaɪz/ **verb** [T] **1** to know and understand that sth is true or that sth has happened: *I'm sorry I mentioned it, I didn't realize how much it upset you.* ● *Didn't you realize (that) you needed to bring money?* **2** to become conscious of sth or that sth has happened, usually some time later: *When I got home, I realized that I had left my keys at the office.* **3** to make sth that you imagined become reality: *His worst fears were realized when he saw the damage caused by the fire.* –realization (also **-isation**) /ˌrɪəlaɪ'zeɪʃn/ **noun** [U]

★**really** /'rɪəli/ **adv 1** actually; in fact: *I couldn't believe it was really happening.* ● *He said he was sorry but I don't think he really meant it.* ● *She wasn't really angry, she was only pretending.* ● *Is it really true?* **2** very; very much: *I'm really tired.* ● *Are you really sure?* ● *I really hope you enjoy yourself.* ● *I really tried but I couldn't do it.* **3** used as a question for expressing surprise, interest, doubt, etc: *'She's left her husband.' 'Really? When did that happen?'* **4** used in negative sentences to make what you are saying less strong: *I don't really agree with that.* **5** used in questions when you are expecting sb to answer 'No': *You don't really expect me to believe that, do you?*

realtor /'rɪəltə/ **noun** (*US*) = **ESTATE AGENT**

reap /riːp/ **verb** [T] to cut and collect a crop (corn, wheat, etc): (*figurative*) *Work hard now and you'll **reap the benefits** later on.*

reappear /ˌriːə'pɪə/ **verb** [I] to appear again or be seen again –reappearance /-rəns/ **noun** [C,U]

reappraisal /ˌriːə'preɪzl/ **noun** [C,U] the new examination of a situation, way of doing sth, etc in order to decide if any changes are necessary

★**rear**¹ /rɪə/ **noun** [sing] **1 the rear** the back part: *Smoking is only permitted at the rear of the bus.* **2** the part of your body that you sit on; bottom –**rear** **adj**: *the rear window/lights of a car*

IDIOM **bring up the rear** to be the last one in a race, a line of people, etc

rear² /rɪə/ **verb** **1** [T] to look after and educate children: *This generation of children will be reared without fear of war.* **2** [T] to breed and look after animals on a farm, etc: *to rear cattle/poultry* **3** [I] **rear (up)** (used about horses) to stand only on the back legs

rearrange /ˌriːəˈreɪndʒ/ **verb** [T] **1** to change the position or order of things: *We've rearranged the living room to make more space.* **2** to change a plan, meeting, etc that has been fixed: *The match has been rearranged for next Wednesday.*

★**reason**¹ /ˈriːzn/ **noun** **1** [C] **a reason (for sth/ for doing sth); a reason why.../that...** a cause or an explanation for sth that has happened or for sth that sb has done: *What's your reason for being so late?* • *Is there any reason why you couldn't tell me this before?* • *He said he couldn't come but he didn't **give a reason**.* • *The reason (that) I'm phoning you is to ask a favour.* • *For some reason they can't give us an answer until next week.* • *She left the job for personal reasons.* **2** [C,U] **(a) reason (to do sth); (a) reason (for sth/for doing sth)** something that shows that it is right or fair to do sth: *I **have reason** to believe that you've been lying.* • *I think we have reason for complaint.* • *You **have every reason** (= you are completely right) to be angry, considering how badly you've been treated.* **3** [U] the ability to think and to make sensible decisions: *Only human beings are capable of reason.* **4** [U] what is right or acceptable: *I tried to persuade him not to drive but he just wouldn't **listen to reason**.* • *I'll pay anything **within reason** for a ticket.*

IDIOM **it stands to reason** (*informal*) it is obvious if you think about it

reason² /ˈriːzn/ **verb** [I,T] to form a judgement or opinion, after thinking about sth in a logical way

PHRASAL VERB **reason with sb** to talk to sb in order to persuade him/her to behave or think in a more reasonable way

★**reasonable** /ˈriːznəbl/ **adj** **1** fair, practical and sensible: *I think it's reasonable to expect people to keep their promises.* • *I tried to be reasonable even though I was very angry.* **2** acceptable and appropriate in a particular situation: *It was a lovely meal and the bill was very reasonable!* •➤ opposite **unreasonable** **3** quite good, high, big, etc but not very: *His work is of a reasonable standard.*

reasonably /ˈriːznəbli/ **adv** **1** fairly or quite (but not very): *The weather was reasonably good but not brilliant.* **2** in a sensible and fair way

reasoning /ˈriːzənɪŋ/ **noun** [U] the process of thinking about sth and making a judgement or decision: *What's the reasoning behind his sudden decision to leave?*

reassure /ˌriːəˈʃɔː/ **verb** [T] to say or do sth in order to stop sb worrying or being afraid: *The mechanic reassured her that the engine was fine.* –**reassurance** /-ˈʃɔːrəns/ **noun** [U,C] advice or help that you give to sb to stop him/her worrying or being afraid: *I need some reassurance that I'm doing things the right way.* –**reassuring adj** –**reassuringly adv**

rebate /ˈriːbeɪt/ **noun** [C] a sum of money that is given back to you because you have paid too much: *to get a tax rebate*

rebel¹ /ˈrebl/ **noun** [C] **1** a person who fights against his/her country's government because he/she wants things to change **2** a person who refuses to obey people in authority or to accept rules: *At school he had a reputation as a rebel.*

rebel² /rɪˈbel/ **verb** [I](**rebelling**; **rebelled**) **rebel (against sb/sth)** to fight against authority, society, a law, etc: *She rebelled against her parents by marrying a man she knew they didn't approve of.*

rebellion /rɪˈbeljən/ **noun** [C,U] **1** an occasion when some of the people in a country try to change the government, using violence **2** the action of fighting against authority or refusing to accept rules: *Voting against the leader of the party was an act of open rebellion.*

rebellious /rɪˈbeljəs/ **adj** not doing what authority, society, etc wants you to do: *rebellious teenagers*

reboot /ˌriːˈbuːt/ **verb** [I,T] (*computing*) if you reboot a computer or if it reboots, you turn it off and then turn it on again immediately

rebound /rɪˈbaʊnd/ **verb** [I] **rebound (from/ off sth)** to hit sth/sb and then go in a different direction: *The ball rebounded off a defender and went into the goal.* –**rebound** /ˈriːbaʊnd/ **noun** [C]

rebuff /rɪˈbʌf/ **noun** [C] an unkind refusal of an offer or suggestion –**rebuff verb** [T]

rebuild /ˌriːˈbɪld/ **verb** [T] (*pt, pp* **rebuilt** /ˌriːˈbɪlt/) to build sth again: *Following the storm, a great many houses will have to be rebuilt.*

rebuke /rɪˈbjuːk/ **verb** [T] (*formal*) to speak angrily to sb because he/she has done sth wrong –**rebuke noun** [C]

recall /rɪˈkɔːl/ **verb** [T] **1** to remember sth (a fact, event, action, etc) from the past: *I don't recall exactly when I first met her.* • *She couldn't recall meeting him before.* **2** to order sb to return; to ask for sth to be returned: *The company has recalled all the fridges that have this fault.*

recap /ˈriːkæp/ (*spoken*) (also written **recapitulate** /ˌriːkəˈpɪtʃuleɪt/) **verb** [I,T] (**recapping**; **recapped**) to repeat or look again at the main points of sth to make sure that they have been understood: *Let's quickly recap what we've done in today's lesson, before we finish.*

recapture /ˌriːˈkæptʃə/ **verb** [T] **1** to win

back sth that was taken from you by an enemy or a competitor: *Government troops have recaptured the city.* **2** to catch a person or animal that has escaped **3** to create or experience again sth from the past: *The film brilliantly recaptures life in the 1930s.*

recede /rɪ'siːd/ **verb** [I] **1** to move away and begin to disappear: *The coast began to recede into the distance.* **2** (used about a hope, fear, chance, etc) to become smaller or less strong **3** (used about a man's hair) to fall out and stop growing at the front of the head: *He's got a receding hairline.* ⋯➤ picture at **hair**

★**receipt** /rɪ'siːt/ **noun 1** [C] a **receipt (for sth)** a piece of paper that is given to show that you have paid for sth: *Keep the receipt in case you want to exchange the shirt.* **2** [U] (*formal*) receipt (of sth) the receiving of sth

★**receive** /rɪ'siːv/ **verb** [T] **1** receive sth (from sb/sth) to get or accept sth that sb sends or gives to you: *I received a letter from an old friend last week.* • *to receive a phone call/a prize* **2** to experience a particular kind of treatment or injury: *We received a warm welcome from our hosts.* • *He received several cuts and bruises in the accident.* **3** (often passive) to react to sth new in a particular way: *The film has been well received by the critics.*

receiver /rɪ'siːvə/ **noun** [C] **1** (also **handset**) the part of a telephone that is used for listening and speaking

> To answer or make a telephone call you **pick up** or **lift** the receiver. To end a telephone call you **put down** or **replace** the receiver or you **hang up**.

2 a piece of television or radio equipment that changes electronic signals into sounds or pictures

★**recent** /'riːsnt/ **adj** that happened or began only a short time ago: *In recent years there have been many changes.* • *This is a recent photograph of my daughter.*

★**recently** /'riːsntli/ **adv** not long ago: *She worked here until quite recently.* • *Have you seen Paul recently?*

> **Recently** can refer to both a point in time and a period of time. If it refers to a point in time, use the past simple tense: *He got married recently.* If it refers to a period, use the present perfect or present perfect continuous tense: *I haven't done anything interesting recently.* • *She's been working hard recently.* **Lately** can only refer to a period of time. It is used only with the present perfect or present perfect continuous tense: *I've seen a lot of films lately.* • *I've been spending too much money lately.*

receptacle /rɪ'septəkl/ **noun** [C] (*formal*) a container

★**reception** /rɪ'sepʃn/ **noun 1** [U] the place inside the entrance of a hotel or office building where guests or visitors go when they first arrive: *Leave your key at/in reception if you go out, please.* • *the reception desk* **2** [C] a formal party to celebrate sth or to welcome an important person: *Their wedding reception was held at a local hotel.* • *There will be*

an official reception at the embassy for the visiting ambassador. **3** [sing] the way people react to sth: *The play got a mixed reception* (= some people liked it, some people didn't). **4** [U] the quality of radio or television signals: *TV reception is very poor where we live.*

receptionist /rɪ'sepʃənɪst/ **noun** [C] a person who works in a hotel, office, etc answering the telephone and dealing with visitors and guests when they arrive: *a hotel receptionist*

receptive /rɪ'septɪv/ **adj** receptive (to sth) ready to listen to new ideas, suggestions, etc

recess /rɪ'ses/ **noun 1** [C,U] a period of time when Parliament, committees, etc do not meet **2** [U] (*US*) a short break during a trial in a court of law ⋯➤ Look at the note at **interval**. **3** [C] part of a wall that is further back than the rest, forming a space **4** [C] a part of a room that receives very little light

recession /rɪ'seʃn/ **noun** [C,U] a period when the business and industry of a country is not successful: *The country is now in recession.* • *How long will the recession last?*

recharge /ˌriː'tʃɑːdʒ/ **verb** [I,T] to fill a battery with electrical power; to fill up with electrical power: *He plugged the drill in to recharge it.* ⋯➤ Look at **charge**. –**rechargeable** adj: *rechargeable batteries*

★**recipe** /'resəpi/ **noun** [C] **1** a **recipe (for sth)** the instructions for cooking or preparing sth to eat. A recipe tells you what to use (the **ingredients**) and what to do: *a recipe for chocolate cake* **2** a **recipe for sth** the way to get or produce sth: *Putting Dave in charge of the project is a recipe for disaster.*

recipient /rɪ'sɪpiənt/ **noun** [C] (*formal*) a person who receives sth

reciprocal /rɪ'sɪprəkl/ **adj** involving two or more people or groups who agree to help each other or to behave in the same way towards one another: *The arrangement is reciprocal. They help us and we help them.*

recital /rɪ'saɪtl/ **noun** [C] a formal public performance of music or poetry: *a piano recital* ⋯➤ Look at **concert**.

recite /rɪ'saɪt/ **verb** [I,T] to say aloud a piece of writing, especially a poem or a list, from memory

reckless /'rekləs/ **adj** not thinking about possible bad or dangerous results that could come from your actions: *reckless driving* –**recklessly adv**

reckon /'rekən/ **verb** [T] (*informal*) **1** to think; to have an opinion about sth: *She's very late now. I reckon (that) she isn't coming.* • *I think she's forgotten. What do you reckon?* **2** to calculate sth approximately: *I reckon the journey will take about half an hour.*

PHRASAL VERBS **reckon on sth** to expect sth to happen and therefore to base a plan or action on it: *I didn't book in advance because I wasn't reckoning on tickets being so scarce.*
reckon (sth) up to calculate the total amount or number of sth
reckon with sb/sth to think about sb/sth as a possible problem

reclaim /rɪ'kleɪm/ verb [T] **1** reclaim sth (from sb/sth) to get back sth that has been lost or taken away: *Reclaim your luggage after you have been through passport control.* **2** to get back useful materials from waste products **3** to make wet land suitable for use

recline /rɪ'klaɪn/ verb [I] to sit or lie back in a relaxed and comfortable way –reclining adj: *The car has reclining seats at the front.*

recognition /ˌrekəg'nɪʃn/ noun **1** [U] the fact that you can identify sb/sth that you see: *When I arrived no sign of recognition showed on her face at all.* **2** [U,sing] the act of accepting that sth exists, is true or is official **3** [U] a public show of respect for sb's work or actions: *She has received public recognition for her services to charity.* ● *Please accept this gift in recognition of the work you have done.*

recognizable (also **recognisable**) /'rekəgnaɪzəbl; ˌrekəg'naɪzəbl/ adj recognizable (as sb/sth) that can be identified as sb/sth: *He was barely recognizable with his new short haircut.* –recognizably /-əbli/ adv

★**recognize** (also **-ise**) /'rekəgnaɪz/ verb [T] **1** to know again sb/sth that you have seen or heard before: *I recognized him but I couldn't remember his name.* **2** to accept that sth is true **3** to accept sth officially: *My qualifications are not recognized in other countries.* **4** to show officially that you think sth that sb has done is good

recoil /rɪ'kɔɪl/ verb [I] to quickly move away from sb/sth unpleasant: *She recoiled in horror at the sight of the corpse.*

recollect /ˌrekə'lekt/ verb [I,T] to remember sth, especially by making an effort: *I don't recollect exactly when it happened.*

recollection /ˌrekə'lekʃn/ noun **1** [U] recollection (of sth/doing sth) the ability to remember: *I have no recollection of promising to lend you money.* **2** [C,usually pl] something that you remember: *I have only vague recollections of the town where I spent my early years.*

★**recommend** /ˌrekə'mend/ verb [T] **1** recommend sb/sth (to sb) (for/as sth) to say that sb/sth is good and that sb should try or use him/her/it: *Which film would you recommend?* ● *Could you recommend me a good hotel?* ● *We hope that you'll recommend this restaurant to all your friends.* ● *Doctors don't always recommend drugs as the best treatment for every illness.* **2** to tell sb what you strongly believe he/she should do: *I recommend that you get some legal advice.* ● *I wouldn't recommend (your) travelling on your own. It could be dangerous.* •➔ Look at **suggest.**

recommendation /ˌrekəmen'deɪʃn/ noun **1** [C,U] saying that sth is good and should be tried or used: *I visited Seville on a friend's recommendation and I really enjoyed it.* **2** [C] a statement about what should be done in a particular situation: *In their report on the crash, the committee make several recommendations on how safety could be improved.*

recompense /'rekəmpens/ verb [T] (*formal*) recompense sb (for sth) to give

money, etc to sb for special efforts or work or because you are responsible for a loss he/she has suffered: *The airline has agreed to recompense us for the damage to our luggage.* –recompense noun [sing,U]: *Please accept this cheque in recompense for our poor service.*

reconcile /'rekənsaɪl/ verb [T] **1** reconcile sth (with sth) to find a way of dealing with two ideas, situations, statements, etc that seem to be opposite to each other: *She finds it difficult to reconcile her career ambitions with her responsibilities to her children.* **2** (often passive) reconcile sb (with sb) to make people become friends again after an argument: *After years of not speaking to each other, she and her parents were eventually reconciled.* **3** reconcile yourself to sth to accept an unpleasant situation because there is nothing you can do to change it –reconciliation /ˌrekənsɪli'eɪʃn/ noun [sing,U]: *The negotiators are hoping to bring about a reconciliation between the two sides.*

reconnaissance /rɪ'kɒnɪsns/ noun [C,U] the study of a place or area for military reasons: *The plane was shot down while on a reconnaissance mission over enemy territory.*

reconsider /ˌriːkən'sɪdə/ verb [I,T] to think again about sth, especially because you may want to change your mind: *Public protests have forced the government to reconsider their policy.*

reconstruct /ˌriːkən'strʌkt/ verb [T] **1** to build again sth that has been destroyed or damaged **2** to get a full description or picture of sth using the facts that are known: *The police are trying to reconstruct the victim's movements on the day of the murder.* –reconstruction /-'strʌkʃn/ noun [C,U]: *a reconstruction of the crime using actors*

★**record**[1] /'rekɔːd/ noun **1** [C] a record (of sth) a written account of what has happened, been done, etc: *The teachers keep records of the children's progress.* ● *medical records* ● *It's on record that he was out of the country at the time of the murder.* **2** [sing] the facts, events, etc that are known (and sometimes written down) about sb/sth: *The police said that the man had a criminal record* (= he had been found guilty of crimes in the past). ● *This airline has a bad safety record.* **3** [C] (also **album**) a thin, round piece of plastic which can store music so that you can play it when you want **4** [C] the best performance or the highest or lowest level, etc ever reached in sth, especially in sport: *Who holds the world record for high jump?* ● *She's hoping to break the record for the 100 metres.* ● *He did it in record time* (= very fast).

IDIOMS **off the record** (used about sth sb says) not to be treated as official; not intended to be made public: *She told me off the record that she was going to resign.*

put/set the record straight to correct a mistake by telling sb the true facts

★**record**[2] /rɪ'kɔːd/ verb **1** [T] to write down or film facts or events so that they can be referred to later and will not be forgotten: *He*

r

recorded everything in his diary. • *At the inquest the coroner* **recorded** *a* **verdict** *of accidental death.* **2** [I,T] to put music, a film, a programme, etc onto a CD or cassette so that it can be listened to or watched again later: *Quiet, please! We're recording.* • *The band has recently recorded a new album.* • *There's a concert I would like to record from the radio this evening.*

'**record-breaking** adj (only *before* a noun) the best, fastest, highest, etc ever: *We did the journey in record-breaking time.*

recorder /rɪˈkɔːdə/ noun [C] **1** a machine for recording sound and/or pictures: *a tape/cassette/video recorder* **2** a type of musical instrument that is often played by children. You play it by blowing through it and covering the holes in it with your fingers. ••> Look at the note at **piano.** ••> picture at **music**

recording /rɪˈkɔːdɪŋ/ noun **1** [C] sound or pictures that have been put onto a cassette, CD, film, etc: *the Berlin Philharmonic's recording of Mahler's Sixth symphony* **2** [U] the process of making a cassette, record, film, etc: *a recording session/studio*

'**record player** noun [C] a machine that you use for playing records

recount /rɪˈkaʊnt/ verb [T] (*formal*) to tell a story or describe an event

recourse /rɪˈkɔːs/ noun [U] (*formal*) having to use sth or ask sb for help in a difficult situation: *She made a complete recovery without recourse to surgery.*

★**recover** /rɪˈkʌvə/ verb **1** [I] recover (from sth) to become well again after you have been ill: *It took him two months to recover from the operation.* **2** [I] recover (from sth) to get back to normal again after a bad experience, etc: *The old lady never really recovered from the shock of being mugged.* **3** [T] recover sth (from sb/sth) to find or get back sth that was lost or stolen: *Police recovered the stolen goods from a warehouse in South London.* **4** [T] to get back the use of your senses, control of your emotions, etc

★**recovery** /rɪˈkʌvəri/ noun **1** [usually sing,U] recovery (from sth) a return to good health after an illness or to a normal state after a difficult period of time: *to make a good/ quick/speedy/slow recovery* • *She's on the road to recovery* (= getting better all the time) *now.* • *the prospects of economic recovery* **2** [U] recovery (of sth/sb) getting back sth that was lost, stolen or missing

recreation /ˌrekriˈeɪʃn/ noun [U,sing] enjoying yourself and relaxing when you are not working; a way of doing this: *recreation activities such as swimming or reading*

recrimination /rɪˌkrɪmɪˈneɪʃn/ noun [C,usually pl,U] an angry statement accusing sb of sth, especially in answer to a similar statement from him/her: *bitter recriminations*

recruit¹ /rɪˈkruːt/ noun [C] a person who has just joined the army or another organization

recruit² /rɪˈkruːt/ verb [I,T] to find new people to join a company, an organization, the armed forces, etc: *to recruit young people*

to the teaching profession –**recruitment** noun [U]

rectangle /ˈrektæŋgl/ noun [C] a shape with four straight sides and four angles of 90 degrees (**right angles**). Two of the sides are longer than the other two. ••> synonym **oblong** ••> picture at **shape** –**rectangular** /rekˈtæŋgjələ/ adj

rectify /ˈrektɪfaɪ/ verb [T] (*pres part* **rectifying**; *3rd pers sing pres* **rectifies**; *pt, pp* **rectified**) (*formal*) to correct sth that is wrong

recuperate /rɪˈkuːpəreɪt/ verb [I] (*formal*) recuperate (from sth) to get well again after an illness or injury –**recuperation** /rɪˌkuːpəˈreɪʃn/ noun [U]

recur /rɪˈkɜː/ verb [I] (**recurring**; **recurred**) to happen again or many times: *a recurring problem/illness/nightmare* –**recurrence** /rɪˈkʌrəns/ noun [C,U] –**recurrent** /rɪˈkʌrənt/ adj

recycle /ˌriːˈsaɪkl/ verb [T] **1** to put used objects and materials through a process so that they can be used again: *recycled paper* • *Aluminium cans can be recycled.* **2** to keep used objects and materials and use them again: *Don't throw away your plastic carrier bags – recycle them!* –**recyclable** adj: *Most plastics are recyclable.*

★**red** /red/ noun [C,U], adj (**redder**; **reddest**) **1** (of) the colour of blood: *red wine* • *She was dressed in red.*

> We use **crimson, maroon** and **scarlet** to describe different shades of red.

2 a colour that some people's face becomes when they are embarrassed, angry, shy, etc: *He went bright red when she spoke to him.* • *to turn/be/go red in the face* **3** (used about a person's hair or an animal's fur) (of) a colour between red, orange and brown: *She's got red hair and freckles.*

IDIOMS **be in the red** to have spent more money than you have in the bank, etc: *I'm £500 in the red at the moment.* ••> opposite **be in the black**

catch sb red-handed → CATCH¹

a red herring an idea or subject which takes people's attention away from what is really important

see red (*informal*) to become very angry

red 'card noun [C] (in football) a card that is shown to a player who is being sent off the field for doing sth wrong ••> Look at **yellow card.**

the ˌred 'carpet noun [sing] a piece of red carpet that is put outside to receive an important visitor; a special welcome for an important visitor: *I didn't expect to be given the red carpet treatment!*

redcurrant /ˌredˈkʌrənt/ noun [C] a small red berry that you can eat: *redcurrant jelly*

redden /ˈredn/ verb [I,T] to become red or to make sth red

> **Go red** or **blush** are more common.

reddish /ˈredɪʃ/ adj fairly red in colour

redeem /rɪˈdiːm/ verb [T] **1** to prevent sth from being completely bad: *The redeeming*

feature of the job is the good salary.
2 redeem yourself to do sth to improve people's opinion of you, especially after you have done sth bad

redemption /rɪˈdempʃn/ **noun** [U] (according to the Christian religion) the action of being saved from evil

IDIOM **beyond redemption** too bad to be saved or improved

redevelop /ˌriːdɪˈveləp/ **verb** [T] to build or arrange an area, a town, a building, etc in a different and more modern way: *They're redeveloping the city centre.* –**redevelopment noun** [U]

redhead /ˈredhed/ **noun** [C] a person, usually a woman, who has red hair

ˌred-ˈhot adj (used about a metal) so hot that it turns red

redial /riːˈdaɪəl/ **verb** [I,T] to call the same number on a telephone that you have just called

redistribute /ˌriːdɪˈstrɪbjuːt; riːˈdɪs-/ **verb** [T] to share sth out among people in a different way from before –**redistribution** /ˌriːdɪs-trɪˈbjuːʃn/ **noun** [U]

ˌred-ˈlight district noun [C] a part of a town where there are a lot of people, especially women, who earn money by having sex with people

ˌred ˈpepper noun [C] = PEPPER¹(2) ∙➤ picture on page C3

ˌred ˈtape noun [U] official rules that must be followed and papers that must be filled in, which seem unnecessary and often cause delay and difficulty in achieving sth

★**reduce** /rɪˈdjuːs/ **verb** [T] **1 reduce sth (from sth) (to sth); reduce sth (by sth)** to make sth less or smaller in quantity, price, size, etc: *The sign said 'Reduce speed now'.* ∙➤ opposite **increase 2 reduce sb/sth (from sth) to sth** (often passive) to force sb/sth into a particular state or condition, usually a bad one: *One of the older boys reduced the small child to tears.*

★**reduction** /rɪˈdʌkʃn/ **noun 1** [C,U] reduction (in sth) that action of making sth or of becoming less or smaller: *a sharp reduction in the number of students* **2** [C] the amount by which sth is made smaller, especially in price: *There were massive reductions in the June sales.*

redundant /rɪˈdʌndənt/ **adj 1** (used about employees) no longer needed for a job and therefore out of work: *When the factory closed 800 people were made redundant.* **2** not necessary or wanted –**redundancy** /-dənsi/ **noun** [C,U] (*pl* **redundancies**): *redundancy pay*

reed /riːd/ **noun** [C] **1** a tall plant, like grass, that grows in or near water ∙➤ picture on page C2 **2** a thin piece of wood at the end of some musical instruments which produces a sound when you blow through it ∙➤ picture at **music**

reef /riːf/ **noun** [C] a long line of rocks, plants, etc just below or above the surface of the sea: *a coral reef*

reek /riːk/ **verb** [I] **reek (of sth)** to smell strongly of sth unpleasant: *His breath reeked of tobacco.* –**reek noun** [sing]

reel¹ /riːl/ **noun** [C] a round object that thread, wire, film for cameras, etc is put around: *a cotton reel* ● *a reel of film* ∙➤ Look at **spool.** ∙➤ picture at **garden** and **knit**

reel² /riːl/ **verb** [I] **1** to walk without being able to control your legs, for example because you are drunk or you have been hit **2** to feel very shocked or upset about sth: *His mind was still reeling from the shock of seeing her again.*

PHRASAL VERB **reel sth off** to say or repeat sth from memory quickly and without having to think about it: *She reeled off a long list of names.*

ref abbr reference: *ref no 3456*

★**refer** /rɪˈfɜː/ **verb** (**referring**; **referred**) **1** [I] **refer to sb/sth (as sth)** to mention or talk about sb/sth: *When he said 'some students', do you think he was referring to us?* ● *She always referred to Ben as 'that nice man'.* **2** [I] **refer to sb/sth** to describe or be connected with sb/sth: *The term 'adolescent' refers to young people between the ages of 12 and 17.* **3** [I] **refer to sb/sth** to find out information by asking sb or by looking in a book, etc: *If you don't understand a word you may refer to your dictionaries.* **4** [T] **refer sb/sth to sb/sth** to send sb/sth to sb/sth else for help or to be dealt with: *The doctor has referred me to a specialist.*

referee /ˌrefəˈriː/ **noun** (also *informal* **ref**) [C] **1** the official person in sports such as football who controls the match and prevents players from breaking the rules ∙➤ A similar official in sports such as tennis is called an **umpire. 2** (*Brit*) a person who gives information about your character and ability, usually in a letter, for example when you are hoping to be chosen for a job: *Her teacher agreed to act as her referee.* –**referee verb** [I,T]

★**reference** /ˈrefrəns/ **noun 1** [C,U] (a) reference (to sb/sth) a written or spoken comment that mentions sb/sth: *The article made a direct reference to a certain member of the royal family.* **2** [U] looking at sth for information: *The guidebook might be useful for future reference.* **3** [C] a note, especially in a book, that tells you where certain information came from or can be found **4** [C] (*abbr* **ref**) (used on business letters, etc) a special number that identifies a letter, etc: *Please quote our reference when replying.* **5** [C] a statement or letter describing a person's character and ability that is given to a possible future employer: *My boss gave me a good reference.*

IDIOM **with reference to sb/sth** (*formal*) about or concerning sb/sth: *I am writing with reference to your letter of 10 April...*

ˈreference book noun [C] a book that you use to find a piece of information: *dictionaries, encyclopedias and other reference books*

referendum /ˌrefəˈrendəm/ **noun** [C,U] (*pl* **referendums** or **referenda** /-də/) an occasion when all the people of a country can vote on a particular political question: *to hold a referendum*

refill /ˌriːˈfɪl/ **verb** [T] to fill sth again: *Can I refill your glass?* –refill /ˈriːfɪl/ **noun** [C]: *a refill for a pen*

refine /rɪˈfaɪn/ **verb** [T] **1** to make a substance pure and free from other substances: *to refine sugar/oil* **2** to improve sth by changing little details: *to refine a theory*

refined /rɪˈfaɪnd/ **adj 1** (used about a substance) that has been made pure by having other substances taken out of it: *refined sugar/oil/flour* **2** (used about a person) polite; having very good manners ••➤ opposite for senses 1 and 2 **unrefined 3** improved and therefore producing a better result

refinement /rɪˈfaɪnmənt/ **noun 1** [C] a small change that improves sth: *The new model has electric windows and other refinements.* **2** [U] good manners and polite behaviour

refinery /rɪˈfaɪnəri/ **noun** [C] (*pl* **refineries**) a factory where a substance is made pure by having other substances taken out of it: *an oil/sugar refinery*

★**reflect** /rɪˈflekt/ **verb 1** [T] to send back light, heat or sound from a surface: *The windows reflected the bright morning sunlight.* **2** [T] **reflect sb/sth (in sth)** (usually passive) to show an image of sb/sth on the surface of sth such as a mirror, water or glass: *She caught sight of herself reflected in the shop window.* **3** [T] to show or express sth: *His music reflects his interest in African culture.* **4** [I] **reflect (on/upon) sth** to think, especially deeply and carefully, about sth

<u>PHRASAL VERB</u> **reflect (well, badly, etc) on sb/sth** to give a particular impression of sb/sth: *It reflects badly on the whole school if some of its pupils misbehave in public.*

★**reflection** (*Brit also* **reflexion**) /rɪˈflekʃn/ **noun 1** [C] an image that you see in a mirror, in water or on a shiny surface: *He admired his reflection in the mirror.* **2** [U] the sending back of light, heat or sound from a surface **3** [C] a thing that shows what sb/sth is like: *Your clothes are a reflection of your personality.* **4** [sing] **a reflection on/upon sb/sth** something that causes people to form a good or bad opinion about sb/sth: *Parents often feel that their children's behaviour is a reflection on themselves.* **5** [U,C] careful thought about sth: *a book of his **reflections** on fatherhood*

<u>IDIOM</u> **on reflection** after thinking again: *I think, on reflection, that we were wrong.*

reflective /rɪˈflektɪv/ **adj 1** (*written*) (used about a person, mood, etc) thinking deeply about things: *a reflective expression* **2** (used about a surface) sending back light or heat: *Wear reflective strips when you're cycling at night.* **3** reflective (of sth) showing what sth is like

reflector /rɪˈflektə/ **noun** [C] **1** a surface that sends back (reflects) light, heat or sound that hits it **2** a small piece of glass or plastic on a bicycle or on clothing that can be seen at night when light shines on it

reflex /ˈriːfleks/ **noun 1** [C] (also **'reflex action**) a sudden movement or action that you make without thinking: *She put her hands out as a reflex to stop her fall.* **2 reflexes** [pl] the ability to act quickly when necessary: *A good tennis player needs to have excellent reflexes.*

reflexion (*Brit*) = **REFLECTION**

reflexive /rɪˈfleksɪv/ **adj, noun** [C] (*grammar*) (a word or verb form) showing that the person who performs an action is also affected by it: *In 'He cut himself', 'cut' is a **reflexive verb** and 'himself' is a **reflexive pronoun**.*

★**reform** /rɪˈfɔːm/ **verb 1** [T] to change a system, the law, etc in order to make it better: *to reform the examination system* **2** [I,T] to improve your behaviour; to make sb do this: *Our prisons aim to reform criminals, not simply to punish them.* –reform **noun** [C,U]

reformer /rɪˈfɔːmə/ **noun** [C] a person who tries to change society and make it better

refrain¹ /rɪˈfreɪn/ **verb** [I] (*formal*) **refrain (from sth/doing sth)** to stop yourself doing sth; to not do sth: *Please refrain from smoking in the hospital.*

refrain² /rɪˈfreɪn/ **noun** [C] (*formal*) a part of a song which is repeated, usually at the end of each verse ••➤ synonym **chorus**

refresh /rɪˈfreʃ/ **verb** [T] to make sb/sth feel less tired or less hot and full of energy again: *He looked refreshed after a good night's sleep.*
<u>IDIOM</u> **refresh your memory (about sb/sth)** to remind yourself about sb/sth: *Could you refresh my memory about what we said on this point last week?*

refreshing /rɪˈfreʃɪŋ/ **adj 1** pleasantly new or different: *It makes **a refreshing change** to meet somebody who is so enthusiastic.* **2** making you feel less tired or hot: *a refreshing swim/shower/drink*

refreshment /rɪˈfreʃmənt/ **noun 1 refreshments** [pl] light food and drinks that are available at a cinema, theatre or other public place **2** [U] (*formal*) the fact of making sb stronger and less tired or hot; food or drink that helps to do this

refrigerate /rɪˈfrɪdʒəreɪt/ **verb** [T] to make food, etc cold in order to keep it fresh –refrigerator (*formal*) = **FRIDGE**

refuge /ˈrefjuːdʒ/ **noun** [C,U] **refuge (from sb/sth)** protection from danger, trouble, etc; a place that is safe: *We had to **take refuge** under a tree while it rained.* ● *a refuge for the homeless*

★**refugee** /ˌrefjuˈdʒiː/ **noun** [C] a person who has been forced to leave his/her country for political or religious reasons, or because there is a war, not enough food, etc: *a refugee camp* ••➤ Look at **fugitive** and **exile**.

refund /ˈriːfʌnd/ **noun** [C] a sum of money that is paid back to you, especially because you have paid too much or you are not happy with sth you have bought: *to claim/demand/get a refund* –refund /rɪˈfʌnd; ˈriːfʌnd/ **verb** [T] –refundable **adj**: *The deposit is not refundable.*

★**refusal** /rɪ'fjuːzl/ **noun** [U,C] **(a)** refusal (of sth); (a) refusal (to do sth) saying or showing that you will not do, give or accept sth: *I can't understand her refusal to see me.*

★**refuse**¹ /rɪ'fjuːz/ **verb** [I,T] to say or show that you do not want to do, give, or accept sth: *He refused to listen to what I was saying.* ● *My application for a grant has been refused.* •➤ opposite **agree**

refuse² /'refjuːs/ **noun** [U] (*formal*) things that you throw away; rubbish: *the refuse collection* (= when dustbins are emptied)

regain /rɪ'geɪn/ **verb** [T] to get sth back that you had lost: *to regain consciousness*

regal /'riːgl/ **adj** very impressive; typical of or suitable for a king or queen

★**regard**¹ /rɪ'gɑːd/ **verb** [T] **1** regard sb/sth as sth; regard sb/sth (with sth) to think of sb/sth (in the way mentioned): *Do you regard this issue as important?* ● *Her work is highly regarded* (= people have a high opinion of it). ● *In some villages newcomers are regarded with suspicion.* **2** (*formal*) to look at sb/sth for a while
   IDIOM **as regards sb/sth** (*formal*) in connection with sb/sth: *What are your views as regards this proposal?*

regard² /rɪ'gɑːd/ **noun** **1** [U] regard to/for sb/sth attention to or care for sb/sth: *He shows little regard for other people's feelings.* **2** [U, sing] (a) regard (for sb/sth) a feeling of admiration for sb/sth: respect: *She obviously has great regard for your ability.* **3** regards [pl] (used especially to end a letter politely) kind thoughts; best wishes: *Please give my regards to your parents.*
   IDIOM **in/with regard to sb/sth; in this/that/one regard** (*formal*) about sb/sth; connected with sb/sth: *With regard to the details – these will be finalized later.*

regarding /rɪ'gɑːdɪŋ/ **prep** (*formal*) about or in connection with: *Please write if you require further information regarding this matter.*

regardless /rɪ'gɑːdləs/ **adv**, **prep** regardless (of sb/sth) paying no attention to sb/sth; treating problems and difficulties as unimportant: *I suggested she should stop but she carried on regardless.* ● *Everybody will receive the same, regardless of how long they've worked here.*

regatta /rɪ'gætə/ **noun** [C] an event at which there are boat races

reggae /'regeɪ/ **noun** [U] a type of West Indian music with a strong rhythm

★**regime** /reɪ'ʒiːm/ **noun** [C] a method or system of government, especially one that has not been elected in a fair way: *a military/fascist regime*

regiment /'redʒɪmənt/ **[C,with sing or pl verb]** a group of soldiers in the army who are commanded by a particular officer (a colonel) –**regimental** /ˌredʒɪ'mentl/ **adj**

regimented /'redʒɪmentɪd/ **adj** (*formal*) (too) strictly controlled

★**region** /'riːdʒən/ **noun** [C] **1** a part of the country or the world; a large area of land: *desert/tropical/polar regions* ● *This region of France is very mountainous.* •➤ Look at the note at **district**. **2** an area of your body
   IDIOM **in the region of sth** about or approximately: *There were somewhere in the region of 30000 people at the rally.*

regional /'riːdʒənl/ **adj** connected with a particular region: *regional accents* •➤ Look at **local**, **international** and **national**.

★**register**¹ /'redʒɪstə/ **verb** **1** [I,T] to put a name on an official list: *You should register with a doctor nearby.* ● *All births, deaths and marriages must be registered.* **2** [I,T] to show sth or to be shown on a measuring instrument: *The thermometer registered 32°C.* ● *The earthquake registered 6.4 on the Richter scale.* **3** [T] to show feelings, opinions, etc: *Her face registered intense dislike.* **4** [I,T] (often used in negative sentences) to notice sth and remember it; to be noticed and remembered: *He told me his name but it didn't register.* **5** [T] to send a letter or package by special (registered) post

★**register**² /'redʒɪstə/ **noun** **1** [C] an official list of names, etc or a book that contains this kind of list: *The teacher calls the register first thing in the morning.* ● *the electoral register* (= of people who are able to vote in an election) **2** [C,U] the type of language (formal or informal) that is used in a piece of writing

registered 'post noun [U] (*Brit*) a postal service that you pay extra for. If your letter or parcel is lost the post office will make a payment to you.

'register office = **REGISTRY OFFICE**

registrar /ˌredʒɪ'strɑː; 'redʒɪstrɑː/ **noun** [C] **1** a person whose job is to keep official lists, especially of births, marriages and deaths **2** a person who is responsible for keeping information about the students at a college or university

registration /ˌredʒɪ'streɪʃn/ **noun** [U] putting sb/sth's name on an official list: *Registration for evening classes will take place on 8 September.*

regi'stration number noun [C] the numbers and letters on the front and back of a vehicle that are used to identify it

registry /'redʒɪstri/ **noun** [C] (*pl* registries) a place where official lists are kept

'registry office (also **register office**) **noun** [C] an office where a marriage can take place and where births, marriages and deaths are officially written down •➤ Look at the note at **wedding**.

★**regret**¹ /rɪ'gret/ **verb** [T] (**regretting**; **regretted**) **1** to feel sorry that you did sth or that you did not do sth: *I hope you won't regret your decision later.* ● *Do you regret not taking the job?* **2** (*formal*) used as a way of saying that you are sorry for sth: *I regret to inform you that your application has been unsuccessful.*

★**regret**² /rɪ'gret/ **noun** [C,U] a feeling of sadness about sth that cannot now be changed: *Do you have any regrets that you didn't go to university?* –**regretful** /-fl/ **adj**: *a regretful look/smile* –**regretfully** /-fəli/ **adv**

r

regrettable /rɪˈgretəbl/ **adj** that you should feel sorry or sad about: *It is regrettable that the police were not informed sooner.* –regrettably **adv**

★**regular**¹ /ˈregjələ/ **adj 1** having the same amount of space or time between each thing or part: *a regular heartbeat ● Nurses checked her blood pressure at regular intervals.* ● *The fire alarms are tested on a regular basis.* ● *We have regular meetings every Thursday.* ··➤ opposite **irregular 2** done or happening often: *The doctor advised me to take regular exercise.* ● *Accidents are a regular occurrence on this road.* **3** going somewhere or doing sth often: *a regular customer ● We're regular visitors to Britain.* **4** normal or usual: *Who is your regular dentist?* **5** not having any individual part that is different from the rest: *regular teeth/features ● a regular pattern* ··➤ opposite **irregular 6** fixed or permanent: *a regular income/job ● a regular soldier/army* **7** (*especially US*) standard, average or normal: *Regular or large fries?* **8** (*grammar*) (used about a noun, verb, etc) having the usual or expected plural, verb form, etc: *'Walk' is a regular verb.* ··➤ opposite **irregular** –regularly **adv**: *to have a car serviced regularly* –regularity /ˌregjuˈlærəti/ **noun** [U,C]: *My car breaks down with increasing regularity.*

regular² /ˈregjələ/ **noun** [C] **1** (*informal*) a person who goes to a particular shop, bar, restaurant, etc very often **2** a person who usually does a particular activity or sport **3** a permanent member of the army, navy, etc

regulate /ˈregjuleɪt/ **verb** [T] **1** to control sth by using laws or rules **2** to control a machine, piece of equipment, etc: *You can regulate the temperature in the car with this dial.*

★**regulation** /ˌregjuˈleɪʃn/ **noun 1** [C, usually pl] an official rule that controls how sth is done: *to observe/obey the safety regulations ● The plans must comply with EU regulations.* **2** [U] the control of sth by using rules: *state regulation of imports and exports*

rehabilitate /ˌriːəˈbɪlɪteɪt/ **verb** [T] to help sb to live a normal life again after an illness, being in prison, etc –rehabilitation /ˌriːəˌbɪlɪˈteɪʃn/ **noun** [U]: *a rehabilitation centre for drug addicts*

rehearsal /rɪˈhɜːsl/ **noun** [C,U] the time when you practise a play, dance, piece of music, etc before you perform it to other people: *a dress rehearsal* (= when all the actors wear their stage clothes) –rehearse /rɪˈhɜːs/ **verb** [I,T] **rehearse** (for sth)

reign /reɪn/ **verb** [I] **1 reign** (**over sb/sth**) (used about a king or queen) to rule a country: (*figurative*) *the reigning world champion* **2 reign** (**over sb/sth**) to be in charge of a business or organization **3** to be present as the most important quality of a particular situation: *Chaos reigned after the first snow of the winter.* –reign **noun** [C]

reimburse /ˌriːɪmˈbɜːs/ **verb** [T] (*formal*) to pay money back to sb: *The company will*

reimburse you in full for your travelling expenses.

rein /reɪn/ **noun** [C, usually pl] a long thin piece of leather that is held by the rider and used to control a horse's movements ··➤ picture at **horse**

reincarnation /ˌriːɪnkɑːˈneɪʃn/ **noun 1** [U] the belief that people who have died can live again in a different body: *Do you believe in reincarnation?* **2** [C] a person or animal whose body is believed to contain the soul of a dead person: *He believes he is the reincarnation of an Egyptian princess.* ··➤ Look at **incarnation**.

reindeer /ˈreɪndɪə/ **noun** [C] (*pl* **reindeer**) a type of large brownish wild animal that eats grass and lives in Arctic regions

reinforce /ˌriːɪnˈfɔːs/ **verb** [T] to make sth stronger: *Concrete can be reinforced with steel bars.*

reinforcement /ˌriːɪnˈfɔːsmənt/ **noun 1** [U] making sth stronger: *The sea wall is weak in places and needs reinforcement.* **2 reinforcements** [pl] extra people who are sent to make an army, navy, etc stronger

reinstate /ˌriːɪnˈsteɪt/ **verb** [T] **1 reinstate sb** (**in/as sth**) to give back a job or position that was taken from sb: *He was cleared of the charge of theft and reinstated as Head of Security.* **2** to return sth to its former position or role –reinstatement **noun** [U]

★**reject**¹ /rɪˈdʒekt/ **verb** [T] to refuse to accept sb/sth: *The plan was rejected as being impractical.* –rejection **noun** [C,U]: *Gargi got a rejection from Leeds University.* ● *There has been total rejection of the new policy.*

reject² /ˈriːdʒekt/ **noun** [C] a person or thing that is not accepted because he/she/it is not good enough: *Rejects are sold at half price.*

rejoice /rɪˈdʒɔɪs/ **verb** [I] (*formal*) **rejoice** (**at/over sth**) to feel or show great happiness –rejoicing **noun** [U]: *There were scenes of rejoicing when the war ended.*

rejuvenate /rɪˈdʒuːvəneɪt/ **verb** [T] (often passive) to make sb/sth feel or look younger –rejuvenation /rɪˌdʒuːvəˈneɪʃn/ **noun** [U]

relapse /rɪˈlæps/ **verb** [I] to become worse again after an improvement: *to relapse into bad habits* –relapse /ˈriːlæps/ **noun** [C]: *The patient had a relapse and then died.*

★**relate** /rɪˈleɪt/ **verb** [T] **1 relate A to/with B** to show or make a connection between two or more things: *The report relates heart disease to high levels of stress.* **2** (*formal*) **relate sth** (**to sb**) to tell a story to sb: *He related his side of the story to a journalist.*
PHRASAL VERB **relate to sb/sth 1** to be concerned or involved with sth **2** to be able to understand how sb feels: *Some teenagers find it hard to relate to their parents.*

related /rɪˈleɪtɪd/ **adj related** (**to sb/sth**) **1** connected with sb/sth: *The rise in the cost of living is directly related to the price of oil.* **2** of the same family: *We are related by marriage.*

★**relation** /rɪˈleɪʃn/ **noun 1 relations** [pl] relations (**with sb**); relations (**between A and B**) the way that people, groups, countries, etc feel about or behave towards each other: *The police officer stressed that good relations with the community were essential.* **2** [U] relation (between sth and sth); relation (to sth) the connection between two or more things: *There seems to be little relation between the cost of the houses and their size.* • *Their salaries bear no relation to the number of hours they work.* **3** [C] a member of your family: *a close/distant relation* ••➤ synonym **relative**

➤ Note the expressions: *'What relation are you to each other?'* and *'Are you any relation to each other?'*

IDIOM in/with relation to sb/sth **1** concerning sb/sth: *Many questions were asked, particularly in relation to the cost of the new buildings.* **2** compared with: *Prices are low in relation to those in other parts of Europe.*

★**relationship** /rɪˈleɪʃnʃɪp/ noun [C] **1** a relationship (with sb/sth); a relationship (between A and B) the way that people, groups, countries, etc feel about or behave towards each other: *The relationship between the parents and the school has improved greatly.* **2** a relationship (with sb); a relationship (between A and B) a friendly or loving connection between people: *to have a relationship with sb* • *He'd never been in a serious relationship before he got married.* • *The film describes the relationship between a young man and an older woman.* • *Do you have a close relationship with your brother?* **3** a relationship (to sth); a relationship (between A and B) the way in which two or more things are connected: *Is there a relationship between violence on TV and the increase in crime?* **4** a relationship (to sb); a relationship (between A and B) a family connection: *'What is your relationship to Bruce?' 'He's married to my cousin.'*

★**relative¹** /ˈrelətɪv/ adj **1** relative (to sth) when compared to sb/sth else: *the position of the earth relative to the sun* • *They live in relative luxury.* **2** (grammar) referring to an earlier noun, phrase or sentence: *In the phrase 'the lady who lives next door', 'who' is a relative pronoun.*

➤ For more information about relative pronouns and clauses, look at the **Quick Grammar Reference** section at the back of this dictionary.

★**relative²** /ˈrelətɪv/ noun [C] a member of your family: *a close/distant relative* ••➤ synonym **relation**

relatively /ˈrelətɪvli/ adv to quite a large degree, especially when compared to others: *Spanish is a relatively easy language to learn.*

★**relax** /rɪˈlæks/ verb **1** [I] to rest while you are doing sth enjoyable, especially after work or effort: *This holiday will give you a chance to relax.* • *They spent the evening relaxing in front of the television.* **2** [I] to become calmer and less worried: *Relax – everything's going to be OK!* **3** [I,T] to become or make sb/sth become less hard or tight: *A hot bath will*

relax you after a hard day's work. • *Don't relax your grip on the rope!* **4** [T] to make rules or laws less strict

★**relaxation** /ˌriːlækˈseɪʃn/ noun **1** [C,U] something that you do in order to rest, especially after work or effort: *Everyone needs time for rest and relaxation.* **2** [U] making sth less strict, tight or strong

★**relaxed** /rɪˈlækst/ adj not worried or tense: *The relaxed atmosphere made everyone feel at ease.*

relaxing /rɪˈlæksɪŋ/ adj pleasant, helping you to rest and become less worried: *a quiet relaxing holiday*

relay¹ /ˈriːleɪ; ˈriːˈleɪ/ verb [T] (pt, pp **relayed**) **1** to receive and then pass on a signal or message: *Instructions were relayed to us by phone.* **2** (Brit) to put a programme on the radio or television

relay² /ˈriːleɪ/ (also ˈrelay race) noun [C] a race in which each member of a team runs, swims, etc one part of the race

★**release¹** /rɪˈliːs/ verb [T] **1** release sb/sth (from sth) to allow sb/sth to be free: *He's been released from prison.* • (figurative) *His firm released him for two days a week to go on a training course.* **2** to stop holding sth so that it can move, fly, fall, etc freely: *1000 balloons were released at the ceremony.* • (figurative) *Crying is a good way to release pent-up emotions.* **3** to move sth from a fixed position: *He released the handbrake and drove off.* **4** to allow sth to be known by the public: *The identity of the victim has not been released.* **5** to make a film, record, etc available so the public can see or hear it: *Their new single is due to be released next week.*

★**release²** /rɪˈliːs/ noun [C,U] **1** (a) release (of sth) (from sth) the freeing of sth or the state of being freed: *The release of the hostages took place this morning.* • *I had a great feeling of release when my exams were finished.* **2** a book, film, record, piece of news, etc that has been made available to the public; the act of making sth available to the public: *a press release* • *The band played their latest release.* • *The film won't be/go on release until March.*

relegate /ˈrelɪɡeɪt/ verb [T] to put sb/sth into a lower level or position: *The team finished bottom and were relegated to the second division.* –**relegation** /ˌrelɪˈɡeɪʃn/ noun [U]

relent /rɪˈlent/ verb [I] **1** to finally agree to sth that you had refused: *Her parents finally relented and allowed her to go to the concert.* **2** to become less determined, strong, etc: *The heavy rain finally relented and we went out.*

relentless /rɪˈlentləs/ adj not stopping or changing: *the relentless fight against crime* –**relentlessly** adv: *The sun beat down relentlessly.*

★**relevant** /ˈreləvənt/ adj relevant (to sb/sth) **1** connected with what is happening or being talked about: *Much of what was said was not directly relevant to my case.* **2** important and useful: *Many people feel that poetry is no longer relevant in today's world.* ••➤ opposite

r

[I] **intransitive**, a verb which has no object: *He laughed.*   [T] **transitive**, a verb which has an object: *He ate an apple.*

irrelevant –relevance **noun** [U]: *I honestly can't see the relevance of what he said.*

★**reliable** /rɪˈlaɪəbl/ **adj** that you can trust: *Japanese cars are usually very reliable.* ● *Is he a reliable witness?* ▸ opposite **unreliable** ▸ verb **rely** –reliability /rɪˌlaɪəˈbɪləti/ **noun** [U] –reliably /-əbli/ **adv**: *I have been reliably informed that there will be no trains tomorrow.*

reliance /rɪˈlaɪəns/ **noun** [U] reliance on sb/ sth **1** being able to trust sb/sth: *Don't place too much reliance on her promises.* **2** not being able to live or work without sb/sth; being dependent on sb/sth ▸ verb **rely**

reliant /rɪˈlaɪənt/ **adj** reliant on sb/sth not being able to live or work without sb/sth: *They are totally reliant on the state for financial support.* ▸ verb **rely** ▸ Look at self-**reliant**.

relic /ˈrelɪk/ **noun** [C] an object, tradition, etc from the past that still survives today

★**relief** /rɪˈliːf/ **noun 1** [U,sing] relief (from sth) the feeling that you have when sth unpleasant stops or becomes less strong: *What a relief! That awful noise has stopped.* ● *It was a great relief to know they were safe.* ● *to breathe a sigh of relief* ● *To my relief, he didn't argue with my suggestion at all.* **2** [U] the removal or reduction of pain, worry, etc: *These tablets provide pain relief for up to four hours.* **3** [U] money or food that is given to help people who are in trouble or difficulty: *disaster relief for the flood victims* **4** [U] a reduction in the amount of tax you have to pay

relieve /rɪˈliːv/ **verb** [T] to make an unpleasant feeling or situation stop or get better: *This injection should relieve the pain.* ● *We played cards to relieve the boredom.*

PHRASAL VERB **relieve sb of sth** (*formal*) to take sth away from sb: *to relieve sb of responsibility*

★**relieved** /rɪˈliːvd/ **adj** pleased because your fear or worry has been taken away: *I was very relieved to hear that you weren't seriously hurt.*

★**religion** /rɪˈlɪdʒən/ **noun 1** [U] the belief in a god or gods and the activities connected with this **2** [C] one of the systems of beliefs that is based on a belief in a god or gods: *the Christian/Hindu/Muslim/Sikh religion*

★**religious** /rɪˈlɪdʒəs/ **adj 1** connected with religion: *religious faith* **2** having a strong belief in a religion: *a deeply religious person*

religiously /rɪˈlɪdʒəsli/ **adv 1** very carefully or regularly: *She stuck to the diet religiously.* **2** in a religious way

relinquish /rɪˈlɪŋkwɪʃ/ **verb** [T] (*formal*) to stop having or doing sth ▸ **Give up** is more common.

relish¹ /ˈrelɪʃ/ **verb** [T] to enjoy sth or to look forward to sth very much: *I don't relish the prospect of getting up early tomorrow.*

relish² /ˈrelɪʃ/ **noun 1** [U] (*written*) great enjoyment: *She accepted the award with obvious relish.* **2** [U,C] a thick, cold sauce made from fruit and vegetables

relive /ˌriːˈlɪv/ **verb** [T] to remember sth and imagine that it is happening again

reload /ˌriːˈləʊd/ **verb** [I,T] to put sth into a machine again: *to reload a gun* ● *to reload a disk into a computer*

reluctant /rɪˈlʌktənt/ **adj** reluctant (to do sth) not wanting to do sth because you are not sure it is the right thing to do –reluctance **noun** [U]: *Tony left with obvious reluctance.* –reluctantly **adv**

★**rely** /rɪˈlaɪ/ **verb** [I] (*pres part* relying; *3rd pers sing pres* relies; *pt, pp* relied) rely on/ upon sb/sth (to do sth) **1** to need sb/sth and not be able to live or work properly without him/her/it: *The old lady had to rely on other people to do her shopping for her.* **2** to trust sb/sth to work or behave well: *Can I rely on you to keep a secret?* ▸ noun **reliance** ▸ Look at **reliable** and **reliant**.

★**remain** /rɪˈmeɪn/ **verb** [I] **1** to stay or continue in the same place or condition: *to remain silent/standing/seated* ● *Josef went to live in America but his family remained behind in Europe.* **2** to be left after other people or things have gone: *They spent the two remaining days of their holidays buying presents to take home.* **3** to still need to be done, said or dealt with: *It remains to be seen* (= we do not know yet) *whether we've made the right decision.* ● *Although he seems very pleasant, the fact remains that I don't trust him.*

remainder /rɪˈmeɪndə/ **noun** (usually **the remainder**) [sing,with sing or pl verb] the people, things, etc that are left after the others have gone away or been dealt with; the rest

remains /rɪˈmeɪnz/ **noun** [pl] **1** what is left behind after other parts have been used or taken away: *The builders found the remains of a Roman mosaic floor.* **2** (*formal*) a dead body (sometimes one that has been found somewhere a long time after death): *Human remains were discovered in the wood.*

remand /rɪˈmɑːnd/ **noun** [U] (*Brit*) the time before a prisoner's trial takes place: *a remand prisoner* –remand **verb** [T]: *The man was remanded in custody* (= sent to prison until the trial).

IDIOM **on remand** (used about a prisoner) waiting for the trial to take place

★**remark** /rɪˈmɑːk/ **verb** [I,T] remark (on/upon sb/sth) to say or write sth; to comment: *A lot of people have remarked on the similarity between them.* ▸ Look at **observation** and **comment**. –remark **noun** [C]

remarkable /rɪˈmɑːkəbl/ **adj** unusual and surprising in a way that people notice: *That is a remarkable achievement for someone so young.* –remarkably /-əbli/ **adv**

remedial /rɪˈmiːdiəl/ **adj 1** aimed at improving or correcting a situation **2** helping people who are slow at learning sth: *remedial English classes*

remedy¹ /ˈremədi/ **noun** [C] (*pl* remedies) a remedy (for sth) **1** something that makes you better when you are ill or in pain: *Hot*

r

lemon with honey is a good remedy for colds.
2 a way of solving a problem: *There is no easy remedy for unemployment.*

remedy[2] /'remədi/ *verb* [T] (*pres part* **remedying**; *3rd pers sing pres* **remedies**; *pt, pp* **remedied**) to change or improve sth that is wrong or bad: *to remedy an injustice*

*★**remember** /rɪ'membə/ *verb* [I,T] **1** remember (sb/sth); remember (doing sth); remember that... to have sb/sth in your mind or to bring sb/sth back into your mind: *We arranged to go out tonight – remember?* ● *As far as I can remember, I haven't seen him before.* ● *I'm sorry. I don't remember your name.* ● *Do you remember the night we first met?* ● *Remember that we're having visitors tonight.* ● *Can you remember when we bought the stereo?* **2** remember (sth/to do sth) to not forget to do what you have to do: *I remembered to buy the coffee.* ● *Remember to turn the lights off before you leave.*

> Notice that if you remember **to do** something, you don't forget to do it. If you remember **doing** something, you have a picture or memory in your mind of doing it: *I remember leaving my keys on the table last night.* ● *Remember to take your keys when you go out.*

IDIOM remember me to sb used when you want to send good wishes to a person you have not seen for a long time: *Please remember me to your wife.* ⚫➤ Look at the note at **remind.**

remembrance /rɪ'membrəns/ *noun* [U] (*formal*) thinking about and showing respect for sb who is dead: *a service **in remembrance of** those killed in the war*

*★**remind** /rɪ'maɪnd/ *verb* [T] **1** remind sb (about/of sth); remind sb (to do sth/that...) to help sb to remember sth, especially sth important that he/she has to do: *Can you remind me of your address?* ● *He reminded the children to wash their hands.* ● *Remind me what we're supposed to be doing tomorrow.* **2** remind sb of sb/sth to cause sb to remember sb/sth: *That smell reminds me of school.* ● *You remind me of your father.*

> You **remember** something by yourself. If somebody or something **reminds** you of something he/she/it causes you to remember it: *Did you remember to phone Ali last night?* ● *Remind me to phone Ali later.*

reminder /rɪ'maɪndə/ *noun* [C] something that makes you remember sth: *We received a reminder that we hadn't paid the electricity bill.*

reminisce /ˌremɪ'nɪs/ *verb* [I] reminisce (about sb/sth) to talk about pleasant things that happened in the past

reminiscent /ˌremɪ'nɪsnt/ *adj* (not before a noun) that makes you remember sb/sth; similar to: *His suit was reminiscent of an old army uniform.*

remnant /'remnənt/ *noun* [C] a piece of sth that is left after the rest has gone: *These few trees are the remnants of a huge forest.*

remorse /rɪ'mɔːs/ *noun* [U] remorse (for sth/ doing sth) a feeling of sadness because you have done sth wrong: *She was filled with remorse for what she had done.* ⚫➤ Look at **guilt.** –**remorseful** /-fl/ *adj*

remorseless /rɪ'mɔːsləs/ *adj* **1** showing no pity **2** not stopping or becoming less strong: *a remorseless attack on sb* –**remorselessly** *adv*

remote /rɪ'məʊt/ *adj* **1** remote (from sth) far away from where other people live: *a remote island in the Pacific* **2** far away in time: *the remote past/future* **3** not very great: *I haven't the remotest idea who could have done such a thing.* ● *a remote possibility* **4** not very friendly or interested in other people: *He seemed rather remote.* –**remoteness** *noun* [U]

re,mote con'trol *noun* **1** [U] a system for controlling sth from a distance: *The doors can be opened by remote control.* **2** (also **remote**) [C] a piece of equipment for controlling sth from a distance

remotely /rɪ'məʊtli/ *adv* (used in negative sentences) to a very small degree; at all: *I'm not remotely interested in your problems.*

removal /rɪ'muːvl/ *noun* **1** [U] the action of taking sb/sth away: *the removal of restrictions/regulations/rights* **2** [C,U] the activity of moving from one house to live in another: *a removal van*

*★**remove** /rɪ'muːv/ *verb* [T] (*formal*) **1** remove sb/sth (from sth) to take sb/sth off or away: *Remove the saucepan from the heat.* ● *This washing powder will remove most stains.* ● *to remove doubts/fears/problems* ● *I would like you to remove my name from your mailing list.* ● *He had an operation to remove the tumour.* ⚫➤ Take off, out, etc is less formal. **2** remove sb (from sth) to make sb leave his/her job or position

removed /rɪ'muːvd/ *adj* (not before a noun) far or different from sth: *Hospitals today are far removed from what they were fifty years ago.*

remover /rɪ'muːvə/ *noun* [C,U] a substance that cleans off paint, dirty marks, etc: *make-up remover*

render /'rendə/ *verb* [T] (*written*) **1** to cause sb/sth to be in a certain condition: *She was rendered speechless by the attack.* **2** to give help, etc to sb: *to render sb a service/render a service to sb*

rendezvous /'rɒndɪvuː; -deɪ-/ *noun* [C] (*pl* **rendezvous** /-vuːz/) **1** a rendezvous (with sb) a meeting that you have arranged with sb: *He had a secret rendezvous with Daniela.* **2** a place where people often meet: *The cafe is a popular rendezvous for students.*

renew /rɪ'njuː/ *verb* [T] **1** to start sth again: *renewed outbreaks of violence* ● *to renew a friendship* **2** to give sb new strength or energy: *After a break he set to work with renewed enthusiasm.* **3** to make sth valid for a further period of time: *to renew a contract/ passport/library book* –**renewal** /-'njuːəl/ *noun* [C,U]: *When is your passport due for renewal?*

renewable /rɪ'njuːəbl/ *adj* **1** (used about

sources of energy) that will always exist: *renewable resources such as wind and solar power* ··➤ opposite **non-renewable 2** that can be continued or replaced with a new one for another period of time

renounce /rɪ'naʊns/ **verb** [T] (*formal*) to say formally that you no longer want to have sth or to be connected with sth ··➤ **noun** renunciation

renovate /'renəveɪt/ **verb** [T] to repair an old building and put it back into good condition –**renovation** /ˌrenə'veɪʃn/ **noun** [C,U]: *The house is in need of complete renovation.*

renown /rɪ'naʊn/ **noun** [U] (*formal*) fame and respect that you get for doing sth especially well –**renowned** **adj** renowned (for/as sth): *The region is renowned for its food.*

★**rent**[1] /rent/ **noun** [U,C] money that you pay regularly for the use of land, a house or a building: *a high/low rent* ● *She was allowed to live there rent-free until she found a job.* ● *Is this house for rent* (= available to rent)?

★**rent**[2] /rent/ **verb** [T] **1 rent sth (from sb)** to pay money for the use of land, a building, a machine, etc: *Do you own or rent your television?* ● *to rent a flat* ··➤ Look at the note at **hire**[i](1). **2 rent sth (out) (to sb)** to allow sb to use land, a building, a machine, etc for money: *We could rent out the small bedroom to a student.* ··➤ Look at **hire**[i](3). **3** (*US*) = **HIRE**[1](1) **4** (*US*) = **HIRE**[1](3)

rental /'rentl/ **noun** [C,U] money that you pay when you rent a telephone, television, etc

renunciation /rɪˌnʌnsi'eɪʃn/ **noun** [U] (*formal*) saying that you no longer want sth or believe in sth ··➤ verb **renounce**

reorganize (also **-ise**) /ri'ɔːgənaɪz/ **verb** [I,T] to organize sth again or in a new way –**reorganization** (also **-isation**) /riˌɔːgənaɪ'zeɪʃn/ **noun** [C,U]

Rep **abbr** (in US politics) **1** Representative (in Congress) **2** Republican (Party)

rep /rep/ (*informal*) (also **representative**) **noun** [C] a person whose job is to travel round a particular area and visit companies, etc, to sell the products of the firm for which he/she works: *a sales rep*

★**repair**[1] /rɪ'peə/ **verb** [T] to put sth old or damaged back into good condition: *These cars can be expensive to repair.* ● *How much will it cost to have the TV repaired?* ··➤ synonyms **fix**, **mend** ··➤ Look at **irreparable**.

repair[2] /rɪ'peə/ **noun** [C,U] something that you do to mend sth that is damaged: *The school is closed for repairs to the roof.* ● *The road is in need of repair.* ● *The bridge is under repair.* ● *The bike was damaged beyond repair so I threw it away.*
[IDIOM] **in good, bad, etc repair** in a good, bad, etc condition

repatriate /ˌriː'pætrieɪt/ **verb** [T] to send sb back to his/her own country –**repatriation** /riːˌpætri'eɪʃn/ **noun** [C,U]

repay /rɪ'peɪ/ **verb** [T] (*pt, pp* **repaid** /rɪ'peɪd/) **1** **repay sth (to sb)**; **repay (sb) sth** to pay back money that you owe to sb: *to repay a debt/loan* ● *When will you repay the*

money to them? ● *When will you repay them the money?* **2** **repay sb (for sth)** to give sth to sb in return for help, kindness, etc: *How can I ever repay you for all you have done for me?*

repayable /rɪ'peɪəbl/ **adj** that you can or must pay back: *The loan is repayable over three years.*

repayment /rɪ'peɪmənt/ **noun** **1** [U] paying sth back: *the repayment of a loan* **2** [C] money that you must pay back to sb/sth regularly: *I make monthly repayments on my loan.*

repeal /rɪ'piːl/ **verb** [T] (*formal*) to officially make a law no longer valid

★**repeat**[1] /rɪ'piːt/ **verb 1** [I,T] repeat (sth/yourself) to say, write or do sth again or more than once: *Don't repeat the same mistake again.* ● *Could you repeat what you just said?* ● *The essay is quite good, but you repeat yourself several times.* ● *Raise and lower your left leg ten times, then repeat with the right.* **2** [T] repeat sth (to sb) to say or write sth that sb else has said or written or that you have learnt: *Please don't repeat what you've heard here to anyone.* ● *Repeat each sentence after me.* ··➤ **noun** repetition

repeat[2] /rɪ'piːt/ **noun** [C] something that is done, shown, given, etc again: *I think I've seen this programme before – it must be a repeat.*

repeated /rɪ'piːtɪd/ **adj** (only *before* a noun) done or happening many times: *There have been repeated accidents on this stretch of road.* –**repeatedly** **adv**: *I've asked him repeatedly not to leave his bicycle there.*

repel /rɪ'pel/ **verb** [T] (**repelling**; **repelled**) **1** to send or push sb/sth back or away **2** to make sb feel disgusted: *The dirt and smell repelled her.* ··➤ **noun** repulsion

repellent[1] /rɪ'pelənt/ **noun** [C,U] a chemical substance that is used to keep insects, etc away: *a mosquito repellent*

repellent[2] /rɪ'pelənt/ **adj** causing a strong feeling of disgust: *a repellent smell*

repent /rɪ'pent/ **verb** [I,T] (*formal*) repent (of) (sth) to feel and show that you are sorry about sth bad that you have done: *to repent of your sins* ● *He repented his hasty decision.* –**repentance** **noun** [U] /-əns/ –**repentant** /-ənt/ **adj**

repercussion /ˌriːpə'kʌʃn/ **noun** [C, usually pl] an unpleasant effect or result of sth you do: *His resignation will have serious repercussions.*

repertoire /'repətwɑː/ **noun** [C] **1** all the plays or music that an actor or a musician knows and can perform: *He must have sung every song in his repertoire last night.* **2** all the things that a person is able to do

repetition /ˌrepə'tɪʃn/ **noun** [C,U] doing sth again; sth that you do or that happens again: *to learn by repetition* ● *Let's try to avoid a repetition of what happened last Friday.* ··➤ verb **repeat**

repetitive /rɪ'petətɪv/ (also **repetitious** /ˌrepə'tɪʃəs/) **adj** not interesting because the same thing is repeated many times

★**replace** /rɪ'pleɪs/ *verb* [T] **1** replace sb/sth (as/with sb/sth) to take the place of sb/sth; to use sb/sth in place of another person or thing: *Teachers will never be replaced by computers in the classroom.* **2** replace sth (with sb/sth) to exchange sb/sth for sb/sth that is better or newer: *We will replace any goods that are damaged.* **3** to put sth back in the place where it was before: *Please replace the books on the shelves when you have finished with them.* ·➤ **Put back** is more common and less formal.

replaceable /rɪ'pleɪsəbl/ *adj* that can be replaced ·➤ opposite **irreplaceable**

replacement /rɪ'pleɪsmənt/ *noun* **1** [U] exchanging sb/sth for sb/sth that is better or newer: *The carpets are in need of replacement.* **2** [C] a person or thing that will take the place of sb/sth: *Mary is leaving next month so we must advertise for a replacement for her.*

replay¹ /'riːpleɪ/ *noun* [C] **1** (*Brit*) a sports match that is played again because neither team won the first time **2** something on the television, on a film or a cassette tape that you watch or listen to again: *Now let's see an action replay of that tremendous goal!*

replay² /ˌriːˈpleɪ/ *verb* [T] **1** to play a sports match, etc again because neither team won the first time **2** to play again sth that you have recorded: *They kept replaying the goal over and over again.*

replica /'replɪkə/ *noun* [C] a replica (of sth) an exact copy of sth

★**reply** /rɪ'plaɪ/ *verb* [I,T] (*pres part* **replying**; *3rd pers sing pres* **replies**; *pt, pp* **replied**) reply (to sb/sth) (with sth) to say, write or do sth as an answer to sb/sth: *I wrote to Sue but she hasn't replied.* ● *'Yes, I will,' she replied.* ● *to reply to a question* ·➤ Look at the note at **answer¹**. –reply *noun* [C,U] (*pl* **replies**): *Al nodded in reply to my question.*

★**report¹** /rɪ'pɔːt/ *verb* **1** [I,T] report (on sb/sth) (to sb/sth); report sth (to sb) to give people information about what you have seen, heard, etc: *Several people reported seeing/having seen the boy.* ● *Several people reported that they had seen the boy.* ● *The company reported huge profits last year.* ● *Call me if you have anything new to report.* **2** [I,T] report (on) sth (in a newspaper or on the television or radio) to write or speak about sth that has happened: *The paper sent a journalist to report on the events.* **3** [T] report sb (to sb) (for sth) to tell a person in authority about an accident, a crime, etc or about sth wrong that sb has done: *All accidents must be reported to the police.* ● *The boy was reported missing early this morning.* **4** [I] report (to sb/sth) for sth to tell sb that you have arrived: *On your arrival, please report to the reception desk.* **5** [T] (*formal*) be reported to be/as sth used to say that you have heard sth said, but you are not sure if it is true: *The 70-year-old actor is reported to be/as being comfortable in hospital.*

PHRASAL VERBS **report back (on sth) (to sb)** to give information to sb about sth he/she has

asked you to find out about: *One person in each group will then report back on what you've decided to the class.*

report to sb (not used in the continuous tenses) to have sb as your manager in the company or organization that you work for

➤ Although this verb is not used in the continuous tenses, it is common to see the present participle (= -*ing* form): *A new team was put together for the project, reporting to Michael Nolan.*

★**report²** /rɪ'pɔːt/ *noun* [C] **1** a report (on/of sth) a written or spoken description of what you have seen, heard, done, studied, etc: *newspaper reports* ● *a report on the company's finances* ● *a first-hand report* (= from the person who saw what happened) **2** a written statement about the work of a student at school, college, etc: *to get a good/bad report*

re,ported 'speech = INDIRECT SPEECH

➤ Look at the **Quick Grammar Reference** section at the back of this dictionary.

reporter /rɪ'pɔːtə/ *noun* [C] a person who writes about the news in a newspaper or speaks about it on the television or radio ·➤ Look at **journalist**.

★**represent** /ˌreprɪ'zent/ *verb* [T] **1** to act or speak in the place of sb else; to be the representative of a group or country: *You will need a lawyer to represent you in court.* ● *It's an honour for an athlete to represent his or her country.* **2** to be equal to sth; to be sth: *These results represent a major breakthrough in our understanding of cancer.* **3** to be a picture, sign, example, etc of sth: *The yellow lines on the map represent minor roads.* **4** to describe sb/sth in a particular way

★**representation** /ˌreprɪzen'teɪʃn/ *noun* **1** [U,C] the way that sb/sth is shown or described; something that shows or describes sth: *The article complains about the representation of women in advertising.* ·➤ Look at **proportional representation**. **2** [U] (*formal*) having sb to speak for you

representative¹ /ˌreprɪ'zentətɪv/ *adj* representative (of sb/sth) typical of a larger group to which sb/sth belongs: *Tonight's audience is not representative of national opinion.*

representative² /ˌreprɪ'zentətɪv/ *noun* [C] **1** a person who has been chosen to act or speak for sb else or for a group **2** (*formal*) = REP

repress /rɪ'pres/ *verb* [T] **1** to control an emotion or to try to prevent it from being shown or felt: *She tried to repress her anger.* **2** to limit the freedom of a group of people –repression /rɪ'preʃn/ *noun* [U]: *protests against government repression*

repressed /rɪ'prest/ *adj* **1** (used about a person) having emotions and desires that he/she does not show or express **2** (used about an emotion) that you do not show: *repressed anger/desire*

repressive /rɪ'presɪv/ *adj* that limits people's freedom: *a repressive government*

reprieve /rɪ'priːv/ verb [T] to stop or delay the punishment of a prisoner who was going to be punished by death –**reprieve** noun [C]: *The judge granted him a last-minute reprieve.*

reprimand /'reprɪmɑːnd/ verb [T] reprimand sb (for sth) to tell sb officially that he/she has done sth wrong –**reprimand** noun [C]: *a severe reprimand*

reprisal /rɪ'praɪzl/ noun [C,U] punishment, especially by military force, for harm that one group of people does to another

reproach /rɪ'prəʊtʃ/ verb [T] reproach sb (for/with sth) to tell sb that he/she has done sth wrong; to blame sb: *You've nothing to reproach yourself for. It wasn't your fault.* –**reproach** noun [C,U]: *His behaviour is beyond reproach* (= cannot be criticized). ● *Alison felt his reproaches were unjustified.* –**reproachful** /-fl/ adj: *a reproachful look* –**reproachfully** /-fəli/ adv

★**reproduce** /ˌriːprə'djuːs/ verb 1 [T] to produce a copy of sth: *It is very hard to reproduce a natural environment in the laboratory.* 2 [I] (used about people, animals and plants) to produce young

★**reproduction** /ˌriːprə'dʌkʃn/ noun 1 [U] the process of producing babies or young: *sexual reproduction* 2 [U] the production of copies of sth: *Digital recording gives excellent sound reproduction.* 3 [C] a copy of a painting, etc

reproductive /ˌriːprə'dʌktɪv/ adj connected with the production of young animals, plants, etc: *the male reproductive organs*

reproof /rɪ'pruːf/ noun [C,U] (formal) something that you say to sb when you do not approve of what he/she has done

reptile /'reptaɪl/ noun [C] an animal that has cold blood and a skin covered in scales, and whose young come out of eggs, for example crocodiles and snakes

➤ Compare **amphibian**.

★**republic** /rɪ'pʌblɪk/ noun [C] a country that has an elected government and an elected leader (president): *the Republic of Ireland* ••➤ Look at **monarchy**.

republican /rɪ'pʌblɪkən/ noun [C] 1 a person who supports the system of an elected government and leader 2 **Republican** a member of the Republican Party ••➤ Look at **Democrat**. –**republican** adj

the Re'publican Party noun [sing] one of the two main political parties of the US ••➤ The other party is the Democratic Party, whose members are called **Democrats**.

repudiate /rɪ'pjuːdieɪt/ verb [T] to say that you refuse to accept or believe sth: *to repudiate a suggestion/an accusation/responsibility*

repulsive /rɪ'pʌlsɪv/ adj that causes a strong feeling of disgust ••➤ verb **repel** –**repulsion** noun [U]

reputable /'repjətəbl/ adj that is known to be good ••➤ opposite **disreputable**

★**reputation** /ˌrepju'teɪʃn/ noun [C] a reputation (for/as sth) the opinion that people in general have about what sb/sth is like: *to*

have a good/bad reputation ● *Adam has a reputation for being late.* ••➤ synonym **name**

reputed /rɪ'pjuːtɪd/ adj generally said to be sth, although it is not certain: *He's reputed to be the highest-paid sportsman in the world.* –**reputedly** adv

★**request**[1] /rɪ'kwest/ noun [C,U] request (for sth/that...) an act of asking for sth: *a request for help* ● *I'm going to make a request for a larger desk.* ● *to grant/turn down a request* ● *Single rooms are available on request.*

request[2] /rɪ'kwest/ verb [T] (formal) request sth (from/of sb) to ask for sth: *Passengers are requested not to smoke on this bus.* ● *to request a loan from the bank* ••➤ **Request** is more formal than **ask**.

★**require** /rɪ'kwaɪə/ verb [T] 1 to need sth: *a situation that requires tact and diplomacy* ••➤ **Require** is more formal than **need**. 2 (often passive) to officially demand or order sth: *Passengers are required by law to wear seat belts.*

requirement /rɪ'kwaɪəmənt/ noun [C] something that you need or that you must do or have: *university entrance requirements*

★**rescue** /'reskjuː/ verb [T] rescue sb/sth (from sb/sth) to save sb/sth from a situation that is dangerous or unpleasant: *He rescued a child from drowning.* –**rescue** noun [C,U]: *Ten fishermen were saved in a daring sea rescue.* ● *Blow the whistle if you're in danger, and someone should come to your rescue.* ● *rescue workers/boats/helicopters* –**rescuer** noun [C]

★**research** /rɪ'sɜːtʃ/ noun [U] research (into/on sth) a detailed and careful study of sth to find out more information about it: *to do research into sth* ● *scientific/medical/historical research* ● *We are carrying out market research to find out who our typical customer is.* –**research** verb [I,T] research (into/on) (sth): *They're researching ways of reducing traffic in the city centre.*

researcher /rɪ'sɜːtʃə/ noun [C] a person who does research

resemble /rɪ'zembl/ verb [T] to be or look like sb/sth else: *Laura resembles her brother.* –**resemblance** /rɪ'zembləns/ noun [C,U] (a) resemblance (between A and B); (a) resemblance (to sb/sth): *a family resemblance* ● *The boys bear no resemblance to their father.*

resent /rɪ'zent/ verb [T] to feel angry about sth because you think it is unfair: *I resent his criticism.* ● *Louise bitterly resented being treated differently from the men.* –**resentful** /-fl/ adj –**resentment** noun [sing,U]: *to feel resentment towards sb/sth*

reservation /ˌrezə'veɪʃn/ noun 1 [C] a seat, table, room, etc that you have booked: *We have reservations in the name of Petrovic.* ● *I'll phone the restaurant to make a reservation.* 2 [C,U] a feeling of doubt about sth (such as a plan or an idea): *I have some reservations about letting Julie go out alone.*

★**reserve**[1] /rɪ'zɜːv/ verb [T] reserve sth (for sb/sth) 1 to keep sth for a special reason or to use at a later time: *The car park is reserved for hotel guests only.* **2** to ask for a seat, table, room, etc to be available at a future time; to book: *to reserve theatre tickets*

reserve² /rɪˈzɜːv/ **noun 1** [C,usually pl] something that you keep for a special reason or to use at a later date: *The US has huge oil reserves.* **2** [C] an area of land where the plants, animals, etc are protected by law: *a nature reserve* • *He works as a warden on a game reserve in Kenya.* **3** [U] the quality of being shy or keeping your feelings hidden: *It took a long time to break down her reserve and get her to relax.* **4** [C] (in sport) a person who will play in a game if one of the usual members of the team cannot play

IDIOM **in reserve** that you keep and do not use unless you need to: *Keep some money in reserve for emergencies.*

reserved /rɪˈzɜːvd/ **adj** shy and keeping your feelings hidden •➤ opposite **unreserved**

reservoir /ˈrezəvwɑː/ **noun** [C] a large lake where water is stored to be used by a particular area, city, etc

reside /rɪˈzaɪd/ **verb** [I] (*formal*) **reside (in/ at...)** to have your home in or at a particular place

residence /ˈrezɪdəns/ **noun 1** [U] the state of having your home in a particular place: *The family applied for permanent residence in the United States.* • *a hall of residence for college students* • *Some birds have taken up residence in our roof.* **2** [C] (*formal*) a house, especially an impressive or important one

★**resident** /ˈrezɪdənt/ **noun** [C] **1** a person who lives in a place: *local residents* **2** a person who is staying in a hotel: *The hotel bar is open only to residents.* –**resident adj**

residential /ˌrezɪˈdenʃl/ **adj 1** (used about a place or an area) that has houses rather than offices, large shops or factories: *They live in a quiet residential area.* **2** that provides a place for sb to live: *This home provides residential care for the elderly.*

residue /ˈrezɪdjuː/ **noun** [C,usually sing] (*formal*) what is left after the main part of sth is taken or used: *The washing powder left a white residue on the clothes.*

resign /rɪˈzaɪn/ **verb 1** [I,T] **resign (from/as) (sth)** to leave your job or position: *He's resigned as chairman of the committee.* **2** [T] **resign yourself to sth/doing sth** to accept sth that is unpleasant but that you cannot change: *Jamie resigned himself to the fact that she was not coming back to him.*

resignation /ˌrezɪɡˈneɪʃn/ **noun 1** [C,U] **resignation (from sth)** a letter or statement that says you want to leave your job or position: *to hand in your resignation* • *a letter of resignation* **2** [U] the state of accepting sth unpleasant that you cannot change

resigned /rɪˈzaɪnd/ **adj** **resigned (to sth/ doing sth)** accepting sth that is unpleasant but that you cannot change: *Ben was resigned to the fact that he would never be an athlete.*

resilient /rɪˈzɪliənt/ **adj** strong enough to deal with illness, a shock, change, etc –**resilience noun** [U]

resist /rɪˈzɪst/ **verb 1** [I,T] to try to stop sth happening or to stop sb from doing sth; to fight back against sth/sb: *The government are resisting pressure to change the law.* • *to resist arrest* **2** [T] to stop yourself from having or doing sth that you want to have or do: *I couldn't resist telling Nadia what we'd bought for her.*

resistance /rɪˈzɪstəns/ **noun** [U] **1** **resistance (to sb/sth)** trying to stop sth from happening or to stop sb from doing sth; fighting back against sb/sth: *The government troops overcame the resistance of the rebel army.* **2** **resistance (to sth)** the power in a person's body not to be affected by disease

resistant /rɪˈzɪstənt/ **adj** **resistant (to sth) 1** not wanting sth and trying to prevent sth happening: *resistant to change* **2** not harmed or affected by sth: *This watch is water-resistant.*

resolute /ˈrezəluːt/ **adj** having or showing great determination: *a resolute refusal to change* •➤ **Determined** is more common. –**resolutely adv**

resolution /ˌrezəˈluːʃn/ **noun 1** [U] the quality of being firm and determined **2** [U] solving or settling a problem, dispute, etc **3** [C] a formal decision that is taken after a vote by a group of people: *The UN resolution condemned the invasion.* **4** [C] a firm decision to do or not to do sth

resolve /rɪˈzɒlv/ **verb** (*formal*) **1** [T] to find an answer to a problem: *Most of the difficulties have been resolved.* **2** [I,T] to decide sth and be determined not to change your mind: *He resolved never to repeat the experience.*

resort¹ /rɪˈzɔːt/ **noun** [C] a place where a lot of people go to on holiday: *a seaside/ski resort*

IDIOM **in the last resort; (as) a last resort** ➔ **LAST¹**

resort² /rɪˈzɔːt/ **verb** [I] **resort to sth/doing sth** to do or use sth bad or unpleasant because you feel you have no choice: *After not sleeping for three nights I finally resorted to sleeping pills.*

resounding /rɪˈzaʊndɪŋ/ **adj** (only *before* a noun) **1** very loud: *resounding cheers* **2** very great: *a resounding victory/win/defeat/success*

resource /rɪˈsɔːs; -ˈzɔːs/ **noun** [C,usually pl] a supply of sth, a piece of equipment, etc that is available for sb to use: *Russia is rich in natural resources such as oil and minerals.*

resourceful /rɪˈzɔːsfl; -ˈsɔːs-/ **adj** good at finding ways of doing things

★**respect¹** /rɪˈspekt/ **noun 1** [U] **respect (for sb/sth)** the feeling that you have when you admire or have a high opinion of sb/sth: *I have little respect for people who are arrogant.* • *to win/lose sb's respect* •➤ Look at **self-respect.** **2** [U] **respect (for sb/sth)** polite behaviour or care towards sb/sth that you think is important: *We should all treat older*

r

people with more respect. ‣ opposite **disrespect 3** [C] a detail or point: *In what respects do you think things have changed in the last ten years?* • *Her performance was brilliant in every respect.*

IDIOMS **with respect to sth** (*formal*) about or concerning

pay your respects → PAY¹

★**respect²** /rɪ'spekt/ *verb* [T] **1** respect sb/sth (for sth) to admire or have a high opinion of sb/sth: *I respect him for his honesty.* **2** to show care for or pay attention to sb/sth: *We should respect other people's cultures and values.* —**respectful** *adj* respectful (to/towards sb): *The crowd listened in respectful silence.* ‣ opposite **disrespectful** —**respectfully** /-fəli/ *adv*

respectable /rɪ'spektəbl/ *adj* **1** considered by society to be good, proper or correct: *a respectable family* • *He combed his hair and tried to look respectable for the interview.* **2** quite good or large: *a respectable salary* —**respectability** /rɪˌspektə'bɪləti/ *noun* [U]

respective /rɪ'spektɪv/ *adj* (only *before* a noun) belonging separately to each of the people who have been mentioned

respectively /rɪ'spektɪvli/ *adv* in the same order as sb/sth that was mentioned

respiration /ˌrespə'reɪʃn/ *noun* [U] (*formal*) breathing

respite /'respaɪt/ *noun* [sing,U] respite (from sth) a short period of rest from sth that is difficult or unpleasant: *There was a brief respite from the fighting.*

★**respond** /rɪ'spɒnd/ *verb* [I] **1** (*formal*) respond (to sb/sth) (with/by sth) to say or do sth as an answer or reaction to sth: *He responded to my question with a nod.* • *Owen responded to the manager's criticism by scoring two goals.* ‣ **Respond** is more formal than **answer** or **reply**. **2** respond (to sb/sth) to have or show a good or quick reaction to sb/sth: *The patient did not respond well to the new treatment.*

★**response** /rɪ'spɒns/ *noun* [C,U] (a) response (to sb/sth) an answer or reaction to sb/sth: *I've sent out 20 letters of enquiry but I've had no responses yet.* • *The government acted in response to economic pressure.*

★**responsibility** /rɪˌspɒnsə'bɪləti/ *noun* (*pl* **responsibilities**) **1** [U,C] responsibility (for sb/sth); responsibility (to do sth) a duty to deal with sth so that it is your fault if sth goes wrong: *I refuse to take responsibility if anything goes wrong.* • *It is John's responsibility to make sure the orders are sent out on time.* • *I feel that I have a responsibility to help them – after all, they did help me.* • *Who has responsibility for the new students?* **2** [U] the fact of sth being your fault; blame: *No group has yet admitted responsibility for planting the bomb.*

IDIOM **shift the blame/responsibility (for sth) (onto sb)** → SHIFT¹

★**responsible** /rɪ'spɒnsəbl/ *adj* **1** (not before a noun) responsible (for sb/sth); responsible (for doing sth) having the job or duty

of dealing with sb/sth, so that it is your fault if sth goes wrong: *The school is responsible for the safety of the children in school hours.* • *The manager is responsible for making sure the shop is run properly.* **2** (not before a noun) responsible (for sth) being the person whose fault sth is: *Who was responsible for the accident?* **3** (not before a noun) responsible (to sb/sth) having to report to sb/sth with authority, or to sb who you are working for, about what you are doing: *Members of Parliament are responsible to the electors.* **4** (used about a person) that you can trust to behave well and in a sensible way: *Marisa is responsible enough to take her little sister to school.* ‣ opposite **irresponsible 5** (used about a job) that is important and that should be done by a person who can be trusted

★**responsibly** /rɪ'spɒnsəbli/ *adv* (used about sb's way of behaving) that you can trust; sensible

responsive /rɪ'spɒnsɪv/ *adj* paying attention to sb/sth and reacting in a suitable or positive way: *By being responsive to changes in the market, the company has had great success.*

★**rest¹** /rest/ *verb* **1** [I] to relax, sleep or stop after a period of activity or because of illness; to not use a part of your body for a period of time: *We've been walking for hours. Let's rest here for a while.* **2** [T] to not use a part of your body for a period of time because it is tired or painful: *Your knee will get better as long as you rest it as much as you can.* **3** [I,T] rest (sth) on/against sth to place sth in a position where it is supported by sth else; to be in such a position: *She rested her head on his shoulder and went to sleep.*

IDIOM **let sth rest** to not talk about sth any longer

PHRASAL VERB **rest on sb/sth** to depend on sb/sth or be based on sth: *The whole theory rests on a very simple idea.*

★**rest²** /rest/ *noun* **1** [C,U] a period of relaxing, sleeping or doing nothing: *I can't walk any further! I need a rest.* • *I'm going upstairs to **have a rest** before we go out.* • *Try not to worry now.* **Get some rest** *and think about it again tomorrow.* • *I sat down to **give my bad leg a rest.* **2** [sing,with sing or pl verb] the rest (of sb/sth) the part that is left; the ones that are left: *We had lunch and spent the rest of the day on the beach.* • *She takes no interest in what happens in the rest of the world.* • *They were the first people to arrive. The rest came later.* • *The rest of our bags are still in the car.*

IDIOM **at rest** not moving: *Do not open the door until the vehicle is at rest.*

come to rest to stop moving: *The car crashed through a wall and came to rest in a field.*

put/set your/sb's mind at rest → MIND¹

★**restaurant** /'restrɒnt/ *noun* [C] a place where you can buy and eat a meal: *a fast food/hamburger restaurant* • *a Chinese/an Italian/a Thai restaurant* ‣ Look at **cafe** and **takeaway**.

restful /'restfl/ adj giving a relaxed, peaceful feeling: *I find this piece of music very restful.*

restless /'restləs/ adj **1** unable to relax or be still because you are bored, nervous or impatient: *The children always get restless on long journeys.* **2** (used about a period of time) without sleep or rest –**restlessly** adv

restoration /ˌrestə'reɪʃn/ noun **1** [C,U] the return of sth to its original condition; the things that are done to achieve this: *The house is in need of restoration.* **2** [U] the return of sth to its original owner: *the restoration of stolen property to its owner*

restore /rɪ'stɔː/ verb [T] restore sb/sth (to sb/sth) **1** to put sb/sth back into his/her/its former condition or position: *She restores old furniture as a hobby.* • *In the recent elections, the former president was restored to power.* **2** (*formal*) restore sth to sb to give sth that was lost or stolen back to sb

restrain /rɪ'streɪn/ verb [T] restrain sb/sth (from sth/doing sth) to keep sb or sth under control; to prevent sb or sth from doing sth: *I had to restrain myself from saying something rude.*

restrained /rɪ'streɪnd/ adj not showing strong feelings

restraint /rɪ'streɪnt/ noun **1** [U] the quality of behaving in a calm or controlled way: *It took a lot of restraint on my part not to hit him.* • *Soldiers have to exercise self-restraint even when provoked.* **2** [C] a restraint (on sb/sth) a limit or control on sth: *Are there any restraints on what the newspapers are allowed to publish?*

restrict /rɪ'strɪkt/ verb [T] restrict sb/sth (to sth/doing sth) to put a limit on sb/sth: *There is a plan to restrict the use of cars in the city centre.*

restricted /rɪ'strɪktɪd/ adj controlled or limited: *There is only restricted parking available.*

restriction /rɪ'strɪkʃn/ noun restriction (on sth) **1** [C] something (sometimes a rule or law) that limits the number, amount, size, freedom, etc of sb/sth: *parking restrictions in the city centre* • *The government is to impose tighter restrictions on the number of immigrants permitted to settle in this country.* **2** [U] the action of limiting the freedom of sb/sth: *This ticket permits you to travel anywhere, without restriction.*

restrictive /rɪ'strɪktɪv/ adj limiting; preventing people from doing what they want

'rest room noun [C] (*US*) a public toilet in a hotel, shop, restaurant, etc •➤ Look at the note at **toilet.**

★**result**[1] /rɪ'zʌlt/ noun **1** [C] something that happens because of sth else; the final situation at the end of a series of actions: *The traffic was very heavy and as a result I arrived late.* • *This wasn't really the result that I was expecting.* **2** [C,U] a good effect of an action: *He has tried very hard to find a job, until now without result.* • *The treatment is beginning to show results.* **3** [C] the score at the end of a game, competition or election: *Do*

you know today's football results? • *The results of this week's competition will be published next week.* • *The result of the by-election was a win for the Liberal Democrats.* **4** [C,usually pl] the mark given for an exam or test: *When do you get your exam results?* **5** [C] something that is discovered by a medical test: *I'm still waiting for the result of my X-ray.* • *The result of the test was negative.*

result[2] /rɪ'zʌlt/ verb [I] result (from sth) to happen or exist because of sth: *Ninety per cent of the deaths resulted from injuries to the head.*

PHRASAL VERB **result in sth** to cause sth to happen; to produce as an effect: *There has been an accident on the motorway, resulting in long delays.*

resume /rɪ'zuːm; -'zjuː-/ verb [I,T] to begin again or continue after a pause or interruption: *Normal service will resume as soon as possible.*

resumé /'rezjumeɪ/ noun (*US*) = **CV**

resumption /rɪ'zʌmpʃn/ noun [sing,U] (*written*) beginning again or continuing after a pause or interruption

resurrect /ˌrezə'rekt/ verb [T] to bring back sth that has not been used or has not existed for a long time: *From time to time they resurrect old programmes and show them again on television.*

resurrection /ˌrezə'rekʃn/ noun **1** [U] bringing back sth that has not existed or not been used for a long time **2 the Resurrection** [sing] (in the Christian religion) the return to life of Jesus Christ

resuscitate /rɪ'sʌsɪteɪt/ verb [T] to bring sb who has stopped breathing back to life: *Unfortunately, all efforts to resuscitate the patient failed.* –**resuscitation** /rɪˌsʌsɪ'teɪʃn/ noun [U]: *mouth-to-mouth resuscitation*

retail /'riːteɪl/ noun [U] the selling of goods to the public in shops, etc •➤ Look at **wholesale.**

retailer /'riːteɪlə/ noun [C] a person or company who sells goods to the public in a shop

retain /rɪ'teɪn/ verb [T] (*formal*) to keep or continue to have sth; not to lose: *Despite all her problems, she has managed to retain a sense of humour.* •➤ noun **retention**

retaliate /rɪ'tælieɪt/ verb [I] retaliate (against sb/sth) to react to sth unpleasant that sb does to you by doing sth unpleasant in return: *They have announced that they will retaliate against anyone who attacks their country.* –**retaliation** /rɪˌtæli'eɪʃn/ noun [U] retaliation (against sb/sth) (for sth): *The terrorist group said that the shooting was in retaliation for the murder of one of its members.*

retarded /rɪ'tɑːdɪd/ adj slower to develop than normal

retention /rɪ'tenʃn/ noun [U] the action of keeping sth or of being kept •➤ verb **retain**

rethink /ˌriː'θɪŋk; ˌriː'θɪŋk/ verb [I,T] (*pt, pp* **rethought** /-'θɔːt/) to think about sth again because you probably need to change it: *The* *government has been forced to rethink its economic policy.*

★retire /rɪˈtaɪə/ verb [I] **1** retire (from sth) to leave your job and stop working usually because you have reached a certain age: *Injury forced her to retire from professional athletics.* **2** (*formal*) to leave and go to a quiet or private place

★retired /rɪˈtaɪəd/ adj having stopped work permanently: *a retired teacher*

★retirement /rɪˈtaɪəmənt/ noun **1** [C,U] the act of stopping working permanently: *She has decided to take early retirement.* • *The former world champion has announced his retirement from the sport.* **2** [sing,U] the situation or period after retiring from work: *We all wish you a long and happy retirement.*

> A **pension** is the regular money received by somebody who has retired. It comes from the government, his/her former employer or both. A **pensioner** or an **old-age pensioner** is a person who has retired because of age.

retiring /rɪˈtaɪərɪŋ/ adj (used about a person) shy and quiet

retort /rɪˈtɔːt/ verb [T] to reply quickly to what sb says, in an angry or amusing way: *'Who asked you for your opinion?' she retorted.* –retort noun [C]: *an angry retort*

retrace /rɪˈtreɪs/ verb [T] to repeat a past journey, series of events, etc: *If you retrace your steps, you might see where you dropped the ticket.*

retract /rɪˈtrækt/ verb [I,T] (*formal*) to say that sth you have said is not true: *When he appeared in court, he retracted the confession he had made to the police.*

retreat¹ /rɪˈtriːt/ verb [I] **1** (used about an army, etc) to move backwards in order to leave a battle or in order not to become involved in a battle: *The order was given to retreat.* •➤ opposite **advance 2** to move backwards; to go to a safe or private place: (*figurative*) *She seems to retreat into a world of her own sometimes.*

retreat² /rɪˈtriːt/ noun **1** [C,U] the action of moving backwards, away from a difficult or dangerous situation: *The invading forces are now in retreat.* •➤ opposite **advance 2** [C] a private place where you can go when you want to be quiet or to rest: *a religious retreat*

retribution /ˌretrɪˈbjuːʃn/ noun [U] (*written*) retribution (for sth) punishment for a crime

retrieve /rɪˈtriːv/ verb [T] **1** retrieve sth (from sb/sth) to get sth back from the place where it was left or lost: *Police divers retrieved the body from the canal.* **2** (*computing*) to find information that has been stored: *The computer can retrieve all the data about a particular customer.* **3** to make a bad situation or a mistake better; to put sth right: *The team was losing two-nil at half-time but they managed to retrieve the situation in the second half.* –retrieval /-vl/ noun [U]

retrospect /ˈretrəspekt/ noun
IDIOM **in retrospect** thinking about sth that

happened in the past, often seeing it differently from the way you saw it at the time: *In retrospect, I can see what a stupid mistake it was.*

retrospective /ˌretrəˈspektɪv/ adj **1** looking again at the past: *a retrospective analysis of historical events* **2** (used about laws, decisions, payments, etc) intended to take effect from a date in the past: *Is this new tax law retrospective?* –retrospectively adv

★return¹ /rɪˈtɜːn/ verb **1** [I] return (to/from...) to come or go back to a place: *I leave on the 10th July and return on the 25th.* • *I shall be returning to this country in six months.* • *When did you return from Italy?* • *He left his home town when he was 18 and never returned.* **2** [I] return (to sth/doing sth) to go back to the former or usual activity, situation, condition, etc: *The strike is over and they will return to work on Monday.* • *It is hoped that train services will return to normal soon.* **3** [I] to come back; to happen again: *If the pain returns, make another appointment to see me.* **4** [T] return sth (to sb/sth) to give, send, put or take sth back: *I've stopped lending him things because he never returns them.* • *Application forms must be returned by 14 March.* **5** [T] to react to sth that sb does, says or feels by doing, saying, or feeling sth similar: *I've phoned them several times and left messages but they haven't returned any of my calls.* • *We'll be happy to return your hospitality if you ever come to our country.* **6** [T] (in sport) to hit or throw the ball back

★return² /rɪˈtɜːn/ noun **1** [sing] a return (to/from...) coming or going back to a place or to a previous activity, situation or condition: *I'll contact you on my return from holiday.* • *He has recently made a return to form (= started playing well again).* **2** [U] giving, sending, putting or taking sth back: *I demand the immediate return of my passport.* **3** [C] (in sport) the act of hitting or throwing the ball back: *She hit a brilliant return.* **4** [C,U] (a) return (on sth) the profit from a business, etc: *This account offers high returns on all investments.* **5** [C] (*Brit also* re,turn 'ticket, *US* round trip; round trip ticket) a ticket to travel to a place and back again: *A day return to Oxford, please.* • *Is the return fare cheaper than two singles?* •➤ opposite **single** or **one-way 6** (also the re'turn key) [sing] the button on a computer that you press when you reach the end of a line or of an instruction
IDIOMS **by return (of post)** (*Brit*) immediately; by the next post
in return (for sth) as payment or in exchange (for sth); as a reaction to sth: *Please accept this present in return for all your help.*

returnable /rɪˈtɜːnəbl/ adj that can or must be given or taken back: *a non-returnable deposit*

reunion /riːˈjuːniən/ noun **1** [C] a party or occasion when friends or people who worked together meet again after they have not seen each other for a long time: *The college holds an annual reunion for former students.* **2** [C,U] a reunion (with sb/between A and B) coming together again after being apart: *The released hostages had an emotional reunion with their families at the airport.*

reunite /ˌriːjuːˈnaɪt/ *verb* [I,T] reunite (A with/and B) to come together again; to join two or more people, groups, etc together again: *The missing child was found by the police and reunited with his parents.*

Rev *abbr* Reverend

rev¹ /rev/ *verb* [I,T] (**revving; revved**) rev (sth) (up) when an engine revs or when you rev it, it turns quickly and noisily

rev² /rev/ *noun* [C] (*informal*) (used when talking about an engine's speed) one complete turn: *4 000 revs per minute* ••➤ Look at **revolution.**

★**reveal** /rɪˈviːl/ *verb* [T] **1** reveal sth (to sb) to make sth known that was secret or unknown before: *He refused to reveal any names to the police.* **2** to show sth that was hidden before: *The X-ray revealed a tiny fracture in her right hand.*

revealing /rɪˈviːlɪŋ/ *adj* **1** allowing sth to be known that was secret or unknown before: *This book provides a revealing insight into the world of politics.* **2** allowing sth to be seen that is usually hidden, especially sb's body: *a very revealing swimsuit*

revel /ˈrevl/ *verb* (**revelling; revelled**; *US* **reveling; reveled**)
PHRASAL VERB revel in sth/doing sth to enjoy sth very much: *He likes being famous and revels in the attention he gets.*

revelation /ˌrevəˈleɪʃn/ *noun* **1** [C] something that is made known, that was secret or unknown before, especially sth surprising: *This magazine is full of revelations about the private lives of the stars.* **2** [sing] a thing or a person that surprises you and makes you change your opinion about sb/sth

revenge /rɪˈvendʒ/ *noun* [U] revenge (on sb) (for sth) something that you do to punish sb who has hurt you, made you suffer, etc: *He made a fool of me and now I want to get my revenge.* • *He wants to take revenge on the judge who sent him to prison.* • *The shooting was in revenge for an attack by the nationalists.* ••➤ Look at **vengeance.** –**revenge** *verb* [T] revenge yourself on sb: *She revenged herself on her enemy.* ••➤ Look at **avenge.**

revenue /ˈrevənjuː/ *noun* [U,pl] money regularly received by a government, company, etc: *Revenue from income tax rose last year.*

reverence /ˈrevərəns/ *noun* [U] (*formal*) reverence (for sb/sth) a feeling of great respect

Reverend (also **reverend**) /ˈrevərənd/ *adj* (*abbr* **Rev**) the title of a Christian priest

reverent /ˈrevərənt/ *adj* (*formal*) showing respect

reversal /rɪˈvɜːsl/ *noun* [U,C] the action of changing sth to the opposite of what it was before; an occasion when this happens: *The government insists that there will be no rever-*

sal of policy. • *The decision taken yesterday was a complete reversal of last week's decision.*

★**reverse¹** /rɪˈvɜːs/ *verb* **1** [T] to put sth in the opposite position to normal or to how it was before: *Today's results have reversed the order of the top two teams.* **2** [T] to exchange the positions or functions of two things or people: *Jane and her husband have reversed roles – he stays at home now and she goes to work.* **3** [I,T] to go backwards in a car, etc; to make a car go backwards: *It will probably be easier to reverse into that parking space.* • *He reversed his brand new car into a wall.*
IDIOM reverse (the) charges (*Brit*) to make a telephone call that will be paid for by the person who receives it: *Phone us when you get there, and reverse the charges.* • *a reverse charge call*

➤ The US expression is to **call collect.**

★**reverse²** /rɪˈvɜːs/ *noun* **1** [sing] the reverse (of sth) the complete opposite of what was said just before, or of what is expected: *Of course I don't dislike you – quite the reverse (=* I like you very much). • *This course is the exact reverse of what I was expecting.* **2** (also re‚verse 'gear) [U] the control in a car, etc that allows it to move backwards: *Leave the car in reverse while it's parked on this hill.* • *Where's reverse in this car?*
IDIOM in reverse in the opposite order, starting at the end and going backwards to the beginning

★**reverse³** /rɪˈvɜːs/ *adj* opposite to what is expected or has just been described
IDIOM in/into reverse order starting with the last one and going backwards to the first one: *The results will be announced in reverse order.*

reversible /rɪˈvɜːsəbl/ *adj* (used about clothes) that can be worn with either side on the outside: *a reversible coat*

revert /rɪˈvɜːt/ *verb* [I] revert (to sth) to return to a former state or activity: *The land will soon revert to jungle if it is not farmed.* • *If the experiment is unsuccessful we will revert to the old system.*

★**review¹** /rɪˈvjuː/ *noun* **1** [C,U] the examining or considering again of sth in order to decide if changes are necessary: *There will be a review of your contract after the first six months.* • *The system is in need of review.* **2** [C] a look back at sth in order to check, remember, or be clear about sth: *a review of the major events of the year* **3** [C] a newspaper or magazine article, or an item on television or radio, in which sb gives an opinion on a new book, film, play, etc: *The film got bad reviews.*

review² /rɪˈvjuː/ *verb* [T] **1** to examine or consider sth again in order to decide if changes are necessary: *Your salary will be reviewed after one year.* **2** to look at or think about sth again to make sure that you understand it: *Let's review what we've done in class this week.* **3** to write an article or to talk on television or radio, giving an opinion on a new book, film, play, etc: *In this week's edition our film critic reviews the latest films.*

reviewer /rɪˈvjuːə/ noun [C] a person who writes about new books, films, etc

★**revise** /rɪˈvaɪz/ verb **1** [T] to make changes to sth in order to correct or improve it: *The book has been revised for this new edition.* • *I revised my opinion of him when I found out that he had lied.* **2** [I,T] (*Brit*) revise (for sth) to read or study again sth that you have learnt, especially when preparing for an exam: *I can't come out tonight. I'm revising for my exam.* • *None of the things I had revised came up in the exam.*

revision /rɪˈvɪʒn/ noun **1** [C,U] the changing of sth in order to correct or improve it: *It has been suggested that the whole system is in need of revision.* **2** [U] (*Brit*) the work of reading or studying again sth you have learnt, especially when preparing for an exam: *I'm going to have to do a lot of revision for History.*

revival /rɪˈvaɪvl/ noun **1** [C,U] the act of becoming or making sth strong or popular again: *economic revival* • *a revival of interest in traditional farming methods* **2** [C] a new performance of a play that has not been performed for some time: *a revival of the musical 'The Sound of Music'*

revive /rɪˈvaɪv/ verb [I,T] **1** to become or to make sb/sth strong or healthy again; to come or to bring sb back to life or consciousness: *Hopes have revived for an early end to the fighting.* • *I'm very tired but I'm sure a cup of coffee will revive me.* • *Attempts were made to revive him but he was already dead.* **2** to become or to make sth popular again; to begin to do or use sth again: *Public interest in athletics has revived now that the national team is doing well.* • *to revive an old custom*

revolt /rɪˈvəʊlt/ verb **1** [I] revolt (against sb/sth) to protest in a group, often violently, against the person or people in power: *A group of generals revolted against the government.* **2** [T] to make sb feel disgusted or ill: *The sight and smell of the meat revolted him.* •➤ noun revulsion –**revolt** noun [C,U]: *The people rose in revolt against the corrupt government.*

revolting /rɪˈvəʊltɪŋ/ adj extremely unpleasant; disgusting: *What a revolting colour/smell.*

★**revolution** /ˌrevəˈluːʃn/ noun **1** [C,U] action taken by a large group of people to try to change the government of a country, especially by violent action: *the French Revolution of 1789* • *a country on the brink of revolution* **2** [C] a revolution (in sth) a complete change in methods, opinions, etc, often as a result of progress: *the Industrial Revolution* **3** [C,U] a movement around sth; one complete turn around a central point (for example in a car engine): *400 revolutions per minute* •➤ Look at **rev²**.

revolutionary¹ /ˌrevəˈluːʃənəri/ adj **1** connected with or supporting political revolution: *the revolutionary leaders* **2** producing great changes; very new and different: *a revolutionary new scheme to ban cars from the city centre*

revolutionary² /ˌrevəˈluːʃənəri/ noun [C] (*pl* **revolutionaries**) a person who starts or supports action to try to change the government of a country, especially by using violent action

revolutionize (also **-ise**) /ˌrevəˈluːʃənaɪz/ verb [T] to change sth completely, usually improving it: *a discovery that could revolutionize the treatment of mental illness*

revolve /rɪˈvɒlv/ verb [I] to move in a circle around a central point: *The earth revolves around the sun.*

PHRASAL VERB **revolve around sb/sth** to have sb/sth as the most important part: *Her life revolves around the family.*

revolver /rɪˈvɒlvə/ noun [C] a type of small gun with a container for bullets that turns round

revolving /rɪˈvɒlvɪŋ/ adj that goes round in a circle: *revolving doors*

revulsion /rɪˈvʌlʃn/ noun [U] a feeling of disgust (because sth is extremely unpleasant) •➤ verb **revolt**

★**reward¹** /rɪˈwɔːd/ noun reward (for sth/doing sth) **1** [C,U] something that you are given because you have done sth good, worked hard, etc: *Winning the match was just reward for all the effort.* **2** [C] an amount of money that is given in exchange for helping the police, returning sth that was lost, etc: *Police are offering a reward for information leading to a conviction.*

reward² /rɪˈwɔːd/ verb [T] reward sb (for sth/for doing sth) (often passive) to give sth to sb because he/she has done sth good, worked hard, etc: *Eventually her efforts were rewarded and she got a job.*

rewarding /rɪˈwɔːdɪŋ/ adj (used about an activity, job, etc) giving satisfaction; making you happy because you think it is important, useful, etc

rewind /ˌriːˈwaɪnd/ verb [T] (*pt, pp* **rewound**) to make a video or cassette tape go backwards: *Please rewind the tape at the end of the film.* –**rewind** noun [U] •➤ Look at **fast forward**.

rewrite /ˌriːˈraɪt/ verb [T] (*pt* **rewrote** /-ˈrəʊt/; *pp* **rewritten** /-ˈrɪtn/) to write sth again in a different or better way

rhetoric /ˈretərɪk/ noun [U] (*formal*) a way of speaking or writing that is intended to impress or influence people but is not always sincere –**rhetorical** /rɪˈtɒrɪkl/ adj –**rhetorically** /-kli/ adv

rhe,torical 'question noun [C] a question that does not expect an answer

rheumatism /ˈruːmətɪzəm/ noun [U] an illness that causes pain in muscles and where your bones join together (the joints)

rhino /ˈraɪnəʊ/ (*pl* **rhinos**) (*informal*) = **RHINOCEROS**

rhinoceros /raɪˈnɒsərəs/ noun [C] (*pl* **rhinoceros** or **rhinoceroses**) a large animal from Africa or Asia, with a thick skin and with one or two horns on its nose

rhubarb /ˈruːbɑːb/ noun [U] a plant with long

[C] **countable**, a noun with a plural form: *one book, two books*   [U] **uncountable**, a noun with no plural form: *some sugar*

red parts (stalks) that can be cooked and eaten as fruit

rhyme¹ /raɪm/ **noun 1** [C] a word that has the same sound as another **2** [C] a short piece of writing, or something spoken, in which the word at the end of each line sounds the same as the word at the end of the line before it •➤ Look at **nursery rhyme**. **3** [U] the use of words in a poem or song that have the same sound, especially at the ends of lines: *All of his poetry was written in rhyme.*

rhyme² /raɪm/ **verb 1** [I] **rhyme (with sth)** to have the same sound as another word; to contain lines that end with words that sound the same: *'Tough' rhymes with 'stuff'.* **2** [T] **rhyme sth (with sth)** to put together words that have the same sound

⋆**rhythm** /'rɪðəm/ **noun** [C,U] a regular repeated pattern of sound or movement: *I'm not keen on the tune but I love the rhythm.* • *He's a terrible dancer because he has no sense of rhythm.* • *He tapped his foot in rhythm with the music.* –**rhythmic** /'rɪðmɪk/ (also **rhythmical** /'rɪðmɪkl/) **adj**: *the rhythmic qualities of African music* –**rhythmically** /-kli/ **adv**

rib /rɪb/ **noun** [C] one of the curved bones that go round your chest: *He's so thin that you can see his ribs.* •➤ picture on page C5

ribbon /'rɪbən/ **noun** [C,U] a long, thin piece of material that is used for tying or decorating sth: *a present wrapped in a blue ribbon* •➤ picture at **hat** and **wrap**

⋆**rice** /raɪs/ **noun** [U] short, thin, white or brown grain from a plant that grows on wet land in hot countries. We cook and eat rice: *boiled/fried/steamed rice* •➤ picture at **cereal**

⋆**rich** /rɪtʃ/ **adj 1** having a lot of money or property; not poor: *a rich family/country* • *one of the richest women in the world* •➤ Look at **wealthy**. •➤ opposite **poor 2 the rich noun** [pl] people with a lot of money or property **3 rich in sth** containing a lot of sth: *Oranges are rich in vitamin C.* **4** (used about food) containing a lot of fat, oil, sugar or cream and making you feel full quickly: *a rich chocolate cake* **5** (used about soil) containing the substances that make it good for growing plants in **6** (used about colours, sounds or smells) strong and deep –**richness noun** [U]

riches /'rɪtʃɪz/ **noun** [pl] (*formal*) a lot of money or property •➤ synonym **wealth**

richly /'rɪtʃli/ **adv 1** in a generous way: *She was richly rewarded for her hard work.* **2** in a way that people think is right: *His promotion was richly deserved.*

rickety /'rɪkəti/ **adj** likely to break; not strongly made: *a rickety old fence* • *rickety furniture*

ricochet /'rɪkəʃeɪ/ **verb** [I] (*pt, pp* **ricocheted** /-ʃeɪd/) **ricochet (off sth)** (used about a moving object) to fly away from a surface after hitting it: *The bullet ricocheted off the wall and grazed his shoulder.*

⋆**rid** /rɪd/ **verb** [T] (*pres part* **ridding**; *pt, pp* **rid**) (*formal*) **rid yourself/sb/sth of sb/sth** to

make yourself/sb/sth free from sb/sth that is unpleasant or not wanted: *He was unable to rid himself of his fears and suspicions.* • (*Brit*) *He was a nuisance and we're well rid of him* (= it will be much better without him).

IDIOM get rid of sb/sth to make yourself free of sb/sth that is annoying you or that you do not want; to throw sth away: *Let's get rid of that old chair and buy a new one.*

riddance /'rɪdns/ **noun**

IDIOM good riddance (to sb/sth) (*spoken*) used for expressing pleasure or satisfaction that sb/sth that you do not like has gone

ridden¹ /raɪd/ *past participle of* RIDE¹

ridden² /'rɪdn/ **adj** (*formal*) (usually in compound adjectives) full of: *She was guilt-ridden.* • *She was ridden with guilt.*

riddle /'rɪdl/ **noun** [C] **1** a difficult question that you ask people for fun that has a clever or amusing answer **2** a person, thing or event that you cannot understand or explain

riddled /'rɪdld/ **adj riddled with sth** full of sth, especially sth unpleasant: *This essay is riddled with mistakes.*

⋆**ride¹** /raɪd/ **verb** (*pt* **rode** /rəʊd/; *pp* **ridden** /'rɪdn/) **1** [I,T] to sit on a horse and control it as it moves: *We rode through the woods and over the moor.* • *Which horse is Dettori riding in the next race?* •➤ **Go riding** is a common way of talking about riding a horse for pleasure in British English: *She goes riding every weekend.* In US English **go horseback riding** is used. **2** [I,T] to sit on a bicycle, motorbike, etc and control it as it moves: *She jumped onto her motorbike and rode off* (= went away). • *Can John ride a bicycle yet?* **3** [I] (*especially US*) to travel as a passenger in a bus, car, etc –**rider noun** [C]

⋆**ride²** /raɪd/ **noun** [C] **1** a short journey on a horse or bicycle, or in a car, bus, etc: *It's only a short bus/train ride into Warwick.* • *We went for a bike ride on Saturday.* **2** used to describe what a journey or trip is like: *a smooth/bumpy/comfortable ride* **3** a large machine at an amusement park which you pay to go on for amusement or excitement; an occasion when you go on one of these: *My favourite fairground ride is the roller coaster.*

IDIOM take sb for a ride (*informal*) to cheat or trick sb

ridge /rɪdʒ/ **noun** [C] **1** a long, narrow piece of high land along the top of hills or mountains **2** a line where two surfaces meet at an angle

ridicule /'rɪdɪkjuːl/ **noun** [U] unkind laughter or behaviour that is intended to make sb/sth appear silly: *He had become an object of ridicule.* –**ridicule verb** [T]: *The idea was ridiculed by everybody present.*

⋆**ridiculous** /rɪ'dɪkjələs/ **adj** very silly or unreasonable: *They're asking a ridiculous* (= very high) *price for that house.* –**ridiculously adv**

riding /'raɪdɪŋ/ (*US* '**horseback riding**) **noun** [U] the sport or hobby of riding a horse: *riding boots* • *a riding school*

rife /raɪf/ **adj** (not before a noun) (*formal*)

I] **intransitive**, a verb which has no object: *He laughed.* [T] **transitive**, a verb which has an object: *He ate an apple.*

r

(used especially about bad things) very common: *Rumours are rife that his wife has left him.*

rifle¹ /'raɪfl/ **noun** [C] a long gun that you hold against your shoulder to shoot with ••> We **load**, **aim** and **fire** a rifle.

rifle² /'raɪfl/ **verb** [I,T] **rifle (through)** sth to search sth usually in order to steal from it: *I caught him rifling through the papers on my desk.*

rift /rɪft/ **noun** [C] **1** a serious disagreement between friends, groups, etc that stops their relationship from continuing: *a growing rift between the brothers* **2** a very large crack or opening in the ground, a rock, etc

rig¹ /rɪg/ **verb** [T] (**rigging**; **rigged**) to arrange or control an event, etc in an unfair way, in order to get the result you want: *They claimed that the competition had been rigged.*
PHRASAL VERB rig sth up to make sth quickly, using any materials you can find: *We tried to rig up a shelter using our coats.*

rig² /rɪg/ = OIL RIG

rigging /'rɪgɪŋ/ **noun** [U] the ropes, etc that support a ship's sails

★**right¹** /raɪt/ **adj 1** correct; true: *I'm afraid that's not the right answer.* • *Have you got the right time?* • *You're quite right – the film does start at 7 o'clock.* • *You were right about the weather – it did rain.* • '*You're Chinese, aren't you?*' '*Yes, that's right.*' **2** right (for sb/sth) best; most suitable: *I hope I've made the right decision.* • *I am sure we've chosen the right person for the job.* • *I would help you to wash the car, but I'm not wearing the right clothes.* **3** (used about behaviour, actions, etc) fair; morally and socially correct: *It's not right to pay people so badly.* • *What do you think is the right thing to do?* ••> opposite for senses 1, 2 and 3 **wrong 4** healthy or normal; as it should be: *The car exhaust doesn't sound right – it's making a funny noise.* • *I don't know what it is, but something's just not right.* **5** on or of the side of the body that faces east when a person is facing north: *Most people write with their right hand.* • *He's blind in his right eye.* ••> opposite **left 6** (*Brit spoken*) (used for emphasizing sth bad) real or complete: *I'll look a right idiot in that hat!* –**rightness noun** [U]
IDIOMS get/start off on the right/wrong foot (with sb) → FOOT¹
get on the right/wrong side of sb → SIDE¹
on the right/wrong track → TRACK¹
put/set sth right to correct sth or deal with a problem: *There's something wrong with the lawnmower. Do you think you'll be able to put it right?*
right (you are)! (*spoken*) yes, I will or yes, I agree; OK: '*See you later.*' '*Right you are!*'
(as) right as rain completely healthy and normal

★**right²** /raɪt/ **adv 1** exactly; directly: *The train was right on time.* • *He was sitting right beside me.* **2** correctly; in the way that it should happen or should be done: *Have I spelt your name right?* • *Nothing seems to be going*

right *for me at the moment.* ••> opposite **wrong 3** all the way; completely: *Did you watch the film right to the end?* • *There's a high wall that goes right round the house.* **4** to the right side: *Turn right at the traffic lights.* ••> opposite **left 5** immediately: *Wait here a minute – I'll be right back.* **6** (*spoken*) (used for preparing sb for sth that is about to happen) get ready; listen: *Have you got your seat belts on? Right, off we go.*
IDIOMS right/straight away → AWAY
right now at this moment; exactly now: *We can't discuss this right now.*
serve sb right → SERVE

★**right³** /raɪt/ **noun 1** [U] what is morally good and fair: *Does a child of ten really understand the difference between right and wrong?* • *You did right to tell me what happened.* ••> opposite **wrong 2** [sing] the right side or direction: *We live in the first house on the right.* • *Take the first right and then the second left* ••> opposite **left 3** [U,C] the right (to sth/to do sth) a thing that you are allowed to do according to the law; a moral authority to do sth: *Freedom of speech is one of the basic human rights.* • *civil rights* (= the rights each person has to political and religious freedom, etc) • *animal rights campaigner.* • *Everyone has the right to a fair trial.* • *You have no right to tell me what to do.* **4 the Right** [sing,with sing or pl verb] the people or political parties who are against social change
IDIOMS be in the right to be doing what is correct and fair: *You don't need to apologize. You were in the right and he was in the wrong.*
by rights according to what is fair or correct: *By rights, half the profit should be mine.*
in your own right because of what you are yourself and not because of other people
within your rights (to do sth) acting in a reasonable or legal way: *You are quite within your rights to demand to see your lawyer.*

right⁴ /raɪt/ **verb** [T] to put sb/sth/yourself back into a normal position: *The boat tipped over and then righted itself again.*
IDIOM right a wrong to do sth to correct an unfair situation or sth bad that you have done

'right angle noun [C] an angle of 90°: *A square has four right angles.*

righteous /'raɪtʃəs/ **adj** (*formal*) that you think is morally good or fair: *righteous anger/indignation* ••> Look at **self-righteous**.

rightful /'raɪtfl/ **adj** (only *before* a noun) (*formal*) legally or morally correct; fair –**rightfully** /-fəli/ **adv**

'right-hand adj (only *before* a noun) of or on the right of sb/sth: *The postbox is on the right-hand side of the road.* • *in the top right hand corner of the screen*

,right-'handed adj using the right hand for writing, etc and not the left

,right-hand 'man noun [sing] the person

you depend on most to help and support you in your work: *the President's right-hand man*

rightly /'raɪtli/ *adv* correctly or fairly: *He's been sacked and quite rightly, I believe.*

right of 'way *noun* (*pl* **rights of way**) **1** [C,U] (*especially Brit*) a path across private land that the public may use; legal permission to go into or through another person's land: *Walkers have right of way through the farmer's field.* **2** [U] (used in road traffic) the fact that a vehicle in a particular position is allowed to drive into or across a road before another vehicle in a different position: *He should have stopped – I had the right of way.*

right 'wing *noun* [sing, with sing or pl verb] the people in a political party who are against social change –**right-wing** *adj*: *a right-wing government* •➤ opposite **left-wing**

rigid /'rɪdʒɪd/ *adj* **1** not able or not wanting to change or be changed **2** difficult to bend; stiff: *a rucksack with a rigid frame* • *She was rigid with fear.* –**rigidity** *noun* [U] –**rigidly** *adv*: *The speed limit must be rigidly enforced.*

rigorous /'rɪɡərəs/ *adj* done very carefully and with great attention to detail: *Rigorous tests are carried out on the drinking water.* –**rigorously** *adv*

rigour (*US* **rigor**) /'rɪɡə/ *noun* (*formal*) **1** [U] doing sth carefully with great attention to detail: *The tests were carried out with rigour.* **2** [U] the quality of being strict: *the full rigour of the law* **3** [C, usually pl] difficult conditions

rim /rɪm/ *noun* [C] an edge at the top or outside of sth that is round: *the rim of a cup* •➤ picture at **cup**

rind /raɪnd/ *noun* [C,U] the thick hard skin on the outside of some fruits, some types of cheese, meat etc

> We say the **rind** or **peel** of a lemon or an orange. A fruit with a softer covering like a banana has a **skin**.

★**ring**[1] /rɪŋ/ *noun* **1** [C] a piece of jewellery that you wear on your finger: *a gold/diamond/wedding ring* • an engagement ring •➤ picture at **jewellery 2** [C] (usually in compound nouns) a round object of any material with a hole in the middle: *curtain rings* • *a key ring* (= for holding keys) **3** [C] a round mark or shape: *The coffee cup left a ring on the table top.* • *Stand in a ring and hold hands.* **4** [C] the space with seats all around it where a performance, boxing match, etc takes place: *a circus/boxing ring* **5** (*US* **burner**) [C] one of the round parts on the top of an electric or gas cooker on which you can put pans **6** [C] a number of people who are involved in sth that is secret or not legal together: *a spy/drugs ring* **7** [C] the sound made by a bell; the action of ringing a bell: *There was a ring at the door.* **8** [sing] a ring of sth a particular quality that words or sounds have: *What the man said had a ring of truth about it* (= sounded true).

IDIOM **give sb a ring** (*Brit informal*) to telephone sb: *I'll give you a ring in the morning.*

★**ring**[2] /rɪŋ/ *verb* (*pt* **rang** /ræŋ/; *pp* **rung** /rʌŋ/) **1** [I,T] (*especially US* **call**) ring (sb/sth) (up) to telephone sb/sth: *What time will you ring tomorrow?* • *I rang up yesterday and booked the hotel.* • *Ring the station and ask what time the next train leaves.* •➤ synonym **phone 2** [I,T] to make a sound like a bell or to cause sth to make this sound: *Is that the phone ringing?* • *We rang the door bell but nobody answered.* **3** [I] ring (for sb/sth) to ring a bell in order to call sb, ask for sth, etc: *'Did you ring, sir?' asked the stewardess.* • *Could you ring for a taxi, please?* **4** [I] (used about words or sounds) to have a certain effect when you hear them: *Her words didn't ring true* (= you felt that you could not believe what she said). **5** [I] ring (with sth) to be filled with loud sounds: *The music was so loud it made my ears ring.* **6** [T] (*pt, pp* **ringed**) (often passive) to surround sb/sth **7** [T] (*US* **circle**) (*pt, pp* **ringed**) to draw a circle around sth

IDIOM **ring a bell** to sound familiar or to remind you, not very clearly, of sb/sth: *'Do you know Chris Oliver?' 'Well, the name rings a bell.'*

PHRASAL VERBS **ring (sb) back** (*Brit*) to telephone sb again or to telephone sb who has telephoned you: *I can't talk now – can I ring you back?*

ring in (*Brit*) to telephone a television or radio show, or the place where you work: *Mandy rang in sick this morning.*

ring out to sound loudly and clearly

ringleader /'rɪŋliːdə/ *noun* [C] a person who leads others in crime or in causing trouble: *The ringleaders were jailed for 15 years.*

'ring road *noun* [C] (*Brit*) a road that is built all around a town so that traffic does not have to go into the town centre •➤ Look at **bypass**[1].

rink /rɪŋk/ = **SKATING RINK**

rinse /rɪns/ *verb* [T] to wash sth in water in order to remove soap or dirt: *Rinse your hair thoroughly after each shampoo.* –**rinse** *noun* [C]

riot /'raɪət/ *noun* [C] a situation in which a group of people behave in a violent way in a public place, often as a protest: *Further riots have broken out in Manchester.* –**riot** *verb* [I]: *There is a danger that the prisoners will riot if conditions do not improve.* –**rioter** *noun* [C]

IDIOM **run riot 1** to behave in a wild way without any control: *At the end of the football match, the crowd ran riot.* **2** (used about your imagination, feelings, etc) to allow sth to develop and continue without trying to control it

riotous /'raɪətəs/ *adj* **1** wild or violent; lacking in control **2** wild and full of fun

RIP /ˌɑːr aɪ 'piː/ *abbr* (used on graves) rest in peace

rip[1] /rɪp/ *verb* (**ripping; ripped**) **1** [I,T] to tear or be torn quickly and suddenly: *Oh no! My dress has ripped!* • *He ripped the letter in half/two and threw it in the bin.* • *The blast of the bomb ripped the house apart.* **2** [T] to

remove sth quickly and violently often by pulling it: *He ripped the poster from the wall.*
PHRASAL VERBS **rip through sth** to move very quickly and violently through sth: *The house was badly damaged when fire ripped through the first floor.*

rip sb off (*informal*) to cheat sb by charging too much money for sth

rip sth up to tear sth into small pieces

rip² /rɪp/ **noun** [C] a long tear (in material, etc)

★**ripe** /raɪp/ **adj 1** (used about fruit, grain, etc) ready to be picked and eaten **2 ripe (for sth)** ready for sth or in a suitable state for sth –**ripen** /-ən/ **verb** [I,T]

'**rip-off noun** [C] (*informal*) something that costs a lot more than it should: *The food in that restaurant is a complete rip-off!*

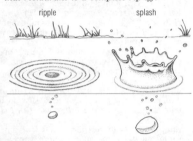

ripple   splash

ripple /'rɪpl/ **noun** [C] **1** a very small wave or movement on the surface of water **2** [usually sing] **a ripple (of sth)** a sound that gradually becomes louder and then quieter again; a feeling that gradually spreads through a person or a group of people: *a ripple of laughter* –**ripple verb** [I,T]

★**rise¹** /raɪz/ **noun 1** [C] **a rise (in sth)** an increase in an amount, a number or a level: *There has been a **sharp rise** in the number of people out of work.* •➤ opposite **drop** or **fall 2** [C] (*US* **raise**) an increase in the money you are paid for the work you do: *I'm hoping to **get a rise** next April.* • *a 10% **pay rise*** **3** [sing] **the rise (of sth)** the process of becoming more powerful or important: *The rise of fascism in Europe.* • *her meteoric **rise to fame/power***
IDIOM **give rise to sth** (*formal*) to cause sth to happen or exist

★**rise²** /raɪz/ **verb** [I] (*pt* **rose** /rəʊz/; *pp* **risen** /'rɪzn/) **1** to move upwards, to become higher, stronger or to increase: *Smoke was rising from the chimney.* • *The temperature has risen to nearly forty degrees.* •➤ opposite **fall 2** (*written*) to get up from a chair, bed, etc: *The audience rose and applauded the singers.* **3** (used about the sun, moon, etc) to appear above the horizon: *The sun rises in the east and sets in the west.* •➤ opposite **set 4** to become more successful, powerful, important, etc: *He **rose through the ranks** to become managing director.* • *She **rose to power** in the 90s.* **5** to be seen above or higher than sth else **6** to come from: *Shouts of protest rose from the crowd.* **7 rise (up) (against**

sb/sth) to start fighting against your ruler, government, etc –**rising adj**: *the rising cost of living* • *a rising young rock star*
IDIOM **rise to the occasion, challenge, task,** etc to show that you are able to deal with a problem, etc successfully

★**risk¹** /rɪsk/ **noun 1** [C,U] **(a) risk (of sth/ that...); (a) risk (to sb/sth)** a possibility of sth dangerous or unpleasant happening; a situation that could be dangerous or have a bad result: *Don't **take** any **risks** when you're driving.* • *You could drive a car without insurance, but it's **not worth the risk.*** • *Scientists say these pesticides **pose a risk** to wildlife.* • *If we don't leave early enough we **run the risk** of missing the plane.* • *Small children are most **at risk** from the disease.* **2** [sing] a person or thing that might cause danger: *If he knows your real name he's a security risk.*
IDIOMS **at your own risk** having the responsibility for whatever may happen: *This building is in a dangerous condition – enter at your own risk.*

at the risk of (sth/doing sth) even though there could be a bad effect: *He rescued the girl at the risk of his own life.*

★**risk²** /rɪsk/ **verb** [T] **1** to take the chance of sth unpleasant happening: *If you don't work hard now you risk failing your exams.* **2** to put sth or yourself in a dangerous position: *The man had to **risk his life** to save the little boy.*

risky /'rɪski/ **adj** (**riskier; riskiest**) involving the possibility of sth bad happening; dangerous

ritual /'rɪtʃuəl/ **noun** [C,U] an action, ceremony or process which is always done the same way: (*a*) *religious ritual* –**ritual adj** –**ritually adv**

rival¹ /'raɪvl/ **noun** [C] a person or thing that is competing with you: *It seems that we're rivals for the sales manager's job.*

rival² /'raɪvl/ **verb** [T] (**rivalling; rivalled:** *US* **rivaling; rivaled**) **rival sb/sth (for/in sth)** to be as good as sb/sth: *Nothing rivals skiing for sheer excitement.*

rivalry /'raɪvlri/ **noun** [C,U] (*pl* **rivalries**) **rivalry (with sb); rivalry (between A and B)** competition between people, groups, etc: *There was a lot of rivalry between the sisters.*

★**river** /'rɪvə/ **noun** [C] a large, natural flow of water that goes across land and into the sea: *the River Nile* • *He sat down on the bank of the river to fish.*

➤ A river **flows** into the sea. Where it joins the sea is the river **mouth**. A boat sails **on** the river. We walk, sail, etc **up** or **down** river.

riverside /'rɪvəsaɪd/ **noun** [sing] the land next to a river: *a riverside hotel*

rivet¹ /'rɪvɪt/ **noun** [C] a metal pin for fastening two pieces of metal together

rivet² /'rɪvɪt/ **verb** [T] (usually passive) to keep sb very interested: *I was riveted by her story.* –**riveting adj**

---

rm abbr room

roach /rəʊtʃ/ (US) = COCKROACH

★**road** /rəʊd/ noun **1** [C] a way between places, with a hard surface which cars, buses, etc can drive along: *Turn left off the main* (= important) *road.* • *road signs*

➤ Roads (US highways) connect towns and villages: *a road map of Slovakia.* A road in a town, city or village that has buildings at the side is often called a **street**. **Street** is not used for roads outside towns: *a street map of London.* A wide street, often with trees or buildings along it, is called an **avenue**. **Motorways** (US **freeways/ expressways**) are roads with two **carriage-ways**, each with two or three **lanes**, that are built for traffic travelling fast over long distances, avoiding towns. **A-roads** are big important roads that link towns. **B-roads** are smaller country roads. **M** on a map stands for **motorway**.

2 Road (abbr **Rd**) [sing] used in names of roads, especially in towns: *60 Marylebone Road, London*

IDIOMS **by road** in a car, bus, etc: *It's going to be a terrible journey by road – let's take the train.*

on the road travelling: *We were on the road for 14 hours.*

roadblock /'rəʊdblɒk/ noun [C] a barrier put across a road by the police or army to stop traffic

roadside /'rəʊdsaɪd/ noun [C, usually sing] the edge of a road: *a roadside cafe*

'**road tax** noun [C,U] (Brit) a tax which the owner of a vehicle has to pay to be allowed to drive it on public roads

the roadway /'rəʊdweɪ/ noun [sing] the part of the road used by cars, etc; not the side of the road

roadworks /'rəʊdwɜːks/ noun [pl] work that involves repairing or building roads

roadworthy /'rəʊdwɜːði/ adj in good enough condition to be driven on the road

roam /rəʊm/ verb [I,T] to walk or travel with no particular plan or aim: *Gangs of youths were roaming the streets looking for trouble.*

roar /rɔː/ verb **1** [I,T] to make a loud, deep sound: *She roared with laughter at the joke.* • *The lion opened its huge mouth and roared.* **2** [I] to shout very loudly **3** [I] **roar along, down, past**, etc to move in the direction mentioned, making a loud, deep sound: *A motorbike roared past us.* –**roar** noun [C]: *the roar of heavy traffic on the motorway* • *roars of laughter*

roaring /'rɔːrɪŋ/ adj **1** making a very loud noise **2** (used about a fire) burning very well **3** very great: *a roaring success*

roast[1] /rəʊst/ verb **1** [I,T] to cook or be cooked in an oven or over a fire: *a smell of roasting meat* • *to roast a chicken* •➤ Look at the note at **cook**. **2** [T] to heat and dry sth: *roasted peanuts* –**roast** adj (only before a noun): *roast beef/potatoes/chestnuts*

roast[2] /rəʊst/ noun [C,U] a piece of meat

that has been cooked in an oven **2** [C] (especially US) an outdoor meal at which food is cooked over a fire •➤ Look at **barbecue**.

★**rob** /rɒb/ verb [T] (**robbing; robbed**) **rob sb/sth (of sth) 1** to take money, property, etc from a person or place illegally: *to rob a bank* •➤ Look at the note at **steal**. **2** **rob sb/sth (of sth)** to take sth away from sb/sth that he/ she/it should have: *His illness robbed him of the chance to play for his country.*

★**robber** /'rɒbə/ noun [C] a person who steals from a place or a person, especially using violence or threats •➤ Look at the note at **thief**.

robbery /'rɒbəri/ noun [C,U] (pl **robberies**) the crime of stealing from a place or a person, especially using violence or threats: *They were found guilty of armed robbery* (= using a weapon).

robe /rəʊb/ noun [C] **1** a long, loose piece of clothing, especially one worn at ceremonies **2** (US) = DRESSING GOWN

robin /'rɒbɪn/ noun [C] a small brown bird with a bright red chest

robot /'rəʊbɒt/ noun [C] a machine that works automatically and can do some tasks that a human can do: *These cars are built by robots.*

robust /rəʊ'bʌst/ adj strong and healthy

★**rock**[1] /rɒk/ noun **1** [U] the hard, solid material that forms part of the surface of the earth: *layers of rock formed over millions of years* **2** [C, usually pl] a large mass of rock that sticks out of the sea or the ground: *The ship hit the rocks and started to sink.* **3** [C] a single large piece of rock: *The beach was covered with rocks that had broken away from the cliffs.* **4** [C] (US) a small piece of rock that can be picked up; a stone: *The boy threw a rock at the dog.* **5** (also '**rock music**) [U] a type of pop music with a very strong beat, played on electric guitars, etc: *I prefer jazz to rock.* • *a rock singer/band* •➤ Look at **classical**, **jazz** and **pop**. **6** [U] (Brit) a type of hard sweet made in long, round sticks

IDIOM **on the rocks 1** (used about a marriage, business, etc) having problems and likely to fail **2** (used about drinks) served with ice but no water: *whisky on the rocks*

rock[2] /rɒk/ verb **1** [I,T] to move backwards and forwards or from side to side; to make sb/sth do this: *boats rocking gently on the waves* • *He rocked the baby in his arms to get her to sleep.* **2** [T] to shake sth violently: *The city was rocked by a bomb blast.* **3** [T] to shock sb

IDIOM **rock the boat** to do sth that causes problems or upsets people: *They employ mainly quiet people who won't complain and rock the boat.*

'**rock and 'roll** (also **rock 'n' roll**) noun [U] a type of music with a strong beat that was most popular in the 1950s

'**rock 'bottom** noun [U] the lowest point: *He hit rock bottom when he lost his job and his wife left him.* • *rock-bottom prices* '**rock climbing** noun [U] the sport of climbing rocks and mountains with ropes, etc

rocket¹ /'rɒkɪt/ noun [C] **1** a vehicle that is used for travel into space: *a space rocket* • *to launch a rocket* **2** a weapon that travels through the air and that carries a bomb ••➤ synonym **missile** **3** an object that shoots high into the air and explodes in a beautiful way when you light it with a flame ••➤ picture at **firework**

rocket² /'rɒkɪt/ verb [I] to increase or rise very quickly: *Prices have rocketed recently.*

rocky /'rɒki/ adj covered with or made of rocks: *a rocky road/coastline*

rod /rɒd/ noun [C] (often in compounds) a thin straight piece of wood, metal, etc: *a fishing rod*

rode *past tense* of **RIDE**¹

rodent /'rəʊdnt/ noun [C] a type of small animal, such as a rat, a rabbit, a mouse, etc, which has strong sharp front teeth

rodeo /'rəʊdiəʊ; rəʊ'deɪəʊ/ noun [C] (*pl* **rodeos**) a competition or performance in which people show their skill in riding wild horses, catching cows, etc

roe /rəʊ/ noun [U] the eggs of a fish that we eat

rogue /rəʊg/ adj behaving differently from other similar people or things, often causing damage: *a rogue gene/program*

★**role** /rəʊl/ noun [C] **1** the position or function of sb/sth in a particular situation: *Parents play a vital role in their children's education.* **2** a person's part in a play, film, etc: *She was chosen to play the role of Cleopatra.* • *a leading role in the film*

'**role play** noun [C,U] an activity, used especially in teaching, in which a person acts a part

rolls

toilet roll   roll of film

★**roll**¹ /rəʊl/ noun [C] **1** something made into the shape of a tube by turning it round and round itself: *a roll of film/ wallpaper* **2** bread baked in a round shape for one person to eat ••➤ picture at **bread** **3** moving or making sth move by turning it over and over: *Everything depended on one roll of the dice.* **4** an official list of names: *the electoral roll* (= the list of people who can vote in an election) **5** a long, low sound: *a roll of drums* **6** a movement from side to side

★**roll**² /rəʊl/ verb **1** [I,T] to move by turning over and over; to make sth move in this way: *The apples fell out of the bag and rolled everywhere.* • *He tried to roll the rock up the hill.* **2** [I] to move smoothly, often on wheels: *The car began to roll back down the hill.* • *Tears were rolling down her cheeks.* **3** [I,T] roll (sth) (over) to turn over and over; to make sth do this: *The horse was rolling in the dirt.* • *The car rolled over in the crash.* • *We rolled the log over to see what was underneath.* **4** [I,T] roll (sth) (up) to make sth into the shape of a

ball or tube: *He was rolling himself a cigarette.* • *The insect rolled up when I touched it.* ••➤ opposite **unroll** **5** [T] roll sth (out) to make sth become flat by moving sth heavy over it: *Roll out the pastry thinly.* **6** [I] to move from side to side: *The ship began to roll in the storm.*

IDIOM **be rolling in money/in it** (*slang*) to have a lot of money

PHRASAL VERBS **roll in** (*informal*) to arrive in large numbers or amounts: *Offers of help have been rolling in.*

roll up (*informal*) (used about a person or a vehicle) to arrive, especially late

roller /'rəʊlə/ noun [C] **1** a piece of equipment or part of a machine that is shaped like a tube and used, for example, to make sth flat or to help sth move: *a roller blind on a window* **2** [usually pl] small plastic tubes that are used to make sb's hair curly

Rollerblade™ /'rəʊləbleɪd/ noun [C] a boot with one row of narrow wheels on the bottom: *a pair of Rollerblades* ••➤ picture at **skate** –**rollerblade** verb [I] ••➤ **Go rollerblading** is a common way of talking about rollerblading for pleasure: *We go rollerblading every weekend.*

'**roller coaster** noun [C] a narrow metal track that goes up and down and round tight bends, and that people ride on in a special vehicle for fun

'**roller skate** (also **skate**) noun [C] a type of shoe with small wheels on the bottom: *a pair of roller skates* ••➤ picture at **skate** –'**roller skate** verb [I] –'**roller skating** noun [U]

'**rolling pin** noun [C] a piece of wood, etc in the shape of a tube, that you use for making pastry flat and thin before cooking ••➤ picture at **kitchen**

Roman /'rəʊmən/ adj **1** connected with ancient Rome or the Roman Empire: *Roman coins* • *the Roman invasion of Britain* **2** connected with the modern city of Rome –**Roman** noun [C]

the ,**Roman** '**alphabet** noun [sing] the letters A to Z, used especially in Western European languages

,**Roman** '**Catholic** (also **Catholic**) noun [C], adj (a member) of the Christian Church which has the Pope as its head: *She's (a) Roman Catholic.* ••➤ Look at **Protestant**.

,**Roman** **Ca'tholicism** (also **Catholicism**) noun [U] the beliefs of the Roman Catholic Church

romance /rəʊ'mæns/ noun **1** [C] a love affair: *The film was about a teenage romance.* **2** [U] a feeling or atmosphere of love or of sth new, special and exciting **3** [C] a novel about a love affair: *historical romances*

,**Roman** '**numerals** noun [pl] the letters used by the ancient Romans as numbers

➤ Roman numerals, for example IV (=4) and X (=10), are still used sometimes. For example they may be found numbering the pages and chapters of books or on some clocks.

r

[C] **countable**, a noun with a plural form: *one book, two books*   [U] **uncountable**, a noun with no plural form: *some sugar*

★**romantic**¹ /rəʊˈmæntɪk/ **adj 1** having a quality that strongly affects your emotions or makes you think about love; showing feelings of love: *a romantic candlelit dinner* ● *He isn't very romantic – he never says he loves me.* **2** involving a love affair: *Reports of a romantic relationship between the two film stars have been strongly denied.* **3** having or showing ideas about life that are emotional rather than real or practical: *He has a romantic idea that he'd like to live on a farm in Scotland.* –**romantically** /-kli/ **adv**

romantic² /rəʊˈmæntɪk/ **noun** [C] a person who has ideas that are not based on real life or that are not very practical

romanticize (also -**ise**) /rəʊˈmæntɪsaɪz/ **verb** [I,T] to make sth seem more interesting, exciting, etc than it really is

romp /rɒmp/ **verb** [I] (used about children and animals) to play in a happy and noisy way –**romp noun** [C]

   IDIOM **romp home/to victory** to win easily: *United romped to a 4-0 victory over Juventus.*

★**roof** /ruːf/ **noun** [C] (*pl* roofs) **1** the part of a building, vehicle, etc which covers the top of it: *a flat/sloping/tiled roof* ● *the roof of a car* ● *The library and the sports hall are under one roof* (= in the same building). ··► picture on page C7 **2** the highest part of the inside of sth: *The roof of the cave had collapsed.* ● *The soup burned the roof of my mouth.*

   IDIOM **a roof over your head** somewhere to live: *I might not have any money, but at least I've got a roof over my head.*

'**roof rack noun** [C] a structure that you fix to the roof of a car and use for carrying luggage or other large objects ··► picture at **rack**

rooftop /ˈruːftɒp/ **noun** [C,usually pl] the outside of the roofs of buildings: *From the tower we looked down over the rooftops of the city.*

★**room** /ruːm; rʊm/ **noun 1** [C] a part of a house or building that has its own walls, floor and ceiling: *a sitting/dining/living room* ● *I sat down in the waiting room until the doctor called me.* ● *I'd like to book a double room for two nights next month.* **2** [U] room (for sb/ sth); room (to do sth) space; enough space: *These chairs take up too much room.* ● *I threw away my old clothes to make room in the wardrobe for some new ones.* ● *There were so many people that there wasn't any room to move.* ··► Look at **space** and the note at **place**¹. **3** [U] room for sth the opportunity or need for sth: *There's room for improvement in your work* (= it could be much better). ● *The lack of time gives us very little room for manoeuvre.*

roomful /ˈruːmfʊl; ˈrʊm-/ **noun** [C] a large number of people or things in a room

'**room-mate noun** [C] a person that you share a room with in a flat, etc

roomy /ˈruːmi/ **adj** (**roomier; roomiest**) having plenty of space: *a roomy house/car*

roost /ruːst/ **noun** [C] a place where birds rest or sleep –**roost verb** [I]

rooster /ˈruːstə/ (*US*) = **COCK**¹(1)

★**root**¹ /ruːt/ **noun 1** [C] the part of a plant that grows under the ground and takes in water and food from the soil: *The deep roots of these trees can cause damage to buildings.* ● *root vegetables such as carrots and parsnips* ··► picture on page C2 **2** [C] the part of a hair or tooth that is under the skin and that attaches it to the rest of the body **3 roots** [pl] the place where you feel that you belong, because you grew up there, live there or your relatives once lived there **4** [C] the basic cause or origin of sth: *Let's try and get to the root of the problem.* ··► Look at **square root**.

root² /ruːt/ **verb**

   PHRASAL VERBS **root about/around (for sth)** to search for sth by moving things: *What are you rooting around in my desk for?*

root for sb to give support to sb who is in a competition, etc

root sth out to find and destroy sth bad completely

★**rope**¹ /rəʊp/ **noun** [C,U] very thick, strong string that is used for tying or lifting heavy things, climbing up, etc: *We need some rope to tie up the boat with.* ··► picture at **cable**

   IDIOM **show sb/know/learn the ropes** to show sb/know/learn how a job should be done

rope² /rəʊp/ **verb** [T] rope A to B/A and B together to tie sb/sth with a rope

   PHRASAL VERBS **rope sb in (to do sth)** (*informal*) to persuade sb to help in an activity, especially when he/she does not want to: *I've been roped in to help at the school play.*

rope sth off to put ropes round or across an area in order to keep people out of it

rosary /ˈrəʊzəri/ **noun** [C] (*pl* **rosaries**) a string of small round pieces of wood, etc used for counting prayers

rosé /ˈrəʊzeɪ/ **noun** [U] pink wine

rose¹ *past tense of* **RISE**²

★**rose**² /rəʊz/ **noun** [C] a flower with a sweet smell, that grows on a bush that usually has sharp points (**thorns**) growing on it ··► picture on page C2

rosette /rəʊˈzet/ **noun** [C] a decoration made from long pieces of coloured material (**ribbons**) that you wear on your clothes. Rosettes are given as prizes or worn to show that sb supports a particular political party. ··► picture at **medal**

roster /ˈrɒstə/ (*especially US*) = **ROTA**

rostrum /ˈrɒstrəm/ **noun** [C] a platform that sb stands on to make a public speech, etc

rosy /ˈrəʊzi/ **adj** (**rosier; rosiest**) **1** pink and pleasant in appearance: *rosy cheeks* **2** full of good possibilities: *The future was looking rosy.*

rot /rɒt/ **verb** [I,T] (**rotting; rotted**) to go bad or make sth go bad as part of a natural process: *Too many sweets will rot your teeth!* ··► synonym **decay** –**rot noun** [U]

rota /ˈrəʊtə/ [C] (*US also* **roster**) **noun** a list of people who share a certain job or task and the times that they are each going to do it: *We organize the cleaning on a rota.*

r

rotary /ˈrəʊtəri/ **adj** moving in circles round a central point

rotate /rəʊˈteɪt/ **verb** [I,T] **1** to turn in circles round a central point; to make sth do this: *The earth rotates on its axis.* **2** to happen in turn or in a particular order; to make sth do this: *We rotate the duties so that nobody is stuck with a job they don't like.*

rotation /rəʊˈteɪʃn/ **noun** [C,U] **1** movement in circles around a central point: *one rotation every 24 hours* **2** happening or making things happen in a particular order: *The company is chaired by all the members in rotation.*

rotor /ˈrəʊtə/ **noun** [C] a part of a machine that turns round, for example the long metal parts (blades) that go round on top of a type of aircraft (a helicopter)

rotten /ˈrɒtn/ **adj** **1** (used about food and other substances) old and not fresh enough or good enough to use: *rotten vegetables* **2** (*informal*) very unpleasant: *That was a rotten thing to say!* **3** (*spoken*) used to emphasize that you are angry: *You can keep your rotten job!*

rouge /ruːʒ/ **noun** [U] (*old-fashioned*) a red powder or cream used for giving more colour to the cheeks

★**rough¹** /rʌf/ **adj** **1** not smooth or level: *rough ground* •➤ opposite **smooth** or **soft 2** violent; not calm or gentle: *You can hold the baby, but don't be rough with him.* • *The sea was rough and half the people on the boat were seasick.* •➤ opposite **calm 3** made or done quickly or without much care; approximate: *a rough estimate* • *Can you give me a rough idea of what time you'll be arriving?* **4** (*informal*) looking or feeling ill: *You look a bit rough – are you feeling all right?* –**roughness noun** [U]

IDIOM **be rough (on sb)** be unpleasant or bad luck for sb

rough² /rʌf/ **noun**

IDIOMS **in rough** done quickly without worrying about mistakes, as a preparation for the finished piece of work or drawing

take the rough with the smooth to accept difficult or unpleasant things in addition to pleasant things

rough³ /rʌf/ **adv** in a rough way: *One of the boys was told off for playing rough.*

IDIOM **live/sleep rough** to live or sleep outdoors, usually because you have no home or money

rough⁴ /rʌf/ **verb**

IDIOM **rough it** to live without all the comfortable things that you usually have: *You have to rough it a bit when you go camping.*

roughage /ˈrʌfɪdʒ/ **noun** [U] the types or parts of food (fibre) which help your stomach to deal with other foods

roughen /ˈrʌfn/ **verb** [T] to make sth less smooth or soft

★**roughly** /ˈrʌfli/ **adv 1** in a violent way; not gently: *He grabbed her roughly by her arm.* **2** not exactly; approximately: *It took roughly three hours, I suppose.*

roulette /ruːˈlet/ **noun** [U] a game in which a ball is dropped onto a moving wheel that has holes with numbers on them. The players bet on which number hole the ball will be in when the wheel stops.

★**round¹** /raʊnd/ **adj** having the shape of a circle or a ball: *a round table*

IDIOM **in round figures/numbers** given to the nearest 10, 100, 1000, etc; not given in exact numbers

★**round²** /raʊnd/ **adv, prep**

➤ For special uses with many verbs, for example **come round**, **get round**, **go round**, etc see the verb entries.

1 in a circle or curve; on all sides of sth: *He had a bandage right round his head.* • *We sat round the table, talking late into the night.* • *We were just talking about Ravi and he came round the corner.* • *How long would it take to walk round the world?* • (*figurative*) *It wasn't easy to see a way round the problem* (= a way of solving it). **2** in a full circle: *The wheels spun round and round but the car wouldn't move.* **3** turning to look or go in the opposite direction: *Don't look round but the teacher's just come in.* • *She turned the car round and drove off.* **4** from one place, person, etc to another: *Pass the photographs round for everyone to see.* • *I've been rushing round all day.* **5** in or to a particular area or place: *Do you live round here?* • *I'll come round to see you at about 8 o'clock.* **6** in or to many parts of sth: *Let me show you round the house.* • *He spent six months travelling round Europe.*

IDIOMS **round about (sth)** in the area near a place; approximately: *We hope to arrive round about 6.*

the other way round in the opposite way or order: *My appointment's at 3 and Lella's is at 3.15 – or was it the other way round?*

➤ **Around** has the same meaning as **round** and is more common in US English.

★**round³** /raʊnd/ **noun** [C] **1** a number or series of events, etc: *a further round of talks with other European countries* **2** a regular series of visits, etc, often as part of a job: *The postman's round takes him about three hours.* • *Dr Adamou is on his daily round of the wards.* **3** a number of drinks (one for all the people in a group): *It's my round* (=it's my turn to buy the drinks). **4** one part of a game or competition: *Parma will play Real Madrid in the next round.* **5** (in golf) one game, usually of 18 holes: *to play a round of golf* **6** a bullet or a number of bullets, fired from a gun: *He fired several rounds at us.* **7** a short, sudden period of loud noise: *The last speaker got the biggest round of applause.*

round⁴ /raʊnd/ **verb** [T] to go round sth: *The police car rounded the corner at high speed.*

PHRASAL VERBS **round sth off** to do sth that completes a job or an activity: *We rounded off the meal with coffee and chocolates.*

round sb/sth up to bring sb/sth together in one place: *The teacher rounded up the children.*

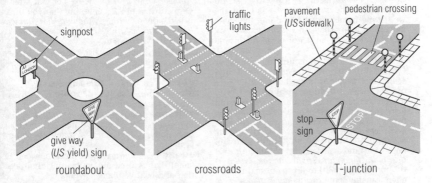

signpost • traffic lights • pavement (US sidewalk) • pedestrian crossing • stop sign

give way (US yield) sign

roundabout   crossroads   T-junction

round sth up/down to increase/decrease a number, price, etc to the nearest whole number

roundabout¹ /'raʊndəbaʊt/ **noun** [C] **1** a circle where several roads meet, that all the traffic has to go round in the same direction **2** a round platform made for children to play on. They sit or stand on it and sb pushes it round. •➤ picture at **swing** **3** = **MERRY-GO-ROUND**

roundabout² /'raʊndəbaʊt/ **adj** longer than is necessary or usual; not direct: *We got lost and came by rather a roundabout route.*

rounders /'raʊndəz/ **noun** [U] a British game that is similar to baseball

round 'trip noun [C] **1** a journey to a place and back again: *It's a four-mile round trip to the centre of town.* **2** (US) = **RETURN²**(5)

rouse /raʊz/ **verb** [T] **1** (*formal*) to make sb wake up: *She was sleeping so soundly that I couldn't rouse her.* **2** to make sb/sth very angry, excited, interested, etc

rousing /'raʊzɪŋ/ **adj** exciting and powerful: *a rousing speech*

rout /raʊt/ **verb** [T] to defeat sb completely –**rout noun** [C]

★**route** /ruːt/ **noun** [C] **1** a route (from A) (to B) a way from one place to another: *What is the most direct route from Bordeaux to Lyon?* ● *I got a leaflet about the bus routes from the information office.* **2** a route to sth a way of achieving sth: *Hard work is the only route to success.*

★**routine¹** /ruː'tiːn/ **noun** **1** (C,U) the usual order and way in which you regularly do things: *Make exercise part of your daily routine.* **2** [U] tasks that have to be done again and again and so are boring **3** [C] a series of movements, jokes, etc that are part of a performance: *a dance/comedy routine*

routine² /ruː'tiːn/ **adj** **1** normal and regular; not unusual or special: *The police would like to ask you some routine questions.* **2** boring; not exciting: *It's a very routine job, really.*

routinely /ruː'tiːnli/ **adv** regularly; as part of a routine: *The machines are routinely checked every two months.*

★**row¹** /rəʊ/ **noun** [C] **1** a line of people or things: *a row of books* ● *The children were all standing in a row at the front of the class.* **2** a line of seats in a theatre, cinema, etc: *Our seats were in the back row.* ● *a front-row seat*
IDIOM **in a row** one after another; without a break: *It rained solidly for four days in a row.*

row² /rəʊ/ **verb** **1** [I,T] to move a boat through the water using long thin pieces of wood with flat parts at the end (oars): *We often go rowing on the lake.* **2** [T] to carry sb/sth in a boat that you row: *Could you row us over to the island?* •➤ Look at **paddle**. –**row noun** [sing]

★**row³** /raʊ/ **noun** **1** [C] a row (about/over sth) a noisy argument or serious disagreement between two or more people, groups, etc: *When I have a row with my girlfriend, I always try to make up as soon as possible.* ● *A row has broken out between the main parties over education.* **2** [sing] a loud noise: *What a row! Could you be a bit quieter?* –**row verb** [I] **row (with sb) (about/over sth)**: *Pete and I are always rowing about money!*

rowdy /'raʊdi/ **adj** noisy and likely to cause trouble: *a rowdy group of football fans* ● *rowdy behaviour* –**rowdily adv** –**rowdiness noun** [U]

'rowing boat (US **rowboat** /'rəʊbəʊt/) **noun** [C] a small boat that you move through the water using long thin pieces of wood with flat parts at the end (oars) •➤ picture at **boat**

★**royal** /'rɔɪəl/ **adj** **1** connected with a king or queen or a member of their family: *the royal family* **2** (used in the names of organizations) supported by a member of the royal family –**royal noun** [C] (*informal*): *the Queen, the Princes and other royals*

Royal 'Highness noun [C] used when you are speaking to or about a member of the royal family

royalty /'rɔɪəlti/ **noun** (*pl* **royalties**) **1** [U] members of the royal family **2** [C] an amount of money that is paid to the person who wrote a book, piece of music, etc every time his/her work is sold or performed: *The author earns a 2% royalty on each copy sold.*

rpm /ˌɑː piː 'em/ **abbr** revolutions per minute: *engine speed 2500 rpm*

RSI /ˌɑːr es 'aɪ/ **noun** [U] repetitive strain injury; pain and swelling, especially in the wrists and hands, caused by doing the same movement many times in a job or an activity

RSVP /ˌɑːr es viː 'piː/ **abbr** (used on invitations) please reply

Rt Hon abbr Right Honourable: a title for Cabinet ministers in the government and some other people in important positions

★**rub** /rʌb/ **verb** (**rubbing**; **rubbed**) **1** [I,T] to move your hand, a cloth, etc backwards and forwards on the surface of sth while pressing firmly: *Ralph rubbed his hands together to keep them warm.* ● *The cat rubbed against my leg.* **2** [T] rub sth in (to sth) to put a cream, liquid, etc onto a surface by rubbing: *Apply a little of the lotion and rub it into the skin.* **3** [I] rub (on/against sth) to press on/against sth, often causing pain or damage: *These new shoes are rubbing my heels.* –**rub noun** [C]

IDIOMS **rub salt into the wound/sb's wounds** to make a situation that makes sb feel bad even worse

rub shoulders with sb to meet and spend time with famous people: *As a journalist you rub shoulders with the rich and famous.*

PHRASAL VERBS **rub it/sth in** to keep reminding sb of sth embarrassing that he/she wants to forget: *I know it was a stupid mistake, but there's no need to rub it in!*

rub off (on/onto sb) (used about a good quality) to be passed from one person to another: *Let's hope some of her enthusiasm rubs off onto her brother.*

rub sth off (sth) to remove sth from a surface by rubbing: *He rubbed the dirt off his boots.*

rub sth out to remove the marks made by a pencil, chalk, etc using a rubber, cloth, etc: *That answer is wrong. Rub it out.*

★**rubber** /'rʌbə/ **noun 1** [U] a strong substance that can be stretched and does not allow water to pass through it, used for making tyres, boots, etc. Rubber is made from the juice of a tropical tree or is produced using chemicals: *a rubber ball* ● *rubber gloves* ● *foam rubber* **2** [C] (*especially US* **eraser**) a small piece of rubber that you use for removing pencil marks from paper; soft material used for removing chalk marks or pen marks from a board

,**rubber 'band** (also e,lastic 'band) **noun** [C] a thin circular piece of rubber that is used for holding things together: *Her hair was tied back with a rubber band.* ••➤ picture on page S6

,**rubber 'stamp noun** [C] a person or group who gives official approval to sth without thinking about it first ••➤ picture on page S6 –**rubber-stamp verb** [T]: *The committee have no real power – they just rubber-stamp the chairman's ideas.*

rubbery /'rʌbəri/ **adj** like rubber: *This meat is rubbery.*

★**rubbish** /'rʌbɪʃ/ (*US* **garbage**; **trash**) **noun** [U] **1** things that you do not want any more; waste material: *The dustmen collect the rubbish every Monday.* ● *a rubbish bin* ● *It's only*

rubbish – throw it away. ••➤ Look at **waste**. ••➤ picture at **bin 2** something that you think is bad, silly or wrong: *I thought that film was absolute rubbish.* ● *Don't talk such rubbish.*

'**rubbish tip** = **TIP¹**(4)

rubble /'rʌbl/ **noun** [U] pieces of broken brick, stone, etc, especially from a damaged building

rubella /ruːˈbelə/ = **GERMAN MEASLES**

ruby /'ruːbi/ **noun** [C] (*pl* **rubies**) a type of precious stone that is red

rucksack /'rʌksæk/ **noun** [C] (*Brit*) a bag that you use for carrying things on your back ••➤ synonyms **backpack** or **pack** ••➤ picture at **bag**

rudder /'rʌdə/ **noun** [C] a piece of wood or metal that is used for controlling the direction of a boat or plane

★**rude** /ruːd/ **adj 1** rude (to sb) (about sb/sth) not polite: *She was very rude to me about my new jacket.* ● *It's rude to interrupt when people are speaking.* ● *I think it was rude of them not to phone and say that they weren't coming.* ••➤ Look at **impolite**. **2** connected with sex, using the toilet, etc in a way that might offend people: *a rude joke/word/gesture* **3** sudden and unpleasant: *If you're expecting any help from him, you're in for a rude shock.* –**rudely adv** –**rudeness noun** [U]

rudimentary /ˌruːdɪˈmentri/ **adj** very basic or simple

ruffle /'rʌfl/ **verb** [T] **1** ruffle sth (up) to make sth untidy or no longer smooth: *to ruffle sb's hair* **2** (often passive) to make sb annoyed or confused

rug /rʌg/ **noun** [C] **1** a piece of thick material that covers a small part of a floor

➤ Compare **carpet** and **mat**.

••➤ picture on page C7 **2** a large piece of thick cloth that you put over your legs or around your shoulders to keep warm, especially when travelling

rugby /'rʌgbi/ **noun** [U] a form of football that is played by two teams of 13 or 15 players with a roundish ball that can be carried, kicked or thrown

➤ **Rugby League** is played with 13 players in a team, **Rugby Union** with 15 players.

••➤ Look at **league**.

rugged /'rʌgɪd/ **adj 1** (used about land) rough, with a lot of rocks and not many plants **2** (used about a man) strong and attractive **3** strong and made for difficult conditions

★**ruin¹** /'ruːɪn/ **verb** [T] **1** to damage sth so badly that it loses all its value, pleasure, etc: *a ruined building* ● *The bad news ruined my week.* ● *That one mistake ruined my chances of getting the job.* **2** to cause sb to lose all his/her money, hope of being successful, etc: *The cost of the court case nearly ruined them.*

ruin² /'ruːɪn/ **noun 1** [U] the state of being destroyed or very badly damaged: *The city was in a state of ruin.* **2** [U] the cause or state of having lost all your money, hope of being successful, etc: *Many small companies are facing financial ruin.* **3** [C] the parts of a building that are left standing after it has been destroyed or badly damaged: *the ruins of the ancient city of Pompeii*

IDIOMS go to rack and ruin → **RACK¹**

in ruin(s) badly damaged or destroyed: *After the accident her life seemed to be in ruins.*

ruinous /'ru:məs/ **adj** causing serious problems, especially with money

★**rule¹** /ru:l/ **noun 1** [C] an official statement that tells you what you must or must not do in a particular situation or when playing a game: *to **obey/break a rule*** • *Do you know the rules of chess?* • *It's **against the rules** to smoke in this area.* • *The company have strict **rules and regulations** governing employees' dress.*

> A **law** is stronger. You can be officially punished if you break it.

2 [C] a piece of advice about what you should do in a particular situation: *When you run a marathon, the **golden rule** is: don't start too fast.* **3** [sing] what is usual: *Large families are the exception rather than the rule nowadays.* • *As a general rule, women live longer than men.* • *I don't read much as a rule.* **4** [C] (in a language) a description of what is usual or correct: *What is the rule for forming the past tense?* **5** [U] government; control: *The country is **under** military rule.*

IDIOMS bend the rules → **BEND¹**

a rule of thumb a simple piece of practical advice, not involving exact details or figures

work to rule a form of protest by workers in which they follow the rules of their employment very closely so that their work takes longer than usual

★**rule²** /ru:l/ **verb** [I,T] **1** rule (over sb/sth) to have the power over a country, group of people, etc: *Julius Caesar ruled over a vast empire.* • *(figurative) His whole life was ruled by his ambition to become President.* **2** rule (on sth); rule (in favour of/against sb/sth) to make an official decision: *The judge will rule on whether or not the case can go ahead.*

PHRASAL VERB rule sb/sth out to say that sb/sth is not possible, cannot do sth, etc; to prevent sth: *The government has ruled out further increases in train fares next year.*

★**ruler** /'ru:lə/ **noun** [C] **1** a person who rules a country, etc **2** a straight piece of wood, plastic, etc marked with centimetres, that you use for measuring sth or for drawing straight lines •→ picture on page S6

ruling¹ /'ru:lɪŋ/ **adj** (only *before* a noun) with the most power in an organization, country, etc: *the ruling political party*

ruling² /'ru:lɪŋ/ **noun** [C] an official decision

rum /rʌm/ **noun** [U,C] a strong alcoholic drink that is made from the juice of a plant from which sugar is made (**sugar cane**)

rumble /'rʌmbl/ **verb** [I] to make a deep heavy sound: *I was so hungry that my stomach was rumbling.* –rumble **noun** [sing]: *a rumble of thunder*

rummage /'rʌmɪdʒ/ **verb** [I] to move things and make them untidy while you are looking for sth: *Nina rummaged through the drawer looking for the tin-opener.*

★**rumour** (*US* rumor) /'ru:mə/ **noun** [C,U] (a) rumour (about/of sb/sth) (a piece of) news or information that many people are talking about but that is possibly not true: *I didn't start the rumour about Barry's operation.* • *Rumour has it* (= people are saying) *that Lena has resigned.* • *to confirm/deny a rumour* (= to say that it is true/not true)

rumoured (*US* rumored) /'ru:məd/ **adj** reported or said, but perhaps not true: *They are rumoured to be getting divorced.*

rump /rʌmp/ **noun** [C] the back end of an animal: *rump steak* (= meat from the rump)

★**run¹** /rʌn/ **verb** [I,T] (*pres part* running; *pt* ran /ræn/; *pp* run) **1** [I,T] to move using your legs, going faster than a walk: *I had to run to catch the bus.* • *I often go running in the evenings* (= as a hobby). • *I ran nearly ten kilometres this morning.* **2** [I,T] to move, or move sth, quickly in a particular direction: *I've been running around after the kids all day.* • *The car ran off the road and hit a tree.* • *She ran her finger down the list of passengers.* **3** [I] to lead from one place to another; to be in a particular position: *The road runs along the side of a lake.* **4** [T] to organize or be in charge of sth; to provide a service: *She runs a restaurant.* • *They run English courses all the year round.* **5** [I,T] to operate or function; to make sth do this: *The engine is running very smoothly now.* • *We're running a new computer program today.* **6** [I] to operate at a particular time: *All the trains are running late this morning.* • *We'd better hurry up – we're running behind schedule.* **7** [T] to use and pay for a vehicle: *It costs a lot to run a car.* **8** [I] to continue for a time: *My contract has two months left to run.* • *The play ran for nearly two years in a London theatre.* **9** [I,T] (used about water or other liquid) to flow; to make water flow: *When it's really cold, my nose runs.* • *I can hear a tap running somewhere.* • *to run a bath/a tap* **10** [I] run with sth to be covered with flowing water: *My face was running with sweat.* **11** [I] (used about the colour in material, etc) to spread, for example when the material is washed: *Don't put that red shirt in the washing machine. It might run.* **12** [I] run (for sth) to be one of the people hoping to be chosen (a candidate) in an election: *He's running for president.* **13** [T] to publish sth in a newspaper or magazine: *'The Independent' is running a series of articles on pollution.* **14** [T] run a test/check (on sth) to do a test or check on sth: *They're running checks on the power supply to see what the problem is.*

IDIOMS be running at to be at a certain level

run for it to run in order to escape

> For other idioms containing **run**, look at the entries for the nouns, adjectives, etc, for example **run in the family** is at **family**.

PHRASAL VERBS run across sb/sth to meet or

r

find sb/sth by chance

run after sb/sth to try to catch sb/sth

run away to escape from somewhere: *He's run away from home.*

run sb/sth down 1 to hit a person or an animal with your vehicle: *She was run down by a bus.* **2** to criticize sb/sth: *He's always running her down in front of other people.*

run (sth) down to stop functioning gradually; to make sth do this: *Turn the lights off or you'll run the battery down.*

run into sb to meet sb by chance

run into sth to have difficulties or a problem: *If you run into any problems, just let me know.*

run (sth) into sb/sth to hit sb/sth with a car, etc: *He ran his car into a brick wall.*

run sth off to copy sth, using a machine

run off with sth to take or steal sth

run out (of sth) to finish your supply of sth; to come to an end: *We've run out of coffee.* • *Time is running out.* • *My passport runs out next month.*

run sb/sth over to hit a person or an animal with your vehicle: *The child was run over as he was crossing the road.*

run through sth to discuss or read sth quickly: *She ran through the names on the list.*

★ **run²** /rʌn/ *noun* **1** [C] an act of running on foot: *I go for a three-mile run every morning.* • *The prisoner tried to make a run for it* (= to escape on foot). **2** [C] a journey by car, train, etc: *The bus driver was picking up kids on the school run.* **3** [sing] a series of similar events or sth that continues for a very long time: *We've had a run of bad luck recently.* **4** [sing] **a run on sth** a sudden great demand for sth **5** [C] a point in the games of baseball and cricket

IDIOMS **in the long run →** LONG¹

on the run hiding or trying to escape from sb/sth: *The escaped prisoner is still on the run.*

runaway¹ /ˈrʌnəweɪ/ *adj* **1** out of control: *a runaway horse/car/train* **2** happening very easily: *a runaway victory*

runaway² /ˈrʌnəweɪ/ *noun* [C] a person, especially a child, who has left or escaped from somewhere

run-'down *adj* **1** (used about a building or place) in bad condition: *a run-down block of flats* **2** very tired and not healthy

rung¹ /rʌŋ/ *noun* [C] one of the bars that form the steps of a ladder •➤ picture at **ladder**

rung² *past participle* of **RING²**

runner /ˈrʌnə/ *noun* [C] **1** a person or animal that runs, especially in a race: *a long-distance runner* **2** a person who takes guns, drugs, etc illegally from one country to another

runner-'up *noun* [C] (*pl* **runners-up**) the person or team that finished second in a race or competition

★ **running¹** /ˈrʌnɪŋ/ *noun* [U] **1** the action or sport of running: *How often do you go running?* • *running shoes* **2** the process of managing a business or other organization: *She's not involved in the day-to-day running of the*

office. • *the running costs of a car* (= petrol, insurance, repairs, etc)

IDIOM **in/out of the running (for sth)** (*informal*) having/not having a good chance of getting or winning sth

★ **running²** /ˈrʌnɪŋ/ *adj* **1** used after a number and a noun to say that sth has happened a number of times in the same way without a change: *Our school has won the competition for four years running.* **2** (only *before* a noun) flowing or available from a tap (used about water): *There is no running water in the cottage.* **3** (only *before* a noun) not stopping; continuous: *a running battle between two rival gangs*

running 'commentary *noun* [C] a spoken description of sth while it is happening

runny /ˈrʌni/ *adj* (*informal*) **1** containing more liquid than is usual or than you expected: *runny jam* **2** (used about your eyes or nose) producing too much liquid: *Their children always seem to have runny noses.*

'run-up *noun* [sing] **1** the period of time before a certain event: *the run-up to the election* **2** (in sport) a run that people do in order to be going fast enough to do an action

runway /ˈrʌnweɪ/ *noun* [C] a long piece of ground with a hard surface where aircraft take off and land at an airport

rupture /ˈrʌptʃə/ *noun* [C,U] **1** a sudden bursting or breaking **2** (*formal*) the sudden ending of good relations between two people or groups –**rupture** *verb* [I,T]: *Her appendix ruptured and she had to have emergency surgery.*

rural /ˈrʊərəl/ *adj* connected with the country, not the town •➤ Look at **urban** and **rustic**.

ruse /ruːz/ *noun* [C] a trick or clever plan

★ **rush¹** /rʌʃ/ *verb* **1** [I,T] to move or do sth with great speed, often too fast: *I rushed back home when I got the news.* • *Don't rush off – I want to talk to you.* • *The public rushed to buy shares in the new company.* **2** [T] to take sb/sth to a place very quickly: *He suffered a heart attack and was rushed to hospital.* **3** [I,T] **rush (sb) (into sth/into doing sth)** to do sth or make sb do sth without thinking about it first: *Don't let yourself be rushed into marriage.* • *Don't rush me – I'm thinking!*

IDIOM **be rushed/run off your feet →** FOOT¹

★ **rush²** /rʌʃ/ *noun* **1** [sing] a sudden quick movement: *At the end of the match there was a rush for the exits.* • *I was so nervous, all my words came out in a rush.* **2** [sing,U] a situation in which you are in a hurry and need to do things quickly: *I can't stop now. I'm in a terrible rush.* • *Don't hurry your meal. There's no rush.* **3** [sing] **a rush (on sth)** a time when many people try to get sth: *There's been a rush to buy petrol before the price goes up.* **4** [sing] a time when there is a lot of activity and people are very busy: *We'll leave early to avoid the rush.* **5** [C] a type of tall grass that grows near water •➤ picture on page C2

[C] **countable**, a noun with a plural form: *one book, two books*   [U] **uncountable**, a noun with no plural form: *some sugar*

'**rush hour** noun [C] the times each day when there is a lot of traffic because people are travelling to or from work: *rush-hour traffic*

rust /rʌst/ noun [U] a reddish-brown substance that forms on the surface of iron, etc, caused by the action of air and water –**rust** verb [I,T]: *Some parts of the car had rusted.*

rustic /'rʌstɪk/ adj typical of the country or of country people; simple: *The whole area is full of rustic charm.* •➤ Look at **rural** and **urban**.

rustle /'rʌsl/ verb [I,T] to make a sound like dry leaves or paper moving: *There was a rustling noise in the bushes.* –**rustle** noun [sing]
PHRASAL VERB **rustle sb/sth up** (*informal*) to find sb or prepare sth in a short time: *to rustle up a quick snack*

★**rusty** /'rʌsti/ adj **1** (used about metal objects) covered with a brownish substance (**rust**) as a result of being in contact with water and air: *rusty tins* **2** (used about a skill) not as good as it was because you have not used it for a long time: *My French is rather rusty.*

rut /rʌt/ noun [C] a deep track that a wheel makes in soft ground
IDIOM **be in a rut** to have a boring way of life that is difficult to change

ruthless /'ruːθləs/ adj (used about people and their behaviour) hard and cruel; determined to get what you want and showing no pity to others: *a ruthless dictator* –**ruthlessly** adv –**ruthlessness** noun [U]

rye /raɪ/ noun [U] a plant that is grown in colder countries for its grain, which is used to make flour and also an alcoholic drink (**whisky**) •➤ picture at **cereal**

....

S s

....

S, s[1] /es/ noun [C] (*pl* **S's**; **s's**) the nineteenth letter of the English alphabet: *'School' begins with (an) 'S'.*

S[2] abbr **1** small (size) **2** (*US* **So**) south(ern): *S Yorkshire*

sabbath /'sæbəθ/ (also **the Sabbath**) noun [sing] the day of the week for rest and prayer in certain religions (Sunday for Christians, Saturday for Jews)

sabotage /'sæbətɑːʒ/ noun [U] damage that is done on purpose and secretly in order to prevent an enemy or competitor being successful, for example by destroying machinery, roads, bridges, etc: *industrial/ economic/military sabotage* –**sabotage** verb [T]

saccharin /'sækərɪn/ noun [U] a very sweet substance that can be used instead of sugar

sachet /'sæʃeɪ/ noun [C] a small plastic or paper packet that contains a small amount of liquid or powder: *a sachet of shampoo/sugar/ coffee* •➤ picture at **container**

sack[1] /sæk/ noun [C] a large bag made from a rough heavy material, paper or plastic, used for carrying or storing things: *sacks of flour/ potatoes*
IDIOMS **get the sack** (*Brit*) to be told by your employer that you can no longer continue working for him/her (usually because you have done sth wrong): *Tony got the sack for poor work.*

give sb the sack (*Brit*) to tell an employee that he/she can no longer continue working for you (because of bad work, behaviour, etc): *Tony's work wasn't good enough and he was given the sack.*

sack[2] /sæk/ (*especially US* **fire**) verb [T] to tell an employee that he/she can no longer work for you (because of bad work, bad behaviour, etc): *Her boss has threatened to sack her if she's late again.*

sacred /'seɪkrɪd/ adj **1** connected with God, a god or religion: *The Koran is the sacred book of Muslims.* **2** too important and special to be changed or harmed: *a sacred tradition*

sacrifice[1] /'sækrɪfaɪs/ noun [U,C] **1** giving up sth that is important or valuable to you in order to get or do sth that seems more important; sth that you give up in this way: *If we're going to have a holiday this year, we'll have to **make** some **sacrifices**.* **2** sacrifice (to sb) the act of offering sth to a god, especially an animal that has been killed in a special way; an animal, etc that is offered in this way

sacrifice[2] /'sækrɪfaɪs/ verb **1** [T] sacrifice sth (for sb/sth) to give up sth that is important or valuable to you in order to get or do sth that seems more important: *She is not willing to sacrifice her career in order to have children.* **2** [I,T] to kill an animal and offer it to a god, in order to please the god

sacrilege /'sækrəlɪdʒ/ noun [U,sing] treating a religious object or place without the respect that it deserves

★**sad** /sæd/ adj (**sadder**; **saddest**) **1** sad (to do sth); sad (that...) unhappy or causing sb to feel unhappy: *We are very sad to hear that you are leaving.* • *I'm very sad that you don't trust me.* • *That's one of the saddest stories I've ever heard!* • *a sad poem/song/film* **2** bad or unacceptable: *It's a sad state of affairs when your best friend doesn't trust you.* –**sadden** /'sædn/ verb [T] (*formal*): *The news of your father's death saddened me greatly.* –**sadness** noun [C,U]

saddle /'sædl/ noun [C] **1** a seat, usually made of leather, that you put on a horse so that you can ride it •➤ picture at **horse** **2** a seat on a bicycle or motorbike •➤ picture on page S9 –**saddle** [T] verb
PHRASAL VERB **saddle sb with sth** to give sb a responsibility or task that he/she does not want

sadism /'seɪdɪzəm/ noun [U] getting pleasure, especially sexual pleasure, from hurting other people
➤ Compare **masochism**.

sadist /ˈseɪdɪst/ **noun** [C] a person who gets pleasure, especially sexual pleasure, from hurting other people –**sadistic** /səˈdɪstɪk/ **adj** –**sadistically** /-kli/ **adv**

sadly /ˈsædli/ **adv 1** unfortunately: *Sadly, after eight years of marriage they had grown apart.* **2** in a way that shows unhappiness **3** in a way that is wrong: *If you think that I've forgotten what you did, you're **sadly mistaken**.*

sae /ˌes eɪ ˈiː/ **abbr** stamped addressed envelope

safari /səˈfɑːri/ **noun** [C,U] (*pl* **safaris**) a trip to see or hunt wild animals, especially in East Africa: *to be/go on safari*

★**safe¹** /seɪf/ **adj 1** (not before a noun) safe **(from sb/sth)** free from danger; not able to be hurt: *She didn't **feel safe** in the house on her own.* ● *Do you think my car will be safe in this street?* ● *Keep the papers where they will be safe from fire.* **2 safe (to do sth); safe (for sb)** not likely to cause danger, harm or risk: *Don't sit on that chair, it isn't safe.* ● *I left my suitcase in a **safe place** and went for a cup of coffee.* ● *Is this drug safe for children?* ● *She's a very safe driver.* ● *It's not safe to walk alone in the streets at night here.* ● *Is it safe to drink the water here?* ● *I think **it's safe to say** that the situation is unlikely to change for some time.* **3** (not before a noun) not hurt, damaged or lost: *After the accident he checked that all the passengers were safe.* ● *After five days the child was found, **safe and sound**.* –**safely adv**: *I rang my parents to tell them I had arrived safely.*

IDIOMS **in safe hands** with sb who will take good care of you

on the safe side not taking risks; being very careful

safe² /seɪf/ **noun** [C] a strong metal box or cupboard with a special lock that is used for keeping money, jewellery, documents, etc in

safeguard /ˈseɪfɡɑːd/ **noun** [C] a safeguard **(against sb/sth)** something that protects against possible dangers –**safeguard verb** [T]: *to safeguard sb's interests/rights/privacy*

★**safety** /ˈseɪfti/ **noun** [U] the state of being safe; not being dangerous or in danger: *In the interests of safety, smoking is forbidden.* ● *road safety* (= the prevention of road accidents) ● *New safety measures have been introduced on trains.*

ˈ**safety belt** = SEAT BELT

ˈ**safety net noun** [C] **1** a net that is placed to catch sb who is performing high above the ground if he/she falls **2** an arrangement that helps to prevent disaster (usually with money) if sth goes wrong

ˈ**safety pin noun** [C] a metal pin with a point that is bent back towards the head, which is covered so that it cannot be dangerous. •► picture at **pin**

ˈ**safety valve noun** [C] a device in a machine that allows steam, gas, etc to escape if the pressure becomes too great

sag /sæɡ/ **verb** [I] (**sagging**; **sagged**) to hang or to bend down, especially in the middle

saga /ˈsɑːɡə/ **noun** [C] a very long story; a long series of events

Sagittarius /ˌsædʒɪˈteəriəs/ **noun** [C,U] the ninth sign of the zodiac, the Archer

said *past tense, past participle of* SAY¹

★**sail¹** /seɪl/ **verb 1** [I] (used about a boat or ship and the people on it) to travel on water in a ship or boat of any type: *I stood at the window and watched the ships sailing by.* ● *to sail round the world* **2** [I,T] to travel in and control a boat with sails, especially as a sport: *My father is teaching me to sail.* ● *I've never sailed this kind of yacht before.* •► When we are talking about spending time sailing a boat for pleasure, we say **go sailing**: *We often go sailing at weekends.* **3** [I] to begin a journey on water: *When does the ship sail?* ● *We sail for Santander at six o'clock tomorrow morning.* **4** [I] to move somewhere quickly in a smooth or proud way: *The ball sailed over the fence and into the neighbour's garden.* ● *Mary sailed into the room, completely ignoring all of us.*

IDIOM **sail through (sth)** to pass a test or exam easily

sail² /seɪl/ **noun 1** [C] a large piece of strong material that is fixed onto a ship or boat. The wind blows against the sail and moves the ship along. **2** [sing] a trip on water in a ship or boat with a sail **3** [C] any of the long parts that the wind moves round that are attached to a building (**windmill**) •► picture at **windmill**

IDIOM **set sail** → SET¹

sailboard /ˈseɪlbɔːd/ = WINDSURFER(1)

sailing /ˈseɪlɪŋ/ **noun** [U] the sport of being in, and controlling, small boats with sails

ˈ**sailing boat** (*US* **sailboat**) **noun** [C] a boat with a sail or sails

★**sailor** /ˈseɪlə/ **noun** [C] a person who works on a ship or a person who sails a boat

★**saint** /seɪnt; snt/ **noun** [C] **1** a very good or religious person who is given special respect after death by the Christian church

> When it is used as a title **saint** is written with a capital letter: *Saint Patrick*. In the names of places, churches, etc the short form **St** is usually used: *St Andrew's Church*. Before names **saint** is pronounced /snt/. Look at **patron saint**.

2 a very good, kind person

sake /seɪk/ **noun** [C]

IDIOMS **for Christ's/God's/goodness'/ Heaven's/pity's, etc sake** (*spoken*) used to emphasize that it is important to do sth or to show that you are annoyed: *For goodness' sake, hurry up!* ● *Why have you taken so long, for God's sake?* •► **For God's sake** and especially **for Christ's sake** are stronger and may offend some people.

for the sake of sb/sth; for sb's/sth's sake in order to help sb/sth: *Don't go to any trouble for my sake.* ● *They only stayed together for the sake of their children/for their children's sake.*

S

★**salad** /'sæləd/ noun [C,U] a mixture of vegetables, usually not cooked, that you often eat together with other foods: *All main courses are served with chips or salad.* ·➤ picture on page C4

★**salary** /'sæləri/ noun [C,U] (*pl* **salaries**) the money that a person receives (usually every month) for the work he/she has done: *My salary is paid directly into my bank account.* ● *a high/low salary* ·➤ Look at the note at **pay²**.

★**sale** /seɪl/ noun **1** [C,U] the action of selling or being sold; the occasion when sth is sold: *The sale of alcohol to anyone under the age of 18 is forbidden.* ● *a sale of used toys* **2 sales** [pl] the number of items sold: *Sales of personal computers have increased rapidly.* ● *The company reported excellent sales figures.* **3 sales** [U] (also '**sales department**) the part of a company that deals with selling its products: *Jodie works in sales/in the sales department.* ● *a sales representative/sales rep* **4** [C] a time when shops sell things at prices that are lower than usual: *The sale starts on December 28th.* ● *I got several bargains in the sales.* ·➤ Look at **car boot sale** and **jumble sale**.
▢IDIOMS **for sale** offered for sb to buy: *This painting is not for sale.* ● *I see our neighbours have put their house up for sale.*
on sale 1 available for sb to buy, especially in shops: *This week's edition is on sale now at your local newsagents.* **2** (*US*) offered at a lower price than usual

'**sales clerk** (also **clerk**) (*US*) = **SHOP ASSIST-ANT**

salesman /'seɪlzmən/ noun [C] (*pl* **-men** /-men/) a man whose job is selling things to people

salesperson /'seɪlzpɜːsn/ noun [C] (*pl* **salespeople** /'seɪlzpiːpl/) a person whose job is selling things to people, especially in a shop

saleswoman /'seɪlzwʊmən/ noun [C] (*pl* **-women** /-wɪmɪn/) a woman whose job is selling things to people

salient /'seɪliənt/ adj (only *before* a noun) most important or noticeable

saliva /sə'laɪvə/ noun [U] the liquid that is produced in the mouth ·➤ Look at **spit**.

salmon /'sæmən/ noun [C,U] (*pl* **salmon**) a large fish with silver skin and pink meat that we eat: *smoked salmon*

salmonella /,sælmə'nelə/ noun [U] a type of bacteria that causes food poisoning

salon /'sælɒn/ noun [C] a shop where you can have beauty or hair treatment or where you can buy expensive clothes

saloon /sə'luːn/ (*US* **sedan**) noun [C] a car with a fixed roof and a separate area (**boot**) for luggage ·➤ picture at **car**

★**salt¹** /sɔːlt/ noun [U] a common white substance that is found in sea water and the earth. Salt is used in cooking for flavouring

food: *Season with salt and pepper.* ● *Add a pinch* (= a small amount) *of salt.* –**salt** adj: *salt water*
▢IDIOMS **rub salt into the wound/sb's wounds** ➤ **RUB**
take sth with a pinch of salt ➤ **PINCH²**

salt² /sɔːlt/ verb [T] (usually passive) to put salt on or in sth: *salted peanuts*

'**salt water** adj living in the sea: *a salt water fish*

➤ Fish that live in rivers are **freshwater** fish.

salty /'sɔːlti/ adj having the taste of or containing salt: *I didn't like the meat, it was too salty.*

salute /sə'luːt/ noun [C] **1** an action that a soldier, etc does to show respect, by holding his/her hand to the forehead: *to give a salute* **2** something that shows respect for sb: *The next programme is a salute to one of the world's greatest film stars.* –**salute** verb [I,T]: *The soldiers saluted as they marched past the general.*

salvage¹ /'sælvɪdʒ/ noun [U] saving things that have been or are likely to be lost or damaged, especially in an accident or a disaster; the things that are saved: *a salvage operation/company/team*

salvage² /'sælvɪdʒ/ verb [T] **salvage sth (from sth)** to manage to rescue sth from being lost or damaged; to rescue sth or a situation from disaster: *They salvaged as much as they could from the house after the fire.*

salvation /sæl'veɪʃn/ noun **1** [U] (in the Christian religion) being saved from the power of evil **2** [U,sing] a thing or person that rescues sb/sth from danger, disaster, etc

★**same** /seɪm/ adj, adv, pron **1 the same... (as sb/sth); the same...that...** not different, not another or other; exactly the one or ones that you have mentioned before: *My brother and I had the same teacher at school.* ● *They both said the same thing.* ● *I'm going to wear the same clothes as/that I wore yesterday.* ● *This one looks exactly the same as that one.* **2 the same... (as sb/sth); the same...that...** exactly like the one already mentioned: *I wouldn't buy the same car again* (= the same model of car). ● *We treat all the children in the class the same.* ● *I had the same experience as you some time ago.* ● *All small babies look the same.* ● *Is there another word that means the same as this?*

➤ We cannot say *a same ...*To express this idea we use **the same sort of**: *I'd like the same sort of job as my father.*

▢IDIOMS **all/just the same** in spite of this/that; anyway: *I understand what you're saying. All the same, I don't agree with you.* ● *I don't need to borrow any money but thanks all the same for offering.*
at the same time 1 together; at one time: *I can't think about more than one thing at the same time.* **2** on the other hand; however: *It's a very good idea but at the same time it's*

rather risky.

much the same → MUCH

on the same wavelength able to understand sb because you have similar ideas and opinions

(the) same again (*spoken*) a request to be served or given the same drink as before

same here (*spoken*) the same thing is also true for me: *'I'm bored.' 'Same here.'*

(the) same to you (*spoken*) used as an answer when sb says sth rude to you or wishes you sth: *'You idiot!' 'Same to you!'* ● *'Have a good weekend.' 'The same to you.'*

sample /'sɑːmpl/ **noun** [C] a small number or amount of sb/sth that is looked at, tested, examined, etc to find out what the rest is like: *The interviews were given to a **random sample** of shoppers.* ● *to take a blood sample* ● *a free sample of shampoo* ••➤ synonym **specimen** –**sample verb** [T]: *You are welcome to sample any of our wines before making a purchase.*

sanatorium /ˌsænə'tɔːriəm/ (*US* **sanatarium** /ˌsænə'teəriəm/) **noun** [C] a type of hospital where patients who need a long period of treatment for an illness can stay

sanction[1] /'sæŋkʃn/ **noun** 1 [C, usually pl] **sanctions (against sb)** an official order that limits business, contact, etc with a particular country, in order to make it do sth, such as obeying international law: *The sanctions against those countries have now been lifted.* 2 [U] (*formal*) official permission to do or change sth 3 [C] a punishment for breaking a rule or law

sanction[2] /'sæŋkʃn/ **verb** [T] to give official permission for sth

sanctuary /'sæŋktʃuəri/ **noun** (*pl* **sanctuaries**) 1 [C] a place where birds or animals are protected from being hunted 2 [C,U] a place where sb can be safe from enemies, the police, etc

★**sand** /sænd/ **noun** 1 [U] a powder consisting of very small grains of rock, found in deserts and on beaches ••➤ picture on page C8 2 **the sands** [pl] a large area of sand

sandal /'sændl/ **noun** [C] a type of light, open shoe that people wear when the weather is warm ••➤ picture at **shoe**

sandcastle /'sændkɑːsl/ **noun** [C] a pile of sand that looks like a castle, made by children playing on a beach

'sand dune = DUNE

sandpaper /'sændpeɪpə/ **noun** [U] strong paper with sand on it that is used for rubbing surfaces in order to make them smooth

★**sandwich**[1] /'sænwɪdʒ/ **noun** [C] two slices of bread with food between them: *a ham/cheese sandwich* ••➤ picture on page C4

sandwich[2] /'sænwɪdʒ/ **verb** [T] **sandwich sb/sth (between sb/sth)** to place sb/sth in a very narrow space between two other things or people

sandy /'sændi/ **adj** covered with or full of sand

sane /seɪn/ **adj** 1 (used about a person) mentally normal; not crazy: *No sane person would*

do anything like that. 2 (used about a person or an idea, a decision, etc) sensible; showing good judgement ••➤ opposite **insane** ••➤ noun **sanity**

sang *past tense* of SING

sanitarium (*US*) = SANATORIUM

sanitary /'sænətri/ **adj** connected with the protection of health, for example how human waste is removed: *Sanitary conditions in the refugee camps were terrible.* ••➤ Look at **insanitary**.

'sanitary towel (*US* **'sanitary napkin**) **noun** [C] a thick piece of soft material that women use to absorb blood lost during their period (3) ••➤ Look at **tampon**.

sanitation /ˌsænɪ'teɪʃn/ **noun** [U] the equipment and systems that keep places clean, especially by removing human waste

sanity /'sænəti/ **noun** [U] 1 the state of having a normal healthy mind 2 the state of being sensible and reasonable ••➤ opposite **insanity** ••➤ adjective **sane**

sank *past tense* of SINK[1]

Santa Claus /'sæntə klɔːz/ = FATHER CHRISTMAS

sap[1] /sæp/ **noun** [U] the liquid in a plant or tree

sap[2] /sæp/ **verb** [T] (**sapping**; **sapped**) **sap (sb of) sth** to make sb/sth weaker; to destroy sth gradually: *Years of failure have sapped (him of) his confidence.*

sapling /'sæplɪŋ/ **noun** [C] a young tree ••➤ picture on page C2

sapphire /'sæfaɪə/ **noun** [C,U] a bright blue precious stone

sarcasm /'sɑːkæzəm/ **noun** [U] the use of words or expressions to mean the opposite of what they actually say. People use sarcasm in order to criticize other people or to make them look silly. ••➤ Look at **ironic**. –**sarcastic** /sɑː'kæstɪk/ **adj**: *a sarcastic comment* –**sarcastically** /-kli/ **adv**

sardine /ˌsɑː'diːn/ **noun** [C] a type of very small silver-coloured fish that we cook and eat: *a tin of sardines*

sari /'sɑːri/ **noun** [C] a dress that consists of a long piece of shiny cloth (silk) or cotton that women, particularly Indian women, wear around their bodies ••➤ picture on page C6

sash /sæʃ/ **noun** [C] a long piece of material that is worn round the waist or over the shoulder, often as part of a uniform

Sat *abbr* Saturday: *Sat 2 May*

sat *past tense, past participle* of SIT

Satan /'seɪtn/ **noun** [sing] a name for the Devil ••➤ Look at **devil**.

satchel /'sætʃəl/ **noun** [C] a bag, often carried over the shoulder, used by schoolchildren for taking books to and from school

satellite /'sætəlaɪt/ **noun** [C] 1 an electronic device that is sent into space and moves around the earth or another planet for a particular purpose: *a weather/communications satellite* 2 a natural object that moves round a bigger object in space

'satellite dish (also **dish**) **noun** [C] a large,

circular piece of equipment that people have on the outside of their houses, that receives signals from a satellite (1) so that they can receive satellite television

satellite television (also **satellite TV**) noun [U] television programmes that are broadcast using a satellite (1)

satin /'sætɪn/ noun [U] a type of cloth that is smooth and shiny: *a satin dress/ribbon*

satire /'sætaɪə/ noun **1** [U] the use of humour to attack a person, an idea or behaviour that you think is bad or silly **2** [C] a satire (on sb/sth) a piece of writing or a play, film, etc that uses satire: *a satire on political life* –satirical /sə'tɪrɪkl/ adj: *a satirical magazine* –satirically /-kli/ adv

★**satisfaction** /ˌsætɪs'fækʃn/ noun [U,C] the feeling of pleasure that you have when you have done, got or achieved what you wanted; sth that gives you this feeling: *Roshni stood back and looked at her work with a sense of satisfaction.* ● *We finally found a solution that was to everyone's **satisfaction**.* ● *She was about to **have the satisfaction** of seeing her book in print.* ••➤ opposite **dissatisfaction**

★**satisfactory** /ˌsætɪs'fæktəri/ adj good enough for a particular purpose; acceptable: *This piece of work is not satisfactory. Please do it again.* ••➤ opposite **unsatisfactory** –satisfactorily /-tərəli/ adv: *Work is progressing satisfactorily.*

satisfied /'sætɪsfaɪd/ adj satisfied (with sb/ sth) pleased because you have had or done what you wanted: *a satisfied smile* ● *a satisfied customer* ••➤ opposite **dissatisfied**

★**satisfy** /'sætɪsfaɪ/ verb [T] (*pres part* **satisfying**; *3rd pers sing pres* **satisfies**; *pt, pp* **satisfied**) **1** to make sb pleased by doing or giving him/her what he/she wants: *No matter how hard I try, my piano teacher is never satisfied.* **2** to have or do what is necessary for sth: *Make sure you **satisfy** the entry **requirements** before you apply to the university.* ● *I had a quick look inside the parcel just to **satisfy** my **curiosity**.* **3** satisfy sb (that...) to show or give proof to sb that sth is true or has been done: *Once the police were satisfied that they were telling the truth, they were allowed to go.*

satisfying /'sætɪsfaɪɪŋ/ adj pleasing, giving satisfaction: *I find it satisfying to see people enjoying something I've cooked.*

satsuma /sæt'suːmə/ noun [C] a type of small orange

saturate /'sætʃəreɪt/ verb [T] **1** to make sth extremely wet: *Her clothes were completely saturated.* **2** to fill sth so completely that it is impossible to add any more: *The market is saturated with cheap imports.* –saturation /ˌsætʃə'reɪʃn/ noun [U]

★**Saturday** /'sætədeɪ; -di/ noun [C,U] (*abbr* **Sat**) the day of the week after Friday

➤ Days of the week are always written with a capital letter. For examples of how to use the days of the week in sentences, look at **Monday**.

Saturn /'sætɜːn; -tən/ noun [sing] the planet that is sixth in order from the sun and that has rings around it

★**sauce** /sɔːs/ noun [C,U] a thick hot or cold liquid that you eat on or with food: *The chicken was served in a delicious sauce.* ● *ice cream with chocolate sauce* ••➤ picture on page C4 ••➤ Look at **gravy**.

★**saucepan** /'sɔːspən/ noun [C] a round metal pot with a handle that is used for cooking things on top of a cooker ••➤ picture at **pan**

★**saucer** /'sɔːsə/ noun [C] a small round plate that you put under a cup ••➤ picture at **cup**

sauna /'sɔːnə/ noun [C] **1** a type of bath where you sit in a room that is very hot: *to have a sauna* **2** the room that you sit in to have a sauna

saunter /'sɔːntə/ verb [I] to walk without hurrying

★**sausage** /'sɒsɪdʒ/ noun [C,U] a mixture of meat cut into very small pieces, spices, etc that is made into a long thin shape. Some sausage is eaten cold in slices; other types are cooked and then served whole: *garlic/ liver sausage* ● *We had sausages and chips for lunch.* ••➤ picture on page C4

savage /'sævɪdʒ/ adj very cruel or violent: *He was the victim of a savage attack.* ● *The book received savage criticism.* –savage verb [T]: *The boy died after being savaged by a dog.* –savagely adv –savagery /'sævɪdʒri/ noun [U]

★**save¹** /seɪv/ verb **1** [T] save sb/sth (from sth/from doing sth) to keep sb/sth safe from death, harm, loss, etc: *to save sb's **life*** ● *to save sb from drowning* ● *We are trying to save the school from closure.* **2** [I,T] save (sth) (up) (for sth) to keep or not spend money so that you can use it later: *I'm saving up for a new bike.* ● *Do you manage to save any of your wages?* **3** [T] to keep sth for future use: *I'll be home late so please save me some dinner.* ● *Save that box. It might come in useful.* ● *If you get there first, please save me a seat.* **4** [I,T] save (sb) (sth) (on) sth to avoid wasting time, money, etc: *It will save you twenty minutes on the journey if you take the express train.* ● *You can save on petrol by getting a smaller car.* ● *This car will save you a lot on petrol.* **5** [T] save (sb) sth/doing sth to avoid, or make sb able to avoid, doing sth unpleasant or difficult: *If you make an appointment it will save you waiting.* **6** [T] to store information in a computer by giving it a special instruction: *Don't forget to save the file before you close it.* **7** [T] to stop a goal being scored in sports such as football, hockey, etc

IDIOMS keep/save sth for a rainy day → **RAINY**
save face to prevent yourself losing the respect of other people

save² /seɪv/ noun [C] (in football, etc) the action of preventing a goal from being scored: *The goalkeeper made a great save.*

saver /'seɪvə/ noun [C] **1** a person who saves money for future use: *The rise in interest rates is good news for savers.* **2** (often used in compounds) a thing that helps you save time, money, or the thing mentioned

saving /'seɪvɪŋ/ **noun 1** [C] **a saving (of sth) (on sth)** an amount of time, money, etc that you do not have to use or spend: *The sale price represents a saving of 25% on the usual price.* **2 savings** [pl] money that you have saved for future use: *All our savings are in the bank.*

saviour (*US* **savior**) /'seɪvɪə/ **noun** [C] a person who rescues or saves sb/sth from danger, loss, death, etc

savoury (*US* **savory**) /'seɪvəri/ **adj** (used about food) having a taste that is not sweet ••➤ Look at **sweet.**

saw¹ *past tense of* SEE

★ **saw²** /sɔː/ **noun** [C] a tool that is used for cutting wood, etc. A saw has a long flat metal part (a **blade**) with sharp teeth on it, and a handle at one or both ends ••➤ picture at **tool** –**saw verb** [I,T] (*pt* **sawed**; *pp* **sawn** /sɔːn/) *to saw through the trunk of a tree* ● *He sawed the log up into small pieces.*

> In US English the past participle is **sawed.**

sawdust /'sɔːdʌst/ **noun** [U] very small pieces of wood that fall like powder when you are cutting a large piece of wood

sax /sæks/ (*informal*) = SAXOPHONE

saxophone /'sæksəfəʊn/ (also *informal* **sax**) **noun** [C] a metal musical instrument that you play by blowing into it. Saxophones are especially used for playing modern music, for example jazz: *This track features Dexter Gordon on sax.* ••➤ Look at the note at **piano.** ••➤ picture at **music**

★ **say¹** /seɪ/ **verb** [T] (*3rd pers sing pres* **says** /sez/; *pt, pp* **said** /sed/) **1 say sth (to sb); say that...; say sth (about sb)** to speak or tell sb sth, using words: *'Please come back,' she said.* ● *The teacher said we should hand in our essays on Friday.* ● *I said goodbye to her at the station.* ● *We can ask him, but I'm sure he'll say no.* ● *He said to his mother that he would phone back later.* ● *They just sat there without saying anything.* ● *'This isn't going to be easy,' she said to herself* (= she thought). ● *'What time is she coming?' 'I don't know – she didn't say.'* ● *It is said that cats can sense the presence of ghosts.*

> **Say** or **tell? Say** is often used with the actual words that were spoken or before **that** in indirect speech: *'I'll catch the 9 o'clock train,' he said.* ● *He said that he would catch the 9 o'clock train.* Notice that you say sth **to** sb: *He said to me that he would catch the 9 o'clock train.* **Tell** is always followed by a noun or pronoun, showing who you were speaking to: *He told me that he would catch the 9 o'clock train.* **Tell,** not **say,** can also be used when you are talking about giving orders or advice: *I told them to hurry up.* ● *She's always telling me what I ought to do.*

2 to express an opinion on sth: *I wouldn't say she's unfriendly – just shy.* ● *What is the artist trying to say in this painting?* ● *Well, what do you say? Do you think it's a good idea?*

● *It's hard to say what I like about the book.* ● *'When will it be finished?' 'I couldn't say* (= I don't know).*' **3** (used about a book, notice, etc) to give information: *What time does it say on that clock?* ● *The map says the hotel is just past the railway bridge.* ● *The sign clearly says 'No dogs'.* **4 say sth (to sb)** to show a feeling, a situation, etc without using words: *His angry look said everything about the way he felt.* **5** to imagine or guess sth about a situation; to suppose: *We will need, say, £5000 for a new car.* ● *Say you don't get a place at university, what will you do then?*

IDIOMS **go without saying** to be clear, so that you do not need to say it: *It goes without saying that the children will be well looked after at all times.*

have a lot, nothing, etc to say for yourself to have a lot, nothing, etc to say in a particular situation: *Late again! What have you got to say for yourself?*

I must say (*spoken*) used to emphasize your opinion: *I must say, I didn't believe him at first.*

I wouldn't say no (*spoken*) used to say that you would like sth: *'Coffee?' 'I wouldn't say no.'*

Say when (*spoken*) used to tell sb to say when you have poured enough drink in his/her glass or put enough food on his/her plate

that is to say... which means...: *We're leaving on Friday, that's to say in a week's time.*

say² /seɪ/ **noun** [sing,U] **(a) say (in sth)** the authority or right to decide sth: *I'd like to have some say in the arrangements for the party.*

IDIOM **have your say** to express your opinion: *Thank you for your comments. Now let somebody else have their say.*

saying /'seɪɪŋ/ **noun** [C] a well-known phrase that gives advice about sth or says sth that many people believe is true: *'Love is blind' is an old saying.* ••➤ Look at **proverb.**

scab /skæb/ **noun** [C,U] a mass of dried blood that forms over a part of the body where the skin has been cut or broken ••➤ Look at **scar.**

scaffold /'skæfəʊld/ **noun** [C] a platform on which criminals were killed in past times by hanging

scaffolding /'skæfəldɪŋ/ **noun** [U] long metal poles and wooden boards that form a structure which is put next to a building so that people who are building, painting, etc can stand and work on it

scald /skɔːld/ **verb** [T] to burn sb/sth with very hot liquid: *I scalded my arm badly when I was cooking.* –**scald noun** [C] –**scalding adj:** *scalding hot water*

★ **scale¹** /skeɪl/ **noun 1** [C,U] the size of sth, especially when compared to other things: *We shall be making the product on a large scale next year.* ● *At this stage it is impossible to estimate the full scale of the disaster.* **2** [C] a series of marks on a tool or piece of equipment that you use for measuring sth: *The ruler has one scale in centimetres and one*

scales

kitchen scales   bathroom scales

scale in inches. **3** [C] a series of numbers, amounts, etc that are used for measuring or fixing the level of sth: *The earthquake measured 6.5 on the Richter scale.* ● *the new pay scale for nurses* **4** [C] the relationship between the actual size of sth and its size on a map or plan: *The map has a scale of one centimetre to a kilometre.* ● *a scale of 1: 50 000* (= one to fifty thousand) ● *We need a map with a larger scale.* ● *a scale model* **5 scales** [pl] a piece of equipment that is used for weighing sb/sth: *I weighed it on the kitchen scales.* **6** [C] a series of musical notes which go up or down in a fixed order. People play or sing scales to improve their technical ability: *the scale of C major* **7** [C] one of the small flat pieces of hard material that cover the body of some fish and animals: *the scales of a snake* •➤ picture on page C1

scale² /skeɪl/ **verb** [T] to climb up a high wall, steep cliff, etc

PHRASAL VERB **scale sth up/down** to increase/ decrease the size, number, importance, etc of sth: *Police have scaled up their search for the missing boy.*

scalp /skælp/ **noun** [C] the skin on the top of your head that is under your hair

scalpel /'skælpəl/ **noun** [C] a small knife that is used by doctors (**surgeons**) when they are doing operations

scamper /'skæmpə/ **verb** [I] (used especially about a child or small animal) to run quickly

scan /skæn/ **verb** [T] (**scanning; scanned**) **1** to look at or read every part of sth quickly until you find what you are looking for: *Vic scanned the list until he found his own name.* **2** (used about a machine) to examine what is inside a person's body or inside an object such as a suitcase: *Machines scan all the luggage for bombs and guns.* –**scan noun** [C]: *The scan showed the baby was in the normal position.*

scandal /'skændl/ **noun 1** [C,U] an action, a situation or behaviour that shocks people; the public feeling that is caused by such behaviour: *The chairman resigned after being involved in a financial scandal.* ● *There was no suggestion of scandal in his private life.* ● *The poor state of school buildings is a real scandal.* **2** [U] talk about sth bad or wrong that sb has or may have done: *to spread scandal about sb*

scandalize (also **-ise**) /'skændəlaɪz/ **verb** [T] to cause sb to feel shocked by doing sth that he/she thinks is bad or wrong

scandalous /'skændələs/ **adj** very shocking

or wrong: *It is scandalous that so much money is wasted.*

Scandinavia /,skændɪ'neɪvɪə/ **noun** [sing] the group of countries in northern Europe that consists of Denmark, Norway and Sweden. Sometimes Finland and Iceland are also said to be part of Scandinavia. –**Scandinavian adj**

scanner /'skænə/ **noun** [C] an electronic machine that can look at, record or send images or electronic information: *The scanner can detect cancer at an early stage.* ● *I used the scanner to send the document by e-mail.*

scant /skænt/ **adj** (only *before* a noun) not very much; not as much as necessary

scanty /'skænti/ **adj** too small in size or amount: *We didn't learn much from the scanty information they gave us.* –**scantily adv**: *I realized I was too scantily dressed for the cold weather.*

scapegoat /'skeɪpgəʊt/ **noun** [C] a person who is punished for things that are not his/her fault: *When Alison was sacked she felt she had been made a scapegoat for all the company's problems.*

*★**scar** /skɑ:/ **noun** [C] a mark on the skin that is caused by a cut that skin has grown over: *The operation didn't leave a very big scar.* •➤ Look at **scab.** –**scar verb** [I,T] (**scarring; scarred**): *William's face was scarred for life in the accident.*

*★**scarce** /skeəs/ **adj** not existing in large quantities; hard to find: *Food for birds and animals is scarce in the winter.* •➤ opposite **plentiful** –**scarcity** /'skeəsəti/ **noun** [C,U] (*pl* **scarcities**): *(a) scarcity of food/jobs/ resources*

scarcely /'skeəsli/ **adv 1** only just; almost not: *There was scarcely a car in sight.* ● *She's not a friend of mine. I scarcely know her.* •➤ Look at **hardly. 2** used to suggest that sth is not reasonable or likely: *You can scarcely expect me to believe that after all you said before.*

*★**scare¹** /skeə/ **verb 1** [T] to make a person or an animal frightened: *The sudden noise scared us all.* ● *It scares me to think what might happen.* **2** [I] to become frightened: *I don't scare easily, but when I saw the gun I was terrified.*

PHRASAL VERB **scare sb/sth away/off** to make a person or animal leave or stay away by frightening them: *Don't make any noise or you'll scare the birds away.*

scare² /skeə/ **noun** [C] **1** a feeling of being frightened: *It wasn't a serious heart attack but it gave him a scare.* **2** a situation where many people are afraid or worried about sth: *Last night there was a bomb scare in the city centre.*

scarecrow /'skeəkrəʊ/ **noun** [C] a very simple model of a person that is put in a field to frighten away the birds

*★**scared** /skeəd/ **adj** scared (**of sb/sth**); scared (**of doing sth/to do sth**) frightened: *Are you scared of the dark?* ● *She's scared of*

---

walking home alone. ● *Everyone was too scared to move.*

scarf /skɑ:f/ **noun** [C] (*pl* **scarfs** /skɑ:fs/ or **scarves** /skɑ:vz/) **1** a long thin piece of cloth, usually made of wool, that you wear around your neck to keep warm ‧‧➤ picture on page C6 **2** a square piece of cloth that women wear around their neck or shoulders or over their heads to keep warm or for decoration

scarlet /'skɑ:lət/ **adj, noun** [U] (of) a bright red colour

scary /'skeəri/ **adj** (**scarier; scariest**) (*informal*) frightening: *a scary ghost story* ● *It was a bit scary driving in the mountains at night.*

scathing /'skeɪðɪŋ/ **adj** expressing a very strong negative opinion about sb/sth; very critical: *a scathing attack on the new leader* ● *scathing criticism*

scatter /'skætə/ **verb 1** [I] (used about a group of people or animals) to move away quickly in different directions **2** [T] to drop or throw things in different directions over a wide area: *The wind scattered the papers all over the room.*

scattered /'skætəd/ **adj** spread over a large area or happening several times during a period of time: *There will be sunny intervals with scattered showers today.*

scavenge /'skævɪndʒ/ **verb** [I,T] to look for food, etc among waste and rubbish –**scavenger noun** [C]: *Scavengers steal the food that the lion has killed.*

SCE /ˌes si: 'i:/ **abbr** Scottish certificate of Education. Pupils in Scotland take the SCE at Standard grade at the age of about 16 and at Higher grade at about 17.

scenario /sə'nɑːriəʊ/ **noun** [C] (*pl* **scenarios**) **1** one way that things may happen in the future: *A likely scenario is that the company will get rid of some staff.* **2** a description of what happens in a play or film

★**scene** /si:n/ **noun 1** [C] the place where sth happened: *the scene of a crime/an accident* ● *An ambulance was **on the scene** in minutes.* **2** [C] an occasion when sb expresses great anger or another strong emotion in public: *There was quite a scene when she refused to pay the bill.* **3** [C] one part of a book, play, film, etc in which the events happen in one place: *The first scene of 'Hamlet' takes place on the castle walls.* **4** [C,U] what you see around you in a particular place: *Her new job was no better, but at least it would be a **change of scene***. **5 the scene** [sing] the way of life or the present situation in a particular area of activity: *The political scene in Eastern Europe is very confused.* ● *the fashion scene*

scenery /'si:nəri/ **noun** [U] **1** the natural beauty that you see around you in the country: *The scenery is superb in the mountains.* **2** the furniture, painted cloth, boards, etc that are used on the stage in a theatre: *The scenery is changed during the interval.*

➤ We say that an area of the country has beautiful **scenery** when it is attractive to

look at. The **landscape** of a particular area is the way the features of it are arranged: *Trees and hedges are a typical feature of the British landscape.* ● *an urban landscape* (= in a city or town). You have a **view** of something when you look out of a window or down from a high place: *There was a marvellous view of the sea from our hotel room.* Look also at the note at **country** (3).

scenic /'si:nɪk/ **adj** having beautiful scenery

scent /sent/ **noun 1** [C,U] a pleasant smell: *This flower has no scent.* **2** [C,U] the smell that an animal leaves behind and that some other animals can follow **3** [U] (*especially Brit*) a liquid with a pleasant smell that you wear on your skin to make it smell nice; perfume **4** [sing] the feeling that sth is going to happen: *The scent of victory was in the air.* –**scent verb** [T]: *The dog scented a rabbit and shot off.* –**scented adj**

sceptic (*US* **skeptic**) /'skeptɪk/ **noun** [C] a person who doubts that sth is true, right, etc –**sceptical** (*US* **skeptical**) /-kl/ **adj** sceptical (of/about sth): *Many doctors are sceptical about the value of alternative medicine.*

scepticism (*US* **skepticism**) /'skeptɪsɪzəm/ **noun** [U] a general feeling of doubt about sth; a feeling that you are not likely to believe sth

schedule[1] /'ʃedjuːl/ **noun 1** [C,U] a plan of things that will happen or of work that must be done: *Max has a busy schedule for the next few days.* ● *to be ahead of/behind schedule* (= to have done more/less than was planned) **2** (*US*) = **TIMETABLE**

schedule[2] /'ʃedjuːl/ **verb** [T] **schedule sth (for sth)** to arrange for sth to happen or be done at a particular time: *We've scheduled the meeting for Monday morning.* ● *The train was scheduled to arrive at 10.07.*

scheme[1] /ski:m/ **noun** [C] **1** a scheme (to do sth/for doing sth) an official plan or system for doing or organizing sth: *a new scheme to provide houses in the area* ● *a local scheme for recycling newspapers* **2** a clever plan to do sth: *He's thought of a new scheme for making money fast.* ‧‧➤ Look at **colour scheme**.

scheme[2] /ski:m/ **verb** [I,T] to make a secret or dishonest plan: *She felt that everyone was scheming to get rid of her.*

schizophrenia /ˌskɪtsə'fri:niə/ **noun** [U] a serious mental illness in which a person confuses the real world and the world of the imagination and often behaves in strange and unexpected ways –**schizophrenic** /ˌskɪtsə'frenɪk/ **adj, noun** [C]

scholar /'skɒlə/ **noun** [C] **1** a person who studies and has a lot of knowledge about a particular subject **2** a person who has passed an exam or won a competition and has been given some money (**a scholarship**) to help pay for his/her studies: *a British Council scholar* ‧‧➤ Look at **student**.

scholarship /'skɒləʃɪp/ **noun 1** [C] an amount of money that is given to a person who has passed an exam or won a competition, in order to help pay for his/her studies: *to win a scholarship to Yale* **2** [U] serious study of an academic subject

★**school** /skuːl/ **noun 1** [C] the place where children go to be educated: *Where did you go to school?* • *They're building a new school in our area.* • *Do you have to wear school uniform?* • *Was your school co-educational* (= for boys and girls) *or single-sex?* **2** [U] the time you spend at a school; the process of being educated in a school: *Their children are still at school.* • *Children start school at 5 years old in Britain and can leave school at 16.* • *School starts at 9 o'clock and finishes at about 3.30.* • *After school we usually have homework to do.*

> You are talking about **school** (no ' **the**') when you are talking about going there for the usual reason (that is, as a pupil or teacher): *Where do your children go to school?* • *I enjoyed being at school.* • *Do you walk to school?* You talk about **the school** if you are talking about going there for a different reason (for example, as a parent): *I have to go to the school on Thursday to talk to John's teacher.* You must also use **a** or **the** when more information about the school is given: *Rani goes to the school in the next village.* • *She teaches at a school for children with learning difficulties.*

3 [sing, with sing or pl verb] all the pupils and teachers in a school: *The whole school cheered the winner.* **4** (used to form compounds) connected with school: *children of school age* • *The bus was full of schoolchildren.* • *It is getting increasingly difficult for school-leavers to find jobs.* • *Schoolteachers have been awarded a 2% pay rise.* • *I don't have many good memories of my schooldays.* **5** [C] a place where you go to learn a particular subject: *a language/driving/drama/business school* **6** [C] (*US*) a college or university **7** [C] a department of a university that teaches a particular subject: *the school of geography at Leeds University* **8** [C] a group of writers, painters, etc who have the same ideas or style: *the Flemish school of painting* **9** [C] a large group of fish swimming together

IDIOM **a school of thought** the ideas or opinions that one group of people share: *There are various schools of thought on this matter.*

schooling /ˈskuːlɪŋ/ **noun** [U] the time that you spend at school; your education

★**science** /ˈsaɪəns/ **noun 1** [U] the study of and knowledge about the physical world and natural laws: *Modern science has discovered a lot about the origin of life.* • *Fewer young people are studying science at university.* **2** [C] one of the subjects into which science can be divided: *Biology, chemistry and physics are all sciences.*

> The study of people and society is called **social science**.

‚science ˈfiction **noun** [U] books, films, etc

about events that take place in the future, often involving travel in space

★**scientific** /ˌsaɪənˈtɪfɪk/ **adj 1** connected with or involving science: *We need more funding for scientific research.* • *scientific instruments* **2** (used about a way of thinking or of doing sth) careful and logical: *a scientific study of the way people use language* –**scientifically** /-kli/ **adv**: *Sorting out the files won't take long if we do it scientifically.*

★**scientist** /ˈsaɪəntɪst/ **noun** [C] a person who studies or teaches science, especially biology, chemistry or physics

scissors

blade

nail clippers

★**scissors** /ˈsɪzəz/ **noun** [pl] a tool for cutting things that consists of two long, flat, sharp pieces of metal that are joined together •> **Scissors** is a plural noun: *These scissors are blunt.* We CANNOT say 'a scissors': we must say **a pair of scissors**.

scoff /skɒf/ **verb 1** [I] **scoff (at sb/sth)** to speak about sb/sth in a way that shows you think that he/she/it is stupid or ridiculous **2** [T] (*Brit informal*) to eat a lot of sth quickly

scold /skəʊld/ **verb** [I,T] **scold sb (for sth/for doing sth)** to speak angrily to sb because he/she has done something bad or wrong •> **Tell off** is more common.

scone /skɒn; skəʊn/ **noun** [C] a small, simple cake, usually eaten with butter on

scoop¹ /skuːp/ **noun** [C] **1** a tool like a spoon used for picking up ice cream, flour, grain, etc **2** the amount that one scoop contains **3** an exciting piece of news that is reported by one newspaper, television or radio station before it is reported anywhere else

scoop² /skuːp/ **verb** [T] **1** **scoop sth (out/up)** to make a hole in sth or to take sth out by using a scoop or sth similar: *Scoop out the middle of the pineapple.* **2** **scoop sb/sth (up)** to move or lift sb/sth using a continuous action: *He scooped up the child and ran.* **3** to win a big or important prize: *The film has scooped all the awards this year.* **4** to get a story before all other newspapers, TV stations, etc

scooter /ˈskuːtə/ **noun** [C] **1** a light motorbike with a small engine •> picture at **motorbike 2** a child's toy with two wheels that you stand on and move by pushing one foot against the ground

scope /skəʊp/ **noun 1** [U] **scope (for sth/to do sth)** the chance or opportunity to do sth: *The job offers plenty of scope for creativity.* **2** [sing] the variety of subjects that are being discussed or considered: *The government was unwilling to extend the scope of the inquiry.*

scorch /skɔːtʃ/ **verb** [T] to burn sth so that its colour changes but it is not destroyed: *I scorched my blouse when I was ironing it.*

scorching /ˈskɔːtʃɪŋ/ **adj** very hot: *It was absolutely scorching on Tuesday.*

S

★score¹ /skɔː/ **noun 1** [C] the number of points, goals, etc that sb/sth gets in a game, competition, exam, etc: *What was the final score?* ● *The score is 3-2 to Liverpool.* ● *The top score in the test was 80%.* **2 scores** [pl] very many: *Scores of people have written to offer their support.* **3** [C] the written form of a piece of music
IDIOM **on that score** as far as that is concerned: *Ian will be well looked after. Don't worry on that score.*

★score² /skɔː/ **verb** [I,T] to get points, goals, etc in a game, competition, exam, etc: *The team still hadn't scored by half-time.* ● *Louise scored the highest marks in the exam.*

scoreboard /'skɔːbɔːd/ **noun** [C] a large board that shows the score during a game, competition, etc

scorn¹ /skɔːn/ **noun** [U] **scorn (for sb/sth)** the strong feeling that you have when you do not respect sb/sth

scorn² /skɔːn/ **verb** [T] **1** to feel or show a complete lack of respect for sb/sth: *The President scorned his critics.* **2** to refuse to accept help or advice, especially because you are too proud: *The old lady scorned all offers of help.* –**scornful** /-fl/ **adj**: *a scornful look/smile/remark* –**scornfully** /-fəli/ **adv**

Scorpio /'skɔːpiəʊ/ **noun** (*pl* **Scorpios**) [C,U] the eighth sign of the zodiac, the Scorpion

scorpion

scorpion /'skɔːpiən/ **noun** [C] a creature which looks like a large insect and lives in hot countries. A scorpion has a long curved tail with a poisonous sting in it.

Scot /skɒt/ **noun** [C] a person who comes from Scotland

Scotch /skɒtʃ/ **noun** [U,C] a strong alcoholic drink (whisky) that is made in Scotland; a glass of this ••➤ Look at the note at **Scottish**.

Scots /skɒts/ **adj** of or connected with people from Scotland ••➤ Look at the note at **Scottish**.

Scotsman /'skɒtsmən/ **noun** [C] a man who comes from Scotland

Scottish /'skɒtɪʃ/ **adj** of or connected with Scotland, its people, culture, etc

➤ **Scots** is usually only used about the people of Scotland: *a Scots piper*. **Scottish** is used about Scotland and about both people and things that come from Scotland: *Scottish law/dancing/music* ● *She speaks with a strong Scottish accent.* ● *the Scottish Highlands*. **Scotch** is used for whisky and some kinds of food, but not for people

scoundrel /'skaʊndrəl/ **noun** [C] (*old-fashioned*) a man who behaves very badly towards other people, especially by being dishonest

scour /'skaʊə/ **verb** [T] **1** to clean sth by rubbing it hard with sth rough: *to scour a dirty pan* **2** to search a place very carefully because you are looking for sb/sth

scourge /skɜːdʒ/ **noun** [C] a person or thing that causes a lot of trouble or suffering: *Raul was the scourge of the United defence.*

scout /skaʊt/ **noun** [C] **1 Scout** (also **Boy 'Scout**) a member of an organization (the Scouts) that teaches boys how to look after themselves and encourages them to help others. Scouts do sport, learn useful skills, go camping, etc. ••➤ Look at **Guide**. **2** a soldier who is sent in front of the rest of the group to find out where the enemy is or which is the best route to take

scowl /skaʊl/ **noun** [C] a look on your face that shows you are angry or in a bad mood ••➤ Look at **frown**. –**scowl verb** [I]

scrabble /'skræbl/ **verb** [I] to move your fingers or feet around quickly, trying to find sth or get hold of sth: *She scrabbled about in her purse for some coins.*

scramble /'skræmbl/ **verb** [I] **1** to climb quickly up or over sth using your hands to help you; to move somewhere quickly: *He scrambled up the hill and over the wall.* ● *He scrambled to his feet* (= off the ground) *and ran off into the trees.* ● *The children scrambled into the car.* **2 scramble (for sth/to do sth)** to fight or move quickly to get sth which a lot of people want: *People stood up and began scrambling for the exits.* ● *Everyone was scrambling to get the best bargains.* –**scramble noun** [sing]

scrambled 'egg noun [U] eggs mixed together with milk and then cooked in a pan

scrap¹ /skræp/ **noun 1** [C] a small piece of sth: *a scrap of paper/cloth* ● *scraps of food* **2** [U] something that you do not want any more but that is made of material that can be used again: *The old car was sold for scrap.* ● *scrap paper* **3** [C] (*informal*) a short fight or argument

scrap² /skræp/ **verb** [T] (**scrapping**; **scrapped**) to get rid of sth that you do not want any more: *I think we should scrap that idea.*

scrapbook /'skræpbʊk/ **noun** [C] a large book with empty pages that you can stick pictures, newspaper articles, etc in

scrape¹ /skreɪp/ **verb 1** [T] **scrape sth (down/out/off)** to remove sth from a surface by moving a sharp edge across it firmly: *Scrape all the mud off your boots before you come in.* **2** [T] **scrape sth (against/along/on sth)** to damage or hurt sth by rubbing it against sth rough or hard: *Mark fell and scraped his knee.* ● *Sunita scraped the car against the wall.* **3** [I,T] **scrape (sth) against/along/on sth** to rub (sth) against sth and make a sharp unpleasant noise: *The branches scraped against the window.* **4** [T] to manage to get or win sth with difficulty: *I just scraped a pass in the maths exam.*
PHRASAL VERBS **scrape by** to manage to live on the money you have, but with difficulty: *We can just scrape by on my salary.*
scrape through (sth) to succeed in doing sth

with difficulty: *to scrape through an exam* (= just manage to pass it)
scrape sth together/up to get or collect sth together with difficulty

scrape² /skreɪp/ **noun** [C] **1** the action or unpleasant sound of one thing hard against another **2** damage or an injury caused by rubbing against sth rough: *I got a nasty scrape on my knee.* **3** (*informal*) a difficult situation that was caused by your own stupid behaviour

'**scrap heap** **noun** [C] a large pile of objects, especially metal, that are no longer wanted
IDIOM **on the scrap heap** not wanted any more: *Many of the unemployed feel that they are on the scrap heap.*

scrappy /'skræpi/ **adj** not organized or tidy and so not pleasant to see: *a scrappy essay/football match*

★**scratch¹** /skrætʃ/ **verb** **1** [I,T] **scratch (at sth)** to rub your skin with your nails, especially because it is irritating you (**itching**): *Don't scratch at your insect bites or they'll get worse.* ● *Could you scratch my back for me?* ● *She sat and scratched her head as she thought about the problem.* **2** [I,T] to make a mark on a surface or a slight cut on a person's skin with sth sharp: *The cat will scratch if you annoy it.* ● *The table was badly scratched.* **3** [I] to make a sound by rubbing a surface with sth sharp: *The dog was scratching at the door to go outside.* **4** [T] to use sth sharp to make or remove a mark: *He scratched his name on the top of his desk.* ● *I tried to scratch the paint off the table.*

★**scratch²** /skrætʃ/ **noun 1** [C] a cut, mark or sound that was made by sb/sth sharp rubbing a surface: *There's a scratch on the car door.* ·➤ picture at **blob 2** [sing] an act of scratching part of the body because it is irritating you (**itching**): *The dog had a good scratch.*
IDIOMS **from scratch** from the very beginning: *I'm learning Spanish from scratch.*
(be/come) up to scratch (*informal*) to be/become good enough

scrawl /skrɔːl/ **verb** [I,T] to write sth quickly in an untidy and careless way: *He scrawled his name across the top of the paper.* –**scrawl noun** [sing]: *Her signature was just a scrawl.* ·➤ Look at **scribble**.

★**scream¹** /skriːm/ **verb** [I,T] **scream (sth) (out) (at sb)** to cry out loudly in a high voice because you are afraid, excited, angry, in pain, etc: *She saw a rat and screamed out.* ● *'Don't touch that,' he screamed.* ● *She screamed at the children to stop.* ● *He screamed with pain.* ● *He clung to the edge of the cliff, screaming for help.* ·➤ Look at **shout**.

scream² /skriːm/ **noun 1** [C] a loud cry in a high voice: *a scream of pain* **2** [sing] (*informal*) a person or thing that is very funny: *Sharon's a real scream.*

screech /skriːtʃ/ **verb** [I,T] to make an unpleasant loud, high sound: *'Get out of here,'*

she screeched at him. ·➤ Look at **shriek**.
–**screech noun** [sing]: *the screech of brakes*

★**screen¹** /skriːn/ **noun 1** [C] a flat vertical surface that is used for dividing a room or keeping sb/sth out of sight: *The nurse pulled the screen round the bed.* **2** [C] the glass surface of a television or computer where the picture or information appears ·➤ picture on page S7 **3** [C] the large flat surface on which films are shown **4** [sing] films and television: *Some actors look better in real life than on screen.*

screen² /skriːn/ **verb** [T] **1 screen sb/sth (off) (from sb/sth)** to hide or protect sb/sth from sb/sth else: *The bed was screened off while the doctor examined him.* ● *to screen your eyes from the sun* **2 screen sb (for sth)** to examine or test sb to find out if he/she has a particular disease or if he/she is suitable for a particular job: *All women over 50 should be screened for breast cancer.* ● *The Ministry of Defence screens all job applicants.* **3** to show sth on television or in a cinema

'**screen saver noun** [C] a computer program that replaces what is on the screen with a moving image if the computer is not used for certain amount of time

★**screw¹** /skruː/ **noun** [C] a thin pointed piece of metal used for fixing two things, for example pieces of wood, together. You turn a screw with a special tool (a **screwdriver**). ·➤ picture at **bolt** and **tool**

screw² /skruː/ **verb 1** [T] **screw sth (on, down, etc)** to fasten sth with a screw or screws: *The bookcase is screwed to the wall.* ● *The lid is screwed down so you can't remove it.* **2** [I,T] to fasten sth, or to be fastened, by turning: *The legs screw into holes in the underside of the seat.* ● *Make sure that you screw the top of the jar on tightly.* **3 screw sth (up) (into sth)** to squeeze sth, especially a piece of paper, into a tight ball: *He screwed the letter up into a ball and threw it away.*
PHRASAL VERBS **screw (sth) up** (*slang*) to make a mistake and cause sth to fail: *You'd better not screw up this deal.*
screw your eyes, face, etc up to change the expression on your face by nearly closing your eyes, in pain or because the light is strong

★**screwdriver** /'skruːdraɪvə/ **noun** [C] a tool that you use for turning screws ·➤ picture at **tool**

scribble /'skrɪbl/ **verb** [I,T] **1** to write sth quickly and carelessly: *to scribble a note down on a pad* ·➤ Look at **scrawl**. **2** to make marks with a pen or pencil that are not letters or pictures: *The children had scribbled all over the walls.* –**scribble noun** [C,U]

script /skrɪpt/ **noun 1** [C] the written form of a play, film, speech, etc: *Who wrote the script for the movie?* **2** [C,U] a system of writing: *Arabic/Cyrillic/Roman script*

scripture /'skrɪptʃə/ **noun** [U] (also **the scriptures** [pl]) the holy books of religion, such as the Bible

S

scroll¹ /skrəʊl/ **noun** [C] a long roll of paper with writing on it

scroll² /skrəʊl/ **verb** [I] scroll (up/down) to move text up and down or left and right on a computer screen

scrollbar /'skrəʊlbɑː/ **noun** [C] a tool on a computer screen that you use to move the text up and down or left and right ••➤ picture on page S7

scrounge /skraʊndʒ/ **verb** [I,T] (*informal*) scrounge (sth) (from/off sb) to get sth by asking another person to give it to you instead of making an effort to get it for yourself: *Lucy is always scrounging money off her friends.*

scrub¹ /skrʌb/ **verb** [I,T] (scrubbing; scrubbed) **1** scrub (sth) (down/out) to clean sth with soap and water by rubbing it hard, often with a brush: *to scrub (down) the floor/walls* **2** scrub (sth) (off/out); scrub (sth) (off sth/out of sth) to remove sth or be removed by scrubbing: *to scrub the dirt off the walls* • *I hope these coffee stains will scrub out.*

scrub² /skrʌb/ **noun 1** [sing] an act of cleaning sth by rubbing it hard, often with a brush: *This floor needs a good scrub.* **2** [U] small trees and bushes that grow in an area that has very little rain

scruff /skrʌf/ **noun**

[IDIOM] **by the scruff (of the/your neck)** by the back of the/your neck

scruffy /'skrʌfi/ **adj** dirty and untidy: *He always looks so scruffy.* • *scruffy jeans*

scrum /skrʌm/ **noun** [C] the part of a game of rugby when several players put their heads down in a circle and push against each other to try to get the ball

scruples /'skruːplz/ **noun** [pl] a feeling that stops you from doing sth that you think is morally wrong: *I've got no scruples about asking them for money* (= I don't think it's wrong).

scrupulous /'skruːpjələs/ **adj 1** very careful or paying great attention to detail: *a scrupulous investigation into the causes of the disaster* **2** careful to do what is right or honest ••➤ opposite **unscrupulous** –scrupulously **adv**: *scrupulously clean/honest/tidy*

scrutinize (also -ise) /'skruːtɪnaɪz/ **verb** [T] to look at or examine sth carefully: *The customs official scrutinized every page of my passport.* –scrutiny /'skruːtəni/ **noun** [U]: *The police kept all the suspects under close scrutiny.*

scuba-diving /'skuːbə daɪvɪŋ/ **noun** [U] swimming under water using special equipment for breathing: *to go scuba-diving* ••➤ picture at **dive**

scuff /skʌf/ **verb** [T] to make a mark on your shoes or with your shoes, for example by kicking sth or by rubbing your feet along the ground

scuffle /'skʌfl/ **noun** [C] a short, not very violent fight

sculptor /'skʌlptə/ **noun** [C] a person who

makes figures or objects (sculptures) from stone, wood, etc

sculpture /'skʌlptʃə/ **noun 1** [U] the art of making figures or objects from stone, wood, clay, etc **2** [C,U] a work or works of art that were made in this way

scum /skʌm/ **noun** [U] **1** a dirty or unpleasant substance on the surface of a liquid **2** (*slang*) an insulting word for people that you have no respect for: *Drug dealers are scum.*

scurry /'skʌri/ **verb** [I] (*pres part* scurrying; *3rd pers sing pres* scurries; *pt, pp* scurried) to run quickly with short steps; to hurry

scuttle /'skʌtl/ **verb** [I] to run quickly with short steps or with the body close to the ground: *The spider scuttled away when I tried to catch it.*

scythe /saɪð/ **noun** [C] a tool with a long handle and a long, curved piece of metal with a very sharp edge (a blade). You use a scythe to cut long grass, corn etc.

SE **abbr** south-east(ern): *SE Asia*

★**sea** /siː/ **noun 1** (often **the sea**) [U] the salt water that covers large parts of the surface of the earth: *The sea is quite calm/rough today.* • *Do you live by the sea?* • *to travel by sea* • *There were several people swimming in the sea.* ••➤ picture on page C8 **2** (often **Sea**) [C] a particular large area of salt water. A sea may be part of the ocean or may be surrounded by land: *the Mediterranean Sea* • *the Black Sea* ••➤ Look at **ocean. 3** [sing] (also **seas** [pl]) the state or movement of the waves of the sea: *The boat sank in heavy* (= rough) *seas off the Scottish coast.* **4** [sing] a large amount of sb/sth close together

[IDIOM] **at sea 1** sailing in a ship: *They spent about three weeks at sea.* **2** not understanding or not knowing what to do

the 'seabed noun [sing] the floor of the sea

seafood /'siːfuːd/ **noun** [U] fish and shellfish from the sea that we eat

the 'sea front [sing] the part of a town facing the sea: *The hotel is right on the sea front.* • *to walk along the sea front* ••➤ picture on page C8

seagull /'siːgʌl/ = **GULL**

tusk

walrus

seal   flipper

seal¹ /siːl/ **noun** [C] **1** a grey animal with short fur that lives in and near the sea and that eats fish. Seals have no legs and swim with the help of short flat arms (flippers). **2** an official design or mark that is put on a document, an envelope, etc to show that it is genuine or that it has not been opened **3** a small piece of paper, metal, plastic, etc on a packet, bottle, etc that you must break before you can open it **4** something that stops air or liquid from getting in or out of something: *The seal has worn and oil is escaping.*

seal² /siːl/ **verb** [T] **1** seal sth (up/down) to close or fasten a package, envelope, etc: *The parcel was sealed with tape.* • *to seal (down) an envelope* **2** seal sth (up) to fill a hole or cover sth so that air or liquid does not get in or out: *The food is packed in sealed bags to keep it fresh.* **3** (*formal*) to make sth sure, so that it cannot be changed or argued about: *to seal an agreement*

PHRASAL VERB **seal sth off** to stop any person or thing from entering or leaving an area or building: *The building was sealed off by the police.*

'sea level noun [U] the average level of the sea, used for measuring the height of places on land: *The town is 500 metres above sea level.*

'sea lion noun [C] a type of large animal that lives in the sea and on land and uses two flat arms (flippers) to move through the water

seam /siːm/ **noun** [C] **1** the line where two pieces of cloth are sewn together ••➤ picture on page C6 **2** a layer of coal under the ground

seaman /'siːmən/ **noun** [C] (*pl* -men /-mən/) a sailor

seance (also **séance**) /'seɪɑːns/ **noun** [C] a meeting at which people try to talk to the spirits of dead people

★**search** /sɜːtʃ/ **verb** [I,T] search (sb/sth) (for sb/sth); search (through sth) (for sth) to examine sth/sth carefully because you are looking for something; to look for sth that is missing: *The men were arrested and searched for drugs.* • *Were your bags searched at the airport?* • *They are still searching for the missing child.* • *She searched through the papers on the desk, looking for the letter.* –search **noun** [C,U]: *the search for the missing boy* • *She walked round for hours in search of her missing dog.*

searcher /'sɜːtʃə/ **noun** [C] **1** a person who is looking for sb/sth **2** a program that allows you to look for particular information on a computer

searching /'sɜːtʃɪŋ/ **adj** (used about a look, question, etc) trying to find out the truth: *The customs officers asked a lot of searching questions about our trip.*

'search party noun [C] a group of people who look for sb who is lost or missing

'search warrant noun [C] an official piece of paper that gives the police the right to search a building, etc

seashell /'siːʃel/ **noun** [C] the empty shell of a small animal that lives in the sea

seashore /'siːʃɔː/ (usually **the seashore**) **noun** [U] the part of the land that is next to the sea: *We were looking for shells on the seashore.*

seasick /'siːsɪk/ **adj** feeling sick or vomiting because of the movement of a boat or ship: *to feel/get/be seasick* ••➤ Look at **airsick, carsick** and **travel-sick.**

seaside /'siːsaɪd/ (often **the seaside**) **noun** [sing] an area on the coast, especially one where people go on holiday: *to go to the seaside* • *a seaside town*

★**season¹** /'siːzn/ **noun** [C] **1** one of the periods of different weather into which the year is divided: *In cool countries, the four seasons are spring, summer, autumn and winter.* • *the dry/rainy season* **2** the period of the year when sth is common or popular or when sth usually happens or is done: *the holiday/football season*

IDIOMS **in season 1** (used about fresh foods) available in large quantities **2** (used about a female animal) ready to have sex
out of season 1 (used about fresh foods) not available in large quantities **2** (used about a place where people go on holiday) at the time of year when it is least popular with tourists

season² /'siːzn/ **verb** [T] to add salt, pepper, spices, etc to food in order to make it taste better –seasoning **noun** [C,U]: *Add seasoning to the soup and serve with bread.*

seasonal /'siːzənl/ **adj** happening or existing at a particular time of the year: *There are a lot of seasonal jobs in the summer.*

seasoned /'siːznd/ **adj** having a lot of experience of sth: *a seasoned traveller*

'season ticket noun [C] a ticket that allows you to make a particular journey by bus, train, etc or to go to a theatre or watch a sports team as often as you like for a fixed period of time

★**seat¹** /siːt/ **noun** [C] **1** something that you sit on: *Please take a seat* (= sit down). • *the back/driving/passenger seat of a car* ••➤ picture at **motorbike** and on page S9 **2** the part of a chair, etc that you sit on **3** a place in a theatre, on a plane, etc where you pay to sit: *There are no seats left on that flight.* **4** a place on a council or in a parliament that you win in an election: *to win/lose a seat*

IDIOMS **be in the driving seat** to be the person, group, etc that has the most powerful position in a particular situation
take a back seat → **BACK²**

seat² /siːt/ **verb** [T] **1** (often passive) (*formal*) to sit down: *Please be seated.* **2** to have seats or chairs for a particular number of people

'seat belt (also **'safety belt**) **noun** [C] a strap that is fixed to the seat in a car or plane and that you wear around your body so that you are not thrown forward if there is an accident: *to fasten/unfasten your seat belt* ••➤ Look at **belt.** ••➤ picture on page S9

seating /'siːtɪŋ/ **noun** [U] the seats or chairs in a place or the way that they are arranged: *The conference hall has seating for 500 people.*

seaweed /'siːwiːd/ **noun** [U] a plant that grows in the sea. There are many different types of seaweed.

sec /sek/ **noun** [C] (*informal*) = **SECOND²**(2)

secluded /sɪ'kluːdɪd/ **adj** far away from other people, roads, etc; very quiet: *a secluded beach/garden* –seclusion /sɪ'kluːʒn/ **noun** [U]

★**second¹** /'sekənd/ **pron, determiner, adv, noun** 2nd: *We are going on holiday in the second*

S

week in July. ● *Birmingham is the second largest city in Britain after London.* ● *She poured herself a second cup of coffee.* ● *Our team finished second.* ● *I came second in the competition.* ● *Queen Elizabeth the Second* ● *the second of January* ● *January the second*

IDIOMS **second nature (to sb)** something that has become a habit or that you can do easily because you have done it so many times: *With practice, typing becomes second nature.*

second thoughts a change of mind or opinion about sth; doubts that you have when you are not sure if you have made the right decision: *On second thoughts, let's go today, not tomorrow.* ● *I'm starting to have second thoughts about accepting her offer.*

★**second²** /'sekənd/ noun **1** [C] one of the 60 parts into which a minute is divided **2** (also *informal* **sec**) [C] a short time: *Wait a second, please.* **3** [U] the second of the four or five speeds (**gears**) that a car can move forward in: *Once the car's moving, put it in second.* **4** [C, usually pl] something that has a small fault and that is sold at a lower price: *The clothes are all seconds.* **5** [C] (*formal*) a second (in sth) the second-best result in a British university degree: *to get an upper/ lower second in physics*

second³ /'sekənd/ verb [T] to support sb's suggestion or idea at a meeting so that it can then be discussed and voted on

★**secondary** /'sekəndri/ adj **1** less important than sth else: *Other people's opinions are secondary – it's my opinion that counts.* **2** caused by or developing from sth else

secondary school noun [C] (*Brit*) a school for children aged from eleven to eighteen

second-'best¹ adj not quite the best but the next one after the best: *the second-best time in the 100 metres race* ·➤ Look at **best**.

second-'best² noun [U] something that is not as good as the best, or not as good as you would like: *I'm not prepared to accept second-best.*

second 'class¹ noun [U] **1** (also **'standard class**) ordinary accommodation in a train, boat, plane, etc **2** the way of sending letters, etc that is cheaper but that takes longer than first class – **second-'class** adv: *to travel second-class* ● *to send a letter second-class*

second-'class² adj **1** (also **'standard class**) used about ordinary accommodation in a train, plane, etc: *a second-class ticket* ● *a second-class compartment* **2** (used about a university degree) of the level that is next after first-class: *a second-class honours degree in geography* **3** of little importance: *Old people should not be treated as second-class citizens.*

second 'cousin noun [C] the child of your mother's or father's cousin

second 'floor noun [C] the floor in a building that is two floors above the lowest floor: *I live on the second floor.* ● *a second-floor flat*

➤ In US English the second floor is next above the lowest.

the 'second hand noun [C] the hand on some clocks and watches that shows seconds

second-'hand adj, adv **1** already used or owned by sb else: *a second-hand car* ● *I bought this camera second-hand.* ·➤ Look at **old**. **2** (used about news or information) that you heard from sb else, and did not see or experience yourself ·➤ Look at **hand**.

second 'language noun [C] a language that is not your native language but which you learn because it is used, often for official purposes, in your country: *French is the second language of several countries in Africa.*

secondly /'sekəndli/ adv (used when you are giving your second reason or opinion) also: *Firstly, I think it's too expensive and secondly, we don't really need it.*

second-'rate adj of poor quality: *a second-rate poet*

secrecy /'si:krəsi/ noun [U] being secret or keeping sth secret: *I must stress the importance of secrecy in this matter.*

★**secret¹** /'si:krət/ noun **1** [C] something that is not or must not be known by other people: *to keep a secret* ● *to let sb in on/tell sb a secret* ● *I can't tell you where we're going – it's a secret.* ● *It's no secret that they don't like each other* (= everybody knows). **2** [sing] the secret (of/to sth/doing sth) the only way or the best way of doing or achieving sth: *What is the secret of your success* (= how did you become so successful)*?*

IDIOM **in secret** without other people knowing: *to meet in secret*

★**secret²** /'si:krət/ adj **1** secret (from sb) that is not or must not be known by other people: *We have to keep the party secret from Carmen.* ● *a secret address* ● *a secret love affair* **2** used to describe actions that you do not tell anyone about: *a secret drinker* ● *She's got a secret admirer.* –**secretly** adv: *The government secretly agreed to pay the kidnappers.*

secret 'agent (also **agent**) noun [C] a person who tries to find out secret information especially about the government of another country ·➤ Look at **spy**.

secretarial /ˌsekrə'teəriəl/ adj involving or connected with the work that a secretary does: *secretarial skills/work*

★**secretary** /'sekrətri/ noun [C] (*pl* **secretaries**) **1** a person who works in an office. A secretary types letters, answers the telephone, keeps records, etc: *the director's personal secretary* **2** an official of a club or society who is responsible for keeping records, writing letters, etc **3** (*US*) the head of a government department, chosen by the President **4** (*Brit*) = **SECRETARY OF STATE**(1)

Secretary of 'State noun [C] **1** (also **Secretary**) (in Britain) the head of one of the main government departments: *the Secretary of State for Defence* **2** (in the US) the head of the government department that deals with foreign affairs

secrete /sɪ'kri:t/ verb [T] **1** (used about a part of a plant, animal or person) to produce a liquid **2** (*formal*) to hide sth in a secret place

secretion /sɪˈkriːʃn/ **noun** (*formal*) [C,U] a liquid that is produced by a plant or an animal; the process by which the liquid is produced: *The frog covers itself in a poisonous secretion for protection.*

secretive /ˈsiːkrətɪv/ **adj** liking to keep things secret from other people: *Wendy is very secretive about her private life.* –secretively **adv** –secretiveness **noun** [U]

the ˌsecret ˈservice noun [sing] the government department that tries to find out secret information about other countries and governments

sect /sekt/ **noun** [C] a group of people who have a particular set of religious or political beliefs. A sect has often broken away from a larger group.

★**section** /ˈsekʃn/ **noun** [C] **1** one of the parts into which something is divided: *the string section of an orchestra* ● *the financial section of a newspaper* ● *The library has an excellent reference section.* **2** a view or drawing of sth as if it was cut from the top to the bottom so that you can see the inside: *The illustration shows a section through a leaf.*

sector /ˈsektə/ **noun** [C] **1** a part of the business activity of a country: *The manufacturing sector has declined in recent years.* ● *the public/private sector* **2** a part of an area or of a large group of people: *the Christian sector of the city*

secular /ˈsekjələ/ **adj** not concerned with religion or the church

secure¹ /sɪˈkjʊə/ **adj 1** free from worry or doubt; confident: *Children need to feel secure.* ● *to be financially secure* ➙ opposite **insecure 2** not likely to be lost; safe: *Business is good so his job is secure.* ● *a secure investment* **3** not likely to fall or be broken; firmly fixed: *That ladder doesn't look very secure.* **4** secure (against/from sth) well locked or protected: *Make sure the house is secure before you go to bed.* –securely **adv**: *All doors and windows must be securely fastened.*

secure² /sɪˈkjʊə/ **verb** [T] **1** secure sth (to sth) to fix or lock sth firmly: *The load was secured with ropes.* ● *Secure the rope to a tree or a rock.* **2** secure sth (against/from sth) to make sth safe: *The sea wall needs strengthening to secure the town against flooding.* **3** to obtain or achieve sth, especially by having to make a big effort: *The company has secured a contract to build ten planes.*

★**security** /sɪˈkjʊərəti/ **noun** (*pl* **securities**) **1** [U] the state of feeling safe and being free from worry; protection against the difficulties of life: *Children need the security of a stable home environment.* ● *financial/job security* ➙ opposite **insecurity 2** [U] things that you do to protect sb/sth from attack, danger, thieves, etc: *Security was tightened at the airport before the president arrived.* ● *The robbers were caught on the bank's security cameras.* **3** [U] the section of a large company or organization that deals with the pro-

tection of buildings, equipment and staff: *If you see a suspicious bag, contact airport security immediately.* **4** [C,U] something of value that you use when you borrow money. If you cannot pay the money back then you lose the thing you gave as security

sedan /sɪˈdæn/ **noun** [C] (*US*) = **SALOON**

sedate¹ /sɪˈdeɪt/ **adj** quiet, calm and well-behaved

sedate² /sɪˈdeɪt/ **verb** [T] to give sb a drug or medicine to make him/her feel calm or want to sleep: *The lion was sedated and treated by a vet.* –sedation /sɪˈdeɪʃn/ **noun** [U]: *The doctor put her under sedation.*

sedative /ˈsedətɪv/ **noun** [C] a drug or medicine that makes you feel calm or want to sleep ➙ Look at **tranquillizer**.

sedentary /ˈsedntri/ **adj** involving a lot of sitting down; not active: *a sedentary lifestyle/job*

sediment /ˈsedɪmənt/ **noun** [C,U] a thick substance that forms at the bottom of a liquid

seduce /sɪˈdjuːs/ **verb** [T] **1** seduce sb (into sth/doing sth) to persuade sb to do sth he/she would not usually agree to do: *Special offers seduce customers into spending their money.* **2** to persuade sb to have sex with you –seduction /sɪˈdʌkʃn/ **noun** [C,U]

seductive /sɪˈdʌktɪv/ **adj 1** sexually attractive: *a seductive smile* **2** attractive in a way that makes you want to have or do sth: *a seductive argument/opinion* (= one which you are tempted to agree with)

★**see** /siː/ **verb** (*pt* **saw** /sɔː/; *pp* **seen** /siːn/) **1** [I,T] to become conscious of sth, using your eyes; to use the power of sight: *It was so dark that we couldn't see.* ● *On a clear day you can see for miles.* ● *Have you seen my wallet anywhere?* ● *I've just seen a mouse run under the cooker.* ● *He looked for her but couldn't see her in the crowd.* ➙ Look at the note at **look**¹. **2** [T] to look at or watch a film, play, television programme, etc: *Did you see that programme on sharks last night?* ● *Have you seen Spielberg's latest film?* **3** [T] to find out sth by looking, asking or waiting: *Go and see if the postman has been yet.* ● *We'll wait and see what happens before making any decisions.* ● *'Can we go swimming today, Dad?' 'I'll see.'* ● *I saw in the paper that they're building a new theatre.* **4** [T] to spend time with sb; to visit sb: *I saw Alan at the weekend; we had dinner together.* ● *You should see a doctor about that cough.* **5** [I,T] to understand sth; to realize sth: *Do you see what I mean?* ● *She doesn't see the point in spending so much money on a car.* ● *'You have to key in your password first.' 'Oh, I see.'* **6** [T] to have an opinion about sth: *How do you see the situation developing?* **7** [T] to imagine sth as a future possibility: *I can't see her changing her mind.* **8** [T] to do what is necessary in a situation; to make sure that sb does sth: *I'll see that he gets the letter.* **9** [T] to go out with sb, for example to help or protect him/her: *He asked me if he could see me home, but I said no.* ● *I'll see you to the door.* **10** [T] to be the

S

time when an event happens: *Last year saw huge changes in the education system.*
IDIOMS as far as I can see → FAR²
as far as the eye can see → FAR²
let me see; let's see → LET
see eye to eye (with sb) to agree with sb; to have the same opinion as sb: *We don't always see eye to eye on political matters.*
see if... to try to do sth: *I'll see if I can find time to do it.* ● *See if you can undo this knot.*
see you around (*informal*) used for saying goodbye to sb you have made no arrangement to see again
see you (later) used for saying goodbye to sb you expect to see soon or later that day
you see used for giving a reason: *She's very unhappy. He was her first real boyfriend, you see.*
PHRASAL VERBS see about sth/doing sth to deal with sth: *I've got to go to the bank to see about my traveller's cheques.*
see sb off to go with sb to the railway station, the airport, etc in order to say goodbye to him/her
see through sb/sth to be able to see that sb/sth is not what he/she/it appears: *The police immediately saw through his story.*
see to sb/sth to do what is necessary in a situation; to deal with sb/sth: *I'll see to the travel arrangements and you book the hotel.*
★**seed** /siːd/ **noun 1** [C,U] the small hard part of a plant from which a new plant of the same kind can grow: *a packet of sunflower seeds* ●▸ picture on pages C2 and C3 **2** [C] the start of a feeling or event that continues to grow **3** [C] a player in a sports competition, especially tennis, who is expected to finish in a high position
seeded /ˈsiːdɪd/ **adj** (used about a player or a team in a sports competition) expected to finish in a high position
seedless /ˈsiːdləs/ **adj** having no seeds: *seedless grapes*
seedling /ˈsiːdlɪŋ/ **noun** [C] a very young plant or tree that has grown from a seed
seedy /ˈsiːdi/ **adj** dirty and unpleasant; possibly connected with illegal or immoral activities: *a seedy hotel/neighbourhood*
seeing /ˈsiːɪŋ/ (also **seeing that; seeing as**) **conj** (*informal*) because; as: *Seeing as we're going the same way, I'll give you a lift.*
seek /siːk/ **verb** [T] (*pt, pp* **sought** /sɔːt/) (*formal*) **1** to try to find or get sth: *Politicians are still seeking a peaceful solution.* **2** seek sth (from sb) to ask sb for sth: *You should seek advice from a solicitor about what to do next.* **3** seek (to do sth) to try to do sth: *They are still seeking to find a peaceful solution to the conflict.* **4** -seeking (used to form compound adjectives) looking for or trying to get the thing mentioned: *attention-seeking behaviour* ● *a heat-seeking missile*
★**seem** /siːm/ **verb** [I] seem (to sb) (to be) sth; seem (like) sth (not in the continuous tenses) to give the impression of being or doing sth; to appear: *Emma seems (like) a very nice girl.* ● *Emma seems to be a very nice girl.*

● *It seems to me that we have no choice.* ● *You seem happy today.* ● *This machine doesn't seem to work.*
seeming /ˈsiːmɪŋ/ **adj** (only *before* a noun) appearing to be sth: *Despite her seeming enthusiasm, Sandra didn't really help much.* –**seemingly** **adv**: *a seemingly endless list of complaints*
seen *past participle* of **SEE**
seep /siːp/ **verb** [I] (used about a liquid) to flow very slowly through sth: *Water started seeping in through small cracks.*
ˈ**see-saw** **noun** [C] an outdoor toy for children that consists of a long piece of wood that is balanced in the middle. One child sits on each end of the see-saw and one goes up while the other is down.
seethe /siːð/ **verb** [I] **1** to be very angry: *I was absolutely seething.* **2** seethe (with sth) to be very crowded: *The streets were seething with people.*
segment /ˈsegmənt/ **noun** [C] **1** a section or part of sth: *I've divided the sheet of paper into three segments.* ● *a segment of the population* **2** one of the parts into which an orange can be divided ●▸ picture on page C3
segregate /ˈsegrɪgeɪt/ **verb** [T] segregate sb/sth (from sb/sth) to separate one group of people or things from the rest: *The two groups of football fans were segregated to avoid trouble.* ●▸ Look at **integrate**. –**segregation** /ˌsegrɪˈgeɪʃn/ **noun** [U]: *racial segregation* (= separating people of different races)
seize /siːz/ **verb** [T] **1** to take hold of sth suddenly and firmly; to grab sth: *The thief seized her handbag and ran off with it.* ● (*figurative*) *to seize a chance/an opportunity* **2** to take control or possession of sb/sth: *The police seized 50 kilos of illegal drugs.* **3** (usually passive) (used about an emotion) to affect sb suddenly and very strongly: *I felt myself seized by panic.*
PHRASAL VERBS seize (on/upon) sth to make use of a good and unexpected chance: *He seized on a mistake by the goalkeeper and scored.*
seize up (used about a machine) to stop working because it is too hot, does not have enough oil, etc
seizure /ˈsiːʒə/ **noun 1** [U] using force or legal authority to take control or possession of sth: *the seizure of 30 kilos of heroin by police* **2** [C] a sudden strong attack of an illness, especially one affecting the brain
seldom /ˈseldəm/ **adv** not often; rarely: *There is seldom snow in Athens.* ● *I very seldom go to the theatre.*
select¹ /sɪˈlekt/ **verb** [T] to choose sb/sth from a number of similar things: *The best candidates will be selected for interview.* ●▸ **Select** is more formal than **choose** and suggests that a lot of care is taken when making the decision.
select² /sɪˈlekt/ **adj** (*formal*) **1** carefully chosen as the best of a group: *A university*

*education is no longer the privilege of **a select few**.* **2** used or owned by rich people

selection /sɪ'lekʃn/ **noun 1** [U] choosing or being chosen: *The manager is responsible for team selection.* **2** [C] a number of people or things that have been chosen: *a selection of hits from the fifties and sixties* **3** [C] a number of things from which you can chose: *This shop has a very good selection of toys.*

selective /sɪ'lektɪv/ **adj 1** careful when choosing: *She's very selective about who she invites to her parties.* **2** concerning only some people or things; not general: *selective schools/education* –**selectively adv**

self /self/ **noun** [C] (*pl* **selves** /selvz/) a person's own nature or qualities: *It's good to see you back to **your old self** again* (= feeling well or happy again). ● *Her spiteful remark revealed her **true self** (= what she was really like).*

self-addressed 'envelope = STAMPED ADDRESSED ENVELOPE

self-as'sured adj = ASSURED –**self-as'surance noun** = ASSURANCE(2)

self-'catering adj (*Brit*) (used about a holiday or a place to stay) where meals are not provided for you so you cook them yourself

self-'centred (*US* **self-centered**) **adj** thinking only about yourself and not about other people ●► Look at **selfish**.

self-con'fessed adj admitting that you are sth or do sth that most people consider to be bad

self-'confident adj feeling sure about your own value and abilities ●► Look at **confident**. –**self-'confidence noun** [U]: *Many women lack the self-confidence to apply for senior jobs.*

self-'conscious adj too worried about what other people think about you –**self-consciously adv** –**self-consciousness noun** [U]

self-con'tained adj (*Brit*) (used about a flat, etc) having its own private entrance, kitchen and bathroom: *a self-contained apartment*

self-con'trol noun [U] the ability to control your emotions and appear calm even when you are angry, afraid, excited, etc: *to lose/keep your self-control*

self-de'fence (*US* **self de'fense**) **noun** [U] the use of force to protect yourself or your property: *Lee is learning karate for self-defence.* ● *to shoot sb **in self-defence** (= because they are going to attack you)*

self-des'truct verb [I] to destroy him/her/itself –**self-destructive adj** –**self-destruction noun** [U]

self-'discipline noun [U] the ability to make yourself do sth difficult or unpleasant: *It takes a lot of self-discipline to give up smoking.*

self-em'ployed adj working for yourself and earning money from your own business

self-es'teem noun [U] a good opinion of your own character and abilities: *a man with high/low self-esteem*

self-'evident adj that does not need any proof or explanation; clear

self-ex'planatory adj clear and easy to understand; not needing to be explained: *The book's title is self-explanatory.*

self-in'dulgent adj allowing yourself to have or do things you enjoy (sometimes when it would be better to stop yourself) –**self-indulgence noun** [C,U]

self-'interest noun [U] thinking about what is best for yourself rather than for other people

★**selfish** /'selfɪʃ/ **adj** thinking only about your own needs or wishes and not about other people's: *a selfish attitude* ● *I'm sick of your selfish behaviour!* ●► opposite **unselfish** or **selfless** ●► Look at **self-centred**. –**selfishly adv** –**selfishness noun** [U]

selfless /'selfləs/ **adj** thinking more about other people's needs or wishes than your own

self-'made adj having become rich or successful by your own efforts: *a self-made millionaire*

self-'pity /ˌself 'pɪti/ **noun** [U] the state of thinking too much about your own problems or troubles and feeling sorry for yourself

self-'portrait noun [C] a picture that you draw or paint of yourself

self-'raising flour (*US* **self-rising flour**) **noun** [U] flour that contains a substance that makes cakes, etc rise during cooking ●► Look at **plain flour**.

self-re'liant adj not depending on help from anyone else ●► Look at **reliant**.

self-re'spect noun [U] a feeling of confidence and pride in yourself: *Old people need to keep their dignity and self-respect.* ●► Look at **respect**. –**self-respecting adj** (often in negative sentences): *No self-respecting language student (= nobody who is serious about learning a language) should be without this book.*

self-'righteous adj believing that you are always right and other people are wrong, so that you are better than other people ●► Look at **righteous**. –**self-righteously adv** –**self-righteousness noun** [U]

self-'sacrifice noun [U] giving up what you need or want, in order to help others

self-'service adj (used about a shop, petrol station, restaurant, etc) where you serve yourself and then pay at a special desk (**a cash desk**)

self-suf'ficient adj able to produce or provide everything that you need without help from or having to buy from others

★**sell** /sel/ **verb** (*pt, pp* **sold** /səʊld/) **1** [I,T] sell (sb) (sth) (at/for sth); sell (sth) (to sb) (at/for sth) to give sth to sb who pays for it and is then the owner of it: *We are going to sell our car.* ● *I sold my guitar to my neighbour for £200.* ● *Would you sell me your ticket?* ● *I offered them a lot of money but they wouldn't sell.* **2** [T] to offer sth for people to buy: *Excuse me, do you sell stamps?* ● *to sell insurance/advertising space* **3** [I,T] to be bought by

S

people in the way or in the numbers mentioned; to be offered at the price mentioned: *These watches sell at £1000 each in the shops but you can have this one for £500.* ● *Her books sell well abroad.* ● *This newspaper sells over a million copies a day.* **4** [T] to make people want to buy sth: *They rely on advertising to sell their products.* ●► noun for senses 1 to 4 is **sale 5** [T] **sell sth/yourself to sb** to persuade sb to accept sth; to persuade sb that you are the right person for a job, position, etc: *Now we have to try and sell the idea to the management.*

IDIOM **be sold on sth** (*informal*) to be very enthusiastic about sth

PHRASAL VERBS **sell sth off** to sell sth in order to get rid of it, often at a low price: *The shops sell their remaining winter clothes off in the spring sales.*

sell out; be sold out (used about tickets for a concert, football game, etc) to be all sold: *All the tickets sold out within two hours* ● *The concert was sold out weeks ago.*

sell out (of sth); be sold out (of sth) to sell all of sth so that no more is/are available to be bought: *I'm afraid we've sold out of bread.*

sell up to sell everything you own, especially your house, your business, etc (in order to start a new life, move to another country, etc)

'sell-by date noun [C] (*Brit*) the date printed on food containers, packets, etc after which the food should not be sold: *This milk is past its sell-by date.*

seller /'selə/ noun [C] **1** (often in compounds) a person or business that sells: *a bookseller* ● *a flower seller* **2** something that is sold, especially in the amount or way mentioned: *This magazine is a big seller in the 25-40 age group.* ●► Look at **best seller**.

Sellotape™ /'seləteɪp/ noun [U] (*Brit*) a type of clear tape that is sold in rolls and used for sticking things ●► Look at **tape**. –**sellotape** verb [T]

selves plural of **SELF**

semblance /'semblans/ noun [sing, U] (*formal*) (a) **semblance of sth** the appearance of being sth or of having a certain quality

semen /'si:men/ noun [U] the liquid that is produced by the male sex organs containing the seed (**sperm**) necessary for producing babies or young

semi /'semi/ noun [C] (*pl* **semis** /'semiz/) (*Brit informal*) a house that is joined to another one with a shared wall between them, forming a pair of houses

semicircle /'semis3:kl/ noun [C] one half of a circle; something that is arranged in this shape: *I want you all to sit in a semicircle.* ●► picture at **circle**

semicolon /,semi'kəʊlən/ noun [C] a mark (;) used in writing for separating parts of a sentence or items in a list

,semi-de'tached adj (used about a house) joined to another house with a shared wall on one side forming a pair of houses

semi-final /,semi'faɪnl/ noun [C] one of the two games in a sports competition which decide which players or teams will play each other in the final ●► Look at **quarter-final** and **final**. –**semi-finalist** /-'faɪnəlɪst/ noun [C]

seminar /'semɪnɑ:/ noun [C] **1** a class at a university, college, etc in which a small group of students discuss or study a subject with a teacher: *I've got a seminar on Goethe this morning.* **2** a meeting for business people in which working methods, etc are taught or discussed: *a one-day management seminar*

Sen abbr (in US politics) Senator

senate /'senət/ (often **the Senate**) noun [C, with sing or pl verb] one of the two groups of elected politicians who make laws in the government in some countries, for example the US ●► Look at **Congress** and **House of Representatives**.

senator /'senətə/ (often **Senator**) noun [C] (*abbr* **Sen**) a member of a group of elected politicians (**the Senate**) who make laws in the government in some countries, for example the US: *Senator McCarthy*

★**send** /send/ verb [T] (*pt, pp* **sent** /sent/) **1** **send sth (to sb/sth)**; **send (sb) sth** to make sth go or be taken somewhere, especially by mail, radio, etc: *to send a letter/parcel/message/fax to sb* ● *Don't forget to send me a postcard.* **2** to tell sb to go somewhere or to do sth; to arrange for sb to go somewhere: *My company is sending me on a training course next month.* ● *She sent the children to bed early.* ● *to send sb to prison* ● *I'll send someone round to collect you at 10.00.* **3** to cause sb/sth to move in a particular direction, often quickly or as a reaction that cannot be prevented: *I accidentally pushed the table and sent all the drinks flying.* **4** **send sb (to/into sth)** to make sb/sth have a particular feeling or enter a particular state: *The movement of the train sent me to sleep.*

IDIOM **give/send sb your love** → **LOVE**[1]

PHRASAL VERBS **send for sb/sth** to ask for sb to come to you; to ask for sth to be brought or sent to you: *Quick! Send for an ambulance!*

send sth in to send sth to a place where it will be officially dealt with: *I sent my application in three weeks ago but I still haven't had a reply.*

send off (for sth); send away (to sb) (for sth) to write to sb and ask for sth to be sent to you: *Let's send off for some holiday brochures.*

send sb off (used in a sports match) to order a player who has broken a rule to leave the field and not to return: *Beckham was sent off for a foul in the first half.*

send sth off to post sth: *I'll send the information off today.*

send sth out 1 to send sth to a lot of different people or places: *We sent out the invitations two months before the wedding.* **2** to produce sth, for example light, heat, sound, etc

send sb/sth up (*Brit informal*) to make sb/sth look ridiculous or silly especially by copying him/her/it in a way that is intended to be amusing

---

[C] **countable**, a noun with a plural form: *one book, two books*   [U] **uncountable**, a noun with no plural form: *some sugar*

The Human Body

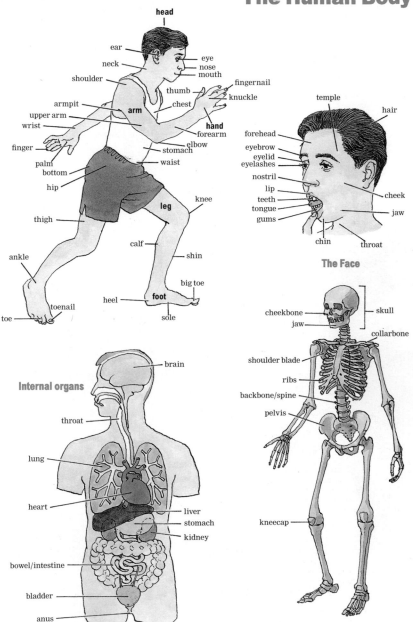

head

ear
neck
shoulder
armpit
upper arm
arm
wrist
finger
palm
bottom
hip
thigh
ankle
toenail
toe

eye
nose
mouth
thumb
fingernail
knuckle
chest
hand
forearm
elbow
stomach
waist
knee
leg
calf
shin
big toe
heel
foot
sole

temple
hair
forehead
eyebrow
eyelid
eyelashes
nostril
lip
teeth
tongue
gums
chin
cheek
jaw
throat

The Face

Internal organs

brain
throat
lung
heart
liver
stomach
kidney
bowel/intestine
bladder
anus

cheekbone
jaw
collarbone
skull
shoulder blade
ribs
backbone/spine
pelvis
kneecap

The Skeleton

Clothes

turban
jacket
tie
suit
trousers (*US* pants)

sari

bow tie
shirt
waistcoat (*US* vest)
trousers (*US* pants)

T-shirt
dungarees *US* overalls)

scarf
dress

jacket
cagoule
scarf
blazer
pocket
coat

top
collar
blouse
sleeve
button
zip (*US* zipper)
cuff

anorak (*Brit*)
hood

cardigan

leggings
polo neck
V-neck
sweater (*Brit also* jumper)

mittens
gloves
hem
seam
skirt

flies
waistband
shorts
sweatshirt

belt
swimsuit/ swimming costume

swimming trunks

tights (*US* pantyhose)
stockings
socks
bikini

The House

Postcards

Seaside

Dear Penny

Having a great time at the seaside. Yesterday we went to the beach. I paddled but the kids were brave enough to swim (the sea was freezing!). Had an ice cream on the pier then walked along the promenade. The harbour's very pretty – might go for a boat trip tomorrow.

See you soon,
love Kate & family

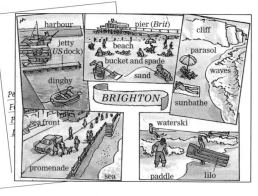

harbour | pier (*Brit*) | cliff
jetty (*US* dock) | beach | parasol
dinghy | bucket and spade | sand | waves
BRIGHTON | sunbathe
sea front | waterski
promenade | sea | paddle | lilo

Mountains

Hi Linda

Been hiking up Bear Mountain. From the top you could see for miles. The lake looked tiny from up there. Had lunch in a log cabin then caught the cable car back down – couldn't walk another step. I'd love to go skiing here in the winter. Bet you wish you were here!

Barry

Lind
27 L
Putn
Lond
UK

Welcome to Bear Mountain

peak
mountain
cabin | valley
cable car | cable
hiker | waterfall
backpack/rucksack
lake
footpath/track/trail

City

Dear All

I'm exhausted. Spent this morning in the Natural History Museum then went shopping. Found a great market with loads of interesting stalls. Right now I'm sitting at a cafe in the main square watching the world go by. Don't want to come home!

best wishes
Rachel

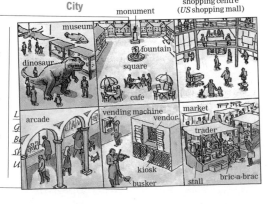

shopping centre (*US* shopping mall)
monument
museum
fountain
dinosaur
square
cafe
arcade | vending machine | vendor | market
trader
kiosk
busker | stall | bric-a-brac

senile /'si:naɪl/ *adj* behaving in a confused and strange way, and unable to remember things because of old age: *I think she's going senile.* –**senility** /sə'nɪləti/ *noun* [U]

senior[1] /'si:niə/ *adj* **1** senior (to sb) having a high or higher position in a company, organization, etc: *a senior lecturer/officer/manager* • *He's senior to me.* **2** (often **Senior**) (*abbr* **Snr; Sr**) (*especially US*) used after the name of a man who has the same name as his son, to avoid confusion **3** (*Brit*) (used in schools) older **4** (*US*) connected with the final year at high school or college ••➤ Look at **junior**[1].

senior[2] /'si:niə/ *noun* [C] **1** somebody who is older or of a higher position (than one or more other people): *My oldest sister is ten years my senior.* • *She felt undervalued, both by her colleagues and her seniors.* **2** (*Brit*) one of the older students at a school **3** (*US*) a student in the final year of school, college or university: *high school seniors* ••➤ Look at **junior**[2].

senior citizen = OLD-AGE PENSIONER

seniority /ˌsi:ni'ɒrəti/ *noun* [U] the position or importance that a person has in a company, organization, etc in relation to others: *The names are listed below in order of seniority.*

sensation /sen'seɪʃn/ *noun* **1** [C] a feeling that is caused by sth affecting your body or part of your body: *a pleasant/unpleasant/tingling sensation* **2** [U] the ability to feel when touching or being touched: *For some time after the accident he had no sensation in his legs.* **3** [C,usually *sing*] a general feeling or impression that is difficult to explain: *I had the peculiar sensation that I was floating in the air.* **4** [C,usually *sing*] great excitement, surprise or interest among a group of people; sb/sth that causes this excitement: *The young American caused a sensation by beating the top player.*

sensational /sen'seɪʃənl/ *adj* **1** causing, or trying to cause, a feeling of great excitement, surprise or interest among people: *This magazine specializes in sensational stories about the rich and famous.* **2** (*informal*) extremely good or beautiful; very exciting –**sensationally** *adv*

★**sense**[1] /sens/ *noun* **1** [U] the ability to think or act in a reasonable or sensible way; good judgement: *At least he had the sense to stop when he realized he was making a mistake.* • *I think there's a lot of sense in what you're saying.* ••➤ Look at **common sense**. **2** [U,*sing*] the ability to understand sth; the ability to recognize what sth is or what its value is: *She seems to have lost all sense of reality.* • *I like him – he's got a great sense of humour.* • *I'm always getting lost. I've got absolutely no sense of direction.* **3** [U] sense (in doing sth) the reason for doing sth; purpose: *There's no sense in going any further – we're obviously lost.* • *What's the sense in making things more difficult for yourself?* **4** [U,*sing*] a natural ability to do or produce sth well: *Good business sense made her a millionaire.*

• *He's got absolutely no dress sense* (= he dresses very badly). **5** [*sing*] a feeling or consciousness of sth: *I felt a tremendous sense of relief when the exams were finally over.* • *She only visits her family out of a sense of duty.* **6** [C] one of the five natural physical powers of sight, hearing, smell, taste and touch, that people and animals have: *I've got a cold and I've lost my sense of smell.* • *Dogs have an acute sense of hearing.* **7** [C] (used about a word, phrase, etc) a meaning: *This word has two senses.*

IDIOMS **come to your senses** to finally realize that you should do sth because it is the most sensible thing to do

in a sense in one particular way but not in other ways; partly: *In a sense you're right, but there's more to the matter than that.*

make sense 1 to be possible to understand; to have a clear meaning: *What does this sentence mean? It doesn't make sense to me.* **2** (used about an action) to be sensible or logical: *I think it would make sense to wait for a while before making a decision.*

make sense of sth to manage to understand sth that is not clear or is difficult to understand: *I can't make sense of these instructions.*

talk sense → TALK[1](6)

sense[2] /sens/ *verb* [T] (not used in the continuous tenses) to realize or become conscious of sth; to get a feeling about sth even though you cannot see it, hear it, etc: *I sensed that something was wrong as soon as I went in.*

➤ Although this verb is not used in the continuous tenses, it is common to see the present participle (= -ing form): *Sensing a scandal, the tabloid photographers rushed to the star's hotel.*

senseless /'sensləs/ *adj* **1** having no meaning or purpose **2** unconscious: *He was beaten senseless.*

sensibility /ˌsensə'bɪləti/ *noun* (*pl* **sensibilities**) **1** [U,C] the ability to understand and experience deep feelings, for example in art, literature, etc **2** **sensibilities** [pl] a person's feelings, especially when he/she is easily offended

★**sensible** /'sensəbl/ *adj* (used about people and their behaviour) able to make good judgements based on reason and experience; practical: *a sensible person/decision/precaution* • *Stop joking and give me a sensible answer.* • *I think it would be sensible to leave early, in case there's a lot of traffic.* ••➤ opposite **silly** or **foolish** –**sensibly** /-əbli/ *adv*: *Let's sit down and discuss the matter sensibly.*

➤ Compare **sensible** and **sensitive**. **Sensible** is connected with common sense, reasonable action and good judgement. **Sensitive** is connected with feelings and emotions and with the five senses of sight, hearing, touch, smell and taste.

★**sensitive** /'sensətɪv/ *adj* **1** sensitive (to sth) showing that you are conscious of and able to understand people's feelings, problems, etc: *It*

S

wasn't very sensitive of you to keep mentioning her boyfriend. You know they've just split up. ● **to be sensitive to sb's feelings/wishes 2 sensitive (about/to sth)** easily upset, offended or annoyed, especially about a particular subject: *She's still a bit sensitive about her divorce.* ● *He's very sensitive to criticism.* ••➤ opposite for senses 1 and 2 **insensitive 3** (used about a subject, a situation, etc) needing to be dealt with carefully because it is likely to cause anger or trouble: *This is a sensitive period in the negotiations between the two countries.* **4 sensitive (to sth)** easily hurt or damaged; painful, especially if touched: *a new cream for sensitive skin* ● *My teeth are very sensitive to hot or cold food.* **5** (used about a scientific instrument, a piece of equipment, etc) able to measure very small changes ••➤ Look at the note at **sensible**. –**sensitively** adv: *The investigation will need to be handled sensitively.* –**sensitivity** /ˌsensə'tɪvəti/ **noun** [U]: *I think your comments showed a complete lack of sensitivity.*

sensual /'senʃuəl/ **adj** connected with physical or sexual pleasure: *the sensual rhythms of Latin music* –**sensuality** /ˌsenʃu'æləti/ **noun** [U]

sensuous /'senʃuəs/ **adj** giving pleasure to the mind or body through the senses: *the sensuous feel of pure silk* –**sensuously** adv –**sensuousness** noun [U]

sent past tense, past participle of **SEND**

★**sentence**[1] /'sentəns/ **noun** [C] **1** (*grammar*) a group of words containing a subject and a verb, etc. When a sentence is written it begins with a big (**capital**) letter and ends with a full stop. ••➤ Look at **phrase**. **2** the punishment given by a judge to sb who has been found guilty of a crime: *20 years in prison was a very harsh sentence.*

sentence[2] /'sentəns/ **verb** [T] **sentence sb (to sth)** (used about a judge) to tell sb who has been found guilty of a crime what the punishment will be: *The judge sentenced her to three months in prison for shoplifting.*

sentiment /'sentɪmənt/ **noun** **1** [C,U] (*formal*) (often plural) an attitude or opinion that is often caused or influenced by emotion: *His comments expressed my sentiments exactly.* **2** [U] feelings such as pity, romantic love, sadness, etc that influence sb's action or behaviour (sometimes in situations where this is not appropriate): *There's no room for sentiment in business.*

sentimental /ˌsentɪ'mentl/ **adj 1** producing or connected with emotions such as romantic love, pity, sadness, etc which may be too strong or not appropriate: *How can you be sentimental about an old car!* ● *a sentimental love song* **2** connected with happy memories or feelings of love rather than having any financial value: *The jewellery wasn't worth much but it had great sentimental value to me.* –**sentimentality** /ˌsentɪmen'tæləti/ **noun** [U] –**sentimentally** /-təli/ **adv**

sentry /'sentri/ **noun** [C] (*pl* **sentries**) a sol-

dier who stands outside a building and guards it

separable /'sepərəbl/ **adj** able to be separated ••➤ opposite is **inseparable**

★**separate**[1] /'seprət/ **adj 1 separate (from sth/sb)** apart; not together: *You should always keep your cash and credit cards separate.* **2** different; not connected: *We stayed in separate rooms in the same hotel.*

★**separate**[2] /'sepəreɪt/ **verb 1** [I,T] **separate (sb/sth) (from sb/sth)** to stop being together; to cause people or things to stop being together: *I think we should separate into two groups.* ● *The friends separated at the airport.* ● *I got separated from my friends in the crowd.* **2** [T] **separate sb/sth (from sb/sth)** to keep people or things apart; to be between people or things with the result that they are apart: *The two sides of the city are separated by the river.* **3** [I] to stop living together as a couple with your wife, husband or partner: *His parents separated when he was still a baby.*

separated /'sepəreɪtɪd/ **adj** not living together as a couple any more: *My wife and I are separated.*

separately /'seprətli/ **adv** apart; not together: *Shall we pay separately or all together?*

★**separation** /ˌsepə'reɪʃn/ **noun 1** [C,U] the action of separating or being separated; a situation or period of being apart **2** [C] an agreement where a couple decide not to live together any more: *a trial separation*

Sept abbr September: *2 Sept 1920*

★**September** /sep'tembə/ **noun** [U,C] (*abbr* **Sept**) the ninth month of the year, coming after August

➤ To see how the months are used in sentences, look at the examples and the note at **January**.

septic /'septɪk/ **adj** infected with poisonous bacteria: *The wound went septic.*

sequel /'siːkwəl/ **noun** [C] **a sequel (to sth) 1** a book, film, etc that continues the story of the one before **2** something that happens after, or is the result of, a previous event

sequence /'siːkwəns/ **noun 1** [C] a number of things (actions, events, etc) that happen or come one after another: *Complete the following sequence: 1, 4, 8, 13, ...* **2** [U] the order in which a number of things happen or are arranged: *The photographs are in sequence.*

serene /sə'riːn/ **adj** calm and peaceful: *a serene smile* –**serenely** adv –**serenity** /sə'renəti/ **noun** [U]

sergeant /'saːdʒənt/ **noun** [C] (*abbr* **Sgt**) **1** an officer with a low position in the army or air force **2** an officer with a middle position in the police force

serial /'sɪəriəl/ **noun** [C] a story in a magazine or on television or radio that is told in a number of parts over a period of time: *the first part of a six-part drama serial* ••➤ Look at the note at **series**. –**serialize** (also -**ise**) /-rɪəlaɪz/ **verb** [T]

ˈserial number noun [C] the number marked on sth to identify it and to distinguish it from other things of the same type

★series /ˈsɪəriːz/ noun [C] (pl series) 1 a number of things that happen one after another and are of the same type or connected: a series of events ● There has been a series of burglaries in this district recently. 2 a number of programmes on radio or television which have the same main characters and each tell a complete story

> Compare series and serial. In a series each part is a different, complete story involving the same main characters. In a serial the same story continues in each part.

★serious /ˈsɪəriəs/ adj 1 bad or dangerous: a serious accident/illness/offence ● Pollution is a very serious problem. ● Her condition is serious and she's likely to be in hospital for some time. 2 needing to be treated as important, not just for fun: Don't laugh, it's a serious matter. ● a serious discussion 3 serious (about sth/about doing sth) (used about a person) not joking; thoughtful: Are you serious about starting your own business (= are you really going to do it)? ● He's terribly serious. I don't think I've ever seen him laugh. ● You're looking very serious. Was it bad news? –seriousness noun [U]

★seriously /ˈsɪəriəsli/ adv 1 in a serious way: Three people were seriously injured in the accident. ● My mother is seriously ill. ● It's time you started to think seriously about the future. 2 used at the beginning of a sentence for showing that you are not joking or that you really mean what you are saying: Seriously, I do appreciate all your help. ● Seriously, you've got nothing to worry about. 3 used for expressing surprise at what sb has said and asking if it is really true: 'I'm 40 today.' 'Seriously? You look a lot younger.'

IDIOM take sb/sth seriously to treat sb or sth as important: You take everything too seriously! Relax and enjoy yourself.

sermon /ˈsɜːmən/ noun [C] a speech on a religious or moral subject that is given as part of a service in church

serrated /səˈreɪtɪd/ adj having a row of points in V-shapes along the edge: a knife with a serrated edge

servant /ˈsɜːvənt/ noun [C] a person who is paid to work in sb's house, doing work such as cooking, cleaning, etc ••> Look at civil servant.

★serve /sɜːv/ verb 1 [T] to give food or drink to sb during a meal; to take an order and then bring food or drink to sb in a restaurant, bar, etc: Breakfast is served from 7.30 to 9.00 am. 2 [T] (used about an amount of food) to be enough for a certain number of people: According to the recipe, this dish serves four. 3 [I,T] (in a shop) to take a customer's order; to give help, sell goods, etc: There was a long queue of people waiting to be served. 4 [I,T] to be useful or suitable for a particular purpose: The judge said the punishment would serve as

a warning to others. ● It's an old car but it will serve our purpose for a few months. 5 [I,T] to perform a duty or provide a service for the public or for an organization: During the war, he served in the Army. ● She became a nurse because she wanted to serve the community. 6 [T] to spend a period of time in prison as punishment: He is currently serving a ten-year sentence for fraud. 7 [I,T] (in tennis and similar sports) to start play by hitting the ball

IDIOMS first come, first served → FIRST²

serve sb right used when sth unpleasant happens to sb and you do not feel sorry for him/her because you think it is his/her own fault: 'I feel sick.' 'It serves you right for eating so much.'

server /ˈsɜːvə/ noun [C] a computer that stores information that a number of computers can share ••> Look at client.

★service¹ /ˈsɜːvɪs/ noun 1 [C] a system or organization that provides the public with sth that it needs; the job that an organization does: There is a regular bus service to the airport. ● the postal service ● the National Health Service ● We offer a number of financial services. ••> Look at Civil Service. 2 [U] (also the services) [pl] the armed forces; the army, navy or air force; the work done by the people in them: They both joined the services when they left school. ● Do you have to do military service in your country? 3 [U,C] work done for sb; help given to sb: He left the police force after thirty years' service. 4 [U] the work or the quality of work done by sb when serving a customer: I enjoyed the meal but the service was terrible. ● Is service included in the bill? 5 [C] the checks, repairs, etc that are necessary to make sure that a machine is working properly: We take our car for a service every six months. 6 [C] a religious ceremony, usually including prayers, singing, etc: a funeral service 7 [C] (in tennis and similar sports) the first hit of the ball at the start of play; a player's turn to serve (7) 8 services [pl] a place at the side of a motorway where there is a petrol station, a shop, toilets, a restaurant, etc

service² /ˈsɜːvɪs/ verb [T] to examine and, if necessary, repair a car, machine, etc: All cars should be serviced at regular intervals.

ˈservice station = SERVICE¹(8)

serviette /ˌsɜːviˈet/ noun [C] a square of cloth or paper that you use when you are eating to keep your clothes clean and to clean your mouth or hands on ••> synonym napkin

session /ˈseʃn/ noun 1 [C] a period of doing a particular activity: The whole tape was recorded in one session. ● She has a session at the gym every week. 2 [C,U] a formal meeting or series of meetings of a court of law, parliament, etc

★set¹ /set/ verb (pres part setting; pt, pp set) 1 [T] to put sb/sth or to be in a particular place or position: I set the box down carefully on the floor. 2 [T] (often passive) to make the action of a book, play, film, etc take place in a particular time, situation, etc: *The film is set in 16th century Spain.* **3** [T] to cause a particular state or event; to start sth happening: *The new government set the prisoners free.* ● *The rioters set a number of cars on fire.* **4** [T] to prepare or arrange sth for a particular purpose: *I set my alarm for 6.30.* ● *to set the table* (= put the plates, knives, forks, etc on it) **5** [T] to decide or arrange sth: *Can we set a limit of two hours for the meeting?* ● *They haven't set the date for their wedding yet.* **6** [T] to do sth good that people have to try to copy or achieve: *Try to set a good example to the younger children.* ● *He has set a new world record.* ● *They set high standards of customer service.* **7** [T] to give sb a piece of work or a task: *We've been set a lot of homework this weekend.* ● *I've set myself a target of four hours' study every evening.* **8** [I] to become firm or hard: *The concrete will set solid/hard in just a few hours.* **9** [T] to fix a precious stone, etc in a piece of jewellery **10** [T] to fix a broken bone in the correct position so that it can get better: *The doctor set her broken leg.* **11** [I] (used about the sun) to go down below the horizon in the evening ●➤ opposite **rise**

IDIOMS **set foot (in/on sth)** to visit, enter or arrive at/in a place: *No woman has ever set foot in the temple.*

put/set sth right → **RIGHT**[1]

set sail to begin a journey by sea: *Columbus set sail for India.*

set your heart on sth; have your heart set on sth → **HEART**

put/set your/sb's mind at rest → **MIND**[1]

set eyes on sb/sth to see sb/sth: *He loved the house the moment he set eyes on it.*

PHRASAL VERBS **set about sth** to start doing sth, especially dealing with a problem or task: *How would you set about tackling this problem?*

set sth aside to keep sth to use later: *I try to set aside part of my wages every week.*

set sb/sth back to delay sb/sth: *The bad weather has set our plans back six weeks.*

set forth (*formal*) to start a journey

set sth forth (*formal*) to show or tell sth to sb or to make sth known

set in to arrive and remain for a period of time: *I'm afraid that the bad weather has set in.*

set off to leave on a journey: *We set off at 3 o'clock this morning.*

set sth off to do sth which starts a reaction: *When this door is opened, it sets off an alarm.*

set out to leave on a journey

set out to do sth to decide to achieve sth: *He set out to prove that his theory was right.*

set (sth) up to start a business, organization, system, etc: *The company has set up a new branch in Wales.*

★**set²** /set/ *noun* [C] **1** a number of things that belong together: *a set of kitchen knives* ● *In the first set of questions, you have to fill in the gap.* ● *a set of instructions* ● *a spare set of keys* ● *a chess set* **2** a piece of equipment for

receiving television or radio signals: *a television set* **3** the scenery that is made for a play or film **4** (in tennis) a group of games forming part of a match: *China won the volleyball final by three sets to one.*

set³ /set/ *adj* **1** placed in a particular position: *deep-set eyes* ● *Our house is quite set back from the road.* **2** fixed and not changing; firm: *There are no set hours in my job.* ● *I'll have the set menu* (= with a fixed price and limited choice of dishes). **3** (used about a book, text, etc) that everyone must study for an exam: *We have to study three set texts for French.* **4** **set (for sth); set (to do sth)** ready, prepared or likely to do sth: *Okay, I'm set – let's go!* ● *I was all set to leave when the phone rang.* ● *The Swiss team look set for victory.*

IDIOMS **be set against sth/doing sth** to be determined that sth will not happen or that you will not do sth

be set on sth/doing sth to be determined to do sth: *She's set on a career in acting.*

setback /'setbæk/ *noun* [C] a difficulty or problem that stops you progressing as fast as you would like: *She suffered a major setback when she missed the exams through illness.*

settee /se'ti:/ *noun* [C] a long soft seat with a back and arms that more than one person can sit on ●➤ synonym **sofa**

setting /'setɪŋ/ *noun* [C] **1** the position sth is in; the place and time in which sth happens: *The hotel is in a beautiful setting, close to the sea.* **2** one of the positions of the controls of a machine: *Cook it in the oven on a moderate setting.*

settle /'setl/ *verb* **1** [I,T] to put an end to an argument or disagreement: *They settled the dispute without going to court.* ● *They settled out of court.* ● *We didn't speak to each other for years, but we've settled our differences now.* **2** [T] to decide or arrange sth finally: *Everything's settled. We leave on the nine o'clock flight on Friday.* **3** [I] to go and live permanently in a new country, area, town, etc: *A great many immigrants have settled in this country.* **4** [I,T] to put yourself or sb else into a comfortable position: *I settled in front of the television for the evening.* ● *She settled herself beside him on the sofa.* **5** [I,T] to become or to make sb/sth calm or relaxed: *The baby wouldn't settle.* **6** [T] to pay money that you owe: *to settle a bill/a debt* **7** [I] to land on a surface and stop moving: *A flock of birds settled on the roof.*

PHRASAL VERBS **settle down 1** to get into a comfortable position, sitting or lying **2** to start having a quieter way of life, especially by staying in the same place or getting married: *She had a number of jobs abroad before she eventually settled down.* **3** to become calm and quiet: *Settle down! It's time to start the lesson.*

settle down to sth to start doing sth which involves all your attention: *Before you settle down to your work, could I ask you something?*

settle for sth to accept sth that is not as good

as what you wanted: *We're going to have to settle for the second prize.*

settle in/into sth to start feeling comfortable in a new home, job, etc: *How are the children settling in at their new school?*

settle on sth to choose or decide sth after considering many different things

settle up (with sb) to pay money that you owe to sb

settled /'setld/ *adj* **1** not changing or not likely to change: *More settled weather is forecast for the next few days.* **2** comfortable; feeling that you belong (in a home, a job, a way of life, etc): *We feel very settled here.*

settlement /'setlmənt/ *noun* [C,U] **1** an official agreement that ends an argument; the act of reaching an agreement: *a divorce settlement* • *the settlement of a dispute* **2** a place that a group of people have built and live in, where few or no people lived before; the process of people starting to live in a place: *There is believed to have been a prehistoric settlement on this site.* • *the settlement of the American West*

settler /'setlə/ *noun* [C] a person who goes to live permanently in a place where not many people live: *the first white settlers in Australia*

★**seven** /'sevn/ *number* **1** 7

➤ For examples of how to use numbers in sentences, look at **six**.

2 (used to form compound adjectives) having seven of the thing mentioned: *a seven-sided coin*

★**seventeen** /ˌsevn'tiːn/ *number* 17

➤ For examples of how to use numbers in sentences, look at **six**.

seventeenth /ˌsevn'tiːnθ/ *pron*, *determiner*, *adv* 17th •➤ Look at the examples at **sixth**.

seventh¹ /'sevnθ/ *noun* [C] the fraction ⅐; one of seven equal parts of sth •➤ Look at the examples at **sixth**.

seventh² /'sevnθ/ *pron*, *determiner*, *adv* 7th •➤ Look at the examples at **sixth**.

seventieth /'sevntiəθ/ *pron*, *determiner*, *adv* 70th •➤ Look at the examples at **sixth**.

★**seventy** /'sevnti/ *number* 70

➤ For examples of how to use numbers in sentences, look at **sixty**.

sever /'sevə/ *verb* [T] **1** to cut sth into two pieces; to cut sth off: *The builders accidentally severed a water pipe.* • *His hand was almost severed in the accident.* **2** to end a relationship or communication with sb: *He has severed all links with his former friends.*

★**several** /'sevrəl/ *pron*, *determiner* more than two but not very many; a few: *It took her several days to recover from the shock.* • *There were lots of applications for the job – several of them from very well-qualified people.* • *I don't think it's a good idea for several reasons.*

severe /sɪ'vɪə/ *adj* **1** causing sb to suffer, be upset or have difficulties: *Such terrible crimes deserve the severest punishment.* • *I think your criticism of her work was too severe.* **2** extremely bad or serious: *The company is*

in *severe financial difficulty.* • *He suffered severe injuries in the fall.* • *severe weather conditions* –**severely** *adj*: *The roof was severely damaged in the storm.* • *The report severely criticizes the Health Service.* –**severity** /sɪ'verəti/ *noun* [U]: *I don't think you realize the severity of the problem.*

★**sew** /səʊ/ *verb* [I,T] (*pt* **sewed**; *pp* **sewn** /səʊn/ or **sewed**) sew (sth) (on) to join pieces of cloth, or to join sth to cloth, using a needle and thread and forming stitches: *I can't sew.* • *A button's come off my shirt – I'll have to sew it back on.* •➤ picture at **knit**

PHRASAL VERB **sew sth up 1** to join two things by sewing; to repair sth by sewing two things together: *The surgeon sewed up the wound.* **2** to arrange sth so that it is certain to happen or be successful

sewage /'suːɪdʒ/ *noun* [U] the waste material from people's bodies that is carried away from their homes in water in large underground pipes (sewers)

sewer /'suːə/ *noun* [C] an underground pipe that carries human waste to a place where it can be treated

sewing /'səʊɪŋ/ *noun* [U] **1** using a needle and thread to make or repair things: *I always take a sewing kit when I travel.* • *a sewing machine* **2** something that is being sewn

sewn *past participle* of **sew**

★**sex** /seks/ *noun* **1** [U] the state of being either male or female: *Applications are welcome from anyone, regardless of sex or race.* • *Do you mind what sex your baby is?* •➤ synonym **gender 2** [C] one of the two groups consisting of all male people or all female people: *the male/female sex* • *He's always found it difficult to get on with the opposite sex* (= women). **3** (also *formal* **intercourse**; **sexual intercourse**) [U] the physical act in which the sexual organs of two people touch and which can result in a woman having a baby: *to have sex with somebody* • *sex education in schools*

sexism /'seksɪzəm/ *noun* [U] the unfair treatment of people, especially women, because of their sex; the attitude that causes this –**sexist** /'seksɪst/ *adj*: *a sexist attitude to women* • *sexist jokes*

★**sexual** /'sekʃuəl/ *adj* connected with sex: *sexual problems* • *the sexual organs* • *a campaign for sexual equality* (= to get fair and equal treatment for both men and women)

➤ Compare **sexy**.

–**sexually** /'sekʃəli/ *adv*: *to be sexually attracted to sb*

ˌsexual ˈintercourse (*formal*) = **sex**(3)

sexuality /ˌsekʃu'æləti/ *noun* [U] the nature of sb's sexual activities or desires

sexy /'seksi/ *adj* (**sexier**; **sexiest**) (*informal*) sexually attractive or exciting: *Do you find the lead singer sexy?* • *a sexy dress*

Sgt *abbr* sergeant

sh /ʃ/ *exclamation* used to tell sb to stop making noise: *Sh! People are trying to sleep in here.*

S

shabby /'ʃæbi/ **adj 1** in bad condition because of having been used or worn too much: *a shabby suit* **2** (used about people) dressed in an untidy way; wearing clothes that are in bad condition **3** (used about the way that sb is treated) unfair; not generous –**shabbily** adv: *a shabbily-dressed man* • *She felt she'd been treated shabbily by her employers.*

shack /ʃæk/ **noun** [C] a small building, usually made of wood or metal, that has not been built well

— shade

— shadow

★**shade¹** /ʃeɪd/ **noun 1** [U] an area that is out of direct sunlight and is darker and cooler than areas in the sun: *It was so hot that I had to go and sit in the shade.* **2** [C] something that keeps out light or makes it less bright: *a lampshade* **3 shades** [pl] (*informal*) = **SUNGLASSES** **4** [C] a shade (of sth) a type of a particular colour: *a shade of green* **5** [C] a small difference in the form or nature of sth: *a word with various shades of meaning* **6** [sing] a shade a little bit

shade² /ʃeɪd/ **verb** [T] **1** to protect sth from direct light; to give shade to sth: *The sun was so bright that I had to shade my eyes.* **2 shade sth (in)** to make an area of a drawing darker, for example with a pencil: *The trees will look more realistic once you've shaded them in.*

★**shadow¹** /'ʃædəʊ/ **noun 1** [C] a dark shape on a surface that is caused by sth being between the light and that surface: *The dog was chasing its own shadow.* • *The shadows lengthened as the sun went down.* ⋯▸ picture at **shade 2** [U] an area that is dark because sth prevents direct light from reaching it: *His face was in shadow.* **3** [sing] a very small amount of sth: *I know without a shadow of doubt that he's lying.*
IDIOM **cast a shadow (across/over sth)** → CAST¹

shadow² /'ʃædəʊ/ **verb** [T] to follow and watch sb's actions: *The police shadowed the suspect for three days.*

shadow³ /'ʃædəʊ/ **adj** (in British politics) belonging to the biggest political party that is not in power, with special responsibility for a particular subject, for example education or defence. Shadow ministers would probably become government ministers if their party won the next election: *the shadow Cabinet*

shadowy /'ʃædəʊi/ **adj 1** dark and full of shadows: *a shadowy forest* **2** difficult to see because there is not much light: *A shadowy figure was coming towards me.* **3** that not much is known about; mysterious

shady /'ʃeɪdi/ **adj 1** giving shade; giving protection from the sun: *I found a shady spot under the trees and sat down.* **2** (*informal*) not completely honest or legal

shaft /ʃɑːft/ **noun** [C] **1** a long, narrow hole in which sth can go up and down or enter or leave: *a lift shaft* • *a mine shaft* **2** a bar that connects parts of a machine so that power can pass between them

shaggy /'ʃægi/ **adj 1** (used about hair, material, etc) long, thick and untidy **2** covered with long, thick, untidy hair: *a shaggy dog*

★**shake¹** /ʃeɪk/ **verb** (*pt* **shook** /ʃʊk/; *pp* **shaken** /'ʃeɪkən/) **1** [I,T] to move from side to side or up and down with short, quick movements: *I was so nervous that I was shaking.* • *The whole building shakes when big lorries go past.* • (*figurative*) *His voice shook with emotion as he described the accident.* • *Shake the bottle before taking the medicine.* • *She shook him to wake him up.* **2** [T] to disturb or upset sb/sth: *The scandal has shaken the whole country.* **3** [T] to cause sth to be less certain; to cause sb to doubt about sth: *Nothing seems to shake her belief that she was right.*
IDIOMS **shake sb's hand/shake hands (with sb)/shake sb by the hand** to take sb's hand and move it up and down (when you meet sb, to show that you have agreed on sth, etc) ⋯▸ picture on page S8
shake your head to move your head from side to side, as a way of saying no ⋯▸ picture on page S8
PHRASAL VERB **shake sb/sth off** to get rid of sb/sth; to remove sth by shaking: *I don't seem to be able to shake off this cold.* • *Shake the crumbs off the tablecloth.*

shake² /ʃeɪk/ **noun** [C] the action of shaking sth or being shaken

'shake-up noun [C] a complete change in the structure or organization of sth

shaky /'ʃeɪki/ **adj** (**shakier**; **shakiest**) **1** shaking or feeling weak because you are frightened or ill **2** not firm; weak or not very good: *The table's a bit shaky so don't put anything heavy on it.* • *They've had a shaky start to the season losing most of their games.* –**shakily** adv

★**shall** /ʃəl; *strong form* ʃæl/ **modal verb** (*negative* **shall not**; *short form* **shan't** /ʃɑːnt/) **1** used for asking for information or advice: *What time shall I come?* • *Where shall we go for our holiday?* **2** used for offering to do sth: *Shall I help you carry that box?* • *Shall we drive you home?* **3 shall we** used for suggesting that you do sth with the person or people that you are talking to: *Shall we go out for a meal this evening?*

▶ For more information about modal verbs, look at the **Quick Grammar Reference** section at the back of this dictionary.

4 (*formal*) used with 'I' and 'we' in future tenses, instead of 'will': *I shall be very happy to see him again.* • *We shan't be arriving until ten o'clock.* • *At the end of this year, I shall have been working here for five years.* **5** (*formal*) used for saying that sth must happen or will definitely happen: *In the rules it says that a player shall be sent off for using bad language.*

shallow/deep

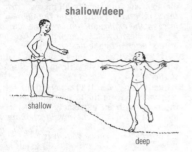

shallow

deep

★**shallow** /'ʃæləʊ/ **adj 1** not deep; with not much distance between top and bottom: *The sea is very shallow here.* • *a shallow dish* **2** not having or showing serious or deep thought: *a shallow person/book* ••▶ opposite for both senses **deep** –**shallowness noun** [U]

★**shame¹** /ʃeɪm/ **noun 1** [U] the unpleasant feeling of guilt and embarrassment that you get when you have done sth stupid or morally wrong; the ability to have this feeling: *She was **filled with shame** at the thought of how she had lied to her mother.* • *His actions have **brought shame on** his whole family.* • *He doesn't care how he behaves in public. He's got no shame!* ••▶ adjective **ashamed 2 a shame** [sing] a fact or situation that makes you feel disappointed: *It's **a shame** about Adam failing his exams, isn't it?* • *What a shame you have to leave so soon.* • *It would be a shame to miss an opportunity like this.*

shame² /ʃeɪm/ **verb** [T] to make sb feel shame for sth bad that he/she has done

shameful /'ʃeɪmfl/ **adj** which sb should be feel bad about; shocking: *a shameful waste of public money* –**shamefully adv**

shameless /'ʃeɪmləs/ **adj** not feeling embarrassed about doing sth bad; having no shame: *a shameless display of greed and bad manners* –**shamelessly adv**

★**shampoo** /ʃæm'puː/ **noun 1** [C,U] a liquid that you use for washing your hair; a similar liquid for cleaning carpets, cars, etc: *shampoo for greasy/dry/normal hair* **2** [C] the action of washing sth with shampoo –**shampoo verb** [T] (*pres part* **shampooing**; *3rd pers sing pres* **shampoos**; *pt, pp* **shampooed**)

shamrock /'ʃæmrɒk/ **noun** [C,U] a plant

with three leaves, which is the national symbol of Ireland

shandy /'ʃændi/ **noun** [C,U] (*pl* **shandies**) a drink that is a mixture of beer and a sweet, colourless, non-alcoholic drink with bubbles (lemonade)

shan't *short for* **SHALL NOT**

shanty town /'ʃænti taʊn/ **noun** [C] an area, usually on the edge of a big city, where poor people live in bad conditions in buildings that they have made themselves

shapes

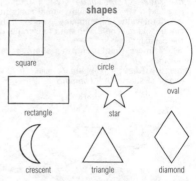

square   circle

oval

rectangle   star

crescent   triangle   diamond

★**shape¹** /ʃeɪp/ **noun 1** [C,U] the form of the outer edges or surfaces of sth; an example of sth that has a particular form: *a round/square/rectangular shape* • *a cake **in the shape of** a heart* • *clothes to fit people of **all shapes and sizes*** • *Squares, circles and triangles are all different shapes.* • *I could just make out a dark shape in the distance.* • *The country is roughly square **in shape**.* **2** **-shaped** (used to form compound adjectives) having the shape mentioned: *an L-shaped room* **3** [U] the physical condition of sb/sth; the good or bad state of sb/sth: *She was **in such bad shape** (= so ill) that she had to be taken to hospital.* • *I go swimming regularly to keep **in shape**.* **4** [sing] **the shape (of sth)** the organization, form or structure of sth

IDIOMS **out of shape 1** not in the usual or correct shape: *My sweater's gone out of shape now that I've washed it.* **2** not physically fit: *You're out of shape. You should get more exercise.*

take shape to start to develop well: *Plans to expand the company are beginning to take shape.*

★**shape²** /ʃeɪp/ **verb** [T] **1 shape sth (into sth)** to make sth into a particular form: *Shape the mixture into small balls.* **2** to influence the way in which sth develops; to cause sth to have a particular form or nature: *His political ideas were shaped by his upbringing.*

shapeless /'ʃeɪpləs/ **adj** not having a clear shape: *a shapeless dress*

★**share¹** /ʃeə/ **verb 1** [T] **share sth (out)** to divide sth between two or more people: *We shared the pizza out between the four of us.* **2** [I,T] **share (sth) (with sb)** to have, use, do

S

or pay sth together with another person or other people: *I share a flat with four other people.* ● *I shared my sandwiches with Jim.* ● *We share the same interests.* **3** [T] **share sth (with sb)** to tell sb about sth; to allow sb to know sth: *Sometimes it helps to share your problems.*

★**share²** /ʃeə/ **noun 1** [sing] **share (of sth)** a part or amount of sth that has been divided between several people: *We each pay a share of the household bills.* ● *I'm willing to take my share of the blame.* **2** [C, usually pl] **shares (in sth)** one of many equal parts into which the value of a company is divided, that can be sold to people who want to own part of the company

IDIOM **(more than) your fair share of sth** → **FAIR¹**

shareholder /ˈʃeəhəʊldə/ **noun** [C] an owner of shares in a company

shark

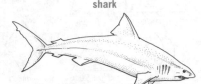

shark /ʃɑːk/ **noun** [C] (*pl* **sharks** or **shark**) a large, often dangerous, sea fish that has a lot of sharp teeth

★**sharp¹** /ʃɑːp/ **adj 1** having a very thin but strong edge or point; that can cut or make a hole in sth easily: *a sharp knife* ● *sharp teeth* ●➤ opposite **blunt 2** (used about a change of direction or level) very great and sudden: *a sharp rise/fall in inflation* ● *This is a sharp bend so slow down.* **3** clear and definite: *the sharp outline of the hills* ● *a sharp contrast between the lives of the rich and the poor* **4** able to think, act, understand, see or hear quickly: *a sharp mind* ● *You must have sharp eyes if you can read that sign from here.* **5** (used about actions or movements) quick and sudden: *One short sharp blow was enough to end the fight.* **6** (used about words, comments, etc) said in an angry way; intended to upset sb or be critical **7** (used about pain) very strong and sudden: *a sharp pain in the chest* ●➤ opposite **dull 8** (used about sth that affects the senses) strong; not mild or gentle, often causing an unpleasant feeling: *a sharp taste* ● *a sharp wind* **9** (symbol ♯) (in music) half a note higher than the stated note: *in the key of C sharp minor* ●➤ Look at **flat¹**(5) **10** (in music) slightly higher than the correct note: *That last note was sharp. Can you sing it again?* ●➤ Look at **flat¹**(6) –**sharply** /ˈʃɑːpli/ **adv:** *The road bends sharply to the left.* ● *Share prices fell sharply this morning.* –**sharpness noun** [U]

sharp² /ʃɑːp/ **adv 1** (used about a time) exactly, punctually: *Be here at three o'clock sharp.* **2** turning suddenly: *Go to the traffic lights and turn sharp right.* **3** (in music)

slightly higher than the correct note ●➤ Look at **flat¹**(6).

sharp³ /ʃɑːp/ **noun** [C] (*symbol* ♯) (in music) a note that is half a note higher than the note with the same letter ●➤ Look at **flat²**(2).

sharpen /ˈʃɑːpən/ **verb** [I,T] to become or to make sth sharp or sharper: *to sharpen a knife* ● *This knife won't sharpen.*

sharpener /ˈʃɑːpnə/ **noun** [C] an object or tool that is used for making sth sharp: *a pencil/knife sharpener*

shatter /ˈʃætə/ **verb 1** [I,T] (used about glass, etc) to break into very small pieces: *I dropped the glass and it shattered on the floor.* ● *The force of the explosion shattered the windows.* **2** [T] to destroy sth completely: *Her hopes were shattered by the news.*

shattered /ˈʃætəd/ **adj 1** very shocked and upset **2** (*informal*) very tired: *I'm absolutely shattered.*

★**shave¹** /ʃeɪv/ **verb** [I,T] **shave (sth) (off)** to remove hair from the face or another part of the body with an extremely sharp piece of metal (**a razor**): *I cut myself shaving this morning.* ● *When did you shave off your moustache?* ● *to shave your legs*

PHRASAL VERB **shave sth off (sth)** to cut a very small amount from sth: *We'll have to shave a bit off the door to make it close properly.*

shave² /ʃeɪv/ **noun** [C, usually sing] the action of shaving: *to have a shave* ● *I need a shave.*

IDIOM **a close shave/thing** → **CLOSE³**

shaven /ˈʃeɪvn/ **adj** having been shaved: *clean-shaven* (= not having a beard or moustache)

shaver /ˈʃeɪvə/ (also **electric razor**) **noun** [C] an electric tool that is used for removing hair from the face or another part of the body

shawl /ʃɔːl/ **noun** [C] a large piece of cloth that is worn by a woman round her shoulders or head or that is put round a baby

★**she** /ʃiː/ **pron** (the subject of a verb) the female person who has already been mentioned: *'What does your sister do?' 'She's a dentist.'* ● *I asked her a question but she didn't answer.*

shear /ʃɪə/ **verb** [T] (*pt* **sheared**; *pp* **sheared** or **shorn**) to cut the wool off a sheep

shears /ʃɪəz/ **noun** [pl] a tool that is like a very large pair of scissors and that is used for cutting things in the garden: *a pair of shears* ●➤ picture at **garden**

sheath /ʃiːθ/ **noun** [C] (*pl* **sheaths** /ʃiːðz/) a cover for a knife or other sharp weapon ●➤ picture at **spear**

she'd /ʃiːd/ *short for* **SHE HAD, SHE WOULD**

shed¹ /ʃed/ **noun** [C] a small building that is used for keeping things or animals in: *a garden shed* ● *a bicycle shed* ● *a cattle shed* ●➤ picture on page C7

shed² /ʃed/ **verb** [T] (*pres part* **shedding**; *pt, pp* **shed**) **1** to lose sth because it falls off: *This snake sheds its skin every year.* ● *Autumn is coming and the trees are beginning to shed their leaves.* **2** to get rid of or

S

remove sth that is not wanted

IDIOMS shed blood (*written*) to kill or injure people

shed light on sth to make sth clear and easy to understand

shed tears to cry

★ **sheep** /ʃiːp/ noun [C] (*pl* sheep) an animal that is kept on farms and used for its wool or meat

➤ A male sheep is a **ram**, a female sheep is a **ewe** and a young sheep is a **lamb**. When sheep make a noise they **bleat**. This is written as **baa**. The meat from sheep is called **lamb** or **mutton**. Look at the note at **meat**.

•➤ picture at **goat**

sheepdog /ˈʃiːpdɒg/ noun [C] a dog that has been trained to control sheep

sheepish /ˈʃiːpɪʃ/ adj feeling or showing embarrassment because you have done sth silly: *a sheepish grin* –**sheepishly** adv

sheepskin /ˈʃiːpskɪn/ noun [U] the skin of a sheep, including the wool, from which coats, etc are made: *a sheepskin rug/jacket*

sheer /ʃɪə/ adj **1** (only *before* a noun) used to emphasize the size, degree or amount of sth: *It's sheer stupidity to drink and drive.* ● *It was **sheer luck** that I happened to be in the right place at the right time.* ● *Her success is due to **sheer hard work**.* ● *I only agreed out of sheer desperation.* **2** very steep; almost vertical: *Don't walk near the edge. It's **a sheer drop** to the sea.*

★ **sheet** /ʃiːt/ noun [C] **1** a large piece of material used on a bed •➤ picture at **bed 2** a piece of paper that is used for writing, printing, etc on: *a sheet of notepaper* ● *Write each answer on a separate sheet.* •➤ Look at **balance sheet**. **3** a flat, thin piece of any material, especially a square or rectangular one: *a sheet of metal/glass* **4** a wide, flat area of sth: *The road was covered with **a sheet of ice**.*

sheikh (also **sheik**) /ʃeɪk/ noun [C] an Arab ruler

★ **shelf** /ʃelf/ noun [C] (*pl* shelves /ʃelvz/) a long flat piece of wood, glass, etc that is fixed to a wall or in a cupboard, used for putting things on: *I put up a shelf in the kitchen.* ● *I reached up and took down the book from the top shelf.* ● *a bookshelf* •➤ picture on page C7

she'll /ʃiːl/ short for SHE WILL

★ **shell** /ʃel/ noun **1** [C,U] a hard covering that protects eggs, nuts and some animals: *Some children were collecting shells on the beach.* ● *a piece of eggshell* ● *Tortoises have a hard shell.* •➤ picture at **nut**, **shellfish** and **snail 2** [C] the walls or hard outer structure of sth: *The body shell of the car is made in another factory.* **3** [C] a metal container that explodes when it is fired from a large gun

IDIOMS come out of your shell to become less shy and more confident when talking to other people

go, retreat, etc into your shell to suddenly become shy and stop talking

shell² /ʃel/ verb [T] **1** to take the hard outer layer (shell) off a nut or other kind of food: *to*

shell peas **2** to fire metal containers (shells) full of explosives from a large gun

shellfish

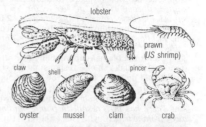
lobster
prawn (US shrimp)
claw
shell
pincer
oyster   mussel   clam   crab

shellfish /ˈʃelfɪʃ/ noun (*pl* shellfish) **1** [C] a type of animal that lives in water and has a shell **2** [U] these animals eaten as food

★ **shelter¹** /ˈʃeltə/ noun **1** [U] shelter (from sth) protection from danger or bad weather: *to give somebody food and shelter* ● *We looked around for somewhere to **take shelter** from the storm.* **2** [C] a small building that gives protection, for example from bad weather or attack: *a bus shelter* ● *an air-raid shelter*

shelter² /ˈʃeltə/ verb **1** [I] shelter (from sth) to find protection or a safe place: *Let's shelter from the rain under that tree.* **2** [T] shelter sb/sth (from sb/sth) to protect sb/sth; to provide a safe place away from harm or danger: *The trees shelter the house from the wind.*

sheltered /ˈʃeltəd/ adj **1** (used about a place) protected from bad weather **2** protected from unpleasant things in your life: *We had a sheltered childhood, living in the country.*

shelve /ʃelv/ verb [T] to decide not to continue with a plan, etc, either for a short time or permanently: *Plans for a new motorway have been shelved.*

shelves /ʃelvz/ *plural* of SHELF

shelving /ˈʃelvɪŋ/ noun [U] a set of shelves

shepherd¹ /ˈʃepəd/ noun [C] a person whose job is to look after sheep

shepherd² /ˈʃepəd/ verb [T] to guide and look after people so that they do not get lost

sheriff /ˈʃerɪf/ noun [C] an officer of the law in a US county

sherry /ˈʃeri/ noun [C,U] (*pl* sherries) a type of strong Spanish wine; a glass of this wine

she's /ʃiːz; ʃiz/ short for SHE IS, SHE HAS

shield¹ /ʃiːld/ noun [C] **1** (in past times) a large piece of metal or wood that soldiers carried to protect themselves **2** riot shield a piece of equipment made of strong plastic, that the police use to protect themselves from angry crowds **3** a person or thing that is used to protect sb/sth especially by forming a barrier: *The metal door acted as a shield against the explosion.* **4** an object or drawing in the shape of a shield, sometimes used as a prize in a sports competition •➤ picture at **medal**

shield² /ʃiːld/ verb [T] shield sb/sth (against/from sb/sth) to protect sb/sth from

S

shift¹ /ʃɪft/ verb [I,T] **1** to move or be moved from one position or place to another: *She shifted uncomfortably in her chair.* • *He shifted his desk closer to the window.* **2** to change your opinion of or attitude towards sth: *Public attitudes towards marriage have shifted over the years.*

IDIOM **shift the blame/responsibility (for sth) (onto sb)** to make sb else responsible for sth you should do or for sth bad you have done

shift² /ʃɪft/ noun **1** [C] a shift (in sth) a change in your opinion of or attitude towards sth: *There has been a shift in public opinion away from war.* **2** [C, with sing or pl verb] (in a factory, etc) one of the periods that the working day is divided into; the group who work during this period: *The night shift has/have just gone off duty.* • *to work in shifts* • *shift work/workers* • *to be on the day/night shift* **3** [sing] one of the keys that you use for writing on a computer, etc, that allows you to write a big (capital) letter: *the shift key*

shifty /ˈʃɪfti/ adj (used about a person or his/her appearance) giving the impression that you cannot trust him/her: *shifty eyes*

shilling /ˈʃɪlɪŋ/ noun [C] **1** the basic unit of money in some countries, for example Kenya **2** a British coin worth five pence that was used in past times

shimmer /ˈʃɪmə/ verb [I] to shine with a soft light that seems to be moving: *Moonlight shimmered on the sea.*

shin /ʃɪn/ noun [C] the bone down the front part of your leg from your knee to your foot •▸ picture on page C5

★**shine**¹ /ʃaɪn/ verb (pt, pp shone /ʃɒn/) **1** [I] to send out or to reflect light; to be bright: *I could see a light shining in the distance.* • *The sea shone in the light of the moon.* **2** [T] to direct a light at sb/sth: *The policeman shone a torch on the stranger's face.*

shine² /ʃaɪn/ noun [sing] **1** a bright effect caused by light hitting a polished surface **2** the act of polishing sth so that it shines

shingle /ˈʃɪŋgl/ noun [U] small pieces of stone lying in a mass on a beach

'shin pad noun [C] a thick piece of material used to protect the shin when playing some sports

shiny /ˈʃaɪni/ adj (shinier; shiniest) causing a bright effect when in the sun or in light: *The shampoo leaves your hair soft and shiny.* • *a shiny new car*

★**ship**¹ /ʃɪp/ noun [C] a large boat used for carrying passengers or cargo by sea: *to travel by ship* • *to launch a ship*

> A **boat** is smaller than a ship. A **liner** is used to carry people for long distances called **voyages** and a **ferry** is used for short distances called **crossings**.

ship² /ʃɪp/ verb [T] (shipping; shipped) to send or carry sth by ship or by another type of transport

shipbuilder /ˈʃɪpbɪldə/ noun [C] a person or company who makes or builds ships –shipbuilding noun [U]

shipment /ˈʃɪpmənt/ noun **1** [U] the carrying of goods from one place to another **2** [C] a quantity of goods that are sent from one place to another

shipping /ˈʃɪpɪŋ/ noun [U] **1** ships in general or considered as a group **2** the carrying of goods from one place to another: *a shipping company*

shipwreck /ˈʃɪprek/ noun [C,U] an accident at sea in which a ship is destroyed by a storm, rocks, etc and sinks ••▸ A person or a ship that has suffered such an accident has been shipwrecked.

shipyard /ˈʃɪpjɑːd/ noun [C] a place where ships are repaired or built

shirk /ʃɜːk/ verb [I,T] to avoid doing sth that is difficult or unpleasant, especially because you are too lazy: *to shirk your responsibilities*

★**shirt** /ʃɜːt/ noun [C] a piece of clothing made of cotton, etc, worn on the upper part of the body

> A shirt usually has a **collar** at the neck, long or short **sleeves**, and **buttons** down the front.

••▸ picture on page C6

shiver /ˈʃɪvə/ verb [I] to shake slightly, especially because you are cold or frightened: *shivering with cold/fright* –shiver noun [C]: *The thought sent a shiver down my spine.*

shoal /ʃəʊl/ noun [C] a large group of fish that feed and swim together

★**shock**¹ /ʃɒk/ noun **1** [C,U] the feeling that you get when sth unpleasant happens suddenly; the situation that causes this feeling: *The sudden noise gave him a shock.* • *The bad news came as a shock to her.* • *I'm still suffering from shock at the news.* • *His mother is in a state of shock.* **2** [U] a serious medical condition of extreme weakness caused by damage to the body: *He was in/went into shock after the accident.* **3** [C] a violent shaking movement (caused by a crash, explosion, etc) **4** [C] = ELECTRIC SHOCK

★**shock**² /ʃɒk/ verb **1** [T] to cause an unpleasant feeling of surprise in sb: *We were shocked by his death.* • *I'm sorry, I didn't mean to shock you when I came in.* **2** [I,T] to make sb feel disgusted or offended: *These films deliberately set out to shock.* –shocked adj: *a shocked expression/look*

shocking /ˈʃɒkɪŋ/ adj **1** that offends or upsets people; that is morally wrong: *a shocking accident* • *shocking behaviour/news* **2** (especially Brit informal) very bad

shod past tense, past participle of SHOE²

shoddy /ˈʃɒdi/ adj **1** made carelessly or with poor quality materials: *shoddy goods* **2** dishonest or unfair –shoddily adv

S

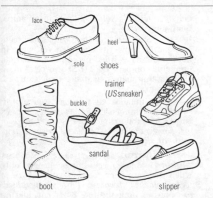

lace
heel
sole   shoes
trainer
(US sneaker)
buckle
sandal
boot   slipper

★**shoe**¹ /ʃuː/ **noun** [C] **1** a type of covering for the foot, usually made of leather or plastic: *a pair of shoes* • *running shoes* • *What size are your shoes/What is your shoe size?* • *I tried on a nice pair of shoes but they didn't fit.* **2** =HORSESHOE

IDIOM **in my, your, etc place/shoes** → PLACE¹

shoe² /ʃuː/ **verb** [T] (*pt, pp* **shod** /ʃɒd/) to fit a shoe on a horse

shoelace /ˈʃuːleɪs/ (*especially US* **shoestring**) **noun** [C] a long thin piece of material like string used to fasten a shoe: *to tie/untie a shoelace*

shoestring /ˈʃuːstrɪŋ/ (*especially US*) = SHOELACE

IDIOM **on a shoestring** using very little money: *to live on a shoestring*

shone *past tense, past participle* of SHINE¹

shoo /ʃuː/ **interj** (usually said to animals or small children) Go away! –**shoo** **verb** [T] (*pt, pp* **shooed**) shoo sb/sth away, off, out, etc to make sb/sth go away by saying 'shoo' and waving your hands

shook *past tense* of SHAKE¹

★**shoot**¹ /ʃuːt/ **verb** (*pt, pp* **shot** /ʃɒt/) **1** [I,T] shoot (sth) (at sb/sth) to fire a gun or another weapon: *Don't shoot!* • *She shot an arrow at the target, but missed it.* **2** [T] to injure or kill sb/sth with a gun: *The policeman was shot in the arm.* • *The soldier was shot dead.* **3** [I,T] to hunt and kill birds and animals with a gun as a sport: *He goes shooting at the weekends.* ••► Look at **hunting**. **4** [I,T] to move somewhere quickly and suddenly; to make sth move in this way: *The car shot past me at 100 miles per hour.* **5** [I] (of pain) to go very suddenly along part of your body: *The pain shot up my leg.* • *shooting pains in the chest* **6** [I,T] to make a film or photograph of sth: *They shot the scene ten times.* **7** [I] shoot (at sth) (in football, etc) to try to kick or hit the ball into the goal: *He should have shot instead of passing.* ••► noun **shot**

PHRASAL VERBS **shoot sb/sth down** to make sb/sth fall to the ground by shooting him/her/it: *The helicopter was shot down by a missile.*

shoot up to increase by a large amount; to grow very quickly: *Prices have shot up in the past year.*

shoot² /ʃuːt/ **noun** [C] a new part of a plant or tree

'**shooting star** **noun** [C] a piece of rock that burns with a bright light as it travels through space

★**shop**¹ /ʃɒp/ (*US* **store**) **noun** [C] a building or part of a building where things are bought and sold: *a cake/shoe shop* • *a corner shop* (= a local shop, usually at the corner of a street) • *When do the shops open?* • *a butcher's/baker's shop*

➤ We usually say **at the butcher's**, etc instead of 'at the butcher's shop', etc.

IDIOM **talk shop** → TALK¹

★**shop**² /ʃɒp/ **verb** [I] (**shopping; shopped**) shop (for sth) to go to a shop or shops in order to buy things: *He's shopping for some new clothes.*

➤ **Go shopping** is more common than **shop**: *We go shopping every Saturday.*

–**shopper** **noun** [C]

PHRASAL VERB **shop around (for sth)** to look at the price and quality of an item in different shops before you decide where to buy it

'**shop assistant** (*US* '**sales clerk**; **clerk**) **noun** [C] a person who works in a shop

'**shop** '**floor** **noun** [sing] (*Brit*) an area of a factory where things are made; the people who make things in a factory

shopkeeper /ˈʃɒpkiːpə/ (*US* '**storekeeper**) **noun** [C] a person who owns or manages a small shop

shoplifter /ˈʃɒplɪftə/ **noun** [C] a person who steals sth from a shop while pretending to be a customer ••► Look at the note at **thief**.

shoplifting /ˈʃɒplɪftɪŋ/ **noun** [U] the crime of stealing goods from a shop while pretending to be a customer: *He was arrested for shoplifting.* ••► Look at **lift**¹(6).

★**shopping** /ˈʃɒpɪŋ/ **noun** [U] **1** the activity of going to the shops and buying things: *We always do the shopping on a Friday night.* • *a shopping basket/bag/trolley* **2** (*especially Brit*) the things that you have bought in a shop

'**shopping centre** (*US* '**shopping mall**; **mall**) **noun** [C] a place where there are many shops, either outside or in a covered building ••► picture on page C8

★**shore** /ʃɔː/ **noun** [C,U] the land at the edge of a sea or lake

➤ **Ashore** means the same as 'on shore'.

shorn *past participle* of SHEAR

★**short**¹ /ʃɔːt/ **adj, adv 1** not measuring much from one end to the other: *a short line/distance/dress* • *This essay is rather short.* • *short hair* ••► opposite **long** ••► verb **shorten 2** less than the average height: *a short, fat man* ••► opposite **tall 3** not lasting a long time; brief: *a short visit/film* • *She left a short time ago.* • *to have a short memory* (= to only remember things that have happened

recently) ••➤ opposite **long** ••➤ verb **shorten**
4 short (of/on sth) not having enough of
what is needed: *Because of illness, the team is
two players short.* • *Good secretaries are in
short supply* (= there are not enough of
them). • *We're a bit short of money at the
moment.* • *Your essay is a bit short on detail.*
••➤ noun **shortage 5** suddenly: *She stopped
short when she saw the accident.* **6** short for
sth used as a shorter way of saying sth or as
an abbreviation: *'Bill' is short for 'William'.*
7 short (with sb) (used about a person)
speaking in an impatient and angry way to
sb ••➤ adverb **shortly**

IDIOMS **cut sth/sb short** to not allow sb to
finish speaking; to interrupt
fall short (of sth) to not be enough; to not
reach sth: *The pay rise fell short of the workers' demands.*
for short as a short form: *She's called 'Diana',
or 'Di' for short.*
go short (of sth) to be without enough (of
sth): *He made sure his family never went short
of food.*
in the long/short term → TERM¹
in short in a few words; briefly
run short (of sth) to have used up most of sth
so there is not much left: *We're running short
of coffee.*
short of sth/doing sth apart from; except for:
*Nothing short of a miracle will save the busi-
ness now.*
stop short of sth/doing sth → STOP¹

short² /ʃɔːt/ *noun* [C] **1** (*informal*) = SHORT
CIRCUIT **2** (*especially Brit*) a small strong alcoholic drink: *I prefer wine to shorts.*

shortage /ˈʃɔːtɪdʒ/ *noun* [C] a situation
where there is not enough of sth: *a food/
housing/water shortage* • *a shortage of
trained teachers*

,**short 'circuit** (also *informal* **short**) *noun*
[C] a bad electrical connection that causes a
machine to stop working —,**short-'circuit**
verb [I,T]: *The lights short-circuited.*

shortcoming /ˈʃɔːtkʌmɪŋ/ *noun* [C,usually
pl] a fault or weakness

,**short 'cut** *noun* [C] a quicker, easier or more
direct way to get somewhere or to do sth: *He
took a short cut to school through the park.*

shorten /ˈʃɔːtn/ *verb* [I,T] to become shorter
or to make sth shorter

shortfall /ˈʃɔːtfɔːl/ *noun* [C] **shortfall (in sth)**
the amount by which sth is less than you
need or expect

shorthand /ˈʃɔːthænd/ *noun* [U] a method of
writing quickly that uses signs or short
forms of words: *to write in shorthand* • *a
shorthand typist*

shortlist /ˈʃɔːtlɪst/ *noun* [C,usually sing] a list
of the best people for a job, etc who have been
chosen from all the people who want the job:
She's one of the four people on the shortlist.
—**shortlist** *verb*: *Six candidates were shortlisted
for the post.*

,**short-'lived** *adj* lasting only for a short time

shortly /ˈʃɔːtli/ *adv* **1** soon; not long: *The

manager will see you shortly.* **2** in an impatient, angry way

★**shorts** /ʃɔːts/ *noun* [pl] **1** a type of short trousers ending above the knee that you wear in
hot weather, while playing sports, etc
••➤ picture on page C6 **2** (*US*) a piece of loose
clothing that men wear under their trousers:
boxer shorts

➤ Notice that, because **shorts** is a plural
word, we cannot say, for example, 'a new
short'. The following are possible: *I need to
get some new shorts.* • *I need to get a new
pair of shorts.*

,**short-'sighted** *adj* **1** (*especially US* ,near-
'sighted) able to see things clearly only
when they are very close to you: *I have to
wear glasses because I'm short-sighted.*
••➤ opposite **long-sighted 2** not considering
what will probably happen in the future: *a
short-sighted attitude/policy*

,**short-'staffed** *adj* (used about an office, a
shop, etc) not having enough people to do the
work

,**short 'story** *noun* [C] a piece of writing that
is shorter than a novel

,**short-'term** *adj* lasting for a short period of
time from the present: *short-term plans/mem-
ory*

★**shot¹** /ʃɒt/ *noun* [C] **1** a shot (at sb/sth) an
act of firing a gun, etc, or the noise that this
makes: *to take a shot at the target* • *The
policeman fired a warning shot into the air.*
2 (in sport) the action of kicking, throwing or
hitting a ball in order to score a point or a
goal: *Owen scored with a low shot into the
corner of the net.* • *Good shot!* **3** a photograph
or a picture in a film: *I got some good shots of
the runners as they crossed the line.* **4** [usually
sing] (*informal*) a shot (at sth/at doing sth) a
try at doing sth; an attempt: *Let me have a
shot at it* (= let me try to do it). • *Just give it
your best shot* (= try as hard as you can). **5** a
small amount of a drug that is put into your
body using a needle **6** (often **the shot**) a
heavy metal ball that is thrown as a sport
(the shot-put)

IDIOMS **a long shot** → LONG¹
call the shots/tune → CALL¹
like a shot (*informal*) very quickly; without
stopping to think about it: *If someone invited
me on a free holiday, I'd go like a shot.*

shot² *past tense, past participle* of SHOOT¹

shotgun /ˈʃɒtɡʌn/ *noun* [C] a long gun that is
used for shooting small animals and birds

★**should** /ʃəd; *strong form* ʃʊd/ *modal verb*
(*negative* **should not**; *short form* **shouldn't**
/ˈʃʊdnt/) **1** (used for saying that it is right or
appropriate for sb to do sth, or for sth to
happen) ought to: *The police should do something about street crime in this area.* • *Children shouldn't be left on their own.* • *I'm
tired. I shouldn't have gone to bed so late/I
should have gone to bed earlier.* **2** used for
giving or for asking for advice: *You should
try that new restaurant.* • *Do you think I
should phone him?* • *What should I do?*

3 used for saying that you expect sth is true or will happen: *It's 4.30. They should be in New York by now.* ● *It should stop raining soon.* **4** (*Brit formal*) used with 'I/we' instead of 'would' in 'if' sentences: *I should be most grateful if you could send me…* **5** (*formal*) used after 'if' and 'in case' to refer to a possible event or situation: *If you should decide to accept, please phone us.* ● *Should you decide to accept…* **6** used as the past tense of 'shall' when we report what sb says: *He asked me if he should come today* (= he asked 'Shall I come today?'). **7** I should imagine, say, think, etc used to give opinions that you are not certain about

➤ For more information about modal verbs, look at the **Quick Grammar Reference** section at the back of this dictionary.

★**shoulder**[1] /ˈʃəʊldə/ *noun* **1** [C] the part of your body between your neck and the top of your arm: *I asked him why he'd done it but he just shrugged his shoulders* (= raised his shoulders to show that he did not know or care). ● *She fell asleep with her head on his shoulder.* ••➤ picture on page C5 **2** -**shouldered** (used to form compound adjectives) having the type of shoulders mentioned: *a broad-shouldered man* **3** [C] a part of a dress, coat, etc that covers the shoulders ••➤ Look at **hard shoulder**.

IDIOMS **a shoulder to cry on** used to describe a person who listens to your problems and understands how you feel
have a chip on your shoulder → **CHIP**[1]
rub shoulders with sb → **RUB**

shoulder[2] /ˈʃəʊldə/ *verb* [T] **1** to accept the responsibility for sth: *to shoulder the blame/responsibility for sth* **2** to push sb/sth with your shoulder

'**shoulder bag** *noun* [C] a type of bag that you carry over one shoulder with a long strap ••➤ synonym **handbag**

'**shoulder blade** *noun* [C] either of the two large flat bones on each side of your back, below your shoulders ••➤ picture on page C5

★**shout** /ʃaʊt/ *verb* **1** [I] shout (at/to sb); shout out to speak or cry out in a very loud voice: *There's no need to shout – I can hear you.* ● *The teacher shouted angrily at the boys.* ● *to shout out in pain/excitement* **2** [T] shout sth (at/to sb); shout sth out to say sth in a loud voice: *'Careful,' she shouted.* ● *The students kept shouting out the answers, so we stopped playing in the end.* ● *The captain shouted instructions to his team.* ••➤ Look at **scream**. –**shout** *noun* [C]

PHRASAL VERB **shout sb down** to shout so that sb who is speaking cannot be heard: *The speaker was shouted down by a group of protesters.*

shove /ʃʌv/ *verb* [I,T] (*informal*) to push with a sudden, rough movement: *Everybody in the crowd was pushing and shoving.* ● *The policeman shoved the thief into the back of the police car.* –**shove** *noun* [C,usually sing]: *to give sb/sth a shove*

shovel /ˈʃʌvl/ *noun* [C] a tool used for picking up and moving earth, snow, sand, etc ••➤ Look also at **spade**. ••➤ picture at **garden** –**shovel** *verb* [I,T] (**shovelling**; **shovelled**; (*US*) **shoveling** **shoveled**)

★**show**[1] /ʃəʊ/ *verb* (*pt* showed; *pp* shown /ʃəʊn/ or showed) **1** [T] show sb/sth (to sb); show sb (sth) to let sb see sb/sth: *I showed the letter to him.* ● *I showed him the letter.* ● *She showed me what she had bought.* ● *They're showing his latest film at our local cinema.* ● *She was showing signs of stress.* ● *This white T-shirt really shows the dirt.* ● *The picture showed him arguing with a photographer.* **2** [T] to make sth clear; to give information about sth: *Research shows that most people get too little exercise.* ● *This graph shows how prices have gone up in the last few years.* **3** [I] to be able to be seen; to appear: *I tried not to let my disappointment show.* **4** [T] to help sb to do sth by doing it yourself; to explain sth: *Can you show me how to put the disk in the computer?* **5** [T] to lead sb to or round a place; to explain how to go to a place: *I'll come with you and show you the way.* ● *Shall I show you to your room?* ● *A guide showed us round the museum.*

PHRASAL VERBS **show (sth) off** (*informal*) to try to impress people by showing them how clever you are or by showing them sth that you are proud of: *John was showing off by driving his new car very fast.*

show up (*informal*) to arrive, especially when sb is expecting you: *I thought you'd never show up.*

show (sth) up to allow sth to be seen: *The sunlight shows up those dirty marks on the window.*

show sb up (*informal*) to make sb embarrassed about your behaviour or appearance: *He showed her up by shouting at the waiter.*

★**show**[2] /ʃəʊ/ *noun* **1** [C] a type of entertainment performed for an audience: *a TV comedy show* ● *a quiz show* **2** [C,U] an occasion when a collection of things are brought together for people to look at: *a dog show* ● *a fashion show* ● *Paintings by local children will be on show at the town hall next week.* **3** [C,U] something that a person does or has in order to make people believe sth that is not true: *Although she hated him, she put on a show of politeness.* ● *His bravery is all show* (= he is not as brave as he pretends to be). **4** [sing] an occasion when you let sb see sth: *a show of emotion/gratitude/temper*

'**show business** (also *informal* **showbiz** /ˈʃəʊbɪz/) *noun* [U] the business of entertaining people, in the theatre, in films, on television, etc: *He's been in show business since he was five years old.*

showdown /ˈʃəʊdaʊn/ *noun* [C] a final argument, meeting or fight at the end of a long disagreement: *The management are preparing for a showdown with the union.*

★**shower**[1] /ˈʃaʊə/ *noun* [C] **1** a piece of equipment that produces a spray of water that you stand under to wash; the small room or part of a room that contains a shower: *The shower* *doesn't work.* • *She's in the shower.* • *I'd like a room with a shower, please.* ‣ picture on page C7 **2** an act of washing yourself by standing under a shower: *I'll just have a quick shower then we can go out.* **3** a short period of rain ‣ Look at **rain** and **acid rain**. **4** a lot of very small objects that fall or fly through the air together: *a shower of sparks/broken glass*

shower² /'ʃaʊə/ *verb* **1** [I,T] **shower (down) on sb/sth; shower sb with sth** to cover sb/sth with a lot of small falling objects: *Ash from the volcano showered down on the town.* • *People suffered cuts after being showered with broken glass.* **2** [I] to wash yourself under a shower: *I came back from my run, showered and got changed.*

showing /'ʃəʊɪŋ/ *noun* **1** [C] an act of showing a film, etc: *The second showing of the film begins at 8 o'clock.* **2** [sing] how sb/sth behaves; how successful sb/sth is: *On its present showing, the party should win the election.*

showjumping /'ʃəʊdʒʌmpɪŋ/ *noun* [U] a competition in which a person rides a horse over a series of fences (**jumps**)

shown *past participle* of **SHOW¹**

'show-off *noun* [C] a person who tries to impress others by showing them how clever he/she is, or by showing them sth he/she is proud of: *She's such a show-off, always boasting about how good she is at this and that.*

showroom /'ʃəʊruːm; -rɒm/ *noun* [C] a type of large shop where customers can look at goods such as cars, furniture and electrical items that are on sale

shrank *past tense* of **SHRINK**

shrapnel /'ʃræpnəl/ *noun* [U] small pieces of metal that fly around when a bomb explodes

shred¹ /ʃred/ *noun* **1** [C] a small thin piece of material that has been cut or torn off: *His clothes were torn to shreds by the rose bushes.* **2** a **shred of sth** [sing] (in negative sentences) a very small amount of sth: *There wasn't a shred of truth in her story.*

shred² /ʃred/ *verb* [T] (**shredding; shredded**) to tear or cut sth into shreds: *shredded cabbage*

shrewd /ʃruːd/ *adj* able to make good decisions because you understand a situation well: *a shrewd thinker/decision* –**shrewdly** *adv*

shriek /ʃriːk/ *verb* **1** [I] to make a short, loud, noise in a high voice: *She shrieked in fright.* • *The children were shrieking with laughter.* **2** [T] to say sth loudly in a high voice: '*Stop it!' she shrieked.* ‣ Look at **screech**. –**shriek** *noun* [C]

shrill /ʃrɪl/ *adj* (used about a sound) high and unpleasant: *a shrill cry*

shrimp /ʃrɪmp/ *noun* [C] a small sea creature with a shell and a lot of legs that turns pink when you cook it

> **Shrimps** are smaller than **prawns**.

‣ picture at **shellfish**

shrine /ʃram/ *noun* [C] a place that is important to a particular person or group of people

for religious reasons or because it is connected with a special person

'Oh no! My T-shirt has **shrunk**!'

'Oh no! My T-shirt has **stretched**!'

shrink /ʃrɪŋk/ *verb* (*pt* **shrank** /ʃræŋk/ or **shrunk** /ʃrʌŋk/; *pp* **shrunk**) **1** [I,T] to become smaller or make sth smaller: *My T-shirt shrank in the wash.* • *Television has shrunk the world.* • *The rate of inflation has shrunk to 4%.* **2** [I] to move back because you are frightened or shocked: *We shrank back against the wall when the dog appeared.*

PHRASAL VERB **shrink from sth/doing sth** to not want to do sth because you find it unpleasant

shrivel /'ʃrɪvl/ *verb* [I,T] (**shrivelling; shrivelled**; *US* **shriveling; shriveled**) **shrivel (sth) (up)** to become smaller, especially because of dry conditions: *The plants shrivelled up and died in the hot weather.*

shroud¹ /ʃraʊd/ *noun* [C] a cloth or sheet that is put round a dead body before it is buried

shroud² /ʃraʊd/ *verb* [T] **shroud sth (in sth)** (usually passive) to cover or hide sth

Shrove Tuesday /ˌʃrəʊv 'tjuːzdeɪ; -di/ *noun* [C] the day before a period of forty days (**Lent**) during which some Christians do not eat certain foods

> In some countries the period before Shrove Tuesday is celebrated as **carnival**. In Britain many people eat **pancakes** on this day.

shrub /ʃrʌb/ *noun* [C] a small bush

shrubbery /'ʃrʌbəri/ *noun* [C] (*pl* **shrubberies**) an area where a lot of small bushes have been planted

S

shrug /ʃrʌg/ verb [I,T] (**shrugging; shrugged**) to lift your shoulders as a way of showing that you do not know sth or are not interested: *'Who knows?' he said and shrugged.* ● *'It doesn't matter to me,' he said, shrugging his shoulders.* •➤ picture on page S8 –**shrug** noun [C]: *I asked him if he was sorry and he just answered with a shrug.*

PHRASAL VERB **shrug sth off** to not allow sth to affect you in a bad way: *An actor has to learn to shrug off criticism.*

shrunk → **SHRINK**

shudder /ʃʌdə/ verb [I] to suddenly shake hard, especially because of an unpleasant feeling or thought: *Just to think about the accident makes me shudder.* ● *The engine shuddered violently and then stopped.* –**shudder** noun [C]

shuffle¹ /ʃʌfl/ verb **1** [I] to walk by sliding your feet along instead of lifting them off the ground: *The child shuffled past, wearing her mother's shoes.* **2** [I,T] to move your body or feet around because you are uncomfortable or nervous: *The audience were so bored that they began to shuffle in their seats.* **3** [I,T] to mix a pack of playing cards before a game: *It's your turn to shuffle.* ● *She shuffled the cards carefully.*

shuffle² /ʃʌfl/ noun [C,usually sing] **1** a way of walking without lifting your feet off the ground **2** an act of shuffling cards

shun /ʃʌn/ verb [T] (**shunning; shunned**) (*written*) to avoid sb/sth; to keep away from sb/sth: *She was shunned by her family when she married him.*

★**shut¹** /ʃʌt/ verb (*pres part* **shutting;** *pt, pp* **shut**) **1** [I,T] to make sth closed; to become closed: *Could you shut the door, please?* ● *I can't shut my suitcase.* ● *Shut your books, please.* ● *He shut his eyes and tried to go to sleep.* ● *This window won't shut properly.* ● *The doors open and shut automatically.* **2** [I,T] (used about a shop, restaurant, etc) to stop doing business for the day; to close: *What time do the shops shut on Saturday?* **3** [T] to prevent sb/sth from leaving a place; to close a door on sth: *She shut herself in her room and refused to come out.* ● *Tony shut his fingers in the door of the car.*

PHRASAL VERBS **shut sb/sth away** to keep sb/ sth in a place where people cannot find or see him/her/it

shut (sth) down (used about a factory, etc) to close for a long time or for ever: *Financial problems forced the business to shut down.*

shut sb/sth off (from sth) to keep sb/sth apart from sth: *He shuts himself off from the rest of the world.*

shut sb/sth out to keep sb/sth out: *He tried to shut out all thoughts of the accident.*

shut (sb) up (*informal*) **1** to stop talking; to be quiet: *I wish you'd shut up!* **2** to make sb stop talking

shut sb/sth up (in sth) to put sb/sth somewhere and stop him/her leaving: *He was shut up in prison for nearly ten years.*

shut² /ʃʌt/ adj (not before a noun) **1** in a closed position: *Make sure the door is shut properly before you leave.*

➤ Remember that we can use **closed** before a noun: *a closed door*, but not **shut**.

2 not open to the public: *The restaurant was shut so we went to one round the corner.*

IDIOM **keep your mouth shut** → **MOUTH¹**

shutter /ʃʌtə/ noun [C] **1** a wooden or metal cover that is fixed outside a window and that can be opened or shut. A shop's shutter usually slides down from the top of the shop window. •➤ picture at **curtain 2** the part at the front of a camera that opens for a very short time to let light in so that a photograph can be taken

shuttle /ʃʌtl/ noun [C] a plane, bus or train that travels regularly between two places

shuttlecock /ʃʌtlkɒk/ noun [C] (in the sport of badminton) the small, light object that is hit over the net •➤ picture on page S2

★**shy¹** /ʃaɪ/ adj **1** nervous and uncomfortable about meeting and speaking to people; showing that sb feels like this: *She's very shy with strangers.* ● *a shy smile* **2** shy (of/about sth/ doing sth) frightened to do sth or to become involved in sth: *She's not shy of telling people what she thinks.* –**shyly** adv –**shyness** noun [U]: *He didn't overcome his shyness till he had left school.*

shy² /ʃaɪ/ verb (*pres part* **shying;** *3rd pers sing pres* **shies;** *pt, pp* **shied**) [I] (used about a horse) to suddenly move back or sideways in fear

PHRASAL VERB **shy away from sth/from doing sth** to avoid doing sth because you are afraid

sibling /ˈsɪblɪŋ/ noun [C] (*formal*) a brother or a sister •➤ In ordinary language we use **brother(s)** and **sister(s)**: *Have you got any brothers and sisters?*

★**sick¹** /sɪk/ adj **1** not well; ill: *a sick child* ● *Do you get paid for days when you're off sick* (= from work)? ● *You're too ill to work today – you should phone in sick.*

➤ Note that **be sick** in British English usually means 'to bring up food from the stomach; vomit'.

2 the sick noun [pl] people who are ill **3** feeling ill in your stomach so that you may bring up food through your mouth (vomit): *I feel sick – I think it was that fish I ate.* ● *Don't eat any more or you'll make yourself sick.* •➤ Look at **nausea, travel-sick, seasick, airsick** and **carsick**. **4** sick of sb/sth feeling bored or annoyed because you have had too much of sb/sth: *I'm sick of my job.* ● *I'm sick of tidying up your mess!* **5** sick (at/about sth) very annoyed or disgusted by sth: *He felt sick at the sight of so much waste.* **6** (*informal*) mentioning disease, suffering, death, etc in a cruel or disgusting way: *He offended everyone with a sick joke about blind people.*

IDIOMS **be sick** to bring up food from the stomach; vomit: *It's common for women to be sick in the first months of pregnancy.*

make sb sick to make sb very angry: *Oh, stop complaining. You make me sick!*

S

sick to death of sb/sth feeling tired of or annoyed by sb/sth: *I'm sick to death of his grumbling.*

sick² /sɪk/ **noun** [U] food that sb has brought up from his/her stomach; vomit: *There was sick all over the car seat.*

sicken /'sɪkən/ **verb** [T] to make sb feel disgusted: *The sight of people fighting sickens me.* –**sickening** adj: *His head made a sickening sound as it hit the road.*

'**sick leave noun** [U] a period spent away from work, etc because of illness: *Mike's been off on sick leave since March.*

sickly /'sɪkli/ **adj 1** (used about a person) weak and often ill: *a sickly child* **2** unpleasant; causing you to feel ill: *the sickly smell of rotten fruit*

sickness /'sɪknəs/ **noun 1** [U] the state of being ill: *A lot of workers are absent because of sickness.* **2** [U] a feeling in your stomach that may make you bring up food through your mouth: *Symptoms of the disease include sickness and diarrhoea.* **3** [C,U] a particular type of illness: *pills for seasickness* ● *Sleeping sickness is carried by the tsetse fly.*

★ **side¹** /saɪd/ **noun** [C] **1** one of the flat outer surfaces of sth: *A cube has six sides.* **2** -**sided** (used to form compound adjectives) having the number of sides mentioned: *a six-sided coin* **3** one of the surfaces of sth except the top, bottom, front or back: *I went round to the side of the building.* ● *The side of the car was damaged.* **4** the edge of sth, away from the middle: *Make sure you stay at the side of the road when you're cycling.* ● *We moved to one side to let the doctor get past.* **5** the area to the left or right of sth; the area in front of or behind sth: *We live (on) the other side of the main road.* ● *It's more expensive to live on the north side of town.* ● *In Japan they drive on the left-hand side of the road.* ● *She sat at the side of his bed/at his bedside.* **6** either of the two flat surfaces of sth thin: *Write on both sides of the paper.* **7** the right or the left part of your body, especially from under your arm to the top of your leg: *She lay on her side.* ● *The soldier stood with his hands by his sides.* **8** either of two or more people or groups who are fighting, playing, arguing, etc against each other: *The two sides agreed to stop fighting.* ● *the winning/losing side* ● *Whose side are you on?* (= Who do you want to win?) **9** what is said by one person or group that is different from what is said by another: *I don't know whose side of the story to believe.* **10** your mother's or your father's family: *There is no history of illness on his mother's side.*

IDIOMS **get on the right/wrong side of sb** to please/annoy sb: *He tried to get on the right side of his new boss.*

look on the bright side → **LOOK¹**

on/from all sides; on/from every side in/from all directions

on the big, small, high, etc side (*informal*) slightly too big, small, high, etc

on the safe side → **SAFE¹**

put sth on/to one side; leave sth on one side to leave or keep sth so that you can use it or deal with it later: *You should put some money to one side for the future.*

side by side next to each other; close together: *They walked side by side along the road.*

take sides (with sb) to show that you support one person rather than another in an argument: *Parents should never take sides when their children are quarrelling.*

side² /saɪd/ **verb**

PHRASAL VERB **side with sb (against sb)** to support sb in an argument

sideboard /'saɪdbɔːd/ **noun** [C] a type of low cupboard about as high as a table, that is used for storing plates, etc in a room that is used for eating (**dining room**) •► picture on page C7

sideburns /'saɪdbɜːnz/ **noun** [pl] hair that grows down a man's face in front of his ears

'**side effect noun** [C] **1** the unpleasant effect that a drug may have in addition to its useful effects: *Side effects of the drug include nausea and dizziness.* **2** an unexpected effect of sth that happens in addition to the intended effect: *One of the side effects when the chemical factory closed was that fish returned to the river.*

sideline /'saɪdlaɪn/ **noun 1** [C] something that you do in addition to your regular job, especially to earn extra money: *He's an engineer, but he repairs cars as a sideline.* **2** **sidelines** [pl] the lines that mark the two long sides of the area used for playing sports such as football, tennis, etc; the area behind this

IDIOM **on the sidelines** not involved in an activity; not taking part in sth

sidelong /'saɪdlɒŋ/ **adj** directed from the side; sideways: *a sidelong glance*

'**side road noun** [C] a small road which joins a bigger main road

'**side street noun** [C] a narrow or less important street near a main street

sidetrack /'saɪdtræk/ **verb** [T] (usually passive) to make sb forget what he/she is doing or talking about and start doing or talking about sth less important

sidewalk /'saɪdwɔːk/ (*US*) = **PAVEMENT**

sideways /'saɪdweɪz/ **adv, adj 1** to, towards or from one side: *He jumped sideways to avoid being hit.* **2** with one of the sides at the top: *We'll have to turn the sofa sideways to get it through the door.*

sidle /'saɪdl/ **verb** [I] **sidle up/over (to sb/sth)** to move towards sb/sth in a nervous way, as if you do not want anyone to notice you

siege /siːdʒ/ **noun** [C,U] a situation in which an army surrounds a town for a long time or the police surround a building so that nobody can get in or out

siesta /si'estə/ **noun** [C] a short sleep or rest that people take in the afternoon, especially in hot countries: *to have/take a siesta*

sieve /sɪv/ **noun** [C] a type of kitchen tool that has a metal or plastic net, used for separating solids from liquids or very small pieces of food from large pieces: *Pour the soup through a sieve to get rid of any lumps.* ⋯▸ picture at **kitchen** –**sieve** *verb* [T]: *to sieve flour*

sift /sɪft/ *verb* **1** [T] to pass flour, sugar or a similar substance through a kitchen tool (a sieve) in order to remove any lumps: *to sift flour/sugar* **2** [I,T] sift (through) sth to examine sth very carefully: *It took weeks to sift through all the evidence.*

★**sigh** /saɪ/ *verb* **1** [I] to let out a long, deep breath that shows you are tired, sad, disappointed, etc: *She sighed with disappointment at the news.* **2** [T] to say sth with a sigh: *'I'm so tired,' he sighed.* **3** [I] to make a long sound like a sigh –**sigh** *noun* [C]
   IDIOM heave a sigh → **HEAVE¹**

★**sight¹** /saɪt/ *noun* **1** [U] the ability to see: *He lost his sight in the war* (= he became blind). ● *My grandmother has very poor sight.* **2** -**sighted** (used to form compound adjectives) having eyes that are weak in a particular way: *I'm short-sighted/long-sighted.* **3** [sing] the sight of sb/sth the act of seeing sb/sth: *I feel ill at the sight of blood.* **4** [U] a position where sb/sth can be seen: *They waited until the plane was in/within sight and then fired.* ● *When we get over this hill the town should come into sight.* ● *She didn't let the child out of her sight.* **5** [C] something that you see: *The burned-out building was a terrible sight.* **6** sights [pl] places of interest that are often visited by tourists: *When you come to New York I'll show you the sights.* **7** a sight [sing] (*informal*) a person or thing that looks strange or amusing **8** [C, usually pl] the part of a gun that you look through in order to aim it
   IDIOMS at first glance/sight → **FIRST¹**
   catch sight/a glimpse of sb/sth → **CATCH¹**
   in sight likely to happen or come soon: *A peace settlement is in sight.*
   lose sight of sb/sth → **LOSE**
   on sight as soon as you see sb/sth: *The soldiers were ordered to shoot the enemy on sight.*

sight² /saɪt/ *verb* [T] to see sb/sth, especially after looking out for him/her/it

sighting /'saɪtɪŋ/ *noun* [C] an occasion when sb/sth is seen: *the first sighting of a new star*

sightseeing /'saɪtsiːɪŋ/ *noun* [U] visiting the sights of a city, etc as a tourist: *We did some sightseeing in Rome.*

sightseer /'saɪtsiːə/ *noun* [C] a person who visits the sights of a city, etc as a tourist ⋯▸ Look at **tourist.**

★**sign¹** /saɪn/ *noun* [C] **1** sign (of sth) something that shows that sb/sth is present, exists or may happen: *The patient was showing some signs of improvement.* ● *As we drove into the village there wasn't a sign of life anywhere* (= we couldn't see anyone). **2** a piece of wood, paper, etc that has writing or a picture on it that gives you a piece of information, an instruction or a warning: *What does that sign say?* ● *a road sign* ● *Follow the signs to Banbury.* ⋯▸ picture at **roundabout** **3** a movement that you make with your head,

hands or arms that has a particular meaning: *I made a sign for him to follow me.* ● *I'll give you a sign when it's time for you to speak.* **4** a type of shape, mark or symbol that has a particular meaning: *In mathematics, a cross is a plus sign.* **5** (also sign of the 'zodiac) one of the twelve divisions or symbols of the zodiac: *I'm a Leo. What sign are you?*

★**sign²** /saɪn/ *verb* **1** [I,T] to write your name on a letter, document, etc to show that you have written it or that you agree with what it says: *'Could you sign here, please?'* ● *I forgot to sign the cheque.* ● *The two presidents signed the treaty.* ⋯▸ noun signature **2** [T] sign sb (up) to get sb to sign a contract to work for you: *Real Madrid have signed two new players.* **3** [I] to communicate using sign language
   PHRASAL VERBS sign in/out to write your name to show you have arrived at or left a hotel, club, etc
   sign up (for sth) to agree formally to do sth: *I've signed up for evening classes.*

★**signal** /'sɪɡnəl/ *noun* [C] **1** a sign, action or sound that sends a particular message: *When I give (you) the signal, run!* **2** an event, action or fact that shows that sth exists or is likely to happen: *The fall in unemployment is a clear signal that the economy is improving.* **3** a set of lights used to give information to train drivers **4** a series of radio waves, etc that are sent out or received: *a signal from a satellite* –**signal** *verb* [I,T] (signalling; signalled; *US* signaling; signaled): *She was signalling wildly that something was wrong.*

signatory /'sɪɡnətri/ *noun* [C] (*pl* signatories) signatory (to sth) one of the people or countries that sign an agreement, etc

★**signature** /'sɪɡnətʃə/ *noun* [C] a person's name, written by that person and always written in the same way: *I couldn't read his signature.* ⋯▸ verb sign

significance /sɪɡ'nɪfɪkəns/ *noun* [U] the importance or meaning of sth: *Few people realized the significance of the discovery.*

★**significant** /sɪɡ'nɪfɪkənt/ *adj* **1** important or large enough to be noticed: *Police said that the time of the murder was extremely significant.* ● *There has been a significant improvement in your work.* **2** having a particular meaning: *It could be significant that he took out life insurance shortly before he died.* –**significantly** *adv*: *Attitudes have changed significantly since the 1960s.*

signify /'sɪɡnɪfaɪ/ *verb* [T] (*pres part* signifying; *3rd pers sing pres* signifies; *pt, pp* signified) (*formal*) **1** to be a sign of sth; to mean: *What do those lights signify?* **2** to express or indicate sth: *They signified their agreement by raising their hands.*

'**sign language** *noun* [U] a language used especially by people who cannot hear or speak, using the hands to make signs instead of spoken words

signpost /'saɪnpəʊst/ *noun* [C] a sign at the side of a road that gives information about

S

directions and distances to towns ••➤ picture at **roundabout**

Sikh /siːk/ noun [C] a member of one of the religions of India (**Sikhism**) that developed from Hinduism but teaches that there is only one god –**Sikhism** /'siːkɪzəm/ noun [U]

★**silence** /'saɪləns/ noun **1** [U] no noise or sound at all: *There must be silence during examinations.* **2** [C,U] a period when nobody speaks or makes a noise: *My question was met with an awkward silence.* ● *We ate in silence.* **3** [U] not making any comments about sth –**silence verb** [T]

silencer /'saɪlənsə/ (*US* **muffler**) noun [C] **1** a device which is fixed to the long tube under a vehicle (**exhaust pipe**) to reduce the noise made by the engine ••➤ picture at **motorbike 2** the part of a gun that reduces the noise when it is fired

★**silent** /'saɪlənt/ adj **1** where there is no noise; making no noise; very quiet: *The house was empty and silent.* **2** silent (on/about sth) refusing to speak about sth: *The policeman told her she had the right to remain silent.* **3** not using spoken words: *a silent prayer/protest* **4** (of a letter) not pronounced: *The 'b' in 'comb' is silent.* –**silently adv**

silhouette /ˌsɪluˈet/ noun [C] the dark solid shape of sb/sth seen against a light background –**silhouetted adj**

silicon chip /ˌsɪlɪkən 'tʃɪp/ noun [C] (*computing*) a piece of a chemical element (**silicon**) that is used in computers, etc

silk /sɪlk/ noun [U] the soft smooth cloth that is made from threads produced by an insect (a **silkworm**): *a silk shirt/dress*

silky /'sɪlki/ adj smooth, soft and shiny; like silk: *silky hair*

sill /sɪl/ noun [C] a shelf that is at the bottom of a window, either inside or outside: *a window sill*

★**silly** /'sɪli/ adj (**sillier, silliest**) **1** not showing thought or understanding; foolish: *a silly mistake* ● *Don't be so silly!* ••➤ opposite **sensible 2** appearing ridiculous, so that people will laugh: *I'm not wearing that hat – I'd look silly in it.* –**silliness noun** [U]

silt /sɪlt/ noun [U] sand, soil or mud that collects at the sides or on the bottom of a river

★**silver¹** /'sɪlvə/ noun [U] **1** (*symbol* **Ag**) a valuable grey-white metal that is used for making jewellery, coins, etc: *a silver spoon/necklace* ● *That's a nice ring. Is it silver?* **2** coins made from silver or sth that looks like silver **3** objects that are made of silver, for example knives, forks, spoons, dishes: *The thieves stole some jewellery and some valuable silver.*
IDIOM every cloud has a silver lining → **CLOUD¹**

★**silver²** /'sɪlvə/ adj **1** having the colour of silver: *a silver sports car* **2** celebrating the 25th anniversary of sth: *They're celebrating their silver wedding this year.* ••➤ Look at **diamond** and **golden**.

ˌsilver 'medal (also **silver**) noun [C] a small flat round piece of silver that is given to the

person or team that comes second in a sports competition: *to win a silver medal at the Olympic Games* ••➤ Look at **gold medal** and **bronze medal**. –ˌsilver 'medallist noun [C]

ˌsilver 'wedding noun [C] the 25th anniversary of a wedding ••➤ Look at the 25th anniversary of a wedding ••➤ Look at **golden wedding** and **diamond wedding**.

silvery /'sɪlvəri/ adj having the appearance or colour of silver: *an old lady with silvery hair*

★**similar** /'sɪmələ/ adj similar (to sb/sth); similar (in sth) like sb/sth but not exactly the same: *Our houses are very similar in size.* ● *Your handwriting is very similar to mine.* ••➤ opposite **different** or **dissimilar** –**similarly adv**: *The plural of 'shelf' is 'shelves'. Similarly, the plural of 'wolf' is 'wolves'.*

similarity /ˌsɪməˈlærəti/ noun (*pl* **similarities**) **1** [U,sing] similarity (to sb/sth); similarity (in sth) the state of being like sb/sth but not exactly the same: *She bears a remarkable/striking similarity to her mother.* **2** [C] a similarity (between A and B); a similarity (in/of sth) a characteristic that people or things have which makes them similar: *Although there are some similarities between the two towns, there are a lot of differences too.* ● *similarities in/of style*

simmer /'sɪmə/ verb [I,T] to cook gently in a liquid that is almost boiling

★**simple** /'sɪmpl/ adj **1** easy to understand, do or use; not difficult or complicated: *This dictionary is written in simple English.* ● *a simple task/method/solution* ● *I can't just leave the job. It's not as simple as that.* **2** without decoration or unnecessary extra things; plain and basic: *a simple black dress* ● *The food is simple but perfectly cooked.* **3** (used about a person or a way of life) natural and not complicated: *a simple life in the country* **4** not intelligent; slow to understand **5** used for saying that the thing you are talking about is the only thing that is important or true: *I'm not going to buy it for the simple reason that* (= only because) *I haven't got enough money.*

simplicity /sɪmˈplɪsəti/ noun [U] **1** the quality of being easy to understand, do or use: *We all admired the simplicity of the plan.* **2** the quality of having no decoration or unnecessary extra things; being natural and not complicated: *I like the simplicity of her paintings.*

simplify /'sɪmplɪfaɪ/ verb [T] (*pres part* **simplifying**; *3rd pers sing pres* **simplifies**; *pt, pp* **simplified**) to make sth easier to do or understand; to make sth less complicated: *The process of applying for visas has been simplified.* –**simplification** /ˌsɪmplɪfɪˈkeɪʃn/ noun [C,U]

simplistic /sɪmˈplɪstɪk/ adj making a problem, situation, etc seem less difficult and complicated than it really is

simply /'sɪmpli/ adv **1** used to emphasize how easy or basic sth is: *Simply add hot water and stir.* **2** (used to emphasize an adjective) completely; absolutely: *That meal was simply excellent.* **3** in a way that makes sth easy to understand: *Could you explain it more simply?* **4** in a simple, basic way; without decoration or unnecessary extra things: *They live simply, with very few luxuries.* **5** only; just: *There's no need to get angry. The whole problem is simply a misunderstanding.*

simulate /ˈsɪmjuleɪt/ *verb* [T] to create certain conditions that exist in real life using computers, models, etc, usually for study or training purposes: *The astronauts trained in a machine that simulates conditions in space.* –**simulation** /ˌsɪmjuˈleɪʃn/ *noun* [C,U]: *a computer simulation of a nuclear attack*

simultaneous /ˌsɪmlˈteɪniəs/ *adj* happening or done at exactly the same time as sth else –**simultaneously** *adv*

sin /sɪn/ *noun* [C,U] an action or way of behaving that is not allowed by a religion: *He believes it is a sin for two people to live together without being married.* –**sin** *verb* [I] (**sinning; sinned**) –**sinner** *noun* [C]

★**since** /sɪns/ *adv, conj, prep* **1** from a particular time in the past until a later time in the past or until now: *My parents bought this house in 1975 and we've been living here ever since.* • *I've been working in a bank ever since I left school.* • *It was the first time they'd won since 1974.* • *I haven't seen him since last Tuesday.* • *She has had a number of jobs since leaving university.*

> We use both **since** and **for** to talk about how long something has been happening. We use **since** when we are talking about the *beginning* of the period of time, and **for** when we are talking about the *length* of the period of time: *I've known her since 1997.* • *I've known her for three years.*

2 at a time after a particular time in the past: *We were divorced two years ago and she has since married someone else.* **3** because; as: *Since they've obviously forgotten to phone me, I'll have to phone them.*

★**sincere** /sɪnˈsɪə/ *adj* **1** (used about a person) really meaning or believing what you say; not pretending: *Do you think she was being sincere when she said she admired me?* **2** (used about a person's feelings, beliefs or behaviour) true; showing what you really mean or feel: *Please accept our sincere thanks/apologies.* ••➤ opposite **insincere** –**sincerely** *adv*: *I am sincerely grateful to you for all your help.* • *Yours sincerely, ...* (= at the end of a formal letter) –**sincerity** /sɪnˈserəti/ *noun* [U] ••➤ opposite **insincerity**

sinful /ˈsɪnfl/ *adj* breaking a religious law; immoral

★**sing** /sɪŋ/ *verb* [I,T] (*pt* **sang** /sæŋ/; *pp* **sung** /sʌŋ/) to make musical sounds with your voice: *He always sings when he's in the bath.* • *The birds were singing outside my window.* • *She sang all her most popular songs at the concert.* –**singing** *noun* [U]: *singing lessons*

singe /sɪndʒ/ *verb* [I,T] (*pres part* **singeing**) to burn the surface of sth slightly, usually by accident; to be burned in this way

singer /ˈsɪŋə/ *noun* [C] a person who sings, or whose job is singing, especially in public: *an opera singer*

★**single¹** /ˈsɪŋɡl/ *adj* **1** (only *before* a noun) only one: *He gave her a single red rose.* • *I managed to finish the whole job in a single afternoon.* • *I went to a single-sex* (= for boys only or girls only) *school.* **2** (only *before* a noun) used to emphasize that you are talking about each individual item of a group or series: *You answered every single question correctly. Well done!* **3** not married: *Are you married or single?* • *a single man/woman* **4** (only *before* a noun) for the use of only one person: *I'd like to book a single room, please.* ••➤ Look at the note at **bed¹**. **5** (also **one-way**) (only *before* a noun) (used about a ticket or the price of a ticket) for a journey to a particular place, but not back again: *How much is the single fare to Rome?* ••➤ Look at **return²**(5).

IDIOM in single file → **FILE¹**

single² /ˈsɪŋɡl/ *noun* **1** [C] a ticket for a journey to a particular place, but not back again: *Two singles to Hull, please.* ••➤ Look at **return²**(5). **2** [C] a CD, tape, etc that has only one song on each side; the main song on this tape or CD: *Catatonia's new single* ••➤ Look at **album**. **3** [C] a bedroom for one person in a hotel, etc ••➤ Look at **double¹**(5). **4 singles** [pl] people who are not married and do not have a romantic relationship with sb else **5 singles** [pl] a game of tennis, etc in which one player plays against one other player ••➤ Look at **doubles**.

single³ /ˈsɪŋɡl/ *verb*

PHRASAL VERB single sb/sth out (for sth) to give special attention or treatment to one person or thing from a group: *She was singled out for criticism.*

single-'handed *adj, adv* on your own with nobody helping you

single-'minded *adj* having one clear aim or goal which you are determined to achieve –**single-mindedness** *noun* [U]

single 'parent *noun* [C] a person who looks after his/her child or children without a husband, wife or partner: *a single-parent family*

singly /ˈsɪŋɡli/ *adv* one at a time; individually: *You can buy the tapes either singly or in packs of three.*

singular /ˈsɪŋɡjələ/ *adj* **1** (*grammar*) in the form that is used for talking about one person or thing only: *'Table' is a singular noun; 'tables' is a plural noun.* ••➤ Look at **plural**. **2** (*written*) unusual –**singular** *noun* [sing] (*grammar*) : *The word 'clothes' has no singular.* • *What's the singular of 'people'?*

sinister /ˈsɪnɪstə/ *adj* seeming evil or dangerous; making you feel that sth bad will happen: *There's something sinister about him. He frightens me.*

★**sink¹** /sɪŋk/ *verb* (*pt* **sank** /sæŋk/; *pp* **sunk** /sʌŋk/) **1** [I,T] to go down or make sth go down under the surface of liquid or a soft substance: *If you throw a stone into water, it sinks.* • *My feet sank into the mud.* ••➤ picture at **float 2** [I] (used about a person) to move downwards, usually by falling or sitting down: *I came home and sank into a chair, exhausted.* **3** [I] to get lower; to fall to a lower position or level: *We watched the sun sink slowly below the horizon.* **4** [I] to decrease in value, number, amount, strength, etc

IDIOM **your heart sinks** → **HEART**

PHRASAL VERBS **sink in** (used about information, an event, an experience, etc) to be completely understood or realized: *It took a long time for the terrible news to sink in.*

sink in; sink into sth (used about a liquid) to go into sth solid; to be absorbed

★ **sink²** /sɪŋk/ *noun* [C] a large open container in a kitchen, with taps to supply water, where you wash things ·► picture on page C7 ·► Look at **washbasin**.

sinus /'saɪnəs/ *noun* [C] (often plural) one of the spaces in the bones of your face that are connected to your nose: *I've got a terrible cold and my sinuses are blocked.* ● *a sinus infection*

sip /sɪp/ *verb* [I,T] (**sipping; sipped**) to drink, taking only a very small amount of liquid into your mouth at a time: *We sat in the sun, sipping lemonade.* –**sip** *noun* [C]

siphon (also **syphon**) /'saɪfn/ *verb* [T] **1 siphon sth into/out of sth; siphon sth off/out** to remove a liquid from a container, often into another container, through a tube **2 siphon sth off; siphon sth (from/out of sb/sth)** to take money from a company illegally over a period of time

★ **sir** /sɜː/ *noun* **1** [sing] used as a polite way of speaking to a man whose name you do not know, for example in a shop or restaurant, or to show respect: *I'm afraid we haven't got your size, sir.* ·► Look at **madam**. **2** [C] used at the beginning of a formal letter to a male person or male people: *Dear Sir...* ● *Dear Sirs...* ·► Look at **Madam**. **3** /sə/ [sing] the title that is used in front of the name of a man who has received one of the highest British honours

siren /'saɪrən/ *noun* [C] a device that makes a long, loud sound as a warning or signal: *an air-raid siren* ● *Three fire engines raced past, sirens wailing.*

★ **sister** /'sɪstə/ *noun* [C] **1** a girl or woman who has the same parents as another person: *I've got one brother and two sisters.* ● *We're sisters.* ·► Look at **half-sister** and **stepsister**. In English there is no common word that means 'both brothers and sisters': *Have you got any brothers and sisters?* The word **sibling** is very formal. **2** (often **Sister**) (*Brit*) a female hospital nurse in a high position **3 Sister** a member of certain female religious groups; a nun **4** (usually used as an adjective) a thing that belongs to the same type or group as sth else: *We have a sister company in Japan.* **5** (*informal*) a woman who you feel close to because she is a member of the same society, group, etc as you

'sister-in-law *noun* [C] (*pl* **sisters-in-law**) **1** the sister of your husband or wife **2** the wife of your brother

★ **sit** /sɪt/ *verb* (*pres part* **sitting**; *pt, pp* **sat** /sæt/) **1** [I] to rest your weight on your bottom, for example in a chair: *We sat in the garden all afternoon.* ● *She was sitting on the sofa, talking to her mother.* **2** [T] **sit sb (down)** to put sb into a sitting position; make sb sit down: *He picked up his daughter and sat her down on a chair.* ● *She sat me down and offered me a cup of tea.* **3** [I] to be in a particular place or position: *The letter sat on the table for several days before anybody opened it.* **4** [T] (*Brit*) to take an exam: *If I fail, will I be able to sit the exam again?* **5** [I] (*formal*) (used about an official group of people) to have a meeting or series of meetings

IDIOM **sit on the fence** to avoid saying which side of an argument you support

PHRASAL VERBS **sit about/around** (*informal*) to spend time doing nothing active or useful: *We just sat around chatting all afternoon.*

sit back to relax and not take an active part in what other people are doing: *Sit back and take it easy while I make dinner.*

sit down to lower your body into a sitting position: *He sat down in an armchair.*

sit sth out 1 to stay in a place and wait for sth unpleasant or boring to finish **2** to not take part in a dance, game, etc

sit through sth to stay in your seat until sth boring or long has finished

sit up 1 to move into a sitting position when you have been lying down or to make your back straight: *Sit up straight and concentrate!* **2** to not go to bed although it is very late: *We sat up all night talking.*

sitcom /'sɪtkɒm/ (also *formal* ,**situation 'comedy**) *noun* [C,U] a funny programme on television that shows the same characters in different amusing situations each week

site /saɪt/ *noun* [C] **1** a piece of land where a building was, is or will be situated: *a building/construction site* ● *The company is looking for a site for its new offices.* **2** a place where sth has happened or that is used for sth: *the site of a famous battle* –**site** *verb* [T] (*written*)

sitting /'sɪtɪŋ/ *noun* [C] **1** a period of time during which a court of law or a parliament meets and does its work **2** a time when a meal is served in a school, hotel, etc to a number of people at the same time: *Dinner will be in two sittings.*

'sitting room (*Brit*) = **LIVING ROOM**

situated /'sɪtʃueɪtɪd/ *adj* in a particular place or position: *The hotel is conveniently situated close to the beach.*

★ **situation** /,sɪtʃu'eɪʃn/ *noun* [C] **1** the things that are happening in a particular place or at a particular time: *The situation in the north of the country is extremely serious.* ● *Tim is in a difficult situation at the moment.* ● *the economic/financial/political situation* **2** (*written*) the position of a building, town, etc in relation to the area around it **3** (*written, old-fashioned*) a job: *Situations Vacant* (= the part of a newspaper where jobs are advertised)

'sit-up *noun* [C] an exercise for the stomach muscles in which you lie on your back with your legs bent, then lift the top half of your body from the floor: *to do sit-ups* •➤ picture on page S2

★**six** /sɪks/ *number* **1** 6: *The answers are on page six.* • *There are six of us for dinner tonight.* • *They have six cats.* • *My son is six (years old) next month.* • *a birthday card with a big six on it* **2 six-** (in compounds) having six of the thing mentioned: *She works a six-day week.*

➤ For more information about numbers in dates, measurements, prices, etc, look at the special section on numbers at the back of this dictionary.

★**sixteen** /ˌsɪks'tiːn/ *number* 16

➤ For examples of how to use numbers in sentences, look at **six**.

sixteenth /ˌsɪks'tiːnθ/ *pron*, *determiner*, *adv* 16th •➤ Look at the examples at **sixth**.

sixth¹ /sɪksθ/ *pron*, *determiner*, *adv* 6th: *I've had five cups of tea already, so this is my sixth.* • *This is the sixth time I've tried to phone him.*

➤ For more information about numbers in dates, measurements, prices, etc, look at the special section on numbers at the back of this dictionary.

sixth² /sɪksθ/ *noun* [C] the fraction ⅙; one of six equal parts of sth

'sixth form *noun* [C, usually sing, with sing or pl verb] (*Brit*) the final two years at secondary school for students from the age of 16 to 18 who are studying for A level exams –**'sixth-former** *noun* [C]

sixtieth /'sɪkstiəθ/ *pron*, *determiner*, *adv* 60th •➤ Look at the examples at **sixth**.

★**sixty** /'sɪksti/ *number* **1** 60: *Sixty people went to the meeting.* • *There are sixty pages in the book.* • *He retired at sixty.*

➤ For examples of how to use numbers in sentences, look at **six**.

2 the sixties [pl] the numbers, years or temperatures between 60 and 69; the 60s: *I don't know the exact number of members, but it's in the sixties.* • *The most famous pop group of the sixties was The Beatles.* • *The temperature tomorrow will be in the high sixties.*

IDIOM **in your sixties** between the age of 60 and 69: *I'm not sure how old she is but I should think she's in her sixties.* • *in your early/mid/late sixties*

➤ For more information about numbers in dates, measurements, prices, etc, look at the special section on numbers at the back of this dictionary.

★**size¹** /saɪz/ *noun* **1** [U] how big or small sth is: *I was surprised at the size of the hotel. It was enormous!* • *The planet Uranus is about four times the size of* (= as big as) *Earth.*

➤ When we ask about the size of something, we usually say, 'How big...?': *How big is your house?* We say, 'What size...?' when we ask about the size of something that is pro-

duced in a number of fixed measurements: *What size shoes do you take?* • *What size are you?* (= when buying clothes)

2 [C] one of a number of fixed measurements in which sth is made: *Have you got this dress in a bigger size?* • *I'm a size 12.* • *What size pizza would you like? Medium or large?* **3 -sized** (*also* **-size**) (used to form compound adjectives) of the size mentioned: *a medium-sized flat* • *a king-size bed*

size² /saɪz/ *verb*
PHRASAL VERB **size sb/sth up** to form an opinion or judgement about sb/sth

sizeable (*also* **sizable**) /'saɪzəbl/ *adj* quite large: *a sizeable sum of money*

sizzle /'sɪzl/ *verb* [I] to make the sound of food frying in hot fat

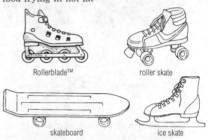

Rollerblade™   roller skate

skateboard   ice skate

skate¹ /skeɪt/ *noun* [C] **1** (*also* **ice skate**) a boot with a thin sharp metal part on the bottom that is used for moving on ice **2** =ROLLER SKATE **3** a large flat sea fish that can be eaten

skate² /skeɪt/ *verb* [I] **1** (*also* **ice-skate**) to move on ice wearing special boots (**ice skates**): *Can you skate?* • *They skated across the frozen lake.* •➤ **Go skating** is a common way of talking about skating for pleasure **2** =ROLLER SKATE –**skater** *noun* [C]

skateboard /'skeɪtbɔːd/ *noun* [C] a short narrow board with small wheels at each end that you can stand on and ride as a sport •➤ picture at **skate** –**skateboarding** *noun* [U]: *When we were children we used to go skateboarding in the park.*

skating /'skeɪtɪŋ/ *noun* **1** (*also* **ice skating**) [U] the activity or sport of moving on ice wearing special boots: *Would you like to go skating this weekend?* **2** = ROLLER SKATING

'skating rink (*also* **ice rink; rink**) *noun* [C] a large area of ice, or a building containing a large area of ice, that is used for skating on

★**skeleton¹** /'skelɪtn/ *noun* [C] the structure formed by all the bones in a human or animal body: *the human skeleton* • *a dinosaur skeleton*

skeleton² /'skelɪtn/ *adj* (used about an organization, a service, etc) having the smallest number of people that is necessary for it to operate

skeptic, skeptical, skepticism (*US*) = SCEPTIC, SCEPTICAL, SCEPTICISM

sketch /sketʃ/ *noun* [C] **1** a simple, quick

drawing without many details: *He drew a* **rough sketch** *of the new building on the back of an envelope.* **2** a short funny scene on television, in the theatre, etc: *The drama group did a sketch about a couple buying a new house.* **3** a short description without any details –**sketch verb** [I,T]: *I sat on the grass and sketched the castle.*

sketchy /'sketʃi/ **adj** not having many or enough details

goggles
pole
downhill skiing
binding
boot
ski
cross-country skiing
snowboarding
snowboard

ski¹ /skiː/ **verb** [I] (*pres part* **skiing**; *pt, pp* **skied**) to move over snow on skis: *When did you learn to ski?* ● *They* **go skiing** *every year.* –**ski adj**: *a ski resort/instructor/slope/suit* –**skiing noun** [U]: *alpine/downhill/cross-country skiing*

ski² /skiː/ **noun** [C] one of a pair of long, flat, narrow pieces of wood or plastic that are fastened to boots and used for sliding over snow: *a pair of skis*

skid /skɪd/ **verb** [I] (**skidding**; **skidded**) (usually used about a vehicle) to suddenly slide forwards or sideways without any control: *I skidded on a patch of ice and hit a tree.* –**skid noun** [C]: *The car went into a skid and came off the road.*

skier /'skiːə/ **noun** [C] a person who skis: *Mina's a good skier.*

★**skilful** (*US* **skillful**) /'skɪlfl/ **adj 1** (used about a person) very good at doing sth: *a skilful painter/politician* ● *He's very skilful with his hands.* **2** done very well: *skilful guitar playing* –**skilfully** /-fəli/ **adv**

★**skill** /skɪl/ **noun 1** [U] the ability to do sth well, especially because of training, practice, etc: *It takes great skill to make such beautiful jewellery.* ● *This is an easy game to play. No skill is required.* **2** [C] an ability that you need in order to do a job, an activity, etc well: *The course will help you to develop your reading and listening skills.* ● *management skills* ● *Typing is a skill I have never mastered.*

skilled /skɪld/ **adj 1** (used about a person) having skill; skilful: *a skilled worker* **2** (used about work, a job etc) needing skill or skills; done by people who have been trained: *a highly skilled job* ● *Skilled work is difficult to find in this area.* ·❯ opposite **unskilled**

skim /skɪm/ **verb** (**skimming**; **skimmed**) **1** [T] **skim sth (off/from sth)** to remove sth from the surface of a liquid: *to skim the cream off the milk* **2** [I,T] to move quickly over or past sth, almost touching it or touching it slightly: *The plane flew very low, skimming the tops of the buildings.* **3** [I,T] **skim (through/over) sth** to read sth quickly in order to get the main idea, without paying attention to the details and without reading every word: *I usually just skim through the newspaper in the morning.*

,**skimmed 'milk noun** [U] milk from which the cream has been removed

skimp /skɪmp/ **verb** [I] **skimp (on sth)** to use or provide less of sth than is necessary

skimpy /'skɪmpi/ **adj** using or having less than is necessary; too small or few

★**skin¹** /skɪn/ **noun** [C,U] **1** the natural outer covering of a human or animal body: *to have (a) fair/dark/sensitive skin* ● *skin cancer* **2** -**skinned** (used to form compound adjectives) having the type of skin mentioned: *My sister's very dark-skinned.* **3** (often in compounds) the skin of a dead animal, with or without its fur, used for making things: *a sheepskin jacket* ● *a bag made of crocodile skin* **4** the natural outer covering of some fruits or vegetables; the outer covering of a sausage: (a) *banana/tomato skin* ·❯ Look at the note at **rind**. ·❯ picture on page C3 **5** the thin solid surface that can form on a liquid: *A skin had formed on top of the milk.*

IDIOMS **by the skin of your teeth** (*informal*) (used to show that sb almost failed to do sth) only just: *I ran into the airport and caught the plane by the skin of my teeth.*

have a thick skin → THICK¹

skin-deep (used about a feeling or an attitude) not as important or as strongly felt as it appears to be; superficial: *I knew his concern about me was only skin-deep.*

skin² /skɪn/ **verb** [T] (**skinning**; **skinned**) to remove the skin from sth

IDIOM **keep your eyes peeled/skinned (for sb/sth) → EYE¹**

skinny /'skɪni/ **adj** (used about a person) too thin ·❯ Look at the note at **thin**.

,**skin'tight adj** (used about a piece of clothing) fitting very tightly and showing the shape of the body

skip¹ /skɪp/ **verb** (**skipping**; **skipped**) **1** [I] to move along quickly and lightly in a way that is similar to dancing, with little jumps and steps, from one foot to the other: *A little girl came skipping along the road.* ● *Lambs were skipping about in the field.* **2** [I] to jump over a rope that you or two other people hold at each end, turning it round and round over the head and under the feet: *Some girls were skipping in the playground.* **3** [T] to not do sth that you usually do or should do: *I got up rather late, so I skipped breakfast.* **4** [T] to miss the next thing that you would normally read, do, etc: *I accidentally skipped one of the questions in the test.*

skip² /skɪp/ **noun** [C] **1** a small jumping movement **2** a large, open metal container for rubbish, often used during building work

skipper /'skɪpə/ **noun** [C] (*informal*) the captain of a boat or ship, or of a sports team

'skipping rope **noun** [C] a rope, often with handles at each end, that you turn over your head and then jump over, for fun or for exercise

skirmish /'skɜːmɪʃ/ **noun** [C] a short fight between groups of people

★**skirt**¹ /skɜːt/ **noun** [C] a piece of clothing that is worn by women and girls and that hangs down from the waist •➤ Look at **culottes**. •➤ picture on page C6

skirt² /skɜːt/ **verb** [I,T] to go around the edge of sth

PHRASAL VERB skirt round sth to avoid talking about sth in a direct way: *The manager skirted round the subject of our pay increase.*

skittles /'skɪtlz/ **noun** [U] a game in which players try to knock down as many bottle-shaped objects (**skittles**) as possible by throwing or rolling a ball at them

skive /skaɪv/ **verb** [I] (*Brit informal*) **skive** (**off**) to not work when you should

skulk /skʌlk/ **verb** [I] to stay somewhere quietly and secretly, hoping that nobody will notice you, especially because you are planning to do sth bad

★**skull** /skʌl/ **noun** [C] the bone structure of a human or animal head: *She suffered a fractured skull in the fall.* •➤ picture on page C5

★**sky** /skaɪ/ **noun** [C,usually sing,U] (*pl* **skies**) the space that you can see when you look up from the earth, and where you can see the sun, moon and stars: *a cloudless/clear blue sky* • *I saw a bit of blue sky between the clouds.* • *I saw a plane high up in the sky.*

sky-'high **adj, adv** very high

skyline /'skaɪlaɪn/ **noun** [C] the shape that is made by tall buildings, etc against the sky: *the Manhattan skyline*

skyscraper /'skaɪskreɪpə/ **noun** [C] an extremely tall building

slab /slæb/ **noun** [C] a thick, flat piece of sth: *huge concrete slabs* •➤ picture on page C7

slack /slæk/ **adj** **1** loose; not tightly stretched: *Leave the rope slack.* **2** (used about a period of business) not busy; not having many customers: *Trade is very slack here in winter.* **3** not carefully or properly done: *Slack security made terrorist attacks possible.* **4** (used about a person) not doing your work carefully or properly: *You've been rather slack about your homework lately.*

slacken /'slækən/ **verb** [I,T] **1** to become or make sth less tight: *The rope slackened and he pulled his hand free.* **2** **slacken** (**sth**) (**off**) to become or make sth slower or less active: *He slackened off his pace towards the end of the race.*

slacks /slæks/ **noun** [pl] trousers (especially not very formal ones): *a pair of slacks*

slag¹ /slæg/ **verb**

PHRASAL VERB slag sb off (*informal*) to say cruel or critical things about sb

slag² /slæg/ **noun** [U] the waste material that is left after metal has been removed from rock

'slag heap **noun** [C] a hill made of slag

slain *past participle* of **SLAY**

slalom /'slɑːləm/ **noun** [C] (in skiing, canoeing, etc) a race along a course on which competitors have to move from side to side between poles

slam /slæm/ **verb** (**slamming**; **slammed**) **1** [I,T] to shut or make sth shut very loudly and with great force: *I heard the front door slam.* • *She slammed her book shut and rushed out of the room.* **2** [T] to put sth somewhere very quickly and with great force: *He slammed the book down on the table and stormed out.* •➤ Look at **grand slam**.

slander /'slɑːndə/ **noun** [C,U] a spoken statement about sb that is not true and that is intended to damage the good opinion that other people have of him/her; the legal offence of making this kind of statement –**slander** **verb** [T] –**slanderous** /-dərəs/ **adj**

★**slang** /slæŋ/ **noun** [U] very informal words and expressions that are more common in spoken language. Slang is sometimes used only by a particular group of people (for example students, young people, criminals) and often stays in fashion for a short time. Some slang is not polite: *'Fag' is slang for 'cigarette' in British English.*

slant¹ /slɑːnt/ **verb 1** [I] to be at an angle, not vertical or horizontal: *My handwriting slants backwards.* • *That picture isn't straight – it's slanting to the right.* **2** [T] (usually passive) to describe information, events, etc in a way that supports a particular group or opinion –**slanting** **adj**: *She has beautiful slanting eyes.*

slant² /slɑːnt/ **noun 1** [sing] a position at an angle, not horizontal or vertical: *The sunlight fell on the table at a slant.* **2** [C] a way of thinking, writing, etc about sth, that sees things from a particular point of view

slap¹ /slæp/ **verb** [T] (**slapping**; **slapped**) **1** to hit sb/sth with the inside of your hand when it is flat: *She slapped him across the face.* • *People slapped him on the back and congratulated him on winning.* •➤ picture on page S8 **2** to put sth onto a surface quickly and carelessly –**slap** **noun** [C]: *I gave him a slap across the face.*

slap² /slæp/ (*also* ,**slap 'bang**) **adv** (*informal*) used to show that sth happens accidentally at a bad time or place: *I hurried round the corner and walked slap into someone coming the other way.*

slapdash /'slæpdæʃ/ **adj** careless, or done quickly and carelessly: *slapdash building methods* • *He's a bit slapdash about doing his homework on time.*

slapstick /'slæpstɪk/ **noun** [U] a type of humour that is based on simple physical jokes, for example people falling over or hitting each other

'slap-up **adj** (*Brit informal*) (used about a meal) very large and very good

slash /slæʃ/ **verb 1** [I,T] **slash** (**at**) **sb/sth** to

S

make or try to make a long cut in sth with a violent movement **2** [T] to reduce an amount of money, etc very much: *The price of coffee has been slashed by 20%.*

slat /slæt/ **noun** [C] one of a series of long, narrow pieces of wood, metal or plastic, used in furniture, fences etc

slate /sleɪt/ **noun 1** [U] a type of dark grey rock that can easily be split into thin flat pieces **2** [C] one of the thin flat pieces of slate that are used for covering roofs

slaughter /'slɔːtə/ **verb** [T] **1** to kill an animal, usually for food **2** to kill a large number of people at one time, especially in a cruel way: *Men, women and children were slaughtered and whole villages destroyed.* •➤ Look at the note at **kill**. –**slaughter noun** [U]

slaughterhouse /'slɔːtəhaʊs/ (also **abattoir**) **noun** [C] a place where animals are killed for food

slave¹ /sleɪv/ **noun** [C] (in past times) a person who was owned by another person and had to work for him/her *without pay*: *the abolition of slavery in America* **slavery noun** [U]:

slave² /sleɪv/ **verb** [I] **slave (away)** to work very hard

slay /sleɪ/ **verb** [T] (*pt* **slew** /sluː/; *pp* **slain** /sleɪn/) (*old-fashioned*) to kill violently; to murder

sleazy /'sliːzi/ **adj** (used about a place or a person) unpleasant and probably connected with criminal activities: *a sleazy nightclub*

sledge /sledʒ/ (*US also* **sled** /sled/) **noun** [C] a vehicle without wheels that is used for travelling on snow. Large sledges are often pulled by dogs, and smaller ones are used for going down hills, for fun or as a sport •➤ Look at **bobsleigh** and **toboggan**. •➤ picture at **sleigh** –**sledge verb** [I]

sleek /sliːk/ **adj 1** (used about hair or fur) smooth and shiny because it is healthy **2** (used about a vehicle) having an elegant, smooth shape: *a sleek new sports car*

★**sleep**¹ /sliːp/ **noun 1** [U] the natural condition of rest when your eyes are closed and your mind and body are not active or conscious: *Most people need at least seven hours' sleep every night.* • *I didn't get much sleep last night.* • *Do you ever talk in your sleep?* • *I couldn't get to sleep last night.* **2** [sing] a period of sleep: *You'll feel better after a good night's sleep.* • *I sometimes have a short sleep in the afternoon.*

IDIOMS **go to sleep 1** to start sleeping: *He got into bed and soon went to sleep.* **2** (used about an arm, leg, etc) to lose the sense of feeling in it

put (an animal) to sleep to kill an animal that is ill or injured because you want to stop it suffering

★**sleep**² /sliːp/ **verb** (*pt, pp* **slept** /slept/) **1** [I] to rest with your eyes closed and your mind and body not active: *Did you sleep well?* • *I only slept for a couple of hours last night.* • *I slept solidly from 10 last night till 11 this morning.*

➤ **Asleep** is usually used to describe sb who is sleeping: *The baby's asleep.* **Go to sleep** is the verb we use to mean 'start to sleep': *I was reading in bed last night, and I didn't go to sleep until about one o'clock.*

2 [T] (used about a place) to have enough beds for a particular number of people

IDIOM **sleep/live rough** → **ROUGH**³

PHRASAL VERBS **sleep in** to sleep until later than usual in the morning because you do not have to get up

➤ Compare **oversleep**.

sleep together; sleep with sb to have sex with sb (usually when you are not married to or living with that person)

sleeper /'sliːpə/ **noun** [C] **1** (with an adjective) a person who sleeps in a particular way. If you are a light sleeper you wake up easily: *a light/heavy sleeper* **2** a bed on a train; a train with beds

'**sleeping bag noun** [C] a large soft bag that you use for sleeping in when you go camping, etc

'**sleeping pill noun** [C] a medicine in solid form that you swallow to help you sleep: *to take a sleeping pill*

sleepless /'sliːpləs/ **adj** (used about a period, usually the night) without sleep –**sleeplessness noun** [U] •➤ Look at **insomnia**.

sleepwalk /'sliːpwɔːk/ **verb** [I] to walk around while you are asleep

sleepy /'sliːpi/ **adj 1** tired and ready to go to sleep: *These pills might make you feel a bit sleepy.* **2** (used about a place) very quiet and not having much activity –**sleepily adv**

sleet /sliːt/ **noun** [U] a mixture of rain and snow •➤ Look at the note at **weather**.

★**sleeve** /sliːv/ **noun** [C] **1** one of the two parts of a piece of clothing that cover the arms or part of the arms: *a blouse with long sleeves* •➤ picture on page C6 **2** -**sleeved** (used to form compound adjectives) with sleeves of a particular kind: *a short-sleeved shirt*

sleeveless /'sliːvləs/ **adj** without sleeves: *a sleeveless sweater*

sleigh

sledge
(*US also* sled)

sledge
(*US also* sled)

sleigh /sleɪ/ **noun** [C] a vehicle without wheels that is used for travelling on snow

S

and that is usually pulled by horses ••> Look at **bobsleigh**.

slender /'slendə/ *adj* **1** (used about a person or part of sb's body) thin in an attractive way: *long slender fingers* **2** smaller in amount or size than you would like: *My chances of winning are very slender*.

slept *past tense, past participle of* **SLEEP¹**

slew *past tense of* **SLAY**

★**slice¹** /slaɪs/ *noun* [C] **1** a flat piece of food that is cut from a larger piece: *a thick/thin slice of bread* ● *Cut the meat into thin slices.* ••> picture at **bread** ••> picture at **cake** **2** a part of sth: *The directors have taken a large slice of the profits.*

★**slice²** /slaɪs/ *verb* **1** [T] to cut into thin flat pieces: *Peel and slice the apples.* ● *a loaf of sliced bread* **2** [I,T] to cut sth easily with sth sharp: *He sliced through the rope with a knife.* ● *The glass sliced into her hand.* **3** [T] (in ball sports) to hit the ball on the bottom or side so that it does not travel in a straight line

slick¹ /slɪk/ *adj* **1** done smoothly and well, and seeming to be done without any effort **2** clever at persuading people but perhaps not completely honest

slick² /slɪk/ = **OIL SLICK**

★**slide¹** /slaɪd/ *verb* (*pt, pp* slid /slɪd/) **1** [I,T] to move or make sth move smoothly along a surface: *She fell over and slid along the ice.* ● *The doors slide open automatically.* **2** [I,T] to move or make sth move quietly without being noticed: *I slid out of the room when nobody was looking.* ● *She slid her hand into her pocket and took out a gun.* **3** [I] (used about prices, values, etc) to go down slowly and continuously **4** [I] to move gradually towards a worse situation: *The company slid into debt and eventually closed.*

★**slide²** /slaɪd/ *noun* [C] **1** a small piece of glass that you put sth on when you want to examine it under a piece of equipment that makes things appear much bigger (a **microscope**) **2** a large toy consisting of a ladder and a long piece of metal, plastic, etc. Children climb up the ladder then slide down the other part. ••> picture at **swing** **3** a continuous slow fall, for example of prices, values, levels, etc **4** a small piece of photographic film in a plastic or cardboard frame ••> Look at **transparency**.

★**slight** /slaɪt/ *adj* **1** very small; not important or serious: *I've got a slight problem, but it's nothing to get worried about.* ● *a slight change/difference/increase/improvement* ● *I haven't the slightest idea* (= no idea at all) *what you're talking about.* **2** (used about a person's body) thin and light: *His slight frame is perfect for a long-distance runner.*

IDIOM **not in the slightest** not at all: *'Are you angry with me?' 'Not in the slightest.'*

★**slightly** /'slaɪtli/ *adv* **1** a little: *I'm slightly older than her.* **2** a slightly-built person is small and thin

★**slim¹** /slɪm/ *adj* (**slimmer; slimmest**) **1** thin in an attractive way: *a tall, slim woman* ••> Look at the note at **thin**. **2** not as big as

you would like: *Her chances of success are very slim.*

slim² /slɪm/ *verb* [I] (**slimming; slimmed**) to become or try to become thinner and lighter by eating less food, taking exercise, etc ••> Look at **diet**.

slime /slaɪm/ *noun* [U] a thick unpleasant liquid: *The pond was covered with slime and had a horrible smell.*

slimy /'slaɪmi/ *adj* **1** covered with slime **2** (used about a person) pretending to be friendly, in a way that you do not trust or like

sling¹ /slɪŋ/ *noun* [C] a piece of cloth that you put under your arm and tie around your neck to support a broken arm, wrist, etc ••> picture at **bandage**

sling² /slɪŋ/ *verb* [T] (*pt, pp* slung) **1** to put or throw sth somewhere in a rough or careless way **2** to put sth into a position where it hangs loosely

slingshot /'slɪŋʃɒt/ (*US*) = **CATAPULT¹**

slink /slɪŋk/ *verb* [I] (*pt, pp* slunk) to move somewhere slowly and quietly because you do not want anyone to see you, often when you feel guilty or embarrassed

★**slip¹** /slɪp/ *verb* (**slipping; slipped**) **1** [I] **slip (over); slip (on sth)** to slide accidentally and fall or nearly fall: *She slipped over on the wet floor.* ● *His foot slipped on the top step and he fell down the stairs.* **2** [I] to slide accidentally out of the correct position or out of your hand: *This hat's too big. It keeps slipping down over my eyes.* ● *The glass slipped out of my hand and smashed on the floor.* **3** [I] to move or go somewhere quietly, quickly, and often without being noticed: *While everyone was dancing we slipped away and went home.* **4** [T] **slip sth (to sb); slip (sb) sth** to put sth somewhere or give sth to sb quietly and often without being noticed: *She picked up the money and slipped it into her pocket.* **5** [I,T] **slip into/out of sth; slip sth on/off** to put on or take off a piece of clothing quickly and easily: *I slipped off my shoes.* **6** [I] to fall a little in value, level, etc

IDIOMS **let sth slip** → **LET**

slip your mind to be forgotten: *I'm sorry, the meeting completely slipped my mind.*

PHRASAL VERBS **slip out** to accidentally say sth or tell sb sth: *I didn't intend to tell them. It just slipped out.*

slip up (*informal*) to make a mistake

slip² /slɪp/ *noun* [C] **1** a small mistake, usually made by being careless or not paying attention: *to make a slip* **2** a small piece of paper: *I made a note of her name on* **a slip of paper.** ● (*Brit*) *There seems to be a mistake on my* **payslip** (= the piece of paper from your employer each month showing how much money you have been paid and how much tax, etc has been taken off). **3** an act of sliding accidentally and falling or nearly falling **4** a thin piece of clothing that is worn by a woman under a dress or skirt

IDIOMS **give sb the slip** (*informal*) to escape from sb who is following or trying to catch

---

[I] **intransitive**, a verb which has no object: *He laughed.*　　　　　[T] **transitive**, a verb which has an object: *He ate an apple.*

you

a **slip of the tongue** something that you say that you did not mean to say

,**slipped** '**disc** noun [C] a painful injury caused when one of the flat things (**discs**) between the bones in your back (**spine**) moves out of its correct position

slipper /'slɪpə/ noun [C] a light soft shoe that is worn inside the house: *a pair of slippers* •➤ picture at **shoe**

slippery /'slɪpəri/ (also *informal* **slippy**) adj (used about a surface or an object) difficult to walk on or hold because it is smooth, wet, etc: *a slippery floor*

'**slip road** (*US* **entrance/exit ramp**) noun [C] a road that leads onto or off a motorway

slit[1] /slɪt/ noun [C] a long narrow cut or opening: *a long skirt with a slit up the back*

slit[2] /slɪt/ verb [T] (**slitting**; *pt, pp* **slit**) to make a long narrow cut in sth: *She slit the envelope open with a knife.*

slither /'slɪðə/ verb [I] to move by sliding from side to side along the ground like a snake: *I saw a snake slithering down a rock.*

slob /slɒb/ noun [C] (*informal*) (used as an insult) a very lazy or untidy person

slog[1] /slɒg/ verb [I] (**slogging**; **slogged**) **1** (*informal*) slog (away) (at sth); slog (through sth) to work hard for a long period at sth difficult or boring: *I've been slogging away at this homework for hours.* **2** slog down, up, along, etc to walk or move in a certain direction with a lot of effort

slog[2] /slɒg/ noun [sing] a period of long, hard, boring work or a long, tiring journey

slogan /'sləʊgən/ noun [C] a short phrase that is easy to remember and that is used in politics or advertising: *Anti-government slogans had been painted all over the walls.* • *an advertising slogan*

slop /slɒp/ verb [I,T] (**slopping**; **slopped**) (used about a liquid) to pour over the edge of its container; to make a liquid do this: *He filled his glass too full and beer slopped onto the table.*

★**slope** /sləʊp/ noun **1** [C] a surface or piece of land that goes up or down: *The village is built on a slope.* • *a steep/gentle slope* • *The best ski slopes are in the Alps.* **2** [sing] the amount that a surface is not level; the fact of not being level –slope verb [I]: *The road slopes down to the river.* • *a sloping roof*

sloppy /'slɒpi/ adj **1** that shows lack of care, thought or effort; untidy: *a sloppy worker/writer/dresser* • *a sloppy piece of work* **2** (used about clothes) not tight and without much shape **3** (*Brit informal*) showing emotions in a silly embarrassing way: *I can't stand sloppy love songs.* •➤ A more formal word is **sentimental**.

slosh /slɒʃ/ verb (*informal*) **1** [I] (used about a liquid) to move around noisily inside a container **2** [T] to pour or drop liquid somewhere in a careless way

sloshed /slɒʃt/ adj (*slang*) drunk

slot[1] /slɒt/ noun [C] **1** a straight narrow opening in a machine, etc: *Put your money into the slot and take the ticket.* •➤ picture at **telephone 2** a place in a list, system, organization, etc: *The single has occupied the Number One slot for the past two weeks.*

slot[2] /slɒt/ verb [I,T] (**slotting**; **slotted**) to put sth into a particular space that is designed for it; to fit into such a space: *He slotted a tape into the VCR.* • *The video slotted in easily.*

IDIOM **fall/slot into place** ➔ **PLACE**[1]

'**slot machine** noun [C] a machine with an opening for coins that sells drinks, cigarettes, etc or on which you can play games

slouch /slaʊtʃ/ verb [I] to sit, stand or walk in a lazy way, with your head and shoulders hanging down

slovenly /'slʌvnli/ adj (*old-fashioned*) lazy, careless and untidy

★**slow**[1] /sləʊ/ adj, adv **1** moving, doing sth or happening without much speed; not fast: *The traffic is always very slow in the city centre.* • *Haven't you finished your homework yet? You're being very slow!* • *Progress was slower than expected.* • *a slow driver/walker/reader* •➤ opposite **fast**

➤ It is possible to use **slow** as an adverb, but **slowly** is much more common. However, **slow** is often used in compounds: *slow-moving traffic*. The comparative forms **slower** and **more slowly** are both common: *Could you drive a bit slower/more slowly, please?*

2 slow to do sth; slow (in/about) doing sth not doing sth immediately: *She was rather slow to realize what was going on.* • *They've been rather slow in replying to my letter!* **3** not quick to learn or understand: *He's the slowest student in the class.* **4** not very busy; with little action: *Business is very slow at the moment.* **5** (not before a noun) (used about watches and clocks) showing a time that is earlier than the real time: *That clock is five minutes slow* (= it says it is 8.55 when the correct time is 9.00). –**slowness** noun [U]

IDIOM **quick/slow on the uptake** ➔ **UPTAKE**

★**slow**[2] /sləʊ/ verb [I,T] to start to move, do sth or happen at a slower speed; to cause sth to do this: *He slowed his pace a little.*

PHRASAL VERB **slow (sb/sth) down/up** to start to move, do sth or happen at a slower speed; to cause sb/sth to do this: *Can't you slow down a bit? You're driving much too fast.* • *These problems have slowed up the whole process.*

★**slowly** /'sləʊli/ adv at a slow speed; not quickly: *He walked slowly along the street.*

,**slow** '**motion** noun [U] (in a film or on television) a method of making action appear much slower than in real life: *They showed the winning goal again, this time in slow motion.*

sludge /slʌdʒ/ noun [U] a thick, soft unpleasant substance; mud

slug /slʌg/ noun [C] a small black or brown animal with a soft body and no legs, that moves slowly along the ground and eats garden plants •➤ picture at **snail**

sluggish /'slʌgɪʃ/ **adj** moving or working more slowly than normal in a way that seems lazy

slum /slʌm/ **noun** [C] an area of a city where living conditions are extremely bad, and where the buildings are dirty and have not been repaired for a long time

slump¹ /slʌmp/ **verb** [I] **1** (used about economic activity, prices, etc) to fall suddenly and by a large amount: *Shares in BP slumped 33p to 181p yesterday.* • *The newspaper's circulation has slumped by 30%.* **2** to fall or sit down suddenly when your body feels heavy and weak, usually because you are tired or ill

slump² /slʌmp/ **noun** [C] **1** a slump (in sth) a sudden large fall in sales, prices, the value of sth, etc: *a slump in house prices* **2** a period when a country's economy is doing very badly and a lot of people do not have jobs: *The British car industry is in a slump.*

slung *past tense, past participle* of **SLING²**

slunk *past tense, past participle* of **SLINK**

slur¹ /slɜː/ **verb** [T] (**slurring**; **slurred**) to pronounce words in a way that is not clear, often because you are drunk

slur² /slɜː/ **noun** [C] a slur (on sb/sth) an unfair comment or an insult that could damage people's opinion of sb/sth

slurp /slɜːp/ **verb** [I,T] (*informal*) to drink noisily

slush /slʌʃ/ **noun** [U] **1** snow that has been on the ground for a time and that is now a dirty mixture of ice and water **2** (*informal*) films, books, feelings, etc that are considered to be silly because they are too romantic and emotional –**slushy adj**

sly /slaɪ/ **adj 1** (used about a person) acting or done in a secret or dishonest way, often intending to trick people •➤ synonym **cunning 2** (used about an action) suggesting that you know sth secret: *a sly smile/look* –**slyly adv**

smack /smæk/ **verb** [T] to hit sb with the inside of your hand when it is flat, especially as a punishment: *I never smack my children.* –**smack noun** [C]: *You're going to get a smack if you don't do as I say!*

PHRASAL VERB **smack of sth** to make you think that sb/sth has an unpleasant attitude or quality

★**small** /smɔːl/ **adj, adv 1** not large in size, number, amount, etc: *a small car/flat/town* • *a small group of people* • *a small amount of money* • *She's painted the picture far too small.* • *That dress is too small for you.* **2** young: *He has a wife and three small children.* • *When I was small we lived in a big old house.* **3** not important or serious; slight: *Don't worry. It's only a small problem.*

➤ **Small** is the most usual opposite of **big** or **large**. **Little** is often used with another adjective to express an emotion, as well as the idea of smallness: *a horrible little man*

• *a lovely little girl* • *a nice little house.* The comparative and superlative forms **smaller** and **smallest** are common, and small is often used with words like 'rather', 'quite' and 'very': *My flat is smaller than yours.* • *The village is quite small.* • *a very small car.* **Little** is not often used with these words and does not usually have a comparative or superlative form.

IDIOM **in a big/small way** ➔ **WAY¹**

‚small ˈad (*Brit informal*) = **CLASSIFIED ADVERTISEMENT**

‚small ˈchange noun [U] coins that have a low value

the ˈsmall hours noun [pl] the early morning hours soon after midnight

smallpox /'smɔːlpɒks/ **noun** [U] a serious infectious disease that causes a high temperature and leaves marks on the skin. In past times many people died from smallpox.

the ˈsmall print (*US* **the ˈfine print**) **noun** [U] the important details of a legal document, contract, etc that are usually printed in small type and are therefore easy to miss: *Make sure you read the small print before you sign anything.*

‚small-ˈscale adj (used about an organization or activity) not large; limited in what it does

ˈsmall talk noun [U] polite conversation, for example at a party, about unimportant things: *We had to make small talk for half an hour.*

★**smart¹** /smɑːt/ **adj 1** (*especially Brit*) (used about a person) having a clean and tidy appearance: *You look smart. Are you going somewhere special?* **2** (*especially Brit*) (used about a piece of clothing, etc) good enough to wear on a formal occasion: *a smart suit* **3** clever; intelligent: *He's not smart enough to be a politician.* **4** (*especially Brit*) fashionable and usually expensive: *a smart restaurant/hotel* **5** (used about a movement or action) quick and usually done with force –**smartly adv**: *She's always smartly dressed.*

smart² /smɑːt/ **verb** [I] **1** smart (from sth) to feel a stinging pain in your body **2** smart (from/over sth) to feel upset or offended because of a criticism, failure, etc

ˈsmart card noun [C] a plastic card, for example a credit card, on which information can be stored in electronic form

smarten /'smɑːtn/ **verb** (*especially Brit*)
PHRASAL VERB **smarten (yourself/sb/sth) up** to make yourself/sb/sth look tidy and more attractive

★**smash¹** /smæʃ/ **verb 1** [I,T] to break sth, or to be broken violently and noisily into many pieces: *The glass smashed into a thousand pieces.* • *The police had to smash the door open.* **2** [I,T] smash (sth) against, into, through, etc to move with great force in a particular direction; to hit sth very hard: *The car smashed into a tree.* • *He smashed his fist through the window.* **3** [T] smash sth (up) to

S

crash a vehicle, usually causing a lot of damage **4** [T] (in tennis) to hit a ball that is high in the air downwards very hard over the net

smash² /smæʃ/ **noun 1** [sing] the action or the noise of sth breaking violently **2** [C] (in tennis, etc) a way of hitting a ball that is high in the air downwards and very hard over the net **3** (also **smash 'hit**) [C] (*informal*) a song, play, film, etc that is very successful

smear¹ /smɪə/ **verb** [T] smear sth on/over sth/sb; smear sth/sb with sth to spread a sticky substance across sth/sb: *Her face was smeared with blood.*

smear² /smɪə/ **noun** [C] **1** a dirty mark made by spreading a substance across sth **2** something that is not true that is said or written about an important person and that is intended to damage people's opinion about him/her, especially in politics: *He was the victim of a **smear campaign**.*

★**smell¹** /smel/ **verb** (*pt, pp* **smelt** /smelt/ or **smelled** /smeld/) **1** [I] smell (of sth) to have a particular smell: *Dinner smells good!* • *This perfume smells of roses.* • *His breath smelt of whisky.* **2** [I] to have a bad smell: *Your feet smell.* **3** [T] to notice or recognize sb/sth by using your nose: *He could smell something burning.* • *Can you smell gas?* • *I could still smell her perfume in the room.*

➤ We do not use **smell** or other verbs of the senses (for example **taste**, **see**, **hear**) in the continuous tenses (for example in the continuous tenses). Instead we often use **can**, for example: *I can smell smoke.*

4 [T] to put your nose near sth and breathe in so that you can discover or identify its smell: *I smelt the milk to see if it had gone off.* **5** [I] to be able to smell: *I can't smell properly because I've got a cold.*

★**smell²** /smel/ **noun 1** [C] the impression that you get of sth by using your nose; the thing that you smell: *What's that smell?* • *a sweet/musty/fresh/sickly smell* • *a strong/faint smell of garlic* **2** [sing] an unpleasant smell: *Ugh! What's that smell?*

➤ **Stink**, **stench**, **odour** and **pong** are all words for unpleasant smells. **Aroma**, **fragrance**, **perfume** and **scent** refer to pleasant smells.

3 [U] the ability to sense things with the nose: *Dogs have a very good **sense of smell**.* **4** [C] the action of putting your nose near sth to smell it: *Have a smell of this milk; is it all right?*

smelly /'smeli/ **adj** (*informal*) having a bad smell: *smelly feet*

★**smile¹** /smaɪl/ **noun** [C] an expression on your face in which the corners of your mouth turn up, showing happiness, pleasure, etc: *to have a smile on your face* • *'It's nice to see you,' he said with a smile.* ••➤ Look at **beam**, **grin** and **smirk**.

★**smile²** /smaɪl/ **verb 1** [I] smile (at sb/sth) to make a smile appear on your face: *to smile sweetly/faintly/broadly* • *She smiled at the camera.* **2** [T] to say or express sth with a smile: *I smiled a greeting to them.*

smirk /smɜːk/ **noun** [C] a unpleasant smile which you have when you are pleased with yourself or think you are very clever –**smirk verb** [I]

smog /smɒg/ **noun** [U] dirty, poisonous air that can cover a whole city

★**smoke¹** /sməʊk/ **noun 1** [U] the grey, white or black gas that you can see in the air when something is burning: *Thick smoke poured from the chimney.* • *a room full of cigarette smoke* **2** [C,usually sing] an action of smoking a cigarette, etc

★**smoke²** /sməʊk/ **verb 1** [I,T] to breathe in smoke through a cigarette, etc and let it out again; to use cigarettes, etc in this way, as a habit: *Do you mind if I smoke?* • *I used to smoke 20 cigarettes a day.* **2** [I] to send out smoke: *The oil in the pan started to smoke.* –**smoker noun** [C]: *She's a **chain smoker** (= she finishes one cigarette and then immediately lights another).* ••➤ opposite **non-smoker** –**smoking noun** [U]: *My doctor has advised me to give up smoking.* • *Would you like a table in the smoking or non-smoking section?*

smoked /sməʊkt/ **adj** (used of certain types of food) given a special taste by being hung for a period of time in smoke from wood fires: *smoked salmon/ham/cheese*

smoky /'sməʊki/ **adj 1** full of smoke; producing a lot of smoke: *a smoky room/fire* **2** with the smell, taste or appearance of smoke

smolder (*US*) = **SMOULDER**

★**smooth¹** /smuːð/ **adj 1** having a completely flat surface with no lumps or holes or rough areas: *smooth skin* • *a smooth piece of wood* ••➤ opposite **rough 2** (of a liquid mixture) without lumps: *Stir the sauce until it is smooth.* ••➤ opposite **lumpy 3** without difficulties: *The transition from the old method to the new has been very smooth.* **4** (of a journey in a car, etc) with an even, comfortable movement: *You get a very smooth ride in this car.* ••➤ opposite **bumpy 5** too pleasant or polite to be trusted ••➤ We use this word in a critical way, usually about a man: *I don't like him. He's far too smooth.* –**smoothness noun** [U]

IDIOM take the rough with the smooth → **ROUGH²**

smooth² /smuːð/ **verb** [T] smooth sth (away, back, down, out, etc) to move your hands in the direction mentioned over a surface to make it smooth

smoothly /'smuːðli/ **adv** without any difficulty: *My work has been going quite smoothly.*

smother /'smʌðə/ **verb** [T] **1** smother sb (with sth) to kill sb by covering his/her face so that he/she cannot breathe: *She was smothered with a pillow.* **2** smother sth/sb in/with sth to cover sth/sb with too much of sth **3** to stop a feeling, etc from being expressed **4** to stop sth burning by covering it: *to smother the flames with a blanket*

smoulder (*US* **smolder**) /'sməʊldə/ **verb** [I] to burn slowly without a flame: *a cigarette smouldering in an ashtray.*

smudge /smʌdʒ/ **verb 1** [T] to make sth dirty or untidy by touching it: *Leave your painting to dry or you'll smudge it.* **2** [I] to become untidy, without a clean line around it: *Her lipstick smudged when she kissed him.* –**smudge noun** [C]

smug /smʌg/ **adj** too pleased with yourself: *Don't look so smug.* ••▸ We use this word in a critical way. –**smugly adv**: *He smiled smugly as the results were announced.* –**smugness noun** [U]

smuggle /'smʌgl/ **verb** [T] to take things into or out of a country secretly in a way that is not allowed by the law; to take a person or a thing secretly into or out of a place: *The drugs had been smuggled through customs.* –**smuggler noun** [C]: *a drug smuggler*

★**snack** /snæk/ **noun** [C] food that you eat quickly between main meals: *I had a snack on the train.* –**snack verb** [I] (*informal*) **snack on sth**

'snack bar noun [C] a type of small cafe where you can buy a small quick meal like a sandwich

snag¹ /snæg/ **noun** [C] a small difficulty or disadvantage that is often unexpected or hidden: *His offer is very generous – are you sure there isn't a snag?*

snag² /snæg/ **verb** [T] (**snagging; snagged**) to catch a piece of clothing, etc on sth sharp and tear it

snail   slug

shell

snail /sneɪl/ **noun** [C] a type of animal with a soft body and no legs that is covered by a shell. Snails move very slowly.

'snail mail noun [U] (*informal*) used by people who use e-mail to describe the system of sending letters by ordinary post

★**snake¹** /sneɪk/ **noun** [C] a type of long thin animal with no legs that slides along the ground by moving its body from side to side

snake² /sneɪk/ **verb** [I] (*written*) to move like a snake in long curves from side to side

★**snap¹** /snæp/ **verb** (**snapping; snapped**) **1** [I,T] to break or be broken suddenly, usually with a sharp noise: *The top has snapped off my pen.* ● *The branch snapped.* ● *I snapped my shoelace when I was tying it.* **2** [I,T] to move or be moved into a particular position, especially with a sharp noise: *She snapped the bag shut and walked out.* **3** [I,T] **snap (sth) (at sb)** to speak or say sth in a quick angry way: *Why do you always snap at me?* **4** [I] to try to bite sb/sth: *The dog snapped at the child's hand.* **5** [I,T] (*informal*) to take a quick photograph of sb/sth: *A tourist snapped the plane as it crashed.* **6** [I] to suddenly be unable to control your feelings any longer: *Suddenly something just snapped and I lost my temper with him.*

IDIOM snap your fingers to make a sharp noise by moving your middle finger quickly against your thumb, especially when you want to attract sb's attention

PHRASAL VERB snap sth up to buy or take sth quickly, especially because it is very cheap

snap² /snæp/ **noun 1** [C] a sudden sharp sound of sth breaking **2** (also **snapshot**) [C] a photograph that is taken quickly and in an informal way: *I showed them some holiday snaps.* **3** [U] (*Brit*) a card game where players call out 'Snap' when two cards that are the same are put down by different players

snap³ /snæp/ **adj** (*informal*) (only *before* a noun) done quickly and suddenly, often without any careful thought: *a snap decision/ judgement*

snare /sneə/ **noun** [C] a device (**trap**) used to catch birds or small animals –**snare verb** [T]

snarl /snɑːl/ **verb** [I,T] **snarl (sth) (at sb)** (used about an animal) to make an angry sound while showing the teeth: *The dog snarled at the stranger.* –**snarl noun** [C,usually sing]

snatch¹ /snætʃ/ **verb 1** [I,T] to take sth with a quick rough movement: *A boy snatched her handbag and ran off.* ••▸ Look at **grab**. It is similar in meaning. **2** [T] to take or get sth quickly using the only time or chance that you have: *I managed to snatch some sleep on the train.*

PHRASAL VERB snatch at sth to try to take hold of sth suddenly: *The man snatched at my wallet but I didn't let go of it.*

snatch² /snætʃ/ **noun 1** [sing] a sudden movement that sb makes when trying to take hold of sth **2** [C,usually pl] a short part or period of something: *I heard snatches of conversation from the next room.*

sneak¹ /sniːk/ **verb 1** [I] **sneak into, out of, past, etc sth; sneak in, out, away, etc** to go very quietly in the direction mentioned, so that no one can see or hear you: *The prisoner sneaked past the guards.* ● *Instead of working, he sneaked out to play football.* **2** [T] (*informal*) to do or take sth secretly: *I tried to sneak a look at the test results in the teacher's bag.*

PHRASAL VERB sneak up (on sb/sth) to go near sb very quietly, especially so that you can surprise him/her

sneak² /sniːk/ **noun** [C] (*informal*) a person, especially a child, who tells sb about the bad things sb has done ••▸ This word is used in a critical way.

sneaker /'sniːkə/ (*US*) = **PLIMSOLL, TRAINER**(1)

sneaking /'sniːkɪŋ/ **adj** (used about feelings) not expressed; secret: *I've a sneaking suspicion that he's lying.*

sneer /snɪə/ **verb** [I] **sneer (at sb/sth)** to show that you have no respect for sb/sth by the expression on your face or the way that you speak: *She sneered at his attempts to speak French.* –**sneer noun** [C]

sneezing

coughing

He's blowing his nose.

sneeze /sniːz/ verb [I] to make air come out of your nose suddenly and noisily in a way that you cannot control, for example because you have a cold: *Dust makes me sneeze.* –**sneeze** noun [C]

snide /snaɪd/ adj (used about an expression or comment) critical in an unpleasant way

sniff /snɪf/ verb **1** [I] to breathe air in through the nose in a way that makes a sound, especially because you have a cold or you are crying: *Stop sniffing and blow your nose.* **2** [I,T] sniff (at) sth to smell sth by sniffing: *'I can smell gas,' he said, sniffing the air.* ● *The dog sniffed at the bone.* –**sniff** noun [C]: *Have a sniff of this milk and tell me if it's still OK.*

sniffle /ˈsnɪfl/ verb [I] to make noises by breathing air suddenly up your nose, especially because you have a cold or you are crying

snigger /ˈsnɪɡə/ verb [I] snigger (at sb/sth) to laugh quietly and secretly in an unpleasant way –**snigger** noun [C]

snip¹ /snɪp/ verb [I,T] (**snipping**; **snipped**) snip (sth) (off, out, in, etc) to cut using scissors, with a short quick action: *He sewed on the button and snipped off the ends of the cotton.* ● *to snip a hole in sth*

snip² /snɪp/ noun [C] **1** a small cut made with scissors: *She made a small snip in the cloth.* **2** (*Brit informal*) something that is much cheaper than expected

snippet /ˈsnɪpɪt/ noun [C] a small piece of sth, especially information or news

snivel /ˈsnɪvl/ verb [I] (**snivelling**; **snivelled**: *US* **sniveling**; **sniveled**) to keep crying quietly in a way that is annoying

snob /snɒb/ noun [C] a person who thinks he/she is better than sb of a lower social class and who admires people who have a high social position: *He's such a snob – he wears his Oxford University tie all the time.* –**snobbish** adj –**snobbishly** adv –**snobbishness** noun [U]

snobbery /ˈsnɒbəri/ noun [U] behaviour or attitudes typical of people who think they are better than other people in society, for example because they have more money, better education, etc: *To say that 'all pop music is rubbish' is just snobbery.*

snog /snɒɡ/ verb [I,T] (**snogging**; **snogged**) (*Brit informal*) (used about a couple) to kiss each other for a long period of time –**snog** noun [sing]

snooker /ˈsnuːkə/ noun [U] a game in which two players try to hit a number of coloured balls into pockets at the edges of a large table using a long stick (cue): *to play snooker* •➤ Look at **billiards** and **pool**.

snoop /snuːp/ verb [I] snoop (around); snoop (on sb) to look around secretly and without permission in order to find out information, etc: *She suspected that her neighbours visited just to snoop on her.*

snooty /ˈsnuːti/ adj (*informal*) acting in a rude way because you think you are better than other people

snooze /snuːz/ verb [I] (*informal*) to have a short sleep, especially during the day –**snooze** noun [C,usually sing]: *I had a bit of a snooze on the train.* •➤ Look at **nap**.

snore /snɔː/ verb [I] to breathe noisily through your nose and mouth while you are asleep: *She heard her father snoring in the next room.* –**snore** noun [C]: *He's got the loudest snore I've ever heard.*

snorkel /ˈsnɔːkl/ noun [C] a short tube that a person swimming just below the surface of the water can use to breathe through

> We use **go snorkelling** to talk about swimming like this.

•➤ picture at **dive**

snort /snɔːt/ verb [I] **1** (used about animals) to make a noise by blowing air through the nose and mouth **2** (used about people) to blow out air noisily as a way of showing that you do not like sth, or that you are impatient –**snort** noun [C]

snot /snɒt/ noun [U] (*informal*) the liquid produced by the nose

snout /snaʊt/ noun [C] the long nose of certain animals: *a pig's snout* •➤ picture at **badger**

⋆**snow**¹ /snəʊ/ noun [U] small, soft, white pieces of frozen water that fall from the sky in cold weather: *Three inches of snow fell during the night.* ● *The snow melted before it could settle* (= stay on the ground). •➤ Look at the note at **weather**.

⋆**snow**² /snəʊ/ verb [I] (used about snow) to fall from the sky: *It snowed all night.*

snowball¹ /ˈsnəʊbɔːl/ noun [C] a lump of snow that is pressed into the shape of a ball and used by children for playing

snowball² /ˈsnəʊbɔːl/ verb [I] to quickly grow bigger and bigger or more and more important

snowboard /ˈsnəʊbɔːrd/ noun [C] a type of board that you fasten to both your feet and use for moving down mountains that are covered with snow –**snowboarding** noun [U]: *Have you ever been snowboarding?* •➤ picture at **ski**

snowdrift /ˈsnəʊdrɪft/ noun [C] a deep pile of snow that has been made by the wind: *The car got stuck in a snowdrift.*

snowdrop /ˈsnəʊdrɒp/ noun [C] a type of small white flower that appears at the end of winter •➤ picture on page C2

,**snowed 'in** adj not able to leave home or travel because the snow is too deep

S

[C] **countable**, a noun with a plural form: *one book, two books*   [U] **uncountable**, a noun with no plural form: *some sugar*

snowed 'under *adj* with more work, etc than you can deal with

snowfall /'snəʊfɔːl/ *noun* **1** [C] the snow that falls on one occasion: *heavy snowfalls* **2** [U] the amount of snow that falls in a particular place

snowflake /'snəʊfleɪk/ *noun* [C] one of the small, soft, white pieces of frozen water that fall together as snow

snowman /'snəʊmæn/ *noun* [C] (*pl* **-men** /-men/) the figure of a person made out of snow

snowplough (*US* **snowplow**) /'snəʊ plaʊ/ *noun* [C] a vehicle that is used to clear snow away from roads or railways ••▸ Look at **plough**.

snowy /'snəʊi/ *adj* with a lot of snow: *snowy weather* • *a snowy scene*

Snr (also **Sr**) *abbr* (*especially US*) Senior

snub /snʌb/ *verb* [T] (**snubbing**; **snubbed**) to treat sb rudely, for example by refusing to look at or speak to him/her –**snub** *noun* [C]: *When they weren't invited to the party, they felt it was a snub.*

snuff /snʌf/ *noun* [U] (especially in past times) tobacco which people breathe up into the nose in the form of a powder

snuffle /'snʌfl/ *verb* [I] (used about people and animals) to make a noise through your nose: *The dog snuffled around the lamp post.*

snug /snʌg/ *adj* **1** warm and comfortable: *a snug little room* • *The children were snug in bed.* **2** fitting sb/sth closely: *Adjust the safety belt to give a snug fit.* –**snugly** *adv*

snuggle /'snʌgl/ *verb* [I] **snuggle (up to sb)**; **snuggle (up/down)** to get into a position that makes you feel safe, warm and comfortable, usually next to another person: *She snuggled up to her mother.* • *I snuggled down under the blanket to get warm.*

★**so¹** /səʊ/ *adv* **1** used to emphasize an adjective or adverb, especially when this produces a particular result: *She's so ill (that) she can't get out of bed.* • *He was driving so fast that he couldn't stop.* • *You've been so kind. How can I thank you?* ••▸ Look at the note at **such**. **2** used in negative sentences for comparing people or things: *She's not so clever as we thought.* **3** used in place of something that has been said already, to avoid repeating it: *Are you coming by plane? If so,* (= if you are coming by plane) *I can meet you at the airport.* • *'I failed, didn't I?' 'I'm afraid so.'*

> ➤ In formal language, you can refer to actions that somebody has mentioned using **do** with **so**: *He asked me to write to him and I did so* (= I wrote to him).

4 (not with verbs in the negative) also, too: *He's a teacher and so is his wife.* • *'I've been to New York.' 'So have I.'* • *I like singing and so does Helen.*

> ➤ For negative sentences, look at **neither**.

5 used to show that you agree that sth is true, especially when you are surprised: *'It's getting late.' 'So it is. We'd better go.'* **6** (*for-*

mal) (used when you are showing sb sth) in this way; like this: *It was a black insect, about so big* (= using your hands to show the size). • *Fold the paper in two diagonally, like so.*

IDIOMS **and so on (and so forth)** used at the end of a list to show that it continues in the same way: *They sell pens, pencils, paper and so on.*

I told you so used to tell sb that he/she should have listened to your advice: *'I missed the bus.' 'I told you so. I said you needed to leave earlier.'*

it (just) so happens (used to introduce a surprising fact) by chance: *It just so happened that we were going the same way, so he gave me a lift.*

just so → JUST¹

or so (used to show that a number, time, etc is not exact) approximately; about: *A hundred or so people came to the meeting.*

so as to do sth with the intention of doing sth; in order to do sth

so much for used for saying that sth was not helpful or successful: *So much for that diet! I didn't lose any weight at all.*

that is so (*formal*) that is true

★**so²** /səʊ/ *conj* **1** with the result that; therefore: *She felt very tired so she went to bed early.* **2 so (that)** with the purpose that; in order that: *She wore dark glasses so (that) nobody would recognize her.* **3** used to show how one part of a story follows another: *So what happened next?*

IDIOM **so what?** (*informal*) (showing that you think sth is not important) Who cares?: *'It's late.' 'So what? We don't have to go to school tomorrow.'*

soak /səʊk/ *verb* **1** [I,T] to become or make sth completely wet: *Leave the dishes to soak for a while.* • *The dog came out of the river and shook itself, soaking everyone.* **2** [I] **soak into/through sth**; **soak in** (used about a liquid) to pass into or through sth: *Blood had soaked through the bandage.*

PHRASAL VERB **soak sth up** to take sth in (especially a liquid): *I soaked the water up with a cloth.*

soaked /səʊkt/ *adj* (not before a noun) extremely wet: *I got soaked waiting for my bus in the rain.*

soaking /'səʊkɪŋ/ (also **soaking 'wet**) *adj* extremely wet

'so-and-so *noun* [C] (*pl* **so-and-so's**) (*informal*) **1** a person who is not named: *Imagine a Mrs So-and-so telephones. What would you say?* **2** a person that you do not like: *He's a bad-tempered old so-and-so.*

★**soap** /səʊp/ *noun* [U] a substance that you use for washing and cleaning: *He washed his hands with soap.* • *a bar of soap* • *soap powder* (= for washing clothes) –**soapy** *adj*

'soap opera (also *informal* **soap**) *noun* [C] a story about the lives and problems of a group of people which continues several times a week on television or radio ••▸ Look at **opera**.

soar /sɔː/ *verb* [I] **1** to fly high in the air **2** to

[I] **intransitive**, a verb which has no object: *He laughed.*   [T] **transitive**, a verb which has an object: *He ate an apple.*

rise very fast: *Prices are soaring because of inflation.*

sob /sɒb/ **verb** [I] (**sobbing**; **sobbed**) to cry while taking in sudden, sharp breaths; to speak while you are crying: *The child was sobbing because he'd lost his toy.* –**sob** **noun** [C]: *It was heartbreaking to listen to her sobs.*

sober¹ /'səʊbə/ **adj** **1** (of a person) not affected by alcohol: *He'd been drunk the first time he'd met her, but this time he was **stone-cold sober**.* **2** not funny; serious: *a sober expression* • *Her death is a sober reminder of just how dangerous drugs can be.* **3** (of a colour) not bright or likely to be noticed: *a sober grey suit*

sober² /'səʊbə/ **verb**
PHRASAL VERB **sober (sb) up** to become or make sb become normal again after being affected by alcohol: *I need a cup of black coffee to sober me up.* • *There's no point talking to him until he's sobered up.*

sobering /'səʊbərɪŋ/ **adj** making you feel serious: *It is **a sobering thought** that over 25 million people have been killed in car accidents.*

Soc **abbr** Society: *Amateur Dramatic Soc*

so-called **adj** **1** used to show that the words you describe sb/sth with are not correct: *Her so-called friends only wanted her money.* **2** used to show that a special name has been given to sb/sth

soccer /'sɒkə/ (*especially US*) = **FOOTBALL**(1)

sociable /'səʊʃəbl/ **adj** enjoying being with other people; friendly

★**social** /'səʊʃl/ **adj** **1** connected with society and the way it is organized: *social problems/ issues/reforms* **2** concerning the position of people in society: *We share the same social background.* **3** connected with meeting people and enjoying yourself: *a social club* • *She has a busy social life.* • *Children have to develop their social skills when they start school.* **4** (used about animals) living in groups –**socially** /-ʃəli/ **adv**: *We work together but I don't know him socially.*

socialism /'səʊʃəlɪzəm/ **noun** [U] the political idea that is based on the belief that all people are equal and that money and property should be equally divided ••➤ Look at **communism**, **Marxism** and **capitalism**. –**socialist** **adj**, **noun** [C]: *socialist beliefs/policies/writers* • *Tony was a socialist when he was younger.*

social 'science **noun** [C,U] the study of people in society

social se'curity (*US* **welfare**) **noun** [U] money paid regularly by the government to people who are poor, old, ill, or who have no job: *to live on social security*

social 'services **noun** [pl] a group of services organized by local government to help people who have money or family problems

social work **noun** [U] work that involves giving help and advice to people with money or family problems –**social worker** **noun** [C]

★**society** /sə'saɪəti/ **noun** (*pl* **societies**) **1** [C,U] the people in a country or area,

thought of as a group, who have shared customs and laws: *a civilized society* • *Society' attitude to women has changed considerably this century.* • *The role of men in society is changing.* **2** [C] an organization of people who share a particular interest or purpose; a club: *a drama society*

sociologist /ˌsəʊsi'ɒlədʒɪst/ **noun** [C] a student of or an expert in sociology

sociology /ˌsəʊsi'ɒlədʒi/ **noun** [U] the study of human societies and social behaviour –**sociological** /ˌsəʊsiə'lɒdʒɪkl/ **adj**

★**sock** /sɒk/ **noun** [C] a piece of clothing that you wear on your foot and lower leg, inside your shoe: *a pair of socks* ••➤ picture on page C6
IDIOM **pull your socks up** (*Brit*) to start working harder or better than before

socket /'sɒkɪt/ **noun** [C] **1** (also **power point** or **plug**) a place in a wall where a piece of electrical equipment can be connected to the electricity supply ••➤ picture at **plug** **2** a hole in a piece of electrical equipment where another piece of equipment can be connected **3** a hole that sth fits into: *your eye socket*

soda /'səʊdə/ **noun** **1** (also **'soda water**) [U] water that has bubbles in it and is usually used for mixing with other drinks: *a whisky and soda* **2** [C] (*US*) = **FIZZY DRINK**

sofa /'səʊfə/ **noun** [C] a comfortable seat with a back and arms for two or more people to sit on: *a sofa bed* (= a sofa that you can open out to make a bed) ••➤ synonym **settee** ••➤ picture on page C7

★**soft** /sɒft/ **adj** **1** not hard or firm: *a soft bed/ seat* • *The ground is very soft after all that rain.* ••➤ opposite **hard** **2** smooth and pleasant to touch; not rough: *soft skin/hands* • *a soft towel* ••➤ opposite **rough** **3** (used about sounds, voices, words, etc) quiet or gentle; not loud or angry: *She spoke in a soft whisper.* ••➤ opposite **loud** or **harsh** **4** (used about light, colours etc) gentle and pleasant: *The room was decorated in soft pinks and greens.* ••➤ opposite **bright** **5** (used about people) kind and gentle, sometimes too much so: *A good manager can't afford to be too soft.* ••➤ opposite **hard** or **strict** **6** (used about illegal drugs) less dangerous and serious than the type of illegal drugs which can kill people

➤ Compare **hard drug**.

–**softly** **adv**: *He closed the door softly behind him.* –**softness** **noun** [U]
IDIOM **have a soft spot for sb/sth** (*informal*) to have good or loving feelings towards sb/ sth

soft 'drink **noun** [C] a cold drink that contains no alcohol

soften /'sɒfn/ **verb** **1** [I,T] to become softer or gentler; to make sb/sth softer or gentler: *a lotion to soften the skin* **2** [T] to make sth less shocking and unpleasant: *Her letter sounded too angry so she softened the language.* • *The air bag softened the impact of the crash.*

soft-'hearted adj kind and good at understanding other people's feelings ••> opposite **hard-hearted**

soft 'option noun [C] the easier thing to do of two or more possibilities, but not the best one: *The government has taken the soft option of agreeing to their demands.*

soft-'spoken adj having a gentle, quiet voice: *He was a kind, soft-spoken man.*

software /'spftweə/ noun [U] (*computing*) the programs and other operating information used by a computer: *There's a lot of new educational software available now.* ••> Look at **hardware.**

soggy /'spgi/ adj very wet and soft and so unpleasant

★ **soil¹** /sɔɪl/ noun **1** [C,U] the substance that plants, trees, etc grow in; earth: *poor/dry/ acid/sandy soil* ••> Look at the note at **ground¹.** ••> picture on page C2 **2** [U] (*written*) the land that is part of a country

soil² /sɔɪl/ verb [T] (*formal*) (often passive) to make sth dirty

solace /'splas/ noun [U,sing] (*written*) solace (in sth) a person or thing that makes you feel better or happier when you are sad or disappointed: *to find/seek solace in sb/sth*

solar /'səʊlə/ adj (only *before* a noun) **1** connected with the sun: *a solar eclipse* (= when the sun is blocked by the moon) **2** using the sun's energy: *solar heating/power*

the 'solar system noun [sing] the sun and the planets that move around it

sold *past tense, past participle* of **SELL**

★ **soldier** /'səʊldʒə/ noun [C] a member of an army: *The soldiers marched past.*

sole¹ /səʊl/ adj (only *before* a noun) **1** only; single: *His sole interest is football.* **2** belonging to one person only; not shared −**solely** adv: *I agreed to come solely because of your mother.*

sole² /səʊl/ noun **1** [C] the bottom surface of your foot ••> picture on page C5 **2** [C] the part of a shoe or sock that covers the bottom surface of your foot ••> picture at **shoe 3** [C,U] (*pl* **sole**) a flat sea fish that we eat

solemn /'spləm/ adj **1** (used about a person) very serious; not happy or smiling: *Her solemn face told them that the news was bad.* **2** sincere; done or said in a formal way: *to make a solemn promise* −**solemnity** /sə'lemnəti/ noun [U] −**solemnly** adv: *'I have something very important to tell you,' she began solemnly.*

solicit /sə'lɪsɪt/ verb **1** [T] (*formal*) to ask sb for money, help, support, etc: *They tried to solicit support for the proposal.* **2** [I,T] (used about a woman who has sex for money) to go to sb, especially in a public place, and offer sex in return for money

solicitor /sə'lɪsɪtə/ noun [C] (*Brit*) a lawyer whose job is to give legal advice, prepare legal documents and arrange the buying and selling of land, etc ••> Look at the note at **lawyer.**

★ **solid¹** /'splɪd/ adj **1** hard and firm; not in the form of liquid or gas: *It was so cold that the village pond had frozen solid.* **2** having no holes or empty spaces inside; not hollow: *a solid mass of rock* **3** strong, firm and well-made: *a solid little car* • (*figurative*) *They built up a solid friendship over the years.* **4** of good enough quality; that you can trust: *The police cannot make an arrest without solid evidence.* **5** (only *before* a noun) made completely of one substance, both on the inside and outside: *a solid gold chain* **6** (*spoken*) without a break or pause: *I was so tired that I slept for twelve solid hours/twelve hours solid.* −**solidity** /sə'lɪdəti/ noun [U]

solid² /'splɪd/ noun [C] **1** a substance or object that is hard; not a liquid or gas: *Liquids become solids when frozen.* • *The baby is not yet on solids* (= solid food). **2** an object that has length, width and height, not a flat shape: *A cube is a solid.*

solidarity /,splɪ'dærəti/ noun [U] solidarity (with sb) the support of one group of people for another, because they agree with their aims: *Many local people expressed solidarity with the strikers.*

solidify /sə'lɪdɪfaɪ/ verb [I] (*pres part* **solidifying**; *3rd pers sing pres* **solidifies**; *pt, pp* **solidified**) to become hard or solid

solidly /'splɪdli/ adv **1** strongly: *a solidly built house* **2** without stopping: *It rained solidly all day.*

solitaire /,splɪ'teə/ noun [U] **1** a game for one person in which you remove pieces from a special board by moving other pieces over them until you have only one piece left **2** (*US*) = **PATIENCE**(2)

solitary /'splətri/ adj **1** done alone, without other people: *Writing novels is a solitary occupation.* **2** (used about a person or an animal) enjoying being alone; frequently spending time alone: *She was always a solitary child.* **3** (only *before* a noun) one on its/his/her own with no others around: *a solitary figure walking up the hillside* ••> synonym **lone 4** (only *before* a noun) (usually in negative sentences or questions) only one; single: *I can't think of a solitary example* (= not even one).

solitary con'finement noun [U] a punishment in which a person in prison is kept completely alone in a separate cell away from the other prisoners

solitude /'splɪtjuːd/ noun [U] the state of being alone, especially when you find this pleasant: *She longed for peace and solitude.*

➤ Compare **loneliness** and **isolation.**

solo¹ /'səʊləʊ/ noun [C] (*pl* **solos**) a piece of music for only one person to play or sing ••> Look at **duet.** −**soloist** noun [C]

solo² /'səʊləʊ/ adj, adv **1** (done) alone; by yourself: *a solo flight* • *to fly solo* **2** connected with or played as a musical solo: *a solo artist* (= a singer who is not part of a group)

soluble /'spljəbl/ adj **1** soluble (in sth) that will dissolve in liquid: *These tablets are soluble in water.* **2** (*formal*) (used about a problem, etc) that has an answer; that can be solved ••> opposite **insoluble**

★**solution** /sə'lu:ʃn/ **noun 1** [C] a solution (to sth) a way of solving a problem, dealing with a difficult situation, etc: *a solution to the problem of unemployment* **2** [C] the solution (to sth) the answer (to a game, competition etc): *The solution to the quiz will be published next week.* **3** [C,U] (a) liquid in which sth solid has been dissolved: *saline solution*

★**solve** /sɒlv/ **verb** [T] **1** to find a way of dealing with a problem or difficult situation: *The government is trying to solve the problem of inflation.* ● *The police have not managed to solve the crime.* ● *to solve a mystery* **2** to find the correct answer to a competition, a problem in mathematics, a series of questions, etc: *to solve a puzzle/equation/riddle* ••➤ noun **solution** ••➤ adjective **soluble**

solvent /'sɒlvənt/ **noun** [C,U] a liquid that can dissolve another substance

sombre (*US* **somber**) /'sɒmbə/ **adj 1** dark in colour; dull **2** sad and serious –**sombrely** adv

★**some** /səm; *strong form* sʌm/ **determiner, pron 1** (before uncountable nouns and plural countable nouns) a certain amount of or a number of: *We need some butter and some potatoes.* ● *I don't need any more money – I've still got some.*

➤ In negative sentences and in questions we use **any** instead of **some**: *Do we need any butter?* ● *I need some more money. I haven't got any.* But look at **2** for examples of questions where **some** is used.

2 used in questions when you expect or want the answer 'yes': *Would you like some more cake?* ● *Can I take some of this paper?* **3** some (of sb/sth) used when you are referring to certain members of a group or certain types of a thing, but not all of them: *Some pupils enjoy this kind of work, some don't.* ● *Some of his books are very exciting.* ● *Some of us are going to the park.* **4** used with singular countable nouns for talking about a person or thing without saying any details: *I'll see you again some time, I expect.* ● *There must be some mistake.* ● *I read about it in some newspaper or other.*

★**somebody** /'sʌmbədi/ (also **someone**) **pron** a person who is not known or not mentioned by name: *How are you? Somebody said that you'd been ill.* ● *She's getting married to someone she met at work.* ● *There's somebody at the door.* ● *I think you should talk to someone else* (= another person) *about this problem.*

➤ **Somebody**, **anybody** and **everybody** are used with a singular verb but are often followed by a plural pronoun (except in formal language where 'his/her' or 'him/her' must be used): *Somebody has left their coat behind.* ● *Has anyone not brought their books?* ● *I'll see everybody concerned and tell them the news.* The difference between **somebody** and **anybody** is the same as the difference between **some** and **any**. Look at the note at **some**.

'**some day** adv (also **someday**) at a time in the future that is not yet known: *I hope you'll come and visit me some day.*

★**somehow** /'sʌmhaʊ/ **adv 1** in a way that is not known or certain: *The car's broken down but I'll get to work somehow.* ● *Somehow we had got completely lost.* **2** for a reason you do not know or understand: *I somehow get the feeling that I've been here before.*

★**someone** /'sʌmwʌn/ = **SOMEBODY**

someplace /'sʌmpleɪs/ (*US*) = **SOMEWHERE**

somersault /'sʌməsɔːlt/ **noun** [C] a movement in which you roll right over with your feet going over your head

★**something** /'sʌmθɪŋ/ **pron 1** a thing that is not known or not named: *I've got something in my eye.* ● *Wait a minute – I've forgotten something.* ● *Would you like something else* (= another thing) *to drink?*

➤ The difference between **something** and **anything** is the same as the difference between **some** and **any**. Look at the note at **some**.

2 a thing that is important, useful or worth considering: *There's something in what your mother says.* ● *I think you've got something there – I like that idea.* **3** (*informal*) used to show that a description, an amount, etc is not exact: *a new comedy series aimed at thirty-somethings* (= people between thirty and forty years old).

IDIOMS or something (*informal*) used for showing that you are not sure about what you have just said: *'What's his job?' 'I think he's a plumber, or something.'*

something like similar to: *A loganberry is something like a raspberry.*

something to do with connected or involved with: *The programme's something to do with the environment.*

★**sometime** (also **some time**) /'sʌmtaɪm/ **adv** at a time that you do not know exactly or have not yet decided: *I'll phone you sometime this evening.* ● *I must go and see her sometime.*

★**sometimes** /'sʌmtaɪmz/ **adv** on some occasions; now and then: *Sometimes I drive to work and sometimes I go by bus.* ● *I sometimes watch television in the evenings.*

somewhat /'sʌmwɒt/ **adv** rather; to some degree: *We missed the train, which was somewhat unfortunate.*

★**somewhere** /'sʌmweə/ (*US also* **someplace**) **adv 1** at, in, or to a place that you do not know or do not mention by name: *I've seen your glasses somewhere downstairs.* ● *'Have they gone to France?' 'No, I think they've gone somewhere else* (= to another place) *this year.'*

➤ The difference between **somewhere** and **anywhere** is the same as the difference between **some** and **any**. Look at the note at **some**.

2 used when you do not know an exact time, number, etc: *Your ideal weight should probably be somewhere around 70 kilos.*

son /sʌn/ **noun** [C] a male child •➤ Look at **daughter**.

sonata /sə'nɑːtə/ **noun** [C] a piece of music written for the piano, or for another instrument together with the piano

song /sɒŋ/ **noun 1** [C] a piece of music with words that you sing: *a folk/love/pop song* **2** [U] songs in general; music for singing: *to burst/break into song* (= to suddenly start singing) **3** [U,C] the musical sounds that birds make: *birdsong*

songwriter /'sɒŋraɪtə/ **noun** [C] a person whose job is to write songs

sonic /'sɒnɪk/ **adj** (*technical*) connected with sound waves

son-in-law **noun** [C] (*pl* **sons-in-law**) the husband of your daughter

soon /suːn/ **adv 1** in a short time from now; a short time after sth else has happened: *It will soon be dark.* • *He left soon after me.* • *We should arrive at your house soon after twelve.* • (*spoken*) *See you soon.* **2** early; quickly: *Don't leave so soon. Stay for tea.* • *How soon can you get here?*

IDIOMS **as soon as** at the moment (that); when: *Phone me as soon as you hear some news.* • *I'd like your reply **as soon as possible** (= at the earliest possible moment).*

no sooner...than (*written*) immediately when or after: *No sooner had I shut the door than I realized I'd left my keys inside.*

➤ Note the word order here. The verb follows immediately after 'No sooner', and the subject comes after that.

sooner or later at some time in the future; one day

soot /sʊt/ **noun** [U] black powder that comes from burning things and collects in chimneys

soothe /suːð/ **verb** [T] **1** to make sb calmer or less upset; to comfort sb **2** to make a part of the body or a feeling less painful: *The doctor gave me some skin cream to soothe the irritation.* –**soothing** **adj**: *soothing music* • *a soothing massage* –**soothingly** **adv**

sophisticated /sə'fɪstɪkeɪtɪd/ **adj 1** having or showing a lot of experience of the world and social situations; knowing about fashion, culture, etc **2** (used about machines, systems, etc) advanced and complicated **3** able to understand difficult or complicated things: *Voters are much more sophisticated these days.* –**sophistication** /sə,fɪstɪ'keɪʃn/ **noun** [U]

soppy /'sɒpi/ **adj** (*informal*) full of unnecessary emotion; silly: *a soppy romantic film*

soprano /sə'prɑːnəʊ/ **noun** [C] (*pl* **sopranos** /-nəʊz/) the highest singing voice; a woman, girl, or boy with this voice

sordid /'sɔːdɪd/ **adj 1** unpleasant; not honest or moral: *We discovered the truth about his sordid past.* **2** very dirty and unpleasant

sore¹ /sɔː/ **adj** (used about a part of the body) painful, especially when touched: *to have a sore throat* • *My feet were sore from walking so far.* –**soreness** **noun** [U]: *a cream to reduce soreness and swelling*

IDIOMS **a sore point** a subject that is likely to make sb upset or angry when mentioned

stand/stick out like a sore thumb to be extremely obvious, especially in a negative way: *A big new office block would stand out like a sore thumb in the old part of town.*

sore² /sɔː/ **noun** [C] a painful, often red place on your body where the skin is cut or infected

sorely /'sɔːli/ **adv** (*formal*) very much; seriously: *You'll be sorely missed when you leave.*

sorrow /'sɒrəʊ/ **noun** (*formal*) **1** [U] a feeling of great sadness because sth bad has happened **2** [C] a very sad event or situation –**sorrowful** **adj** –**sorrowfully** **adv**

sorry¹ /'sɒri/ **adj** (**sorrier**; **sorriest**) **1** (not before a noun) sorry (to see, hear, etc); sorry that... sad or disappointed: *I was sorry to hear that you've been ill.* • *I am sorry that we have to leave so soon.* • *'Simon's mother died last week.' 'Oh, I am sorry.'* **2** (not before a noun) sorry (for/about sth); sorry (to do sth/that...) used for excusing yourself for sth that you have done: *I'm awfully sorry for spilling that coffee.* • *I'm sorry I've kept you all waiting.* • *I'm sorry to disturb you so late in the evening, but I wonder if you can help me.* **3** (not before a noun) used for politely saying 'no' to sth, disagreeing with sth or introducing bad news: *'Would you like to come to dinner on Friday?' 'I'm sorry, I'm busy that evening.'* • *I'm sorry, I don't agree with you. I think we should accept the offer.* • *I'm sorry to tell you that your application has been unsuccessful.* **4** (only *before* a noun) very bad: *The house was in a sorry state when we first moved in.* • *They were a sorry sight when they finally got home.*

IDIOM **be/feel sorry for sb** to feel sadness or pity for sb: *I feel very sorry for the families of the victims.* • *Stop feeling sorry for yourself!*

sorry² /'sɒri/ **interj 1** used for making excuses, apologizing, etc: *Sorry, I didn't see you standing behind me.* • *Sorry I'm late – the bus didn't come on time.* • *He didn't even say sorry* (= apologize)! **2** (*especially Brit*) used for asking sb to repeat sth that you have not heard correctly): *'My name's Dave Harries.' 'Sorry? Dave who?'* **3** (used for correcting yourself when you have said sth wrong): *Take the second turning, sorry, the third turning on the right.*

sort¹ /sɔːt/ **noun 1** [C] a sort of sb/sth a type or kind: *What sort of music do you like?* • *She's got all sorts of problems at the moment.* • *There were snacks – peanuts, olives, that sort of thing.* **2** [sing] (*especially Brit*) a particular type of character; a person •➤ synonym **kind**

IDIOMS **a sort of sth** (*informal*) a type of sth; sth that is similar to sth: *Can you hear a sort of ticking noise?*

sort of (*spoken*) rather; in a way: *'Do you see what I mean?' 'Sort of.'* • *I'd sort of like to go, but I'm not sure.*

sort² /sɔːt/ **verb** [T] **1** sort sth (into sth) to put things into different groups or places, according to their type, etc; to separate things of one type from others: *I'm just sorting these papers into the correct files.* **2** (*especially Brit informal*) (often passive) to find an answer to a problem or difficult situation; to organize sth/sb: *I'll have more time when I've got things sorted at home.*

PHRASAL VERBS **sort sth out 1** to find an answer to a problem; to organize sth: *I haven't found a flat yet but I hope to sort something out soon.* **2** to tidy or organize sth: *The toy cupboard needs sorting out.*

sort through sth to look through a number of things, in order to find sth that you are looking for or to put them in order

so-so /ˌsəʊ 'səʊ/ **adj, adv** (*informal*) all right but not particularly good/well: *'How are you?' 'So-so.'*

soufflé /'suːfleɪ/ **noun** [C,U] a type of food made mainly from egg whites, flour and milk, beaten together and baked until it rises

sought *past tense, past participle of* SEEK

'sought after adj that people want very much, because it is of high quality or rare

soul /səʊl/ **noun 1** [C] the spiritual part of a person that is believed to continue to exist after the body is dead **2** [C,U] the inner part of a person containing his/her deepest thoughts and feelings: *There was a feeling of restlessness deep in her soul.* •➤ Look at **spirit**. **3** [C] (*old-fashioned*) (used with adjectives) a particular type of person **4** [sing] (in negative statements) a person: *There wasn't a soul in sight* (= there was nobody). • *Promise me you won't tell a soul.* **5** (also **'soul music**) [U] a type of popular African American music: *a soul singer*

IDIOM **heart and soul** ➔ HEART

soulful /'səʊlfl/ **adj** having or showing deep feeling: *a soulful expression*

soulless /'səʊlləs/ **adj** without feeling, warmth or interest: *soulless industrial towns*

★**sound¹** /saʊnd/ **noun 1** [C,U] something that you hear or that can be heard: *the sound of voices* • *a clicking/buzzing/scratching sound* • *After that, he didn't make a sound.* • *She opened the door without a sound.* • *Light travels faster than sound.* • *sound waves* **2** [U] what you can hear coming from a television, radio, etc: *Can you turn the sound up/down?*

IDIOM **by the sound of it/things** judging from what sb has said or what you have read about sb/sth: *She must be an interesting person, by the sound of it.*

★**sound²** /saʊnd/ **verb 1** [I] (not usually in the continuous tenses) to give a particular impression when heard or read about; to seem: *That sounds like a child crying.* • *She sounded upset and angry on the phone.* • *You sound like your father when you say things like that!* • *He sounds a very nice person from his letter.* • *Does she sound like the right person for the job?* • *It doesn't sound as if/though he's very reliable.* •➤ In spoken English, people often use 'like' instead of 'as if' or 'as though', especially in US English, but this is considered incorrect in written British

English. **2 -sounding** (used to form compound adjectives) seeming to be of the type mentioned, from what you have heard or read: *a Spanish-sounding surname* **3** [T] to cause sb to make a sound; to give a signal by making a sound: *to sound the horn of your car* • *A student on one of the upper floors sounded the alarm.*

PHRASAL VERB **sound sb out (about sth)** to ask sb questions in order to find out what he/she thinks or intends

★**sound³** /saʊnd/ **adj, adv 1** sensible; that you can depend on and that will probably give good results: *sound advice* • *a sound investment* **2** healthy and strong; in good condition: *The structure of the bridge is basically sound.* •➤ opposite **unsound** –**soundness noun** [U]

IDIOM **be sound asleep** to be deeply asleep

'sound effect noun [C, usually pl] a sound that is made artificially, for example the sound of the wind, and used in a play, film or computer game to make it more realistic

soundly /'saʊndli/ **adv** completely or deeply: *The children were sleeping soundly.*

soundproof /'saʊndpruːf/ **adj** made so that no sound can get in or out: *a soundproof room*

soundtrack /'saʊndtræk/ **noun** [C] the recorded sound and music from a film or computer game •➤ Look at **track**.

★**soup** /suːp/ **noun** [U,C] liquid food made by cooking meat, vegetables, etc in water: *a tin of chicken soup* •➤ picture on page C4

★**sour** /'saʊə/ **adj 1** having a sharp taste like that of a lemon: *This sauce is quite sour* **2** (used especially about milk) tasting or smelling unpleasant because it is no longer fresh: *This cream has gone sour.* **3** (used about people) angry and unpleasant: *a sour expression* • *a sour-faced old woman* –**sour verb** [T] (*formal*) *The disagreement over trade tariffs has soured relations between the two countries.* –**sourly adv** –**sourness noun** [U]

IDIOMS **go/turn sour** to stop being pleasant or friendly: *Their relationship turned sour after a few months.*

sour 'grapes pretending to not want sth that in fact you secretly want, because you cannot have it

★**source** /sɔːs/ **noun** [C] a place, person or thing where sth comes or starts from or where sth is obtained: *Britain's oil reserves are an important source of income.* • *This word has its source in Greek.* • *The television is a great source of entertainment.* • *Police have refused to reveal the source of their information.*

★**south¹** /saʊθ/ (also **the south**) **noun** [sing] (*abbr* **S**) **1** the direction that is on your right when you watch the sun rise; one of the four main directions that we give names to (the points of the compass): *warm winds from the south* • *Which way is south?* • *We live to the south of* (= further south than) *London* •➤ picture at **north 2 the South** the southern part of any country, city, region or the world: *Nice is in the South of France.* •➤ Look at **north, east** and **west**.

S

south² /saʊθ/ *adj, adv* **1** (also **South**) (only *before* a noun) in the south: *the south coast of Cornwall* **2** to or towards the south: *The house faces south.* ● *We live just south of Birmingham.* **3** (used about a wind) coming from the south

southbound /'saʊθbaʊnd/ *adj* travelling or leading towards the south

,**south-'east¹** (also **the South-East**) *noun* [sing] (*abbr* **SE**) the direction or a region that is halfway between south and east ••➤ picture at **north**

,**south-'east²** *adj, adv* in, from or to the south-east of a place or country: *the south-east coast of Spain*

,**south-'easterly** *adj* **1** towards the south-east: *in a south-easterly direction* **2** (used about a wind) coming from the south-east

,**south-'eastern** *adj* (only *before* a noun) connected with the south-east of a place or country: *the south-eastern states of the US*

,**south-'eastward(s)** *adv* towards the south-east

southerly /'sʌðəli/ *adj* **1** to, towards or in the south: *Keep going in a southerly direction.* **2** (used about a wind) coming from the south

★**southern** (also **Southern**) /'sʌðən/ *adj* of, in or from the south of a place: *a man with a southern accent* ● *Greece is in Southern Europe.*

southerner (also **Southerner**) /'sʌðənə/ *noun* [C] a person who was born in or lives in the southern part of a country ••➤ opposite **northerner**

the ,South 'Pole *noun* [sing] the point on the Earth's surface which is furthest south ••➤ picture at **earth**

southward /'saʊθwəd/ (also **southwards**) *adj, adv* towards the south

,**south-'west¹** (also **the South-West**) *noun* [sing] (*abbr* **SW**) the direction or region halfway between south and west ••➤ picture at **north**

,**south-'west²** *adj, adv* in, from or to the south-west of a place or country: *the south-west coast of France* ● *Our garden faces south-west.*

,**south-'westerly** *adj* **1** towards the south-west: *in a south-westerly direction* **2** (used about a wind) coming from the south-west

,**south-'western** *adj* (only *before* a noun) connected with the south-west of a place or country

,**south-'westward(s)** *adv* towards the south-west: *Follow the B409 south-westward for twenty miles.*

souvenir /,su:və'nɪə/ *noun* [C] something that you keep to remind you of somewhere you have been on holiday or of a special event: *I brought back a menu as a souvenir of my trip.*

sovereign¹ /'sɒvrɪn/ *noun* [C] a king or queen

sovereign² /'sɒvrɪn/ *adj* **1** (used about a country) not controlled by any other country;

independent **2** having the highest possible authority

sovereignty /'sɒvrənti/ *noun* [U] the power that a country has to control its own government

sow¹ /saʊ/ *noun* [C] an adult female pig ••➤ Look at the note at **pig**.

sow² /səʊ/ *verb* [T] (*pt* **sowed**; *pp* **sown** /səʊn/ or **sowed**) **sow** A (in B); **sow** B (with A) to plant seeds in the ground: *to sow seeds in pots* ● *to sow a field with wheat*

soya bean /'sɔɪə biːn/ (*US* **soy bean** /'sɔɪ biːn/) *noun* [C] a type of bean that can be cooked and eaten or used to make many different kinds of food, for example flour, oil and a sort of milk

,**soy 'sauce** (also ,**soya 'sauce**) *noun* [U] a dark brown sauce that is made from soya beans and that you add to food to make it taste better

spa /spɑː/ *noun* [C] a place where mineral water comes out of the ground and where people go to drink this water because it is considered to be healthy

★**space¹** /speɪs/ *noun* **1** [C,U] **space (for sb/sth) (to do sth)** an area or space that is empty or not used: *Is there enough space for me to park the car there?* ● *Shelves would take up less space than a cupboard.* ● *a parking space* ● *We're a bit short of space.* ● *There's a space here for you to write your name.* ● *Leave a space after the comma.* ••➤ Look at **room** and the note at **place¹**. **2** [U] (also ,**outer 'space**) (often used to form compound nouns) the area which surrounds the planet Earth and the other planets and stars: *space travel* ● *a spaceman/spacewoman* (= a person who travels in space) ● *a spacecraft/spaceship* **3** [C,usually sing] a period of time: *Priti had been ill three times in/within the space of four months.* ● *He's achieved a lot in a short space of time.* **4** [U] time and freedom to think and do what you want: *I need some space to think.*

space² /speɪs/ *verb* [T] **space sth (out)** to arrange things so that there are empty spaces between them

spacious /'speɪʃəs/ *adj* having a lot of space; large in size –**spaciousness** *noun* [U]

spade /speɪd/ *noun* **1** [C] a tool that you use for digging ••➤ picture at **dig** and **garden**. Look at **shovel**. **2 spades** [pl] the group (suit) of playing cards with pointed black symbols on them: *the king of spades* ••➤ Look at the note and picture at **card**. **3** [C] one of the cards from this suit: *Have you got a spade?*

spaghetti /spə'geti/ *noun* [U] a type of Italian food (**pasta**) made from flour and water that looks like long strings: *How long does spaghetti take to cook?* ••➤ picture on page C4

span¹ /spæn/ *noun* [C] **1** the length of sth from one end to the other: *the wingspan of a bird* **2** the length of time that sth lasts or continues: *Young children have a short attention span.*

span² /spæn/ *verb* [T] (**spanning**; **spanned**)

S

[I] **intransitive**, a verb which has no object: *He laughed.*   [T] **transitive**, a verb which has an object: *He ate an apple.*

1 to form a bridge over sth **2** to last or continue for a particular period of time

spank /spæŋk/ **verb** [T] to hit a child on his/her bottom with an open hand as a punishment

★ **spanner** /'spænə/ (*US* **wrench**) **noun** [C] a metal tool with an end shaped for turning small metal rings (**nuts**) and pins (**bolts**) that are used for holding things together •➤ picture at **tool**

★ **spare**¹ /speə/ **adj 1** not needed now but kept because it may be needed in the future: *The spare tyre is kept in the boot.* • *a spare room* **2** not used for work: *What do you do in your spare time?* **3** not being used; free: *There were no seats spare so we had to stand.* –spare **noun** [C]: *The fuse has blown. Where do you keep your spares?*

spare² /speə/ **verb** [T] **1** spare sth (for sb); spare (sb) sth to be able to give sth to sb: *I suppose I can spare you a few minutes.* **2** spare sb (from) sth/doing sth to save sb from having an unpleasant experience: *You could spare yourself waiting if you book in advance.* **3** spare no effort, expense, etc to do sth as well as possible without limiting the money, time, etc involved: *No expense was spared at the wedding.* • *He spared no effort in trying to find a job.* **4** spare sb/sth (from sth) to not hurt or damage sb/sth
IDIOM to spare more than is needed: *There's no time to spare. We must leave straight away.*

,spare 'part **noun** [C] a part for a machine, engine, etc that you can use to replace an old part which is damaged or broken

sparing /'speərɪŋ/ **adj** (*formal*) using only a little of sth; careful –sparingly **adv**

spark¹ /spɑːk/ **noun 1** [C] a very small bright piece of burning material: *A spark set fire to the carpet.* **2** [C] a flash of light that is caused by electricity: *A spark ignites the fuel in a car engine.* **3** [C,U] an exciting quality that sb/sth has

spark² /spɑːk/ **verb**
PHRASAL VERB spark sth off to cause sth: *Eric's comments sparked off a tremendous argument.*

sparkle /'spɑːkl/ **verb** [I] to shine with many small points of light: *The river sparkled in the sunlight.* –sparkle **noun** [C,U]

sparkling /'spɑːklɪŋ/ **adj 1** shining with many small points of light: *sparkling blue eyes* **2** (used about a drink) containing bubbles of gas: *sparkling wine/mineral water* •➤ picture at **bubble**

'spark plug **noun** [C] a small piece of equipment in an engine that produces a bright flash of electricity (a spark) to make the fuel burn and start the engine

sparrow /'spærəʊ/ **noun** [C] a small brown and grey bird that is common in many parts of the world

sparse /spɑːs/ **adj** small in quantity or amount: *a sparse crowd* • *He just had a few sparse hairs on his head.* –sparsely **adv**: *a sparsely populated area* –sparseness **noun** [U]

spartan /'spɑːtn/ **adj** (*formal*) very simple and not comfortable: *spartan living conditions*

spasm /'spæzəm/ **noun** [C,U] a sudden movement of a muscle that you cannot control: *He had painful muscular spasms in his leg.*

spat past tense, past participle of **SPIT**¹

spate /speɪt/ **noun** [sing] a large number or amount of sth happening at one time: *There has been a spate of burglaries in the area recently.*

spatial /'speɪʃl/ **adj** (*formal*) connected with the size or position of sth

spatter /'spætə/ **verb** [T] spatter sb/sth (with sth); spatter sth (on sb/sth) to cover sb/sth with small drops of sth wet

spatula /'spætjələ/ **noun** [C] a tool with a wide flat part used in cooking for mixing and spreading things •➤ picture at **kitchen**

★ **speak** /spiːk/ **verb** (*pt* spoke /spəʊk/; *pp* spoken /'spəʊkən/) **1** [I] speak (to sb) (about sth); speak (of sth) to talk or say things: *I'd like to speak to the manager, please.* • *Could you speak more slowly?* • *I was so angry I could hardly speak.*

➤ **Speak** and **talk** have almost the same meaning but we use **talk** more informally, to show that two or more people are having a conversation, and **speak** to show that only one person is saying something, especially in a formal situation: *I'd like to speak to the manager, please.* • *We talked all night.* • *The head teacher spoke to the class about university courses.*

2 [T] (not used in the continuous tenses) to know and be able to use a language: *Does anyone here speak German?* • *She speaks (in) Greek to her parents.* • *a French-speaking guide* **3** [I] speak (on/about sth) to make a speech to a group of people **4** [I] (*informal*) be speaking (to sb) to be friendly with sb again after an argument
IDIOMS be on speaking terms (with sb) to be friendly with sb again after an argument: *Thankfully they are back on speaking terms again.*

so to speak used when you are describing sth in a way that sounds strange: *She turned green, so to speak, after watching a television programme about the environment.*

speak for itself to be very clear so that no other explanation is needed: *The statistics speak for themselves.*

speak/talk of the devil → **DEVIL**

speak your mind to say exactly what you think, even though you might offend sb
PHRASAL VERBS speak for sb to express the thoughts or opinions of sb else

speak out (against sth) to say publicly that you think sth is bad or wrong

speak up to speak louder

speaker /'spiːkə/ **noun** [C] **1** a person who makes a speech to a group of people: *Tonight's speaker is a well-known writer and journalist.* **2** a person who speaks a particular language: *She's a fluent Russian speaker.* **3** = **LOUDSPEAKER**(1)

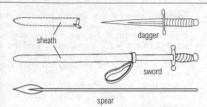

sheath

dagger

sword

spear

spear /spɪə/ **noun** [C] a long pole with a sharp point at one end, used for hunting or fighting

spearhead /'spɪəhed/ **noun** [C,usually sing] a person or group that begins or leads an attack –**spearhead verb** [T]

spearmint /'spɪəmɪnt/ **noun** [U] a type of leaf with a strong fresh taste that is used in sweets, etc: *spearmint chewing gum* •➤ Look at **peppermint**.

★**special**[1] /'speʃl/ **adj 1** not usual or ordinary; important for some particular reason: *a special occasion* • *Please take special care of it.* • *Are you doing anything special tonight?* **2** (only *before* a noun) for a particular purpose: *Andy goes to a special school for the deaf.* • *There's a special tool for doing that.*

special[2] /'speʃl/ **noun** [C] something that is not of the usual or ordinary type: *an all-night election special on TV* • *I'm going to cook one of my specials tonight.*

specialist /'speʃəlɪst/ **noun** [C] a person with special or deep knowledge of a particular subject: *She's a specialist in diseases of cattle.* • *I have to see a heart specialist.* • *to give specialist advice*

speciality /ˌspeʃi'æləti/ **noun** [C] (*pl* **specialities**) (*US* **specialty** /'speʃəlti/; *pl* **specialties**) **1** an area of study or a subject that you know a lot about **2** something made by a person, place, business, etc that is very good and that he/she/it is known for: *The cheese is a speciality of the region.*

specialize (also **-ise**) /'speʃəlaɪz/ **verb** [I] **specialize (in sth)** to give most of your attention to one subject, type of product, etc: *This shop specializes in clothes for taller men.* –**specialization** (also **-isation**) /ˌspeʃəlaɪ'zeɪʃn/ **noun** [U]

specialized (also **-ised**) /'speʃəlaɪzd/ **adj 1** to be used for a particular purpose: *a specialized system* **2** having or needing deep or special knowledge of a particular subject: *We have specialized staff to help you with any problems.*

specially /'speʃəli/ (also **especially**) **adv 1** for a particular purpose or reason: *I made this specially for you.* **2** particularly; very; more than usual: *The restaurant has a great atmosphere but the food is not specially good.* • *It's not an especially difficult exam.*

specialty (*US*) = **SPECIALITY**

★**species** /'spiːʃiːz/ **noun** [C] (*pl* **species**) a group of plants or animals that are all the same and that can breed together: *This conservation group aims to protect endangered species.* • *a rare species of frog*

★**specific** /spə'sɪfɪk/ **adj 1** specific (about sth) detailed or exact: *You must give the class specific instructions on what they have to do.* • *Can you be more specific about what the man was wearing?* **2** particular; not general: *Everyone has been given a specific job to do.* –**specifically** /-kli/ **adv**: *a play written specifically for radio*

specification /ˌspesɪfɪ'keɪʃn/ **noun** [C,U] detailed information about how sth is or should be built or made

specify /'spesɪfaɪ/ **verb** [T] (*pres part* **specifying**; *3rd pers sing pres* **specifies**; *pt, pp* **specified**) to say or name sth clearly or in detail: *The fire regulations specify the maximum number of people allowed in.*

specimen /'spesɪmən/ **noun** [C] **1** an example of a particular type of thing, especially intended to be studied by experts or scientists **2** a small amount of sth that is tested for medical or scientific purposes: *Specimens of the patient's blood were tested in the hospital laboratory.* •➤ synonym **sample**

speck /spek/ **noun** [C] a very small spot or mark: *a speck of dust/dirt*

specs /speks/ (*informal*) = **GLASSES**

spectacle /'spektəkl/ **noun** [C] something that is impressive or shocking to look at

spectacles /'spektəklz/ (*formal*) = **GLASSES**

spectacular /spek'tækjələ/ **adj** very impressive to see: *The view from the top of the hill is quite spectacular.* –**spectacularly adv**

★**spectator** /spek'teɪtə/ **noun** [C] a person who is watching an event, especially a sporting event

spectre (*US* **specter**) /'spektə/ **noun** [C] **1** something unpleasant that people are afraid might happen in the future: *the spectre of unemployment* **2** (*old-fashioned*) = **GHOST**

spectrum /'spektrəm/ **noun** [C,usually sing] (*pl* **spectra** /'spektrə/) **1** the set of seven colours into which white light can be separated: *You can see the colours of the spectrum in a rainbow.* **2** all the possible varieties of sth: *The speakers represented the whole spectrum of political opinions.*

speculate /'spekjuleɪt/ **verb 1** [I,T] speculate (about/on sth); speculate that... to make a guess about sth: *to speculate about the result of the next election* **2** [I] to buy and sell with the aim of making money but with the risk of losing it: *to speculate on the stock market* –**speculation** /ˌspekju'leɪʃn/ **noun** [U,C] –**speculator noun** [C]

sped *past tense, past participle* of **SPEED**[2]

★**speech** /spiːtʃ/ **noun 1** [C] a formal talk that you give to a group of people: *The Chancellor is going to* **make a speech** *to city businessmen.* **2** [U] the ability to speak: *He lost the* **power of speech** *after the accident.* • *freedom of speech* (= being allowed to express your opinions openly) **3** [U] the particular way of speaking of a person or group of people: *She's doing a study of children's speech.* **4** [C] a group of words that one person must say in a play

S

speechless /'spiːtʃləs/ **adj** not able to speak, for example because you are shocked, angry, etc

★**speed**¹ /spiːd/ **noun 1** [U] fast movement: *I intend to start the race slowly and gradually* **pick up speed**. ● *The bus was travelling* **at speed** *when it hit the wall.* **2** [C,U] the rate at which sb/sth moves or travels: *The car was travelling* **at a speed of** *140 kilometres an hour.* ● *to travel* **at top/high/full/maximum speed.**

speed² /spiːd/ **verb** [I] (*pt, pp* **sped** /sped/) **1** to go or move very quickly: *He sped round the corner on his bicycle.* **2** (only used in the continuous tenses) to drive a car, etc faster than the legal speed limit: *The police said she had been speeding.*

PHRASAL VERB **speed (sth) up** (*pt, pp* **speeded**) to go or make sth go faster: *The new computer system should speed up production in the factory.*

speedboat /'spiːdbəʊt/ **noun** [C] a small fast boat with an engine

speeding /'spiːdɪŋ/ **noun** [U] driving a car, etc faster than the legal speed limit

'speed limit noun [C,usually sing] the highest speed that you may drive without breaking the law on a particular road: *He was going way* **over the speed limit** *when the police stopped him.*

speedometer /spiː'dɒmɪtə/ **noun** [C] a piece of equipment in a vehicle that tells you how fast you are travelling •➤ picture on page S9

speedway /'spiːdweɪ/ **noun** [U] the sport of racing motorbikes around a roundish track made of a dirty black substance

speedy /'spiːdi/ **adj** fast; quick: *a speedy response/reply* –**speedily adv** –**speediness noun** [U]

★**spell**¹ /spel/ **verb** (*pt, pp* **spelled** /speld/ or **spelt** /spelt/) **1** [I,T] to write or say the letters of a word in the correct order: *I could never spell very well at school.* ● **How do you spell** *your surname?* ● *His name is spelt P-H-I-L-I-P.* **2** [T] (used about a set of letters) to form a particular word: *If you add an 'e' to 'car' it spells 'care'.* **3** [T] to mean sth; to have sth as a result: *Another poor harvest would* **spell disaster** *for the region.*

PHRASAL VERB **spell sth out 1** to write or say the letters of a word or name in the correct order: *I have an unusual name, so I always have to spell it out to people.* **2** to express sth in a very clear and direct way

spell² /spel/ **noun** [C] **1** a short period of time: *a spell of cold weather* **2** (especially in stories) magic words or actions that cause sb to be in a particular state or condition

spelling /'spelɪŋ/ **noun 1** [C,U] the way that letters are arranged to make a word: *'Center' is the American spelling of 'centre'.* **2** [U] the ability to write the letters of a word correctly: *Roger is very poor at spelling.*

spelt *past tense, past participle* of **SPELL**¹

★**spend** /spend/ **verb** (*pt, pp* **spent** /spent/) **1** [I,T] **spend (sth) (on sth)** to give or pay money for sth: *How much do you spend on food each week?* ● *You shouldn't go on spending like that.* **2** [T] **spend sth (on sth/doing sth)** to pass time: *I spent a whole evening writing letters.* ● *I'm spending the weekend at my parents' house.* ● *He spent two years in Rome.* ● *I don't want to spend too much time on this project.*

spending /'spendɪŋ/ **noun** [U] the amount of money that is spent by a government or an organization

sperm /spɜːm/ **noun 1** [C] (*pl* **sperm** or **sperms**) a cell that is produced in the sex organs of a male and that can join with a female egg to produce young **2** [U] the liquid that contains sperms

sphere /sfɪə/ **noun** [C] **1** any round object shaped like a ball •➤ picture at **cube 2** an area of interest or activity –**spherical** /'sferɪkl/ **adj**

spice¹ /spaɪs/ **noun 1** [C,U] a substance, especially a powder, that is made from a plant and used to give flavour to food: *I use a lot of herbs and spices in my cooking.* ● *Pepper and paprika are two common spices.* •➤ Look at **spice. 2** [U] excitement and interest: *to add spice to a situation* –**spicy adj**: *Do you like spicy food?*

spice² /spaɪs/ **verb** [T] **spice sth (up) (with sth) 1** to add spice to food: *He always spices his cooking with lots of chilli powder.* **2** to add excitement to sth

spider /'spaɪdə/ **noun** [C] a type of small animal like an insect with eight legs. Spiders make (**spin**) special nets (**webs**) to catch insects for food.

spike /spaɪk/ **noun** [C] a piece of metal, wood, etc that has a sharp point at one end

spill

He's **spilled** his milk.

★**spill** /spɪl/ **verb** [I,T] (*pt, pp* **spilt** /spɪlt/ or **spilled**) **1** (used especially about a liquid) to accidentally come out of a container; to make a liquid, etc do this: *The bag split, and sugar spilled everywhere.* ● *Some water had spilled out of the bucket onto the floor.* ● *I've spilt some coffee on the desk.* **2** [I] **spill out, over, into, etc** to come out of a place suddenly and go in different directions: *The train stopped and everyone spilled out.*
–**spill noun** [C]: *Many seabirds died as a result of the oil spill.*

IDIOM **spill the beans** (*informal*) to tell a person about sth that should be a secret

★**spin**¹ /spɪn/ **verb** (**spinning**; *pt, pp* **spun** /spʌn/) **1** [I,T] **spin (sth) (round)** to turn or to make sth turn round quickly: *Mary spun*

round when she heard someone call her name.
● **to spin a ball/coin/wheel 2** [I,T] to make thread from a mass of wool, cotton, etc: *A spider spins a web.* **3** [T] to remove water from clothes that have just been washed in a washing machine by turning them round and round very fast

PHRASAL VERB **spin sth out** to make sth last as long as possible

spin² /spɪn/ noun [C,U] **1** an act of making sth spin: *She put a lot of spin on the ball.* **2** (especially in politics) a way of talking publicly about a difficult situation, a mistake, etc that makes it sound positive for you

IDIOM **go/take sb for a spin** to go/take sb out in a car or other vehicle

spinach /'spɪnɪtʃ; -ɪdʒ/ noun [U] a plant with large dark green leaves that can be cooked and eaten as a vegetable ••➤ picture on page C3

spinal /'spaɪnl/ adj connected with the bones of your back (the spine) ••➤ synonym **backbone**

'spin doctor noun [C] (especially in politics) a person who finds ways of talking about difficult situations, mistakes, etc in a positive way

spin 'dryer noun [C] (*Brit*) a machine that removes water from wet clothes by turning them round and round very fast –**spin-dry** verb [T]

spine /spaɪn/ noun [C] **1** the bones of the back of a person or animal; the backbone **2** one of the sharp points like needles, on some plants and animals: *Porcupines use their spines to protect themselves.* ••➤ Look at **prickle. 3** the narrow part of the cover of a book that you can see when it is on a shelf

spineless /'spaɪnləs/ adj weak and easily frightened

'spin-off noun [C] a spin-off (from/of sth) something unexpected and useful that develops from sth else

spinster /'spɪnstə/ noun [C] (*old-fashioned*) a woman, especially an older woman, who has never been married

➤ Nowadays **single** is the most usual word that is used to describe a man or a woman who is not married.

••➤ Look at **bachelor.**

spiral /'spaɪrəl/ noun [C] a long curved line that moves round and round away from a central point –**spiral** adj: *a spiral staircase* –**spiral** verb [I] (**spiralling; spiralled**: *US* **spiraling; spiraled**)

spire /'spaɪə/ noun [C] a tall pointed tower on the top of a church

★ **spirit¹** /'spɪrɪt/ noun **1** [sing] the part of a person that is not physical; your thoughts and feelings, not your body: *the power of the human spirit to overcome difficulties* **2** [C] the part of a person that many people believe still exists after his/her body is dead; a ghost or a being without a body: *It was believed that people could be possessed by evil spirits.* ••➤ Look at **soul. 3** [C] the mood, attitude or

state of mind of sb/sth: *to be in high/low spirits* (= in a happy/sad mood) **4** -**spirited** (used to form compound adjectives) having the mood or attitude of mind mentioned: *a group of high-spirited teenagers* **5** **spirits** [pl] (*especially Brit*) strong alcoholic drinks, for example whisky and vodka **6** [U] energy, strength of mind or determination: *The group had plenty of team spirit.* **7** [sing] the typical or most important quality of sth: *the pioneer spirit* ● *The painting perfectly captures the spirit of the times.*

spirit² /'spɪrɪt/ verb
PHRASAL VERB **spirit sb/sth away/off** to take sb/sth away secretly

spirited /'spɪrɪtɪd/ adj full of energy, determination and courage

spiritual /'spɪrɪtʃuəl/ adj **1** concerning deep thoughts, feelings or emotions rather than the body or physical things: *spiritual development/growth/needs* ••➤ Look at **material. 2** concerning the Church or religion: *a spiritual leader* –**spiritually** /-tʃuəli/ adv

spiritualism /'spɪrɪtʃuəlɪzəm/ noun [U] the belief that people who have died can get messages to living people, usually through a special person (a medium) –**spiritualist** noun [C]

★ **spit¹** /spɪt/ verb [I,T] (**spitting**; *pt, pp* **spat** /spæt/)

➤ In US English the past tense and past participle can also be **spit.**

spit (sth) (out) to force liquid, food, etc out from your mouth: *He took one sip of the wine and spat it out.*

spit² /spɪt/ noun **1** [U] (*informal*) the liquid in your mouth ••➤ Look at **saliva. 2** [C] a long, thin piece of land that sticks out into the sea, a lake, etc **3** [C] a long thin metal stick that you put through meat to hold it when you cook it over a fire: *chicken roasted on a spit*

★ **spite** /spaɪt/ noun [U] the desire to hurt or annoy sb: *He stole her letters out of spite.* –**spite** verb [T]

IDIOM **in spite of** used to show that sth happened although you did not expect it: *In spite of all her hard work, Sue failed her exam.* ••➤ synonym **despite**

spiteful /'spaɪtfl/ adj behaving in a cruel or unkind way in order to hurt or upset sb: *He's been saying a lot of spiteful things about his ex-girlfriend.* –**spitefully** adv /-fəli/

★ **splash¹** /splæʃ/ verb [I,T] (used about a liquid) to fall or to make liquid fall noisily or fly in drops onto a person or thing: *Rain splashed against the windows.* ● *The children were splashing each other with water.* ● *Be careful not to splash paint onto the floor.*
PHRASAL VERB **splash out (on sth)** (*Brit informal*) to spend money on sth that is expensive and that you do not really need

splash² /splæʃ/ noun [C] **1** the sound of liquid hitting sth or of sth hitting liquid: *Paul jumped into the pool with a big splash.* **2** a small amount of liquid that falls onto sth: *splashes of oil on the cooker* ••➤ picture at

S

ripple 3 a small bright area of colour: *Flowers add a splash of colour to a room.*

splatter /'splætə/ **verb** [I,T] (used about a liquid) to fly about in large drops and hit sb/sth noisily: *The paint was splattered all over the floor.* • *Heavy rain splattered on the roof.*

splay /spleɪ/ **verb** [I,T] **splay (sth) (out)** (to cause sth) to spread out or become wide apart at one end: *splayed fingers*

splendid /'splendɪd/ **adj 1** very good; excellent: *What a splendid idea!* **2** very impressive: *the splendid royal palace* –**splendidly adv**

splendour (*US* **splendor**) /'splendə/ **noun** [U] very impressive beauty

splint /splɪnt/ **noun** [C] a piece of wood or metal that is tied to a broken arm or leg to keep it in the right position

splinter /'splɪntə/ **noun** [C] a small thin sharp piece of wood, metal or glass that has broken off a larger piece: *I've got a splinter in my finger.* –**splinter verb** [I,T]

★**split**[1] /splɪt/ **verb** (*pres part* **splitting**; *pt, pp* **split**) **1** [I,T] **split (sb) (up) (into sth)** to divide or to make a group of people divide into smaller groups: *Let's split into two groups.* **2** [T] **split sth (between sb/sth)**; **split sth (with sb)** to divide or share sth: *We split the cost of the meal between the six of us.* **3** [I,T] **split (sth) (open)** to break or make sth break along a straight line: *My jeans have split.*

IDIOMS **split the difference** (used when agreeing on a price) to agree on an amount or figure that is halfway between the two amounts or figures already mentioned

split hairs to pay too much attention in an argument to details that are very small and not important •➤ Usually used in a critical way.

PHRASAL VERB **split up (with sb)** to end a marriage or relationship: *He's split up with his girlfriend.*

split[2] /splɪt/ **noun** [C] **1** a disagreement that divides a group of people **2** a long cut or hole in sth

,**split-'second noun** [C] a very short period of time

splutter /'splʌtə/ **verb 1** [I,T] to speak with difficulty for example because you are very angry or embarrassed **2** [I] to make a series of sounds like a person coughing –**splutter noun** [C]

★**spoil** /spɔɪl/ **verb** [T] (*pt, pp* **spoilt** /spɔɪlt/ or **spoiled** /spɔɪld/) **1** to change sth good into sth bad, unpleasant, useless, etc; to ruin sth: *The new office block will spoil the view.* • *Our holiday was spoilt by bad weather.* • *Eating between meals will spoil your appetite.* **2** to do too much for sb, especially a child, so that you have a bad effect on his/her character: *a spoilt child* **3** **spoil sb/yourself** to do sth special or nice to make sb/yourself happy

spoils /spɔɪlz/ **noun** [pl] (*written*) things that have been stolen by thieves, or taken in a war or battle: *the spoils of war*

spoilsport /'spɔɪlspɔːt/ **noun** [C] (*informal*) a person who tries to stop other people enjoying themselves, for example by not taking part in an activity

spoke[1] /spəʊk/ **noun** [C] one of the thin pieces of metal that connect the centre of a wheel (the hub) to the outside edge (the rim) •➤ picture on page S9

spoke[2] *past tense of* **SPEAK**

spoken *past participle of* **SPEAK**

spokesman /'spəʊksmən/ **noun** [C] (*pl* -**men** /-mən/) a person who is chosen to speak for a group or organization

★**spokesperson** /'spəʊkspɜːsn/ **noun** [C] (*pl* **spokespersons** or **spokespeople** /'spəʊkspiːpl/) a person who is chosen to speak for a group or organization •➤ **Spokesperson** is now often preferred to 'spokesman' or 'spokeswoman' because it can be used for a man or a woman.

spokeswoman /'spəʊkswʊmən/ **noun** [C] (*pl* -**women** /-wɪmɪn/) a woman who is chosen to speak for a group or organization

sponge[1] /spʌndʒ/ **noun** [C,U] **1** a piece of artificial or natural material that is soft and light and full of holes and can hold water easily, used for washing yourself or cleaning sth •➤ picture at **bucket 2** =**SPONGE CAKE**

sponge[2] /spʌndʒ/ **verb** [T] to remove or clean sth with a wet sponge1(1) or cloth PHRASAL VERB **sponge off sb** (*informal*) to get money, food, etc from sb without paying or doing anything in return

'**sponge bag** (also '**toilet bag**) **noun** [C] (*Brit*) a small bag in which you put soap, toothpaste, etc (**toiletries**) when you are travelling

'**sponge cake** (also **sponge**) **noun** [C,U] a light cake made with eggs, flour and sugar, and usually no fat

sponsor /'spɒnsə/ **noun** [C] **1** a person or an organization that helps to pay for a special sports event, etc (usually so that it can advertise its products) •➤ Look at **patron**. **2** a person who agrees to pay money to a charity if sb else completes a particular activity –**sponsor verb** [T]: *a sponsored walk to raise money for children in need* –**sponsorship noun** [U]: *Many theatres depend on industry for sponsorship.*

spontaneous /spɒn'teɪniəs/ **adj** done or happening suddenly; not planned: *a spontaneous burst of applause* –**spontaneously adv** –**spontaneity** /,spɒntə'neɪəti/ **noun** [U]

spooky /'spuːki/ **adj** (*informal*) strange and frightening: *It's spooky being in the house alone at night.*

spool /spuːl/ **noun** [C] a round object which thread, film, wire, etc are put around •➤ Look at **reel**.

★**spoon** /spuːn/ **noun** [C] an object with a round end and a long handle that you use for eating, mixing or serving food: *Give each person a knife, fork and spoon.* • *a wooden spoon for cooking* •➤ picture at **kitchen** –**spoon verb** [T]

S

spoonful /'spu:nfʊl/ **noun** [C] the amount that one spoon can hold: *Add two spoonfuls of sugar.*

sporadic /spə'rædɪk/ **adj** not done or happening regularly –**sporadically** /-kli/ **adv**

★**sport** /spɔ:t/ **noun 1** [U] a physical game or activity that you do for exercise or because you enjoy it: *John **did** a lot of **sport** when he was at school.* • *Do you like sport?* **2** [C] a particular game or type of sport: *What's your favourite sport?* • ***winter sports*** (= skiing, skating, etc) –**sporting** **adj**: *a major sporting event*

'sports car **noun** [C] a low, fast car often with a roof that you can open

sportsman /'spɔ:tsmən/ **noun** [C] (*pl* -**men** /-mən/) a man who does a lot of sport or who is good at sport: *a keen sportsman*

sportsmanlike /'spɔ:tsmənlaɪk/ **adj** behaving in a fair, generous and polite way when you are playing a game or doing sport

sportsmanship /'spɔ:tsmənʃɪp/ **noun** [U] the quality of being fair, generous and polite when you are playing a game or doing sport

sportswoman /'spɔ:tswʊmən/ **noun** [C] (*pl* -**women** /-wɪmɪn/) a woman who does a lot of sport or who is good at sport

★**spot**¹ /spɒt/ **noun** [C] **1** a small round mark on a surface: *Leopards have dark spots.* • *a blue skirt with red spots on it* ••➤ adjective **spotted** **2** a small dirty mark on sth: *grease/ rust spots* **3** a small red or yellow lump that appears on your skin: *Many teenagers **get** spots.* ••➤ adjective **spotty** **4** a particular place or area: *a quiet/lonely/secluded spot* **5** [usually sing] *a spot of sth* (*Brit informal*) a small amount of sth **6** =**SPOTLIGHT**(1)

IDIOMS **have a soft spot for sb/sth →** **SOFT**
on the spot 1 immediately: *Paul was caught stealing money and was dismissed on the spot.* **2** at the place where sth happened or where sb/sth is needed: *The fire brigade were on the spot within five minutes.*
put sb on the spot to make sb answer a difficult question or make a difficult decision without having much time to think

spot² /spɒt/ **verb** [T] (**spotting; spotted**) (not used in the continuous tenses) to see or notice sb/sth, especially suddenly or when it is not easy to do: *I've spotted a couple of spelling mistakes.*

➤ Although this verb is not used in the continuous tenses, it is common to see the present participle (= -*ing* form): *Spotting a familiar face in the crowd, he began to push his way towards her.*

'spot 'check **noun** [C] a check that is made suddenly and without warning on a few things or people chosen from a group

spotless /'spɒtləs/ **adj** perfectly clean

spotlight /'spɒtlaɪt/ **noun 1** (also **spot**) [C] a lamp that can send a single ray of bright light onto a small area. Spotlights are often used in theatres. ••➤ picture at **light 2 the spot-**

light [sing] the centre of public attention or interest: *to be **in the spotlight***

'spot 'on **adj** (*Brit informal*) (not before a noun) exactly right: *Your estimate was spot on.*

spotted /'spɒtɪd/ **adj** (used about clothes, cloth, etc) covered with round shapes of a different colour: *a spotted blouse*

spotty /'spɒti/ **adj** having small red or yellow lumps on your skin

spouse /spaʊs/ **noun** [C] (*written*) your husband or wife ••➤ **Spouse** is a formal or official word, used on forms, documents, etc.

spout¹ /spaʊt/ **noun** [C] a tube or pipe through which liquid comes out: *the spout of a teapot*

spout² /spaʊt/ **verb** [I,T] **1** to send out a liquid with great force; to make a liquid do this **2** (*informal*) **spout (on/off) (about sth)** to say sth, using a lot of words, in a way that is boring or annoying

sprain /spreɪn/ **verb** [T] to injure part of your body, especially your wrist or the thinnest part of your leg (**ankle**), by suddenly bending or turning it: *to sprain your ankle* –**sprain** **noun** [C]

sprang *past tense* of **SPRING**²

sprawl /sprɔ:l/ **verb** [I] **1** to sit or lie with your arms and legs spread out in an untidy way: *People lay sprawled out in the sun.* **2** to cover a large area of land –**sprawling** **adj**: *the sprawling city suburbs*

spray¹ /spreɪ/ **noun** **1** [U] liquid in very small drops that is sent through the air: *clouds of spray from the waves* **2** [C,U] liquid in a special container (**an aerosol**) that is forced out under pressure when you push a button: *hairspray* ••➤ picture at **container**

spray² /spreɪ/ **verb** [I,T] (used about a liquid) to be forced out of a container or sent through the air in very small drops; to send a liquid out in this way: *The crops are regularly sprayed with pesticide.*

★**spread**¹ /spred/ **verb** (*pt, pp* **spread**) **1** [I,T] to affect a larger area or a bigger group of people; to make sth do this: *The fire spread rapidly because of the strong wind.* • *Rats and flies **spread disease**.* • *to **spread rumours** about sb* **2** [T] **spread sth (out) (on/over sth)** to open sth that has been folded so that it covers a larger area; to move things so that they cover a larger area: *Spread the map out on the table so we can all see it!* **3** [T] **spread A on/over B; spread B with A** to cover a surface with a layer of a soft substance: *to spread jam on bread* • *to spread bread with jam* **4** [T] **spread sth (out) (over sth)** to separate sth into parts and divide them between different times or people: *You can* *spread your repayments over a period of three years.*

PHRASAL VERB spread (sb/yourself) out to move away from the others in a group of people in order to cover a larger area: *The police spread out to search the whole area.*

spread² /spred/ noun **1** [U] an increase in the amount or number of sth that there is, or in the area that is affected by sth: *Dirty drinking water encourages the spread of disease.* **2** [C,U] a soft food that you put on bread **3** [C] a newspaper or magazine article that covers one or more pages: *a double-page spread*

spreadsheet /'spredʃi:t/ noun [C] (*computing*) a computer program for working with rows of numbers, used especially for doing accounts

spree /spri:/ noun [C] (*informal*) a short time that you spend doing sth you enjoy, often doing too much of it: *to go on a shopping/spending spree*

sprig /sprɪg/ noun [C] a small piece of a plant with leaves on it

★ **spring¹** /sprɪŋ/ noun **1** [C,U] the season of the year between winter and summer when the weather gets warmer and plants begin to grow: *Daffodils bloom in spring.* **2** [C] a long piece of thin metal or wire that is bent round and round. After you push or pull a spring it goes back to its original shape and size: *bed springs* ••▸ picture at **coil 3** [C] a place where water comes up naturally from under the ground: *a hot spring* **4** [C] a sudden jump upwards or forwards

spring² /sprɪŋ/ verb [I] (*pt* **sprang** /spræŋ/; *pp* **sprung** /sprʌŋ/) **1** to jump or move quickly: *When the alarm went off, Ray sprang out of bed.* • *to spring to your feet* (= stand up suddenly) • (*figurative*) *to spring to sb's defence/assistance* (= to quickly defend or help sb) **2** (used about an object) to move suddenly and violently: *The branch sprang back and hit him in the face.* **3** to appear or come somewhere suddenly: *Tears sprang to her eyes.* • *Where did you just spring from?*

IDIOM come/spring to mind → **MIND¹**

PHRASAL VERBS spring from sth (*written*) to be the result of: *The idea for the book sprang from an experience she had while travelling in India.*

spring sth on sb (*informal*) to do or say sth that sb is not expecting

spring up to appear or develop quickly or suddenly: *Play areas for children are springing up everywhere.*

springboard /'sprɪŋbɔːd/ noun [C] **1** a low board that bends and that helps you jump higher, for example before you jump into a swimming pool **2** a springboard (for/to sth) something that helps you start an activity, especially by giving you ideas

spring-'clean verb [T] to clean a house, room, etc very well, including the parts that you do not usually clean

spring 'onion noun [C,U] a type of small onion with a long green central part and leaves. ••▸ picture on page C3

springtime /'sprɪŋtaɪm/ noun [U] (*written*) the season of spring

springy /'sprɪŋi/ adj going quickly back to its original shape or size after being pushed, pulled, etc: *soft springy grass*

sprinkle /'sprɪŋkl/ verb [T] sprinkle A (on/onto/over B); sprinkle B (with A) to throw drops of water or small pieces of sth over a surface: *to sprinkle sugar on a cake* • *to sprinkle a cake with sugar*

sprinkler /'sprɪŋklə/ noun [C] a device with holes in it that sends out water in small drops. Sprinklers are used in gardens, to keep the grass green, and in buildings, to stop fires from spreading.

sprint /sprɪnt/ verb [I,T] to run a short distance as fast as you can –**sprint** noun [C]

sprout¹ /spraʊt/ verb [I,T] (used about a plant) to begin to grow or to produce new leaves: *The seeds are sprouting.*

sprout² /spraʊt/ noun [C] **1** = **BRUSSELS SPROUT 2** a new part that has grown on a plant

spruce /spru:s/ verb

PHRASAL VERB spruce (sb/yourself) up to make sb/yourself clean and tidy

sprung *past participle* of **SPRING²**

spud /spʌd/ noun [C] (*informal*) a potato

spun *past participle* of **SPIN¹**

spur¹ /spɜː/ noun [C] **1** a piece of metal that a rider wears on the back of his/her boots to encourage the horse to go faster ••▸ picture at **horse 2** a spur (to sth) something that encourages you to do sth or that makes sth happen more quickly: *My poor exam results acted as a spur to make me study harder.*

IDIOM on the spur of the moment without planning; suddenly

spur² /spɜː/ verb [T] (**spurring**; **spurred**) spur sb/sth (on/onto sth) to encourage sb or make him/her work harder or faster: *The letter spurred me into action.* • *We were spurred on by the positive feedback from customers.*

spurn /spɜːn/ verb [T] (*formal*) to refuse sth that sb has offered to you: *to spurn an offer of friendship*

spurt /spɜːt/ verb **1** [I,T] (used about a liquid) to come out quickly with great force; to make a liquid do this: *Blood spurted from the wound.* **2** [I] to suddenly increase your speed or effort –**spurt** noun [C]

spy¹ /spaɪ/ noun [C] (*pl* **spies**) a person who tries to get secret information about another country, person or organization

spy² /spaɪ/ verb (*pres part* **spying**; *3rd pers sing pres* **spies**; *pt, pp* **spied**) **1** [I] to try to get secret information about sb/sth ••▸ Look at **espionage. 2** [T] (*formal*) to see

IDIOM spy on sb/sth to watch sb/sth secretly: *The man next door is spying on us.*

spyhole /'spaɪhəʊl/ noun [C] a small hole in a door for looking at the person on the other side before deciding to let him/her in

sq abbr **1** =**SQUARE²**(6): *10 sq cm* **2 Sq** = **SQUARE¹**(2): *6 Hanover Sq*

S

squabble /'skwɒbl/ verb [I] squabble (over/ about sth) to argue in a noisy way about sth that is not very important –squabble noun [C]

squad /skwɒd/ noun [C,with sing or pl verb] a group of people who work as a team: *He's a policeman with the drugs squad.*

squadron /'skwɒdrən/ noun [C,with sing or pl verb] a group of military aircraft or ships

squalid /'skwɒlɪd/ adj very dirty, untidy and unpleasant: *squalid housing conditions*

squall /skwɔːl/ noun [C] a sudden storm with strong winds

squalor /'skwɒlə/ noun [U] the state of being very dirty, untidy or unpleasant: *to live in squalor*

squander /'skwɒndə/ verb [T] squander sth (on sth) to waste time, money, etc: *He squanders his time on TV and computer games.*

★**square**[1] /skweə/ noun [C] **1** a shape that has four sides of the same length and four angles of 90 degrees (right angles): *There are 64 squares on a chess board.* ••➤ picture at **shape 2** (also **Square**) (*abbr* **Sq**) an open space in a town or city that has buildings all around it: *Protesters gathered in the town square.* • *Trafalgar Square* ••➤ picture on page C8 **3** the number that you get when you multiply another number by itself: *Four is the square of two.* ••➤ Look at **square root**.

★**square**[2] /skweə/ adj, adv **1** having four straight sides of the same length and corners of 90°: *a square tablecloth* **2** shaped like a square or forming an angle of about 90°: *a square face* • *square shoulders* **3** (not before a noun) not owing any money: *Here is the money I owe you. Now we're (all) square.* **4** (not before a noun) having equal points (in a game, etc): *The teams were all square at half-time.* **5** fair or honest, especially in business matters: *a square deal* **6** (*abbr* sq) used for talking about the area of sth: *If a room is 5 metres long and 4 metres wide, its area is 20 square metres.* **7** (used about sth that is square in shape) having sides of a particular length: *The picture is twenty centimetres square* (= each side is twenty centimetres long). **8** (also **squarely**) in an obvious and direct way: *to look sb square in the eye* • *I think the blame falls squarely on her.*

IDIOM **a square meal** a good meal that makes you feel satisfied

square[3] /skweə/ verb [I,T] square (sth) with sb/sth to agree with sth; to make sure that sb/sth agrees with sth: *Your conclusion doesn't really square with the facts.* • *If you want time off you'll have to square it with the boss.*

PHRASAL VERB **square up (with sb)** to pay sb the money that you owe him/her

squared /skweəd/ adj (used about a number) multiplied by itself: *Four squared is sixteen.* ••➤ Look at **square root**.

square 'root noun [C] a number that produces another particular number when it is multiplied by itself: *The square root of sixteen is four.* ••➤ Look at **square**, **squared** and **root**.

squash[1] /skwɒʃ/ verb **1** [T] to press sth so that it is damaged, changes shape or becomes flat: *The fruit at the bottom of the bag will get squashed.* • *Move up – you're squashing me!* ••➤ picture at **squeeze 2** [I,T] to go into a place, or move sb/sth to a place, where there is not much space: *We all squashed into the back of the car.* **3** [T] to destroy sth because it is a problem: *to squash sb's suggestion/plan/ idea*

squash[2] /skwɒʃ/ noun **1** [C,usually sing] a lot of people in a small space: *We can get ten people around the table, but it's a bit of a squash.* **2** [U,C] (*Brit*) a drink that is made from fruit juice and sugar. You add water to squash before you drink it: *orange squash* **3** [U] a game for two people, played in a special room (court). You play squash by hitting a small rubber ball against any one of the walls of the room: *a squash racket*

squat[1] /skwɒt/ verb [I] (**squatting; squatted**) **1** to rest with your weight on your feet, your legs bent and your bottom just above the ground ••➤ picture at **kneel 2** to go and live in an empty building without permission from the owner

squat[2] /skwɒt/ adj short and fat or thick: *a squat ugly building*

squatter /'skwɒtə/ noun [C] a person who is living in an empty building without the owner's permission

squawk /skwɔːk/ verb [I] (used especially about a bird) to make a loud unpleasant noise –squawk noun [C]

squeak /skwiːk/ noun [C] a short high noise that is not very loud: *the squeak of a mouse* • *She gave a little squeak of surprise.* –squeak verb [I,T] –squeaky adj: *a squeaky floorboard* • *a squeaky voice*

squeal /skwiːl/ verb [I,T] to make a loud high noise because of pain, fear or enjoyment: *The baby squealed in delight at the new toy.* –squeal noun [C]

➤ A **squeal** is louder and longer than a **squeak** but it is not as loud as a **scream**.

squeamish /'skwiːmɪʃ/ adj easily upset by unpleasant sights, especially blood

★**squeeze**[1] /skwiːz/ verb **1** [T] squeeze sth (out) ; squeeze sth (from/out of sth) to press sth hard for a particular purpose: *She squeezed his hand as a sign of affection.* • *to squeeze a tube of toothpaste* • *Squeeze a lemon/the juice of a lemon into a glass.* • *I squeezed the water out of the cloth.* **2** [I,T] squeeze (sb/sth) into, through, and etc ; squeeze (sb/sth) through, in, past, etc to force sb/sth into or through a small space: *We can squeeze another person into the back of the car.* • *There was just room for the bus to squeeze past.*

squeeze[2] /skwiːz/ noun **1** [C] an act of pressing sth firmly: *He gave her hand a squeeze and told her he loved her.* **2** [C] the amount of liquid that you get from squeezing an orange, a lemon, etc: *a squeeze of lemon* **3** [sing] a situation where there is not much space: *It*

S

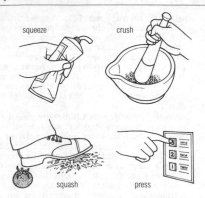

squeeze crush

squash press

*was **a tight squeeze** to get everybody around the table.* **4** [C, usually sing] an effort to use less money, time, etc, especially with the result that there is not enough

squelch /skweltʃ/ **verb** [I] to make the sound your feet make when you are walking in deep wet mud

squid /skwɪd/ **noun** [C,U] (*pl* **squid** or **squids**) a sea animal that we eat with a long soft body and ten long parts (tentacles) ••➤ picture at **octopus**

squiggle /'skwɪgl/ **noun** [C] (*informal*) a quickly drawn line that goes in all directions

squint /skwɪnt/ **verb** [I] **1** squint (at sth) to look at sth with your eyes almost closed: *to squint in bright sunlight* **2** to have eyes that appear to look in different directions at the same time –**squint noun** [C]

squirm /skwɜːm/ **verb** [I] to move around in your chair because you are nervous, uncomfortable, etc

squirrel /'skwɪrəl/ **noun** [C] a small red or grey animal with a long thick tail that lives in trees and eats nuts

squirt /skwɜːt/ **verb** [I,T] If a liquid squirts or if you squirt it, it is suddenly forced out of sth in a particular direction: *I cut the orange and juice squirted out.* • *She squirted water on the flames.* • *He squirted me with water.* –**squirt noun** [C]: *a squirt of lemon juice*

Sr *abbr* = **SNR**

St *abbr* **1** =**SAINT**: *St Peter* **2** =**STREET**: *20 Swan St* **3 st** (*Brit*) stone; a measure of weight

stab¹ /stæb/ **verb** [T] (**stabbing**; **stabbed**) to push a knife or other pointed object into sb/sth: *The man had been stabbed in the back.* • *He stabbed a potato with his fork.*

stab² /stæb/ **noun** [C] **1** an injury that was caused by a knife, etc: *He received stab wounds to his neck and back.* **2** a sudden sharp pain

IDIOM **have a stab at sth/doing sth** (*informal*) to try to do sth

stabbing¹ /'stæbɪŋ/ **noun** [C] an occasion when sb is injured or killed with a knife or other sharp object

stabbing² /'stæbɪŋ/ **adj** (only *before* a noun) (used about a pain) sudden and strong

stability /stə'bɪləti/ **noun** [U] the state or quality of being steady and not changing: *After so much change we now need a period of stability.* • *The ladder is slightly wider at the bottom for greater stability.* ••➤ opposite **instability** ••➤ adjective **stable**

stabilize (also **-ise**) /'steɪbəlaɪz/ **verb** [I,T] to become or to make sth firm, steady and unlikely to change: *The patient's condition has stabilized.* ••➤ Look at **destabilize**.

stable¹ /'steɪbl/ **adj** steady, firm and unlikely to change: *This ladder doesn't seem very stable.* • *The patient is in a stable condition.* ••➤ opposite **unstable** ••➤ noun **stability**

stable² /'steɪbl/ **noun** [C] a building where horses are kept

stack¹ /stæk/ **noun** [C] **1** a tidy pile of sth: *a stack of plates/books/chairs* **2** (*informal*) (often plural) a lot of sth: *I've still got stacks of work to do.*

stack² /stæk/ **verb** [T] stack sth (up) to put sth into a tidy pile: *Could you stack those chairs for me?*

stacked /stækt/ **adj** full of piles of things: *The room was stacked high with books.*

★**stadium** /'steɪdiəm/ **noun** [C] (*pl* **stadiums** or **stadia** /-diə/) a large structure, usually with no roof, where people can sit and watch sport

★**staff** /stɑːf/ **noun** [C, usually sing, U] the group of people who work for a particular organization: *hotel/library/medical staff* • *Two members of staff will accompany the students on the school trip.* • *The hotel has over 200 people on its staff.* • *full-time/part-time staff* • *a staffroom* (= in a school) ••➤ **Staff** is usually used in the singular but with a plural verb: *The staff all speak good English.* –**staff verb** [T] (usually passive): *The office is staffed 24 hours a day.*

stag /stæg/ **noun** [C] the male of a type of large wild animal that eats grass (deer) ••➤ picture at **deer**

★**stage¹** /steɪdʒ/ **noun 1** [C] one part of the progress or development of sth: *The first stage of the course lasts for three weeks.* • *I suggest we do the journey in two stages.* • *At this stage it's too early to say what will happen.* **2** [C] a platform in a theatre, concert hall, etc on which actors, musicians, etc perform **3** [sing,U] the world of theatre; the profession of acting: *Her parents didn't want her to go on the stage.* • *an actor of stage and screen*

stage² /steɪdʒ/ **verb** [T] **1** to organize a performance of a play, concert, etc for the public **2** to organize an event: *They have decided to stage a 24-hour strike.*

stage 'manager noun [C] the person who is responsible for the stage, lights, scenery, etc during a theatre performance

stagger /'stægə/ **verb** [I] to walk with short steps as if you could fall at any moment, for example because you are ill, drunk or carrying sth heavy: *He staggered across the finishing line and collapsed.*

staggered /'stægəd/ **adj 1** (*informal*) very

S

surprised: *I was absolutely staggered when I heard the news.* **2** (used about a set of times, payments, etc) arranged so that they do not all happen at the same time: *staggered working hours* (= when people start and finish work at different times)

staggering /'stægərɪŋ/ **adj** that you find difficult to believe –**staggeringly adv**

stagnant /'stægnənt/ **adj 1** (used about water) not flowing and therefore dirty and having an unpleasant smell **2** (used about business, etc) not active; not developing: *a stagnant economy*

stagnate /stæg'neɪt/ **verb** [I] **1** to stop developing, changing or being active: *a stagnating economy* **2** (used about water) to be or become stagnant –**stagnation** /stæg'neɪʃn/ **noun** [U]

'stag night (also **'stag party**) **noun** [C] a party for men only that is given for a man just before his wedding day

➤ Compare **hen party**.

staid /steɪd/ **adj** serious, old-fashioned and rather boring

★**stain** /steɪn/ **verb** [I,T] to leave a coloured mark that is difficult to remove: *Don't spill any of that red wine – it'll stain the carpet.* –**stain noun** [C]: *The blood had left a stain on his shirt.* •➤ picture at **blob**

,stained 'glass noun [U] pieces of coloured glass that are used in church windows, etc: *a stained-glass window*

,stainless 'steel noun [U] a type of steel that does not change colour or get damaged by water (rust): *a stainless steel pan*

★**stair** /steə/ **noun 1 stairs** [pl] a series of steps inside a building that lead from one level to another: *a flight of stairs* • *I heard somebody coming down the stairs.* • *She ran up the stairs.* •➤ Look at **downstairs** and **upstairs**.

➤ Compare **stair** and **step**. **Stairs** or **flights of stairs** are usually inside buildings. **Steps** are usually outside buildings and made of stone or concrete.

•➤ picture on page C7 **2** [C] one of the steps in a series inside a building

staircase /'steəkeɪs/ (also **stairway**) **noun** [C] a set of stairs with rails on each side that you can hold on to •➤ Look at **escalator**. •➤ picture on page C7

stake¹ /steɪk/ **noun 1** [C] a wooden or metal pole with a point at one end that you push into the ground **2** [C] a part of a company, etc that you own, usually because you have put money into it: *Foreign investors now have a 20% stake in the company.* **3 stakes** [pl] the things that you might win or lose in a game or in a particular situation: *We play cards for money, but never for very high stakes.*
IDIOM at stake in danger of being lost; at risk: *He thought very carefully about the decision because he knew his future was at stake.*

stake² /steɪk/ **verb** [T] **stake sth (on sth)** to put your future, etc in danger by doing sth, because you hope that it will bring you a

good result: *He is staking his political reputation on this issue.*
IDIOM **stake a/your claim (to sth)** to say that you have a right to have sth
PHRASAL VERB **stake sth out 1** to clearly mark an area of land that you are going to use **2** to make your position, opinion, etc clear to everyone: *In his speech, the President staked out his position on tax reform.* **3** to watch a place secretly for a period of time: *The police had been staking out the house for months.*

★**stale** /steɪl/ **adj 1** (used about food or air) old and not fresh any more: *The bread will go stale if you don't put it away.* **2** not interesting or exciting any more •➤ Look at **fresh**.

stalemate /'steɪlmeɪt/ **noun** [sing,U] **1** a situation in an argument in which neither side can win or make any progress **2** (in chess) a position in which a game ends without a winner because neither side can move

stalk¹ /stɔːk/ **noun** [C] one of the long thin parts of a plant which the flowers, leaves or fruit grow on •➤ picture on page C3

stalk² /stɔːk/ **verb 1** [T] to move slowly and quietly towards an animal in order to catch or kill it: *a lion stalking its prey* **2** [T] to follow a person over a period of time in a frightening or annoying way: *The actress claimed the man had been stalking her for two years.* **3** [I] to walk in an angry way

stall¹ /stɔːl/ **noun 1** [C] a small shop with an open front or a table with things for sale: *a market stall* • *a bookstall at the station* •➤ picture on page C8 **2 stalls** [pl] the seats nearest the front in a theatre or cinema **3** [C, usually sing] a situation in which a vehicle's engine suddenly stops because it is not receiving enough power: *The plane went into a stall and almost crashed.*

stall² /stɔːl/ **verb** [I,T] **1** (used about a vehicle) to stop suddenly because the engine is not receiving enough power; to make a vehicle do this accidentally: *The bus often stalls on this hill.* • *I kept stalling the car.* **2** to avoid doing sth or to try to stop sth happening until a later time

stallion /'stæliən/ **noun** [C] an adult male horse, especially one that is kept for breeding •➤ Look at the note at **horse**.

stalwart /'stɔːlwət/ **adj** always loyal to the same organization, team, etc: *a stalwart supporter of the club* –**stalwart noun** [C]

stamina /'stæmɪnə/ **noun** [U] the ability to do sth that involves a lot of physical or mental effort for a long time: *You need a lot of stamina to run long distances.*

stammer /'stæmə/ **verb** [I,T] to speak with difficulty, repeating sounds and pausing before saying things correctly: *He stammered an apology and left quickly.* –**stammer noun** [sing]: *to have a stammer*

★**stamp¹** /stæmp/ **noun** [C] **1** (also **postage stamp**) a small piece of paper that you stick onto a letter or package to show that you have paid for it to be posted: *a first-class/second-class stamp* • *Barry's hobby is collecting stamps.*

S

➤ In the British postal system, there are two types of stamp for posting letters, etc to other parts of Britain, **first-class** stamps and **second-class** stamps. Letters with first-class stamps are more expensive and arrive more quickly.

2 a small object that prints some words, a design, the date, etc when you press it onto a surface: *a date stamp* **3** the mark made by stamping sth onto a surface: *Have you got any visa stamps in your passport?* • (*figurative*) *The government has given the project its stamp of approval.* **4** the stamp of sth [usually sing] something that shows a particular quality or that sth was done by a particular person

stamp² /stæmp/ **verb 1** [I,T] **stamp (on sth)** to put your foot down very heavily and noisily: *He stamped on the spider and squashed it.* • *It was so cold that I had to stamp my feet to keep warm.* • *She stamped her foot in anger.* **2** [I] to walk with loud heavy steps: *She stamped around the room, shouting angrily.* **3** [T] **stamp A (on B); stamp B (with A)** to print some words, a design, the date, etc by pressing a small object (a stamp) onto a surface: *to stamp a passport*
PHRASAL VERB **stamp sth out** to put an end to sth completely: *The police are trying to stamp out this kind of crime.*

stamped addressed 'envelope (also **self-addressed 'envelope) noun** [C] (*abbr* **sae**) an empty envelope with your own name and address and a stamp on it that you send to a company, etc when you want sth sent back to you

stampede /stæm'pi:d/ **noun** [C] a situation in which a large number of animals or people start running in the same direction, for example because they are frightened or excited –**stampede verb** [I]

stance /stæns; stɑːns/ **noun** [C, usually sing] **1 stance (on sth)** the opinions that sb expresses publicly about sth: *the Prime Minister's stance on foreign affairs* **2** the position in which somebody stands, especially when playing a sport

★**stand¹** /stænd/ **verb** [I,T] (*pt, pp* **stood** /stʊd/) **1** [I] to be on your feet, not sitting or lying down; to be upright: *He was standing near the window.* • *Stand still – I'm trying to draw you!* • *Only a few houses were left standing after the earthquake.* **2** [I] **stand (up)** to rise to your feet from another position: *He stood up when I entered the room.* **3** [T] to put sb/sth in a particular place or position: *We stood the mirror against the wall while we decided where to hang it.* **4** [I] to be or to stay in a particular position or situation: *The castle stands on a hill.* • *The house has stood empty for ten years.* **5** [I] (used about an offer, a decision, etc) to stay the same as before, without being changed: *Does your decision still stand?* • *The world record has stood for ten years.* **6** [I] **stand (at) sth** to be of a particular height, level, amount, etc: *The world*

record stands at 6·59 metres. • *The building stands nearly 60 metres high.* **7** [I] **stand (on sth)** to have an opinion or view about sth **8** [I] **stand to do sth** to be in a situation where you are likely to do sth: *If he has to sell the company, he stands to lose a lot of money.* **9** [I] **stand (for/as sth)** to be one of the people hoping to be chosen in an election (a candidate): *She's standing for the European Parliament.* **10** [T] (in negative sentences and questions, with *can/could*) to not like sb/sth at all; to hate sb/sth: *I can't stand that woman – she's so rude.* • *I couldn't stand the thought of waiting another two hours so I went home.* **11** [T] (used especially with *can/could*) to be able to survive difficult conditions: *Camels can stand extremely hot and cold temperatures.* •➤ synonym **bear** or **take**
PHRASAL VERBS **stand around** to stand somewhere not doing anything: *A lot of people were just standing around outside.*
stand aside to move to one side: *People stood aside to let the police pass.*
stand back to move back: *The policeman told everybody to stand back.*
stand by 1 to be present, but do nothing in a situation: *How can you stand by and let them treat their animals like that?* **2** to be ready to act: *The police are standing by in case there's trouble.*
stand for sth 1 to be a short form of sth: *What does BBC stand for?* **2** to support sth (such as an idea or opinion): *I hate everything that the party stands for.*
stand in (for sb) to take sb's place for a short time
stand out to be easily seen or noticed
stand up to be or become vertical: *You'll look taller if you stand up straight.*
stand sb up (*informal*) to not appear when you have arranged to meet sb, especially a boyfriend or girlfriend
stand up for sb/sth to say or do sth which shows that you support sb/sth: *I admire him. He really stands up for his rights.*
stand up to sb/sth to defend yourself against sb/sth who is stronger or more powerful

★**stand²** /stænd/ **noun** [C] **1** a table or object that holds or supports sth, often so that people can buy it or look at it: *a newspaper/ hamburger stand* • *a company stand at a trade fair* **2** a large structure where people can watch sport from seats arranged in rows that are low near the front and high near the back **3** a stand (on/against sth) to take action to defend yourself or sth that you have a strong opinion about: *The workers have decided to take/make a stand against further job losses.*

★**standard¹** /'stændəd/ **noun** [C] **1** a level of quality: *We complained about the low standard of service in the hotel.* • *This work is not up to your usual standard.* **2** a level of quality that you compare sth else with: *By European standards this is a very expensive city.* • *He is a brilliant player by any standard.* **3** [usually pl] a level of behaviour that is

S

morally acceptable: *Many people are worried about falling standards in modern society.*

standard² /'stændəd/ **adj 1** normal or average; not special or unusual: *He's got long arms, so standard sizes of shirt don't fit him.* **2** that people generally accept as normal and correct: *standard English*

standardize (also **-ise**) /'stændədaɪz/ **verb** [T] to make things that are different the same: *Safety tests on old cars have been standardized throughout Europe.* –**standardization** (also **standardisation**) /ˌstændədaɪˈzeɪʃn/ **noun** [U]

standard of 'living noun [C] the amount of money and level of comfort that a particular person or group has: *There is a higher standard of living in the north than in the south.*

> An expression with a similar meaning is **living standards**. This is used in the plural: *Living standards have improved.*

standby /'stændbaɪ/ **noun 1** [C] (*pl* **standbys**) a thing or person that can be used if needed, for example if sb/sth is not available or in an emergency: *We always keep candles as a standby in case there is a power cut.* **2** [U] the state of being ready to do sth immediately if needed or if a ticket becomes available: *Ambulances were on standby along the route of the marathon.* • *We were put on standby for the flight to Rome.* –**standby adj** (only *before* a noun): *a standby ticket/passenger*

standing¹ /'stændɪŋ/ **noun** [U] **1** the position that sb/sth has, or how people think of him/her/it: *The agreement has no legal standing.* ••> synonym **status 2** the amount of time during which sth has continued to exist

standing² /'stændɪŋ/ **adj** that always exists; permanent

standing 'order noun [C] an instruction to your bank to make a regular payment to sb from your account

standpoint /'stændpɔɪnt/ **noun** [C] a particular way of thinking about sth ••> synonym **point of view**

standstill /'stændstɪl/ **noun** [sing] a situation when there is no movement, progress or activity: *The traffic is at/has come to a complete standstill.*

IDIOM **grind to a halt/standstill** → **GRIND¹**

stank *past tense of* **STINK**

staple /'steɪpl/ **noun** [C] a small thin piece of bent wire that you push through pieces of paper using a special tool in order to hold them together (**stapler**) ••> picture on page S6 –**staple verb** [T]: *Staple the letter to the application form.* –**stapler noun** [C]

staple 'diet noun [C,usually sing] the main food that a person or animal normally eats: *a staple diet of rice and fish*

★**star¹** /stɑː/ **noun 1** [C] a large ball of burning gas in outer space that you see as a small point of light in the sky at night: *It was a clear night and the stars were shining brightly.* **2** [C] a shape, decoration, mark, etc with five or six points sticking out in a regu-

lar pattern: *I've marked the possible candidates on the list with a star.* ••> picture at **shape 3** [C] a mark that represents a star that is used for telling you how good sth is, especially a hotel or restaurant: *a five-star hotel* **4** [C] a famous person in acting, music or sport: *a pop/rock/film/movie star* • *a football/tennis star* **5 stars** [pl] = **HOROSCOPE**

star² /stɑː/ **verb** (**starring**; **starred**) **1** [I] **star (in sth)** to be one of the main actors in a play, film, etc: *Gwyneth Paltrow is to star in a new romantic comedy.* **2** [T] to have sb as a star: *The film stars Kate Winslett.*

starboard /'stɑːbəd/ **noun** [U] the side of a ship that is on the right when you are facing towards the front of it ••> opposite **port**

starch /stɑːtʃ/ **noun** [C,U] **1** a white substance that is found in foods such as potatoes, rice and bread **2** a substance that is used for making cloth rigid

stardom /'stɑːdəm/ **noun** [U] the state of being a famous person in acting, music or sport: *She shot to stardom in a Broadway musical.*

★**stare** /steə/ **verb** [I] **stare (at sb/sth)** to look at sb or sth for a long time because you are surprised, shocked, etc: *Everybody stared at his hat.* • *He didn't reply, he just stared into the distance.*

stark¹ /stɑːk/ **adj 1** very empty and without decoration and therefore not attractive: *a stark landscape* **2** unpleasant and impossible to avoid: *He now faces the stark reality of life in prison.* **3** very different to sth in a way that is easy to see

stark² /stɑːk/ **adv** completely; extremely: *stark naked* • *Have you gone stark raving mad?*

starlight /'stɑːlaɪt/ **noun** [U] the light that is sent out by stars in the sky

starry /'stɑːri/ **adj** full of stars: *a starry night*

★**start¹** /stɑːt/ **verb 1** [I,T] **start (sth/to do sth/doing sth)** to begin doing sth: *Turn over your exam papers and start now.* • *We'll have to start (= leave) early if we want to be in Dover by 10.00* • *Prices start at £5.* • *After waiting for an hour, the customers started to complain.* • *She started playing the piano when she was six.* • *What time do you have to start work in the morning?* **2** [I,T] to begin or to make sth begin to happen: *What time does the concert start?* • *I'd like to start the meeting now.* • *The police think a young woman may have started the fire.* ••> Look at the note at **begin.** **3** [I,T] **start (sth) (up)** (used about a machine, etc) to work; to make an engine, a car, etc begin to work: *The car won't start.* • *We heard an engine starting up in the street.* • *He got onto his motor bike, started the engine and rode away.* **4** [I,T] **start (sth) (up)** to create a company, an organization, etc; to begin to exist: *They've decided to start their own business.* • *There are a lot of new companies starting up in that area now.* **5** [I] to make a sudden, quick movement because you are surprised or afraid: *A loud noise outside*

S

made me start.

IDIOMS **get/start off on the right/wrong foot (with sb)** → **FOOT¹**

to start (off) with 1 used for giving your first reason for sth: *'Why are you so angry?' 'Well, to start off with, you're late, and secondly you've lied to me.'* **2** in the beginning; at first: *Everything was fine to start with, but the marriage quickly deteriorated.*

set/start the ball rolling → **BALL**

PHRASAL VERBS **start off** to begin in a particular way: *I'd like to start off by welcoming you all to Leeds.*

start on sth to begin doing sth that needs to be done

start out to begin your life, career, etc in a particular way that changed later: *She started out as a teacher in Glasgow.*

start over (*US*) to begin again

★ **start²** /stɑːt/ **noun 1** [C, usually sing] the point at which sth begins: *The chairman made a short speech at the start of the meeting.* ● *I told you it was a bad idea from the start.* **2** [C, usually sing] the action or process of starting: *to make a fresh start* (= do sth again in a different way) **3 the start** [sing] the place where a race begins: *The athletes are now lining up at the start.* **4** [C, usually sing] an amount of time or distance that you give to a weaker person at the beginning of a race, game, etc

➤ Compare **head start**.

5 [C, usually sing] a sudden quick movement that your body makes because you are surprised or afraid: *She woke up with a start.*

IDIOMS **for a start** (*spoken*) (used to emphasize your first reason for sth): *'Why can't we go on holiday?' 'Well, for a start we can't afford it...'*

get off to a good, bad, etc start to start well, badly, etc

get off to a flying start → **FLYING**

starter /'stɑːtə/ (*US usually* **appetizer**) **noun** [C] a small amount of food that is served before the main course of a meal

'**starting point noun** [C] starting point (for sth) **1** an idea or topic that you use to begin a discussion with **2** the place where you begin a journey

startle /'stɑːtl/ **verb** [T] to surprise sb/sth in a way that slightly shocks or frightens him/her/it: *The gunshot startled the horses.* –**startled adj** –**startling** /'stɑːtlɪŋ/ **adj**

starvation /stɑːˈveɪʃn/ **noun** [U] suffering or death because there is not enough food: *to die of starvation*

★ **starve** /stɑːv/ **verb** [I,T] to suffer or die because you do not have enough food to eat; to make sb/sth suffer or die in this way: *Millions of people are starving in the poorer countries of the world.* ● *That winter many animals starved to death.*

IDIOMS **be starved of sth** to suffer because you are not getting enough of sth that you need: *The children had been starved of love and affection for years.*

be starving (*informal*) to be extremely hungry

★ **state¹** /steɪt/ **noun 1** [C] the mental, emotional or physical condition that sb/sth is in at a particular time: *the state of the economy* ● *He is in a state of shock.* ● *The house is in a terrible state.* **2** (also **State**) [C] a country considered as an organized political community controlled by one government: *Pakistan has been an independent state since 1947.* ••➤ Look at the note at **country. 3** (especially **the State**) [U] the government of a country: *affairs/matters of state* ● *the relationship between the Church and the State* ● *a state-owned company* ● *She went to a state school.* ● *heads of State* (= government leaders) **4** (also **State**) [C] an organized political community forming part of a country: *the southern States of the US*

➤ Compare **county** and **province**.

5 [U] the formal ceremonies connected with high levels of government or with the leaders of countries: *The Queen is going on a state visit to China.* **6 the States** [pl] (*informal*) the United States of America: *We lived in the States for about five years.*

IDIOMS **be in/get into a state** (*especially Brit informal*) to be or become very nervous or upset: *Now don't get into a state! I'm sure everything will be all right.*

state of affairs a situation: *This state of affairs must not be allowed to continue.*

state of mind mental condition: *She's in a very confused state of mind.*

★ **state²** /steɪt/ **verb** [T] to say or write sth, especially formally: *Your letter states that you sent the goods on 31 March, but we have never received them.*

stately /'steɪtli/ **adj** formal and impressive: *a stately old building*

,**stately 'home noun** [C] (*Brit*) a large old house that has historical interest and can be visited by the public

★ **statement** /'steɪtmənt/ **noun** [C] **1** something that you say or write, especially formally: *The Prime Minister will make a statement about the defence cuts today.* **2** = **BANK STATEMENT**

statesman /'steɪtsmən/ **noun** [C] (*pl* -**men** /-mən/) an important and experienced politician who has earned public respect

static¹ /'stætɪk/ **adj** not moving, changing or developing: *House prices are static.*

static² /'stætɪk/ **noun** [U] **1** sudden noises that disturb radio or television signals, caused by electricity in the atmosphere **2** (also ,**static elec'tricity**) electricity that collects on a surface: *My hair gets full of static when I brush it.*

★ **station¹** /'steɪʃn/ **noun** [C] **1** (also **railway station**) a building on a railway line where trains stop so that passengers can get on and off **2** (usually in compound nouns) a building from which buses begin and end journeys **3** (usually in compound nouns) a building where a particular service or activity is based: *a police/fire station* ● *a petrol station* ● *a power station* (= where electricity is gen-

S

erated) **4** (often in compound nouns) a radio or television company and the programmes it sends out: *a local radio/TV station* ● *He tuned in to another station.* •➤ Look at **channel**.

station² /'steɪʃn/ **verb** [T] (often passive) to send sb, especially members of the armed forces, to work in a place for a period of time

stationary /'steɪʃənri/ **adj** not moving: *He crashed into the back of a stationary vehicle.*

stationer's /'steɪʃənəz/ **noun** [sing] a shop that sells writing equipment, such as paper, pens, envelopes, etc

★**stationery** /'steɪʃənri/ **noun** [U] writing equipment, for example pens, pencils, paper, envelopes •➤ picture on page S6

'**station wagon** (*US*) = **ESTATE CAR**

statistics /stə'tɪstɪks/ **noun 1** [pl] numbers that have been collected in order to provide information about sth: *Statistics indicate that 90% of homes in this country have a television.* ● *crime statistics* **2** [U] the science of collecting and studying these numbers –**statistical** /stə'tɪstɪkl/ **adj**: *statistical information* –**statistically** /-kli/ **adv**

★**statue** /'stætʃuː/ **noun** [C] a figure of a person or animal that is made of stone or metal and usually put in a public place •➤ picture at **column**

stature /'stætʃə/ **noun** [U] (*written*) **1** the importance and respect that sb has because people have a high opinion of his/her skill or of what he/she has done **2** the height of a person: *He's quite small in stature.*

status /'steɪtəs/ **noun 1** [U] the legal position of a person, group or country: *Please indicate your name, age and marital status* (= whether you are married or single). ● *They were granted refugee status.* **2** [sing] your social or professional position in relation to other people: *Teachers don't have a very high status in this country.* •➤ synonym **standing 3** [U] a high social position: *The new job gave him much more status.*

the status quo /ˌsteɪtəs 'kwəʊ/ **noun** [sing] the situation as it is now, or as it was before a recent change

'**status symbol noun** [C] something that a person owns that shows that he/she has a high position in society and a lot of money

statute /'stætʃuːt/ **noun** [C] (*formal*) a law or a rule

statutory /'stætʃətri/ **adj** (*formal*) decided by law: *a statutory right*

staunch /stɔːntʃ/ **adj** believing in sb/sth or supporting sb/sth very strongly; loyal

stave /steɪv/ **verb**
PHRASAL VERB **stave sth off** to stop sth unpleasant from happening now, although it may happen at a later time; to delay sth: *to stave off hunger/illness/inflation/bankruptcy*

★**stay¹** /steɪ/ **verb** [I] **1** to continue to be somewhere and not go away: *Patrick stayed in bed until 11 o'clock.* ● *I can't stay long.* ● *Stay on this road until you get to Wells.* ● *Pete's staying late at the office tonight.* **2** to continue to

be in a particular state or situation without change: *I can't stay awake any longer.* ● *I don't know why they stay together* (= continue to be married or in a relationship).

> **Remain** and **stay** are similar in meaning but **remain** is more formal.

3 to live in a place temporarily as a visitor or guest: *We stayed with friends in France.* ● *Which hotel are you staying at?* ● *Can you stay for lunch?* ● *Why don't you stay the night?*

IDIOM **stay put** (*informal*) to continue in one place; to not leave
PHRASAL VERBS **stay behind** to not leave a place after other people have gone: *I'll stay behind and help you wash up.*
stay in to remain at home and not go out: *I'm going to stay in and watch TV.*
stay on (at...) to continue studying, working, etc somewhere for longer than expected or after other people have left
stay out to continue to be away from your house, especially late at night
stay up to go to bed later than usual: *I'm going to stay up to watch the late film.*

stay² /steɪ/ **noun** [C] a period of time that you spend somewhere as a visitor or guest: *Did you enjoy your stay in Crete?*

STD /ˌes tiː 'diː/ **abbr 1** (*Brit*) subscriber trunk dialling; the system by which you can make long-distance telephone calls direct **2** sexually transmitted disease

★**steady¹** /'stedi/ **adj** (**steadier**; **steadiest**) **1** developing, growing or happening gradually and at a regular rate: *a steady increase/ decline* **2** staying the same; not changing and therefore safe: *a steady job/income* **3** firmly fixed, supported or balanced; not shaking or likely to fall down: *You need a steady hand to take good photographs.* ● *He held the ladder steady as she climbed up it.* –**steadily** **adv**: *Unemployment has risen steadily since April 1998.*

steady² /'stedi/ **verb** [I,T] (*pres part* **steadying**; *3rd pers sing pres* **steadies**; *pt, pp* **steadied**) to stop yourself/sb/sth from moving, shaking or falling; to stop moving, shaking or falling: *She thought she was going to fall, so she put out a hand to steady herself.* ● *He had to steady his nerves/voice before beginning his speech.*

steak /steɪk/ **noun** [C,U] a thick flat piece of meat or fish: *a piece of steak* ● *a cod/salmon steak* •➤ Look at **chop²**. •➤ picture on page C4

★**steal** /stiːl/ **verb** (*pt* **stole** /stəʊl/; *pp* **stolen** /'stəʊlən/) **1** [I,T] steal (sth) (from sb/sth) to take sth from a person, shop, etc without permission and without intending to return it or pay for it: *The terrorists were driving a stolen car.* ● *We found out she had been stealing from us for years.*

> You **steal** things, but you **rob** a person or place: *My camera has been stolen!* ● *I've been robbed!* ● *to rob a bank*

•➤ Look also at the note at **thief**. **2** [I] steal

away, in, out, etc to move somewhere secretly and quietly

stealth /stelθ/ noun [U] (*formal*) behaviour that is secret or quiet –**stealthy** adj: *a stealthy approach/movement* –**stealthily** adv

★ **steam**¹ /sti:m/ noun [U] the hot gas that is produced by boiling water: *Steam was rising from the coffee.* ● *a steam engine* (= that uses the power of steam)

IDIOMS **let off steam** (*informal*) to get rid of energy or express strong feeling by behaving in a noisy or wild way

run out of steam to gradually lose energy or enthusiasm

steam² /sti:m/ verb **1** [I] to send out steam: *a bowl of steaming hot soup* **2** [T] to place food over boiling water so that it cooks in the steam; to cook in this way: *steamed vegetables/fish* ● *Leave the potatoes to steam for 30 minutes.*

IDIOM **be/get steamed up** (*informal*) to be or become very angry or worried about sth

PHRASAL VERB **steam (sth) up** to cover sth or become covered with steam: *My glasses have steamed up.*

steamroller /'sti:mrəʊlə/ noun [C] a big heavy vehicle with wide heavy wheels that is used for making the surface of a road flat

★ **steel**¹ /sti:l/ noun [U] a very strong metal that is made from iron mixed with another substance (carbon). Steel is used for making knives, tools, machines, etc.

steel² /sti:l/ verb [T] **steel yourself** to prepare yourself to deal with sth difficult or unpleasant: *Steel yourself for a shock.*

steelworks /'sti:lwɜ:ks/ noun [C, with sing or pl verb] (*pl* **steelworks**) a factory where steel is made

★ **steep** /sti:p/ adj **1** (used about a hill, mountain, street, etc) rising or falling quickly; at a sharp angle: *I don't think I can cycle up that hill. It's too steep.* **2** (used about an increase or fall in sth) very big **3** (*informal*) too expensive –**steeply** adv: *House prices have risen steeply this year.* –**steepness** noun [U]

steeped /sti:pt/ adj **steeped in sth** having a lot of; full of sth: *a city steeped in history*

steeple /'sti:pl/ noun [C] a tower on the roof of a church, often with a pointed top (spire)

★ **steer** /stɪə/ verb **1** [I,T] to control the direction that a vehicle is going in: *Can you push the car while I steer?* ● *to steer a boat/ship/bicycle/motorbike*

➤ **Steer** means to control the direction of a vehicle. If you **ride** a bicycle/motorbike or **sail** a boat you steer it and you are also in control of everything else.

2 [T] to take control of a situation and try to influence the way it develops: *She tried to steer the conversation away from the subject of money.*

IDIOM **keep/stay/steer clear (of sb/sth)** → CLEAR²

steering /'stɪərɪŋ/ noun [U] the parts of a vehicle that control the direction that it moves in: *a car with power steering*

'**steering wheel** (also **wheel**) noun [C] the wheel that the driver turns in a vehicle to control the direction that it moves in ••➤ picture on page S9

★ **stem**¹ /stem/ noun [C] **1** the main long thin part of a plant above the ground from which the leaves or flowers grow ••➤ picture on page C2 **2** (*grammar*) the main part of a word onto which other parts are added: *'Writ-' is the stem of the words 'write', 'writing', 'written' and 'writer'.*

stem² /stem/ verb [T] (**stemming**; **stemmed**) to stop sth that is increasing or spreading

PHRASAL VERB **stem from sth** (not used in the continuous tenses) to be the result of sth

➤ Although this verb is not used in the continuous tenses, it is common to see the present participle (= -ing form): *He was treated for depression stemming from his domestic and business difficulties.*

stench /stentʃ/ noun [C,sing] a very unpleasant smell

★ **step**¹ /step/ noun [C] **1** the action of lifting one foot and putting it down in a different place: *Nick took a step forward and then stopped.* ● *I heard steps outside the window.* ● *We were obviously lost so we decided to retrace our steps* (= go back the way we had come). **2** one action in a series of actions that you take in order to achieve sth: *This will not solve the problem completely, but it is a step in the right direction.* **3** one of the surfaces on which you put your foot when you are going up or down stairs: *on the top/bottom step* ••➤ Look at the note at **stair**.

IDIOMS **in/out of step (with sb/sth)** moving/ not moving your feet at the same time as other people when you are marching, dancing, etc

step by step (used for talking about a series of actions) moving slowly and gradually from one action or stage to the next: *clear step-by-step instructions*

take steps to do sth to take action in order to achieve sth

watch your step 1 to be careful about where you are walking **2** to be careful about how you behave

★ **step**² /step/ verb [I] (**stepping**; **stepped**) **1** to lift one foot and put it down in a different place when you are walking: *Be careful! Don't step in the mud.* ● *to step forward/back* ● *Ouch! You stepped on my foot!* **2** to move a short distance; to go somewhere: *Could you step out of the car please, sir?* ● *I stepped outside for a minute to get some air.*

PHRASAL VERBS **step down** to leave an important job or position and let sb else take your place

step in to help sb in a difficult situation or to become involved in a dispute

step sth up to increase the amount, speed, etc of sth: *The Army has decided to step up its security arrangements.*

step- /step-/ (used in compound nouns)

related as a result of one parent marrying again

stepbrother /'stepbrʌðə/ **noun** [C] the son from an earlier marriage of sb who has married your mother or father

➤ Compare **half-brother**.

stepchild /'steptʃaɪld/ **noun** [C] (*pl* **step-children**) the child from an earlier marriage of your husband or wife

stepdaughter /'stepdɔːtə/ **noun** [C] the daughter from an earlier marriage of your husband or wife

stepfather /'stepfɑːðə/ **noun** [C] the man who has married your mother when your parents are divorced or your father is dead

stepladder /'steplædə/ **noun** [C] a short ladder with two parts, one with steps, that are joined together at the top so that it can stand on its own and be folded up when you are not using it.

stepmother /'stepmʌðə/ **noun** [C] the woman who has married your father when your parents are divorced or your mother is dead

'**stepping stone noun** [C] **1** one of a line of flat stones that you can step on in order to cross a river **2** something that allows you to make progress or helps you to achieve sth

stepsister /'stepsɪstə/ **noun** [C] the daughter from an earlier marriage of sb who has married your mother or father

➤ Compare **half-sister**.

stepson /'stepsʌn/ **noun** [C] the son from an earlier marriage of your husband or wife

stereo /'steriəʊ/ (*pl* **stereos**) **noun 1** (also '**stereo system**) [C] a machine that plays CDs or cassettes, or a radio that has two boxes (**speakers**) so that you hear separate sounds from each: *a car/personal stereo* •➤ picture on page S9 **2** [U] the system for playing recorded music, speech etc in which the sound is divided in two parts: *This pro-gramme is broadcast in stereo.* •➤ Look at **mono**. –**stereo adj**: *a stereo television*

stereotype /'steriətaɪp/ **noun** [C] a fixed idea about a particular type of person or thing, which is often not true in reality –**stereotype verb** [T]: *In advertisements, women are often stereotyped as housewives.*

sterile /'steraɪl/ **adj 1** not able to produce young animals or babies **2** completely clean and free from bacteria: *All equipment used during a medical operation must be sterile.* **3** not producing any useful result: *a sterile discussion/argument* –**sterility** /stə'rɪləti/ **noun** [U] –**sterilization** (also **sterilisation**) /ˌsterəlaɪ'zeɪʃn/ **noun** [U]

sterilize (also **-ise**) /'sterəlaɪz/ **verb** [T] **1** to make sb/sth completely clean and free from bacteria **2** (usually passive) to perform an operation on a person or an animal so that they cannot have babies

sterling[1] /'stɜːlɪŋ/ **noun** [U] the system of money that is used in Britain, that uses the pound as its basic unit

sterling[2] /'stɜːlɪŋ/ **adj** of very high quality: *sterling work*

stern[1] /stɜːn/ **adj** very serious; not smiling: *a stern expression/warning* –**sternly adv**

stern[2] /stɜːn/ **noun** [C] the back end of a ship or boat •➤ Look at **bow**[3].

stethoscope

stethoscope

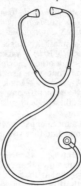

/'steθəskəʊp/ **noun** [C] the piece of equipment that a doctor uses for listening to your breathing and heart

stew /stjuː/ **noun** [C,U] a type of food that you make by cooking meat and/or vegetables in liquid for a long time –**stew verb** [I,T]

steward /'stjuːəd/ **noun** [C] **1** a man whose job is to look after passengers on an aircraft, a ship or a train **2** (*Brit*) a person who helps to organize a large public event, for example a race

stewardess /ˌstjuːə'des; 'stjuːə-/ **noun** [C] **1** a woman whose job is to look after passengers on an aircraft •➤ synonym **air hostess** **2** a woman who looks after the passengers on a ship or train

★**stick**[1] /stɪk/ **verb** (*pt, pp* **stuck** /stʌk/) **1** [I,T] stick (sth) in/into (sth) to push a pointed object into sth; to be pushed into sth: *Stick a fork into the meat to see if it's ready.* **2** [I,T] to fix sth to sth else by using a special substance (**glue**); to become fixed to sth else: *I stuck a stamp on an envelope.* **3** [T] (*informal*) to put sth somewhere, especially quickly or carelessly: *Stick your bags in the bedroom.* • *Just at that moment James stuck his head round the door.* **4** [I] stick (in sth) (used about sth that can usually be moved) to become fixed in one position so that it cannot be moved: *The car was stuck in the mud.* • *This drawer keeps sticking.* **5** [T] (*informal*) (often in negative sentences and questions) to stay in a difficult or unpleasant situation: *I can't stick this job much longer.*

IDIOMS poke/stick your nose into sth → **NOSE**[1]
stick/put your tongue out → **TONGUE**

PHRASAL VERBS stick around (*informal*) to stay somewhere, waiting for sth to happen or for sb to arrive

stick at sth (*informal*) to continue working at sth even when it is difficult

stick by sb (*informal*) to continue to give sb help and support even in difficult times

stick out (*informal*) to be very noticeable and easily seen: *The new office block really sticks out from the older buildings around it.*

stick (sth) out to be further out than sth else; to push sth further out than sth else: *The boy's head was sticking out of the window.*

S

stick it/sth out (*informal*) to stay in a difficult or unpleasant situation until the end

stick to sth (*informal*) to continue with sth and not change to anything else

stick together (*informal*) (used about a group of people) to stay friendly and loyal to each other

stick up to point upwards: *You look funny. Your hair's sticking up!*

stick up for yourself/sb/sth (*informal*) to support or defend yourself/sb/sth: *Don't worry. I'll stick up for you if there's any trouble.*

★**stick²** /stɪk/ *noun* [C] **1** a small thin piece of wood from a tree **2** (*especially Brit*) = **WALKING STICK 3** (in hockey and some other sports) a long thin piece of wood that you use for hitting the ball: *a hockey stick* ••▶ Look at **bat²**, **club²**(2) and **racket¹**. ••▶ picture on page S2 **4** a long thin piece of sth: *a stick of celery/dynamite*

sticker /'stɪkə/ *noun* [C] a piece of paper with writing or a picture on one side that you can stick onto sth

★**sticky** /'stɪki/ *adj* (**stickier**; **stickiest**) **1** used for describing a substance that easily becomes joined to things that it touches, or sth that is covered with this kind of substance: *These sweets are very sticky.* ● *sticky tape* **2** (*informal*) (used about a situation) difficult or unpleasant

★**stiff¹** /stɪf/ *adj* **1** (used about material, paper, etc) firm and difficult to bend or move: *My new shoes feel rather stiff.* ● *The door handle is stiff and I can't turn it.* **2** (used about parts of the body) not easy to move: *My arm feels really stiff after playing tennis yesterday.* **3** (used about a liquid) very thick; almost solid: *Beat the egg whites until they are stiff.* **4** more difficult or stronger than usual: *The firm faces stiff competition from its rivals.* ● *a stiff breeze/wind* **5** (used about sb's behaviour) not relaxed or friendly; formal **6** (used about an alcoholic drink) strong: *a stiff whisky* –**stiffness** *noun* [U]

stiff² /stɪf/ *adv* (*informal*) extremely: *to be bored/frozen/scared/worried stiff*

stiffen /'stɪfn/ *verb* **1** [I] (used about a person) to suddenly stop moving and hold your body very straight, usually because you are afraid or angry **2** [I,T] to become rigid; to make sth rigid so that it will not bend

stiffly /'stɪfli/ *adv* in an unfriendly formal way: *He smiled stiffly.*

stifle /'staɪfl/ *verb* **1** [T] to stop sth happening, developing or continuing: *Her strict education had stifled her natural creativity.* ● *to stifle a yawn/cry/giggle* **2** [I,T] to be or to make sb unable to breathe because it is very hot and/or there is no fresh air: *Richard was almost stifled by the smoke.* –**stifling** /'staɪflɪŋ/ *adj*: *The heat was stifling.*

stigma /'stɪgmə/ *noun* [C,U] bad and often unfair feelings that people in general have about a particular illness, way of behaving, etc: *There is still a lot of stigma attached to being unemployed.*

★**still¹** /stɪl/ *adv* **1** continuing until now or until the time you are talking about and not finishing: *Do you still live in London?* ● *It's still raining.* ● *I've eaten all the food but I'm still hungry.* ● *In 1997 Zoran was still a student.* **2** in addition; more: *There are still ten days to go until my holiday.* **3** in spite of what has just been said: *He had a bad headache but he still went to the party.* **4** used for making a comparative adjective stronger: *It was very cold yesterday, but today it's colder still.* ● *There was still more bad news to come.*

★**still²** /stɪl/ *adj, adv* **1** not moving: *Stand still! I want to take a photograph!* ● *Children find it hard to keep/stay still for long periods.* **2** quiet or calm: *The water was perfectly still.* **3** (used about a drink) not containing gas: *still mineral water* ••▶ Look at **fizzy** and **sparkling**. ••▶ picture at **bubble** –**stillness** *noun* [U]

still³ /stɪl/ *noun* [C] a single photograph that is taken from a film or video

stillborn /'stɪlbɔːn/ *adj* (used about a baby) dead when it is born

stilt /stɪlt/ *noun* [C] **1** one of two long pieces of wood, with places to rest your feet on, on which you can walk above the ground: *Have you tried walking on stilts?* **2** one of a set of poles that support a building above the ground or water

stilted /'stɪltɪd/ *adj* (used about a way of speaking or writing) not natural or relaxed; too formal

stimulant /'stɪmjələnt/ *noun* [C] a drug or medicine that makes you feel more active

stimulate /'stɪmjuleɪt/ *verb* [T] **1** to make sth active or more active: *Exercise stimulates the blood circulation.* ● *The government has decided to cut taxes in order to stimulate the economy.* **2** to make sb feel interested and excited about sth: *The lessons don't really stimulate him.* –**stimulation** /ˌstɪmjuˈleɪʃn/ *noun* [U]

stimulating /'stɪmjuleɪtɪŋ/ *adj* interesting and exciting: *a stimulating discussion*

stimulus /'stɪmjələs/ *noun* [C,U] (*pl* **stimuli** /-laɪ/) something that causes activity, development or interest: *Books provide children with ideas and a stimulus for play.*

★**sting¹** /stɪŋ/ *verb* [I,T] (*pt, pp* **stung** /stʌŋ/) **1** (used about an insect, plant, etc) to make a person or animal feel a sudden pain by pushing sth sharp into his/her skin and sending poison into him/her: *Ow! I've been stung by a bee!* ● *Be careful. Those plants sting.* **2** to make sb/sth feel a sudden, sharp pain: *Soap stings if it gets in your eyes.* **3** to make sb feel very hurt and upset because of sth you say

★**sting²** /stɪŋ/ *noun* [C] **1** the sharp pointed part of some insects and animals that is used for pushing into the skin of a person or an animal and putting in poison ••▶ picture at **scorpion 2** the pain that you feel when an animal or insect pushes its sting into you: *I got a wasp sting on the leg.* **3** a sharp pain that feels like a sting

stink /stɪŋk/ *verb* [I] (*pt* **stank** /stæŋk/ or

stunk /stʌŋk/; *pp* **stunk**) (*informal*) stink (of sth) **1** to have a very strong and unpleasant smell: *It stinks in here – open a window!* ● *to stink of fish* **2** to seem to be very bad, unpleasant or dishonest: *The whole business stinks of corruption.* –**stink** *noun* [C]

stint /stɪnt/ *noun* [C] a fixed period of time that you spend doing sth: *He did a brief stint in the army after leaving school.*

stipulate /'stɪpjuleɪt/ *verb* [T] (*formal*) to say exactly and officially what must be done: *The law stipulates that all schools must be inspected every three years.* –**stipulation** /ˌstɪpju'leɪʃn/ *noun* [C,U]

★**stir**[1] /stɜː/ *verb* (**stirring**; **stirred**) **1** [T] to move a liquid, etc round and round, using a spoon, etc: *She stirred her coffee with a teaspoon.* **2** [I,T] to move or make sb/sth move slightly: *She heard the baby stir in the next room.* **3** [T] to make sb feel a strong emotion: *The story stirred Carol's imagination.* ● *a stirring speech*

PHRASAL VERB **stir sth up** to cause problems, or to make people feel strong emotions: *He's always trying to stir up trouble.* ● *The article stirred up a lot of anger among local residents.*

stir[2] /stɜː/ *noun* **1** [C] the action of stirring: *Give the soup a stir.* **2** [sing] something exciting or shocking that everyone talks about

stirrup /'stɪrəp/ *noun* [C] one of the two metal objects that you put your feet in when you are riding a horse ●▸ picture at **horse**

★**stitch**[1] /stɪtʃ/ *noun* [C] **1** one of the small lines of thread that you can see on a piece of material after it has been sewn ●▸ picture at **knit 2** one of the small pieces of thread that a doctor uses to sew your skin together if you cut yourself very badly, or after an operation: *How many stitches did you have in your leg?* **3** one of the small circles of wool that you put round a needle when you are knitting **4** [usually sing] a sudden pain that you get in the side of your body when you are running

IDIOM **in stitches** (*informal*) laughing so much that you cannot stop

stitch[2] /stɪtʃ/ *verb* [I,T] to sew

★**stock**[1] /stɒk/ *noun* **1** [U,C] the supply of things that a shop, etc has for sale: *We'll have to order extra stock if we sell a lot more this week.* ● *I'm afraid that book's out of stock at the moment. Shall I order it for you?* ● *I'll see if we have your size in stock.* **2** [C] an amount of sth that has been kept ready to be used: *Food stocks in the village were very low.* **3** [C,U] a share that sb has bought in a company, or the value of a company's shares: *to invest in stocks and shares* **4** [C,U] a liquid that made by boiling meat, bones, vegetables, etc in water, used especially for making soups and sauces

IDIOM **take stock (of sth)** to think about sth very carefully before deciding what to do next

stock[2] /stɒk/ *verb* [T] **1** (usually used about a shop) to have a supply of sth: *They stock food from all over the world.* **2** to fill a place with

sth: *a well-stocked library*

PHRASAL VERB **stock up (on/with sth)** to collect a large supply of sth for future use: *to stock up with food for the winter*

stock[3] /stɒk/ *adj* (only *before* a noun) (used for describing sth that sb says) used so often that it does not have much meaning: *He always comes out with the same stock answers.*

stockbroker /'stɒkbrəʊkə/ (also **broker**) *noun* [C] a person whose job it is to buy and sell shares in companies for other people

'stock exchange *noun* [C] **1** a place where shares in companies are bought and sold: *the Tokyo Stock Exchange* **2** (also **'stock market**) the business or activity of buying and selling shares in companies ●▸ Look at **exchange**.

stocking /'stɒkɪŋ/ *noun* [C] one of a pair of thin pieces of clothing that fit tightly over a woman's feet and legs: *a pair of stockings* ●▸ Look at **tights**. ●▸ picture on page C6

stockist /'stɒkɪst/ *noun* [C] a shop that sells goods made by a particular company

stocktaking /'stɒkteɪkɪŋ/ *noun* [U] the activity of counting the total supply of things that a shop or business has at a particular time: *They close for an hour a month to do the stocktaking.*

stocky /'stɒki/ *adj* (used about a person's body) short but strong and heavy

stoic /'stəʊɪk/ (also **stoical** /-kl/) *adj* (*formal*) suffering pain or difficulty without complaining –**stoically** /-kli/ *adv* –**stoicism** /'stəʊɪsɪzəm/ *noun* [U]

stole *past tense* of **STEAL**

stolen *past participle* of **STEAL**

stolid /'stɒlɪd/ *adj* (used about a person) showing very little emotion or excitement –**stolidly** *adv*

★**stomach**[1] /'stʌmək/ (also *informal* **tummy**) *noun* [C] **1** the organ in your body where food goes after you have eaten it: *He went to the doctor with stomach pains.* ●▸ picture on page C5 **2** the front part of your body below your chest and above your legs: *She turned over onto her stomach.* ●▸ picture on page C5

stomach[2] /'stʌmək/ *verb* [T] (*informal*) (usually in negative sentences and questions) to be able to watch, listen to, accept, etc sth that you think is unpleasant: *I can't stomach too much violence in films.*

'stomach-ache *noun* [C,U] a pain in your stomach: *I've got terrible stomach-ache.* ●▸ Look at the note at **ache**.

stomp /stɒmp/ *verb* [I] (*informal*) to walk with heavy steps

★**stone** /stəʊn/ *noun* **1** [U] a hard solid substance that is found in the ground: *The house was built of grey stone.* ● *a stone wall* **2** [C] a small piece of rock: *The boy picked up a stone and threw it into the river.* **3** [C] = **PRECIOUS STONE 4** [C] the hard seed inside some fruits, for example peaches, plums, cherries and olives **5** [C] (*pl* **stone**) a measure of weight; 6·35 kilograms. There are 14 pounds in a stone: *I weigh eleven stone two* (= 2 pounds).

S

stoned /stəʊnd/ **adj** (*slang*) not behaving or thinking normally because of drugs or alcohol

stony /'stəʊni/ **adj 1** (used about the ground) having a lot of stones in it, or covered with stones **2** not friendly: *There was a stony silence as he walked into the room.*

stood *past tense, past participle* of **STAND**[1]

★**stool** /stu:l/ **noun** [C] a seat that does not have a back or arms: *a piano stool*

stoop /stu:p/ **verb** [I] to bend your head and shoulders forwards and downwards: *He had to stoop to get through the low doorway.*
–**stoop noun** [sing]: *to walk with a stoop*
PHRASAL VERB **stoop to sth/doing sth** to do sth bad or wrong that you would normally not do

★**stop**[1] /stɒp/ **verb** (**stopping**; **stopped**)
1 [I,T] to finish moving or make sth finish moving: *He walked along the road for a bit, and then stopped.* • *Does this train stop at Didcot?* • *My watch has stopped.* • *I stopped someone in the street to ask the way to the station.* **2** [I,T] to no longer continue or make sth not continue: *I think the rain has stopped.* • *It's stopped raining now.* • *Stop making that terrible noise!* • *The bus service stops at midnight.* • *We tied a bandage round his arm to stop the bleeding.*

> If you **stop to do** something, you stop in order to do it: *On the way home I stopped to buy a newspaper.* If you **stop doing** something you do not do it any more: *Stop talking and listen to me!*

3 [T] **stop sb/sth (from) doing sth** to make sb/sth end or finish an activity; prevent sb/sth from doing sth: *They've built a fence to stop the dog getting out.* • *I'm going to go and you can't stop me.* **4** [I,T] **stop (for sth); stop (and do/to do sth)** to end an activity for a short time in order to do sth: *Shall we stop for lunch now?* • *Let's stop and look at the map.* • *We stopped work for half an hour to have a cup of coffee.*
IDIOMS **stop at nothing** to do anything to get what you want, even if it is wrong or dangerous

stop short of sth/doing sth to almost do sth, but then decide not to do it at the last minute
PHRASAL VERBS **stop off (at/in...)** to stop during a journey to do sth

stop over (at/in...) to stay somewhere for a short time during a long journey

★**stop**[2] /stɒp/ **noun** [C] **1** an act of stopping or state of being stopped: *Our first stop will be in Edinburgh.* • *Production at the factory will come to a stop at midnight tonight.* • *I managed to bring the car to a stop just in time.* **2** the place where a bus, train, etc stops so that people can get on and off: *a bus stop* • *I'm getting off at the next stop.*
IDIOMS **pull out all the stops** → **PULL**[1]

put a stop to sth to prevent sth bad or unpleasant from continuing

stopgap /'stɒpgæp/ **noun** [C] a person or a thing that does a job for a short time until sb/sth permanent can be found

stopover /'stɒpəʊvə/ **noun** [C] a short stop in a journey

stoppage /'stɒpɪdʒ/ **noun** [C] **1** a situation in which people stop working as part of a protest **2** (in sport) an interruption in a game for a particular reason

stopper /'stɒpə/ **noun** [C] an object that you put into the top of a bottle in order to close it

stopwatch /'stɒpwɒtʃ/ **noun** [C] a watch which can be started and stopped by pressing a button, so that you can measure exactly how long sth takes

storage /'stɔːrɪdʒ/ **noun** [U] the keeping of things until they are needed; the place where they are kept: *This room is being used for storage at the moment.*

★**store**[1] /stɔː/ **noun** [C] **1** a large shop: *She's a sales assistant in a large department store.* • *a furniture store* ••► Look at **chain store**. **2** (US) = **SHOP**[1](1) **3** a supply of sth that you keep for future use; the place where it is kept: *a good store of food for the winter* • *Police discovered a weapons store in the house.*
IDIOMS **in store (for sb/sth)** going to happen in the future: *There's a surprise in store for you when you get home!*

set...store by to consider sth to be important: *Nick sets great store by his mother's opinion.*

★**store**[2] /stɔː/ **verb** [T] to keep sth or a supply of sth for future use: *to store information on a computer*

storekeeper /'stɔːkiːpə/ (US) = **SHOPKEEPER**

storeroom /'stɔːruːm; -rʊm/ **noun** [C] a room where things are kept until they are needed

storey (US **story**) /'stɔːri/ **noun** [C] (*pl* **storeys**; US **stories**) one floor or level of a building: *The building will be five storeys high.* • *a two-storey house* • *a multi-storey car park*

stork /stɔːk/ **noun** [C] a large white bird with a long beak, neck and legs. Storks often make their homes (**nests**) on the top of buildings.

★**storm**[1] /stɔːm/ **noun** [C] very bad weather, with a lot of rain, strong winds, etc: *Look at those black clouds. I think there's going to be a storm.* • *a hailstorm/snowstorm/sandstorm/ thunderstorm*

> **Storm** is the general word for very bad weather. A very strong wind is a **gale**. A storm with very strong winds is a **hurricane**. A storm with a very strong circular wind is called a **cyclone**, **tornado**, **typhoon** or **whirlwind**. A very bad snowstorm is a **blizzard**.

storm[2] /stɔːm/ **verb 1** [I] to enter or leave somewhere in a very angry and noisy way: *He threw down the book and stormed out of the room.* **2** [T] to attack a building, town, etc suddenly and violently in order to take control of it

stormy /'stɔːmi/ **adj 1** used for talking about very bad weather, with strong winds, heavy rain, etc: *a stormy night* • *stormy weather* **2** involving a lot of angry argument and strong feeling: *a stormy relationship*

S

★**story** /'stɔːri/ **noun** [C] (*pl* **stories**) **1** a story (about sb/sth) a description of people and events that are not real: *I'll **tell** you **a** story about the animals that live in that forest.* ● *I always read the children **a** bedtime story.* ● *a detective/fairy/ghost/love story* **2** an account, especially a spoken one, of sth that has happened: *The police didn't believe his story.* **3** a description of true events that happened in the past: *He's writing his life story.* **4** an article or report in a newspaper or magazine: *The plane crash was the front-page story in most newspapers.* **5** (*US*) = STOREY

stout /staʊt/ **adj 1** (used about a person) rather fat **2** strong and thick: *stout walking boots*

stove /stəʊv/ **noun** [C] **1** the top part of a cooker that has gas or electric rings: *He put a pan of water to boil on the stove.* **2** a closed metal box in which you burn wood, coal, etc for heating: *a wood-burning stove*

stow /stəʊ/ **verb** [T] **stow sth (away)** to put sth away in a particular place until it is needed

stowaway /'stəʊəweɪ/ **noun** [C] a person who hides in a ship or plane so that he/she can travel without paying

straddle /'strædl/ **verb** [T] **1** (used about a person) to sit or stand with your legs on each side of sth: *to straddle a chair* **2** (used about a building, bridge, etc) to be on both sides of sth

straggle /'strægl/ **verb** [I] **1** to walk, etc more slowly than the rest of the group: *The children straggled along behind their parents.* **2** to grow, spread or move in an untidy way or in different directions: *Her wet hair straggled across her forehead.* –**straggler** **noun** [C] –**straggly** **adj**: *long straggly hair*

★**straight¹** /streɪt/ **adj 1** with no bends or curves; going in one direction only: *a straight line* ● *He's got dark, straight hair.* ● *Keep your back straight!* ● *He was so tired he couldn't walk **in a straight line**.* ●> picture at **hair** and **line 2** (not before a noun) in an exactly horizontal or vertical position: *That picture isn't straight.* **3** honest and direct: *Politicians never give **a** straight answer.* ● *Are you being straight with me?* **4** tidy or organized as it should be: *It took ages to **put the room straight** after we'd decorated it.* **5** (*informal*) attracted to people of the opposite sex; heterosexual ●> opposite **gay 6** (*informal*) used to describe a person who you think is too serious and boring

IDIOMS **get sth straight** to make sure that you understand sth completely

keep a straight face to stop yourself from smiling or laughing

put/set the record straight → RECORD¹

★**straight²** /streɪt/ **adv 1** not in a curve or at an angle; in a straight line: *Go **straight on** for about two miles until you come to some traffic lights.* ● *He was looking **straight ahead**.* ● *to **sit up straight** (= with a straight back)* **2** without stopping; directly: *I took the*

children straight home after school. ● *to walk straight past sb/sth* ● *I'm going straight to bed when I get home.* ● *He joined the army straight from school.* **3** in an honest and direct way: *Tell me straight, doctor – is it serious?*

IDIOMS **go straight** to become honest after being a criminal

right/straight away → AWAY

straight out in an honest and direct way: *I told Asif straight out that I didn't want to see him any more.*

straighten /'streɪtn/ **verb** [I,T] **straighten (sth) (up/out)** to become straight or to make sth straight: *The road straightens out at the bottom of the hill.* ● *to straighten your tie*

PHRASAL VERBS **straighten sth out** to remove the confusion or difficulties from a situation

straighten up to make your body straight and vertical

straightforward /ˌstreɪt'fɔːwəd/ **adj 1** easy to do or understand; simple: *straightforward instructions* **2** honest and open: *a straightforward person*

strain¹ /streɪn/ **noun 1** [U] pressure that is put on sth when it is pulled or pushed by a physical force: *Running downhill puts strain on the knees.* ● *The rope finally broke **under the strain**.* **2** [C,U] worry or pressure caused by having too much to deal with: *to be **under a lot of strain** at work* **3** [C] something that makes you feel worried and tense: *I always find exams a terrible strain.* **4** [C,U] an injury to part of your body that is caused by using it too much **5** [C] one type of animal, plant or disease that is slightly different from the other types

strain² /streɪn/ **verb 1** [I,T] to make a great effort to do sth: *I was straining to see what was happening.* ● *Bend down as far as you can without straining.* **2** [T] to injure a part of your body by using it too much: *Don't read in the dark. You'll strain your eyes.* ● *I think I've strained a muscle in my neck.* **3** [T] to put a lot of pressure on sth: *Money problems have strained their relationship.* **4** [T] to separate a solid and a liquid by pouring them into a special container with small holes in it: *to strain tea/vegetables/spaghetti*

strained /streɪnd/ **adj 1** not natural or friendly: *Relations between the two countries are strained.* **2** worried because of having too much to deal with: *Martin looked tired and strained.*

strait /streɪt/ **noun 1** [C, usually pl] a narrow piece of sea that joins two larger seas: *the straits of Gibraltar* **2 straits** [pl] a very difficult situation, especially one caused by having no money: *The company is in financial straits.*

IDIOM **be in dire straits** → DIRE

straitjacket (also **straightjacket**) /'streɪt-dʒækɪt/ **noun** [C] a piece of clothing like a jacket with long arms which is put on people who are considered dangerous to prevent them from behaving violently

strand /strænd/ **noun** [C] **1** a single piece of

cotton, wool, hair, etc **2** one part of a story, situation or idea

stranded /'strændɪd/ **adj** left in a place that you cannot get away from: *We were left stranded when our car broke down in the mountains.*

★**strange** /streɪndʒ/ **adj 1** unusual or unexpected: *A very strange thing happened to me on the way home.* ● *a strange noise* **2** that you have not seen, visited, met, etc before: *a strange town* ● *My mother told me not to talk to strange men.*

> We do not use **strange** to talk about a person or thing that comes from a different country. Look at **foreign**.

–**strangely adv**: *The streets were strangely quiet.* ● *Tim's behaving very strangely at the moment.* –**strangeness noun** [U]

★**stranger** /'streɪndʒə/ **noun** [C] **1** a person that you do not know: *I had to ask a complete stranger to help me with my suitcase.*

> We do not use **stranger** to talk about a person who comes from a different country. Look at **foreigner**.

2 a person who is in a place that he/she does not know: *I'm a stranger to this part of the country.*

strangle /'stræŋgl/ **verb** [T] **1** to kill sb by squeezing his/her neck or throat with your hands, a rope, etc ••➤ synonym **throttle** ••➤ Look at **choke**. **2** to prevent sth from developing

★**strap** /stræp/ **noun** [C] a long narrow piece of leather, cloth, plastic, etc that you use for carrying sth or for keeping sth in position: *I managed to fasten my watch strap but now I can't undo it.* ••➤ pictures at **bag**, **binoculars** and **clock** –**strap verb** [T] (**strapping**; **strapped**): *The racing driver was securely strapped into the car.*

strategic /strə'tiːdʒɪk/ (also **strategical**) **adj 1** helping you to achieve a plan; giving you an advantage: *They made a strategic decision to sell off part of the company.* **2** connected with a country's plans to achieve success in a war or in its defence system **3** (used about bombs and other weapons) intended to be fired at the enemy's country rather than be used in battle –**strategically** /-kli/ **adv**: *The island is strategically important.*

strategy /'strætədʒi/ **noun** (*pl* **strategies**) **1** [C] a plan that you use in order to achieve sth: *What's your strategy for this exam?* **2** [U] the action of planning how to do or achieve sth: *military strategy*

★**straw** /strɔː/ **noun 1** [U] the long, straight, central parts (**stems**) of plants, for example wheat, that are dried and then used for animals to sleep on or for making baskets, covering a roof, etc: *a straw hat* ••➤ picture on page C4 **2** [C] one piece of straw **3** [C] a long plastic or paper tube that you can use for drinking through ••➤ picture at **container**

IDIOM **the last/final straw** the last in a series of bad things that happen to you and that

makes you decide that you cannot accept the situation any longer

strawberry /'strɔːbəri/ **noun** [C] (*pl* **strawberries**) a small soft red fruit with small white seeds on it: *strawberries and cream*

stray[1] /streɪ/ **verb** [I] **1** to go away from the place where you should be: *The sheep had strayed onto the road.* **2** to not keep to the subject you should be thinking about or discussing: *My thoughts strayed for a few moments.*

stray[2] /streɪ/ **noun** [C] a dog, cat, etc that does not have a home –**stray adj** (only *before* a noun): *a stray dog*

streak[1] /striːk/ **noun** [C] **1** streak (of sth) a thin line or mark: *The cat had brown fur with streaks of white in it.* **2** a part of a person's character that sometimes shows in the way he/she behaves: *Vesna's a very caring girl, but she does have a selfish streak.* **3** a continuous period of bad or good luck in a game of sport: *The team is on a losing/winning streak at the moment.*

streak[2] /striːk/ **verb** [I] (*informal*) to run fast

streaked /striːkt/ **adj** streaked (with sth) having lines of a different colour: *black hair streaked with grey*

★**stream**[1] /striːm/ **noun** [C] **1** a small river: *I waded across the shallow stream.* **2** the continuous movement of a liquid or gas: *a stream of blood* **3** a continuous movement of people or things: *a stream of traffic* **4** a large number of things which happen one after another: *a stream of letters/telephone calls/questions*

stream[2] /striːm/ **verb** [I] **1** (used about a liquid, gas or light) to flow in large amounts: *Tears were streaming down his face.* ● *Sunlight was streaming in through the windows.* **2** (used about people or things) to move somewhere in a continuous flow: *People were streaming out of the station.*

streamer /'striːmə/ **noun** [C] a long piece of coloured paper that you use for decorating a room before a party, etc

streamline /'striːmlaɪn/ **verb** [T] **1** to give a vehicle, etc a long smooth shape so that it will move easily through air or water **2** to make an organization, process, etc work better by making it simpler –**streamlined adj**

★**street** /striːt/ **noun** [C] **1** a road in a town, village or city that has shops, houses, etc on one or both sides: *to walk along/down the street* ● *to cross the street* ● *I met Karen in the street this morning.* ● *a narrow street* ● *a street map of Rome* ••➤ Look at the note at **road**. **2** **Street** (*abbr* **St**) [sing] used in the names of streets: *64 High Street* ● *The post office is in Sheep Street.*

IDIOMS **the man in the street** → **MAN**[1]

streets ahead (of sb/sth) (*informal*) much better than sb/sth

(right) up your street (*informal*) (used about an activity, subject, etc) exactly right for you because you know a lot about it, like it very much, etc

S

*★**strength** /streŋθ/ **noun 1** [U] the quality of being physically strong; the amount of this quality that you have: *He pulled with all his strength but the rock would not move.* • *I didn't have the strength to walk any further.* **2** [U] the ability of an object to hold heavy weights or not to break or be damaged easily: *All our suitcases are tested for strength before they leave the factory.* **3** [U] the power and influence that sb has: *Germany's economic strength* **4** [U] how strong a feeling or opinion is **5** [C,U] a good quality or ability that sb/sth has: *His greatest strength is his ability to communicate with people.* • *the strengths and weaknesses of a plan* ••➤ opposite **weakness**

IDIOMS **at full strength** (used about a group) having all the people it needs or usually has: *Nobody is injured, so the team will be at full strength for the game.*

below strength (used about a group) not having the number of people it needs or usually has

on the strength of as a result of information, advice, etc

strengthen /'streŋθn/ **verb** [I,T] to become stronger or to make sth stronger: *exercises to strengthen your muscles* ••➤ opposite **weaken**

strenuous /'strenjuəs/ **adj** needing or using a lot of effort or energy: *Don't do strenuous exercise after eating.* • *She's making a strenuous effort to be on time every day.* –**strenuously** *adv*

*★**stress**¹ /stres/ **noun 1** [C,U] worry and pressure that is caused by having too much to deal with: *He's been under a lot of stress since his wife went into hospital.* ••➤ Look at **trauma**. **2** [U] stress (on sth) the special attention that you give to sth because you think it is important: *We should put more stress on preventing crime.* **3** [C,U] (a) stress (on sth) the force that you put on a particular word or part of a word when you speak: *In the word 'dictionary' the stress is on the first syllable, 'dic'.* **4** [C,U] a physical force that may cause sth to bend or break: *Heavy lorries put too much stress on this bridge.*

stress² /stres/ **verb** [T] to give sth special force or attention because it is important: *The minister stressed the need for a peaceful solution.* • *Which syllable is stressed in this word?* ••➤ synonym **emphasize**

stressful /'stresfl/ **adj** causing worry and pressure: *a stressful job*

*★**stretch**¹ /stretʃ/ **verb 1** [I,T] to pull sth so that it becomes longer or wider; to become longer or wider in this way: *The artist stretched the canvas tightly over the frame.* • *My T-shirt stretched when I washed it.* ••➤ picture at **shrink 2** [I,T] stretch (sth) (out) to push out your arms, legs, etc as far as possible: *He switched off the alarm clock, yawned and stretched.* • *She stretched out on the sofa and fell asleep.* • *She stretched out her arm to take the book.* ••➤ picture on page S2 **3** [I] to cover a large area of land or a long period of time: *The long white beaches stretch for miles along the coast.* **4** [T] to make use of

all the money, ability, time, etc that sb has available for use: *The test has been designed to really stretch students' knowledge.*

IDIOM **stretch your legs** to go for a walk after sitting down for a long time

stretch² /stretʃ/ **noun** [C] **1** a stretch (of sth) an area of land or water: *a dangerous stretch of road* **2** [usually sing] the action of making the muscles in your arms, legs, back, etc as long as possible: *Stand up, everybody, and have a good stretch.*

IDIOM **at a stretch** without stopping: *We travelled for six hours at a stretch.*

at full stretch ➤ **FULL**¹

stretcher /'stretʃə/ **noun** [C] a piece of cloth supported by two poles that is used for carrying a person who has been injured

*★**strict** /strɪkt/ **adj 1** not allowing people to break rules or behave badly: *Samir's very strict with his children.* • *I went to a very strict school.* **2** that must be obeyed completely: *I gave her strict instructions to be home before 9.00.* **3** exactly correct; accurate: *a strict interpretation of the law*

strictly /'strɪktli/ **adv** in a strict way: *Smoking is strictly forbidden.*

IDIOM **strictly speaking** to be exactly correct or accurate: *Strictly speaking, the tomato is not a vegetable. It's a fruit.*

stride¹ /straɪd/ **verb** [I] (*pt* strode /strəʊd/; *pp* stridden /'strɪdn/) to walk with long steps, often because you feel very confident or determined: *He strode up to the house and knocked on the door.*

stride² /straɪd/ **noun** [C] a long step

IDIOMS **get into your stride** to start to do sth in a confident way and well after an uncertain beginning

make great strides to make very quick progress

take sth in your stride to deal with a new or difficult situation easily and without worrying

strident /'straɪdnt/ **adj** (used about a voice or a sound) loud and unpleasant

strife /straɪf/ **noun** [U] (*written*) trouble or fighting between people or groups

*★**strike**¹ /straɪk/ **noun** [C] **1** a period of time when people refuse to go to work, usually because they want more money or better working conditions: *a one-day strike* • *Union members voted to go on strike.* **2** a sudden military attack, especially by aircraft

*★**strike**² /straɪk/ **verb** (*pt, pp* struck /strʌk/) **1** [T] (*formal*) to hit sb/sth: *The stone struck her on the head.* • *The boat struck a rock and began to sink.*

➤ **Hit** is more common: *The stone hit her on the head.*

2 [I,T] to attack and harm sb/sth suddenly: *The earthquake struck Kobe in 1995.* • *The building had been struck by lightning.* **3** [I] to stop work as a protest: *The workers voted to strike for more money.* **4** [T] strike sb (as sth) to give sb a particular impression: *Does anything here strike you as unusual?* • *He*

S

strikes me as a very caring man. **5** [T] (used about a thought or an idea) to come suddenly into sb's mind: *It suddenly struck me that she would be the ideal person for the job.* **6** [T] to produce fire by rubbing sth, especially a match, on a surface: *She struck a match and lit her cigarette.* **7** [I,T] (used about a clock) to ring a bell so that people know what time it is. **8** [T] to discover gold, oil, etc in the ground

IDIOMS **strike a balance (between A and B)** to find a middle way between two extremes

strike a bargain (with sb) to make an agreement with sb

within striking distance near enough to be reached or attacked easily

PHRASAL VERBS **strike back** to attack sb/sth that has attacked you

strike up sth (with sb) to start a conversation or friendship with sb

striker /'straɪkə/ noun [C] **1** a person who has stopped working as a protest **2** (in football) a player whose job is to score goals

striking /'straɪkɪŋ/ adj very noticeable; making a strong impression: *There was a striking similarity between the two men.* –**strikingly** adv

★**string¹** /strɪŋ/ noun **1** [C,U] a piece of long, strong material like very thin rope, that you use for tying things: *a ball/piece/length of string* ● *The key is hanging on a string.* ••➤ picture at **cable 2** [C] one of the pieces of thin wire, etc that produce the sound on some musical instruments: *A guitar has six strings.* ••➤ picture at **music 3** [C] one of the pieces of thin material that is stretched across the thing (racket) that you use to hit the ball in tennis and other sports **4** the **strings** [pl] the instruments in an orchestra that have strings **5** [C] **a string of sth** a line of things that are joined together on the same piece of thread: *a string of beads* **6** [C] **a string of sth** a series of people, things or events that follow one after another: *a string of visitors*

IDIOMS **(with) no strings attached; without strings** with no special conditions

pull strings → PULL¹

string² /strɪŋ/ verb [T] (*pt, pp* **strung** /strʌŋ/) **string sth (up)** to hang up a line of things with a piece of string, etc

PHRASAL VERBS **string sb/sth out** to make people or things form a line with spaces between each person or thing

string sth together to put words or phrases together to make a sentence, speech, etc

stringent /'strɪndʒənt/ adj (used about a law, rule, etc) very strict

★**strip¹** /strɪp/ noun [C] a long narrow piece of sth: *a strip of paper*

strip² /strɪp/ verb (**stripping; stripped**) **1** [I,T] **strip (sth) (off)** to take off your clothes; to take off sb else's clothes: *The doctor asked him to strip to the waist.* ● *I was stripped and searched at the airport by two customs officers.* **2** [T] **strip sb/sth (of sth)** to take sth away from sb/sth: *They stripped the house of all its furniture.* **3** [T] **strip sth (off)**

to remove sth that is covering a surface: *to strip the paint off a door* ● *to strip wallpaper*

★**stripe** /straɪp/ noun [C] a long narrow line of colour: *Zebras have black and white stripes.* –**striped** /straɪpt/ adj: *a red and white striped dress*

stripper /'strɪpə/ noun [C] a person whose job is to take off his/her clothes in order to entertain people

striptease /'strɪptiːz/ noun [C,U] entertainment in which sb takes off his/her clothes, usually to music

strive /straɪv/ verb [I] (*pt* **strove** /strəʊv/; *pp* **striven** /'strɪvn/) (*formal*) **strive (for sth/to do sth)** to try very hard to do or get sth: *to strive for perfection*

strode *past tense* of **STRIDE¹**

★**stroke¹** /strəʊk/ noun **1** [C] one of the movements that you make when you are writing or painting: *a brush stroke* **2** [C] one of the movements that you make when you are swimming, rowing, playing golf, etc: *Woods won by three strokes* (= hits of the ball in golf). **3** [C,U] (used in compounds) one of the styles of swimming: *I can do backstroke and breaststroke, but not front crawl.* ••➤ Look at **crawl. 4** [C] a sudden illness which attacks the brain and can leave a person unable to move part of his/her body, speak clearly, etc: *to have a stroke* **5** [sing] a stroke of sth a sudden successful action or event: *It was a stroke of luck finding your ring on the beach, wasn't it?*

IDIOMS **at a/one stroke** with a single action

not do a stroke (of work) to not do any work at all

stroke² /strəʊk/ verb [T] **1** to move your hand gently over sb/sth: *She stroked his hair affectionately.* ● *to stroke a dog* **2** to move sth somewhere with a smooth movement

stroll /strəʊl/ noun [C] a slow walk for pleasure: *to go for a stroll along the beach* –**stroll** verb [I]

★**strong** /strɒŋ/ adj **1** (used about a person) physically powerful; able to lift or carry heavy things: *I need someone strong to help me move this bookcase.* ● *to have strong arms/muscles* **2** (used about an object) not easily broken or damaged: *That chair isn't strong enough for you to stand on.* **3** (used about a natural force) powerful: *strong winds/currents/sunlight* **4** having a big effect on the mind, body or senses: *a strong smell of garlic* ● *strong coffee* ● *a strong drink* (= with a lot of alcohol in it) ● *I have the strong impression that they don't like us.* **5** (used about opinions and beliefs) very firm; difficult to fight against: *There was strong opposition to the idea.* ● *strong support* for the government's plan **6** powerful and likely to succeed: *She's a strong candidate for the job.* ● *a strong team* **7** (used after a noun) having a particular number of people ••➤ noun **strength** for all senses –**strongly** adv: *The directors are strongly opposed to the idea.* ● *to feel very strongly about sth*

IDIOMS **going strong** (*informal*) continuing,

even after a long time: *The company was formed in 1851 and is still going strong.*

sb's strong point something that a person is good at: *Maths is not my strong point.*

ˌstrong-'minded **adj** having firm ideas or beliefs

stroppy /'strɒpi/ **adj** (*Brit slang*) (used about a person) easily annoyed and difficult to deal with

strove *past tense* of **STRIVE**

struck *past tense, past participle* of **STRIKE²**

★structure¹ /'strʌktʃə/ **noun 1** [C,U] the way that the parts of sth are put together or organized: *the political and social structure of a country* ● *the grammatical structures of a language* **2** [C] a building or sth that has been built or made from a number of parts: *The old office block had been replaced by a modern glass structure.* –structural /'strʌktʃərəl/ **adj**

structure² /'strʌktʃə/ **verb** [T] to arrange sth in an organized way: *a carefully-structured English course*

★struggle¹ /'strʌgl/ **verb** [I] **1** struggle (with sth/for sth/to do sth) to try very hard to do sth, especially when it is difficult: *We struggled up the stairs with our heavy suitcases.* ● *Maria was struggling with her English homework.* ● *The country is struggling for independence.* **2** struggle (with sb/sth); struggle (against sth) to fight in order to prevent sth or to escape from sb: *He shouted and struggled but he couldn't get free.* ● *A passer-by was struggling with one of the robbers on the ground.* ● *He has been struggling against cancer for years.*

PHRASAL VERB struggle on to continue to do sth although it is difficult: *I felt terrible but managed to struggle on to the end of the day.*

struggle² /'strʌgl/ **noun** [C] **1** a fight in which sb tries to do or get sth when this is difficult: *All countries should join together in the struggle against terrorism.* ● *He will not give up the presidency without a struggle.* ● *a struggle for independence* **2** [usually sing] sth that is difficult to achieve: *It will be a struggle to get there on time.*

strum /strʌm/ **verb** [I,T] (**strumming**; **strummed**) to play a guitar by moving your hand up and down over the strings

strung *past tense, past participle* of **STRING²**

strut /strʌt/ **verb** [I] (**strutting**; **strutted**) to walk in a proud way

stub /stʌb/ **noun** [C] the short piece of a cigarette or pencil that is left after the rest of it has been used

stubble /'stʌbl/ **noun** [U] **1** the short parts of corn, wheat, etc that are left standing after the rest has been cut **2** the short hairs that grow on a man's face when he has not shaved for some time •➤ picture at **hair**

stubborn /'stʌbən/ **adj** not wanting to do what other people want you to do; refusing to change your plans or decisions: *She's too stubborn to apologize.* •➤ synonym **obstinate** •➤ Look at **pig-headed.** –stubbornly **adv**: *He stubbornly refused to apologize so he was sacked.* –stubbornness **noun** [U]

stuck¹ *past tense, past participle* of **STICK²**

stuck² /stʌk/ **adj 1** not able to move: *This drawer's stuck. I can't open it at all.* ● *We were stuck in traffic for over two hours.* **2** not able to continue with an exercise, etc because it is too difficult: *If you get stuck, ask your teacher for help.*

stud /stʌd/ **noun 1** [C] a small piece of metal that sticks out from the rest of the surface that it is fixed to: *a black leather jacket with studs all over it* **2** [C] a small, round, solid piece of metal that you wear through a hole in your ear or other part of the body **3** [C] one of the pieces of plastic or metal that stick out from the bottom of football, etc boots and that help you stand up on wet ground **4** [C,U] a number of high quality horses or other animals that are kept for breeding young animals; the place where these horses, etc are kept: *a stud farm*

studded /'stʌdɪd/ **adj 1** covered or decorated with small pieces of metal that stick out from the rest of the surface **2** studded (with sth) containing a lot of sth

★student /'stjuːdnt/ **noun** [C] a person who is studying at a college or university: *Paola is a medical student at Bristol University.* ● *a full-time/part-time student* ● *a postgraduate/ research student*

➤ Compare **pupil.** Look also at **scholar**, **graduate** and **undergraduate.**

studied /'stʌdid/ **adj** (*formal*) carefully planned or done, especially when you are trying to give a particular impression

★studio /'stjuːdiəʊ/ **noun** [C] (*pl* **studios**) **1** a room where an artist or photographer works **2** a room or building where films or television programmes are made, or where music, radio programmes, etc are recorded: *a film/ TV/recording studio*

studious /'stjuːdiəs/ **adj** (used about a person) spending a lot of time studying

studiously /'stjuːdiəsli/ **adv** with great care

★study¹ /'stʌdi/ **noun** (*pl* **studies**) **1** [U] the activity of learning about sth: *One hour every afternoon is left free for individual study.* ● *Physiology is the study of how living things work.* **2** **studies** [pl] the subjects that you study: *business/media/Japanese studies* **3** [C] a piece of research that examines a question or a subject in detail: *They are doing a study of the causes of heart disease.* **4** [C] a room in a house where you go to read, write or study

★study² /'stʌdi/ **verb** (*pres part* **studying**; *3rd pers sing pres* **studies**; *pt, pp* **studied**) **1** [I,T] study (sth/for sth) to spend time learning about sth: *to study French at university* ● *Leon has been studying hard for his exams.* **2** [T] to look at sth very carefully: *to study a map*

★stuff¹ /stʌf/ **noun** [U] (*informal*) **1** used to refer to sth without using its name: *What's that green stuff at the bottom of the bottle?* ● *The shop was burgled and a lot of stuff was stolen.* ● *They sell stationery and stuff (like that).* ● *I'll put the swimming stuff in this*

S

bag. **2** used to refer in general to things that people do, say, think, etc: *I've got lots of stuff to do tomorrow so I'm going to get up early.* ● *I don't believe all that stuff about him being robbed.* ● *I like reading and stuff.*

stuff² /stʌf/ *verb* **1** [T] stuff sth (with sth) to fill sth with sth: *The pillow was stuffed with feathers.* ● *red peppers stuffed with rice* **2** [T] (*informal*) stuff sth into sth to put sth into sth else quickly or carelessly: *He quickly stuffed a few clothes into a suitcase.* **3** [I,T] (*informal*) stuff yourself (with sth) to eat too much of sth: *Barry just sat there stuffing himself with sandwiches.* ● *I can't eat any more – I'm stuffed.* **4** [T] to fill the body of a dead bird or animal with special material so that it looks as if it is alive: *They've got a stuffed crocodile in the museum.*

stuffing /'stʌfɪŋ/ *noun* [U] **1** a mixture of small pieces of food that you put inside a chicken, vegetable, etc before you cook it **2** the material that you put inside cushions, soft toys, etc

stuffy /'stʌfi/ *adj* **1** (used about a room) too warm and having no fresh air **2** (*informal*) (used about a person) formal and old-fashioned

stumble /'stʌmbl/ *verb* [I] **1** stumble (over/on sth) to hit your foot against sth when you are walking or running and almost fall over **2** stumble (over/through sth) to make a mistake when you are speaking, playing music, etc: *The newsreader stumbled over the name of the Russian tennis player.*
PHRASAL VERB stumble across/on sb/sth to meet or find sb/sth by chance

'stumbling block *noun* [C] something that causes trouble or a difficulty, so that you cannot achieve what you want: *Money is still the stumbling block to settling the dispute.*

stump¹ /stʌmp/ *noun* [C] the part that is left after sth has been cut down, broken off, etc: *a tree stump*

stump² /stʌmp/ *verb* [T] (*informal*) to cause sb to be unable to answer a question or find a solution for a problem: *I was completely stumped by question 14.*

stun /stʌn/ *verb* [T] (**stunning; stunned**) **1** to make a person or animal unconscious or confused by hitting him/her/it on the head **2** to make a person very surprised by telling him/her some unexpected news: *His sudden death stunned his friends and colleagues.* –stunned *adj*

stung *past tense, past participle* of **STING¹**

stunk *past participle* of **STINK**

stunning /'stʌnɪŋ/ *adj* (*informal*) very attractive, impressive or surprising: *a stunning view*

stunt¹ /stʌnt/ *noun* [C] **1** something that you do to get people's attention: *a publicity stunt* **2** a very difficult or dangerous thing that sb does to entertain people or as part of a film: *Some actors do their own stunts, others use a stunt man.*

stunt² /stʌnt/ *verb* [T] to stop sb/sth growing

or developing properly: *A poor diet can stunt a child's growth.*

stuntman /'stʌntmæn/ *noun* [C] (*pl* -men /mæn/) a person who does sth dangerous in a film in the place of an actor

stupendous /stjuː'pendəs/ *adj* very large or impressive: *a stupendous achievement*

★**stupid** /'stjuːpɪd/ *adj* **1** not intelligent or sensible: *Don't be so stupid, of course I'll help you!* ● *He was stupid to trust her.* ● *a stupid mistake/suggestion/question* **2** (only *before* a noun) (*informal*) used to show that you are angry or do not like sb/sth: *I'm tired of hearing about his stupid car.* –stupidity /stjuː-'pɪdəti/ *noun* [U] –stupidly *adv*

stupor /'stjuːpə/ *noun* [sing,U] the state of being nearly unconscious or being unable to think properly

sturdy /'stɜːdi/ *adj* (**sturdier; sturdiest**) strong and healthy; that will not break easily: *sturdy legs* ● *sturdy shoes* –sturdily *adv* –sturdiness *noun* [U]

stutter /'stʌtə/ *verb* [I,T] to have difficulty when you speak, so that you keep repeating the first sound of a word –stutter *noun* [C]: *to have a stutter*

sty (also **stye**) /staɪ/ *noun* [C] (*pl* **sties** or **styes**) **1** a painful spot on the skin that covers the eye (the eyelid) **2** = **PIGSTY**

★**style** /staɪl/ *noun* **1** [C,U] the way that sth is done, built, etc: *a new style of architecture* ● *The writer's style is very clear and simple.* ● *an American-style education system* **2** [C,U] the fashion, shape or design of sth: *We stock all the latest styles.* ● *I like your new hairstyle.* **3** [U] the ability to do things in a way that other people admire: *He's got no sense of style.*

stylish /'staɪlɪʃ/ *adj* fashionable and attractive: *She's a stylish dresser.*

suave /swɑːv/ *adj* (usually used about a man) confident, elegant and polite, sometimes in a way that does not seem sincere

subconscious /ˌsʌb'kɒnʃəs/ (also **unconscious**) *noun* [sing] the subconscious the hidden part of your mind that can affect the way that you behave without you realizing –subconscious *adj*: *the subconscious mind* ● *Many advertisements work at a subconscious level.* –subconsciously *adv*

subdivide /ˌsʌbdɪ'vaɪd/ *verb* [I,T] to divide or be divided into smaller parts –subdivision /'sʌbdɪvɪʒn/ *noun* [C,U]

subdue /səb'djuː/ *verb* [T] to defeat sb/sth or bring sb/sth under control

subdued /səb'djuːd/ *adj* **1** (used about a person) quieter and with less energy than usual **2** not very loud or bright: *subdued laughter/ lighting*

★**subject¹** /'sʌbdʒɪkt/ *noun* [C] **1** a person or thing that is being considered, shown or talked about: *What subject is the lecture on?* ● *What are your views on this subject?* ● *I've tried several times to bring up/raise the subject of money.* **2** an area of knowledge that you study at school, university, etc: *My favourite subjects at school are Biology and*

S

French. **3** (*grammar*) the person or thing that does the action described by the verb in a sentence: *In the sentence 'The cat sat on the mat', 'the cat' is the subject.* •➤ Look at **object**. **4** a person from a particular country, especially one with a king or queen; a citizen: *a British subject*
IDIOM **change the subject** → **CHANGE¹**

subject² /səb'dʒekt/ **verb**
PHRASAL VERB **subject sb/sth to sth** to make sb/sth experience sth unpleasant: *He was subjected to verbal and physical abuse from the other boys.*

subject³ /'sʌbdʒɪkt/ **adj subject to sth 1** likely to be affected by sth: *The area is subject to regular flooding.* • *Smokers are more subject to heart attacks than non-smokers.* **2** depending on sth as a condition: *The plan for new housing is still subject to approval by the minister.* **3** controlled by or having to obey sb/sth

subjective /səb'dʒektɪv/ **adj** based on your own tastes and opinions instead of on facts: *Try not to be so subjective in your essays.* •➤ opposite **objective** –**subjectively adv**

'**subject matter noun** [U] the ideas or information contained in a book, speech, painting, etc

subjunctive /səb'dʒʌŋktɪv/ **noun** [sing] the form of a verb in certain languages that expresses doubt, possibility, a wish, etc –**subjunctive adj**

sublime /sə'blaɪm/ **adj** (*formal*) of extremely high quality that makes you admire sth very much –**sublimely adv**

submarine /ˌsʌbmə'riːn/ **noun** [C] a type of ship that can travel under the water as well as on the surface

submerge /səb'mɜːdʒ/ **verb** [I,T] to go or make sth go under water: *The fields were submerged by the floods.* –**submerged adj**

submission /səb'mɪʃn/ **noun 1** [U] the accepting of sb else's power or control because he/she has defeated you **2** [U,C] the action of giving a plan, document, etc to an official organization so that it can be studied and considered; the plan, document, etc that you send

submissive /səb'mɪsɪv/ **adj** ready to obey other people and do whatever they want

submit /səb'mɪt/ **verb** (**submitting**; **submitted**) **1** [T] **submit sth (to sb/sth)** to give a plan, document, etc to an official organization so that it can be studied and considered: *to submit an application/ complaint/claim* **2** [I] **submit (to sb/sth)** to accept sb/sth's power or control because he/she has defeated you

subordinate¹ /sə'bɔːdɪnət/ **adj subordinate (to sb/sth)** having less power or authority than sb else; less important than sth else –**subordinate noun** [C]: *the relationship between superiors and their subordinates*

subordinate² /sə'bɔːdɪneɪt/ **verb** [T] to treat one person or thing as less important than another

su,bordinate 'clause noun [C] (*grammar*)
a group of words that is not a sentence but that adds information to the main part of the sentence: *In the sentence 'We left early because it was raining', 'because it was raining' is the subordinate clause.*

subscribe /səb'skraɪb/ **verb** [I] **1 subscribe (to sth)** to pay for a newspaper or magazine to be sent to you regularly **2** (*formal*) **subscribe to sth** to agree with an idea, belief, etc: *I don't subscribe to the view that all war is wrong.*

subscriber /səb'skraɪbə/ **noun** [C] a person who pays to receive a newspaper or magazine regularly or to use a particular service: *subscribers to satellite and cable television*

subscription /səb'skrɪpʃn/ **noun** [C] an amount of money that you pay, usually once a year, to receive a newspaper or magazine regularly or to belong to an organization

subsequent /'sʌbsɪkwənt/ **adj** (*formal*) (only *before* a noun) coming after or later: *I thought that was the end of the matter but subsequent events proved me wrong.* –**subsequently adv**: *The rumours were subsequently found to be untrue.*

subservient /səb'sɜːviənt/ **adj 1 subservient (to sb/sth)** too ready to obey other people **2** (*formal*) **subservient (to sth)** considered to be less important than sb/sth else –**subservience noun** [U]

subside /səb'saɪd/ **verb** [I] **1** to become calmer or quieter: *The storm seems to be subsiding.* **2** (used about land, a building, etc) to sink down into the ground –**subsidence** /'sʌbsɪdns; səb'saɪdns/ **noun** [U]

subsidiary¹ /səb'sɪdiəri/ **adj** connected with sth but less important than it

subsidiary² /səb'sɪdiəri/ **noun** [C] (*pl* **subsidiaries**) a business company that belongs to and is controlled by another larger company

subsidize (also **-ise**) /'sʌbsɪdaɪz/ **verb** [T] (used about a government, etc) to give money in order to keep the cost of a service low: *Public transport should be subsidized.*

subsidy /'sʌbsədi/ **noun** [C,U] (*pl* **subsidies**) money that the government, etc pays to help an organization or to keep the cost of a service low: *agricultural/state/housing subsidies*

subsist /səb'sɪst/ **verb** [I] (*formal*) **subsist (on sth)** to manage to live with very little food or money –**subsistence noun** [U]

★**substance** /'sʌbstəns/ **noun 1** [C] a solid or liquid material: *poisonous substances* • *The cloth is coated in a new waterproof substance.* **2** [U] importance, value or truth: *The commissioner's report gives substance to these allegations.* **3** [U] the most important or main part of sth: *What was the substance of his argument?*

substandard /ˌsʌb'stændəd/ **adj** of poor quality; not as good as usual or as it should be

substantial /səb'stænʃl/ **adj 1** large in amount: *The storms caused substantial damage.* • *a substantial sum of money* **2** large or strong* •➤ opposite **insubstantial**

S

substantially /səbˈstænʃəli/ adv **1** very much; greatly: *House prices have fallen substantially.* **2** generally; in most points

substitute /ˈsʌbstɪtjuːt/ noun [C] a substitute (for sb/sth) a person or thing that takes the place of sb/sth else: *One player was injured so the substitute was sent on to play.* –**substitute** verb [T] substitute sth/sb (for sb/sth): *You can substitute margarine for butter.* –**substitution** /ˌsʌbstɪˈtjuːʃn/ noun [C,U]

subtitle /ˈsʌbtaɪtl/ noun [C, usually pl] the words at the bottom of the picture on television or at the cinema. The subtitles translate the words of a foreign film or programme or show the words that are spoken, to help people with hearing problems.

subtle /ˈsʌtl/ adj **1** not very noticeable; not very strong or bright: *subtle colours* ● *I noticed a subtle difference in her.* **2** very clever; and using indirect methods to achieve sth: *Advertisements persuade us to buy things in very subtle ways.* –**subtlety** /ˈsʌtlti/ noun [C,U] (*pl* subtleties) –**subtly** /ˈsʌtli/ adv

★**subtract** /səbˈtrækt/ verb [T] subtract sth (from sth) to take one number or quantity away from another: *If you subtract five from nine you get four.* •➤ opposite **add** –**subtraction** /səbˈtrækʃn/ noun [C,U]

★**suburb** /ˈsʌbɜːb/ noun [C] an area where people live that is outside the central part of a town or city: *Most people live **in the suburbs** and work in the centre of town.* –**suburban** /səˈbɜːbən/ adj •➤ People often think of life in the suburbs as dull, so **suburban** sometimes means 'dull and uninteresting'. –**suburbia** /səˈbɜːbiə/ noun [U]

subversive /səbˈvɜːsɪv/ adj trying to destroy or damage a government, religion or political system by attacking it secretly and in an indirect way: *subversive literature/activities* –**subversive** noun [C] –**subversion** /səbˈvɜːʃn/ noun [U]

subvert /səbˈvɜːt/ verb [T] to try to destroy or damage a government, religion or political system by attacking it secretly and in an indirect way

subway /ˈsʌbweɪ/ noun [C] **1** a tunnel under a busy road or railway that is for people who are walking (**pedestrians**) **2** (*US*) = **UNDERGROUND**[3]

★**succeed** /səkˈsiːd/ verb **1** [I] succeed (in sth/doing sth) to manage to achieve what you want; to do well: *Our plan succeeded.* ● *A good education will help you succeed in life.* ● *to succeed in passing an exam* •➤ opposite **fail** [I,T] to have a job or important position after sb else: *Tony Blair succeeded John Major as Prime Minister in 1997.*

★**success** /səkˈses/ noun **1** [U] the fact that you have achieved what you want; doing well and becoming famous, rich, etc: *Hard work is **the key to success**.* ● *Her attempts to get a job for the summer have not **met with** much success* (= she hasn't managed to do it). ● *What's the secret of your success?* **2** [C] the thing that you achieve; sth that becomes very popular: *He really tried to **make a success of** the business. ● The film 'Titanic' was a huge success* •➤ opposite **failure**

★**successful** /səkˈsesfl/ adj having achieved what you wanted; having become popular, rich, etc: *a successful attempt to climb Mount Everest* ● *a successful actor* –**successfully** /-fəli/ adv

succession /səkˈseʃn/ noun **1** [C] a number of people or things that follow each other in time or order; a series: *a succession of events/problems/visitors* **2** [U] the right to have an important position after sb else

IDIOM **in succession** following one after another: *There have been three deaths in the family in quick succession.*

successor /səkˈsesə/ noun [C] a person or thing that comes after sb/sth else and takes his/her/its place •➤ Look at **predecessor**.

succinct /səkˈsɪŋkt/ adj said clearly, in a few words –**succinctly** adv

succulent /ˈsʌkjələnt/ adj (used about fruit, vegetables and meat) containing a lot of juice and tasting very good

succumb /səˈkʌm/ verb [I] (*formal*) succumb (to sth) to stop fighting against sth

★**such** /sʌtʃ/ determiner, pron **1** (used for referring to sb/sth that you mentioned earlier) of this or that type: *I don't believe in ghosts. There's **no such thing**. ● The economic situation is such that we all have less money to spend.* **2** used for emphasizing the degree of sth: *It was such a fascinating book that I couldn't put it down. ● It seems such a long time since we last met.*

➤ You use **such** before a noun or before a noun that has an adjective in front of it: *Simon is such a bore!* ● *Susan is such a boring woman.* You use **so** before an adjective that is used without a noun: *Don't be so boring.* Compare: *It was so cold we stayed at home.* ● *It was such a cold night that we stayed at home.*

3 used to describe the result of sth: *The statement was worded **in such a way that** it did not upset anyone.*

IDIOMS **as such** as the word is usually understood; exactly: *It's not a promotion as such, but it will mean more money.*

such as for example: *Fatty foods such as chips are bad for you.*

★**suck** /sʌk/ verb **1** [I,T] to pull a liquid into your mouth: *to suck milk up through a straw* •➤ picture at **blow** **2** [I,T] to have sth in your mouth and keep touching it with your tongue: *He was noisily sucking (on) a sweet.* **3** [T] to pull sth in a particular direction, using force: *Vacuum cleaners suck up the dirt.*

sucker /ˈsʌkə/ noun [C] **1** (*informal*) a person who believes everything that you tell him/her and who is easy to trick or persuade to do sth **2** a part of some plants, animals or insects that is used for helping them stick onto a surface

suction /ˈsʌkʃn/ noun [U] the action of removing air or liquid from a space or container so that sth else can be pulled into it or so that two surfaces can stick together: *A vacuum cleaner works by suction.*

★**sudden** /'sʌdn/ **adj** done or happening quickly, or when you do not expect it: *a sudden decision/change* –**suddenly adv**: *Suddenly, everybody started shouting.* –**suddenness noun** [U]

IDIOMS **all of a sudden** quickly and unexpectedly: *All of a sudden the lights went out.*

sudden death a way of deciding who wins a game where the score is equal by playing one more point or game

suds /sʌdz/ **noun** [pl] the bubbles that you get when you mix soap and water

sue /su:/ **verb** [I,T] **sue (sb) (for sth)** to go to a court of law and ask for money from sb because he/she has done sth bad to you, or said sth bad about you: *to sue sb for libel/ breach of contract/damages*

suede /sweɪd/ **noun** [U] a type of soft leather which does not have a smooth surface and feels a little like cloth

suet /'su:ɪt/ **noun** [U] a type of hard animal fat that is used in cooking

★**suffer** /'sʌfə/ **verb 1** [I,T] **suffer (from sth); suffer (for sth)** to experience sth unpleasant, for example pain, sadness, difficulty, etc: *Mary often suffers from severe headaches.* • *Our troops suffered heavy losses.* • *He made a rash decision and now he's suffering for it.* **2** [I] to become worse in quality: *My work is suffering as a result of problems at home.* –**sufferer noun** [C]: *asthma sufferers* –**suffering noun** [U]

sufficient /sə'fɪʃnt/ **adj** (*formal*) as much as is necessary; enough: *We have sufficient oil reserves to last for three months.* •➤ opposite **insufficient** –**sufficiently adv**

suffix /'sʌfɪks/ **noun** [C] (*grammar*) a letter or group of letters that you add at the end of a word, and that changes the meaning of the word or the way it is used: *To form the noun from the adjective 'sad', add the suffix 'ness'.* •➤ Look at **prefix.**

suffocate /'sʌfəkeɪt/ **verb** [I,T] to die because there is no air to breathe; to kill sb in this way –**suffocating adj** –**suffocation** /ˌsʌfə'keɪʃn/ **noun** [U]

★**sugar** /'ʃʊɡə/ **noun 1** [U] a sweet substance that you get from certain plants: *Do you take sugar in tea?* •➤ picture on page C4 **2** [C] (in a cup of tea, coffee, etc) the amount of sugar that a small spoon can hold; a lump of sugar

sugary /'ʃʊɡəri/ **adj** very sweet

★**suggest** /sə'dʒest/ **verb** [T] **1 suggest sth (to sb); suggest doing sth; suggest that...** to mention a plan or an idea that you have for sb to discuss or consider: *Can anybody suggest ways of raising more money?* • *Tony suggested going out for a walk.* • *Tony suggested (that) we go out for a walk.* • *Tony suggested a walk.* **2 suggest sb/sth (for/as sth)** to say that a person, thing or place is suitable: *Who would you suggest for the job?*

➤ You cannot 'suggest somebody something'.

•➤ Look at **recommend. 3** to say or show sth in an indirect way: *Are you suggesting the accident was my fault?*

★**suggestion** /sə'dʒestʃən/ **noun 1** [C] a plan or idea that sb mentions for sb else to discuss and consider: *May I make a suggestion?* • *Has anyone got any suggestions for how to solve this problem?* **2** [U] putting an idea into a person's mind; giving advice about what to do **3** [sing] a slight amount or sign of sth

suggestive /sə'dʒestɪv/ **adj 1 suggestive (of sth)** making you think of sth; being a sign of sth: *Your symptoms are more suggestive of an allergy than a virus.* **2** making you think about sex: *a suggestive dance/remark/posture* –**suggestively adv**

suicidal /ˌsu:ɪ'saɪdl/ **adj 1** (used about a person) wanting to kill himself/herself: *to feel suicidal* **2** likely to have a very bad result; extremely dangerous

★**suicide** /'su:ɪsaɪd/ **noun** [U,C] the act of killing yourself deliberately: *Ben has tried to commit suicide several times.* • *There have been three suicides by university students this year.*

★**suit¹** /su:t/ **noun** [C] **1** a formal set of clothes that are made of the same material, consisting of a jacket and either trousers or a skirt: *He always wears a suit and tie to work.* •➤ picture on page C6 **2** an article of clothing or set of clothes that you wear for a particular activity: *a tracksuit/swimsuit* **3** one of the four sets of thirteen playing cards (**hearts, clubs, diamonds** and **spades**) that form a pack •➤ Look at the note and picture at **card.**

IDIOM **follow suit → FOLLOW**

★**suit²** /su:t/ **verb** [T] (not used in the continuous tenses) **1** to be convenient or useful for sb/sth: *Would Thursday at 9.30 suit you?* • *He will help around the house, but only when it suits him.* **2** (used about clothes, colours, etc) to make you look attractive: *That dress really suits you.*

★**suitable** /'su:təbl/ **adj suitable (for sb/sth); suitable (to do sth)** right or appropriate for sb/sth: *The film isn't suitable for children.* • *I've got nothing suitable to wear for a wedding.* •➤ opposite **unsuitable** –**suitability** /ˌsu:tə'bɪləti/ **noun** [U] –**suitably adv**

★**suitcase** /'su:tkeɪs/ (also **case**) **noun** [C] a box with a handle that you use for carrying your clothes, etc in when you are travelling •➤ picture at **bag**

suite /swi:t/ **noun** [C] **1** a set of rooms, especially in a hotel: *the honeymoon/penthouse suite* • *a suite of rooms/offices* •➤ Look at **en suite. 2** a set of two or more pieces of furniture of the same style or covered in the same material: *a three-piece suite* (= a sofa and two armchairs)

suited /'su:tɪd/ **adj suited (for/to sb/sth)** appropriate or right for sb/sth

sulfur (*US*) = **SULPHUR**

sulk /sʌlk/ **verb** [I] to refuse to speak or smile because you want people to know that you are angry about sth –**sulky adj** –**sulkily /-ɪli/ adv**

sullen /'sʌlən/ **adj** looking bad-tempered and not wanting to speak to people: *a sullen face/ expression/glare* –**sullenly adv**

sulphur (*US* **sulfur**) /'sʌlfə/ **noun** [U] (*symbol* **S**) a natural yellow substance with a strong unpleasant smell

sultan (also **Sultan**) /'sʌltən/ **noun** [C] the ruler in some Muslim countries

sultana /sʌl'tɑːnə/ **noun** [C] a dried grape with no seeds in it that is used in cooking ••➤ Look at **raisin**.

sultry /'sʌltri/ **adj 1** (used about the weather) hot and uncomfortable **2** (used about a woman) behaving in a way that makes her sexually attractive

★**sum**¹ /sʌm/ **noun** [C] **1** an amount of money: *The industry has spent huge **sums of money** modernizing its equipment.* **2** [usually sing] **the sum (of sth)** the amount that you get when you add two or more numbers together: *The sum of two and five is seven.* **3** a simple problem that involves calculating numbers: *to **do sums** in your head*

sum² /sʌm/ **verb** (**summing**; **summed**)

PHRASAL VERBS **sum (sth) up** to describe in a few words the main ideas of what sb has said or written: *To sum up*, there are three options here...

sum sb/sth up to form an opinion about sb/sth: *He summed the situation up immediately.*

summary¹ /'sʌməri/ **noun** [C] (*pl* **summaries**) a short description of the main ideas or points of sth but without any details: *A brief summary of the experiment is given at the beginning of the report.* ••➤ synonym **précis** –**summarize** (also **-ise**) /'sʌməraɪz/ **verb** [T]: *Could you summarize the story so far?*

summary² /'sʌməri/ **adj** (*formal*) done quickly and without taking time to think about whether it is the right thing to do or following the right process: *a summary judgment*

★**summer** /'sʌmə/ **noun** [C,U] one of the four seasons of the year, after spring and before autumn. Summer is the warmest season of the year: *Is it very hot here in summer?* ● *a summer's day* –**summery adj**: *summery weather* ● *a summery dress*

summertime /'sʌmətaɪm/ **noun** [U] the season of summer: *It's busy here in the summertime.*

summing-'up noun [C] (*pl* **summings-up**) a speech in which a judge gives a short description (**summary**) of what has been said in a court of law before a decision (**verdict**) is reached

summit /'sʌmɪt/ **noun** [C] **1** the top of a mountain **2** an important meeting or series of meetings between the leaders of two or more countries

summon /'sʌmən/ **verb** [T] **1** (*formal*) to order a person to come to a place: *The boys were summoned to the head teacher's office.* **2** **summon sth (up)** to find strength, courage or some other quality that you need even

though it is difficult to do so: *She couldn't summon up the courage to leave him.*

summons /'sʌmənz/ **noun** [C] (*pl* **summonses**) an order to appear in a court of law

Sun³ **abbr** Sunday: *Sun 5 April*

★**sun**¹ /sʌn/ **noun 1 the sun** [sing] the star that shines in the sky during the day and that gives the earth heat and light: *The sun rises in the east and sets in the west.* ● *the rays of the sun* **2** [sing,U] light and heat from the sun: *Don't sit **in the sun** too long.* ● *Too much sun can be harmful.*

IDIOM **catch the sun** → **CATCH**¹

sun² /sʌn/ **verb** [T] (**sunning**; **sunned**) **sun yourself** sit or lie outside when the sun is shining in order to enjoy the heat

sunbathe /'sʌnbeɪð/ **verb** [I] to take off most of your clothes and sit or lie in the sun in order to make your skin go darker (**get a tan**) ••➤ picture on page C8 ••➤ Look at **bathe**.

sunbeam /'sʌnbiːm/ **noun** [C] a line (**ray**) of sunlight

sunburn /'sʌnbɜːn/ **noun** [U] red painful skin caused by spending too long in the sun –**sunburned** (also **sunburnt**) **adj**

★**Sunday** /'sʌndeɪ; -di/ **noun** [C,U] (*abbr* **Sun**) the day of the week after Saturday

➤ Days of the week are always written with a capital letter. For examples of how to use the days of the week in sentences, look at **Monday**.

sundial /'sʌndaɪəl/ **noun** [C] a type of clock used in past times that uses the shadow of a pointed piece of metal to show what the time is

sundry /'sʌndri/ **adj** (only *before* a noun) of various kinds that are not important enough to be named separately

IDIOM **all and sundry** (*informal*) everyone

sunflower /'sʌnflaʊə/ **noun** [C] a very tall plant with large yellow flowers, often grown for its seeds and their oil, which is used in cooking

sung *past participle* of **SING**

sunglasses /'sʌnɡlɑːsɪz/ (also ˌdark 'glasses, *informal* shades) **noun** [pl] a pair of glasses with dark glass in them to protect your eyes from bright sunlight

sunk *past participle* of **SINK**¹

sunken /'sʌŋkən/ **adj 1** below the water: *a sunken ship* **2** (used about cheeks or eyes) very far into the face as a result of illness or age **3** at a lower level than the surrounding area: *a sunken bath/garden*

sunlight /'sʌnlaɪt/ **noun** [U] the light from the sun

sunlit /'sʌnlɪt/ **adj** having bright light from the sun: *a sunlit terrace*

sunny /'sʌni/ **adj** (**sunnier**; **sunniest**) having a lot of light from the sun: *a sunny garden* ● *a sunny day*

sunrise /'sʌnraɪz/ **noun** [U] the time when the sun comes up in the morning: *to get up **at** sunrise* ••➤ Look at **dawn** and **sunset**.

S

sunset /'sʌnset/ *noun* [C,U] the time when the sun goes down in the evening: *The park closes **at sunset**.* • *a beautiful sunset*

sunshine /'sʌnʃaɪn/ *noun* [U] heat and light from the sun: *We sat down **in the sunshine** and had lunch.*

sunstroke /'sʌnstrəʊk/ *noun* [U] an illness that is caused by spending too much time in very hot, strong sunlight: *Keep your head covered or you'll **get sunstroke**.*

suntan /'sʌntæn/ (also **tan**) *noun* [C] when you have a suntan, your skin is darker than usual because you have spent time in the sun: *to have/get a suntan* • *suntan oil* –**suntanned** (also **tanned**) *adj*

★**super** /'su:pə/ *adj (informal)* **1** (often used to form compounds) bigger, better, stronger than other things of the same type: *a new super computer* • *superglue* **2** (*old-fashioned*) very good; wonderful: *We had a super time.*

superb /su:'pɜ:b/ *adj* extremely good, excellent –**superbly** *adv*

supercilious /ˌsu:pə'sɪliəs/ *adj* showing that you think that you are better than other people: *a supercilious smile* –**superciliously** *adv*

superficial /ˌsu:pə'fɪʃl/ *adj* **1** not studying or thinking about sth in a deep or complete way: *a superficial knowledge of the subject* **2** only on the surface, not deep: *a superficial wound/cut/burn* **3** (used about people) not caring about serious or important things: *He's a very superficial sort of person.* –**superficiality** /ˌsu:pə,fɪʃi'æləti/ *noun* [U] –**superficially** /-ʃəli/ *adv*

superfluous /su:'pɜ:fluəs/ *adj* more than is wanted; not needed

superhuman /ˌsu:pə'hju:mən/ *adj* greater than is usual for human beings: *superhuman strength*

superimpose /ˌsu:pərɪm'pəʊz/ *verb* [T] **superimpose sth (on sth)** to put sth on top of sth else so that what is underneath can still be seen: *The old street plan was superimposed on a map of the modern city.*

superintendent /ˌsu:pərɪn'tendənt/ *noun* [C] **1** a police officer with a high position: *Detective Superintendent Waters* **2** a person who looks after a large building

★**superior¹** /su:'pɪəriə/ *adj* **1** **superior (to sb/sth)** better than usual or than sb/sth else: *He is clearly superior to all the other candidates.* •➤ opposite **inferior 2 superior (to sb)** having a more important position: *a superior officer* **3** thinking that you are better than other people –**superiority** /su:,pɪəri'ɒrəti/ *noun* [U]

superior² /su:'pɪəriə/ *noun* [C] a person of higher position: *Report any accidents to your superior.* •➤ opposite **inferior**

superlative /su:'pɜ:lətɪv/ *noun* [C] the form of an adjective or adverb that expresses its highest degree: *'Most beautiful', 'best' and 'fastest' are all superlatives.*

★**supermarket** /'su:pəma:kɪt/ *noun* [C] a very large shop that sells food, drink, goods used in the home, etc

supernatural /ˌsu:pə'nætʃrəl/ *adj* **1** that cannot be explained by the laws of science: *a creature with supernatural powers* **2 the supernatural** *noun* [sing] events, forces or powers that cannot be explained by the laws of science: *I don't believe in the supernatural.*

supersede /ˌsu:pə'si:d/ *verb* [T] to take the place of sb/sth which existed or was used before and which has become old-fashioned: *Steam trains were gradually superseded by electric trains.*

supersonic /ˌsu:pə'sɒnɪk/ *adj* faster than the speed of sound

superstar /'su:pəsta:/ *noun* [C] a singer, film star, etc who is very famous and popular

superstition /ˌsu:pə'stɪʃn/ *noun* [C,U] a belief that cannot be explained by reason or science: *According to superstition, it's unlucky to walk under a ladder.* –**superstitious** /ˌsu:pə'stɪʃəs/ *adj*: *I never do anything important on Friday the 13th – I'm superstitious.*

superstore /'su:pəstɔ:/ *noun* [C] a very large shop that sells food or a wide variety of one particular type of goods

supervise /'su:pəvaɪz/ *verb* [I,T] to watch sb/sth to make sure that work is being done properly or that people are behaving correctly: *Your job is to supervise the building work.* –**supervision** /ˌsu:pə'vɪʒn/ *noun* [U]: *Children should not play here without supervision.* –**supervisor** *noun* [C]

supper /'sʌpə/ *noun* [C,U] (*old-fashioned*) the last meal of the day, either the main meal of the evening or a small meal that you eat quite late, not long before you go to bed

supple /'sʌpl/ *adj* that bends or moves easily; not stiff: *Children are generally far more supple than adults.* –**suppleness** *noun* [U]

supplement /'sʌplɪmənt/ *noun* [C] something that is added to sth else: *You have to pay a small supplement if you travel on a Saturday.* –**supplement** *verb* [T] **supplement sth (with sth)**: *to supplement your diet with vitamins* –**supplementary** /ˌsʌplɪ'mentri/ *adj*: *supplementary exercises at the back of the book*

supplier /sə'plaɪə/ *noun* [C] a person or company that supplies goods

★**supply¹** /sə'plaɪ/ *verb* [T] (*pres part* **supplying**; *3rd pers sing pres* **supplies**; *pt, pp* **supplied**) **supply sth (to sb)**; **supply sb (with sth)** to give or provide sth: *The farmer supplies eggs to the surrounding villages.* • *He supplies the surrounding villages with eggs.*

supply² /sə'plaɪ/ *noun* (*pl* **supplies**) [C] a store or amount of sth that is provided or available to be used: *The water supply was contaminated.* • *Food supplies were dropped by helicopter.* • *In many parts of the country water is **in short supply** (= there is not much of it).*

★**support¹** /sə'pɔ:t/ *verb* [T] **1** to help sb by saying that you agree with him/her/it, and sometimes giving practical help such as

S

money: *Several large companies are support-ing the project.* ● *Which political party do you support?* **2** to give sb the money he/she needs for food, clothes, etc: *Jim has to support two children from his previous marriage.* **3** to carry the weight of sb/sth: *Large columns support the roof.* **4** to show that sth is true or correct: *What evidence do you have to support what you say?* **5** to have a particular sports team as your favourite: *Which football team do you support?*

★**support²** /sə'pɔːt/ **noun 1** [U] **support (for sb/sth)** help and encouragement that you give to a person or thing: *public support for the campaign* ● *Steve spoke **in support of** the proposal.* **2** [C,U] something that carries the weight of sb/sth or holds sth firmly in place: *a roof support* ● *She held on to his arm for support.* **3** [U] money to buy food, clothes, etc: *She has no job, no home and no means of support.*

IDIOM **moral support** → MORAL¹

supporter /sə'pɔːtə/ **noun** [C] a person who supports a political party, sports team, etc: *football supporters*

supportive /sə'pɔːtɪv/ **adj** giving help or support to sb in a difficult situation: *Everyone was very supportive when I lost my job.*

★**suppose** /sə'pəʊz/ **verb** [T] **1** to think that sth is probable: *What do you suppose could have happened?* ● *I don't suppose that they're coming now.* **2** to pretend that sth will hap-pen or is true: *Suppose you won the lottery. What would you do?* **3** used to make a sugges-tion, request or statement less strong: *I don't suppose you'd lend me your car tonight, would you?* **4** used when you agree with sth, but are not very happy about it: *'Can we give Andy a lift?' 'Yes, I suppose so, if we must.'*

IDIOM **be supposed to do sth 1** to be expected to do sth or to have to do sth: *The train was supposed to arrive ten minutes ago.* ● *This is secret and I'm not supposed to talk about it.* **2** (*informal*) to be considered or thought to be sth: *This is supposed to be the oldest building in the city.*

supposedly /sə'pəʊzɪdli/ **adv** according to what many people believe

supposing /sə'pəʊzɪŋ/ **conj** if sth happens or is true; what if: *Supposing the plan goes wrong, what will we do then?*

supposition /ˌsʌpə'zɪʃn/ **noun** [C,U] an idea that a person thinks is true but which has not been shown to be true

suppress /sə'pres/ **verb** [T] **1** to stop sth by using force **2** to stop sth from being seen or known: *to suppress the truth* **3** to stop your-self from expressing your feelings, etc: *to suppress laughter/a yawn* –**suppression** /sə'preʃn/ **noun** [U]

supremacy /suː'preməsi/ **noun** [U] **suprem-acy (over sb/sth)** the state of being the most powerful

supreme /suː'priːm/ **adj** the highest or greatest possible

supremely /suː'priːmli/ **adv** extremely

surcharge /'sɜːtʃɑːdʒ/ **noun** [C] an extra amount of money that you have to pay for sth

★**sure** /ʃɔː/ **adj, adv 1** (not before a noun) hav-ing no doubt about sth; certain: *You must be sure of your facts before you make an accus-ation.* ● *I'm not sure what to do next.* ● *Craig was sure that he'd made the right decision.* ● *I think I had my bag when I got off the bus but I'm not sure.*

➤ **Sure** and **certain** are very similar in meaning. However they are used in a slightly different way. Compare: *It is cer-tain that there will be an election next year.* ● *There is sure to be an election next year.*

2 (not before a noun) **sure of sth; sure to do sth** that you will definitely get or do, or that will definitely happen: *If you go and see them you can be sure of a warm welcome.* ● *If you work hard you are sure to pass the exam.* ●➤ opposite **unsure 3** that you can be certain of: *A noise like that is a sure sign of engine trouble.* **4** (*informal*) used to say 'yes' to sb *'Can I have a look at your newspaper?' 'Sure.'*

IDIOMS **Be sure to do sth** Don't forget to do sth: *Be sure to write and tell me what happens.*

for sure without doubt: *Nobody knows for sure what happened.*

make sure 1 to find out whether sth is in a particular state or has been done: *I must go back and make sure I closed the window.* **2** to take the action that is necessary: *Make sure you are back home by 11 o'clock.*

sure enough as was expected: *I expected him to be early, and sure enough he arrived five minutes before the others.*

sure of yourself confident about your opinions, or about what you can do

sure (thing) (*US informal*) yes: *'Can I borrow this book?' 'Sure thing.'*

★**surely** /'ʃɔːli/ **adv 1** without doubt: *This will surely cause problems.* **2** used for expressing surprise at sb else's opinions, plans, actions etc: *Surely you're not going to walk home in this rain?* ● *'Meena's looking for another job.' 'Surely not.'* **3** (*US informal*) yes; of course

surf¹ /sɜːf/ **noun** [U] the white part on the top of waves in the sea

surf² /sɜːf/ **verb** [I] to stand or lie on a special board (a **surfboard**) and ride on a wave towards the shore

IDIOM **surf the net** to use the Internet

★**surface¹** /'sɜːfɪs/ **noun 1** [C] the outside part of sth: *the earth's surface* ● *Teeth have a hard surface called enamel.* ● *This tennis court has a very uneven surface.* **2 the surface** [sing] the top part of an area of water: *leaves float-ing on the surface of a pond* **3** [C] the flat top part of a piece of furniture, used for working on: *a work surface* ● *kitchen surfaces* **4** [sing] the qualities of sb/sth that you see or notice that are not hidden: *Everybody seems very friendly but there are a lot of tensions below/beneath the surface.*

surface² /'sɜːfɪs/ **verb 1** [I] to come up to the surface of water **2** [I] to appear again: *All the old arguments surfaced again in the discus-sion.* **3** [T] to cover the surface of sth

'surface mail noun [U] letters, packages, etc that go by road, rail or sea, not by air ••➤ Look at **airmail**.

surfeit /'sɜːfɪt/ noun [sing] (*written*) a surfeit (of sth) too much of sth

surfer /'sɜːfə/ noun [C] a person who rides on waves standing on a special board

surge /sɜːdʒ/ noun [C,usually sing] a surge (of/in sth) **1** a sudden strong movement in a particular direction by a large number of people or things: *a surge forward* • *a surge* (= an increase) *in the demand for electricity* **2** a sudden strong feeling –surge verb [I]: *The crowd surged forward.*

surgeon /'sɜːdʒən/ noun [C] a doctor who performs medical operations (surgery): *a brain surgeon*

surgery /'sɜːdʒəri/ noun (*pl surgeries*) **1** [U] medical treatment in which your body is cut open so that part of it can be removed or repaired: *to undergo surgery* ••➤ Look at **plastic surgery** and **operation**. **2** [C,U] the place or time when a doctor or dentist sees patients: *Surgery hours are from 9.00 to 11.30.*

surgical /'sɜːdʒɪkl/ adj connected with medical operations: *surgical instruments* –surgically /-kli/ adv

surly /'sɜːli/ adj unfriendly and rude: *a surly expression*

surmount /sə'maʊnt/ verb [T] to deal successfully with a problem or difficulty ••➤ Look at **insurmountable**.

surname /'sɜːneɪm/ (also **last name**) noun [C] the name that you share with other people in your family: *'What's your surname?' 'Jones.'* ••➤ Look at the note at **name**.

surpass /sə'pɑːs/ verb [T] (*formal*) to do sth better than sb/sth else or better than expected: *The success of the film surpassed all expectations.*

surplus /'sɜːpləs/ noun [C,U] an amount that is extra or more than you need: *the food surplus in Western Europe* –surplus adj: *They sell their surplus grain to other countries.*

surprise¹ /sə'praɪz/ noun **1** [U] the feeling that you have when sth happens that you do not expect: *They looked up in surprise when she walked in.* • *To my surprise they all agreed with me.* **2** [C] something that you did not expect or know about: *What a pleasant surprise to see you again!* • *The news came as a complete surprise.* • *a surprise visit/attack/party*

IDIOM **take sb by surprise** to happen or do sth when sb is not expecting it

surprise² /sə'praɪz/ verb [T] **1** to make sb feel surprised: *It wouldn't surprise me if you get the job.* **2** to attack or find sb suddenly and unexpectedly

surprised /sə'praɪzd/ adj feeling or showing surprise: *I was very surprised to see Cara there. I thought she was still abroad.*

surprising /sə'praɪzɪŋ/ adj that causes surprise: *It's surprising how many adults can't read or write.* –surprisingly adv: *Surprisingly few people got the correct answer.*

surreal /sə'riːəl/ (also **surrealistic** /sə,riːə'lɪstɪk/) adj very strange; with images mixed together in a strange way like in a dream: *a surreal film/painting/situation*

surrender /sə'rendə/ verb **1** [I,T] surrender (to sb) to stop fighting and admit that you have lost ••➤ synonym **yield** **2** [T] (*formal*) surrender sb/sth (to sb) to give sb/sth to sb else: *The police ordered them to surrender their weapons.* –surrender noun [C,U]

surreptitious /,sʌrəp'tɪʃəs/ adj done secretly: *I had a surreptitious look at what she was writing.* –surreptitiously adv

surrogate /'sʌrəgət/ noun [C], adj (a person or thing) that takes the place of sb/sth else: *a surrogate mother* (= a woman who has a baby and gives it to another woman who cannot have children)

★**surround** /sə'raʊnd/ verb [T] surround sb/ sth (by/with sth) to be or go all around sb/ sth: *The garden is surrounded by a high wall.* • *Troops have surrounded the parliament building.*

surrounding /sə'raʊndɪŋ/ adj (only *before* a noun) that is near or around sth

surroundings /sə'raʊndɪŋz/ noun [pl] everything that is near or around you; the place where you live: *to live in pleasant surroundings* • *animals living in their natural surroundings* (= not in zoos) ••➤ Look at **environment**.

surveillance /sɜː'veɪləns/ noun [U] the careful watching of sb who may have done sth wrong: *The building is protected by surveillance cameras.*

survey¹ /'sɜːveɪ/ noun [C] **1** a study of the opinions, behaviour, etc of a group of people: *Surveys have shown that more and more people are getting into debt.* • *to carry out/ conduct/do a survey* **2** the action of examining an area of land and making a map of it **3** the action of examining a building in order to find out if it is in good condition

survey² /sə'veɪ/ verb [T] **1** to look carefully at the whole of sth: *We stood at the top of the hill and surveyed the countryside.* **2** to carefully measure and make a map of an area of land **3** to examine a building carefully in order to find out if it is in good condition

★**survive** /sə'vaɪv/ verb **1** [I,T] to continue to live or exist in or after a difficult or dangerous situation: *More than a hundred people were killed in the crash and only five passengers survived.* • *How can she survive on such a small salary?* • *to survive a plane crash* • *Not many buildings survived the bombing.* **2** [T] to live longer than sb/sth –survival /sə'vaɪvl/ noun [U]: *A heart transplant was his only chance of survival.* –survivor noun [C]: *There were five survivors of the crash.*

susceptible /sə'septəbl/ adj (not before a noun) susceptible to sth easily influenced, damaged or affected by sb/sth: *People in a new country are highly susceptible to illness.*

★**suspect¹** /sə'spekt/ verb [T] **1** to believe that sth may happen or be true, especially sth

S

bad: *The situation is worse than we first suspected.* ● *Nobody suspected that she was thinking of leaving.* ·➤ Look at **unsuspecting. 2** to not be sure that you can trust sb or believe sth: *I rather suspect his motives for offering to help.* **3 suspect sb (of sth/of doing sth)** to believe that sb is guilty of sth: *I suspect Laura of taking the money.* ● *She strongly suspected that he was lying.* ·➤ noun suspicion

suspect[2] /'sʌspekt/ **noun** [C] a person who is thought to be guilty of a crime: *The suspects are being questioned by police.*

suspect[3] /'sʌspekt/ **adj** possibly not true or not to be trusted: *to have suspect motives* ● *a suspect parcel* (= that may contain a bomb)

suspend /sə'spend/ **verb** [T] **1 suspend sth (from sth) (by/on sth)** to hang sth from sth else: *The huge skeleton is suspended from the museum's ceiling on chains.* **2** to stop or delay sth for a time: *Some rail services were suspended during the strike.* ● *The young man was given a **suspended sentence** (= he will not go to prison unless he commits another crime).* **3 suspend sb (from sth)** to send sb away from his/her school, job, position, etc for a period of time, usually as a punishment: *He was suspended from school for a week for stealing.* ·➤ noun suspension

suspender /sə'spendə/ **noun 1** [C,usually pl] (*Brit*) a short piece of elastic that women use to hold up the thin pieces of clothing that fit closely over a woman's legs and feet (**stockings**) **2 suspenders** [pl] (*US*) = **BRACE**[1](2)

suspense /sə'spens/ **noun** [U] the feeling of excitement or worry that you have when you feel sth is going to happen, when you are waiting for news, etc: *Don't keep us **in suspense**. Tell us what happened.*

suspension /sə'spenʃn/ **noun 1** [C,U] not being allowed to do your job or go to school for a period of time, usually as a punishment: *suspension on full pay* **2** [U] delaying sth for a period of time ·➤ verb suspend **3 the suspension** [U] the parts that are connected to the wheels of a car, etc that make it more comfortable to ride in

★**suspicion** /sə'spɪʃn/ **noun 1** [C,U] a feeling or belief that sth is wrong or that sb has done sth wrong: *I always treat smiling politicians with suspicion.* ● *She was arrested **on suspicion of** murder.* ● *He is **under suspicion** of being involved in drug smuggling.* **2** [C] a feeling that sth may happen or be true: *I have a suspicion that he's forgotten he invited us.* ·➤ verb suspect

★**suspicious** /sə'spɪʃəs/ **adj 1 suspicious (of/about sb/sth)** feeling that sb has done sth wrong, dishonest or illegal: *We became suspicious of his behaviour and alerted the police.* **2** that makes you feel that sth is wrong, dishonest or illegal: *The old man died **in suspicious circumstances**.* ● *It's very suspicious that she was not at home on the evening of the murder.* ● *a suspicious-looking person* –**suspiciously adv**: *to behave suspiciously*

sustain /sə'steɪn/ **verb** [T] **1** to keep sb/sth

alive or healthy: *Oxygen sustains life.* **2** to make sth continue for a long period of time without becoming less: *It's hard to sustain interest for such a long time.* **3** (*formal*) to experience sth bad: *to sustain damage/an injury/a defeat*

SW abbr south-west(ern): *SW Australia*

swagger /'swægə/ **verb** [I] to walk in a way that shows that you are too confident or proud –**swagger noun** [sing]

★**swallow** /'swɒləʊ/ **verb 1** [T] to make food, drink, etc go down your throat to your stomach: *It's easier to swallow pills if you take them with water.* ·➤ picture at **lick 2** [I] to make a movement in your throat, often because you are afraid or surprised, etc: *She swallowed hard and tried to speak, but nothing came out.* **3** [T] to accept or believe sth too easily: *You shouldn't swallow everything they tell you!* **4** [T] to accept an insult, etc without complaining: *I find her criticisms very hard to swallow.* **5** [T] **swallow sth (up)** to use all of sth, especially money: *The rent swallows up most of our monthly income.* –**swallow noun** [C **IDIOM** hard to swallow → **HARD**[1]

swam *past tense of* **SWIM**

swamp[1] /swɒmp/ **noun** [C,U] an area of soft, wet land

swamp[2] /swɒmp/ **verb** [T] **1** to cover or fill sth with water: *The fishing boat was swamped by enormous waves.* **2 swamp sb/sth (with sth)** (usually passive) to give sb so much of sth that he/she cannot deal with it: *We've been swamped with applications for the job.* ·➤ synonym **inundate**

swan /swɒn/ **noun** [C] a large, usually white bird with a very long neck that lives on lakes and rivers ·➤ picture at **duck**

★**swap** (also **swop**) /swɒp/ **verb** [I,T] (**swapping**; **swapped**) **swap (sth) (with sb)**; **swap A for B** to give sth for sth else; to exchange: *When we finish these books shall we swap* (= you have my book and I'll have yours) ● *Would you swap seats with me?* ● *I'd swap my job for hers any day.* –**swap noun** [sing]: *Let's **do a swap**.* **IDIOM** change/swap places (with sb) → **PLACE**[1]

swarm[1] /swɔːm/ **noun** [C] **1** a large group of insects, especially bees, moving around together: *a swarm of bees/locusts/flies* **2** a large number of people moving together

swarm[2] /swɔːm/ **verb** [I] to fly or move in large numbers **PHRASAL VERB** swarm with sb/sth to be too crowded or full

swat /swɒt/ **verb** [T] (**swatting**; **swatted**) to hit sth, especially an insect, with sth flat

sway /sweɪ/ **verb 1** [I] to move slowly from side to side: *The trees were swaying in the wind.* **2** [T] to influence sb: *Many people were swayed by his convincing arguments.*

★**swear** /sweə/ **verb** (*pt* **swore** /swɔː/; *pp* **sworn** /swɔːn/) **1** [I] **swear (at sb/sth)** to use rude or bad language: *He hit his thumb with the hammer and swore loudly.* ● *There's no point in swearing at the car just because it* *won't start!* •➤ Look at **curse**. **2** [I,T] **swear (to do sth); swear that...** to make a serious promise: *When you give evidence in court you have to swear to tell the truth.* • *Will you swear not to tell anyone?*

PHRASAL VERBS **swear by sth** to believe completely in the value of sth

swear sb in (usually passive) to make sb say officially that he/she will accept the responsibility of a new position: *The President will be sworn in next week.*

'swear word (also *old-fashioned* **oath**) **noun** [C] a word that is considered rude or bad and that may offend people

sweat /swet/ **verb** [I] **1** to produce liquid through your skin because you are hot, ill or afraid **2 sweat (over sth)** to work hard: *I've been sweating over that problem all day.* –**sweat noun** [C,U]: *He stopped digging and wiped the sweat from his forehead.* • *He woke up in a sweat.* •➤ Look at **perspiration**.

IDIOM **work/sweat your guts out** → **GUT¹**

sweater /'swetə/ **noun** [C] a warm piece of clothing with long sleeves, often made of wool, which you wear on the top half of your body

> **Sweater, jumper, pullover** and **jersey** are all words for the same piece of clothing. They are often made from wool or a similar material. A **sweatshirt** is usually made from cotton and may be worn informally or for sport. A **cardigan** fastens down the front.

•➤ picture on page C6

sweatshirt /'swetʃɜːt/ **noun** [C] a warm piece of cotton clothing with long sleeves, which you wear on the top half of your body •➤ picture on page C6

sweaty /'sweti/ **adj 1** wet with sweat: *I was hot and sweaty after the match and needed a shower.* **2** causing you to sweat: *a hot sweaty day*

swede /swiːd/ **noun** [C,U] a large, round, yellow vegetable that grows under the ground •➤ picture on page C3

★**sweep¹** /swiːp/ **verb** (*pt, pp* **swept** /swept/) **1** [I,T] to clean the floor, etc by moving dust, dirt, etc away with a brush: *to sweep the floor* • *I'm going to sweep the leaves off the path.* •➤ Look at the note at **clean²**. **2** [T] to remove sth from a surface using your hand, etc: *He swept the books angrily off the table.* **3** [I,T] to move quickly and smoothly over the area or in the direction mentioned: *Fire swept through the building.* **4** [T] to move or push sb/sth with a lot of force: *The huge waves swept her overboard.* • *He was swept along by the huge crowd.* **5** [I] to move in a way that impresses or is intended to impress people: *Five big black Mercedes swept past us.* **6** [I,T] to move over an area, especially in order to look for sth: *The army were sweeping the fields for mines.* • *His eyes swept quickly over the page.*

PHRASAL VERBS **sweep (sb/sth) aside** to not allow sb/sth to affect your progress or plans

sweep sth out to remove dirt and dust from

the floor of a room or building using a brush

sweep over sb (used about a feeling) to suddenly affect sb very strongly

sweep (sth) up to remove dirt, dust, leaves, etc using a brush

sweep² /swiːp/ **noun** [C] **1** [usually sing] the action of moving dirt and dust from a floor or surface using a brush: *I'd better give the floor a sweep.* **2** a long, curving shape or movement: *He showed us which way to go with a sweep of his arm.* **3** a movement over an area, especially in order to look for sth **4** =**CHIMNEY SWEEP**

IDIOM **a clean sweep** → **CLEAN¹**

sweeper /'swiːpə/ **noun** [C] **1** a person or thing that cleans surfaces with a brush: *He's a road sweeper.* • *Do you sell carpet sweepers?* **2** (in football) the defending player who plays behind the other defending players

sweeping /'swiːpɪŋ/ **adj 1** (used about statements, etc) too general and not accurate enough: *He made a sweeping statement about all politicians being dishonest.* **2** having a great and important effect: *sweeping reforms*

★**sweet¹** /swiːt/ **adj 1** containing, or tasting as if it contains, a lot of sugar: *Children usually like sweet things.* • *This cake's too sweet.* •➤ Look at **savoury**. **2** (used especially about children and small things) attractive; cute: *a sweet little kitten* • *Isn't that little girl sweet?* **3** having or showing a kind character: *a sweet smile* • *It's very sweet of you to remember my birthday!* **4** (used about a smell or a sound) pleasant –**sweetness noun** [U]

IDIOM **have a sweet tooth** to like eating sweet things

★**sweet²** /swiːt/ **noun 1** [C, usually pl] (*US* **candy** [U]) a small piece of boiled sugar, chocolate, etc, often sold in a packet: *He was sucking a sweet.* • *a sweet shop* **2** [C,U] sweet food served at the end of a meal •➤ Look at **pudding** and **dessert**.

'sweet corn noun [U] yellow grains from a tall plant (**maize**) that taste sweet and are eaten as a vegetable •➤ picture on page C3

sweeten /'swiːtn/ **verb** [T] to make sth sweet by adding sugar, etc

sweetener /'swiːtnə/ **noun** [C,U] a substance used instead of sugar for making food or drink sweet: *artificial sweeteners*

sweetheart /'swiːthɑːt/ **noun** [C] **1** used when speaking to sb, especially a child, in a very friendly way: *Do you want a drink, sweetheart?* **2** (*old-fashioned*) a boyfriend or girlfriend

sweetly /'swiːtli/ **adv** in an attractive, kind or pleasant way: *She smiled sweetly.* • *sweetly-scented flowers*

★**swell¹** /swel/ **verb** (*pt* **swelled** /sweld/; *pp* **swollen** /'swəʊlən/ or **swelled**) **1** [I,T] **swell (up)** to become or to make sth bigger, fuller or thicker: *After the fall her ankle began to swell up.* • *Heavy rain had swollen the rivers.* **2** [I,T] to increase or make sth increase in number or size: *The crowd swelled to 600 by the end of the evening.* **3** [I] (*written*) (used about feelings or sound) to

S

suddenly become stronger or louder: *Hatred swelled inside him.*

swell² /swel/ **noun** [sing] the slow movement up and down of the surface of the sea

★**swelling** /'swelɪŋ/ **noun 1** [C] a place on your body that is bigger or fatter than usual because of an injury or illness: *I've got a nasty swelling under my eye.* **2** [U] the process of becoming swollen: *The disease often causes swelling of the ankles and knees.*

sweltering /'sweltərɪŋ/ **adj** (*informal*) much too hot: *It was sweltering in the office today.*

swept past tense, past participle of **SWEEP¹**

swerve /swɜːv/ **verb** [I] to change direction suddenly: *The car swerved to avoid the child.* –**swerve noun** [C]

swift /swɪft/ **adj** happening without delay; quick: *a swift reaction/decision/movement* ● *a swift runner* –**swiftly adv**

swig /swɪg/ **verb** [I,T] (**swigging**; **swigged**) (*informal*) to take a quick drink of sth, especially alcohol –**swig noun** [C]

swill /swɪl/ **verb** [T] swill sth (out/down) to wash sth by pouring large amounts of water, etc into, over or through it

★**swim** /swɪm/ **verb** (*pres part* **swimming**; *pt* **swam** /swæm/; *pp* **swum** /swʌm/) **1** [I,T] to move your body through water: *How far can you swim?* ● *Hundreds of tiny fish swam past.*

> ➤ **Go swimming** is a common way of talking about swimming for pleasure: *We go swimming every Saturday.* We can also say **go for a swim** when we are talking about one particular occasion: *I went for a swim this morning.*

••➤ picture on page S2 **2** [I] be swimming (in/with sth) to be covered with a lot of liquid: *The salad was swimming in oil.* **3** [I] to seem to be moving or turning: *The floor began to swim before my eyes and I fainted.* **4** [I] (used about your head) to feel confused: *My head was swimming with so much new information.* –**swim noun** [sing]: *to go for/ have a swim* –**swimmer noun** [C]: *a strong/ weak swimmer*

'**swimming bath noun** [C] (also **swimming baths** [pl]) a public swimming pool, usually indoors

★'**swimming pool** (also **pool**) **noun** [C] a pool that is built especially for people to swim in: *an indoor/outdoor/open-air swimming pool*

'**swimming trunks noun** [pl] a piece of clothing like shorts that a man wears to go swimming: *a pair of swimming trunks* ••➤ picture on page C6

swimsuit /'swɪmsuːt/ (also '**swimming costume**) **noun** [C] a piece of clothing that a woman wears to go swimming ••➤ Look at **bikini.** ••➤ picture on page C6

swindle /'swɪndl/ **verb** [T] swindle sb/sth (out of sth) to trick sb in order to get money, etc –**swindle noun** [C]: *a tax swindle*

swine /swaɪn/ **noun 1** [C] (*informal*) a very unpleasant person **2** [pl] (*old-fashioned*) pigs

★**swing¹** /swɪŋ/ **verb** (*pt, pp* **swung** /swʌŋ/ **1** [I,T] to move backwards and forwards or from side to side while hanging from sth; to make sb/sth move in this way: *The rope was swinging from a branch.* ● *She sat on the wall, swinging her legs.* **2** [I,T] to move or make sb/sth move in a curve: *The door swung open and Rudi walked in.* ● *He swung the child up onto his shoulders.* **3** [I] to move or change from one position or situation towards the opposite one: *She swung round when she heard the door open.* ● *His moods swing from one extreme to the other.* **4** [I,T] swing (at sb/sth) to try to hit sb/sth

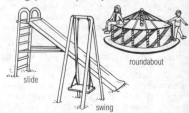

slide

roundabout

swing

★**swing²** /swɪŋ/ **noun 1** [sing] a swinging movement or rhythm: *He took a swing at the ball.* **2** [C] a seat, a piece of rope, etc that is hung from above so that you can swing backwards and forwards on it: *Some children were playing on the swings.* **3** [C] a change from one position or situation towards the opposite one

IDIOM in full swing → **FULL¹**

swipe /swaɪp/ **verb 1** [I,T] (*informal*) swipe (at) sb/sth to hit or try to hit sb/sth by moving your arm in a curve: *He swiped at the wasp with a newspaper but missed.* **2** [T] (*informal*) to steal sth **3** [T] to pass the part of a plastic card on which information is stored through a special machine for reading it: *The receptionist swiped my credit card and handed me the slip to sign.* –**swipe noun** [C]: *She took a swipe at him with her handbag.*

'**swipe card noun** [C] a small plastic card on which information is stored which can be read by an electronic machine

swirl /swɜːl/ **verb** [I,T] to move or cause sth to make fast circular movements: *Her long skirt swirled round her legs as she danced.* ● *He swirled some water round in his mouth and spat it out.* –**swirl noun** [C]

★**switch¹** /swɪtʃ/ **noun** [C] **1** a small button or sth similar that you press up or down in order to turn on electricity: *a light switch* **2** a sudden change: *a switch in policy*

★**switch²** /swɪtʃ/ **verb** [I,T] **1** switch (sth) (over) (to sth); switch (between A and B) to change or be changed from one thing to another: *I'm fed up with my glasses – I'm thinking of switching over to contact lenses* ● *Press these two keys to switch between documents on screen.* ● *The match has been switched from Saturday to Sunday.* **2** switch (sth) (with sb/sth); switch (sth) (over/round) to exchange positions, activities, etc: *This* *week you can have the car and I'll go on the bus, and next week we'll switch over.* ● *Someone switched the signs round and everyone went the wrong way.*

PHRASAL VERBS **switch (sth) off/on** to press a switch in order to start/stop electric power: *Don't forget to switch off the cooker.*

switch (sth) over to change to a different television programme

switchboard /'swɪtʃbɔːd/ noun [C] the place in a large company, etc where all the telephone calls are connected

swivel /'swɪvl/ verb [I,T] (**swivelling; swivelled**; *US* **swiveling; swiveled**) swivel (sth) (round) to turn around a central point; to make sth do this: *She swivelled round to face me.* ● *He swivelled his chair towards the door.*

swollen¹ *past participle of* SWELL¹

swollen² /'swəʊlən/ adj thicker or wider than usual: *Her leg was badly swollen after the accident.*

swoop /swuːp/ verb [I] **1** to fly or move down suddenly: *The bird swooped down on its prey.* **2** (used especially about the police or the army) to visit or capture sb/sth without warning: *Police swooped at dawn and arrested the man.* –**swoop** noun [C] **a swoop (on sb/sth)**

swop = SWAP

sword /sɔːd/ noun [C] a long, very sharp metal weapon, like a large knife ●➤ picture at **spear**

swore *past tense of* SWEAR

sworn *past participle of* SWEAR

swot¹ /swɒt/ verb [I,T] (**swotting; swotted**) swot (up) (for/on sth); swot sth up to study sth very hard, especially to prepare for an exam: *She's swotting for her final exams.*

swot² /swɒt/ noun [C] (*informal*) a person who studies too hard

swum *past participle of* SWIM

swung *past tense, past participle of* SWING¹

syllable /'sɪləbl/ noun [C] a word or part of a word which contains one vowel sound: *'Mat' has one syllable and 'mattress' has two syllables.* ● *The stress in 'international' is on the third syllable.*

syllabus /'sɪləbəs/ noun [C] (*pl* **syllabuses**) a list of subjects, etc that are included in a course of study ●➤ Look at **curriculum.**

★**symbol** /'sɪmbl/ noun [C] **1** a symbol (of sth) a sign, object, etc which represents sth: *The cross is the symbol of Christianity.* **2** a symbol (for sth) a letter, number or sign that has a particular meaning: *O is the symbol for oxygen.*

symbolic /sɪm'bɒlɪk/ (also **symbolical** /-kl/) adj used or seen to represent sth: *The white dove is symbolic of peace.* –**symbolically** adv /-kli/

symbolism /'sɪmbəlɪzəm/ noun [U] the use of symbols to represent things, especially in art and literature

symbolize (also **-ise**) /'sɪmbəlaɪz/ verb [T] to represent sth: *The deepest notes in music*

are often used to symbolize danger or despair.

symmetric /sɪ'metrɪk/ (also **symmetrical** /-rɪkl/) adj having two halves that match each other exactly in size, shape, etc –**symmetrically** /-kli/ adv

symmetry /'sɪmətri/ noun [U] the state of having two halves that match each other exactly in size, shape, etc

★**sympathetic** /ˌsɪmpə'θetɪk/ adj **1** sympathetic (to/towards sb) showing that you understand other people's feelings, especially their problems: *When Suki was ill, everyone was very sympathetic.* ● *I felt very sympathetic towards him.*

> In English, **sympathetic** does not mean 'friendly and pleasant'. If you want to express this meaning, you say a person is **nice**: *I met Alex's sister yesterday. She's very nice.*

2 sympathetic (to sb/sth) being in agreement with or supporting sth/sb: *I explained our ideas but she wasn't sympathetic to them.* –**sympathetically** /-kli/ adv

sympathize (also **-ise**) /'sɪmpəθaɪz/ verb [I] sympathize (with sb/sth) **1** to feel sorry for sb; to show that you understand sb's problems: *I sympathize with her, but I don't know what I can do to help.* **2** to support sb/sth: *I find it difficult to sympathize with his opinions.*

sympathizer /'sɪmpəθaɪzə/ noun [C] a person who agrees with and supports an idea or aim

★**sympathy** /'sɪmpəθi/ noun (*pl* **sympathies**) **1** [U] sympathy (for/towards sb) an understanding of other people's feelings, especially their problems: *Everyone* ***feels*** *great* ***sympathy*** *for the victims of the attack.* ● *I don't expect any sympathy from you.* ● *I* ***have*** *no* ***sympathy*** *for Mark – it's his own fault.* **2** sympathies [pl] feelings of support or agreement

IDIOM **in sympathy (with sb/sth)** in agreement, showing that you support or approve of sb/sth: *Taxi drivers stopped work in sympathy with the striking bus drivers.*

symphony /'sɪmfəni/ noun [C] (*pl* **symphonies**) a long piece of music written for a large orchestra

symptom /'sɪmptəm/ noun [C] **1** a change in your body that is a sign of illness: *The symptoms of flu include a headache, a high temperature and aches in the body.* **2** a sign (that sth bad is happening or exists) –**symptomatic** /ˌsɪmptə'mætɪk/ adj

synagogue /'sɪnəgɒg/ noun [C] a building where Jewish people go to pray or to study their religion

synchronize (also **-ise**) /'sɪŋkrənaɪz/ verb [T] to make sth happen or work at the same time or speed: *We synchronized our watches to make sure we agreed what the time was.*

syndicate /'sɪndɪkət/ noun [C] a group of people or companies that work together in order to achieve a particular aim

S

[I] **intransitive**, a verb which has no object: *He laughed.*   [T] **transitive**, a verb which has an object: *He ate an apple.*

syndrome /'sɪndrəʊm/ **noun** [C] **1** a group of signs or changes in the body that are typical of an illness: *Down's syndrome* • *Acquired Immune Deficiency Syndrome (Aids)* **2** a set of opinions or a way of behaving that is typical of a particular type of person, attitude or social problem

synonym /'sɪnənɪm/ **noun** [C] a word or phrase that has the same meaning as another word or phrase in the same language: *'Big' and 'large' are synonyms*. –synonymous /sɪ'nɒnɪməs/ **adj** (*figurative*) synonymous (with sth)

syntax /'sɪntæks/ **noun** [U] the system of rules for the structure of a sentence in a language

synthesizer (also **-iser**) /'sɪnθəsaɪzə/ **noun** [C] an electronic musical instrument that can produce a wide variety of different sounds

synthetic /sɪn'θetɪk/ **adj** made by a chemical process; not natural: *synthetic materials/fibres* –synthetically /-kli/ **adv**

syphon = SIPHON

syringe /sɪ'rɪndʒ/ **noun** [C] a plastic or glass tube with a needle that is used for taking a small amount of blood out of the body or for putting drugs into the body

syrup /'sɪrəp/ **noun** [U] a thick sweet liquid, often made by boiling sugar with water or fruit juice: *peaches in syrup* •➤ Look at **treacle**.

★**system** /'sɪstəm/ **noun 1** [C] a set of ideas or rules for organizing sth; a particular way of doing sth: *We have a new computerized system in the library.* • *The government is planning to reform the education system.* **2** [C] a group of things or parts that work together: *a central heating system* • *a transport system* **3** [C] the body of a person or animal; parts of the body that work together: *the central nervous system* **4 the system** [sing] (*informal*) the traditional methods and rules of a society: *You can't beat the system* (= you must accept these rules).
> IDIOM **get sth out of your system** (*informal*) to do sth to free yourself of a strong feeling or emotion

systematic /ˌsɪstə'mætɪk/ **adj** done using a fixed plan or method: *a systematic search* –systematically /-kli/ **adv**

Tt

T, t¹ /tiː/ **noun** [C] (*pl* **T's**; **t's**) the twentieth letter of the English alphabet: *'Table' begins with (a) 'T'.*

t² (*US* **tn**) **abbr** ton(s), tonne(s): *5t coal*

ta /taː/ **interj** (*Brit informal*) thank you

tab /tæb/ **noun** [C] **1** a small piece of cloth, metal or paper that is fixed to the edge of sth to help you open, hold or identify it: *You ope. the tin by pulling the metal tab.* **2** the mone that you owe for food, drink, etc in a bar, caf or restaurant; the bill
> IDIOM **keep tabs on sb/sth** (*informal*) t watch sb/sth carefully; to check sth

★**table** /'teɪbl/ **noun** [C] **1** a piece of furnitur with a flat top supported by legs: *a dining bedside/coffee/kitchen table* • *Could you lay set the table for lunch?* (= put the knives forks, plates, etc on it) • *Let me help yo clear the table* (= remove the dirty plates etc at the end of a meal).
> ➤ We put things **on the table** but we sit at **the table** (= around the table).

••➤ picture on page C7 **2** a list of facts or figures, usually arranged in rows and col umns down a page: *Table 3 shows the results*

tablecloth /'teɪblklɒθ/ **noun** [C] a piece or cloth that you use for covering a table, espe cially when having a meal

'**table manners** **noun** [pl] behaviour that is considered correct while you are having a meal at a table with other people

tablespoon /'teɪblspuːn/ **noun** [C] **1** a large spoon used for serving or measuring food **2** (also '**tablespoonful**) the amount that a tablespoon holds: *Add two tablespoons of sugar.*

★**tablet** /'tæblət/ **noun** [C] a small amount of medicine in solid form that you swallow: *Take two tablets every four hours.* ••➤ picture at **bandage**

'**table tennis** (also *informal* **ping-pong**) **noun** [U] a game with rules like tennis in which you hit a light plastic ball across a table with a small round bat

tabloid /'tæblɔɪd/ **noun** [C] a newspaper with small pages, a lot of pictures and short articles, especially about famous people

taboo /tə'buː/ **noun** [C] (*pl* **taboos**) something that you must not say or do because it might shock, offend or embarrass people –taboo **adj**: *a taboo subject/word*

tacit /'tæsɪt/ **adj** (*formal*) understood but not actually said –tacitly **adv**

tack¹ /tæk/ **noun 1** [sing] a way of dealing with a particular situation: *If people won't listen we'll have to try a different tack.* **2** [C] a small nail with a sharp point and a flat head

tack² /tæk/ **verb** [T] **1** to fasten sth in place with tacks¹(2) **2** to fasten cloth together temporarily with long stitches that can be removed easily
> PHRASAL VERB **tack sth on (to sth)** to add sth extra on the end of sth

★**tackle¹** /'tækl/ **verb 1** [T] to make an effort to deal with a difficult situation or problem: *The government must tackle the problem of rising unemployment.* • *Firemen were brought in to tackle the blaze.* **2** [I,T] (used in football, etc) to try to take the ball from sb in the other team **3** [T] to stop sb running away by pulling him/her down **4** [T] **tackle sb about sth** to speak to sb about a difficult subject: *I'm* *going to tackle him about the money he owes me.*

tackle² /'tækl/ noun **1** [C] the action of trying to get the ball from another player in football, etc **2** [U] the equipment you use in some sports, especially fishing: *fishing tackle*

tacky /'tæki/ adj (*informal*) **1** cheap and of poor quality and/or not in good taste: *a shop selling tacky souvenirs* **2** (used about paint, etc) not quite dry; sticky

tact /tækt/ noun [U] the ability to deal with people without offending or upsetting them: *She handled the situation with great tact and diplomacy.*

tactful /'tæktfl/ adj careful not to say or do things that could offend people –**tactfully** /-fəli/ adv

★**tactic** /'tæktɪk/ noun **1** [C,usually pl] the particular method you use to achieve sth: *We must decide what our tactics are going to be at the next meeting.* ● *I don't think this tactic will work.* **2 tactics** [pl] the skilful arrangement and use of military forces in order to win a battle

tactical /'tæktɪkl/ adj **1** connected with the particular method you use to achieve sth: *a tactical error* ● *tactical discussions/planning* **2** designed to bring a future advantage: *a tactical decision* –**tactically** /-kli/ adv

tactless /'tæktləs/ adj saying and doing things that are likely to offend and upset other people: *It was rather tactless of you to ask her how old she was.* –**tactlessly** adv

tadpole /'tædpəʊl/ noun [C] a young form of a greenish animal that can live in water and on land (a frog) when it has a large black head and a long tail ·➤ picture at **frog**

tag¹ /tæg/ noun [C] **1** (often used to form compound nouns) a small piece of card, material, etc fastened to sth to give information about it; a label: *How much is this dress? There isn't a price tag on it.* ·➤ picture at **label 2** (*grammar*) = **QUESTION TAG**

tag² /tæg/ verb [T] (**tagging**; **tagged**) to fasten a tag onto sb/sth

PHRASAL VERB **tag along** to follow or go somewhere with sb, especially when you have not been invited

★**tail**¹ /teɪl/ noun **1** [C] the part at the end of the body of an animal, bird, fish, etc: *The dog barked and wagged its tail.* ·➤ picture at **horse**, **otter** and **scorpion 2** [C] the back part of an aircraft, spacecraft, etc **3 tails** [pl] a man's formal coat that is short at the front but with a long, divided piece at the back, worn especially at weddings **4 tails** [pl] the side of a coin that does not have the head of a person on it: *'We'll toss a coin to decide,' said my father. 'Heads or tails?'* **5** [C] (*informal*) a person who is sent to follow sb secretly to get information about him/her

IDIOM **make head or tail of sth** → **HEAD**¹

tail² /teɪl/ verb [T] to follow sb closely, especially to watch where he/she goes

PHRASAL VERB **tail away/off** (*especially Brit*) to become smaller and weaker

tailor¹ /'teɪlə/ noun [C] a person whose job is to make clothes, especially for men

tailor² /'teɪlə/ verb [T] (usually passive) **1 tailor sth to/for sb/sth** to make or design sth for a particular person or purpose: *programmes tailored to the needs of specific groups* **2** to make clothes: *a well-tailored coat*

tailor-'made adj tailor-made (for sb/sth) made for a particular person or purpose and therefore very suitable

taint /teɪnt/ noun [usually sing] (*formal*) the effect of sth bad or unpleasant that spoils the quality of sb/sth: *the taint of corruption.* –**taint** verb [T] (usually passive): *Her reputation was tainted by the scandal.*

★**take** /teɪk/ verb [T] (*pt* **took** /tʊk/; *pp* **taken** /'teɪkən/) **1** to carry or move sb/sth; to go with sb from one place to another: *Take your coat with you – it's cold.* ● *Could you take this letter home to your parents?* ● *The ambulance took him to hospital.* ● *I'm taking the children swimming this afternoon.* ·➤ picture at **borrow 2** to put your hand round sth and hold it (and move it towards you): *She held out the keys, and I took them.* ● *He took a sweater out of the drawer.* ● *She took my hand /me by the hand.* **3** to remove sth from a place or a person, often without permission: *Who's taken my pen?* ● *My name had been taken off the list.* ● *The burglars took all my jewellery.* **4** to accept or receive sth: *If you take my advice you'll forget all about him.* ● *Do you take credit cards?* ● *What coins does the machine take?* ● *I'm not going to take the blame for the accident.* ● *She's not going to take the job.* **5** to capture a place by force; to get control of sth/sb: *The state will take control of the company.* **6** to understand sth or react to sth in a particular way: *She took what he said as a compliment.* ● *I wish you would take things more seriously.* **7** to get a particular feeling from sth: *He takes great pleasure in his grandchildren.* ● *When she failed the exam she took comfort from the fact that it was only by a few marks.* **8** to be able to deal with sth difficult or unpleasant: *I can't take much more of this heat.* ·➤ synonym **stand 9** to need sth/sb: *It took three people to move the piano.* ● *How long did the journey take?* ● *It took a lot of courage to say that.* **10** to swallow sth: *Take two tablets four times a day.* ● *Do you take sugar in tea?* **11** to write or record sth: *She took notes during the lecture.* ● *The police officer took my name and address.* **12** to photograph sth: *I took some nice photos of the wedding.* **13** to measure sth: *The doctor took my temperature/pulse/blood pressure* **14** (not used in the continuous tenses) to have a certain size of shoes or clothes: *What size shoes do you take?* **15** (not used in the continuous tenses) to have enough space for sb/sth: *How many passengers can this bus take?* **16** used with nouns to say that sb is performing an action: *Take a look at this article* (= look at it). ● *We have to take a decision* (= decide). **17** to study a subject for an exam; to do an exam: *I'm taking the advanced exam this summer.* **18** take sb **(for sth)** to give lessons to sb: *Who takes you for History?* (= who is your teacher) **19** to use a form of transport; to use a particular route: *I always take the train to York.* ● *Which road do you take to Hove?* ● *Take the second turning on the right.* **20** (not used in the continuous tenses) (*grammar*) to have or need a word to go with it in a sentence or other structure: *The verb 'depend' takes the preposition 'on'.*

IDIOMS **be taken with sb/sth** to find sb/sth attractive or interesting

I take it (that...) (used to show that you understand sth from a situation, even though you have not been told) I suppose: *I take it that you're not coming?*

take it from me believe me

take a lot out of sb to make sb very tired

take a lot of/some doing to need a lot of work or effort

➤ For other idioms containing **take**, look at the entries for the nouns, adjectives, etc, for example **take place** is at **place**[1].

PHRASAL VERBS **take sb aback** to surprise or shock sb

take after sb (not used in the continuous tenses) to look or behave like an older member of your family, especially a parent

take sth apart to separate sth into the different parts it is made of

take sth away 1 to cause a feeling, etc to disappear: *These aspirins will take the pain away.* **2** to buy cooked food at a restaurant, etc and carry it out to eat somewhere else, for example at home ••➤ noun **takeaway**

take sb/sth away (from sb) to remove sb/sth: *She took the scissors away from the child.*

take sth back 1 to return sth to the place that you got it from **2** to admit that sth you said was wrong

take sth down 1 to remove a structure by separating it into the pieces it is made of: *They took the tent down and started the journey home.* **2** to write down sth that is said

take sb in 1 to make sb believe sth that is not true: *I was completely taken in by her story.* **2** to invite sb who has no home to live with you

take sth in to understand what you see, hear or read: *There was too much in the museum to take in at one go.*

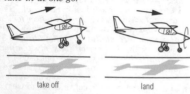

take off   land

take off 1 (used about an aircraft) to leave the ground and start flying ••➤ opposite **land** **2** (used about an idea, a product, etc) to become successful or popular very quickly or suddenly

take sb off to copy the way sb speaks or

behaves in an amusing way

take sth off 1 to remove sth, especially clothes: *Come in and take your coat off.* **2** to have the period of time mentioned as a holiday: *I'm going to take a week off.*

take on to start to employ sb: *The firm is taking on new staff.*

take sth on to accept a responsibility or decide to do sth: *He's taken on a lot of extra work.*

take sb out to go out with sb (for a social occasion): *I'm taking Sarah out for a meal tonight.*

take sth out to remove sth from inside your body: *He's having two teeth taken out.*

take sth out (of sth) to remove sth from sth: *He took a notebook out of his pocket.* ● *I need to take some money out of the bank.*

take it out on sb to behave badly towards sb because you are angry or upset about sth, even though it is not this person's fault

take (sth) over to get control of sth or responsibility for sth: *The firm is being taken over by a large company.* ● *Who's going to take over as assistant when Tim leaves?*

take to sb/sth to start liking sb/sth

take to sth/doing sth to begin doing sth regularly as a habit

take sth up to start doing sth regularly (for example as a hobby): *I've taken up yoga recently.*

take up sth to use or fill an amount of time or space: *All her time is taken up looking after the new baby.* ••➤ synonym **occupy**

take sb up on sth 1 to say that you disagree with sth that sb has just said, and ask him/her to explain it: *I must take you up on that last point.* **2** (*informal*) to accept an offer that sb has made

take sth up with sb to ask or complain about sth: *I'll take the matter up with my MP.*

takeaway /ˈteɪkəweɪ/ (*US* **takeout; carry-out**) *noun* [C] **1** a restaurant that sells food that you can eat somewhere else **2** the food that such a restaurant sells: *Let's have a takeaway.*

take-off *noun* [U,C] the moment when an aircraft leaves the ground and starts to fly: *The plane is ready for take-off.* ••➤ opposite **landing**

takeover /ˈteɪkəʊvə/ *noun* [C] the act of taking control of sth: *They made a takeover bid for the company.* ● *a military takeover of the government*

takings /ˈteɪkɪŋz/ *noun* [pl] the amount of money that a shop, theatre, etc gets from selling goods, tickets, etc

talcum powder /ˈtælkəm paʊdə/ (also **talc** /tælk/) *noun* [U] a soft powder which smells nice. People often put it on their skin after a bath.

tale /teɪl/ *noun* [C] **1** a story about events that are not real: *fairy tales* **2** a report or description of sb/sth that may not be true: *I've heard tales of people seeing ghosts in that house.*

★**talent** /ˈtælənt/ *noun* [C,U] (a) talent (for sth) a natural skill or ability: *She has a talent for*

painting. ● *His work shows great talent.*
–**talented** adj: *a talented musician*

★**talk¹** /tɔːk/ **verb 1** [I] **talk (to/with sb) (about/of sb/sth)** to say things; to speak in order to give information or to express feelings, ideas, etc: *I could hear them talking downstairs.* ● *Can I talk to you for a minute?* ● *Nasreen is not an easy person to talk to.* ● *We need to talk about the plans for the weekend.* ● *He's been talking of going to Australia for some time now.* ● *Dr Hollis will be talking about Japanese Art in her lecture.* •➤ Look at the note at **speak**. **2** [I,T] to discuss sth serious or important: *We can't go on like this. We need to talk.* ● *Could we* **talk business** *after dinner?* **3** [I] to discuss people's private lives: *His strange lifestyle started the local people talking.* •➤ synonym **gossip 4** [I] to give information to sb, especially when you do not want to

IDIOMS **know what you are talking about**
→ **KNOW¹**
talk sense to say things that are correct or sensible: *He's the only politician who talks any sense.*
talk/speak of the devil → **DEVIL**
talk shop to talk about your work with the people you work with, outside working hours

PHRASAL VERBS **talk down to sb** to talk to sb as if he/she is less intelligent or important than you
talk sb into/out of doing sth to persuade sb to do/not to do sth: *She tried to talk him into buying a new car.*
talk sth over (with sb) to discuss sth with sb, especially in order to reach an agreement or make a decision

★**talk²** /tɔːk/ **noun 1** [C] **a talk (with sb) (about sth)** a conversation or discussion: *Tim and I had a long talk about the problem.* **2 talks** [pl] formal discussions between governments: *The Foreign Ministers of the two countries will meet for talks next week.* ● *arms/pay/ peace talks* **3** [C] **a talk (on sth)** a formal speech on a particular subject; a lecture: *He's giving a talk on 'Our changing world'.* **4** [U] (*informal*) things that people say that are not based on facts or reality: *He says he's going to resign but it's just talk.* •➤ Look also at **small talk**.

talkative /ˈtɔːkətɪv/ **adj** liking to talk a lot

★**tall** /tɔːl/ **adj 1** (used about people or things) of more than average height; not short: *a tall young man* ● *a tall tree/tower/chimney* ● *Nick is taller than his brother.* •➤ opposite **short 2** used to describe the height of sb/sth: *Claire is five feet tall.* ● *How tall are you?* •➤ noun **height**

➤ **Tall** and **high** have similar meanings. We use **tall** to describe the height of people and trees (*He is six foot three inches tall.* ● *A tall oak tree stands in the garden.*) and other narrow objects (*the tall skyscrapers of Manhattan*). We use **high** to describe the measurement of sth (*The fence is two metres high.*) and the distance of sth from the ground (*a room with high ceilings*).

tambourine /ˌtæmbəˈriːn/ **noun** [C] a musical instrument that has a circular frame covered with plastic or skin, with metal discs round the edge. To play it, you hit it or shake it with your hand. •➤ picture at **music**

tame¹ /teɪm/ **adj 1** (used about animals or birds) not wild or afraid of people: *The birds are so tame they will eat from your hand.* **2** boring; not interesting or exciting: *After the big city, you must find village life very tame.*

tame² /teɪm/ **verb** [T] to bring sth wild under your control; to make sth tame

tamper /ˈtæmpə/ **verb**
PHRASAL VERB **tamper with sth** to make changes to sth without permission, especially in order to damage it

tampon /ˈtæmpɒn/ **noun** [C] a tightly-rolled piece of cotton material that a woman puts inside her body to absorb the blood that she loses once a month •➤ Look at **sanitary towel**.

tan¹ /tæn/ **noun 1** = **SUNTAN 2** [U] a colour between yellow and brown –**tan** adj

tan² /tæn/ **verb** [I,T] (**tanning**; **tanned**) (used about a person's skin) to become brown as a result of spending time in the sun: *Do you tan easily?* –**tanned** adj: *You're looking very tanned – have you been on holiday?*

tandem /ˈtændəm/ **noun** [C] a bicycle with seats for two people, one behind the other
IDIOM **in tandem (with sb/sth)** working together with sth/sb else; happening at the same time as sth else

tangent /ˈtændʒənt/ **noun** [C] a straight line that touches a curve but does not cross it
IDIOM **go off at a tangent**; (*US*) **go off on a tangent** to suddenly start saying or doing sth that seems to have no connection with what has gone before

tangerine /ˌtændʒəˈriːn/ **noun 1** [C] a fruit like a small sweet orange with a skin that is easy to take off **2** [U], **adj** (of) a deep orange colour

tangible /ˈtændʒəbl/ **adj** that can be clearly seen to exist: *There are tangible benefits in the new system.* •➤ opposite **intangible**

tangle /ˈtæŋgl/ **noun** [C] a confused mass, especially of threads, hair, branches, etc that cannot easily be separated from each other: *My hair's full of tangles.* ● *This string's in a tangle.* –**tangled** adj: *The wool was all tangled up.*

★**tank** /tæŋk/ **noun** [C] **1** a container for holding liquids or gas; the amount that a tank will hold: *a water/fuel/petrol/fish tank* ● *We drove there and back on one tank of petrol.* •➤ picture at **dive** and **motorbike 2** a large, heavy military vehicle covered with strong metal and armed with guns, that moves on special wheels

tanker /ˈtæŋkə/ **noun** [C] a ship or lorry that carries oil, petrol, etc in large amounts: *an oil tanker*

tannoy /ˈtænɔɪ/ **noun** [C] a system used for given spoken information in a public place: *They announced* **over the tannoy** *that our flight was delayed.*

t

tantalizing (also **tantalising**) /'tæntəlaɪ-zɪŋ/ **adj** making you want sth that you cannot have or do; tempting: *A tantalizing aroma of cooking was coming from the kitchen.* –**tantalizingly** (also **tantalisingly**) **adv**

tantrum /'tæntrəm/ **noun** [C] a sudden explosion of anger, especially by a child

⋆**tap**[1] /tæp/ **verb** (**tapping**; **tapped**) **1** [I,T] tap (at/on sth); tap sb/sth (on/with sth) to touch or hit sb/sth quickly and lightly: *Their feet were tapping in time to the music.* ● *She tapped me on the shoulder.* ··➤ picture on page S8 **2** [I,T] tap (into) sth to make use of a source of energy, knowledge, etc that already exists: *to tap the skills of young people* **3** [T] to fit a device to sb's telephone so that his/her calls can be listened to secretly

⋆**tap**[2] /tæp/ **noun** [C] **1** (*US* **faucet**) a type of handle that you turn to let water, gas, etc out of a pipe or container: *Turn the hot/cold tap on/off.* ··➤ picture at **plug 2** a light hit with your hand or fingers **3** a device that is fitted to sb's telephone so that his/her calls can be listened to secretly

'**tap dance noun** [C] a style of dancing in which you tap the rhythm of the music with your feet, wearing special shoes with pieces of metal on them –'**tap-dance verb** [I]

⋆**tape**[1] /teɪp/ **noun 1** [U] a thin band of plastic material used for recording sound, pictures or information: *I've got the whole concert on tape* (= recorded). **2** [C] a cassette which is used for recording or playing music, videos, etc: *a blank tape* (= a tape which is empty) ● *to rewind a tape* **3** [U] a long narrow band of plastic, etc with a sticky substance on one side that is used for sticking things together, covering electric wires, etc: *sticky/adhesive tape* ··➤ Look at **Sellotape. 4** [C,U] a narrow piece of cloth that is used for tying things together or as a label ··➤ Look at **red tape. 5** [C] a piece of material stretched across a race track to mark where the race finishes

tape[2] /teɪp/ **verb** [T] **1** to record sound, music, television programmes, etc using a cassette **2** tape sth (up) to fasten sth by sticking or tying sth with tape[1](3)

'**tape measure** (also '**measuring tape**) **noun** [C] a long thin piece of plastic, cloth or metal with centimetres, etc marked on it. It is used for measuring things. ··➤ Look at **tape.**

'**tape recorder noun** [C] a machine that is used for recording and playing sounds on tape

tapestry /'tæpəstri/ **noun** [C,U] (*pl* **tapestries**) a piece of heavy cloth with pictures or designs sewn on it in coloured thread

'**tap water noun** [U] water that comes through pipes and out of taps, not water sold in bottles

tar /tɑ:/ **noun** [U] **1** a thick black sticky liquid that becomes hard when it is cold. Tar is obtained from coal and is used for making roads, etc. ··➤ Look at **Tarmac. 2** a similar substance formed by burning tobacco: *low-tar cigarettes*

⋆**target**[1] /'tɑ:gɪt/ **noun** [C] **1** a result that you try to achieve: *Our target is to finish the job by Friday.* ● *So far we're right on target* (= making the progress we expected). ● *a target area/audience/group* (= the particular area, audience, etc that a product, programme, etc is aimed at) **2** a person, place or thing that you try to hit when shooting or attacking: *Doors and windows an easy target for burglars.* **3** a person or thing that people criticize, laugh at, etc: *The education system has been the target of heavy criticism.* **4** an object, often a round board with circles on it, that you try to hit in shooting practice: *to aim at/hit/miss a target*

target[2] /'tɑ:gɪt/ **verb** [T] (usually passive) target sb/sth; target sth at/on sb/sth to try to have an effect on a particular group of people; to try to attack sb/sth: *The product is targeted at teenagers.*

tariff /'tærɪf/ **noun** [C] **1** a tax that has to be paid on goods coming into a country **2** a list of prices, especially in a hotel

Tarmac™ /'tɑ:mæk/ **noun 1** [U] a black material used for making the surfaces of roads ··➤ Look at **tar. 2 the tarmac** [sing] an area covered with a Tarmac surface, especially at an airport

tarnish /'tɑ:nɪʃ/ **verb 1** [I,T] (used about metal, etc) to become or to make sth less bright and shiny **2** [T] to spoil the good opinion people have of sb/sth

tarpaulin /tɑ:'pɔ:lɪn/ **noun** [C,U] strong material that water cannot pass through, which is used for covering things to protect them from the rain

tart[1] /tɑ:t/ **noun 1** [C,U] an open pie filled with sweet food such as fruit or jam ··➤ picture on page C4 **2** [C] (*Brit informal*) a woman who dresses or behaves in a way that people think is immoral

tart[2] /tɑ:t/ **verb**

PHRASAL VERB **tart sb/sth up** (*Brit informal*) to decorate and improve the appearance of sb/sth

tartan /'tɑ:tn/ **noun** [U,C] **1** a traditional Scottish pattern of coloured squares and lines that cross each other **2** material made from wool with this pattern on it

⋆**task** /tɑ:sk/ **noun** [C] a piece of work that has to be done, especially an unpleasant or difficult one: *Your first task will be to type these letters.* ● *to perform/carry out/undertake a task*

⋆**taste**[1] /teɪst/ **noun 1** [sing] the particular quality of different foods or drinks that allow you to recognize them when you put them in your mouth; flavour: *I don't like the taste of this coffee.* ● *a sweet/bitter/sour/salty taste* **2** [U] the ability to recognize the flavour of food or drink: *I've got such a bad cold that I seem to have lost my sense of taste.* **3** [C,usually sing] a taste (of sth) a small amount of sth to eat or drink that you have in order to see what it is like: *Have a taste of this cheese to see if you like it.* **4** [sing] a short experience of sth: *That was my first taste of success.*

5 [U] the ability to decide if things are suitable, of good quality, etc: *He has excellent* **taste in** *music.* **6** [sing] a taste (for sth) what a person likes or prefers: *She has developed a taste for modern art.*

IDIOM **(be) in bad, poor, etc taste** (used about sb's behaviour) (to be) unpleasant and not suitable: *Some of his comments were in very bad taste.*

★**taste²** /teɪst/ *verb* **1** [I] taste (of sth) to have a particular flavour: *The pudding tasted of oranges.* ● *to taste sour/sweet/delicious* **2** [T] to notice or recognize the flavour of food or drink: *Can you taste the garlic in this soup?* **3** [T] to try a small amount of food and drink; to test the flavour of sth: *Can I taste a piece of that cheese to see what it's like?*

tasteful /ˈteɪstfl/ *adj* (used especially about clothes, furniture, decorations, etc) attractive and well-chosen: *tasteful furniture* ••➤ opposite **tasteless** –**tastefully** /-fəli/ *adv*

tasteless /ˈteɪstləs/ *adj* **1** having little or no flavour: *This sauce is rather tasteless.* ••➤ opposite **tasty 2** likely to offend people: *His joke about the funeral was particularly tasteless.* **3** (used especially about clothes, furniture, decorations, etc) unattractive; not well-chosen ••➤ opposite **tasteful**

tasty /ˈteɪsti/ *adj* (**tastier**; **tastiest**) having a good flavour: *spaghetti with a tasty mushroom sauce*

tattered /ˈtætəd/ *adj* old and torn; in bad condition: *a tattered coat*

tatters /ˈtætəz/ *noun*
IDIOM **in tatters** badly torn or damaged; ruined: *Her dress was in tatters.*

tattoo /təˈtuː/ *noun* [C] (*pl* **tattoos**) a picture or pattern that is marked permanently on sb's skin –**tattoo** *verb* [T] (tattooing; tattooed): *She had his name tattooed on her left hand.*

tatty /ˈtæti/ *adj* (*informal*) in bad condition: *tatty old clothes*

taught *past tense, past participle* of **TEACH**

taunt /tɔːnt/ *verb* [T] to try to make sb angry or upset by saying unpleasant or cruel things –**taunt** *noun* [C]

Taurus /ˈtɔːrəs/ *noun* [C,U] the second sign of the zodiac, the Bull

taut /tɔːt/ *adj* (used about rope, wire, etc) stretched very tight; not loose

tavern /ˈtævən/ *noun* [C] (*old-fashioned*) a pub

★**tax** /tæks/ *noun* [C,U] (a) tax (on sth) the money that you have to pay to the government so that it can provide public services: *income tax* ● *There used to be a tax on windows.* –**tax** *verb* [T] (often passive): *Alcohol, cigarettes and petrol are heavily taxed.*

taxable /ˈtæksəbl/ *adj* on which you have to pay tax: *taxable income*

taxation /tækˈseɪʃn/ *noun* [U] **1** the system by which a government takes money from people so that it can pay for public services: *direct/indirect taxation* **2** the amount of money that people have to pay in tax: *to increase/reduce taxation* ● *high/low taxation*

,tax-'free *adj* on which you do not have to pay tax

★**taxi¹** /ˈtæksi/ (also 'taxicab *especially US* cab) *noun* [C] a car with a driver whose job is to take you somewhere in exchange for money: *Shall we go by bus or get/take a taxi?*

➤ The amount of money that you have to pay (your **fare**) is shown on a **meter**.

taxi² /ˈtæksi/ *verb* [I] (used about an aircraft) to move slowly along the ground before or after flying

taxing /ˈtæksɪŋ/ *adj* difficult; needing a lot of effort: *a taxing exam*

'taxi rank *noun* [C] a place where taxis park while they are waiting to be hired

TB /ˌtiː ˈbiː/ *abbr* tuberculosis

tbsp *abbr* tablespoonful(s): *Add 3 tbsp sugar.*

★**tea** /tiː/ *noun* **1** [U] a hot drink made by pouring boiling water onto the dried leaves of the tea plant or of some other plants; a cup of this drink: *a cup/pot of tea* ● *weak/strong tea* ● *herb/mint/camomile tea* ● *Two teas and one coffee, please.* ••➤ picture on page C4 **2** [U] the dried leaves that are used for making tea: *a packet of tea* **3** [C,U] (*especially Brit*) a small afternoon meal of sandwiches, cakes, etc and tea to drink, or a cooked meal eaten at 5 or 6 o'clock: *The kids have their tea as soon as they get home from school.*

IDIOM **(not) sb's cup of tea** ➔ **CUP¹**

'tea bag *noun* [C] a small paper bag with tea leaves in it, that you use for making tea ••➤ picture on page C4

★**teach** /tiːtʃ/ *verb* (*pt, pp* **taught** /tɔːt/) **1** [I,T] teach sb (sth/to do sth); teach sth (to sb) to give sb lessons or instructions so that he/she knows how to do sth: *My mother taught me to play the piano.* ● *Jeremy is teaching us how to use the computer.* ● *He teaches English to foreign students.* ● *I teach in a primary school.* **2** [T] to make sb believe sth or behave in a certain way: *The story teaches us that history often repeats itself.* ● *My parents taught me always to tell the truth.* **3** [T] to make sb have a bad experience so that he/she is careful not to do the thing that caused it again: *A week in prison? That'll teach him to drink and drive!*
IDIOM **teach sb a lesson** to make sb have a bad experience so that he/she will not do the thing that caused it again

★**teacher** /ˈtiːtʃə/ *noun* [C] a person whose job is to teach, especially in a school or college: *He's a teacher at a primary school.* ● *a maths/chemistry/music teacher* ••➤ Look at **head¹**(6).

teaching /ˈtiːtʃɪŋ/ *noun* **1** [U] the work of a teacher: *My son went into teaching and my daughter became a doctor.* ● *teaching methods* **2** [C, usually pl] ideas and beliefs that are taught by sb/sth: *the teachings of Gandhi*

'tea cloth (*Brit*) = **TEA TOWEL**

teacup /ˈtiːkʌp/ *noun* [C] a cup that you drink tea from

t

'tea leaves noun [pl] the small leaves that are left in a cup after you have drunk the tea

★**team¹** /tiːm/ noun [C] **1** a group of people who play a sport or game together against another group: *a football team* • *Are you **in/on the team**?* **2** a group of people who work together: *a team of doctors*

> When **team** is used in the singular, it can be followed by either a singular or a plural verb: *The team play/plays two matches every week.*

team² /tiːm/ verb

PHRASAL VERB **team up (with sb)** to join sb in order to do sth together: *I teamed up with Elena to plan the project.*

teamwork /'tiːmwɜːk/ noun [U] the ability of people to work together: *Teamwork is a key feature of the training programme.*

teapot /'tiːpɒt/ noun [C] a container that you use for making tea in and for serving it •➤ picture on page C4

★**tear¹** /tɪə/ noun [C, usually pl] a drop of water that comes from your eye when you are crying, etc: *I was **in tears** (= crying) at the end of the film.* • *The little girl **burst into tears** (= suddenly started to cry).*
IDIOM **shed tears** → SHED²

tear

'Oh no! I've torn my shirt!'

She **tore up** the letter.

★**tear²** /teə/ verb (pt **tore** /tɔː/; pp **torn** /tɔːn/) **1** [I,T] to damage sth by pulling it apart or into pieces; to become damaged in this way: *I tore my shirt on that nail.* • *She tore the letter in half.* • *I tore a page out of my notebook.* • *This material doesn't tear easily.* **2** [T] to remove sth by pulling violently and quickly: *Paul tore the poster down from the wall.* • *He tore the bag out of her hands.* **3** [T] to make a hole in sth by force **4** [I] **tear along, up, down, past,** etc to move very quickly in a particular direction: *An ambulance went tearing past.* –**tear** noun: [C] *You've got a tear in the back of your trousers.*
IDIOM **wear and tear** → WEAR²

PHRASAL VERBS **tear sth apart 1** to pull sth violently into pieces **2** to destroy sth completely: *The country has been torn apart by the war.*

tear yourself away (from sb/sth) to make yourself leave sb/sth or stop doing sth

be torn between A and B to find it difficult to choose between two things or people

tear sth down (used about a building) to destroy it: *They tore down the old houses and built a shopping centre.*

tear sth up to pull sth into pieces, especially sth made of paper: *'I hate this photograph,' she said, tearing it up.*

tearful /'tɪəfl/ adj crying or nearly crying

'tear gas noun [U] a type of gas that hurts the eyes and throat, and is used by the police, etc to control large groups of people

tease /tiːz/ verb [I,T] to laugh at sb either in a friendly way or in order to upset him/her: *Don't pay any attention to those boys. They're only teasing.* • *They teased her about being fat.*

teaspoon /'tiːspuːn/ noun [C] **1** a small spoon used for putting sugar in tea, coffee, etc **2** (also **teaspoonful** /-fʊl/) the amount that a teaspoon can hold

'tea towel (also **tea cloth**) noun [C] a small towel that is used for drying plates, knives, forks, etc

★**technical** /'teknɪkl/ adj **1** connected with the practical use of machines, methods, etc in science and industry: *The train was delayed due to a technical problem.* **2** connected with the skills involved in a particular activity or subject: *This computer magazine is too technical for me.*

technicality /ˌteknɪ'kæləti/ noun [C] (pl **technicalities**) one of the details of a particular subject or activity

technically /'teknɪkli/ adv **1** according to the exact meaning, facts, etc: *Technically, you should pay by May 1st, but it doesn't matter if it's a few days late.* **2** in a way that involves detailed knowledge of the machines, etc that are used in industry or science: *The country is technically not very advanced.* **3** used about sb's practical ability in a particular activity: *He's a technically brilliant dancer.*

technician /tek'nɪʃn/ noun [C] a person whose work involves practical skills, especially in industry or science: *a laboratory technician*

★**technique** /tek'niːk/ noun **1** [C] a particular way of doing sth: *new techniques for teaching languages* • *marketing/management techniques* **2** [U] the practical skill that sb has in a particular activity: *He's a naturally talented runner, but he needs to work on his technique.*

★**technology** /tek'nɒlədʒi/ noun [C,U] (pl **technologies**) the scientific knowledge and/or equipment that is needed for a particular industry, etc: *developments in com-*

puter technology –technological /,teknə-
lɒdʒɪkl/ **adj**: *technological developments*
–technologist /tek'nɒlədʒɪst/ **noun** [C]: *Tech-
nologists are developing a computer that can
perform surgery.*

teddy /'tedi/ (also **'teddy bear**) **noun** [C] (*pl*
teddies) a toy for children that looks like a
bear

tedious /'tiːdiəs/ **adj** boring and lasting for a
long time: *a tedious train journey*

teem /tiːm/ **verb** [I] **teem with sth** (used
about a place) to have a lot of people or
things moving about in it: *The streets were
teeming with people.*

teenage /'tiːneɪdʒ/ **adj** (only *before* a noun)
1 between 13 and 19 years old: *teenage children* **2** typical of or suitable for people
between 13 and 19 years old: *teenage maga-
zines/fashion*

teenager /'tiːneɪdʒə/ **noun** [C] a person aged
between 13 and 19 years old: *Her music is very
popular with teenagers.* ••► Look at **adolescent**.

teens /tiːnz/ **noun** [pl] the period of a person's
life between the ages of 13 and 19: *to be **in**
your early/late teens*

teeshirt /'tiːʃɜːt/ = **T-SHIRT**

teeth *plural* of **TOOTH**

teethe /tiːð/ **verb** [I] (usually in the *–ing*
forms) (used about a baby) to start growing
its first teeth

'teething troubles (also **'teething problems**) **noun** [pl] the problems that can develop
when a person, system, etc is new: *We've just
installed this new software and are having a
few teething troubles with it.*

teetotal /tiː'təʊtl/ **adj** (not before a noun)
(used about a person) never drinking alcohol
–teetotaller (*US* **teetotaler**) /-tlə/ **noun** [C]

TEFL /'tefl/ **abbr** Teaching English as a Foreign Language

tel **abbr** telephone (number): *tel 01865 56767*

telecommunications /,telikə,mjuːnɪ-
'keɪʃnz/ **noun** [pl] the technology of sending
signals, images and messages over long distances by radio, telephone, television, etc

telegram /'telɪɡræm/ **noun** [C] a message
that is sent by a system (telegraph) that uses
electrical signals and that is then printed and
given to sb

telegraph /'telɪɡrɑːf/ **noun** [U] a method of
sending messages over long distances, using
wires that carry electrical signals

'telegraph pole noun [C] a tall wooden pole
that is used for supporting telephone wires

telemarketing /'telɪmɑːkɪtɪŋ/ = **TELESALES**

telepathy /tə'lepəθi/ **noun** [U] the communication of thoughts between people's minds
without using speech, writing or other normal methods

telephone

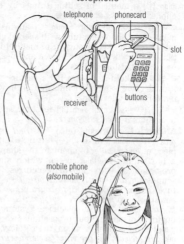

★**telephone** /'telɪfəʊn/ (also *informal*
phone) **noun 1** [U] an electrical system for
talking to sb in another place by speaking
into a special piece of equipment: *Can I contact you by telephone?* ● *to make a phone
call* ● *What's your telephone number?*
••► It is more common to use **phone** rather
than **telephone**, especially when you are
speaking. **2** [C] the piece of equipment that
you use when you talk to sb by telephone:
Could I use your telephone? ● *a mobile phone*
(= one that you can carry around) ● *a public
telephone*

► When you make a telephone call you first
dial the number. The telephone **rings** and
the person at the other end **answers** it. If
he/she is already using the telephone, it is
engaged. When you finish speaking you
hang up or **put the phone down**. The number that you dial before the telephone number if you are telephoning a different area
or country is called the **code**: *'What's the
code for Spain?'*

–telephone (also phone) **verb** [I,T]: *Sarah
phoned. She's going to be late.* ● *I'll phone you
later.*
IDIOM **on the phone/telephone → PHONE**

'telephone box (also **'phone box**; **'call
box**) **noun** [C] a small covered place in a
street, etc that contains a telephone for public use

'telephone directory (also *informal*
'phone book) **noun** [C] a book that gives a
list of the names, addresses and telephone
numbers of the people in a particular area

'telephone exchange (also **exchange**)
noun [C] a place belonging to a telephone company where telephone lines are connected to
each other

t

telesales /'teliseɪlz/ (also **telemarketing**) **noun** [U] a method of selling things by telephone: *He works in telesales.*

telescope /'telɪskəʊp/ **noun** [C] an instrument in the shape of a tube with special glass inside it. You look through it to make things that are far away appear bigger and nearer. •➤ picture at **binoculars**

teletext /'telitekst/ **noun** [U] a service that provides news and other information in written form on television

televise /'telɪvaɪz/ **verb** [T] to show sth on television: *a televised concert*

★**television** /'telɪvɪʒn/ (also **TV**, *Brit informal* **telly**) **noun 1** (also **'television set**) [C] a piece of electrical equipment in the shape of a box. It has a glass screen which shows programmes with moving pictures and sounds: *to turn the television on/off* •➤ picture on page C7 **2** [U] the programmes that are shown on a television set: *Paul's watching television.* **3** [U] the electrical system and business of sending out programmes so that people can watch them on their television sets: *a television presenter/series/documentary* ● *cable/satellite/terrestrial/digital television* ● *She works in television.* IDIOM **on television** being shown by television; appearing in a television programme: *What's on television tonight?*

★**tell** /tel/ **verb** (*pt, pp* **told** /təʊld/) **1** [T] **tell sb (sth/that…); tell sb (about sth); tell sth to sb** to give information to sb by speaking or writing: *She told me her address but I've forgotten it.* ● *He wrote to tell me that his mother had died.* ● *Tell us about your holiday.* ● *to tell the truth/a lie* ● *to tell a story* ● *Excuse me, could you tell me where the station is?* ● *He tells that story to everyone he sees.* •➤ Look at the note at **say**. **2** [T] **tell sb to do sth** to order or advise sb to do sth: *The policewoman told us to get out of the car.* **3** [I,T] to know, see or judge (sth) correctly: *'What do you think Jenny will do next?' 'It's hard to tell.'* ● *I could tell that he had enjoyed the evening.* ● *You can never tell what he's going to say next.* ● *I can't tell the difference between Dan's sisters.* **4** [T] (used about a thing) to give information to sb: *This book will tell you all you need to know.* **5** [I] to not keep a secret: *Promise you won't tell!* **6** [I] **tell (on sb/sth)** to have a noticeable effect: *I can't run as fast as I could – my age is beginning to tell!* IDIOMS **all told** with everybody or everything counted and included

(I'll) tell you what (*informal*) used to introduce a suggestion: *I'll tell you what – let's ask Diane to take us.*

I told you (so) (*informal*) I warned you that this would happen

tell A and B apart ➜ **APART**

tell the time to read the time from a clock or watch

PHRASAL VERBS **tell sb off (for sth/for doing sth)** to speak to sb angrily because he/she has done sth wrong: *The teacher told me off for not doing my homework.*

tell on sb to tell a parent, teacher, etc about sth bad that sb has done

telling /'telɪŋ/ **adj 1** showing, without intending to, what sb/sth is really like: *The number of homeless people is a telling comment on today's society.* **2** having a great effect: *That's quite a telling argument.*

'tell-tale **adj** giving information about sth secret or private: *He said he was fine, but there were tell-tale signs of worry on his face.*

telly /'teli/ (*pl* **tellies**) (*Brit informal*) = **TELEVISION**

temp¹ /temp/ **noun** [C] (*informal*) a temporary employee, especially in an office, who works somewhere for a short period of time when sb else is ill or on holiday –**temp verb** [I]

temp² *abbr* temperature: *temp 15 °C*

temper /'tempə/ **noun 1** [C,U] if you have a temper you get angry very easily: *Be careful of Paul. He's got quite a temper!* ● *You must learn to control your temper.* **2** [C] the way you are feeling at a particular time: *It's no use talking to him when he's in a bad temper.* •➤ synonym **mood**

IDIOMS **in a temper** feeling very angry and not controlling your behaviour

keep/lose your temper to stay calm/to become angry •➤ Look at **bad-tempered**.

temperament /'temprəmənt/ **noun** [C,U] a person's character, especially as it affects the way he/she behaves and feels: *to have an artistic/a fiery/a calm temperament*

temperamental /ˌtemprə'mentl/ **adj** often and suddenly changing the way you behave or feel

temperate /'tempərət/ **adj** (used about a climate) not very hot and not very cold

★**temperature** /'temprətʃə/ **noun 1** [C,U] how hot or cold sth is: *Heat the oven to a temperature of 200°C.* ● *a high/low temperature* ● *an increase in temperature* **2** [C] how hot or cold a person's body is

IDIOMS **have a temperature** (used about a person) to be hotter than normal because you are ill

take sb's temperature to measure the temperature of sb's body with a special instrument (a thermometer)

temple /'templ/ **noun** [C] **1** a building where people pray to a god or gods: *a Buddhist/ Hindu temple* **2** one of the flat parts on each side of your forehead •➤ picture on page C5

tempo /'tempəʊ/ **noun** (*pl* **tempos** /'tempəʊz/) **1** [sing,U] the speed of an activity or event **2** [C,U] the speed of a piece of music: *a fast/slow tempo*

★**temporary** /'temprəri/ **adj** lasting for a short time; not permanent: *a temporary job* ● *This arrangement is only temporary.* –**temporarily** /'temprərəli/ **adv**

★**tempt** /tempt/ **verb** [T] **tempt sb (into sth/ into doing sth); tempt sb (to do sth)** to try to persuade or attract sb to do sth, even if it is wrong: *His dream of riches had tempted him into a life of crime.* ● *She was tempted to stay in bed all morning.*

temptation /temp'teɪʃn/ **noun 1** [U] a feeling that you want to do sth, even if you know that it is wrong: *I managed to resist the temptation to tell him what I really thought.* • *She wanted a cigarette badly, but didn't give in to temptation.* **2** [C] a thing that attracts you to do sth wrong or silly: *All that money is certainly a big temptation.*

tempting /'temptɪŋ/ **adj** attractive in a way that makes you want to do or have sth: *a tempting offer*

★**ten** /ten/ **number** 10

➤ For examples of how to use numbers in sentences, look at **six**.

tenacious /tə'neɪʃəs/ **adj** not likely to give up or let sth go; determined –**tenacity** /tə'næsəti/ **noun** [U]

tenancy /'tenənsi/ **noun** [C,U] (*pl* **tenancies**) the use of a room, flat, building or piece of land, for which you pay rent to the owner: *a six-month tenancy* • *It says in the tenancy agreement that you can't keep pets.*

tenant /'tenənt/ **noun** [C] a person who pays money (rent) to the owner of a room, flat, building or piece of land so that he/she can live in it or use it

➤ The owner is called a **landlord** or **landlady**.

★**tend** /tend/ **verb 1** [I] **tend to do sth** to usually do or be sth: *Women tend to live longer than men.* • *There tends to be a lot of heavy traffic on that road.* • *My brother tends to talk a lot when he's nervous.* **2** [I] used for giving your opinion in a polite way: *I tend to think that we shouldn't interfere.* **3** [I,T] (*formal*) **tend (to) sb/sth** to look after sb/sth: *Paramedics tended (to) the injured.*

tendency /'tendənsi/ **noun** [C] (*pl* **tendencies**) **a tendency (to do sth/towards sth)** something that a person or thing usually does; a way of behaving: *They both have a tendency to be late for appointments.* • *The dog began to show vicious tendencies.* • *She seems to have a tendency towards depression.*

tender[1] /'tendə/ **adj 1** kind and loving: *tender words/looks/kisses* **2** (used about food) soft and easy to cut or bite; not tough: *The meat should be nice and tender.* **3** (used about a part of the body) painful when you touch it

IDIOM **at a tender age; at the tender age of…** when still young and without much experience: *She went to live in London at the tender age of 15.* –**tenderly adv** –**tenderness noun** [U]

tender[2] /'tendə/ **verb** [I,T] (*written*) to offer or give sth formally: *After the scandal the Foreign Minister was forced to tender her resignation.* –**tender** (also **bid**) **noun** [C]: *Several firms submitted a tender for the catering contract.*

tendon /'tendən/ **noun** [C] a strong, thin part inside your body that joins a muscle to a bone

tenement /'tenəmənt/ **noun** [C] a large building that is divided into small flats, especially in a poor area of a city

★**tennis** /'tenɪs/ **noun** [U] a game for two or four players who hit a ball over a net using a

piece of equipment (a racket) that is held in one hand: *Let's play tennis.* • *to have a game of tennis* • *a tennis match*

➤ In tennis you can play **singles** (a game between two people) or **doubles** (a game between two teams of two people).

tenor /'tenə/ **noun** [C] **1** a fairly high singing voice for a man; a man with this voice: *Pavarotti is a famous Italian tenor.*

➤ Tenor is between **alto** and **baritone**.

2 a musical instrument that plays notes within the same limits as a tenor voice: *a tenor saxophone*

tenpin bowling /ˌtenpɪn 'bəʊlɪŋ/ **noun** [U] a game in which you roll a heavy ball towards ten objects (tenpins) and try to knock them down

★**tense**[1] /tens/ **adj 1** (used about a person) not able to relax because you are worried or nervous: *She looked pale and tense.* **2** (used about a muscle or a part of the body) tight; not relaxed **3** (used about an atmosphere or situation) in which people feel worried and not relaxed

tense[2] /tens/ **verb** [I,T] **tense (up)** to have muscles that have become hard and not relaxed

★**tense**[3] /tens/ **noun** [C,U] (*grammar*) a form of a verb that shows if sth happens in the past, present or future

➤ For more information about verb tenses, look at the **Quick Grammar Reference** section at the back of this dictionary.

tension /'tenʃn/ **noun 1** [C,U] the condition of not being able to relax because you are worried or nervous: *I could hear the tension in her voice as she spoke.* **2** [C,U] bad feeling and lack of trust between people, countries, etc: *There are signs of growing tensions between the two countries.* **3** [U] (used about a rope, muscle, etc) the state of being stretched tight; how tightly sth is stretched: *The massage relieved the tension in my neck.*

tent

★**tent** /tent/ **noun** [C] a small structure made of cloth that is held up by poles and ropes. You use a tent to sleep in when you go camping: *to put up/take down a tent*

tentacle /'tentəkl/ **noun** [C] one of the long thin soft parts like legs that some sea animals have: *An octopus has eight tentacles.* •➤ picture at **octopus**

tentative /'tentətɪv/ **adj 1** (used about plans,

etc) uncertain; not definite **2** (used about a person or his/her behaviour) not confident about what you are saying or doing: *a tentative smile/suggestion* –**tentatively adv**

tenterhooks /'tentəhʊks/ **noun** [pl]
IDIOM (be) on tenterhooks to be in a very nervous or excited state because you are waiting to find out what is going to happen

★**tenth**[1] /tenθ/ **pron, determiner, adv** 10th
••➤ Look at the examples at **sixth**.

★**tenth**[2] /tenθ/ **noun** [C] the fraction ¹/₁₀; one of ten equal parts of sth ••➤ Look at the examples at **sixth**.

tenuous /'tenjuəs/ **adj** very weak or uncertain: *The connection between Joe's story and what actually happened was tenuous.*

tenure /'tenjə/ **noun** [U] a legal right to live in a place, hold a job, use land, etc for a certain time

tepid /'tepɪd/ **adj** (used about liquids) only slightly warm

★**term**[1] /tɜːm/ **noun 1** [C] a word or group of words with a particular meaning: *What exactly do you mean by the term 'racist'?* ● *a technical term in computing* **2 terms** [pl] in terms of ...; in ...terms used for showing which particular way you are thinking about sth or from which point of view: *The flat would be ideal in terms of size, but it is very expensive.* **3 terms** [pl] the conditions of an agreement: *Under the terms of the contract you must give a week's notice.* ● *Both sides agreed to the peace terms.* **4** [C] a period of time into which a school or university year is divided: *the autumn/spring/summer term* ● *an end-of-term test* **5** [C] a period of time for which sth lasts: *The US President is now in his second term of office.*
IDIOMS be on equal terms (with sb) → **EQUAL**[1]
be on good, friendly, etc terms (with sb) to have a friendly relationship with sb
come to terms with sth to accept sth unpleasant or difficult
in the long/short term over a long/short period of time in the future

★**term**[2] /tɜːm/ **verb** [T] to describe sb/sth by using a particular word or expression: *the period of history that is often termed the 'Dark Ages'*

terminal[1] /'tɜːmɪnl/ **adj** (used about an illness) slowly causing death: *terminal cancer* –**terminally** /-nəli/ **adv**: *a terminally ill patient*

terminal[2] /'tɜːmɪnl/ **noun** [C] **1** a large railway station, bus station or building at an airport where journeys begin and end: *the bus terminal* ● *Which terminal are you flying from?* **2** the computer that one person uses for getting information from a central computer or for putting information into it

terminate /'tɜːmɪneɪt/ **verb** [I,T] (*formal*) to end or to make sth end: *to terminate a contract/an agreement* –**termination noun** [U]

terminology /ˌtɜːmɪ'nɒlədʒi/ **noun** [U] the special words and expressions that are used in a particular profession, subject or activity

terminus /'tɜːmɪnəs/ **noun** [C] (*pl* **termin-**

uses /-nəsɪz/) the last stop or station at the end of a bus route or railway line

terrace /'terəs/ **noun 1** [C] a flat area of stone next to a restaurant or large house where people can have meals, sit in the sun, etc ••➤ Look at **patio**, **veranda** and **balcony**. **2** [C] (*Brit*) a line of similar houses that are all joined together **3** [C, usually pl] one of a series of steps that are cut into the side of a hill so that crops can be grown there **4 terraces** [pl] the wide steps that people stand on to watch a football match

terraced /'terəst/ **adj 1** (*Brit*) (used about a house) forming part of a line of similar houses that are all joined together **2** (used about a hill) having steps cut out of it so that crops can be grown there

terrain /tə'reɪn/ **noun** [U] land of the type mentioned: *mountainous/steep/rocky terrain*

★**terrible** /'terəbl/ **adj 1** very unpleasant; causing great shock or injury: *a terrible accident* ● *terrible news* ● *What a terrible thing to do!* **2** ill or very upset: *I feel terrible. I think I'm going to be sick.* ● *He felt terrible when he realized what he had done.* **3** very bad; of poor quality: *a terrible hotel/book/memory/driver* **4** (only *before* a noun) used to emphasize how bad sth is: *in terrible pain/trouble* ● *The room was in a terrible mess.*

★**terribly** /'terəbli/ **adv 1** very: *I'm terribly sorry.* **2** very badly: *I played terribly.* ● *The experiment went terribly wrong.*

terrier /'teriə/ **noun** [C] a type of small dog

terrific /tə'rɪfɪk/ **adj 1** (*informal*) extremely nice or good; excellent: *You're doing a terrific job!* **2** (only *before* a noun) very great: *I've got a terrific amount of work to do.* –**terrifically** /-kli/ **adv**: *terrifically expensive*

★**terrified** /'terɪfaɪd/ **adj** terrified (of sb/sth) very afraid: *I'm absolutely terrified of snakes.* ● *What's the matter? You look terrified.*

terrify /'terɪfaɪ/ **verb** [T] (*pres part* **terrifying**; *3rd pers sing pres* **terrifies**; *pt, pp* **terrified**) to frighten sb very much

territorial /ˌterə'tɔːriəl/ **adj** (only *before* a noun) connected with the land or area of sea that belongs to a country: *territorial waters*

territory /'terətri/ **noun** (*pl* **territories**) **1** [C,U] an area of land that belongs to one country: *to fly over enemy territory* **2** [C,U] an area that an animal has as its own **3** [U] an area of knowledge or responsibility: *Computer programming is Frank's territory.*

terror /'terə/ **noun 1** [U] very great fear: *He screamed in terror as the rats came towards him.* **2** [C] a person or thing that makes you feel afraid: *the terrors of the night* **3** [U] violence and the killing of ordinary people for political purposes: *a campaign of terror* **4** [C] a person or animal, especially a child, that is difficult to control: *Joey's a little terror.*

terrorism /'terərɪzəm/ **noun** [U] the killing of ordinary people for political purposes: *an act of terrorism* –**terrorist** /'terərɪst/ **noun** [C], **adj**

terrorize (also **-ise**) /'terəraɪz/ **verb** [T] to make sb feel frightened by using or threatening to use violence against him/her: *The* *gang has terrorized the neighbourhood for months.*

terse /tɜːs/ **adj** said in few words and in a not very friendly way: *a terse reply*

tertiary /'tɜːʃəri/ **adj** (used about education) at university or college level: *a tertiary college*

TESL /'tesl/ **abbr** Teaching English as a Second Language

★**test¹** /test/ **noun** [C] **1** a short exam to measure sb's knowledge or skill in sth: *We have a spelling test every Friday.*

> When you **take** a test you can either **pass** it (succeed) or **fail** it (not succeed).

2 a short medical examination of a part of your body: *to have an eye test* **3** an experiment to find out if sth works or to find out more information about it: *Tests show that the new drug is safe and effective.* • *to carry out/perform/do a test* **4** a situation or event that shows how good, strong, etc sb/sth is

IDIOM **put sb/sth to the test** to do sth to find out how good, strong, etc sb/sth is

★**test²** /test/ **verb** [T] **1** test sb/sth (for sth); test sth (on sb/sth) to try, use or examine sth carefully to find out if it is working properly or what it is like: *These cars have all been tested for safety.* • *Do you think drugs should be tested on animals?* **2** to examine a part of the body to find out if it is healthy: *to have your eyes tested* **3** test sb (on sth) to examine sb's knowledge or skill in sth: *We're being tested on irregular verbs this morning.*

testament /'testəmənt/ **noun** [C, usually sing] (*written*) a testament (to sth) something that shows that sth exists or is true

testicle /'testɪkl/ **noun** [C] one of the two roundish male sex organs that produce the male cells (sperm) that are needed for making young

testify /'testɪfaɪ/ **verb** [I,T] (*pres part testifying*; *3rd pers sing pres testifies*; *pt, pp testified*) to make a formal statement that sth is true, especially in a court of law

testimony /'testɪməni/ **noun** (*pl testimonies*) **1** [C,U] a formal statement that sth is true, especially one that is made in a court of law **2** [U,sing] (*formal*) something that shows that sth else exists or is true

'**test tube** **noun** [C] a thin glass tube that is used in chemical experiments

tetanus /'tetənəs/ **noun** [U] a serious disease that makes your muscles, especially the muscles of your face, hard and impossible to move. You can get tetanus by cutting yourself on sth dirty.

tether¹ /'teðə/ **verb** [T] to tie an animal to sth with a rope, etc

tether² /'teðə/ **noun** [C]

IDIOM **at the end of your tether → END¹**

★**text** /tekst/ **noun 1** [U] the main written part of a book, newspaper, etc (not the pictures, notes, index, etc) **2** [C] the written form of a speech, interview, etc: *The newspaper printed the complete text of the interview.* **3** [C] a book or a short piece of writing that people study as part of a literature or language course: *a*

set text (= one that has to be studied for an examination)

textbook /'tekstbʊk/ **noun** [C] a book that teaches a particular subject and that is used especially in schools: *a history textbook*

textile /'tekstaɪl/ **noun** [C] any cloth made in a factory: *cotton textiles* • *the textile industry*

texture /'tekstʃə/ **noun** [C,U] the way that sth feels when you touch it: *a rough/smooth/coarse texture* • *This cheese has a very creamy texture.*

★**than** /ðən; *strong form* ðæn/ **conj, prep 1** used when you are comparing two things: *He's taller than me.* • *He's taller than I am.* • *London is more expensive than Madrid.* • *You speak French much better than she does/than her.* **2** used with 'more' and 'less' before numbers, expressions of time, distance, etc: *I've worked here for more than three years.* **3** used after 'would rather' to say that you prefer one thing to another: *I'd rather play tennis than football.*

★**thank** /θæŋk/ **verb** [T] thank sb (for sth/for doing sth) to tell sb that you are grateful: *I'm writing to thank you for the present you sent me.* • *I'll go and thank him for offering to help.*

> **Thank you** and **thanks** are both used for telling somebody that you are grateful for something. **Thanks** is more informal: *Thank you very much for your letter.* • *'How are you, Rachel?' 'Much better, thanks.'* You can also use **thank you** and **thanks** to accept something that somebody has offered to you: *'Stay for dinner.' 'Thank you. That would be nice.'* When you want to refuse something you can say **no, thank you** or **no, thanks**: *'Would you like some more tea?' 'No, thanks.'*

IDIOM **thank God/goodness/heavens** used for expressing happiness that sth unpleasant has stopped or will not happen: *Thank goodness it's stopped raining.*

thankful /'θæŋkfl/ **adj** thankful (for sth/to do sth/that...) (not before a noun) pleased and grateful: *I was thankful to hear that you got home safely.* • *I was thankful for my thick coat when it started to snow.*

thankfully /-fəli/ **adv 1** used for expressing happiness that sth unpleasant did not or will not happen ·•> synonym **fortunately**: *Thankfully, no one was injured in the accident.* **2** in a pleased or grateful way: *I accepted her offer thankfully.*

thankless /'θæŋkləs/ **adj** involving hard work that other people do not notice or thank you for

★**thanks** /θæŋks/ **noun** [pl] words which show that you are grateful: *I'd like to express my thanks to all of you for coming here today.*

IDIOMS **thanks to sb/sth** because of sb/sth: *We're late, thanks to you!*
a vote of thanks → VOTE¹

Thanksgiving (Day) /ˌθæŋksˈgɪvɪŋ deɪ/ **noun** [U,C] a public holiday in the US and in Canada ·•> note on next page

---

[I] **intransitive**, a verb which has no object: *He laughed.* [T] **transitive**, a verb which has an object: *He ate an apple.*

➤ Thanksgiving Day is on the fourth Thursday in November in the US and on the second Monday in October in Canada. It was originally a day when people thanked God for the harvest.

'**thank you** noun [C] an expression of thanks

★**that** /ðæt/ **determiner, pron, conj, adv 1** (*pl* **those** /ðəʊz/) used to refer to a person or thing, especially when he/she/it is not near the person speaking: *I like that house over there.* ● *What's that in the road?* ● *'Could you pass me the book?' 'This one?' 'No, that one over there.'* **2** (*pl* **those** /ðəʊz/) used for talking about a person or thing already known or mentioned: *That was the year we went to Spain, wasn't it?* ● *Can you give me back that money I lent you last week?* **3** /ðət; *strong form* ðæt/ (used for introducing a relative clause) the person or thing already mentioned: *I'm reading the book that won the Booker prize.* ● *The people that live next door are French.*

➤ When **that** is the object of the verb in the relative clause, it is often left out: *I want to see the doctor (that) I saw last week.* ● *I wore the dress (that) I bought in Paris.*

4 /ðət; *strong form* ðæt/ used after certain verbs, nouns and adjectives to introduce a new part of the sentence: *She told me that she was leaving.* ● *I hope that you feel better soon.* ● *I'm certain that he will come.* ● *It's funny that you should say that.*

➤ **That** is often left out in this type of sentence: *I thought you would like it.*

5 (used with adjectives, adverbs) as much as that: *30 miles? I can't walk that far.*

IDIOMS **that is (to say)** used when you are giving more information about sb/sth: *I'm on holiday next week. That's to say, from Tuesday.*

that's that there is nothing more to say or do: *I'm not going and that's that.*

thatched /θætʃt/ **adj** (used about a building) having a roof made of dried grass (straw)

thaw /θɔː/ **verb** [I,T] **thaw (sth) (out)** to become or to make sth become soft or liquid again after freezing: *Is the snow thawing?* ● *Always thaw chicken thoroughly before you cook it.* ●➤ Look at **melt**. –**thaw** noun [C, usually sing]

★**the** /ðə; ði; *strong form* ðiː/ **definite article 1** used for talking about a person or thing that is already known or that has already been mentioned: *I took the children to the dentist.* ● *We met the man who bought your house.* ● *The milk is in the fridge.* **2** used when there is only one of sth: *The sun is very strong today.* ● *Who won the World Cup?* ● *the government* **3** used with numbers and dates: *This is the third time I've seen this film.* ● *Friday the thirteenth* ● *I grew up in the sixties.* **4** used with adjectives to name a group of people: *the French* ● *the poor* **5** (*formal*) used with a singular noun when you are talking generally about sth: *The dolphin is an intelligent animal.* **6** with units of

measurement, meaning 'every': *Our car does forty miles to the gallon.* **7** with musical instruments: *Do you play the piano?* **8** the well-known or important one: *'My best friend at school was Tony Blair.' 'You mean the Tony Blair?'*

➤ 'The' is pronounced /ðiː/ in this sense.

9 the...the... used for saying that the way in which two things change is connected: *The more you eat, the fatter you get.*

➤ For more information about articles, look at the **Quick Grammar Reference** section at the back of this dictionary.

★**theatre** /ˈθɪətə/ (*US* **theater**) noun **1** [C] a building where you go to see plays, shows, etc: *How often do you go to the theatre?* **2** [U] plays in general; drama: *He's studying modern Russian theatre.* **3** [sing,U] the work of acting in or producing plays: *He's worked in (the) theatre for thirty years.* **4** [U] = OPERATING THEATRE

theatrical /θiˈætrɪkl/ **adj 1** (only *before* a noun) connected with the theatre **2** (used about behaviour) dramatic and exaggerated because you want people to notice it

theft /θeft/ **noun** [C,U] the crime of stealing sth: *There have been a lot of thefts in this area recently.* ● *The woman was arrested for theft.* ●➤ Look at the note at **thief**.

★**their** /ðeə/ **determiner 1** of or belonging to them: *The children picked up their books and walked to the door.* **2** (*informal*) used instead of *his* or *her*: *Has everyone got their book?*

★**theirs** /ðeəz/ **pron** of or belonging to them: *Our flat isn't as big as theirs.*

★**them** /ðəm; *strong form* ðem/ **pron** (the object of a verb or preposition) **1** the people or things mentioned earlier: *I'll phone them now.* ● *'I've got the keys here.' 'Oh good. Give them to me.'* ● *We have students from several countries but most of them are Italian.* ● *They asked for your address so I gave it to them.*

➤ 'Them' is sometimes written **'em** to represent the way that it is said in informal speech.

2 (*informal*) him or her: *If anyone phones, tell them I'm busy.*

theme /θiːm/ **noun** [C] the subject of a talk, a piece of writing or a work of art: *The theme of today's discussion will be 'Our changing cities'.*

'**theme park** noun [C] a park with a lot of things to do, see, ride on, etc, which are all based on a single idea

★**themselves** /ðəmˈselvz/ **pron 1** used when the people or things who do an action are also affected by it: *Helen and Sarah seem to be enjoying themselves.* ● *People often talk to themselves when they are worried.* **2** used to emphasize 'they': *They themselves say that the situation cannot continue.* ● *Did they paint the house themselves?* (= or did sb else do it for them?)

IDIOM **(all) by themselves 1** alone: *The boys*

are too young to go out by themselves. •➤ Look at the note at **alone**. **2** without help: *The children cooked the dinner all by themselves.*

★**then** /ðen/ *adv* **1** (at) that time: *In 1990? I was at university then.* • *I spoke to him on Wednesday, but I haven't seen him since then.* • *They met in 1941 and remained close friends from then on.* • *I'm going tomorrow. Can you wait until then?* • *Phone me tomorrow – I will have decided by then.* **2** next; after that: *I'll have a shower and get changed, then we'll go out.* • *There was silence for a minute. Then he replied.* **3** used to show the logical result of a statement or situation: 'I don't feel at all well.' 'Why don't you go to the doctor then?' • *If you don't do any work then you'll fail the exam.* **4** (*spoken*) (used after words like *now, okay, right,* etc to show the beginning or end of a conversation or statement): *Now then, are we all ready to go?* • *Right then, I'll see you tomorrow.*

IDIOMS **then/there again → AGAIN**
there and then; then and there →THERE

thence /ðens/ *adv* (*old-fashioned*) from there

theology /θiˈɒlədʒi/ *noun* [U] the study of religion –**theological** /ˌθiːəˈlɒdʒɪkl/ *adj*

theoretical /ˌθɪəˈretɪkl/ *adj* **1** based on ideas and principles, not on practical experience: *A lot of university courses are still too theoretical these days.* **2** that may possibly exist or happen, although it is unlikely: *There is a theoretical possibility that the world will end tomorrow.* •➤ Look at **practical**. –**theoretically** /-kli/ *adv*

★**theory** /ˈθɪəri/ *noun* (*pl* **theories**) **1** [C] an idea or set of ideas that try to explain sth: *the theory about how life on earth began* **2** [U] the general idea or principles of a particular subject: *political theory* • *the theory and practice of language teaching* **3** [C] an opinion or a belief that has not been shown to be true
IDIOM **in theory** as a general idea which may not be true in reality: *Your plan sounds fine in theory, but I don't know if it'll work in practice.*

therapeutic /ˌθerəˈpjuːtɪk/ *adj* **1** helping you to relax and feel better: *I find listening to music very therapeutic.* **2** helping to cure an illness: *therapeutic drugs*

therapy /ˈθerəpi/ *noun* [U] treatment to help or cure a mental or physical illness, usually without drugs or medical operations: *to have/undergo therapy* –**therapist** /ˈθerəpɪst/ *noun* [C]: *a speech therapist*

★**there** /ðeə/ *adv, pron* **1** used as the subject of 'be', 'seem', 'appear', etc to say that sth exists: *Is there a god?* • *There's a man at the door.* • *There wasn't much to eat.* • *There's somebody singing outside me* • *There seems to be a mistake here.* **2** in, at or to that place: *Could you put the table there, please?* • *I like Milan. My husband and I met there.* • *Have you been to Bonn? We're going there next week.* • *Have you looked under there?* **3** used for calling attention to sth: *Oh look, there's Kate!* • *Hello there! Can anyone hear me?* **4** at that point (in

a conversation, story, etc): *Could I interrupt you there for a minute?* **5** available if needed: *Her parents are always there if she needs help.*
IDIOMS **be there for sb** to be available to help and support sb when he/she has a problem: *Whenever I'm in trouble, my sister is always there for me.*
then/there again → AGAIN
there and then; then and there immediately; at that time and place
there you are 1 used when you give sth to sb: *There you are. I've bought you a newspaper.* **2** used when you are explaining sth to sb: *Just press the switch and there you are!*

thereabouts /ˌðeərəˈbaʊts/ (*US* **thereabout** /ˌðeərəˈbaʊt/) *adv* (usually *after or*) somewhere near a number, time or place: *There are 100 students, or thereabouts.* • *She lives in Sydney, or thereabouts.*

thereafter /ˌðeərˈɑːftə/ *adv* (*written*) after that

thereby /ˌðeəˈbaɪ/ *adv* (*written*) in that way

therefore /ˈðeəfɔː/ *adv* for that reason: *The new trains have more powerful engines and are therefore faster.* •➤ synonym **thus**

therein /ˌðeərˈɪn/ *adv* (*written*) because of sth that has just been mentioned

thereupon /ˌðeərəˈpɒn/ *adv* (*written*) immediately after that and often as the result of sth

thermal¹ /ˈθɜːml/ *adj* **1** connected with heat: *thermal energy* **2** (used about clothes) made to keep you warm in cold weather: *thermal underwear*

thermal² /ˈθɜːml/ *noun* **1 thermals** [pl] clothes, especially underwear, made to keep you warm in cold weather **2** [C] a flow of rising warm air

★**thermometer** /θəˈmɒmɪtə/ *noun* [C] an instrument for measuring the temperature of sb's body or of a room

Thermos™ /ˈθɜːməs/ (also **'Thermos flask**) *noun* [C] a type of container used for keeping a liquid hot or cold

thermostat /ˈθɜːməstæt/ *noun* [C] a device that controls the temperature in a house or machine by switching the heat on and off as necessary

thesaurus /θɪˈsɔːrəs/ *noun* [C] (*pl* **thesauruses**) a book that contains lists of words and phrases with similar meanings

these → THIS

thesis /ˈθiːsɪs/ *noun* [C] (*pl* **theses** /ˈθiːsiːz/) **1** a long piece of writing on a particular subject that you do as part of a university degree: *He did his thesis on Japanese investment in Europe.* •➤ Look at **dissertation**. **2** an idea that is discussed and presented with evidence in order to show that it is true

★**they** /ðeɪ/ *pron* (the subject of a verb) **1** the people or things that have been mentioned: *We've got two children. They're both boys.* • *'Have you seen my keys?' 'Yes, they're on the table.'* **2** people in general or people whose identity is not known or stated: *They say it's going to be a mild winter.* **3** (*informal*) used instead of *he* or *she*: *Somebody phoned for you but they didn't leave their name.*

they'd /ðeɪd/ *short for* THEY HAD, THEY WOULD

they'll /ðeɪl/ *short for* THEY WILL

they're /ðeə/ *short for* THEY ARE

they've /ðeɪv/ *short for* THEY HAVE

★**thick¹** /θɪk/ **adj 1** (used about sth solid) having a large distance between its opposite sides; not thin: *a thick black line* ● *a thick coat/book* ● *These walls are very thick.* **2** used for saying what the distance is between the two opposite sides of something: *The ice was six centimetres thick.* **3** having a lot of things close together: *a thick forest* ● *thick hair* **4** (used about a liquid) that does not flow easily: *thick cream* ● *This paint is too thick.* ••➤ opposite for senses 1 to 4 thin **5** (used about fog, smoke, etc) difficult to see through: *There'll be a thick fog tonight.* ● *thick clouds of smoke* **6** thick (with sth) containing a lot of sth/smb close together: *The air was thick with dust.* ● *The streets were thick with shoppers.* **7** (used about sb's accent) very strong **8** (*informal*) slow to learn or understand; stupid –**thick adv**: *Snow lay thick on the ground.* –**thickly adv**: *Spread the butter thickly.* ● *a thickly wooded area*

IDIOM **have a thick skin** to be not easily upset or worried by what people say about you

thick² /θɪk/ **noun**

IDIOMS **in the thick of sth** in the most active or crowded part of sth; very involved in sth **through thick and thin** through difficult times and situations

thicken /ˈθɪkən/ **verb** [I,T] to become or to make sth thicker

thickness /ˈθɪknəs/ **noun** [C,U] the quality of being thick or how thick sth is

thick-'skinned adj not easily worried or upset by what other people say about you: *Politicians have to be thick-skinned.*

★**thief** /θiːf/ **noun** [C] (*pl* **thieves** /θiːvz/) a person who steals things from another person

➤ A **thief** is a general word for a person who steals things, usually secretly and without violence. The name of the crime is **theft**. A **robber** steals from a bank, shop, etc and often uses violence or threats. A **burglar** steals things by breaking into a house, shop, etc, often at night, and a **shoplifter** goes into a shop when it is open and takes things without paying. A **mugger** steals from sb in the street and uses violence or threats. Look also at the note at **steal**.

thigh /θaɪ/ **noun** [C] the top part of your leg, above your knee ••➤ picture on page C5

thimble /ˈθɪmbl/ **noun** [C] a small metal or plastic object that you wear on the end of your finger to protect it when you are sewing

★**thin¹** /θɪn/ **adj** (**thinner**; **thinnest**) **1** (used about sth solid) having a small distance between the opposite sides; not thick: *a thin book/shirt* ● *a thin slice of meat* **2** having

very little fat on the body; not fat: *You need to eat more. You're too thin!*

➤ **Thin**, **skinny**, **slim** and **underweight** all have a similar meaning. **Thin** is the most general word for describing people who have very little flesh on their bodies. **Slim** is used to describe people who are thin in an attractive way: *You're so slim! How do you do it?* If you say sb is **skinny**, you mean that he/she is too thin and not attractive. **Underweight** is a much more formal word, and is often used for describing people who are too thin in a medical sense: *The doctor says I'm underweight.*

3 (used about a liquid) that flows easily; not thick: *a thin sauce* **4** (used about mist, smoke, etc) not difficult to see through **5** having only a few people or things with a lot of space between them: *The population is rather thin in this part of the country.* ••➤ opposite for senses 1, 3 and 4 thick –**thin adv**: *Don't slice the onion too thin.* –**thinly adv**: *thinly sliced bread* ● *thinly populated areas*

IDIOMS **thin on the ground** ➤ GROUND¹ **through thick and thin** ➤ THICK² **vanish, etc into thin air** to disappear completely **wear thin** ➤ WEAR¹

★**thin²** /θɪn/ **verb** [I,T] (**thinning**; **thinned**) **thin (sth) (out)** to become thinner or fewer in number; to make sth thinner: *The trees thin out towards the edge of the forest.* ● *Thin the sauce by adding milk.*

★**thing** /θɪŋ/ **noun 1** [C] an object that is not named: *What's that red thing on the table?* ● *A pen is a thing you use for writing with.* ● *I need to get a few things at the shops.* **2** [C] a quality or state: *There's no such thing as a ghost* (= it doesn't exist). ● *The best thing about my job is the way it changes all the time.* **3** [C] an action, event or statement: *When I get home the first thing I do is have a cup of tea.* ● *A strange thing happened to me yesterday.* ● *What a nice thing to say!* **4** [C] a fact, subject, etc: *He told me a few things that I didn't know before.* **5 things** [pl] clothes or tools that belong to sb or are used for a particular purpose: *I'll just go and pack my things.* ● *We keep all the cooking things in this cupboard.* **6 things** [pl] the situation or conditions of your life: *How are things with you?* **7** [C] used for expressing how you feel about a person or an animal: *You've broken your finger? You poor thing!* **8 the thing** [sing] exactly what is wanted or needed: *That's just the thing I was looking for!*

IDIOMS **a close shave/thing** ➤ CLOSE³ **be a good thing (that)** to be lucky that: *It's a good thing you remembered your umbrella.* **do your own thing** to do what you want to do, independently of other people **first/last thing** as early/late as possible: *I'll telephone her first thing tomorrow morning.* ● *I saw him last thing on Friday evening.* **for one thing** used for introducing a reason for something: *I think we should go by train. For one thing it's cheaper.*

have a thing about sb/sth (*informal*) to have strong feelings about sb/sth

to make matters/things worse → WORSE

take it/things easy → EASY²

★**think** /θɪŋk/ **verb** (*pt, pp* **thought** /θɔːt/)
1 [I,T] think (sth) (of/about sb/sth); think that... to have a particular idea or opinion about sth/sb; to believe: *'Do you think (that) we'll win?' 'No, I **don't think** so.'* ● *'Sue's coming tomorrow, isn't she?' 'Yes, I **think** so.'* ● *I think (that) they've moved to York but I'm not sure.* ● *What did you think of the film?* ● *What do you think about going out tonight?* ● *Gary's on holiday, I think.* **2** [I] **think (about sth)** to use your mind to consider sth or to form connected ideas: *Think before you speak.* ● *What are you thinking about?* ● *He had to think hard* (= a lot) *about the question.* **3** [I] **think of/about doing sth; think that...** to intend or plan to do sth: *We're thinking of moving house.* ● *I think I'll go for a swim.* **4** [I] to form an idea of sth; to imagine sth: *Just think what we could do with all that money!* **5** [I] **think about/of sb** to consider the feelings of sb else: *She never thinks about anyone but herself.* **6** [T] to remember sth; to have sth come into your mind: *Can you think where you left the keys?* ● *I didn't think to ask him his name.* **7** [T] to expect sth: *The job took longer than we thought.* **8** [I] to think in a particular way: *If you want to be successful, you have to **think big**.* ● *We've got to **think positive**.* –**think noun:** [sing] *I'm not sure. I'll have to **have a think** about it.*

IDIOMS **think better of (doing) sth** to decide not to do sth; to change your mind

think highly, a lot, not much, etc of sb/sth to have a good, bad, etc opinion of sb/sth: *I didn't think much of that film.*

think the world of sb to love and admire sb very much

PHRASAL VERBS **think of sth** to create an idea in your imagination: *Who first thought of the plan?*

think sth out to consider carefully all the details of a plan, idea, etc: *a well-thought-out scheme*

think sth over to consider sth carefully: *I'll think your offer over and let you know tomorrow.*

think sth through to consider every detail of sth carefully: *He made a bad decision because he didn't think it through.*

think sth up to create sth in your mind; to invent: *to think up a new advertising slogan*

thinker /'θɪŋkə/ **noun** [C] **1** a person who thinks about serious and important subjects **2** a person who thinks in a particular way: *a quick/creative/clear thinker*

thinking¹ /'θɪŋkɪŋ/ **noun** [U] **1** using your mind to think about sth: *We're going to have to do some quick thinking.* **2** ideas or opinions about sth: *This accident will make them change their thinking on safety matters.* ●➤ Look at **wishful thinking**.

thinking² /'θɪŋkɪŋ/ **adj** intelligent and using your mind to think about important subjects

★**third¹** /θɜːd/ **pron, determiner, adv** 3rd ●➤ Look at the examples at **sixth**.

third² /θɜːd/ **noun** [C] **1** the fraction ⅓; one of three equal parts of sth **2** (*Brit*) a result in final university exams, below first and second class degrees

thirdly /'θɜːdli/ **adv** used to introduce the third point in a list: *We have made savings in three areas: firstly, defence, secondly, education and thirdly, health.*

,third 'party **noun** [C] a person who is involved in a situation in addition to the two main people involved

the ,Third 'World noun [sing] the poorer countries of Asia, Africa and South America

thirst /θɜːst/ **noun 1** [U,sing] the feeling that you have when you want or need a drink: *Cold tea really quenches your thirst.* ● *to die of thirst* **2** [sing] **a thirst for sth** a strong desire for sth ●➤ Look at **hunger**.

★**thirsty** /'θɜːsti/ **adj** (**thirstier**; **thirstiest**) wanting or needing a drink: *I'm thirsty. Can I have a drink of water, please?* ●➤ Look at **hungry**. –**thirstily adv**

★**thirteen** /,θɜː'tiːn/ **number** 13

➤ For examples of how to use numbers in sentences, look at **six**.

thirteenth /,θɜː'tiːnθ/ **pron, determiner, adv** 13th ●➤ Look at the examples at **sixth**.

thirtieth /'θɜːtiəθ/ **pron, determiner, adv** 30th ●➤ Look at the examples at **sixth**.

★**thirty** /'θɜːti/ **number** 30

➤ For examples of how to use numbers in sentences, look at **sixty**.

★**this** /ðɪs/ **determiner, pron** (*pl* **these** /ðiːz/)
1 used for talking about sb/sth that is close to you in time or space: *Have a look at this photo.* ● *These boots are really comfortable. My old ones weren't.* ● *Is this the book you asked for?* ● *These are the letters to be filed, not those over there.* ● *This chair's softer than that one, so I'll sit here.* **2** used for talking about sth that was mentioned or talked about earlier: *Where did you hear about this?* **3** used for introducing sb or showing sb sth: *This is my wife, Claudia, and these are our children, David and Vicky.* ● *It's easier if you do it like this.* **4** (used with days of the week or periods of time) of today or the present week, year, etc: *Are you busy this afternoon?* ● *this Friday* (= the Friday of this week) **5** (*informal*) (used when you are telling a story) a certain: *Then this woman said...* –**this adv:** *The road is not usually this busy.*

IDIOM **this and that; this, that and the other** various things: *We chatted about this and that.*

thistle /'θɪsl/ **noun** [C] a wild plant with purple flowers and sharp points (**prickles**) on its leaves ●➤ picture on page C2

thong /θɒŋ/ (*US*) = FLIP-FLOP

thorn /θɔːn/ **noun** [C] one of the hard sharp points on some plants and bushes, for example on rose bushes ●➤ picture on page C2

thorny /ˈθɔːni/ *adj* **1** causing difficulty or disagreement: *a thorny problem/question* **2** having thorns

★**thorough** /ˈθʌrə/ *adj* **1** careful and complete: *The police made a thorough search of the house.* **2** doing things in a very careful way, making sure that you look at every detail: *Pam is slow but she is very thorough.* –**thoroughness** *noun* [U]

thoroughly /ˈθʌrəli/ *adv* **1** in a careful and complete way: *to study a subject thoroughly* **2** completely; very much: *We thoroughly enjoyed our holiday.*

those *plural* of **THAT**(1,2)

★**though** /ðəʊ/ *conj, adv* **1** in spite of the fact that; although: *Though he had very little money, Alex always managed to dress smartly.* ● *She still loved him even though he had treated her so badly.* **2** but: *I'll come as soon as I can, though I can't promise to be on time.* **3** (*informal*) however: *I quite like him. I don't like his wife, though.* ⸱⸱➤ Look at the note at **although**.

  IDIOMS   **as if** → **AS**
as though → **AS**

thought[1] *past tense, past participle* of **THINK**

★**thought**[2] /θɔːt/ *noun* **1** [C] an idea or opinion: *What are your thoughts on this subject?* ● *The thought of living alone filled her with fear.* ● *I've just had a thought* (= an idea). **2** [U] the power or process of thinking: *I need to give this problem some thought.* **3 thoughts** [pl] a person's mind and all the ideas that are in it: *You are always in my thoughts.* **4** [sing] a feeling of care or worry: *They sent me flowers. What a kind thought!* **5** [U] particular ideas or a particular way of thinking: *a change in medical thought on the subject*

  IDIOMS   **deep in thought/conversation** → **DEEP**[1]

a school of thought → **SCHOOL**
second thoughts → **SECOND**[1]

thoughtful /ˈθɔːtfl/ *adj* **1** thinking deeply: *a thoughtful expression* **2** thinking about what other people want or need: *It was very thoughtful of you to send her some flowers.* –**thoughtfully** /-fəli/ *adv* –**thoughtfulness** *noun* [U]

thoughtless /ˈθɔːtləs/ *adj* not thinking about what other people want or need or what the result of your actions will be ⸱⸱➤ synonym **inconsiderate** –**thoughtlessly** *adv* –**thoughtlessness** *noun* [U]

★**thousand** /ˈθaʊznd/ *number* 1000

➤ Notice that you use **thousand** in the singular when you are talking about a number. You use **thousands** when you mean 'a lot': *There were over 70 000 spectators at the match.* ● *Thousands of people attended the meeting.*
For examples of how to use numbers in sentences, look at **six**. For more information about numbers look at the special section on numbers at the back of this dictionary.

thousandth[1] /ˈθaʊznθ/ *determiner* 1000th

thousandth[2] /ˈθaʊznθ/ *noun* [C] the fraction ¹/₁₀₀₀; one of a thousand equal parts of sth

thrash (sth) /θræʃ/ *verb* **1** [T] to hit sb/sth many times with a stick, etc as a punishment **2** [I,T] **thrash (sth) (about/around)** to move or make sth move wildly without any control **3** [T] to defeat sb easily in a game, competition, etc

  PHRASAL VERB   **thrash sth out** to talk about sth with sb until you reach an agreement

thrashing /ˈθræʃɪŋ/ *noun* [C] **1** the action of hitting sb/sth many times with a stick, etc as a punishment **2** (*informal*) a bad defeat in a game

★**thread**[1] /θred/ *noun* **1** [C,U] a long thin piece of cotton, wool, etc that you use for sewing or making cloth: *a needle and thread* ⸱➤ picture at **cable 2** [C] the connection between ideas, the parts of a story, etc: *I've lost the thread of this argument.*

thread[2] /θred/ *verb* [T] **1** to put sth long and thin, especially thread, through a narrow opening or hole: *to thread a needle* ● *He threaded the belt through the loops on the trousers.* **2** to join things together by putting them onto a string, etc

  IDIOM   **thread your way through sth** to move through sth with difficulty, going around things or people that are in your way

threadbare /ˈθredbeə/ *adj* (used about material or clothes) old and very thin

★**threat** /θret/ *noun* **1** [C] a warning that sb may hurt, kill or punish you if you do not do what he/she wants: *to make threats against sb* ● *He keeps saying he'll resign, but he won't carry out his threat.* **2** [U,sing] the possibility of trouble or danger: *The forest is under threat from building developments.* **3** [C] a person or thing that may damage sth or hurt sb; something that indicates future danger

★**threaten** /ˈθretn/ *verb* **1** [T] **threaten sb (with sth); threaten (to do sth)** to warn that you may hurt, kill or punish sb if he/she does not do what you want: *The boy threatened him with a knife.* ● *She was threatened with dismissal.* ● *The man threatened to kill her if she didn't tell him where the money was.* **2** [I,T] to seem likely to do sth unpleasant: *The wind was threatening to destroy the bridge.* –**threatening** *adj* –**threateningly** *adv*

★**three** /θriː/ *number* 1 3 **2** (used to form compound adjectives) having three of the thing mentioned: *a three-legged stool* ⸱➤ Look at **third**.

➤ For examples of how to use numbers in sentences, look at **six**.

three-di·men·sion·al (also **3-D**) *adj* having length, width and height: *a three-dimensional model*

threshold /ˈθreʃhəʊld/ *noun* [C] **1** the ground at the entrance to a room or building **2** the level at which sth starts to happen: *Young children have a low boredom threshold.* **3** the time when you are just about to start sth or find sth: *We could be on the threshold of a scientific breakthrough.*

[C] **countable**, a noun with a plural form: *one book, two books*   [U] **uncountable**, a noun with no plural form: *some sugar*

threw *past tense of* **THROW**

thrift /θrɪft/ **noun** [U] the quality of being careful not to spend too much money –**thrifty adj**

thrill /θrɪl/ **noun** [C] a sudden strong feeling of pleasure or excitement –**thrill verb** [T]: *His singing thrilled the audience.* –**thrilled adj**: *He was absolutely thrilled with my present.* –**thrilling adj**

thriller /ˈθrɪlə/ **noun** [C] a play, film, book, etc with a very exciting story, often about a crime

thrive /θraɪv/ **verb** [I] (*pt* **thrived** or **throve** /θrəʊv/; *pp* **thrived**) to grow or develop well –**thriving adj**: *a thriving industry*

★**throat** /θrəʊt/ **noun** [C] **1** the front part of your neck: *The attacker grabbed the man by the throat.* •➤ picture on page C5 **2** the back part of your mouth and the passage down your neck through which air and food pass: *She got a piece of bread stuck in her throat.* • *I've got a sore throat.* •➤ picture on page C5
IDIOMS **clear your throat** → **CLEAR³**
have/feel a lump in your throat → **LUMP¹**

throb /θrɒb/ **verb** [I] (**throbbing**; **throbbed**) to make strong regular movements or noises; to beat strongly: *Her finger throbbed with pain.* –**throb noun** [C]

throne /θrəʊn/ **noun 1** [C] the special chair where a king or queen sits **2 the throne** [sing] the position of being king or queen

throng¹ /θrɒŋ/ **noun** [C] (*written*) a large crowd of people

throng² /θrɒŋ/ **verb** [I,T] (*written*) (used about a crowd of people) to move into or fill a particular place

throttle¹ /ˈθrɒtl/ **verb** [T] to hold sb tightly by the throat and stop him/her breathing •➤ synonym **strangle**

throttle² /ˈθrɒtl/ **noun** [C] the part in a vehicle that controls the speed by controlling how much fuel goes into the engine

★**through** /θruː/ **prep, adv 1** from one end or side of sth to the other: *We drove through the centre of London.* • *to look through a telescope* • *She cut through the rope.* • *to push through a crowd of people* **2** from the beginning to the end of sth: *Food supplies will not last through the winter.* • *We're halfway through the book.* • *He read the letter through and handed it back.* **3** past a limit, stage or test: *He lifted the rope to let us through.* • *She didn't get through the first interview.* **4** because of; with the help of: *Errors were made through bad organization.* • *David got the job through his uncle.* **5** (also **thru**) (*US*) until, and including: *They are staying Monday through Friday.* **6** (*Brit*) connected by telephone: *Can you put me through to extension 5678, please?*
PHRASAL VERB **be through (with sb/sth)** to have finished with sb/sth

throughout /θruːˈaʊt/ **adv, prep 1** in every part of sth: *The house is beautifully decorated throughout.* • *The match can be watched live on television throughout the world.* **2** from the beginning to the end of sth: *We didn't enjoy the holiday because it rained throughout.*

throve *past tense of* **THRIVE**

★**throw** /θrəʊ/ **verb** (*pt* **threw** /θruː/; *pp* **thrown** /θrəʊn/) **1** [I,T] throw (sth) (to/at sb); throw sb sth to send sth from your hand through the air by moving your hand or arm quickly: *How far can you throw?* • *Throw the ball to me.* • *Throw me the ball.* • *Don't throw stones at people.* **2** [T] to put sth somewhere quickly or carelessly: *He threw his bag down in a corner.* • *She threw on a sweater and ran out of the door.* **3** [T] to move your body or part of it quickly or suddenly: *Jenny threw herself onto the bed and sobbed.* • *Lee threw back his head and roared with laughter.* **4** [T] to cause sb to fall down quickly or violently: *The bus braked and we were thrown to the floor.* **5** [T] to put sb in a particular (usually unpleasant) situation: *We were thrown into confusion by the news.* **6** [T] (*informal*) to make sb feel upset, confused or surprised: *The question threw me and I didn't know what to reply.* **7** [T] to send light or shade onto sth: *The tree threw a long shadow across the lawn.* –**throw noun** [C] *It's your throw* (= it's your turn to throw the dice in a board game, etc). • *a throw of 97 metres*
PHRASAL VERBS **throw sth away 1** (also **throw sth out**) to get rid of rubbish or sth that you do not want: *I threw his letters away.* **2** to waste or not use sth useful: *to throw away a good opportunity*
throw sth in (*informal*) to include sth extra without increasing the price
throw sb out to force sb to leave a place
throw sth out 1 to decide not to accept sb's idea or suggestion **2** = **THROW STH AWAY**(1)
throw up (*informal*) to vomit; to be sick
throw sth up 1 to vomit food **2** to produce or show sth **3** to leave your job, career, studies, etc

thru (*US*) = **THROUGH**(5)

thrust¹ /θrʌst/ **verb** [I,T] (*pt, pp* **thrust**) **1** to push sb/sth suddenly or violently; to move quickly and suddenly in a particular direction: *The man thrust his hands deeper into his pockets.* • *She thrust past him and ran out of the room.* **2** to make a sudden forward movement with a knife, etc
PHRASAL VERB **thrust sb/sth upon sb** to force sb to accept or deal with sb/sth

thrust² /θrʌst/ **noun 1 the thrust** [sing] the main part or point of an argument, policy, etc **2** [C] a sudden strong movement forward

thud /θʌd/ **noun** [C] the low sound that is made when a heavy object hits sth else: *Her head hit the floor with a dull thud.* –**thud verb** [I] (**thudding**; **thudded**)

thug /θʌg/ **noun** [C] a violent person who may harm other people

★**thumb¹** /θʌm/ **noun** [C] **1** the short thick finger at the side of each hand •➤ picture on page C5 **2** the part of a glove, etc that covers your thumb(1)
IDIOMS **a rule of thumb** → **RULE¹**
stand/stick out like a sore thumb → **SORE¹**
the thumbs up/down a sign or an expression that shows approval/disapproval

t

[I] **intransitive**, a verb which has no object: *He laughed.*   [T] **transitive**, a verb which has an object: *He ate an apple.*

under sb's thumb (used about a person) completely controlled by sb: *She's got him under her thumb.*

thumb² /θʌm/ **verb** [I,T] **thumb (through) sth** to turn the pages of a book, etc quickly

  IDIOM **thumb a lift** to hold out your thumb to cars going past, to ask sb to give you a free ride •➤ Look at the note at **hitchhike**.

thumbtack /'θʌmtæk/ (*US*) = **DRAWING PIN**

thump /θʌmp/ **verb 1** [T] to hit sb/sth hard with sth, usually your closed hand (**fist**): *He started coughing and Jo thumped him on the back.* **2** [I,T] to make a loud sound by hitting sth or by beating hard: *His heart was thumping with excitement.* –**thump noun** [C]

thunder¹ /'θʌndə/ **noun** [U] the loud noise in the sky that you can hear when there is a storm: *a clap/crash/roll of thunder*

> ➤ Thunder can usually be heard after a flash of **lightning**.

thunder² /'θʌndə/ **verb** [I] **1** (used with *it*) to make a loud noise in the sky during a storm: *The rain poured down and it started to thunder.* **2** to make a loud deep noise like thunder: *Traffic thundered across the bridge.*

thunderstorm /'θʌndəstɔːm/ **noun** [C] a storm with loud noises and flashes of light in the sky (**thunder** and **lightning**)

Thur (also **Thurs**) **abbr** Thursday: *Thurs 26 June*

★**Thursday** /'θɜːzdeɪ, -di/ **noun** [C,U] (*abbr* **Thur, Thurs**) the day of the week after Wednesday

> ➤ Days of the week are always written with a capital letter. For examples of how to use the days of the week, look at **Monday**.

★**thus** /ðʌs/ **adv** (*formal*) **1** like this; in this way: *Thus began the series of incidents which changed her life.* **2** because of or as a result of this •➤ synonym **therefore**

thwart /θwɔːt/ **verb** [T] **thwart sth; thwart sb (in sth)** to stop sb doing what he/she planned to do; to prevent sth happening: *to thwart sb's plans/ambitions/efforts* • *She was thwarted in her attempt to gain control.*

thyme /taɪm/ **noun** [U] a plant that is used in cooking (**a herb**) and has small leaves and a sweet smell

tic /tɪk/ **noun** [C] a sudden quick movement of a muscle, especially in your face or head, that you cannot control: *He has a nervous tic.*

tick¹ /tɪk/ **verb 1** [I] (used about a clock or watch) to make regular short sounds **2** (*US* **check**) [T] to put a mark (✓) next to a name, an item on a list, etc to show that sth has been dealt with or chosen: *Please tick the appropriate box.*

> ➤ In British English you tick an answer, a piece of writing, etc that is **correct** and a put a cross (✗) next to sth that is wrong. In US English, you tick (check) sth to show that sth is **wrong**.

  IDIOM **what makes sb/sth tick** the reasons why sb behaves or sth works in the way he/she/it does: *He has a strong interest in people and what makes them tick.*

  PHRASAL VERBS **tick away/by** (used about time) to pass

tick sb/sth off to put a mark (✓) next to a name an item on a list, etc to show that sth has been done or sb has been dealt with

tick over (*informal*) (usually in the continuous tenses) **1** (used about an engine) to run slowly while the vehicle is not moving **2** to keep working slowly without producing or achieving very much

tick² /tɪk/ **noun** [C] **1** (*US* **check mark**; **check**) a mark (✓) next to an item on a list that shows that sth has been done or next to an answer to show that it is either correct or wrong: *Put a tick after each correct answer.*

tick (*US* check mark)

> ➤ In US English a check mark next to an answer in a piece of writing, etc shows that sth is **wrong**. In British English it shows that sth is **correct** and a cross (✗) is used to indicate a mistake.

2 (also **ticking**) the regular short sound that a watch or clock makes when it is working **3** (*Brit informal*) a moment

★**ticket** /'tɪkɪt/ **noun** [C] **1** **a ticket (for/to sth)** a piece of paper or card that shows you have paid for a journey, or allows you to enter a theatre, cinema, etc: *two tickets for the Cup Final* • *a single/return ticket to London* • *a ticket office/machine/collector* •➤ Look at **season ticket**. **2** a piece of paper or a label in a shop that shows the price, size, etc of sth that is for sale •➤ picture at **label 3** an official piece of paper that you get when you have parked illegally or driven too fast telling you that you must pay money as a punishment (a fine): *a parking ticket*

  IDIOM **just the job/ticket → JOB**

tickle /'tɪkl/ **verb 1** [T] to touch sb lightly with your fingers or with sth soft so that he/she laughs: *She tickled the baby's toes.* **2** [I,T] to produce or to have an uncomfortable feeling in a part of your body: *My nose tickles/is tickling.* • *The woollen scarf tickled her neck.* **3** [T] (*informal*) to amuse and interest sb: *That joke really tickled me.* –**tickle noun** [C]

ticklish /'tɪklɪʃ/ **adj** if a person is ticklish, he/she laughs when sb touches him/her in a sensitive place: *Are you ticklish?*

tidal /'taɪdl/ **adj** connected with the regular rise and fall of the sea (**tides**)

tidal wave **noun** [C] a very large wave in the sea which destroys things when it reaches the land, and is often caused by movements under the surface of the earth (an **earthquake**)

tide¹ /taɪd/ **noun** [C] **1** the regular change in the level of the sea caused by the moon and the sun. At *high tide* the sea is closer to the land, at *low tide* it is farther away and more of the beach can be seen: *The tide is coming in/going out.* ·➤ Look at **ebb**. **2** [usually sing] the way that most people think or feel about sth at a particular time: *It appears that the tide has turned in the government's favour.*

tide² /taɪd/ *verb*

PHRASAL VERB **tide sb over** to give sb sth to help him/her through a difficult time

★**tidy¹** /'taɪdi/ *adj* (**tidier**; **tidiest**) **1** (*especially Brit*) arranged with everything in good order; neat: *If you keep your room tidy it is easier to find things.* **2** (used about a person) liking to keep things in good order; neat: *Mark is a very tidy boy.* ·➤ opposite **untidy** –**tidily** *adv* –**tidiness** *noun* [U]

★**tidy²** /'taɪdi/ *verb* [I,T] (*pres part* **tidying**; *3rd pers sing pres* **tidies**; *pt, pp* **tidied**) tidy (sb/sth/yourself) (up) to make sb/sth/yourself look in order and well arranged: *We must tidy this room up before the visitors arrive.*

PHRASAL VERB **tidy sth away** to put sth into the drawer, cupboard, etc where it is kept so that it cannot be seen

★**tie¹** /taɪ/ *noun* [C] **1** (*US also* **necktie**) a long thin piece of cloth worn round the neck, especially by men, with a knot at the front. A tie is usually worn with a shirt: *a striped silk tie* ·➤ Look at **bow tie**. ·➤ picture on page C6 **2** [usually pl] a strong connection between people or organizations: *personal/emotional ties* ● *family ties* **3** something that limits your freedom **4** a situation in a game or competition in which two or more teams or players get the same score: *There was a tie for first place.*

★**tie²** /taɪ/ *verb* (*pres part* **tying**; *3rd pers sing pres* **ties**; *pt, pp* **tied**) **1** [T] to fasten sb/sth or fix sb/sth in position with rope, string, etc; to make a knot in sth: *The prisoner was tied to a chair.* ● *Kay tied her hair back with a ribbon.* ● *to tie sth in a knot* ● *to tie your shoelaces* ·➤ opposite **untie 2** [T] tie sb (to sth/to doing sth) (usually passive) to limit sb's freedom and make him/her unable to do everything he/she wants to: *I don't want to be tied to staying in this country permanently.* **3** [I] tie (with sb) (for sth) to have the same number of points as another player or team at the end of a game or competition: *England tied with Italy for third place.*

IDIOM **your hands are tied** → **HAND¹**

PHRASAL VERBS **tie sb/yourself down** to limit sb's/your freedom: *Having young children really ties you down.*

tie in (with sth) to agree with other facts or information that you have; to match: *The new evidence seems to tie in with your theory.*

tie sb/sth up 1 to fix sb/sth in position with rope, string, etc: *The dog was tied up in the back garden.* **2** (usually passive) to keep sb busy: *Mr Jones is tied up in a meeting.*

tier /tɪə/ *noun* [C] one of a number of levels

tiger /'taɪgə/ *noun* [C] a large wild cat that has yellow fur with black lines (**stripes**). Tigers live in parts of Asia.

➤ A female tiger is called a **tigress** and a baby is called a **cub**.

·➤ picture at **lion**

★**tight** /taɪt/ *adj, adv* **1** fixed firmly in position and difficult to move or unfasten: *a tight knot*
● *Keep a **tight grip/hold** on this rope.*
● *Hold tight so that you don't fall off.*

➤ **Tightly**, not **tight**, is used before a past participle: *The van was packed tight with boxes.* ● *The van was tightly packed with boxes.*

2 (used about clothes) fitting very closely in a way that is often uncomfortable: *These shoes hurt. They're too tight.* ● *a tight-fitting skirt* ·➤ opposite **loose 3** controlled very strictly and firmly: *Security is very tight at the airport.* **4** stretched or pulled hard so that it cannot be stretched further: *The rope was stretched tight.* **5** not having much free time or space: *My schedule this week is very tight.* **6** -tight (used to form compound adjectives) not allowing sth to get in or out: *an airtight/watertight container* –**tightly** *adv*: *Screw the lid on tightly.* ● *She kept her eyes tightly closed.* –**tightness** *noun* [U]

tighten /'taɪtn/ *verb* [I,T] tighten (sth) (up) to become or to make sth tight or tighter: *His grip on her arm tightened.* ● *He tightened the screws as far as they would go.*

IDIOM **tighten your belt** to spend less money because you have less than usual available

PHRASAL VERB **tighten up (on) sth** to cause sth to become stricter: *to tighten up security/a law*

tightrope /'taɪtrəʊp/ *noun* [C] a rope or wire that is stretched high above the ground on which people walk, especially as a form of entertainment

tights /taɪts/ (*US* **pantyhose**) *noun* [pl] a piece of thin clothing, usually worn by women, that fits tightly from the waist over the legs and feet: *a pair of tights* ·➤ Look at **stocking**. ·➤ picture on page C6

★**tile** /taɪl/ *noun* [C] one of the flat, square objects that are arranged in rows to cover roofs, floors, bathroom walls, etc ·➤ picture on page C7 –**tile** *verb* [T]: *a tiled bathroom*

till¹ /tɪl/ (*informal*) = **UNTIL**

till² /tɪl/ (*also* '**cash register**) *noun* [C] the machine or drawer where money is kept in a shop, etc: *Please pay at the till.*

tilt /tɪlt/ *verb* [I,T] to move, or make sth move, into a position with one end or side higher than the other: *The front seats of the car tilt forward.* ● *She tilted her head to one side.* –**tilt** *noun* [sing]

timber /'tɪmbə/ *noun* **1** (*especially US* **lumber**) [U] wood that is going to be used for building **2** [C] a large piece of wood: *roof timbers*

★**time¹** /taɪm/ *noun* **1** [U,sing] a period of minutes, hours, days, etc: *As time passed and there was still no news, we got more worried.* ● *You're wasting time – get on with your work!* ● *I'll go by car to save time.* ● *free/spare time* ● *We haven't got time to stop now.*

● *I've been waiting **a long time**.* ● *Learning a language **takes time**.* **2** [U,C] **time (to do sth); time (for sth)** the time in hours and minutes shown on a clock; the moment when sth happens or should happen: *What's the time?/What time is it?* ● *Can you tell me the times of trains to Bristol, please?* ● *It's time to go home.* ● ***By the time** I get home, Alex will have cooked the dinner.* ● ***This time tomorrow** I'll be on the plane.* ● *It's time for lunch.* **3** [sing] a system for measuring time in a particular part of the world: *eleven o'clock local time* **4** [C] an occasion when you do sth or when sth happens: *I phoned them three times.* ● *I'll do it better **next time**.* ● ***Last time** I saw him, he looked ill.* ● ***How many times** have I told you not to touch that?* **5** [C] an event or an occasion that you experience in a certain way: ***Have a good time** tonight.* ● *We had a terrible time at the hospital.* **6** [C] a period in the past; a part of history: *In Shakespeare's times, few people could read.* ● *The 19th century was a time of great industrial change.* **7** [C,U] the number of minutes, etc, taken to complete a race or an event: *What was his time in the hundred metres?*

IDIOMS **(and) about time (too); (and) not before time** (*spoken*) used to say that sth should already have happened

ahead of your time → AHEAD

all the time/the whole time during the period that sb was doing sth or that sth was happening: *I searched everywhere for my keys and they were in the door all the time.*

at the same time → SAME

at a time on each occasion: *The lift can hold six people at a time.* ● *She ran down the stairs two at a time.*

at one time in the past; previously

at the time at a particular moment or period in the past; then: *I agreed at the time but later changed my mind.*

at times sometimes; occasionally: *At times I wish we'd never moved house.*

before your time before you were born

behind the times not modern or fashionable

bide your time → BIDE

buy time → BUY¹

for the time being just for the present; not for long

from time to time sometimes; not often

give sb a hard time → HARD¹

have a hard time doing sth → HARD¹

have no time for sb/sth to not like sb/sth: *I have no time for lazy people.*

have the time of your life to enjoy yourself very much

in the course of time → COURSE

in good time early; at the right time

in the nick of time → NICK¹

in time (for sth/to do sth) not late; with enough time to be able to do sth: *Don't worry. We'll get to the station in time for your train.*

It's about/high time (*spoken*) used to say that you think sb should do sth very soon: *It's about time you told him what's going on.*

kill time, an hour, etc → KILL¹

once upon a time → ONCE

on time not too late or too early; punctual: *The train left the station on time.*

one at a time → ONE¹

take your time to do sth without hurrying

tell the time → TELL

time after time; time and (time) again again and again; repeatedly

time² /taɪm/ **verb** [T] **1** (often passive) to arrange to do sth or arrange for sth to happen at a particular time: *Their request was badly timed* (= it came at the wrong time). ● *She timed her arrival for shortly after three.* **2** to measure how long sb/sth takes: *Try timing yourself when you write your essay.*

'**time-consuming adj** that takes or needs a lot of time

'**time lag** = LAG²

timeless /'taɪmləs/ **adj** (*formal*) that does not seem to be changed by time or affected by changes in fashion

'**time limit noun** [C] a time during which sth must be done: *We have to **set a time limit** for the work.*

timely /'taɪmli/ **adj** happening at exactly the right time

timer /'taɪmə/ **noun** [C] a person or machine that measures time: *an oven timer*

times¹ /taɪmz/ **prep** (*symbol* **×**) used when you are multiplying one figure by another: *Three times four is twelve.*

times² /taɪmz/ **noun** [pl] used for comparing things: *Tea is **three times as/more** expensive in Spain than in England.*

timetable /'taɪmteɪbl/ (*US* **schedule**) **noun** [C] a list that shows the times at which sth happens: *a bus/train/school timetable*

timid /'tɪmɪd/ **adj** easily frightened; shy and nervous –**timidity noun** [U] –**timidly adv**

timing /'taɪmɪŋ/ **noun** [U] **1** the time when sth is planned to happen: *The manager was very careful about the timing of his announcement.* **2** the skill of doing sth at exactly the right time: *The timing of her speech was perfect.*

★ **tin** /tɪn/ **noun 1** [U] (*symbol* **Sn**) a soft silver-white metal that is often mixed with other metals **2** (also **tin can**; *especially US* **can**) [C] a closed metal container in which food, paint, etc is stored and sold; the contents of one of these containers: *a tin of peas/beans/soup* ● *a tin of paint/varnish* ••➤ picture at **container** **3** [C] a metal container with a lid for keeping food in: *a biscuit/cake tin* –**tinned adj**: *tinned peaches/peas/soup*

tinfoil /'tɪnfɔɪl/ = FOIL¹

tinge /tɪndʒ/ **noun** [C,usually sing] a small amount of a colour or a feeling: *a tinge of sadness* –**tinged adj** tinged (with sth): *Her joy at leaving was tinged with regret.*

tingle /'tɪŋgl/ **verb** [I] (used about a part of the body) to feel as if a lot of small sharp points are pushing into it: *His cheeks tingled as he came in from the cold.* –**tingle noun** [usually sing]: *a tingle of excitement/anticipation/fear*

tinker /'tɪŋkə/ **verb** [I] tinker (with sth) to try

to repair or improve sth without having the proper skill or knowledge

tinkle /'tɪŋkl/ **verb** [I] to make a light high ringing sound, like that of a small bell –**tinkle noun** [C,usually sing]

'**tin-opener** (*especially US* **can-opener**) **noun** [C] a tool that you use for opening a tin of food

tinsel /'tɪnsl/ **noun** [U] long strings of shiny coloured paper, used as a decoration to hang on a Christmas tree

tint /tɪnt/ **noun** [C] a shade or a small amount of a colour: *white paint with a pinkish tint* –**tint verb** [T]: *tinted glasses ● She had her hair tinted.*

★**tiny** /'taɪni/ **adj** (**tinier; tiniest**) very small: *the baby's tiny fingers*

★**tip**[1] /tɪp/ **noun** [C] **1** the thin or pointed end of sth: *the tips of your toes/fingers ● the tip of your nose ● the southernmost tip of South America* **2** a tip (on/for sth/doing sth) a small piece of useful advice about sth practical: *useful tips on how to save money* **3** a small amount of extra money that you give to sb who serves you, for example in a restaurant: *to leave a tip for the waiter ● I gave the porter a $5 tip.* **4** (*Brit*) (also '**rubbish tip**) a place where you can take rubbish and leave it ••➤ synonym **dump** **5** (*Brit informal*) a place that is very dirty or untidy

IDIOMS (**have sth**) **on the tip of your tongue** to be sure you know sth but to be unable to remember it for the moment

the tip of the iceberg only a small part of a much larger problem

tip[2] /tɪp/ **verb** (**tipping; tipped**) **1** [I,T] tip (sth) (up) to move so that one side is higher than the other; to make sth move in this way: *When I stood up, the bench tipped up and the person on the other end fell off.* **2** [T] to make sth come out of a container by holding or lifting it at an angle: *Tip the dirty water down the drain. ● The child tipped all the toys onto the floor.* **3** [I,T] to give a waiter, etc a small amount of extra money (in addition to the normal charge) to thank him/her: *She tipped the taxi driver generously.* **4** [T] tip sb/sth (as sth/to do sth) to think or say that sb/sth is likely to do sth: *This horse is tipped to win the race. ● He is widely tipped as the next Prime Minister.*

PHRASAL VERBS **tip sb off** to give sb secret information

tip (sth) up/over to fall or turn over; to make sth do this: *An enormous wave crashed into the little boat and it tipped over.*

'**tip-off noun** [C] secret information that sb gives, for example to the police, about an illegal activity that is going to happen: *Acting on a tip-off the police raided the house.*

'**tiptoe**[1] /'tɪptəʊ/ **noun**

IDIOM **on tiptoe** standing or walking on the ends of your toes with your heels off the ground, in order not to make any noise or to reach sth high up

tiptoe[2] /'tɪptəʊ/ **verb** [I] to walk on your toes with your heels off the ground

tire[1] /'taɪə/ **verb** [I,T] to feel that you need to rest or sleep; to make sb feel like this

PHRASAL VERBS **tire of sth/sb** to become bored or not interested in sth/sb any more

tire sb/yourself out to make sb/yourself very tired; to exhaust sb/yourself: *The long walk tired us all out.*

tire[2] (*US*) = **TYRE**

★**tired** /'taɪəd/ **adj** feeling that you need to rest or sleep: *She was tired after a hard day's work. ● I was completely tired out* (= exhausted) *after all that.* –**tiredness noun** [U]

IDIOM **be tired of sb/sth/doing sth** to be bored with or annoyed by sb/sth/doing sth: *I'm tired of this game. Let's play something else. ● I'm sick and tired of listening to the same thing again and again.*

tireless /'taɪələs/ **adj** putting a lot of hard work and energy into sth over a long period of time without stopping or losing interest

tiresome /'taɪəsəm/ **adj** (*formal*) that makes you angry or bored; annoying

tiring /'taɪərɪŋ/ **adj** making you want to rest or sleep: *a tiring journey/job*

tissue /'tɪʃu:; 'tɪsju:/ **noun 1** [U,pl] the mass of cells that form the bodies of humans, animals and plants: *muscle/brain/nerve/scar tissue ● Radiation can destroy the body's tissues.* **2** [C] a thin piece of soft paper that you use to clean your nose and throw away after you have used it: *a box of tissues* **3** (also **tissue paper**) [U] thin soft paper that you use for putting around things that may break

tit /tɪt/ **noun** [C] (*slang*) a woman's breast ••➤ Some people find this word offensive.

IDIOM **tit for tat** something unpleasant that you do to sb because he/she has done sth to you

titbit /'tɪtbɪt/ (*US* **tidbit**) **noun** [C] **1** a small but very nice piece of food **2** an interesting piece of information

★**title** /'taɪtl/ **noun** [C] **1** the name of a book, play, film, picture, etc: *I know the author's name but I can't remember the title of the book.* **2** a word that shows a person's position, profession, etc: *'Lord', 'Doctor', 'Reverend', 'Mrs' and 'General' are all titles.* **3** the position of being the winner of a competition, especially a sports competition: *Sue is playing this match to defend her title* (= to remain champion).

titled /'taɪtld/ **adj** having a word, for example 'Duke', 'Lady', etc before your name that shows that your family has an important position in society

'**title-holder noun** [C] the person or team who won a sports competition the last time it took place; the current champion

'**title role noun** [C] the main character in a film, book, etc whose name is the same as the title

titter /'tɪtə/ **verb** [I] to laugh quietly, especially in an embarrassed or nervous way –**titter noun** [C]

'**T-junction noun** [C] a place where two roads join to form the shape of a T ••➤ picture at **roundabout**

t

★to /tə; *before vowels* tu:; tu; *strong form* tu:/ **prep, adv 1** in the direction of; as far as: *She's going to London.* ● *Turn to the left.* ● *Pisa is to the west of Florence.* ● *He has gone to school.* **2** used to show the end or limit of a series of things or period of time: *from Monday to Friday* ● *from beginning to end* **3** used to show the person or thing that receives sth: *Give that to me.* ● *I am very grateful to my parents.* ● *What have you done to your hair?* ● *Sorry, I didn't realize you were talking to me.* **4** (nearly) touching sth; directed towards sth: *He put his hands to his ears.* ● *They sat back to back.* ● *She made no reference to her personal problems.* **5** reaching a particular state: *The meat was cooked to perfection.* ● *His speech reduced her to tears* (= made her cry). **6** used to introduce the second part of a comparison: *I prefer theatre to opera.* **7** (used for expressing quantity) for each unit of money, measurement, etc: *How many dollars are there to the euro?* **8** (used to say what time it is) before: *It's ten to three* (= ten minutes before three o'clock). **9** used to express sb's opinion or feeling about sth: *To me, it was the wrong decision.* ● *It sounded like a good idea to me.* ● *I don't think our friendship means anything to him.* **10** used for expressing a reaction or attitude to sth: *To my surprise, I saw two strangers coming out of my house.* ● *His paintings aren't really to my taste.* **11** used with verbs to form the infinitive: *I want to go home now.* ● *Don't forget to write.* ● *I didn't know what to do.* **12** /tu:/(used about a door) in or into a closed position: *Push the door to.*
IDIOM **to and fro** backwards and forwards

toad /təʊd/ *noun* [C] a small cold-blooded animal that has a rough skin and lives both on land and in water ●➤ picture at **frog**

toadstool /'təʊdstuːl/ *noun* [C] a type of small wild plant (a **fungus**) that is usually poisonous, with a round top and a thin supporting part ●➤ Look at **mushroom** and **fungus**.

toast /təʊst/ *noun* **1** [U] a thin piece of bread that is heated on both sides to make it brown: *a piece/slice of toast* **2** [C] **a toast (to sb/sth)** an occasion at which a group of people wish sb happiness, success, etc, by drinking a glass of wine, etc at the same time: *I'd like to propose a toast to the bride and groom.* ●➤ Look at **drink**. –**toast** *verb* [T]

toaster /'təʊstə/ *noun* [C] an electrical machine for making bread turn brown by heating it on both sides

tobacco /tə'bækəʊ/ *noun* [U] the substance that people smoke in cigarettes and pipes (the dried leaves of the tobacco plant)

tobacconist /tə'bækənɪst/ *noun* **1** [C] a person who sells cigarettes, matches, etc **2** (also **the tobacconist's**) [sing] a shop where you can buy cigarettes, matches, etc

toboggan /tə'bɒgən/ *noun* [C] a type of flat board with flat pieces of metal underneath, that people use for travelling down hills on snow for fun

➤ A **toboggan** is a small **sledge**. Look also at **bobsleigh**.

★today /tə'deɪ/ *noun* [U], **adv 1** (on) this day: *Today is Monday.* ● *What shall we do today.* ● *School ends a week today* (= on this day next week). ● *Where is today's paper?* **2** (in the present age; these days: *Young people today have far more freedom.* ●➤ synonym **nowadays**

toddle /'tɒdl/ *verb* [I] **1** to walk with short steps like a very young child **2** (*informal*) to walk or go somewhere

toddler /'tɒdlə/ *noun* [C] a young child who has only just learnt to walk

★toe¹ /təʊ/ *noun* [C] **1** one of the small parts like fingers at the end of each foot ●➤ picture on pages C1 and C5 **2** the part of a sock, shoe, etc that covers your toes

toe² /təʊ/ *verb* (*pres part* **toeing**; *pt, pp* **toed**)
IDIOM **toe the (party) line** to do what sb in authority tells you to do, even if you do not agree with him/her

TOEFL /'təʊfl/ *abbr* Test of English as a Foreign Language; the examination for foreign students who want to study at an American university

toenail /'təʊneɪl/ *noun* [C] one of the hard flat parts that cover the end of your toes ●➤ picture on page C5

toffee /'tɒfi/ *noun* [C,U] a hard sticky sweet that is made by cooking sugar and butter together

★together¹ /tə'geðə/ *adv* **1** with or near each other: *Can we have lunch together?* ● *They walked home together.* ● *I'll get all my things together tonight because I want to leave early.* ● *Stand with your feet together.* **2** so that two or more things are mixed or joined to each other: *Mix the butter and sugar together.* ● *Tie the two ends together.* ● *Add these numbers together to find the total.* **3** at the same time: *Don't all talk together.*
IDIOMS **get your act together →** **ACT²**
together with in addition to; as well as: *I enclose my order together with a cheque for £15.*

together² /tə'geðə/ *adj* (*informal*) (used about a person) organized, capable: *I'm not very together this morning.*

togetherness /tə'geðənəs/ *noun* [U] a feeling of friendship

toil /tɔɪl/ *verb* [I] (*formal*) to work very hard or for a long time at sth –**toil** *noun* [U]

★toilet /'tɔɪlət/ *noun* [C] a large bowl with a seat, connected to a water pipe, that you use when you need to get rid of waste material from your body; the room containing this: *I need to go to the toilet* (= use the toilet).

➤ In their houses, people usually refer to the **toilet** or, informally, the **loo**. **Lavatory** and **WC** are formal and old-fashioned words. In public places the toilets are called the **Ladies** or the **Gents**. In US English people talk about the **bathroom** in their houses and the **restroom**, **ladies' room** or **men's room** in public places.

[C] **countable**, a noun with a plural form: *one book, two books*   [U] **uncountable**, a noun with no plural form: *some sugar*

•➤ picture on page C7

'toilet bag (also **sponge bag**) *noun* [C] a bag that you use when travelling to carry things such as soap, toothpaste, etc (**toiletries**)

'toilet paper (also **toilet tissue**) *noun* [U] soft, thin paper that you use to clean yourself after going to the toilet

toiletries /'tɔɪlətriz/ *noun* [pl] things such as soap or toothpaste that you use for washing, cleaning your teeth, etc

➤ When you travel, you usually carry your toiletries in a **sponge bag** or **toilet bag**.

'toilet roll *noun* [C] a long piece of toilet paper rolled round a tube •➤ picture at **roll**

token¹ /'təʊkən/ *noun* [C] **1** a round piece of metal, plastic, etc that you use instead of money to operate some machines or as a form of payment **2** (*Brit*) a piece of paper that you can use to buy sth of a certain value in a particular shop. Tokens are often given as presents: *a £10 book/CD/gift token* •➤ Look at **voucher**. **3** something that represents or is a symbol of sth: *Please accept this gift as a token of our gratitude.*

token² /'təʊkən/ *adj* (only *before* a noun) **1** done, chosen, etc in a very small quantity, and only in order not to be criticized: *There is a token woman on the board of directors.* **2** small, but done or given to show that you are serious about sth and will keep a promise or an agreement: *a token payment*

told *past tense, past participle* of **TELL**

tolerable /'tɒlərəbl/ *adj* **1** quite good, but not of the best quality **2** of a level that you can accept or deal with, although unpleasant or painful: *Drugs can reduce the pain to a tolerable level.* •➤ opposite **intolerable**

tolerant /'tɒlərənt/ *adj* tolerant (**of/towards sb/sth**) the ability to allow or accept sth that you do not like or agree with •➤ opposite **intolerant** –**tolerance** *noun* [U] tolerance (**of/ for sb/sth**): *religious/racial tolerance* •➤ opposite **intolerance**

tolerate /'tɒləreɪt/ *verb* [T] **1** to allow or accept sth that you do not like or agree with: *In a democracy we must tolerate opinions that are different from our own.* **2** to accept or be able to deal with sb/sth unpleasant without complaining: *The noise was more than she could tolerate.* –**toleration** /ˌtɒləˈreɪʃn/ = **TOLERANCE**

toll /təʊl/ *noun* **1** [C] money that you pay to use a road or bridge: *motorway tolls* • *a toll bridge* **2** [C, usually sing] the amount of damage done or the number of people who were killed or injured by sth: *The official death toll has now reached 5000.*

IDIOM **take a heavy toll/take its toll (on sth)** to cause great loss, damage, suffering, etc

★**tomato** /təˈmɑːtəʊ/ *noun* [C] (*pl* **tomatoes**) a soft red fruit that is often eaten without being cooked in salads, or cooked as a vegetable: *tomato juice/soup/sauce* •➤ picture on page C3

tomb /tuːm/ *noun* [C] a large place, usually built of stone under the ground, where the body of an important person is buried: *the tombs of the Pharaohs* •➤ Look at **grave**.

tomboy /'tɒmbɔɪ/ *noun* [C] a young girl who likes the same games and activities that are traditionally considered to be for boys

tombstone /'tuːmstəʊn/ *noun* [C] a large flat stone that lies on or stands at one end of the place where a person is buried (a grave) and shows the name, dates, etc of the dead person •➤ Look also at **gravestone** and **headstone**.

tomcat /'tɒmkæt/ (also **tom**) *noun* [C] a male cat

★**tomorrow** /təˈmɒrəʊ/ *noun* [U], *adv* **1** (on) the day after today: *Today is Friday so tomorrow is Saturday.* • *See you tomorrow.* • *I'm going to bed. I've got to get up early tomorrow morning.* • *a week tomorrow* (= a week from tomorrow)

➤ Notice that we say 'tomorrow morning', 'tomorrow afternoon', etc not 'tomorrow in the morning', etc. Look at the note at **morning**.

2 the future: *The schoolchildren of today are tomorrow's workers.*

ton /tʌn/ *noun* **1** [C] a measure of weight; 2240 pounds

➤ Do not confuse **ton** and **tonne**. A ton is the same as 1·016 tonnes.
In US English a ton is 2000 pounds.

2 tons [pl] (*informal*) a lot: *I've got tons of homework to do.*

tone¹ /təʊn/ *noun* **1** [C,U] the quality of a sound or of sb's voice, especially expressing a particular emotion: *'Do you know each other?' she asked in a casual tone of voice.* **2** [sing] the general quality or style of sth: *The tone of the meeting was optimistic.* **3** [C] a shade of a colour: *warm tones of red and orange* **4** [C] a sound that you hear on the telephone: *Please speak after the tone* (= an instruction on an answering machine).

tone² /təʊn/ *verb* [T] tone sth (**up**) to make your muscles, skin, etc firmer, especially by doing exercise

PHRASAL VERB **tone sth down** to change sth that you have said, written, etc, to make it less likely to offend

ˌtone-'deaf *adj* not able to sing or hear the difference between notes in music

tongs /tɒŋz/ *noun* [pl] a tool that looks like a pair of scissors but that you use for holding or picking things up •➤ picture at **kitchen**

★**tongue** /tʌŋ/ *noun* **1** [C] the soft part inside your mouth that you can move. You use your tongue for speaking, tasting things, etc. •➤ picture on page C5 **2** [C,U] the tongue of some animals, cooked and eaten **3** [C] (*formal*) a language: *your mother tongue* (= the language you learned as a child)

IDIOMS **on the tip of your tongue** → **TIP¹**
put/stick your tongue out to put your tongue outside your mouth as a rude sign to sb
a slip of the tongue → **SLIP²**
(with) tongue in cheek done or said as a joke; not intended seriously

---

[I] **intransitive**, a verb which has no object: *He laughed.*   [T] **transitive**, a verb which has an object: *He ate an apple.*

'tongue-tied *adj* not saying anything because you are shy or nervous

'tongue-twister *noun* [C] a phrase or sentence with many similar sounds that is difficult to say correctly when you are speaking quickly

tonic /'tɒnɪk/ *noun* **1** (also **'tonic water**) [U,C] a type of water with bubbles in it and a rather bitter taste that is often added to alcoholic drinks: *a gin and tonic* **2** [C,U] a medicine or sth you do that makes you feel stronger, healthier, etc, especially when you are very tired: *A relaxing holiday is a wonderful tonic.*

★**tonight** /tə'naɪt/ *noun* [U], *adv* (on) the evening or night of today: *Tonight is the last night of our holiday.* ● *What's on TV tonight?* ● *We are staying with friends tonight and travelling home tomorrow.*

tonne /tʌn/ *noun* [C] a measure of weight; 1000 kilograms •➤ Look at **ton**.

tonsil /'tɒnsl/ *noun* [C] one of the two soft lumps in your throat at the back of your mouth: *She had to* **have** *her* **tonsils out** (= removed in a medical operation).

tonsillitis /ˌtɒnsə'laɪtɪs/ *noun* [U] an illness in which the tonsils become very sore and swollen

too/enough

Tom's sweater is **not big enough**.

Kevin's sweater is **too big**.

★**too** /tuː/ *adv* **1** (used before adjectives and adverbs) more than is good, allowed, possible, etc: *These boots are too small.* ● *It's far too cold to go out without a coat.* ● *It's too long a journey for you to make alone.*

➤ Notice that you cannot say 'It's a too long journey'.

2 (not with negative statements) in addition; also: *Red is my favourite colour but I like blue, too.* ● *Phil thinks you're right and I do too.*

➤ Notice that at the end of a clause you use **too** for agreement with positive statements and **either** for agreement with negative statements: *I like eating out and Rakesh does too.* ● *I don't like cooking and Rakesh doesn't either.*

3 used to add sth which makes a situation even worse: *Her purse was stolen. And on her birthday too.* **4** (usually used in negative sentences) very: *The weather is not too bad today.*

took *past tense of* TAKE

tools

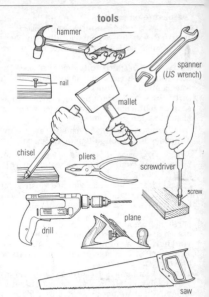

hammer

nail

spanner (*US* **wrench**)

mallet

chisel

pliers

screwdriver

screw

drill

plane

saw

★**tool** /tuːl/ *noun* [C] a piece of equipment such as a hammer, that you hold in your hand(s) and use to do a particular job: *Hammers, screwdrivers and saws are all carpenter's tools.* ● *garden tools* ● *a tool kit* (= a set of tools in a box or a bag)

➤ A tool is usually something you can hold in your hand, for example a spanner or hammer. An **implement** is often used outside, for example for farming or gardening. A **machine** has moving parts and works by electricity, with an engine, etc. An **instrument** is often used for technical or delicate work: *a dentist's instruments.* A **device** is a more general word for a piece of equipment that you consider to be useful and that is designed to do one particular task: *The machine has a safety device which switches the power off if there is a fault.*

toolbar /'tuːlbɑː/ *noun* [C] a row of symbols on a computer screen that show the different things that the computer can do •➤ picture on page S7

toot /tuːt/ *noun* [C] the short high sound that a car horn makes –**toot** *verb* [I,T]: *Toot your horn to let them know we're here.*

★**tooth** /tuːθ/ *noun* [C] (*pl* **teeth** /tiːθ/) **1** one of the hard white things in your mouth that you use for biting: *She's got beautiful teeth.*

➤ You **brush/clean** your teeth to remove bits of food. If a tooth is **decayed**, the dentist may **fill** it or **extract** it/**take** it **out**. If you have had all your teeth out, you can have **false teeth** or **dentures**.

•➤ picture on page C5. •➤ Look at **wisdom tooth**. **2** one of the long narrow pointed parts of an object such as a comb

IDIOMS **by the skin of your teeth** → **SKIN¹**

gnash your teeth → **GNASH**

grit your teeth → **GRIT²**

have a sweet tooth → **SWEET¹**

toothache /'tuːθeɪk/ **noun** [U,C,usually sing] a pain in your tooth or teeth ••> Look at the note at **ache**.

toothbrush /'tuːθbrʌʃ/ **noun** [C] a small brush with a handle that you use for cleaning your teeth ••> picture at **brush**

toothpaste /'tuːθpeɪst/ **noun** [U] a substance that you put on your toothbrush and use for cleaning your teeth

toothpick /'tuːθpɪk/ **noun** [C] a short pointed piece of wood that you use for getting pieces of food out from between your teeth

★**top¹** /tɒp/ **noun 1** [C] the highest part or point of sth: *The flat is at the top of the stairs.*
• *Snow was falling on the mountain tops.*
• *Start reading at the top of the page.* ••> opposite **foot 2** [C] the flat upper surface of sth: *a desk/table/bench top* **3** [sing] **the top (of sth)** the highest or most important position: *to be at the top of your profession* **4** [C] the cover that you put onto sth in order to close it: *Put the tops back on the pens or they will dry out.*

➤ A **top** or a **cap** is often small and round. You often take it off by turning: *a bottle top* • *Unscrew cap to open.* A **lid** may be larger. You can lift it off: *a saucepan lid* • *Put the lid back on the box.*

••> picture at **container 5** [C] a piece of clothing that you wear on the upper part of your body: *a tracksuit/bikini/pyjama top* • *I need a top to match my new skirt.* ••> picture on page C6 **6** [C] a child's toy that turns round very quickly on a point

IDIOMS **at the top of your voice** as loudly as possible

get on top of sb (*informal*) to be too much for sb to manage or deal with: *I've got so much work to do. It's really getting on top of me.*

off the top of your head (*informal*) just guessing or using your memory without preparing or thinking about sth first

on top 1 on or onto the highest point: *a mountain with snow on top* **2** in control; in a leading position: *Josie always seems to come out on top.*

on top of sb/sth 1 on, over or covering sb/sth else: *Books were piled on top of one another.* • *The remote control is on top of the TV.* **2** in addition to sb/sth else: *On top of everything else, the car's broken down.* **3** (*informal*) very close to sb/sth: *We were all living on top of each other in that tiny flat.*

over the top; OTT (*especially Brit informal*) exaggerated or done with too much effort

★**top²** /tɒp/ **adj** highest in position or degree: *one of Britain's top businessmen* • *at top speed* • *the top floor of the building* • *She got top marks for her essay.*

top³ /tɒp/ **verb** [T] (**topping; topped**) **1** to be higher or greater than a particular amount

2 to be in the highest position on a list because you are the most important, successful, etc **3 top sth (with sth)** (usually passive) to put sth on the top of sth: *cauliflower topped with cheese sauce*

PHRASAL VERB **top (sth) up** to fill sth that is partly empty

top 'hat noun [C] the tall black or grey hat that a man wears on formal occasions ••> picture at **hat**

top-'heavy adj heavier at the top than the bottom and likely to fall over

★**topic** /'tɒpɪk/ **noun** [C] a subject that you talk, write or learn about

topical /'tɒpɪkl/ **adj** connected with sth that is happening now; that people are interested in at the present time

topless /'tɒpləs/ **adj, adv** (used about a woman) not wearing any clothes on the upper part of the body so that her breasts are not covered

topmost /'tɒpməʊst/ **adj** (only *before* a noun) highest: *the topmost branches of the tree*

topping /'tɒpɪŋ/ **noun** [C,U] something such as cream or a sauce that is put on the top of food to decorate it or make it taste nicer

topple /'tɒpl/ **verb 1** [I] **topple (over)** to become less steady and fall down: *Don't add another book to the pile or it will topple over.* **2** [T] to cause a leader of a country, etc to lose his/her position of power or authority

top 'secret adj that must be kept very secret, especially from other governments

★**torch** /tɔːtʃ/ **noun** [C] **1** (*US* **flashlight**) a small electric light that you carry in your hand: *Shine the torch under the sofa and see if you can find my ring.* ••> picture at **light 2** a long piece of wood with burning material at the end that you carry to give light: *the Olympic torch*

tore *past tense* of **TEAR²**

torment /'tɔːment/ **noun** [U,C] great pain and suffering in your mind or body; sb/sth that causes this: *to be in torment* –**torment** /tɔː'ment/ **verb** [T]

torn *past participle* of **TEAR²**

tornado /tɔː'neɪdəʊ/ **noun** [C] (*pl* **tornadoes**) a violent storm with a very strong wind that blows in a circle ••> Look at the note at **storm**.

torpedo /tɔː'piːdəʊ/ **noun** [C] (*pl* **torpedoes**) a bomb, shaped like a long narrow tube, that is fired from a type of ship that travels under the water (a **submarine**) and explodes when it hits another ship

torrent /'tɒrənt/ **noun** [C] a strong fast flow of sth, especially water: *The rain was coming down in torrents.*

torrential /tə'renʃl/ **adj** (used about rain) very great in amount

torso /'tɔːsəʊ/ **noun** [C] (*pl* **torsos**) the main part of your body, not your head, arms and legs

t

turtle

tortoise (*US* turtle)

tortoise /ˈtɔːtəs/ (*US* **turtle**) **noun** [C] a small animal with a hard shell that moves very slowly. A tortoise can pull its head and legs into its shell to protect them.

tortuous /ˈtɔːtʃuəs/ **adj 1** complicated, not clear and simple **2** (used about a road, etc) with many bends

torture /ˈtɔːtʃə/ **noun** [U,C] **1** the action of causing sb great pain either as a punishment or to make him/her say or do sth: *His confession was extracted under torture.* **2** mental or physical suffering: *It's torture having to sit here and listen to him complaining for hours.* –**torture** **verb** [T]: *Most of the prisoners were tortured into making a confession.* ● *She was tortured by the thought that the accident was her fault.* –**torturer** **noun** [C]

Tory /ˈtɔːri/ **noun** [C], **adj** (*pl* **Tories**) a member or supporter of the British Conservative Party; connected with this party: *the Tory Party conference* ··➤ Look at the note at **party**.

toss /tɒs/ **verb 1** [T] to throw sth lightly and carelessly: *Bob opened the letter and tossed the envelope into the bin.* **2** [I,T] to move, or make sb/sth move up and down or from side to side: *He lay tossing and turning in bed, unable to sleep.* ● *The ship was tossed about by huge waves.* **3** [T] to move your head back quickly especially to show you are annoyed or impatient: *I tried to apologise but she just tossed her head and walked away.* **4** [I,T] **toss (up) (for sth)** to throw a coin into the air in order to decide sth, by guessing which side of the coin will land facing upwards: *to toss a coin* ··➤ Look at **heads** and **tails**. These are the names of the two sides of a coin and we say 'heads or tails?' when we are guessing which side will face upwards. –**toss** **noun** [C]
▪ IDIOM **win/lose the toss** to guess correctly/wrongly which side of a coin will face upwards when it lands: *Ms Hingis won the toss and chose to serve first.*

tot¹ /tɒt/ **noun** [C] **1** (*informal*) a very small child **2** (*especially Brit*) a small glass of a strong alcoholic drink

tot² /tɒt/ **verb** (**totting**; **totted**)
▪ PHRASAL VERB **tot (sth) up** (*informal*) to add numbers together to form a total

★**total¹** /ˈtəʊtl/ **adj** being the amount after everyone or everything is counted or added together; complete: *What was the total number of people there?* ● *a total failure* ● *They ate in total silence.*

total² /ˈtəʊtl/ **noun** [C] the number that you get when you add two or more numbers or amounts together –**total** **verb** [T] (totalling; totalled; *US* totaling; totaled): *His debts totalled more than £10000.*
▪ IDIOM **in total** when you add two or more numbers or amounts together: *The appeal raised £4 million in total.*

★**totally** /ˈtəʊtəli/ **adv** completely: *I totally agree with you.*

totter /ˈtɒtə/ **verb** [I] to stand or move in a way that is not steady, as if you are going to fall, especially because you are drunk, ill or weak

★**touch¹** /tʌtʃ/ **verb 1** [T] to put your hand or fingers onto sb/sth: *It's very delicate so don't touch.* ● *He touched her gently on the cheek.* ● *The police asked us not to touch anything.* **2** [I,T] (used about two or more things, surfaces, etc) to be or move so close together that there is no space between them: *They were sitting so close that their shoulders touched.* ● *This bicycle is too big. My feet don't touch the ground.* **3** [T] to make sb feel sad, sorry for sb, grateful, etc ··➤ Look at the adjective **touched**. **4** [T] (in negative sentences) to be as good as sb/sth in skill, quality, etc: *He's a much better player than all the others. No one else can touch him.*
▪ IDIOM **touch wood**; **knock on wood** → **WOOD**
▪ PHRASAL VERBS **touch down** (used about an aircraft) to land
touch on/upon sth to mention or refer to a subject for only a short time

★**touch²** /tʌtʃ/ **noun 1** [C, usually sing] the action of putting your hands or fingers onto sb/sth: *I felt the touch of her hand on my arm.* **2** [U] the way sth feels when you touch it: *Marble is cold to the touch.* **3** [U] one of the five senses: the ability to feel things and know what they are like by putting your hands or fingers on them: *The sense of touch is very important to blind people.* **4** [C] a small detail that is added to improve sth: *The flowers in our room were a nice touch.* ● *She's just putting the finishing touches to the cake.* **5** [sing] a way or style of doing sth: *She prefers to write her letters by hand for a more personal touch.* **6** [sing] **a touch (of sth)** a small amount of sth
▪ IDIOMS **in/out of touch (with sb)** being/not being in contact with sb by speaking or writing to him/her: *During the year she was abroad, they kept in touch by letter.*
in/out of touch with sth having/not having recent information about sth: *We're out of touch with what's going on.*
lose touch → **LOSE**
lose your touch → **LOSE**

touched /tʌtʃt/ **adj** (not before a noun) **touched (by) sth; touched that...** made to feel sad, sorry for sb, grateful, etc: *We were very touched by the plight of the refugees.* ● *I was touched that he offered to help.*

touching /ˈtʌtʃɪŋ/ **adj** that makes you feel sad, sorry for sb, grateful, etc

ˈtouch screen **noun** [C] (*computing*) a computer screen which shows information when you touch it: *touch screen technology*

touchy /'tʌtʃi/ **adj 1 touchy (about sth)** easily upset or made angry: *He's a bit touchy about his weight.* **2** (used about a subject, situation, etc) that may easily upset people or make them angry: *Don't mention the exam. It's a very touchy subject.*

★**tough** /tʌf/ **adj 1** difficult; having or causing problems: *It will be a tough decision to make.* ● *He's had a tough time of it* (= a lot of problems) *recently.* **2 tough (on/with sb/sth)** strict; not feeling sorry for anyone: *The government plans to get tough with people who drink and drive.* ● *Don't be too tough on them – they were only trying to help.* **3** strong enough to deal with difficult conditions or situations: *You need to be tough to go climbing in winter.* **4** (used especially about meat) difficult to cut and eat **5** not easily broken, torn or cut; very strong: *a tough pair of boots* **6** (*informal*) **tough (on sb)** unfortunate for sb in a way that seems unfair: *It's tough on her that she lost her job.* –**toughness** **noun** [U]

toughen /'tʌfn/ **verb** [I,T] **toughen (sb/sth) (up)** to make sb/sth tough

★**tour** /tʊə/ **noun 1** [C] **a tour (of/round/around sth)** a journey that you make for pleasure during which you visit many places: *to go on a ten-day coach tour of/around Scotland* ● *a sightseeing tour* ● *a tour operator* (= a person or company that organizes tours) ••➤ Look at the note at **travel**. **2** [C] a short visit around a city, famous building, etc: *a guided tour round St Paul's Cathedral* **3** [C,U] an official series of visits that singers, musicians, sports players, etc make to different places to perform, play, etc: *The band is currently on tour in America.* ● *a concert/cricket tour* –**tour verb** [I,T]: *We toured southern Spain for three weeks.*

tourism /'tʊərɪzəm/ **noun** [U] the business of providing and arranging holidays and services for people who are visiting a place: *The country's economy relies heavily on tourism.*

tourist /'tʊərɪst/ **noun** [C] a person who visits a place for pleasure ••➤ Look at **sightseer**.

tournament /'tɔːnəmənt/ **noun** [C] a competition in which many players or teams play games against each other

tousled /'taʊzld/ **adj** (used about hair) untidy, often in an attractive way

tow /təʊ/ **verb** [T] to pull a car or boat behind another vehicle, using a rope or chain: *My car was towed away by the police.* –**tow noun** [sing,U]

IDIOM **in tow** (*informal*) following closely behind: *He arrived with his wife and five children in tow.*

★**towards** /tə'wɔːdz/ (also **toward** /tə'wɔːd/) **prep 1** in the direction of sb/sth: *I saw Ken walking towards the station.* ● *She had her back towards me.* ● *a first step towards world peace* **2** near or nearer a time or date: *It gets cool towards evening.* ● *The shops get very busy towards Christmas.* **3** (used when you are talking about your feelings about sb/sth) in relation to: *Patti felt very protective towards her younger brother.* ● *What is your*

attitude towards this government? **4** as part of the payment for sth: *The money will go towards the cost of a new minibus.*

★**towel** /'taʊəl/ **noun** [C] a piece of cloth or paper that you use for drying sb/sth/yourself: *a bath/hand/beach towel* ● *kitchen/paper towels* ••➤ Look at **sanitary towel** and **tea towel**.

★**tower** /'taʊə/ **noun** [C] a tall narrow building or part of a building such as a church or castle: *the Eiffel Tower* ● *a church tower*

'tower block **noun** [C] (*Brit*) a very tall building consisting of flats or offices

★**town** /taʊn/ **noun 1** [C] a place with many streets and buildings. A town is larger than a village but smaller than a city: *Romsey is a small market town.* ● *After ten years away, she decided to move back to her home town* (= the town where she was born and spent her childhood). **2 the town** [sing] all the people who live in a town: *The whole town is talking about it.* **3** [U] the main part of a town, where the shops, etc are: *I've got to go into town this afternoon.*

IDIOMS **go to town (on sth)** (*informal*) to do sth with a lot of energy and enthusiasm; to spend a lot of money on sth

(out) on the town (*informal*) going to restaurants, theatres, clubs, etc for entertainment, especially at night

,town 'council **noun** [C] (*Brit*) a group of people who are responsible for the local government of a town

,town 'hall **noun** [C] a large building that contains the local government offices and often a large room for public meetings, concerts, etc ••➤ Look at **hall**.

toxic /'tɒksɪk/ **adj** poisonous

★**toy**[1] /tɔɪ/ **noun** [C] an object for a child to play with: *The little boy continued playing with his toy cars.* ● *a toy soldier/farm* ● *a toyshop*

toy[2] /tɔɪ/ **verb**

PHRASAL VERB **toy with sth 1** to think about doing sth, perhaps not very seriously: *She's toying with the idea of going abroad for a year.* **2** to move sth about without thinking about what you are doing, often because you are nervous or upset: *He toyed with his food but hardly ate any of it.*

trace[1] /treɪs/ **verb** [T] **1 trace sb/sth (to sth)** to find out where sb/sth is by following marks, signs or other information: *The wanted man was traced to an address in Amsterdam.* **2 trace sth (back) (to sth)** to find out where sth came from or what caused it; to describe the development of sth: *She traced her family tree back to the 16th century.* **3** to make a copy of a map, plan, etc by placing a piece of transparent paper (**tracing paper**) over it and drawing over the lines

★**trace**[2] /treɪs/ **noun 1** [C,U] a mark, an object or a sign that shows that sb/sth existed or happened: *traces of an earlier civilization* ● *The man disappeared/vanished without trace.* **2** [C] **a trace (of sth)** a very small amount of sth: *Traces of blood were found under her fingernails.*

★**track¹** /træk/ **noun 1** [C] a natural path or rough road: *Follow the dirt track through the wood.* ••► picture on page C8 **2** [C, usually pl] marks that are left on the ground by a person, an animal or a moving vehicle: *The hunter followed the tracks of a deer.* ● *tyre tracks* ••► Look at **footprint**. **3** [C,U] the two metal rails on which a train runs: *The train stopped because there was a tree across the track.* **4** [C] a piece of ground, often in a circle, for people, cars, etc to have races on: *a running track* **5** [C] one song or piece of music on a cassette, CD or record: *the first track from her latest album* ••► Look at **soundtrack**.

> IDIOMS **keep/lose track of sb/sth** to have/not have information about what is happening or where sb/sth is
>
> **off the beaten track** → **BEAT¹**
>
> **on the right/wrong track** having the right/ wrong idea about sth: *That's not the answer but you're on the right track.*

track² /træk/ **verb** [T] to follow the movements of sb/sth: *to track enemy planes on a radar screen*

> PHRASAL VERB **track sb/sth down** to find sb/ sth after searching for him/her/it

'**track event noun** [C] a sports event that consists of running round a track in a race, rather than throwing sth or jumping ••► Look at **field event**.

'**track record noun** [sing] all the past successes or failures of a person or organization

tracksuit /'træksuːt/ **noun** [C] a warm pair of soft trousers and a matching jacket that you wear for sports practice

tractor /'træktə/ **noun** [C] a large vehicle that is used on farms for pulling heavy pieces of machinery

★**trade¹** /treɪd/ **noun 1** [U] the buying or selling of goods or services between people or countries: *an international trade agreement* ● *Trade is not very good* (= not many goods are sold) *at this time of year.* **2** [C] a particular type of business: *the tourist/building/ retail trade* **3** [C,U] a job for which you need special skill, especially with your hands: *Jeff is a plumber by trade.* ● *to learn a trade* ••► Look at the note at **work**.

★**trade²** /treɪd/ **verb 1** [I] **trade (in sth) (with sb)** to buy or sell goods or services: *We no longer trade with that country.* ● *to trade in luxury goods* ● *to trade in stocks and shares* **2** [T] **trade sth (for sth)** to exchange sth for sth else: *He traded his CD player for his friend's bicycle.* –**trading noun** [U]

> PHRASAL VERB **trade sth in (for sth)** to give sth old in part payment for sth new or newer: *We traded in our old car for a van.*

trademark /'treɪdmɑːk/ **noun** [C] (*abbr* **TM**) a special symbol, design or name that a company puts on its products and that cannot be used by any other company

trader /'treɪdə/ **noun** [C] a person who buys and sells things, especially goods in a market or company shares ••► picture on page C8

tradesman /'treɪdzmən/ **noun** [C] (*pl* **-men**

/-mən/) a person who brings goods to people's homes to sell them or who has a shop

,**trade 'union** (also ,**trades 'union**; **union**) **noun** [C] an organization for people who all do the same type of work. Trade unions try to get better pay and working conditions for their members.

★**tradition** /trə'dɪʃn/ **noun** [C,U] a custom, belief or way of doing sth that has continued from the past to the present: *religious/cultural/literary traditions* ● *By tradition*, *the bride's family pays the costs of the wedding.* –**traditional** /-ʃənl/ **adj**: *It is traditional in Britain to eat turkey at Christmas.* –**traditionally** /-ʃənəli/ **adv**

★**traffic** /'træfɪk/ **noun** [U] **1** all the vehicles that are on a road at a particular time: *heavy/light traffic* ● *We got stuck in traffic and were late for the meeting.* **2** the movement of ships, aircraft, etc: *air traffic control* **3** **traffic (in sth)** the illegal buying and selling of sth: *the traffic in drugs/firearms* –**traffic** [I] (*pres part* **trafficking**; *pt, pp* **trafficked**) **traffic (in sth)**: *He was arrested for trafficking in drugs.*

'**traffic island** (also **island**) **noun** [C] a higher area in the middle of the road, where you can stand and wait for the traffic to pass when you want to cross

'**traffic jam noun** [C] a long line of cars, etc that cannot move or that can only move very slowly: *to be stuck in a traffic jam.*

'**traffic light noun** [C, usually pl] a sign with three coloured lights (red, amber and green) that is used for controlling the traffic where two or more roads meet ••► picture at **roundabout**

'**traffic warden noun** [C] (*Brit*) a person whose job is to check that cars are not parked in the wrong place or for longer than is allowed

tragedy /'trædʒədi/ **noun** (*pl* **tragedies**) **1** [C,U] a very sad event or situation, especially one that involves death: *It's a tragedy that he died so young.* **2** [C] a serious play that has a sad ending: *Shakespeare's 'King Lear' is a tragedy.* ••► Look at **comedy**.

tragic /'trædʒɪk/ **adj 1** that makes you very sad, especially because it involves death: *It's tragic that she lost her only child.* ● *a·tragic accident* **2** (*written*) (only *before* a noun) (used about literature) in the style of tragedy: *a tragic actor/hero* –**tragically** /-kli/ **adv**

trail¹ /treɪl/ **noun** [C] **1** a series of marks in a long line that is left by sb/sth as he/she/it moves: *a trail of blood/footprints* **2** a track, sign or smell that is left behind and that you follow when you are hunting sb/sth: *The dogs ran off on the trail of the fox.* **3** a path through the country ••► picture on page C8

trail² /treɪl/ **verb 1** [I,T] to pull or be pulled along behind sb/sth: *The skirt was too long and trailed along the ground.* **2** [I] to move or walk slowly behind sb/sth else, usually because you are tired or bored: *It was impossible to do any shopping with the kids trailing*

[C] **countable**, a noun with a·plural form: *one book, two books*   [U] **uncountable**, a noun with no plural form: *some sugar*

around after me. **3** [I,T] **trail (by/in sth)** (usually used in the continuous tenses) to be in the process of losing a game or a competition: *At half-time Liverpool were trailing by two goals to three.* **4** [I] (used about plants or sth long and thin) to grow over sth and hang downwards; to lie across a surface: *Computer wires trailed across the floor.*

PHRASAL VERB **trail away/off** (used about sb's voice) to gradually become quieter and then stop

trailer /ˈtreɪlə/ **noun** [C] **1** a type of container with wheels that is pulled by vehicle: *a car towing a trailer with a boat on it* **2** (*US*) = **CARAVAN**(1) **3** (*especially Brit*) a series of short pieces taken from a film and used to advertise it ·✦ Look at **clip**.

★**train**¹ /treɪn/ **noun** [C] **1** a type of transport that is pulled by an engine along a railway line. A train is divided into sections for people (**carriages** and **coaches**) and for goods (**wagons**): *a passenger/goods/freight train* ● *a fast/slow/express train* ● *to catch/take/get the train to London* ● *the 12 o'clock train to Bristol* ● *to get on/off a train* ● *Hurry up or we'll miss the train.* ● *You have to change trains at Reading.*

➤ Note that we say **by train** when speaking in general. We say **on the train** when we mean during one particular train journey: *Miranda travels to work by train.* ● *Yesterday she fell asleep on the train and missed her station.*

2 [usually sing] a series of thoughts or events that are connected: *A knock at the door interrupted my train of thought.*

★**train**² /treɪn/ **verb 1** [T] **train sb (as sth/to do sth)** to teach a person to do sth which is difficult or which needs practice: *The organization trains guide dogs for the blind.* ● *There is a shortage of trained teachers.* **2** [I] **train (as/in sth) (to do sth)** to learn how to do a job: *She trained as an engineer.* ● *He's not trained in anything.* ● *He's training to be a doctor.* **3** [I,T] **train (for sth)** to prepare yourself, especially for a sports event, by practising; to help a person or an animal to do this: *I'm training for the London Marathon.* ● *to train racehorses* **4** [T] **train sth (at/on sb/sth)** to point a gun, camera, etc at sb/sth –**training noun** [U]: *to be in training for the Olympics*

trainee /ˌtreɪˈniː/ **noun** [C] a person who is being taught how to do a particular job

trainer /ˈtreɪnə/ **noun** [C] **1** (*US* **sneaker**) [usually pl] a shoe that you wear for doing sport or as informal clothing ·✦ Look at **plimsoll**. ·✦ picture at **shoe** and on page S2 **2** a person who teaches people or animals how to do a particular job or skill well, or to do a particular sport: *teacher trainers* ● *a racehorse trainer*

trainspotter /ˈtreɪnspɒtə/ **noun** [C] (*Brit*) **1** a person who collects the numbers of railway engines as a hobby **2** a person who has a boring hobby or who is interested in the

details of a subject that other people find boring –**trainspotting noun** [U]

trait /treɪt/ **noun** [C] a quality that forms part of your character or personality

traitor /ˈtreɪtə/ **noun** [C] **a traitor (to sb/sth)** a person who is not loyal to his/her country, friends, etc

➤ A traitor **betrays** his/her friends, country, etc and the crime against his/her country is called **treason**.

tram /træm/ (*US* **streetcar**; **trolley**) **noun** [C] a type of bus that works by electricity and that moves along special rails in the road carrying passengers

tramp¹ /træmp/ **noun 1** [C] a person who has no home or job and who moves from place to place **2** [sing] the sound of people walking with heavy or noisy steps

tramp² /træmp/ **verb** [I,T] to walk with slow heavy steps, especially for a long time

trample /ˈtræmpl/ **verb** [I,T] **trample on/over sb/sth** to walk on sb/sth and damage or hurt him/her/it: *The boys trampled on the flowers.*

trampoline /ˈtræmpəliːn/ **noun** [C] a piece of equipment for jumping up and down on, made of a piece of strong material fixed to a metal frame by springs

trance /trɑːns/ **noun** [C] a mental state in which you do not notice what is going on around you: *to go/fall into a trance*

tranquil /ˈtræŋkwɪl/ **adj** (*formal*) calm and quiet

tranquillizer (also **-iser**; *US also* **tranquilizer**) /ˈtræŋkwɪlaɪzə/ **noun** [C] a drug that is used for making people feel calm or to help them sleep ·✦ Look at **sedative**.

transaction /trænˈzækʃn/ **noun** [C] a piece of business that is done between people: *financial transactions*

transatlantic /ˌtrænzətˈlæntɪk/ **adj** to or from the other side of the Atlantic Ocean; across the Atlantic: *a transatlantic flight/voyage*

transcend /trænˈsend/ **verb** [T] (*formal*) to go further than the usual limits of sth

transcript /ˈtrænskrɪpt/ (also **transcription**) **noun** [C] a written or printed copy of what sb has said: *a transcript of the interview/trial*

transfer¹ /trænsˈfɜː/ **verb** (**transferring**; **transferred**) **1** [I,T] **transfer (sb/sth) (from…) (to…)** to move, or to make sb/sth move, from one place to another: *He's transferring to our Tokyo branch next month.* ● *I'd like to transfer £1000 from my deposit account* (= in a bank). ● *Transfer the data onto a disk.* **2** [T] to officially arrange for sth to belong to, or be controlled by, sb else: *She transferred the property to her son.* –**transferable** /-ˈfɜːrəbl/ **adj**: *This ticket is not transferable* (= may only be used by the person who bought it).

transfer² /ˈtrænsfɜː/ **noun 1** [C,U] moving or being moved from one place, job or state to another: *Paul is not happy here and has asked*

t

for a transfer. **2** [U] changing to a different vehicle or route during a journey: *Transfer from the airport to the hotel is included.* **3** [C] *(US)* a ticket that allows you to continue your journey on another bus or train **4** [C] *(especially Brit)* a piece of paper with a picture or writing on it that you can stick onto another surface by pressing or heating it

transform /træns'fɔ:m/ *verb* [T] transform sb/sth (from sth) (into sth) to change sb/sth completely, especially in a way which improves sb/sth –transformation /ˌtrænsfə-'meɪʃn/ *noun* [C,U]

transfusion /træns'fju:ʒn/ *noun* [C] the action of putting new blood into a person's body instead of his/her own because he/she is ill: *a blood transfusion*

transistor /træn'zɪstə/ *noun* [C] a small piece of electronic equipment that is used in computers, radios, televisions, etc

transit /'trænzɪt/ *noun* [U] **1** the act of being moved or carried from one place to another: *The goods had been damaged in transit.* **2** going through a place on the way to somewhere else

transition /træn'zɪʃn/ *noun* [C,U] (a) transition (from sth) (to sth) a change from one state or form to another: *the transition from childhood to adolescence* –transitional /-ʃənl/ *adj*: *a transitional stage/period*

transitive /'trænsətɪv/ *adj* (*grammar*) (used about a verb) that has a direct object: *In this dictionary transitive verbs are marked* [T]. ••➤ opposite **intransitive**

> ➤ For more information about transitive verbs, look at the **Quick Grammar Reference** section at the back of this dictionary.

★**translate** /træns'leɪt/ *verb* [I,T] translate (sth) (from sth) (into sth) to change sth written or spoken from one language to another: *This book has been translated from Czech into English.* ••➤ Look at **interpret.** –translation /træns'leɪʃn/ *noun* [C,U]: *a word-for-word translation* ● *an error in translation*

translator /træns'leɪtə/ *noun* [C] a person who changes sth that has been written or spoken from one language to another ••➤ Look at **interpreter.**

transmission /trænz'mɪʃn/ *noun* **1** [U] sending sth out or passing sth on from one person, place or thing to another: *the transmission of television pictures by satellite* ● *the transmission of a disease/virus* **2** [C] a TV or radio programme **3** [U,C] the system in a car, etc by which power is passed from the engine to the wheels

transmit /trænz'mɪt/ *verb* [T] (**transmitting; transmitted**) **1** to send out television or radio programmes, electronic signals, etc: *The match was transmitted live all over the world.* **2** to send or pass sth from one person or place to another: *a sexually transmitted disease*

transmitter /trænz'mɪtə/ *noun* [C] a piece of equipment that sends out electronic signals, television or radio programmes, etc

transparency /træns'pærənsi/ *noun* [C] (*pl* **transparencies**) a piece of plastic on which you can write or draw or that has a picture, etc on it that you look at by putting it on a special machine (**projector**) and shining light through it: *a transparency for the overhead projector* ••➤ Look at **slide²**(4).

★**transparent** /træns'pærənt/ *adj* that you can see through: *Glass is transparent.* ••➤ opposite **opaque**

transplant¹ /træns'plɑ:nt/ *verb* [T] **1** to take out an organ or other part of sb's body and put it into another person's body **2** to move a growing plant and plant it somewhere else ••➤ Look at **graft.**

transplant² /'trænsplɑ:nt/ *noun* [C] a medical operation in which an organ, etc is taken out of sb's body and put into another person's body: *to have a heart/liver/kidney transplant*

★**transport** /'trænspɔ:t/ (*especially US* **transportation**) *noun* [U] **1** the action of carrying or taking people or goods from one place to another: *road/rail/sea transport* **2** vehicles that you travel in; a method of travel: *Do you have your own transport (for example a car)?*
● *I travel to school by public transport.*
● *His bike is his only means of transport.* –transport /træn'spɔ:t/ *verb* [T]

transvestite /trænz'vestaɪt/ *noun* [C] a person, especially a man, who enjoys dressing like a member of the opposite sex

★**trap¹** /træp/ *noun* [C] **1** a piece of equipment that you use for catching animals: *a mousetrap* ● *The rabbit's leg was caught in the trap.* **2** a clever plan that is designed to trick sb: *She walked straight into the trap.* **3** an unpleasant situation from which it is hard to escape

★**trap²** /træp/ *verb* [T] (**trapping; trapped**) **1** (often passive) to keep sb in a dangerous place or a bad situation from which he/she cannot escape: *The door closed behind them and they were trapped.* ● *Many people are trapped in low-paid jobs.* **2** to catch and keep or store sth: *Special glass panels trap heat from the sun.* **3** to force sb/sth into a place or situation from which he/she/it cannot escape: *Police believe this new evidence could help trap the killer.* **4** to catch an animal, etc in a trap **5** trap sb (into sth/into doing sth) to make sb do sth by tricking him/her: *She had been trapped into revealing her true identity.*

trapdoor /'træpdɔ:/ *noun* [C] a small door in a floor or ceiling

trapeze /trə'pi:z/ *noun* [C] a wooden or metal bar hanging from two ropes high above the ground, used by entertainers (**acrobats**)

trappings /'træpɪŋz/ *noun* [pl] clothes, possessions, etc which are signs of a particular social position

trash /træʃ/ *(US)* = **RUBBISH**

'trash can *(US)* = **DUSTBIN**

trashy /'træʃi/ *adj* of poor quality: *trashy novels*

trauma /'trɔ:mə/ *noun* [C,U] (an event that causes) a state of great shock or sadness: *the*

trauma of losing your parents ··▸ Look at
stress. –traumatic /trɔːˈmætɪk/ **adj**

★**travel** /ˈtrævl/ **noun 1** [U] the action of going
from one place to another: *air/rail/space
travel* • *a travel bag/clock/iron* (= designed
to be used when travelling) **2 travels** [pl]
time spent travelling, especially to places
that are far away

> ➤ **Travel** is an uncountable word and you
can only use it to talk about the general
activity of moving from place to place: *Foreign travel is very popular these days*. When
you talk about going from one particular
place to another, you use **journey**. A journey can be long: *the journey across Canada*
or short, but repeated: *the journey to work*.
A **tour** is a circular journey or walk during
which you visit several places. You may go
on a tour round a country, city, place of
interest, etc: *a three-week tour around Italy*
• *a guided tour of the castle*. You often use
trip when you are thinking about the whole
visit (including your stay in a place and the
journeys there and back): *They're just back
from a trip to Japan. They had a wonderful
time*. (but: *'How was the journey back?'
'Awful – the plane was delayed!'*) A **trip** may
be short: *a day trip*, or longer: *a trip round
the world*, and can be for business or pleasure: *How about a shopping trip to London
this weekend?* • *He's on a business trip to
New York to meet a client*. An **excursion** is a
short organized trip that you go on with a
group of people: *The holiday includes a full-
day excursion by coach to the capital*. You **go
on** a journey/tour/trip/excursion.

★**travel¹** /ˈtrævl/ **verb** (**travelling; travelled**:
US **traveling; traveled**) **1** [I] to go from one
place to another, especially over a long distance: *Charles travels a lot on business*. • *to
travel abroad* • *to travel by sea/air/car* • *to
travel to work* • *travelling expenses* **2** [T] to
make a journey of a particular distance: *They
travelled 60 kilometres to come and see us*.
IDIOM **travel light** to take very few things
with you when you travel

'**travel agency noun** [C] (*pl* **travel agencies**) a company that makes travel arrangements for people (booking tickets, flights,
hotels, etc)

'**travel agent noun 1** [C] a person whose job
is to make travel arrangements for people
2 the travel agent's [sing] the shop where
you can go to make travel arrangements, buy
tickets, etc

traveller (*US* **traveler**) /ˈtrævlə/ **noun** [C]
1 a person who is travelling or who often
travels **2** (*Brit*) a person who travels around
the country in a large vehicle and does not
have a permanent home anywhere ··▸ Look
at **gypsy**.

'**traveller's cheque** (*US* '**traveler's
check**) **noun** [C] a cheque that you can
change into foreign money when you are
travelling in other countries

'**travel-sick adj** feeling sick or vomiting
because of the movement of the vehicle you

are travelling in ··▸ Look at **airsick**, **carsick**
and **seasick**.

★**tray** /treɪ/ **noun** [C] **1** a flat piece of wood,
plastic, metal, etc with slightly higher edges
that you use for carrying food, drink, etc on
2 a flat container with low edges in which
you put papers, etc on a desk

treacherous /ˈtretʃərəs/ **adj 1** (used about
a person) that you cannot trust and who may
do sth to harm you: *He was weak, cowardly
and treacherous*. **2** dangerous, although seeming safe

treachery /ˈtretʃəri/ **noun** [U] the act of
causing harm to sb who trusts you

treacle /ˈtriːkl/ (*US* **molasses**) **noun** [U] a
thick, dark, sticky liquid that is made from
sugar ··▸ Look at **syrup**.

tread¹ /tred/ **verb** (*pt* **trod** /trɒd/; *pp* **trodden** /ˈtrɒdn/) **1** [I] **tread (on/in/over sb/sth)**
to put your foot down while you are walking:
Don't tread in the puddle! • *He trod on my
foot and didn't even say sorry!* **2** [T] **tread sth
(in/into/down)** to press down on sth with
your foot: *This wine is still made by treading
grapes in the traditional way*.

tread² /tred/ **noun 1** [sing] the sound you
make when you walk; the way you walk
2 [C,U] the pattern on the surface of a tyre on
a vehicle which is slightly higher than the
rest of the surface

treason /ˈtriːzn/ **noun** [U] the criminal act of
causing harm to your country, for example
by helping its enemies ··▸ Look at the note at
traitor.

★**treasure¹** /ˈtreʒə/ **noun 1** [U] a collection of
very valuable objects, for example gold, silver, jewellery, etc: *to find buried treasure*
2 [C] something that is very valuable

treasure² /ˈtreʒə/ **verb** [T] to consider sb/sth
to be very special or valuable: *I will treasure
those memories forever*.

'**treasure hunt noun** [C] a game in which
people try to find a hidden prize by following
special signs (**clues**) which have been left in
different places

treasurer /ˈtreʒərə/ **noun** [C] the person who
looks after the money and accounts of a club
or an organization

the Treasury /ˈtreʒəri/ **noun** [sing, with sing
or pl verb] the government department that
controls public money

★**treat¹** /triːt/ **verb** [T] **1 treat sb/sth (with/as/
like sth)** to act or behave towards sb/sth in a
particular way: *Teenagers hate being treated
like children*. • (*spoken*) *They treat their
workers like dirt* (= very badly). • *You
should treat older people with respect*. • *to
treat sb badly/fairly/well* **2 treat sth as sth**
to consider sth in a particular way: *I decided
to treat his comment as a joke*. **3** to deal with
or discuss sth in a particular way: *The article
treats this question in great detail*. **4 treat
sb/sth (for sth)** to use medicine or medical
care to try to make a sick or injured person
well again: *The boy was treated for burns at
the hospital*. **5 treat sth (with sth)** to put a

chemical substance onto sth in order to protect it from damage, clean it, etc **6 treat sb/ yourself (to sth)** to pay for sth or give sb/ yourself sth that is very special or enjoyable: *Clare treated the children to an ice cream* (= she paid for them).

treat² /triːt/ **noun** [C] something special or enjoyable that you pay for or give to sb/ yourself: *I've brought some cream cakes as a treat.* • *It's a real treat for me to stay in bed late.*

IDIOM **trick or treat → TRICK**

★**treatment** /ˈtriːtmənt/ **noun 1** [U,C] treatment (for sth) the use of medicine or medical care to cure an illness or injury; sth that is done to make sb feel and look good: *to require hospital/medical treatment* **2** [U] the way that you behave towards sb or deal with sth: *The treatment of the prisoners of war was very harsh.* **3** [U,C] treatment (for sth) a process by which sth is cleaned, protected from damage, etc

treaty /ˈtriːti/ **noun** [C] (*pl* **treaties**) a written agreement between two or more countries: *to sign a peace treaty*

treble¹ /ˈtrebl/ **verb** [I,T] to become or to make sth three times bigger: *Prices have trebled in the past ten years.* –**treble determiner**: *This figure is treble the number five years ago.*

treble² /ˈtrebl/ **noun** [C] **1** a high singing voice, especially that of a young boy **2** a boy who has a high singing voice

★**tree** /triː/ **noun** [C] a tall plant that can live for a long time. Trees have a thick wooden central part from which branches grow: *an oak/apple/elm tree* ••➤ picture on page C2

trek /trek/ **noun** [C] **1** a long hard walk, lasting several days or weeks, usually in the mountains **2** (*informal*) a long walk –**trek verb** [I] (**trekking; trekked**)

➤ We use **go trekking** to talk about walking long distances for pleasure

tremble /ˈtrembl/ **verb** [I] **tremble (with sth)** to shake, for example because you are cold, frightened, etc: *She was pale and trembling with shock.* • *His hand was trembling as he picked up his pen to sign.* –**tremble noun** [C]

tremendous /trəˈmendəs/ **adj 1** very large or great: *a tremendous amount of work* **2** (*informal*) very good: *It was a tremendous experience.*

tremendously /trəˈmendəsli/ **adv** very; very much: *tremendously exciting* • *Prices vary tremendously from one shop to another.*

tremor /ˈtremə/ **noun** [C] a slight shaking movement: *There was a tremor in his voice.*

trench /trentʃ/ **noun** [C] **1** a long narrow hole dug in the ground for water to flow along **2** a long deep hole dug in the ground for soldiers to hide in during enemy attacks

trend /trend/ **noun** [C] a trend (towards sth) a general change or development: *The current trend is towards smaller families.* • *He always followed the latest trends in fashion.*

IDIOM **set a/the trend** to start a new style or fashion

trendy /ˈtrendi/ **adj** (*informal*) fashionable

trespass /ˈtrespəs/ **verb** [I] to go onto sb's land or property without permission –**trespasser noun** [C]

★**trial** /ˈtraɪəl/ **noun** [C,U] **1** the process in a court of law where a judge, etc listens to evidence and decides if sb is guilty of a crime or not: *a fair trial* • *He was on trial for murder.* **2** an act of testing sb/sth: *New drugs must go through extensive trials.* • *a trial period* of three months

IDIOM **trial and error** trying different ways of doing sth until you find the best one

,**trial 'run noun** [C] an occasion when you practise doing sth in order to make sure you can do it correctly later on

★**triangle** /ˈtraɪæŋgl/ **noun** [C] **1** a shape that has three straight sides: *a right-angled triangle* ••➤ picture at **shape 2** a metal musical instrument in the shape of a triangle that you play by hitting it with a metal stick ••➤ picture at **music**

triangular /traɪˈæŋgjələ/ **adj** shaped like a triangle

tribe /traɪb/ **noun** [C] a group of people that have the same language and customs and that have a leader (a chief): *tribes living in the Amazonian rainforest* –**tribal** /ˈtraɪbl/ **adj**: *tribal art*

tribunal /traɪˈbjuːnl/ **noun** [C] a type of court with the authority to decide who is right in particular types of dispute or disagreement: *an industrial tribunal*

tributary /ˈtrɪbjətri/ **noun** [C] (*pl* **tributaries**) a small river that flows into a larger river

tribute /ˈtrɪbjuːt/ **noun 1** [C,U] **tribute (to sb)** something that you say or do to show that you respect or admire sb/sth, especially sb who has died: *A special concert was held as a tribute to the composer.* **2** [sing] a **tribute (to sb/sth)** a sign of how good sb/sth is: *The success of the festival is a tribute to the organizers.*

IDIOM **pay tribute to sb/sth → PAY¹**

★**trick** /trɪk/ **noun** [C] **1** something that you do to make sb believe sth that is not true or a joke that you play to annoy sb: *The thieves used a trick to get past the security guards.* **2** something that confuses you so that you see, remember, understand, etc things in the wrong way: *It was a trick question* (= one in which the answer looks easy, but actually is not) **3** an action that uses special skills to make people believe sth which is not true or real as a form of entertainment: *The magician performed a trick in which he made a rabbit disappear.* • *a card trick* **4** [usually sing] a clever or the best way of doing sth –**trick verb** [T]: *I'd been tricked and I felt like a fool.*

IDIOMS **do the job/trick → JOB**

play a joke/trick on sb → JOKE¹

trick or treat (*especially US*) a tradition in which children dressed as ghosts, etc go to people's houses on the evening of October 31st (Hallowe'en) and threaten to do sth bad to them if they do not give them sweets, etc: *to go trick or treating*

PHRASAL VERBS **trick sb into sth/doing sth** to persuade sb to do sth by making him/her believe sth that is not true: *He tricked me into lending him money.*

trick sb out of sth to get sth from sb by making him/her believe sth that is not true: *Stella was tricked out of her share of the money.*

trickery /'trɪkəri/ **noun** [U] the use of dishonest methods to trick sb in order to get what you want

trickle /'trɪkl/ **verb** [I] **1** (used about a liquid) to flow in a thin line: *Raindrops trickled down the window.* **2** to go somewhere slowly and gradually –**trickle noun** [C,usually sing]: *a trickle of water*

tricky /'trɪki/ **adj** (**trickier**; **trickiest**) difficult to do or deal with: *a tricky situation*

tricycle /'traɪsɪkl/ **noun** [C] a bicycle that has one wheel at the front and two at the back

trifle /'traɪfl/ **noun 1 a trifle** [sing] (*formal*) slightly; rather **2** [C] something that is of little value or importance **3** [C,U] (*Brit*) a type of cold sweet food (**dessert**) made from cake and fruit covered with a sweet yellow sauce (**custard**) and cream

trifling /'traɪflɪŋ/ **adj** very small or unimportant

trigger¹ /'trɪgə/ **noun** [C] **1** the part of a gun that you press to fire it: *to pull the trigger* **2** the cause of a particular reaction or event, especially a bad one

trigger² /'trɪgə/ **verb** [T] **trigger sth (off)** to make sth happen suddenly: *Her cigarette smoke had triggered off the fire alarm.*

trillion /'trɪljən/ **number** one million million

> For examples of how to use numbers in sentences, look at **six**. For more information about numbers look at the special section on numbers at the back of this dictionary.

trilogy /'trɪlədʒi/ **noun** [C] (*pl* **trilogies**) a group of three novels, plays, etc that form a set

trim¹ /trɪm/ **verb** [T] (**trimming**; **trimmed**) **1** to cut a small amount off sth so that it is tidy: *to trim your hair/fringe/beard* • *The hedge needs trimming.* **2 trim sth (off sth)** to cut sth off because you do not need it: *Trim the fat off the meat.* **3 trim sth (with sth)** to decorate the edge of sth with sth –**trim noun** [C,usually sing]: *My hair needs a trim.*

trim² /trɪm/ **adj 1** (used about a person) looking thin, healthy and attractive **2** well cared for; tidy

trimming /'trɪmɪŋ/ **noun 1 trimmings** [pl] extra things which you add to sth to improve its appearance, taste, etc **2** [C,U] material that you use for decorating the edge of sth

trio /'triːəʊ/ **noun** (*pl* **trios**) **1** [C,with sing or pl verb] a group of three people who play music or sing together **2** [C] a piece of music for three people to play or sing

★**trip¹** /trɪp/ **noun** [C] a journey to a place and back again, either for pleasure or for a particular purpose: *How was your trip to Turkey?* • *We had to make several trips to move all the furniture.* • *to go on a business/shopping trip* •➤ Look at the note at **travel**. –**tripper noun** [C]: *Brighton was full of day trippers* (= people on trips that last for one day) *from London.*

★**trip²** /trɪp/ **verb** (**tripping**; **tripped**) **1** [I] trip (over/up); trip (over/on sth) to catch your foot on sth when you are walking and fall or nearly fall: *Don't leave your bag on the floor. Someone might trip over it.* • *She tripped up on a loose paving stone.* **2** [T] trip sb (up) to catch sb's foot and make him/her fall or nearly fall: *Linda stuck out her foot and tripped Barry up.*

PHRASAL VERB **trip (sb) up** to make a mistake; to make sb say sth that he/she did not want to say: *The journalist asked a difficult question to try to trip the politician up.*

triple /'trɪpl/ **adj** (only *before* a noun) having three parts, happening three times or containing three times as much as usual: *You'll receive triple pay if you work over the New Year.* –**triple verb** [I,T]

triplet /'trɪplət/ **noun** [C] one of three children or animals that are born to one mother at the same time •➤ Look at **twin**.

tripod /'traɪpɒd/ **noun** [C] a piece of equipment with three legs that you use for putting a camera, etc on •➤ picture at **camera**

★**triumph¹** /'traɪʌmf/ **noun** [C,U] a great success or victory; the feeling of happiness that you have because of this: *The team returned home in triumph.* • *The new programme was a triumph with the public.*

triumph² /'traɪʌmf/ **verb** [I] triumph (over sb/sth) to achieve success; to defeat sb/sth: *France triumphed over Brazil in the final.*

triumphant /traɪ'ʌmfənt/ **adj** feeling or showing great happiness because you have won or succeeded at sth: *a triumphant cheer* –**triumphantly adv**

trivial /'trɪviəl/ **adj** of little importance; not worth considering: *a trivial detail/problem* –**triviality** /ˌtrɪvi'æləti/ **noun** [C,U] (*pl* trivialities)

trivialize (also **-ise**) /'trɪviəlaɪz/ **verb** [T] to make sth seem less important, serious, etc than it really is

trod *past tense* of **TREAD¹**

trodden *past participle* of **TREAD¹**

trolleys

luggage trolley (*US* luggage cart)   shopping trolley (*US* shopping cart)

trolley /'trɒli/ **noun** [C] **1** (*US* **cart**) a piece of equipment on wheels that you use for carrying things: *a supermarket/shopping/luggage trolley* **2** (*Brit*) a small table with wheels that is used for carrying or serving food and drinks: *a tea/sweet/drinks trolley* **3** (*US*) = TRAM

trombone /trɒmˈbəʊn/ *noun* [C] a large metal (**brass**) musical instrument that you play by blowing into it and moving a long tube backwards and forwards ••> Look at the note at **piano**. ••> picture at **music**

troop /truːp/ *noun* **1 troops** [pl] soldiers **2** [C] a large group of people or animals –**troop** *verb* [I]: *When the bell rang everyone trooped into the hall.*

trophy /ˈtrəʊfi/ *noun* [C] (*pl* **trophies**) a large silver cup, etc that you get for winning a competition or race ••> picture at **medal**

tropic /ˈtrɒpɪk/ *noun* **1** [C, usually sing] one of the two lines around the earth that are 23° 27' north (**the Tropic of Cancer**) and south (**the Tropic of Capricorn**) of the line around the middle of the earth (**the equator**) ••> picture at **earth 2 the tropics** [pl] the part of the world that is between these two lines, where the climate is hot and wet –**tropical** /-kl/ *adj*: *tropical fruit*

trot¹ /trɒt/ *verb* (**trotting**; **trotted**) [I] **1** (used about a horse and its rider) to move forward at a speed that is faster than a walk ••> Look at **canter** and **gallop**. **2** (used about a person or an animal) to walk fast, taking short quick steps

PHRASAL VERB **trot sth out** (*informal*) to repeat an old idea rather than thinking of sth new to say: *to trot out the same old story*

trot² /trɒt/ *noun* [sing] a speed that is faster than a walk

IDIOM **on the trot** (*informal*) one after another; without stopping: *We worked for six hours on the trot.*

★**trouble¹** /ˈtrʌbl/ *noun* **1** [U,C] trouble (with sb/sth) (a situation that causes) a problem, difficulty or worry: *If I don't get home by 11 o'clock I'll be in trouble.* • *I'm having trouble getting the car started.* • *I'm having trouble with my car.* • *financial troubles* • *Marie is clever. The trouble is she's very lazy.* **2** [U] extra work or effort: *Let's eat out tonight. It will save you the trouble of cooking.* • *Why don't you stay the night with us. It's no trouble.* • *I'm sorry to put you to so much trouble.* **3** [C,U] a situation where people are fighting or arguing with each other: *There's often trouble in town on Saturday night after the bars have closed.* **4** [U] illness or pain: *back/heart trouble*

IDIOMS **ask for trouble** → ASK
get into trouble to get into a situation which is dangerous or in which you may be punished
go to a lot of trouble (to do sth) to put a lot of work or effort into sth: *They went to a lot of trouble to make us feel welcome.*
take trouble over/with sth; take trouble to do sth/doing sth to do sth with care

take the trouble to do sth to do sth even though it means extra work or effort

trouble² /ˈtrʌbl/ *verb* [T] **1** to make sb worried, upset, etc: *Is there something troubling you?* **2** (*formal*) trouble sb (for sth) (used when you are politely asking sb for sth or to do sth) to disturb sb: *Sorry to trouble you, but would you mind answering a few questions?* ••> synonym **bother**

troublemaker /ˈtrʌblmeɪkə/ *noun* [C] a person who often deliberately causes trouble

troublesome /ˈtrʌblsəm/ *adj* causing trouble, pain, etc over a long period of time

trough /trɒf/ *noun* [C] **1** a long narrow container from which farm animals eat or drink **2** a low area or point, between two higher areas

★**trousers** /ˈtraʊzəz/ (*US* **pants**) *noun* [pl] a piece of clothing that covers the whole of both your legs

➤ Note that, because **trousers** is a plural word, we cannot say, for example, 'a new trouser'. The following are possible: *I need some new trousers.* • *I need a new pair of trousers.* Before another noun the form **trouser** is used: *a trouser suit* (= a woman's suit consisting of a jacket and trousers).

••> picture on page C6

trout /traʊt/ *noun* [C,U] (*pl* **trout**) a type of fish that lives in rivers and that we eat

truant /ˈtruːənt/ *noun* [C] a child who stays away from school without permission –**truancy** /-ənsi/ *noun* [U]

IDIOM **play truant**; (*US*) **play hooky** to stay away from school without permission

truce /truːs/ *noun* [C] an agreement to stop fighting for a period of time ••> Look at **ceasefire**.

★**truck** /trʌk/ *noun* [C] **1** (*especially US*) = LORRY: *a truck driver* ••> picture at **vehicle 2** (*Brit*) an section of a train that is used for carrying goods or animals: *a cattle truck*

trudge /trʌdʒ/ *verb* [I] to walk with slow, heavy steps, for example because you are very tired

★**true** /truː/ *adj* **1** right or correct: *Is it true that Adam is leaving?* • *I didn't think the film was at all true to life* (= it didn't show life as it really is). • *Read the statements and decide if they are true or false.* ••> opposite **untrue** or **false 2** real or genuine, often when this is different from how sth seems: *The novel was based on a true story.* ••> opposite **false 3** having all the typical qualities of the thing mentioned: *How do you know when you have found true love?* **4** true (to sb/sth) behaving as expected or as promised: *He was true to his word* (= he did what he had promised). • *She has been a true friend to me.* ••> noun **truth**

IDIOMS **come true** to happen in the way you hoped or dreamed: *My dream has come true!*
too good to be true used to say that you cannot believe that sth/sb is as good as it/he/she seems
true to form typical; as usual

[C] **countable**, a noun with a plural form: *one book, two books*   [U] **uncountable**, a noun with no plural form: *some sugar*

truly /ˈtruːli/ *adv* **1** (used to emphasize a feeling, statement) really; completely: *We are truly grateful to you for your help.* **2** used to emphasize that sth is correct or accurate: *I cannot truly say that I was surprised at the news.*

> **Yours truly** is often used at the end of a formal letter.

IDIOM **well and truly** → **WELL¹**

trump /trʌmp/ *noun* [C] (in some card games) a card of the chosen set (suit) that has a higher value than cards of the other three sets during a particular game: *Spades are trumps.*

'trump card *noun* [C] a special advantage you have over other people that you keep secret until you can surprise them with it: *It was time for her to play her trump card.*

trumpet /ˈtrʌmpɪt/ *noun* [C] a metal (brass) musical instrument that you play by blowing into it. There are three buttons on it which you press to make different notes. ··➤ Look at the note at **piano**. ··➤ picture at **music**

truncheon /ˈtrʌntʃən/ (*Brit*) (also **baton**) *noun* [C] (*old-fashioned*) a short thick stick that a police officer carries as a weapon

trundle /ˈtrʌndl/ *verb* [I,T] to move, or make sth heavy move, slowly and noisily: *A lorry trundled down the hill.*

trunk /trʌŋk/ *noun* **1** [C] the thick central part of a tree that the branches grow from ··➤ picture on page C2 **2** [C] (*US*) = **BOOT¹**(2) **3** [C] an elephant's long nose ··➤ picture at **elephant** **4 trunks** [pl] = **SWIMMING TRUNKS** **5** [C] a large box that you use for storing or transporting things **6** [usually sing] the main part of your body (not including your head, arms and legs)

★**trust¹** /trʌst/ *noun* **1** [U] **trust (in sb/sth)** the belief that sb is good, honest, sincere, etc and will not try to harm or trick you: *Our marriage is based on love and trust.* • *I should never have put my trust in him.* ··➤ Look at **distrust** and **mistrust**. **2** [C,U] a legal arrangement by which a person or organization looks after money and property for sb else until that person is old enough to control it

IDIOM **take sth on trust** to believe what sb says without having proof that it is true: *I can't prove it. You must take it on trust.*

★**trust²** /trʌst/ *verb* [T] **trust sb (to do sth); trust sb (with sth)** to believe that sb is good, sincere, honest, etc and that he/she will not trick you or try to harm you: *He said the car was safe but I just don't trust him.* • *You can't trust her with money.* • *I don't trust that dog. It looks dangerous.* ··➤ Look at **mistrust** and **distrust**.

IDIOM **Trust sb (to do sth)** (*spoken*) it is typical of sb to do sth: *Trust Alice to be late. She's never on time!*

trustee /trʌˈstiː/ *noun* [C] a person who looks after money or property for sb else

trusting /ˈtrʌstɪŋ/ *adj* believing that other people are good, sincere, honest, etc

trustworthy /ˈtrʌstwɜːði/ *adj* that you can depend on to be good, sincere, honest, etc

★**truth** /truːθ/ *noun* (*pl* **truths** /truːðz/) **1 the truth** [sing] what is true; the facts: *Please tell me the truth.* • *Are you telling me the whole truth about what happened?* • *The truth is, we can't afford to live here any more.* **2** [U] the state or quality of being true: *There's a lot of truth in what she says.* **3** [C] a fact or idea that is believed by most people to be true: *scientific/universal truths* ··➤ adjective **true**

truthful /ˈtruːθfl/ *adj* **1 truthful (about sth)** (used about a person) who tells the truth; honest: *I don't think you're being truthful with me.* **2** (used about a statement) true or correct: *a truthful account* –**truthfully** /-fəli/ *adv*

★**try¹** /traɪ/ *verb* (*pres part* **trying**; *3rd pers sing pres* **tries**; *pt, pp* **tried**) **1** [I] **try (to do sth)** to make an effort to do sth: *I tried to phone you but I couldn't get through.* • *She was trying hard not to laugh.* • *She'll try her best to help you.* • *I'm sure you can do it if you try.*

> **Try and** is more informal than **try to**. It cannot be used in the past tense: *I'll try and get there on time.* • *I tried to get there on time, but I was too late.*

2 [T] **try (doing) sth** to do, use or test sth in order to see how good or successful it is: *'I've tried everything but I can't get the baby to sleep.' 'Have you tried taking her out in the car?'* • *Have you ever tried raw fish?* • *We tried the door but it was locked.* **3** [T] **try sb (for sth)** to examine sb in a court of law in order to decide if he/she is guilty of a crime or not: *He was tried for murder.*

IDIOM **try your hand at sth** to do sth such as an activity or a sport for the first time

PHRASAL VERBS **try sth on** to put on a piece of clothing to see if it fits you properly: *Can I try these jeans on, please?*

try sb/sth out to test sb/sth to find out if he/she/it is good enough

try² /traɪ/ *noun* [C] (*pl* **tries**) an occasion when you try to do sth; an attempt: *I don't know if I can move it by myself, but I'll give it a try.*

trying /ˈtraɪɪŋ/ *adj* that makes you tired or angry: *a trying journey*

'T-shirt (also **teeshirt**) *noun* [C] a shirt with short sleeves and without buttons or a collar ··➤ picture on page C6

tsp *abbr* teaspoonful(s): *Add 1 tsp salt.*

tub /tʌb/ *noun* [C] **1** a large round container **2** a small plastic container with a lid that is used for holding food: *a tub of margarine/ice cream* ··➤ picture at **container**

tuba /ˈtjuːbə/ *noun* [C] a large metal (brass) musical instrument that makes a low sound ··➤ Look at the note at **piano**. ··➤ picture at **music**

★**tube** /tjuːb/ *noun* **1** [C] a long empty pipe: *Blood flowed along the tube into the bottle.* • *the inner tube of a bicycle tyre* ··➤ Look at **test tube**. **2** [C] a tube (of sth) a long thin

t

container with a lid at one end made of soft plastic or metal. Tubes are used for holding thick liquids that can be squeezed out of them: *a tube of toothpaste* •➤ picture at **container 3 the tube** [sing] (*Brit informal*) = **UNDERGROUND³**

tuberculosis /tjuːˌbɜːkjuˈləʊsɪs/ *noun* [U] (*abbr* **TB**) a serious disease that affects the lungs

tubing /ˈtjuːbɪŋ/ *noun* [U] a long piece of metal, rubber, etc in the shape of a tube

TUC /ˌtiː juː ˈsiː/ *abbr* the Trades Union Congress; the association of British trades unions

tuck /tʌk/ *verb* [T] **1 tuck sth in, under, round, etc (sth)** to put or fold the ends or edges of sth into or round sth else so that it looks tidy: *Tuck your shirt in – it looks untidy like that.* **2 tuck sth (away)** to put sth into a small space, especially to hide it or to keep it safe: ● *The letter was tucked behind a pile of books.*

PHRASAL VERBS **tuck sth away 1** (only in the passive form) to be situated in a quiet place; to be hidden *The house was tucked away among the trees.* **2** to hide sth somewhere; to keep sth in a safe place *He tucked his wallet away in his inside pocket.*

tuck sb in/up to make sb feel comfortable in bed by pulling the covers up around him/her

tuck in; tuck into sth (*especially Brit spoken*) to eat with pleasure

Tue (also **Tues**) *abbr* Tuesday: *Tues 9 March*

★**Tuesday** /ˈtjuːzdeɪ; -di/ *noun* [C,U] (*abbr* **Tue**; **Tues**) the day of the week after Monday

➤ Days of the week are always written with a capital letter. For examples of how to use the days of the week in sentences, look at **Monday**.

tuft /tʌft/ *noun* [C] a small amount of hair, grass, etc growing together

tug¹ /tʌɡ/ *verb* [I,T] (**tugging**; **tugged**) tug (**at/on sth**) to pull sth hard and quickly, often several times: *The little boy tugged at his father's trouser leg.*

tug² /tʌɡ/ *noun* [C] **1** a sudden hard pull: *She gave the rope a tug.* **2** (also **tugboat**) a small powerful boat that is used for pulling ships into a port, etc

tuition /tjuˈɪʃn/ *noun* [U] tuition (**in sth**) teaching, especially to a small group of people: *private tuition in Italian* ● *tuition fees* (= the money that you pay to be taught, especially in a college or university)

tulip /ˈtjuːlɪp/ *noun* [C] a brightly-coloured flower, shaped like a cup, that grows in the spring •➤ picture on page C2

tumble /ˈtʌmbl/ *verb* [I] **1** to fall down suddenly but without serious injury: *He tripped and tumbled all the way down the steps.* **2** to fall suddenly in value or amount: *House prices have tumbled.* **3** to move in a particular direction in an untidy way: *She opened her suitcase and all her things tumbled out of it.* –**tumble** *noun* [C]

PHRASAL VERB **tumble down** to fall down; to collapse: *The walls of the old house were tumbling down.*

tumble-'dryer (also **tumble-drier**) *noun* [C] (*Brit*) a machine that dries clothes by moving them about in hot air

tumbler /ˈtʌmblə/ *noun* [C] a tall glass for drinking out of with straight sides and no handle

tummy /ˈtʌmi/ *noun* [C] (*pl* **tummies**) (*informal*) = **STOMACH¹**

tumour (*US* **tumor**) /ˈtjuːmə/ *noun* [C] a mass of cells that are not growing normally in the body as the result of a disease: *a brain tumour*

tumultuous /tjuˈmʌltʃuəs/ *adj* very noisy, because people are excited: *tumultuous applause*

tuna /ˈtjuːnə/ (also **'tuna fish**) *noun* [C,U] (*pl* **tuna**) a large sea fish that we eat: *a tin of tuna*

★**tune¹** /tjuːn/ *noun* [C,U] a series of musical notes that are sung or played to form a piece of music: *The children played us a tune on their recorders.*

IDIOMS **call the shots/tune** → **CALL¹**
change your tune → **CHANGE¹**
in/out of tune 1 at/not at the correct musical level (**pitch**): *You're singing out of tune.* **2** having/not having the same opinions, interests, feelings, etc as sb/sth

tune² /tjuːn/ *verb* **1** [T] to make small changes to the sound a musical instrument makes so that it is at the correct musical level (**pitch**): *to tune a piano/guitar* **2** [T] to make small changes to an engine so that it runs well **3** [I] **tune (in) to sth** to listen to a particular radio station: *Stay tuned to this station for the latest news.*

PHRASAL VERBS **tune in (to sth)** to move the controls of a radio or television so that you can listen to or watch a particular station

tune up to make small changes to a group of musical instruments so that they sound pleasant when played together

tuneful /ˈtjuːnfl/ *adj* (used about music) pleasant to listen to

tunic /ˈtjuːnɪk/ *noun* [C] **1** a piece of women's clothing, usually without sleeves, that is long and not tight **2** (*Brit*) the jacket that is part of the uniform of a policeman, soldier, etc

★**tunnel** /ˈtʌnl/ *noun* [C] a passage under the ground: *The train disappeared into a tunnel.* –**tunnel** *verb* [I,T] (**tunnelling**; **tunnelled**: *US* **tunneling**; **tunneled**)

turban /ˈtɜːbən/ *noun* [C] a covering for the head worn especially by Sikh and Muslim men. A turban is made by folding a long piece of cloth around the head. •➤ picture on page C6

turbulent /ˈtɜːbjələnt/ *adj* **1** in which there is a lot of change, disorder and disagreement, and sometimes violence **2** (used about water or air) moving in a violent way –**turbulence** *noun* [U]

turf¹ /tɜːf/ *noun* [U,C] (a piece of) short thick grass and the layer of soil underneath it

turf² /tɜːf/ **verb** [T] to cover ground with turf
[PHRASAL VERB] **turf sb out (of sth)** (*Brit informal*) to force sb to leave a place

turkey /'tɜːki/ **noun** [C,U] a large bird that is kept on farms. Turkeys are usually eaten at Christmas in Britain and at Thanksgiving in the US.
[IDIOM] **cold turkey** → **COLD¹**

turmoil /'tɜːmɔɪl/ **noun** [U,sing] a state of great noise or confusion: *His mind was in (a) turmoil.*

★**turn¹** /tɜːn/ **verb 1** [I,T] to move or make sth move round a fixed central point: *The wheels turned faster and faster.* ● *She turned the key in the lock.* ● *Turn the steering wheel to the right.* **2** [I,T] to move your body, or part of your body, so that you are facing in a different direction: *He turned round when he heard my voice.* ● *She **turned** her **back** on me* (= she deliberately moved her body to face away from me). **3** [I,T] to change the position of sth: *I turned the box upside down.* ● *He turned the page and started the next chapter.* ● *Turn to page 33 in your books.* **4** [T] to point or aim sth in a particular direction: *She turned her attention back to the television.* **5** [I,T] to change direction when you are moving: *Go straight on and **turn left** at the church.* ● *The car **turned the corner.*** **6** [I,T] (to cause) to become: *He **turned** very red when I asked him about the money.* ● *These caterpillars will turn into butterflies.* **7** [T] (not used in the continuous tenses) to reach or pass a particular age or time: *It's turned midnight.*

➤ For idioms containing **turn**, look at the entries for the nouns, adjectives, etc, for example **turn a blind eye** is at **blind**.

[PHRASAL VERBS] **turn (sth) around/round** to change position or direction in order to face the opposite way, or to return the way you came: *This road is a dead end. We'll have to turn round and go back to the main road.* ● *He turned the car around and drove off.*
turn away to stop looking at sb/sth: *She turned away in horror at the sight of the blood.*
turn sb away to refuse to allow a person to go into a place
turn back to return the same way that you came: *We've come so far already, we can't turn back now.*
turn sb/sth down to refuse an offer, etc or the person who makes it: *Why did you turn that job down? ● He asked her to marry him, but she turned him down.*
turn sth down to reduce the sound or heat that sth produces: *Turn the television down!*
turn off (sth) to leave one road and go on another
turn sth off to stop the flow of electricity, water, etc by moving a switch, tap, etc: *He turned the TV off.*
turn sth on to start the flow of electricity, water, etc by moving a switch, tap, etc: *to turn the lights on*
turn out (for sth) to be present at an event
turn out (to be sth) to be in the end: *The*

weather turned out fine. ● *The house that they had promised us turned out to be a tiny flat.*
turn sth out to move the switch, etc on a light or a source of heat to stop it: *Turn the lights out before you go to bed.*
turn over 1 to change position so that the other side is facing out or upwards: *He turned over and went back to sleep.* **2** (used about an engine) to start or to continue to run **3** (*Brit*) to change to another programme when you are watching television
turn sth over 1 to make sth change position so that the other side is facing out or upwards: *You may now turn over your exam papers and begin.* **2** to keep thinking about sth carefully: *She kept turning over what he'd said in her mind.*
turn to sb/sth to go to sb/sth to get help, advice, etc
turn up 1 to arrive; to appear: *What time did they finally turn up?* **2** to be found, especially by chance: *I lost my glasses a week ago and they haven't turned up yet.*
turn sth up to increase the sound or heat that sth produces: *Turn the heating up – I'm cold.*

★**turn²** /tɜːn/ **noun** [C] **1** the action of turning sb/sth round: *Give the screw another couple of turns to make sure it is really tight.* **2** a change of direction in a vehicle: *to make a **left/right turn*** ● *a U-turn* (= when you turn round in a vehicle and go back in the opposite direction) **3** (*Brit* **turning**) a bend or corner in a road, river, etc: *Take the next turn on the left.* **4** [usually sing] the time when sb in a group of people should or is allowed to do sth: *Please wait in the queue until it is your turn.* ● *Whose turn is it to do the cleaning?* •➤ synonym **go 5** an unusual or unexpected change: *The patient's condition has **taken a turn for the worse*** (= suddenly got worse).
[IDIOMS] **(do sb) a good turn** to do sth helpful for sb
in turn one after the other: *I spoke to each of the children in turn.*
take turns (at sth) to do sth one after the other to make sure it is fair
the turn of the century/year the time when a new century/year starts
wait your turn → **WAIT¹**

turning /'tɜːnɪŋ/ (*Brit*) (also **turn**) **noun** [C] a place where one road leads off from another: *We must have taken a wrong turning.*

'turning point noun [C] a turning point (in sth) a time when an important change happens, usually a good one

turnip /'tɜːnɪp/ **noun** [C,U] a round white vegetable that grows under the ground •➤ picture on page C3

'turn-off noun [C] the place where a road leads away from a larger or more important road: *This is the turn-off for York.*

turnout /'tɜːnaʊt/ **noun** [C,usually sing] the number of people who go to a meeting, sports event, etc

turnover /'tɜːnəʊvə/ **noun** [sing] a turnover (of sth) **1** the amount of business that a company does in a particular period of time: *The* firm has an annual turnover of $50 million. **2** the rate at which workers leave a company and are replaced by new ones: *a high turnover of staff*

turnstile /'tɜːnstaɪl/ noun [C] a metal gate that moves round in a circle when it is pushed, and allows one person at a time to enter a place

turpentine /'tɜːpəntaɪn/ noun [U] a clear liquid with a strong smell that you use for removing paint or for making paint thinner

turquoise /'tɜːkwɔɪz/ adj, noun **1** [C,U] a blue or greenish-blue precious stone **2** [U] (of) a greenish-blue colour

turret /'tʌrət/ noun [C] a small tower on the top of a large building

turtle /'tɜːtl/ noun [C] **1** a reptile with a thick shell that lives in the sea **2** (*US*) = **TORTOISE** ••➤ picture at **tortoise**

tusk /tʌsk/ noun [C] one of the two very long pointed teeth of an elephant, etc. Elephants' tusks are made of a hard, white substance like bone (**ivory**). ••➤ picture at **elephant** and **seal**

tussle /'tʌsl/ noun [C] (*informal*) a tussle (for/over sth) a fight, for example between two or more people who want to have the same thing

tut /tʌt/ (also ,tut-'tut) interj the way of writing the sound that people make to show disapproval of sb/sth

tutor /'tjuːtə/ noun [C] **1** a private teacher who teaches one person or a very small group **2** (*Brit*) a teacher who is responsible for a small group of students at school, college or university. A tutor advises students on their work or helps them if they have problems in their private life.

tutorial /tjuːˈtɔːriəl/ noun [C] a lesson at a college or university for an individual student or a small group of students

tuxedo /tʌkˈsiːdəʊ/ (*pl* tuxedos /-dəʊz/) (also *informal* tux) (*US*) = **DINNER JACKET**

★**TV** /ˌtiː ˈviː/ abbr = **TELEVISION**

twang /twæŋ/ noun [C] the sound that is made when you pull a tight piece of string, wire or elastic and then let it go suddenly –twang verb [I,T]

tweed /twiːd/ noun [U] thick woollen cloth with a rough surface used for making clothes

tweezers /'twiːzəz/ noun [pl] a small tool consisting of two pieces of metal that are joined at one end. You use tweezers for picking up or pulling out very small things: *a pair of tweezers*

★**twelfth** /twelfθ/ pron, determiner, adv 12th ••➤ Look at the examples at **sixth**.

★**twelve** /twelv/ number 12 ••➤ Look at **dozen**. For examples of how to use numbers in sentences, look at **six**.

★**twentieth** /'twentiəθ/ pron, determiner, adv 20th ••➤ Look at the examples at **sixth**.

★**twenty** /'twenti/ number 20

> ➤ For examples of how to use numbers in sentences, look at **sixty**.

★**twice** /twaɪs/ adv two times: *I've been to Egypt twice – once last year and once in 1994.* ● *The film will be shown twice daily.* ● *Take the medicine twice a day.* ● *Prices have risen twice as fast in this country as in Japan.*

twiddle /'twɪdl/ verb [I,T] (*Brit*) twiddle (with) sth to keep turning or moving sth with your fingers, often because you are nervous or bored

twig /twɪg/ noun [C] a small thin branch on a tree or bush ••➤ picture on page C2

twilight /'twaɪlaɪt/ noun [U] the time after the sun has set and before it gets completely dark ••➤ Look at **dusk**.

★**twin** /twɪn/ noun [C] **1** one of two children or animals that are born to one mother at the same time: *They're very alike. Are they twins?* ● *a twin brother/sister* ● *identical twins* ••➤ Look at **twin**. **2** one of a pair of things that are the same or very similar: *twin engines* ● *twin beds* ••➤ Look at the note at **bed**[1].

twinge /twɪndʒ/ noun [C] **1** a sudden short pain: *He suddenly felt a twinge in his back.* **2** a twinge (of sth) a sudden short feeling of an unpleasant emotion

twinkle /'twɪŋkl/ verb [I] **1** to shine with a light that seems to go on and off: *Stars twinkled in the night sky.* **2** (used about your eyes) to look bright because you are happy –twinkle noun [sing]

,twin 'town noun [C] one of two towns in different countries that have a special relationship: *Grenoble is Oxford's twin town.*

twirl /twɜːl/ verb [I,T] twirl (sb/sth) (around/round) to turn round and round quickly; to make sb/sth do this

★**twist**[1] /twɪst/ verb **1** [I,T] to bend or turn sth into a particular shape, often one it does not go in naturally; to be bent in this way: *She twisted her long hair into a knot.* ● *Her face twisted in anger.* ● *He twisted his ankle while he was playing squash.* **2** [I] to turn a part of your body while the rest stays still: *She twisted round to see where the noise was coming from.* ● *He kept twisting his head from side to side.* **3** [T] to turn sth around in a circle with your hand: *She twisted the ring on her finger nervously.* ● *Most containers have twist-off caps.* **4** [I] (used about a road, etc) to change direction often: *a narrow twisting lane* ● *The road twists and turns along the coast.* **5** [I,T] twist (sth) (round/around sth) to put sth round another object; to be round another object: *The telephone wire has got twisted round the table leg.* **6** [T] to change the meaning of what sb has said: *Journalists often twist your words.*

IDIOM **twist sb's arm** (*informal*) to force or persuade sb to do sth

twist[2] /twɪst/ noun [C] **1** the action of turning sth with your hand, or of turning part of your body: *She killed the chicken with one twist of its neck.* **2** an unexpected change or development in a story or situation **3** a place where a road, river, etc bends or changes direction: *the twists and turns of the river* **4** something that has become or been bent into a particular shape: *Straighten out the wire so that there are no twists in it.*

twit /twɪt/ **noun** [C] (*Brit informal*) a stupid person

twitch /twɪtʃ/ **verb** [I,T] to make a quick sudden movement, often one that you cannot control; to cause sth to make a sudden movement: *The rabbit twitched and then lay still.*
• *He twitched his nose.* –**twitch noun** [C]: *He has a nervous twitch.*

twitter /'twɪtə/ **verb** [I] (used about birds) to make a series of short high sounds

★**two** /tu:/ **number 1** 2 •→ Look at **second**. For examples of how to use numbers in sentences, look at **six**. **2 two-** (used to form compound adjectives) having two of the thing mentioned: *a two-week holiday*
IDIOMS be in two minds (about sth/about doing sth) → **MIND¹**
in two in or into two pieces: *The plate fell on the floor and broke in two.*

tycoon /taɪ'ku:n/ **noun** [C] a person who is very successful in business or industry and who has become rich and powerful

★**type¹** /taɪp/ **noun 1** [C] a type (of sth) a group of people or things that share certain qualities and that are part of a larger group; a kind or sort: *Which type of paint should you use on metal?* • *Spaniels are a type of dog.*
• *You meet all types of people in this job.* • *the first building of its type in the world* • *I love this type/these types of movie.* **2** [C] a person of a particular kind: *He's the careful type.*
• *She's not the type to do anything silly.*
•→ Look at **typical**. **3 -type** (used to form compound adjectives) having the qualities, etc of the group, person or thing mentioned: *a ceramic-type material* • *a police-type badge*
4 [U] letters that are printed or typed

★**type²** /taɪp/ **verb** [I,T] to write sth by pressing keys on a machine that have letters on: *Can you type?* • *to type a letter* –**typing noun** [U]: *typing skills*

typewriter /'taɪpraɪtə/ **noun** [C] a machine that you use for writing in print

typewritten /'taɪprɪtn/ **adj** written using a typewriter or computer

typhoid /'taɪfɔɪd/ **noun** [U] a serious disease that can cause death. People get typhoid from bad food or water.

typhoon /taɪ'fu:n/ **noun** [C] a violent tropical storm with very strong winds •→ Look at the note at **storm**.

★**typical** /'tɪpɪkl/ **adj typical (of sb/sth) 1** having or showing the usual qualities of a particular person, thing or type: *a typical Italian village* • *There's no such thing as a typical American* (= they are all different). •→ opposites **untypical** and **atypical 2** behaving in the way you expect: *It was absolutely typical of him not to reply to my letter.*

★**typically** /'tɪpɪkli/ **adv 1** in a typical case; that usually happens in this way: *Typically it is the girls who offer to help, not the boys.* **2** in a way that shows the usual qualities of a

particular person, type or thing: *typically British humour*

typify /'tɪpɪfaɪ/ **verb** [T] (*pres part* **typifying**; *3rd pers sing pres* **typifies**; *pt, pp* **typified**) to be a typical mark or example of sb/sth: *This film typified the Hollywood westerns of that time.*

typist /'taɪpɪst/ **noun** [C] a person who works in an office typing letters, etc

tyranny /'tɪrəni/ **noun** [U] the cruel and unfair use of power by a person or small group to control a country or state –**tyrannical** /tɪ'rænɪkl/ **adj**: *a tyrannical ruler* –**tyrannize** (also **-ise**) /'tɪrənaɪz/ **verb** [I,T]

tyrant /'taɪrənt/ **noun** [C] a cruel ruler who has complete power over the people in his/her country •→ Look at **dictator**.

★**tyre** (*US* **tire**) /'taɪə/ **noun** [C] the thick rubber ring that fits around the outside of a wheel: *a flat tyre* (= a tyre with no air in it) •→ picture on page S9

· ·

U u

· ·

U, u¹ /ju:/ **noun** [C] (*pl* **U's**; **u's** /ju:z/) the twenty-first letter of the English alphabet: *'Ulcer' begins with (a) 'U'.*

U² /ju:/ **abbr** (*Brit*) (used about films that are suitable for anyone, including children) universal

udder /'ʌdə/ **noun** [C] the part of a female cow, etc that hangs under its body and produces milk

UEFA /ju:'eɪfə/ **abbr** the Union of European Football Associations: *the UEFA cup*

UFO (also **ufo**) /,ju: ef 'əʊ/ **abbr** an unidentified flying object •→ Look at **flying saucer**.

ugh /ɜ:/ **interj** used in writing to express the sound that you make when you think sth is disgusting

★**ugly** /'ʌgli/ **adj** (**uglier**; **ugliest**) **1** unpleasant to look at or listen to; unattractive: *The burn left an ugly scar on her face.* • *an ugly modern office block* **2** (used about a situation) dangerous or threatening –**ugliness noun** [U]

UHT /,ju: eɪtʃ 'ti:/ **abbr** used about foods such as milk that are treated to last longer: *UHT milk*

UK /,ju: 'keɪ/ **abbr** the United Kingdom; England, Scotland, Wales and N Ireland: *a UK citizen*

ulcer /'ʌlsə/ **noun** [C] a painful area on your skin or inside your body. Ulcers may produce a poisonous substance and sometimes bleed: *a mouth/stomach ulcer*

ulterior /ʌl'tɪəriə/ **adj** that you keep hidden or secret: *Why is he suddenly being so nice to me? He must have an ulterior motive.*

ultimate¹ /'ʌltɪmət/ **adj** (only *before* a noun)
1 being or happening at the end; last or final:

u

Our ultimate goal is complete independence. **2** the greatest, best or worst

ultimate² /'ʌltɪmət/ **noun** [sing] (*informal*) **the ultimate (in sth)** the greatest or best: *This new car is the ultimate in comfort.*

ultimately /'ʌltɪmətli/ **adv 1** in the end: *Ultimately, the decision is yours.* **2** at the most basic level; most importantly

ultimatum /ˌʌltɪ'meɪtəm/ **noun** [C] (*pl* **ultimatums**) a final warning to sb that, if he/she does not do what you ask, you will use force or take action against him/her: *I gave him an ultimatum – either he paid his rent or he was out.*

ultra- /'ʌltrə/ (in compounds) extremely: *ultra-modern*

ultraviolet /ˌʌltrə'vaɪələt/ **adj** of a type of light that causes your skin to turn darker and that can be dangerous in large amounts

umbilical cord /ʌmˌbɪlɪkl 'kɔːd/ **noun** [C] the tube that connects a baby to its mother before it is born

★**umbrella** /ʌm'brelə/ **noun** [C] an object that you open and hold over your head to keep yourself dry when it is raining: *to put an umbrella up/down*

umpire /'ʌmpaɪə/ **noun** [C] a person who watches a game such as tennis or cricket to make sure that the players obey the rules ••➤ Look at **referee**. –**umpire verb** [I,T]

umpteen /ˌʌmp'tiːn/ **pron, determiner** (*informal*) very many; a lot –**umpteenth** /ˌʌmp'tiːnθ/ **pron, determiner:** *For the umpteenth time – phone if you're going to be late!*

UN /ˌjuː 'en/ **abbr** the United Nations Organization

★**unable** /ʌn'eɪbl/ **adj** unable to do sth not having the time, knowledge, skill, etc to do sth; not able to do sth: *She lay there, unable to move.* ••➤ noun **inability**

unacceptable /ˌʌnək'septəbl/ **adj** that you cannot accept or allow ••➤ opposite **acceptable** –**unacceptably** /-bli/ **adv**

unaccompanied /ˌʌnə'kʌmpənɪd/ **adj** alone, without sb/sth else with you: *Unaccompanied children are not allowed in the bar.*

unaffected /ˌʌnə'fektɪd/ **adj 1** not changed by sth **2** behaving in a natural way without trying to impress anyone ••➤ opposite **affected**

unaided /ʌn'eɪdɪd/ **adv** without any help

unanimous /ju'nænɪməs/ **adj 1** (used about a group of people) all agreeing about sth: *The judges were unanimous in their decision.* **2** (used about a decision, etc) agreed by everyone: *The jury reached a unanimous verdict of guilty.* –**unanimously adv**

unarmed /ʌn'ɑːmd/ **adj** having no guns, knives, etc; not armed ••➤ opposite **armed**

unashamed /ˌʌnə'ʃeɪmd/ **adj** not feeling sorry or embarrassed about sth bad that you have done ••➤ opposite **ashamed** –**unashamedly** /-'ʃeɪmədli/ **adv**

unassuming /ˌʌnə'sjuːmɪŋ/ **adj** not wanting

people to notice how good, important, etc you are

unattached /ˌʌnə'tætʃt/ **adj 1** not connected to sb/sth else **2** not married; without a regular partner

unattended /ˌʌnə'tendɪd/ **adj** not watched or looked after: *Do not leave children unattended.*

unauthorized /ʌn'ɔːθəraɪzd/ **adj** done without permission

unavoidable /ˌʌnə'vɔɪdəbl/ **adj** that cannot be avoided or prevented ••➤ opposite **avoidable** –**unavoidably** /-əbli/ **adv**

unaware /ˌʌnə'weə/ **adj** (not before a noun) unaware (of sb/sth) not knowing about or not noticing sb/sth: *She seemed unaware of all the trouble she had caused.* ••➤ opposite **aware**

unawares /ˌʌnə'weəz/ **adv** by surprise; without expecting sth or being prepared for it: *I was taken completely unawares by his suggestion.*

unbalanced /ʌn'bælənst/ **adj 1** (used about a person) slightly crazy **2** not fair to all ideas or sides of an argument ••➤ opposite **balanced**

unbearable /ʌn'beərəbl/ **adj** too unpleasant, painful, etc for you to accept ••➤ synonym **intolerable** ••➤ opposite **bearable** –**unbearably** /-əbli/ **adv:** *It was unbearably hot.*

unbeatable /ʌn'biːtəbl/ **adj** that cannot be defeated or improved on: *unbeatable prices*

unbeaten /ʌn'biːtn/ **adj** that has not been beaten or improved on

unbelievable /ˌʌnbɪ'liːvəbl/ **adj** very surprising; difficult to believe ••➤ opposite **believable** ••➤ Look at **incredible**. –**unbelievably** /-əbli/ **adj:** *His work was unbelievably bad.*

unblemished /ʌn'blemɪʃt/ **adj** not spoiled, damaged or marked in any way: *The new party leader has an unblemished reputation.*

unborn /ˌʌn'bɔːn/ **adj** not yet born

unbroken /ʌn'brəʊkən/ **adj 1** continuous; not interrupted: *a period of unbroken silence* **2** that has not been beaten: *His record for the 1500 metres remains unbroken.*

uncalled-for /ʌn'kɔːld fɔː/ **adj** (used about behaviour or comments) not fair and not appropriate: *That comment was quite uncalled-for.*

uncanny /ʌn'kæni/ **adj** very strange; that you cannot easily explain: *an uncanny coincidence*

★**uncertain** /ʌn'sɜːtn/ **adj 1** uncertain (about/of sth) not sure; not able to decide: *She was still uncertain of his true feelings for her.* **2** not known exactly or not decided: *He's lost his job and his future seems very uncertain.* ••➤ opposite **certain** –**uncertainly adv** –**uncertainty noun** [C,U] (*pl* **uncertainties**): *Today's decision will put an end to all the uncertainty.* ••➤ opposite **certainty**

unchanged /ʌn'tʃeɪndʒd/ **adj** staying the same; not changed

uncharacteristic /ˌʌnkærəktə'rɪstɪk/ **adj**

[C] **countable**, a noun with a plural form: *one book, two books*   [U] **uncountable**, a noun with no plural form: *some sugar*

not typical or usual ••➤ opposite **characteristic** –**uncharacteristically** /-kli/ **adv**

★**uncle** /'ʌŋkl/ **noun** [C] the brother of your father or mother; the husband of your aunt: *Uncle Steven*

★**uncomfortable** /ʌn'kʌmftəbl/ **adj 1** not pleasant to wear, sit in, lie on, etc: *uncomfortable shoes* **2** not able to sit, lie, etc in a position that is pleasant **3** feeling or causing worry or embarrassment: *I felt very uncomfortable when they started arguing in front of me.* ••➤ opposite **comfortable** –**uncomfortably** /-əbli/ **adv**

uncommon /ʌn'kɒmən/ **adj** unusual ••➤ opposite **common**

uncompromising /ʌn'kɒmprəmaızıŋ/ **adj** refusing to discuss or change a decision

unconcerned /ˌʌnkən'sɜːnd/ **adj** unconcerned (about/by/with sth) not interested in sth or not worried about it ••➤ opposite **concerned**

unconditional /ˌʌnkən'dıʃənl/ **adj** without limits or conditions: *an unconditional surrender* ••➤ opposite **conditional** –**unconditionally** /-ʃənəli/ **adv**

★**unconscious** /ʌn'kɒnʃəs/ **adj 1** in a state that is like sleep, for example because of injury or illness: *He was found lying unconscious on the kitchen floor.* **2** unconscious of sb/sth not knowing or aware of sb/sth **3** done, spoken, etc without you thinking about it or realizing it: *The article was full of unconscious humour.* ••➤ opposite **conscious 4 the unconscious noun** [sing] = **SUBCONSCIOUS** –**unconsciously adv** –**unconsciousness noun** [U]

uncontrollable /ˌʌnkən'trəʊləbl/ **adj** that you cannot control: *I suddenly had an uncontrollable urge to laugh.* –**uncontrollably** /-əbli/ **adv**

uncountable /ʌn'kaʊntəbl/ **adj** (*grammar*) an uncountable noun cannot be counted and so does not have a plural. In this dictionary uncountable nouns are marked '[U]'. ••➤ opposite **countable**

➤ For more information about uncountable nouns, look at the **Quick Grammar Reference** section at the back of this dictionary.

uncover /ʌn'kʌvə/ **verb** [T] **1** to remove the cover from sth ••➤ opposite **cover 2** to find out or discover sth: *Police have uncovered a plot to murder a top politician.*

undecided /ˌʌndɪ'saɪdɪd/ **adj 1** not having made a decision: *I'm still undecided about whether to take the job or not.* **2** without any result or decision ••➤ opposite **decided**

undeniable /ˌʌndɪ'naɪəbl/ **adj** clear, true or certain –**undeniably** /-əbli/ **adv**

★**under** /'ʌndə/ **prep, adv 1** in or to a position that is below sth: *We found him hiding under the table.* ● *The dog crawled under the gate and ran into the road.*

➤ Compare **under, below, beneath** and **underneath**. You use **under** to say that one thing is directly under another thing. There may be a space between the two things: *The cat is asleep under the table* or one thing

may be touching or covered by the other thing: *I think your letter is under that book.* You can use **below** to say that one thing is in a lower position than another thing: *They live on the floor below us.* ● *The skirt comes down to just below the knee.* You use **under** (not **below**) to talk about movement from one side of something to the other side: *We swam under the bridge.* You can use **beneath** in formal writing to say that one thing is directly under another thing, but **under** is more common. You can use **underneath** in place of **under** when you want to emphasize that something is being covered or hidden by another thing: *Have you looked underneath the sofa as well as behind it?*

2 below the surface of sth; covered by sth: *Most of an iceberg is under the water.* ● *He was wearing a vest under his shirt.* **3** less than a certain number; younger than a certain age: *People working under 20 hours a week will pay no extra tax.* ● *Nobody under eighteen is allowed to buy alcohol.* **4** governed or controlled by sb/sth: *The country is now under martial law.* **5** according to a law, agreement, system, etc: *Under English law you are innocent until you are proved guilty.* **6** experiencing a particular feeling, process or effect: *He was jailed for driving under the influence of alcohol.* ● *a building under construction* ● *The manager is under pressure to resign.* ● *I was under the impression that Bill was not very happy there.* **7** using a particular name: *to travel under a false name* **8** found in a particular part of a book, list, etc: *You'll find some information on rugby under 'team sports'.*

under- /'ʌndə/ (in compounds) **1** lower in level or position: *an under-secretary* **2** not enough: *undercooked food*

underclothes /'ʌndəkləʊðz/ **noun** [pl] = **UNDERWEAR**

undercover /ˌʌndə'kʌvə/ **adj** working or happening secretly: *an undercover reporter/ detective*

undercut /ˌʌndə'kʌt/ **verb** [T] (*pres part* **undercutting**; *pt, pp* **undercut**) to sell sth at a lower price than other shops, etc

underdog /'ʌndədɒg/ **noun** [C] a person, team, etc who is weaker than others, and not expected to be successful: *San Marino were the underdogs, but managed to win the game 2-1.*

underestimate /ˌʌndər'estɪmeɪt/ **verb** [T] **1** to guess that the amount, etc of sth will be less than it really is **2** to think that sb/sth is not as strong, good, etc as he/she/it really is: *Don't underestimate your opponent. He's a really good player.* ••➤ opposite **overestimate** –**underestimate** /-mət/ **noun** [C]

underfoot /ˌʌndə'fʊt/ **adv** under your feet; where you are walking: *It's very wet underfoot.*

undergo /ˌʌndə'gəʊ/ **verb** [T] (*pt* **underwent** /-'went/; *pp* **undergone** /-'gɒn/) to have a

u

difficult or unpleasant experience: *She underwent a five-hour operation.*

undergraduate /ˌʌndə'grædʒuət/ noun [C] a university student who has not yet taken his/her first degree •➤ Look at **graduate** and **postgraduate**.

*★**underground**[1] /'ʌndəgraʊnd/ adj 1** under the surface of the ground: *an underground car park* **2** secret or illegal: *an underground radio station*

*★**underground**[2] /ˌʌndə'graʊnd/ adv 1** under the surface of the ground: *The cables all run underground.* **2** into a secret place: *She went underground to escape from the police.*

*★**underground**[3] /'ʌndəgraʊnd/ (*US* **subway**) noun [sing] a railway system under the ground

> In London the underground railway is called **the underground** or **the tube**.

undergrowth /'ʌndəgrəʊθ/ noun [U] bushes and plants that grow around and under trees

underhand /ˌʌndə'hænd/ adj secret or not honest

*★**underline** /ˌʌndə'laɪn/ verb [T] **1** to draw a line under a word, etc **2** to show sth clearly or to emphasize sth: *This accident underlines the need for greater care.*

underlying /ˌʌndə'laɪɪŋ/ adj important but hidden: *the underlying causes of the disaster*

undermine /ˌʌndə'maɪn/ verb [T] to make sth weaker: *The public's confidence in the government has been undermined by the crisis.*

*★**underneath** /ˌʌndə'niːθ/ prep, adv under; below: *The coin rolled underneath the chair.* •➤ Look at the note at **under**.

the underneath /ˌʌndə'niːθ/ noun [sing] the bottom or lowest part of something: *There is a lot of rust on the underneath of the car.*

underpants /'ʌndəpænts/ (*Brit also* **pants**) noun [pl] a piece of clothing that men or boys wear under their trousers

underpass /'ʌndəpɑːs/ noun [C] a road or path that goes under another road, railway, etc

underpay /ˌʌndə'peɪ/ verb [T] (*pt, pp* **underpaid**) to pay sb too little •➤ opposite **overpay**

underprivileged /ˌʌndə'prɪvəlɪdʒd/ adj having less money, rights, opportunities, etc than other people in society •➤ opposite **privileged**

underrate /ˌʌndə'reɪt/ verb [T] to think that sb/sth is less clever, important, good, etc than he/she/it really is •➤ opposite **overrate**

undershirt /'ʌndəʃɜːt/ noun (*US*) = **VEST**(1)

*★**understand** /ˌʌndə'stænd/ verb (*pt, pp* **understood** /-'stʊd/) **1** [I,T] to know or realize the meaning of sth: *I'm not sure that I really understand.* • *I didn't understand the instructions.* • *Please speak more slowly. I can't understand you.* • *Do you understand what I'm asking you?* **2** [T] to know how or why sth happens or why it is important: *I can't understand why the engine won't start.* • *As far as I understand it, the changes won't*

affect *us.* **3** [T] to know sb's character and why he/she behaves in a particular way: *It's easy to understand why she felt so angry.* **4** [T] (*formal*) to have heard or been told sth IDIOMS **give sb to believe/understand (that)** → **BELIEVE**

make yourself understood to make your meaning clear: *I can just about make myself understood in Russian.*

understandable /ˌʌndə'stændəbl/ adj that you can understand –**understandably** /-əbli/ adv: *She was understandably angry at the decision.*

*★**understanding**[1] /ˌʌndə'stændɪŋ/ noun **1** [U, sing] the knowledge that sb has of a particular subject or situation: *A basic understanding of physics is necessary for this course.* • *He has little understanding of how computers work.* **2** [C, usually sing] an informal agreement: *I'm sure we can **come to/reach an understanding** about the money I owe him.* **3** [U] the ability to know why people behave in a particular way and to forgive them if they do sth wrong or bad **4** [U] the way in which you think sth is meant: *My understanding of the arrangement is that he will only phone if there is a problem.*

IDIOM **on the understanding that...** only if...; because it was agreed that...: *We let them stay in our house on the understanding that it was only for a short period.*

*★**understanding**[2] /ˌʌndə'stændɪŋ/ adj showing kind feelings towards sb; sympathetic

understate /ˌʌndə'steɪt/ verb [T] to say that sth is smaller or less important than it really is •➤ opposite **overstate** –**understatement** noun [C]: *'Is she pleased?' 'That's an understatement. She's delighted.'*

understudy /'ʌndəstʌdi/ noun [C] (*pl* **understudies**) an actor who learns the role of another actor and replaces him/her if he/she is ill

undertake /ˌʌndə'teɪk/ verb [T] (*pt* **undertook** /-'tʊk/; *pp* **undertaken** /-'teɪkən/) **1** to decide to do sth and start doing it: *The company is undertaking a major programme of modernization.* **2** to agree or promise to do sth

undertaker /'ʌndəteɪkə/ (also **funeral director**; *US also* **mortician**) noun [C] a person whose job is to prepare dead bodies to be buried and to arrange funerals

undertaking /ˌʌndə'teɪkɪŋ/ noun [C, usually sing] **1** a piece of work or business: *Buying the company would be a risky undertaking.* **2** undertaking (that.../to do sth) a formal or legal promise to do sth

undertone /'ʌndətəʊn/ noun [C] a feeling, quality or meaning that is not expressed in a direct way

IDIOM **in an undertone; in undertones** in a quiet voice

undervalue /ˌʌndə'væljuː/ verb [T] to place too low a value on sb/sth

underwater /ˌʌndə'wɔːtə/ adj, adv existing, happening or used below the surface of water: *underwater exploration* • *an underwater camera* • *Can you swim underwater?*

★**underwear** /'ʌndəweə/ noun [U] clothing that is worn next to the skin under other clothes

> **Underclothes** has the same meaning and is a plural noun.

underweight /ˌʌndə'weɪt/ adj weighing less than is normal or correct ••➤ Look at the note at **thin**. ••➤ opposite **overweight**

the underworld /'ʌndəwɜːld/ noun [sing] people who are involved in organized crime

undesirable /ˌʌndɪ'zaɪərəbl/ adj unpleasant or not wanted; likely to cause problems ••➤ opposite **desirable**

undid *past tense* of **UNDO**

undignified /ʌn'dɪgnɪfaɪd/ adj causing you to look foolish and to lose the respect of other people ••➤ opposite **dignified**

undivided /ˌʌndɪ'vaɪdɪd/ adj
IDIOMS **get/have sb's undivided attention** to receive all sb's attention
give your undivided attention (to sb/sth) to give all your attention to sb/sth

★**undo** /ʌn'duː/ verb [T] (*3rd pers sing pres* **undoes**; *pt* **undid**; *pp* **undone**) **1** to open sth that was tied or fastened: *to undo a knot/ zip/button* **2** to destroy the effect of sth that has already happened: *His mistake has undone all our good work.*

undone /ˌʌn'dʌn/ adj **1** open; not fastened or tied: *I realized that my zip was undone.* **2** not done: *I left the housework undone.*

undoubted /ʌn'daʊtɪd/ adj definite; accepted as being true –**undoubtedly** adv

★**undress** /ʌn'dres/ verb **1** [I] to take off your clothes ••➤ **Get undressed** is more commonly used than **undress**: *He got undressed and had a shower.* **2** [T] to take off sb's clothes ••➤ opposite **dress** –**undressed** adj

undue /ˌʌn'djuː/ adj more than is necessary or reasonable: *The police try not to use undue force when arresting a person.* –**unduly** adv: *She didn't seem unduly worried by their unexpected arrival.*

unearth /ʌn'ɜːθ/ verb [T] to dig sth up out of the ground; to discover sth that was hidden: *Archaeologists have unearthed a Roman tomb.*

unearthly /ʌn'ɜːθli/ adj strange or frightening: *an unearthly scream*
IDIOM **at an unearthly hour** (*informal*) extremely early in the morning

unease /ʌn'iːz/ (also **uneasiness**) noun [U] a worried or uncomfortable feeling ••➤ opposite **ease**

uneasy /ʌn'iːzi/ adj **1** **uneasy (about sth/ doing sth)** worried; not feeling relaxed or comfortable **2** not settled; unlikely to last: *an uneasy compromise* –**uneasily** adv

uneconomic /ˌʌniːkə'nɒmɪk; ˌʌnek-/ adj (used about a company, etc) not making or likely to make a profit; unprofitable ••➤ opposite **economic**

uneconomical /ˌʌniːkə'nɒmɪkl; ˌʌnek-/ adj

wasting money, time, materials, etc ••➤ opposite **economical** –**uneconomically** /-kli/ adv

★**unemployed** /ˌʌnɪm'plɔɪd/ adj **1** not able to find a job; out of work: *She has been unemployed for over a year.* ••➤ synonym **jobless** ••➤ opposite **employed** **2** **the unemployed** noun [pl] people who cannot find a job

★**unemployment** /ˌʌnɪm'plɔɪmənt/ noun [U] **1** the situation of not being able to find a job: *The number of people claiming unemployment benefit* (= money given by the state) *has gone up.* ••➤ opposite **employment** **2** the number of people who are unemployed: *The economy is doing very badly and unemployment is rising.* ••➤ synonym **joblessness** ••➤ Look at **the dole**.

unending /ʌn'endɪŋ/ adj having or seeming to have no end

unequal /ʌn'iːkwəl/ adj **1** not fair or balanced: *an unequal distribution of power* **2** different in size, amount, level, etc ••➤ opposite **equal** –**unequally** adv

uneven /ʌn'iːvn/ adj **1** not completely smooth, level or regular: *The sign was painted in rather uneven letters.* ••➤ opposite **even** **2** not always of the same level or quality –**unevenly** adv: *The country's wealth is unevenly distributed.*

★**unexpected** /ˌʌnɪk'spektɪd/ adj not expected and therefore causing surprise –**unexpectedly** adv: *I got there late because I was unexpectedly delayed.*

★**unfair** /ˌʌn'feə/ adj **1** **unfair (on/to sb)** not dealing with people as they deserve; not treating each person equally: *This law is unfair to women.* • *The tax is unfair on people with low incomes.* **2** not following the rules and therefore giving an advantage to one person, team, etc ••➤ opposite **fair** –**unfairly** adv –**unfairness** noun [U]

unfaithful /ʌn'feɪθfl/ adj **unfaithful (to sb/ sth)** having a sexual relationship with sb who is not your husband, wife or partner ••➤ opposite **faithful** –**unfaithfulness** noun [U]

unfamiliar /ˌʌnfə'mɪliə/ adj **1** **unfamiliar (to sb)** that you do not know well: *an unfamiliar part of town* **2** **unfamiliar (with sth)** not having knowledge or experience of sth: *I'm unfamiliar with this author.* ••➤ opposite **familiar**

unfashionable /ʌn'fæʃnəbl/ adj not popular at a particular time: *unfashionable ideas/ clothes* ••➤ opposite **fashionable** ••➤ Look also at **old-fashioned**.

unfavourable (*US* **unfavorable**) /ʌn-'feɪvərəbl/ adj **1** showing that you do not like or approve of sb/sth **2** not good and likely to cause problems or make sth difficult ••➤ opposite **favourable** ••➤ Look also at **adverse**.

unfit /ʌn'fɪt/ adj **1** **unfit (for sth/to do sth)** not suitable or not good enough for sth: *His*

u

ð **then** | s **so** | z **zoo** | ʃ **she** | ʒ **vision** | h **how** | m **man** | n **no** | ŋ **sing** | l **leg** | r **red** | j **yes** | w **wet**

criminal past makes him unfit to be a polit-
ician. **2** not in good physical health, especially because you do not get enough exercise
•◦➤ opposite **fit**

unfold /ʌnˈfəʊld/ *verb* [I,T] **1** to open out and
become flat; to open out sth that was folded:
The sofa unfolds into a spare bed. • *I unfolded
the letter and read it.* •◦➤ opposite **fold (up)**
2 to become known, or to allow sth to become
known a little at a time

unforeseen /ˌʌnfɔːˈsiːn/ *adj* not expected:
an unforeseen problem

unforgettable /ˌʌnfəˈgetəbl/ *adj* making
such a strong impression that you cannot
forget it

★**unfortunate** /ʌnˈfɔːtʃənət/ *adj* **1** not lucky
•◦➤ opposite **fortunate 2** that you feel sorry
about –**unfortunately** *adv*: *I'd like to help you
but unfortunately there's nothing I can do.*

unfounded /ʌnˈfaʊndɪd/ *adj* not based on or
supported by facts: *unfounded allegations*

★**unfriendly** /ʌnˈfrendli/ *adj* unfriendly (to/
towards sb) unpleasant or not polite to sb
•◦➤ opposite **friendly**

ungainly /ʌnˈgeɪnli/ *adj* moving in a way
that is not smooth or elegant

ungrateful /ʌnˈgreɪtfl/ *adj* not feeling or
showing thanks to sb •◦➤ opposite **grateful**
–**ungratefully** /-fəli/ *adv*

unguarded /ʌnˈgɑːdɪd/ *adj* **1** not protected
or guarded **2** saying more than you wanted to
•◦➤ opposite **guarded**

unhappily /ʌnˈhæpɪli/ *adv* **1** sadly **2** unfortunately •◦➤ opposite **happily**

★**unhappy** /ʌnˈhæpi/ *adj* (**unhappier**; **un-
happiest**) **1** unhappy (about sth) sad: *She's
terribly unhappy about losing her job.* • *He
had a very unhappy childhood.* **2** unhappy
(about/at/with sth) not satisfied or pleased;
worried: *They're unhappy at having to accept
a pay cut.* •◦➤ opposite **happy** –**unhappiness**
noun [U]

unhealthy /ʌnˈhelθi/ *adj* **1** not having or
showing good health: *He looks pale and
unhealthy.* **2** likely to cause illness or poor
health: *unhealthy conditions* **3** not natural: *an
unhealthy interest in death* •◦➤ opposite
healthy

unheard /ʌnˈhɜːd/ *adj* (not before a noun)
not listened to or given any attention: *My
suggestions went unheard.*

un'heard-of *adj* not known; never having
happened before

unicorn /ˈjuːnɪkɔːn/ *noun* [C] an animal that
only exists in stories, that looks like a white
horse with one horn growing out of its forehead

unidentified /ˌʌnaɪˈdentɪfaɪd/ *adj* whose
identity is not known: *An unidentified body
has been found in the river.*

★**uniform¹** /ˈjuːnɪfɔːm/ *noun* [C,U] the set of
clothes worn at work by the members of
certain organizations or groups and by some
schoolchildren: *I didn't know he was a policeman because he wasn't in uniform.* –**uni-
formed** *adj*

uniform² /ˈjuːnɪfɔːm/ *adj* not varying; the
same in all cases or at all times –**uniformity**
/ˌjuːnɪˈfɔːməti/ *noun* [U]

unify /ˈjuːnɪfaɪ/ *verb* [T] (*pres part* **unifying**;
3rd pers sing pres **unifies**; *pt, pp* **unified**) to
join separate parts together to make one unit,
or to make them similar to each other
–**unification** /ˌjuːnɪfɪˈkeɪʃn/ *noun* [U]

unilateral /ˌjuːnɪˈlætrəl/ *adj* done or made
by one person who is involved in sth without
the agreement of the other person or people:
a unilateral declaration of independence
•◦➤ Look at **multilateral**. –**unilaterally** /-rəli/
adv

uninhabitable /ˌʌnɪnˈhæbɪtəbl/ *adj* not
possible to live in •◦➤ opposite **habitable**

uninhabited /ˌʌnɪnˈhæbɪtɪd/ *adj* (used
about a place or a building) with nobody
living in it •◦➤ opposite **inhabited**

uninhibited /ˌʌnɪnˈhɪbɪtɪd/ *adj* behaving in
a free and natural way, without worrying
what other people think of you •◦➤ opposite
inhibited

unintelligible /ˌʌnɪnˈtelɪdʒəbl/ *adj* impossible to understand •◦➤ opposite **intelligible**

uninterested /ʌnˈɪntrəstɪd/ *adj* uninterested (in sb/sth) having or showing no interest in sb/sth: *She seemed uninterested in
anything I had to say.* •◦➤ opposite **interested**

➤ Compare **disinterested**, it has a different
meaning.

★**union** /ˈjuːniən/ *noun* **1** [U,sing] the action of
joining or the situation of being joined **2** [C] a
group of states or countries that have joined
together to form one country or group: *the
European Union* **3** =**TRADE UNION 4** [C] an
organization for a particular group of people:
the Athletics Union

the ˌUnion ˈJack *noun* [C] the national flag
of the United Kingdom, with red and white
crosses on a dark blue background

★**unique** /juˈniːk/ *adj* **1** not like anything else;
being the only one of its type: *Shakespeare
made a unique contribution to the world of
literature.* **2** unique to sb/sth connected with
only one place, person or thing: *This dance is
unique to this region.* **3** very unusual

unisex /ˈjuːniseks/ *adj* designed for and used
by both sexes: *unisex fashions*

unison /ˈjuːnɪsn/ *noun*
IDIOM in unison saying, singing or doing the
same thing at the same time as sb else: *'No,
thank you,' they said in unison.*

★**unit** /ˈjuːnɪt/ *noun* [C] **1** a single thing which
is complete in itself, although it can be part
of sth larger: *The book is divided into ten
units.* **2** a fixed amount or number used as a
standard of measurement: *a unit of currency*
3 a group of people who perform a certain
function within a larger organization: *the
intensive care unit of a hospital* **4** a small
machine that performs a particular task or
that is part of a larger machine: *The heart of
a computer is the central processing unit.* **5** a
piece of furniture that fits with other pieces

of furniture and has a particular use: *matching kitchen units* ••→ picture on page C7

unite /juːˈnaɪt/ *verb* **1** [I,T] to join together and act in agreement; to make this happen: *Unless we unite, our enemies will defeat us.* **2** [I] unite **(in sth/in doing sth)** to join together for a particular purpose: *We should all unite in seeking a solution to this terrible problem.*

united /juːˈnaɪtɪd/ *adj* joined together by a common feeling or aim

the U,nited ˈKingdom *noun* [sing] (*abbr* **UK**) England, Scotland, Wales and Northern Ireland

> **The UK** includes England, Scotland, Wales and Northern Ireland, but *not* the Republic of Ireland (Eire), which is a separate country. **Great Britain** is England, Scotland and Wales only. **The British Isles** include England, Scotland, Wales, Northern Ireland and the Republic of Ireland.

the U,nited ˈNations *noun* [sing, with sing or pl verb] (*abbr* **UN**) the organization formed to encourage peace in the world and to deal with problems between countries

the U,nited ˈStates (of Aˈmerica) *noun* [sing, with sing or pl verb] (*abbr* **US**; **USA**) a large country in North America made up of 50 states and the District of Columbia

unity /ˈjuːnəti/ *noun* [U] the situation in which people are in agreement and working together

★**universal** /ˌjuːnɪˈvɜːsl/ *adj* connected with, done by or affecting everyone in the world or everyone in a particular group: *The environment is a universal issue.* –**universally** /-səli/ *adv*

the universe /ˈjuːnɪvɜːs/ *noun* [sing] everything that exists, including the planets, stars, space, etc

★**university** /ˌjuːnɪˈvɜːsəti/ *noun* [C] (*pl* **universities**) an institution that provides the highest level of education, in which students study for degrees and in which academic research is done: *Which university did you go to?* • *I did History at university.* • *a university lecturer*

> We use the expressions **at university** and **go to university** without *a* or *the* when we mean that somebody attends the university as a student: *He's hoping to go to university next year but not if somebody goes there for any other reason: I'm going to a conference at the university in July.*

★**unkind** /ˌʌnˈkaɪnd/ *adj* unpleasant and not friendly: *That was an unkind thing to do.* • *The zoo was accused of being unkind to its animals.* ••→ opposite **kind** –**unkindly** *adv* –**unkindness** *noun* [C,U]

unknown¹ /ˌʌnˈnəʊn/ *adj* **1** unknown **(to sb)** that sb does not know; without sb knowing: *Unknown to the boss, she went home early.* **2** not famous or familiar to other people: *an unknown actress* ••→ opposite **well-known** or **famous**

IDIOM **an unknown quantity** a person or thing that you know very little about

unknown² /ˌʌnˈnəʊn/ *noun* **1** (usually **the unknown**) [sing] a place or thing that you know nothing about: *a fear of the unknown* **2** [C] a person who is not well known

unleaded /ˌʌnˈledɪd/ *adj* not containing lead: *unleaded petrol*

★**unless** /ənˈles/ *conj* if…not; except if: *I was told that unless my work improved, I would lose the job.* • *'Would you like a cup of coffee?' 'Not unless you've already made some.'* • *Unless anyone has anything else to say, the meeting is closed.* • *Don't switch that on unless I'm here.*

★**unlike** /ˌʌnˈlaɪk/ *adj, prep* **1** in contrast to; different from: *She's unlike anyone else I've ever met.* • *He's extremely ambitious, unlike me.* • *This is an exciting place to live, unlike my home town.* **2** not typical of; unusual for: *It's unlike him to be so rude – he's usually very polite.*

★**unlikely** /ʌnˈlaɪkli/ *adj* (**unlikelier**; **unlikeliest**) **1** unlikely **(to do sth/that…)** not likely to happen; not expected; not probable: *I suppose she might win but I think it's very unlikely.* • *It's highly unlikely that I'll have any free time next week.* ••→ opposite **likely** **2** difficult to believe: *an unlikely excuse* ••→ synonym **improbable**

unlimited /ʌnˈlɪmɪtɪd/ *adj* without limit; as much or as great as you want ••→ opposite **limited**

★**unload** /ˌʌnˈləʊd/ *verb* **1** [I,T] unload **(sth) (from sth)** to take things that have been transported off or out of a vehicle: *We unloaded the boxes from the back of the van.* **2** [I,T] (used about a vehicle) to have the things removed that have been transported: *Parking here is restricted to vehicles that are loading or unloading.* ••→ opposite **load** **3** [T] (*informal*) unload **sb/sth (on/onto sb)** to get rid of sth you do not want or to pass it to sb else: *He shouldn't try and unload the responsibility onto you.*

unlock /ˌʌnˈlɒk/ *verb* [I,T] to open the lock on sth using a key; to be opened with a key: *I can't unlock this door.* • *This door won't unlock.* ••→ opposite **lock**

★**unlucky** /ˌʌnˈlʌki/ *adj* (**unluckier**; **unluckiest**) having or causing bad luck: *They were unlucky to lose because they played so well.* • *Thirteen is often thought to be an unlucky number.* ••→ opposite **lucky** –**unluckily** *adv*

unmarried /ˌʌnˈmærɪd/ *adj* not married; single ••→ opposite **married**

unmistakable /ˌʌnmɪˈsteɪkəbl/ *adj* that cannot be confused with anything else; easy to recognize: *She had an unmistakable French accent.* –**unmistakably** /-əbli/ *adv*

unmoved /ˌʌnˈmuːvd/ *adj* not affected emotionally: *The judge was unmoved by the boy's sad story, and sent him to jail.*

unnatural /ʌnˈnætʃrəl/ *adj* different from what is normal or expected ••→ opposite **nat-**

u

ural –**unnaturally** /-rəli/ **adv**: *It's unnaturally quiet in here.*

★**unnecessary** /ˌʌn'nesəsəri/ **adj** more than is needed or acceptable: *We should try to avoid all unnecessary expense.* •➤ Look at **needless**, it has a different meaning. •➤ opposite **necessary** –**unnecessarily** /ˌʌnˌnesə'serəli/ **adv**: *His explanation was unnecessarily complicated.*

unnoticed /ˌʌn'nəʊtɪst/ **adj** not noticed or seen: *He didn't want his hard work to go unnoticed.*

unobtrusive /ˌʌnəb'truːsɪv/ **adj** avoiding being noticed; not attracting attention –**unobtrusively adv**: *He tried leave as unobtrusively as possible.*

unofficial /ˌʌnə'fɪʃl/ **adj** not accepted or approved by a person in authority: *an unofficial strike* • *Unofficial reports say that four people died in the explosion.* •➤ opposite **official** –**unofficially** /-ʃəli/ **adv**

unorthodox /ʌn'ɔːθədɒks/ **adj** different from what is generally accepted, usual or traditional •➤ opposite **orthodox**

unpack /ˌʌn'pæk/ **verb** [I,T] to take out the things that were in a bag, suitcase, etc: *When we arrived at the hotel we unpacked and went to the beach.* •➤ opposite **pack**

unpaid /ˌʌn'peɪd/ **adj** **1** not yet paid: *an unpaid bill* **2** not receiving money for work done: *an unpaid assistant* **3** (used about work) done without payment: *unpaid overtime*

★**unpleasant** /ʌn'pleznt/ **adj** **1** causing you to have a bad feeling; not nice: *This news has come as an unpleasant surprise.* •➤ opposite **pleasant** **2** unfriendly; impolite: *There's no need to get unpleasant, we can discuss this in a friendly way.* –**unpleasantly adv**

unplug /ˌʌn'plʌg/ **verb** [T] (**unplugging**; **unplugged**) to remove a piece of electrical equipment from the electricity supply: *Could you unplug the cassette recorder, please?* •➤ opposite **plug sth in**

unpopular /ˌʌn'pɒpjələ/ **adj** unpopular (with sb) not liked by many people: *Her methods made her very unpopular with the staff.* •➤ opposite **popular** –**unpopularity** /ˌʌnˌpɒpju'lærəti/ **noun** [U]

unprecedented /ʌn'presɪdentɪd/ **adj** never having happened or existed before •➤ Look at **precedent**.

unprovoked /ˌʌnprə'vəʊkt/ **adj** (used especially about an attack) not caused by anything the person who is attacked has said or done •➤ opposite **provoked**

unqualified /ˌʌn'kwɒlɪfaɪd/ **adj** **1** not having the knowledge or not having passed the exams that you need for sth: *I'm unqualified to offer an opinion on this matter.* •➤ opposite **qualified** **2** complete; absolute: *an unqualified success*

unquestionable /ʌn'kwestʃənəbl/ **adj** certain; that cannot be doubted •➤ opposite **questionable** –**unquestionably** /-əbli/ **adv**: *She is unquestionably the most famous opera singer in the world.*

unravel /ʌn'rævl/ **verb** (**unravelling**; **unravelled**; *US* **unraveling**; **unraveled**) [I,T] **1** to unfasten or remove the knots from a piece of string, thread, etc; to come unfastened in this way: *I unravelled the tangled string and wound it into a ball.* **2** (used about a complicated story, etc) to become or to make sth become clear

unreal /ˌʌn'rɪəl/ **adj** **1** very strange and seeming more like a dream than reality: *Her voice had an unreal quality about it* **2** not connected with reality: *Some people have unreal expectations of marriage.*

unreasonable /ʌn'riːznəbl/ **adj** unfair; expecting too much: *I think she is being totally unreasonable.* • *He makes unreasonable demands on his staff.* •➤ opposite **reasonable** –**unreasonably** /-əbli/ **adv**

unrelenting /ˌʌnrɪ'lentɪŋ/ **adj** continuously strong, not becoming weaker or stopping

unreserved /ˌʌnrɪ'zɜːvd/ **adj** **1** (used about seats in a theatre, etc) not kept for the use of a particular person •➤ opposite **reserved** **2** without limit; complete: *The government's action received the unreserved support of all parties.* –**unreservedly** /ˌʌnrɪ'zɜːvɪdli/ **adv**

unrest /ʌn'rest/ **noun** [U] a situation in which people are angry or not happy and likely to protest or fight: *social unrest*

unrivalled (*US* **unrivaled**) /ʌn'raɪvld/ **adj** much better than any other of the same type: *His knowledge of Greek theology is unrivalled.*

unroll /ʌn'rəʊl/ **verb** [I,T] to open from a rolled position: *He unrolled the poster and stuck it on the wall.* •➤ opposite **roll up**

unruly /ʌn'ruːli/ **adj** difficult to control; without discipline: *an unruly crowd* –**unruliness noun** [U]

unsavoury (*US* **unsavory**) /ˌʌn'seɪvəri/ **adj** unpleasant; not morally acceptable: *His friends are all unsavoury characters.*

unscathed /ʌn'skeɪðd/ **adj** not hurt, without injury: *He came out of the fight unscathed.*

unscrew /ˌʌn'skruː/ **verb** [T] **1** to remove the screws from sth **2** to open or remove sth by turning it: *Could you unscrew the top of this bottle for me?*

unscrupulous /ʌn'skruːpjələs/ **adj** being dishonest, cruel or unfair in order to get what you want •➤ opposite **scrupulous**

unsightly /ʌn'saɪtli/ **adj** very unpleasant to look at; ugly: *an unsightly new building*

unskilled /ˌʌn'skɪld/ **adj** not having or needing special skill or training: *an unskilled job/worker* •➤ opposite **skilled**

unsolicited /ˌʌnsə'lɪsɪtɪd/ **adj** not asked for: *unsolicited praise/advice*

unsound /ˌʌn'saʊnd/ **1** in poor condition; weak: *The building is structurally unsound.* **2** based on wrong ideas and therefore mistaken •➤ opposite **sound**

unstable /ʌn'steɪbl/ **adj** **1** likely to fall down or move; not firmly fixed **2** likely to change or fail: *a period of unstable government* **3** (used about a person's moods or behaviour) likely to change suddenly or often •➤ opposite **stable** •➤ noun **instability**

unstuck /ˌʌn'stʌk/ adj no longer stuck together or stuck down: *The label on the parcel is about to come unstuck.*

IDIOM **come unstuck** to fail badly; to be unsuccessful: *His plan came unstuck when he realized he didn't have enough money.*

unsuitable /ˌʌn'su:təbl/ adj not right or appropriate for sb/sth: *This film is unsuitable for children under 12.* •➤ opposite **suitable**

unsure /ˌʌn'ʃɔ:/ adj **1** unsure of yourself not feeling confident about yourself: *He's young and still quite unsure of himself.* **2** unsure (about/of sth) not certain; having doubts: *I didn't argue because I was unsure of the facts.* •➤ opposite **sure** or **certain**

unsuspecting /ˌʌnsə'spektɪŋ/ adj not realizing that there is danger •➤ Look at **suspect** and **suspicious**.

untangle /ˌʌn'tæŋgl/ verb [T] to separate threads which have become tied together in a confused way: *The wires got mixed up and it took me ages to untangle them.*

unthinkable /ʌn'θɪŋkəbl/ adj impossible to imagine or accept: *It was unthinkable that he would never see her again.*

unthinking /ʌn'θɪŋkɪŋ/ adj done, said, etc without thinking carefully –**unthinkingly** adv

★**untidy** /ʌn'taɪdi/ adj **1** not tidy or well arranged: *an untidy bedroom • untidy hair* **2** (used about a person) not keeping things tidy or in good order: *My flatmate is so untidy!* •➤ opposite **tidy** or **neat** –**untidily** adv –**untidiness** noun [U]

untie /ʌn'taɪ/ verb [T] (*pres part* **untying**; *3rd pers sing pres* **unties**; *pt, pp* **untied**) to remove a knot; to free sb/sth that is tied by a rope, etc •➤ opposite **tie up** or **fasten**

until /ən'tɪl/ (also **till**) prep, conj up to the time or the event mentioned: *The restaurant is open until midnight. • Until that moment she had been happy. • She waited until he had finished. • We won't leave until the police get here* (= we won't leave before they come).

➤ We can use **until** in both formal and informal English. **Till** is more common in informal English and is not usually used at the beginning of a sentence. Make sure that you only use **till**/ **until** to talk about a time. We use **as far as** to talk about distance: *I walked as far as the shops.* We use **up to** to talk about a number: *You can take up to 20 kilos of luggage.*

untold /ˌʌn'təʊld/ adj very great; so big, etc that you cannot count or measure it: *untold suffering*

untoward /ˌʌntə'wɔ:d/ adj (used about an event, etc) unexpected and unpleasant: *The security guard noticed nothing untoward.*

untruth /ʌn'tru:θ/ noun [C] (*pl* **untruths** /-'tru:ðz/) (*written*) something that is not true; a lie –**untruthful** /-fl/ adj

untypical /ʌn'tɪpɪkl/ adj not typical or usual: *an untypical example* •➤ opposite **typical**. •➤ Compare **atypical**.

unused¹ /ˌʌn'ju:zd/ adj that has not been used

unused² /ˌʌn'ju:st/ adj unused to sth/to doing sth not having any experience of sth: *She was unused to getting such a lot of attention.*

★**unusual** /ʌn'ju:ʒuəl; -ʒəl/ adj **1** not expected or normal: *It's unusual for Joe to be late.* •➤ opposite **usual 2** interesting because it is different: *What an unusual hat!*

unusually /ʌn'ju:ʒuəli; -ʒəli/ adv **1** in a way that is not normal or typical of sb/sth: *Unusually for her, she forgot his birthday.* •➤ opposite **usually 2** more than is common; extremely

unveil /ˌʌn'veɪl/ verb [T] to show sth new to the public for the first time: *The President unveiled a memorial to those who died in the war.*

unwanted /ˌʌn'wɒntɪd/ adj not wanted: *an unwanted gift*

unwarranted /ʌn'wɒrəntɪd/ adj that is not deserved or for which there is no good reason: *unwarranted criticism*

unwell /ʌn'wel/ adj (not before a noun) ill; sick: *to feel unwell*

unwieldy /ʌn'wi:ldi/ adj difficult to move or carry because it is too big, heavy, etc

unwilling /ʌn'wɪlɪŋ/ adj not wanting to do sth but often forced to do it by other people •➤ opposite **willing**

unwind /ˌʌn'waɪnd/ verb (*pt, pp* **unwound** /-'waʊnd/) **1** [I,T] if you unwind sth or if sth unwinds, it comes away from sth that it had been put round: *The bandage had unwound.* **2** [I] (*informal*) to relax, especially after working hard: *After a busy day, it takes me a while to unwind.* •➤ Look at **wind³**.

unwise /ˌʌn'waɪz/ adj showing a lack of good judgement; foolish: *It would be unwise to tell anyone about our plan yet.* •➤ opposite **wise** –**unwisely** adv

unwitting /ʌn'wɪtɪŋ/ adj not realizing sth; not intending to do sth: *an unwitting accomplice to the crime* –**unwittingly** adv

unwrap /ʌn'ræp/ verb [T] (**unwrapping**; **unwrapped**) to take off the paper, etc that covers or protects sth

unzip /ˌʌn'zɪp/ verb [I,T] (**unzipping**; **unzipped**) if a bag, piece of clothing, etc unzips, or you unzip it, you open it by pulling on the device that fastens the opening (the zip) •➤ opposite **zip (up)**

★**up** /ʌp/ prep, adv

➤ For special uses with many verbs, for example **pick sth up**, look at the verb entries.

1 at or to a high or higher level or position: *The monkey climbed up the tree. • I carried her suitcase up to the third floor. • Put your hand up if you know the answer. • I walked up the hill.* **2** in or into a vertical position: *Stand up, please. • Is he* (= out of bed) *up yet?* **3** used for showing an increase in sth: *Prices have gone up. • Turn the volume up.* **4** used with verbs of closing or covering: *Do up your coat. It's cold. • She tied the parcel up with*

u

string. ● *I found some wood to **cover up** the hole.* **5** to the place where sb/sth is: *She ran up to her mother and kissed her.* ● *A car drove up and two men got out.* **6** coming or being put together: *The teacher collected up our exam papers.* ● *Asif and Joe teamed up in the doubles competition.* **7** (used about a period of time) finished: *Stop writing. Your time's up.* **8** into pieces: *We chopped the old table up and used it for firewood.* ● *She tore **up** the letter and threw it away.* **9** used for showing that an action continues until it is completed: *Eat up, everybody, I want you to finish everything on the table.* ● *Can you help me **clean up** the kitchen?* **10** in a particular direction: *I live just **up the road**.* ● *Move up a little and let me sit down.* **11** in or to the north: *My parents have just moved **up north**.* ● *When are you going up to Scotland?* **12** (used about computers) working; in operation: *Are the computers back up yet?* **13** (*informal*) used for showing that sth is spoiled: *I really messed up when I told the interviewer I liked sleeping.*

IDIOMS **be up for sth 1** to be available to be bought or chosen: *That house is up for sale.* ● *How many candidates are up for election?* **2** (*informal*) to be enthusiastic about doing sth: *Is anyone up for a swim?*

be up to sb to be sb's responsibility: *I can't take the decision. It's not up to me.*

not up to much (*informal*) not very good: *The programme wasn't up to much.*

up against sth/sb facing sth/sb that causes problems

up and down backwards and forwards, or rising and falling: *He was nervously walking up and down outside the interview room.*

up and running (used about sth new) working well

up to sth 1 as much/many as: *We're expecting up to 100 people at the meeting.* **2** as far as now: *Up to now, things have been easy.* **3** capable of sth: *I don't feel up to cooking this evening. I'm too tired.* **4** doing sth secret and perhaps bad: *What are the children up to? Go and see.*

what's up? (*informal*) what's the matter?

upbringing /'ʌpbrɪŋɪŋ/ **noun** [sing] the way a child is treated and taught how to behave by his/her parents: *a strict upbringing*

update /ˌʌp'deɪt/ **verb** [T] **1** to make sth more modern **2** to put the latest information into sth; to give sb the latest information: *Our database of addresses is updated regularly.* –**update** /'ʌpdeɪt/ **noun** [C]: *an update on a news story* (= the latest information)

upgrade /ˌʌp'greɪd/ **verb** [T] to change sth so that it is of a higher standard: *Upgrading your computer software can be expensive.* –**upgrade** /'ʌpgreɪd/ **noun** [C]

upheaval /ʌp'hiːvl/ **noun** [C,U] a sudden big change, especially one that causes a lot of trouble

uphill /ˌʌp'hɪl/ **adj, adv 1** going towards the top of a hill ●➤ opposite **downhill 2** needing a lot of effort: *It was an uphill struggle to find a job.*

uphold /ʌp'həʊld/ **verb** [T] (*pt, pp* **upheld** /-'held/) to support a decision, etc especially when other people are against it

upholstered /ʌp'həʊlstəd/ **adj** (used about a chair, etc) covered with a soft thick material

upholstery /ʌp'həʊlstəri/ **noun** [U] the thick soft materials used to cover chairs, car seats, etc

upkeep /'ʌpkiːp/ **noun** [U] **1** the cost or process of keeping sth in a good condition: *The landlord pays for the upkeep of the building.* **2** the cost or process of providing children or animals with what they need to live

upland /'ʌplənd/ **adj** consisting of hills and mountains –**upland noun** [C,usually pl]

uplifting /ˌʌp'lɪftɪŋ/ **adj** producing a feeling of hope and happiness: *an uplifting speech*

upon /ə'pɒn/ **prep** (*formal*) = **ON**

★**upper** /'ʌpə/ **adj** in a higher position than sth else; situated above sth: *He had a cut on his upper lip.* ●➤ opposite **lower**

IDIOM **get, have, etc the upper hand** to get into a stronger position than another person; to gain control over sb

ˌ**upper 'case noun** [U] letters that are written or printed in their large form; capital letters: *'BBC' is written in upper case.* ●➤ opposite **lower case**

uppermost /'ʌpəməʊst/ **adj** in the highest or most important position: *Concern for her family was **uppermost in her mind**.*

★**upright** /'ʌpraɪt/ **adj, adv 1** in or into a vertical position: *I was so tired I could hardly stay upright.* ●➤ synonym **erect 2** honest and responsible

IDIOM **bolt upright → BOLT³**

uprising /'ʌpraɪzɪŋ/ **noun** [C] a situation in which a group of people start to fight against the people in power in their country

uproar /'ʌprɔː/ **noun** [U,sing] a lot of noisy, confusion, anger, etc; an angry discussion about sth: *The meeting ended **in uproar**.*

uproot /ˌʌp'ruːt/ **verb** [T] to pull up a plant by the roots: *Strong winds had uprooted the tree.*

ups /ʌps/ **noun**

IDIOM **ups and downs** both good times and bad times: *We're happy together but we've had our ups and downs.*

★**upset¹** /ˌʌp'set/ **verb** [T] (*pres part* **upsetting**; *pt, pp* **upset**) **1** to make sb worry or feel unhappy: *The pictures of starving children upset her.* **2** to make sth go wrong: *to upset someone's plans* **3** to knock sth over: *I upset a cup of tea all over the tablecloth.* **4** to make sb ill in the stomach

★**upset²** /ˌʌp'set/ **adj 1** worried and unhappy: *She was looking very upset about something.* **2** slightly ill: *I've got **an upset stomach**.*

➤ Note that the adjective is pronounced /'ʌpset/ when it comes before a noun and /ˌʌp'set/ in other positions in the sentence.

upset³ /'ʌpset/ **noun 1** [C,U] a situation in which there are unexpected problems or difficulties: *The company survived the recent upset* *in share prices.* **2** [C] a slight illness in your stomach: *a stomach upset* **3** [C,U] a situation that causes worry and sadness: *She's had a few upsets recently.* ● *It had been the cause of much emotional upset.*

upshot /'ʌpʃɒt/ **noun** [sing] **the upshot (of sth)** the final result, especially of a conversation or an event

★**upside down** /ˌʌpsaɪd 'daʊn/ **adv 1** with the top part turned to the bottom: *You're holding the picture upside down.* ··▸ picture at **back 2** (*informal*) in or into a very untidy state: *I had to* **turn** *the house* **upside down** *looking for my keys.*

★**upstairs** /ˌʌp'steəz/ **adv** to or on a higher floor of a building: *to go upstairs* ● *She's sleeping upstairs.* ··▸ opposite **downstairs** –**upstairs** /'ʌpsteəz/ **adj**: *an upstairs window* – **the upstairs noun** [sing] (*informal*): *We're going to paint the upstairs.*

upstream /ˌʌp'striːm/ **adv, adj** in the direction that a river flows from: *He found it hard work swimming upstream.* ··▸ opposite **downstream**

upsurge /'ʌpsɜːdʒ/ **noun** [C,usually sing] an **upsurge (in sth)** a sudden increase of sth

uptake /'ʌpteɪk/ **noun**
> IDIOM **quick/slow on the uptake** quick/slow to understand the meaning of sth: *I gave him a hint but he's slow on the uptake.*

uptight /ˌʌp'taɪt/ **adj** (*informal*) nervous and not relaxed: *He gets uptight before an exam.*

★**up-to-'date adj 1** modern **2** having the most recent information

up-to-the-'minute adj having the most recent information possible

upturn /'ʌptɜːn/ **noun** [C] an **upturn (in sth)** an improvement in sth: *an upturn in support for the government* ··▸ opposite **downturn**

upturned /ˌʌp'tɜːnd/ **adj 1** pointing upwards: *an upturned nose* **2** turned upside down

★**upward** /'ʌpwəd/ **adj** moving or directed towards a higher place: *an upward trend in exports* (= an increase) ··▸ opposite **downward** –**upward** (also **upwards** /-wədz/) **adv**

'upwards of prep more than the number mentioned: *They've invited upwards of a hundred guests.*

uranium /jʊ'reɪniəm/ **noun** [U] (*symbol* **U**) a metal that can be used to produce nuclear energy: *Uranium is highly radioactive.*

Uranus /'jʊərənəs; jʊ'reɪnəs/ **noun** [sing] the planet that is seventh in order from the sun

★**urban** /'ɜːbən/ **adj** connected with a town or city: *urban development* ··▸ Look at **rural**.

★**urge¹** /ɜːdʒ/ **verb** [T] **1 urge sb (to do sth); urge sth** to advise or try hard to persuade sb to do sth: *I urged him to fight the decision.* ● *Drivers are urged to take care on icy roads.* ● *Police urge caution on the icy roads.* **2** to force sb/sth to go in a certain direction: *He urged his horse over the fence.*
> PHRASAL VERB **urge sb on** to encourage sb: *The captain urged his team on.*

urge² /ɜːdʒ/ **noun** [C] a strong need or desire: *sexual/creative urges*

★**urgent** /'ɜːdʒənt/ **adj** needing immediate attention: *an urgent message* –**urgency** /-dʒənsi/ **noun** [U]: *a matter of the greatest urgency* –**urgently adv**: *I must see you urgently.*

urinate /'jʊərɪneɪt/ **verb** [I] (*formal*) to pass urine from the body

urine /'jʊərɪn; -raɪn/ **noun** [U] the yellowish liquid that is passed from your body when you go to the toilet

urn /ɜːn/ **noun** [C] **1** a special container, used especially to hold the powder (**ashes**) that is left when a dead person has been burnt (**cremated**) **2** a large metal container used for making a large quantity of tea or coffee and for keeping it hot

US /ˌjuː 'es/ **abbr** the United States (of America)

★**us** /əs; *strong form* ʌs/ **pron** (used as the object of a verb, or after *be*) me and another person or other people; me and you: *Come with us.* ● *Leave us alone.* ● *Will you write to us?*

USA /ˌjuː es 'eɪ/ **abbr** the United States of America

usable /'juːzəbl/ **adj** that can be used

usage /'juːsɪdʒ/ **noun 1** [U] the way that sth is used; the amount that sth is used **2** [C,U] the way that words are normally used in a language: *a guide to English grammar and usage*

★**use¹** /juːz/ **verb** [T] (*pres part* **using**; *pt, pp* **used** /juːzd/) **1 use sth (as/for sth); use sth (to do sth)** to do sth with a machine, an object, a method, etc for a particular purpose: *Could I use your phone?* ● *The building was used as a shelter for homeless people.* ● *A gun is used for shooting with.* ● *What's this used for?* ● *We used the money to buy a house.* ● *Use your imagination!* ● *That's a word I never use.* **2** to need or to take sth: *Don't use all the milk.* **3** to treat sb/sth in an unfair way in order to get sth that you want
> PHRASAL VERB **use sth up** to use sth until no more is left

★**use²** /juːs/ **noun 1** [U] the action of using sth or of being used: *The use of computers is now widespread.* ● *She kept the money for use in an emergency.* **2** [C,U] the purpose for which sth is used: *This machine has many uses.* **3** [U] the ability or permission to use sth: *He lost the use of his hand after the accident.* ● *She offered them the use of her car.* **4** [U] the advantage of sth; how useful it is: *It's no use studying for an exam at the last minute.* ● *What's the use of trying?* ● *Will this jumper* **be of use** *to you or should I get rid of it?*
> IDIOMS **come into/go out of use** to start/stop being used regularly or by a lot of people: *E-mail came into widespread use in the 1990s.*
> **make use of sth/sb** to use sth/sb in a way that will give you an advantage

★**used adj 1** /juːzd/ that has had another owner before: *a garage selling used cars* ··▸ Another word with the same meaning is **second-hand**. **2** /juːst/ **used to sth/to doing sth** familiar with sth; accustomed to sth: *He's used to the heat.* ● *I'll never* **get used to** *getting up so early.*

u

★**used to** /'juːst tə; *before a vowel and in final position* 'juːst tuː/ **modal verb** for talking about sth that happened often or continuously in the past or about a situation which existed in the past: *She used to live with her parents* (= but she doesn't now). ● *You used to live in Glasgow, didn't you?* ● *Did you use to smoke?* ● *He didn't use to speak to me.*

➤ We usually use **did** to form negatives and questions with **use to**: *I didn't use to like jazz.* ● *Did she use to be in your class?* Be careful not to confuse **used to** + infinitive, which only refers to the past, with **be used to (doing) sth**, which can refer to the past, present or future. Compare: *I used to live on my own* (= but now I don't). ● *I'm used to living on my own* (= I am accustomed to it).

★**useful** /'juːsfl/ **adj** having some practical use; helpful: *a useful tool* ● *useful advice* –**usefully** /-fəli/ **adv** –**usefulness noun** [U]

IDIOM **come in useful** to be of practical help in a certain situation: *Don't throw that box away – it might come in useful for something.*

★**useless** /'juːsləs/ **adj 1** that does not work well, that does not achieve anything: *This new machine is useless.* ● *It's useless complaining/to complain – you won't get your money back.* **2** (*informal*) **useless (at sth/at doing sth)** (used about a person) weak or not successful at sth: *I'm useless at sport.* –**uselessly adv** –**uselessness noun** [U]

★**user** /'juːzə/ **noun** [C] (often in compounds) a person who uses a service, machine, place, etc: *users of public transport* ● *drug users*

‚**user-'friendly adj** (used about computers, books, machines, etc) easy to understand and use

usher¹ /'ʌʃə/ **noun** [C] a person who shows people to their seats in a theatre, church, etc

usher² /'ʌʃə/ **verb** [T] to take or show sb where to go: *I was ushered into an office.*

PHRASAL VERB **usher sth in** to be the beginning of sth new or to make sth new begin: *The agreement ushered in a new period of peace for the two countries.*

★**usual** /'juːʒuəl; -ʒəl/ **adj** usual **(for sb/sth) (to do sth)** happening or used most often: *It's usual for her to work at weekends.* ● *He got home later than usual.* ● *I sat in my usual seat.* ●➤ opposite **unusual**

IDIOM **as usual** in the way that has often happened before: *Here's Dylan, late as usual!*

usually /'juːʒuəli; -ʒəli/ **adv** in the way that is usual; most often: *She's usually home by six.* ● *Usually, we go out on Saturdays.*

utensil /juː'tensl/ **noun** [C] a type of tool that is used in the home: *kitchen/cooking utensils* ●➤ picture at **kitchen**

uterus /'juːtərəs/ **noun** [C] (*pl* **uteruses**; in scientific use **uteri** /-raɪ/) (*formal*) the part of a woman or female animal where a baby develops before it is born

➤ A less formal word is **womb**.

utility /juː'tɪləti/ **noun** (*pl* **utilities**) **1** [C] (*especially US*) a service provided for the public, such as a water, gas or electricity supply:

the administration of public utilities **2** [U] (*formal*) the quality of being useful **3** [C] (*computing*) a program or part of a program that does a particular task: *a utility program*

u'**tility room noun** [C] a small room in some houses, often next to the kitchen, where people keep large pieces of kitchen equipment, such as a washing machine

utilize (also **-ise**) /'juːtəlaɪz/ **verb** [T] (*formal*) to make use of sth: *to utilize natural resources*

utmost¹ /'ʌtməʊst/ **adj** (*formal*) (only *before* a noun) greatest: *a message of the utmost importance*

utmost² /'ʌtməʊst/ **noun** [sing] the greatest amount possible: *Resources have been exploited to the utmost.* ● *I will do my utmost* (= try as hard as possible) *to help.*

Utopia (also **utopia**) /juː'təʊpiə/ **noun** [C,U] a place or state that exists only in the imagination, where everything is perfect –**Utopian** (also **utopian**) /-piən/ **adj**

utter¹ /'ʌtə/ **adj** (only *before* a noun) complete; total: *He felt an utter fool.* –**utterly adv**: *It's utterly impossible.*

utter² /'ʌtə/ **verb** [T] to say sth or make a sound with your voice: *She did not utter a word* (= she did not say anything) *in the meeting.* –**utterance** /'ʌtərəns/ **noun** [C] (*formal*)

U-turn /'juː tɜːn/ **noun** [C] **1** a type of movement where a car, etc turns round so that it goes back in the direction it came from **2** (*informal*) a sudden change from one plan or policy to a completely different or opposite one ●●➤ Look at **about turn**.

V, v¹ /viː/ **noun** [C] (*pl* **V's**; **v's**) **1** the twenty-second letter of the English alphabet: *'Velvet' begins with (a) 'V'.* **2** the shape of a V: *a V-neck sweater*

v² **abbr 1** (also **vs**) versus; against: *Liverpool vs Everton* **2** **V** volt(s): *a 9V battery* **3** verse **4** (*informal*) very: *v good*

vacancy /'veɪkənsi/ **noun** [C] (*pl* **vacancies**) **1** a vacancy **(for sb/sth)** a job that is available for sb to do: *We have a vacancy for a secretary in our office.* **2** a room in a hotel, etc that is available: *The sign outside the hotel said 'No Vacancies'.*

★**vacant** /'veɪkənt/ **adj 1** (used about a house, hotel room, seat, etc) not being used; empty **2** (used about a job in a company, etc) that is available for sb to take: *the 'Situations Vacant' page* (= the page of a British newspaper where jobs are advertised) **3** showing no sign of intelligence or understanding: *a* *vacant expression* –**vacantly** adv: *She stared at him vacantly.*

vacate /veɪˈkeɪt; vəˈkeɪt; 'veɪkeɪt/ **verb** [T] (*formal*) to leave a building, a seat, a job, etc so that it is available for sb else

vacation /vəˈkeɪʃn/ **noun 1** [C] (*Brit*) any of the periods of time when universities or courts of law are closed: *the Christmas/Easter vacation* **2** [C,U] (*US*) (a) holiday: *The boss is on vacation.* ·➤ Look at the note at **holiday**.

vaccinate /ˈvæksɪneɪt/ **verb** [T] **vaccinate sb (against sth)** (often passive) to protect a person or an animal against a disease by giving him/her/it a mild form of the disease with a needle which is put under the skin (**an injection**): *Were you vaccinated against measles as a child?* ·➤ **Immunize** and **inoculate** have similar meanings. –**vaccination** /ˌvæksɪˈneɪʃn/ **noun** [C,U]

vaccine /ˈvæksiːn/ **noun** [C] a mild form of a disease that is put into a person or an animal's blood using a needle (**an injection**) in order to protect the body against that disease

vacuum¹ /ˈvækjuəm/ **noun** [C] **1** a space that is completely empty of all substances, including air or other gases: *vacuum-packed foods* (= in a pack from which most of the air has been removed) **2** [usually sing] a situation from which sth is missing or lacking **3** (*informal*) = **VACUUM CLEANER**

vacuum² /ˈvækjuəm/ **verb** [I,T] to clean sth using a vacuum cleaner

vacuum cleaner

'vacuum cleaner (also *informal* **vacuum**) **noun** [C] an electric machine that cleans carpets, etc by sucking up dirt ·➤ Look at **cleaner**.

vagina /vəˈdʒaɪnə/ **noun** [C] the passage in the body of a woman or female animal that connects the outer sex organs to the part where a baby grows (**womb**)

vagrant /ˈveɪɡrənt/ **noun** [C] a person who has no home and no job, especially one who asks people for money

vague /veɪɡ/ **adj 1** not clear or definite: *He was very vague about how much money he'd spent.* • *a vague shape in the distance* **2** (used about a person) not thinking or understanding clearly: *She looked vague when I tried to explain.* –**vagueness noun** [U]

vaguely /ˈveɪɡli/ **adv 1** in a way that is not clear; slightly: *Her name is vaguely familiar.* **2** without thinking about what is happening: *He smiled vaguely and walked away.*

★**vain** /veɪn/ **adj 1** useless; failing to produce the result you want: *She turned away in a vain attempt to hide her tears.* **2** (used about a person) too proud of your own appearance, abilities, etc: *He's so vain – he looks in every mirror he passes.* –**vainly** adv ·➤ noun **vanity**

IDIOM **in vain** without success: *The firemen tried in vain to put out the fire.*

valentine /ˈvæləntaɪn/ **noun** [C] **1** (also '**valentine card**) a card that you send, usually without putting your name on it, to sb you love

➤ It is traditional to send these cards on **St Valentine's Day** (14 February).

2 the person you send this card to

valiant /ˈvæliənt/ **adj** (*formal*) full of courage and not afraid –**valiantly** adv

★**valid** /ˈvælɪd/ **adj 1** valid (for sth) that is legally or officially acceptable: *This passport is valid for one year only.* **2** based on what is logical or true; acceptable: *I could raise no valid objections to the plan.* • *Jeff's making a perfectly valid point.* ·➤ opposite **invalid** –**validity** /vəˈlɪdəti/ **noun** [U]

★**valley** /ˈvæli/ **noun** [C] the low land between two mountains or hills, which often has a river flowing through it ·➤ picture on page C8

★**valuable** /ˈvæljuəbl/ **adj 1** worth a lot of money: *Is this ring valuable?* **2** very useful: *a valuable piece of information* ·➤ opposite **valueless** or **worthless**. Be careful. **Invaluable** means 'very useful'.

valuables /ˈvæljuəblz/ **noun** [pl] the small things that you own that are worth a lot of money, such as jewellery, etc: *Please put your valuables in the hotel safe.*

valuation /ˌvæljuˈeɪʃn/ **noun** [C] a professional judgement about how much money sth is worth

★**value¹** /ˈvælju/ **noun 1** [U,C] the amount of money that sth is worth: *The thieves stole goods with a total value of $10000.* • *to go up/down in value* ·➤ Look at **face value**. **2** [U] (*Brit*) how much sth is worth compared with its price: *The hotel was good/excellent value* (= well worth the money it cost). • *Package holidays give the best value for money.* **3** [U] the importance of sth: *to be of great/little/no value to sb* • *This bracelet is of great sentimental value to me.* **4 values** [pl] beliefs about what is the right and wrong way for people to behave; moral principles: *a return to traditional values* • *Young people have a different set of values and expectations.*

value² /ˈvælju/ **verb** [T] (*pres part* **valuing**) **1 value sb/sth (as sth)** to think sb/sth is very important: *Sandra has always valued her independence.* • *I really value her as a friend.* **2** (usually passive) **value sth (at sth)** to decide the amount of money that sth is worth: *The house was valued at $150000.*

valueless /ˈvæljuːləs/ **adj** without value or use; worthless ·➤ opposite **valuable**. ·➤ Look at **invaluable**, it has a different meaning.

valve /vælv/ **noun** [C] a device in a pipe or tube which controls the flow of air, liquid or gas, letting it move in one direction only: *a radiator valve* • *the valve on a bicycle tyre* ·➤ picture on page S9

V

vampire /'væmpaɪə/ noun [C] (in horror stories) a dead person who comes out at night and drinks the blood of living people

★**van** /væn/ noun [C] a road vehicle that is used for transporting things ••➤ A **van** is smaller than a **lorry** and is always covered. ••➤ picture at **vehicle**

vandal /'vændl/ noun [C] a person who damages sb else's property intentionally and for no purpose –**vandalism** /-dəlɪzəm/ noun [U]: *acts of vandalism* –**vandalize** (also **-ise**) /'vændəlaɪz/ verb [T] (usually passive): *All the phone boxes in this area have been vandalized.*

vanilla /və'nɪlə/ noun [U] a substance from a plant that is used for giving flavour to sweet food: *vanilla ice cream*

★**vanish** /'vænɪʃ/ verb [I] **1** to disappear suddenly or in a way that you cannot explain: *When he turned round, the two men had vanished without trace.* **2** to stop existing: *This species of plant is vanishing from our countryside.*

vanity /'vænəti/ noun [U] the quality of being too proud of your appearance, or abilities ••➤ adjective **vain**

vantage point /'vɑːntɪdʒ pɔɪnt/ noun [C] a place from which you have a good view of sth: (*figurative*) *From our modern vantage point, we can see why the Roman Empire collapsed.*

vapour (*US* **vapor**) /'veɪpə/ noun [C,U] a mass of very small drops of liquid in the air, for example steam: *water vapour*

variable /'veəriəbl/ adj not staying the same; often changing –**variability** /,veəriə-'bɪləti/ noun [U]

variant /'veəriənt/ noun [C] a slightly different form or type of sth

★**variation** /,veəri'eɪʃn/ noun **1** [C,U] (a) variation (in sth) a change or difference in the amount or level of sth: *There was a lot of variation in the examination results.* • *There may be a slight variation in price from shop to shop.* **2** [C] a variation (on/of sth) a thing that is slightly different from another thing in the same general group: *All her films are just variations on a basic theme.*

varied /'veərid/ adj having many different kinds of things or activities: *I try to make my classes as varied as possible.*

★**variety** /və'raɪəti/ noun (*pl* **varieties**) **1** [sing] a variety (of sth) a number of different types of the same thing: *There is a wide variety of dishes to choose from.* **2** [U] the quality of not being or doing the same all the time: *There's so much variety in my new job. I do something different every day!* **3** [C] a variety (of sth) a type of sth: *a new variety of apple called 'Perfection'*

★**various** /'veəriəs/ adj several different: *I decided to leave London for various reasons.*

varnish /'vɑːnɪʃ/ noun [U] a clear liquid that you paint onto hard surfaces, especially wood, to protect them and make them shine ••➤ Look at **nail varnish**. –**varnish** verb [T]

★**vary** /'veəri/ verb (*pres part* **varying**; *3rd pers sing pres* **varies**; *pt, pp* **varied**) **1** [I] vary (in sth) (used about a group of similar things) to be different from each other: *The hotel bedrooms vary in size from medium to very large.* **2** [I] vary (from...to...) to be different or to change according to the situation, etc: *The price of the holiday varies from £500 to £1200, depending on the time of year.* **3** [T] to make sth different by changing it often in some way: *I try to vary my work as much as possible so I don't get bored.*

★**vase** /vɑːz/ noun [C] a container that is used for holding cut flowers

vasectomy /və'sektəmi/ noun [C] (*pl* **vasectomies**) (*medical*) a medical operation to stop a man being able to have children

★**vast** /vɑːst/ adj extremely big: *a vast sum of money* • *a vast country* –**vastly** adv: *a vastly improved traffic system*

VAT (also **Vat**) /,viː eɪ 'tiː; væt/ abbr value added tax: *prices include VAT*

vault¹ /vɔːlt/ noun [C] **1** a room with a strong door and thick walls in a bank, etc that is used for keeping money and other valuable things safe **2** a room under a church where dead people are buried: *a family vault* **3** a high roof or ceiling in a church, etc, made from a number of arches joined together at the top

vault² /vɔːlt/ verb [I,T] vault (over) sth to jump over or onto sth in one movement, using your hands or a pole to help you: *The boy vaulted over the wall.*

VCR /,viː siː 'ɑː/ abbr video cassette recorder

VDU /,viː diː 'juː/ noun [C] visual display unit; a screen on which you can see information from a computer

veal /viːl/ noun [U] the meat from a young cow (calf) ••➤ Look at the note at **meat**.

veer /vɪə/ verb [I] (used about vehicles) to change direction suddenly: *The car veered across the road and hit a tree.*

veg¹ /vedʒ/ noun [U] (*Brit informal*) vegetables: *a fruit and veg stall*

veg² /vedʒ/ verb (*Brit slang*)
PHRASAL VERB **veg out** to relax and do nothing that needs thought or effort: *I'm just going to go home and veg out in front of the telly.*

vegan /'viːgən/ noun [C] a person who does not eat meat or any other animal products at all ••➤ Look at **vegetarian**. –**vegan** adj

★**vegetable** /'vedʒtəbl/ (also *informal* **veg**; **veggie**) noun [C] a plant or part of a plant that we eat. Potatoes, beans and onions are vegetables: *vegetable soup*

vegetarian /,vedʒə'teəriən/ (*Brit informal* **veggie**) noun [C] a person who does not eat meat or fish ••➤ Look at **vegan**. –**vegetarian** adj: *a vegetarian cookery book*

vegetation /,vedʒə'teɪʃn/ noun [U] (*formal*) plants in general; all the plants that are found in a particular place: *tropical vegetation*

veggie /'vedʒi/ noun [C] (*informal*) **1** (*Brit*)

V

VEGETARIAN 2 =**VEGETABLE** –**veggie adj**: *a veggie burger*

vehement /'vi:əmənt/ **adj** showing very strong (often negative) feelings, especially anger: *a vehement attack on the government*

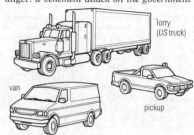

'lorry
(*US* truck)

van

pickup

★**vehicle** /'vi:əkl/ **noun** [C] **1** something which transports people or things from place to place, especially on land, for example cars, bicycles, lorries and buses: *Are you the owner of this vehicle?* **2** something which is used for communicating particular ideas or opinions: *This newspaper has become a vehicle for Conservative opinion.*

veil /veɪl/ **noun** [C] a piece of thin material for covering the head and face of a woman: *a bridal veil*

vein /veɪn/ **noun 1** [C] one of the tubes which carry blood from all parts of your body to your heart ••➤ Look at **artery**. **2** [sing,U] a particular style or quality: *After a humorous beginning, the programme continued in a more serious vein.*

Velcro™ /'velkrəʊ/ **noun** [U] a material for fastening parts of clothes together. Velcro is made of a man-made material (**nylon**) and is used in small pieces, one rough and one smooth, that can stick together and be pulled apart.

velocity /və'lɒsəti/ **noun** [U] (*technical*) the speed at which sth moves

velvet /'velvɪt/ **noun** [U] a kind of cloth made of cotton or other material, with a soft thick surface on one side only: *black velvet trousers*

vendetta /ven'detə/ **noun** [C] a serious argument or dispute between two people or groups which lasts for a long time

'**vending machine noun** [C] a machine from which you can buy drinks, cigarettes, etc by putting coins in it ••➤ picture on page C8

vendor /'vendə/ **noun** [C] (*formal*) a person who is selling sth ••➤ Look at **purchaser**. ••➤ picture on page C8

veneer /və'nɪə/ **noun 1** [C,U] a thin layer of wood or plastic that is stuck onto the surface of a cheaper material, especially wood, to give it a better appearance **2** [sing] (*formal*) a **veneer (of sth)** a part of sb's behaviour or of a situation which hides what it is really like underneath: *a thin veneer of politeness*

venetian blind /vəˌni:ʃn 'blaɪnd/ **noun** [C] a covering for a window that is made of horizontal pieces of flat plastic, etc which can be turned to let in as much light as you want

vengeance /'vendʒəns/ **noun** [U] (*written*) **vengeance (on sb)** the act of punishing or harming sb in return for sth bad he/she has done to you, your friends or family: *He felt a terrible desire for vengeance on the people who'd destroyed his career.* ••➤ Look at **revenge**.

  IDIOM **with a vengeance** to a greater degree than is expected or usual: *After a week of good weather winter returned with a vengeance.*

venison /'venɪsn/ **noun** [U] the meat from a large wild animal (**deer**)

venom /'venəm/ **noun** [U] **1** the poisonous liquid that some snakes, spiders, etc produce when they bite or sting you **2** extreme anger or hatred and a desire to hurt sb: *She shot him a look of pure venom.* –**venomous** /'venəməs/ **adj**

vent /vent/ **noun** [C] an opening in the wall of a room or machine which allows air to come in, and smoke, steam or smells to go out: *an air vent* ● *a heating vent*

ventilate /'ventɪleɪt/ **verb** [T] to allow air to move freely in and out of a room or building: *The office is badly ventilated.* –**ventilation** /ˌventɪ'leɪʃn/ **noun** [U]: *There was no ventilation in the room except for one tiny window.*

venture[1] /'ventʃə/ **noun** [C] a project which is new and possibly dangerous, because you cannot be sure that it will succeed: *a business venture*

venture[2] /'ventʃə/ **verb** [I] to do sth or go somewhere new and dangerous, when you are not sure what will happen: *He ventured out into the storm to look for the lost child.* ● *The company has decided to venture into computer production as well as design.*

venue /'venju:/ **noun** [C] the place where people meet for an organized event, for example a concert or a sporting event

Venus /'vi:nəs/ **noun** [sing] the planet that is second in order from the sun and nearest to the earth

veranda (also **verandah**) /və'rændə/ (*US also* **porch**) **noun** [C] a platform joined to the side of a house, with a roof and floor but no outside wall ••➤ Look at **balcony**, **patio** and **terrace**.

★**verb** /vɜ:b/ **noun** [C] (*grammar*) a word or group of words that is used to indicate that sth happens or exists, for example *bring, happen, be, do.* ••➤ Look at **phrasal verb**.

verbal /'vɜ:bl/ **adj** (*formal*) **1** connected with words, or the use of words: *verbal skills* **2** spoken, not written: *a verbal agreement/ warning* –**verbally** /'vɜ:bəli/ **adv**

★**verdict** /'vɜ:dɪkt/ **noun** [C] **1** the decision that is made by a specially chosen group of people (**the jury**) in a court of law, which states if a person is guilty of a crime or not: *The jury returned a verdict of 'not guilty'.* ● *Has the jury reached a verdict?* **2** a **verdict (on sb/**

sth) a decision that you make or an opinion that you give after testing sth or considering sth carefully: *The general verdict was that the restaurant was too expensive.*

verge¹ /vɜːdʒ/ noun [C] (*Brit*) the narrow piece of land at the side of a road, railway line, etc that is usually covered in grass
> IDIOM on the verge of sth/doing sth very near to doing sth, or to sth happening: *He was on the verge of a nervous breakdown.* • *Scientists are on the verge of discovering a cure.*

verge² /vɜːdʒ/ verb
> PHRASAL VERB verge on sth to be very close to an extreme state or condition: *What they are doing verges on the illegal.*

verify /'verɪfaɪ/ verb [T] (*pres part* **verifying**; *3rd pers sing pres* **verifies**; *pt, pp* **verified**) (*formal*) to check or state that sth is true: *to verify a statement* –**verification** /ˌverɪfɪ'keɪʃn/ noun [U]

vermin /'vɜːmɪn/ noun [pl] small wild animals (for example rats) that carry disease and destroy plants and food

versatile /'vɜːsətaɪl/ adj **1** (used about an object) having many different uses: *a versatile tool that drills, cuts or polishes* **2** (used about a person) able to do many different things: *She's so versatile! She can dance, sing, act and play the guitar!*

★**verse** /vɜːs/ noun **1** [U] writing arranged in lines which have a definite rhythm and often finish with the same sound (**rhyme**): *He wrote his valentine's message in verse.* **2** [C] a group of lines which form one part of a song or poem: *This song has five verses.*

★**version** /'vɜːʃn/ noun [C] **1** a thing which has the same basic content as sth else but which is presented in a different way: *Have you heard the live version of this song?* **2** a person's description of sth that has happened: *The two drivers gave very different versions of the accident.*

versus /'vɜːsəs/ prep **1** (*abbr* **v, vs**) used in sport for showing that two teams or people are playing against each other: *England versus Argentina* **2** used for showing that two ideas or things that are opposite to each other, especially when you are trying to choose one of them: *It's a question of quality versus price.*

★**vertical** /'vɜːtɪkl/ adj going straight up at an angle of 90° from the ground: *a vertical line* • *The cliff was almost vertical.*
> ➤ Compare **horizontal** and **perpendicular**.
•➤ picture at **line** –**vertically** /-kli/ adv

★**very** /'veri/ adv, adj **1** used with an adjective or adverb to make it stronger: *very small* • *very slowly* • *I don't like milk very much.* • *'Are you hungry?' 'Not very.'*
> ➤ We use **very** with superlative adjectives: *very best, youngest, etc* but with comparative adjectives we use **much** or **very much**: *much better; very much younger*

2 used to emphasize a noun: *We climbed to the very top of the mountain* (= right to the top). • *You're the very person I wanted to talk to* (= exactly the right person).

vessel /'vesl/ noun [C] **1** (*written*) a ship or large boat **2** (*old-fashioned*) a container for liquids, for example a bottle, cup or bowl: *ancient drinking vessels*

★**vest** /vest/ noun [C] **1** (*US* **undershirt**) a piece of clothing that you wear under your other clothes, on the top part of your body **2** (*US*) = **WAISTCOAT**

vested interest /ˌvestɪd 'ɪntrest/ noun [C] a strong and often secret reason for doing sth that will bring you an advantage of some kind, for example more money or power

vestige /'vestɪdʒ/ noun [C] a small part of sth that is left after the rest of it has gone: *the last vestige of the old system* •➤ synonym **trace**

★**vet**¹ /vet/ (also *formal* **'veterinary surgeon** *US* **veterinarian**) noun [C] a doctor for animals: *We took the cat to the vet/to the vet's.*

vet² /vet/ verb [T] (**vetting**; **vetted**) to do careful and secret checks before deciding if sb/sth can be accepted or not: *All new employees at the Ministry of Defence are carefully vetted* (= somebody examines the details of their past lives).

veteran /'vetərən/ noun [C] **1** a person who has served in the army, navy or air force, especially during a war **2** a person who has very long experience of a particular job or activity

veterinary /'vetənri/ adj connected with the medical treatment of sick or injured animals: *a veterinary practice* •➤ Look at **vet**.

veto /'viːtəʊ/ verb [T] (*pres part* **vetoing**; *3rd pers sing pres* **vetoes**; *pt, pp* **vetoed**) to refuse to give official permission for an action or plan, when other people have agreed to it: *The Prime Minister vetoed the proposal to reduce taxation.* –**veto** noun [C,U] (*pl* **vetoes**): *the right of veto*

vexed /vekst/ adj causing difficulty, worry, and a lot of discussion: *the vexed question of our growing prison population*

via /'vaɪə/ prep **1** going through a place: *We flew from Paris to Sydney via Bangkok.* **2** by means of sth; using sth: *These pictures come to you via our satellite link.*

viable /'vaɪəbl/ adj that can be done; that will be successful: *I'm afraid your idea is just not commercially viable.* –**viability** /ˌvaɪə'bɪləti/ noun [U]

viaduct /'vaɪədʌkt/ noun [C] a long, high bridge which carries a railway or road across a valley

vibrant /'vaɪbrənt/ adj **1** full of life and energy; exciting: *a vibrant city/atmosphere/personality* **2** (used about colours) bright and strong

vibrate /vaɪ'breɪt/ verb [I] to make continuous very small and fast movements from side to side: *When a guitar string vibrates it makes a sound.* –**vibration** /vaɪ'breɪʃn/ noun [C,U]

vicar /'vɪkə/ noun [C] a priest of the Church of England. A vicar looks after a church and

V

the people in the surrounding area (parish)
•➤ Look at **minister**.

vicarage /'vɪkərɪdʒ/ *noun* [C] the house where a vicar lives

vice /vaɪs/ *noun* **1** [U] criminal activities involving sex or drugs **2** [C] a moral weakness or bad habit: *Greed and envy are terrible vices.* • *My only vice is smoking.* •➤ Look at **virtue**. **3** (*US* **vise**) [C] a tool that you use to hold a piece of wood, metal, etc firmly while you are working on it: (*figurative*) *He held my arm in a vice-like* (= very firm) *grip.*

vice- /vaɪs/ (used to form compound nouns) having a position second in importance to the position mentioned: *Vice-President* • *the vice-captain*

vice versa /ˌvaɪs 'vɜːsə/ *adv* in the opposite way to what has just been said: *Anna ordered fish and Maria chicken – or was it vice versa?*

vicinity /və'sɪnəti/ *noun*
IDIOM **in the vicinity (of sth)** (*formal*) in the surrounding area: *There's no bank in the immediate vicinity.*

vicious /'vɪʃəs/ *adj* **1** cruel; done in order to hurt sb/sth: *a vicious attack* **2** (used about an animal) dangerous; likely to hurt sb –**viciously** *adv*
IDIOM **a vicious circle** a situation in which one problem leads to another and the new problem makes the first problem worse

★**victim** /'vɪktɪm/ *noun* [C] a person or animal that is injured, killed or hurt by sb/sth: *a murder victim* • *The children are often the innocent victims of a divorce.*

victimize (also -**ise**) /'vɪktɪmaɪz/ *verb* [T] to punish or make sb suffer unfairly –**victimization** (also -**isation**) /ˌvɪktɪmaɪ'zeɪʃn/ *noun* [U]

victor /'vɪktə/ *noun* [C] (*formal*) the person who wins a game, competition, battle, etc

Victorian /vɪk'tɔːriən/ *adj* **1** connected with the time of the British queen Victoria (1837-1901): *Victorian houses* **2** having attitudes that were typical in the time of Queen Victoria –**Victorian** *noun* [C]

★**victory** /'vɪktəri/ *noun* [C,U] (*pl* **victories**) success in winning a battle, game, competition, etc: *Keane led his team to victory in the final.* –**victorious** /vɪk'tɔːriəs/ *adj*: *the victorious team*
IDIOM **romp home/to victory** → ROMP

★**video** /'vɪdiəʊ/ *noun* (*pl* **videos**) **1** [U] the system of recording moving pictures and sound by using a camera, and showing them using a machine (a **video recorder**) connected to a television: *We recorded the wedding on video.* • *The film is coming out on video in May.* **2** (also ˌvideo casˈsette) [C] a tape or cassette on which you record moving pictures and sound or on which a film or television programme has been recorded: *Would you like to see the video we made on holiday?* • *To rent a video* **3** =VIDEO RECORDER –**video** *verb* [T] (*3rd pers sing pres* **videos**; *pres part* **videoing**; *pt, pp* **videoed**): *We hired a camera to video the school play.*

ˈvideo recorder (also video; ˌvideo casˈsette recorder) *noun* [C] (*abbr* VCR) a machine that is connected to a television on which you can record or play back a film or television programme

videotape /'vɪdiəʊteɪp/ *noun* [C] = VIDEO(2) –**videotape** *verb* [T] = VIDEO: *a videotaped interview*

★**view¹** /vjuː/ *noun* **1** [C] a **view (about/on sth)** an opinion or a particular way of thinking about sth: *He expressed the view that standards were falling.* • *In my view, she has done nothing wrong.* • *She has strong views on the subject.* **2** [U] the ability to see sth or to be seen from a particular place: *The garden was hidden from view behind a high wall.* • *to come into view* • *to disappear from view* **3** [C] what you can see from a particular place, especially beautiful natural scenery: *There are breathtaking views from the top of the mountain.* • *a room with a sea view* •➤ Look at the note at **scenery**.
IDIOMS **have, etc sth in view** (*formal*) to have sth as a plan or idea in your mind
in full view (of sb/sth) → FULL¹
in view of sth because of sth; as a result of sth: *In view of her apology we decided to take no further action.*
a point of view → POINT¹
with a view to doing sth (*formal*) with the aim or intention of doing sth

★**view²** /vjuː/ *verb* [T] (*formal*) **1** **view sth (as sth)** to think about sth in a particular way: *She viewed holidays as a waste of time.* **2** to watch or look at sth: *Viewed from this angle, the building looks much taller than it really is.*

viewer /'vjuːə/ *noun* [C] a person who watches television

viewpoint /'vjuːpɔɪnt/ *noun* [C] a way of looking at a situation; an opinion: *Let's look at this problem from the customer's viewpoint.* •➤ synonym **point of view**

vigil /'vɪdʒɪl/ *noun* [C,U] a period when you stay awake all night for a special purpose: *All night she kept vigil over the sick child.*

vigilant /'vɪdʒɪlənt/ *adj* (*formal*) careful and looking out for danger –**vigilance** /-əns/ *noun* [U]

vigilante /ˌvɪdʒɪ'lænti/ *noun* [C] a member of a group of people who try to prevent crime or punish criminals in a community, especially because they believe the police are not doing this

vigour (*US* **vigor**) /'vɪgə/ *noun* [U] strength or energy: *After the break we started work again with renewed vigour.* –**vigorous** /'vɪgərəs/ *adj*: *vigorous exercise* –**vigorously** *adv*

vile /vaɪl/ *adj* very bad or unpleasant: *She's in a vile mood.* • *a vile smell*

villa /'vɪlə/ *noun* [C] **1** a house that people rent and stay in on holiday **2** a large house in the country, especially in Southern Europe

★**village** /'vɪlɪdʒ/ *noun* **1** [C] a group of houses with other buildings, for example a shop, school, etc, in a country area. A village is smaller than a town: *a small fishing village* • *the village shop* **2** [sing, with sing or pl verb] all the people who live in a village: *All the village is/are taking part in the carnival.*

villager /'vɪlɪdʒə/ **noun** [C] a person who lives in a village

villain /'vɪlən/ **noun** [C] **1** an evil person, especially in a book or play: *In most of his films he has played villains, but in this one he's a good guy.* ••► Look at **hero**. **2** (*informal*) a criminal: *The police caught the villains who robbed the bank.*

vindictive /vɪn'dɪktɪv/ **adj** wanting or trying to hurt sb without good reason: *a vindictive comment/person* –**vindictiveness noun** [U]

vine /vaɪn/ **noun** [C] the plant that grapes grow on

vinegar /'vɪnɪɡə/ **noun** [U] a liquid with a strong sharp taste that is made from wine. Vinegar is often mixed with oil and put onto salads.

vineyard /'vɪnjəd/ **noun** [C] a piece of land where grapes are grown

vintage¹ /'vɪntɪdʒ/ **noun** [C] the wine that was made in a particular year: *1999 was an excellent vintage.*

vintage² /'vɪntɪdʒ/ **adj 1** (used about wine) that was produced in a particular year and district: *a bottle of vintage champagne* **2** of very high quality: *a vintage performance by Robert De Niro*

vinyl /'vaɪnl/ **noun** [C,U] a strong plastic that can bend easily and is used for making wall, floor and furniture coverings, book covers, etc

viola /vi'əʊlə/ **noun** [C] a musical instrument with strings, that you hold under your chin and play with a long thin object (a bow) made of wood and hair: *A viola is like a large violin.* ••► Look at the note at **piano**.

violate /'vaɪəleɪt/ **verb** [T] (*formal*) **1** to break a rule, an agreement, etc: *to violate a peace treaty* **2** not to respect sth; to spoil or damage sth: *to violate sb's privacy/rights* –**violation** /ˌvaɪə'leɪʃn/ **noun** [C,U]: *(a) violation of human rights*

★**violence** /'vaɪələns/ **noun** [U] **1** behaviour which harms or damages sb/sth physically: *They threatened to **use violence** if we didn't give them the money.* • *an **act of violence*** **2** great force or energy: *the violence of the storm*

★**violent** /'vaɪələnt/ **adj 1** using physical strength to hurt or kill sb; caused by this behaviour: *The demonstration started peacefully but later turned violent.* • *a violent death* • *violent crime* **2** very strong and impossible to control: *He has a violent temper.* • *a violent storm/collision* –**violently adv**: *The ground shook violently and buildings collapsed in the earthquake.*

violet /'vaɪələt/ **noun 1** [C] a small plant that grows wild or in gardens and has purple or white flowers and a pleasant smell ••► picture on page C2 **2** [U] a bluish purple colour –**violet adj**

★**violin** /ˌvaɪə'lɪn/ **noun** [C] a musical instrument with strings, that you hold under your chin and play with a long thin object (a bow) made of wood and hair ••► Look at the note at **piano**. In informal English a violin is some-

times called a **fiddle**. ••► picture at **music**

VIP /ˌviː aɪ 'piː/ **abbr** (*informal*) very important person: *the VIP lounge at the airport* • *give someone the VIP treatment* (= treat sb especially well)

virgin¹ /'vɜːdʒɪn/ **noun** [C] a person who has never had sex

virgin² /'vɜːdʒɪn/ **adj** that has not yet been used, touched, damaged, etc: *virgin forest*

virginity /və'dʒɪnəti/ **noun** [U] the state of never having had sex: *to lose your virginity*

Virgo /'vɜːɡəʊ/ **noun** [C,U] the sixth sign of the zodiac, the Virgin

virile /'vɪraɪl/ **adj** (used about a man) strong and having great sexual energy

virility /və'rɪləti/ **noun** [U] a man's sexual power and energy

virtual /'vɜːtʃuəl/ **adj** (only *before* a noun) **1** being almost or nearly sth: *The country is in a state of virtual civil war.* **2** made to appear to exist by computer: *virtual reality* –**virtually** /-tʃuəli/ **adv**: *The building is virtually finished.*

★**virtue** /'vɜːtʃuː/ **noun 1** [U] behaviour which shows high moral standards: *to lead a life of virtue* ••► synonym **goodness 2** [C] a good quality or habit: *Patience is a great virtue.* ••► Look at **vice**. **3** [C,U] the virtue (of sth/of being/doing sth) an advantage or a useful quality of sth: *This new material **has the virtue** of being strong as well as very light.* IDIOM **by virtue of** (*formal*) by means of sth or because of sth

virtuoso /ˌvɜːtʃu'əʊsəʊ/ **noun** [C] (*pl* **virtuosos** or **virtuosi**) a person who is extremely skilful at sth, especially playing a musical instrument

virtuous /'vɜːtʃuəs/ **adj** behaving in a morally good way

virulent /'vɪrələnt; 'vɪrjələnt/ **adj 1** (used about a poison or a disease) very strong and dangerous: *a particularly virulent form of influenza* **2** (*formal*) very strong and full of anger: *a virulent attack on the leader*

★**virus** /'vaɪrəs/ **noun** [C] (*pl* **viruses**) **1** a living thing, too small to be seen without a special instrument (microscope), that causes disease in people, animals and plants: *HIV, the virus that is thought to cause Aids* • *to catch a virus* ••► Look at **bacteria** and **germ**. **2** (*computing*) instructions that are put into a computer program in order to stop it working properly and destroy information

visa /'viːzə/ **noun** [C] an official mark or piece of paper that shows you are allowed to enter, leave or travel through a country: *His passport was full of visa stamps.* • *a tourist/work/student visa*

vise (*US*) = **vice**(3)

visibility /ˌvɪzə'bɪləti/ **noun** [U] the distance that you can see in particular light or weather conditions: *In the fog visibility was down to 50 metres.* • *poor/good visibility*

★**visible** /'vɪzəbl/ **adj** that can be seen or noticed: *The church tower was visible from* *the other side of the valley.* ● *a visible improvement in his work* ●➤ opposite **invisible** –visibly /-əbli/ *adv*: *Rosa was visibly upset.*

★**vision** /'vɪʒn/ *noun* **1** [U] the ability to see; sight: *to have good/poor/normal/perfect vision* **2** [C] a picture in your imagination: *They have a vision of a world without weapons.* ● *I **had visions of** being left behind, but in fact the others had waited for me.* **3** [C] a dream or similar experience often connected with religion **4** [U] the ability to make great plans for the future: *a leader of great vision* **5** [U] the picture on a television or cinema screen: *a temporary loss of vision*

visionary /'vɪʒənri/ *adj* having great plans for the future: *a visionary leader* –**visionary** *noun* [C]

★**visit** /'vɪzɪt/ *verb* [I,T] to go to see a person or place for a period of time: *I don't live here. I'm just visiting.* ● *We often visit relatives at the weekend.* ● *She's going to visit her son in hospital.* ● *When you go to London you must visit the Science Museum.* –**visit** *noun* [C]: *The Prime Minister is **on a visit** to Germany.* ● *We had a flying* (= very short) *visit from Richard on Sunday.*

★**visitor** /'vɪzɪtə/ *noun* [C] a person who visits sb/sth: *visitors to London from overseas*

visor /'vaɪzə/ *noun* [C] **1** the part of a hard hat (a helmet) that you can pull down to protect your eyes or face **2** a piece of plastic, cloth, etc on a hat or in a car, which stops the sun shining into your eyes ●➤ picture at **hat**

★**visual** /'vɪʒuəl/ *adj* connected with seeing: *the visual arts* (= painting, sculpture, cinema, etc) –**visually** /'vɪʒuəli/ *adv*: *The film is visually stunning.*

ˌ**visual 'aid** *noun* [C] a picture, film, map, etc that helps a pupil to learn sth

visualize (also -ise) /'vɪʒuəlaɪz/ *verb* [T] to imagine or have a picture in your mind of sb/sth: *It's hard to visualize what this place looked like before the factory was built.*

★**vital** /'vaɪtl/ *adj* **1** very important or necessary: *Practice is vital if you want to speak a language well.* ● *vital information* **2** full of energy; lively –**vitally** /'vaɪtəli/ *adv*: *vitally important*

vitality /vaɪˈtæləti/ *noun* [U] the state of being full of energy

★**vitamin** /'vɪtəmɪn/ *noun* [C] one of several substances that are found in certain types of food and that are important for growth and good health: *Oranges are rich in vitamin C.*

vivacious /vɪˈveɪʃəs/ *adj* (used about a person, usually a woman) full of energy; lively and happy

vivid /'vɪvɪd/ *adj* **1** having or producing a strong, clear picture in your mind: *vivid dreams/memories* **2** (used about light or a colour) strong and very bright: *the vivid reds and yellows of the flowers* –**vividly** *adv*

vivisection /ˌvɪvɪˈsekʃn/ *noun* [U] doing scientific experiments on live animals

vixen /'vɪksn/ *noun* [C] the female of a type of reddish wild dog (fox)

viz /vɪz/ *abbr* (often read out as 'namely') that is to say; in other words

★**vocabulary** /vəˈkæbjələri/ *noun* (*pl* **vocabularies**) **1** [C,U] all the words that sb knows or that are used in a particular book, subject, etc: *He has an amazing vocabulary for a five-year-old.* ● *There are many ways to increase your English vocabulary.* **2** [sing] all the words in a language: *New words are always coming into the vocabulary.*

vocal /'vəʊkl/ *adj* **1** (only *before* a noun) connected with the voice: *vocal cords* (= the muscles in the back of your throat that move to produce the voice) **2** expressing your ideas or opinions loudly or freely: *a small but vocal group of protesters*

vocalist /'vəʊkəlɪst/ *noun* [C] a singer, especially in a band: *a lead/backing vocalist*

vocation /vəʊˈkeɪʃn/ *noun* [C,U] a type of work or a way of life that you believe to be especially suitable for you: *Peter has finally found his vocation in life.*

vocational /vəʊˈkeɪʃənl/ *adj* connected with the skills, knowledge, etc that you need to do a particular job: *vocational training*

vociferous /vəˈsɪfərəs/ *adj* (*formal*) expressing your opinions or feelings in a loud and confident way –**vociferously** *adv*

vodka /'vɒdkə/ *noun* [U] a strong clear alcoholic drink originally from Russia

vogue /vəʊg/ *noun* [C,U] a vogue (for sth) a fashion for sth: *a vogue for large cars* ● *That hairstyle is **in vogue** at the moment.*

★**voice¹** /vɔɪs/ *noun* **1** [C] the sounds that you make when you speak or sing; the ability to make these sounds: *He had a bad cold and **lost his voice*** (= could not speak for a period of time). ● *to speak in a loud/soft/low/hoarse voice* ● *to lower/raise your voice* (= speak more quietly/loudly) ● *Shh! **Keep your voice down!*** ● *Alan is 13 and his **voice is breaking*** (= becoming deep and low like a man's). **2** -**voiced** (used to form compound adjectives) having a voice of the type mentioned: *husky-voiced* **3** [sing] a voice (in sth) (the right to express) your ideas or opinions: *The workers want more of a voice in the running of the company.* **4** [C] a particular feeling, attitude or opinion that you have or express: *You should listen to the voice of reason and apologise.* **5** [sing] (*grammar*) the form of a verb that shows if a sentence is active or passive: *'Keats wrote this poem' is in the **active voice.*** ● *'This poem was written by Keats' is in the **passive voice.***

> For more information about the passive voice, look at the **Quick Grammar Reference** section at the back of this dictionary.

ɪᴅɪᴏᴍ **at the top of your voice → TOP¹**

voice² /vɔɪs/ *verb* [T] to express your opinions or feelings: *to voice complaints/criticisms*

void¹ /vɔɪd/ *noun* [C,usually sing] (*formal*) a

V

large empty space: *Her death left a void in their lives.*

void² /vɔɪd/ *adj* **1** (used about a ticket, contract, decision, etc) that can no longer be accepted or used: *The agreement was declared void.* **2** (*formal*) **void (of sth)** completely lacking sth: *This book is totally void of interest for me.*

vol *abbr* **1** (*pl* **vols**) volume (of a book): *The Complete Works of Byron, Vol 2* **2** volume: *vol 333 ml*

volatile /'vɒlətaɪl/ *adj* **1** that can change suddenly and unexpectedly: *a highly volatile situation which could easily develop into rioting* ● *a volatile personality* **2** (used about a liquid) that can easily change into a gas

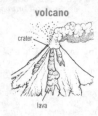

volcano
crater
lava

volcano /vɒl-'keɪnəʊ/ *noun* [C] (*pl* **volcanoes; volcanos**) a mountain with a hole (**crater**) at the top through which steam, hot melted rock (**lava**), fire, etc sometimes come out: *an active/dormant/extinct volcano* ● *When did the volcano last erupt?* –**volcanic** /vɒl'kænɪk/ *adj*: *volcanic rock/ash*

★**volley** /'vɒli/ *noun* [C] **1** (in tennis, etc) a hit or kick of the ball before it touches the ground: *a forehand/backhand volley* **2** a number of stones, bullets, etc that are thrown or shot at the same time: *The soldiers fired a volley over the heads of the crowd.* **3** a lot of questions, insults, etc that are directed at one person very quickly, one after the other: *a volley of abuse* –**volley** *verb* [I,T]: *Rios volleyed the ball into the net.*

volleyball /'vɒlibɔːl/ *noun* [U] a game in which two teams of six players hit a ball over a high net with their hands while trying not to let the ball touch the ground on their own side

volt /vəʊlt/ *noun* [C] (*abbr* v) a unit for measuring electrical force

voltage /'vəʊltɪdʒ/ *noun* [C,U] an electrical force measured in units (**volts**)

★**volume** /'vɒljuːm/ *noun* **1** [U,C] the amount of space that sth contains or fills: *What is the volume of this sphere?* ●➤ Look at **area**(2). **2** [C,U] the large quantity or amount of sth: *the sheer volume* (= the large amount) *of traffic on the roads* ● *I've got volumes of work to get through.* **3** [U,sing] how loud a sound is: *to turn the volume on a radio up/down* ● *a low/high volume* **4** [C] (*abbr* **vol**) a book, especially one of a set or series: *The dictionary comes in three volumes.*

★**voluntary** /'vɒləntri/ *adj* **1** done or given because you want to do it, not because you have to do it: *He took voluntary redundancy and left the firm last year.* ●➤ opposite **compulsory 2** done or working without payment: *She does some voluntary work at the hospital.* **3** (used about movements of the body) that you can control ●➤ opposite **involuntary** –**voluntarily** /'vɒləntrəli; ˌvɒlən'terəli/ *adv*: *She left the job voluntarily, she wasn't sacked.*

★**volunteer¹** /ˌvɒlən'tɪə/ *noun* [C] **1** a person who offers or agrees to do sth without being forced or paid to do it: *Are there any volunteers to do the washing up?* **2** a person who joins the armed forces without being ordered to ●➤ Look at **conscript²**.

★**volunteer²** /ˌvɒlən'tɪə/ *verb* **1** [I,T] **volunteer (sth); volunteer (to do sth)** to offer sth or to do sth which you do not have to do or for which you will not be paid: *They volunteered their services free.* ● *She frequently volunteers for extra work because she really likes her job.* ● *One of my friends volunteered to take us all in his car.* **2** [I] **volunteer (for sth)** to join the armed forces without being ordered **3** [T] to give information, etc or to make a comment or suggestion without being asked to: *I volunteered a few helpful suggestions.*

vomit /'vɒmɪt/ *verb* [I,T] to bring food, etc up from the stomach and out of the mouth ●➤ In everyday British English we say **be sick**. –**vomit** *noun* [U]

★**vote¹** /vəʊt/ *noun* **1** [C] **a vote (for/against sb/sth)** a formal choice in an election or at a meeting, which you show by holding up your hand or writing on a piece of paper: *The votes are still being counted.* ● *There were 10 votes for, and 25 against the motion.* **2** [C] **a vote (on sth)** a method of deciding sth by asking people to express their choice and finding out what most people want: *The democratic way to decide this would be to take a vote.* ● *Let's have a vote/put it to the vote.* **3** **the vote** [sing] the total number of votes in an election: *She obtained 30% of the vote.* **4** **the vote** [sing] the legal right to vote in political elections: *Women did not get the vote in this country until the 1920s.*

IDIOMS **cast a/your vote →** CAST¹

a vote of thanks a short speech to thank sb, usually a guest at a meeting, dinner, etc: *The club secretary proposed a vote of thanks to the guest speaker.*

★**vote²** /vəʊt/ *verb* **1** [I,T] **vote (for/against sb/sth); vote (on sth); vote to do sth** to show formally a choice or opinion by marking a piece of paper or by holding up your hand: *Who did you vote for in the last general election?* ● *46% voted in favour of* (= for) *the proposed change.* ● *Very few MPs voted against the new law.* ● *After the debate we'll vote on the motion.* ● *They voted to change the rules of the club.* ● *I voted Liberal Democrat.* **2** [T] (usually passive) to choose sb for a particular position or prize: *He was voted best actor at the Oscars.* –**voter** *noun* [C]

vouch /vaʊtʃ/ *verb* [I] **vouch for sb/sth** to say that a person is honest or good or that sth is true or genuine

voucher /'vaʊtʃə/ *noun* [C] (*Brit*) a piece of paper that you can use instead of money to pay for all or part of sth ●➤ Look at **token**.

V

vow /vaʊ/ **noun** [C] a formal and serious promise (especially in a religious ceremony): *to keep/break your **marriage vows*** –**vow verb** [T]: *We vowed never to discuss the subject again.*

★**vowel** /'vaʊəl/ **noun** [C] any of the sounds represented in English by the letters a, e, i, o or u ••► Look at **consonant**.

voyage /'vɔɪɪdʒ/ **noun** [C] a long journey by sea or in space: *a voyage to Jupiter* –**voyager noun** [C]

VSO /ˌviː es 'əʊ/ **abbr** (*Brit*) Voluntary Service Overseas; a scheme for people to go to work in developing countries

vulgar /'vʌlgə/ **adj 1** not having or showing good judgement about what is attractive or appropriate; not polite or well-behaved: *vulgar furnishings* ● *a vulgar man/woman* **2** rude or likely to offend people: *a vulgar joke* –**vulgarity** /vʌl'gærəti/ **noun** [C,U] (*pl* vulgarities)

vulnerable /'vʌlnərəbl/ **adj** vulnerable (to sth/sb) weak and easy to hurt physically or emotionally: *Poor organization left the troops vulnerable to enemy attack.* ••► opposite **invulnerable** –**vulnerability** /ˌvʌlnərə'bɪləti/ **noun** [U]

vulture /'vʌltʃə/ **noun** [C] a large bird with no feathers on its head or neck that eats dead animals

W w

W, w[1] /'dʌblju:/ **noun** [C] (*pl* W's; w's) the twenty-third letter of the English alphabet: *'Water' begins with (a) 'W'.*

W[2] **abbr 1** watt(s): *a 60W light bulb* **2** west(ern): *W Cumbria*

wacky (also **whacky**) /'wæki/ **adj** (*informal*) amusing or funny in a slightly crazy way

wad /wɒd/ **noun** [C] **1** a large number of papers, paper money, etc folded or rolled together: *He pulled a wad of £20 notes out of his pocket.* **2** a mass of soft material that is used for blocking sth or keeping sth in place: *The nurse used a wad of cotton wool to stop the bleeding.*

waddle /'wɒdl/ **verb** [I] to walk with short steps, moving the weight of your body from one side to the other, like a duck

wade /weɪd/ **verb** [I] to walk with difficulty through fairly deep water, mud, etc

PHRASAL VERB **wade through sth** to deal with or read sth that is boring and takes a long time

wafer /'weɪfə/ **noun** [C] a very thin, dry biscuit often eaten with ice cream

waffle[1] /'wɒfl/ **noun 1** [C] a flat cake with a pattern of squares on it that is often eaten warm with a sweet sauce (syrup) **2** [U] (*Brit informal*) language that uses a lot of words but that does not say anything important or interesting: *The last two paragraphs of your essay are just waffle.*

waffle[2] /'wɒfl/ **verb** [I] (*Brit informal*) waffle (on) (about sth) to talk or write for much longer than necessary without saying anything important or interesting

waft /wɒft/ **verb** [I,T] to move, or make sth move, gently through the air: *The smell of her perfume wafted across the room.*

wag /wæg/ **verb** [I,T] (**wagging**; **wagged**) to shake up and down or move from side to side; to make sth do this: *The dog wagged its tail.*

★**wage**[1] /weɪdʒ/ **noun** [sing] (also **wages** *pl*) the regular amount of money that you earn for a week's work: *a weekly wage of £200* ● *What's the national **minimum wage** (= the lowest wage that an employer is allowed to pay by law)?*

➤ **Wage** in the singular is mainly used to talk about the amount of money paid or when the word is combined with another, for example 'wage packet', 'wage rise', etc. **Wages** in the plural means the money itself: *I have to pay the rent out of my wages.* Look at the note at **pay**[2].

wage[2] /weɪdʒ/ **verb** [T] wage sth (against/on sb/sth) to begin and then continue a war, battle, etc: *to wage war on your enemy*

waggle /'wægl/ **verb** [I,T] (*informal*) to move up and down or from side to side with quick, short movements; to make sth do this

wagon /'wægən/ **noun** [C] (*US* **freight car**) an open railway truck used for carrying goods or animals: *coal transported in goods wagons*

waif /weɪf/ **noun** [C] a small thin person, usually a child, who seems to have nowhere to live

wail /weɪl/ **verb 1** [I,T] to cry or complain in a loud, high voice, especially because you are sad or in pain **2** [I] (used about things) to make a sound like this: *sirens wailing in the streets outside* –**wail noun** [C]: *a wail of anguish/despair/distress* ● *the wail of sirens*

★**waist** /weɪst/ **noun** [C,usually sing] **1** the narrowest part around the middle of your body: *She put her arms around his waist.* ••► picture on page C5 **2** the part of a piece of clothing that goes round the waist: *The trousers are too baggy round the waist.*

waistband /'weɪstbænd/ **noun** [C] the narrow piece of material at the waist of a piece of clothing, especially trousers or a skirt ••► picture on page C6

waistcoat /'weɪskəʊt/ (*US* **vest**) **noun** [C] a piece of clothing with buttons down the front and no sleeves that is often worn over a shirt and under a jacket as part of a man's suit ••► picture on page C6

waistline /'weɪstlaɪn/ **noun** [C,usually sing] **1** (used to talk about how fat or thin a person is) the measurement or size of the body

W

around the waist **2** the place on a piece of clothing where your waist is

★**wait¹** /weɪt/ verb [I] **1** wait (for sb/sth) (to do sth) to stay in a particular place, and not do anything until sb/sth arrives or until sth happens: *Wait here. I'll be back in a few minutes.* ● *Have you been waiting long?* ● *If I'm a bit late, can you wait for me?* ● *I'm waiting to see the doctor.*

  ➤ Compare **wait** and **expect**: *I was expecting him to be there at 7.30 but at 8 I was still waiting.* ● *I'm waiting for the exam results but I'm not expecting to pass.* If you **wait**, you stay in one place and pass the time doing nothing, until sth happens or sb arrives: *I waited outside the theatre until they arrived.* If you **expect** sth, you think or believe that sth will very probably happen and you spend your time doing other things before it happens: *I'm expecting you to get a good grade in your exam.*

2 to be left or delayed until a later time: *Is this matter urgent or can it wait?*
IDIOMS **can't wait/can hardly wait** used when you are emphasizing that sb is very excited and enthusiastic about doing sth: *The kids can't wait to see their father again.*
keep sb waiting to make sb wait or be delayed, especially because you arrive late: *I'm sorry if I've kept you waiting.*
wait and see to be patient and find out what will happen later (perhaps before deciding to do sth): *We'll just have to wait and see – there's nothing more we can do.*
wait your turn to wait until the time when you are allowed to do sth
PHRASAL VERBS **wait behind** to stay in a place after others have left it: *She waited behind after class to speak to her teacher.*
wait in to stay at home because you are expecting sb to come or sth to happen
wait on sb to serve food, drink etc to sb, usually in a restaurant
wait up (for sb) to not go to bed because you are waiting for sb to come home

★**wait²** /weɪt/ noun [C,usually sing] a wait (for sth/sb) a period of time when you wait
IDIOM **lie in wait (for sb)** → LIE²

★**waiter** /'weɪtə/ noun [C] a man whose job is to serve customers at their tables in a restaurant, etc

'**waiting list** noun [C] a list of people who are waiting for sth, for example a service or medical treatment, that will be available in the future: *to put your name on a waiting list*

'**waiting room** noun [C] a room where people can sit while they are waiting, for example for a train, or to see a doctor or dentist

★**waitress** /'weɪtrəs/ noun [C] a woman whose job is to serve customers at their tables in a restaurant, etc

waive /weɪv/ verb [T] (*formal*) to say officially that a rule, etc need not be obeyed; to say officially that you no longer have a right

to sth: *In your case, we will waive your tuition fees.*

★**wake¹** /weɪk/ verb [I,T] (*pt* **woke** /wəʊk/; *pp* **woken** /'wəʊkən/) wake (sb) (up) to stop sleeping; to make sb stop sleeping: *I woke early in the morning and got straight out of bed.* ● *Wake up! It's nearly 8 o'clock!* ● *Could you wake me at 7.30, please?* •➤ adjective **awake**
PHRASAL VERBS **wake sb up** to make sb become more active or full of energy: *She always has a coffee to wake her up when she gets to work.*
wake up to sth to realize sth; to notice sth

wake² /weɪk/ noun [C] **1** an occasion before a funeral when people meet to remember the dead person, traditionally held at night to watch over the body before it is buried **2** the track that a moving ship leaves behind on the surface of the water
IDIOM **in the wake of sb/sth** following or coming after sb/sth: *The earthquake left a trail of destruction in its wake.*

waken /'weɪkən/ verb [I,T] (*formal, old-fashioned*) to stop sleeping or to make sb/sth stop sleeping: *She wakened from a deep sleep.*

★**walk¹** /wɔːk/ verb **1** [I] to move or go somewhere by putting one foot in front of the other on the ground, but without running: *The door opened and Billy walked in.* ● *I walk to work every day.* ● *He walks with a limp.* ● *Are the shops within walking distance* (= near enough to walk to)? **2** [I] to move in this way for exercise or pleasure •➤ We often use **go walking** to talk about taking long walks for pleasure: *We often go walking in the Alps in the summer.* Look at the note at **walk²**. **3** [T] to go somewhere with sb/sth on foot, especially to make sure he/she gets there safely: *I'll walk you home if you don't want to go on your own.* ● *He walked me to my car.* **4** [T] to take a dog out for exercise: *I'm just going to walk the dog.* –**walker** noun [C]: *She's a fast walker.* ● *This area is very popular with walkers.*
PHRASAL VERBS **walk off with sth 1** to win sth easily: *She walked off with all the prizes.* **2** to steal sth; to take sth that does not belong to you by mistake: *When I got home I realized that I had walked off with her pen.*
walk out (of sth) to leave suddenly and angrily: *She walked out of the meeting in disgust.*
walk out on sb (*informal*) to leave sb for ever: *He walked out on his wife and children after 15 years of marriage.*
walk (all) over sb (*informal*) **1** to treat sb badly, without considering his/her needs or feelings: *I don't know why she lets her husband walk all over her like that.* **2** to defeat sb completely: *He played brilliantly and walked all over his opponent.*
walk up (to sb/sth) to walk towards sb/sth, especially in a confident way

★**walk²** /wɔːk/ noun **1** [C] going somewhere on foot for pleasure, exercise, etc: *We went for a walk in the country.* ● *I'm just going to take the dog for a walk.* ● *The beach is five min-*

utes' walk/a five-minute walk from the hotel.

➤ We use **go for a walk** when we are talking about a short walk that we take for pleasure. We use **go walking** to talk about a long walk that may last several hours or days.

2 [C] a path or route for walking for pleasure: *From here there's a lovely walk through the woods.* **3** [sing] a way or style of walking: *He has a funny walk.* **4** [sing] the speed of walking: *She slowed to a walk.*

IDIOM **a walk of life** a person's job or position in society: *She has friends from all walks of life.*

walkie-talkie /ˌwɔːki ˈtɔːki/ **noun** [C] (*informal*) a small radio that you can carry with you to send or receive messages

'**walking stick** (also **stick**) **noun** [C] a stick that you carry and use as a support to help you walk

➤ Compare **crutch**.

•➤ picture at **bandage**

walkover /ˈwɔːkəʊvə/ **noun** [C] an easy win or victory in a game or competition

★**wall** /wɔːl/ **noun** [C] **1** a solid, vertical structure made of stone, brick, etc that is built round an area of land to protect it or to divide it: *There is a high wall all around the prison.* **2** one of the sides of a room or building joining the ceiling and the floor: *He put the picture up on the wall.*

IDIOM **up the wall** (*informal*) crazy or angry: *That noise is driving me up the wall.*

walled /wɔːld/ **adj** surrounded by a wall

★**wallet** /ˈwɒlɪt/ (*US* **billfold**) **noun** [C] a small, flat, folding case in which you keep paper money, plastic cards, etc •➤ Look at **purse**.

wallop /ˈwɒləp/ **verb** [T] (*informal*) to hit sb/sth very hard

wallow /ˈwɒləʊ/ **verb** [I] **wallow (in sth)** **1** (used about people and large animals) to lie and roll around in water, etc in order to keep cool or for pleasure: *I spent an hour wallowing in the bath.* **2** to take great pleasure in sth (a feeling, situation, etc): *to wallow in self-pity* (= to think about your unhappiness all the time and seem to be enjoying it)

wallpaper /ˈwɔːlpeɪpə/ **noun** [U] paper that you stick to the walls of a room to decorate or cover them –**wallpaper verb** [I,T]

ˌ**wall-to-'wall** **adj** (only *before* a noun) (used especially about a carpet) covering the floor of a room completely

wally /ˈwɒli/ **noun** [C] (*pl* **wallies**) (*Brit slang*) a silly person; a fool

walnut /ˈwɔːlnʌt/ **noun 1** [C] a nut that we eat, with a hard brown shell that is in two halves •➤ picture at **nut** **2** (also **walnut tree**) [C] the tree on which these nuts grow **3** [U] the wood of the walnut tree, used in making furniture

walrus /ˈwɔːlrəs/ **noun** [C] a large animal that lives in or near the sea in Arctic regions. It is similar to another sea animal (**seal**) but the walrus has two long outer teeth (**tusks**). •➤ picture at **seal**

waltz[1] /wɔːls/ **noun** [C] an elegant dance that you do with a partner, to music which has a rhythm of three beats; the music for this dance: *a Strauss waltz*

waltz[2] /wɔːls/ **verb 1** [I,T] to dance a waltz: *They waltzed around the floor.* • *He waltzed her round the room.* **2** [I] (*informal*) to go somewhere in a confident way: *You can't just waltz in and expect your meal to be ready for you.*

wan /wɒn/ **adj** looking pale and ill or tired

wand /wɒnd/ **noun** [C] a thin stick that people hold when they are doing magic tricks: *I wish I could wave a magic wand and make everything better.*

★**wander** /ˈwɒndə/ **verb 1** [I,T] to walk somewhere slowly with no particular sense of direction or purpose: *We spent a pleasant day wandering around the town.* • *He was found in a confused state, wandering the streets.* **2** [I] **wander (away/off) (from sb/sth)** to walk away from a place where you ought to be or the people you were with: *We must stay together while visiting the town so I don't want anybody to wander off.* • *Don't wander away from the main road.* **3** [I] (used about sb's mind, thoughts, etc) to stop paying attention to sth; to be unable to stay on one subject: *The lecture was so boring that my attention began to wander.*

wane[1] /weɪn/ **verb** [I] **1** (*written*) to become gradually weaker or less important: *My enthusiasm was waning rapidly.* **2** (used about the moon) to appear slightly smaller each day after being full and round

wane[2] /weɪn/ **noun**

IDIOM **on the wane** (*written*) becoming smaller, less important or less common: *The singer's popularity seems to be on the wane these days.*

wangle /ˈwæŋgl/ **verb** [T] (*informal*) to get sth that you want by persuading sb or by having a clever plan: *Somehow he wangled a day off to meet me.*

wanna /ˈwɒnə/ a way of writing 'want to' or 'want a', which is considered to be bad style, to show that sb is speaking in an informal way: *I wanna go home now.* •➤ Look at the note at **gonna**.

★**want**[1] /wɒnt/ **verb** [T] (not used in the continuous tenses) **1 want sth (for sth); want (sb) to do sth; want sth (to be) done** to have a desire or a wish for sth: *He wants a new bike.* • *What do they want for breakfast?* • *I don't want to discuss it now.* • *I want you to stop worrying about it.* • *The boss wants this letter typed.* • *I don't want Emma going out on her own at night.* • *They want Bhanot as captain.*

➤ **Want** and **would like** are similar in meaning, but 'would like' is more polite: *'I want a drink!' screamed the child.* • *'Would you like some more tea, Mrs Atwal?'*

2 (*informal*) used to say that sth needs to be done: *The button on my shirt wants sewing on.* • *The house wants a new coat of paint.*

3 (*informal*) (used to give advice to sb) should or ought to: *He wants to be more careful about what he tells people.* **4** (usually passive) to need sb to be in a particular place or for a particular reason: *Mrs Lewis, you are wanted on the phone.* ● *She is wanted by the police* (= the police are looking for her because she is suspected of committing a crime). **5** to feel sexual desire for sb

> Although this verb is not used in the continuous tenses, it is common to see the present participle (= -*ing* form): *She kept her head down, not wanting to attract attention.*

★**want²** /wɒnt/ noun (*formal*) **1 wants** [pl] sth you need or want: *All our wants were satisfied.* **2** [sing] a lack of sth: *He's suffering due to a want of care.*

IDIOM **for (the) want of sth** because of a lack of sth; because sth is not available: *I took the job for want of a better offer.*

wanting /'wɒntɪŋ/ adj (*formal*) **wanting (in** sth) (not before a noun) **1** not having enough of sth; lacking: *The children were certainly not wanting in enthusiasm.* **2** not good enough: *The new system was found wanting.*

wanton /'wɒntən/ adj (*formal*) (used about an action) done in order to hurt sb or damage sth for no good reason: *wanton vandalism*

★**war** /wɔ:/ noun **1** [U,C] a state of fighting between different countries or groups within countries using armies and weapons: *The Prime Minister announced that the country was at war.* ● *to declare war on another country* (= announce that a war has started) ● *When war broke out* (= started), *thousands of men volunteered for the army.* ● *a civil war* (= fighting between different groups in one country) ● *to go to war against sb* ● *to fight a war* **2** [C,U] very aggressive competition between groups of people, companies, countries, etc: *a price war among oil companies* **3** [U,sing] **war (against/on sb/sth)** efforts to end or get rid of sth: *We seem to be winning the war against organized crime.*

'war crime noun [C] a cruel act that is committed during a war and that is against the international rules of war

★**ward¹** /wɔ:d/ noun [C] **1** a separate part or room in a hospital for patients with the same kind of medical condition: *the maternity/psychiatric/surgical ward* **2** (*Brit*) one of the sections into which a town is divided for elections **3** a child who is under the protection of a court of law; a child whose parents are dead and who is cared for by another adult (guardian): *The child was made a ward of court.*

ward² /wɔ:d/ verb

PHRASAL VERB **ward sb/sth off** to protect or defend yourself against danger, illness, attack, etc

warden /'wɔ:dn/ noun [C] **1** a person whose job is to check that rules are obeyed or to look after the people in a particular place: *a traffic warden* (= a person who checks that cars are not parked in the wrong place)

2 (*especially US*) the person in charge of a prison

warder /'wɔ:də/ noun [C] (*Brit*) a person whose job is to guard prisoners •➤ Look at **guard**.

wardrobe /'wɔ:drəʊb/ noun [C] **1** a large cupboard in which you can hang your clothes •➤ picture on page C7 **2** a person's collection of clothes: *I need a whole new summer wardrobe.*

ware /weə/ noun **1** [U] (used in compounds) made from a particular type of material or suitable for a particular use: *glassware* ● *kitchenware* **2 wares** [pl] (*old-fashioned*) goods offered for sale

warehouse /'weəhaʊs/ noun [C] a building where large quantities of goods are stored before being sent to shops

warfare /'wɔ:feə/ noun [U] methods of fighting a war; types of war: *guerrilla warfare*

warily, wariness → WARY

warlike /'wɔ:laɪk/ adj liking to fight or good at fighting: *a warlike nation*

★**warm¹** /wɔ:m/ adj **1** having a pleasant temperature that is fairly high, between cool and hot: *It's quite warm in the sunshine.* ● *I jumped up and down to keep my feet warm.* •➤ Look at the note at **cold¹**. **2** (used about clothes) preventing you from getting cold: *Take plenty of warm clothes.* **3** friendly, kind and pleasant: *I was given a very warm welcome.* **4** creating a pleasant, comfortable feeling: *warm colours* –the warm **noun** [sing]: *It's awfully cold out here – I want to go back into the warm.* –**warmly** adv: *warmly dressed* ● *She thanked him warmly for his help.*

★**warm²** /wɔ:m/ verb [I,T] **warm (sb/sth) (up)** to become or to make sb/sth become warm or warmer: *It was cold earlier but it's beginning to warm up now.* ● *I sat in front of the fire to warm up.*

PHRASAL VERBS **warm to/towards sb** to begin to like sb that you did not like at first

warm to sth to become more interested in sth

warm up to prepare to do an activity or sport by practising gently: *The team warmed up before the match.*

warm-'hearted adj kind and friendly

warmth /wɔ:mθ/ noun [U] **1** a fairly high temperature or the effect created by this, especially when it is pleasant: *She felt the warmth of the sun on her face.* **2** the quality of being kind and friendly: *I was touched by the warmth of their welcome.*

★**warn** /wɔ:n/ verb [T] **1 warn sb (of sth); warn sb (about sb/sth)** to tell sb about sth unpleasant or dangerous that exists or might happen, so that he/she can avoid it: *When I saw the car coming I tried to warn him, but it was too late.* ● *The government is warning the public of possible terrorist attacks.* ● *He warned me about the danger of walking home alone at night.* **2 warn (sb) against doing sth; warn sb (not to do sth)** to advise sb not to do sth: *The radio warned people against going out during the storm.* ● *I warned you not to trust him.*

warning /'wɔ:nɪŋ/ **noun** [C,U] something that tells you to be careful or tells you about sth, usually sth bad, before it happens: *Your employers can't dismiss you without warning.* ● *You could have given me some warning that your parents were coming to visit.*

warp /wɔ:p/ **verb 1** [I,T] to become bent into the wrong shape, for example as a result of getting hot or wet; to make sth become like this: *The window frame was badly warped and wouldn't shut.* **2** [T] to influence sb so that he/she starts behaving in an unusual or shocking way: *His experiences in the war had warped him.* –**warped adj**

warpath /'wɔ:pɑ:θ/ **noun**

IDIOM (be/go) **on the warpath** (*informal*) to be very angry and want to fight or punish sb

warrant¹ /'wɒrənt/ **noun** [C] an official written statement that gives sb permission to do sth: *a search warrant* (= a document that allows the police to search a house)

warrant² /'wɒrənt/ **verb** [T] (*formal*) to make sth seem right or necessary; to deserve sth: *I don't think her behaviour warrants such criticism.*

warranty /'wɒrənti/ **noun** [C,U] (*pl* **warranties**) a written statement that you get when you buy sth, which promises to repair or replace it if it is broken or does not work: *Fortunately my stereo is still under warranty.* ·➤ Look at **guarantee.**

warrior /'wɒriə/ **noun** [C] (*old-fashioned*) a person who fights in a battle; a soldier

warship /'wɔ:ʃɪp/ **noun** [C] a ship for use in war

wart /wɔ:t/ **noun** [C] a small hard dry lump that sometimes grows on the face or body

wartime /'wɔ:taɪm/ **noun** [U] a period of time during which there is a war

wary /'weəri/ **adj** wary (of sb/sth) careful because you are uncertain or afraid of sb/sth: *Since becoming famous, she has grown wary of journalists.* –**warily** /-rəli/ **adv**

was → BE

★**wash¹** /wɒʃ/ **verb 1** [I,T] to clean sb/sth/ yourself with water and often soap: *to wash your hands/face/hair* ● *That shirt needs washing.* ● *Wash and dress quickly or you'll be late!* ● *I'll wash* (= wash the dishes), *you dry.* ·➤ Look at the note at **clean².** **2** [I,T] (used about water) to flow or carry sth/sb in the direction mentioned: *I let the waves wash over my feet.* ● *The current washed the ball out to sea.* **3** [I] to be able to be washed without being damaged: *Does this material wash well, or does the colour come out?*

IDIOM **wash your hands of sb/sth** to refuse to be responsible for sb/sth any longer: *They washed their hands of their son when he was sent to prison.*

PHRASAL VERBS **wash sb/sth away** (used about water) to carry sb/sth away: *The floods had washed away the path.*

wash (sth) off to (make sth) disappear by washing: *The writing has washed off and now I can't read it.* ● *Go and wash that make-up off!*

wash out to be removed from a material by washing: *These grease marks won't wash out.* **wash sth out** to wash sth or the inside of sth in order to remove dirt: *I'll just wash out this bowl and then we can use it.*

wash (sth) up 1 (*Brit*) to wash the plates, knives, forks, etc after a meal: *Whose turn is it to wash up?* **2** (*US*) to wash your face and hands: *Go and wash up quickly and put on some clean clothes.* **3** (often passive) (used about water) to carry sth to land and leave it there: *Police found the girl's body washed up on the beach.*

★**wash²** /wɒʃ/ **noun 1** [C, usually sing] an act of cleaning or being cleaned with water: *I'd better go and have a wash before we go out.* **2** [sing] the waves caused by the movement of a ship through water

IDIOM **in the wash** (used about clothes) being washed: *'Where's my red T-shirt?' 'It's in the wash.'*

washable /'wɒʃəbl/ **adj** that can be washed without being damaged

washbasin /'wɒʃbeɪsn/ (also **basin**) **noun** [C] a large bowl for water that has taps and is fixed to a wall, in a bathroom, etc ·➤ Look at **sink.** ·➤ picture at **plug**

washed 'out adj tired and pale: *They arrived looking washed out after their long journey.*

★**washing** /'wɒʃɪŋ/ **noun** [U] **1** clothes that need to be washed or are being washed: *Could you put the washing in the machine?* ● *a pile of dirty washing* **2** the act of cleaning clothes, etc with water: *I usually do the washing on Mondays.*

'washing machine noun [C] an electric machine for washing clothes ·➤ picture on page C7

'washing powder noun [U] soap in the form of powder for washing clothes

washing-'up noun [U] **1** the work of washing the plates, knives, forks, etc after a meal: *I'll do the washing-up.* ● *washing-up liquid* **2** plates, etc that need washing after a meal: *Put the washing-up next to the sink.*

washout /'wɒʃaʊt/ **noun** [C] (*informal*) an event that is a complete failure, especially because of rain

washroom /'wɒʃru:m; -rʊm/ **noun** [C] (*US*) a toilet, especially in a public building

wasn't short for WAS NOT

wasp /wɒsp/ **noun** [C] a small black and yellow flying insect that can sting ·➤ picture at **insect**

wastage /'weɪstɪdʒ/ **noun** [U] (*formal*) using too much of sth in a careless way; the amount of sth that is wasted

★**waste¹** /weɪst/ **verb** [T] **1** waste sth (on sb/ sth); waste sth (in doing sth) to use or spend sth in a careless way or for sth that is not necessary: *She wastes a lot of money on cigarettes.* ● *He wasted his time at university because he didn't work hard.* ● *She wasted no time in decorating her new room* (= she did it

W

immediately). **2** (usually passive) to give sth to sb who does not value it: *Expensive wine is wasted on me. I don't even like it.*

★**waste²** /weɪst/ *noun* **1** [sing] a waste (of sth) using sth in a careless and unnecessary way: *The seminar was **a waste of time** – I'd heard it all before.* ● *It seems a waste to throw away all these old newspapers.* **2** [U] material, food, etc that is not needed and is therefore thrown away: *nuclear waste* ● *A lot of household waste can be recycled and reused.* •➤ Look at **rubbish**. **3** wastes [pl] (*formal*) large areas of land that are not lived in and not used: *the wastes of the Sahara desert*

IDIOM **go to waste** to not be used and so thrown away and wasted: *I can't bear to see good food going to waste!*

waste³ /weɪst/ *adj* (only *before* a noun) **1** (used about land) not used or not suitable for use; not looked after: *There's an area of waste ground outside the town where people dump their rubbish.* **2** no longer useful; that is thrown away: *waste paper* ● *waste material*

wasted /ˈweɪstɪd/ *adj* **1** not necessary or successful: *a wasted journey* **2** very thin, especially because of illness **3** (*slang*) suffering from the effects of drugs or alcohol

wasteful /ˈweɪstfl/ *adj* using more of sth than necessary; causing waste

waste-ˈpaper basket *noun* [C] a basket etc, in which you put paper, etc which is to be thrown away •➤ picture at **bin**

★**watch¹** /wɒtʃ/ *verb* **1** [I,T] to look at sb/sth for a time, paying attention to what happens: *I watched in horror as the car swerved and crashed.* ● *I'm watching to see how you do it.* ● *We **watch** television most evenings.* ● *Watch what she does next.* ● *I watched him open the door and walk away.* **2** [T] to take care of sth for a short time: *Could you watch my bag for a second while I go and get a drink?* **3** [T] watch sb/sth (for sth) to be careful about sb/sth; to pay careful attention to sth/sb: *You'd better **watch what you say** to her. She gets upset very easily.* ● *Watch those two boys – they're acting suspiciously.*

IDIOM **watch your step** → **STEP¹**

PHRASAL VERBS **watch out** to be careful because of possible danger or trouble: *Watch out! There's a car coming.* ● *If you don't watch out you'll lose your job.*

watch out for sb/sth to look carefully and be ready for sb/sth: *Watch out for snakes if you walk through the fields.*

watch over sb/sth to look after or protect sb/sth: *For two weeks she watched over the sick child.*

★**watch²** /wɒtʃ/ *noun* **1** [C] a type of small clock that you usually wear around your wrist: *a digital watch* ● *My watch is a bit fast/slow* (= shows a time that is later/earlier than the correct time). •➤ Look at **clock**. **2** [sing,U] the action of watching sb/sth in case of possible danger or problems: *Tour companies have to **keep a close watch on** the political situation in the region.*

watchdog /ˈwɒtʃdɒg/ *noun* [C] a person or group whose job is to make sure that large companies respect people's rights: *a consumer watchdog*

watchful /ˈwɒtʃfl/ *adj* careful to notice things

★**water¹** /ˈwɔːtə/ *noun* **1** [U] the clear liquid that falls as rain and is in rivers, seas and lakes: *a glass of water* ● *All the rooms have hot and cold running water.* ● *drinking water* ● *tap water*

➤ When water is heated to 100°Celsius, it **boils** and becomes **steam**. When steam touches a cold surface, it **condenses** and becomes water again. When water is cooled below 0°Celsius, it **freezes** and becomes **ice**.

2 [U] a large amount of water, especially the water in a lake, river or sea: *Don't go too near the edge or you'll fall in the water!* ● *After the heavy rain several fields were **under water**.* **3** [U] the surface of an area of water: *Can you swim **under water**?* ● *I can see my reflection in the water.* **4** waters [pl] the water in a particular sea, lake, etc or near a particular country: *The ship was still in British waters.*

IDIOMS **keep your head above water** → **HEAD¹**

pass water → **PASS¹**

water² /ˈwɔːtə/ *verb* **1** [T] to give water to plants **2** [I] (used about the eyes or mouth) to fill with liquid: *The smoke in the room was starting to **make my eyes water**.* ● *These menus will really **make your mouth water**.*

PHRASAL VERB **water sth down 1** to add water to a liquid in order to make it weaker **2** to change a statement, report, etc so that the meaning is less strong or direct

watercolour /ˈwɔːtəkʌlə/ *noun* **1** watercolours [pl] paints that are mixed with water, not oil **2** [C] a picture that has been painted with watercolours

watercress /ˈwɔːtəkres/ *noun* [U] a type of plant with small round green leaves which have a strong taste and are often eaten in salads

waterfall /ˈwɔːtəfɔːl/ *noun* [C] a river that falls down from a cliff, rock, etc •➤ picture on page C8

ˈwatering can *noun* [C] a container with a long tube on one side which is used for pouring water on plants •➤ picture at **garden**

waterlogged /ˈwɔːtəlɒgd/ *adj* **1** (used about the ground) extremely wet: *Our boots sank into the waterlogged ground.* **2** (used about a boat) full of water and likely to sink

watermelon /ˈwɔːtəmelən/ *noun* [C,U] a large, round fruit with a thick, green skin. It is pink or red inside with a lot of black seeds. •➤ picture on page C3

waterproof /ˈwɔːtəpruːf/ *adj* that does not let water go through: *a waterproof jacket*

watershed /ˈwɔːtəʃed/ *noun* [C] an event or time which is important because it marks the beginning of sth new or different

waterski /ˈwɔːtəskiː/ *verb* [I] to move across the surface of water standing on narrow

---

[C] **countable**, a noun with a plural form: *one book, two books*   [U] **uncountable**, a noun with no plural form: *some sugar*

boards (**waterskis**) and being pulled by a boat ••➤ picture on page C8

watertight /'wɔːtətaɪt/ **adj 1** made so that water cannot get in or out: *a watertight container* **2** (used about an excuse, opinion, etc) impossible to prove wrong; without any faults: *His alibi was absolutely watertight.*

waterway /'wɔːtəweɪ/ **noun** [C] a canal, river, etc along which boats can travel

watery /'wɔːtəri/ **adj 1** containing mostly water: *watery soup* • *A watery liquid came out of the wound.* **2** weak and pale: *watery sunshine* • *a watery smile*

watt /wɒt/ **noun** [C] a unit of electrical power: *a 60-watt light bulb*

★**wave¹** /weɪv/ **noun** [C] **1** a line of water moving across the surface of water, especially the sea, that is higher than the rest of the surface: *We watched the waves roll in and break on the shore.* ••➤ Look at **tidal wave.** ••➤ picture on page C8 **2** a sudden increase or spread of a feeling or type of behaviour: *There has been a wave of sympathy for the refugees.* • *a crime wave* • *The pain came in waves.* ••➤ Look at **heatwave. 3** a large number of people or things suddenly moving or appearing somewhere: *There is normally a wave of tourists in August.* **4** a movement of sth, especially your hand, from side to side in the air: *With a wave of his hand, he said goodbye and left.* **5** the form that some types of energy such as sound, light, heat, etc take when they move: *sound waves* • *shock waves from the earthquake* ••➤ Look at **long wave, medium wave** and **short wave. 6** a gentle curve in your hair ••➤ Look at **perm.**

★**wave²** /weɪv/ **verb 1** [I,T] to move your hand from side to side in the air, usually to attract sb's attention or as you meet or leave sb: *She waved to me as the train left the station.* • *I leant out of the window and waved goodbye to my friends.* ••➤ picture on page S8 **2** [T] **wave sth (at sb); wave sth (about)** to hold sth in the air and move it from side to side: *The crowd waved flags as the President came out.* • *She was talking excitedly and waving her arms about.* **3** [T] **wave sb/sth away, on, through,** etc to move your hand in a particular direction to show sb/sth which way to go: *There was a policeman in the middle of the road, waving us on.* **4** [I] to move gently up and down or from side to side: *The branches of the trees waved gently in the breeze.*

PHRASAL VERBS **wave sth aside** to decide not to pay attention to sb/sth because you think he/she/it is not important

wave sb off to wave to sb who is leaving

waveband /'weɪvbænd/ **noun** [C] a set of radio waves of similar length

wavelength /'weɪvleŋθ/ **noun** [C] **1** the distance between two sound waves **2** the length of wave on which a radio station sends out its programmes

IDIOM **on the same wavelength** ➔ **SAME**

waver /'weɪvə/ **verb** [I] **1** to become weak or uncertain, especially when making a decision or choice: *He never wavered in his sup-*

port for her. **2** to move in a way that is not firm or steady: *His hand wavered as he reached for the gun.*

wavy /'weɪvi/ **adj** having curves; not straight: *wavy hair* • *a wavy line* ••➤ picture at **hair** and **line**

wax /wæks/ **noun** [U] **1** a substance made from fat or oil that melts easily and is used for making candles, polish, etc ••➤ picture at **candle 2** a yellow substance that is found in your ears

★**way¹** /weɪ/ **noun 1** [C] **a way (to do sth/of doing sth)** a particular method, style or manner of doing sth: *What is the best way to learn a language?* • *I've discovered a brilliant way of saving paper!* • *They'll have to find the money one way or another.* • *He always does things his own way.* • *She smiled in a friendly way.* **2** [C, usually sing] the route you take to reach somewhere; the route you would take if nothing were stopping you: *Can you tell me the way to James Street?* • *Which way should I go to get to the town centre?* • *If you lose your way, phone me.* • *We stopped on the way to Leeds for a meal.* • *Can I drive you home? It's on my way.* • *Get out of my way!* • *Can you move that box – it's in my/the way.* **3** [sing] a direction or position: *Look this way!* • *That painting is the wrong way up* (= with the wrong edge at the top). • *Shouldn't you be wearing that hat the other way round?* (= facing in the other direction) • *He thought I was older than my sister but in fact it's the other way round* (= the opposite of what he thought). ••➤ Look at **back to front. 4** [C] a path, road, route, etc that you can travel along ••➤ Look at **highway, motorway** and **railway. 5** [sing] a distance in space or time: *It's a long way from London to Edinburgh.* • *The exams are still a long way off.* • *We came all this way to see him and he's not at home!*

IDIOMS **be set in your ways** to be unable to change your habits, attitudes, etc

by the way (used for adding sth to the conversation) on a new subject: *Oh, by the way, I saw Mario in town yesterday.*

change your ways ➔ **CHANGE¹**

get/have your own way to get or do what you want, although others may want sth else

give way to break or fall down: *The branch of the tree suddenly gave way and he fell.*

give way (to sb/sth) 1 to stop or to allow sb/sth to go first: *Give way to traffic coming from the right.* ••➤ picture at **roundabout 2** to allow sb to have what he/she wants although you did not at first agree with it: *We shall not give way to the terrorists' demands.*

go a long way ➔ **LONG¹**

go out of your way (to do sth) to make a special effort to do sth

have a long way to go ➔ **LONG¹**

the hard way ➔ **HARD¹**

in a/one/any way; in some ways to a certain degree but not completely: *In some ways I prefer working in a small office.*

in a big/small way used for expressing the

size or importance of an activity: *'Have you done any acting before?' 'Yes, but in a very small way (= not very much).'*
in the way 1 blocking the road or path: *I can't get past. There's a big lorry in the way.* **2** not needed or wanted: *I felt rather in the way at my daughter's party.*
learn the hard way → LEARN
no way (*informal*) definitely not: *'Can I borrow your car?' 'No way!'*
under way having started and making progress: *Discussions between the two sides are now under way.*
a/sb's way of life the behaviour and customs that are typical of a person or group of people

way² /weɪ/ **adv** (*informal*) very far; very much: *I finally found his name way down at the bottom of the list.* ● *Matt's got way more experience than me.*

WC /ˌdʌblju: 'siː/ **abbr** toilet

★**we** /wiː/ **pron** the subject of a verb; used for talking about the speaker and one or more other people: *We're going to the cinema.* ● *We are both very pleased with the house.*

★**weak** /wiːk/ **adj 1** (used about the body) having little strength or energy; not strong: *The child was weak with hunger.* ● *Her legs felt weak.* **2** that cannot support a lot of weight; likely to break: *That bridge is too weak to take heavy traffic.* **3** not having economic success: *a weak currency/economy/market* **4** easy to influence; not firm or powerful: *He is too weak to be a good leader.* ● *a weak character* **5** (used about an argument, excuse, etc) not easy to believe: *She made some weak excuse about washing her hair tonight.* **6** not easy to see or hear; not definite or strong: *a weak voice* ● *She gave a weak smile.* **7** (used about liquids) containing a lot of water, not strong in taste: *weak coffee* ● *I like my tea quite weak.* **8 weak (at/in/on sth)** not very good at sth: *He's weak at Maths.* ● *His maths is weak.* ● *a weak team* ∙→ opposite for all senses **strong** –**weakly adv**

★**weaken** /ˈwiːkən/ **verb** [I,T] **1** to become less strong; to make sb/sth less strong: *The illness had left her weakened.* ● *The building had been weakened by the earthquake.* ∙→ opposite **strengthen 2** to become less certain or firm about sth: *She eventually weakened and allowed him to stay.*

ˈ**weak form noun** [C] a way of pronouncing a word when it is not emphasized

★**weakness** /ˈwiːknəs/ **noun 1** [U] the state of being weak: *He thought that crying was a sign of weakness.* **2** [C] a fault or lack of strength, especially in a person's character: *It's important to know your own strengths and weaknesses.* ∙→ opposite for senses 1 and 2 **strength 3** [C, usually sing] **a weakness for sth/sb** a particular and often foolish liking for sth/sb: *I have a weakness for chocolate.*

★**wealth** /welθ/ **noun 1** [U] a lot of money, property, etc that sb owns; the state of being rich: *They were a family of enormous wealth.* ∙→ synonym **riches 2** [sing] **a wealth of sth** a

large number or amount of sth: *a wealth of information/experience/talent*

★**wealthy** /ˈwelθi/ **adj** (**wealthier**; **wealthiest**) having a lot of money, property, etc; rich

wean /wiːn/ **verb** [T] to gradually stop feeding a baby or young animal with its mother's milk and start giving it solid food

★**weapon** /ˈwepən/ **noun** [C] an object which is used for fighting or for killing people, such as a gun, knife, bomb, etc

★**wear¹** /weə/ **verb** (*pt* **wore** /wɔː/; *pp* **worn** /wɔːn/) **1** [T] to have clothes, jewellery, etc on your body: *He was wearing a suit and tie.* ● *I wear glasses for reading.* **2** [T] to have a certain look on your face: *His face wore a puzzled look.* **3** [I,T] to become or make sth become thinner, smoother or weaker because of being used or rubbed a lot: *These tyres are badly worn.* ● *The soles of his shoes had worn smooth.* **4** [T] to make a hole, path, etc in sth by rubbing, walking, etc: *Put some slippers on or you'll wear a hole in your socks!* **5** [I] to last for a long time without becoming thinner or damaged: *This material wears well.*
IDIOM **wear thin** to have less effect because of being used too much: *We've heard that excuse so often that it's beginning to wear thin.*
PHRASAL VERBS **wear (sth) away** to damage sth or to make it disappear over a period of time, by using or touching it a lot; to disappear or become damaged in this way: *The wind had worn the soil away.*
wear (sth) down to become or to make sth smaller or smoother: *The heels on these shoes have worn right down.*
wear sb/sth down to make sb/sth weaker by attacking, persuading, etc: *They wore him down with constant arguments until he changed his mind.*
wear off to become less strong or to disappear completely: *The effects of the drug wore off after a few hours.*
wear (sth) out to become too thin or damaged to use any more; to cause sth to do this: *Children's shoes wear out very quickly.*
wear sb out to make sb very tired: *She wore herself out walking home with the heavy bags.*
∙→ Look at **worn-out**.

★**wear²** /weə/ **noun** [U] **1** wearing or being worn; use as clothing: *You'll need jeans and jumpers for everyday wear.* **2** (usually in compounds) used especially in shops to describe clothes for a particular purpose or occasion: *casual/evening/sports wear* ● *children's wear* **3** long use which damages the quality or appearance of sth: *The engine is checked regularly for signs of wear.*
IDIOMS **wear and tear** the damage caused by ordinary use
the worse for wear → WORSE

weary /ˈwɪəri/ **adj** very tired, especially after you have been doing sth for a long time: *He gave a weary smile.* –**wearily** /ˈwɪərəli/ **adv** –**weariness noun** [U]

★**weather¹** /ˈweðə/ **noun** [U] the climate at a certain place and time, how much wind, rain, sun, etc there is and how hot or cold it is: *What's the weather like where you are?* ● *hot/warm/sunny/fine weather* ● *cold/wet/windy/wintry weather* ● *I'm not going for a run in this weather!*

➤ **Rain** is drops of water that fall from the clouds. **Snow** is frozen rain. It is soft and white and often settles on the ground. **Sleet** is rain that is not completely frozen. **Hail** is rain frozen to ice. When it is only raining very slightly it is **drizzling**. When it is raining very hard it is **pouring**. **Fog** is like a cloud at ground level. It makes it difficult to see very far ahead. **Mist** is a thin type of fog. Look also at **storm**.

[IDIOMS] **make heavy weather of sth** → HEAVY **under the weather** (*informal*) not very well

weather² /'weðə/ *verb* **1** [I,T] to change or make sth change in appearance because of the effect of the sun, air or wind: *The farmer's face was weathered by the sun.* **2** [T] to come safely through a difficult time or experience: *Their company managed to weather the recession and recover.*

'**weather-beaten** *adj* (used especially about a person's face or skin) made rough and damaged by the sun and wind

'**weather forecast** (also **forecast**) *noun* [C] a description of the weather that is expected for the next day or next few days •➤ Look at **weather**.

weave /wiːv/ *verb* [I,T] (*pt* **wove** /wəʊv/ or in sense 2 **weaved**; *pp* **woven** /'wəʊvn/ or in sense 2 **weaved**) **1** to make cloth, etc by passing threads under and over a set of threads that is fixed to a frame (**loom**): *woven cloth* **2** to change direction often when you are moving so that you are not stopped by anything: *The cyclist weaved in and out of the traffic.*

web /web/ *noun* [C] a type of fine net that a spider makes in order to catch small insects: *A spider spins webs.* •➤ Look at **cobweb**.

Wed *abbr* Wednesday: *Wed 4 May*

we'd /wiːd/ *short for* WE HAD, WE WOULD

★**wedding** /'wedɪŋ/ *noun* [C] a marriage ceremony and often the meal or party that follows it (the reception): *I've been invited to their wedding.* ● *a wedding dress/guest/present* ● *a wedding ring* (= one that is worn on the third finger to show that a person is married)

➤ **Marriage** is the word for the state of being married to somebody. It can also be used for the ceremony, with the same meaning as **wedding**. The man who is getting married is the **bridegroom**, the woman is the **bride**. Other important people at the ceremony are the **best man** and the **bridesmaids**. A wedding can take place in church (a **church wedding**) or in a **registry office**. A couple celebrate their **silver wedding** when they have been married for 25 years, their **golden wedding** after 50 and their **diamond wedding** after 60.

wedge¹ /wedʒ/ *noun* [C] a piece of wood, etc with one thick and one thin pointed end that you can push into a small space, for example to keep things apart: *The door was kept open with a wedge.*

wedge² /wedʒ/ *verb* [T] **1** to force sth apart or to prevent sth from moving by using a wedge: *to wedge a door open* **2** to force sth/sb to fit into a small space: *The cupboard was wedged between the table and the door.*

★**Wednesday** /'wenzdeɪ; -di/ *noun* [C,U] (*abbr* **Wed**) the day of the week after Tuesday

➤ Days of the week are always written with a capital letter. For examples of how to use the days of the week in sentences, look at **Monday**.

wee /wiː/ (also '**wee-wee**) *noun* [C,U] (*informal*) (used by young children or when you are talking to them) water that you pass from your body; urine –**wee** *verb* [I]

weed¹ /wiːd/ *noun* **1** [C] a wild plant that is not wanted in a garden because it prevents other plants from growing properly **2** [U] a mass of very small green plants that floats on the surface of an area of water

weed² /wiːd/ *verb* [I,T] to remove weeds from a piece of ground, etc

[PHRASAL VERB] **weed sth/sb out** to remove the things or people that you do not think are good enough: *He weeded out all the letters with spelling mistakes in them.*

weedy /'wiːdi/ *adj* (*informal*) small and weak: *a small weedy man*

★**week** /wiːk/ *noun* [C] **1** a period of seven days, especially from Monday to Sunday or from Sunday to Saturday: *We arrived last week.* ● *He left two weeks ago.* ● *I haven't seen her for a week.* ● *I go there twice a week.* ● *They'll be back in a week/in a week's time.*

➤ In British English, a period of two weeks is usually called a **fortnight**.

2 the part of the week when people go to work, etc, usually from Monday to Friday: *She works hard during the week so that she can enjoy herself at the weekend.* ● *I work a 40-hour week.*

[IDIOMS] **today, tomorrow, Monday, etc week** seven days after today, tomorrow, Monday, etc

week in, week out every week without a rest or change: *He's played for the same team week in, week out for 20 years.*

a week yesterday, last Monday, etc seven days before yesterday, Monday, etc

★**weekday** /'wiːkdeɪ/ *noun* [C] any day except Saturday or Sunday: *I only work on weekdays.*

★**weekend** /ˌwiːk'end/ *noun* [C] Saturday and Sunday: *What are you doing at the weekend?* •➤ **At the weekend** is used in British English. In US English you say **on the weekend**.

★**weekly¹** /'wiːkli/ *adj, adv* happening or appearing once a week or every week: *a weekly report* ● *We are paid weekly.*

weekly² /'wiːkli/ *noun* [C] (*pl* **weeklies**) a newspaper or magazine that is published every week

W

weep /wi:p/ *verb* [I,T] (*pt, pp* **wept** /wept/) (*formal*) to let tears fall because of strong emotion; to cry: *She wept at the news of his death.*

★**weigh** /weɪ/ *verb* **1** [T] to measure how heavy sth is, especially by using a machine (scales): *I weigh myself every week.* ● *Can you weigh this parcel for me, please?* **2** [T] to have or show a certain weight: *I weigh 56 kilos.* ● *How much does this weigh?* **3** [T] **weigh sth (up)** to consider sth carefully: *You need to weigh up your chances of success.* **4** [T] **weigh sth (against sb/sth)** to consider if one thing is better, more important, etc than another or not: *We shall weigh the advantages of the plan against the risks.* **5** [I] **weigh against (sb/sth)** to be considered as a disadvantage when sb/sth is being judged: *She didn't get the job because her lack of experience weighed against her.*

PHRASAL VERBS **weigh sb down** to make sb feel worried and sad: *He felt weighed down by all his responsibilities.*
weigh sb/sth down to make it difficult for sb/sth to move (by being heavy): *I was weighed down by heavy shopping.*
weigh on sb/sth to make sb worry

➤ We also say **weigh on sb's mind**: *That problem has been weighing on my mind for a long time.*

weigh sb/sth up to consider sb/sth carefully and form an opinion: *I weighed up my chances and decided it was worth applying.*

★**weight¹** /weɪt/ *noun* **1** [U] how heavy sth/sb is; the fact of being heavy: *The doctor advised him to* ***lose weight*** (= become thinner and less heavy). ● *He's* ***put on weight*** (= got fatter). ● *The weight of the snow broke the branch.* **2** [C] a heavy object: *The doctor has told me not to lift heavy weights.* **3** [C] a piece of metal that weighs a known amount that can be used to measure an amount of sth, or that can be lifted as a form of exercise: *a 500-gram weight* ● *She lifts weights in the gym as part of her daily training.* •➤ picture on page S2 **4** [sing] something that you are worried about: *Telling her the truth took* ***a weight off his mind.***

IDIOMS **carry weight** ➤ CARRY
pull your weight ➤ PULL¹

weight² /weɪt/ *verb* [T] **1 weight sth (down) (with sth)** to hold sth down with a heavy object or objects: *to weight down a fishing net* **2** (usually passive) to organize sth so that a particular person or group has an advantage/disadvantage: *The system is* ***weighted in favour of/against*** *people with children.*

weightless /'weɪtləs/ *adj* having no weight, for example when travelling in space –**weightlessness** *noun* [U]

weightlifting /'weɪtlɪftɪŋ/ *noun* [U] a sport in which heavy metal objects are lifted

'**weight training** *noun* [U] the activity of lifting heavy objects (weights) as a form of exercise: *I do weight training to keep fit.*

weighty /'weɪti/ *adj* (**weightier; weightiest**) serious and important: *a weighty question*

weir /wɪə/ *noun* [C] a type of wall that is built across a river to stop or change the direction of the flow of water

weird /wɪəd/ *adj* strange and unusual: *a weird noise/experience* –**weirdly** *adv*

★**welcome¹** /'welkəm/ *verb* [T] **1** to be friendly to sb when he/she arrives somewhere: *Everyone came to the door to welcome us.* **2** to be pleased to receive or accept sth: *I've no idea what to do next, so I'd welcome any suggestions.* –**welcome** *noun* [C]: *Let's give a warm welcome to our next guest.*

★**welcome²** /'welkəm/ *adj* **1** received with pleasure; giving pleasure: *You're always welcome here.* ● *welcome news* **2** **welcome to sth/to do sth** allowed to do sth: *You're welcome to use my bicycle.* **3** used to say that sb can have sth that you do not want yourself: *Take the car if you want. You're welcome to it. It's always breaking down.* –**welcome** *interj*: *Welcome to London!* ● *Welcome home!*

IDIOMS **make sb welcome** to receive sb in a friendly way
you're welcome (*spoken*) you don't need to thank me: *'Thank you for your help.' 'You're welcome.'*

weld /weld/ *verb* [I,T] to join pieces of metal by heating them and pressing them together

★**welfare** /'welfeə/ *noun* [U] **1** the general health, happiness of a person, an animal or a group: *The doctor is concerned about the child's welfare.* **2** the help and care that is given to people who have problems with health, money, etc: *education and welfare services* **3** (*US*) = SOCIAL SECURITY

,**welfare** '**state** *noun* [sing] a system organized by a government to provide free services and money for people who have no job, who are ill, etc; a country that has this system

we'll /wi:l/ *short for* WE SHALL, WE WILL

★**well¹** /wel/ *adv* (**better; best**) **1** in a good way: *You speak English very well.* ● *I hope your work is going well.* ● *You passed your exam! Well done!* ● *He took it well when I told him he wasn't on the team.* •➤ opposite **badly 2** completely or fully: *Shake the bottle well before opening.* ● *How well do you know Henry?* **3** very much: *They arrived home well past midnight.* ● *She says she's 32 but I'm sure she's well over 40.* ● *This book is* ***well worth*** *reading.* **4** (used with *can, could, may* or *might*) probably or possibly: *He might well be right.* **5** (used with *can, could, may* or *might*) with good reason: *I can't very well refuse to help them after all they've done for me.* ● *'Where's Bill?' 'You may well ask!'* (= *I don't know either)'*

IDIOMS **as well (as sb/sth)** in addition to sb/sth: *Can I come as well?* ● *He's worked in Japan as well as Italy.* •➤ Look at the note at **also.**
augur well/ill for sb/sth ➤ AUGUR
bode well/ill (for sb/sth) ➤ BODE
do well 1 to be successful: *Their daughter*

W

has done well at university. **2** to be getting better after an illness: *Mr Singh is doing well after his operation.*

do well to do sth used to say that sth is the right and sensible thing to do: *He would do well to check the facts before accusing people.*

may/might (just) as well used for saying that sth is the best thing you can do in the situation, even though you may not want to do it: *I may as well tell you the truth – you'll find out anyway.*

mean well → MEAN¹

well and truly completely: *We were well and truly lost.*

well/badly off → OFF¹

★**well²** /wel/ **adj** (**better** /'betə/, **best** /best/) (not before a noun) **1** in good health: *'How are you?' 'I'm very well, thanks.'* ● *This medicine will make you feel better.* ● *Get well soon* (= written in a card that you send to somebody who is ill). **2** in a good state: *I hope all is well with you.*

[IDIOMS] **all very well (for sb)** (*informal*) used for showing that you are not happy or do not agree with sth: *It's all very well for her to criticize* (= it's easy for her to criticize) *but it doesn't help the situation.*

(just) as well (to do sth) sensible; a good idea: *It would be just as well to ask his permission.* ●● Look at **it is just as well (that)** at **just**.

★**well³** /wel/ **interj 1** used for showing surprise: *Well, thank goodness you've arrived.* **2** used for expressing uncertainty: *'Do you like it?' 'Well, I'm not really sure.'* **3** used when you begin the next part of a story or when you are thinking about what to say next: *Well, the next thing that happened was...* ● *Well now, let me see...* **4** used to show that you are waiting for sb to say sth: *Well? Are you going to tell us what happened?* **5** used to show that you want to finish a conversation: *Well, it's been nice talking to you.* **6** (also **oh well**) used for showing that you know there is nothing you can do to change a situation: *Oh well, there's nothing we can do about it.*

well⁴ /wel/ **noun** [C] **1** a deep hole in the ground from which water is obtained: *to draw water from a well* **2** =OIL WELL

well⁵ /wel/ **verb** [I] **well (out/up)** (used about a liquid) to come to the surface: *Tears welled up in her eyes*

,**well-'balanced adj 1** (used about a person) calm and sensible **2** (used about a meal, etc) containing enough of the healthy types of food your body needs: *a well-balanced diet*

,**well-be'haved adj** behaving in a way that most people think is correct

'**well-being noun** [U] a state of being healthy and happy

,**well 'done adj** (used about meat, etc) cooked for a long time

➤ Compare **rare** and **medium**.

,**well-'dressed adj** wearing attractive and fashionable clothes

,**well-'earned adj** that you deserve, especially because you have been working hard: *a well-earned holiday*

,**well-'fed adj** having good food regularly

,**well-in'formed adj** knowing a lot about one or several subjects

wellington /'welɪŋtən/ (also *informal* **welly** /'weli/) **noun** [C] (*pl* **wellingtons**; **wellies**) (*Brit*) one of a pair of long rubber boots that you wear to keep your feet and the lower part of your legs dry: *a pair of wellingtons*

,**well-'kept adj** looked after very carefully so that it has a tidy appearance: *a well-kept garden*

,**well-'known adj** known by a lot of people; famous ●● opposite **unknown**

,**well-'meaning adj** (used about a person) wanting to be kind or helpful, but often not having this effect

,**well-'meant adj** intended to be kind or helpful but not having this result

,**well-to-'do adj** having a lot of money, property, etc; rich

'**well-wisher noun** [C] somebody who hopes that a person or thing will be successful: *She received lots of letters from well-wishers before the competition.*

★**Welsh** /welʃ/ **adj** from Wales ●● Look at the section on geographical names at the back of this dictionary.

went *past tense* of **GO¹**

wept *past tense, past participle* of **WEEP**

we're /wɪə/ *short for* **WE ARE**

were → BE

★**west** /west/ **noun** [sing] (*abbr* **W**) **1** (also **the west**) the direction you look towards in order to see the sun go down; one of the four main directions that we give names to (the points of the compass): *Which way is west?* ● *Rain is spreading from the west.* ● *There's a road to the west of here.* ●● picture at **north** **2** the west; the West the part of any country, city, etc that is further to the west than other parts: *I live in the west of Scotland.* ● *The climate in the West is much wetter than the East.* **3** the West [sing] the countries of North America and Western Europe —**west adj, adv** in, to or towards the west: *The island is five miles west of here.* ● *to travel west* ● *West London*

westbound /'westbaʊnd/ **adj** travelling or leading towards the west: *the westbound carriageway of the motorway*

westerly /'westəli/ **adj 1** to, towards or in the west: *in a westerly direction* **2** (used about winds) coming from the west

★**western¹** (also **Western**) /'westən/ **adj 1** in or of the west: *western France* **2** from or connected with the western part of the world, especially Europe or North America

western² /'westən/ **noun** [C] a film or book about life in the past in the west of the United States

westerner /'westənə/ **noun** [C] a person who was born or who lives in the western part of

W

the world, especially Europe or North America: *Westerners arriving in China usually experience culture shock.*

westernize (also **-ise**) /'westənaɪz/ **verb** [T] (usually passive) to make a country or people more like Europe and North America: *Young people in our country are becoming westernized through watching American television programmes.*

the West Indies **noun** [pl,with sing or pl verb] a group of islands in the Caribbean Sea that consists of the Bahamas, the Antilles and the Leeward and Windward Islands –**West Indian** **noun** [C]: *The West Indians won their match against Australia.* –**West Indian** **adj**

westward /'westwəd/ **adj** towards the west: *in a westward direction* –**westward** (also **westwards**) **adv**: *to fly westwards*

★**wet**[1] /wet/ **adj** (**wetter**; **wettest**) **1** covered in a liquid, especially water: *wet clothes/ hair/grass/roads* ● *Don't get your feet wet.*

> ➤ **Moist** means slightly wet. **Damp** is used to describe things that are slightly wet and feel unpleasant because of it: *Don't sit on the grass. It's damp.*

2 (used about the weather, etc) with a lot of rain: *a wet day* **3** (used about paint, etc) not yet dry or hard: *The ink is still wet.* ●➤ opposite for sense **1**, **2**, and **3** **dry** **4** (used about a person) without energy or enthusiasm –the wet **noun** [sing]: *Come in out of the wet* (= the rainy weather).

IDIOMS a **wet blanket** (*informal*) a person who spoils other people's fun, especially because he or she refuses to take part in sth

wet through extremely wet

wet[2] /wet/ **verb** [T] (*pres part* **wetting**; *pt, pp* **wet** or **wetted**) **1** to make sth wet **2** (used especially of young children) to make yourself or your bed, clothes, etc wet by letting a yellowish liquid (**urine**) escape from your body

wet suit **noun** [C] a rubber suit that covers the whole of the body, used by people doing sports in the water or swimming under the water

we've /wi:v/ *short for* **WE HAVE**

whack /wæk/ **verb** [T] (*informal*) to hit sb/ sth hard

whale

whale /weɪl/ **noun** [C] a very large animal that lives in the sea and looks like a very large fish

whaling /'weɪlɪŋ/ **noun** [U] the hunting of whales

wharf /wɔ:f/ **noun** [C] (*pl* **wharves** /wɔ:vz/) a platform made of stone or wood at the side of a river where ships and boats can be tied up

★**what** /wɒt/ **determiner, pron** **1** used for asking for information about sb/sth: *What time is it?* ● *What kind of music do you like?* ● *She asked him what he was doing.* ● *What's their phone number?* ●➤ Look at the note at **which**. **2** the thing or things that have been mentioned or said: *What he says is true.* ● *I haven't got much, but you can borrow what money I have.* **3** used for emphasizing sth: *What strange eyes she's got!* ● *What a kind thing to do!* **4** used to express surprise or to tell sb to say or repeat sth: *'I've asked Alice to marry me.' 'What!'*

IDIOMS **how/what about...?** ➔ **ABOUT**[2]

what for for what purpose or reason: *What's this little switch for?* ● *What did you say that for* (= why did you say that)?

what if...? what would happen if...?: *What if the car breaks down?*

★**whatever** /wɒt'evə/ **adj, adv, pron** **1** any or every; anything or everything: *You can say whatever you like.* ● *He took whatever help he could get.* **2** used to say that it does not matter what happens or what sb does, because the result will be the same: *I still love you, whatever you may think.* ● *Whatever she says, she doesn't really mean it.* **3** (used for expressing surprise or worry) what: *Whatever could have happened to them?* **4** (also **whatsoever**) at all: *I've no reason whatever to doubt him.* ● *'Any questions?' 'None whatsoever.'*

IDIOMS **or whatever** (*informal*) or any other or others of a similar kind: *You don't need to wear anything smart – jeans and a sweater or whatever.*

whatever you do used to emphasize that sb must not do sth: *Don't touch the red switch, whatever you do.*

★**wheat** /wi:t/ **noun** [U] **1** a type of grain which can be made into flour **2** the plant which produces this grain: *a field of wheat* ●➤ picture at **cereal**

★**wheel**[1] /wi:l/ **noun** **1** [C] one of the circular objects under a car, bicycle, etc that turns when it moves: *His favourite toy is a dog on wheels.* ● *By law, you have to carry a spare wheel in your car.* **2** [usually sing] = **STEERING WHEEL**: *Her husband was at the wheel* (= he was driving) *when the accident happened.* ●➤ picture on page S9

wheel[2] /wi:l/ **verb** **1** [T] to push along an object that has wheels; to move sb about in/on a vehicle with wheels: *He wheeled his bicycle up the hill.* ● *She was wheeled back to her bed on a trolley.* **2** [I] to fly round in circles: *Birds wheeled above the ship.* **3** [I] to turn round suddenly: *Eleanor wheeled round, with a look of horror on her face.*

wheelbarrow /'wi:lbærəʊ/ (also **barrow**) **noun** [C] a type of small open container with one wheel and two handles that you use outside for carrying things ●➤ picture at **garden**

wheelchair /'wi:ltʃeə/ **noun** [C] a chair with large wheels that a person who cannot walk can move or be pushed about in

wheel clamp (*Brit*) = **CLAMP**[1](2)

wheeze /wi:z/ **verb** [I] to breathe noisily, for example if you have a chest illness

when /wen/ **adv, conj 1** at what time: *When did she arrive?* ● *I don't know when she arrived.* **2** used for talking about the time at which sth happens or happened: *Sunday is the day when I can relax.* ● *I last saw her in May, when she was in London.* ● *He jumped up when the phone rang.*

> Notice that we use the present tense after 'when' if we are talking about a future time: *I'll call you when I'm ready.*

3 since; as; considering that: *Why do you want more money when you've got enough already?*

> **When** is used for talking about something that you think or know will happen, but **if** is used for something you are not sure will happen. Compare: *I'll ask her when she comes* (= you are sure that she will come). ● *I'll ask her if she comes* (= you are not sure whether she will come or not).

whenever /wen'evə/ **conj, adv 1** at any time; no matter when: *You can borrow my car whenever you want.* ● *Don't worry. You can give it back the next time you see me, or whenever.* **2** (used when you are showing that you are surprised or impatient) when: *Whenever did you find time to do all that cooking?*

where /weə/ **adv, conj 1** in or to what place or position: *Where can I buy a newspaper?* ● *I asked him where he lived.* **2** in or to the place or situation mentioned: *the town where you were born* ● *She ran to where they were standing.* ● *Where possible, you should travel by bus, not taxi.* ● *We came to a village, where we stopped for lunch.* ● *Where maths is concerned, I'm hopeless.*

whereabouts¹ /ˌweərə'baʊts/ **adv** where; in or near what place: *Whereabouts did you lose your purse?*

whereabouts² /'weərəbaʊts/ **noun** [pl] the place where sb/sth is: *The whereabouts of the stolen painting are unknown.*

whereas /ˌweər'æz/ **conj** used for showing a fact that is different: *He eats meat, whereas she's a vegetarian.* ••> synonym **while**

whereby /weə'baɪ/ **adv** (*written*) by which; because of which: *These countries have an agreement whereby foreign visitors can have free medical care.*

whereupon /ˌweərə'pɒn/ **conj** (*written*) after which: *He fell asleep, whereupon she walked quietly from the room.*

wherever /weər'evə/ **conj, adv 1** in or to any place: *You can sit wherever you like.* ● *She comes from Desio, wherever that is* (= I don't know where it is). **2** everywhere, in all places that: *Wherever I go, he goes.* **3** used for showing surprise: *Wherever did you learn to cook like that?*

IDIOM or wherever or any other place: *The students might be from Sweden, Denmark or wherever.*

whet /wet/ **verb** (**whetting; whetted**)

IDIOM whet sb's appetite to make sb want

more of sth: *Our short stay in Dublin whetted our appetite to spend more time there.*

whether /'weðə/ **conj 1** (used after verbs like 'ask', 'doubt', 'know', etc) if: *He asked me whether we would be coming to the party.* **2** used for expressing a choice or doubt between two or more possibilities: *I can't make up my mind whether to go or not.*

> **Whether** and **if** can both be used in sense 1. Only **whether** can be used before 'to' + verb: *Have you decided whether to accept the offer yet?* Only **whether** can be used after a preposition: *the problem of whether to accept the offer.*

IDIOM whether or not used to say that sth will be true in either of the situations that are mentioned: *We shall play on Saturday whether it rains or not.* ● *Whether or not it rains, we shall play on Saturday.*

which /wɪtʃ/ **determiner, pron 1** used in questions to ask sb to be exact, when there are a number of people or things to choose from: *Which hand do you write with?* ● *Which is your bag?* ● *She asked me which book I preferred.* ● *I can't remember which of the boys is the older.*

> **Which** or **what**? We use **which** when there is only a limited group or number to choose from: *Which car is yours? The Ford or the Volvo* (= there are only two cars there)*?* We use **what** when the group is not limited: *What car would you choose* (= of all the makes of the car that exist)*, if you could have any one you wanted?* ● *What is your name?*

2 used for saying exactly what thing or things you are talking about: *Cars which use unleaded petrol are more eco-friendly.* ● (*formal*) *The situation in which he found himself was very difficult.*

> In less formal English we would write: *The situation which he found himself in was very difficult.* In the final example, 'which' is often left out: *The situation he found himself in...*

3 used for giving more information about a thing or animal: *My first car, which I bought as a student, was a Renault.* ••> Note that there is a comma before 'which' and at the end of the part of the sentence which it introduces. **4** used for making a comment on what has just been said: *We had to wait 16 hours for our plane, which was really annoying.* ••> Note that there is a comma before 'which'.

whichever /wɪtʃ'evə/ **determiner, pron 1** any person or thing; it does not matter which one you choose: *You can choose whichever book you want.* **2** used for expressing surprise) which: *You're very late. Whichever way did you come?*

whiff /wɪf/ **noun** [usually sing] a whiff (of sth) a smell, especially one which only lasts for a short time: *He caught a whiff of her perfume.*

while¹ /waɪl/ (also *formal* **whilst** /waɪlst/) **conj 1** during the time that; when: *He always phones while we're having lunch.* **2** at the same time as: *He always listens to the radio while he's driving to work.* **3** (*formal*) used when you are contrasting two ideas: *Some countries are rich, while others are extremely poor.* •➤ synonym **whereas**

★**while**² /waɪl/ *noun* [sing] a (usually short) period of time: *Let's sit down here for a while.*
IDIOMS **once in a while** → **ONCE**
worth sb's while → **WORTH**¹

while³ /waɪl/ *verb*
PHRASAL VERB **while sth away** to pass time in a lazy or relaxed way: *We whiled away the evening chatting and listening to music.*

whim /wɪm/ *noun* [C] a sudden idea or desire to do sth (often sth that is unusual or not necessary): *We bought the house on a whim.*

whimper /'wɪmpə/ *verb* [I] to cry softly, especially with fear or pain –**whimper** *noun* [C]

whine /waɪn/ *verb* **1** [I,T] to complain about sth in an annoying, crying voice: *The children were whining all afternoon.* **2** [I] to make a long high unpleasant sound because you are in pain or unhappy: *The dog is whining to go out.* –**whine** *noun* [C]

whip¹ /wɪp/ *noun* [C] **1** a long thin piece of leather, etc with a handle, that is used for making animals go faster and for hitting people as a punishment: *He cracked the whip and the horse leapt forward.* **2** (in Britain and the US) an official of a political party who makes sure that all members vote on important matters

whip² /wɪp/ *verb* (**whipping; whipped**) **1** [T] to hit a person or an animal hard with a whip, as a punishment or to make him/her/it go faster or work harder **2** [I] (*informal*) to move quickly, suddenly or violently: *She whipped round to see what had made the noise behind her.* **3** [T] to remove or pull sth quickly and suddenly: *He whipped out a pen and made a note of the number.* **4** [T]**whip sth (up)** to mix the white part of an egg, cream, etc until it is light and thick: *whipped cream* **5** [T] (*Brit informal*) to steal sth: *Who's whipped my pen?*
PHRASAL VERBS **whip through sth** (*informal*) to do or finish sth very quickly
whip sb/sth up to deliberately try to make people excited or feel strongly about sth: *to whip up excitement*
whip sth up (*informal*) to prepare food quickly: *to whip up a quick snack*

whir (*especially US*) = **WHIRR**

whirl¹ /wɜːl/ *verb* [I,T] to move, or to make sb/sth move, round and round very quickly in a circle: *The dancers whirled round the room.* • (*figurative*) *I couldn't sleep. My mind was whirling after all the excitement.*

whirl² /wɜːl/ *noun* [sing] **1** the action or sound of sth moving round and round very quickly: *the whirl of the helicopter's blades* **2** a state of confusion or excitement: *My head's in a whirl – I'm so excited.* **3** a number of events or activities happening one after the other: *The next few days passed in a whirl of activity.*
IDIOM **give sth a whirl** (*informal*) to try sth to see if you like it or can do it

whirlpool /'wɜːlpuːl/ *noun* [C] a place in a river or the sea where currents in the water move very quickly round in a circle

whirlwind /'wɜːlwɪnd/ *noun* [C] a very strong circular wind that forms a tall column of air moving round and round in a circle as it travels across the land or the sea •➤ Look at the note at **storm**.

whirr (*especially US* **whir**) /wɜː/ *verb* [I] to make a continuous low sound like the parts of a machine moving: *The noise of the fan whirring kept me awake.* –**whirr** (*especially US* **whir**) *noun* [C,usually sing]

whisk¹ /wɪsk/ *noun* [C] a tool that you use for beating eggs, cream, etc very fast •➤ picture at **kitchen**

whisk² /wɪsk/ *verb* [T] **1** to beat or mix eggs, cream, etc very fast using a fork or a whisk: *Whisk the egg whites until stiff.* **2** to take sb/sth somewhere very quickly: *The prince was whisked away in a black limousine.*

whisker /'wɪskə/ *noun* [C] one of the long thick hairs that grow near the mouth of some animals such as a mouse, cat, etc •➤ picture on page C1

whisky /'wɪski/ *noun* (*pl* **whiskies**)
➤ In the US and Ireland the spelling is **whiskey**.
1 [U] a strong alcoholic drink that is made from grain and is sometimes drunk with water and/or ice: *Scotch whisky* **2** [C] a glass of whisky

★**whisper** /'wɪspə/ *verb* [I,T] to speak very quietly into sb's ear, so that other people cannot hear what you are saying –**whisper** *noun* [C]: *to speak in a whisper*

★**whistle**¹ /'wɪsl/ *noun* [C] **1** a small metal or plastic tube that you blow into to make a long high sound or music: *The referee blew his whistle to stop the game.* **2** the sound made by blowing a whistle or by blowing air out between your lips: *United scored just moments before the final whistle.* • *He gave a low whistle of surprise.*

★**whistle**² /'wɪsl/ *verb* **1** [I,T] to make a musical or a high sound by forcing air out between your lips or by blowing a whistle: *He whistled a tune to himself.* **2** [I] to move somewhere quickly making a sound like a whistle: *A bullet whistled past his head.*

★**white**¹ /waɪt/ *adj* **1** of the very light colour of fresh snow or milk: *a white shirt* • *white coffee* (= with milk) **2** (used about a person) belonging to or connected with a race of people who have pale skin **3 white (with sth)** (used about a person) very pale because you are ill, afraid, etc: *to be white with shock/anger/fear* • *She went white as a sheet when they told her.*
IDIOM **black and white** → **BLACK**¹

★**white**² /waɪt/ *noun* **1** [U] the very light colour of fresh snow or milk: *She was dressed in white.* **2** [C,usually pl] a member of a race of people with pale skin **3** [C,U] the part of an egg that surrounds the yellow part (**yolk**) and that becomes white when it is cooked: *Beat* *the whites of four eggs.* •➤ picture at **egg 4** [C] the white part of the eye

[IDIOM] **in black and white** → **BLACK²**

'white-collar *adj* (used about work) done in an office not a factory; (used about people) who work in an office •➤ Look at **blue-collar**.

'white 'elephant *noun* [sing] something that you no longer need and that is not useful any more, although it cost a lot of money

the 'White House *noun* [sing] **1** the large house in Washington D.C. where the US president lives and works **2** used to refer to the US president and the other people in the government who work with him/her

'white 'lie *noun* [C] a lie that is not very harmful or serious, especially one that you tell because the truth would hurt sb

whitewash¹ /'waɪtwɒʃ/ *noun* [U] **1** a white liquid that you use for painting walls **2** [sing] trying to hide unpleasant facts about sb/sth: *The opposition claimed the report was a whitewash.*

whitewash² /'waɪtwɒʃ/ *verb* [T] **1** to paint whitewash onto a wall **2** to try to hide sth bad or wrong that you have done

'white-water 'rafting *noun* the sport of travelling down a fast rough section of a river, lake, etc in a rubber boat

whizz¹ (*especially US* whiz)/wɪz/ *verb* [I] (*informal*) to move very quickly, often making a high continuous sound: *The racing cars went whizzing by.*

whizz² (*especially US* whiz)/wɪz/ *noun* [sing] a person who is very good and successful at sth: *She's a whizz at crosswords.* • *He's our new marketing whizz-kid* (= a young person who is very good at sth).

★**who** /huː/ *pron* **1** used in questions to ask sb's name, identity, position, etc: *Who was on the phone?* • *Who's that woman in the grey suit?* • *She wondered who he was.* **2** used for saying exactly which person or what kind of person you are talking about: *I like people who say what they think.* • *That's the man who I met at Ann's party.* • *The woman who I work for is very nice.*

➤ In the last two examples (= when 'who' is the object, or when it is used with a preposition) 'who' can be left out: *That's the man I met at Ann's party.* • *The woman I work for is very nice.*

3 used for giving extra information about sb: *My mother, who's over 80, still drives a car.* •➤ Note that the extra information you give is separated from the main clause by commas. Look at the note at **whom**.

who'd /huːd/ *short for* **WHO HAD, WHO WOULD**

★**whoever** /huː'evə/ *pron* **1** the person or people who; any person who: *I want to speak to whoever is in charge.* **2** it does not matter who: *I don't want to see anybody – whoever it is.* **3** (used for expressing surprise) who: *Whoever could have done that?*

★**whole¹** /həʊl/ *adj* **1** complete; full: *I drank a whole bottle of water.* • *Let's just forget the whole thing.* • *She wasn't telling me the whole truth.* **2** not broken or cut: *Snakes swallow their prey whole* (= in one piece). •➤ *adverb* **wholly**

whole² /həʊl/ *noun* [sing] **1** a thing that is complete or full in itself: *Two halves make a whole.* **2** the whole of sth all that there is of sth: *I spent the whole of the morning cooking.*

[IDIOMS] **as a whole** as one complete thing or unit and not as separate parts: *This is true in Britain, but also in Europe as a whole.*

on the whole generally, but not true in every case: *On the whole I think it's a very good idea.*

wholefood /'həʊlfuːd/ *noun* [U] **wholefoods** [pl] food that is considered healthy because it does not contain artificial substances and is produced as naturally as possible

wholehearted /ˌhəʊl'hɑːtɪd/ *adj* complete and enthusiastic: *to give sb your wholehearted support* –**wholeheartedly** *adv*

wholemeal /'həʊlmiːl/ (*also* **wholewheat**) *adj* (made from) flour that contains all the grain including the outside layer (**husk**): *wholemeal bread/flour*

wholesale /'həʊlseɪl/ *adv, adj* (adjective only *before* a noun) **1** connected with buying and selling goods in large quantities, especially in order to sell them again and make a profit: *They get all their building materials wholesale.* • *wholesale goods/prices* •➤ Look at **retail**. **2** (usually about sth bad) very great; on a very large scale: *the wholesale slaughter of wildlife*

wholesome /'həʊlsəm/ *adj* **1** good for your health: *simple wholesome food* **2** having a moral effect that is good: *clean wholesome fun*

who'll /huːl/ *short for* **WHO WILL**

wholly /'həʊlli/ *adv* completely; fully: *George is not wholly to blame for the situation.*

★**whom** /huːm/ *pron* (*formal*) used instead of 'who' as the object of a verb or preposition: *Whom did you meet there?* • *He asked me whom I had met.* • *To whom am I speaking?*

➤ The use of **whom** instead of **who** is very formal. We usually express a sentence such as: *He asked me with whom I had discussed it.'* as '*He asked me who I had discussed it with.'* (Note the position of the preposition at the end.)

whooping cough /'huːpɪŋ kɒf/ *noun* [U] a serious disease, especially of children, which makes them cough loudly and not be able to breathe easily

whoops /wʊps/ *interj* used when you have, or nearly have, a small accident: *Whoops! I nearly dropped the cup.*

whoosh /wʊʃ/ the sudden movement and sound of air or water going past very fast –**whoosh** *verb* [I]

who're /'huːə/ *short for* **WHO ARE**

who's /huːz/ *short for* **WHO IS, WHO HAS**

★**whose** /huːz/ *determiner, pron* **1** (used in questions to ask who sth belongs to or whom?): *Whose car is that?* • *Whose is that car?*

W

● *Those are nice shoes – I wonder whose they are.* **2** (used to say exactly which person or thing you mean, or to give extra information about a person or thing) of whom; of which: *That's the boy whose mother I met.* ● *My neighbours, whose house is up for sale, are splitting up.* ●•➤ When using 'whose' to give extra information about a person or thing, you should separate that part of the sentence from the main clause with commas.

who've /huːv/ *short for* WHO HAVE

★**why** /waɪ/ **adv 1** for what reason: *Why was she so late?* ● *I wonder why they went.* ● *'I'm not staying any longer.' 'Why not?'* **2** used for giving or talking about a reason for sth: *The reason why I'm leaving you is obvious.* ● *I'm tired and that's why I'm in such a bad mood.* IDIOMS why ever used to show that you are surprised or angry: *Why ever didn't you phone?*

why not? used for making or agreeing to a suggestion: *Why not phone her tonight?* ● *'Shall we go out tonight?''Yes, why not?'*

wick /wɪk/ **noun** [C] the piece of string that burns in the middle of a candle ●•➤ picture at **candle**

★**wicked** /'wɪkɪd/ **adj 1** morally bad; evil **2** (*informal*) slightly bad but in a way that is amusing and/or attractive: *a wicked sense of humour* –**wickedly adv** –**wickedness noun** [U]

★**wide**[1] /waɪd/ **adj 1** measuring a lot from one side to the other: *The road was not wide enough for two cars to pass.* ● *a wide river* ●•➤ opposite **narrow** ●•➤ noun width ●•➤ Look at the note at **broad**. **2** measuring a particular distance from one side to the other: *The box was only 20 centimetres wide.* ● *How wide is the river?* **3** including a large number or variety of different people or things; covering a large area: *You're the nicest person in the whole wide world!* ● *a wide range/choice/variety* of goods ● *a manager with wide experience of industry* **4** fully open: *The children's eyes were wide with excitement.* **5** not near what you wanted to touch or hit: *His first serve was wide* (for example in tennis). –**widely: adv** *Their opinions differ widely.* ● *Steve travelled widely in his youth.*

★**wide**[2] /waɪd/ **adv** as far or as much as possible; completely: *Open your mouth wide.* ● *It was late but she was still wide awake.* ● *The front door was wide open.*

widen /'waɪdn/ **verb** [I,T] to become wider; to make sth wider: *The road widens just up ahead.*

,**wide-'ranging adj** covering a large area or many subjects: *a wide-ranging discussion*

widespread /'waɪdspred/ **adj** found or happening over a large area; affecting a large number of people: *The storm has caused widespread damage.*

widow /'wɪdəʊ/ **noun** [C] a woman whose husband has died and who has not married again –**widowed** /'wɪdəʊd/ **adj**: *She's been widowed for ten years now.*

widower /'wɪdəʊə/ **noun** [C] a man whose wife has died and who has not married again

★**width** /wɪdθ/ **noun 1** [C,U] the amount that sth measures from one side or edge to the other: *The room is eight metres in width.* ● *The carpet is available in two different widths.* ●•➤ adjective wide ●•➤ picture at **length 2** [C] the distance from one side of a swimming pool to the other ●•➤ Look at **length** and **breadth**.

wield /wiːld/ **verb** [T] **1** to have and use power, authority, etc: *She wields enormous power in the company.* **2** to hold and be ready to use a weapon: *Some of the men were wielding knives.*

wiener /'wiːnər/ (*US*) = FRANKFURTER

★**wife** /waɪf/ **noun** [C] (*pl* **wives** /waɪvz/) the woman to whom a man is married

wig /wɪg/ **noun** [C] a covering made of real or false hair that you wear on your head

wiggle /'wɪgl/ **verb** [I,T] (*informal*) to move from side to side with small quick movements; to make sth do this: *You have to wiggle your hips in time to the music.* –**wiggle noun** [C]

wigwam /'wɪgwæm/ **noun** [C] a type of tent that was used by some Native Americans in past times

★**wild**[1] /waɪld/ **adj 1** (used about animals or plants) living or growing in natural conditions, not looked after by people: *wild animals/flowers/strawberries* **2** (used about an area of land) in its natural state; not changed by people: *the wild plains of Siberia* **3** (used about a person or his/her behaviour or emotions) without control or discipline; slightly crazy: *The crowd went wild with excitement.* ● *They let their children run wild* (= behave in an uncontrolled way). **4** not carefully planned; not sensible or accurate: *She made a wild guess.* ● *wild accusations/rumours* **5** (*informal*) wild (about sb/sth) liking sb/sth very much: *I'm not wild about their new house.* **6** (used about the weather) with strong winds; stormy: *It was a wild night last night.* –**wildly adv** –**wildness noun** [U]

wild[2] /waɪld/ **noun 1 the wild** [sing] a natural environment that is not controlled by people: *the thrill of seeing elephants in the wild* **2 the wilds** [pl] places that are far away from towns, where few people live: *They live somewhere out in the wilds.*

wilderness /'wɪldənəs/ **noun** [C, usually sing] **1** a large area of land that has never been used for building on or for growing things: *The Antarctic is the world's last great wilderness.* **2** a place that people do not take care of or control: *Their garden is a wilderness.*

wildlife /'waɪldlaɪf/ **noun** [U] birds, plants, animals, etc that are wild and live in a natural environment

wilful (*US also* **willful**) /'wɪlfl/ **adj 1** done deliberately although the person doing it knows that it is wrong: *wilful damage/neglect* **2** doing exactly what you want, no matter what other people think or say: *a wilful child* –**wilfully** /-fəli/ **adv**

will¹ /wɪl/ **modal verb** (*short form* **'ll**; *negative* **will not**; *short form* **won't** /wəʊnt/) **1** used in forming the future tenses: *He'll be here soon.* ● *I'm sure you'll pass your exam.* ● *I'll be sitting on the beach this time next week.* ● *Next Sunday, they'll have been in England for a year.* **2** used for showing that sb is offering sth or wants to do sth, or that sth is able to do sth: *'We need some more milk.' 'OK, I'll get it.'* ● *Why won't you tell me where you were last night?* ● *My car won't start.* **3** used for asking sb to do sth: *Will you sit down, please?* **4** used for ordering sb to do sb: *Will you all be quiet!* **5** used for saying that you think sth is probably true: *That'll be the postman at the door.* ● *He'll have left work by now, I suppose.* **6** (only in positive sentences) used for talking about sth annoying that sb always or very often does

> You must put extra stress on 'will' and the short form cannot be used when you want to show that you are annoyed: *He will keep interrupting me when I'm trying to work.* For more information about modal verbs, look at the **Quick Grammar Reference** section at the back of this dictionary.

★**will²** /wɪl/ **noun 1** [C,U] the power of the mind to choose what to do; a feeling of strong determination: *Both her children have got very strong wills.* ● *My father seems to have lost the will to live.* **2 -willed** (used to form compound adjectives) having the type of will mentioned: *a strong-willed/weak-willed person* **3** [sing] what sb wants to happen in a particular situation: *My mother doesn't want to sell the house and I don't want to go against her will.* **4** [C] a legal document in which you write down who should have your money and property after your death: *You really ought to make a will.* ● *Gran left us some money in her will.*

IDIOM of your own free will → FREE¹

will³ /wɪl/ **verb** [T] to use the power of your mind to do sth or to make sth happen: *He willed himself to carry on to the end of the race.*

★**willing** /'wɪlɪŋ/ **adj 1** willing (to do sth) (not before a noun) happy to do sth; having no reason for not doing sth: *Are you willing to help us?* ● *She's perfectly willing to lend me her car.* ● *I'm not willing to take any risks.* **2** ready or pleased to help and not needing to be persuaded; enthusiastic: *a willing helper/volunteer* ●▸ opposite **unwilling** –willingly **adv** –willingness **noun** [U,sing]

willow /'wɪləʊ/ (also **'willow tree**) **noun** [C] a tree with long thin branches that hang down which grows near water

'will power noun [U] determination to do sth; strength of mind: *It takes a lot of will power to give up smoking.*

willy /'wɪli/ **noun** [C] (*pl* **willies**) (*informal*) a word used to refer to the male sex organ (penis)

willy-nilly /ˌwɪli 'nɪli/ **adv 1** in a careless way without planning: *Don't spend your money willy-nilly.* **2** if you want to or not

wilt /wɪlt/ **verb** [I] (used about a plant or flower) to bend and start to die, because of heat or a lack of water

wily /'waɪli/ **adj** clever at getting what you want ●▸ synonym **cunning**

wimp /wɪmp/ **noun** [C] (*informal*) a weak person who has no courage or confidence –wimpish **adj**

★**win** /wɪn/ **verb** (*pres part* **winning**; *pt, pp* **won** /wʌn/) **1** [I,T] to be the best, first or strongest in a race, game, competition, etc: *to win a game/match/championship* ● *I never win at table tennis.* ● *Which party do you think will win the next election?* **2** [T] to get money, a prize, etc as a result of success in a competition, race, etc: *We won a trip to Australia.* ● *Who won the gold medal?* ● *He won the jackpot in the lottery.*

> Note that we **earn** (not **win**) money at our job: *I earn £15000 a year.*

3 [T] to get sth by hard work, great effort, etc: *Her brilliant performance won her a great deal of praise.* ● *to win support for a plan* –win **noun**: [C] *We have had two wins and a draw so far this season.* –winning **adj**: *The winning ticket is number 65.*

IDIOMS win/lose the toss → TOSS

you can't win (*informal*) there is no way of being completely successful or of pleasing everyone: *Whatever you do you will upset somebody. You can't win.*

PHRASAL VERB win sb over/round (to sth) to persuade sb to support or agree with you: *They're against the proposal at the moment, but I'm sure we can win them over.*

wince /wɪns/ **verb** [I] to make a sudden quick movement (usually with a part of your face) to show you are feeling pain or embarrassment

winch /wɪntʃ/ **noun** [C] a machine that lifts or pulls heavy objects using a thick chain, rope, etc –winch **verb** [T]: *The injured climber was winched up into a helicopter.*

★**wind¹** /wɪnd/ **noun 1** [C,U] air that is moving across the surface of the earth: *There was a strong wind blowing.* ● *A gust of wind blew his hat off.* ● *gale-force/strong/high winds* **2** [U] the breath that you need for doing exercise or playing a musical instrument: *She stopped running to get her wind back.* **3** [U] gas that is formed in your stomach: *The baby cries when he has wind.* **4** [U] the group of instruments in an orchestra that you blow into to produce the sound

IDIOM get wind of sth to hear about sth that is secret

wind² /wɪnd/ **verb** [T] **1** to cause sb to have difficulty in breathing: *The punch in the stomach winded me.* **2** to help a baby get rid of painful gas in the stomach by rubbing or gently hitting its back

★**wind³** /waɪnd/ **verb** (*pt, pp* **wound** /waʊnd/) **1** [I] (used about a road, path, etc) to have a lot of bends or curves in it: *The path winds down the cliff to the sea.* **2** [T] to put sth long round sth else several times: *She wound the*

W

bandage around his arm. **3** [T] to make sth work or move by turning a key, handle, etc: *He wound the car window down.* ● *Wind the tape on a bit to the next song.*

PHRASAL VERBS **wind down** (about a person) to rest and relax after a period of hard work, worry, etc ••➤ Look at **unwind**.

wind up to find yourself in a place or situation that you did not intend to be in: *We got lost and wound up in a dangerous-looking part of town.*

wind sb up to annoy sb until he/she becomes angry

wind sth up to finish, stop or close sth: *The company was losing money and was soon wound up.*

windfall /'wındfɔːl/ **noun** [C] an amount of money that you win or receive unexpectedly

winding /'waɪndɪŋ/ **adj** with bends or curves in it: *a winding road through the hills*

'wind instrument noun [C] a musical instrument that you play by blowing through it

windmill

windmill /'wınd-mıl/ **noun** [C] a tall building or structure with long parts (sails) that turn in the wind. In past times windmills were used for making flour from grain, but now they are used mainly for producing electricity.

sail

★**window** /'wındəʊ/ **noun** [C] **1** the opening in a building, car, etc that you can see through and that lets light in. A window usually has glass in it: *Open the window. It's hot in here.* ● *a shop window* ● *These windows need cleaning.* ••➤ picture on page C7 **2** an area on a computer screen that has a particular type of information in it ••➤ picture on page S7 **3** a time when you have not arranged to do anything and so are free to meet sb, etc: *I'm busy all Tuesday morning, but I've got a window from 2 until 3.*

windowpane /'wındəʊpeın/ **noun** [C] one piece of glass in a window

'window-shopping noun [U] looking at things in shop windows without intending to buy anything

'window sill (also **'window ledge**) **noun** [C] the narrow shelf at the bottom of a window, either inside or outside ••➤ picture at **curtain**

windpipe /'wındpaıp/ **noun** [C] the tube that takes air from the throat to the lungs

windscreen /'wındskriːn/ (*US* **windshield** /'wınd∫iːld/) **noun** [C] the window in the front of a vehicle ••➤ picture on page S9

'windscreen wiper (also **wiper** *US* **'windshield wiper**) **noun** [C] one of the two moving arms (blades) that remove water, snow, etc from the front window of a car (the windscreen) ••➤ picture on page S9

windsurf /'wındsɜːf/ **verb** [I] to move over

water standing on a special board with a sail ••➤ We usually say **go windsurfing**: *Have you ever been windsurfing?* –windsurfing **noun** [U]

windsurfer /'wındsɜːfə/ **noun** [C] **1** (also **sailboard**) a board with a sail that you stand on as it moves over the surface of the water, pushed by the wind **2** a person who rides on a board like this

windswept /'wındswept/ **adj 1** (used about a place) that often has strong winds: *a windswept coastline* **2** looking untidy because you have been in a strong wind: *windswept hair*

windy /'wındi/ **adj** (**windier; windiest**) with a lot of wind: *a windy day*

★**wine** /waın/ **noun** [C,U] an alcoholic drink that is made from grapes, or sometimes other fruit: *sweet/dry wine* ● *German wines*

> Wine is made in three colours; red, white and rosé.

★**wing** /wıŋ/ **noun 1** [C] one of the two parts that a bird, insect, etc uses for flying: *The chicken ran around flapping its wings.* ••➤ picture at **insect 2** [C] one of the two long parts that stick out from the side of a plane and support it in the air **3** [C] a part of a building that sticks out from the main part or that was added on to the main part: *the maternity wing of the hospital* **4** (*US* **fender**) [C] the part of the outside of a car that covers the top of the wheels **5** [C,usually sing] a group of people in a political party that have particular beliefs or opinions: *the right wing of the Conservative Party* ••➤ Look at **left-wing** and **right-wing**. **6** [C] (in football, etc) the part at each side of the area where the game is played: *to play on the wing* **7** (also **winger**) [C] (in football, etc) a person who plays in an attacking position at one of the sides of the field **8 the wings** [pl] (in a theatre) the area at the sides of the stage where you cannot be seen by the audience

IDIOM **take sb under your wing** to take care of and help sb who has less experience than you

wink /wıŋk/ **verb** [I] **wink (at sb)** to close and open one eye very quickly, usually as a signal to sb ••➤ Look at **blink**. –wink **noun** [C]: *He smiled and gave the little girl a wink.* ● *I didn't sleep a wink* (= not at all).

IDIOM **forty winks → FORTY**

★**winner** /'wınə/ **noun** [C] **1** a person or animal that wins a competition, game, race, etc: *The winner of the competition will be announced next week.* **2** (*informal*) something that is likely to be successful: *I think your idea is a winner.* **3** (in sport) a goal that wins a match, a hit that wins a point, etc: *Anelka scored the winner in the last minute.*

winning → WIN

★**winter** /'wıntə/ **noun** [C,U] the coldest season of the year between autumn and spring: *It snows a lot here in winter.* ● *a cold winter's day* ● *We went skiing in France last winter.* –wintry /'wıntri/ **adj**: *wintry weather*

'winter 'sports noun [pl] sports which take

W

place on snow or ice, for example skiing and skating

wintertime /'wɪntətaɪm/ **noun** [U] the period or season of winter

★**wipe¹** /waɪp/ **verb** [T] **1** to clean or dry sth by rubbing it with a cloth, etc: *She stopped crying and wiped her eyes with a tissue.* ● *Could you wipe the table, please?* ••➤ Look at the note at **clean²**. **2 wipe sth from/off sth; wipe sth away/off/up** to remove sth by rubbing it: *He wiped the sweat from his forehead.* ● *Wipe up the milk you spilled.* **3 wipe sth (off) (sth)** to remove sound, information or images from sth: *I accidentally wiped the tape.* ● *I tried to wipe the memory from my mind.*

PHRASAL VERB **wipe sth out** to destroy sth completely: *Whole villages were wiped out in the bombing raids.*

wipe² /waɪp/ **noun** [C] **1** the action of wiping: *He gave the table a quick wipe.* **2** a piece of paper or thin cloth that has been made wet with a special liquid and is used for cleaning sth: *a box of baby wipes*

wiper /'waɪpə/ = **WINDSCREEN WIPER**

★**wire¹** /waɪə/ **noun** [C,U] **1** metal in the form of thin thread; a piece of this: *a piece of wire* ● *Twist those two wires together.* ● *a wire fence* **2** a piece of wire that is used to carry electricity: *telephone wires* ••➤ picture at **cable**

wire² /waɪə/ **verb** [T] **1 wire sth (up) (to sth)** to connect sth to a supply of electricity or to a piece of electrical equipment by using wires: *to wire a plug* ● *The microphone was wired up to a loudspeaker.* **2 wire sth (to sb); wire sb sth** to send money to sb's bank account using an electronic system: *The bank's going to wire me the money.* **3** to join two things together using wire

wiring /'waɪərɪŋ/ **noun** [U] the system of wires that supplies electricity to rooms in a building

wiry /'waɪəri/ **adj** (used about a person) small and thin but strong

wisdom /'wɪzdəm/ **noun** [U] the ability to make sensible decisions and judgements because of your knowledge or experience: *I don't see the wisdom of this plan* (= I do not think that it is a good idea). ••➤ adjective **wise**

'**wisdom tooth** **noun** [C] one of the four teeth at the back of your mouth that appear when you are about 20 years old ••➤ Look at note at **tooth**.

★**wise** /waɪz/ **adj** having the knowledge or experience to make good and sensible decisions and judgements: *a wise choice* ● *It would be wiser to wait for a few days.* –**wisely** **adv**

★**wish¹** /wɪʃ/ **verb** **1** [T] **wish (that)** (often with a verb in the past tense) to want sth that cannot now happen or that probably will not happen: *I wish I had listened more carefully.* ● *I wish that I knew what was going to happen.* ● *I wish I was taller.* ● *I wish I could help you.*

➤ Note that in formal English we use **were** instead of **was** with 'I' or 'he/she': *I wish I were rich.* ● *She wishes she were in a different class.*

2 [I] **wish for sth** to say to yourself that you want sth that can only happen by good luck or chance: *She wished for her mother to get better.* **3** [T] (*formal*) **wish (to do sth)** to want to do sth: *I wish to make a complaint about one of the doctors.* **4** [T] to say that you hope sb will have sth: *I rang him up to wish him a happy birthday.* ● *We wish you all the best for your future career.*

★**wish²** /wɪʃ/ **noun** **1** [C] a feeling that you want to have sth or that sth should happen: *I have no wish to see her ever again.* ● *Doctors should respect the patient's wishes.* **2** [C] a try at making sth happen by thinking hard about it, especially in stories when it often happens by magic: *Throw a coin into the fountain and make a wish.* ● *My wish came true* (= I got what I asked for). **3 wishes** [pl] a hope that sb will be happy or have good luck: *Please give your parents my best wishes.* ● *Best Wishes* (= at the end of a letter)

,**wishful 'thinking** **noun** [U] ideas that are based on what you would like, not on facts ••➤ Look at **thinking**.

wisp /wɪsp/ **noun** [C] **1** a few pieces of hair that are together **2** a small amount of smoke –**wispy** **adj**

wistful /'wɪstfl/ **adj** feeling or showing sadness because you cannot have what you want: *a wistful sigh* –**wistfully** /-fəli/ **adv**

wit /wɪt/ **noun** [U] **1** the ability to use words in a clever and amusing way ••➤ adjective **witty** **2 -witted** (used to form compound adjectives) having a particular type of intelligence: *quick-witted* ● *slow-witted* **3** (also **wits** [pl]) the fact of being clever; intelligence: *The game of chess is essentially a battle of wits.*

IDIOMS **at your wits' end** not knowing what to do or say because you are very worried

keep your wits about you to be ready to act in a difficult situation

witch /wɪtʃ/ **noun** [C] (in past times and in stories) a woman who is thought to have magic powers ••➤ Look at **wizard**.

witchcraft /'wɪtʃkrɑːft/ **noun** [U] the use of magic powers, especially evil ones

★**with** /wɪð; wɪθ/ **prep** **1** in the company of sb/sth; in or to the same place as sb/sth: *I live with my parents.* ● *Are you coming with us?* ● *I talked about the problem with my tutor.* **2** having or carrying sth: *a girl with red hair* ● *a house with a garden* ● *the man with the suitcase* **3** using sth: *Cut it with a knife.* ● *I did it with his help.* **4** used for saying what fills, covers, etc sth: *Fill the bowl with water.* ● *His hands were covered with oil.* **5** in competition with sb/sth; against sb/sth: *He's always arguing with his brother.* ● *I usually play tennis with my sister.* **6** towards, concerning or compared with sb/sth: *Is he angry with us?* ● *There's a problem with my visa.* ● *Compared with Canada, England has mild winters.* **7** including sth: *The price is for* *two people with all meals.* **8** used to say how sth happens or is done: *Open this parcel with care.* ● *to greet sb with a smile* **9** because of sth; as a result of sth: *We were shivering with cold.* ● *With all the problems we've got, we're not going to finish on time.* **10** in the care of sb: *We left the keys with the neighbours.* **11** agreeing with or supporting sb/sth: *We've got everybody with us on this issue.* •➤ opposite **against 12** at the same time as sth: *I can't concentrate with you watching me all the time.* IDIOM be with sb to be able to follow what sb is saying: *I'm not quite with you. Say it again.*

★**withdraw** /wɪð'drɔː/ *verb* (*pt* **withdrew** /-'druː/; *pp* **withdrawn** /-'drɔːn/) **1** [I,T] withdraw (sb/sth) (from sth) to move or order sb to move back or away from a place: *The troops withdrew from the town.* **2** [T] to remove sth or take sth away: *to withdraw an offer/a statement* **3** [T] to take money out of a bank account: *How much would you like to withdraw?* •➤ Look at **deposit. 4** [I] to decide not to take part in sth: *Jackson withdrew from the race at the last minute.*

withdrawal /wɪð'drɔːəl/ *noun* **1** [C,U] moving or being moved back or away from a place: *the withdrawal of troops from the war zone* **2** [C] taking money out of your bank account; the amount of money that you take out: *to make a withdrawal* **3** [U] the act of stopping doing sth, especially taking a drug: *When he gave up alcohol he suffered severe withdrawal symptoms.*

withdrawn /wɪð'drɔːn/ *adj* (used about a person) very quiet and not wanting to talk to other people

wither /'wɪðə/ *verb* **1** [I,T] wither (sth) (away) (used about plants) to become dry and die; to make a plant do this: *The plants withered in the hot sun.* **2** [I] wither (away) to become weaker then disappear: *This type of industry will wither away in the years to come.*

withering /'wɪðərɪŋ/ *adj* done to make sb feel silly or embarrassed: *a withering look*

withhold /wɪð'həʊld/ *verb* [T] (*pt, pp* **withheld** /-'held/) (*formal*) withhold sth (from sb/sth) to refuse to give sth to sb: *to withhold information from the police*

★**within** /wɪ'ðɪn/ *prep, adv* **1** in a period not longer than a particular length of time: *I'll be back within an hour.* ● *She got married, found a job and moved house, all within a week.* **2** within sth (of sth) not further than a particular distance from sth: *The house is within a kilometre of the station.* **3** not outside the limits of sb/sth: *Each department must keep within its budget.* **4** (*formal*) inside sb/ sth: *The anger was still there deep within him.*

★**without** /wɪ'ðaʊt/ *prep, adv* **1** not having or showing sth: *Don't go out without a coat on.* ● *He spoke without much enthusiasm.* ● *If there's no salt we'll have to manage without.* **2** not using or being with sb/sth: *I drink my coffee without milk.* ● *Can you see without your glasses?* ● *Don't leave without me.* **3** used with a verb in the *-ing* form to mean 'not':

She left without saying goodbye. ● *I used her phone without her knowing.*

withstand /wɪð'stænd/ *verb* [T] (*pt, pp* **withstood** /-'stʊd/) (*formal*) to be strong enough not to break, give up, be damaged, etc: *These animals can withstand very high temperatures.*

★**witness¹** /'wɪtnəs/ *noun* [C] **1** (also **eyewitness**) a witness (to sth) a person who sees sth happen and who can tell other people about it later: *There were two witnesses to the accident.* **2** a person who appears in a court of law to say what he/she has seen or what he/she knows about sb/sth: *a witness for the defence/prosecution* **3** a person who sees sb sign an official document and who then signs it himself/herself

IDIOM bear witness (to sth) → BEAR²

witness² /'wɪtnəs/ *verb* [T] **1** to see sth happen and be able to tell other people about it later: *to witness a murder* **2** to see sb sign an official document and then sign it yourself: *to witness a will*

'**witness box** (*US* '**witness-stand**) *noun* [C] the place in a court of law where a witness stands when he/she is giving evidence

witty /'wɪti/ *adj* (**wittier; wittiest**) clever and amusing; using words in a clever way: *a very witty speech* •➤ noun **wit**

wives *plural of* **WIFE**

wizard /'wɪzəd/ *noun* [C] (in stories) a man who is believed to have magic powers •➤ Look at **witch** and **magician**.

wk *abbr* (*pl* **wks**) week

wobble /'wɒbl/ *verb* [I,T] to move from side to side in a way that is not steady; to make sb/sth do this: *Put something under the leg of the table. It's wobbling.* ● *Stop wobbling the desk. I can't write.* –**wobbly** /'wɒbli/ *adj*

woe /wəʊ/ *noun* (*formal*) **1** woes [pl] the problems that sb has **2** [U] (*old-fashioned*) great unhappiness

IDIOM woe betide sb used as a warning that there will be trouble if sb does/does not do a particular thing: *Woe betide anyone who yawns while the boss is talking.*

wok /wɒk/ *noun* [C] a large pan that is shaped like a bowl and used for cooking Chinese food •➤ picture at **pan**

woke *past tense of* **WAKE¹**

woken *past participle of* **WAKE¹**

wolf /wʊlf/ *noun* [C] (*pl* **wolves** /wʊlvz/) a wild animal that looks like a dog and that lives and hunts in a group (**pack**)

★**woman** /'wʊmən/ *noun* [C] (*pl* **women** /'wɪmɪn/) **1** an adult female person: *men, women and children* ● *Would you prefer to see a woman doctor?* **2** -**woman** (in compounds) a woman who does a particular activity: *a businesswoman*

womanhood /'wʊmənhʊd/ *noun* [U] the state of being a woman

womanly /'wʊmənli/ *adj* having qualities considered typical of a woman

womb /wuːm/ *noun* [C] the part of a woman

W

or female animal where a baby grows before it is born •➤ A more formal word is **uterus**.

won *past tense, past participle* of **WIN**

★ **wonder**[1] /'wʌndə/ **verb** **1** [I,T] wonder (about sth) to want to know sth; to ask yourself questions about sth: *I wonder what the new teacher will be like.* • *Vesna's been gone a long time – I wonder if she's all right.* • *It was something that she had been wondering about for a long time.* **2** [T] used as a polite way of asking a question or of asking sb to do sth: *I wonder if you could help me.* • *I was wondering if you'd like to come to dinner at our house.* **3** [I,T] wonder (at sth) to feel great surprise or admiration: *We wondered at the speed with which he worked.* • *'She was very angry.' 'I don't wonder* (= I'm not surprised). *She had a right to be.'*

★ **wonder**[2] /'wʌndə/ **noun** **1** [U] a feeling of surprise and admiration: *The children just stared **in wonder** at the acrobats.* **2** [C] something that causes you to feel surprise or admiration: *the wonders of modern technology*

IDIOMS **do wonders (for sb/sth)** to have a very good effect on sb/sth: *Working in Mexico did wonders for my Spanish.*

it's a wonder (that)… it's surprising that…: *It's a wonder we managed to get here on time, with all the traffic.*

no wonder it is not surprising: *You've been out every evening this week. No wonder you're tired.*

★ **wonderful** /'wʌndəfl/ **adj** extremely good; fantastic: *What wonderful weather!* • *It's wonderful to see you again.* —**wonderfully** /-fəli/ **adv**

won't *short for* **WILL NOT**

★ **wood** /wʊd/ **noun** **1** [U,C] the hard substance that trees are made of: *He chopped some wood for the fire.* • *Pine is a soft wood.* •➤ picture on page C2 **2** [C] (often plural) an area of land that is covered with trees. A wood is smaller than a forest: *a walk in the woods*

IDIOM **touch wood**; (*US*) **knock on wood** an expression that people use (often while touching a piece of wood) to prevent bad luck: *I've been driving here for 20 years and I haven't had an accident yet – touch wood!*

wooded /'wʊdɪd/ **adj** (used about an area of land) having a lot of trees growing on it

wooden /'wʊdn/ **adj** made of wood

woodland /'wʊdlənd/ **noun** [C,U] land that has a lot of trees growing on it: *The village is surrounded by woodland.* • *woodland birds*

woodwind /'wʊdwɪnd/ **noun** [sing,with sing or pl verb] the set of musical instruments that you play by blowing into them

woodwork /'wʊdwɜːk/ **noun** [U] **1** the parts of a building that are made of wood such as the doors, stairs, etc **2** the activity or skill of making things out of wood

woof /wʊf/ **noun** [C] (*informal*) used for describing the sound (a **bark**) that a dog makes

★ **wool** /wʊl/ **noun** [U] **1** the soft thick hair of sheep **2** thick thread or cloth that is made from wool: *The sweater is 50% wool and 50%*

acrylic. •➤ Look at **cotton wool**. •➤ picture at **knit**

woollen (*US* **woolen**) /'wʊlən/ **adj** made of wool: *a warm woollen jumper*

woolly (*US* **wooly**) /'wʊli/ **adj** like wool or made of wool: *The dog had a thick woolly coat.* • *long woolly socks*

★ **word**[1] /wɜːd/ **noun** **1** [C] a sound or letter or group of sounds or letters that expresses a particular meaning: *What's the Greek word for 'mouth'?* • *What does this word mean?* **2** [C] a thing that you say; a short statement or comment: *Could I **have a word** with you in private?* • *Don't say a word about this to anyone.* **3** [sing] a promise: *I **give you my word** that I won't tell anyone.* • *I'll **keep my word** to her and lend her the money.* • *You'll just have to trust him not to **go back on his word**.*

IDIOMS **a dirty word** → **DIRTY**[1]

not breathe a word (of/about sth) (to sb) → **BREATHE**

not get a word in edgeways to not be able to interrupt when sb else is talking so that you can say sth yourself

have, etc the last word → **LAST**[1]

in other words → **OTHER**

lost for words → **LOST**[2]

put in a (good) word for sb to say sth good about sb to sb else: *If you could put in a good word for me I might stand a better chance of getting the job.*

take sb's word for it to believe what sb says without any proof

word for word **1** repeating sth exactly: *Sharon repeated word for word what he had told her.* **2** translating each word separately, not looking at the general meaning: *a word-for-word translation*

word[2] /wɜːd/ **verb** [T] (often passive) to choose carefully the words that you use to express sth: *The statement was carefully worded so that nobody would be offended by it.*

wording /'wɜːdɪŋ/ **noun** [sing] the words that you use to express sth: *The wording of the contract was vague.*

word-'perfect **adj** able to say sth that you have learnt from memory, without making a mistake

word 'processor **noun** [C] a type of small computer that you can use for writing letters, reports, etc. You can correct or change what you have written before you print it out. —**word processing** **noun** [sing]

wore *past tense* of **WEAR**[1]

★ **work**[1] /wɜːk/ **verb** **1** [I,T] work (as sth) (for sb); work (at/on sth); work (to do sth) to do sth which needs physical or mental effort, in order to earn money or to achieve sth: *She's working for a large firm in Glasgow.* • *I'd like to work as a newspaper reporter.* • *Doctors often work extremely long hours.* • *My teacher said that I wouldn't pass the exam unless I worked harder.* • *I hear she's working on a new novel.* • *I'm going to stay in tonight and work at my project.* **2** [T] to make yourself/sb work, especially very hard: *The coach works the players very hard in training.* **3** [I,T] (used

W

about a machine, etc) to function; to make sth function; to operate: *Our telephone hasn't been working for several days.* ● *We still don't really understand how the brain works.* ● *Can you show me how to work the photocopier?* **4** [I] to have the result or effect that you want; to be successful: *Your idea sounds good but I don't think it will really work.* ● *The heat today could work in favour of the African runners.* **5** [I,T] to move gradually to a new position or state: *Engineers check the plane daily, because nuts and screws can* **work loose.** ● *I watched the snail* **work its way** *up the wall.* **6** [I,T] to use materials to make a model, a picture, etc: *He worked the clay into the shape of a horse.* ● *She usually works in/with oils or acrylics.*

IDIOMS **work/perform miracles** → **MIRACLE**
work/sweat your guts out → **GUT¹**
work to rule → **RULE¹**

PHRASAL VERBS **work out 1** to develop or progress, especially in a good way: *I hope things work out for you.* **2** to do physical exercises in order to keep your body fit: *We work out to music at my exercise class.*

work out (at) to come to a particular result or total after everything has been calculated: *If we divide the work between us it'll work out at about four hours each.*

work sb out to understand sb: *I've never been able to work her out.*

work sth out 1 to find the answer to sth; to solve sth: *I can't work out how to do this.* **2** to calculate sth: *I worked out the total cost.* **3** to plan sth: *Have you worked out the route through France?*

work up to sth to develop or progress to sth: *Start with 15 minutes' exercise and gradually work up to 30.*

work sth up to develop or improve sth with effort: *I'm trying to work up the energy to go out.*

work sb/yourself up (into sth) to make sb/ yourself become angry, excited, upset, etc: *He had worked himself up into a state of anxiety about his interview.*

★**work²** /wɜːk/ **noun 1** [U] the job that you do, especially in order to earn money; the place where you do your job: *It is very difficult to* **find work** *in this city.* ● *He's been* **out of work** *(= without a job) for six months.* ● *When do you* **start work?** ● *I'll ask if I can* **leave work** *early today.* ● *I* **go to work** *at 8 o'clock.* ● *The people* **at work** *gave me some flowers for my birthday.* ● *Police work is not as exciting as it looks on TV.*

➤ **Work** is an uncountable noun. In some contexts we must use **job**: *I've found work at the hospital.* ● *I've got a new job at the hospital.* **Employment** is the state of having a paid job and is more formal and official than **work** or **job**: *Many married women are in part-time employment.* **Occupation** is the word used on forms to ask what you are or what job you do: *Occupation: student. Occupation: bus driver.* A **profession** is a job that needs special training and higher edu-

cation: *the medical profession.* A **trade** is a job that you do with your hands and that requires special skill: *He's a carpenter by trade.*

2 [U] something that requires physical or mental effort that you do in order to achieve sth: *Her success is due to sheer* **hard work.** ● *I've got a lot of work to do today.* ● *We hope to* **start work** *on the project next week.* **3** [U] something that you are working on or have produced: *a piece of written work* ● *The teacher marked their work.* ● *Is this all your own work?* **4** [C] a book, painting, piece of music, etc: *an early work by Picasso* ● *the complete works of Shakespeare* **5 works** [pl] the act of building or repairing sth: *The roadworks are causing long traffic jams.* **6 works** [C,with sing or pl verb] (often in compounds) a factory: *The steelworks is/are closing down.*

IDIOM **get/go/set to work (on sth)** to begin; to make a start (on sth)

workable /'wɜːkəbl/ *adj* that can be used successfully; practical: *a workable plan/solution*

workaholic /ˌwɜːkə'hɒlɪk/ *noun* [C] a person who loves work and does too much of it

workbook /'wɜːkbʊk/ *noun* [C] a book with questions and exercises in it that you use when you are studying sth

★**worker** /'wɜːkə/ *noun* [C] **1** (often in compounds) a person who works, especially one who does a particular kind of work: *factory/ office/farm workers* ● *skilled/manual workers* **2** a person who is employed to do physical work rather than organizing things or managing people: *Workers' representatives will meet management today to discuss the pay dispute.* **3** a person who works in a particular way: *a slow/fast worker*

workforce /'wɜːkfɔːs/ *noun* [C,with sing or pl verb] **1** the total number of people who work in a company, factory, etc **2** the total number of people in a country who are able to work: *Ten per cent of the workforce is/are unemployed.*

★**working** /'wɜːkɪŋ/ *adj* (only *before* a noun) **1** employed; having a job: *the problems of childcare for working mothers* **2** connected with your job: *He stayed with the same company for the whole of his working life.* ● *The company offers excellent working conditions.* **3** good enough to be used, although it could be improved: *We are looking for someone with a working knowledge of French.*

IDIOM **in working order** → **ORDER¹**

workings /'wɜːkɪŋz/ *noun* [pl] the way in which a machine, an organization, etc operates: *It's very difficult to understand the workings of the legal system.*

workload /'wɜːkləʊd/ *noun* [C] the amount of work that you have to do: *She often gets home late when she has a heavy workload.*

workman /'wɜːkmən/ *noun* [C] (*pl* **-men** /-mən/) a man who works with his hands, especially at building or making things

workmanlike /'wɜːkmənlaɪk/ *adj* done,

made, etc very well, but not original or exciting: *The leading actor gave a workmanlike performance.*

workmanship /'wɜːkmənʃɪp/ **noun** [U] the skill with which sth is made

,**work of 'art noun** [C] (*pl* **works of art**) a very good painting, book, piece of music, etc •◂➤ Look at **art**.

workout /'wɜːkaʊt/ **noun** [C] a period of physical exercise, for example when you are training for a sport or keeping fit: *She does a twenty-minute workout every morning.*

worksheet /'wɜːkʃiːt/ **noun** [C] a piece of paper with questions or exercises on it that you use when you are studying sth

workshop /'wɜːkʃɒp/ **noun** [C] **1** a place where things are made or repaired **2** a period of discussion and practical work on a particular subject, when people share their knowledge and experience: *a drama/writing workshop*

worktop /'wɜːktɒp/ (also ,**work surface**) **noun** [C] a flat surface in a kitchen, etc that you use for preparing food, etc on •◂➤ picture on page C7

★**world** /wɜːld/ **noun 1 the world** [sing] the earth with all its countries and people: *a map of the world* ● *the most beautiful place in the world* ● *I took a year off work to travel round the world.* ● *She is famous all over the world.* **2** [sing] a particular part of the earth or group of countries: *the western world* ● *the Arab world* ● *the Third World* **3** [sing] the life and activities of people; their experience: *It's time you learned something about the real world!* ● *the modern world* **4** [C] (often in compounds) a particular area of activity or group of people or things: *the world of sport/fashion/politics* ● *the medical/business/animal/natural world* **5** [sing] the people in the world: *The whole world seemed to know the news before me!* **6** [C] a planet with life on it: *Do you believe there are other worlds out there, like ours?*

IDIOMS **do sb a/the world of good** (*informal*) to have a very good effect on sb: *The holiday has done her the world of good.*

in the world used to emphasize what you are saying: *Everyone else is stressed but he doesn't seem to have a care in the world.* ● *There's no need to rush – we've got all the time in the world.* ● *What in the world are you doing?*

the outside world → OUTSIDE²

think the world of sb/sth → THINK

,**world-'famous adj** known all over the world

worldly /'wɜːldli/ **adj 1** connected with ordinary life, not with the spirit: *He left all his worldly possessions to his nephew.* **2** having a lot of experience and knowledge of life and people: *a sophisticated and worldly man*

,**world 'war noun** [C] a war that involves a lot of different countries: *the Second World War* ● *World War One*

worldwide /,wɜːld'waɪd; 'wɜːldwaɪd/ **adj, adv** (happening) in the whole world: *The product*

will be marketed worldwide. ● *The situation has caused worldwide concern.*

the ,World Wide 'Web (also **the Web**) **noun** [sing] (*abbr* **WWW**) the international system of computers that makes it possible for you to see information from around the world on your computer: *web pages* ● *a web site* (= where a company, an organization, etc has information about itself on the Web) •◂➤ Look at **the Internet**.

worm

maggot

worm¹ /wɜːm/ **noun** [C] **1** a small animal with a long thin body and no eyes, bones or legs: *an earthworm* **2 worms** [pl] one or more worms that live inside a person or an animal and may cause disease: *He's got worms.*

worm² /wɜːm/ **verb** [T] **worm your way/yourself along, through, etc** to move slowly or with difficulty in the direction mentioned: *I managed to worm my way through the crowd.*
PHRASAL VERB **worm your way/yourself into sth** to make sb like you or trust you, in order to dishonestly gain an advantage for yourself

worn *past participle* of WEAR¹

,**worn-'out adj 1** too old or damaged to use any more: *My shoes are completely worn-out.* **2** extremely tired: *I think I'll go to bed early.* •◂➤ Look at **wear**.

★**worried** /'wʌrid/ **adj worried (about sb/sth); worried (that...)** thinking that sth bad might happen or has happened: *Don't look so worried. Everything will be all right.* ● *I'm worried sick about the exam.* ● *We were worried stiff* (= extremely worried) *that you might have had an accident.*

★**worry¹** /'wʌri/ **verb** (*pres part* **worrying**; *3rd pers sing pres* **worries**; *pt, pp* **worried**) **1** [I] **worry (about sb/sth)** to think that sth bad might happen or has happened: *Don't worry – I'm sure everything will be all right.* ● *There's nothing to worry about.* ● *He worries if I don't phone every weekend.* **2** [T] **worry sb/yourself (about sb/sth)** to make sb/yourself think that sth bad might happen or has happened: *What worries me is how are we going to get home?* ● *She worried herself sick when he was away in the army.* **3** [T] **worry sb (with sth)** to disturb sb; to bother sb: *I'm sorry to worry you with my problems but I really do need some advice.*

IDIOM **not to worry** it is not important; it doesn't matter

★**worry²** /'wʌri/ **noun** (*pl* **worries**) **1** [U] the state of worrying about sth: *His son has caused him a lot of worry recently.* **2** [C] something that makes you worry; a problem: *Crime is a real worry for old people.* ● *financial worries* –**worrying adj**: *a worrying situation*

W

★**worse** /wɜːs/ *adj, adv* (the comparative of *bad* or of *badly*) **1** not as good or as well as sth else: *My exam results were far/much worse than I thought they would be.* • *She speaks German even worse than I do.* **2** (not before a noun) more ill; less well: *If you get any worse we'll call the doctor.* –**worse** noun [U]: *The situation was already bad but there was worse to come.*

IDIOMS **to make matters/things worse** to make a situation, problem, etc even more difficult or dangerous than before

none the wiser/worse → NONE²

the worse for wear (*informal*) damaged; not in good condition: *This suitcase looks a bit the worse for wear.*

worse luck! (*spoken*) unfortunately: *The dentist says I need three fillings, worse luck!*

worsen /'wɜːsn/ *verb* [I,T] to become worse or to make sth worse: *Relations between the two countries have worsened.*

worship /'wɜːʃɪp/ *verb* (**worshipping**; **worshipped**; *US* **worshiping**; **worshiped**) **1** [I,T] to pray to and show respect for God or a god: *People travel from all over the world to worship at this shrine.* **2** [T] to love or admire sb/sth very much: *She worshipped her husband.* –**worship** noun [U]: *Different religions have different forms of worship.* –**worshipper** noun [C]

★**worst¹** /wɜːst/ *adj, adv* (the superlative of *bad* or of *badly*) the least pleasant or suitable; the least well: *It's been the worst winter that I can remember.* • *A lot of the children behaved badly but my son behaved worst of all!*

worst² /wɜːst/ *noun* [sing] something that is as bad as it can be: *My parents always expect the worst if I'm late.*

IDIOMS **at (the) worst** if the worst happens or if you consider sb/sth in the worst way: *The problem doesn't look too serious. At worst we'll have to make a few small changes.*

if the worst comes to the worst if the worst possible situation happens

★**worth¹** /wɜːθ/ *adj* **1** having a particular value (in money): *How much do you think that house is worth?* **2** worth doing, etc used as a way of recommending or advising: *That museum's well worth visiting if you have time.* • *The library closes in 5 minutes – it's not worth going in.*

➤ We can say either: *It isn't worth repairing the car* OR: *The car isn't worth repairing.*

3 enjoyable or useful to do or have, even if it means extra cost, effort, etc: *It takes a long time to walk to the top of the hill but it's worth the effort.* • *Don't bother cooking a big meal. It isn't worth it – we're not hungry.*

IDIOMS **get your money's worth** → MONEY

worth sb's while helpful, useful or interesting to sb

worth² /wɜːθ/ *noun* [U] **1** the value of sb/sth; how useful sb/sth is: *She has proved her worth as a member of the team.* **2** the amount of sth that the money mentioned will buy: *ten pounds' worth of petrol* **3** the amount of sth

that will last for the time mentioned: *two days' worth of food*

worthless /'wɜːθləs/ *adj* **1** having no value or use: *It's worthless – it's only a bit of plastic!* **2** (used about a person) having bad qualities ••➤ Look at **priceless**, **valuable** and **invaluable**.

worthwhile /ˌwɜːθ'waɪl/ *adj* enjoyable, useful or satisfying enough to be worth the cost or effort: *Working for so little money just isn't worthwhile.*

★**worthy** /'wɜːði/ *adj* (**worthier**; **worthiest**) **1** worthy of sth/to do sth good enough for sth or to have sth: *He felt he was not worthy to accept such responsibility.* **2** that should receive respect, support or attention: *a worthy leader* • *a worthy cause*

★**would** /wəd/ strong form /wʊd/ *modal verb* (*short form* **'d**; *negative* **would not**; *short form* **wouldn't** /'wʊdnt/) **1** used when talking about the result of an event that you imagine: *He would be delighted if you went to see him.* • *She'd be stupid not to accept.* • *I would have done more, if I'd had the time.* **2** used for asking sb politely to do sth: *Would you come this way, please?* **3** used with 'like' or 'love' as a way of asking or saying what sb wants: *Would you like to come with us?* • *I'd love a piece of cake.* **4** to agree or be ready to do sth: *She just wouldn't do what I asked her.* **5** used as the past form of 'will' when you report what sb says or thinks: *They said that they would help us.* • *She didn't think that he would do a thing like that.* **6** used after 'wish': *I wish the sun would come out.* **7** used for talking about things that often happened in the past: *When he was young he would often walk in these woods.* **8** used for commenting on behaviour that is typical of sb: *You would say that. You always support him.* **9** used when you are giving your opinion but are not certain that you are right: *I'd say she's about 40.*

➤ For more information about modal verbs, look at the **Quick Grammar Reference** section at the back of this dictionary.

★**wound¹** /wuːnd/ *noun* [C] an injury to part of your body, especially a cut, often one received in fighting: *a bullet wound*

IDIOM **rub salt into the wound/sb's wounds** → RUB

wound² /wuːnd/ *verb* [T] (*usually passive*) **1** to injure sb's body with a weapon: *He was wounded in the leg during the war.* ••➤ Look at the note at **hurt**. **2** (*formal*) to hurt sb's feelings deeply: *I was wounded by his criticism.* –**wounded** /'wuːndɪd/ *adj*: *a wounded soldier* –**the wounded** noun [pl]: *Paramedics tended to the wounded at the scene of the explosion.*

wound³ *past tense, past participle* of WIND³

wove *past tense* of WEAVE

woven *past participle* of WEAVE

wow /waʊ/ *interj* (*informal*) used for expressing that you are very impressed and surprised by sth: *Wow! What a fantastic boat!*

WP *abbr* word processing; word processor

W

wrangle /'ræŋgl/ **noun** [C] a noisy or complicated argument: *The company is involved in a legal wrangle over copyrights.* –wrangle **verb** [I]

wrap

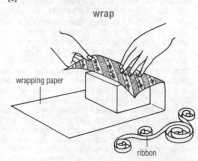

wrapping paper

ribbon

★**wrap** /ræp/ **verb** [T] (**wrapping**; **wrapped**) **1** wrap sth (up) (in sth) to put paper or cloth around sb/sth as a cover: *to wrap up a present* • *The baby was found wrapped in a blanket.* **2** wrap sth round/around sb/sth to tie sth such as paper or cloth around an object or a part of the body: *The man had a bandage wrapped round his head.*

IDIOM be wrapped up in sth to be very involved and interested in sb/sth: *They were completely wrapped up in each other. They didn't notice I was there.*

PHRASAL VERB wrap (sb/yourself) up to put warm clothes on sb/yourself

wrapper /'ræpə/ **noun** [C] the piece of paper or plastic which covers sth when you buy it: *a sweet/chocolate wrapper*

wrapping /'ræpɪŋ/ **noun** [C,U] paper, plastic, etc that is used for covering sth in order to protect it: *Remove the wrapping before heating the pie.*

'**wrapping paper noun** [U] paper which is used for putting round presents •➤ picture at wrap

wrath /rɒθ/ **noun** [U] (*written*) very great anger

wreak /riːk/ **verb** [T] (*formal*) wreak sth (on sb/sth) to cause great damage or harm to sb/sth: *Fierce storms wreak havoc at this time of year.*

wreath /riːθ/ **noun** [C] (*pl* wreaths /riːðz/) a circle of flowers and leaves, especially one that you give to the family of sb who has died

wreck /rek/ **noun 1** [C] a ship that has sunk or been badly damaged at sea: *Divers searched the wreck.* **2** [C] a car, plane, etc which has been badly damaged, especially in an accident: *The car was a wreck but the lorry escaped almost without damage.* **3** [C,usually sing] (*informal*) a person or thing that is in a very bad condition: *He drove so badly I was a nervous wreck when we got there.* –wreck **verb** [T]: *Vandals had wrecked the school hall.* • *The strike wrecked all our holiday plans.*

wreckage /'rekɪdʒ/ **noun** [U] the broken pieces of sth that has been destroyed: *Investi-*

gators searched the wreckage of the plane for evidence.

wrench[1] /rentʃ/ **verb** [T] **1** wrench sb/sth (away, off, etc) to pull or turn sb/sth strongly and suddenly: *They had to wrench the door off the car to get the driver out.* • (*figurative*) *The film was so exciting that I could hardly wrench myself away.* **2** to injure part of your body by turning it suddenly

wrench[2] /rentʃ/ **noun 1** [C] a sudden, violent pull or turn: *With a wrench I managed to open the door.* **2** [sing] the sadness you feel because you have to leave sb/sth **3** [C] (*US*) = SPANNER

wrestle /'resl/ **verb** [I] **1** wrestle (with) sb to fight by trying to get hold of your opponent's body and throw him/her to the ground. People wrestle as a sport: *He managed to wrestle the man to the ground and take the knife from him.* **2** wrestle (with sth) to try hard to deal with sth that is difficult

wrestling /'reslɪŋ/ **noun** [U] a sport in which two people fight and try to throw each other to the ground: *a wrestling match* –wrestler **noun** [C]

wretch /retʃ/ **noun** [C] (*old-fashioned*) a poor, unhappy person: *The poor wretch was clearly starving.*

wretched /'retʃɪd/ **adj 1** very unhappy **2** (*informal*) used for expressing anger: *That wretched dog has chewed up my slippers again!*

wriggle /'rɪgl/ **verb** [I,T] **1** wriggle (about/around) to move about, or to move a part of your body, with short, quick movements, especially from side to side: *The baby was wriggling around on my lap.* • *She wriggled her fingers about in the hot sand.* **2** to move in the direction mentioned by making quick turning movements: *The worm wriggled back into the soil.*

PHRASAL VERB wriggle out of sth/doing sth (*informal*) to avoid sth by making clever excuses: *It's your turn to wash up – you can't wriggle out of it this time!*

wring /rɪŋ/ **verb** [T] (*pt, pp* wrung /rʌŋ/) wring sth (out) to press and squeeze sth in order to remove water from it

wrinkle[1] /'rɪŋkl/ **noun** [C] a small line in sth, especially one on the skin of your face which you get as you grow older: *She's got fine wrinkles around her eyes.* • *Smooth out the wrinkles in the fabric.* •➤ Look at furrow. –wrinkled /'rɪŋkld/ **adj**

wrinkle[2] /'rɪŋkl/ **verb** [I,T] wrinkle (sth) (up) to form small lines and folds in sth: *She wrinkled her nose at the nasty smell.* • *My skirt had wrinkled up on the journey.*

★**wrist** /rɪst/ **noun** [C] the narrow part at the end of your arm where it joins your hand •➤ picture on page C5

wristwatch /'rɪstwɒtʃ/ **noun** [C] a watch on a strap which you wear round your arm near your hand

writ /rɪt/ **noun** [C] a legal order to do or not to do sth, given by a court of law

W

★**write** /raɪt/ **verb** (*pt* **wrote** /rəʊt/; *pp* **written** /'rɪtn/) **1** [I,T] to make words, letters, etc, especially on paper using a pen or pencil: *I can't write with this pen.* ● *Write your name and address on the form.* **2** [T] to create a book, story, song, etc in written form for people to read or use: *Tolstoy wrote 'War and Peace'.* ● *He wrote his wife a poem.* ● *Who wrote the music for that film?* **3** [I,T] write (sth) (to sb); write (sb) sth to write and send a letter, etc to sb: *I've written a letter to my son./I've written my son a letter.* ● *I've written to him.*

➤ In US English we can say: *I've written him.*

She wrote that they were all well and would be home soon. ● *She phones every week and writes occasionally.* **4** [T] write sth (out) (for sb) to fill or complete a form, cheque, document, etc with the necessary information: *I wrote out a cheque for £10.*

PHRASAL VERBS **write back (to sb)** to send a reply to sb

write sth down to write sth on paper, especially so that you can remember it: *Did you write down Jon's address?*

write in (to sb/sth) (for sth) to write a letter to an organization, etc to ask for sth, give an opinion, etc

write off/away (to sb/sth) (for sth) to write a letter to an organization, etc to order sth or ask for sth

write sb/sth off to accept or decide that sb/ sth will not be successful or useful: *Don't write him off yet. He could still win.*

write sth off to accept that you will not get back an amount of money you have lost or spent: *to write off a debt*

write sth out to write the whole of sth on paper: *Can you write out that recipe for me?*

write sth up to write sth in a complete and final form, often using notes that you have made: *to write up lecture notes*

'**write-off** **noun** [C] a thing, especially a vehicle, that is so badly damaged that it is not worth repairing

★**writer** /'raɪtə/ **noun** [C] a person who writes, especially one whose job is to write books, stories, etc

writhe /raɪð/ **verb** [I] to turn and roll your body about: *She was writhing in pain.*

★**writing** /'raɪtɪŋ/ **noun** [U] **1** words that have been written or printed; the way a person writes: *This card's got no writing inside. You can put your own message.* ● *I can't read your writing, it's too small.* **2** the skill or activity of writing words: *He had problems with his reading and writing at school.* **3** the activity or job of writing books, etc: *It's difficult to earn much money from writing.* **4** the books, etc that sb has written or the style in which sb writes: *Love is a common theme in his early writing.*

IDIOM **in writing** in written form: *I'll confirm the offer in writing next week.*

'**writing paper** **noun** [U] paper for writing letters on

written[1] *past participle* of **WRITE**

written[2] /'rɪtn/ **adj** expressed on paper; not just spoken: *a written agreement*

★**wrong**[1] /rɒŋ/ **adj, adv 1** not correct; in a way that is not correct: *the wrong answer* ● *I always pronounce that word wrong.* ● *You've got the wrong number* (= on the telephone). ● *I think you're wrong about Nicola – she's not lazy.* ●➤ opposite **right 2** not the best; not suitable: *That's the wrong way to hold the bat.* ● *I think she married the wrong man.* ● *I like him – I just think he's wrong for the job.* **3** (not before a noun) **wrong (with sb/sth)** causing problems or difficulties; not as it should be: *You look upset. Is something wrong?* ● *What's wrong with the car this time?* ● *She's got something wrong with her leg.* **4** **wrong (to do sth)** not morally right or honest: *It's wrong to tell lies.* ● *The man said that he had done nothing wrong.*

IDIOMS **get on the right/wrong side of sb** → **SIDE**[1]

get sb wrong (*informal*) to not understand sb: *Don't get me wrong! I don't dislike him.*

go wrong 1 to make a mistake: *I'm afraid we've gone wrong. We should have taken the other road.* **2** to stop working properly or to stop developing well: *My computer's gone wrong and I've lost all my work.*

get/start off on the right/wrong foot (with sb) → **FOOT**[1]

on the right/wrong track → **TRACK**[1]

wrong[2] /rɒŋ/ **noun 1** [U] things that are morally bad or dishonest: *Children quickly learn the difference between **right and wrong**.* **2** [C] an action or situation which is not fair: *A terrible wrong has been done. Those men should never have gone to prison.*

IDIOM **in the wrong** (used about a person) having made a mistake; whose fault sth is

wrong[3] /rɒŋ/ **verb** [T] to do sth to sb which is bad or unfair: *I wronged her when I said she was lying.*

wrongful /'rɒŋfl/ **adj** (*formal*) (only *before* a noun) not fair, not legal or not moral: *He sued the company for wrongful dismissal.*

wrongly /'rɒŋli/ **adv** in a wrong or mistaken way: *He was wrongly accused of stealing money.*

➤ The adverb **wrong** is used after a verb or the object of a verb, especially in conversation: *He's spelt my name wrong.* The adverb **wrongly** is especially used before a past participle or a verb: *My name's been wrongly spelt.*

wrote *past tense* of **WRITE**

wrung *past tense, past participle* of **WRING**

wry /raɪ/ **adj** expressing both disappointment and amusement: *'Never mind,' she said with a wry grin. 'At least we got one vote.'* —**wryly** *adv*

wt *abbr* weight: *net wt 500g*

WWW /'dʌblju: dʌblju: dʌblju:/ *abbr* the World Wide Web

X, x /eks/ noun [C] (pl **X's**; **x's**) the twenty-fourth letter of the English alphabet: *'Xylophone' begins with (an) 'X'*.

➤ X is used by teachers to show that an answer is wrong. It is also used instead of the name of a person if you do not know or do not want to say his/her name: *Mr and Mrs X*. At the end of a letter it represents a kiss: *Lots of love, Mary XX*.

xenophobia /ˌzenəˈfəʊbiə/ noun [U] a fear or hatred of foreign people and cultures –**xenophobic** adj

Xerox™ /ˈzɪərɒks/ noun [C] **1** a machine that produces copies of letters, documents, etc **2** a copy produced by such a machine •➤ synonym **photocopy** –**xerox** verb [T]

XL abbr extra large (size)

Xmas /ˈkrɪsməs; ˈeksməs/ noun [C,U] (*informal*) (used as a short form in writing) Christmas: *Happy Xmas* (= written message in a Christmas card)

X-ray noun [C] **1** [usually pl] a kind of light that makes it possible to see inside solid objects, for example the human body, so that they can be examined and a photograph of them can be made **2** a photograph that is made with an X-ray machine: *The X-ray showed that the bone was not broken*. •➤ Look at **ray**. –**X-ray** verb [T]: *She had her chest X-rayed*.

xylophone /ˈzaɪləfəʊn/ noun [C] a musical instrument that consists of a row of wooden bars of different lengths. You play it by hitting these bars with a small hammer. •➤ Look at the note at **piano**. •➤ picture at **music**

Y, y /waɪ/ noun [C] (pl **Y's**; **y's**) the twenty-fifth letter of the English alphabet: *'Yawn begins with (a) 'Y'*.

yacht /jɒt/ noun [C] **1** a boat with sails used for pleasure: *a yacht race* **2** a large boat with a motor, used for pleasure •➤ Look at **dinghy**.

yachting /ˈjɒtɪŋ/ noun [U] the activity or sport of sailing or racing yachts

yachtsman /ˈjɒtsmən/ noun [C] (pl **-men** /-mən/) a person who sails a yacht in races or for pleasure

yachtswoman /ˈjɒtswʊmən/ noun [C] (pl **-women** /-wɪmɪn/) a woman who sails a yacht in races or for pleasure

yank /jæŋk/ verb [I,T] (*informal*) to pull sth suddenly, quickly and hard: *She yanked at the door handle*. –**yank** noun [C]

yap /jæp/ verb [I] (**yapping**; **yapped**) (used about dogs, especially small ones) to make short, loud noises in an excited way

★**yard** /jɑːd/ noun [C] **1** (*Brit*) an area outside a building, usually with a hard surface and a wall or fence around it: *a school/prison yard* •➤ Look at **courtyard** and **churchyard**. **2** (*US*) = **GARDEN**¹(1) **3** (usually in compounds) an area, usually without a roof, used for a particular type of work or purpose: *a shipyard/boatyard* • *a builder's yard*

➤ In British English the piece of land belonging to a house is a **garden** if it has grass, flowers, etc, and a **yard** if it is made of concrete or stone. In US English this piece of land is a **yard** whether it has grass or not. Picture on page C7.

4 (*abbr* **yd**) a measure of length; 0·914 of a metre. There are 3 feet in a yard: *Our house is 100 yards from the supermarket*.

yardstick /ˈjɑːdstɪk/ noun [C] a standard with which things can be compared: *Exam results should not be the only yardstick by which pupils are judged*.

yarn /jɑːn/ noun **1** [U] thread (usually of wool or cotton) that has been prepared (**spun**) and is used for knitting, etc **2** [C] (*informal*) a long story that sb tells, especially one that is invented or exaggerated

★**yawn** /jɔːn/ verb [I] to open your mouth wide and breathe in deeply, especially when you are tired or bored: *I kept yawning all through the lecture*. –**yawn** noun [C]: *'How much longer will it take?' he said with a yawn*.

yd (pl **yds**) abbr yard, a measure of length

yeah /jeə/ interj (*informal*) yes

★**year** /jɜː; jɪə/ noun **1** [C] (also **calendar year**) the period from 1 January to 31 December, 365 or 366 days divided into 12 months or 52 weeks: *last year/this year/next year* • *The population of the country will be 70 million by the year 2010*. • *Interest is paid on this account once a year*. • *a leap year* (= one that has 366 days) • *the New Year* (= the first days of January) **2** [C] any period of 12 months, measured from any date: *She worked here for twenty years*. • *He left school just over a year ago*. • *In a year's time, you'll be old enough to vote*. **3** [C] a period of 12 months in connection with schools, the business world, etc: *the academic/school year* • *the tax/financial year* **4** [C] (*especially Brit*) (used in schools, universities, etc) the level that a particular student is at: *My son is in year ten now*. • *The first-years* (= students in their first year at school/university, etc) *do French as a compulsory subject*. • *He was a year below me at school*. **5** [C,usually pl] (used in connection with the age of sb/sth) a period of 12 months: *He's ten years old today*. • *a six-year-old*

daughter • *This car is nearly five years old.*
• *The company is now in its fifth year.*

➤ Note that you say '*He's ten.*' or '*He's ten years old.*' but NOT '*He's ten years.*' or '*a ten-years-old boy*' Look at the note at **age**.

6 years [pl] a long time: *It happened years ago.* • *I haven't seen him for years.*
IDIOMS **all year round** for the whole year
donkey's years → **DONKEY**
year after year; year in year out every year for many years

★**yearly** /'jɜːli; 'jɪəli/ **adj, adv** (happening) every year or once a year: *The conference is held yearly.*

yearn /jɜːn/ **verb** [I] (*written*) **yearn (for sb/ sth); yearn (to do sth)** to want sb/sth very much, especially sth that you cannot have
–**yearning noun** [C,U]

yeast /jiːst/ **noun** [U] a substance used for making bread rise and for making beer, wine, etc

yell /jel/ **verb** [I,T] **yell (out) (sth); yell (sth) (at sb/sth)** to shout very loudly, often because you are angry, excited or in pain: *She yelled out his name.* • *There's no need to yell at me, I can hear you perfectly well.*
–**yell noun** [C]

★**yellow** /'jeləʊ/ **noun** [C,U], **adj** (of) the colour of lemons or butter: *a pale/light yellow dress* • *a bright shade of yellow* • *the yellows and browns of the autumn leaves*

yellow 'card noun [C] (used in football) a card that is shown to a player as a warning that he/she will be sent off the field if he/she behaves badly again ••➤ Look at **red card**.

yellowish /'jeləʊɪʃ/ **adj** (also **yellowy** /'jeləʊi/) slightly yellow in colour

yellow line noun [C] (*Brit*) a yellow line at the side of a road to show that you can only park there for a limited time: *double yellow lines* (= you must not park there at all)

the Yellow 'Pages™ **noun** [pl] a telephone book (on yellow paper) that lists all the business companies, etc in a certain area in sections according to the goods or services they provide

yelp /jelp/ **verb** [I] to give a sudden short cry, especially of pain –**yelp noun** [C]

★**yes** /jes/ **interj 1** used to give a positive answer to a question, for saying that sth is true or correct or for saying that you want sth: '*Are you having a good time?*' '*Yes, thank you.*' • '*You're married, aren't you?*' '*Yes, I am.*' • '*May I sit here?*' '*Yes, of course.*' • '*More coffee?*' '*Yes, please.*' **2** used for showing you have heard sb or will do what he/she asks: '*Waiter!*' '*Yes, madam.*' **3** used when saying that a negative statement that sb has made is not true: '*You don't care about anyone but yourself.*' '*Yes I do.*' ••➤ opposite **no**
–**yes noun** [C] (*pl* **yeses** /'jesɪz/): *Was that a yes or a no?*

★**yesterday** /'jestədeɪ; 'jestədi/ **adv, noun** [C,U] (on) the day before today: *Did you watch the film on TV yesterday?* • *yesterday morning/ afternoon/evening* • *I posted the form the day*

before yesterday (= if I am speaking on Wednesday, I posted it on Monday). • *Have you still got yesterday's paper?* • *I spent the whole of yesterday walking round the shops.*

★**yet** /jet/ **adv, conj 1** used with negative verbs or in questions for talking about sth that has not happened but that you expect to happen: *Has it stopped raining yet?* • *I haven't seen that film yet.*

➤ In US English you can say: *I didn't see that film yet.*

2 (used with negative verbs) now; as early as this: *You don't have to leave yet - your train isn't for another hour.* **3** from now until the period of time mentioned has passed: *She isn't that old, she'll live for years yet.* **4** (used especially with *may* or *might*) at some time in the future: *With a bit of luck, they may yet win.* **5** (used with superlatives) until now/ until then; so far: *This is her best film yet.* **6** used with comparatives to emphasize an increase in the degree of sth: *a recent and yet more improbable theory* **7** but; in spite of that: *He seems pleasant, yet there's something about him I don't like.*
IDIOMS **as yet** until now: *As yet little is known about the disease.*
yet again (used for expressing surprise or anger that sth happens again) once more; another time: *I found out that he had lied to me yet again.*
yet another used for expressing surprise that there is one more of sth: *They're opening yet another fast food restaurant in the square.*
yet to do, etc that has not been done and is still to do in the future: *The final decision has yet to be made.*

YHA /ˌwaɪ eɪtʃ 'eɪ/ **abbr** (*Brit*) Youth Hostels Association

yield¹ /jiːld/ **verb 1** [T] to produce or provide crops, profits or results: *How much wheat does each field yield?* • *Did the experiment yield any new information?* **2** [I] (*formal*) **yield (to sb/sth)** to stop refusing to do sth or to obey sb: *The government refused to yield to the hostage takers' demands.* ••➤ **Give in** is less formal. **3** [T] **yield sb/sth (up) (to sb/ sth)** to allow sb to have control of sth that you were controlling: *The army has yielded power to the rebels.* **4** [I] (*formal*) to move, bend or break because of pressure: *The dam finally yielded under the weight of the water.* ••➤ **Give way** is less formal. **5** [I] (*US*) **yield (to sb/sth)** to allow other vehicles on a bigger road to go first: *You have to yield to traffic from the left here.* ••➤ **Give way** is used in British English.
PHRASAL VERB **yield to sth** (*formal*) to be replaced by sth, especially sth newer: *Old-fashioned methods have yielded to new technology.* ••➤ **Give way** is less formal.

yield² /jiːld/ **noun** [C] the amount that is produced: *Wheat yields were down 5% this year.* • *This investment has an annual yield of 12%.*

yo /jəʊ/ **interj** (*especially US slang*) used by some people when they see a friend; hello

yob /jɒb/ **noun** [C] (*Brit slang*) a boy or young

y

man who is rude, loud and sometimes violent or aggressive ••➤ Look at **lout** and **hooligan**.

yoga /'jəʊgə/ *noun* [U] a system of exercises for the body that helps you control and relax both your mind and your body

yoghurt (also **yogurt**) /'jɒgət/ *noun* [C,U] a slightly sour, thick liquid food made from milk: *plain/banana/strawberry yoghurt* ••➤ picture on page C4

yoke /jəʊk/ *noun* **1** [C] a long piece of wood fixed across the necks of two animals so that they can pull heavy loads together **2** [sing] something that restricts your freedom and makes your life difficult: *the yoke of parental control*

yolk /jəʊk/ *noun* [C,U] the yellow part in the middle of an egg ••➤ picture at **egg**

yonks /jɒŋks/ *noun* [U] (*slang*) a very long time: *I haven't been to the theatre for yonks.*

★**you** /jə; juː/ *pron* **1** used as the subject or object of a verb, or after a preposition to refer to the person or people being spoken or written to: *You can play the guitar, can't you?* ● *I've told you about this before.* ● *Bring your photos with you.* **2** used with a noun, adjective or phrase when calling sb sth: *You idiot! What do you think you're doing?* **3** used for referring to people in general: *The more you earn, the more tax you pay.* ••➤ **One** has the same meaning but is much more formal and is becoming old-fashioned nowadays: *The more one earns, the more tax one pays.*

you'd /juːd/ *short for* **YOU HAD, YOU WOULD**

you'll /juːl/ *short for* **YOU WILL**

★**young**¹ /jʌŋ/ *adj* (**younger** /'jʌŋgə/, **youngest** /'jʌŋgɪst/) not having lived or existed for very long; not old: *They have two young children.* ● *I'm a year younger than her.* ● *My father was the youngest of eight children.* ● *my younger brothers* ••➤ opposite **old**

IDIOM **young at heart** behaving or thinking like a young person, although you are old

young² /jʌŋ/ *noun* [pl] **1** young animals: *Swans will attack to protect their young.* **2** **the young** young people considered as a group: *The young of today are more ambitious than their parents.*

youngish /'jʌŋɪʃ/ *adj* quite young

youngster /'jʌŋstə/ *noun* [C] a young person: *There is very little entertainment for youngsters in this town.*

★**your** /jə; jɔː/ *determiner* **1** of or belonging to the person or people being spoken to: *What's your flat like?* ● *Thanks for all your help.* ● *How old are your children now?* **2** belonging to or connected with people in general: *When your life is as busy as mine, you have little time to relax.* **3** (*informal*) used for saying that sth is well-known to people in general: *So this is your typical English pub, is it?*

4 (also **Your**) used in some titles: *your Highness*

you're /jɔː; jʊə/ *short for* **YOU ARE**

★**yours** /jɔːz/ *pron* **1** of or belonging to you: *Is this bag yours or mine?* ● *I was talking to a friend of yours the other day.* **2 Yours** used at the end of a letter: *Yours sincerely.../faithfully...* ● *Yours...*

★**yourself** /jɔː'self; jə'self/ *pron* (*pl* **yourselves** /-'selvz/) **1** used when the person or people being spoken to both do an action and are also affected by it: *Be careful or you'll hurt yourself.* ● *Here's some money. Buy yourselves a present.* ● *You're always talking about yourself!* **2** used for emphasis: *You yourself told me there was a problem last week.* ● *Did you repair the car yourselves?* (= or did sb else do it for you?) **3** you: *'How are you?' 'Fine, thanks. And yourself?'* **4** in your normal state; healthy: *You don't look yourself today.*

IDIOM **(all) by yourself/yourselves 1** alone: *Do you live by yourself?* ••➤ Look at the note at **alone**. **2** without help: *You can't cook dinner for ten people by yourself.*

★**youth** /juːθ/ *noun* (*pl* **youths** /juːðz/) **1** [U] the period of your life when you are young, especially the time before a child becomes an adult: *He was quite a good sportsman in his youth.* **2** [U] the fact or state of being young: *I think that her youth will be a disadvantage in this job.* **3** [C] a young person (usually a young man, and often one that you do not have a good opinion of): *a gang of youths* **4** **the youth** [U] young people considered as a group: *the youth of today* ••➤ Look at **age** and **old age**.

youthful /'juːθfl/ *adj* **1** typical of young people: *youthful enthusiasm* **2** seeming younger than you are: *She's a youthful fifty-year-old.*

'youth hostel *noun* [C] a cheap and simple place to stay, especially for young people, when they are travelling

you've /juːv/ *short for* **YOU HAVE**

'yo-yo *noun* [C] (*pl* **yo-yos**) a toy which is a round piece of wood or plastic with a string round the middle. You put the string round your finger and can make the yo-yo go up and down it.

yr (*pl* **yrs**) *abbr* year

yuck /jʌk/ *interj* (*informal*) used for saying that you think sth is disgusting or very unpleasant: *It's filthy! Yuck!* –**yucky** *adj*: *What a yucky colour!*

yummy /'jʌmi/ *adj* (*informal*) tasting very good; delicious: *a yummy cake*

yuppie (also **yuppy**) /'jʌpi/ *noun* [C] (*pl* **yuppies**) a successful young professional person who lives in a city, earns a lot of money and spends it on fashionable things

y

Zz

Z, z /zed/ noun [C] (*pl* **Z's; z's**) the twenty-sixth letter of the English alphabet: *'Zero' begins with (a) 'Z'.*

zany /'zeɪni/ adj funny in an unusual and crazy way: *a zany comedian*

zap /zæp/ verb (**zapping; zapped**) (*informal*) **1** [T] **zap sb/sth (with sth)** to destroy, hit or kill sb, usually with a gun or other weapon: *It's a computer game where you have to zap aliens with a laser.* **2** [I,T] to change television programmes very quickly using an electronic device (remote control)

zeal /ziːl/ noun [U] (*written*) great energy or enthusiasm: *religious zeal*

zealous /'zeləs/ adj using great energy and enthusiasm –**zealously** adv

zebra

zebra /'zebrə/ noun [C] (*pl* **zebra** or **zebras**) an African wild animal that looks like a horse, with black and white lines (stripes) all over its body.

zebra 'crossing noun [C] (*Brit*) a place where the road is marked with black and white lines and people can cross safely because cars must stop to let them do this ••▸ Look at **pedestrian crossing**.

★**zero** /'zɪərəʊ/ noun **1** [C] 0

> For examples of how to use numbers in sentences, look at **six**.

2 [U] freezing point; 0°C: *The temperature is likely to fall to five degrees **below zero** (=* -5°C). **3** [U] the lowest possible amount or level; nothing at all: *zero growth/inflation/profit*

> The figure **0** has several different names in British English. **Zero** is most commonly used in scientific or technical contexts. **Nil** is most commonly used in scores in sport, especially football (when spoken). **Nought** is used when referring to the figure **0** as part of a larger number: *a million is one followed by six noughts.* **O** (pronounced 'oh') is most commonly used when saying numbers such as telephone or flight numbers.

zest /zest/ noun [U,sing] **zest (for sth)** a feeling of enjoyment, excitement and enthusiasm: *She has a great **zest for life**.*

zigzag /'zɪgzæg/ noun [C], adj (consisting of) a line with left and right turns, like a lot of letter W's, one after the other: *The skier came down the slope in a series of zigzags.* ● *a zigzag pattern/line* ••▸ picture at **line** –**zigzag** verb [I] (**zigzagging; zigzagged**)

zinc /zɪŋk/ noun [U] a whitish metal, often put on the surface of iron and steel as protection against water

★**zip** /zɪp/ (*US* **zipper**) noun [C] a device for fastening clothes, bags, etc: *to do up/undo a zip* ••▸ picture at **button** –**zip** verb [T] (**zipping; zipped**) **zip sth (up):** *There was so much in the bag that it was difficult to zip it up.* ••▸ opposite **unzip**

'ZIP code (also **zip code**) (*US*) = **POSTCODE**

the zodiac /'zəʊdɪæk/ noun [sing] a diagram of the positions of the sun, moon and planets, which is divided into twelve equal parts, each with a special name and symbol (the signs of the zodiac)

> The signs of the zodiac are used in **astrology** and **horoscopes** (often called **the stars**) in newspapers and magazines. People often refer to the signs and to the influence that they think these have on a person's personality and future: *Which sign (of the zodiac) are you?*

zone /zəʊn/ noun [C] an area that is different from those around it for example because sth special happens there: *a war zone*

zoo /zuː/ noun [C] (*pl* **zoos**) a park where many kinds of wild animals are kept so that people can look at them and where they are bred, studied and protected

zoology /zəʊ'ɒlədʒi; zuː'ɒl-/ noun [U] the scientific study of animals ••▸ Look at **botany** and **biology**. –**zoological** /ˌzəʊə'lɒdʒɪkl/ adj –**zoologist** /zəʊ'ɒlədʒɪst/ noun [C]

zoom /zuːm/ verb [I] to move or go somewhere very fast: *Traffic zoomed past us.* **PHRASAL VERB** **zoom in (on sb/sth)** (used about a camera) to give a closer view of the object/person being photographed by fixing a special device to the camera (a zoom lens): *The camera zoomed in on the actor's face.* ••▸ picture at **camera**

zoom 'lens noun [C] a device on a camera that can make an object being photographed appear gradually bigger or smaller so that it seems to be getting closer or further away

zucchini /zu'kiːni/ (*pl* **zucchini** or **zucchinis**) (*especially US*) = **COURGETTE**

[C] **countable**, a noun with a plural form: *one book, two books*   [U] **uncountable**, a noun with no plural form: *some sugar*

Reference sections

Verbs: the tenses of regular verbs

The Simple Tenses

Note: The verb forms for I, you, we, and they are the same.
The verb forms for he, she and it are the same.

The present simple

| I look | *do I look?* | I do not look (**don't look**) |
| he looks | *does he look?* | he does not look (**doesn't look**) |

The simple past

| I looked | *did I look?* | I did not look (**didn't look**) |
| he looked | *did he look?* | he did not look (**didn't look**) |

The present perfect

| I have looked (**I've looked**) | *have I looked?* | I have not looked (**haven't looked**) |
| he has looked (**he's looked**) | *has he looked?* | he has not looked (**hasn't looked**) |

The past perfect (pluperfect)

| I had looked (**I'd looked**) | *had I looked?* | I had not looked (**hadn't looked**) |
| he had looked (**he'd looked**) | *had he looked?* | he had not looked (**hadn't looked**) |

The future simple

| I will look (**I'll look**) | *will I look?* | I will not look (won't look) |
| he will look (**he'll look**) | *will he look?* | he will not look (won't look) |

The future perfect

| I will have looked (**I'll have looked**) | *will I have looked?* | I will not have looked (**won't have looked**) |
| he will have looked (**he'll have looked**) | *will he have looked?* | he will not have looked (**won't have looked**) |

The conditional

| I would look (**I'd look**) | *would I look?* | I would not look (**wouldn't look**) |
| he would look (**he'd look**) | *would he look?* | he would not look (**wouldn't look**) |

The conditional perfect

| I would have looked (**would've looked**) | *would I have looked?* | I would not have looked (**wouldn't have looked**) |
| he would have looked (**would've looked**) | *would he have looked?* | he would not have looked (**wouldn't have looked**) |

Verbs: the tenses of regular verbs

The Continuous Tenses

Note: The continuous tenses are sometimes called the progressive tenses. The verb forms for **I**, **you**, **we** and **they** are the same except for where a different form for **you** is shown. The verb forms for **he**, **she** and **it** are the same.

The present continuous

I am looking (**I'm looking**)	*am I looking?*	I am not looking (**I'm not looking**)
you are looking (**you're looking**)	*are you looking?*	you are not looking (**aren't looking**)
he is looking (**he's looking**)	*is he looking?*	he is not looking (**isn't looking**)

The past continuous

I was looking	*was I looking?*	I was not looking (**wasn't looking**)
you were looking	*were you looking?*	you were not looking (**weren't looking**)
he was looking	*was he looking?*	he was not looking (**wasn't looking**)

The present perfect continuous

I have been looking (**I've been looking**)	*have I been looking?*	I have not been looking (**haven't been looking**)
you have been looking (**you've been looking**)	*have you been looking?*	you have not been looking (**haven't been looking**)
he has been looking (**he's been looking**)	*has he been looking?*	he has not been looking (**hasn't been looking**)

The past perfect continuous

I had been looking (**I'd been looking**)	*had I been looking?*	I had not been looking (**hadn't been looking**)
he had been looking (**he'd been looking**)	*had he been looking?*	he had not been looking (**hadn't been looking**)

The future continuous

I will be looking (**I'll be looking**)	*will I be looking?*	I will not be looking (**won't be looking**)
he will be looking (**he'll be looking**)	*will he be looking?*	he will not be looking (**won't be looking**)

The future perfect continuous

I will have been looking (**I'll have been looking**)	*will I have been looking?*	I will not have been looking (**won't have been looking**)
he will have been looking (**he'll have been looking**)	*will he have been looking?*	he will not have been looking (**won't have been looking**)

The conditional continuous

I would be looking (**I'd be looking**)	*would I be looking?*	I would not be looking (**wouldn't be looking**)
he would be looking (**he'd be looking**)	*would he be looking?*	he would not be looking (**wouldn't be looking**)

The conditional perfect continuous

I would have been looking (**would've been looking**)	*would I have been looking?*	I would not have been looking (**wouldn't have been looking**)
he would have been looking (**would've been looking**)	*would he have been looking?*	he would not have been looking (**wouldn't have been looking**)

Verbs

Talking about the present

▶ To describe **an action that is happening now**, you use the **present continuous**:	We're just **having** breakfast. What **are** you **reading**? She's not **listening** to me.
The present continuous is also used to talk about **something that is not yet finished**, even if you are not doing it at the moment when you are talking:	I'm **learning** Japanese. She's **writing** a book about snails.
When something happens often, and you find it annoying, you use the present continuous with **always**:	He's always **asking** silly questions. They're always **coming** round here to borrow something.
Some verbs are not used in the continuous tenses, for example **need**, **want**, **know** etc: ▶ Look also at promise, agree, seem, appear, understand, appreciate. These verbs describe a state, not an action.	I **need** some new shoes. She **hates** her job. They **love** Mexican food. He **wants** to go home. **Do** you **know** Tania Smith?
Other verbs are used in the present continuous when they describe an action, and the present simple when they describe a state:	He's **tasting** the soup. The soup **tastes** salty. She's **being** difficult again. She's a difficult child. What **are** you **thinking** about? Do you **think** I should leave?
▶ To describe **something that is always true,** you use the **present simple**:	Whales **are** mammals. Rice **doesn't grow** in this climate. He **lives** in Spain. What temperature **does** water **boil** at?
You also use the present simple for things that happen regularly:	She **leaves** for school at 8 o'clock. **Does** he **work** in a factory? We **don't** often **go** out for a meal.

Verbs

Talking about the past

▶ To describe **action that finished in the past,** you use the **past simple**:	He **got** up, **paid** the bill, and **left**. I **didn't read** the letter, I just **gave** it to Lee. What **did** you **say** to him?
Often a specific time is mentioned:	**Did** you **speak** to Amy yesterday?
You also use the past simple when you describe **a state that continued for some time, but that is now finished**:	I **went** to school in Scotland. **Did** she really **work** there for ten years? He **didn't grow** up in Canada – he went there as an adult.
It is also used to describe actions that happened regularly in the past:	I often **played** tennis with her. She always **won**. They never **went** to the cinema when they **lived** in the country.

▶ To describe **a state that started in the past and is still happening,** you use the **present perfect**:	They **have lived** here for ten years, and they don't want to move. I**'ve worked** here since 1998. I**'ve known** Caroline for years.
You also often use the present perfect when the time is not mentioned, or is not important:	He**'s written** a book. We**'ve bought** a new computer.
Sometimes the action finished in the past, but the effect is still felt in the present:	He**'s lost** his calculator (and he still hasn't found it).
Notice the use of the present perfect with **since** and **for** to show the duration of an action or state up until the present:	I **have known** about it since Christmas. How long **have** you **known**? She **hasn't bought** any new clothes for years.
In British English, the present perfect is often used with **just**, **ever**, **already**, and **yet**:	I've just **arrived**. **Have** you ever **been** here before? He**'s already packed** his suitcases. **Haven't** you **finished** yet?
or to describe something that happened during a period of time that is not yet finished:	The train **has been** late three times this week. He still **hasn't visited** her.

Verbs

▶ To talk about **an activity that started in the past and is still happening**, or that **has only just finished and its results are visible now**, you use the **present perfect continuous**:	I**'ve been working** since eight o'clock – can I have a break now? My hands are dirty because I**'ve been gardening**. They **haven't been learning** English very long.
▶ To describe **something that was already in progress when something else happened**, you use the **past continuous**:	It **was raining** when I left the house. **Was** he **cooking** dinner when you got home? I **wasn't wearing** a coat and I got very wet.
As with the present continuous, this tense cannot be used with 'state' verbs:	The fresh bread **smelled** wonderful (not ~~was smelling~~)
▶ To describe **something that happened before another action in the past,** you use the **past perfect**:	When I got to the station, the train **had left**. I **had** never **met** Ed before he came to Bath. They **had moved** into the flat three months before Joe lost his job.
▶ To describe **an activity that went on for a period of time further back in the past than something else**, you use the **past perfect continuous**:	My hands were dirty because I **had been gardening**. She **hadn't been working** at the shop very long when they sacked her.

Talking about the future

There are several ways of talking about the future besides the tense that we call 'the future'.

▶ To talk about **future plans where the time is mentioned**, you use the **present continuous**:	He**'s flying** to Japan in August. What **are** you **doing** this evening? I'm not **starting** my new job till next Monday.
▶ To talk about **what you intend to do in the future but have not yet arranged**, you use **be going to** with the infinitive:	I**'m going to phone** Michael tonight. What **are** you **going to do** when you leave school? I**'m not going to be** as strict with my children as my parents were with me.

Verbs

▶ However, to talk about **a decision that you make as you are speaking**, you say **will** with the infinitive:	I can't do this. I**'ll ask** the teacher. I**'ll take** the blue one. We**'ll have** the salad, please.
▶ When you talk about **what you know or think will happen in the future** (but not about your own intentions or plans), you use **will** with the infinitive:	It **will be** 25° tomorrow. She**'ll be** in the office on Monday. **Will** he **pass** the exam, do you think? This job **won't take** long.
However, you use the present simple to refer to a future time after **when**, **as soon as**, **before**, **until**, etc:	Ring me as soon as you **hear** any news. I'll look after Jo until you **get** back. You'll recognize the street when you **see** it.
▶ For **requests, promises,** and **offers,** you also use **will** with the infinitive:	**Will** you **buy** some bread on your way home? We**'ll be** back early, don't worry. I**'ll help** you with your maths.
▶ To talk about **the very near future,** you can use **about to** with the infinitive:	Go and ask him quickly. He's **about to go** out.
▶ To talk about **actions that will continue for a period of time in the future**, you use the **future continuous**:	I**'ll be waiting** near the ticket office. I**'ll be wearing** a green hat. This time next week you**'ll be relaxing** in the sun!
▶ To ask somebody about their **plans or intentions**, you also use **will be + -ing**	How many nights will you **be staying**? **Will** you **be flying** back or going by train?
▶ To talk about **something that will be finished at a particular time in the future**, you use the **future perfect**:	I **will have finished** this work by 3 o'clock. They**'ll have lived** here for four years in May.
▶ To talk about **future plans where something has been officially arranged**, for example on a timetable or programme, you can use the **present simple**:	We **leave** Palma at 10 and **arrive** in Luton at 12.30. School **starts** on 9 September.

Verbs

Transitive and intransitive verbs

[T] Verbs that can have a direct object are called **transitive verbs**.
In this dictionary they are marked [T]. Look up the verb **include**.
> He included four new names on the list.

It is not possible to say:
> ~~He included.~~

[I] Verbs that cannot have a direct object are called **intransitive verbs**.
In this dictionary they are marked [I]. Look up the verb **arrive**.
> We arrived very late at the hotel.

It is not possible to say:
> ~~We arrived the hotel.~~

[I,T] Many verbs can be both intransitive and transitive.
In this dictionary they are marked [I,T]:
> [I] He spoke for two hours. [T] Do you speak Japanese?
> [I] This door only locks from the outside. [T] Have you locked the door?

Some verbs can have two objects, an indirect and a direct object.
Look up the verb **give** and notice the structures that are shown there:
> **give sb sth; give sth to sb**

In a sentence you can say:
> He gave his mother the CDs. *or* He gave the CDs to his mother.

Either or both of the objects can be pronouns:
> He gave her the CDs. He gave her them.
> He gave the CDs to her. He gave them to her.
> He gave them to his mother.

Conditionals

Sentences with **if** express possibilities. There are three main types:

1 If I **write** my essay this afternoon, I **will have** time to go out tonight.
  (It is still morning, and it is probable that I will do this – **present tense** after **if**, **future tense** in the main clause.)

2 If I **wrote** my essay this afternoon, I **would have** time to go out tonight.
  (It is still morning, but I think it is less likely that I will do this – **simple past** after **if**, **conditional tense** in the main clause.)

3 If I **had written** my essay this afternoon, I **would have had** time to go out tonight.
  (It is now evening, and I haven't written my essay: it is now impossible for me to go out – **past perfect** after **if**, **conditional perfect** in the main clause.)

Here are some of the other types of **if** sentence:
Something that is always true, or that always was true in the past:

If you **mix** blue and red, you **get** purple.
  (**Present simple** in both parts of the sentence)

If I **asked** her to come with us, she always **said** no.
  (**Simple past** in both parts of the sentence.)

Verbs: Reported speech

Direct speech to reported speech

Jeff: 'I'm coming home.' → Jeff said he was coming home.

When you report somebody's words using **said**, **asked**, etc, you usually change the tense to one further back in the past:

'I **don't know** whether Jane **wants** to come.'	→ He said he **didn't know** whether Jane **wanted** to come.
'She **is thinking** of staying at home tomorrow.'	→ He said she **was thinking** of staying at home the following day.
'**Have** you **booked** your ticket?'	→ She asked whether he **had booked** his ticket.
'I **finished** my exams yesterday.'	→ He said he **had finished** his exams the day before.
'I**'ll ring** from the station.'	→ He told me he **would ring** from the station.

The modal verbs **should**, **would**, **might**, **could**, **must**, and **ought** are not usually changed:

'We might go to the cinema.' → They said they might go to the cinema.

If the reporting verb (**say**, **ask**, etc) is in the present or present perfect, then the tense of the sentence doesn't usually change.

'I'm going home.' → Barry says he's going home.
Barry's just told me he's going home.

Reporting requests and commands

When you report a request or an order, you usually use an infinitive construction:

'Please will you do the dishes?'	→ She **asked** me **to do** the dishes.
'Don't touch the stove!'	→ She **told** the children **not to touch** the stove.

Reporting questions

Notice that you use **if** or **whether** to report yes/no questions:

'Are you ready?' → She asked **if/whether I was ready**.

With **wh-** questions, the **wh-** word stays in the sentence:

'When are you leaving?' → She asked me **when I was leaving**.

The word order in these sentences is the same as a normal statement, not as in a question:

'Did you see them?' → He asked me **if I had seen** them.

Reporting verbs

Here are some more examples of reported speech using different **reporting verbs**:

'Will you come with me?' 'All right.'	→ She **agreed** to come with me.
'Sorry I didn't phone you.'	→ She **apologized** for not phoning me.
'Did you steal the money?' 'Yes, I did.'	→ He **admitted** (to) stealing the money.
	→ He **admitted** that he'd stolen the money.
'Shall we take a break now'	→ He **suggested** taking a break.
'You should have a holiday.'	→ He **advised** me to have a holiday.
'I'm freezing!'	→ He **complained** that he was freezing.

Verbs: The passive

In an **active** sentence, the subject is the person or thing that performs the action:
  Masked thieves stole a valuable painting from the museum last night.

When you make this into a **passive sentence** the object of the verb becomes the subject:
  A valuable painting was stolen from the museum last night.

You use the passive when you do not know who performed the action, or when this information is not important. It is common in formal writing, for example scientific writing:
  The liquid was heated to 60° and then filtered.

If you want to mention who performed the action, you use by at the end of the sentence:
  The painting was stolen by masked thieves.

Another reason for choosing the passive is when you want to save new information until the end of the sentence for emphasis:
  The picture was painted by Constable.

The passive is made with a form of to be and the past participle of the verb:
  ▶ The painting is valued by experts at 2 million dollars.
  ▶ The theft is being investigated by the police.
  ▶ Other museums have been warned to take extra care.
  ▶ The painting was kept in a special room.
  ▶ The lock had been broken and the cameras had been switched off.
  ▶ This morning everything possible was being done to find the thieves.
  ▶ Staff at the museum will be questioned tomorrow.
  ▶ An international search is to be started.
  ▶ The theft must have been planned with the help of someone inside the museum.

It is possible to put a verb that has two objects into the passive:
  An American millionaire gave **the museum** the painting.
  → **The museum** was given the painting by an American millionaire.
  The director told **the staff** the news this morning.
  → **The staff** were told the news this morning by the director.

Modal verbs

Ability can could be able to
  Can he swim?
  My brother could swim when he was two.
  I couldn't find my keys this morning.
  I could have run faster, but I didn't want the others to get tired.
  She has not been able to walk since the accident.
  He was able to speak to Ann before she left.
  Will people be able to live on the moon one day?

▶ For the difference between 'could' and 'managed to', look at the note at the entry for could.

Verbs: Modal verbs

Possibility could may might
  Could/Might you have lost it on the way home?
  She **may/might/could** be ill. I'll phone her.
  I **may have/might have** left my purse in the shop.
  Amy **might/may** know the answer.
  I **might/may** not go if I'm tired.
  He **might have** enjoyed the party if he'd gone.

Permission can could may may not must not
  Can we come in?
  You **can't** get up until you're better.
  Could we possibly stay at your flat?
  (*written*) Staff **may** take their break between 12 and 2.
  (*formal*) **May** I sit here?
  (*written*) Crockery **may not** be taken out of the canteen.
  (*formal*) You **must not** begin until I tell you.

Obligation ought to/should (*mild*) **have (got) to/must** (*strong*)
  I **ought to/should** go on a diet.
  I **ought to have/should have** asked her first.
  (*written*) All visitors **must** report to reception on arrival.
  I **must** get that report finished today.
  Do you **have to** write your name on the form?
  She **had to** throw the burnt cake away.
  You **will have to** wait, I'm afraid.

Advice ought to should
  Ought I to/Should I write and thank him?
  She **ought to/should** go out more often.
  You **ought to have/should have** gone to bed earlier.
  You **shouldn't** borrow the car without asking.

No necessity don't have to shouldn't have didn't need to needn't have
  You **don't have to** pick us up, we can take a taxi.
  They **didn't have to** go through customs.
  You **shouldn't have** bothered making lunch, we could have bought a sandwich.
  He **didn't need to** have any fillings at the dentist's.
  They **needn't have** waited.

➤ For the difference between 'didn't need to' and 'needn't have',
  look at the note at **need²**.

Requests can could will would
  Can you pass me the dictionary?   **Will** you buy me an ice cream, Mum?
  Could you help me with my translation?   **Would** you type this letter for me, please?

➤ **Could** and **would** are more formal than **can** and **will**.

Offers and suggestions shall will
  Shall I do the washing-up?   I'll take you to the airport.
  Shall we go now?

Nouns

Countable and uncountable nouns

[C] Countable nouns can be singular or plural:
a friend/two friends   one book/five books
In this dictionary they are marked [C].

[U] Uncountable nouns cannot have a plural and are not used with a/an.
They cannot be counted. In this dictionary they are marked [U].
Look up the entries for
rice, money, water, information, advice and **furniture.**
It is possible to say **some rice** but not ~~a rice~~ or ~~two rices~~.
Abstract nouns like **importance, luck, happiness** are usually
uncountable.

[C,U] Some nouns have both countable and uncountable meanings.
In this dictionary they are marked [C,U] or [U,C].
Look up the entries for **cheese, coffee, paper** and **friendship.**

   [U] ▶ Have some cheese!
   [C] They sell a variety of cheeses. (= types of cheese)
   [U] ▶ I don't drink much coffee.
   [C] She ordered too many coffees. (=cups of coffee)
   [U] ▶ I haven't got any more paper.
   [C] Can you buy me a paper? (= a newspaper)
   [U] ▶ Friendship is more important than wealth.
   [C] None of these were lasting friendships. (= relationships)

[sing] Some nouns are only singular: In this dictionary they are marked [sing].
Look up the entries for:
aftermath, dearth, and **brink.**
They cannot be used in the plural but they can be used with a/an or the
in the aftermath of the earthquake
There was a dearth of fresh food.
We are on the brink of disaster.

[pl] Other words are only plural. Look up the entries for **jeans, sunglasses**
and **scissors.** In this dictionary they are marked [pl].
You cannot say ~~a sunglasses~~
To talk about individual items, you say **a pair:**
a pair of sunglasses   two pairs of sunglasses.
Words like **headphones, clothes,** and **goods** can only be used in the plural:
I need to buy some new clothes.
Nouns which describe groups of people, such as **the poor** are plural:
The poor are getting poorer and the rich are getting richer.

Articles

The definite article

You use the definite article, **the**, when you expect the person who is listening to
know which person or thing you are talking about:
      Thank you for the flowers (= the ones that you brought me).
      The teacher said my essay was the best (= our teacher).

Nouns

You use **the** with the names of rivers and groups of islands:
>Which is longer, **the** Rhine or **the** Danube?
>Where are **the** Seychelles?
>Menorca is one of **the** Balearic Islands.

The indefinite article
You use the indefinite article, **a**, (**an** before a vowel sound) when the other person does not know which person or thing you are talking about or when you are not referring to a particular thing or person:
>He's got **a** new bike. (I haven't mentioned it before.)
>Could you bring me **a** knife? (Any knife will be okay.)

You also use **a/an** to talk about a type or class of people or things, such as when you describe a person's job:
>She's **an** accountant.

You use **a(n)** in prices, speeds, etc:
>$100 **a** day
>70 kilometres **an** hour
>50 cents **a** pack
>three times **a** week

No article
You do not use an article when you are talking in general:
>I love flowers (all flowers).
>Honey is sweet (all honey).
>Are nurses well paid here? (nurses in general)

You **do not** use **the** with most names of countries, counties, states, streets, or lakes:
>I'm going to Turkey.
>She's from Yorkshire.
>They live in Iowa.
>a house in Walton Street
>Lake Louise

or with a person's title when the name is mentioned:
>President Kennedy   **but**   **the** President of the United States.

> ➤ Look at the entries for **school**, **university**, **college**, **hospital**, **prison** and **piano** for more information about the use of articles.

The possessive with 's

You can add **'s** to a word or a name to show possession. It is most often used with words for people, countries and animals:
>Ann**'s** job
>the manager**'s** secretary
>my brother**'s** computer
>the children**'s** clothes
>the dog**'s** basket
>Spain**'s** beaches

When the word already ends in a plural **s**, you add an apostrophe after it:
>the boys**'** rooms
>the Smiths**'** house

Nouns

much, many, a lot, a little, a few

Much is used with **uncountable nouns**, usually in negative sentences and questions:
> I haven't got much money left.
> Did you watch much television?

Much is very formal in affirmative sentences:
> There will be much discussion before a decision is made.

Many is used with **countable nouns**, usually in negative sentences and questions:
> There aren't many tourists here in December.
> Are there many opportunities for young people?

In affirmative sentences, it is more formal than **a lot of**:
> Many people prefer to stay at home

A lot of or (*informal*) **lots of** is used with countable and uncountable nouns:
> **A lot of** tourists visit the castle.   He's been here **lots of** times.
> I've spent **a lot of** money.   You need **lots of** patience to make model aircraft.

A little is used with **uncountable nouns**:
> Add a little vinegar.

A few is used with **countable nouns**:
> I've got a few letters to write.

> ➤ **Note**: that in these sentences, the meaning is positive. **Few** and **little** without **a** have a negative meaning:
> **Few** people have ever seen these animals in the wild.
> There is now **little** hope that they can win the championship.

Adjectives

Comparatives and Superlatives

Look at this text. It contains several comparatives and superlatives.
> Temperatures yesterday were **highest** in the south-east. The **sunniest** place was Brighton, and the **wettest** was Glasgow. Tomorrow will be **cooler** than today, but in Scotland it will be a **drier** day. **Better** weather is expected for the weekend, but it will become **more changeable** again next week.

To form comparatives and superlatives:
Adjectives of **one syllable** add -er, -est:

cool	cooler	coolest
high	higher	highest

Adjectives

Adjectives that already end in -e only add -r, -st:

| nice | nicer | nicest |

Some words double the last letter:

| wet | wetter | wettest |
| big | bigger | biggest |

Adjectives of **three syllables** or more take more, most:

| changeable | more changeable | most changeable |
| interesting | more interesting | most interesting |

Some adjectives of **two syllables** are like cool, especially those that end in -er, -y, or -ly:

| clever | cleverer | cleverest |

Words that end in -y change it to -i:

| sunny | sunnier | sunniest |
| friendly | friendlier | friendliest |

Other adjectives of **two syllables** are like interesting:

| harmful | more harmful | most harmful |

Some adjectives have **irregular forms**:

| good | better | best |
| bad | worse | worst |

Adjectives with nouns

Most adjectives can be used before the noun that they describe or after a linking verb:

I need a new bike.   **This bike isn't new**
It's an interesting book.   **She said the film sounded interesting.**

Some adjectives **cannot** come **before** a noun. Look at the entry for asleep and notice how this information is given in the dictionary. You can say:

Don't wake him – he's asleep. but not: ~~an asleep child~~

> ► Look up the entries for **afraid**, **alive**, **ashamed**, **certain**, and **pleased**.

Some adjectives can **only** be used **before** a noun. Look at the entry for the adjective **chief** and notice how this information is given in the dictionary. You can say:

That was the **chief** disadvantage. but not: ~~This disadvantage was chief.~~

> ► Look up the entries for **downright**, **flagrant**, **former** and **main**.

Relative clauses

Defining relative clauses

These phrases **define** or **identify** which person or thing we are talking about:

Which of them is the boss?　　　　The man **who came in late** is the boss.

> **Note** that there is **no comma** before an defining relative clause. The pronouns that we use in these clauses are **who**, **whom**, **that**, and **which**:

When the **subject** is a person:
the man **who** came in late　or　the man **that** came in late

When the **object** is a person:
the girl **that** I saw　or　the girl I saw　or　the girl **whom** I saw (*formal*)

When the **subject** is a thing:
the chair **that** is in the corner　or　the chair **which** is in the corner (*formal*)

When the **object** is a thing:
the book **that** I'm reading　or　the book I'm reading　or
the book **which** I'm reading (*formal*)

> **Notice** that **that**, **who**, and **which** can be left out when the thing or person is the object of the verb.

whose shows that something **belongs** to somebody:
the woman **whose** car broke down　the people **whose** house was burgled

Whose is not usually used to refer to a thing:
the chair ~~whose~~ leg is broken

It is more natural to say:
the chair with the broken leg

Non-defining relative clauses

These phrases **add extra information** about somebody or something which could be left out and the sentence would still make sense. This extra information is separated from the main clause by commas:

The film, which was shot in Mexico, has won an Oscar.

The pronouns that can be used in non-identifying relative clauses are
who for a person; **which** for a thing; **whose** to show belonging

My sister, who is a vegetarian, ordered a cheese salad.
The tickets, which can be bought at the station, are valid for one day.
Lucy, whose car had broken down, arrived by bus.

Irregular verbs

In this list you will find the infinitive form of the verb followed by the past tense and the past participle. Where two forms are given, look up the verb in the main part of the dictionary to see whether there is a difference in the meaning.

Infinitive	Past Tense	Past Participle	Infinitive	Past Tense	Past Participle
arise	arose	arisen	dream	dreamt, dreamed	dreamt,
awake	awoke	awoken			dreamed
be	was/were	been	drink	drank	drunk
bear	bore	borne	drive	drove	driven
beat	beat	beaten	dwell	dwelt, dwelled	dwelt, dwelled
become	became	become	eat	ate	eaten
befall	befell	befallen	fall	fell	fallen
begin	began	begun	feed	fed	fed
bend	bent	bent	feel	felt	felt
beset	beset	beset	fight	fought	fought
bet	bet, betted	bet, betted	find	found	found
bid	bid	bid	flee	fled	fled
bind	bound	bound	fling	flung	flung
bite	bit	bitten	fly	flew	flown
bleed	bled	bled	forbid	forbade, forbad	forbidden
blow	blew	blown	forecast	forecast	forecast
break	broke	broken	foresee	foresaw	foreseen
breed	bred	bred	forget	forgot	forgotten
bring	brought	brought	forgive	forgave	forgiven
broadcast	broadcast	broadcast	forgo	forwent	forgone
build	built	built	forsake	forsook	forsaken
burn	burnt, burned	burnt, burned	freeze	froze	frozen
burst	burst	burst	get	got	got;
bust	bust, busted	bust, busted			(US) gotten
buy	bought	bought	give	gave	given
cast	cast	cast	go	went	gone
catch	caught	caught	grind	ground	ground
choose	chose	chosen	grow	grew	grown
cling	clung	clung	hang	hung, hanged	hung, hanged
come	came	come	have	had	had
cost	cost	cost	hear	heard	heard
creep	crept	crept	hide	hid	hidden
cut	cut	cut	hit	hit	hit
deal	dealt	dealt	hold	held	held
dig	dug	dug	hurt	hurt	hurt
dive	dived; (US) dove	dived	input	input, inputted	input,
do	did	done			inputted
draw	drew	drawn	keep	kept	kept

Irregular verbs

Infinitive	Past Tense	Past Participle	Infinitive	Past Tense	Past Participle
kneel	knelt; (esp US) kneeled	knelt; (esp US) kneeled	put	put	put
			quit	quit	quit
know	knew	known	read	read	read
lay	laid	laid	rebuild	rebuilt	rebuilt
lead	led	led	repay	repaid	repaid
lean	leant, leaned	leant, leaned	rethink	rethought	rethought
leap	leapt, leaped	leapt, leaped	rewind	rewound	rewound
learn	learnt, learned	learnt, learned	rewrite	rewrote	rewritten
leave	left	left	rid	rid	rid
lend	lent	lent	ride	rode	ridden
let	let	let	ring	rang	rung
lie	lay	lain	rise	rose	risen
light	lighted, lit	lighted, lit	run	ran	run
lose	lost	lost	saw	sawed	sawn; (US) sawed
make	made	made			
mean	meant	meant	say	said	said
meet	met	met	see	saw	seen
mislay	mislaid	mislaid	seek	sought	sought
mislead	misled	misled	sell	sold	sold
misread	misread	misread	send	sent	sent
misspell	misspelt, misspelled	misspelt, misspelled	set	set	set
			sew	sewed	sewn, sewed
mistake	mistook	mistaken	shake	shook	shaken
misunder- stand	misunderstood	misunder- stood	shear	sheared	shorn, sheared
mow	mowed	mown, mowed	shed	shed	shed
			shine	shone	shone
outdo	outdid	outdone	shoe	shod	shod
outgrow	outgrew	outgrown	shoot	shot	shot
overcome	overcame	overcome	show	showed	shown, showed
overdo	overdid	overdone			
overhang	overhung	overhung	shrink	shrank, shrunk	shrunk
overhear	overheard	overheard	shut	shut	shut
overpay	overpaid	overpaid	sing	sang	sung
override	overrode	overridden	sink	sank	sunk
overrun	overran	overrun	sit	sat	sat
oversee	oversaw	overseen	slay	slew	slain
oversleep	overslept	overslept	sleep	slept	slept
overtake	overtook	overtaken	slide	slid	slid
overthrow	overthrew	overthrown	sling	slung	slung
pay	paid	paid	slink	slunk	slunk
prove	proved	proved; (US) proven	slit	slit	slit

Irregular verbs

Infinitive	Past Tense	Past Participle	Infinitive	Past Tense	Past Participle
smell	smelt, smelled	smelt, smelled	take	took	taken
sow	sowed	sown, sowed	teach	taught	taught
speak	spoke	spoken	tear	tore	torn
speed	sped, speeded	sped, speeded	tell	told	told
			think	thought	thought
spell	spelt, spelled	spelt, spelled	thrive	thrived, throve	thrived
spend	spent	spent	throw	threw	thrown
spill	spilt, spilled	spilt, spilled	thrust	thrust	thrust
spin	spun	spun	tread	trod	trodden
spit	spat;	spat;	undercut	undercut	undercut
	(US also) spit	(US also) spit	undergo	underwent	undergone
split	split	split	underpay	underpaid	underpaid
spoil	spoilt, spoiled	spoilt, spoiled	understand	understood	understood
spread	spread	spread	undertake	undertook	undertaken
spring	sprang	sprung	undo	undid	undone
stand	stood	stood	unwind	unwound	unwound
steal	stole	stolen	uphold	upheld	upheld
stick	stuck	stuck	upset	upset	upset
sting	stung	stung	wake	woke	woken
stink	stank, stunk	stunk	wear	wore	worn
stride	strode	stridden	weave	wove, weaved	woven, weaved
strike	struck	struck			
string	strung	strung	weep	wept	wept
strive	strove	striven	wet	wet, wetted	wet, wetted
swear	swore	sworn	win	won	won
sweep	swept	swept	wind	wound	wound
swell	swelled	swollen, swelled	withdraw	withdrew	withdrawn
			withhold	withheld	withheld
swim	swam	swum	withstand	withstood	withstood
swing	swung	swung	wring	wrung	wrung
			write	wrote	written

Expressions using numbers

The Numbers

1	one	1st	first
2	two	2nd	second
3	three	3rd	third
4	four	4th	fourth
5	five	5th	fifth
6	six	6th	sixth
7	seven	7th	seventh
8	eight	8th	eighth
9	nine	9th	ninth
10	ten	10th	tenth
11	eleven	11th	eleventh
12	twelve	12th	twelfth
13	thirteen	13th	thirteenth
14	fourteen	14th	fourteenth
15	fifteen	15th	fifteenth
16	sixteen	16th	sixteenth
17	seventeen	17th	seventeenth
18	eighteen	18th	eighteenth
19	nineteen	19th	nineteenth
20	twenty	20th	twentieth
21	twenty-one	21st	twenty-first
22	twenty-two	22nd	twenty-second
30	thirty	30th	thirtieth
40	forty	40th	fortieth
50	fifty	50th	fiftieth
60	sixty	60th	sixtieth
70	seventy	70th	seventieth
80	eighty	80th	eightieth
90	ninety	90th	ninetieth
100	a/one hundred*	100th	hundredth
101	a/one hundred and one*	101st	hundred and first
200	two hundred	200th	two hundredth
1 000	a/one thousand*	1 000th	thousandth
10 000	ten thousand	10 000th	ten thousandth
100 000	a/one hundred thousand*	100 000th	hundred thousandth
1 000 000	a/one million*	1 000 000th	millionth

Examples 697: six hundred and ninety-seven
3 402: three thousand, four hundred and two
80 534: eighty thousand, five hundred and thirty-four

* You use **one hundred**, **one thousand**, etc, instead of **a hundred**, **a thousand**,
when it is important to stress that you mean one (not two, for example).
In numbers over a thousand, you use a comma or a small space: **1,200** or **1200**

Telephone Numbers

In telephone numbers you say each number separately, often with a pause after
two or three numbers:
    509236 five o nine – two three six
You can say **six six** or **double six** for **66**:
    02166 o two one – six six or o two one – double six.
If you are phoning a number in a different town, you have to use the

Expressions using numbers

area code before the number: 01865 is the code for Oxford.
If you are phoning somebody in a large firm, you can ask for their extension number. (01865) 56767 x 4840 (extension 4840)

Fractions and Decimals

½	a half	⅓	a/one third
¼	a quarter	⅖	two fifths
⅛	an/one eighth	7/12	seven twelfths
1/10	a/one tenth	1 ½	one and a half
1/16	a/one sixteenth	2 ⅜	two and three eighths

0.1	(nought) point one	**1.75**	one point seven five
0.25	(nought) point two five	**3.976**	three point nine seven six
0.33	(nought) point three three		

Percentages and Proportions

90% of all households have a television.
Nine out of ten households have a television.
Nine tenths of all households have a television.

Mathematical Expressions

+	plus
-	minus
x	times or multiplied by
÷	divided by
=	equals
%	per cent
3²	three squared
5³	five cubed
6¹⁰	six to the power of ten

Examples
7+6=13 seven plus six equals (or is) thirteen
5x8=40 five times eight equals forty
or five eights are forty
or five multiplied by eight is forty

Temperature

In Britain, temperatures are now usually given in **degrees Celsius**, (although many people are still more familiar with **Fahrenheit**). In the United States, **Fahrenheit** is used, except in science.
To convert **Fahrenheit** to **Celsius**, subtract 32 from the number, then multiply by 5 and divide by 9:

$$68°F -$$
$$32$$
$$= 36 \times$$
$$5$$
$$= 180 \div 9$$
$$= 20°C$$

Expressions using numbers

Examples

Water freezes at 32°F and boils at 212°F.
The maximum temperature this afternoon will be 15°, and the minimum tonight may reach –5° (minus five).
She was running a temperature of 102° last night, and it's still above normal.

Weight

	GB	Metric
	1 ounce (oz)	= 28.35 grams (g)
16 ounces	= 1 pound (lb)	= 0.454 kilogram (kg)
14 pounds	= 1 stone (st)	= 6.356 kilograms
112 pounds	= 1 hundredweight (cwt)	= 50.8 kilograms
20 hundredweight	= 1 ton (t)	= 1.016 tonnes

Examples

The baby weighed 8 lb 2oz (eight pounds two ounces).
For this recipe you need 750g (seven hundred and fifty grams) of flour.

> ➤ **Note:** In the United States, one hundredweight is equal to 100 pounds and one ton is 2 000 lb or 0.907 tonne. Americans do not use stones, so they talk about their weight in pounds: *He weighs 180 pounds*.

Length

	GB	Metric
	1 inch (in)	= 25.4 millimetres (mm)
12 inches	= 1 foot (ft)	= 30.48 centimetres (cm)
3 feet	= 1 yard (yd)	= 0.914 metre (m)
1 760 yards	= 1 mile	= 1.609 kilometres (km)

Examples

300 dots per inch
flying at 7000 feet
The speed limit is 30 mph (**thirty miles per hour**).
The room is 11'x 9'6" (**eleven feet by nine feet six** *or* eleven foot by nine foot six).

Area

	GB	Metric
	1 square inch (sq in)	= 6.452 square centimetres
144 square inches	= 1 square foot (sq ft)	= 929.03 square centimetres
9 square feet	= 1 square yard (sq yd)	= 0.836 square metre
4840 square yards	= 1 acre	= 0.405 hectare
640 acres	= 1 square mile	= 2.59 square kilometres or 259 hectares

Examples

an 80-acre country park
160 000 square miles of the jungle have been destroyed.

Expressions using numbers

Cubic Measure

	GB	Metric
	1 cubic inch (cu in)	= 16 39 cubic centimetres (cc)
1728 cubic inches	= 1 cubic foot (cu ft)	= 0.028 cubic metre
27 cubic feet	= 1 cubic yard	= 0.765 cubic metre

Example
a car with a 1500 cc engine

Capacity

	GB	US	Metric
20 fluid ounces (fl oz)	= 1 pint (pt)	= 1.201 pints	= 0.568 litre (l)
2 pints	= 1 quart (qt)	= 1.201 quarts	= 1.136 litres
4 quarts	= 1 gallon (gall)	= 1.201 gallons	= 4.546 litres

Examples
I drink a litre of water a day.   a quart of orange juice

Times

	In Conversation	In official language
06.00	six o'clock	(o) six hundred (hours)
06.05	five past six	(o) six o five
06.10	ten past six	(o) six ten
06.15	(a) quarter past six	(o) six fifteen
06.20	twenty past six	(o) six twenty
06.30	half past six	(o) six thirty
06.35	twenty-five to seven	(o) six thirty-five
06.40	twenty to seven	(o) six forty
06.45	(a) quarter to seven	(o) six forty-five
06.50	ten to seven	(o) six fifty
06.55	five to seven	(o) six fifty-five
10.12	twelve minutes past ten	ten twelve
13.10	ten past one	thirteen ten
19.56	four minutes to eight	nineteen fifty-six

In US English, **after** is sometimes used instead of 'past' and **of** instead of 'to'.

> ▶ **Note:** The 24-hour clock is used in official language: *The next train is the 07.02 to Marlow. (o seven o two)* In conversation, you can say: *I left at seven in the morning/two in the afternoon/eight in the evening/eleven at night.* a.m. (for times before midday) and p.m. (for times after midday) are used in slightly more formal language: *School starts at 9 a.m.*

Dates

You can write dates in numbers or in numbers and words:
15/4/01 (US 4/15/01)   15 April 2001   April 15th, 2001 (esp US)
You can say:
April the fifteenth, two thousand and one   or   the fifteenth of April, two thousand and one (In US English, April fifteenth, two thousand and one)
Example
She was born on 4 May (May the fourth/the fourth of May).

Map of Britain and Ireland

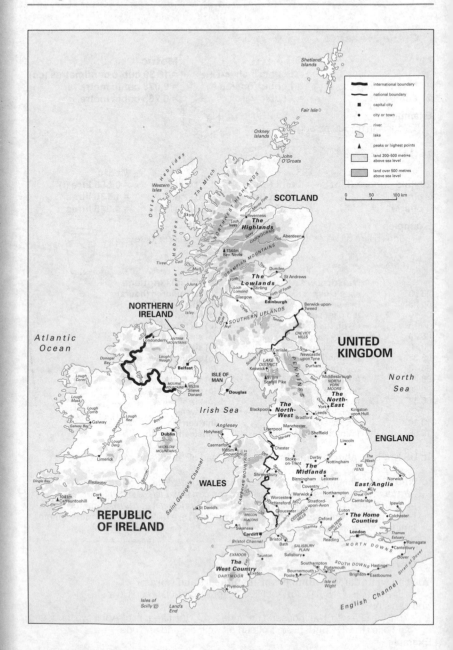

British and Irish place names

Towns and Cities in the United Kingdom and Ireland

Aberdeen /ˌæbəˈdiːn/
Bath /bɑːθ/
Belfast /belˈfɑːst/
Berwick-upon-Tweed
 /ˌberɪk əpɒn ˈtwiːd/
Birmingham /ˈbɜːmɪŋəm/
Blackpool /ˈblækpuːl/
Bournemouth /ˈbɔːnməθ/
Bradford /ˈbrædfəd/
Brighton /ˈbraɪtn/
Bristol /ˈbrɪstl/
Caernarfon /kəˈnɑːvn/
Cambridge /ˈkeɪmbrɪdʒ/
Canterbury /ˈkæntəbəri/
Cardiff /ˈkɑːdɪf/
Carlisle /ˌkɑːˈlaɪl/
Chester /ˈtʃestə/
Colchester /ˈkəʊltʃestə/
Cork /kɔːk/
Coventry /ˈkɒvəntri/
Derby /ˈdɑːbi/
Douglas /ˈdʌɡləs/
Dover /ˈdəʊvə/
Dublin /ˈdʌblɪn/
Dundee /ˌdʌnˈdiː/
Durham /ˈdʌrəm/
Eastbourne /ˈiːstbɔːn/
Edinburgh /ˈedɪnbərə/
Ely /ˈiːli/
Exeter /ˈeksɪtə/
Galway /ˈɡɔːlweɪ/
Glasgow /ˈɡlɑːzɡəʊ/
Gloucester /ˈɡlɒstə/
Hastings /ˈheɪstɪŋz/
Hereford /ˈherɪfəd/
Holyhead /ˈhɒlihed/
Inverness /ˌɪnvəˈnes/
Ipswich /ˈɪpswɪtʃ/
Keswick /ˈkezɪk/

Kingston upon Hull
 /ˌkɪŋstən əpɒn ˈhʌl/
Leeds /liːdz/
Leicester /ˈlestə/
Limerick /ˈlɪmərɪk/
Lincoln /ˈlɪŋkən/
Liverpool /ˈlɪvəpuːl/
London /ˈlʌndən/
Londonderry /ˈlʌndənderi/
Luton /ˈluːtn/
Manchester /ˈmæntʃestə/
Middlesborough /ˈmɪdlzbrə/
Newcastle upon Tyne
 /ˌnjuːkɑːsl əpɒn ˈtaɪn/
Northampton /nɔːˈθæmptən/
Norwich /ˈnɒrɪdʒ/
Nottingham /ˈnɒtɪŋəm/
Oxford /ˈɒksfəd/
Plymouth /ˈplɪməθ/
Poole /puːl/
Portsmouth /ˈpɔːtsməθ/
Ramsgate /ˈræmzɡeɪt/
Reading /ˈredɪŋ/
Salisbury /ˈsɔːlzbəri/
Sheffield /ˈʃefiːld/
Shrewsbury /ˈʃrəʊzbəri/
Southampton /saʊˈθæmptən
St. Andrews /snt ˈændruːz/
St. David's /snt ˈdeɪvɪdz/
Stirling /ˈstɜːlɪŋ/
Stoke-on-Trent /ˌstəʊk ɒnˈt
Stratford-upon-Avon
 /ˌstrætfəd əpɒn ˈeɪvn/
Swansea /ˈswɒnzi/
Taunton /ˈtɔːntən/
Warwick /ˈwɒrɪk/
Worcester /ˈwʊstə/
York /jɔːk/

World map showing capital cities

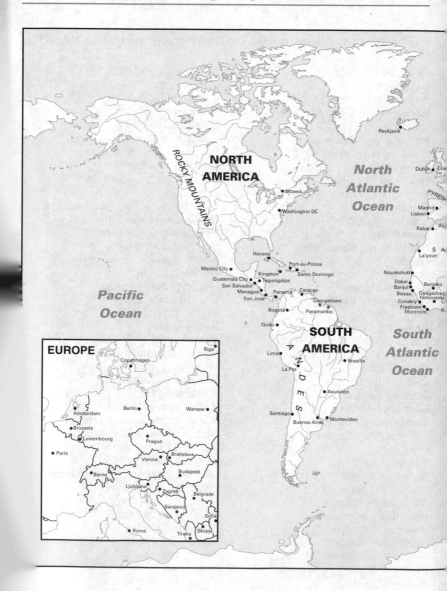

ROCKY MOUNTAINS

NORTH AMERICA

Ottawa
Washington DC

North Atlantic Ocean

Reykjavik

Dublin • Lo

PYREN

Madrid
Lisbon

Rabat • Al

S A
La'youn

Havana
Port-au-Prince
Mexico City
Kingston Santo Domingo
Guatemala City • Tegucigalpa
San Salvador
Managua • Panama Caracas
San Jose
Georgetown
Bogotá Paramaribo
Quito

Nouakchott
Dakar
Banjul Bamako
Bissau Ouagadou
Conakry Yamoussou
Freetown
Monrovia A

Pacific Ocean

SOUTH AMERICA

A
N
D
E
S

Lima
La Paz
Brasília

Asunción

Santiago
Buenos Aires Montevideo

South Atlantic Ocean

EUROPE

Riga

Copenhagen

Berlin Warsaw

Amsterdam
Brussels
Luxembourg
Prague
Paris
Vienna Bratislava
Berne Budapest
Ljubljana Zagreb
Sarajevo Belgrade
Sofia
Rome Tirana Skopje

World map showing capital cities

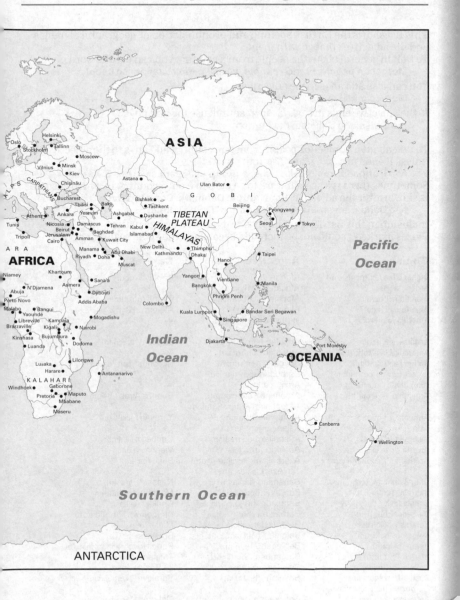

Geographical names

This list shows the English spelling and pronunciation of geographical names and the adjectives that go with them.
To talk in general about the people from a country, you can use the word people:
Moroccan people, French people, Israeli people, Japanese people

You can also add an **-s** to the adjective:
Moroccans, Israelis

If the adjective ends in a /s/, /z/ or /ʃ/ sound, use **the** and no **-s**:
the Swiss, the Chinese, the French

To talk about a number of people from one country, add an **-s** to the adjective, unless it ends in a /s/, /z/ or /ʃ/ sound:
two Germans, some Pakistanis, a group of Japanese, a few Swiss
Sometimes there is a special word for a person from a country, in which case this is shown after the adjective, for example **Denmark: Danish, a Dane**:
two Danes, several Turks, a roomful of Dutchwomen

Inclusion in this list does not imply status as a sovereign nation.
Places marked * could not be included because of the small scale of the map.

Country	Adjective	Capital
Afghanistan /æf'gænɪstɑːn/	Afghan /'æfgæn/	Kabul /'kɑːbʊl/
Africa /'æfrɪkə/	African /'æfrɪkən/	—
Albania /æl'beɪniə/	Albanian /æl'beɪniən/	Tirana /tɪ'rɑːnə/
Algeria /æl'dʒɪəriə/	Algerian /æl'dʒɪəriən/	Algiers /æl'dʒɪəz/
America /ə'merɪkə/	→(the) United States of America	—
Angola /æŋ'gəʊlə/	Angolan /æŋ'gəʊlən/	Luanda /lu:'ændə/
Antarctica /æn'tɑːktɪkə/	Antarctic /æn'tɑːktɪk/	—
Antigua and Barbuda /æn,ti:gə ən bɑː'bju:də/	Antiguan /æn'ti:gən/, Barbudan /bɑː'bjudən/	St Johns* /snt 'dʒɒnz/
(the) Arctic /'ɑːktɪk/	Arctic /'ɑːktɪk/	—
Argentina /,ɑːdʒən'ti:nə/	Argentine /'ɑːdʒəntaɪn/, Argentinian /,ɑːdʒən'tɪniən/	Buenos Aires /,bweɪnəs 'aɪri:z/
Armenia /ɑː'mi:niə/	Armenian /ɑː'mi:niən/	Yerevan /,jerɪ'væn/
Asia /'eɪʃə, 'eɪʒə/	Asian /'eɪʃən, 'eɪʒən/	—
Australia /ɒ'streɪliə/	Australian /ɒ'streɪliən/	Canberra /'kænbərə/
Austria /'ɒstriə/	Austrian /'ɒstriən/	Vienna /vi'enə/
Azerbaijan /,æzəbaɪ'dʒɑːn/	Azerbaijani /,æzəbaɪ'dʒɑːni/, an Azeri /ə'zeəri/	Baku /bæ'ku:/
(the) Bahamas /bə'hɑːməz/	Bahamian /bə'heɪmiən/	Nassau* /'næsaʊ/
Bahrain /bɑː'reɪn/	Bahraini /bɑː'reɪni/	Manama /mə'nɑːmə/
Bangladesh /,bæŋglə'deʃ/	Bangladeshi /,bæŋglə'deʃi/	Dhaka /'dækə/
Barbados /bɑː'beɪdɒs/	Barbadian /bɑː'beɪdiən/	Bridgetown* /'brɪdʒtaʊn/
Belarus /,belə'ru:s/	Belorussian /,belə'rʌʃn/	Minsk /mɪnsk/
Belgium /'beldʒəm/	Belgian /'beldʒən/	Brussels /'brʌslz/
Benin /be'ni:n/	Beninese /,benɪ'ni:z/	Porto Novo /,pɔːtəʊ 'nəʊvəʊ/
Bhutan /bu:'tɑːn/	Bhutanese /,bu:tə'ni:z/	Thimphu /'tɪmpu:/
Bolivia /bə'lɪviə/	Bolivian /bə'lɪviən/	La Paz /læ 'pæz/
Bosnia-Herzegovina /,bɒzniə ,hɜːtsəgə'vi:nə/	Bosnian /'bɒzniən/	Sarajevo /,særə'jeɪvəʊ/
Botswana /bɒt'swɑːnə/	Botswanan /bɒt'swɑːnən/, person: Motswana /mɒt'swɑːnə/, people: Batswana /bæt'swɑːnə/	Gaborone /,gæbə'rəʊni/
Brazil /brə'zɪl/	Brazilian /brə'zɪliən/	Brasilia /brə'zɪliə/

Geographical names

Country	Adjective	Capital
Brunei Darussalam /ˌbruːnaɪ dæˈruːsælæm/	Brunei /bruːˈnaɪ/, Bruneian /bruːˈnaɪən/	Bandar Seri Begawan /ˌbændə ˌserɪ bəˈgɑːwən/
Bulgaria /bʌlˈgeərɪə/	Bulgarian /bʌlˈgeərɪən/	Sofia /ˈsəʊfɪə, səˈfiːə/
Burkina /bɜːˈkiːnə/	Burkinese /bɜːkɪˈniːz/	Ouagadougou /ˌwɑːgəˈduːguː/
Burma /ˈbɜːmə/	Burmese /bɜːˈmiːz/	Yangon /jæŋˈgɒn/
Burundi /bʊˈrʊndi/	Burundian /bʊˈrʊndiən/	Bujumbura /ˌbuːdʒəmˈbʊrə/
Cambodia /kæmˈbəʊdiə/	Cambodian /kæmˈbəʊdiən/	Phnom Penh /nɒm ˈpen/
Cameroon /ˌkæməˈruːn/	Cameroonian /ˌkæməˈruːniən/	Yaoundé /jæˈʊndeɪ/
Canada /ˈkænədə/	Canadian /kəˈneɪdiən/	Ottawa /ˈɒtəwə/
Cape Verde /ˌkeɪp ˈvɜːd/	Cape Verden /ˌkeɪp ˈvɜːdiən/	Praia*/ˈpraɪə/
(the) Central African Republic /ˌsentrəl ˌæfrɪkən rɪˈpʌblɪk/	Central African /ˌsentrəl ˈæfrɪkən/	Bangui /ˈbæŋgiː/
Chad /tʃæd/	Chadian /ˈtʃædiən/	N'Djamena /ˌ(ə)ndʒæˈmeɪnə/
Chile /ˈtʃɪli/	Chilean /ˈtʃɪliən/	Santiago /ˌsæntɪˈɑːgəʊ/
China /ˈtʃaɪnə/	Chinese /tʃaɪˈniːz/	Beijing /beɪˈ(d)ʒɪŋ/
Colombia /kəˈlɒmbiə/	Colombian /kəˈlɒmbiən/	Bogotá /ˌbɒgəˈtɑː/
Comoros /ˈkɒmərəʊz/	Comoran /kəˈmɔːrən/	Moroni* /məˈrəʊni/
Congo /ˈkɒŋgəʊ/	Congolese /ˌkɒŋgəˈliːz/	Brazzaville /ˈbræzəvɪl/
Costa Rica /ˌkɒstə ˈriːkə/	Costa Rican /ˌkɒstə ˈriːkən/	San José /ˌsæn həʊˈzeɪ/
Côte d'Ivoire /ˌkəʊt diːˈvwɑː/	→ (the) Ivory Coast	
Croatia /krəʊˈeɪʃə/	Croatian /krəʊˈeɪʃən/	Zagreb /ˈzɑːgreb/
Cuba /ˈkjuːbə/	Cuban /ˈkjuːbən/	Havana /həˈvænə/
Cyprus /ˈsaɪprəs/	Cypriot /ˈsɪpriət/	Nicosia /ˌnɪkəˈsɪə/
(the) Czech Republic /ˌtʃek rɪˈpʌblɪk/	Czech /tʃek/	Prague /prɑːg/
(the) Democratic Republic of Congo /deməˌkrætɪk rɪˌpʌblɪk əv ˈkɒŋgəʊ/	Congolese /ˌkɒŋgəˈliːz/	Kinshasa /ˌkɪnˈʃɑːsə/
Denmark /ˈdenmɑːk/	Danish /ˈdeɪnɪʃ/, a Dane /deɪn/	Copenhagen /ˌkəʊpənˈheɪg(ə)n/
Djibouti /dʒɪˈbuːti/	Djiboutian /dʒɪˈbuːtiən/	Djibouti /dʒɪˈbuːti/
Dominica /ˌdɒmɪˈniːkə/	Dominican /ˌdɒmɪˈniːkən/	Roseau /rəʊˈzəʊ/
(the) Dominican Republic /dəˌmɪnɪkən rɪˈpʌblɪk/	Dominican /dəˈmɪnɪkən/	Santo Domingo /ˌsæntəʊ dəˈmɪŋgəʊ/
Ecuador /ˈekwədɔː/	Ecuadorian /ˌekwəˈdɔːriən/	Quito /ˈkiːtəʊ/
Egypt /ˈiːdʒɪpt/	Egyptian /iˈdʒɪpʃn/	Cairo /ˈkaɪrəʊ/
El Salvador /el ˈsælvədɔː/	Salvadorean /ˌsælvəˈdɔːriən/	San Salvador /ˌsæn ˈsælvədɔː/
England /ˈɪŋglənd/	English /ˈɪŋglɪʃ/, an Englishman /ˈɪŋglɪʃmən/, an Englishwoman /ˈɪŋglɪʃwʊmən/	London /ˈlʌndən/
Equatorial Guinea /ˌekwəˌtɔːriəl ˈgɪni/	Equatorial Guinean /ˌekwəˌtɔːriəl ˈgɪniən/	Malabo /məˈlɑːbəʊ/
Eritrea /ˌerɪˈtreɪə/	Eritrean /ˌerɪˈtreɪən/	Asmera /æsˈmeərə/
Estonia /eˈstəʊniə/	Estonian /eˈstəʊniən/	Tallinn /ˈtælɪn/
Ethiopia /ˌiːθiˈəʊpiə/	Ethiopian /ˌiːθiˈəʊpiən/	Addis Ababa /ˌædɪs ˈæbəbə/
Europe /ˈjʊərəp/	European /ˌjʊərəˈpiːən/	—
Fiji /ˈfiːdʒiː/	Fijian /fɪˈdʒiːən/	Suva* /ˈsuːvə/
Finland /ˈfɪnlənd/	Finnish /ˈfɪnɪʃ/, a Finn /fɪn/	Helsinki /helˈsɪŋki/
France /frɑːns/	French /frentʃ/, a Frenchman /ˈfrentʃmən/, a Frenchwoman /ˈfrentʃwʊmən/	Paris /ˈpærɪs/
(the) FYROM /ˌfɔːmə ˌjuːgəʊslɑːv rɪˈpʌblɪk əv mæsəˈdəʊniə/	Macedonian /ˌmæsəˈdəʊniən/	Skopje /ˈskɒpjeɪ/
Gabon /gæˈbɒn/	Gabonese /ˌgæbəˈniːz/	Libreville /ˈliːbrəvɪl/
(the) Gambia /ˈgæmbiə/	Gambian /ˈgæmbiən/	Banjul /bænˈdʒuːl/

Geographical names

Country	Adjective	Capital
Georgia /'dʒɔːdʒə/	Georgian /'dʒɔːdʒən/	Tbilisi /ˌtəbɪ'liːsi/
Germany /'dʒɜːməni/	German /'dʒɜːmən/	Berlin /bɜː'lɪn/
Ghana /'gɑːnə/	Ghanian /gɑː'neɪən/	Accra /ə'krɑː/
Great Britain /ˌgreɪt 'brɪtn/	British /'brɪtʃ/, Briton /'brɪtn/	London /'lʌndən/
Greece /griːs/	Greek /griːk/	Athens /'æθɪnz/
Grenada /grə'neɪdə/	Grenadian /grə'neɪdiən/	St George's* /snt 'dʒɔːdʒɪz/
Guatemala /ˌgwætə'mɑːlə/	Guatemalan /ˌgwætə'mɑːlən/	Guatemala City /ˌgwætəˌmɑːlə 'sɪti/
Guinea /'gɪni/	Guinean /'gɪniən/	Conakry /'kɒnəkri/
Guinea-Bissau /ˌgɪni bɪ'saʊ/	Guinean /'gɪniən/	Bissau /bɪ'saʊ/
Guyana /gaɪ'ænə/	Guyanese /ˌgaɪə'niːz/	Georgetown /'dʒɔːdʒtaʊn/
Haiti /'heɪti/	Haitian /'heɪʃn/	Port-au-Prince /ˌpɔːtəʊ'prɪns/
Holland /'hɒlənd/	→(the) Netherlands	
Honduras /hɒn'djʊərəs/	Honduran /hɒn'djʊərən/	Tegucigalpa /teˌguːsɪ'gælpə/
Hungary /'hʌŋgəri/	Hungarian /hʌŋ'geəriən/	Budapest /ˌb(j)uːdə'pest/
Iceland /'aɪslənd/	Icelandic /aɪs'lændɪk/	Reykjavik /'reɪkjəvɪk/
India /'ɪndiə/	Indian /'ɪndiən/	New Delhi /ˌnjuː 'deli/
Indonesia /ˌɪndə'niːziə/	Indonesian /ˌɪndə'niːziən/	Djakarta /dʒə'kɑːtə/
Iran /ɪ'rɑːn/	Iranian /ɪ'reɪniən/	Tehran /teə'rɑːn/
Iraq /ɪ'rɑːk/	Iraqi /ɪ'rɑːki/	Baghdad /bæg'dæd/
Ireland /'aɪələnd/	Irish /'aɪrɪʃ/, an Irishman /'aɪrɪʃmən/, an Irishwoman /'aɪrɪʃwʊmən/	Dublin /'dʌblɪn/
Israel /'ɪzreɪl/	Israeli /ɪz'reɪli/	Jerusalem /dʒə'ruːsələm/
Italy /'ɪtəli/	Italian /ɪ'tæliən/	Rome /rəʊm/
(the) Ivory Coast /ˌaɪvəri 'kəʊst/	Ivorian /aɪ'vɔːriən/	Yamoussoukro /ˌjæmuː'suːkrəʊ/
Jamaica /dʒə'meɪkə/	Jamaican /dʒə'meɪkən/	Kingston /'kɪŋstən/
Japan /dʒə'pæn/	Japanese /ˌdʒæpə'niːz/	Tokyo /'təʊkɪəʊ/
Jordan /'dʒɔːdn/	Jordanian /dʒɔː'deɪniən/	Amman /ə'mɑːn/
Kazakhstan /ˌkæzæk'stɑːn/	Kazakh /kə'zæk/	Astana /'æstənɑː/
Kenya /'kenjə/	Kenyan /'kenjən/	Nairobi /naɪ'rəʊbi/
Kirgyastan ˌkɪəgɪ'stɑːn/	Kirgyz /'kɪəgɪz/	Bishkek /bɪʃ'kek/
Kiribati /ˌkɪrɪ'bæs /	—	Tarawa* /tə'rɑːwə/
Korea, North /ˌnɔːθ kə'rɪə/	North Korean /ˌnɔːθ kə'rɪən/	Pyongyang /pjɒŋ'jæŋ/
Korea, South /ˌsaʊθ kə'rɪə/	South Korean /ˌsaʊθ kə'rɪən/	Seoul /səʊl/
Kuwait /kʊ'weɪt/	Kuwaiti /kʊ'weɪti/	Kuwait City /kʊˌweɪt 'sɪti/
Laos /laʊs/	Laotian /laʊʃn/	Vientiane /ˌvjen'tjɑːn/
Latvia /'lætviə/	Latvian /'lætviən/	Riga /'riːgə/
Lebanon /'lebənən/	Lebanese /ˌlebə'niːz/	Beirut /beɪ'ruːt/
Lesotho /lə'suːtuː/	Sotho /'suːtuː/, person: Mosotho /mə'suːtuː/, people: Basotho /bə'suːtuː/	Maseru /mə'seəru/
Liberia /laɪ'bɪəriə/	Liberian /laɪ'bɪəriən/	Monrovia /mɒn'rəʊviə/
Libya /'lɪbiə/	Libyan /'lɪbiən/	Tripoli /'trɪpəli/
Liechtenstein /'lɪktənstaɪn/	Liechtenstein, a Liechtensteiner /'lɪktənstaɪnə/	Vaduz* /væ'dʊts/
Lithuania /ˌlɪθjuː'eɪniə/	Lithuanian /ˌlɪθjuː'eɪniən/	Vilnius /'vɪlnɪəs/
Luxembourg /'lʌksəmbɜːg/	Luxembourg, a Luxembourger /'lʌksəmbɜːgə/	Luxembourg /'lʌksəmbɜːg/
Madagascar /ˌmædə'gæskə/	Madagascan /ˌmædə'gæskən/, a Malagasy /ˌmælə'gæsi/	Antananarivo /ˌæntəˌnænə'riːvəʊ/
Malawi /mə'lɑːwi/	Malawian /mə'lɑːwiən/	Lilongwe /lɪ'lɒŋweɪ/
Malaysia /mə'leɪziə/	Malaysian /mə'leɪziən/	Kuala Lumpur /ˌkwɑːlə 'lʊmpʊə/
(the) Maldives /'mɔːldiːvz/	Maldivian /mɔː'ldɪviən/	Male* /'mɑːleɪ/
Mali /'mɑːli/	Malian /'mɑːliən/	Bamako /'bæməkəʊ/
Malta /'mɔːltə/	Maltese /mɔː'tiːz/	Valletta* /və'letə/
Mauritania /ˌmɒrɪ'teɪniə/	Mauritanian /ˌmɒrɪ'teɪniən/	Nouakchott /nwæk'ʃɒt/
Mauritius /mə'rɪʃəs/	Mauritian /mə'rɪʃn/	Port Louis* /ˌpɔːt 'luːɪs, -'luːi/

Geographical names

Country	Adjective	Capital
Mexico /'meksɪkəʊ/	Mexican /'meksɪkən/	Mexico /'meksɪkəʊ /
Moldova /mɒl'dəʊvə/	Moldovian /mɒl'dəʊvən/	Chişinău /ˌkɪʃ'naʊ/
Mongolia /mɒŋ'gəʊliə/	Mongolian /mɒŋ'gəʊliən/, a Mongol /'mɒŋgl/	Ulan Bator /ˌuːlɑːn 'bɑːtə/
Montserrat /ˌmɒnsə'ræt/	Montserratian /ˌmɒnsə'reɪʃn/	Plymouth* /'plɪməθ/
Morocco /mə'rɒkəʊ/	Moroccan /mə'rɒkən/	Rabat /rə'bæt/
Mozambique /ˌməʊzæm'biːk/	Mozambiquean /ˌməʊzæm'biːkən/	Maputo /mə'puːtəʊ/
Myanmar /miˌæn'mɑː/	→Burma	
Namibia /nə'mɪbiə/	Namibian /nə'mɪbiən/	Windhoek /'wɪnthʊk/
Nauru /'naʊruː/	Nauruan /naʊ'ruːən/	—
Nepal /nɪ'pɔːl/	Nepalese /ˌnepə'liːz/	Kathmandu /ˌkætmæn'duː/
(the) Netherlands /'neðələndz/	Dutch /dʌtʃ/, a Dutchman /'dʌtʃmən/, a Dutchwoman /'dʌtʃwʊmən/	Amsterdam /ˌæmstə'dæm/
New Zealand /ˌnjuː 'ziːlənd/	New Zealand, a New Zealander /ˌnjuː 'ziːləndə/	Wellington /'welɪŋtən/
Nicaragua /ˌnɪkə'rægjuə/	Nicaraguan /ˌnɪkə'rægjuən/	Managua /mə'nɑːgwə/
Niger /niː'ʒeə/	Nigerian /niː'ʒeəriən/	Niamey /njɑː'meɪ/
Nigeria /naɪ'dʒɪəriə/	Nigerian /naɪ'dʒɪəriən/	Abuja /ə'buːdʒə/
Northern Ireland /ˌnɔːðən 'aɪlənd/	Northern Irish /ˌnɔːðən 'aɪrɪʃ/	Belfast* /bel'fɑːst/
Norway /'nɔːweɪ/	Norwegian /nɔː'wiːdʒən/	Oslo /'ɒzləʊ/
Oman /əʊ'mɑːn/	Omani /əʊ'mɑːni/	Muscat /'mʌskæt/
Pakistan /ˌpɑːkɪ'stɑːn/	Pakistani /ˌpɑːkɪ'stɑːni/	Islamabad /ɪz'lɑːməbæd/
Panama /'pænəmɑː/	Panamanian /ˌpænə'meɪniən/	Panama /'pænəmɑː/
Papua New Guinea /ˌpæpuə ˌnjuː 'gɪni/	Papuan /'pæpuən/	Port Moresby /ˌpɔːt 'mɔːzbi/
Paraguay /'pærəgwaɪ/	Paraguayan /ˌpærə'gwaɪən/	Asunción /ə,sʊnsɪ'ɒn/
Peru /pə'ruː/	Peruvian /pə'ruːviən/	Lima /'liːmə/
(the) Philippines /'fɪlɪpiːnz/	Philippine /'fɪlɪpiːn/, a Filipino /ˌfɪlɪ'piːnəʊ/	Manila /mə'nɪlə/
Poland /'pəʊlənd/	Polish /'pəʊlɪʃ/, a Pole /pəʊl/	Warsaw /'wɔːsɔː/
Portugal /'pɔːtʃʊgl/	Portuguese /ˌpɔːtʃʊ'giːz/	Lisbon /'lɪzbən/
Qatar /kæ'tɑː, 'kʌtə/	Qatari /kæ'tɑːri/	Doha /'dəʊhɑː/
Romania /ru'meɪniə/	Romanian /ru'meɪniən/	Bucharest /ˌbuːkə'rest/
Russia /'rʌʃə/	Russian /'rʌʃn/	Moscow /'mɒskəʊ/
Rwanda /ru'ændə/	Rwandan /ru'ændən/	Kigali /kɪ'gɑːli/
San Marino /ˌsæn mə'riːnəʊ/	San Marinese /ˌsæn mærɪ'niːz/	San Marino* /ˌsæn mə'riːnəʊ/
Sao Tomé and Principe /ˌsaʊ təˌmeɪ ən 'prɪnsɪpeɪ/	Sao Tomean /ˌsaʊ tə'meɪən/	Sao Tomé* /ˌsaʊ tə'meɪ/
Saudi Arabia /ˌsaʊdi ə'reɪbiə/	Saudi /'saʊdi/, Saudi Arabian /ˌsaʊdi ə'reɪbiən/	Riyadh /riː'ɑːd/
Scotland /'skɒtlənd/	Scottish /'skɒtɪʃ/, Scots /skɒts/, a Scot /skɒt/, a Scotsman /'skɒtsmən/, a Scotswoman /'skɒtswʊmən/	Edinburgh* /'edɪnbərə/
Senegal /ˌsenɪ'gɔːl/	Senegalese /ˌsenɪgə'liːz/	Dakar /'dækɑː/
(the) Seychelles /seɪ'ʃelz/	Seychellois /ˌseɪʃel'wɑː/	Victoria* /vɪk'tɔːriə/
Sierra Leone /siˌerə li'əʊn/	Sierra Leonean /siˌerə li'əʊniən/	Freetown /'friːtaʊn/
Singapore /ˌsɪŋə'pɔː/	Singaporean /ˌsɪŋə'pɔːriən/	Singapore /ˌsɪŋə'pɔː/
Slovakia /sləʊ'vɑːkiə/	Slovak /'sləʊvæk/	Bratislava /ˌbrætɪ'slɑːvə/
Slovenia /sləʊ'viːniə/	Slovene /'sləʊviːn/, Slovenian /sləʊ'viːniən/	Ljubljana /lju:'bljɑːnə/
(the) Solomon Islands /'sɒləmən aɪləndz/	Solomon Islander /'sɒləmən aɪləndə/	Honiara* /ˌhəʊnɪ'ɑːrə/

Geographical names

Country	Adjective	Capital
Somalia /sə'mɑːliə/	Somali /sə'mɑːli/	Mogadishu /ˌmɒgə'dɪʃuː/
South Africa /ˌsaʊθ 'æfrɪkə/	South African /ˌsaʊθ 'æfrɪkən/	Pretoria /prɪ'tɔːriə/
Spain /speɪn/	Spanish /'spænɪʃ/, a Spaniard /'spænɪəd/	Madrid /mə'drɪd/
Sri Lanka /sri 'læŋkə/	Sri Lankan /sri 'læŋkən/	Colombo /kə'lʌmbəʊ/
St Kitts and Nevis /snt ˌkɪts ən 'niːvɪs/	Kittitian /kɪ'tɪʃn/, Nevisian /niː'vɪsɪən/	Basseterre* /bæs'teə/
St Lucia /snt 'luːʃə/	St Lucian /snt 'luːʃən/	Castries* /kæ'striːs/
St Vincent and the Grenadines /snt ˌvɪnsnt ən ðə 'grenədiːnz/	Vincentian /vɪn'senʃɪən/	Kingstown* /'kɪŋztaʊn/
Sudan /suː'dɑːn/	Sudanese /ˌsuːdə'niːz/	Khartoum /kɑː'tuːm/
Suriname /ˌsʊərɪ'næm/	Surinamese /ˌsʊərɪnæ'miːz/	Paramaribo /ˌpærə'mærɪbəʊ/
Swaziland /'swɑːzilænd/	Swazi /'swɑːzi/	Mbabane /ˌ(ə)mbɑː'bɑːni/
Sweden /'swiːdn/	Swedish /'swiːdɪʃ/, a Swede /swiːd/	Stockholm /'stɒkhəʊm/
Switzerland /'swɪtsələnd/	Swiss /swɪs/	Berne /bɜːn/, /beən/
Syria /'sɪriə/	Syrian /'sɪriən/	Damascus /də'mɑːskəs/
Taiwan /taɪ'wɑːn/	Taiwanese /ˌtaɪwə'niːz/	Taipei /taɪ'peɪ/
Tajikistan /tæˌdʒiːkɪ'stɑːn/	Tajik /tæ'ʒiːk/	Dushanbe /duː'ʃænbeɪ/
Tanzania /ˌtænzə'niːə/	Tanzanian /ˌtænzə'niːən/	Dodoma /dəʊ'dəʊmə/
Tibet /tɪ'bet/	Tibetan /tɪ'betn/	Lhasa* /'lɑːsə/
Thailand /'taɪlænd/	Thai /taɪ/	Bangkok /bæŋ'kɒk/
Togo /'təʊgəʊ/	Togolese /ˌtəʊgə'liːz/	Lomé /'ləʊmeɪ/
Tonga /'tɒŋə, 'tɒŋgə/	Tongan /'tɒŋən, 'tɒŋgən/	Nuku'alofa* /ˌnuːkuə'ləʊfə/
Trinidad and Tobago /ˌtrɪnɪdæd ən tə'beɪgəʊ/	Trinidadian /ˌtrɪnɪ'dædiən/, Tobagonian /ˌtəʊbə'gəʊniən/	Port-of-Spain* /ˌpɔːt əv 'speɪn/
Tunisia /tjuː'nɪziə/	Tunisian /tjuː'nɪziən/	Tunis /'tjuːnɪs/
Turkey /'tɜːki/	Turkish /'tɜːkɪʃ/, a Turk /tɜːk/	Ankara /'æŋkərə/
Turkmenistan /tɜːkˌmenɪ'stɑːn/	Turkmen /'tɜːkmen/	Ashgabat /'æʃgəbæt/
Tuvalu /tuː'vɑːluː/	Tuvaluan /ˌtuːvə'luːən/	Funafuti* /ˌfuːnə'fuːti/
Uganda /juː'gændə/	Ugandan /juː'gændən/	Kampala /kæm'pɑːlə/
Ukraine /juː'kreɪn/	Ukrainian /juː'kreɪniən/	Kiev /'kiːef/
(the) United Arab Emirates /juːˌnaɪtɪd ˌærəb 'emɪrəts/	Emirian /e'mɪriən/	Abu Dhabi /ˌæbuː 'dɑːbi/
(the) United Kingdom /juːˌnaɪtɪd 'kɪŋdəm/	British /'brɪtɪʃ/, a Briton /'brɪtn/	London /'lʌndən/
(the) United States of America /juːˌnaɪtɪd ˌsteɪts əv ə'merɪkə/	American /ə'merɪkən/	Washington DC /ˌwɒʃɪŋtən diː 'siː/
Uruguay /'jʊərəgwaɪ/	Uruguayan /ˌjʊərə'gwaɪən/	Montevideo /ˌmɒntɪvɪ'deɪəʊ/
Uzbekistan /ʊzˌbekɪ'stɑːn/	Uzbek /'ʊzbek/	Tashkent /tæʃ'kent/
Vanuatu /ˌvænu'ɑːtuː/	Vanuatan /ˌvænu'ɑːtən/	Vila* /'viːlə/
Venezuela /ˌvenə'zweɪlə/	Venezuelan /ˌvenə'zweɪlən/	Caracas /kə'rækəs/
Vietnam /viˌet'næm/	Vietnamese /viˌetnə'miːz/	Hanoi /hæ'nɔɪ/
Wales /weɪlz/	Welsh /welʃ/, a Welshman /'welʃmən/, a Welshwoman /'welʃwomən/	Cardiff* /'kɑːdɪf/
(the) West Indies /ˌwest 'ɪndiz/	West Indian /ˌwest 'ɪndiən/	—
Western Sahara /ˌwestən sə'hɑːrə/	Sahrawian /sɑː'rɑːwɪən/, Sahrawi /sɑː'rɑːwi/	La'youn /lɑː'juːn/
Western Samoa /ˌwestən sə'məʊə/	Samoan /sə'məʊən/	Apia* /'æpiə/
(the) Yemen Republic /ˌjemən rɪ'pʌblɪk/	Yemeni /'jeməni/	Sana'a /sæ'nɑː/
Yugoslavia /ˌjuːgəʊ'slɑːviə/	Yugoslavian /ˌjuːgəʊ'slɑːviən/	Belgrade /bel'greɪd/
Zambia /'zæmbiə/	Zambian /'zæmbiən/	Lusaka /luː'sɑːkə/
Zimbabwe /zɪm'bɑːbwi/	Zimbabwean /zɪm'bɑːbwiən/	Harare /hə'rɑːri/

Workbook key

Part One:

How good a dictionary user are you?

1 B	2 C	3 A	4 B
5 C	6 B	7 B	8 C
9 A	10 B	11 C	12 A
13 B	14 B	15 C	16 A
17 C	18 A	19 B	20 C

Matching exercise:

adj/noun/verb/adv	part of speech (3)
look forward to sth/doing sth	phrasal verb (8)
It began to **rain heavily**.	example (5)
(be) above board	idiom (7)
–heavily	derivative (6)
/fə'netɪks/	pronunciation (2)
the meaning of the word	definition (4)

Part Two:

Finding the right word

1

cheap factory dig happy funny child encourage optimism old

2

bank	2	noun, verb
film	2	noun, verb
light	4	noun, adjective, verb, adverb
blind	3	adjective, verb, noun
warm	2	adjective, verb

Finding the right meaning

film¹	(1)
chocolate	(3)
break¹	(3)
light²	(4)
return¹	(4)

Picture crossword

Across

1 whiskers; **4** fangs; **7** shed; **8** dungarees; **12** radish; **13** cardigan; **14** kebab; **16** busker; **18** thistle; **20** stem; **21** sapling; **22** straw; **23** lung

Down

2 scale; 3 pelvis; **5** segment; **6** parasol; **9** sparkling; **10** pod; **11** cagoule; **15** cellar; **17** cabin; **19** loft; **20** sole

Sounding people out

nervous /'nɜːvəs/; bad-tempered /ˌbæd 'tempəd /; generous /'dʒenərəs /; outgoing /'aʊtgəʊɪŋ/; mean /miːn /; tidy /'taɪdi/; nosy /'nəʊsi/; considerate /kən'sɪdərət/; silly /'sɪli/; modest /'mɒdɪst/; mystery adjective = narrow-minded

Wordsearch

1	sieve	11 liver
2	stapler	12 Wellington
3	spade	13 swarm
4	cockroach	14 lobster
5	saddle	15 drake
6	aubergine	16 acorn
7	Ghana	17 Spaniard
8	oboe	18 dreadlocks
9	orchid	19 purr
10	sari	20 doe

Adjectives, nouns & opposites

2 **adj** absent, **opposite** present; **noun** absence, **opposite** presence
absence from

3 satisfied; dissatisfied; satisfaction; dissatisfaction
dissatisfaction with

4 accurate; inaccurate; accuracy; inaccuracy
inaccuracies

5 grateful; ungrateful; gratitude; ingratitude
gratitude for

6 poor; rich or wealthy; poverty; wealth
poverty

7 compatible; incompatible; compatibility; incompatibilty
compatible with

8 strong; weak; strength; weakness
weaknesses

Workbook key

Spot the error

example: *believe*
embarrassed
lying
made a mistake
received
(surprised) at
had (fallen)
badly/seriously (hurt)
fell
from freezing
to (retire)

Sentence Transformations:

1 I'm off to the shop because we're running out of milk.
2 We're thinking of/about buying a new car.
3 I really enjoyed myself in Australia.
4 James suggested going out and celebrating that night.
5 A man is being questioned in connection with the robbery.
6 He might not have got my message.
7 There's hardly any money left in our account.
8 It was such a boring party that we left early.
9 I'm dying to meet her new boyfriend.
10 If I had arrived earlier I would have caught the train.

Fill in the missing words

1	weighing	9	on
2	in/with	10	for
3	from	11	than
4	from	12	in
5	have been	13	of
6	on	14	become
7	by	15	alone
8	off/away from		

Study pages key

S2 Sports and Hobbies

Exercise 1

play	do	go + -ing	make	no other verb
golf	gymnastics	hiking	models	draw
netball	athletics	cycling	clothes	sew
darts	crosswords	windsurfing		
the piano	judo	climbing		
snooker				
squash				
chess				
badminton				

Exercise 2

1	racket, shuttlecock	6	trainers
2	(golf) clubs	7	cue
3	racket	8	bat
4	(hockey) stick	9	jodhpurs
5	helmet	10	basket

S10 Pronunciation and spelling

ə	ɪ	ʌ	ɜː
certain	mountain	other	bird
chocolate	biscuit	blood	earth
control	busy	country	expert
famous	language	money	heard
moustache	married	one	journey
pleasure	minute	won	nurse
woman	orange		work
	package		
	packet		
	pretty		
	women		

beard /ˈbɪəd/
beautiful /ˈbjuːtɪfl/
break /breɪk/
breakfast /ˈbrekfəst/
comfortable /ˈkʌmftəbl/
cupboard /ˈkʌbəd/
friend /frend/
fruit /fruːt/
government /ˈgʌvənmənt/
guide /gaɪd/
heart /hɑːt/

iron /ˈaɪən/
naked /ˈneɪkɪd/
queue /kjuː/
restaurant /ˈrestrɒnt/
sausage /ˈsɒsɪdʒ/
sew /səʊ/
stomach /ˈstʌmək/
suit /suːt/
tired /ˈtaɪəd/
vegetable /ˈvedʒtəbl/

gh

gh silent: night, although, daughter, higher, thorough

gh pronounced as /f/: cough, rough, enough, tough

gh pronounced as /g/: ghetto, ghost

double consonants

fatter	opening	kidnapped
hoping	listening	beaten
stopped	planned	equalled
writing	visited	offering
written	biggest	happened
winning	referring	developing
whining	preferable	

S12 Phrasal Verbs

back = **in return**   on = **continuing**
off = **separate, no longer attached**

Which particle?

1 back   2 off   3 on   4 back   5 on   6 off

Formal to informal language

2 Tell the boss exactly what you think. Don't worry – I'll **back you up**.

3 You'll never guess who I just **bumped into** in the street just now!

4 I'm trying to **cut down** on the amount of coffee I drink each day.

5 I'll have to **put** the meeting **off** until next week.

6 The flight is at 8.00 so we'll have to **set off** very early for the airport.

7 I think the baby really **takes after** his mother.

8 I was so pleased when my dad finally **gave up** smoking.

9 It's amazing how some people manage to **bring up** their children alone.

10 Have we got time to **drop in on** Elena on the way home?

Opposites

1 f   2 i   3 c   4 j   5 b   6 e   7 d
8 a   9 h   10 g

turn sth on – turn sth off
pick sth up – put sth down
put sth on – take sth off
cheer sb up – get sb down
check in – check out
pull over – pull out
pack sth in – take sth up
pick sb up – drop sb off
add sth on – take sth away
sit down – stand up

S14 Idioms

Exercise 1

a chest (**4**)	e feet (**2**)	i head; heels (**8**)
b head (**6**)	f heart (**7**)	j back (**10**)
c nose (**5**)	g eye (**9**)	k mind (**1**)
d eyes (**11**)	h arm (**3**)	

Exercise 2

1 keep an eye on
2 poking/sticking her nose in
3 head over heels in love
4 got cold feet
5 get it off your chest
6 twist her arm
7 make up your mind
8 bit my head off
9 behind her back
10 are up to our eyes in

S16 Informal English

Types of people

1 a moron, a twit, a prat, a wally
2 a spoilsport, a wet blanket
3 a sucker
4 a doormat, a pushover
5 a creep
6 a layabout, a slob
7 a babe, a hunk
8 a scream
9 a swot
10 a wimp
11 a loony, a psycho, a lunatic
12 a crook
13 a globetrotter
14 a pest, a pain
15 a loner
16 an anorak, a trainspotter
17 a big mouth
18 a big-head
19 a yob
20 a has-been

Informal to formal English

These days, I'm so **poor** that I've had to move out of my flat. I'm £3,000 **overdrawn** and I had to find a way of **stopping** my bank manager **annoying** me. Still, **taking an optimistic view**, at least I don't have to **pay** much for rent now because a **friend** of mine is letting me stay at his **house** until things start to **improve**. The only thing is, he and his girlfriend are **having problems** and their rows are driving me **mad**. The last one was about where they should go on holiday. I mean, James is OK, but he's a bit of **a weak person** and **the most important thing is**, Claire

Study pages key

always gets what she wants, so what's the point of him refusing to change his mind about where they go on holiday? I'm probably making the atmosphere worse by being there when the couple want to be alone, which must make things difficult for them. I suppose I should organize myself properly and find a job.

S17 US English

Exercise 1

1	automobile	1	flat
2	license plate	2	wardrobe
3	windshield	3	lift
4	trunk	4	dustbin/rubbish bin
5	tire	5	fridge/refrigerator
6	hood	6	curtains
7	fender	7	toilet
8	gas tank	8	tap
		9	ground floor

Exercise 2

1 the motorway = the freeway/expressway
2 a petrol station = a gas station
3 the casualty department = the emergency room/ER
4 the cinema = the movie theater
5 car park = parking lot
6 the chemist's = the drugstore
7 an off-licence = a liquor store
8 flat = apartment
9 a tube station = a subway station
10 the pavement = the sidewalk

S18 Letter writing

Important phrases

1 d   2 f   3 e   4 h   5 b   6 j   7 a   8 g   9 c
10 k   11 i

Informal and formal letters

3rd June, 2000
Dear Mrs Maclennan
1 was recommended/has been recommended
2 to enquire
3 are planning
4 reserving
   I would be grateful if you could
5 is required
   I look forward to hearing from you
   Yours sincerely

S20 Essay writing

1 Despite the fact that (or Although) thousands die on the roads every year, little is being done to improve safety.
2 First of all (or Firstly), limits should be imposed on the power of car engines.
3 There are three main causes of accidents: excessive speed, carelessness and alcohol.
4 On the whole, results have been poor – in fact, the Transport Minister called them 'disastrous'.
5 Because of the number of fatal accidents, the road is called 'the motorway of death'.
6 Car manufacturers are reluctant to accept this, however.
7 Stricter laws on drink-driving have not led to fewer deaths, either.
8 Although there are heavy fines for speeding, many drivers still take the risk.

S22 Confusable words

Exercise 1

1	view	6	as
2	prescription	7	for; ago
3	sensitive	8	job
4	nice	9	currently
5	dead	10	lonely

Exercise 2

1	amazing	6	✗ worrying
2	embarrassed	7	✗ relaxing; ✗ refreshed
3	revolting	8	✓; ✗ frightening
4	moving	9	✓; ✗ boring
5	tiring; exhausted	10	✗ disappointing; ✗ satisfied

Exercise 3

1	taught	11	lend
2	take	12	bring
3	miss	13	Going; getting
4	looks	14	explain
5	damaged; hurt	15	waste
6	laid; lay	16	rose
7	stole	17	robbed
8	(have) left	18	seemed
9	tell	19	grew up
10	Raise	20	managed to

Study pages key

S24 Words that go together

Which adverb?

highly unlikely	drink heavily
gravely ill	fail miserably
bitterly cold	frozen stiff
bitterly disappointed	sleep soundly
badly hurt	bored stiff
glaringly obvious	

Which adjective?

1	a sharp increase	5	a heavy fine
2	a wild guess	6	fierce competition
3	in minute detail	7	full responsibility
4	by sheer luck		

Which verb?

1	broke his promise	5	tell the difference
2	caught fire	6	committed suicide
3	formed a queue	7	drives me crazy
4	achieved her ambition	8	draw the curtains

1	give	11	having
2	doing	12	gave
3	make	13	take
4	make	14	took
5	do	15	made
6	had/having	16	give
7	taking	17	make
8	gave	18	make
9	take/have	19	make
10	took	20	making

S27 Prepositions

in summer/July
on holiday
at times
in the middle
at New Year/Christmas
at the seaside
at the moment
in the newspaper
on the phone
at night
on a trip
at random
in a strange way
at the same time
at your own pace
on the bus/your bike
on the left
on TV/video/the radio
at the front/the back
in the mountains
on the way here
I was covered in mud.
She's hopeless at maths.

He smiled at her.
I'd like some information on museums.
Do you believe in ghosts?
I can't concentrate on my work.
Everything depends on this exam.

S28 Verb patterns

He promised to write me a letter./He promised (that) he would write me a letter.
She suggested taking regular exercise/She suggested (that) I take regular exercise.
I thanked them for looking after me.
He let me borrow his car for the day.

1	stealing	6	to speak
2	(from) hitting	7	meeting
3	to open	8	joining
4	seeing	9	doing
5	to meet	10	being

S32 Word Formation

Exercise 1

mono- bi- tri- quad- penta- hexa- septa- octa- nona- deca- cent- kilo-

Exercise 2

illegible, unattractive, harmless, irresponsible, impatient, irrelevant, disobedient, useful, uncomfortable, atypical or untypical, non-alcoholic, unsuccessful

Exercise 3

1	readable	6	simplify
2	traditionally	7	achievement
3	extra-large	8	transatlantic
4	brownish	9	poisonous
5	illegal	10	northward

Exercise 4

1 beauty – beautiful, beautifully
2 please – pleased, pleasing, pleasant, unpleasant
3 sense – senseless, sensible, sensitive, insensitive, nonsense
4 patient – impatient, patience, impatience, patiently, impatiently
5 collect – collection, collector
6 excite – excited, unexcited, exciting, unexciting, excitement
7 responsible – responsibly, irresponsible, responsibility
8 rely – reliable, unreliable, reliably, reliance, reliability
9 behave – behaviour, misbehave, misbehaviour
10 real – reality, really, unreal

Pronunciation

If two pronunciations for one word are given, both are acceptable. The first form given is considered to be more common.

/-/ A hyphen is used in alternative pronunciations when only part of the pronunciation changes. The part that remains the same is replaced by the hyphen.
accent /'æksent; -sənt/

/'/ This mark shows that the syllable after it is said with more force (stress) than other syllables in the word or group of words. For example any /'eni/ has a stress on the first syllable; depend /dɪ'pend/ has a stress on the second syllable.

/ˌ/ This mark shows that a syllable is said with more force than other syllables in a word but with a stress that is not as strong as for those syllables marked /'/. So in the word pronunciation /prəˌnʌnsi'eɪʃn/ the main stress is on the syllable /'eɪʃn/ and the secondary stress is on the syllable /ˌnʌn/.

Strong and weak forms

Some very common words, for example an, as, that, of, have two or more pronunciations: a strong form and one or more weak forms. In speech the weak forms are more common. For example from is /frəm/ in He comes from Spain. The strong form occurs when the word comes at the end of a sentence or when it is given special emphasis. For example from is /frɒm/ in Where are you from? and in The present's not from John, it's for him.

Pronunciation in derivatives and compounds

Many derivatives are formed by adding a suffix to the end of a word. These are pronounced by simply saying the suffix after the word. For example slowly /'sləʊli/ is said by adding the suffix -ly /-li/ to the word slow /sləʊ/.

However, where there is doubt about how a derivative is pronounced, the phonetic spelling is given. The part that remains the same is represented by a hyphen.

accidental /ˌæksɪ'dentl/; accidentally /-təli/

In compounds (made up of two or more words) the pronunciation of the individual words is not repeated. The dictionary shows how the compound is stressed using the marks /'/ and /ˌ/. In 'air steward the stress is on the first word. In ˌair ˌtraffic con'troller there are secondary stresses on air and on the first syllable of traffic, and the main stress is on the second syllable of controller.